The Oxford Handbook of Social Neuroscience

OXFORD LIBRARY OF PSYCHOLOGY

Editor-in-Chief PETER E. NATHAN

The Oxford Handbook of Social Neuroscience

Edited by

Jean Decety

John T. Cacioppo

UNIVERSITY PRESS

OXFORD
UNIVERSITY PRESS

Oxford University Press, Inc., publishes works that further
Oxford University's objective of excellence
in research, scholarship, and education.

Oxford New York
Auckland   Cape Town   Dar es Salaam   Hong Kong   Karachi
Kuala Lumpur   Madrid   Melbourne   Mexico City   Nairobi
New Delhi   Shanghai   Taipei   Toronto

With offices in
Argentina   Austria   Brazil   Chile   Czech Republic   France   Greece
Guatemala   Hungary   Italy   Japan   Poland   Portugal   Singapore
South Korea   Switzerland   Thailand   Turkey   Ukraine   Vietnam

Copyright © 2011 by Oxford University Press

Published by Oxford University Press, Inc.
198 Madison Avenue, New York, New York 10016
www.oup.com

Oxford is a registered trademark of Oxford University Press

Library of Congress Cataloging-in-Publication Data
CIP data on file
ISBN 978-0-19-534216-1

9 8 7 6 5 4 3 2 1

Printed in China

SHORT CONTENTS

OXFORD LIBRARY OF PSYCHOLOGY

The *Oxford Library of Psychology*, a landmark series of handbooks, is published by Oxford University Press, one of the world's oldest and most highly respected publishers, with a tradition of publishing significant books in psychology. The ambitious goal of the *Oxford Library of Psychology* is nothing less than to span a vibrant, wide-ranging field and, in so doing, to fill a clear market need.

Encompassing a comprehensive set of handbooks, organized hierarchically, the *Library* incorporates volumes at different levels, each designed to meet a distinct need. At one level are a set of handbooks designed broadly to survey the major subfields of psychology; at another are numerous handbooks that cover important current focal research and scholarly areas of psychology in depth and detail. Planned as a reflection of the dynamism of psychology, the *Library* will grow and expand as psychology itself develops, thereby highlighting significant new research that will impact on the field. Adding to its accessibility and ease of use, the *Library* will be published in print and, later on, electronically.

The *Library* surveys psychology's principal subfields with a set of handbooks that capture the current status and future prospects of those major subdisciplines. This initial set includes handbooks of social and personality psychology, clinical psychology, counseling psychology, school psychology, educational psychology, industrial and organizational psychology, cognitive psychology, cognitive neuroscience, methods and measurements, history, neuropsychology, personality assessment, developmental psychology, and more. Each handbook undertakes to review one of psychology's major subdisciplines with breadth, comprehensiveness, and exemplary scholarship. In addition to these broadly-conceived volumes, the *Library* also includes a large number of handbooks designed to explore in depth more specialized areas of scholarship and research, such as stress, health and coping, anxiety and related disorders, cognitive development, or child and adolescent assessment. In contrast to the broad coverage of the subfield handbooks, each of these latter volumes focuses on an especially productive, more highly focused line of scholarship and research. Whether at the broadest or most specific level, however, all of the *Library* handbooks offer synthetic coverage that reviews and evaluates the relevant past and present research and anticipates research in the future. Each handbook in the *Library* includes introductory and concluding chapters written by its editor to provide a roadmap to the handbook's table of contents and to offer informed anticipations of significant future developments in that field.

An undertaking of this scope calls for handbook editors and chapter authors who are established scholars in the areas about which they write. Many of the nation's and world's most productive and best-respected psychologists have agreed to edit *Library* handbooks or write authoritative chapters in their areas of expertise.

For whom has the *Oxford Library of Psychology* been written? Because of its breadth, depth, and accessibility, the *Library* serves a diverse audience, including graduate students in psychology and their faculty mentors, scholars, researchers, and practitioners in psychology and related fields. Each will find in the *Library* the information they seek on the subfield or focal area of psychology in which they work or are interested.

Befitting its commitment to accessibility, each handbook includes a comprehensive index, as well as extensive references to help guide research. And because the *Library* was designed from its inception as an online as well as a print resource, its structure and contents will be readily and rationally searchable online. Further, once the *Library* is released online, the handbooks will be regularly and thoroughly updated.

In summary, the *Oxford Library of Psychology* will grow organically to provide a thoroughly informed perspective on the field of psychology, one that reflects both psychology's dynamism and its increasing interdisciplinarity. Once published electronically, the *Library* is also destined to become a uniquely valuable interactive tool, with extended search and browsing capabilities. As you begin to consult this handbook, we sincerely hope you will share our enthusiasm for the more than 500-year tradition of Oxford University Press for excellence, innovation, and quality, as exemplified by the *Oxford Library of Psychology.*

Peter E. Nathan
Editor-in-Chief
Oxford Library of Psychology

ABOUT THE EDITORS

Jean Decety
Jean Decety, Ph.D., is Irving B. Harris Professor of Psychology and Psychiatry at the University of Chicago. He is the co-Director of the Brain Research Imaging Center at the University of Chicago Medical Center. He received his Ph.D. in Neurobiology from the University of Claude Bernard (Lyon, France) in 1989.

John T. Cacioppo
John T. Cacioppo, Ph.D., is the Tiffany and Margaret Blake Distinguished Service Professor and Director of the Center for Cognitive and Social Neuroscience Social Psychology Program at the University of Chicago. He received his Ph.D. in Social Psychology from Ohio State University in 1977.

CONTRIBUTORS

Reginald B. Adams, Jr.
Department of Psychology
The Pennsylvania State University
University Park, PA

Ralph Adolphs
Division of Humanities and Social
Sciences
California Institute of Technology
Pasadena, CA

David G. Amaral
Department of Psychiatry &
Behavioral Sciences
University of California
Davis, CA

Franco Amati
Cognitive Neuroimaging Laboratory
Montclair University
Montclair, NJ

Daniel L. Ames
Department of Psychology
Princeton University
Princeton, NJ

David M. Amodio
Department of Psychology and
Center for Neural Science
New York University
New York, NY

Craig A. Anderson
Department of Psychology
Iowa State University
Ames, IA

Sylvain Baillet
Departments of Neurology
and Biophysics
Froedtert & The Medical College of
Wisconsin
Milwaukee, WI

Kira Bailey
Department of Psychology
Iowa State University
Ames, IA

Aron K. Barbey
Cognitive Neuroscience Section
National Institute of Neurological
Disorders and Stroke
Bethesda, MD
Department of Psychology
Georgetown University
Washington, DC

John A. Bargh
Department of Psychology
Yale University
New Haven, CT

Simon Baron-Cohen
Department of Psychiatry
University of Cambridge
Cambridge, UK

Joseph W. Barter
Genes, Cognition, and
Psychosis Program
National Institute of
Mental Health
Bethesda, MD

Bruce D. Bartholow
Department of
Psychological Sciences
University of Missouri
Columbia, MO

Melissa D. Bauman
Department of Psychiatry &
Behavioral Sciences
University of California
Davis, CA

Janelle Beadle
Department of Neurology and Program
of Neuroscience
University of Iowa
Iowa City, IA

Jennifer S. Beer
Department of Psychology
University of Texas at Austin
Austin, TX

Pascal Belin
Voice Neurocognition Laboratory
Institute of Neuroscience and Psychology
University of Glasgow
Glasgow, UK

Matthew K. Belmonte
National Brain Research Center
Manesar, India

Gary G. Berntson
Department of Psychology
Ohio State University
Columbus, OH

Kent Berridge
Department of Psychology
University of Michigan
Ann Arbor, MI

Sylvie Berthoz
Inserm U669 &
Institut Mutualiste Montsouris
Paris, France

Meghana Bhatt
City of Hope
Duarte, CA

Wendy Birmingham
Department of Psychology & Health
Psychology Program
University of Utah
Salt Lake City, UT

James Blair
Department of Health &
Human Services
National Institute of Mental Health
Bethesda, MD

Sarah-Jayne Blakemore
Royal Society University Research Fellow
UCL Institute of Cognitive Neuroscience
London, UK

Eliza Bliss-Moreau
Department of Psychiatry & Behavioral
Sciences
University of California
Davis, CA

Jos A. Bosch
School of Sport and Exercise Sciences
University of Birmingham, UK
Mannheim Institute of Public
Health, Social and Preventive
Medicine (MIPH)
University of Heidelberg, Germany

Victoria Burns
School of Sport and Exercise Sciences
University of Birmingham
UK

John T. Cacioppo
Department of Psychology
University of Chicago
Chicago, IL

Colin F. Camerer
Division of Humanities and Social Sciences
California Institute of Technology
Pasadena, CA

McKenzie Carlisle
Department of Psychology &
Health Psychology Program
University of Utah
Salt Lake City, UT

Laura L. Carstensen
Department of Psychology
Stanford University
Stanford, CA

C. Sue Carter
Department of Psychiatry
University of Illinois at Chicago
Chicago, IL

Bhismadev Chakrabarti
School of Psychology and Clinical
Language Sciences
University of Reading
Reading, UK

Thierry Chaminade
CNRS and Aix-Marseille University
Marseille, France

Joan Y. Chiao
Department of Psychology
Northwestern University
Chicago, IL

Markus Christen
Institute of Biomedical Ethics
University of Zurich
Switzerland

James A. Coan
Department of Psychology
University of Virginia
Charlottesville, VA

Paul T. Costa, Jr.
Laboratory of Personality and Cognition
National Institute on Aging
Baltimore, MD

William A. Cunningham
Department of Psychology
Ohio State University
Columbus, OH

Paul W. Czoty
Department of Physiology &
Pharmacology
Wake Forest University School of Medicine
Winston-Salem, NC

Ricardo de Oliveira-Souza
Cognitive and Behavioral
Neuroscience Unit
Institute D'Or for Research and Education
Rio de Janeiro, Brazil

Frans B. M. de Waal
Living Links Center, Yerkes National
Primate Research Center and
Department of Psychology
Emory University
Atlanta, GA

Jean Decety
Department of Psychology and
Department of Psychiatry and Behavioral
Neuroscience
University of Chicago
Chicago, IL

Mauricio R. Delgado
Department of Psychology
Rutgers University
Newark, NJ

Kathryn E. Demos
Department of Psychological
and Brain Sciences
Dartmouth College
Hanover, NH

Sally S. Dickerson
Department of Psychology
and Social Behavior
University of California Irvine
Irvine, CA

Cheryl L. Dickter
Department of Psychology
College of William and Mary
Williamsburg, VA

Robin Dunbar
Institute of Cognitive &
Evolutionary Anthropology
University of Oxford
Oxford, UK

Jiska Eelen
Department of Psychology
Katholieke Universiteit Leuven
Belgium

Naomi I. Eisenberger
Department of Psychology
University of California
Los Angeles
Los Angeles, CA

Christopher G. Engeland
Center for Wound Healing and
Tissue RegenerationUniversity of
Illinois at Chicago
Chicago, IL

Martha J. Farah
Center for Cognitive Neuroscience
University of Pennsylvania
Philadelphia, PA

Susan T. Fiske
Department of Psychology
Princeton University
Princeton, NJ

Nathan A. Fox
Department of Human Development
University of Maryland
College Park, MD

Hiroki Fukui
Department of Forensic
Psychiatry
National Center of Neurology
and Psychiatry
Tokyo, Japan

Valeria Gazzola
Department of Neuroscience
University Medical Center
Groningen
Groningen, the Netherlands

Andrea L. Glenn
Department of Psychology
University of Pennsylvania
Philadelphia, PA

Marie Gomot
Inserm U930
Université François Rabelais de Tours
Tours, France

Jean-Philippe Gouin
Department of Psychology
Ohio State University
Columbus, OH

Jordan Grafman
Traumatic Brain Injury
Research Laboratory
Kessler Foundation
West Orange, NJ

Tara L. Gruenewald
Department of Medicine/Geriatrics
University of California Los Angeles
Los Angeles, CA

Ingrid Johnsen Haas
Department of Psychology
Ohio State University
Columbus, OH

Jonathan G. Hakun
Department of Psychology
Michigan State University
East Lansing, MI

Liisa V. Hantsoo
Department of Psychology
Ohio State University
Columbus, OH

Louise C. Hawkley
Department of Psychology
University of Chicago
Chicago, IL

Todd F. Heatherton
Department of Psychological
and Brain Sciences
Dartmouth College
Hanover, NH

Rachel S. Herz
Department of Psychiatry
and Human Behavior
Brown University
Providence, RI

Catherine A. Hynes
School of Psychology
University of Queensland
Brisbane, Australia

Marco Iacoboni
David Geffen School of Medicine
University of California
Los Angeles
Los Angeles, CA

Tiffany A. Ito
Department of Psychology and
Neuroscience
University of Colorado
Boulder, CO

Andrew Jahn
Department of Psychological
and Brain Sciences
Indiana University Bloomington, IN

Vanessa Janowski
Division of Humanities and
Social Sciences
California Institute of Technology
Pasadena, CA

Yoko Kamio
Department of Child & Adolescent
Mental Health
National Center of Neurology
and Psychiatry
Tokyo, Japan

Ina Maria Kaufmann
University Research Priority Program
Ethics
University of Zurich
Zurich, Switzerland

Mitsuo Kawato
ATR Brain Information
Communication
Research Laboratory Group
Kyoto, Japan

Julian Paul Keenan
Cognitive Neuroimaging Laboratory
Montclair University
Montclair, NJ

Margaret E. Kemeny
Department of Psychiatry
University of California
San Francisco
San Francisco, CA

Christian Keysers
Netherlands Institute for Neuroscience
Royal Netherlands Academy
of Arts and Sciences
Amsterdam, the Netherlands

Janice K. Kiecolt-Glaser
Department of Psychiatry
Ohio State University College
of Medicine
Columbus, OH

Michael L. Kirwan
Department of Human
Development
University of Maryland
College Park, MD

Hedy Kober
Department of Psychiatry
Yale University
New Haven, CT

Patricia K. Kuhl
Institute for Learning & Brain Sciences
University of Washington
Seattle, WA

Daniel D. Langleben
Department of Psychiatry University of
Pennsylvania School of Medicine
Philadelphia, PA

Lauren A. Leotti
Department of Psychology
Rutgers University
Newark, NJ

Martin A. Lindquist
Department of Statistics
Columbia University
New York, NY

Michael V. Lombardo
Department of Psychiatry
University of Cambridge
Cambridge, UK

Christopher J. Machado
Department of Psychiatry &
Behavioral Sciences
University of California
Davis, CA

C. Neil Macrae
School of Psychology
University of Aberdeen
Scotland, UK

Marcus Maringer
Department of Psychology
University of Amsterdam
the Netherlands

Svenja Matusall
Chair of Science Studies
Eidgenössische Technische
Hochschule (ETH) Zurich
Zurich, Switzerland

Robert R. McCrae
809 Evesham St.
Baltimore, MD

Werner Mende
Berlin-Brandenburg Academy
of Sciences and Humanities
Berlin, Germany

Peter Mende-Siedlecki
Department of Psychology
Princeton University
Princeton, NJ

Jorge Moll
Cognitive and Behavioral Neuroscience Unit
Institute D'Or for Research and
Education
Rio de Janeiro, Brazil

Drake Morgan
Department of Psychiatry
University of Florida
Gainesville, FL

Ezequiel Morsella
Department of Psychology (SFSU)
and Neurology (UCSF) San Francisco
State University, and University of
California, San Francisco
San Francisco, CA

Michael A. Nader
Department of Physiology &
Pharmacology
Wake Forest University School of Medicine
Winston-Salem, NC

Anthony J. Nelson
Department of Psychology
The Pennsylvania State University
University Park, PA

Paula M. Niedenthal
Department of Psychology
CNRS and the University of
Clermont-Ferrand
Clermont-Ferrand, France

Greg J. Norman
Department of Psychology
University of Chicago
Chicago, IL

Howard C. Nusbaum
Department of Psychology
University of Chicago
Chicago, IL

Kevin N. Ochsner
Department of Psychology
Columbia University
New York, NY

Hanna Oh
Department of Engineering
The Cooper Union
New York, NY

Lisa A. Parr
Division of Psychiatry and
Behavioral Sciences
Yerkes National Primate Research Center
Altanta, GA

Tomáš Paus
The Rotman Research Institute
University of Toronto
Toronto, Ontario, Canada

Stephen W. Porges
Department of Psychiatry
University of Illinois at
Chicago
Chicago, IL

Lydia Pouga
Inserm U960
Cognitives Neurosciences Lab
Ecole Normale Supérieure
Paris, France

Stephanie D. Preston
Department of Psychology
University of Michigan
Ann Arbor, MI

Joëlle Proust
Research
Institut Jean-Nicod
Paris, France

Susanne Quadflieg
Department of Psychology
University of Louvain
Belgium

Adrian Raine
Department of Criminology,
Psychiatry, and Psychology
University of Pennsylvania
Philadelphia, PA

Kyle G. Ratner
Department of Psychology
New York University
New York, NY

Gregory R. Samanez-Larkin
Department of Psychology
Stanford University
Stanford, CA

David Seelig
Department of Neuroscience
University of Pennsylvania
School of Medicine
Philadelphia, PA

Simone G. Shamay-Tsoory
Department of Psychology
University of Haifa
Israel

Tal Shany-Ur
Department of Neurology
University of California
San Francisco
San Francisco, CA

Shlomi Sher
Department of Psychology
University of California
San Diego, CA

Tania Singer
Department of Social Neuroscience
Max Planck Institute for Human
Cognitive and Brain Sciences
Stephanstraße
Leipzig, Germany

Timothy W. Smith
Department of Psychology &
Health Psychology Program
University of Utah
Salt Lake City, UT

Valerie E. Stone
School of Psychology
University of Queensland
Brisbane, Australia, and
Answers About Brain Injury, LLC
Golden, CO

Angelina R. Sutin
Laboratory of Personality
and Cognition
National Institute on Aging
Baltimore, MD

Shelley E. Taylor
Department of Psychology
University of California
Los Angeles, CA

Marc Thioux
Netherlands Institute for Neuroscience
Royal Netherlands Academy of
Arts and Sciences
Amsterdam, the Netherlands

Shozo Tobimatsu
Department of Clinical Neurophysiology
Graduate School of Medical Sciences
Kyushu University
Fukuoka, Japan

Alexander T. Todorov
Departments of Neurology and
Psychology
Princeton University
Princeton, NJ

Daniel Tranel
Department of Neurology and Psychology
University of Iowa
Iowa City, IA

Bert N. Uchino
Department of Psychology &
Health Psychology Program
University of Utah
Salt Lake City, UT

Tor D. Wager
Department of Psychology
Columbia University
New York, NY

Dylan D. Wagner
Department of Psychological and
Brain Sciences
Dartmouth College
Hanover, NH

Bridget M. Waller
Department of Psychology
University of Portsmouth
Portsmouth, UK

Kathleen Wermke
Center for Pre-Speech Development &
Developmental Disorders
University Würzburg
Berlin, Germany

Michele Wessa
Department of Cognitive &
Clinical Neuroscience
Central Institute of Mental Health
Mannheim, Germany

Robert West
Department of Psychology
Iowa State University
Ames, IA

Lauren K. White
Department of Human
Development
University of Maryland
College Park, MD

Bruno Wicker
Institut de Neurosciences
Cognitives de la Méditerrannée
CNRS, Université de
la méditerranée
Marseille, France

Piotr Winkielman
Department of Psychology
University of California
San Diego, CA

Roland Zahn
School of Psychological Sciences
University of Manchester
Manchester, UK

Leslie A. Zebrowitz
Department of Psychology
Brandeis University
Waltham, MA

Yi Zhang
Department of Psychology
Brandeis University
Waltham, MA

Caroline F. Zink
Genes, Cognition, and
Psychosis Program
National Institute of
Mental Health
Bethesda, MD

CONTENTS

PART 1

Foundational Principles and Methods

An Introduction to Social Neuroscience

John T. Cacioppo *and* Jean Decety

Abstract

Social neuroscience is the interdisciplinary field devoted to the study of neural, hormonal, cellular, and genetic mechanisms, and to the study of the associations and influences between social and biological levels of organization. The current *Handbook* represents the first comprehensive review of contemporary research in the field. This introductory chapter begins with a brief background on studies of the mind in the 20th century. It then discusses the mechanisms underlying complex behavior and the three principles of social neuroscience (i.e., multiple determinism, nonadditive determinism, and reciprocal determinism). An overview of the eight sections of this *Handbook* is presented.

Keywords: social neuroscience, brain mechanisms, complex behavior, determinism, social factors

Social species, by definition, create emergent organizations beyond the individual—structures ranging from dyads and families to groups and cultures. These emergent social structures evolved hand in hand with neural, hormonal, cellular, and genetic mechanisms to support them because the consequent social behaviors helped these organisms survive, reproduce, and care for offspring sufficiently long that they too reproduced, thereby ensuring their genetic legacy. Social neuroscience is the interdisciplinary field devoted to the study of these neural, hormonal, cellular, and genetic mechanisms, and to the study of the associations and influences between social and biological levels of organization. Humans are fundamentally a social species whose social environment has shaped our genes, brains, and bodies, and our biology has fundamentally shaped the social environments we have created. Social neuroscience, therefore, provides an overarching paradigm in which to investigate human

behavior and biology, and to determine where we as a species fit within a broader biological context. The current *Handbook* represents the first comprehensive review of contemporary research in the field.

Background

During much of the 20th century, the individual was treated as the fundamental unit of analysis, and the brain was treated as a solitary information-processing organ. This is an entirely understandable starting point. The brain, the organ of the mind, is housed deep within the cranial vault, where it is protected and isolated from others, as are the neural, hormonal, and genetic processes of interest to most biological scientists. Even cognition, emotion, and behavior can be thought of as beginning with the neurobiological events within individual organisms, events that can be isolated and examined. It should be no surprise, therefore, that the study of the mind by biological, behavioral, and cognitive scientists in the 20th century tended to focus on single organisms, organs, cells, intracellular processes, and genes.

Further contributing to this backdrop is the well-tested premise that investigation of the mechanisms upon which psychological operations and behavior are based is best addressed at as small a scale as possible. As Llinás (1989) noted:

> . . . the brain, as complex as it is, can only be understood from a cellular perspective. This perspective has been the cornerstone of neurosciences over the past 100 years (p. vii).

An implication drawn from this perspective is that the contributions of the social world to behavior and biology are largely irrelevant with respect to the basic development, structure, or processes of the brain and behavior, and, therefore, they are of little interest. To the extent that social factors were suspected of being relevant, their consideration was thought to be so complicated that they should be considered at some later date, if at all, once the basic mechanisms underlying human biology and behavior had been determined.

The approach of social scientists throughout most of the 20th century was no less focused than that of biologists. World wars, a great depression, and civil injustices made it amply clear that social and cultural forces were too important to address to await the full explication of cellular and molecular mechanisms. Moreover, from the perspective of the social sciences, social factors ranging from mother-infant attachment to culture defined and shaped who we were as a species. As a consequence, biological events and processes were routinely ignored in the social sciences.

Mechanisms Underlying Complex Behavior Exist at Multiple Levels of Organization

It is now recognized that cognitive, affective, and behavioral processes occur unconsciously, with only a subset of the end products reaching awareness (e.g., Wilson & Bar-Anan, 2008). Theoretical models have been developed that specify structures and processes of the mind, as have behavioral paradigms that permit the isolation of posited structures and processes for empirical analysis. These theoretical specifications and paradigms are critically important for understanding the biological basis of mental and behavioral processes because the brain and genes are too complex to identify their functions without theory to guide the process of empirical exploration and discovery. For instance, any given

behavior can be ambiguous as to its origins. One may eat because one is hungry, out of habit because it is mealtime, or as a social occasion in which the consumption of food is the norm. The identification of which genes, gene transcripts, proteins, cells, cell assemblies, brain regions, and neural networks are relevant to a given behavior is advanced by the empirical isolation of the underlying psychological component processes. The classic work on the neural substrates of classical conditioning, which proved so productive because behavioral paradigms for isolating specific forms of learning were so well specified, is a case in point.

For most of the 20th century, investigations of the brain mechanisms underlying these psychological processes were limited in animals to methods such as brain lesions, electrophysiological recording, and neurochemistry, and in humans to post-mortem examinations, observations of the occasional unfortunate individual who suffered trauma to or disorders of the brain, electroencephalography, and event-related brain potential recording in response to specific cognitive or behavioral tasks (Raichle, 2000; Sarter, Berntson, & Cacioppo, 1996). Developments in multimodal structural, hemodynamic, and electrophysiological brain imaging acquisition and analysis techniques; more sophisticated specifications and analyses of focal brain lesions; focused experimental manipulations of brain activity using transcranial magnetic stimulation and pharmacological agents; the integration of neuroimaging, psychophysiological, neuroendocrine, and genetic assessments; and emerging visualization and quantitative techniques that integrate anatomical and functional connectivity—in addition to information about neural processes at different scales of organization—are creating new opportunities for scientific investigations of the working human brain. Despite the increased sophistication and data yield from recent advances that make it possible to observe at various levels of analysis the operation of the working brain, an atheoretical exploration alone is not likely to yield many major discoveries of the working mind and behavior. It is simply too complex to understand the neural basis of specific mental processes without well-designed tasks that isolate those processes:

> . . . the task of functional brain imaging becomes clear: identify regions and their temporal relationships associated with the performance of a well-designed task. The brain instantiation of the task will emerge from an understanding of the elementary

operations performed within such a network (Raichle, 2000, p. 34).

Moreover, the emergent structures that characterize social species are not simply late irrelevant add-ons, but rather they were shaped by and shaped basic neural, hormonal, cellular, and genetic mechanisms, and they are important for normal mental and physical development and functioning. Across social species, individual members do not fare well when living solitary lives. Social isolation decreases the lifespan of the fruit fly; promotes the development of obesity and type 2 diabetes in mice; delays the positive effects of running on adult neurogenesis and increases the activation of the sympathoadrenomedullary response to acute stressors in rats; decreases the expression of genes regulating glucocorticoid response in the frontal cortex of piglets; decreases open field activity, increases basal cortisol concentrations, and decreases lymphocyte proliferation to mitogens in pigs; increases the 24-hour urinary catecholamines levels and evidence of oxidative stress in the aortic arch of the rabbit; increases the morning rise in cortisol in squirrel monkeys; and profoundly disrupts social development in rhesus monkeys. Humans, born to the longest period of total dependency of any species and dependent on conspecifics across the lifespan to survive and prosper, fare poorly both mentally and physically, especially when they *perceive* they are socially isolated. The mechanism suggested initially for the finding in humans was that isolated individuals engage in poorer health behaviors. This hypothesis is not generally supported by the data in humans and does not account for the effects of isolation in nonhuman social species (cf. Cacioppo & Hawkley, 2009).

It is estimated that hominids have walked the earth for the past 7 million years. *Homo sapiens* have evolved within approximately the last 1% of that period, and only the last 5% to 10% of this brief span has brought an array of human achievements that we now take for granted. Humans were not the first bipedal creatures or the first to use tools, but humans, apparently uniquely, contemplate the history of the earth, the reach of the universe, the origin of the species, the genetic blueprint of life, and the physical basis of their own unique mental existence. The attributes of *Homo sapiens* responsible for our success as a species are debatable, but the number of genes and the size of the human brain are themselves insufficient explanations (Cacioppo et al., 2007). Estimates among biologists a decade ago were that 100,000 genes were needed for the

cellular processes responsible for human social behavior, but humans have only about a quarter that number of genes. The prefrontal cortex is thought to be particularly important for critical behaviors such as executive function and working memory, yet the ratio of prefrontal to total cortical gray matter is no greater in humans than it is in nonhuman primates. Although humans may have more cortical neurons than most mammals, they have barely more than whales and elephants. The specialized capacities of humans may result from the increased number and processing capacity of synapses in the brain, greater cell-packing density, greater connectivity, and higher neural-conduction velocities, raising the brain's overall information-processing capacity. Other specialized capacities of humans range from hands with fingers and thumbs to theory of mind and language. Together, these properties support complex and coordinated collective enterprises.

Our brains are not solitary information processing devices any more than the cell phone is a solitary information-processing device. The cell phone has been designed to connect to other cell phones, and its very existence and function depends on connection with other such devices. Our brains have evolved to connect to other minds, and our remarkable accomplishments as a species reflect our collective ability, as instantiated in each individual brain, rather than our individual might.

Social neuroscience emerged in the early 1990s as a new interdisciplinary academic field devoted to understanding how biological systems implement social processes and behavior, capitalizing on biological concepts and methods to inform and refine theories of social processes and behavior, and using social and behavioral concepts and data to inform and refine theories of neural organization and function (Cacioppo & Berntson, 1992). Social neuroscience as an approach has faced skeptics representing two diametric positions in the social and biological sciences.

The first is the view that social neuroscience deals in dualistic reasoning:

> Historically, the question of the relation of the body to the mind was, at best, opaque; the mental attributes of humans were only vaguely related to the attributes of the brain. Despite the increase in our knowledge of brain morphology and function at the end of the nineteenth century and the beginning of the twentieth century, there was still a feeling among many scholars that the nature of

human reason might be related to some new and wonderful knowledge totally alien to that which is accessible through the scientific method (Llinás, 1989, p. vii).

The scientific study of the brain mechanisms underlying social processes and behavior is premised on the rejection of René Descartes' contention that because the body existed in time and space and the mind had no spatial dimension, the body and mind were made of completely different stuff. Instead, social neuroscientists have developed theoretical constructs and models to provide a means of understanding highly complex activity without needing to specify each individual action's simplest components, thereby providing an efficient means of describing the behavior of a complex system. Chemists who work with the periodic table on a daily basis use recipes rather than the periodic table to cook not because food preparation cannot be reduced to chemical expressions but because it is not cognitively efficient to do so. The scientist who uses theoretical constructs is no more a dualist than a chemist who uses both culinary and chemical levels of analysis to understand what it takes to develop fine cuisine.

A second set of skeptics has argued that any reductionist account of mental or behavioral phenomena falls outside the purview of the behavioral and social sciences (e.g., Coltheart, 2006; Kihlstrom, 2006). However, social neuroscience is *not* a substitute for the behavioral or social sciences, it is an interdisciplinary field that draws on these sciences as well as on the neurosciences to provide a single, integrative paradigm in which to investigate complex human behavior across levels of organization, from the molecular to the molar.

The field of social neuroscience is grounded in three simple principles (Cacioppo & Berntson, 1992). The first, the principle of *multiple determinism*, specifies that a target event at one level of organization can have multiple antecedents within or across levels of organization. On the biological level, for instance, researchers identified the contribution of individual differences in the endogenous opioid receptor system in drug use, whereas on the social level investigators have noted the important role of social context. Both operate, and our understanding of drug abuse is incomplete if either level is excluded. Similarly, immune functions were once considered to reflect specific and nonspecific physiological responses to pathogens or tissue damage. It is now clear that immune responses are heavily influenced by central nervous processes that are affected by

social interactions. It is clear that an understanding of immunocompetence will be inadequate in the absence of considerations of social and behavioral factors. The implication is that major advances in the neurosciences and the social sciences can result from increasing the scope of the analysis to include the contributions of factors and processes from both perspectives.

An important corollary to this principle is that the mapping between elements across levels of organization becomes more complex (e.g., many-to-many) as the number of intervening levels of organization increases. One implication is that the likelihood of complex and potentially obscure mappings increases as one skips levels of organization. This is one reason that going from the genotype to endophenotypes and from endophenotypes to phenotypes has proven to be more productive than going directly from the genotype to phenotype.

The second principle is of *nonadditive determinism*, which specifies that properties of the whole are not always readily predictable from the properties of the parts. Consider an illustrative study by Haber and Barchas (1984), who investigated the effects of amphetamine on primate behavior. The behavior of nonhuman primates was examined following the administration of amphetamine or placebo. No clear pattern emerged between the drug and placebo conditions until each primate's position in the social hierarchy was considered. When this social factor was taken into account, amphetamine was found to increase dominant behavior in primates high in the social hierarchy and to increase submissive behavior in primates low in the social hierarchy. The importance of this study derives from its demonstration of how the effects of physiological changes on social behavior can appear unreliable until the analysis is extended across levels of organization. A strictly physiological (or social) analysis, regardless of the sophistication of the measurement technology, may not have revealed the orderly relationship that existed.

The third principle is of *reciprocal determinism*, which specifies that there can be mutual influences between biological and social factors in determining behavior. For example, not only has the level of testosterone in nonhuman male primates been shown to promote sexual behavior, but the availability of receptive females influences the level of testosterone in nonhuman primates. Accordingly, comprehensive accounts of these behaviors cannot be achieved if the biological or the social level of organization is considered unnecessary or irrelevant.

Mounting evidence for the importance of the relationship between social events and biological events has prompted biological, cognitive, and social scientists to collaborate more systematically, with a common view that the understanding of mind and behavior could be enhanced by an integrative analysis that encompasses levels of organization ranging from culture to genes. Indeed, there has been a dramatic growth in social neuroscience over the past two decades. Subareas within the broad perspective of social neuroscience include computational social neuroscience, social cognitive neuroscience, social affective neuroscience, cultural neuroscience, neuroeconomics, social developmental neuroscience, and comparative social neuroscience. Work in each of these fields is represented in this *Handbook*.

One can ask whether social constructs, once reduced to their neural, hormonal, and genetic components, will be relegated to the junk pile of excess theoretical baggage. Such a question reflects the conflation of different levels of analysis and what has been called a category error (Ryle, 2000). The job of science is to align adjacent scientific fields to specify the bridging laws that link different levels of analysis (Cacioppo & Tassinary, 1990; Nagel, 1961), not to reduce and eliminate higher levels of analysis. Indeed, the constructs developed by behavioral and social scientists provide a means of understanding highly complex activity without needing to specify each individual action by its simplest components, thereby providing a cognitively efficient approach to describing complex systems. The efficiency of expression is not the only issue: The concepts defining fine cuisine are not part of the discipline of chemistry. The theoretical terms of the behavioral and social sciences are similarly valuable in relation to those of biology, but can be informed and refined through integration with theories and methods from the neurosciences. The field of social neuroscience, therefore, represents a new paradigm that embraces animal as well as human studies, patient as well as nonpatient studies, computational as well as empirical analyses, and neural as well as behavioral research.

Like any new field, social neuroscience faces problems and challenges that must be confronted and addressed. Doing so will make it possible to provide more comprehensive accounts for the basic structures, processes, and behaviors of humans and other complex social species. The purpose of this *Handbook of Social Neuroscience* is to stimulate just such interactions by providing a review of representative research in the field, acknowledging contemporary problems and challenges, and identifying fertile paradigms and areas of future inquiry.

Our goal in constituting this *Handbook* is to provide a representative rather than exhaustive coverage of the field. The *Handbook* nevertheless includes 67 chapters which are partitioned into eight related sections. The first section outlines a brief history and some of the most important foundational principles and methods underlying the field, laying the groundwork for the chapters to follow.

Social and emotional processes are closely intertwined in humans and other social species, and the second section focuses on different aspects of social motivation and emotion. Humans are a highly symbolic, meaning-making species, and our social environment contributed to our development and expansion of our cognitive capacities. The third section, therefore, focuses on processes of social cognition such as self-other distinctions, face perception, and impression formation. The fourth section addresses some of the same issues but moves from a focus on the effects of social stimuli on an individual's brain and biology—that is, intrapersonal processes—to interpersonal processes. The fifth section continues to scale up the level of organization to focus on group processes, while still focusing on the underlying neural, hormonal, cellular, and genetic mechanisms that influence and are influenced by them.

The final third of the *Handbook* moves from a focus on processes across levels of organization (intrapersonal to group) to a focus on problems and applications. The sixth section, for instance, deals with social influences on health and clinical syndromes, ranging from the health effects of social isolation to the social underpinnings of various psychopathologies. As complex social behavior comes under the scrutiny of the neurosciences, new insights are provided for addressing applied problems. The seventh section addresses illustrative applications that have benefitted from a social neuroscientific approach. The final section addresses a set of societal implications from the perspective of social neuroscience.

We would like to thank all of our colleagues who contributed to the *Handbook*. By providing an authoritative reference in the field of social neuroscience, we hope this volume proves useful to scholars and students and facilitates training, developments, and progress in the field.

References

Cacioppo, J. T., Amaral, D. G., Blanchard, J. J., Cameron, J. L., Sue Carter, C., Crews, D., et al. (2007). Social neuroscience: Progress and implications for mental health. *Perspectives on Psychological Science, 2*(2), 99–123.

Cacioppo, J. T. & Berntson, G. G. (1992). Social psychological contributions to the decade of the brain: Doctrine of multilevel analysis. *American Psychologist, 47*(8), 1019–1028.

Cacioppo, J. T. & Hawkley, L. C. (2009). Perceived social isolation and cognition. *Trends in Cognitive Sciences, 13*(10), 447–454.

Cacioppo, J. T. & Tassinary, L. G. (1990). Inferring psychological significance from physiological signals. *American Psychologist, 45*, 16–28.

Coltheart, M. (2006). What has functional neuroimaging told us about the mind (so far)? *Cortex, 42*, 323–331.

Haber, S. N. & Barchas, P. R. (1984). The regulatory effect of social rank on behavior after amphetamine administration. In P. R. Barchas (Ed.), *Social hierarchies: Essays toward a sociophysiological perspective*. Westport, CT: Greenwood Press

Kihlstrom, J. F. (2006). Does neuroscience constrain social-psychological theory? *Dialogue, 21*(16–17).

Llinás, R. R. (1989). *The biology of the brain: From neurons to networks*. New York: W.H. Freeman.

Nagel, E. (1961). The structure of science. *American Journal of Physics, 29*, 716.

Raichle, M. E. (2000). A brief history of human functional brain mapping. In A. W. Toga & J. C. Mazziotta (Eds.), *Brain mapping: The systems* (pp. 33–77). San Diego, CA: Academic Press.

Ryle, G. (2000). *The concept of mind*. Chicago, IL: Chicago University Press.

Sarter, M., Berntson, G. G., & Cacioppo, J. T. (1996). Brain imaging and cognitive neuroscience – Toward strong inference in attributing function to structure. *American Psychologist, 51*(1), 13–21.

Wilson, T. D. & Bar-Anan, Y. (2008). Psychology. The unseen mind. *Science, 321*(5892), 1046–1047.

The Emergence of Social Neuroscience as an Academic Discipline

Svenja Matusall, Ina Maria Kaufmann, *and* Markus Christen

Abstract

The term 'social neuroscience' combines two topics of scientific enquiry—the 'social' and the 'brain'—whose relation can be analyzed from two different perspectives: either from a broader historical one focusing on the emergence of modern brain research even before neuroscience was formed, or from a narrower one, based on a conceptual idea of how disciplines and research fields are characterized in contemporary science. This chapter analyzes the latter aspect, although it begins with some remarks on the former perspective. The analysis is made from the 'external' perspective of history and sociology of science intending to reconstruct origins, properties, and discourses that lead to today's understanding of social neuroscience as a disciplinary field.

Keywords: history of neuroscience, social brain, social neuroscience, academic discipline, bibliometry, impact analysis, science studies, interdisciplinarity, discipline building

The Social and the Brain—Some Basic Clarifications

The term "social neuroscience" combines two topics of scientific enquiry—the "social" and the "brain"—whose relation can be analyzed from two different perspectives: a broader historical one focusing on the emergence of modern brain research even before neuroscience was formed (the term "neuroscience" was first used in its modern sense by Ralph Gerhard in the late 1950s, Adelman & Smith, 2004), or from a narrower one, based on a conceptual idea of how disciplines and research fields are characterized in contemporary science. This chapter analyzes the latter aspect, although we begin with some remarks on the former perspective. Our analysis is made from the "external" perspective of history and sociology of science intending to reconstruct origins, properties, and discourses that lead to today's

understanding of social neuroscience as a disciplinary field.

The advent of modern brain research in the beginning of the 19th century was accompanied with a conceptual shift concerning the understanding of the brain's role in mediating human behavior. Whereas Cartesian dualism assigned to the brain the role of being an executor of the soul—the brain as the "organ of the soul" had been the dominant paradigm for about 150 years—the work of Franz Josef Gall (and others) established a new significance to the brain as the originator and elicitor of the various expressions of human nature (Hagner, 1997). This shift was not only the precondition for introducing many modern neuroscientific concepts (Clarke & Jacyna, 1987), it also made it in principle possible to relate brain functions to human behavior and its social consequences like criminality, immorality, or gender and racial differences. This assumption of a relation between brain and behavior was also the basis of 19th century phrenology. Thus, the "social brain" was already present in the 19th century—but not in the sense that the interplay between neural mechanisms and social behavior was a topic of research. Phrenologists like Gall and neuroanatomists like Theodor Meynert or Paul Flechsig only located cognitive and social properties in the brain. However, one cannot claim that the early social brain was just considered to be a placeholder for immovable human character traits that determine individual behavior in its social environment. There was indeed a debate on how social circumstances influence human character dispositions (e.g., in the philosophy of Karl Marx), although no systematic attempt to relate social entities with brain structures and their mutual development was made. Allowedly, in the late 19th century, a research tradition began with John Hughlings Jackson (cf. his *Croonian Lectures on Evolution and Dissolution of the Nervous System, 1884*) to study the evolution of the human brain and its capacities. This tradition, however—that included Walter Cannon, James Papez and Paul MacLean—was marginalized for the best part of the 20th century until it was rediscovered by evolutionary psychology in the 1980s, especially with the social brain hypothesis (see e.g., Brothers, 1990 or Dunbar, 1998). These scientists were not interested in social behavior themselves but their focus on evolutionary structures of the brain and/or emotions made them important predecessors for social neuroscience's conceptualizations of the brain.

In that sense, the "social" and the "brain" engaged in a complex relationship long before "social neuroscience" emerged in today's understanding. In particular, one has to distinguish between the "social brain" as an epistemic object—whose history is interwoven with the emergence of modern brain research and that is both a natural and a cultural object (Hagner, 2004)—and "social neuroscience" as an attempt to understand the mutual development and interplay of social and neuronal entities. Furthermore, it would be a mistake to describe the emergence of social neuroscience as a direct consequence of developments that lead to different notions of the social brain. These developments—now and then—have to be interpreted in a broader cultural and historical context. For example, the attempt of Constantin von Monakow—a leading figure in brain research in the early 20th century—to develop a brain-based theory of human conscience and morality (von Monakow, 1950) or

Kurt Goldstein's holistic notion of brain and organism (Goldstein, 1934/1995) cannot be interpreted without taking into account the fundamental trauma World War I caused among European intelligentsia (Harrington, 1996). Understanding the various attempts to explain social phenomena by neuronal functions requires the comprehension of the conditions and contexts under which scientific research took place.

Thus, analyzing the emergence of social neuroscience as an academic discipline goes hand in hand with describing the boundary conditions in which scientists today work and scientific fields develop. In particular, one has to take into account that the concept of "discipline" itself changes in time. Although the attributes of disciplines—journals, academic societies, courses, conference series, labs/departments, curriculae, and in particular the emergence of a more or less coherent body of knowledge related to a specific set of scientific questions and practices (Stichweh, 1992, 2001)—basically remain the same, the dynamics of their development have changed. Two examples may clarify this point: The increased competition for funding requires researchers to carve out territories in the scientific landscape and to promote their broader significance towards the public more pronouncedly. Furthermore, today's information technologies substantially ease the formation of journals and social organization of scientists. Thus, the number of scientific fields declaring themselves as disciplines increased substantially in the last few decades (Stichweh, 2003).

This brief portrait of social neuroscience cannot take into account all these aspects that influence the forming of an academic discipline in today's scientific system. In this contribution, we will use qualitative and quantitative (in particular: bibliometric) tools to sketch and critically examine the main definitions of the field given by its exponents, to describe the founding phase of social neuroscience (which we localize in the 1990s) and to present its differentiation and impact on other fields in this decade. Methodological issues are described in the appendix.

"Social Neuroscience" and the Search for Explanatory Connections between Biological and Social Entities

Social neuroscience today holds many attributes of a discipline—i.e., journals, academic societies, courses, conference series, and labs/research groups (see below). Besides these structural attributes, the commitment on a specific set of scientific questions and (to a lesser degree) methods, that allow the growth of a coherent body of knowledge (although it will certainly also contain competing hypotheses) is crucial for the emergence of a discipline. This commitment is usually formalized in a definition of the field and the debate about this definition is an inherent part of the process of discipline formation. Handbooks—such as this inaugural handbook of social neuroscience—play a major role in this "stabilization" of the definition of a discipline.

In this section, we first clarify ways of attributing the term social to different sets of entities; second, we list programmatic definitions of social neuroscience (or branches of social neuroscience) given by exponents of the field in review papers, introductions to textbooks, and journal editorials; and third, we discuss these definitions critically. One has to be aware that these definitions reflect the spectrum of legitimate research questions and the setting of priorities, i.e., broader definitions (as given in this handbook) leave space for more "branches" within social neuroscience. Furthermore, the set of questions and methods considered as characteristic for social neuroscience is by no means uncontested within the field at this point. The ongoing debates on these issues indicate that social neuroscience is not yet a stable discipline, but has the more diffuse character of being a disciplinary field in which various disciplinary traditions merge.

Social Entities

What are the classes of entities that should be called "social"? The possibilities span from including all species whose members are in a considerable relation over time (e.g., all species that exchange DNA), up to restricting the term for humans alone. In the history of science, all positions find their advocates—although in recent time a consensus emerged that also animals can be called "social species." From a historical point of view, one has to take into account that regarding the content of the term "social," different priorities can be set—and these priorities are related to dominating paradigms of societal organization. For example, the highly functional differentiation of social insect states has been taken as a positive example for societal organization (Geiger, 1933) as well as a reference point for satirical descriptions of society, exemplified in Bernard Mandeville's famous *The Fable of the Bees*. The remarkable observation that today's characterizations of the content of the term "social" often sets priorities on "positive" issues like cooperation, empathy, care, etc., probably reflects dominating

guiding principles of western societies. This indicates that the term "social" is tricky and its relation to biological entities is often contaminated with specific ideals of societal organization—an aspect that we cannot outline further at this place.

However, it is plausible to assume that possible ambiguities in the definition of social neuroscience are partly explained by differences in attributing the term "social" to biological species and (relatedly) the content of this term. The larger the class of species considered as being social species, the smaller is the discriminative power of the term social—and discussions on this issue are widespread in several disciplines. An example is the debate on "animal culture" in primatology (Laland & Galef, 2009). We will come back to this issue in the third part of this section.

Finally, we add that the search for explanatory connections between biological and social entities has found various occurrences in Western thinking for quite a few centuries before social neuroscience came into existence. Anthropologist Marshall Sahlins argues that

"... since Hobbes, at least, the competitive and acquisitive characteristics of Western man have been confounded with Nature, and the Nature thus fashioned in the human image has been in turn reapplied to the explanation of Western man. (...) Human society is natural, and natural societies are curiously human. Adam Smith produces a social version of Thomas Hobbes, Charles Darwin a naturalized version of Adam Smith; William Graham Sumner thereupon reinvents Darwin as society, and Edward O. Wilson reinvents Sumner as nature" (Sahlins, 1976, p. 93).

Since Darwin, he says, the motion of this pendulum has accelerated with new and more refined notions of humans as species and species as human in every decade. The most recent undertaking in that respect (before social neuroscience) was sociobiology with its focus on the relation between genes and social behavior beginning in the 1940s. The critical appraisal of sociobiology showed some limitations of the scope on social entities from the vantage point of evolution, i.e., natural selection, adaptation, and fitness. This perspective made it difficult for social sciences and humanities to take part in this endeavor that called itself "integrative," since this focus on biology may not be very helpful for explaining complex cultural, social, or philosophical questions. However, there are ways of thinking about human social behavior, taking into account evolutionary perspectives without taking biology or "nature" as the basis of human developments. The concepts of "Evolution in Four Dimensions" (Jablonka & Lamb, 2005) or the dual inheritance model (e.g., Tomasello, 1999) both consider the reciprocity of human-made environments and evolution. The concept of evolution in four dimensions argues that next to the genetic inheritance system, three more dimensions and the interactions between all dimensions are crucial for human evolution: the epigenetic, the behavioral, and the symbolic inheritance systems. The dual inheritance model argues that to live culturally is a biological, inherited capacity. In the course of evolution, human-shaped culture again influenced biological evolution by shaping the environment humans had to adapt themselves to (Rose & Rose, 2009). It would be worthwhile but beyond the scope of this contribution to investigate parallels in the current acknowledgement of social neuroscience with the earlier discussions on the relevance of sociobiology and other attempts in order to understand social behavior.

Proposed Definitions

The term *social neuroscience* was coined in 1992 by John Cacioppo and Gary Bernston. In their paper on social psychology's contribution to the decade of the brain, they sketch programmatic principles for understanding mental and behavioral phenomena and their underlying (neuro-)biological processes, called "Doctrine of Multilevel Analysis." They claim that although the brain is the essential component of social beings, the nature of brain, behavior, and society is too complex to be reduced merely to neural processes and that theories of social behavior require the consideration of both social and biological levels of organization. The examples they use in their argumentation (emerging e.g., from behavioral genetics, drug abuse research, and cancer research) demonstrate that the term "social" includes also nonhuman social species. Moreover, the understanding of these phenomena indeed requires a "multilevel integrative analysis," i.e., the integration of knowledge and theories gained both about the elements on each structural level (by its associated discipline) and about the relational features of these elements *across* the levels. This multilevel analysis should follow the principles of multiple determinism (one event may have multiple causes on different levels), nonadditive determinism (the whole may be different from the sum of its parts), and reciprocal determinism (mutual influences between factors on different

levels) to take into account the complexities of the phenomena studied. Both neuroscience and social psychology should benefit from cooperation in developing a more general psychological theory (pp. 1026–7). Thus, the project of social neuroscience is described as a cooperative project between researchers emerging from two different scientific disciplines (social psychology and neuroscience) in order to avoid the pitfalls of reductionism—an aspect, that is again emphasized in their 2005 textbook ("the broader the collaboration between different disciplines, the better the understanding of mind and behavior," p. xiii).

Coming from a different research tradition and almost a decade later, Kevin Ochsner and Matthew Lieberman (2001) use the term "social cognitive neuroscience" for describing an interdisciplinary approach integrating data from three levels of analysis: the *social level*, characterized by the experience and behavior of motivated people in personally relevant contexts; the *cognitive level*, characterized by information processing mechanisms underlying phenomena on the social level; and the *neural level*, on which those brain systems are analyzed, that instantiate the processes on the cognitive level. However, their emphasis is on the *cognitive* level, since social psychology and cognitive neuroscience both are concerned with describing psychological processes in terms of information processing, and the emphasis regarding the biological basis is on the *neural* level. In this way, compared to the former proposal of Cacioppo and Bernston, they have a narrower view of the field, also by setting their focus on *human* social behavior—a specification that is reflected by their term *social cognitive neuroscience*, which would only be a branch of social neuroscience defined according to Cacioppo and Bernston. In his historical overview of social cognitive neuroscience, Ochsner (2007) himself argues that this research field is distinct from social neuroscience, focusing on human social cognition, while social neuroscience integrated approaches linking social variables to psychophysiological, endocrine, and immunological parameters both in humans and in animals.

We add three additional short proposals made in the last few years for defining social neuroscience: First, in the editorial of the launching issue of *Social Neuroscience*—one of the two journals of the field—it is stated,

"social neuroscience may be broadly defined as the exploration of the neurological underpinnings of the processes traditionally examined by, but not limited to, social psychology" (Decety & Keenan, 2006, p. 1).

Thus, they clarify their disciplinary counterpart although indicating an openness concerning the research traditions dealing with "the social." Second, Eddy Harmon-Jones and Piotr Winkielman (2007) define social neuroscience as

"an integrative field that examines how nervous (. . .), endocrine and immune systems are involved in socio-cultural processes. Social neuroscience is nondualist in its view of humans, yet it is also nonreductionistic and emphasizes the importance of understanding how the brain and body influence social processes as well as how social processes influence the brain and body. In other words, social neuroscience is a comprehensive attempt to understand mechanisms that underlie social behavior by combining biological and social approaches" (p. 4).

Third, in 2005, a workshop supported by National Institute of Mental Health brought together a group of researchers in order to discuss the scope and the future of social neuroscience (Cacioppo et al., 2007). The workshop outlined the "epistemic frame" in which social neuroscience should operate: "constitutive reductionism, a systematic approach to investigating the parts to better understand the whole" (p. 101). Thus, social neuroscience should also aim to find the "bridging principles" (following the terminology of Nagel, 1961) between the organizational levels used to describe and explain social behavior. In the workshop, the following topics were identified as "most active areas of research" within social neuroscience: brain-imaging studies in normal children and adults; animal models of social behavior; studies of stroke patients; imaging studies of psychiatric patients; and research on social determinants of peripheral neural, neuroendocrine, and immunological processes. Studies in these fields should give insight, e.g., into developmental processes, psychopathologies, the role of hormones, and of social contexts on social behavior, group processes, and the evolution of the social brain.

This short overview demonstrates that social neuroscience has the potential to include a large number of research topics, which can be classified along three classes of levels of analysis: the social, the cognitive, and the biological. In each class, many levels of organization can be distinguished, yet the questions about which levels are present, which are relevant, and what are the bridging principles between those, constitute one major scientific challenge for social neuroscience. In the following, we present only a selection of research topics proposed in the literature.

First, on the social level, Todorov, Harris, and Fiske (2006) claim the existence of a "core social motive" that belongs to a social group. From this motive, the cognitive motives "understanding" and "controlling" as well as the affective motives "self-enhancing" and "trusting" would emerge (p. 78). Another important research topic is the individual or a group of individuals being in a social world (Lieberman, 2007). It is claimed that individuals aim to create a "coherent" social world, requiring the coordination of activities with those around us, the use of feedback from others to understand ourselves, and the development of self-theories and attitudes towards social groups (p. 270–1). Thus, several research topics are identified in order to understand interpersonal relationships—one of the main concerns of social neuroscience.

Second, on the cognitive level, social neuroscience is concerned with social perception and cognition; the latter requiring the ability to "understand others" and to "understand oneself." The research frame of understanding others includes theory of mind, empathy, cheating and bargaining, fairness, and justice. The research frame of understanding oneself includes recognizing oneself (through the lens of others), reflecting oneself, self-knowledge, and self-concept. Other research topics on the cognitive level are self-regulation (intentional and unintentional, emotion processing, motivation, attitudes, stereotypes, and prejudices) (for overviews see e.g., Liebermann, 2007; Todorov et al., 2006; Blakemore, Winston, & Frith, 2004).

Third, research on the biological level includes a variety of different topics. On the neural level, it tackles the identification of core processing (automatic vs. controlled; internally-focused vs. externally focused; Lieberman 2007, p. 261), the relations and interactions of different brain regions (e.g. prefrontal cortex and amygdala), the structure of brain regions, the localization of brain activities related to social behavior, or the impact of mirror neurons. Research on the genetic level may be particularly helpful for understanding psychiatric disorders. On the neuroendocrinological level the influence of hormones on social behavior, but also the influence of social context on hormone production, is investigated (Cacioppo et al., 2007, pp. 104–106).

The separation in levels is helpful to distinguish where the various research interests of social neuroscience come from and it may also be helpful to start an investigation at the level from which the question originates. The aim of social neuroscience, however, is to integrate all levels and thus to get a deeper and broader understanding of social behavior. To give two examples of cross-level research: In 1999, Michael Meaney and colleagues investigated the influence of maternal care and deprivation on stress in offspring and the nongenetic transmission of certain modes of behavior from one generation to another in rats (Francis et al., 1999). And four years later, Caspi et al. (2003) presented a long-term study investigating the gene-environment interaction in depression. As Blakemore et al. observed, social neuroscience does not avoid the classic nature-nurture debate (Blakemore et al., 2006, pp. 219–20). With its methods and concepts this field may overcome the assumed bias between these two poles of Western thought.

After reviewing these programmatic papers, it remains still open whether social neuroscience will indeed reciprocally investigate behavior, interactions, and structures on the one hand and biological structures and functions on the other hand or whether it will set its priorities on the "biological" side and take neural, hormonal, and genetic aspects as pivot points for its investigations. There are indeed very different questions that can be asked within social neuroscience. Furthermore, different opinions on the relevance of nonhuman research in social neuroscience can be observed—an aspect that also depends on the understanding of the term "social" and the willingness to integrate an evolutionary perspective when understanding social behavior, that goes along with enlarging the focus on other social species—in particular other primates.

Critical Appraisal

We focus our critical appraisal of these self-definitions of social neuroscience on two noticeable aspects. First, the exponents of the field stress the importance of the fact that the interactions of social beings create "emergent" structures and processes, whose understanding requires the cooperation of different disciplines, whereas an "individualistic" approach focusing on the single organism (or brain) is not sufficient. This "integrative view"—a central point in the definition of social neuroscience along Cacioppo and Berntson—of social neuroscience is typical for a specific understanding of science that recently gained importance in several scientific fields, e.g., in the emergence of complexity theory in the late 1980s (Cowan, Pines, & Meltzer, 1994). It is based on a *topos* of modern science that understands nature

(and society) as a hierarchy of structures, whereas this hierarchical order results from the evolutionary dynamics that explain the natural history of the world (Bonner, 1988). Within this framework, the term "emergence" is prevalent, but often obscure in its function. Originally introduced by John Stuart Mill ("emergent properties" as an antonym of "resultant properties"), it gained popularity in evolutionary theories of the 1920s by offering an alternative in the dispute between mechanists and vitalists; but the concept was demystified by the critique of Ernest Nagel in the 1960s, turning it to a rather weak concept within the reductionism debate (Nagel, 1961). The concept of emergence regained interest first in the context of the mind-body problem in the 1970s and later in complexity theory in the 1980s. This rebound, however, does not mean that the difficult conceptual issues that go along with "emergent organizations" and the like have been solved (Bunge, 2003). From a theoretical point of view, the issues of epistemic, ontological, and methodological reductionism associated with (social) neuroscience are complex (for a detailed discussion see Bennett & Hacker, 2003).

In neuroscience, it is quite common to establish a new discipline as resulting from the equitable cooperation of existing ones (see the example of the Neuroscience Research Program, Swazey, 1992). However, whether this equality in terms of methodology and epistemic standards is theoretically sound and reflects the reality of scientific practice may be questionable. Phrases in titles of social neuroscience papers like "the neural basis of . . ." or "neural foundations of . . ." could imply that the epistemic order is not as equally as pictured in the above definitions and motivate the suspicion that the non-reductionist wording may be more declarative than descriptive. At least, the issues of the methodological and epistemic equality of the disciplines involved in the formation of social neuroscience and the various problems of reductionism that emerge with the "neurological underpinning" of social and cognitive entities require a detailed analysis.

Second, the epistemological question what "social" means in social neurosciences remains open. Currently, in neuroscience, the concept of "social" is a relatively static factor in experimentation (Cromby, 2007, p. 163), whereas in social sciences it is a highly contested term. Depending on what theory is referred to it can be anything from the sum of individual actions to power relations—factors that form a society. There is indeed a danger that the concept of a "society"—with its structures, constraints, inequalities, and possibilities—disappears, if inter-actions, emotions, actions, and behaviors are all located within neural structures of individuals or the evolutionary make-up of "social species." The methodological framework of social neuroscience is considerably (with the exception of genetic and hor-monal studies, that can include larger populations) limited to inter-individual interactions in small groups—although an enlarged scope of interest including cultural phenomena can be observed recently (Chiao, 2009). Currently, most of the enti-ties on the social level relevant for social neurosci-ence (e.g., "core social motives," "trust between individuals," "attitudes towards social groups") rep-resent only a minor fraction of possible entities on this level. Surely, methodological constraints explain the selection to some degree. But maybe it is not a coincidence that the investigation of social interac-tions via social structures or collective processes is replaced by the investigation of processes that take place within individuals at the same time when, in a broader societal setting, collectivist solutions have been replaced by more individual solutions (e.g., in welfare). Paul Rabinow (1999) described this development as the transformation towards a "biosociality"—social structures become less impor-tant while identities are more and more based on individual (i.e., genetic) attributes than on social or group attributes. The approach towards studying the social via communal genetic make-up or indi-viduals' brains is rather different from studying the external conditions for a social structure. In this approach, sociality becomes something innate and thus every normal individual is capable of behaving sociably. (Consequently, deviant behavior is defined by the lack sociality in individuals, e.g., in autism or psychopathy).

The Roots of Modern Social Neuroscience in the 1990s

The period of the emergence of social neuroscience was not the first time that human social behavior became a relevant issue in brain research (see above). However, if the growth of the annual fraction of neuroscientific publications using a social terminol-ogy relative to the whole body of neuroscientific publication is taken as a first proxy for the scien-tific dynamic of the field, a steady and remarkable increase can be detected beginning in the early 1990s (Figure 2.1, for methodological issues see the appendix). This indicates a growing interest in the social brain in contemporary neuroscience and we take this observation (together with the qualitative

analysis of social neuroscience publications) as evi-dence for our hypothesis, that social neuroscience as an academic discipline emerged in the 1990s and stabilized in this decade. In this section, we first sketch changes in the "thought style" (Ludwik Fleck, 1979) during the last few decades within life sciences generally and neuroscience specifically that helped to prepare the ground for social neuroscience. Second, we identify main methodological and con-ceptual innovations that characterize the emerging social neuroscience. Third, we use a quantitative approach to identify high-impact papers of emerg-ing social neuroscience published between 1990 and 1999 and discuss their disciplinary roots and cross-disciplinary impact.

Changing Thought Styles

The bacteriologist and sociologist of science Ludwik Fleck introduces the term "thought style" to define the sum of factors that shape the way of thinking in a certain (scientific) community at a certain time (Fleck, 1979). Accordingly, Fleck defines a scien-tific fact

> "as a thought stylized conceptual relation which can be investigated from the point of view of history and from that of psychology, both individual and collective, but which cannot be substantively reconstructed in toto simply from these points of view" (p. 83).

Seen in this way, a scientific fact is what a given group perceives as true on the basis of scientific cog-nition at a given time. But it cannot be explained only by looking at this group. Other factors like social, economic, or political circumstances have to be taken into consideration, because they are inter-dependent with the scientific knowledge. A fact is built upon a common basis of preconditions and notions, which change over time. This is the pre-condition for development in scientific and other kinds of thinking.

To give an example: The nature-nurture debate can be seen as a debate oscillating between two thought styles regarding the causal role of biological respectively social entities for human behavior. This debate, which can be traced far back in Western intellectual history, became most prevalent with the rise of genetics in the second half of the 20th cen-tury and was severely fought over in psychology (Lewontin et al., 1984; Lewontin, 2000). Novel attempts regarding this discussion usually claim to "bridge the gap" but whether these are indeed a syn-thesis that can abstract from the subtle influences of

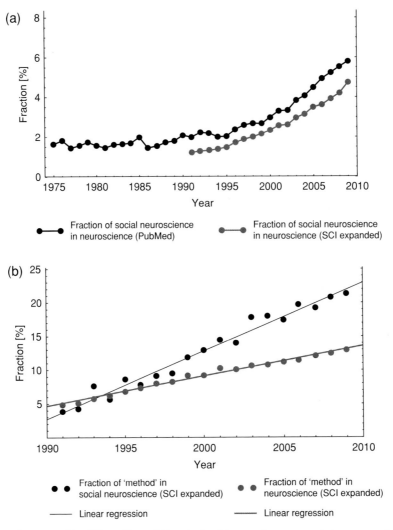

Fig. 2.1 Publication Dynamics of Social Neuroscience: a) Growth of social neuroscience papers relative to neuroscience papers measured in two different publication databases: A steady increase is identifiable beginning in the mid-1990s. b) Growth of "methodology papers" within social neuroscience compared to neuroscience in general (only measured based on SCI expanded). The slope of the linear approximation in former is 2.27 times larger than in latter, indicating an increased importance of non-invasive imaging methodologies for social neuroscience compared to neuroscience in general.

an intellectual climate remains open. Sociobiology and its follower, evolutionary psychology, attempted this synthesis (e.g., Barkow, Cosmides, & Tooby, 1992)—but at the same time discredited social science approaches towards human behavior (Rose & Rose, 2000). Thus, although the polarity of the nature-nurture debate probably has been outdated on the level of scientific explanations of some phenomena (e.g., in genetics the gene-environment interaction, see Fox Keller, 2008), it still may correctly describe thought styles that promote specific approaches towards the project of explaining human behavior and constrain others. The last few decades have seen an increased interest in enterprises that were looking for biological underpinnings of social

behavior and for including a notion of sociality (or at least environment) in investigations of human nature (e.g., epigenetics or plasticity of the brain)—indicating an assemblage of intra- and extra-scientific factors that was friendly to emerging social neuroscience. Within the broad scope of social neuroscience, some approaches attempt to overcome the bias between nature and nurture by focusing on epigenetics and gene-environment interaction (see above).

Yet, a change in thought styles could not only be observed in this broader cultural and scientific context. Also within brain research a series of conceptual shifts took place. In the mid-20th century, the information perspective (Aspray, 1985) became dominant in neuroscience: Processes in molecular biology, developmental biology, and neuroscience have been considered increasingly as processes in which information is "read," "transformed," "computed," or "stored" (Kay, 2000). This information perspective on biological processes was part of the cognitive turn within neuroscience and psychology (Gardner, 1985). The cognitive turn reflects a challenge to the prevailing behavioral model of human functioning, which had dismissed the need to examine interior mental processes and looked for lawful relationships in learning experiments. This new dominating thought style of cognition marginalized specific questions within neuroscience, in particular the role of emotions (LeDoux, 2000). This changed again during the 1980s, when (among other developments) the neuroanatomy of fear conditioning had been analyzed in animal models. In the 1990s, interests in neuroscience (and various other fields) were increasingly directed towards emotions, indicating the emergence of a new thought style that paved the ground for social neuroscience.

Innovations

A friendly intellectual climate both in neuroscience as well as in the broader context alone is not sufficient for a new discipline to emerge. Innovations both on the conceptual and the methodological and technological level (see e.g., Cambrosio, 2009; Rheinberger, 2007) are required to enable a sufficient number of scientists to start working on similar questions. For social neuroscience, at least three such innovations can be identified: the study of higher cognitive functions with imaging technologies; the combination of tools of cognitive neuroscience and neuroendocrinology with methods of behavioral research in animals, social psychology, and behavioral economics (e.g., games); and the discovery of mirror neurons in macaque monkeys.

We have to remember that other methodologies—in particular lesion research in animals and humans and studies about the biological underpinning of animal (social) behavior like affiliation and pair bonding—also play an important role in the course of the development of social neuroscience. As these methodologies and their associated research fields have historical origins that are (partly) many decades old (e.g., the fact that the use of full metal jacket bullets in the First World War made head-shot soldiers survive their injuries and allowed significant progress in lesion research in humans), it is difficult to assess, since when these research fields should be associated with the endeavor of social neuroscience.

These methodologies have existed for several decades without leading to the emergence of social neuroscience as a distinct disciplinary field. Hence, in the following, we will focus on the three mentioned innovations that are strongly connected with conceptualizing research in the framework of social neuroscience.

The importance of (functional) imaging technologies must be emphasized here. Imaging technologies (in particular fMRI and PET, but also EEG-based methods like event-related potentials) are a crucial tool in social neuroscience research—a point that is also confirmed by our bibliometric analysis: Although the fraction of papers with a vocabulary reflecting imaging methodologies generally increase within the neuroscience publication body, the annual increase of such publications within the social neuroscience publication body is considerably larger (Figure 2.1). Furthermore, this technology has been used in 62% of all non-review papers (95 out of 153) of the most often cited papers analyzed by us (see next section). Imaging technologies provide both the means for testing hypotheses and a catalyst for the emergence of new theories, although there are important constraints when using such technologies (Cacioppo et al., 2003; Logothetis, 2008). This enables social neurosciences to take the powerful position in contemporary public discourse they have (Hagner, 1996; Beaulieu, 2001, 2002), although it only is one of several methods used. Without doubt, using imaging technologies is demanding and requires diligence for each of the four stages of the process (experimental design, measurement, data analysis, data presentation; see Dumit, 2004). The recent debate on dealing with the selection bias may serve as an example for the methodological challenges associated with imaging (Miller, 2008; Abbott, 2009).

A second methodological innovation is the combination of methods emerging from genetics, neuroendocrinology, and neuroimaging with experimental paradigms drawn from social psychology and behavioral economics (e.g., experimental games). These studies are not limited to humans and demonstrate the extension of concepts like "fairness" usually restricted to human beings, to other social species (e.g., in Brosnan & De Waal, 2003; Tomasello & Warneken, 2006).

The discovery of mirror neurons in the frontal area F5 macaque monkeys (di Pellegrino et al., 1992; Rizzolatti, Fadiga, Gallese, & Fogassi, 1996) was a third important step towards conceptualizing and, in particular, popularizing the social brain and its capacities like theory of mind or empathy—two prominent topics in social neuroscience (for review see Jackson & Decety, 2004; Gallese, Keysers, & Rizzolatti, 2004; Iacoboni, 2009). In popular scientific publications, mirror neurons have become a prominent theme in explaining various aspects of human social behavior. In the scientific literature, however, mirror neurons are less predominant and recently, both the existence of mirror neurons in humans (Lingnau, Gesierich, & Caramazza, 2009) as well as their explanatory power for understanding social capacities has been increasingly criticized (e.g. Hickock, 2008; Jacob, 2008).

Pioneers

For a more detailed view on the developments in the 1990s, we performed a bibliometric analysis to identify the top 100 papers published between 1990 and 1999 that contained those terms of our social neuroscience vocabulary, for which the number of the associated papers showed the most significant increase

during that period (see appendix for further explanations). In this way, the 100 most highly cited papers that reflect the scientific production within the emerging social neurosciences have been identified. The majority of these papers were published in the late 1990s and originated from North America (mostly the U.S.) and the United Kingdom (Figure 2.2). Based on these quantitative results, social neuroscience can be identified as a scientific discipline emerging in the Anglo-Saxon academic culture that gets appreciation in the second half of the 1990s.

By performing an impact analysis, we identified the disciplinary origins and disciplinary appreciations of these papers within eight disciplinary clusters (Figure 2.3). The analysis reveals two aspects. First, regarding their origins, not only "neuroscience," but also "psychology" and "psychiatry" are important disciplinary origins (these three clusters include 73% of all entries). Compared to the decade 2000–2009, a much smaller fraction has been published in journals classified as "multidisciplinary sciences"

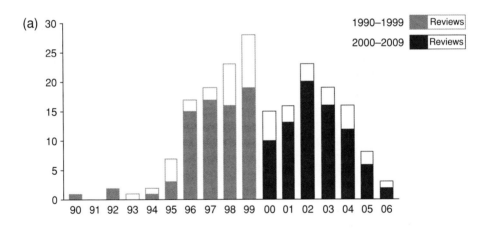

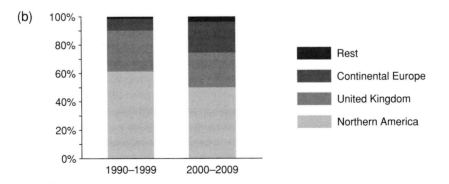

Fig. 2.2 Top 100 Papers in Terms of Citation of the Decades 1990–1999 and 2000–2009: a) The distribution of the total 200 most-cited papers in social neuroscience of the decades 1990–1999 and 2000–2009 clusters around 1996–2004: 87.5% of all papers were published in these years. 23 (first decade) resp. 29 (second decade) publications are classified as "review papers." b) The geographic origin of the top 100 papers of the first decade is more centered in the Anglo-Saxon academic culture (89.7%) compared to the second decade (74.3%).

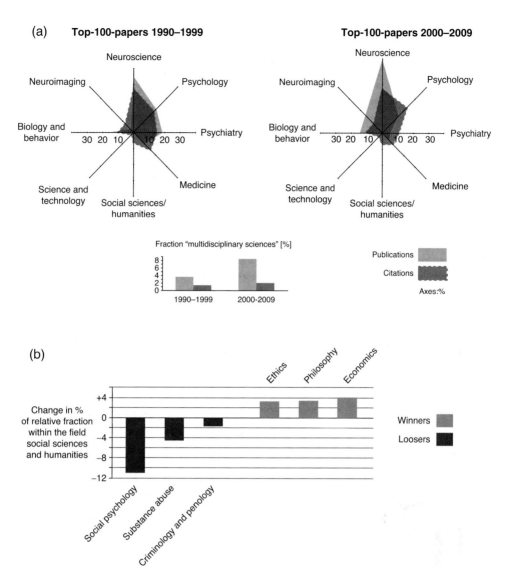

Fig. 2.3 Impact Analysis for Top 100 Papers of the Decades 1990–1999 and 2000–2009: a) The top 100 papers in social neuroscience of the second decade have a different impact profile than those of the first decade and show a larger net-transfer to other disciplinary clusters: 27.9% compared to 17.6%. This is partly explained by the larger fraction of papers from the second decade published in interdisciplinary journals. b) Top 3 winning and losing subject areas forming the cluster "social sciences and humanities" when comparing the appreciation of social neuroscience papers of the 1990s and the 2000s. The papers gained interest in core fields of social science and humanities, namely economics, philosophy, and ethics.

(in particular journals like *Science, Nature,* and *PNAS*). When looking at the distribution of the papers between the dominant journals (Figure 2.4; for the concept of "dominant journal" see appendix), the relevance of psychiatry as a field for publishing and thus promoting the emergence of the field is striking. Just as remarkable is the fact that none of these journals (*Biological Psychiatry, American Journal of Psychiatry, Neuropsychologia, Psychiatry Research—Neuroimaging*) is classified as dominant in the decade 2000 to 2009.

Second, regarding their impact, the analysis reveals a comparably low transfer to other clusters. The overlap of the distributions "publications" and "citations" along the eight axes for the papers emerging from the first decade is considerably larger compared to 2000–2009. This also results from the fact that the "disciplinary basis" (measured in terms of items originating from different disciplinary clusters) was larger in that time. Some impact of these papers on the cluster "social sciences and humanities" can be detected, although it is rather low and does not

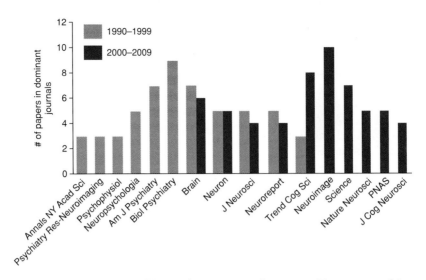

Fig. 2.4 Dominant Journals for Top 100 Papers of the Decades 1990–1999 and 2000–2009: Top 100 papers of the second decade are to a large degree published in other journals than those of the first decade. 55 (first decade) resp. 58 papers appeared in these dominant journals. The chart only includes those papers that define the category "dominant journal," that is, one cannot conclude that, for example, no top 100 paper of the first decade was published in *Science*.

increase much in the decade 2000–2009. However, within this cluster, some changes are remarkable. Regarding impact, the subject categories "social psychology" (the justification for attributing the subject category "social psychology" to the disciplinary cluster "social sciences and humanities" is given in the appendix) and (to a lesser degree) "substance abuse" and "criminology and penology" are considerably more important in the 1990s than later. This again reveals that questions related to psychiatric issues were more important in the 1990s than later. Interesting is that publications are surprisingly often cited in papers in the cluster "neuroimaging," indicating that the early papers may also have had some effect on developing this methodology.

The Establishment of Social Neuroscience as an Academic Discipline

In the years 2000 to 2009, social neuroscience obtained various attributes of a discipline: People started to use the term to describe their own work, departments created positions for social neuroscience and after a while, journals (*Social Neuroscience*, first issue: March 2006; and *Social Cognitive and Affective Neuroscience*, first issue: June 2006) and conferences using this label were formed. Researchers who worked rather independently on issues such stereotyping, empathy, emotion processing, or mentalizing in the 1990s, now began to meet. They first met in a coincidental manner before becoming more organized, meeting for workshops

and pre-conferences of meetings of both the Society for Personality and Social Psychology and the Cognitive Neuroscience Society. For example, in 2001, a first conference using the term "social cognitive neuroscience" took place in Los Angeles. In 2004, the conference "Social Neuroscience: People Thinking About People" accompanied the establishment of the University of Chicago Center for Cognitive and Social Neuroscience. Since 2007, the Social Affective Neuroscience Conference takes place annually. A dinner to discuss the challenges and opportunities in the interdisciplinary field of social neuroscience at the Society for Neuroscience meeting (Chicago, November 2009) resulted to meetings led by John Cacioppo and Jean Decety with social neuroscientists, psychologists, neuroscientists, and neurologists in Argentina, Chile, The Netherlands, Japan, China, Hong Kong, Singapore, South Korea, Australia, and New Zealand. It was noted that, as a social species, humans create emergent organizations beyond the individual—structures that range from dyads, families, and groups to cities, civilizations, and international alliances. These emergent structures evolved hand in hand with neural, hormonal, cellular, and genetic mechanisms to support them because the consequent social behaviors helped humans survive, reproduce, and care for offspring sufficiently long that they too survived to reproduce, thereby ensuring their genetic legacy. Social neuroscience was defined broadly as the interdisciplinary study of the neural, hormonal, cellular, and genetic mechanisms underlying the emergent structures that define social species. Thus, among the participants in these meetings were scientists who used a wide variety of methods in studies of animals as well as humans and patients as well as normal participants. The consensus also emerged that a Society for Social Neuroscience should be established to give scientists from diverse disciplines and perspectives the opportunity to meet, communicate with, and benefit from the work of each other. The international, interdisciplinary Society for Social Neuroscience (http://S4SN.org) was launched at the conclusion of these consultations in Auckland, New Zealand on January 20, 2010, and the inaugural meeting for the Society was specified as the day prior to the 2010 Society for Neuroscience meeting (San Diego, CA). In this section, we first characterize the field and its impact by qualitative and quantitative methods and discuss whether specific topics gain more cross-disciplinary attention than others. Second, we speculate about the effect of thematic differentiations within social neuroscience and their effect on the stability of this research field.

Topics and Impact

The large variety of topics addressed in this handbook itself is a portrait of social neuroscience demonstrating a broad spectrum of research topics. Using our approach for identifying the top 100 papers published 2000 and 2009, we see indeed changes regarding the origin and appreciation of these papers. Not surprisingly, most papers have been published in the early years of this decade. In respect of their geographical origin, the concentration in North America and the United Kingdom is less pronounced, although still clearly present (Figure 2.2). The transfer between the disciplinary clusters, however, is clearly stronger than in the 1990s (Figure 2.3): Almost two-thirds of the papers fall into the clusters "neuroscience" or "neuroimaging," whereas they show increased appreciation by psychology, psychiatry, medicine and, to a lesser degree, in social sciences and humanities. The number of papers that appeared in journals like *Science* and *Nature* (classified as "multidisciplinary sciences") doubled, which partly explains the increased cross-disciplinary transfer. Finally, the characteristics of the dominating journals also changed: Psychiatric journals are no longer represented, whereas the importance of imaging methodologies is emphasized by the fact that 10 of the top 100 papers appeared in *NeuroImage*.

The three winners in terms of citations within the disciplinary cluster "social sciences and humanities"

are the subject categories "economics," "philosophy," and "ethics." Thus, although the general impact within this cluster did not increase much compared to the 1990s (from 6.0% to 7.3%), social neuroscience obtained more appreciation in disciplines that are closer to the core of social sciences and humanities compared to the 1990s. In that sense it is justified to claim that social neuroscience gained attention within the fields whose knowledge and research traditions they want to use and influence. However, one has to take into account that this quantitative analysis cannot reveal whether this appreciation is positive or critical.

Finally, we broadened our impact analysis to four subjects (taking all 200 papers into account) that fall into the thematic range of social neuroscience and that received a comparable number of citations (Figure 2.5): papers on moral issues (moral decision making, moral emotions etc.), papers on psychopathy and sociopathy, papers on empathy and papers on trust, cooperation and punishment (i.e., attributes of social interactions). Their impact was calculated separately and compared to the mean impact of all 200 papers along the eight axes (black line). Regarding the first two issues, papers on psychopathy and sociopathy had the largest impact within psychiatry, whereas moral issues had most impact in social sciences and humanities—actually, these issues had the strongest impact within this cluster of all issues we analyzed. Regarding the second two issues, papers on empathy were by the majority cited within psychology, whereas papers of the group trust-cooperation-punishment had a highest appreciation within social sciences and humanities.

In summary, the quantitative impact analysis of the most highly cited papers that characterize the formation (1990s) and establishing (2000s) phases of social neuroscience reveals the following:

• The disciplinary basis of social neuroscience narrowed over time: being comparably strongly founded in neuroscience, psychology, and psychiatry (73% of all entries) in the 1990s, neuroscience (and neuroimaging) became dominant clusters (~60%) for publications in the 2000s.

• The interest in "anormal" social being (e.g., psychopaths) shifted to an interest in issues of "normal" social behavior.

• Although the impact in the disciplinary cluster "social sciences and humanities" is not that large, social neuroscience results gained more attention in core disciplines of this cluster.

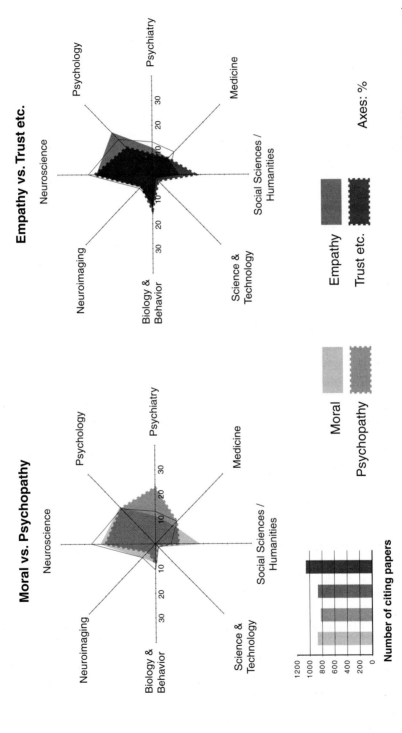

Fig. 2.5 Impact Analysis for Selected Topics of Social Neuroscience: Impact analysis for four selected topics "moral," "psychopathy/sociopathy," "empathy," and "trust, cooperation, punishment" that gained a similar total number of citations of all 200 papers along the eight disciplinary clusters. The black line in the graph indicates the total number of citing papers. The black line in the graph indicates the total number of cited papers.

We have to remind the limits of such quantitative approaches. First, we clarify that the search for the top 100 papers has been limited to the Science Citation Index (SCI) expanded database. Due to this constraint, the focus is on contributions with a (neuro-)scientific origin as defined by the Institute for Scientific Information (ISI), neglecting papers from journals classified as emerging from social sciences and humanities. This choice was made intentionally in order to assess the impact of social neuroscience papers with a "scientific" publication origin. We are aware that this does not generate a complete picture of a disciplinary field that intends to merge different disciplinary traditions. Second, although the ISI database is rather large, a well-known selection bias for English journals and conference proceedings distorts in particular the appreciation of social neuroscience papers in humanities, where language diversity is higher. Furthermore, citations in monographs—an important publication category in humanities—are not captured. The method thus probably underestimates the impact of social neuroscience papers in social science and humanities. Additionally, one may also include the impact of social neuroscience in grey literature and media reports, which was beyond the scope of this contribution. Third, an additional limitation is that the methodology does not assess the type of appreciation—i.e., whether the social neuroscience papers are cited with affirmative or critical intention. This aspect requires a qualitative approach.

Is Social Neuroscience a Stable Discipline?

We close this chapter by some considerations regarding the stability of social neuroscience as a discipline (or disciplinary field). This question emerges, as the domain of the "social" offers potentially enormous opportunities for research from a neuroscientific point of view—but also for the establishment of new and fruitful research questions that emerge in the boundary zones of classical disciplines. This huge reservoir for potential research questions results from both the vagueness and the restrictedness concerning the domain of social entities that are considered valuable research objects in social neuroscience. This may lead to a differentiation within social neuroscience that can already be observed: Neuroeconomics, neuromarketing, neurofinance, neuropedagogy, moral neuroscience and many more subfields have emerged in the last few years—a process of disciplinary differentiation that is not undisputed both in social neuroscience and in neuroscience in general.

This process raises two questions: First, one has to ask what effect such a "neuralization" of social research topics may have on the existing disciplines within social sciences: Will it influence these fields regarding methodology and epistemic standards? Will it require new curriculae—taking into account the fact that most students in social sciences are not trained to become social scientists but to become professionals in companies, governmental institutions, etc.? Today, the position of these established disciplines within social science towards social neuroscience often lies between ignoring and hostility—a third one is slowly emerging that is asking how traditional disciplines in the social sciences can benefit from neuroscientific knowledge.

Secondly, and this is important for social neuroscience itself: Is there a danger of fragmentation—given its general goal to understand mechanisms that underlie social behavior—by combining biological and social approaches? May this new attempt to understand social phenomena from a generalized perspective end up in a plethora of neuro-xxx-fields, each of which is struggling with its own problems regarding methodology? The alternative would be that social neuroscience helps to widen the perspectives of psychology, neuroscience, and other disciplines by integrating questions and methods from all of them. Given the historical experience, this process will probably go hand-in-hand with the emergence of new types of problems that are considered as relevant and it will require changes both regarding the training of new students and funding schemes that are more open for interdisciplinary research. In this way, the future development of social neuroscience is embedded in broader changes the university and research system currently undergoes.

We want to thank the editors for their critical remarks on preliminary versions and Michael Hagner for his helpful comments.

Appendix
Publication Quantification and Social Neuroscience Vocabulary Identification

The numbers of publications in neuroscience ("neuro"), in neuroscience methods ("method"), and in social neuroscience ("social") were estimated by identifying publications that include specific words or word stems in title or abstract within the databases SCI expanded (accessible via ISI Web of Knowledge) and PubMed. The Boolean search expression for the set "neuro" was: neuro* OR neural OR brain* OR amygdala OR cerebellum OR cortical OR cortex OR hippocampus (= NEURO). The "method" set included all noninvasive imaging technologies mentioned in Huesing, Jaencke, & Tag (2006), a reference study on impact assessment of neuroimaging (including TMS, although this method is used to stimulate neural tissue). The Boolean search expression for the set "method" was: NEURO AND ("brain imaging" OR "computer tomography" OR "functional magnetic resonance imaging" OR "functional MRI" OR fMRI OR "magnetic resonance imaging" OR MRI OR "positron emission tomography" OR PET OR SPECT OR Electroencephalography OR EEG OR Magnetoencephalography OR MEG OR "diffusion tensor tomography" OR "diffusion tensor imaging" OR "voxel-based morphometry" OR "deformation-based morphometry" OR "tensor-based morphometry" OR "near infrared spectroscopy" OR "transcranial magnetic stimulation" OR TMS) (= METHOD). The Boolean search expression for the set "social" was: NEURO AND (social* OR socio* OR cultura* OR emotion* OR econom*) (= SOCIAL). "Methods" papers within the set "social" were identified by the Boolean search expression NEURO AND METHOD AND SOCIAL. In all cases, the number of publications published in the time span of one year (from 01.01.XXXX to 31.12.XXXX) was evaluated. In PubMed, the time span was 1975–2008, in SCI expanded, the time span was 1991–2008, as before 1991, the entries in SCI expanded did not include the abstracts. The analysis was performed on September 11th 2009.

The social neuroscience vocabulary was identified by following the intuition that the number of social neuroscience publications with those expressions shows a considerable increase in the last two decades—i.e., the expressions refer to topics that gain interest when time elapsed. The vocabulary was constructed as follows. In the first step, by analyzing 20 review papers, books, or known high impact papers of social neuroscience, 57 expressions or word stems that may be typical for social neuroscience publications were identified, i.e., expression referring to topics (aggression, disgust, etc.) or methodologies (ultimatum game, TMS, etc.). In the second step, the distribution of logarithmized mean relative frequencies of publications containing an expression X within the sets "neuro" and "social" were evaluated. By defining a cut-off criterion (excluding the left and right tail of the distribution), expressions that generally appear very often or very rare within the sets "neuro" and "social" were excluded (12 expressions). In the third step, for the remaining expressions, the annual frequency of publications within the set "social" normalized with the total number of publications within "social" of the same year was evaluated in the database SCI expanded and the time span 1991–2008. Furthermore, a more sophisticated analysis was performed by identifying the frequency of these expressions in the sets Neuro in general, evaluating the distribution of frequencies and defining a cut-off criterion based on these distributions in order to identify very frequent terms. An example of such a Boolean expression is "aggression AND SOCIAL AND NEURO." This led to a time series showing the frequency of publications containing an expression X relative to all social neuroscience publications. In this way, the remaining 45 expression have been classified into three groups: 1) expressions that show a steady or stepwise increase in the 1990s (21 expressions), 2) expressions that show this increase between 2000 and 2009 (14 expressions), and 3) expressions whose frequency did not increase considerably in the last two decades (10 expressions). The class 1 expressions are: amygdala, antisocial, autis*, disgust, embarrassment, emotion regulation, empathy, executive function, fMRI/functional MRI/functional magnetic resonance imaging, guilt, justice, orbitofrontal cortex, personality, prefrontal cortex, psychopath*, social cognition, social learning, sociopath*, theory of mind, utilities (= SET1). The class 2 expressions are: agency, aggression, altruism, cognitive control, cooperation, dilemma, face*, fairness, mirror neuro*, moral*, neuroeconom*, shame,

TMS/transcranial magnetic stimulation, ultimatum game (=SET2). The analysis was performed on October 27th/28th 2008.

Identification of Top 100 Papers

The Top 100 Papers in terms of citation for the period 1990–1999 and 2000–2009 were identified as follows. Using the Boolean search expression NEURO AND SOCIAL AND SET1 resp. SET2 (the expressions in SET 1/SET2 were concatenated using OR), an ordered list of the 500 top cited papers of each group, was created. The analysis was performed on September 16th 2009. From these lists, three independent coders selected those papers classified as "social neuroscience papers"—in particular by excluding papers where not a single reference to neuroscience is made (in terms of methodology, topic, etc.), papers that exclusively refer to animal behavior (without any linkage to human social behavior), and papers whose main focus is in finding or understanding psychiatric diseases like depression, schizophrenia, etc. By this exclusion we set the focus on neuroscientific explanations of normal human social behavior. Papers on which the coders came to divergent conclusions were individually discussed and finally classified based on mutual agreement. The geographical origin of these papers was evaluated using the corresponding function of SCI expanded.

The dominant journals were evaluated as follows: For each group of papers, a list of journals sorted in descending order by the number of top 100 papers published in that journal was created. Those journals on top of the list that contained more than 50% of all publications were classified as "dominant," whereas the cut-off was made after those journals that had the same number of publications. For example, for the papers of the time span 2000–2009, three journals had 5 resp. 4 papers each. Up to the group of 5-paper journals, the total numbers of papers was 46. By including the three 4-paper journals, the total sum reached 58 and was thus above 50%.

Impact Analysis

In the SCI database, each publication is related to one or several ISI subject categories based on the journal the publication has been published in. This allows a so-called impact analysis (Christen, 2008) which compares pooled subject categories of a set of publications and the set of publications that cite former. In order to evaluate the impact of social neuroscience publications in other disciplines, we created eight so-called disciplinary clusters that pool the SCI subject categories in a way suitable for our analysis. These subject categories are (in parentheses are listed those ISI subject categories that include >90% of all entries for the citation analysis. They are sorted according to their contribution of all entries of a single disciplinary cluster. For the first subject category, its fraction of all entries in each cluster both for the 1990–1999 and 2000–2009 data is specified as well):

- **Neuroscience** (neuroscience: 100%/100%)
- **Neuroimaging** (neuroimaging: 52%/52%; radiology, nuclear medicine & medical imaging)
- **Biology & Behavior** (behavioral sciences: 54%/54%; physiology; biochemistry & molecular biology; biology; zoology; genetics & heredity)
- **Psychology** (psychology, experimental: 47%/40%; psychology; psychology, multidisciplinary; psychology, developmental, psychology, biological)
- **Psychiatry** (psychiatry: 79%/78%; psychology, clinical)

- **Medicine** (clinical neurology: 47%/48%; pharmacology & pharmacy; endocrinology & metabolism; pediatrics; rehabilitation; medicine, general & internal; ophthalmology; anesthesiology; geriatrics & gerontology; medicine, research & experimental; surgery; public, environmental & occupational health; gerontology; gastroenterology & hepatology; obstetrics & gynecology)
- **Social Sciences & Humanities** (psychology, social: 31%/20%; substance abuse; linguistics; social science, interdisciplinary; philosophy; law; economics; social sciences, biomedical; ethics; history & philosophy of sciences; criminology & penology; business; education, special; management; social issues; anthropology; sociology; nutrition & diethetics; communication; sport sciences; political sciences; medical ethics; education & educational research)
- **Science & Technology** (computer science & artificial intelligence: 41%/41%; engineering, electrical & electronic; food sciences & technology; computer science, theory & methods; engineering, biomedical; computer science, interdisciplinary applications; computer science & cybernetics; robotics; biophysics; automation & control systems)

Both for the top 100 papers of 1990–1999 and for 2000–2000, all of their subject categories as well as the subject categories of all papers that cite these top 100 papers (excluding self-citation) were evaluated using the corresponding functionality of the SCI database. All entries of the subject category "multidisciplinary sciences" were excluded and were displayed separately, as those entries refer to journals like *Science, Nature,* and *PNAS* that cannot be attributed to the clusters defined above. In the spider diagram (Figure 2.5), the axes have been arranged in order to express disciplinary closeness as optimal as possible (the circular sequence is: neuroscience—psychology—psychiatry—medicine—social science & humanities—science & technology—biology & behavior—neuroimaging). For each axis, the fraction of the pooled subject categories of each disciplinary cluster compared to all entries is shown. The net transfer is the sum of all negative (or positive) differences of the percentages of publication vs. citation for all eight clusters.

The impact analysis for the four specified topics was made using all 200 top cited papers of the time span 1990–2009. Those papers were attributed by three independent coders to 17 topics. Papers in which the coders came to divergent conclusions were individually discussed and finally classified based on mutual agreement. Then, for each topic, the number of citations the papers of a single topic was evaluated. We chose four topics with comparable numbers of citations for the impact analysis: "moral behavior/moral decision making/moral emotions" (6 papers, 880 citations); "psychopathology/sociopathology" (7 papers, 1059 citations); "empathy" (6 papers, 825 citations) and "trust/cooperation/punishment" (5 papers, 867 citations). The citation analysis was then performed analogously as described above.

Data collection: Svenja Matusall, Ina Maria Kaufmann, Markus Christen; data analysis: Markus Christen; writing: Svenja Matusall, Markus Christen

References

Abbott, A. (2009). Brain imaging skewed. *Nature, 458,* 1087.

Adelman, G. & Smith, B.H. (2004). *Encyclopedia of neuroscience,* 3rd ed. Amsterdam: Elsevier.

Aspray, W. (1985). The scientific conceptualization of information: A survey. *Annals of the History of Computing, 7*(2), 117–140.

Barkow, J., Cosmides, L., & Tooby, J. (eds.) (1992). *The adapted mind: Evolutionary psychology and the generation of culture.* Oxford: Oxford University Press.

Beaulieu, A. (2001). Voxels in the brain: Neuroscience, informatics and changing notions of objectivity. *Social Studies of Science, 31*(5), 635–680.

Beaulieu, A. (2002). Images are not the (only) truth: Brain mapping, visual knowledge, and iconoclasm. *Science, Technology, & Human Values, 27*(1), 53–86.

Bennett, M.R. & Hacker, P.M.S. (2003). *Philosophical foundations of neuroscience.* Malden, MA: Blackwell Publishing.

Blakemore, S.-J., Winston, J., & Frith, U. (2004). Social cognitive neuroscience: Where are we heading? *Trends in Cognitive Sciences, 8*(5), 216–222.

Bonner, J. T. (1988). *The evolution of complexity by means of natural selection.* Princeton: Princeton University Press.

Brosnan, S.F. & De Waal, F.B. (2003): Monkeys reject unequal pay. *Nature, 425,* 297–299.

Brothers, L. (1990). The social brain: A project for integrating primate behaviour and neurophysiology in a new domain. *Concepts Neuroscience, 1,* 27–251.

Bunge, M. (2003). *Emergence and convergence: Qualitative novelty and the unity of knowledge.* Toronto: University of Toronto Press.

Cacioppo, J., Berntson, G.G., Lorig, T.S., Norris, C.J., Rickett, E., & Nusbaum, H. (2003). Just because you're imaging the brain doesn't mean you can stop using your head: A primer and set of first principles. *Journal of Personality and Social Psychology, 85*(4), 650–661.

Cacioppo, J., Amaral, D., Blanchard, J., Cameron, J., Carter, C.S., Crews, D., et al. (2007). Social neuroscience: Progress and implications for mental health. *Perspectives on Psychological Science, 2,* 99–123.

Cacioppo, J. & Berntson, G. (1992). Social psychological contributions to the decade of the brain. Doctrine of multilevel analysis. *American Psychologist, 47*(8), 1019–1028.

Cacioppo, J. & Berntson, G. (eds.) (2005). *Social neuroscience. Key readings.* New York: Psychology Press.

Cambrosio, A. (2009). Decentering life. *BioSocieties, 4*(2–3), 318–321.

Caspi, A., Sugden, K., Moffitt, T.E., Taylor, A., Craig, I.W., Harrington, H., et al. (2003). Influence of life stress on depression: Moderation by a polymorphism in the 5-HTT gene. *Science, 301,* 386–389.

Chiao, J.Y. (ed.) (2009). Cultural neuroscience: Cultural influences on brain function. *Progress in Brain Research.* Amsterdam: Elsevier.

Christen, M. (2008). Varieties of publication patterns in neuroscience at the cognitive turn. *Journal of the History of the Neurosciences, 17,* 207–225.

Clarke, E. & Jacyna, L.S. (1987). *Nineteenth-century origins of neuroscientific concepts.* Berkeley: University of California Press.

Cowan, G.A., Pines, D., & Meltzer, D. (1994): *Complexity. metaphors, models, and reality.* Perseus Books: Cambridge.

Cromby, J. (2007). Integrating social science with neuroscience: Potentials and problems. *BioSocieties, 2,* 149–169.

Decety, J. & Keenan, J. (2006). Social neuroscience: A new journal. *Social Neuroscience, 1*(1), 1–4.

Dumit, J. (2004). *Picturing personhood: Brain scans and biomedical identity*. Princeton: Princeton University Press.

Dunbar, R. (1998). The social brain hypothesis. *Evolutionary Anthropology*, 6(5), 178–190.

Fleck, L. (1979). *The genesis and development of a scientific fact*. Chicago: University of Chicago Press (German Original 1935).

Francis, D., Diorio, J., Liu, D., & Meaney, M.J. (1999). Nongenomic transmission across generations of maternal behavior and stress responses in the rat. *Science*, 286, 1155–1158.

Fox Keller, E. (2008). Nature and the natural. *Biosocieties*, 3, 117–124.

Gallese, V., Keysers, C., & Rizzolatti, G. (2004). A unifying view of the basis of social cognition. *Trends in Cognitive Sciences*, 8(9), 396–403.

Gardner, H.E. (1985). *The mind's new science: A history of the cognitive revolution*. New York: Basic Books.

Geiger, T. (1933). *Soziologische Kritik der eugenischen Bewegung*. Berlin: Schoetz.

Goldstein, K. (1934). *Der Aufbau des Organismus. Einführung in die Biologie unter besonderer Berücksichtigung der Erfahrungen am kranken Menschen*. Frankfurt/Main: Fischer, 259–286. The organism: A holistic approach to biology derived from pathological data in man. New York: Zone Books.)

Hagner, M. (1996). Der Geist bei der Arbeit. Überlegungen zur visuellen Repräsentation cerebraler Prozese. Borck, C. (ed.): *Anatomien medizinischen Wissens. Medizin Macht Moleküle*. Frankfurt: Fischer.

Hagner, M. (1997). *Homo cerebralis. Der Wandel vom Seelenorgan zum Gehirn*. Berlin: Berlin Verlag. (English translation in preparation, Stanford University Press).

Hagner, M. (2004). *Geniale Gehirne. Zur Geschichte der Elitenhirnforschung*. Göttingen: Wallstein.

Harmon-Jones, E. & Winkielman, P. (2004) (ed.). *Social neuroscience. Integrating biological and psychological explanations of social behavior*. New York: Guilford Publishing.

Harrington, A. (1996). *Reenchanted science. Holism in German culture from Wilhelm II to Hitler*. Princeton: Princeton University Press.

Hickock, G. (2008). Eight problems for the mirror neuron theory of action understanding in monkeys and humans. *Journal of Cognitive Neuroscience*, 21(7), 1229–1243.

Huesing, B., Jaencke, L., & Tag, B. (2006). *Impact assessment of neuroimaging*. Zürich/Singen: Hochschulverlag ETH Zürich.

Hughlings Jackson, J. (1884): The Croonian lectures on evolution and dissolution of the nervous system. *The British Medical Journal*, 1(1213), 591–593.

Iacoboni, M. (2009). Imitation, empathy, and mirror neurons. *Annual Review of Psychology*, 60, 653–670.

Jablonka, E. & Lamb, M. (2005). *Evolution in four dimensions. Genetic, epigenetic, behavioral, and symbolic variation in the history of life*. Cambridge, MA: MIT Press.

Jacob, P. (2008): What do mirror neurons contribute to human social cognition? *Mind & Language*, 23(2), 190–223.

Jackson, P. & Decety, J. (2004). Motor cognition: A new paradigm to study self-other interactions. *Current Opinion in Neurobiology*, 14 (2), 259–263.

Kay, L.E. (2000) *Who wrote the book of life? A history of the genetic code*. Stanford: Stanford University Press.

Laland, K.N. & Galef, B.G. (2009): *The question of animal culture*. Cambridge, MA: Harvard University Press.

LeDoux, J.E. (2000). Emotion circuits in the brain. *Annual Review of Neuroscience*, 23, 155–184.

Lewontin, R., Rose, S., & Kamin, L. (1984). *Not in our genes: Biology, ideology, and human nature*. New York: Pantheon.

Lewontin, R. (2000). *The triple helix: Gene, organism, and environment*. Cambridge, MA: Harvard University Press.

Lieberman, M. (2007). Social cognitive neuroscience: A review of core processes. *Annual Review of Psychology*, 58, 259–289.

Lingnau, A., Gesierich, B., & Caramazza, A. (2009): Asymmetric fMRI adaptation reveals no evidence for mirror neurons in humans. *PNAS*, 106(24), 9925–9930.

Logothetis, N.K. (2008): What we can do and what we cannot do with fMRI. *Nature*, 453, 869–878.

Meaney, M.J. (2001). Nature, nurture, and the disunity of knowledge. *Annals of the New York Academy of Sciences*, 935, 50–61.

Miller, G. (2008). Growing pains for fMRI. *Science*, 320, 1412–1414.

Nagel, E. (1961); *The structure of science. Problems in the logic of scientific explanation*. London, Henley: Routledge & Kegan Paul.

Ochsner, K. (2007) Social cognitive neuroscience: Historical development, core principles, and future promise. A. Kruglanksi & E.T. Higgins. (Eds.) *Social psychology: A handbook of basic principles*. 2nd Ed. Guilford Press: New York, 39–66.

Ochsner, K. & Lieberman, M. (2001). The emergence of social cognitive neuroscience. *American Psychologist*, 56(9), 717–734.

di Pellegrino, G., Fadiga, L., Fogassi, L., Gallese, V., & Rizzolatti, G. (1992). Understanding motor events: A neurophysiological study. *Experimental Brain Research*, 91, 176–180.

Rabinow, P. (1999). Artificiality and enlightenment: From sociobiology to biosociality. In M. Biagioli (ed.), *The science studies reader*. New York: Routledge.

Rheinberger, H.-J. (2007): Wie werden aus Spuren Daten, und wie verhalten sich Daten zu Fakten? *Nach Feierabend. Zürcher Jahrbuch für Wissenschaftsgeschichte 3: Daten* (pp. 117–125). Berlin und Zürich: Diphanes.

Rizzolatti, G. Fadiga, L., Gallese, V. & Fogassi, L. (1996). Premotor cortex and the recognition of motor actions. *Cognitive Brain Research*, 3, 131–141.

Rose, H. & Rose, S. (eds.) (2000). *Alas, poor Darwin! Arguments against evolutionary psychology*. New York: Harmony Books.

Rose, H. & Rose, S. (2009). The changing face of human nature. *Daedalus*, Summer 2009, 7–20.

Sahlins, M. (1976): *The use and abuse of biology. An anthropological critique of sociobiology*. Ann Arbor: University of Michigan Press.

Stichweh, R. (1992). The sociology of scientific disciplines: On the genesis and stability of the disciplinary structure of modern science. *Science in Context*, 5, 3–15.

Stichweh, R. (2001). *History of scientific disciplines. International encyclopedia of the social and behavioral sciences*, Volume 20. Oxford: Elsevier, 13727–13731.

Stichweh, R. (2003). *Differentiation of scientific disciplines: Causes and consequences. Encyclopedia of life support systems*. Paris: UNESCO.

Swazey, J.P. (1992). Forging a neuroscience community: A brief history of the neurosciences research program. In: F. G. Worden, J. P. Swazey, & G. Adelman (eds.), *The neurosciences, paths of discovery* (pp. 103–120). Cambridge, MA: MIT Press.

Todorov, A., Harris, L.T., & Fiske S.F. (2006). Toward socially inspired social neuroscience. *Brain Research, 1079*, 76–85.

Tomasello, M. (1999). *The cultural origins of human cognition*. Cambridge, MA; Harvard University Press.

Tomasello, M. & Warneken, F. (2006). Altruistic helping in human infants and young chimpanzees. *Science, 311*, 1301–1303.

Von Monakow, C. (1950). *Gehirn und Gewissen: Psychobiologische Aufsätze*. Zurich: Conzett und Huber.

Evolutionary Basis of the Social Brain

Robin Dunbar

Abstract

Primates have unusually large brains for body size compared to all other vertebrates. Given the extraordinary cost of neural material, this raised a pressing question about why primates (in particular) should be willing to incur such high costs. This chapter begins by considering the various hypotheses aimed at addressing this question. It then discusses what social behavior can tell us about cognition and how cognition interfaces between brain and behavior.

Keywords: primates, brain size, social brain hypothesis, cognition, social behavior

Introduction

It is now three and a half decades since Jerison (1973) pointed out that primates have unusually large brains for body size compared to all other vertebrates. Given the extraordinary cost of neural material (the "expensive tissue hypothesis": Aiello & Wheeler, 1995; see also Mink, Blumenschine, & Adams, 1981; Kaufman, 2003; Isler & van Schaik, 2006; Karbowski, 2007), this raised a pressing question about why primates (in particular) should be willing to incur such high costs. Initial proposals inevitably focused on ecological correlates of brain size, generally speaking within taxonomic orders. Noting that frugivores have larger brains than folivores among both primates and insectivores (Harvey, Clutton-Brock, & Mace., 1980), many early analyses emphasized the cognitive demands of foraging, either through mental mapping (reflecting either the need to track ephemeral food sources such as fruiting trees or the increased home range size consequent on both

frugivory and larger body size) or through the demands of embedded foraging (extracting food from some kind of matrix) (Clutton-Brock & Harvey, 1980; Gibson, 1986). More recently, the role of innovations and tool use has been given rather more prominence (Reader & Laland, 2002; Lefebvre, Reader, & Sol, 2004), reflecting instrumental skills that seem to have direct implications for extinction risk, at least among birds (Sol, Timmermans & Lefebvre, 2002, 2005a,b; Sol, Székely, Liker, & Lefebvre, 2007; Shultz, Bradbury, Evans, Gregory & Blackburn, 2005). All of these emphasize the impact that enhanced cognitive abilities have on individual survival, thus influencing fitness directly.

However, an alternative suggestion was that the explanation for the unusually large brains of primates (in particular) lay in the fact that they seemed to differ from other mammals mainly in respect of social skills (Jolly, 1966; Humphrey, 1976; Kummer, 1982). This suggestion was later picked up in the form of the Machiavellian intelligence hypothesis proposed by Byrne & Whiten (1988). Unfortunately, perhaps, the term Machiavellian was taken by many to imply that primates behaved with human-like devious political intent, something that was never intended in the original proposal. As a result, subsequent explorations have tried to refocus this proposal by naming it the social brain hypothesis (Brothers, 1990; Barton & Dunbar, 1997; Dunbar, 1998). More recently still, a version of the innovations hypothesis has also surfaced in the social context as a consequence of the suggestion that innovations may be inherited through social learning as opposed to trial-and-error learning by individuals (Reader & Laland, 2002).

Meanwhile, neurobiologists have tended to emphasize ontogenetic explanations for large brain size. These have focused either on the developmental or energetic implications of diet (Martin, 1981; Hofman, 1983) or on longevity (Barrickman, Bastian, Isler, van Schaik, 2007) and the role of neurogenesis (Finlay & Darlington, 1995; Finlay, Darlington, & Nicastro, 2001). Large brains (and hence enhanced cognitive abilities) are viewed as being a by-product of basic biological processes (scaling effects of energy demand or the time available to grow a large brain). Finlay et al. (2001) make

this argument explicit in showing that brain volume is essentially a function of the number of neurogenic cycles that can be fitted into the time available for brain growth.

Figure 3.1 summarizes these various hypotheses, their inter-relationships, and how they influence fitness. The ontogenetic hypotheses differ from the ecological and social hypotheses in that, in general, they assume no functional consequences selecting for large brains; rather, large brains, and all that follows therefrom, is simply a by-product of changes elsewhere in the biological system—body size (with its implications for scaling effects on energy), gestation, or longevity (with their implications for neurogenesis). In contrast, all the ecological and social hypotheses assume that large brains are a consequence of selection for enhanced cognitive abilities. They differ in whether they view foraging (instrumental knowledge acquired by trial-and-error learning) or social skills as the crucial function of cognition that imposed the selection pressure for enhanced competencies, and in terms of whether they see food (survival and/or fertility) or predation risk (survival alone) as the rate-limiting factor in population dynamics. Most of these hypotheses focus on foraging skills, and thus food-finding as the limiting constraint, because ecologists traditionally tend to

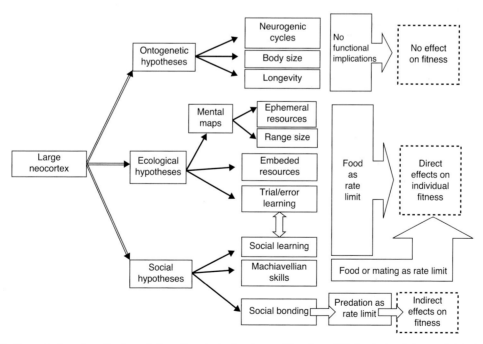

Fig. 3.1 Alternative hypotheses for the evolution of large brains in primates. Hypotheses differ in whether their central claim is about ontogeny, ecological or social processes, on whether they view food or predation as the rate-limiting process in population dynamics, and on whether they view the fitness benefits from large brains as being direct or indirect.

prioritize nutrient cycling as the critical factor that limits animal populations (see also Dunbar, Korstjens, & Lehmann, 2009).

Although the three social hypotheses (social learning, Machiavellian, and social brain *sensu stricto*) all count as forms of the social brain hypothesis, there is an important distinction between the Machiavellian and social learning hypotheses, on the one hand, and the social brain hypothesis *sensu stricto* on the other. The former assume that the fitness consequences of social skills arise directly at the level of the individual: Skills that allow others to be exploited or which facilitate acquisition of foraging skills or knowledge from other group members enhance the actor's fitness by allowing it either to gain advantages over other group members (the Machiavellian intelligence hypothesis) or to survive more effectively through improved foraging ability (social learning hypothesis). Enhanced social cognitive skills consequent on having a larger brain thus, once again, affect fitness directly by influencing an individual's chances of surviving and/or reproducing (the latter either through the effect that food has on fertility or through skills that allow an individual to outwit its opponents in the competition for resources or matings). In contrast, the social brain hypothesis *sensu stricto* focuses on a more complex process whereby social skills influence an individual's fitness only indirectly (Dunbar, 1998). Here, an individual's fitness is maximized by how well the group solves the problems that directly affect fitness, and this in turn is a consequence of how well bonded it is (this in turn being a consequence of the individual members' social cognitive skills). In this case, the functional explanation is a two-step process: some ecological benefit requires large, coherent social groups, and these in turn require enhanced social (and thus cognitive) skills. In this case, large brain size and/or enhanced cognitive abilities do not influence individual survival directly, but rather indirectly through an intermediate social cognitive goal (how well the group is bonded). The various explanations thus differ (1) in terms of whether they envisage any function at all for large brains, (2) whether the rate-limiting process is considered to be survival (longevity) or fertility, and hence whether the fitness-limiting function that has to be solved is food-finding or predation risk, (3) whether this ecological constraint is solved by individual trial-and-error learning or through some social process, and (4) whether the cognition involved is concerned directly or only indirectly with fitness.

Testing Between the Hypotheses

Over the years, evidence has been adduced for all of the hypotheses listed in Figure 3.1. However, individual hypotheses have invariably been tested in isolation, usually in the form of bivariate correlations between some behavioral trait and some measure of brain size. This makes it difficult to be certain that the correlation between brain size and the implied fitness benefit is real, and not due to both being independently correlated with a third variable. This is especially problematic for the ontogenetic hypotheses, because in fact these turn out to be constraints rather than *bona fide* evolutionary explanations (Dunbar & Shultz, 2007a). Those (mainly ontogenetic) hypotheses which suggest that social or other cognitive skills are purely a by-product of a capacity to develop a large brain (thanks to spare maternal energy or an extended life history) face the problem that brain is amongst the most energetically expensive tissues in the body (the "expensive tissue hypothesis": Aiello & Wheeler, 1995). Since this creates a steep gradient up which evolution has to push the species in order to evolve a larger brain, it is biologically implausible to suggest that there is no corresponding benefit acting as a selection factor favoring larger brains. By the same token, explanations that have suggested that large group size might be a by-product of having a large brain for, say, enhanced foraging skills (all the ecological hypotheses, plus the social learning and Machiavellian social hypotheses) likewise run into the problem that large groups incur enormous costs for their members. These come in the form of significant time costs for foraging and much larger day journeys and home ranges (Dunbar et al., 2009), as well as massive costs for females in terms of disrupted menstrual cycle endocrinology and thus infertility (Dunbar, 2010a). Without some benefit from being in larger groups these costs will invariably ensure that group size remains small.

In short, it seems that only the social brain hypothesis itself is free of these kinds of anomalies. Indeed, only the social brain hypothesis explicitly requires a direct relationship between some aspect of brain size and social group size. Although the social learning hypothesis offers some grounds for a possible relationship between group size and brain size (more group members presumably means more opportunities for social learning), there is no explicit reason why having a large group should be essential for social learning. Moreover, as with all the other ecological hypotheses, the social learning hypothesis does not, of itself, require that groups be any more than loose aggregations. In contrast, the social brain hypothesis explicitly points to the bondedness of social groups as the crucial intermediate step between brain size and the ecological problem driving brain size evolution (namely, predation risk). And it is in their near-unique form of bondedness that primate societies differ from those of other species of mammals (Shultz & Dunbar, 2007; Dunbar & Shultz, 2007b, 2010).

So far, the only coherent attempt to pitch the various hypotheses into direct competition with each other is that by Dunbar & Shultz (2007a), who used path analysis to compare alternative models predicting social group size across the primates. They found that the best predictors were habit (diurnal vs. nocturnal lifestyles) and neocortex size, with predation risk as the ultimate factor selecting for large groups. They were able to show that all other variables considered were either energetic or developmental constraints on the evolution of large neocortices (lifespan, body size, total brain size, diet, and metabolic rate) or consequences of having a large group (day journey length and home-range size). Thus, the path analysis allows the various hypotheses for large brains to be assigned to roles (causes, constraints, and consequences) within a general system model. In effect, the causal sequence is that predation risk drives the need for large groups, and this in turn necessitates a large neocortex to facilitate large stable groups, and the need to evolve a large neocortex (and hence brain) requires a number of critical energetic and life history constraints to be resolved because, as Finlay et al. (2001) point out, brain tissue can be laid down only at a constant rate determined by the natural cycles of neurogenesis. Larger brains require more growth time, hence necessitating a longer period of gestation and lactation to complete brain growth (in turn, necessitating a longer lifespan) and greater total energy intake (to fuel the larger number of cells).

With this much established, the primary evidence to support the social brain hypothesis is an explicit correlation between social group size and relative neocortex size. This relationship is extremely robust: Three separate brain datasets based on entirely different samples and methodologies confirm that mean species group size is linearly related to neocortex volume on a double-log plot (Figure 3.2). Although it might have been suggested that the original result (Dunbar, 1992a) was weak because the database it used (Stephan et al., 1981) was based on a very small number of specimens (often just 1–2 individuals) per species, the fact that all three datasets

(one at least of which has large samples per species) exhibit the same pattern proves the hypothesis is robust. More importantly, it does not seem to matter whether we use absolute or relative neocortex size (compare Figure 3.2a with Figure 3.2b and 3.2c), or whether or not we use formal comparative methods to partial out the effects of phylogeny (or, indeed, which phylogenetic methods one uses) (Barton, 1996; Dunbar & Shultz, 2007a; Shultz & Dunbar, 2007; Pérez-Barbería, Shultz, & Dunbar, 2007). Note also that all three graphs in Figure 3.2 exhibit the same pattern of separate socio-cognitive grades for prosimians, monkeys, and apes.

There have, more recently, been a number of attempts to generalize this relationship to other taxa, including whales (Marino, 1996), insectivores (Dunbar & Bever, 1998, carnivores (Finarelli & Flynn, 2009), ungulates (Pérez-Barbería & Gordon, 2005; Shultz & Dunbar, 2006), bats (Pitnick, Jones, & Wilkinson, 2006), and even birds (Beauchamp & Fernandez-Juricic, 2004; Garamszegi, Eens, Erritzoe, & Møller, 2004), with mixed results (albeit in most cases thanks to muddled methodologies as much as anything). The reason for this will become apparent (see below), but in the meantime it may be noted that the only really robust attempt to test the social brain hypothesis across taxonomic groups has been that by Pérez-Barbería et al. (2007) who used powerful new statistical methods to show that there was a significant co-evolutionary relationship between sociality and brain/neocortex volume in carnivores and ungulates, as well as primates: When one trait changed (from less social to more social) in the phylogenetic tree, the other trait usually changed too (from small brain size to large).

Finally, we may note that, in Figure 3.2, the value for mean community size in humans (~150, from Dunbar [1992b] and Zhou, Sornette, Hill, & Dunbar [2005]) fits neatly onto the end of the ape distribution. Humans seem to be just as cognitively constrained in the size of their core social groups as other primates are. Like other primates (Kudo & Dunbar, 2001; Hill, Bentley, & Dunbar, 2008), humans live in multi-layered societies in which the layers are scaled with each other (Zhou et al., 2005; Hamilton, Milne, Walker, Burger, & Brown, 2007; Roberts, 2009). In one respect, this hierarchical scaling of grouping levels begs the question as to the level at which the cognitive constraint implied by the correlation with neocortex size acts. It remains unclear, for example, whether the cognitive constraint acts on total group size, with the layers reflecting some form of structuring to relationships

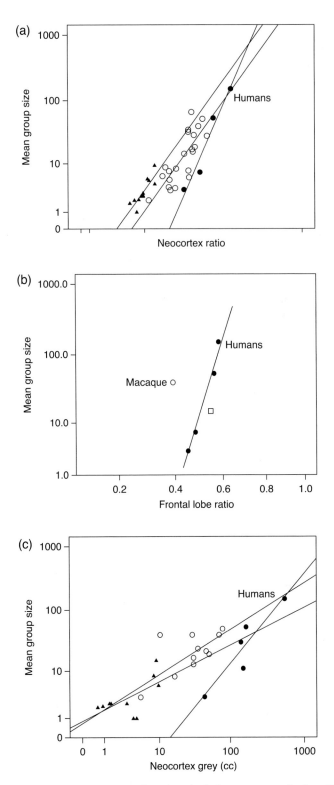

Fig. 3.2 Mean social group size plotted against neocortex volume for individual primate genera, for three different brain datasets. (a) neocortex ratio (histological data: Stephan et al. [1981], (b) frontal lobe ratio [frontal lobe volume divided by rest of brain] (histological data: Fuster [1988]) and (c) absolute neocortex grey matter volume (MRI data: Bush & Allman [2000]). All three show grades that separate prosimians (where present) (triangles, dotted line), monkeys (open circles, dashed line) and apes, including gibbons (solid circles, solid line). In Figure 3.2(b), the open square is the orangutan, with community sizes estimated from figures

(Continued)

within this, or whether the constraint acts on the size of the inner most layer (in human terms, intimate and close friends), with the layering reflecting a small world effect (i.e., a friends-of-friends effect).

What Can Social Behavior Tell Us About Cognition?

Quite what cognitive mechanisms mediate the relationship between brain size and social group size, and how they do this, is, however, far from clear (Healy & Rowe, 2007; Behrens, Hunt, & Rushworth, 2009). Nonetheless, more fine-grained analysis of some of the behavioral patterns associated with large neocortices may at least allow us to point to the kinds of things that might be involved. Neocortex ratio has, for example, been shown to be correlated with the complexity of male mating strategies (Pawłowski, Lowen, & Dunbar, 1998), the size of grooming cliques (Kudo & Dunbar, 2001), the proportion of play that is social (as opposed to instrumental or solitary) (Lewis, 2001), and the relative frequency of tactical deception (Byrne & Corp, 2004); in addition, species that regularly use coalitions (a near-unique hallmark of primate sociality) have significantly larger neocortices for body size than species that do not (Dunbar & Shultz, 2007a). These behavioral phenomena are all considered cognitively demanding, though exactly what this means has yet to be elucidated (Dunbar, 2009).

However, perhaps the most interesting pointer to the cognitive demands of sociality may be the fact that the social brain takes a rather different form in species other than primates. Across a broad range of mammals and birds, social group size does not correlate with brain (or neocortex) size. Instead, the best predictor of brain size is pair-bonded monogamy (Shultz & Dunbar, 2007). Indeed, one can still detect a signature for monogamy within the primate brain data: When social group size is partialed out, species that have monogamous mating and social systems have larger neocortices than species that have other social arrangements across all three main taxonomic groupings (prosimians, monkeys, and apes) (Dunbar, 2010b). That this has something to do with pair bonding rather than

biparental care per se is indicated by the fact that, among birds, relative brain size is significantly larger in species that pair for life than in those that pair with a new mate each breeding season (annual pair bonders) (Shultz & Dunbar, 2007, 2010a). It seems that something about pair-bonded monogamy makes it cognitively very demanding. In effect, what primates seem to have done is to generalize the cognitive capacities that underpin pair bonding to other members of the group (thereby essentially creating "friendships": Silk, 2002, Dunbar & Shultz, 2010). Since the number of friends is limited only by the size of the group, the correlation between group size and neocortex volume is a natural outcome.

But why should pair bonds be so cognitively demanding? One plausible reason is that pair-bonded individuals have to be able to factor their mate's needs and requirements into their calculations about their own behavior. In effect, a pair bond is an implicit social contract in which two individuals cooperate on a particular task (reproduction). Their ability to achieve that goal must depend on their willingness to avoid actions that destabilize or threaten the relationship. This is perhaps most obvious in the case of birds: There is little to be gained by one member of the pair spending all its time feeding away from the nest if its mate is forced to abandon the eggs to cooling or nest predators in order to avoid starvation. Hence, in order to ensure that their mates satisfy their own biological needs, pair members must be able to incorporate the mate's perspective into their own strategic decisions. This is not necessarily theory of mind (ToM) of the kind that seems to be so defining of the human condition, but it is surely a step on the way, and this may be crucial both in understanding why sociality is cognitively demanding *and* in how we eventually get to the level of social cognition that we find in humans. Understanding a partner's perspective might thus be the key precursor for the kinds of full-blown theory of mind we find in humans, and thus the critical selection pressure that kicked off the secondary evolution of brains that were larger than minimally necessary for successful survival.

At a minimal level, for example, baboons (as a representative member of the cognitively and socially

Fig. 3.2 (Continued) given by Mackinnon (1974) and Singleton and van Schaik (2001). Data for human community size from Dunbar (1992b). Note that these grades cut across conventional taxonomic boundaries, and appear to delineate socio-cognitive rather than taxonomic grades (see also Lehmann, Korstjens, & Dunbar, 2007). Each of the grades is a significant correlation (one-tailed tests, without phylogenetic control): (a) prosimians [includes *Tarsier*]: $r = 0.433$, $p = 0.042$, $N = 17$; monkeys: $r = 0.669$, $p = 0.0005$, $N = 21$; hominoids: $r = 0.955$, $p = 0.023$, $N = 4$; (b) hominoids: $r = 0.958$, $p = 0.021$, $N = 4$; (c) prosimians: $r = 0.789$, $p = 0.010$, $N = 8$; monkeys: $r = 0.645$, $p = 0.012$, $N = 12$; hominoids: $r = 0.966$, $p = 0.004$, $N = 5$.

advanced monkeys) appear to be able to integrate at least two levels of information (rank and matriline membership) about another individual into their understanding of that individual's social position within the group (Bergman, Beehner, Cheney, & Seyfarth, 2003). Baboons' abilities to manage their relationships so as to maintain a network of friends that can be counted on to act as reliable allies is crucial to their ability to reproduce successfully, especially for females (Dunbar, 1984, 1989, 2010a; Silk, Alberts, & Altmann, 2003, Silk et al., 2009; Crockford, Wittig, Whitten, Seyfarth, & Cheney, 2008). In this respect, primate (and especially anthropoid primate) sociality seems to be very different from that in other birds and mammals: it depends on intensely bonded relationships that seem to be all but unique (Shultz & Dunbar, 2007; Dunbar & Shultz, 2010). This seems to mark a shift from groups as lose aggregations to groups as congregations that are robust and stable across time.

It is worth noting here that socialization probably plays at least as important a role as pure computational power (in so far as this is reflected in neocortex volume). Joffe (1997) showed that, while the best predictor of total brain size in primates is the period of parental investment (gestation plus lactation), the best predictor of *neocortex* volume (and especially neocortex volume excluding primary visual cortex) is the length of the period of socialization (the period between weaning and puberty). In other words, the hardware seems to require considerable investment in software programming through socialization and practice in order for it to be able to manage large numbers of social relationships. Lewis's (2001) finding that social play correlates with relative neocortex size also points to the importance of socialization.

How Cognition Interfaces Between Brain and Behavior

But what kind of cognition is involved? There has been a general assumption that primates are marked out as different by some kind of specialized social cognition evolved to support these more unique aspects of primate sociality—although, with the exception of the phenomenon known as theory of mind (ToM) in humans, quite what that might be has never been clear. Moreover, while ToM (formally equivalent to second order intentionality) has been a useful benchmark for exploring social cognition and has been studied in considerable detail, it is a threshold achieved by 3–5 year olds and of limited real interest for what adults can do.

Similarly, although there has been considerable interest in social cognition in the recent neuroimaging literature, these studies have all been concerned with judgments (e.g., of trustworthiness) or reward responses in simple dyadic contexts (e.g., Knoch, Pascual-Leone, Meyer, Treyer, & Fehr, 2006; Behrens et al., 2009; Lebreton, Barnes, Miettunen, Peltonen, Ridler, Veijola et al., 2009). While clearly providing valuable insights into how such judgments are made, these do not really capture the richness of the social world in which humans and other primates live (Dunbar, 2009). Nor do they engage with the question of just how and why humans differ from other primates.

Nonetheless, taking ToM as representative of the kinds of specialized social cognition that lie at the heart of primate sociality may offer us some insight into these questions. While we have shown that normal adult humans are typically capable of coping with fifth order intentional mentalizing (Kinderman, Dunbar, & Bentall, 1998; Stiller & Dunbar, 2007), there is a general agreement among those who work on primate cognition that only great apes can rise above first order intentionality. Even then, the evidence for ToM in great apes is not as compelling as it is for human children. Call & Tomasello (1999), for example, found that chimpanzees failed an analogue false belief task that children passed with ease; in contrast, a more comprehensive series of experiments by O'Connell & Dunbar (2003) suggested that chimpanzees were about as competent as 3–4 years old human children and, more importantly, were significantly better than autistic adults (who lacked formal ToM). On the other hand, there is considerable evidence that chimpanzees can engage in perspective-taking (e.g., Hare, Call, Agnetta, & Tomasello, 2000; Hare, Call, & Tomasello, 2001), and compelling evidence that orangutans can make appropriate inferences about intentions (Cartmill & Byrne, 2007). If we accept that monkeys are limited to first order intentionality, great apes to second, and adult humans to fifth, then it turns out that these values plot linearly against absolute frontal lobe grey matter volume (Figure 3.3). Importantly, frontal lobe volumes for all monkeys and apes fall into two clear clusters. This suggests that the scale of social cognition that a species can achieve might be dictated, in part at least, by some aspect of neocortex volume, and frontal lobe volume in particular. In line with this, Joffe & Dunbar (1997) found that social group size in primates is predicted much more reliably if some of the more dorsal areas of the neocortex (principally, primary visual cortex) is removed.

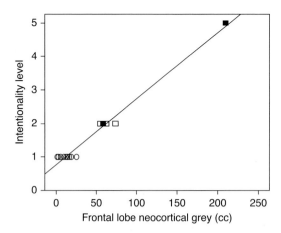

Fig. 3.3 Intentionality competencies (highest achievable level of intentionality) plotted against frontal lobe grey matter volume in 13 species of New and Old World monkeys (open circles), 4 great ape species (open square) and adult humans (solid square). Humans and chimpanzees are the only two species that have been formally tested for these competencies using formal false belief tasks, but there is compelling evidence for orangutans, so bonobos and gorillas are assumed to be at the same level; monkeys are generically considered to be capable only of first order intentionality. Note the close clustering of frontal lobe volumes with no overlap for the two non-human taxa, and the fact that these values yield an unexpectedly tight linear relationship between intentionality and frontal lobe volume.

Compiled from Bush and Allmann (2004), Rilling and Insel (1999).

This claim is reinforced by a recent finding from neuroimaging studies that intentional competencies in normal human adults correlate with both the gross volume of orbitofrontal region of the frontal lobe (Powell, Lewis, Dunbar, García-Fiñana, & Roberts, 2010) and, in a voxel-based morphometric study, with the volume of core units within this region that are known to be associated with ToM (Lewis, Rezaie, Brown, Roberts, & Dunbar, in press). These findings become important in the light of the fact that we have been able to show that, in humans, performance on these kinds of mentalizing tasks correlates with the size of an individual's social network of close friends (Stiller & Dunbar, 2007; Lewis et al., in press). Thus, there seems to be a three-way correlation between the size of core brain regions involved in mentalizing, social cognitive competencies, and the number of friends that can be maintained.

The literature on ToM has broadly been divided over what these capacities might actually involve. One tends to the view that social cognition represents a novel form of cognition instantiated in a specialized module (or perhaps a distributed network of sub-modules) (see Gallagher & Frith, 2003; Frith & Frith, 2003, 2007; Saxe, 2006); the other is that

ToM and its ancillary components are simply by-products of executive function competencies (Ozonoff, 1995; Sommerville & Decety, 2006; Decety & Lamm, 2007). From a purely evolutionary point of view, the latter is the more congenial, if only because it makes it easier to see how one might get the transitions from non-primates to primates to humans. On this view, ToM is simply how we experience the underlying executive function competences when we can bring these to bear on a particular problem at a sufficient scale, this being simply a function of the computational power of the relevant brain regions (notably the frontal lobes, since these are considered to be the main locus of executive function: Stuss, Eskes, & Foster, 1994; Kolb & Wishaw, 1996; Miller & Cohen, 2001; Thompson, Cannon, Narr, van Erp, Poutanen, Huttunen et al., 2001; Ardila, 2008). The tentative evidence in Figure 3.3 for a relationship between mentalizing competences and frontal lobe volume fits well with this suggestion. If mentalising is a function of executive cogition, then the critical link between brain volume, executive cognition and social cognition may be provided by the recent finding that executive function competencies in primates correlate with relative neocortex volume (Shultz & Dunbar, 2010b).

References

Aiello, L. & Wheeler, P. (1995). The expensive-tissue hypothesis: The brain and the digestive system in human and primate evolution. *Curr Anthropol, 36*, 199–221.

Ardila, A. (2008). On the evolutionary origins of executive function. *Brain Cogn, 68*, 92–99.

Barrickman, N.L., Bastian, M.L., Isler, K., & van Schaik, C.P. (2007) Life history costs and benefits of encephalization: A comparative test using data from long-term studies of primates in the wild. *J Hum Evol, 54*, 568–590.

Barton, R.A. (1996). Neocortex size and behavioural ecology in primates. *Proc R Soc Lond, 263B*, 173–177.

Barton, R.A. & Dunbar, R.I.M. (1997) Evolution of the social brain. In: A. Whiten & R. Byrne (eds.), *Machiavellian Intelligence II* (pp. 240–263). Cambridge: Cambridge University Press.

Beauchamp, G. & Fernandez-Juricic, E. (2004). Is there a relationship between forebrain size and group size in birds? *Evol Ecol Res, 6*, 833–842.

Behrens, T.E.J., Hunt, L.T., & Rushworth, M.F.S. (2009). Then computation of social behaviour. *Science, 324*, 1160–1164.

Bergman, T.J., Beehner, J.C., Cheney, D.L., & Seyfarth, R.M. (2003). Hierarchical classification by rank and kinship in baboons. *Science, 302*, 1234–1236.

Brothers, L. (1990). The social brain: A project for integrating primate behavior and neurophysiology in a new domain. *Concepts Neurosci, 1*, 27–51.

Bush, E.C. & Allman, J.M. (2004). The scaling of frontal cortex in primates and carnivores. *PNAS, 101*, 3962–3966.

Byrne, R.W. & Corp, N. (2004). Neocortex size predicts deception rate in primates. *Proc R Soc Lond*, *271*, 1693–1699.

Byrne, R.W. & Whiten, A. (eds.). (1988). *Machiavellian Intelligence*. Oxford: Oxford University Press.

Call, J. & Tomasello, M. (1999). A nonverbal theory of mind test: The performance of children and apes. *Child Develop*, *70*, 381–395.

Cartmill, E.A. & Byrne, R.B. (2007). Orangutans modify their gestural signaling according to their audience's comprehension. *Curr Biol*, *17*, 1–4.

Clutton-Brock, T.H. & Harvey, P.H. (1980). Primates, brains and ecology. *J Zool Lond*, *190*, 309–323.

Crockford, C., Wittig, R.M., Whitten, P.L., Seyfarth, R.M., & Cheney, D.L. (2008). Social stressors and coping mechanisms in wild female baboons (*Papio hamadryas ursinus*). *Hormones Behav*, *53*, 254–265.

Decety, J. & Lamm, C. (2007). The role of the right temporoparietal junction in social interaction: How low-level computational processes contribute to meta-cognition. *Neuroscient*, *13*, 580–593.

Dunbar, R.I.M. (1984). *Reproductive decisions: An economic analysis of gelada baboon social strategies*. Princeton, NJ: Princeton University Press.

Dunbar, R.I.M. (1989). Reproductive strategies of female gelada baboons. In: A. Rasa, C. Vogel, & E. Voland (eds.), *Sociobiology of sexual and reproductive strategies* (pp. 74–92). London: Chapman & Hall.

Dunbar, R.I.M. (1992a) Neocortex size as a constraint on group size in primates. *J. Human Evol*, *22*, 469–493.

Dunbar, R.I.M. (1992b). Coevolution of neocortex size, group size and language in humans. *Behav Brain Sci*, *16*, 681–735.

Dunbar, R.I.M. (1998). The social brain hypothesis. *Evol Anthrop*, *6*, 178–190.

Dunbar, R.I.M. (2003). Why are apes so smart? In: P. Kappeler & M. Pereira (eds.), *Primate life histories and socioecology* (pp. 285–298). Chicago: Chicago University Press.

Dunbar, R.I.M. (2009). Darwin and the ghost of Phineas Gage: Neuro-evolution and the social brain. *Cortex*, *45*, 1119–1125.

Dunbar, R.I.M. (2010a). Brain and behaviour in primate evolution. In: P. H. Kappeler & J. Silk (eds.), *Mind the gap: Tracing the origins of human universals*, pp. 315–330. Cambridge, MA: MIT Press.

Dunbar, R.I.M. (2010b). The social brain and its implications. In: U. Frey, C. Störmer, & K. Willführ (eds.), *Homo novus: A human without illusions*, pp. 65–77. Berlin: Springer Verlag.

Dunbar, R.I.M. & Bever, J. (1998). Neocortex size predicts group size in carnivores and some insectivores. *Ethology*, *104*, 695–708.

Dunbar, R.I.M. & Shultz, S. (2007a). Understanding primate brain evolution. *Phil Trans R Soc Lond*, *362B*, 649–658.

Dunbar, R.I.M. & Shultz, S. (2007b). Evolution in the social brain. *Science*, *317*, 1344–1347.

Dunbar, R.I.M. & Shultz, S. (2010). Bondedness and sociality. *Behaviour*, *147*, 775–803.

Dunbar, R.I.M., Korstjens, A.H., & Lehmann, J. (2009). Time as an ecological constraint. *Biol Rev*, *84*, 413–429.

Finarelli, J.A. & Flynn, J.J. (2009). Brain-size evolution and sociality in Carnivora. *Proc Natl Acad Sci USA* 106: 9345–9349.

Finlay, B.L. & Darlington, R.B. (1995). Linked regularities in the development and evolution of mammalian brains. *Science*, *268*, 1578–1584.

Finlay, B.L., Darlington, R.B., & Nicastro, N. (2001). Developmental structure in brain evolution. *Behav Brain Sci*, *24*, 263–308.

Frith, C.D. & Frith, U. (2007). Social cognition in humans. *Curr Biol*, *17*, R724–R732.

Frith, U. & Frith, C.D. (2003). Development and neurophysiology of mentalising. *Phil Trans R Soc Lond*, *358B*, 459–473.

Fuster, J.M. (1988). *The prefrontal cortex: anatomy, physiology and neuropsychology of the frontal lobe*. New York: Lippincott Williams & Wilkins.

Gallagher, H.L. & Frith, C.D. (2003). Functional imaging of "theory of mind." *Trends Cogn Sci*, 7, 77–83.

Garamszegi, L.Z., Eens, M., Erritzoe, J., & Møller, A.P. (2004). Sperm competition and sexually size dimorphic brains in birds. *Proc R Soc Lond*, *272B*, 159–166.

Gibson, K.R. (1986). Cognition, brain size and the extraction of embedded food resources. In: J.G. Else & P.C. Lee (eds.), Primate ontogeny, cognition and social behaviour (pp. 93–104). Cambridge: Cambridge University Press.

Hamilton, M.J., Milne, B.T., Walker, R.S., Burger, O., & Brown, J.H. (2007). The complex structure of hunter-gatherer social networks. *Proc R Soc Lond*, *274B*, 2195–2202.

Hare, B., Call, J., Agnetta, B., & Tomasello, M. (2000). Chimpanzees know what conspecifics do and do not see. *Anim Behav*, *59*, 771–785.

Hare, B., Call, J., & Tomasello, M. (2001). Do chimpanzees know what conspecifics know? *Anim Behav*, *61*, 139–151.

Harvey, P.H., Clutton-Brock, T.H., & Mace, G.A. (1980). Brain size and ecology in small mammals and primates. *PNAS*, *77*, 4387–4389.

Healy, S.D. & Rowe, C. (2007). A critique of comparative studies of brain size. *Proc R Soc Lond*, *274B*, 453–464.

Hill, R.A., Bentley, A., & Dunbar, R.I.M. (2008). Network scaling reveals consistent fractal pattern in hierarchical mammalian societies. *Biol Lets*, *4*, 748–751.

Hofman, M.A. (1983). Energy metabolism, brain size and longevity in mammals. *Q Rev Biol*, *58*, 495–512.

Humphrey, N.L. (1976). The social function of intellect. In: P.P.G. Bateson & R.A. Hinde (eds.), *Growing points in ethology* (pp. 303–317). Cambridge: Cambridge University Press.

Isler, K. & van Schaik, C.P. (2006) Metabolic costs of brain size evolution. *Biol Letters*, *2*, 557–560.

Jerison, H.J. (1973). *Evolution of the brain and intelligence*. London: Academic Press.

Joffe, T. H. (1997). Social pressures have selected for an extended juvenile period in primates. *J Human Evol*, *32*, 593–605.

Joffe, T.H. & Dunbar, R.I.M. (1997). Visual and socio-cognitive information processing in primate brain evolution. *Proc Roy Soc Lond*, *264B*, 1303–1307.

Jolly, A. (1966). Lemur social behaviour and primate intelligence. *Science*, *153*, 501–506.

Karbowski, J. (2007). Global and regional brain metabolic scaling and its functional consequences. *BMC Biology*, *5*, 18–46.

Kaufman, J.A. (2003). On the expensive tissue hypothesis: Independent support from highly encephalised fish. *Curr Anthropol*, *44*, 705–706.

Kinderman, P., Dunbar, R.I.M., & Bentall, R.P. (1998). Theory-of-mind deficits and causal attributions. *Brit J Psych*, *89*, 191–204.

Knoch, D., Pascual-Leone, A., Meyer, K., Treyer, V., & Fehr, E. (2006). Diminishing reciprocal fairness by disrupting the right prefrontal cortex. *Science*, *314*, 829–832.

Kolb, B. & Wishaw, I.Q. (1996). *Fundamentals of human neuropsychology*. 4th ed. San Francisco: W.H. Freeman.

Kudo, H. & Dunbar, R.I.M. (2001) Neocortex size and social network size in primates. *Anim Behav*, *62*, 711–722.

Kummer, H. (1982). Social knowledge in free-ranging primates. In: D. Griffin (ed.), *Animal mind—human mind* (pp. 113–130). Berlin: Springer.

Lebreton, M., Barnes, A., Miettunen, J., Peltonen, L., Ridler, K., Veijola, J., et al. (2009). The brain structural disposition to social interaction. *Eur J Neurosci*, *29*, 2247–2252.

Lefebvre, L., Reader, S.M., & Sol, D. (2004). Brains, innovations and evolution in birds and primates. *Brain Behav Evol*, *63*, 233–246.

Lehmann, J., Korstjens, A.H., & Dunbar, R.I.M. (2007). Group size, grooming and social cohesion in primates. *Anim Behav*, *74*, 1617–1629.

Lewis, K. (2001) A comparative study of primate play behaviour: Implications for the study of cognition. *Folia Primatol*, *71*, 417–421.

Lewis, P., Rezaie, R., Brown, R., Roberts, R., & Dunbar, R.I.M. (in press). Orbitofrontal volume predicts understanding of others and social success. *Neuroimage*.

Mackinnon, J. (1974). The behaviour and ecology of wild orangutans (*Pongo pygmaeus*). *Anim Behav*, *22*, 3–74.

Marino, L. (1996). What can dolphins tell us about primate evolution? *Evol Anthrop*, *5*, 81–86.

Martin, R.D. (1981). Relative brain size and metabolic rate in terrestrial vertebrates. *Nature*, *293*, 57–60.

Miller, E.K. & Cohen, J.D. (2001). An integrative theory of prefrontal cortex function. *Ann Rev Neurosci*, *24*, 167–202.

Mink, J.W., Blumenschine, R.J., & Adams, D.B. (1981). Ratio of central nervous system to body metabolism in vertebrates– its constancy and functional basis. *Am J Physiol*, *241*, R203–R212.

O'Connell, S. & Dunbar, R.I.M. (2003). A test for comprehension of false belief in chimpanzees. *Evol Cognition*, *9*, 131–139.

Ozonoff, S. (1995). Executive functions in autism. In: E. Schopler & G.B. Mesibov (eds.), *Learning and cognition in austism* (pp. 199–218). New York: Plenum Press.

Pawłowski, B.P., Lowen, C.B., & Dunbar, R.I.M. (1998) Neocortex size, social skills and mating success in primates. *Behaviour*, *135*, 357–368.

Pérez-Barbería, F.J. & Gordon, I.J. (2005). Gregariousness increases brain size in ungulates. *Oecologia*, *145*, 41–52.

Pérez-Barbería, F.J., Shultz, S., & Dunbar, R.I.M. (2007) Evidence for intense coevolution of sociality and brain size in three orders of mammals. *Evolution*, *61*, 2811–2821.

Pitnick, S., Jones, K.E., & Wilkinson, G.S. (2006). Mating system and brain size in bats. *Proc R Soc Lond*, *273B*, 719–724.

Powell, J., Lewis, P., Dunbar, R.I.M., García-Fiñana, M., & Roberts, N. (2010). Quantitative neural correlates of social cognitive competences. *Neuropsychologia*, *00*, 000–000.

Reader, S.M. & Laland, K. (2002). Social intelligence, innovation and advanced brain size in primates. *Proc Natl Acad Sci USA*, *99*, 4436–4441.

Rilling, J.K. & Insel, T.R. (1999). The primate bneocortex in comparative perspective using magnetic resonance imaging. *J Human Evol*, *37*, 191–223.

Roberts, S.B.G. (2009). Constraints on social networks. In: R.I.M. Dunbar, C. Gamble, & J.A.G. Gowlett (eds.), *Social brain, distributed mind* (pp. 117–137). Oxford: Oxford University Press.

Saxe, R. (2006). Why and how to study theory of mind with fMRI. *Brain Research*, *1079*, 57–65.

Shultz, S. & Dunbar, R.I.M. (2006). Both social and ecological factors predict ungulate brain size. *Proc. R. Soc. Lond*, *273B*, 207–215.

Shultz, S. & Dunbar, R.I.M. (2007). The evolution of the social brain: Anthropoid primates contrast with other vertebrates. *Proc R Soc Lond B*, *274*, 2429–2436.

Shultz, S. & Dunbar, R.I.M. (2010a). Social bonds in birds are associated with brain size and contingent on the correlated evolution of life-history and increased parental investment. *Biol. J. Linn. Soc*, *100*, 111–123.

Shultz, S. & Dunbar, R.I.M. (2010b). Species differences in executive function correlate with hippocampus volume and neocortex ratio across non human primates. *J. Comp. Psychol*, *124*, 252–260.

Shultz, S., Bradbury, R., Evans, K., Gregory, R., & Blackburn, T. (2005). Brain size and resource specialisation predict longterm population trends in British birds. *Proc. R. Soc. Lond*, *272B*, 2305–2311.

Silk, J.B. (2002). The "F"-word in primatology. *Behaviour*, *139*, 421–446.

Silk, J.B., Alberts, S.C., & Altmann, J. (2003). Social bonds of female baboons enhance infant survival. *Science*, *302*, 1232–1234.

Silk, J.B., Beehner, J.C., Bergman, T.J., Crockford, C., Engh, A.L., Moscovice, L.R., et al. (2009). The benefits of social capital: Close social bonds among female baboons enhance offspring survival. *Proc R Soc Lond*, *276B*, 3099–3104.

Singleton, I. & van Schaik, C.P. (2001). Orangutan home range size and its determinants in a Sumatran swamp forest. *Int J Primat*, *22*, 877–911.

Sol, D., Timmermans, S. & Lefebvre, L. (2002). Behavioural flexibility and invasion success in birds. *Anim Behav*, *63*, 495–502.

Sol, D., Lefebvre, L., & Rodriguez-Teijeiro, D. J. (2005a). Brain size, innovative propensity and migratory behaviour in temperate Palaeartic birds. *Proc R Soc B*, *272*, 1433–1441.

Sol, D., Duncan, R.P., Blackburn, T.M., Cassey, P., & Lefebrve, L. (2005b). Big brains, enhanced cognition and response of birds to novel environments. *Proc Nat Acad Sci USA*, *102*, 5460–5465.

Sol, D., Székely, T., Liker, A., & Lefebvre, L. (2007). Big-brained birds survive better in nature. *Proc R Soc Lond*, *274*, 763–769.

Sommerville, J.A. & Decety, J. (2006). Weaving the fabric of social interaction: articulating developmental psychology and cognitive neuroscience in the domain of motor cognition. *Psychonom Bull Rev*, *13*, 179–200.

Stephan, H., Frahm, H. & Baron, G. (1981). New and revised data on bolumes of brain structures in insectivores and primates. *Folia primatol*, *35*, 1–29.

Stiller, J. & Dunbar, R.I.M. (2007). Perspective-taking and social network size in humans. *Social Networks*, *29*, 93–104.

Stuss, D.T., Eskes, G.A., & Foster, J.K. (1994). Experimental neuropsychological studies of frontal lobe functions. In: F. Boller & J. Grafman (eds.), *Handbook of neuropsychology*, Vol. 9 (pp. 149–185). Amsterdam: Elsevier.

Thompson, P.M., Cannon, T.D., Narr, K.L., van Erp, T., Poutanen, V.-P., Huttunen, M., et al., L (2001). Genetic influences on brain structure. *Nature Neurosci, 4,* 1253–1258.

Wittig, R.M., Crockford, C., Lehmann, J., Whitten, P.L., Seyfarth, R.M., & Cheney, D.L. (2008). Focused grooming networks and stress alleviation in wild female baboons. *Hormones Behav, 54,* 170–177.

Zhou, W-X., Sornette, D., Hill, R.A., & Dunbar, R.I.M. (2005). Discrete hierarchical organization of social group sizes. *Proc R Soc Lond, 272B,* 439–444.

The Evolution of Social Cognition

Lisa A. Parr *and* Bridget M. Waller

Abstract

This chapter discusses several issues important for understanding the evolution of social cognition, defined simply as the collection of skills that are important, and perhaps unique, to living in groups. These skills are not limited to but may include social recognition, recognition of social communication signals, like facial expressions, following gaze/perspective taking, and understanding others' intentions. Social cognition can be fully understood through careful examination of the communicative patterns that occur between individuals, each with unique relationship history. In this view, social cognition is best described as a form of distributed cognition, an emergent property of unique relationships within a social environment.

Keywords: communication, emotion, facial expression, cooperation, empathy, theory of mind, homology, brain size, social function, social complexity, social affordance, primates, evolution, social cognition

Introduction

Sociality can be defined as the quality of dynamic interactions among group-living individuals. Despite the fact that almost all biological organisms are social, living in groups is a special category of sociality that produces a paradox for the individual. On one hand, groups provide important benefits that come from strength in numbers: the more individuals, the more eyes to detect predators and the more bodies to defend territories. On the other hand, with more individuals comes greater competition over valuable, limited resources and ultimately more inter-individual conflict. Numerous branches of biology have attempted to disentangle the delicate interplay between the costs and benefits of group living, leading to many important theories about ecological constraints on group size, including the distribution

of food resources, species' migration patterns, territoriality, and interspecies conflicts (Krause & Ruxton, 2002). Some of these have focused on the importance of sophisticated social skills, or social cognition, as strategies that evolved to help individuals manage the increasing competition that is inherent with larger group sizes. Initially, this view focused on a Machiavellian style of intelligence (termed "Machiavellian" intelligence) in which individuals deceived and manipulated group members to gain an advantage in accessing scarce and valuable resources (Byrne & Whiten, 1988).

The Machiavellian view of social cognition focuses heavily on the success of the individual and their strategies to succeed in a social environment. But researchers also acknowledged that it could be equally as adaptive to engage in more egalitarian strategies that emphasize social communication, cooperation, food sharing, and the reconciliation of interpersonal conflicts (de Waal, 1982; Humphrey, 1976; Jolly, 1966). This egalitarian view focuses more on the interactions between individuals, where altruism and cooperation function to help individuals maintain strong and healthy relationships. Recent studies using economic games such as the Prisoner's Dilemma have highlighted the inherently altruistic nature of humans. In these games, the two players can individually profit the most by cheating on their partners but, despite this selfish strategy leading to the most economic gains, players typically cooperate for the sake of their relationship, even when they never directly see one another, e.g., they play the game through a computer interface (review, Fehr & Fischbacher, 2003). Moreover, players will willingly forgo their individual benefits for the opportunity to punish cheaters, suggesting that the more Machiavellian approach is unlikely to be sustained in a social environment (Barrett & Henzi, 2005). Thus it seems that altruistic and egalitarian behaviors can arise through evolutionary processes where important benefits are conferred to individuals by living in groups and thus maintaining the stability of these groups is essential (Clutton-Brock, 2002).

This chapter discusses several issues important for understanding the evolution of social cognition, defined simply as the collection of skills that are important, and perhaps unique, to living in groups. These skills are not limited to, but may include, social recognition and recognition of social communication signals, like facial expressions, following gaze/perspective taking, and understanding others' intentions. First, in order to understand the evolution of a trait or behavior (either when or why a trait first appeared in a phylogenetic lineage), a comparative approach is essential. For example, to understand whether any of the skills important for social cognition are unique to humans, they must be thoroughly investigated in other closely related species, such as the chimpanzee, that last shared a common ancestor with humans approximately 6 million years ago. Human studies define social cognition as the ability to understand the intentions, desires, and beliefs of others, also known as theory of mind (ToM). As will be argued, methodological and conceptual constraints make this an extremely elusive skill to study empirically in nonverbal animals. Because of this, whether chimpanzees or other nonhuman primates have ToM-like socio-cognitive skills remains one of the most highly debated topics in comparative evolutionary psychology. This leads to the

second point: The comparative approach is aided by deconstructing complex behavior (typically found only in humans), like social cognition, into more basic elements, or building blocks (such as those described above). In this way, the presence or absence of these elemental units of behavior (traits) can be examined in many species and the evolution of species-unique behaviors can be more readily illuminated. One of the most essential elements of social cognition is individual recognition: Group members must have the ability to recognize one another and their quality of social relationships, whether this broadly reflects the discrimination of conspecifics versus heterospecifics, or to more specialized classes of individuals such as group mate, kin, alliance partner, etc. This is extremely important as different relationships afford different patterns of behavioral interaction. Particularly among species with flexible social systems, like chimpanzees and humans, the ability to recognize specific individuals against a backdrop of changing social dynamics is a critical element of social cognition and leads to the formation of long-lasting, inter-individual relationships.

Finally, and perhaps most importantly for the evolution of social cognition, members of the same species must be able to communicate with each other, sharing information about their motivation, intentions, and emotions, and understanding these qualities in others. This communication occurs through a diverse array of facial expressions, body postures, gestures, and vocalizations that can be studied from an evolutionary perspective by comparing similar behaviors across related primate species, including humans. It is through careful examination of the communicative patterns that occur between individuals, each with unique relationship history, that social cognition can be fully understood. In this view, social cognition is best described as a form of distributed cognition, an emergent property of unique relationships within a social environment.

A Comparative Approach to Studying Social Cognition

In order to understand the evolution of a particular trait/behavior and whether it is unique to humans, researchers must take a comparative/phylogenetic approach. For example, a uniquely human trait is present in humans, but not found in their closest living relative, the chimpanzee. Traits present in both humans and chimpanzees, but not in Old World monkeys, are most likely homologous, having evolved through the descent from a common ancestor (last shared by humans and great apes approximately 6 million years ago). Traits present in monkeys and humans, but not found in great apes, would represent analogous, not homologous, traits (those arising through convergent or parallel evolutionary processes and unrelated to common descent). It is only through the identification of species-unique and species-shared characteristics that the evolutionary trajectory of traits may be more fully understood. However, as speciation is a process that necessarily changes characteristics over time, homologous traits are subject to change long after two species diverge from a common ancestor and these changes may affect many aspects of the trait including physical appearance, function, or both. Therefore, in attempting to identify homologous traits across species, it is crucial that researchers not focus their level of comparison too narrowly. A broad, multifaceted level of comparison would prove more informative for detecting homologies, especially when traits appear different at a single level.

In 1963, Nobel Prize-winning ethologist Niko Tinbergen proposed a multifaceted framework for addressing evolutionary questions about traits or behaviors. He suggested that behavior can be evaluated at four independent levels of explanation: causation, ontogeny, phylogeny, and function. *Causation* refers to the conditions required for the behavior to be expressed; its immediately eliciting context. *Ontogeny* examines when during development these traits emerge. *Phylogeny* refers to when during evolutionary history these traits emerge, and *function* refers to the how the behavior increases the reproductive success or inclusive fitness of the individual. Broadly, these four levels of explanation can be divided into two main questions, *proximate* (causation/ontogeny) referring to "how" traits emerge and *ultimate* (phylogenetic/function) referring to "why" they emerge. Using the structure provided by these different levels of analysis, researchers have been able to describe similarities and differences in traits/behaviors across species with a greater detail and precision than previously afforded.

A well-studied example comes from studies of a facial expression called the bared-teeth display, which is common to many mammalian species and has been studied extensively in nonhuman primates (van Hooff, 1967). An initial proximate assessment reveals that the bared-teeth display is highly conserved across all species studied thus far: It is produced by similar changes in the underlying facial musculature (Waller et al, 2006; Waller, Parr, Gothard, Burrows, & Fuglevand, 2008) and innervated by a similarly arranged facial motor nucleus in the brainstem (Sherwood, 2005). Other proximate causations, however, appear to differ: The social and emotional contexts that elicit the bared-teeth display are quite varied. In some species it occurs during contexts of high negative arousal (rhesus macaques: de Waal & Luttrell, 1985) while in others it occurs during calmer and perhaps affiliative interactions (stumptail macaques: Thierry, Demaria, Preuschoft, & Desportes, 1989; chimpanzees: Waller & Dunbar, 2005). These differences appear to be regulated by the overall social organization and temperament of the species (Preuschoft & van Hooff, 1997). Despotic species, e.g., rhesus macaques, use the bared-teeth display as a formal signal of submission, given by subordinate monkeys to dominant ones, while more egalitarian species, e.g., stump-tail macaques and chimpanzees, use the expression as a signal of appeasement. In humans, the homologous expression is the smile and has a similar function to facilitate social appeasement (Mehu & Dunbar, 2008). At the ultimate level, however, the specific use and meaning of the expression is similar across species in reducing conflict and increasing social bonding (Preuschoft & van Hooff, 1997). Thus, when attempting to understand the evolution of a particular behavior, it is essential to examine it at different levels of explanation as many species-specific factors can influence the expression of homologous behaviors over time.

Studying Social Cognition in Nonhuman Primates

As mentioned earlier, the majority of studies on social cognition in humans focus on its highest level of expression, theory of mind (ToM), or mental perspective taking. This asks specifically what individuals know about the mental states, intentions, desires, and beliefs of others, and acknowledges that the thoughts, desires, and beliefs of others can differ from one's own (Beer & Ochsner, 2006; Premack & Woodruff, 1978; Wimmer & Perner, 1983). Human infants do not develop ToM until they are around 4 or 5 years old, well after the onset of basic language skills. The hallmark test of ToM is the false-belief task (Wimmer & Perner, 1983) in which children are presented with a scenario where a protagonist hides candy in a particular location and then leaves the room. Another individual then moves that candy to a new location. When the protagonist re-enters the room, the child is asked where s/he will look for the candy. Prior to ~4 years, the child will say in the new location, where the candy currently exists, but after ~4 years, the child understands that the protagonist's knowledge about the candy's location differs from the child's own knowledge, i.e., the protagonist didn't see the candy moved. Because the false-belief task requires verbal instruction about whose perspective to take, it cannot be fully adapted for use with nonverbal organisms, such as nonhuman primates or preverbal infants.

Instead, studies of social cognition in nonhuman primates (chimpanzees) have almost exclusively placed a dominant and subordinate individual in competition over a food reward (Hare et al., 2000). In a typical set up, a dominant and subordinate individual are positioned on opposite sides looking into a room that contains two small barriers. Food is placed next to the barriers so that one piece is visible only to the subordinate and the other piece is visible to both individuals. When allowed access into the room, the subordinate avoids the food that both can see and only attempts to take the food that is hidden from the dominant (Hare et al., 2000). In a second study, both the dominant and subordinate witness food being hidden next to a single barrier, so that after baiting it is only visible to the subordinate (Hare et al., 2001). The food is then moved to a new location when a) only the subordinate sees the move, similar to the condition in the false-belief task, and b) when both the dominant and subordinate can see the move. In this experiment, the subordinate only attempts to retrieve the food in condition a, when only they saw it moved (Hare et al., 2001). The explanation for both experiments is that chimpanzees have knowledge that seeing things means knowing things, so the subordinate only tries to obtain the food that it knows the dominant has not seen.

While the data from these studies are intriguing, the only dependent variable measured is the proportion of trials in which the subordinate successfully takes the food where the critical comparison is between attempts to take food that the dominant can see (around 30% of trials) versus food that the dominant cannot see or did not see moved (around 45% of the trials) (Hare et al., 2001). Thus, the interpretation is hinged on unobservable processes and although the data are suggested to reveal the chimpanzee's ability to use advanced socio-cognitive strategies, no measures of social behavior or interactions are made. The problem does not lie with the design of Hare and colleagues' study, because it is remarkably clever in it simplicity, but that ToM

involves unobservable thoughts and so cannot be directly measured in nonverbal animals. Therefore, the authors can only conclude that chimpanzee social cognition ". . . is based on a representational understanding of the behavior of others . . ." such as basic visual orientation skills, but does not translate into visual, or mental, perspective taking (Hare et al., 2001, p. 149).

The reason for this detailed example is to emphasize the importance of a more systematic approach to understanding the evolution of social cognition and whether it shares homologous features among related primates, including humans. The only way to do this when the behavior in question is as complex as social cognition/ToM is to break the behavior down into simpler elements. Using Tinbergen's (1963) framework (described above), researchers can examine these basic elements at multiple evolutionary levels, e.g., whether the behaviors look similar, emerge at similar stages of development, have phylogenetic continuity, and serve a similar adaptive function. This alternative approach enables social cognition to be studied using observable events/behaviors distributed between individuals within the context of their unique relationship, rather than unobservable, private thoughts or beliefs. In the experiments described above, for example, before even attempting to take a piece of food, the subordinate chimpanzee must first recognize the identity of the dominant, recall the status of their relationship, remember the outcome of previous interactions, competitive or otherwise, and then evaluate their own internal motivation to obtain food (see social affordances below), taking the specific context into account before deciding on a behavioral path. While this may seem like a complex sequence of evaluations, for which ToM-like skills would be extremely useful, a more detailed examination reveals a series of relatively straightforward individual and social evaluations based on key skills that collectively are necessary for social cognition to take place, but individually can be explained through relatively simple cognitive processes.

Building Blocks of Social Cognition: Knowledge of Individual Relationships and their Social Affordances
Recognition of Individuals and Relationships
Social organization is highly varied across the primate taxa, taking on a wide array of compositions that range from monogamous pairs to large multi-male, multi-female communities. Despite the precise

composition of individuals, there are several key behavioral elements that are necessary for primate societies to thrive. Already it has been suggested that one of the most basic, yet important, elements of social cognition is individual recognition across a variety of categorical levels. One must be able to recognize conspecifics from other species (Pascalis et al., 2002), and members of one's own (ingroup) versus another group (outgroup) (Macrae & Bodenhausen, 2000). Within one's group, there are means for discriminating kin versus unrelated individuals and studies have shown that this can involve visual/facial cues alone (Parr & de Waal, 1999). Even more complex is the recognition of specific individuals, friends, foes, and alliance partners and these particular classes of relationship can change frequently over the course of an individual's lifetime. The ability to discriminate among different individuals from a variety of different relationship categories enables adaptive prosocial behavior to transcend small kin groups, because key social benefits can be paid back (reciprocal altruism) to unrelated individuals. As will be discussed below, it is not just overall group size, but the complexity of social relationships that has been implicated in driving the evolution of large brain size and social intelligence among primates, particularly humans and great apes (Shultz & Dunbar, 2007).

Among nonhuman primates, several interesting studies have demonstrated not only knowledge about one's own relationships, but knowledge about the relationships among others, or third-party relationships. Chimpanzees produce distinct scream vocalizations that vary according to their role in the conflict and screams given after receipt of severe aggression were more exaggerated but only when there was a conspecific nearby the victim who outranked the aggressor and thus could potentially intervene (Slocombe & Zuberbuhler, 2007). Capuchin monkeys appear to use triadic awareness when selecting alliance partners. Data suggest that, in addition to selecting individuals more dominant to themselves and of the highest rank available, they select an individual with whom them have the highest quality of social relationship (reflected by greater ratio of cooperative/affiliative to agonistic interactions) compared to their opponent (Perry, Carrett, & Manson, 2004). Several studies in a variety of primate species have also documented kin-directed third-party affiliations (Aureli & de Waal, 2000). These involve affiliative behaviors directed at the kin of a former opponent rather than the opponent themselves, suggesting that these interventions function to

repair the relationship among conflicting individuals when the risk of resumed aggression is too great for them to reconcile directly (e.g., Wittig, Crockford, Wikberg, Seyfarth, & Cheney, 2007). The recognition of different categories of individuals effectively increases the overall number of partners that one can socialize with, and the variety of different relationships that one can have over the course of one's lifetime.

Recognition of Social Affordances

Also essential for the evolution of social cognition is that individuals have a basic understanding of how their own behavior and physical skills enable them to interact with the world around them, particularly the social world. This is similar to the concept of environmental affordances proposed by ecological psychology, only pertaining specifically to the social environment (Gibson, 1979). Environmental affordances refer to the physical and relational properties of objects in an environment that lend themselves to be acted upon. An object sitting on the ground "affords" pushing while a hole in a fence "affords" poking. Social affordances involve characteristics of individuals that provide information about social interactions, or important aspects of an environment. For example, to a subordinate individual, a dominant's posture affords a submissive one in return. An individual's gaze affords important information about location, body posture affords information about intended direction of movement, and facial expression affords important information about an individual's subsequent behavioral tendencies (van Hooff, 1967).

What is also essential here is an appreciation of the rules that govern social interactions and an individual's motivation to obtain particular goals in the face of these societal rules. If one is satiated, for example, it is unlikely that they will challenge another group member for food, so there are rules about the costs and benefits of one's own behavior. As already mentioned, humans will punish cheaters in a cooperation task by willingly foregoing their own individual gains in order to ensure cheaters get nothing, thus there are rules about cooperation and defection (Fehr & Fischbacher, 2003). Similar rules may also apply to nonhuman primates, where capuchin monkeys cease to cooperate in an exchange task if they observe an unfair distribution of payoffs (Brosnan & de Waal, 2003). Chimpanzees groom more with individuals that previously shared food with them, suggesting rules about reciprocity (de Waal, 1997), and prescriptive rules regarding age-dependent regulation of play intensity and the use of play signals have been reported among chimpanzees (Flack et al., 2004). Although the concept of social affordances is more complex than can be addressed here, it is important to mention because selection operates on the adaptive properties of behavior, not on the thoughts or beliefs an individual may have leading to the production of the behavior. In the social domain, this does not simply involve stimulus response contingency learning, but incorporates information about the identity of the social partner and the societal rules that constrain how one can interact with others. In the example above, when playing with a younger juvenile in the presence of their mother, chimpanzees will perform more play signals, perhaps functioning to appease the mother and preventing her intervention, thus affording more intense play interactions (Flack et al., 2004). Therefore, to understand social cognition, it is essential to understand what features of the social environment an individual is attending to, e.g., specific individuals, behavioral cues, and social affordances, whether this information is accurately perceived, and an individual's motivation for engaging in subsequent interactions.

Social Cognition Is Afforded Through Social Communication

Communication is one of the most important components of social cognition, forming a fundamental building block on which social interactions and the evolution of socio-cognitive strategies may be formed (e.g., the use of bared-teeth displays to reduce aggression and facilitate affiliative interactions). Among primates, visual cues and vocal cues (facial expressions, gestures, body postures, and vocalizations) are the most prominent categories of communicative behaviors that, when used together, create a dynamic repertoire of flexible signals from which highly elaborate communication systems have emerged (Partan & Marler, 1999). Spontaneous communication often changes the behavior of individuals during ongoing social interactions, implying that meaningful information transfer has occurred. Lip-smacking in white-faced capuchins, for example, increases affiliative behavior between the sender and receiver, indicating that this expression can functionally change the quality of their social interaction (de Marco et al., 2008). Likewise, performing a bared-teeth expression after a conflict reduces the likelihood of subsequent agonistic behavior and thus functions to appease a potential aggressor (Preuschoft & van Hooff, 1997; Waller & Dunbar, 2005).

Whether the individual performing the display "intends" to influence the other does not change the fact that the production of these signals has predictive consequences for subsequent interactions, enabling individuals to modify their behavior in an ongoing flexible manner. This communication is the cornerstone of primate social cognition and without it, individuals would be unable to successfully navigate their complex social environment or balance the competitive and cooperative interactions inherent in large groups. In this sense, social cognition is afforded by a detailed, structured, yet flexible communication system.

The majority of research on animal social cognition, however, has primarily examined what an animal understands about gaze direction or pointing cues used by humans to indicate the location of a desired object or hidden food (e.g., Call et al., 2003; Kaminski et al., 2005). As these experiments involve interspecies interactions, critics have argued that they are inherently unnatural, as chimpanzees do not typically learn from human demonstrators. In their classic study, Povinelli and Eddy (1996) found that although chimpanzees can develop rules so as to react appropriately to human gaze and pointing gestures, e.g., only attempt to interact with the human whose eyes are visible, this appeared to be unrelated to any actual understanding of the human's intention. More importantly, however, there is little evidence for the spontaneous use of such gestures, like pointing, among nonlanguage-trained chimpanzees, suggesting that these are not even species-typical signals. A recent study, for example, showed that language-trained apes were readily able to exchange/barter goods with a human experimenter using specific symbols, but they failed to do so with one another (Brosnan & Beran, 2009). Thus, in order to fully understand social cognition, it is essential to disentangle (both theoretically and empirically) the difference between cognitive abilities (what a chimp is able to learn in captivity when interacting with humans) and socio-communicative skills (the interactions chimpanzees have with each other to convey information).

There remain, however, several outstanding issues, primarily what cues are relevant for social communication, when animals use these cues during spontaneous interactions, and whether social communication provides any means to further understand others' mental states. The most appropriate way to examine these issues is to study intraspecific communication within a typical social context, as this is the environment most similar to the situation in which the interplay between cognition and communication evolved. This, however, is not often done, in part because it is both extremely difficult and time consuming to conduct observational studies of spontaneous communicative behavior. The behaviors themselves occur infrequently and if antecedent conditions are considered, they must be captured at their onset, requiring an observational data collection procedure (focal animal sampling) that is extremely time consuming, as only one animal can be studied at a given time. As is so often the case, there is a trade-off between experimental control that comes through structured laboratory studies and accessing the spontaneous manner in which animals behave. For similar reasons, the ethology of human communication is also a much neglected area of research focus. These obstacles are one reason for the divide between studies of animal cognition, in the sense of what is *understood*, from the manner by which it comes to be understood, in the sense of what cues are important and how they are exchanged. To truly understand the social cognition of other animals we need to contextualize their communication and analyze how social interaction is based on an exchange of information through specific species-typical behavior.

The Importance of Facial Expressions

Facial expressions have been studied quite extensively in some species of nonhuman primates and many of these appear to be homologous to basic emotional expressions in humans. Parr and colleagues (2007), for example, showed that 4 of 5 prototypical expressions in chimpanzees have clear counterparts to human expressions in terms of their component muscle movements, those corresponding to anger (bulging lip face), smile (bared-teeth face), screaming (scream), and laughter (playface) (see Figure 4.1). The bared-teeth display is morphologically similar in many species of primates (Preuschoft & van Hooff, 1997), but variations can occur as in the case of the gorilla, where the upper teeth are often visible (Palagi et al., 2007). Other primate expressions are not found in humans and specific variants may be unique to each species. Lip smacking, for example, is an affinitive display common to many species (e.g., capuchins: de Marco et al., 2008; and macaques: Preuschoft & van Hooff, 1997), but not found in the human repertoire.

Some have attempted to trace how nonhuman primate behavioral repertoires have changed across phylogeny (Andrews, 1963; Chevalier-Skolnikoff, 1973), or in relation to socioecological or life-history characteristics (Preuschoft & van Hooff, 1997; Dobson, 2009), thus trying to ascertain which forces are driving selection for changes in facial expression. In his seminal book, Huber (1931) adopted a linear approach suggesting that the facial musculature (and thus facial expression) changed across phylogeny according to an ascending scale,

Play face   Joy   Bulging-lip face   Mad face

Bared-teeth display   Happy   Scream   Surprise/excited

Fig. 4.1 A comparison of human and chimpanzee facial expressions. Adapted from Parr (2010) with kind permission of Elsevier.

with human facial expression repertoires at the pinnacle of evolutionary success. Evolution, however, is not a directed process and humans do not represent the endpoint of an ascending evolutionary trajectory (Hodos & Campbell, 1969). Indeed, recent dissections of the facial musculature in primates have demonstrated remarkable similarity across many species (Burrows & Smith, 2003; Burrows et al., 2006). Thus, it may be more appropriate to adopt a socioecological approach and examine specific *needs* for expressions. Dobson (2009) performed such an analysis and found that species living in larger groups had greater facial mobility and that facial expression, per se, may aid group cohesion. Thus, increasing group size may be one explanation for increased facial mobility and/or expressiveness among primates.

Like any complex skill, social intelligence requires cognitive resources and humans are not only one of the most social species, but they have the largest brains of any mammal. Numerous theorists (see Dunbar) have speculated that this increase in brain size is directly related to the cognitive demands stemming from life in complex social groups, as opposed to complex physical environments. This idea, referred to as the social brain hypothesis (Dunbar, 1998), holds strongest for anthropoid primates in which relative brain size (the ratio of neocortex size to overall brain size) is positively correlated with many important features of sociality, including mean group size, number of females, size of grooming cliques, frequency of coalition formation, male mating strategies, social play, frequency of social learning, and tactical deception (reviewed by Dunbar & Shultz, 2007). Interestingly, residual brain volume is higher in mammalian and avian species that form pair bonds, or are monogamous, compared to species that have polygamous mating systems. Moreover, pair-bonded species spend more time engaged in social activities than species with other mating systems, even after controlling for group size (Shultz & Dunbar, 2007). Thus, the selection pressure for larger brains may have originated with the socio-cognitive demands stemming from monogamous relationships and then generalized to nonreproductive social relationships among the anthropoid primates because of their intense sociality (Shultz & Dunbar, 2007).

In addition to brain size, numerous other specializations appear to have emerged in hominoids to cope with increased sociality and like the work of Dobson suggests, many of these appear to involve specializations for facial mobility and expressive signaling.

Phylogenetic specializations have been reported in the facial nucleus in the pons of the brainstem where the facial nucleus volume (compared to medullary volume) is larger in apes and humans compared to other monkey species (Sherwood et al., 2005). This region is particularly important in providing input (via the facial nerve, cranial nerve VII) to the mimetic facial muscles involved in social communication. The cytoarchitecture of the face area of the primary motor cortex also differs such that the neurons in layer III that form cortico-cortical connections were less dense in great apes and humans compared to other Old World monkey species. This suggests greater space for interneuronal signaling which may provide greater voluntary control of facial expressions during social interactions (see Dobson, 2009 above).

Summary: Social Cognition Involves more than Theory of Mind

An overemphasis on ToM as the hallmark of social cognition in both human and nonhuman primate species may actually be the result of our own inherent Cartesian biases about the relationship between large brains and complex societies (Barrett, Henzi & Rendall, 2007); however, just because primates live in complex social groups and have large brains does not confirm the presence of selection pressures to drive the evolution of advanced socio-cognitive strategies and counter-strategies, e.g., Machiavellian intelligence. Instead, as has been argued in this chapter, the ability to solve complex social problems can often be explained through an examination of basic skills, such as individual recognition, understanding of social affordances, and social communication. These skills enable a species like the chimpanzee to engage in seemingly complex social interactions by detecting regularities in ongoing behavior and then forming general heuristics about the outcome of those behaviors based on an accumulation of social knowledge (Povinelli & Vonk, 2003). These behavioral regularities can then come to provide important information to others who may act to enforce them, e.g., execution of prescriptive rules, creating the appearance of understanding others' intentions and desires. A cognitive strategy that deals with general heuristics as opposed to rigid response patterns is likely to prevail in a complex social environment where the behavior of others is largely unpredictable (Byrne & Bates, 2007), and opportunities for learning through standard mechanisms are unavailable (Flack et al., 2004). This gives the individual a flexible set of options for responding that can be influenced by a number of different, and sometimes novel, factors. This type of behavioral flexibility is a defining feature of primate social complexity. Perhaps more importantly, by narrowly focusing on ToM as the standard for studying social cognition, researchers overlook other important and equally complex social skills. As stated above, this narrow focus may cloud the identification of homologous traits and, perhaps more importantly, bias an understanding of the function and meaning of the behaviors themselves, obscuring its importance for the society as a whole.

References

Andrew, R. J. (1963). The origin and evolution of the calls and facial expressions of the primates. *Behaviour, 20,* 1–109.

Aureli, F. & de Waal, F. B. M. (2000). *Natural conflict resolution.* Los Angeles: University of California Press.

Barrett, L. & Henzi, P. (2005). The social nature of primate cognition. *Proceedings of the Royal Society: B, 272,* 1865–1875.

Barrett, L., Henzi, P., & Rendall, D. (2007). Social brains, simple minds: Does social complexity really require cognitive complexity? *Philosophical transactions of the Royal Society, 362,* 561–575.

Beer, J. & Ochsner, K. N. (2006). Social cognition: A multi level analysis. *Brain Research, 1079,* 98–105.

Brosnan, S. F. & de Waal, F. B. M. (2003). Monkeys reject unequal pay. *Nature, 425,* 297–299.

Brosnan, S. F. & Beran, M. J. (2009). Trading behavior between conspecifics in chimpanzees, Pan troglodytes. *Journal of Comparative Psychology, 123,* 181–194.

Burrows, A. M. & Smith, T. D. (2003). Muscles of facial expression in Otolemur, with a comparison to Lemuroidea. *Anatomical Record Part A, 274A,* 827–836.

Burrows, A., Waller, B. M. & Parr, L. A. & Bonar, C. J. (2006). Muscles of facial expression in the chimpanzee (Pan troglodytes): Descriptive, comparative, and phylogenetic contexts. *Journal of Anatomy, 208,* 153–168.

Byrne, R. W. & Bates, L. A. (2007). Sociality, evolution and cognition. *Current Biology, 17,* R714–R723.

Byrne, R. W. & Whiten, A. (1988). *Machiavellian intelligence: Social expertise and the evolution of intellect in monkeys, apes and humans.* Oxford: Oxford University Press.

Call, J., Bräuer, J., Kaminski, J., & Tomasello, M. (2003). Domestic dogs are sensitive to the attentional state of humans. *Journal of Comparative Psychology, 117,* 257–263.

Chevalier-Skolnikoff, S. (1973). Facial expression of emotion in nonhuman primates. In P. Ekman (Ed.), *Darwin and facial expressions* (pp. 11–89). New York: Academic Press.

Clutton-Brock, T. H. (2002). Breeding together: Kin selection and mutualism in cooperative vertebrates. *Science, 293,* 2446–2449.

De Marco, A., Petit, O., & Visalberghi, E. (2008). The repertoire and the social function of the facial displays in white-faced capuchins (Cebus capucinus). *Folia Primatologica, 29,* 469–486.

de Waal, F. B. M. (1997). The chimpanzee's service economy: Food for grooming. *Evolution & Human Behavior, 18,* 1–12.

de Waal, F. B. M. (1982). *Chimpanzee politics: Power and sex among apes.* London: Jonathon Cape.

de Waal, F. B. M. & Luttrell, L. (1985). The formal hierarchy of rhesus monkeys: An investigation of the bared teeth display. *American Journal of Primatology, 9,* 73–85.

Dobson, S. D. (2009) Socioecological correlates of facial mobility in nonhuman anthropoids. *American Journal of Physical Anthropology, 139,* 413–420.

Dobson, S. D. (2009) Allometry of facial mobility in anthropoid primates: implications for the evolution of facial expression. *American Journal of Physical Anthropology, 138,* 70–81.

Dunbar, R. I. M. & Shultz, S. (2007). Evolution in the social brain. *Science, 317,* 1344–1347.

Dunbar, R. I. M. (1998). The social brain hypothesis. *Evolutionary Anthropology, 6,* 178–190.

Fehr, E. & Fischbacher, U. (2003). The nature of human altruism. *Nature, 425,* 785–791.

Flack, J. C., Jeannotte, L. A., & de Waal, F. B. M. (2004). Play signaling and the perception of social rules by juvenile chimpanzees (Pan troglodytes). *Journal of Comparative Psychology, 118,* 149–159.

Gibson, J. J. (1979). *The Ecological Approach to Visual Perception.* Boston: Houghton-Mifflin.

Hare, B., Call, J., & Tomasello, M. (2001). Do chimpanzees know what conspecifics know? *Animal Behaviour, 61,* 139–151.

Hare, B., Call, J., Agnetta, B., & Tomasello, M. (2000). Chimpanzees know what conspecifics do and do not see. *Animal Behaviour, 59,* 771–785.

Hodos, W. & Campbell, C. B. G. (1969). Scala naturae: Why there is no theory in comparative psychology. *Psychological Review, 76,* 337–350.

Huber, E. (1931). *Evolution of facial musculature and facial expression.* Oxford: Oxford University Press.

Humphrey, N. K. (1976). The social function of intellect. In: P. P. G. Bateson & R. A. Hinde (Eds.), *Growing points in ethology* (pp. 303–317). Cambridge: Cambridge University Press.

Jolly, A. (1966). Lemur social behavior and primate social intelligence. *Science, 153,* 501–506.

Kaminski, J., Riedel, J., Call, J., & Tomasello, M. (2005) Domestic goats (Capra hircus) follow gaze direction and use social cues in an object choice task. *Animal Behaviour, 69,* 11–18.

Macrae, C. N. & Bodenhausen, G. V. (2000). Social cognition: Thinking categorically about others. *Annual Review of Psychology, 51,* 93–120.

Mehu, M. & Dunbar, R. I. M. (2008). The relationship between smiling and laughter in humans (Homo sapiens): Testing the Power Asymmetry Hypothesis. *Folia Primatologica, 79,* 269–280.

Palagi, E., Antonacci, D., & Cordoni, G. (2007). Fine-tuning of social play in juvenile lowland gorillas (Gorilla gorilla). *Developmental Psychobiology, 49,* 433–445.

Parr, L. A. (2010). Emotion and social cognition in primates. In: M. D. Breed & J. Moore (Eds.), *Encyclopedia of Animal Behavior, Volume 1* (pp. 621–627). Oxford: Academic Press.

Parr, L. A. & de Waal, F. B. M. (1999). Visual kin recognition in chimpanzees. *Nature, 399,* 647–648.

Parr, L. A., Waller, B. M., Vick, S. J., & Bard, K. A. (2007). Classifying chimpanzee facial expressions by muscle action. *Emotion, 7,* 172–181.

Partan, S. & Marler, P. (1999). Communication goes multimodal. *Science, 283,* 1272–1273.

Pascalis, O., de Haan, M., & Nelson, C.A. (2002). Is face processing species-specific during the first year of life? *Science, 296*, 1321–1323.

Perry, S., Carrett, H. C., & Manson, J. H. (2004). White-faced capuchin monkeys show triadic awareness in their choice of allies. *Animal Behaviour, 67*, 165–170.

Povinelli, D. J. & Eddy, T. J. (1996). What young chimpanzees know about seeing. *Monographs of the Society for Research on Child Development, 61*, 1–152.

Povinelli, D. J. & Vonk, J. (2003). Chimpanzee minds: Suspiciously human? *Trends in Cognitive Science, 7*, 157–160.

Premack, D. & Woodruff, G. (1978). Does the chimpanzee have a theory of mind? *Behavioral and Brain Sciences, 4*, 515–526.

Preuschoft, S. & van Hooff, J.A.R.A.M. (1997). The social function of "smile" and "laughter": Variations across primate species and societies. In: U. Segerstrale & P. Mobias (Eds.), *Nonverbal Communication: Where Nature Meets Culture* (pp. 252–281). New Jersey: Erlbaum.

Sherwood, C. C. (2005). Comparative anatomy of the facial motor nucleus in mammals, with an analysis of neuron numbers in primates. *The Anatomical Record, Part A, 287A*, 1067–1079.

Shultz, S. & Dunbar, R. I. M. (2007). The evolution of the social brain: anthropoid primates contrast to other vertebrates. *Proceedings of the Royal Society of London B, 274*, 2429–2436.

Slocombe, K. & Zuberbuhler, K. (2007). Chimpanzees modify recruitment screams as a function of audience composition. *Proceedings of the National Academy of Sciences, 104*, 17228–17233.

Thierry, B., Demaria, C., Preuschoft, S., & Desportes, C. (1989). Structural convergence between silent bared-teeth display and relaxed open-mouth display in the Tonkean macaque (Macaca tonkeana). *Folia Primatologica, 52*, 178–184.

Tinbergen, N. (1963). On aims and methods of ethology. *Zeitshrift für Tierpsychologie, 20*, 410–433.

Van Hooff, J. A. R. A. M. (1967). The facial displays of the Catarrhine monkeys and apes. In D. Morris (Ed.), *Primate ethology* (pp. 7–68). Chicago: Aldine.

Waller, B. M. & Dunbar, R. I. M. (2005). Differential behavioral effects of silent bared teeth display and relaxed open mouth display in chimpanzees (Pan troglodytes). *Ethology, 111*, 129–142.

Waller, B. M., Parr, L. A., Gothard, K. M., Burrows, A. M., & A. J. Fuglevand. (2008). Mapping the contribution of single muscles to facial movements in the Rhesus Macaque. *Physiology and Behaviour, 95*, 93–100.

Waller, B. M., Vick, S. J., Parr, L. A., Bard, K. A., Smith Pasqualini, M. C., Gothard, K. et al. (2006). Intramuscular stimulation of facial muscles in humans and chimpanzees: Duchenne revisited. *Emotion, 6*, 367–382.

Wimmer, H. & Perner, J. (1983). Beliefs about beliefs: Representation and constraining function of wrong beliefs in young children's understanding of deception. *Cognition, 13*, 41–68.

Wittig, R. M, Crockford, C., Wikberg, E., Seyfarth, R. M., & Cheney, D. L. (2007). Kin-mediated reconciliation substitutes for direct reconciliation in female baboons. *Proceedings of Biological Science, 274*, 1109–1115.

Wimmer, H. & Perner, J. (1978). Belief about beliefs: Representation and constraining function of wrong beliefs in young children's understanding of deception. *Cognition, 13*, 103–128.

Social Neuroscience:
A Neuropsychological Perspective

Janelle Beadle *and* Daniel Tranel

Abstract

This chapter discusses the human lesion approach for understanding the mechanisms of social processes. It begins with a description of the lesion method, which allows researchers to explore the association between focal damage to a particular brain region and impairment in a clearly defined cognitive-behavioral function. In humans, the lesion method is used to study individuals who have incurred focal brain damage naturally as a result of external insult (e.g., car accident, bullet wound) or due to specific kinds of disease or damage (e.g., cerebrovascular disease, surgical treatment of epilepsy, tumor resection). The chapter goes on to present some notable examples of lesion-method research in the field of social neuroscience.

Keywords: human lesion approach, social processes, cognitive behavior, social neuroscience, lesion method research

Introduction

In 1992, the term social neuroscience was used in an influential paper emphasizing the importance of investigating and explaining social behavior through multiple levels of analysis, including not only social psychological constructs but also neural systems (Cacioppo & Bernston, 1992). By now, social neuroscience is a burgeoning field that has literally exploded in size and scope over the past several years, spawning new journals, new specialty areas, and dedicated textbooks such as the one in which this chapter appears.

It is interesting to consider briefly why this might be the case. A few contributing factors would seem to include: (1) During the 1990s, the World Wide Web became a widely available and highly accessible tool. This development gave social an entirely new meaning, expanding virtually overnight and by many orders of magnitude the realm of interactions that persons can have with each other. (2) The decade of the '90s also witnessed the emergence of functional neuroimaging, especially functional magnetic resonance imaging (fMRI), as a readily available and widely used tool in cognitive neuroscience. This development paved the way for entire species of researchers—who often would have identified previously with groups such as social and/or physiological psychology—to deem themselves neuroscientists. (3) We also note that studying the myriad functions that fall under the rubric of social has enormous intuitive appeal and almost automatic vernacular intrigue. Discovering the brain's "moral compass" has a charm to it that is hard to match with, say, discovering the neural basis of visual attention. (4) Finally, the past two decades have witnessed a rediscovery of emotion, and the reinsertion of emotion into the lineup of topics considered acceptable as proper domains of neuroscientific inquiry. Much of this resurgence can be traced to the influential and paradigm-shifting theoretical framework that Antonio Damasio explicated in a series of books published in the mid to late 1990s, especially *Descartes' Error* (1994) and *The Feeling of What Happens* (1999). Emotion is tightly intertwined with all manner of social processes and functions, a fact underscored by the numerous studies that have shown similar neural systems underpinning emotional and social processes. Hence, the reinstatement of emotion as a popular topic of neuroscientific investigation has also catalyzed the rapid expansion of the field of social neuroscience.

In short, the neuroscientific study of social processes has become increasingly fashionable and more and more widely practiced. This has led to a whole host of exciting new discoveries, many of whose importance for neuroscience and for the fundamental understanding of human health and disease is immediately obvious. As one prominent example, researchers studying the neural basis of loneliness (a state of psychological suffering due to perceived social isolation) have discovered that lonely people are more likely to experience a variety of negative health issues and diseases, including impairments in sleep, depression, cardiovascular disease, and even Alzheimer's disease (Cacioppo et al., 2002; Hawkley, Masi, Berry, & Cacioppo, 2006; Paul, Ayis, & Ebrahim, 2006). As the baby boomer population grows older, researchers have also become very interested in the effects of aging on brain systems involved in social functioning, and how these changes may affect real-world decision making.

Along with this, recent work has highlighted related changes in the domain of emotion. For example, older adults are less able than younger adults to recognize stimuli with negative content (e.g., Moreno, Borod, Welkowitz, & Alpert, 1993; Sullivan & Ruffman, 2004) and may experience negative emotion with less frequency and intensity (e.g., Gross, Carstensen, Pasupathi, Tsai, Skorpen, & Hsu, 1997). This functional change may be a consequence of neurological changes—for example, reduced brain activity has been found in the amygdala of older adults (in comparison to younger adults) when they are viewing negatively valenced pictures (Mather et al., 2004). There is evidence that some older adults may have difficulty making advantageous financial decisions, and this has been documented in the laboratory (Denburg, Tranel, & Bechara, 2005) as well as in real-world settings such

as targeting of older persons through telemarketing (American Association of Retired Persons [AARP], 1996). It is thought that aging-related changes in decision-making behavior may be a result of degeneration to particular brain structures, with the prefrontal cortex being most often implicated (Denburg et al., 2007). Thus, this domain of inquiry is not only important and interesting in its own right; it is also highly relevant to the fundamental knowledge base that is necessary for conquering diseases and promoting health. We would also note that many variables that are social in kind, are modifiable and amenable to intervention and change (unlike, say, genetic variables), and this means that there is enormous potential for developing programs that could prevent or alter the course of disease. Hence, scientific knowledge in this domain has enormous practical potential.

Against this background, it is interesting to ponder the role of traditional neuropsychological approaches to the study of social neuroscience. This is especially intriguing in the wake of the tsunami of functional imaging studies that has hit the literature over the past decade, and that continues more or less unabated. Does traditional neuropsychology have anything to contribute in this context? What are some of the important questions that neuropsychology can answer, and might even be positioned uniquely to answer? We have prepared the following chapter with these overarching questions in mind.

At the outset, we would like to point out that the lesion method remains a fundamental and indispensable scientific approach to the study of brain-behavior relationships in cognitive neuroscience, and we and others have underscored this message in several recent articles (e.g., Chatterjee, 2005; Fellows, Heberlein, Morales, Shivde, Waller, & Wu, 2005; Hernandez, Denburg, & Tranel, 2009; Koenigs, Tranel, & Damasio, 2007; Poldrack, 2006; Rorden & Karnath, 2004). What investigators like Brenda Milner (Milner, 1972) gleaned from a single case of profound anterograde amnesia can now be systematically studied in sufficiently large groups of such patients and where careful experimental control over neuropsychological and neuroanatomical variables is possible. Historically, lesion studies have often provided the first source of evidence for specific brain-behavior relationships (e.g., hippocampus and memory in patient H.M.) that are later validated with converging evidence from other methods. Today, as in decades past, findings from lesion studies still continue to inspire and set the agenda for other approaches. Also, the lesion method remains an ideal approach for fleshing out clinical and real-world observations and characterizations of behavioral phenomena. The lesion method also affords a means to test, at the systems level, the *necessity* of a particular structure in (not just correlated with or involved in) a cognitive process and provides uniquely complementary information to results from imaging and animal studies.

We can be more specific. While the lesion method has both shared and unique inferential pitfalls with other methods, the lesion method, in neurological patients, confers particular investigational and inferential advantages relative to other approaches (e.g., fMRI, animal studies). An obvious but often overlooked advantage is the possibility of conducting in-depth experiments on higher order cognitive abilities whose temporal and social characteristics are not currently amenable to other approaches. Especially in the domain of social processes, the core behaviors under scrutiny are decidedly human and decidedly social (other people are often involved). Many of the relevant experiments concern linguistic descriptions and high-level, face-to-face social interactions among people.

To be sure, there are challenges associated with studying social behaviors in laboratory settings and there are limitations on the extent to which real-world conditions can be simulated in the laboratory. But the confines of a magnetic resonance scanner introduce even more restrictions (e.g., difficulty implementing online social interactive tasks requiring expressive and pragmatic language use such as gesture, scanner noise). Studying the behaviors of patients with acquired brain damage provides an accessible and ecologically valid means of establishing brain-behavior relationships related to the domains of social functioning. Moreover, data from lesion studies of neurological patients are uniquely positioned to facilitate the translation of scientific knowledge into clinical application, as the research participants are in many cases the same individuals who would benefit from such clinical interventions.

To fully understand the mechanisms of social behavior, a multilevel approach that incorporates a variety of scientific methods which measure both macro- and micro-structural levels of a specific behavior should be used (Cacioppo & Bernston, 1992; Sarter, Bernston, & Cacioppo, 1996; Cacioppo, Bernston, Sheridan, & McClintock, 2000). A very complex social behavior can be explained succinctly at the level of higher-order cognitive mechanisms through social-psychological constructs which specify the mediating and moderating roles of various aspects of the individual's personality, life experience, and interaction with social groups over time. This same social behavior can be further understood by examining the individual's genetic makeup and determining how their genes may have interacted with their environment over time. For example, the interaction of genes that predispose an individual for developing a disease in combination with a socially distressing environment can increase the overall risk of a disease. As one instance, men with a positive family history of hypertension who also had high cardiovascular reactivity (high cardiac reactivity to stress) and significant life stressors showed higher levels of blood pressure than those who had a positive family history of hypertension but did not have high cardiovascular reactivity or significant life stress (Light et al., 1999). Functional neuroimaging serves as a useful tool to examine normal, healthy human brain function at the level of brain systems. Through functional neuroimaging, researchers are able to discern the network of brain areas involved in a specific psychological process in an online fashion. While the human lesion method is used to investigate the *necessity* of a brain region for a particular function, functional neuroimaging adds additional information by specifying the network of brain areas *involved* in a particular brain function. However, like all scientific techniques, there are limitations to the functional neuroimaging approach. Although the BOLD response is on the order of 6 to 8 seconds, it still does not reflect the time course of a neuron's action potential. Another limitation of this method is that it is difficult to design an appropriate control task that accounts for all mechanistic aspects of an experimental task except for the one process that is specific to the experimental task. Another type of methodology—the animal lesion study—can directly complement a human lesion study through the method of experimentally lesioning a particular focal brain area of interest in the animal which can then be compared to the outcome of a similar naturally occurring lesion in a human lesion study. However, one limitation of animal lesion studies specific to the domain of social neuroscience is that although animals do engage in many of the same social behaviors as humans, it is difficult to measure their personal experience. Despite this limitation, research has examined some social behaviors that are shared by humans and animals such as communication with others through distress vocalizations (Carden & Hofer, 1990) and participation in conflict between social groups (Keeley, 1996;

Goodall et al., 1979), making it a relevant methodology to study social behavior.

In short, a multilevel approach is the most optimal way to fully understand the mechanisms of social processes, and the human lesion approach provides an extremely valuable method by which to obtain information about social processes. We are excited to outline in this chapter the specific reasons why this is the case. In the following section, we take up that venture, and elaborate some of the nuts and bolts of the modern practice of the lesion method. The chapter then moves to a section in which we present some especially notable examples of lesion-method research in the field of social neuroscience.

The Lesion Method

As already alluded to, the lesion method in cognitive neuroscience confers a number of distinct advantages over other approaches, and it stands alone among experimental methods in that it can determine the necessity of a given brain region for a specific function. Using the lesion method, researchers can explore the association between focal damage to a particular brain region and impairment in a clearly defined cognitive-behavioral function. In this way, a hypothesis about a particular brain-behavior relationship can be tested. If damage to a particular brain region results in impairment to a particular cognitive-behavioral function, it is concluded that the brain region is necessary (albeit not necessarily sufficient) for that function. There are variations across laboratories in the way the lesion method is conducted, and the following describes how this method is practiced in our laboratory (H. Damasio & A. Damasio, 2003).

In humans, the lesion method is used to study individuals who have incurred focal brain damage naturally as a result of external insult (e.g., car accident, bullet wound) or due to specific kinds of disease or damage (e.g., cerebrovascular disease, surgical treatment of epilepsy, tumor resection). Lesion studies often examine patients whose lesions were caused by stroke, herpes simplex encephalitis, surgical ablation of benign tumors, specific cases of head trauma, or surgical treatment of epilepsy. Naturally occurring lesions do not affect each region of the brain equally. Rather, different types of brain insults tend to produce damage preferentially in certain areas of the brain. For example, herpes simplex encephalitis tends to affect limbic system structures; surgical treatment of epilepsy typically involves the anterior-mesial temporal lobes; and cerebrovascular accidents more commonly affect the perisylvian regions fed by the middle cerebral artery.

Case Study vs. Group Study Approach
CASE STUDY APPROACH

In its origin, the lesion method was a case study approach which involved the study of a patient with a particular lesion and a particular behavioral deficit. More recently, the lesion method has evolved to include group studies of patients who have lesions in similar locations or similar behavioral deficits (where either the common lesion site or the common behavioral deficit can be used as the independent variable). However, the case study method is still a valuable technique, especially to document rare and theoretically significant cases that help the scientific community to better understand the functional organization of the brain (Editorial, 2004). Patients who fall under the rubric of a case study tend to have a rare (typically focal) lesion or a behavioral deficit that is clear, specific, and stable over time. The behavioral performance of the patient often does not overlap with, or even come close to overlapping with, that of the group of comparison participants. Oftentimes, the magnitude of the difference between the patient's performance and the performance of healthy comparison participants is standardized in the form of a z-score (Editorial, 2004). To demonstrate the specificity of the deficit, the patient should show normal performance on a variety of other neuropsychological measures that do not tap into the processing demands required by the deficient ability.

A case study shares many similar methodological considerations to a group study. The patient should have a focal, specific lesion. A direct comparison should be made to a group of brain-damaged patients who have a focal lesion in a different location but with a similar size, etiology, and chronicity (time since lesion onset), with similar demographic characteristics (e.g., sex, age), and with similar performance on other measures of cognitive functioning (e.g., IQ, memory, language) that do not directly relate to the behavioral deficit being measured. In many cases, the patient should also be compared to a group of normal, healthy comparison participants matched on similar demographic and cognitive characteristics. (A comparison of "target" lesion patients to brain-damaged *and* healthy comparison participants is ideal, however, there are many examples of exceptions to this, whereby one or the other of these comparison groups is sufficient. And in some cases, the behavioral profile of the target patient is so obvious and so far from normal that a comparison group is unnecessary.) Anatomical information about the patient's lesion should be described and quantified using statistical imaging analysis techniques (see below for discussion).

A recent case study serves as an example of how the examination of a patient with a rare lesion can aid in our understanding of an important neuroanatomical circuit (Feinstein et al., 2009). This study describes the case of Roger, a man with a rare lesion encompassing virtually the entire limbic system. Since brain injury typically only affects part of the limbic system, this study is unique in that the damage includes more or less the entire system. The study serves as a useful model of the case study approach, as exemplified in its nuanced description of Roger's cognitive and emotional functioning which is measured through standardized neuropsychological measurement, rigorously designed experimental tests, and rich anecdotal observations. A holistic picture of Roger's functioning becomes evident, and it is revealed that his primary deficits are a temporally graded retrograde amnesia (spanning 10 years before the brain injury to onset) that affects both episodic and semantic memory, as well as a severe anterograde amnesia for declarative verbal and nonverbal information. In contrast, Roger shows predominantly spared function on tests of intelligence, language, and visual function. The patient's brain damage is carefully described by a trained neuroanatomist, who delineates the damage to each portion of the limbic system as well as explicitly noting any damage that has occurred outside of the limbic system. An in-depth description of the neuroanatomy of the patient's lesion in a case study is critical to its functional interpretation, as even focal lesions can produce damage to regions outside the area of interest. (And we would add that this component of case reports is often underreported and underspecified, which, ultimately, does a disservice to the field because it becomes impossible to compare cases across laboratories, reconcile discrepant findings, and the like.) A compelling example of such a predicament is the case of Phineas Gage, where, because the patient never came to autopsy (and obviously was not studied with modern neuroimaging tools), there has continued a vigorous (and, ultimately, unsolvable) debate about the particulars of his lesion—for example, was it bilateral? Which prefrontal structures were damaged? (Damasio, Grabowski, Frank, Galaburda, & Damasio, 1994; Macmillan, 2000; Ratiu & Talos, 2004).

GROUP STUDY APPROACH

The traditional group study approach examines a sample of patients with a specific lesion location or behavioral deficit. To begin with, it is often important that all patients in the study have a lesion that is the chronic phase of recovery (at least three months after the onset) and that the lesion is stable (non-progressing). Mixing patients with evolving lesions and patients with stable lesions creates noise and adds to the chances of not finding reliable brain-behavior relationships. Selection of patients for the target group (or patients with damage to the region of interest) is based upon the degree to which the patient's lesion matches the following criteria: location, size, laterality (right-sided, left-sided, bilateral) and etiology (cause: stroke, surgery to remove epileptic foci, tumor resection, etc.). Oftentimes, researchers attempt to restrict the etiology of their sample, such as including only cases of lesions due to cerebrovascular disease or surgical resection of benign tumors, in order to reduce the effect of how different types of brain insults can cause different effects in the brain. Next, a comparison group is selected, comprised by patients who have focal damage to a brain region outside the target region but of similar size, etiology, and chronicity. Finally, another comparison group comprised by healthy, normal participants is selected. The two comparison groups are matched to the target group on particular demographic characteristics (e.g., age, sex, education, handedness) as well as general cognitive functions (e.g., intelligence, language, memory).

A more recent type of group study approach— the voxel-wise symptom-lesion analysis—employs an exploratory analysis that examines all voxels in the brain to determine which particular brain-damaged region is most significantly associated with a cognitive deficit. This methodology can be used when the researchers do not have an a priori hypothesis of the relationship between a brain area and a function. Patients with a variety of different lesion locations and sizes are included in the sample and a particular cognitive or emotional function of interest is examined. The scores of the patients in the sample on the cognitive/emotional function are represented along a continuum (if possible, depending on the fidelity of the measurement). An example of this type of approach is seen in a study that uses a voxel-wise analysis to examine the neural correlates of naming and recognition of concrete entities (Rudrauf, Mehta, Bruss, Tranel, Damasio, & Grabowski, 2008).

There are advantages to both the case study and group study approach when studying lesion-deficit relationships. The primary advantage of the case study approach is that it allows the researcher to further understand the brain's functional organization. If a small, focal lesion results in a specific behavioral deficit, it can be concluded that a specific brain area is necessary for a given function. This same conclusion can not be made in group studies where there is overlapping damage to a particular region because it is unclear what role the damage to the other areas may play. Another advantage of the case study approach is that it allows a more precise anatomical description of lesion location and extent. For a single case study it is not necessary, as in the group approach, to average across the lesions of a group of patients when performing the anatomical analysis. A limitation of the case study approach is that as a result of individual variability in brain structure and function, personality characteristics, cognitive abilities, and other idiosyncratic factors, a focal lesion to a particular brain area may produce a behavioral deficit in some individuals but not others. Another limitation of the case study approach is that some lesions may produce a behavioral deficit that is functionally relevant yet is subtle and thus undetectable due to a lack of power. Group studies that involve a large sample of patients with damage to a particular brain region help to ameliorate some of these issues by providing greater power to detect a difference between the target patient group and a comparison group. Another advantage of group studies is that the neural correlates of a particular function can be explored without having an a priori prediction of the particular brain regions involved in the function. This type of analysis can be accomplished through voxel-based analyses where the role that each and every voxel in the brain may play in a specific behavioral function is considered (at least insofar as what the lesion sampling has covered; see the next section for more details about this issue).

MULTIPLE CASE STUDY APPROACH

A powerful approach, that blends some of the strengths of the case study method with those of the group approach, is the multiple case study design. This entails the selection of a number of patients who, typically, have demonstrated a very robust, severe impairment in a particular function and have a focal lesion to a particular region of the brain. This type of approach affords more statistical power than a case study because a greater number of patients are investigated; moreover, the reliability of the finding

is more certain. At the same time, this approach may allow the researcher to have greater specificity in determining the lesion-deficit relationship than in a group study approach, because it focuses on those patients with the most severe impairment rather than on patients with functional deficits that vary along a spectrum of severity as in group studies. Also, because all of the cases are presented individually in some depth, the investigators can include and consider nuances and idiosyncrasies of the patients that would be left out or masked by group means in a group-level approach. An example of this approach is described in a multiple case study of six patients with a consistent, severe impairment in their knowledge of locative prepositions (e.g., *in, on, around*) and brain damage to the left posterior frontal operculum, white matter subjacent to this region, and the white matter located underneath the inferior parietal operculum (described in Study 2, Tranel & Kemmerer, 2004). The patients all showed significant impairments in their naming of actions, and some of the patients also had deficits in naming concrete entities (e.g., persons, animals, fruits). However, the researchers found a double dissociation between naming and conceptual knowledge, because the patients' conceptual knowledge for actions and concrete entities was mostly intact. In summary, the multiple case study approach is a useful, statistically powerful way to examine the lesion-deficit relationship in instances where there are multiple patients with severe impairments in a particular function and focal brain damage to a particular region of the brain, but where individual details of the cases are important and can be preserved in the presentation of the data.

Lesion Method Analysis Techniques

An important component of the lesion method is the description and quantification of the anatomy of the patient's lesion in order to examine the association between a specific brain region and a cognitive or emotional function. The development of magnetic resonance imaging (MRI) technology has allowed researchers to image the structure of the brain, making regions of brain damage visible to the naked eye as well as quantifiable by various measurement techniques. Through the examination of MRI images, researchers are able to determine the location and size of gray and white matter lesions. Methods have been developed to image a single patient's brain as well as to compare lesion characteristics across a group of patients with brain damage. Our laboratory uses the Brainvox system which allows for three-dimensional visualization and analysis of MRI images of patients with lesions (Frank, Damasio, & Grabowski, 1997). Using the MAP-3 tool within Brainvox, lesions from each patient are manually transferred to the shared space of a normal reference brain, taking into account proximity to sulcal and gyral landmarks.

Statistical analysis of group lesion studies typically involves either region of interest analysis (ROI) or voxel-wise analysis. ROI analysis is primarily utilized when there is a specific (a priori) hypothesis about a brain region's involvement in a particular function. The target participant group is selected on the basis of specific, focal damage that is (relatively) isolated to a region of interest. Another comparison group of patients is then selected, who have circumscribed brain damage to regions outside of the target region of interest. Participants are then dichotomized on the basis of having a target lesion (yes/no) and having a behavioral deficit (yes/no). Statistical tests compare these four groups: lesion/deficit, lesion/no-deficit, no-lesion/deficit, and no-lesion/no-deficit. An advantage of ROI analysis is that fewer statistical comparisons need to be conducted than in voxel-wise analysis, and therefore there is higher statistical power to be able to detect differences between groups.

When there is no a priori prediction about the involvement of a particular brain area for a function or if the researcher wants to do an exploratory investigation of which brain areas might be involved in a particular function, a voxel-wise analysis is a better fit. In this type of analysis, the relationship between a lesion and a deficit at each voxel in the brain is examined. Consequently, using voxel-wise analysis, there is better spatial resolution than in the ROI method to detect exactly which region of the brain results in a deficit for the function of interest. This is different from the ROI method which examines a clearly defined anatomical region as a whole rather than examining it at a more fine-grained voxel-wise level. A limitation of the voxel-wise approach is that because there are thousands of voxels in the brain, numerous statistical comparisons need to be performed and therefore there is a concern about how multiple comparisons may result in a high false positive rate. In this case, it is difficult to determine whether the voxels implicated in the deficit are truly related to the deficit or if they have occurred due to random chance. However, there are statistical methods available to help account for the effect of multiple comparisons.

The ROI approach has been used frequently in our laboratory to examine the relationship between a lesion to a particular brain region and a deficit in a particular function (e.g., Damasio, Grabowski, Tranel, Hichwa, & Damasio, 1996; Damasio, Tranel, Grabowski, Adolphs, & Damasio, 2004). A lesion overlap difference map (M3) is created that examines the overlap between a lesion and a functional deficit at the level of each voxel to determine areas of maximum overlap of lesion and deficit. More specifically, an M3 lesion-deficit analysis is performed such that at each voxel, the number of subjects with a lesion (L) and deficit (D) specified as N_{LD} is subtracted by the number of subjects with a lesion (L) and no deficit (~D) specified as N_{L-D}. This can be expressed as a joint probability such that the proportion of lesion subjects with a deficit is subtracted by the number of lesion subjects without a deficit and then multiplied by the number of subjects in the entire sample:

$$(1a) \quad M3 = \left[N \, Prop \, (L,D) - Prop \, (L, {\sim}D) \right]$$

A statistical assumption of the null hypothesis is that the two variables of interest are independent of each other. Applied to this specific case, this means that the presence of a lesion at a specific location does not influence the rate at which a deficit will appear. Based upon this assumption, equation 1a can be transformed so that it is expressed as the joint probability of two independent variables:

$$(1b) \quad Prop \, (L,D) - Prop \, (L, {\sim}D)$$
$$= Prop \, (L) \, Prop \, (D) - Prop \, (L) \, Prop \, ({\sim}D)$$

Furthermore, this equation can be transformed by factoring out Prop (L) to result in the final product:

$$(1c) \quad M3 = Prop(L)[P(D) - P({\sim}D)]N$$

The M3 method is limited in its ability to make statistical inferences in certain cases. This becomes particularly evident when there is no relationship between the lesion location and a particular functional deficit. The arithmetic outcome is shifted based upon the difference between the proportion of subjects with a deficit versus no deficit. In addition, the outcome is highly dependent on the number of lesions at a particular voxel location and the number of subjects in the sample. Consequently, the resulting outcome becomes inflated locally (due to the proportion of lesions at that particular voxel) or globally (due to the number of subjects in the sample.) Another important issue to consider is that the lesion coverage at each voxel is heterogeneous due to the natural occurrence of lesions in some areas but not others. An alternative approach to M3 is the "lesion proportion difference" measure called PM3, which is the proportion of subjects with a lesion among those with a deficit minus the proportion of subjects with a lesion among those with no deficit (utilized in Karnath, Fruhmann Berger, Zopf, & Kuker, 2004; described in Rudrauf et al., 2008). This method advances the M3 method by centering the probability distribution corresponding to the null hypothesis around zero, accounting for uneven numbers of subjects who have deficits in comparison to subjects who have no deficits and cancelling the global effect of the number of subjects in the sample. The PM3 is defined as:

$$PM3 = (NLD / ND) - (NL \sim D / N \sim D)$$
$$= Prop(L \mid D) - Prop(L \mid \sim D)$$

It is important to note that methods like MAP3 and PM3 methods are purely descriptive in nature because they are not thresholded at a specific statistical criterion (Rudrauf et al., 2008). Instead, these methods typically employ a uniform cutoff to determine which scores truly indicate a deficit based upon the consideration of false positives (Damasio et al., 2004).

Methods have been developed to conduct inferential statistical analyses in group lesion studies. In the context of the M3 and PM3 methods, novel techniques have been devised for threshold methods that were initially only descriptive in nature (Rudrauf et al., 2008). Statistical methods are typically tailored to the characteristics of the data being examined. If the behavioral impairment is expressed in a binary manner (e.g., presence or absence of an emotion-processing deficit), a binomial test is most appropriate (reviewed in Rorden, Karnath, & Bonilha, 2007.) The most frequently used binomial test is the Yates corrected chi-square test, an approximation of the Fisher exact test. However, this statistical test may not be entirely appropriate for lesion data and therefore an alternative statistical test, called the Liebermeister test (Liebermeister, 1877), has been suggested. This test is similar to the Fisher exact test in its calculation but it offers better sensitivity (Seneta & Phipps, 2001).

If a behavioral impairment instead exists on a continuum, typically a t-test or an analysis of variance (ANOVA) is used (Bates et al., 2003). However, in the case of voxel-wise analysis, the t-test or ANOVA may not be the most effective statistical test to use (discussed in Rorden et al., 2007). Voxel-wise analysis involves the computation of a statistical test comparing each and every voxel, resulting in thousands of tests. Consequently, it is difficult to determine whether the statistical assumptions of a t-test are upheld for each test. These include that the data are normally distributed, represented on an interval scale and that the two groups of interest have comparable variance. The t-test is also not suitable when the mean is not representative of the sample, as in cases where the sample is skewed. Finally, oftentimes behavioral deficits are measured by scales that do not accurately represent an interval. For example, in a scale that is not expressed on an interval, the difference between two points on the scale may not mean the same thing as the difference between two other points on the scale. Typically when these assumptions are violated, researchers use a Wilcoxon-Mann-Whitney test (Mann & Whitney, 1947; Wilcoxon, 1945) or the robust rank order test (Fligner & Policello, 1981). However, these tests are not always entirely appropriate for lesion data because they assume that the data have a similar shape and range and that they are drawn from symmetrical distributions. A more recently developed test—the Brunner-Munzel test—(Brunner & Munzel, 2000) helps to remedy some of these problems by using a rank order test that is assumption free. When there are at least 10 observations in each group, it generates a statistic that is normal, and when the groups are smaller than 10 it uses an additional permutation test to approximate the precise p value (Neubert & Brunner, 2007).

When conducting voxel-wise analyses, it is important to account for the effect of multiple comparisons, or in other words, to control for family-wise error rate (the chance of making a Type 1 error). The Bonferroni correction is a frequently used method that conservatively controls for family-wise error. Because the comparisons in voxel-wise analysis are not independent, some researchers have asserted that this method is too conservative because of its acceptance of a higher Type II error than is necessary to produce the least amount of Type I error. An alternative to this method is the false discovery rate (FDR) thresholding approach, which is thought to provide better power than the Bonferroni correction while still controlling for the ratio of false alarms to hits (for application to lesion method see: Bates et al., 2003; Friston, 2000; Rorden & Karnath, 2004).

Limitations of the Lesion Method

Although the lesion-deficit approach is a powerful methodology, there are limitations that derive from both issues of practicality as well as functional resolution. One limitation of the lesion method is practical, and has to do with access to patients. The lesion method is often conducted within the context of a medical center because scientists will need access to neurological patients. Other necessities include neuropsychological testing facilities and structural imaging facilities. It helps to have a continuous referral of new patients from clinicians. Another limitation of the lesion method is a consequence of the functional resolution of the method. Typically, even small, focal lesions may not affect a single functional unit of the brain but rather may affect brain tissue that is involved in multiple functions. Lesion overlap analysis or voxel-wise studies aid in providing more precision, but there are limitations in these methods as well. A related issue derives from the fact that certain cognitive functions may recruit more than one brain area. Consequently, damage to a single brain area may not necessarily completely impair function because the individual is able to rely on other brain structures in the functional system. Furthermore, individual differences in the function and anatomy of the brain may become more pronounced after lesion onset, thus making it difficult to make general conclusions about the function of a particular brain area across subjects.

Another important limitation of the lesion method derives from the fact that when researchers conduct the lesion method in humans, the lesions are not made experimentally (as in animal research),

and lesions do not occur in all areas of the brain with equal frequency. In particular, there are specific regions of the brain that are frequently affected by brain injury and other regions that are rarely affected. For example, in cases of traumatic brain injury due to an automobile accident or a concussion, portions of the frontal lobes (especially orbital) and temporal lobes are most often affected. Cerebrovascular accidents such as ischemic or hemorrhagic strokes typically affect perisylvian regions fed by the middle cerebral artery. Herpes simplex encephalitis damages limbic system structures (especially medial temporal and cingulate regions) and surgical treatment for epilepsy involves the removal of portions of the anterior mesial temporal lobes. A pictorial representation of the brain regions sampled in one of our lesion studies (Rudrauf et al., 2008) is presented in Figure 5.1.

Another limitation has to do with connectivity. In general, lesion studies have not accounted very well for the effect of white matter damage that often occurs as a result of brain injury, and that can obviously produce functional deficits. It is important to recognize that the brain functions as a system of interconnected parts, including gray matter as well as the white matter fiber tracts that connect various cortical regions (Friston, 2000). In the past, researchers have been limited by technological constraints that made it difficult to consider the effects of gray and white matter damage simultaneously. Recently, progress on this issue has been facilitated by the advent of diffusion tensor imaging (DTI), which

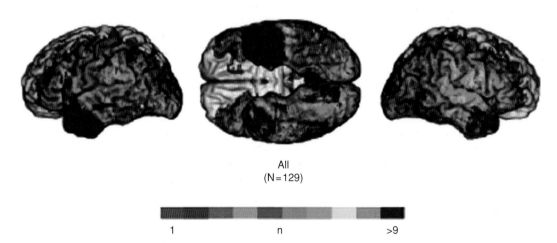

All
(N=129)

1   n   >9

Fig. 5.1 Voxel-wise approach to the lesion method in humans, showing a "lesion coverage map." The lesion coverage at each voxel based on a sample of 129 patients with brain damage is represented on a reference brain, and keyed by the color bar (ranging from 1 lesion to 9 or more at any given voxel). Left lateral, ventral, and right lateral views are depicted.
Reproduced from Rudrauf, D., Mehta, S., Bruss, J., Tranel, D., Damasio, H., & Grabowski, T. J. (2008), with permission of Elsevier.

enables the visualization and even some degree of quantification of damage to white matter fiber tracts (Jones, 2008). Novel statistical techniques that allow researchers to utilize probability maps of the various types of fiber tracts (projection, commissural, and association) that are registered to a normal reference brain atlas have also facilitated analyses of connectivity issues. One particular method that uses this approach is generalized lesion-symptom mapping (GLSM), which incorporates information about white matter fiber tracts from DTI-based tractographic atlases in order to conduct lesion-deficit analyses at both a tract-wise and voxel-wise level (Rudrauf, Mehta, & Grabowski, 2008). In a study illustrating the validity of this approach, the researchers choose to examine a fiber tract system that has been very well documented both anatomically and functionally—the geniculo-calcarine visual pathway. The researchers compared the results of a gray matter analysis alone versus an analysis of gray matter and white matter damage in 149 patients with right homonymous visual field deficits following focal brain damage. The analysis revealed that although analysis of gray matter alone implicated several regions in the temporal lobe, when fiber tract information was included only damage to the optic radiations predicted the visual field defects. This example illustrates the importance of considering the effects of white matter damage on functional deficits. Consideration of the connectivity of brain regions may lead to a more accurate understanding of the association between a lesion and a deficit.

Application of the Lesion Method to Social Neuroscience

In what follows, we present several examples from the recent literature, in which the lesion method has been used in particularly compelling fashion to tackle issues in the field of social neuroscience. Again, we would underscore that these examples provide notable illustrations of how the lesion method can inform questions in this field in ways that are especially convincing and in some respects, unattainable with other methods.

Moral Judgment

Philosophers have debated the mechanisms of moral judgment for many years, but only recently has the field of neuroscience attempted to examine the neural underpinnings of moral judgment through functional neuroimaging and lesion studies (Greene, Sommerville, Nystrom, Darley, & Cohen, 2001; Koenigs et al., 2007). Although moral

decision-making theory has been long dominated by cognitive models that describe moral decision making as a process of rational deliberation, more recently researchers have hypothesized that moral judgments may also be a consequence of emotional responses (Valdesolo & DeSteno, 2006). Some evidence for this idea stems from behavioral work that has shown that an induction of an affective state can change how someone makes a moral decision (Valdesolo & DeSteno, 2006) as well as descriptions of how moral decision making is impaired in neurological populations with emotional disturbances (Eslinger, Grattan, Damasio, & Damasio, 1992). Additional evidence for the role of emotion in moral judgment derives from functional neuroimaging studies which conclude that there is heightened brain activity in areas related to emotional functioning, in particular the ventromedial prefrontal cortex (VMPC), when healthy, normal participants make moral decisions (Greene et al., 2001).

To further the understanding of the neural correlates of moral judgments and the role of emotion in moral reasoning, a lesion study was conducted using a region of interest approach to examine whether the ventromedial prefrontal cortex was necessary to make normal moral judgments (Koenigs et al., 2007). The study examined moral judgments in a target group of six patients with focal brain damage to the ventromedial prefrontal cortex, and severe acquired impairments in social emotional processing. The lesions in the target group were overlayed on a reference brain to convey the commonality of damage in the ventromedial prefrontal region (Figure 5.2.) The behavior of the target group was compared to a group of 12 patients with brain damage to regions outside of the target region of interest as well as a group of 12 normal comparison participants. Both groups were matched to the target group on education, sex, handedness, and age (and, for the brain-damaged group, chronicity of lesion). Participants made moral judgments by deciding whether they would engage in a behavior depicted in two critical types of scenarios: "personal" scenarios (highly emotional vignettes requiring a participant to choose between an emotionally distressing act that will save several people or a less emotional act that will only save one person) and "impersonal" scenarios (vignettes in which the participant must choose between saving one versus many people from a more distant, impersonal vantage point). Strikingly, a greater proportion of patients with damage to the ventromedial prefrontal cortex made utilitarian judgments for a subset of

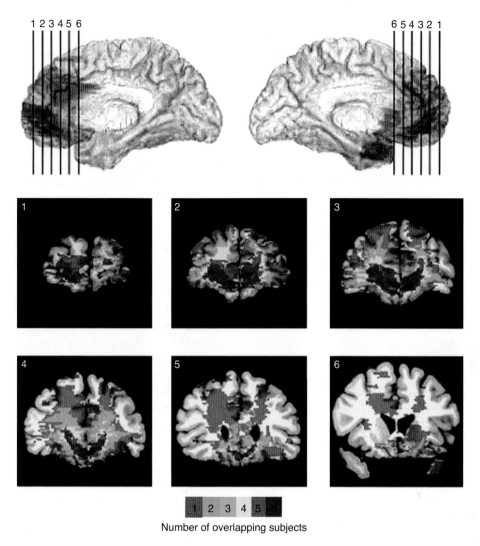

Fig. 5.2 Lesion overlap map of VMPC patients who participated in a moral judgment study. The lesions of 6 VMPC patients are displayed in mesial views and coronal slices. The color bar indicates the number of overlapping lesions at each voxel.
Reproduced from Koenigs, M., Young, L., Adolphs, R., Tranel, D., Cushman, F., Hauser, M., et al. (2007), with permission of Nature Publishing Group.

"personal" scenarios. After closer examination, it was revealed that this subset of personal scenarios also produced high disagreement among the comparison groups; these scenarios were denoted as "high-conflict personal scenarios" by Koenigs and colleagues. The high-conflict personal scenarios pitted two very difficult choices against each other. However, one of the choices was clearly more emotionally salient. For example, in one decision you must either smother your baby to save several other people or let the baby cry and several people will be killed. In these emotionally charged scenarios, the patients with damage to the VMPC made the utilitarian choice—i.e., they chose to smother their own baby to save the lives of several others. It is well documented that patients with damage to the

VMPC have a severe reduction in their capacity for social emotions (e.g., compassion, empathy, guilt). Consequently, their utilitarian choices may be the result of an inactive emotional system that prevents them from experiencing the emotional distress and disgust that normal, healthy individuals experience when engaging in morally reprehensible acts.

Empathy

Empathy, which refers to the ability to understand and adopt the feelings of other individuals, is an inherently social construct, centering on our ability to relate to other people. Although the construct of empathy has been studied for several decades in the field of psychology, within the field of social neuroscience researchers are just beginning to understand the neural systems that subserve the experience of empathy (Eslinger, 1998; Preston & de Waal, 2002; Singer, 2006). Most of this research has focused on the neural correlates of empathic function in normal, healthy adults. The numerous neuroscientific theories of empathy that have emerged contain a common theme: empathy for others occurs through the embodied simulation of our own emotional experiences and the sensory and motor responses that make up these experiences such as hugging, crying, or smiling (e.g., Bastiaansen, Thioux, & Keysers, 2009). At a more basic level, studies have shown that similar neural mechanisms are involved in personal sensory experience and the observation of the sensory experience of others. For example, in a functional neuroimaging study, the anterior insula and nearby frontal operculum were activated in the observation of another person expressing food-related disgust or pleasure and the experience of personally tasting food from these various categories (Jabbi, Swart, & Keysers, 2007). The same brain areas were involved in viewing facial expressions of the emotion of disgust and then smelling disgusting odors (Wicker, Keysers, Plailly, Royet, Gallese, & Rizzolatti, 2003). Similarly, the personal experience of physical pain (e.g., a moderately painful electric stimulation), and the knowledge that another person (a loved one) is experiencing this same type of pain, also recruit the anterior insula as well as the anterior cingulate (Singer, Seymour, O'Doherty, Kaube, Dolan, & Frith, 2004). Results from these studies have pointed to a neural circuit important for empathy, which includes secondary somatosensory and premotor cortices used to simulate the sensory and motor components of others' experiences, and the anterior insula and the anterior cingulate, which are involved in experiencing the emotions others (Singer, 2006; Bastiaansen et al., 2009). There is also evidence that the right hemisphere may be preferentially involved in empathy, although this could be modulated by sex so that women show a right hemisphere preference more so than men (e.g., Rueckert & Naybar, 2008).

Many different neurological and psychiatric illnesses result in (and, for some psychiatric diseases, may in part be caused by) poor empathy. Examples include patients with brain damage to the ventromedial prefrontal cortex, frontotemporal dementia, autism, psychopathy, and schizophrenia (Eslinger, 1998; Rankin et al., 2006; Blair, 2008; Shamay-Tsoory, Shur, Harari, & Levkovitz, 2007). In addition, recent research has found that healthy older adults may experience decreased empathy in

comparison to younger adults (Bailey, Henry, & Von Hippel, 2008; Schieman & Van Gundy, 2000). In particular, a small number of studies have found that older adults experience lower cognitive empathy, or the ability to adopt the mental perspective (or "put oneself in the shoes") of another person (Bailey et al., 2008). In patients with focal brain damage, empathy has primarily been measured through anecdotal reports of family members or through questionnaires rated by the patient or family members of the patient that assess empathy as a general tendency in daily life (Eslinger, 1998; Shamay-Tsoory, Tomer, Berger, & Aharon-Peretz, 2003; Shamay-Tsoory, Tomer, Berger, Goldsher, & Aharon-Peretz, 2005). These studies have implicated the orbitofrontal and ventromedial prefrontal cortices as brain regions that are necessary for empathy.

There are two primary limitations to the research that has examined empathy in patients with neurological disease: Empathy has not been measured implicitly and "online," and empathic experience in real time has not been measured. Explicit measurement of empathy may be problematic because previous studies have shown that patients with brain damage (particularly those with damage to the frontal lobe) are able to use their intact social "factual" knowledge to reason their way through the questionnaires. Moreover, such patients are notorious for having poor insight, making their self-reports of rather questionable validity in the first place. Thus, such patients may give the impression of being normal when they clearly are not (Barrash, Tranel, & Anderson, 2000; Saver & Damasio, 1991.) Implicit measurement may aid in the understanding of empathy because it allows the researcher to measure the construct of empathy in a way that is more naturalistic and less likely to produce socially desirable responses. One example of a way in which to measure empathy implicitly would be to assess behavior in a live empathy-provoking situation and measure whether patients respond similarly to normal individuals.

We designed a study which attempts to address some of the limitations of previous work to further understand the neural underpinnings of empathy. This study assessed online empathic experience both implicitly and explicitly. Participants included patients with adult-onset brain damage to the ventromedial prefrontal cortex. The study contained two parts: first, the induction of online empathy and second, the assessment of empathy through implicit and explicit measurements. The participants' behavior on a social economic decision-making game that they played against other people served as an implicit measure of prosocial behavior. Explicit measurement of empathy occurred through the self-report assessment of the patient's current empathic state at regular intervals throughout the experiment as well as the measurement of trait empathy, or empathy as a general tendency.

In order to understand how empathy was induced in this experiment, the context of this naturalistic deception experiment must first be understood. Participants were told that they would be playing an economic game (where they would make decisions about money) against a series of two different opponents through a hands-free intercom system. The participant played against one opponent at a time and this opponent was located in a separate testing room. The "opponent" was actually a voice recording of a community theater actor of a similar age to the patient. During the course of the experiment, unbeknownst to the participant, a naturalistic neutral emotion induction and empathic induction would occur. Right before the neutral induction the participant rated their current feelings which served as a baseline for their empathic feelings during the experiment. Participants were asked to, "Indicate to what extent you feel this way right now, that is, at the present moment," on a scale from 1 (very slightly or not at all) to 5 (extremely). The two items designed to assess empathic concern included "sympathetic" and "compassionate."

Both inductions occurred in an implicit manner. The neutral induction occurred by the participant overhearing through the intercom a conversation of neutral content between the research assistant and the participant's opponent as they talked about the events of their day (actually a voice recording). Following this induction, the participant rated their online feelings and then played the game against their first opponent. After the first game, the participant rated their current feelings again which served as a baseline of their feelings before the empathic induction took place. This second baseline was measured to determine their current feelings immediately before the empathic induction. Following this, the empathic induction took place and this included the participant overhearing a conversation between the research assistant and the second opponent who revealed that today was the anniversary of his son's death (in a voice recording).

The game played in the current study was the Repeated Fixed Opponent variant of the Ultimatum Game (UG). The UG is a well-studied social economic decision-making game that has been used in contexts ranging from marketing to neuroscience (Kahneman, Knetsch, & Thaler, 1986; Sanfey, Rilling, Aronson, Nystrom, & Cohen, 2003; Koenigs & Tranel, 2007). This game poses a common bargaining scenario whereby a seller makes a final offer (often called an ultimatum) to a buyer (e.g. "The loaf of bread costs $3—take it or leave it") and the buyer can either accept it, or reject it and leave it on the bargaining table. We designed our experiment so that the participant would make an offer to their opponent that could range from $1–9 (e.g. "You get $5 and I get $5"). Their opponent (actually a series of voice recordings) would then choose to either accept or reject the offer. If the offer is accepted, both persons receive the proposed division of money but if the offer is rejected, neither person receives any money. In the traditional 1-Shot version of the UG, in which the participant plays against a different opponent over every round, offers that are less than half of the total are often rejected, and offers that are 20% or less than the total are rejected at a rate of about 50% (Guth, Schmittberger, & Schwarze, 1982). Rationally, it may not be clear why a person would *ever* reject an offer, because some money is better than no money. However, theorists have proposed that rejections may occur due to the prevalent awareness of the norm of fairness which exists across many cultures (Roth, Prasnikar, Okuno-Fujiwara, & Zamir, 1991; Fehr & Fischbacher, 2003) and violations of this norm provoke anger (Pillutla & Murnighan, 1996). This response of negative emotion due to unfair behavior fits nicely in the context of findings that this game engages the insula, in which functional brain activity covaries as a response of the fairness of the offer (Sanfey et al., 2003), and with findings that the ventromedial prefrontal cortex (which plays a role in emotion regulation) is important for normal behavior during the UG (Koenigs & Tranel, 2007).

THE REPEATED FIXED OPPONENT UG

In the Repeated Fixed Opponent UG, the participant plays against the same "fixed" opponent for several rounds as compared to the 1-Shot version in which a participant plays against a different opponent for each round. This version of the UG was chosen for three reasons: (1) It allows for an effective empathic induction, (2) it allows for the empathic induction to be believable, (3) it allows for a measurement of social interaction over time rather than at just one time point.

The Repeated Fixed Opponent version of the UG has not been studied much, and particularly has not been studied in older adults. Prior to conducting the empathy experiment with patients with damage to the ventromedial prefrontal cortex, we conducted a pilot study to further understand how younger and older adults play the Repeated Fixed Opponent UG. The participants in this study included twenty pairs of healthy, normal younger adults (N = 40) aged 24–45 years and twenty pairs of healthy, normal older adults (N = 40) aged 55–81 years. Age-matched pairs (younger vs. younger, older vs. older) played against each other. In this pilot study, the pairs included two real opponents (rather than voice recordings as described in the previous study) and participants were located in two different testing rooms and made their offers and responses orally through a hands-free intercom system.

When participants were offered a share of equal to or greater than half of the total, the older and younger groups behaved similarly, accepting virtually all offers. However, when participants were made offers of less than half of the total, an age difference in behavior emerged. Older adults rejected offers of less than half of the total at a significantly higher rate than younger adults (Figure 5.3). Since there is evidence that one aspect of empathy—cognitive empathy—may be decreased in late life, the study next investigated whether there was an association between empathy as a general tendency and rejection rate of offers less than half of the total. Cognitive empathy was measured using the Perspective Taking subscale of the Interpersonal Reactivity Index, a well-studied self-report measure of trait empathy (Davis, 1980). A significant

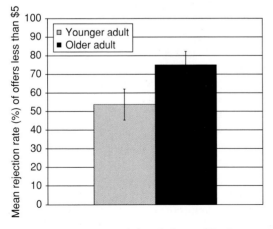

Fig. 5.3 Mean rejection rate (%) on the Repeated Fixed Opponent Ultimatum Game for all offers less than half of the total (less than $5) as a function of age group (younger adult, older adult). Error bars reflect standard error of the mean.

inverse relationship was found between empathy and rejection rate of offers less than half the total, with high rejection rates being associated with low levels of empathy. Due to a decreased capacity to adopt the mental state of others, older adults may not realize how their high rejection behavior may cause the other person to become upset and may instead be focused on their own emotions.

THE ONLINE EMPATHIC RESPONSE OF PATIENTS WITH DAMAGE TO THE VENTROMEDIAL PREFRONTAL CORTEX

During the online empathic induction, patients with damage to the ventromedial prefrontal cortex reported that they experienced moderate empathic concern towards their opponent. In particular, while undergoing the online induction, the patients' responses ranged from "a little" empathic concern to "quite a bit" of empathic concern with the modal response being "moderate" empathic concern. In comparison to their feelings of empathic concern in the control (neutral) condition, patients reported greater empathic concern during the online empathy condition (modal response = 1 point change from neutral to empathic condition). At an individual subject level, the number of patients with damage to the ventromedial prefrontal cortex that endorsed feelings of "moderate" to "quite a bit" of empathy during the empathic condition was greater than that of the neutral condition. In summary, patients with damage to the ventromedial prefrontal cortex reported that they experienced online empathic concern for another person.

However, a strikingly different pattern emerged in the implicit measure of empathic behavior (the Ultimatum Game.) The patients did not show an increase in empathic behavior during the empathy condition, but rather behaved very similarly in both the neutral and empathic conditions (Figure 5.4). In the neutral condition, patients with damage to the ventromedial prefrontal cortex gave an average of $4.43 (SD = .56) out of $10 to their opponent, and in the empathic condition the patients gave virtually an identical amount of $4.45 (SD = .74). Consequently, although the patients reported an increase in their online experience of empathy during the empathic condition, they did not show empathic behavior.

The preliminary results of this study indicate that patients with damage to the ventromedial prefrontal cortex do not experience online empathy towards others. An implicit measure of empathic behavior (the Ultimatum Game) demonstrated that

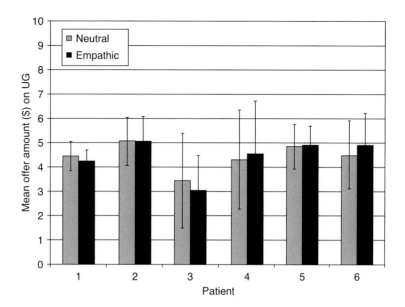

Fig. 5.4 Mean offer amount ($) given by each patient with ventromedial prefrontal damage (N = 6) on a measure of empathic behavior (the Repeated Fixed Opponent Ultimatum Game) as a function of induction type (neutral, empathic). Error bars reflect standard deviation.

patients did not show empathy towards a person who was suffering (the man who had lost his son). Although the patients did rate that they felt some level of empathy during the induction, these ratings may be more reflective of social desirability effects than actual empathic feelings. A previous study found that patients are able to access factual social knowledge, which enables them to appear emotionally and socially competent on a number of off-line tasks—in short, to "talk a good game" (Saver & Damasio, 1991), while in real-world settings these patients demonstrate clear social impairments (e.g., Anderson, Barrash, Bechara, & Tranel, 2006).

Sex Differences

At a large-scale macroscopic level, the brains of men and women are very similar. Closer inspection, though, reveals some striking differences between men and women in the ways in which various brain structures relate to cognitive and behavioral functions. Obviously, it is important for both men and women to be able to navigate the social world effectively, but individuals of each sex may have somewhat different goals. To begin with, women bear children, and this central and basic function likely sets the agenda for the individual and societal goals of many women. Men do not bear children and may often be driven by an agenda that emphasizes the acquisition and maintenance of resources and power. The ventromedial prefrontal cortex and amygdala are especially important for social-emotional processing. Recent evidence suggests that

the left-sided and right-sided components of these structures may serve different functions in men versus women.

THE VENTROMEDIAL PREFRONTAL CORTEX

To investigate whether sex plays a role in the functional asymmetry of the ventromedial prefrontal cortex (VMPC), we examined same sex pairs with unilateral lesions of similar location and extent in the VMPC, but located in a different hemisphere (Tranel, Damasio, Denburg, & Bechara, 2005). The participants included two male pairs and one female pair, and each pair had one patient with unilateral damage to the right side and another patient with unilateral damage to the left side. An additional two women with right-sided damage to the VMPC were included and although an exact left-sided match for these women could not be found, these two patients were compared to the males with right-sided damage. Three key functions of the VMPC were examined: social conduct, emotional processing/personality, and decision making. Structured rating scales were completed by collaterals (family members/friends of the patient) and neuropsychologists to assess social conduct. Social conduct was determined by the degree of change from pre- to post- brain injury in the domains of social status, employment status, and interpersonal functioning. Emotional processing and personality were assessed through self-report ratings of the patient on the Beck Depression Inventory and Minnesota Multiphasic Personality Inventory-2 as well as the Iowa Scales of Personality Change. Decision making was measured by the Iowa Gambling Task (IGT), which represents a decision-making environment that is similar to the real world in that it takes into account factors such as reward, punishment, and uncertainty.

A functional asymmetry in the VMPC was demonstrated as a result of sex. Males showed impaired function only when they had incurred right-sided unilateral damage to the VMPC but not when they had left-sided unilateral damage. The reverse pattern was seen in females: Females with left-sided unilateral damage to the VMPC showed severe functional impairments, but females with right-sided unilateral damage to the VMPC did not. This finding was interpreted to mean that the two genders may rely on differential strategies in the domains of social conduct, emotional processing/personality, and decision making. Such evidence suggests that the right VMPC and amygdala in men and the left VMPC and amygdala in women are important for social-emotional functioning, possibly reflecting differing social strategies and divergent social goals. Potentially, the left-sided dominance observed in women reflects a need for expertise in interpersonal relationships (and this could be related to factors such as the need to bear and rear children, maintenance of in-group cohesion, etc.), whereas the right-sided dominance observed in men could reflect a need for expertise in intergroup relations (e.g., warfare, out-group relations, leverage of critical resources, etc.).

THE AMYGDALA

The amygdala plays an important role in the detection of emotional signals in the social environment. It is involved in recognition of emotional facial expressions (Adolphs, 2002, 2003), processing social information (Hariri, Tessitore, Mattay, Fera, & Weinberger, 2002) and the enhancement of emotional information in memory (Buchanan & Adolphs, 2004; LaBar & Cabeza, 2006). The role of the amygdala extends to the domain of real-world decision making where it detects emotional signals in the environment in order to guide behavior. Additional convergent evidence comes from the finding that patients with bilateral damage to the amygdala are impaired on a task of complex decision making, the Iowa Gambling Task (Bechara, Damasio, Damasio, & Lee, 1999). Not only is the amygdala crucial for social and emotional functioning, but its hemispheric-related functionality may differ between the sexes. For example, during the encoding of emotionally arousing material, the relationship between amygdala activation and memory for emotional material was the strongest in the right

amygdala in males but in the left amygdala in females (Cahill et al., 2001; Canli & Gabrieli, 2004). We have studied whether there is sex-related functional asymmetry of the amygdala through the investigation of four patients with unilateral damage to the amygdala (Tranel & Bechara, 2009).

A case-matched lesion approach was utilized whereby a pair of men with unilateral amygdala damage (1 right amygdala, 1 left amygdala) were contrasted and a pair of women with unilateral amygdala damage (1 right amygdala, 1 left amygdala) were contrasted. Neuroanatomical analysis revealed that the four patients all had major damage to the amygdala unilaterally. The patients were assessed on the domains of social conduct, emotional processing/personality, and decision making through the same procedures specified in Tranel and colleagues (2005). We found preliminary evidence for a sex-related asymmetry of the amygdala: The man with right-sided damage to the amygdala showed severe impairments in social/emotional functioning (but the man with left-sided damage to the amygdala did not), whereas the woman with left-sided damage to the amygdala showed impairments in these domains, but the woman with right-sided damage did not. These results are considered to be preliminary because this is the first study of its kind and the sample size was small. However, the strength of these findings lies in the specificity of the case-based matching that allows for a direct comparison of how damage to the right or left amygdala affects socio-emotional function while accounting for shared nonspecific factors across patients, such as taking neurological medicine and going through brain surgery.

Altogether, the studies summarized in this section provide intriguing evidence that there is a sex-related functional asymmetry in the ventromedial prefrontal cortex and the amygdala, two areas crucial for socio-emotional functioning. The directionality of this pattern is the same in both brain areas: males-right, females-left. This work emphasizes the importance of examining the effect of sex on the functional architecture of the brain, particularly within the domain of social and emotional functioning. Evolutionarily, sex-related functional differences in the brain's emotion system may have developed based upon the differential needs the physical and social environment placed on each sex. For example, left-sided dominance may have evolved in women because of their involvement in raising children and maintaining unity within their social group, whereas right-sided dominance may have been more beneficial to men in their need to moderate relations between tribes and compete for resources.

Concluding Comments

As the field of social neuroscience came into existence and rapidly grew into a major subdiscipline within cognitive neuroscience, it has, not surprisingly, attracted a large and growing number of constituents. This has fueled, in turn, a welter of new data, elaborate new theoretical frameworks, and, as with many of the challenging topics in cognitive neuroscience, a whole host of new questions. Many of these questions have profound practical significance. For example: Are utilitarian social decisions best made by eschewing emotion and using cold, hard reasoning? How do social emotions such as empathy and embarrassment shape and influence interpersonal interactions? Is social isolation a risk factor for neurological disease? Are there differences between men and women in the manner in which neural structures are specialized for social processing? These and many similar kinds of questions will shape the research agenda in this field for years to come.

The lesion method in social neuroscience has played a major role in pushing the field forward, and it will continue to be a key contributor. The lesion method, especially as exemplified by critical case studies, has often opened entirely new avenues of work, for example, by raising important and provocative questions about putative brain-behavior relationships (e.g., Is the ventromedial prefrontal cortex necessary for social emotions and moral reasoning?). The modern practice of the lesion method has capitalized on powerful new tools for lesion-deficit analysis (e.g., voxel-based lesion-symptom mapping), as well as unique patient resources (e.g., the Neurological Patient Registry at the University of Iowa), to yield robust conclusions about brain-behavior relationships. It is our hope that this knowledge will catalyze breakthroughs in understanding the more fundamental neural mechanisms behind cognition and behavior. In turn, progress towards the diagnosis, treatment, cure, and prevention of neurological and psychiatric disease may be realized.

Not so long ago, the rubric of social neuroscience was yet to be invented (cf. Cacioppo & Bernston, 1992). Now, this topic has become so popular and fashionable that it can be the hinge point for a dedicated Handbook, such as the one in which this chapter appears. As this happens, it is interesting to witness how frequently the modern literature ends up recapitulating themes that were articulated so eloquently by the forefathers of our field, especially William James (1918) and Charles Darwin (see 1989). For example, those scientists from many generations past clearly recognized and appreciated the central role that emotion plays in human existence and social interaction, and we are very pleased that our contemporaries have become similarly enamored. In a world that is ever more social, this development can only be a good thing, and we have every reason to be sanguine that social neuroscience will mature into a cornerstone field within cognitive neuroscience.

Authors' note:
This chapter was supported by NINDS P50 NS19632 and NIDA R01 DA022549.

References

Adolphs, R. (2002). Recognizing emotion from facial expressions: Psychological and neurological mechanisms. *Behavioral and Cognitive Neuroscience Reviews, 1*, 21–61.

Adolphs, R. (2003). Cognitive neuroscience of human social behavior. *Nature Reviews Neuroscience, 4*, 165–178.

American Association of Retired Persons. (1996). *Telemarketing fraud and older Americans: An AARP Survey.* Washington, DC: AARP.

Anderson, S. W., Barrash, J., Bechara, A., & Tranel, D. (2006). Impairments of emotion and real-world complex behavior following childhood- or adult-onset damage to ventromedial prefrontal cortex. *Journal of the International Neuropsychological Society, 12*, 224–235.

Bailey, P. E., Henry, J. D., & Von Hippel, W. (2008). Empathy and social functioning in late adulthood. *Aging & Mental Health, 12*, 499–503.

Barrash, J., Tranel, D., & Anderson, S.W. (2000). Acquired personality disturbances associated with bilateral damage to the ventromedial prefrontal region. *Developmental Neuropsychology, 18*, 355–381.

Bastiaansen, J. A. C. J., Thioux, M., & Keysers, C. (2009). Evidence for mirror systems in emotions. *Philosophical Transactions of the Royal Society: Biological Sciences, 364*, 2391–2404.

Bates, E., Wilson, S. M., Saygin, A. P., Dick, F., Sereno, M. I., Knight, R. T., et al. (2003). Voxel-based lesion-symptom mapping. *Nature Neuroscience, 6*, 448–450.

Bechara, A., Damasio, H., Damasio, A.R., & Lee, G.P. (1999). Different contribution of the human amygdala and ventromedial prefrontal cortex to decision making. *Journal of Neuroscience, 19*, 5473–5481.

Blair, R. J. R. (2008). Fine cuts of empathy and the amygdala: Dissociable deficits in psychopathy and autism, *The Quarterly Journal of Experimental Psychology, 61*, 157–170.

Brunner, E. & Munzel, U. (2000). The nonparametric Behrens–Fisher problem: Asymptotic theory and small-sample approximation. *Biometrical Journal, 42*, 17–25.

Buchanan, T. W. & Adolphs, R. (2004). The neuroanatomy of emotional memory in humans. In D. Reisberg & P. Hertel (Eds.), *Memory and emotion*. New York: Oxford University Press.

Cacioppo, J. T. & Bernston, G. G. (1992). Social psychological contributions to the decade of the brain. Doctrine of multilevel analysis. *American Psychologist, 47*, 1019–1028.

Cacioppo, J. T., Bernston, G. G., Sheridan, J. F., & McClintock, M. K. (2000). Multilevel integrative analyses of human behavior: Social neuroscience and the complementing nature of social and biological approaches. *Psychological Bulletin, 126*, 829–843.

Cacioppo, J. T., Hawkley, L. C., Berntson, G. G., Ernst, J. M., Gibbs, A. C., Stickgold, R., et al. (2002). Do lonely days invade the nights? Potential social modulation of sleep efficiency. *Psychological Science, 13*, 384–387.

Cahill, L., Haier, R.J., White, N.S., Fallon, J., Kilpatrick, L., Lawrence, C., et al. (2001). Sex-related difference in amygdala activity during emotionally influenced memory storage. *Neurobiology of Learning and Memory, 75*, 1–9.

Canli, T. & Gabrieli, J. (2004). Imaging gender differences in sexual arousal. *Nature Neuroscience, 7*, 325–326.

Carden, S. E. & Hofer, M. A. (1990). Independence of benzodiazepine and opiate actions in the suppression of isolation and distress in rat pups. *Behavioral Neuroscience, 104*, 160–166.

Chatterjee, A. (2005). A madness to the methods in cognitive neuroscience? *Journal of Cognitive Neuroscience, 17*, 847–849.

Damasio, A.R. (1994). *Descartes' error: Emotion, reason, and the human brain*. New York: G. P. Putnam Press.

Damasio, A.R. (1999). *The feeling of what happens: Body and emotion in the making of consciousness*. New York: Harcourt Brace.

Damasio, H. & Damasio, A.R. (2003). The lesion method in behavioral neurology and neuropsychology. In T.E. Feinberg & M. J. Farah (Eds.), *Behavioral neurology and neuropsychology* (2nd ed., pp. 71–83). New York: McGraw Hill.

Damasio, H., Grabowski, T., Frank, R., Galaburda, A. M., & Damasio, A. R. (1994). The return of Phineas Gage: Clues about the brain from the skull of a famous patient. *Science, 264*, 1102–1105.

Damasio, H., Grabowski, T. J., Tranel, D., Hichwa, R. D., & Damasio, A. R. (1996). A neural basis for lexical retrieval. *Nature, 380*, 499–505.

Damasio, H., Tranel, D., Grabowski, T., Adolphs, R., & Damasio, A. (2004). Neural systems behind word and concept retrieval. *Cognition, 92*, 179–229.

Darwin, C. (1871). *The expression of the emotions in man and animals*. P. Ekman & P. Prodger (3rd ed., 1998). NY, New York: Oxford University Press.

Davis, M. H. (1980). Individual differences in empathy: A multidimensional approach. *Dissertation Abstracts International, 40*, 3480.

Denburg, N. L., Cole, C. A., Hernandez, M., Yamada, T. H., Tranel, D., Bechara, A., et al. (2007). The orbitofrontal cortex, real-world decision making, and normal aging. *Annals of the New York Academy of Sciences, 1121*, 480–498.

Denburg, N. L., Tranel, D., & Bechara, A. (2005). The ability to decide advantageously declines prematurely in some normal older persons. *Neuropsychologia, 43*, 1099–1106.

Editorial. (2004). When once is enough. *Nature Neuroscience, 7*, 93.

Eslinger, P. J. (1998). Neurological and neuropsychological bases of empathy. *European Neurology, 39*, 193–199.

Eslinger, P. J., Grattan, L. M., Damasio, H., & Damasio, A. R. (1992). Developmental consequences of childhood frontal lobe damage. *Archives of Neurology, 49*, 764–769.

Fehr, E., & Fischbacher, U. (2003). The nature of human altruism. *Nature, 425*, 785–791.

Fellows, L. K., Heberlein, A. S., Morales, D. A., Shivde, G., Waller, S., & Wu, D. H. (2005). Method matters: An empirical study of impact in cognitive neuroscience. *Journal of Cognitive Neuroscience, 17*, 850–858.

Feinstein, J.S., Rudrauf, D., Khalsa, S.S., Cassell, M.D., Bruss, J., Grabowski, T.J., et al. (2009). Bilateral limbic system destruction in man. *Journal of Clinical and Experimental Neuropsychology, 17*, 1–19.

Fligner, M. A., & Policello, G. E. (1981). Robust rank procedure for the Behrens–Fisher problem. *Journal of the American Statistical Association, 76*, 162–168.

Frank, R. J., Damasio, H., & Grabowski, T. J. (1997). Brainvox: An interactive, multimodal visualization and analysis system for neuroanatomical imaging. *NeuroImage, 5*, 13–30.

Friston, K. J. (2000). The labile brain. I. neuronal transients and nonlinear coupling. *Philosophical Transactions of the Royal Society of London. Series B, Biological Sciences, 355*, 215–236.

Goodall, J., Bandura, A., Bergmann, E., Busse, C., Matama, H., Mpongo, E., et al. (1979). Inter-community interactions in the chimpanzee population of the Gombe National Park. In D. A. Hamburg & E. R. McCown (Eds.), *The great apes* (pp. 13–53). Menlo Park, CA: Benjamin/Cummings.

Greene, J. D., Sommerville, R. B., Nystrom, L. E., Darley, J. M., & Cohen, J. D. (2001). An fMRI investigation of emotional engagement in moral judgment. *Science, 293*, 2105–2108.

Gross, J. J., Carstensen, L. L., Pasupathi, M., Tsai, J., Skorpen, C. G., & Hsu, A. Y. (1997). Emotion and aging: Experience, expression, and control. *Psychology and Aging, 12*, 590–599.

Guth, W., Schmittberger, R., & Schwarze, B. (1982). An experimental analysis of ultimatum bargaining. *Journal of Economic Behavior and Organization, 3*, 367–388.

Hariri, A. R., Tessitore, A., Mattay, V. S., Fera, F., & Weinberger, D. R. (2002). The amygdala response to emotional stimuli: A comparison of faces and scenes. *NeuroImage, 17*, 317–323.

Hawkley, L. C., Masi, C. M., Berry, J. D., & Cacioppo, J. T. (2006). Loneliness is a unique predictor of age-related differences in systolic blood pressure. *Psychology and Aging, 21*, 152–164.

Hernandez, M., Denburg, N. L., & Tranel, D. (2009). Decision-making, aging, and the ventromedial prefrontal cortex. In J. C. Dreher & L. Tremblay (Eds.), *Handbook of reward and decision making* (pp. 291–306). Amsterdam: Elsevier Press.

Jabbi, M. Swart, M., & Keysers, C. (2007). Empathy for positive and negative emotions in the gustatory cortex. *Neuroimage, 34*, 1744–1753.

James, W. (1918). *The principles of psychology*. New York: H. Holt and Company.

Jones, D. K. (2008). Studying connections in the living human brain with diffusion MRI. *Cortex, 44*, 936–952.

Kahneman, D., Knetsch, J. L., & Thaler, R. (1986). Fairness as a constraint on profit seeking: Entitlements in the market. *American Economic Review, 76*, 728–741.

Karnath, H. O., Fruhmann Berger, M., Zopf, R., & Kuker, W. (2004). Using SPM normalization for lesion analysis in spatial neglect. *Brain, 127*, E10.

Keeley, L. (1996). *War before civilization*. New York: Oxford University Press.

Koenigs, M. & Tranel, D. (2007). Irrational economic decision-making after ventromedial prefrontal damage: Evidence from the ultimatum game. *The Journal of Neuroscience, 27*, 951–956.

Koenigs, M., Tranel, D., & Damasio, A.R. (2007). The lesion method in cognitive neuroscience. In J. T. Cacioppo, L. G. Tassinary, & G.G. Berntson (Eds.), *Handbook of psychophysiology* (3rd ed. pp. 139–156). Cambridge, MA: Cambridge University Press.

Koenigs, M., Young, L., Adolphs, R., Tranel, D., Cushman, F., Hauser, M., et al. (2007). Damage to the prefrontal cortex increases utilitarian moral judgments. *Nature, 446,* 908–911.

LaBar, K.S. & Cabeza, R. (2006). Cognitive neuroscience of emotional memory. *Nature Reviews Neuroscience, 7,* 54–64.

Liebermeister, C. (1877). Über wahrscheinlichkeitsrechnung in anwendung auf therapeutische statistik. *Sammlung Klinischer Vorträge, 110,* 935–962.

Light, K. C., Girdler, S. S., Sherwood, A., Bragdon, E. E., Brownley, K. A., West, S. G., et al. (1999). High stress responsivity predicts later blood pressure only in combination with positive family history and high life stress. *Hypertension, 33,* 1458–1464.

Macmillan, M. (2000). *An odd kind of fame.* Stories of Phineas Gage. Cambridge, MA: The MIT Press.

Mann, H. B. & Whitney, D. R. (1947). On a test of whether one of two random variables is stochastically larger than the other. *Annals of Mathematical Statistics, 18,* 50–60.

Mather, M., Canli, T., English, T., Whitfield, S., Wais, P., Ochsner, K., et al. (2004). Amygdala responses to emotionally valenced stimuli in older and younger adults. *Psychological Science, 15,* 259–263.

Milner, B. (1972). Disorders of learning and memory after temporal lobe lesions in man. *Clinical Neurosurgery, 19,* 421–446.

Moreno, C., Borod, J. C., Welkowitz, J., & Alpert, M. (1993). The perception of facial emotion across the adult life span. *Developmental Neuropsychology, 9,* 305–314.

Neubert, K. & Brunner, E. (2007). A studentized permutation test for the nonparametric Behrens–Fisher problem. *Computational Statistics & Data Analysis, 51,* 5192–5204.

Paul, C., Ayis, S., & Ebrahim, S. (2006). Psychological distress, loneliness and disability in old age. *Psychology, Health & Medicine, 11,* 221–232.

Pillutla, M. M. & Murnighan, J. K. (1996). Unfairness, anger, and spite: Emotional rejections of ultimatum offers. *Organizational Behavior and Human Decision Processes, 68,* 208–224.

Poldrack, R. A. (2006). Can cognitive processes be inferred from neuroimaging data? *Trends in Cognitive Sciences, 10,* 59–63.

Preston, S. D. & de Waal, F. B. M. (2002). Empathy: Its ultimate and proximate bases. *Behavioral and Brain Sciences, 25,* 1–72.

Rankin, K. P., Gorno-Tempini, M. C., Allison, S. C., Stanley, C. M., Glenn, S., Weiner, M. W., et al. (2006). Structural anatomy of empathy in neurodegenerative disease. *Brain, 129,* 2945–2956.

Ratiu, P. & Talos, I. F. (2004). Images in clinical medicine. The tale of Phineas Gage, digitally remastered. *The New England Journal of Medicine, 351,* e21.

Rorden, C. & Karnath, H. O. (2004). Using human brain lesions to infer function: A relic from a past era in the fMRI age? *Nature Reviews Neuroscience, 5,* 813–819.

Rorden, C., Karnath, H.O., & Bonilha, L. (2007). Improving lesion-symptom mapping. *Journal of Cognitive Neuroscience, 19,* 1081–1088.

Roth, A. E., Prasnikar, V., Okuno-Fujiwara, M., & Zamir, S. (1991). Bargaining and market behavior in Jerusalem, Ljubljana, Pittsburgh, and Tokyo: An experimental study. *American Economic Review, 81,* 1068–1095.

Rudrauf, D., Mehta, S., Bruss, J., Tranel, D., Damasio, H., & Grabowski, T. J. (2008). Thresholding lesion overlap difference maps: Application to category-related naming and recognition deficits. *NeuroImage, 41,* 970–984.

Rudrauf, D., Mehta, S., & Grabowski, T. J. (2008). Disconnection's renaissance takes shape: Formal incorporation in group-level lesion studies. *Cortex, 44,* 1084–1096.

Rueckert, L. & Naybar, N. (2008). Gender differences in empathy: The role of the right hemisphere. *Brain and Cognition, 67,* 162–167.

Sanfey, A. G., Rilling, J. K., Aronson, J. A., Nystrom, L. E., & Cohen, J. D. (2003). The neural basis of economic decision-making in the ultimatum game. *Science, 300,* 1755–1758.

Sarter, M., Bernston, G. G., & Cacioppo, J. T. (1996). Brain imaging and cognitive neuroscience. Toward strong inference in attributing function to structure. *The American Psychologist, 51,* 13–21.

Saver, J. L. & Damasio, A. R. (1991). Preserved access and processing of social knowledge in a patient with acquired sociopathy due to ventromedial frontal damage. *Neuropsychologia, 29,* 1241–1249.

Schieman, S. & Van Gundy, K. (2000). The personal and social links between age and self-reported empathy. *Social Psychology Quarterly, 63,* 152–174.

Seneta, E. & Phipps, M. C. (2001). On the comparison of two observed frequencies. *Biometrical Journal, 43,* 23–43.

Shamay-Tsoory, S. G., Shur, S., Harari, H., & Levkovitz, Y. (2007). Neurocognitive basis of impaired empathy in schizophrenia. *Neuropsychology, 21,* 431–438.

Shamay-Tsoory, S. G., Tomer, R., Berger, B. D., & Aharon-Peretz, J. (2003). Characterization of empathy deficits following prefrontal brain damage: The role of the right ventromedial prefrontal cortex. *Journal of Cognitive Neuroscience, 15,* 324–337.

Shamay-Tsoory, S. G., Tomer, R., Berger, B. D., Goldsher, D., & Aharon-Peretz, J. (2005). Impaired "Affective Theory of Mind" is associated with right ventromedial prefrontal damage. *Cognitive and Behavioral Neurology, 18,* 55–67.

Singer, T. (2006). The neuronal basis and ontogeny of empathy and mind reading: Review of literature and implications for future research. *Neuroscience and Biobehavioral Reviews, 30,* 855–863.

Singer, T., Seymour, B., O'Doherty, J., Kaube, H., Dolan, R., & Frith, C. D. (2004). Empathy for pain involves the affective but not sensory components of pain. *Science, 303,* 1157–1162.

Sullivan, S. & Ruffman, T. (2004). Emotion recognition deficits in the elderly. *The International Journal of Neuroscience, 114,* 403–432.

Tranel, D. & Bechara, A. (2009). Sex-related functional asymmetry of the amygdala: Preliminary evidence using a case-matched lesion approach. *Neurocase, 15,* 217–234.

Tranel, D., Damasio, H., Denburg, N.L., & Bechara, A. (2005). Does gender play a role in functional asymmetry of ventromedial prefrontal cortex? *Brain, 128,* 2872–2881.

Tranel, D. & Kemmerer, D. (2004). Neuroanatomical correlates of locative prepositions. *Cognitive Neuropsychology, 21,* 719–749.

Valdesolo, P. & DeSteno, D. (2006). Manipulations of emotional context shape moral judgment. *Psychological Science*, *17*, 476–477.

Wicker, B., Keysers, C., Plailly, J., Royet, J. P., Gallese, V., & Rizzolatti, G. (2003.) Both of us disgusted in my insula: The common neural basis of seeing and feeling disgust. *Neuron*, *40*, 655–664.

Wilcoxon, F. (1945). Individual comparisons by ranking methods. *Biometrics Bulletin*, *1*, 80–83.

Essentials of Functional Magnetic Resonance Imaging

Tor D. Wager *and* Martin A. Lindquist

Abstract

This chapter provides an introductory overview of functional magnetic resonance imaging (fMRI) study design, analysis, and inference from start to finish. The first section discusses the kinds of questions that fMRI studies can productively answer. The second section discusses issues surrounding data acquisition, including how to choose scanning parameters that are appropriate for the specific scientific questions asked. The third section focuses on fMRI data processing, and the fourth section discusses statistical analysis and inference. The final section discusses how to localize and interpret results, including which kinds of inferences are likely to be valid and which are not.

Keywords: fMRI, neuroimaging, brain imaging, data analysis, data collection

In the last twenty years, neuroimaging techniques have opened up new frontiers in the study of the physical basis of the mind. As a result, established disciplines such as cognitive psychology, personality and social psychology, psychophysiology, and psychiatry have incorporated direct investigation of human brain activity. In addition, new fields have emerged that blend existing approaches with neuroscientific techniques. For example, cognitive neuroscience, affective neuroscience, social cognitive neuroscience, and neuroeconomics all draw heavily on neuroimaging. From the many neuroimaging techniques available, functional magnetic resonance imaging (fMRI) has emerged as a primary research tool in these disciplines. It is particularly appealing because it is both widely available to researchers in psychological and other behavioral sciences and also provides dynamic, second-by-second images of metabolic activity across the whole brain, striking a balance between spatial and temporal resolution.

Any effort to understand the brain substrates of psychology must involve converging evidence from multiple methods. A strength of fMRI is that it complements a number of other techniques. It complements lesion studies by providing images of dynamic activity changes in the intact, functioning brain. It complements electroencephalography (EEG) and magnetoencephalography (MEG) by providing enhanced ability to localize the sources of activity changes in the brain (Dale et al., 2000; Menon, Ford, Lim, Glover, & Pfefferbaum, 1997). It complements positron emission tomography (PET) studies by providing more information about the timing of brain activity changes in relation to task demands and behavior and permitting analyses of individual subjects. It complements brain stimulation studies in humans by providing hypotheses about which regions play a necessary role in mental processes. Finally, it complements invasive electrophysiological studies in nonhuman animals by providing a whole-brain "bird's eye" view of areas likely to show altered electrophysiological activity. Currently, fMRI is the only technique that can provide whole-brain, second-by-second coverage of functional activity. In addition, it can be easily integrated with other MR-based methods, including imaging of brain structure and white-matter tract integrity, in the same imaging session. Images from each of these methods are shown in Figure 6.1.

This chapter is intended to provide an introductory overview of fMRI study design, analysis, and inference from start to finish. It complements previous, more detailed overviews (Wager, Hernandez, Jonides, & Lindquist, 2007; Wager, Lindquist, & Hernandez, in press) by providing a brief tour through the different stages of an fMRI study, highlighting key considerations at each step for those planning to conduct fMRI studies or interested in reading and evaluating them. Each phase of an fMRI study, from conceiving the goals of the study to interpreting and describing the results, is like a link in a chain; the overall study is generally only

as valuable as the weakest link. In the first section, we discuss the kinds of questions that fMRI studies can effectively answer. The ability to ask appropriate questions is the first "link" in obtaining useful results. We also address questions about the particulars of the study, such as appropriate sample size and fMRI-specific experimental design. In the second section we discuss issues surrounding data acquisition, including how to choose scanning parameters that are appropriate for the specific scientific questions. In the third section we discuss fMRI data processing, and in the following section we discuss statistical analysis and inference. Finally, we discuss how to localize and interpret results, including which kinds of inferences are likely to be valid and which are not.

Conceiving and Designing an fMRI Experiment

FMRI studies, like most other studies, start with a scientific question. As fMRI provides a measure of brain activity,[1] questions that concern mind-brain

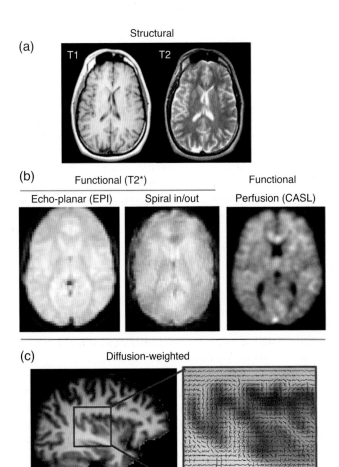

(a)

Structural

T1   T2

(b)

Functional (T2*)

Echo-planar (EPI)   Spiral in/out

Functional

Perfusion (CASL)

(c)   Diffusion-weighted

Fig. 6.1 Different kinds of MRI-based images. (a) The same slice of brain imaged with two different structural imaging methods: T1-weighted (left), which appear brighter for tissues with relatively little water content, and T2-weighted, with brighter signal in tissues with high T2 decay. (b) Three kinds of functional images: echo-planar (left) and spiral (center) blood-oxygen-level-dependent (BOLD) images, and a perfusion-related image acquired with continuous arterial spin labeling. (c) Diffusion tensor imaging allows researchers to measure directional diffusion and reconstruct the fiber tracts of the brain. This provides a way to study how different brain areas are connected.

relationships are most likely to be answerable. To ask whether there are different roles for different parts of prefrontal cortex in emotion generation, for example, is a challenging but addressable topic. However, to use fMRI (or PET, EEG, etc.) to ask what participants are thinking as they generate emotion is an order of magnitude more complex, and it is not clear that fMRI can provide much useful information (Cacioppo & Tassinary, 1990; Coltheart, 2006; Poldrack, 2006; Sarter, Berntson, & Cacioppo, 1996). However, those fMRI studies that do bear on psychological theory can be particularly informative.

The ability to make inferences about the mind from fMRI activity depends on having brain measures or outcomes that are interpretable in terms of psychological processes. For example, part of the medial occipital cortex is often called *primary visual cortex* or V1, and because of a long history of research in neuroscience, activity in this region is often considered a marker for early visual sensory processes. Evidence for activity in V1 during mental imagery was critical in resolving a debate over whether imagery is a sensory process or a purely conceptual one (Kosslyn, Thompson, Kim, & Alpert, 1995). In this study, when participants imagined a larger letter, they showed more extensive activity in parts of V1 mapped to the peripheral visual field than when they imagined a smaller letter. Likewise, evidence from multiple modalities for attention effects in V1 and its thalamic inputs helped resolve a debate about whether attention involves "early" selection (O'Connor, Fukui, Pinsk, & Kastner, 2002; Roelfsema, Lamme, & Spekreijse, 1998). However, despite these two examples, plausible biological markers of psychological processes are still extremely rare; developing them is a major goal for the field of neuroimaging.

Goals of an fMRI Study

Functional MRI studies are performed for a great variety of reasons, some geared towards basic understanding of brain-behavioral relationships and others for particular practical applications. However, they tend to fall within several broad families described in detail below. Explicitly defining the goals of a study help in evaluating whether the design and implementation are likely to serve them at each step in the process.

STRUCTURE-FUNCTION MAPPING

The most common use of fMRI to date is *structure-function mapping,* which is best defined as an exploratory, or hypothesis-building, approach. Such "brain mapping" studies are necessary for the development of biological markers and understanding the boundaries of the psychological categories they represent. This process is largely exploratory when an area of study is new and few precise hypotheses are available and moves towards testing of particular alternatives in particular regions or networks as evidence accumulates from many studies.

PROCESS DISSOCIATION AND ASSOCIATION

A second use of fMRI is for *process dissociation or association.* The question of which mental processes are similar to one another, and which are different, is central to our understanding of the organization of the mind. Neuropsychologists and neuroscientists have long sought to "carve nature at its joints," and identify the key types of mental processes and tasks that are of the same kind. Categorization of mental abilities has also been central in the field of psychometrics and aptitude testing. The basic logic in both areas is that performance measures that are inter-correlated share some common mechanisms, and capacity limitations, that are not shared by tasks in other categories. Neuroimaging activation has been used as a "molar" measure of association, much as correlations are used in psychometric testing: If two or more tasks produce dissociable activation patterns, they must have different mechanisms.

Dissociation occurs when a brain region is more active in Task A than Task B. A double dissociation occurs when each task activates one region more than the other task. Double dissociations are a powerful tool because they imply that the two tasks utilize different processes, and that one task is not a subset of the other. For example, in one study from our laboratory, we found that different types of task switching, or switching attention from one feature or object to another, differentially activated a set of regions thought to be involved in the control of attention (Wager, Jonides, Smith, & Nichols, 2005). Four types of switches were dissociable—each produced higher brain activity in some regions than the others—paralleling behavioral findings that performance switch costs are more highly correlated for similar types of switches than dissimilar types (Wager, Jonides, & Smith, 2006).

There is no perfect method for making inferences about mental structure, and dissociation logic is no exception. While we believe that process dissociation is a useful conceptual tool, we note two important caveats. First, double dissociations in neuroimaging data can be produced in trivial ways. Imagine a study of two tasks: (1) perceiving an intensely painful stimulus, and (2) perceiving a moderately painful stimulus. In this thought experiment, we will assume that (2) is a subset of (1), so there are no "different mechanisms." Task 1 is likely to produce more activation in the insula and cingulate cortex, thereby producing a dissociation. It is also likely to produce greater de-activation in the visual sensory cortex, so that Task 2 shows greater activity in these areas. In this case, we have observed a double dissociation, but not because there were unique processes related to moderate pain. Additional controls are necessary. Stronger evidence for unique processes would be provided if we could demonstrate *separate modifiability*: regions activated in each task that are not affected at all by the other task (Sternberg, 2001).

The second important caveat is that questions about similarity and dissociation are always relative to the spatial sensitivity of the measure. Typical blood oxygenation level-dependent (BOLD) studies use "voxels" (volumetric pixels, a basic unit of sampling resolution) of about 27 mm^3, which means that signal is averaged across several million neurons at best. No matter where a voxel is in the brain, different neurons within this population are almost sure to encode different stimulus properties and respond to different tasks, as even a cursory look at the primate electrophysiology literature will reveal. Thus, studies that activate the same areas only do so at a particular spatial resolution. If physical pain and pain empathy activate overlapping voxels in the cingulate and insula, they engage the same processes only insofar as there is a single, general role for these structures across tasks—it does not mean that they activate the same neurons. And even if the same neurons are active, they may play different functional roles in different tasks because they participate in different networks. In one study, for example (Zaki et al., 2007), we found that physical pain and pain empathy produced overlapping activation of the cingulate and insula, but that they could be distinguished by the connectivity of these regions with brainstem areas (for physical pain) or temporal and medial frontal regions (for pain empathy).

PREDICTION AND PSYCHOLOGICAL INFERENCE
A third class of goals concerns the use of fMRI data for a variety of practical and scientific purposes: Diagnosing early-onset Alzheimer's; identifying subgroups of patients who will respond differently to treatment; predicting words, thoughts, and intentions from patterns of brain activity; and detecting deception are but a few examples. The incorporation of fMRI-based measures into medical diagnosis

and treatment, law, and policy decisions at many levels is in its infancy. Though the potential is clearly evident, great care must be taken not to over generalize a limited set of results to broader contexts without rigorous validation.

A core issue is that fMRI is inherently suited to making inferences about brain responses given that participants are engaging in a particular task state that varies over time. It can say little about the reverse type of inference, inference about psychological state given a particular pattern of brain response. For example, imagine a participant performing an ideal lie-detection task in an ideal scanner. Because conditions are ideal, the insula is activated when the participant is lying with 100% reliability. Would we then be able to use insula activity as a lie detector, to infer when the participant was lying? Not necessarily. Frustration, or anxiety, may also activate the insula—and as long as *anything besides lying* activates the insula, there is a plausible alternative inference. Formal analysis techniques geared towards prediction provide quantitative estimates of the accuracy of such "reverse" psychological inference, and this is an exciting area of rapid development in fMRI-based research. However, it is important to note that even in the ideal case these techniques can only provide evidence that distinguishes a process from a limited set of well-defined alternatives. Thus, it might be possible to predict whether a given image is "familiar" or "unfamiliar" (the basis of many common tests of deception) given only those two alternatives, but it is much more difficult to rule out other, less well-specified alternatives—"unfamiliar but anxiety-provoking," "unfamiliar but salient"—and to detect and avoid the use of countermeasures. Thus, the prospect of using fMRI for prediction and psychological inference is both exciting and challenging.

Design Structure: Kinds of Designs
Most published studies to date either focus on structure-function mapping or process association/dissociation, either across the brain or in specific anatomical regions of interest. The most common way of doing this is through a *subtraction design*. Essentially, researchers construct two (or more) task conditions that are matched, ideally, on all sensory and psychological features except one process of interest. If we denote the experimental and control conditions as conditions A and B, respectively, the subtraction contrast [A–B] will isolate the process of interest. It is rarely possible to match features perfectly, and in this case areas showing a significant

[A–B] difference will have multiple interpretations. For example, some of our work compares moderately intense thermal pain with non-painful warmth (Wager, Scott, & Zubieta, 2007). The subtraction contrast identifies brain regions that respond to and encode the sensation of pain, but likely also includes areas involved in attentional orienting and action tendencies.

Three primary variants of the subtract design are used to permit more specific inference. In *parametric variation* designs, fMRI is used to test whether brain activity increases linearly as the involvement of a particular psychological process is incrementally varied (Buchel, Holmes, Rees, & Friston, 1998). (Other functional forms, including searching for quadratic or monotonic relationships, are also possible). Figure 6.2 shows some examples. Such designs can provide more convincing inferences because they incorporate more specific predictions about a particular process. Parametric modulators can be task conditions such as task difficulty (Figure 6.2, left; Dagher, Owen, Boecker, & Brooks, 1999) or time (Buchel, Morris, Dolan, & Friston, 1998); measured variables such as reaction time (Grinband, Hirsch, & Ferrera, 2006) or subjective value (Figure 6.2, right) (Hare, Camerer, & Rangel, 2009); or psychological model-derived processes such as prediction errors (McClure, Berns, & Montague, 2003).

With *factorial designs*, multiple types of events are included in the design, and main effects and interactions between factors are tested. Factorial designs are particularly compatible with process association and dissociation inferences, described above, because they independently vary two or more factors that may influence brain activity.

Finally, *multiple subtraction designs* compare a task with multiple control conditions, each designed to control for a separate, potentially confounded process (Price & Friston, 1997).

The underlying goal of these three techniques is essentially the same: to characterize which brain areas predict/respond to/differentiate one set of task conditions from another. The vast majority of studies use these design types to provide more specific inferences in process association/dissociation designs, but they can do little to circumvent the limitation posed by the spatial resolution of fMRI, which integrates signals across millions of neurons into a single voxel.

A growing trend in the fMRI literature is to try to circumvent some of the spatial limitations by using two kinds of techniques: *fMRI adaptation designs* and *pattern classification-compatible designs*. The logic of fMRI adaptation studies is that repetition of a particular stimulus often produces neural fatigue, in the sense that the second repetition will produce a smaller response (Grill-Spector & Malach, 2001). If two trial types, A and B, activate the same neurons, then there should be cross-trial habituation, i.e., the response to B when it follows A should be reduced. If they activate different neurons, there should be no cross-trial habituation. A full discussion of these designs is beyond the scope of this chapter, but briefly, it is important to consider three things: First, vascular responses show

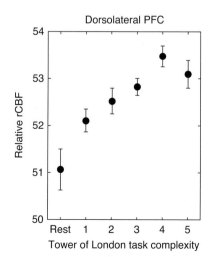
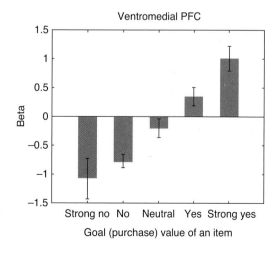

Fig. 6.2 Parametric variation designs can provide more convincing inferences because they incorporate more specific predictions about a particular process. Parametric "modulators" can be task conditions such as task difficulty (Dagher et al., 1999; left), subjective value (Hare et al., 2009; right), or other measured or experimental variables.

nonlinear habituation independent of neural activity or mental processes (Vazquez et al., 2006; Wager, Vazquez, Hernandez, & Noll, 2005). Second, even if two stimuli activate the *same neuron,* they can produce different degrees of habituation (Sawamura, Orban, & Vogels, 2006). Finally, though interpretations of fMRI-adaptation effects are often cast in terms of neuronal firing, global processes related to memory may play an important role as well (Henson, 2003).

Pattern classification is an analysis technique that is naturally suited to prediction and reverse inference, and many dozens of studies now employ these techniques to predict a variety of psychological states or events from patterns of fMRI data (Mitchell et al., 2004). Predictive techniques are also increasingly being used to address questions about structure-function mapping and process overlap through *information-based mapping* (Haynes & Rees, 2006). The logic behing information-based mapping is that even if two tasks activate the same gross anatomical region (e.g., the insula), the activation may reflect different populations of interdigitated neurons. If the spatial distribution of clumps of neurons that respond more to one task than the other are suitably distinct and the spatial resolution of the fMRI study is high enough, then the two tasks should produce different patterns of relative activity across local voxels. If so, then the machine learning techniques discussed above can be used to test association or dissociation. An algorithm might be trained to discriminate between Task and Control conditions for Task A (i.e., [Task A–Control A]). If the predictive map that results can subsequently be used to discriminate Task vs. Control for Task B, there is evidence for shared processes at a finer spatial scale.

To close this section, let's return to the main goal of dissociation/association logic, which is to test whether mental processes share common and/or distinct neural substrates. Ultimately, fMRI can only provide inferences about brain signals, and their relationship to mental processes or mechanisms requires an additional conceptual leap, equating the similarity of *brain* mechanisms to similarity of the underlying *mental* process. Our study of physical pain and pain empathy highlights one aspect of this issue. Even if the same neurons respond to physical and social pain, if these neurons are part of different functional networks, are these shared neurons part of the same mental process? Imagine a conference call with some work colleagues. You are a "neuron," and together you form a "network" that accomplishes a particular task. Now imagine that after this call, you have another conference call with some old college friends. You are involved in both; does that mean that the two networks accomplish, even to a small degree, the same task? Not necessarily.

The initial stages of any study involve grappling with these issues and making critical decisions about the study questions and how fMRI can provide useful answers. Once you have made some preliminary decisions on these issues, you are ready to implement a detailed design for your fMRI study. This is the subject of the next section.

Practical fMRI Design

There are many considerations in designing an fMRI study, and they may vary with the study goals. Here, we provide an overview of some of the general considerations. Some principles of experimental design are not unique to fMRI—for example, it is always critical to avoid confounding the comparisons you are interested in with effects of time, practice, fatigue, task history, and other factors. Functional MRI is uniquely challenging in this respect, however, because unlike traditional psychological outcome measures, fMRI activity is potentially sensitive to *any* differences among task conditions in what the participant sees, hears, thinks, or imagines.

HOW MANY SUBJECTS, AND FOR HOW LONG? POWER AND SAMPLE SIZE

This seemingly simple question is actually quite complex. There is a tradeoff between scanning more subjects and the fMRI time spent per subject. The optimal balance depends on the relative balance of within-subjects noise (error) and between-subjects noise (individual differences) in each region of interest in the brain. The within-subjects effect size can be decomposed into multiple factors: (1) the effect size of the "neural" effect, including the neural effect magnitude, time on task, fatigue, and habituation; (2) the inherent scanner noise, considering autocorrelation (slow drift) and physiological noise; (3) the number of independent data points collected, considering that sequential fMRI scans are nonindependent (autocorrelated); (4) the accuracy of the model of neural signal and BOLD hemodynamics used in the analysis; and (5) correlations in the predicted response among conditions of interest. The between-subjects effect size depends on: (1) the within-subjects effect size; (2) the magnitude of individual differences in the comparison of interest; (3) the magnitude of individual differences in the BOLD response, including in the magnitude, shape, and fit to the assumed hemodynamic model; and (4) the accuracy of inter-subject registration (i.e., normalization or warping) or other method for matching brain areas across subjects for analysis. The bottom line is this: The greater the within-subjects noise, the more likely it is that it will pay off to scan fewer subjects for longer. The greater the between-subjects noise, the more likely it is that your money will be best spent on additional subjects.

It can be daunting to consider each of these issues in detail, as information on many of them may not be obtainable until *after* you've run the study. The best way to determine how many subjects to run, and consequently how much money and time you will have to spend to run the study, is to estimate the within-subjects and between-subjects variation from existing data and perform a power analysis (Mumford & Nichols, 2008). If you can estimate the within- and between-subjects error, then the reference curves in Figure 6.3 can provide a guide to optimal choices (see the figure legend for more details). However, often these estimates are not available. As a rule of thumb, if a group analysis is the goal, scan subjects for at least 10 minutes in

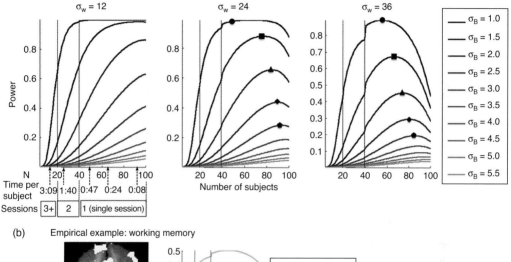

(a) Power for fixed number of scan hours, considering tradeoff of sample size (N) vs. scan time per subject, for an allocation of 60 scan hours

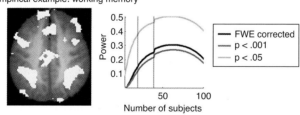

(b) Empirical example: working memory

Fig. 6.3 The optimal number of subjects for a fixed total cost varies systematically based on the ratio of within-subjects error and between-subjects differences. (a) Statistical power (on the y-axis) as a function of the sample size/scan time per subject tradeoff (on the x-axis). The lines in each graph show different levels of between-subjects variation (inter-individual differences) and the three panels show three different levels of within-subjects noise. When within-subjects noise is low (left panel), it is always better to run more subjects, even when very little time is spent imaging each subject. However, as the within-subjects noise increases (middle and right panels), it becomes optimal to increase the acquisition time for each participant. As the inter-individual differences increase (shown by increasingly light-shaded lines), the optimal ratio shifts towards more subjects with less time per subject. The points marked on the graphs show approximately optimal tradeoff points. Of course, the usefulness of these curves for planning future studies depends on having reasonable estimates for within-subjects and between-subjects error, which vary depending on the scanner noise, experimental design, paradigm, and brain region. (b) An example of the sample size/run time tradeoff from a working memory study in our laboratory. We identified regions of interest showing reliable increases or decreases relative to rest (left panel), and then calculated the average effect size and power across voxels for an independent 3-back vs. 2-back comparison. The average effect size was d = 0.23. The average within-subject standard deviation per observation was 66, and the average between-subject standard deviation was 2.48. The optimal allocation of 60 scan hours for these values was N = 62, with 28 min of functional time per subject in a single session (in our calculations, 30 min per session was allocated for subject setup and structural imaging). The power curve is shown in the right panel.

cognitive tasks. If additional time is free, scan them for longer—but if it is costly, the time and money is usually best spent scanning more subjects. If you care about obtaining significance maps within individual subjects, instead scan fewer subjects for longer.

Two other points are worth mentioning in connection with the basics of designing a study. First, subjects tend to get sleepy in the scanner after 30 minutes or so of lying still and listening to the repetitive sounds of the scanner (believe it or not!). After 60 minutes or so, many participants will experience pain on pressure points, and they will move more than usual. These factors may provide additional reasons to limit functional time to reasonably short periods. Second, it is a good idea to build positive controls into your task design— comparisons that are known to strongly activate particular brain regions, such as early visual cortex for visual stimulation–rest or motor cortex activation for movement–rest. These comparisons can serve as benchmarks for effect sizes in other studies and, if the expected results are not found, signal basic errors in data processing and analysis that might otherwise go undetected. Positive controls are a standard part of experimental research in biology, but sadly, too few functional imaging studies employ them. Those that do are usually more compelling.

POWERFUL VS. INFORMATIVE DESIGNS: MAKING TRADEOFFS

Now, we turn to the nuts and bolts of experimental design: choosing the task conditions, when and for how long to present them, and what comparisons to make. The first neuroimaging designs were block designs, and they are still commonly used today. An example is shown in the top panel of Figure 6.4. Here, stimuli (or task conditions) of the same type are grouped together in time, and stimulation/performance within a block is typically as continuous as possible, to maximize the time on the task of interest. If stimulation can be continuous, stimulus history is not an important factor, and blocking stimuli does not change the nature of the task in undesirable ways, then a design with two block types (e.g., visual stimulation and rest) alternated every 16–20 sec is maximally powerful (Liu, 2004; Skudlarski, Constable, & Gore, 1999; Wager & Nichols, 2003). In addition, block designs are relatively robust to mis-specification of the shape of the neural input and hemodynamic response functions (HRF), as we describe in more detail below.

Block designs with more conditions (including parametric variation and factorial designs) may be informative, in that there are more conditions to compare and there is potentially more leverage on how to interpret activations. However, multiple-condition

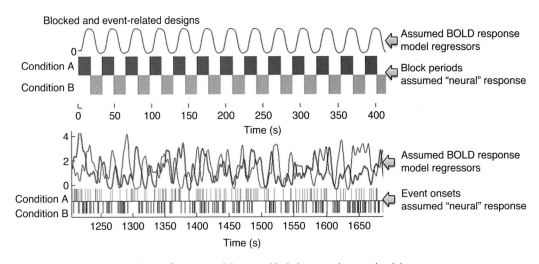

Fig. 6.4 The two most common classes of experimental design are block designs and event-related designs. In a block design (top), experimental conditions are separated into extended time intervals, or blocks, of the same type. In an event-related design (bottom), the stimulus consists of short discrete events whose timing and order can be randomized.

designs can also be less powerful, for two reasons. First, less time is spent imaging any one condition, so activation estimates will be less stable. Second, alternations across blocks occur more slowly in time. The noise in fMRI is high at low frequencies, meaning that the signal drifts slowly over time. High-pass filters are typically used to remove noise, but they cannot be used if the conditions of interest also vary slowly. Because a 16 sec alternation frequency closely matches the frequency of the hemodynamic response in most areas of the brain, it is nearly perfectly efficient. Thus, all things being equal, a two-condition block design with 16 sec blocks is the most powerful and robust design.

Event-related designs

These are a popular alternative, for several reasons. First, not all designs can be implemented as block designs without changing the nature of the task. For example, in a stop-signal task, the subject is asked to respond as fast as possible to a visual stimulus, but stop if an auditory tone is presented just after stimulus onset. Blocking "stop" trials would dramatically change how difficult it is to stop, because participants could anticipate and adapt to the trial structure. Second, event-related designs are more interpretable in one important, fundamental sense: They allow activity to be linked with more credibility to individual event types. Activation in block designs could be a "state" effect that occurs throughout a block, in between trials, or only on certain trials (e.g., errors), making interpretation more difficult. Event-related designs can isolate trials or even parts of trials (Ollinger, Shulman, & Corbetta, 2001). They can also permit analysis of activity modulated by performance variables such as reaction time on a trial-by-trial basis, as discussed above, and estimation of the shape and timing of the HRF in response to each event type in each voxel (Bellgowan, Saad, & Bandettini, 2003). As with block designs, the most statistically powerful designs involve only two event types, in order to maximize time on task and minimize low-frequency variation in the design.

A third reason why simpler event-related designs are more powerful is that fewer event types means less *multicolinearity*, a standard but largely insurmountable problem in statistical analysis that can dramatically reduce power and lead to effects which are unstable even when significant. Multicolinearity occurs when the linear model regressor (the predicted fMRI signal) for one event type can be predicted by a combination of the other regressors. Fewer event types mean, on average, less multicolinearity. Of course, designs with more event types may offer more interesting psychological inferences, if they are appropriately powered.

As mentioned above, event-related designs are also less robust. This is because the BOLD response to brief neural events is not an instantaneous one; it is determined by slow changes in blood oxygenation, flow, and volume, as illustrated in Figure 6.5. A brief burst of neural firing typically produces a slow hemodynamic response (HR) that peaks about 5–6 sec post-stimulus and returns to baseline after 20–30 sec, as shown in Figure 6.6. As discussed in the analysis section below, fMRI analyses typically assume a fixed shape for the HR and use it to develop predictors for what BOLD responses to various types of events are expected to look like (shown in Figure 6.6B). These predictors are fit to the observed fMRI time series from each voxel in each subject. One problem is that the hemodynamic response varies across brain regions, subjects, and tasks (Aguirre, Zarahn, & D'Esposito, 1998; Schacter, Buckner, Koutstaal, Dale, & Rosen, 1997; Summerfield et al., 2006). Event-related designs are sensitive to the difference between the assumed and actual hemodynamic responses, whereas block designs are less sensitive.

The slow HR is an important factor that shapes other elements of fMRI design as well. It acts like a low-pass filter, smoothing out rapid changes in the signal. If you present events too close together, the HR will blur the rapid rise and fall in your experimental design into what looks like a flat line. Because the linear modeling approach depends on this rise and fall—it fits the shapes of the regressors to the shape of the rise and fall in the data—this blurring dramatically decreases power. On the other hand, if you present events too far apart, you create little variation in the regressors (and the data) across time because very little time is spent on-task. Thus, optimal designs are those that present events fairly close together. Alternating two event-types every four seconds or so in a randomized fashion is optimal for a randomized event-related design.

The four-second rule of thumb takes into consideration another important factor: nonlinearity. In building predictors of fMRI signal, it is typically assumed that each event produces a discrete response that is the same for all events, and that the total signal is the sum of responses to individual events. If this were strictly true, you could present 1000 spider pictures in 1 second and get a response 1000 times as large as if you had presented only one photo!

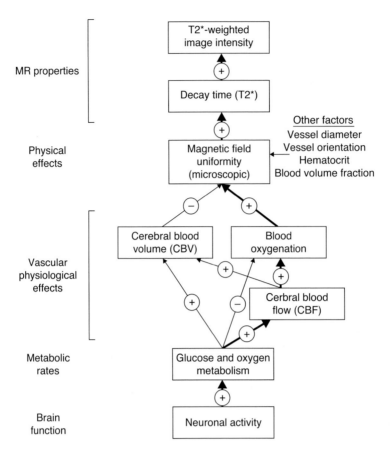

Fig. 6.5 Influences on T$_2$*-weighted signal in BOLD fMRI imaging.
Courtesy Dr. Doug Noll.

Obviously, the response is not linear. In fact, the largest sources of nonlinearity are neural habituation and vascular saturation. Neurons often stop responding as strongly after a few hundred milliseconds (and some respond only to stimulus onset or offset), and blood vessels dilate and lose elasticity. The effect of both is that the BOLD response reaches a ceiling as stimulation intensity or frequency increases (Vazquez & Noll, 1998; Birn, Saad, & Bandettini, 2001; Friston, Mechelli, Turner, & Price, 2000; Wager, Vazquez et al., 2005). Four seconds' delay between brief events is enough to prevent most nonlinear interactions between successive events (Miezin, Maccotta, Ollinger, Petersen, & Buckner, 2000).

Rest intervals and "jitter."
Standard BOLD fMRI can provide comparisons of relative activity between conditions, but it cannot provide absolute measures of blood flow. When designing an experiment, it is important to plan for all the comparisons that you want to make. This includes comparisons with rest or a comparable

"low-level" control condition. Let's say you're conducting an experiment comparing activity during viewing of faces and scenes ("places"). You'd like to compare [Faces–Places] and identify face-specific brain regions. But you would also like to know whether your face-specific regions *increase* in response to faces. Some regions that show a [Face–Place] difference might do so because they *decrease* in response to places. To test for increases during face processing, you must test for increases relative to some other, third control condition, e.g., [Face–Rest]. If you are interested in this comparison, your design must contain a third condition—most commonly, rest. How much time you spend sampling the rest condition depends on how much you care about [Face–Rest] as opposed to [Face–Place]. An optimal design for the former involves spending as much time sampling face presentation and rest as possible, with equal allocation of time between them. For the latter, an optimal design involves heavy and balanced sampling of face and place presentation. Thus, the experimental design

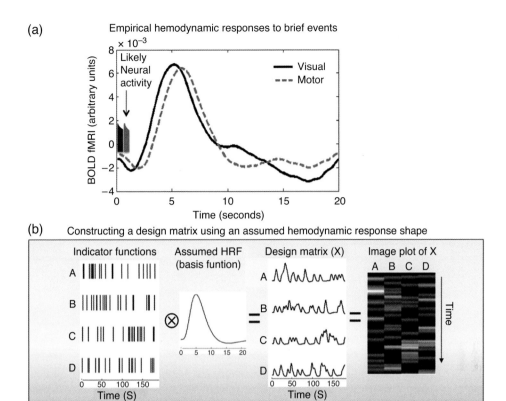

(a) Empirical hemodynamic responses to brief events

(b) Constructing a design matrix using an assumed hemodynamic response shape

Fig. 6.6 (A) Empirical hemodynamic response functions (HRFs) from primary visual and motor cortices, adapted from Lindquist, Zhang, Glover, & Shepp (2008), with permission of Elsevier. Data were sampled at a high time-resolution using a recently developed acquisition technique (100 ms, with whole-brain coverage at 12 mm spatial resolution), permitting visualization of fine-grained details of the HRF, including the initial dip in signal due to blood oxygenation decreases. Participants saw a contrast-reversing checkerboard (visual) for 100 ms and made a button-press response an average of 250 ms later. The signal in the visual cortex proceeds the signal in the motor cortex throughout the duration of the HRF. (B) In an fMRI experiment with four conditions (A, B, C, and D), the stimulus function is convolved with a canonical HRF to obtain two sets of predicted BOLD responses. The responses are placed into the columns of a design matrix X and used to compute whether there is significant signal corresponding to the two conditions in a particular time course.

should consider the relative importance of different comparisons in the study.

In an event-related design, rest intervals are often included between events in the form of an inter-trial interval or inter-stimulus interval (ITI or ISI). Rapid and regular alternations between stimuli and rest will not provide an efficient design, for the same reason that rapid alternation between two event types (e.g., Face and Place) will not be efficient; the BOLD HR will essentially smooth out the differences between conditions and make it impossible to detect anything. For this reason, event-related designs usually use variable-length ITIs, also known as jitter. Jitter is important because it de-correlates predicted responses to events that would otherwise be collinear. How much jitter is appropriate? A rule of thumb, shown to be near-optimal, is to use short ITIs (e.g., 4 sec) for 50% the trials, with exponentially

decreasing frequency as ITI increases; thus, 25% of the trials might use a 6 sec ITI, 12.5% might use an 8 sec ITI, and so on.

Another important consideration is which type of low-level control condition to use. Many researchers believe that the resting state is a privileged state against which to compare functional activation (Raichle et al., 2001). However, other researchers point out that rest involves active processes that likely include self-monitoring and memory retrieval (among others), and that individuals may vary dramatically in which processes they engage at rest. Stark and Squire (2001), for example, found that activity in the medial temporal lobes was substantially higher during rest than during some low-level cognitive tasks. The memory tasks they used "activated" relative to a low-level cognitive control condition, but "de-activated" relative to rest. Thus, it may sometimes be more appropriate to compare tasks to low-level baseline tasks during which mental activity can be more precisely experimentally controlled (Johnson et al., 2005). There is currently no universally accepted "right answer."

Optimized experimental designs

What constitutes an optimal experimental design depends on the psychological nature of the task, as well as on the specific comparisons (contrasts) of interest in the study. In fMRI studies, the delay and shape of the BOLD response, scanner drift and nuisance factors such as physiological noise, and other factors also play important roles in design optimality. Not all designs with the same number of trials for a given set of conditions are equal, and the spacing and ordering of events is critical (Josephs & Henson, 1999; Liu, 2004; Smith, Jenkinson, Beckmann, Miller, & Woolrich, 2007; Wager & Nichols, 2003).

Several computer algorithms are available for constructing statistically optimized designs (e.g., Wager & Nichols, 2003), particularly for event-related designs. These programs generally operate on the spacing, frequency, and order of stimulus presentation during the experiment. They incorporate assumptions about the HRF shape and linearity or non-linearity of the response, information about the comparisons of interest in the study, and other design and analysis choices such as the frequency of image collection and data filtering options. One important point is that there is a substantial tradeoff in power between *detecting* activation differences between conditions (i.e., an [A–B] contrast) using an assumed HRF shape and estimating the *shape* of evoked activations with a more flexible model (Liu, Frank, Wong, & Buxton, 2001). For detecting activation differences, a block design alternating between two blocks (A and B) with a block length of 16 sec each is statistically most efficient. For HRF shape estimation, a useful toolbox for optimizing the event ordering is based on M-sequences, or sequences which are orthogonal to themselves shifted in time (Buracas & Boynton, 2002). Random event-related designs fall somewhere in between blocked and event-related designs, but are non-optimal on both. Computer-aided designs can produce substantially better results than random event-related designs on both measures.

Acquiring Data

Functional MRI is a multidisciplinary venture, and considerable physics and engineering knowledge goes into the data acquisition. Thus, it is a good idea to make friends with a physicist or two and send them birthday cards (though we note that Dr. Doug Noll graciously provided us with Figure 6.5 without one). Image acquisition is rapidly developing, and cutting-edge research continues to push towards better image quality, lower noise and artifacts, higher temporal and spatial resolution, and, as a consequence, more meaningful results. Commercial manufacturers have increasingly made stable fMRI acquisition protocols available, and these standard acquisition procedures may be adequate for many studies. But even seemingly routine imaging requires careful selection of acquisition parameters. How many slices will you collect? In what orientation? How large will the voxels be? How rapidly will images be acquired? Will you be able to obtain signal in key brain areas such as the amygdala, orbitofrontal cortex, and medial temporal cortices? This section will help you talk to your physicist collaborator and design an acquisition scheme that is suitable for your study.

Just as with the experimental design, the key to setting up an appropriate data acquisition protocol lies in understanding some basic tradeoffs and considering them in relation to the goals of your particular study. We first provide a bit of background, and then some considerations on these choices. Terms with specific meaning in MR physics are in italics.

MR Basics

Both structural (*T1-* or *T2-weighted*) and functional (*T2*/susceptibility weighted* or *perfusion-weighted*) MRI images are obtained using the same scanner, though it is programmed differently depending on the image type. In all cases, a subject is placed in a strong magnetic field, usually 1.5 to 7 Tesla, generated by a coil of wire wrapped around a tube. The person being imaged lies in the center of the tube, or the *bore*. The field is always on, and anything attracted to magnets can be pulled into the bore of the magnet with irresistible force, even when the imaging control console is shut down. Therefore, it is extremely important not to bring metal objects, or anyone who might have metal in their body, near the scanner.

During imaging, the participant is exposed to a radiofrequency (RF) electromagnetic field pulse delivered through a second coil (commonly called *the head coil*) that typically surrounds the participant's head. Unlike PET, this does not involve exposure to radioactive material, and there are no known risks to repeating this procedure. The main magnetic field (B_0, *b-naught*" aligns the spins of protons in hydrogen atoms (*the spins*) in the brain along its axis. When the RF pulse is delivered, these protons absorb the energy at a very specific frequency band that depends on the field strength and become *excited*. The nuclei then emit the energy at the same frequency as they *relax*. Different tissue types have different *relaxation times*, which creates the contrast between gray matter, white matter, and cerebrospinal fluid (CSF) in the images.

There are several kinds of relaxation that are used to create contrast in images: T_1, T_2, and T_2^*. These letters are used to denote the relaxation rate associated with each. T_1 is the rate at which spins relax back to the main magnetic field. T_1-weighted images have values across the image sensitive to the differences in T_1 across gray matter, white matter, and CSF, and they provide excellent detailed images of brain anatomy. T_2 refers to how quickly the energy applied from the RF pulse dissipates, which also depends on the tissue type. T_2-weighted images also provide excellent anatomical structure and additional detail in some subcortical and brainstem nuclei. Regions such as the substantia nigra, with high iron content (which is magnetic), have very fast T_2 relaxation and appear as dark spots in T_2-weighted images, providing anatomical definition in these regions. Finally, T_2^* is the rate of attenuation of the magnetic field applied by the RF pulse. T_2^* depends additionally on local inhomogeneities in magnetic susceptibility that are caused by changes in blood flow and oxygenation.

As the spins relax, the returned energy is detected by the *receiver coil*, generally the same coil that produced the RF field. This energy is detected as a one-dimensional series of fluctuations over time; however, due to Nobel prize-winning work by Paul Lauterbur and Peter Mansfield, it is possible to reconstruct a three-dimensional (3-D) image from these signals. This is done by applying *gradients*, magnets that change the strength of the magnetic field in systematic ways across space so that the frequency and the phase of the signals detected by the receive coil encode the location of the signal in the brain. *Pulse sequences*, or software programs that implement particular patterns of RF and gradient manipulations, are designed to acquire data that can be used to reconstruct images of the brain. There are various types of pulse sequences, including *echo-planar imaging* (EPI) and *spiral imaging*. With a standard EPI sequence, 3-D localization is done by selectively exciting tissue in one two-dimensional (2-D) slice of brain at a time (*slice*

selection) and applying gradients to encode the location of the signal within the 2-D slice. It should be noted that the MR signal is not acquired voxel by voxel; rather, the acquired data is collected in the frequency domain, or *k-space*. The data can be converted from k-space to *image space* (an image that looks like a brain) by applying a *Fourier transform*.

BOLD Signal

T_2^*-weighted imaging is used to obtain measures of regional brain activity. The most popular method uses the blood oxygenation level-dependent (BOLD) signal (Kwong et al., 1992; Ogawa et al., 1992), which takes advantage of the difference in T_2^* between oxygenated and deoxygenated hemoglobin. As neural activity increases, so does metabolic demand for oxygen and nutrients. As oxygen is extracted from the blood, the hemoglobin becomes paramagnetic, which creates small distortions in the B_0 field that cause a T_2^* decrease (i.e., a faster decay of the signal). Increases in deoxyhemoglobin can lead to a decrease in BOLD signal, often referred to as the "initial dip" (Figure 6.6A). The initial decrease in signal is followed by an increase, due to an overcompensation in blood flow that tips the balance towards oxygenated hemoglobin (and less signal loss due to dephasing). This ultimately leads to a higher BOLD signal that gives the positive rise that characterizes the hemodynamic response.

Arterial Spin Labeling (ASL)

Arterial spin labeling is a family of techniques that provides an alternative to BOLD imaging (Williams, Detre, Leigh, & Koretsky, 1992). ASL uses pulse sequences sensitive to blood volume or cerebral perfusion (or cerebral blood flow, CBF), a quantifiable physiological measure that is more directly related to neuronal metabolism than BOLD. In typical ASL experiments, two images are collected: one following a radio-frequency tagging period during which transverse magnetization ("label") is imparted to protons, and the other after a control period during which the tag clears and the system is allowed to return to equilibrium. Subtraction of these two images yields a signal that is proportional to the amount of label that is in the tissue (which is sensitive to blood flow), and can be used to quantify the cerebral perfusion rate. ASL may be used to quantify and study baseline cerebral blood flow without comparison to an active state, which is desirable for many kinds of studies of special populations (aging populations, children, those with schizophrenia, mood disorders, etc.). Because the measurements are stable over time, ASL can be used to compare conditions across long time periods, facilitating the study of phenomena such as emotional states, drug effects, and learning.

Study-Specific Acquisition Choices

There are a number of ways to optimize fMRI acquisition to maximize the chances of achieving the goals of a particular study, but each option comes with associated costs, as summarized in Table 6.1. Below, we discuss several options and their costs and benefits. If you have access to multiple scanners, one choice may involve which *field strength* to use, typically either 1.5 T or 3.0 T. Higher field strength means lower thermal noise, the inherent noise in the excitation and measurement of spins, and a higher BOLD contrast-to-noise ratio (CNR). But higher fields are not always better, because *susceptibility artifacts* are greater at higher field strengths. Susceptibility artifacts are decreases and/or spatial distortions in the signal that occur due to local inhomogeneity in the magnetic field not related to blood flow, often at the boundaries between tissue and sinus spaces at the bottom of the brain, including orbitofrontal cortex, ventromedial prefrontal cortex, amygdala, and the medial temporal lobes. Minimizing susceptibility artifacts is an important consideration if signal in these areas is of interest. Some approaches are to use "z-shimming" during acquisition to make the field more homogenous (Constable & Spencer, 1999), improved reconstruction algorithms (Noll, Fessler, & Sutton, 2005),

"unwarping" algorithms that measure EPI distortion by measuring inhomogeneity in the magnetic field and attempting to correct it (Andersson, Hutton, Ashburner, Turner, & Friston, 2001), and use of magnetic inserts in the mouths of participants that act as shims (Wilson & Jezzard, 2003). However, choices of standard acquisition parameters can also have a great impact on susceptibility and other signal characteristics. We describe some of these choices, and their impact, below.

One way of minimizing susceptibility artifacts is to shorten the TE, the *echo time* between delivery of the RF excitation pulse and reading out the signal. There is an optimal TE for T2* sensitivity (typically about 40 msec for 1.5 T, and 25 msec for 3.0 T), and it grows shorter as the field strength increases, because signal loss (*dephasing*) due to inhomogeneity occurs at a faster rate. Shortening the TE, say to 25 msec at 1.5 T, will decrease susceptibility, but also decrease BOLD contrast and thus the BOLD signal-to-noise ratio. For high-susceptibility areas such as the amygdala and orbitofrontal cortex, this is likely to be advantageous, but it will reduce sensitivity for other brain areas. This tradeoff, and others described below, must be evaluated with respect to the particular goals of your study.

Another way to reduce susceptibility artifacts is to scan using smaller voxels, and, in particular, thinner slices. Current typical voxel sizes are 3 x 3 x 3 mm. Collecting thinner slices reduces the inhomogeneity gradient across space within a voxel, and lower inhomogeneity means less susceptibility

Table 6.1 Costs and benefits of optimized fMRI acquisition

	Higher field strength	Shorter TE	Smaller voxels	Longer TR	Accelerated imaging
Brain coverage			−	+	+
Contrast/noise	+	−	−	+	−
BOLD signal/noise	+	−	−	+	−*
Spatial resolution			+	+	+
Temporal resolution			−	−	+
Susceptibility artifact reduction	−	+		−	+
Resistance to motion/physiological artifacts	−			−	+

Note: Analysis options are shown in columns, and their effects shown in rows. Characteristics listed in rows are advantageous, but there are inherent tradeoffs in the data acquisition process that make it impossible to have one's cake and eat it too. Minus signs (−) mean "disadvantageous" and plus signs (+) mean "advantageous".
*there is reduced signal to noise but more images, so the benefits and costs may balance.

artifact. This is obviously advantageous for increasing the spatial resolution, which improves localization ability. However, it comes at a cost to CNR, which decreases proportional to the voxel volume (there are fewer spins to detect in a given voxel), and thereby reduces sensitivity to experimental effects. Thus, the CNR for a 1 x 1 x 1 voxel acquisition scheme is 27 times lower that the standard 3 mm acquisition. Another problem with smaller voxels is that it takes longer to acquire an image across the whole brain. Researchers interested in high-resolution fMRI studies may opt for increased spatial resolution and reduced susceptibility, but these benefits come at a cost to statistical power and brain coverage.

These tradeoffs may be less extreme if the repetition time (TR) to acquire images is lengthened. A typical TR is on the order of 2 sec, meaning that an image volume is acquired every 2 sec. Longer TRs decrease the temporal resolution, but permit more brain coverage (more slices) with smaller voxel sizes. For TRs in the range of 0.5–2.5 sec, the cost of reduced temporal resolution is minimal, as the BOLD hemodynamic response lag is on the order of 6 sec. However, there is a danger in event-related designs: If trials are locked to the TR, the peak of the BOLD response will fall somewhere in between the samples. This issue can be avoided by "jittering" the events with respect to image acquisition. Other problems with longer TRs, however, are harder to overcome. A chief one is that even small head movements (or brain movement due to breathing and heart-beat) during the acquisition of a volume can induce inhomogeneity that creates large artifacts in the data. In addition, motion during volume acquisition causes inaccuracies in image preprocessing, as slice timing acquisition and motion correction algorithms do not adjust for the shift in slice locations within the volume.

A relatively recent development is the use of *accelerated imaging*, which involves sub-sampling k-space, i.e., acquiring a volume more quickly by only sampling some frequencies. This reduces the BOLD signal/noise ratio, but allows image acquisition to be accelerated. Some common acceleration schemes are SENSE and GRAPPA. The acceleration factor (i.e., the *SENSE factor*) determines how much faster images are acquired: An acceleration factor of 2 decreases the TR by ½, 3 by 1/3, etc. This can be done without loss in spatial resolution due to advances in *parallel imaging*, the simultaneous use of multiple RF receive coils to collect data. Many fMRI systems are now equipped with 8-channel

head coils, and 32-channel coils are also commercially available. Because the coils are smaller, they must be positioned closer to the head surface, and they produce a signal/noise benefit primarily on the brain surface.

In summary, tradeoffs between all these factors make different acquisition schemes optimal for different study goals (Table 6.1). A good strategy is to work with a physicist to test different combinations of parameters before the study, balancing the coverage, spatial and temporal resolution, and susceptibility artifacts.

As a starting point for a customized acquisition scheme, we provide two examples. A typical whole-brain acquisition for our group is ~35 slices with TR = 2 sec, 3 x 3 x 3 mm voxels, and an 8-channel coil with SENSE factor 2. For experiments in which signal in the orbitofrontal cortex and amygdala is of interest, an alternate scheme might be 15 slices at TR = 1 sec, with 1.5 x 1.5 x 1.5 mm voxels but coverage only of the areas of interest.

Analyzing Data

There are several common objectives in the statistical analysis of fMRI data. These vary from simply localizing regions of the brain activated by a certain task to determining distributed networks that correspond to brain function and making predictions about psychological or disease states. In the following section we discuss the standard approach towards preprocessing fMRI data, the general linear model (GLM), and emerging techniques for modeling brain connectivity.

Preprocessing fMRI Data

Prior to analysis, fMRI data typically undergoes a series of preprocessing steps aimed at reconstructing images from the raw data, identifying and removing artifacts, and validating model assumptions. A common pipeline is shown in Figure 6.7. The goals of preprocessing are to minimize the influence of data acquisition and physiological artifacts, validate statistical assumptions, and standardize the locations of brain regions across subjects in order to achieve increased validity and sensitivity in group analysis.

Preprocessing is necessary to justify numerous assumptions made in later data analysis: that all voxels in a brain volume were acquired simultaneously; that each data point in a specific voxel's time series only consists of signal from that voxel (i.e., that the participant did not move in between measurements); and that each voxel is located in the same anatomical region for all subjects. Without

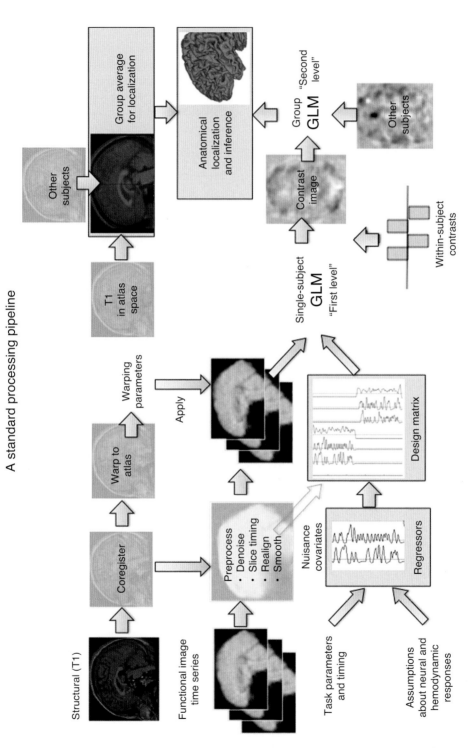

Fig. 6.7 A data analysis pipeline that shows the major processing steps for a functional MRI study. This is the pipeline currently used in our laboratory.

preprocessing the data prior to analysis, none of these assumptions would hold and the resulting statistical analysis would be invalid.

The major steps in fMRI preprocessing are reconstruction, data visualization and artefact reduction, slice acquisition timing correction, realignment, co-registration of structural and functional images, registration or nonlinear warping to a template (also called normalization), and smoothing. Each step is described below.

IMAGE RECONSTRUCTION

The first stage of preprocessing is image reconstruction. The raw MR signal is acquired in k-space and the data is subsequently transformed into brain volumes; each consisting of a number of uniformly spaced volume elements, or voxels, whose intensity represents the spatial distribution of the nuclear spin density within that particular voxel. There are a variety of approaches to sampling the data (e.g., echo-planar, spiral), each with its own benefits relating to speed, signal-to-noise ratio, and ease of reconstruction, and different options for reconstruction depending on the image sampling scheme. For a more complete discussion see Lindquist (Lindquist, 2008).

VISUALIZATION AND ARTIFACT REDUCTION

Neuroimaging data contain artifacts that arise from a number of sources, including head movement, reconstruction and interpolation processes, and brain movement and vascular effects related to periodic physiological fluctuations. Functional MRI data often contains transient spike artifacts and slow drift over time related to a variety of sources, including magnetic gradient instability, RF interference, and movement-induced inhomogeneities in the magnetic field. These artifacts will likely violate the assumption of normally and identically distributed errors; unless dealt with, the consequences include reduced power in group analysis and increased false positives in single-subject inference.

A first line of defense is to examine the data using exploratory techniques and diagnose problems, which can then be addressed using a variety of artifact prevention or reduction techniques. There are many possible sources of artifacts, some that signal fundamental problems with the scanner setup (e.g., RF leaks) and others that are inevitable and whose impact can be minimized during analysis. However, because fMRI data involves hundreds of thousands of measurements over time, visualizing the data is not trivial. A popular approach is to extract principal components or independent components from the whole-brain time series and visualize them. Multiple packages, such as FSL's Melodic software, the Group ICA of Functional MRI (GIFT) toolbox, fMRIstat software, and others provide ways of doing this.

Some ICA/PCA packages also provide the capability to remove components deemed artifactual from the data, and there is increasing interest in using such methods to "de-noise" fMRI data (Nakamura et al., 2006; Tohka et al., 2007). One central difficulty is determining which components to remove. Many components are likely to involve a mix of task-related and artifact-related signals, and there is no guarantee that removing a component will increase the accuracy or precision of estimates of task-related effects.

Another popular approach is the estimation and inclusion of physiological artifacts from known sources, including participant head motion, heartbeat, respiration, and fluctuations in CO^2 concentration with breathing. Several recent papers show benefits of estimating a canonical "cardiac response function," "respiration response function," and de-noising of fMRI data by combining heartbeat and respiration measures with these functions during scanning (Chang, Cunningham, & Glover, 2009).

One all-too-common artifact that cannot be corrected by model-based physiological correction is gradient artifacts or "spikes" in the data that can affect one or more slices. A growing number of laboratories have developed procedures for identifying such artifacts and minimizing their influence, either through robust estimation techniques or simply removing, interpolating, or Windsorizing them (i.e., adjusting extreme values only into a more reasonable range). A sensible approach, which we prefer, is to identify spikes and create dummy regressors (which model only that time point) for inclusion in the statistical analysis. Toolboxes such as AFNI's 3ddespike, ArtRepair (Mazaika, Hoeft, Glover, & Reiss, 2009), and others may also be useful.

A potential issue with all of these approaches is that single-subject inferences may be inaccurate (i.e., p-values may be wrong) if variance is removed from the data without accounting for it in the subsequent statistical analysis. Any removal of components or known physiological effects should be accompanied by an appropriate reduction in the degrees of freedom in the statistical model. If covariates are entered in a regression analysis, this reduction is automatically performed. But if filtering or de-noising is done *before* analysis, it is more difficult

to produce valid single-subject p-values, particularly if components are removed rather than covariates specified a priori.

SLICE TIMING CORRECTION

When analyzing 3D fMRI data, it is typically assumed that the entire brain volume is measured simultaneously. In reality, because the volume consists of multiple slices that are sampled sequentially, and therefore at different time points, similar time courses from different slices will be temporally shifted relative to one another. Thus, it is common practice to correct the signal intensity in all voxels, so they can be considered to be sampled at the same point in the acquisition period. This can be done by interpolating the signal intensity at the chosen time point from the same voxel in previous and subsequent acquisitions. A number of interpolation techniques exist (e.g., bilinear and sinc interpolation) with varying degrees of accuracy and speed. Sinc interpolation is the slowest, but generally the most accurate. Some researchers do not use slice timing, as it adds interpolation error to the data, and instead use more flexible hemodynamic models to account for variations in acquisition time.

MOTION CORRECTION

An important issue involved in any fMRI study is the proper handling of any subject movement that may have taken place during data acquisition. Even small amounts of head motion can be a major source of error if not treated correctly. All typical analyses assume that each voxel contains signal in the same brain area from image to image. When movement occurs, the signal from a specific voxel will come from different areas of the brain, blurring the signal and creating edge artifacts. Even worse, head movement creates alterations in the magnetic field that can result in large susceptibility artifacts. The first step in correcting for motion, and a partial solution for the first problem above, is to find the best possible alignment between the input image and some target image (e.g., the first image or the mean image). A rigid body transformation involving six variable parameters is used. This allows the input image to be translated (shifted in the x, y, and z directions) and rotated (altered roll, pitch, and yaw) to match the target image. Usually, the matching process is performed by minimizing some cost function (e.g., the sums of squared differences) that assesses similarity between the two images. Once the parameters that achieve optimal realignment are determined, the image is re-sampled using interpolation to create new motion-corrected voxel values. This procedure is repeated for each brain volume.

Realignment corrects adequately for small movements of the head, but it does not correct for the more complex spin-history artifacts (i.e., movement x magnetic field homogeneity interactions) created by the motion. The parameters at each time point are saved for later inspection and are often included in the analysis as covariates of no interest; however, even this additional step does not completely remove artifacts created by head motion. Residual artifacts remain in the data and contribute to noise. Sometimes this noise is correlated with task contrasts of interest, which can create false results in single-subject analyses. Because these artifacts typically differ in sign and magnitude across subjects, group analyses are usually robust to such artifacts in terms of false positives (though there are exceptions), but movement artifacts can severely compromise power.

CO-REGISTRATION

Functional MRI data is typically of low spatial resolution and provides relatively little anatomical detail. Therefore, high-resolution structural images are used for warping and localization. The transformations (warps) estimated from structural images are typically applied to the functional images, which are then analyzed, so accurate registration of structural and functional images is critical. Co-registration aligns structural and functional images, or in general, different types of images of the same brain. Because functional and structural images are collected using different sequences and different tissue classes have different average intensities, using a least squares difference method to match images is typically not appropriate. Instead, an affine transformation can be used that maximizes the *mutual information* among the two images, or the degree that knowing the intensity of one can be used to predict the intensity of the other (Cover & Thomas, 1991). Typically, a single structural image is co-registered to the first or mean functional image.

NORMALIZATION

For group analysis, each voxel must lie within the same brain structure for each individual subject. Of course, individual brains differ in their shapes and features, but there are similarities shared by every non-pathological brain. Normalization attempts to register each subject's anatomy to a standardized stereotaxic space defined by a template brain (e.g., the Talairach or Montreal Neurological

Institute [MNI] brain). In this scenario, it is common to use nonlinear transformations to match local features. One begins by estimating a smooth continuous mapping between the points in an input image with those in the target image. Next, the mapping is used to re-sample the input image so that it is warped onto the target image, resulting in a normalized image that can be compared with similarly normalized images obtained from other subjects. The main benefits of normalizing data are that spatial locations can be reported and interpreted in a consistent manner, results can be generalized to a larger population, and results can be compared across studies and subjects. Drawbacks are that it reduces spatial resolution and may introduce errors due to interpolation.

SMOOTHING

It is common practice to spatially smooth fMRI data prior to analysis. Smoothing typically involves convolving the functional images with a Gaussian kernel, described by the full width of the kernel at half its maximum height (FWHM). Common values vary between 4–12mm FWHM.

FMRI data are smoothed for several reasons. First, it may improve inter-subject registration and overcome limitations in the spatial normalization by blurring any residual anatomical differences. Second, it ensures that the assumptions of random field theory (RFT), commonly used to correct for multiple-comparisons, are valid. A rough estimate of the amount of smoothing required to meet the assumptions of RFT is a FWHM of 3 times the voxel size (e.g., 9mm for 3mm voxels), but the required value may be much higher for small samples (e.g., < 20 subjects in a group analysis; Nichols & Hayasaka, 2003). Third, if the spatial extent of a region of interest is larger than the spatial resolution, smoothing may reduce random noise in individual voxels and increase the signal-to-noise ratio within the region.

The process of spatially smoothing an image is equivalent to applying a low-pass filter to the sampled k-space data prior to reconstruction. This implies that much of the acquired data is discarded as a byproduct of smoothing, and spatial resolution is sacrificed without gaining any benefits. Additionally, acquiring an image with high spatial resolution and then smoothing the image is not the same as directly acquiring a low resolution image. The signal-to-noise ratio during acquisition increases as the square of the voxel volume, so acquiring small voxels means that signal is lost that can never be recovered. Hence, it is optimal in terms of sensitivity to acquire images at the desired resolution and not employ smoothing.

Previously, many investigators also *temporally smoothed* their data. This procedure removes high-frequency signals from the data. However, this approach has largely been replaced by more standard time series models (e.g., autoregressive modeling). There is no expected benefit to temporal smoothing on sensitivity, as it further decreases the temporal resolution of the data.

The General Linear Model

The general linear model (GLM) is a linear analysis method that subsumes many basic analysis techniques, including t-tests, ANOVA, and multiple regression (Worsley & Friston, 1995). It is by far the most common approach for assessing task–brain activity relationships in the neuroimaging literature. The GLM can be used to estimate whether the brain responds to a single type of event, to compare different types of events, to assess correlations between brain activity and behavioral performance or other psychological variables, and perform several types of tests of functional and effective connectivity. The GLM is appropriate when multiple predictor variables are used to explain variability in a single, continuously distributed outcome variable. The predictors are related to psychological events, and the outcome variable is signal in a brain voxel or region of interest. The analysis is typically "massively univariate," meaning that the analyst performs a separate GLM analysis at every voxel in the brain, and summary statistics are saved in maps of statistic values across the brain.

GLM MODEL BASICS

Functional MRI analysis typically proceeds in three stages: The "first level" analysis, in which activation parameter estimates for each condition (event type), voxel, and individual are obtained. Differences in activation parameter estimates across conditions, or contrasts, are then estimated for each individual in a second stage. Finally, a group analysis is conducted on contrast values to test whether the observed activation differences between conditions are likely to exist in the population. This is typically referred to as "second level" analysis.

First-level analysis

In the first level analysis, separate GLM models are estimated on the time series data for each voxel within each individual. For a single subject, the fMRI time course from one voxel is the outcome variable (y). Activity is modeled as the sum of a series of independent predictors (x1, x2, etc.) related to task conditions and other nuisance covariates of no interest (e.g., head movement estimates). For each task condition or event type of interest, a time series of the predicted shape of the signal response is constructed, using prior information about the shape of the vascular response to a brief impulse of neural activity. An example is shown in Figure 6.6B. The vectors of predicted time series values for each task condition are collated into the columns of the design matrix, X. The GLM fitting procedure estimates the amplitude for each column of X, so that the sum of fitted values across all predictors' best fits the data. These amplitudes are regression slopes, denoted $\hat{\beta}$ (the "hat" denotes an estimate of a theoretical constant value). It also estimates a time series of error values, ε, that cannot be explained by the model. The model is thus described by the equation:

$$y = X\beta + \varepsilon \quad (5)$$

where β is a k x 1 vector of regression slopes, X is an n x k model matrix, y is an n x 1 vector containing the observed data, k is number of regressors, and ε is an n x 1 vector of unexplained error values. Error values are assumed to be independent and follow a normal distribution with mean 0 and standard deviation σ. The estimated $\hat{\beta}$s correspond to the estimated magnitude of activation for each psychological condition described in the columns of X.

One of the advantages of the GLM is that there exists an algebraic solution for $\hat{\beta}$ that minimizes the squared error. The estimation yields a series of maps of $\hat{\beta}$s across voxels for each subject. Those $\hat{\beta}$s are used as estimates of the BOLD response amplitude for each condition or event type.

Contrasts
Differences among conditions can be assessed using contrasts, or linear combinations of the βs. For example, imagine that Condition A and Condition B shown in Figure 6.4 reflect periods of auditory and visual stimulation, respectively. The contrast [A–B] estimates the activation difference for auditory-visual stimulation, and it can be tested by applying a linear contrast vector c (i.e., calculating $c\beta$). In this case c = [1 –1]. In general, multiple contrasts can be specified, and they are usually calculated after estimating the model and saved as subject-specific contrast images, with one image per contrast.

Contrasts can be used to estimate signal magnitudes in response to a single condition (i.e., c = [1 0]), an average over multiple conditions (c = [1 1]), or a difference in magnitude across conditions (c = [1 –1]). Hypothesis testing is performed in the usual manner by testing individual model parameters or contrasts using a t-test. Contrast images are usually entered as data for a group analysis, as described below. In addition, another kind of contrast, the F-contrast, can be used to test the significance of a subset of parameters (e.g., do a set of nuisance covariates explain a significant amount of variation in the data?). However, F-contrast images are not suitable for group analysis.

Group analysis
Though making inferences about single subjects is common in some areas (i.e., fMRI of early visual processes), most researchers are interested in generalizing their results to a population of unobserved individuals—science is, after all, about generalizable knowledge. To achieve this goal requires a group analysis. The group analysis consists of specifying a second-level GLM model, this time using as the data (y) a set of contrast images for a single contrast, one per subject. The simplest design matrix is an intercept term (all values constant), which performs a one-sample t-test of whether contrast values are non-zero at each voxel. However, it is possible to specify designs that implement a two-sample t-test (e.g., regressors with 1 or –1), regression relating individual differences in a continuous predictor to contrast values, ANOVA, and other designs. One common, critical-to-avoid error is including multiple images per subject in the group analysis without specifying an appropriate second-level error model. In this case, the group analysis includes repeated measures, and correlated errors across repeated measures must be dealt with appropriately.

The two-stage first- and second-level analysis scheme implements a particular form of a mixed-effects model, a model containing both fixed and random effects. Levels of variables treated as fixed effects are assumed to be invariant (e.g., males and females; visual and auditory modalities), and no inferences are made about previously unobserved levels. Levels of variables treated as random effects, by comparison, are assumed to be randomly sampled from a larger population, and the model permits inferences to new, unobserved levels. The variable "subject identity" is a classic example of a variable that should be treated as a random effect, and this is what the analysis described above does.

However, the two-stage analysis makes an assumption that is often violated: It assumes that the contrast standard error is the same across all subjects, which implies identical design matrices and residual variances. This is rarely if ever true in practice, which has led to the development and increasing popularity of full mixed-effects models. Such models incorporate both first-level (within-subjects) and second-level (between-subjects) effects into one model, and in so doing can relax the assumption of homogenous standard errors and appropriately weight the contribution of each subject's estimates to the group estimates in proportion to their precision. The larger a subject's standard error, the less reliable their estimate, and the less that subject should contribute to the group results. Fitting this type of model requires estimating variance components at each level. Typically, separate error variances are estimated for (1) measurement error within-subjects (and model mis-fitting), and (2) the inter-individual differences among subjects. Restricted maximum likelihood (ReML) is a popular type of estimate of variance components based on the residuals. Since variance estimates and model fits (s) are inter-dependent, iterative algorithms such as EM are used to estimate ReML variance components. Though the full mixed-effects model is correct in more cases and is advantageous, Mumford and Nichols have recently reported that the simple two-stage analysis is valid and performs reasonably well (Mumford & Nichols, 2009).

MODEL-BUILDING

The most challenging aspect of using the GLM is the creation of realistic predictions of task-related signals to include in the columns of X. To build the model, researchers start with an "indicator" vector representing the neuronal activity for each condition sampled at the resolution of the fMRI experiment (Figure 6.6B). This vector has zero value except during hypothesized neural activation periods, where the signal is assigned a value of 1. Each indicator vector is convolved with a canonical HRF to yield a predicted time course related to that event, which forms a column of the X. If the canonical HRF fits the shape of the BOLD response to psychological events, this simple approach has great sensitivity to detect differences. However, if the canonical HRF does not fit, there is at best a drop in power, and at worst false positives and misinterpretation of results (Lindquist & Wager, 2007; Loh, Lindquist, & Wager, 2008). As an alternative, the same "neural" indicator vector can be convolved

with multiple canonical waveforms and entered into multiple columns of X for a single event type (Figure 6.8). These reference waveforms are called basis functions, and the predictors for an event type constructed using different basis functions can combine linearly to better fit the evoked BOLD responses. The ability of a basis set to capture variations in hemodynamic responses depends on both the number and shape of the reference waveforms. There is a fundamental trade-off between flexibility to model variations and power. This is because each parameter is estimated with error, and flexible models can tend to model noise and thus produce noisier parameter estimates. For a critical evaluation of various basis sets see Lindquist and Wager (2007b) and Lindquist, Loh, Atlas, and Wager (2008c).

Additional predictors are typically added to account for other sources of variation in the data. One kind of predictor is the parametric modulator (Figure 6.9). These are increasingly used to model trial-to-trial variation in a psychological process, as discussed above. Another kind is nuisance covariates, which are included to reduce noise and to prevent signal changes related to head movement and physiological (e.g., respiration) artifacts from influencing the contrast estimates. In fMRI, the signal typically drifts slowly over time, so that the most power is in the lowest temporal frequencies and the noise is autocorrelated. Un-modeled physiological artifacts may give rise to much of this autocorrelated noise (Lund, Madsen, Sidaros, Luo, & Nichols, 2005). In addition to modeling known physiological artifacts, covariates that implement high-pass filtering, or removal of signal frequencies below a specified cutoff, can also be added at this stage. This characteristic has prompted the widespread use of high-pass filters that removes fluctuations below a specified frequency cutoff from the data. High-pass filtering is often performed in the GLM analysis by adding covariates of no interest (e.g. low-frequency cosines). Of course, care must be taken to ensure that the fluctuations induced by the task design are not in the range of frequencies removed by the filter.

Multiple Comparisons

The results of fMRI studies are usually summarized in a statistical parametric map (SPM). These maps describe brain activation by color-coding voxels whose t-values (or comparable statistics) exceed a certain statistical threshold for significance. The implication is that these voxels are activated by the experimental task. When constructing such a map

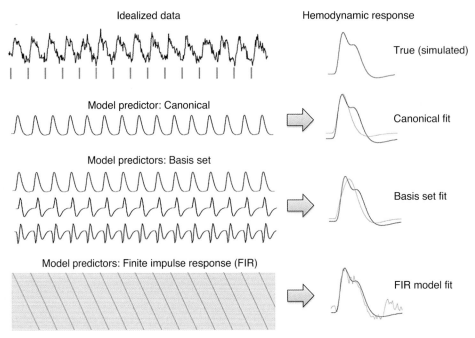

Fig. 6.8 Design matrices using basis sets. The same "neural" indicator vector can be convolved with multiple canonical waveforms and entered into multiple columns of X for a single event type. These reference waveforms are basis functions, and the predictors for an event type constructed using different basis functions can combine linearly to better fit the evoked BOLD responses. The ability of a basis set to capture variations in hemodynamic responses depends on both the number and shape of the reference waveforms. There is a fundamental tradeoff between flexibility to model variations and power. This is because each parameter is estimated with error, and flexible models can tend to model noise and thus produce noisier parameter estimates. For a critical evaluation of various basis sets see Lindquist and Wager (2007) and Lindquist, Loh, Atlas, and Wager (2008). Here, the top panel shows an idealized data time series and event onsets (vertical lines). The panels below depict regressors for three different kinds of models (with time on the x-axis): One assuming a canonical hemodynamic response (top), one using a common basis set with a canonical waveform and two derivatives (middle), and a finite impulse response (FIR) basis set that assumes almost nothing about the shape of the response. At the right is shown an idealized, but non-canonical, hemodynamic response (solid lines), with the fitted response for each model superimposed (light gray lines).

it is important to carefully consider the appropriate threshold to use when declaring a voxel active. In a typical experiment, up to 100,000 hypothesis tests (one for each voxel) are performed simultaneously, and it is crucial to correct for multiple comparisons. Several approaches towards controlling the false positive rate have been used; the fundamental difference between methods lies in whether they control the family-wise error rate (FWER) or the false discovery rate (FDR).

Methods that control the FWER based on the effect size in each voxel—e.g., random field theory, "height" thresholds, and Bonferroni correction—tend to give over-conservative results (Hayasaka & Nichols, 2004). They tend to correct for more spatial comparisons than are actually made because voxels are, as a whole, positively inter-correlated across the brain. These methods provide the gold standard for performing a whole-brain analysis, and interpreting any region that is significant with

FWER correction can typically be considered truly "activated." (However, the commonly used "extent-based" correction in SPM is under-conservative and should be used with caution.) They are not optimal for estimating which voxels show true effects and which do not—i.e., balancing false positives and false negatives—because there is typically extremely low power, or a low chance of detecting an effect in any single truly activated voxel. Basic power calculations suggest that even with large effect sizes (d = 1), typical sample-sizes yield voxel-wise FWER-corrected power rates of only around 5% (see Figure 6.10).

The false discovery rate (FDR) controls the proportion of false positives among all rejected tests (Genovese, Lazar, and Nichols, 2002). Controlling the FDR at q < .05 (by convention, q is used instead of p) implies that on average only 5% of the significant results are expected to be false positives. The FDR controlling procedure is adaptive in the

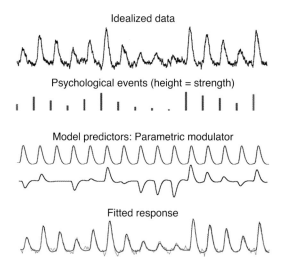

Idealized data

Psychological events (height = strength)

Model predictors: Parametric modulator

Fitted response

Fig. 6.9 Example of a parametric modulator design. The top panel shows an idealized data time series and event onsets (vertical lines). The strength or intensity of a psychological process varies from trial to trial, as depicted by the relative heights of the lines. The middle panels show the predictors for a single event type. The upper panel shows the regressor for the average response, and the lower panel shows the modulatory effect, created by convolving with a variable-amplitude "neural" (impulse) function after centering the amplitude. Centering makes the modulator more orthogonal to the mean response, and gives each parameter a unique psychological interpretation (mean trial effect and effects of the modulating variable.)

sense that the larger the signal, the lower the threshold. If there are no effects anywhere in the brain except in one voxel, the FDR-corrected threshold will be equivalent to the FWER-corrected threshold for that voxel. If there are highly significant effects everywhere in the brain except one voxel in question,

the FDR-corrected threshold will be equal to the uncorrected p-value threshold (e.g., $p < .05$). Researchers are increasingly using FDR correction because it provides an often reasonable balance between true and false positives in small-sample studies. However, its major limitation is that it does not allow one to infer that any specific findings are not false positives. It is reasonable to infer that most of the findings are true positives, but does not provide information about which ones are not.

Assessing Brain Connectivity

To date, human brain mapping has been primarily used to provide maps that show which regions of the brain are activated by specific tasks. Recently, there has been an increased interest in augmenting this type of analysis with connectivity studies that describe how various brain regions interact and how these interactions depend on experimental conditions. It is common practice in the analysis of neuroimaging data to make the distinction between *functional* and *effective connectivity* (Friston, 1994). Functional connectivity is defined as the undirected association between two or more fMRI time series, while effective connectivity is the directed influence of one brain region on the physiological activity recorded in other brain regions; it implies both causality and directness. It implies causality because the models used to assess effective connectivity are usually directional, and directness in the sense that effective connectivity measures attempt to partial out indirect influences from other regions.

Functional connectivity is a statement about observed associations among regions and/or other

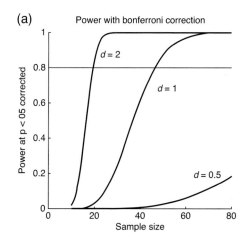

(a)

Power with bonferroni correction

$d = 2$

$d = 1$

$d = 0.5$

Power at p < 05 corrected

Sample size

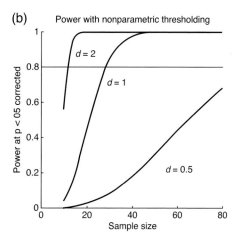

(b)

Power with nonparametric thresholding

$d = 2$

$d = 1$

$d = 0.5$

Power at p < 05 corrected

Sample size

Fig. 6.10 (a) Power curves—calculated for effect sizes of 0.5, 1, and 2—for a whole-brain search with 200,000 voxels and FWE correction at $p < .05$ using the Bonferroni method. (b) Same results using nonparametric permutation testing which takes into account the spatial smoothness in the data.

performance and physiological variables—for example, the correlation between time series in two regions (bivariate connectivity). Simple functional connectivity analyses usually compare correlations between ROIs, sometimes in a task-dependent fashion, or between a "seed" region of interest and voxels throughout the brain. Multivariate analysis methods are also used to reveal networks of multiple interconnected regions. Popular methods include Principal Components Analysis (PCA) (Andersen, 1999), Partial Least Squares (PLS) (McIntosh, 1996), and Independent Components Analysis (ICA) (Calhoun, 2001; McKeown, 1998). Connectivity between two or more regions may result from direct influences (i.e., functional links between regions) or indirect effects due to common input from a third variable. None of these methods are able to address issues of causality or the common influences of other variables.

Functional connectivity methods can be applied at different levels of analysis, with different interpretations at each level. Connectivity across time series data can reveal networks that are dynamically co-activated over time (either "intrinsically," regardless of task state, or in a task-dependent fashion), and is closest to the concept of communication among regions, though it does not conclusively demonstrate that. Connectivity across single-trial response estimates (Rissman, Gazzaley, & D'Esposito, 2004) can identify coherent networks of task-related activations. Whereas these levels are only accessible to fMRI and EEG/MEG, which provide relatively rich time series data, other levels of analysis may be examined in PET studies as well. Connectivity across subjects can reveal patterns of coherent individual differences, which may result from communication among regions but also from differences in strategy use or other genetically determined or learned differences among individuals. Finally, connectivity across studies can reveal tendencies for studies to co-activate within sets of regions, which may be influenced by any of the factors mentioned above, and also differences among tasks or other study-level variables.

Effective connectivity analysis, on the other hand, is model-dependent. Typically, a small set of regions and a proposed set of connections are specified a priori, and tests of fit are used to compare a small number of alternative models and assess the statistical significance of individual connections. Because connections may be specified directionally (with hypothesized causal influences of one area on another), the model implies causal relationships. Because there are many possible models, the choice of regions and connections must be anatomically motivated. Most effective connectivity depends on two models: a neuroanatomical model that describes which areas are connected, and a mathematical model that describes how areas are connected. Common methods include Structural Equation Modeling (SEM) (McIntosh & Gonzalez-Lima, 1994) and Dynamic Causal Modeling (DCM) (Friston, Harrison, & Penny, 2003). While "effective connectivity" methods have become increasingly popular, it is important to keep in mind that the conclusions about direct influences and causality obtained using these models are only as good as the specified models. Any misspecification of the underlying model will almost certainly lead to erroneous conclusions. In particular, the exclusion of important lurking variables (brain regions involved in the network but not included in the model) can completely change the fit of the model and thereby affect both the direction and strength of the connections. Great care always needs to be taken when interpreting the results of these methods.

The distinction between functional and effective connectivity is not entirely clear (Horwitz, 2003). If the discriminating features of an "effective connectivity" analysis are a directional model in which causal influences are specified, and the willingness to make claims about direct vs. indirect connections, then many analyses, including multiple regression, might count as effective connectivity. While many researchers use both SEM and DCM to ascribing causality in relationships among brain regions, it is important to keep in mind that the tests performed in both techniques are based on model fit rather than on the causality of the effect. Similarly, Granger causality (Roebroeck, Formisano, & Goebel, 2005) is another approach that is typically considered to test effective connectivity, though neither causal influences nor direct vs. indirect effects are tested within the basic model framework. Causality is tested strictly in the sense of temporal relationships, rather than on whether activity in a brain region is necessary or sufficient for activity in another. In the end, it is not the label of "functional" or "effective" that is important, but the specific assumptions and robustness and validity of inference afforded by each method.

When performing connectivity and correlation studies it is tempting to make statements regarding causal links between different brain regions. The idea of causality is a very deep and important philosophical issue (Pearl, 2000; Rubin, 1974).

Often a cavalier attitude is taken in attributing causal effects and the differentiation between explanation and causation is often blurred. Properly randomized experimental designs permit causal inferences of task manipulations on brain activity. However, in neuroimaging and EEG/MEG studies, all the brain variables are observed, and none are manipulated. Therefore, we do not recommend making strong conclusions about causality and "direct" influences among brain regions using these methods, because the validity of such conclusions is very difficult to verify. The combination of neuroimaging and TMS or related forms of brain stimulation (Bohning et al., 1997) may provide more reliable causal inferences about the effects of activating one brain region on another. By stimulating the brain, experimental manipulation of one brain area can be achieved and its causal effects on other brain regions thus examined. However, the problem remains of assessing which effects are "direct" as opposed to mediated by other intervening regions.

One way of circumventing some of the issues with making claims about directness and causality is not to make them. In recent work, we have taken the approach of fitting mediation models, which are inherently directional, but using them as a means for discovery and modeling of functional pathways rather than as a basis for claims that one brain region is directly influencing another one (Wager, Davidson, Hughes, Lindquist, & Ochsner, 2008). We have used formal mediation tests from path analysis to identify brain voxels that mediate the relationship between activity in one brain area (an "initial variable," X) and either another area or a behavioral or physiological outcome of interest (Y, e.g., performance). The areas that are significant mediators are likely to be part of a functional pathway or network that relates the initial variable to the outcome—i.e., there is an X-M-Y pathway. If all the variables are observed rather than experimentally manipulated, we feel more comfortable avoiding inferences about the direction of causality.

In contrast to mediation effects, another type of effect commonly tested in fMRI analyses is moderation or modulation. Mediation provides evidence for a pathway connecting more than two variables and tests the product of two constituent effects. Moderation, by contrast, is an interaction test: A significant moderation effect implies that the level of a moderator (e.g., high vs. low) influences connectivity between Region 1 and Region 2.

The path modeling framework can also be used to localize brain mediators or moderators of

experimental independent variables, which permits stronger claims about causality. For example, a mediation analysis could be used to localize voxels that mediate effects of an experimental design variable (e.g., Task A – Control B) on a behavioral or physiological outcome of interest (e.g., performance). The causality of the task-to-brain relationship, at least, can be established with relative confidence.

A particular kind of moderation effect, the "psychophysiological interaction" (Friston et al., 1997) has been popularized in the fMRI literature and is included in the SPM software. In this analysis, the interaction between an independent task variable and a "seed" brain region is calculated, and a search over all voxel time-series is conducted for correlates of that interaction. A common interpretation is that the task condition moderates the connectivity between the seed and other significant regions. While the effect of the task on the brain is likely causal, it is difficult to establish which of the two brain regions (seed or result) is the moderator, and which is moderated. The interaction can be interpreted in multiple ways.

Many researchers have now attempted to use the timing of responses across the brain to infer causality, and many such approaches are actively being developed. Variants of Granger causal models (Granger, 1969) are an example, as they can localize relationships between brain regions that have different relative timing. However, because of the potentially substantial variability in hemodynamic responses across the brain, these differences may be due to vascular differences rather than neural timing differences. In addition, temporal precedent does not necessitate causality: A rooster crowing every morning "Granger causes" the sun to rise, because it is reliably associated with and precedes the sunrise, but does not actually cause the sun to rise according to either commonsense or formal notions of causality. Interactions between task variables and timing (e.g., demonstrating that Region 1 precedes Region 2 more in Task A than in Task B) provide potentially stronger inferences, but there are alternative explanations. First, if both regions respond to Task A, but not Task B, any hemodynamic latency difference is likely to create a latency x task interaction in a Granger model. In addition, with all of the path and Granger models discussed above, one cannot know whether there is not another, unmeasured variable (e.g., system-wide release of a neuromodulator such as dopamine or opioids) that is responsible for creating the observed functional/effective connectivity.

Conclusions

In this chapter, we have reviewed the essential elements of conducting an fMRI study, including conceiving and designing an experiment, acquiring data, and analyzing the data with univariate and multivariate statistical models. In closing, we would like to emphasize a few points. First, FMRI-based cognitive and affective neuroscience is a rapidly growing area. There are many perspectives and techniques, and these are changing continuously. As of this writing, there are literally hundreds of published, freely available toolboxes for fMRI data analysis. Many of these are collected on the NIH-funded Neuroimaging Informatics Tools and Resources Clearinghouse (NITRC; http://www.nitrc.org/). We hope that this brief introduction will provide some pointers towards further study and some practical advice. Second, fMRI is a collaborative endeavor, and there are very few individuals (if any!) who fully understand every aspect of the process. An fMRI "dream team" would likely include a psychologist, physicist, statistician, computer scientist, engineer, neuroscientist, and neuroanatomist, each of whom would contribute unique and complimentary knowledge. We believe that fMRI should be played like a team sport, with consultation obtained and credit given on each of the various aspects to the extent practicable.

The challenges inherent in the complexity of data collection and analysis are formidable, but progress is being made on every front. Over the past 10 years, we have seen a marked increase in the quality of fMRI studies. The data quality is increasing because scanners are becoming more sensitive and more stable. Best-practice procedures for study design and analysis are beginning to emerge, and more groups use valid analysis techniques on larger samples. And finally, data analysis techniques from several fields are being brought to bear in creative and powerful ways, providing qualitatively new views on the function of the human brain. Given the pace and complexity of recent advancements, it is exciting to think of what developments lie ahead.

Authors' note:
Parts of this chapter are adapted from: Wager, T. D., Hernandez, L., Jonides, J., & Lindquist, M. (2007). Elements of functional neuroimaging. In J. T. Cacioppo, L. G. Tassinary & G. G. Berntson (Eds.), *Handbook of Psychophysiology* (4th ed., pp. 19–55), Cambridge: Cambridge University Press. We would like to thank Dr. Doug Noll for providing Figure 6.5 and for helpful comments on the manuscript, and Ted Yanagahara for creating Figure 6.1C.

Note

1 Brain "activity" or "activation" is typically used to refer to Blood Oxygen Level Dependent (BOLD) signal, a complex set of changes usually coupled to the ratio of oxygen demand and blood flow in local blood vessels. A number of more detailed descriptions of BOLD physiology have been published elsewhere (Buxton, Wong, & Frank, 1998; Etkin & Wager, 2007; Logothetis, Pauls, Augath, Trinath, & Oeltermann, 2001), so we will not cover that in detail here. In addition to BOLD, perfusion imaging can be used to obtain more direct measures of local cerebral blood flow (CBF), and spectroscopy and other non-BOLD techniques can provide other types of measures. However, BOLD signal is relatively robust and is almost universally used in psychological studies.

References

Aguirre, G. K., Zarahn, E., & D'Esposito, M. (1998). The variability of human, BOLD hemodynamic responses. *Neuroimage, 8*(4), 360–369.

Andersen, AH, G. D., Avison, MJ. (1999). Principal component analysis of the dynamic response measured by fMRI: a generalized linear systems framework. Magnetic Resonance in Medicine, 17(6), 785–815.

Andersson, J. L., Hutton, C., Ashburner, J., Turner, R., & Friston, K. (2001). Modeling geometric deformations in EPI time series. *Neuroimage, 13*(5), 903–919.

Bellgowan, P. S., Saad, Z. S., & Bandettini, P. A. (2003). Understanding neural system dynamics through task modulation and measurement of functional MRI amplitude, latency, and width. *Proc Natl Acad Sci U S A, 100*(3), 1415–1419.

Birn, R. M., Saad, Z. S., & Bandettini, P. A. (2001). Spatial heterogeneity of the nonlinear dynamics in the FMRI BOLD response. *Neuroimage, 14*(4), 817–826.

Bohning, D. E., Pecheny, A. P., Epstein, C. M., Speer, A. M., Vincent, D. J., Dannels, W., et al. (1997). Mapping transcranial magnetic stimulation (TMS) fields in vivo with MRI. *Neuroreport, 8*(11), 2535–2538.

Buchel, C., Holmes, A. P., Rees, G., & Friston, K. J. (1998). Characterizing stimulus-response functions using nonlinear regressors in parametric fMRI experiments. *Neuroimage, 8*(2), 140–148.

Buchel, C., Morris, J., Dolan, R. J., & Friston, K. J. (1998). Brain systems mediating aversive conditioning: An event-related fMRI study. *Neuron, 20*(5), 947–957.

Buracas, G. T. & Boynton, G. M. (2002). Efficient design of event-related fMRI experiments using M-sequences. *Neuroimage, 16*(3 Pt 1), 801–813.

Buxton, R. B., Wong, E. C., & Frank, L. R. (1998). Dynamics of blood flow and oxygenation changes during brain activation: The balloon model. *Magn Reson Med, 39*(6), 855–864.

Cacioppo, J. T. & Tassinary, L. G. (1990). Inferring psychological significance from physiological signals. *Am Psychol, 45*(1), 16–28.

Calhoun, V. D., Adali, T., Pearlson, G. D. and Pekar, J. J. (2001). Spatial and temporal independent component analysis of functional MRI data containing a pair of task-related waveforms. *Human Brain Mapping, 13*, 43–53.

Chang, C., Cunningham, J. P., & Glover, G. H. (2009). Influence of heart rate on the BOLD signal: the cardiac response function. *Neuroimage, 44*(3), 857–869.

Coltheart, M. (2006). What has functional neuroimaging told us about the mind (so far)? *Cortex, 42*(3), 323–331.

Constable, R. T. & Spencer, D. D. (1999). Composite image formation in z-shimmed functional MR imaging. *Magn Reson Med, 42*(1), 110–117.

Cover, T. M. & Thomas, J. A. (1991). Elements of information theory. In (pp. 18–26). New York: Wiley.

Dagher, A., Owen, A. M., Boecker, H., & Brooks, D. J. (1999). Mapping the network for planning: a correlational PET activation study with the Tower of London task. *Brain, 122 (Pt 10)*, 1973–1987.

Dale, A. M., Liu, A. K., Fischl, B. R., Buckner, R. L., Belliveau, J. W., Lewine, J. D., et al. (2000). Dynamic statistical parametric mapping combining fMRI and MEG for high-resolution imaging of cortical activity. *Neuron, 26* (1), 55–67.

Etkin, A. & Wager, T. D. (2007). Functional neuroimaging of anxiety: A meta-analysis of emotional processing in PTSD, social anxiety disorder, and specific phobia. *Am J Psychiatry,* 164(10), 1476–1488.

Friston, K. (1994). Functional and effective connectivity in neuroimaging: a synthesis. Human Brain Mapping, 2, 56–78.

Friston, K., Harrison, L, & Penny, W. (2003). Dynamic causal modelling. *Neuroimage, 19*, 1273–1302.

Friston, K. J., Buechel, C., Fink, G. R., Morris, J., Rolls, E., & Dolan, R. J. (1997). Psychophysiological and modulatory interactions in neuroimaging. *Neuroimage, 6*(3), 218–229.

Friston, K. J., Mechelli, A., Turner, R., & Price, C. J. (2000). Nonlinear responses in fMRI: The Balloon model, Volterra kernels, and other hemodynamics. *Neuroimage, 12*(4), 466–477.

Granger, C. W. J. (1969). Investigating causal relations by econometric models and cross-spectral methods. *Econometrica 37*, 424–438.

Grill-Spector, K. & Malach, R. (2001). fMRI-adaptation: A tool for studying the functional properties of human cortical neurons. *Acta Psychol (Amst), 107*(1–3), 293–321.

Grinband, J., Hirsch, J., & Ferrera, V. P. (2006). A neural representation of categorization uncertainty in the human brain. *Neuron, 49*(5), 757–763.

Hare, T. A., Camerer, C. F., & Rangel, A. (2009). Self-control in decision-making involves modulation of the vmPFC valuation system. *Science, 324*(5927), 646–648.

Haynes, J. D. & Rees, G. (2006). Decoding mental states from brain activity in humans. *Nature Reviews Neuroscience, 7*(7), 523–534.

Henson, R. N. (2003). Neuroimaging studies of priming. *Prog Neurobiol, 70*(1), 53–81.

Horwitz, B. (2003). The elusive concept of brain connectivity. *Neuroimage, 19*, 466–470.

Johnson, M. K., Raye, C. L., Mitchell, K. J., Greene, E. J., Cunningham, W. A., & Sanislow, C. A. (2005). Using fMRI to investigate a component process of reflection: prefrontal correlates of refreshing a just-activated representation. *Cogn Affect Behav Neurosci, 5*(3), 339–361.

Josephs, O. & Henson, R. N. (1999). Event-related functional magnetic resonance imaging: modelling, inference and optimization. *Philos Trans R Soc Lond B Biol Sci, 354*(1387), 1215–1228.

Kosslyn, S. M., Thompson, W. L., Kim, I. J., & Alpert, N. M. (1995). Topographical representations of mental images in primary visual cortex. *Nature, 378*(6556), 496–498.

Kwong, K. K., Belliveau, J. W., Chesler, D. A., Goldberg, I. E., Weisskoff, R. M., Poncelet, B. P., et al. (1992). Dynamic magnetic resonance imaging of human brain activity during primary sensory stimulation. *Proc Natl Acad Sci U S A, 89*(12), 5675–5679.

Lindquist, M., Zhang, C.-H., Glover, G. H., & Shepp, L. (2008). Rapid three-dimensional functional magnetic resonance imaging of the negative BOLD response. *Journal of Magnetic Resonance, 191*, 100–111.

Lindquist, M. A. (2008). The statistical analysis of fMRI data. *Statistical Science, 23*(4), 439–464.

Lindquist, M. A. & Wager, T. D. (2007). Validity and power in hemodynamic response modeling: A comparison study and a new approach. *Hum Brain Mapp, 28*(8), 764–784.

Liu, T. T. (2004). Efficiency, power, and entropy in event-related fMRI with multiple trial types. Part II: Design of experiments. *Neuroimage, 21*(1), 401–413.

Liu, T. T., Frank, L. R., Wong, E. C., & Buxton, R. B. (2001). Detection power, estimation efficiency, and predictability in event-related fMRI. *Neuroimage, 13*(4), 759–773.

Logothetis, N. K., Pauls, J., Augath, M., Trinath, T., & Oeltermann, A. (2001). Neurophysiological investigation of the basis of the fMRI signal. *Nature, 412*(6843), 150–157.

Loh, J. M., Lindquist, M. A., & Wager, T. D. (2008). Residual analysis for detecting mis-modeling in fMRI. *Statistica Sinica, To appear.*

Lund, T. E., Madsen, K. H., Sidaros, K., Luo, W. L., & Nichols, T. E. (2005). Non-white noise in fMRI: Does modelling have an impact? *Neuroimage.*

Mazaika, P. K., Hoeft, F., Glover, G. H., & Reiss, A. L. (2009). Methods and software for fMRI analysis of clinical subjects. *NeuroImage, 47*, 58–58.

McClure, S. M., Berns, G. S., & Montague, P. R. (2003). Temporal prediction errors in a passive learning task activate human striatum. *Neuron, 38*(2), 339–346.

McIntosh, A. & Gonzalez-Lima, F. (1994). Structural equation modeling and its application to network analysis in functional brain imaging. *Human Brain Mapping, 2*, 2–22.

McIntosh, A. R., Bookstein, F.L., Haxby, J.V., & Grady, C.L. (1996). Spatial pattern analysis of functional brain images using partial least squares. *NeuroImage, 3*, 143–157.

McKeown, M. J. & Makeig, S. (1998). Analysis of fMRI data by blind separation into independent spatial components. *Human Brain Mapping, 6*, 160–188.

Menon, V., Ford, J. M., Lim, K. O., Glover, G. H., & Pfefferbaum, A. (1997). Combined event-related fMRI and EEG evidence for temporal-parietal cortex activation during target detection. *Neuroreport, 8*(14), 3029–3037.

Miezin, F. M., Maccotta, L., Ollinger, J. M., Petersen, S. E., & Buckner, R. L. (2000). Characterizing the hemodynamic response: effects of presentation rate, sampling procedure, and the possibility of ordering brain activity based on relative timing. *Neuroimage, 11*(6 Pt 1), 735–759.

Mitchell, T. M., Hutchinson, R., Niculescu, R. S., Pereira, F., Wang, X., Just, M., et al. (2004). Learning to decode cognitive states from brain images. *Machine Learning, 57*(1), 145–175.

Mumford, J. A. & Nichols, T. (2009). Simple group fMRI modeling and inference. *Neuroimage, 47*(4), 1469–1475.

Mumford, J. A. & Nichols, T. E. (2008). Power calculation for group fMRI studies accounting for arbitrary design and temporal autocorrelation. *Neuroimage, 39*(1), 261–268.

Nakamura, W., Anami, K., Mori, T., Saitoh, O., Cichocki, A., & Amari, S. (2006). Removal of ballistocardiogram artifacts from simultaneously recorded EEG and fMRI data using independent component analysis. *IEEE Trans Biomed Eng, 53*(7), 1294–1308.

Noll, D. C., Fessler, J. A., & Sutton, B. P. (2005). Conjugate phase MRI reconstruction with spatially variant sample density correction. *IEEE Trans Med Imaging, 24*(3), 325–336.

O'Connor, D. H., Fukui, M. M., Pinsk, M. A., & Kastner, S. (2002). Attention modulates responses in the human lateral geniculate nucleus. *Nature Neuroscience, 5*(11), 1203–1209.

Ogawa, S., Tank, D. W., Menon, R., Ellermann, J. M., Kim, S. G., Merkle, H., et al. (1992). Intrinsic signal changes accompanying sensory stimulation: Functional brain mapping with magnetic resonance imaging. *Proc Natl Acad Sci U S A, 89*(13), 5951–5955.

Ollinger, J. M., Shulman, G. L., & Corbetta, M. (2001). Separating processes within a trial in event-related functional MRI. *Neuroimage, 13*(1), 210–217.

Pearl, J. (2000). *Causality: models, reasoning, and inference.* Cambridge, U.K.; New York: Cambridge University Press.

Poldrack, R. A. (2006). Can cognitive processes be inferred from neuroimaging data? *Trends Cogn Sci, 10*(2), 59–63.

Price, C. J. & Friston, K. J. (1997). Cognitive conjunction: A new approach to brain activation experiments. *Neuroimage, 5*(4 Pt 1), 261–270.

Raichle, M. E., MacLeod, A. M., Snyder, A. Z., Powers, W. J., Gusnard, D. A., & Shulman, G. L. (2001). A default mode of brain function. *Proc Natl Acad Sci U S A, 98*(2), 676–682.

Rissman, J., Gazzaley, A., & D'Esposito, M. (2004). Measuring functional connectivity during distinct stages of a cognitive task. *Neuroimage, 23*(2), 752–763.

Roebroeck, A., Formisano, E., & Goebel, R. (2005). Mapping directed influence over the brain using Granger causality and fMRI. *Neuroimage, 25*(1), 230–242.

Roelfsema, P. R., Lamme, V. A. F., & Spekreijse, H. (1998). Object-based attention in the primary visual cortex of the macaque monkey. *Nature, 395*(6700), 376–381.

Rubin, D. B. (1974). Estimating causal effects of treatments in randomized and nonrandomized studies. *Journal of Educational Psychology, 66*(5), 688–701.

Sarter, M., Berntson, G. G., & Cacioppo, J. T. (1996). Brain imaging and cognitive neuroscience. Toward strong inference in attributing function to structure. *Am Psychol, 51*(1), 13–21.

Sawamura, H., Orban, G. A., & Vogels, R. (2006). Selectivity of neuronal adaptation does not match response selectivity: A single-cell study of the FMRI adaptation paradigm. *Neuron, 49*(2), 307–318.

Schacter, D. L., Buckner, R. L., Koutstaal, W., Dale, A. M., & Rosen, B. R. (1997). Late onset of anterior prefrontal activity during true and false recognition: an event-related fMRI study. *Neuroimage, 6*(4), 259–269.

Skudlarski, P., Constable, R. T., & Gore, J. C. (1999). ROC analysis of statistical methods used in functional MRI: Individual subjects. *Neuroimage, 9*(3), 311–329.

Smith, S., Jenkinson, M., Beckmann, C., Miller, K., & Woolrich, M. (2007). Meaningful design and contrast estimability in FMRI. *Neuroimage, 34*(1), 127–136.

Stark, C. E. & Squire, L. R. (2001). When zero is not zero: The problem of ambiguous baseline conditions in fMRI. *Proc Natl Acad Sci U S A, 98*(22), 12760–12766.

Sternberg, S. (2001). Separate modifiability, mental modules, and the use of pure and composite measures to reveal them. *Acta Psychol (Amst), 106*(1–2), 147–246.

Summerfield, C., Greene, M., Wager, T., Egner, T., Hirsch, J., & Mangels, J. (2006). Neocortical connectivity during episodic memory formation. *PLoS Biol, 4*(5), e128.

Tohka, J., Foerde, K., Aron, A. R., Tom, S. M., Toga, A. W., & Poldrack, R. A. (2007). Automatic independent component labeling for artifact removal in fMRI. *Neuroimage.*

Vazquez, A. L., Cohen, E. R., Gulani, V., Hernandez-Garcia, L., Zheng, Y., Lee, G. R., et al. (2006). Vascular dynamics and BOLD fMRI: CBF level effects and analysis considerations. *Neuroimage, 32*(4), 1642–1655.

Wager, T. D., Davidson, M. L., Hughes, B. L., Lindquist, M. A., & Ochsner, K. N. (2008). Prefrontal-subcortical pathways mediating successful emotion regulation. *Neuron, 59*(6), 1037–1050.

Wager, T. D., Hernandez, L., Jonides, J., & Lindquist, M. (2007). Elements of functional neuroimaging. In J. T. Cacioppo, L. G. Tassinary, & G. G. Berntson (Eds.), *Handbook of psychophysiology* (4th ed., pp. 19–55). Cambridge: Cambridge University Press.

Wager, T. D., Jonides, J., & Smith, E. E. (2006). Individual differences in multiple types of shifting attention. *Memory & Cognition, 34*(8), 1730–1743.

Wager, T. D., Jonides, J., Smith, E. E., & Nichols, T. E. (2005). Towards a taxonomy of attention-shifting: Individual differences in fMRI during multiple shift types. *Cogn Affect Behav Neurosci, 5*(2), 127–143.

Wager, T. D., Lindquist, M., & Hernandez, L. (in press). Essentials of functional neuroimaging. In J. Cacioppo & G. G. Berntson (Eds.), *Handbook of neuroscience for the behavioral sciences.*

Wager, T. D. & Nichols, T. E. (2003). Optimization of experimental design in fMRI: A general framework using a genetic algorithm. *Neuroimage, 18*(2), 293–309.

Wager, T. D., Scott, D. J., & Zubieta, J. K. (2007). Placebo effects on human mu-opioid activity during pain. *Proc Natl Acad Sci U S A, 104*(26), 11056–11061.

Wager, T. D., Vazquez, A., Hernandez, L., & Noll, D. C. (2005). Accounting for nonlinear BOLD effects in fMRI: Parameter estimates and a model for prediction in rapid event-related studies. *Neuroimage, 25*(1), 206–218.

Williams, D. S., Detre, J. A., Leigh, J. S., & Koretsky, A. P. (1992). Magnetic resonance imaging of perfusion using spin inversion of arterial water. *Proc Natl Acad Sci U S A, 89*(1), 212–216.

Wilson, J. L. & Jezzard, P. (2003). Utilization of an intra-oral diamagnetic passive shim in functional MRI of the inferior frontal cortex. *Magn Reson Med, 50*(5), 1089–1094.

Worsley, K. J. & Friston, K. J. (1995). Analysis of fMRI time-series revisited—again. *Neuroimage, 2*(3), 173–181.

Zaki, J., Ochsner, K. N., Hanelin, J., Wager, T. D., & Mackey, S. C. (2007). Different circuits for different pain: Patterns of functional connectivity reveal distinct networks for processing pain in self and others. *Social Neuroscience, 2*, 276–291.

Electromagnetic Brain Mapping Using MEG and EEG

Sylvain Baillet

Abstract

This chapter describes how electroencephalography (EEG) and magnetoencephalography (MEG) offer complementary alternatives to typical neuroimaging studies. It briefly reviews the basic methods of sensor data analysis, which focus on the chronometry of so-called brain events. It further emphasizes how MEG and EEG may be utilized as neuroimaging techniques, that is, how they are capable to map dynamic brain activity and functional connectivity with fair spatial resolution and unique rapid time scales.

Keywords: neuroimaging, techniques & methods, event-related brain responses, neural oscillations, evoked potentials & fields, induced brain activity, ongoing brain activity, brain networks, coherence & synchrony, functional connectivity

Introduction

Accessing brain activity non-invasively using neuroimaging techniques has been possible for about two decades and has continued to thrive from the technical and methodological standpoints (Friston, 2009b). With the ubiquitous availability of magnetic resonance imaging (MRI) scanners in major hospitals and research centers, functional MRI (fMRI) has certainly become the modality of choice to approach the human brain in action. A well-documented and thoroughly discussed limitation of fMRI, however, sits in the very physiological origins of the signals accessible to the analysis. Indeed, fMRI is essentially sensitive to local fluctuations in blood oxygen levels and flow, which connection to cerebral activity is the object of very active scientific investigations and sometimes, controversies (Logothetis & Pfeuffer, 2004; Logothetis & Wandell, 2004; Eijsden, Hyder, Rothman, &

Shulman, 2009). A more fundamental limitation of fMRI and metabolic techniques such as positron emission tomography (PET) is the lack of temporal resolution. In essence, the physiological changes captured by these techniques fluctuate within a typical time scale of several hundreds of milliseconds at best, which makes them excellent at mapping the regions involved in task performance or resting states (Fox & Raichle, 2007), but incapable of resolving the flow of rapid brain activity that unfolds with time. Metaphorically speaking, metabolic and hemodynamic techniques perform as very sensitive cameras that are able to capture low-intensity signals using long aperture durations, hence a sluggish temporal resolution. This basic limitation has become salient as new neuroscience questions emerge to investigate the brain as an ensemble of complex networks that form, reshape, and flush information dynamically (Varela, Lachaux, Rodriguez, &

Martinerie, 2001; Sergent & Dehaene, 2004; Werner, 2007).

An additional, though seemingly minor, limitation of these modalities consists in their operational environment: Most scanners are installed in hospitals, with typically limited access time but more importantly, necessitate that subjects lie supine in a narrow tunnel, with loud noises generated by the MRI acquisition processes. Such non-ecological environment is certainly detrimental to the subject's comfort and therefore, limits the possibilities in terms of stimulus presentation and real-time interaction with participants, which are central issues in social neuroscience studies.

This chapter therefore describes how electroencephalography (EEG) and magnetoencephalography (MEG) offer complementary alternatives to typical neuroimaging studies in that respect. We will briefly review the basic, though very rich, methods of sensor data analysis, which focus on the chronometry of so-called brain events. We will further emphasize how MEG and EEG may be utilized as neuroimaging techniques; that is, how they are capable to map dynamic brain activity and functional connectivity with fair spatial resolution and unique rapid time scales. EEG recordings have been made possible in the MRI environment, therefore leading to multimodal data acquisition and analysis (Laufs, Daunizeau, Carmichael, & Kleinschmidt, 2008). This has brought up interesting discussions and results on for example, rapid phenomena such as epileptiform events and the electrophysiological counterpart of BOLD resting-state fluctuations (Mantini, Perrucci, Gratta, Romani, & Corbetta, 2007). MEG and EEG data acquired with high-density sensor arrays also stand by themselves as functional neuroimaging techniques: This is the realm of electromagnetic brain mapping (Salmelin & Baillet, 2009). It is indeed interesting to note that MEG instruments are being installed in prominent functional neuroimaging clinical and research centers that are willing to expand their investigations beyond the static, functional cartography of the brain. This chapter offers a pragmatic review of this rapidly evolving field.

MEG/EEG Principles and Instrumentation
Physiological Sources of Electromagnetic Fields
All electrical currents produce electromagnetic fields, and our body is inundated by currents of all sorts. The muscles and the heart are two well-known and strong sources of electrophysiological currents,

qualified as "animal electricity" by early scientists like Luigi Galvani, who were able to evidence such phenomena more than 200 years ago. The brain also sustains ionic current flows within and across cell assemblies, with neurons as the strongest generators. The architecture of the neural cell—as decomposed into dendritic branches and tree, soma and axon—conditions the paths taken by the tiny intracellular currents flowing within the cell. The relative complexity and large variety of these current pathways can be simplified by looking at the cell from some distance: Indeed, these elementary currents instantaneously sum into a net primary current flow, which can be well described as a small, straight electrical dipole conducting current from a source to a sink (Figure 7.1). Intracellular current sources are twofold in a neuron: 1) axon potentials, which generate fast discharges of currents, and 2) slower excitatory and inhibitory post-synaptic potentials (E/I PSPs), which create an electrical imbalance between the basal, apical dendritic tree and/or the cell soma. Each of these two categories of current sources generates electromagnetic fields, which can be well captured by local electrophysiological recording techniques. The amount of current being generated by a single cell is, however, too small to be detected several centimeters away and outside the head. Detecting electrophysiological traces noninvasively is conditioned to two main factors: 1) that the architecture of the cell is propitious to give rise to a large net current, and 2) that neighboring cells would drive their respective intracellular currents with a sufficient degree of group synchronization so that they build up and reach levels detectable at some distance. Fortunately, a great share of neural cells possesses a longitudinal geometry; these are the pyramidal cells in neocortical layers II/III and V. Also, neurons are grouped into assemblies of tightly interconnected cells. Therefore, it is likely that PSPs be identically distributed across a given assembly, with the immediate benefit that they build up efficiently to drive larger levels of currents, which in turn generate electromagnetic fields that are strong enough to be detected outside the head (Figure 7.1).

Neurons in assemblies are also likely to fire volleys of action potentials with a fair degree of synchronization. However, the very short duration of each action potential firing—typically a few milliseconds—makes it very unlikely that they sufficiently overlap in time to sum up to a massive current flow. Though smaller in amplitude, PSPs sustain with typical durations—a few tens to hundreds of milliseconds—that make temporal and

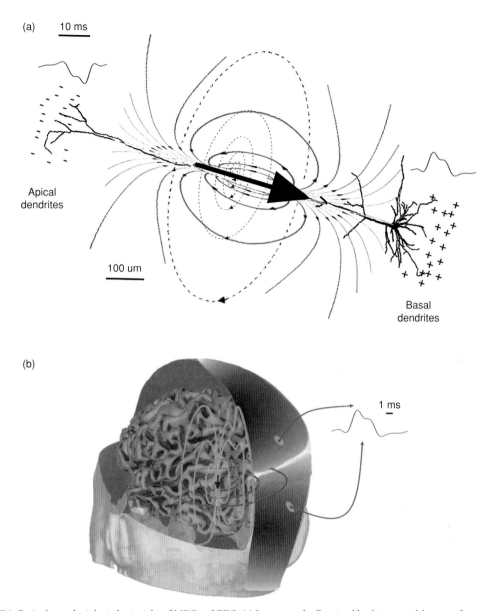

Fig. 7.1 Basic electrophysiological principles of MEG and EEG. (a) Large neural cells—just like this pyramidal neuron from cortex layer V—drive ionic electrical currents. These latter are essentially impressed by the difference in electrical potentials between the basal and apical dendrites or the cell body, which is due to a blend of excitatory and inhibitory post-synaptic potentials (PSP), which are slow (>10 ms) relative to axon potentials firing and therefore sum up efficiently at the scale of synchronized neural ensembles. These primary currents can be modeled using an equivalent current dipole, here represented by a large black arrow. The electrical circuit of currents is closed within the entire head volume by secondary volume currents shown with the dark plain lines. Additionally, magnetic fields are generated by the primary and secondary currents. The magnetic field lines induced by the primary currents are shown using dashed lines arranged in circles about the dipole source. (b) At a larger spatial scale, the mass effect of currents due to neural cells sustaining similar PSP mixtures add up locally and behave also as a current dipole (shown in red). This primary generator induces secondary currents (shown in yellow) that travel through the head tissues. They eventually reach the scalp surface where they can be detected using pairs of electrodes in EEG. Magnetic fields (in green) travel more freely within tissues and are less distorted than current flows. They can be captured using arrays of magnetometers in MEG. The distribution of blue and red colors on the scalp illustrates the continuum of magnetic and electric fields and potentials distributed at the surface of the head.

amplitude-overlap build up more efficiently within the cell ensemble.

Interestingly, although PSPs were thought originally to impress only rather slow fluctuations of currents, recent experimental and modeling evidence demonstrate they are capable of also generating fast spiking activity (Murakami & Okada, 2006). One might assume that these latter may be at the origins of the very high-frequency brain oscillations (that is, up to 1 KHz) captured by MEG (Cimatti et al., 2007). Indeed, mechanisms of active ion channeling within dendrites would further contribute to larger amplitudes of primary currents than initially predicted (Murakami & Okada, 2006). Hence, neocortical columns consisting of as few as 50,000 pyramidal cells with an individual current density of 0.2 pA.m would induce a net current density of 10 nA.m at the assembly level. This is the typical source strength that can be detected using MEG and EEG. Other neural cell types, such as Purkinje and stellate cells are structured with less favorable morphology and/or density than pyramidal cells. It is therefore expected that their contribution to MEG/EEG surface signals is less than neocortical regions. Published models and experimental data, however, report regularly on the detection of cerebellar and deeper brain activity using MEG or EEG (Tesche, 1996, Jerbi, et al., 2007, Attal et al., 2009).

Cellular currents are therefore the primary contributors to MEG/EEG surface signals. These current generators operate in a conductive medium and therefore impress a secondary type of current that circulates through the head tissues (including the skull bone) and loops back to close the electrical circuit (Figure 7.1). Consequently, it is key to the methods attempting to localize the primary current sources to discriminate these latter from the contributions of secondary currents to the measurements. Modeling the electromagnetic properties of head tissues is critical in that respect. Before reviewing this important aspect of the MEG/EEG realm, we shall first discuss the basics of MEG/EEG instrumentation.

Instrumentation

EEG instrumentation

Basic EEG sensing technology is extremely mature and relatively cost-effective, thanks to its wide distribution in the clinical world. The basic principles of EEG consist of the measurement of differences in electrical potentials between couples of electrodes. Two typical set-ups are available: 1) Bipolar electrode montages, where electrodes are arranged in pairs. Hence, electrical potential differences are measured relatively within each electrode pairs. 2) Monopolar electrode montages, where voltage differences are measured relatively to a unique reference electrode. Electrodes may be manufactured using multiple possible materials: Silver/silver chloride compounds are the most common and excel in most aspects of the required specifications—low impedance (from 1 to 20 KΩ) and relatively wide frequency responses (from direct currents to ideally the KHz range). The contact with the skin is critical to signal quality. Skin preparation is essential and the time required is commensurate to the number of electrodes used in the montage. The skin needs to be lightly abraded and cleansed before a special conductive medium—a paste, generally—is applied between the skin and the electrode.

Advanced EEG solutions are constantly being proposed to research investigators and include essentially: 1) A greater number of sensors (up to 256, typically; see Figure 7.4); 2) Faster sampling rates (up to 5KHz or higher on all channels); 3) Facilitated electrode positioning and preparation (with spongy electrolyte contacts or active "dry" electrodes); and 4) Multimodal compatibility (whereby EEG can be recorded concurrently to MEG or fMRI). In that respect, EEG remains one of the very few brain sensing technologies that is capable of bridging multiple environments: from very high to ultra-low magnetic fields, and may also be used in ambulatory mode. The ideal EEG laboratory, however, requires that recordings take place in a room with walls containing conducting materials, as a Faraday cage, for the reduction of electrostatic interferences.

Though electrodes may be glued to the subject's skin, more practical solutions exist for short-term subject monitoring: Electrodes are inserted into elastic caps or nets that can be adapted to the subject's head in a reasonable amount of time (Figure 7.2).

Subject preparation is indeed a factor of importance when using EEG. Electrode application to position digitization—an optional step if source imaging is not required by the experiment—requires about 30 minutes from well-trained operators. Conductivity bridges, impedance drifts—due to degradation of the contact gel—and relative subject discomfort (when using caps on hour-long recordings) are also important factors to consider when designing an EEG experiment. Most advanced EEG systems integrate tools for the online verification of

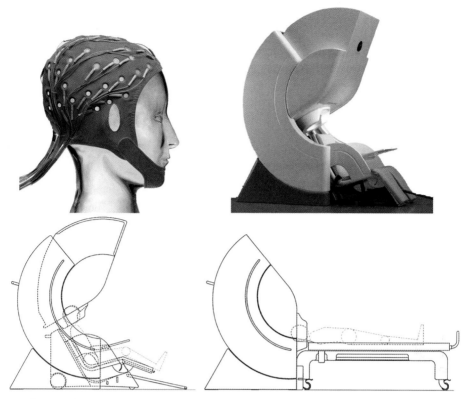

Fig. 7.2 Typical MEG and EEG Equipment. Top left: An elastic EEG cap with 60 electrodes. Top right: A MEG system, which can be operated both in seated upright (bottom left) and supine horizontal (bottom right) positions. EEG recordings can be performed concurrently with the MEG's, using magnetically compatible electrodes and wires.
Illustrations adapted courtesy of Elekta.

electrode impedances. Typical amplitudes of ongoing EEG signals range between 0.1 to 5 μV.

MEG instrumentation

Heart biomagnetism was the first to be evidenced experimentally by Baule and McFee (1963) and Russian groups, followed in Chicago, and then in Boston by David Cohen, who contributed significant technological improvements in the late 1960s. The first low-noise MEG recording followed immediately in 1971 when Cohen reported on spontaneous oscillatory brain activity (α-rhythm), just like Hans Berger did with EEG about 40 years before. The seminal technique was revolutionized in 1969 by the introduction of extremely sensitive current detectors developed by James Zimmerman at the Massachusetts Institute of Technology: the superconducting quantum interference devices (SQUIDs). Once coupled to magnetic pick-up coils, these detectors are able to capture the minute variations of electrical currents induced by the flux of magnetic fields through the coil. Magnetometers—a pick-up coil paired with a current detector—are

therefore the building blocks of MEG-sensing technology. Because of the very small scale of the magnetic fields generated by the brain, signal-to-noise ratio (SNR) is a key issue in MEG technology. The supraconducting sensing technology involved requires cooling at –269°C (–452F). About 70 liters of liquid helium are necessary on a weekly basis to keep the system up to performance. Liquid nitrogen is not considered as an alternative because of the relatively higher thermal noise levels it would allow in the circuitry of current detectors. Ancillary refrigeration—for example, using liquid nitrogen just like in MR systems—is not an option either, for the main reason that MEG sensors need to be located as close to the head as possible. Hence, interleaving another container between the helium-cooled sensors and the subject would increase the distance between the sources and the measurement locations, therefore decreasing SNR. Some MEG sites currently experiment solutions to recycle some of the helium that naturally boils off from the MEG gantry. This approach is optimal if gas liquefaction equipment is available in the proximity of the

MEG site. Under the best circumstances, this technique allows the recuperation and re-utilization of about 60% to 90% of the original helium volume.

Thermal insulation is obviously a challenge in terms of safety of the subject, limited boil-off rate, and minimal distance to neural sources. The technology involved uses thin sheets of fiberglass separated with vacuum, which brings the pick-up coils only a couple of centimeters away from the head surface, with total comfort to the subject. The MEG instrument therefore consists of a rigid helmet containing the sensors, supplemented by a reservoir of liquid helium. Though the MEG equipment is obviously not ambulatory, most commercial systems can operate with subjects in seated (upright) and horizontal (supine) positions (Figure 7.2). Having these options is usually well-appreciated by investigators in terms of alternatives for stimulus presentation, subject comfort, and so forth.

Working with ultra-sensitive sensors is problematic, though, as these latter are very good at picking up all sorts of nuisances and electromagnetic perturbations generated by external sources. The magnetically-shielded room (MSR) has been an early major improvement to MEG sensing technology. All sites in urban areas contain the MEG equipment inside the walls of an MSR, which is built from a variety of metallic alloys. Most metals are successful at capturing radio-frequency perturbations. Mu-metal (a nickel-iron alloy) is one particular material of choice: Its high magnetic permeability makes it very effective at screening external static or low-frequency magnetic fields. The attenuation of electromagnetic perturbations through the MSR walls is colossal and makes MEG recordings possible, even in noisy environments like hospitals (even near MRI suites) and in the vicinity of road traffic.

Stimulus presentation in the MSR, especially when it requires external devices, needs to be considered carefully to avoid introducing supplementary electromagnetic perturbations. Fortunately, MEG centers can benefit from most of the equipment available to fMRI studies, as it is specified along the same constraints regarding magnetic compatibility. Therefore, audio and video presentations can be performed using electrostatic transducers and beams of videoprojection. Electrical stimulation for somatosensory mapping generates artifacts of short durations that do not overlap with the earliest brain responses (>20ms latency). They can be advantageously replaced by air puffs delivery.

As timing is critical in MEG (and EEG), all stimulation solutions need to be driven through a computer with well-characterized timing features. For instance, some electrostatic transducers eventually conduct sound through air tubes, thereby with delays in the tens of milliseconds range that need to be properly characterized. Refresh rates of video presentation need to be as short as possible to ensure quasi-immediate display.

The technology involved in MEG sensing, the weekly helium refills, and the materials building the MSR, make MEG a costly piece of equipment. Exciting recent developments, however, contribute to constant progress in cost-effectiveness, practicality, and the future of MEG sensing science.

Active shielding solutions, for instance, are available commercially. They consist in picking-up the external magnetic fields from outside the MSR and compensate for their contribution to MEG sensors in real time. The immediate benefit is in MSRs of reduced size and weight and in consequence, price.

The depletion of the global stock of helium is a well-documented fact that concerns multiple technology fields, beyond MEG (MRI refrigeration, space rocket propulsion, state-of-the-art video and TV displays and yes, party balloons among others). The immediate consequence of this looming shortage is a steady price increase, hence growing operational costs for MEG. Though alternative helium resources may well not be exploited as of today, the future of biomagnetism is certainly in alternative sensing technologies. High-temperature magnetometers are being developed and are based on radically-different principles than the low-temperature physics of current MEG systems (Savukov & Romalis, 2005; Pannetier-Lecoeur et al., 2009). SNR and sensitivity to the lower frequency range of the electromagnetic spectrum have long been issues with these emerging technologies, which were primarily designed for nuclear magnetic resonance measurements. It appears they now have considerably matured and are ready for MEG prototyping at a larger scale.

Today's MEG commercial systems are organized in whole-head sensor arrays arranged in a rigid helmet covering most of the head surface but not the face area. MEG signals are recorded from about 300 channels, which sometimes consist of pairs of magnetometers to form physical gradiometers (Hämäläinen, Hari, Ilmoniemi, Knuutila, & Lounasmaa, 1993). These latter are less sensitive to far-field sources, which are supposed to originate from distant generators (e.g., road traffic, elevators, heartbeats). An important benefit of MEG systems is the possibility to record EEG from dense arrays of electrodes (>60) simultaneously, thereby completing the electromagnetic signature of neural currents. Additional analog channels are usually available for miscellaneous recordings (heart monitoring (ECG), muscle activity (EMG), eye movements (EOG), respiration, skin conductance, subject's responses, etc.). Sampling rate can reach up to 5KHz on all channels with a typical instrumental noise level limited to a few $fT/\sqrt{Hz}$. One femto-Tesla (1fT) is 10^{-15} T. Ongoing brain signals measured with MEG are on the range of about 10–50 $fT/\sqrt{Hz}$ (Figure 7.3), with a relatively rapid decay in amplitude as frequency increases.

MEG has substantial benefits with respect to EEG: 1) While EEG is strongly degraded by the heterogeneity in conductivity within head tissues (e.g., insulating skull vs. conducting scalp), this effect is extremely limited in MEG, resulting in greater spatial discrimination of neural contributions. This has important implications for source modeling as we shall see below. 2) Subject preparation time is reduced considerably; 3) Measures are absolute, that is, they are not dependent on the choice of a reference; 4) Subject's comfort is improved as there is no direct contact of the sensors on the skin. Installation of new MEG systems

is presently steadily growing within research and clinical centers (about 200 worldwide).

MEG/EEG experiments can be run with the subjects in supine or seated positions. A caveat, however, concerns EEG recording in supine position, which may rapidly lead to subject discomfort because occipital electrodes become painful pressure points. The quiet, room-size, and fairly open environment of the MSR and Faraday cages (relatively to MRI bores), make it friendlier to most subjects. Care givers may accompany subjects during the experiment.

Scenarios of Most Typical MEG/EEG Sessions

A successful MEG or EEG study is a combination of quality instrumentation, careful paradigm design, and well-understood preprocessing and analysis methods integrated in efficient software tools. We shall review these latter aspects in this section.

Subject Preparation

We have already discussed the basics of EEG preparation to ensure that contact of electrodes with skin is of quality and stable. Additional precautions

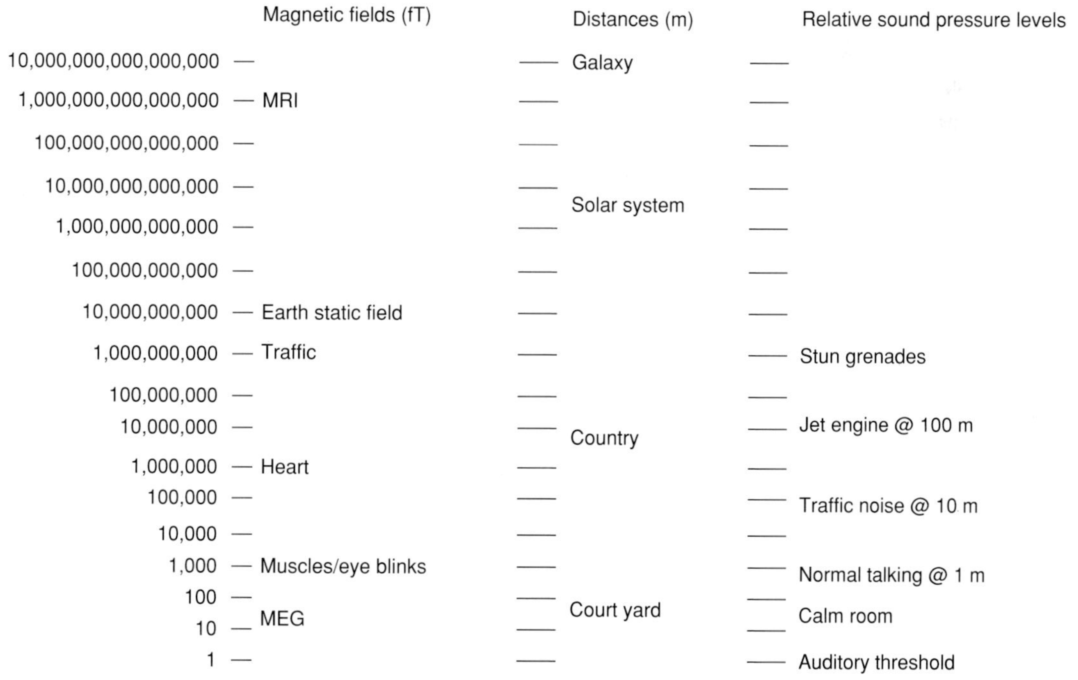

Magnetic fields (fT)		Distances (m)	Relative sound pressure levels
10,000,000,000,000,000	—	— Galaxy	—
1,000,000,000,000,000	— MRI	—	—
100,000,000,000,000	—	—	—
10,000,000,000,000	—	— Solar system	—
1,000,000,000,000	—	—	—
100,000,000,000	—	—	—
10,000,000,000	— Earth static field	—	—
1,000,000,000	— Traffic	—	— Stun grenades
100,000,000	—	—	—
10,000,000	—	— Country	— Jet engine @ 100 m
1,000,000	— Heart	—	—
100,000	—	—	— Traffic noise @ 10 m
10,000	—	—	—
1,000	— Muscles/eye blinks	—	— Normal talking @ 1 m
100	—	— Court yard	— Calm room
10	— MEG	—	
1	—	—	— Auditory threshold

Fig. 7.3 Scales of magnetic fields in a typical MEG environment (in femto-Tesla) compared to equivalent distance measures (in meters) and relative sound pressure levels. A MEG instrument probe therefore deals with a range of environmental magnetic fields of about 10 to 12 orders of magnitude, most of which consist of nuisances and perturbations masking the brain activity.

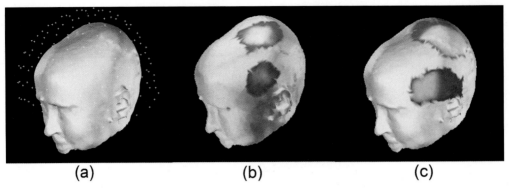

Fig. 7.4 On the benefits of a larger number of sensors: (a) 3D rendering of a subject's scalp surface with crosshair markers representing the locations of 151 axial gradiometers as MEG sensors (coil locations are from the VSM MedTech 151 Omega System). (b) Interpolated field topography onto the scalp surface 50 ms following the electric stimulation of the right index finger. The fields reveal a strong and focal dipolar structure above the contralateral central cortex. (c) The number of channels has been evenly reduced to 27. Though the dipolar pattern is still detected, its spatial extension is more smeared—hence the intrinsic spatial resolution of the measurements has been degraded—due to the effect of interpolation between sensors, which are now quite distant from the maxima of the evoked magnetic field pattern.

should be taken for an MEG recording session as any magnetic material carried by the subject would cause major MEG artifacts. It is therefore recommended that the subject's compatibility with MEG be rapidly checked by recording and visually inspecting their spontaneous resting activity, prior to EEG preparation and proceeding any further into the experiment. Large artifacts due to metallic and magnetic parts (coins, credit cards, some dental retainers, body piercing, bra supports, etc.) or particles (make-up, hair spray, tattoos) can be readily and visually detected as they cause major low-frequency deflections in MEG traces. They are usually emphasized with respiration and/or eye blinks and/or jaw movements. Some causes of artifacts may not be easily circumvented: Research volunteers may have participated in an fMRI study, sometimes months before the MEG session. Previous participation to an MRI session is likely to have caused strong, long-term magnetization of, for example, dental retainers, which generally brings the MEG session to a premature close. Onsite demagnetization may be attempted using "degaussing" techniques—usually using a conventional magnetic tape eraser, which attenuates and scrambles magnetization—with limited chances of success, though.

Subjects are subsequently encouraged to change, to wear a gown or scrubs before completing their preparation. If EEG is recorded with MEG, electrode preparation should follow the conventional principles of good EEG practice. Additional leads for EOG, ECG, or EMG may then be positioned. In state-of-the-art MEG systems, head-positioning

(HPI) coils are taped to the subject's head to detect its position with respect to the sensor array while recording. This is critical as, though head motion is not encouraged, it is very likely to occur within and in between runs, especially with young children and some patients. The HPIs drive a current at some higher (about 300Hz) frequency that is readily detected by the MEG sensors at the beginning of each run. Each of the HPI coils can then be localized within seconds with millimeter accuracy. Some MEG systems feature the possibility for continuous head-position monitoring during the very recording and off-line head movement compensation (Wehner, Hämäläinen, Mody, & Ahlfors, 2008).

Head-positioning is made possible after the locations of the HPI coils are digitized prior to sitting the subject under the MEG array (Figure 7.5). The distance between HPI pairs is then checked for consistency by the MEG system, which is a fundamental step in the quality control of the recordings. Noisy sensors or environment and badly secured HPI taping are sources of discrepancies between the moment of subject preparation and the actual MEG recordings and should be attended. If advanced source analysis is required, additional 3D digitization of anatomical fiducial points is necessary to ensure that subsequent registration to the subject's MRI anatomical volume is successful and accurate (see below). A minimum of 3 fiducial points should be localized: they usually sit by the nasion and left and right peri-auricular points (Figure 7.5). To reduce ambiguity in the detection of these points in the MR volume data, they can be marked using

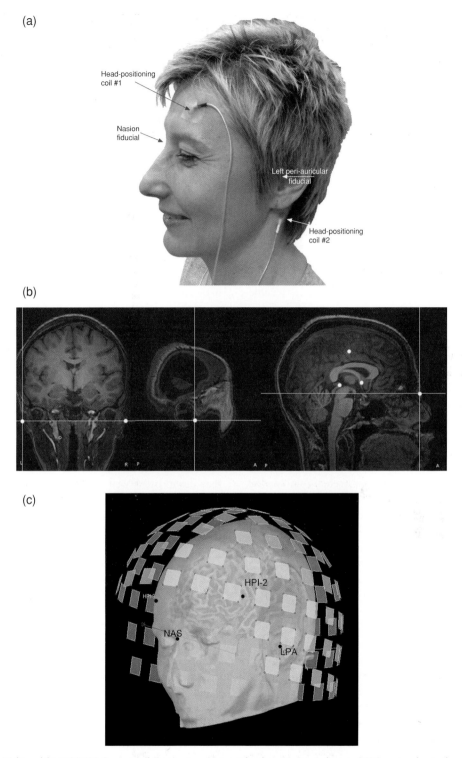

Fig. 7.5 Multimodal MEG/MRI Geometrical Registration. (a) 3 to 5 head-positioning indicators (HPI) are taped onto the subject's scalp. Their positions, together with 3 additional anatomical fiducials (nasion, left and right peri-auricular points [NAS, LPA, and RPA, respectively]) are digitized using a magnetic pen digitizer. (b) The anatomical fiducials need to be detected and marked in the subject's anatomical MRI volume data: They are shown as white dots in this figure, together with 3 optional, additional points defining the anterior and posterior commissures and the interhemispheric space, for the definition of Talairach coordinates. (c) These anatomical landmarks henceforth define a geometrical referential in which the MEG sensor locations and the surface envelopes of the head tissues (e.g., the scalp and brain surface, segmented from the MRI volume) are co-registered. MEG sensors are shown as squares positioned about the head. The anatomical fiducials and HPI locations are marked using dark dots.

vitamin E pills or any other solid marker that is readily visible in T1-weighted MR images, if MRI is scheduled right after the MEG session. Digitization of EEG electrode locations is also mandatory for accurate, subsequent source analysis. Overall, about 15 minutes are required for subject preparation for an MEG-only session, which can extend up to about 45 minutes if simultaneous high-density EEG is required.

Paradigm Design

The time dimension accessible to MEG/EEG offers some considerable variety in the design of experimental paradigms for testing virtually any basic neuroscience hypothesis. Managing this new dimension is sometimes puzzling for investigators with an fMRI neuroimaging background as MEG/EEG allows them to manipulate experimental parameters and presentations in the real time of the brain, not at the much slower pace of hemodynamic responses.

In a nutshell, MEG/EEG experimental design is conditioned on the type of brain responses of foremost interest to the investigator: evoked, induced, or sustained. The most common experimental design by far is the interleaved presentation of transient stimuli representing multiple conditions to be tested. In this design, stimuli of various categories and valences (pictures, sounds, somatosensory electric pulses or air puffs, or their combination, etc.) are presented in sequence with various interstimulus interval (ISI) durations. ISIs are typically much shorter than in fMRI paradigms and range from a few tens of milliseconds to a few seconds.

The benefit of the high temporal resolution of MEG/EEG is twofold in that respect: 1) It allows investigators to detect and categorize the chronometry of effects occurring after stimulus presentation (evoked or induced brain responses), and 2) it provides leverage to the investigator to manipulate the timing of stimulus presentation to emphasize the very dynamics of brain processes.

The first category of experimental designs is the most typical and has a long history of scientific investigations in the characterization of the specificity of certain brain responses to certain stimulus categories (sounds, faces, words, novelty detection, etc.) as we shall discuss in greater details below.

The second category of designs aims at pushing the limits of the dynamics of brain processes: A typical situation would consist in better understanding how brain processes unfold and may be conditional to a hierarchy of sequences in the treatment

of stimulus information from, for example, primary sensory areas to its cognitive evaluation. This may be well exemplified by paradigms such as oddball rapid serial visual presentation (RSVP; Kranczioch, Debener, Herrmann, & Engel, 2006; and see Figure 7.6), or when investigating time-related effects such as the attentional blink (Sergent, Baillet, & Dehaene, 2005; Dux & Marois, 2009). Steady-state brain responses triggered by sustained stimulus presentations belong also to this category. Here, a stimulus with specific temporal encoding (e.g., visual pattern reversals or sound modulations at a well-defined frequency) is presented and may trigger brain responses locked to the stimulus presentation rate or some harmonics. This approach is sometimes called "frequency-tagging" (of brain responses). This has lead to a rich literature of steady-state brain responses in the study of multiple brain systems (Ding, Sperling, & Srinivasan, 2006; Bohórquez & Ozdamar, 2008; Parkkonen, Andersson, Hämäläinen, & Hari, 2008; Vialatte, Maurice, Dauwels, & Cichocki, 2009) and new strategies for brain computer interfaces (see e.g., Mukesh, Jaganathan, & Reddy, 2006).

As a beneficial rule of thumb for stimulus presentation in MEG/EEG paradigms, it is important to randomize the ISI durations as much as possible for most paradigms, to minimize the effect of stimulus occurrence expectancy from the subjects. Indeed, this latter triggers brain activity patterns that have been well characterized in multiple EEG studies (Clementz, Barber, & Dzau, 2002; Mnatsakanian & Tarkka, 2002) and which may bias both the subsequent MEG/EEG and behavioral responses (e.g., reaction times) to stimulation.

Data Acquisition

A typical MEG/EEG session usually consists of several runs. A run is a series of experimental trials. A trial is an experimental event whereby a stimulus has been presented to a subject, or the subject has performed a predefined action, within a certain condition of the paradigm. Trials and runs certainly vary in duration and length depending on experimental contingencies, but it is certainly good advice to try to keep these numbers relatively low. It is most beneficial to the subject's comfort and vigilance to keep the duration of a run under 10 minutes, and preferably 5 minutes. Longer runs augment the participant's fatigue, which most commonly results in more frequent eye blinks, head movements, and poorer compliance to the task instructions. For the same reasons, it is not recommended that a full session lasts longer than about 2 hours. Communication with

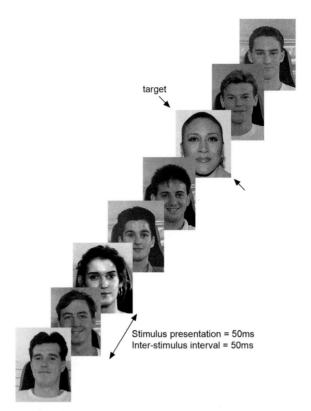

target

Stimulus presentation = 50ms
Inter-stimulus interval = 50ms

Fig. 7.6 A Typical Event-Related Paradigm Design for MEG/EEG. The experiment consists of the detection of a visual "oddball." Pictures of faces are presented very rapidly to the participants every 100ms, for a duration of 50ms and an ISI of 50ms. In about 15% of the trials, a face known to the participant is presented. This is the target stimulus and the participant needs to count the number of times he/she has seen the target individual among the unknown, distracting faces. Here, the experiment consisted of 4 runs of about 200 trials, resulting in a total of 120 target presentations. Typical surface data and source imaging for this paradigm are displayed in Fig. 7.8 and 7.13, respectively.

the subject is made possible at all times via two-way intercom and video monitoring.

Setting the data sampling rate is the first parameter to decide upon when starting an MEG/EEG acquisition. Most recent systems can reach up to 5 KHz per channel, which is certainly doable but leads to large data files that may be cumbersome to manipulate off-line. The sampling rate parameter is critical as it conditions the span of the frequency spectrum of the data. Indeed, this latter is limited in theory to half the sampling rate, while good practice would rather consider it be limited to about one-third of the sampling frequency.

As we shall see below, a vast majority of studies target brain responses that are evoked by stimulation and revealed after trial averaging. Most of these responses have a typical half-cycle of about 20ms and above, hence a characteristic frequency reaching up to 100Hz. A sampling rate of 300 to 600Hz would therefore be a safe choice. As briefly discussed above, high-frequency oscillatory responses in the brain

have, however, been evidenced in the somatosensory cortex and may reach up to about 900Hz (Cimatti et al., 2007). They therefore necessitate higher sampling rates of about 3 to 5KHz. Storage and file handling issues may arise though, as every minute of recording corresponds to about 75MB of data, sampled at 1 KHz on 300 MEG and 60 EEG channels.

During acquisition, MEG and EEG operators shall proceed to basic quality controls of the recordings. So called "bad channels" may be readily detected because of evident larger noise amounts in the traces, and shall be addressed (by, e.g., posing more gel under the electrode or tuning the deficient MEG channel).

Filters may be applied during the recording, though only with caution. Indeed, band-pass filters for display only are innocuous to subsequent analysis, but most MEG/EEG instruments feature filters that are applied definitely to the actual data being recorded. The investigator shall be well aware of these parameters, which may transform into roadblocks to the analysis of some components of interest in the signals. A typical example is a low-pass filter applied at 40Hz, which prohibits subsequent access to any upper frequency ranges. Notch filters are usually applied during acquisition to attenuate power line contamination at 50 or 60Hz, though without preventing possible nuisances at some harmonics. Low-pass anti-aliasing filters are generally applied by default during acquisition—before analog-to-digital conversion of signals—and their cut-off frequency is conditioned to the data sampling rate: it is conventionally set to about a third of the sampling frequency.

As a general recommendation, it is suggested to keep filtering to the minimum required during acquisition—that is, anti-aliasing and optionally, a high-pass filter set at about 0.3Hz to attenuate slow DC drifts, if of no interest to the experiment—because much can be performed off-line during the pre-processing steps of signal analysis, which we shall review now.

Data Pre-processing

The frequency spectrum of MEG/EEG data is rich and complex. Multiple processes take place simultaneously and engage neural populations at various spatial, temporal and frequency scales (Varela et al., 2001). The purpose of data pre-processing is to enhance the levels of signals of interest, while attenuating nuisances or even rejecting some episodes in the recordings that are tarnished by artifacts. In the following subsections, it is presupposed that the investigator is able to specify—even at a crude level of details—the basic temporal and frequency properties of the signals of interest carrying the effects being tested in the experiment. In a nutshell, it is important to target upfront a well-defined range of brain dynamics in the course of the design of the paradigm and of the analysis pipeline.

Digital Filtering

As briefly discussed above, data filtering is a conceptually simple, though powerful, technique to extract signals within a predefined frequency band of interest. This off-line data pre-processing step is the realm of digital filtering: an important and sophisticated subfield of electrical engineering (Hamming, 1983). Applying a filter to the data presupposes that the information carried by signals will be mostly preserved, to the benefit of attenuating other frequency components of supposedly no interest.

Not every digital filter is suitable to the analysis of MEG/EEG traces. Indeed, the performances of filters are defined from basic characteristics such as the attenuation outside the bandpass of the frequency response, stability, computational efficiency, and most importantly, the introduction of phase delays. This latter is a systematic by-product of filtering and some filters may be particularly inappropriate in that respect: Infinite impulse response (IIR) digital filters are usually more computationally efficient than finite impulse response (FIR) alternatives, but with the inconvenience of introducing non-linear, frequency-dependent phase delays; hence, some non-equal delays in the temporal domain at all frequencies, which is unacceptable for MEG/EEG signal analysis where timing and phase measurements are crucial. FIR filters delay signals in the time domain equally at all frequencies, which can be conveniently compensated for by applying the filter twice: once forward and once backward on the MEG/EEG time series (Oppenheim, Schafer, & Buck, 1999) (Figure 7.7). Note, however, some possible edge effects of the FIR filter at the beginning and end of the time series, and the necessity of a large number of time samples when applying filters with low high-pass cut-off frequencies (as the length of the filter's FIR increases). Hence, it is generally advisable to apply digital high-pass filters on longer episodes of data, such as on the original "raw" recordings, before these latter are chopped into epochs of shorter durations about each trial for further analysis.

Bringing more details to the discussion would reach outside the scope of this book. The investigator should nevertheless be well aware of the potential pitfalls of analysis techniques in general, and of digital filters in particular. Although commercial software tools are well equipped with adequate filter functions, in-house or academic software solutions should be first evaluated with great caution.

Advanced Data Correction Techniques

Despite all the precautions to obtain clean signals from EEG and MEG sensors, electrophysiological traces are likely to be contaminated by a wide variety of artifacts. These include other sources than the brain and primarily the eyes, the heart, muscles (head or limb motion, muscular tension due to postural discomfort or fatigue), electromagnetic perturbations from other devices used in the experiment, leaking power line contamination, and so forth. The key challenge is that most of these factors of nuisance contribute to MEG/EEG recordings with significantly more power than ongoing brain signals (a factor of about 50 for heartbeats, eye-blinks and

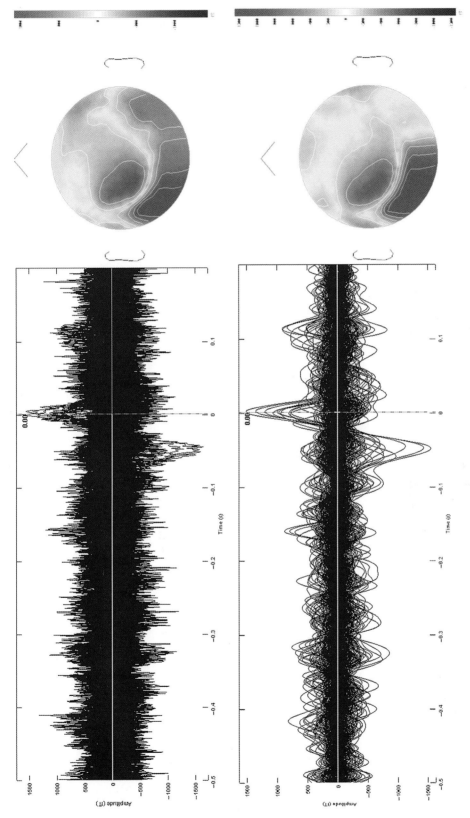

Fig. 7.7 Digital band-pass filtering applied to spontaneous MEG data during an interictal epileptic spike event (total epoch of 700ms duration, sampled at 1KHz). The time series of 306 MEG sensors are displayed using a butterfly plot, whereby all waveforms are overlaid within the same axes. The top row displays the original data with digital filters applied during acquisition between 1.5 and 330Hz. The bottom row is a pre-processed version of the same data, band-passed filtered between 2 and 30Hz. Note how this version of the data better reveals the epileptic event occurring about time t=0ms. The corresponding sensor topographies of MEG measures are displayed to the right. The gray scale display represents the intensity of the magnetic field captured at each sensor location and interpolated over a flattened version of the MEG array (nose pointing upwards). Note also how digital band-pass filtering strongly alters the surface topography of the data, by revealing a simpler dipolar pattern over the left temporo-occipital areas of the array.

movements, see Figure 7.3). Whether experimental trials contaminated by artifacts need to be discarded requires that these latter be properly detected in the first place.

The literature of methods for tackling noise detection, attenuation, and correction is too immense to be properly covered in this chapter. In a nutshell, the chances of detecting and correcting artifacts are higher when these latter are monitored by a dedicated measurement. Hence, electrophysiological monitoring (ECG, EOG, EMG, etc.) is strongly encouraged in most experimental settings. These additional recordings may be used as artifact templates for visual or automatic inspection of the MEG/EEG data. Some MEG solutions use additional magnetic sensors located away from the subject's head to capture the environmental magnetic fields inside the MSR. Adaptive filtering techniques may then be applied quite effectively (Haykin, 1996).

For steady-state perturbations, which are thought to be independent of the brain processes of interest, empirical statistics obtained from a series of representative events (e.g., eye-blinks, heartbeats) are likely to properly capture the nuisance they systematically generate in the MEG/EEG recordings. Approaches like principal or independent component analysis (PCA and ICA, respectively) have proven to be effective in that respect for both conventional MEG/EEG and simultaneous EEG/fMRI recordings (Nolte & Hämäläinen, 2001; Pérez, Guijarro, & Barcia, 2005; Delorme, Sejnowski, & Makeig, 2007; Koskinen & Vartiainen, 2009). Modality-specific noise attenuation techniques, like signal space separation and alike (SSS), have been proposed for MEG (Taulu, Kajola, & Simola, 2004). They basically consist of designing software spatial filters that attenuate sources of nuisance that originate from outside a virtual spherical volume designed to contain the subject's head within the MEG helmet.

Ultimately, the decision of whether episodes contaminated by well-identified artifacts need to be discarded or corrected belongs to the investigator. Some scientists design their paradigms so that the number of trials is large enough that a few may be discarded without putting the analysis to jeopardy.

Epoch Averaging: Evoked Responses Across Trials

An enduring tradition of MEG/EEG signal analysis consists of enhancing brain responses that are evoked by a stimulus or an action, by averaging the data about each event—defined as an epoch—across trials. The underlying assumption is that there exist some consistent brain responses that are time-locked and so-called "phase-locked" to a specific event (again, e.g., the presentation of a stimulus or a motor action). Hence, it is straightforward to enhance these responses by proceeding to epoch averaging across trials, under the assumption that the rest of the data is inconsistent in time or phase with respect to the event of interest. This simple practice has permitted a vast number of contributions to the field of event-related potentials (in EEG, ERP) and fields (in MEG, ERF) (Handy, 2004; Niedermeyer & Silva, 2004).

Trial averaging necessitates that epochs be defined about each event of interest (e.g., the stimulus onset, or the subject's response). An epoch has a certain duration, usually defined with respect to the event of interest (pre- and post-event). Averaging epochs across trials can be conducted for each experimental condition at the individual and the group levels. This latter practice is called "grand-averaging" and has been made possible originally because electrodes are positioned on the subject's scalp according to montages, which are defined with respect to basic, reproducible geometrical measures taken on the head. The international 10–20 system was developed as a standardized electrode positioning and naming nomenclature to allow direct comparison of studies across the EEG community (Niedermeyer & Silva, 2004). Standardization of sensor placement does not exist in the MEG community, as the sensor arrays are specific to the device being used and subject heads fit differently under the MEG helmet. Therefore, grand or even inter-run averaging is not encouraged in MEG at the sensor level without applying movement compensation techniques, or without at least checking that limited head displacements occurred between runs. Note, however, that trial averaging may be performed on the source time series of the MEG or EEG generators. In this latter situation, typical geometrical normalization techniques such as those used in fMRI studies need to be applied across subjects and are now a more consistent part of the MEG/EEG analysis pipeline.

Once proper averaging has been completed, measures can be taken on ERP/ERF components. Components are defined as waveform elements that emerge from the baseline of the recordings. They may be characterized in terms of, for example, relative latency, topography, amplitude, and duration with respect to baseline or a specific test condition (Figure 7.8). Once again, the ERP/ERF literature is immense and cannot be summarized in these lines. Multiple reviews and textbooks are available and describe in great details the specificity and sensitivity of event-related components. In the context of social neuroscience, let us just cite some recent MEG and EEG studies concerning: emotion face perception (Vuilleumier & Pourtois, 2007), gaze (George & Conty, 2008; Holmes, Mogg, Garcia, & Bradley, 2010), visual induction of emotions (Rudrauf et al., 2009) and imitation tasks (Biermann-Ruben et al., 2008), among many others.

Phase-locked ERP/ERF components capture only the part of task-related brain responses that repeat consistently in latency and phase with respect to an event. One might, however, question the physiological origins and relevance of such components in the framework of oscillatory cell assemblies, as a possible mechanism ruling the most basic electrophysiological processes (Gray, König, Engel, & Singer, 1989; Silva, 1991; David & Friston, 2003;

Vogels, Rajan, & Abbott, 2005). This has lead to a fair amount of controversy, whereby evoked components would rather be considered as artifacts of event-related, induced phase resetting of ongoing brain rhythms, mostly in the alpha frequency range ([8,12]Hz) (Makeig et al., 2002). Under this assumption, epoch averaging would only provide a secondary and poorly specific window on brain processes: this is certainly quite severe. Indeed, event-related amplitude modulations—hence, not phase effects—of ongoing alpha rhythms have been reported as major contributors to the slower event-related components captured by ERP/ERFs (Mazaheri & Jensen, 2008). Some authors associate these modulations of event-related amplitudes to local enhancements/reductions of event-related synchronization/desynchronization (ERS/ERD) within cell assemblies. The underlying assumption is that as the activity of more cells tends to be synchronized, the net ensemble activity will build up to an increase in signal amplitude (Pfurtscheller & Silva, 1999).

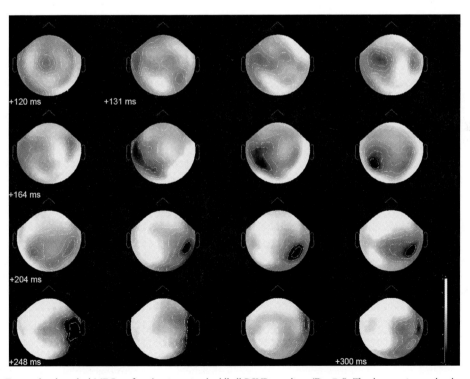

Fig. 7.8 Event-related, evoked MEG surface data in a visual oddball RSVP paradigm (Fig. 7.6). The data was interpolated between sensors and projected on a flattened version of the MEG channel array. Shades of gray represent the inward and outward magnetic fields picked-up outside the head during the [120,300] ms time interval following the presentation of the target face object. The spatial distribution of magnetic fields over the sensor array is usually relatively smooth and reveals some characteristic shape patterns that indicate that brain activity is rapidly changing and propagating during the time window. A much clearer insight can be provided by source imaging, as illustrated in Fig. 7.13.

Epoch Averaging: Induced Responses Across Trials

Massive event-related cell synchronization is not guaranteed to take place with consistent temporal phase with respect to the onset of the event. It is therefore relatively easy to imagine that averaging trials when such phase jitters occur across event repetitions would lead to decreased effect sensitivity. This assumption can be further elaborated in the theoretical and experimental framework of distributed, synchronized cell assemblies during perception and cognition (Varela et al., 2001; Tallon-Baudry, 2009). The seminal works by Gray and Singer in cat vision have shown that synchronization of oscillatory responses of spatially distributed cell ensembles is a way to establish relations between features in different parts of the visual field (Gray et al., 1989). These authors evidenced that these phenomena take place in the gamma range ([40,60]Hz)—that is, an upper frequency range—of the event-elated responses. These results have been confirmed by a large number of subsequent studies in animals and implanted electrodes in humans, which all demonstrated that these event-related responses could only be captured with an approach to epoch averaging that would be robust to phase jitters across trials (Tallon-Baudry, Bertrand, Delpuech, & Permier, 1997; Rodriguez et al., 1999).

More evidence of gamma-range brain responses detected with EEG and MEG scalp techniques are being reported as analysis techniques are being refined and distributed to a greater community of investigators (Hoogenboom, Schoffelen, Oostenveld, Parkes, & Fries, 2006). It is striking to note that as a greater number of investigations are conducted, the frequency range of gamma responses of interest is constantly expanding and now reaches between [30,100]Hz and above. As a caveat, this frequency range is also most favorable to contamination from muscle activity, such as phasic contractions or micro-saccades, which may also happen to be task-related (Yuval-Greenberg & Deouell, 2009; Melloni, Schwiedrzik, Wibral, Rodriguez, & Singer, 2009). Therefore, great precautions must be brought to rule out possible confounds in that matter.

An additional interesting feature of gamma responses for neuroimagers is that there is a growing body of evidence showing that they tend to be more specifically coupled to the hemodynamics responses captured in fMRI than other components of the electrophysiological responses (Niessing et al., 2005; Lachaux et al., 2007; Koch, Werner, Steinbrink, Fries, & Obrig, 2009).

Because induced responses are mostly characterized by phase jitters across trials, averaging MEG/EEG traces in the time domain would be detrimental to the extraction of induced signals from the ongoing brain activity (David & Friston, 2003). A typical approach to the detection of induced components once again builds on the hypothesis of systematic emission of event-related oscillatory bursts limited in time duration and frequency range. Time-frequency decomposition (TFD) is a methodology of choice in that respect, as it proceeds to the estimation of instantaneous power in the time-frequency domain of time series. TFD is insensitive to variations of the signal phase when computing the average signal power across trials. TFD is a very active field of signal processing and one of the core tools for TFD is wavelet signal decomposition. Wavelets feature the possibility to perform the spectral analysis of non-stationary signals, the spectral properties and contents of which are evolving with time (Mallat, 1998). This is typical of phasic electrophysiological responses for which Fourier spectral analysis is not adequate because it is based on signal stationarity assumptions (Kay, 1988).

Hence, even though the typical statistics of induced MEG/EEG signal analysis is the trial mean (i.e., sample average), it is performed with a different measure: the estimation of short-term signal power, decomposed in time and frequency bins. Several academic and commercial software solutions are now available to perform such analysis (and the associated inference statistics) on electrophysiological signals.

New Trends and Methods: Connectivity/ Complexity Analysis

The analysis of brain connectivity is a rapidly evolving field of neuroscience, with significant contributions from new neuroimaging techniques and methods (Bandettini, 2009). While structural and functional connectivity has been emphasized with MRI-based techniques (Johansen-Berg & Rushworth, 2009; Friston, 2009a), the time resolution of MEG/EEG offers a unique perspective on the mechanisms of rapid neural connectivity engaging cell assemblies at multiple temporal and spatial scales.

We may summarize the research taking place in that field by mentioning two approaches that have developed somewhat distinctly in the recent years, though we might predict they will ultimately converge with forthcoming research efforts. We shall note that most of the methods summarized below are also applicable to the analysis of MEG/EEG source connectivity and are not restricted to the analysis of sensor data. We further emphasize that connectivity analysis is easily fooled by confounds in the data, such as volume conduction effects—that is, smearing of scalp MEG/EEG data due to the distance from brain sources to sensors and the conductivity properties of head tissues, as we shall discuss below—which need to be carefully evaluated in the course of the analysis (Nunez et al., 1997; Marzetti, Gratta, & Nolte, 2008).

The first strategy has inherited directly from the compelling intracerebral recording results demonstrating that cell synchronization is a central feature of neural communication (Gray et al., 1989). Signal analysis techniques dedicated to the estimation of signal interdependencies in the broad sense have been largely applied to MEG/EEG sensor traces. Contrarily to what is appropriate to the analysis of fMRI's slow hemodynamics, simple correlation measures in the time domain are thought not to be able to capture the specificity of electrophysiological signals, which components are defined over a fairly large frequency spectrum. Coherence measures are certainly amongst the most investigated techniques in MEG/EEG, because they are designed to be sensitive to simultaneous variations of power that are specific to each frequency bin of the signal spectrum (Nunez et al., 1997). There is, however, a competitive assumption that neural signals may synchronize their phases, without the necessity of simultaneous, increased power modulation (Varela et al., 2001). Wavelet-based techniques have therefore been developed to detect episodes of phase synchronization between signals (Lachaux, Rodriguez, Martinerie, & Varela, 1999; Rodriguez et al., 1999).

Connectivity analysis has also been recently studied through the concept of causality, whereby some neural regions would influence others in a non-symmetric, directed fashion (Gourévitch, Bouquin-Jeannès, & Faucon, 2006). The possibilities to investigate directed influence between not only pairs, but larger sets of time series (i.e., MEG/EEG sensors or brain regions) are vast and are therefore usually ruled by parametric models. These latter may either be related to the definition of the time series (i.e., through auto-regressive modeling for Granger-causality assessment, Lin et al., 2009), or to the very underlying structure of the connectivity between neural assemblies (i.e., through structural equation modeling, Astolfi et al., 2005; and dynamic causal modeling, David et al., 2006; Kiebel, Garrido, Moran, & Friston, 2008).

The second approach to connectivity analysis pertains to the emergence of complex networks studies and associated methodology. Complex networks science is a recent branch of applied mathematics that provides quantitative tools to identify and characterize patterns of organization among large inter-connected networks such as the Internet, air transportation systems, and mobile telecommunication. In neuroscience, this strategy, rather, concerns the identification of global characteristics of connectivity within the full array of brain signals captured at the sensor or source levels. With this methodology, the concept of the brain *connectome* has recently emerged, and encompasses new challenges for integrative neurosciences and the technology, methodology, and tools involved in neuroimaging, to better embrace spatially-distributed dynamical neural processes at multiple spatial and temporal scales (Sporns, Tononi, & Kötter, 2005; Deco, Jirsa, Robinson, Breakspear, & Friston, 2008). From the operational standpoint, brain "connectomics" is contributing both to theoretical and computational models of the brain as a complex system (Honey, Kötter, Breakspear, & Sporns, 2007; Izhikevich & Edelman, 2008), and experimentally, by suggesting new indices and metrics—such as nodes, hubs, efficiency, modularity, and so forth—to characterize and scale the functional organization of the healthy and diseased brain (Bassett & Bullmore, 2009). This type of approach is very promising, and calls for large-scale validation and maturation to connect with the well-explored realm of basic electrophysiological phenomena.

Electromagnetic Source Imaging

The quantitative analysis of MEG/EEG sensor data is a source of vast possibilities to characterize time-resolved brain activity. Some studies, however, may require a more direct assessment of the anatomical origins of the effects detected at the sensor level. It is also likely that some effects may not even be revealed using scalp measures because of severe mixing and smearing due to the relative large distance from sources to sensors and volume conduction effects.

Electromagnetic source imaging addresses this issue by characterizing these latter elements (the head shape and size, relative position and properties of sensors, noise statistics, etc.) in a principled manner and by suggesting a model for the generators responsible for the signals in the data. Ultimately, models of electrical source activity are produced and need to be analyzed in a multitude of dimensions: amplitude maps, time/frequency properties, connectivity, and so forth, using statistical assessment techniques. The rest of this chapter details most of the steps required, while skipping technical details, which can be found in the references cited.

MEG/EEG Source Estimation as a Modeling Problem

FORWARD AND INVERSE MODELING

From a methodological standpoint, MEG/EEG source modeling is referred to as an "inverse problem," a ubiquitous concept, well known to physicists and mathematicians in a wide variety of scientific fields: from medical imaging to geophysics and particle physics (Tarantola, 2004). The inverse problem framework helps conceptualize and formalize the fact that, in experimental sciences, models are confronted to observations to draw specific scientific conclusions and/or estimate some parameters that were originally unknown. Parameters are quantities that might be changed without fundamentally violating and thereby invalidating the theoretical model. Predicting observations from a model with a given set of parameters is called solving the *forward* modeling problem. The reciprocal situation where observations are used to estimate the values of some model parameters is the *inverse* modeling problem.

In the context of brain functional imaging in general, and MEG/EEG in particular, we are essentially interested in identifying the neural sources of external signals observed outside the head (noninvasively). These sources are defined by their locations in the brain and their amplitude variations in time. These are the essential unknown parameters that MEG/EEG source estimation will reveal, which is a typical incarnation of an inverse modeling problem.

Forward modeling in the context of MEG/EEG consists of predicting the electromagnetic fields and potentials generated by any arbitrary source model, that is, for any location, orientation, and amplitude of the flow of neural currents. In general, MEG/EEG forward modeling considers that some parameters are known and fixed: the geometry of the head, conductivity of tissues, sensor locations, and so forth. This will be discussed in the next section.

As an illustration, take a single current dipole as a model for the global activity of the brain at a specific latency of an MEG averaged evoked response. We might choose to let the dipole location, orientation, and amplitude as the set of free parameters to be inferred from the sensor observations. We need to specify some parameters to solve the forward modeling problem consisting in predicting how a single current dipole generates magnetic fields on the sensor array in question. We might therefore choose to specify that the head geometry will be approximated as a single sphere, with its center at some given coordinates (see Figure 7.9).

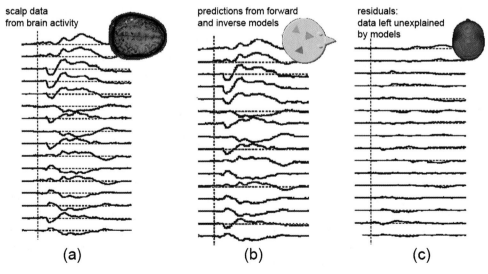

Fig. 7.9 Modeling illustrated: (a) Some unknown brain activity generates variations of magnetic fields and electric potentials at the surface of the scalp. This is illustrated by time series representing measurements at each sensor lead. (b) Modeling of the sources and of the physics of MEG and EEG. As naively represented here, forward modeling consists of a simplification of the complex geometry and electromagnetic properties of head tissues. Source models are presented with colored arrow heads. Their free parameters—for example, location, orientation, and amplitude—are adjusted during the inverse modeling procedure to optimize some quantitative index. This is illustrated here in (c), where the residuals—that is, the absolute difference between the original data and the measures predicted by a source model—are minimized.

A fundamental principle is that, whereas the forward problem has a unique solution in classical physics (as dictated by the causality principle), the inverse problem might accept multiple solutions, which are models that equivalently predict the observations.

In MEG and EEG, the situation is critical: It has been demonstrated theoretically by von Helmoltz back in the XIXth century that the general inverse problem that consists in finding the sources of electromagnetic fields outside a volume conductor has an infinite number of solutions. This issue of non-uniqueness is not specific to MEG/EEG: Geophysicists, for instance, are also confronted with non-uniqueness in trying to determine the distribution of mass inside a planet by measuring its external gravity field. Hence, theoretically, an infinite number of source models equivalently fit any MEG and EEG observations. Fortunately, this question has been addressed with the mathematics of ill-posedness and inverse modeling, which formalize the necessity of bringing additional contextual information to complement a basic theoretical model.

Hence, the inverse problem is a true *modeling* problem. This has both philosophical and technical impacts on approaching the general theory and the practice of inverse problems (Tarantola, 2004). For instance, it will be important to obtain measures of uncertainty on the estimated values of the model parameters. Indeed, we want to avoid situations where a large set of values for some of the parameters produce models that equivalently account for the experimental observations. If such a situation arises, it is important to be able to question the quality of the experimental data and maybe, falsify the theoretical model.

Ill-posed inverse problems
The non-uniqueness of the solution is a situation where an inverse problem is said to be *ill-posed*. In the reciprocal situation where there is no value for the system's parameters to account for the observations, the data are said to be inconsistent (with the model). Another critical situation of ill-posedness is when the model parameters do not depend continuously on the data. This means that even tiny changes on the observations (e.g., by adding a small amount of noise) trigger major variations in the estimated values of the model parameters. This is critical to any experimental situations, and in MEG/EEG in particular, where estimated brain source amplitudes are sought not to "jump" dramatically from millisecond to millisecond.

The epistemology and early mathematics of ill-posedness have been paved by Jacques Hadamard (1902), where he somehow radically stated that problems that are not uniquely solvable are of no interest whatsoever. This statement is obviously unfair to important questions in science such as gravitometry, the backwards heat equation, and surely MEG/EEG source modeling.

The modern view on the mathematical treatment of ill-posed problems was initiated in the 1960s by Andrei N. Tikhonov and the introduction of the concept of *regularization*, which spectacularly formalized a *Solution of Ill-Posed Problems* (Tikhonov & Arsenin, 1977). Tikhonov suggested that some mathematical manipulations on the expression of ill-posed problems could make them turn well-posed in the sense that a solution would exist and possibly be unique. More recently, this approach found a more general and intuitive framework using the theory of probability, which naturally refers to the uncertainty and contextual a priori inherent to experimental sciences (see e.g., Tarantola, 2004).

As of 2010, more than 2000 journal articles referred in the U.S. National Library of Medicine publication database to the query "(MEG OR EEG) AND source." This abundant literature may be considered ironically as only a small sample of the infinite number of solutions to the problem, but it is rather a reflection of the many different ways MEG/EEG source modeling can be addressed by considering additional information of various natures.

Such a large number of reports on a single, technical issue has certainly been detrimental to the visibility and credibility of MEG/EEG as a brain mapping technique within the larger functional brain mapping audience, where the fMRI inverse problem is reduced to the well-posed estimation of the BOLD signal (though it is subject to major detection issues).

Today, it seems that a reasonable degree of technical maturity has been reached by electromagnetic brain imaging using MEG and/or EEG. All methods reduce to only a handful of classes of approaches, which are now well identified. Methodological research in MEG/EEG source modeling is now moving from the development of inverse estimation techniques to statistical appraisal and the identification of functional connectivity. In these respects, it is now joining the concerns shared by other functional brain imaging communities (Salmelin & Baillet, 2009).

Modeling the Electromagnetics of Head Tissues

Models of neural generators

MEG/EEG forward modeling requires two basic models that are bound to work together in a complementary manner: a physical model of neural sources, and a model that predicts how these sources generate electromagnetic fields outside the head. The canonical source model of the net primary intracellular currents within a neural assembly is the electric current dipole. The adequacy of a simple, equivalent current dipole (ECD) model as a building block of cortical current distributions was originally motivated by the shape of the scalp topography of MEG/EEG-evoked activity observed (Figure 7.8). This latter consists essentially of (multiple) so-called "dipolar distributions" of inward/outward magnetic fields and positive/negative electrical potentials. From a historical standpoint, dipole modeling applied to EEG and MEG surface data was a spin-off from the considerable research on quantitative electrocardiography, where dipolar field patterns are also omnipresent, and where the concept of ECD was contributed as early as the 1960s (Geselowitz, 1964).

However, although cardiac electrophysiology is well captured by a simple ECD model because there is not much questioning about source localization, the temporal dynamics and spatial complexity of brain activity may be more challenging. Alternatives to the ECD model exist in terms of the compact, parametric representation of distributed source currents. They consist either of higher-order source models called *multipoles* (Jerbi, Mosher, Baillet, & Leahy, 2002; Jerbi et al., 2004)—also derived from cardiographic research (Karp, Katila, Saarinen, Siltanen, & Varpula, 1980)—or densely distributed source models (Wang, Williamson, & Kaufman, 1992). In the latter case, a large number of ECDs are distributed in the entire brain volume or on the cortical surface, thereby forming a dense grid of elementary sites of activity, the intensity distribution of which is determined from the data.

To understand how these elementary source models generate signals that are measurable using external sensors, further modeling is required for the geometrical and electromagnetic properties of head tissues and the properties of the sensor array.

Modeling the sensor array

The details of the sensor geometry and pick-up technology are dependent on the manufacturer of the array. We may, however, summarize some fundamental principles in the following lines.

We have already reviewed how the sensor locations can be measured with state-of-the-art MEG and EEG equipment. If this information is missing, sensor locations may be roughly approximated from montage templates, but this will be detrimental to the accuracy of the source estimates (Schwartz, Poiseau, Lemoine, & Barillot, 1996). This is critical with MEG, as the subject is relatively free to position his/her head within the sensor array. Typical 10/20 EEG montages offer less degrees of freedom in that respect. Careful consideration of this geometrical registration issue using the solutions discussed above (HPI, head digitization, and anatomical fiducials) should provide satisfactory performances in terms of accuracy and robustness.

In EEG, the geometry of electrodes is considered as point-like. Advanced electrode modeling should include the true shape of the sensor (that is, a "flat" cylinder), but it is generally acknowledged that the spatial resolution of EEG measures is coarse enough to neglect this factor. One important piece of information, however, is the location of the reference electrode—that is, nasion, central, linked mastoids, and so forth—as it defines the physics of a given set of EEG measures. If this information is missing, the EEG data can be re-referenced with respect to the instantaneous arithmetic average potential (Niedermeyer & Silva, 2004).

In MEG, the sensing coils may also be considered point-like as a first approximation, though some analysis software packages include the exact sensor geometry in modeling. The computation of the total magnetic flux induction captured by the MEG sensors can be more accurately modeled by the geometric integration within their surface area. Gradiometer arrangements are readily modeled by applying the arithmetic operation they mimic, combining the fields modeled at each of its magnetometers.

Recent MEG systems include sophisticated online noise-attenuation techniques, such as higher-order gradient corrections and signal space projections. They contribute significantly to the basic model of data formation and therefore need to be taken into account (Nolte & Curio, 1999).

Modeling head tissues

Predicting the electromagnetic fields produced by an elementary source model at a given sensor array requires another modeling step, which concerns a large part of the MEG/EEG literature. Indeed, MEG/EEG "head modeling" studies the influence of the head geometry and electromagnetic properties of head tissues on the magnetic fields and electrical potentials measured outside the head.

Given a model of neural currents, the physics of MEG/EEG are ruled by the theory of electrodynamics (Feynman, 1964), which reduces in MEG to Maxwell's equations, and to Ohm's law in EEG, under quasistatic assumptions. These latter consider that the propagation delay of the electromagnetic waves from brain sources to the MEG/EEG sensors is negligible. The reason is the relative proximity of MEG/EEG sensors to the brain with respect to the expected frequency range of neural sources (up to 1 KHz) (Hämäläinen et al., 1993). This is a very important, simplifying assumption, which has immediate consequences on the computational aspects of MEG/EEG head modeling.

Indeed, the equations of electro and magnetostatics determine that there exist analytical, closed-form solutions to MEG/EEG head modeling when the head geometry is considered as spherical. Hence, the simplest, and consequently by far most popular, model of head geometry in MEG/EEG consists of concentric spherical layers: with one sphere per major category of head tissue (scalp, skull, cerebrospinal fluid, and brain).

The spherical head geometry has further attractive properties for MEG in particular. Quite remarkably indeed, spherical MEG head models are insensitive to the number of shells and their respective conductivity: A source within a single homogeneous sphere generates the same MEG fields as when located inside a multilayered set of concentric spheres with different conductivities. The reason for this is that conductivity only influences the distribution of secondary volume currents that circulate within the head volume and which are impressed by the original primary neural currents. The analytic formulation of Maxwell's equations in the spherical geometry shows that these secondary currents do not generate any magnetic field outside the volume conductor (Sarvas, 1987). Therefore, in MEG, only the location of the center of the spherical head geometry matters. The respective conductivity and radius of the spherical layers have no influence on the measured MEG fields. This is not the case in EEG, where the location, radii, and respective conductivity of each spherical shell influence the surface electrical potentials.

This relative sensitivity to tissue conductivity values is a general, important difference between EEG and MEG.

A spherical head model can be optimally adjusted to the head geometry, or restricted to regions of interest, for example, parieto-occipital regions for visual studies. Geometrical registration to MRI anatomical data improves the adjustment of the best-fitting sphere geometry to an individual head.

Another remarkable consequence of the spherical symmetry is that radially oriented brain currents produce no magnetic field outside a spherically symmetric volume conductor. For this reason, MEG signals from currents generated within the gyral crest or sulcal depth are attenuated, with respect to those generated by currents flowing perpendicularly to the sulcal walls. This is another important contrast between MEG and EEG's respective sensitivity to source orientation (Hillebrand & Barnes, 2002).

Finally, the amplitude of magnetic fields decreases faster than electrical potentials' with the distance from the generators to the sensors. Hence, it has been argued that MEG is less sensitive to mesial and subcortical brain structures than EEG. Experimental and modeling efforts have shown, however, that MEG can detect neural activity from deeper brain regions (Tesche, 1996; Attal et al., 2009).

Though spherical head models are convenient, they are poor approximations of the human head shape, which has some influence on the accuracy of MEG/EEG source estimation (Fuchs, Drenckhahn, Wischmann, & Wagner, 1998). More realistic head geometries have been investigated and all require solving Maxwell's equations using numerical methods. Boundary element (BEM) and finite element (FEM) methods are generic numerical approaches to the resolution of continuous equations over discrete space. In MEG/EEG, geometric tessellations of the different envelopes forming the head tissues need to be extracted from the individual MRI volume data to yield a realistic approximation of their geometry (Figure 7.10).

In BEM, the conductivity of tissues is supposed to be homogeneous and isotropic within each envelope. Therefore, each tissue envelope is delimited using surface boundaries defined over a triangulation of each of the segmented envelopes obtained from MRI.

FEM assumes that tissue conductivity may be anisotropic (such as the skull bone and the white matter); therefore, the primary geometric element needs to be an elementary volume, such as a tetrahedron (Marin, Guerin, Baillet, Garnero, & Meunier, 1998).

The main obstacle to a routine usage of BEM, and more pregnantly of FEM, is the surface or volume tessellation phase. Because the head geometry is

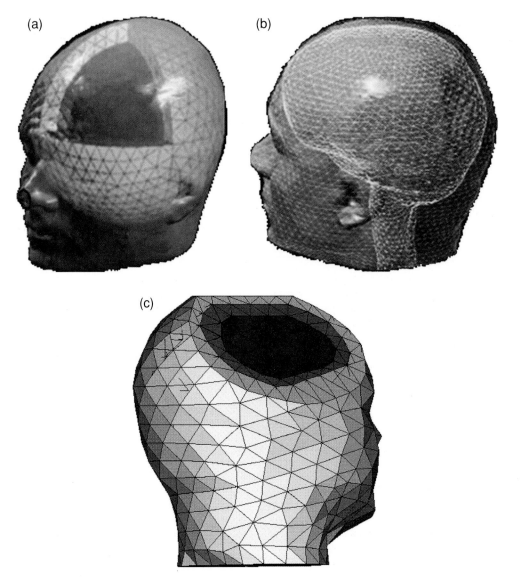

Fig. 7.10 Three approaches to MEG/EEG head modeling: (a) Spherical approximation of the geometry of head tissues, with analytical solution to Maxwell's and Ohm's equations; (b) Tessellated surface envelopes of head tissues obtained from the segmentation of MRI data; (c) An alternative to (b) using volume meshes—here built from tetrahedra. In both (b) and (c) Maxwell's and Ohm's equations need to be solved using numerical methods: BEM and FEM, respectively.

intricate and not always well defined from conventional MRI due to signal drop-outs and artifacts, automatic segmentation tools sometimes fail to identify some important tissue structures. The skull bone, for instance, is invisible on conventional T1-weighted MRI. Some image processing techniques, however, can estimate the shape of the skull envelope from high-quality T1-weighted MRI data (Dogdas, Shattuck, & Leahy, 2005). However, the skull bone is a highly anisotropic structure, which is difficult to model from MRI data. Recent progress using MRI diffusion-tensor imaging (DTI) helps

reveal the orientation of major white fiber bundles, which is also a major source of conductivity anisotropy (Haueisen et al., 2002).

Computation times for BEM and FEM remain extremely long (several hours on a conventional workstation), and are detrimental to rapid access to source localization following data acquisition. Both algorithmic (Huang, Mosher, & Leahy, 1999; Kybic, Clerc, Faugeras, Keriven, & Papadopoulo, 2005) and pragmatic (Ermer, Mosher, Baillet, & Leah, 2001; Darvas, Ermer, Mosher, & Leahy, 2006) solutions to this problem have, however, been proposed to make realistic head models more operational. They are available in some academic software packages.

Finally, let us close this section with an important caveat: Realistic head modeling is bound to the correct estimation of tissues conductivity values. Though solutions for impedance tomography using MRI (Tuch, Wedeen, Dale, George, & Belliveau, 2001) and EEG (Goncalves et al., 2003) have been suggested, they remain to be matured before entering the daily practice of MEG/EEG. So far, conductivity values from ex-vivo studies are conventionally integrated in most spherical and realistic head models (Geddes & Baker, 1967).

MEG/EEG Source Modeling

For clarity purposes, we will not attempt to formalize in a general, overly technical way, the classes of approaches to MEG/EEG source estimation. Rather, we will adopt a pragmatic standpoint, observing that two main chapels have developed quite separately: the localization and the imaging approaches respectively (Salmelin & Baillet, 2009). Our purpose here is to mark methodological landmarks and emphasize differences, similarities, and their respective assets.

Source localization vs. source imaging

The *localization* approach to MEG/EEG source estimation considers that brain activity at any time instant is generated by a relatively small number (a handful, at most) of brain regions. Each source is therefore represented by an elementary model, such as an ECD, that captures local distributions of neural currents. Ultimately, each elementary source is back projected or constrained to the subject's brain volume or an MRI anatomical template, for further interpretation. In a nutshell, localization models are essentially compact, in terms of number of generators involved and their surface extension (from point-like to small cortical surface patches).

The alternative *imaging* approaches to MEG/EEG source modeling were originally inspired by the plethoric research in image restoration and reconstruction in other domains (early digital imaging, geophysics, and other biomedical imaging techniques). The resulting image source models do not yield small sets of local elementary models but rather the distribution of "all" neural currents. This results in stacks of images where brain currents are estimated wherever elementary current sources had been previously positioned. This is typically achieved using a dense grid of current dipoles over the entire brain volume or limited to the cortical gray matter surface. These dipoles are fixed in location and generally, orientation, and are homologous to pixels in a digital image. The imaging procedure consists of the estimation of the amplitudes of all these elementary currents at once. Hence, contrary to the localization model, there is no intrinsic sense of distinct, active source regions per se. Explicit identification of activity issued from discrete brain regions usually necessitates complementary analysis, such as empirical or inference-driven amplitude thresholding, to discard elementary sources of non-significant contribution according to the statistical appraisal. In that respect, MEG/EEG source images are very similar in essence to the activation maps obtained in fMRI, with the benefit of time resolution, however (see Figure 7.11).

The following subsections further detail these two respective approaches.

Dipole fitting: The localization approach

As discussed above, early quantitative source localization research in electro and magnetocardiography had promoted the equivalent current dipole as a generic model of massive electrophysiological activity. Before efficient estimation techniques and software were available, electrophysiologists would empirically solve the MEG/EEG forward and inverse problems to characterize the neural generators responsible for experimental effects detected on the scalp sensors.

This approach is exemplified in Wood, Cohen, Cuffin, Yarita, and Allison (1985), where terms such as "waveform morphology" and "shape of scalp topography" are used to discuss the respective sources of MEG and EEG signals. This empirical approach to localization has considerably benefited from the constant increase in the number of sensors of MEG and EEG systems (Figure 7.4).

Indeed, surface interpolation techniques of sensor data have gained considerable popularity in MEG and EEG research (Perrin, Pernier, Bertrand, Giard, & Echallier, 1987): Investigators now can routinely access surface representations of their data on an approximation of the scalp surface—as a disc, a sphere—or on the very head surface extracted from the subject's MRI. Wood et al. (1985)—like many others—used the distance between the minimum and maximum magnetic distribution of the dipolar-looking field topography to infer the putative depth of a dipolar source model of the data.

Computational approaches to source localization attempt to mimic the talent of electrophysiologists, with a more quantitative benefit though. We have

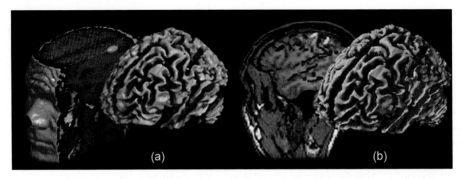

Fig. 7.11 Inverse modeling: the localization (a) vs. imaging (b) approaches. Source modeling through localization consists in decomposing the MEG/EEG generators in a handful of elementary source contributions; the simplest source model in this situation being the equivalent current dipole (ECD). This is illustrated here from experimental data testing the somatotopic organization of primary cortical representations of hand fingers. The parameters of the single ECD have been adjusted on the [20, 40] ms time window following stimulus onset. The ECD was found to localize along the contralateral central sulcus as revealed from the 3D rendering obtained after the source location has been registered to the individual anatomy. In the imaging approach, the source model is spatially distributed using a large number of ECDs. Here, a surface model of MEG/EEG generators was constrained to the individual brain surface extracted from T1-weighted MR images. Elemental source amplitudes are interpolated onto the cortex, which yields an image-like distribution of the amplitudes of cortical currents.

seen that the current dipole model has been adopted as the canonical equivalent generator of the electrical activity of a brain region considered as a functional entity. Localizing a current dipole in the head implies that 6 unknown parameters be estimated from the data: 3 for location per se, 2 for orientation, and 1 for amplitude. Therefore, characterizing the source model by a restricted number of parameters was considered as a possible solution to the ill-posed inverse problem and has been attractive to many MEG/EEG scientists. Without additional prior information besides the experimental data, the number of unknowns in the source estimation problem needs to be smaller than that of the instantaneous observations for the inverse problem to be well posed, in terms of uniqueness of a solution. Therefore, recent high-density systems with about 300 sensors would theoretically allow the unambiguous identification of 50 (300/6) dipolar sources; a number that would probably satisfy the modeling of brain activity in many neuroscience questions.

It appears, however, that most research studies using MEG/EEG source localization bear a more conservative profile, using many fewer dipole sources (typically <5). The reasons for this are both technical and proper to MEG/EEG brain signals as we shall now discuss.

Numerical approaches to the estimation of unknown source parameters are generally based on the widely used least-squares (LS) technique, which attempts to find the set of parameter values that minimize the (square of the) difference between observations and predictions from the model (Figure 7.9). Biosignals such as MEG/EEG traces are naturally contaminated by nuisance components (e.g., environmental noise and physiological artifacts), which shall not be explained by the model of brain activity. These components, however, contribute to some uncertainty on the estimation of the source model parameters. As a toy example, let us consider noise components that are independent and identically distributed on all 300 sensors. One would theoretically need to adjust as many additional free parameters in the inverse model as the number of noise components to fully account for all possible experimental (noisy) observations. However, we would end up handling a problem with 300 additional unknowns, adding to the original 300 source parameters, with only 300 data measures available.

Hence, and to avoid confusion between contributions from nuisances and signals of true interest, the MEG/EEG scientist needs to determine the respective parts of interest (the signal) versus perturbation (noise) in the experimental data. The preprocessing steps we have reviewed in the earlier sections of this chapter are therefore essential to identify, attenuate, or reject some of the nuisances in the data, prior to proceeding to inverse modeling.

Once the data has been preprocessed, the basic LS approach to source estimation aims at minimizing the deviation of the model predictions from the data: that is, the part in the observations that are left unexplained by the source model.

Let us suppose for the sake of further demonstration that the data is idealistically clean from any noisy disturbance, and that we are still willing to fit 50 dipoles (hence 300 parameters) to 300 data points. This is in theory an ideal case where there are as many unknowns as there are instantaneous data measures. However, we shall discuss that unknowns in the models do not all share the same type of dependency to the data. In the case of a dipole model, doubling the amplitude of the dipole doubles the amplitude of the sensor data. Dipole source amplitudes are therefore said to be linear parameters of the model. Dipole locations, however, do not depend linearly on the data: The amplitude of the sensor data is altered non-linearly with changes in depth and position of the elementary dipole source. It is considered that small, local displacements of brain activity can be efficiently modeled by a rotating dipole source at some fixed location. Though source orientation is a non-linear parameter, replacing a free-rotating dipole by a triplet of 3 orthogonal dipoles with fixed orientations is a way to express any arbitrary source orientation by a set of 3—hence, linear—amplitude parameters. Non-linear parameters are more difficult to estimate in practice than linear unknowns. The optimal set of source parameters defined from the LS criterion exists and is theoretically unique when sources are constrained to be dipolar (see e.g., Badia, 2004). However, in practice, non-linear optimization may be trapped by suboptimal values of the source parameters corresponding to a so-called local minimum of the LS objective. Therefore, the practice of multiple dipole fitting is very sensitive to initial conditions, for example, the values assigned to the unknown parameters to initiate the search, and to the number of sources in the model, which increases the possibility of the optimization procedure to be trapped in local, suboptimal LS minima.

In summary, even though localizing a number of elementary dipoles corresponding to the amount of instantaneous observations is theoretically well posed, we are facing two issues that will drive us to reconsider the source-fitting problem in practice: 1) The risk of overfitting the data, meaning that the inverse model may account for the noise components in the observations, and 2) nonlinear searches that tend to be trapped in local minima of the LS objective.

A general rule of thumb when the data is noisy and the optimization principle is ruled by nonlinear dependency is to keep the complexity of the estimation as low as possible. Taming complexity starts with reducing the number of unknowns so that the estimation problem becomes overdetermined.

In experimental sciences, overdeterminacy is not as critical as underdeterminacy. From a pragmatic standpoint, supplementary sensors provide additional information and allow the selection of subsets of channels, which may be less contaminated by noise and artifacts.

The early MEG/EEG literature is abundant in studies reporting on single dipole source models. The somatotopy of primary somatosensory brain regions (Okada, Tanenbaum, Williamson, & Kaufman, 1984; Meunier, Lehéricy, Garnero, & Vidailhet, 2003), primary, tonotopic auditory (Zimmerman, Reite, & Zimmerman, 1981), and visual (Lehmann, Darcey, & Skrandies, 1982) responses are examples of such studies where the single dipole model contributed to the better temporal characterization of primary brain responses.

Later components of evoked fields and potentials usually necessitate more elementary source to be fitted. However, this may be detrimental to the numerical stability and significance of the inverse model. The spatio-temporal dipole model was therefore developed to localize the sources of scalp waveforms that were assumed to be generated by multiple and overlapping brain activations (Scherg & Cramon, 1985). This spatio-temporal model and associated optimization expect that an elementary source is active over a certain duration—with amplitude modulations— while remaining at the same location with the same orientation. This is typical of the introduction of prior information in the MEG/EEG source estimation problem, and this will be further developed in the imaging techniques discussed below.

The number of dipoles to be adjusted is also a model parameter that needs to be estimated. However, it leads to difficult, and usually impractical, optimization (Waldorp, Huizenga, Nehorai, Grasman, & Molenaar, 2005). Therefore, the number of elementary sources in the model is often qualitatively assessed by expert users, which may question the reproducibility of such user-dependent analyses. Hence, special care should be brought to the evaluation of the stability and robustness of the estimated source models. With all that in mind, source localization techniques have proven to be effective, even on complex experimental paradigms (see e.g., Helenius, Parviainen, Paetau, & Salmelin, 2009).

Signal classification and spatial filtering techniques are efficient alternative approaches in that respect. They have gained considerable momentum in the MEG/EEG community in recent years. They are discussed in the following subsection.

Scanning techniques: Spatial filters, beamformers, and signal classifiers

The inherent difficulties to source localization with multiple generators and noisy data have led signal processors to develop alternative approaches, most notably in the glorious field of radar and sonar in the 1970s. Rather than attempting to identify discrete sets of sources by adjusting their nonlinear location parameters, scanning techniques have emerged and proceeded by systematically sifting through the brain space to evaluate how a predetermined elementary source model would fit the data at every voxel of the brain volume. For this local model evaluation to be specific of the brain location being scanned, contributions from possible sources located elsewhere in the brain volume need to be blocked. Hence, these techniques are known as *spatial-filters* and *beamformers* (the simile is a virtual beam being directed and "listening" exclusively at some brain region).

These techniques have triggered tremendous interest and applications in array signal processing and have percolated the MEG/EEG community at several instances (e.g., Spencer, Leahy, Mosher, & Lewis, 1992; Hillebrand, Singh, Holliday, Furlong & Barnes 2005). At each point of the brain grid, a narrow-band spatial filter is formed and evaluates the contribution to data from an elementary source model—such as a single or a triplet of current dipoles—while contributions from other brain regions are ideally muted, or at least attenuated. Veen and Buckley (1988) provide a detailed technical introduction to beamformers and excellent further reading.

It is sometimes claimed that beamformers do not solve an inverse problem: This is a bit overstated. Indeed, spatial filters do require a source and a forward model that will be both confronted to the observations. Beamformers scan the entire expected source space and systematically test the prediction of the source and forward models with respect to observations. These predictions compose a distributed score map, which should not be misinterpreted as a current density map. More technically—though no details are given here—the forward model needs to be inverted by the beamformer as well. It only proceeds iteratively by sifting through each source grid point and estimating the output of the corresponding spatial filter. Hence, beamformers and spatial filters are truly avatars of inverse modeling.

Beamforming is therefore a convenient method to translate the source localization problem into a signal detection issue. As every method that tackles a complex estimation problem, there are drawbacks to the technique:

1. Beamformers depend on the covariance statistics of the noise in the data. These latter may be estimated from the data through sample statistics. However, the number of independent data samples that are necessary for the robust—and numerically stable—estimation of covariance statistics is proportional to the square of the number of data channels, that is, of sensors. Hence beamformers ideally require long, stationary episodes of data, such as sweeps of ongoing, unaveraged data and experimental conditions where behavioral stationarity ensures some form of statistical stationarity in the data (e.g., ongoing movements). Cheyne, Bakhtazad, and Gaetz (2006) have suggested that event-related brain responses can be well captured by beamformers using sample statistics estimated across single trials.

2. They are more sensitive to errors in the head model. The filter outputs are typically equivalent to local estimates of SNR. However, this latter is not homogeneously distributed everywhere in the brain volume: MEG/EEG signals from activity in deeper brain regions or gyral generators in MEG have weaker SNR than in the rest of the brain. The consequence is side lobe leakages from interfering sources nearby, which impede filter selectivity and therefore, the specificity of source detection (Wax & Anu, 1996).

3. Beamformers may be fooled by simultaneous activations occurring in brain regions outside the filter pass-band that are highly correlated with source signals within the pass-band. External sources are interpreted as interferences by the beamformer, which blocks the signals of interest because they bear the same sample statistics as the interference.

Signal processors had long identified these issues and consequently developed multiple signal classification (MUSIC) as an alternative technique (Schmidt, 1986). MUSIC assumes that signal and noise components in the data are uncorrelated. Strong theoretical results in information theory show that these components live in separate, high-dimensional data subspaces, which can be identified using, for example, a PCA of the data time series (Golub, 1996). Mosher, Baillet, and Leahy (1999) provide an extensive review of signal classification approaches to MEG and EEG source localization.

However, the practical aspects of MUSIC and its variations remain limited by their sensitivity in the accurate definition of the respective signal and noise subspaces. These techniques may be fooled by background brain activity, which signals share similar properties with the event-related responses of interest. An interesting side application of MUSIC-like powerful discrimination ability, though, has been developed in epilepsy spike-sorting (Ossadtchi et al., 2004).

In summary, spatial-filters, beamformers, and signal classification approaches bring us closer to a distributed representation of the brain electrical activity. As a caveat, the results generated by these techniques are not an estimation of the current density everywhere in the brain. They represent a score map of a source model—generally a current dipole—that is evaluated at the points of a pre-defined spatial lattice, which sometimes leads to misinterpretations. The localization issue now becomes a signal detection problem within the score map (Mosher, Baillet, & Leahy, 2003). The imaging approaches we are about to introduce now, push this detection problem further by estimating the brain current density globally.

Distributed source imaging
Source imaging approaches have developed in parallel to the techniques discussed above. Imaging source models consist of distributions of elementary sources, generally with fixed locations and orientations, which amplitudes are estimated at once. MEG/EEG source images represent estimations of the global neural current intensity maps, distributed within the entire brain volume or constrained at the cortical surface.

Source image supports consist of either a 3D lattice of voxels or of the nodes of the triangulation of the cortical surface. These latter may be based on a template, or preferably obtained from the subject's individual MRI and confined to a mask of the grey matter. Multiple academic software packages perform the necessary segmentation and tessellation processes from high-contrast T1-weighted MR image volumes.

As discussed earlier in this chapter, the cortically constrained image model derives from the assumption that MEG/EEG data originates essentially from large cortical assemblies of pyramidal cells, with currents generated from post-synaptic potentials flowing orthogonally to the local cortical surface. This orientation constraint can either be strict (Dale & Sereno, 1993) or relaxed by authorizing some controlled deviation from the surface normal (Lin, Belliveau, Dale, & Hamalainen, 2006).

In both cases, reasonable spatial sampling of the image space requires several thousands (typically 10,000) of elementary sources, as depicted Figure 7.12. Consequently, though the imaging inverse problem consists in estimating only linear parameters, it is dramatically underdetermined.

Just like in the context of source localization where for example, the number of sources is a restrictive prior as a remedy to ill-posedness, imaging models need to be complemented by a priori information. This is properly formulated with the mathematics of regularization as we shall now briefly review.

Adding priors to the imaging model can be adequately formalized in the context of Bayesian inference where solutions to inverse modeling satisfy both the fit to observations—given some probabilistic model of the nuisances—and additional priors. From a parameter estimation perspective, the maximum of the a posteriori probability distribution of source intensity, given the observations could be considered as the "best possible model." This maximum a posteriori (MAP) estimate has been extremely successful in the digital image restoration and reconstruction communities. Geman and Geman (1984) is a masterpiece reference of the genre. The MAP is obtained in Bayesian statistics through the optimization of the mixture of the likelihood of the noisy data—that is, of the predictive power of a given source model—with the a priori probability of a given source model.

We do not want to detail the mathematics of Bayesian inference any further here as this would reach outside the objectives of this chapter. Specific recommended further reading includes Demoment (1989) for a Bayesian discussion on regularization and Baillet, Mosher, and Leahy (2001) for an introduction to MEG/EEG imaging methods, also in the Bayesian framework.

From a practical standpoint, the priors on the source image models may take multiple faces: promote current distributions with high spatial and temporal smoothness; penalize models with currents of unrealistic, non-physiologically plausible amplitudes; favor the adequation with an fMRI activation maps; or prefer source image models made of piecewise homogeneous active regions, and so forth. An appealing benefit from well-chosen priors is that it may ensure the uniqueness of the optimal solution to the imaging inverse problem, despite its original underdeterminacy.

Because relevant priors for MEG/EEG imaging models are plethoric, it is important to understand

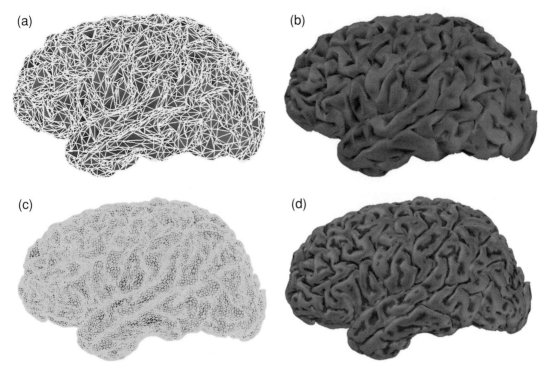

Fig. 7.12 The cortical surface, tessellated at two resolutions, using: (a,b) 10,034 vertices (20,026 triangles with 10 mm^2 average surface area) and (c,d) 79,124 vertices (158,456 triangles with 1.3 mm^2 average surface area).

that the associated source estimation methods usually belong to the same technical background. Also, the selection of image priors can be seen as arbitrary and subjective an issue as the selection of dipoles in the source localization techniques we have reviewed previously. Comprehensive solutions for this model selection issue are now emerging and will be briefly reviewed further below.

The free parameters of the imaging model are the amplitudes of the elementary source currents distributed on the brain's geometry. The non-linear parameters (e.g., the elementary source locations) now become fixed priors as provided by anatomical information. The model estimation procedure and the very existence of a unique solution strongly depend on the mathematical nature of the image prior.

A widely-used prior in the field of image reconstruction considers that the expected source amplitudes be as small as possible on average. This is the well-described minimum-norm (MN) model. Technically speaking, we are referring to the L2-norm; the objective cost function ruling the model estimation is quadratic in the source amplitudes, with a unique analytical solution (Tarantola, 2004). The computational simplicity and uniqueness of the

MN model has been very attractive in MEG/EEG early on (Wang et al., 1992).

The basic MN estimate is problematic though, as it tends to favor the most superficial brain regions (e.g., the gyral crowns) and underestimate contributions from deeper source areas (such as sulcal fundi) (Fuchs, Wagner, Köhler, & Wischmann, 1999).

As a remedy, a slight alteration of the basic MN estimator consists of weighting each elementary source amplitude by the inverse of the norm of its contribution to sensors. Such depth weighting yields a weighted MN (WMN) estimate, which still benefits from uniqueness and linearity in the observations as the basic MN (Lin, Witzel, et al., 2006).

Despite their robustness to noise and simple computation, it is relevant to question the neurophysiological validity of MN priors. Indeed–though reasonably intuitive–there is no evidence that neural currents would systematically match the principle of minimal energy. Some authors have speculated that a more physiologically relevant prior would be that the norm of spatial derivatives (e.g., surface or volume gradient or Laplacian) of the current map be minimized (see LORETA method in Pascual-Marqui, Michel, and Lehmann (1994)). As a general rule of thumb however, all MN-based source imaging approaches overestimate the smoothness of the spatial distribution of neural currents. Quantitative and qualitative empirical evidence, however, demonstrate spatial discrimination of reasonable range at the sub-lobar brain scale (Darvas, Pantazis, Kucukaltun-Yildirim, & Leahy, 2004; Sergent et al., 2005) (Figure 7.13).

Most of the recent literature in regularized imaging models for MEG/EEG consists of struggling to improve the spatial resolution of the MN-based models (see Baillet, Mosher, & Leahy, 2001, for a review) or to reduce the degree of arbitrariness involved in selecting a generic source model a priori (Mattout, Phillips, Penny, Rugg, & Friston, 2006; Stephan, Penny, Daunizeau, Moran, & Friston, 2009). This results in notable improvements in theoretical performances, though with higher computational demands and practical optimization issues.

As a general principle, we are facing the dilemma of knowing that all priors about the source images are certainly abusive, hence that the inverse model is approximative, while hoping it is just not *too* approximative. This discussion is recurrent in the general context of estimation theory and model selection as we shall discuss in the next section.

Appraisal of MEG/EEG Source Models

Throughout this chapter, we have been dealing with modeling, and modeling implies dealing with uncertainty. MEG/EEG source estimation has uncertainty everywhere: Data are complex and contaminated with various nuisances, source models are simplistic, head models have approximated geometries and conductivity properties, the choice of priors has its share of subjectivity, and so forth.

It is therefore reasonable to question how sensitive the numerical methods at stake are to these possible sources of errors and bias. This concerns the appraisal of the source model, which general methodology has been adapted to MEG/EEG just recently and is now achieving significant maturity.

Confidence intervals. We have discussed how fitting dipoles to a data time segment may be quite sensitive to initial conditions and therefore, subjective. Similarly, imaging source models suggest that each brain location is active, potentially. It is therefore

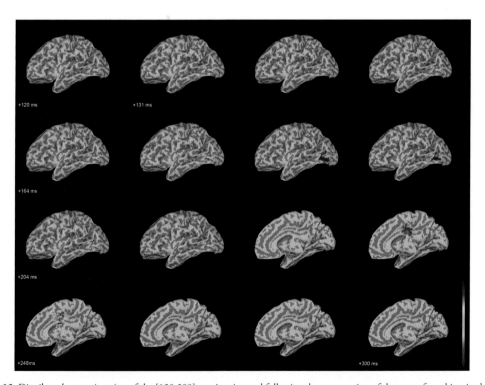

Fig. 7.13 Distributed source imaging of the [120,300] ms time interval following the presentation of the target face object in the visual RSVP oddball paradigm described in Fig. 7.6. The images show a slightly smoothed version of one participant's cortical surface. Colors encode the contrast of MEG source amplitudes between responses to target versus control faces. Visual responses are detected by 120ms and rapidly propagate anteriorly. By 250 ms onwards, strong anterior mesial responses are detected in the cingular cortex. These latter are the main contributors of the brain response to target detection.

important to evaluate the confidence one might acknowledge to a given model. In other words, we are now looking for error bars that would define a confidence interval about the estimated values of a source model.

Signal processors have developed a principled approach to what they have coined as "detection and estimation theories" (Kay, 1993). The main objective consists of understanding how certain one can be about the estimated parameters of a model, given a model for the noise in the data. The basic approach consists of considering the estimated parameters (e.g., source locations) as distributed through random variables. Parametric estimation of error bounds on the source parameters consists of estimating their bias and variance.

Bias is an estimation of the distance between the true value and the expectancy of estimated parameter values due to perturbations. The definition of variance follows immediately. Cramer-Rao lower bounds (CRLB) on the estimator's variance can be explicitly computed using an analytical solution to the forward model and given a model for perturbations (e.g., with distribution under a normal law). In a nutshell, the tighter the CRLB, the more confident one can be about the estimated values. Mosher, Spencer, Leahy, and Lewis, (1993) have investigated this approach using extensive Monte-Carlo simulations, which evidenced a resolution of a few millimeters for single dipole models. These results were later confirmed by phantom studies (Leahy, Mosher, Spencer, Huang, & Lewine, 1998; Baillet, Riera, et al., 2001). CRLB increased markedly for two-dipole models, thereby demonstrating their extreme sensitivity and instability.

Recently, non-parametric approaches to the determination of error bounds have greatly benefited from the commensurable increase in computational power. Jack-knife and bootstrap techniques proved to be efficient and powerful tools to estimate confidence intervals on MEG/EEG source parameters, regardless of the nature of perturbations and of the source model.

These techniques are all based on data resampling approaches and have proven to be exact and efficient when a large-enough number of experimental replications are available (Davison & Hinkley, 1997). This is typically the case in MEG/EEG experiments where protocols are designed on multiple trials. If we are interested, for example, in knowing about the confidence interval on a source location in a single-dipole model from evoked averaged data, the bootstrap will generate a large number (typically >500)

of surrogate average datasets, by randomly choosing trials from the original set of trials and averaging them all together. Because the trial selection is random and from the complete set of trials, the corresponding sample distribution of the estimated parameter values is proven to converge toward the true distribution. A pragmatic approach to the definition of a confidence interval thereby consists in identifying the interval containing, for example, 95% of the resampled estimates (see Figure 7.14; Baryshnikov, Veen, & Wakai, 2004; Darvas et al., 2005; McIntosh & Lobaugh, 2004).

Statistical inference

Questions like: "How different is the dipole location between these two experimental conditions?" and "Are source amplitudes larger in such condition than in a control condition?" belong to statistical inference from experimental data. The basic problem of interest here is hypothesis testing, which is supposed to potentially invalidate a model under investigation. Here, the *model* must be understood at a higher hierarchical level than when talking about, for example, an MEG/EEG source model. It is supposed to address the neuroscience question that has motivated data acquisition and the experimental design (Guilford & Fruchter, 1978).

In the context of MEG/EEG, the population samples that will support the inference are either trials or subjects, for hypothesis testing at the individual and group levels, respectively.

As in the case of the estimation of confidence intervals, both parametric and non-parametric approaches to statistical inference can be considered. There is no space here for a comprehensive review of tools based on parametric models. They have been and still are extensively studied in the fMRI and PET communities—and recently adapted to EEG and MEG (Kiebel, Tallon-Baudry, & Friston, 2005)—and popularized with software toolboxes such as SPM (Friston, Ashburner, Kiebel, Nichols, & Penny, 2007).

Non-parametric approaches such as permutation tests have emerged for statistical inference applied to neuroimaging data (Nichols & Holmes, 2002; Pantazis, Nichols, Baillet, & Leahy, 2005). Rather than applying transformations to the data to secure the assumption of normally-distributed measures, non-parametric statistical tests take the data as they are and are robust to departures from normal distributions.

In brief, hypothesis testing forms an assumption about the data that the researcher is interested about

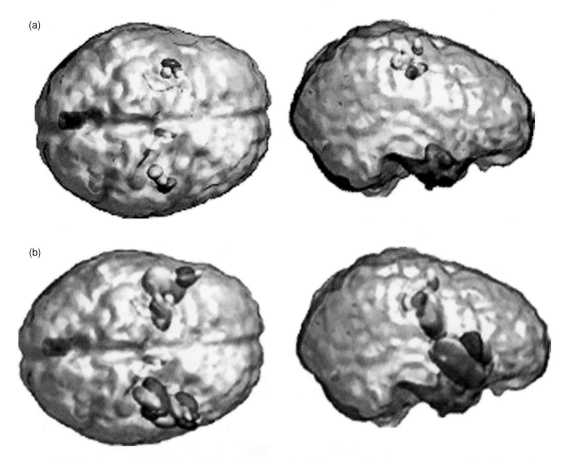

(a)

(b)

Fig. 7.14 The bootstrap procedure yields nonparametric estimates of confidence intervals on source parameters. This is illustrated here with data from a study of the somatotopic cortical representation of hand fingers. Ellipsoids represent the resulting 95% confidence intervals on the location of the ECD, as a model of the 40 ms (a) and 200 ms (b) brain response following hand-finger stimulation. Ellipsoid gray levels encode for the stimulated fingers. While in (a) the respective confidence ellipsoids do not overlap between fingers, they considerably increase in volume for the secondary responses in (b), thereby demonstrating that a single ECD is not a proper model of brain currents at this later latency. Note similar evaluations may be drawn from imaging models using the same resampling methodology. These considerations naturally lead us to statistical inference, which questions hypothesis testing.

questioning. This basic hypothesis is called the null hypothesis, H0, and is traditionally formulated to translate no significant finding in the data, for example, "There are no differences in the MEG/EEG source model between two experimental conditions." The statistical test will express the significance of this hypothesis and evaluate the probability that the statistics in question would be obtained just by chance. In other words, the data from both conditions are interchangeable under the H0 hypothesis. This is literally what permutation testing does. It computes the sample distribution of estimated parameters under the null hypothesis and verifies whether a statistic of the original parameter estimates was likely to be generated under this law.

We shall now review rapidly the principles of multiple hypotheses testing from the same sample of measurements, which induces errors when multiple parameters are being tested at once. This issue pertains to statistical inference both at the individual and group levels. Samples therefore consist of repetitions (trials) of the same experiment in the same subject, or of the results from the same experiment within a set of subjects, respectively. This distinction is not crucial at this point. We shall, however, point at the issue of spatial normalization of the brain across subjects either by applying normalization procedures (Ashburner & Friston, 1997) or by the definition of a generic coordinate system onto the cortical surface (Fischl, Sereno, & Dale, 1999; Mangin et al., 2004) (Figure 7.5).

The outcome of a test will evaluate the probability p that the statistics computed from the data samples be issued from complete chance as expressed by the null hypothesis. The investigator needs to fix a threshold on p a priori, above which H0 cannot be rejected, thereby corroborating H0. Tests are designed to be computed once from the data sample so that the error—called the type I error—consisting in accepting H0 while it is invalid stays below the predefined p-value.

If the same data sample is used several times for several tests, we multiply the chances that we commit a type I error. This is particularly critical when running tests on sensor or source amplitudes of an imaging model as the number of tests is on the order of 100 and even 10,000, respectively. In this latter case, a 5% error over 10,000 tests is likely to generate 500 occurrences of false positives by wrongly rejecting H0. This is obviously not desirable and this is the reason why this so-called family-wise error rate (FWER) should be kept under control.

Parametric approaches to address this issue have been elaborated using the theory of random fields and have gained tremendous popularity through the SPM software (Friston et al., 2007). These techniques have been extended to electromagnetic source imaging but are less robust to departure from normality than nonparametric solutions. The FWER in nonparametric testing can be controlled by using, for example, the statistics of the maximum over the entire source image or topography at the sensor level (Pantazis et al., 2005).

The emergence of statistical inference solutions adapted to MEG/EEG has brought electromagnetic source localization and imaging to a considerable degree of maturity that is quite comparable to other neuroimaging techniques (see Figure 7.15 for an example). Most software solutions now integrate sound solutions to statistical inference for MEG and EEG data, and this is a field that is still growing rapidly.

Emergent approaches for model selection
While there is a long tradition of considering inverse modeling as an optimization problem—that is, designate *the* solution to an inverse problem as the source model corresponding to the putative global maximum of some adequacy functional—there are situations where, for empirical and/or theoretical reasons, the number of possible solutions is just too large to ensure this goal can be reached. This kind of situation calls for a paradigm shift in the approach

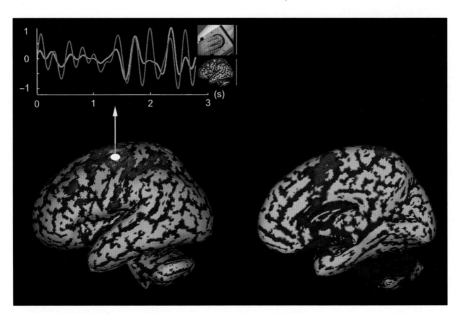

Fig. 7.15 MEG functional connectivity and statistical inference at the group level illustrated: Jerbi et al. (2007) have revealed a cortical functional network involved in hand movement coordination at low frequency (4Hz). The statistical group inference first consisted of fitting for each trial in the experiment, a distributed source model constrained to the individual anatomy of each of the 14 subjects involved. The brain area with maximum coherent activation with instantaneous hand speed was identified within the contralateral sensorimotor area (white dot). The traces at the top illustrate excellent coherence in the [3,5]Hz range between these measurements (hand speed in green and M1 motor activity in blue). Secondly, the search for brain areas with activity in significant coherence with M1 revealed a larger distributed network of regions. All subjects were coregistered to a brain surface template in Talairach normalized space with the corresponding activations interpolated onto the template surface. A nonparametric t-test contrast was completed using permutations between rest and task conditions (p<0.01).

to inverse modeling, which animates vivid discussions in the concerned scientific communities (Tarantola, 2006).

In MEG and EEG more specifically, we have admitted that picking a number of dipoles for localization purposes or an imaging prior to insure uniqueness of the solution has its (large) share of arbitrariness. Just like nonparametric statistical methods have benefited from the tremendous increase of cheap computational power, Monte-Carlo simulation methods are powerful computational numerical approaches to the general problem of model selection.

Indeed, a relevant question would be to let the data help the researcher decide whether any element from a general class of models would properly account for the data, with possibly predefined confidence intervals on the admissible model parameters.

These approaches are currently emerging from the MEG/EEG literature and have considerable potential (David et al., 2006; Mattout et al., 2006; Daunizeau et al., 2006). It is likely, however, that the critical ill-posedness of the source modeling problem be detrimental to the efficiency of establishing tight bounds on the admissible model parameters. Further, these techniques are still extremely demanding in terms of computational resources.

Conclusions: A Pragmatic Point of View

Throughout this chapter, we have stumbled into many pitfalls imposed by the ill-posed nature of the MEG/EEG source estimation problem. We have tried to give a pragmatic point of view on these difficulties.

It is indeed quite striking that despite all these shortcomings, MEG/EEG source analysis is able to reveal exquisite relative spatial resolution when localization approaches are used appropriately, and—though being of relative limited absolute spatial resolution—imaging models help the researchers tell a story on the cascade of brain events that have been occurring in controlled experimental conditions. From one millisecond to the next, imaging models are able to reveal tiny alterations in the topography of brain activations at the scale of a few millimeters.

An increasing number of groups from other neuroimaging modalities have come to realize that beyond mere cartography, temporal and oscillatory brain responses are essential keys to the understanding and interpretation of the basic mechanisms ruling information processing amongst neural assemblies. The growing number of EEG systems installed in MR magnets and the steady increase in MEG equipments demonstrate an active and dynamic scientific community, with exciting perspectives for the future of multidisciplinary brain research.

References

Ashburner, J. & Friston, K. (1997). Multimodal image coregistration and partitioning–a unified framework. *Neuroimage*, *6*(3), 209–217.

Astolfi, L., Cincotti, F., Babiloni, C., Carducci, F., Basilisco, A., & Rossini, P. M. (2005). Estimation of the cortical connectivity by high-resolution EEG and structural equation modeling: Simulations and application to finger tapping data. *IEEE Trans Biomed Eng*, *52*(5), 757–768.

Attal, Y., Bhattacharjee, M., Yelnik, J., Cottereau, B., Lefèvre, J., & Okada, Y. (2009). Modelling and detecting deep brain activity with MEG and EEG. *IRBM–Biomed. Eng. & Res.*, *30*(3), 133–138.

Badia, A. E. (2004). Summary of some results on an EEG inverse problem. *Neurol Clin Neurophysiol*, *2004*, 102.

Baillet, S., Mosher, J., & Leahy, R. (2001). Electromagnetic brain mapping. *IEEE Signal Processing Magazine*, *18*(6), 14–30.

Baillet, S., Riera, J. J., Marin, G., Mangin, J. F., Aubert, J., & Garnero, L. (2001). Evaluation of inverse methods and head models for EEG source localization using a human skull phantom. *Phys Med Biol*, *46*(1), 77–96.

Bandettini, P. A. (2009). What's new in neuroimaging methods? *Ann N Y Acad Sci*, *1156*, 260–293.

Baryshnikov, B. V., Veen, B. D. V., & Wakai, R. T. (2004). Maximum likelihood dipole fitting in spatially colored noise. *Neurol Clin Neurophysiol*, *2004*, 53.

Bassett, D. S. & Bullmore, E. T. (2009). Human brain networks in health and disease. *Curr Opin Neurol*, *22*(4), 340–347.

Baule, G. & McFee, R. (1963). Detection of the magnetic field of the heart. *Am Heart J*, *66*, 95–96.

Biermann-Ruben, K., Kessler, K., Jonas, M., Siebner, H. R., Bäumer, T., & Münchau, A. (2008). Right hemisphere contributions to imitation tasks. *Eur J Neurosci*, *27*(7), 1843–1855.

Bohórquez, J. & Ozdamar, O. (2008). Generation of the 40-hz auditory steady-state response (assr) explained using convolution. *Clin Neurophysiol*, *119*(11), 2598–2607.

Cheyne, D., Bakhtazad, L., & Gaetz, W. (2006). Spatiotemporal mapping of cortical activity accompanying voluntary movements using an event-related beamforming approach. *Human Brain Mapping*, *27*(3), 213–229.

Cimatti, Z., Schwartz, D. P., Bourdain, F., Meunier, S., Bleton, J. P., & Vidailhet, M. (2007). Time-frequency analysis reveals decreased high-frequency oscillations in writer's cramp. *Brain*, *130*(Pt 1), 198–205.

Clementz, B. A., Barber, S. K., & Dzau, J. R. (2002). Knowledge of stimulus repetition affects the magnitude and spatial distribution of low-frequency event-related brain potentials. *Audiol Neurootol*, *7*(5), 303–314.

Dale, A. & Sereno, M. (1993). Improved localization of cortical activity by combining EEG and MEG with MRI cortical surface reconstruction: A linear approach. *Journal of Cognitive Neuroscience*, *5*, 162–176.

Darvas, F., Ermer, J. J., Mosher, J. C., & Leahy, R. M. (2006). Generic head models for atlas-based EEG source analysis. *Hum Brain Mapp*, *27*(2), 129–143.

Darvas, F., Pantazis, D., Kucukaltun-Yildirim, E., & Leahy, R. M. (2004). Mapping human brain function with MEG and EEG: methods and validation. *Neuroimage, 23*, S289–S299.

Darvas, F., Rautiainen, M., Pantazis, D., Baillet, S., Benali, H., & Mosher, J. C. (2005). Investigations of dipole localization accuracy in MEG using the bootstrap. *Neuroimage, 25*(2), 355–368.

Daunizeau, J., Mattout, J., Clonda, D., Goulard, B., Benali, H., & Lina, J. M. (2006). Bayesian spatio-temporal approach for EEG source reconstruction: Conciliating ECD and distributed models. *IEEE Trans Biomed Eng, 53*(3), 503–516.

David, O. & Friston, K. J. (2003). A neural mass model for MEG/EEG: Coupling and neuronal dynamics. *Neuroimage, 20*(3), 1743–1755.

David, O., Kiebel, S. J., Harrison, L. M., Mattout, J., Kilner, J. M., & Friston, K. J. (2006). Dynamic causal modeling of evoked responses in EEG and MEG. *Neuroimage, 30*(4), 1255–1272.

Davison, A. C. A. C. & Hinkley, D. V. (1997). *Bootstrap methods and their application.* Cambridge: Cambridge University Press.

Deco, G., Jirsa, V. K., Robinson, P. A., Breakspear, M., & Friston, K. (2008). The dynamic brain: From spiking neurons to neural masses and cortical fields. *PLoS Comput Biol, 4*(8), e1000092.

Delorme, A., Sejnowski, T., & Makeig, S. (2007). Enhanced detection of artifacts in EEG data using higher-order statistics and independent component analysis. *Neuroimage, 34*(4), 1443–1449.

Demoment, G. (1989). Image reconstruction and restoration: Overview of common estimation structures and problems. *IEEE Transactions on Acoustics, Speech, and Signal Processing* [see also IEEE Transactions on Signal Processing], *37*(12), 2024–2036.

Ding, J., Sperling, G., & Srinivasan, R. (2006). Attentional modulation of ssvep power depends on the network tagged by the flicker frequency. *Cereb Cortex, 16*(7), 1016–1029.

Dogdas, B., Shattuck, D. W., & Leahy, R. M. (2005). Segmentation of skull and scalp in 3-d human MRI using mathematical morphology. *Hum Brain Mapp, 26*(4), 273–285.

Dux, P. E. & Marois, R. (2009). The attentional blink: A review of data and theory. *Atten Percept Psychophys, 71*(8), 1683–1700.

Eijsden, P. van, Hyder, F., Rothman, D. L., & Shulman, R. G. (2009). Neurophysiology of functional imaging. *Neuroimage, 45*(4), 1047–1054.

Ermer, J. J., Mosher, J. C., Baillet, S., & Leah, R. M. (2001). Rapidly recomputable EEG forward models for realistic head shapes. *Phys Med Biol, 46*(4), 1265–1281.

Feynman, R. P. (1964). *The Feynman lectures on physics (volume 2).* Reading, Massachusetts: Addison-Wesley.

Fischl, B., Sereno, M. I., & Dale, A. M. (1999). Cortical surface-based analysis. ii: Inflation, flattening, and a surface–based coordinate system. *Neuroimage, 9*(2), 195–207.

Fox, M. D. & Raichle, M. E. (2007). Spontaneous fluctuations in brain activity observed with functional magnetic resonance imaging. *Nat Rev Neurosci, 8*(9), 700–711.

Friston, K. (2009a). Causal modelling and brain connectivity in functional magnetic resonance imaging. *PLoS Biol, 7*(2), e33.

Friston, K. J. (2009b). Modalities, modes, and models in functional neuroimaging. *Science, 326*(5951), 399–403.

Friston, K., Ashburner, J., Kiebel, S., Nichols, T., & Penny, W. (Eds.) (2007). *Statistical parametric mapping: The analysis of functional brain images* Salt Lake City: Academic Press.

Fuchs, M., Drenckhahn, R., Wischmann, H. A., & Wagner, M. (1998). An improved boundary element method for realistic volume-conductor modeling. *IEEE Trans Biomed Eng, 45*(8), 980–997.

Fuchs, M., Wagner, M., Köhler, T., & Wischmann, H. A. (1999). Linear and nonlinear current density reconstructions. *J Clin Neurophysiol, 16*(3), 267–295.

Geddes, L. A. & Baker, L. E. (1967). The specific resistance of biological material—a compendium of data for the biomedical engineer and physiologist. *Med Biol Eng, 5*(3), 271–293.

Geman, S. & Geman, D. (1984). Stochastic relaxation, Gibbs distributions and the Bayesian restoration of images. *IEEE Trans. Patt. Anal. Machine Intell, 6*(6), 712–741.

George, N. & Conty, L. (2008). Facing the gaze of others. *Neurophysiol Clin, 38*(3), 197–207.

Geselowitz, D. B. (1964). Dipole theory in electrocardiography. *Am J Cardiol, 14*, 301–306.

Golub, G. H. & van Loan, C. F. (1996). *Matrix computations* (3rd ed.). Baltimore, MD: Johns Hopkins University Press.

Goncalves, S. I., Munck, J. C. de, Verbunt, J. P. A., Bijma, F., Heethaar, R. M., & daSilva, F. L. (2003). In vivo measurement of the brain and skull resistivities using an EIT-based method and realistic models for the head. *IEEE Transactions on Biomedical Engineering, 50*(6), 754–767.

Gourévitch, B., Bouquin-Jeannès, R. L., & Faucon, G. (2006). Linear and nonlinear causality between signals: Methods, examples and neurophysiological applications. *Biol Cybern, 95*(4), 349–369.

Gray, C. M., König, P., Engel, A. K., & Singer, W. (1989). Oscillatory responses in cat visual cortex exhibit intercolumnar synchronization which reflects global stimulus properties. *Nature, 338*(6213), 334–337.

Guilford, P., J. & Fruchter, B. (1978). *Fundamental statistics in psychology and education.* (6th ed.). New York: McGraw-Hill.

Hadamard, J. (1902). Sur les problemes aux derivees partielles et leur signification physique. *Princeton University Bulletin*, 49–52.

Hämäläinen, M., Hari, R., Ilmoniemi, R., Knuutila, J., & Lounasmaa, O. (1993). Magnetoencephalography: Theory, instrumentation and applications to the noninvasive study of human brain function. *Rev. Mod. Phys., 65*, 413–497.

Hamming, R. W. (1983). *Digital filters.* Englewood Cliffs, NJ: Prentice Hall.

Handy, T. C. (2004). *Event-related potentials: A methods handbook (Bradford books).* Cambridge, MA: The MIT Press.

Haueisen, J., Tuch, D. S., Ramon, C., Schimpf, P. H., Wedeen, V. J., & George, J. S. (2002). The influence of brain tissue anisotropy on human EEG and MEG. *Neuroimage, 15*(1), 159–166.

Haykin, S. (1996). *Adaptive filter theory.* London: Prentice-Hall.

Helenius, P., Parviainen, T., Paetau, R., & Salmelin, R. (2009). Neural processing of spoken words in specific language impairment and dyslexia. *Brain, 132*(Pt 7), 1918–1927.

Hillebrand, A. & Barnes, G. R. (2002). A quantitative assessment of the sensitivity of whole-head MEG to activity in the adult human cortex. *NeuroImage, 16*, 638–650.

Hillebrand, A., Singh, K. D., Holliday, I. E., Furlong, P. L., & Barnes, G. R. (2005). A new approach to neuroimaging with magnetoencephalography. *Hum Brain Mapp, 25*(2), 199–211.

Holmes, A., Mogg, K., Garcia, L. M., & Bradley, B. P. (2010). Neural activity associated with attention orienting triggered by gaze cues: A study of lateralized ERPS. *Soc Neurosci*, 1–11.

Honey, C. J., Kötter, R., Breakspear, M., & Sporns, O. (2007). Network structure of cerebral cortex shapes functional connectivity on multiple time scales. *Proc Natl Acad Sci U S A*, *104*(24), 10240–10245.

Hoogenboom, N., Schoffelen, J. M., Oostenveld, R., Parkes, L. M., & Fries, P. (2006). Localizing human visual gamma-band activity in frequency, time and space. *Neuroimage*, *29*(3), 764–773.

Huang, M. X., Mosher, J. C., & Leahy, R. M. (1999). A sensor-weighted overlapping-sphere head model and exhaustive head model comparison for MEG. *Phys Med Biol*, *44*(2), 423–440.

Izhikevich, E. M. & Edelman, G. M. (2008). Large-scale model of mammalian thalamocortical systems. *Proc Natl Acad Sci U S A*, *105*(9), 3593–3598.

Jerbi, K., Baillet, S., Mosher, J. C., Nolte, G., Garnero, L., & Leahy, R. M. (2004). Localization of realistic cortical activity in MEG using current multipoles. *Neuroimage*, *22*(2), 779–793.

Jerbi, K., Lachaux, J., NDiaye, K., Pantazis, D., Leahy, R., & Garnero, L. (2007). Coherent neural representation of hand speed in humans revealed by MEG imaging. *Proc Natl Acad Sci U S A*, *104*(18), 7676–7681.

Jerbi, K., Mosher, J. C., Baillet, S., & Leahy, R. M. (2002). On MEG forward modelling using multipolar expansions. *Phys Med Biol*, *47*(4), 523–555.

Johansen-Berg, H. & Rushworth, M. F. S. (2009). Using diffusion imaging to study human connectional anatomy. *Annu Rev Neurosci*, *32*, 75–94.

Karp, P. J., Katila, T. E., Saarinen, M., Siltanen, P., & Varpula, T. T. (1980). The normal human magnetocardiogram. ii. A multipole analysis. *Circ Res*, *47*(1), 117–130.

Kay, S. M. (1988). *Modern spectral estimation*. Englewood Cliffs, NJ: Prentice Hall.

Kay, S. M. (1993). *Fundamentals of statistical signal processing: Estimation theory*. Englewood Cliffs, NJ: Prentice Hall.

Kiebel, S. J., Garrido, M. I., Moran, R. J., & Friston, K. J. (2008). Dynamic causal modelling for EEG and MEG. *Cogn Neurodyn*, *2*(2), 121–136.

Kiebel, S. J., Tallon-Baudry, C., & Friston, K. J. (2005). Parametric analysis of oscillatory activity as measured with EEG/MEG. *Hum Brain Mapp*, *26*(3), 170–177.

Koch, S. P., Werner, P., Steinbrink, J., Fries, P., & Obrig, H. (2009). Stimulus-induced and state-dependent sustained gamma activity is tightly coupled to the hemodynamic response in humans. *J Neurosci*, *29*(44), 13962–13970.

Koskinen, M. & Vartiainen, N. (2009). Removal of imaging artifacts in EEG during simultaneous EEG/fMRI recording: Reconstruction of a high-precision artifact template. *Neuroimage*, *46*(1), 160–167.

Kranczioch, C., Debener, S., Herrmann, C. S., & Engel, A. K. (2006). EEG gamma-band activity in rapid serial visual presentation. *Exp Brain Res*, *169*(2), 246–254.

Kybic, J., Clerc, M., Faugeras, O., Keriven, R., & Papadopoulo, T. (2005). Fast multipole acceleration of the MEG/EEG boundary element method. *Phys Med Biol*, *50*(19), 4695–4710.

Lachaux, J. P., Fonlupt, P., Kahane, P., Minotti, L., Hoffmann, D., & Bertrand, O. (2007). Relationship between task-related gamma oscillations and bold signal: New insights from combined fMRI and intracranial EEG. *Hum Brain Mapp*, *28*(12), 1368–1375.

Lachaux, J. P., Rodriguez, E., Martinerie, J., & Varela, F. J. (1999). Measuring phase synchrony in brain signals. *Hum Brain Mapp*, *8*(4), 194–208.

Laufs, H., Daunizeau, J., Carmichael, D. W., & Kleinschmidt, A. (2008). Recent advances in recording electrophysiological data simultaneously with magnetic resonance imaging. *Neuroimage*, *40*(2), 515–528.

Leahy, R. M., Mosher, J. C., Spencer, M. E., Huang, M. X., & Lewine, J. D. (1998). A study of dipole localization accuracy for MEG and EEG using a human skull phantom. *Electroencephalogr Clin Neurophysiol*, *107*(2), 159–173.

Lehmann, D., Darcey, T. M., & Skrandies, W. (1982). Intracerebral and scalp fields evoked by hemiretinal checkerboard reversal, and modeling of their dipole generators. *Adv Neurol*, *32*, 41–48.

Lin, F. H., Belliveau, J. W., Dale, A. M., & Hamalainen, M. S. (2006). Distributed current estimates using cortical orientation constraints. *Human Brain Mapping*, *27*(1), 1–13.

Lin, F. H., Hara, K., Solo, V., Vangel, M., Belliveau, J. W., Stufflebeam, S. M. (2009). Dynamic granger-geweke causality modeling with application to interictal spike propagation. *Hum Brain Mapp*, *30*(6), 1877–1886.

Lin, F. H., Witzel, T., Ahlfors, S. P., Stufflebeam, S. M., Belliveau, J. W., & Hämäläinen, M. S. (2006). Assessing and improving the spatial accuracy in MEG source localization by depth-weighted minimum-norm estimates. *Neuroimage*, *31*(1), 160–171.

Logothetis, N. K. & Pfeuffer, J. (2004). On the nature of the bold fMRI contrast mechanism. *Magn Reson Imaging*, *22*(10), 1517–1531.

Logothetis, N. K. & Wandell, B. A. (2004). Interpreting the BOLD signal. *Annu Rev Physiol*, *66*, 735–769.

Makeig, S., Westerfield, M., Jung, T. P., Enghoff, S., Townsend, J., & Courchesne, E. (2002). Dynamic brain sources of visual evoked responses. *Science*, *295*(5555), 690–694.

Mallat, S. (1998). *A wavelet tour of signal processing*. San Diego: Academic Press.

Mangin, J. F., Rivière, D., Coulon, O., Poupon, C., Cachia, A., Cointepas, Y. (2004). Coordinate-based versus structural approaches to brain image analysis. *Artif Intell Med*, *30*(2), 177–197.

Mantini, D., Perrucci, M. G., Gratta, C. D., Romani, G. L., & Corbetta, M. (2007). Electrophysiological signatures of resting state networks in the human brain. *Proc Natl Acad Sci U S A*, *104*(32), 13170–13175.

Marin, G., Guerin, C., Baillet, S., Garnero, L., & Meunier, G. (1998). Influence of skull anisotropy for the forward and inverse problem in EEG: Simulation studies using FEM on realistic head models. *Hum Brain Mapp*, *6*(4), 250–269.

Marzetti, L., Gratta, C. D., & Nolte, G. (2008). Understanding brain connectivity from EEG data by identifying systems composed of interacting sources. *Neuroimage*, *42*(1), 87–98.

Mattout, J., Phillips, C., Penny, W. D., Rugg, M. D., & Friston, K. J. (2006). MEG source localization under multiple constraints: An extended bayesian framework. *Neuroimage*, *30*(3), 753–767.

Mazaheri, A. & Jensen, O. (2008). Asymmetric amplitude modulations of brain oscillations generate slow evoked responses. *J Neurosci*, *28*(31), 7781–7787.

McIntosh, A. R. & Lobaugh, N. J. (2004). Partial least squares analysis of neuroimaging data: Applications and advances. *Neuroimage*, *23 Suppl 1*, S250–S263.

Melloni, L., Schwiedrzik, C. M., Wibral, M., Rodriguez, E., & Singer, W. (2009). Response to: Yuval-Greenberg et al., "Transient induced gamma-band response in EEG as a manifestation of miniature saccades." *Neuron* 58, 429–441. *Neuron*, *62*(1), 8–10; author reply 10–12.

Meunier, S., Lehéricy, S., Garnero, L., & Vidailhet, M. (2003). Dystonia: Lessons from brain mapping. *Neuroscientist*, *9*(1), 76–81.

Mnatsakanian, E. V. & Tarkka, I. M. (2002). Task-specific expectation is revealed in scalp-recorded slow potentials. *Brain Topogr*, *15*(2), 87–94.

Mosher, J., Baillet, S., & Leahy, R. (2003). Equivalence of linear approaches in bioelectromagnetic inverse solutions. In *Proceedings of the 2003 IEEE workshop on statistical signal processing* (pp. 294–297). San Antonio.

Mosher, J. C., Baillet, S., & Leahy, R. M. (1999). EEG source localization and imaging using multiple signal classification approaches. *J Clin Neurophysiol*, *16*(3), 225–238.

Mosher, J. C., Spencer, M. E., Leahy, R. M., & Lewis, P. S. (1993). Error bounds for EEG and MEG dipole source localization. *Electroencephalogr Clin Neurophysiol*, *86*(5), 303–321.

Mukesh, T. M. S., Jaganathan, V., & Reddy, M. R. (2006). A novel multiple frequency stimulation method for steady state VEP-based brain computer interfaces. *Physiol Meas*, *27*(1), 61–71.

Murakami, S. & Okada, Y. (2006). Contributions of principal neocortical neurons to magnetoencephalography and electroencephalography signals. *J Physiol*, *575*(Pt 3), 925–936.

Nichols, T. E. & Holmes, A. P. (2002). Nonparametric permutation tests for functional neuroimaging: A primer with examples. *Hum Brain Mapp*, *15*(1), 1–25.

Niedermeyer, E. & daSilva, F. L. (2004). *Electroencephalography: Basic principles, clinical applications, and related field* (5th ed.). Philadelphia: Lippincott Williams & Wilkins.

Niessing, J., Ebisch, B., Schmidt, K. E., Niessing, M., Singer, W., & Galuske, R. A. W. (2005). Hemodynamic signals correlate tightly with synchronized gamma oscillations. *Science*, *309*(5736), 948–951.

Nolte, G. & Curio, G. (1999). The effect of artifact rejection by signal-space projection on source localization accuracy in MEG measurements. *IEEE Trans Biomed Eng*, *46*(4), 400–408.

Nolte, G. & Hämäläinen, M. S. (2001). Partial signal space projection for artefact removal in MEG measurements: A theoretical analysis. *Phys Med Biol*, *46*(11), 2873–2887.

Nunez, P. L., Srinivasan, R., Westdorp, A. F., Wijesinghe, R. S., Tucker, D. M., & Silberstein, R. B. (1997). EEG coherency. i: Statistics, reference electrode, volume conduction, laplacians, cortical imaging, and interpretation at multiple scales. *Electroencephalogr Clin Neurophysiol*, *103*(5), 499–515.

Okada, Y. C., Tanenbaum, R., Williamson, S. J., & Kaufman, L. (1984). Somatotopic organization of the human somatosensory cortex revealed by neuromagnetic measurements. *Exp Brain Res*, *56*(2), 197–205.

Oppenheim, A. V., Schafer, R. W., & Buck, J. R. (1999). *Discrete-time signal processing* (2nd ed.). Englewood Cliffs, NJ: Prentice-Hall.

Ossadtchi, A., Baillet, S., Mosher, J. C., Thyerlei, D., Sutherling, W., & Leahy, R. M. (2004). Automated interictal spike detection and source localization in magnetoencephalography using independent components analysis and spatio-temporal clustering. *Clin Neurophysiol*, *115*(3), 508–522.

Pannetier-Lecoeur, M., Fermon, C., Dyvorne, H., Jacquinot, J., Polovy, H., & Walliang, A. (2009). Magnetoresistive-superconducting mixed sensors for biomagnetic applications. *Journal of Magnetism and Magnetic Materials*, In Press, Corrected Proof.

Pantazis, D., Nichols, T. E., Baillet, S., & Leahy, R. M. (2005). A comparison of random field theory and permutation methods for the statistical analysis of MEG data. *Neuroimage*, *25*(2), 383–394.

Parkkonen, L., Andersson, J., Hämäläinen, M., & Hari, R. (2008). Early visual brain areas reflect the percept of an ambiguous scene. *Proc Natl Acad Sci U S A*, *105*(51), 20500–20504.

Pascual-Marqui, R. D., Michel, C. M., & Lehmann, D. (1994, Oct). Low resolution electromagnetic tomography: A new method for localizing electrical activity in the brain. *Int J Psychophysiol*, *18*(1), 49–65.

Perrin, F., Pernier, J., Bertrand, O., Giard, M. H., & Echallier, J. F. (1987). Mapping of scalp potentials by surface spline interpolation. *Electroencephalogr Clin Neurophysiol*, *66*(1), 75–81.

Pfurtscheller, G. & daSilva, F. H. L. (1999). Event-related EEG/MEG synchronization and desynchronization: Basic principles. *Clin Neurophysiol*, *110*(11), 1842–1857.

Pérez, J. J., Guijarro, E., & Barcia, J. A. (2005). Suppression of the cardiac electric field artifact from the heart action evoked potential. *Med Biol Eng Comput*, *43*(5), 572–581.

Rodriguez, E., George, N., Lachaux, J. P., Martinerie, J., Renault, B., & Varela, F. J. (1999). Perception's shadow: Long-distance synchronization of human brain activity. *Nature*, *397*(6718), 430–433.

Rudrauf, D., Lachaux, J. P., Damasio, A., Baillet, S., Hugueville, L., Martinerie, J. (2009). Enter feelings: Somatosensory responses following early stages of visual induction of emotion. *Int J Psychophysiol*, *72*(1), 13–23.

Salmelin, R. & Baillet, S. (2009). Electromagnetic brain imaging. *Hum Brain Mapp*, *30*(6), 1753–1757.

Sarvas, J. (1987). Basic mathematical and electromagnetic concepts of the biomagnetic inverse problem. *Phys Med Biol*, *32*(1), 11–22.

Savukov, I. M. & Romalis, M. V. (2005). NMR detection with an atomic magnetometer. *Phys Rev Lett*, *94*(12), 123001.

Scherg, M. & vonCramon, D. (1985). Two bilateral sources of the late AEP as identified by a spatio-temporal dipole model. *Electroencephalogr Clin Neurophysiol*, *62*(1), 32–44.

Schmidt, R. O. (1986). Multiple emitter location and signal parameter estimation. *IEEE Transactions on Antennas and Propagation*, *34*, 276–280.

Schwartz, D., Poiseau, E., Lemoine, D., & Barillot, C. A. (1996). Registration of MEG/EEG data with MRI: Methodology and precision issues. *Brain Topography*, *9*, 101–116.

Sergent, C., Baillet, S., & Dehaene, S. (2005). Timing of the brain events underlying access to consciousness during the attentional blink. *Nature Neuroscience*, *8*(10), 1391–1400.

Sergent, C. & Dehaene, S. (2004). Neural processes underlying conscious perception: Experimental findings and a global neuronal workspace framework. *J Physiol Paris*, *98*(4–6), 374–384.

Silva, F. L. da. (1991). Neural mechanisms underlying brain waves: From neural membranes to networks. *Electroencephalogr Clin Neurophysiol*, *79*(2), 81–93.

Spencer, M., Leahy, R., Mosher, J., & Lewis, P. (1992). Adaptive filters for monitoring localized brain activity from surface potential time series. In IEEE (Ed.), *Conference record of the twenty-sixth asilomar conference on signals, systems and computers* (Vol. 1, pp. 156–161).

Sporns, O., Tononi, G., & Kötter, R. (2005). The human connectome: A structural description of the human brain. *PLoS Comput Biol, 1*(4), e42.

Stephan, K. E., Penny, W. D., Daunizeau, J., Moran, R. J., & Friston, K. J. (2009). Bayesian model selection for group studies. *Neuroimage, 46*(4), 1004–1017.

Tallon-Baudry, C. (2009). The roles of gamma-band oscillatory synchrony in human visual cognition. *Front Biosci, 14*, 321–332.

Tallon-Baudry, C., Bertrand, O., Delpuech, C., & Permier, J. (1997). Oscillatory gamma-band (30–70 hz) activity induced by a visual search task in humans. *J Neurosci, 17*(2), 722–734.

Tarantola, A. (2004). *Inverse problem theory and methods for model parameter estimation*. Philadelphia, USA: SIAM Books.

Tarantola, A. (2006, Aug). Popper, bayes and the inverse problem. *Nat Phys, 2*(8), 492–494.

Taulu, S., Kajola, M., & Simola, J. (2004). Suppression of interference and artifacts by the signal space separation method. *Brain Topogr, 16*(4), 269–275.

Tesche, C. D. (1996). MEG imaging of neuronal population dynamics in the human thalamus. *Electroencephalogr Clin Neurophysiol Suppl, 47*, 81–90.

Tikhonov, A. & Arsenin, V. (1977). *Solutions of ill-posed problems*. Washington, D.C: Winston & sons.

Tuch, D. S., Wedeen, V. J., Dale, A. M., George, J. S., & Belliveau, J. W. (2001). Conductivity tensor mapping of the human brain using diffusion tensor MRI. *Proc Natl Acad Sci U S A, 98*(20), 11697–11701.

Varela, F., Lachaux, J. P., Rodriguez, E., & Martinerie, J. (2001). The brainweb: Phase synchronization and large-scale integration. *Nature Reviews Neuroscience, 2*(4), 229–239.

Veen, B. D. van & Buckley, K. M. (1988). Beamforming: A versatile approach to spatial filtering. *ASSP Magazine, IEEE* [see also IEEE Signal Processing Magazine], *5*, 4–24.

Vialatte, F. B., Maurice, M., Dauwels, J., & Cichocki, A. (2009). Steady-state visually evoked potentials: Focus on essential paradigms and future perspectives. *Prog Neurobiol.*

Vogels, T. P., Rajan, K., & Abbott, L. F. (2005). Neural network dynamics. *Annu Rev Neurosci, 28*, 357–376.

Vuilleumier, P. & Pourtois, G. (2007). Distributed and interactive brain mechanisms during emotion face perception: Evidence from functional neuroimaging. *Neuropsychologia, 45*(1), 174–194.

Waldorp, L. J., Huizenga, H. M., Nehorai, A., Grasman, R. P. P. P., & Molenaar, P. C. M. (2005). Model selection in spatio-temporal electromagnetic source analysis. *IEEE Trans Biomed Eng, 52*(3), 414–420.

Wang, J. Z., Williamson, S. J., & Kaufman, L. (1992). Magnetic source images determined by a lead-field analysis: The unique minimum-norm least-squares estimation. *IEEE Trans Biomed Eng, 39*(7), 665–675.

Wax, M. & Anu, Y. (1996). Performance analysis of the minimum variance beamformer. *IEEE Transactions on Signal Processing, 44*, 928–937.

Wehner, D. T., Hämäläinen, M. S., Mody, M., & Ahlfors, S. P. (2008). Head movements of children in MEG: Quantification, effects on source estimation, and compensation. *Neuroimage, 40*(2), 541–550.

Werner, G. (2007). Brain dynamics across levels of organization. *J Physiol Paris, 101*(4–6), 273–279.

Wood, C. C., Cohen, D., Cuffin, B. N., Yarita, M., & Allison, T. (1985). Electrical sources in human somatosensory cortex: Identification by combined magnetic and potential recordings. *Science, 227*(4690), 1051–1053.

Yuval-Greenberg, S. & Deouell, L. Y. (2009). The broadband-transient induced gamma-band response in scalp EEG reflects the execution of saccades. *Brain Topogr, 22*(1), 3–6.

Zimmerman, J. T., Reite, M., & Zimmerman, J. E. (1981). Magnetic auditory evoked fields: dipole orientation. *Electroencephalogr Clin Neurophysiol, 52*(2), 151–156.

Psychoneuroimmunology in vivo: Methods and Principles

Jos A. Bosch, Christopher G. Engeland, *and* Victoria E. Burns

Abstract

This chapter provides a primer and practical guide for social scientists who wish to study the effects of social interactions on immune function. It focuses on three widely employed in vivo (i.e., 'whole body') assessment methods of immune function, namely, the responses to vaccination, the rate of wound healing, and the control of latent virus infections. The focus on these three in vivo approaches has a strong conceptual and empirical basis. Conceptually, in vivo assessment is the only approach that provides an unambiguous answer regarding the health-relevant impact of social factors on immune function. The empirical basis for focusing on the aforementioned three in vivo assessment methods is straightforward: These three approaches are the only in vivo methods for which meta-analyses show a robust effect which is reproducible across research laboratories.

Keywords: psychoneuroimmunology, wound healing, vaccination, reactivation, latent viruses, methods, review, stress

Introduction

Social interaction and a need to belong are intrinsic to human existence, and it is hardly surprising therefore that the most stressful experiences are typically those that strain or break social connections (Cacioppo & Hawkley, 2003; Hawkley, Browne, & Cacioppo, 2005; House, Landis, & Umberson, 1988). There is good evidence that the reported health benefits of social integration and, conversely, the health risks of social isolation, involve a direct effect of neurocognitive processes on peripheral physiology (Cacioppo & Hawkley, 2003; Cacioppo et al., 2002; Hawkley, Bosch, Engeland, Marucha, & Cacioppo, 2006; Hawkley & Cacioppo, 2003). One research area that has attracted considerable attention in this regard is psychoneuroimmunology (PNI); the study of the bidirectional communication between the brain and the immune system (Glaser & Kiecolt-Glaser, 2005; Kiecolt-Glaser, McGuire, Robles, & Glaser, 2002; Segerstrom & Miller, 2004; Zorrilla et al., 2001). Research efforts in this area have accrued substantial evidence to support the idea that social factors influence the immune system, and, as a corollary, increase susceptibility to a range of pathological conditions that are critically dependent on immune system function. Examples are infections, inflammatory disorders, cardiovascular diseases, and healing of wounds (Cohen & Herbert, 1996; Krantz & McCeney, 2002; Rozanski, Blumenthal, & Kaplan, 1999; Walburn, Vedhara, Hankins, Rixon, & Weinman, 2009). An equally extensive literature shows that activation of the immune system, in turn, induces a constellation of behavioral and psychological symptoms—denoted as sickness behavior—of which generalized dysphoria and social disengagement are the most prominent characteristics (Dantzer, O'Connor, Freund, Johnson, & Kelley, 2008). The aim of the present chapter is to provide a primer and practical guide for social scientists who wish to study the effects of social interactions on immune function in vivo.

Immunologists have developed countless assessment methods that enable them to study multiple aspects of immune function in isolation. However, the research questions of immunologists do not necessarily align with those of social scientists. The latter are typically not interested in the intricacies of a particular aspect of immunity, but hope to obtain a global measure of immune function that has external and criterion validity. Therefore this chapter will focus on three widely employed in vivo (i.e., "whole body") assessment methods of immune function, namely, the responses to vaccination, the rate of wound healing, and the control of latent virus infections. The focus on these three in vivo approaches has a strong conceptual and empirical basis. Conceptually, in vivo assessment is the only approach that provides an unambiguous answer regarding the health-relevant impact of social factors on immune function. This contrasts with more commonly employed in vitro, or "test tube", techniques. Immunologists have devised such in vitro techniques to conveniently study the behavior of immune cells in a controlled environment outside the body. For such in vitro assays a sample of blood (and sometimes also tissue) is taken to the laboratory where it can be exposed to a variety of experimental conditions. For example, immunologists who study the ability of immune cells to migrate to their targets, such as bacteria, have developed migration assays to observe and quantify cell movement. Likewise, immunologists who study cell division employ so-called proliferation assays, and immunologists who study events that trigger inflammation may use the blood to measure responses to various signal molecules like cytokines. Although extremely useful for answering certain specialized questions, such isolated testing, removed from, for example, the hormonal milieu in which immune responses are ordinarily generated, provides scant information about the overall status of the highly integrated and complex immune system. Moreover, the blood contains only 2% of all immune cells (the other 98% are in the various tissues). As such, the in vitro approach has limited application to overall understanding of the relationship between societal, social, psychological, and behavioral factors and susceptibility to disease. In vivo methods are

therefore the approach that yields the best external and criterion validity.

The empirical basis for focusing on the aforementioned three in vivo assessment methods is straightforward: These three approaches are the only in vivo methods for which meta-analyses show a robust effect that is reproducible across laboratories (Segerstrom & Miller, 2004; Walburn et al., 2009). The average effect sizes of vaccination studies yield an $R = -.22$ (indicating lower vaccination responses with increased levels of stress) (Segerstrom & Miller, 2004). The averaged effect size found in studies on the association between psychological stress and wound healing ($N = 22$) generated an impressive $R = -.44$ (Walburn et al., 2009). Finally, the effect sizes reported for latent viral reactivation are between $R = .18$ and $R = .44$, depending on virus and stressor type (Segerstrom & Miller, 2004).

In addition to conceptual and statistical arguments, the choice for a particular immunological assessment method will be driven by practical considerations. Table 8.1 lists several of these considerations, such as costs, training, and effort.

Introduction to the Immune System
The Chronology of an Immune Response
The immune system is an extremely versatile defense system that protects against micro-organisms and other foreign invaders like toxins, it also regulates repair processes in response to tissue damage, and it protects against neoplasms (cancers). When successful, this system establishes a state of immunity against infection and disease (Latin: *immunitas*, freedom from). It consists of an enormous variety of cells and molecules, capable of highly specific recognition and elimination of a seemingly limitless number of threats to our body. These cells and molecules act together in a dynamic network, which complexity rivals that of the nervous system. Importantly, the immune system does not operate autonomously. It is, amongst others, influenced by central nervous system processes and their neuro-hormonal outflows, which, in turn, are shaped by social and psychological factors. Despite its immense complexity, it is possible to make a breakdown of main activities and present the immune response in a more-or-less chronological order.

The white blood cells, or leukocytes, are the principal effectors of the immune response. An immune response is typically initiated when these cells detect an anomalous event, which may be invasion of a foreign organism or substance (e.g., bacterium, virus,

Table 8.1 Comparison of the Three in vivo Methods

	Vaccination	Wound healing	Viral reactivation
Clinical relevance	Intermediate	High	Low
Costs	Intermediate Determination of specific antibodies costs $20–$40 per sample (but much cheaper if assays are in-house). Each vaccine costs between $20–$60 (sometimes paid by medical insurance or employer)	High Participants are typically compensated generously. Investment in equipment and skills training is needed. Is typically done in surgical practice or hospital setting.	Low Commercial assays cost $4–$8 per sample (cheaper if technique is in-house). Standard laboratory equipment used, noncomplicated techniques
Training	Moderate Vaccine delivery typically by certified person (e.g., nurse). Requires venous blood taking	Substantial Experimental and observational wounds require involvement of highly trained individual, typically MD or specialized nurse. Tape stripping can be done by trained researcher. May involve venous blood taking. Training needed of personnel to standardize wound assessment and scoring.	Minor Requires venous blood taking (finger-prick can be alternative)
Labor	Moderate Vaccine administration and 1 or 2 follow-up sessions	Substantial Wound placement requires preparation and can take 1–4 hours per person. Frequent follow-up appointments to monitor healing	Minor Repeated blood taking in longitudinal studies may complicate study design

toxin), or dysfunction of bodily cells (e.g., damage, death, mutation). Initially, the immune response involves so-called "innate" immune cells; a subset of leukocytes which utilize recognition molecules that enable them to detect a broad range of anomalies. Their primary function is to initiate inflammation locally at the site where the anomaly is detected; for example, the location of microbial invasion, tissue damage, or neoplastic growth. Inflammation denotes a coherent set of biochemical and cellular reactions that aim to recruit other immune cells to the site, to aid in the destruction of whatever anomaly was detected. The inflammatory process involves the release of various hazardous substances and cytokines, which are the signaling molecules of the immune system. The inflammatory cytokines affect the surrounding blood vessels by making them leaky, to allow influx of protective serum proteins, and making them sticky, so that blood-borne leukocytes can easily migrate out of the blood into the site of nascent inflammation. These biochemical and cellular events accumulate in a classic set of clearly noticeable symptoms; the tissue swells, becomes red, warm, and painful, and functions less well.

The inflammatory response is a very aggressive and damaging reaction, which is therefore supposed to be swift and to remain local. However, when the inflamed area is large or the inflammatory response severe, the inflammatory recreation induces a body-wide, or "systemic," reaction. A primary objective of this systemic response is to contain the inflammation within its local site, for example, by neutralizing cytokines and chemicals that leak out and may hereby cause damage to other tissues. Another function is to initiate physiological and behavioral reactions that may further aid in recovery. Such physiological responses involve, amongst others, the release of various stress hormones that suppress excessive inflammation and support enhanced metabolic needs. The behavioral responses, subsumed under the term sickness behavior, form the most obvious example of how the immune system and brain interact. Sickness behavior involves a general sense of malaise and dysphoria, accompanied by symptoms such as fatigue, lack of appetite, listlessness, and social withdrawal. These symptoms are mediated by locally produced inflammatory cytokines, which are relayed to the brain via afferent neural pathways and in an endocrine fashion via release in the circulation.

While the inflammatory response is characterized by an influx of immune cells, a small set of cells migrate away of the site of inflammation, in order to recruit reinforcements. These cells are antigen-presenting cells. An "antigen" is jargon used to describe any type of molecule that triggers an immune response. Thus, an antigen could, for example, be a viral or bacterial protein, or a fragment from a mutated or cancerous cell. Antigen-presenting cells pick up local antigen and presenting it elsewhere to alert other immune cells about the presence of an anomalous event. "Elsewhere" means the lymphoid organs: specialized organs in which a large number of immune cells congregate to exchange information about various immunological events throughout the body, and to prepare an adequate response. Using military metaphors, these organs are sometimes dubbed the "army barracks and head quarters" of the immune system. When lymphoid immune cells, or lymphocytes, are presented with antigen, the ones best capable of responding to that specific antigen selectively divide, or proliferate. Hereby these cells increase their numbers from tens to millions in several days. After this proliferation phase, the lymphocytes migrate out of the lymphoid tissues to eliminate the source of antigen elsewhere in the body. This second wave of immune cells is called the adaptive immune response, because these lymphocytes are specifically adapted to the antigen that started the cascade of immune responses.

The adaptive immunological response, generated from within the lymphoid organs, is fundamentally different from the innate immune response in two ways. First, adaptive immunity involves the ability to identify and attack antigen in a highly specialized manner. Thus, rather than eliminating antigen by initiating a broad-spectrum inflammatory response, which often causes bystander damage to healthy tissue, lymphocytes (the cells that effectuate the adaptive immune response) are capable of operating with surgical precision. A second difference is that after the antigen is cleared, lymphocytes retain a pool of long-lived memory lymphocytes. These memory cells mount a very rapid immune response upon a subsequent antigen encounter and hereby provide lifelong protection against disease. Thus, when triggered by the same antigen, the innate immune cells will rigidly mount the exact same inflammatory response, while the lymphocytes act fast and antigen-specific, such that inflammation, and thus any symptoms of disease, can be prevented. This protective memory response is utilized by vaccines, which is why they prevent infectious disease.

One particular feature of the adaptive immune response needs special mentioning: the production of antibodies. Antibodies, or "immunoglobulins," are serum proteins that have the ability to bind and neutralize specific antigenic molecules. Antibodies are produced by the B cells, which are named after the fact that these cells mature in the bone marrow. Whereas all other immune cells need to physically interact with the relevant antigens, B cells can conveniently secrete their antigen-specific receptors, which are the antibodies, and hereby exert their immunological actions in an endocrine fashion. Relevant to the scope of this chapter, the measurement of antibody levels has proven to be an extremely useful tool for monitoring immune responses. For example, the response to a vaccine can be monitored by quantifying serum antibody levels that B cells generate in response to a vaccine antigen (e.g., influenza or hepatitis B virus particles). Likewise, because memory B cells produce antibodies many years after an infection, detection of antigen-specific antibodies is used to establish if exposure to particular antigens, for example, via infection or vaccination, has occurred at some point in life.

CONTAMINATION, INFECTION, AND DISEASE

In everyday usage the above terms are used interchangeably, but for immunologists these terms have very specific meaning. For example, in its everyday use, having a cold or the flu is commonly referred to as having an infection, and most people also make no clear distinction between "being infected" or "being contaminated." However, among immunologists the word contamination is reserved for the mere exposure to a microorganism, and an infection defines a situation whereby a micro-organism is able to invade and replicate in bodily tissues. Most contaminations do not develop into an infection. In turn, most infections do not result in significant clinical symptoms, that is, disease. A seminal study by Cohen et al. (1991) illustrates the importance of distinguishing between the three concepts. For this study, healthy volunteers were contaminated with a cold virus which was administered via nose drops. In subsequent days it was tested if the virus was able to replicate by measuring viral particles in a nasal rinse, which signifies infection, and it was further tested whether the cold virus caused any disease symptoms such as sneezing or nasal congestion (i.e., disease). Since everyone was exposed to the virus by nose drops, 100% of participants were contaminated. However, despite a 100% contamination rate, only 82% of participants showed signs of infection. Significantly, of the study participants who became infected, only 38% also developed a cold (Cohen et al., 1991).

Measuring Immune Responses in vivo
Vaccination Studies
PRINCIPLE AND RELEVANCE
Vaccines are one of the most successful public health interventions of all time. By exposing recipients to a non-harmful version of an infectious agent, such as a virus or bacteria, their immune system is "tricked" into making antibodies that will protect them against a subsequent attack. The extent of this antibody response reflects the culmination of a series of interactions of different immune cell types in different immune compartments of the body, all occurring within a dynamic neuroendocrine milieu. As such, vaccination response provides an accurate reflection of the true functional status of the immune system and is a very useful in vivo marker for use in psychoneuroimmunology research.

IMMUNE RESPONSE TO VACCINATION
The infectious agent, or antigen, contained in the vaccine is recognized by professional antigen-presenting cells, and displayed on their cell surface for presentation to T cells. If a specific T cell recognizes this antigen, it becomes activated and divides many times. These T cells are now able to activate B cells that have recognized and presented the same antigen. With this T-cell help, the B cells can now also divide and become plasma cells which produce lots of antigen-specific antibodies. These antibodies can be measured in serum, providing a quantifiable measure of the final product of this cascade of reactions. Higher levels of specific antibodies suggest that the person is more protected against the illness (Couch & Kasel, 1983). Any psychological intervention that improves antibody responses would, therefore, have clear clinical implications. In addition though, the antibody response to vaccination can be used as an indicator of the immune system's *general* ability to respond to an antigen. Except in specialist circumstances (Cohen & Herbert, 1996), it is not possible to control contact with infections; early research was often confounded with variations in antigen exposure. Vaccination offers an opportunity to safely administer a set dose of antigen at a selected time point, and to assess immune status both pre- and post-exposure. As such, this approach yields results that are scientifically robust and have easily interpretable clinical implications for both vaccination efficacy and susceptibility to infection.

PSYCHOSOCIAL FACTORS AND ANTIBODY RESPONSE TO VACCINATION
Psychological stress has been associated with a reduced antibody response to a variety of vaccinations, and in a diverse range of populations, such as young healthy adults, community-dwelling older adults, and caregivers (Burns, Carroll, Ring, & Drayson, 2003; Cohen, Miller, & Rabin, 2001; Glaser & Kiecolt-Glaser, 2005). More recently, poorer antibody responses were found in participants with higher rates of neuroticism (Phillips, Carroll, Burns, & Drayson, 2005) and loneliness (Pressman et al., 2005), whereas social support (Gallagher, Phillips, Ferraro, Drayson, & Carroll, 2008a, 2008b; Phillips, Burns, Carroll, Ring, & Drayson, 2005) and positive affect (Marsland, Cohen, Rabin, & Manuck, 2006) both predict better antibody responses. As such, there is now a considerable body of evidence demonstrating that the magnitude of the antibody response to vaccination is associated with a wide range of psychosocial factors. The degree of control over antigen exposure permitted by vaccination studies also permits the systematic investigation of interventions designed to enhance immune function. For example, recent studies have demonstrated that antibody response to vaccination can be enhanced by mindfulness meditation (Davidson et al., 2003) and cognitive-behavioral stress management (Vedhara et al., 2003).

There remain, however, key challenges still to address, particularly regarding the elucidation of the mechanisms underlying these associations and their clinical implications (Burns et al., 2003; Cohen et al., 2001; Glaser & Kiecolt-Glaser, 2005). Utilizing the full potential of the different methodologies available within the vaccination model should enable researchers to provide answers to these remaining questions.

METHODOLOGICAL CONSIDERATIONS IN VACCINATION STUDIES

There are a wide range of technical decisions for the psychoneuroimmunology researcher to navigate. Choices made at the study design stage have important implications for the theoretical and clinical conclusions that can be drawn later. It is important, therefore, to consider carefully the different options, which can be divided into (1) the choice of vaccination, (2) the assessment protocol, and (3) the type of assay used.

Choice of Vaccination

Vaccines differ in terms of the type of antibody response they elicit, the relative novelty of the antigen (i.e., whether the participants are likely to have been exposed to the antigen before), and the typical efficacy of the vaccination in the general population. For example, as outlined above, most vaccines contain protein antigens and require both T cells and B cells to work together to produce an antibody response; these are known as "thymus-dependent" responses. However, a minority of vaccines are targeted against polysaccharide antigens and elicit antibody responses known as "thymus-independent" responses, which don't require T-cell help. By comparing the relative susceptibility of thymus-dependent and independent responses, the investigator can start to unravel which aspects of the immune system are most affected by psychosocial factors. For example, if an intervention changes the response to a thymus-dependent, but not -independent, vaccine, it could be surmised that the effect is likely to be due to changes in T-cell function.

The novelty of the vaccine antigen is also an important factor. The first time the immune system encounters an antigen, it produces a slower, "primary" immune response. In contrast, if it is a familiar antigen, a more rapid and effective "secondary" immune response is generated. Hepatitis B provides a particularly neat model in this context. In the United Kingdom, most young, healthy adults will not have been exposed to the hepatitis B virus

either naturalistically or through previous vaccination. The vaccine protocol involves three doses over a six month period; this allows the assessment of the initial primary response to the first vaccination, and then secondary responses to the subsequent doses. Some researchers attempt to circumvent the issues of naturalistic exposure or previous vaccination entirely, by using a non-clinical vaccination such as keyhole limpet hemocyanin (KLH). KLH is a novel protein, derived from the giant keyhole limpet (a tropical sea snail), and elicits a primary immune response. Although the lack of naturalistic exposure has clear benefits for study design, there are some questions over the clinical relevance of measuring the antibody response to a non-harmful protein. In contrast, use of the influenza vaccine in this type of research is hampered by the confounding effects of naturalistic exposure. However, it has clear clinical relevance, particularly for older adults who experience high levels of influenza-related morbidity and mortality. Overall, by selecting vaccinations according to whether they induce a primary or secondary response, it is possible to investigate which aspects of the immune response are most susceptible to psychophysiological processes.

Finally, vaccines differ in their efficacy, and there is preliminary evidence that this may impact upon their susceptibility to psychosocial factors such as stress. Studies using the influenza vaccine often find that only one of the three strains contained within the vaccine appears to be affected by stress (Miller et al., 2004; Phillips et al., 2006). Moreover, it has also been argued that strains which evoke robust antibody responses are less susceptible to psychosocial influence, whereas less immunogenic strains are more vulnerable to such effects (Cohen et al., 2001). In sum, these various theoretical and clinical implications should be considered when the choice of vaccination is made, in order to maximize the eventual impact of the research findings.

Timing of Assessment and Antibody Subclass

One of the key benefits of the vaccination model, compared to examining the response to naturalistic infection, is the ability to measure the antibody status at baseline, prior to antigen exposure, and then again post-vaccination in order to assess the magnitude of the response over a set period. The baseline measurement allows the researcher to control for previous exposure to the antigen; this is important as pre-vaccination antibody levels are a strong predictor of the subsequent response. The amount of time between vaccination and follow-up assessment will, again, depend on the interests of the researcher. The main antibody subclass generated by vaccination is immunoglobulin (Ig) G, and this typically peaks at four to six weeks post-vaccination. However, a primary immune response will elicit an antibody subclass known as immunoglobulin (Ig) M, peaking at around one week post-vaccination. Both the IgM and IgG responses have been shown recently to be susceptible to psychosocial influence, such as social support (Gallagher et al., 2008a, 2008b), although this warrants further attention in a wider range of vaccines.

Assay Type

The choice of assay is a more practical consideration that can impact on the costs and labor involved in determining the antibody levels. Again, it will depend on the type of vaccine used. For example, a common method for assessing the response to influenza vaccine is the hemagglutination inhibition (HAI) assay. Influenza virus binds red blood cells together in vitro in a process known as hemagglutination; this assay measures the ability of specific antibodies to inhibit this binding. The outcome is an antibody "titre"; the higher the titre, the greater the antibody concentration. However, the HAI assay is unable to distinguish between different antibody subclasses.

An enzyme-linked immunosorbent assay (ELISA) is the most common method used to assess specific antibody levels. In brief, the antigen (e.g., viral particles) is adhered to the base of a small plastic well and the serum sample is added. Any antibody specific for that antigen (e.g., the antibodies produced in response to flu virus vaccine) binds to it, and hereby becomes also immobilized to the plastic. By simply washing the plastic well, the rest of the serum, and with it all antibody that is not specific to the antigen, is rinsed away. A molecule is then added that binds an enzyme to the antibody, which is thereby tagged and can thus be quantified. This is done through a series of chemical reactions targeting the enzyme, upon which a color response is generated; the greater the antibody concentration, the deeper the color of the response. This reaction can subsequently be quantified by passing the colored well through a light-sensitive sensor. This ELISA is relatively quick and simple to perform, and can be adapted to measure different antibody types (or subclasses). However, as with the HAI assay, antibodies against only one antigen at a time can be assessed at a time. As vaccines such as influenza and pneumococcal contain multiple antigens,

assessment of the antibody response to each strain can be time consuming.

A recent advance has been the development of multiplex systems, such as Luminex, which allow simultaneous assessment of the antibody response to multiple antigens. Instead of adhering the antigen to the base of a small well, the system uses up to 100 sets of tiny color-coded beads; each set can be associated with a different antigen. A "cocktail" of relevant beads can be mixed with the serum, whereby any specific antibodies will adhere to the appropriate beads. Similar technology to the ELISA is then used to create a color change. When the sample is passed through the Luminex machine, it is possible to determine the extent of the color change for each of the different bead types. This information can then be translated into a specific antibody level for each of the separate antigens contained in the vaccine. The benefits of this type of assay are clearly demonstrated by the work of Gallagher and colleagues (Gallagher, Phillips, Drayson, & Carroll, 2009; Gallagher et al., 2008a, 2008b), who assessed antibody responses against multiple pneumococcal serotypes in a single assay. As psychosocial effects have largely been found with polyvalent vaccinations where a number of similar acting antigenic strains are administered in one vaccine, this type of technology is likely to be crucial in comparing the relative susceptibility of different strains.

Wound Healing Studies
PRINCIPLE AND RELEVANCE
Impaired healing is a common medical complication and its treatment costs U.S. Health Services over 9 billion dollars annually (Ashcroft, Mills, & Ashworth, 2002). These costs are largely associated with delays in wound closure, which increase infection rates and the risk of medical complications (Robson, 1997). As a result, numerous models have been developed to examine and better characterize tissue repair and regeneration. Several of these models have been used in the context of stress and social isolation (for a review see Engeland & Marucha, 2009). Such stress studies were motivated by the observation that psychosocial stressors delay surgical recovery (Kiecolt-Glaser, Marucha, Malarkey, Mercado, & Glaser, 1995; Walburn et al., 2009). For example, Broadbent et al. (Broadbent, Petrie, Alley, & Booth, 2003) obtained Perceived Stress Scale scores from 47 patients just prior to their undergoing a hernia operation. Higher stress scores predicted lower IL-1 levels in wound fluid, as well as slower recovery times and greater pain. Thus,

pre-operative stress appears to alter inflammatory responses and worsen surgical outcomes. In addition to studies showing that negative psychological factors can have a detrimental effect, there is evidence that interventions aimed at reducing stress, such as massage therapy, relaxation techniques, and psycho-education also reduce the negative effects of stress on surgical outcomes (Devine, 1992; Field et al., 1998; Holden-Lund, 1988).

A problem with surgical outcome studies is that the induced wounds are not standardized for parameters such as size, shape, depth, time, and duration of surgery. This obviously complicates the assessment of healing rates and surgical outcomes. To circumvent this problem, standardized wound models have been developed, which standardize for wound size, conditions, location, and time of placement. Most of these models typically also minimize pain, and not just for ethical concerns: McGuire et al. (McGuire et al., 2006) reported that acute and especially persistent pain after gastric bypass surgery related to slower closure of standardized 2mm dermal wounds. This observation is consistent with what has been reported for analgesics, which tend to have a positive effect (Beilin et al., 2003), indicating that pain itself is a stressor that may impact healing outcomes (see review by Engeland & Graham, in press).

ORAL WOUND HEALING
Marucha et al. (Marucha, Kiecolt-Glaser, & Favagehi, 1998) developed a standardized model of oral mucosal healing in which a 3.5mm diameter wound is placed on the hard palate of the mouth using a biopsy punch and scalpel. Videographs of the wound are obtained at the time of wounding and then daily until healed. These oral wounds take about 7–9 days to heal, although this is longer in slower healers (e.g., older women) (Engeland, Bosch, Cacioppo, & Marucha, 2006). Although subject attrition can be problematic due to the requirement of daily videographs, soliciting subjects that work or live near the research facility generally overcomes this issue.

To create a reference for photographic assessment, a 6mm diameter standard template is placed around the wound (this template essentially is a small a piece of paper with a 6mm punch hole). All wounds are calculated as a ratio to this standard to control for photographic artifacts such as angle and magnification errors. Wound ratios are then calculated as a ratio to the original wound size (ratio) on day 0. To further increase standardization, the same clinician should create all wounds, and wound sizes

(surface area) should be assessed in a blinded manner with well-trained raters (as validated by inter-rater correspondence). Canvas is a software program that allows quantification of wound size from pictures (e.g., Bosch, Engeland, Cacioppo, & Marucha, 2007; Engeland et al., 2006).

Using this mucosal wound model, delayed healing has been demonstrated in women, in the aged, and in dysphoric individuals (Bosch et al., 2007; Engeland et al., 2006). Longitudinal studies, whereby participants were wounded more than once, have shown delayed healing during final examinations as compared to summer vacation (Marucha et al., 1998). In this study, university students were found to heal 40% slower during examinations than during summer vacation (Marucha et al., 1998).

DERMAL WOUND HEALING MODELS
Punch biopsies
The principle of a dermal punch biopsy wound is identical to the oral punch biopsy wounds as described above. In the first psychological study using this model, Kiecolt-Glaser et al. (1995) placed 3.5mm punch biopsy wounds on the arms of 13 Alzheimer's caregivers and 13 age-matched controls. Alzheimer's caregivers took 24% (9 days) longer than controls to heal. As skin is much slower to heal (the wounds in the aforementioned study took 4–7 weeks to heal), pictures are not taken daily, but weekly or bi-weekly. Preferably, such wounds are placed in an "out of the way" area (e.g., inner side of the upper non-dominant arm) so that possible small remaining blemishes/scars are less noticeable. Wound closure is determined by photography of the wound or the response to hydrogen peroxide. The latter is caused by interaction with certain plasma enzymes, such as catalases, and the absence of foaming thus indicates that the wound is sealed. Experience for our laboratory suggests that photography is the more objective and reliable measure of the two, also because hydrogen peroxide itself causes tissue damage and thereby delays wound healing. In other studies, high resolution ultrasound scanning has been used to determine the width at the base of such wounds. This is considered a more accurate marker of wound healing progress than assessing surface area by photography/videography. Ultrasound scanning has the additional advantage that also assessment of the subdermal tissue can be made, thereby also obtaining information of important sub-surface processes such as vascularization. Using this method, Ebrecht et al.

(2004) demonstrated that cortisol levels and perceived stress each predicted dermal healing rates in young men.

In both dermal and mucosal wound studies it is not uncommon to place additional excisional wounds (typically 1 x 5 x 1.5mm deep) proximal to the punch biopsy. From these, wounds biopsies (2 x 5 x 1.5mm deep) can be obtained at various time points. This allows for the determination of gene expression in wounded tissue using real-time PCR or gene microarrays (Marucha, Engeland; personal communication).

Blister wounds and tape stripping

A blister model of wound healing has as the advantage that it is less invasive than the placement of excisional wounds, and it is convenience for sampling of wound fluid from the "blister chamber" for further analyses. Briefly, a vacuum of 350 mm Hg is applied through a pump and regulator for 1–1.5h until blisters form. In this way, a set of sterile blisters, typically 8mm in diameter, is created. The fluid is then drained from each blister with a syringe and the epidermis is removed with scissors. A plastic plate is then placed over the blister and the wells are filled with approximately 1 ml of autologous serum (i.e., serum from the participant) and sealed with tape. Wound fluid can then be sampled at various time points by syringe, allowing one sample per blister. Using this model, negative effects on local inflammation and healing have been reported for higher perceived stress, conflictive interactions, and anger expression (Glaser et al., 1999; Gouin, Kiecolt-Glaser, Malarkey, & Glaser, 2008; Kiecolt-Glaser et al., 2005; Roy et al., 2005).

A relatively non-invasive measure of skin integrity involves tape stripping. The epithelium provides an essential barrier to pathogens and limits the loss of water from the body. Cellophane tape is repeatedly applied and removed from an area of epidermis, commonly to the forearm, to disrupt this skin barrier. Barrier recovery is assessed using an evaporimeter to measure trans-epidermal water loss (TEWL) over time. A main methodological challenge is to accurately measure the amount of evaporation, which is low, and to exclude measurement error due to environmental influences such as room temperature and humidity. Slower recovery times of barrier function have been related to interview stress (Trier Social Stress Test), university examinations, and sleep deprivation (Altemus, Rao, Dhabhar, Ding, & Granstein, 2001; Garg et al.,

2001; Robles, 2007; Robles, Brooks, & Pressman, 2009).

THE POST HEALING PERIOD

Once wound closure is complete, the underlying architecture continues to be remodeled for weeks to months and sometimes even years. Thus, even if wounds close at similar rates there may be differences in tensile wound strength and wound architecture. These parameters may be evaluated by obtaining small biopsies of "healed" tissue. Assessing wound strength requires a tensiometer for determining the shearing force needed to rip the tissue apart. However, this requires a relatively large biopsy so is only done in animals. To examine the underlying wound architecture, histology can be performed on very small biopsy samples using Picrosirius red staining (see Junqueira, Bignolas, & Brentani, 1979). Wounds which have healed less well will have collagen fibrils that are thinner in diameter and more poorly organized with less cross-linking (less of a basket-weave pattern) (Ashcroft et al., 1997; Jorgensen, Sorensen, Kallehave, Vange, & Gottrup, 2002; Junqueira et al., 1979). Compared to normal tissue, healed tissue is less strong, its architecture is less well organized, and it is more prone to future injury. Patients reporting higher worry about an upcoming surgical operation had lower levels of matrix metalloproteinase-9 (Broadbent et al., 2003), an enzyme that regulates tissue strength and appearance post-healing. Hence, stress can affect matrix degradation processes, linking stress to later stages of healing.

COMPARING DERMAL AND ORAL WOUND HEALING

As a final note, we may add that dermal and mucosal tissues are inherently different, and the healing of these types of wounds should be viewed separately. Mucosal tissues heal faster, with less inflammation, and with little to no scarring in comparison to dermal wounds (Szpaderska, Zuckerman, & DiPietro, 2003). The gender advantage between these tissues is also reversed. Women have been shown to heal dermal wounds faster (Ashcroft et al., 1997; Ashcroft et al., 2002; Ashcroft et al., 2003; Gilliver & Ashcroft, 2007; Jorgensen et al., 2002; Mills, Ashworth, Gilliver, Hardman, & Ashcroft, 2005), whereas Engeland et al. (2006; Engeland, Sabzehei, & Marucha, 2009) have shown that oral mucosal wounds heal faster in men. Finally, stress inhibits early inflammation in dermal wounds (Broadbent et al., 2003; Glaser et al., 1999; Kiecolt-Glaser et al.,

2005; Kiecolt-Glaser et al., 1995), but in mucosal wounds stress causes hyper-inflammation of the tissue (unpublished observations). Thus, although stress appears to delay healing in both tissue types, mechanistic differences are apparent.

Monitoring Reactivation of Latent Herpes Viruses

HERPES INFECTIONS AND LATENCY

While the immune system is able to eradicate most infections, a number of micro-organisms have developed ways to escape this fate. The herpes viruses are particularly well known for this ability to persist within their human host (Cohrs & Gilden, 2001; Croen, 1991). In healthy individual these viruses typically elicit mild (e.g., cold sores, fatigue) or no disease symptoms at all. However, in immune-suppressed patients (e.g., those with AIDS or using immune suppressive drugs), these viruses can elicit very severe complications (Nester, Anderson, Roberts Jr., & Nester, 2008).

Viruses, herpes viruses no exception, essentially consist of nothing more than a strand of genetic material covered by a protein shell. These viral particles enter bodily cells and nest themselves in the DNA of host cells. A characteristic of herpes viruses is that they remain dormant in the cellular genome; a state denoted as latency, interrupted by brief periods of reactivation whereby the virus replicates and infects other cells. These peaks of reactivation are often opportunistically chosen. For example, the DNA of cytomegalovirus (CMV) contains a small strand that acts as a sensor for immune suppressive signals, which include stress hormones (Prosch et al., 2000).

Herpes viruses have been extremely successful in colonizing humans. Their typical infection rates range between 30% and 90%, depending on the virus, and are in part related to factors such as age, socio-economic status, topographical location, sexual experience, and early life exposures (e.g., higher infection rates in children that attended day care) (Arvin, Campadelli-Fiume, & Roizman, 2007). Although eight herpes viruses have thus far been identified, research into the effects of psychosocial factors and reactivation has largely been limited to four subtypes: herpes simplex virus 1 (HSV-1), which causes cold sores; herpes simplex 2 (HSV-2), which causes genital lesions; varizella zoster virus (VZV), which causes chicken pox and shingles; Epstein-Barr virus (EBV), which causes glandular fever; and CMV, which in most individuals does not cause symptoms. Several of these viruses have been associated with more serious long term effects,

although these effects are relatively rare. For example, EBV is a primary cause of Burkitt lymphoma, a form of leukemia. In recent years CMV has been identified as a cause of immune senescence, that is, it accelerates the normal age-related decline in immune function (Arvin et al., 2007).

PRINCIPLE AND RELEVANCE

Apart from generating relatively mild clinical symptoms after a first infection (e.g., glandular fever in case of EBV infection, chicken pox after VZV infection), herpes viruses rarely generate any symptoms during latency. Even the main exception to this rule, HSV-1 and HSV-2, which are respectively responsible for recurrent oral and genital lesions, typically cause symptoms that, although a painful nuisance, are rarely serious (Arvin et al., 2007). So why study reactivation of these viruses? The interest is not so much related to the pathological consequences these viruses, but is related the opportunity they provide to study immune competence in vivo. Thus, the virus is used as the proverbial "canary in the coalmine," whereby reactivation of the virus is indicative of impaired immune competence. That said, we may add that some herpes viruses can cause clinical problems later in life, such as shingles in case of VZV infection, and that herpes viruses have intrinsic oncogenic properties. For example, EBV is associated with Burkitt lymphoma, nasopharyngeal carcinoma, diffuse oligoclonal B-cell lymphoma, and Hodgkin's disease (Arvin et al., 2007). Other pathologies have also been associated with latent viruses, including chronic fatigue syndromes, arthrosclerosis, and inflammatory disorders. Although these consequences are sometimes invoked as an additional justification for research, they are rarely the primary focus.

Latent herpes viruses reactivate under a variety of social and non-social stressors, and this observation is remarkably consistent across the different herpes virus types studied so far, whereby meta-analysis shows low to intermediate effect sizes (R between .18 and .44, depending on stressor type and virus) (Segerstrom & Miller, 2004). Factors that are linked with viral reactivation include loneliness, lower socio-economic status, social isolation, poor marital quality, caregiver stress, depression, anxiety, academic examinations, and space flights (Dalkvist, Wahlin, Bartsch, & Forsbeck, 1995; Friedman, Katcher, & Brightman, 1977; Glaser, Kiecolt-Glaser, Speicher, & Holliday, 1985; Glaser, Pearl, Kiecolt-Glaser, & Malarkey, 1994; Irwin et al., 1998; Katcher, Brightman, Luborsky, & Ship, 1973;

Kiecolt-Glaser et al., 1988; Logan, Lutgendorf, Hartwig, Lilly, & Berberich, 1998; McDade et al., 2000; Mehta, Stowe, Feiveson, Tyring, & Pierson, 2000; Miller, Freedland, Duntley, & Carney, 2005; Pariante et al., 1997; Pierson, Stowe, Phillips, Lugg, & Mehta, 2005; Stowe, Mehta, Ferrando, Feeback, & Pierson, 2001; Stowe et al., 2009; Stowe, Pierson, & Barrett, 2001; Tingate, Lugg, Muller, Stowe, & Pierson, 1997). Such reactivation is taken as evidence that the immune system has a reduced ability to keep the virus under control, an assumption that is strongly supported by experimental animal studies and, in case of herpes simplex 1 and 2 infections, is also consistent with an increase in negative clinical outcomes such as cold sores (Chida & Mao, 2009).

ASSESSMENT OF VIRAL REACTIVATION

There are a number of techniques available to detect viral reactivation. For the purpose of this overview we omitted techniques that require expensive equipment or a specialized virology laboratory. This, then, also implies omission of the gold standard: isolation and quantification of viral particles in tissue culture. Conveniently, however, there are good alternative techniques available that deliver very reliable and valid results, which can be done using standard laboratory equipment, and which require only a modest amount of training. These techniques grossly fall into two categories: (1) detection of antibody levels in serum that are produced in response to the virus, and (2) direct quantification of viral nucleotides (i.e., the genetic material of the virus).

Quantification of virus-specific antibody levels: principle and considerations

Probably the most commonly used method to assess viral activity is the quantification of plasma concentration of antibodies specific for (or, as immunologists call it, "directed against") the virus of interest. In previously infected individuals, antiviral antibodies are always present in serum (hence the term 'seropositive') and levels are tightly regulated by the immune system. However, a dysfunction of the immune system permits viral reactivation and leads to increased levels of antiviral antibodies. Thus, when virus replication is detected by the immune system, an immunological response is mounted which includes production of antibodies by B lymphocytes (see earlier introduction into immunology). For instance, the well-documented age-related declines in cellular immunity are associated with increased herpes virus antibodies (Glaser, Strain, et al., 1985). As a result, the level of specific

antibodies produced to a virus can be used as an indirect measure of viral replication. Note that while in the context of vaccination research elevated antibodies are a good thing (i.e., a marker of an effective immune response); in the context of viral replication elevated antibody levels rather signify impaired immunity.

The typical assay used to detect specific antibodies is the ELISA (see section on vaccination responses for a description of this assay) or one of the many variations on this method. Although a straightforward laboratory technique, which will require little more than a week to master, there are several specific issues that can be tricky. First, commercial assays vary greatly in their measurement range. This aspect is not essential in clinical situations whereby the aim is to merely detect a positive or negative serostatus: In that situation the physician merely is interested to know if antibodies can be found or not. However, in a research context whereby antibody levels do matter, one may opt for an assay that has a large measurement range to avoid ceiling effects. Second, commercially available assays, even when FDA approved, vary considerable in quality (e.g., specificity, sensitivity). Luckily, there are a large number of comparative studies published that tested the quality of various assays (e.g., (Ashley, 2002; Bhatia et al., 2004; Gartner et al., 2003), and careful scrutiny of this literature should precede any purchase.

A critical issue for the ELISA methods is the specificity of the response. Commercial ELISAs differ in the type of antigen that is used to capture antibodies directed against the same virus. For example, some assays use whole virus as an antigen, while others use purified viral proteins, synthetic protein, or recombinant viral proteins (a technology whereby proteins are generated from a segment of DNA placed in a micro-organism) (Gartner et al., 2003). These differences imply that results are sometimes difficult to compare between assays.

The use of different assay antigens may also be intentional. For example, distinct ELISAs are being used, often in parallel, to detect EBV-specific antibodies against different components of the virus, such as the EBV-viral capsid antigen (VCA) or the EBV-early antigen. The VCA proteins are antigens released during productive viral replication, while incomplete reactivation is indicated by increased antibodies to the early antigen. Hence, distinct antigens signify distinct aspects of viral replication (Stowe et al., 2009). Assay specificity is specifically relevant for the distinction between HSV-1, which causes oral lesions, and HSV-2, which causes genital lesions. These two herpes simplex variants show considerable molecular overlap, and only tests which distinguish HSV-2 from HSV-1 on the basis of the glycoprotein antigens gG1 and gG2 have yielded acceptable accuracy (Ashley, 2002; Cherpes, Ashley, Meyn, & Hillier, 2003).

Another issue pertains to the type of virus-specific antibody that is being detected by the assay. Available assays quantify IgG antibody or IgM antibody; these antibody subclasses provide different information about the nature of the infection. IgG antibody levels will rise upon re-infection or in response to viral reactivation during latency. In contrast, a recent new (or "primary") infection will cause a selective rise in IgM antibody levels: upon primary infection one can detect IgM but no or only little IgG. This aspect can be useful in studies on determinants of viral exposure, such as sexual behavior, whereby differentiation between IgG and IgM can help distinguish newly infected cases from old established infections.

The fact that most assays require blood can be problematic in social science studies, which typically take place outside hospital or laboratory settings and do not involved trained personnel certified for bloodletting. Bloodletting by using a finger prick might be an option in such research. A study by McDade shows that collecting blood obtained by finger prick correlates well with the values obtained from venous obtained plasma (McDade et al., 2000). Moreover, this study provided evidence that finger blood can be stored on pieces of absorbent paper at room temperature for several weeks and still yield a reasonable retest reliability (r = .77 with reference assay, McDade et al., 2000). Moreover, for some, herpes virus viral particles can be detected in saliva (e.g., EBV) or urine (e.g., CMV) (Stowe et al., 2007; Tingate et al., 1997).

Other methods
Serum antibodies respond slowly to reactivation (within 2–6 days) and show a very long half-life (IgG half-life is 23 days). Whereas this stability has benefits in some research situations (e.g., little interference by circadian variation), this is certainly not an advantage in clinical situations where viral infection or reactivation can be deadly. In this context the temporal resolution of antibody responses is too low; the clinician needs to know on a daily basis if the patient reactivates and whether the treatment with antiviral drugs has its intended effect (Bhatia et al., 2004; Strick & Wald, 2006).

A number of alternatives to the ELISA method have become available, of which the quantitative polymerase chain reaction (qPCR) is the most frequently employed (Bhatia et al., 2004; Mendelson, Aboudy, Smetana, Tepperberg, & Grossman, 2006; Strick & Wald, 2006).

Quantitative PCR is a technique that allows sensitive quantification of DNA, including viral DNA. Hence the technique can be employed to detect and quantify viral particles in various fluids including serum, urine, and saliva (Mendelson et al., 2006; Stowe et al., 2007; Strick & Wald, 2006; Tingate et al., 1997). Regrettably, this technique is not yet universally applicable. For example, while qPCR is very useful in immunosuppressed patients, who have high levels of viral products in serum, in healthy individuals viral levels are often too low to be reliably detected. Likewise, while some viruses can be detected in urine (e.g., CMV) or saliva (e.g., EBV), other viruses cannot (Stowe et al., 2007; Tingate et al., 1997). A final caveat is that qPCR results and serum antibody levels do not always correspond. For example, serological diagnosis of EBV reactivation failed to correlate with viral load, determined by qPCR, in immunosuppressed patients (Gartner et al., 2000) and healthy individuals (Hoffmann et al., 2010).

References

Altemus, M., Rao, B., Dhabhar, F. S., Ding, W., & Granstein, R. D. (2001). Stress-induced changes in skin barrier function in healthy women. *J Invest Dermatol*, *117*(2), 309–317.

Arvin, A. M., Campadelli-Fiume, G., & Roizman, B. (2007). *Human herpesviruses: Biology, therapy, and immunoprophylaxis*. Cambridge: Cambridge University Press.

Ashcroft, G. S., Dodsworth, J., van Boxtel, E., Tarnuzzer, R. W., Horan, M. A., Schultz, G. S., et al. (1997). Estrogen accelerates cutaneous wound healing associated with an increase in TGF-beta1 levels. *Nat Med*, *3*(11), 1209–1215.

Ashcroft, G. S., Mills, S. J., & Ashworth, J. J. (2002). Ageing and wound healing. *Biogerontology*, *3*(6), 337–345.

Ashcroft, G. S., Mills, S. J., Lei, K., Gibbons, L., Jeong, M. J., Taniguchi, M., et al. (2003). Estrogen modulates cutaneous wound healing by downregulating macrophage migration inhibitory factor. *J Clin Invest*, *111*(9), 1309–1318.

Ashley, R. L. (2002). Performance and use of HSV type-specific serology test kits. *Herpes*, *9*(2), 38–45.

Beilin, B., Shavit, Y., Trabekin, E., Mordashev, B., Mayburd, E., Zeidel, A., et al. (2003). The effects of postoperative pain management on immune response to surgery. *Anesth Analg*, *97*(3), 822–827.

Bhatia, J., Shah, B. V., Mehta, A. P., Deshmukh, M., Sirsat, R. A., & Rodrigues, C. (2004). Comparing serology, antigenemia assay and polymerase chain reaction for the diagnosis of cytomegalovirus infection in renal transplant patients. *J Assoc Physicians India*, *52*, 297–300.

Bosch, J. A., Engeland, C. G., Cacioppo, J. T., & Marucha, P. T. (2007). Depressive symptoms predict mucosal wound healing. *Psychosom Med*, *69*(7), 597–605.

Broadbent, E., Petrie, K. J., Alley, P. G., & Booth, R. J. (2003). Psychological stress impairs early wound repair following surgery. *Psychosom Med*, *65*(5), 865–869.

Burns, V. E., Carroll, D., Ring, C., & Drayson, M. (2003). Antibody response to vaccination and psychosocial stress in humans: relationships and mechanisms. *Vaccine*, *21*(19–20), 2523–2534.

Cacioppo, J. T. & Hawkley, L. C. (2003). Social isolation and health, with an emphasis on underlying mechanisms. *Perspect Biol Med*, *46*(3 Suppl), S39–52.

Cacioppo, J. T., Hawkley, L. C., Crawford, L. E., Ernst, J. M., Burleson, M. H., Kowalewski, R. B., et al. (2002). Loneliness and health: Potential mechanisms. *Psychosom Med*, *64*(3), 407–417.

Cherpes, T. L., Ashley, R. L., Meyn, L. A., & Hillier, S. L. (2003). Longitudinal reliability of focus glycoprotein G-based type-specific enzyme immunoassays for detection of herpes simplex virus types 1 and 2 in women. *J Clin Microbiol*, *41*(2), 671–674.

Chida, Y. & Mao, X. (2009). Does psychosocial stress predict symptomatic herpes simplex virus recurrence? A meta-analytic investigation on prospective studies. *Brain Behav Immun*, *23*(7), 917–925.

Cohen, S. & Herbert, T. B. (1996). Health psychology: Psychological factors and physical disease from the perspective of human psychoneuroimmunology. *Annu Rev Psychol*, *47*, 113–142.

Cohen, S., Miller, G. E., & Rabin, B. S. (2001). Psychological stress and antibody response to immunization: A critical review of the human literature. *Psychosom Med*, *63*(1), 7–18.

Cohen, S., Tyrrell, D. A., & Smith, A. P. (1991). Psychological stress and susceptibility to the common cold. *N Engl J Med*, *325*(9), 606–612.

Cohrs, R. J. & Gilden, D. H. (2001). Human herpesvirus latency. *Brain Pathol*, *11*(4), 465–474.

Couch, R. B. & Kasel, J. A. (1983). Immunity to influenza in man. *Annu Rev Microbiol*, *37*, 529–549.

Croen, K. D. (1991). Latency of the human herpesviruses. *Annu Rev Med*, *42*, 61–67.

Dalkvist, J., Wahlin, T. B., Bartsch, E., & Forsbeck, M. (1995). Herpes simplex and mood: A prospective study. *Psychosom Med*, *57*(2), 127–137.

Dantzer, R., O'Connor, J. C., Freund, G. G., Johnson, R. W., & Kelley, K. W. (2008). From inflammation to sickness and depression: When the immune system subjugates the brain. *Nat Rev Neurosci*, *9*(1), 46–56.

Davidson, R. J., Kabat-Zinn, J., Schumacher, J., Rosenkranz, M., Muller, D., Santorelli, S. F., et al. (2003). Alterations in brain and immune function produced by mindfulness meditation. *Psychosom Med*, *65*(4), 564–570.

Devine, E. C. (1992). Effects of psychoeducational care for adult surgical patients: A meta-analysis of 191 studies. *Patient Educ Couns*, *19*(2), 129–142.

Ebrecht, M., Hextall, J., Kirtley, L. G., Taylor, A., Dyson, M., & Weinman, J. (2004). Perceived stress and cortisol levels predict speed of wound healing in healthy male adults. *Psychoneuroendocrinology*, *29*(6), 798–809.

Engeland, C. G., Bosch, J. A., Cacioppo, J. T., & Marucha, P. T. (2006). Mucosal wound healing: The roles of age and sex. *Arch Surg*, *141*(12), 1193–1197; discussion 1198.

Engeland, C. G., & Graham, J. E. (in press) Psychoneuroimmunological aspects of wound healing and the role of pain. In: Upton D (Ed). Psychological Impact of Pain in Patients with Wounds. Wounds UK Ltd, A Schofield Healthcare Media Company, London

Engeland, C. G. & Marucha, P. T. (2009). Wound healing and stress. In R. D. Granstein & T. A. Luger (Eds.), *Neuroimmunology of the skin: Basic science to clinical relevance* (pp. 233–247). Berlin: Springer.

Engeland, C. G., Sabzehei, B., & Marucha, P. T. (2009). Sex hormones and mucosal wound healing. *Brain Behav Immun*, *23*(5), 629–635.

Field, T., Peck, M., Krugman, S., Tuchel, T., Schanberg, S., Kuhn, C., et al. (1998). Burn injuries benefit from massage therapy. *J Burn Care Rehabil*, *19*(3), 241–244.

Friedman, E., Katcher, A. H., & Brightman, V. J. (1977). Incidence of recurrent herpes labialis and upper respiratory infection: A prospective study of the influence of biologic, social and psychologic predictors. *Oral Surg Oral Med Oral Pathol*, *43*(6), 873–878.

Gallagher, S., Phillips, A. C., Drayson, M. T., & Carroll, D. (2009). Parental caregivers of children with developmental disabilities mount a poor antibody response to pneumococcal vaccination. *Brain Behav Immun*, *23*(3), 338–346.

Gallagher, S., Phillips, A. C., Ferraro, A. J., Drayson, M. T., & Carroll, D. (2008a). Psychosocial factors are associated with the antibody response to both thymus-dependent and thymus-independent vaccines. *Brain Behav Immun*, *22*(4), 456–460.

Gallagher, S., Phillips, A. C., Ferraro, A. J., Drayson, M. T., & Carroll, D. (2008b). Social support is positively associated with the immunoglobulin M response to vaccination with pneumococcal polysaccharides. *Biol Psychol*, *78*(2), 211–215.

Garg, A., Chren, M. M., Sands, L. P., Matsui, M. S., Marenus, K. D., Feingold, K. R., et al. (2001). Psychological stress perturbs epidermal permeability barrier homeostasis: Implications for the pathogenesis of stress-associated skin disorders. *Arch Dermatol*, *137*(1), 53–59.

Gartner, B. C., Hess, R. D., Bandt, D., Kruse, A., Rethwilm, A., Roemer, K., et al. (2003). Evaluation of four commercially available Epstein-Barr virus enzyme immunoassays with an immunofluorescence assay as the reference method. *Clin Diagn Lab Immunol*, *10*(1), 78–82.

Gartner, B. C., Kortmann, K., Schafer, M., Mueller-Lantzsch, N., Sester, U., Kaul, H., et al. (2000). No correlation in Epstein-Barr virus reactivation between serological parameters and viral load. *J Clin Microbiol*, *38*(6), 2458.

Gilliver, S. C. & Ashcroft, G. S. (2007). Sex steroids and cutaneous wound healing: The contrasting influences of estrogens and androgens. *Climacteric*, *10*(4), 276–288.

Glaser, R. & Kiecolt-Glaser, J. K. (2005). Stress-induced immune dysfunction: Implications for health. *Nat Rev Immunol*, *5*(3), 243–251.

Glaser, R., Kiecolt-Glaser, J. K., Marucha, P. T., MacCallum, R. C., Laskowski, B. F., & Malarkey, W. B. (1999). Stress-related changes in proinflammatory cytokine production in wounds. *Arch Gen Psychiatry*, *56*(5), 450–456.

Glaser, R., Kiecolt-Glaser, J. K., Speicher, C. E., & Holliday, J. E. (1985). Stress, loneliness, and changes in herpesvirus latency. *J Behav Med*, *8*(3), 249–260.

Glaser, R., Pearl, D. K., Kiecolt-Glaser, J. K., & Malarkey, W. B. (1994). Plasma cortisol levels and reactivation of latent Epstein-Barr virus in response to examination stress. *Psychoneuroendocrinology*, *19*(8), 765–772.

Glaser, R., Strain, E. C., Tarr, K. L., Holliday, J. E., Donnerberg, R. L., & Kiecolt-Glaser, J. K. (1985). Changes in Epstein-Barr virus antibody titers associated with aging. *Proc Soc Exp Biol Med*, *179*(3), 352–355.

Gouin, J. P., Kiecolt-Glaser, J. K., Malarkey, W. B., & Glaser, R. (2008). The influence of anger expression on wound healing. *Brain Behav Immun*, *22*(5), 699–708.

Hawkley, L. C., Bosch, J. A., Engeland, C. G., Marucha, P. T., & Cacioppo, J. T. (2007). Loneliness, dysphoria, stress and immunity: A role for cytokines. In N. P. Plotnikoff, R. E. Faith & A. J. Murgo (Eds.), *Cytokines, stress and immunity* (2nd ed., pp. 67–85). Boca Raton: CRC press.

Hawkley, L. C., Browne, M. W., & Cacioppo, J. T. (2005). How can I connect with thee? Let me count the ways. *Psychol Sci*, *16*(10), 798–804.

Hawkley, L. C. & Cacioppo, J. T. (2003). Loneliness and pathways to disease. *Brain Behav Immun*, *17*, S98–S105.

Hoffmann, D., Wolfarth, B., Horterer, H. G., Halle, M., Reichhuber, C., Nadas, K., et al. (2010). Elevated Epstein-Barr virus loads and lower antibody titers in competitive athletes. *J Med Virol*, *82*(3), 446–451.

Holden-Lund, C. (1988). Effects of relaxation with guided imagery on surgical stress and wound healing. *Res Nurs Health*, *11*(4), 235–244.

House, J. S., Landis, K. R., & Umberson, D. (1988). Social relationships and health. *Science*, *241*, 540–545.

Irwin, M., Costlow, C., Williams, H., Artin, K. H., Chan, C. Y., Stinson, D. L., et al. (1998). Cellular immunity to varicella-zoster virus in patients with major depression. *J Infect Dis*, *178 Suppl 1*, S104–108.

Jorgensen, L. N., Sorensen, L. T., Kallehave, F., Vange, J., & Gottrup, F. (2002). Premenopausal women deposit more collagen than men during healing of an experimental wound. *Surgery*, *131*(3), 338–343.

Junqueira, L. C., Bignolas, G., & Brentani, R. R. (1979). Picrosirius staining plus polarization microscopy, a specific method for collagen detection in tissue sections. *Histochem J*, *11*(4), 447–455.

Katcher, A. H., Brightman, V., Luborsky, L., & Ship, I. (1973). Prediction of the incidence of recurrent herpes labialis and systemic illness from psychological measurements. *J Dent Res*, *52*(1), 49–58.

Kiecolt-Glaser, J. K., Kennedy, S., Malkoff, S., Fisher, L., Speicher, C. E., & Glaser, R. (1988). Marital discord and immunity in males. *Psychosom Med*, *50*(3), 213–229.

Kiecolt-Glaser, J. K., Loving, T. J., Stowell, J. R., Malarkey, W. B., Lemeshow, S., Dickinson, S. L., et al. (2005). Hostile marital interactions, proinflammatory cytokine production, and wound healing. *Arch Gen Psychiatry*, *62*(12), 1377–1384.

Kiecolt-Glaser, J. K., Marucha, P. T., Malarkey, W. B., Mercado, A. M., & Glaser, R. (1995). Slowing of wound healing by psychological stress. *Lancet*, *346*(8984), 1194–1196.

Kiecolt-Glaser, J. K., McGuire, L., Robles, T. F., & Glaser, R. (2002). Psychoneuroimmunology and psychosomatic medicine: back to the future. *Psychosom Med*, *64*(1), 15–28.

Krantz, D. S. & McCeney, M. K. (2002). Effects of psychological and social factors on organic disease: A critical assessment of research on coronary heart disease. *Annu Rev Psychol*, *53*, 341–369.

Logan, H. L., Lutgendorf, S., Hartwig, A., Lilly, J., & Berberich, S. L. (1998). Immune, stress, and mood markers related to recurrent oral herpes outbreaks. *Oral Surg Oral Med Oral Pathol Oral Radiol Endod*, *86*(1), 48–54.

Marsland, A. L., Cohen, S., Rabin, B. S., & Manuck, S. B. (2006). Trait positive affect and antibody response to hepatitis B vaccination. *Brain Behav Immun*, *20*(3), 261–269.

Marucha, P. T., Kiecolt-Glaser, J. K., & Favagehi, M. (1998). Mucosal wound healing is impaired by examination stress. *Psychosom Med*, *60*(3), 362–365.

McDade, T. W., Stallings, J. F., Angold, A., Costello, E. J., Burleson, M., Cacioppo, J. T., et al. (2000). Epstein-Barr virus antibodies in whole blood spots: A minimally invasive method for assessing an aspect of cell-mediated immunity. *Psychosom Med*, *62*(4), 560–567.

McGuire, L., Heffner, K., Glaser, R., Needleman, B., Malarkey, W., Dickinson, S., et al. (2006). Pain and wound healing in surgical patients. *Ann Behav Med*, *31*(2), 165–172.

Mehta, S. K., Stowe, R. P., Feiveson, A. H., Tyring, S. K., & Pierson, D. L. (2000). Reactivation and shedding of cytomegalovirus in astronauts during spaceflight. *J Infect Dis*, *182*(6), 1761–1764.

Mendelson, E., Aboudy, Y., Smetana, Z., Tepperberg, M., & Grossman, Z. (2006). Laboratory assessment and diagnosis of congenital viral infections: Rubella, cytomegalovirus (CMV), varicella-zoster virus (VZV), herpes simplex virus (HSV), parvovirus B19 and human immunodeficiency virus (HIV). *Reprod Toxicol*, *21*(4), 350–382.

Miller, G. E., Cohen, S., Pressman, S., Barkin, A., Rabin, B. S., & Treanor, J. J. (2004). Psychological stress and antibody response to influenza vaccination: when is the critical period for stress, and how does it get inside the body? *Psychosom Med*, *66*(2), 215–223.

Miller, G. E., Freedland, K. E., Duntley, S., & Carney, R. M. (2005). Relation of depressive symptoms to C-reactive protein and pathogen burden (cytomegalovirus, herpes simplex virus, Epstein-Barr virus) in patients with earlier acute coronary syndromes. *Am J Cardiol*, *95*(3), 317–321.

Mills, S. J., Ashworth, J. J., Gilliver, S. C., Hardman, M. J., & Ashcroft, G. S. (2005). The sex steroid precursor DHEA accelerates cutaneous wound healing via the estrogen receptors. *J Invest Dermatol*, *125*(5), 1053–1062.

Nester, E. W., Anderson, D. G., Roberts Jr., C. E., & Nester, M. T. (2008). *Microbiology: A human perspective* (6th ed.). New York: McGraw-Hill.

Pariante, C. M., Carpiniello, B., Orru, M. G., Sitzia, R., Piras, A., Farci, A. M., et al. (1997). Chronic caregiving stress alters peripheral blood immune parameters: The role of age and severity of stress. *Psychother Psychosom*, *66*(4), 199–207.

Phillips, A. C., Burns, V. E., Carroll, D., Ring, C., & Drayson, M. (2005). The association between life events, social support, and antibody status following thymus-dependent and thymus-independent vaccinations in healthy young adults. *Brain Behav Immun*, *19*(4), 325–333.

Phillips, A. C., Carroll, D., Burns, V. E., & Drayson, M. (2005). Neuroticism, cortisol reactivity, and antibody response to vaccination. *Psychophysiology*, *42*(2), 232–238.

Phillips, A. C., Carroll, D., Burns, V. E., Ring, C., Macleod, J., & Drayson, M. (2006). Bereavement and marriage are associated with antibody response to influenza vaccination in the elderly. *Brain Behav Immun*, *20*(3), 279–289.

Pierson, D. L., Stowe, R. P., Phillips, T. M., Lugg, D. J., & Mehta, S. K. (2005). Epstein-Barr virus shedding by astronauts during space flight. *Brain Behav Immun*, *19*(3), 235–242.

Pressman, S. D., Cohen, S., Miller, G. E., Barkin, A., Rabin, B. S., & Treanor, J. J. (2005). Loneliness, social network size, and immune response to influenza vaccination in college freshmen. *Health Psychol*, *24*(3), 297–306.

Prosch, S., Wendt, C. E., Reinke, P., Priemer, C., Oppert, M., Kruger, D. H., et al. (2000). A novel link between stress and human cytomegalovirus (HCMV) infection: sympathetic hyperactivity stimulates HCMV activation. *Virology*, *272*(2), 357–365.

Robles, T. F. (2007). Stress, social support, and delayed skin barrier recovery. *Psychosom Med*, *69*(8), 807–815.

Robles, T. F., Brooks, K. P., & Pressman, S. D. (2009). Trait positive affect buffers the effects of acute stress on skin barrier recovery. *Health Psychol*, *28*(3), 373–378.

Robson, M. C. (1997). Wound infection. A failure of wound healing caused by an imbalance of bacteria. *Surg Clin North Am*, *77*(3), 637–650.

Roy, S., Khanna, S., Yeh, P. E., Rink, C., Malarkey, W. B., Kiecolt-Glaser, J., et al. (2005). Wound site neutrophil transcriptome in response to psychological stress in young men. *Gene Expr*, *12*(4–6), 273–287.

Rozanski, A., Blumenthal, J. A., & Kaplan, J. (1999). Impact of psychological factors on the pathogenesis of cardiovascular disease and implications for therapy. *Circulation*, *99*(16), 2192–2217.

Segerstrom, S. C. & Miller, G. E. (2004). Psychological stress and the human immune system: A meta-analytic study of 30 years of inquiry. *Psychol Bull*, *130*(4), 601–630.

Stowe, R. P., Kozlova, E. V., Yetman, D. L., Walling, D. M., Goodwin, J. S., & Glaser, R. (2007). Chronic herpesvirus reactivation occurs in aging. *Exp Gerontol*, *42*(6), 563–570.

Stowe, R. P., Mehta, S. K., Ferrando, A. A., Feeback, D. L., & Pierson, D. L. (2001). Immune responses and latent herpesvirus reactivation in spaceflight. *Aviat Space Environ Med*, *72*(10), 884–891.

Stowe, R. P., Peek, M. K., Perez, N. A., Yetman, D. L., Cutchin, M. P., & Goodwin, J. S. (2009). Herpesvirus reactivation and socioeconomic position: A community-based study. *J Epidemiol Community Health*.

Stowe, R. P., Pierson, D. L., & Barrett, A. D. (2001). Elevated stress hormone levels relate to Epstein-Barr virus reactivation in astronauts. *Psychosom Med*, *63*(6), 891–895.

Strick, L. B. & Wald, A. (2006). Diagnostics for herpes simplex virus: Is PCR the new gold standard? *Mol Diagn Ther*, *10*(1), 17–28.

Szpaderska, A. M., Zuckerman, J. D., & DiPietro, L. A. (2003). Differential injury responses in oral mucosal and cutaneous wounds. *J Dent Res*, *82*(8), 621–626.

Tingate, T. R., Lugg, D. J., Muller, H. K., Stowe, R. P., & Pierson, D. L. (1997). Antarctic isolation: Immune and viral studies. *Immunol Cell Biol*, *75*(3), 275–283.

Vedhara, K., Bennett, P. D., Clark, S., Lightman, S. L., Shaw, S., Perks, P., et al. (2003). Enhancement of antibody responses to influenza vaccination in the elderly following a cognitive-behavioural stress management intervention. *Psychother Psychosom*, *72*(5), 245–252.

Walburn, J., Vedhara, K., Hankins, M., Rixon, L., & Weinman, J. (2009). Psychological stress and wound healing in humans: A systematic review and meta-analysis. *J Psychosom Res*, *67*(3), 253–271.

Zorrilla, E. P., Luborsky, L., McKay, J. R., Rosenthal, R., Houldin, A., Tax, A., et al. (2001). The relationship of depression and stressors to immunological assays: a meta-analytic review. *Brain Behav Immun*, *15*(3), 199–226.

PART 2

Motivation and Emotion

The Neurobiology of Social Bonding and Attachment

C. Sue Carter *and* Stephen W. Porges

Abstract

Sociality is characterized by interactions between two or more individuals. These interactions may be either negative or positive. Negative social behaviors include agonistic or aggressive interactions. Positive social interactions include both nonselective social aggregations and gregarious behavior and selective social interactions and pair bonds. This chapter highlights our current understanding of the neurobiology of social interactions, including those selective behaviors that are necessary for the formation and expression of social bonds.

Keywords: social behavior, social attachment, maternal behavior, social isolation, autonomic nervous system, parasympathetic nervous system, vagus, oxytocin, vasopressin, corticotropin releasing factor (CRF), adrenal hormones, cortisol/corticosterone, sex differences, dopamine, opioids

Background

The terms "bonding," and the related concept of "attachment," are used in several different ways within various behavioral disciplines (reviewed Carter et al., 2006). Attachment theory, influenced by John Bowlby (1969, 1973, 1980) and his followers (Ainsworth, Blehar, Waters, & Wall, 1978), distinguishes between attachment and bonding, and focuses on the relationship between a child and another individual (usually the mother or caretaker). In this context, standardized behavioral paradigms have been developed. In these paradigms the responses of a child to the presence or absence of its primary caretaker are used to classify individual differences in attachment. These categories of attachment also may predict behavioral or emotional responses in later life. In the context of classical attachment theory the "attachment figure" and the "affectional bond" cannot be replaced. However, "bonds" are seen as relatively long-lived ties to unique individuals, and multiple bonds may be formed and broken.

Another, more physiological, perspective on attachment is found in the work of Myron Hofer (1996, 2006). Hofer identified the concept of "hidden regulators," through which the social behavior of one individual may influence or help maintain the physiological state of another. From this point of view the concept of "attachment" is used to define underlying processes that maintain social relationships, and which are disturbed when the attachment figure is lost. These broader definitions incorporate the interactions among various homeostatic systems including temperature regulation, food intake, and stress buffering. An infant may use its caretaker to help with all of these functions, and it is recognized that responses to one system can cross over to affect others. Parallels have been noted between maternal separation and the loss of an adult partner, including in both cases stages of reactions to loss that can range from agitation to withdrawal and shut-down. As described below, the physiological processes underlying the reaction to separation and loss may be best understood in the context of the evolution of the mammalian nervous system, including the autonomic nervous system (Porges, 2007).

Contemporary neurobiological work on social bonds has focused on the mother-infant bond and more recently on bonds between two adults. Both "bonding" and "attachment" have been used to describe a process through which selective relationships or "bonds" develop between an infant and its mother (Keverne & Kendrick, 1991; Kendrick, 2000). Selective social relationships also can be formed between adults, especially between male-female pairs that tend to form the core of family groups in socially monogamous species, such as prairie voles (Carter, DeVries, & Getz, 1995).

The Consequences of Social Bonds or Their Absence

It is useful to differentiate between the causes versus the consequences of social bonds. The wide-ranging health consequences of social bonds are often described by the response to separation or by the consequences of the failure to form bonds during early life. The widespread effects of social bonds or their absence are experienced because the underlying biology of social bonds relies on neurobiological systems that are essential for homeostasis, including systems that regulate digestion, sleep, and the immune system (Henry & Wang, 1998). One level of coordination among these systems is the autonomic nervous system, including the tenth cranial nerve, also known as the vagus. The vagus nerve is the peripheral representation of the parasympathetic nervous system and coordinates most peripheral systems and their functions including the digestive and immune systems. The same neuropeptides, described below, that are essential for social bonding, also modulate vagal function, allowing an integration of social experiences with growth and restoration in the face of disease or challenge.

Social bonds are protective in the face of both emotional and physical challenges. When positive social relationships are not present, either because attachments were not formed or because bonds are broken, the risk for mental and physical illness increases (Shear & Shair, 2005). The presence or absence of social bonds is an important predictor of speed of recovery and subsequent longevity following illnesses as diverse as cancer and cardiovascular disease (Cacioppo & Hawkley, 2003). Inconsistent early social experiences or the absence of social bonds might be expected to predict in later life the capacity to form relationships, as well as stress management and general health; however, human experiments testing this hypothesis are uncommon. A variety of mental illnesses, such as autism and depression, also are characterized by dysfunctional social behaviors. These diverse relationships suggest that an understanding of the mechanisms of social bonding also will lead to the discovery of endogenous protective mechanisms responsible for mental and physical health.

How are Social Bonds Measured?

Social bonds are hypothetical constructs. However, for the purposes of neurobiological research operational definitions are necessary (Carter, 1998). Positive sociality is sometimes defined by the absence of defensive or aggressive behavior. The selectivity that defines social bonding involves more than simply a failure to avoid another individual, but also is measured by active behavioral processes including preferential and positive behaviors, such as selective contact, toward a familiar partner. In humans, self-report and expressed emotions or "feelings" can be used to define a social bond. In addition, autonomic or neuroendocrine changes in the presence or absence of a social partner may index social bonds. However, physiological measures are difficult to collect and to interpret in humans, especially under the intimate conditions associated with social bond formation in humans. Physiological measures are most valuable when studied in context and in conjunction with other measures. For example, changes in heart rate or "stress" hormones are not specific to pair bonding, and are sensitive to changes in physical activity, thermoregulation, states of fear, or a myriad of other processes.

In animal studies, social bonds are typically measured by choice behaviors between a familiar partner or a comparable stranger. Peaceful physical contact over a prolonged period of time is an especially sensitive indicator of pair bonding in animals (Williams, Catania, & Carter, 1992). Alternatively, social bonds can be assessed by the debilitating effects of separation on behavior and physiology (e.g., Grippo, Lamb, Carter, & Porges, 2007b). Willingness to defend a mate or a territory also has been used as a defining feature of pair bonding. In socially monogamous mammals, such as prairie voles, aggression toward intruders is triggered following prolonged cohabitation and mating (Winslow, Hastings, Carter, Harbaugh, & Insel, 1993; Bowler, Cushing, & Carter, 2002). This form of selective and defensive aggression, interpreted as mate guarding, also has been used as an index of pair-bond formation.

Although "pair bond" implies a relationship between two partners, the tendency or willingness to form social bonds may extend to more than a single partner. The capacity or tendency to form either one or more social bonds varies across species, and in some cases may lead to extended family groups. As in humans, studies of social behavior in animals are best conducted with knowledge of the history and social context of the individual, as well as the evolutionary processes that produce the neural substrates for a given behavior.

How are Social Bonds Formed?

The capacity to engage in social behavior and subsequently to form social bonds is an emergent property of the mammalian nervous system (Bowlby, 1973; Porges, 1998). Social behaviors and the ability to develop social bonds vary across species, among individuals, and may be sexually dimorphic. Physiological processes, including autonomic and emotional states can facilitate or inhibit the capacity to form social bonds. However, because of the evolved nature of the mammalian nervous system, the basic neuroendocrine processes leading to pair-bond formation are shared among various mammals, including humans.

The central nervous system, including sensory organs, the brain, and the cranial nerves regulating the muscles of the face and head, and the various branches of the autonomic nervous system are involved in all aspects of sociality (Porges, 2007). The first step in pair-bond formation is social engagement and then individual recognition. The nervous system perceives and interprets available social cues as either positive, signaling possible approach, or negative, often followed by avoidance or withdrawal. An initial step in social engagement comes with the perception of the traits of another, often based on visual cues, followed by dynamic social stimuli (facial expression, gestures, vocal intonations, odors, and touch). In modern society, humans also may interact at a distance using correspondence, the telephone, and Internet. Irrespective of the sensory system that is used, the formation of social bonds relies on ancient neural, autonomic, and endocrine processes.

Social Engagement: A Necessary Prerequisite for Establishing a Social Bond

The prevalent theoretical positions assume that the bonding participants are in close proximity. In the Bowlby-Ainsworth conceptualization the bond is evaluated by separating the pair. In the Hofer conceptualization the relationship is part of a biobehavioral homeostatic process. However, missing from these perspectives are neural mechanisms regulating attractiveness and spontaneous engagement that bring the participants into close proximity. To develop a social bond, individuals have to be in close proximity (or be perceived as such). This is true for the models focusing on both mother-infant attachment and the strong bonds associated with social monogamy. Both models test the strength and features of the relationship through separation paradigms. There are, of course, major differences between the contexts in which mother-infant attachment and the social bonds of reproductive partners are established and tested. One specific difference is the contrast in mobility between the mother-infant and reproductive partner dyads. In the mother-infant dyad there is an imbalance because the infant may have limited abilities to move toward or away from the mother. However, in the reproductive partner dyad, both adults may exhibit approach or avoidance behaviors.

Although proximity is critical to the establishment of social bonds, proximity is measured by the ability to navigate across physical distance via voluntary behavior. If social bonds were solely dependent upon voluntary motor behaviors, then the newborn infant would be greatly disadvantaged because the neural regulation of the spinal motor pathways are immature at birth and take several years to fully develop. However, in mammals not all muscles are driven by corticospinal pathways. Unlike the striated muscles controlling the trunk and limbs, in primates and especially humans, corticobulbar pathways regulate the striated muscles of the face and head. In humans, myelination of corticobulbar pathways begins between 24 and 28 weeks' gestation (Sarnat, 2003) and is sufficiently developed at birth to be available to the full-term infant, allowing babies to signal their caregiver (e.g., vocalizations, grimace) and to engage the social (e.g., gaze, smile) and nutrient (e.g., sucking) aspects of their world. Thus, the neural regulation of muscles, such as those of the face and head, that provide important elements of social cueing, can facilitate social interactions between an infant and a caregiver. Thus, social interactions are possible not only between adults, but also in the newborn, which function collectively as an integrated social engagement system (Porges, 2003).

The muscles of the face and head influence both the expression and receptivity of social cues and can effectively reduce or increase social distance. Neural regulation of these muscles can reduce social distance by making eye contact, expressing prosody in voice, displaying contingent facial expressions, and modulating tension in the middle ear muscles to improve the extraction of human voice from background sounds. Alternatively, by reducing the muscle tone to these muscles, the eyelids droop, prosody is lost, and positive and contingent facial expressions are diminished. The ability to extract human voice from background sounds is compromised and the awareness of the social engagement behaviors of others may be lost. Thus, the neural regulation of the striated muscles of the face and head function both as an active social engagement system that reduces psychological distance, and as a filter that can influence the perception of the engagement behaviors of others.

Special visceral efferent pathways mediate the neural regulation of the striated muscles of the face and head. From both clinical and research perspectives, the striated muscles of the face and head provide potent information regarding the behavioral dimensions used to express as well as to evaluate the strength of attachment or the stress to the social bond. For example, facial expressivity and prosody of vocalizations have been used as clinical indicators as well as quantifiable responses of separation distress (Newman, 1988).

Maternal Behavior May be the Physiological Prototype for Social-Bond Formation

Mammals produce young that are nutritionally dependent, for at least some part of their lives, on the mother. Studies of maternal behavior provided clues regarding the neuroendocrine mechanisms necessary for the formation or expression of social bonds between adults.

The neuroendocrine processes associated with birth and lactation normally are involved in maternal bonding (Keverne & Kendrick, 1991), as well as other forms of social bonding (Williams, Insel, Harbaugh, & Carter, 1994). Neuropeptide hormones including oxytocin (OT) and arginine vasopressin (AVP) have been implicated in the regulation of birth and maternal behavior, as well as in the formation of social bonds. Oxytocin and AVP are small

peptides consisting of nine amino acids. The major sources of OT and AVP are hypothalamic cells, including processes that release these peptides within the brain, as well as separate processes that secrete OT and AVP into the bloodstream at the posterior pituitary (Landgraf & Neumann, 2004). Oxytocin and AVP are usually not made in the same cells, but may have dynamic interactions with each other's receptors in the regulation of behavioral states and emotions. Oxytocin has only one known receptor (OTR), while AVP has three receptor subtypes. Centrally administered AVP, acting on the V1a receptor subtype, has been implicated in social bonding (Winslow et al., 1993). Following, mating males of socially monogamous species become intensively but selectively aggressive toward strangers, providing some degree of mate guarding. V1a receptor stimulation also has a role in the regulation of both sympathetic and parasympathetic activity, providing another level of integration among social physiology, emotional responses, and social behavior. Thus, the observed effect of AVP on social bonding may be mediated through shifts in autonomic regulation.

In comparison to maternal behavior, less is known about the neurobiology of male parental or alloparental behavior. However, several studies implicate AVP in these behaviors (Bester-Meredith, Young, & Marler, 1999; Wang, Liu, Young, & Insel, 2000). In comparison to males, alloparental behavior in female prairie voles is less likely to be spontaneous, and females that have not given birth may attack pups. However, following birth, maternal behavior is seen in virtually every female prairie vole. It is likely, as in rats, that the postpartum maternal behavior of female voles reflects the dependence of females on OT (Olazabal & Young, 2006). This is one of many examples of evidence for sex differences in the regulation of social behaviors. Oxytocin and other hormones of parturition appear to be of particular importance to female parental behavior, while AVP has a critical role in male parental behavior; however, both OT and AVP may be capable of influencing these behaviors in both sexes (Bales, Kim, Lewis-Reese, & Carter, 2004).

Stress and Gender Differences in Pair Bonding

Another clue to the physiology of selective social behaviors comes from the fact that the events that reliably lead to social bond formation may involve mobilization, and in some cases shared fear-inducing experiences, followed by a sense of perceived safety.

This sense of safety may be enhanced by the presence of another individual. However, for birth and lactation to be successful these events usually occur in a setting of safety; extremely high levels of stress or fear can inhibit either. In addition, a normal birth is usually followed by positive maternal responses to the newborn. Based on animal models it seems likely that an essential aspect of maternal behavior is the capacity to overcome neophobia and social anxiety (Fleming & Luebke, 1981; Numan, 2007). A similar model may apply in the formation of adult social bonds (Carter, 1998). Social bonds are associated with an increased sense of safety and a reduction in fear and anxiety. This may be in part due to the capacity of OT and under some conditions also of AVP to be anxiolytic; by reducing anxiety these peptides may permit or facilitate social engagement and eventual bonding. Sex differences in steroid and peptide hormones, either during development or in adulthood, may be important in explaining sex differences in the factors that regulate social bonding, as well as disorders such as autism that are highly sexually dimorphic (Carter, 2007).

AVP is androgen dependent, especially in the amygdala and bed nucleus of the stria terminalis with a male-bias in AVP projections to the lateral septum (De Vries & Panzica, 2006). In males, increases in *endogenous* AVP in these brain regions may be of importance to pair-bond formation, possibly allowing social bonds to form under stressful conditions when adrenal steroids and AVP are elevated. In females, in contrast, pair-bond formation (with a male partner) was inhibited by exposure to a stressor or exogenous corticosterone (DeVries, Taymans, & Carter, 1996).

Sex differences in the relative importance of specific neuropeptides or their receptors are consistent with sex differences in reproductive strategies (Koolhaas, Everts, de Ruiter, de Boer, & Bohus, 1998). In general, during reproduction males need the capacity to show active responses, including high levels of arousal and physical activity. Defense of a social partner and higher levels of vigilance are consistent with the behavioral effects of AVP within the central nervous system, where AVP plays a role in regulating physiological and behavioral activation, such as increased blood pressure and reactivity to stressors. Specifically, AVP plays a role in the central regulation of baroreceptor reflexes, raising the set point to potentiate sympathetic excitation. The consequences of this change would include an increase in blood pressure and heart rate, and increased ability to mobilize. However, the effects of AVP on anxiety or mobilization appear to be dose dependent; at lower, more physiological levels AVP may reduce fear, while higher levels of AVP may be associated with increased anxiety and vigilance. Exogenous AVP can facilitate the formation of a partner preference in prairie voles of both sexes (Cho, DeVries, Williams, & Carter, 1999). Females, with less central AVP synthesis, are somewhat more dependent on OT and are more likely to show behavioral patterns that require immobility, including those associated with birth, lactation, and female sexual postures such as lordosis. In contrast, males, possibly with more reliance on AVP, may show a more active set of coping responses.

The Effect of Social Isolation

Experiments in animals provide an opportunity to examine in more depth the physiological consequences of the absence of social companionship. Studies in prairie voles capitalize on the fact that this species has a human-like parasympathetic (i.e., vagal) control of the heart, with high levels of parasympathetic activity, unique in rodents (Grippo, Lamb, Carter, & Porges, 2007a). In prairie voles, separation from a partner, followed by prolonged isolation, was associated with increases in heart rate, decreases in parasympathetic function, increased reactivity to stressors, and increases in measures used to index anhedonia and depression (Grippo et al., 2007b). When a bond is disrupted by separating members of a pair, increases in both central and peripheral measures of OT have been measured, especially in females (Grippo, Gerena et al., 2007). Elevations in OT may provide physiological compensation and coping against negative consequences of isolation. This elevation of OT also holds the potential to partially compensate for the loss in homeostatic regulation, normally mediated via social interactions (e.g., Hofer, 1996). In prairie voles, chronic OT injections were capable of preventing or reversing the cardiac and behavioral effects following prolonged separation (i.e., isolation) from a cage mate (Grippo, Trahanas et al., 2009).

Possible Mechanisms for Behavioral Effects of Oxytocin

The amygdala and its connections play a role in the integration of reactions to various kinds of sensory stimuli, including approach and avoidance. In human males, intranasal administration of OT inhibited the activity of the amygdala, especially after exposure to fear-associated stimuli; intranasal OT also altered down-stream connections to brainstem structures involved in the regulation of the autonomic nervous system (Kirsch et al., 2005). Arginine vasopressin, acting centrally (in areas including the bed nucleus of the stria terminalis [BNST], amygdala, and lateral septum), may elevate vigilance and defensiveness, possibly serving in some cases as an antagonist to the effects of OT. Behaviors mediated by the central amygdala may mediate stimulus-specific fear, while the BNST has been implicated in experiences related to anxiety. Other peptides, including CRF, released during "stressful" experiences (and possibly chronically) may be anxiogenic, acting in the extended amygdala including the BNST, to influence responses to dangerous or threatening cues. At least some of the fear-associated or defensive actions of CRF or AVP can be counteracted by OT. For example, it has been shown that OT, via receptors in the periaqueductal gray (PAG) (Ogawa, Kow, & Pfaff, 1992), in addition to reducing sympathetic stress responses, may dampen nociception (e.g., Lund et al., 2002). Oxytocin also may regulate the most primitive defensive response system, characterized by immobilization. This phylogenetically ancient neural system includes the dorsal motor nucleus of the vagus, which expresses high levels of OT receptors and has OT inputs (Rinaman, 1998), and regulates the unmyelinated vagus (see Porges, 2003). Thus, OT may be involved in processes that reduce fear and anxiety, raise pain thresholds, and dampen both the sympathetic and parasympathetic defense responses.

Support for this hypothesis comes from several recent studies in humans showing that intranasal OT increased the willingness of human males to "trust" others (Kosfeld, Heinrichs, Zak, Fischbacher, & Fehr, 2005) and be "generous" (Zak, Stanton, & Ahmadi, 2007), at least as measured in computerized testing. Similar studies suggested that intranasal OT also increased the capacity to detect subtle emotional cues in pictures of human eyes (Domes, Heinrichs, Michel, Berger, & Herpertz, 2007; Domes et al., 2007; Heinrichs, von Dawans, & Domes, 2009).

At least one site of action for exogenous OT is the amygdala. In men, OT inhibited fear-induced activation of the amygdala (Kirsch et al., 2005). In contrast, in women the effects of OT appeared to be in the opposite direction; that is, OT treatment enhanced the response of the amygdala to fearful stimuli (Domes et al., 2010). The effects of intranasal AVP also have been examined in humans, with different consequences from those for OT. Men given AVP showed increases in activity in corregator muscles, a component of frowning, and also rated

neutral facial expression as more "unfriendly." Of interest, women given AVP smiled more and reported more positive, affiliative responses to unfamiliar neutral faces (Thompson, George, Walton, Orr, & Benson, 2006). Reasons for these sex differences are not well understood, but are consistent with a general pattern of sex differences in both reactions to social stimuli and also to OT and AVP (Carter, 2007).

Taken together, animal and human studies suggest that OT may act on sociality through neural mechanisms that involve the autonomic nervous system and promote a sense of safety that facilitates approach behaviors. Simultaneously, at least in men, OT appears to dampen fear and avoidance behaviors. Under stressful social conditions in which avoidance or escape are not an option, then a more primitive immobilization strategy, based upon ancient neural systems, may emerge. This primitive system is associated with a phylogenetically ancient unmyelinated vagal pathway that triggers bradycardia, apnea, vasovagal syncope, and defecation as adaptive survival strategies to reduce metabolic demands and feign death. Although this system functions adaptively for reptiles, amphibia, and fish, the effects of immobilization and metabolic shut-down can be lethal for mammals. The novel neurophysiological properties of OT also might permit physical immobility without fear in prosocial settings, permitting sleep, digestion, growth, restoration, and reproduction (see Porges, 1998). Moreover, OT may act through related mechanisms to promote survival under conditions of subordination or inescapable fear (Ebner, Bosch, Krömer, Singewald & Neumann, 2005). For example, during subordination, the capacity to immobilize and not struggle, or even form social bonds toward a dominant partner, becomes part of an adaptive system.

Opioids and Pair Bonding

Several other neurochemical systems, including those that rely on endogenous opioids, have been implicated in both maternal care and the selective sociality that emerges over time, especially in primate mothers. Both the initial retrieval of a young infant and selective social behaviors, typical of later maternal responsivity, can be inhibited by blocking opioid receptors with naloxone; however, naloxone-treated mothers were still capable of suckling their young (Keverne, Nevison, & Martel, 1997). An even more pronounced neglect of the young is seen in sheep following blockade of opioid receptors in the postpartum period (Martel, Nevison, Rayment, Simpson,

& Keverne, 1993), possibly because the maternal behavior of sheep, in comparison to primates, is more dependent on subcortical processes.

Separation distress on the part of infants also may be regulated by opioids. In guinea pigs, which are precocial at birth, opiate injection diminished distress vocalizations (Herman & Panksepp, 1978). Interestingly, infant rats did not show the expected decline in crying following opiate treatments (Winslow & Insel, 1991). However, in rats (Insel & Winslow; 1991; Winslow & Insel, 1993) and also in squirrel monkeys, separation distress calls were inhibited by OT or AVP (Winslow & Insel, 1991). Details of the sources of species variation in these responses, as well as the more general role of opioids in social bonding, remain to be investigated. However, because the endogenous opioids also play a role in the regulation of the release of OT and AVP, they may influence social behaviors indirectly. In addition, the effects of OT and other parturition-related hormones on the hypothalamic-pituitary-adrenal (HPA) axis can be inhibited by the endogenous opioids (Landgraf & Neumann, 2004). Each of these might be expected to influence the expression and timing of social behavior.

Dopamine and Pair Bonding

Dopamine has a central role in both maternal behavior (Champagne et al., 2004) and pair-bond formation (Aragona et al., 2006; Aragona & Wang, 2007). Dopamine also has been associated with behavioral activation and incentive seeking (Salamone, Correa, Farrar, & Mingote, 2007; Berridge, 2007), which can be elements of social-bond formation.

In lactating female rats, suckling by pups as well as exposure to exogenous OT can activate the medial prefrontal cortex (mPFC) and nucleus accumbens (NAcc), as indexed by fMRI (Febo, Numan, & Ferris, 2005; Ferris et al., 2005). In sheep, olfactory cues and inputs to the mPFC, which are relayed through the NAcc, are critical to allowing positive discriminatory responses toward a ewe's own lamb, versus a stranger (Broad, Hinton, Keverne, & Kendrick, 2002). Interactions between OT and dopamine in the NAcc also have been implicated in maternal behavior in prairie voles (Olazabal & Young, 2006).

Dopamine is released during mating (Gingrich, Liu, Cascio, Wang, & Insel, 2000), which in prairie voles facilitates the onset of pair bonding (Williams et al., 1992). The formation of social bonds is regulated at least in part by dopamine transmission in striatal tissue including the NAcc. Oxytocin receptors are especially abundant in the shell of the NAcc in socially monogamous species, including prairie voles; but not in nonmonogamous voles (Lim & Young, 2004). Interactions between OT and dopamine in the NAcc play a role in pair bonding in female prairie voles (Hammock & Young, 2005). Administration of a general dopamine receptor antagonist in the NAcc blocked mating-induced partner preferences and treatment with a dopamine agonist facilitated pair bonding, supporting an essential role for dopamine in pair-bond formation (Aragona et al., 2006). The action of dopamine on social-bond formation and maintenance of these bonds is mediated through different subtypes of dopamine receptors. D2 receptors are necessary for pair-bond formation. In contrast, D1 receptors play a role in the maintenance of social bonds, including an increase in selective, defensive aggression, which can help to protect the pair bond. The effect of dopamine on pair bonding in prairie voles is specific to D2 receptors in the shell of the NAcc, via an inhibitory signaling cascade that requires cyclic AMP (Aragona & Wang, 2007).

The NAcc also is a major input to the ventral pallidum and there is evidence that AVP and dopamine may interact in the ventral pallidum to facilitate pair bonding, possibly by reinforcing the bond, but also possibly by helping overcome fear or anxiety. To date, these studies have focused on males, so whether this action of AVP applies to females remains to be studied. Prairie voles, in comparison to nonmonogamous vole species, have high levels of V1a receptors in the ventral pallidum. Blocking the V1a receptor in this region inhibited partner preference formation in male prairie voles (Lim & Young, 2004). In addition, up-regulation of V1a receptors in the ventral pallidum (using a viral vector) facilitated pair bonding in male prairie voles (Pitkow et al., 2001), and over-expression of the prairie vole V1a receptor in the ventral pallidum of montane voles, a species that does not usually form pair bonds, also facilitated partner preferences (Lim, Murphy, & Young, 2004). Species-specific microsatellites in the promoter region of the gene for the V1a receptor may alter the expression of this receptor, especially in brain regions necessary for pair bonding; these findings may help to explain species or individual differences in the capacity to form pair bonds (Hammock, 2007).

"Stress" Hormones and Pair bonding

Corticotropin releasing factor (CRF) is another neuropeptide that has been implicated in birth, maternal behavior, anxiety, and adult social bonding.

The effects of CRF on pair bonding in prairie voles are dose-dependent, and thus far have only been studied in males (DeVries, Guptaa, Cardillo, Cho, & Carter, 2002). However, CRF receptors are sexually dimorphic (at least in prairie voles), which also might contribute to sex differences in pair-bond formation. Corticotropin RF and AVP are both associated with increased release of corticosterone. It is possible that a cocktail of "stress" hormones may facilitate pair bonding in males. Corticotropin RF, administered directly into the NAcc also is capable of facilitating pair bonding in male prairie voles, but not nonmonogamous vole species (Lim et al., 2007). Species differences exist in CRF receptors, with higher levels of the CRF type 2 receptor and lower levels of CRF type 1 receptor in the NAcc in social monogamous species of voles. CRF also may modulate the release of dopamine, possibly accounting indirectly for the effects of CRF on pair bonding.

Social Recognition and Engagement

The basic elements in the formation of a new social bond include engagement to reduce physical distance and recognition of another individual as either familiar or unfamiliar, followed in time by a preference for the familiar individual. While the ventral vagal complex, including the source nuclei of the myelinated vagus, and special visceral efferent pathways regulating the striated muscles of the face and head are involved in social engagement strategies, both OT and AVP have been implicated in social recognition memory. For example, mice mutant for either the gene for OT (Young, 2002) or the OT receptor (Takayanagi, et al., 2005), or the gene for the AVP V1a receptor (Bielsky, Hu, Szegda, Westphal, & Young, 2004) show indications of reductions in social recognition. V1a receptors in the lateral septum have been specifically implicated in social recognition in male mice (Bielsky, Hu, & Young, 2005). The lateral septum projects to the NAcc and through this connection might be relevant to social bonding in pair bonding species. Increasing either OT or AVP by exogenous administration has the capacity to increase sociality in general, although both peptides may be important to allow the formation of selective social bonds (Cho et al., 1999).

The Autonomic Nervous System is Regulated by Neuroendocrine Factors That are Also Necessary for Social Behavior

As the autonomic nervous system evolved from its reptilian origins, new autonomic mechanisms

emerged that supported the metabolic needs of the more complex mammalian nervous system and concurrent social behaviors. Autonomic function is necessary for all forms of affective and emotional experience, including the interactive and contingent behaviors that are essential to social bonding. The capacity of neuropeptides, including OT and AVP to regulate the autonomic nervous system is central to the capacity of these peptides to regulate sociality (Figure 9.1).

Of particular importance to mammalian sociality are the changes in the autonomic nervous system that occurred in the phylogenetic transition from reptiles to mammals. Specifically, a new myelinated vagus evolved, including a medullary source nucleus known as the nucleus ambiguus (NA). The NA is considered part of the ventral vagal complex (VVC) which contains source nuclei for nerves of the face and head, and is ventral to the more primitive dorsal vagal complex (DVC) which contains the dorsal motor nucleus of the vagus (Porges, 2007). The myelinated vagus is linked in the VVC of the brainstem to the source nuclei regulating the striated muscles of the head and face. Thus, the primary features of emotion and affect (i.e., neural regulation of facial muscles and the heart) are regulated by this system.

The vagal source nuclei and their respective efferent pathways (i.e., myelinated vagus originating in the NA of the VVC and unmyelinated vagus originating in the DVC) are paired with vagal afferents that terminate in the nucleus of the solitary tract (NTS). Approximately 80% of the vagal fibers are afferent and carry information from viscera to the brainstem. Output from the NTS contributes to the regulation of higher brain functions including modulation of arousal and bodily state. Oxytocin receptors are highly abundant in the DVC, while the NA and NTS contain receptors for both OT and AVP (e.g., Yarkov, Montero, Lemus, Roces de Alvarez-Buylla, & Alverez-Buylla, 2001). The DVC and the unmyelinated vagus have been implicated in various types of conditioning such as taste aversion (e.g., nausea) and passive avoidance. Oxytocin may act to protect the autonomic nervous system from "surging," creating states associated with syncope, nausea, and defecation. Thus, vagal systems may be modulated by various neuropeptides, including OT and AVP. The vagal systems can thus dampen both sympathoadrenal and DVC (unmyelinated) vagal reactivity, calm anxiety and fear, and concurrently promote proximity and the subsequent formation of social bonds.

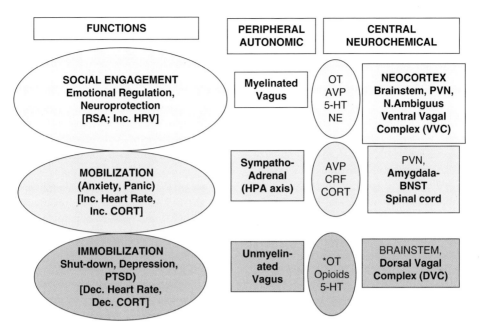

FUNCTIONS	PERIPHERAL AUTONOMIC		CENTRAL NEUROCHEMICAL
SOCIAL ENGAGEMENT Emotional Regulation, Neuroprotection [RSA; Inc. HRV]	**Myelinated Vagus**	OT AVP 5-HT NE	**NEOCORTEX** Brainstem, PVN, N.Ambiguus Ventral Vagal Complex (VVC)
MOBILIZATION (Anxiety, Panic) [Inc. Heart Rate, Inc. CORT]	**Sympatho-Adrenal (HPA axis)**	AVP CRF CORT	PVN, Amygdala-BNST Spinal cord
IMMOBILIZATION Shut-down, Depression, PTSD) [Dec. Heart Rate, Dec. CORT]	**Unmyelinated Vagus**	*OT Opioids 5-HT	BRAINSTEM, Dorsal Vagal Complex (DVC)

Fig. 9.1 Neuropeptides, including OT, AVP, CRF and endogenous opioids, as well as neurotransmitters such as 5-HT and NE, influence behavior and emotions through direct actions on the brain, as well as indirect effects on different components of the autonomic nervous system and the hypothalamic-pituitary-adrenal (HPA) axis. OT= oxytocin; AVP = arginine vasopressin; CRF = corticotropin releasing factor; 5-HT = serotonin; NE = norepinephrine; CORT = cortisol or corticosterone. PVN = paraventricular nucleus of the hypothalamus; a major source nucleus for synthesis of OT, AVP, and CRF. BNST = bed nucleus of the stria terminalis, considered part of the extended amygdala and a target for the actions of OT, AVP, and CRF. PTSD = post traumatic stress disorder. RSA = respiratory sinus arrhythmia, an index of myelinated vagal activity. HRV = heart rate variability. DVC = dorsal vagal complex. VVC = ventral vagal complex. OT, 5-HT, and endogenous opioids, acting in the brainstem, may be protective during or against shutting-down and immobilization.

In attempts to explain positive social behaviors, we and others have previously focused on the anxiolytic properties of OT (Carter, 1998; Neumann, 2007; Uvnas-Moberg, 1998). However, alternative interpretations may exist. Anxiety can be viewed a natural adaptive response to a "fear" of shut-down (i.e., syncope, bradycardia, apnea), mobilizing the individual to allow a physiological state that is incompatible with shutting down. Oxytocin may shift the response to the given "stimulus" from physiological shutdown to allow a state of calmness. However, in contrast to typical anxiolytic drugs that block or dampen this "reactivity," OT may not simply be dampening reactivity, but rather OT may alter neurobiological cues to permit immobilization as an adaptive response. In this context, OT is changing the detection of immobilization as life threat to that of safety.

Developmental Factors can Alter Social Bonding

Neuroendocrine systems involved in social bonding undergo long-lasting functional modifications as a function of early experience. This epigenetic model may help to explain the origins of traits that have been called personality or temperament, as well as individual differences in behavior. Understanding of these systems also may offer insights into the development of pathological or maladaptive behaviors.

Genetic differences are one source of variance in social behavior, including the tendency to form social bonds (Lim et al., 2004; Lim, Murphy, et al. 2004; Hammock, 2007). However, genetic differences (at least those known at present) are not sufficient to explain individual variations in social behaviors. Among the behaviors and neural systems that are changed by early experience are those necessary for pair bond formation. For example, female prairie voles that were deliberately maintained with minimal disturbance during the preweaning period did not in later life form pair bonds (Bales, van Westerhuyzen, et al., 2007).

Manipulations of OT and AVP in the postnatal period also are capable of programming individual differences in sociality (Carter, 2003). In female prairie voles, exposure to exogenous OT during neonatal life has a dose-dependent capacity to facilitate later pair bonds (Bales & Carter, 2003; Bales, Lewis-Reese, et al., 2007) and enhanced subsequent hypothalamic synthesis of OT (Yamamoto et al. 2004). In contrast, even brief neonatal exposure to an OT receptor antagonist (OTA) disrupted subsequent social behaviors, including the tendency to form social bonds, to exhibit parental behaviors, and to manage anxiety or stress. OTA treatment also disrupted the expression of the AVP V1a receptor, with consequences that were particularly dramatic in males (Bales, Plotsky, et al., 2007). Many of the consequences of early peptide manipulations on the nervous system were sexually dimorphic and mapped to sex differences in behavior. The androgen-dependence of hypothalamic AVP and the sexually dimorphic capacity of an OTA to down regulate both AVP receptors and AVP, may help to explain the fact that exposure to OTA was especially disruptive to male behavior. Conversely, in males (but not females), early OT exposure upregulated V1a receptors in the ventral pallidum (Bales, Plotsky, et al., 2007), consistent with the finding that increases in AVP V1a receptors in the ventral pallidum can facilitate pair bonding in male prairie voles (Lim, Murphy, et al., 2004).

Early Experiences and Social Bonding

The biological mechanisms underlying traits, including the capacity to form affiliative bonds, are dynamic and capable of being influenced by early experience (Carter, Boone, Pournajafi-Nazarloo, & Bales, 2009). The effects are often on the same systems that regulate sociality in adulthood. For example, physiological and behavioral changes associated with pregnancy, birth, lactation, and the management of infants during the postpartum period can produce long-lasting changes in behavior. The use of exogenous OT (i.e., Pitocin) to induce or augment labor and more recently the use of OT antagonists, also hold the potential to influence the parent and offspring. Even apparently simple decisions, such as the amount of time that an infant is touched or receives other forms of social stimulation, can retune the developing mammalian nervous system (Meaney, Szyf, & Seckl,. 2007).

The degree to which these findings might generalize to human behavior is not known. However, there is growing evidence that early experiences, including physiological and behavioral changes associated with pregnancy, birth, lactation, and the management of infants during the postpartum

period, have the capacity to produce long-lasting changes in behavior. Human breast milk contains OT and related hormones, which may be eliminated in infant formulas. Moreover, sucking behavior engages the same neural circuits involved in social engagement (Porges, 2003). Thus the decision to breastfeed, with both nutritional and behavioral consequences may represent more than an endocrine manipulation for the newborn. Breastfeeding could also be a neural exercise in the social context of nursing that will strengthen the bond with the mother through the joint mechanisms of increasing OT and possibly dopamine as well, while at the same time enhancing the neural regulation of the ventral vagal complex.

In summary, the mechanisms responsible for social bonding and attachment in infancy rely on the same neuroendocrine and autonomic systems that regulate adult social behaviors. However, the neurobiological processes that underlie the development of later social behaviors may be particularly sensitive to experiences in early life, including exposure to exogenous hormones, such as Pitocin during birth, and decisions such as breast versus bottle feeding or time spent holding a baby. The capacity of these systems to be modified by early experience can be adaptive, but also presents special challenges to the human parent, whose child-rearing decisions may be translate into long-lasting biological changes with behavioral consequences throughout the lifespan.

References

Ainsworth, M. D. S., Blehar, M. C., Waters, E. & Wall, S. (1978). *Patterns of attachment: A psychological study of the strange situation.* Hillsdale, NJ: Erlbaum.

Aragona, B. J., Liu, Y., Yu, Y. J., Curtis, J. T., Detwiler, J. M., Insel, T. R. et al. (2006). Nucleus accumbens dopamine differentially mediates the formation and maintenance of monogamous pair bonds. *Nat. Neurosci., 9,* 33–39.

Aragona, B. J. & Wang, Z. (2007). Opposing regulation of pair bond formation by cAMP signaling within the nucleus accumbens shell. *J. Neurosci., 27,* 13352–12256.

Bales, K. L., Kim, A. J., Lewis-Reese, A. D., & Carter, C. S. (2004). Both oxytocin and vasopressin may influence alloparental care in male prairie voles. *Horm. Behav., 45,* 354–361.

Bales, K. L., van Westerhuyzen, J. A., Lewis-Reese, A. D., Grotte, N.D., Lanter, J. A., & Carter, C. S. (2007). Oxytocin has dose-dependent developmental effects of pair-bonding and alloparental care in female prairie voles. *Horm. Behav., 52,* 274–279.

Bales, K. L., Lewis-Reese, A. D., Pfeifer, L. A., Kramer, K. M., & Carter, C. S. (2007). Early experience affects the traits of monogamy in a sexually dimorphic manner. *Dev. Psychobiol., 49,* 335–342.

Bales, K. L., Plotsky, P. M., Young, L. J., Lim, M. M., Grotte, N., Ferrer, E. et al. (2007). Neonatal oxytocin manipulations have long-lasting, sexually dimorphic effects on vasopressin receptors. *Neuroscience, 144*, 38–45.

Berridge, K. C. (2007). The debate over dopamine's role in reward: The case for incentive salience. *Psychopharmacology (Berl), 191*, 391–431.

Bester-Meredith, J. K., Young, L. J., & Marler, C. A. (1999). Species differences in paternal behavior and aggression in *Peromyscus* and their associations with vasopressin immunoreactivity and receptors, *Horm. Behav., 36*, 25–38.

Bielsky, I. F., Hu, S. B., Szegda, K. L., Westphal, H. & Young, L. J. (2004). Profound impairment in social recognition and reduction in anxiety-like behavior in vasopressin V1a receptor knockout mice. *Neuropsychopharmacology, 29*, 483–493.

Bielsky, I. F., Hu, S. B., & Young, L. J. (2005). Sexual dimorphism in the vasopressin system: Lack of an altered behavioral phenotype in female V1a receptor knockout mice. *Behav. Brain Res,. 164*, 132–136.

Bowlby, J. (1969). *Attachment and loss, Volume I. Attachment.* New York: Basic Books, Inc.

Bowlby, J. (1973). *Attachment and loss, Volume II. Separation: Anxiety and anger.* New York: Basic Books, Inc.

Bowlby, J. (1980). *Attachment and loss, Volume III. Loss.* New York: Basic Books, Inc.

Bowler, C. M., Cushing, B. S., & Carter, C.S. (2002). Social factors regulate female-female aggression and affiliation in prairie voles. *Physiol. Behav., 76*, 559–566.

Broad, K. D., Hinton, M. R., Keverne, E. B., & Kendrick, K. M. (2002). Involvement of the medial prefrontal cortex in mediating behavioural responses to odour cues rather than olfactory recognition memory. *Neuroscience, 114*, 715–729.

Cacioppo, J. T. & Hawkley, L. C. (2003). Social isolation and health, with an emphasis on underlying mechanisms. *Perspect. Biol Med., 46*, S39–S52.

Carter, C. S. (1998). Neuroendocrine perspectives on social attachment and love. *Psychoneuroendocrinology, 23*, 779–818.

Carter, C. S. Developmental consequences of oxytocin. *Physiol. Behav., 79*, 383–397.

Carter, C. S. (2007). Sex differences in oxytocin and vasopressin: Implications for autism spectrum disorders? *Behav. Brain Res., 176*, 170–186.

Carter, C. S., DeVries, A. C., & Getz, L. L. (1995). Physiological substrates of mammalian monogamy: The prairie vole model. *Neurosci. Biobehav. Rev., 19*, 303–314.

Carter, C. S., Ahnert, L., Grossmann, K., Hrdy, S. B., Lamb, M., Porges, S.W., et al. (Eds.) (2006). *Attachment and bonding: A new synthesis.* Cambridge: MIT Press.

Carter, C. S., Boone, E. M., Pournajafi-Nazarloo, H., & Bales, K. L. (2009). Consequences of early experiences and exposure to oxytocin and vasopressin are sexually dimorphic. *Devel. Neurosci., 31*, 332–341.

Champagne, F. A., Chretien, P., Stevenson, C. W., Zhang, T. Y., Gratton, A., & Meaney, M. J. (2004). Variations in nucleus accumbens dopamine associated with individual differences in maternal behaviour in the rat. *J. Neurosci., 24*, 4113–4123.

Cho, M. M., DeVries, A. C., Williams, J. R., & Carter, C. S. (1999). The effects of oxytocin and vasopressin on partner preferences in male and female prairie voles (*Microtus ochrogaster*). *Behav. Neurosci., 5*, 1071–1080.

DeVries, A. C., DeVries, M. B., Taymans, S. E., & Carter, C. S. (1996). The effects of stress on social preferences are sexually dimorphic in prairie voles. *Proc. Natl. Acad. Sci. USA, 93*, 11980–11984.

DeVries, A. C., Guptaa, T, Cardillo, S., Cho, M., & Carter, C. S. (2002). Corticotropin-releasing factor induced social preferences in male prairie voles. *Psychoneuroendocrinology, 27*, 705–714.

De Vries, G. J. & Panzica, G. C. (2006). Sexual differentiation of central vasopressin and vasotocin systems in vertebrates: Different mechanisms, similar endpoints. *Neuroscience, 138*, 947–955.

Domes, G., Heinrichs, M., Michel, A., Berger, C., & Herpertz, S. C. (2007). Oxytocin improves "mind-reading" in humans. *Biol. Psychiat., 61*, 731–733.

Domes, G., Heinrichs, M., Glascher, J., Buchel, C., Braus, D. F., & Herpertz, S. C. (2007). Oxytocin attenuates amygdala responses to emotional faces regardless of valence. *Biol. Psychiat., 62*, 1187–190.

Domes, G., Lischke, A., Berger, C., Grossmann, A., Hauenstein, K., Heinrichs, M., et al. (2010). Effects of intranasal oxytocin on emotional face processing in women. *Psychoneuroendocrinology, 35*, 83–93.

Ebner, K., Bosch, O. J., Krömer, S. A., Singewald, N., & Neumann, I. D. (2005). Release of OT in the rat central amygdala modulates stress-coping behavior and the release of excitatory amino acids. *Neuropsychopharmacology, 30*, 223–230.

Febo, M., Numan, M., & Ferris, C. F. (2005). Functional magnetic resonance imaging shows oxytocin activates brain regions associated with mother-pup bonding during suckling. *J. Neurosci., 25*, 11637–11644.

Ferris, C. F., Kulkani, P., Sullivan, J. M., Harder, J. A., Messenger, T. L., & Febo, M. (2005). Pup suckling is more rewarding than cocaine: Evidence from functional magnetic resonance imaging and three dimensional computational analysis. *J. Neurosci., 25*, 149–156.

Fleming, A. S. & Luebke, C. (1981). Timidity prevents the nulliparous female from being a good mother. *Physiol. Behav., 27*, 863–868.

Gingrich, B. S., Liu, Y., Cascio, C., Wang, Z., & Insel, T. R. (2000). Dopamine D2 receptors in the nucleus accumbens are important for social attachment in female prairie voles (*Microtus ochrogaster*). *Behav. Neurosci., 114*, 173–183.

Grippo, A. J., Lamb, D. G., Carter, C. S., & Porges, S. W. (2007a). Cardiac regulation in the socially monogamous prairie vole. *Physiol. Behav., 90*, 386–393.

Grippo, A. J., Lamb, D. G., Carter, C. S., & Porges, S. W. (2007b). Social isolation disrupts autonomic regulation of the heart and influences negative affective behaviors. *Biol. Psychiat., 62*, 1162–1170.

Grippo, A. J., Gerena, D, Huang, J, Kumar, N., Shah, M., Ughreja, R., et al. (2007). Social isolation induces behavioral and neuroendocrine disturbances relevant to depression in female and male prairie voles. *Psychoneuroendocrinology, 32*, 966–980.

Grippo, A. J., Trahanas, D. M., Zimmermann, R.R. 2nd, Porges, S.W., & Carter, C. S. (2009). Oxytocin protects against negative behavioral and autonomic consequences of long-term social isolation. *Psychoneuroendocrinology, 34*, 1542–1553.

Hammock, E. A. (2007). Gene regulation as a modulator of social preference in voles. *Adv. Genet., 59*, 107–127.

Hammock, E. A. & Young, L. J. (2005). Microsatellite instability generates diversity in brain and sociobehavioral traits. *Science, 308*, 1630–1634.

Henry, J. P. & Wang, S. (1998). Effects of early stress on adult affiliative behavior. *Psychoneuroendocrinology*, *23*, 863–876.

Herman, B. H. & Panksepp, J. (1978). Effects of morphine and naloxone on separation distress and approach attachment: Evidence of opiate mediation of social effect. *Pharmacol. Biochem. Behav.*, *9*, 213–220.

Heinrichs, M., von Dawans, B., & Domes, G. (2009). Oxytocin, vasopressin and human social behavior. *Front. Neuroendocrinol.*, *30*, 548–557.

Hofer, M. A. (1996). On the nature and consequences of early loss. *Psychosom. Med.*, *58*, 570–581.

Hofer, M. A. (2006). Psychobiological roots of early attachment. *Curr. Direct. Psychol. Sci.*, *15*, 84–88.

Insel, T. R. & Winslow, J. T. (1991). Central administration of oxytocin modulates the infant rat's response to social isolation. *Eur. J. Pharmacol.*, *203*, 149–152.

Kendrick, K. M. (2000). Oxytocin, motherhood and bonding. *Exp. Physiol.*, *85S*, 111S–124S.

Keverne, E. B. & Kendrick, K. M. (1991). Morphine and corticotropin releasing factor potentiate maternal acceptance in multiparous ewes after vaginocervical stimulation. *Brain Res.*, *540*, 55–62.

Keverne, E. B., Nevison, C. M., & Martel, F. L. (1997). Early learning and the social bond. *Ann. N.Y. Acad. Sci.*, *807*, 329–339.

Kirsch, P., Esslinger, C., Chen, Q., Mier, D., Lis, S., Siddhanti, S., et al. (2005). Oxytocin modulates neural circuitry for social cognition and fear in humans. *J. Neurosci.*, *25*, 11489–11493.

Koolhaas, J. M., Everts, H., de Ruiter, A. J., de Boer, S. F. & Bohus, B. (1998). Coping with stress in rats and mice: Differential peptidergic modulation of the amygdala-lateral septum complex. *Prog. Brain Res.*, *119*, 437–448.

Kosfeld, M., Heinrichs, M., Zak, P. J., Fischbacher, U., & Fehr, E. (2005). Oxytocin increases trust in humans. *Nature*, *435*, 673–676.

Landgraf, R. & Neumann, I. D. (2004). Vasopressin and oxytocin release within the brain: A dynamic concept of multiple and variable modes of neuropeptide communication. *Front. Neuroendocrin.*, *25*, 150–176.

Lim, M. M. & Young, L. J. (2004). Vasopressin-dependent neural circuits underlying pair bond formation in the monogamous prairie vole. *Neuroscience*, *125*, 35–45.

Lim, M. M., Wang, Z., Olazábal, D. E., Ren, X., Terwilliger, E. F. & Young, L. J. (2004). Enhanced partner preference in a promiscuous species by manipulating the expression of a single gene. *Nature*, *429*, 754–757.

Lim, M. M., Murphy, A. Z., & Young, L. J. (2004). Ventral striatopallidal oxytocin and vasopressin V1a receptors in the monogamous prairie vole (*Microtus ochrogaster*). *J. Comp. Neurol.*, *468*, 555–570.

Lim, M. M., Liu, Y., Ryabinin, A. E., Bai, Y., Wang, Z. & Young, L. J. (2007). CRF receptors in the nucleus accumbens modulate partner preference in prairie voles. *Horm. Behav.*, *51*, 508–515.

Lund, I., Ge, Y., Yu, L. C., Uvnas-Moberg, K., Wang, J., Yu, C., et al. (2002). Repeated massage-like stimulation induces long-term effects on nociception: Contribution of oxytocinergic mechanisms. *Eur. J. Neurosci.*, *16*, 333–338.

Martel, F. L., Nevison, C. M. Rayment, F. D., Simpson, M. D. A., & Keverne, E. B. (1993). Opioid receptor blockade reduces maternal affect and social grooming in rhesus monkeys. *Psychoneuroendocrinology*, *18*, 307–321.

Meaney, M. J., Szyf, M., & Seckl, J. R. (2007). Epigenetic mechanisms of perinatal programming of hypothalamic-pituitary-adrenal function and health. *Trends Mol. Med.*, *13*, 269–277.

Neumann, I. D. (2007). Stimuli and consequences of dendritic release of oxytocin within the brain. *Biochem. Soc. Trans.*, *35*, 1252–1257.

Newman, J. D. (1988). *The physiological control of mammalian vocalizations*. New York: Plenum.

Numan, M. (2007). Motivational systems and the neural circuitry of maternal behavior in the rat. *Dev. Psychobiol.*, *49*, 12–21.

Olazabal, D. E. & Young L. J. (2006). Oxytocin receptors in the nucleus accumbens facilitate "spontaneous" maternal behavior in adult female prairie voles. *Neuroscience*, *141*, 559–568.

Ogawa, S., Kow, L. M., & Pfaff, D. W. (1992). Effects of lordosis-relevant neuropeptides on midbrain periaqueductal gray neuronal activity in vitro. *Peptides*, *13*, 965–975.

Pitkow, L. J., Sharer, C. A., Ren, X., Insel, T. R., Terwilliger, E. F., & Young, L. J. (2001). Facilitation of affiliation and pair-bond formation by vasopressin receptor gene transfer into the ventral forebrain of a monogamous vole. *J. Neurosci.*, *21*, 7392–7396.

Porges, S. W. (1998). Love: An emergent property of the mammalian autonomic nervous system. *Psychoneuroendocrinology*, *23*, 837–862.

Porges, S. W. (2003). Social engagement and attachment: A phylogenetic perspective. *Ann. N. Y. Acad Sci.*, *1008*, 31–47.

Porges, S. W. (2007). The polyvagal perspective. *Biol. Psychol.*, *74*, 116–143.

Rinaman, L. (1998). Oxytocinergic inputs to the nucleus of the solitary tract and dorsal motor nucleus of the vagus in neonatal rats. *J. Comp. Neurol.*, *399*, 101–109.

Salamone, J. D., Correa, M., Farrar, A., & Mingote, S. M. (2007). Effort-related functions of nucleus accumbens dopamine and associated forebrain circuits. *Psychopharmacology (Berl)*, *191*, 461–482.

Sarnat, H. B. (2003). Functions of the corticospinal and corticobulbar tracts in the human newborn. *J. Ped. Neurol.*, *1*, 3–8.

Shear, K. & Shair, H. (2005). Attachment, loss, and complicated grief. *Dev. Psychobiol.*, *47*, 253–267.

Takayanagi, Y., Yoshida, M., Bielsky, I. F., Ross, H. E., Kawamata, M., Onaka, T., et al. (2005). Pervasive social deficits, but normal parturition, in oxytocin receptor-deficient mice. *Proc. Natl. Acad. Sci. U S A*, *102*, 16096–16101.

Thompson, R. R., George, K., Walton, J. C., Orr, S. P., & Benson J. (2006). Sex-specific influences of vasopressin on human social communication. *Proc. Natl. Acad. Sci. U S A*, *103*, 7889–7894.

Uvnas-Moberg, K. (1998). Oxytocin may mediate the benefits of positive social interaction and emotions. *Psychoneuroendocrinology*, *23*, 819–835.

Wang, Z. X., Liu, Y., Young, L .J., & Insel, T. R. (2000). Hypothalamic vasopressin gene expression increases in both males and females postpartum in a biparental rodent. *J. Neuroendocrin.*, *12*, 111–120.

Williams, J. R., Catania, K. C., & Carter, C. S. (1992). Development of partner preferences in female prairie voles (*Microtus ochrogaster*): The role of social and sexual experience. *Horm. Behav.*, *26*, 339–349.

Williams, J. R., Insel, T. R., Harbaugh, C. R., & Carter, C. S. (1994). Oxytocin centrally administered facilitates formation of a partner preference in female prairie voles *(Microtus ochrogaster)*. *J. Neuroendocrinol.*, *6*, 247–250.

Winslow, J. T., Hastings, N., Carter, C. S., Harbaugh, C. R., & Insel, T.R. (1993). A role for central vasopressin in pair bonding in monogamous prairie voles. *Nature*, *365*, 545–548.

Winslow, J. T. & Insel, T. R. (1991). Endogenous opioids: Do they modulate the rat pup's response to social isolation? *Behav. Neurosci.*, *105*, 253–263.

Winslow, J. T. & Insel, T. R. (1991). Vasopressin modulates male squirrel monkeys' behaviour during social separation. *Eur. J. Pharmacol.*, *200*, 95–101.

Winslow, J. T. & Insel, T. R. (1993). Effects of central vasopressin administration to infant rats. *Eur. J. Pharmacol.*, *233*, 101–107.

Yamamoto, Y., Cushing, B. S., Kramer, K. M., Epperson, P. D., Hoffman, G. E., & Carter, C. S. (2004). Neonatal manipulations of oxytocin alter expression of oxytocin and vasopressin immunoreactive cells in the paraventricular nucleus of the hypothalamus in a gender-specific manner. *Neuroscience*, *125*, 947–955.

Yarkov, A., Montero, S., Lemus, M., Roces de Alvarez-Buylla, E., & Alverez-Buylla, R. (2001). Arginine-vasopressin in nucleus of the tractus solitarius induces hyperglycemia and brain glucose retention. *Brain Res.*, *902*, 212–222.

Young, L. J. (2002). The neurobiology of social recognition, approach, and avoidance. *Biol. Psychiat.*, *5*, 18–26.

Zak, P. J., Stanton, A. A., & Ahmadi, S. (2007). Oxytocin increases generosity in humans. *PLoS ONE*, *2*: e1128.

Social Neuroscience of Evaluative Motivation

Greg J. Norman, John T. Cacioppo, *and* Gary G. Berntson

Abstract

Recent theoretical and technological advances now allow for neuroscientifically relevant
conceptualizations of motivation. Such models, grounded in solid evidence regarding evolutionary
development and neuroanatomical organization and function, have the potential to improve the precision
and scope of motivational concepts and theories, resolve theoretical disputes, and generate novel and
testable behavioral hypotheses. Derived from evidence spanning three centuries of research, this chapter
reviews one such approach based on the heterarchical organization of the central nervous system and its
implications for motivational processes underlying approach and withdrawal. Through the utilization of
this multilevel approach, theoretical and conceptual bridges are able to close many gaps between
neuroscience and social psychology that have plagued integrative conceptualizations of behavior.

Keywords: motivation, motivational systems, neurobehavioral organization, central nervous system,
evolutionary development

Introduction

One particular consequence of the evolutionary
development of locomotion approximately 3 billion
years ago has been the necessity to decide, at some
level, what environmental stimuli to approach and
what to avoid. Over millennia, organisms have
evolved complex nervous systems capable of performing computations that incorporate an innate
evaluation of how particular actions may influence
their reproductive fitness. Through this evolutionary process, organisms have developed motivational
systems that encourage particular activities (i.e.,
copulation, foraging for food, avoiding predation)
which promote survival and minimize negative consequences, ultimately leading to an increased probability of passing genetic information to subsequent
generations. Motivational concepts have been central
to explanations of psychological and behavioral

data and have served as a basis for many psychological theories over the past century (Berridge,
2004; Cofer, 1964). Although theories of motivation have been diverse, they all seek to account for
or conceptualize psychological or behavioral data
that are otherwise enigmatic. In particular, they
seek to capture those behavioral determinants that
are not readily discernible from a structural or contextual perspective. Why, for example, does an
organism eat at one time (when food deprived)
and not at another (when sated), under otherwise
comparable conditions? Why do some organisms
seek social affiliation with others, and become
distressed if separated? Neither of these can be
considered simple reflexes, as organisms will go to
great effort and engage in arbitrary behavior in order
to achieve the desired goal. Motivational theories
are routinely conceptualized entirely at a single

level of organization in a rather top-down fashion. This reliance on top-down models of motivation even occurs in cases where fairly well-described neurobiological neural substrates exist, such as in thirst and hunger. Although this single-level approach to theory building has yielded important results, the question arises as to whether a multi-level, interdisciplinary approach to neurobehavioral organization may offer meaningful insights into, or constraints on, motivational concepts and theories (Berntson & Cacioppo, 2004; Cacioppo & Berntson, 1993). The present chapter will consider some neurobiological aspects of motivational systems and their neuraxial organization in hopes of providing a foundation for future integrative neurobehavioral and neuropsychological models of motivation.

Levels of Organization

In his essay *"Evolution and dissolution of the nervous system,"* John Hughlings Jackson (1884) laid groundwork for integrative and multilevel characterizations of neuroarchitectural organization. Jackson posited that the evolutionary development of more complex neuronal organization does not entail the replacement of lower, more primitive levels; rather, Jackson argued that evolutionary pressures have selected for the re-representation and elaboration of existing functions at progressively higher levels of the nervous system. Indeed, the nervous system is characterized by a hierarchical organizational pattern comprised of simple reflex-like circuits at the lowest levels (brainstem and spinal cord) and distributed neural networks for more integrative processing at higher levels (for reviews see Berntson, Boysen, & Cacioppo, 1993; Berntson & Cacioppo, 2000; Berridge, 2004). Through parallel processing at various levels of the neuraxis, these interacting hierarchical structures allow neural systems to rapidly respond to threatening stimuli through low-level processing (e.g., startle reflex) while more rostral neural substrates permit elaborated processing of potential outcomes and future responses. Based on hierarchical interconnections, higher level systems may depend heavily on lower level systems for the transmission and preliminary processing of stressful stimuli.

Additional complexities exist beyond strict hierarchical organization patterns, as descending projections from the highest levels of the neuraxis are able to bypass intermediate levels and directly synapse onto lower level structures, such as the brainstem

(See Figure 10.1; Wakana, Jiang, Nagae-Poetscher, van Zijl, & Mori, 2004; Porter, 1987). This organizational pattern, previously described as a neural heterarchy (Berntson & Cacioppo, 2000), contains the components of hierarchical systems, as higher levels are in continuous communication with lower systems via intermediate levels, but has the additional capacity to interact over widely separated levels via direct connections with the lowest levels. The capacity for direct interactions across widely separated organizational levels appears to be, at least in part, a recent evolutionary development. For example, within the primary motor cortex, thought to represent the highest level of motor responses, differentiated regions are able to entirely bypass intermediate levels. In conjunction with the well-described cortical projections to spinal motor interneurons in mammals, recent reports have demonstrated a "new" area within the primary motor cortex, present only in higher primates, with direct access to spinal motoneurons (Rathelot & Strick, 2009). The highest and most recently developed levels of the cortical motor system are able to directly interact with the lowest most primitive levels allowing for novel patterns of motor output that are essential for flexible, highly skilled movements (Rathelot & Strick, 2009). Thus, there continues to be an evolutionary re-presentation and elaboration occurring even within the highest levels of the neuraxis. In addition to somatomotor systems, this pattern of organization is also apparent in the central regulation of the autonomic nervous system (Berntson & Cacioppo, 2000; Critchley et al., 2005).

As illustrated in Figure 10.2, baroreceptor reflexes are composed of a tightly organized brainstem-mediated reflex system that serves to maintain blood pressure homeostasis. Increases in blood pressure activate specialized cardiovascular mechanoreceptors, which then feed back into brainstem reflex circuitry leading to reciprocal increases in vagal cardiac output and decreases in sympathetic cardiac and vascular tone. These responses collectively lead to decreases in heart rate, cardiac output, and vascular tone, which synergistically compensate for alterations in blood pressure. In contrast to lower-level, homeostatic reflexive regulatory processes, higher-level systems, for example with even mild psychological stress, are capable of overriding the baroreflex to yield concurrent increases in blood pressure and heart rate. This nonhomeostatic modulation of cardiovascular function affords the basic autonomic support for behavioral action. It appears to arise in part from descending inhibition of brainstem baroreflex networks as well as through long descending projections from higher neurobehavioral

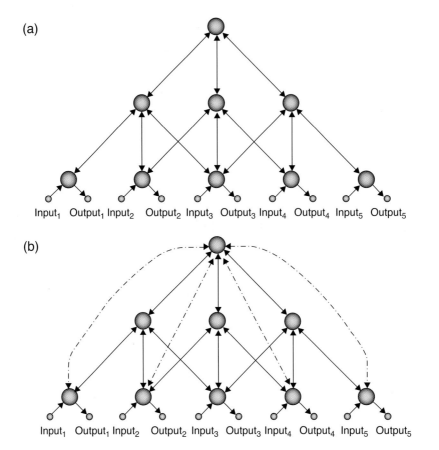

(a)

Input₁ Output₁ Input₂ Output₂ Input₃ Output₃ Input₄ Output₄ Input₅ Output₅

(b)

Input₁ Output₁ Input₂ Output₂ Input₃ Output₃ Input₄ Output₄ Input₅ Output₅

Fig. 10.1 Hierarchical and heterarchical organizations. A heterarchy differs from a hierarchy in the existence of long ascending and descending pathways that span intermediate levels. Properties of the levels in both classes of organizations lie along the illustrated continua of processing mode, integrative capacity, and output repertoire. As illustrated, heterarchical organizations have greater integrative capacity and output flexibility as the long ascending and descending projections provide inputs and outputs that are not constrained by intermediate levels.

substrates that project monosynaptically onto lower autonomic source nuclei (see Figure 10.2). In this fashion, cortical and limbic structures are able to bypass intermediate hierarchical elements and directly control lower levels in a heterarchical fashion (see Berntson et al., 1994).

Levels of Function: Lower levels and Spinal Reflexes

Spinal reflex networks represent the lowest and most primitive levels of organization within the central nervous systems. The evolution of the nervous system proceeded in parallel with the evolutionary increase in complexity and tissue differentiation within organisms, and the associated need to integrate internal functions and motor actions. Within the ventral horn of the spinal cord resides all lower motor neurons controlling the skeletal muscles of

the trunk and limbs, and all somatosensory information from these structures enters the nervous system at the level of the cord. In addition to serving as the final common pathway for central influences on the musculature, the spinal cord also contains primitive integrative organizations. These reflex networks regulate simple stimulus-response relations, and represent the lowest level in the neuraxial heterarchy. Although spinal networks may have limited functions, they offer considerable advantages for the study of neurobehavioral relations, precisely because of their simplicity. Spinal circuits reveal the basic functional architecture that characterizes neural organizations at all levels of the neuraxis (for historical introduction, see Sherrington, 1906). Higher level neural networks evidence similar organizational schemes and adhere to the common functional principles seen at lower levels, but

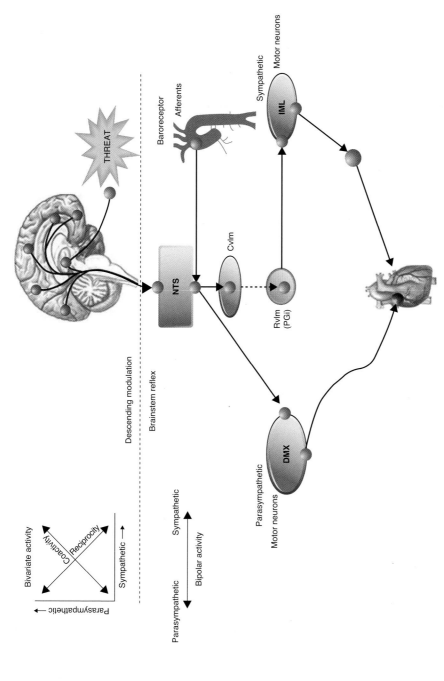

Fig. 10.2 Below dotted line: Summary of brainstem systems underlying the baroreceptor cardiac reflex. Baroreceptor afferents project to nucleus tractus solitarius (NTS), which in turn leads to activation of parasympathetic motor neurons in the nucleus ambiguous (nA) and dorsal motor nucleus of the vagus (DMX). The NTS also activates the caudal ventrolateral medulla (Cvlm) which in turn inhibits the rostral ventrolateral medulla (Rvlm), leading to a withdrawal of excitatory drive on the sympathetic motor neurons in the intermediolateral cell column of the spinal cord (IML). The activation patterns of the relatively rigid brainstem circuitry can be characterized by the bipolar scale ranging from parasympathetic to sympathetic dominance. **Above dotted line:** Expansion of the baroreflex circuit through descending heterarchical projections from rostral neural areas such as the medial prefrontal cortex, hypothalamus, and amygdala. The heterarchical projections allow for the overriding of the baroreflex to yield concurrent increases in blood pressure and heart rate. Thus, bivariate models of autonomic function are necessary to account for the observed patterns of activation driven by more rostral neural structures.

these schemes and principles may be more difficult to discern and anatomical systems and functional relations may be more elaborate and distributed (Berntson & Cacioppo, 2008; Cacioppo & Decety, 2009).

Of particular relevance to the study of the neural substrates of motivation are the most basic neural responses to environment stimuli, cutaneous spinal reflexes. One such group of basic neural responses is the flexor (pain) withdrawal reflexes to noxious stimuli. Flexor withdrawal reflexes are among the most salient and powerful, the earliest to develop, and the most resistant to disruption (termed the *negativity bias*, see below). Such properties represent an important functional and organization manifestation inherent within all levels of the nervous system; powerful mechanisms exist that serve to protect the organism from danger by encouraging escape and/or avoidance from potentially noxious stimuli or contexts. The potency of these protective responses is readily apparent in the overwhelming motivational effects of pain which arise from higher neuraxial levels but depend on lower levels for signal transmission and motor output.

Motivational constructs are generally not invoked to account for spinal flexor withdrawal reflexes, as an adequate explanation can be found in the structure of the relatively simple underlying neural circuits and their interactions. Nevertheless, such behaviors represent a well-conserved primitive pre-motivational disposition to avoid particular classes of stimuli that can serve as a model for conceptualizing higher-level adaptive behaviors which entail clear motivational properties. Moreover, motivational processes do manifest in variations in threshold and magnitude of flexor withdrawal responses. In fact, higher level motivational influences can enhance (e.g., fear-potentiated startle/withdrawal) or completely suppress spinal withdrawal reflexes (e.g., in self-administration of insulin).

Flexor reflexes contrast with another class, the extensor reflexes. These reflexes foster extension reactions to mild-moderate cutaneous stimulation that promote engagement with the environment (e.g., support, locomotion, exploration responses) or acquisition and consumption of objects (grasping, mouthing, etc). The opposing actions of flexor and extensor reflexes are similar to elementary approach/withdrawal reflexes of simple invertebrates having only a primitive nervous system, and illustrate a general pattern of evaluative bivalence in the organization of lower level circuits. The direct

neural circuits underlying these bivalent response systems are distinct and independent, this relative independence, however, is physically constrained by flexor and extensor muscle insertion and articulation actions at the joints. In addition to physical constraints, there exist inhibitory neural interactions between the flexor and extensor circuits. Inhibitory interneuronal circuits exert mutual reciprocal inhibition between flexor and extensor motor neurons—a principle of neural organization that Sherrington termed *reciprocal innervation* (Sherrington, 1906). Reciprocal innervation is the property by which spinal reflex networks that activate a specific outcome (e.g., limb flexion) also tend to inhibit opponent (e.g., extensor) muscles, which synergistically promotes the target response.

An understanding of the integrative outputs of spinal approach/withdrawal circuits provides the basic neuroarchitectural organization for models of higher level evaluative processes. Although higher level systems are more flexible and elaborated, the basic architectural features of lower level systems also provide the general structure-skeletal framework for higher re-representative systems. For example, flexor withdrawal and extensor approach reflexes are not symmetrical in strength, as flexor withdrawal reflexes are significantly more potent than their antagonistic extensor (approach) reflexes. As will be considered below, a homologous asymmetry in the strength of evaluative systems is also apparent at higher levels of the neuraxis where avoidance reactions (anxiety, fear) tend to have a stronger hold on affect when compared to approach reactions (incentive, reward). The asymmetry in the strength of spinal reflexes makes adaptive sense, as a single failure of the avoidance system can lead to subsequent injury or death. Thus, natural selection may have tuned the avoidance system for preferential control of behavior. The bias towards avoidance reactions represents a reoccurring theme at all levels of the neuraxis and has been termed the *negativity bias* (Cacioppo, Gardner, & Berntson, 1999; Cacioppo, Larsen, Smith, & Berntson, 2004).

Despite this negativity bias, flexor/withdrawal reflexes are not always dominant over their opponent processes as extensor/approach reflexes can take precedence over withdrawal processes at lower levels of stimulation or activation. This disposition toward approach behaviors in the context of low levels of activation has been termed the *positivity offset* (see Figure 10.3; Cacioppo & Berntson, 1999;

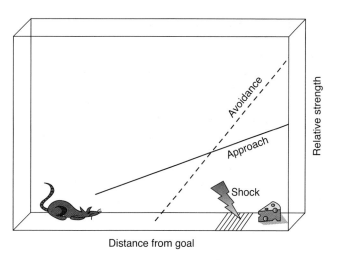

Fig. 10.3 Approach-Avoidance conflict representing negativity bias and positivity offset. Approach (solid line) and avoidance (dashed line) gradients as a function of distance from the goal. Goal items include food (positive incentive) and shock (negative incentive). The avoidance gradient has a steeper slope, and predominates proximal to the goal box (negativity bias), whereas at more remote loci, the approach gradient is higher than the avoidance gradient (positivity offset). The intersection of the gradients represents the maximal conflict point, where approach and avoidance dispositions are equivalent.

Cacioppo et al., 2004), and characterizes the operations of evaluative/motivational dispositions at multiple levels of the neuraxis. As we will consider below, the asymmetry of neurobehavioral dispositions can lead to a context-dependent outcome in that approach dispositions may predominate at lower levels of evaluative activation but can be trumped by avoidance or withdrawal (negativity bias) at higher levels of evaluative activation (Figure 10.3).

Levels of Function: Intermediate Levels—Decerebration

In accordance with Jackson's view on the evolution of the nervous system, the primitive approach/withdrawal dispositions characteristic of spinal reflexes are substantially developed and elaborated at the level of the brainstem. Classical demonstrations of the functional capacity of brainstem networks come from studies of experimental isolation of the brainstem and spinal cord (decerebration) and from cases of human decerebration (Berntson & Micco, 1976; Berntson, Tuber, Ronca, & Bachman, 1983; Ronca et al., 1985; Yates, Jakus, & Miller, 1993; Harris, Kelso, Flatt, Bartness, & Grill, 2006). Decerebrates show highly organized escape, avoidance, and defensive behaviors in response to aversive stimuli as well as approach/ingestive responses to palatable tastes (Berntson, Boysen, & Cacioppo, 1993; Berntson & Micco, 1976). Similarly, considerable functional capacity is also apparent in cases of human decerebration (anencephaly and hydranencephaly), generally the result of a failure of cell migration early in the development of the nervous system. Although these infants typically do not survive for more than a few weeks after birth, they show a relatively intact array of infantile reflexes, including flexor and extensor reflexes, stepping reflexes, and a wide range of brainstem reflexes including tonic neck reflexes and suckling reflexes, among others.

Similar to spinal flexor and extensor reflexes, the basic brainstem substrates for approach and avoidance appear to be distinct and at least partially independent (Berntson et al., 1993; Berridge & Grill, 1984; Steiner, 2001). Brainstem neurobehavioral substrates are more complex and elaborate than the relatively rigid and tightly organized reflex networks at the level of the spinal cord, and both decerebrate animals (Norman, Buchwald, & Villablanca, 1977; Mauk & Thompson, 1987) and humans (Tuber, Berntson, Bachman, & Allen, 1980; Berntson et al., 1983) have been shown to display neural plasticity and associative learning.

Among the more thoroughly studied of brainstem processes are those supporting approach–avoidance action dispositions related to taste hedonics. Similar to the organization of the spinal cord, the neuroarchitecture underlying approach and avoidance dispositions appear to operate in parallel and under separate control in brainstem circuitry (Berntson, Boysen, & Cacioppo, 1993; Berridge & Grill, 1984; Steiner, 2001; Berridge, 2004). Taste hedonics and associated intake/rejection responses offer a prime example of brainstem evaluative systems. Orofacial displays to taste, represented by stereotyped, reflex-like negative rejection/ejection responses to aversive stimuli (gaping, tongue protrusion) and positive intake responses (smiling, licking, swallowing) are well conserved in mammals. Such responses can be seen early in development and are readily apparent in decerebrate organisms. The positive and negative responses to gustatory stimuli mirror the reflexes of the spinal cord in that they reflect opposing patterns of approach/avoidance dispositions. Similar to spinal reflexes, the behavioral output of these systems cannot be interpreted as lying along a single bipolar continuum extending from approach (highly positive) to avoidance (highly negative). Although this depiction can be useful, it belies the underlying complexity of hedonic processes as experimental evidence suggests that gustatory approach/withdrawal systems are partially independent and do not converge on a single hedonic integrator (Berridge & Kringelbach, 2008).

Just as one can tighten extensor and flexor muscles simultaneously, intake and rejection responses are not incompatible and can become coactive. For example, although the probability of rejection responses to a glucose solution increases following the addition of a bitter compound, this can occur without a reciprocal reduction in probability of intake responses. Similarly, increasing both bitter and sweet concurrently leads to increases in both intake and rejection responses (Berridge & Grill, 1984). Thus, it is clear that taste preference, as measured by behavioral consumption and represented on a bipolar scale, does not always represent the underlying bivariate hedonic state (see evaluative space section below, Figure 10.6). This does not rule out interactions between the approach/avoidance responses, of course, but suggests that the mixing positive and negative valences of hedonic stimuli do not simply yield a null average of the two, or a state of indifference (Berridge & Grill, 1984).

Levels of Function: Higher Level Re-representations

As one moves from the lower to the highest levels of the neuraxis, the re-representation and elaboration of processes essential to motivation becomes increasingly apparent. While brainstem and spinal structure are remarkably sensitive to aversive and hedonic stimuli, they lack much of the behavioral flexibility and adaptability of higher level systems. Although decerebrates may ingest palatable foods, they do not display typical goal seeking behavior in the absence of a food stimulus, but rather are prisoners to immediate environmental conditions and contexts (see Berntson, Boysen, & Cacioppo, 1993; Berntson & Micco, 1976). It is with the development of more rostral brain structures (limbic system and neocortex) that one begins to see the emergence of goal-directed behaviors that reflect anticipatory processes and expectancies that are characteristic of higher organisms. Moreover, while lower pre-motivational

substrates may entail simple approach/withdrawal dispositions, higher motivational processes become further differentiated and nuanced.

Berridge (2008) characterizes the "liking" aspects of motivation as those which entail the hedonic and response-eliciting properties of a stimulus or motivational context. These are apparent in the orofacial intake/ingestive responses to positive hedonic tastes as described above for the decerebrate organism. The decerebrate, however, largely lacks what Berridge terms the "wanting" aspects of motivation, which entail an attentional focus on and goal-seeking behaviors directed toward a desired stimuli, state, or context. This latter aspect of motivational processes is heavily dependent on the increased computational capacity of higher levels of the neuraxis and is mediated by more elaborate neural circuitry. It should not be surprising that the neuroarchitecture of higher evaluative processes entails more complex and distributed networks, which are not as clearly delimited nor as cleanly dichotomized into positive and negative substrates as is the case with lower level representations. Indeed, many computational, attentional, and memorial processes may be routinely deployed for both positive and negative evaluative processing. Indeed, even systems underlying positive hedonics, reward, and approach may play a role in aversive contexts in guiding behavior toward a (positive) safety context or outcome (Ikemoto & Panksepp, 1999).

In line with Jackson's concept of evolutionary re-representation, it is important to note that various organizing principles are inherent to all levels of the neuraxis. Similar to findings with pre-motivational spinal reflexes, within higher level systems the magnitude of a response to negative stimuli has been suggested to be generally larger than to positive stimuli (Baumeister, Bratslavsky, Finkenauer, & Vohs, 2001; Pratto & John, 1991). This negativity bias can be seen in diverse attentional paradigms such as identification of negative versus positive emotional faces, and in event-related potential markers of the early stages of evaluative processing (Cacioppo et al., 2004; Öhman & Mineka, 2001). However, while this negativity bias has been considered obligatory at spinal levels, it may be subject to modulation by higher level motivational and evaluative processes (Smith et al., 2006; Berntson & Cacioppo, 2008).

Levels of Function: Higher Levels and the Elaboration of Approach and Avoidance Systems

Although the findings mentioned above are consistent with a differentiation of positive and negative neural substrates at higher levels of the neuraxis, similar to that seen at lower levels, there are added complexities in higher substrates. For example, the nucleus accumbens (nACC), a structure historically associated with reward, contains subcomponents with important phenomenological and computational distinctions. The "liking" (positive hedonic effect, reward) and "wanting" (incentive salience, goal-striving) aspects of hedonic states are mediated by distinct anatomical regions of the nACC (Berridge, 1996; Pecina & Berridge, 2005; Berridge, this volume). Moreover, the neural architecture mediating the "wanting" is far more distributed throughout the neuraxis, a development likely a result of the importance of motivational drive on evolutionary fitness. "Wanting" and "liking" are further differentiated by their neurochemical substrates. The motivational drive to attain a particular goal, "wanting," can be either increased or decreased through manipulation of endogenous dopaminergic signaling without altering "liking" responses (Berridge et al., 2008; this volume). Conversely, "liking" responses appear to be more dependent on opioid, cannabinoids, and GABAergic signaling (Berridge & Kringelbach, 2008). Such complexities caution against the overly simplistic ascription of discrete neural loci to the mediation of complex neuropsychological phenomena (Cacioppo & Decety, 2009). Nevertheless, there remain clear differentiations between higher neural substrates mediating approach and avoidance motivational systems.

Similar to the increased flexibility and processing capacity underlying reward and incentive salience, rostral neuroaxial systems exist that allow organisms to avoid particular stimuli that present a threat to existence. The amygdala is one of the most well-studied neural structures and since the classic studies of Walter Rudolf Hess (1954) on brain stimulation in the waking animal, this structure has been implicated in fear and negative affect. In general accord with animal studies, imaging studies in humans have reported amygdala activation during emotion, especially with negative emotions (Critchley et al., 2005; Sabatinelli, Bradley, Fitzsimmons, & Lang, 2005; Zald & Pardo, 1997), and patients with amygdala damage have been reported to show attenuated negative affect (Tranel, Gullickson, Koch, & Adolphs, 2006) and deficits in emotional memory (Buchanan, Tranel, & Adolphs, 2006; LaBar & Cabeza, 2006; Phelps, 2006; Phelps & LeDoux, 2005). In a recent study, Berntson, Bechara, Damasio, Tranel, and Cacioppo (2007) found that patients with amygdala damage were

similar to control and normative groups in the ability to recognize and appropriately label the valence of particular stimuli. Additionally, when asked to rate the emotional arousal to each stimulus, amygdala lesions patients were comparable to control groups in their ratings of neutral and positive pictures. However, when tested on the ratings of emotional arousal to negative stimuli, amygdala patients showed a selective decrease in emotional arousal to negative stimuli, thus highlighting the multifaceted nature of higher level systems (Figure 10.4).

Similar to the motivational systems mediating reward, the neural substrates underlying the motivational drive to avoid threats, namely fear and anxiety, are increasingly re-represented within the neuraxis. Fear is generally held to be a reaction to an explicit threatening stimulus, with escape or avoidance the outcome of increased cue proximity (see Figure 10.3). Anxiety is considered a more general state of distress, typically longer lasting, prompted by less explicit or more generalized cues, and involving physiological arousal but often without organized functional behavior (Berntson, Sarter, & Cacioppo, 1998; Lang, Davis, & Ohman, 2000).

As mentioned above, the amygdala appears to be a vital structure in subcortical circuits that allow for rapid detection and response to threat (Ledoux, 1996; Ohman & Mineka, 2001). These circuits allow more elaborated processing of threat-related cues than do lower-level brainstem substrates, but remain highly efficient, as they can operate without the need for extensive cortical processing and outside of conscious awareness (Tooby & Cosmides, 1990; Larson et al., 2006; Ledoux, 1996; Ohman & Mineka, 2001). Although the amygdala may also participate in classical thalamocortical-limbic circuits, direct thalamo-amygdaloid pathways are a sufficient substrate for fear reactions and simple fear conditioning, providing for a "quick and dirty transmission route" (LeDoux, 2000; Figure 10.5). Highlighting the multilevel nature of aversive processing, the thalamo-amygdaloid subcortical circuit may support simple fear conditioning and fear reactions even in the absence of awareness ("blindsight") following visual cortical injuries (see Weiskrantz, 1986; de Gelder, Vroomen, Pourtois, & Weiskrantz, 1999; Pegna, Khateb, Lazeyras, & Seghier, 2005). Recent research supports this heterarchical organization as auditory fear conditioning induces plasticity in amygdala neurons prior to apparent changes in cortical areas suggesting that early plasticity in amygdala neurons results from direct thalamoamygdala projections (Quirk, Repa,

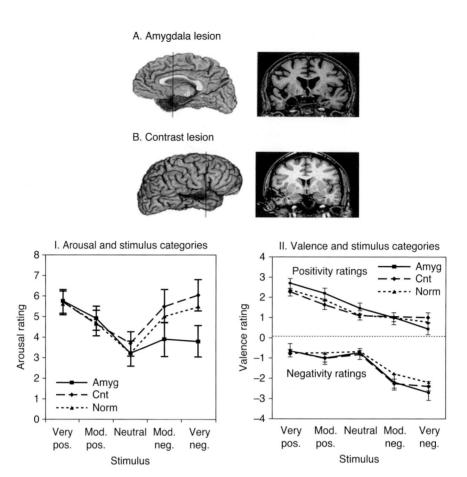

Fig. 10.4 Lesions and arousal and valence ratings in the evaluative picture-rating study. Top: (A). Illustrative bilateral lesion of the amygdala secondary to herpes simplex encephalitis. (B) Example of one of the smaller lesion in the lesion contrast group that spared the amygdala. Bottom: Mean (s.e.m.) arousal (I) and valence (II) ratings across stimulus categories, for patients with amygdala lesions (Amyg) compared with the clinical contrast group (Cnt) and normative control data (Norm). All groups effectively discriminated the stimulus categories and applied valence ratings accordingly. All groups also displayed comparable arousal functions to positive stimuli, but the amygdala group showed diminished arousal selectively to the negative stimuli. Adapted from Berntson et al. (2007) with permission of Oxford Journals.

& LeDoux, 1995; Quirk, Armony, & LeDoux, 1997; Ohman & Mineka, 2001). The more direct, efficient, but relatively limited thalamo-amygdaloid and the more elaborated, integrative, and flexible thalamo-cortical-amygdaloid circuits represent distinct heterarchical levels of processing of immediate threat (Figure 10.5).

While the amygdala appears to be especially critical for simple fear conditioning and fear potentiation of startle (LeDoux, 2003; Phelps & LeDoux, 2005; Walker, Toufexis, & Davis, 2003), its role in anxiety remains less clear. Indeed, while inactivation of the central nucleus of the amygdala interferes with both the learning and expression components of fear conditioning (Wilensky, Schafe, Kristensen, & LeDoux, 2006), it fails to attenuate anxiety like behavior in mice (Walker & Davis, 1997). Rather, the bed nucleus of the stria terminalis (BNST) and the medial prefrontal cortex may be more specifically involved in anxiety-like reactions to longer-lasting, more generalized threat cues. Lesions of the BNST, for example, disrupt light-induced startle potentiation, which has been suggested to be a model for anxiety, but largely spare simple conditioned fear-potentiated startle (Walker & Davis, 1997; Walker, Toufexis, & Davis, 2003). Further, lesions of the basal forebrain cortical cholinergic pathway or its termination in the medial prefrontal cortex disrupt anxiety-like responses, but spare simple fear conditioning (Berntson et al., 1998; Hart, Sarter, & Berntson, 1999). Whereas cortical systems may not be necessary in explicit fear responses, they appear

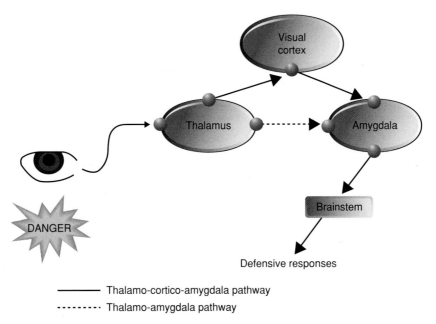

Thalamo-cortico-amygdala pathway
-------- Thalamo-amygdala pathway

Fig. 10.5 Schematic representation of the classical thalamo-cortical visual pathway, where afferent information is conveyed to the cortex via the relay nucleus of the thalamus (lateral geniculate nucleus). Also illustrated is an alternative thalamo-amygdala route, which can bypass the cortex and mediate rapid fear and defensive responses to certain classes of aversive stimuli (see LeDoux, 2003).

to be critical for the processing of more complex stimuli and contextual fear conditioning (Knox & Berntson, 2006; LeDoux, 2000; Phillips & LeDoux, 1992; Stowell, Berntson, & Sarter, 2000).

Extending such findings, Gray and McNaughton (2000) have incorporated much of the above information into a two-dimensional defense system model which makes clear anatomical, behavioral, and functional distinctions between fear and anxiety. The first dimension is a qualitative distinction between systems controlling defensive avoidance (fear) and defensive approach (anxiety). The model notes that the two states often display opposite characteristics where fear produces speed toward or away from a stimulus while anxiety produces slowness, caution, and deliberation (Gray & McNaughton, 2000; McNaughton & Corr, 2004, 2008). The second dimension is based on functional and organizational distinctions inherent to the neuroarchitectural substrates involved in fear and anxiety. These distinctions are characterized in a hierarchical manor where substantial overlap between the two systems exists at caudal levels (periaqueductal gray & medial hypothalamus) at a gross anatomical level, although differentiation within these general areas likely exists (see Berntson, 2006). As one moves rostrally, further differentiation may

emerge (e.g., anterior cingulate for defensive avoidance and posterior cingulate for defensive approach), but the more significant perspective concerns the level of requisite processing (see McNaughton & Corr, 2008).

The multiple heterarchical levels represent at least partially distinct processing substrates, and may function in at least partial independence from other levels (Berntson, Sarter, & Cacioppo, 1998). Generally, however, different levels are in close reciprocal communication and are capable of shifting from approach to avoidance defensive strategies quickly and can even display coactivation of approach/avoidance substrates (Gray & McNaughton, 2000; Larsen, McGraw, Mellers, & Cacioppo, 2004). As described above, higher neural systems can inhibit or override lower-level substrates, but more typically, complex interactions and recurrent processing may occur across levels. Indeed, Cunningham and Zelazo (2007) have utilized this information in constructing what they have termed the iterative-reprocessing model. A central component of this model is the appreciation of the reciprocal, recurrent communications across distinct spatial and temporal dimensions of neural processing. Lower-level substrates, such as the hypothalamus, may provide affectively laden information regarding the valance and the arousal dimensions of a particular stimulus or context that serve to guide higher evaluative processing substrates. According to this model, higher level pre-frontal cortical systems are then able to utilize this information to subsequently modulate processing at lower levels of neuraxial organization (see Cunningham, this volume). The multiplicity in heterarchical levels may preclude simple isomorphic mappings between affect in the psychological domain and neural substrates in the biological domain (Berntson, 2006; Cacioppo & Decety, 2009).

Levels of Function: Higher levels and Evaluative Space

As discussed above, theories of evaluative and motivational processes historically have often been derived exclusively from psychological and behavioral data, leading to the conceptualization of affective states as lying along a bipolar continuum extending from positive to negative. It is now clear, however, that varying degrees of positive and negative evaluative activation can coexist yielding a state of ambivalence (Larsen et al., 2004). Rewards and punishments in a task may lead to relatively selective activation of positive and negative evaluative states, respectively. This may comport with a

bipolar model of affective reactions. Ambivalence, however, is apparent in situations in which reward is obtained but is less than possible or expected (disappointing wins) or in which losses are incurred, but are less than could have been (relieving losses). This ambivalence is characterized by concurrent activation of both positive and negative evaluative states, and is not consistent with a bipolar model of affective space. Based upon these kinds of findings and on neurobehavioral understandings of the relative independence of the approach and avoidance systems, Cacioppo and Berntson have described an alternative, bivariate model of affect. As depicted in Figure 10.6, this model, termed The Evaluative Space Model (ESM) subsumes the bipolar conceptualization as the reciprocal diagonal, but also captures independent activations of positive and negative substrates as well as states of ambivalence associated with the coactivity diagonal (Cacioppo & Berntson, 1994; Cacioppo, Garnder, & Berntson, 1997; Cacioppo, Larsen, Smith, & Berntson, 2004). The ESM can account for dynamic changes in both approach and avoidance dispositions such as that depicted in Figure 10.3, where an organism is motivated to approach a highly rewarding stimulus while aversion systems are simultaneously working to avoid harm. The ESM

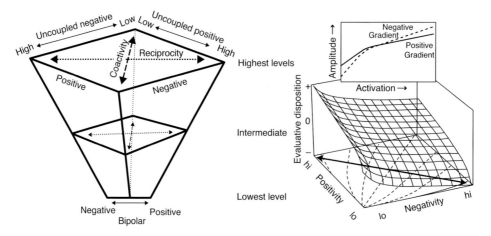

Fig. 10.6 Bivariate evaluative space. Left: The bivariate evaluative plane. The Y axis represents the level of activation of positive evaluative processes, and the X axis represents the level of activation of the negative evaluative processes. The reciprocity diagonal represents the classical bipolar model of valence which extends from high positivity (left) to high negativity (right) along a single evaluative continuum. The coactivity diagonal represents an alternative mode where both evaluative dimensions are coactivated (conflict, ambivalence). The arrows outside of the box represent uncoupled changes in positive or negative evaluative processing. This evaluative plane provides a more comprehensive model of evaluative processes that subsumes the bipolar model as one reciprocal. The evaluative space at the most rostral levels is characterized by its flexibility to operate in bivariate as well as bipolar modes. As one moves downward to intermediate levels, bivariate modes of operation are less apparent and at the lowest levels bipolar activation is typical. Right: A three-dimensional depiction of evaluative space, where the surface overlying the bivariate plane represents the net approach/avoidance disposition for any location on the evaluative plane. The insert on this figure illustrates activation functions along the positivity and negativity axes. Differences in the slopes and intercepts of these functions depict the positivity offset (higher intercept) and negativity bias (higher slope).

represents a more comprehensive model of affective space, and illustrates how multilevel analyses, including neuroevolutionary and neurobehavioral frameworks, can guide and constrain theories and models of higher neuropsychological functioning. It further illustrates the importance of cognitive, affective, and behavioral data in understanding neurobehavioral organizations. Indeed, it is this mutual synergy that constitutes the power of multilevel interdisciplinary efforts at understanding both biological and psychological phenomena.

Summary

Recent theoretical and technological advances now allow for neuroscientifically relevant conceptualizations of motivation. Such models, grounded in solid evidence regarding evolutionary development and neuroanatomical organization and function, have the potential to improve the precision and scope of motivational concepts and theories, resolve theoretical disputes, and generate novel and testable behavioral hypotheses. Derived from evidence spanning three centuries of research, the present chapter has reviewed one such approach based on the heterarchical organization of the central nervous system and its implications for motivational processes underlying approach and withdrawal. Through the utilization of this multilevel approach, theoretical and conceptual bridges are able to close many gaps between neuroscience and social psychology that have plagued integrative conceptualizations of behavior.

References

Baumeister, R. F., Bratslavsky, E., Finkenauer, C., & Vohs, K. D. (2001). Bad is stronger than good. *Review of General Psychology, 5*, 323–370.

Berntson, G. G. (2006). Reasoning about brains. In J. T. V. Cacioppo, P. S. Visser, & C. L. Pickett, (Eds.), *Social neuroscience: People thinking about thinking people.* Cambridge, Massachusetts: The MIT Press.

Berntson, G. G. & J. T. Cacioppo, (Eds.). (2004). *Multilevel analyses and reductionism: Why social psychologists should care about neuroscience and vice versa.* Cambridge: MIT Press.

Berntson, G. G., Bechara, A., Damasio, H., Tranel, D., & Cacioppo, J. T. (2007). Amygdala contribution to selective dimensions of emotion. *Soc Cogn Affect Neurosci, 2*(2), 123–129.

Berntson, G. G., Boysen, S. T., & Cacioppo, J. T. (1993). Neurobehavioral organization and the cardinal principle of evaluative bivalence. *Ann N Y Acad Sci, 702*, 75–102.

Berntson, G. G., Cacioppo, J. T., Binkley, P. F., Uchino, B. N., Quigley, K. S., & Fieldstone, A. (1994). Autonomic cardiac control. III. Psychological stress and cardiac response in autonomic space as revealed by pharmacological blockades. *Psychophysiology, 31*(6), 599–608.

Berntson, G. G. & Cacioppo, J. T. (2000). *From homeostasis to allodynamic regulation.* Cambridge: University Press.

Berntson, G. G. & Micco, D. J. (1976). Organization of brainstem behavioral systems. *Brain Res Bull, 1*(5), 471–483.

Berntson, G. G., Sarter, M., & Cacioppo, J. T. (1998). Anxiety and cardiovascular reactivity: The basal forebrain cholinergic link. *Behav Brain Res, 94*(2), 225–248.

Berntson, G. G., Tuber, D. S., Ronca, A. E., & Bachman, D. S. (1983). The decerebrate human: associative learning. *Exp Neurol, 81*(1), 77–88.

Berntson, G. G & Cacioppo, J. T. (2008). The functional neuroarchitecture of evaluative processes. In A. Elliot (Ed.) *Handbook of approach and avoidance motivation.* (pp. 307–321) New York: Lawrence Erlbaum.

Berridge, K. C. (1996). Food reward: Brain substrates of wanting and liking. *Neurosci Biobehav Rev, 20*(1), 1–25.

Berridge, K. C. (2004). Motivation concepts in behavioral neuroscience. *Physiol Behav, 81*(2), 179–209.

Berridge, K. C. & Grill, H. J. (1984) Isohedonic tastes support a two-dimensional hypothesis of palatability. *Appetite, 5*(3), 221–223.

Berridge, K. C. & Kringelbach, M. L. (2008). Affective neuroscience of pleasure: Reward in humans and animals. *Psychopharmacology (Berl), 199*(3), 457–480.

Buchanan, T. W., Tranel, D., & Adolphs, R. (2006). Memories for emotional autobiographical events following unilateral damage to medial temporal lobe. *Brain, 129*(Pt 1), 115–127.

Cacioppo, J. T., & Berntson, G. G. (1994). Relationship between attitudes and evaluative space: A critical review, with emphasis on the separability of positive and negative substrates. *Psychol Bull, 115*, 401–423.

Cacioppo, J. T. & Decety, J. (2009). What are the brain mechanisms on which psychological processes are based? *Perspectives on Psychological Science, 4*, 10–18.

Cacioppo, J. T., Gardner, W. L., & Berntson, G. G. (1997). Beyond bipolar conceptualizations and measures: The case of attitudes and evaluative space. *Pers Soc Psychol Rev, 1*(1), 3–25.

Cacioppo, J. T., Gardner, W. L., & Berntson, G. G. (1999). The affect system has parallel and integrative processing components: Form follows function. *Journal of Personality and Social Psychology, 76*, 839–855.

Cacioppo, J. T., Larsen, J. T., Smith, N. K., & Berntson, G. G. (2004). The affect system: What lurks below the surface of feelings. In N. H. F. A.R. Manstead & A.H. Fischer (Eds.), *Feelings and emotions: The Amsterdam conference.* New York: Cambridge University Press.

Cofer, C. N. & Appley, M. H (1964). *Motivation: Theory and research.* New York John Wiley & Sons.

Critchley, H. D., Rotshtein, P., Nagai, Y., O'Doherty, J., Mathias, C. J., & Dolan, R. J. (2005). Activity in the human brain predicting differential heart rate responses to emotional facial expressions. *Neuroimage, 24*(3), 751–762.

Cunningham, W. A. & Zelazo P. D. (2007). Attitudes and evaluations: a social cognitive neuroscience perspective. *Trends in Cognitive Sciences, 11*(3), 97–104.

de Gelder, B., Vroomen, J., Pourtois, G., & Weiskrantz, L. (1999). Non-conscious recognition of affect in the absence of striate cortex. *Neuroreport, 10*(18), 3759–3763.

Gray, J. A. & McNaughton, N. (2000). *The Neuropsychology of Anxiety: An enquiry into the functions of the septo-hippocampal system.* Oxford: Oxford University Press.

Harris, R. B., Kelso, E. W., Flatt, W. P., Bartness, T. J., & Grill, H. J. (2006). Energy expenditure and body composition of chronically maintained decerebrate rats in the fed and fasted condition. *Endocrinology, 147*(3), 1365–1376.

Hess, W. R. (1954). *Diencephalon: Autonomic and extrapyramidal functions.* New York: Grune and Stratton.

Ikemoto, S. & Panksepp, J. (1999). The role of nucleus accumbens dopamine in motivated behavior: a unifying interpretation with special reference to reward-seeking. *Brain Res Brain Res Rev, 31*(1), 6–41.

Jackson, J. H. (1884). *Evolution and dissolution of the nervous system (Croonian Lectures).* New York: Basic Books.

Knox, D. & Berntson, G. G. (2006). Effect of nucleus basalis magnocellularis cholinergic lesions on fear-like and anxiety-like behavior. *Behav Neurosci, 120*(2), 307–312.

LaBar, K. S. & Cabeza, R. (2006). Cognitive neuroscience of emotional memory. *Nat Rev Neurosci, 7*(1), 54–64.

Lang, P. J., Davis, M., & Ohman, A. (2000). Fear and anxiety: animal models and human cognitive psychophysiology. *J Affect Disord, 61*(3), 137–159.

Larson, C. L., Schaefer, H. S., Siegle, G. J., Jackson, C. A., Anderle, M. J., & Davidson, R. J. (2006). Fear is fast in phobic individuals: Amygdala activation in response to fear-relevant stimuli. *Biol Psychiatry, 60*(4), 410–417.

Larsen, J. T., McGraw, A. P., Mellers, B. A., & Cacioppo, J. T. (2004). The agony of victory and the thrill of defeat: Mixed emotional reactions to disappointing wins and relieving losses. *Psychological Science, 15*, 325–330.

LeDoux, J. (2003). The emotional brain, fear, and the amygdala. *Cell Mol Neurobiol, 23*(4–5), 727–738.

LeDoux, J. E. (1996). *The emotional brain: The mysterious underpinnings of emotional life. New York*: Simon and Schuster.

LeDoux, J. E. (2000). Emotion circuits in the brain. *Annu Rev Neurosci, 23*, 155–184.

Mauk, M. D. & Thompson, R. F. (1987). Retention of classically conditioned eyelid responses following acute decerebration. *Brain Res, 403*(1), 89–95.

McNaughton, N. & Corr, P. J. (2004). A two-dimensional neuropsychology of defense: Fear/anxiety and defensive distance. *Neurosci Biobehav Rev, 28*(3), 285–305.

McNaughton, N. & Corr, P. (2008). Central theories of motivation and emotion. In G. G. Berntson & J. T. Cacioppo (Eds.). *Handbook of neuroscience for the behavioral sciences.* John Wiley and Sons.

Norman, R. J., Buchwald, J. S., & Villablanca, J. R. (1977). Classical conditioning with auditory discrimination of the eye blink in decerebrate cats. *Science, 196*(4289), 551–553.

Ohman, A. & Mineka, S. (2001). Fears, phobias, and preparedness: Toward an evolved module of fear and fear learning. *Psychol Rev, 108*(3), 483–522.

Pecina, S., Smith, K. S., & Berridge, K. C. (2006). Hedonic hot spots in the brain. *Neuroscientist, 12*(6), 500–511.

Pegna, A. J., Khateb, A., Lazeyras, F., & Seghier, M. L. (2005). Discriminating emotional faces without primary visual cortices involves the right amygdala. *Nat Neurosci, 8*(1), 24–25.

Pecina, S. & Berridge, K.C. (2005) Hedonic hot spot in nucleus accumbens shell: where do mu-opioids cause increased hedonic impact of sweetness? *J. Neurosci., 25*(50), 11777–11786.

Phelps, E.A. (2006). Emotion and cognition: insights from studies of the human amygdala. *Annu. Rev. Psychol. 57*, 27–53.

Phelps, E. A. & LeDoux, J. E. (2005). Contributions of the amygdala to emotion processing: From animal models to human behavior. *Neuron, 48*(2), 175–187.

Phillips, R. G. & LeDoux, J. E. (1992). Differential contribution of amygdala and hippocampus to cued and contextual fear conditioning. *Behav Neurosci, 106*(2), 274–285.

Porter, R. (1987). Functional studies of motor cortex. *Ciba Found Symp*, 132, 83–97.

Pratto, F. & Oliver, P. J. (1991). Automatic Vigilance: The Attention-Grabbing Power of Negative Social Information. *J Pers Soc Psychol, 61*, 380–91.

Quirk, G. J., Armony, J. L., & LeDoux, J. E. (1997). Fear conditioning enhances different temporal components of tone-evoked spike trains in auditory cortex and lateral amygdala. *Neuron, 19*(3), 613–624.

Quirk, G. J., Repa, C., & LeDoux, J. E. (1995). Fear conditioning enhances short-latency auditory responses of lateral amygdala neurons: Parallel recordings in the freely behaving rat. *Neuron, 15*(5), 1029–1039.

Rathelot, J. A. & Strick, P. L. (2009). Subdivisions of primary motor cortex based on cortico-motoneuronal cells. *Proc Natl Acad Sci U S A, 106*(3), 918–923.

Ronca, A. E., Berntson, G. G., & Tuber, D. S. (1985). Cardiac orienting and habituation to auditory and vibrotactile stimuli in the infant decerebrate rat. *Dev Psychobiol, 18*(6), 545–558.

Sabatinelli, D., Bradley, M. M., Fitzsimmons, J. R., & Lang, P. J. (2005). Parallel amygdala and inferotemporal activation reflect emotional intensity and fear relevance. *Neuroimage, 24*(4), 1265–1270.

Sherrington, C. S. (1906). *The integrative action of the nervous system.* New Haven: Yale University Press.

Smith, N. K., Larsen, J. T., Chartrand, T. L., Cacioppo, J. T., Katafi asz, H. A., & Moran, K. E. (2006). Being bad isn't always good: Evaluative context moderates the attention bias toward negative information. *Journal of Personality and Social Psychology, 90*, 210–220.

Steiner, J. E., Glaser, D., Hawilo, M. E., & Berridge, K. C. (2001). Comparative expression of hedonic impact: Affective reactions to taste by human infants and other primates. *Neurosci Biobehav Rev, 25*(1), 53–74.

Stowell, J. R., Berntson, G. G., & Sarter, M. (2000). Attenuation of the bidirectional effects of chlordiazepoxide and FG 7142 on conditioned response suppression and associated cardiovascular reactivity by loss of cortical cholinergic inputs. *Psychopharmacology (Berl), 150*(2), 141–149.

Tooby, J. & Cosmides, L. (1990). The past explains the present: Emotional adaptations and the structure of ancestral environment. *Ethology and Sociobiology, 11*, 375–424.

Tranel, D., Gullickson, G., Koch, M., & Adolphs, R. (2006). Altered experience of emotion following bilateral amygdala damage. *Cogn Neuropsychiatry, 11*(3), 219–232.

Tuber, D. S., Berntson, G. G., Bachman, D. S., & Allen, J. N. (1980). Associative learning in premature hydranencephalic and normal twins. *Science, 210*(4473), 1035–1037.

Wakana, S., Jiang, H., Nagae-Poetscher, L. M., van Zijl, P. C., & Mori, S. (2004). Fiber tract-based atlas of human white matter anatomy. *Radiology, 230*(1), 77–87.

Walker, D. L. & Davis, M. (1997). Double dissociation between the involvement of the bed nucleus of the stria terminalis and the central nucleus of the amygdala in startle increases produced by conditioned versus unconditioned fear. *J Neurosci, 17*(23), 9375–9383.

Walker, D. L., Toufexis, D. J., & Davis, M. (2003). Role of the bed nucleus of the stria terminalis versus the amygdala in fear, stress, and anxiety. *Eur J Pharmacol, 463*(1–3), 199–216.

Weiskrantz, L. (1986). *Blindsight: A case study and implications.* Oxford: Oxford University Press.

Wilensky, A. E., Schafe, G. E., Kristensen, M. P., & LeDoux, J. E. (2006). Rethinking the fear circuit: The central nucleus of the amygdala is required for the acquisition, consolidation, and expression of Pavlovian fear conditioning. *J Neurosci, 26*(48), 12387–12396.

Yates, B. J., Jakus, J., & Miller, A. D. (1993). Vestibular effects on respiratory outflow in the decerebrate cat. *Brain Res, 629*(2), 209–217.

Zald, D. H. & Pardo, J. V. (1997). Emotion, olfaction, and the human amygdala: Amygdala activation during aversive olfactory stimulation. *Proc Natl Acad Sci U S A, 94*(8), 4119–4124.

Processing Social and Nonsocial Rewards in the Human Brain

Lauren A. Leotti *and* Mauricio R. Delgado

Abstract

Converging evidence from the animal literature, clinical studies, and neuroimaging research highlights a specific set of brain structures as integral for reward processing and for learning associations between behaviors and their consequences. The existence of a biologically based reward system underscores the importance of reward information for adaptively learning about the environment and for motivating goal-directed behavior. This chapter presents a general overview of the human reward system. First, it provides an overview of the anatomy involved in reward processing. Next, it discusses the basic findings related to the affective and motivational components of reward, and their influences on cognition and behavior. Finally, it discusses how rewards are processed in a social context and the potential implications for learning and behavior.

Keywords: human reward system, reward processing, motivation, cognition, social rewards

Reward is the experience, or the anticipation of, positive consequences of an action. At the most basic level, our behavior is motivated by a desire to seek pleasure and to avoid pain. As a result, rewards are important for motivating behavior consistent with both immediate and long-term goals. Immediate goals include fulfillment of our basic biological needs. These goals are typically met with primary rewards, also known as primary reinforcers, which include water, food, and sex. However, reward is not limited to the fulfillment of biological needs, as we clearly experience reward in things such as monetary riches. These types of rewards, or secondary reinforcers, acquire rewarding properties through their associations with primary reinforcers, and are important for achieving long-terms goals related to the fulfillment of biological and psychological needs.

Converging evidence from the animal literature, clinical studies, and neuroimaging research highlight a specific set of brain structures as integral for reward processing and for learning associations between behaviors and their consequences. The existence of a biologically based reward system underscores the importance of reward information for adaptively learning about the environment and for motivating goal-directed behavior. In this chapter we present a general overview of the human reward system. First, we provide an overview of the anatomy involved in reward processing. Next, we discuss the basic findings related to the affective and motivational components of reward, and their influences on cognition and behavior. Finally, we discuss how rewards are processed in a social context and the potential implications for learning and behavior.

Neural Circuitry Underlying Reward Processing

Overview

While various brain regions have been implicated in one or more aspects of reward processing, a network involving cortical-basal ganglia connections has been consistently linked with reward-related activity that aids goal-directed behavior. This network includes, but is not limited to, cortical regions, such as the orbitofrontal cortex (OFC), medial prefrontal cortex (mPFC), and subcortical regions such as the caudate, putamen, and nucleus accumbens, which collectively make up the striatum (see Figure 11.1). The anatomy of this corticostriatal network supports the notion of an integrated reward system in the brain. First, many of the brain regions are targets of midbrain dopamine projections, and thus receive modulatory input from the neurotransmitter that has been frequently implicated in reward processing. Second, the constituent brain regions are known to be highly interconnected, thus promoting communication of reward-related information throughout the brain. Much of our knowledge about the anatomy of the reward system is derived from animal research; however, research suggests that considerable overlap in neural circuits implicated in reward processing in human and nonhuman primates exist (for a review, see Haber & Knutson, 2010).

Dopamine Pathways

Several lines of research have provided support for the important role of dopamine in reward processing. Dopamine-producing neurons originate primarily in the substantia nigra and in the adjacent ventral tegmental area (VTA). In animals, direct stimulation of the VTA itself is rewarding, as evidenced by the reinforcement of behaviors that result in stimulation of this region (Corbett & Wise, 1980; Mora & Myers, 1977; Phillips, Brooke, & Fibiger, 1975; Phillips, Mora, & Rolls, 1979; Wise & Rompre, 1989). Additionally, the reinforcing effects of addictive drugs depend on sustained dopamine activity in these pathways (Di Chiara, 1995; Koob, 1992; Wise & Hoffman, 1992). Dopaminergic neurons in the midbrain demonstrate increased firing rates in response to unexpected rewards (Ljungberg, Apicella, & Schultz, 1992; Romo & Schultz, 1990; Schultz, 1986; Schultz & Romo, 1990). Similar patterns of neuronal firing have been observed in neurons in the OFC and striatum (Apicella, Ljungberg, Scarnati, & Schultz, 1991; P. Apicella, Scarnati, Ljungberg, & Schultz, 1992; P. Apicella, Scarnati, & Schultz, 1991; Bowman, Aigner, & Richmond, 1996; Hikosaka & Watanabe, 2000; Hikosaka, Sakamoto, & Usui, 1989; Lavoie & Mizumori, 1994; Niki, Sakai, & Kubota, 1972; Niki & Watanabe, 1979; Rosenkilde, Bauer, & Fuster, 1981; Schoenbaum, Chiba, & Gallagher, 1998; Shidara, Aigner, & Richmond, 1998; Tremblay & Schultz, 1999, 2000; Watanabe, 1989), suggesting that reward-related information is processed throughout the corticostriatal system and modulated by several major dopamine pathways. Dopaminergic neurons in the substantia nigra project largely to the striatum to form the nigrostriatal dopamine pathway, which is primarily involved in

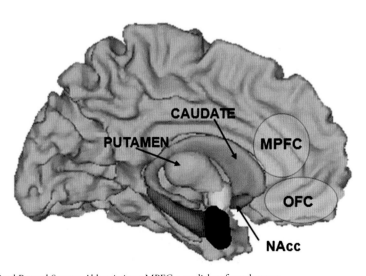

Fig. 11.1 Corticostriatal Reward System. Abbreviations: MPFC = medial prefrontal cortex; OFC = orbital frontal cortex; NAcc = nucleus accumbens.

motor control. Dopaminergic neurons originating in the VTA can either project to the striatum and limbic regions (such as the amygdala and hippocampus) to form the mesolimbic dopamine pathway, or project to the cortex, to form the mesocortical dopamine pathways. These pathways function as the major reward pathways in the brain.

Dopamine is not involved in detecting rewards per se, however; instead it is thought to provide a teaching signal for learning about rewards. This was demonstrated in a seminal paper by Schultz, Dayan, and Montague (1997) which reported phasic increases in dopaminergic cells of nonhuman primates to the delivery of unexpected rewards and to cues that signaled upcoming rewards. Upon further consideration, it was suggested that these cells were coding the differences in expected and experienced outcomes, also known as prediction errors. Positive prediction errors (reward experienced is greater than anticipated reward) result in a phasic increase in firing of dopaminergic neurons, whereas negative prediction errors (reward experienced is less than anticipated reward) result in phasic dips in firing rates. This is supported by a recent study by Bayer and Glimcher (2005) which found that midbrain dopamine neurons in awake primates increase their firing rates in response to positive prediction errors, but stop firing altogether if a reward is expected but does not occur. Thus, dopamine is believed to serve as a teaching signal that is critical for reward learning.

Orbital Frontal Cortex (OFC)

The human OFC refers to the portion of the prefrontal cortex (PFC) that receives projections from the magnocellular medial nucleus of the mediodorsal thalamus (Fuster, 1997) and includes Brodmann areas (BA) 11, 13, and 47/12. The anatomical boundaries of the human OFC and mPFC are not entirely clear because there is evidence of overlap (Ongur & Price, 2000), particularly with a region sometimes referred to as the ventromedial PFC (vmPFC), which has been linked with general emotional processing attributed to changing values, such as risky decision making (Bechara, Damasio, Damasio, & Anderson, 1994; Damasio, 1994), representation of goal values (Rangel, Camerer, & Montague, 2008), and extinction or inhibition of conditioned fear (Delgado, Li, Schiller, & Phelps, 2008; Phelps, Delgado, Nearing, & LeDoux, 2004; Schiller et al., 2008). While BA 11, 13, and 47/12 have also been attributed to the mPFC, the more medial region also encompasses areas 14, 24, 25, and 32. Because the OFC and mPFC receive input

from all of the sensory modalities as well as visceromotor information (Ongur & Price, 2000), they are positioned to play a key role in multisensory integration of information. Additionally, the OFC has strong reciprocal connections with other regions involved in the reward network, such as the dorsal and ventral striatum (Eblen & Graybiel, 1995; Haber, Kunishio, Mizobuchi, & Lynd-Balta, 1995; Rolls, 1999), as well as with other brain regions involved in emotional and motivational processing, including the amygdala (Amaral & Price, 1984; Carmichael & Price, 1995; Cavada, Company, Tejedor, Cruz-Rizzolo, & Reinoso-Suarez, 2000), anterior cingulate cortex (Carmichael & Price, 1996; Cavada et al., 2000; Van Hoesen, Morecraft, & Vogt, 1993), hippocampus (Cavada et al., 2000), hypothalamus (Rolls, 1999), insula (Mesulam & Mufson, 1982), and periaqueductal gray (Rempel-Clower & Barbas, 1998). In general, research suggests the OFC and mPFC play a key role in coding the magnitude or expected value of rewards, independent of stimulus type. A more detailed discussion of the role of the OFC in reward processing is provided in subsequent sections of the chapter.

Striatum

The striatum is the primary input structure of the basal ganglia and is composed of three structures: the caudate, putamen, and the nucleus accumbens (NAcc). As mentioned above, there are strong reciprocal connections between the striatum and the PFC, as well as the amygdala, hippocampus, and midbrain (Bar-Gad, Morris, & Bergman, 2003; Haber, 2003; Parent & Hazrati, 1995; Robbins & Everitt, 1996). The striatum is functionally divided into a dorsal component, consisting of the caudate and putamen, and a ventral component, consisting of the nucleus accumbens as well as the more ventral regions of the caudate and putamen. The dorsal striatum connects primarily with dorsolateral regions of the PFC principally involved in higher cognitive and motor functions (Fudge & Haber, 2002; Haber, Kim, Mailly, & Calzavara, 2006), while the ventral striatum connects primarily with ventral regions of the PFC and limbic regions thought to be involved in emotion and motivational processes (Groenewegen & Uylings, 2000).

Affective and Motivational Influences of Reward
Overview
Goal-directed behavior depends on both affective and motivational components of reward processing.

Reward can be defined in terms of the hedonic value associated with a stimulus, learned via conditioning, when the stimulus elicits or is paired with a positive feeling. This affective component of reward is critical for learning about stimuli in the environment, and consequently for defining how our interactions with these stimuli will advance or deter our current or future goals. Rewards can also be described in terms of their reinforcing properties (i.e., the motivational incentive to engage in a specific behavior), based on the expected value of the action's consequences. The ability to evaluate and predict behaviors that will result in future reward is essential to promote adaptive behavior and to guide future decisions.

Affective Components of Reward

From a rich animal literature, we have learned that the OFC/MPFC and the striatum are implicated in the affective evaluation of reward. Neurophysiology studies have demonstrated that neurons in the OFC and striatum respond to rewards across sensory modalities (Schultz, 2000; Thorpe, Rolls, & Maddison, 1983; Tremblay & Schultz, 1999; Wallis & Miller, 2003; Watanabe, 1996), further being able to distinguish between stimuli differing in reward magnitude or desirability (Cromwell & Schultz, 2003; Hassani, Cromwell, & Schultz, 2001; Roesch & Olson, 2004; Tremblay & Schultz, 1999; Wallis & Miller, 2003). The results of human neuroimaging studies have been largely consistent with the animal findings, supporting the role of the corticostriatal system in reward processing.

Evidence from the neuroimaging literature suggests that the OFC is involved in coding the expected value of a stimulus, since activity in this region linearly increases as a function of the magnitude or subjective value of reward. This pattern of activity has been observed in response to primary reinforcers such as food and drink (de Araujo, Kringelbach, Rolls, & McGlone, 2003; de Araujo, Rolls, Kringelbach, McGlone, & Phillips, 2003; Kringelbach, O'Doherty, Rolls, & Andrews, 2003; Plassmann, O'Doherty, & Rangel, 2007), pleasant odors (Rolls, Kringelbach, & de Araujo, 2003), touch (Rolls, O'Doherty et al., 2003), sexually appetitive stimuli (Arnow et al., 2002; Redoute et al., 2000), pleasant qualities of music (Blood, Zatorre, Bermudez, & Evans, 1999), and attractive faces (Aharon et al., 2001; O'Doherty, Winston et al., 2003; Winston, O'Doherty, & Dolan, 2003), as well as to secondary reinforcers such as monetary reward (Elliott, Newman, Longe, & William Deakin, 2004; Galvan

et al., 2006; Knutson, Fong, Bennett, Adams, & Hommer, 2003; O'Doherty, Critchley, Deichmann, & Dolan, 2003; O'Doherty, Kringelbach, Rolls, Hornak, & Andrews, 2001; Tobler, O'Doherty, Dolan, & Schultz, 2007; Yacubian et al., 2006).

Some studies suggest there may be functional dissociations within the OFC along a medial-lateral dimension and along an anterior-posterior dimension (Kringelbach & Rolls, 2004). In their meta-analysis, Kringelbach and Rolls found that the medial OFC tended to be more involved in monitoring reward values, whereas the lateral OFC tended to be activated more in response to punishments. This finding suggests that the medial OFC may be important for learning about rewards and maintaining goal-related behavior, and the more lateral regions of the OFC may serve a distinct role in signaling when reward contingencies have changed to indicate that behavior must be adapted. The meta-analysis also revealed that primary reinforcers (e.g. taste, odor) tended to activate more posterior regions of the OFC, closer to the primary sensory cortices, whereas more abstract and complex reinforcers (e.g., monetary rewards) tended to activate more anterior regions of the OFC. These functional dissociations are a source of great debate, however, as other studies find OFC activity is primarily linked with valence or goal values irrespective of localization or type of stimuli (Anderson et al., 2003; Plassmann et al., 2007).

Within the human striatum, various neuroimaging experiments have highlighted activity in both dorsal and ventral components during delivery and anticipation of rewards. Such modulation of striatum activity is observed across various types of reward stimuli, including primary reinforcers such as food/drink (O'Doherty, Deichmann, Critchley, & Dolan, 2002; O'Doherty, Rolls, Francis, Bowtell, & McGlone, 2001), addictive drugs (Breiter et al., 1997), and sexually appetitive stimuli (Arnow et al., 2002; Redoute et al., 2000), as well as secondary reinforcers, such as verbal performance feedback (Elliott, Frith, & Dolan, 1998; Nieuwenhuis, Slagter, von Geusau, Heslenfeld, & Holroyd, 2005), appreciation of beauty (Aharon et al., 2001), and humor (Mobbs, Greicius, Abdel-Azim, Menon, & Reiss, 2003), and of course, monetary rewards (Breiter, Aharon, Kahneman, Dale, & Shizgal, 2001; Delgado, Nystrom, Fissell, Noll, & Fiez, 2000; Knutson, Adams, Fong, & Hommer, 2001; Knutson & Cooper, 2005). Additionally, many studies have found that the striatum responds not only to reward delivery but also to the anticipation of its delivery (Kirsch et al., 2003; Knutson et al., 2001; Knutson & Cooper, 2005; O'Doherty et al., 2002). Like the OFC, the striatum also differentiates between rewards and punishments and demonstrates greater activity as a function of increasing reward magnitude or preference during the anticipation and delivery of rewards (Delgado, Locke, Stenger, & Fiez, 2003; Delgado et al., 2000; Delgado, Stenger, & Fiez, 2004; Kirsch et al., 2003).

Influences on the Affective Evaluation of Rewards

Activity in reward-related regions may depend on several contextual and person variables that can influence the expectations and experience of rewards. For example, the perception of risk, or uncertainty of reward outcome, can influence the subjective value of an anticipated reward and associated activity in reward regions, including the OFC and striatum (Critchley, Mathias, & Dolan, 2001; Hsu, Bhatt, Adolphs, Tranel, & Camerer, 2005; Huettel, Song, & McCarthy, 2005; Kuhnen & Knutson, 2005; Spicer et al., 2007; Tobler et al., 2007). The effects of risk on reward processing may depend on the experienced variability in reward history (Huettel et al., 2005), as well as individual differences in sensitivity to risk (Hsu, Krajbich, Zhao, & Camerer, 2009; Tobler et al., 2007).

Reward processing is also dependent on the temporal delay of reward delivery. In other words, future rewards are often valued less than immediate rewards (Frederick, Loewenstein, & O'Donoghue, 2002; Green & Myerson, 2004; Laibson, 1997). Perhaps not surprisingly, corticostriatal circuitry typically associated with reward processing is also affected by the temporal delay of reward (Kable & Glimcher, 2007; McClure, Ericson, Laibson, Loewenstein, & Cohen, 2007; McClure, Laibson, Loewenstein, & Cohen, 2004). For instance, McClure and colleagues (2004) found that activity in both the ventral striatum and OFC significantly decreased when participants anticipated delayed relative to immediate rewards. Based on their findings, the authors concluded that these brain regions may be part of an impulsive response system that is selective to immediate rewards and insensitive to future rewards. Findings from a later study conducted by Kable and Glimcher (2007) suggest that activity in the ventral striatum and MPFC actually reflects differences in subjective value of rewards, regardless of whether they are immediately available or delayed. To reconcile these competing views, it has been proposed

that a single reward value is computed in these corticostriatal circuits, but that immediate and delayed outcomes might contribute different types of information into the eventual computation of value (Rangel et al., 2008).

Explicit knowledge about the cultural status of a reward (e.g., price or brand name status) also may influence the perceived pleasantness of rewards. Using a variant of the classic "Pepsi challenge," McClure and colleagues found that explicitly stated preferences for Coke® brand over Pepsi® brand correlated with increased activity in response to tasting Coke relative to Pepsi (McClure, Li, et al., 2004). Further, the authors found that when subjects knew that Coke had been delivered, relative to the condition when they were unsure whether the liquid delivered was Coke or Pepsi, there was greater BOLD activity in reward-related brain regions, including the midbrain. In a related study, Plassmann and colleagues (2008) presented subjects with a taste test between two wines, which were actually identical samples but labeled with different prices. Not only did the subjects report liking the pricier wine more, but they actually demonstrated increased signal in the OFC when tasting the wine that was believed to be more expensive. These studies suggest that top-down processes can modulate the experience of reward.

Motivational Components of Reward

To engage in goal-directed behavior, it is critical that the brain's reward mechanisms do more than simply respond to what is pleasurable—rather, the motivational saliency of the stimulus or event should also be integrated in the calculation of value. Indeed, certain regions within the corticostriatal reward network explicitly code for *actions* that are most adaptive in a given context, as opposed to coding for expected values of actions' outcomes. Specifically, the dorsal striatum has most consistently been shown to respond preferentially to the anticipation and delivery of rewards that are contingent on an individual's behavior. The firing rates of a subset of neurons in the monkey caudate and putamen, for instance, have been linked with the expected value of an action (e.g., choose left vs. choose right), rather than with the reward value itself, or with the selection of an action, independent of its reward outcome (Samejima, Ueda, Doya, & Kimura, 2005).

In humans, rewards that are instrumentally delivered activate the striatum to a greater extent than do rewards that are passively received or based on noncontingent actions (Bjork & Hommer, 2007; Elliott et al., 2004; O'Doherty et al., 2004; Tricomi, Delgado, & Fiez, 2004). Increased activity in the dorsal striatum is also observed when there is greater motivational incentive to perform a task (Delgado et al., 2004) or in response to highly salient stimuli (Zink, Pagnoni, Martin-Skurski, Chappelow, & Berns, 2004). Additionally, perceived agency, or the perception of control over an action and its consequences, may augment the perceived motivational value of reward, as studies have found greater activity in the striatum for rewards that were the consequence of a personal choice, as opposed to a forced-choice (Coricelli et al., 2005; Tricomi et al., 2004). Collectively, neuroimaging evidence suggests the dorsal striatum plays an important role in monitoring consequences of behavior, which is important for guiding future decision making (Balleine, Delgado, & Hikosaka, 2007; Delgado, 2007; Montague & Berns, 2002; O'Doherty, 2004).

Because the reward system signals behaviors that are motivationally relevant to goal achievement, reward processing within the corticostriatal network should depend on motivational context. In other words, rewards should engage the corticostriatal network most when the motivational incentive is highest. An elegant study by Gottfried and colleagues (2003) illustrated this point using an appetitive conditioning and stimulus devaluation procedure. In their study, OFC activity in hungry participants increased in response to cues predictive of pleasant food-related odors relative to neutral cues. After participants were fed to satiation, OFC activity was selectively decreased in response to the conditioned stimulus that predicted the odor related to the recently consumed meal, but did not change for the other conditioned stimulus. Presumably, satiation reduced the motivational incentive for one appetitive stimulus, and consequently reduced expectations of reward for that stimulus.

Influences of Reward Components on Learning and Decision-making

In general, reward contingencies are not deterministic, nor are they fixed. Rather, expectations about stimulus-reward contingencies must be learned probabilistically through trial and error, and expectations of reward must be updated in response to changes in the environment in order to achieve and maintain goal-directed behavior. Dopaminergic modulation within the corticostriatal network involved in reward processing may play a critical role in adaptively updating reward expectancies

by responding to changes in stimulus-reward contingencies, and thus providing a teaching signal indicating the necessity to learn new associations between stimuli, actions, and reward outcomes (Schultz, 2000). These updates in reward expectancies, or reward prediction errors, allow individuals to learn from past behaviors and to modulate future behaviors based on the outcomes of past decisions.

Above, we discussed evidence supporting the roles of the OFC and ventral striatum in coding expected reward values of stimuli, and the role of the dorsal striatum in coding expected reward values of actions. These findings suggest that the distinct regions may play dissociable roles in reward learning. In a series of microdialysis studies, for instance, dopamine levels in the dorsal striatum have been shown to be elevated when rats are presented with a conditioned stimulus in which cocaine delivery is contingent upon a behavior (i.e., drug-seeking behavior), but not when a non-contingent stimulus is presented (Ito, Dalley, Howes, Robbins, & Everitt, 2000; Ito, Dalley, Robbins, & Everitt, 2002). In contrast, non-contingent presentations of a conditioned stimulus led to increases in dopamine levels in the ventral striatum. These results are consistent with other rodent research that has quantified dorsomedial striatum as a critical structure for action-outcome learning during instrumental conditioning (Yin, Knowlton, & Balleine, 2006; Yin, Ostlund, Knowlton, & Balleine, 2005). Lesions to the OFC result in impairments updating stimulus-reward information, resulting in reward reversal deficits (Butter, 1969; Jones & Mishkin, 1972), and lesions to the striatum have been associated with impairments in stimulus-response learning (Robbins, Cador, Taylor, & Everitt, 1989). Additionally, patients with disrupted striatal function, as observed in Parkinson's disease, are slower during initial learning of associative paradigms (Myers et al., 2003) showing deficits during a feedback-based learning task, as opposed to intact learning during a non-feedback version of the same paradigm (Shohamy, Myers, Onlaor, & Gluck, 2004).

Consistent with the animal and neuropsychological literatures, several neuroimaging studies have linked the dorsal striatum with action-outcome processing (Delgado, Miller, Inati, & Phelps, 2005; O'Doherty et al., 2004; Tricomi et al., 2004) and the ventral striatum with stimulus-outcome processing (O'Doherty et al., 2004). Other studies have found that the OFC and ventral striatum are correlated with reward prediction errors during classical conditioning, or associative learning, whereas the dorsal striatum is more highly associated with prediction errors during instrumental conditioning, when rewards are contingent upon behavior (McClure, Berns, & Montague, 2003; O'Doherty, Dayan, Friston, Critchley, & Dolan, 2003; O'Doherty et al., 2004; Yacubian et al., 2006). However, there is evidence that the OFC codes for reward prediction but not reward prediction errors, and that activity in the OFC is critical for signaling downstream prediction errors in the corticostriatal network (Takahashi et al., 2009). Such findings are consistent with the actor-critic theory (O'Doherty et al., 2004), such that the ventral striatum and OFC act as "critics" to maintain reward-related information of stimuli, important for predicting future rewards, whereas the dorsal striatum is the "actor," maintaining reward-related information about specific actions, to optimize future behaviors leading to potential rewards.

If the corticostriatal reward network is integral for reward-learning, activity within this network should be modulated by changes to perceived value of stimuli or actions that occur during learning. To address this question, Delgado et al. (2005) acquired functional brain images while participants performed a probabilistic reward-learning task (see Figure 11.2). Participants learned to associate cues with a probability (100, 67, or 50%) that a card would be high or low value, which would inform their choices when guessing whether the card was high or low. The dorsal striatum was activated most during the initial early stages of learning (i.e., the first few trials) when feedback was most valuable. As learning progressed, however, the response to rewards decreased in the striatum, as the 100% cue became predictable. In contrast, rewards or positive feedback attained in trials where the cues were more probabilistic (e.g., 67%) did not differ between early and late stages of learning, suggesting that the striatum is active when reward feedback is valuable for informing predictions. Other studies have found that individual differences in striatal activity during learning predict the extent to which individuals demonstrate learning behaviorally, by making choices that optimize available rewards (Haruno et al., 2004; Schonberg, Daw, Joel, & O'Doherty, 2007). Collectively, these data suggest that the human striatum is an integral component of a circuit involved in learning and updating current rewards with the purpose of guiding action that will maximize reward consumption.

The Social Brain: The Value of "Social" Rewards
Overview
Humans, along with other animals, are social beings. Social rewards are powerful because they address the needs to belong and be validated (Steele, 1988). These motives are fundamental. Developmental research shows that infants deprived of affectionate human contact (but whose physical needs are met) show overwhelming grief, are susceptible to illness and early death, and fail to physically develop (Hollenbeck et al., 2004; Spitz, 1966). People deprived of social support (which largely operates by satisfying needs to belong and to be validated) are more susceptible to mental and physical illnesses (Taylor, 1999). Because messages of acceptance or rejection are so important, people are highly alert to signs of exclusion. Indeed, even apparently trivial forms of social ostracism can lead to increased sadness and hostility (Williams, 1997; Williams, Cheung, & Choi, 2000). The neural mechanisms underlying the emotional pain of rejection are, significantly, similar to those moderating physical pain (Eisenberger, Lieberman, & Williams, 2003; Macdonald & Leary, 2005). In sum, people are highly attuned to social signals of approval and disapproval, because such signals address core needs and motives. As a result, positive social interactions may be experienced as both pleasant and reinforcing.

Neuroimaging Studies of Social Rewards
A rapidly growing neuroimaging literature is pointing to the corticostriatal reward network also being responsible for processing social rewards. This is illustrated by a recent study by Izuma and colleagues (2008) showing that activity in the striatum increases in response to both monetary rewards and to positive social feedback about the quality of one's reputation. Other recent studies suggest that circuits involved in basic reward processing are engaged by various types of social rewards, such as experiencing socially driven emotions like fairness, pride, and gratitude, as well as engaging in prosocial behaviors. For example, evidence suggests that experiencing pride in one's own actions recruits the ventral MPFC, while the experience of gratitude for another's actions recruits the VTA. An early study using the prisoner's dilemma paradigm found greater activation of the caudate and MPFC when partners cooperated with each other relative to other conditions when one of the players defected (Rilling et al., 2002). In another study using the related

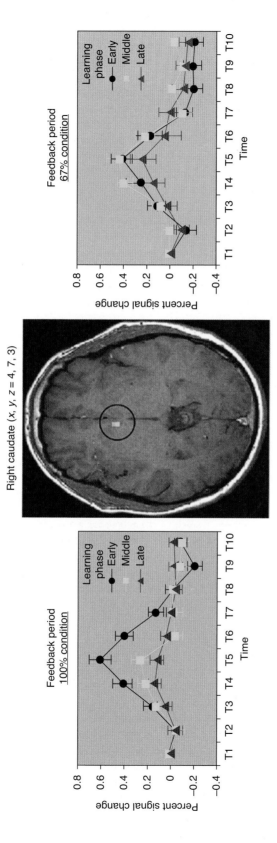

Fig. 11.2 The figure demonstrates the interaction between learning phase (early, middle, and late) and time during the feedback period on activity in the right caudate nucleus. Larger responses to the positive feedback or reward are observed in the early phases of learning for both deterministic (100%) and probabilistic (67%) conditions. In later phases of learning, activity in the right caudate decreased for positive feedback that were completely predictable (100%) but did not for feedback which was still informative (67%). Figure adapted from Delgado et al. (2005) with permission from Elsevier.

ultimatum game, subjective feelings of fairness were associated with greater activity in the ventral striatum, as well as in the OFC and MPFC (Tabibnia, Satpute, & Lieberman, 2008). Additionally, a study by Moll et al. (2006) found that the dorsal and ventral striatum respond not only to receiving monetary rewards, but also to the choice to donate money to charity. These findings suggest that positive social interactions, regardless of whether you are the giver or the receiver, involve reward-related processes.

We may experience reward in certain social interactions because we have learned to associate them with positive outcomes relevant to our short and long-term goals. Learning about social rewards requires integration of information over multiple social interactions to relate social information to actions and outcomes. For example, we learn to trust others based on previous experiences with those individuals, just as we learn that to associate that certain stimuli are associated with positive or negative outcomes. Though research investigating the neural substrates of social reward processing is relatively new, there is growing evidence that learning about social rewards involves similar neural circuitry as does learning about nonsocial rewards. King-Casas et al. (2005) demonstrated that benevolent offers in a trust game are associated with increased activity in the caudate. In that study, activity in the caudate peaked earlier in the trial as the intention to trust a partner increased, potentially reflecting a prediction error for social rewards. Activation of the striatum has been observed when participants are presented with the mere face of previous trust game cooperators (Singer, Kiebel, Winston, Dolan, & Frith, 2004), suggesting either that the face itself is rewarding due to its association with positive outcome in the trust game, or that the face serves as a "trustworthiness" signal that may encourage future social interaction. There is some evidence that learning to trust others through experience may be influenced by neuromodulators, such as oxytocin, which has been shown to prevent the reduction of activity in the striatum to partners who prove to be untrustworthy, in turn fostering more trust-like behavior by investors who were administered with oxytocin (Baumgartner, Heinrichs, Vonlanthen, Fischbacher, & Fehr, 2008).

These studies imply that like nonsocial rewards, learning about social rewards (e.g., whether or not to trust someone) depends on feedback-based learning mechanisms. However, the recruitment of these learning mechanisms may depend on how social information is acquired (i.e., whether perceptions of a partner's trustworthiness were developed through repeated experiences with the partner, or perception of trustworthiness is based on explicit knowledge of partner's character). Prior knowledge about a partner's moral character, for example, has been shown to reduce the reliance on feedback-based learning during the trust game (Delgado, Frank, & Phelps, 2005). Specifically, neural signals in the striatum differentiated between positive and negative feedback during multiple trust game interactions with morally "neutral" partners, when no prior information was available and learning depended on trial by trial experiences. This is consistent with previous results suggesting the striatum is important for feedback learning (e.g., Delgado, 2007) and this type of learning is also displayed during social interactions where reputations are built (King-Casas et al., 2005). Interestingly, the same differentiation between positive and negative feedback was not observed when interacting with "good" or "bad" partners, when previous information was available. Thus, prior explicit knowledge may exert top-down influences on our reward processes and potentially bias how we acquire and update information about social rewards.

Modulation of Reward Processes by Social Context

Not only do we experience social events as rewarding, but our experience of rewards may be modulated by the social context. The tendency to engage in social comparison may change the perceived subjective value of rewards. For example, one could imagine that a student would be very happy after receiving an A grade on an exam, but that same student may not feel as pleased with his grade if he learned that a peer received an A+ on the same exam. The effects of social comparison on experienced reward may explain phenomena such as envy and schadenfreude, or experiencing pleasure in others' misfortunes, which has been correlated with activity in the ventral striatum (Takahashi et al., 2009). Other recent neuroimaging studies have demonstrated that activity in reward circuits systematically varies depending on whether rewards are won or lost in a social versus nonsocial context (Delgado, Schotter, Ozbay, & Phelps, 2008), and how rewards compare to those experienced by a hierarchically superior or inferior opponent (Zink et al., 2008). In addition to social comparison, other information about the social context can influence individuals' perceptions of reward. For example, delivery of punishment to those who have violated social norms activates the dorsal striatum, suggesting that delivery of justice is rewarding (de Quervain et al., 2004). Together, these studies illustrate how social context can modulate how individuals perceive the value of rewards.

Shared Neural Substrates for Reward Processing

Collectively, the findings discussed above suggest that positive social interactions recruit reward systems in the brain. Research has just begun to investigate whether social rewards share the same neural substrates as nonsocial rewards (e.g., Izuma et al., 2008). The availability of social information, along with the anticipation and experience of social interaction, are factors that challenge current understanding of how the brain processes reward-related information and how it uses such information to make decisions in a number of ways. For example, social feedback, such as a negative business transaction resulting from a social interaction, may share similar properties (e.g., valence, magnitude) with non-social feedback (e.g., negative business transaction resulting from lottery), but its influence on behavior may be exaggerated and potentially lead to aberrant social behavior characteristic of some mental disorders (e.g., avoid future social interactions). Thus, one research topic of great interest over the next few years will be to continue to understand how social rewards are valued in the brain and how they compare with non-social rewards.

An initial probing of whether social and non-social rewards share a common neural currency could be achieved by comparing the existing neuroimaging literature where individuals process either nonsocial or social rewards. To accomplish this, we compared reward-related activations reported in 27 fMRI studies (see Table 11.1) using a qualitative analysis approach. Specifically, we created activity maps for clusters showing main effects of reward, including contrasts of reward versus punishment (or baseline) and contrasts of reward magnitude (high vs. low). Individual maps were created for studies investigating primary rewards (10 studies, 83 clusters), monetary rewards (12 studies, 94 clusters), and social rewards (6 studies, 30 clusters). Clusters reported in individual studies were represented in the activity maps by 5mm spheres, centered at the peak activation (Montreal Neurological Institute, or MNI coordinates).

Combining these maps to form a conjunction map of the intersection of activity across studies and reward types, we found that an area of the ventral striatum was consistently reported across domains (see Figure 11.3). Although this analysis is not exhaustive in its inclusion of reward-related studies and the approach provides a rather conservative estimate of co-activation that is not quantitatively derived, it still manages to identify the ventral striatum as a key player in reward processing across social and nonsocial rewards. Thus, these findings provide promising evidence of a common neural currency for rewards, regardless of stimulus type, further supporting the role of the striatum in reward processing. Future studies incorporating a variety of incentives (i.e., social and nonsocial feedback) within the same design will allow for better characterization of common and distinct circuits between social and nonsocial rewards. Identifying a common neural substrate of rewards has considerable implications for understanding variations in normal social and nonsocial decision making as well as for determining potential causes and treatments for maladaptive behaviors across social and nonsocial domains.

Future Directions

Over the past decade, neuroimaging research has allowed for significant advances toward understanding

Table 11.1 Studies Included in Comparative Analysis

Reward	Studies
Primary	Aharon et al., 2001; Arnow et al., 2002; Blood et al.,1999; Kringelbach, O'Doherty, Rolls, & Andrews, 2003; O'Doherty et al., 2004; O'Doherty, Rolls, et al., 2001; O'Doherty, Winston, et al., 2003; Redoute et al., 2000; Rolls, Kringelbach, & de Araujo, 2003; Rolls, O'Doherty, et al., 2003
Secondary	Bjork & Hommer, 2007; Delgado et al., 2000; Delgado, Schotter, et al., 2008; Elliott et al., 2004; Galvan et al., 2006; Galvan et al., 2007; Izuma et al., 2008; Knutson et al., 2003; Kuhnen & Knutson, 2005; O'Doherty, Critchley, et al., 2003; O'Doherty, Kringelbach, et al., 2001; Yacubian et al., 2006
Social	Izuma et al., 2008; King-Casas et al., 2005; Moll et al., 2006; Rilling et al., 2002; Tabibnia et al., 2008; Takahashi, Kato, et al., 2009

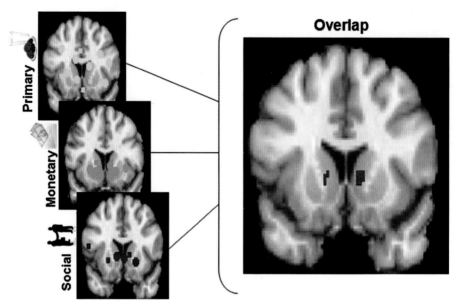

Fig. 11.3 Primary, monetary, and social rewards representations in the human striatum. Comparing activity across multiple fMRI studies investigating reward processes, we found that the striatum was active across reward types, suggesting a common neural currency for rewards. Coronal sections coordinate Y = 15.

the human reward system. Nonetheless, certain fundamental questions remain unanswered. Of utmost importance is an understanding of whether positively and negatively valenced reinforcers have different influences on the multiple corticostriatal loops that mediate goal-directed behavior in humans. While an extensive literature has focused on the processing of appetitive stimuli, magnified even more by the recent focus on neuroeconomic processes (for a review, see Sanfey, Loewenstein, McClure, & Cohen, 2006), aversive processing is a topic that also merits attention, as similar if not more costly influences on behavior can be observed.

Currently there is some suggestion that the same circuitry involved in processing appetitive or rewarding stimuli may also underlie the processing of aversive stimuli. An extensive animal literature suggests that the experience and even anticipation of aversive stimuli results in elevated dopamine levels in the dorsal and ventral striatum (Abercrombie, Keefe, DiFrischia, & Zigmond, 1989; Kalivas & Duffy, 1995; McCullough & Salamone, 1992; Murphy, Pezze, Feldon, & Heidbreder, 2000; Pezze, Heidbreder, Feldon, & Murphy, 2001; Robinson, Becker, Young, Akil, & Castaneda, 1987; Wilkinson, 1997; Young, 2004; Young, Ahier, Upton, Joseph, & Gray, 1998; Young, Joseph, & Gray, 1993). In addition, a number of human neuroimaging studies report activation of the striatum in response to

the anticipation of aversive stimuli, such as shock (Buchel, Dolan, Armony, & Friston, 1999; Buchel, Morris, Dolan, & Friston, 1998; LaBar, Gatenby, Gore, LeDoux, & Phelps, 1998; Phelps et al., 2004; Shin et al., 2005; Whalen et al., 1998), thermal pain (Ploghaus et al., 2000; Seymour, Daw, Dayan, Singer, & Dolan, 2007), and monetary loss (Delgado, Li et al., 2008; Seymour et al., 2007; Tom, Fox, Trepel, & Poldrack, 2007). Research that examines how aversive stimuli affect learning and behavior will have important implications for understanding maladaptive behavior in personal, as well as interpersonal, domains. For example, patients with generalized social phobia show a greater engagement of MPFC in response to negative feedback regarding the self (e.g., "you are unattractive") compared to other (e.g., "he is unattractive"), suggesting that the perception of negative social feedback can influence approach/avoid responses in this population (Blair et al., 2008). Thus, it will be critical for future studies to address the impact of appetitive and aversive stimuli on social and nonsocial behavior and learning processes within corticostriatal networks.

Additionally, further research is necessary to determine how responses to appetitive stimuli can be regulated and controlled. An individual's ability to regulate responses to both appetitive and aversive stimuli is important for behavioral control and optimal decision-making. In theory, signals from the reward system are important for learning about goal-directed behavior. However, reward signals from the corticostriatal network may lead to maladaptive behaviors, such as compulsive drug use, since activity in the striatum has been linked to drug craving (Breiter et al., 1997; Sinha et al., 2005), and risk-seeking behavior (Potenza & Winters, 2003). Failures in the ability to regulate appetitive responding may be important for explaining the exaggerated response to rewards and decreased ability to learn from feedback that has been observed in adolescents, as well as in patients with disorders characterized by impulse control, including addiction and other psychiatric disorders (Beck et al., 2009; Galvan et al., 2006; Heinz et al., 2004). Emotion regulation strategies, which are known to be useful for regulating negative emotional responses (see Ochsner & Gross, 2005), have recently been demonstrated as effective in reducing striatal responses to appetitive stimuli (Delgado, Gillis, & Phelps, 2008; Staudinger, Erk, Abler, & Walter, 2009). It will be important to identify the efficacy of different types of regulation strategies, as well as the mechanisms underlying their effects on the corticostriatal reward system.

Although this chapter has focused on a corticostriatal network, emphasizing the roles of the striatum and OFC, other brain regions may play critical roles in the reward system, and the relationship of these regions to the corticostriatal reward circuitry needs to better understood. For example, both animal neurophysiological studies and human neuroimaging studies have implicated regions such as the amygdala, insula, and anterior cingulate cortex in reward processing (Behrens, Hunt, & Rushworth, 2009; Berridge & Kringelbach, 2008) These regions are all highly interconnected with the OFC and striatum, and may serve as critical components of reward processing, yet, compared to the OFC and striatum, less is known about their precise functions within human reward processing. Further research is necessary to identify the specific roles of these regions, and to better understand how they interact with key regions of the corticostriatal reward circuitry.

More generally, we need to gain a better understanding of functional dissociations within the corticostriatal reward network. Given the variability in neuroimaging techniques and experimental paradigms used across studies, as well as the inherent limitations to the methodologies, it is difficult to ascertain the precision of reported activations, and thus, even more difficult to identify whether there is a shared neural substrate. However, future studies that also incorporate recent advances in methodologies will likely lead to greater insight into this question and others as researchers continue to probe the human reward system.

Acknowledgments

This work was supported by a National Institute of Mental Health grant (MH084081).

References

Abercrombie, E. D., Keefe, K. A., DiFrischia, D. S., & Zigmond, M. J. (1989). Differential effect of stress on in vivo dopamine release in striatum, nucleus accumbens, and medial frontal cortex. *J Neurochem*, *52*(5), 1655–1658.

Aharon, I., Etcoff, N., Ariely, D., Chabris, C. F., O'Connor, E., & Breiter, H. C. (2001). Beautiful faces have variable reward value: fMRI and behavioral evidence. *Neuron*, *32*(3), 537–551.

Amaral, D. G. & Price, J. L. (1984). Amygdalo-cortical projections in the monkey (Macaca fascicularis). *J Comp Neurol*, *230*(4), 465–496.

Anderson, A. K., Christoff, K., Stappen, I., Panitz, D., Ghahremani, D. G., Glover, G., et al. (2003). Dissociated neural representations of intensity and valence in human olfaction. *Nat Neurosci*, *6*(2), 196–202.

Apicella, P., Ljungberg, T., Scarnati, E., & Schultz, W. (1991). Responses to reward in monkey dorsal and ventral striatum. *Exp Brain Res*, *85*(3), 491–500.

Apicella, P., Scarnati, E., Ljungberg, T., & Schultz, W. (1992). Neuronal activity in monkey striatum related to the expectation of predictable environmental events. *J Neurophysiol*, *68*(3), 945–960.

Apicella, P., Scarnati, E., & Schultz, W. (1991). Tonically discharging neurons of monkey striatum respond to preparatory and rewarding stimuli. *Exp Brain Res*, *84*(3), 672–675.

Arnow, B. A., Desmond, J. E., Banner, L. L., Glover, G. H., Solomon, A., Polan, M. L., et al. (2002). Brain activation and sexual arousal in healthy, heterosexual males. *Brain*, *125*(Pt 5), 1014–1023.

Balleine, B. W., Delgado, M. R., & Hikosaka, O. (2007). The role of the dorsal striatum in reward and decision-making. *J Neurosci*, *27*(31), 8161–8165.

Bar-Gad, I., Morris, G., & Bergman, H. (2003). Information processing, dimensionality reduction and reinforcement learning in the basal ganglia. *Prog Neurobiol*, *71*(6), 439–473.

Baumgartner, T., Heinrichs, M., Vonlanthen, A., Fischbacher, U., & Fehr, E. (2008). Oxytocin shapes the neural circuitry of trust and trust adaptation in humans. *Neuron*, *58*(4), 639–650.

Bayer, H. M. & Glimcher, P. W. (2005). Midbrain dopamine neurons encode a quantitative reward prediction error signal. *Neuron*, *47*(1), 129–141.

Bechara, A., Damasio, A. R., Damasio, H., & Anderson, S. W. (1994). Insensitivity to future consequences following damage to human prefrontal cortex. *Cognition*, *50*(1–3), 7–15.

Beck, A., Schlagenhauf, F., Wustenberg, T., Hein, J., Kienast, T., Kahnt, T., et al. (2009). Ventral striatal activation during reward anticipation correlates with impulsivity in alcoholics. *Biol Psychiatry*, *66*(8), 734–742.

Behrens, T. E., Hunt, L. T., & Rushworth, M. F. (2009). The computation of social behavior. *Science, 324*(5931), 1160–1164.

Berridge, K. C., & Kringelbach, M. L. (2008). Affective neuroscience of pleasure: Reward in humans and animals. *Psychopharmacology (Berl), 199*(3), 457–480.

Bjork, J. M. & Hommer, D. W. (2007). Anticipating instrumentally obtained and passively-received rewards: A factorial fMRI investigation. *Behav Brain Res, 177*(1), 165–170.

Blair, K., Geraci, M., Devido, J., McCaffrey, D., Chen, G., Vythilingam, M., et al. (2008). Neural response to self- and other referential praise and criticism in generalized social phobia. *Arch Gen Psychiatry, 65*(10), 1176–1184.

Blood, A. J., Zatorre, R. J., Bermudez, P., & Evans, A. C. (1999). Emotional responses to pleasant and unpleasant music correlate with activity in paralimbic brain regions. *Nat Neurosci, 2*(4), 382–387.

Bowman, E. M., Aigner, T. G., & Richmond, B. J. (1996). Neural signals in the monkey ventral striatum related to motivation for juice and cocaine rewards. *J Neurophysiol, 75*(3), 1061–1073.

Breiter, H. C., Aharon, I., Kahneman, D., Dale, A., & Shizgal, P. (2001). Functional imaging of neural responses to expectancy and experience of monetary gains and losses. *Neuron, 30*(2), 619–639.

Breiter, H. C., Gollub, R. L., Weisskoff, R. M., Kennedy, D. N., Makris, N., Berke, J. D., et al. (1997). Acute effects of cocaine on human brain activity and emotion. *Neuron, 19*(3), 591–611.

Buchel, C., Dolan, R. J., Armony, J. L., & Friston, K. J. (1999). Amygdala-hippocampal involvement in human aversive trace conditioning revealed through event-related functional magnetic resonance imaging. *J Neurosci, 19*(24), 10869–10876.

Buchel, C., Morris, J., Dolan, R. J., & Friston, K. J. (1998). Brain systems mediating aversive conditioning: An event-related fMRI study. *Neuron, 20*(5), 947–957.

Butter, C. (1969). Perseveration and extinction in discrimination reversal tasks following selective frontal ablations in Macaca mulatta. *Physiol Behav, 4*, 163–171.

Carmichael, S. T. & Price, J. L. (1995). Limbic connections of the orbital and medial prefrontal cortex in macaque monkeys. *J Comp Neurol, 363*(4), 615–641.

Carmichael, S. T., & Price, J. L. (1996). Connectional networks within the orbital and medial prefrontal cortex of macaque monkeys. *J Comp Neurol, 371*(2), 179–207.

Cavada, C., Company, T., Tejedor, J., Cruz-Rizzolo, R. J., & Reinoso-Suarez, F. (2000). The anatomical connections of the macaque monkey orbitofrontal cortex. A review. *Cereb Cortex, 10*(3), 220–242.

Corbett, D. & Wise, R. A. (1980). Intracranial self-stimulation in relation to the ascending dopaminergic systems of the midbrain: A moveable electrode mapping study. *Brain Res, 185*(1), 1–15.

Coricelli, G., Critchley, H. D., Joffily, M., O'Doherty, J. P., Sirigu, A., & Dolan, R. J. (2005). Regret and its avoidance: A neuroimaging study of choice behavior. *Nat Neurosci, 8*(9), 1255–1262.

Critchley, H. D., Mathias, C. J., & Dolan, R. J. (2001). Neural activity in the human brain relating to uncertainty and arousal during anticipation. *Neuron, 29*(2), 537–545.

Cromwell, H. C. & Schultz, W. (2003). Effects of expectations for different reward magnitudes on neuronal activity in primate striatum. *J Neurophysiol, 89*(5), 2823–2838.

Damasio, A. R. (1994). *Descartes' error*. New York: Avon.

de Araujo, I. E. T., Kringelbach, M. L., Rolls, E. T., & McGlone, F. (2003). Human cortical responses to water in the mouth, and the effects of thirst. *Journal of Neurophysiology, 90*, 1865–1876.

de Araujo, I. E. T., Rolls, E. T., Kringelbach, M. L., McGlone, F., & Phillips, N. (2003). Taste-olfactory convergence, and the representation of the pleasantness of flavour, in the human brain. *European Journal of Neuroscience, 18*, 2059–2068.

de Quervain, D. J., Fischbacher, U., Treyer, V., Schellhammer, M., Schnyder, U., Buck, A., et al. (2004). The neural basis of altruistic punishment. *Science, 305*(5688), 1254–1258.

Delgado, M. R. (2007). Reward-related responses in the human striatum. *Ann N Y Acad Sci, 1104*, 70–88.

Delgado, M. R., Frank, R. H., & Phelps, E. A. (2005). Perceptions of moral character modulate the neural systems of reward during the trust game. *Nat Neurosci, 8*(11), 1611–1618.

Delgado, M. R., Gillis, M. M., & Phelps, E. A. (2008). Regulating the expectation of reward via cognitive strategies. *Nat Neurosci, 11*(8), 880–881.

Delgado, M. R., Li, J., Schiller, D., & Phelps, E. A. (2008). The role of the striatum in aversive learning and aversive prediction errors. *Philos Trans R Soc Lond B Biol Sci, 363*(1511), 3787–3800.

Delgado, M. R., Locke, H. M., Stenger, V. A., & Fiez, J. A. (2003). Dorsal striatum responses to reward and punishment: Effects of valence and magnitude manipulations. *Cogn Affect Behav Neurosci, 3*(1), 27–38.

Delgado, M. R., Miller, M. M., Inati, S., & Phelps, E. A. (2005). An fMRI study of reward-related probability learning. *Neuroimage, 24*(3), 862–873.

Delgado, M. R., Nystrom, L. E., Fissell, C., Noll, D. C., & Fiez, J. A. (2000). Tracking the hemodynamic responses to reward and punishment in the striatum. *J Neurophysiol, 84*(6), 3072–3077.

Delgado, M. R., Schotter, A., Ozbay, E. Y., & Phelps, E. A. (2008). Understanding overbidding: Using the neural circuitry of reward to design economic auctions. *Science, 321*(5897), 1849–1852.

Delgado, M. R., Stenger, V. A., & Fiez, J. A. (2004). Motivation-dependent Responses in the Human Caudate Nucleus. *Cereb Cortex, 14*(9), 1022–1030.

Di Chiara, G. (1995). The role of dopamine in drug abuse viewed from the perspective of its role in motivation. *Drug Alcohol Depend, 38*(2), 95–137.

Eblen, F. & Graybiel, A. M. (1995). Highly restricted origin of prefrontal cortical inputs to striosomes in the macaque monkey. *J Neurosci, 15*(9), 5999–6013.

Eisenberger, N. I., Lieberman, M. D., & Williams, K. D. (2003). Does rejection hurt? An FMRI study of social exclusion. *Science, 302*(5643), 290–292.

Elliott, R., Frith, C. D., & Dolan, R. J. (1998). Differential neural response to positive and negative feedback in planning and guessing tasks. *Neuropsychologia, 35*(10), 1395–1404.

Elliott, R., Newman, J. L., Longe, O. A., & William Deakin, J. F. (2004). Instrumental responding for rewards is associated with enhanced neuronal response in subcortical reward systems. *Neuroimage, 21*(3), 984–990.

Frederick, S., Loewenstein, G., & O'Donoghue, T. (2002). Time discounting and time preference: A critical review. *Journal of Economic Literature, 40*, 351–401.

Fudge, J. L. & Haber, S. N. (2002). Defining the caudal ventral striatum in primates: Cellular and histochemical features. *J Neurosci*, *22*(23), 10078–10082.

Fuster, V. (1997). Human lesion studies. *Ann N Y Acad Sci, 811*, 207–224; discussion 224–205.

Galvan, A., Hare, T. A., Parra, C. E., Penn, J., Voss, H., Glover, G., et al. (2006). Earlier development of the accumbens relative to orbitofrontal cortex might underlie risk-taking behavior in adolescents. *J Neurosci, 26*(25), 6885–6892.

Gottfried, J. A., O'Doherty, J., & Dolan, R. J. (2003). Encoding predictive reward value in human amygdala and orbitofrontal cortex. *Science, 301*(5636), 1104–1107.

Green, L. & Myerson, J. (2004). A discounting framework for choice with delayed and probabilistic rewards. *Psychol Bull, 130*(5), 769–792.

Groenewegen, H. J. & Uylings, H. B. M. (2000). The prefrontal cortex and the integration of sensory, limbic and autonomic information. *Prog Brain Res, 126*, 3–28.

Haber, S. N. (2003). The primate basal ganglia: Parallel and integrative networks. *J Chem Neuroanat, 26*(4), 317–330.

Haber, S. N., Kim, K. S., Mailly, P., & Calzavara, R. (2006). Reward-related cortical inputs define a large striatal region in primates that interface with associative cortical connections, providing a substrate for incentive-based learning. *J Neurosci, 26*(32), 8368–8376.

Haber, S. N. & Knutson, B. (2010). The reward circuit: Linking primate anatomy and human imaging. *Neuropsychopharmacology, 35*(1), 4–26.

Haber, S. N., Kunishio, K., Mizobuchi, M., & Lynd-Balta, E. (1995). The orbital and medial prefrontal circuit through the primate basal ganglia. *J Neurosci, 15*(7 Pt 1), 4851–4867.

Haruno, M., Kuroda, T., Doya, K., Toyama, K., Kimura, M., Samejima, K., et al. (2004). A neural correlate of reward-based behavioral learning in caudate nucleus: A functional magnetic resonance imaging study of a stochastic decision task. *J Neurosci, 24*(7), 1660–1665.

Hassani, O. K., Cromwell, H. C., & Schultz, W. (2001). Influence of expectation of different rewards on behavior-related neuronal activity in the striatum. *J Neurophysiol, 85*(6), 2477–2489.

Heinz, A., Siessmeier, T., Wrase, J., Hermann, D., Klein, S., Grusser, S. M., et al. (2004). Correlation between dopamine D(2) receptors in the ventral striatum and central processing of alcohol cues and craving. *Am J Psychiatry, 161*(10), 1783–1789.

Hikosaka, K. & Watanabe, M. (2000). Delay activity of orbital and lateral prefrontal neurons of the monkey varying with different rewards. *Cerebral Cortex, 10*, 263–271.

Hikosaka, O., Sakamoto, M., & Usui, S. (1989). Functional properties of monkey caudate neurons. III. Activities related to expectation of target and reward. *J Neurophysiol, 61*(4), 814–832.

Hollenbeck, A. R., Nannis, E. D., Strope, B. E., Hersh, S. P., Levine, A. S., & Pizzo, P. A. (2004). Children with serious illness: Behavioral correlates of separation and isolation. *Child Psychiatry and Human Development, 11*, 3–11.

Hsu, M., Bhatt, M., Adolphs, R., Tranel, D., & Camerer, C. F. (2005). Neural systems responding to degrees of uncertainty in human decision-making. *Science, 310*(5754), 1680–1683.

Hsu, M., Krajbich, I., Zhao, C., & Camerer, C. (2009). Neural response to reward anticipation under risk is nonlinear in probabilities. *Science, 29*(7), 2231–2237.

Huettel, S. A., Song, A. W., & McCarthy, G. (2005). Decisions under uncertainty: probabilistic context influences activation of prefrontal and parietal cortices. *J Neurosci, 25*(13), 3304–3311.

Ito, R., Dalley, J. W., Howes, S. R., Robbins, T. W., & Everitt, B. J. (2000). Dissociation in conditioned dopamine release in the nucleus accumbens core and shell in response to cocaine cues and during cocaine-seeking behavior in rats. *J Neurosci, 20*(19), 7489–7495.

Ito, R., Dalley, J. W., Robbins, T. W., & Everitt, B. J. (2002). Dopamine release in the dorsal striatum during cocaine-seeking behavior under the control of a drug-associated cue. *J Neurosci, 22*(14), 6247–6253.

Izuma, K., Saito, D. N., & Sadato, N. (2008). Processing of social and monetary rewards in the human striatum. *Neuron, 58*(2), 284–294.

Jones, B. & Mishkin, M. (1972). Limbic lesions and the problem of stimulus-reinforcement associations. *Experimental Neurology, 36*(2), 362–377.

Kable, J. W. & Glimcher, P. W. (2007). The neural correlates of subjective value during intertemporal choice. *Nat Neurosci, 10*(12), 1625–1633.

Kalivas, P. W. & Duffy, P. (1995). Selective activation of dopamine transmission in the shell of the nucleus accumbens by stress. *Brain Res, 675*(1–2), 325–328.

King-Casas, B., Tomlin, D., Anen, C., Camerer, C. F., Quartz, S. R., & Montague, P. R. (2005). Getting to know you: Reputation and trust in a two-person economic exchange. *Science, 308*(5718), 78–83.

Kirsch, P., Schienle, A., Stark, R., Sammer, G., Blecker, C., Walter, B., et al. (2003). Anticipation of reward in a nonaversive differential conditioning paradigm and the brain reward system: An event-related fMRI study. *Neuroimage, 20*(2), 1086–1095.

Knutson, B., Adams, C. M., Fong, G. W., & Hommer, D. (2001). Anticipation of increasing monetary reward selectively recruits nucleus accumbens. *J Neurosci, 21*(16), RC159.

Knutson, B. & Cooper, J. C. (2005). Functional magnetic resonance imaging of reward prediction. *Curr Opin Neurol, 18*(4), 411–417.

Knutson, B., Fong, G. W., Bennett, S. M., Adams, C. M., & Hommer, D. (2003). A region of mesial prefrontal cortex tracks monetarily rewarding outcomes: Characterization with rapid event-related fMRI. *Neuroimage, 18*(2), 263–272.

Koob, G. F. (1992). Neural mechanisms of drug reinforcement. *Ann N Y Acad Sci, 654*, 171–191.

Kringelbach, M. L., O'Doherty, J., Rolls, E. T., & Andrews, C. (2003). Activation of the human orbitofrontal cortex to a liquid food stimulus is correlated with its subjective pleasantness. *Cereb Cortex, 13*(10), 1064–1071.

Kringelbach, M. L. & Rolls, E. T. (2004). The functional neuroanatomy of the human orbitofrontal cortex: Evidence from neuroimaging and neuropsychology. *Prog Neurobiol, 72*(5), 341–372.

Kuhnen, C. M. & Knutson, B. (2005). The neural basis of financial risk taking. *Neuron, 47*(5), 763–770.

LaBar, K. S., Gatenby, J. C., Gore, J. C., LeDoux, J. E., & Phelps, E. A. (1998). Human amygdala activation during conditioned fear acquisition and extinction: A mixed-trial fMRI study. *Neuron, 20*(5), 937–945.

Laibson, D. I. (1997). Golden eggs and hyperbolic discounting. *Quarterly Journal of Economics, 112*, 443–477.

Lavoie, A. M. & Mizumori, S. J. (1994). Spatial, movement- and reward-sensitive discharge by medial ventral striatum neurons of rats. *Brain Res, 638*(1–2), 157–168.

Ljungberg, T., Apicella, P., & Schultz, W. (1992). Responses of monkey dopamine neurons during learning of behavioral reactions. *J Neurophysiol, 67*(1), 145–163.

Macdonald, G. & Leary, M. R. (2005). Why does social exclusion hurt? The relationship between social and physical pain. *Psychol Bull, 131*, 202–223.

McClure, S. M., Berns, G. S., & Montague, P. R. (2003). Temporal prediction errors in a passive learning task activate human striatum. *Neuron, 38*(2), 339–346.

McClure, S. M., Ericson, K. M., Laibson, D. I., Loewenstein, G., & Cohen, J. D. (2007). Time discounting for primary rewards. *J Neurosci, 27*(21), 5796–5804.

McClure, S. M., Laibson, D. I., Loewenstein, G., & Cohen, J. D. (2004). Separate neural systems value immediate and delayed monetary rewards. *Science, 306*(5695), 503–507.

McClure, S. M., Li, J., Tomlin, D., Cypert, K. S., Montague, L. M., & Montague, P. R. (2004). Neural correlates of behavioral preference for culturally familiar drinks. *Neuron, 44*(2), 379–387.

McCullough, L. D. & Salamone, J. D. (1992). Anxiogenic drugs beta-CCE and FG 7142 increase extracellular dopamine levels in nucleus accumbens. *Psychopharmacology (Berl), 109*(3), 379–382.

Mesulam, M. M. & Mufson, E. J. (1982). Insula of the old world monkey. III: Efferent cortical output and comments on function. *J Comp Neurol, 212*(1), 38–52.

Mobbs, D., Greicius, M. D., Abdel-Azim, E., Menon, V., & Reiss, A. L. (2003). Humor modulates the mesolimbic reward centers. *Neuron, 40*(5), 1041–1048.

Moll, J., Krueger, F., Zahn, R., Pardini, M., de Oliveira-Souza, R., & Grafman, J. (2006). Human fronto-mesolimbic networks guide decisions about charitable donation. *Proc Natl Acad Sci U S A, 103*(42), 15623–15628.

Montague, P. & Berns, G. (2002). Neural economics and the biological substrates of valuation. *Neuron, 36*(2), 265.

Mora, F. & Myers, R. D. (1977). Brain self-stimulation: Direct evidence for the involvement of dopamine in the prefrontal cortex. *Science, 197*(4311), 1387–1389.

Murphy, C. A., Pezze, M., Feldon, J., & Heidbreder, C. (2000). Differential involvement of dopamine in the shell and core of the nucleus accumbens in the expression of latent inhibition to an aversively conditioned stimulus. *Neuroscience, 97*(3), 469–477.

Myers, C. E., Shohamy, D., Gluck, M. A., Grossman, S., Kluger, A., Ferris, S., et al. (2003). Dissociating hippocampal versus basal ganglia contributions to learning and transfer. *J Cogn Neurosci, 15*(2), 185–193.

Nieuwenhuis, S., Slagter, H. A., von Geusau, N. J., Heslenfeld, D. J., & Holroyd, C. B. (2005). Knowing good from bad: Differential activation of human cortical areas by positive and negative outcomes. *Eur J Neurosci, 21*(11), 3161–3168.

Niki, H., Sakai, M., & Kubota, K. (1972). Delayed alternation performance and unit activity of the caudate head and medial orbitofrontal gyrus in the monkey. *Brain Res, 38*(2), 343–353.

Niki, H. & Watanabe, M. (1979). Prefrontal and cingulate unit activity during timing behavior in the monkey. *Brain Res, 171*(2), 213–224.

O'Doherty, J. P. (2004). Reward representations and reward-related learning in the human brain: Insights from neuroimaging. *Curr Opin Neurobiol, 14*(6), 769–776.

O'Doherty, J. P., Critchley, H., Deichmann, R., & Dolan, R. J. (2003). Dissociating valence of outcome from behavioral control in human orbital and ventral prefrontal cortices. *J Neurosci, 23*(21), 7931–7939.

O'Doherty, J. P., Dayan, P., Friston, K., Critchley, H., & Dolan, R. J. (2003). Temporal difference models and reward-related learning in the human brain. *Neuron, 38*(2), 329–337.

O'Doherty, J. P., Dayan, P., Schultz, J., Deichmann, R., Friston, K., & Dolan, R. J. (2004). Dissociable roles of ventral and dorsal striatum in instrumental conditioning. *Science, 304*(5669), 452–454.

O'Doherty, J. P., Deichmann, R., Critchley, H. D., & Dolan, R. J. (2002). Neural responses during anticipation of a primary taste reward. *Neuron, 33*(5), 815–826.

O'Doherty, J. P., Kringelbach, M. L., Rolls, E. T., Hornak, J., & Andrews, C. (2001). Abstract reward and punishment representations in the human orbitofrontal cortex. *Nat Neurosci, 4*(1), 95–102.

O'Doherty, J. P., Rolls, E. T., Francis, S., Bowtell, R., & McGlone, F. (2001). Representation of pleasant and aversive taste in the human brain. *J Neurophysiol, 85*(3), 1315–1321.

O'Doherty, J. P., Winston, J., Critchley, H., Perrett, D., Burt, D. M., & Dolan, R. J. (2003). Beauty in a smile: The role of medial orbitofrontal cortex in facial attractiveness. *Neuropsychologia, 41*(2), 147–155.

Ochsner, K. N. & Gross, J. J. (2005). The cognitive control of emotion. *Trends Cogn Sci, 9*(5), 242–249.

Ongur, D. & Price, J. L. (2000). The organization of networks within the orbital and medial prefrontal cortex of rats, monkeys and humans. *Cereb Cortex, 10*(3), 206–219.

Parent, A. & Hazrati, L. N. (1995). Functional anatomy of the basal ganglia. I. The cortico-basal ganglia-thalamo-cortical loop. *Brain Res Brain Res Rev, 20*(1), 91–127.

Pezze, M. A., Heidbreder, C. A., Feldon, J., & Murphy, C. A. (2001). Selective responding of nucleus accumbens core and shell dopamine to aversively conditioned contextual and discrete stimuli. *Neuroscience, 108*(1), 91–102.

Phelps, E. A., Delgado, M. R., Nearing, K. I., & LeDoux, J. E. (2004). Extinction learning in humans: role of the amygdala and vmPFC. *Neuron, 43*(6), 897–905.

Phillips, A. G., Brooke, S. M., & Fibiger, H. C. (1975). Effects of amphetamine isomers and neuroleptics on self-stimulation from the nucleus accumbens and dorsal noradrenergic bundle. *Brain Res, 85*(1), 13–22.

Phillips, A. G., Mora, F., & Rolls, E. T. (1979). Intracranial self-stimulation in orbitofrontal cortex and caudate nucleus of rhesus monkey: Effects of apomorphine, pimozide, and spiroperidol. *Psychopharmacology (Berl), 62*(1), 79–82.

Plassmann, H., O'Doherty, J., & Rangel, A. (2007). Orbitofrontal cortex encodes willingness to pay in everyday economic transactions. *J Neurosci, 27*(37), 9984–9988.

Plassmann, H., O'Doherty, J., Shiv, B., & Rangel, A. (2008). Marketing actions can modulate neural representations of experienced pleasantness. *Proc Natl Acad Sci U S A, 105*(3), 1050–1054.

Ploghaus, A., Tracey, I., Clare, S., Gati, J. S., Rawlins, J. N., & Matthews, P. M. (2000). Learning about pain: The neural substrate of the prediction error for aversive events. *Proc Natl Acad Sci U S A, 97*(16), 9281–9286.

Potenza, M. N. & Winters, K. C. (2003). The neurobiology of pathological gambling: Translating research findings into clinical advances. *J Gambl Stud, 19*(1), 7–10.

Rangel, A., Camerer, C., & Montague, P. R. (2008). A framework for studying the neurobiology of value-based decision making. *Nat Rev Neurosci, 9*(7), 545–556.

Redoute, J., Stoleru, S., Gregoire, M. C., Costes, N., Cinotti, L., Lavenne, F., et al. (2000). Brain processing of visual sexual stimuli in human males. *Hum Brain Mapp, 11*(3), 162–177.

Rempel-Clower, N. L. & Barbas, H. (1998). Topographic organization of connections between the hypothalamus and prefrontal cortex in the rhesus monkey. *J Comp Neurol, 398*(3), 393–419.

Rilling, J., Gutman, D., Zeh, T., Pagnoni, G., Berns, G., & Kilts, C. (2002). A neural basis for social cooperation. *Neuron, 35*(2), 395–405.

Robbins, T. W., Cador, M., Taylor, J. R., & Everitt, B. J. (1989). Limbic-striatal interactions in reward-related processes. *Neurosci Biobehav Rev, 13*(2–3), 155–162.

Robbins, T. W. & Everitt, B. J. (1996). Neurobehavioural mechanisms of reward and motivation. *Curr Opin Neurobiol, 6*(2), 228–236.

Robinson, T. E., Becker, J. B., Young, E. A., Akil, H., & Castaneda, E. (1987). The effects of footshock stress on regional brain dopamine metabolism and pituitary beta-endorphin release in rats previously sensitized to amphetamine. *Neuropharmacology, 26*(7A), 679–691.

Roesch, M. R. & Olson, C. R. (2004). Neuronal activity related to reward value and motivation in primate frontal cortex. *Science, 304*(5668), 307–310.

Rolls, E. T. (1999). *The brain and emotion.* Oxford; New York: Oxford University Press.

Rolls, E. T., Kringelbach, M. L., & de Araujo, I. E. (2003). Different representations of pleasant and unpleasant odours in the human brain. *Eur J Neurosci, 18*(3), 695–703.

Rolls, E. T., O'Doherty, J., Kringelbach, M. L., Francis, S., Bowtell, R., & McGlone, F. (2003). Representations of pleasant and painful touch in the human orbitofrontal and cingulate cortices. *Cereb Cortex, 13*(3), 308–317.

Romo, R. & Schultz, W. (1990). Dopamine neurons of the monkey midbrain: Contingencies of responses to active touch during self-initiated arm movements. *J Neurophysiol, 63*(3), 592–606.

Rosenkilde, C. E., Bauer, R. H., & Fuster, J. M. (1981). Single cell activity in ventral prefrontal cortex of behaving monkeys. *Brain Res, 209*(2), 375–394.

Samejima, K., Ueda, Y., Doya, K., & Kimura, M. (2005). Representation of action-specific reward values in the striatum. *Science, 310*(5752), 1337–1340.

Sanfey, A. G., Loewenstein, G., McClure, S. M., & Cohen, J. D. (2006). Neuroeconomics: cross-currents in research on decision-making. *Trends Cogn Sci, 10*(3), 108–116.

Schiller, D., Cain, C. K., Curley, N. G., Schwartz, J. S., Stern, S. A., Ledoux, J. E., et al. (2008). Evidence for recovery of fear following immediate extinction in rats and humans. *Learn Mem, 15*(6), 394–402.

Schoenbaum, G., Chiba, A. A., & Gallagher, M. (1998). Orbitofrontal cortex and basolateral amygdala encode expected outcomes during learning. *Nat Neurosci, 1*(2), 155–159.

Schonberg, T., Daw, N. D., Joel, D., & O'Doherty, J. P. (2007). Reinforcement learning signals in the human striatum distinguish learners from nonlearners during reward-based decision making. *J Neurosci, 27*(47), 12860–12867.

Schultz, W. (1986). Responses of midbrain dopamine neurons to behavioral trigger stimuli in the monkey. *J Neurophysiol, 56*(5), 1439–1461.

Schultz, W. (2000). Multiple reward signals in the brain. *Nat Rev Neurosci, 1*(3), 199–207.

Schultz, W., Dayan, P., & Montague, P. R. (1997). A neural substrate of prediction and reward. *Science, 275*(5306), 1593–1599.

Schultz, W. & Romo, R. (1990). Dopamine neurons of the monkey midbrain: Contingencies of responses to stimuli eliciting immediate behavioral reactions. *J Neurophysiol, 63*(3), 607–624.

Seymour, B., Daw, N., Dayan, P., Singer, T., & Dolan, R. (2007). Differential encoding of losses and gains in the human striatum. *J Neurosci, 27*(18), 4826–4831.

Shidara, M., Aigner, T. G., & Richmond, B. J. (1998). Neuronal signals in the monkey ventral striatum related to progress through a predictable series of trials. *J Neurosci, 18*(7), 2613–2625.

Shin, L. M., Wright, C. I., Cannistraro, P. A., Wedig, M. M., McMullin, K., Martis, B., et al. (2005). A functional magnetic resonance imaging study of amygdala and medial prefrontal cortex responses to overtly presented fearful faces in posttraumatic stress disorder. *Arch Gen Psychiatry, 62*(3), 273–281.

Shohamy, D., Myers, C. E., Onlaor, S., & Gluck, M. A. (2004). Role of the basal ganglia in category learning: How do patients with Parkinson's disease learn? *Behav Neurosci, 118*(4), 676–686.

Singer, T., Kiebel, S. J., Winston, J. S., Dolan, R. J., & Frith, C. D. (2004). Brain responses to the acquired moral status of faces. *Neuron, 41*(4), 653–662.

Sinha, R., Lacadie, C., Skudlarski, P., Fulbright, R. K., Rounsaville, B. J., Kosten, T. R., et al. (2005). Neural activity associated with stress-induced cocaine craving: A functional magnetic resonance imaging study. *Psychopharmacology (Berl), 183*(2), 171–180.

Spicer, J., Galvan, A., Hare, T. A., Voss, H., Glover, G., & Casey, B. (2007). Sensitivity of the nucleus accumbens to violations in expectation of reward. *Neuroimage, 34*(1), 455–461.

Spitz, R. (1966). *The first year of life: A psychoanalytic study of normal and deviant development of object relations.* Oxford: International Universities Press.

Staudinger, M. R., Erk, S., Abler, B., & Walter, H. (2009). Cognitive reappraisal modulates expected value and prediction error encoding in the ventral striatum. *Neuroimage, 47*(2), 713–721.

Steele, C. (1988). The psychology of self-affirmation: Sustaining the integrity of the self. In L. Berkowitz (Ed.), *Advances in experimental social psychology. Social psychological studies of the self: Perspectives and programs.* (Vol. 21). San Diego, CA: Academic Press.

Tabibnia, G., Satpute, A. B., & Lieberman, M. D. (2008). The sunny side of fairness: Preference for fairness activates reward circuitry (and disregarding unfairness activates self-control circuitry). *Psychol Sci, 19*(4), 339–347.

Takahashi, H., Kato, M., Matsuura, M., Mobbs, D., Suhara, T., & Okubo, Y. (2009). When your gain is my pain and your pain is my gain: Neural correlates of envy and schadenfreude. *Science, 323*(5916), 937–939.

Takahashi, Y. K., Roesch, M. R., Stalnaker, T. A., Haney, R. Z., Calu, D. J., Taylor, A. R., et al. (2009). The orbitofrontal cortex and ventral tegmental area are necessary for learning from unexpected outcomes. *Neuron, 62*(2), 269–280.

Taylor, S. E. (1999). *Health psychology* (4th ed.). Boston: McGraw-Hill.

Thorpe, S. J., Rolls, E. T., & Maddison, S. (1983). The orbitofrontal cortex: Neuronal activity in the behaving monkey. *Exp Brain Res, 49*(1), 93–115.

Tobler, P. N., O'Doherty, J. P., Dolan, R. J., & Schultz, W. (2007). Reward value coding distinct from risk attitude-related uncertainty coding in human reward systems. *J Neurophysiol, 97*(2), 1621–1632.

Tom, S. M., Fox, C. R., Trepel, C., & Poldrack, R. A. (2007). The neural basis of loss aversion in decision-making under risk. *Science, 315*(5811), 515–518.

Tremblay, L. & Schultz, W. (1999). Relative reward preference in primate orbitofrontal cortex. *Nature, 398*(6729), 704–708.

Tremblay, L. & Schultz, W. (2000). Modifications of reward expectation-related neuronal activity during learning in primate orbitofrontal cortex. *J Neurophysiol, 83*(4), 1877–1885.

Tricomi, E. M., Delgado, M. R., & Fiez, J. A. (2004). Modulation of caudate activity by action contingency. *Neuron, 41*(2), 281–292.

Van Hoesen, G. W., Morecraft, R. J., & Vogt, B. A. (1993). Connections of the monkey cingulate cortex. In B. A. Vogt & M. Gabriel (Eds.), *The neurobiology of the cingulate cortex and limbic thalamus: A comprehensive handbook* (pp. 249–284). Boston: Birkhauser.

Wallis, J. D. & Miller, E. K. (2003). Neuronal activity in primate dorsolateral and orbital prefrontal cortex during performance of a reward preference task. *Eur J Neurosci, 18*(7), 2069–2081.

Watanabe, M. (1989). The appropriateness of behavioral responses coded in post-trial activity of primate prefrontal units. *Neurosci Lett, 101*(1), 113–117.

Watanabe, M. (1996). Reward expectancy in primate prefrontal neurons. *Nature, 382*(6592), 629–632.

Whalen, P. J., Rauch, S. L., Etcoff, N. L., McInerney, S. C., Lee, M. B., & Jenike, M. A. (1998). Masked presentations of emotional facial expressions modulate amygdala activity without explicit knowledge. *J Neurosci, 18*(1), 411–418.

Wilkinson, L. S. (1997). The nature of interactions involving prefrontal and striatal dopamine systems. *J Psychopharmacol, 11*(2), 143–150.

Williams, K. D. (1997). Social ostracism. In R. M. Kowalski (Ed.), *Aversive interpersonal behaviors* (pp. 133–170). New York, NY: Plenum Press.

Williams, K. D., Cheung, C. K. T., & Choi, W. (2000). Cyberostracism: Effects of being ignored over the Internet. *Journal of Personality and Social Psychology 79*, 748–762.

Winston, J. S., O'Doherty, J., & Dolan, R. J. (2003). Common and distinct neural responses during direct and incidental processing of multiple facial emotions. *Neuroimage, 20*(1), 84–97.

Wise, R. A. & Hoffman, D. C. (1992). Localization of drug reward mechanisms by intracranial injections. *Synapse, 10*(3), 247–263.

Wise, R. A. & Rompre, P. P. (1989). Brain dopamine and reward. *Annu Rev Psychol, 40*, 191–225.

Yacubian, J., Glascher, J., Schroeder, K., Sommer, T., Braus, D. F., & Buchel, C. (2006). Dissociable systems for gain- and loss-related value predictions and errors of prediction in the human brain. *J Neurosci, 26*(37), 9530–9537.

Yin, H. H., Knowlton, B. J., & Balleine, B. W. (2006). Inactivation of dorsolateral striatum enhances sensitivity to changes in the action-outcome contingency in instrumental conditioning. *Behav Brain Res, 166*(2), 189–196.

Yin, H. H., Ostlund, S. B., Knowlton, B. J., & Balleine, B. W. (2005). The role of the dorsomedial striatum in instrumental conditioning. *Eur J Neurosci, 22*(2), 513–523.

Young, A. M. (2004). Increased extracellular dopamine in nucleus accumbens in response to unconditioned and conditioned aversive stimuli: studies using 1 min microdialysis in rats. *J Neurosci Methods, 138*(1–2), 57–63.

Young, A. M., Ahier, R. G., Upton, R. L., Joseph, M. H., & Gray, J. A. (1998). Increased extracellular dopamine in the nucleus accumbens of the rat during associative learning of neutral stimuli. *Neuroscience, 83*(4), 1175–1183.

Young, A. M., Joseph, M. H., & Gray, J. A. (1993). Latent inhibition of conditioned dopamine release in rat nucleus accumbens. *Neuroscience, 54*(1), 5–9.

Zink, C. F., Pagnoni, G., Martin-Skurski, M. E., Chappelow, J. C., & Berns, G. S. (2004). Human striatal responses to monetary reward depend on saliency. *Neuron, 42*(3), 509–517.

Zink, C. F., Tong, Y., Chen, Q., Bassett, D. S., Stein, J. L., & Meyer-Lindenberg, A. (2008). Know your place: Neural processing of social hierarchy in humans. *Neuron, 58*(2), 273–283.

Emotion, Consciousness, and Social Behavior

Piotr Winkielman, Kent Berridge, *and* Shlomi Sher

Abstract

This chapter focuses on the relation of emotion to consciousness and the implication of this relation for social behavior. The chapter is structured as follows. First, it briefly shows that the traditional perspectives on human emotions view them as necessarily conscious. Second, it shows evidence that emotions can be unconsciously triggered. Third, it shows that there are cases of truly "unconscious" or "unfelt" emotion. Fourth, it addresses some challenges to these ideas. Fifth, it addresses the relation between conscious and unconscious components of emotion. Reflecting the focus of this book, the chapter discusses neuroscience research that identifies structures and functions associated with conscious and unconscious aspects of emotions and considers their implications for social behavior.

Keywords: emotion, affect, consciousness, unconscious, subliminal stimuli, subjective experience, phenomenology, affective influence

One of the most fascinating topics in social neuroscience is the operation of emotions. This chapter focuses on the relation of emotion to consciousness and the implication of this relation for social behavior. That is, we will ask questions like the following: Which components of emotion are necessarily conscious and which can operate without conscious awareness? Can emotions be triggered with unconscious stimuli? Can they drive social behavior? And what about the emotional reaction itself? Can it remain unconscious while it has meaningful impact on behavior? What are the neural and psychological mechanisms underlying unconscious emotions? And what mechanisms support conscious feelings? To clarify, by conscious feelings we mean the experiential, first-person, phenomenological "what-is-it-like" aspect of emotion. In common language, it is what a depression sufferer refers to when saying: "I am feeling blue" or what a substance user refers to when saying "I am feeling so good."

Though questions about the role of consciousness may seem "philosophical," they address important aspects of psychology and neurobiology and the answers are relevant for both theoretical and practical understanding of social behavior. Let us give a few examples. First, consider the task of understanding and changing attitudes—the basis of social relations. This task requires figuring out the interplay between their conscious and unconscious elements. For example, can "dislikes" or even "hatred" remain unconscious and drive stereotypic or aggressive behavior? If so, how do we make them conscious? Researchers and the public care whether people's emotional reactions can be driven by unattended emotional pictures and words that might influence emotions and decisions without ever being

explicitly detected. For example, recall the controversy about the advertisement produced by GW Bush's 2000 campaign against Al Gore which contained a briefly flashed word "RATS"—a fragment of the word "bureaucrats" (Berke, 2000). The critics' concern was that forming an association with pestilential rodents might lead viewers to unconsciously form a negative view of a public health care plan. Second, consider the task of understanding the validity of people's reports of their own emotion. Shall we trust people's self-reports of happiness or rather establish their well-being via behavioral measures (e.g., smiling, stress hormones)? Psychiatrists also care whether it is better to diagnose a patient's anxiety or depression via their reports of conscious feeling or via observation of the patient's actions. Activists thinking about issues of animal consciousness or fetal consciousness care what kind of organisms can feel conscious pleasure or pain (e.g., the "fish pain" debate in the UK, and the abortion debate in the US). Neurologists care whether emotional behavior (e.g., withdrawal from a noxious stimulation) of post-accident patients suspected of being in a vegetative state signifies a conscious state or can occur in the absence of consciousness.

Our chapter aims to show that answers to these difficult questions are beginning to emerge from psychology and neuroscience. The chapter is structured as follows. First, we briefly show that the traditional perspectives on human emotions view them as necessarily conscious. Second, we show evidence that emotions can be unconsciously triggered. Third, and most importantly, we show that there are cases of truly "unconscious" or "unfelt" emotion. Fourth, we address some challenges to these ideas. Fifth, we address the relation between conscious and unconscious components of emotion. Reflecting the focus of this book, throughout our chapter we discuss neuroscience research that identifies structures and functions associated with conscious and unconscious aspects of emotions and consider their implications for social behavior.

Emotion as a Conscious Experience

Let us start with some terminological clarifications. It is common to define emotion as a state characterized by loosely coordinated changes in the following five components: (i) *feeling*—changes in subjective experience, (ii) *cognition*—changes in attentional, perceptual, and inferential processes (appraisals), (iii) *action*—changes in the predisposition for or execution of specific responses, (iv) *expression*—changes in the facial, vocal, postural appearance,

and (v) *physiology*—changes in the central and peripheral nervous systems.

It is also useful to distinguish "*affect*" and "*emotion*." The term "affect" describes a state identified primarily by valence (positive/negative). The term "emotion" describes a state that can be identified by more than its valence, and includes specific types of negative states such as fear, guilt, anger, sadness, or disgust, and specific positive states, such as happiness, love, or pride. Throughout this chapter, we will primarily use the term emotion. This is because we believe that our arguments also apply to specific emotion states, even though the empirical evidence for our position has been obtained so far primarily in the domain of affect. We will return to this issue later.

Theories of Emotion: Feeling as a Central Component

Theorists have long recognized that there are many components of emotion. Yet, psychologists and philosophers of emotion typically have considered feeling as central or even a necessary component. This is true for many historical figures (e.g., Freud, 1950, James, 1884). It is also true for many contemporary theorists in psychology (e.g., Clore, 1994). For example, one definition of "affect" says that the term "primarily refers to hedonic experience, the experience of pleasure and pain" (Frijda, 1999 p., 194). Interestingly, some emotion theorists grounded in animal research and clinical neuroscience typically do not consider subjective experience as a central or necessary component of emotion (Damasio, 1999; LeDoux, 1996; but see Panksepp, 2005).

Emotion Research in Psychology: Feeling as a Central Agenda

The feeling component is emphasized not only in theories, but also in research on human emotion. In social psychological studies, for example, the presence of an emotion is typically determined by self-reports of feelings (e.g., mood questionnaires). When studies collect multiple measures of emotion, including physiological ones, self-report is often considered as the "gold standard" for determining whether emotion had occurred (Larsen & Frederickson, 1999). There is also a lot of substantive interest in the nature of feelings. For example, some of the debates in emotion literature concern the contribution of bodily responses to subjective feelings (Niedenthal, Barsalou, Winkielman, Ric, & Krauth-Gruber, 2005) or the simultaneous co-existence of positive and negative feelings (Cacioppo,

Larsen, Smith, & Berntson, 2004). Most importantly, conscious feeling is seen as a central causal force in emotional impact on social behavior. For example, a popular social psychological model, tellingly called "feeling-as-information," proposes that emotions influence behavior because people use subjective experience as a heuristic shortcut to judgment (Schwarz & Clore, 2003).

Unconscious Emotion

As we have just shown, conscious feeling has a central place in both the theoretical thinking and empirical practice of human emotion research. However, do emotions always require consciousness? Can one meaningfully talk about "unfelt" or "unconscious" emotions? Over the last several years, researchers have increasingly started to consider these possibilities. Note that in most studies below, researchers investigated rather undifferentiated affective reactions, rather than qualitatively differentiated emotion (we'll return to this issue).

Unconscious Elicitation of Affect

The first challenge to the role of consciousness in emotion came from demonstrations that subliminal stimuli can trigger affective reactions. One example comes from research on the mere-exposure effect, or the increase in liking for repeated items (Kunst-Wilson & Zajonc, 1980). In one study, participants were first subliminally exposed to several repeated neutral stimuli consisting of random visual patterns. Later, those participants reported feeling more positive than participants exposed to non-repeated stimuli (Monahan, Murphy, & Zajonc, 2000). An example of a subliminal induction of negative affect comes from studies in which subliminal stimuli, such as gory scenes embedded in a movie, or snakes presented to phobic participants, led to an increase in self-reported anxiety (Öhman & Soares, 1994; Robles, Smith, Carver, & Wellens, 1987).

Note that in the just-described studies the presence of the affective reaction is determined by asking people to self report. However, unconscious stimuli can also elicit an affective reaction detectable using physiological measures. For example, skin-conductance response, an indicator of sympathetic arousal, can be triggered by subliminally presented emotional words (Lazarus & McCleary, 1951) and by pictures of fear-relevant objects (Öhman et al., 2000). Similarly, subliminal facial expressions activate the amygdala, a structure involved in assigning affective significance to the stimulus (Whalen, et al., 1998), and elicit facial reactions detectable with

electromyography (Dimberg, Thunberg, & Elmehed, 2000). We will return to these interesting findings later.

Unconscious Affective States

The above studies suggest that emotional reactions can be triggered unconsciously. However, they were not designed to test whether the emotional state can be unconscious. First, most studies used self-report as a measure of affect, which by definition requires that the emotion is conscious. Second, in the physiological studies, self-reports of emotion experience were either not collected or collected after the measure of affective reactions. As a result, it is not clear if the reaction registered in physiology was itself conscious or not. Third, because these studies did not measure behavioral consequences, it is possible that any emotion reaction was weak or inconsequential. Still, the physiological studies are suggestive and raise the possibility that, under the right conditions, people may have genuine affective reactions that are not manifested in their conscious experience.

Several years ago, we offered theoretical arguments and empirical support for the idea of unconscious emotion (Berridge & Winkielman, 2003; Winkielman & Berridge, 2004). Our views were in agreement with several authors in psychology, including those who emphasize the relative automaticity of emotional processing (e.g., Kihlstrom, 1999); separability of expressive (verbal), physiological, and behavioral components of emotion (Lang, 1968); and fallibility of the meta-cognitive processes (Lambie & Marcel, 2002). Our views also aligned with several authors in affective neuroscience who emphasize the role of deep brain structures in generating unconscious elements of fear, anger, happiness, or sadness (e.g., Damasio, 1999; LeDoux, 1996).

In the next several sections, we review the main theoretical and empirical arguments that continue to support the idea that emotion may exist independent of conscious experience and offer some updated arguments and evidence. First, we present some functional and evolutionary considerations. Second, we review evidence from research on the emotional brain. Third, we discuss relevant psychological studies. After that, we address theoretical and empirical challenges to the notion of unconscious emotion and address some outstanding issues.

Functional and Evolutionary Considerations

Does the capacity for emotional behavior evolutionarily precede, follow, or co-occur with the capacity for conscious feeling? This is a difficult question as it involves making historical assumptions about the conjunction of two complex mental faculties—emotion and consciousness (Hayes & Huber, 2001). It is more manageable to ask whether evolutionarily basic affective reactions require conscious processing. Consider simple positive-negative reactions that animals produce to stimuli, such as predators, prey, strangers, con-specifics, food, drink, or mates (Konorski, 1967). The function of these affective reactions is to allow animals to react appropriately to favorable or unfavorable events by adjusting sensory apparatus (e.g., prioritizing certain stimuli), physiology (e.g., cardiovascular and hormonal changes), and action (e.g., priming of motor programs). From a design standpoint, it would be inefficient (and disadvantageous) if performing this basic function required the organism to possess a cognitive apparatus capable of consciousness (Cosmides & Tooby, 2000). Even in humans, conscious mechanisms are often too slow and imprecise for coordinating critical approach-avoidance responses. Most importantly, consciousness is often unnecessary. The disconnected (and presumably unconscious) spinal cord will reflexively withdraw the leg from a noxious stimulus delivered to the sole of the foot. Furthermore, many relatively complex coordination functions in organisms are efficiently performed without experiential representation. For example, decorticated rats, given proper female stimulation, will perform mounts, intromissions, and ejaculations that are similar to control rats (Whishaw, Kolb, 1985). In humans, one example of this is the automatic coupling between the cardiovascular, respiratory, and digestive systems (Porges, 1997). In short, it is reasonable to assume that at least basic affective reactions can be performed without mechanisms responsible for conscious feelings (LeDoux, 1996).

One standard challenge psychologists sometimes offer to the above arguments is that brute positive/negative reactions should not be called "affective." For example, paramecia can approach some stimuli, but it makes little sense to use the term "positive affect" for an organism that does not even have neurons. Further, even in more complex organisms, many reactions to favorable or unfavorable stimuli are more aptly classified as "reflexes" than "affective behaviors." For example, when a spider jumps to kills a prey, it makes little sense to explain this behavior by positing an underlying state of "negative affect." We agree, and along with most authors, require that to count as affective, the behavior should meet several criteria. First, the organism must be able to assess the input in terms of "valence." Second, this assessment must lead to a temporary state that involves several reasonably synchronized components (i.e., perceptual, hormonal, cardiovascular, muscular). Importantly, these criteria do not require the organism to explicitly represent its goals or explicitly make emotional "judgments"—only to respond in a coherent way to challenges and opportunities in its environment. Given these criteria, affect perhaps should *not* be assigned to reflexes, or to creatures like paramecia. But, it should be assigned to organisms that respond bivalently in a coherent, multisystem fashion to appropriate challenges and opportunities, even if these organisms have limited consciousness. For example, under these criteria, reptiles are capable of affect because they show coherent cardiovascular, hormonal, perceptual, and behavioral responses to favorable and unfavorable stimuli (Cabanac, 1999). In fact, there are many structural homologies between reptiles and mammalian limbic system (Martinez-Garcia, Martinez-Marcos, & Lanuza, 2002) and there are also remarkable similarities in the affective neurochemistry in birds, fish, reptiles, and mammals (Goodson & Bass, 2001).

In short, the available data suggest that vertebrates are capable of coordinated, multisystem responses to emotionally-relevant stimuli, with homologous neural circuitry regulating these responses across a diversity of vertebrate groups. Thus, while there are obvious differences in the neural substrates required for conscious experience across these groups, there is nonetheless remarkable consistency in other components of affective response. It therefore seems logical to propose that neural components of emotional processing can function in a way that is largely uncoupled from the neural components of consciousness.

Neural basis of Emotional Processing: Review of Relevant Areas

The just-presented evolutionary arguments are consistent with research on modern mammalian brains. As we discuss next, both subcortical and cortical structures participate in affective processes. The location of the most important structures of the generalized emotional brain is indicated in Figure 12.1. Below, we provide a brief overview of what is known about the roles of those structures in generating positive and negative affect. However, we remind the reader that our presentation here is highly simplified and does not capture the multiple roles these structures play in both affect and cognition, and

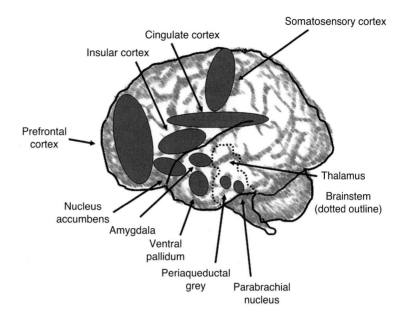

Fig. 12.1 Generalized Emotional Brain in Mammals.

Somatosensory cortex

Cingulate cortex

Insular cortex

Prefrontal cortex

Thalamus

Brainstem (dotted outline)

Nucleus accumbens

Amygdala

Ventral pallidum

Periaqueductal grey

Parabrachial nucleus

their complex neuroanatomy and neurochemistry (see Berridge, 2003). In the next section, we will consider functional patterns of activity across these areas that may correspond to conscious and unconscious emotion.

Subcortical Networks and Basic Affective Reactions

The subcortical structures involved in causing basic affective reactions range from the "mere" brainstem to the complex network of the "extended amygdala" (Berridge, 2003). Let us illustrate with a few examples the critical role of these structures in both positive and negative affect.

Brainstem

In both animals and humans the brainstem modulates basic affective responses. For example, in the domain of positive affect, research highlights the importance of the parabrachial nucleus (PBN). The PBN receives signals ascending from many sensory modalities, including visceral signals regarding internal bodily functions, and also taste sensations from the tongue. Not surprisingly, PBN plays a role in generating positive responses to tasty foods. For example, when a rat's PBN is tweaked by microinjections that activate its benzodiazepine/GABA receptors, the rat produces greater "liking" reactions to sugar, such as tongue protrusions and lip licking (Berridge & Pecina, 1995). In the domain of negative affect, research highlights the importance of the periaqueductal gray (PAG). In animals, the PAG mediates defensive reactions to threatening stimuli (Pankseep,

1998), and in both animals and humans, the PAG mediates responses to pain (Willis & Westlund, 1997). Importantly, the PAG does not simply compile incoming information to relay to the forebrain, but forms reciprocal connections with subcortical forebrain structures, thereby providing an anatomical basis for sensory stimuli to be processed by the PAG in a context-dependent and coordinated fashion (Pankseep, 1998).

A particularly poignant demonstration of the importance of brainstem to basic affective reactions is offered by a cruel experiment of nature. As a result of a birth defect, some infants have a congenitally malformed brain, possessing only a brainstem, but no cortex and little else of the forebrain (i.e., no amygdala, nucleus accumbens, etc). Yet, in these anencephalic infants, the sweet taste of sugar still elicits facial expressions that resemble normal "liking" reactions, such as lip sucking and smiles, whereas bitter tastes elicit facial expressions that resemble "disliking" reactions, such as mouth gapes and nose wrinkling (Steiner, 1973). In this context, it is also interesting that positive facial expressions to sweetness are emitted by various apes and monkeys and even rats (Berridge, 2000; Steiner et al., 2001). The pattern of positive facial expression becomes increasingly less similar to humans as the taxonomic distance increases between a species and us. But all of these species share some reaction components that are homologous to ours, suggesting common evolutionary ancestry and a similar neural mechanism that may be anchored in the brainstem.

Extended Amygdala

The term "extended amygdala" designates a configuration including the central and medial nuclei of amygdala, the bed nucleus of the stria terminalis, and other structures, and which works in close concert with parallel limbic circuits such as the mesolimbic nucleus accumbens and ventral pallidum system (Heimer & Van Hoesen, 2006). Recent years have witnessed an explosion of research highlighting the role of extended amygdala in basic affective reactions.

Amygdala

The amygdala consists of a set of almond-shaped nuclei located in the medial temporal lobe, just anterior to the hippocampus. The amygdala is reciprocally connected to a variety of areas. This includes visual thalamus and visual cortex, allowing for affective modification of perception; the dorsolateral prefrontal cortex, allowing for upstream and downstream regulation of affect state; and subcortical structures, allowing affective influence on sympathetic and parasympathetic regulation of cardiovascular activity, respiration, hormone levels, and basic muscular reactions. The role of the amygdala in perceptual and learning aspects of emotion has been confirmed in animal research as well as human neuroimaging and lesion studies. Thus, patients with congenital or acquired amygdala damage show impairments in conditioned fear responses, fear-potentiated startle, and arousal-enhanced perception and memory (Whalen & Phelps, 2009). Remarkably, patients with damage to the amygdala show little, if any, impairment in their subjective experience of emotion, at least as measured by the magnitude and frequency of self-reported positive or negative affect assessed on the PANAS scale (Anderson & Phelps, 2002). This suggests a relative independence of the amygdala from the mechanisms underlying generation of feelings.

The relative separation of the amygdala from the mechanisms involving a generation of a conscious feeling response is also suggested by research on patients with autism, who are known to have anatomical irregularities in the amygdala (Schumann & Amaral, 2009). These patients show atypical patterns of physiological responses to affective stimuli (e.g., potentiation of startle responses by both positive and negative stimuli) but a typical pattern of self-reported feeling reactions to emotional stimuli (Wilbarger, McIntosh, & Winkielman, 2009, see Winkielman, McIntosh, & Oberman, 2009 for review).

As mentioned earlier, there is some evidence that amygdala activation can occur without conscious perception of the stimulus. Thus, fMRI studies show that the amygdala can be activated with facial expressions that are not consciously perceived, including expressions of fear and anger presented subliminally (Morris, Öhman, & Dolan, 1999; Whalen et al., 1998), under condition of binocular suppression (Williams et al., 2004), or presented to a patient's blind visual field (Morris, et al, 2001). A component of these effects may involve a direct pathway from the visual thalamus to the amygdala. However, the human amygdala is richly interconnected with the visual cortex and probably receives the majority of input this way, thus challenging the popular notion of the "low-road" to emotion in typical humans (Pessoa & Adolphs, 2010).

Importantly, these studies should not be read as indicating a full independence of amygdala from attention. For example, in one study, none of the affect-related activations observed when attention was focused on happy or angry faces survived when attention was allocated to other items in the same displays (Pessoa, 2005). This suggests that attention can modulate amygdala responses to emotional stimuli under some conditions, and sometimes dramatically. Yet, it is not entirely clear how general these effects of attention are. Critically, it might be that attention (which amplifies neural signals) might be a prerequisite for any processing—conscious or unconscious (see Koch & Tsuchiya, 2007 for distinction between attention and consciousness). Finally, it is important to remember that the levels of amygdala activation revealed in an fMRI study supply only a crude measure of what the amygdala may or may not be computing.

Ventral Pallidum

The ventral pallidum borders on the lateral hypothalamus at its front and lateral sides. It is a major target of the limbic nucleus accumbens (Smith et al., 2009). The ventral pallidum also feeds subcortical affective signals forward into corticolimbic loops by projecting to the orbitofrontal and ventromedial areas of prefrontal cortex via a relay in the medial dorsal thalamus. In rats, this structure is involved in producing positive reactions to tasty foods, as suggested by the facts that (i) ventral pallidal neurons fire to tasty rewards, (ii) behavioral "liking" reactions to sweetness are increased by opioid drug microinjections in ventral pallidum, and (iii) excitotoxin lesions of ventral pallidum abolish hedonic reactions and cause aversive reactions (e.g., gaping and headshakes) to be elicited even by normally palatable foods (Cromwell & Berridge, 1993; Smith et al., 2009; Tindell et al., 2006). Ventral pallidum may also be crucial to sexual and social pair-bonding in rodents (Insel & Fernald, 2004). Less is known regarding the role of ventral pallidum in affect for humans, as the structure is too small to study in brain-imaging studies. However, there are a few intriguing observations. For example, electrical stimulation of the adjacent structure, globus pallidus, has been reported to sometimes induce bouts of affective mania that can last for days (Miyawaki, Perlmutter, Troster, Videen, & Koller, 2000). Also, the induction of a state of sexual or competitive arousal in normal men was found to be accompanied by increased blood flow in the ventral globus pallidus (Rauch et al., 1999).

Nucleus Accumbens

The nucleus accumbens lies at the front of the subcortical forebrain and is rich in dopamine and opioid neurotransmitter systems. The accumbens is often portrayed as a reward and pleasure "center" (as often as the amygdala is portrayed as a "center" of fear). In fact, activation of dopamine projections to the accumbens and related targets has been viewed by many neuroscientists as a neural "common currency" for reward. There is actually evidence that dopamine contributions to the accumbens reflect not "pleasure," or "liking" of the stimulus, but rather an incentive salience, or "wanting" of the stimulus (Berridge & Robinson, 1998). However, for the purpose of our argument here it is only important to highlight the role of accumbens in positive affective reactions. For example, in rats, brain microinjections of drug droplets that activate opioid receptors in nucleus accumbens cause increased "liking" for sweetness, as well as increased "wanting" (Pecina & Berridge, 2000; 2005). In humans, the accumbens activates to drug cues, sex cues, and also to other desired stimuli, including foods, drinks, and even money (Knutson et al., 2001; Knutson et al. 2008).

Cortical Networks

One cannot talk about the emotional brain of mammals without discussing the cortex. In fact, when human subjects spontaneously recall emotional events, a host of cortical structures activate, including the prefrontal cortex, the insula, the somatosensory cortices, and the cingulate cortex (Damasio et al., 2000). The approximate location of those structures is shown in Figure 12.1.

PREFRONTAL CORTEX

The prefrontal cortex lies, not surprisingly, at the very front of the brain. The ventral or bottom one-third of the prefrontal cortex is called the orbitofrontal cortex and is most elaborately developed in humans and other primates. There is some evidence that subcortical projections to the prefrontal cortex contribute to conscious affective experience. For example, the intense feeling of pleasure experienced by heroin users appears to involve accumbens-to-cortex signals that are relayed to cortical regions via the ventral pallidum and thalamus (Wise, 1996). In another example, self-reports of "excitement" in typical participants are related to the degree of activation in the nucleus accumbens and prefrontal cortex (Knutson et al., 2004). The orbitofrontal cortex contains a special zone in its midanterior region that specifically codes positive pleasure, and where fMRI activation tracks changes in a food sensory pleasure induced by sensory-specific satiety (Kringelbach, 2005; 2010). The prefrontal cortex is not only directly involved in conscious emotional experience but also participates in affective reactions by modulating lower brain structures via descending projections (Damasio, 1999; Phan, Wager, Taylor, & Liberzon, 2004). For example, the orbitofrontal cortex projects back to the accumbens (Davidson, Jackson, & Kalin, 2000) and the dorsolateral prefrontal cortex projects back to the amygdala (Ochsner & Gross, 2004).

SOMATOSENSORY CORTEX AND INSULA

The primary (S1) and secondary (S2) somatosensory cortex is located behind the central sulcus. The somatosensory cortex is responsible for monitoring the state of the body, including sensations (e.g., touch) and proprioception (i.e., state of muscles and joints). The insula is located near the bottom of the somatosensory cortex, almost at the intersection of the frontal, parietal, and temporal lobes. The insula receives inputs from limbic structures, such as the amygdala, and cortical structures, such as the prefrontal cortex and posterior parietal cortex and the anterior cingulate, and appears particularly important for interoception, or monitoring the state of internal organs (Craig, 2003; Critchley et al., 2004).

There is evidence that the somatosensory cortex and the insula may jointly contribute to emotional experience by representing the current body state (Craig, 2009). For example, neuroimaging studies show that recall of emotional memories is associated with extensive activation of the somatosensory cortex (Damasio et al., 2000). In another example, lesions to the right somatosensory cortex are associated with impaired perception of facial expressions as well as impaired touch perception (Adolphs et al., 2000). Finally, human studies show involvement of insula in pain (Peyron et al., 2000), disgust (Wicker et al., 2003), and appreciation of sweet tastes and related rewards (O'Doherty et al., 2002). These findings are generally consistent with the so called "embodiment" approach to emotion, which emphasizes the representational role of the central and peripheral representations of the body (e.g., Niedenthal et al., 2005).

CINGULATE CORTEX

The cingulate cortex consists of a longitudinal strip running front to back along the midline on each hemisphere of the brain, just above the corpus callosum. Again, it is a richly interconnected structure thought to interface between the limbic system and prefrontal cortex (Craig, 2009 above). The cingulate cortex has been implicated in human clinical conditions such as pain, depression, anxiety, and other distressing states (Davidson, Abercrombie, Nitschke, & Putnam, 1999; Peyron et al., 2000). Interestingly, some research suggests that emotion experience is associated with the dorsal anterior region of the cingulate cortex, whereas more reflective parts of the awareness are associated with the rostral anterior region (Lane, 2000).

Functional Organization of Conscious States

As the foregoing review indicates, a host of subcortical and cortical structures is involved in the production of emotional responses to valenced stimuli. This raises the important question: How does neural activity in these structures relate to the complexity and consciousness of the corresponding emotional state? A simple (and probably over-simplistic) viewpoint would identify the subjective component of emotion with activity in the cortical components of the neural emotion network. Subcortical structures would then be mediating only the nonconscious components of the emotional response. From this viewpoint, evidence for "unconscious emotion" would be explained by the autonomous operation of (a subset of) the subcortical components of the network, in the absence of direct cortical involvement. In a more nuanced (and more realistic) perspective, however, cortical representations of emotion may themselves be conscious or unconscious, and the neural basis of conscious emotion is expected to essentially involve interactions between cortical and subcortical structures in the network. Conscious emotion may emerge, for example, as the cortex hierarchically re-represents and feeds back on subcortical processes that inform it. On such view, conscious emotion is not "localizable" to particular structures at either level. Adopting this perspective, the question becomes: What qualitative patterns of functional organization across the areas reviewed above are likely to underlie conscious and unconscious emotion? In this section, we address this question in the context of a general "global workspace" model of the functional organization of conscious states.

Global Workspace

Attempts to functionally distinguish conscious from unconscious cognitive processing commonly focus, at the input side, on integration, and on flexibility of response at the output side. In this framework, a conscious representation characteristically (i) involves a unified interpretation coherently integrating information from multiple sensory modalities and other systems (e.g., vision, touch, introception, working and long-term memory), and (ii) supports a coherent suite of actions ranging over arbitrary response mappings and implemented by arbitrary motor effectors (e.g., a button-press with the right index finger, a verbal response in, say, English, Polish or German, the coded eye movements of a locked-in patient). Included among the coherent suite of actions in (ii) is the subject's adamant verbal report about the qualitative character of his/her subjective experience—as well as a wealth of possible meta-cognitive reports about the contents of current cognition (cf. Schooler, 2002 on "meta-consciousness").

Consciousness, in this functional approach, is uniquely associated with a massive integrated choreography of representation and response. While conscious experience has sometimes been speculatively identified with a putative choreographer residing at a specific brain locus (e.g., the pineal gland of Descartes, 1649; cf. Dennett, 1991), it is presently more popular to identify conscious experience (somehow) with the neural choreography itself. The "neural correlate of consciousness" is then expected to be a pattern of coordinated neural activity across perceptual, associative, and premotor areas all working (somehow) on the same page.

This general idea is neatly captured in Baars' (1993, 1997) influential metaphor of a "global workspace." Cognition is comprised of a collection of semi-independent specialized processors, each capable of rapidly performing a limited set of nonconscious computations. Information becomes conscious when the output of a subset of the processors is globally broadcast to the entire network of processors. Broadcasting a common pool of information allows the network of processors, coherently but slowly, to collectively deal with novel contingencies for which no single processor is adequately specialized. Consistent with this idea, several specific instances of unconscious processing are believed to involve the same dedicated cortical sites that are critical for conscious processing of similar information, but without sustained orchestrated activation across distant brain areas. For example, numerous studies have found evidence for semantic priming from visually masked words, even when subjects are unable to report the identity of the words (e.g., Merikle & Daneman, 1998). In neuroimaging experiments, unconsciously masked words produce sustained activity (albeit at reduced levels) in the same specialized cortical region of the left temporal lobe that is strongly and specifically activated by consciously visible words. However, when subjects are not conscious of the word stimuli, sustained activity is *not* seen across a slew of word non-specific areas strongly activated by conscious word stimuli (Dehaene et al., 2001).

Vegetative State

The idea that specialized cortical processors can operate autonomously in the absence of conscious awareness is dramatically illustrated in the vegetative state. Vegetative patients have preserved sleep/wake cycles but are deemed to lack awareness of self and environment. The condition, reviewed in Jennett (2002), is typically caused by widespread damage to the cerebral cortex and/or its underlying white matter. Recent experimental evidence suggests that apparent unawareness in the vegetative state may stem from a failure to integrate locally processed information into a unified brain-wide representation. For example, Laureys and colleagues (2002) delivered noxious tactile stimuli to vegetative patients as well as control subjects while changes in regional cerebral blood flow were measured. Both patients and controls showed stimulus-specific activity in primary thalamic and cortical somatosensory areas contralateral to the noxious stimulus. In addition, the noxious stimuli activated a widely distributed array of higher-order "association areas" in both hemispheres of conscious control brains, but not in apparently unconscious vegetative brains.

This principle of largely intact local processors against a background of blocked global representation may, we suggest, likewise explain atypical fragments of coordinated behavior which are occasionally observed in vegetative patients, and which have been associated with relatively preserved activity in isolated neural mini-networks. These stereotyped behavioral fragments sometimes involve a strong affective component. For example, Plum et al. (1998) described a vegetative patient, exhibiting no clear behavioral signs of meaningful awareness for self or environment, in whom the following behavioral pattern was repeatedly demonstrated:

> "When anyone makes a loud noise or attempts to examine, feed or bathe him, he immediately expresses clenched-teeth, rigid extremities, and produces a high pitched noise that sounds like a maximal screaming rage. During these attacks his skin color flushes, and his blood pressure rises" (pp. 1931).

The authors likened this coordinated response pattern to the "sham rage" which Cannon (1927) was able to elicit in brainstem-transected cats. While metabolic levels were severely reduced throughout this patient's cerebrum, the reduction was less marked in a network of brain areas the authors conjectured to be involved in affective response. Further evidence that autonomous neural subnetworks can operate in the absence of global integration and conscious awareness comes from the study of NREM parasomnias (non-rapid eye movement, slow wave sleep). In a SPECT imaging study of presumably unconscious ambulation during sleepwalking, isolated activity was observed in a mini-network including the thalamus, cerebellum, and posterior cingulate cortex—while global activity was significantly depressed throughout most of the cortex (Bassetti et al., 2000).

Recall that "affect" and "emotion" were earlier defined as complex coordinated syndromes of valence-based subjective, physiological, and behavioral components. In the global workspace framework, consciousness itself is viewed as equivalent to, or closely linked with, the system-wide integration of many component processors, ranging widely over modalities, dimensions, and response mappings. In this setting, the binary question—Can emotion be unconscious?—is seen to approximate a more continuous question: To what extent can various subsets of processors in the neural emotion network operate in an internally coherent fashion, without themselves being integrated with the various other processors in the global workspace? How big can a coherent network of affective processors become—and hence how elaborate can affect-congruent behaviors and physiological reactions become—without being recruited into the coherent brain-wide network of activity that is the presumed neural correlate of normal subjective experience?

The next section describes experimental evidence suggesting that affect-congruent responses can reach a remarkably high level of coherence and complexity in the absence of conscious awareness. But first, we briefly note the broad reach of this question—how much integration is possible outside the conscious global workspace—in the affective neuroscience of consciousness.

Sleep Murders and Other Dissociations

The question of "complex yet unconscious emotional actions" is posed in an especially striking form by the numerous putative instances of "sleep-murder" (reviewed in Broughton et al., 1994). In one important Canadian medico-legal case, Kenneth Parks was acquitted of murder and attempted murder after a defense that attributed his actions to "noninsane automatism"—several sleep experts argued, and the jury accepted, that Parks left his home, drove 10–15 minutes to his in-law's house, and assaulted them in an elaborate unconscious automatism during an episode of sleepwalking (Broughton et al., 1994). For a case in which a highly similar sleepwalking defense was rejected by an American jury see Cartwright, 2004. For other examples of remarkably complex behavior during apparent sleepwalking, see Schenck and Mahowald (1995) and Siddiqui et al. (2009).

The question of complex unconscious actions also arises in the longstanding debate between "credulous" and "skeptical" views (Sutcliffe, 1961) of putative functional dissociations in experimental hypnosis (Knox et al., 1974) and dissociative identity disorder (Putnam, 1989). What is the maximum possible level of sub-total neural integration—and correspondingly, how much internal coherence can complex behavioral and physiological responses exhibit in the absence of unified conscious awareness?

Experimental Psychology

Thought the neuroscientific evidence for the possibility of unconscious emotion is rather compelling, it is not enough. After all, much of it comes from animal studies and studies of brain-damaged patients, thus it is unclear how it applies to typical individuals. Further, in many laboratory studies physiology (rather than behavior) is the primary dependent variable. Thus, it is unclear whether physiological activations observed in well-controlled empirical studies have meaningful behavioral consequences. Fortunately, in recent years, psychology has begun to explore these questions with a variety of paradigms, often using a combination of behavioral and physiological methods.

Unconscious Affective Reactions to Facial Expressions

What about ordinary people with fully intact brains? Can they have "unconscious emotions" too? There are now several studies which explored unconscious emotion using subliminal facial expressions. In one of the initial studies, participants were asked to rate neutral Chinese ideographs preceded by subliminal happy or angry faces (Winkielman, Zajonc, & Schwarz, 1997). During the task, some participants were asked to monitor changes in their conscious feelings. They were also told not to use their feelings as a source of their preference ratings. Those participants were given instructions containing plausible alternative explanations for why their feelings might change (e.g., background music, flashing pictures). In effect, these instructions encouraged corrective attributions that typically eliminate the contaminating influence of conscious feelings on evaluative judgments (Clore, 1994). However, even for participants who knew to disregard their "contaminated" feelings, the subliminal happy faces increased, and subliminal angry faces decreased preference ratings. Most relevant to the question of unconscious emotion, participants did not remember experiencing any changes in their mood when asked after the experiment about their emotions.

A more compelling evidence for unconscious emotion would show that cognitively able and motivated participants are *unable to report a conscious feeling* at the same time their behavior reveals the *presence of an affective reaction*. Ideally, the affective reaction should be strong enough to change even behavior that has real consequences for the individual. To obtain such evidence, Winkielman, Berridge, and Wilbarger (2005) assessed consumption behavior after exposing participants to several subliminal emotional facial expressions (happy, neutral, or angry). Each of the subliminal expressions was masked by a clearly visible neutral face on which participants performed a simple gender detection task. Immediately after the subliminal affect induction, some participants rated their feelings (mood and arousal) and then consumed a fruit beverage. Other participants performed consumption behavior and feeling ratings in opposite order. In Study 1, the consumption behavior involved pouring themselves a cup of a novel drink from a pitcher and then drinking it. In Study 2, participants were asked to take a small sip of the drink and rate it on different dimensions (e.g., monetary value). In both studies, there was no evidence of any change in conscious mood or arousal, regardless of whether participants rated their feelings on a simple scale from positive to negative or on a multi-item scale asking about specific emotions. Yet participants' consumption behavior and drink ratings were influenced by those subliminal affective stimuli, especially when participants were thirsty. Specifically, after happy faces thirsty participants poured significantly more drink from the pitcher and drank more from their cup than after angry faces (Study 1). Thirsty participants were also willing to pay about twice as much more for the drink after happy, rather than angry expressions (Study 2). That is, subliminal emotional faces evoked affective reactions that altered participants' consumption behavior and evaluation of the beverage, but produced no mediating change in their conscious feelings at the moment the affective reactions were caused. Since participants rated their feelings of mood immediately after the subliminal affect induction, these results cannot be explained by the failure of affective memory.

One can wonder, however, whether such unconscious emotional reactions can drive a more complex social behavior. After all, a decision to pour and drink a novel beverage is relatively simple and could be driven by activation of basic approach-avoidance tendencies. Would an abstract and cognitive incentive, such as an investment prospect that requires an active decision whether to allocate money, also be increased in attractiveness by a subliminal positive prime, similar to the drink? To address this concern, we have recently used the same priming paradigm but asked participants to make more complex financial decisions (for overview, see Winkielman, Knutson, Paulus, & Trujillo, 2007). For example, in one study participants decided whether to gamble $1 for a 50% chance of winning $2.50 or whether to simply pocket the dollar. Participants primed with subliminal happy faces were more likely to choose the investment than participants primed with angry faces, presumably reflecting a more favorable evaluation of the bet.

One can wonder, however, to what extent the reactions elicited by unconscious affective faces are truly "affective," in the sense of involving "hot"

representation of valence in the systems traditionally associated with emotion. Perhaps they are only "evaluative," in the sense of activation of certain meaning components (Clore, 1994). Our recent studies addressed this concern in two ways. First, as mentioned earlier, physiological and neuroimaging studies suggest that subliminal angry and fearful faces activate the amygdala and related limbic structures. Thus, one should be able to find psychophysiological traces of emotion in the just-described ideograph-rating and drinking studies. Indeed, we found that subliminal emotional facial expressions cause weak but detectable changes in response of low-level physiological systems. Specifically, we found congruent facial EMG responses (smiling to happy faces and frowning to angry faces) and emotion-congruent startle modulation, suggesting that the primes activate emotional channels that produce valenced expressions (Starr, Linn, & Winkielman, 2007). Another way to distinguish between the cold "evaluative" and "hot" affective aspects of emotion is by the use of different materials for emotion induction. Specifically, affective words have long been known to prime evaluative processes (e.g., as assessed by priming). On the other hand, affective pictures are more efficient than words in eliciting physiological reactions, which reflect changes in core affective systems (Larsen, Norris, & Cacioppo, 2003). This is true even if words and pictures are matched on self-reported valence and frequency. Consistent with these observations, we found that subliminal (and supraliminal) emotional facial expressions influence consumption in an affect-congruent way, whereas words do not (Starr, Winkielman, & Gogolushko, 2008). Thus, it appears that even though the reaction induced by the emotional facial expressions is unconscious, it works via modification of a low-level emotional response, rather via high-level evaluative priming. In sum, we propose that all these results demonstrate unconscious affect in the strong sense—a genuine affective process strong enough to alter behavior, but of which people are simply not aware.

Challenges and Limits to Unconscious Emotion

Findings like the one just described constitute some evidence for the independence of affect and conscious experience. But, there are several challenges to be met.

How does unconscious affect work?

One challenge involves specifying the mechanisms by which affect can influence behavior towards an object without eliciting conscious feelings. One possibility is that unconscious affect directly modulates the object's ability to trigger affective and motivational responses via a "front-end" or perceptual-attentional mechanism. That is, instead of triggering feelings, the affect could modify the position of the relevant target object on the organism's "incentive landscape." For example, we speculate that subliminal facial expressions might activate the amygdala, which then might project to the adjacent accumbens and related structures responsible for processing of incentives (Berridge, 2003; Rolls, 1999; Whalen et al., 1998). Altered neuronal activity in the nucleus accumbens (constituting unconscious "liking") could then change the human affective reaction to the sight of an incentive (drink, money) leading to differential behaviors, all without eliciting conscious feelings (see Winkielman et al., 2008 for a more comprehensive discussion).

Affect or emotion?
There is now decent evidence for *unconscious affect*—changes in general positivity–negativity. But what about *unconscious emotion*—categorically different states such as fear, anger, disgust, sadness, joy, love, shame, guilt, or pride? Some skeptics doubt this possibility based on the argument that emotional states require sophisticated cognitive differentiation. For example, an emotion such as guilt requires entertaining several beliefs such as "I did something wrong to another person, I was responsible, I could have done something to prevent it." This argument may hold for higher-order social emotion, but not for basic emotions. After all, animals, even reptiles, appear to show categorically different reactions to situations demanding different emotional response (e.g., fear, rage, rejection, Pankseep, 1998). It is also interesting that human neuroimaging studies reveal unique patterns of amygdala activation to consciously presented facial expressions of fear, anger, sadness, and disgust (Phan et al., 2002; Whalen, 1998). If future research shows that, say, masked facial expressions of fear, anger, sadness, or disgust can create different physiological reactions with different behavioral consequences, all without eliciting conscious feelings, then there might indeed be processes fully deserving the label "unconscious emotion." So far, we are not aware of such studies, but we believe the empirical challenges lie more in how to make the disgust or sadness stimuli convincingly "invisible" (which is difficult for faces but especially for complex pictures), rather than with the emotional reaction of disgust or sadness being

necessarily conscious. In fact, there are some intriguing hints from a series of studies using subliminal words related to guilt and sadness—two negative but qualitatively different emotions (Zemack-Rugar, Bettman, & Fitzsimons, 2007). When participants were primed with subliminal guilt words, they showed less indulgence in their behavior than participants primed with sad words. Unfortunately, it is unclear in these studies whether the words induced actual emotions (there was no evidence of any feeling changes on the self-report level, but also no physiological measure of actual emotion). Still, these results at least raise a possibility that basic triggers of social emotions can operate unconsciously.

Unnoticed, unverbalized, or unconscious affect?
Another challenge comes from the difficulty of conclusively establishing the absence of feelings (as far as one can ever prove absence). The problem stems from the very nature of reporting on phenomenal states. Several writers pointed out the difference between the primary "experiencing" consciousness and the secondary "reflecting" consciousness (Lambie & Marcel, 2002; Schooler, 2002). Future research should address to what extent the absence of self-reported feelings in human studies represents a genuine absence of phenomenology, or inability to reflect on that phenomenology. Several writers have suggested that these questions could be addressed by providing participants with training in (i) introspection; (ii) use of beepers, ratings scales, or momentary-affect dials; or (iii) alternative, non-verbal ways of expressing emotion (Bartoshuk, 2000; Lambie & Marcel, 2002; Nielsen & Kaszniak, 2007; Schooler & Schreiber, 2004). Finally, neuroscience may be of help. If it's possible in the future to reliably identify a neural correlate of subjective experience, the presence of conscious feelings could be suggested by changes in relevant neural activation.

Conscious and Unconscious Emotion in Social Behavior

In the preceding section we have presented a variety of arguments for "unfelt" affect and emotion. So are conscious feelings just like "icing on the cake"—nice, but not necessary? We do not believe so. In the following section we offer some speculation on the role of conscious feelings in emotion, and the relation between conscious and unconscious components of emotion. We especially emphasize the critical role of conscious feelings in social behavior.

What Good is Conscious Feeling?

In general, there are several benefits for a mental state to be conscious. Consciousness allows the organism to go beyond simple, habitual reactions and design novel, complex, context-sensitive forms of responding. So, in many ways, an emotion system that has access to consciousness is going to be a more sophisticated one. Consciousness also allows control. The organism can stop undesirable responses and promote the desirable ones, and decide how and when to respond. Obviously, this control function has tremendous social consequences (Ochsner & Gross, 2004). Conscious access to feelings also plays a communicative and motivational function. Thus, conscious feelings give internal feedback about how well the organism is doing with the current pursuits, telling it to maintain or change its path. More importantly, being aware of one's emotion and able to communicate it to others seems crucial for basic social coordination. Feelings also come with psychological immediacy and urgency, making the organism "care" about its fate in a way that may not be available to any other mechanism (Searle, 1997). This extends from simple hedonic states, such as pain and pleasure, to complex emotions. Thus, pangs of guilt propel us to make amends, whereas green eyes of jealousy alert us to trespasses of our mates (Frank, 1998). Again, this function appears critical in making emotions social.

What Makes Emotion Unconscious or Conscious?

Given the many benefits, why then are humans sometimes unaware of their emotion? We suppose that a variety of neuroscientific and psychological factors play a role. Most of these factors probably apply regardless of whether the process is emotional or cognitive. Earlier in this chapter, we speculated that under some circumstances relevant neural processes could simply bypass the circuitry for subjective experience and feed directly into behavioral circuitry. That is, sometimes emotion can be unconscious for the same reason why vision can be unconscious. As documented in research on "vision for perception vs. vision for action" (Goodale & Milner, 2004) and in research on "blindsight" (Weiscranz, 1996), the relevant information can feed into the action system without ever reaching brain areas responsible for subjective experience. Further, sometimes rudimentary affective processes may be like other neural processes, such as thermoregulation, which are designed to run unconsciously and to

elicit conscious experience only rarely, when there is an important reason for intervention. Another important factor might be the brain's inability to construct a coherent percept, as when alternative sources of activation compete for interpretation (Crick & Koch, 2003).

Other factors preventing the emergence of conscious representation are more psychological. Thus, the input might be too weak or too brief, as amply demonstrated in the work on backward masking (Enns & DiLollo, 2000). Or, the input may be strong, but inconsistent with the perceivers' expectations and thus escape attentional processing, as demonstrated in research on change blindness (Simons & Chabris, 1999). Or, the input may not make sense in the context of the current situation (Dennett, 1991). Yet, in all these cases, the input may be sufficient to influence behavior.

Unfortunately, there is little empirical work on factors that determine the emergence of conscious emotional feelings. Future work could make some progress by, for example, systematically examining what determines whether subliminal stimuli elicit conscious mood. As we discussed earlier, in our work, subliminal facial expressions did not elicit feeling (Winkielman et al., 2008). However, many studies observed feeling changes after subliminal bloody pictures (Robles, Smith, Carver, & Wellens, 1987) or mere-exposed ideographs (Monahan, Murphy, & Zajonc, 2000). These findings suggest that perhaps simple or highly practiced stimuli, like happy and angry faces used in our studies, are less likely to elicit feelings than more complex or novel stimuli, like visual scenes or ideographs. The impact on feelings could also depend on the individual's sensitivity to a particular emotion inducer. For example, subliminally presented snakes increased conscious anxiety in phobic, but not typical, participants (Öhman & Soares, 1994). Similarly, introspectively sensitive participants are better at detecting impact of subliminal stimuli and use their own reactions in behavior (Katkin, Wiens, & Öhman, 2001). Another interesting factor is the salience of the self representation. That is, when the self is salient, a change in an affective state might lead to a reportable conscious feeling, rather than be channeled to a representation of an external object (Lambie & Marcel, 2002). In sum, the emergence of conscious feelings may be determined by a host of stimulus, personal, and motivational factors. Though little is known at this point, it seems clear that the question of when and how emotion becomes conscious can be fruitfully empirically investigated, especially now given all the new experimental and neuroscientific techniques.

Concluding Summary

In this chapter we argued that understanding the relation between emotion and consciousness is important for many basic theoretical and practical questions of social neuroscience. We showed that evidence from many domains supports the idea of "unconscious emotion." Not only can basic emotional reactions be elicited with unconscious stimuli, but the affective reaction itself can remain unconscious. Yet, we also believe that conscious subjective experience plays a major role in human social behavior and should continue as a central topic of emotion research. It is only through the understanding of the relation between conscious and unconscious components that we will be able to fully capture the role of emotion in social life.

References

Adolphs, R., Damasio, H., Tranel, D., Cooper, G., & Damasio, A. R. (2000). A role for somatosensory cortices in the visual recognition of emotion as revealed by 3-D lesion mapping. *Journal of Neuroscience, 20*, 2683–2690.

Anderson, A. K. & Phelps, E. A. (2002). Is the human amygdala critical for the subjective experience of emotion? Evidence of intact dispositional affect in patients with lesions of the amygdala. *Journal of Cognitive Neuroscience, 14*, 709–720.

Baars, B. (1993). How does a serial, integrated and very limited stream of consciousness emerge from a nervous system that is mostly unconscious, distributed, parallel, and of enormous capacity? In G.R. Bock & J. Marsh (Eds.). *Experimental and theoretical studies of consciousness* (pp. 282–290), New York: Wiley.

Baars, B. J. (1997). *In the theater of consciousness: The workspace of the mind*. New York: Oxford University Press.

Bartoshuk, L. M. (2000). Psychophysical advances aid the study of genetic variation in taste. *Appetite, 34*, 105.

Bassetti, C., Vella, S., Donati, F., Wielepp, P., & Weder, B. (2000). SPECT during sleepwalking. *The Lancet, 346*, 484–485.

Berke, R. L (September 12, 2000). Democrats See, and Smell, Rats in G.O.P. Ad. New York Times.

Berridge, K. C. (2000). Measuring hedonic impact in animals and infants: Microstructure of affective taste reactivity patterns. *Neuroscience & Biobehavioral Reviews, 24*, 173–198

Berridge, K. C. (2003). Comparing the emotional brain of humans and other animals. In R. J. Davidson, H. H. Goldsmith, & K. Scherer (Eds.), *Handbook of affective sciences* (pp. 25–51), Oxford: Oxford University Press.

Berridge, K. C. & Pecina, S. (1995). Benzodiazepines, appetite, and taste palatability. *Neuroscience and Biobehavioral Reviews, 19*, 121–131.

Berridge, K. C. & Robinson, T. E. (1998). What is the role of dopamine in reward: Hedonic impact, reward learning, or incentive salience? *Brain Research—Brain Research Reviews, 28*, 309–369.

Berridge, K. C. & Winkielman, P. (2003). What is an unconscious emotion: The case for unconscious "liking." *Cognition and Emotion, 17*, 181–211.

Broughton, R., Billings, R., Cartwright, R., Doucette, D., Edmeads, J., Edwardh, M., et al. (1994). Homicidal somnambulism: A case report. *Sleep, 17*, 253–264.

Cabanac, M. (1999). Emotion and phylogeny. *Journal of Consciousness Studies, 6*, 176–190.

Cacioppo, J. T., Larsen, J. T., Smith, N. K., & Berntson, G. G. (2004). The affect system: What lurks below the surface of feelings? In A. S. R. Manstead, N. H. Frijda, & A. H. Fischer (Eds.), *Feelings and emotions: The Amsterdam conference*. New York: Cambridge University Press.

Cannon, W. B. (1927). *Bodily changes in pain, hunger, fear and rage*, 2nd ed. New York: D. Appleton & Co.

Cartwright, R. (2004). Sleepwalking violence: A sleep disorder, a legal dilemma, and a psychological challenge. *American Journal of Psychiatry, 161*, 1149–1158.

Clore, G. L. (1994). Why emotions are never unconscious. In P. Ekman & R. J. Davidson (Eds.), *The nature of emotion: Fundamental questions* (pp. 285–290). New York: Oxford University Press.

Cosmides, L. & Tooby, J. (2000). Evolutionary psychology and the emotions. In M. Lewis & J. Haviland-Jones (Eds.) *Handbook of emotion* (2nd ed.) pp. 91–115. New York: Guilford Press.

Craig, A. D. (2003). Interoception: The sense of the physiological condition of the body. *Current Opinion in Neurobiology, 13*, 500–505.

Craig, A. D. (2009). How do you feel—now? The anterior insula and human awareness. *Nature Reviews Neuroscience, 10*, 59–70.

Crick, F. & Koch, C. (2003). A framework for consciousness. *Nature Neuroscience, 6*, 119–126

Critchley H. D., Wiens, S., Rotshtein, P., Oehman, A., & Dolan, R. J. (2004). Neural systems supporting interoceptive awareness. *Nature Neuroscience, 2*, 189–195.

Cromwell, H. C. & Berridge, K. C. (1993). Where does damage lead to enhanced food aversion: The ventral pallidum/ substantia innominata or lateral hypothalamus? *Brain Research, 624*, 1–2, 1–10.

Damasio, A. R. (1999). *The feeling of what happens: Body and emotion in the making of consciousness*. New York: Harcourt Brace.

Damasio, A. R., Grabowski, T. J., Bechara, A., Damasio, H., Ponto, L. L., Parvizi, J., et al. (2000). Subcortical and cortical brain activity during the feeling of self-generated emotions. *Nature Neuroscience, 3*, 1049–1056.

Davidson, R. J., Jackson, D. C., & Kalin, N. H. (2000). Emotion, plasticity context, and regulation: Perspectives from affective neuroscience. *Psychological Bulletin, 126*, 890–909.

Dehaene, S., Naccache, L., Cohen, L., Le Bihan, D., Mangin, J.-F., Poline, J.-B., et al. (2001). Cerebral mechanisms of word masking and unconscious repetition priming. *Nature Neuroscience, 4*, 752–758.

Dennett, D. C. (1991). *Consciousness explained*. Boston: Little, Brown and Co.

Descartes, R. (1649). The Passions of the soul. In J. Cottingham, R. Stroothoff, & D. Murdoch, (Trans.) (1985). *The philosophical writings of Descartes*, Volume 1. Cambridge: Cambridge University Press.

Dimberg, U., Thunberg, M., & Elmehed, K. (2000). Unconscious facial reactions to emotional facial expressions. *Psychological Science, 11*, 86–89.

Drogosz, M. & Nowak, A. (2006). A neural model of mere exposure: The EXAC mechanism. *Polish Psychological Bulletin, 37,* 7–15.

Enns, J. T. & DiLollo, V. (2000). What's new in visual masking. *Trends in Cognitive Sciences, 4,* 345–352.

Frank, R. (1988). *Passions within reason. The strategic role of the emotions.* New York: Norton.

Freud, S. (1950). *Collected papers* (J. Riviere, Trans. Vol. 4). London: Hogarth Press and The Institute of Psychoanalysis.

Frijda, N. H. (1999). Emotions and hedonic experience. In D. Kahneman, E. Diener, & N. Schwarz (Eds.), *Well-being: The foundations of hedonic psychology* (pp. 190–210). New York: Russell Sage Foundation.

Goodale, M. A. & Milner, M. A. (2004). *Sight unseen: An exploration of conscious and unconscious vision.* Oxford: Oxford University Press.

Goodson, J. L. & Bass, A. H. (2001). Social behavior functions and related anatomical characteristics of vasotocin/vasopressin systems in vertebrates. *Brain Research Reviews, 35,* 246–265.

Heimer, L. & Van Hoesen, G. W. (2006). The limbic lobe and its output channels: Implications for emotional functions and adaptive behavior. *Neuroscience & Biobehavioral Reviews, 30,* 126–147.

Heyes, C. M. & L. Huber, (Eds.) (2001). *Evolution of cognition.* Cambridge, MA: MIT Press.

Insel, T. R. & Fernald, R. D. (2004). How the brain processes social information: Searching for the social brain. *Annual Reviews: Neuroscience, 27,* 697–722

James, W. (1884). *What is an emotion. Mind, 9,* 188–205.

Jennett, B. (2002). *The vegetative state: Medical facts, ethical and legal dilemmas.* Cambridge: Cambridge University Press.

Katkin, E. S., Wiens, S., & Öhman, A. (2001). Nonconscious fear conditioning, visceral perception, and the development of gut feelings. *Psychological Science, 12,* 366–370.

Kihlstrom, J. F. (1999). The psychological unconscious. In L. A. Pervin & O. P. John (Eds.), *Handbook of personality: Theory and research* (2 ed., pp. 424–442). New York: The Guilford Press.

Knox, V. J, Morgan, A. H., & Hilgard, E. 1974. Pain and suffering in ischemia: The paradox of hypnotically suggested anesthesia as contradicted by reports from the "hidden observer." *Archives of General Psychiatry, 30,* 840–847.

Knutson, B., Adams, C. M., Fong, G. W., & Hommer, D. (2001). Anticipation of increasing monetary reward selectively recruits nucleus accumbens. *Journal of Neuroscience, 21,* 1–5.

Knutson, B., Bjork, J. M., Fong, G. W., Hommer, D. W., Mattay, V. S., & Weinberger, D. R. (2004). *Amphetamine modulates human incentive processing. Neuron, 43,* 261–269.

Knutson, B., Wimmer, G. E., Kuhnen, C. M., & Winkielman, P. (2008). Nucleus accumbens activation mediates the influence of reward cues on financial risk taking. *NeuroReport, 19,* 509–513.

Koch, C. & Tsuchiya. N. (2007) Attention and consciousness: Two distinct brain processes, *Trends in Cognitive Sciences, 11,* 16–22.

Konorski, J. (1967). *Integrative activity of the brain: An interdisciplinary approach.* Chicago: University of Chicago Press.

Kringelbach, M. L. (2005). The human orbitofrontal cortex: Linking reward to hedonic experience. *Nat Rev Neurosci, 6,* 691–702.

Kringelbach, M. L. (2010). The hedonic brain: A functional neuroanatomy of human pleasure. In: M.L. Kringelbach & K.C. Berridge (Eds.), *Pleasures of the brain* (pp. 202–221). Oxford: Oxford University Press.

Lambie, J. A. & Marcel, A. J. (2002). Consciousness and the varieties of emotion experience: A theoretical framework. *Psychological Review, 109,* 219–259.

Lane, R. D. (2000). Neural correlates of conscious emotional experience. In R. D. Lane and L. Nadel (Eds.), *Cognitive neuroscience of emotion* (pp. 345–370). New York, NY: Oxford University Press.

Lang, P. J. (1968). Fear reduction and fear behavior: Problems in treating a construct. In: J. Schlien, J. (Ed.), *Research in psychotherapy III.* Washington DC: APA.

Larsen, R. J. & Fredrickson, B. L. (1999). Measurement issues in emotion research. In D. Kahneman, E. Diener, & N. Schwarz (Eds.) *Well-being: Foundations of hedonic psychology* (pp. 40–60). New York: Russell Sage.

Larsen, J. T., Norris, C. J., & Cacioppo, J. T. (2003). Effects of positive affect and negative affect on electromyographic activity over zygomaticus major and corrugator supercilii. *Psychophysiology, 40,* 776–785.

Laureys, S., Faymonville, M. E., Peigneux, P., Damas, P., Lambermont, B., Del Fiore, G., et al. (2002). Cortical processing of noxious somatosensory stimuli in the persistent vegetative state. *NeuroImage, 17,* 732–741.

Lazarus, R. S. & McCleary, R. A. (1951). Autonomic discrimination without awareness: A study of subception. *Psychological Review, 58,* 113–122.

LeDoux, J. (1996). *The emotional brain: The mysterious underpinnings of emotional life.* New York: Simon & Schuster.

Martinez-Garcia, F, Martinez-Marcos, A, & Lanuza, E. (2002). The pallial amygdala of amniote vertebrates: Evolution of the concept, evolution of the structure. *Brain Research Bulletin, 57,* 463–469.

Merikle, P. M. & Daneman, M. (1998). Psychological investigations of unconscious perception. *Journal of Consciousness Studies, 5,* 5–18.

Miyawaki, E., Perlmutter, J. S., Troster, A. I., Videen, T. O., & Koller, W. C. (2000). The behavioral complications of pallidal stimulation: A case report. *Brain & Cognition, 42,* 417–434.

Monahan, J. L., Murphy, S. T., & Zajonc, R. B. (2000). Subliminal mere exposure: Specific, general and diffuse effects. *Psychological Science, 11,* 462–466.

Morris, J.S., DeGelder, B., Weiskrantz, L. & Dolan, R.J. (2001) Differential extrageniculostriate and amygdala responses to presentation of emotional faces in a cortically blind field. *Brain, 124,* 1241–1252.

Morris, J. S., Öhman, A., & Dolan, R. J. (1999). A subcortical pathway to the right amygdala mediating "unseen" fear. *Proceedings of the National Academy of Sciences, 96,* 1680–1685.

Niedenthal, P. M., Barsalou, L., Winkielman, P., Krauth-Gruber, S., & Ric, F. (2005). Embodiment in attitudes, social perception, and emotion. *Personality and Social Psychology Review, 9,* 184-211.

Nielsen, L. & Kaszniak, A.W. (2007). Conceptual, theoretical, and methodological issues in inferring subjective emotion experience: recommendations for researchers. In J. A. Coan and J. J. B. Allen (Eds.), *The handbook of emotion elicitation and assessment.* New York, NY: Oxford University Press.

Ochsner, K. N. & Gross, J. J. (2004). Thinking makes it so: A social cognitive neuroscience approach to emotion regulation. In R. F. Baumeister & K. D. Vohs (Eds.), *Handbook of*

self-regulation: Research, theory, and applications (pp. 229–255). New York: Guilford Press.

O'Doherty, J., Deichmann, R., Critchley H. D., & Dolan R. J. (2002). Neural responses during anticipation of a primary taste reward. *Neuron, 33*, 815–826.

Öhman, A., Flykt, A., & Lundqvist, D. (2000). Unconscious emotion: Evolutionary perspectives, psychophysiological data and neuropsychological mechanisms. In R. D. Lane, L. Nadel & G. Ahern (Eds.), *Cognitive neuroscience of emotion* (pp. 296–327). New York: Oxford University Press.

Öhman, A. & Soares, J. J. F. (1994). "Unconscious anxiety": Phobic responses to masked stimuli. *Journal of Abnormal Psychology, 103*, 231–240.

Panksepp, J. (1998). *Affective neuroscience: The foundations of human and animal emotions.* Oxford, U.K.: Oxford University Press.

Panksepp, J. (2005). Affective consciousness: Core emotional feelings in animals and humans. *Consciousness & Cognition, 14*, 19–69.

Pecina, S. & Berridge, K. C. (2000). Opioid eating site in accumbens shell mediates food intake and hedonic "liking": Map based on microinjection Fos plumes. *Brain Research, 863*, 71–86.

Peciña, S. & Berridge, K. C. (2005). Hedonic hot spot in nucleus accumbens shell: Where do mu-opioids cause increased hedonic impact of sweetness? *Journal of Neuroscience, 25*, 11777–11786.

Pessoa, L. (2005). To what extent are emotional visual stimuli processed without attention and awareness? *Current Opinion in Neurobiology, 15*, 188–196.

Pessoa, L. & Adolphs, R. (2010). Emotion processing and the amygdala: from a 'low road' to 'many roads' of evaluating biological significance. *Nature Reviews Neuroscience*, November;11:773–83.

Peyron, R., Laurent, B., & Garcia-Larrea, L. (2000). Functional imaging of brain responses to pain. A review and meta-analysis. *Clinical Neurophysiology, 30*, 263–288.

Phan, K. L, Wagner, T, Taylor, S. F., & Liberzon, I. (2002). Functional neuroanatomy of emotion: A meta-analysis of emotion activation studies in PET and fMRI. *Neuroimage, 16*, 331–348.

Plum, F., Schiff, N., Ribary, U., & Llinas, R. (1998). Coordinated expression in chronically unconscious persons. *Philosophical Transactions of the Royal Society, B: Biological Sciences, 353*, 1929–1933.

Porges, S. W. (1997). Emotion: An evolutionary by-product of the neural regulation of the autonomic nervous system. In C. S. Carter, B. Kirkpatrick, & I.I. Lederhendler (Eds.), *The integrative neurobiology of affiliation*, Annals of the New York Academy of Sciences, 807, 62–77.

Putnam, F. W. (1989). *Diagnosis and treatment of multiple personality disorder.* New York: Guilford Press.

Rauch, S. L., Shin, L. M., Dougherty, D. D., Alpert, N. M., Orr, S. P., Lasko, M., et al. (1999). Neural activation during sexual and competitive arousal in healthy men. *Psychiatry Research, 91*, 1–10.

Robles, R., Smith, R., Carver, C. S. & Wellens, A. R. (1987). Influence of subliminal images on the experience of anxiety. *Personality and Social Psychology Bulletin, 13*, 399–410.

Rolls, E. T. (1999). *The brain and emotion.* Oxford: Oxford University Press.

Russell, J. A. (2003). Core affect and the psychological construction of emotion. *Psychological Review, 110*, 145–172.

Schenck, C. & Mahowald, M. (1995). Polysomnographically documented case of adult somnambulism with long distance automobile driving and frequent nocturnal violence: Parasomnia with continuing danger as a non-insane automatism? *Sleep*, 18, 765–772.

Schooler, J. W. (2002). Re-representing consciousness: Dissociations between experience and meta-consciousness. *Trends in Cognitive Sciences, 6*, 339–344.

Schooler, J. W. & Schreiber, C. A. (2004). Consciousness, meta-consciousness, and the paradox of introspection. *Journal of Consciousness Studies, 11*, 17–29.

Schumann C. M. & Amaral D. G. (2009). The human amygdala and autism. In: P. Whalen and E. Phelps (Eds.), *The human amygdala.*(pp. 362-381) New York: Guilford Press, New York.

Schwarz, N. & Clore, G. L. (2003). Mood as information: 20 years later. *Psychological Inquiry, 14*, 296–303.

Searle, J. (1997). *The mystery of consciousness.* New York, New York Review Press.

Siddiqui, F., Osuna, E., & Chokroverty, S. (2009). Writing emails as part of sleepwalking after increase in Zolpidem. *Sleep Medicine*, 10, 262–264.

Simons, D. J. & Chabris, C. F. (1999). Gorillas in our midst: Sustained inattentional blindness for dynamic events. *Perception, 28*, 1059–1074.

Smith, K. S., Tindell, A. J., Aldridge, J. W., & Berridge, K. C., (2009). Ventral pallidum roles in reward and motivation. *Behavioral Brain Research, 196*, 155–167.

Starr, M. J., Lin, J., & Winkielman, P. (2007). *The impact of unconscious facial expressions on consumption behavior involves changes in positive affect: Evidence from EMG and appetitive reflex-modulation.* Poster presented at 47th Annual Meeting of Society for Psychophysiological Research. Savannah, GA.

Starr, M. J., Winkielman, P., & Gogolushko, K. (2008). *Influence of affective pictures and words on consumption behavior and facial expressions.* Poster presented at Society for Psychophysiological Research, Austin, TX.

Steiner, J. E. (1973). The gustofacial response: Observation on normal and anencephalic newborn infants. *Symposium on Oral Sensation and Perception, 4*, 254–278.

Steiner, J. E., Glaser, D., Hawilo, M. E., & Berridge, K. C. (2001). Comparative expression of hedonic impact: Affective reactions to taste by human infants and other primates. *Neuroscience and Biobehavioral Reviews, 25*, 53–74.

Sutcliffe, J. P. (1961). "Credulous" and "skeptical" views of hypnotic phenomena: Experiments on esthesia, hallucination, and delusion. *Journal of Abnormal and Social Psychology, 62*, 189–200.

Tindell, A. J., Smith, K. S., Pecina, S., Berridge, K. C., & Aldridge, J.W. (2006). Ventral pallidum firing codes hedonic reward: When a bad taste turns good. *J Neurophysiol, 96*, 2399–2409.

Watson, D. & Tellegen, A. (1985). Toward a consensual structure of mood. *Psychological Bulletin, 98*, 219–235.

Weiskrantz, L. (1996). Blindsight revisited. *Current Opinion in Neurobiology, 6*, 215–220.

Whalen, P. J. (1998) Fear, vigilance and ambiguity: Initial neuroimaging studies of the human amygdala. *Current Directions in Psychological Science, 7*, 177–188.

Whalen, P and Phelps, E. (2009), The Human Amygdala., New York: Guilford Press, New York.

Whalen, P. J., Rauch, S. L., Etcoff, N. L., McInerney, S. C., Lee, M. B., & Jenike, M. A. (1998). Masked presentations of emotional facial expressions modulate amygdala activity without explicit knowledge. *Journal of Neuroscience*, *18*, 411–418.

Whishaw, I. Q. & Kolb, B. (1985). The mating movements of male decorticate rats: Evidence for subcortically generated movements by the male but regulation of approaches by the female. *Behavioural Brain Research*, *17*, 171–191.

Wicker, B., Keysers C., Plailly J., Royet J-P., Gallese V. and Rizzolatti G. (2003). Both of us disgusted in my insula: The common neural basis of seeing and feeling disgust. *Neuron*, *40*, 655–664.

Wilbarger, J. L., McIntosh, D. N., & Winkielman, P. (2009). Startle modulation in autism: Positive affective stimuli enhance startle response. *Neuropsychologia*, *47*, 1323–1331.

Williams, M. A., Morris, A. P., McGlone, F., Abbott, D. F., & Mattingley, J. B. (2004). Amygdala responses to fearful and happy facial expressions under conditions of binocular suppression. *Journal of Neuroscience*, *24*, 2898–2904.

Willis, W. D. & Westlund, K. N. (1997). Neuroanatomy of the pain system and of the pathways that modulate pain. *Journal of Clinical Neurophysiology*, *14*, 2–31.

Winkielman, P. & Berridge, K. C. (2004). Unconscious emotion. *Current Directions in Psychological Science*, *13*, 120–123.

Winkielman, P., Berridge, K. C., & Wilbarger, J. L. (2005). Unconscious affective reactions to masked happy versus angry faces influence consumption behavior and judgments of value. *Personality and Social Psychology Bulletin*, *1*, 121–135.

Winkielman, P., Knutson, B., Paulus, M. P., & Trujillo, J. T. (2007). Affective influence on decisions: Moving towards the core mechanisms. *Review of General Psychology*, *11*, 179–192.

Winkielman, P., McIntosh, D. N., & Oberman, L. (2009). Embodied and disembodied emotion processing: Learning from and about typical and autistic individuals. *Emotion Review*, *2*, 178–190.

Winkielman, P., Zajonc, R. B., & Schwarz, N. (1997). Subliminal affective priming resists attributional interventions. *Cognition and Emotion*, *11*, 433–465.

Wise, R. A. (1996). Addictive drugs and brain stimulation reward. *Annual Review of Neuroscience*, *19*, 319–340.

Zemack-Rugar, Y., Bettman, J. R., & Fitzsimons, G. J. (2007). The effects of nonconsciously priming emotion concepts on behavior. *Journal of Personality and Social Psychology*, *93*, 927–939.

Attitudes

William A. Cunningham, Ingrid Johnsen Haas, *and* Andrew Jahn

Abstract

This chapter reviews social neuroscience research that links social psychological attitudes and evaluative processes to their presumed neural bases. The chapter is organized into four parts. The first section discusses how attitude representations are transformed into evaluative states that can be used to guide thought and action. The next two sections address the related processes of attitude learning and change. The final section discusses applications of these concepts for the study of prejudice and political behavior.

Keywords: attitudes, evaluation, reinforcement, conditioning, amygdala, striatum, orbitofrontal cortex, prefrontal cortex, prejudice

The concepts of attitude and evaluation have been central to social psychology for nearly a century. This should not be surprising, as the ubiquitous act of assigning positive or negative valence is crucial for survival, be it in guiding immediate behavior toward or away from an object, or in anticipation of future rewards or punishments. Through accumulated experience, these evaluative judgments can be consolidated in memory to form a summary attitude, which can be recalled to guide future behavior. These summary attitudes, though imperfect at times, allow for the construction of quick evaluative judgments when similar stimuli or situations occur. For example, once we learn that someone is untrustworthy, we can avoid that person in future situations without needing to re-evaluate all of our previous interactions with the individual. Thus, attitudes enable us to predict the value of objects and the behavior of others, allowing us to adapt to the world through experience and make advantageous decisions.

In this chapter, we review social neuroscience research that links social psychological attitudes and evaluative processes to their presumed neural bases. The chapter is organized into four parts. In the first section, we discuss how attitude representations are transformed into evaluative states that can be used to guide thought and action. In the next two sections, we address the related processes of attitude formation and change. In the last section, we discuss applications of these concepts for the study of prejudice and political behavior.

Attitude Expression

The processes of attitude expression involve the translation of attitudinal representations into an active evaluation that can be used to inform thoughts and behavior (see Cunningham & Zelazo, 2007). Whereas an attitude refers to a relatively stable set of representations (only some of which may be active at any time), an evaluation reflects the current processing state of the evaluative system (which is determined by the aspects of the attitude that are currently active). Evaluative processes help determine the motivational significance of a stimulus as well as its expected reward or punishment value. In order to do so, these processes draw upon preexisting attitudes, as well as novel information about the stimulus, contextual information, and current goal states. Evaluative states arise out of dynamic interactions between these elements. Encountered or imagined stimuli (e.g., people, objects, or abstract concepts) elicit relatively automatic evaluations, but these initial "gut reactions" can be modulated by an increasing number of higher-level cognitive and reflective processes (Cunningham & Zelazo, 2007). These higher-order reflective processes send information back to the lower-order processes, allowing for a re-evaluation of the affective response and, if necessary, a different affective interpretation of the same stimuli. This allows for the foregrounding of more relevant and congruent affective representations and the backgrounding of irrelevant or incongruent contextual information in order to achieve a more nuanced evaluation congruent with the current context and/or goals.

When considering the brain regions involved in generating these evaluative predictions, the amygdala has received the most attention. Ever since the classic work of Kluver and Bucy (1937; see also Weiskrantz, 1956) demonstrated that lesions to the temporal lobes led to a decrease in avoidance of potentially threatening stimuli, a common framework for understanding amygdala function has been fear detection and conditioning (see next section). Research using functional magnetic resonance imaging (fMRI) in humans has shown that the amygdala is involved in the detection of threat in many stimulus modalities, including the perception of visual facial expressions of fear (Adolphs et al., 1999; Calder, Keane, Manes, Antoun, & Young, 2000; Morris et al., 1998), cognitive representations of fear (Phelps et al., 2001), threat-related words (Isenberg et al., 1999), and aversive odors (Zald & Pardo, 1997). Given this body of research, Freese and Amaral (2009) have suggested that the amygdala detects danger and then automatically directs behavioral responses.

An examination of the anatomic connections with the amygdala suggests that this region is well suited for automatic vigilance and organized response functions (Davis & Whalen, 2001). Specifically, the amygdala has widespread connections to areas associated with perceptual processing and autonomic/ visceral activation (see Freese & Amaral, 2009, for a review). Thus, following amygdala activation, greater attention can be directed to the stimulus while the body prepares for immediate action. Furthermore, the amygdala has multiple connections to areas of prefrontal cortex (Aggleton, Burton, & Passingham, 1980), receiving from and relaying information to areas of orbitofrontal, insular, and lateral prefrontal cortices (Amaral & Price, 1984; Stefanacci & Amaral, 2000). These connections allow information processed in the amygdala to be used by regions involved in more deliberate forms of decision-making. Through reciprocal connections, amygdala activation can be modulated to take into consideration the entire state of the organism. Thus, following amygdala activation, multiple brain systems are dynamically reorganized (or given the opportunity to reorganize) to appropriately deal with the current environment.

One critical aspect of amygdala function concerns the speed at which it can evaluate the rapid stream of incoming information. Many models of amygdala function suggest that it operates relatively automatically and unconsciously, and current research has provided support for this idea. For example, conscious awareness of a valenced stimulus does not appear to be necessary to produce amygdala activation. In a conceptual replication of previous research on supraliminal face processing (Morris et al., 1996), Whalen and colleagues (1998) demonstrated that subliminal presentations of emotionally fearful faces led to amygdala activation. In addition, Morris, Öhman, and Dolan (1998) found that after participants were classically conditioned to associate particular angry faces with an aversive stimulus, the amygdala showed greater activity to these conditioned faces than to the control faces, using both subliminal and supraliminal presentations. Using depth electrodes, Kawasaki and colleagues (2001) found that the processing of valence (greater neural firing to valenced as opposed to neutral stimuli) occurred 200 milliseconds after stimulus presentation in single-cell recordings of the human amygdala. Taken together, these studies indicate that the human amygdala responds rapidly to valenced stimuli, even when they are presented outside conscious awareness.

However, the suggestion that the amygdala's role in evaluation is valence specific has been called into question. Specifically, several studies have since shown that the amygdala is sensitive not only to fearful or negative information, but also to positive information (Hamann, Ely, Hoffman, & Kilts,

2002; Hamann & Mao, 2002; Garavan et al., 2001; Liberzon et al., 2003), leading to at least two competing theoretical positions. First, it is possible that the amygdala provides evaluative information about both positive and negative stimuli. According to this view, the amygdala is active whenever generating both positive or negative evaluations. Alternatively, amygdala activation may reflect some process associated with evaluative processing other than valence, such as stimulus intensity or arousal. Hamann and colleagues (2002) replicated the finding that the amygdala responds not only to positive and negative stimuli, but also to unusual or interesting stimuli, suggesting that it serves a more general function than just processing valence. Further, studies that have independently manipulated valence and intensity (Anderson et al., 2003; Small et al., 2003), or used statistical methods to separate the contributions of the two (Cunningham, Raye, & Johnson, 2004), have provided evidence that amygdala activity appears to be associated more with processing affective intensity than with processing any particular valence. Consistent with this idea, patients with bilateral amygdala damage have impaired recognition of emotional arousal, while recognition of valence remains intact (Adolphs, Russell, & Tranel, 1999; see Berntson, Bechara, Damasio, Tranel, & Cacioppo, 2007 for a more nuanced perspective).

One explanation for these findings has been to suggest that amygdala activation may reflect the processing of motivationally relevant stimuli, perhaps recruiting additional resources to facilitate appropriate interactions with the stimulus (e.g., Sander, Grafman, & Zalla, 2003). According to this view, a primary early function of attitudes is to inform us about what is important in any particular situation—then modulate the appropriate second-order perceptual, attentional, autonomic, or cognitive/conceptual processes that allow us to deal with the challenges or opportunities that are present. If this is the case, then amygdala activation should vary as a function of the goals of the organism.

To examine the motivational flexibility of and top-down influences on amygdala activation, Cunningham, Raye, and Johnson (2005) presented participants with positively and negatively valenced stimuli during fMRI scanning. After scanning, participants completed an individual differences measure of their prevention- and promotion-focus orientation (i.e., participants indicated whether they were more motivated by negative or positive stimuli, respectively; Higgins, 1997). Consistent with this idea, among participants who were more promotion focused, greater activation was observed in the amygdala, anterior cingulate gyrus, and extrastriate cortex for positive stimuli. For more prevention-focused participants, greater activation was observed in these same regions for negative stimuli.

In addition, a recent experimental study has provided evidence that situational motives shape amygdala processing in a dynamic fashion (Cunningham, Van Bavel, & Johnsen, 2008). In this study, participants were presented with famous names and asked to focus on either the positive or negative aspects of the person (e.g., ignoring everything bad, how good is this person?). Activity in bilateral amygdala and insula was found to vary as a function of evaluative fit. That is, when focusing on negativity, greater amygdala and insula activity was associated with participants' negativity ratings of the names, but not positivity ratings (recorded after scanning). The opposite pattern was found for the positive-focus condition, such that greater activity was observed in these same regions to ratings of positivity than negativity. Taken together, these studies suggest that chronic and situational motivational concerns can modulate the processing of valenced information to generate situationally appropriate evaluations. These studies demonstrate the power of top-down processes to modulate lower-order processes and provide a new understanding of amygdala function.

Beyond the Amygdala

Although most attention has been directed toward the amygdala, evaluative processes are associated with a much larger circuit involving additional cortical and subcortical regions. Among the more critical subcortical regions associated with evaluation is the ventral striatum, and more specifically the nucleus accumbens (NAcc). Linking NAcc activity to evaluation more closely, studies of economic decision making have shown that NAcc activity is not only correlated with, but is even sometimes a better predictor of, a participant's choice to buy a particular product than is self-report (Knutson et al, 2007).[1] Critically, whereas the amygdala activation appears to be associated with the evaluation of both positive and negative stimuli, the NAcc is primarily involved in the anticipation of positive outcomes and/or receipt of incentives or rewards (Breiter, Aharon, & Kahneman, 2001; Cardinal et al., 2002; Knutson et al., 2001). That is, while the amygdala may not be valence specific, the NAcc may allow for dissociated representations of positive and negative evaluation (see Cacioppo & Berntson, 1994 for a detailed review of evidence of dissociated processing of positive and negative valence).

Whereas activity in the amygdala has been shown to play a role in directing attention towards motivationally significant stimuli and automatically preparing for behavior, little evidence has been found to suggest that this activation leads to the experience of subjective preference. That is, although activation in the amygdala is correlated with objective attitude ratings (Cunningham et al., 2003, 2004), the actual subjective pleasantness associated with receiving (or displeasure associated with not receiving) an expected outcome is correlated with activation in orbitofrontal cortex (OFC; Kringelbach, 2005). Orbitofrontal cortex activity is evident for primary rewards such as food or drink (Kringelbach, O'Doherty, Rolls, & Andrews, 2003; Rolls, 2000), as well as symbolic rewards, such as money (Tom, Fox, Trepel, & Poldrack, 2007; Elliott, Newman, Longe, & William Deakin, 2003; Knutson et al., 2003). Orbitofrontal cortex activity has also been linked to the evaluation of the relative appropriateness of one's responses, activating both to receiving rewards and avoiding punishments (Cunningham, Mowrer, & Kesek, 2009; Kim, Shimojo, & O'Doherty, 2006). Specifically, activity in the medial OFC is typically related to evaluations of positive or rewarding information, whereas activity in the lateral OFC is related to evaluations of negative or punishing information (see Kringelbach & Rolls, 2004 for a review). Thus, while the amygdala and nucleus accumbens may provide information regarding expected outcomes following the perception of a stimulus, the OFC represents the current subjective evaluation.

Because the OFC receives input from multiple sensory modalities, it may play an important role in providing a common metric for representing and comparing disparate aspects of evaluative information (Montague & Berns, 2002; Murray, O'Doherty, & Schoenbaum, 2007; Rolls, 2000; Padoa-Schioppa & Assad, 2006; Wallis & Miller, 2003). Thus, the evaluative connotation of a friendship, a new car, or the ideals of egalitarianism can be reduced to a common evaluative dimension and directly compared across stimulus type. In this sense, whereas relatively more limbic regions may encode and retrieve objective S-R associations, the conversion from attitude to subjective evaluation (which can vary as a function of different contextual factors) may require the OFC. Specifically, activity in medial OFC is typically related to evaluations of positive or rewarding information, whereas activity

in lateral OFC is related to evaluations of negative or punishing information (Anderson et al., 2003; Kringelbach & Rolls, 2004; O'Doherty et al., 2003; but see Northoff et al., 2000).

To the extent that the amygdala and nucleus accumbens provide information regarding expected outcomes following the perception of a stimulus, and the OFC represents the current state of the organism, the dense reciprocal connections between amygdala and OFC allow for a comparison of expected rewards and punishments with current experience. Support for this idea comes from research demonstrating large OFC activations following violations of expectancies (Nobre et al., 1999) and the inability of patients with OFC damage to update representations when predictions and outcomes are incongruent (Rolls et al., 2004; Fellows & Farah, 2003). Thus, whereas subcortical systems provide a low–resolution estimate of likely outcomes, regions of the OFC may be involved in integrating amygdala output with current experience, allowing the current context to play a role in shaping the evaluation (e.g., Blair, 2004; Beer, Heery, Keltner, Scabini, & Knight, 2003; Rolls, 2000; Rolls, Hornak, Wade, & McGrath, 1994).

Constructing More Elaborated Evaluations

In many cases, the evaluation resulting from processing in the amygdala and OFC will be sufficient to produce a behavioral response. In other cases, however, this joint processing may lead to conflict or uncertainty about the stimulus or a predicted outcome. The presence of conflict triggers anterior cingulate cortex activation (see Bush, Luu, & Posner, 2000; Carter et al., 1998), which may then signal the need for additional processing of the stimulus in regions of the lateral prefrontal cortex involved in cognitive control (see Bunge & Zelazo, 2006; MacDonald, Cohen, Stenger, & Carter, 2000; Ridderinkhof, Ullsperger, Crone, & Nieuwenhuis, 2004). This additional processing in the lateral prefrontal cortex allows for regulation of affect in a top-down fashion by deliberately amplifying or suppressing the processing of certain aspects of the stimulus, changing the input to the system for subsequent processing. Reprocessing will likely modify the current evaluation by modulating activity in lower-order regions (e.g., Cunningham, Johnson et al., 2004; Ochsner, Bunge, Gross, & Gabrieli, 2002; Ochsner et al., 2004).

More complex networks of processing allow for more complex construals of a stimulus. This occurs because more information about a stimulus can be integrated into the construal and because these networks support the formulation and use of higher-order rules for deliberately selecting certain aspects of a stimulus or context to which to attend (Bunge & Zelazo, 2006; Cunningham & Zelazo, 2007). The selection function of prefrontal cortex may foreground specific aspects of information (and background others). Further, prefrontal cortex may also play a role in keeping current goals and contextual demands/constraints in mind, which is important for fulfilling the competing goals of minimizing error while minimizing processing load (e.g., Cunningham, Zelazo, Packer, & Van Bavel, 2007). This characterization of the prefrontal cortex is consistent with its hypothesized role in allowing for higher levels of reflective consciousness via reprocessing (Zelazo, 2004) and in the monitoring and control of cognition and behavior (e.g., Carver & Scheier, 2001; Shallice, 1982; Stuss & Benson, 1986). Taken together, the dynamic interactions among different brain regions support a flexible and complex process of evaluation that unfolds over time and exists on a continuum from relatively automatic (and simple) to relatively reflective (and complex).

Attitude Formation

The goal of an adaptive learning system is to develop appropriate and accurate estimates of the future value of certain stimuli. As such, attitudes reflect our previous experience with the environment and the learning that accompanies our ongoing positive and negative experiences. To the extent that positive experiences accompany the presence of particular stimuli or following a particular behavior, a more positive attitude will develop (and negative attitudes will develop for negative experiences). The next time that we encounter that same (or similar) situation, our evaluative system can infer that a similar positive (or negative) experience will occur. In general, attitudes that follow direct experience are likely to develop more quickly and result in stronger predictions (Fazio & Zanna, 1981).

The assumptions of reinforcement conditioning can be best summarized by Thorndike's law of effect (1911), which states that an organism will be more likely to repeat actions associated with a reward, and less likely to repeat actions associated with a punishment or negative stimulus. Whereas classical conditioning establishes an evaluative association between one's previous experiences and the attitude object, instrumental conditioning forms associations between hedonic outcomes and the behavior

that produced them. Furthermore, instrumental conditioning involves a fundamentally different set of interactions between the cortical structures and neurotransmitters comprising the instrumental response, which are discussed in detail below.

The most well-known example of both classical and instrumental conditioning is that of fear conditioning (Watson & Rayner, 1920), and among the brain structures believed to be involved in fear conditioning, the amygdala has received the most attention (Davis, 1992; Adolphs, Tranel, Damasio, & Damasio, 1995; LeDoux, Cicchetti, Xagoraris, & Romanski, 1990). For example, during fMRI, the amygdala is active while learning evaluative contingencies (LaBar, Gatenby, Gore, LeDoux, & Phelps, 1998), and patients with amygdala lesions do not show fear conditioning (LaBar, LeDoux, Spencer, & Phelps, 1995). Although much of the learning literature assigns the amygdala a critical role in fear conditioning, recent research has also demonstrated an important association between the amygdala and the processing of reward-related and novel information (see Murray, 2007 for a review). For example, studies of appetitive conditioning on rats with amygdala lesions have shown that the amygdala is necessary for learning some approach behaviors (Cardinal, Parkinson, Lachenal, et al., 2002; Everitt et al., 1999). The human amygdala exhibits a similar pattern of reward processing. Among hungry participants conditioned to associate a visual cue with the odor of a pleasant-smelling food, the amygdala is more active in response to seeing this conditioned visual stimulus than in participants whose hunger has been sated (Gottfried, O'Doherty, & Dolan, 2003). Taken together, these studies suggest that the amygdala plays an active role in conditioned responses regardless of valence (Everitt, Cardinal, Hall, Parkinson, & Robbins, 2000).

Beyond the Amygdala

As in the attitude expression literature, it is a mistake to ascribe too much function to the amygdala. In particular, areas of the striatum and prefrontal cortex also play important roles in reinforcement learning. One prominent theory of striatal contributions to reinforcement learning is that of the actor/critic model (Sutton & Barto, 1998; but see Khamassi et al., 2005), in which the ventral and dorsal striatum serve distinct functions in generating evaluative representations. According to this model, the ventral striatum plays the role of the "critic," generating predictions about the likely reward value of a particular stimulus. The ventral striatum updates representations to the extent that the prediction and the actual outcome differ (the temporal difference error), which is relayed to the dorsal striatum. This dorsal region (the "actor") then processes this information and makes certain stimulus-response associations more or less likely, depending on the hedonic outcome previously experienced.

To empirically test these roles for dorsal and ventral striatum in humans, O'Doherty and colleagues (2004) hypothesized that these regions would also show differences in activation in response to the amount of control participants had in choosing a particular reward. Two groups were formed, one involving instrumental learning and the other classical learning. In the instrumental learning condition, participants were able to choose which stimuli they preferred based on expected value (i.e., the hedonic value of the reward multiplied by the probability of receiving it), while in the classical learning condition a computer chose the stimuli and the participants had to guess which stimulus was chosen. Ventral striatum activity was observed across both conditions, consistent with its role in appraising predicted value. Dorsal striatum activity, on the other hand, was positively correlated with the prediction error signal during instrumental conditioning. This result supports the hypothesis that this region serves in an "actor" role in exhibiting greater prediction-error-related activity when rewards are chosen during instrumental conditioning, as opposed to classical conditioning.

Although the computations provided by the basal ganglia may appear sufficient for outcome reinforcement learning, current neurobiologically constrained computational models of reinforcement learning and decision-making indicate that the orbitofrontal cortex (OFC) plays a complementary role to the basal ganglia system (see Frank & Claus, 2006). Specifically, the OFC appears to be necessary for representing current reward states (Knutson, Fong, Bennett, Adams, & Hommer, 2003; O'Doherty, Kringelbach, Rolls, Hornak, & Andrews, 2001) and updating representations when stimulus contingencies change (Chudasama & Robbins, 2003; Fellows & Farah, 2003). As noted earlier, the OFC may provide a representation of reward magnitude currently being received, which can then be used to flexibly guide behavior and update representations in basal ganglia. That is, the computations of hedonic state from the OFC may provide a powerful input to the comparison between

predicted and received outcomes to generate prediction error signals.

While conditioning forms a critical part of the formation of attitudes, there are several instances where attitudes can form in the absence of direct experience. For example, people can learn the evaluative association of a stimulus without any direct experience with the aversive stimulus per se (e.g., Bandura, 1977). People can learn by observing others' responses, or by simply being told that something is good or bad, helpful or harmful. To illustrate this point, Phelps et al. (2001) verbally instructed participants that they would receive at least one shock during the course of an fMRI experiment when a particular stimulus was presented. Although no shocks were ever received during scanning, the authors observed left amygdala activation when the threatening stimulus was presented. The verbally created association between the stimulus and the potentially aversive outcome was therefore sufficient to elicit an amygdala response. Evidence for the amygdala's potential role in observational learning was provided in a follow-up study. Participants that simply watched someone else receiving shocks during a conditioning task had greater amygdala activated to the conditioned stimuli (Olsson, Nearing, & Phelps, 2007). Lastly, the social status of a person has been shown to alter brain activity without direct experience. When playing a trust game, participants has less striatum activity to partners who were portrayed to be trustworthy or untrustworthy when compared to neutral partners (Delgado, Frank, & Phelps, 2005). This suggests that social knowledge may have the ability to supersede conditioned knowledge (and the conditioning process).

Overall, these findings highlight an exciting array of possibilities for learning and attitude formation beyond simple classical conditioning. The ability to mentally empathize and learn from observation produces neural effects similar to those produced through classical conditioning alone. We can dislike groups of people who we have never met, have an aversion to new situations, or have abstract opinions for which we would be willing to die. For such attitudes, conditioning may only play a small part in the development and maintenance of attitude representations.

Attitude Change
Changing circumstances can necessitate the reversal of previously learned associations between stimuli and their hedonic value. This attitude reversal can

occur when current evaluations are no longer useful, or when they turn out to be harmful; for example, a positive evaluation toward a seemingly delicious piece of food must update rapidly if it induces vomiting once ingested. This will result in a more negative evaluation the next time that the food is encountered, suggesting that the attitude has changed.

In exploring how this reversal learning occurs, however, it is useful to make a distinction between ingrained attitudes that are activated more automatically, and more flexible evaluations that can be reversed relatively quickly. This distinction has been categorized as an interaction between the temporary, or short-term, and the permanent, or long-term, aspects of attitude reversal (Frank & Claus, 2006). Both are relative to the number of interactions an organism has had with a certain stimulus or situation. In the case of temporary attitude change, for example, updating and potential reversal of an attitude can occur from situation to situation, while in permanent or long-term attitude change, the reversal occurs over several interactions that are contrary to a previously held attitude.

Although we have focused thus far on the role of the OFC in representing received rewards and helping to provide a reinforcement signal for learning, the OFC is also involved in the updating of evaluative representations either because the representation is no longer appropriate (e.g., extinction) or because the context or situation requires a different response (e.g., Blair, 2004; Beer, Heery, Keltner, Scabini, & Knight, 2003; Rolls, 2000; Rolls, Hornak, Wade, & McGrath, 1994). One way that these processes can be achieved is by providing a complementary predictive reward signal to the basal ganglia that updates more rapidly. Whereas the basal ganglia learning systems slowly incorporate changes in reward contingencies across time and situation, the OFC can update more quickly, using recent experiences to guide an evaluative signal. While the OFC rapidly evaluates and processes sensory information (Kringelbach & Rolls, 2003, 2004), it is argued that this region is also critical in evaluating the associations between environmental stimuli and reinforcement.

Due to these properties, it is possible the OFC plays a key role in reversing or extinguishing previously learned behavior-reward associations (Rolls, 2000). Evidence supporting this hypothesis is illustrated by experiments looking at the effects of learning and reversal in clinical patients with lesions in these prefrontal areas. In one such study by Fellows and Farah (2003), evaluative reversal was examined in patients with OFC lesions. Patients with either ventromedial OFC (vmOFC) or dorsolateral OFC (dlOFC) lesions performed a simple decision-making task where the reward and loss contingencies of two decks of cards were reversed in the middle of the experiment. While dlOFC lesion patients performed equally to controls on the card game, vmOFC patients performed significantly worse following reversal of the contingencies of the decks. For the worst performers, maximal lesion overlap was observed in the left posteromedial orbitofrontal cortex. These results suggest that attitude reversal, which requires rapid updating, recruits areas of the vmOFC to make these behavioral changes.

Neuroimaging investigations examining these prefrontal regions have corroborated these results in healthy subjects, and have revealed an important distinction between the medial and lateral regions of the OFC in influencing the behavioral response to rewarding and punishing outcomes. In an fMRI investigation by O'Doherty and colleagues (2001), two abstract fractal representations were presented in which participants had to discover through trial and error which fractal was associated with greater gains over multiple trials. Selecting the correct fractal would display a monetary reward on the screen, while an incorrect choice would display the amount lost. The values of the fractals were then switched partway through each trial block, and blood oxygen-level dependent (BOLD) activity was examined during this switch. Immediately after the reversal, medial OFC activity was significantly associated with the BOLD signal following a rewarding stimulus (i.e., the actual receipt of the reward), while lateral OFC activity showed a similar correlation following a punishing stimulus. In both cases, activity in these OFC regions was correlated with the magnitude of the reward or punishment. Based on previous findings, the authors suggested that there are limited and weak connections between the medial and lateral OFC, while within each of these regions there exist several strong and robust neural connections. Therefore, it is useful to categorize the medial and lateral OFC as separate structures contributing to the updating of the relative hedonic values of rewarding and punishing stimuli, respectively.

While the OFC has been shown to play an important role in rapidly updating and reversing attitudes, the basal ganglia, due to its role in forming habits and unconscious motor responses (Jog, Kubota, Connolly, Hillegaart, & Graybiel, 1999;

Packard & McGaugh, 1996), is thought to be involved in updating attitudes and evaluations over the long term, and is strongly modulated by dopamine (DA; Gerfen, 2000). For example, increased DA during positive reinforcement leads to an increased probability for the action that produced the reinforcement (Frank & Claus, 2006; Houk, Adams, & Barto, 1995). The structure of the dopamine pathway itself supports this inference, as it projects to the basal ganglia and medial region of the frontal cortex, experiencing phasic increases in DA when events are better than expected, and phasic decreases in DA when events are worse than expected (Schultz, Dayan, & Montague, 1997). Evidence for the basal ganglia's role in habit formation also comes from lesion studies showing that lesions to a specific part of the striatum affect the learning of habitual responses. For example, lesions to the dorsolateral striatum in rats led to decreased habitual responding, and an increased sensitivity to reward cues when learning stimulus-response associations (Yin, Ostlund, Knowlton, & Belleine, 2005).

Although the basal ganglia and OFC appear to represent two different modes of learning and forming attitudes, we hypothesize that both are influenced by the same information and differ as a function of their learning rates. The basal ganglia is influenced by all positive and negative events providing information about the relative hedonic value of a particular stimulus or behavior, leading to predictions about the reward outcome of a behavior over a relatively long period of time (Jog et al., 1999). When these predictions are violated, as posited by the actor/critic model (O'Doherty et al., 2004), an updating of representations takes place in order to reflect this new information. However, this process takes relatively longer than that of the OFC, which is able to update its representations rapidly on a trial-to-trial basis. Eventually, then, the evaluations stored by the basal ganglia could become the basis for the relatively automatic representations held in working memory by the OFC, leading to these representations becoming the same in both areas, until additional information is encountered and processed by the basal ganglia. This model also possibly explains why, under cognitive load, the representation stored by the basal ganglia takes prominence. The OFC, which contains many of the higher-order cognitive areas required for nuanced and critical thinking, also requires significant cognitive resources to manipulate any attitudes or representations in working memory. Thus, the more automatic and readily accessible attitudes of the basal ganglia will tend to predominate in these cognitively demanding situations.

Yet, not all attitudes can be represented as simple stimulus-evaluation or stimulus-response associations. As noted earlier, evaluations can be highly context dependent and can sometimes lead to conflict, as when both positive and negative characteristics are associated with the attitude object, resulting in a state known as ambivalence (Cacioppo & Berntson, 1994). Thus, although in most situations the OFC can help generate an unambiguous evaluation constrained by a situation, this sometimes fails, and more elaborate "higher-order" attitudes need to be developed to organize attitude representations. That is, by deliberately weighting some information more than others, individuals can form a more integrated evaluation. Unlike inhibition, which drives inconvenient information out of mind, these integrated evaluations yield more complex activations, and may represent and account for inconsistencies. The evaluations that result from this type of processing are similar to what Petty and Cacioppo (1984) call an "elaborated attitude," which is known to be relatively stable and resistant to change. In this sense, these evaluations can be thought of as "resolved ambivalence."

In terms of the underlying brain systems for such a process, the anterior cingulate cortex (ACC) has been shown to play a key role in modulating the activity of both of these areas in attitude reversal. In particular, the ACC is involved in conflict monitoring and evaluating the appropriateness of behavior in specific situations. Largely guided by contextual cues, the ACC assists in modifying behavior to maximize hedonic reward (Bush, Luu, & Posner, 2000; Carter et al., 1998; Holroyd & Coles, 2002). The ACC is thought to signal the need for additional processing in areas of the lateral prefrontal cortex that can reorganize representations in a more abstracted form (Hazy, Frank, & O'Reilly, 2007; Rougier, Noelle, Braver, Cohen, & O'Reilly, 2005). Through repeated re-organization of the same information, a second-level representation can be generated that can be used for subsequent judgments and behavior.

Prejudice

An early focus for the social neuroscience study of attitudes has been the domain of prejudice. Initial studies demonstrated a role for the amygdala in the processing of other-race faces. Hart and colleagues (2000) demonstrated that, for White participants, amygdala activation to supraliminal Black faces habituated more slowly than White faces; the reverse pattern was found for Black participants. They concluded that all faces are processed immediately for their threat value, but that ingroup faces are deemed safe more quickly than outgroup faces. The role of the amygdala in intergroup perception was further expanded upon by Phelps and colleagues (2000), who showed that greater amygdala activation to Black than White faces was correlated with an indirect measure of race bias that reflects a preference for one race over the other—the Implicit Association Test (IAT; Greenwald et al., 1998). Interestingly, for White participants, neither of these studies showed greater overall amygdala activation to Black faces relative to White faces.

One potential explanation for not finding the expected greater amygdala activation to Black than White faces is that control processes may inhibit or reconstrue an activated emotional response. That is, higher-level cognitive functions may moderate automatically activated attitudes. Thus, for participants viewing long blocks of Black or White faces (as in Hart et al., 2000 and Phelps et al., 2000), there is greater opportunity for control processes to dampen or attenuate any automatic effects that would otherwise be observed. Consistent with this hypothesis, Cunningham and colleagues (2004) found that the majority of White participants had greater amygdala activation to Black than to White faces (which were randomly intermixed), but only when the faces were presented briefly and masked such that participants did not report seeing the faces. For faces that could be clearly seen and thus consciously processed, decreased amygdala activation for Black relative to White faces was accompanied by activation in areas of the PFC and the anterior cingulate gyrus—areas associated with cognitive control.

Interestingly, it appears that mental activities that counteract prejudiced thoughts may diminish control in other situations. According to Baumeister, Bratslavsky, Muraven, and Tice (1998), self-regulation is a limited resource, and any act of control not only uses up resources at the time of control, but also for some time afterward while the system recuperates. Richeson and Shelton (2003) found that after non-prejudiced White participants interacted with a Black individual—a task that may require cognitive control for participants who harbor prejudice but want to act or appear egalitarian—they subsequently performed worse on the Stroop task, a task that requires cognitive control for incompatible

trials (e.g., reporting that the word green is in a red print color). In a follow-up fMRI study, Richeson and colleagues (2003) scanned White participants while they viewed Black and White faces. Afterward, participants performed the Stroop task. As in Cunningham and colleagues (2004), greater activation was observed in the right lateral PFC while participants viewed Black compared with White faces. Furthermore, the degree of right PFC activity while viewing Black faces during the fMRI task predicted subsequent Stroop performance, with those with the most right PFC activity during fMRI performing the worst on the Stroop task. Presumably, the cognitive cost of control was manifested in the subsequent cognitive task. This pattern of findings provides support for the idea that nonprejudiced participants attempt to regulate their emotional responses to Black faces.

In light of these findings (and the work discussed earlier), the amygdala should not be considered a source of prejudice, but as a component in a larger framework of competing automatic and controlled processes which modulate the expression of prejudice. For example, Phelps, Cannistraci, and Cunningham (2003) reported on a patient who, despite bilateral amygdala damage, still showed evidence of automatic race biases on an indirect measure of automatic associations, suggesting that automatic evaluative responses are possible without an amygdala. This is consistent with the position that the amygdala is better characterized as a responsive component to motivationally relevant stimuli, instead of strictly negative, fearful, or threatening stimuli (Canli et al., 2005; Cunningham et al., 2004, 2008; Mather et al., 2004).

In the processing of social groups, and people or objects in general, other areas are associated with processing emotional intensity and valence, notably, the right prefrontal and orbitofrontal cortex. While explicit acts of hate and more overt forms of discrimination are the most salient features of prejudice, they often overshadow a complementary form of prejudice in the form of positive associations toward ingroup members. Indeed, the history of intergroup conflict provides strong evidence that "ingroup love" is a more common root of discrimination than "outgroup hate" (Brewer, 1999). Moreover, in contexts where discrimination arises as a result of differential evaluations of two groups, ingroup bias can lead to the same patterns of discrimination as outgroup derogation. Take, for example, racial discrimination in the context of a hiring decision: ingroup bias and outgroup derogation would both lead a White candidate to be hired over a Black candidate. Although these decisions are the result of different affective processes, the result is identical—the candidates receive unequal levels of treatment and discrimination ensues.

Recent research has begun to examine the neural processes involved in these ingroup and outgroup biases. In one study, participants were randomly assigned to a novel mixed-race team without a history of contact or conflict with an outgroup team (Van Bavel, Packer, & Cunningham, 2008). Following assignment, participants spent three minutes memorizing the team membership of 24 faces, and these faces were presented during fMRI scanning. Unlike previous research that has found greater amygdala activation to Black than White faces, this study found greater amygdala activation to team ingroup than outgroup faces, regardless of race. Although this may seem counterintuitive if one takes the view that the amygdala responds only (or primarily) to threatening stimuli, it is consistent with the view that amygdala activation reflects the processing of the affective nature of motivationally significant stimuli (Anderson & Phelps, 2001; Cunningham et al., 2008). In many cases, negative or threatening stimuli take this role; however, in some situations positive stimuli can have greater motivational significance. The results from this study imply that, in the absence of intergroup conflict and outgroup derogation, the ingroup may be motivationally primary (see also, Allport, 1954). This suggestion was bolstered by finding additional activations in reward processing regions, such as the striatum and orbitofrontal cortex, that show greater activation to ingroup than outgroup faces and that significantly correlated with self-reported preferences for ingroup (vs. outgroup) members.

Political Attitudes

As social neuroscience investigations have begun to inform our understanding of basic social psychological processes, researchers have started to apply these findings to improve our understanding of political behavior. Although research in this area has typically focused on replicating previous evaluative effects in the domain of political judgment (e.g., Kaplan, Freedman, & Iacoboni, 2007), other research has taken into consideration that fact that the evaluation of political candidates differs from other evaluative categories in that people rarely have direct exposure to the candidate, and the evaluation is often influenced by group membership and political ideology (Westen, Blagov, Harenski, Kilts, &

Hamann, 2006). Though undecided voters may be relatively more open to new information, once people have made a decision about which political candidate to support in an election they have a tendency to minimize the influence of any new information that may be inconsistent. For example, once one has decided to support candidate X, he or she may not want to learn about any inconsistencies in candidate X's statements. On this view, motivated reasoning helps to maintain attitudes in the face of inconsistent information (e.g., Rahn, 1993), and as such, the study of political attitudes may allow for a better understanding of the motivational components of attitude acquisition, expression, and change.

Although motivated reasoning often prevents attitude change, there are situations in which attitudes about political candidates may, and perhaps should, change. Voters who are uncertain, have weak or ambivalent attitudes, or those who are low on identification with a political party may be more likely to show attitude change in response to new information about a political candidate (e.g., Lavine, 2001; Lodge & Taber, 2005; McGraw, Hasecke, & Conger, 2003). Unlike attitude change resulting from direct experience, attitude change here likely involves the integration of new semantic information or inferred group membership to generate new attitudes. Thus, attitude change should be expected to require more prefrontal components that may serve to shape attitude representations. Consistent with this idea, when exposed to negative political advertising, participants who showed greater activation in the dorsolateral prefrontal cortex also showed greater negative attitude change (Kato, et al., 2009). This pattern of results supports the hypothesis that, unlike reversal learning in simple conditioning, attitude change for more abstracted information like political attitudes may require a reorganization of information mediated by the prefrontal cortex (O'Reilly, Noelle, Braver, & Cohen, 2002).

Political evaluation is often considered to be a deliberate act, where people weigh various options and develop a coherent political ideology. Yet, political ideology can also operate relatively automatically, coloring and shaping our perceptions of people and the information that they present. For instance, while people with low political expertise may be more open to new information, people with high political expertise and identification are more likely to interpret new information in terms of automatically accessible schemas. Knutson, Wood, Spampinato, and Grafman (2006) demonstrated that, in contrast to people who were less politically involved, highly politically identified participants had less lateral prefrontal cortex activity when responding to politically relevant stimuli. These data suggest that highly identified people engaged with particular information in a less deliberate fashion. As such, political experts may be able to rely on already established schemas to make quick evaluations, which may allow them to automatically interpret and incorporate consistent information into existing schemas.

Political ideology can also function as a social identity and guide our perceptions of others. For example, in one study participants were asked to think about the opinions and preferences of a person who had a similar or dissimilar political affiliation (Mitchell, Macrae, & Banaji, 2006). It was assumed that participants who more strongly identified with a certain political party would process a similar-minded person as an ingroup member, and therefore activate brain areas that have been linked to self-referential processing. For example, liberals were expected to be able to understand the mental states of another liberal more than a conservative, and the converse was expected for conservatives. Considering the mental state of a similar other led to activity in ventral areas of the medial prefrontal cortex (PFC), whereas considering the mental state of a dissimilar other led to activity in more dorsal areas of the medial PFC. Interestingly, individuals who strongly self-categorized with a political group, as measured by the IAT, had greater ventral medial PFC activity to politically similar others and less dorsal medial PFC activity to dissimilar others. Because regions of the medial PFC have previously been implicated in building mental models of other minds and simulating the thoughts and feelings of other people (a process called mentalizing; Mitchell, 2006), with more ventral areas being more involved in the processing of self-relevant information (Kelley et al., 2002), the authors concluded that although similar and dissimilar others both recruit regions involved in understanding others, similar others were more likely to be processed like the self.

Summary

Although understanding attitudes presents a considerable challenge for scientists, there is a rich history of relevant theoretical ideas and findings from social and cognitive psychology and intriguing new findings from social cognitive neuroscience. Borrowing from the literatures on reinforcement learning and affective processing, we can appreciate the intricate neural systems that attitudes operate upon. Interestingly, many of the same brain regions that are involved in expression, formation, and change appear to be identical, suggesting a unified set of dynamic processes that can give rise to multiple attitudinal phenomena. As such, evaluation may reflect the current processing of an integrated information processing system at any given time. The particular ways in which information is constrained, weighed, and integrated as evaluations are constructed online from attitudes and the exact computations of the various brain regions involved in these processes will require more in-depth investigation.

More importantly, much of this research has examined relatively simple learning paradigms, or responses to relatively simple attitude stimuli (i.e., an aversive task, shock, or facial expression). Although attitudes can be formed under several of these types of situations, we have suggested that they are much more likely to be formed by a complex interaction of social and contextual factors. Using neuroimaging techniques, we are just beginning to uncover how different brain regions contribute to the formation and change of attitudes, and particularly how these can be applied to important social issues such as prejudice and political behavior. A more thorough investigation of the interplay between attitudes, the situation, and the mind is crucial for a deeper understanding of attitudes, both whence they came from and where they are going.

Note

1 Although the NAcc is correlated with buying behavior, it is unclear from these fMRI studies whether this is the result of the motivational dopaminergic "wanting" or the more hedonic opioid "liking" subdivisions of the NAcc (Berridge, Robinson, & Aldridge, 2009).

References

Adolphs, R., Russell, J. A., & Tranel, D. (1999). A role for the human amygdala in recognizing emotional arousal from unpleasant stimuli. *Psychological Science, 10*, 167–171.

Adolphs, R., Tranel, D., Damasio, H., & Damasio, A. R. (1995). Fear and the human amygdala. *Journal of Neuroscience, 15*, 5879–5891.

Adolphs, R., Tranel, D., Hamann, S., Young, A. W., Calder, A. J., Phelps, E. A., et al. (1999). Recognition of facial emotion in nine individuals with bilateral amygdala damage. *Neuropsychologia, 37*, 1111–1117.

Aggleton, J. P., Burton, M. J., & Passingham, R. E. (1980). Cortical and subcortical afferents to the amygdala of the rhesus monkey (macaca mulatta). *Brain Research, 190*, 347–368.

Allport, G. W. (1954). *The nature of prejudice.* Cambridge, MA: Addison-Wesley.

Amaral, D. G. & Price, J. L. (2004). Amygdalo-cortical projections in the monkey (macaca fascicularis). *The Journal of Comparative Neurology, 230*, 465–496.

Anderson, A. K., Christoff, K., Steppen, I., Panltz, D., Ghahremani, D. G., Glover, G., et al. (2003). Dissociated neural representations of intensity and valence in human olfaction. *Nature Neuroscience, 6*, 196–202.

Anderson, A. K., & Phelps, E. A. (2001). Lesions of the human amygdala impair enhanced perception of emotionally salient events. *Nature, 411*, 305–309.

Bandura, A. (1977). *Social learning theory.* Englewood Cliffs, NJ: Prentice Hall.

Beer, J. S., Heery, E. A., Keltner, D., Scabini, D., & Knight, R. T. (2003). The regulatory function of self–conscious emotion: Insights from patients with orbitofrontal damage. *Journal of Personality and Social Psychology, 85*, 589–593.

Berntson, G. G., Bechara, A., Damasio, H., Tranel, D., & Cacioppo, J. T. (2007). Amygdala contribution to selective dimensions of emotion. *Social Cognitive and Affective Neuroscience, 2*, 123–129.

Berridge, K. C., Robinson, T. E. & Aldridge, J. W. (2009). Dissecting components of reward: "Liking," "wanting," and learning. *Current Opinion in Pharmacology, 9*, 65–73.

Blair, R. J. R. (2004). The roles of orbital frontal cortex in the modulation of antisocial behavior. *Brain and Cognition, 55*, 198–208.

Breiter, H. C., Aharon, I., Kahneman, D., Dale, A. & Shizgal, P. (2001). Functional imaging of neural responses to expectancy and experience of monetary gains and losses. *Neuron, 30*, 619–639.

Brewer, M. B. (1999). The psychology of prejudice: Ingroup love or outgroup hate? *Journal of Social Issues, 55*, 429–444.

Bunge, S. A. & Zelazo, P. D. (2006). A brain-based account of the development of rule use in childhood. *Current Directions in Psychological Science, 15*, 118–121.

Bush, G., Luu, P., Posner, M. I. (2000). Cognitive and emotional influences in anterior cingulated cortex. *Trends in Cognitive Science, 4*, 215–222.

Caacioppo, J. T., & Berntson, G. G. (1994). Relationship between attitudes and evaluative space: A critical review, with emphasis on the separability of positive and negative substrates. *Psychological Bulletin, 115*, 401–423.

Calder, A. J., Keane, J., Manes, F., Antoun, N., & Young, A. W. (2000). Impaired recognition and experience of disgust following brain injury. *Nature Neuroscience, 3*, 1077–1078.

Canli, T., Congdon, E., Gutknecht, L., Constable, R. T., & Lesch, K. P. (2005). Amygdala responsiveness is modulated by tryptophan hydroxylase-2 gene variation. *Journal of Neural Transmission, 112*, 1479–1485.

Cardinal, R. N., Parkinson, J. A., Lachenal, G., Halkerston, K. M., Rudarakanchana, N., Hall, J., et al. (2002). Effects of selective excitotoxic lesions of the nucleus accumbens core, anterior cingulated cortex, and central nucleus of the amygdala on autoshaping performance in rats. *Behavioral Neuroscience, 116*, 553–567.

Carter, C. S., Braver, T. S., Barch, D. M., Botvinick, M. M., Noll, D., & Cohen, J. D. (1998). Anterior cingulate cortex, error detection, and the online monitoring of performance. *Science, 1*, 747–749.

Carver, C. S. & Scheier, M. F. (2001). *On the self-regulation of behavior.* Cambridge, MA: Cambridge University Press.

Chudasama, Y. & Robbins, T. W. (2003). Dissociable contributions of the orbitofrontal and infralimbic cortex to Pavlovian autoshaping and discrimination reversal learning: Further evidence for the functional heterogeneity of the rodent frontal cortex. *The Journal of Neuroscience, 23*, 8771–8780.

Cools, R. (2005). Dopaminergic modulation of cognitive function—Implications for l-DOPA treatment in Parkinson's disease. *Neuroscience and Biobehavioral Reviews, 30*, 1–23.

Cunningham, W. A., Kesek, A., Mowrer, S.M. (2009). Distinct orbitofrontal regions encode stimulus and choice valuation. *Journal of Cognitive Neuroscience.* 21, 1956–1966.

Cunningham, W. A., Johnson, M. K., Gatenby, J. C., Gore, J. C., & Banaji, M. R. (2003). Neural components of social evaluation. *Journal of Personality and Social Psychology, 85*, 639–649.

Cunningham, W. A., Raye, C. L., & Johnson, M. K. (2004). Implicit and explicit evaluation: fMRI correlates of valence, emotional intensity, and control in the processing of attitudes. *Journal of Cognitive Neuroscience, 16*, 1717–1729.

Cunningham, W. A., Raye, C. L., & Johnson, M. K. (2005). Neural correlates of evaluation associated with promotion and prevention regulatory focus. *Cognitive, Affective, & Behavioral Neuroscience, 5*, 202–211.

Cunningham, W. A., Van Bavel, J. J., & Johnsen, I. R. (2008). Affective flexibility: Evaluative processing goals shape amygdala activity. *Psychological Science, 19*, 152–160.

Cunningham, W. A. & Zelazo, P. D. (2007). Attitudes and evaluations: A social cognitive neuroscience perspective. *Trends in Cognitive Sciences, 11*, 97–104.

Cunningham, W. A., Zelazo, P. D., Packer, D. J., & Van Bavel, J. J. (2007). The iterative reprocessing model: A multilevel framework for attitudes and evaluation. *Social Cognition, 25*, 736–760.

Davis, M. (1992). The role of the amygdala in fear and anxiety. *Annual Review of Neuroscience, 15*, 353–375.

Davis, M. & Whalen, P. J. (2001). The amygdala: Vigilance and emotion. *Molecular Psychiatry, 6*, 13–34.

Delgado, M. R., Frank, R. H., & Phelps, E. A. (2005). Perceptions of moral character modulate the neural systems of reward during the trust game. *Nature Neuroscience, 8*, 1611–1618.

Elliott, R., Newman, J. L., Longe, O. A., & William Deakin, J. F. (2003). Differential response patterns in the striatum and orbitofrontal cortex to financial reward in humans: A parametric functional magnetic resonance imaging study. *The Journal of Neuroscience, 23*, 303–307.

Everitt, B. J., Cardinal, R. N., Hall, J., Parkinson, J. A., & Robbins, T. R. (2000). Differential involvement of amygdala subsystems in appetitive conditioning and drug addiction. In J. P. Aggleton (Ed.), *The amygdala: A functional analysis* (pp. 353–390). Oxford: Oxford UP.

Everitt, B. J., Parkinson, J. A., Olmstead, M. C., Arroyo, M. Robledo, P. & Robbins, T. W. (1999). Associative processes in addiction and reward: The role of amygdala-ventral striatal subsystems. *Annals of the New York Academy of Sciences, 877*, 412–438.

Fazio, R. H., & Zanna, M. P. (1981). Direct experience and attitude-behavior consistency. In L. Berkowitz (Ed.), *Advances in Experimental Social Psychology* (Vol. 14, pp. 161–202). New York: Academic Press.

Fellows, L. K. & Farah, M. J. (2003). Ventromedial frontal cortex mediates affective shifting in humans: Evidence from a reversal learning paradigm. *Brain, 126*, 1830–1837.

Frank, M. J. & Claus, E. D. (2006). Anatomy of a decision: Striato-orbitofrontal interactions in reinforcement learning, decision making and reversal. *Psychological Review, 113,* 300–326.

Frank, M. J., Moustafa, A. A., Haughey, H. M., Curran, T., & Hutchison, K. E. (2007). Genetic triple dissociation reveals multiple roles for dopamine in reinforcement learning. *Proceedings of the National Academy of Sciences, 41,* 16311–16316.

Freese, J. & Amaral, D. (2009) Neuroanatomy of the primate amygdala. In P. Whalen & E. Phelps, (Eds.). *The human amygdale* (pp. 3–42). New York: Guilford.

Garavan, H., Pendergrass, J. C., Ross, T. J., Stein, E. A., & Risinger, R. C. (2001). Amygdala response to both positive and negatively valenced stimuli. *NeuroReport, 12,* 2779–2783.

Gawronski, B. & Bodenhausen, G. V. (2006). Associative and propositional processes in evaluation: An integrative review of implicit and explicit attitude change. *Psychological Bulletin, 132,* 692–731.

Gerfen, C. R. (2000). Molecular effects of dopamine on striatal projection pathways. *Trends in Neurosciences, 23,* 64–70.

Gottfried, J. A., O'Doherty, J., & Dolan, R. J. (2003). Encoding predictive reward value in human amygdala and orbitofrontal cortex. *Science, 22,* 1104–1107.

Greenwald, A. G., McGhee, D. E., & Schwartz, J. L. K. (1998). Measuring individual differences in implicit cognition: The implicit association test. *Journal of Personality and Social Psychology, 74,* 1464–1480.

Hamann, S. B., Ely, T., D., Hoffman, J. M., & Kilts, C. D. (2002). Activation of the human amygdala in positive and negative emotion. *Psychological Science, 13,* 135–141.

Hamann, S. B. & Mao, H. (2002). Positive and negative emotional verbal stimuli elicit activity in the left amygdala. *Brain Imaging, 13,* 15–19.

Hart, A. J., Whalen, P. J., Shin, L. M., McInerney, S. C., Fischer, H., & Rauch, S. L. (2000). Differential response in the human amygdala to racial outgroup vs. ingroup face stimuli. *Brain Imaging, 11,* 2351–2354.

Hazy, T. E., Frank, M. J. & O'Reilly, R. C. (2007). Towards an executive without a homunculus: Computational models of the prefrontal cortex/basal ganglia system. *Philosophical Transactions of the Royal Society B, 362,* 1601–1613.

Higgins, E. T. (1997). Beyond pleasure and pain. *American Psychologist, 52,* 1280–1300.

Holroyd, C. B. & Coles, M. G. H. (2002). The neural basis of human error processing: Reinforcement learning, dopamine, and error-related negativity. *Psychological Review, 109,* 679–709.

Houk, J. C., Adams, J. L., & Barto, A. G. (1995). A model of how the basal ganglia generate and use neural signals that predict reinforcement. In J. C. Houk, J. L. Davis, & D. G. Beiser (Eds.), *Models of information processing in the basal ganglia* (pp. 249–270). Cambridge, MA: MIT Press.

Hutchison, W. D., Davis, K. D., Lozano, A. M., Tasker, R. R., & Dostrovsky, J. O. (1999). Pain-related neurons in the human cingulate cortex. *Nature Neuroscience, 2,* 403–405.

Isenberg, N., Silbersweig, D., Engelien, A., Emmerich, S., Malavade, K., Beattie, B., et al. (1999). Linguistic threat activates the human amygdala. *Proceedings of the National Academy of Sciences, 96,* 10456–10459.

Jog, M. S., Kubota, Y., Connolly, C. I., Hillegaart, V., & Graybiel, A. M. (1999). Building neural representations of habits. *Science, 286,* 1745–1749.

Kaplan, J. T., Freedman, J., & Iacoboni, M. (2007). Us versus them: Political attitudes and party affiliation influence neural responses to faces of presidential candidates. *Neuropsychologia, 45,* 55–64.

Kato, J., Ide, H., Kabashima, I., Kadota, H., Takano, K., & Kansaku, K. (2009). Neural correlates of attitude change following positive and negative advertisements. *Frontiers in Behavioral Neuroscience, 3,* 1–13.

Kawasaki, H., Kaurfman, O., Damasio. H., Damasio, A. R., Granner, M., Bakken, H., et al. (2001). Single-neuron responses to emotional visual stimuli recorded in human ventral prefrontal cortex. *Nature Neuroscience, 4,* 15–16.

Kelley, A. E. & Berridge, K. C. (2002). The neuroscience of natural rewards: Relevance to addictive drugs. *The Journal of Neuroscience, 22,* 3306–3311.

Khamassi, M., Lacheze, L., Girard, B., Berthoz, A., & Guillot, A. (2005). Actor-critic models of reinforcement learning in the basal ganglia. *Adaptive Behavior, 13,* 131–148.

Kim, H., Shimojo, S., & O'Doherty, J. P. (2006). Is avoiding an aversive outcome rewarding? Neural substrates of avoidance learning in the human brain. *PLoS Biology, 4,* 1453–1461.

Kluver, H. & Bucy, P.C. (1937). Psychic blindness and other symptoms following bilateral temporal lobectomy in rhesus monkeys. *American Journal of Psychology, 119,* 352–353.

Knutson, B., Adams, C. M., Fong, G. W., & Hommer, D. (2001). Anticipation of increasing monetary reward selectively recruits nucleus accumbens. *The Journal of Neuroscience, 21,* 159–164.

Knutson, B., Fong, G. W., Bennett, S. M., Adams, C. M., & Hommer, D. (2003). A region of mesial prefrontal cortex tracks monetarily rewarding outcomes: Characterization with rapid event-related fMRI. *Neuroimage, 18,* 263–272.

Knutson, B., Scott, R., Wimmer, G. E., Prelec, D., & Loewenstein, G. (2007). Neural predictors of purchases. *Neuron, 53,* 147–156.

Knutson, K. M., Wood, J. N., Spampinato, M. V., & Grafman, J. (2006). Politics on the brain: An fMRI investigation. *Social Neuroscience, 1,* 25–40.

Kringelbach, M. L. (2005). The human orbitofrontal cortex: Linking reward to hedonic experience. *Nature Reviews Neuroscience, 6,* 691–702.

Kringelbach, M. L., O'Doherty, J., Rolls, E. T., & Andrews, C. (2003). Activation of the human orbitofrontal cortex to a liquid food stimulus is correlated with its subjective pleasantness. *Cerebral Cortex, 13,* 1064–1071.

Kringelbach, M. L. & Rolls, E. T. (2003). Neural correlates of rapid reversal learning in a simple model of human social interaction. *NeuroImage, 20,* 1371–1383.

Kringelbach, M. L. & Rolls, E. T. (2004). The functional neuroanatomy of the human orbitofrontal cortex: Evidence from neuroimaging and neuropsychology. *Progress in Neurobiology, 72,* 341–372.

LaBar, K. S., Gatenby, C., Gore, J. C., LeDoux, J. E., Phelps, E. A. (1998). Human amygdala activation during conditioned fear acquisition and extinction: A mixed trial fMRI study. *Neuron, 20,* 937–945.

LaBar, K. S., LeDoux, J. E., Spencer, D. D., & Phelps, E. A. (1995). Impaired fear conditioning following unilateral temporal lobectomy in humans. *Journal of Neuroscience, 15,* 6846–6855.

Lavine, H. (2001). The electoral consequences of ambivalence toward presidential candidates. *American Journal of Political Science, 45,* 915–929.

LeDoux, J. E., Cicchetti, P., Xagoraris, A., & Romanski, L. M. (1990). The lateral amygdaloid nucleus: Sensory interface of the amygdala in fear conditioning. *Journal of Neuroscience, 10*, 1062–1069.

Liberzon, I., Phan, K. L., Decker, L. R., & Taylor, S. F. (2003). Extended amygdala and emotional salience: A PET activation study of positive and negative affect. *Neuropsychopharmacology, 28*, 726–733.

Lodge, M. & Taber, C. S. (2005). The automaticity of affect for political leaders, groups, and issues: An experimental test of the hot cognition hypothesis. *Political Psychology, 26*, 455–482.

MacDonald, A. W., Cohen, J. D., Stenger, V. A., & Carter, C. S. (2000). Dissociating the role of the dorsolateral prefrontal and anterior cingulate cortex in cognitive control. *Science, 288*, 1835–1838.

Mather, M., Canli, T., English, T., Whitfield, S., Wais, P., Ochsner, K., Gabrieli, J. D. E., & Carstensen, L. L. (2004). Amygdala responses to emotionally valenced stimuli in older and younger adults. *Psychological Science, 15*, 259–263.

McGraw, K. M., Hasecke, E., & Conger, K. (2003). Ambivalence, uncertainty, and processes of candidate evaluation. *Political Psychology, 24*, 421–448.

Mitchell, J. P., Macrae, C. N., & Banaji, M. R. (2006). Dissociable medial prefrontal contributions to judgments of similar and dissimilar others. *Neuron, 50*, 655–663.

Montague, P. & Berns, G. (2002). Neural economics and the biological substrates of valuation. *Neuron, 36*, 265–284.

Morris, J. S., Ohman, A., & Dolan, R. J. (1998). Conscious and unconscious emotional learning in the amygdala. *Nature, 393*, 467–470.

Muraven, M., Tice, D. M., Baumeister, R. F. (1998). Self-control as a limited resource. *Journal of Personality and Social Psychology, 74*, 774–789.

Murray, E. A. (2007). The amygdala, reward and emotion. *TRENDS in Cognitive Sciences, 11*, 489–497.

Murray, E. A., O'Doherty, J. P., & Schoenbaum, G. (2007). What we know and do not know about the functions of the orbitofrontal cortex after 20 years of cross-species studies. *The Journal of Neuroscience, 271*, 8166–8169.

Nobre, A., Coull, J., Frith, C., Mesulam, M. (1999). Orbitofrontal cortex is activated during breaches of expectation in tasks of visual attention. *Nature Neuroscience, 2*, 11–12.

Northoff, G., Richter, A., Gessner, M., Schlagenhauf, F., Fell, J., Baumgart, F., et al. (2000). Functional dissociation between medial and lateral prefrontal cortical spatiotemporal activation in negative and positive emotions: A combined fMRI/MEG study. *Cerebral Cortex, 10*, 93–107.

Morris, J. S., Frith, C. D., Perrett, D. I., Rowland, D., Young, A. W., Calder, A. J., et al. (1996). A differential neural response in the human amygdala to fearful and happy facial expressions. *Nature, 383*, 812–815.

Ochsner, K. N., Bunge, S. A., Gross, J. J., & Gabrieli, J. D. E. (2002). Rethinking feelings: An fMRI study of the cognitive regulation of emotion. *Journal of Cognitive Neuroscience, 14*, 1215–1229.

Ochsner, K. N., Knierim, K., Ludlow, D. H., Hanelin, J., Ramachandran, T., Glover, G., et al. (2004). Reflecting upon feelings: An fMRI study of neural systems supporting the attribution of emotion to self and other. *Journal of Cognitive Neuroscience, 16*, 1746–1772.

O'Doherty, J., Critchley, H., Deichmann, R., & Dolan, R. J. (2003). Dissociating valence of outcome from behavioral control in human orbital and ventral prefrontal cortices. *The Journal of Neuroscience, 23*, 7931–7939.

O'Doherty, J., Dayan, P., Schultz, J., Deichmann, R., Friston, K., & Dolan, R. J. (2004). Dissociable roles of ventral and dorsal striatum in instrumental conditioning. *Science, 16*, 452–454.

O'Doherty, J., Kringelbach, M. L., Rolls, E. T., Hornak, J., & Andrews, C. (2001). Abstract reward and punishment representations in the human orbitofrontal cortex. *Nature Neuroscience, 4*, 95–102.

Ohman, A. (2005). The role of the amygdala in human fear: Automatic detection of threat. *Psychoneuroendocrinology, 30*, 953–958.

Olsson, A., Nearing, K. I., & Phelps, E. A. (2007). Learning fears by observing other: The neural systems of social fear transmission. *Social Cognitive and Affective Neuroscience, 2*, 3–11.

O'Reilly, R. C., Noelle, D. C., Braver, T. S., & Cohen, J. D. (2002). Prefrontal cortex and dynamic categorization tasks: Representational organization and neuromodulatory control. *Cerebral Cortex, 12*, 246–257.

Packard, M. G. & McGaugh, J. L. (1996). Inactivation of hippocampus or caudate nucleus with lidocaine differentially affects expression of place and response learning. *Neurobiology of Learning and Memory, 65*, 65–72.

Padoa-Schioppa, C. & Assad, J. A. (2006). Neurons in the orbitofrontal cortex encode economic value. *Nature, 441*, 223–226.

Petty, R. E. & Cacioppo, J. T. (1984). The effects of involvement on response to argument quantity and quality: Central and peripheral routes to persuasion. *Journal of Personality and Social Psychology, 46*, 69–81.

Phelps, E. A., Cannistraci, C. J., & Cunningham, W. A. (2003). Intact performance on an indirect measure of race bias following amygdala damage. *Neuropsychologia, 41*, 203–208.

Phelps, E. A., O'Connor, K. J., Cunningham, W. A., Funayama, E. S., Gatenby, J. C., Gore, J. C., et al. (2000). Performance on indirect measures of race evaluation predicts amygdala activation. *Journal of Cognitive Neuroscience, 12*, 729–738.

Phelps, E. A., O'Connor, K. J., Gatenby, J. C., Gore, J. C., Grillon, C., & Davis, M. (2001). Activation of the left amygdala to a cognitive representation of fear. *Nature Neuroscience, 4*, 437–441.

Rahn, W. M. (1993). The role of partisan stereotypes in information processing about political candidates. *American Journal of Political Science, 37*, 472–496.

Richeson, J. A., Baird, A. A., Gordon, H. L., Heatherton, T. F., Wyland, C. L., Trawalter, S., et al. (2003). An fMRI investigation of the impact of interracial contact on executive function. *Nature Neuroscience, 6*, 1323–1328.

Ridderinkhof, K. R., Ullsperger, M., Crone, E. A., & Nieuwenhuis, S. (2004). The role of the medial frontal cortex in cognitive control. *Science, 206*, 443–447.

Rolls, E. T. (2000). The orbitofrontal cortex and reward. *Cerebral Cortex, 10*, 284–294.

Rolls, E. T. (2004). The functions of the orbitofrontal cortex. *Brain and Cognition, 55*, 11–29.

Rolls, E. T., Hornak, J., Wade, D., & McGrath, J. (1994). Emotion-related learning in patients with social and emotional changes associated with frontal lobe damage. *Journal of Neurology, Neurosurgery, and Psychiatry, 57*, 1518–1524.

Rolls, E. T., McCabe, C., & Redoute, J. (2008). Expected value, reward outcome, and temporal difference error representations in a probabilistic decision task. *Cerebral Cortex*, *18*, 652–663.

Rougier, N.P., Noelle, D., Braver, T.S., Cohen, J.D. & O'Reilly, R.C. (2005). Prefrontal cortex and the flexibility of cognitive control: Rules without symbols. *Proceedings of the National Academy of Sciences*, *102*, 7338–7343.

Roskos-Ewoldsen, D. R. & Fazio, R. H. (1992). On the orienting value of attitudes. *Journal of Personality and Social Psychology*, *63*, 198–211.

Sander, D., Grafman, J., & Zalla, T. (2003). The human amygdala: An evolved system for relevance detection. *Reviews in the Neurosciences*, *14*, 303–316.

Schultz, W., Dayan, P., & Montague, P. R. (1997). A neural substrate of prediction and reward. *Science*, *275*, 1593–1599.

Shallice, T. (1982). Specific impairments of planning. *Philosophical Transactions of the Royal Society of London*, *298*, 199–209.

Small, D. M., Gregory, M. D., Mak, Y. E., Gitelman, D., Mesulam, M. M., & Parrish, T. (2003). Dissociation of neural representation of intensity and affective valuation in human gustation. *Neuron*, *39*, 701–711.

Stefanacci, L. & Amaral, D. G. (2000). Topographic organization of cortical inputs to the lateral nucleus of the macaque monkey amygdala: A retrograde tracing study. *The Journal of Comparative Neurology*, *421*, 52–79.

Stuss, D. T. & Benson, D. F. (1986). The frontal lobes and control of cognition and memory. In E. Perecman (Ed.), *The frontal lobes revisited* (pp. 144–158). New York: Raven.

Sutton, R. S. & Barto, A. G. *Reinforcement learning*. MIT Press, Cambridge, MA, 1998.

Tom, S. M., Fox, C. R., Trepel, C., & Poldrack, R. A. (2007). The neural basis of loss aversion in decision-making under risk. *Science*, *26*, 515–518.

Thorndike, E. (1911). *Animal intelligence: Experimental studies*. New York: Macmillan.

Van Bavel, J. J., Packer, D. J., & Cunningham, W. A. (2008). The neural substrates of in-group bias: A functional magnetic resonance imaging investigation. *Psychological Science*, *19*, 1131–1139.

Wallis, J. D. & Miller, E. K. (2003). Neuronal activity in primate dorsolateral and orbital prefrontal cortex during performance of a reward preference task. *European Journal of Neuroscience*, *18*, 2069–2081.

Watson, J.B., & Rayner, R. (1920). Conditioned emotional reactions. *Journal of Experimental Psychology*, *3*, 1–14.

Weiskrantz, L. (1956). Behavioral changes associated with ablation of the amygdaloid complex in monkeys. *Journal of Comparative Physiological Psychology*, *49*, 381–391.

Westen, D., Blagov, P. S., Harenski, K., Kilts, C., & Hamann, S. (2006). Neural bases of motivated reasoning: An fMRI study of emotional constraints on partisan political judgment in the 2004 U.S. presidential election. *Journal of Cognitive Neuroscience*, *18*, 1947–1958.

Whalen, P. J., Rauch, S. L., Etcoff, N. L., McInerney, S. C., Lee, M. B., & Jenike, M. A. (1998). Masked presentations of emotional facial expressions modulate amygdala activity without explicit knowledge. *The Journal of Neuroscience*, *18*, 411–418.

Yin, H. H., Ostlund, S. B., Knowlton, B. J., & Balleine, B. W. (2005). The role of the dorsomedial striatum in instrumental conditioning. *European Journal of Neuroscience*, *22*, 513–523.

Zald, D. H. & Pardo, J. V. (1997). Emotion, olfaction, and the human amygdala: Amygdala activation during aversive olfactory stimulation. *Proceedings of the National Academy of Sciences*, *94*, 4119–4124.

Zelazo, P. D. (2003). The development of conscious control in childhood. *Trends in Cognitive Sciences*, *8*, 12–17.

The Emotion-Attention Interface: Neural, Developmental, and Clinical Considerations

Michael L. Kirwan, Lauren K. White, *and* Nathan A. Fox

Abstract

This chapter provides a basic foundation of the neuroscience, behavior, and development of attention processes and the role that different aspects of attention play in social and emotional behavior. It begins with a brief overview of Posner's model of attention. It then discusses the normative development of the orienting system and impairments in this system that have been identified in autism and anxiety disorders. The following section reviews the normative development of the executive attention system before shifting to selective deficits in the aforementioned clinical populations. The chapter concludes by discussing future directions for research on the interface between emotion and attention.

Keywords: attention, orienting, disengagement, executive attention, development, anxiety, autism

Introduction

For some years now, researchers have studied the development of adaptive social behavior from infancy through childhood and have attempted to identify those factors that converge to orient a child's trajectory towards social competence or not. These studies indicate that the interface between emotion and attention plays a particularly important role in the emergence and direction of social behavior. Facility in particular attention processes (such as orienting or executive attention) appear to play an important role in the development of social competence: the ability to act appropriately in social interactive contexts. As well, a child's affective state or temperamental disposition may affect the way stimuli are attended to and understood. For example, children with a fearful temperament attend to stimuli differently than those without

this temperament and these differences in attention affect social behavior. This bi-directional interaction between attention and emotion has also been grounded in the studies of brain-behavior interaction. The human neuroscience literature, which first described the circuits involved in basic attention processes, now provides evidence for links between affect and its regulation by attention.

This chapter attempts to provide a basic foundation of the neuroscience, behavior, and development of attention processes and the role that different aspects of attention play in social and emotional behavior. We take a developmental approach, examining the emergence of attention processes and their links to social and emotional behavior, and we use two clinical conditions as examples where there has been a good deal of work on the emotion-attention interface: anxiety and autism. Our goal is to provide the reader with a comprehensive overview of the development of components of attention and their role in the development of social behavior in typical and atypical populations.

Over a century has passed since William James famously claimed, "Everyone knows what attention is" (James, 1890). Current research has helped us to understand that attention is not a unitary construct, but rather an amalgam of dissociable processes, each with their own dedicated neural architecture, that allows us to navigate our everyday surroundings (Rafal & Robertson, 1995). As these processes have been parsed and classified in the literature, two dimensions of attention have been discussed at length—one focuses on the *type* of attention being observed (i.e., orienting, shifting, inhibiting) and the other focuses on the *cause* of this attention (i.e., stimulus-driven vs. top-down).

One model of attention that has integrated both of these accounts is that described by Posner and colleagues (e.g. Posner, 1992, 1995; Posner & Petersen, 1990; Rothbart & Posner, 2001). According to this model, the multitude of attentional processes can be broken down into three functional systems (orienting, alerting, and executive attention) that are subserved by two neuroanatomical networks (one anterior and one posterior). These systems are important in the development of self-regulation (Carlson & Wang, 2007; Johnson, Posner, & Rothbart, 1991; McConnell & Bryson, 2005; Rueda, Posner, & Rothbart, 2005; Sheese, Rothbart, Posner, White, & Fraundorf, 2008), and aberrant attentional processes have been observed in both autistic (Corbett, Constantine, Hendren, Rocke, & Ozonoff, 2009; Landry & Bryson, 2004; Lopez, Lincoln, Ozonoff, & Lai, 2005; Zwaigenbaum, et al., 2005) and anxious (Amir, Elias, Klumpp, & Przeworski, 2003; Bar-Haim, Lamy, Pergamin, Bakermans-Kranenburg, & van IJzendoorn, 2007; Fox, Russo, Bowles, & Dutton, 2001; Salemink, van den Hout, & Kindt, 2007; White, McDermott, Degnan, Henderson, & Fox, in press) populations. This chapter will begin with a brief overview of Posner's model of attention. Next, we discuss the normative development of the orienting system and impairments in this system that have been identified in autism and anxiety disorders. The following section will review the normative development of the executive attention system before shifting to selective deficits in the aforementioned clinical populations. Finally, we end by discussing future directions for research on the interface between emotion and attention.

Posner Model of Attention
Alerting, Orienting, and Executive Attention

The Posner model (e.g. Posner, 1992, 1995; Posner & Petersen, 1990; Rothbart & Posner, 2001) describes three distinct *types* of attention that can enhance processing—orienting, alerting, and executive attention. Although these three systems appear to be fairly independent (Fan, McCandliss, Sommer, Raz, & Posner, 2002), there has been some evidence of interactions between the systems (Callejas, Lupianex, & Tudela, 2004; Fernandez-Duque & Posner, 2001; Raz & Buhle, 2006). While this chapter deals largely with orienting and executive attention, the complete model should be clearly defined in order to understand the possible links between the systems.

The alerting system is involved in achieving, increasing, and maintaining an alert state and can help prepare an individual to process stimuli that are of high priority in their environment (Posner & Petersen, 1990; Raz & Buhle, 2006). Alerting can either be in the form of a general alert state or an alert state that is specific to the processing of task-related information. Although increased alerting is associated with increased processing of a target as indexed by faster reaction times, it carries with it a trade-off. These faster reaction times are often accompanied by decreases in response effectiveness as indexed by lower accuracy rates. This suggests that although increased alertness may lead to the selection of a target for further processing, it appears to do so without a sufficient amount of information (Posner & Petersen, 1990).

The orienting system selects certain information in the environment, either by involuntary or voluntary means, in which to attend. By way of this selection, certain stimuli in the environment are processed more efficiently or take priority in subsequent processing (Posner & Petersen, 1990). The act of orienting involves several steps: the *disengagement* of attention from one location, the *shifting* of attention toward a second location, and the *re-engaging* of attention to the new location (Posner & Petersen, 1990). Orienting includes exogenous (involuntary) orienting, when the onset of a cue automatically captures one's attention (e.g., a sudden flash of light), and endogenous (voluntary) orienting, when one voluntarily focuses attention to specific stimuli (e.g., attending to a peer's facial expression after you just told a joke) (Raz & Buhle, 2006). Though it is often considered under the umbrella of orienting, disengagement refers specifically to the cessation of gaze fixation or attention fixation that is required prior to a gaze shift. This chapter will often use the term "disengagement" to refer to both covert attention shifts and gaze shifts, though the relations between these two shifts has been the subject of some debate (Hutton, 2008). However, there is evidence for a high degree of overlap in their underlying anatomy (Nobre, Gitelman, Dias, & Mesulam, 2000), as well as evidence that visual attention must be disengaged in order for gaze to be reoriented (Fischer & Breitmeyer, 1987).

The executive attention system involves the voluntary control of attention (Rothbart & Posner, 2006) and often serves to regulate the other more involuntary attention processes mentioned above. This system is thought to be involved in filtering out unimportant or irrelevant information; monitoring; planning; flexibly switching attention between tasks or other types of information; generating novel responses; and overriding dominant responses in favor of performing a subdominant response (Miyake, et al., 2000; Posner & Fan, 2004; Smith & Jonides, 1999). These functions of the executive system are thought to play a crucial role in the regulation of thoughts, emotions, and behaviors (Rothbart, Ellis, & Posner, 2004), and exert strong influence over other attention process (e.g., the orienting system).

Posterior and Anterior Attention Networks

These attention systems are also often characterized as deriving from different areas of the brain, known as the anterior and posterior attention networks (Posner & Petersen, 1990). Animal and lesion studies have localized the posterior network to the superior colliculus, the pulvinar region of the thalamus, and the posterior parietal lobe (Munoz, 2002; Posner & Petersen, 1990; Rafal & Robertson, 1995), while the anterior network consists of the supplementary motor area, the basal ganglia, the dorsolateral prefrontal cortex, and the anterior cingulate cortex (Fan, McCandliss, Fossella, Flombaum, & Posner, 2005; Posner & DiGirolamo, 1998; Rothbart & Posner, 2001). Whereas the posterior attention network is thought to underlie the more reactive tendencies or involuntary processes of orienting, the anterior attention network is thought to underlie the more voluntary aspects of attention, such as the executive attention system and the regulation of involuntary processes (Posner & Raichle, 1994; Posner & Rothbart, 1998). This regulation from the anterior attention network occurs through multiple pathways to the posterior network, and the anterior network often helps to control or direct the

posterior attention network to attend to psychologically or behaviorally relevant information. In addition, the anterior attention system is believed to have important interconnections with frontal approach-withdrawal motivation systems, as well as the limbic system (Derryberry et al., 2002).

Posterior Attention System
Development of Attention Orienting and Disengagement
INFANCY

The ability to flexibly orient one's attention to salient information in the environment appears to develop by four months of age, a finding that has been confirmed in a number of paradigms (see Colombo, 2001 for review). By three months of age, infants can orient to discrepant elements in stationary displays (Catherwood, Skoien, Green, & Holt, 1996; Colombo, Ryther, Frick, & Gifford, 1995), though this ability has been shown as early as two months depending on stimulus properties (Salapatek, 1975). Between 6 and 14 weeks, infants also develop the ability to orient to small moving stimuli (Dannemiller, 1994; Dannemiller & Freedland, 1993). Infants have also been shown to orient to a previously cued spatial location by four months (Johnson, Posner, & Rothbart, 1994; Johnson & Tucker, 1996) and can be trained to orient attention to a location at the same age (Johnson et al., 1991).

In contrast to the early development of orienting, infants between one and two months of age show a marked *inability* to disengage their attention once it is fixated in both the gap-overlap task (Atkinson, Hood, Wattam-Bell, & Braddick, 1992; Butcher, Kalverboer, & Geuze, 2000; Johnson et al., 1991) and social situations (Kaye & Fogel, 1980; van Wulfften Palthe, 1986); a phenomenon that has alternately been referred to as "sticky fixation" (Hood, 1995), "blank looking" (Bronson, 1982), "tropistic fixation" (Caron, Caron, Minichiello, Weiss, & Friedman, 1977), or "obligatory attention" (Stechler & Latz, 1966). However, significant incremental gains in both frequency and latency of disengagement have been observed over the first few months of life (Atkinson et al., 1992). By four months of age, the mechanism for disengagement of attention appears to be well established, and although there is much inter-individual difference in facility of disengagement at this age (Butcher et al., 2000; Finlay & Ivinskis, 1984), prolonged staring becomes much less frequent and shifts of attention and gaze occur more easily than at earlier ages (Butcher et al., 2000; Hicks & Richards, 1998; Hood & Atkinson, 1993; Johnson et al., 1991). After four months, this process continues to mature at a slower rate, such that disengagement of attention in the infant is qualitatively similar to adult disengagement by six months of age (Hood & Atkinson, 1993; Matsuzawa & Shimojo, 1997).

Several hypotheses have been proposed to explain this early deficit in attention disengagement and its subsequent recovery (Hood et al., 1996; Johnson, 1990; Posner, Rothbart, & Rosicky, 1994), but all have agreed on two central ideas. First, in order for an attention shift to occur, the tendency to maintain focus of attention must be overcome by the tendency to shift attention, and second, the observed difficulties in attention disengagement are the result of maturational differences between brain regions that maintain focused attention and regions that control the shifting of attention. It has been posited that the regions controlling this disengagement are part of the posterior attention system (Posner & Petersen, 1990; Schiller, 1985), which receive magnocellular inputs from the lateral geniculate that project to the parietal cortex. This system matures more slowly than the anterior, parvocellular system. Functional maturity of the posterior attention system has been observed using PET in three-month-old infants (Chugani, Phelps, & Mazziota, 1987) and these differences in maturation have been viewed as a possible explanation for early, age-related differences in attention disengagement (Hunnius, Geuze, & van Geert, 2006).

Gains in the ability to disengage and reorient attention have also been related to social and emotional development in the infant (Johnson et al., 1991; McConnell & Bryson, 2005), where better control of one's orienting system appears to aid in an infants' self-regulation. In one study by Johnson, Posner, and Rothbart (1991), four-month-old infants who disengaged their attention more easily were reported as less distress-prone and more soothable by their parents. Another study by McConnell and Bryson (2005) found similar results. In their study, longer disengagement latencies significantly correlated with increased fear at four months and both greater distress and less smiling at six months. Even in early observational studies of one-month-old infants, their level of obligatory attention was associated with increased levels of distress (Stechler & Latz, 1966; Tennes, Emde, Kisley, & Metcalf, 1972). Interestingly, an infant's ability to disengage from a stimulus is related to the emotional valence of that stimulus. Several studies have also found that seven-month-old infants both attend longer to and disengage less frequently from fearful faces as compared to happy, neutral, and novel faces (Peltola, Leppanen, Palokangas, & Hietanen, 2008; Peltola, Leppanen, Vogel-Farley, Hietanen, & Nelson, 2009), suggesting the importance of threat-related emotional stimuli very early in development. Disengagement may also be important for the development of social looking (Butcher & Kalverboer, 1997) and joint attention (Hood, Willen, & Driver, 1998), as research has found that infants as young as three months can follow the gaze of a centrally presented image of an adult face.

CHILDHOOD, ADOLESCENCE, AND ADULTHOOD

Reflecting its development in early infancy, the reflexive orienting observed in children is qualitatively similar to that of adolescents (MacPherson, Klein, & Moore, 2003) and adults (Rueda, Fan, et al., 2004) when measured by spatial cueing paradigms. Uncued prosaccade paradigms have shown similar results (Klein & Foerster, 2001). One study by Ristic and Kingstone (2009), however, has cast further light on this issue. Using a sample of three- to six-year-old children and adults, they compared the two groups on a task that required both reflexive and volitional orienting. While reflexive orienting alone appears to mature early in development, their task investigated the combined effects of reflexive and volitional orienting. Interestingly, they found the effects on reaction-time facilitation to be additive in young children but superadditive in adults, suggesting that while reflexive attention may mature early, its interaction with volitional attention takes longer to develop.

In contrast to the literature on orienting, there exists a current paucity of research on attention disengagement using children between one and six years of age. Beyond this window, however, several studies have examined the development of disengagement with gap and overlap conditions in pro- and antisaccade paradigms. In the first of these studies, Ross and Ross (1983) compared a group of 8- to 11-year-old children with adults on a gap-overlap paradigm. Their results indicated that under conditions where disengagement was not required (gap trials) the two groups did not differ in their saccadic latencies. However, on the trials requiring disengagement (overlap trials), children showed significantly longer saccadic latencies than adults.

Fischer, Biscaldi, and Gezeck (1997) further clarified the developmental trajectory of attention disengagement by testing a large sample (n = 281) of subjects ages 8 to 70 on both a prosaccade overlap (PO) task and an antisaccade gap (AG) task. In the task assessing disengagement (PO), saccadic latency decreased significantly from the youngest age groups through the ages of 15 to 20, followed by a slight increase after age 30. This finding was partially replicated by Klein and Foerster (2001). They found that saccadic latency in a prosaccade overlap task significantly decreases from early (6–7) to late (10–11) childhood, but not significantly from late childhood to adulthood (18–26). However, this lack of a difference between their 10–11 and 18–26 groups may be due to methodological issues, as they had both fewer subjects and fewer age bins than Fischer and colleagues.

Several studies have also examined attention disengagement in younger and older adult populations. Pratt, Abrams, and Chasteen (1997) tested a group of 18- to 22-year-old students and a group of 60- to 83-year-old adults on a gap-overlap test, finding that the older group had longer saccadic latencies than the younger group in both gap and overlap trials. Importantly, the gap effect was larger in the older group, who showed relatively slower latencies on the overlap trials compared to the gap trials than the younger group. This finding has been replicated by Fahle and Wegner (2000), who attribute the age-related slowing of reaction times to difficulty disengaging attention rather than a predominantly motor-related problem.

Attention Orienting and Disengagement in Clinical Populations

AUTISM

In some of the earliest clinical descriptions of autism, the features of the disorder have been described in terms of three constellations of symptoms: abnormalities in social interactions, deficits in communication, and insistence on sameness (Kanner, 1943). Atypical eye gaze is one well-documented social abnormality that has been found in both autistic infants and children (Dawson, Meltzoff, Osterling, Rinaldi, & Brown, 1998; Phillips, Baroncohen, & Rutter, 1992), but recent research has begun to investigate whether these gaze-related abnormalities are specific to the social domain. In general, these attentional findings tend to fall into three categories: social orienting, nonsocial orienting, and disengagement impairment.

Social orienting impairment refers to autistic children's failure to spontaneously orient to naturally occurring social stimuli in their environments (Dawson et al., 1998). This is usually assessed by children's response to their name being called or their spontaneous orienting towards others' faces. A number of studies have demonstrated that children who are eventually diagnosed with autism show much less social orienting in home videos from their first birthday than do non-autistic children (Osterling & Dawson, 1994; Osterling, Dawson, & Munson, 2002; Werner, Dawson, Osterling, & Dinno, 2000). This finding has been replicated with three- to five-year-old children in the laboratory setting (Dawson et al., 1998; Dawson et al., 2004; Leekam, Lopez, & Moore, 2000).

With regard to nonsocial orienting, the literature on autistic populations is much less concordant. One study by Leekam and colleagues (2000) found that autistic preschoolers showed deficits in orienting towards adults who made a bid for their attention but not towards objects that made similar bids. Ioracci and Burack (2004) showed similar intact nonsocial orienting using a prosaccade task. However, several other researchers have shown autistic populations to be deficient in cross-modal orienting (Courchesne et al., 1994), slower in visual attention orienting (Casey et al., 1995; Townsend, Courchesne, & Egaas, 1996), and impaired in orienting to cued spatial locations (Wainwright-Sharp & Bryson, 1993).

The final cluster of attentional findings in autistic populations involves deficits in attention disengagement. In one such study, Landry and Bryson (2004) compared autistic children to age-matched children with Down syndrome and normal controls on a gap-overlap task. Their results showed that the autistic group took significantly longer than both the Down syndrome and control groups on overlap (disengage) trials, but not on gap trials. The autistic group also showed a much higher percentage of trials where they failed to disengage from the central stimulus (18.0%) compared to the control group (7.7%) and the Down syndrome group (0.8%). These impairments in disengagement have also been shown in the developmentally normal infant siblings of children with autism spectrum disorders (Elsabbagh et al., 2009).

A further longitudinal study by Zwaigenbaum and colleagues (2005) measured attention disengagement in the infant siblings of autistic children at both six and twelve months finding no difference between the groups at six months. Interestingly, however, of the 20 siblings assessed, all of those who showed longer latencies to disengage attention at 12 months compared to 6 months (25%, n = 5) were classified on the autism spectrum at 24 months.

These patterns of impaired disengagement have also been found in autistic adults using the gap-overlap task. In a study by Kawakubo and colleagues (2007), autistic adults showed significantly longer saccadic reaction times on overlap trials compared to normal controls, but showed no difference on gap trials. Electroencephalographic results also indicated that autistic adults displayed a significantly higher pre-saccadic positivity during the period of 100 to 70 ms before saccade onset, the amplitude of which was significantly correlated with severity of clinical symptoms. As a whole, these studies suggest that impaired disengagement of attention may be an early behavioral indicator of autism spectrum disorders, as well as a persistent symptom throughout the lifespan.

ANXIETY

Perturbations in orienting have also been documented in anxiety, and are thought to play a causal role in the development of the disorder (MacLeod, Rutherford, Campbell, Ebsworthy, & Holker, 2002). These perturbations in attention are indexed by a facilitation to orient attention toward threatening information in the environment and a difficulty to disengage attention away from a source of threat (Cisler, Bacon, & Williams, 2009). Such patterns have been found when the threat is mild or ambiguous (Frenkel, Lamy, Algom, & Bar-Haim, 2008; Richards et al., 2002) and using both subliminal and supraliminal stimulus presentations (Hunt, Keogh, & French, 2006; Mogg, Bradley, Williams, & Mathews, 1993). The dot-probe task is a commonly used task to assess attention biases to threat in anxious individuals. In this task, a neutral and a threatening stimulus are presented simultaneously, followed by a neutral target probe appearing in the location of one of the previously viewed stimuli. Anxious individuals show facilitated target detection when the target appears in the location of the threatening stimulus compared to target detection when the target appears in the location of the neutral stimulus; a pattern not found in non-anxious individuals. Using different modifications of the dot-probe task, this finding has been replicated in many different clinical anxiety disorders, as well as nonclinical anxiety (see Bar-Haim et al., 2007 for review), and level of attention bias to threat has been shown to predict treatment effectiveness in children (Legerstee et al., 2009).

Despite the well-documented finding that orienting processes in anxious individuals prioritize the processing of threat, the nature of such bias remains under debate. The attention bias documented in the dot-probe task could arise in part from facilitation in orienting toward threat or slowed disengagement of attention away from threat. To try to tease apart the source of such bias, several recent studies have employed methodologies that examine both orienting towards and disengagement from threat in anxious populations (Carlson & Reinke, 2008; Koster, Crombez, Van Damme, Verschuere, & De Houwer, 2004; Koster, Crombez, Verschuere, & De Houwer, 2004; Koster, Crombez, Verschuere, Van Damme, & Wiersema, 2006; Salemink et al., 2007). Using a modified dot-probe task with the addition of a neutral-neutral stimulus display, facilitation of orienting toward threat can be calculated by subtracting reaction times from trials in which the probe replaced the location of the threat stimulus when another neutral stimulus was present from trials in which the two neutral stimuli were present. On the other hand, disengagement on this task can be measured by subtracting the reaction times on trials in which the target appeared in the location of the previously viewed neutral stimulus when a threat stimulus had also been presented from reaction times on trials in which no threat stimulus was present. Koster et al. (2006) found that compared to low-trait anxious individuals, high-trait anxious individuals showed greater attention bias toward both moderate and high levels of threat. Looking at the indices for facilitation and disengagement, results revealed that difficulties disengaging from threat appeared to be the main cause for the documented attention bias. In a similar study, Salemink et al. (2007) also showed that attention bias to threat in anxious individuals appears to be caused by difficulties disengaging from threat, where the index of disengagement difficulties positively related to level of anxiety ratings. However, in a recent study using masked presentation of threat stimuli on a modified dot-probe task, facilitated orienting and not disengagement of attention appeared to be the basis of attention bias to threat (Carlson & Reinke, 2008). Using eye tracking during a dot-probe task, under high-stress conditions, socially anxious individuals showed facilitated orienting toward emotional faces compared to neutral faces; however, this finding did not remain under no-stress conditions (Garner, Mogg, & Bradley, 2006). Taken together, there appears to be some evidence to suggest that facilitated orienting toward threat underlies the attention bias characteristic of anxious children and adults. However, the majority of research using variants of the dot-probe task and emotional spatial cueing paradigms indicate that this attention bias to threat is largely an effect of difficulties disengaging from threat (Fox, Russo, & Dutton, 2002; Georgiou, et al., 2005; Salemink, et al., 2007).

Recent research suggests that the perturbations witnessed in anxious individuals' orienting processes are not specific to threat-related processing, but that anxiety is linked to a general impoverished orienting system. Using the Attention Network Task (Fan et al., 2002), in which informative spatial cues are presented to facilitate task performance, under neutral conditions anxious individuals show a decreased ability to use the spatial cues to orient their attention towards a specific location (Moriya & Tanno, 2008). Using a neutral version of a spatial-cueing paradigm with short (100) and long (800) SOA between cue and target onset, anxious and nonanxious individuals did not differ in their ability to disengage attention from invalid cues at the long SOA (Poy, Eixarch, & Avila, 2003). However, group differences were detected at the short SOA; compared to non-anxious controls, anxious individuals showed greater difficulty disengaging away from peripheral cues. Taken together, a deficiency in one's general ability to disengage attention, not only under the presence of threat, may be a behavioral feature associated with anxiety.

Impaired orienting may be a risk factor in the development of anxiety (Lonigan, Vasey, Phillips, & Hazen, 2004; Mathews & MacLeod, 2002). A pattern of biased attentional processing of threat, if present over the course of development, likely predisposes a child to dramatic increases in emotional vulnerability. Whether this pattern of biased orienting is due to threat-related impairments or a more general impoverished orienting system, the perturbed processing leads to amplifications in the amount of threat-related information that is processed. The resulting bias in attentional processing of threat increases a child's vulnerability to experience stress and anxiety (Lonigan & Vasey, 2009).

Anterior Attention System
Development of Executive Attention
Many of the changes that occur in the posterior attention system over development arise in part from the maturation of the anterior attention system (Ruff & Rothbart, 1996). For example, while the ability to disengage attention relies on a complex interplay of involuntary and voluntary attention processes (Raz & Buhle, 2006), as a child's executive attention system develops they have better voluntary control

over their orienting system. The anterior attention network encompasses the skills that underlie the executive attention system (Posner, 1992, 1995; Posner & Petersen, 1990; Rothbart & Posner, 2001). This system is recruited during behavioral and cognitive monitoring, conflict detection, and planning, and reflects the ability to flexibly switch attention between different attentional and response sets, filter out unimportant or irrelevant information, generate novel responses, and inhibit dominant responses (Rothbart & Posner, 2006; Rueda et al., 2005). The dramatic development of the executive attention system parallels rapid changes in a child's ability to regulate their emotions (Posner & Rothbart, 2000; Rothbart, Ellis, Rueda, & Posner, 2003) and adaptive social behaviors (Hughes, 1998; Hughes, Dunn, & White, 1998), and deficits in the executive attention network have been implicated in the development of psychopathology and developmental disorders (e.g., Hill, 2004; Muris, Mayer, van Lint, & Hofman, 2008).

INFANCY
Developmental research has shown a striking lack of executive attention functions in infants and toddlers (Ruff & Rothbart, 1996), with dramatic behavioral and neural maturation in this network from the early preschool years until late childhood (Casey et al., 1995; Casey, Trainor, Giedd, et al., 1997; Posner & Rothbart, 1998; Rueda, Fan, et al., 2004). However, many of the tasks used to assess executive attention in children place high demands on a child's verbal and motor abilities, making them inappropriate for use in young children and infants. Using novel tasks that require minimal motor or language skills, research has been able to successfully measure early executive attention in infants and young toddlers (Rothbart et al., 2003; Sheese et al., 2008).

Using a task in which young children had to make a simple response to the identity of a stimulus, a response that was either conflicting to the location of the stimulus (spatially incongruent) or nonconflicting (spatially congruent), two-year-olds showed high accuracy on the no-conflict trials. However, on the spatially conflicting trials their accuracy was extremely low (Gerardi-Caulton, 2000). Interestingly, just one year later three-year-olds were performing significantly better on the high-conflict trials. Using sequential looking paradigms, Posner, Rothbart and colleagues have examined early executive attention in infants and young toddlers (Rothbart et al., 2003; Sheese et al., 2008). In these paradigms, visual stimuli are presented in a recurring sequence as a participant's reflexive saccades (eye movements that are made to a location after stimulus onset) and anticipatory saccades (eye movements made to a location prior to stimulus onset) are examined. When ambiguity is added to the visual sequence, as is the case with a 1-2-1-3 pattern, where the number references a location in space, the participant must learn and disambiguate the sequential pattern. For instance, after a stimulus has been presented in location one, the following stimulus could appear in location two or location three. A child's ability at two years of age to learn the ambiguous pattern (as indexed by their anticipatory eye movements) is related to parental reports of self-regulation and an ability to resolve conflict using a modified Stroop paradigm. Prior to age two, a similar paradigm has detected the presence of an early executive attention system in six- and seven-month olds, where the level of anticipatory eye movements is related to various self-regulatory measures (Sheese et al., 2008).

CHILDHOOD, ADOLESCENCE, AND ADULTHOOD

Dramatic improvements in a child's executive attention system occur over the preschool years (Diamond, 2002; Rueda et al., 2005), and such improvements are thought to continue into adolescence (Luna & Sweeney, 2004; Rubia et al., 2000), not reaching full maturity until early adulthood (Luna et al., 2001). Even during the developmental period from 3- to 5-years of age, children show rapid improvement in many aspects of executive attention. Using the Dimensional Change Card Sort Task (Frye, Zelazo, & Palfai, 1995), an assessment of attention shifting in which a child must sort a series of cards that vary on two dimensions (i.e., shape and color), 3-year-olds do just fine when asked to sort the cards by one dimension (e.g., color). However, when asked to switch sorting rules and sort by the second dimension (e.g., shape), 3-year-olds continue to sort by the first dimension (Zelazo, 2006; Zelazo, Frye, & Rapus, 1996). By 4 and 5 years of age children become much better at flexibly shifting their attention to sort by the second sorting rule. Using a flanker-based paradigm in which the participants had to indicate the direction of a central stimulus, which was either congruent or incongruent to the direction of flanker stimuli, Reuda et al. (2004) showed significant improvement in children's performance on incongruent trials between 4 to 7 years of age. Interestingly, however, by 7 years of age

children did not significantly differ from adults' performance on this task.

During adolescence, improvements on already existing cognitive functions as well as increased consistency in the proper implementation of such functions occur (Luna & Sweeney, 2004). Rapid maturation of the prefrontal cortex is thought to underlie these improvements from childhood (Casey, Trainor, Orendi, et al., 1997) to adolescence and adulthood (Luna et al., 2001), where diffuse brain activation becomes much more focal during tasks that activate the executive attention system.

Executive Attention in Clinical Populations
AUTISM
Executive attention deficits are thought to be a key characteristic in autism spectrum disorders. Several studies have shown that the level of impairment in executive attention functions is related the level of clinical symptoms (Lopez et al., 2005; South, Ozonoff, & McMahon, 2007). Of particular importance is the notion that the deficits in executive attention observed in autism spectrum disorder likely underlie deficits in other domains such as joint attention (e.g., McEvoy, Rogers, & Pennington, 1993) and theory of mind (e.g., Ozonoff, Pennington, & Rogers, 1991)—key impairments in autistic individuals.

The ability to flexibly shift attention, thoughts, and behaviors appears to be a specific executive attention deficit associated with autism. In a recent meta-analysis, Willcutt and colleagues (2008) found a large effect-size difference in attention flexibility between individuals with autism spectrum disorder and controls. Using a Wisconsin Card Sorting Task in which subjects must sort cards according to varying dimensions (e.g., shape and color) where, unbeknownst to the subject, the sorting rule changes during the task, individuals with autism spectrum disorder showed deficits in the ability to adapt to the new sorting rules (Corbett et al., 2009). Using the DCCS, similar difficulties in attention shifting have been found in autistic children and adolescents with either mild or severe impairments (Colvert, Custance, & Swettenham, 2002; Zelazo, Jacques, Burack, & Frye, 2002). Although an attention-control deficit is often found in individuals with autism spectrum disorder, it should be noted that there have been some inconsistencies in this area of research (see Geurts, Corbett, & Solomon, 2009 for review).

An inability to inhibit context-inappropriate behaviors, an outcome of a poor inhibitory control system, has also been theoretically implicated in autism spectrum disorder (Kana, Keller, Minshew, & Just, 2007). However, compared to control groups, autistic children and adults do not show deficits on the Stroop task (e.g., Christ, Holt, White, & Green, 2007; Ozonoff, 1997), a commonly used task to measure inhibitory control. Interestingly, however, group differences have been documented using a go-no-go task (e.g., Christ et al., 2007; Ozonoff, Strayer, McMahon, & Filloux, 1994). Despite the mixed behavioral findings on inhibitory control deficits in individuals with autism spectrum disorder, Kana and colleagues (2007) found that autistic individuals showed less brain activation in areas typically associated with inhibitory control (i.e., anterior cingulate cortex) during both a simple and complex inhibitory task compared to a control group, despite a lack in behavioral differences. This suggests that autistic individuals may not rely on the typical neural networks associated with inhibitory control, but employ other cognitive strategies to inhibit certain responses.

Autistic individuals show perturbations in their conflict and behavior monitoring (Henderson, et al., 2006; Vlamings, Jonkman, Hoeksma, van Engeland, & Kemner, 2008). Moreover, it has been suggested that these perturbations play a role in autistic symptomotology (Mundy, 2003). Henderson and colleagues (2006) found that compared to controls, high functioning autistic individuals showed longer error-related negativity (ERN) latencies, suggesting a less-efficient monitoring system in autistic individuals. However, the high functioning autistic group was significantly less accurate on the task compared to control group, leaving the possibility that the ERN differences detected in this study were a function of task performance, not a behavior monitoring difference per se. Although there were no main effects of group on ERN amplitude, when divided by verbal ability, autistic children with higher verbal ability had larger ERNs than a control group matched on verbal scores. Another study examining the relation between ERN and autism showed that compared to a control group, individuals with autism spectrum disorder showed decreased ERNs (Vlamings et al., 2008). Recent neuroimaging research has shown structural and functional abnormalities in the anterior cingulate cortex, a region of the brain thought to play a critical role in conflict and behavior monitoring, in autistic individuals (Dichter & Belger, 2007; Gomot et al., 2006; Kennedy, Redcay, & Courchesne, 2006). This underlying neural abnormality in the ACC is

thought to result in improper monitoring, likely influencing the rigid and inflexible behaviors observed in autistic individuals (Thakkar et al., 2008).

ANXIETY

The executive attention networks play an important role in adaptive emotion regulation (Rothbart et al., 2003; Rothbart & Sheese, 2007). Perturbations in this network are linked to poor emotional outcomes and developmental psychopathology, playing a particularly influential role in the development of anxiety (Muris et al., 2008; Rothbart & Posner, 2006).

Voluntary attention control, including the ability to flexibly focus and shift attention, appears to play a significant role in anxious symptomotology (Bishop, Jenkins, & Lawrence, 2007; Muris, Meesters, & Rompelberg, 2007). One phenomenon that likely underlies this association is the influence attention control has on the biased processing of threat, an output from the posterior attention system (Derryberry & Reed, 2002; Lonigan et al., 2004). For example, children with negative temperamental reactivity (e.g., behavioral inhibition or high negative affect) have been shown to automatically process negative emotional information in the environment, even when such information is irrelevant (Lonigan & Vasey, 2009; Perez-Edgar et al., 2010a). However, an individual's voluntary attention control has been shown to help diminish such an attention bias, likely leading to more positive emotional outcomes (Derryberry & Reed, 1994; Lonigan & Vasey, 2009). Using a dot-probe task, Derryberry and Reed (2002) found that with short stimulus durations (250 ms), trait anxious individuals showed a bias to attend to threatening information. However, at longer stimulus durations, presumably allowing the influence of top-down control processes, self-reported attention control moderated the link between anxiety and attention bias towards threat. That is, anxious individuals with poor attention control still showed an attention bias at the longer stimulus presentation, but anxious individuals with high levels of attention control no longer showed such bias. This finding has been replicated using laboratory assessments of attentional control (Reinholdt-Dunne, Mogg, & Bradley, 2009) and in children (Lonigan & Vasey, 2009; Lonigan et al., 2004). The ability to efficiently control attention likely serves as a protective factor for the development of anxiety by reducing an individual's attention biases towards threat, a processing bias causally linked to anxiety (e.g., MacLeod et al., 2002).

Anxiety is also associated with the inability to control attentional focus (Bishop, 2009; Perez-Edgar et al., 2010b). In a longitudinal study, Perez-Edgar and colleagues (2010b) found that 9-month-olds with a poor ability to ignore irrelevant distracters in the environment were more likely to be behaviorally inhibited later in childhood. Moreover, the ability to flexibly focus attention moderated the link between behavioral inhibition and aspects of adolescent anxiety during a social situation, such that early behavioral inhibition was only related to increased social anxiety for children with poor attention focus. Using an emotional Stroop task in which individuals must ignore irrelevant emotional stimuli in a group of 4- to 11-year-old children, increased interference from the irrelevant emotional distracters was related to increased shyness and anxiety (Perez-Edgar & Fox, 2003). A recent neuroimaging study showed a similar pattern of results in anxious adults; under conditions in which task load was low (where irrelevant distracters can more readily compete for attentional resources), individuals with high levels of trait anxiety showed a deficient ability to properly recruit the neural networks that would afford an individual with adequate attention focus, allowing the individual to more readily filter out irrelevant distracting stimuli (Bishop, 2009). Thus, the inability to efficiently filter out irrelevant stimuli, whether they are neutral or emotional information, likely puts a child at increased risk for social and emotional difficulties.

In a longitudinal study examining emotional development and the ability to flexibly shift attention, Eisenberg and colleagues (Eisenberg, Shepard, Fabes, Murphy, & Guthrie, 1998) found children with poor attention-shifting abilities had greater behavioral and emotional problems later in childhood. However, this association was only present for children high in negative emotionality, suggesting that children with more reactive temperaments and executive attention deficits may be at increased risk for the development of anxiety. Anxious individuals also show a decreased ability to use information in their environment to exert top-down control to shift attention (Ansari, Derakshan, & Richards, 2008; Wieser, Pauli, & Muhlberger, 2009). Using an anti-saccade task in which a cue stimulus signals whether a participant must look toward or away from a target, most individuals show an improvement in performance when trial types (saccade or anti-saccade) are randomized (Hodgson, Golding,

Molyva, Rosenthal, & Kennard, 2004). This benefit in performance is thought to result in part by cue stimulus presentation prior to each trial, from which participants can recruit top-down attention control to shift performance between trial types. Interestingly, however, on a neutral anti-saccade task anxious participants do not show such benefit in performance (Ansari et al., 2008). Similar results have been shown on an anti-saccade task using emotional and neutral stimuli (Wieser et al., 2009). Thus, it appears that anxious individuals may have an inability to recruit voluntary attention control to shift their attention in their environment.

Inhibitory control plays a crucial role in the successful regulation of behaviors and emotions (Carlson & Wang, 2007; Rothbart et al., 2003). In a recent study examining the relations between children's inhibitory control and emotional regulation as assessed through both parental report and laboratory assessment, a child's inhibitory control was related to their ability to inhibit an emotional response when such response was situationally inappropriate (Carlson & Wang, 2007). The relation between the two constructs held for both parental reports and laboratory assessments. Interestingly, however, children with moderate levels of inhibitory control seemed to be the best at regulating emotions, with children in the top and bottom quadrants of inhibitory control being the worst at inhibiting inappropriate emotional responses. This suggests that very high and low levels of inhibitory control may be harmful to adaptive emotional development (Carlson & Wang, 2007). Similar findings have been shown in children high in temperamental behavioral inhibition (Thorell, Bohlin, & Rydell, 2004; White et al., in press). Inhibitory control (as measured by Day Night and Pointing Stroop tasks) was found to moderate the relation between 24-month behavioral inhibition and anxiety problems in preschool years (White et al., in press). Results showed that children with both high levels of behavioral inhibition and inhibitory control were at increased risk for anxiety problems. The authors interpreted this finding to suggest that in children with fearful temperaments already showing constrained behaviors and attention, high levels of inhibitory control may result in over control (e.g., Carver, 2005), intensifying fear and withdrawal behaviors. Additionally, high inhibitory control may increase anxious cognitions. In anxious adults, high inhibitory control was associated with increased worry and anxious symptomotology (Price & Mohlman, 2007). Having too much restraint or control over the modification of one's behaviors and emotions may result in increased anxiety.

A marked improvement in the ability to deal with conflict occurs over development. However, individual differences in this ability appear to have a strong influence on a child's risk for anxiety problems (Hajcak, McDonald, & Simons, 2003; McDermott et al., 2008). In a recent study by Henderson (2010), a child's self-reported shyness was associated with measures of social anxiety and a negative attribution style only for children showing enhanced N2 responses on a laboratory flanker task—an ERP index of conflict sensitivity. In similar studies examining cognitive monitoring, greater ERNs—an ERP component reflecting an individuals' error response and monitoring (Dehaene, Posner, & Tucker, 1994)—are associated with increased trait anxiety and worry (Hajcak et al., 2003). In a group of 8- to 14-year-old children, anxious children showed increased ERNs compared to their nonanxious peers (Ladouceur, Dahl, Birmaher, Axelson, & Ryan, 2006). Behavioral inhibition in adolescents is also associated with increased ERNs (McDermott et al., 2008). Interestingly, within the high behaviorally inhibited adolescents, the size of an individual's ERN was related to their level of anxiety, such that behaviorally inhibited adolescents with the largest ERNs were most at risk for anxiety problems. Similar to the inhibitory control findings, increased conflict and error response sensitivity may put a child at risk for increased problems in anxiety.

Future Directions

There has been a good deal of interest recently in the area of training of attention and its role in facilitating changes in social behavior. New research methods manipulating attention processing have found a causal link between attention bias and elevated emotional vulnerability in a stressful situation (Eldar, Ricon, & Bar-Haim, 2008; MacLeod et al., 2002; Salemink et al., 2007). Macleod and colleagues (2002) used a modified dot-probe paradigm, manipulating the contingency between the threat stimuli and the target probe so as they were always in the same location. Pre- and post- training attention bias scores showed that the paradigm was successful in inducing attention bias; participants in the train-to-negative group showed an attention bias to threat in a test phase. Directly after the attention bias was induced, increases in anxiety levels were not found. However, after participants underwent a stress induction, participants in the train

towards threat condition reported increased anxiety scores. Eldar, Ricon, and Bar-Haim (2008) have documented similar findings in children. Using a similar paradigm to MacLeod and colleagues (2002), they showed that children who had their attention trained towards threat showed an attention bias to threat in a subsequent test phase. Similar to the adult findings, children in the train-to-threat condition reported elevated levels of anxious behaviors after a stress induction compared to their pre-training anxiety levels. The authors also found children trained towards threat showed increased stress behaviors during the stress task compared to the group trained away from threat. Similar training studies find that attention training away from threat is related to decreased emotional vulnerability in anxious adults (Mathews & MacLeod, 2002) and anxious children (Bar-Haim, Morag, & Glickman, in press). These studies represent the next phase in expanding the emotion-attention interface. They show the promise of using experimental methods manipulating aspects of attention to induce changes in social behavior, and they lend themselves to examining the changes in underlying brain circuitry that may be affected by training and thus may underlie changes in social behavior.

References

Amir, N., Elias, J., Klumpp, H., & Przeworski, A. (2003). Attentional bias to threat in social phobia: Facilitated processing of threat or difficulty disengaging attention from threat? *Behav Res Ther*, *41*(11), 1325–1335.

Ansari, T. L., Derakshan, N., & Richards, A. (2008). Effects of anxiety on task switching: Evidence from the mixed antisaccade task. *Cogn Affect Behav Neurosci*, *8*(3), 229–238.

Atkinson, J., Hood, B., Wattam-Bell, J., & Braddick, O. (1992). Changes in infants' ability to switch visual attention in the first three months of life. *Perception*, *21*(5), 643–653.

Bar-Haim, Y., Morag, I., Glickman, S. (in press). Training anxious children to disengage attention from threat: A randomized controlled trial. *Journal of Child Psychology and Psychiatry*.

Bar-Haim, Y., Lamy, D., Pergamin, L., Bakermans-Kranenburg, M. J., & van IJzendoorn, M. H. (2007). Threat-related attentional bias in anxious and nonanxious individuals: A meta-analytic study. *Psychological Bulletin*, *133*(1), 1–24.

Bishop, S. J. (2009). Trait anxiety and impoverished prefrontal control of attention. *Nat Neurosci*, *12*(1), 92–98.

Bishop, S. J., Jenkins, R., & Lawrence, A. D. (2007). Neural processing of fearful faces: Effects of anxiety are gated by perceptual capacity limitations. *Cerebral Cortex*, *17*, 1595–1603.

Bronson, G. W. (1982). *The scanning patterns of human infants: Implications for visual learning*. Norwood, NJ: Ablex.

Butcher, P. R. & Kalverboer, A. F. (1997). The early development of visuo-spatial attention and its impact on social looking. *Early Development and Parenting*, *6*(1), 15–26.

Butcher, P. R., Kalverboer, A. F., & Geuze, R. H. (2000). Infant's shifts of gaze from a central to a peripheral stimulus: A longitudinal study of development between 6 and 26 weeks. *Infant Behav Dev*, *23*, 3–21.

Callejas, A., Lupiánex, J., & Tudela, P. (2004). The three attentional networks: On their independence and interactions. *Brain and Cognition*, *54*, 225–227.

Carlson, J. M. & Reinke, K. S. (2008). Masked fearful faces modulate the orienting of covert spatial attention. *Emotion*, *8*(4), 522–529.

Carlson, S. M. & Wang, T. S. (2007). Inhibitory control and emotion regulation in preschool children. *Cognitive Development*, *22*, 489–510.

Caron, A., Caron, R., Minichiello, M. D., Weiss, S. J., & Friedman, S. L. (1977). Constraints on the use of the familiarization-novelty method in the assessment of infant discrimination. *Child Dev*, *48*, 747–762.

Carver, C. S. (2005). Impulse and constraint: Perspectives from personality psychology, convergence with theory in other areas, and potential for integration. *Pers Soc Psychol Rev*, *9*(4), 312–333.

Casey, B. J., Cohen, J. D., Jezzard, P., Turner, R., Noll, D. C., Trainor, R. J., et al. (1995). Activation of prefrontal cortex in children during a nonspatial working memory task with functional MRI. *Neuroimage*, *2*(3), 221–229.

Casey, B. J., Trainor, R., Giedd, J., Vauss, Y., Vaituzis, C. K., Hamburger, S., et al. (1997). The role of the anterior cingulate in automatic and controlled processes: A developmental neuroanatomical study. *Dev Psychobiol*, *30*(1), 61–69.

Casey, B. J., Trainor, R. J., Orendi, J. L., Schubert, A. B., Nystrom, L. E., Gledd, J. N., et al. (1997). A developmental functional MRI study of prefrontal activation during performance of a Go-No-Go task. *Journal of Cognitive Neuroscience*, *9*(6), 835–847.

Catherwood, D., Skoien, P., Green, V., & Holt, C. (1996). Assessing the primary moments in infant encoding of compound visual stimuli. *Infant Behav Dev*, *19*, 1–11.

Christ, S. E., Holt, D. D., White, D. A., & Green, L. (2007). Inhibitory control in children with autism spectrum disorder. *J Autism Dev Disord*, *37*(6), 1155–1165.

Chugani, H. T., Phelps, M. E., & Mazziota, J. C. (1987). Positron emission tomography study of human brain functional development. *Ann Neurol*, *22*, 487–497.

Cisler, J. M., Bacon, A. K., & Williams, N. L. (2009). Phenomenological characteristics of attentional biases towards threat: A critical review. *Cognitive Therapy and Research*, *33*(2), 221–234.

Colombo, J. (2001). The development of visual attention in infancy. *Annu Rev Psychol*, *52*, 337–367.

Colombo, J., Ryther, J. S., Frick, J. E., & Gifford, J. J. (1995). Visual pop-out in infants: Evidence for preattentive search in 3- and 4-month-olds. *Psychonom Bull Rev*, *2*, 266–268.

Colvert, E., Custance, D., & Swettenham, J. (2002). Rule-based reasoning and theory of mind in autism: A commentary on the work of Zelazo, Jacques, Burack, and Frye. *Infant and Child Development*, *11*, 197–200.

Corbett, B. A., Constantine, L. J., Hendren, R., Rocke, D., & Ozonoff, S. (2009). Examining executive functioning in children with autism spectrum disorder, attention deficit hyperactivity disorder and typical development. *Psychiatry Res*, *166*(2–3), 210–222.

Courchesne, E., Townsend, J., Akshoomoff, N. A., Saitoh, O., Yeung-Courchesne, R., Lincoln, A. J., et al. (1994). Impairment in shifting attention in autistic and cerebellar patients. *Behav Neurosci*, *108*(5), 848–865.

Dannemiller, J. L. (1994). Reliability of motion detection by young infants measured with a new signal detection paradigm. *Infant Behav Dev*, *17*, 101–105.

Dannemiller, J. L. & Freedland, R. L. (1993). Motion-based detection by 14-week-old infants. *Vision Res*, *33*(5–6), 657–664.

Dawson, G., Meltzoff, A. N., Osterling, J., Rinaldi, J., & Brown, E. (1998). Children with autism fail to orient to naturally occurring social stimuli. *J Autism Dev Disord*, *28*(6), 479–485.

Dawson, G., Toth, K., Abbott, R., Osterling, J., Munson, J., Estes, A., et al. (2004). Early social attention impairments in autism: Social orienting, joint attention, and attention to distress. *Dev Psychol*, *40*(2), 271–283.

Dehaene, S., Posner, M. I., & Tucker, D. M. (1994). Localization of a neural system for error detection and compensation. *Psychological Science*, *5*, 303–305.

Derryberry, D. & Reed, M. A. (1994). Temperament and attention: Orienting toward and away from positive and negative signals. *J Pers Soc Psychol*, *66*(6), 1128–1139.

Derryberry, D. & Reed, M. A. (2002). Anxiety-related attentional biases and their regulation by attentional control. *Journal of Abnormal Psychology*, *111*, 225–236.

Diamond, A. (2002). Normal development of prefrontal cortex from birth to young adulthood: Cognitive functions, anatomy, and biochemistry. In D. Stuss & R. Knight (Eds.), *Principles of frontal lobe function* (pp. 466–503). New York: Oxford University Press.

Dichter, G. S. & Belger, A. (2007). Social stimuli interfere with cognitive control in autism. *Neuroimage*, *35*(3), 1219–1230.

Eisenberg, N., Shepard, S. A., Fabes, R. A., Murphy, B. C., & Guthrie, I. K. (1998). Shyness and children's emotionality, regulation, and coping: Contemporaneous, longitudinal, and across-context relations. *Child Development*, *69*, 767–790.

Eldar, S., Ricon, T., & Bar-Haim, Y. (2008). Plasticity in attention: Implications for stress response in children. *Behav Res Ther*, *46*(4), 450–461.

Elsabbagh, M., Volein, A., Holmboe, K., Tucker, L., Csibra, G., Baron-Cohen, S., et al. (2009). Visual orienting in the early broader autism phenotype: Disengagement and facilitation. *J Child Psychol Psychiatry*, *50*(5), 637–642.

Fahle, M. & Wegner, A.-J. (2000). Age dependence of sensory and motor components in saccades. *Neuroophthalmology*, *24*(3), 427–440.

Fan, J., McCandliss, B. D., Fossella, J., Flombaum, J. I., & Posner, M. I. (2005). The activation of attentional networks. *Neuroimage*, *26*(2), 471–479.

Fan, J., McCandliss, B. D., Sommer, T., Raz, A., & Posner, M. I. (2002). Testing the efficiency and independence of attentional networks. *J Cogn Neurosci*, *14*(3), 340–347.

Fernandez-Duque, D. & Posner, M. I. (2001). Brain imaging of attentional networks in normal and pathological states. *J Clin Exp Neuropsychol*, *23*(1), 74–93.

Finlay, D. & Ivinskis, A. (1984). Cardiac and visual responses to moving stimuli presented either successively or simultaneously to the central and peripheral visual fields in 4-month-old infants. *Dev Psychol*, *20*, 29–36.

Fischer, B., Biscaldi, M., & Gezeck, S. (1997). On the development of voluntary and reflexive components in human saccade generation. *Brain Res*, *754*(1–2), 285–297.

Fischer, B. & Breitmeyer, B. (1987). Mechanisms of visual attention revealed by saccadic eye movements. *Neuropsychologia*, *25*(1A), 73–83.

Fox, E., Russo, R., Bowles, R., & Dutton, K. (2001). Do threatening stimuli draw or hold visual attention in subclinical anxiety? *J Exp Psychol Gen, 130*(4), 681–700.

Fox, E., Russo, R., & Dutton, K. (2002). Attentional bias for threat: Evidence for delayed disengagement from emotional faces. *Cogn Emot, 16*(3), 355–379.

Frenkel, T. I., Lamy, D., Algom, D., & Bar-Haim, Y. (2008). Individual differences in perceptual sensitivity and response bias in anxiety: Evidence from emotional faces. *Cogn Emot, 23*(4), 688–700.

Frye, D., Zelazo, P. D., & Palfai, T. (1995). Theory of mind and rule-based reasoning. *Cognitive Development, 10*, 483–527.

Garner, M., Mogg, K., & Bradley, B. P. (2006). Orienting and maintenance of gaze to facial expressions in social anxiety. *J Abnorm Psychol, 115*(4), 760–770.

Georgiou, G. A., Bleakley, C., Hayward, J., Russo, R., Dutton, K., Eltiti, S., et al. (2005). Focusing on fear: Attentional disengagement from emotional faces. *Vis cogn, 12*(1), 145–158.

Gerardi-Caulton, G. (2000). Sensitivity to spatial conflict and the development of self-regulation in children 24–26 months of age. *Developmental Science, 3*(4), 397–404.

Geurts, H. M., Corbett, B., & Solomon, M. (2009). The paradox of cognitive flexibility in autism. *Trends Cogn Sci, 13*(2), 74–82.

Gomot, M., Bernard, F. A., Davis, M. H., Belmonte, M. K., Ashwin, C., Bullmore, E. T., et al. (2006). Change detection in children with autism: An auditory event-related fMRI study. *Neuroimage, 29*(2), 475–484.

Hajcak, G., McDonald, N., & Simons, R. F. (2003). Anxiety and error-related brain activity. *Biol Psychol, 64*(1–2), 77–90.

Henderson, H., Schwartz, C., Mundy, P., Burnette, C., Sutton, S., Zahka, N., et al. (2006). Response monitoring, the error-related negativity, and differences in social behavior in autism. *Brain Cogn, 61*(1), 96–109.

Henderson, H. A. (2010). Electrophysiological correlates of cognitive control and the regulation of shyness in children. *Dev Neuropsychol, 35*(2), 177–193.

Hicks, J. M. & Richards, J. E. (1998). The effect of stimulus movement and attention on peripheral stimulus localization by 8- to 26-week-old infants. *Infant Behav Dev, 21*, 571–589.

Hill, E. L. (2004). Executive dysfunction in autism. *Trends Cogn Sci, 8*(1), 26–32.

Hodgson, T. L., Golding, C., Molyva, D., Rosenthal, C. R., & Kennard, C. (2004). Eye movement during task switching: Reflexive, symbolic, and affective contributions to response selection. *Cognitive Neuroscience, 16*(318–330).

Hood, B. M. (1995). Shifts of visual attention in the human infant: A neuroscientific approach. In C. Rovee-Collier & L. P. Lipsitt (Eds.), *Advances in infancy research* (Vol. 9, pp. 163–216). Norwood, NJ: Ablex.

Hood, B. M. & Atkinson, J. (1993). Disengaging visual attention in the infant and adult. *Infant Behav Dev, 16*, 405–422.

Hood, B. M., Murray, L., King, F., Hooper, R., Atkinson, J., & Braddick, O. (1996). Habituation changes in early infancy: Longitudinal measures from birth to 6 months. *J Reprod Infant Psychol, 14*, 177–185.

Hood, B. M., Willen, J. D., & Driver, J. (1998). Adult's eyes trigger shifts of visual attention in human infants. *Psychol Sci, 9*(2), 131–134.

Hughes, C. (1998). Executive function in preschoolers: Links with theory of mind and verbal ability. *British Journal of Developmental Psychology, 16*, 233–253.

Hughes, C., Dunn, J., & White, A. (1998). Trick or treat?: Uneven understanding of mind and emotion and executive dysfunction in "hard-to-manage" preschoolers. *J Child Psychol Psychiatry, 39*(7), 981–994.

Hunnius, S., Geuze, R. H., & van Geert, P. (2006). Associations between the developmental trajectories of visual scanning and disengagement of attention in infants. *Infant Behav Dev, 29*(1), 108–125.

Hunt, C., Keogh, E., & French, C. C. (2006). Anxiety sensitivity: The role of conscious awareness and selective attentional bias to physical threat. *Emotion, 6*(3), 418–428.

Hutton, S. B. (2008). Cognitive control of saccadic eye movements. *Brain Cogn, 68*(3), 327–340.

Iarocci, G. & Burack, J. A. (2004). Intact covert orienting to peripheral cues among children with autism. *J Autism Dev Disord, 34*(3), 257–264.

James, W. (1890). *The principles of psychology*. New York: H. Holt and Company.

Johnson, M. H. (1990). Cortical maturation and the development of visual attention in early infancy. *J Cog Neurosci, 2*, 81–95.

Johnson, M. H., Posner, M. I., & Rothbart, M. K. (1991). Components of visual orienting in early infancy—contingency learning, anticipatory looking, and disengaging. *Journal of Cognitive Neuroscience, 3*(4), 335–344.

Johnson, M. H., Posner, M. I., & Rothbart, M. K. (1994). Facilitation of saccades toward a covertly attented location in early infancy. *Psychol Sci, 5*, 90–93.

Johnson, M. H. & Tucker, L. A. (1996). The development and temporal dynamics of spatial orienting in infants. *J Exp Child Psychol, 63*(1), 171–188.

Kana, R. K., Keller, T. A., Minshew, N. J., & Just, M. A. (2007). Inhibitory control in high-functioning autism: Decreased activation and underconnectivity in inhibition networks. *Biol Psychiatry, 62*(3), 198–206.

Kanner, L. (1943). Autistic disturbances of affective contact. *Nervous Child, 2*, 217–250.

Kawakubo, Y., Kasai, K., Okazaki, S., Hosokawa-Kakurai, M., Watanabe, K., Kuwabara, H., et al. (2007). Electrophysiological abnormalities of spatial attention in adults with autism during the gap overlap task. *Clin Neurophysiol, 118*(7), 1464–1471.

Kaye, K. & Fogel, A. (1980). The temporal structure of face to face communication between mothers and infants. *Dev Psychol, 16*, 454–464.

Kennedy, D. P., Redcay, E., & Courchesne, E. (2006). Failing to deactivate: Resting functional abnormalities in autism. *Proc Natl Acad Sci U S A, 103*(21), 8275–8280.

Klein, C. & Foerster, F. (2001). Development of prosaccade and antisaccade task performance in participants aged 6 to 26 years. *Psychophysiology, 38*(2), 179–189.

Koster, E. H., Crombez, G., Van Damme, S., Verschuere, B., & De Houwer, J. (2004). Does imminent threat capture and hold attention? *Emotion, 4*(3), 312–317.

Koster, E. H., Crombez, G., Verschuere, B., & De Houwer, J. (2004). Selective attention to threat in the dot probe paradigm: Differentiating vigilance and difficulty to disengage. *Behav Res Ther, 42*(10), 1183–1192.

Koster, E. H., Crombez, G., Verschuere, B., Van Damme, S., & Wiersema, J. R. (2006). Components of attentional bias to threat in high trait anxiety: Facilitated engagement, impaired disengagement, and attentional avoidance. *Behav Res Ther, 44*(12), 1757–1771.

Ladouceur, C. D., Dahl, R. E., Birmaher, B., Axelson, D. A., & Ryan, N. D. (2006). Increased error-related negativity (ERN) in childhood anxiety disorders: ERP and source localization. *J Child Psychol Psychiatry*, *47*(10), 1073–1082.

Landry, R. & Bryson, S. E. (2004). Impaired disengagement of attention in young children with autism. *J Child Psychol Psychiatry*, *45*(6), 1115–1122.

Leekam, S. R., Lopez, B., & Moore, C. (2000). Attention and joint attention in preschool children with autism. *Dev Psychol*, *36*(2), 261–273.

Legerstee, J. S., Tulen, J. H., Kallen, V. L., Dieleman, G. C., Treffers, P. D., Verhulst, F. C., et al. (2009). Threat-related selective attention predicts treatment success in childhood anxiety disorders. *J Am Acad Child Adolesc Psychiatry*, *48*(2), 196–205.

Lonigan, C. J. & Vasey, M. W. (2009). Negative affectivity, effortful control, and attention to threat-relevant stimuli. *J Abnorm Child Psychol*, *37*(3), 387–399.

Lonigan, C. J., Vasey, M. W., Phillips, B. M., & Hazen, R. A. (2004). Temperament, anxiety, and the processing of threat-relevant stimuli. *Journal of Clinical Child and Adolescent Psychology*, *33*, 8–20.

Lopez, B. R., Lincoln, A. J., Ozonoff, S., & Lai, Z. (2005). Examining the relationship between executive functions and restricted, repetitive symptoms of autistic disorder. *J Autism Dev Disord*, *35*(4), 445–460.

Luna, B. & Sweeney, J. A. (2004). The emergence of collaborative brain function: fMRI studies of the development of response inhibition. *Ann N Y Acad Sci*, *1021*, 296–309.

Luna, B., Thulborn, K. R., Munoz, D. P., Merriam, E. P., Garver, K. E., Minshew, N. J., et al. (2001). Maturation of widely distributed brain function subserves cognitive development. *Neuroimage*, *13*(5), 786–793.

MacLeod, C., Rutherford, E., Campbell, L., Ebsworthy, G., & Holker, L. (2002). Selective attention and emotional vulnerability: Assessing the causal basis of their association through the experimental manipulation of attentional bias. *J Abnorm Psychol*, *111*(1), 107–123.

MacPherson, A. C., Klein, R. M., & Moore, C. (2003). Inhibition of return in children and adolescents. *J Exp Child Psychol*, *85*(4), 337–351.

Mathews, A. & MacLeod, C. (2002). Induced processing biases have causal effects on anxiety. *Cognition and Emotion*, *16*(3), 331–354.

Matsuzawa, M. & Shimojo, S. (1997). Infants' fast saccades in the gap paradigm and development of visual attention. *Infant Behav Dev*, *20*, 449–455.

McConnell, B. A. & Bryson, S. E. (2005). Visual attention and temperament: Developmental data from the first 6 months of life. *Infant Behav Dev*, *28*(4), 537–544.

McDermott, J. M., Perez-Edgar, K., Henderson, H. A., Chronis-Tuscano, A., Pine, D. S., & Fox, N. A. (2008). A history of childhood behavioral inhibition and enhanced response monitoring in adolescence are linked to clinical anxiety. *Biol Psychiatry*.

McEvoy, R. E., Rogers, S. J., & Pennington, B. F. (1993). Executive function and social communication deficits in young autistic children. *J Child Psychol Psychiatry*, *34*(4), 563–578.

Miyake, A., Friedman, N., Emerson, M. J., Witzki, A. H., Howerter, A., & Wager, T. D. (2000). The unity and diversity of executive functions and their contributions to complex "frontal lobe" tasks: A latent variable analysis. *Cognit Psychol*, *41*(1), 49–100.

Mogg, K., Bradley, B. P., Williams, R., & Mathews, A. (1993). Subliminal processing of emotional information in anxiety and depression. *Journal of Abnormal Psychology*, *102*, 304–311.

Moriya, J. & Tanno, Y. (2008). Relationships between negative emotionality and attentional control in effortful control. *Personality and Individual Differences*, *44*(6), 1348–1355.

Mundy, P. (2003). Annotation: The neural basis of social impairments in autism: the role of the dorsal medial-frontal cortex and anterior cingulate system. *J Child Psychol Psychiatry*, *44*(6), 793–809.

Munoz, D. P. (2002). Saccadic eye movements: Overview of neural circuitry. *Prog Brain Res*, *140*, 89–96.

Muris, P., Mayer, B., van Lint, C., & Hofman, S. (2008). Attentional control and psychopathological symptoms in children. *Personality and Individual Differences*, *44*, 1495–1505.

Muris, P., Meesters, C., & Rompelberg, L. (2007). Attention control in middle childhood: Relations to psychopathological symptoms and threat perception distortions. *Behav Res Ther*, *45*(5), 997–1010.

Nobre, A. C., Gitelman, D. R., Dias, E. C., & Mesulam, M. M. (2000). Covert visual spatial orienting and saccades: Overlapping neural systems. *Neuroimage*, *11*(3), 210–216.

Osterling, J. & Dawson, G. (1994). Early recognition of children with autism: A study of first birthday home videotapes. *J Autism Dev Disord*, *24*(3), 247–257.

Osterling, J. A., Dawson, G., & Munson, J. A. (2002). Early recognition of 1-year-old infants with autism spectrum disorder versus mental retardation. *Dev Psychopathol*, *14*(2), 239–251.

Ozonoff, S. (1997). Components of executive function in autism and other disorders. In J. Russell (Ed.), *Autism as an executive disorder* (pp. 179–211). Oxford: Oxford University Press.

Ozonoff, S., Pennington, B. F., & Rogers, S. J. (1991). Executive function deficits in high-functioning autistic individuals: Relationship to theory of mind. *J Child Psychol Psychiatry*, *32*(7), 1081–1105.

Ozonoff, S., Strayer, D. L., McMahon, W. M., & Filloux, F. (1994). Executive function abilities in autism and Tourette syndrome: An information processing approach. *J Child Psychol Psychiatry*, *35*(6), 1015–1032.

Peltola, M. J., Leppanen, J. M., Palokangas, T., & Hietanen, J. K. (2008). Fearful faces modulate looking duration and attention disengagement in 7-month-old infants. *Dev Sci*, *11*(1), 60–68.

Peltola, M. J., Leppanen, J. M., Vogel-Farley, V. K., Hietanen, J. K., & Nelson, C. A. (2009). Fearful faces but not fearful eyes alone delay attention disengagement in 7-month-old infants. *Emotion*, *9*(4), 560–565.

Perez-Edgar, K. & Fox, N. A. (2003). Individual differences in children's performance during an emotional Stroop task: A behavioral and electrophysiological study. *Brain Cogn*, *52*(1), 33–51.

Perez-Edgar, K., Bar-Haim, Y., McDermott, J. M., Chronis-Tuscano, A., Pine, D. S., & Fox, N. A. (2010a). Attention biases to threat and behavioral inhibition in early childhood shape adolescent social withdrawal. *Emotion*, *10*(3), 349–357.

Perez-Edgar, K., McDermott, J. N., Korelitz, K., Degnan, K. A., Curby, T. W., Pine, D. S., et al. (2010b). Patterns of sustained attention in infancy shape the developmental trajectory of social behavior from toddlerhood through adolescence. *Dev Psychol*, *46*(6), 1723–1730.

Phillips, W., Baroncohen, S., & Rutter, M. (1992). The role of eye contact in goal detection—Evidence from normal infants and children with autism or mental handicap. *Development and Psychopathology*, 4(3), 375–383.

Posner, M. I. (1992). Attention as a cognitive and neural system. *Curr Dir Psychol Sci*, 1(1), 11–14.

Posner, M. I. (1995). Attention in cognitive neuroscience: An overview. In M. S. Gazzaniga (Ed.), *Cognitive neurosciences* (pp. 615–624). Cambridge, MA: MIT Press.

Posner, M. I. & DiGirolamo, G. J. (1998). Executive attention: Conflict, target detection and cognitive control. In R. Parasuraman, (Ed.), *The attentive brain* (pp. 401–423). Cambridge: MIT Press.

Posner, M. I. & Fan, J. (2004). *Attention as an organ system.* Cambridge UK: Cambridge University Press.

Posner, M. I., & Petersen, S. E. (1990). The attention system of the human brain. *Annu Rev Neurosci*, 13, 25–42.

Posner, M. I. & Raichle, M. E. (1994). *Images of mind.* New York: Scientific American Library.

Posner, M. I. & Rothbart, M. K. (1998). Attention, self-regulation, and consciousness. *Philos Trans R Soc Lond B Biol Sci*, 21, 27–43.

Posner, M. I. & Rothbart, M. K. (2000). Developing mechanisms of self-regulation. *Development and Psychopathology*, 12, 427–441.

Posner, M. I., Rothbart, M. K., & Rosicky, J. (1994). Orienting in normal and pathological development. *Dev Psychopathol*, 6, 635–652.

Poy, R., Eixarch, M. C., & Avila, C. (2003). On the relationship between attention and personality: Covert visual orienting of attention in anxiety and impulsivity. *Pers Individ Dif*, 36(6), 1471–1481.

Pratt, J., Abrams, R. A., & Chasteen, A. L. (1997). Initiation and inhibition of saccadic eye movements in younger and older adults: An analysis of the gap effect. *J Gerontol B Psychol Sci Soc Sci*, 52(2), P103–107.

Price, R. B. & Mohlman, J. (2007). Inhibitory control and symptom severity in late life generalized anxiety disorder. *Behav Res Ther*, 45(11), 2628–2639.

Rafal, R. & Robertson, L. (1995). The neurology of visual attention. In M. S. Gazzaniga (Ed.), *The cognitive neurosciences* (pp. 625–648). Cambridge, MA: MIT Press.

Raz, A. & Buhle, J. (2006). Typologies of attentional networks. *Nat Rev Neurosci*, 7(5), 367–379.

Reinholdt-Dunne, M. L., Mogg, K., & Bradley, B. (2009). Effects of anxiety and attention control on processing pictorial and linguistic emotional information. *Behaviour Research and Therapy*.

Richards, A., French, C. C., Calder, A. J., Webb, B., Fox, R., & Young, A. W. (2002). Anxiety-related bias in the classification of emotionally ambiguous facial expressions. *Emotion*, 2(3), 273–287.

Ristic, J. & Kingstone, A. (2009). Rethinking attentional development: Reflexive and volitional orienting in children and adults. *Dev Sci*, 12(2), 289–296.

Ross, S. M. & Ross, L. E. (1983). The effects of onset and offset warning and post-target stimuli on the saccade latency of children and adults. *J Exp Child Psychol*, 36(2), 340–355.

Rothbart, M. K., Ellis, L. K., & Posner, M. I. (2004). Temperament and self-regulation. In R. F. Baumeister & K. D. Vohs (Eds.), *Handbook of self-regulation: Research, theory, and applications* (pp. 357–370). New York: Guilford Press.

Rothbart, M. K., Ellis, L. K., Rueda, M. R., & Posner, M. I. (2003). Developing mechanisms of temperamental effortful control. *Journal of Personality*, 71, 1113–1143.

Rothbart, M. K. & Posner, M. I. (2001). Mechanism and variation in the development of attentional networks. In C. A. Nelson & M. Luciana (Eds.), *Handbook of developmental cognitive neuroscience* (1st ed., pp. 353–363). Cambridge, MA: MIT Press.

Rothbart, M. K. & Posner, M. I. (2006). Temperament, attention, and developmental psychopathology. In D. Cicchetti & D. J. Cohen (Eds.), *Developmental psychopathology: Developmental neuroscience* (2nd ed., Vol. 2, pp. 465–501). Hoboken, N.J.: John Wiley & Sons, Inc.

Rothbart, M. K. & Sheese, B. E. (2007). Temperament and emotion regulation. In J. J. Gross (Ed.), *Handbook of emotion regulation*. New York: Guilford Press.

Rubia, K., Overmeyer, S., Taylor, E., Brammer, M., Williams, S. C., Simmons, A., et al. (2000). Functional frontalisation with age: Mapping neurodevelopmental trajectories with fMRI. *Neurosci Biobehav Rev*, 24(1), 13–19.

Rueda, M. R., Fan, J., McCandliss, B. D., Halparin, J. D., Gruber, D. B., Lercari, L. P., et al. (2004). Development of attentional networks in childhood. *Neuropsychologia*, 42(8), 1029–1040.

Rueda, M. R., Posner, M. I., & Rothbart, M. K. (2005). The development of executive attention: Contributions to the emergence of self-regulation. *Dev Neuropsychol*, 28(2), 573–594.

Rueda, M. R., Posner, M. I., Rothbart, M. K., & Davis-Stober, C. P. (2004). Development of the time course for processing conflict: An event-related potentials study with 4 year olds and adults. *BMC Neurosci*, 5, 39.

Ruff, H. A. & Rothbart, M. K. (1996). *Attention in early development: Themes and variations.* New York: Oxford University Press.

Salapatek, P. (1975). Pattern perception and early infancy. In L. Cohen & P. Salapatek (Eds.), *Infant perception: From sensation to cognition* (Vol. 2, pp. 133–248). New York: Academic.

Salemink, E., van den Hout, M. A., & Kindt, M. (2007). Selective attention and threat: Quick orienting versus slow disengagement and two versions of the dot probe task. *Behav Res Ther*, 45(3), 607–615.

Schiller, P. H. (1985). The neural control of visually guided eye movements. In J. E. Richards (Ed.), *Cognitive neuroscience of attention: A developmental perspective* (pp. 3–50). Mahwah, NJ: Erlbaum.

Sheese, B. E., Rothbart, M. K., Posner, M. I., White, L. K., & Fraundorf, S. H. (2008). Executive attention and self-regulation in infancy. *Infant Behav Dev*, 31(3), 501–510.

Smith, E. E. & Jonides, J. (1999). Storage and executive processes in the frontal lobes. *Science*, 283, 1657–1661.

South, M., Ozonoff, S., & McMahon, W. M. (2007). The relationship between executive functioning, central coherence, and repetitive behaviors in the high-functioning autism spectrum. *Autism*, 11(5), 437–451.

Stechler, G. & Latz, E. (1966). Some observations on attention and arousal in the human infant. *J Am Acad Child Psychiatry*, 5, 517–525.

Tennes, K., Emde, R., Kisley, A., & Metcalf, D. (1972). The stimulus barrier in early infancy: An exploration of some formulations of John Benjamin. In R. R. Holt & E. Peterfreund (Eds.), *Psychoanalysis and contemporary science*. New York: Macmillan.

Thakkar, K. N., Polli, F. E., Joseph, R. M., Tuch, D. S., Hadjikhani, N., Barton, J. J., et al. (2008). Response monitoring, repetitive behaviour and anterior cingulate abnormalities in autism spectrum disorders (ASD). *Brain*, *131*(Pt 9), 2464–2478.

Thorell, L., Bohlin, G., & Rydell, A. (2004). Two types of inhibitory control: Predictive relations to social functioning. *International Journal of Behavioral Development*, *28*(3), 193–203.

Townsend, J., Courchesne, E., & Egaas, B. (1996). Slowed orienting of covert visual-spatial attention in autism: Specific deficits associated with cerebellar and parietal abnormality. *Development and Psychopathology*, *8*(3), 563–584.

van Wulfften Palthe, T. (1986). *Neural maturation and early social behavior: A longitudinal study of mother-infant interaction.* Groningen, The Netherlands: Van Denderen.

Vlamings, P. H., Jonkman, L. M., Hoeksma, M. R., van Engeland, H., & Kemner, C. (2008). Reduced error monitoring in children with autism spectrum disorder: An ERP study. *Eur J Neurosci*, *28*(2), 399–406.

Wainwright-Sharp, J. A. & Bryson, S. E. (1993). Visual orienting deficits in high-functioning people with autism. *J Autism Dev Disord*, *23*(1), 1–13.

Werner, E., Dawson, G., Osterling, J., & Dinno, N. (2000). Brief report: Recognition of autism spectrum disorder before one year of age: A retrospective study based on home videotapes. *J Autism Dev Disord*, *30*(2), 157–162.

White, L. K., McDermott, J. M., Degnan, K. A., Henderson, H. A., & Fox, N. A. (in press). Behavioral inhibition and anxiety: The moderating roles of inhibitory control and attention shifting. *Journal of Abnormal Child Psychology.*

Wieser, M. J., Pauli, P., & Muhlberger, A. (2009). Probing the attentional control theory in social anxiety: An emotional saccade task. *Cogn Affect Behav Neurosci*, *9*(3), 314–322.

Willcutt, E., Sonuga-Barke, E., Nigg, J. T., & Sergeant, J. (2008). Recent developments in neuropsychological models of childhood psychiatric disorders. In T. Banaschewski & L. A. Rohde (Eds.), *Biological child psychiatry. Recent trends and developments. Adv Biol Psychiatry* (Vol. 24, pp. 195–226). Basel: Karger.

Zelazo, P. D. (2006). The dimensional change card sort (DCCS): A method of assessing executive function in children. *Nature Protocols*, *1*, 297–301.

Zelazo, P. D., Frye, D., & Rapus, T. (1996). An age-related dissociation between knowing rules and using them. *Cognitive Development*, *11*, 37–63.

Zelazo, P. D., Jacques, S., Burack, J. A., & Frye, D. (2002). The relation between theory of mind and rule use: Evidence from persons with autism-spectrum disorders. *Infant and Child Development*, *11*, 171–195.

Zwaigenbaum, L., Bryson, S., Rogers, T., Roberts, W., Brian, J., & Szatmari, P. (2005). Behavioral manifestations of autism in the first year of life. *Int J Dev Neurosci*, *23*(2–3), 143–152.

The Neuroscience of Personality Traits: Descriptions and Prescriptions

Angelina R. Sutin, Robert R. McCrae, *and* Paul T. Costa, Jr.

Abstract

This chapter offers an overview of current knowledge on personality traits and specific recommendations about how it might inform and advance research in neuroscience. It begins by describing one central model in trait psychology, the five-factor model, and the relation between traits and similar constructs—specifically, temperament and mood. It then discusses several core features that suggest a biological basis for these traits and very briefly reviews theories on their biological origins. Next, it reviews recent research on one biological aspect of traits, their resting-state neural correlates. Finally, the chapter ends with future directions for the neuroscience of personality traits with an eye to how personality psychology can inform theoretical and practical approaches to neuroimaging research on individual differences.

Keywords: personality, neuroscience research, five-factor model, traits, temperament, mood

In the past twenty years, personality traits have come to be recognized as central constructs in understanding human nature, with profound, pervasive, and enduring influences on people's adjustment and behavior (Ozer & Benet-Martínez, 2006). They have also been shown to be deeply rooted in biology, presumably mediated by the structure and functioning of the brain. Personality psychologists need neuroscience, and especially neuroimaging techniques, to develop more adequate theories of how personality is shaped and how it might be altered. At the same time, neuroscientists interested in human behavior and experience can profit from the findings and methods of contemporary personality psychology. This chapter is intended to offer an overview of current knowledge on personality traits and specific recommendations

about how it might inform and advance research in neuroscience.

Personality, most broadly defined, is an individual's characteristic ways of thinking, feeling, and behaving. Since antiquity, philosophers and scientists alike have developed systems for classifying people based on their psychological traits. It has only been within the last century, however, that the rigorous study of traits has revealed five robust factors that are easily observable in the self and others, stable across the lifespan, heritable, and universal. Much is known about the behavioral correlates of these stable individual differences; with technological advances in non-invasive neuroimaging techniques, attention has now turned to identifying their biological origins and how such traits may modulate the neural mechanisms responsible for individual differences in emotional, interpersonal, experiential, attitudinal, and motivational styles.

In this chapter, we first describe one central model in trait psychology, the five-factor model (McCrae & John, 1992), and the relation between traits and similar constructs—specifically, temperament and mood. We then discuss several core features that suggest a biological basis for these traits and very briefly review theories on their biological origins. Next, we review recent research on one biological aspect of traits, their resting-state neural correlates. Finally, we end with future directions for the neuroscience of personality traits with an eye to how personality psychology can inform theoretical and practical approaches to neuroimaging research on individual differences.

Five-Factor Model of Personality

Within the five-factor model (FFM), personality traits are hierarchically ordered around five broad dimensions: Neuroticism, Extraversion, Openness to Experience, Agreeableness, and Conscientiousness. Individuals high on Neuroticism (versus emotional stability) have a general tendency to experience negative affects, such as fear, sadness, and guilt; find controlling their urges difficult, and cope poorly with stress. Extraverts, in contrast, are prone to feeling positive emotions; tend to have cheerful dispositions; and are sociable, active, and assertive. Openness to Experience refers to the experiential component of personality; and captures an individual's cognitive flexibility, need for variety, and depth of emotional experience. Agreeableness contrasts altruism, sympathy, and trust with egocentrism, skepticism, and competitiveness. Finally, conscientious individuals are typically characterized as hard working, disciplined, orderly, and deliberate.

Research conducted over several decades has demonstrated the predictive utility of these five factors. For example, Neuroticism and Extraversion are consistently related (in opposite directions) to subjective well-being and quality of life (Costa & McCrae, 1980). Open and agreeable individuals tend to be less prejudiced (Ekehammar & Akrami, 2007); conscientious individuals tend to perform well in both the classroom (Noftle & Robins, 2007) and on the job (Barrick & Mount, 1991). Further, high Neuroticism and low Conscientiousness predict a variety of health-risk behaviors, such as smoking and drug use (Terracciano, Löckenhoff, Crum, Bienvenu, & Costa, 2008), and health outcomes, such as longevity (Terracciano, Löckenhoff, Zonderman, Ferrucci, & Costa, 2008).

Neuroscience researchers are most likely to be familiar with aspects of personality traditionally described as *temperaments*. When used to describe infants, temperament can mean anything from individual differences in sleeping and eating patterns to mood to sensory sensitivity. In adulthood, temperament commonly refers to the emotional components and emotion regulation aspects of personality. However, it has become clear that dimensions of temperament identified in adulthood correspond closely to the dimensions of the FFM (Evans & Rothbart, 2007). For example, although each are defined in slightly different ways, temperament constructs such as Negative Affectivity and Harm Avoidance are essentially equivalent to FFM Neuroticism: All refer to susceptibility to negative emotions. Similarly, the content domains of Positive Emotionality and Reward Dependence are similar to that of Extraversion, and Constraint and Persistence are roughly similar to Conscientiousness. Their conceptual and empirical overlap has led some to argue that personality and adult temperament should be considered the same thing (Costa & McCrae, 2000).

Personality traits can, however, be distinguished from the state fluctuations in mood and emotions that might be studied by fMRI techniques. Moods and emotions generally refer to what the individual is feeling at a specific or limited moment in time. Traits, in contrast, refer to the propensity to experience such emotions. For example, individuals high on Neuroticism have a general tendency to feel negative affects such as fear, anxiety, and shame. When faced with an anxiety-provoking situation, their experience of fear and anxiety will likely be more rapid in onset, more intense, and longer lasting than that of an individual low in Neuroticism. Similarly, individuals high in Extraversion more readily experience positive emotions and mood states. Experimental evidence bears this out: Individuals high in Neuroticism tend to be more susceptible to negative mood inductions, whereas extraverts tend to be more susceptible to positive ones (Larson & Ketelaar, 1991).

Biological Origins of Personality

Just as people have tried to classify personality traits since antiquity, so too have they searched for their biological origins. There are at least four characteristics of FFM-defined traits that suggest that personality should have a biological basis: Traits are consensually valid, stable across the life course, heritable, and universal. We consider each point in turn.

First, the expression of each trait is readily observable and observers are fairly accurate in their evaluation of another's traits. That is, an individual who rates herself high in Neuroticism will likely also be rated high in Neuroticism by others who know her. Acquaintances as diverse as parents, partners, and peers, who do not know each other but know the individual in very different contexts, can agree on what the individual's personality is like (Funder, Kolar, & Blackman, 1995). Thus, similarity of trait expression across a variety of contexts leads to agreement among disparate observers. This consensual validation of traits across life contexts suggests that behavioral consistency is driven by characteristics of the individual rather than simply the demands of the situation.

Second, traits are stable across the adult life course: An individual's score on Extraversion at age 25 may be the best predictor of his Extraversion score at age 65. Numerous studies with retest intervals ranging from 6 to over 20 years reveal uniformly high stability coefficients (Terracciano, Costa, & McCrae, 2006). Despite modest mean-level changes, the relative ordering of individuals tends to remain the same. Our extravert, for example, may be somewhat less extraverted at age 65 than at age 25, but he is still likely to be more extraverted than other 65 year olds. High stability, however, does not mean that personality does not change over time. Maturational trends suggest that Neuroticism, Extraversion, and Openness decrease across middle adulthood, whereas Agreeableness and conscientiousness increase. These age-related trends in the mean levels of personality traits recur across cultures despite different generational histories, which suggest an intrinsic maturation of personality relatively independent of the environment (McCrae et al., 1999).

Third, a large body of evidence suggests that the five factors (Bouchard, 1994), and their more circumscribed facets (Jang, McCrae, Livesley, Angleitner, & Riemann, 1998), are heritable. At the factor level, behavioral genetics studies consistently find that approximately 50% of the variance in measures of each trait is attributable to genetics. The remaining variance has been estimated to be due to nonshared environmental influences (such as different peer groups or differences in the prenatal environment) and error of measurement. Notably, the shared environment, such as having the same parents or socioeconomic status (SES), does not contribute significantly to adult personality.

Finally, the five factors are universal. Across gender, different age groups, and cultures with presumably radically different environments, the same five-factor structure is recovered (McCrae, Terracciano, et al., 2005). Traits apparently function in much the same way around the world. Cross-observer agreement is routinely found in American, European, and Asian samples (for a review, see McCrae et al., 2004). Similar maturational trends are observed in both Eastern and Western cultures (McCrae et al., 1999). Even the pattern of sex differences in traits, although small in magnitude, is found across a wide range of cultures (Costa, Terracciano, & McCrae, 2001). Finally, similar heritability estimates are also found around the world (Jang et al., 1998).

The universality of FFM traits implies biological mechanisms that, independent of cultural and societal influences, contribute significantly to personality. Such findings led to the development of Five-Factor Theory (McCrae & Costa, 2008), which postulates that FFM traits are deeply rooted in biology. However, that theory is silent on the specific genes, brain structures, and physiological mechanisms responsible for the development and functions of personality traits. Other personality psychologists, however, have attempted to identify the biological underpinning of dispositional traits, taking both bottom-up and top-down approaches.

Many early theories on the biological basis of personality, such as Eysenck's (1967), Gray's (1981), and Cloninger's (1993), remain influential today. These theorists made admirable attempts at identifying the molecular and/or neural basis of personality, but evidence tends not to support their core assumptions. For example, Cloninger hypothesized that each trait is closely associated with a neurotransmitter system. Accumulated evidence, however, indicates that single neurotransmitter systems do not underlie these personality dimensions (for a review, see Paris, 2005) and there is not a one-to-one relation between neurotransmitter systems and FFM-defined traits (e.g., Terracciano et al., 2009). It seems likely that these efforts at theorizing were premature, given the extraordinary complexity of the brain and our still-limited knowledge of its functioning. Yet, these theories, based on an antiquated understanding of how the brain works, continue to be popular because they offer testable, theory-driven hypotheses. Instead of devising grand theories of the mechanisms that give rise to complex behaviors, a more fruitful approach may be to begin by documenting the biological correlates of each trait, much as we have documented their behavioral correlates.

Resting-state Neural Correlates of Personality

Regardless of how traits come to be, everything that a person thinks, feels, and believes must arise from the brain. That is, traits may be purely genetic in origin, purely environmental in origin, or some combination of the two, but neural activity, in some way, must be responsible for their expression. As such, some observable patterns should be apparent for each trait. We next turn to what this may look like when the brain is at rest.

Even when the brain is not actively engaged in a task, stable patterns of activity can be measured reliably. Individual differences in this resting-state activity have been linked to a variety of affective and psychiatric disorders, such as major depression (Dunn et al., 2002) and schizophrenia (Malaspina et al., 2004). Likewise, individual differences in normal personality functioning may have stable patterns of resting-state neural activity. In fact, traits may be more strongly related to resting-state activity than activity during a task because the demands of a task may overwhelm the association between personality and activity.

Investigators are beginning to chart the resting-state correlates of personality traits across varying neuroimaging methodologies. Given its association with mood and anxiety disorders, much of this work has focused on Neuroticism. The diversity of techniques, scales, and samples, however, has painted a complex picture of the resting-state neural correlates of this trait. For example, measuring activity with positron emission tomography (PET), Deckersbach and colleagues (2006) found a negative association between Neuroticism and activity in the left insular cortex and the left superior temporal gyrus (Broadmann Area (BA) 22) using the Five Factor Index; Kim, Hwang, Park, and Kim (2008) found a negative correlation between Neuroticism and the medial prefrontal gyrus (BA 10), right inferior frontal gyrus (BA 48), and the precentral and postcentral gyrus (BA 4/3) using the Eysenck Personality Questionnaire; and Hakamata and colleagues (2006) found a positive correlation between Harm Avoidance (a construct related to Neuroticism) and the right thalamus and negative correlations with the right posterior cingulate gyrus, bilateral middle temporal gyrus (BA 21), and the left middle frontal gyrus (BA 11), among others, using the Temperament and Character Inventory. Differences in conceptualizations and measures of Neuroticism and in demographic characteristics (e.g., mixed-sex samples, differences in age) may have contributed to these divergent findings.

A focus on the neural correlates of the two factors of Neuroticism and Extraversion is hardly surprising given that these are the factors most closely tied to emotions and to psychopathology. Personality, however, is more than just these emotional components. Openness to Experience, for example, captures individual differences in cognitive flexibility, need for variety, and depth of motional experience (Costa & McCrae, 1992). Like Neuroticism, Openness is likely correlated with activity in specific regions of the brain when at rest.

Using a robust design, we examined the resting-state correlates of this experiential trait in a sample of older adults (> 55 years; Sutin, Beason-Held, Resnick, & Costa, 2009). Participants (N = 100) underwent resting-state PET scans twice, approximately two years apart, and also completed the NEO Personality Inventory (NEO-PI-R), a standard, comprehensive, and well-validated measure (Costa & McCrae, 1992) of FFM personality traits, twice, within two years of each scan. We used conjunction analyses to identify correlations that replicated across the two assessments. Our goal was to identify only the strongest and most reliable associations. Further, although the psychological correlates of personality generally do not differ by sex, mounting evidence points to sex differences in brain structure (Cosgrove, Mazure, & Staley, 2007), volume (Carne, Vogrin, Litewka, & Cook, 2006), and metabolic activity at rest (Gur et al., 1995). And, just as the neural mechanisms responsible for performance on a task may differ by sex (Cahill, 2006), so too may the neural correlates of traits. Thus, we took this potential for sex differences into account and directly tested whether the neural correlates of Openness were different for men and women.

Open individuals are able to store and manipulate information with ease (DeYoung, Peterson, & Higgins, 2005), which may contribute to their characteristic cognitive flexibility. It is of note then, that Openness correlated with areas associated with working memory and attention, two mechanisms necessary for such flexibility (MacDonald, Cohen, Stenger, & Carter, 2000). These correlates, however, were sex-specific: Openness correlated positively with the dorsolateral prefrontal cortex (DL-PFC) among the women and with the anterior cingulate cortex (ACC) among the men. These correlates are consistent with neuropsychological models of Openness that implicate the PFC and ACC in the neural underpinnings of this trait (DeYoung et al.

2005). This divergence suggests that the two sexes rely on different neural pathways for the operations that define the trait Openness to Experience.

We also found common neural correlates of Openness to Experience in addition to the sex-specific ones. Both men and women high in Openness had greater activity in their orbitofrontal cortex (OFC) compared to men and women low in Openness. The OFC is implicated in a variety of processes integral to this trait, including sensory integration, the processing of emotional information, and emotion recognition and differentiation (Petrides, 2007; Viskontas, Possin, & Miller, 2007). Working together, activation of the DL-PFC and ACC may orient open individuals to exploration and novelty, whereas activity in the OFC may reward such tendencies.

Our findings provide evidence that when the brain is not actively engaged in a task, traits are associated with unique, stable patterns of resting-state neural activity. They also point to the need for large-sample studies that consider men and women separately, because assuming that men and women are interchangeable potentially obscures sex-specific associations. It should be noted, however, that the brain undergoes both structural and functional changes as it ages; future research will tell whether these differences hold across the life course. In addition, although we focused specifically on PET, other neuroimaging techniques, such as fMRI, tensor diffusion imaging (TDI), and single photon emission computed tomography (SPECT), are often used to examine the relation between personality and aspects of brain function and structure. Integration across methodologies will surely lead to a more nuanced picture of the neural mechanisms associated with each of the traits.

Integrating Personality and Neuroscience

In this final section, we offer future directions for the integration of personality and neuroscience research. We pay particular attention to how methodologies traditionally used in personality can contribute to the design of neuroscience studies. We also consider how neuroscience can contribute to our understanding of personality traits.

Sample Size

Personality research requires large samples, as effect sizes tend to be in the small-to-moderate range. Large samples are needed to guarantee adequate power to detect such effects. Studies of biological correlates of personality, from genes to hormones to neural activity, have generally used small samples due to the sheer cost of biological assessments. Studies of traits using 20 subjects, however, are unlikely to reveal meaningful, replicable differences between people. Molecular geneticists tackle this limitation by pooling their data into large databases. This approach allows for meta-analyses on data from as many as 80,000 subjects (e.g., Willer et al., 2009); the benefit of such an approach is clear. Although several attempts have been made to create similar databases for neuroimaging data (e.g., fMRIdc; BrainMap), they have met with limited success so far.

Personality traits, however, may present an ideal subject for neuroimaging meta-analyses. Different studies generally use experimental conditions that are peculiar to the hypothesis they are testing, and thus cannot easily be combined with other data sets. But most studies also include baseline measures, and it is precisely these that are most directly relevant to studies of enduring personality traits. Neuroimaging studies routinely collect information on age and gender; if they also included assessments of personality, data on traits and baseline brain activity could readily be pooled.

Personality Assessment

Neuroimaging researchers invest a great deal of time and money in scanning; they likewise need to invest in maximizing the quality of their personality assessments. It is worth emphasizing that the cost and effort associated with collecting personality data is trivial compared to the effort needed to collect imaging data. For the convenience of both subjects and researchers, it is important to note that the personality assessment does not need to be obtained at the time of the scan. That is, subjects can fill out the questionnaire before they come in for the scan, take the questionnaire home with them and return it by mail or at a later date, or even fill it out years later. The stability of personality traits in adulthood suggests that when the assessment takes place is of secondary importance. An exception, of course, would be if the target population suffers from a neurodegenerative disease or other disorder that also has an effect on personality (Costa & McCrae, in press).

More important than the timing of the assessment, however, is that the scale be reliable and valid. Researchers have many theoretically grounded, empirically tested personality inventories to choose from. For example, the NEO-PI-R gives a detailed personality assessment of the five factors and their facets, whereas instruments such as the NEO Five-Factor Inventory (Costa & McCrae, 1992) or the

Big Five Inventory (John, Naumann, & Soto, 2008) are available for shorter assessments of personality at the global factor level. Using standard measures will help facilitate pooling data across studies, as well as reduce error variance and ensure appropriate measurement of the construct of interest. It should be noted that it is cost efficient to measure the full range of personality traits (all five factors and preferably specific traits) in every study, even if the researcher's chief interest is in one or two traits. Routine reporting of findings for all five factors would contribute to cumulative knowledge on the neuroscience of personality traits.

Useful information about personality can also come from sources other than the subject him- or herself. Observer ratings using standardized instruments, for example, are another valid source of information that is free of some of the biases associated with self-reports. Such ratings can profitably be used if the subjects are unable to report on their own personality traits (as in studies of patients with dementia). Used in conjunction with self-reports, observer ratings may help cross-validate findings. We took such an approach in the study of resting-state neural correlates of Openness described above; a subsample of the men (N = 11) also had peer ratings of personality on the observer rating version of the NEO-PI-R. We correlated these ratings with the areas associated with self-reported Openness. As in the analysis of self-report data, observer ratings were positively correlated with blood flow to the right insula (r = .64, p < .05) and negatively with blood flow to the left cuneus (r = −.63, p < .05). Such multiple assessments, through either observer ratings or repeated administration of the same measure, tend to increase reliability, leading to more robust findings that are less dependent on chance or state-specific effects (Kendler, Neale, Kessler, Heath, & Eaves, 1993; Riemann, Angleitner, & Strelau, 1997).

Neuroscience

In a similar vein, researchers could also take multiple assessments of neural activity/functioning, such as the two longitudinal PET assessments used in our Openness study. Multiple neuroimaging assessments should likewise help reduce state-specific effects, and, given their variability, may be even more important than multiple personality assessments. Further, integrating structural and functional measurements could strengthen conclusions that can be drawn from such measurements. For example, if individuals high in Conscientiousness

had thicker cortical structures in a particular region, this thickness could be included as a covariate in functional analyses. Adjusting for differences in brain structure may reveal better estimates of functional activity (Devlin & Poldrack, 2007). Future research could also consider adding genetic variants, as such variants appear to modulate the association between neural activity and traits (e.g., Williams et al., 2009).

As a complement to neuroimaging studies, research on patient populations may shed additional light on the association between personality and specific brain regions (Beer & Lombardo, 2007). For example, patients with OFC lesions typically show impaired reward processing (Berlin, Rolls, & Kischka, 2004). As described above, for individuals high on Openness, chronic activity in the OFC may serve, in part, to reward their exploration and novelty. Thus, damage to this area of the brain may be associated with lower Openness. Patients with OFC lesions could be compared to patients with other lesions and matched controls to test whether Openness is lower in patients with OFC damage. If OFC damage is associated with lower Openness, such evidence makes a stronger case for the role of the OFC in trait Openness. Interestingly, one patient study found that those with either OFC lesions or lesions to other areas of their prefrontal cortex (PFC) scored lower on Openness compared with healthy matched controls (Berlin et al., 2004). Further, the patients with other PFC lesions were primarily women with DL-PFC lesions. Thus, this patient study provides additional support for the OFC and DL-PFC activity implicated in Openness. Through neuroimaging studies of healthy participants, specific regions associated with each personality factor could be identified. Then, the personality of patients with damage to those specific regions could be compared to that of matched controls to examine whether personality differs in the expected direction.

The longitudinal methodologies frequently used in personality research could also be incorporated into neuroscience studies of personality. Intrinsic maturation of personality across the lifespan is likely mirrored by functional and/or structural changes in the brain. Knowledge of personality's developmental course will help facilitate this research. For example, personality develops most rapidly between the ages of 18 and 30; thus, effects may be most apparent during this period. Maturation, however, does continue into old age, albeit at a slower rate. Longitudinal studies may be able to identify changes in brain activity that predate changes in the expression of personality. Or perhaps as the brain ages, changes in blood flow to other areas of the brain compensate for changes in specific structures, much the same as it does for cognitive functioning (Beason-Held, Kraut, & Resnick, 2008).

Knowledge of the content domain of traits and their correlates will help inform design and level of analysis. For example, individuals high on Neuroticism are particularly reactive to emotional cues, such as facial expressions. These individuals are susceptible to negative emotional states and thus they should be reactive to negative facial expressions, but not positive ones. In contrast, extraverts are highly susceptible to positive emotions, and thus Extraversion should be related to positive facial expressions and unrelated to negative ones. Current research on Neuroticism, Extraversion, and facial expressions support this divergence: Neuroticism, but not Extraversion, is associated with sustained activity in the medial prefrontal cortex following presentation of sad faces (Haas, Constable, & Canli, 2008), whereas during the processing of happy faces, individuals high in Extraversion, but not Neuroticism, show greater activation of the amygdala (Canli, Sivers, Whitfield, Gotlib, & Gabrieli, 2002).

One of the many challenges facing investigators interested in the neural correlates of personality is how to "activate" personality in the scanner. Many affective paradigms easily lend themselves to the confines of the scanner and this may partly account for the disproportionate focus on Neuroticism and Extraversion compared to the other three FFM traits. Inducing positive or negative mood, the processing of facial expressions and emotional discrimination tasks are all simple procedures that adapt well to the scanner and get at the emotional core of Neuroticism and Extraversion. But, Neuroticism and Extraversion are more than just negative and positive affect, and more generally, personality is more than just Neuroticism and Extraversion. For investigators interested in the neural dynamics underlying the expression of traits, new paradigms need to be devised that capture the nature of the trait in the scanner. For example, aesthetic chills—transient emotional responses to the experience of beauty—are a nearly universal marker of Openness to Experience (McCrae, 2007) that can be induced in the scanner (Blood & Zatorre, 2001). Developing paradigms based on each trait's behavioral markers may be one fruitful avenue for activating traits in the scanner.

Finally, neuroscience may also contribute to our understanding of the mechanisms associated with traits. For example, in our research, we found that Openness to Experience was associated with resting-state activity in the ACC for men and in the DL-PFC for women (Sutin et al., 2009). The ACC is an area associated with attentional control, conflict detection, and the monitoring of internal states that require adjustments in control (Kerns et al., 2004), whereas the DL-PFC is an area associated with the active manipulation of information held in storage (i.e., working memory; Smith & Jonides, 1999). These divergent neural mechanisms suggest that men and women high on Openness may rely on different processes for their cognitive flexibility. Men may focus their attention on novel aspects of the environment, whereas women may take in more from their environment and then manipulate the information once encoded. Based on the neural findings, it would be interesting to test whether there are sex differences in the association between Openness and behavioral measures of attention and working memory.

The ancient Greeks ascribed personality traits to the four humors, each tied to a specific organ. As such, the biology of personality has long roots, but has yet to reach maturity. With improved noninvasive techniques and more cost-effective technologies, personality neuroscience is set to make rapid advances in identifying the responsible biological mechanisms. Grounding this research in the vast literature of the FFM will hasten its ascent.

Acknowledgment

Preparation of this chapter was supported entirely by the Intramural Research Program of the NIH, National Institute on Aging.

References

Barrick, M. R. & Mount, M. K. (1991). The Big 5 personality dimensions and job-performance: A meta-analysis. *Personnel Psychology, 44*, 1–26.

Beason-Held, L. L., Kraut, M. A., & Resnick, S. M. (2008). II. Temporal patterns of longitudinal change in aging brain function. *Neurobiology of Aging, 29*, 497–513.

Beer, J. S. & Lombardo, M. V. (2007). Patient and neuroimaging methodologies in the study of personality and social processes. In R. W. Robins, R. C. Fraley, & R. F. Krueger (Eds.), *Handbook of research methods in personality psychology* (pp. 360–369). New York: Guilford.

Berlin, H. A., Rolls, E. T., & Kischka, U. (2004). Impulsivity, time perception, emotion and reinforcement sensitivity in patients with orbitofrontal cortex lesions. *Brain, 127*, 1108–1126.

Blood, A. J. & Zatorre, R. J. (2001). Intensely pleasurable responses to music correlate with activity in brain regions implicated in reward and emotion. *Proceedings of the National Academy of Sciences of the United States of America, 98,* 11818–11823.

Bouchard, T. J. (1994). Genes, environment, and personality. *Science, 264,* 1700–1701.

Cahill, L. (2006). Why sex matters for neuroscience. *Nature Reviews Neuroscience, 7,* 477–484.

Canli, T., Sivers, H., Whitfield, S. L., Gotlib, I. H., & Gabrieli, J. D. E. (2002). Amygdala response to happy faces as a function of extraversion. *Science, 296,* 2191.

Carne, R. P., Vogrin, S., Litewka, L., & Cook, M. J. (2006). Cerebral cortex: An MRI-based study of volume and variance with age and sex. *Journal of Clinical Neuroscience, 13,* 60–72.

Cloninger, C. R., Svrakic, D. M., & Przybeck, T. R. (1993). A psychobiological model of temperament and character. *Archives of General Psychiatry, 50,* 975–990.

Cosgrove, K. P., Mazure, C. M., & Staley, J. K. (2007). Evolving knowledge of sex differences in brain structure, function, and chemistry. *Biological Psychiatry, 62,* 847–855.

Costa, P. T., Jr. & McCrae, R. R. (1980). Influence of extraversion and neuroticism on subjective well-being: Happy and unhappy people. *Journal of Personality and Social Psychology, 38,* 668–678.

Costa, P. T., Jr. & McCrae, R. R. (1992). *Revised NEO Personality Inventory (NEO-PI-R) and the NEO Five-Factor Inventory (NEO-FFI) professional manual.* Odessa, FL: Psychological Assessment Resources.

Costa, P. T., Jr. & McCrae, R. R. (2000). A theoretical context for adult temperament. In T. D. Wachs & G. A. Kohnstamm (Eds.), *Temperament in context* (pp. 1–21). Hillsdale: Erlbaum.

Costa, P. T., Jr. & McCrae, R. R. (in press). Contemporary personality psychology. In C. E. Coffey & J. L. Cummings (Eds.), *Textbook of geriatric neuropsychiatry* (3rd ed.). Washington, DC: American Psychiatric Press.

Costa, P. T., Jr., Terracciano, A., & McCrae, R. R. (2001). Gender differences in personality traits across cultures: Robust and surprising findings. *Journal of Personality and Social Psychology, 81,* 322–331.

Deckersbach, T., Miller, K. K., Klibanski, A., Fischman, A., Dougherty, D. D., Blais, M. A., et al. (2006). Regional cerebral brain metabolism correlates of neuroticism and extraversion. *Depression and Anxiety, 23,* 133–138.

Devlin, J. T. & Poldrack, R. A. (2007). In praise of tedious anatomy. *NeuroImage, 37,* 1033–1041.

DeYoung, C. G., Peterson, J. B., & Higgins, D. M. (2005). Sources of Openness/Intellect: Cognitive and neuropsychological correlates of the fifth factor of personality. *Journal of Personality, 73,* 825–858.

Dunn, R. T., Kimbrell, T. A., Ketter, T. A., Frye, M. A., Willis, M. W., Luckenbaugh, D. A., et al. (2002). Principal components of the beck depression inventory and regional cerebral metabolism in unipolar and bipolar depression. *Biological Psychiatry, 51,* 387–399.

Ekehammar, B. & Akrami, N. (2007). Personality and prejudice: From big five personality factors to facets. *Journal of Personality, 75,* 899–926.

Evans, D. E. & Rothbart, M. K. (2007). Developing a model for adult temperament. *Journal of Research in Personality, 41,* 868–888.

Eysenck, H. J. (1967). *The biological basis of personality.* Springfield: Thomas.

Funder, D. C., Kolar, D. C., & Blackman, M. C. (1995). Agreement among judges of personality: Interpersonal relations, similarity, and acquaintanceship. *Journal of Personality and Social Psychology, 69,* 656–672.

Gray, J. A. (1981). A critique of Eysenck's theory of personality. In H. J. Eysenck (Ed.), *A model for personality.* Berlin: Springer-Verlag.

Gur, R. C., Mozley, L. H., Mozley, P. D., Resnick, S. M., Karp, J. S., Alavi, A., et al. (1995). Sex differences in regional cerebral glucose metabolism during a resting state. *Science, 267,* 528–531.

Haas, B. W., Constable, R. T., & Canli, T. (2008). Stop the sadness: Neuroticism is associated with sustained medial prefrontal cortex response to emotional facial expressions. *NeuroImage, 42,* 385–392.

Hakamata, Y., Iwase, M., Iwata, H., Kobayashi, T., Tamaki, T., Nishio, M., et al. (2006). Regional brain cerebral glucose metabolism and temperament: A positron emission tomography study. *Neuroscience Letters, 396,* 33–37.

Jang, K. L., McCrae, R. R., Livesley, W. J., Angleitner, A., & Riemann, R. (1998). Heritability of facet-level traits in a cross-cultural twin sample: Support for a hierarchical model of personality. *Journal of Personality and Social Psychology, 74,* 1556–1565.

John, O. P., Naumann, L. P., & Soto, C. J. (2008). Paradigm shift to the integrative Big Five trait taxonomy: History, measurement, and conceptual issues. In O. P. John, R. W. Robins & L. A. Pervin (Eds.), *Handbook of personality: Theory and research* (3rd ed., pp. 114–158). New York: Guilford.

Kendler, K. S., Neale, M. C., Kessler, R. C., Heath, A. C., & Eaves, L. J. (1993). The lifetime history of major depression in women: Reliability of diagnosis and heritability. *Archives of General Psychiatry, 50,* 863–870.

Kerns, J. G., Cohen, J. D., MacDonald Iii, A. W., Cho, R. Y., Stenger, V. A., & Carter, C. S. (2004). Anterior cingulate conflict monitoring and adjustments in control. *Science, 303,* 1023–1026.

Kim, S. H., Hwang, J. H., Park, H. S., & Kim, S. E. (2008). Resting brain metabolic correlates of neuroticism and extraversion in young men. *NeuroReport, 19,* 883–886.

Larson, R. J. & Ketelaar, T. (1991). Personality and susceptibility to positive and negative emotional states. *Journal of Personality and Social Psychology, 61,* 132–140.

MacDonald, A. W., Cohen, J. D., Stenger, V. A., & Carter, C. S. (2000). Dissociating the role of the dorsolateral prefrontal and anterior cingulate cortex in cognitive control. *Science, 288,* 1835–1838.

Malaspina, D., Harkavy-Friedman, J., Corcoran, C., Mujica-Parodi, L., Printz, D., Gorman, J. M., et al. (2004). Resting neural activity distinguishes subgroups of schizophrenia patients. *Biological Psychiatry, 56,* 931–937.

McCrae, R. R. (2007). Aesthetic chills as a universal marker of openness to experience. *Motivation and Emotion, 31,* 5–11.

McCrae, R. R., Costa Jr, P. T., Martin, T. A., Oryol, V. E., Rukavishnikov, A. A., Senin, I. G., et al. (2004). Consensual validation of personality traits across cultures. *Journal of Research in Personality, 38,* 179–201.

McCrae, R. R., Costa Jr, P. T., Pedroso de Lima, M., Simões, A., Ostendorf, F., Angleitner, A., et al. (1999). Age differences in personality across the adult life span: Parallels in five cultures. *Developmental Psychology, 35,* 466–477.

McCrae, R. R. & Costa, P. T. (2008). The Five-Factor Theory of personality. In O. P. John, R. W. Robins & L. A. Pervin

(Eds.), *Handbook of personality: Theory and research* (3rd ed.). New York: Guilford Press.

McCrae, R. R. & John, O. P. (1992). An introduction to the five-factor model and its applications. *Journal of Personality*, *60*, 175–215.

McCrae, R. R., Terracciano, A., & 78 Members of the Personality Profiles of Cultures Project. (2005). Universal features of personality traits from the observer's perspective: Data from 50 cultures. *Journal of Personality and Social Psychology*, *88*, 547–561.

Noftle, E. E. & Robins, R. W. (2007). Personality predictors of academic outcomes: Big Five correlates of GPA and SAT Scores. *Journal of Personality and Social Psychology*, *93*, 116–130.

Ozer, D. J. & Benet-Martínez, V. (2006). Personality and the prediction of consequential outcomes. *Annual Review of Psychology*, *57*, 401–421.

Paris, J. (2005). Neurobiological dimensional models of personality: A review of the models of Cloninger, Depue, and Siever. *Journal of Personality Disorders*, *19*, 156–170.

Petrides, M. (2007). The orbitofrontal cortex: Novelty, deviation from expectation, and memory, *Annals of the New York Academy of Sciences* (Vol. 1121, pp. 33–53).

Riemann, R., Angleitner, A., & Strelau, J. (1997). Genetic and environmental influences on personality: A study of twins reared together using the self- and peer report NEO-FFI scales. *Journal of Personality*, *65*, 449–475.

Smith, E. E. & Jonides, J. (1999). Storage and executive processes in the frontal lobes. *Science*, *283*, 1657–1661.

Sutin, A. R., Beason-Held, L. L., Resnick, S. M., & Costa, P. T. (2009). Sex differences in the resting-state neural correlates of Openness to Experience among older adults. *Cerebral Cortex*.

Terracciano, A., Balaci, L., Thayer, J., Scally, M., Kokinos, S., Ferrucci, L., et al. (2009). Variants of the serotonin transporter gene and NEO-PI-R Neuroticism: No association in the BLSA and SardiNIA samples. *American Journal of Medical Genetics Part B: Neuropsychiatric Genetics*.

Terracciano, A., Costa Jr, P. T., & McCrae, R. R. (2006). Personality plasticity after age 30. *Personality and Social Psychology Bulletin*, *32*, 999–1009.

Terracciano, A., Löckenhoff, C. E., Crum, R. M., Bienvenu, O. J., & Costa Jr, P. T. (2008). Five-factor model personality profiles of drug users. *BMC Psychiatry*, *8*.

Terracciano, A., Löckenhoff, C. E., Zonderman, A. B., Ferrucci, L., & Costa Jr, P. T. (2008). Personality predictors of longevity: Activity, emotional stability, and conscientiousness. *Psychosomatic Medicine*, *70*, 621–627.

Viskontas, I. V., Possin, K. L., & Miller, B. L. (2007). Symptoms of frontotemporal dementia provide insights into orbitofrontal cortex function and social behavior, *Annals of the New York Academy of Sciences* (Vol. 1121, pp. 528–545).

Willer, C. J., Speliotes, E. K., Loos, R. J. F., Li, S., Lindgren, C. M., Heid, I. M., et al. (2009). Six new loci associated with body mass index highlight a neuronal influence on body weight regulation. *Nature Genetics*, *41*, 25–34.

Williams, L. M., Gatt, J. M., Kuan, S. A., Dobson-Stone, C., Palmer, D. M., Paul, R. H., et al. (2009). A polymorphism of the MAOA gene is associated with emotional brain markers and personality traits on an antisocial Index. *Neuropsychopharmacology*.

Emotion Recognition

Ralph Adolphs *and* Vanessa Janowski

Abstract

The ability to infer other people's emotional states is a hallmark of human social behavior. Emotion recognition plays a crucial role in our social lives not only because it enables us to understand and predict other people's actions, but also because it provides us with a mirror of their evaluations of us. This chapter begins with an overview of emotion recognition with a focus on vision. It then provides an update on recognizing emotion from facial expressions, the largest topic in the literature. It concludes with a summary of visual emotion recognition from cues other than facial expressions, and ends with brief speculations on how emotion recognition may be changing in light of electronic media and the Internet, a topic ripe for further investigation.

Keywords: emotion recognition, amygdala, patient SM, insula, body posture, basic emotions, fear recognition, facial expression, bubbles method

Introduction

The ability to infer other people's emotional states is hallmark of human social behavior. Emotion recognition plays a crucial role in our social lives not only because it enables us to understand and predict other people's actions, but also because it provides us with a mirror of their evaluations of ourselves. Here we provide two ingredients: First, we provide an overview of emotion recognition with a focus on vision; second, we provide an update on recognizing emotion from facial expressions, the largest topic in the literature (Adolphs, 2002; Heberlein & Adolphs, 2007; Atkinson & Adolphs, 2005). We conclude with a summary of visual emotion recognition from cues other than facial expressions, and end with brief speculations on how emotion recognition may be changing in light of electronic media and the Internet, a topic ripe for further investigation.

Before beginning our review, we summarize briefly what we mean by "emotion recognition." The term has generally been applied to judging how people feel from observations of their actions and other bodily signals, such as tone of voice, body posture, and facial expression. The emotions that have been investigated the most intensely have focused on those that can be recognized the most reliably from facial expressions—the so-called "basic" emotions of happiness, surprise, fear, anger, disgust, and sadness (contempt is also sometimes added) (Ekman, 1973). In large part this is due to the ease of constructing stimuli (pictures of facial expressions) to investigate this topic; yet it is patently apparent that more complex emotions, such as the social emotions (guilt, shame, pride, jealousy, etc.) play equally (or more) important roles in everyday life, and like basic emotions they can be recognized (although less reliably so from the face alone). We therefore emphasize the recognition of basic emotions in this review. This is the aspect of emotion recognition representing the bulk of research and about which the most is known regarding neurological underpinnings.

A second important clarification concerns the term "recognition." Unlike what colloquial usage might suggest, we do not recognize emotions simply by reading them off the faces we look at. Instead, a substantial amount of inference and attribution is required, and this is context-dependent. The simplest view of information processing outlines a serial flow from initial perception of informative stimuli (such as perception of facial features and their configuration), to association of these with their emotional and social meaning (a set of inferential processes that reflect diverse abilities including associations, inferential reasoning, and empathic simulation). Of course, things are more complicated than that: Emotion recognition unfolds over time, and initial perception and attention to salient features in a face will be influenced by context and recognition.

Emotion recognition, then, is the collection of processes by which we attempt to reconstruct the internal emotional state of another person from whatever cues we have available—their facial expression, their tone of voice, their actions, and additional contextual and historical information. There is a final aspect of emotion recognition that needs to be emphasized at the outset: it is active. We often probe people in order to evoke responses that can tell us how they feel. This ranges from merely glancing at them and registering their response to overtly asking them how they feel. As yet, there is little neuroscience research that takes this reciprocity into account, but it is a direction of paramount importance for the future.

Emotion recognition from Facial Expressions
Recognition of Identity and Emotion
Faces are perhaps the most viewed item in our lives, and they are a special object to which we preferentially direct our attention even as infants (Johnson, 2005). We can glean many different kinds of information from faces, including identity, gender, age, emotion, and more complex social attributes. Two processes that have received the most neuroscientific attention are the recognition of identity and emotion. The former, identifying the static configuration of faces (although there is recent work also investigating how faces change slowly over time; see

Preminger et al., 2009), is thought to rely primarily on the fusiform gyrus, lateral inferior occipital gyrus, and superior temporal gyrus, while the latter, involving the processing of dynamic changes in faces, relies on the superior temporal gyrus and sulcus (Haxby, Hoffman, & Gobbini, 2000; Puce, Allison, McCarthy, 1999; Allison, Puce, McCarthy, 2000;) as well as right somatosensory cortices, including the insula and supramarginal gyrus (Adolphs, Damasio, Tranel, Cooper, & Damasio, 2000).

The evidence for separate processes in the case of identity and emotion lies in different brain regions being necessary to process face identity or emotion, evidence for which has been found in lesion studies (Adolphs, Tranel, Damasio, & Damasio, 1994; Calder, Keane, Manes, Antoun, & Young, 2000; Tranel, Damasio, & Damasio, 1988). However, there are several difficulties with this view. First, the evidence is not all that compelling upon closer scrutiny; for instance, emotion recognition and identity recognition tasks have not generally been matched with respect to difficulty. Other models have argued that the processes underlying the recognition of identity and emotion are not entirely independent but based on shared representations (Calder & Young, 2005). There is neurobiological evidence supporting this idea from both neuroimaging (Ganel et al., 2005) and electrophysiological data. For instance, we have found evidence that both emotion and identity information are encoded early in the ventral temporal cortex, whereas lateral and superior temporal cortex encodes information about emotional expression at later latencies (Tsuchiya et al., 2008). However, both of these studies in humans leave open the likely possibility that individual neurons within these cortical regions are disproportionately specialized to process identity or emotion, an issue that could not be resolved in the prior studies.

Cortical Processing of Faces
More broadly, the fusiform gyrus and surrounding cortex, which has come to be called the fusiform face area, is relatively more active when viewing faces than any other kind of stimulus (Kanwisher, 2000; Kanwisher, McDermott, Chun, 1997), though it has also be shown to be active in subordinate-level categorization not necessarily involving faces (for example, when categorizing a leopard as a mammal) (Tarr & Gauthier, 2000), a finding that continues to fuel a debate about the domain-specificity of face processing. The orbitofrontal cortex, in particular on the right side, has also been shown to play a role

in the recognition of emotions from both faces and voices (Hornak, Rolls, & Wade, 1996). It appears to be more active when identifying a particular emotion as opposed to simply passively viewing it, whereas the converse appears to be true for the amygdala (Hariri, Mattay, Tessitore, Fera, & Weinberger, 2003). These findings from humans are complemented by studies in monkeys at the single-cell level. It has been known for some time that there are neurons in the inferotemporal cortex of monkeys (in regions homologous to those of the fusiform face area in humans) with responses remarkably selective for complex objects (Tanaka, 2003), faces (Gross, Rocha-Miranda, & Bender, 1972) and even very specific orientations and aspects of faces (Perrett, Mistlin, & Chitty, 1987). There have also been reports of some segregation of neurons with responses tuned more to emotional expression in a face, and others with responses tuned more to identity of the face (Hasselmo, Rolls, & Baylis, 1989). More recent studies have found a network of patches of cortical regions in the temporal (Tsao, Freiwald, Tootell, & Livingstone, 2006) and frontal (Tsao et al., 2008) cortex in the macaque that contain neurons with a very high selectivity for faces. These face patches are connected in specific ways that are beginning to give us an overview of the information flow of face processing (Moeller, Freiwald, & Tsao, 2008). Similarly, very high response specificity to complex objects, including the identity of specific faces, has been found in single-unit recording in the human temporal lobe; moreover, these responses can encode high-level abstract categories that show considerable invariance from the actual stimuli themselves (Kreiman et al., 2000).

These brain structures—the amygdala, fusiform, superior temporal, and orbitofrontal cortices—interact for more detailed processing of emotions in faces (Figure 16.3). For instance, the orbitofrontal cortex provides feedback to the amygdala that is thought to provide contextual modulation, and the amygdala modulates the processing of emotional faces in posterior cortical regions. Vuilleumier et al. (2004) found evidence that the amygdala enhances processing in visual cortices as well as the fusiform face area when looking at fearful faces compared to neutral faces. It is likely that these aspects of connectivity contribute substantially to individual differences in emotion recognition in the healthy population, and that they also contribute to alterations in emotion processing in neuropsychiatric illness. Considerable interest in this regard has been focused on the connectivity between medial

prefrontal cortices and the amygdala. For instance, this connectivity, both structurally and functionally, has been linked to genetic polymorphisms in serotonin neurotransmission that are known to underlie risk of psychopathology (Pezawas et al., 2005).

One current puzzle concerns whether and to what extent brain regions might be specialized for processing specific emotions, rather than emotion in general. There is the strongest evidence in regard to the emotions of disgust and fear, which have been linked to the insula and the amygdala, respectively. While there are some data regarding specific brain regions in processing specific emotions (such as depression, happiness, or anxiety), there is little consistent data regarding anatomical specificity in particular for emotion recognition. In fact, this is debated even for structures such as the amygdala, for which fMRI studies have shown that there is not a clear-cut pattern for any emotion (Fitzgerald, Angstadt, Jelsone, Nathan, & Phan, 2006). Another fruitful approach to emotion recognition may be to ask which particular strategies might underlie the recognition of certain emotions, or which specific facial features carry diagnostic information. With respect to the former question, it is important to note that simply asking subjects to recognize different emotions (typically by matching to a list of the words for the emotions) confounds emotion recognition with various aspects of task difficulty (some emotions are more familiar than others, some more confusable than others, some recognized at a more subordinate level of categorization than others, and so on). For instance, asking subjects to recognize happiness in facial expressions typically produces accuracy rates near 100% for two simple reasons: All these faces carry a single uniquely diagnostic feature, the smile, and they also are recognized at a more superordinate category level ("happiness") than the many different negative emotions ("unhappiness"); see Adolphs (2002) for a review.

With respect to the second issue, the particular facial features, this has been analyzed recently in some detail using a novel method called "bubbles" (Gosselin & Schyns, 2001). This technique randomly samples small parts of a face to show to subjects as stimuli (Figure 16.1A). On each trial, the participant is asked to make an emotion discrimination (e.g., between fear and happiness), and the accuracy on each trial is regressed onto the location of the regions of the face that were shown in the stimuli. From this regression, across many trials, one can extract a statistical map of which regions of the face were reliably correlated with accurate emotion discrimination, revealing the features within faces that viewers used to identify the different emotions (Figure 16.1B). Fear recognition has been shown to be impaired in patients with amygdala damage (Adolphs, Tranel, Damasio, & Damasio, 1994). However, as with the functional imaging studies implicating the amygdala in fear recognition, there are numerous exceptions to this finding, many of which may reflect alternative strategies on relatively unconstrained tasks or individual differences in such strategies. Recent studies have argued that the amygdala serves a more abstract and instrumental role in seeking out potentially important information, a role that may not be at all specific to social or emotional information but instead contributes more broadly to allocating processing resources when there is ambiguity (Hsu, Bhatt, Adolphs, Tranel, & Camerer, 2005; Whalen, 2007), when vigilance is required (Whalen, 1999), or when the environment is unpredictable (Herry et al., 2007). With respect to processing facial expressions of fear, one recent story that ties these diverse threads together came from a study in which emotion recognition was combined with eye tracking. In that study (Adolphs et al., 2005), a patient with bilateral amygdala lesions was found to be impaired in recognizing emotional facial expressions of fear because she failed to direct her gaze and visual attention to the eye region of faces—which are normally the most important in order to recognize fear.

However, when this patient was explicitly directed to look at the eyes, her impairment in recognizing fear on the experimental task disappeared (Figure 16.2). Thus, perhaps the amygdala is involved not only in the emotional responses to faces, but also in guiding attention and gaze to emotionally salient regions of the face, biasing cognition depending on the relative social and emotional valence. Further lending support to this hypothesis is another study that has shown that the amygdala response to emotional faces is modulated by eye gaze (Adams, Gordon, Baird, Ambady, & Kleck, 2003), as well as by evidence that the amygdala is recruited in the modulation of visual attention by emotional stimuli (Anderson & Phelps, 2001).

CONSCIOUS AND NON-CONSCIOUS PROCESSING OF FACES

The amygdala's role in processing emotion from faces, revealed in the above study, has been supported by a number of other studies. For instance, it is activated by viewing just the eyes from faces, and more activated when viewing eyes in fearful faces, even under conditions of subliminal presentation (Whalen et al., 2004). In fact, this aspect of face processing has the best evidence for being privileged and rapid. When the "bubbles" method was used in combination with EEG measures, it was found that the N170, a well-documented electrophysiological signature of initial face processing, was driven in its

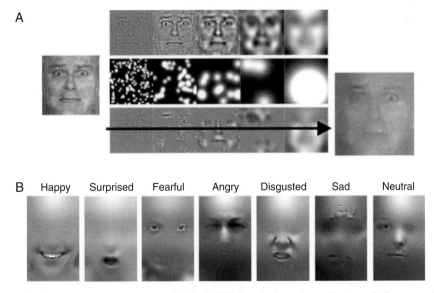

Fig. 16.1 Facial features used to recognize emotions. (A) The "bubbles" method samples small regions of a face space, often within different spatial frequency bands, to produce a sparse face stimulus (bottom right). From this task, classification images are calculated that show the regions within faces within which there was a statistically significant association between viewers' ability to discriminate a particular emotion from all the others (B).

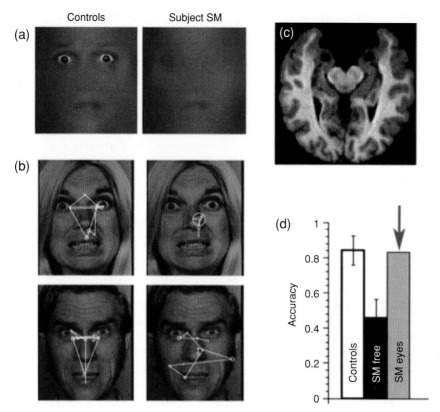

Fig. 16.2 Bilateral amygdala lesions impair the use of the eyes and gaze to the eyes during emotion judgment. Data are from patient SM, who has complete bilateral amygdala lesions and is impaired in recognizing fear. Using sparsely revealed faces to identify face areas used during emotion judgment, patient SM (brain shown in c) differed from controls such that controls exhibited much greater use of the eyes than SM, while SM did not rely more on any area of the face than did controls (a). While looking at whole faces, SM exhibited abnormal face gaze (b), making far fewer fixations to the eyes than did controls. When SM was instructed to look at the eyes (d, "SM eyes") in a whole face, she could do this, resulting in a remarkable recovery in ability to recognize the facial expression of fear compared to her accuracy prior to this instruction (d, "SM free").
Modified from Adolphs (2008) with permission of Elsevier.

earliest components by the eye region of faces, with a subsequent sweep of inputs triggered by lower regions of the face (Schyns, Petro, & Smith, 2007). The eyes within faces are also the feature that most rapidly overcomes interocular suppression in experiments using continuous flash suppression. In these studies, a flashing checkerboard pattern is shown into one eye, while a static face stimulus is shown to the other eye; the conscious percept is initially only of the flashing checkerboard, which completely suppresses perception of the face. However, after some time, or with experimental changes in contrast, the face begins to peek through into consciousness: In this case, the eyes become visible first (Yang, Zald, & Blake, 2007). The amygdala has been linked to such experiments as well, as it is activated by facial expressions of fear under conditions of continuous flash suppression. Indeed, the fMRI signal in the amygdala looks equivalent whether in response

to conscious (non-suppressed) faces or to invisible faces suppressed with continuous flash suppression (Jiang & He, 2006).

Early visual processing occurs along two pathways, a subcortical pathway via the superior colliculus and pulvinar to the amygdala and a cortical route through the thalamus and striate cortices to the temporal cortex. The former pathway is thought to mediate rapid, coarse, and often non-conscious processing of highly salient stimuli, while the latter is a slower route subserving conscious object recognition (Johnson, 2005). This idea is supported by several findings. For example, some individuals with blindsight, in which individuals are blind due to damage to the primary visual cortex but remain able to respond to visual stimuli, are able to discriminate emotions in faces well above chance, even though these individuals do not have a conscious experience of seeing these faces (Morris, de Gelder,

Weiskrantz, & Dolan, 2001; de Gelder, Vroomen, Pourtois, Weiskrantz, 1999). This leads to the hypothesis that subcortical processing of emotional visual stimuli by the amygdala and brainstem nuclei may be separate from conscious vision (Johnson, 2005). Yet there are problems with this view as well: Visual response latencies in the amygdala are typically no shorter than in the visual cortex, the role of the amygdala in nonconscious processing continues to be debated, and there is no anatomical evidence for a direct and fast route of subcortical input to the amygdala (see Adolphs, 2008 for a review).

Much of the evidence for nonconscious and subcortical processing of emotional visual stimuli has come from studies with healthy subjects. Morris, Ohman, and Dolan (1999) used aversive conditioning for angry faces and reported that unconsciously viewed angry faces increased right amygdala activation, while consciously viewed angry faces increased left amygdala activation, and another study has shown facial reactions when faces were shown subliminally (Dimberg, Thunberg, & Elmehed, 2000). However, Phillips et al. (2004) did not find any significant amygdala activation to unconsciously presented angry facial stimuli. Rogowska and Yurgelun-Todd (2009) showed gender differences during unconsciously presented fearful faces. While both males and females activated the right amygdala, females had stronger brain activation for affectively negative pictures was in the cingulate, a region known to mediate affective response, and in the fusiform gyrus, an area associated with face recognition. These results suggest that it is also important to take gender differences into account when emotional paradigms are used in functional brain imaging and in interpreting responses to affective stimuli.

Thus, the evidence in favor of the subcortical pathway to the amygdala being responsible for unconscious emotion perception has not been entirely clear-cut. Several researchers suggested that the amygdala activation found in some studies might be due to the amygdala's involvement in processing through the cortical route (Pessoa, Kastner, & Ungerleider, 2002; Rolls, 1999), or simply due to subjects reporting they did not see a stimulus when in fact they had. To address this, several more recent studies have used binocular rivalry to more effectively control for the visual stimulus shown and found that the left amygdala, though not the inferotemporal cortex, was more active when unconsciously viewing suppressed fearful faces than

non-face objects (Pasley, Mayes, & Schultz, 2004), and another study using the same technique found increased amygdala activation to both fearful and happy faces compared to neutral faces, though when the faces were consciously viewed, only the right amygdala was significantly more active (Williams et al., 2004). All these findings do argue that the amygdala may play a role in privileged processing of especially salient features, such as the eyes. However, it is also consistent with the idea that the primary input to the amygdala, and likely the target of its modulating output, is cortex rather than subcortical nuclei.

THE INSULA, SOMATOSENSORY CORTICES, AND SIMULATION

The insula, involved in processing interoceptive information and intimately connected with the amygdala, has been shown to be important in recognizing disgust, much like the amygdala has been associated with fear (Calder, Lawrence, & Young, 2001). Patients with damage to the insula, basal ganglia, or with Huntington's disease have been shown to be impaired in the recognition of disgust (Calder et al., 2000; Calder, Lawrence, & Young, 2001; Sprengelmeyer et al., 1996), and the ability to feel disgust has also been shown to be impaired in patients with left insula and basal ganglia damage (Calder et al., 2001; Adolphs, Tranel, & Damasio, 2002). As with the amygdala and fear, however, this association is not absolute—some patients with damage to these areas remain able to recognize disgust, and questions remain regarding the precise selectivity of these areas. For example, in the study done by Calder and colleagues (Calder et al., 2000), a patient with left insula and basal ganglia damage was impaired in recognizing disgust from facial as well as auditory stimuli, though he was able to distinguish disgusting photographs as such. In another study, a patient with bilateral insula damage but no basal ganglia damage was impaired in recognition of disgust from stimuli (Adolphs, Tranel, & Damasio, 2003).

There is some evidence for disproportionate involvement of certain brain structures in the recognition of anger as well. Impairment in the recognition of anger in faces has been in turn shown in people with damage to the ventral striatum (Calder et al., 2004) and has been variably linked to the amygdala and regions of the prefrontal cortex (Harmer, Thilo, Rothwell, & Goodwin, 2001; Hornak et al., 1996). Finally, there are also individual differences as well as effects of gender in emotion recognition (Wager, Phan, Liberzon, & Taylor, 2003).

What is the mechanism by which the above structures participate in emotion recognition? As we noted in the introduction, many different strategies come into play in recognizing emotions; often these differ between the tasks used in different studies, and they may also differ as a consequence of individual differences in emotion recognition ability. We would like to highlight two different mechanisms, which can be tied to the amygdala and the insula, respectively: an instrumental role in guiding attention and modulating visual cortex function, and an empathic role in which emotional responses evoked in the viewer contribute to emotion recognition through

simulation. The first mechanism was outlined above and is illustrated in the data shown in Figure 16.2. The second mechanism has received much recent attention from cognitive neuroscientists (and prior to that from psychologists (Chartrand & Bargh, 1999) and philosophers (Goldman & Sripada, 2005)). Emotions motivate behavior, and thus simulating other people's emotions provides us with one strategy for predicting what they are likely to do. A complementary strategy is to simulate aspects of the premotor representations that would normally accompany goal-directed behavior, a mechanism supported by finding representations, at the systems and cellular level (Gallese et al., 2004; Rizzolatti & Craighero, 2004), that are engaged

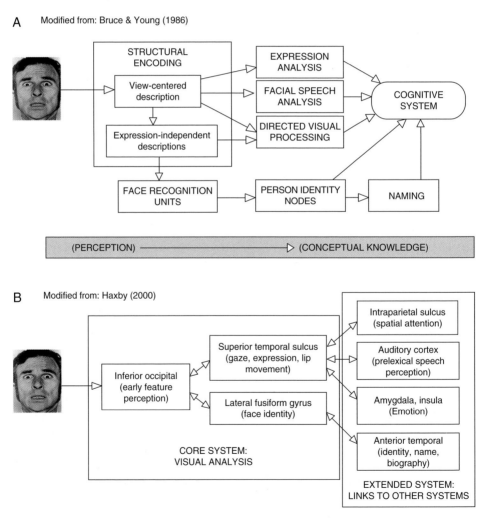

Fig. 16.3 Processing of emotion in faces. (A) A model of emotional face processing modified from Bruce and Young (1986) indicates separate processes underlying emotion and identity recognition in faces, and emphasizes the computational aspects of the processes involved in naming specific types of information. (B) A model of face processing from Haxby (2000) emphasizes the neuroanatomical aspects, separating into the perceptual processing of emotions in the superior temporal gyrus and identity in the fusiform gyrus, and shows the two-way interactions between areas involved in specific functions.

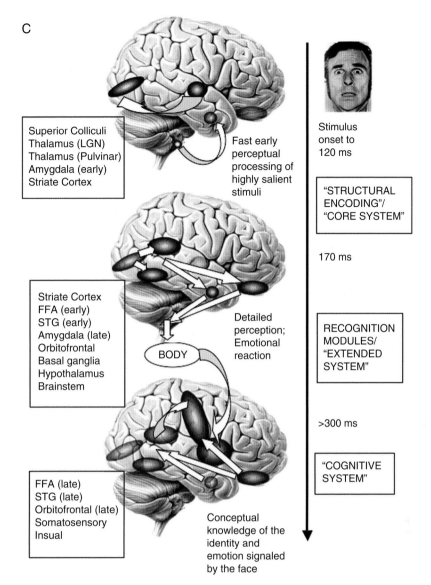

C

Superior Colliculi
Thalamus (LGN)
Thalamus (Pulvinar)
Amygdala (early)
Striate Cortex

Fast early
perceptual
processing of
highly salient
stimuli

Stimulus
onset to
120 ms

"STRUCTURAL
ENCODING"/
"CORE SYSTEM"

170 ms

Striate Cortex
FFA (early)
STG (early)
Amygdala (late)
Orbitofrontal
Basal ganglia
Hypothalamus
Brainstem

BODY

Detailed
perception;
Emotional
reaction

RECOGNITION
MODULES/
"EXTENDED
SYSTEM"

>300 ms

FFA (late)
STG (late)
Orbitofrontal (late)
Somatosensory
Insual

"COGNITIVE
SYSTEM"

Conceptual
knowledge of the
identity and
emotion signaled
by the face

Fig. 16.3 (Continued) (C) The processing of emotional facial expressions involves different regions at particular points in time relative to a stimulus onset. While the same brain structures may be involved in diverse aspects of processing at various points in time, studies involving electrocorticogram recordings have provided better temporal and spatial resolution. Reproduced from Adolphs (2002) *Behav Cognit Neurosci Rev*.

both when we plan to execute an action ourselves and when we observe another person carry out the same action. Moreover, these "mirror" representations are at the high level of goal-oriented intentional action, as they can abstract from the particulars of any specific perceptual input (Fogassi et al., 2005). Together, our ability to simulate motivational and premotor representations of other people has been hypothesized to ground our ability to know about other minds (Gallese, 2007), although deliberative reasoning no doubt also plays a role. It is also interesting to note that monkeys have mirror neurons,

but do not imitate or appear to know about other minds, indicating that additional enabling mechanisms, possibly including enculturation, are required for mere mirroring at the neural level to generate knowledge of other minds (Iriki, 2006). While it has historically sometimes been seen as distinct from simulation, "theory of mind" ability, broadly construed, is aimed at this single goal: to understand the internal states that predict the behavior of other people.

How does this simulation strategy relate to the insula? The idea is that the insula represents internal bodily states in ourselves, and can therefore also represent vicariously the inferred bodily states in other people (Craig, 2008). The insula is activated by a large array of interoception-based emotional states, not only disgust. It is activated in anger, in pain, as well as in pleasurable emotional states (Craig, 2002). The strongest evidence for its role in simulation mechanisms such as those described above comes from two findings. First, as alluded to earlier, patients with insula lesions can have parallel impairments both in feeling disgust themselves as well as in recognizing it in others. Secondly, the insula is activated when we observe disgusted facial expressions in others, and this is a region within the insula that overlaps with our own experience of disgust (Wicker et al., 2003). It is also activated when we empathize with another person's pain (Singer et al., 2004). An intriguing finding has been obtained also for recognition of sadness. For example, one's perception of sadness in faces is increased with constricted pupils, which in turn activate an empathic pupillary response in the viewer and activate the insula (Harrison, Singer, Rothstein, Dolan, & Critchley, 2006; Demos, Kelley, Ryan, Davis, & Whalen, 2008).

A similar role can be assigned to other somatosensory cortices: They could serve to construct a representation of the presumptive somatic state of the observed other person that forms the basis for their emotional experience. In one study (Adolphs et al., 2000), we found that lesions of the right somatosensory cortex impaired the visual recognition of facial emotion across several negatively valenced emotions (it remains unclear if the differential impairment of certain emotions in that study reflects genuine emotion specificity or results from some other factor, such as the differential difficulty recognizing certain emotions in the task). That the somatosensory cortex on the right side was involved more than the left may be related to aspects of lateralized processing of emotion (which is complex and still incompletely understood), such as that the left side of the face is on average more expressive, or expressive earlier, than the right due to differential neural control (Borod et al., 1998). This lesion study is supported by a study that used transcranial magnetic stimulation (TMS) to transiently inactivate the right somatosensory cortex (Pourtois et al., 2004), as well as by an fMRI study showing activation in the right somatosensory cortex when viewing facial expressions of emotion (Winston et al., 2003). However, all these findings fall short of establishing a "mirror-neuron" correlate in humans to the one that has been found in monkeys, since the methods used cannot resolve responses at the level of single neurons.

There is a single finding to date of neuronal responses in humans suggesting a mirroring-like response for emotion empathy. This was a recording done in neurosurgical patients who had electrodes in the anterior cingulate cortex. A neuron was found that responded both to the administration of a painful stimulus to the subject, as well as to the observation of pain in another person (Hutchison, Davis, Lozano, Tasker, & Dostrovsky, 1999). The anterior cingulate cortex likely also participates in emotion recognition, although its role so far has been investigated most explicitly with respect to behavioral motivation and task monitoring.

The above mechanism of recognizing emotions through some sort of simulation, perhaps based on an empathic reaction in the viewer, is related to a very large literature on theory of mind, simulation, and empathy. Theory of mind, or the ability to attribute mental states to others and understand that they may have different beliefs, goals, and intentions from one's own, draws on the medial frontal cortex, inferior parietal cortex, as well as the temporoparietal junction and areas of the superior temporal sulcus. There is considerable experimental evidence for the idea that we are able to understand others and make inferences about their mental states by simulating those states in some way (Goldman & Sripada, 2005; Ames et al., 2008). Some studies have shown that this understanding is mediated by how similar we feel to the other person, an effect found in the medial prefrontal cortex (Mitchell et al., 2005; Mitchell et al., 2006). There is also evidence that the MFC may be further subdivided into the inferior MFC, activated when thinking about one's own emotions and beliefs as well as those of someone close to us, and the superior MFC, activated more when thinking about the mental states of unknown others (Amodio & Frith, 2006). This raises the likely possibility that while substrates for representing our own emotional states and those of other people draw on an overlapping set of neural regions, they are not identical—at a minimum, they must of course allow us to distinguish our own emotions from those of others, even if we use the former in part to figure out the latter.

Hein and Singer (2006) propose that there are in fact two different pathways to understanding another person's mind: 1) empathy and embodiment of another's emotions and 2) theory of mind, mentalizing, or cognitive perspective taking. They find that while brain regions activated by empathy include the ACC, somatosensory and insular cortices, and limbic areas; brain areas that are activated by theory of mind include the mediofrontal cortex (MFC), superior temporal sulcus (STS), temporo-parietal junction (TPJ) and temporal poles. In a lesion study, Samson et al. (2004) showed that the left TPJ, in addition to the frontal lobes, is necessary to reason about others' beliefs, a finding supported by evidence from Saxe and Kanwisher (2003) and Saxe and Powell (2006), who implicate the TPJ bilaterally. Yet there is debate regarding the conclusion that the TPJ is specific to theory-of-mind processing: It is engaged also in lower-level processing of agency and attentional mechanisms (Decety & Lamm, 2007), and recent data suggest a parcellation within the TPJ such that some sectors may be more specialized for processing theory-of-mind whereas others mediate exogenous attention (Scholz et al., 2009). There are thus several different aspects of "simulating" another person, some more based on emotional empathic responses, and some more strategic and less emotional; there are also aspects of simulation that may map onto emotional and cognitive empathy constructs (Preston & deWaal, 2002).

Other Visual Signals—Body Posture and Movement

While many of the emotion recognition studies to date deal with faces, there is also a growing body of literature on emotion recognition from other visual cues. We are able to recognize distinct expressions of the six basic emotions—happiness, sadness, fear, anger, surprise, and disgust—from static body postures (Atkinson et al., 2004) as well as by whole body movement (Atkinson et al., 2004, Dittrich et al., 1996). Thus far, such studies have identified several brain areas involved in emotion processing in body posture and movement—the amygdala, fusiform, and somatosensory cortices.

The amygdala appears to play a role in seeking out potentially salient social information not only in faces, but also in other visual signals in a social setting. In a study with macaques, the amygdala has been found to contain cells responsive to complex body movements (Brothers, Ring, & Kling, 1990). Similarly, de Gelder et al. (2004) found that looking at fearful body postures leads to increased activation in regions known to process emotions, including the amygdala, orbitofrontal cortex, posterior cingulate, anterior insula and nucleus accumbens, as well as areas related to the representation of action and movement. The authors hypothesize that viewing a fearful body thus causes the brain to prepare for action. Adolphs and Tranel (2003) showed that bilateral amygdala damage impairs the recognition

of negative emotions such as anger in static images of social scenes when both faces and bodies are included, but not when faces are obscured and subjects rely exclusively on body posture cues. Another study using point-light walkers found that patients with lesions to the right somatosensory cortex in particular were impaired in recognizing emotions (Heberlein et al., 2004), a result that corresponds to impairments in recognizing emotions from static facial expressions discussed earlier. These findings paint a somewhat more complex picture than was the case for emotion recognition from facial expressions. Just as we can recognize emotion from faces, we can do so with remarkable accuracy and speed from body movements, even in the absence of face information. But the neural substrates of this ability may be more distributed than is the case with faces. While several cortical regions and the amygdala are involved as evidenced by their activation in neuroimaging studies, it is not clear how necessary a role they play, since amygdala damage seems to spare recognition of emotion from body movements (Atkinson et al., 2007).

The STS has also been shown to play a role in gaze, facial movements, and other biological movements, both in humans and monkeys (Allison, Puce, & McCarthy, 2000), and lesions to the STS have been shown to impair judgments of gaze direction in monkeys. Similarly, the STS has been found to be preferentially activated both in monkeys and humans when observing meaningful hand gestures related to speech or perception of body movements (Allison, Puce, & McCarthy, 2000), and another study found that the STS may be important in the perception of emotional expressions (Narumoto et al., 2001).

Emotion Recognition in the Future

An intriguing extension of the above reviewed studies is into the age of the Internet, videoconferencing, email, and text messaging. The stimulus base for our social interactions and for inferring emotional states of other people has changed dramatically in the past decade. With respect to the neural substrates, there are two fundamental possibilities. One possibility is that recognizing emotion from more symbolic cues recruits the same set of brain structures as does emotion recognition from facial expressions and other biologically basic cues. One would certainly expect this to be the case for some stimuli, such as emoticons. One could also expect this to be the case for lexical stimuli (words, sentences), since we have had these for some time and it is clear from both psychological and neurobiological studies that they are quite capable of eliciting emotion processing with a potency that can approach that of direct images. The presumptive mechanism that underlies this ability likely draws on the efficacy with which these stimuli can trigger imagery depicting whatever the words describe, and such images can then be processed in the same way as visual stimuli would be. An alternative possibility is that words can bypass visual processing altogether and go straight to higher-order processing of the associated emotional meaning. These two alternatives raise some interesting predictions that could be tested. One would expect emotion recognition from sentences through the intermediate of imagery to involve the amygdala in directing attention to aspects of the images, or to their creation. On the other hand, if high-level meaning is derived from the sentences in the absence of imagery, the amygdala may play less of a role. In either case, simulation routines that rely on structures such as the insula would be predicted to come into play.

A second possibility is that emotion recognition in the age of the Internet is quite different in many respects from emotion recognition from real people. Some of these differences are patent; the question is if they force different neural processing. For instance, the real-time reciprocity that we noted in the introduction is generally omitted, or greatly slowed. In general, one would expect emotion recognition from indirect channels to be slower and be guided by more strategic, controlled processing.

References

Adams, R. B., Gordon, H. L., Baird, A. A., Ambady, N., & Kleck, R. E. (2003). Effects of gaze on amygdala sensitivity to anger and fear in faces. *Science, 300,* 1536.

Adolphs, R. (2002). Recognizing emotion from facial expressions: Psychological and neurological mechanisms. *Behav Cognit Neurosci Rev, 1,* 21–61.

Adolphs, R. (2006). Perception and emotion: How we recognize facial expressions. *Current Directions in Psychological Science, 15*(5).

Adolphs, R., Damasio, H., Tranel, D., Cooper, G., & Damasio, A. R. (2000). A role for somatosensory cortices in the visual recognition of emotion as revealed by 3-D lesion mapping. *The Journal of Neuroscience, 20,* 2683–2690.

Adolphs, R., Gosselin, F., Buchanan, T. W., Tranel, D., Schyns, P. G., & Damasio, A. (2005). A mechanism for impaired fear recognition after amygdala damage. *Nature, 433,* 68–72.

Adolphs, R., Tranel, D., & Damasio, H. (2002). Neural systems for recognizing emotion from prosody. *Emotion, 2,* 23–51.

Adolphs, R., Tranel, D., & Damasion, A. R. (2003). Dissociable neural systems for recognizing emotions. *Brain and Cognition, 52,* 61–69.

Adolphs, R., Tranel, D., Damasio, H., & Damasio, A. (1994). Impaired recognition of emotion in facial expressions following bilateral damage to the human amygdala. *Nature, 372,* 669–672.

Adolphs, R. (2002). Neural systems for recognizing emotion. *Current Opinion in Neurobiology, 12*(2), 169–177.

Adolphs, R. (2008). Fear, faces and the human amygdala. *Current Opinion in Neurobiology, 18,* 1–7.

Adolphs, R. & Tranel, D. (2003). Amygdala damage impairs emotion recognition from scenes only when they contain facial expressions. *Neuropsychologia, 41*(10), 1281–1289.

Adolphs, R., Tranel, D., & Baron-Cohen, S. (2002). Amygdala damage impairs recognition of social emotions from facial expressions. *Journal of Cognitive Neuroscience, 14,* 1264–1274.

Allison, T., Puce, A., & McCarthy, G. (2000). Social perception from visual cues: Role of the STS region. *Trends Cognit Sci, 4,* 267–278.

Ames, D., Jenkins, A., Mahzarin, R., & Mitchell, J. (2008). Taking another person's perspective increases self-referential neural processing. *Psychological Science, 19*(7).

Amodio, D. & Frith, C. Meeting of minds: The medial frontal cortex and social cognition. *Nature Reviews Neuroscience, 7.*

Anderson, A. K. & Phelps, E.A. (2001). Lesions of the human amygdala impair enhanced perception of emotionally salient events. *Nature, 411,* 305–309.

Atkinson, A. P., Dittrich, W. H., Gemmell, A. J., & Young, A. W. (2004). Emotion perception from dynamic and static body expressions in point-light and full-light displays. *Perception, 33,* 717–746.

Atkinson, A. P. & Adolphs, R. (2005). Visual emotion perception: Mechanisms and processes. In L. Feldman-Barrett, P. M. Niedenthal, & P. Winkielman (Eds.), *Emotion and consciousness,* New York: Guilford Press.

Atkinson, A. P., Heberlein, A. S., & Adolphs, R. (2007). Spared ability to recognize fear from static and moving whole-body cues following bilateral amygdala damage. *Neuropsychologia, 45,* 2772–2782.

Baron-Cohen, S., et al. (1995). Are children with autism blind to the mentalistic significance of the eyes? *Br. J. Dev. Psychol. 13,* 379–398.

Baron-Cohen, S., et al. (1999). Social intelligence in the normal and autistic brain: An fMRI study. *Eur. J. Neurosci., 11,* 1891–1898.

Baron-Cohen, S., Wheelwright, S., & Jolliffe, T. (1997). Is there are a "language of the eyes"? Evidence from normal adults and adults with autism or Asperger syndrome. *Visual Cognition, 4,* 311–332.

Borod, J. C., Koff, E., Yecker, S., Santschi, C., & Schmidt, J. (1998). Facial asymmetry during emotional expression: Gender, valence and measurement technique. *Psychophysiology, 36,* 1209–1215.

Brothers, L., Ring, B., & Kling, A. (1990). Response of neurons in the macaque amygdala to complex social stimuli. *Behav. Brain Res., 41,* 199–213.

Bruce, V. & Young, A. (1986). Understanding face recognition. *British Journal of Psychology, 77,* 305–327.

Calder, A. J., Lawrence, A. D., & Young, A. W. (2001). Neuropsychology of fear and loathing. *Nature Reviews Neuroscience, 2,* 352–363.

Calder, A. J., Keane, J., Manes, F., Antoun, N., & Young, A. W. (2000). Impaired recognition and experience of disgust following brain injury. *Nature Neuroscience, 3,* 1077–1078.

Calder, A. J., Keane, J., Lawrence, A.D., & Manes, F. (2004). Impaired recognition of anger following damage to the ventral striatum. *Brain, 127,* 1958–1969.

Calder, A. & Young, A. (2005). Understanding the recognition of facial identity and facial expression. *Nature Reviews Neuroscience*, 6, 641–651.

Chartrand, T. L. & Bargh, J. A. (1999). The chameleon effect: The perception-behavior link and social interaction. *Journal of Personality and Social Psychology*, 76(6), 893–910.

Craig, A. D. (2002). How do you feel? Interoception: The sense of the physiological condition of the body. *Nature Reviews Neuroscience*, 3, 655–666.

Craig, A. D. (2008). Interoception and emotion: A neuroanatomical perspective. In J. M. H.-J. M. Lewis & L. Feldman-Barrett (Eds.), *Handbook of emotions, 3rd Edition* (pp. 272–288). New York: Guilford Press.

de Gelder, B., Vroomen, J., Pourtois, G., & Weiskrantz, L. (1999). Non-conscious recognition of affect in the absence of striate cortex. *Neuroreport*, 10, 3759–3763.

de Gelder, B., Snyder, J., Greve, D., Gerard, G., & Hadjikhani, N. (2004). Fear fosters flight: A mechanism for fear contagion when perceiving emotion expressed by a whole body. *PNAS*, 101(47), 16701–16706.

Decety, J. & Lamm, C. (2007). The role of the right temporoparietal junction in social interaction: How low-level computational processes contribute to meta-cognition.

Demos, K. E., Kelley, W. M., Ryan, S. L., Davis, F. C., & Whalen, P. J. (2008). Human amygdala sensitivity to the pupil size of others. *Cerebral Cortex*, 18, 2729–2734.

Dimberg, U., Thunberg, M., & Elmehed, K. (2000). Unconscious facial reactions to emotional facial expressions. *Psychological Science*, 11, 86–89.

Dittrich, W. H., Troscianko, T., Lea, S. E. G., & Morgan, D. (1996). Perception of emotion from dynamic light-point displays represented in dance. *Perception*, 25, 727–738.

Ekman, P. (Ed.). (1973). *Darwin and facial expression: A century of research in review*. New York: Academic Press.

Fogassi, L., Ferrari, P. F., Gesierich, B., Rozzi, S., Chersi, F., & Rizzolatti, G. (2005). Parietal lobe: From action organization to intention understanding. *Science*, 308, 662–667.

Gallese, V. (2007). Before and below "theory of mind": Embodied simulation and the neural correlates of social cognition. *Philos Trans R Soc Lond B Biol Sci*, 362, 659–669.

Gallese, V., Keysers, C., & Rizzolatti, G. (2004). A unifying view of the basis of social cognition. *Trends Cogn Sci*, 8, 396–403.

Ganel, T., Valyear, K. F., Goshen-Gottstein, Y., & Goodale, M. A. (2005). The involvement of the "fusiform face area" in processing facial expression. *Neuropsychologia*, 43, 1645–1654.

Goldman, A. I. & Sripada, C. S. (2005). Simulationist models of face-based emotion recognition. *Cognition*, 94(3), 193–213.

Gosselin, F. & Schyns, P. G. (2001). Bubbles: A technique to reveal the use of information in recognition. *Vision Research*, 41, 2261–2271.

Gross, C. G., Rocha-Miranda, C. E., & Bender, D. B. (1972). Visual properties of neurons in inferotemporal cortex of the Macaque. *Journal of Neurophysiology*, 35, 96–111.

Fitzgerland, D. A., Angstadt, M., Jelsone, L., Nathan, P. J., & Phan, K. L. (2006). Beyond threat: Amygdala reactivity across multiple expressions of facial affect. *Neuroimage*, 30, 1441–1448.

Hariri, A. R., Mattay, V. S., Tessitore, A., Fera, F., & Weinberger, D. R. (2003). Neocortical modulation of the amygdala response to fearful stimuli. *Biological Psychiatry*, 53, 494–501.

Harmer, C. J., Thilo, K. V., Rothwell, J. C., & Goodwin, G. M. (2001). Transcranial magnetic stimulation of medial-frontal cortex impairs the processing of angry facial expressions. *Nature Neuroscience*, 4, 17–18.

Harrison, N. A., Singer, T., Rothstein, P., Dolan, R. J., & Critchley, H. D. (2006). Pupillary contagion: Central mechanisms engaged in sadness processing. *Social Cognitive and Affective Neuroscience*, 1, 5–17.

Hasselmo, M. E., Rolls, E. T., & Baylis, G. C. (1989). The role of expression and identity in the face-selective responses of neurons in the temporal visual cortex of the monkey. *Behav. Brain Res*, 32, 203–218.

Haxby, J. V., Hoffman, E. A., & Gobbini, M. I. (2000). The distributed human neural system for face perception. *Trends in Cognitive Science*, 4, 223–233.

Heberlein, A. S., Adolphs, R., Tranel, D., & Damasio, H. (2004). Cortical regions for judgments of emotions and personality traits from point-light walkers. *Journal of Cognitive Neuroscience*, 16, 1143–1158.

Heberlein, A. & Adolphs, R. (2007). Neurobiology of emotion recognition: Current evidence for shared substrates. In E. Harmon-Jones & P. Winkielman (Eds.), *Social neuroscience* (pp. 31–55). New York: Guilford Press.

Hein, G. & Singer, T. (2006). I feel how you feel but not always: The empathic brain and its modulation. *Current Opinion in Neurobiology*, 18.

Herry, C., Bach, D. R., Esposito, F., DiSalle, F., Perrig, W. J., Scheffler, K., et al. (2007). Processing of temporal unpredictability in human and animal amygdala. *The Journal of Neuroscience*, 27, 5958–5966.

Hornak, J., Rolls, E. T., & Wade, D. (1996). Face and voice expression identification in patients with emotional and behavioral changes following ventral frontal lobe damage. *Neuropsychologia*, 34, 247–261.

Hsu, M., Bhatt, M., Adolphs, R., Tranel, D., & Camerer, C. F. (2005). Neural systems responding to degrees of uncertainty in human decision-making. *Science*, 310, 1680–1683.

Hutchison, W. D., Davis, K. D., Lozano, A. M., Tasker, R. R., & Dostrovsky, J. O. (1999). Pain-related neurons in the human cingulate cortex. *Nature Neuroscience*, 2, 403–405.

Iriki, A. (2006). The neural origins and implications of imitation, mirror neurons and tool use. *Curr Opin Neurobiol*, 16, 660–667.

Jiang, Y. & He, S. (2006). Cortical responses to invisible faces: Dissociating subsystems for facial-information processing. *Current Biology*, 16, 2023–2029.

Johnson, M. H. (2005). Subcortical face processing. *Nature Reviews Neuroscience*, 6, 766–774.

Kanwisher, N., McDermott, J., & Chun, M. M. (1997). The fusiform face area: A module in human extrastriate cortex specialized for face perception. *J Neurosci*, 17, 4302–4311.

Kanwisher, N. (2000). Domain specificity in face perception. *Nat Neurosci*, 3, 759–763.

Kreiman, G., Koch, C., & Fried, I. (2000). Category-specific visual responses of single neurons in the human medial temporal lobe. *Nature Neurosci*, 3.

Mitchell, J. P., Banaji, M. R., & Macrae, C. N. (2005). The link between social cognition and self-referential thought in the medial prefrontal cortex. *J Cogn Neurosci*, 17, 1306–1315.

Mitchell, J., Macrae, C. & Mahzarin, R. (2006). Dissociable medial prefrontal contributions to judgments of similar and dissimilar others. *Neuron*, 50.

Moeller, S., Freiwald, W. A., & Tsao, D. Y. (2008). Patches with links: A unified system for processing faces in the macaque temporal lobe. *Science*, 320, 1355–1359.

Morris, J. S., Ohman, A., & Dolan, R. J. (1999). A subcortical pathway to the right amygdala mediating "unseen" fear. *Proceedings of the National Academy of Sciences, 96*, 1680–1685.

Morris, J. S., deGelder, B., Weiskrantz, L., & Dolan, R. J. (2001). Differential extrageniculostriate and amygdala responses to presentation of emotional faces in a cortically blind field. *Brain, 124*, 1241–1252.

Narumoto, J., Okada, T., Sadato, N., Fukui, K., & Yonekura, Y. (2001). Attention to emotion modulates fMRI activity in human right superior temporal sulcus. *Cognitive Brain Research, 12*, 225–231.

Pasley, B. N., Mayes, L. C., & Schultz, R. T. (2004). Subcortical discrimination of unperceived objects during binocular rivalry. *Neuron, 42*, 163–172.

Perrett, D. I., Mistlin, A. J., & Chitty, A. J. (1987). Visual neurons responsive to faces. *Trends in Neurosciences, 10*, 358–364.

Pessoa, L., Kastner, S., & Ungerleider, L.G. (2002). Attentional control of the processing of neutral and emotional stimuli. *Cognitive Brain Research, 15*, 31–45.

Pezawas, L., Meyer-Lindenberg, A., Drabant, E. M., Verchinski, B. A., Munoz, K. E., Kolachana, B. S., et al. (2005). 5-HTTLPR polymorphism impacts human cingulate-amygdala interactions: A genetic susceptibility mechanism for depression. *Nature Neuroscience, 8*, 828–834.

Phillips, M. L., Williams, L. M., Heining, M., Herba, C. M., Russell, T., Andrew, C., et al. (2004). Differential neural responses to overt and covert presentations of facial expressions of fear and disgust. *NeuroImage, 21*, 1484–1496.

Pourtois, G., Sander, D., Andres, M., Grandjean, D., Reveret, L., Olivier, E., et al. (2004). Dissociable roles of the human somatosensory and superior temporal cortices for processing social face signals. *European Journal of Neuroscience, 20*(12), 3507–3515.

Preminger, S., Blumenfeld, B., Sagi, D., & Tsodyks, M. (2009). Mapping dynamic memories of gradually changing objects. *PNAS, 106*, 5371–5376.

Preston, S., & deWaal, F. (2002). Empathy: Its ultimate and proximate bases. *Behavioral and Brain Sciences, 25*(1), 1–20.

Puce, A., Allison, T., & McCarthy, G. (1999). Electrophysiological studies of human face perception. III. Effects of top-down processing on face-specific potentials. *Cereb Cortex, 9*, 445–458.

Rizzolatti, G. & Craighero, L. (2004). The mirror-neuron system. *Annu Rev Neurosci, 27*, 169–192.

Rogowska, J., & Yurgelun-Todd, D. (2009). Gender differences in healthy control subjects during masked facial affect processing. *ESMRMB 26th Annual Scientific Meeting*, October 1–3, Antalya, Turkey.

Rolls, E. T. (1999). *The brain and emotion*. New York: Oxford University Press.

Samson, D., Apperly, I. A., Chiavarino, C., & Humphreys, G. (2004). Left temporoparietal junction is necessary for representing someone else's belief. *Nature Neuroscience, 7*(5).

Saxe, R. & Kanwisher, N. (2003). People thinking about thinking people: The role of the temporo-parietal junction in "theory of mind." *Neuroimage, 19*.

Saxe, R. & Powell, L. (2006). It's the thought that counts. *Psychological Science, 17*(8).

Scholz, J., Triantafyllou, C., Whitfield-Gabrieli, S., Brown, E. N., & Saxe, R. (2009). Distinct regions of right temporo-parietal junction are selective for theory of mind and exogenous attention. *PLoS One, 4*, e4869.

Schyns, P. G., Petro, L. S., & Smith, M. L. (2007). Dynamics of visual information integration in the brain for categorization facial expressions. *Current Biology, 17*, 1580–1585.

Singer, T., Seymour, B., O'Doherty, J., Kaube, H., Dolan, R. J., & Frith, C. D. (2004). Empathy for pain involves the affective but not sensory components of pain. *Science, 303*, 1157–1162.

Sprengelmeyer, R., Young, A. W., Calder, A. J., Karnat, A., Lange, H., Hoemberg, V., et al. (1996). Loss of disgust. Perception of faces and emotions in Huntington's disease. *Brain, 119*, 1647–1666.

Sprengelmeyer, R., Young, A. W., Pundt, I., Sprengelmeyer, A., Calder, A. J., Berrios, G., et al. (1997). Disgust implicated in obsessive-compulsive disorder. *Proc R Soc London Ser B, 264*, 1767–1773.

Tanaka, K. (2003). Columns for complex visual object features in the inferotemporal cortex: Clustering of cells with similar but slightly different stimulus selectivities. *Cereb Cortex, 13*, 90–99.

Tarr, M. J. & Gauthier, I. (2000). FFA: A flexible fusiform area for subordinate level visual processing automatized by expertise. *Nat Neurosci, 3*, 764–769.

Tranel, D., Damasio, A. R., & Damasio, H. (1988). Intact recognition of facial expression, gender, and age in patients with impaired recognition of face identity. *Neurology, 38*, 690–696.

Tsao, D. Y., Freiwald, W. A., Tootell, R. B. H., & Livingstone, M. S. (2006). A cortical region consisting entirely of face-selective cells. *Science, 311*, 670–674.

Tsao, D. Y., Schweers, N., Moeller, S. M., & Freiwald, W. A. (2008). Patches of face-selective cortex in the macaque frontal lobe. *Nat Neurosci, 11*, 877–879.

Tsuchiya, N., Kawasaki, H., Oya, H., Howard, M. H., & Adolphs, R. (2008). Decoding face information in time, frequency and space from direct intracranial recordings of the human brain. *PLoS One, 3*, e3892.

Vuilleumier, P., Richardson, M. P., Armony, J. L., Driver, J., & Dolan, R. J. (2004). Distant influences of amygdala lesion on visual cortical activation during emotional face processing. *Nature Neuroscience, 7*, 1271–1278.

Wager, T. D., Phan, K. L., Liberzon, I., & Taylor, S. F. (2003). Valence, gender, and lateralization of functional brain anatomy in emotion: A meta-analysis of findings from neuroimaging. *Neuroimage, 19*, 513–531.

Whalen, P. J. (1999). Fear, vigilance, and ambiguity: Initial neuroimaging studies of the human amygdala. *Current Directions in Psychological Science, 7*, 177–187.

Whalen, P. J., Kagan, J., Cook, R. G., Davis, F. C., Kim, H., Polis, S., McLaren, D. G., Somerville, L. H., McLean, A. A., Maxwell, J. S., & Johnstone, T. (2004). Human amygdala responsivity to masked fearful eye whites. *Science, 306*, 2061.

Whalen, P. J. (2007). The uncertainty of it all. *TICS, 11*, 499–500.

Wicker, B., Keysers, C., Plailly, J., Royet, J. P., Gallese, V., & Rizzolatti, G. (2003). Both of us disgusted in my insula: The common neural basis of seeing and feeling disgust. *Neuron, 40*(3), 655–664.

Winston, J. S., O'Doherty, J., & Dolan, R. J. (2003). Common and distinct neural responses during direct and incidental processing of multiple facial emotions. *NeuroImage, 20*(1), 84–97.

Yang, E., Zald, D., & Blake, R. (2007). Fearful expressions gain preferential access to awareness during continuous flash suppression. *Emotion, 7*, 882–886.

Odor-Evoked Memory

Rachel S. Herz

Abstract

The experience of a memory evoked by an odor and the ability to remember odors are two different cognitive-perceptual processes. The latter is the ability to recognize and/or identify that you have smelled a particular odor before. For example, we recognize dozens of odors each day—the scent from the nearby Starbucks or the laboratory floor cleaner. These olfactory experiences are similar to recognizing other sensory semantic cues, the sound of a coffee maker, the sight of your daughter's mitten, or the feel of your dog's tail against your leg. These sensory recognitions do not bring back any particular memory event. By contrast, a memory evoked by an odor occurs when an odor triggers the recollection of a specific episodic event from one's past typically having little to do with the odor itself. For example, a perfume evokes the memory of a relative. Episodic odor-evoked memories can also invoke memory for the door – you smell a perfume and recognize it as being Chanel No. 5. However, odor-evoked memory is when this simple perfume recognition evolves into a full blown episodic memory experience of your favorite aunt. Odor-evoked memories are typified by various characteristics. This chapter examines these characteristics and the possible uniqueness of odor-evoked memory among memory experiences.

Keywords: sense of smell, odor-evoked memory, olfaction, neuroanatomy, episodic memory

Most people believe that their sense of smell has minimal impact on the critical aspects of existence; however, they are mistaken. Olfaction is deeply involved in every aspect of our lives from the obvious (e.g. food experiences, smoke detection) to the subtle (e.g., our sense of self, social relationships). The subtle aspects of olfactory perception and cognition are most germane to social neuroscience, and odor-evoked memory is a critical facet. The emotionality and evocativeness elicited by odor-evoked memory (see detailed discussion below) is responsible for giving us a sense of *self*, of who and where we are, in time and place, present and past. Moreover,

through both neuroanatomy and neuroevolution, the physiology of olfaction is uniquely tied to our emotions, motivations, associations, and social perceptions. Our sense of smell gives us the texture of our emotional life and is the fabric that knits together our hedonic, personal, and interpersonal experiences. Thus, for any comprehensive investigation into what it means to be human, especially within the context of social neuroscience, an understanding of olfaction and odor-evoked memory is essential.

The experience of a memory evoked by an odor and the ability to remember odors are two different cognitive-perceptual processes. The latter is the ability to recognize and/or identify that you have smelled a particular odor before. We recognize dozens of odors each day—the scent from the nearby Starbucks, the laboratory floor cleaner, the newly opened package of printer paper, your tuna fish sandwich. These olfactory experiences are similar to recognizing other sensory semantic cues such as the sound of a coffee maker, the sight of your daughter's mitten, or the feel of your dog's tail against your leg. These sensory recognitions do not bring back any particular memory event. By contrast, a memory evoked by an odor occurs when an odor triggers the recollection of a specific episodic event from one's past typically having little to do with the odor itself. There are instances when memory for odors and odor-evoked memory overlap, such as when you smell a perfume and recognize it as being Chanel No. 5 or the one that your favorite aunt wore. However, odor-evoked memory is when this simple perfume recognition evolves into a full blown autobiographical memory of your favorite aunt. An episodic memory experience that is typified by various characteristics. The specific characteristics of odor-evoked memory and their possible unique status among memory experiences is the focus of the present chapter. Though related in general nature, this chapter will not address the topic of odors in context-dependent memory.

History of Methodology and Findings

For those who study odor-evoked memory, much has been made of the most frequently cited literary example of this phenomenon: the passage from the first chapter of *Swann's Way*, where Marcel Proust recounts how the aroma arising from a madelèine biscuit soaked with linden tea brought back a long-forgotten recollection.

> ". . . No sooner had the warm liquid, and the crumbs with it, touched my palate than a shudder ran through my whole body, and I stopped, intent upon the extraordinary changes that were taking place. An exquisite pleasure had invaded my senses, but individual, detached with no suggestion of its origin. . . . Whence could it have come to me, this all powerful joy? I was conscious that it was connected with the taste of the tea and cake but that it infinitely transcended those savors . . .
> . . . all of Combrey with its environment has come forth from my cup of tea."[1]

Many of the characteristics of this memory description, such as its vividness, emotionality, age

and phenomenology, have been used as the criteria upon which to judge the distinctiveness of odor-evoked-memory (Jellinek, 2004). A common assertion is also that odors are "the best cues" to memory.

The special attributes of odor-evoked-memory and a determination of whether odors are in fact the best cues to memory was first examined shortly after Proust's famous description (Laird, 1935). However, a comprehensive analysis of this topic has only begun within the last twenty years. The first empirical investigations of odor-evoked memory relied on descriptive measures and self-report for detailing their qualities and characteristics. The results of these studies indicated that odor-evoked memories are markedly intense/vivid and emotional and frequently bring back memories of long ago events. (Laird, 1935; Herz & Cupchik, 1992). However, these studies focused only on odor-evoked memories and did not compare them to other memory experiences. Thus, whether odor-evoked memory is truly different from, or better than, other memory experiences could not be ascertained. Moreover, since most people pay little attention to olfactory information compared with other modes of sensory and cognitive processing, the surprise that a memory is actually being evoked by a scent may augment the apparent salience of odor-evoked memory (Herz, 2007). In order to assess whether odor-evoked memory is different or special, a cross-modal approach must be used, where memories elicited by stimuli presented in various sensory modalities are compared.

In the first cross-modal odor memory experiment, Rubin, Groth, and Goldsmith (1984) gave participants 15 familiar stimuli (e.g., coffee, band-aids, cigarettes) to assess in either olfactory, verbal, or picture form. For each item, the participant described the memory that was evoked, and rated it on several scales: age of memory, vividness, emotionality at time of event, emotionality at time of recall, how many times it had been thought of, and when it was last recalled (prior to the experiment). From these measures, the only statistically reliable findings were that memories evoked by odors were *thought of* and *talked about* less often than memories evoked by words and pictures. There was a trend for odor-evoked memories to be more emotional, but the effect was not statistically consistent.

A decade later, Hinton and Henley (1993) compared subjects' free-associations to verbal, olfactory and visual versions of six familiar everyday items (coffee, tobacco, carnations, orange, Ivory soap, pine). Confirming the intuition that odors have a special capacity to elicit hedonic responses, they found that the free associations elicited by odors were more emotional than the free associations elicited by words or visual versions of the same items. Moreover, when the free association resembled an autobiographical recollection it was most often elicited by an odor cue. This suggests that associations elicited by odors are more hedonically toned and personally involving than those elicited by other sensory stimuli.

A more comprehensive approach, involving a paired-associate (PA) cross-modal paradigm, was developed by Herz and Cupchik (1995). In these experiments, a series of familiar source objects (cues) were presented to participants in either olfactory, verbal, visual, or tactile form (e.g., the smell of popcorn, the word "popcorn," seeing popcorn, or feeling popcorn) while participants viewed emotionally evocative pictures. Participants were told that the aim of the experiment was to evaluate the effects of different environmental cues on the perception of pictures. No mention of memory or memory testing was ever made. Two days later, however, when participants returned to the laboratory, they were given a surprise cued recall test for their picture experiences, and the accuracy and emotionality of their memories were assessed.

Figure 17.1 illustrates the results from one of the many experiments we conducted using this paradigm. Memories evoked by odors are significantly more emotionally arousing than memories elicited by the same item in other sensory forms, but the accuracy and content detail of memories does not vary as a function of cue-type (Herz & Cupchik, 1995; Herz, 1998). That is, odor-evoked memories are experienced as more emotionally intense than other memory experiences, but odors do not elicit more accurate memories than other sensory cues.

Naturalistic autobiographical memory experiments are contrasted with laboratory studies by having participants recall memories from their own personal past compared to memory for information presented during an experiment. In the first naturalistic odor-evoked memory experiment, Aggelton and Waskett (1999) compared relevant and irrelevant odors as cues to recall for the event of having visited a Viking museum exhibit. Museum visitors who had been to the Viking exhibit approximately 6.5 yrs earlier, were presented with seven odors that had been used in the exhibit (e.g., burnt wood, rope/tar, fish-market) and seven that had not (e.g. coffee, rose, disinfectant). The results demonstrated that odors which were present during the Viking exhibit led to more detailed memory for the exhibit than those that weren't. This result suggests that odors specifically linked to past events evoke memories for those events. However, it can also be argued that the odors of the Viking exhibit were more unusual and specific than the control odors and thus a general sense of what Viking exhibits are like might have been conjured by those odors.

A more general issue is that the unimodal (odor cue only) memory method can only generate descriptive data, as it non-comparative. Moreover, participants' reports may be colored by a personal investment in their memories and conventional beliefs in the special nature of odor-evoked recall. The cross-modal autobiographical method, where a memory cue in several sensory forms is presented and the participant is asked to recall a past associated event, is superior in that it actually compares odor-evoked memory against memories elicited by other sensory stimuli. However, when simply implemented as such it suffers from the problem that memory selection is confounded with memory recollection. That is, because the memory cue is provided prior to the selection of a memory, the

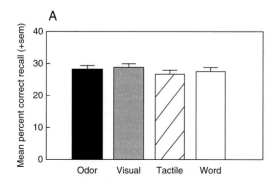
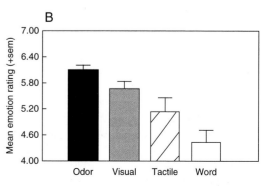

Fig. 17.1 (A) Mean Recall Accuracy by Cue-Type. (B) Mean Rated Memory Emotionality by Cue-Type.

cue itself may influence what particular autobiographical memory individuals choose to recall, and accordingly odors may lead to choosing more emotional memories than other sensory memory cues.

In an effort to remedy this problem Chu and Downes (2002) developed a double-cuing method where participants first retrieved a memory to a verbal cue (e.g., ginger) and then retrieved it again with either the same verbal cue "ginger" (label group), or an odor cue that either corresponded (e.g., ginger odor—congruent group) or did not (e.g., cinnamon odor—incongruent group) to the original verbal cue. Memories were evaluated in each condition for various qualitative measures, including how: personal, pleasant, embarrassing, vivid, and unique they were. Results revealed that when re-cued with the congruent odor, memories were rated as higher on every scale compared to when memories when re-cued with the same verbal cue or with an incongruent odor. Using a similar procedure, Maylor, Carter, and Hallett (2002) asked both young and old adults (mean age 21 and 84 yrs, respectively) first to retrieve a memory to a word cue (e.g., coffee) and then a few minutes later retested them with the same word cue either accompanied, or not, by the relevant odor (e.g., coffee word + coffee odor or coffee word only). Their results showed that all participants recalled more memories when the re-test phase was accompanied by odor cues. However, qualitative features of the memories were not assessed in this study.

We also developed a two-stage protocol involving initial verbal cuing (Herz & Schooler, 2002). Individuals were given a verbal odor name (e.g., "Coppertone suntan lotion") and were then asked to think of a memory from their past and to rate it on a variety of dimensions. They were then given either a visual (a photograph of a Coppertone bottle) or an olfactory (the odor of Coppertone) version of the cue, and were asked to think about their memory again. Selecting the memories in response to verbal names prior to the introduction of the sensory cues allowed for matching of the memories selected in the two cue conditions. Any differences in the quality of the memories that were subsequently observed could therefore be attributed to the effects of the cues on memory *recollection* rather than memory *selection*. We found that compared to visual re-cues, memories that were re-evoked by odors were reliably experienced as more emotional and that participants stated they were more brought back to the original time and place of the memory episode (Herz & Schooler, 2002).

Using the same two-stage protocol, a further study was conducted in which olfactory, visual, and auditory cues were introduced after the memory was initially retrieved by a word (Herz, 2004). This study differed from the first in that it followed a within-subjects design where each participant experienced all the memory cues in all sensory formats. The results from this second experiment confirmed that memories recalled by odors were significantly more emotional and evocative (participants were brought back to the original time and place) than memories re-called by the same cue presented verbally, visually, or auditorily. Notably, as in our laboratory-based studies, there were no differences in evaluations for the content features of memory (vividness, specificity) as a function of cue-type found in either study (Herz & Schooler, 2002; Herz, 2004).

The results from these diverse experiments indicate that odor-evoked memories are more emotional and evocative than memories elicited by other cues. These data also demonstrate that received wisdom regarding the "specialness" of odor-evoked memories cannot account for the results. At a deeper, theoretical level, these findings further indicate that the distinguishing emotional quality of odor-evoked memories is due to processes that occur during sensory recollection, and are not due to memory selection. That is, the emotional punch of odor-evoked memory occurs during the memory retrieval process, and is not simply due to odors themselves eliciting more emotional experiences. This is further supported by laboratory experiments where each cue was tested for its emotionality during the encoding phase of the experiment as well as the retrieval phase and no differences in emotional potency were observed for any of the cues at encoding (Herz & Cupchik, 1995; Herz, 1998). In sum, the processes that make odor-evoked memories distinctively emotional occur and are a product of retrieval.

In support of the view that retrieval confers specific attributes to memory, positron emission tomography research has revealed that encoding and retrieval are subserved by different neural areas, with encoding a function primarily of the left dorsal prefrontal cortex, and retrieval a function of the right prefrontal cortex (Cabeza & Nyberg, 2000; Tulving, Kapur, Craik, Moscovitch, & Houle, 1994). In this regard it is noteworthy that both olfaction and emotion are primarily processed in the right hemisphere (Ross, Homan, & Buck, 1994; Zatorre, Jones-Gotman, Evans, & Meyer, 1992). Moreover, returning to Proust's own account, the emotional salience of his famed episode was connected to the retrieval of his odor-evoked memory, not the original mundane Sunday visits to his aunt's house.

In keeping with technological advancements in cognitive research, we have also used functional magnetic resonance imaging (fMRI) to compare regions of activation during recall triggered by olfactory and visual cues (Herz, Eliassen, Beland, & Souza, 2003). In our experiment we used perfumes as the cross-modal stimulus. Prior to the main experiment, potential female (only) volunteers were interviewed to determine whether a specific perfume could be identified that elicited a positive autobiographical memory. The criterion for admission as a participant of the experiment was the ability to recall a positive, personal memory in which both the smell and sight of a perfume figured. For example, one participant stated that her memory was:

A trip to Paris when I was in 4th grade and me sitting and watching my mother while she was getting ready to go out and the "Opium" perfume that she used which was on her vanity.

Individuals who met these criteria were invited to participate in the main experiment and one to two months later were scheduled for fMRI testing.

Testing followed a block design in which three blocks of 16 trials were administered consisting of four stimuli and clean air. Participants were exposed to two experimental stimuli: the smell and sight of the specific perfume they had previously identified as being emotionally meaningful to them (EO and EV); and two control stimuli: (CO and CV) the smell and sight, respectively, of a perfume that they were not familiar with (an unmarketed perfume that was the same for all participants). The first trial of every block and between each stimulus trial was an air-only trial.

Functional MRI analyses revealed significantly greater activation in the amygdala and hippocampal regions during recall to the odor of the personally significant perfume (EO) than to any other cue. This is particularly noteworthy because odors generally elicit activation in limbic structures. Thus the present finding was due to the emotionality of memory that was elicited and was not an olfactory artifact. Furthermore, subsequent behavioral testing confirmed that participants experienced the greatest emotion responses to their personally meaningful fragrance (see Figure 17.2). This result is the first and to our knowledge only neurobiological demonstration that the subjective experience of the emotional potency of odor-evoked memory is specifically correlated with heightened activation in the amygdala-hippocampal region during recall.

Distinguishing Characteristics of Odor-Evoked Memory

Several defining features of odor-evoked memory have emerged through the scientific investigations of the past several decades that echo those claimed from popular literature and anecdote. In particular, odor-evoked memories are reported as being more potent than other memory experiences on some or all of the following characteristics: vividness, emotionality, evocativeness (being brought back to the original time and place), rarity (rarely thought of compared to other memories), age (memories from

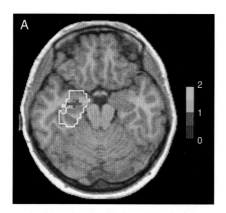 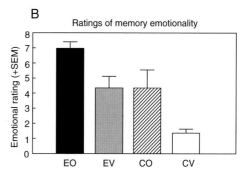

Fig. 17.2 (A) Activation for the Experimental Odor (EO) in the amygdala. The positive activation difference for the comparison EO vs. EV + CO + CV is shown. EO = Experimental Odor; EV = Experimental Visual; CO = Control Odor; CV = Control Visual. The slice shown is at Z = −16 mm inferior to anterior commissure (AC). The maximum intensity difference of 1.65 (MR units) appeared at 14, 8,−16, relative to the AC, corresponding to left hemisphere Broadmann's areas 28 and 34. (B) Mean emotion ratings given during memory elicitation to each stimulus.

early life), and by being the "best" cues to memory. An analysis of the validity of these claims is undertaken below.

Vividness

Anecdotal descriptions of odor-evoked memory typically include mention of their high "vividness." A problem for empirically determining the strength of this characteristic, however, is that the term "vividness" is colloquially ambiguous and can mean the clarity and intensity of visual imagery in a memory, as well, or in addition to, the emotional vividness (i.e., intensity) of a memory. The connotative ambiguity of the term "vividness" may account for the discrepancies in the data that have been obtained in tests of this measure. Herz and Cupchik (1995) and Herz (1998) found no differences in the number of memory details recalled comparing odors to visual, verbal, and tactile versions of the same memory cue item. By contrast, using a verbal cuing procedure, Chu and Downes (2002) found that re-recollection with an odor cue led to higher ratings of memory vividness and more memory detail compared to memories re-cued by verbal or visual items. Methodological differences may account for this difference as the Herz experiments used laboratory controlled to-be-remembered images as the memory items, rather than autobiographical memory events, and a recuing method was not employed.

However, in Herz and Schooler (2002) and Herz (2004) a recuing method was used and autobiographical memories were tested, yet no differences in rated memory vividness were obtained. Similarly, Rubin et al. (1984) did not find any effect for memory vividness in their cross-modal autobiographical memory study. It appears most likely that the differences in results for memory "vividness" are due to the meaning of "vividness" that was presumed by the participants. That is, whether the connotation implied emotional vividness as opposed to the vividness of visual imagery in the memory. Differences in the methodology of Chu and Downes (2002) in contrast to Rubin et al. (1984), Herz and Schooler (2002), and Herz (2004), may have led participants to presume different meanings in each case; the former invoking more emotional construal and the later experiments suggesting a visual imagery connotation. For example, Chu and Downes (2002) asked participants to rate their memories on a variety of terms: pleasant, painful, anxious, embarrassing, vivid, and unique; all of which could be interpreted as relating to emotional quality. By contrast,

in Rubin et al. (1984) and the Herz experiments, participants were asked to rate their memories on a series of dimensions where the emotion-related items and the imagery-accuracy items were more distinctly separated. Notably, Chu and Downes (2002) reported that odors led to recall of specifically more emotional detail than did verbal labels. This further supports the possibility that their vividness measure was interpreted in emotional terms. Another issue is that there is no neuroanatomical or functional evidence or reason for why odors should elicit memories of greater visual vividness or object detail than memories evoked by visual or verbal cues (see discussion of neuroanatomy and neuroevolution below).

Emotionality and Evocativeness

An odor that you have smelled before immediately elicits a liking or disliking response. This hedonic response is due to the emotional associations that have been acquired to the odor (Bartoshuk, 1991; Engen, 1988; Herz, 2001). Often, these associations are generalized and cannot be precisely linked to one past episodic event. However, there are occasions where both liking and the memory event are precisely tied to a particular odor. For example, a woman once told me that she hated the scent of roses because the first time she ever smelled a rose was at her mother's funeral. Thus, the scent of rose for her is both highly disliked and a specific recollection of a very upsetting past event.

As previously mentioned, my laboratory has extensively tested the emotional potency of odor-evoked memory using a cross-modal paradigm. Across a range of experiments, designed to test both experimentally constrained and personal autobiographical memories, we have consistently found that memories recalled to odors are experienced as significantly more emotional than memories triggered by any other sensory cue (Herz, 1998; Herz et al., 2003; Herz, 2004; Herz & Cupchik, 1995; Herz & Schooler, 2002). These findings have recently been replicated by others comparing odors with visual and verbal cues (e.g., Bonfigli, Kodilja, & Zanuttini, 2002; Willander & Larsson, 2007).

We have also obtained neurobiological evidence for the heightened emotional potency of odor-evoked memory using fMRI. Memories triggered by the scent of a personally meaningful odor elicited significantly greater activation in brain areas directly linked to emotion and emotional-memory processing (amygdala-hippocampal complex) than memories of the same event triggered by the visual version of the memory cue or a nonmeaningful odor and visual cue (Herz et al., 2003).

Of further interest, music is renowned as an emotionally evocative stimulus and it is often reported that music evokes poignant memories (Royet et al., 2000). Herz (1998) used a PA paradigm with odors, visual stimuli, and music of comparative novelty, pleasantness, and complexity as memory cues and assessed the physiological emotion correlate of heart rate in addition to self-report measures. Results showed that memories elicited by odors were accompanied by greater heart rate increases than those elicited by music, and that this was not an artifact of the act of sniffing. These data indicate that physiological indices of emotion are also higher during recall elicited by odors than with other emotional stimuli such as music.

The "evocativeness" of a memory is defined by the degree to which one has the feeling of being brought back to the original time and place of the episodic event (Herz & Schooler, 2002). Only four studies to date have examined memory evocativeness elicited by odors in contrast to memories elicited by other stimuli. Herz and Schooler (2002) and Herz (2004) showed that autobiographical memories re-cued by olfactory, visual, and auditory variants of verbal memory items (e.g., "fresh cut grass") led to the greatest feelings of being brought back in time and place when triggered by odors. In two subsequent experiments by Willander and Larsson (2006; 2007), it was shown that odor-evoked memories were accompanied by a stronger feeling of being brought back in time than memories elicited by verbal and picture cues of the same items (e.g., tobacco, black-current, soap). The feeling of being transported back to the original memory event exemplifies one's emotional connection to the memory experience, and as such evocativeness can be viewed as a dimension of memory emotionality. These findings strongly substantiate the claim that odors are unique among memory cues for eliciting singularly potent emotional recall. Moreover, no experimental studies to date have reported that odor-evoked memories are *not* emotional.

Neuroanatomy and Neuroevolution:
Why should odors elicit uniquely emotional memories? The answer lies in neuroanatomy and neuroevolution. When we inhale, aromatic molecules travel into the nose and land on two patches of mucus membrane at the back of each nostril (the olfactory epithelia) where the receptors for odor

sensation are located. The interaction between an odorant and the receptors then leads to a specific pattern of receptor activation. The gross neuroanatomy shows that the axons of the olfactory receptors enter the brain through the cribriform plate (a bony structure at the level of the eyebrow) and bundle together to form the olfactory nerve. The olfactory nerve transmits information to the olfactory bulb from where neural impulses are then immediately relayed to the amygdala-hippocampal complex of the limbic system and thereafter to higher cognitive areas. In the case of a specific odor, the particular pattern of receptor activity translates to specific neural activity that is associated for the individual in emotional and meaningful terms (including whether it is an unfamiliar and unmeaningful/unemotional odor).

Unlike any of our other senses, olfactory efferents have a direct and immediate connection with the neural substrates of emotion and memory processing (Cahill, Babinsky, Markowitsch, & McGaugh, 1995; Turner, Mishkin, & Knapp, 1980). Only two synapses separate the olfactory nerve from the amygdala, a structure critical for the expression and experience of emotion (Aggleton & Mishkin, 1986) and human emotional memory (Cahill et al., 1995); and only three synapses separate the olfactory nerve from the hippocampus, involved in associative learning, short-term and long-term memory transfer, and in various declarative memory functions (Eichenbaum, 2001; Schwerdtfeger, Buhl, & Gemroth, 1990; Staubli, Ivy, & Lynch, 1984). Furthermore, olfactory information does not need to be mediated through the thalamus (a principal integration locus for sensory information) the way all other sensory information is, but rather is instantly relayed to the amygdala-hippocampal complex. Classical conditioning of specific cues to emotion is also mediated by the amygdala (LeDoux, 1998), and the olfactory cortex and amygdala have been shown to play a major role in stimulus reinforcement association learning (see Rolls, 1999). Moreover, the orbitofrontal cortex, where olfaction is processed, is the cortical area responsible for assigning affective value to stimuli and for determining the reinforcement (approach-avoid) value of stimuli in general (Davidson, Putnam, & Larson, 2000; Quirk & Gehlert, 2003). None of our other senses have this direct and intimate connection with the areas of the brain that process emotion, associative learning, and memory. Figure 17.3 illustrates the encoding pathway between initial odor sensation and subsequent neurological processing.

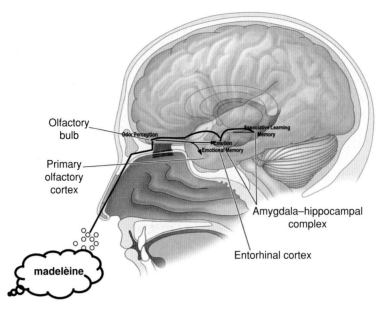

Olfactory
bulb

Odor Perception

Associative Learning
Memory

Emotion
Emotional Memory

Primary
olfactory
cortex

Amygdala–hippocampal
complex

Entorhinal cortex

madelèine

Fig. 17.3 Schematic showing the neural route from odor sensation through to odor perception, emotion and emotional memory processing (amygdala), associative learning, and memory elicitation (hippocampus).

In addition to the distinctive neuroanatomical connection between olfaction and emotion, olfaction and emotion are deeply connected by neuro-evolution. The structures of the limbic system (e.g., the amygdala and hippocampus) evolved from neural tissue that was originally olfactory cortex. The basic substrates of the brain that process emotion and learning evolved from an area that was first dedicated to processing the sense of smell. Something to ponder is whether, or how, we would experience emotion if we didn't have a sense of smell. Furthermore, the informational significance of emotion and olfaction are functionally the same. The most immediate responses we have to an odor are simple binary opposites: like or dislike; approach or avoid. Emotions convey the same message: Approach what is good, joyful, loving; avoid what is bad, fearsome, or liable to cause grief. Thus, emotions and olfaction are functionally analogous. Both enable the organism to react appropriately to its environment, maximizing its chances for survival and reproductive success. In my opinion, the human emotional system may be a highly evolved, cognitive version of the basic behavioral motivations instigated by the olfactory system in animals (Herz, 2000; 2007).

Old and Rare

As with antiques whose value increases with their age and rarity, odor-evoked memories appear to be uniquely precious compared to memories elicited by other stimuli. In Laird's (1935) early experimental

account of odor-evoked memory, "old" was included as a distinguishing feature of the recollections. That is, the memories people recalled were from events long ago in their past.

The clustering of memories from a specific life stage is referred to as a "memory bump." Traditionally, it has been found that when older adults recall episodic memories to verbal and visual cues their recollections predominate on events which occurred in their second and third decades of life; the period of adolescence and early adulthood. The question as to whether odor-evoked memories also cluster in this life phase or from earlier in time, as suggested by Laird, has only been investigated in a few studies.

In their pioneering experiment, Rubin et al. (1984) were unable to find any differences among college students in the age distribution for odor-evoked memories compared to memories elicited by photographs or verbal labels. Likewise, Goddard, Pring, and Felmingham (2005) compared memories elicited by words, pictures, and odors in young adults and found no differences in the age distribution of memories. However, in studies where older cohorts have been tested, an earlier bump by approximately ten years has been found for memories elicited by odors compared to memories elicited by words. Chu and Downes (2000) found that among older participants (average age 69 yrs), a bump for odor-evoked memories emerged between the ages of 6–10, compared with the bump for label-cued events which was found between the ages of 11–20. Most recently, Willander and Larsson (2006; 2007) have confirmed that the memory bump for odor-evoked memories is earlier than for memories triggered by other cues. Testing adults between the ages of 65–80 years (mean age 74 yrs), they found a significant clustering of memories from the first decade of life elicited by odors compared to verbally evoked memories which peaked in early adulthood.

Old memories may also be more likely to be rare memories—that is, infrequently relived compared to other episodic experiences. Rubin et al. (1984) found that odor-evoked memories were talked about and thought of less often than memories evoked by verbal or visual items. Similarly, Willander and Larsson (2006) reported that odor-evoked memories were thought about less often than memories evoked by pictures and that fewer memories were elicited by odors than by verbal cues (Willander & Larsson, 2007). These findings support the idea that odors evoke memories that are more rare and infrequently relived compared to memories triggered by other stimuli.

Why should the temporal distribution of odor-evoked memories be concentrated in the first years of life compared to the memory bump in later development observed for verbal and visual memory? One possibility is that the clustering of odor-evoked recollections in early life is due to the fact that odors evoke the first experiences that have been associated to them, and since most new experiences occur in early childhood this could explain why associations to odors predominantly evoke events from these years. Schroers, Prigot, and Fagan (2007) found that odors could serve as memory cues for three month old infants. Infants who learned to move a mobile in the presence of a distinctive odor (coconut or cherry) later showed that they remembered how to move the mobile when tested in the presence of the same odor either 1 or 5 days later, thus demonstrating that odor-evoked memory is established at the earliest moments in childhood. Infants who were retested without their odor cue (an alternate odor or no odor) did not show any retention for the mobile task.

In addition to the fact that many olfactory associations occur during childhood, it is known that proactive interference is particularly strong in odor memory and that it is difficult to associate an odor to a new experience once an initial association has been made (Lawless & Engen, 1977). By contrast, retroactive interference is stronger than proactive interference for visual and verbal information.

Memories recalled to odors might therefore center on first associations because proactive interference inhibits later memories from being formed. Conversely, for verbal and visual cues, newer memories tend to erase first associations and hence recollections center around more recent experiences and those that were formative to the development of the person as a whole—the second and third decades of life. Additionally, the relative low frequency of encountering odors that trigger episodic memories and consequently the reduced rewriting of these memories through repeated recollections may be a further reason for the preservation of first associations and the early memory bump observed. In this regard it would be important to know whether memories for events from later in life that are triggered by odors, are to odors which are less likely to be encountered (more rare) than those which trigger earlier recollections.

The low frequency of encountering olfactory cues that are linked to a specific event compared to memories triggered by other cue-types may generally explain why odor-evoked memories are rare—they are infrequently thought of because they infrequently occur. The number of occasions over a lifespan in which one encounters the specific odor cue to an episodic memory is likely to be much less than the times one encounters non-olfactory memory cues. Indeed the low probability of encountering an olfactory memory cue may shed light on one way in which odors can be considered "the best" cues to memory.

Best Cues to Memory

The claim is often made that odors are the best cues to memory; however, research negates this assertion if "better" refers to memory accuracy (e.g., Herz, 1998; 2004). Numerous experiments have demonstrated that odors do not bring back more accurate or more content-rich memories than other sensory stimuli. Rather, it seems that the emotional saliency and evocativeness of odor-evoked memories makes them feel more real and leads to the false impression that such memories are especially accurate (Herz, 1998). The confidence that one's recollections are true, which is so hard to resist when memories are colored by emotional experience, is similar to what often emerges during eyewitness testimony in the courtroom. Eyewitnesses recalling emotionally charged episodes are often extremely confident that their recollections are accurate, but research shows that these memories are often incorrect (Busey, Tunnicliff, Loftus, & Loftus, 2000).

There is, however, one way in which odors may be better memory cues. They may be more likely to elicit events which otherwise would never be remembered. That is, odors may unlock memories whose only "mental tag" may be the odor that was present when the memory was encoded. This again might be due to the low frequency by which certain odors are encountered. A specific odor may be explicitly tied to one event in life and no other because that scent was only encountered in that particular situation, whereas visual or verbal versions of the same cue are multiply encountered in various iterations of similar events. For example, a particular brand of dish soap may have a very distinctive odor, but the sight of various brands of dish soap bottles, which one is repeatedly exposed to, are all relatively similar. In other words, due to redundancy and interference with multiple experiences, visual and verbal representations of critical memory cues lose their ability to trigger the memory of a particular episode. Whereas, due to the very low frequency of encountering certain specific scents, odors can remain faithful memory cues to a specific past episode. Upon reflection, one realizes that it is very uncommon for a deeply significant odor-evoked memory to be triggered by an everyday odor.

In sum, resistance to being overwritten (proactive interference) and the high distinctiveness of certain scents can combine to make odors faithfully and directly tied to particular events like no other cue. The ability to elicit a memory that might otherwise never be retrieved may be the one feature that makes odors "better" memory cues.

Phenomenology

One of the central characteristics of Proust's madelèine and linden tea-triggered recollection that has not been put to experimental scrutiny is the phenomenology of his memory experience. That is, the temporal order of its unfolding. In Proust's multipage description, the emotion that the odor elicited came well before awareness of the content to which that emotion was connected. That is, the temporal unfolding of his memory was first emotional and then only after a number of minutes, and pages, did the visual and concrete content to which that memory was attached become apparent (Herz, 2007; Jellinek, 2004). Memories that are cued by other stimuli occur in the reverse order. First you visualize some concrete aspect of the event and then you perform an (often instantaneous) emotional appraisal of the event whereupon you feel the emotions connected to it. For example, you hear a piece of music that reminds you of a special date from your past. The first aspect of that memory is the visual recapitulation of that event which you then analyze as being positive, sad, funny, embarrassing, and so forth, and your emotional experience follows suit. By contrast, when an odor evokes a memory, the first experience is an emotional sensation after which the event from whence that emotion comes from emerges. In other words, the experiential order of odor-evoked memory appears to follow the temporal sequence of the neuranatomical pathways that are involved; sensory-perceptual → limbic-emotional → higher cognitive structures.

The bottom-up versus top-down temporal unfolding of odor-evoked memory may distinguish it from other memory experiences. However, before any claims for this feature of odor-evoked memory can be made the phenomenology of odor-evoked memory needs to be experimentally explored. Although doing so presents various experimental difficulties, it is not outside the realm of testability especially if combined with neuroimaging techniques. In an ideal investigation of this phenomenon, autobiographical memories could be re-cued by visual, auditory, and olfactory versions of the same memory triggers during simultaneous neuroimaging and behavioral testing. The qualitative experience and temporal sequence of brain areas that become activated when memories are triggered by odors versus various different stimuli could thereby be discerned.

Conclusions

Rigorous empirical research has been conducted in the field of odor-evoked memory over the past several decades and major strides have been made in experimentally defining the anecdotal aspects of this distinctive memory experience. Among the features of odor-evoked memory that have been experimentally verified, the most notable is the uniquely emotional and evocative nature of odor-evoked memory. There is also clear evidence that memories elicited by odors tend to be from an earlier time of life and are more rarely relived than memories elicited by other stimuli. The degree of visual imagery in odor-evoked memory does not appear to be higher than with any other stimuli, although if vividness is interpreted as emotional intensity, then this description may be apt. Odors also do not seem to be the best cues to memory, if "best" refers to accuracy. Here, again, the feeling that odors are superior reminders is based on their unique emotional potency. However, it may be the case that odors are more likely to trigger memories that otherwise would never be recalled, and this may be the one feature that makes odors "better" memory triggers than other stimuli. Whether this is a true defining feature of odor-evoked memory awaits experimental investigation. Additionally, the phenomenological experience of odor-evoked memory as first emotional and then cognitive, which is opposite in sequence to memories cued by other stimuli, currently remains speculative and needs to be scientifically explored.

The reasons for the special and unique qualities of odor-evoked memory are due to the privileged neuroanatomical relationship between olfactory processing and the structures that subserve emotion, memory, and associative learning as well as the particular cognitive-perceptual characteristics of olfaction, such as distinctiveness, low frequency, and proactive interference. In sum, the odor-evoked memory research to date shows that it has a number of unique features and that odor-evoked memory is likely a different memory system from than that which subserves visual and verbal memory (Herz & Engen, 1996).

The neuroanatomy of olfaction not only makes it the gateway to our emotional and memorial experiences but it is also the sensory system that epitomizes our approach-avoidance responses. Approach-avoid is the foundation for all of our social interactions. Studying olfaction, thus, not only gives us insight into our selves and our past but also illuminates the core of social-emotional perception and cognition. The many special features of olfaction and how it can serve as a model for understanding the basic elements of social neuroscience awaits future research and eager investigators.

Note

1 From: Proust, M. (1928). *Swann's Way*, The Modern Library, Inc: New York. page 62.

References

Aggleton, J. P. & Mishkin, M. (1986). The amygdala: Sensory gateway to the emotions. In R. Plutchik & H. Kellerman (Eds.), *Emotion: Theory, research and experience. Vol 3: Biological foundations of emotion*. Orlando: Academic Press.

Aggleton, J.P. & Waskett, L. (1999). The ability of odours to serve as state-dependent cues for real-world memories: Can Viking smells aid the recall of Viking experiences? *British Journal of Psychology, 90*, 1–7.

Bartoshuk, L.M. (1991). Taste, smell and pleasure. In R. C. Bolles (Ed.). *The hedonics of taste* (pp. 15–28). Hillsdale, New Jersey: Lawrence Erlbaum.

Bonfigli, L., Kodilja, R., & Zanuttini, L. (2002). Verbal versus olfactory cues: Affect in elicited memories. *Perceptual and Motor Skills, 94*, 9–20.

Busey, T. A., Tunnicliff, J., Loftus, G. R., & Loftus, E. F. (2000). Accounts of the confidence-accuracy relation in recognition memory, *Psychonomic Bulletin and Review, 7*, 26–48.

Cabeza, R. & Nyberg, L. (2000). Imaging Cognition II: An empirical review of 275 PET and fMRI studies. *Journal of Cognitive Neuroscience, 12*, 1–47.

Cahill, L., Babinsky, R., Markowitsch, H. J., & McGaugh, J. L. (1995). The amygdala and emotional memory. *Nature, 377*, 295–296.

Chu, S. & Downes, J. J. (2000). Long live Proust: The odour-cued autobiographical memory bump. *Cognition, 75*, B41–B50.

Chu, S. & Downes, J. J. (2002). Proust nose best: Odors are better cues of autobiographical memory. *Memory & Cognition, 30*(4), 511–518.

Davidson, R. J., Putnam, K. M., & Larson, C. L. (2000). Dysfunction in the neural circuitry of emotion regulation—a possible prelude to violence. *Science, 289*, 591–594.

Eichenbaum, H. (2001). The hippocampus and declarative memory: Cognitive mechanisms and neural codes. *Behavioural Brain Research, 127*, 199–207.

Engen, T. (1988). The acquisition of odor hedonics. In S. Van Toller & G. H. Dodd (Eds.), *Perfumery: The psychology and biology of fragrance*. New York: Chapman & Hall.

Goddard, L., Pring, L., & Felmingham, N. (2005). The effects of cue modality on the quality of personal memories retrieved. *Memory, 13*, 79–86.

Herz, R. S. (1998). Are odors the best cues to memory? A cross-modal comparison of associative memory stimuli. *Annals of the New York Academy of Sciences, 855*, 670–674.

Herz, R. S. (2000). Scents of time. *The Sciences (July/August)*, 34–39.

Herz, R. S. (2001). Ah, sweet skunk: Why we like or dislike what we smell. *Cerebrum, Vol. 3*(4), 31–47.

Herz, R. S. (2004). A comparison of autobiographical memories triggered by olfactory, visual and auditory stimuli. *Chemical Senses, 29*, 217–224.

Herz, R. (2007). *The scent of desire: Discovering our enigmatic sense of smell*. New York: William Morrow.

Herz, R. S. & Cupchik, G. C. (1992). An experimental characterization of odor-evoked memories in humans. *Chemical Senses, 17*, 519–528.

Herz, R. S. & Cupchik, G. C. (1995). The emotional distinctiveness of odor-evoked memories. *Chemical Senses, 20*, 517–528.

Herz, R. S. & Engen, T. (1996). Odor memory: Review and analysis. *Psychonomic Bulletin and Review, 3*, 300–313.

Herz, R. S., Eliassen, J. C., Beland, S. L., & Souza, T. (2003). Neuroimaging evidence for the emotional potency of odor-evoked memory. *Neuropsychologia, 42*, 371–378.

Herz, R. S. & Schooler, J. W. (2002). A naturalistic study of autobiographical memories evoked to olfactory versus visual cues. *American Journal of Psychology, 115*, 21–32.

Hinton, P. B. & Henley, T. B. (1993). Cognitive and affective components of stimuli presented in three modes. *Bulletin of the Psychonomic Society, 31*, 595–598.

Jellinek, J. S. (2004). Proust remembered: Has Proust's account of odor-cue autobiographical memory recall really been investigated? *Chemical Senses, 29*, 455–458.

Laird, D. A. (1935). What can you do with your nose? *Scientific Monthly, 41*, 126–130.

Lawless, H. & Engen, T. (1977). Associations to odors: Interference, mnemonics and verbal labeling. *Journal of*

Experimental Psychology: Human Learning and Memory, 3, 52–59.

LeDoux, J. (1998). Fear and the brain: Where have we been and where are we going? *Biological Psychiatry, 44*, 1229–1238.

Maylor, E. A., Carter, S. M., & Hallett, E. L. (2002). Preserved olfactory cuing of autobiographical memories in old age. *Journal of Gerontology: Psychological Sciences, 57B*, 41–46.

Proust, M. (1928). *Swann's way*. New York: Modern Library.

Quirk, G. L. & Gehlert, D. R. (2003). Inhibition in the amygdala: Key to pathological states? *Annals of the New York Academy of Sciences, 985*, 263–272.

Rolls, E. T. (1999). *The brain and emotion*. Oxford: Oxford University Press.

Royet, J. P., Zald, D., Versace, R., Costes, N., Lavenne, F., Koenig, O., et al. (2000). Emotional responses to pleasant and unpleasant olfactory, visual, and auditory stimuli: A positron emission tomography study. *Journal of Neuroscience, 20*, 7752–7759.

Ross, E. D., Homan, R. W., & Buck, R. (1994). Differential hemispheric lateralization of primary and social emotions. *Neuropsychiatry, Neuropsychology, and Behavioral Neurology, 7*, 1–19.

Rubin, D. C., Groth, E., & Goldsmith, D. J. (1984). Olfactory cueing of autobiographical memory. *American Journal of Psychology, 97*, 493–507.

Schroers, M., Prigot, J. & Fagen, J. (2007). The effect of salient odor context on memory retrieval in young infants. *Infant Behavior & Development, 30*, 685–689.

Schwerdtfeger, W. L., Buhl, E. H., & Gemroth, P. (1990). Disynaptic olfactory input to the hippocampus mediated by stellate cells in the entorhinal cortex. *Journal of Comparative Neurology, 194*, 519–534.

Staubli, U., Ivy, G., & Lynch, G. (1984). Hippocampal denervation causes rapid forgetting of olfactory information in rats. *Proceedings of the National Academy of Sciences USA, 81*, 5885–5887.

Tulving, E., Kapur, S. Craik, F. I. M., Moscovitch, M., & Houle, S. (1994). Hemispheric encoding/retrieval asymmetry in episodic memory: positron emission tomography findings. *Proceedings of the National Academy of Sciences USA, 91*, 2016–2020.

Turner, B. H., Mishkin, M., & Knapp, M. (1980). Organization of the amygdalopetal projections from modality-specific cortical association areas in the monkey. *Journal of Comparative Neurology, 191*, 515–543.

Willander, J. & Larsson, M. (2006). Smell your way back to childhood: Autobiographical odor memory. *Psychonomic Bulletin & Review, 13*, 240–244.

Willander, J. & Larsson, M. (2007). Olfaction and emotion: The case of autobiographical memory. *Memory & Cognition, 35*, 1659–1663.

Zatorre, R. J., Jones-Gotman, M., Evans, A. C., & Meyer, E. (1992). Functional localization and lateralization of human olfactory cortex. *Nature, 360*, 339–340.

Emotion Regulation: Neural Bases and Beyond

Peter Mende-Siedlecki, Hedy Kober, *and* Kevin N. Ochsner

Abstract

This chapter provides a brief background on emotion regulation and describes in detail two classes of emotion regulation strategies. Towards that end, the remainder of the chapter is organized into three parts. In the first, it defines what we mean by emotion and emotion regulation, and introduces our approach to understanding them at multiple levels of analysis. In the second, it reviews current research on two kinds of cognitive strategies for regulating emotion: attention deployment and cognitive change. Finally, it considers the implications of this review for future research on emotion regulation.

Keywords: emotion regulation, emotion, cognitive strategies, attention deployment, cognitive change

Life is full of both profound tragedies and routine setbacks, and the emotions elicited by these events can interfere with our everyday lives. However, we humans possess an astonishing faculty for regulating these emotions and adapting to the situations from which they arise. Whether it's positively reframing an undesirable situation to make it more manageable or steering oneself away from a potential threat, the ability to successfully regulate one's emotions is a key aspect of mental health. Indeed, individual differences in emotion regulation have implications for well being, and chronic regulatory failure is associated with disorders ranging from depression to addiction (Davidson, Putnam, & Larson, 2000; Ochsner & Gross, 2005). In this chapter, we will provide a brief background on emotion regulation and describe in detail two classes of emotion regulation strategies. Towards that end, the remainder of this chapter is organized into three parts. In the first, we define what we mean by emotion and emotion regulation, and introduce our approach to understanding them at multiple levels of analysis. In the second, we review current research on two kinds of cognitive strategies for regulating emotion. Finally, we consider the implications of this review for future research on emotion regulation.

The Playing Field

In sports, it's always important to know the rules of the game before one begins to play. In reviewing the literature on emotion regulation, it is much the same: Before diving into the literature, it's important to clearly define the terms and limits of what is to be considered.

What is Emotion?

To understand the process of emotion regulation, one must first understand what regulatory processes are targeting. Emotions can be thought of as responses to adaptive challenges that involve changes in physiology, behavior, and experience (Cacioppo, Berntson, Larsen, Poehlmann, & Ito, 2000; Ochsner & Barrett, 2001; Scherer, Schorr, & Johnstone, 2001). This response is triggered by an appraisal of the significance of the challenge to one's current goals, wants, or needs. This emotion-generative cycle, where appraisals generate responses, may repeat as the output of one cycle contributes to the input for the next.

Neuroimaging studies of emotion have identified several subcortical structures that play key roles in triggering emotional responses, with the amygdala and striatum foremost among them (Kober et al., 2008; Wager, Davidson, Hughes, Lindquist, & Ochsner, 2008). The amygdala is commonly associated with the detection of arousing stimuli in general and potential threats in particular (Phelps, 2006; Whalen, 1998), while the striatum is thought to be important for learning about the rewarding or reinforcing properties of a stimulus (Kelley, 2004).

The Process Model of Emotion Regulation

With roots in prior work on ego defense, stress and coping, and delay of gratification (Ochsner & Gross, 2005), current research has progressed from the study of general constructs to investigating questions about particular behavioral and experiential consequences of successful regulation, different strategies that may be employed, and which brain systems are involved with which strategies.

A process model of emotion regulation put forth by James Gross guides much of this work. According to this model, the emotion regulatory impact of different forms of emotion regulation can be understood in terms of how they impact specific stages of the emotion generation process. Some kinds of strategies, such as *situation selection* or *situation modification*, entail avoiding or changing the emotion-eliciting event itself. Other kinds of strategies, such as *attention deployment* and *cognitive change*, involve changing how one attends to and appraises the meaning of the emotion-eliciting event. The final kind of strategy, known as *response modulation*, involves controlling how one responds behaviorally to an emotion, such as suppressing the expression of an emotion (Gross, 1998).

To make this concrete, consider the example of a painful breakup. An individual struggling with undesirable negative emotions may choose to cut themselves off entirely from their former partner (*situation selection*), or they might only associate with that former partner in contexts that are deemed emotionally "safe," for instance, in a group setting (*situation modification*). Alternatively, this individual may select more internal means of easing the pain associated with their breakup. They may choose to distract themselves from their emotional turmoil by throwing themselves into their work or hobbies (*attention deployment*), or they might attempt to rethink their perspective on the breakup, ultimately deciding that it was the best outcome for both parties involved (*cognitive change*). Finally, the individual could choose to "keep a stiff upper lip"—suppressing the expression of their emotion so that no one else can tell what they are feeling (*response modulation*).

Current behavioral research has sought to compare and contrast the consequences of deploying different kinds of emotion regulatory strategies. For example, it has been found that response modulation strategies such as expressive suppression may diminish facial and bodily movements associated with emotion, despite little change in subjective report of that emotional experience and potentially dangerous increases in physiological markers of arousal (Gross, 1998; Roberts, Levenson, & Gross, 2008). By contrast, cognitive change strategies such as reappraisal have been shown to decrease subjective report of emotional experience, absent of unwanted physical or social disadvantages, and may be associated with decreased stress reactivity, compared to a more suppressive style of regulation (Moore, Zoellner, & Mollenholt, 2008). Further, the tendency to reappraise rather than to suppress is associated with better interpersonal functioning, more positive emotion, less negative emotion, and greater well-being (Gross & John, 2003).

Levels of Analysis

Our approach to describing the mechanisms underlying emotion and emotion regulation draws on the theories and methods of social psychology on the one hand, and cognitive and affective neuroscience on the other. This *social cognitive and affective neuroscience* approach (Ochsner, 2007; Ochsner & Barrett, 2001) seeks to describe the mechanisms underlying emotion and emotion regulation at three levels of analysis. The first is the social level, at which we describe specific kinds of behaviors and experiences that are of interest. The second is the cognitive, or information processing level, at which we describe the mental representations and psychological processes that give rise to the phenomenon in question. The third is the neural level, at which we describe the neural systems whose computations embody processes at the cognitive level.

One benefit of this multi-level approach is that it helps clarify which levels of analysis are addressed by our terminology. In the case of emotion regulation this is especially important, because some terms can ambiguously refer to multiple levels of analysis. For example, the term *suppression* has been used in at least three ways. First, *suppression* is often used to describe behavioral attempts to keep an emotion or thought out of awareness or to keep a given action from being executed (Gross & Levenson, 1993; Wegner, Schneider, Carter, & White, 1987). In this case, the term *suppression* refers to the social-level task given to participants. In the second, *suppression* refers not to the specific behaviors in which participants engage, but rather to the goal of reducing the occurrence of a thought or emotion, which can be achieved by various means, including cognitive change (Phan et al., 2005; Urry et al., 2006). When used in this way, the meaning of the term *suppression* shades between references to explicit social-level goals consciously held by participants and cognitive-level processes used to achieve those goals. Finally, in the third, *suppression* is used specifically to refer only to hypothetical cognitive processes that achieve the goal of keeping emotions or thoughts out of awareness (Freud, 1900/1980).

So which is it? Is suppression a social level goal, a social level behavior, or a cognitive process? For present purposes, we treat *suppression* as a social-level strategy that involves goals and specific behaviors designed to attain them. In like fashion, the strategies described under Gross's process model of emotion regulation also are described at the social level in terms of the goals and behaviors used to attain them.

In the following review, our goal is to carefully distinguish between and describe the relations among the three levels, while neither conflating nor confusing them. The data from functional neuroimaging studies allow us to do this in two ways. By measuring brain activity elicited while subjects are participating in behavioral tasks, we have two dependent measures—one at a neural level and one at the social level—that we can use to gain leverage on theories of the psychological processes that connect them. This is, of course, a difficult task because no task is process-pure and no brain structure uniquely participates in one psychological process (Kosslyn, 1994). Nevertheless, we argue that attempting to triangulate on core processes using two kinds of data (as when conducting functional imaging studies) can provide novel insights not obtainable using just one type of data (e.g., behavior-only studies; Ochsner, 2007).

Current Work: From Attention Deployment to Cognitive Change

With the above considerations in mind, this chapter focuses on reviewing neuroimaging studies of two kinds of cognitive strategies: attention deployment and cognitive change. We focus on these two strategies because they are associated with clearly defined social-level behavioral strategies that can be studied in an imaging environment, and because—perhaps not coincidentally—they have been the focus of the largest amount of work.

Attention Deployment

Attention deployment refers to the use of control processes to modify emotional responses by devoting less conscious attention to the emotional content of a given stimulus. This diversion of attention has been shown, in turn, to promote decreases in reported emotion, as well as decreases in activity in areas associated with the processing of affective responses, such as the amygdala and the anterior insula (Ochsner & Gross, 2005).

In general usage, attention deployment strategies may not be associated with an explicit regulatory goal. Although they promote a reduction in behavioral and neural markers of an emotional response, the need to split attention across multiple tasks may end up having a beneficial, albeit not necessarily intended, emotion regulatory effect. In this sense, the regulatory effects of attention deployment are "implicit," because they occur in the absence of explicit awareness of a goal and subsequent attempts to regulate emotion.

We have divided the various types of attention deployment strategies into three classes—those that alter the emotional response through a distracting task or secondary stimulus (*distraction*), those that direct attention away from the emotional content of a stimulus towards some other perceptual feature (*selective attention*), and those that involve an explicit semantic judgment of the stimulus that focuses attention on a single dimension of meaning (*selective construal*).

DISTRACTION

Distraction is an emotion regulation strategy that recruits various cognitive processes—such as those involved in shifting attention and mediating conflict—towards the goal of modulating affect. Studies of distraction typically involve diminishing participants' attention to emotional stimuli by using an unrelated distractor task that participants must complete simultaneously with exposure to an emotionally evocative event. Though these studies typically use pain as an elicitor of negative emotion, some recent studies have attempted to test the regulatory effects of distraction on the experience of emotion associated with other stimuli—for instance, the anticipation of subsequent negative stimuli, such as aversive photos.

Distraction consistently has been shown to produce decreases in both subjective report of pain and activity in areas associated with pain processing—the so-called "pain matrix," encompassing the secondary somatosensory cortex, the insula, portions of the anterior cingulate cortex, and the thalamus (Jones, 1998). Studies that report these modulations have asked participants to complete a verbal attention task distraction during cold pressor pain (e.g., pain caused by immersing a participant's arm in ice cold water) (Frankenstein, Richter, McIntyre, & Remy, 2001), a self-distraction task during thermal pain (Tracey et al., 2002), the Stroop task during thermal pain (Bantick et al., 2002; Valet et al., 2004), a rapid serial visual-processing task distraction during capsaicin-induced hyperalgesia (Wiech et al., 2005), a multisource interference task distraction during transcutaneous electrical nerve stimulation (Seminowicz & Davis, 2007), and an auditory distractor task during visceral pain (Dunckley et al., 2007). In addition, two studies have reported activations in the periaqueductal gray—an area associated with pain analgesia (Wager et al., 2004)—associated with distraction during the experience of pain (Tracey et al., 2002; Valet et al., 2004).

Several of these studies have also observed activations in the dorsal anterior cingulate cortex (ACC) and the lateral prefrontal cortex (PFC) during distraction (Bantick et al., 2002; Frankenstein et al., 2001; Seminowicz & Davis, 2007; Valet et al., 2004), areas typically associated with cognitive control. However, as these regions have also been associated with working memory and other executive functions (Wager & Smith, 2003), it should be noted that these activations could be attributable to either the conscious regulation of pain, participation in the distractor tasks themselves, or some combination of the two.

Similar results were reported in the few studies that examined distraction's impact on the experience of non-pain-related negative emotion. For example, distraction from anxious anticipation of subsequent negative emotion by means of an N-back task resulted in decreases in amygdala activity compared to the attended condition and increases in activity in the ventrolateral PFC (Erk, Abler, & Walter, 2006). Similar recruitment of the left lateral PFC was observed in association with self-distraction during pain-related anxiety (Kalisch, Wiech, Herrmann, & Dolan, 2006). Interestingly, although the authors of the latter study suggest a left-distraction/right-reappraisal lateralization of function in the brain, to date, no studies have directly compared distraction-based emotion regulation and cognitive reappraisal-based emotion regulation.

SELECTIVE ATTENTION

Selective attention strategies draw on cognitive processes used to shift and engage attention to effect modulations in affective responding. Neuroimaging studies of this strategy typically involve paradigms where participants are instructed to focus on the non-emotional portions of an affective stimulus or combination of stimuli. Though this manipulation can be associated with an increase in attentional load, it does not constitute a distractor task, per se. Studies of distraction, as discussed above, typically shift participants' attention by means of some cognitive task or other-modal cue.

Selectively directing attentional resources away from the emotional content of a stimulus has been shown to modulate affective responding, as well as affective processing at the neural level. For instance, amygdala activity in response to fear faces was decreased when participants judged the orientation of a set of bars on either side of the image, compared to simply attending to the faces (Pessoa, McKenna, Gutierrez, & Ungerleider, 2002). This task is distinguished from a distraction paradigm in that the faces and bars are not presented in competing sensory modalities. They are two visual stimuli presented side-by-side and for such a brief amount of time that they could be said to constitute a single composite stimulus.

Another study produced similar results in response to the presentation of pairs of fear faces and houses—amygdala activity was significantly lower when low trait-anxiety subjects attended to houses, as opposed to fear faces (Bishop, Duncan, & Lawrence, 2004). In a later study, participants were presented letter strings superimposed over fear faces and asked to make easy or difficult judgments of the strings. Amygdala activity in response to fear faces was significantly lower while under high perceptual load compared to low perceptual load (Bishop, Jenkins, & Lawrence, 2007). Finally, recent work using EEG suggests that the late positive potential (LPP), a measure of attention to emotional stimuli, is affected by similar manipulations.

When attention is selectively directed to nonarousing portions of aversive images, the LPP is reduced (Dunning & Hajcak, 2009; Hajcak, Dunning, & Foti, 2009).

However, several other studies examining the effects of selective attention on emotional experience have produced discrepant results. For instance, in studies using similar face versus house matching tasks, the amygdala was activated irrespective of attention to fear faces (Anderson, Christoff, Panitz, De Rosa, & Gabrieli, 2003; Vuilleumier, Armony, Driver, & Dolan, 2001). Additionally, a similar pattern of amygdala activity was observed in a comparison of attended versus ignored anger prosody (Sander et al., 2005). However, though attention failed to modulate amygdala activity in this study, the orbitofrontal cortex (OFC) showed greater activity during the attended than the ignored condition. Further, this activity was strongly correlated with an individual difference measure of proneness to anxiety, suggesting that individual differences may contribute to the degree that such manipulations modulate affective processing.

One potential source of inconsistency in these studies of selective attention is the varying degree of attentional demand between tasks. For instance, the participants in the studies by Vuilleumier et al. (2001) and Anderson et al. (2003) performed at a higher rate of success than the subjects in the study described by Pessoa and colleagues (Pessoa et al., 2002). In a later study, Pessoa et al. included task difficulty as a variable, and found that amygdala activity was greater for fear faces as opposed to neutral faces only when the bar-orientation task was least difficult (Pessoa, Padmala, & Morland, 2005). Although this indicates a relationship between attentional demand and modulation of the emotional experience, in the absence of a way to quantify attentional load on the same metric across different studies and tasks, these results still do not resolve why no attention-related amygdala modulation was observed in Vuilleumier et al. (2001) and Anderson et al. (2003), the putatively "easier" tasks.

That being said, the correlation reported between proneness to anxiety and OFC activity during the attended condition is of note (Sander et al., 2005), especially in light of findings in several studies by Bishop and colleagues (2004). In their 2004 study, the face versus house matching task produced no attentional modulation of amygdala activity in the high trait-anxiety subjects (Bishop et al., 2004). Later, it was observed that high state anxiety was associated with increased amygdala activity to fear faces under low perceptual load, and further, that high trait anxiety was associated with less dorsal ACC, dorsolateral PFC, and ventrolateral PFC activity during low perceptual load. Further research should be conducted to clarify the relationship between attentional focus and individual differences in level of anxiety, which might modulate sensitivity to unattended affective stimuli.

SELECTIVE CONSTRUAL

Selective construal strategies can be thought of as a specific type of selective attention in which attention is directed to an alternative dimension of semantic meaning, rather than an alternative perceptual aspect of a stimulus. Such studies typically ask participants to make judgments about some aspect of the meaning or content of emotional stimuli that is orthogonal to its emotional content.

Somewhat confusingly, depending on the study, construal along either emotional or non-emotional dimensions both have been shown to modulate affect and activation in areas related to affective processing (e.g., the amygdala). On one hand, consider that several of these studies have shown a relative decrease in amygdala activation as a result of directly judging the emotional, rather than the perceptual features of a stimulus. Such judgments include matching of aversive scenes or emotional faces in terms of their affective as opposed to perceptual qualities, (Hariri, Bookheimer, & Mazziotta, 2000; Hariri, Mattay, Tessitore, Fera, & Weinberger, 2003; Lieberman et al., 2007; Lieberman, Hariri, Jarcho, Eisenberger, & Bookheimer, 2005) and active rating of emotional responses versus passive viewing of emotionally charged photos (Taylor, Phan, Decker, & Liberzon, 2003). Furthermore, a recent behavioral study yielded evidence that these effects can even be conserved over time. Pairing aversive images with affective labels—which presumably directs participants to construe them in terms of their affective meaning—was associated with greater decreases in physiological responses to those images after an eight-day period, than those images that had been unpaired (Tabibnia, Lieberman, & Craske, 2008). These effects have been accompanied by activity in the ACC (Hariri et al., 2000; Hariri et al., 2003; Taylor et al., 2003), as well as prefrontal activations, including right ventrolateral PFC (Hariri et al., 2000; Hariri et al., 2003; Lieberman et al., 2007) and right dorsomedial PFC (Taylor et al., 2003). However, a later study comparing active rating versus passive viewing of sad and happy films (a paradigm similar to Taylor et al., 2002) did not observe a decrease in self-report of emotion or neural indicators of emotional processing, though active rating once again produced activity in the ACC (Hutcherson et al., 2005).

On the other hand, many studies of selective construal have failed to observe any modulation in affective processing areas. In paradigms similar to those described above, no significant differences were observed in amygdala activity when participants make gender as opposed to affect judgments of happy, disgusted, fearful, and sad faces, (Gorno-Tempini et al., 2001; Winston, O'Doherty, & Dolan, 2003), emotion versus age judgments of famous individuals with negative associations (Cunningham, Johnson, Gatenby, Gore, & Banaji, 2003), and trustworthiness versus age judgments of differentially trustworthy faces (Winston, Strange, O'Doherty, & Dolan, 2002).

One potential explanation for these discrepant results is a difference in the stimuli used across studies. Whereas studies that do not observe amygdala modulation typically use lower-intensity, lower-arousal stimuli, such as expressive Ekman faces (Gorno-Tempini et al., 2001; Winston et al., 2003), several studies that *do* observe amygdala modulation use highly aversive, high-arousal images from the International Affective Picture System (Hariri et al., 2003; Taylor et al., 2003). Among the differences between these two kinds of stimuli that could be responsible for the discrepant results, one possibility is that faces have significance that systems like the amygdala have evolved to detect, regardless of attentional engagement. Alternatively, high arousal stimuli may elicit more amygdala activity overall and thus may have more "room to fall" when attentional resources drop.

Another factor is that studies of selective construal have used two similar, but functionally different paradigms. The first group of studies compares two different *tasks* (matching vs. labeling, (Hariri et al., 2000; Hariri et al., 2003)), while the second group compares two different *judgments* (e.g., gender vs. valence assessments; Cunningham et al., 2003; Gorno-Tempini et al., 2001; Winston et al., 2003; Winston et al., 2002). This raises the possibility that the attentional demands of the match task may simply be greater than those of the label task, while emotional and gender judgments impose similar attentional load, at least in some cases. Therefore, this increased load may account for the amygdala deactivations observed in the former studies as opposed to the latter. Indeed, Lieberman et al. (2007) controlled for these differences, and observed the greatest amygdala deactivations in the "affect label" condition, as compared to "affect match," "gender label," or "gender match." All in all, the variability in these results speaks to a need for further clarity in future studies of selective construal strategies.

SUMMARY

In general, studies of attention deployment strategies have been rather limited in terms of their scope. Most of these studies have been focused on the regulation of affective perception, rather than affective responding. This has resulted in paradigms that produce interesting results, but sometimes fail to achieve a certain level of construct or ecological validity. On the one hand, while pain-related stimuli are certainly arousing and affective, they don't represent the kind of multidimensional emotional experiences of every day life. On the other hand, fear faces, such as those used in studies of selective attention and selective construal, lack inherent affective significance in the experimental environment. While they may have significance for survival in everyday life (e.g., in our evolutionary context, a fear face may have indicated a need to run away from a predator in the African savannah, and still communicates the presence of potential dangers), they may be too abstracted from the survival goals of a subject in a neuroimaging study to elicit a meaningful level of emotional response. Clearly, we need to find a middle ground. Future work in this area should employ more self-relevant stimuli in an effort to make this so.

Furthermore, the relatively stark delineation of stimuli used to study these three types of strategies makes a comparison between forms of attention deployment rather problematic. To reiterate, studies of distraction focus predominantly on pain-related stimuli, while, for the most part, studies of selective attention and selective construal use emotional face stimuli. To truly parcellate which attention-deployment strategies are most efficient at regulating which emotions—and furthermore, which neural mechanisms facilitate this regulation—a direct comparison of these strategies must be performed within subjects, using the same emotionally evocative stimuli.

Cognitive Change

Research addressing the use of cognitive change to regulate emotional responses usually focuses on changes in emotional experience brought about by either the cognitive manipulation of current emotional states or the cognitive generation of new emotional states. In general, while the strategies used to achieve these ends have similar functional goals as attention-deployment strategies (e.g., modulation of affect), they are more dependent upon higher cognitive faculties like mental imagery, memory, and response selection (Ochsner & Gross, 2005).

REAPPRAISAL

Reappraisal is an umbrella term that encompasses various sub-strategies used to mentally transform the meaning of a stimulus, thereby changing one's affective response to it. In this way, reappraisal can be used to increase, decrease, or maintain an emotional response, in some cases by fundamentally altering one's personal relationship to it. To achieve these varied ends, reappraisal draws upon a wide array of cognitive processes including those involved in working memory, language, response inhibition, and control of response conflicts. Studies of reappraisal examine the behavioral and neural consequences of modifying responses to emotionally arousing stimuli. These studies often, but not always, involve an explicit goal to regulate emotion, whereby participants are instructed to actively construe emotional stimuli in a different way in order to change their emotional state. The majority of these studies have focused on decreasing feelings of negative affect, although current research has begun to examine the use of similar strategies with positive or discrete types of emotion as well (Kim & Hamann, 2007; Kober, Kross, Hart, Mischel, & Ochsner, in press).

In a typical study, participants are presented with an emotionally charged stimulus and instructed to think about it through a particular cognitive frame that changes the meaning or affective value of the stimulus. The different means of reappraising can be thought of as sub-strategies that exert different kinds of change on the lens through which a stimulus is viewed. Two sub-strategies in particular have received the most attention. The first is *reinterpretation*, which involves re-thinking the event, actors, and context of an image. The second is *distancing*, which involves viewing an image from the perspective of a detached (objective) third-person observer. In addition, various other reappraisal-like sub-strategies have been studied that combine elements of reappraisal with other strategies. For example, "cognitive substitution," described below, involves aspects of both reappraisal and distraction as participants generate and focus on emotions related to a cue, but that are different than those typically associated with it.

REINTERPRETATION

Cognitive strategies focused on reinterpretation typically involve a rethinking or reimagining of the outcomes, dispositions, or intentions associated with an affective stimulus in such a way that changes the initial emotional response to that stimulus. For example, a participant may be presented with an image of a crying child that initially evokes feelings of sadness or fear for the distressed child, but when given the cue to reinterpret, the participant may imagine that the child will soon be found and comforted by her mother and the situation will resolve itself positively (Ochsner, Bunge, Gross, & Gabrieli, 2002).

Reinterpretation-based reappraisal has been shown to modulate amygdala activity associated with emotions elicited by normatively aversive images (Johnstone, van Reekum, Urry, Kalin, & Davidson, 2007; Kim & Hamann, 2007; Ochsner et al., 2002; Ochsner et al., 2004; Phan et al., 2005; Urry et al., 2006; van Reekum et al., 2007), images of moral violations (Harenski & Hamann, 2006), and positive images (Kim & Hamann, 2007). Reinterpretation typically is associated with increased activity in a network of regions associated with cognitive control, including dorsolateral PFC, dorsomedial PFC, and dorsal ACC. Some recent work has examined the connectivity between areas of the PFC and amygdala, observing an inverse relationship between ventrolateral PFC activity and amygdala activity (Urry et al., 2006), a relationship between the ventrolateral PFC and the amygdala mediated by the ventromedial PFC (Johnstone et al., 2007), and both positive and negative mediations of ventrolateral PFC activity and reappraisal success by striatum and amygdala activity, respectively (Wager et al., 2008).

Until recently, no study had directly compared either the behavioral or neural effects of an attentional control-based strategy with those of a cognitive change-based strategy. McRae and colleagues sought to make this comparison, examining both the emotional consequences and neural underpinnings of distraction versus reappraisal within the same subjects (McRae et al., 2010). Consistent with prior work, reappraisal and distraction both downregulated behavioral ratings of negative emotion, as well as activation in the amygdala. In addition, both conditions produced increased activity in PFC and ACC. In the critical comparison between reappraisal and distraction, reappraisal led to greater drops in subjective report of negative affect, as well as greater increases in medial PFC and anterior temporal regions—areas typically associated with processing the semantic content of affective stimuli. By contrast, distraction was observed to induce significantly greater drops in amygdala activity and significantly greater increases in PFC and attention-related parietal areas.

DISTANCING

The reappraisal sub-strategy known as distancing draws on cognitive processes similar to those involved in reinterpretation, although in this case in an effort to assume a personally, and hence emotionally, removed perspective. In studies of distancing, participants are instructed to act as third-person observers while perceiving emotionally arousing stimuli. For instance, if presented with a gory photo of an accident, one might take the viewpoint of detached, clinical observer not personally connected to the events or individuals depicted in the photo (Ochsner et al., 2004).

Distancing-based strategies have been shown to modulate amygdala activity associated with emotions elicited by sad films (Levesque et al., 2003), erotic photos (Beauregard, Levesque, & Bourgouin, 2001), aversive images (Ochsner et al., 2004), pain anticipation (Kalisch et al., 2005), threatening images (Eippert et al., 2007), and negative images with social content, specifically (Koenigsberg et al., in press). Though distancing strategies differ qualitatively from reinterpretation strategies, they activate a similar set of areas: dorsomedial PFC, dorsolateral PFC, and dorsal ACC, suggesting that they rely on a largely similar set of underlying processes. In direct comparisons of reinterpretation and distancing (Kim & Hamann, 2007; Ochsner et al., 2004), it was reported that generally, reinterpretation recruits lateral PFC regions more strongly than distancing and conversely, distancing recruits medial PFC regions more strongly than reinterpretation. This differentiation falls in line with previous research linking the lateral and medial aspects of the PFC to processes involved in working memory/selective attention (Knight, Staines, Swick, & Chao, 1999; Miller & Cohen, 2001; Ochsner et al., 2004; Smith & Jonides, 1999) and self-reflection on affective states (Gusnard, Akbudak, Shulman, & Raichle, 2001; Lane, Fink, Chau, & Dolan, 1997; Lieberman, 2007; Simpson, Drevets, Snyder, Gusnard, & Raichle, 2001), respectively.

Several studies have also examined the effect of *reducing* psychological distance—i.e., feeling closer to—an emotional stimulus. In such studies, participants are asked to fully immerse themselves in an aversive image and imagine that the emotional events depicted are happening to them (Eippert et al., 2007; Ochsner et al., 2004). Neurally speaking, immersion yields similar results to other forms of cognitive change, activating such areas as dorsomedial PFC, dorsolateral PFC, and ventrolateral PFC. Critically, immersion strategies typically increase amygdala activity. When immersion was directly compared with distancing, immersion was associated with greater medial PFC and posterior cingulate activity, while distancing produces more lateral PFC and OFC activity (Ochsner et al., 2004).

SUMMARY

Consistently, cognitive change strategies have been observed to modulate both self-report of emotion and affective processing. In turn, these modulations have been typically linked to activity in the PFC and dorsal ACC. The relative regularity of these results over the course of many studies is encouraging, and speaks to the use of strongly evocative stimuli and discrete regulatory strategies. As we begin to know more and more about what areas of the brain are involved in such regulatory processes, we can expand our scope to examine the differences between specific strategies, as well as investigate how and why regulation fails in certain populations.

As work progresses, however, there comes a crucial need for regularity and specificity of terminology—if our goal as a field is to develop an understanding of the unique brain systems that implement different strategies. Studies that offer their participants a variety of qualitatively different strategies and suggest that they simply use the strategy that works best (Johnstone et al., 2007; Kim & Hamann, 2007; Urry et al., 2006) pose a potential problem, because though the implicit goal of emotion regulation is constant, at any given moment, we cannot be sure what subjects are actually doing to dampen or heighten their emotional responses.

Conclusions and Future Directions

With all the progress that has been made on understanding the cognitive and neural mechanisms of emotion regulation, there is still much that remains unclear. Indeed, for every question answered, two more seem to crop up in its place. In this section we consider work on strategies related to, but that do not fit perfectly in the preceding review, critically sum up what the review has told us, and consider issues that future work might fruitfully explore.

Hybrid Strategies

There are many cognitive regulatory strategies that combine key elements of attention deployment or cognitive change strategies. Cognitive substitution is one such combination, drawing upon aspects of distraction, selective attention, and reappraisal to effect a change in the emotional experience of an affective stimulus by replacing the initial appraisal of that stimulus with an unrelated, but preferential emotional experience.

Several studies have examined the effects of supplanting the initial emotional response with an entirely new emotional experience, like thinking of a positive memory during a sad film (Cooney, Joormann, Atlas, Eugene, & Gotlib, 2007) or thinking of something calming during reward expectation or shock expectation (Delgado, Gillis, & Phelps, 2008; Delgado, Nearing, LeDoux, & Phelps, 2008). In these studies, the cognitive substitution strategy has modulated activity in key processing areas—the amygdala (Delgado, Nearing, et al., 2008) and the ventral striatum (Delgado, Gillis, et al., 2008)—and has been associated with dorsolateral, ventrolateral, and ventromedial PFC activity.

It should be noted that some studies of attention deployment can be thought of as potentially falling under this hybrid category; for instance, the Kalisch et al. (2005) study of self-distraction's effect on the experience of pain-related anxiety. As previously mentioned, in this study participants were instructed to distract themselves by thinking of anything that would get their minds off the pain they were about to experience. The neuroimaging results from this study—activity in the left lateral PFC—further suggest a similarity.

Critical Summary

To different degrees, attention deployment and cognitive change strategies have been shown to modulate both subjective reports and neural signatures of various emotional responses. Whereas reappraisal-based cognitive change strategies such as reinterpretation and distancing consistently have been shown to modulate affective processing and experience, results have been more mixed for attention deployment strategies, such as selective attention and selective construal. Ultimately, though similar brain regions are associated with supporting these strategies, including the PFC and the ACC, many questions remain about differential recruitment of these areas across various strategies of emotion regulation.

Future Directions

With the preceding review in mind, there are numerous directions for future work. Here we consider four of the most salient.

DEFINING BOUNDARIES

Moving forward, researchers must be careful to differentiate between qualitatively different forms of regulation. Consider, for example, that in the cognitive change literature, multiple studies couch reinterpretation or distancing strategies in terms of "suppression" (Levesque et al., 2003; Phan et al., 2005, respectively) or cue their subjects to implement a reinterpretation strategy with the word "suppress" (Koenigsberg et al., in press; Urry et al., 2006; van Reekum et al., 2007). As suppression comprises a very different, response-focused form of emotion regulation, characterized by a modulation of the behavioral response to an emotional stimulus (Gross, 1998), rather than an internal reframing of affective meaning of that stimulus, we must maintain consistency in the usage and definition of these key terms.

Researchers also should guard against spillover between strategies when instructing participants to regulate. For instance, in a direct comparison between reappraisal and suppression strategies—an important contrast, to be sure—what was billed as a reappraisal strategy ultimately took the form of a combination of perspective-taking frames and changes in selective attention (Goldin, McRae, Ramel, & Gross, 2008). Indeed, every strategy involves combinations of processes of multiple kinds. Our point here is simply to say that instructional sets should be kept clearly oriented towards one *strategy* or another, so as to know to what we can attribute observed effects—the multiple processes engaged by one strategy or the combination of two different strategies.

Similar issues exist in studies of attention deployment. As previously discussed, discrepant results have been observed in studies of both selective attention and selective construal, due to inconsistencies between paradigms. For instance, a lack of clarity in operationalizing attentional load has produced a set of studies that observe modulation of affective processing due to attentional shifts (Pessoa et al., 2002; Bishop et al. 2004), and a competing set of studies that observe no such modulation (Vuillumier et al., 2001; Anderson et al., 2003). In addition, because the lines between distraction and selective attention are sometimes blurred in the descriptions researchers give of their own work, we must be sure to test differences in psychological processes, not simply semantics.

CRITICAL COMPARISONS

As our understanding of various emotion regulatory strategies grows, comparisons between different strategies along the regulatory continuum become crucial. This will afford us more clarity regarding the component processes that comprise different regulation strategies. It is critical that we build on general statements regarding "the modulation of affective processing" by pursuing specific information about how different types of strategies utilize different psychological processes to modulate emotional experiences. Studies like those that compare reappraisal and distraction (McRae et al., in press) and reappraisal and suppression (Goldin et al., 2008) are beginning to address these important issues.

BROADENING THE SCOPE

As our understanding of attention deployment and cognitive change grows, it's important to consider new avenues of emotion regulation. It's critical that we use stimuli that a) truly evoke emotion and b) cover a diversity of emotions. Real-life emotional experiences cannot be totally understood by simply accounting for valence—there's more to life than negative and positive events. Fear, sadness, anger, and consummatory desire are all emotions that, from time to time, call for regulation. Studies that have begun to examine the behavioral and neural circumstances of such regulation (Delgado et al., 2008; Kober et al., 2010) are adding depth to our field and deepening our knowledge of emotion regulation.

We can also explore new avenues of regulation. For instance, two recent studies have examined a cognitive change strategy modeled on mindfulness-based meditation practices. When employing this "acceptance" strategy, subjects viewed their negative emotions as transient mental events that would soon pass. In one study, while subjects "accepted" their negative autobiographical memories, this strategy evoked left lateral PFC activity and modulated both subjective report of negative emotion, as well as subgenual cingulated and medial PFC activity (Kross, Davidson, Weber, & Ochsner, 2009). The acceptance strategy has also been observed to down-regulate activity in the right amygdala and right anterior insula, in response to both highly aversive images and thermal pain, respectively (Kober et al., in prep). Additionally, a correlational analysis

between "accept" activity and acceptance success scores revealed bilateral activations in lateral PFC, suggesting a neural similarity to reappraisal strategies like reinterpretation.

INDIVIDUAL DIFFERENCES

The model discussed in this chapter provides a framework for testing hypotheses about the ranges of both normal and abnormal emotion regulatory abilities. For instance, recent research has investigated the impact of gender on reappraisal (McRae et al., 2008), ruminative tendencies on reappraisal (Ray et al., 2005), dispositional mindfulness on selective construal abilities (Creswell et al., 2007), and anxious tendencies on selective attention abilities (Bishop et al., 2004, Bishop et al., 2007). Learning how these individual differences affect our capability for effective emotion regulation will fill in the gaps in our knowledge, and ultimately shed light on why we so frequently fail in our attempts to regulate. Studies like these serve to better crystallize our understanding of emotion regulation as a dynamic process, dependent on myriad person-specific and situation-specific factors.

From there, it becomes imperative that we also study emotion regulation in the context of dysfunction, as well. Investigations of the influence of certain disorders on regulative capabilities, such as depression (Beauregard et al., 2001; Johnstone et al., 2007), social anxiety (Goldin et al., 2009), and borderline personality disorder (Koenigsberg et al., in press), have revealed abnormal patterns of PFC activity and amygdala modulation in abnormal populations. Future research should continue to interrogate the relationship between such disorders and regulatory failures.

References

Anderson, A. K., Christoff, K., Panitz, D., De Rosa, E., & Gabrieli, J. D. (2003). Neural correlates of the automatic processing of threat facial signals. *Journal of Neuroscience, 23*(13), 5627–5633.

Bantick, S. J., Wise, R. G., Ploghaus, A., Clare, S., Smith, S. M., & Tracey, I. (2002). Imaging how attention modulates pain in humans using functional MRI. *Brain, 125*(Pt 2), 310–319.

Beauregard, M., Levesque, J., & Bourgouin, P. (2001). Neural correlates of conscious self-regulation of emotion. *Journal of Neuroscience, 21*(18), RC165.

Bishop, S. J., Duncan, J., & Lawrence, A. D. (2004). State anxiety modulation of the amygdala response to unattended threat-related stimuli. *J. Neurosci., 24*(46), 10, 364–10368.

Bishop, S. J., Jenkins, R., & Lawrence, A. D. (2007). Neural processing of fearful faces: Effects of anxiety are gated by perceptual capacity limitations. *Cereb. Cortex, 17*(7), 1595–1603.

Cacioppo, J. T., Berntson, G. G., Larsen, J. T., Poehlmann, K. M., & Ito, T. A. (2000). The psychophysiology of emotion. In R. Lewis & J. M. Haviland-Jones (Eds.), *The handbook of emotion* (2 ed., pp. 173–191). New York: Guilford.

Cooney, R. E., Joormann, J., Atlas, L. Y., Eugene, F., & Gotlib, I. H. (2007). Remembering the good times: Neural correlates of affect regulation. *NeuroReport*, *18*(17), 1771–1774.

Cunningham, W. A., Johnson, M. K., Gatenby, J. C., Gore, J. C., & Banaji, M. R. (2003). Neural components of social evaluation. *Journal of Personality and Social Psychology*, *85*, 639–649.

Davidson, R. J., Putnam, K. M., & Larson, C. L. (2000). Dysfunction in the neural circuitry of emotion regulation—a possible prelude to violence. *Science*, *289*(5479), 591–594.

Delgado, M. R., Gillis, M. M., & Phelps, E. A. (2008). Regulating the expectation of reward via cognitive strategies. *Nat Neurosci*, *11*(8), 880–881.

Delgado, M. R., Nearing, K. I., LeDoux, J. E., & Phelps, E. A. (2008). Neural circuitry underlying the regulation of conditioned fear and its relation to extinction. *59*(5), 829–838.

Dunckley, P., Aziz, Q., Wise, R. G., Brooks, J., Tracey, I., & Chang, L. (2007). Attentional modulation of visceral and somatic pain. *Neurogastroenterology and Motility*, *19*(7), 569–577.

Dunning, J. P. & Hajcak, G. (2009). See no evil: Directing visual attention within unpleasant images modulates the electrocortical response. *Psychophysiology*, *46*(1), 28–33.

Eippert, F., Veit, R., Weiskopf, N., Erb, M., Birbaumer, N., & Anders, S. (2007). Regulation of emotional responses elicited by threat-related stimuli. *Hum Brain Mapp*, *28*(5), 409–423.

Erk, S., Abler, B., & Walter, H. (2006). Cognitive modulation of emotion anticipation. *Eur J Neurosci*, *24*(4), 1227–1236.

Frankenstein, U. N., Richter, W., McIntyre, M. C., & Remy, F. (2001). Distraction modulates anterior cingulate gyrus activations during the cold pressor test. *Neuroimage*, *14*(4), 827–836.

Freud, S. (1900/1980). *The interpretation of dreams*. New York; Avon Books.

Goldin, P. R., Manber, T., Hakimi, S., Canli, T., & Gross, J. J. (2009). Neural bases of social anxiety disorder: Emotional reactivity and cognitive regulation during social and physical threat. *Arch Gen Psychiatry*, *66*(2), 170–180.

Goldin, P. R., McRae, K., Ramel, W., & Gross, J. J. (2008). The neural bases of emotion regulation: Reappraisal and suppression of negative emotion. *Biological Psychiatry*, *63*(6), 577–586.

Gorno-Tempini, M. L., Pradelli, S., Serafini, M., Pagnoni, G., Baraldi, P., Porro, C., et al. (2001). Explicit and incidental facial expression processing: An fMRI study. *Neuroimage*, *14*(2), 465–473.

Gross, J. J. (1998). Antecedent- and response-focused emotion regulation: Divergent consequences for experience, expression, and physiology. *Journal of Personality and Social Psychology*, *74*(1), 224–237.

Gross, J. J. & John, O. P. (2003). Individual differences in two emotion regulation processes: Implications for affect, relationships, and well-being. *Journal of Personality and Social Psychology*, *85*, 348–362.

Gross, J. J. & Levenson, R. W. (1993). Emotional suppression: Physiology, self-report, and expressive behavior. *Journal of Personality and Social Psychological*, *64*(6), 970–986.

Gusnard, D. A., Akbudak, E., Shulman, G. L., & Raichle, M. E. (2001). Medial prefrontal cortex and self-referential mental activity: Relation to a default mode of brain function. *Proceedings of the National Academy of Sciences U S A*, *98*(7), 4259–4264.

Hajcak, G., Dunning, J. P., & Foti, D. (2009). Motivated and controlled attention to emotion: Time-course of the late positive potential. *Clinical Neurophysiology: Official Journal of the International Federation of Clinical Neurophysiology*, *120*(3), 505–510.

Harenski, C. L. & Hamann, S. (2006). Neural correlates of regulating negative emotions related to moral violations. *Neuroimage*, *30*(1), 313–324.

Harenski, C. L., Kim, S. H., & Hamann, S. (2009). Neuroticism and psychopathy predict brain activation during moral and nonmoral emotion regulation. *Cogn Affect Behav Neurosci.*, *9*(1), 1–15.

Hariri, A. R., Bookheimer, S. Y., & Mazziotta, J. C. (2000). Modulating emotional responses: Effects of a neocortical network on the limbic system. *Neuroreport*, *11*(1), 43–48.

Hariri, A. R., Mattay, V. S., Tessitore, A., Fera, F., & Weinberger, D. R. (2003). Neocortical modulation of the amygdala response to fearful stimuli. *Biol Psychiatry*, *53*(6), 494–501.

Hutcherson, C. A., Goldin, P. R., Ochsner, K. N., Gabrieli, J. D., Barrett, L. F., & Gross, J. J. (2005). Attention and emotion: Does rating emotion alter neural responses to amusing and sad films? *Neuroimage*, *27*(3), 656–668.

Johnstone, T., van Reekum, C. M., Urry, H. L., Kalin, N. H., & Davidson, R. J. (2007). Failure to regulate: Counterproductive recruitment of top-down prefrontal-subcortical circuitry in major depression. *J. Neurosci.*, *27*(33), 8877–8884.

Jones, A. (1998). The pain matrix and neuropathic pain. *Brain*, *121*(5), 783–784.

Kalisch, R., Wiech, K., Critchley, H. D., Seymour, B., O'Doherty, J. P., Oakley, D. A., et al. (2005). Anxiety reduction through detachment: Subjective, physiological, and neural effects. *Journal of Cognitive Neuroscience*, *17*(6), 874–883.

Kalisch, R., Wiech, K., Herrmann, K., & Dolan, R. J. (2006). Neural correlates of self-distraction from anxiety and a process model of cognitive emotion regulation. *J Cogn Neurosci*, *18*(8), 1266–1276.

Kelley, A. E. (2004). Ventral striatal control of appetitive motivation: Role in ingestive behavior and reward-related learning. *Neuroscience & Biobehavioral Reviews*, *27*(8), 765–776.

Kim, S. H. & Hamann, S. (2007). Neural correlates of positive and negative emotion regulation. *Journal of Cognitive Neuroscience*, *19*(5), 1–23.

Knight, R. T., Staines, W. R., Swick, D., & Chao, L. L. (1999). Prefrontal cortex regulates inhibition and excitation in distributed neural networks. *Acta Psychological (Amst)*, *101*(2–3), 159–178.

Kober, H., Barrett, L. F., Joseph, J., Bliss-Moreau, E., Lindquist, K., & Wager, T. D. (2008). Functional grouping and cortical-subcortical interactions in emotion: A meta-analysis of neuroimaging studies. *NeuroImage*, *42*(2), 998–1031.

Kober, H., Kross, E., Hart, C. L., Mischel, W., & Ochsner, K. N. (2010). Regulation of craving by cognitive strategies in cigarette smokers. *Drugs and Alcohol Dependence*, *106*(1), 52–55.

Kober, H., Mende-Siedlecki, P., Buhle, J., Hughes, B., Kross, E., Wager, T., & Ochsner, K.N. (in prep). Mindfulness-induced changes in the experiences of pain and negative emotion.

Koenigsberg, H. W., Fan, J., Ochsner, K. N., Liu, X., Guise, K., Pizzarello, S., et al. (in press). Neural correlates of using distancing to regulate emotional responses to social cues. *Neuropsychologia, 48*(6), 1813–1822.

Kosslyn, S. M. (1994). *Image and brain: The resolution of the imagery debate.* Cambridge, Mass: MIT Press.

Kross, E., Davidson, M., Weber, J., & Ochsner, K. N. (2009). Coping with emotions past: The neural bases of regulating affect associated with negative autobiographical memories. *Biological Psychiatry, 65*(5), 361–366.

Lane, R. D., Fink, G. R., Chau, P. M., & Dolan, R. J. (1997). Neural activation during selective attention to subjective emotional responses. *Neuroreport, 8*(18), 3969–3972.

Levesque, J., Eugene, F., Joanette, Y., Paquette, V., Mensour, B., Beaudoin, G., et al. (2003). Neural circuitry underlying voluntary suppression of sadness. *Biol Psychiatry, 53*(6), 502–510.

Lieberman, M. D. (2007). Social cognitive neuroscience: A review of core processes. *Annu Rev Psychol, 58*, 259–289.

Lieberman, M. D., Eisenberger, N. I., Crockett, M. J., Tom, S. M., Pfeifer, J. H., & Way, B. M. (2007). Putting feelings into words: Affect labeling disrupts amygdala activity in response to affective stimuli. *Psychol Sci, 18*(5), 421–428.

Lieberman, M. D., Hariri, A., Jarcho, J. M., Eisenberger, N. I., & Bookheimer, S. Y. (2005). An fMRI investigation of race-related amygdala activity in African-American and Caucasian-American individuals. *Nat Neurosci, 8*(6), 720–722.

McRae, K., Ochsner, K. N., Mauss, I. B., Gabrieli, J. D. E., & Gross, J. J. (2008). Gender differences in emotion regulation: An fMRI study of cognitive reappraisal. *Group Processes Intergroup Relations, 11*(2), 143–162.

McRae, K., Hughes, B., Chopra, S., Gabrieli, J. D. E., Gross, J. J., & Ochsner, K. N. (2010). The neural bases of distraction and reappraisal. *Journal of Cognitive Neuroscience, 22*(2), 248–262.

Miller, E. K. & Cohen, J. D. (2001). An integrative theory of prefrontal cortex function. *Annu Review Neuroscience, 24*, 167–202.

Moore, S. A., Zoellner, L. A., & Mollenholt, N. (2008). Are expressive suppression and cognitive reappraisal associated with stress-related symptoms? *Behaviour Research and Therapy, 46*(9), 993–1000.

Ochsner, K. N. (2007). Social cognitive neuroscience: Historical development, core principles, and future promise. In A. Kruglanksi & E. T. Higgins (Eds.), *Social psychology: A handbook of basic principles* (2nd ed., pp. 39–66). New York: Guilford Press.

Ochsner, K. N. & Barrett, L. F. (2001). A multiprocess perspective on the neuroscience of emotion. In T. J. Mayne & G. A. Bonanno (Eds.), *Emotions: Current issues and future directions* (pp. 38–81). New York: The Guilford Press.

Ochsner, K. N., Bunge, S. A., Gross, J. J., & Gabrieli, J. D. E. (2002). Rethinking feelings: An fMRI study of the cognitive regulation of emotion. *Journal of Cognitive Neuroscience, 14*(8), 1215–1229.

Ochsner, K. N. & Gross, J. J. (2005). The cognitive control of emotion. *Trends in Cognitive Sciences, 9*(5), 242–249.

Ochsner, K. N., Knierim, K., Ludlow, D., Hanelin, J., Ramachandran, T., & Mackey, S. (2004). Reflecting upon feelings: An fMRI study of neural systems supporting the attribution of emotion to self and other. *Journal of Cognitive Neuroscience, 16*(10), 1746–1772.

Pessoa, L., McKenna, M., Gutierrez, E., & Ungerleider, L. G. (2002). Neural processing of emotional faces requires attention. *Proc Natl Academy Science U S A, 99*(17), 11,458–11463.

Pessoa, L., Padmala, S., & Morland, T. (2005). Fate of unat-tended fearful faces in the amygdala is determined by both attentional resources and cognitive modulation. *Neuroimage, 28*(1), 249–255.

Phan, K. L., Fitzgerald, D. A., Nathan, P. J., Moore, G. J., Uhde, T. W., & Tancer, M. E. (2005). Neural substrates for voluntary suppression of negative affect: A functional magnetic resonance imaging study. *Biol Psychiatry, 57*(3), 210–219.

Phelps, E. A. (2006). Emotion and cognition: Insights from studies of the human amygdala. *Annu Rev Psychol, 57*, 27–53.

Roberts, N. A., Levenson, R. W., & Gross, J. J. (2008). Cardiovascular costs of emotion suppression cross ethnic lines. *International Journal of Psychophysiology, 70*(1), 82–87.

Sander, D., Grandjean, D., Pourtois, G., Schwartz, S., Seghier, M. L., Scherer, K. R., et al. (2005). Emotion and atten-tion interactions in social cognition: Brain regions involved in processing anger prosody. *NeuroImage, 28*(4), 848–858.

Scherer, K. R., Schorr, A., & Johnstone, T. (Eds.). (2001). *Appraisal processes in emotion: Theory, methods, research.* New York, NY: Oxford University Press.

Seminowicz, D. A. & Davis, K. D. (2007). Interactions of pain intensity and cognitive load: The brain stays on task. *Cereb. Cortex, 17*(6), 1412–1422.

Simpson, J. R., Jr., Drevets, W. C., Snyder, A. Z., Gusnard, D. A., & Raichle, M. E. (2001). Emotion-induced changes in human medial prefrontal cortex: II. During anticipatory anxiety. *Proceedings of the National Academy of Sciences U S A, 98*(2), 688–693.

Smith, E. E. & Jonides, J. (1999). Storage and executive pro-cesses in the frontal lobes. *Science, 283*(5408), 1657–1661.

Tabibnia, G., Lieberman, M. D., & Craske, M. G. (2008). The lasting effect of words on feelings: Words may facilitate expo-sure effects to threatening images. *Emotion, 8*(3), 307–317.

Taylor, S. F., Phan, K. L., Decker, L. R., & Liberzon, I. (2003). Subjective rating of emotionally salient stimuli modulates neural activity. *Neuroimage, 18*(3), 650–659.

Tracey, I., Ploghaus, A., Gati, J. S., Clare, S., Smith, S., Menon, R. S., et al. (2002). Imaging attentional modulation of pain in the periaqueductal gray in humans. *Journal of Neuroscience, 22*(7), 2748–2752.

Urry, H. L., van Reekum, C. M., Johnstone, T., Kalin, N. H., Thurow, M. E., Schaefer, H. S., et al. (2006). Amygdala and ventromedial prefrontal cortex are inversely coupled during regulation of negative affect and predict the diurnal pattern of cortisol secretion among older adults. *J Neurosci, 26*(16), 4415–4425.

Valet, M., Sprenger, T., Boecker, H., Willoch, F., Rummeny, E., Conrad, B., et al. (2004). Distraction modulates connectiv-ity of the cingulo-frontal cortex and the midbrain during pain—an fMRI analysis. *Pain, 109*(3), 399–408.

van Reekum, C. M., Johnstone, T., Urry, H. L., Thurow, M. E., Schaefer, H. S., Alexander, A. L., et al. (2007). Gaze fixations predict brain activation during the voluntary regulation of pic-ture-induced negative affect. *Neuroimage, 36*(3), 1041–1055.

Vuilleumier, P., Armony, J. L., Driver, J., & Dolan, R. J. (2001). Effects of attention and emotion on face processing in the human brain: An event-related fMRI study. *Neuron, 30*(3), 829–841.

Wager, T. D., Davidson, M. L., Hughes, B. L., Lindquist, M. A., & Ochsner, K. N. (2008). Prefrontal-subcortical pathways mediating successful emotion regulation. *Neuron, 59*(6), 1037–1050.

Wager, T. D., Rilling, J. K., Smith, E. E., Sokolik, A., Casey, K. L., Davidson, R. J., et al. (2004). Placebo-induced changes in FMRI in the anticipation and experience of pain. *Science*, *303*(5661), 1162–1167.

Wager, T. D. & Smith, E. E. (2003). Neuroimaging studies of working memory: A meta-analysis. *Cogn Affect Behav Neurosci*, *3*(4), 255–274.

Wegner, D. M., Schneider, D. J., Carter, S. R., & White, T. L. (1987). Paradoxical effects of thought suppression. *Journal of Personality & Social Psychology*, *53*(1), 5–13.

Whalen, P. J. (1998). Fear, vigilance, and ambiguity: Initial neuroimaging studies of the human amygdala. *Current Directions in Psychological Science*, *7*(6), 177–188.

Wiech, K., Seymour, B., Kalisch, R., Enno Stephan, K., Koltzenburg, M., Driver, J., et al. (2005). Modulation of pain processing in hyperalgesia by cognitive demand. *NeuroImage*, *27*(1), 59–69.

Winston, J. S., O'Doherty, J., & Dolan, R. J. (2003). Common and distinct neural responses during direct and incidental processing of multiple facial emotions. *Neuroimage*, *20*(1), 84–97.

Winston, J. S., Strange, B. A., O'Doherty, J., & Dolan, R. J. (2002). Automatic and intentional brain responses during evaluation of trustworthiness of faces. *Nature Neuroscience*, *5*(3), 277–283.

PART 3

Social Cognition

Brain Development during Childhood and Adolescence[*]

Tomáš Paus

Abstract

This chapter discusses brain development during childhood and adolescence, based on findings obtained with magnetic resonance imaging (MRI). MRI contributed a wealth of information about the adolescent brain, documenting, in particular, its continuing structural maturation and beginning to elucidate interesting changes in its functional organization. Several large-scale MR-based studies of childhood and adolescence are under way, promising to deliver new insights into neural mechanisms underlying cognitive and emotional development during adolescence and, most importantly, to identify possible genetic and environmental influences on brain maturation and on cognitive and socio-emotional development during childhood and adolescence.

Keywords: brain development, adolescent brain, magnetic resonance imaging, neuroimaging, brain structure, brain function

Basic Brain Anatomy and Neurochemistry

Based on embryonic and evolutionary development, the mammalian brain is typically divided into the forebrain, midbrain, and hindbrain. The *forebrain* consists of the cerebrum (the cerebral cortex and basal ganglia) and diencephalon (thalamus, hypothalamus, and other grey-matter nuclei). The *midbrain* includes the substantia nigra and tectum (superior and inferior colliculi). The *hindbrain* consists of the cerebellum, pons, and medulla oblongata.

The *cerebral cortex* is the outermost layer of the cerebrum; it is a 2–4 mm thick sheath of grey matter, with two-thirds of the cortex being buried in the cerebral sulci (or folds). The surface area of the cortex increases with increasing brain size more than one would expect from a simple geometric relationship between the surface and volume; this is particularly the case for the prefrontal cortex (Toro et al., 2008). The outermost area, the neocortex, has six cortical layers that differ in the mixture of the different types of neurons (e.g., pyramidal and granular cells); based on the so-called cytoarchitecture, a number of cortical areas can be distinguished (e.g., Brodmann, 1909). The archicortex, which includes the hippocampus, is evolutionarily older and has only three cortical layers.

Brain tissue can be divided into grey and white matter; this distinction is simply based on the visual appearance of a fresh brain. *Grey matter* consists of a number of cellular elements, including the cell

---

[*] This chapter was published first in Lerner RM and Steinberg L (Eds) *Handbook of Adolescent Psychology, 3rd Edition*. John Wiley and Sons, pp. 95–115, 2009.

bodies of nerve cells (neurons) and their tree-like extensions (dendrites), glial cells (e.g., astrocytes, microglia), and blood vessels. The adult human brain contains over 100 billion neurons (Sholl, 1956). Figure 19.1 provides a breakdown of the relative number of various cellular elements found in the mouse cerebral cortex (Braitenberg & Schüz, 1998). *White matter* owes its appearance to the high content of a fatty substance called myelin that wraps around axons, the long projections of neurons. The white matter of a 20-year-old man contains a staggering 176,000 km of myelinated axons (Marner et al., 2003).

Transmission of information from one neuron to the next involves several steps. Local excitatory and inhibitory postsynaptic potentials (EPSPs and IPSPs) are continuously being summed at the axonal hillock and, once a threshold value is reached, an action potential is generated. The action potential then travels along the axon and, at the synapse, causes a release of neurotransmitters. The so-called conduction velocity is higher in myelinated versus non-myelinated axons and in axons with larger versus smaller diameter (Hursh, 1939; Rushton, 1951; Schmidt-Nielsen, 1990).

Neurotransmitters are chemicals that either relay action potentials or modulate (e.g., amplify or moderate) this process. Neurotransmitters include amino acids (e.g., glutamate and gamma amino-butyric acid [GABA]), monoamines (e.g., dopamine, serotonin, norepinephrine), acetylcholine, and many neuropeptides (e.g., oxytocin). Glutamate and GABA are the main excitatory and inhibitory neurotransmitters, respectively, and dopamine is one of the most studied neuromodulators. The action of a particular neurotransmitter is mediated by a receptor; a given neurotransmitter can bind to a number of receptor subtypes that are found in different brain regions, or different layers of the cerebral

cortex, with varied densities (Eickhoff, Schleicher, Scheperjans, Palomero-Gallagher, & Zilles, 2007; Zilles, *Palomero-Gallagher, & Schleicher*, 2004). The very complex interaction between different neurotransmitters released at any given time at the synapse determines the number of EPSPs and IPSPs generated on the post-synaptic membrane and, in turn, firing of the neuron.

The basic principles of the brain's functional organization are those of *specialization and integration*. Information is computed in highly specialized but often spatially segregated regions of the cortex and sub-cortical grey-matter nuclei. This information is, in turn, integrated by being shared across the various cortical and subcortical regions via cortico-cortical and cortico-subcortical projections. Hence the importance of structural and functional connectivity.

Magnetic Resonance Imaging

Magnetic resonance imaging (MRI) is the only method that allows the researcher to map both structure and function of the human brain in a non-invasive manner. For this reason, this chapter focuses on findings obtained with MRI. It should be noted that other techniques, namely electroencephalography (EEG) and magnetoencephalography (MEG), have high temporal resolution and are therefore particularly useful for evaluating developmental changes in the *speed* of neural processing. We have compared the different brain-mapping techniques and described the basic principles guiding their use in studies of brain-behavior relationship elsewhere (Paus, 2003).

Magnetic resonance imaging revolutionized the way we can study structure and function of the human brain in living human beings throughout the entire life span (Bushong, 2003). The principles of MRI are relatively straightforward. In most

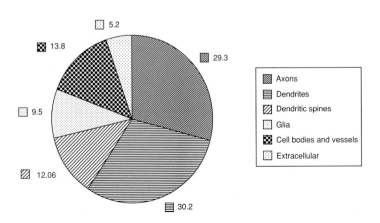

Fig. 19.1 Cellular composition of the cerebral cortex. Compiled from Braitenberg, V. & Schüz, A. (1998).

applications, the MR signal is based on magnetic properties of the hydrogen atoms, which are a component of the most abundant substance in the human body, water. By placing the human body in a strong static magnetic field (B_0; 0.5 to 7.0 T) and applying a brief pulse of electromagnetic energy, we can make the little dipoles formed by the hydrogen nuclei rotate away from their axes and, in turn, measure the time it takes for the nuclei to "relax" back to their original position. By changing slightly the static magnetic field at different positions along/across the B_0, we can establish the spatial origin of the signal and, eventually, create a 3-dimensional (3D) image of the measurement. What is measured depends on the combination of various imaging parameters or, in the terminology of the MR physicists, on the acquisition sequence.

Imaging Brain Structure

For imaging *brain structure*, the most common acquisition sequences include T1-weighted (T1W) and T2-weighted (T2W) images, diffusion-tensor images (DTI) and magnetization-transfer images (MT). The T1W and T2W images are typically used for quantifying the volume of grey and white matter (both global and regional), and estimating the cortical thickness or other morphological properties of the cerebral cortex, such as its folding. Using DTI and MT imaging, one can assess different properties of white matter, again, both globally and regionally. The various features of brain structure that can be extracted from these four types of images are described below. In addition to the above sequences, less common but often even more informative acquisitions include T1 and T2 relaxometry (i.e., measurement of the actual relaxation times; Roberts & Mikulis, 2007) and magnetic resonance spectroscopy (MRS; Hope & Moorcraft, 1991).

Imaging Brain Function

For imaging *brain function*, the most common MR parameter to measure is the blood oxygenation-level dependent (BOLD) signal. The BOLD signal reflects the proportion of oxygenated and de-oxygenated blood in a given brain region at a given moment. A strong correlation between the amount of synaptic activity and regional cerebral blood flow is the reason why the BOLD signal is a good, albeit indirect, measure of brain "function" (Logothetis, Pauls, Augath, Trinath, & Oeltermann, 2001). In the majority of functional MRI (fMRI) studies, one measures *changes* in BOLD signal in response to various sensory, motor, or cognitive stimuli.

Therefore, only brain regions that are likely to respond to such stimuli can be examined using a given paradigm.

Imaging Neurotransmission

For imaging *neurotransmission*, one must resort to positron emission tomography (PET). To assess the distribution of a particular receptor, a small amount of a specific radioactive tracer is injected into the blood stream. Mainly for reasons of radiation safety, this approach is not used in studies of healthy children and adolescents. Therefore, our knowledge of age-related changes in neurotransmitter systems during development relies on *post mortem* data and studies carried out in experimental animals.

Computational Neuroanatomy

As pointed out above, the different acquisition sequences capture various properties of grey and white matter and, in turn, provide a wealth of information that can be extracted from the images using an ever-growing array of computational algorithms. Here, I provide an overview of the most common techniques used in developmental studies.

Computational analysis of high-resolution structural brain MR images (typically T1W and T2W images) is used to extract in a fully automatic fashion two types of measurements: (1) Voxel- or vertex-wise features derived for each X, Y, and Z (i.e., three-dimensional) location (e.g., grey- and white-matter "density" maps, cortical thickness, cortical folding); and (2) Volumetric measures (volumes of grey or white matter in particular brain regions, or the area of specific brain structures, etc).

Density maps are generated by (1) registering T1W images with a template brain (e.g., the average MNI-305 atlas; Evans et al., 1993); (2) classifying the brain tissue into grey matter (GM), white matter (WM) and cerebrospinal fluid (CSF); and (3) smoothing the binary 3-D images (i.e., GM, WM, and CSF) to generate 3-D maps of GM/WM "density." These maps are then used in voxel-wise analyses of age- or group-related differences in GM or WM density (see Ashburner & Friston, 2000, for a methodological overview).

Cortical thickness can be measured, for example, using FreeSurfer; this is a set of automated tools for reconstruction of the brain cortical surface (Fischl & Dale, 2000). For every subject, FreeSurfer segments the cerebral cortex, white matter, and other subcortical structures, and then computes triangular meshes that recover the geometry and the topology of the pial surface and the grey/white interface of the left and right hemispheres. The local cortical thickness is measured based on the difference between the position of equivalent vertices in the pial and grey/white surfaces. A correspondence between the cortical surfaces across subjects then is established using a nonlinear alignment of the principal sulci in each subject's brain with an average brain (Fischl, Sereno, Tootell, & Dale, 1999). Local estimates of *cortical folding* can be obtained by measuring, for every point x on the cortical surface, the area contained in a small sphere centered at x. If the brain were lissencephalic (i.e., without convolutions), the area inside the sphere would be approximately that of the disc. Using this approach, one can estimate the local degree of folding throughout the cortex (Toro et al., 2008).

The *volume of brain tissues* (grey matter or white matter) can be estimated by registering nonlinearly the native T1W images to a labeled template brain on which lobes (or other pre-defined brain regions) have been defined a priori (usually traced by an expert). Information about anatomical boundaries from the template brain can then be back-projected onto each subject's brain, in native space, and intersected with the tissue-classification map. One can then count the number of grey and white matter voxels belonging to a given anatomical region, such as the frontal lobe (Collins, Neelin, Peters, & Evans, 1994, Collins, Holmes, Peters, & Evans, 1995). More sophisticated algorithms are often developed to segment small structures with poorly defined boundaries, such as the hippocampus and amygdala (Chupin et al., 2007).

In addition to the density maps and volumetric measurements of white-matter structures, such as the corpus callosum, two other techniques are used to evaluate structural properties of white matter: diffusion tensor imaging (DTI) and magnetic transfer (MT) imaging. Using *diffusion tensor imaging*, one can estimate local differences in the magnitude (apparent diffusion coefficient, ADC) and directionality (fractional anisotropy, FA) of the (fast) diffusion of water in the extra-cellular space around the axons (in most common acquisition protocols). The more unidirectional the water diffusion is in a given fiber tract, the higher the FA value in that location. It is assumed that FA varies as a function of structural properties of white matter, such as myelination and fiber arrangement of a given white-matter tract (e.g., Laule et al., 2007; Mädler, Drabycz, Kolind, Whittall, & Mackay, 2008). Values of FA can be calculated, for example, using FMRIB's Diffusion Toolbox (http://www.fmrib.

ox.ac.uk/fsl). The Tract-based spatial-statistics (TBSS) can be used to compare statistically the FA values between individuals by aligning the individual subjects to the average white-matter tract "skeleton" (Smith et al., 2006).

The *magnetization transfer ratio* (MTR) is another measure employed for the assessment of white-matter properties; it provides information on the macromolecular content and structure of the tissue (McGowan, 1999). Given that the macromolecules of myelin are the dominant source of MT signal in white matter (Kucharczyk, Macdonald, Stanisz, & Henkelman, 1994; Schmierer, Scaravilli, Altmann, Barker, & Miller, 2004), one can use MTR as an index of myelination. Note, however, that myelin is not likely to be the sole factor influencing MTR (see Laule et al., 2007). The MT ratio is calculated as the percent signal change between two acquisitions, MT pulse on and off (Pike, 1996). To obtain mean MTR values for white matter, one can calculate MTR across all WM voxels constituting a given lobar volume of WM in that subject.

The above techniques provide a wealth of information about structural properties of the human brain. The next section will review findings obtained with some of these approaches in studies of typically developing children and adolescents.

Brain Structure

Over the last 10 years, a number of investigators used some of the above techniques of MR-based computational neuroanatomy in large samples of typically developing children and adolescents and provided a rather coherent picture of the development of brain structure between the age of 4 and 20 years (see Table 19.1 for an overview).

Age Differences in White Matter

The initial MR studies of brain development, from birth to young adulthood, clearly showed age-related increases in both global and regional volumes of white matter (reviewed in Paus, 2001). Using data acquired in the largest MR study of brain development to date (n = 897 scans obtained in 601 individuals, 5 to 25 years of age), Lenroot and Giedd (2006) described a quadratic age-related growth of WM volumes constituting the four cerebral lobes and a linear growth of the corpus callosum. The WM growth showed a clear sexual dimorphism in that it was steeper in boys compared with girls. We have replicated the latter finding in a large adolescent sample (n = 408, age 12 to 18 years) and shown that it can be, in part, attributed to the

Table 19.1 Age-related Changes in Brain Structure during Childhood and Adolescence

Source*	Year	Age	n	Design	Measures
Giedd/Rapoport Nature Neuroscience	1999	4 to 21 yr	145	Cross-sectional/ Longitudinal	GM and WM lobar volumes
Paus/Evans Science	1999	4 to 17 yr	111	Cross-sectional	WM density
Courchesne/Press Radiology	2000	19 months to 80 yr	116	Cross-sectional	GM volume, GM/WM ratio, brain size
de Bellis/Boring Cerebral Cortex	2001	6 to 17 yr	118	Cross-sectional	GM and WM volumes, corpus callosum
Schneider/Martin Neuroradiology	2004	1 day to 16 yr	52	Cross-sectional	FA, D'
Ben Bashat/Assaf J Magn Reson Imaging	2005	4 months to 23 yr	36	Cross-sectional	FA, displacement, probability (at high b value)
Schmithorst/Holland Human Brain Mapping	2005	5 to 18 yr	47	Cross-sectional	FA, MD, performance
Shaw/Giedd Nature	2006	5 to 21 yr	307	Cross-sectional/ Longitudinal	Cortical thickness
Lerch/Evans Neuroimage	2006	5 to 19 yr	292	Cross-sectional	Cortical thickness, inter-regional similarity
Niogi/McCandliss Neuropsychologia	2006	6 to 10 yr	31	Cross-sectional	FA, performance
Wallace/Giedd J Child Psychol Psychiatry	2006	5 to 18 yr	512	Cross-sectional., twins	GM, WM and brain volumes
Sowell/Toga Cereb Cortex	2007	7 to 87 yr	176	Cross-sectional	Cortical thickness, brain size
Shaw/Giedd Lancet Neurology	2007	5 to 19 yr	239	Cross-sectional/ Longitudinal	Cortical thickness, entorhinal cortex
Bonekamp/Horska Neuroimage	2007	5 to 19 yr	40	Cross-sectional	FA, ADC
Gilmore/Gerig Journal of Neuroscience	2007	38 to 48 weeks**	74	Cross-sectional	GM and WM "cortical" volume, global volumes
Lenroot/Giedd Neuroimage	2007	3 to 27 yr	387	Cross-sectional/ Longitudinal	GM and WM volumes, corpus callosum, caudate nucleus
Whitford/Williams Human Brain Mapping	2007	10 to 30 yr	138	Cross-sectional	GM and WM volumes, resting EEG
Wilke/Holland Exp Brain Res	2007	5 to 18 yr	200	Cross-sectional	GM and WM volumes, VBM
Paus/Pausova Neuroimage	2008	12 to 18 yr	300	Cross-sectional	Corpus callosum: Volume and MTR
Toro/Paus Neuropsychopharmacology	2008	12 to 18 yr	314	Cross-sectional	Cortical thickness
Shaw/Wise Journal of Neuroscience	2008	4 to 33 yr	375	Cross-sectional/ Longitudinal	Cortical thickness

(Continued)

Table 19.1   (Cont'd) Age-related Changes in Brain Structure during Childhood and Adolescence

Source*	Year	Age	n	Design	Measures
Paus/Pausova Social Neuroscience	2008	12 to 18 yr	295	Cross-sectional	Cortical thickness, inter-regional similarity
Schmitt/Giedd Cerebral Cortex	2008	5 to 19 yr	600	Cross-sectional, twins	Cortical thickness, inter-regional similarity
Wood/Nopoulos Social Cog Affective Neurosci	2008	7 to 17 yr	74	Cross-sectional	Cortical volume, orbitofrontal cortex and gyrus rectus
Qiu/Khong Neuroimage	2008	7 to 26 yr	75	Cross-sectional	FA, MD
Schmithorst/Dardzinski Human Brain Mapping	2008	5 to 18 yr	105	Cross-sectional	FA, MD
Lebel/Beaulieu Neuroimage	2008	5 to 30 yr	202	Cross-sectional	FA, MD
Muetzel/Luciana Neuroimage	2008	9 to 24 yr	92	Cross-sectional	FA, MD in corpus callosum, performance
Ding/Fiehler Am J Neuroradiol	2008	0.2 to 39 yr	55	Cross-sectional	FA, T2 in corpus callosum
Eckert/Binder Neuroimage	2008	10.8 to 12 yr	39	Cross-sectional	GM density
Colibazzi/Peterson Human Brain Mapping	2008	7 to 57 yr	107	Cross-sectional	Hippocampus, amygdala, global volumes
Wells/Horska Brain Cogn	2008	5 to 18 yr	48	Cross-sectional	Temporal lobe volume
Perrin/Paus Journal of Neuroscience	2008	12 to 18 yr	408	Cross-sectional	WM volume and MTR
Lotfipour/Paus Archives of General Psychiatry	2009	12 to 18 yr	314	Cross-sectional	Cortical thickness, orbitofrontal cortex
Shaw/Rapoport Archives of General Psychiatry	2009	4 to 21 yr	358	Cross-sectional/ Longitudinal	Cortical thickness
Schmitt/Giedd Neuroimage	2009	5 to 19 yr	600	Cross-sectional, twins	Cortical thickness
Lenroot/Giedd Human Brain Mapping	2009	5 to 19 yr	600	Cross-sectional, twins	Cortical thickness
Ostby/Walhovd Journal of Neuroscience	2009	8 to 31 yr	171	Cross-sectional	Cortical thickness, subcortical volumes
Lebel/Beaulieu Human Brain Mapping	2009	5 to 30	183	Cross-sectional	FA in arcuate fasciculus, performance
Hasan/Ewing-Cobbs Brain Res	2009	7 to 59	99	Cross-sectional	FA, MD in corpus callosum
Hasan/Ewing-Cobbs Brain Res	2009	7 to 76	108	Cross-sectional	FA, MD in uncinate fasciculus
Skak Madsen/Jernigan Neuropsychologia	2009	7 to 13	65	Cross-sectional	FA, MD, performance
Olson/Luciana J Cog Neurosci	2009	9 to 23 yr	79	Cross-sectional	FA, MD, performance

(Continued)

Table 19.1   (Cont'd) Age-related Changes in Brain Structure during Childhood and Adolescence

Source*	Year	Age	n	Design	Measures
Peper/Hulshoff Pol Psychoneuroendocrinology	2009	10 to 15 yr	78	Cross-sectional	GM and WM density, global volumes
Herve/Paus Human Brain Mapping	2009	12 to 18 yr	409	Cross-sectional	GM density, corticospinal tract
Neufang/Konrad Cerebral Cortex	2009	8 to 15 yr	46	Cross-sectional	GM density
Toro/Paus Brain Function and Structure	2009	12 to 18 yr	331	Cross-sectional	Hippocampus, Amygdala, global volumes
Lotfipour/Paus Molecular Psychiatry	2009	12 to 18 yr	423	Cross-sectional	Striatum volume
Paus/Pausova Hormones and Behavior	2009	12 to 18 yr	419	Cross-sectional	WM and GM volumes, GM density
Perrin/Paus Neuroimage	2009	12 to 18 yr	408	Cross-sectional	WM volumes, WM density and MTR

*First/Last Author, Journal
**Post-conception

rise of testosterone levels, especially in male adolescents with an "efficient" (vis-à-vis transcriptional activity) variant of the androgen-receptor gene (Figure 19.2; Perrin et al., 2008a). In addition to the age-related increases in the overall volume of white matter, there are several interesting regional variations. These include age-related increases in white matter density in the internal capsule and the putative arcuate fasciculus (Paus et al., 1999), regional variations in the growth of the corpus callosum where the splenium continues to increase whereas the genu does not (Giedd et al., 1996c, 1999b; Pujol, 1993), and an age-related increase in the white matter volume of the left inferior frontal gyrus in boys but not girls (Blanton et al., 2004).

Diffusion tensor imaging (DTI) has been employed more recently to assess age-related changes in magnitude and directionality of the diffusion of water in the human brain during childhood and adolescence. Several studies have described age-related increases and decreases in fractional anisotropy (FA) and mean diffusivity (MD), respectively (reviewed in Cascio et al., 2007). In one of the largest studies to date, Lebel et al. (2008; n = 202, 5 to 30 years) described maturational trajectories of FA and MD that differed significantly across various fiber tracts (Figure 19.3). Others pointed out sex differences in developmental trajectories of FA during childhood and adolescence in certain fiber tracts, such as the arcuate fasciculus (Schmithorst et al., 2008; n = 106, 6 to 20 years; FA increasing in girls but decreasing in boys; no such difference for MD). Although FA and MD usually show an inverse relationship, this is far from uniform across the developing brain. For example, in the same group of children and adolescents (n = 31, 6 to 17 years), some fiber tracts (e.g., the inferior fronto-occipital fasciculus) showed concomitant age-related increase/decrease in FA/MD while other tracts (e.g., CST) showed only a decrease in MD without any change in FA (Eluvathingal et al., 2007). The above examples illustrate both the value of DTI-based studies of WM maturation during adolescence, as well as challenges related to their interpretation (see below).

Age Differences in Gray Matter

The monotonic nature of the developmental changes in brain maturation observed for white matter does not appear to hold in the case of grey matter. Grey matter volume in the frontal and parietal lobes appears to peak at between 10 and 12 years, and decreases slightly afterwards; in the temporal lobes the peak occurs around the age of 16 years (Giedd et al., 1999a). Other investigators found similar age-related grey matter "loss" in the frontal, parietal, and temporal lobes; it appears to start around puberty in the sensorimotor areas and spreads

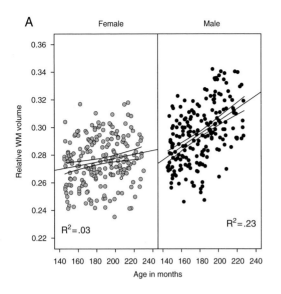

A

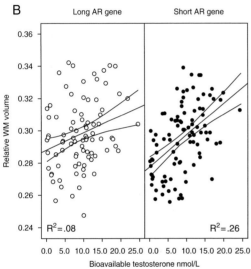

B

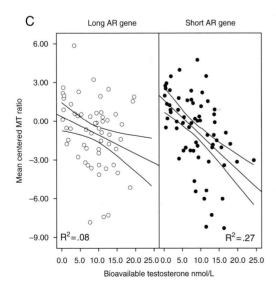

C

Fig. 19.2 A, Relative (brain-volume corrected) volume of white matter (WM) plotted as a function of age in female (left) and male (right) adolescents; B, Relative volume of WM plotted as a function of plasma levels of bioavailable testosterone in male adolescents with low (short AR gene) and high (long AR gene) number of CAG repeats in the androgen-receptor gene. C, Magnetization Transfer (MT) Ratio in WM plotted as a function of plasma levels of bioavailable testosterone in male adolescents with low (short AR gene) and high (long AR gene) number of CAG repeats in the androgen-receptor gene.

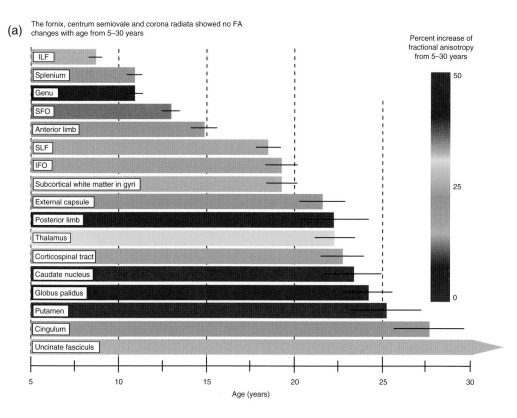

(a) The fornix, centrum semiovale and corona radiata showed no FA changes with age from 5–30 years

Percent increase of fractional anisotropy from 5–30 years

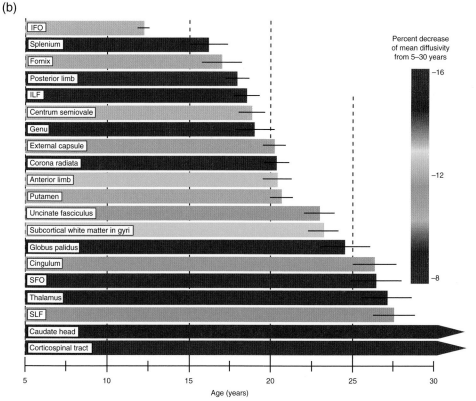

(b)

Percent decrease of mean diffusivity from 5–30 years

Fig. 19.3 Magnitude and timing of developmental changes in fractional anisotropy (a) and mean diffusivity (b).

Adapted from Lebel, C., Walker, L., Leemans, A., Phillips, L., Beaulieu, C. (2008) with permission from Elsevier.

forward over the frontal cortex and back over the parietal and then temporal cortex (Gogtay et al., 2004; Sowell et al., 2001). The dorsolateral prefrontal cortex and the posterior part of the superior temporal gyrus appear to "lose" grey matter last of all (Gogtay et al., 2004). More recently, similar age-related "loss" of the cortical grey matter has been observed using cortical thickness as the parameter of interest (Shaw et al., 2006). It has been often suggested that such age-related changes in cortical grey-matter during adolescence reflect "synaptic pruning." Whether or not this might be the case is discussed later.

Structure-Function Correlation

Knowledge of the functional organization of the human brain, gleaned from lesion studies and functional imaging work, provides a foundation for the initial functional interpretations of the above structural observations. For example, changes in white-matter volume along the arcuate fasciculus and in the left inferior frontal gyrus are likely to correlate with changes in language, while the late maturational changes in grey matter within the prefrontal cortex and the superior temporal gyrus/ sulcus may be related, respectively, to executive functions and processing of biological motion (see below). Only a handful of studies have acquired structural and functional (e.g., neuropsychological assessment) datasets in the same group of individuals, however. In these studies, significant correlations were found between IQ and grey matter volume of the prefrontal cortex (Reiss, Abrams, Singer, Ross & Denckla, 1996), between IQ and fractional anisotropy in the white matter of the frontal lobes (Schmithorst, Wilke, Dardzinski, & Holland, 2005), between IQ and cortical thickness (Shaw et al., 2006), between reading skills and fractional anisotropy in the left temporo-parietal white matter (Beaulieu et al., 2005, Deutsch et al., 2005) and between the performance in vocabulary and phonological tests and FA in the arcuate fasciculus (Lebel & Beaulieu, 2009). We have shown that the degree of similarity in cortical thickness across a network of regions typically engaged during action observation (Grosbras et al., 2007) varies as a function of resistance to peer influences (Paus et al., 2008).

Brain Function

Functional imaging studies pose both technical (reviewed in Davidson, Thomas, & Casey, 2003) and conceptual challenges. The latter involve a confounding interaction between age and performance. In other words, when studying age-related changes in brain activity during the performance of a given task, how do we interpret fMRI findings against the background of concomitant age-related differences in task performance? Is brain activity different because the behavior (performance) is different, or *vice versa*? One of the approaches used to overcome this issue is that of matching subjects either by age or by performance, and examining the differences in fMRI response in these matched groups; this approach has been used extensively in studies of verb generation, for example (Brown et al., 2004; Schlaggar et al., 2002). In the domain of executive function, Kwon, Reiss, and Menon (2002) used this approach in a study of visuo-spatial working memory and found age-related (from age 7 to 22 years) increases in the BOLD signal in the prefrontal and parietal cortex even after factoring out inter-individual differences in performance. Similar BOLD increases were also observed in these regions during the performance of a variety of tasks involving some form of response inhibition, including the Stroop task (Adleman et al., 2002), anti-saccade task (Luna et al., 2001), the stop task (Rubia et al., 2000) and, to a certain extent, during performance on a go/no-go task (Tamm, Menon & Reiss, 2002) and the Eriksen flanker task (Bunge et al., 2002).

During adolescence, high demands are placed not only on the executive systems but also on the interplay between cognitive and affect-related processes. Such cognition-emotion interactions are particularly crucial in the context of peer-peer interactions and the processing of verbal and nonverbal cues. It is therefore of interest to note that the cortex of the superior temporal sulcus (STS) contains a set of regions engaged during the processing of nonverbal cues such as those carried by eye and mouth movements (e.g., Puce et al., 1998), hand movements/actions (e.g., Beauchamp, Lee, Haxby, & Martin, 2002; Decety et al., 1997; Grezes et al., 1999), or body movements (e.g., Bonda, Petrides, Ostry, & Evans, 1996). As suggested by Allison, Puce, and McCarthy (2000), feedforward and feedback interactions between the STS and amygdala may be critical for the discrimination of various facial expressions and for the attentional enhancement of the neural response to socially salient stimuli. Consistent with such an "amplification" mechanism, Kilts and colleagues (2003) observed a significantly stronger neural response to dynamic, as compared with static, facial expressions of anger in both the STS and amygdala. My colleagues and I have also observed a strong BOLD response in the amygdala not only while adult subjects viewed video clips of angry hand movements or angry faces, but also during viewing of (dynamic) neutral facial expressions (Grosbras & Paus, 2006). Although basic aspects of face perception are in place shortly after birth (Goren et al., 1975), both the quantity and quality of face processing continues to increase throughout adolescence (e.g., Carey, 1992; Taylor et al., 1999, McGivern et al., 2002). Developmental fMRI studies of the processing of facial expressions are consistent with this pattern. For example, happy, but not sad, faces elicit significant BOLD response in the amygdala in adolescent subjects (Yang, Menon, Reid, Gotlib, & Reiss, 2003). Studies of fearful facial expressions suggest that an increase in the BOLD signal in the amygdala can be detected in adolescents (Baird et al., 1999) but it is relatively weak (Thomas et al., 2001).

Adolescence has been traditionally associated with risk-taking and sensation-seeking behavior (reviewed in Steinberg, 2008). In this context, several investigators have used functional MRI to examine possible differences between children, adolescents, and young adults in brain activity while they experienced gains or losses of various rewards. Given its role in reward and motivation (Robbins & Everitt, 1996), the nucleus accumbens (or ventral striatum) has been the focus of the majority of these studies. If adolescents were "driven" by rewards, one would expect heightened engagement of this structure during tasks that involve reward seeking. This appeared to be the case in some (Ernst et al., 2005; Galvan et al., 2006) but not other (Bjork et al., 2004) studies. In the latter report, Bjork and colleagues (2004) described an age-related increase (from 12 to 28 years) in the BOLD signal in the nucleus accumbens during anticipation of gains; this was the case even when self-reported level of excitement was taken into account. It is worthwhile pointing out that, in the same study, self-reported excitement was positively correlated with the BOLD signal in the accumbens even when age was taken into account. This observation highlights the importance of multidimensional approach to the interpretation of fMRI findings (see below for a more detailed discussion).

The aforementioned studies evaluated age-related differences in the presence and/or magnitude in task-related changes in the BOLD signal. As pointed out above, however, information computed in the various specialized and spatially segregated regions must be integrated to give rise to behaviors as complex as the choice of an appropriate action in an emotionally laden context. Hence, it is also important in imaging studies to evaluate possible age differences in functional connectivity (i.e., whether there are age differences in patterns of activation). Only a handful of investigators have included such assessments in their analyses. In a study of memory encoding, Menon et al. (2005) observed an age-related *decrease* in the fMRI signal between 11 and 19 years in the left medial temporal lobe while subjects viewed a series of novel photographs of natural outdoor scenes, as compared with viewing the same scene repeatedly (control condition). They then used voxel-wise regression analysis to identify brain regions that showed correlation in the fMRI signal with that measured in two subregions of the left medial temporal lobe, namely the hippocampus and the entorhinal cortex. This analysis revealed an age-related *increase* in the correlation between activation in the left entorhinal cortex and the left dorsolateral prefrontal cortex. This work nicely illustrates the importance of including the analysis of functional connectivity in developmental studies; although the fMRI signal decreased in one of the memory-relevant structures (entorhinal cortex), the hypothesized interaction between this structure and other brain regions (prefrontal cortex) actually increased.

In a different developmental study, Schmithorst and Holland (2006) investigated the relationship between intelligence and functional connectivity in a large sample of typically developing children and adolescents, aged 5 to 18 years. They measured fMRI signal during a task requiring the child to generate silently appropriate verbs in response to hearing nouns, every 5 seconds. After identifying brain regions engaged during this task, as compared with simply tapping fingers in response to a warble tone, they correlated fMRI signal in all such voxels with the subjects' full-scale intelligence quotient (FSIQ). This analysis revealed a positive fMRI-FSIQ correlation in five regions of the left hemisphere: Broca's area, the middle temporal gyrus, the anterior cingulate, the precuneus, and the medial frontal gyrus (putative supplementary motor area). Next, the authors computed the connectivity coefficient, defined as a weighted sum of the pairwise covariances between these regions. Using this coefficient as a measure of functional connectivity, Schmithorst and Holland found several age and gender differences in the relationship between intelligence and connectivity. In boys, functional connectivity appeared to increase as a function of intelligence between 5 and 9 years; no such relationship was present in older boys (10 to 12 years), and a negative correlation was observed in the oldest boys (13 to 18 years). In girls, on the other hand, no relationship was found in younger girls (age 5 to 13 years) but a strong positive correlation between functional connectivity and intelligence was clearly present in older girls (13 to 18 years). It is of note that the above effects were found in the time series measured during both the verb-generation and the control task, while some other effects were only found in the verb-generation task. As the authors point out, the observed gender differences in the relationship between intelligence and functional connectivity are consistent with some structural findings in adults, such as significant correlations between intelligence and regional white-matter volumes in women but grey-matter volumes in men (Haier, Jung, Yeo, Head, & Alkire, 2005).

My colleagues and I have investigated functional connectivity in the context of possible neural substrate of resistance to peer influences (RPI) in early adolescence (Grosbras et al., 2007). In these studies, we asked whether the probability with which an adolescent follows the goals set by peers or those set by himself/herself might depend on the interplay between the three neural systems: the fronto-parietal network (responsible for bottom-up imitation of actions), the STS network (responsible for processing social cues), and the prefrontal network (responsible for top-down regulation of actions). In the scanner, we asked 10-year-old children to watch brief video clips containing face or hand/arm actions, executed in neutral or angry ways, while measuring changes in fMRI signals. Outside the scanner, we administered a questionnaire assessing resistance to peer influence (Steinberg & Monahan, 2007). We found that children with high versus low scores on the resistance-to-peer-influence measure showed stronger inter-regional correlations in brain activity across the three networks while watching angry hand-actions. The pattern of inter-regional correlations identified by this method included both: (i) regions involved in action observation—the fronto-parietal as well as temporo-occipital systems; and (ii) regions in the prefrontal cortex.

Overall, studies of functional connectivity during childhood and adolescence are in their infancy. The three examples given above illustrate the power of this approach but also indicate that large numbers of subjects of both sex in different age groups may be necessary to reach valid conclusions.

Acquiring high-resolution structural MRI and/or DTI in the same individuals would greatly facilitate the identification of possible similarities, and differences, between functional, effective, and structural connectivity in the same sample (reviewed in Paus, 2007). As I discuss in the following section, interpretation of fMRI data is challenging and should be approached cautiously.

Interpreting Imaging-based Evidence of Brain Maturation

A number of conceptual frameworks have been put forward to interpret some of the findings reviewed above vis-à-vis underlying neurobiology. Unfortunately, the indirect nature of the available measures makes it very difficult to verify the validity of some of these propositions. Here I will raise questions about some of the underlying assumptions implicit in these frameworks in order to clarify the distinction between established facts and hypotheses.

Cortical Grey-Matter and Synaptic Pruning

It is the case that MR-based estimates of the volume of cortical GM and cortical thickness appear to decrease during adolescence. This has been often interpreted as an indication of "synaptic pruning," a process by which "redundant" synapses overproduced in the early years of life are being eliminated (see Purves, White, & Riddle, 1996, for a critical appraisal of neural Darwinism).

The initial evidence for accelerated synaptic pruning during post-natal development came from *post mortem* studies by Huttenlocher, who described a decrease in the number of dendritic spines in the human cerebral cortex during childhood and adolescents (Huttenlocher, 1984; Huttenlocher & de Courten, 1987). It should be noted that these initial studies were limited by the low number of specimens available for the different stages of human development. A more definite evidence of synapse elimination during adolescence was provided by studies carried out by Rakic and colleagues in non-human primates (e.g., Bourgeois & Rakic 1993; Rakic, Bourgeois, Eckenhoff, Zecevic, & Goldman-Rakic, 1986). They observed a dramatic decrease (about a 45% loss) in the number of synapses in the visual cortex during puberty (between the age of 2.5 and 5 years), whether expressed as a number of synapses per neuron or per cubic mm of neuropil (unmyelinated nerve fibers). But is it likely that this decrease in synaptic density translate into a decrease in cortical volume? Bourgeois and Rakic (1993) commented that

> "changes in the density of synapses affect very little either the volume or surface of the cortex because the total volume of synaptic boutons . . . is only a very small fraction of the cortical volume" and concluded that ". . . a decline of synaptic number during puberty should have a rather small effect on the overall volume of the cortex" (Bourgeois & Rakic, 1993).

If the number of synapses per se is unlikely to change the cortical volume/thickness, then what other cellular elements could affect it? As illustrated in Figure 19.1, about 10% of the (mouse) cortex is occupied by glial cells and about 60% by neuropil, the latter consisting of dendritic and axonal processes. It is conceivable that a reduced number of synapses, and a corresponding decrease in metabolic requirements, would be accompanied by a reduction in the number of glial cells, leading to a decrease in the cortical grey matter volume or thickness. But it is perhaps even more likely that the apparent loss of grey matter reflects an increase in the degree of myelination of intra-cortical axons. As shown in Figure 19.4 (Top: qualitative data from Kaes, 1907; Bottom: quantitative data from Conel, 1939–1967), myelination of intra-cortical fibers progresses gradually from birth to adulthood. The higher the number of myelinated fibers in the cortex, the less "grey" the cortex would appear on regular T1-weighted images. Such a "partial-volume" effect could result in an apparent loss of cortical grey-matter (see also Paus, 2005).

White Matter and Myelination

Given the well-documented histology-based increase in the degree of myelination during the first two decades of human life (e.g., Yakovlev & Lecours, 1967), it is perhaps not surprising that any changes in the volume or "density" of white matter revealed by computational analyses of T1-weighted images are attributed to changes in myelination. Again, assumptions based on previous knowledge are influencing interpretation of new data. Quite often, articles reporting age-related changes in myelination have merely measured volumes of white matter.

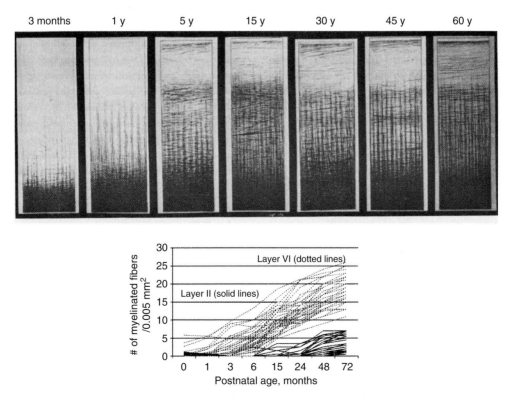

Fig. 19.4 *Top.* Post-mortem intracortical myelin-stain data from Kaes (1907). *Bottom.* Plot of Conel's uncorrected post-mortem data on layer II (dashed lines) and layer VI (solid lines) myelinated fiber density (no. per 0.005 mm2) versus postnatal age (months) for the Von Economo areas he studied.

Adapted from Shankle et al. (1998) with permission from PNAS. Copyright 1998, National Academy of Sciences, USA.

Is this only a matter of semantics, or could other, myelination-independent, processes affect the volume and/or other features of white matter?

Figure 19.2 provides a clear example of dissociation between age-related changes in the volume of white matter during adolescence and changes in magnetic transfer ratio (MTR), an indirect index of the amount of myelin in white matter. Although white-matter volume increased with age during adolescence among males (Figure. 19.2A), MTR values decreased thus indicating a decrease in the amount of myelin in the unit of volume (Perrin et al., 2008a). Furthermore, in male adolescents, WM volume (Figure. 19.2B) and MT ratio (Figure. 19.2C) varied as a function of testosterone level, in particular in individuals with an "efficient" variant (short allele) of androgen-receptor gene. If not increases in myelin, what could be driving the observed increase in white matter volume during male adolescence? Our tentative answer is that this may be due to changes in axonal caliber; the larger the caliber, the fewer axons fit in the same unit of the imaged volume, producing a relative decrease in the myelination index. Furthermore, axons of larger (internal) diameter tend to have a relatively thinner myelin sheath, resulting in a higher g ratio (ratio between internal and external [internal + myelin sheath] diameter, see Paus, 2010a, Paus & Toro, 2009). Although more work is needed to confirm this initial observation, it serves as a reminder that most of the MR sequences from which inferences are often drawn are not specific enough to interpret MR-based findings as reflecting a single neurobiological process, such as myelination.

Functional "Activations"

Interpretations of group differences in task-related brain activity indexed by the BOLD signal are fraught with difficulties. When evaluating differences between, for example, children and adolescents performing a "reward" task, one can observe a number of possible outcomes. Compared with children, adolescents may "activate" additional brain regions, show stronger "activations" in the same brain regions, or present a more focused "pattern" of activations. How should we interpret such findings? Cautiously, with a number of factors in mind.

We should first consider the possibility that the two groups may differ in the task performance and/or strategy employed to solve the task at hand. As noted earlier, when age-related differences in fMRI response are found, these can be removed by matching participants of different ages on their

performance (e.g., Kwon et al., 2002; Schlaggar et al., 2002). Clearly, the more sensitive the performance measure used and the higher the number of participants, the easier it would be to deal with this potential confounder.

The next factor to consider is the emotional and motivational state of the participant. Depending on the familiarity with the task, scanning environment, or the duration of the scanning session, participants are likely to experience varied levels of anxiety and arousal in the scanner. These and other external factors may have different effects on participants of different ages. In addition to minimizing the effect of such confounders, one could collect measures of autonomic (e.g., heart rate, pupil diameter) or central (EEG) arousal during scanning and include these as covariates in subsequent analyses of fMRI data.

Importantly, state-related changes are accompanied by release of neurotransmitters, such as dopamine and norepinephrine (Arnsten & Li, 2005), that modulate task-related changes in brain "activation." In fact, age-related differences in dopaminergic neurotransmission have often been invoked when interpreting fMRI findings obtained in the context of reward processing, often comparing adolescents with young adults. Two recent post mortem studies reported, however, that there are no differences between adolescents (14 to 18 years) and young adults (20 to 24 years) in the levels of different dopamine receptors or in the activity of enzymes involved in the synthesis (tyrosine hydroxylase) and metabolism (COMT) of dopamine in the prefrontal cortex (Turnbridge et al., 2007; Weickert et al., 2007).

At the analytical level, it is of course essential to support claims about the presence or absence of "activations" by proper statistical analysis. It is not sufficient to demonstrate that a particular brain region shows a statistically significant increase in the BOLD signal in one group while it fails to reach the threshold in another group. One should also be aware of possible imaging artefacts. For example, when counting the number of "activated" voxels and/or regions, a possibility exists that any subtle misregistrations of images acquired over time may give rise to apparent "activations" that may mimic true changes in brain activity; for example, small "nodding" movements of the head may affect midline structures, such as the anterior cingulate cortex. On the other hand, subtle misregistration may lead to an apparent decrease in the magnitude of the BOLD response at a "peak" location. Again, age may modulate the probability of such confounders.

Overall, interpretation of findings obtained with functional MRI is challenging and needs to take into account both the experimental design and physiology underlying the fMRI signal. Even when all possible experimental variables are perfectly controlled, the indirect nature of the BOLD signal and the complexity of the underlying neurophysiology prevent one to draw conclusions about developmental processes such as synaptic pruning or dopaminergic neurotransmission.

Brain Images and Causality

The use of structural and functional neuroimaging provides a powerful tool for the study of brain maturation and cognitive development during adolescence. In addition to the need to keep in mind the many specific challenges associated with the interpretation of structural and functional findings discussed in the previous section, one also needs to be cautious about the general meaning of "brain images." In particular, we should not confuse a manifestation with a cause.

Observing a difference between children and adolescents in the size (or "activation") of a particular structure simply points to a possible neural mechanism mediating the effect of age on a given behavior; it is not the "cause" of this behavior. For example, a stronger activation of the ventral striatum during the performance of a "reward" task by adolescents, as compared with adults, should not be interpreted as "causing" the adolescent's reward-seeking behavior; it merely indicates possible age-related differences in the probability of engaging this structure during this particular task. In this sense, neuroimaging-based assessment should be treated in the same way, and at the same level, as any other quantitative phenotype describing cognitive, emotional, endocrine, or physiological characteristics of an individual. To look for causes of a given behavior and its higher or lower probability during adolescence, we need to turn our attention to the individual's environment and his/her genes.

Role of Genes and Environment in Shaping the Brain

It is clear that both genes and experience influence many structural features of the human brain. In a special issue of *Human Brain Mapping* (2007) on genomic imaging (Glahn, Thompson, & Paus, 2007), a number of articles reported high heritability of regional volumes of grey matter estimated from twin studies carried out in adults, as well as in children and adolescents. At a single-gene level, several previous reports revealed differences between (adult) individuals with different allelic variations in brain morphology (e.g., Pezawas et al., 2004 [BDNF], 2005 [5-HTTLPR]).

Findings of genetic influences on brain morphology are often seen as the consequence of a *direct* effect of the genes on brain structure, perhaps occurring as early as *in utero*. But it is also possible, if fact quite likely, that these effects are mediated by the different levels of *functional* engagement of given neural circuits in individuals with different genes and experiences. Several studies have confirmed that a repeated (functional) engagement of a particular neural circuit leads to changes in its structural properties, which can be detected in vivo with MR (e.g., in musicians: Gaser & Schlaug, 2003: Sluming et al., 2002; London taxi drivers: Maguire et al., 2000; bilingual subjects: Mechelli et al., 2004; initially inexperienced jugglers: Draganski et al., 2004). Although determining directionality of such structure-function relationships is impossible in the majority of current studies (with the exception of the "juggler" study), the existing animal experimental literature confirms the possibility of experience impacting brain structure (e.g., Sirevaag & Greenough, 1988). For example, we have recently described a positive relationship between the number of different drugs tried by an adolescent during his/her lifetime and the thickness of the orbitofrontal cortex and suggested that this relationship arose via experience-related (drug seeking/drug use) plasticity. We reasoned that, if this were to be the case, individuals with the more "efficient" variant of the BDNF gene (i.e., val-val homozygotes) would show this relationship whereas those with the less "efficient" variant (i.e., met carriers) would not; this was the case (Lotfipour et al., 2009).

Overall, there is an increasing body of evidence that challenges a simple, deterministic view of genes influencing the brain directly and, in turn, the individual's behavior. As indicated by a number of studies on the effect of experience on brain structure, MRI-derived anatomical measures may very well reflect a cumulative effect of the differential experience (behavior), acting in the context of a particular genetic background, rather than the other way around. This point speaks directly to the issue of biological determinism. Quite often, we view developmental changes in brain structure as (biological) prerequisites of a particular cognitive ability. For example, the common logic assumes that cognitive/executive control of behavior emerges in full only after the prefrontal cortex reaches the adult-like level of structural maturity. But given the role of experience in shaping the brain, it might also be that high demands on cognitive control faced, for example, by young adolescents assuming adult roles due to family circumstances, may facilitate structural maturation of their prefrontal cortex. This scenario, if proven correct, will move us away from the "passive" view of brain development into one that emphasizes active role of the individual and his/her environment in modulating the "biological" developmental processes.

Conclusions

The second decade of human brain development is as dynamic as the preceding one; the human brain continues to grow and change both in a structural and functional sense. Magnetic resonance imaging has contributed a wealth of information about the adolescent brain; documenting, in particular, its continuing structural maturation and beginning to elucidate interesting changes in its functional organization. Several large-scale MR-based studies of childhood and adolescence are under way, promising to deliver new insights into neural mechanisms underlying cognitive and emotional development during adolescence and, most importantly, to identify possible genetic and environmental influences on brain maturation and on cognitive and socio-emotional development during childhood and adolescence (reviewed in Paus 2010b). Together with other techniques not covered in this chapter, such as electro- and magneto-encephalography, we are continuing to learn a great deal about the developing brain in space and time.

Acknowledgments

The author's work in supported by the Canadian Institutes of Health Research, the Royal Society (U.K.), and the National Institutes of Health (U.S.A.). I am grateful to our collaborators, students, and research fellows for their intellectual contributions and hard work.

References

Adleman, N. E., Menon, V., Blasey, C. M., White, C. D., Warsofsky, I. S., Glover, G. H., et al. (2002). A developmental fMRI study of the Stroop color-word task. *Neuroimage, 16*, 61–75.

Allison, T., Puce, A., & McCarthy, G. (2000). Social perception from visual cues: Role of the STS region. *Trends Cogn. Sci. 4*, 267–278.

Angold, A., Costello, E. J., Erkanli, A., & Worthman, C. M. (1999). Pubertal changes in hormone levels and depression in girls. *Psychol Med., 29*(5), 1043–1053.

Angold, A., Costello, E. J., & Worthman C. M. (1998). Puberty and depression: The roles of age, pubertal status and pubertal timing. *Psychol Med., 28*(1):51–61.

Ankney, C. D. (1992). Differences in brain size. *Nature, 13*, 358(6387):6532.

Arnsten, A. F. & Li, B. M. (2005). Neurobiology of executive functions: Catecholamine influences on prefrontal cortical functions. *Biol Psychiatry, 57*, 1377–1384.

Ashburner, J. & Friston, K.J. (2000). Voxel-based morphometry—the methods. *Neuroimage, 11*(6 Pt 1), 805–821.

Baird, A. A., Gruber, S. A., Fein, D. A., Maas, L. C., Steingard, R. J., Renshaw, P.F., et al. (1999) Functional magnetic resonance imaging of facial affect recognition in children and adolescents. *J Am Acad Child Adolesc Psychiatry, 38*, 195–199.

Beauchamp, M. S., Lee, K. E., Haxby, J. V., & Martin, A. (2003). FMRI responses to video and point-light displays of moving humans and manipulable objects. *J Cogn Neurosci, 15*(7), 991–1001.

Beauchamp, M. S., Lee, K. S., Haxby, J. V., & Martin, A. (2002). Parallel visual motion processing streams for manipulable objects and human movements. *Neuron, 34*, 149–159.

Beaulieu, C., Plewes, C., Paulson, L. A., Roy, D., Snook, L., Concha, L., et al. (2005). Imaging brain connectivity in children with diverse reading ability. *Neuroimage, 25*(4), 1266–1271.

Beaulieu, C. (2002). The basis of anisotropic water diffusion in the nervous system—a technical review. *NMR Biomed, 15*, 435–455.

Bermudez, P. & Zatorre, R. J. (2001). Sexual dimorphism in the corpus callosum: Methodological considerations in MRI morphometry. *Neuroimage, 13*(6 Pt 1), 1121–1130.

Bjork, J. M., Knutson, B., Fong, G.W., Caggiano, D.M., Bennett, S.M., & Hommer, D.W. (2004). Incentive-elicited brain activation in adolescents: Similarities and differences from young adults. *J Neurosci, 24*, 1793–1802.

Bjork, J. M., Smith, A. R., Danube, C, L., & Hommer, D. W. (2007). Developmental differences in posterior mesofrontal cortex recruitment by risky rewards. *J Neurosci, 27*, 4839–4849.

Blanton, R. E., Levitt, J. G., Peterson, J. R., Fadale, D., Sporty, M. L., Lee, M., et al. (2004). Gender differences in the left inferior frontal gyrus in normal children. *Neuroimage, 22*, 626–636.

Bonda, E., Petrides, M., Ostry, D., & Evans, A. (1996) Specific involvement of human parietal systems and the amygdala in the perception of biological motion. *J. Neurosci, 16*, 3737–3744.

Bourgeois JP, Rakic P. Changes of synaptic density in the primary visual cortex of the macaque monkey from fetal to adult stage. *J Neurosci.* 1993 Jul;13(7):2801–20.

Braitenberg, V. (2001). Brain size and number of neurons: An exercise in synthetic neuroanatomy. *J Comput Neurosci, 10*, 71–77.

Braitenberg, V. & Schüz, A. (1998). Cortex: Statistics and geometry of neuronal connectivity. 2nd thoroughly revised edition of: *Anatomy of the cortex. Statistics and geometry* (1991), 249, Springer Verlag, Tiergarten 17, 69121 Heidelberg, Germany.

Brodmann, K. (1909/1994). *Localisation in the cerebral cortex*, Smith-Gordon, London, UK.

Brown, T. T., Lugar, H. M., Coalson, R. S., Miezin, F. M., Petersen, S. E., & Schlaggar, B.L. (2004). Developmental changes in human cerebral functional organization for word generation. *Cereb Cortex.*

Bunge, S. A., Dudukovic NM, Thomason ME, Vaidya CJ, Gabrieli JD. (2002) Immature frontal lobe contributions to cognitive control in children: Evidence from fMRI. *Neuron, 33*, 301–311.

Bushong, S. C. (2003). *Magnetic resonance imaging*, 3rd edition. Mosby Inc.

Carey, S. (1992) Becoming a face expert. *Philos. Trans. R. Soc. Lond. B Biol. Sci., 335*, 95–102.

Carne, R. P., Vogrin, S., Litewka, L., & Cook, M. J. (2006). Cerebral cortex: An MRI-based study of volume and variance with age and sex. *J Clin Neurosci, 13*(1), 60–72.

Cascio CJ, Gerig G, Piven J. (2007) Diffusion tensor imaging: Application to the study of the developing brain. *J Am Acad Child Adolesc Psychiatry. 46*:213–23.

Casey, B. J., Cohen, J. D., Jezzard, P., Turner, R., Noll, D. C., Trainor, R. J., et al. (1995). Activation of prefrontal cortex in children during a nonspatial working memory task with functional MRI. *Neuroimage, 2*, 221–229.

Casey, B. J., Thomas, K. M., Davidson, M. C., Kunz, K., & Franzen, P. L. (2002). Dissociating striatal and hippocampal function developmentally with a stimulus-response compatibility task. *J Neurosci, 22*, 8647–8652.

Caviness, V. S. Jr, Kennedy, D. N., Richelme, C., Rademacher, J., & Filipek, P.A. (1996). The human brain age 7–11 years: A volumetric analysis based on magnetic resonance images. *Cereb Cortex, 6*(5), 726–736.

Chang, F. L. & Greenough, W.T. (1982). Lateralized effects of monocular training on dendritic branching in adult split-brain rats. *Brain Res, 232*(2), 283–292.

Chupin, M., Hammers, A., Bardinet, E., Colliot, O., Liu, R. S. N., Duncan, J. S., et al. (2007). Fully automatic segmentation of the hippocampus and the amygdala from MRI using hybrid prior knowledge. *MICCAI, 4791*, 875–882.

Cocosco, C. A., Zijdenbos, A. P., & Evans, A. C. (2003). A fully automatic and robust MRI tissue classification method. *Med Imag Anal, 7*, 513–527.

Collins, D. L., Holmes, C. J., Peters, T. M. & Evans, A. C. (1995). Automatic 3D model-based neuroanatomical segmentation. *Human Brain Mapping, 3*, 190–208.

Collins, D. L., Neelin, P., Peters, T. M., & Evans, A. C. (1994). Automatic 3D intersubject registration of MR volumetric data in standardized Talairach space. *J Comput Assist Tomogr, 18*, 192–205.

Conel, J. L. (1967) *Postnatal development of the human cerebral cortex: The cortex of the seventy-two-month infant (Vol. 8).* Cambridge, MA: Harvard University Press.

Cowell, P. E., Allen, L. S., Zalatimo, N. S., & Denenberg, V. H. (1992). A developmental study of sex and age interactions in the human corpus callosum. *Brain Res Dev Brain Res, 66*(2), 187–192.

Davidson, M. C., Thomas, K. M., & Casey, B. J. (2003). Imaging the developing brain with fMRI. *Ment Retard Dev Disabil Res Rev, 9*, 161–167.

Davey Smith, G., Ebrahim, S., Lewis, S., Hansell, A. L., Palmer, L. J., & Burton, P. R. (2005). Genetic epidemiology and public health: Hope, hype, and future prospects. *Lancet, 366*, 1484–1498.

De Bellis, M. D., Keshavan, M. S., Beers, S. R., Hall, J., Frustaci, K., Masalehdan, A., et al. (2001). Sex differences in brain maturation during childhood and adolescence. *Cereb Cortex, 11*(6), 552–557.

Decety, J. et al. (1997) Brain activity during observation of actions. Influence of action content and subject's strategy. *Brain, 120*, 1763–1777.

Dekaban, A. S. (1978). Changes in brain weights during the span of human life: Relation of brain weights to body heights and body weights. *Ann Neurol, 4*(4), 345–356.

Deutsch, G. K., Dougherty, R. F., Bammer, R., Siok, W. T., Gabrieli, J. D., & Wandell, B. (2005). Children's reading performance is correlated with white matter structure measured by diffusion tensor imaging. *Cortex, 41*(3), 354–363.

Draganski, B., Gaser, C., Busch, V., Schuierer, G., Bogdahn, U., & May, A. (2004). Neuroplasticity: Changes in grey matter induced by training. *Nature, 427*, 311–312.

Eickhoff, S. B., Schleicher, A., Scheperjans, F., Palomero-Gallagher, N., & Zilles, K. (2007). Analysis of neurotransmitter receptor distribution patterns in the cerebral cortex. *Neuroimage, 34*(4), 1317–1330.

Eluvathingal TJ, Hasan KM, Kramer L, Fletcher JM, Ewing-Cobbs L. (2007) Quantitative diffusion tensor tractography of association and projection fibers in normally developing children and adolescents. *Cereb Cortex. 17*:2760–8.

Erickson, S. L., Akil, M., Levey, A.I., & Lewis, D. A. (1998). Postnatal development of tyrosine hydroxylase- and dopamine transporter-immunoreactive axons in monkey rostral entorhinal cortex. *Cereb Cortex, 8*, 415–427.

Ernst, M., Nelson, E. E., Jazbec, S., McClure, E. B., Monk, C. S., Leibenluft, E., et al. (2005). Amygdala and nucleus accumbens in responses to receipt and omission of gains in adults and adolescents. *Neuroimage, 25*, 1279–1291.

Evans, A. C., Collins, D. L., Mills, S. R., Brown, E. D., Kelly, R. L., & Peters, T. M. (1993). 3D statistical neuroanatomical models from 305 MRI volumes, *Proc. IEEE-Nuclear Science Symposium and Medical Imaging Conference*, 1813–1817.

Evans, A. C. & Brain Development Cooperative Group. (2006). The NIH MRI study of normal brain development. *NeuroImage, 30*, 184–2002.

Fischl, B. & Dale, A. M. (2000). Measuring the thickness of the human cerebral cortex from magnetic resonance images. *Proc Natl Acad Sci U S A, 97*(20).

Fischl, B., Sereno, M. I., Tootell, R. B., & Dale, A. M. (1999). High-resolution intersubject averaging and a coordinate system for the cortical surface. *Hum Brain Mapp, 8*(4), 272–284.

Galvan, A., Hare, T. A., Parra, C. E., Penn, J., Voss, H., Glover, G., et al. (2006). Earlier development of the accumbens relative to orbitofrontal cortex might underlie risk-taking behavior in adolescents. *J Neurosci, 26*, 6885–6892.

Gaser, C. & Schlaug, G. (2003). Brain structures differ between musicians and non-musicians. *J Neurosci, 23*(27), 9240–9245.

Gazzaniga, M. S. (2004). *The cognitive neurosciences III.* New York: MIT Press.

Giedd, J. N., Blumenthal, J., Jeffries, N. O., Castellanos, F. X., Liu, H., Zijdenbos, A., et al. (1999). Brain development during childhood and adolescence: A longitudinal MRI study. *Nature Neuroscience, 2*, 861–863.

Giedd, J. N., Blumenthal, J., Jeffries, N. O., Rajapakse, J. C., Vaituzis, A. C., Liu, H., et al. (1999). Development of the human corpus callosum during childhood and adolescence: a longitudinal MRI study. *Progress in Neuro-Psychopharmacology & Biological Psychiatry, 23*, 571–588.

Giedd, J. N., Rumsey, J. M., Castellanos, F. X., Rajapakse, J. C., Kaysen, D., Vaituzis, A. C., et al. (1996). A quantitative MRI study of the corpus callosum in children and adolescents. *Developmental Brain Research, 91*, 274–280.

Giedd, J. N., Snell, J. W., Lange, N., Rajapakse, J. C., Casey, B. J., Kozuch, P. L., et al. (1996). Quantitative magnetic resonance imaging of human brain development: Ages 4–18. *Cerebral Cortex, 6*, 551–560.

Giedd, J. N., Vaituzis, A. C., Hamburger, S. D., Lange, N., Rajapakse, J. C., Kaysen, D., et al. (1996). Quantitative MRI of the temporal lobe, amygdala and hippocampus in normal human development: Ages 4–18 years. *The Journal of Comparative Neurology, 366*, 223–230.

Giedd, J. N. (2004). Structural magnetic resonance imaging of the adolescent brain. *Ann N Y Acad Sci, 1021*, 77–85.

Giedd, J. N., Clasen, L. S., Lenroot, R., Greenstein, D., Wallace, G. L., Ordaz, S., et al. (2006). Puberty-related influences on brain development. *Mol Cell Endocrinol, 254–255*, 154–62.

Giedd, J. N., Clasen, L. S., Wallace, G. L., Lenroot, R. K., Lerch, J. P., Wells, E. M., et al. (2007). XXY (Klinefelter syndrome): A pediatric quantitative brain magnetic resonance imaging case-control study. *Pediatrics, 119*, e232–240.

Glahn, D. C., Paus, T., Thompson, P. M. (2007). Imaging genomics: Mapping the influence of genetics on brain structure and function. *Human Brain Mapping, 28*, 461–463.

Gogtay, N., Giedd, J. N., Lusk, L., Hayashi, K. M., Greenstein, D., Vaituzis, A. C., et al. (2004). Dynamic mapping of human cortical development during childhood through early adulthood. *Proc Natl Acad Sci U S A, 101*, 8174–8179.

Good, C. D., Johnsrude, I., Ashburner, J., Henson, R. N., Friston, K. J., & Frackowiak, R. S. (2001). Cerebral asymmetry and the effects of sex and handedness on brain structure: A voxel-based morphometric analysis of 465 normal adult human brains. *Neuroimage, 14*(3), 685–700.

Goren, C.C. Sarty M, Wu PY. (1975). Visual following and pattern discrimination of face-like stimuli by newborn infants. *Pediatrics, 56*, 544–549.

Grezes, J., et al. (1999). The effects of learning and intention on the neural network involved in the perception of meaningless actions. *Brain, 122*, 1875–1887.

Grosbras, M. H. & Paus, T. (2006). Brain networks involved in viewing angry hands or faces. *Cerebral Cortex, 16*, 1087–1096.

Grosbras, M. H., Osswald, K., Jansen, M., Toro, R., McIntosh, A. R., Steinberg, L., et al. (2007). Neural mechanisms of resistance to peer influence in early adolescence. *Journal of Neuroscience, 27*, 8040–8045.

Gur, R. C., Gunning-Dixon, F., Bilker, W. B., & Gur, R. E. (2002). Sex differences in temporo-limbic and frontal brain volumes of healthy adults. *Cereb Cortex, 12*(9), 998–1003.

Hagmann, P., Cammoun, L., Martuzzi, R., Maeder, P., Clarke, S., Thiran, J. P., et al. (2006). Hand preference and sex shape the architecture of language networks. *Hum Brain Mapp.*

Haier, R. J., Jung, R. E., Yeo, R. A., Head, K., & Alkire, M. T. (2005). The neuroanatomy of general intelligence: Sex matters. *Neuroimage, 25*(1), 320–327.

Hall, J. A. (1978). Gender effects in decoding nonverbal cues. *Psychological Bulletin, 85*, 845–857.

Herba, C. & Phillips, M. (2004). Annotation: Development of facial expression recognition from childhood to adolescence: Behavioural and neurological perspectives. *J Child Psychol Psychiatry, 45*(7), 1185–1198.

Hope, P. L. & Moorcraft, J. (1991). Magnetic resonance spectroscopy. *Clin Perinatol, 18*(3), 535–548.

Hursh, J. B. (1939). Conduction velocity and diameter of nerve fibers. *American Journal of Physiology, 127*, 131–139.

Huttenlocher, P. R. (1984). Synapse elimination and plasticity in developing human cerebral cortex. *Am J Ment Defic, 88*: 488–496.

Huttenlocher, P. R. & de Courten, C. (1987). The development of synapses in striate cortex of man. *Hum Neurobiol, 6*, 1–9.

Huttenlocher, P. R. & Dabholkar, A. S. (1997). Regional differences in synaptogenesis in human cerebral cortex. *J Comp Neurol, 387*, 167–178.

Hwang, S. J., Ji, E. K., Lee, E. K., Kim, Y. M., Shin da, Y., Cheon, Y. H., et al. (2004). Gender differences in the corpus callosum of neonates. *Neuroreport, 15*(6), 1029–1032.

Joffe, T. H., Tarantal, A. F., Rice, K., Leland, M., Oerke, A. K., Rodeck, C., et al. (2005). Fetal and infant head circumference sexual dimorphism in primates. *Am J Phys Anthropol, 126*(1), 97–110.

Kaes, T. (1907). *Die Grosshirnrinde des Menschen in ihren Massen und ihrem Fasergehalt.* Gustav Fisher, Jena.

Kimura, D. (1996) Sex, sexual orientation and sex hormones influence human cognitive function. *Curr Opin in Neurobiol, 6*, 259–263.

Kilts, C. D. (2003) Dissociable neural pathways are involved in the recognition of emotion in static and dynamic facial expressions. *Neuroimage, 18*, 156–168.

Klingberg, T., Vaidya, C. J., Gabrieli, J. D. E., Moseley, M. E., & Hedehus, M. (1999). Myelination and organization of the frontal white matter in children: A diffusion tensor MRI study. *NeuroReport, 10*, 2817–2821.

Kucharczyk, W., Macdonald, P. M., Stanisz, G. J., & Henkelman, R. M. (1994). Relaxivity and magnetization transfer of white matter lipids at MR imaging: Importance of cerebrosides and pH. *Radiology, 192*, 521–529.

Kwon, H., Reiss, A. L., & Menon, V. (2002). Neural basis of protracted developmental changes in visuo-spatial working memory. *Proc Natl Acad Sci U S A, 99*, 13336–13341.

Laule, C., Vavasour, I. M., Kolind, S. H., Li, D. K., Traboulsee, T. L., Moore, G. R., et al. (2007) Magnetic resonance imaging of myelin. *Neurotherapeutics, 4*, 460–484.

Lebel C, Beaulieu C. Lateralization of the arcuate fasciculus from childhood to adulthood and its relation to cognitive abilities in children. Hum Brain Mapp. 2009 Nov;30(11): 3563–73.

Lebel C, Walker L, Leemans A, Phillips L, Beaulieu C. (2008) Microstructural maturation of the human brain from childhood to adulthood. *Neuroimage.* 40:1044–55.

Le Bihan, D. (2003). Looking into the functional architecture of the brain with diffusion MRI. *Nat Rev Neurosci, 4*, 469–480.

Lenroot, R. K. & Giedd, J. N. (2006). Brain development in children and adolescents: insights from anatomical magnetic resonance imaging. *Neurosci Biobehav Rev,. 30*, 718–729.

Logothetis, N. K., Pauls, J., Augath, M., Trinath, T., & Oeltermann, A. (2001). Neurophysiological investigation of the basis of the fMRI signal. *Nature, 412*, 150–157.

Lotfipour S, Ferguson E, Leonard G, Perron M, Pike GB, Richer L, Séguin JR, Toro R, Veillette S, Pausova Z., Paus T. Orbitofrontal Cortex and Drug Use during Adolescence: Role of Prenatal Exposure to Maternal Smoking and BDNF Genotype. *Archives of General Psychiatry* 66:1244–1252, 2009.

Luders, E., Steinmetz, H., & Jancke, L. (2002). Brain size and grey matter volume in the healthy human brain. *Neuroreport, 13*(17), 2371–2374.

Luna, B. et al. (2001) Maturation of widely distributed brain function subserves cognitive development. *Neuroimage, 13,* 786–793.

Mädler, B., Drabycz, S. A., Kolind, S. H., Whittall, K. P., & Mackay, A. L. (2008). Is diffusion anisotropy an accurate monitor of myelination? Correlation of multicomponent T(2) relaxation and diffusion tensor anisotropy in human brain. *Magn Reson Imaging,* [Epub ahead of print].

Maguire, E. A., Gadian, D. G., Johnsrude, I. S., Good, C. D., Ashburner, J., Frackowiak, R. S., et al. (2000). Navigation-related structural change in the hippocampi of taxi drivers. *Proc Natl Acad Sci U S A,. 97*(8), 4398–4403.

Marner, L., et al. (2003) Marked loss of myelinated nerve fibers in the human brain with age. *J Comp Neurol, 462,* 144–152.

Matsuzawa, J., Matsui, M., Konishi, T., Noguchi, K., Gur, R. C., Bilker, W., et al. (2001). Age-related volumetric changes of brain gray and white matter in healthy infants and children. *Cereb Cortex, 11*(4), 335–342.

McGivern, R.F. Andersen J, Byrd D, Mutter KL, Reilly J. (2002) Cognitive efficiency on a match to sample task decreases at the onset of puberty in children. *Brain Cogn, 50,* 73–89.

McGowan, J. C. (1999) The physical basis of magnetization transfer imaging. *Neurology, 53*(5 Suppl 3), S3–S7.

Mechelli, A., Crinion, J. T., Noppeney, U., O'Doherty, J., Ashburner, J., Frackowiak, R. S., et al. (2004). Neurolinguistics: Structural plasticity in the bilingual brain. *Nature, 431*(7010), 757.

Menon, V., Boyett-Anderson, J. M., & Reiss, A. L. Maturation of medial temporal lobe response and connectivity during memory encoding. *Brain Res Cogn Brain Res, 25*(1), 379–385.

Paus, T. (2003). Principles of functional neuroimaging. In: R. B. Schiffer, S. M. Rao, & B. S. Fogel (Eds.) *Neuropsychiatry, Second Edition* (pp. 63–90). Philadelphia: Lippincott, Williams & Wilkins.

Paus, T. (2005). Mapping brain maturation and cognitive development during adolescence. *Trends Cogn Sci, 9*(2), 60–68.

Paus, T. (2007). Maturation of structural and functional connectivity in the human brain In: V. Jirsa & A. R. McIntosh, (Eds.). *Handbook of brain connectivity,* Springer-Verlag.

Paus T. Growth of White Matter in the Adolescent Brain: Myelin or Axon. *Brain and Cognition* 72:26–35, 2010a.

Paus T. Population Neuroscience: Why and how. *Human Brain Mapping* 31:891–903, 2010b.

Paus T and Toro R. Could sex differences in white matter be explained by g ratio? *Frontiers in Neuroanatomy* 3:14, 2009.

Paus, T., Collins, D. L., Evans, A. C., Leonard, G., Pike, B., & Zijdenbos, A. (2001). Maturation of white matter in the human brain: A review of magnetic-resonance studies. *Brain Research Bulletin, 54,* 255–266.

Paus, T., Marrett, S., Worsley K. J., & Evans, A. C. (1995). Extra-retinal modulation of cerebral blood-flow in the human visual cortex: Implications for saccadic suppression. *Journal of Neurophysiology, 74,* 2179–2183.

Paus, T., Otaky, N., Caramanos, Z., MacDonald, D., Zijdenbos, A., D'Avirro, D., et al. (1996a). In vivo morphometry of the intrasulcal gray matter in the human cingulate, paracingulate, and superior-rostral sulci: hemispheric asymmetries, gender differences and probability maps. *J Comp Neurol, 376,* 664–673.

Paus, T., Zijdenbos, A., Worsley, K., Collins, D. L., Blumenthal, J., Giedd, J. N., et al. (1999). Structural maturation of neural pathways in children and adolescents: in vivo study. *Science, 283,* 1908–1911.

Paus, T., Tomaiuolo, F., Otaky, N., MacDonald, D., Petrides, M., Atlas, J., et al. (1996b). Human cingulate and paracingulate sulci: Pattern, variability, asymmetry, and probabilistic map. *Cerebral Cortex, 6,*.

Paus T, Toro R, Leonard G, Lerner J, Lerner RM, Perron M, Pike GB, Richer L, Steinberg, Veillette S, Pausova Z. Morphological properties of the action-observation cortical network in adolescents with low and high resistance to peer influence. *Social Neuroscience* 3:303–316, 2008.

Pausova, Z., Paus, T., Abrahamowicz, M., Almerigi, J., Arbour, N., Bernard, M., et al. (2007). Maternal smoking and the offspring brain and body during adolescence: Design of the Saguenay Youth Study. *Human Brain Mapping, 28,* 502–518.

Perrin, J. S., Leonard, G., Perron, M., Pike, G. B., Pitiot, A., Richer, L., et al. (2008a). Growth of white matter in the adolescent brain: Role of testosterone and androgen receptor.

Perrin, J. S., Herve, P. Y., Pitiot, A., Totman, J., & Paus, T. (2008b). Brain structure and the female menstrual cycle. *Neuroimage Supplement, 1,* 41:638 M–PM.

Peters, M., Jancke, L., Staiger, J. F., Schlaug, G., Huang, Y., & Steinmetz, H. (1998). Unsolved problems in comparing brain sizes in Homo sapiens. *Brain Cogn, 37,* 254–285.

Pezawas, L., Verchinski, B. A., Mattay, V. S., Callicott, J. H., Kolachana, B. S., Straub, R. E., et al. (2004). The brain-derived neurotrophic factor val66met polymorphism and variation in human cortical morphology. *J Neurosci, 24*(45), 10099–10102.

Pezawas, L., Meyer-Lindenberg, A., Drabant, E. M., Verchinski, B. A., Munoz, K. E., Kolachana, B. S., et al. (2005).5- HTTLPR polymorphism impacts human cingulate-amygdala interactions: A genetic susceptibility mechanism for depression. *Nat Neurosci, 8*(6), 828–834.

Pfefferbaum, A., Mathalon, D. H., Sullivan, E. V., Rawles, J. M., Zipursky, R. B., & Lim, K. O. (1994). A quantitative magnetic resonance imaging study of changes in brain morphology from infancy to late adulthood. *Archives of Neurology, 51,* 874–887.

Pike, G. B. (1996) Pulsed magnetization transfer contrast in gradient echo imaging: A two-pool analytic description of signal response. *Magn Reson Med, 36,* 95–103.

Puce, A. et al. (1998) Temporal cortex activation in humans viewing eye and mouth movements. *J Neurosci, 8,* 2188–2199.

Pujol, J., Lopez, A., Deus, J., Cardoner, N., Vallejo, J., Capdevila, A., et al. (2002). Anatomical variability of the anterior cingulate gyrus and basic dimensions of human personality. *Neuroimage, 15*(4), 847–855.

Pujol, J., Vendrell, P., Junque, C., Marti-Vilalta, J. L., & Capdevila A. (1993). When does human brain development end? Evidence of corpus callosum growth up to adulthood. *Annals of Neurology, 34,* 71–75.

Purves, D., White, L. E., & Riddle, D. R. (1996). Is neural development Darwinian? *Trends Neurosci, 19,* 460–464.

Rakic, P., Bourgeois, J. P., Eckenhoff, M. F., Zecevic, N., & Goldman-Rakic, P. S. (1986). Concurrent overproduction of synapses in diverse regions of the primate cerebral cortex. *Science, 232,* 232–235.

Rauch, R. A. & Jinkins, J. R. (1994). Analysis of cross-sectional area measurements of the corpus callosum adjusted for brain size in male and female subjects from childhood to adulthood. *Behav Brain Res, 64*(1–2), 65–78.

Rees, G., Friston, K., & Koch, C. A direct quantitative relationship between the functional properties of human and macaque V5. *Nat Neurosci, 3,* 716–723.

Reiss, A. L., Abrams, M. T., Singer, H. S., Ross, J. L., & Denckla, M. B. (1996). Brain development, gender and IQ in children. A volumetric imaging study. *Brain, 119*, 1763–1774.

Robbins, T. W. & Everitt, B. J. (1996). Neurobehavioural mechanisms of reward and motivation. *Curr Opin Neurobiol, 6*, 228–236.

Roberts, T. P., Mikulis, D. Neuro MR: principles. *J Magn Reson Imaging, 26*(4), 823–837.

Rosenberg, D. R. & Lewis, D. A. (1995). Postnatal maturation of the dopaminergic innervation of monkey prefrontal and motor cortices: A tyrosine hydroxylase immunohistochemical analysis. *J Comp Neurol, 358*, 383–400.

Rubia, K. et al. (2000) Functional frontalisation with age: Mapping neurodevelopmental trajectories with fMRI. *Neurosci. Biobehav. Rev, 24*, 13–19.

Rushton, W. A. H. (1951). A theory of the effects of fibre size in the medullated nerve. *Journal of Physiology, 115*, 101–122.

Schlaggar, B. L., Brown, T. T., Lugar, H. M., Visscher, K. M., Miezin, F. M., & Petersen, S.E. (2002). Functional neuroanatomical differences between adults and school-age children in the processing of single words. *Science, 296*, 1476–1479.

Schmidt-Nielsen K. (1997). *Animal physiology: Adaptation and environment.* 5th Edition. Cambridge: Cambridge University Press.

Schmierer, K., Scaravilli, F., Altmann, D. R., Barker, G. J., & Miller, D. H. (2004). Magnetization transfer ratio and myelin in postmortem multiple sclerosis brain. *Ann Neurol, 56*, 407–415.

Schmierer, K., Wheeler-Kingshott, C. A., Tozer, D. J., Boulby, P. A., Parkes, H. G., Yousry, T. A., et al. (2008). Quantitative magnetic resonance of postmortem multiple sclerosis brain before and after fixation. *Magn Reson Med, 59*, 268–277.

Schmithorst, V. J. & Holland, S. K. (2006). Functional MRI evidence for disparate developmental processes underlying intelligence in boys and girls. *Neuroimage, 31*, 1366–1379.

Schmithorst, V. J., Wilke, M., Dardzinski, B. J., & Holland, S. K. (2005). Cognitive functions correlate with white matter architecture in a normal pediatric population: A diffusion tensor MRI study. *Hum Brain Mapp,*.

Schmithorst, V. J., Wilke, M., Dardzinski, B. J., & Holland, S. K. (2002). Correlation of white matter diffusivity and anisotropy with age during childhood and adolescence: A cross-sectional diffusion-tensor MR imaging study. *Radiology, 222*(1), 212–218.

Schmithorst VJ, Holland SK, Dardzinski BJ. (2008) Developmental differences in white matter architecture between boys and girls. *Hum Brain Mapp. 29*:696–710.

Shankle WR, Romney AK, Landing BH, Hara J. Developmental patterns in the cytoarchitecture of the human cerebral cortex from birth to 6 years examined by correspondence analysis. Proc Natl Acad Sci U S A. 1998 Mar 31;95(7):4023–8.

Shaw, P., Greenstein, D., Lerch, J., Clasen, L., Lenroot, R., Gogtay, N., et al. (2006). Intellectual ability and cortical development in children and adolescents. *Nature, 440*(7084), 676–679.

Sholl, D. A. (1956). *The organization of the cerebral cortex.* London: Methuen & Co. Ltd.

Sirevaag, A. M. & Greenough, W. T. (1988). A multivariate statistical summary of synaptic plasticity measures in rats exposed to complex, social and individual environments. *Brain Res,. 441*(1–2), 386–392.

Skullerud, K. (1985). Variations in the size of the human brain. Influence of age, sex, body length, body mass index, alcoholism, Alzheimer changes, and cerebral atherosclerosis. *Acta Neurol Scand Suppl, 102*, 1–94.

Sluming, V., Barrick, T., Howard, M., Cezayirli, E., Mayes, A., & Roberts, N. (2002). Voxel-based morphometry reveals increased gray matter density in Broca's area in male symphony orchestra musicians. *Neuroimage, 17*(3), 1613–1622.

Smith, S. M., et al. (2006). Tract-based spatial statistics: Voxelwise analysis of multi-subject diffusion data. *NeuroImage, 31*, 1487–1505.

Snook, L., Paulson, L. A., Roy, D., Phillips, L., & Beaulieu, C. Diffusion tensor imaging of neurodevelopment in children and young adults. *Neuroimage, 26*(4), 1164–1173.

Sowell, E. R., Thompson, P. M., Tessner, K. D., & Toga, A. W. (2001). Mapping continued brain growth and gray matter density reduction in dorsal frontal cortex: Inverse relationships during post-adolescent brain maturation. *J Neurosci, 21*, 8819–8829.

Steinberg, L. (2008). A neurobehavioral perspective on adolescent risk-taking. *Dev Rev, 28*, 78–106.

Steinberg, L. & Monahan, K. (2007). Age differences in resistance to peer influence *Developmental Psychology, 43*, 1531–1543.

Steinmetz, H., Jancke, L., Kleinschmidt, A., Schlaug, G., Volkmann, J., & Huang, Y. (1992). Sex but no hand difference in the isthmus of the corpus callosum. *Neurology, 42*(4), 749–752.

Steinmetz, H., Staiger, J. F., Schlaug, G., Huang, Y., & Jancke, L. (1995). Corpus callosum and brain volume in women and men. *Neuroreport, 6*(7), 1002–1004.

Suzuki, M., Hagino, H., Nohara, S., Zhou, S. Y., Kawasaki, Y., Takahashi, T., et al. (2005). Male-specific volume expansion of the human hippocampus during adolescence. *Cereb Cortex, 15*(2), 187–193.

Talairach, J. & Tournoux, P. (1988) *Co-planar stereotaxic atlas of the human brain.* New York: Thieme Medical Publishers.

Tamm, L., Menon, V., & Reiss, A. L. (2002). Maturation of brain function associated with response inhibition. *J Am Acad Child Adolesc Psychiatry, 41*, 1231–1238.

Taylor, M. J. et al. (1999). ERP evidence of developmental changes in processing of faces. *Clin. Neurophysiol, 110*, 910–915.

Thomas, K. M., Drevets, W. C., Whalen, P. J., Eccard, C. H., Dahl, R. E., Ryan, N. D., et al. (2001). Amygdala response to facial expressions in children and adults. *Biol Psychiatry, 49*, 309–316.

Toro, R., Perron, M., Pike, B., Richer, R., Veillette, S., Pausova, Z., et al. (2008). Brain size and folding of the human cerebral cortex. *Cerebral Cortex*, [Epub ahead of print].

Tunbridge, E. M., Weickert, C. S., Kleinman, J. E., Herman, M. M., Chen, J., Kolachana, B. S., et al. (2007). Catechol-o-methyltransferase enzyme activity and protein expression in human prefrontal cortex across the postnatal lifespan. *Cereb Cortex, 17*, 1206–1212.

Weickert, C. S., Webster, M. J., Gondipalli, P., Rothmond, D., Fatula, R. J., Herman, M. M., et al. (2007). Postnatal alterations in dopaminergic markers in the human prefrontal cortex. *Neuroscience, 144*, 1109–1119.

Yakovlev, P. I. & Lecours, A. R. (1967). In A. Minkowski (Ed.). *Regional development of the brain in early life* (pp. 3–70). Oxford: Blackwell Scientific.

Yang, T. T., Menon, V., Reid, A. J., Gotlib, I. H., & Reiss, A.L. (2003). Amygdalar activation associated with happy facial expressions in adolescents: A 3-T functional MRI study. *J Am Acad Child Adolesc Psychiatry, 42*, 979–985.

Yucel, M., Stuart, G. W., Maruff, P., Velakoulis, D., Crowe, S. F., Savage, G., et al. (2001). Hemispheric and gender-related differences in the gross morphology of the anterior cingulate/paracingulate cortex in normal volunteers: An MRI morphometric study. *Cereb Cortex, 11*(1):17–25.

Zijdenbos, A. P., Forghani, R., & Evans, A. C. (2002). Automatic "pipeline" analysis of 3D MRI data for clinical trials: Application to multiple sclerosis *IEEE Trans Med Imag, 21*, 1280–1291.

Zilles, K., Palomero-Gallagher, N., & Schleicher, A. (2004). Transmitter receptors and functional anatomy of the cerebral cortex. *J Anat, 205*, 417–432.

An Overview of Self-Awareness and the Brain

Julian Paul Keenan, Hanna Oh, *and* Franco Amati

Abstract

This chapter shows how the key to understanding self-awareness over the course of evolution and human development relies in the understanding of how the self resides in the complexities of the brain. From the social neuroscience perspective, the brain has developed specialized mechanisms for processing information about the social environment, including the ability to understand ourselves, to know how others respond to us, and to regulate our actions in order to avoid being dismissed from our social groups. The neural correlates of self-awareness are largely unknown, though it is apparent that the frontal lobes play a crucial role. There are two basic approaches for studying the brain regions involved in self-awareness: studying the impaired brain and imaging the healthy brain using devices such as PET, MRI, and fMRI. The brain regions involved in self-recognition, self-awareness, self-assessment, and theory of mind are discussed.

Keywords: Self-awareness, self-recognition, neuroimaging, consciousness, mirror-recognition, frontal cortex, transcranial magnetic stimulation.

Self-awareness

Synthesizing the domains of social and biological science hinges on a clear understanding of how the self interacts with others. In this way, the study of self-awareness is vital to the field of social neuroscience. Before one can grasp the concept of group, civilization, family, or culture, a firm reference point for the self must exist. Without a concept of self, humans are virtually inept at navigating the complex social environment. This self-reference point is our personal identity and it depends critically on consciousness.

Consciousness has been a central topic in the study of philosophy and psychology for centuries. Despite this fascination, not a single theory regarding consciousness has definitively explained it.

We may say that it arises from the physical brain, but little has been found about the mechanisms that underlie these processes. Therefore, the problem of consciousness still remains as one of the biggest unsolved mysteries in science. Understanding consciousness is not only important for interpreting human behavior, but is fundamental for ultimately understanding the nature of human beings.

The search for the nature of consciousness has likely been ongoing since the reflective human life began. It would be impossible to track down the origin, but a noticeable approach to the question began with the ancient Greek scholars. Although important arguments regarding human nature and the mind go back to Socrates (b. 470 BC) and Plato (b. ca. 428 BC), who emphasized the importance of introspection in order to understand true virtue, it was René Descartes (1596–1650) who began the close examination of consciousness and the relationship between the mind and body. His theories on self-awareness and consciousness are considered significant even today. Descartes believed in the duality of the mind and body. That is, he insisted that there exists a nonphysical mind distinct from the body. Moreover, he argued that conscious introspection could provide true knowledge of oneself that could not be obtained from empirical observation. His ideas are epitomized in one of his famous quotes, "*Cogito, ergo sum*" or "I think, therefore I am." This implies that the self exists and knows its existence because it can think and meditate on its own existence (Keenan, Gallup, & Falk, 2003). Descartes believed that humans are the only creatures with a soul, thus, the only beings capable of reflecting upon existence.

Descartes also developed physiological approaches to understanding consciousness. He believed that the pineal gland was not only involved in sensation, imagination, memory, and bodily movements but also housed the soul. Thus, it was where the mind and body met to form consciousness. His claim was based on the fact that the pineal gland was not lateralized, therefore was not separated from left to right (Keenan et al., 2003). Although the theory was later proven incorrect, Descartes' notion that consciousness could be localized in a certain part of the brain is quite significant. Indeed, this can be considered the first attempt to grasp the nature of consciousness in neuroscience.

In addition to the philosophers, like Descartes, many other great thinkers and scientists suggested new theories to explain consciousness. Sigmund Freud (1856–1939) mainly worked to understand the cause of conscious thought and behavior. He concluded that much of one's memories and experiences, in other words, the self, were repressed. In contradiction to Descartes' notion that every mental state had a conscious aspect, Freud's theory expanded the idea of self, enabling us to understand diverse behaviors as a product of unconsciousness (Lewis, 2006). That is, the self can act, plan, know, and believe based on unconscious beliefs and desires (Chalmers, 1996; Lewis, 2006). Carl Jung (1875–1961) proposed a concept of the collective unconscious. He insisted that there was an unconscious mind or common self shared by all humans, which included ideas such as science, religion, and morality. Also, Jean Piaget (1896–1980) believed in the malleability of self throughout the developmental process. He posited that a child moves from a phase of egocentrism, in which there is no discrimination between the self and the world, to more advanced stages of abstract logic and self-awareness (Piaget, 1970). This is just a handful of significant examples of psychologists who examined the relationship between self-awareness and consciousness, and there are vast numbers of studies devoted to the refining of concepts that these individuals originated.

Definition of Self-awareness

Consciousness has many definitions but the three most commonly used are: (1) the ability to be aware of external or internal stimuli, (2) self-awareness or internal knowledge of oneself, and (3) mutual knowledge or ability to connect with mental states of others (Keenan et al., 2003). It is difficult to define a true and universally accepted meaning for consciousness but for the purpose of this chapter, we will use the second definition. Thus, "consciousness" and "self-awareness" are sometimes used interchangeably.

We often find ourselves narrating and objectively assessing our own thoughts and judgments. We constantly "feel" something and this "feeling" influences our behavior. These feelings are part of a self-reflective process that is so fundamental to human experience that we take it for granted. However familiar, the concept of self-awareness is elusive, and in order to understand it we need to investigate and converge findings from different fields such as philosophy, psychology, neuroscience, and psychopathology (Kircher & David, 2003). Keenan, Gallup, and Falk (2003) defined self-awareness as, "the ability to reflect on one's own mental state and the capacity to regard the self as a different entity from others" (p. 5). In addition, Duval and Wicklund (1972) suggested objective self-awareness, which leads to self-evaluation, the active process of identifying and collecting information of the self. Indeed, there are two types of self-awareness: (1) private self-awareness, which involves awareness of one's own mental states such as emotions, perceptions, motives, and sensations; and (2) public self-awareness, the ability to comprehend how other people view oneself (A. Johnson et al., 2005; Morin, 2004).

Self-awareness ensures one to continue to exist as the same person across time and allows one to be a creator of one's thoughts and actions (Kircher & David, 2003). We feel that our bodies exist in what we call the present; however, we also have the awareness to extend this existence to previous events of the past, and possible events of the future. Many philosophers of the mind refer to this quality as the diachronic quality of self, or an autobiographical self (Dennet, 1992; Strawson, 1997; Gallagher, 2000). It also leads to understanding that one exists as an independent and unique entity (Morin, 2004). Thus, self-awareness enables one to develop uniquely human qualities such as self-regulation, self-conscious emotions,* and theory of mind, which will be discussed later in the chapter (A. Johnson et al., 2005; Keenan, Gallup, & Falk, 2003; Morin, 2004).

Private Self-awareness

Self-awareness can be examined in various ways, but one major approach is through the self-recognition test using a mirror. In fact, an attempt to prove self-awareness through mirror-test has been performed for more than 150 years (Keenan et al., 2003). In order to recognize oneself in the mirror, a concept of the self is necessary (Kircher & David, 2003). Therefore, researchers such as Charles Darwin and Gordon Gallup suggested that the ability to recognize oneself in the mirror is an indication of self-awareness in animals (Kircher & David, 2003).

Charles Darwin (1809–1882) can be regarded as one of the first scientific researchers to utilize the mirror in order to study higher-order cognitive abilities (Keenan et al., 2003). When Darwin presented two orangutans with a mirror, they reacted as if they were looking at other animals (Keenan et al., 2003). These animals couldn't recognize their faces in the mirrors and Darwin concluded that the animals are not capable of mirror self-recognition. In 1877, five years after publishing these results, Darwin published another paper, a diary of his observations from the birth of his first child. In these articles, he described children's reactions to mirrors and proposed that their ability for self-recognition was an indication of higher intellect (Keenan et al., 2003).

Gordon Gallup performed similar mirror-tests in search for the evolution of self-consciousness. Indeed, he performed various mirror self-recognition test on primates as well as human infants. Compared to Darwin's studies, Gallup's research employed clear measures and observable determinants of the self (Keenan et al., 2003). Gallup (1970) reported that after several days of mirror exposure, chimpanzees learned to use mirrors to explore parts of themselves. In additional studies that followed, Gallup anesthetized the chimpanzees and marked them

with red, odorless, and tactile-free dye on their faces (Gallup, 1970). After recovery from anesthesia, the chimpanzees virtually never touched the marks without any mirror present; however, they started examining and touching these marks when the mirror was reintroduced (Gallup, 1970). Moreover, the chimpanzees who never saw themselves in the mirror before the mark didn't respond to the change when the mirror was introduced later (Gallup, 1970). Using the same method, Gallup also tested the monkeys, but they did not make mark-directed touches when re-exposed to the mirror (Gallup, 1970). These results indicate that the chimpanzee has mirror self-recognition whereas the monkey does not. In this paper, Gallup further argued that in order to have self-face recognition, one must possess a persistent sense of one's own appearance as well as an ability to model oneself in one's own mind (Gallup, 1970; Keenan, Gallup, & Falk, 2003).

Indeed, Gallup believed that self-recognition in a mirror was possible only if the animal had self-awareness. However, B. F. Skinner argued that passing the mirror-test does not provide any proof of the existence of self-awareness in animals. That is, an animal could pass the test without having an inner cognitive model of self (Keenan et al., 2003). Robert Epstein, Robert Lanza, and B. F. Skinner (1981), by training the pigeons to peck the dots on their bodies using the mirror, proved that any animal could pass the test by simple training. Additionally, Ferrari and Sternberg (1998) suggested that animals such as chimpanzees could recognize themselves in mirrors without realizing that they were unique, unduplicated selves, which also disputes Gallup's theory. Recent studies have also reported self-recognition abilities in bottlenose dolphins (Marten & Psarakos, 1995), elephants (Plontik, DeWaal, & Reiss, 2006), and even tool-using birds called magpies (Prior, Schwarz, & Gunterkun, 2008). Self-recognition in nonmammalian species has been explained as an ability that may have evolved independently in different classes of vertebrates with separate evolutionary histories (Prior, Schwarz, & Gunterkun, 2008). This then leads researchers to the important question: Does self-recognition necessarily imply self-awareness?

The research on infant development can provide some insights to the above question. In the reports on his children, Darwin (1877) described a child's reaction to a mirror:

> "He was, however, puzzled at the age of seven months, when being outdoors he saw me on the

inside of a large plate-glass window, and seemed in doubt whether or not it was an image."

As Darwin pointed out, newly born infants don't seem to have an ability to recognize themselves in a mirror. Empirical evidence was given with the mirror self-recognition test done by Lewis and Brooks-Gunn (1979). Using experiments similar to Gallup's, but using children as the test subjects, they concluded that infants do not demonstrate mark-directed responses until they are in the middle of the second year (Lewis & Brooks-Gunn, 1979). In fact, 75 percent of all infants pass the test at the age of 18 months and all infants pass the test by the age of two (Keenan, Gallup, & Falk, 2003; Lewis, 1992). This evidence has been used to argue that infants under the age of 18 months have no sense of self (Ferrari & Sternberg, 1998).

There are several behaviors that emerge by the age of two that suggest the formation of self-awareness. First is the use of self-pronouns such as "I," "my," "mine," or the child's name along with an object and predicate such as "My book" or "I sit" (Ferrari & Sternberg, 1998). Self-descriptive utterances are rarely present during the first few months of the second year but by age 2 they are observable, and by 27 to 28 months when sophisticated phrases such as "I do it myself" can be observed (Ferrari & Sternberg, 1998). The research suggests that the increase in descriptions of the child's activity are not simply due to the increased skill of language use, since most children showed the sharpest decline in describing objects when they started displaying an increase in self-descriptions (Ferrari & Sternberg, 1998). Indeed, it is more likely that the two-year-olds do not begin to talk about themselves because they can use verbs but because they become aware of themselves and their ability to achieve goals through their actions (Ferrari & Sternberg, 1998).

It is also around the age of two when children begin to feel and express self-conscious emotions such as pride, shame, guilt, and embarrassment (Lewis, 2006). These emotions are referred to as self-related emotions and are important indicators of self-awareness. Self-related emotions often require one to examine oneself from a third-person perspective (Keenan et al., 2003). In addition, these emotions play a central role in motivating and regulating people's thoughts, feelings, and behaviors (Tracy & Robins, 2007). More importantly, they can act as driving forces for people to work hard in order to achieve certain goals and to behave in morally and socially appropriate ways (Tracy & Robins, 2007).

For example, in order to experience pride, one needs to compare or evaluate one's behavior against some standard, rule, or goal (Lewis, 2006). To experience guilt and shame, one needs to be aware that the self has not met some type of internal or external standard (Keenan et al., 2003). Embarrassment often requires evaluating one's public self-representations (Tracy & Robins, 2007). The balance between these emotions is also important. That is, a person with high self-esteem tends to experience pride but not shame, whereas a person with low self-esteem reflects the opposite pattern (Tracy & Robins, 2007). Also, narcissism is known as a defense against excessive shame (Tracy & Robins, 2007).

Self-related emotions can often be observed late in the second year. Children begin to smile whenever they master certain tasks or goals, which can be a good indication of pride (Ferrari & Sternberg, 1998). They also become embarrassed when they trip and fall or display feelings of guilt after breaking an object (Keenan et al., 2003). Critical self-evaluations continue to increase as children get older. As a child becomes more aware of the opinions and evaluations of others, self-conscious feelings can dominate social life well into adolescent development (Blakemore, 2008). All of these self-related emotions require having an objective view of the self and the ability to internalize the thoughts of others. Moreover, regulation of self-conscious emotions becomes increasingly important (Tracy & Robins, 2007), which mainly involves the self-evaluation process.

Public Self-awareness

Self-understanding can result in a well-defined self-concept, which can influence, for instance, the formation of a consistent and desirable self-image (Sedikides, 1993). The knowledge of the self, however, is not something that can be easily obtained, because one needs to perform dual roles, both as an observer and a subject of inspection (Djikic, Peterson, & Zelazo, 2005). It also requires the ability to understand how other people view us, by going beyond our own representations of the world and assuming another person's perspective (A. Johnson et al., 2005; Jeannerod & Anquetil, 2008).

The social environment can be the most abundant source of self-information. There is strong evidence to indicate that people's self-concepts are deeply shaped by values, beliefs, and practices of the society to which they belong (Morin, 2004). More general social identity characteristics such as race, gender, and age can also influence one's self-representation along with interpersonal relationships (Lockwood & Matthews, 2007). In the case of infant development, face-to-face communication and imitation play crucial roles in forming public self-awareness. These interactions allow a gradual understanding that the self can produce effects in the social environment to reinforce the uniqueness of the self in society (Morin, 2004). Moreover, from the interactions with the caregiver, infants learn to anticipate intentional behavior in other people (Morin, 2004).

One of the most valuable sources of self-information consists of feedback given by others on one's personal characteristics and behaviors. People often pay close attention to how other people view and assess them. These appraisals from the environment allow a person to learn about the self (Morin, 2004). They can also be used to develop internal standards for self-evaluation. In addition, they can trigger self-observation, especially when the information does not fit one's current self-concept (Morin, 2004). Studies suggest that people not only construct their self-image using direct feedback from others, but are also influenced by how they think others view them (Morin, 2004). This often involves a social comparison process of the self to another person. By comparing oneself to the inferior other, an individual can feel superior, successful and satisfied (Lockwood & Matthews, 2007). However, finding out that another person is more competent or more attractive than oneself can often be discouraging (Lockwood & Matthews, 2007) and may lead to low self-esteem and depression. In order to reduce the damage done by such comparisons, people usually adopt biased processing of self-related information. That is, people have a tendency to readily accept positive information about the self whereas negative or threatening information goes through a more critical evaluation process and is often disregarded (Epley & Whitchurch, 2008). This positive illusion, which is called "self-enhancement bias," arises in order to compensate for the gap between the way the individual perceives oneself and others (Kwan, John, Kenny, Bond, & Robins, 2004). Thus, although social feedback is valid, it is not always an accurate source of self-information and even in the face of truth people can misinterpret the information (Morin, 2004) and form overly positive self-concepts during the process of introspection.

Other stimuli that can trigger public self-awareness involve the visual perception of the self prompted by devices such as mirrors, video cameras, and pictures (Morin, 2004). Observing oneself in the mirror or seeing oneself on video provides information about the public self, such as appearances, expressions, and mannerisms (Morin, 2004). This adds to the knowledge about the physical self enabling one to create an accurate self-image. Critically, the difference between the real self-image and the ideal self would likely involve the initiation of perspective taking and self-awareness (Morin, 2004).

Theory of Mind

Self-awareness is strongly related to self-recognition, self-evaluation, and self-conscious emotions; however, the most beneficial aspect of self-awareness is the ability to reflect on the thoughts of others. If one can understand one's own thoughts through introspection, one can also infer other people's thoughts based on one's own mental state. This process is called perspective taking or theory of mind (Premack & Woodruff, 1978). In terms of human development, self-awareness precedes the development of theory of mind, and thus, self-awareness may be necessary in order to employ theory of mind (A. Johnson et al., 2005; Baron-Cohen, 1991). Indeed, theory of mind represents one of the most advanced forms of cognitive activities, and it is a skill that emerges relatively late in human development (Keenan et al., 2003; Meldtzoff, 1995; Baron-Cohen, 1991).

It has been suggested that children at the age of 4 fully develop an ability to understand other people's thoughts and intentions (Ferrari & Sternberg, 1998). Children around this age begin to successfully attribute false-beliefs and can pass tests aimed at measuring theory of mind (Wimmer, & Perner, 1983; Gopnik & Astington, 1988; Baron-Cohen, 1999). It is interesting to note that self-pronouns appears around 20 to 24 months of age and second- and third-person pronouns appear about two months later (Imbens-Bailey & Pan, 2001; Lewis, 2006). Thus, it seems reasonable to assume that a child gains an understanding of the self before gaining an understanding of someone else's mental states (Keenan et al., 2003). Moreover, people with self-awareness deficits, for example, the populations with schizophrenia, autism, and Asperger's syndrome, do not seem to possess theory of mind (A. Johnson et al., 2005; Andreasen, et al; 1994, Leslie, 1991; Baron-Cohen, 1999). Finally, there are indications that animals, such as the chimpanzee and the orangutan, who possess a sense of self also have theory of mind, whereas animals like the monkey who could not pass mirror self-recognition test also failed to pass theory of mind tasks (A. Johnson et al., 2005; Keenan, Gallup, & Falk, 2003).

In addition, it has been discovered that there is a positive relationship between self-awareness and deception ability (A. Johnson et al., 2005). Because intentional deception requires understanding of the mental state of another, it is necessary for one to possess theory of mind in order to successfully deceive others (A. Johnson et al., 2005). For instance, people with schizotypal personality traits who lack self-awareness also demonstrate deception deficits (Barnacz, Johnson, Constantino, & Keenan, 2004). Furthermore, cognitive-emotional deficits may lead to decreases in deception use or ability (A. Johnson et al., 2005).

Based on the above findings, it is possible to make two important conclusions related to the development of self-awareness. First, while passing the mirror test indicates self-awareness, it does not necessarily imply full understanding of the self (Keenan et al., 2003). Second, self-awareness, as defined as the awareness of one's own mind, may lead to greater understanding of mental states of others (Gallup, 1998). With these inferences in place, we can begin to realize that a key to understanding self-awareness over the course of evolution and human development lies in the understanding of how the self resides in the complexities of the brain.

Brain and Self-awareness

From the social neuroscience perspective, the brain has developed specialized mechanisms for processing information about the social environment, including the ability to understand ourselves, to know how others respond to us, and to regulate our action in order to avoid being dismissed from our social groups (Heatherton, Krendl, Macrae, & Kelley, 2007). The neural correlates of self-awareness are largely unknown though it is apparent that the frontal lobes play a crucial role. There are two basic approaches for studying the brain regions involved in self-awareness: studying the impaired brain and imaging the healthy brain using devices such as PET, MRI, and fMRI (Heatherton et al., 2007; Keenan, Gallup, & Falk, 2003). Here the brain regions involved in self-recognition, self-awareness, self-assessment, and theory of mind will be discussed.

Self-recognition

Examining the ability to recognize one's own face is useful in understanding the location of self-awareness

and consciousness in the brain because the test does not require language (Keenan et al., 2003). Self-recognition appears first in the infant development followed by self-awareness and theory of mind. Also, it has been suggested that these three processes are closely related. Thus, it seems logical to study self-face recognition to study how the brain gives rise to the understanding of the self as well as others.

Most of the recent studies in self-face recognition were carried out by using morphed faces of the participants' self and others such as friends, co-workers, strangers, and famous people. Earlier research (e.g., Keenan et al. 1999; Keenan, Freund, Hamilton, Ganis, & Pascual-Leone, 2000; Keenan, Ganis, & Pascual-Leone, 2000) used the laterality of hand responses in order to predict the dominant hemisphere of the brain involved in the process, whereas the recent experiments (e.g., Kaplan, Aziz-Zadeh, Uddin, & Iacoboni, 2008; Kircher et al., 2001; Uddin, Kaplan, Molnar-Szakacs, Zaidel, & Iacoboni, 2005) primarily used fMRI brain-imaging technique to precisely locate the brain regions that are activated.

Markowitsch et al. (1997) observed decreased blood flow in the right frontal and temporal areas by studying the brain of a patient who had episodic amnesia. Indeed, many neuroimaging studies suggest that self-related memory is correlated with activity in the right frontal lobes (Keenan, Ganis, et al., 2000). When subjects were exposed to pictures of self and others, it was found that upright and inverted self-images were identified more rapidly than non-self faces when subjects responded with their left hand (Keenan et al., 1999). In addition, when compared to morphed images composed of a familiar face, the participants identified images less often as being famous if the images were composed of self, but only when responding with their left hands (Keenan, Ganis, et al., 2000). These results in left-hand preference in self-recognition process suggest a preferential role of the right hemisphere in processing self-related material (Keenan, Ganis, et al., 2000). In addition, disruption of self-face recognition was observed by briefly inactivating the functions of right hemisphere through the Wada tests and transcranial magnetic stimulation (TMS) (Keenan et al., 2001).

The research conducted by using fMRI study also supports the involvement of right hemisphere during self-face recognition by presenting more precise results with specific locations of activation. When subjects were shown photographs of their own face, the inferior frontal gyrus, inferior parietal lobe, and inferior occipital cortex in the right hemisphere were activated (Kaplan et al., 2008; Uddin et al., 2005). Moreover, listening to one's own voice showed increased blood flow in the right inferior frontal gyrus, which implies that the preference for self-related stimuli in the right inferior frontal gyrus is not restricted to visual stimuli (Kaplan et al., 2008). The results presented above are consistent with the theory that right prefrontal cortex is involved in self-recognition.

Self-awareness

Extensive evidence from neuroimaging and patient research indicates that the prefrontal cortex plays a vital role in self-awareness (e.g., Morin 2004; Heatherton et al., 2007). The famous case of Phineas Gage, who suffered profound frontal lobe damage due to a large iron rod misfired through his head, demonstrates the important role of frontal lobe in self-awareness. It has been reported that the accident caused significant changes in his personality as well as behavior; formerly described by friends as polite and hardworking, Gage became capricious and volatile after the accident (Heatherton et al., 2007). This provides strong evidence that the frontal lobe is responsible for the regulation of emotion and behavior.

The frontal lobes are known to integrate multi-modality information and perform a variety of higher cognitive and emotional functions (Andreasen et al., 1994). The study of patients with brain damage demonstrates an important involvement of the prefrontal cortex in self-awareness. Schizophrenic patients demonstrate a disruption of self and often have significant deficits in formulating concepts and organizing their thinking and behavior (Andreasen et al., 1994; Keenan, Gallup, & Falk, 2003). That is, while self-stimuli (e.g., mirror recognition and self-photograph recognition) provoke a strong reaction in normal people, schizophrenics tend to make blunt responses (Keenan et al., 2003). Andreasen et al. (1994) reported that relative decrease in brain tissue was found in the frontal lobes in schizophrenia. In addition, Vogeley et al. (1999) indicated a decrease in metabolic rate in the prefrontal regions and pointed out that the dysfunction of the prefrontal cortex may be the neural correlate for the schizophrenic subsyndromes. Patients with Alzheimer's disease often demonstrate the loss of self-face recognition, which indicates loss of self-awareness. A decrease in blood flow to the prefrontal cortex was observed (Starkstein et al., 1994) and the disease is known to often involve neurological

deterioration of the frontal lobes. Moreover, patients with frontotemporal lobar degeneration, a neuro-degenerative disease that selectively atrophies the frontal lobes, temporal lobes, and amygdala, exhibit gradual decline in self-awareness and social dexterity (Sturm, Ascher, Miller, & Levenson, 2008). These patients sometimes show dramatic personality changes and also exhibit deficits in their ability to recognize others' emotions as well as having self-conscious emotions (Sturm, 2008). Thus, it is reasonable to predict that self-awareness is mainly mediated by the prefrontal lobes.

Self-evaluation

Sedikides (1993) categorized self-evaluation process into three primary routes: self-assessment, self-verification, and self-enhancement. Self-assessment refers to gathering of objective self-relevant information (i.e., taking exams such as IQ test or GRE); self-verification is a process of trying to reconfirm one's pre-existing self-concept by seeking feedback that already exists in one's self-image; self-enhancement involves positive biasing of self-relevant information (Sedikides, 1993). Thus, self-evaluation requires analyzing the self by combining internal self-image and public self-representation. Many studies have proven that among three major self-evaluation processes, the self-enhancement motivation plays the most powerful role in determining and forming the self-concept (e.g., Epley & Whitchurch, 2008; Guenther & Alicke, 2007; Sedikides, 1993).

Little is known about the neural mechanisms underlying self-enhancement bias since there is no direct and accurate way to measure the neurological correlation between the brain and self-evaluation. However, through neuroimaging and patient population studies, it is possible to predict certain brain regions that are involved in the process. Indeed, many studies have indicated a possible role for self-evaluation in the medial prefrontal cortex (MPFC) (Kwan et al., 2007). For instance, fMRI studies have reported the activation of the MPFC during self-evaluation (Zhu, Zhang, Fan, & Han, 2007). During self and other judgment trials, significantly greater activation of MPFC was observed during "self" trials than "other" trials using fMRI (Heatherton et al., 2007). Moreover, depressed individuals, who exhibit less or no self-enhancement motivation than non-depressed individuals, showed decreased blood flow to the MPFC in PET studies (Barrios et al., 2008). Indeed, there is considerable evidence that the MPFC may be involved in networks associated with self-evaluation and general self-reflection (S. Johnson et al., 2005; M. Johnson et al., 2006; Barrios et al., 2008). It is important to note, however, that activation of this network may not be exclusive to the self, or at least not in all individuals. Using fMRI, Yaoi and colleagues (2009) found common neural activation patterns between the dorsal MPFC, left middle temporal gyrus, left angular gyrus, precuneus, and right cerebellum for evaluating characteristics of both the self as well as close and distant others. Their work also suggests that the neural basis of self may fluctuate with cultural or individual differences in processing personal attributes, supporting the notion that biases in self-evaluation likely depend on ones social environment (Yaoi et al., 2009). Hence, the self-referencing bias may differ in the brain from one cultural context to the next.

Additional evidence that strongly supports the involvement of the MPFC in the self-evaluation process, mainly self-enhancement, was suggested by the recent research using transcranial magnetic stimulation (TMS) (Barrios et al., 2008; Kwan et al., 2007). TMS produces temporary functional lesions in a neuronal network by briefly obstructing brain processing in certain regions during a cognitive task (Kwan et al., 2007). Therefore, it is useful in demonstrating how certain parts of the brain are associated with differential behavior (Pascual-Leone, Walsh, & Rothwell, 2000). In order to induce natural self-enhancement behavior, participants were asked to rate their best friend and themselves on a number of desirable and undesirable traits (Barrios et al., 2008; Kwan et al., 2007). Taylor and Brown (1988) suggested that mentally healthy individuals have a tendency to have unrealistically positive views of the self, exaggerated perceptions of personal control, and unrealistic optimism. Thus, nondepressed and mentally healthy individuals are likely to indicate more desirable ratings for themselves as compared to their best friend during the baseline condition (sham TMS). The results indicated that TMS delivery to the MPFC decreased participants' tendency to self-enhance compared to the sham TMS condition (Barrios et al., 2008; Kwan et al., 2007). Based on these studies, it is possible to predict that the MPFC plays a critical role in self-evaluation.

Mirror Neurons: Theory of Mind
Imitation is the most commonly used technique of learning during development and is central to the development of fundamental social skills such as reading facial expressions and body languages as well as understanding the intentions and desires of other people (Iacoboni & Dapretto, 2006). Mirror neurons, originally found in area F5 of the monkey premotor cortex, are a particular class of visuomotor neurons, which appear to play a fundamental role in both action understanding and imitation (Rizzolatti & Craighero, 2004). In addition, mirror neurons seem to be involved in mind-reading ability, the ability to detect specific mental states of others such as their perceptions, goals, beliefs, and expectations (Gallese & Goldman, 1998). The discovery of the mirror neuron system, thus, has inspired the series of studies regarding the neural correlates of imitation as well as theory of mind.

Mirror neurons are premotor and parietal cells in the brain that fire when the animal performs goal-directed actions as well as when it observes goal-directed actions performed by others (Blakemore, 2006; Iacoboni & Dapretto, 2006; Rizzolatti & Craighero, 2004). In primates, mirror neurons have been identified in the posterior part of the inferior frontal cortex and the anterior part of the inferior parietal lobule (Iacoboni & Dapretto, 2006; Rizzolatti & Craighero, 2004). In humans, premotor and parietal cortices are found to be activated both by the perception of action and by the execution of action (Blakemore, 2006). The anatomical proximity of the mirror neuron system to frontoparietal systems, which are involved in various forms of sensorimotor integration, suggests that mirror neurons are also connected to some form of sensorimotor integration (Iacoboni & Dapretto, 2006). Imitation is one of the important forms of sensorimotor integration and, therefore, it can be concluded that there are strong links between imitation and mirror neurons in humans (Iacoboni & Dapretto, 2006).

Imitative behavior is critical for the development of social cognitive skills (Iacoboni & Dapretto, 2006). For instance, empathy, which requires the ability to understand and share other people's emotion, occurs by imitating the facial expressions and body postures of other people. Thus, given the role of mirror neurons, it is reasonable to predict that mirror neurons are involved in empathy (Iacoboni & Dapretto, 2006). Moreover, it has been found that the mirror neuron system does not simply provide representation of the actions of others, but also that it codes the intention associated with the observed action (Iacoboni & Dapretto, 2006). This neural mechanism for intention understanding can be served as the basis for understanding the mental states of others (Iacoboni & Dapretto, 2006). Indeed, it has been proposed that mirror neurons play a crucial role in mind-reading; in other words, theory of mind (Gallese & Goldman, 1998). Finally, mirror neurons are activated when individuals are looking at the pictures of themselves, which is an implication that they are also involved in a self-recognition process (Iacoboni & Dapretto, 2006; Uddin et al., 2005).

Based on the knowledge that the mirror neuron systems are closely related to social cognitive skills including theory of mind, it is possible to predict that dysfunction of mirror neurons may lead to deficits in social behavior. It has been suggested that the main cause of autism originates from a mirror neuron system dysfunction (Iacoboni & Dapretto, 2006). Autistic children have problems in imitating behaviors, facial gestures, and voices (Gallese, 2006). Thus, autism can be explained by defective embodied simulation likely originated by a malfunctioning of the mirror neuron systems (Gallese, 2006). This hypothesis can be further supported by the recent finding that the brains of autistic individuals show abnormal thinning of the grey matter in cortical areas that are part of the mirror neuron system (Gallese, 2006).

In light of such evidence, researchers must remain cautious to conclude that imitation relies solely on the mirror neuron system. For example, a recent meta-analysis highlights that the superior and inferior parietal lobules as well as the dorsal portion of the premotor cortex are also commonly implicated in imitation, particularly of hand and finger actions (Molenberghs et al., (2009). Therefore, the role that mirror neurons play in mind-reading abilities might extend to additional regions that demonstrate overlap between self and other activation. Furthermore, research has suggested that simulation in the mirror neuron system is sufficient for understanding motor acts; however, fully understanding an agent's social and communicative intention may require more in regards to social perception (Jacob & Jeannerod, 2004). Additionally, referring to the mirror neuron system as the crucial neural dysfunction in autism is considered premature by some researchers (Southgate & Hamilton, 2008). Instead, the breakdown of social imitative behavior could involve several different cognitive systems that reside both within and just outside of the mirror neuron system (Southgate & Hamilton, 2009). More research is needed to further specify the links between mirror neurons, imitation, and self-other distinctions in the brain. More experimental evidence is necessary to solidify the theories and resolve some of the current ambiguities.

Overall, a better understanding of the cognitive and neural processes underlying self-awareness is vital to the study of social neuroscience. In a field that values the complex interaction of biological and social forces, research on self-awareness not only sheds light on how we interact with others, but also offers us some insight into the deeper questions of human nature and consciousness. From the earliest musings on what it means to be introspective, to the latest empirical evidence regarding the social brain, psychologists, neuroscientists, and philosophers alike can all appreciate that a major part of understanding our world comes from understanding the self.

References

Andreasen, N. C., Flashman, L., Flaum, M., Arndt, S., Swayze, V., O'Leary, D. S., et al. (1994). Regional brain abnormalities in schizophrenia measured with magnetic resonance imaging. *The Journal of American Medical Association*, *272*(22), 1763–1769.

Barnacz, A., Johnson, A., Constantino, P., & Keenan, J. P. (2004). Schizotypal personality traits and deception: The role of self-awareness. *Schizophrenia Research*, *70*, 115–116.

Baron Cohen, S. (1991). Precursors to a theory of mind: understanding attention in others. In A. Whiten, (Eds.), *Natural theories of mind: Evolution, development, and simulation of everyday mind reading* (pp 233–251). Oxford: Basil Blackwell.

Baron Cohen, S. (1999). Social intelligence in the normal and autistic brain: An fMRI study. *European Journal of Neuroscience*, *11*, 1891–1898.

Barrios, V., Kwan, V. S., Ganis, G., Gorman, J., Romanowski, J., & Keenan J. P. (2008). Elucidating the neural correlates of egoistic and moralistic self-enhancement. *Conscious and Cognition*, *17*(2), 451–456.

Blakemore, S. (2006). When the other influences the self. In G. Knoblich (Ed.), *Human body perception from the inside out* (pp. 413–425). Oxford Oxfordshire: Oxford University Press.

Blakemore, S-J. (2008) The social brain in adolescence. *Nature Reviews*, *9*, 267–277.

Chalmers, D. (1996). *The conscious mind*. Oxford Oxfordshire: Oxford University Press.

Darwin, C. (1877). *A biographical sketch of an infant*.

Dennett, D. (1992). The self as a center of narrative gravity. In F. Kessel, P. Cole, & D. Johnson (Eds.), *Self and consciousness multiple perspectives*. Hilsdale: Erlbaum.

Djikic, M., Peterson, J. B., & Zelazo, P. D. (2005). Attentional biases and memory distortions in self-enhancers. *Personality and Individual Differences*, *38*, 559–568.

Duval, S. & Wicklund, R. A. (1972). *A theory of objective self awareness*. New York: Academic Press.

Epley, N. & Whitchurch, E. (2008). Mirror, mirror on the wall: Enhancement in self-recognition. *Personality and Social Psychology Bulletin*, *34*(9), 1159–1170.

Epstein, R., Lanza, R., & Skinner, B. F. (1981). "Self-awareness" in the pigeon. *Science*, *212*, 695–696.

Ferrari, M. & Sternberg, R. J. (1998). *Self-awareness: Its nature and development.* New York: The Guilford Press.

Gallagher, S. (2000) Philosophical conceptions of the self: Implications for cognitive science. *Trends in Cognitive Science, 4,* 14–216.

Gallese, V. (2006). Intentional attunement: A neurophysiological perspective on social cognition and its disruption in autism. *Cognitive Brain Research, 1079*(1), 15–24.

Gallese, V. & Goldman, A. (1998). Mirror neurons and the simulation theory of mind-reading. *Trends in Cognitive Sciences, 2*(12), 493–501.

Gallup, G. G., Jr. (1970). Chimpanzees: Self-recognition. *Science, 167,* 86–87.

Gallup, G. G., Jr. (1998). Self-awareness and the evolution of social intelligence. *Behavioral Processes, 42,* 239–247.

Gopnik, A. & Astington, J. W. (1988). Children's understanding of representational change and it's relation to the understanding of false-beliefs and appearance-reality distinction. *Child Development, 59,* 26–37.

Guenther, C. L. & Alicke, M. D. (2007). Self-enhancement and belief perseverance. *Journal of Experimental Social Psychology, 44,* 706–712.

Heatherton, T. F., Krendl, A. C., Macrae, C. N., & Kelley, W. M. (2007). A social brain sciences approach to understanding self. In C. Sedikides & S. J. Spencer (Eds.). *The self* (pp. 3–20). East Sussex: Psychology Press.

Iacoboni, M. & Dapretto, M. (2006). The mirror neuron system and the consequences of its dysfunction. *Nature Reviews Neuroscience, 7,* 942–951.

Imbens-Bailey, A. & Pan, B. A. (2001). Pragmatics of self- and other-reference in young children. *Social Development, 7*(2), 219–233.

Jacob, P. & Jeannerod, M (2005). The motor theory of social cognition: A critique. *Trends in Cognitive Sciences, 9*(1), 21–25.

Jeannerod, M. & Anquetil, T. (2008). Putting oneself in the perspective of the other: A framework for self-other differentiation. *Social Neuroscience, 3,* 356–367.

Johnson, A. K., Barnacz, A., Yokkaichi, T., Rubio, J., Racioppi, C., Shackelford, T. K., et al. (2005). Me, myself, and lie: The role of self-awareness in deception. *Personality and Individual Differences, 38,* 1847–1853.

Johnson, M. K., Raye, C. L., Mitchell, K. J., Touryan, S. R., Greene, E. J., & Nolen-Hoeksema, S. (2006). Dissociating medial frontal and posterior cingulated activity during self-reflection. *Social Cognitive and Affective Neuroscience, 1*(1), 56.

Johnson, S., Schmitz, T., Kawahara-Baccus, T., Rowley, H., Alexander, A., Lee, J., et al (2005). The cerebral response during subjective choice with and without self-reference. *Journal of Cognitive Neuroscience, 17*(12), 1897–1906.

Kaplan, J. T., Aziz-Zadeh, L., Uddin, L. Q., & Iacoboni, M. (2008). The self across the senses: An fMRI study of self-face and self voice recognition. *Social Cognitive and Affective Neuroscience (SCAN), 3,* 218–223.

Keenan, J. P., Freund, S., Hamilton, R. H., Ganis, G., & Pascual-Leone, A. (2000). Hand response differences in a self-face identification task. *Neuropsychologia, 38,* 1047–1053.

Keenan, J. P., Gallup, G. G., & Falk, D. (2003). *The face in the mirror: the search for the origins of consciousness.* New York: ECCO.

Keenan, J. P., Ganis, G., Freund, S., & Pascual-Leone, A. (2000). Self-face identification is increased with left hand responses. *Laterality, 5*(3), 259–268.

Keenan, J. P., McCutcheon, B., Freund, S., Gallup, G., Sanders, G., & Pascual-Leone, A. (1999). Left hand advantage in a self-face recognition task. *Neuropsychologia, 37,* 1421–1425.

Keenan, J. P., Nelson, A., O'Connor, M., & Pascual-Leone, A. (2001). Self-recognition and the right hemisphere. *Nature, 409*(6818), 305.

Kircher, T. & David, A. S. (2003). Self-consciousness: An integrative approach from philosophy, psychopathology and the neurosciences. In T. Kircher & A. S. David (Eds.), *The self in neuroscience and psychiatry* (pp. 445–474). Cambridge, England: Cambridge University Press.

Kircher T., Senior C., Phillips, M. L., Rabe-Hesketh, S., Benson, P. J., Bullmore, E. T., Brammer, M., et al. (2001). Recognizing one's own face. *Cognition, 78,* B1–B15.

Kwan, V. S., Barrios, V., Ganis, G., Gorman, J., Lange, C., Kumar, M., et al (2007). Assessing the neural correlates of self-enhancement bias: A transcranial magnetic stimulation study. *Experimental Brain Research, 182*(3), 379–385.

Kwan, V. S., John, O. P., Kenny, D. A., Bond, M. H., & Robins, R. W. (2004). Reconceptualizing individual differences in self-enhancement bias: An interpersonal approach. *Psychological Review, 111*(1), 94–110.

Leslie, A.M. (1991). Theory of mind impairment in autism. In A. Whiten, (Ed.). *Natural theories of mind: Evolution, development, and simulation of everyday mind reading* (p 233–251). Oxford: Basil Blackwell.

Lewis, M. (1992). Self-conscious emotions and the development of self. In T. Shapiro & R. N. Emde, et al. (Eds.), *Affect: Psychoanalytic perspectives* (pp. 45–73). Madison, CT: International Universities Press, Inc.

Lewis, M. (2006). The self in self-conscious emotions. *Annals of the New York Academy of Sciences, 818,* 119–142.

Lewis, M. & Brooks-Gunn, J. (1979). *Social cognition and the acquisition of self.* New York: Plenum.

Lockwood, P. & Matthews, J. (2007). The self as a social comparer. In C. Sedikides & S. J. Spencer (Eds.), *The self* (pp. 95–113). East Sussex: Psychology Press.

Markowitsch, H. J., Calabrese, P., Fink, G. R., Durwen, H. F., Kessler, J., Harting, C., et al. (1997). Impaired episodic memory retrieval in a case of probable psychogenic amnesia. *Psychiatry Research, 74,* 119–126.

Marten, K. & Psarakos, S. (1995). Using self-view television to distinguish between self-examination and social behavior in the bottlenose dolphins. *Consciousness and Cognition, 4*(2), 205–224.

Meltzoff, A. (1995). Understanding the intentions of others: Reenactment of intended acts by 18-month old children. *Developmental Psychology, 31,* 838–850.

Molenberghs, P., Cunnington, R., & Mattingly, J. B. (2009). Is the mirror neuron system involved in imitation? A short review and meta-analysis. *Neuroscience and Biobehavioral Reviews, 33,* 975–980.

Morin, A. (2004). A neurocognitive and socioecological model of self-awareness. *Genetic, Social, and General Psychology Monographs, 130,* 197–222.

Pascula-Leone, A., Walsh, V., & Rothwell, J. (2000). Transcranial magnetic stimulation in cognitive neuroscience–virtual lesion, chronometry, and functional connectivity. *Current Opinion in Neurobiology, 10,* 232–237.

Piaget, J. (1970). Piaget's theory. In P.H. Mussen (Ed.) Carmichael's manual of child psychology (3rd ed., Vol. 1, pp. 703–732). New York: Wiley.

Plotnik, J. M., De Wall, F. B., & Reiss, D. (2006). Self-recognition in the Asian elephant. *Proceedings of the National Academy of Sciences, USA*, 103(45).

Premack, D. G. & Woodruff, G. (1978). Does the chimpanzee have a theory of mind? *Behavioral and Brain Sciences*, 1, 515–526.

Prior, H., Schwarz, A., & Gunturkun, O. (2008). Mirror induced behavior in the magpie (pica pica): Evidence of self-recognition. *PLoS Biology*, 6(8), 202.

Rizzolatti, G. & Craighero, L. (2004). The mirror-neuron system. *Annu. Rev. Neurosci.*, 27, 169–192.

Sedikides, C. (1993). Assessment, enhancement, and verification determinants of the self-evaluation process. *Journal of Personality and Social Psychology*, 65(2), 317–338.

Southgate, V. & Hamilton, A. F. (2009). Unbroken mirrors: Challenging a theory of autism. *Trends in Cognitive Sciences*, 12(6), 225–229.

Starkstein, S. E., Migliorelli, R., Tesón, A., Sabe, L., Vázquez, S., Turjanski, M., et al. (1994). Specificity of changes in cerebral blood flow in patients with frontal lobe dementia. *Journal of Neurology, Neurosurgery, and Psychiatry*, 57, 790–796.

Strawson, G. (1997). The self. *The Journal of Consciousness Studies*, 4(5–6), 405–428.

Sturm, V. E., Ascher, E. A., Miller, B. L., & Levenson, R. W. (2008). Diminished self-conscious emotional responding in frontotemporal lobar degeneration patients. *Emotion*, 8(6), 861–869.

Taylor, S. E. & Brown, J. D. (1988). Illusion and well-being: A social psychological perspective on mental health. *Psychological Bulletin*, 103(2), 193–210.

Tracy, J. L. & Robins, R. W. (2007). Self-conscious emotions: Where self and emotion meet. In C. Sedikides & S. J. Spencer (Eds.). *The self* (pp. 187–209). East Sussex: Psychology Press.

Uddin, L. Q., Kaplan, J. T., Molnar-Szakacs, I., Zaidel, E., & Iacoboni, M. (2005). Self-face recognition activates a fronto-parietal "mirror" network in the right hemisphere: An event-related fMRI study. *NeuroImage*, 25, 926–935.

Vogeley, K., Kurthen, M., Falkai, P., & Maier, W. (1999). Essential functions of the human self model are implemented in the prefrontal cortex. *Consciousness and Cognition*, 8(3), 343–363.

Wimmer, H. & Perner, J. (1983). Beliefs about beliefs: representation and constraining function of wrong beliefs in young children's understanding of deception. *Cognition*, 13, 103–128.

Yaoi, K., Osaka, N., & Osaka, M. (2009). Is the self special in the dorsomedial prefrontal cortex. An fMRI study. *Social Neuroscience*, 4(5), 455–463.

Zhu, Y., Zhang, L., Fan, J., & Han, S. (2007). Neural basis of cultural influence on self-representation. *NeuroImage*, 34, 1310–1316.

Susanne Quadflieg *and* C. Neil Macrae

Abstract

This chapter aims to summarize what is currently understood of the neural networks underlying the human experience of being someone. Importantly, given that this experience has many different facets, the neural correlates of a multitude of self-related processes are considered before more general conclusions about the neural self and its potential uniqueness are discussed. The human self comprises a complex collection of components that guide both cognition and behavior. Notwithstanding this complexity, however, we typically experience self as continuous across time and space. Supporting the observation that self is both multifaceted yet unified, recent neuroscientific findings suggest that self-related processing is accomplished by neural networks that are widely distributed in the brain but frequently associated with a common neural signature—activity in the medial prefrontal cortex.

Keywords: neural networks, sense of self, self-recognition, self-related processes

"Is there anything, apart from a really good chocolate cream pie and receiving a large unexpected check in the post, to beat finding yourself?"

– Bill Bryson (*Neither Here Nor There*, 1993)

The possession of a sense of self that persists over time and place has been a central concept in psychological theorizing for over a century (James, 1890). In the last decade, studying the neural implementation of the human self has become particularly en vogue. The tremendous enthusiasm for such research has not even been defeated by the ongoing debate over what the target of this enterprise should be. Rather, by investigating more or less well-circumscribed aspects of the self such as self-recognition,

self-knowledge, and self-memory, researchers have tried to tame this arguably ill-defined entity. As a result, even though many fascinating aspects of the self still await empirical investigation, preliminary data elucidate the neural networks that allow healthy waking humans to experience the world around them from a subjective first-person perspective, and to effortlessly distinguish between "mine" and "not mine"—regardless whether body parts, thoughts, or feelings are concerned. In line with these recent developments, this chapter aims to summarize what is currently understood of the neural networks underlying the human experience of being someone (Metzinger, 2004). Importantly, given that this experience has many different facets (see Box 21.1) the neural correlates of a multitude of self-related processes will be considered before more general conclusions about the neural self and its potential uniqueness will be discussed.

The Embodied Self

It has long been speculated that the ability to recognize oneself in a mirror is an indicator of a rudimentary self-concept (Gallup, 1977; Keenan, Wheeler, Gallup, & Pascual-Leone, 2000). Such speculations are built on observations showing that in humans the onset of mirror recognition abilities around two years of age is accompanied by other developmental milestones indicating increasing self-representational skills, such as synchronic imitation and pretend play (Nielsen & Dissanayake, 2004). Given that the face is commonly considered the most characteristic external physical feature of an individual, the neural correlates of self-recognition have often been investigated by comparing how humans perceive their own versus another person's face. Patient data originally revealed that pathological deficits in visual self-face recognition as found in prosopagnosia, Capgras delusion, and mirror-self misidentification often go along with impairments in the ability to recognize faces of others (for a review, see Brédart & Young, 2004). Although it therefore seems implausible that self-face and other-face recognition are accomplished by completely different neural networks, evidence suggests that the underlying neural substrates can at least be partly dissociated.

Early neuroimaging studies have suggested a right hemisphere preference for self-face processing (e.g., Keenan, Freund, Hamilton, Ganis, & Pascual-Leone, 2000; Keenan, Ganis, Freund, & Pascual-Leone, 2000; Platek, Keenan, Gallup, & Mohamed, 2004; but see Turk et al., 2002 for a left-hemisphere dominance in self-recognition). These studies, however,

have typically presented faces of famous individuals, unfamiliar others, or acquaintances as control stimuli relative to a perceiver's own face. Importantly, one's own face is a highly overlearned, emotionally salient stimulus and its recognition is associated with the activation of knowledge about personal traits and biographical information. As a result, studies of self-face and other-face recognition that compare responses to self versus a nonintimately known other are likely to also reflect differences in these facets of person perception. Thus, observed neural differences may not be indicative of a special self-network, but rather the impact that personal closeness exerts on face recognition. Indeed, it has been shown that perceiving faces of intimate others (i.e., friends and family) elicits a different neural response than the perception of unknown, famous, or familiar but not intimately known faces (Gobbini, Leibenluft, Santiago, & Haxby, 2004; Platek et al., 2006; Sugiura et al., 2005). Thus, the effects of closeness warrant particular attention in the realm of self-recognition.

Neuroimaging data from studies using faces of intimate others as control stimuli are less straightforward than the assumption of a right-hemisphere dominance for self-face recognition would suggest. Besides a dominant right hemispheric activation in response to one's own versus an intimately known other's face (Uddin, Kaplan, Molnar-Szakacs, Zaidel, & Iacoboni, 2005), bilateral activation for self- versus intimate other-recognition has repeatedly been demonstrated (Kircher et al., 2001; Platek et al., 2006; Sugiura et al., 2005). Evidence from an experiment with a split-brain patient also suggests that both hemispheres have a comparable ability to accomplish visual self-face recognition (Uddin, Rayman, & Zaidel, 2005). Thus, although most studies agree that the neural networks implementing self-face and other-face recognition can be partly dissociated, the concrete architecture of a self-face recognition network is still uncertain due to a lack of converging evidence as to the precise neural structures involved. Intriguingly though, it has been demonstrated that being exposed to one's body odor, seeing one's name, and hearing one's name can all facilitate self-face recognition in a reaction time task (Platek, Thomson, & Gallup, 2004). These data suggest that a common neural architecture may contribute toward self-recognition across a wide range of sensory cues. For instance, both seeing one's own face and hearing one's own voice were found to elicit increased activity in the right inferior frontal gyrus compared to perceiving a friend's face and voice (Kaplan, Aziz-Zadeh, Uddin, & Iacoboni, 2008). In addition, activation underlying self-recognition elicited by facial or bodily cues was found to overlap in the right anterior insula and the right dorsal anterior cingulate (Devue et al., 2007). Such preliminary findings suggest that some brain structures may be involved in self-recognition across different self-related cues, thereby suggesting that self may be represented in an abstract manner (but see Sugiura et al., 2008 for counter-evidence).

Investigations targeting the embodied self have not only begun to explore how individuals recognize their own physical appearance (i.e., when encountering self-face or self-body pictures), but also how they experience their own body (Tsakiris, Schütz-Bosbach, & Gallagher, 2007). Converging evidence indicates that monitoring one's bodily sensations such as pain, temperature, touch, muscular and visceral sensations, vasomotor activity, hunger, and thirst is supported by activity in the insula. More specifically, whereas the engagement of the dorsal posterior insula seems to reflect primary interoceptive activity, the anterior insula appears to subserve meta-representations of this activity, creating the capacity to experience and be aware of one's own internal states (for a review, see Craig, 2009). Beyond being aware of oneself as a sentient being, a further fundamental aspect of self-awareness is the experience of one's body as part of the self (Ehrsson, Wiech, Weiskopf, Dolan, & Passingham, 2007). Clinical observations have long fueled the idea that the subjective sense of body ownership (i.e., "that is my hand") is not necessarily a given. Following brain damage, patients have been found to be unaware of body parts, experience body parts as missing, feel body parts as separated from their body, or even misattribute their own body parts as belonging to another person (for a review see Vallar & Ronchi, 2009). Anecdotal evidence

of out-of-body experiences during which individuals have the conscious experience of leaving their physical body also suggests that the normally occurring unity between the mental and bodily self can occasionally break down (Blanke, Landis, Spinelli, & Seeck, 2004; Green, 1968).

One of the favored methods to experimentally investigate such breakdowns is known as the "rubber-hand illusion" (RHI). During the illusion, the synchronous stroking of a seen rubber hand and one's own unseen hand causes the rubber hand to be attributed to one's body such that the perceiver experiences the rubber hand as his or her own (Botvinick & Cohen, 1998). Neurophysiological evidence that the rubber hand is genuinely incorporated into a central representation of one's body was provided by Ehrsson and colleagues (2007) who showed that, by threatening the rubber hand, cortical activity related to the anticipation of pain in interoceptive systems such as the anterior insula could be elicited. Similarly to the RHI, researchers have recently managed to elicit whole-body misattributions comparable to out-of-body experiences in healthy participants (Ehrsson, 2007; Lenggenhager, Tadi, Metzinger, & Blanke, 2007). Interestingly, initial evidence indicates that out-of-body experiences can follow damage to, or electrical stimulation of, the temporo-parietal junction (TPJ), suggesting that by integrating multisensory information the TPJ may play a pivotal role in maintaining a coherent representation of one's own body and the sense of unity between bodily and mental self (Blanke et al., 2004; 2005; Tsakiris, Costantini, & Haggard, 2008; for a review see Blanke & Arzy, 2005).

The Cognitive Self

Besides its embodied nature, the human experience of being someone is fundamentally shaped by our cognitive capacities to store and retrieve autobiographical memories, to form abstract self-knowledge, and to reflect upon our thoughts, attitudes, and preferences. Autobiographical memories (AMs) have been referred to as "personally relevant episodes [that form] the storehouse of our life's experiences ranging from the recent to the very remote" (Maguire, 2001, p. 1441). As self-defining narratives, AMs have the potential to fundamentally shape a person's identity, psychological well-being, and self-development (Conway & Pleydell-Pearce, 2000; McLean, Pasupathi, & Pals, 2007). Comprising both episodic and semantic contents, their inherently self-referential nature distinguishes AMs from other types of long-term knowledge (Brewer, 1986). Although AMs often come to mind involuntarily (Berntsen & Hall, 2004), recent neuroimaging studies have mainly targeted the neural substrates of voluntary AM retrieval. Various constructive processes are thought to underlie intentional AM retrieval, including a controlled and effortful memory search that is reflected in activity in the lateral prefrontal cortex (LPFC, for reviews see Cabeza & Jacques, 2007; Maguire, 2001; Svoboda, McKinnon, & Levine, 2006). The most defining feature of AMs, however, their self-reference has been associated with activity in the medial prefrontal cortex (MPFC; Cabeza & Jacques, 2007; Maguire, 2001; Svoboda et al., 2006). When viewing pictures of familiar locations, for example, individuals displayed stronger MPFC activation towards photographs taken by themselves than by others (Cabeza et al., 2004). Similarly, when participants were asked to recall autobiographical events versus events from a movie, retrieval of self-experienced events was found to elicit increased MPFC activation (Summerfield, Hassabis, & Maguire, 2009). Furthermore, patients suffering from multiple personality disorder were found to display stronger MPFC activation when exposed to traumatic AMs depending on whether these memories "belonged" to their momentarily experienced identity or not (Reinders et al., 2003).

Although it is often suggested that the retrieval of particular AMs critically underlies the ability to reflect about oneself, patient data suggest that self-reflection and retrieving self-knowledge can be possible despite massive AM loss. For instance, for amnesic patients it has been demonstrated that they can judge trait abstractions about themselves ("Am I adventurous?") without being able to remember any particular episodes on which such knowledge is based (Klein, Rozendal, & Cosmides, 2002; Tulving, 1993). Surprisingly, such preserved self-knowledge seems to be consistent with how the patient's personality is perceived by close others. Even more intriguingly, the spared ability to make trait judgments does not generalize to close others. That is, when the target of such judgments is an intimate other (e.g., the patient's child) performance suffers in comparison to that of control participants (Klein, Rozendal, & Cosmides, 2002). These data suggest two important conclusions: (i) self-knowledge does not need to be based on episodic knowledge but can also consist of summary representations that have gained independence from the events on which they were formed; and (ii) self-knowledge may have a special status compared to knowledge about other people.

Both these conclusions seem to be supported by recent neuroimaging studies. As predicted, evidence indicates that self-knowledge is likely to consist of summary representations as well as episode-based representations that are instantiated in separable neural networks. In a study by Lieberman, Jarcho, and Satpute (2004), for instance, participants who were either soccer players or improvisational actors were asked to judge the self-descriptiveness of words related to either soccer or improvisational acting (e.g., "Does the word 'athletic' describe you?"). Based on previous behavioral research, it was assumed that self-judgments rely more strongly on episodic AMs in low-experience than in high-experience domains (Klein, Loftus, Trafton, & Fuhrman, 1992). Indeed, it was found that when judging the self-descriptiveness of words from their low-experience domain, participants displayed increased activation in the LPFC—likely to reflect the associated effortful search for episodic memories on which to base their judgment (Cabeza & Jacques, 2007). In contrast, when assessing words in their high-experience domain, participants displayed increased activation in the ventromedial prefrontal cortex (vMPFC), nucleus accumbens, amygdala, and lateral temporal cortex—brain regions associated with more reflexive processing.

In addition to investigating the different components of self-knowledge, numerous neuroimaging studies have tried to explore how the neural networks underlying self-knowledge may differ from those contributing towards knowledge about others. The dominant paradigm used in these investigations comprises the presentation of short phrases or trait words that participants are asked to judge regarding whether they are self-descriptive or descriptive of another person (e.g., "Does the word 'honest' describe you?" vs. "Does the word 'honest' describe X?"). Using this approach it has been shown that self-judgments are associated with increased activity in the MPFC (Craik et al., 1999; Kelley et al., 2002; Modinos, Ormel, & Aleman, 2009; Pfeifer, Lieberman, & Dapretto, 2007) as long as the other person is a nonintimately known target such as a celebrity (e.g., George Clooney), acquaintance (e.g., class or team mate), or fictional character (e.g., Harry Potter). If the other person is a close friend or family member (e.g., mother), however, self- and other-judgments tend to be indistinguishable in the MPFC (Ochsner et al., 2005; Schmitz, Kawahara-Baccus, & Johnson, 2004; Seger, Stone, & Keenan, 2004; Vanderwahl, Hunyadi, Grupe, Connors, & Schultz, 2008; but see Heatherton et al., 2006).

What these data suggest is that, during person judgments, activation in the MPFC may reflect how much another person is considered to be part of the self. Indeed, a study on the influence of cultural differences on self-other distinctions supports this idea. Social psychologists have long observed that Westerners and East Asians tend to differ in their self conceptions, with the former considering the self more as an autonomous entity, whereas the latter emphasize its interdependence on others (Markus & Kitayama, 1991). Hence, it was expected that Asians would incorporate intimately known others with self more then their Western counterparts. Supporting this observation, it has been demonstrated that when Westerners and Chinese participants were asked to judge the descriptiveness of trait attributes for themselves and their mothers, Westerners but not Chinese displayed increased MPFC activation for self relative to mother judgments (Zhu, Zhang, Fan, & Han, 2007). Similarly, Japanese participants also display comparable MPFC activity when making trait judgments about self and best friend (Yaoi, Osaka, & Osaka, 2009). Intriguingly, Yaoi et al. (2009) also failed to find differences in MPFC activity between self-judgments and judgments concerning a nonintimate other (i.e., a former Japanese prime minister). What this suggests is that cultural forces may exert a considerable impact on the nature of self-referential thought.

Additional insights on AMs and self-knowledge comes from studies which have revealed that information encoded with reference to self can be more easily recalled than information encoded in a self-unrelated manner (Rogers, Kuiper, & Kirker, 1977; for a meta-analysis see Symons & Johnson, 1997). Thus, when participants are shown a series of trait adjectives and are asked to process them with reference to the self or for their general meaning (e.g., "Does the word 'honest' mean the same as 'trustworthy'?") they tend to better recall the self-referenced items in a subsequent surprise memory test (a phenomenon termed the self-reference effect, SRE). Even when information is encoded with reference to another person, this memory advantage for self remains. Supporting the idea that closeness between self and other matters, however, it has been demonstrated that the SRE is attenuated or even eliminated when the target of comparison is an intimate other (Czienskowski & Giljohann, 2002; Symons & Johnson, 1997). Why the self-reference effect emerges is still a matter of great debate. On the one hand, it has been argued that the self is a unique cognitive structure that facilitates the encoding and retrieval of

information (Rogers et al., 1977). On the other hand, however, it has been suggested that the SRE reflects a basic depth-of-processing effect such that the wealth of self-knowledge in memory encourages more elaborative encoding and representation of material (Klein & Loftus, 1988). What is known, however, is that when participants are scanned while judging the self-descriptiveness of a series of trait adjectives, words that are subsequently remembered elicit stronger activation in MPFC during encoding than later forgotten words, indicating that this region contributes to self-related memory advantages (Macrae, Moran, Heatherton, Banfield, & Kelley, 2004).

The Emotional Self

Humans seem to possess a fundamental need to hold a positive self-image (Mezulis, Abramson, Hyde, & Hankin, 2004). For instance, overly positive self-perceptions can be observed when individuals are asked to rate themselves and their best friend on a set of traits. Under such conditions, participants usually produce more desirable and fewer undesirable ratings for themselves than their friend. Intriguingly though, recent evidence suggest that when TMS pulses are delivered to the MPFC to produce a virtual lesion the tendency to self-enhance is decreased—an effect that is not observed when TMS is delivered to control regions (Barrios et al., 2008; Kwan et al., 2007). These data indicate that the MPFC also plays a fundamental role in maintaining positive self-illusions.

The need for a positive self-image is also reflected by the tendency of individuals to consider positive rather than negative information as more self-descriptive (Taylor & Brown, 1988). As a result of this bias, when judging whether a particular trait or attitude describes ourselves, we usually have accompanying emotional reactions depending on whether the description in question denotes a positive or negative attribute. Hence, self-reflection is not a mere cognitive process, but often involves an affective component. Recent neuroimaging studies have tried to investigate whether the cognitive and affective components of self-reflection can be dissociated. Indeed, it has been found that trait attributes that were considered as personally descriptive (relative to nondescriptive) engaged the MPFC and posterior cingulate cortex (PCC) regardless of their valence, whereas increased activity in the ventral anterior cingulate cortex (vACC) was only observed when information considered to be self-descriptive was unfavorable (Moran, Macrae, Heatherton,

Wyland, & Kelley, 2006; Yoshimura et al., 2009). These findings demonstrate that distinct neural circuits in adjacent regions of the prefrontal cortex subserve cognitive and emotional aspects of self-reflection, with the vACC playing a major role in identifying whether self-relevant attributes deviate from our generally positive self-image.

Importantly, a positive self-image can easily be challenged by the behavior of others. The distress experienced in response to being rejected, excluded, or ostracized by others is one of the most intense emotional reactions related to our sense of self. Everyday experience attests that our fundamental need to belong and to establish and maintain pleasant and meaningful connections with others is easily bruised (Baumeiser & Leary, 1995). Intriguingly, neuroimaging data have revealed that the social pain of feeling excluded is based on neural networks similar to those underlying our subjective experience of physical pain. When participants are excluded while playing a virtual ball-tossing game, for instance, they display increased activation in the dorsal ACC (dACC) relative to when they are included in the game (Eisenberger, Lieberman, & Williams, 2003). From studies targeting the processing of physical pain it is well known that the perception of pain in self and other shares important neural commonalities (Ochsner et al., 2008; Singer et al., 2004). Hence, future research will have to clarify whether feeling the pain of social exclusion is self-specific or can also be extended towards the perceived rejection or exclusion of intimate others. Along similar lines, the perception of deceit has been found to elicit increased amygdala activity when individuals observe themselves being deceived relative to perceiving deceit towards an unfamiliar other (Grèzes, Berthoz, & Passingham, 2006). The observed amygdala activation has been associated with greater affective reactions toward self-directed rather than other-directed deceit. Whether, however, amygdala activity in such situations really reflects unique self-relevant affect remains uncertain until investigations can explore which neural processes accompany the perception of deceit in intimate others.

Going beyond the emotional responses elicited by social exclusion and deceit, the human experience of being a sentient self is strongly associated with the experience of a wide range of emotional states (e.g., happy, sad, frightened, excited). Initial neuroimaging data suggest that the neural networks allowing us to draw inferences about our own emotions differ partially from those activated when thinking about the emotional states of others. Ochsner and colleagues (2004) demonstrated that although perceivers can discern equal proportions of pleasant, unpleasant, and neutral affective states in themselves and others depicted in photographic scenes, they seem to do so in different ways. Judging one's own emotional states was found to selectively activate the dorsal MPFC and the right middle temporal gyrus (MTG), whereas judging the emotional states of others recruited the left inferior LPFC and the medial occipital cortex. Unfortunately, at this point, our understanding of the processes contributing toward the observed neural differences is speculative at best. The authors suggest that increased activity in the MTG and dorsal MPFC may reflect heightened self-monitoring during self-judgments, whereas increased activation in the left LPFC and the medial occipital cortex during other-judgments may indicate heightened attention to the external world and to potentially relevant visual cues provided by the pictures. Without question, further research is required to establish how judging one's own emotions may differ from judging the emotions of (unfamiliar and familiar) others.

The Self as a Unifying and Unique Entity

Despite a large collection of distinct processes and representations that contribute towards self, it is important to note that in line with traditional philosophical views, the self acts as a unifier that can bundle the outcome of a variety of bodily, cognitive, and emotional processes. As a consequence, healthy individuals experience the world and themselves from *one* subjective perspective—the so-called first person perspective (1PP). In language, the 1PP is symbolized by the use of first-person pronouns such as "I," "my," "me," and "mine." The 1PP allows representing and integrating multimodal experiences and thoughts into one common framework and has been considered a basic constituent of a "minimal self" (Gallagher, 2000; Vogely & Fink, 2003).

Attempting to uncover the neural correlates of the multimodal 1PP, researchers have instructed participants to adopt either their own perspective (1PP) or that of another person (third person perspective, 3PP) across a wide variety of domains including spatial navigation, action attribution, emotional processing, and mentalizing (for a review see Vogely & Fink, 2003). The observed neural correlates underlying changes of perspectives, however, seem to be quite diverse. For instance, although activity in the inferior parietal cortex has repeatedly been suggested to distinguish between first and third person perspectives, some researchers emphasize its role for judgments from a 1PP (e.g., Vogely & Fink, 2003), whereas others think it is crucial for adopting a 3PP (e.g., Ruby & Decety, 2004). What is known more precisely, however, is that putting ourselves in the shoes of others by trying to project our 1PP onto them (i.e., "How would I feel in his/her place?") can alter how we process information about that person. In particular, activity in the vMPFC seems to reflect the extent that self-projection elicits greater overlap in the cognitive processes engaged during self and other judgments (Ames, Jenkins, Banaji, & Mitchell, 2008). This conclusion is based on a study in which participants were asked to judge the preferences of two individuals, one of which they had previously considered from a first-person perspective (i.e., "Imagine for a moment that you are this person."), and one whom they had considered from a third-person perspective (i.e., "Gather as many clues as you can about what this person might be like"). Replicating previous research, judging one's own preferences was found to recruit the vMPFC more strongly than judging the preferences of the two others. Importantly though, the vMPFC was also found to be sensitive to the perspective another individual had previously been considered from, yielding stronger activity for targets considered from the first- relative to a third-person perspective.

Perhaps not surprisingly, further evidence suggests that how spontaneously we put ourselves in the shoes of others depends on how similar to self we consider them to be. From behavioral research it is known that the more similar we consider another person to ourselves, the more likely we are to use our own thoughts and feelings as a basis for understanding and predicting their behavior (Robbins & Krueger, 2005). In line with this observation, it has been revealed that mentalizing about similar relative to dissimilar others activates a ventral aspect of the MPFC (Mitchell, Banaji, & Macrae, 2005; Mitchell, Macrae, & Banaji, 2006). Using the observation that neural activity in stimulus-sensitive brain regions is typically reduced when a stimulus is repeated, it has also been shown that repetition suppression in the vMPFC is not only produced when individuals repeatedly consider their own mental states but also when perceivers first reflect about a similar other and then about the self (Jenkins, Macrae, & Mitchell, 2008). Such an effect is not observed when self-judgments follow judgments of dissimilar others, suggesting that self-based processing may only be triggered spontaneously when trying to make sense of similar others.

Taken together, accumulating evidence indicates that differences in the neural networks subserving self- and other-processing get diminished the more intimately known another person is or the more similar to oneself he or she is considered. Such findings have an important bearing on the ongoing debate as to whether the representation of self and the processing of self-related information is distinct and unique from the representation and processing of information related to other people (see Gillihan & Farrah, 2005; Legrand & Ruby, 2009). It is noteworthy that there are many observations that attest that under certain circumstances self-processing and other-processing become indistinguishable. For instance, healthy individuals have been found to confuse their own traits and attitudes with those of others (Coats, Smith, Claypool, & Banner, 2000; Smith, Coats, & Walling, 1999), to produce similar memory advantages for self and close others (Czienskowski & Giljohann, 2002; Symons & Johnson, 1997), to get overwhelmed by the emotions of others as if they were their own (Hatfield, Cacioppo, & Rapson, 1994), and to have a hard time learning and keeping in mind that they should distinguish 1PP from 3PP (Mitchell, Robinson, Isaacs, & Nye, 1996; Wellman, Cross, & Watson, 2001). Hence, further research is required to determine which factors (such as similarity, personal closeness, empathic skills) are driving whether self-based processing is used to make sense of a particular other, and whether there is a limit to how much mental and neural overlap between self and other can occur (Decety & Chaminade, 2003; Decety & Grèzes, 2006).

Conclusion

The human self comprises a complex collection of components that guide both cognition and behavior (Boyer et al., 2005; McConnell & Strain, 2007). Notwithstanding this complexity, however, we typically experience self as continuous across time and space. Supporting the observation that self is both multifaceted yet unified, recent neuroscientific findings suggest that self-related processing is accomplished by neural networks that are widely distributed in the brain but frequently associated with a common neural signature—activity in the medial prefrontal cortex. Quite what this activity may be indexing, however, requires clarification and elaboration.

Additional insights may be gained by applying research techniques that enable researchers to investigate synchronized fluctuations of neural activity such as magnetoencephalography (MEG) and electroencephalogram (EEG). The emergence of a consciously experienced self and a genuine first-person perspective has been argued to require meta-cognitive processes which represent and integrate a multitude of internal states into a transparent higher-order self model (Metzinger, 2004). The implementation of such higher-order representations is likely to require dynamic binding of the products of lower-order processes. Initial evidence indicates that such binding may occur through the transient synchronization of discharges of distributed neurons into functionally coherent assemblies (Singer, 2001). What this suggests is that further exploration of binding mechanisms in the brain (e.g., neuronal synchronization) may contribute to our understanding of how the phenomenal unity of the self is created. What remains unquestionable is that the tools of cognitive neuroscience can facilitate understanding of both the structure and function of self, hence elucidate core aspects of human social cognition.

References

Ames, D. L., Jenkins, A. C., Banaji, M. R., & Mitchell, J. P. (2008). Taking another person's perspective increases self-referential neural processing. *Psychological Science, 19*, 642–644.

Barrios, V., Kwan, V. S. Y., Ganis, G., Gorman, J., Romanowski, J., & Keenan, J. P. (2008). Elucidating the neural correlates of egoistic and moralistic self-enhancement. *Consciousness and Cognition, 17*, 451–456.

Baumeister, R. F. & Leary, M. R. (1995). The need to belong: Desire for interpersonal attachment as a fundamental human motivation. *Psychological Bulletin, 117*, 497–529.

Berntsen, D. & Hall, N. M. (2004). The episodic nature of involuntary autobiographical memories. *Memory & Cognition, 32*, 789–803.

Blanke, O. & Arzy, S. (2005). The out-of-body experience: Disturbed self-processing at the temporo-parietal junction. *Neuroscientist, 11*, 16–24.

Blanke, O., Landis, T., Spinelli, L., & Seeck, M. (2004). Out-of-body experience and autoscopy of neurological origin. *Brain, 127*, 243–258.

Blanke, O. & Metzinger, T. (2009). Full-body illusions and minimal phenomenal selfhood. *TRENDS in Cognitive Sciences, 13*, 7–13.

Blanke, O., Mohr, C., Michel, C. M., Pascual-Leone, A., Brugger, P., Seeck, M., et al. (2005). Linking out-of-body experience and self processing to mental own-body imagery at the temporoparietal junction. *Journal of Neuroscience, 25*, 550–557.

Botvinick, M. & Cohen, J. D. (1998). Rubber hand "feels" what eyes see. *Nature, 391*, 756.

Boyer, P., Robbins, P., & Jack, A. I. (2005). Varieties of self-systems worth having. *Consciousness and Cognition, 14*, 647–660.

Brédart, S. & Young, A. W. (2004). Self-recognition in everyday life. *Cognitive Neuropsychiatry, 9*, 183–197.

Brewer, W. F. (1986). What is autobiographical memory? In D. C. Rubin (Ed.), *Autobiographical memory* (pp. 25–49). Cambridge, England: Cambridge University Press.

Cabeza, R. & Jacques, P. S. (2007). Functional neuroimaging of autobiographical memory. *TRENDS in Cognitive Sciences, 11*, 219–227.

Cabeza, R., Prince, S. E., Daselaar, S. M., Greenberg, D., Budde, M., Dolcos, F., et al. (2004). Brain activity during episodic retrieval of autobiographical and laboratory events: An fMRI study using a novel photo paradigm. *Journal of Cognitive Neuroscience, 9*, 1533–1594.

Coats, S., Smith, E. R., Claypool, H. M., & Banner, M. J. (2000). Overlapping mental representations of self and in-group: Reaction time evidence and its relationship with explicit measures of group identification. *Journal of Experimental Social Psychology, 36*, 304–315.

Conway, M. A. & Pleydell-Pearce, C. W. (2000). The construction of autobiographical memories in the self-memory system. *Psychological Review, 107*, 261–288.

Craig, A. D. (2009). How do you feel–now? The anterior insula and human awareness. *Nature Reviews Neuroscience, 10*, 59–70.

Craik, F. I. M., Moroz, T. M., Moscovitch, M., Stuss, D. T., Winocur, G., Tulving, E., et al. (1999). In search of the self: A positron emission tomography study. *Psychological Science, 10*, 26–34.

Czienskowski, U. & Giljohann, S. (2002). Intimacy, concreteness, and the "self-reference effect". *Experimental Psychology, 49*, 73–79.

Decety, J. & Chaminade, T. (2003). When the self represents the other: A new cognitive neuroscience view on psychological identification. *Consciousness and Cognition, 12*, 577–596.

Decety, J. & Grèzes, J. (2006). The power of simulation: Imagining one's own and other's behavior. *Brain Research, 1079*, 4–14.

Decety, J. & Sommerville, J. A. (2003). Shared representations between self and other: A social cognitive neuroscience view. *TRENDS in Cognitive Sciences, 7*, 527–532.

Devue, C., Collette, F., Balteau, E., Degueldre, C., Luxen, A., Maquet, P., et al. (2007). Here I am: The cortical correlates of visual self-recognition. *Brain Research, 1143*, 169–182.

Ehrsson, H. H. (2007). The experimental induction of out-of-body experiences. *Science, 317*, 1048.

Ehrsson, H. H., Wiech, K., Weiskopf, N., Dolan, J. D., & Passingham, R. E. (2007). Threatening a rubber hand that you feel is yours elicits a cortical anxiety response. *Proceedings of the National Academy of Sciences of the USA, 104*, 9828–9833.

Eisenberger, N. I., Lieberman, M. D., & Williams, K. D. (2003). Does rejection hurt? An fMRI study of social exclusion. *Science, 302*, 290–292.

Gallagher, I. (2000). Philosophical conceptions of the self: Implications for cognitive science. *Trends in Cognitive Sciences, 4*, 14–21.

Gallup, G. G. (1977). Self-recognition in primates: a comparative approach to the bidirectional properties of consciousness. *American Psychologist, 32*, 329–338.

Gillihan, S. J. & Farah, M. J. (2005). Is self special? A critical review of evidence from experimental psychology and cognitive neuroscience. *Psychological Bulletin, 131*, 76–97.

Gobbini, M. I., Leibenluft, E., Santiago, N., & Haxby, J. V. (2004). Social and emotional attachment in the neural representation of faces. *NeuroImage, 22*, 1628–1635.

Green, C. E. (1968). *Out-of-the-body experiences*. London: Hamish Hamilton.

Grèzes, J., Berthoz, S., & Passingham, R. E. (2006). Amygdala activation when one is the target of deceit: Did he lie to you or to someone else? *NeuroImage, 30*, 601–608.

Hatfield, E., Cacioppo, J. T., & Rapson, R. L. (1994). *Emotional contagion*. New York: Cambridge University Press.

Heatherton, T. F., Wyland, C. L., Macrae, C. N., Demos, K. E., Denny, B. T., & Kelley, W. K. (2006). Medial prefrontal activity differentiates self from close others. *Social Cognitive and Affective Neuroscience, 1*, 18–25.

James, W. (1890). *The principles of psychology*. New York: Henry Holt and Company.

Jenkins, A. C., Macrae, C. N., & Mitchell, J. P. (2008). Repetition suppression of ventromedial prefrontal activity during judgments of self and others. *Proceedings of the National Academy of Sciences U S A, 105*, 4507–4512.

Kaplan, J. T., Aziz-Zadeh, L., Uddin, L., & Iacoboni, M. (2008). The self across the senses: An fMRI study of self-face and self-voice recognition. *Social Cognitive and Affective Neuroscience, 3*, 218–223.

Keenan, J. P., Freund, S., Hamilton, R. H., Ganis, G., & Pascual-Leone, A. (2000). Hand response differences in a self-face identification task. *Neuropsychologia, 38*, 1047–1053

Keenan, J. P., Ganis, G., Freund, S., & Pascual-Leone, A. (2000). Self-face identification is increased with left hand responses, *Laterality, 5*, 259–268.

Keenan, J. P., Wheeler, M. A., Gallup, Jr., G. G., & Pascual-Leone, A. (2000). Self-recognition and the right prefrontal cortex. *Trends in Cognitive Sciences, 4*, 338–344.

Kelley, W. M., Macrae, C. N., Wyland, C. L., Caglar, S., Inati, S., & Heatherton, T. F. (2002) Finding the self? An event-related fMRI study. *Journal of Cognitive Neuroscience, 14*, 785–794.

Kircher, T. J., Senior, C., Phillips, M. L., Rabe-Hesketh, S., Benson, P. J., Bullmore, E. T., et al. (2001). Recognizing one's own face. *Cognition, 78*, B1–B15.

Klein, S. B. & Loftus, J. (1988). The nature of self-referent encoding: The contributions of elaborative and organizational processes. *Journal of Personality and Social Psychology, 55*, 5–11.

Klein, S. B., Loftus, J., Trafton, J. G., & Fuhrman, R. W. (1992). Use of exemplars and abstractions in trait judgments: A model of trait knowledge about the self and others. *Journal of Personality and Social Psychology, 63*, 739–753.

Klein, S.B., Rozendal, K., & Cosmides, L. (2002). A social–cognitive neuroscience analysis of the self. *Social Cognition, 20*, 105–135.

Kwan, V. S. Y., Barrios, V., Ganis, G., Gorman, J., Lange, C., Kumar, M., et al. (2007). Assessing the neural correlates of self-enhancement bias: A transcranial magnetic stimulation study. *Experimental Brain Research, 182*, 379–385.

Legrand, D. & Ruby, P. (2009). What is self-specific? Theoretical investigation and critical review of neuroimaging results. *Psychological Review, 116*, 252–282.

Lenggenhager, B., Tadi, T., Metzinger, T., & Blanke, O. (2007). Video ergo sum: Manipulating bodily self-consciousness. *Science, 317*, 1096–1099.

Lieberman, M. D., Jarcho, J. M., & Satpute, A. B. (2004). Evidence-based and intuition-based self-knowledge: An fMRI study. *Journal of Personality and Social Psychology, 87*, 421–435.

Macrae, C. N., Moran, J. P., Heatherton, T. F., Banfield, J. F., & Kelley, W. M. (2004). Medial prefrontal activity predicts memory for self. *Cerebral Cortex, 14*, 647–654.

Maguire, E. A. (2001). Neuroimaging studies of autobiographical event memory. *Philosophical Transactions of the Royal Society of London B, 356*, 1441–1451.

Markus, H. R. & Kitayama, S. (1991). Culture and the self: Implication for cognition, emotion and motivation. *Psychological Review, 98*, 224–253.

McConnell, A. R. & Strain, L. M. (2007). Content and structure of the self-concept. In C. Sedikides & S. J. Spencer (Eds.), *The self: Frontiers in social psychology*. New York, NY: Psychology Press.

McLean, K. C., Pasupathi, M., & Pals, J. L. (2007). Selves creating stories creating selves: A process model of self-development. *Personality and Social Psychology Review, 11*, 262–278.

Metzinger, T. (2004). *Being no one. The self-model theory of subjectivity*. Cambridge, MA: MIT Press.

Mezulis, A. H., Abramson, L. Y., Hyde, J. S., & Hankin, B. L. (2004). Is there a universal positivity bias in attributions? A meta-analytic review of individual, developmental, and cultural differences in the self-serving attributional bias. *Psychological Bulletin, 5*, 711–747.

Mitchell, J. P., Banaji, M. R., & Macrae, C. N. (2005). The link between social cognition and self-referential thought in the medial prefrontal cortex. *Journal of Cognitive Neuroscience, 17*, 1306–1315.

Mitchell, J. P., Macrae, C. N., & Banaji, M. R. (2006). Dissociable medial prefrontal contributions to judgments of similar and dissimilar others. *Neuron, 50*, 655–663.

Mitchell, P., Robinson, E. J., Isaacs, J. E., & Nye, R. M. (1996). Contamination in reasoning about false belief: An instance of realist bias in adults but not children. *Cognition, 59*, 1–21.

Modinos, G., Ormel, J., & Aleman, A. (2009). Activation of anterior insula during self-reflection. *Public Library of Science One, 4*, 1–8.

Moran, J. M., Macrae, C. N., Heatherton, T. F., Wyland, C. L., & Kelley, W. M. (2006). Neuroanatomical evidence for distinct cognitive and affective components of self. *Journal of Cognitive Neuroscience, 18*, 1586–1594.

Neisser, U. (1988). Five kinds of self-knowledge. *Philosophical Psychology, 1*, 35–59.

Nielsen, M. & Dissanayake, C. (2004). Pretend play, mirror self-recognition and imitation: A longitudinal investigation through the second year. *Infant Behavior and Development, 27*, 342–365.

Ochsner, K. N., Beer, J. S., Robertson, E. R., Cooper, J. C., Gabrieli, J. D. E., Kihslstrom, J. F., et al. (2005). The neural correlates of direct and reflected self-knowledge. *NeuroImage, 28*, 797–814.

Ochsner, K. N., Knierim, K., Ludlow, D. H., Hanelin, J., Ramachandran, T., Glover, G., et al. (2004). Reflecting upon feelings: An fMRI study of neural systems supporting the attribution of emotion to self and other. *Journal of Cognitive Neuroscience, 16*, 1746–1772.

Ochsner, K. N., Zaki, J., Hanelin, J., Ludlow, D. H., Knierim, K., Ramachandran, T., et al. (2008). Your pain or mine? Common and distinct neural systems supporting the perception of pain in self and other. *Social Cognitive and Affective Neuroscience, 3*, 144–160.

Pfeifer, J. H., Lieberman, M. D., & Dapretto, M. (2007). "I know you are but what am I?!": Neural bases of self- and social knowledge retrieval in children and adults. *Journal of Cognitive Neuroscience, 19*, 1323–1337.

Platek, S. M., Keenan, J. P., Gallup, G. G. Jr., & Mohamed, FB. (2004). Where am I? The neurological correlates of self and other. *Cognitive Brain Research, 19*, 114–122.

Platek, S. M., Loughead, J. W., Gur, R. C., Busch, S., Ruparel, K., Phend, N., et al. (2006). Neural substrates for functionally discriminating self-face from personally familiar faces. *Human Brain Mapping, 27*, 91–98.

Platek, S. M., Thomson, J. W., & Gallup, G. G. (2004). An integrated and intermodal self: Cross modal self-recognition. *Consciousness and Cognition, 13*, 197–210.

Reinders, A. A. T. S., Nijenhuis, E. R. S., Paans, A. M. J., Korf, J., Willemsen, A. T. M., & den Boer, J. A. (2003). One brain, two selves. *NeuroImage, 20*, 2119–2125.

Robbins, J. M. & Krueger, J. I. (2005). Social projection to ingroup and outgroups: A review and meta-analysis. *Personality and Social Psychology Review, 9*, 32–47.

Rogers, T. B., Kuiper, N. A., & Kirker, W. S. (1977). Self-reference and the encoding of personal information. *Journal of Personality and Social Psychology, 35*, 677–688.

Ruby, P. & Decety, J. (2004). How would you feel versus how do you think she would feel? A neuroimaging study of perspective-taking with social emotions. *Journal of Cognitive Neuroscience, 16*, 988–999.

Schmitz, T. W., Kawahara-Baccus, T. N., & Johnson, S. C. (2004). Metacognitive evaluation, self-relevance, and the right prefrontal cortex. *NeuroImage, 22*, 941–947.

Seger, C. A., Stone, M., & Keenan, J. P. (2004). Cortical activations during judgments about the self and an other person. *Neuropsychologia, 42*, 1168–1177.

Singer, W. (2001). Consciousness and the binding problem. *Annals of the New York Academy of Science, 929*, 123–146.

Smith, E. R., Coats, S., & Walling, D. (1999). Overlapping mental representations of self, in-group, and partner: Further response time evidence and a connectionist model. *Personality and Social Psychology Bulletin, 25*, 873–882.

Singer, T., Seymour, B., O'Doherty, J., Kaube, H., Dolan, R. J., & Frith, C. D. (2004). Empathy for pain involves the affective but not sensory components of pain. *Science, 303*, 1157–1162.

Sugiura, M., Sassa, Y., Jeong, H., Horie, K., Sato, S., & Kawashima, R. (2008). Face-specific and domain-general characteristics of cortical responses during self-recognition. *NeuroImage, 42*, 414–422.

Sugiura, M., Watanabe, J., Maeda, Y., Matsue, Y., Fukuda, H., & Kawashima, R. (2005). Cortical mechanisms of visual self-recognition. *NeuroImage, 24*, 143–149.

Summerfield, J. J., Hassabis, D., & Maguire, E. A. (2009). Cortical midline involvement in autobiographical memory. *NeuroImage, 44*, 1188–1200.

Svoboda, E., McKinnon, M. C., & Levine, B. (2006). The functional neuroanatomy of autobiographical memory: A meta-analysis. *Neuropsychologia, 44*, 2189–2208.

Symons, C. S. & Johnson, B. T. (1997). The self-reference effect in memory: A meta-analysis. *Psychological Bulletin, 121*, 371–394.

Taylor, S. E. & Brown, J. D. (1988). Illusion and well-being: A social psychological perspective on mental health. *Psychological Bulletin, 103*, 193–210.

Tsakiris, M., Costantini, M., & Haggard, P. (2008). The role of the right temporo-parietal junction in maintaining a coherent sense of one's body. *Neuropsychologia, 46*, 3014–3018.

Tsakiris, M., Schütz-Bosbach, S., & Gallagher, S. (2007). On agency and body ownership: Phenomenological and neurocognitive reflections. *Consciousness and Cognition, 16*, 645–660.

Tulving, E. (1993). Self–knowledge of an amnesic individual is represented abstractly. In T. K. Srull & R. S. Wyer (Eds.). *Advances in social cognition* (Vol. 5, pp. 147–156). Hillsdale, NJ: Erlbaum.

Turk, D. J., Heatherton, T. F., Kelley, W. M., Funnel, M. G, Gazzaniga, M. S., & Macrae, C. N. (2002). Mike or me? Self-recognition in a split-brain patient. *Nature Neuroscience, 5*, 841–842.

Uddin, L. Q., Kaplan, J. T., Molnar-Szakacs, I., Zaidel, E., & Iacoboni, M. (2005). Self-face recognition activates a frontoparietal "mirror" network in the right hemisphere: an event-related fMRI study. *NeuroImage, 25*, 926–935.

Uddin, L. Q., Rayman, J., & Zaidel, E. (2005). Split-brain reveals separate but equal self-recognition in the two cerebral hemispheres. *Consciousness and Cognition, 14*, 633–640.

Vallar, G. & Ronchi, R. (2009). Somatoparaphrenia: a body delusion. A review of the neuropsychological literature. *Experimental Brain Research, 192*, 533–551.

Vanderwahl, T., Hunyadi, E., Grupe, D. W., Connors, C. M., & Schultz, R. T. (2008). Self, mother, and abstract other: An fMRI study of reflective social processing. *NeuroImage, 41*, 1437–1446.

Vogely, K. & Fink, G. R. (2003). Neural correlates of the first-person-perspective. *TRENDS in Cognitive Sciences, 7*, 38–42.

Wellman, H. M., Cross, D., & Watson, J. (2001). Meta-analysis of theory-of-mind development: the truth about false belief. *Child Development, 72*, 655–684.

Yaoi, K., Osaka, N., & Osaka, M. (2009). Is the self special in the dorsomedial prefrontal cortex? An fMRI study? *Social Neuroscience*, 1–9.

Yoshimura, S., Ueda, K., Suzuki, S., Onoda, K., Okamoto, Y., & Yamawaki, S. (2009). Self-referential processing of negative stimuli within the ventral anterior cingulate gyrus and right amygdala. *Brain and Cognition, 69*, 218–225.

Zhu, Y., Zhang, L., Fan, J., & Han, S. (2007). Neural basis of cultural influence on self-representation. *NeuroImage, 34*, 1310–1316.

Unconscious Action Tendencies: Sources of "Un-Integrated" Action

Ezequiel Morsella *and* John A. Bargh

Abstract

This chapter reviews three classes of unconscious action: actions that can occur when the subject appears to be in an unconscious state or that transpire without any identifiable conscious mediation (first section); actions that are influenced by stimuli of which the subject is unaware (second section); and actions prompted by supraliminal (consciously-experienced) stimuli that influence the subject's consciously-mediated actions in ways that the subject is unaware of (third section). The final section reviews the fundamental difference between conscious and unconscious action tendencies.

Keywords: unconscious action tendencies, unconscious action, consciousness, automaticity, priming, voluntary action, involuntary action, volition, unconsciousness, automatisms, subliminal stimuli, unconscious behavior, subliminal priming, backward masking, involuntary action, reflex, integration consensus, skeletal muscle, rational action, perception-and-action, motor control, unconscious movements.

As revealed in classic research (Festinger, 1957; Heider, 1958; Lewin, 1935), the study of the basic mechanisms giving rise to human action has always informed theories about social phenomena (e.g., conflicted versus non-conflicted action; controlled versus automatic processes; automatic stereotyping; Bargh, 1984). This cross-fertilization of research on action and social psychology continues today, when there is an even greater appreciation of the various kinds of actions that humans are capable of expressing and of the distinct cognitive and neural underpinnings of the different forms of action.

An action such as glancing rightwards, for example, may at times be due to one kind of nervous system event, as when one's attention is grabbed by a stimulus on the right (the visual grasp reflex; Sumner & Husain, 2008); at other times it may be

due to a very different kind of event, as when one voluntarily looks rightwards to check the time on a wall clock. Indistinguishable to most observers, these actions differ at least phenomenologically and even with respect to their cognitive and neurobiological underpinnings (Floyer-Lea & Matthews, 2004; Pacherie, 2000; Puttemans, Wenderoth, & Swinnen, 2005; Raichle et al., 1994). Similarly, voluntary blinking (Bodis-Wollner, Bucher, & Seelos, 1999), saccades (Curtis & D'Esposito, 2003; Munoz & Everling, 2004), breathing (McKay, Evans, Frackowiak, & Corfield, 2003), and swallowing (Kern, Jaradeh, Arndorfer, & Shaker, 2001) differ in various ways from their reflexive counterparts. For instance, reflexive swallowing is believed to involve substantially fewer brain regions than volitional swallowing (Ortinski & Meador, 2004).

In addition, novel and well-learned actions appear to rely on distinct cognitive and neural mechanisms (Floyer-Lea & Matthews, 2004; Pacherie, 2000; Poldrack et al., 2005; Puttemans, Wenderoth, & Swinnen, 2005): A habitual, automatized action requires less attentional and goal-directed processes (and less activation of their associated prefrontal regions; Raichle et al., 1994; Sakai et al., 1998) than when the action was first learned. (See Sumner & Husain, 2008, for a treatment regarding how both kinds of actions may rely on the same neural machinery.) Thus, what appears to be the same action can actually be carried out by vastly different mechanisms, mechanisms which often have different operational principles, phylogenetic origins, and neural underpinnings.

Regardless of the nature of the mechanisms, what matters most from an evolutionary perspective are the consequences of actual, *expressed action*, because natural selection operates at the level of overt (rather than covert) action (Roe & Simpson, 1958). In evolution, what one does is more consequential than what one feels, believes, imagines, or is inclined to do—potentialities that, though intimately related to action, fall outside the jurisdiction of natural selection (Roe & Simpson, 1958). Hence, because overt action can lead to situations that diminish evolutionary fitness and can incur high opportunity costs (the expression of one action oftentimes precludes the expression of other actions), overt action is both risky and costly. Thus, it is beneficial that we are not always compelled to act one way or another but that we can be *inclined* to act in certain ways (Chomsky, 1988) and can also mentally simulate actions in a covert, off-line manner. Knowledge of outcomes can thus be learned without the risks of performing the actions (Bargh & Morsella, 2008). Though inclinations and imagery operate in a realm shielded from that of expressed action, they are still intimately related to action. Thorndike (1905) asserts,

> "The function of thoughts and feelings is to influence actions . . . Thought aims at knowledge, but with the final aim of using the knowledge to guide action" (p. 111).

Sometimes the organism is aware of inclinations and can report about them, as in the case of consciously experienced urges; other times the organism is unaware of such inclinations, as in unconscious action tendencies, the topic of this chapter. In this chapter, we will review three classes of unconscious action: Actions that can occur when the subject

appears to be in an unconscious state or that transpire without any identifiable conscious mediation (first section), actions that are influenced by stimuli of which the subject is unaware (second section), and actions prompted by supraliminal (consciously experienced) stimuli that influence the subject's consciously mediated actions in ways that the subject is unaware of (third section). In the fourth section, we review the fundamental difference between conscious and unconscious action tendencies.

Unconscious Actions

Unconscious events in the nervous system are those processes that, though capable of systematically influencing behavior, cognition, motivation, and emotion, do not influence the organism's subjective experience in such a way that the organism can directly detect, understand, or report the occurrence or nature of these events. Regarding behavior, it is well documented that several kinds of actions can occur while subjects are in what appears to be an unconscious state (Laurey, 2005). For example, actions such as automatic ocular pursuit and some reflexes (e.g., pupillary reflex) can occur in some forms of coma and persistent vegetative states (Klein, 1984; Laurey, 2005; Pilon & Sullivan, 1996), and it seems that licking, chewing, swallowing, and other behaviors can occur unconsciously once the incentive stimulus activates the appropriate receptors (Bindra, 1974; Kern et al., 2001). Research on the kinds of behaviors (automatisms) exhibited during epileptic seizures in which the patient appears to be unconscious, or to not have any conscious control, has revealed that stereotypic actions such as simple motor acts (Kutlu et al., 2005), humming (Bartolomei et al., 2002), spitting (Carmant et al., 1994), and oroalimentary automatisms (Maestro et al., 2008) can occur independently of conscious mediation. (For what it is worth as an anecdote, one of us [EM] recalls with great vividness coming out of general anesthesia and hearing someone repeatedly complain about physical discomfort, only to learn moments later that it was he himself who was the person producing the vociferations.) More complex acts such as written and spoken (nonsense) utterances (Blanken, Wallesch, & Papagno, 1990), sexual behaviors (Spencer, Spencer, Williamson, & Mattson, 1983), and rolling, pedaling, and jumping (Kaido et al., 2006) have also been found to occur in a reflexive manner during seizures. Most dramatically, there are cases in which, during seizures, patients sing recognizable songs (Doherty et al., 2002) or express repetitive affectionate kissing automatisms (Mikati, Comair, & Shamseddine, 2005). Similarly, research on narcolepsy (Zorick, Salis, Roth, & Kramer, 1979) and somnambulism (Plazzi, Vetrugno, Provini, & Montagna, 2005; Schenk & Mahowald, 1995) reveals that complex behaviors (e.g., successfully negotiating objects) can be mediated unconsciously.

Corroborating that such actions can occur unconsciously, following brain injury in which a general awareness is spared, actions can be decoupled from consciousness, as in *blindsight* (Weiskrantz, 1997), in which patients report to be blind but still exhibit visually guided behaviors. Analogously, in blind-smell (Sobel et al., 1999), people can learn to associate odorants with certain environments (e.g., a particular room), even though the concentration of odorants presented during learning was consciously imperceptible. Similarly, in *alien hand syndrome* (Bryon & Jedynak, 1972), *anarchic hand syndrome* (Marchetti & Della Sala, 1998), and *utilization behavior syndrome* (Lhermitte, 1983), brain damage causes hands and arms to function autonomously. These actions include relatively complex goal-directed behavior (e.g., the manipulation of tools; Yamadori, 1997) that are maladaptive and, in some cases, at odds with a patient's reported intentions (Marchetti & Della Sala, 1998).

In addition, Goodale and Milner (2004) report neurological cases in which there is a dissociation between action and conscious perception. Suffering from visual form agnosia, patient D. F. was incapable of reporting the orientation of a tilted slot, but could nonetheless negotiate the slot accurately when inserting an object into it. Other patients with lesions in the ventral-visual system (the "perception pathway"; Goodale & Milner, 2004) cannot identify (recognize) the object, but are still able to reach for it correctly when the experimenter casually asks them to take it. Conversely, patients with lesions in the parietal lobe region are able to correctly identify an object held up to them by an experimenter, but are not able to reach for it correctly based on its spatial orientation (horizontal or vertical). Thus, one group exhibited appropriate action tendencies toward the object in the absence of conscious awareness of what the object was (i.e., action without perception), while the other group was aware of what the object was but could not act towards it appropriately (i.e., perception without action).

Theorists have concluded from this and related studies that two different cortical visual pathways are activated in the course of perception, a dorsal pathway that supports actional responses ("what to do")

and a ventral pathway supporting semantic knowledge regarding the object ("what it is"; see review in Westwood, 2009). Importantly, mounting evidence suggests that it is the dorsal (actional) system that operates largely outside of conscious awareness, while the operation of the ventral system is normally accessible to awareness (Decety & Grèzes, 1999; Jeannerod, 2003). (See Ro, 2008, for recent evidence involving the selective disruption of the pathways by use of transcranial magnetic stimulation.)

Such a dissociation between action and consciousness is evident in the ways that neurologically intact subjects respond to visual illusions (Wraga, Creem, & Proffitt, 2000): Although subjects' self-reports reflect the illusion, such as that one circle appears larger than another in the Ebbinghaus/Titchener illusion, their manual behavior toward the visual objects responsible for the illusion is accurate and does not reflect what subjects report. (For arguments against the notion of perception-action dissociations, see Franz, Gegenfurtner, Bülthoff, & Fahle, 2000; Jeannerod, 2003.) Stottinger and Perner (2006) conclusively demonstrated the dissociation using an illusion (the diagonal illusion) that is free of the kinds of limitations found in previous experiments.

Findings regarding perception-action dissociations corroborate what motor theorists have long known—that one is unconscious of the motor programs guiding action (Rosenbaum, 2002). In addition to action slips and spoonerisms, highly-flexible and "online" adjustments are made unconsciously during an act such as grasping a fruit. Because the spatial relationship between the objects of the world and one's body is seldom fixed (e.g., a fruit is sometimes at left or right), each time an action is performed new motor programs are generated unconsciously to deal with peculiarities of each setting (Rosenbaum, 2002). One is unconscious of these complicated programs (see compelling evidence in Helen & Haggard, 2005) that calculate which muscles should be activated at a given time, but is often aware of their proprioceptive and perceptual consequences (e.g., perceiving the hand grasping; Gray, 2004; Gottlieb & Mazzoni, 2004). (See Berti & Pia, 2006, for a review of motor awareness and its disorders.)

For example, Fourneret and Jeannerod (1998) showed that when one's hand is controlling a computer-drawing device but is prevented from seeing the hand in motion (because it is behind a screen), participants can be easily fooled into thinking that their hand moved one direction when it had actually moved in a different direction (through false feedback on the computer display). Participants reported great confidence that their hand had actually moved in the direction of the line drawn on the screen, when in reality substantial bias had been programmed into the translation of their actual movement into what was displayed. Importantly, this result is obtainable only if participants have little if any conscious access to their actual hand movements. In addition, though the planning of action (e.g., identifying the object that one must act towards) shares resources with conscious perceptual processing, the online, visually guided control of ongoing action does not (Liu, Chua, & Enns, 2008). In short, there is a plethora of findings showing that one is unconscious of the adjustments that are made "online" as one reaches for an object (Fecteau, Chua, Franks, & Enns, 2001; Heath, Neely, Yakimishyn, & Binsted, 2008; Rossetti, 2001).

Dissociations between actions and conscious experience are also evident in compulsions and addiction. For example, though resembling "wanting" because of their repetitive and persistent nature, some addiction-related behaviors are actually unaccompanied by "liking," that is, by the congruent subjective drives (Berridge & Robinson, 1995). Accordingly, research suggests that subjective cravings do not always predict failures in self-control in addiction and that they may not be the only source of drug abuse (Tiffany & Carter, 1998). Automatic processes may also be at play.

Additional evidence that actions of striking complexity can occur without consciousness is evident in the complex reflexive behaviors of the neonate (Berne, 2006) and in the actions exhibited by nonhuman animals. (For a treatment regarding the presence of consciousness in nonhuman animals, see Gray, 2004.) The behavior of most organisms living today—the fly, the Venus fly trap, and perhaps the alligator and its fellow reptiles—is presumably under the guidance of unconscious control. Ethologists have done a thorough job at cataloging the various kinds of intelligent, animal behaviors that appear to occur in a quasi-automatic manner (Gould, 1982). One need only consider the stereotypic egg-retrieving behavior of the goose, the nest-building behavior of the love bird, and the rabbit pup's reflexive nipple-search behavior in response to maternal odor cues (Montigny, Coureaud, & Schaal, 2006). For example, a caged squirrel seems "sated" after expressing digging behaviors toward a nut even though the nut remains unburied and in plain view

(Thorpe, 1964). It remains unclear the degree to which conscious processing is required for these actions (see Gray, 2004).

Unconscious action tendencies are also evident in the classic studies by Benjamin Libet (cf., Libet, 2004). In these experiments, participants are free to make hand movements whenever they choose and are asked only to note when they had made the intention to respond. Libet at the same time was measuring brain activation potentials associated with the instigation of action. This action potential consistently came 200 to 500 milliseconds before the participant's conscious awareness of intending to make the response. (For a related finding involving an even greater span of time, see Soon, Brass, Heinze, & Haynes, 2008.) Current research suggests that the judgment of conscious intention is associated with activity in the presupplementary motor area and the intraparietal sulcus (Berti & Pia, 2006).

In conclusion, there is substantial evidence that complex actions can transpire without conscious mediation. At first glance, these actions are not identifiably less flexible, complex, controlling, deliberative, or action-like than their conscious counterparts (Bargh & Morsella, 2008).

Actions That are Influenced by Stimuli of Which the Subject is Unaware

In an experiment (Logothetis & Schall, 1989), subjects (rhesus monkeys) were trained to "self report" the contents of their conscious experience under conditions of binocular rivalry, a perceptual phenomenon in which visual inputs cannot be resolved into a single percept. In this kind of experiment, subjects are first trained to respond in certain ways when presented with certain visual stimuli (e.g., to button-press when presented with the image of a house). After training, a different visual stimulus is presented to each eye (e.g., an image of a house to one eye and of a tree to the other). Surprisingly, the subject does not consciously perceive both objects (e.g., a tree overlapping a house), but responds as if perceiving only one object at a time (e.g., a house followed by a tree). Each percept occupies consciousness for only a few seconds, even though both images are continuously present and each exerts a nontrivial influence over nervous processing (e.g., activation of the visual system and other brain regions). (For a treatment of the factors that influence the outcome of the visual competition, see Maruya, Yang, & Blake, 2007.) (Interestingly, the self-generated actions [moving a computer mouse] of the subject can influence the duration of suppression during rivalry, even when the object being controlled falls outside of visual awareness; Maruya et al., 2007.) At any given moment, the subject is unaware of the computational processes leading to this bizarre "one at a time" outcome and of the systematic influence that the un-experienced percept has upon neural, cognitive, and even emotional processes. For example, emotion-related amygdala activation increases bilaterally in response to fearful versus neutral faces, even when the face was suppressed because of binocular rivalry (Williams et al., 2004).

Similar responses have been expressed toward stimuli that have been rendered imperceptible ("subliminal") through techniques such as backward masking, in which a stimulus (e.g., a word) is presented for a brief duration (17 msec) and is then followed by a pattern mask (e.g., #####). Under such conditions, subjects report that they were unable to perceive the stimulus. It has been shown that subliminal stimuli can still influence motor responses, attention shifts, emotional responses, and semantic processes (Ansorge, Neumann, Becker, Kalberer, & Cruse, 2007), at least to a certain extent. For example, in a choice response time (RT) task, RTs for responses to subliminal (masked) stimuli are the same as those for responses to supraliminal stimuli (Taylor & McCloskey, 1990). In addition, subjects can select the correct motor response (one of two button presses) when confronted with subliminal stimuli, suggesting that "appropriate programs for two separate movements can be simultaneously held ready for use, and that either one can be executed when triggered by specific stimuli without subjective awareness" (Taylor & McCloskey, 1996, p. 62). (See review in Hallett, 2007.)

The Self-Report Paradox

If humans can perform accurate choice-responses to stimuli of which they are unaware, perhaps monkeys in rivalry experiments, too, are unaware of the stimulus to which they respond motorically. The former is regarded as unconscious action, but the latter for some reason is regarded as conscious "self-report." Yet, both tasks are identical in that each involves a perceptual discrimination that is reflected in overt action. Hence, given the backward masking findings mentioned above, we can no longer be sure that the animals were conscious when responding accurately (and as humans do) to the rivalrous stimuli (though there are good arguments, by analogy, that they were; Gray, 2004). We refer to this as the "self-report paradox": In terms of overt behavior and from an objective standpoint, when does a discrimination constitute "self-report"?

Pessiglione et al. (2007) showed an automatic effort-increase effect in response to increases in incentive or reward on a hand-grip exertion task, both when the reward cue (amount of money to be won on that trial) was presented to conscious awareness as when it was presented subliminally. Neurophysiological recordings also show that the same brain regions are invoked whether the goal pursuit is conscious or unconscious (Pessiglione et al., 2007). In addition, some forms of Pavlovian, evaluative, and operant conditioning may occur unconsciously (Duckworth et al., 2002; Field, 2000; Olson & Fazio, 2001; Olsson & Phelps, 2007; Pessiglione et al., 2008). According to Strahan, Spencer, and Zanna (2002), certain action plans (e.g., eating popcorn) can be influenced by subliminal stimuli only when those plans are already motivated (e.g., when one is hungry). Subliminal stimuli can influence behavioral inclinations such as motivation and emotional states (e.g., as indexed by the skin conductance response; Olsson & Phelps, 2007; Pessiglione et al., 2008.)

Actions Prompted by Supraliminal Stimuli That Influence the Subject's Actions in Ways That the Subject is Unaware of
Unconscious Activation of Action Plans through Supraliminal Stimuli

Ambient, supraliminal stimuli in our immediate environment can exert forms of unconscious "stimulus control," leading to unconscious action tendencies. Consistent with this standpoint, findings suggest that incidental stimuli (e.g., hammers) can automatically set us to physically interact with the world (Tucker & Ellis, 2004; see neuroimaging evidence in Grézes & Decety, 2002; Longcamp, Anton, Roth, & Velay, 2005). For example, perceiving a cylinder unconsciously potentiates one's tendency to perform a power grip (see review in Ellis, 2009). In addition, it has been shown that in choice RT tasks, the mere presence of musical notation influences the responses of musicians but not of nonmusicians (Levine, Morsella, & Bargh, 2007; Stewart et al., 2003).

Unconscious action tendencies are readily evident in classic laboratory paradigms such as the Stroop task (Stroop, 1935) and the flanker task (Eriksen & Schultz, 1979). In the Stroop task, participants name the colors in which stimulus words are written. When they are congruous (e.g., RED presented in red), there is little or no interference (see review in MacLeod & MacDonald, 2000). When the word and color are incongruous (e.g., RED presented in blue), participants must suppress the automatic tendency to word read, leading to increased error rates and RTs (Cohen, Dunbar, & McClelland, 1990). In the Eriksen flanker task (Eriksen & Schultz, 1979), participants are first trained to press one button with one finger when presented with the letter S or M and to press another button with another finger when presented with the letters P or H. After training, participants are instructed to respond to targets that are flanked by distracters. For example, they are instructed to respond to the letter presented in the center of an array (e.g., SSPSS) and to disregard the flanking letters (the distracters). In terms of response time and errors, the least interference is found when the distracters are identical to the target (e.g., SSSSS). Interference is greatest when the distracters are associated with responses that are different from those associated with targets (response interference) and is less when they are different in appearance (stimulus interference) but associated with the same or a similar response. The strong and reliable effect of response interference, reflecting conflict at the response rather than stimulus identification level (van Veen, Cohen, Botvinick, Stenger, & Carter, 2001), suggests that flanking letters can activate response codes to some extent; see Starreveld, Theeuwes, and Mortier (2004). In support of *continuous flow* (Eriksen & Schultz, 1979) and *cascade* (McClelland, 1979; Navarrete & Costa, 2004) models, psychophysiological research shows that, in such response-interference tasks, competition involves simultaneous activation of the brain areas associated with the target- and distracter-related responses (DeSoto, Fabiani, Geary, & Gratton, 2001). This is a case of "activation before selection."

Unconscious Modulation of Behavioral Dispositions through Supraliminal Stimuli

In studies involving supraliminal priming of complex social behavior, it has been demonstrated that many of our complex behaviors occur automatically, determined by causes far removed from our awareness. Behavioral dispositions can be influenced by covert stimuli—when presented with supraliminal words associated with the stereotype "old," people walk slower (Bargh, Chen, & Burrows, 1996); when presented with stimuli associated with the concept "library," people make less noise (Aarts & Dijksterhuis, 2003); and when primed with

"hostility," people become more aggressive (Carver, Ganellen, Froming, & Chambers, 1983).

How may such effects take place? It has been documented that merely hearing action verbs pronounced out loud activates the same brain regions as does witnessing a meaningful action (Jeannerod, 1999) and that both events activate the implicit motor representations needed to carry out that type of behavior (Perani et al., 1999). Motor programs thus appear to be part of the very meaning of action-related verbs (Grèzes & Decety, 2002; Pulvermuller, 2005), and this fact is likely responsible for the many successful behavioral priming demonstrations using verbal stimuli. (For the limitations of this "embodied cognition" standpoint, see Mahon & Caramazza, 2008; Niedenthal, Winkielman, Mondillon, & Vermeulen, 2009.) According to Schacter and Badgaiyan (2001), neuroimaging evidence reveals that the priming of a response is then followed by decreased activation in the brain regions associated with processing that response, which presumably reflects more efficient processing of the response.

These effects have been found not only with verbal stimuli that are semantically related to the goal (as in many studies), but also with material objects. For example, backpacks and briefcases prime cooperation and competitiveness, respectively (Kay, Wheeler, Bargh, & Ross, 2004); candy bars prime tempting hedonic goals (Fisbach, Friedman, & Kruglanski, 2003); dollar bills prime greed (Vohs, Mead, & Goode, 2006); scents such as cleaning fluids prime cleanliness goals (Holland, Hendriks, & Aarts, 2005); sitting in a professor's chair primes social behaviors associated with power (Chen, Lee-Chai, & Bargh, 2001; Custers, Maas, Wildenbeest, & Aarts, 2008); control-related words prime the reduction of prejudice (Araya, Akrami, Ekehammar, & Hedlund, 2002); and the names of close relationship partners (e.g., mother, friend) prime the goals that those partners have for the individual as well as those goals the individual characteristically pursues when with the significant other (Fitzsimons & Bargh, 2003; Shah, 2003). In addition, there is evidence that one can unconsciously process task-irrelevant facial expressions (Preston & Stansfield, 2008) and be automatically vigilant toward negative or harmful stimuli (Öhman, Flykt, & Esteves, 2001; Okon-Singer, Tzelgov, & Henik, 2007) or toward undesirable tendencies such as stereotyping (Glaser, 2007). (See Rakison & Derringer, 2008, for evidence that infants possess an inborn, spider-detecting mechanism.)

Regarding the higher mental processes, automatic effects of environmental stimuli were found to drive evaluation (e.g., Fazio, 1990), stereotyping and prejudice (Devine, 1989), social behavior (e.g., Dijksterhuis & van Knippenberg, 1998), and motivated goal pursuit (e.g., Chartrand & Bargh, 1996)—in each case, without any awareness by the individual of the role played by these external stimuli in the production of his or her behavior. (See Sparrow & Wegner, 2006, for demonstrations of behavior-dependent "unpriming.")

Automatic Imitation

Regarding the effects of social stimuli as primes, it has been demonstrated that people automatically imitate the postures, facial expressions, emotional expressions, and speaking styles of others (e.g., Chartrand & Bargh, 1999; Giles, Coupland, & Coupland, 1991; Hatfield, Cacioppo, & Rapson, 1993). Once informed, subjects report that they are unaware that they had engaged in these imitative behaviors. Not only do people tend to adopt the physical behavior (posture, facial gestures, arm and hand movements) of strangers with whom they interact, without intending to or being aware they are doing so, such unconscious imitation also tends to increase liking and bonding between the individuals—serving as a kind of natural "social glue" (Wiltermuth & Heath, 2009). It has been proposed that automatic imitation is a natural outcome of the basic architecture responsible for perception-to-action mapping (see review in Wilson, 2002).

In neuropsychological populations, imitative response tendencies are displayed dramatically in patients with frontal brain lesions (Brass, Derffuss, Mattes-von Cramon, & von Cramon, 2004). (See Chong, Cunnington, Williams, & Mattingley, 2008, for a treatment of the necessary role of attention in automatic imitation effects.) These automatic imitation effects have been explained by appealing to the notion of *mirror neurons* (Rizzolatti, Sinigaglia, & Anderson, 2008). These neurons become active both when you perceive a given type of action and when you engage in that action yourself (Frith & Wolpert, 2003; Meltzoff & Prinz, 2002). At this high level of encoding, neurons fire with respect to motor acts rather than with respect to the movements that form them. As proposed by several theories (Ashe et al., 1993; Iacoboni & Dapretto, 2006), these neural events seem to be more related to encoding end-state representations, which form part of a "vocabulary" of action representations. In humans, the mirror system encompasses large segments of the premotor cortex and the inferior parietal lobule. Mirror neurons are particularly relevant to "common code" theories of speech perception (e.g., Liberman & Mattingley, 1985). (See Georgopoulos, 2002, regarding shortcomings of the mirror-neuron hypothesis.)

The Difference between Conscious and Unconscious Action Tendencies

In the three sections above, we surveyed the different kinds of unconscious action tendencies that have been well documented in the literature. The mounting evidence leads one to conclude that actions of considerable complexity can transpire even when (a) the actor is unconscious (e.g., automatisms), (b) the actor is conscious but the action is not mediated consciously (e.g., anarchic hand syndrome), (c) the action is influenced or triggered by subliminal stimuli (e.g., backward masking), or (d) the action is influenced by supraliminal stimuli in ways that the actor is unaware of (e.g., supraliminal priming). At first glance, the combined evidence reveals that unconscious actions are not identifiably less flexible, complex, controlling, deliberative, or action-like than their conscious counterparts (Bargh & Morsella, 2008). The principled difference between conscious and unconscious action tendencies is thus less straightforward than what intuition suggests.

Integrated versus Un-integrated Action

Building on a theoretical framework (Morsella, 2005), we propose that the difference between unconscious action and conscious action is that the former is always a case of "un-integrated action," and the latter can be a case of "integrated action." *Integrated action occurs when two (or more) action plans that could normally influence behavior on their own (when existing at that level of activation) are simultaneously co-activated and trying to influence the same skeletal muscle effector.* Thus, integrated action occurs when one holds one's breath, refrains from dropping a hot dish, suppresses the urge to scratch an itch, suppresses a pre-potent response in a laboratory paradigm, or makes oneself breathe faster (Morsella, 2005; Morsella, Krieger, & Bargh, 2009). Suppressing (or over-expressing) a saccade, cough, blink, or some other reflexive behavior is also a case of integrated action. Co-activation can be indexed by behavioral and neural measures; there are several behavioral and neural features that could be used to distinguish integrated from un-integrated action. For example, like any behavior of low strength, conflicted action (a form of integrated action) is easier to perturb than un-conflicted or un-integrated action (Skinner, 1957). Moreover, integrated action is usually accompanied by, or followed by, increases in cognitive control (as in "Gratton effects"; MacLeod & MacDonald, 2000), and it seems to involve the activation of more neural processes than un-integrated action (DeSoto et al., 2001; Ortinski & Meador, 2004).

It is important to note that the level of activation of the plans involved in integrated action is far beyond that of "sub-threshold" activations. For example, in psycholinguistic research, there is substantial evidence that naming "dog" primes the action plan for naming a member of the same category (e.g., "horse"; Levelt, 1989). The level of activation that we are speaking of in our definition of integrated action is far above this threshold—it is at the level of activation at which action plans would not only influence overt action but trigger action.

From this standpoint, conscious mediation is not needed to inhale or withdraw one's hand from a painful stimulus (e.g., un-integrated action plans *x* and *y* can do these things autonomously; Morsella, 2005), but conscious mediation is necessary to curb these actions through the activation of another action plan. This idea is based on a theory proposing that consciousness is a physical state that establishes a form of "cross-talk" that permits otherwise encapsulated systems to influence (specifically) the skeletal muscle system, collectively and adaptively (Morsella, 2005). From this standpoint, skeletal muscle is the "steering wheel" of systems with different operating principles and phylogenetic histories, actional systems that can cross-talk and be integrated only in virtue of conscious states. (According to the theory, the role of these states is limited to skeletal muscle effectors; see Morsella et al., 2009, for an explanation regarding why smooth muscle effectors are not associated with conscious mediation.)

In addition, this view is consistent with the view that conscious action reflects a rational, reflective process (Block, 1995; Johnson & Reeder, 1997). A hallmark of conscious action is its capacity to take various kinds of information into account (Baars, 2002). The answer is also consistent with the *integration consensus* (Morsella, 2005), in which conscious states bring together diverse forms of information in order to guide action adaptively. Irrational action, on the other hand, seems to operate blindly of such considerations. Accordingly, in disorders and phenomena in which action is decoupled from consciousness (e.g., blindsight,

automatisms, tics, spoonerisms, action slips, alien hand syndrome, anarchic hand syndrome, and utilization behavior) actions are perceived as impulsive and often as situationally inappropriate and uncooperative (Chan & Ross, 1997), meaning that they occur without taking other kinds of information into account. Under normal circumstance, such information would activate other action plans that would concurrently modulate overt action. Such co-activation of action plans does not occur when one reflexively looks rightwards, but it does occur when one "voluntarily" looks away from an attention-grabbing stimulus (as in the anti-saccade task; Curtis & D'Esposito, 2003).

Conclusions for Neuroscience: Three Kinds of Binding in the Brain

Research on simple actions and on more complex, social actions (e.g., suppressing the tendency to say something) reveals that, in the nervous system, there are three distinct kinds of integration or "binding." *Perceptual binding* (or *afference binding*) is the binding of perceptual processes and representations. This occurs in intersensory binding, as in the McGurk effect, and in intrasensory, feature binding (e.g., the binding of shape to color; Zeki & Bartels, 1999). Another form of binding, linking perceptual processing to action/motor processing, is known as *efference binding* (Haggard, Aschersleben, Gehrke, & Prinz, 2002). This is kind of stimulus-response binding is what allows one to learn to press a button when presented with a cue in a laboratory paradigm. Responding on the basis of efference binding can occur unconsciously. As mentioned above, Taylor and McCloskey (1990) demonstrated that choice response-times for responses to subliminal stimuli were the same as those for responses to supraliminal stimuli. The third kind of binding, *efference-efference binding*, occurs when two streams of efference binding are trying to influence skeletomotor action at the same time. This occurs in the incongruent conditions of interference paradigms, in which stimulus dimensions activate competing action plans. It also occurs when one holds one's breath, suppresses a prepotent response, or experiences another form of conscious conflict (e.g., suppressing an inappropriate impulse in a social setting). In the present framework, it is the instantiation of conflicting efference-efference binding that requires consciousness (Figure 22.1). Consciousness is the "cross-talk" medium that allows such actional processes to influence action collectively. Absent consciousness, behavior can be influenced by only one of the efference streams,

Fig. 22.1 Three forms of binding in the brain, with only efference-efference binding requiring consciousness. *S* (sensory) signifies "perceptual/afference," and *R* (response) signifies "motor response."

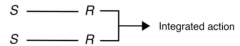

$$S \text{———} S$$

afference binding: e.g., intra- and inter-sensory feature binding, including illusions such as the McGurk effect

$$S \text{———} R$$

efference binding: binding between perceptual and actional codes, as when a supraliminal or subliminal stimulus leads to a button press

$$S \text{———} R$$
$$S \text{———} R$$
→ Integrated action

efference-efference binding: two streams of efference binding are trying to influence skeletomotor action simultaneously, as when holding one's breath or suppressing another action; the binding requires consciousness

leading to unintegrated actions such as unconsciously inhaling while underwater or reflexively removing one's hand from a hot object, but behavior cannot be "integrated," as when one "voluntarily" avoids checking the time on a wall clock in order to focus on the task at hand.

References

Aarts, H. & Dijksterhuis, A. (2003). The silence of the library: Environment, situational norm, and social behavior. *Journal of Personality and Social Psychology, 84*, 18–28.

Ansorge, U., Neumann, O., Becker, S., Kalberer, H., & Cruse, H. (2007). Sensorimotor supremacy: Investigating conscious and unconscious vision by masked priming. *Advances in Cognitive Psychology, 3*, 257–274.

Araya, T., Akrami, N., Ekehammar, B., & Hedlund, L-E. (2002). Reducing prejudice through priming of control-related words. *Experimental Psychology, 49*, 222–227.

Ashe, J., Taira, M., Smyrnis, N., Pellizer, G., Gerorakopoulos, T., Lurito, J. T., et al. (1993). Motor cortical activity preceding a memorized movement trajectory with an orthogonal bend. *Experimental Brain Research, 95*, 118–130.

Baars, B. J. (2002). The conscious access hypothesis: Origins and recent evidence. *Trends in Cognitive Sciences, 6*, 47–52.

Badgaiyan, R. D., Schacter, D. L., & Alpert, N. M. (2001). Priming within and across modalities: Exploring the nature of rCBF increases and decreases. *NeuroImage, 13*, 272–282.

Bargh, J. A. (1984). Automatic and controlled processing of social information. In R. S. Wyer, Jr. & T. K. Srull (Eds.), *Handbook of social cognition* (Vol. 1, pp. 1–41). Hillsdale, NJ: Erlbaum.

Bargh, J. A., Chen, M., & Burrows, L. (1996). Automaticity of social behavior: Direct effects of trait construct and stereotype activation on action. *Journal of Personality and Social Psychology, 71*, 230–244.

Bargh, J. A., & Morsella, E. (2008). The unconscious mind. *Perspectives on Psychological Science, 3*, 73–79.

Bartolomei, F., Wendling, F., Vignal, J. P., Chauvel, P., & Liegeois-Chauvel, C. (2002). Neural networks underlying epileptic humming. *Epilepsia, 43*, 1001–1012.

Berne, S. A. (2006). The primitive reflexes: Considerations in the infant. *Journal of Optometric Vision Development, 37*, 139–145.

Berridge, K. C. & Robinson, T. E. (1995). The mind of an addicted brain: Neural sensitization of wanting versus liking. *Current Directions in Psychological Science, 4*, 71–76.

Berti, A. & Pia, L. (2006). Understanding motor awareness through normal and pathological behavior. *Current Directions in Psychological Science, 15*, 237–240.

Bindra, D. (1974). A motivational view of learning, performance, and behavior modification. *Psychological Review, 81*, 199–213.

Blanken, G., Wallesch, C.-W., & Papagno, C. (1990). Dissociations of language functions in aphasics with speech automatisms (recurring utterances). *Cortex, 26*, 41–63.

Block, N. (1995). On a confusion about a function of consciousness. *Behavioral and Brain Sciences, 18*, 227–287.

Bodis-Wollner, I., Bucher, S. F., & Seelos, K. C. (1999). Cortical activation patterns during voluntary blinks and voluntary saccades. *Neurology, 53*, 1800–1805.

Brass, M., Derffuss, J., Mattes-von Cramon, G., & von Cramon, D. Y. (2004). Imitative response tendencies in patients with frontal brain lesions. *Neuropsychology, 17*, 265–271.

Bryon, S. & Jedynak, C. P. (1972). Troubles du transfert interhemispherique: A propos de trois observations de tumeurs du corps calleux. Le signe de la main etrangere. *Revue Neurologique, 126*, 257–266.

Carmant, L., Riviello, J. J., Thiele, E. A., Kramer, U., Helmers, S. L., Mikati, M., et al. (1994). Compulsory spitting: An unusual manifestation of temporal lobe epilepsy. *Journal of Epilepsy, 7*, 167–170.

Carver, C. S., Ganellen, R. J., Froming, W. J., & Chambers, W. (1983). Modeling: An analysis in terms of category accessibility. *Journal of Experimental Social Psychology, 19*, 403–421.

Chan, J.-L. & Ross, E. D. (1997). Alien hand syndrome: Influence of neglect on the clinical presentation of frontal and callosal variants. *Cortex, 33*, 287–299.

Chartrand, T. L. & Bargh, J. A. (1996). Automatic activation of impression formation and memorization goals: Nonconscious goal priming reproduces effects of explicit task instructions. *Journal of Personality and Social Psychology, 71*, 464–478.

Chartrand, T. L. & Bargh, J. A. (1999). The chameleon effect: The perception-behavior link and social interaction. *Journal of Personality and Social Psychology, 76*, 893–910.

Chen, S., Lee-Chai A. Y., & Bargh J. A. (2001). Relationship orientation as a moderator of the effects of social power. *Journal of Personality and Social Psychology, 80*, 173–187.

Chomsky, N. (1988). *Language and problems of knowledge: The Managua lectures.* Cambridge, MA: MIT Press.

Chong, T., Williams, M. A., Cunnington, R., & Mattingley, J. B. (2008). Selective attention modulates inferior frontal gyrus activity during action observation. *NeuroImage, 40*, 298–307.

Cohen, J. D., Dunbar, K., & McClelland, J. L. (1990). On the control of automatic processes: A parallel distributed processing account of the Stroop effect. *Psychological Review, 97*, 332–361.

Curtis, C. E. & D'Esposito, M. (2003). Success and failure suppressing reflexive behavior. *Journal of Cognitive Neuroscience, 15*, 409–418.

Custers, R., Maas, M., Wildenbeest, M., & Aarts, H. (2008). Nonconscious goal pursuit and the surmounting of physical and social obstacles. *European Journal of Social Psychology, 38*, 1013–1022.

Decety, J. & Grezes, J. (1999). Neural mechanisms subserving the perception of human actions. *Trends in Cognitive Sciences, 3*, 172–178.

DeSoto, M. C., Fabiani, M., Geary, D. C., & Gratton, G. (2001). When in doubt, do it both ways: Brain evidence of the simultaneous activation of conflicting responses in a spatial Stroop task. *Journal of Cognitive Neuroscience, 13*, 523–536.

Devine, P. G. (1989). Stereotypes and prejudice: Their automatic and controlled components. *Journal of Personality and Social Psychology, 56*, 5–18.

Dijksterhuis, A., van Knippenberg, A. (1998). The relation between perception and behavior or how to win a game of Trivial Pursuit. *Journal of Personality and Social Psychology, 74*, 865–877.

Doherty, M. J., Wilensky A. J., Holmes, M. D., Lewis, D. H., Rae, J., & Cohn, G. H. (2002). Singing seizures. *Neurology, 59*, 1435–1438.

Duckworth, K. L., Bargh, J. A., Garcia, M., & Chaiken, S. (2002). The automatic evaluation of novel stimuli. *Psychological Science, 13*, 513–519.

Ellis, R. (2009). Interactions between action and visual objects. In E. Morsella, J. A. Bargh & P. M. Gollwitzer (Eds.), *Oxford handbook of human action* (pp. 214–224). New York: Oxford University Press.

Eriksen, C. W. & Schultz, D. W. (1979). Information processing in visual search: A continuous flow conception and experimental results. *Perception and Psychophysics, 25*, 249–263.

Fazio, R. H. (1990). Multiple processes by which attitudes guide behavior: The MODE model as an integrative framework. In M. P. Zanna (Ed.), *Advances in experimental social psychology* (Vol. 23, pp. 75–109). New York: Academic Press.

Fecteau, J. H., Chua, R., Franks, I., & Enns, J. T. (2001). Visual awareness and the online modification of action. *Canadian Journal of Experimental Psychology, 55*, 104–110.

Festinger, L. (1957). *A theory of cognitive dissonance.* Evanston, IL: Row, Peterson.

Field, A. P. (2000). I like it, but I'm not sure why: Can evaluative conditioning occur without conscious awareness? *Consciousness and Cognition, 9*, 13–36.

Fishbach, A., Friedman, R. S., & Kruglanski, A. W. (2003). Leading us not unto temptation: Momentary allurements elicit overriding goal activation. *Journal of Personality and Social Psychology, 84*, 296–309.

Fitzsimons, G. M. & Bargh, J. A. (2003). Thinking of you: Nonconscious pursuit of interpersonal goals associated with relationship partners. *Journal of Personality and Social Psychology, 84*, 148–163.

Floyer-Lea, A. & Matthews, P. M. (2004). Changing brain networks for visuomotor control with increased movement automaticity. *Journal of Neurophysiology, 92*, 2405–2412.

Fourneret, P. & Jeannerod, M. (1998). Limited conscious monitoring of motor performance in normal subjects. *Neuropsychologia, 36*, 1133–1140.

Franz, V. H., Gegenfurtner, K. R., Bülthoff, H. H., & Fahle, M. (2000). Grasping visual illusions: No evidence for a dissociation between perception and action. *Psychological Science, 11*, 20–25.

Frith, C. & Wolpert, D. (Ed., 2003). *The neuroscience of social interaction.* New York: Oxford University Press.

Georgopoulos, A. P. (2002). Cognitive motor control: Spatial and temporal aspects. *Current Opinion in Biology, 12*, 678–683.

Giles, H., Coupland, J., & Coupland, N. (1991). *Contexts of accommodation: Developments in applied sociolinguistics.* New York: Cambridge University Press.

Glaser, J. (2007). Contrast effects in automatic affect, cognition, and behavior. In D. A. Stapel and J. Suls (Eds.), *Assimilation and contrast in social psychology* (pp. 229–248). New York: Psychology Press.

Goodale, M. & Milner, D. (2004). *Sight unseen: An exploration of conscious and unconscious vision.* New York: Oxford University Press.

Gottlieb, J. & Mazzoni, P. (2004). Neuroscience: Action, illusion, and perception. *Science, 303*, 317–318.

Gould, J. L. (1982). *Ethology: The mechanisms and evolution of behavior.* New York: W. W. Norton.

Gray, J. A. (2004). *Consciousness: Creeping up on the hard problem.* New York: Oxford University Press.

Grézes, J. & Decety, J. (2002). Does visual perception of object afford action? Evidence from a neuroimaging study. *Neuropsychologia, 40*, 212–222.

Haggard, P., Aschersleben, G., Gehrke, J., & Prinz, W. (2002). Action, binding and awareness. In W. Prinz & B. Hommel (Eds.), *Common mechanisms in perception and action: Attention and performance* (Vol. XIX, pp. 266–285). Oxford, UK: Oxford University Press.

Hallett, M. (2007). Volitional control of movement: The physiology of free will. *Clinical Neurophysiology, 117*, 1179–1192.

Hatfield, E., Cacioppo, J. T., & Rapson, R. L. (1993). Emotional contagion. *Current Directions in Psychological Science, 2*, 96–99.

Heath, M., Neely, K. A., Yakimishyn, J., & Binsted, G. (2008). Visuomotor memory is independent of conscious awareness of target features. *Experimental Brain Research, 188*, 517–527.

Heider, F. (1958). *The psychology of interpersonal relations.* New York: John Wiley & Sons.

Holland, R. W., Hendriks, M., & Aarts, H. A. G. (2005). Smells like clean spirit: Nonconscious effects of scent on cognition and behavior. *Psychological Science, 16*, 689–693.

Iacoboni, M. & Dapretto, M. (2006). The mirror neuron system and the consequences of its dysfunction. *Nature Reviews Neuroscience, 7*, 942–951.

Jeannerod, M. (1999). To act or not to act: Perspectives on the representation of actions. *Quarterly Journal of Experimental Psychology, 52A,* 1–29.

Jeannerod, M. (2003). Simulation of action as a unifying concept for motor cognition. In S. H. Johnson-Frey (Ed.), *Taking action: Cognitive neuroscience perspectives on intentional acts.* Cambridge, MA: MIT Press.

Johnson, H. & Haggard, P. (2005). Motor awareness without perceptual awareness. *Neuropsychologia, 43,* 227–237.

Johnson, M. K. & Reeder, J. A. (1997). Consciousness as metaprocessing. In J. D. Cohen & J. W. Schooler (Eds.), *Scientific approaches to consciousness* (pp. 261–293). Mahwah, NJ: Erlbaum.

Kaido, T., Otsuki, T., Nakama, H., Kaneko, Y., Kubota, Y., Sugai, K., et al. (2006). Complex behavioral automatism arising from insular cortex. *Epilepsy and Behavior, 8,* 315–319.

Kay, A. C., Wheeler, S. C., Bargh, J. A., & Ross, L. (2004). Material priming: The influence of mundane physical objects on situational construal and competitive behavioral choice. *Organizational Behavior and Human Decision Processes, 95,* 83–96.

Kern, M. K., Jaradeh, S., Arndorfer, R. C., & Shaker, R. (2001). Cerebral cortical representation of reflexive and volitional swallowing in humans. *American Journal of Physiology: Gastrointestinal and Liver Physiology, 280,* G354–G360.

Klein, D. B. (1984). *The concept of consciousness: A survey.* Lincoln, NE: University of Nebraska Press.

Kutlu, G., Bilir, E., Erdem, A., Gomceli, Y. B., Kurt, G. S., & Serdaroglu, A. (2005). Hush sign: A new clinical sign in temporal lobe epilepsy. *Epilepsy and Behavior, 6,* 452–455.

Laurey, S. (2005). The neural correlate of (un)awareness: Lessons from the vegetative state. *Trends in Cognitive Sciences, 12,* 556–559.

Levelt, W. J. M. (1989). *Speaking: From intention to articulation.* Cambridge, MA: The MIT Press.

Levine, L. R., Morsella, E., & Bargh, J. A. (2007). The perversity of inanimate objects: Stimulus control by incidental musical notation. *Social Cognition, 25,* 265–280.

Lewin, K. (1935). A dynamic theory of personality. New York: McGraw-Hill.

Lhermitte, F. (1983). "Utilization behavior" and its relation to lesions of the frontal lobes. *Brain, 106,* 237–255.

Liberman, A. M., & Mattingly, I. G. (1985). The motor theory of speech perception revised. *Cognition, 21,* 1–36.

Libet, B. (2004). *Mind time: The temporal factor in consciousness.* Cambridge, MA: Harvard University Press.

Liu, G., Chua, R., & Enns, J. T. (2008). Attention for perception and action: Task interference for action planning, but not for online control. *Experimental Brain Research, 185,* 709–717.

Logothetis, N. K. & Schall, J. D. (1989). Neuronal correlates of subjective visual perception. *Science, 245,* 761–762.

Longcamp, M., Anton, J. L., Roth, M., & Velay, J. L. (2005). Premotor activations in response to visually presented single letters depend on the hand used to write: A study on left-handers. *Neuropsychologia, 43,* 1801–1809.

MacLeod, C. M. & McDonald, P. A. (2000). Interdimensional interference in the Stroop effect: Uncovering the cognitive and neural anatomy of attention. *Trends in Cognitive Sciences, 4,* 383–391.

Maestro, I., Carreno, M., Donaire, A., Rumia, J., Conesa, G., Bargallo, N., et al. (2008). Oroalimentary automatisms induced by electrical stimulation of the fronto-opercular

cortex in a patient without automotor seizures. *Epilepsy and Behavior, 13,* 410–412.

Mahon, B. Z. & Caramazza, A. (2008). A critical look at the embodied cognition hypothesis and a new proposal for grounding conceptual content. *Journal of Physiology–Paris, 102,* 59–70.

Marchetti, C. & Della Sala, S. (1998). Disentangling the alien and anarchic hand. *Cognitive Neuropsychiatry, 3,* 191–207.

McClelland, J. L. (1979). On the time-relations of mental processes: An examination of systems of processes in cascade. *Psychological Review, 86,* 287–330.

Mckay, L. C., Evans, K. C., Frackowiak, R. S. J., & Corfield, D. R. (2003). Neural correlates of voluntary breathing in humans determined using functional magnetic resonance imaging. *Journal of Applied Physiology, 95,* 1170–1178.

Meltzoff, A. N., & Prinz, W. (2002). *The imitative mind: Development, evolution, and brain bases.* New York: Cambridge University Press.

Mikati, M. A., Comair, Y. G., & Shamseddine, A. N. (2005). Pattern-induced partial seizures with repetitive affectionate kissing: An unusual manifestation of right temporal lobe epilepsy. *Epilepsy and Behavior, 6,* 447–451.

Montigny, D., Coureaud, G., & Schaal, B. (2006). Rabbit pup response to the mammary pheromenone: From automatism to prandial control. *Physiology and Behavior, 89,* 742–749.

Morsella, E. (2005). The function of phenomenal states: Supramodular interaction theory. *Psychological Review, 112,* 1000–1021.

Morsella, E., Krieger, S. C., & Bargh, J. A. (2009). The function of consciousness: Why skeletal muscles are "voluntary" muscles. In E. Morsella, J. A. Bargh, & P. M. Gollwitzer, *Oxford handbook of human action* (pp. 625–634). Oxford University Press.

Munoz, D. P. & Everling, S. (2004). Look away: The antisaccade task and the voluntary control of eye movement. *Nature Reviews Neuroscience, 5,* 218–228.

Maruya, K., Yang, E., & Blake, R. (2007). Voluntary action influences visual competition. *Psychological Science, 18,* 1090–1098.

Navarrete, E. & Costa, A. (2004). How much linguistic information is extracted from ignored pictures? Further evidence for a cascade model of speech production. *Journal of Memory and Language, 53,* 359–377.

Niedenthal, P. M., Winkielman, P. Mondillon, L., & Vermeulen, N. (2009). Embodiment of emotional concepts: Evidence from EMG measures. *Journal of Personality and Social Psychology, 96,* 1120–1136.

Öhman, A., Flykt, A., & Esteves, F. (2001). Emotion drives attention: Detecting the snake in the grass. *Journal of Experimental Psychology: General, 130,* 466–478.

Okon-Singer, H., Tzelgov, J., & Henik, A. (2007). Distinguishing between automaticity and attention in the processing of emotionally significant stimuli. *Emotion, 7,* 147–157.

Olson, M. A. & Fazio, R. H. (2001). Implicit attitude formation through classical conditioning. *Psychological Science, 12,* 413–417.

Olsson, A. & Phelps, E. A. (2004). Learned fear of "unseen" faces after Pavlovian, observational, and instructed fear. *Psychological Science, 15,* 822–828.

Olsson, A., & Phelps, E. A. (2007). Social learning of fear. *Nature Neuroscience, 10,* 1095–1102.

Ortinski, P., & Meador, K. J. (2004). Neuronal mechanisms of conscious awareness. *Archives of Neurology, 61,* 1017–1020.

Pacherie, E. (2000). The content of intentions. *Mind & Language*, *15*, 400–432.

Perani, D., Cappa, S. F., Schnur, T., Tettamanti, M., Collina, S., Rosa, M. M., et al. (1999). The neural correlates of verb and noun processing: A PET study. *Brain*, *122*, 2337–2344.

Pessiglione, M., Schmidt, L., Draganski, B., Kalisch, R., Lau, H., Dolan, R. J., et al. (2007). How the brain translates money into force: A neuroimaging study of subliminal motivation. *Science. 11*, 904–906.

Pilon, M. & Sullivan, S. J. (1996). Motor profile of patients in minimally responsive and persistent vegetative states. *Brain Injury*, *10*, 421–437.

Plazzi, G., Vetrugno, R., Provini, F., & Montagna, P. (2005). Sleepwalking and other ambulatory behaviors during sleep. *Neurological Sciences*, *26*, S193–S198.

Poldrack, R. A., Sabb, F. W., Foerde, K., Tom, S. M., Asarnow, R. F., Bookheimer, S. Y., et al. (2005). The neural correlates of motor skill automacity. *Journal of Neuroscience*, *25*, 5356–5364.

Preston, S. D. & Stansfield, R. B. (2008). I know how you feel: Task-irrelevant facial expressions are spontaneously processed at a semantic level. *Cognitive, Affective, and Behavioral Neuroscience*, *8*, 54–64.

Pulvermuller, F. (2005). Brain mechanisms linking language and action. *Nature Reviews Neuroscience*, *6*, 576–582.

Puttemans, V., Wenderoth, N., & Swinnen, S. P. (2005). Changes in brain activation during the acquisition of a multifrequency bimanual coordination task: From the cognitive stage to advanced levels of automaticity. *Journal of Neuroscience*, *25*, 4270–4278.

Raichle, M. E., Fiez J. A., Videen T. O., MacLeod A. M., Pardo J. V., Fox P. T., & et al. (1994). Practice-related changes in human brain functional anatomy during nonmotor learning. *Cerebral Cortex*, *4*, 8–26.

Rakison, D. H. & Derringer, J. L. (2008). Do infants possess an evolved spider-detection mechanism? *Cognition*, *107*, 381–393.

Rizzolatti, G., Sinigaglia, C., & Anderson, F. (2008). *Mirrors in the brain: How our minds share actions, emotions, and experience.* New York: Oxford University Press.

Ro, T. (2008). Unconscious vision in action. *Neuropsychologia*, *46*, 379–383.

Roe, A. & Simpson, G. G. (1958). *Behavior and evolution.* New Haven, CT: Yale University Press.

Rosenbaum, D. A. (2002). Motor control. In H. Pashler (Series Ed.) & S. Yantis (Vol. Ed.), *Stevens' handbook of experimental psychology: Vol. 1. Sensation and perception* (3rd ed., pp. 315–339). New York: Wiley.

Rossetti, Y. (2001). Implicit perception in action: Short-lived motor representation of space. In P. G. Grossenbacher (Ed.), *Finding consciousness in the brain: A neurocognitive approach* (pp. 133–181). Netherlands: John Benjamins Publishing.

Spencer, S. S., Spencer, D. D., Williamson, P. D., & Mattson, R. H. (1983). Sexual automatisms in complex partial seizures. *Neurology*, *33*, 527–533.

Shah, J. Y (2003). The motivational looking glass: How significant others implicitly affect goal appraisals. *Journal of Personality and Social Psychology*, *85*, 424–439.

Schacter, D. L. & Addis, D. R. (2007). The cognitive neuroscience of constructive memory: Remembering the past and imagining the future. *Philosophical Transactions of the Royal Society of London, Series B: Biological Sciences*, *362*, 773–786.

Skinner, B. F. (1957). *Verbal behavior.* New York: Appleton-Century-Crofts.

Sobel, N., Prabhakaran, V., Hartley C. A., Desmond J. E., Glover, G. H., Sullivan, E. V., et al. (1999). Blind smell: Brain activation induced by an undetected air-borne chemical. *Brain*, *122*, 209–217.

Soon, C. S., Brass, M., Heinze, H.-J., & Haynes, J.-D. (2008). Unconscious determinants of free decisions in the human brain. *Nature Neuroscience*, *11*, 543–545.

Sparrow, B. & Wegner, D. M. (2006). Unpriming: The deactivation of thoughts through expression. *Journal of Personality and Social Psychology*, *91*, 1009–1019.

Starreveld, P. A., Theeuwes, J., & Mortier, K. (2004). Response selection in visual search: The influence of response compatibility of nontargets. *Journal of Experimental Psychology: Human Perception & Performance*, *30*, 56–78.

Stewart, L., Henson, R., Kampe, K., Walsh, V., Turner, R., & Frith, U. (2003). Brain changes after learning to read and play music. *Neuroimage*, *20*, 71–83.

Stottinger, E. & Perner, J. (2006). Dissociating size representation for action and for conscious judgment: Grasping visual illusions without apparent obstacles. *Consciousness and Cognition: An International Journal, 15,* 269–284.

Strahan, E., Spencer, S. J., & Zanna, M. P. (2002). Subliminal priming and persuasion: Striking while the iron is hot. *Journal of Experimental Social Psychology*, *38*, 556–568.

Stroop, J. R. (1935). Studies of interference in serial verbal reactions. *Journal of Experimental Psychology*, *18*, 643–662.

Sumner, P. & Husain, M. (2008). At the edge of consciousness: Automatic motor activation and voluntary control. *The Neuroscientist*, *14*, 474–486.

Taylor, J. L. & McCloskey, D. I. (1990). Triggering of preprogrammed movements as reactions to masked stimuli. *Journal of Neurophysiology*, *63*, 439–446.

Taylor, J. L. & McCloskey, D. I. (1996). Selection of motor responses on the basis of unperceived stimuli. *Experimental Brain Research*, *110*, 62–66.

Thorndike, E. L. (1905). The functions of mental states. In E. L. Thorndike (Ed.), *The elements of psychology* (pp. 111–119). New York: A. G. Seiler.

Thorpe, W. H. (1964). *Learning and instinct in animals.* Cambridge, MA: Harvard University Press.

Tiffany, S. T. & Carter, B. L. (1998). Is craving the source of compulsive drug use? *Journal of Psychopharmacology*, *12*, 23–30.

Tucker, M. & Ellis, R. (2004). Action priming by briefly presented objects. *Acta Psychologica*, *116*, 185–203.

van Veen, V., Cohen, J. D., Botvinick, M. M., Stenger, V. A., & Carter, C. C. (2001). Anterior cingulate cortex, conflict monitoring, and levels of processing. *Neuroimage*, *14*, 1302–1308.

Vohs, K. D., Mead, N. L., & Goode, M. R. (2006). The psychological consequences of money. *Science*, *314*, 1154–1156.

Weiskrantz, L. (1997). *Consciousness lost and found: A neuropsychological exploration.* New York: Oxford University Press.

Westwood, D. A. (2009). The visual control of object manipulation. In E. Morsella, J. A. Bargh, and P. M. Gollwitzer (Eds.), *Oxford handbook of human action* (pp. 88–103). New York: Oxford University Press.

Williams, M. A., Morris, A. P., McGlone, F., Abbott, D. F., & Mattingley, J. B. (2004). Amygdala responses to fearful and happy facial expressions under conditions of binocular suppression. *Journal of Neuroscience*, *24*, 2898–2904.

Wilson, M. (2002). Six views of embodied cognition. *Psychonomic Bulletin and Review, 9*, 625–636.

Wiltermuth, S. S. & Heath, C. (2009). Synchrony and cooperation. *Psychological Science, 20*, 1–5.

Wraga, M., Creem, S. H., & Proffitt, D. R. (2000). Perception-action dissociations of a walkable Müller-Lyer configuration. *Psychological Science, 11*, 239–243.

Yamadori, A. (1997). Body awareness and its disorders. In M. Ito, Y. Miyashita, & E. T. Rolls (Eds.), *Cognition, computation, and consciousness* (pp. 169–176). Washington, DC: American Psychological Association.

Zeki, S. & Bartels, A. (1999). Toward a theory of visual consciousness. *Consciousness and Cognition, 8*, 225–259.

Zorick, F. J., Salis, P. J., Roth, T., & Kramer, M. (1979). Narcolepsy and automatic behavior. *Journal of Clinical Psychiatry, 40*, 194–197.

The Prefrontal Cortex and Goal-Directed Social Behavior

Aron K. Barbey *and* Jordan Grafman

Abstract

This chapter develops an integrative cognitive neuroscience framework for understanding the social functions of the lateral prefrontal cortex (PFC), reviewing recent theoretical insights from evolutionary psychology and emerging neuroscience evidence to support the importance of this region for orchestrating social behavior on the basis of evolutionarily adaptive social norms. The chapter begins by reviewing the evolutionary foundations of normative social behavior, surveying contemporary research and theory from evolutionary psychology to suggest that widely shared norms of social exchange are the product of evolutionarily adaptive cognitive mechanisms. It then reviews the biology, evolution, and ontogeny of the human PFC, and introduces a cognitive neuroscience framework for goal-directed social behavior on the basis of evolutionarily adaptive social norms represented by the lateral PFC. It examines a broad range of evidence from the social and decision neuroscience literatures demonstrating that evolutionarily adaptive social norms of obligatory, prohibited, and permissible behavior are mediated by the lateral PFC.

Keywords: prefrontal cortex, social functions, cognitive neuroscience framework, goal-directed social behavior, evolution

Introduction

A primary assumption in cognitive neuroscience is that the brain has evolved to solve adaptive problems encountered by our human ancestors. Throughout evolutionary history, a foremost adaptive challenge for our species was living and interacting with other people. To survive and reproduce, our human ancestors had to select mates, form alliances, and compete for limited resources. They also needed to learn social norms and standards of conduct, as violations of these rules might have been severely punished, resulting in banishment from society. Accordingly, just as the brain has evolved mechanisms for perception, memory, language, and thought, it is likely that there are also evolutionarily

adaptive mechanisms that enable humans to coexist with others. Indeed, it is through cooperation that evolution constructs new levels of organization, from genomes and cells to the formation of multicellular organisms, social insects, and complex human societies (Nowak, 2006).

The neuroscientific study of social cognition reflects the interdisciplinary nature of modern science, with investigators from diverse academic disciplines (including anthropology, evolutionary psychology, social psychology, political science, behavioral economics, and decision neuroscience) exploring the unique social nature of human experience through a multifaceted lens (for a social neuroscience review, see Cacioppo et al., 2002). This interdisciplinary enterprise has made considerable progress in understanding the involvement of the prefrontal cortex (PFC) in social cognition (Amodio & Frith, 2006; Barbey, Krueger, & Grafman, 2009; Krueger, Barbey, & Grafman, 2009; Wood & Grafman, 2003). Accumulating evidence suggests that representations within the lateral PFC enable people to orchestrate their thoughts and actions in concert with their intentions to support goal-directed social behavior (Fiddick, Spampinato, & Grafman, 2005; Berthoz, Armony, Blair, & Dolan, 2002; Rilling et al., 2008; Buckholz et al., 2008; Greene, Nystrom, Engell, Darley, & Cohen, 2004; Weissman, Perkins, & Woldorff, 2008; Damasio, Tranel, & Damasio, 1990; Bechara, Damasio, Damasio, & Anderson, 1994; Rolls, Hornak, Wade, & McGrath, 1994; Bechara, Damasio, & Damasio, 2000; LoPresti et al., 2008; Ruby & Decety, 2004). Despite the pivotal role of this region in guiding social interactions, fundamental questions remain concerning the functional organization and forms of social knowledge represented within the lateral PFC. We develop an integrative cognitive neuroscience framework for understanding the social functions of the lateral PFC, reviewing recent theoretical insights from evolutionary psychology and emerging neuroscience evidence to support the importance of this region for orchestrating social behavior on the basis of evolutionarily adaptive social norms.

We begin by reviewing the evolutionary foundations of normative social behavior, surveying contemporary research and theory from evolutionary psychology to suggest that widely shared norms of social exchange are the product of evolutionarily adaptive cognitive mechanisms. We then review the biology, evolution, and ontogeny of the human PFC, and develop a cognitive neuroscience framework for goal-directed social behavior on the basis of evolutionarily adaptive social norms represented by the lateral PFC. We examine a broad range of evidence from the social and decision neuroscience literatures demonstrating that evolutionarily adaptive social norms of obligatory, prohibited, and permissible behavior are mediated by the lateral PFC. Accumulating evidence suggests that behavior-guiding principles for social inference are functionally organized along the dorso-ventral axis of the lateral PFC, whereby obligatory or prohibited action sequences recruit the ventrolateral PFC (vlPFC) (Fiddick et al., 2005; Berthoz et al., 2002; Rilling et al., 2008; Monti, Osherson, Martinez, & Parsons, 2007; Kroger, Nystrom, Cohen, & Johnson-Laird, 2008; Heckers, Zalesak, Weiss,

Ditman, & Titone, 2004; Goel, Buchel, Frith, & Dolan, 2000; Goel & Dolan, 2004; Noveck, Goel, & Smith, 2004) and permissible forms of behavior engage the dorsolateral PFC (dlPFC) (Buckholz et al., 2008; Greene et al., 2004; Weissman et al., 2008; Knoch, Pascual-Leone, Meyer, Treyer, & Fehr, 2006; Thomson, 1976; Volz, Schubotz, & von Cramon, 2004; Kroger et al., 2008). Adaptive behavior guided by both categories of inference recruits the anterolateral PFC (alPFC), which represents the highest level of a rostro-caudal hierarchy characterized by multiple forms of social exchange (Rolls et al., 1994; Bechara et al., 2000; LoPresti et al., 2008; Ruby & Decety, 2004; Badre, 2008; Botvinick, 2008; Koechlin & Summerfield, 2007; Christoff & Keramatian, 2007; Christoff et al., 2001; Christoff, Ream, Geddes, & Gabrieli, 2003; Smith, Keramatian, & Christoff, 2007). We illustrate how this framework supports the integration and synthesis of a diverse body of neuroscience evidence, and draw conclusions about the role of the lateral PFC in social cognition more broadly, contributing to social knowledge networks by representing widely shared norms of social behavior and providing the foundations for moral, ethical, and political systems of value and belief.

Evolutionary Foundations of Social Exchange

Social exchange is an essential aspect of life in all human cultures, promoting the survival of individuals who cooperate for mutual benefit—one providing a benefit to the other conditional on the recipient's providing a benefit in return. From our earliest ancestors to present day, social exchange has facilitated access to sustenance, protection, and mates, and enabled people to live healthier and longer lives (Cohen, 2004; Silk, Alberts, & Altmann, 2003). Social exchange interactions are therefore an important and recurrent human activity occurring over a sufficiently long time period for natural selection to have produced specialized cognitive and neural adaptations (Isaac, 1978; Brosnan & de Waal, 2003). Evolutionary psychologists have proposed that social exchange embodies cognitive mechanisms designed to promote the survival of our species, representing normative social behavior that develops in all healthy humans and is mediated by evolutionarily adaptive neural systems (Maynard Smith, 1982; Cosmides, 1985; 1989; Tooby & Cosmides, 1996; Cosmides & Tooby, 1989; 1992; 2005; Fiddick et al., 2000; Stone, Cosmides, Tooby,

Kroll, & Knight, 2002; Sugiyama, Tooby, & Cosmides, 2002; Trivers, 1971; Axelrod & Hamilton, 1981; Platt & Griggs, 1993; Gigerenzer & Hug, 1992).

An empirical case for this proposal has been established on the basis of behavioral and neuroscience research elucidating the role of evolutionary design features in shaping cognitive and neural mechanisms for social exchange (Cosmides, 1985; 1989; Tooby & Cosmides, 1996; Cosmides & Tooby, 1989; 1992; 2005; Fiddick et al., 2000; Stone et al., 2002; Sugiyama et al., 2002). Game-theoretic models predict that for social exchange to persist within a species, members of the species must detect cheaters (i.e., individuals who do not reciprocate) and direct future benefits to reciprocators rather than cheaters (Trivers, 1971; Axelrod & Hamilton, 1981). Accumulating evidence supports this proposal, demonstrating that the mind embodies functionally specialized cognitive mechanisms for detecting cheaters (Cosmides, 1985; 1989; Tooby & Cosmides, 1996; Cosmides & Tooby, 1989; 1992; 2005; Fiddick et al., 2000; Stone et al., 2002; Sugiyama et al., 2002) that operate according to behavior-guiding principles in the form of a conditional rule: If X provides a requested benefit to Y, then Y will provide a rationed benefit to X. A conditional rule expressing this kind of agreement to cooperate is referred to as a *social contract* and represents a normative standard for social behavior (e.g., the normative belief that mutual cooperation is obligatory and cheating prohibited).

A primary method for investigating conditional reasoning about social contracts is Wason's four-card selection task (Wason, 1966; 1983; Wason & Johnson-Laird, 1972). In the classic version of this task, participants are shown a set of four cards, placed on a table, each of which has a number on one side and a colored patch on the other. The visible faces of the cards show a 3, 8, red, and brown. Participants are then asked which card should be turned over to test the truth of the proposition that "If a card shows an even number on one face, then its opposite face shows a primary color (i.e., red, green, or blue)." Thus, participants in the Wason selection task are asked to identify possible violations of a conditional rule of the form "If P then Q." Conditional rules describing some state of the world using abstract or descriptive content typically elicit a correct response (P and *not-Q*) from only 5 to 30 percent of subjects tested. This finding has been observed even when the rules tested are familiar, or

when participants are taught logic or given incentives (Cosmides, 1985; 1989; Tooby & Cosmides, 1996; Cosmides & Tooby, 1989; 1992; 2005; Fiddick et al., 2000; Stone et al., 2002; Cheng & Holyoak, 1985). In contrast, 65 to 80 percent of participants generate correct responses when the conditional rule expresses a social contract and a violation represents cheating (Cosmides, 1985; 1989; Tooby & Cosmides, 1996; Cosmides & Tooby, 1989; 1992; 2005; Fiddick et al., 2000; Stone et al., 2002). This pattern of performance has been widely observed in industrialized nations (Cosmides, 1985; 1989; Tooby & Cosmides, 1996; Cosmides & Tooby, 1989; 1992; 2005; Fiddick et al., 2000; Stone et al., 2002) and has been found even among isolated, non-literate hunter-horticulturalists (Sugiyama et al., 2002). Cognitive experiments have demonstrated that this improved level of performance is sensitively regulated by the series of variables expected if this were a system optimally designed to reason about obligatory and prohibited forms of social behavior, rather than to support a broader class of inferences (Cosmides, 1985; 1989; Tooby & Cosmides, 1996; Cosmides & Tooby, 1989; 1992; 2005; Fiddick et al., 2000; Stone et al., 2002; Sugiyama et al., 2002; Gigerenzer & Hug, 1992; Cheng & Holyoak, 1985).

Social contracts therefore represent behavior-guiding principles for evolutionarily adaptive forms of social exchange and are critical for drawing inferences about necessary courses of action concerning socially obligatory or prohibited behavior. From an evolutionary perspective, normative standards for necessary forms of social exchange can be distinguished from a broader class of inferences concerning possible or permissible courses of action. Whereas social norms for necessary behavior are central for the organization of society, representing strictly enforced rules for cooperation, the division of labor, and the distribution of resources, social norms for permissible behavior are critical for achieving adaptive goals within society, representing non-punishable courses of action that enable individuals to explore opportunities for reward, formulate plans for achieving social goals, and gain access to available resources (Maynard Smith, 1982; Cosmides, 1985; 1989; Tooby & Cosmides, 1996; Cosmides & Tooby, 1989; 1992; 2005; Fiddick et al., 2000; Stone et al., 2002; Sugiyama et al., 2002; Trivers, 1971; Axelrod & Hamilton, 1981; Platt & Griggs, 1993; Gigerenzer & Hug, 1992; Krueger et al., in press; Krueger, Moll, Zahn,

Heinecke, & Grafman, 2007). Evolutionary adaptations for reasoning about necessary (obligatory or prohibited) versus possible (permissible) courses of action have therefore fundamentally shaped the architecture of the mind, producing functionally distinct cognitive and neural mechanisms for reasoning about necessary and possible states of affairs. While cognitive and neural mechanisms for these forms of inference emerged from goal-directed social behavior (Maynard Smith, 1982; Cosmides, 1985; 1989; Tooby & Cosmides, 1996; Cosmides & Tooby, 1989; 1992; 2005; Fiddick et al., 2000; Stone et al., 2002; Sugiyama et al., 2002; Trivers, 1971; Axelrod & Hamilton, 1981; Platt & Griggs, 1993; Gigerenzer & Hug, 1992), non-social inferences are also shaped by these systems, relying upon an evolutionarily adaptive neural architecture that distinguishes between these two fundamental classes of inference.

An Evolutionarily Adaptive Neural Architecture for Goal-directed Social Behavior

An emerging body of evidence suggests that goal-directed social behavior centrally depends on the PFC, which is particularly important for grouping specific experiences of our interactions with the environment along common themes, that is, as behavior-guiding principles. To this end, our brains have evolved mechanisms for detecting and storing complex relationships between situations, actions, and consequences. By gleaning this knowledge from past experiences, we can develop behavior-guiding principles that allow us to infer which goals are available in similar situations in the future and what actions are likely to bring us closer to them.

We propose that behavior-guiding principles for social inference take the form of evolutionarily adaptive social rules that, when activated, correspond to a dynamic brain state signified by the strength and pattern of neural activity in a local brain region. In this sense, over the course of evolution, the PFC became capable of supporting more complex behaviors. We have labeled these behavior-guiding principles for social inference *structured event complexes* (SECs, Barbey et al., in press; 2009).

An SEC is a goal-oriented set of events that is structured in sequence and represents thematic knowledge, morals, abstractions, concepts, social norms, event features, event boundaries, and grammars. Aspects of SECs are represented independently but are encoded and retrieved as an episode. SECs are encoded and activated on the basis of simulation

mechanisms (Barbey & Patterson, in press; Barbey & Barsalou, 2009; Barsalou, 2008; Barsalou, Niedenthal, Barbey, & Ruppert, 2003; Barsalou, Simmons, Barbey, & Wilson, 2003). It is widely known that experience in the physical and social world activates feature detectors in relevant features maps of the brain (for a review of feature maps in vision, see Zeki, 1993). When a pattern becomes active in a feature map during perception or action, conjunctive neurons in an association area capture the pattern for later cognitive use. Increasing evidence suggests that behavior-guiding principles for social inference are mediated by higher-order association areas localized within the lateral PFC (Figure 23.1).

Decades of neuroscience research have demonstrated that the lateral PFC is comprised of neurons that are exquisitely sensitive to behaviorally informative associations (for a review, see Miller, 2000). This work has focused on the lateral PFC because it represents a site of convergence of the information needed to synthesize multimodal information from a wide range of brain systems. The lateral PFC consists of three major subregions that each emphasize processing of particular information based on their interconnections with specific cortical regions (see Figure 23.2; for a review, see Miller, 2000). Ventrolateral areas are more heavily interconnected with cortical regions for processing information about visual form and stimulus identity (inferior temporal cortex), supporting the categorization of environmental stimuli in the service of goal-directed behavior. Dorsal portions of the lateral

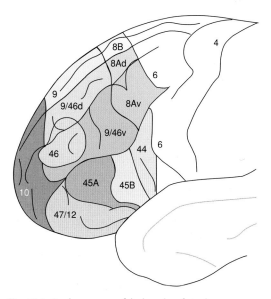

Fig. 23.1 Brodmann map of the lateral prefrontal cortex.
Reproduced with permission from Ramnani & Owen (2004).

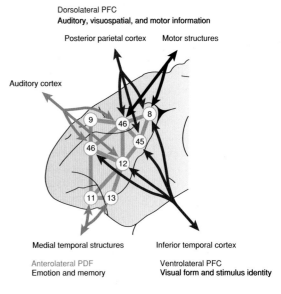

Fig. 23.2 Integrative anatomy of the macaque monkey prefrontal cortex. Numbers refer to subregions within the lateral prefrontal cortex defined by Brodmann. Adapted with permission from Miller (2000).

PFC are heavily interconnected with cortical areas for processing auditory, visuospatial, and motor information, enabling the regulation and control of responses to environmental stimuli. Finally, the anterolateral PFC is indirectly connected (via the ventromedial PFC) with limbic structures that process internal information, such as emotion, memory, and reward (Goldman-Rakic, 1987; Pandya & Barnes, 1987; Fuster, 1989; Barbas & Pandya, 1991. Together, lateral PFC subregions mediate essential elements of the external and internal environment, enabling goal-directed behavior.

Once feature maps within modality-specific regions are captured by a set of conjunctive neurons in the lateral PFC, the set can later activate the pattern in the absence of bottom-up stimulation, producing a simulation of the event sequence (Barbey & Barsalou, 2009; Barsalou, 2008; Barsalou, Niedenthal, et al., 2003; Barsalou, Simmons, et al., 2003). For example, on entering a familiar situation and recognizing it, a simulation that represents the situation becomes active. Typically, not all of the situation is perceived initially. A relevant person, setting, or event may be perceived, which then suggests that a particular situation is about to play out. The simulation can be viewed as a complex configuration of multimodal components that represent the situation (including agents, objects, actions, mental states, and background settings). Because part of this pattern matched the current situation initially, the larger pattern became active in memory. The remaining parts of the pattern—not yet observed in the situation—constitute inferences, namely predictions about what will occur next.

To the extent that the simulation is entrenched in memory, pattern completion is likely to occur automatically. As a situation is experienced repeatedly, its simulated components and the associations linking them increase in potency. Thus when one component is perceived initially, these strong associations complete the pattern automatically. Social norms of behavior represent deeply entrenched simulations, whose learned associations are the product of evolutionarily adaptive cognitive and neural mechanisms. For example, evolutionarily adaptive norms for social exchange concerning obligatory actions (i.e., reciprocal altruism) and prohibited behavior (i.e., cheating) derive from extensive experience spanning our evolutionary history and have therefore fundamentally shaped the cognitive and neural mechanisms that mediate social exchange. The observed role of simulation mechanisms for social inference in non-human primates supports this account (Gil-da-Costa et al., 2004), suggesting that modality-specific simulations represent continuity of social information processing across the species (Barsalou, 2005). According to this framework, social interactions initially match modality-specific representations in one or more simulations that have become entrenched in memory. Once one of these wins the activation process, it provides inferences via pattern completion (Anderson, 1995). Simulations representing necessary (obligatory or prohibited) courses of action motivate expectations concerning specific actions the perceiver and recipient "must" take, whereas simulations for possible (permissible) forms of behavior represent a broader range of outcomes, motivating expectations about courses of action the perceiver and recipient "may" take. The unfolding of inferences about necessary and possible states of affairs—realized as a simulation—represents behavior-guiding principles for the orchestration of social thought and action. The recruitment of specific lateral PFC subregions for social inference is determined by the evolution, development, hierarchical structure, and anatomical connectivity of the PFC.

Research investigating the evolution and ontogeny of the PFC suggests that the lateral PFC initially emerged from ventrolateral prefrontal regions, followed by dorsolateral, and then anterolateral cortices (Figure 23.3; Fuster, 1997; Flechsig, 1901; 1920). From an evolutionary perspective, the emergence of lateral PFC subregions reflects their relative priority for the formation of organized social groups, with the vlPFC signaling the onset of social norms for necessary (obligatory or prohibited) courses of action, providing the foundations for standards of conduct that are central for the organization of society. Social norms for permissible behavior later enabled the representation of a broader range of possible outcomes, supporting the assessment of alternative forms of goal-directed behavior within the

dlPFC. Finally, the evolution of the alPFC enabled processing of higher-order relations and reasoning about complex forms of social behavior involving necessary and possible courses of action. Consistent with its evolutionary development, the ontogeny of the lateral PFC reflects the importance of first representing social norms for necessary behavior (i.e., fundamental rules the child must obey), followed by an understanding of permissible courses of action (e.g., guided by judgments of equity and fairness), and finally higher-order inferences involving both forms of representation (Santrock, 2005).

An emerging body of evidence further demonstrates that the anterior-to-posterior axis of the lateral PFC is organized hierarchically, whereby progressively anterior subregions are associated with higher-order processing requirements for planning and the selection of action (for recent reviews, see Badre, 2008; Botvinick, 2008; Koechlin & Summerfield, 2007; Ramnani & Owen, 2004). Thus, processes within the lateral PFC respect the hierarchical organization of this region, with progressively anterior regions representing simulations that support higher-order inferences incorporating both necessary and possible states of affairs.

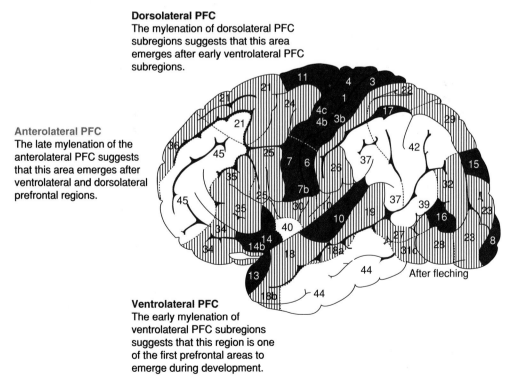

Dorsolateral PFC
The mylenation of dorsolateral PFC subregions suggests that this area emerges after early ventrolateral PFC subregions.

Anterolateral PFC
The late mylenation of the anterolateral PFC suggests that this area emerges after ventrolateral and dorsolateral prefrontal regions.

Ventrolateral PFC
The early mylenation of ventrolateral PFC subregions suggests that this region is one of the first prefrontal areas to emerge during development.

Fig. 23.3 Ontogenetic map of the prefrontal cortex according to Flechsig (1901; 1920). The numeration of the areas indicates the order of their myelination.
Modified with permission from Flechsig (1920).

The connectivity of lateral PFC subregions represents evolutionarily adaptive neural systems for goal-directed social behavior. From an evolutionary perspective, behavior requested by members of high social status represents necessary courses of action that a lower-ranking individual must follow. This provides one explanation for why neural systems for identifying the social status of individuals (based on representations of visual form and stimulus identity) are anatomically connected with ventrolateral prefrontal regions for drawing inferences about necessary courses of action. In contrast, social norms for possible (permissible) behavior are central for achieving adaptive goals within society (Maynard Smith, 1982; Cosmides, 1985; 1989; Tooby & Cosmides, 1996; Cosmides & Tooby, 1989; 1992; 2005; Fiddick et al., 2000; Stone et al., 2002; Sugiyama et al., 2002; Trivers, 1971; Axelrod & Hamilton, 1981; Platt & Griggs, 1993; Gigerenzer & Hug, 1992), providing one explanation for why dorsolateral prefrontal regions for drawing this type of inference are anatomically connected with brain regions for the regulation and control of behavior. Finally, adaptive behavior guided by both categories of inference draws upon higher-order representations that incorporate multiple forms of social exchange and therefore recruits regions of the anterolateral PFC that enable complex representations (e.g., incorporating emotion and memory).

Lateral Prefrontal Contributions to Goal-directed Social Behavior

We review emerging evidence from the social and decision neuroscience literatures demonstrating (1) the involvement of the vlPFC when reasoning about necessary (obligatory or prohibited) courses of action, (2) the recruitment of the dlPFC for drawing inferences about possible (permissible) states of affairs, and (3) activation in the alPFC for higher-order inferences that incorporate both categories of knowledge (Figure 23.4). The simulation architecture underlying these forms of inference further predicts the recruitment of broadly distributed neural systems, incorporating medial prefrontal and posterior knowledge networks representing modality-specific components of experience.

Ventrolateral Prefrontal Cortex

An increasing number of social neuroscience studies have shown that social norms for necessary (obligatory or prohibited) courses of action are represented by the vlPFC (areas 44, 45, and 47; Figure 23.4b). Fiddick et al. (2005) observed activity

within the bilateral vlPFC (area 47) for social exchange reasoning, employing stimuli consisting primarily of social norms for obligatory and prohibited courses of action. Converging evidence is provided by Berthoz et al. (2002), who demonstrated recruitment of the left vlPFC (area 47) when participants detected violations of social norms stories representing obligatory and prohibited courses of action (e.g., the decision to "spit out food made by the host"). Similarly, Rilling et al. (2008) reported activation within the left vlPFC (area 47) when participants detected the violation of obligatory and prohibited norms of social exchange in a Prisoner's dilemma game (i.e., the failure to cooperate).

The decision neuroscience literature further supports this framework, demonstrating the involvement of the vlPFC when drawing conclusions that necessarily follow from the truth of the premises, that is, for *deductive inference*. Although wide consensus in the literature has not yet been reached, an increasing number of studies report consistent findings when common sources of variability are controlled (regarding the linguistic content, linguistic complexity, and deductive complexity of reasoning problems). A recent series of experiments by Monti et al. (2007) controlled for these sources of variability and provided evidence that the left vlPFC (area 47) mediates representations of the logical structure of a deductive argument (e.g., If P or Q, then *Not-R*/*P*/Therefore, *Not-R*), supporting the representation of behavior-guiding principles for necessary forms of behavior within this region. Furthermore, a recent study by Kroger et al. (2008) controlled for the complexity and type of calculations that were performed and also observed activation within the left vlPFC (areas 44 and 45) for deductive reasoning (see also Heckers et al., 2004). Converging evidence is provided by Goel and colleagues (Goel et al., 2000; Goel & Dolan, 2004), who have consistently observed activation within the left vlPFC (areas 44 and 45) for deductive conclusions drawn from categorical syllogisms (e.g., All humans are mortal/Some animals are human/Therefore, some animals are mortal). Finally, Noveck et al. (2004) demonstrated recruitment of the left vlPFC (area 47) for drawing deductive conclusions from conditional statements (e.g., If P then Q/P/Therefore, Q), consistent with the role of this region for representing behavior-guiding principles in the form of a conditional.

Dorsolateral Prefrontal Cortex

Accumulating evidence demonstrates that the dlPFC (areas 46 and 9) represents behavior-guiding

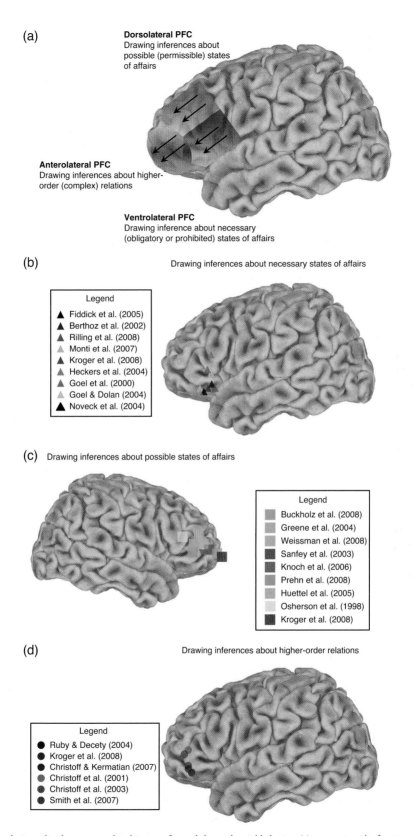

Fig. 23.4 An evolutionarily adaptive neural architecture for goal-directed social behavior. (a) summarizes the functional organization of the lateral PFC, and (b), (c) and (d) illustrate supportive evidence.

principles for evaluating the permissibility or fairness of observed behavior (Figure 23.4c). An early study by Sanfey et al. (2003) reported activity within the right dlPFC (area 46) when participants evaluated the fairness of an offer in an ultimatum game. Knoch et al. (2006) further demonstrated that deactivating this region with repetitive transcranial magnetic stimulation reduced participants' ability to reject unfair offers in the ultimatum game, suggesting that the dlPFC is central for guiding behavior based on evaluations of fairness and permissibility. Converging evidence is provided by Buckholtz et al. (2008), who observed activity within the right dlPFC (area 46) when participants assigned responsibility for crimes and made judgments about appropriate (e.g., equitable or fair) forms of punishment in a legal decision-making task. The work of Greene et al. (2004) further suggests that this region is involved in normative evaluations involving conflicting moral goals. These authors employed moral scenarios similar to the famous trolley problem (Thomson, 1976) and assessed trials in which participants acted in the interest of greater aggregate welfare at the expense of personal moral standards. This contrast revealed reliable activation within the right dlPFC (area 46), suggesting that this region is critical for evaluating the permissibility or fairness of behaviors that conflict with personal moral standards (for additional evidence, see Weissman et al., 2008; Prehn et al., 2008).

Further evidence to support this framework derives from the decision neuroscience literature, which demonstrates the involvement of the dlPFC when drawing conclusions about possible or permissible states of affairs. In contrast to deductive inference, conclusions about possible courses of action reflect uncertainty concerning the actions that "should" be taken and/or the consequences that "might" follow, and are referred to as *inductive inferences*. Volz et al. (2004) found that activation within the right dlPFC (area 9) increased parametrically with the degree of uncertainty held by the participant (see also, Huettel, Song, & McCarthy, 2005). Furthermore, Osherson et al. (1998) observed preferential recruitment of the right dlPFC (area 46) when performance on an inductive reasoning task was directly compared to a matched deductive inference task, supporting the role of this region for reasoning about possible (rather than necessary) states of affairs.

Anterolateral Prefrontal Cortex

A large body of social neuroscience evidence demonstrates that the alPFC (areas 10 and 11)—and the orbitofrontal cortex (OFC) more broadly—is central for social cognition (Figure 23.4d). Studies of patients with lesions confined to the OFC have reported impairments in a wide range of social functions, including the regulation and control of social responses, the perception and integration of social cues, and perspective taking (Rolls et al., 1994; Bechara et al., 2000; LoPresti et al., 2008; Ruby & Decety, 2004). Recent evidence from Stone et al. (2002) further demonstrates that patients with orbitofrontal damage produced selective impairments in reasoning about social contracts, supporting the proposed role of the PFC in social exchange. Bechara et al. (2000) observed profound deficits in the ability of orbitofrontal patients to represent and integrate social and emotional knowledge in the service of decision making. Converging evidence is provided by LoPresti et al. (2008), who demonstrated that the left alPFC (area 11) mediates the integration of multiple social cues (i.e., emotional expression and personal identity), further suggesting that this region supports the integration of multiple classes of social knowledge. Further fMRI evidence was provided by Moll et al. (2006) who reported bilateral recruitment of the OFC (area 11) during a social decision-making task when participants had to evaluate the social contributions of a charitable organization and chose not to make a donation.

Additional support derives from the decision neuroscience literature, which demonstrates that progressively anterior subregions of the lateral PFC (areas 10 and 11) are associated with higher-order processing requirements for thought and action (Barbey, Koenigs, & Grafman, in press; Badre, 2008; Botvinick, 2008; Koechlin & Summerfield, 2007). Ramnani and Owen (2004) reviewed contemporary research and theory investigating the cognitive functions of the alPFC, concluding that this region is central for integrating the outcomes of multiple cognitive operations, consistent with the predicted role of the alPFC for representing higher-order inferences that incorporate both necessary and possible states of affairs (for representative findings, see Kroger et al., 2008; Christoff & Kermatian, 2007; Christoff et al., 2001; 2003; Smith et al., 2007).

Conclusion

We have reviewed converging lines of evidence to support an evolutionarily adaptive neural architecture for goal-directed social behavior within the lateral PFC, drawing upon recent theoretical developments in evolutionary psychology and emerging neuroscience evidence investigating the biology, evolution, ontogeny, and cognitive functions of this region. We have surveyed a broad range of social and decision neuroscience evidence demonstrating that the lateral PFC mediates behavior-guiding principles for specific classes of inference, with the vlPFC recruited when drawing inferences about necessary (obligatory or prohibited) courses of action, engagement of the dlPFC when reasoning about possible (permissible) behavior, and the alPFC recruited when both categories of inference are utilized (Figure 23.4a).

The reviewed findings elucidate the involvement of the lateral PFC in normative dimensions of social interactions and raise questions for future and emerging programs of neuroscience research. One challenge that awaits future research is to address how behavior-guiding principles for necessary (obligatory and prohibited) and possible (permissible) behavior are represented within dual-process theories that distinguish between automatic versus controlled cognitive processes (Lieberman, 2007; Barbey & Sloman, 2007). Future research should further investigate the cognitive operations that are performed within the lateral PFC to support human inference. Does this region (i) contain mechanisms that control the recruitment of representations stored in posterior cortices (Miller, 2000), (ii) serve as an integrative hub for synthesizing modality-specific representations (Pessoa, 2008), or (iii) store unique forms of knowledge (Wood & Grafman, 2003)? Future research should also address the biological, developmental, and evolutionary principles that account for the observed lateralization of behavior-guiding principles for necessary (left hemispheric) versus possible (right hemispheric) courses of action (Figure 23.4). The proposed evolutionary origins and biological basis of behavior-guiding principles for thought and action motivate the question of whether normative standards for human rationality should be constructed from formal mathematical and logical systems, or instead assessed in terms of the evolutionary conditions and ecological contexts that have shaped the development of the human mind (Maynard Smith, 1982; Cosmides, 1985; 1989; Tooby & Cosmides, 1996; Cosmides & Tooby, 1989; 1992; 2005; Fiddick et al., 2000; Stone et al., 2002; Sugiyama et al., 2002; Trivers, 1971; Axelrod & Hamilton, 1981; Platt & Griggs, 1993; Gigerenzer & Hug, 1992). Finally, future research should investigate the role of the lateral PFC in the formation of human belief systems, which structure and organize our understanding of the social world. From evolutionarily adaptive social norms represented within the lateral PFC, belief systems for moral (Moll et al., 2005; Kapogiannis et al., 2009), ethical, and political (Zamboni et al., in press) thought are constructed. By investigating the origins of this knowledge—assessing the formation of normative principles for goal-directed behavior, and their expression in moral, ethical, and political thought—the burgeoning field of social cognitive neuroscience will continue to advance our understanding of the remarkable cognitive and neural architecture from which uniquely human systems of value and belief emerge.

Acknowledgments

The authors are supported by the Intramural Research Program of the National Institute of Neurological Disorders and Stroke. Preparation of this manuscript was based on and adapted from research investigating the role of the prefrontal cortex in goal-directed social behavior (Barbey et al., in press; Barbey et al., 2009).

References

Amodio, D. M. & Frith, C. D. (2006). Meeting of minds: The medial frontal cortex and social cognition. *Nature Reviews Neuroscience, 7,* 268–277.

Anderson, J. A. (1995). *An introduction to neural networks.* Cambridge, MA: MIT Press.

Axelrod, R. & Hamilton, W. D. (1981). The evolution of cooperation. *Science, 211,* 1390–1396.

Badre, D. (2008). Cognitive control, hierarchy, and the rostro-caudal organization of the frontal lobes. *Trends in Cognitive Sciences, 12,* 193–200.

Barbas, H. & Pandya, D. (1991). Patterns of connections of the prefrontal cortex in the rhesus monkey associated with cortical architecture. In H. S. *Levin,* H. M. *Eisenberg* & A. L. *Benton* (Eds.). *Frontal lobe function and dysfunction* (pp. 35–58). New York: Oxford University Press.

Barbey, A. K., Koenigs, M., & Grafman, J. (in press). Orbitofrontal contributions to human working memory. *Cerebral Cortex.*

Barbey, A. K. & Patterson, R. (in press). Neural architecture of explanatory inference in the prefrontal cortex. *Frontiers in Cognitive Science.*

Barbey, A. K. & Barsalou, L. W. (2009). Reasoning and problem solving: Models. In L. Squire, T. Albright, F. Bloom, F. Gage & N. Spitzer (Eds.), *Encyclopedia of neuroscience* (pp. 35–43). Oxford: Academic Press.

Barbey, A. K. & Sloman, S. A. (2007). Base-rate respect: From ecological rationality to dual processes. *Behavioral and Brain Sciences, 30,* 241–297.

Barbey, A. K., Krueger, F., & Grafman, J. (in press). An evolutionarily adaptive neural architecture for goal-directed social behavior. *Trends in Neurosciences.*

Barbey, A. K., Krueger, F., & Grafman, J. (2009). Structured event complexes in the medial prefrontal cortex support counterfactual representations for future planning. *Transactions of the Royal Society: Biological Sciences.*

Barsalou, L. W. (2005). Continuity of the conceptual system across species. *Trends in Cognitive Sciences, 9,* 309–311.

Barsalou, L. W. (2008). Grounded cognition. *Annual Review of Psychology, 59*, 617–645.

Barsalou, L. W., Niedenthal, P. M., Barbey, A. K., & Ruppert, J. (2003). Social embodiment. In B. Ross (Ed.), *The psychology of learning and motivation* (pp. 43–91). San Diego: Academic Press.

Barsalou, L. W., Simmons, W. K., Barbey, A. K., & Wilson, C. D. (2003). Grounding conceptual knowledge in modality-specific systems. *Trends in Cognitive Sciences, 7*, 84–91.

Bechara, A., Damasio, H., & Damasio, A. (2000). Emotion, decision making, and the orbitofrontal cortex. *Cerebral Cortex, 10*, 1047–3211.

Bechara A., Damasio, A. R., Damasio, H., & Anderson, S. W. (1994). Insensitivity to future consequences following damage to human prefrontal cortex. *Cognition, 50*, 7–15.

Berthoz, S., Armony, J. L., Blair, R. J. R. & Dolan, R. J. (2002). An fMRI study of intentional and unintentional (embarrassing) violations of social norms. *Brain, 125*, 1696–1708.

Botvinick, M. M. (2008). Hierarchical models of behavior and prefrontal function. *Trends in Cognitive Sciences, 12*, 201–208.

Brosnan, S. F. & de Waal, F. B. M. (2003). Monkeys reject unequal pay. *Nature, 425*, 297–299.

Buckholtz, J. W., Asplund, C. L., Dux, P. E., Zald, D. H., Gore, J. C., Jones, O. D., et al. (2008). The neural correlates of third-party punishment. *Neuron, 60*, 930–940.

Cacioppo, J. T., Berntson, G. G., Adolphs, R., Carter, C. S., Davidson, R. J., McClintock, M. K., et al. (2002). (Eds.). *Foundations in social neuroscience.* Cambridge, MA: MIT Press.

Cheng, P. & Holyoak, K. (1985). Pragmatic reasoning schemas. *Cognitive Psychology, 17*, 391–416.

Christoff, K. & Keramatian, K. (2007). Abstraction of mental representations: Theoretical considerations and neuroscientific evidence. In: S. A. Bunge & J. D. Wallis, (Eds.), *The neuroscience of rule-guided behavior.* Oxford: Oxford University Press.

Christoff, K., Prabhakaran, V., Dorfman, J., Zhao, Z., Kroger, J. K., Holyoak, K. J., et al. (2001). Rostrolateral prefrontal cortex involvement in relational integration during reasoning. *NeuroImage, 14*, 1136–1149.

Christoff, K., Ream, J. M., Geddes, L. P. T., & Gabrieli, J. D. E. (2003). Evaluating self-generated information: Anterior prefrontal contributions to human cognition. *Behavioral Neuroscience, 117*, 1161–1168.

Cohen, S. (2004). Social relationships and health. *American Psychologist, 59*, 676–684.

Cosmides, L. (1985). *Deduction or Darwinian algorithms? An explanation of the "elusive" content effect on the Wason selection task.* Doctoral dissertation, Department of Psychology, Harvard University.

Cosmides, L. (1989). The logic of social exchange: Has natural selection shaped how humans reason? Studies with the Wason selection task. *Cognition, 31*, 187–276.

Cosmides, L. & Tooby, J. (1989). Evolutionary psychology and the generation of culture: Part II. Case study: A computational theory of social exchange. *Ethology and Sociobiology, 10*, 51–97.

Cosmides, L. & Tooby, J. (1992). Cognitive adaptations for social exchange. In J. Barkow, L. Cosmides & J. Tooby (Eds.), *The adapted mind* (pp. 163–228). New York: Oxford University Press.

Cosmides, L. & Tooby, J. (2005). Social exchange: The evolutionary design of a neurocognitive system. In M. S. Gazzaniga (Ed.), *The new cognitive neurosciences, III.* Cambridge, MA: MIT Press.

Damasio, A. R., Tranel, D., & Damasio, H. (1990). Individuals with sociopathic behavior caused by frontal damage fail to respond autonomically to social stimuli. *Behavioral Brain Research, 41*, 81–94.

Fiddick, L., Cosmides, L., & Tooby, J. (2000). No interpretation without representation: The role of domain-specific representations and inferences in the Wason selection task. *Cognition, 77*, 1–79.

Fiddick, L., Spampinato, M. V., & Grafman, J. (2005). Social contracts and precautions activate different neurological systems: An fMRI investigation of deontic reasoning, *NeuroImage, 28*, 778–786.

Flechsig, P. (1901). Developmental (myelogenetic) localisation of the cerebral cortex in the human subject. *Lancet, 2*, 1027–1029.

Flechsig, P. (1920). *Anatomie des Menschlichen Gehirnsund Ruckenmarks auf Myelogenetischer Grundlage.* Leipzig: Thieme. New York: Basic Books.

Fuster, J. M. (1989). *The prefrontal cortex.* New York: Raven.

Fuster, J. M. (1997). *The prefrontal cortex—Anatomy physiology, and neuropsychology of the frontal lobe.* Philadelphia: Lippincott-Raven.

Gil da Costa, R., Braun, A., Lopes, M., Hauser, M. D., Carson, R. E., Herscovitch, P., et al. (2004) Toward an evolutionary perspective on conceptual representation: Species-specific calls activate visual and affective processing systems. *Proceedings of the National Academy of Sciences, USA, 101*, 17516–17521.

Gigerenzer, G. & Hug, K. (1992). Domain specific reasoning: Social contracts, cheating, and perspective change. *Cognition, 43*, 127–171.

Goel, V. & Dolan, R. J. (2004). Differential involvement of left prefrontal cortex in inductive and deductive reasoning. *Cognition, 93*, B109–B121.

Goel, V., Buchel, C., Frith, C., & Dolan, R. (2000). Dissociation of mechanisms underlying syllogistic reasoning. *NeuroImage, 12*, 504–514.

Goldman-Rakic, P. S. (1987). Circuitry of primate prefrontal cortex and regulation of behavior by representational memory. In F. Plum (Ed.). *Handbook of physiology: The nervous system* (pp. 373–417). Bethesda, MD: American Physiology Society.

Greene, J. D., Nystrom, L. E., Engell, A. D., Darley, J. M., & Cohen, J. D. (2004). The neural bases of cognitive conflict and control in moral judgment. *Neuron, 44*, 389–400.

Heckers, S., Zalesak, M., Weiss, A. P., Ditman, T., & Titone, D. (2004). Hippocampal activation during transitive inference in humans. *Hippocampus, 14*, 153–162.

Huettel, S. A., Song, A. W., & McCarthy, G. (2005). Decisions under uncertainty: Probabilistic context influences activation of prefrontal and parietal cortices. *The Journal of Neuroscience, 25*, 3304–3311.

Isaac, G. (1978). The food-sharing behavior of proto human hominids. *Scientific American, 238*, 90–108.

Kapogiannis, D., Barbey, A. K., Su, M., Zamboni, G., Krueger, F., & Grafman, J. (2009). Cognitive and neural foundations of religious belief. *Proceedings of the National Academy of Sciences of the USA, 106*, 4876–4881.

Knoch, D., Pascual-Leone, A., Meyer, K., Treyer, V., & Fehr, E. (2006). Diminishing reciprocal fairness by disrupting the right prefrontal cortex. *Science, 314*, 829–832.

Koechlin, E. & Summerfield, C. (2007). An information theoretical approach to prefrontal executive function. *Trends in Cognitive Science, 11*, 229–235.

Kroger, J. K., Nystrom, L. E., Cohen, J. D., & Johnson-Laird, P. N. (2008). Distinct neural substrates for deductive and mathematical processing. *Brain Research, 1243*, 86–103.

Krueger, F., Spampinato, M., Barbey, A. K., Huey, T., Morland, T., & Grafman, J. (in press). The role of the frontopolar cortex and inferior parietal cortex in mediating action complexity and duration: A parametric fMRI study. *Neuroreport.*

Krueger F., Barbey A. K., & Grafman, J. (2009). The medial prefrontal cortex mediates social event knowledge. *Trends in Cognitive Sciences, 13*, 103–109.

Krueger, F., Moll, J., Zahn, R., Heinecke, A., & Grafman, J. (2007). Event frequency modulates the processing of daily life activities in human medial prefrontal cortex. *Cerebral Cortex, 17*, 2346–2353.

Lieberman, M. D. (2007). Social cognitive neuroscience: A review of core processes. *Annual Review of Psychology, 58*, 259–289.

LoPresti, M. L., Schon, K., Tricarico, M. D., Swisher, J. D., Celone, K. A., & Stern, C. E. (2008). Working memory for social cues recruits orbitofrontal cortex and amygdala: A functional magnetic resonance imaging study of delayed matching to sample for emotional expressions. *Journal of Neuroscience, 28*, 3718–3728.

Maynard Smith, J. (1982). *Evolution and the theory of games.* Cambridge, England: Cambridge University Press.

Miller, E. K. (2000). The prefrontal cortex and cognitive control. *Nature Reviews Neuroscience, 1*, 59–65.

Moll, J., Zahn, R., de Oliveira-Souza, R., Krueger, F., & Grafman, J. (2005). The neural basis of human moral cognition. *Nature Reviews Neuroscience, 6*, 799–809.

Moll, J., Krueger, F., Zahn, R., Pardini, M., de Oliveira-Souza, R., & Grafman, J. (2006). Human fronto-mesolimbic networks guide decisions about charitable donation. *Proceedings of the National Academy of Sciences, 103*, 15623–15628.

Monti, M. M., Osherson, D. N., Martinez, M. J., & Parsons, L. M. (2007). Functional neuroanatomy of deductive inference: A language-independent distributed network. *NeuroImage, 37*, 1005–1016.

Nowak, M. A. (2006). Five rules for the evolution of cooperation. *Science, 314*, 1560–1563.

Noveck, I. A., Goel, V., & Smith, K. W. (2004). The neural basis of conditional reasoning with arbitrary content. *Cortex, 40*, 613–622.

Osherson, D. N., Perani, D., Cappa, S., Schnur, T., Grassi, F., & Fazio, F. (1998). Distinct brain loci in deductive versus probabilistic reasoning. *Neuropsychologia, 36*, 369–376.

Pandya, D. N. & Barnes, C. L. (1987). Architecture and connections of the frontal lobe. In E. Perecman (Ed.). *The frontal lobes revisited* (pp. 41–72). New York: The IRBN Press.

Pessoa, L. (2008). On the relationship between emotion and cognition. *Nature Reviews Neuroscience, 9*, 148–158.

Platt, R. & Griggs, R. (1993). Darwinian algorithms and the Wason selection task: A factorial analysis of social contract selection task problems. *Cognition, 48*, 163–192.

Prehn, K., Wartenburger, I., Meriau, K., Scheibe, C., Goodenough, O. R., Villringer, A., et al. (2008). Individual differences in moral judgment competence influence neural correlates of socio-normative judgments. *Social Cognitive and Affective Neuroscience, 3*, 33–46.

Ramnani, N. & Owen, A. M. (2004). Anterior prefrontal cortex: Insights into function from anatomy and neuroimaging. *Nature Reviews Neuroscience, 5*, 184–194.

Rilling, J. K., Goldsmith, D. R., Glenn, A. L., Jairam, M. R., Elfenbein, H. A., Dagenais, J. E., et al. (2008). The neural correlates of the affective response to unreciprocated cooperation. *Neuropsychologia, 465*, 1256–1266.

Rolls, E. T., Hornak, J., Wade, D., & McGrath, J. (1994). Emotion-related learning in patients with social and emotional changes associated with frontal lobe damage. *Journal of Neurology, Neurosurgery, and Psychiatry, 57*, 1518–1524.

Ruby, P. & Decety, J. (2004). How would you feel versus how do you think she would feel? A neuroimaging study of perspective-taking with social emotions. *Journal of Neuroscience, 16*, 988–999.

Sanfey, A. G., Rilling, J. K., Aronson, J. A., Nystrom, L. E., & Cohen, J. D. (2003). The neural basis of decision making in the ultimatum game. *Science, 300*, 1755–1758.

Santrock, J. W. (2005). *Children* (8th Ed.). New York: McGraw-Hill.

Silk, J. B., Alberts, S. C. & Altmann, J. (2003). Social bonds of female baboons enhance infant survival. *Science, 302*, 1231–1234.

Smith, R., Keramatian, K., & Christoff, K. (2007). Localizing the rostrolateral prefrontal cortex at the individual level. *NeuroImage, 36*, 1387–1396.

Stone, V., Cosmides, L., Tooby, J., Kroll, N., & Knight, R. (2002). Selective impairment of reasoning about social exchange in a patient with bilateral limbic system damage. *Proceedings of the National Academy of Sciences, 99*(17), 11531–11536.

Sugiyama, L., Tooby, J., & Cosmides, L. (2002). Cross-cultural evidence of cognitive adaptations for social exchange among the Shiwiar of Ecuadorian Amazonia. *Proceedings of the National Academy of Sciences, 99*(17), 11537–11542.

Thomson, J. J. (1976). Killing, letting die, and the trolley problem. *Monist, 59*, 204–217.

Tooby, J. & Cosmides, L. (1996). Friendship and the banker's paradox: Other pathways to the evolution of adaptations for altruism. In W. G. Runciman, J. Maynard Smith, & R. I. M. Dunbar (Eds.), Evolution of social behaviour patterns in primates and man. *Proceedings of the British Academy, 88*, 119–143.

Trivers, R. (1971). The evolution of reciprocal altruism. *Quarterly Review of Biology, 46*, 35–57.

Volz, K. G., Schubotz, R. I., & von Cramon, Y. (2004). Why am I unsure? Internal and external attributions of uncertainty dissociated by fMRI. *NeuroImage, 21*, 848–857.

Wason, P. (1966). Reasoning. In B. M. Foss (Ed.), *New horizons in psychology* (pp. 135–151). Harmondsworth, England: Penguin.

Wason, P. (1983). Realism and rationality in the selection task. In J. St. B. T. Evans (Ed.), *Thinking and reasoning: Psychological approaches* (pp. 44–75). London: Routledge.

Wason, P. & Johnson-Laird, P. (1972). *The psychology of reasoning: Structure and content.* Cambridge, MA: Harvard University Press.

Weissman, D. H., Perkins, A. S. & Woldorff, M. G. (2008). Cognitive control in social situations: A role for the dorsolateral prefrontal cortex. *NeuroImage, 40*, 955–962.

Wood, J. & Grafman, J. (2003). Human prefrontal cortex: Processing and representational perspective. *Nature Reviews Neuroscience, 4*, 139–147.

Zamboni, G., Gozzi, M., Krueger, F., Duhamel, J., Sirigu, A., & Grafman, J. (in press). Individualism, conservatism, and radicalism as criteria for processing political beliefs: A parametric fMRI study. *Social Neuroscience.*

Zeki, S. (1993). *A vision of the brain.* Cambridge, MA: Blackwell Scientific Publications.

Staying in Control: The Neural Basis of Self-Regulation and Its Failure

Dylan D. Wagner, Kathryn E. Demos, *and* Todd F. Heatherton

Abstract

This chapter focuses on the brain systems that underlie both successful and unsuccessful attempts at regulating thoughts, behaviors, desires, and emotions. The prefrontal cortex (PFC) has been theorized to participate in a host of regulatory activities such as top-down processing and executive function. Here, the concern primarily is with its role in self-regulation; that is in controlling social behavior, thoughts, emotions, and in curtailing desires and cravings.

Keywords: self-regulation, emotion regulation, thought suppression, executive function, cognitive control, self, prefrontal cortex, anterior cingulate cortex, neuropsychology

We cannot change habit directly: that notion is magic. But we can change it by modifying conditions, by an intelligent selecting and weighting of the objects which engage attention and which influence the fulfillment of desires. (Dewey, 1922)

Compared to every other species, humans are extraordinarily adept at controlling their thoughts, behaviors, and desires. They don't steal, lie, cheat, or hurt others nearly as much as they could were every impulse left unchecked. That society isn't currently in a state of complete pandemonium is a testament to the importance of self-regulation in maintaining social harmony. Because people are a fundamentally social species, incapable of caring for themselves well into the first decade of life (Gould, 1977; Krogman, 1977), survival has long depended on living in groups. Failing to control impulses that could otherwise disrupt group cohesion (e.g., theft or violence) can lead to group exclusion, which would spell certain death for a social animal (Heatherton &

Vohs, 1998). Thus, the regulation of social behavior is central to our survival and humans undoubtedly evolved brain mechanisms which keep in check acts which could damage their positions in the group.

The central focus of this chapter is on the brain systems that underlie both successful—and unsuccessful—attempts at regulating thoughts, behaviors, desires, and emotions (for a more in-depth examination of emotion regulation we refer the reader to the chapter by Ochsner et al., this volume). The prefrontal cortex (PFC) has been theorized to participate in a host of regulatory activities such as top-down processing (Curtis & D'Esposito, 2003) and executive function (Goldberg, 2001; Miller & Cohen, 2001). Here, the concern primarily is with its role in self-regulation; that is, in controlling social behavior, thoughts, emotions, and in curtailing desires and cravings. This is related to, but distinct from, more general theories of executive function and cognitive control related to response selection, suppression, and conflict detection— abilities thought to be critical for the performance of cognitive tests such as the well known Stroop task or the Wisconsin Card Sorting Task.

Recent years have seen a wealth of new developments in research on the neural basis of self-regulation and cognitive control. These new findings highlight the importance of the prefrontal cortex in the regulation of all aspects of thought and behavior, from lower-order appetitive processes (e.g., food cravings, addictions), to thoughts, emotions, and complex social behaviors.

Frontal Damage and Dysregulation of Behavior

Much of what is known about the role of the prefrontal cortex (PFC) in the initiation and regulation of behavior comes from neuropsychological case studies made over the latter part of the 19th century and up until the present day. While the symptoms of various forms of PFC damage were generally clustered together under the rubric of "prefrontal syndrome," as neurological and neuropsychological techniques improved, it became clear that knowing the precise site of prefrontal damage could explain the different classes of symptoms exhibited by patients with PFC injury. We now understand there to be three regions of the PFC important to self-regulation: the ventromedial PFC (VMPFC), the lateral PFC (ventral and dorsal convexities), and the anterior cingulate cortex (ACC) (Figure 24.1).

Ventromedial PFC Damage

Despite centuries of scattered reports of behavioral changes following damage to the PFC (Lanfranchi, 1315; Platter, 1614) it wasn't until late in the 19th century that the importance of this region to higher cognition and self-control became widely accepted. While the 19th century saw sensory and motor regions being mapped with some accuracy (Ferrier, 1876), the function of the most anterior regions of the prefrontal cortex remained a mystery. The lack of any conclusive deficit following damage to this region led some to call the PFC a "silent area" with no apparent cognitive function. Nevertheless, by the mid 19th century a critical mass of reports on the cognitive and behavioral sequelae of PFC damage led neurologists of the time to the view that the PFC was the seat of higher cognition and self-control.

Perhaps the most dramatic of these early cases is that of Phineas Gage, a twenty-five year-old railroad foreman from Lebanon, New Hampshire who suffered extensive damage to the PFC when a blast charge he was preparing accidentally ignited and propelled his tamping iron—an iron bar roughly one meter long and 3.2 inches in diameter that was used to prepare explosive charges—through his left cheekbone, damaging the left VMPFC and possibly a portion of the ACC (Damasio, Grabowski, Frank, Galaburda, & Damasio, 1994; Harlow, 1848). Physicians of the period were initially incredulous at the possibility that anyone could sustain such

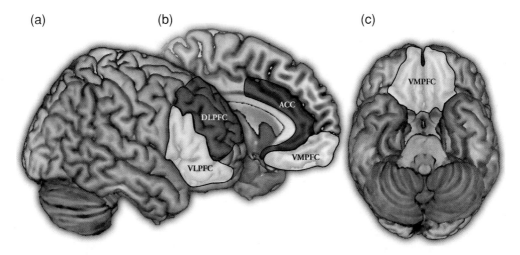

Fig. 24.1 A diagram illustrating the regions important for self-regulation. (a) The dorsolateral and ventrolateral convexities of the lateral prefrontal cortex comprising Brodmann areas 8, 9 and 46 (DLPFC) and 44, 45 and 47 (VLPFC). (b) The anterior cingulate cortex (ACC) comprising Brodmann areas 24, 25 and 32, and the medial portion of the ventromedial prefrontal cortex (VMPFC) consisting of Brodmann areas 11, 12, 25 and the ventral portions of area 10 and 32. (c) The ventral aspect of the VMPFC, comprising the medial portions of Brodmann areas 11, 12 and 25.

a massive trauma to the brain and survive. In Gage's case this was particularly remarkable as not only did he survive the initial injury but he remained fully conscious and lucid. Notwithstanding the large hole atop his head, Gage seemed otherwise unaffected by the blast, conversing casually with both his workers and his physician, John Harlow (Macmillan, 2000). Gage's recovery was complicated by the onset of a serious infection which lasted for 19 days, after which Gage slowly regained his physical strength and was pronounced fully recovered by Harlow some four months later. Following this extraordinary accident, remarkable changes in Gage's personality and behavior were noted. Formerly thought of as honest, reliable, and deliberate (Harlow, 1868), Gage was afterwards described as "gross, profane, coarse, and vulgar, to such a degree that his society was intolerable to decent people" (Anonymous, 1851; attributed to Harlow, see Macmillan, 2000). Had its importance been immediately recognized, the case of Phineas Gage could have been a watershed moment for understanding the importance of the PFC in the regulation of behavior. However, it wasn't until 1878, 17 years after Gage's death and 10 years after Harlow's final definitive report on the psychological changes wrought by Gage's injury (Harlow, 1868), that the neurologist David Ferrier rescued Gage from certain obscurity by making his case the centerpiece of his Goulstonian lecture on cerebral localization given at the Royal College of Physicians in London (Ferrier, 1878).

At the end of the 19th century other cases of dysregulated behavior following PFC damage began to emerge, one of the most notable being a case described by Leonore Welt in 1888 of a patient who survived a severe a brain injury following a fall from a fourth story window. Much like the case of Phineas Gage, the patient developed a marked change in personality and character in the absence of any identifiable intellectual deficit. Following the accident, the patient became a malicious practical joker who was aggressive towards other patients and hospital staff and repeatedly threatened his physicians (Welt, 1888). This particular case is more illuminating than that of Phineas Gage for two reasons. First, it is unmarred by any complications during convalescence—the patient's recovery was swift and uneventful. Second, unlike Gage, the patient's brain was able to be studied shortly after the injury when the patient succumbed to an unrelated infection some months after the accident. Post-mortem examination revealed extensive damage to the right VMPFC along with complete bilateral destruction of the gyrus rectus. In a review of the few extant cases of sudden personality change following PFC injury, Welt noted that common to all cases was damage to the VMPFC (Welt, 1888) and was therefore the first to suggest a critical role for this region in the regulation of behavior.

Since the late 19th century, the evidence for an involvement of the PFC in self-control accumulated at an astounding rate as autopsies became more frequent and neurological theory and practice improved. Case studies and reviews of patients with prefrontal damage owing to tumors, disease, stroke, and head injury all pointed to a role for PFC, and in particular the VMPFC, as being the critical region underlying the often strange examples of disinhibited behavior that these patients exhibited. For instance, Jastrowitz (1888), in a review of patients with PFC tumors, noted a change in overall character that he found difficult to accurately describe but which included a childlike demeanor, an inappropriate jocularity, and an increase in the use of obscene language. These symptoms were later confirmed by Oppenheim (1890), who upon hearing of Jastrowitz's patients examined his own records and found similar personality changes amongst his patients. In particular, Oppenheim noted that many of these patients had tumors which encroached upon the VMPFC. Later reports emphasized behaviors which appear on the surface to be psychopathic, such as: aggressive temperament and antisocial behavior (Rylander, 1939); boasting and self-aggrandizement (Brickner, 1934); inappropriate sexual displays (Ackerly, 1937); disregard of social norms (Blumer & Benson, 1975); verbal and physical aggression (Anderson, Bechara, Damasio, Tranel, & Damasio, 1999); and extremely poor planning and decision making (Eslinger & Damasio, 1985). In most cases patients are aware of the inappropriateness of their actions but nevertheless fail to regulate their behavior in everyday social interactions (Saver & Damasio, 1991). Along with these examples of failures to regulate social behavior, VMPFC lesions have also been associated with disinhibition of primary physiological drives. Hypersexuality and aggressive sexual advances are frequently observed in VMPFC patients (Grafman et al., 1996; Hécaen, 1964; Jarvie, 1954; Rylander, 1939). In addition, excessive overeating (e.g., hyperphagia) can also result from damage to the VMPFC (Erb, Gwirtsman, Fuster, & Richeimer, 1989; Kirschbaum, 1951; Woolley et al., 2007). What emerges from all these cases is that VMPFC damage involves a general dysregulation of social behavior characterized by a disregard of social norms and a lack of interpersonal sensitivity along with difficulty controlling primary physiological drives.

Lateral PFC Damage

In contrast to lesions of the VMPFC, damage to lateral portions of the PFC yield a different profile of deficits characterized by a loss of motivational drive and difficulty adapting to novel situations (e.g., switching task sets). Some of the earliest observations of these deficits came not from patient studies, but from animal lesion experiments carried out in the late 19th century by physiologists such as Bianchi and Ferrier. Ferrier noted, after bilateral ablation of the PFC in monkeys and dogs, that the animals were often "listless" and failed to initiate common behaviors such as searching for food (Ferrier, 1876). Similarly, Bianchi (1895) described incidences of profound apathy and stimulus-bound behavior following lesions of the PFC in monkeys.

Cases of lateral PFC damage in humans are far less common than VMPFC damage. The primary cause of lateral PFC damage comes from ischemic or hemorrhagic stroke while VMPFC damage can arise from any number of sources (e.g., closed-head injuries, stroke, tumors). For this reason, the clinical history of lateral PFC is much more recent than that of VMPFC damage.

Some of the earliest observations of cognitive changes following damage to the lateral PFC were made by the Canadian neurosurgeon Wilder Penfield. Reporting on three patients who had undergone unilateral resections of the PFC, Penfield notes in the first of the cases that the patient's post-operative behavior changed and was characterized by a loss of initiative accompanied by difficulty playing games that require the maintenance of multiple goals (e.g., bridge) (Penfield & Evans, 1935). A more striking example is in the third case he discusses, a patient who underwent a right prefrontal resection to remove a glioma. This particular case is all the more interesting, for the patient was Penfield's sister. Given his intimate knowledge of her personality, Penfield was able to note changes that a clinician might otherwise have missed. Penfield reports that her sense of humor and ability to hold intelligent thoughtful conversations remained unchanged; however, he notes that she now displays a dramatic difficulty in carrying out mundane household tasks, tasks which she previously carried out without difficulty. On the occasion of a small family gathering, he writes:

"When the appointed hour arrived she was in the kitchen, the food was all there, one or two things were on the stove, but the salad was not ready, the meat had not been started and she was distressed and confused by her continued effort alone. It seemed evident that she would never be able to get everything ready at once." (Penfield & Evans, 1935).

Penfield described this difficulty in planning as stemming from "the loss of power of initiative" (Penfield & Evans, 1935) echoing the descriptions of lesioned animals made by Ferrier and Bianchi fifty years earlier. Penfield's observations proved to be quite prescient, as later case studies confirmed both the general apathy and difficulty in planning complex tasks that are the hallmark of lateral PFC damage.

With the advent of more sophisticated neuropsychological tasks, along with modern imaging technology, knowledge of the cognitive sequelae of lateral PFC damage has greatly increased since Penfield's case study. We now know that patients with damage to lateral portions of the PFC experience a wide range of deficits involving the initiation, maintenance, and planning of behavior. In comparison to VMPFC patients, lateral PFC patients show no deficits in social and emotional understanding (Bar-On, Tranel, Denburg, & Bechara, 2003). On neuropsychological tests they exhibit preservative behaviors and fail to adapt to changing task demands (Milner, 1963). They also have difficulty with tasks requiring inhibitory control, such as on the well-known Stroop task, in which subjects are presented with color names printed in a conflicting color of ink (e.g., the word RED written in blue ink) and are asked to name the ink color as quickly as possible. Lateral PFC patients perform poorly on the Stroop task, showing an exaggerated delay in responding and a high error rate (Perret, 1974; Vendrell et al., 1995). In addition, they show deficits on fluency tasks that require patients to generate novel designs (Jones-Gotman & Milner, 1977) in particular they tend to perseverate and repeat the same few designs over and over. Performance on sequencing and planning tasks is also severely compromised (Petrides & Milner, 1982; Shallice, 1982; Shallice & Burgess, 1996). This deficit in planning, while apparent in the lab, is even more remarkable in real-world tasks. A vivid example of this is the multiple errands task devised by Shallice and Burgess (1991). In this task, patients are given instructions to run a number of simple errands, consisting of shopping for items on a list and being at a meeting place for a set time. Patients are told to spend as little money as possible and to not enter a shop unless they intend to buy something. Two observers trailed the patients and made note of their performance. Compared to healthy participants, the patients had an extremely difficult time completing the tasks, often forgetting to purchase items on the list, leaving a shop without paying for an item, and visiting the same shop multiple times (Shallice & Burgess, 1991). This elegant task highlights the many facets of lateral prefrontal function that break down after injury, such as planning ahead, avoiding distractions, sustaining attention, and adapting to novel situations.

Anterior Cingulate Damage

In comparison to VMPFC and lateral PFC damage, ACC lesions are far more rare. Most of our knowledge of ACC function comes not from neuropsychology but from neuroimaging and electrophysiological studies implicating this region in conflict monitoring (Carter et al., 1998; Gehring & Knight, 2000; MacDonald, Cohen, Stenger, & Carter, 2000) and in signaling the need for cognitive control (Kerns et al., 2004). One of the reasons for the relative rarity of patients with focal ACC damage is that, being a midline structure, it is rare for this region to be damaged in closed-head injuries. Patients who have undergone cingulotomies for the treatment of intractable pain or psychiatric disorders (Ballantine, Cassidy, Flanagan, & Marino, 1967; Corkin, 1979; Le Beau & Pecker, 1949; Whitty, Duffield, Tow, & Cairns, 1952) are an important source of information on cingulate function; however, such patients are only infrequently studied with measures of attention that are sensitive to ACC lesions (Cohen, Kaplan, Moser, Jenkins, & Wilkinson, 1999). As such, our knowledge of the cognitive and behavioral effects of focal ACC damage remains limited.

One of the earliest patient series on the psychological effects of cingulotomies noted some personality changes following the procedure (Tow & Whitty, 1953). The most common observation was that patients who were active prior to the surgery lost interest in their hobbies. Moreover, across all patients a common complaint from both patients and family members was of a reduction in energy and "drive." Less frequently reported, but still common, was of a post-operative flattening of emotion (e.g., blunted affect) (Tow & Whitty, 1953). Since then, a number of case studies and reports on large patient series in both stroke and cingulotomy patients have noted a post-surgical reduction in spontaneously generated actions,

difficulty sustaining goal-directed behavior, and blunted affect (Cohen, Kaplan, Moser, Jenkins, & Wilkinson, 1999; Cohen et al., 1999; Cohen, McCrae, & Phillips, 1990; Laplane, Degos, Baulac, & Gray, 1981; Wilson & Chang, 1974). Anecdotally, family members report that patients are passive and apathetic (Cohen et al., 1999). Less frequently reported symptoms of cingulate damage are aggressiveness, social disinhibition, hypersexuality, and bulimia (Devinsky, Morrell, & Vogt, 1995). However, as cases of pure ACC lesions are rare, it's likely that some of these symptoms are due to extra cingulate damage, either in the adjacent MPFC, supplementary motor area (SMA), or the cingulum bundle (e.g., cingulumotomy). For example, when both ACC and SMA are damaged patients may develop akinetic mutism, a syndrome marked by a devastating inability to generate actions or speech (Barris & Schuman, 1953). These patients seldom move, show no sign of emotion or physical pain, eat only when fed, and occasionally will talk, but only when directly asked a question. In cases of pure focal ACC damage without encroachment on the SMA, patients will still exhibit a general apathy but their symptoms are much less catastrophic, compared to akinetic mutism (Laplane, Degos, Baulac, & Gray, 1981).

Functional Neuroanatomy of the Prefrontal Cortex

The clinical cases described above strongly suggest a functional anatomical separation between the VMPFC, lateral PFC, and the ACC (Figure 24.1). The contribution of these three regions to distinct facets of self-regulation and executive function is supported by neuroanatomical evidence of discrete subcortical pathways originating in each of these brain regions (Alexander, Delong, & Strick, 1986). The validity of these divisions is further supported by the observation of distinct behavioral deficits in lesion studies in the monkey (Rosenkilde, 1979). In order to understand how damage to these regions can lead to the remarkable pattern of deficits seen in patients with PFC lesions, we turn now to a consideration of the neuroanatomical circuits of the PFC.

The prefrontal cortex is generally defined as the portion of the frontal cortex anterior to the motor and premotor areas. In humans and great apes, the PFC cortex is disproportionately large relative to other regions of the brain (Rilling, 2006). Moreover, recent findings suggest that it is specifically the white matter volume of the PFC that accounts for this relative size difference; this is especially true in humans, who have the largest PFC white matter volume ratio of all species (Schoenemann, Sheehan, & Glotzer, 2005). The PFC is unique among brain regions in that it shares connections with virtually every system involved in the generation of behavior (e.g., sensory and motor systems, subcortical limbic areas involved in emotion and reward, and medial temporal regions involved in memory). Given this pattern of connectivity, it is little surprise that the PFC has long been considered the locus of self-control.

Ventromedial Prefrontal Cortex

While there are no strict anatomical conventions regarding the VMPFC, all definitions include the gyrus rectus and orbital gyrus and frequently extend to the inferior portion of the medial prefrontal cortex (e.g., the medial portions of Brodmann areas 11, 12, 25 and the ventral portions of 10 and 32) and less frequently to the subgenual ACC. The basis for this division lies in part with the observation that the orbital and medial PFC are cytoarchitecturally similar (Ongur & Price, 2000).

The VMPFC receives visceral and highly processed sensory information from all modalities (Ongur & Price, 2000; Pandya & Barnes, 1987). Of all the regions in the PFC, the VMPFC is the most highly interconnected with limbic areas involved in emotional processing and in particular it shares significant reciprocal connections with the amygdala (Amaral & Price, 1984; Carmichael & Price, 1995). The VMPFC also projects to regions involved in goal-directed behavior and reward in the ventral striatum (e.g., caudate and nucleus accumbens; Haber, Kunishio, Mizobuchi, & Lynd-Balta, 1995). Regions important for visceral and appetitive behaviors such as the hypothalamus, insula, and thalamus project to the VMPFC (Barbas, Saha, Rempel-Clower, & Ghashghaei, 2003; Gabbott, Warner, Jays, & Bacon, 2003). This connectivity pattern is in accord with the neuropsychological evidence implicating the VMPFC in the regulation of affective, social, and appetitive behaviors.

Lateral Prefrontal Cortex

The lateral PFC is composed of both the dorsolateral (Brodmann areas 8, 9 and 46) and ventrolateral (Brodmann Areas 44, 45 and 47) convexities. Unlike the VMPFC and the ACC, the lateral prefrontal cortex has been primarily implicated in cognitive as opposed to affective processes, and unsurprisingly, has no direct links to limbic regions. Instead, the lateral PFC communicates indirectly to limbic areas via its rich connections with the VMPFC and the ACC (McDonald, Mascagni, & Guo, 1996).

Like other areas of PFC, the lateral aspect receives highly processed sensory input. In particular, the topography of the dorsal "what" and ventral "where" visual streams are conserved in the lateral PFC, with the dorsolateral PFC receiving visual input primarily from the parietal cortex and superior temporal visual association areas, and the ventrolateral PFC receiving input from the ventrotemporal association cortex (Barbas, 1988). The lateral PFC projects to secondary motor regions (SMA and premotor cortices; Barbas & Pandya, 1987; Petrides & Pandya, 1999) supporting its role in planning motor movements. Unlike other regions, the neuroanatomical connections of the lateral PFC do not immediately suggest a role for this region in the regulation of social or emotional behavior. In light of previously discussed neuropsychological evidence and recent neuroimaging studies, it has become clear that this region is critical for executive processes important for social and affective control. Unlike the VMPFC, and, as we shall see shortly, the ACC, the lateral PFC has no remarkable interconnections with regions involved in autonomic, arousal, or affective functions. However, the lateral PFC is implicated in a number of executive function processes, namely working memory and response inhibition. These are functions which serve goal-related behavior by allowing us to maintain the current goal in memory, to stay on task, and avoid distracters. Through its rich cortico-cortico connections with ACC and VMPFC, the lateral PFC appears to be involved in maintaining regulation strategies and ensuring that goals are met.

Anterior Cingulate Cortex

The anterior cingulate cortex represents the agranular rostral portion of the cingulate comprising Brodmann areas 24, 25 and 32. The ACC is intimately connected with the lateral PFC and adjacent motor cortices (e.g., premotor and SMA). Its main projections are to the ventral striatum and to limbic structures. Most notably, the ACC receives considerable input from the amygdala (Ongur, An, & Price, 1998; Vogt & Pandya, 1987). However, unlike the VMPFC and lateral PFC, the ACC receives relatively little input from sensory regions (Carmichael & Price, 1995) and instead is intimately connected to regions involved in visceral and autonomic responses (Ongur, An, & Price, 1998).

The ACC can be further subdivided into a perigenual region and a midcingulate region; the former involved in affective processing while the latter is preferentially involved in cognitive tasks. This affective/cognitive dissociation was elegantly demonstrated in a pair of imaging studies which showed activation of the midcingulate ACC for a counting version of the Stroop (Bush et al., 1998) and activation of the perigenual ACC for an emotional version of the same counting Stroop task (Whalen, Bush et al., 1998). These two subdivisions of the ACC also exhibit differential connectivity: the perigenual ACC (area 32, 25 and rostral portion of 24) projects to lateral PFC, VMPFC, insula, and amygdala while the dorsal aspect, corresponding to the midcingulate ACC (area 24) has efferent connection with lateral PFC and motor regions (Ongur & Price, 2000; Pandya, Van Hoesen, & Mesulam, 1981), supporting the notion that the lateral PFC mediates cognitive aspects of control while the VMPFC is more concerned with emotion.

Given this profile of connectivity, it's been suggested that the ACC is ideally situated to initiate new behaviors and regulate established ones (Paus, 2001). In light of the connections that the ACC makes with regions involved in cognitive and emotional regulation, arousal, and motor planning, the remarkable personality changes seen in the ACC-lesioned patients described above (e.g., apathy, blunted affect) appear much less strange.

What Exactly is Worth Regulating?

Based on the neuroanatomical and neuropsychological data described above, three distinct realms of thought and behavior appear worth regulating. They are: appetitive behaviors, such as those that lead us to seek out primary rewards (e.g., food, sex, water, but also cigarettes, drugs, and alcohol); thoughts (e.g., compulsions, stereotypes); and emotions. Although each may rely more on one region of the PFC than another, they all require the full range of executive control functions attributed to the PFC (e.g., working memory, conflict detection). Although patients with damage to the PFC exhibit a wide range of deficits, the most catastrophic are those that affect a patient's ability to maintain relationships with family and function in society. As noted above, damage to the PFC can lead to dysregulation of emotions (both extreme apathy and euphoria), of appetitive behaviors (hyperphagia, hypersexuality), and of thoughts (leading to the violation of social norms). While patients may also exhibit difficulty with planning and focusing attention, it is ultimately the behaviors mentioned above

that are the most damaging to social functioning and to which we now turn.

Regulation of Appetitive Behaviors

Given the potency of rewards, particularly primary ones, it is often a wonder that people are ever able to get out of bed and make it in to work without reaching for another bagel, another cigarette, another gin and tonic, or another bedroom romp. Keeping these appetitive behaviors in check requires considerable effort. For dieters, smokers, alcoholics, and drug addicts, regulating one's cravings can be a constant struggle.

The processing of rewards, particularly natural rewards, relies on a mesolimbic dopamine system consisting of the ventral tegmental area (VTA), the nucleus accumbens (NAcc), and the amygdala. It is a universal feature of all rewards, including drugs of abuse, that they activate dopamine receptors in the NAcc (Boileau et al., 2003; Carelli, Ijames, & Crumling, 2000; Di Chiara & Imperato, 1988; Imperato & Di Chiara, 1986; Pfaus et al., 1990; Schilstrom, Svensson, Svensson, & Nomikos, 1998; Solinas et al., 2002). In neuroimaging research we see convergent evidence in the form of increased activation of the NAcc region to the ingestions of food (Berns, McClure, Pagnoni, & Montague, 2001; O'Doherty, Dayan, Friston, Critchley, & Dolan, 2003) and of drugs of abuse (Breiter et al., 1997; Stein et al., 1998; Zubieta et al., 2005). The involvement of these regions in reward processing and expectation has been well established by numerous electrophysiological (Carelli, King, Hampson, & Deadwyler, 1993; Hollerman, Tremblay, & Schultz, 1998; Mirenowicz & Schultz, 1996), animal lesion (Caine & Koob, 1994; Roberts, Corcoran, & Fibiger, 1977; Taylor & Robbins, 1986), and neuroimaging studies (Cloutier, Heatherton, Whalen, & Kelley, 2008; Delgado, Nystrom, Fissell, Noll, & Fiez, 2000; Elliott, Friston, & Dolan, 2000; Knutson, Taylor, Kaufman, Peterson, & Glover, 2005; Koepp et al., 1998). Moreover, simply viewing images of primary rewards, such as erotic images (Karama et al., 2002) or images of drugs (David et al., 2007; Garavan et al., 2000; Myrick et al., 2008) can lead to activation of mesolimbic reward systems. This "cue-reactivity" paradigm has been instrumental in the study of obesity and drug addiction, repeatedly demonstrating that the obese (Rothemund et al., 2007; Stoeckel et al., 2008), smokers (David et al., 2007; Due, Huettel, Hall, & Rubin, 2002), and drug addicts (Childress et al., 1999; Garavan et al., 2000;

Maas et al., 1998; Wexler et al., 2001) demonstrate greater cue-reactivity than matched controls. Importantly, this cue-related activity predicts self-reported cravings for food or drug items (McClernon, Hiott, Huettel, & Rose, 2005; Myrick et al., 2008; Wang et al., 2004). In addition, individuals who are more sensitive to the rewarding properties of a stimulus, and are therefore more at risk for developing a drug addiction or overeating, show greater cue-related activity in the mesolimbic dopamine system (Beaver et al., 2006). Recent work from our lab has shown that not only is cue-related activity predictive of food craving, but that individuals who demonstrate greater food cue-related activity in NAcc are more likely to gain weight in the following six months (Demos, 2008).

As mentioned above, the ACC and VMPFC are intimately interconnected with the ventral striatum (Haber, Kunishio, Mizobuchi, & Lynd-Balta, 1995), and damage to the VMPFC has also been known to lead to hyperphagia (Erb, Gwirtsman, Fuster, & Richeimer, 1989) and hypersexuality (e.g., Grafman et al., 1996; Hécaen, 1964). Moreover, degenerative diseases of the PFC such as frontotemporal dementia (FTD) have also implicated the VMPFC as being critical for the disinhibited eating behavior that such patients occasionally display (Woolley et al., 2007). Based on this discussion, the prime candidates for regulating craving-related responses in the ventral striatum are the ACC and VMPFC. A number of studies have shown increased recruitment of these regions, in conjunction with lateral PFC in smokers (David et al., 2005), alcoholics (Wrase et al., 2002), drug addicts (Garavan et al., 2000), and the obese (Stoeckel et al., 2008). Although it has been suggested that recruitment of these regions is related to the experience of craving and evaluations of the reward value of a stimulus (Wilson, Sayette, & Fiez, 2004), it is important to note that these regions are also implicated in regulating behavior, which here could mean initiating reward-seeking behavior as much as it could mean initiating avoidance behavior. For example, lateral PFC and ACC are recruited when participants are asked to inhibit arousal when viewing erotic material (Beauregard, Levesque, & Bourgouin, 2001). The ACC was also among regions found to show greater activity when smokers were asked to resist cue-induced craving, compared to when they were asked to increase craving (Brody et al., 2007). An example of the importance of these regions for the regulation of appetitive behaviors comes from a study of successful and non-successful dieters.

In response to food consumption, successful dieters show increased activity in the lateral PFC (i.e., dorsal lateral prefrontal cortex), suggesting that they spontaneously engage self-regulatory strategies in order to curtail food-seeking behavior (DelParigi et al., 2007).

As most people can attest, regulating one's behavior can be a difficult and effortful process, one at which they occasionally, if not often, fail. People seldom intend to eat an entire chocolate cake and wash it down with a bottle of Bollinger, and yet after a few drinks one's resolve shows a marked tendency to go out the window. The phenomena whereby giving into one vice can lead to a wholesale loss of control was first studied by Herman and Mack (1975). In their study, chronic dieters participated in a putative taste-testing session; however, prior to beginning the tasting they were asked to drink a high caloric milkshake. Herman and Mack found that the simple act of breaking their diet, via the milkshake, led dieting participants to engage in disinhibited eating (Herman & Mack, 1975). This basic effect has since been replicated in multiple studies since (Heatherton, Herman, & Polivy, 1991; 1992; Heatherton, Polivy, Herman, & Baumeister, 1993), all of which clearly demonstrate that the act of breaking one's resolve can lead to a general dysregulation of appetitive behavior.

A possible neural mechanism for this breakdown of self-control, one which has been suggested to be at the root of drug addiction, consists of a failure of top-down regulation of the region involved in the representation of reward. According to this theory, mesolimbic reward systems both become hypersensitized to drug cues and become uncoupled from PFC regions involved in top-down regulation (Bechara, 2005; Koob & Le Moal, 1997; 2008).

This theory was put to the test in a study examining food cue-reactivity in the nucleus accumbens in restrained and unrestrained eaters (Demos, Kelley, & Heatherton, 2009). Using a similar milkshake preload as that of Herman and Mack (1975), half of the participants had their diet broken prior to viewing food cues. Restrained eaters whose diet had been broken by the milkshake preload showed increased NAcc food-cue reactivity compared to both the unrestrained eaters and the restrained eaters whose diet had not been broken (Demos, Kelley, & Heatherton, 2009). Interestingly, restrained eaters demonstrated increased recruitment of the lateral PFC (BA45) in response to food cues compared to unrestrained eaters. Moreover, there was no effect of the diet-breaking preload on lateral PFC activity, suggesting that restrained eaters whose diet has been broken are still engaged in self-regulation, but are nevertheless failing to inhibit cue-related activity in reward systems. This phenomenon is mimicked in obese individuals who show enhanced activity in mesolimbic reward systems to images of food compared to matched controls (Stoeckel et al., 2008). Taken together, these findings paint a picture of a dysregulated reward system whereby NAcc, no longer under the influence of top-down control from the PFC, demonstrates an exaggerated response to food cues leading to eventual collapse of self-control.

Regulation of Thought

Damage to regions of the PFC can often lead to a form of acquired sociopathy (Damasio, Tranel, & Damasio, 1990) characterized by a sudden change in personality, whereby formally moral and polite patients suddenly present a range of socially transgressive behaviors (e.g., vulgarity, aggression, rudeness, and other socially inappropriate behaviors). These patients are aware of what constitutes a social or moral transgression (Saver & Damasio, 1991) but nevertheless fail to regulate their social behavior.

Likely everyone has experienced socially inappropriate thoughts or has had to override prejudices; but it is the failure to suppress these thoughts that can lead to anything from mildly inappropriate social transgressions to spectacular displays of bigotry and racism. Unlike other forms of behavioral control, suppressing thoughts does not require one to control overt motor behavior or suppress a prepotent response, and yet people experience thought suppression as being difficult and mentally exhausting. Research on thought suppression and self-regulation has shown that suppressing thoughts is cognitively depleting, making it difficult to exert self-regulation in subsequent tasks (Muraven, Tice, & Baumeister, 1998; Vohs, Baumeister, & Ciarocco, 2005; Wegner, 1989). Similarly, suppressing stereotypes and prejudicial attitudes has also been shown to require similar effort, leaving participants unable to successfully self-regulate in other domains (Richeson & Shelton, 2003).

Despite a wealth of research on the neural correlates of response inhibition and the suppression of prepotent responses, such as in the Stroop task, there have been few attempts to study the neural correlates of thought suppression. In the first study to do so, Wyland and colleagues (2003) had participants engage in a thought-suppression task during imaging with fMRI. Compared to blocks

of unrestrained thought, thought suppression recruited the ACC (Wyland, Kelley, Macrae, Gordon, & Heatherton, 2003). As mentioned above, the ACC is implicated in a number of self-regulatory related processes, namely conflict detection and communicating to the lateral PFC the need for additional cognitive control (see Botvinick, Braver, Barch, Carter, & Cohen, 2001). In this particular case, it may be that ACC activity was indexing failures to suppress thoughts or was instead signaling an increased need for cognitive control. In order to delineate the precise role of ACC in thought suppression, Mitchell et al. (2007) carried out a related study in which participants were instructed to indicate the intrusion of a specific thought via a button press during both periods of thought suppression and periods of unrestrained thought. Critically, the authors employed a state-item design (Visscher et al., 2003) which allowed for separation of regions showing a sustained response during active thought suppression from regions demonstrating transient responses to thought intrusions. Results from this experiment showed that the right lateral PFC demonstrated greater sustained activity during thought suppression compared to epochs of unrestrained thought. The ACC, however, demonstrated transient activity to intrusions of a forbidden thought during periods of thought suppression compared to when that same thought was permissible (e.g., during unrestrained thought epochs). These findings are interpreted as demonstrating that the ACC monitors for conflict and signals the need for additional control, while the lateral PFC is involved in implementing and maintaining cognitive control over the duration of thought suppression periods and is insensitive to temporary failures in thought suppressions (Mitchell et al., 2007).

Over the last twenty years a wealth of social psychological research has demonstrated that racial bias and stereotypes can be automatically activated and that individuals differ in their motivation to engage in deliberate control in suppressing these prejudices (Devine, 1989; Devine, Plant, Amodio, Harmon-Jones, & Vance, 2002; Fiske, 1998; Greenwald, McGhee, & Schwartz, 1998; Payne, 2001). Neuroimaging research on prejudice and racial bias has focused on the relative involvement of the amygdala and PFC regions, the former being implicated in the automatic component of stereotyping, while the PFC is involved in the top-down control of attitudes. The role of the amygdala in the evaluation of racial ingroup and outgroup members is not simply a story of greater amygdala activity for outgroup members. Rather, the response in the amygdala to racial outgroup members is more nuanced, reflecting individual differences in automatic negative evaluations of Blacks as measured by the implicit association test (IAT) (Cunningham et al., 2004; Phelps et al., 2000), the opportunity to engage in top-down control (Cunningham et al., 2004; Richeson et al., 2003), and also perceiver's evaluative goals (Wheeler & Fiske, 2005).

How then does the PFC and amygdala interact to regulate prejudice and racial bias? Cunningham and colleagues (2004) were able to tease apart the roles of the amygdala and PFC in race evaluations by capitalizing on the fact that the amygdala responds to subliminal presentation of affective stimuli (Whalen, Rauch, et al., 1998). Thus, by presenting Black and White faces both implicitly (30ms) and explicitly (525ms), the investigators were able to separately assess conditions in which participants were unlikely to engage in cognitive control (implicit presentation) compared to when participants had the opportunity to regulate their responses (explicit presentation). Their findings demonstrated that the amygdala showed greater activity to Black faces when participants were unaware of any faces. However, when participants were given sufficient time to engage in self-regulation, activity in the amygdala did not differentiate between Black and White faces (Cunningham et al., 2004). Instead, what they found was increased recruitment of lateral PFC regions during the explicit presentation of Black compared to White faces, indicating that participants were engaging in active regulation. Moreover, activity in this region was inversely correlated with activity in the amygdala, indicating that lateral PFC is involved in top-down regulation of amygdala activity during explicit evaluations of Blacks (Cunningham et al., 2004).

While compelling, these results provide only indirect evidence of the role of the PFC in regulating automatic racial biases. Richeson and colleagues (2003) devised a more direct test of the involvement of PFC regions in controlling prejudice by directly relating neural activity in the PFC to the amount of cognitive depletion participants felt after an inter-racial interaction. In their study, Caucasian participants engaged in an inter-racial interaction with an African American confederate that required them to provide their opinion on racially charged political issues (e.g., racial profiling); afterwards participants completed the Stroop task. As expected, participants with greater automatic negative evaluations of Blacks showed increased interference on the Stroop task, indicating that they expended more self-regulatory resources during the inter-racial interaction, leaving them depleted and less able to inhibit their responses during the Stroop task. Importantly, these same participants later completed an ostensibly unrelated fMRI experiment in which they viewed images of Black and White faces. As with the experiment by Cunningham et al. (2004), participants engaged lateral PFC and ACC regions in response to the Black compared to White faces. However, Richeson and colleagues were then able to relate the magnitude of PFC activity to the degree to which participants exhibited increased Stroop interference in the previous inter-racial interaction experiment. Activity in both the lateral PFC and ACC was positively correlated with both increased Stroop interference and with IAT scores (Richeson et al., 2003). Thus, participants who exhibited greater self-regulatory depletion following a face-to-face inter-racial interaction were also more likely to recruit regions of the PFC involved in cognitive control when viewing Black faces.

Emotion Regulation

Many of the antisocial behaviors previously described in VMPFC patients can best be characterized as a failure to appropriately regulate emotions. The ability to effectively control emotions is central to our functioning within society. Failure to do so can lead to aggression, violence, and others forms of antisocial behavior. However, regulating emotions isn't simply a matter of maintaining decorum in polite society, difficulty keeping them in check can also have dire consequences for the individual. Disorders of emotion regulation involve not only aggressive disorders such as antisocial personality disorder, but also encompass debilitating mood disorders such as post-traumatic stress disorder (PTSD) and major depressive disorder (MDD). Depression, in particular, poses a large burden on society and is easily the most prevalent (Kessler, Chiu, Demler, Merikangas, & Walters, 2005) and most costly (Stewart, Ricci, Chee, Hahn, & Morganstein, 2003) mental health disorder.

The neural mechanisms underlying the regulation of emotions have been the subject of much research in the past several years (see Ochsner & Gross, 2005; and the chapter by Ochsner et al., this volume). As might be expected from the earlier discussion of the neuropsychological deficits following damage to the VMPFC, the neuroimaging literature has converged on a model of emotion regulation that consists of top-down modulation of amygdala activity by the VMPFC and lateral PFC (Davidson, Putnam, & Larson, 2000; Ochsner & Gross, 2005). Typically in research of this kind, participants view negatively valenced images and are asked to engage in various emotion regulation strategies, such as suppressing their affective response or engaging in cognitive reappraisal of the negative events depicted in the image. Studies of this kind have revealed a consistent pattern of results whereby regions of the PFC (e.g., VMPFC and lateral PFC) show increased activity when participants are actively regulating their emotions. Conversely, the amygdala, a limbic region consistently involved in affective processing, shows reduced activity during suppression of affective responses. Importantly, activity in these two regions is inversely correlated, a finding which is interpreted as evidence of down-regulation of amygdala activity by the PFC (Ochsner, Bunge, Gross, & Gabrieli, 2002).

This inverse coupling between regions of the PFC and amygdala during emotion regulation has been replicated across numerous studies, although the precise region of the PFC has varied. Results from different studies have converged on three regions: the VMPFC (BA11: Johnstone, van Reekum, Urry, Kalin, & Davidson, 2007; Urry et al., 2006), the LPFC (BA46: Ochsner, Bunge, Gross, & Gabrieli, 2002; BA44: Ochsner et al., 2004; BA47: Hariri, Mattay, Tessitore, Fera, & Weinberger, 2003), and the lateral OFC (BA11: Goldin, McRae, Ramel, & Gross, 2008; Banks, Eddy, Angstadt, Nathan, & Phan, 2007). This pattern of results is mirrored in research on the interpretation of ambiguous facial expressions (e.g., surprise) whereby amygdala activity for negative interpretations of surprised faces is inversely correlated with activity in the MPFC/VMPFC (BA32/25) (Kim, Somerville, Johnstone, Alexander, & Whalen, 2003).

From the above review it's clear that the PFC participates in the active regulation of emotion; however, the variability among studies is perplexing. As noted previously, the lateral PFC has no direct connections with the amygdala and is likely to exert its influence through its many cortico-cortico connections with the VMPFC which itself is highly interconnected with the amygdala. Support for this idea comes from a recent study demonstrating that the VMPFC mediates the relationship between the amygdala and lateral PFC during emotion regulation (Johnstone, van Reekum, Urry, Kalin, & Davidson, 2007).

Dysfunctional responses of brain regions involved in emotion regulation have recently been demonstrated in clinical mood disorders. Johnstone and colleagues (2007) showed that subjects with major depressive disorder failed to recruit the VMPFC during an emotion-regulation task, displaying instead an exaggerated amygdala and VMPFC response in comparison to controls. Similar findings of exaggerated amygdala response to emotional stimuli were found in patients with borderline personality disorder (Donegan et al., 2003). Moreover, two recent studies have found that patients with BPD exhibit a dysfunctional VMPFC–amygdala circuit compared to healthy controls. In the first study, Silbersweig and colleagues (2007) found that BPD patients failed to recruit VMPFC to down-regulate the amygdala in a negative emotion-inhibition task (Silbersweig et al., 2007). In the second study, which examined resting glucose metabolism using FDG-PET, New and colleagues found that that amygdala and VMPFC exhibited correlated glucose metabolism in healthy controls but not in BPD patients, who instead showed no correlation between metabolism in the VMPFC and the amygdala (New et al., 2007).

Another clinical group that demonstrates abnormal limbic and prefrontal responses to negative emotional material is patients with post-traumatic stress disorder (PTSD). Shin and colleagues have shown that the exaggerated amygdala response that is often found in patients with PTSD to traumatic reminders generalizes to negatively valenced material unrelated to their traumatic experience (Shin et al., 2004). Another interesting case of dysfunction between amygdala and prefrontal regions is found in sleep deprivation. Subjects who were sleep deprived for 35 hours demonstrated exaggerated amygdala response to negative images but not to neutral images. Moreover, while control subjects exhibited functional connectivity between amygdala and regions of the MPFC (roughly corresponding to VMPFC but outside of the areas discussed above), sleep deprived subjects showed no such pattern (Yoo, Gujar, Hu, Jolesz, & Walker, 2007).

Taken together, these findings of dysfunctional amygdala–prefrontal circuitry in mood disorders, aggression, and antisocial behavior highlights the importance of emotion regulation for psychological well-being. Indeed, negative affect is one of the main predictors of drug relapse in smokers (Cooney et al., 2007) and alcoholics (Hodgins, el-Guebaly, & Armstrong, 1995).

Self-regulation Relies on a Domain General Resource

There are myriad ways in which the ability to self-regulate can fail. As demonstrated in this chapter, damage to regions of the PFC can lead to deficits in initiating control and inhibiting impulses leading to dramatic changes in personality and behavior which on the surface appear more characteristic of psychopathy than of brain damage. Neuroimaging research has extended prior neuropsychological findings by demonstrating not only the specificity with which the PFC is involved in various aspects of self-regulation, but also in demonstrating that we can use neuroimaging methods to measure the breakdown of control in multiple domains from appetitive behaviors (Demos et al., 2009) to thoughts (Mitchell et al., 2007) to prejudice (Richeson et al., 2003) and finally to emotions (Johnstone, van Reekum, Urry, Kalin, & Davidson, 2007; Yoo, Gujar, Hu, Jolesz, & Walker, 2007).

Although we addressed each of these domains in isolation, there is ample behavioral research demonstrating that the ability to self-regulate relies on a domain-general resource that is exhausted by repeated attempts at self-regulation (Baumeister & Heatherton, 1996; Muraven & Baumeister, 2000; Vohs & Heatherton, 2000). From this standpoint, none of the systems discussed above operates in isolation—regulating emotions can impair our ability to control our diet and vice versa. The interplay between different forms of self-regulation has been shown to have important ramifications for addictive behaviors. For instance, regulating emotions impairs dieters' abilities to restrain themselves from eating (Vohs & Heatherton, 2000) and maintaining diet standards (Hofmann, Rauch, & Gawronski, 2007). Putting participants under high cognitive load has also been shown to impair self-regulation, causing dieters to exhibit unrestrained eating compared to participants under low cognitive load (Ward & Mann, 2000). Similarly, Munraven and colleagues showed that participants who engaged in an effortful thought-suppression manipulation subsequently showed impaired impulse control and drank more alcohol than control participants (Muraven, Collins, & Nienhaus, 2002).

Summary

Knowledge of the neural systems that underlie self-regulation in humans began with Phineas Gage and the prefrontal patients described by Welt (1888) and others (Jastrowitz, 1888; Oppenheim, 1890). As neuropsychological evidence accrued, it became clear that distinct regions of the PFC were involved in separate aspects of self-regulation. The VMPFC, with its rich interconnections with limbic areas involved in emotion and midbrain regions involved in reward, is critical for the control of social, affective, and appetitive behaviors. The lateral PFC, with its role in working memory and executive function, maintains regulatory goals and is crucial for organizing behavior (e.g., planning). Finally, the ACC, sitting at the crossroads of affective, motor, and cognitive networks, is ideally suited to detect when contingencies in the environment demand that we engage in self-regulation.

While there are many kinds of behaviors worth regulating, in this chapter we focused on three general categories of thought and behavior that are considered important for maintaining social harmony; these are: controlling our appetites, regulating our emotions, and suppressing our thoughts. Evidence from animal neurophysiology and functional neuroimaging in humans suggests a general framework whereby the PFC down-regulates stimulus-driven responses in subcortical brain areas involved in affect and reward. When the ability to effectively regulate these responses breaks down, a host of maladaptive behaviors can arise. As we've seen, failure to inhibit cue-related activity is associated with increased weight gain and drug addiction, and failure to down-regulate limbic regions is associated with mood and personality disorders as well as racial bias and prejudice.

Although we've examined each of these realms of self-regulation in isolation, it has become abundantly clear over the last decade that these different forms of self-regulation interact with each other. This has led researchers to examine the possibility that regulating behavior in one domain can impair our ability to engage in other types of self-regulation. Findings from this line of research have shown that regulating emotions can not only break a diet (Vohs & Heatherton, 2000) but can also lead to surprising deficits in unexpected domains, such as managing our impressions of ourselves during interpersonal interactions (Vohs, Baumeister, & Ciarocco, 2005).

Failure to self-regulate is implicated in a variety of negative behaviors such as substance abuse, prejudice, and criminal behavior (see Baumeister & Heatherton, 1996). Conversely, those who are better able to self-regulate demonstrate improved relationships, increased job success, and better mental health (Duckworth & Seligman, 2005; Shoda, 1990; Tangney, Baumeister, & Boone, 2004).

Although we've focused primarily on the neural systems underlying the breakdown of self-control, there are doubtless other factors that come into play. For example, individual differences in self-regulatory ability and executive function (e.g., working memory capacity) might mediate an individual's susceptibility to the effects of cognitive depletion (Shamosh & Gray, 2007). This argument is not simply academic; for instance, individual differences in the ability to delay gratification as an infant are known to be highly predictive of an individual's success decades later (Metcalfe & Mischel, 1999; Mischel, Shoda, & Rodriguez, 1989). Now that the systems underlying self-regulation are relatively well characterized, we can turn to the question of why some people are better self-regulators than others and what are the neural markers of poor self-control.

References

Ackerly, S. (1937). Instinctive, emotional and mental changes following prefrontal lobe extirpation. *American Journal of Psychiatry, 92*, 717–729.

Alexander, G. E., Delong, M. R., & Strick, P. L. (1986). Parallel organization of functionally segregated circuits linking basal ganglia and cortex. *Annual Review of Neuroscience, 9*, 357–381.

Amaral, D. G. & Price, J. L. (1984). Amygdalo-cortical projections in the monkey (Macaca fascicularis). *J Comp Neurol, 230*(4), 465–496.

Anderson, S. W., Bechara, A., Damasio, H., Tranel, D., & Damasio, A. R. (1999). Impairment of social and moral behavior related to early damage in human prefrontal cortex. *Nat Neurosci, 2*(11), 1032–1037.

Anonymous. (1851). Remarkable case of injury. *American Phrenological Journal, 13*, 89.

Ballantine, H. T., Jr., Cassidy, W. L., Flanagan, N. B., & Marino, R., Jr. (1967). Stereotaxic anterior cingulotomy for neuropsychiatric illness and intractable pain. *J Neurosurg, 26*(5), 488–495.

Banks, S. J., Eddy, K. T., Angstadt, M., Nathan, P. J., & Phan, K. L. (2007). Amygdala-frontal connectivity during emotion regulation. *Social Cognitive and Affective Neuroscience, 2*(4), 303–312.

Bar-On, R., Tranel, D., Denburg, N. L., & Bechara, A. (2003). Exploring the neurological substrate of emotional and social intelligence. *Brain, 126*(Pt 8), 1790–1800.

Barbas, H. (1988). Anatomic organization of basoventral and mediodorsal visual recipient prefrontal regions in the rhesus monkey. *J Comp Neurol, 276*(3), 313–342.

Barbas, H. & Pandya, D. N. (1987). Architecture and frontal cortical connections of the premotor cortex (area 6) in the rhesus monkey. *J Comp Neurol, 256*(2), 211–228.

Barbas, H., Saha, S., Rempel-Clower, N., & Ghashghaei, T. (2003). Serial pathways from primate prefrontal cortex to autonomic areas may influence emotional expression. *BMC Neurosci, 4*, 25.

Barris, R. W. & Schuman, H. R. (1953). Bilateral anterior cingulate gyrus lesions: Syndrome of the anterior cingulate gyri. *Neurology, 3*(1), 44–52.

Baumeister, R. F. & Heatherton, T. F. (1996). Self-regulation failure: An overview. *Psychological Inquiry, 7*(1), 1–15.

Beauregard, M., Levesque, J., & Bourgouin, P. (2001). Neural correlates of conscious self-regulation of emotion. *J Neurosci, 21*(18), RC165.

Beaver, J. D., Lawrence, A. D., van Ditzhuijzen, J., Davis, M. H., Woods, A., & Calder, A. J. (2006). Individual differences in reward drive predict neural responses to images of food. *J Neurosci, 26*(19), 5160–5166.

Bechara, A. (2005). Decision making, impulse control and loss of willpower to resist drugs: A neurocognitive perspective. *Nat Neurosci, 8*(11), 1458–1463.

Berns, G. S., McClure, S. M., Pagnoni, G., & Montague, P. R. (2001). Predictability modulates human brain response to reward. *J Neurosci, 21*(8), 2793–2798.

Bianchi, L. (1895). The functions of the frontal lobes. *Brain, 18*(497–530).

Blumer, D. & Benson, D. (1975). Personality changes with frontal and temporal lesions. In D. Benson & D. Blummer (Eds.), *Psychiatric aspects of neurologic disease*. New York: Grune & Stratton.

Boileau, I., Assaad, J. M., Pihl, R. O., Benkelfat, C., Leyton, M., Diksic, M., et al. (2003). Alcohol promotes dopamine release in the human nucleus accumbens. *Synapse, 49*(4), 226–231.

Botvinick, M. M., Braver, T. S., Barch, D. M., Carter, C. S., & Cohen, J. D. (2001). Conflict monitoring and cognitive control. *Psychol Rev, 108*(3), 624–652.

Breiter, H. C., Gollub, R. L., Weisskoff, R. M., Kennedy, D. N., Makris, N., Berke, J. D., et al. (1997). Acute effects of cocaine on human brain activity and emotion. *Neuron, 19*(3), 591–611.

Brickner, R. M. (1934). An interpretation of frontal lobe function based upon the study of a case of partial bilateral frontal lobectomy. *Research Publications of the Association for Research in Nervous and Mental Disease, 13*, 259–351.

Brody, A. L., Mandelkern, M. A., Olmstead, R. E., Jou, J., Tiongson, E., Allen, V., et al. (2007). Neural substrates of resisting craving during cigarette cue exposure. *Biol Psychiatry, 62*(6), 642–651.

Bush, G., Whalen, P. J., Rosen, B. R., Jenike, M. A., McInerney, S. C., & Rauch, S. L. (1998). The counting Stroop: an interference task specialized for functional neuroimaging—validation study with functional MRI. *Hum Brain Mapp, 6*(4), 270–282.

Caine, S. B. & Koob, G. F. (1994). Effects of dopamine D-1 and D-2 antagonists on cocaine self-administration under different schedules of reinforcement in the rat. *J Pharmacol Exp Ther, 270*(1), 209–218.

Carelli, R. M., Ijames, S. G., & Crumling, A. J. (2000). Evidence that separate neural circuits in the nucleus accumbens encode cocaine versus "natural" (water and food) reward. *J Neurosci, 20*(11), 4255–4266.

Carelli, R. M., King, V. C., Hampson, R. E., & Deadwyler, S. A. (1993). Firing patterns of nucleus accumbens neurons during cocaine self-administration in rats. *Brain Res, 626*(1–2), 14–22.

Carmichael, S. T. & Price, J. L. (1995). Limbic connections of the orbital and medial prefrontal cortex in macaque monkeys. *J Comp Neurol, 363*(4), 615–641.

Carter, C. S., Braver, T. S., Barch, D. M., Botvinick, M. M., Noll, D., & Cohen, J. D. (1998). Anterior cingulate cortex, error detection, and the online monitoring of performance. *Science, 280*(5364), 747–749.

Childress, A. R., Mozley, P. D., McElgin, W., Fitzgerald, J., Reivich, M., & O'Brien, C. P. (1999). Limbic activation during cue-induced cocaine craving. *Am J Psychiatry*, *156*(1), 11–18.

Cloutier, J., Heatherton, T. F., Whalen, P. J., & Kelley, W. M. (2008). Are attractive people rewarding? Sex differences in the neural substrates of facial attractiveness. *J Cogn Neurosci*, *20*(6), 941–951.

Cohen, R. A., Kaplan, R. F., Moser, D. J., Jenkins, M. A., & Wilkinson, H. (1999). Impairments of attention after cingulotomy. *Neurology*, *53*(4), 819–824.

Cohen, R. A., Kaplan, R. F., Zuffante, P., Moser, D. J., Jenkins, M. A., Salloway, S., et al. (1999). Alteration of intention and self-initiated action associated with bilateral anterior cingulotomy. *J Neuropsychiatry Clin Neurosci*, *11*(4), 444–453.

Cohen, R. A., McCrae, V., & Phillips, K. (1990). Neurobehavioral consequences of bilateral medial cingulotomy (abstract). *Neurology*, *40*((suppl 1):A198).

Cooney, N. L., Litt, M. D., Cooney, J. L., Pilkey, D. T., Steinberg, H. R., & Oncken, C. A. (2007). Alcohol and tobacco cessation in alcohol-dependent smokers: Analysis of real-time reports. *Psychol Addict Behav*, *21*(3), 277–286.

Corkin, S. (1979). Hidden-figures-test performance: Lasting effects of unilateral penetrating head injury and transient effects of bilateral cingulotomy. *Neuropsychologia*, *17*(6), 585–605.

Cunningham, W. A., Johnson, M. K., Raye, C. L., Gatenby, J. C., Gore, J. C., & Banaji, M. R. (2004). Separable neural components in the processing of black and white faces. *Psychological Science*, *15*(12), 806–813.

Curtis, C. E. & D'Esposito, M. (2003). Success and failure suppressing reflexive behavior. *Journal of Cognitive Neuroscience*, *15*(3), 409–418.

Damasio, A. R., Tranel, D., & Damasio, H. (1990). Individuals with sociopathic behavior caused by frontal damage fail to respond autonomically to social stimuli. *Behav Brain Res*, *41*(2), 81–94.

Damasio, H., Grabowski, T., Frank, R., Galaburda, A. M., & Damasio, A. R. (1994). The return of Gage, Phineas—Clues about the brain from the skull of a famous patient. *Science*, *264*(5162), 1102–1105.

David, S. P., Munafo, M. R., Johansen-Berg, H., Mackillop, J., Sweet, L. H., Cohen, R. A., et al. (2007). Effects of acute nicotine abstinence on cue-elicited ventral striatum/nucleus accumbens activation in female cigarette smokers: A functional magnetic resonance imaging study. *Brain Imaging Behav*, *1*(3–4), 43–57.

David, S. P., Munafo, M. R., Johansen-Berg, H., Smith, S. M., Rogers, R. D., Matthews, P. M., et al. (2005). Ventral striatum/nucleus accumbens activation to smoking-related pictorial cues in smokers and nonsmokers: A functional magnetic resonance imaging study. *Biol Psychiatry*, *58*(6), 488–494.

Davidson, R. J., Putnam, K. M., & Larson, C. L. (2000). Dysfunction in the neural circuitry of emotion regulation—a possible prelude to violence. *Science*, *289*(5479), 591–594.

Delgado, M. R., Nystrom, L. E., Fissell, C., Noll, D. C., & Fiez, J. A. (2000). Tracking the hemodynamic responses to reward and punishment in the striatum. *J Neurophysiol*, *84*(6), 3072–3077.

DelParigi, A., Chen, K., Salbe, A. D., Hill, J. O., Wing, R. R., Reiman, E. M., et al. (2007). Successful dieters have increased neural activity in cortical areas involved in the control of behavior. *Int J Obes (Lond)*, *31*(3), 440–448.

Demos. K. E. (2008). *Restraint and disinhibition in the brain*. Unpublished doctoral dissertation, Dartmouth College, Hanover.

Demos, K. E., Kelley, W. M., Heatherton, T. F. (2009). The neural correlated of dietary restraint violations. Manuscript submitted for publication.

Devine, P. G. (1989). Stereotypes and prejudice—Their automatic and controlled components. *Journal of Personality and Social Psychology*, *56*(1), 5–18.

Devine, P. G., Plant, E. A., Amodio, D. M., Harmon-Jones, E., & Vance, S. L. (2002). The regulation of explicit and implicit race bias: The role of motivations to respond without prejudice. *J Pers Soc Psychol*, *82*(5), 835–848.

Devinsky, O., Morrell, M. J., & Vogt, B. A. (1995). Contributions of anterior cingulate cortex to behaviour. *Brain*, *118*(Pt 1), 279–306.

Dewey, J. (1922). *Human nature and conduct: An introduction to social psychology*. New York: Henry Holt And Company.

Di Chiara, G. & Imperato, A. (1988). Drugs abused by humans preferentially increase synaptic dopamine concentrations in the mesolimbic system of freely moving rats. *Proc Natl Acad Sci U S A*, *85*(14), 5274–5278.

Donegan, N. H., Sanislow, C. A., Blumberg, H. P., Fulbright, R. K., Lacadie, C., Skudlarski, P., et al. (2003). Amygdala hyperreactivity in borderline personality disorder: Implications for emotional dysregulation. *Biol Psychiatry*, *54*(11), 1284–1293.

Duckworth, A. L. & Seligman, M. E. P. (2005). Self-discipline outdoes IQ in predicting academic performance of adolescents. *Psychological Science*, *16*(12), 939–944.

Due, D. L., Huettel, S. A., Hall, W. G., & Rubin, D. C. (2002). Activation in mesolimbic and visuospatial neural circuits elicited by smoking cues: Evidence from functional magnetic resonance imaging. *Am J Psychiatry*, *159*(6), 954–960.

Elliott, R., Friston, K. J., & Dolan, R. J. (2000). Dissociable neural responses in human reward systems. *J Neurosci*, *20*(16), 6159–6165.

Erb, J. L., Gwirtsman, H. E., Fuster, J. M., & Richeimer, S. H. (1989). Bulimia associated with frontal-lobe lesions. *International Journal of Eating Disorders*, *8*(1), 117–121.

Eslinger, P. J. & Damasio, A. R. (1985). Severe disturbance of higher cognition after bilateral frontal lobe ablation: Patient EVR. *Neurology*, *35*(12), 1731–1741.

Ferrier, D. (1876). *The functions of the brain*. London: Smith, Elder & Co.

Ferrier, D. (1878). The Goulstonian Lectures on the localisation of cerebral diseases. *British Medical Journal*, *1*, 443–447.

Fiske, S. T. (1998). Stereotyping, prejudice, and discrimination. *The handbook of social psychology*, *2*, 357–411.

Gabbott, P. L., Warner, T. A., Jays, P. R., & Bacon, S. J. (2003). Areal and synaptic interconnectivity of prelimbic (area 32), infralimbic (area 25) and insular cortices in the rat. *Brain Res*, *993*(1–2), 59–71.

Garavan, H., Pankiewicz, J., Bloom, A., Cho, J. K., Sperry, L., Ross, T. J., et al. (2000). Cue-induced cocaine craving: Neuroanatomical specificity for drug users and drug stimuli. *Am J Psychiatry*, *157*(11), 1789–1798.

Gehring, W. J. & Knight, R. T. (2000). Prefrontal-cingulate interactions in action monitoring. *Nat Neurosci*, *3*(5), 516–520.

Goldberg, E. (2001). *The executive brain: Frontal lobes and the civilized mind*. New York: Oxford University Press.

Goldin, P. R., McRae, K., Ramel, W., & Gross, J. J. (2008). The neural bases of emotion regulation: Reappraisal and suppression of negative emotion. *Biol Psychiatry*, *63*(6), 577–586.

Gould, S. J. (1977). *Ontogeny and phylogeny*. Cambridge, MA: Harvard University Press.

Grafman, J., Schwab, K., Warden, D., Pridgen, A., Brown, H. R., & Salazar, A. M. (1996). Frontal lobe injuries, violence, and aggression: A report of the Vietnam Head Injury Study. *Neurology*, *46*(5), 1231–1238.

Greenwald, A. G., McGhee, D. E., & Schwartz, J. L. (1998). Measuring individual differences in implicit cognition: The implicit association test. *J Pers Soc Psychol*, *74*(6), 1464–1480.

Haber, S. N., Kunishio, K., Mizobuchi, M., & Lynd-Balta, E. (1995). The orbital and medial prefrontal circuit through the primate basal ganglia. *J Neurosci*, *15*(7 Pt 1), 4851–4867.

Hariri, A. R., Mattay, V. S., Tessitore, A., Fera, F., & Weinberger, D. R. (2003). Neocortical modulation of the amygdala response to fearful stimuli. *Biol Psychiatry*, *53*(6), 494–501.

Harlow, J. M. (1848). Passage of an iron rod through the head. *Boston Medical and Surgical Journal*, *39*, 389–393.

Harlow, J. M. (1868). Recovery from the passage of an iron bar through the head. *Publications of the Massachusetts Medical Society*, *2*, 327–347.

Heatherton, T. F. & Baumeister, R. F. (1996). Self-regulation failure: Past, present, and future. *Psychological Inquiry*, *7*(1), 90–98.

Heatherton, T. F., Herman, C. P., & Polivy, J. (1991). Effects of physical threat and ego threat on eating behavior. *J Pers Soc Psychol*, *60*(1), 138–143.

Heatherton, T. F., Herman, C. P., & Polivy, J. (1992). Effects of distress on eating: The importance of ego-involvement. *J Pers Soc Psychol*, *62*(5), 801–803.

Heatherton, T. F., Polivy, J., Herman, C. P., & Baumeister, R. F. (1993). Self-awareness, task failure, and disinhibition: How attentional focus affects eating. *J Pers*, *61*(1), 49–61.

Heatherton, T. F. & Vohs, K. D. (1998). Why is it so difficult to inhibit behavior? *Psychological Inquiry*, *9*(3), 212–216.

Hécaen, H. (1964). Mental symptoms associated with tumors of the frontal lobe. In J. M. Warren & K. Ackert (Eds.), *The frontal granular cortex and behavior* (pp. 335–352). New York: McGraw-Hill.

Herman, C. P. & Mack, D. (1975). Restrained and unrestrained eating. *J Pers*, *43*(4), 647–660.

Hodgins, D. C., el-Guebaly, N., & Armstrong, S. (1995). Prospective and retrospective reports of mood states before relapse to substance use. *J Consult Clin Psychol*, *63*(3), 400–407.

Hofmann, W., Rauch, W., & Gawronski, B. (2007). And deplete us not into temptation: Automatic attitudes, dietary restraint, and self-regulatory resources as determinants of eating behavior. *Journal of Experimental Social Psychology*, *43*(3), 497–504.

Hollerman, J. R., Tremblay, L., & Schultz, W. (1998). Influence of reward expectation on behavior-related neuronal activity in primate striatum. *J Neurophysiol*, *80*(2), 947–963.

Imperato, A. & Di Chiara, G. (1986). Preferential stimulation of dopamine release in the nucleus accumbens of freely moving rats by ethanol. *J Pharmacol Exp Ther*, *239*(1), 219–228.

Jarvie, H. F. (1954). Frontal lobe wounds causing disinhibition: A study of six cases. *Journal of Neurology, Neurosurgery and Psychiatry*, *17*, 14–32.

Jastrowitz, J. (1888). Beitrage zur Lokalisation im Grosshirn und uber deren praktische Verwerthung. *Deutsche Medizinische Wochenschrift*, *14*.

Johnstone, T., van Reekum, C. M., Urry, H. L., Kalin, N. H., & Davidson, R. J. (2007). Failure to regulate: Counterproductive recruitment of top-down prefrontal-subcortical circuitry in major depression. *J Neurosci*, *27*(33), 8877–8884.

Jones-Gotman, M. & Milner, B. (1977). Design fluency: The invention of nonsense drawings after focal cortical lesions. *Neuropsychologia*, *15*(4–5), 653–674.

Karama, S., Lecours, A. R., Leroux, J. M., Bourgouin, P., Beaudoin, G., Joubert, S., et al. (2002). Areas of brain activation in males and females during viewing of erotic film excerpts. *Hum Brain Mapp*, *16*(1), 1–13.

Kerns, J. G., Cohen, J. D., MacDonald, A. W., 3rd, Cho, R. Y., Stenger, V. A., & Carter, C. S. (2004). Anterior cingulate conflict monitoring and adjustments in control. *Science*, *303*(5660), 1023–1026.

Kessler, R. C., Chiu, W. T., Demler, O., Merikangas, K. R., & Walters, E. E. (2005). Prevalence, severity, and comorbidity of 12-month DSM-IV disorders in the National Comorbidity Survey Replication. *Arch Gen Psychiatry*, *62*(6), 617–627.

Kim, H., Somerville, L. H., Johnstone, T., Alexander, A. L., & Whalen, P. J. (2003). Inverse amygdala and medial prefrontal cortex responses to surprised faces. *Neuroreport*, *14*(18), 2317–2322.

Kirschbaum, W. R. (1951). Excessive hunger as a symptom of cerebral origin. *Journal of Nervous and Mental Disease*, *113*, 95–114.

Knutson, B., Taylor, J., Kaufman, M., Peterson, R., & Glover, G. (2005). Distributed neural representation of expected value. *J Neurosci*, *25*(19), 4806–4812.

Koepp, M. J., Gunn, R. N., Lawrence, A. D., Cunningham, V. J., Dagher, A., Jones, T., et al. (1998). Evidence for striatal dopamine release during a video game. *Nature*, *393*(6682), 266–268.

Koob, G. F. & Le Moal, M. (1997). Drug abuse: Hedonic homeostatic dysregulation. *Science*, *278*(5335), 52–58.

Koob, G. F. & Le Moal, M. (2008). Addiction and the brain antireward system. *Annu Rev Psychol*, *59*, 29–53.

Krogman, W. M. (1977). *Child growth*. Ann Arbor: University of Michigan Press.

Lanfranchi, G. (1315). *Chirurgia magna*. London: Marshe.

Laplane, D., Degos, J. D., Baulac, M., & Gray, F. (1981). Bilateral infarction of the anterior cingulate gyri and of the fornices. Report of a case. *J Neurol Sci*, *51*(2), 289–300.

Le Beau, J. & Pecker, J. (1949). La topectomie péricalleuse antérieure dans certaines formes d'agitation psychomotrice au cours de l'épilepsie et de l'arriération mentale. *Rev. neurol.*, *81*, 1039–1041.

Maas, L. C., Lukas, S. E., Kaufman, M. J., Weiss, R. D., Daniels, S. L., Rogers, V. W., et al. (1998). Functional magnetic resonance imaging of human brain activation during cue-induced cocaine craving. *Am J Psychiatry*, *155*(1), 124–126.

MacDonald, A. W., 3rd, Cohen, J. D., Stenger, V. A., & Carter, C. S. (2000). Dissociating the role of the dorsolateral prefrontal and anterior cingulate cortex in cognitive control. *Science*, *288*(5472), 1835–1838.

Macmillan, M. (2000). *An odd kind of fame: Stories of Phineas Gage*. Cambridge: MIT Press.

McClernon, F. J., Hiott, F. B., Huettel, S. A., & Rose, J. E. (2005). Abstinence-induced changes in self-report craving correlate with event-related FMRI responses to smoking cues. *Neuropsychopharmacology*, *30*(10), 1940–1947.

McDonald, A. J., Mascagni, F., & Guo, L. (1996). Projections of the medial and lateral prefrontal cortices to the amygdala: A Phaseolus vulgaris leucoagglutinin study in the rat. *Neuroscience*, *71*(1), 55–75.

Metcalfe, J. & Mischel, W. (1999). A hot/cool-system analysis of delay of gratification: Dynamics of willpower. *Psychological review*, *106*(1), 3–19.

Miller, E. K. & Cohen, J. D. (2001). An integrative theory of prefrontal cortex function. *Annual Review of Neuroscience*, *24*, 167–202.

Milner, B. (1963). Effects of different brain lesions on card sorting. *Arch Neurol*, *9*, 90–100.

Mirenowicz, J. & Schultz, W. (1996). Preferential activation of midbrain dopamine neurons by appetitive rather than aversive stimuli. *Nature*, *379*(6564), 449–451.

Mischel, W., Shoda, Y., & Rodriguez, M. I. (1989). Delay of gratification in children. *Science*, *244*(4907), 933–938.

Mitchell, J. P., Heatherton, T. F., Kelley, W. M., Wyland, C. L., Wegner, D. M., & Neil Macrae, C. (2007). Separating sustained from transient aspects of cognitive control during thought suppression. *Psychol Sci*, *18*(4), 292–297.

Muraven, M., Collins, R. L., & Nienhaus, K. (2002). Self-control and alcohol restraint: An initial application of the self-control strength model. *Psychology of Addictive Behaviors*, *16*(2), 113–120.

Muraven, M. & Baumeister. R.F. (2000), Self-regulation and depletion of limited resources: Does self-control resemble a muscle? *Psychological Bulletin*. *126*(2), 247–259.

Muraven, M., Tice, D. M., & Baumeister, R. F. (1998). Self-control as limited resource: Regulatory depletion patterns. *J Pers Soc Psychol*, *74*(3), 774–789.

Myrick, H., Anton, R. F., Li, X., Henderson, S., Randall, P. K., & Voronin, K. (2008). Effect of naltrexone and ondansetron on alcohol cue-induced activation of the ventral striatum in alcohol-dependent people. *Arch Gen Psychiatry*, *65*(4), 466–475.

New, A. S., Hazlett, E. A., Buchsbaum, M. S., Goodman, M., Mitelman, S. A., Newmark, R., et al. (2007). Amygdala-prefrontal disconnection in borderline personality disorder. *Neuropsychopharmacology*, *32*(7), 1629–1640.

O'Doherty, J. P., Dayan, P., Friston, K., Critchley, H., & Dolan, R. J. (2003). Temporal difference models and reward-related learning in the human brain. *Neuron*, *38*(2), 329–337.

Ochsner, K. N., Bunge, S. A., Gross, J. J., & Gabrieli, J. D. (2002). Rethinking feelings: An FMRI study of the cognitive regulation of emotion. *J Cogn Neurosci*, *14*(8), 1215–1229.

Ochsner, K. N. & Gross, J. J. (2005). The cognitive control of emotion. *Trends Cogn Sci*, *9*(5), 242–249.

Ochsner, K. N., Ray, R. D., Cooper, J. C., Robertson, E. R., Chopra, S., Gabrieli, J. D., et al. (2004). For better or for worse: Neural systems supporting the cognitive down- and up-regulation of negative emotion. *Neuroimage*, *23*(2), 483–499.

Ongur, D., An, X., & Price, J. L. (1998). Prefrontal cortical projections to the hypothalamus in macaque monkeys. *J Comp Neurol*, *401*(4), 480–505.

Ongur, D. & Price, J. L. (2000). The organization of networks within the orbital and medial prefrontal cortex of rats, monkeys and humans. *Cerebral Cortex*, *10*(3), 206–219.

Oppenheim, H. (1890). Zur Pathologie der Grosshirngeschwülste (On the pathology of cerebral tumors). *Archiv für Psychiatrie und Nervenkrankheiten*, *22*, 27–72.

Pandya, D. N. & Barnes, C. L. (1987). Architecture and connections of the frontal lobes. In: Perecman E, editor. *The frontal lobes revisited*, New York: IRBN Press; 1987. p. 41–72.

Pandya, D. N., Van Hoesen, G. W., & Mesulam, M. M. (1981). Efferent connections of the cingulate gyrus in the rhesus monkey. *Exp Brain Res*, *42*(3–4), 319–330.

Paus, T. (2001). Primate anterior cingulate cortex: Where motor control, drive and cognition interface. *Nat Rev Neurosci*, *2*(6), 417–424.

Payne, B. K. (2001). Prejudice and perception: The role of automatic and controlled processes in misperceiving a weapon. *Journal of Personality and Social Psychology*, *81*(2), 181–192.

Penfield, W. & Evans, J. (1935). The frontal lobe in man: A clinical study of maximum removals. *Brain*, *58*, 115–133.

Perret, E. (1974). The left frontal lobe of man and the suppression of habitual responses in verbal categorical behaviour. *Neuropsychologia*, *12*(3), 323–330.

Petrides, M. & Milner, B. (1982). Deficits on subject-ordered tasks after frontal- and temporal-lobe lesions in man. *Neuropsychologia*, *20*(3), 249–262.

Petrides, M. & Pandya, D. N. (1999). Dorsolateral prefrontal cortex: Comparative cytoarchitectonic analysis in the human and the macaque brain and corticocortical connection patterns. *Eur J Neurosci*, *11*(3), 1011–1036.

Pfaus, J. G., Damsma, G., Nomikos, G. G., Wenkstern, D. G., Blaha, C. D., Phillips, A. G., et al. (1990). Sexual behavior enhances central dopamine transmission in the male rat. *Brain Res*, *530*(2), 345–348.

Phelps, E. A., O'Connor, K. J., Cunningham, W. A., Funayama, E. S., Gatenby, J. C., Gore, J. C., et al. (2000). Performance on indirect measures of race evaluation predicts amygdala activation. *Journal of Cognitive Neuroscience*, *12*(5), 729–738.

Platter, F. (1614). *Observationum, in hominis affectibus plerisque, corpori et animo, functionum laesione, dolore, aiave molestia et vitio incommodantibus, libri tres*. Basel: Koenig.

Richeson, J. A., Baird, A. A., Gordon, H. L., Heatherton, T. F., Wyland, C. L., Trawalter, S., et al. (2003). An fMRI investigation of the impact of interracial contact on executive function. *Nat Neurosci*, *6*(12), 1323–1328.

Richeson, J. A. & Shelton, J. N. (2003). When prejudice does not pay: Effects of interracial contact on executive function. *Psychol Sci*, *14*(3), 287–290.

Rilling, J. K. (2006). Human and nonhuman primate brains: Are they allometrically scaled versions of the same design? *Evolutionary Anthropology*, *15*(2), 65–77.

Roberts, D. C., Corcoran, M. E., & Fibiger, H. C. (1977). On the role of ascending catecholaminergic systems in intravenous self-administration of cocaine. *Pharmacol Biochem Behav*, *6*(6), 615–620.

Rosenkilde, C. E. (1979). Functional-heterogeneity of the prefrontal cortex in the monkey—Review. *Behavioral and Neural Biology*, *25*(3), 301–345.

Rothemund, Y., Preuschhof, C., Bohner, G., Bauknecht, H. C., Klingebiel, R., Flor, H., et al. (2007). Differential activation of the dorsal striatum by high-calorie visual food stimuli in obese individuals. *Neuroimage*, *37*(2), 410–421.

Rylander, G. (1939). Personality changes after operations on the frontal lobes. Copenhagen: Munksgaard.

Saver, J. L. & Damasio, A. R. (1991). Preserved access and processing of social knowledge in a patient with acquired sociopathy due to ventromedial frontal damage. *Neuropsychologia, 29*(12), 1241–1249.

Schilstrom, B., Svensson, H. M., Svensson, T. H., & Nomikos, G. G. (1998). Nicotine and food induced dopamine release in the nucleus accumbens of the rat: Putative role of alpha7 nicotinic receptors in the ventral tegmental area. *Neuroscience, 85*(4), 1005–1009.

Schoenemann, P. T., Sheehan, M. J., & Glotzer, L. D. (2005). Prefrontal white matter volume is disproportionately larger in humans than in other primates. *Nature Neuroscience, 8*(2), 242–252.

Shallice, T. (1982). Specific impairments of planning. *Philos Trans R Soc Lond B Biol Sci, 298*(1089), 199–209.

Shallice, T. & Burgess, P. (1996). The domain of supervisory processes and temporal organization of behaviour. *Philos Trans R Soc Lond B Biol Sci, 351*(1346), 1405–1411; discussion 1411–1402.

Shallice, T. & Burgess, P. W. (1991). Deficits in strategy application following frontal lobe damage in man. *Brain, 114 (Pt 2)*, 727–741.

Shamosh, N. & Gray, J. (2007). The relation between fluid intelligence and self-regulatory depletion. *Cognition & Emotion, 21*(8), 1833–1843.

Shin, L. M., Wright, C. I., Cannistraro, P. A., Wedig, M. M., McMullin, K. A., Martis, B., et al. (2004). An fMRI study of amygdala and medial prefrontal cortex responses to overtly presented fearful faces in posttraumatic stress disorder. *Neuropsychopharmacology, 29*, S208–S208.

Shoda, Y. (1990). Predicting adolescent cognitive and self-regulatory competencies from preschool delay of gratification: Identifying diagnostic conditions. *Developmental Psychology, 26*(6), 978–986.

Silbersweig, D., Clarkin, J. F., Goldstein, M., Kernberg, O. F., Tuescher, O., Levy, K. N., et al. (2007). Failure of frontolimbic inhibitory function in the context of negative emotion in borderline personality disorder. *Am J Psychiatry, 164*(12), 1832–1841.

Solinas, M., Ferre, S., You, Z. B., Karcz-Kubicha, M., Popoli, P., & Goldberg, S. R. (2002). Caffeine induces dopamine and glutamate release in the shell of the nucleus accumbens. *J Neurosci, 22*(15), 6321–6324.

Stein, E. A., Pankiewicz, J., Harsch, H. H., Cho, J. K., Fuller, S. A., Hoffmann, R. G., et al. (1998). Nicotine-induced limbic cortical activation in the human brain: A functional MRI study. *Am J Psychiatry, 155*(8), 1009–1015.

Stewart, W. F., Ricci, J. A., Chee, E., Hahn, S. R., & Morganstein, D. (2003). Cost of lost productive work time among US workers with depression. *JAMA, 289*(23), 3135–3144.

Stoeckel, L. E., Weller, R. E., Cook, E. W., 3rd, Twieg, D. B., Knowlton, R. C., & Cox, J. E. (2008). Widespread reward-system activation in obese women in response to pictures of high-calorie foods. *Neuroimage, 41*(2), 636–647.

Tangney, J. P., Baumeister, R. F., & Boone, A. L. (2004). High self-control predicts good adjustment, less pathology, better grades, and interpersonal success. *Journal of Personality, 72*(2), 271–324.

Taylor, J. R. & Robbins, T. W. (1986). 6-Hydroxydopamine lesions of the nucleus accumbens, but not of the caudate nucleus, attenuate enhanced responding with reward-related stimuli produced by intra-accumbens d-amphetamine. *Psychopharmacology (Berl), 90*(3), 390–397.

Tow, P. M. & Whitty, C. W. (1953). Personality changes after operations on the cingulate gyrus in man. *J Neurol Neurosurg Psychiatry, 16*(3), 186–193.

Urry, H. L., van Reekum, C. M., Johnstone, T., Kalin, N. H., Thurow, M. E., Schaefer, H. S., et al. (2006). Amygdala and ventromedial prefrontal cortex are inversely coupled during regulation of negative affect and predict the diurnal pattern of cortisol secretion among older adults. *J Neurosci, 26*(16), 4415–4425.

Vendrell, P., Junque, C., Pujol, J., Jurado, M. A., Molet, J., & Grafman, J. (1995). The role of prefrontal regions in the Stroop Task. *Neuropsychologia, 33*(3), 341–352.

Visscher, K. M., Miezin, F. M., Kelly, J. E., Buckner, R. L., Donaldson, D. I., McAvoy, M. P., et al. (2003). Mixed blocked/event-related designs separate transient and sustained activity in fMRI. *Neuroimage, 19*(4), 1694–1708.

Vogt, B. A. & Pandya, D. N. (1987). Cingulate cortex of the rhesus monkey: II. Cortical afferents. *J Comp Neurol, 262*(2), 271–289.

Vohs, K. D., Baumeister, R. F., & Ciarocco, N. J. (2005). Self-regulation and self-presentation: regulatory resource depletion impairs impression management and effortful self-presentation depletes regulatory resources. *J Pers Soc Psychol, 88*(4), 632–657.

Vohs, K. D. & Heatherton, T. F. (2000). Self-regulatory failure: A resource-depletion approach. *Psychological Science, 11*(3), 249–254.

Wang, G. J., Volkow, N. D., Telang, F., Jayne, M., Ma, J., Rao, M., et al. (2004). Exposure to appetitive food stimuli markedly activates the human brain. *Neuroimage, 21*(4), 1790–1797.

Ward, A. & Mann, T. (2000). Don't mind if I do: Disinhibited eating under cognitive load. *Journal of Personality and Social Psychology, 78*(4), 753–763.

Wegner, D. M. (1989) *White bears and other unwanted thoughts: Suppression, obsession, and the psychology of mental control.* New York: Viking/Penguin.

Welt, L. (1888). Uber charakterveranderungen der menschen infolge von lasionen des stirnhirn. *Deutsch. Arch. f. Klin. Med., 42*, 339–390.

Wexler, B. E., Gottschalk, C. H., Fulbright, R. K., Prohovnik, I., Lacadie, C. M., Rounsaville, B. J., et al. (2001). Functional magnetic resonance imaging of cocaine craving. *Am J Psychiatry, 158*(1), 86–95.

Whalen, P. J., Bush, G., McNally, R. J., Wilhelm, S., McInerney, S. C., Jenike, M. A., et al. (1998). The emotional counting Stroop paradigm: A functional magnetic resonance imaging probe of the anterior cingulate affective division. *Biol Psychiatry, 44*(12), 1219–1228.

Whalen, P. J., Rauch, S. L., Etcoff, N. L., McInerney, S. C., Lee, M. B., & Jenike, M. A. (1998). Masked presentations of emotional facial expressions modulate amygdala activity without explicit knowledge. *J Neurosci, 18*(1), 411–418.

Wheeler, M. E. & Fiske, S. T. (2005). Controlling racial prejudice: Social-cognitive goals affect amygdala and stereotype activation. *Psychol Sci, 16*(1), 56–63.

Whitty, C. W. M., Duffield, J. E., Tow, P. M., & Cairns, H. (1952). Anterior cingulectomy in the treatment of mental disease. *Lancet, 1*(475–481).

Wilson, D. H. & Chang, A. E. (1974). Bilateral anterior cingulectomy for the relief of intractable pain. Report of 23 patients. *Confin Neurol, 36*(1), 61–68.

Wilson, S. J., Sayette, M. A., & Fiez, J. A. (2004). Prefrontal responses to drug cues: A neurocognitive analysis. *Nat Neurosci, 7*(3), 211–214.

Woolley, J. D., Gorno-Tempini, M. L., Seeley, W. W., Rankin, K., Lee, S. S., Matthews, B. R., et al. (2007). Binge eating is associated with right orbitofrontal-insular-striatal atrophy in frontotemporal dementia. *Neurology, 69*(14), 1424–1433.

Wrase, J., Grusser, S. M., Klein, S., Diener, C., Hermann, D., Flor, H., et al. (2002). Development of alcohol-associated cues and cue-induced brain activation in alcoholics. *Eur Psychiatry, 17*(5), 287–291.

Wyland, C. L., Kelley, W. M., Macrae, C. N., Gordon, H. L., & Heatherton, T. F. (2003). Neural correlates of thought suppression. *Neuropsychologia, 41*(14), 1863–1867.

Yoo, S. S., Gujar, N., Hu, P., Jolesz, F. A., & Walker, M. P. (2007). The human emotional brain without sleep—a prefrontal amygdala disconnect. *Curr Biol, 17*(20), R877–878.

Zubieta, J. K., Heitzeg, M. M., Xu, Y., Koeppe, R. A., Ni, L., Guthrie, S., et al. (2005). Regional cerebral blood flow responses to smoking in tobacco smokers after overnight abstinence. *Am J Psychiatry, 162*(3), 567–577.

"Hearing Voices": Neurocognition of the Human Voice

Pascal Belin

Abstract

This chapter examines the neurocognitive bases for voice cognition, focusing on two main questions: Are voices special? That is, how are human voices detected and do they selectively engage neural mechanisms not engaged by nonvocal sounds? And, how is identity information contained in voice—gender and unique identity—processed by the brain? Before addressing these two issues, a brief overview of how voices are produced and their acoustical properties is provided. Evidence suggests that normal human listeners are equipped with sophisticated neural machinery for processing voices and extracting the rich information they contain. Comparable neuronal networks are present in the macaque brain suggesting a long evolutionary history of cerebral voice processing.

Keywords: voice, speech, paralinguistic, identity, affect, fMRI, ERPs, auditory cortex, superior temporal sulcus

Voices are "Auditory Faces"

We live in a world of voices. Every day, we spend a considerable amount of time listening to voices: voices of persons physically present; of persons at remote locations (radio, television, telephone, voice over IP); and also, increasingly, of people that do not exist—synthetic voices. In most cases these voices carry speech: a sophisticated, human-specific use of voice for fast transmission of symbolic information. But voices don't "just" carry speech; they contain much additional information which we appear to be particularly skilled at extracting.

Perceiving the rich information contained in voices plays a central role in our social interactions: Understanding speech is of course essential, but in most cases a deeper understanding of the social context is gained by an accurate perception of *how* things are being said and *who* says them. Studying

that under-explored aspect of voice perception is an important part of the research agenda in social neuroscience.

When we hear a voice, even when linguistic information is not accessible—for example in speech heard through a wall, or in a foreign language, or in inarticulate expressions of emotion such as laughs—we first clearly identify the sound as a voice, that is, we recognize that it has been produced by the vocal apparatus of a fellow human being, and not by an inanimate object or a nonhuman animal. We also are able to extract valuable information on the invariant identity characteristics of the person who produced the vocalization: whether that person is male or female, his/her approximate age and size; we can often identify from novel utterances a person whose voice we already heard. In addition, valuable information on the physiological state of the speaker is available: his/her temporary mood or affective state, but also more subtle information on the speaker's hormonal state and "biological value" conveyed by percepts such as vocal attractiveness.

Because the different types of vocal information (speech, identity, affect) are similar in nature to those conveyed by faces, voices can be considered as "auditory faces." And as for faces, we are endowed with a complex array of cognitive abilities—"voice-cognition" abilities—for extraction and categorization of non-speech vocal information.

These voice-cognition abilities have a much longer evolutionary history than speech perception: Speech "only" appeared some tens of thousand of years ago, while our ancestors have been living in a world of vocalizations for hundreds of millions of years. Many animal species have been shown to possess the ability to identify conspecific individuals from their vocalizations (Charrier, Mathevon, & Jouventin, 2001; Insley, 2000; Rendall, Owren, & Rodman, 1998). Similarly, voice cognition develops much earlier than speech perception during development: For example, newborn babies tested only a few hours after birth are already able to recognize their mother's voice (DeCasper & Fifer, 1980; Ockleford, Vince, Layton, & Reader, 1988). There is even recent evidence of voice discrimination abilities *in utero* by fetuses (Kisilevsky et al., 2003).

Despite the central role played by voice-cognition abilities in our social interactions, research into their cerebral bases has received much less attention than into speech perception or comparable research on face processing. In this chapter we examine the neurocognitive bases for voice cognition, focusing on two main questions: Are voices special? That is, how are human voices detected and do they selectively engage neural mechanisms not engaged by nonvocal sounds? And, how is identity information contained in voice—gender and unique identity—processed by the brain? Before addressing these two issues a brief overview of how voices are produced and their acoustical properties seems necessary.

What is a Voice?

According to the "source/filter" acoustic theory of speech perception (Fant, 1960), vocalizations result from the interaction of a sound source in the larynx with a filter provided by the vocal tract (Fig. 25.1). The sound source consists of quasi-periodic series of pulses generated in the larynx by the successive openings and closings of the vocal folds (Titze, 1993). The rate of vibration of the vocal folds is the fundamental frequency of phonation (f0). The frequency spectrum of this sound source contains energy not only at the f0, but also at all integer multiples of the f0 (harmonics), with decreasing intensity along with frequency. In addition to these quasi-periodic components, the source contains a variable proportion of energy at inharmonic frequencies, caused by temporal or frequency irregularities in vocal-fold vibration (shimmer and jitter; contributing to the "rough" quality of voice) or noise-related aerodynamic turbulences at the vocal folds (contributing to the "breathy" quality of voice).

We never get to hear the vocal source because it is modified by the cavities and tissues located above the larynx (supra-laryngeal vocal tract), that act as a complex, dynamic acoustic filter amplifying energy at certain frequencies. The frequency zones thus amplified, called "formants," depend on both the unique properties of the vocal tract (e.g., its size) and its temporary configuration. Speech phonemes correspond to different positions of the articulators (e.g., tongue, lips) that induce formants at different frequencies. But formant frequencies also depend on the size of the vocal tract, with smaller vocal tracts yielding higher, more dispersed formant frequencies (Fitch, 2000).

The "source" and "filter" components of voice can be modified largely independently of the other—analogous to the eyes and mouth of a face. Speech information is essentially conveyed by the "filter" component of voice, although source-related information (e.g., f0 contour) provides additional linguistic information (e.g., linguistic prosody) or sometimes critical phonetic information in the case of tone languages such as Mandarin. Inter-individual differences in age, gender or hormonal state influence both source and filter component of voice: For instance, men have lower average f0 and formant frequencies then women—although f0 range largely overlaps for men and women. Women use their vocal folds in a more open configuration than men, leading to a higher ratio of low to high frequencies and more aspiration noise in the source (Klatt & Klatt, 1990).

Are Voices Special?

Does hearing voices recruit neuronal networks not—or less—activated by sounds from other categories? The "special" question has already been asked for speech (Liberman & Mattingly, 1989) but also, perhaps more adequately for our purpose, for faces (Farah, 1996). Several lines of evidence converge to the notion that face processing activates specific neuronal networks more than non-facial objects.

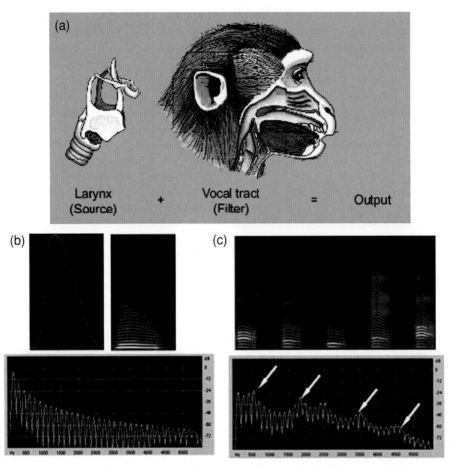

Fig. 25.1 Voice production. a. Vocalizations in human and non-human primates result from the interaction of a source in the larynx with the supralaryngeal vocal tract acting as an acoustic filter. b. The vocal source. Left panel: waveform of a single glottal pulse. Right panel: spectrogram of a sound generated in the larynx by periodic openings and closings of the vocal folds. X-axis: time. Y-axis: frequency. Lower panel: power spectrum of the same sound, showing acoustical energy at all harmonics and monotonically decreasing energy with increasing frequency. X-axis: frequency. Y-axis: power. c. The vocal filter. Upper panel: spectrograms of different phonemes obtained by filtering the glottal source in b. with different configurations of the articulators, resulting in amplification of different frequency bands (formants). X-axis: time. Y-axis: frequency. Lower panel: power spectrum of one of these phonemes. White arrows indicate formant frequencies amplified by vocal tract filtering. X-axis: frequency. Y-axis: power.
From Fitch, W.T. (2000). Reproduced with permission of Elsevier.

These include: behavioral evidence for greater disruption of face than object processing by picture inversion—the "face inversion effect" (Thompson, 1980; Yin, 1969); the observation of patients with impaired face recognition ("prosopagnosia") despite normal object recognition (Assal, 2001; Bodamer, 1947; Farah, Levinson, & Klein, 1995); electrophysiological recordings in macaque superior temporal sulcus (STS) and inferior temporal cortex showing cells with greater response to faces than other objects (Freiwald, Tsao, & Livingstone, 2009; Perrett et al., 1985; Rolls, 2007); evidence for a face-selective electrophysiological "N170" negativity over occipito-temporal cortex (Bentin, Allison, Puce, Perez, & McCarthy, 1996; Puce, Allison, &

McCarthy, 1999; Rossion et al., 1999; but see Thierry, Martin, Downing, & Pegna, 2007); and neuroimaging evidence for greater responses to faces than objects in discrete cortical regions in the human (Haxby, Hoffman, & Ida Gobbini, 2000; Kanwisher, McDermott, & Chun, 1997; Kanwisher & Yovel, 2006; Sergent & Signoret, 1992), and more recently, macaque (Tsao, Freiwald, Knutsen, Mandeville, & Tootell, 2003; Tsao, Freiwald, Tootell, & Livingstone, 2006) brain.

Phonagnosia

What is the corresponding evidence for voices? Clinical studies have shown the existence of patients with selective deficits in voice discrimination or recognition, a deficit termed "phonagnosia" (Assal, Aubert, & Buttet, 1981; Assal, Zander, Kremin, & Buttet, 1976; Neuner & Schweinberger, 2000; Peretz et al., 1994; Van Lancker & Canter, 1982; Van Lancker, Cummings, Kreiman, & Dobkin, 1988). Phonagnosia, like prosopagnosia, has been found to occur most often after posterior right-hemispheric lesions, and is doubly dissociated from receptive aphasia: Patients with receptive aphasia are typically unimpaired at voice recognition and patients with phonagnosia show largely speech perception (Van Lancker & Canter, 1982), demonstrating that voice recognition and speech comprehension rely on partially dissociated neural structures. Interestingly, the first documented case of developmental phonagnosia has recently been described: a woman with above-average IQ showing a selective deficit in voice recognition in the absence of an apparent lesion (Garrido et al., 2009), in analogy with cases of developmental prosopagnosia (Duchaine & Nakayama, 2006). Unfortunately, however, these clinical studies offer little neuro-anatomical detail; they are also much less numerous than comparable studies in prosopagnosic patients, probably owing to the lack of standardized, language-independent batteries of voice-perception tests.

Temporal Voice Areas (TVA) in Auditory Cortex

Neuroimaging techniques such as functional magnetic resonance imaging (fMRI) provide unambiguous evidence for voice selectivity in the human auditory cortex. Using fMRI and a block design, Belin and colleagues revealed discrete, bilateral areas of the auditory cortex showing significantly greater activity in response to voices compared to natural nonvocal sounds such as environmental or musical sounds (Belin, Zatorre, & Ahad, 2002; Belin, Zatorre, Lafaille, Ahad, & Pike, 2000). Although the location of this region, termed the "temporal voice area" (TVA), varied from one participant to the other, it was found in most subjects along the upper bank of the middle part of the STS bilaterally (Figure 25.2), as was the group-averaged maximum of voice sensitivity (Belin, Zatorre, Lafaille, Ahad, & Pike, 2000). Note that the reverse pattern was not found, that is, no region showed a greater response to the nonvocal sounds compared to the vocal ones.

Follow-up experiments using control sound categories such as bells (to control for within-category homogeneity) and scrambled voices (to disrupt frequency spectrum while persevering temporal envelope) suggested a high degree of selectivity of the TVA: Whereas the bilateral TVA responded to all sound categories more to the silent baseline—showing they do not exclusively process vocal sounds—they were significantly more active for the original vocal sounds (Belin, Zatorre, Lafaille, Ahad, & Pike, 2000).

The comparison of responses between speech and nonspeech vocal sounds (e.g., coughs, laughs) reveals an interesting pattern of results: Speech sounds are found to drive the activity of all voice-sensitive regions to a high degree, and yield a much greater response than their scrambled version in most parts of auditory cortex (Belin, Zatorre, & Ahad, 2002). Part of this response recruits anterior

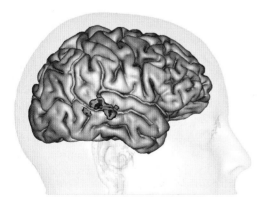
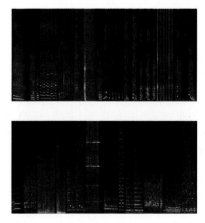

Fig. 25.2 The temporal voice area (TVA). Left panel: rendering of the voice-selective neuronal activity in the TVA on an individual subject's brain anatomy. The TVA are obtained by comparing cerebral activity measured in response to passive stimulation with vocal sounds (upper right panel) vs. non-vocal sounds (lower right panel).

STS regions of the left hemisphere, involved in speech comprehension (Davis & Johnsrude, 2003; Obleser, Zimmermann, Van Meter, & Rauschecker, 2007; Scott, Blank, Rosen, & Wise, 2000). In contrast, vocal sounds devoid of linguistic content, such as laughs, cries, humming, and so forth induce only little activity in the left hemisphere auditory cortex region. It is only in the right anterior temporal lobe regions that those nonspeech vocal sounds drive neuronal activity more than their scrambled counterpart, suggesting that these regions of the right hemisphere are likely to be involved in processing paralinguistic information in voices (Belin, Zatorre, & Ahad, 2002).

The TVA has been observed by several groups since these initial experiments (e.g., Ethofer, Van De Ville, Scherer, & Vuilleumier, 2009; Ethofer et al., 2007; e.g., Gervais et al., 2004; Grandjean et al., 2005). The Voice Neurocognition Laboratory provides stimuli for a 10-min, efficiency-optimized TVA localizer scan that has yielded robust activation of the TVA bilaterally in virtually every single subject so far (URL: http://vnl.psy.gla.ac.uk/resources_main.php).

Species-specificity of the TVA

Are the TVAs species-specific, that is, do they respond to all vocalizations, including animal ones, or do they specifically prefer the human voice? Fecteau et al. (2004) used an event-related design and two categories of animal sounds—a category of mixed animal calls and a homogeneous category of calls from a single species (cats)—to compare the response of the TVA to human voices versus animal vocalizations. Primary auditory cortices showed similar response profiles for the human voices, animal vocalizations, and nonvocal control sounds. At the level of the STS, the TVA showed greater response to the two human vocal sound categories than to the control sounds (Fecteau, Armony, Joanette, & Belin, 2004), replicating earlier findings. However, their response to the two categories of animal vocalizations was not different from the nonvocal controls, suggesting a high degree of species-specificity of the TVA (Fecteau, Armony, Joanette, & Belin, 2004).

A Voice Area in the Macaque Brain

An important corollary question is whether the TVAs are uniquely human: Did the TVAs appear only recently in evolution, perhaps along with the emergence of speech? Or could they also be observed in other animal species, suggesting a longer evolutionary history? Electrophysiological studies in nonhuman primates have provided some evidence of tuning to conspecific vocalizations in some parts of the auditory cortex, particularly its anterior portions (Tian, Reser, Durham, Kustov, & Rauschecker, 2001). But, perhaps because they so far mostly concentrated on core and belt areas of the auditory cortex, these studies have so far not highlighted cortical regions exhibiting strong preferences for conspecific vocalizations over nonvocal sound categories.

The recent development of fMRI studies in macaque monkeys allows a more direct test of the hypothesis of voice selectivity in the macaque auditory cortex. Petkov et al. (2008) used fMRI to measure the activity of awake and anesthetized macaque monkeys in response to auditory stimulation with macaque calls, as well as heterospecific vocalizations and nonvocal control sounds such as environmental sounds (Petkov et al., 2008). They found clear evidence in each macaque for discrete patches of the auditory cortex exhibiting strong preference for macaque calls above other sound categories (Figure 25.3). This greater response to voice was observed predominantly in the bilateral anterior temporal lobe, quite similar to the human results, although more on the superior temporal plane than along the STS (Petkov et al., 2008).

These findings provide strong evidence for a long evolutionary history of voice processing. The fact that voice areas are present in both humans and macaques indicates they were probably already present to some degree in the common ancestors of humans and macaques some 30 million years ago. The differing anatomical locations of the human and macaque TVAs raise the interesting possibility that the TVA may have positioned differently with evolution in the two species (Ghazanfar, 2008); but this finding may also be an artefact related to group averaging in human subjects and to the small macaque sample size studied so far. Interestingly, the TVA showed in both species a greater degree of voice selectivity in the right hemisphere, suggesting that the right hemisphere may have played a greater role than generally considered in the emergence of language.

Are the TVAs Involved in Voice Processing?

That question may seem provocative, but it is an important one. The TVAs show greater response to voices, yet whether they are actually specifically involved in processing vocal information is not established. There is little evidence so far for a causal

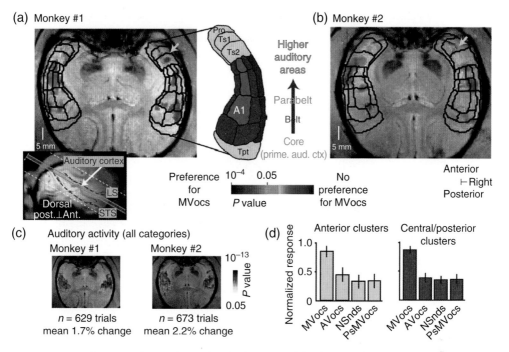

Fig. 25.3 A voice area in the macaque brain. a, b. Combined and coregistered data from six of the experiments with each of two animals. The color code from orange to red indicates voxels with a clear and significant preference for macaque vocalizations. The cyan-to-blue color code identifies voxels with no preference for MVocs. LS, lateral sulcus. The black contours outline the functionally or anatomically parcellated regions obtained independently of the main experiments for each animal; the blow-up identifies fields and regions of auditory cortex. c. The mean auditory cortex activity for each animal as the percentage of signal in relation to the silent baseline across the sound categories. d. Voxel-based normalized response for the anterior clusters (orange arrows, in a, b) and the more distributed central/posterior clusters that prefer MVocs. The MVocs response was significantly higher than the other conditions in these regions of auditory cortex (bars show the mean and the 5 and 95% confidence intervals, bootstrap procedure). A1, field in primary auditory cortex; Tpt, temporoparietal; Pro, proisocortex of the temporal pole.

From Petkov, C.I. et al. (2008). Reproduced with permission from the Nature Publishing Group.

link between activation of the TVA and voice processing. Their preference for voices may conceivably be caused by reasons other than voice processing. For example, as has been argued for face processing in the "fusiform face areas" (FFA), activation of the TVA may reflect expert-level subordinate categorization of different exemplars of a same basic category, rather than voice processing per se. This possibility remains to be examined by studying TVA response to nonvocal sound categories of expertise in populations of auditory experts such as ornithologists.

Abnormal TVA Activation in Autism

At least two studies support the notion that the TVA is indeed involved in processing vocal information. Gervais et al. (2004) examined the TVA in a group of autistic individuals and age-matched normal controls using the same experimental protocol as Belin et al. (2000). Whereas the control group showed typical activation of the TVA when activity

elicited by vocal versus nonvocal sound was compared, the autistic group failed to show activation of the TVA (Gervais et al., 2004). At the individual level, whereas all eight control subjects showed reliable TVA activation, two of the five autistic subjects showed unilateral-only activation of the TVA while the remaining three showed no TVA activation at all (Figure 25.4).

Interestingly, the response to the nonvocal sounds was similar in the two groups, suggesting normal processing of nonvocal sounds in the autistic group. It is only for the vocal sounds that a difference emerged; the autistic sample failing to show the additional TVA activation that controls showed (Gervais et al., 2004). This suggests a potential link between the communicative disorders associated with autism, particularly for vocal sounds (Klin, 1991; Rutherford, Baron-Cohen, & Wheelwright, 2002), and the abnormal activation of the TVA. This possibility received additional support by behavioral results of the study: When subjects were

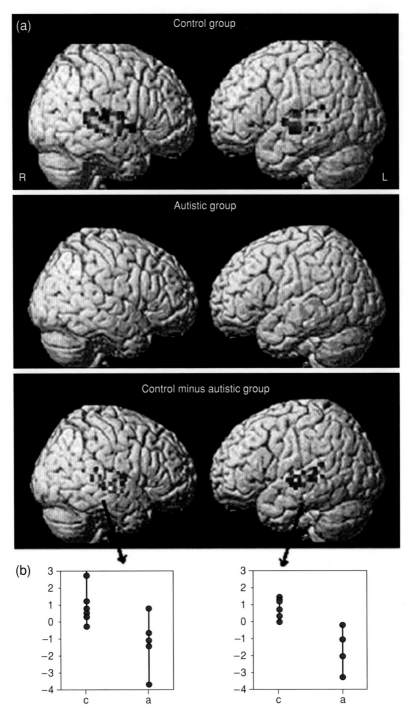

Fig. 25.4 Abnormal cerebral voice processing in autism. a. Location of voice-selective activation in each group (controls: upper panel; individuals with autism: middle panel) and in the direct comparison between groups (lower panel) are shown on a lateral view of both hemispheres. b. Plots illustrate the average voxel effect size for each subject of the two groups in the contrasts "voice vs. non-voice." From Gervais, H. et al. (2004). Reproduced with permission of the Nature Publishing Group.

asked after scanning to recall as many sounds that they had heard as possible, the normal subjects recalled an equal proportion of vocal and nonvocal sounds. In contrast, the autistic subjects recalled an overwhelming (91.5%) proportion of nonvocal sounds, suggesting that the lack of TVA activation was associated at the behavioral level with a bias towards nonvocal sounds. Further experiments are needed to replicate this finding and examine whether manipulating subjects' attention could reduce the abnormal TVA activation of the autistic subjects, as observed for face processing (Hadjikhani et al., 2004).

The Voice Perception Assessment

The above study emphasizes the importance of behavioral measures of voice processing for interpreting the findings of neuroimaging studies. The lack of a standardized, language-independent battery of voice perception similar to those available for face perception has probably hindered the research into the cerebral correlates of voice processing. In an effort to make such a tool available to the scientific community, we have developed the "Voice Perception Assessment" (VPA), an online series of brief tests examining memory for voices, voice discrimination (both with nonvocal control tests), and gender categorization. The VPA is available at: http://vnl.psy.gla.ac.uk/experiments/

Watson et al. (2009) directly examined the link between TVA activation and behavior by correlating brain activity measured with the TVA localizer scan with performance at the VPA in a group of 36 normal participants. A highly significant correlation was found between TVA activation in response to sounds—both vocal and nonvocal—and immediate recall performance at the voice memory test (Watson et al., 2009). Subjects in whom TVA response to sounds (both vocal and nonvocal) was higher correctly recalled more of the voices they had just heard. Interestingly, memory for bell sounds (the control sound category), although similar in the group to memory for voices, was not predicted by TVA activation. These preliminary findings are strong evidence that neuronal populations in the TVA are specifically involved in the encoding of individual voices, but not other sound categories such as bells, for storage in memory. Further studies investigating the link between voice perception performance and cerebral anatomy, for example, using voxel-based morphometry and diffusion tensor imaging, should yield important complementary information.

The Speed of Voice Processing

How fast does the brain differentiate human voices from other sound categories? Only a handful of electrophysiological studies so far have addressed this important issue. Two electroencephalography (EEG) studies using auditory-evoked potentials (AEP) reported a "voice-specific response" (VSR)

with greater amplitude for sung voices than tones played by different musical instruments. The VSR peaked at around 320 ms after stimulus onset and was strongest on the right side (Levy, Granot, & Bentin, 2003; Levy, Hasson, Avidan, Hendler, & Malach, 2001). The authors suggested that this component, different from the "novelty P300," might reflect allocation of attention related to the salience of voice stimuli.

A magnetoencephalography (MEG) study using similar stimuli (Gunji et al., 2003) found no difference in the N1 evoked by voices and instruments respectively, but found a sustained field with greater source strength for the voice stimuli between 300 and 500 ms after onset. They did not observe, however, a magnetic counterpart of the VSR found with ERP, which they attributed to the radial orientation of the sources involved or to the movie-viewing condition used in the MEG but not the ERP study.

The relatively long latencies of the VSR and the magnetic sustained field is surprising, however, given the much shorter latency (from 70 ms postonset) with which the brain discriminates sounds from living versus nonliving sources (Murray, Camen, Gonzalez Andino, Bovet, & Clarke, 2006), or, in the visual modality, the ~170 ms necessary to discriminate faces from nonface objects (Bentin, Allison, Puce, Perez, & McCarthy, 1996; Puce, Allison, & McCarthy, 1999; Rossion et al., 1999).

The "Fronto-temporal Positivity to Voices" (FTPV)

Charest et al. (2009) recently examined whether an earlier voice-specific response could be evidenced. High-density AEPs were recorded from 32 healthy volunteers who listened to 200-ms long stimuli from three sound categories—voices, bird songs, and environmental sounds—while performing a pure-tone detection task. Analyses revealed highly significant voice/nonvoice amplitude differences (Figure 25.5) emerging as early as 164 ms post stimulus onset and peaking around 200 ms on fronto-central (positivity; electrodes FC5 and FC6) and occipital (negativity) electrodes (Charest et al., 2009).

The observation of a "fronto-temporal positivity to voices" (FTPV) in the latency of the auditory P200 component by these two studies is particularly exciting. The finding appears robust, as it is observed in two studies using very different electrode montages, sets of stimuli, and experimental protocols. A reason why it has not been reported before is perhaps that most studies have focused on central

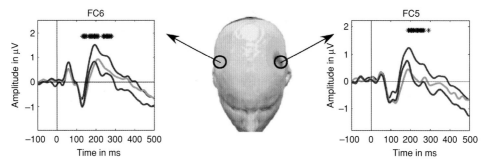

Fig. 25.5 The "Fronto-temporal positivity to voices" (FTPV). Electrophysiological studies reveal that fronto-temporal electrode sites FC5 and FC6 show enhanced evoked potential responses to sounds of human voice (red lines) compared to non-vocal sound categories (blue lines: environmental sounds; green lines: birdsongs) around 200msec after sound stimulus onset. Starts indicate significant amplitude differences as assessed by bootstrapping analyses. The lateral distribution and latency of the FTPV are comparable to those of the face-selective N170 component.

Reproduced from Charest, I. et al. (2009) with permission from the authors.

electrodes, which do not show a marked difference between voice and nonvocal sounds in these two studies. The FTPV thus appears to provide an index of voice processing with latencies and bilateral distribution (although on anterior electrodes) comparable to the face-selective N170 component. Particularly promising is the recent observation of a marked FTPV in 4- to 5-year-old children, suggesting that it could be used as an index of normal voice processing during development (Rogier, Roux, Belin, Bonnet-Brilhault, & Bruneau, 2010).

A Model of Voice Perception

In an effort to understand the functional architecture of cerebral voice processing, we proposed a model of voice perception (Belin, Fecteau, & Bedard, 2004) directly inspired from an influential model of face processing (Bruce & Young, 1986). This model (Figure 25.6) proposes that after low-level analysis in subcortical nuclei and core regions of auditory cortex common to all sound categories, vocal stimuli are further processed in a "structural encoding" stage that may be anatomically localized in the TVA. Vocal information is then processed in three functionally independent pathways: (i) analysis of speech information, known to involve anterior and posterior STS as well as inferior prefrontal regions predominantly in the left hemisphere; (ii) analysis of vocal affective information; and (iii) analysis of vocal identity information, possibly involving "voice recognition units" and a subsequent supra-modal stage of person recognition ("person identity nodes"). The three processing pathways are proposed to interact with one another during normal processing, but each can be selectively impaired.

The model conveys two main ideas. The first idea is that speech is but one type of vocal information: A better understanding of auditory cortex organization, and perhaps insights into the evolution of language (Ghazanfar, 2008), can be gained by considering the voice in its wider role as the carrier of multiple types of information, including (but not always) speech. The second idea is that similar architectures for vocal and facial processing would be a parsimonious principle of cerebral organization, given that voices and faces convey similar types of information that are integrated multi-modally in most situations (Campanella & Belin, 2007).

The model generates a number of predictions, some of which have already received empirical support, for example, the double dissociation between speech perception and voice identity processing in aphasic and phonagnosic patients. Other predictions of the model, such as the multi-modal integration of facial and vocal information between corresponding pathways remain to be tested. Whether its predictions are falsified or not, we hope this model provides a useful heuristic to guide future research.

Cerebral Processing of Identity Information in Voice

Voice carries rich information on the identity of the person who speaks—or simply vocalizes. It is a common observation that when we hear a person speaking (or simply vocalizing), we are able to extract much information on that person's individual characteristics (Kreiman, 1997), such as her gender (Lass, Hughes, Bowyer, Waters, & Bourne, 1976; Mullennix, Johnson, Topcu-Durgun, & Farnsworth, 1995), approximate age (Hartman, 1979; Linville & Rens, 2001), even her size (Lass & Davis, 1976;

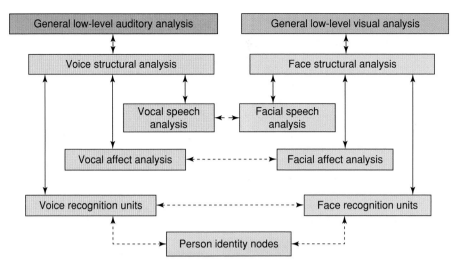

Fig. 25.6 A model of voice perception. The right-hand part of the figure is adapted from Bruce and Young's model of face perception. The left-hand part proposes a similar functional organization for voice processing. Dashed arrows indicate multimodal interactions. Reproduced from Belin, P., Fecteau, S. & Bedard, C. (2004) with permission of Elsevier.

Smith, Patterson, Turner, Kawahara, & Irino, 2005)—although impressions of size from the voice can be misleading (Rendall, Vokey, & Nemeth, 2007). In addition, although a speaker never produces the same sound twice, listeners are quite accurate at extracting invariant features in the vocal signal and build representations of a speaker's identity ("vocal signatures") that can be used to recognize that person from novel utterances. What are the cerebral bases for these voice identity perception abilities?

Processing of Speaker Identity in the Right Anterior Temporal Lobe

Belin and Zatorre (2003) used an fMRI-adaptation paradigm (Grill-Spector, Henson, & Martin, 2006; Grill-Spector & Malach, 2001) to investigate the cerebral basis of speaker identity perception. Normal volunteers were scanned while listening passively to 144 stimuli (12 different syllables spoken by 12 speakers) presented in blocks corresponding to two conditions. In the first condition ("Adapt speaker"), blocks (n = 12) corresponded to the 12 syllables spoken by a single speaker; in the second condition ("Adapt syllable"), blocks corresponded to a single syllable spoken by the 12 different speakers. These two conditions thus used the same 144 stimuli and the same passive listening task; only the order of stimulus presentation differed between the two conditions. So, not much activity difference was expected between these two conditions. But if the brain contains neuronal populations sensitive to a speaker's identity irrespective of the speech information contained

in the voice, these neuronal populations should adapt their activity when the identity of a speaker is repeated in a block. Whereas left and right primary auditory cortices showed similar fMRI signal in the two conditions, a single region (Figure 25.7a,b) showed the expected pattern of significantly less activity in the "Adapt speaker" condition compared to the "Adapt syllable" condition, or, in other words, greater activity when several different voices were heard in a block compared to when a single voice was heard (Belin & Zatorre, 2003). That region was located in the anterior part of the right superior temporal gyrus (STG), close to, and anterior to, the maximum of voice selectivity previously observed (Belin, Zatorre, Lafaille, Ahad, & Pike, 2000).

A superb confirmation of this finding was provided by a study that used a very different design: different stimuli and a "top-down" approach (as opposed to the "bottom-up" approach used by Belin & Zatorre, 2003). In that study (von Kriegstein, Eger, Kleinschmidt, & Giraud, 2003), subjects heard pairs of sentences and were instructed to direct their attention either to the verbal content (sentence discrimination task) or to the speaker pronouncing the sentence (speaker discrimination task). When the two condition were compared to one another, a region showing greatest activity in the "attend speaker" condition compared to the "attend sentence" was found in the right anterior STG (Figure 25.7c), very close to the region observed by Belin and Zatorre (2003). A follow-up study showed that this anterior STG region was functionally connected to

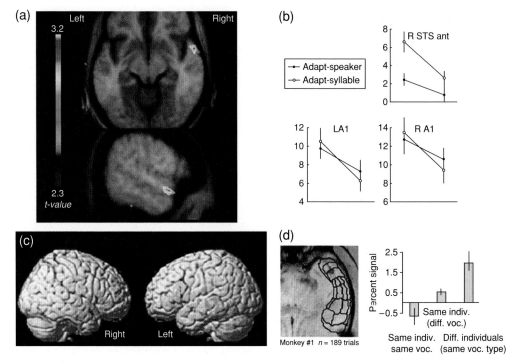

Fig. 25.7 Sensitivity to speaker's vocal identity in right anterior temporal lobe. a, b. A single region of the right anterior temporal lobe shows adaptation to speaker's voice, i.e., reduced activity in the "adapt-speaker" condition (a single voice per block speaking 12 different syllables) compared to the "adapt-syllable" condition (12 different voices per block). Left or right primary auditory cortex responds equally to the two conditions. c. The same region shows greater neuronal activity during listening to sentences when subjects' attention is directed to speaker identity compared to when it is directed to linguistic content. d. The anterior temporal lobe of the macaque also shows adaptation to speaker identity: the regions indicated in red colorscale in the left panel shows reduced activity when the macaque subject listens to different vocalizations from a same (macaque) speaker (middle bar in right-hand graph) compared to vocalizations from several different speakers (right bar).

Panels A & B: Reproduced with permission from Belin, P. & Zatorre, R.J. (2003) with permission of Lippincot Williams & Wilkins.
From von Kriegstein, K., Eger, E., Kleinschmidt, A. & Giraud, A.L. (2003). Panel C: Reproduced with permission from Elsevier.
From Petkov, C.I. et al. (2008). Panel D: Reproduced with permission from the Nature Publishing Group.

the TVA during the speaker identification task (Von Kriegstein & Giraud, 2004).

In their pioneering study of cerebral voice processing in the macaque, Petkov et al. (2008) also investigated the effects of speaker repetition on the cerebral response to voice stimuli (Figure 25.7d). They found that the anterior-most region of the right anterior temporal lobe that showed significant voice-sensitivity also exhibited a pattern of response similar to the one found by Belin and Zatorre (2003): reduced activity in response to stimulation with vocalization from a single macaque individual, as compared to vocalizations from several different individuals (Petkov et al., 2008).

Together, these findings provide compelling evidence for the involvement of right anterior temporal lobe regions in processing information related to the speaker's identity. The fact that these regions show similar speaker sensitivity in the macaque

brain suggests that similar processes were already present in the common ancestor of macaque and humans, some 30 million years ago, indicating a long evolutionary history of speaker-identity processing in the right anterior temporal lobe. Further research is needed to understand how speaker identity is coded in these regions, how they interact with the TVA during speaker identification, and how familiarity with a speaker modulates these responses.

Perception of Gender Information in Voice

As discussed above, there is an important sexual dimorphism in the vocal apparatus of male and female adults affecting both the source and filter aspects of voice production (Titze, 1989). These anatomo-physiological differences results in a number of acoustical differences between the voices of male and female adult speakers (Childers & Wu, 1991;

Wu & Childers, 1991): mean fundamental frequency of phonation (f0) and formant frequencies, for example, both are higher on average in women, and female voices are also characterized by greater aspiration noise (Klatt & Klatt, 1990) and a steeper spectral slope (Hanson & Chuang, 1999). Thus, a number of possibly redundant cues are available to the auditory system to categorize voice gender. However, its task is not as trivial as may appear: Even if average f0 values are higher in women than men, there are important inter-individual differences. Besides, the f0 range of male and female speakers in natural speech show considerable overlap: It is not rare to hear a female voice with a lower f0 than a male voice.

Voice gender categorization is therefore not a straightforward pitch categorization, but rather appears a high-level voice cognition ability that indicates the existence of perceptual representation(s) of voice gender in the listener's brain. These representations were first investigated behaviorally by means of a selective adaptation paradigm and a synthetic male-female continuum (Mullennix, Johnson, Topcu-Durgun, & Farnsworth, 1995): Robust gender adaptation effects were observed for the two adaptors consisting of the male and female endpoints of the continuum, as indicated by a shift of the labeling curve towards the opposite gender. Yet that result was not observed with other adaptors, which the authors interpreted as evidence for an auditory-based representation, as opposed to an abstract, higher-level representation of voice gender (Mullennix, Johnson, Topcu-Durgun, & Farnsworth, 1995). More recently, however, behavioral adaptations effects (shifts in the male-female labeling function) were also observed with natural voice adaptors different from those of the probed continua, suggesting that abstract, higher-level representations of voice gender could nonetheless exist (Schweinberger et al., 2008).

Two functional magnetic resonance imaging (fMRI) studies so far have explored the cerebral correlates of voice gender perception, by comparing cerebral activity measured in normal adults during listening to male versus female voices—as well as f0-modified control voices generated through pitch-shifting (Lattner, Meyer, & Friederici, 2005; Sokhi, Hunter, Wilkinson, & Woodruff, 2005). Despite partially conflicting results, both studies observed greater responses to female than male voices in regions of the auditory cortex, particularly in the right hemisphere. However, these studies used the classical subtraction approach in fMRI, that is,

directly comparing volumes acquired during presentation of male versus female voices to one another, based on the (implicit) assumption that neuronal populations sensitive to male versus female voices would exist and be located in different cortical regions.

Yet, an alternative model is worth investigating: Voice gender could be represented by overlapping neuronal populations sensitive to male versus female voices, respectively. In this case, assuming equal proportions of male- and female-sensitive neurons in a given cortical area/voxel, the subtraction of male- versus female-related cerebral volumes voices would fail to highlight these gender-sensitive neuronal populations since activation would be of equal magnitude in response to male or female voices—although different neurons would be active.

Charest et al. (2009) explored this alternative model of voice gender representation in the fMR-adaptation framework: If a neuronal population sensitive to one voice gender could be adapted by presentation of an adaptor voice of that particular gender, it would respond less to the subsequent presentation of a voice of the same gender, thus yielding a reduced fMRI signal; while subsequent presentation of a voice of a different gender should recruit the previously inactive neuronal population, yielding an increased fMRI signal.

Twenty subjects were scanned while performing a gender categorization task on stimuli drawn from male-female voice continua generated by morphing (Kawahara & Matsui, 2003) between natural male and female voices in 15% steps. An efficiency-optimized adaptation paradigm—the "continuous carry over design (Aguirre, 2007)—in which a long series of stimuli is presented and each stimulus is considered as an adaptor for the following stimulus. Two parametric regressors were used in the analysis: a "physical difference" regressor expressing the difference between two consecutive stimuli in terms of their proportion of female voice; a "perceptual difference" regressor based on subjects' gender categorization responses (Charest, Pernet, Crabbe, & Belin, 2009).

Analyses revealed that regions in which activity was correlated with physical distance were located in the bilateral auditory cortex (Figure 25.8), overlapping strongly with the TVA. In these regions, the more two consecutive stimuli were physically similar, the smaller was the response to the second stimulus; conversely, these regions responded more to a stimulus that was preceded by a stimulus with a larger physical difference, for example, a female

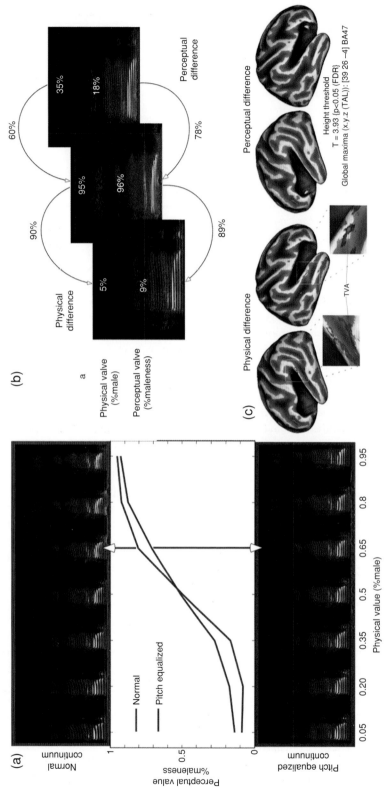

Fig. 25.8 Cerebral sensitivity to voice gender. a. Voice gender continua generated by audio morphing between natural female (left) and male (right) voice samples in steps of 15%. The lower set of spectrograms correspond to pitch-equalized voice gender morphs. Red and blue sigmoid curves in the middle panel represent the gro up-average gender classification responses. b. Stimuli are presented according to the "continuous carry-over design" in a long series of stimuli presented in a pseudo-random order, with each stimulus being a potential adaptor for the next stimulus. Two main regressors are derived: a 'physical distance" regressor, based on the difference in morph steps between two consecutive stimuli; and a "perceptua. distance" regressor, based on subjects' gender ratings. c. Using these two regressors in the analysis reveals hierarchical processing of voice gender, with auditory cortical regions close to the TVA showing sensitivity to physical distance between stimuli; and prefrontal regions sensitive to residual perceptual differences, i.e., in the categorical gender response.

Reproduced with permission from Charest, I., Pernet, C., Crabbe, F. & Belin, P. (2009).

voice following a male voice. Interestingly, the additional portion of the variance explained by subjects' categorical response, that is, the fact that the classification curve is better fitted by a sigmoid rather than a straight line (e.g., voices generated by morphing 20% of a female voice with 80% of a male voice are classified as male more than 80% of the time) corresponded to additional cerebral activity exclusively located in circumscribed, bilateral regions of inferior prefrontal gyri: the more two consecutive stimuli differed in their perceived "genderness" (independently of physical difference that was explained by auditory cortex activity), the greater was inferior prefrontal gyri's activity in response to the second stimulus (Charest, Pernet, Crabbe, & Belin, 2009).

These results suggest a hierarchical model of voice gender cerebral processing, whereby the physical structure of voices is computed in auditory cortex regions overlapping with the TVA—probably instantiated by overlapping neuronal populations sensitive to different vocal features, including gender—and then sent to inferior prefrontal regions to yield a categorical gender response.

Conclusions

The evidence reviewed above indicates that normal human listeners are equipped with sophisticated neural machinery for processing voices and extracting the rich information they contain. Comparable neuronal networks are present in the macaque brain suggesting a long evolutionary history of cerebral voice processing.

Studying the cerebral processing of voices thus appears important not only for a better understanding of the functional architecture of auditory cortex but also for its implications on the evolution of language and speech processing: When our ancestors began to speak, a few dozens of millennia ago, they already possessed highly developed cerebral processes dedicated to processing human voices, a rich basis from which speech-specific processes could emerge. Interestingly, evidence pointing both in humans and macaques for a greater role of right hemispheric structures in voice processing suggests that the right hemisphere may have played a greater role in the evolution of speech perception than is generally assumed.

Studies of cerebral voice processing also have important implications for our understanding of how face and voice information is integrated multimodally during our social interactions, not only for speech comprehension but also in integrating cues on the identity and affective state for person perception.

Much work lies ahead for a precise understanding of the cerebral architecture underlying voice perception and its integration with face processing. In particular, several outstanding questions remained unanswered: Are voices attention-grabbing? Are TVAs affected by auditory expertise? How does voice processing ability relate to anatomical and functional differences in the "vocal brain" between individuals? How is facial and vocal information on a person's identity and affect integrated? We hope that an increasing research effort into cerebral voice processing will soon bring answers to those questions.

Acknowledgments
I thank the collaborators who contributed to this work, particularly Professor Robert J. Zatorre, with whom this story began, and my postgraduate and postdoctoral students: Shirley Fecteau, Guylaine Bélizaire, Jean-Pierre Chartrand, Christine Rosa, Ian Charest, Rebecca Watson, Cyril Pernet, Oliver Baumann, Laetitia Bruckert, Marianne Latinus and Patricia G. Bestelmeyer. The following sources of funding are gratefully acknowledged: Canadian Institutes of Health Research, Natural Sciences and Engineering Research Council of Canada, Fonds de Recherche en Sante du Québec, Canadian Foundation for Innovation, the British Academy, The Royal Society, the Biotechnology and Biological Sciences Research Council, The Medical Research council, the Economic and Social Research Council and France-Télécom.

References
Aguirre, G. K. (2007). Continuous carry-over designs for fMRI. *NeuroImage, 35*, 1480–1494.

Assal, G. (2001). Prosopagnosia. *Bull. Acad. Nat. Méd., 185*(3), 525–536.

Assal, G., Aubert, C., & Buttet, J. (1981). Asymétrie cérébrale et reconnaissance de la voix. *Rev. Neurol., 137*, 255–268.

Assal, G., Zander, E., Kremin, H., & Buttet, J. (1976). Discrimination des voix lors des lesions du cortex cerebral. *Arch. Suisses Neurol. Neurochir. Psychiatr., 119*, 307–315.

Belin, P., Fecteau, S., & Bedard, C. (2004). Thinking the voice: neural correlates of voice perception. *Trends Cogn. Sci., 8*, 129–135.

Belin, P. & Zatorre, R. J. (2003). Adaptation to speaker's voice in right anterior temporal-lobe. *Neuroreport, 14*, 2105–2109.

Belin, P., Zatorre, R. J., & Ahad, P. (2002). Human temporal-lobe response to vocal sounds. *Cogn. Brain Res., 13*, 17–26.

Belin, P., Zatorre, R. J., Lafaille, P., Ahad, P., & Pike, B. (2000). Voice-selective areas in human auditory cortex. *Nature, 403*, 309–312.

Bentin, S., Allison, T., Puce, A., Perez, E., & McCarthy, G. (1996). Electrophysiological studies of face perception in humans. *J. Cogn. Neuro.*, *8*, 551–565.

Bodamer, J. (1947). Die prosop-agnosie. *Arch. Psychiatr. Nerv*, *179*, 6–53.

Bruce, V. & Young, A. (1986). Understanding face recognition. *Br. J. Psychol.*, *77*, 305–327.

Campanella, S. & Belin, P. (2007). Integrating face and voice in person perception. *Trends Cogn. Sci.*, *11*, 535–543.

Charest, I., Pernet, C., Crabbe, F., & Belin, P. (2009). *Investigating the representation of voice gender using a continuous carry-over fMRI design.* Paper presented at the Human Brain Mapping Conference, San Francisco, USA.

Charest, I., Pernet, C. R., Rousselet, G. A., Quiñones, I., Latinus, M., Fillion-Bilodeau, S., et al. (2009). Electrophysiological evidence for an early processing of human voices. *BMC Neurosci.*, *10*, 127.

Charrier, I., Mathevon, N., & Jouventin, P. (2001). Mother's voice recognition by seal pups. *Nature*, *412*, 873.

Childers, D. G. & Wu, K. (1991). Gender recognition from speech. Part II: Fine analysis. *J. Acoust. Soc. Am.*, *90*, 1841–1856.

Davis, M. H. & Johnsrude, I. S. (2003). Hierarchical processing in spoken language comprehension. *J. Neurosci.*, *23*, 3423–3431.

DeCasper, A. J. & Fifer, W. P. (1980). Of human bonding: Newborns prefer their mothers' voices. *Science*, *208*, 1174–1176.

Duchaine, B. C. & Nakayama, K. (2006). Developmental prosopagnosia: A window to content-specific face processing. *Curr. Opin. Neurobiol*, *16*, 166–173.

Ethofer, T., Van De Ville, D., Scherer, K., & Vuilleumier, P. (2009). Decoding of emotional information in voice-sensitive cortices. *Curr. Biol.*

Ethofer, T., Wiethoff, S., Anders, S., Kreifelts, B., Grodd, W., & Wildgruber, D. (2007). The voices of seduction: Cross-gender effects in processing of erotic prosody. *Soc. Cogn. Affect. Neurosci*, *2*, 334–337.

Fant, G. (1960). *Acoustic theory of speech production.* The Hague: Mouton.

Farah, M. J. (1996). Is face recognition "special"? Evidence from neuropsychology. *Behav. Brain Res.*, *76*, 181–189.

Farah, M. J., Levinson, K. L., & Klein, K. L. (1995). Face perception and within-category discrimination in prosopagnosia. *Neuropsychologia*, *33*, 661–674.

Fecteau, S., Armony, J., Joanette, Y., & Belin, P. (2004). Is voice processing species-specific in human auditory cortex? An fMRI study. *Neuroimage*, *23*, 840–848.

Fitch, W. T. (2000). The evolution of speech: A comparative review. *Trends Cogn. Sci.*, *4*, 258–267.

Freiwald, W. A., Tsao, D. Y., & Livingstone, M. S. (2009). A face feature space in the macaque temporal lobe. *Nat. Neurosci.*, *12*, 1187–1196.

Garrido, L., Eisner, F., McGettigan, C., Stewart, L., Sauter, D., Hanley, J. R., et al. (2009). Developmental phonagnosia: A selective deficit of vocal identity recognition. *Neuropsychologia*, *47*, 123–131.

Gervais, H., Belin, P., Boddaert, N., Leboyer, M., Coez, A., Barthélémy, C., et al. (2004). Abnormal voice processing in autism: An fMRI study. *Nat. Neurosci.*, *7*, 801–802.

Ghazanfar, A. A. (2008). Language evolution: Neural differences that make a difference. *Nat. Neurosci.*, *11*, 382–384.

Grandjean, D., Sander, D., Pourtois, G., Schwartz, S., Seghier, M. L., Scherer, K. R., et al. (2005). The voices of wrath: Brain responses to angry prosody in meaningless speech. *Nat. Neurosci.*, *8*, 145–146.

Grill-Spector, K., Henson, R., & Martin, A. (2006). Repetition and the brain: Neural models of stimulus-specific effects. *Trends Cogn. Sci.*, *10*(1), 14–23.

Grill-Spector, K. & Malach, R. (2001). fMR-adaptation: A tool for studying the functional properties of human cortical neurons. *Acta Psychol. (Amst)*, *107*, 293–321.

Gunji, A., Koyama, S., Ishii, R., Levy, D., Okamoto, H., Kakigi, R., et al. (2003). Magnetoencephalographic study of the cortical activity elicited by human voice. *Neurosci. Lett.*, *348*, 13–16.

Hadjikhani, N., Joseph, R. M., Snyder, J., Chabris, C. F., Clark, J., Steele, S., et al. (2004). Activation of the fusiform gyrus when individuals with autism spectrum disorder view faces. *Neuroimage*, *22*, 1141–1150.

Hanson, H. M. & Chuang, E. S. (1999). Glottal characteristics of male speakers: Acoustic correlates and comparison with female data. *J. Acoust. Soc. Am.*, *106*, 1064–1077.

Hartman, D. E. (1979). The perceptual identity and characteristics of aging in normal male adult speakers. *J. Comm. Disord.*, *12*, 53–61.

Haxby, J. V., Hoffman, E. A., & Ida Gobbini, M. (2000). The distributed human neural system for face perception. *Trends Cogn. Sci.*, *4*, 223–233.

Insley, S. J. (2000). Long-term vocal recognition in the northern fur seal. *Nature*, *406*, 404–405.

Kanwisher, N., McDermott, J., & Chun, M. M. (1997). The fusiform face area: A module in human extrastriate cortex specialized for face perception. *J. Neurosci.*, *17*, 4302–4311.

Kanwisher, N. & Yovel, G. (2006). The fusiform face area: A cortical region specialized for the perception of faces. *Philos. Trans. R. Soc. Lond. B Biol. Sci.*, *361*, 2109–2128.

Kawahara, H. & Matsui, H. (2003). Auditory morphing based on an elastic perceptual distance metric in an interference-free time-frequency representation. *Proc. Intern. Conf. Acoust. Speech Signal Proc.*, 256–259.

Kisilevsky, B. S., Hains, S. M., Lee, K., Xie, X., Huang, H., Ye, H. H., et al. (2003). Effects of experience on fetal voice recognition. *Psychol. Sci.*, *14*, 220–224.

Klatt, D. H. & Klatt, L. C. (1990). Analysis, synthesis, and perception of voice quality variations among female and male talkers. *J. Acoust. Soc. Am.*, *87*, 820–857.

Klin, A. (1991). Young autistic children's listening preferences in regard to speech: A possible characterization of the symptom of social withdrawal. *J. Autism Dev. Disord.*, *21*, 29–42.

Kreiman, J. (1997). Listening to voices: Theory and practice in voice perception research. In K. Johnson & J. Mullenix (Eds.), *Talker variability in speech research* (pp. 85–108). New-York: Academic Press.

Lass, N. J. & Davis, M. (1976). An investigation of speaker height and weight identification. *J. Acoust. Soc. Am.*, *60*, 700–703.

Lass, N. J., Hughes, K. R., Bowyer, M. D., Waters, L. T., & Bourne, V. T. (1976). Speaker sex identification from voiced, whispered, and filtered isolated vowels. *J. Acoust. Soc. Am.*, *59*, 675–678.

Lattner, S., Meyer, M. E., & Friederici, A. D. (2005). Voice perception: Sex, pitch, and the right hemisphere. *Hum. Brain Mapp.*, *24*, 11–20.

Levy, D. A., Granot, R., & Bentin, S. (2003). Neural sensitivity to human voices: ERP evidence of task and attentional influences. *Psychophysiology*, *40*, 291–305.

Levy, I., Hasson, U., Avidan, G., Hendler, T., & Malach, R. (2001). Center-periphery organization of human object areas. *Nat. Neurosci.*, *4*, 533–539.

Liberman, A. M. & Mattingly, I. G. (1989). A specialization for speech perception. *Science*, *243*, 489–494.

Linville, S. E. & Rens, J. (2001). Vocal tract resonance analysis of aging voice using long-term average spectra. *J. Voice*, *15*, 323–330.

Mullennix, J. W., Johnson, K. A., Topcu-Durgun, M., & Farnsworth, L. M. (1995). The perceptual representation of voice gender. *J. Acoust. Soc. Am.*, *98*, 3080–3095.

Murray, M. M., Camen, C., Gonzalez Andino, S. L., Bovet, P., & Clarke, S. (2006). Rapid brain discrimination of sounds of objects. *J. Neurosci.*, *26*, 1293–1302.

Neuner, F. & Schweinberger, S. R. (2000). Neuropsychological impairments in the recognition of faces, voices, and personal names. *Brain Cogn.*, *44*, 342–366.

Obleser, J., Zimmermann, J., Van Meter, J., & Rauschecker, J. P. (2007). Multiple stages of auditory speech perception reflected in event-related FMRI. *Cereb. Cortex*, *17*, 2251–2257.

Ockleford, E. M., Vince, M. A., Layton, C., & Reader, M. R. (1988). Responses of neonates to parents' and others' voices. *Early Hum. Dev.*, *18*, 27–36.

Peretz, I., Kolinsky, R., Tramo, M., Labrecque, R., Hublet, C., Demeurisse, G., et al. (1994). Functional dissociations following bilateral lesions of auditory cortex. *Brain*, *117*, 1283–1301.

Perrett, D. I., Smith, P. A., Potter, D. D., Mistlin, A. J., Head, A. S., Milner, A. D., et al. (1985). Visual cells in the temporal cortex sensitive to face view and gaze direction. *Proc. R. Soc. Lond. B Biol. Sci.*, *223*, 293–317.

Petkov, C. I., Kayser, C., Steudel, T., Whittingstall, K., Augath, M., & Logothetis, N. K. (2008). A voice region in the monkey brain. *Nat. Neurosci.*, *11*(2), 367–374.

Puce, A., Allison, T., & McCarthy, G. (1999). Electrophysiological studies of human face perception. III: Effects of top-down processing on face-specific potentials. *Cereb. Cortex*, *9*, 445–458.

Rendall, D., Owren, M. J., & Rodman, P. S. (1998). The role of vocal tract filtering in identity cueing in rhesus monkey (Macaca mulatta) vocalizations. *J. Acoust. Soc. Am.*, *103*, 602–614.

Rendall, D., Vokey, J. R., & Nemeth, C. (2007). Lifting the curtain on the Wizard of Oz: Biased voice-based impressions of speaker size. *J. Exp. Psychol. Hum. Percept. Perform.*, *33*(5), 1208–1219.

Rogier, O., Roux, S., Belin, P., Bonnet-Brilhault F & Bruneau, N. (2010). An electrophysiological correlate of voice processing in 4- to 5-year-old children. *Int. J. Psychophysiol. 75*, 44–7.

Rolls, E. T. (2007). The representation of information about faces in the temporal and frontal lobes. *Neuropsychologia*, *45*, 124–143.

Rossion, B., Campanella, S., Gomez, C. M., Delinte, A., Debatisse, D., Liard, L., et al. (1999). Task modulation of brain activity related to familiar and unfamiliar face processing: An ERP study. *Clin. Neurophysiol.*, *110*(3), 449–462.

Rutherford, M. D., Baron-Cohen, S., & Wheelwright, S. (2002). Reading the mind in the voice: A study with normal adults and adults with Asperger syndrome and high functioning autism. *J. Autism Dev. Disord.*, *32*, 189–194.

Schweinberger, S. R., Casper, C., Hauthal, N., Kaufmann, J. M., Kawahara, H., Kloth, N., et al. (2008). Auditory adaptation in voice perception. *Curr. Biol.*, *18*(9), 684–688.

Scott, S. K., Blank, C. C., Rosen, S., & Wise, R. J. (2000). Identification of a pathway for intelligible speech in the left temporal lobe. *Brain*, *123*, 2400–2406.

Sergent, J. & Signoret, J.-L. (1992). Functional and anatomical decomposition of face processing: Evidence from prosopagnosia and PET study of normal subjects. *Phil. Trans. R. Soc. Lond. B Biol. Sci.*, *335*, 51–61.

Smith, D. R., Patterson, R. D., Turner, R., Kawahara, H., & Irino, T. (2005). The processing and perception of size information in speech sounds. *J. Acoust. Soc. Am.*, *117*, 305–318.

Sokhi, D. S., Hunter, M. D., Wilkinson, I. D., & Woodruff, P. W. (2005). Male and female voices activate distinct regions in the male brain. *Neuroimage*, *27*, 572–578.

Thierry, G., Martin, C. D., Downing, P., & Pegna, A. J. (2007). Controlling for interstimulus perceptual variance abolishes N170 face selectivity. *Nat. Neurosci.*, *10*, 505–511.

Thompson, P. (1980). Margaret Thatcher: A new illusion. *Perception*, *9*, 483–484.

Tian, B., Reser, D., Durham, A., Kustov, A., & Rauschecker, J. P. (2001). Functional specialization in rhesus monkey auditory cortex. *Science*, *292*, 290–293.

Titze, I. R. (1989). Physiologic and acoustic differences between male and female voices. *J. Acoust. Soc. Am.*, *85*, 1699–1707.

Titze, I. R. (1993). Current topics in voice production mechanisms. *Acta Otolaryngol.*, *113*, 421–427.

Tsao, D. Y., Freiwald, W. A., Knutsen, T. A., Mandeville, J. B., & Tootell, R. B. (2003). Faces and objects in macaque cerebral cortex. *Nat. Neurosci.*, *6*, 989–995.

Tsao, D. Y., Freiwald, W. A., Tootell, R. B. H., & Livingstone, M. S. (2006). A cortical region consisting entirely of face-selective cells. *Science*, *311*, 670–674.

Van Lancker, D. R. & Canter, G. J. (1982). Impairment of voice and face recognition in patients with hemispheric damage. *Brain Cog.*, *1*, 185–195.

Van Lancker, D. R., Cummings, J. L., Kreiman, J., & Dobkin, B. H. (1988). Phonagnosia: A dissociation between familiar and unfamiliar voices. *Cortex*, *24*, 195–209.

von Kriegstein, K., Eger, E., Kleinschmidt, A., & Giraud, A. L. (2003). Modulation of neural responses to speech by directing attention to voices or verbal content. *Cogn. Brain Res.*, *17*, 48–55.

Von Kriegstein, K. & Giraud, A. L. (2004). Distinct functional substrates along the right superior temporal sulcus for the processing of voices. *Neuroimage*, *22*, 948–955.

Watson, R., Crabbe, F., Quinones, I., Charest, I., Bestelmeyer, P., Latinus, M., et al. (2009). *Auditory response of the Temporal Voice Areas (TVA) predicts memory performance for voices, but not bells*. Paper presented at the Human Brain Mapping conference, San Francisco, USA.

Wu, K. & Childers, D. G. (1991). Gender recognition from speech. Part I: Coarse analysis. *J. Acoust. Soc. Am.*, *90*, 1828–1840.

Yin, R. K. (1969). Looking at upside-down faces. *J. Exp. Psychol.*, *81*, 141–145.

Intersecting Identities and Expressions: The Compound Nature of Social Perception

Reginald B. Adams, Jr. *and* Anthony J. Nelson

Abstract

This chapter presents a functional approach to social and emotional perception that extends current models of face processing by accounting for the combinatorial nature of social perception. The face is a rich source of social information that requires integrative processing of multiple cues (e.g., facial expression, eye gaze, facial structure). We have seemingly evolved a distributed perceptual system that maximizes both processing efficiency, and the ability to extract ecologically valid social information from a complex and interactive array of facial cues. Based on the functional approach outlined herein, this chapter underscores some of the basic processes necessary for the perception and understanding of compound social cues in the face.

Keywords: social vision, compound social cues, emotion recognition, eye gaze, face perception, facial identity, facial expression, facial maturity, approach/avoidance motivation, social signals, ecological theory, evolutionary psychology, amygdala, superior temporal sulcus, fusiform gyrus

Introduction

The ability to extract social and emotional meaning from nonverbal cues is critical to human interaction. As such, we possess an elaborate system of nonverbal exchange that helps establish and maintain social cohesion, negotiate social hierarchies, attract potential mates, and avoid looming threats. The human face represents the most richly informative and pervasive social stimulus we encounter in our daily lives. We draw strong inferences about others' personalities, inner thoughts, and beliefs from their facial appearance, and do so in what appears to be an effortless, nonreflective, and highly consensual manner (Kenny, Horner, Kashy, & Chu, 1992; Van Overwalle, Drenth, & Marsman, 1999; Willis & Todorov, 2006). We also derive rich social meaning from expressive cues (e.g., eye gaze, facial expression, head posture), which allow for relatively accurate assessments of others' internal mental and emotional states and intentions (Baron-Cohen, Wheelwright, Hill, Raste, & Plumb, 2001; Keltner, Ekman, Gonzaga, & Beer, 2003).

Not surprisingly, we tend to interact face-to-face, and possess what appears to be a natural predilection for face processing. Distinct brain regions in both humans and nonhuman primates appear devoted to processing facial identity (Gross, Bender, & Rocha-Miranda, 1969; Kanwisher, McDermott, & Chun, 1997; Kanwisher, Tong, & Nakayama, 1998; McCarthy, Puce, Gore, & Allison, 1997; cf. Gauthier & Nelson, 2001) and to processing facial expression (Hasselmo, Rolls, & Baylis, 1989; Hoffman & Haxby, 2000; Perrett & Mistlin, 1990; Phillips et al., 1998; Puce, Allison, Bentin, Gore, & McCarthy, 1998). In general, faces are a visually preferred stimulus beginning in infancy and extending through adulthood (Johnson, Dziurawiec, Bartrip, & Morton, 1992; Maurer, 1983; McLuhan, 2001) and are astonishingly well remembered compared to other visual objects (Bruck, Cavanagh, & Ceci, 1991; Phillips, 1979).

To date, there is extensive research on human face processing that has tended to compartmentalize the rich variety of facial cues from which we derive social meaning (e.g., expression, eye gaze, identity), examining them independent of one another, often isolated within separate fields of study. For instance, emotional expression has been most extensively studied within a social psychological framework, and facial identity within a visual cognition framework. Some social cues, such as eye gaze, have been studied extensively within both, but with emphasis on communicative value in social psychology and on perceptual mechanics in vision cognition. Critically, neither parent discipline adequately addresses the combined influences of various cues on social and emotional perception. In this chapter, we focus specifically on how multiple social messages meaningfully combine and interact to form the unified representations that guide our impressions of and responses to others.

The "Social" Face

Behavioral and neuroscientific research has largely treated different *sources* of facial information (e.g., expression versus identity) as being functionally distinct and engaging doubly dissociable processing routes (e.g., Bruce & Young, 1986; Haxby, Hoffman, & Gobbini, 2000; 2002). Certainly given the abundance of visual information supplied by the face, a perceptual system that can parse information and process it in parallel maximizes processing efficiency and minimizes the likelihood of a perceptual bottleneck. What is missed in this approach, however, is an understanding of how various social cues can meaningfully interact in social perception. Thus, the next critical step in our growing understanding of social perception resides in formulating a meaningful interface across disciplines, one that goes beyond the mere cross-application of frameworks. A conceptual merger is required, one that focuses specifically on the intersection of various facial cues in social perception.

The proportionally large size of the human brain relative to other nonhuman primates is thought to be a direct consequence of evolutionary pressures imposed by those who filled our social worlds (Dunbar, 1998). It stands to reason then that our ability to derive social meaning from nonverbal cues

would be an essential function of the visual system. Yet, current models of face processing do not yet incorporate these insights. Notably, expressive- and identity-based facial cues often share underlying social meanings as well as physical resemblances to one another. As such, they should be considered neither cognitively nor perceptually orthogonal. As a result, when processed in combination, their overlapping characteristics should be reflected in the mental and neural operations involved in their perception.

The assumption that "functionally" distinct sources of information are processed along functionally distinct processing routes has also been directly challenged through demonstrations of perceptual *interference* for combinations of various facial cues including: 1) speech patterns and identity (Schweinberger & Soukup, 1998), 2) gender and emotion (Atkinson, Tipples, Burt, & Young, 2005; cf., Le Gal & Bruce, 2002), 3) gender and age judgments (Quinn & Macrae, 2005), 4) gaze and emotion (Ganel, Goshen-Gottstein, & Goodale, 2005; Graham & LaBar, 2007), 5) familiarity and gender judgments (Ganel & Goshen-Gottstein, 2002; 2004), as well as 6) identity and expression at both the behavioral (Baudouin, Martin, Tiberghien, Verlut, & Franck, 2002; Levy & Bentin, 2008; Schweinberger, Burton, & Kelley, 1999) and neural levels (Ganel et al., 2005). That one facial cue can perceptually interfere with the processing of another suggests some level of shared neural machinery.

Further, recent work demonstrates that combinations of facial cues can also yield *facilitative* effects on perceptual processing (e.g., Adams & Kleck, 2003; 2005), suggesting a functional utility to their combined processing. For example, interactions have been found in the processing of eye gaze and emotion such that functionally "congruent" pairings like direct-gaze anger (both approach signals) and averted-gaze fear (both avoidance signals) can be perceived as more intense and recognized more quickly and accurately than incongruent pairings (Adams & Kleck, 2003; 2005; Adams, Ambady, Kleck, & Macrae, 2006; Hess, Adams, & Kleck, 2007, Adams & Franklin, 2009). Differential neural responsivity to these threat-gaze pairs (Adams et al., 2003) and to gaze and head postures has also been found (Chiao, Adams, Tse, Lowenthal, Richeson, & Ambady, 2008). Similar functional interactions have now been reported across a range of social cues including race and emotion (Ackerman et al., 2006; Hugenberg, 2005), race and eye gaze (Adams, Pauker, & Weisbuch, 2010; Richeson, Todd,

Trawalter, & Baird, 2008; Trawalter, Todd, Baird, & Richeson, 2008), gender and emotion (Becker, Kenrick, Neuberg, Blackwell, & Smith, 2007; Hess, Adams, & Kleck, 2004; 2005; cf. LeGal & Bruce, 2002), and gender and age (Quinn & Macrae, 2005). Interactions have also been found for congruent versus incongruent pairings of facial expression, emotional body language, visual scene, and emotional vocal cues, even at the earliest stages of face processing, within 100 ms (Meeren, Hvan, Heijnsbergen, & de Gelder, 2005), and across conscious and nonconscious processing routes (e.g., de Gelder, Morris, & Dolan, 2005).

Examining face processing from such a functional perspective draws together social psychology, vision cognition, and neuroscience, and is grounded in the understanding of a visual system evolved within a social context. To understand the perceptual mechanics of social perception, therefore, we must first consider the social functions they evolved to perform. From this perspective, the combined processing of social cues can be considered adaptive. For example, consider a person with a hypermature (low brow, thin lips, angular) face staring directly at you while expressing anger. Compare this image to a person with "babyish" (high brow, full lips, round) facial features looking away from you while wearing the same expression. Should we expect no differences in the processing of anger displayed on these faces? Four decades of research on facial affect perception suggests that detecting anger in the face ought to be obligatory and thus resistant to other contextual cues. However, given that facial appearance (see Carré, McCormick, & Mondloch, 2009) and gaze direction meaningfully inform the threat conveyed by the face, there is clear adaptive value to processing these cues in a combinatorial manner. Thus, where many current models focus on differentiating the "source" of information (expression versus appearance), and do not consider the social meaning derived from such cues, the current approach outlined here focuses specifically on the underlying meaning conveyed by these cues and their combined ecological relevance to the observer.

The question has been raised as to whether interaction effects like those described above, particularly between eye gaze and emotion, represent low-level perceptual integration or higher-order processing (Engell & Haxby, 2007). Perhaps the most compelling evidence for the latter conclusion is research employing transcranial magnetic stimulation to disrupt neural responses. When applied to the left superior temporal sulcus (STS) eye-gaze

but not emotion processing was disrupted, whereas applying it to the right somatosensory cortex interfered with emotion but not eye-gaze processing (Pourtois et al., 2004). These findings offer compelling evidence that early visual input of eye gaze and emotion involves doubly dissociable neural pathways. This finding should not, however, belittle the functional value of interactive processes. Indeed, recent evidence suggests top-down modulation of even low-level visual processing occurs quite rapidly. For instance, magnocellular projections activate early occipital visual cortex responses projecting to the orbitofrontal cortex, which in turn projects back to the fusiform gyrus and guides simple object recognition (Kveraga, Boshyan, & Bar, 2007). All of this occurs within the first 200 ms of visual input (Kveraga, Ghuman, & Bar, 2007). In this way, top-down processing that is sensitive to meaningful contextual cues can organize even low-level visual processing in a functionally meaningful way.

When considering interactions found between facial identity and expressive cues, however, it becomes important to also consider the potential for low-level perceptual integration due to their shared perceptual properties (i.e., their physical resemblance to one another). In this way, the social meaning derived from facial cues and their perceptual manifestations can be confounded (e.g., Becker et al., 2007). Gender, emotion, and facial maturity offer good examples of facial cues that share both social meaning (e.g., dominance and affiliation) and physical resemblance (e.g., high versus low eye brows). A further extension of this idea is that of functional equivalence, where static facial features and expressive features appear to have evolved to mimic one another. Darwin (1872/1965) first introduced this idea, observing that in animals expressive behaviors often mimic more stable appearance-based features, such as piloerection (see for example, p. 95 and p.104), in a way that functionally exploits innately prepared responses to such cues. Using this same logic, Marsh, Adams, and Kleck (2005) argued that facial expressions in humans (particularly anger and fear) may have similarly evolved to mimic more stable appearance cues related to facial maturity and neotony. Anger is characterized by a low and bulging brow ridge and narrowed eyes, resembling a mature, dominant face, while fear with its raised and arched brow ridge and widened eyes perceptually resembles a submissive, babyface. Gender appearance is similarly associated with facial features that perceptually overlap with facial maturity (see Zebrowitz, 1997), in that "babyish" features (e.g., large, round eyes, full lips) are more typical in women, and "mature" features (e.g., square jaw, pronounced brow) are more typical in men. Such facial appearance is so strongly associated with gender, in fact, that inconsistent pairings of these features can override normal gender stereotypic attributions (Friedman & Zebrowitz, 1992). A similar confound has been demonstrated between gender and emotion cues (Becker et al., 2007; Hess et al., 2005).

Perceptual overlaps have also been demonstrated using computer-based models trained to detect appearance and expression cues in faces (e.g., Said, Sebe, & Todorov, 2009; Zebrowitz, Kikuchi, & Fellous, 2007). In this way, responses to facial cues were necessarily examined without the confound of culturally learned stereotypes or social meanings applied to faces. For instance, Zebrowitz et al. (2007) trained a connectionist model to detect babyfacedness versus maturity in the face, and then applied this model to detecting such cues in surprise, anger, happy, and neutral expressions. They found that the model was fooled into detecting babyfacedness in surprise expressions and maturity in anger expressions due to similarities in height of brow. Additionally, the authors found that objective babyfacedness (as determined by the connectionist model) mediated impressions of surprise and anger in those faces reported by human judges. Similarly, Said and colleagues (2009) employed a Bayesian network trained to detect expressions in faces and then applied this to images of neutral faces that had been rated on a number of personality traits. The authors found that the trait ratings of the faces were meaningfully associated with the perceptual resemblance the faces had with certain expressions. These results speak to a mechanism of perceptual overlap whereby expression and identity cues can trigger similar processing due simply to their physical resemblances.

Thus, as contended by Marsh et al. (2005), it is plausible that expressive cues evolved to take advantage of a perceptual overlap with certain identity-based cues in order to "trick" the perceptual system into responding to them in similar ways. Therefore, expressions that resemble babyfaces, such as fear, may have evolved to elicit a caretaking response in perceivers, whereas anger, an expression that resembles mature faces, may have evolved to signal the message of power and dominance evoked by mature faces. It should perhaps not be at all surprising then to find that combinations of these cues meaningfully influence emotion recognition. Indeed, anger is more readily recognized when displayed on mature faces, and fear when displayed on babyish faces (Adams, 2009). Such effects are likely due to low-level structural encoding in the inferior occipital gyri, before the visual stream splits information related to expressive- versus identity-based processing (see Haxby et al., 2000; 2002).

Evolution of Social Visual Face Processing

One of the foundational tenets of the field of social vision (e.g., Adams, Ambady, Nakayama, & Shimojo, 2010) is that making sense out of other people is an important computational feat the visual system evolved to perform. Arguably, individuals who were able to perceive social meaning from nonverbal cues and to act upon them in an adaptive manner, as well as those who were reliably able to express social meaning to others, were more likely to survive and pass on their genes to subsequent generations. As such, current evolutionary theories of socio-emotional processing focuses on the co-evolution of social expression and perception. Perhaps the most studied aspect of this in face processing is the proposed existence of a universal affect program, which underlies the experience and expression of emotion, along side the corresponding capacity to recognize such emotions when expressed by others (e.g., Ekman & Friesen, 1971). Although Darwin (1872/1965) resisted the notion that facial expressions evolved in response to socio-communicative pressures, current evolutionary theorists do not (e.g., Redican, 1982).

Beginning in the 1970s, primatologists began to examine the evolution of social vision in primates (Brothers, 1997; Premack & Woodruff, 1978; Whiten & Byrne, 1997). In particular, there was a focus on how the environment helped shaped social visual cuing. For instance, Redican (1982) looked at expressive behaviors in arboreal New World monkeys versus terrestrial Old World monkeys. He found that Old World monkeys were more expressive, presumably due to the lack of visual obstruction (i.e., foliage). This work was in line with previous findings by Moynihan (1964), who reported that platyrrhine "night" monkeys, both arboreal and nocturnal, exhibit virtually no capacity for facial expression. Together these findings are consistent with the conclusion that the evolution of complex facial musculature is directly associated with the functional capacity of the face as a mechanism for social signaling. In addition, Dunbar (1998) found that neocortical size is correlated with average communal group size across a variety of primates. He further argued that it was the shift from nocturnal to diurnal living that led to such a heavy reliance on visual perception, from which much more subtly nuanced social meaning could be derived. Taken together, there exists compelling evidence for the co-evolution of the face as a social stimulus, and the brain as a social processor.

Similar to the neo-Darwinian perspectives on the co-evolution of emotional expression and recognition is the ecological approach to vision perception (Gibson, 1979). The ecological approach similarly proposes an interplay between stimulus and perceiver through the notions of behavioral affordances and perceiver attunements. Affordances are defined as opportunities to act on or be acted upon by a stimulus. Gibson argued affordances influence perception in a direct and nonreflective manner (i.e., "direct perception"), requiring no need for symbolic representation or cognitive appraisal. Perceiver attunements are defined as the observer's sensitivity to these affordances. Despite some attunements being innately prepared, there are important differences to be explored across individuals and situations (see Zebrowitz, 2006).

The link between stimulus features and perceiver attunements seems rather intuitive and allows us to expand face processing models to address individual differences, contextual and culture influences, and compound social cue interactions, which are currently missing from models of face perception. In a recent review, Zebrowitz (2006) notes: "A perceived identity, social category, emotion, or psychological trait may each specify the same behavioral affordance" (pg. 668). This observation is consistent the notion of shared signals across facial cues (see Adams, Ambady, Macrae, & Kleck, 2006; Adams & Kleck, 2003; 2005). Put simply, the multiple sources of information contained within the face share underlying meaning as basic signals of motivational intent and thus should be expected to combine in a functional manner to convey social messages.

The Social Visual Brain

Neuroscience has much to contribute in terms of understanding how we process compound nonverbal cues. We can expect that interactivity and overlap in facial cues should be accompanied by interactivity and overlap in the underlying neural structures responsible for processing them. The integration of social information often requires not only quick and efficient processing, but also detailed processing. These seemingly competing forces have benefited from the parallel structure of the visual

system, which confers specialized attunements to different aspects of a stimulus along distinct processing routes.

Parallel visual processing begins as information leaves the retina. Some projections go through a subcortical tract to the colliculus (Leventhal, Rodieck, & Dreher, 1981). The collicular region has been implicated in stimulus localization. It plays an important role in visual orienting and subsequent eye movements (Posner & Petersen, 1990) and feeds information via a subcortical route to the amygdala (through the pulvinar nucleus of the thalamus; Palermo & Rhodes, 2007) constituting the "low road" (LeDoux, 1996) of visual input. This pathway has been implicated in activation of the right amygdala to subliminally presented threats stimuli (Morris, Öhman, & Dolan, 1999; see also Öhman, 2005), and has been found to be most responsive to low spatial frequencies implicating a heavy magnocellular input (Vuilleumier, Armony, Driver, & Dolan, 2003) supporting quick detection of threat.

The remaining majority of projections from the retina go to the lateral geniculate nucleus of the thalamus (LGN; Leventhal, 1979). From there, information on rapid motion proceeds through the magnocellular system (bottom 2 layers of the LGN) while finer detailed, color vision proceeds through the parvocellular system (top 4 layers of the LGN). From there, both systems project to area V1. From V1, projections go along either a ventral, occipito-temporal route, or a dorsal, occipitoparietal route. The ventral, "what" pathway, is implicated in object recognition whereas the dorsal, "where" pathway, is implicated in spatial localization (Mishkin, Ungerleider, & Macko, 1983). Livingstone and Hubel (1987) suggested that the ventral pathway is a rough continuation of the parvocellular system whereas the dorsal pathway is a rough continuation of the magnocellular pathway, while others argue this is not yet clear (e.g., Milner & Goodale, 1996). As vision scientists continue this debate, what is important to note here is that the visual system is composed of parallel and complementary components, maximizing the efficiency of extracting visual information from our environment.

As already indicated, evidence supports that face processing benefits from the parallel structure of the visual system. Invariant facial cues such as facial identity versus changeable aspects of the face such as emotional expression appear to be functionally and neurologically separable. Evidence for this claim includes early behavioral studies (e.g., Etcoff, 1984;

Le Gal & Bruce, 2002), clinical cases showing a dissociation between prosopagnosia (i.e., "face blindness") and expressive agnosia, single-cell recordings in primates (e.g., Hasselmo et al., 1989), and brain imaging studies in humans (e.g., Hoffman & Haxby, 2000). Although the fusiform gyrus and the superior temporal sulcus (STS) both contain cells that are preferentially responsive to facial stimuli (Kanwisher et al., 1997; Kanwisher et al., 1998; Perrett, Rolls, & Caan, 1982), the former appears to be predominant in processing static appearance, whereas the latter appears predominant in the processing "changeable" aspects of the face, including but not limited to emotional expression and eye gaze (Hasselmo et al., 1989; Perrett et al., 1985; Phillips et al., 1998; Puce et al., 1998).

Haxby and colleagues (2000, 2002) offer a neurological model of face processing that high-lights this low-level dissociation, where after an initial period of early perceptual processing in the inferior occipital gyrus, static components of the face (i.e., identity-based cues) are processed in a route that runs through the fusiform gyrus (FG), and changeable components of the face are pro-cessed in a route that runs through the STS. The dissociation between facial expression processing and facial identity recognition arguably reflects the important but independent roles each played in our evolutionary past. The contention that facial identity and emotion are fully dissociable, however, is a strong claim. Essentially, if two cues are pro-cessed in a completely independent manner, vary-ing one cue should by definition exert no influence on the perception of the other cue. Yet, as reviewed above, a growing number of studies using a variety of methodologies are providing opposing evidence to this claim. Various facial cues do appear to influ-ence one another in perceptual processing, includ-ing the two generally regarded as the most distinct: facial identity and expression (see also Calder & Young, 2005; Zebrowitz, 2006 for reviews).

Moving on from early vision areas, visual infor-mation proceeds to what is now commonly referred to as the "extended network" (Haxby et al., 2000; 2002), which includes areas that are highly inter-connected and responsible for the processing of information about an individual (e.g., personality traits and biographical knowledge) and areas associ-ated with the extraction of emotional information. Some of the areas responsible for processing knowl-edge about an individual include the anterior parac-ingulate, posterior STS/TPJ, anterior temporal cortex, and precuneus. Emotion-related areas in the extended network include the amygdala, insula, and striatum (Gobbini & Haxby, 2007). There is some overlap between this "extended network" and what Brothers (1990) previously referred to as the "social brain." For instance, the amygdala, orbitofrontal cortex (OFC), and STS appear to form a three-node pathway important for social processing. Pathways from the STS to the amygdala support adaptive responding (Aggleton, Burton, & Passingham, 1980; Brothers & Ring, 1993) while pathways to the OFC facilitate decision making (Bechara, Damasio, & Damasio, 2000; Schoenbaum, Chiba, & Gallagher, 1999).

Perrett and Mistlin (1990) stated:

"It is probable that the subsystem we have studied in the STS represents an advanced, perhaps final, stage of visual categorization for facial information. Such information from this system may be passed to many other cortical and subcortical systems, each responsible for particular types of reaction, through the extensive set of anatomical connections of the STS" (p. 211).

The STS is, for instance, implicated in the processing of both facial expressions and eye gaze in primates (Hasselmo et al., 1989; Heywood, Cowey, & Rolls, 1992; Perrett & Mistlin, 1990) and in humans (Phillips et al., 1998; Puce et al., 1998), which might explain interactions between these cues in perceptual processing. Notably, there are reciprocal connections between the STS and the amygdala (Aggleton et al., 1980; Palermo & Rhodes, 2007). The amygdala has also been impli-cated in the integration of complex social, emo-tional, and behavioral information (Emery & Amaral, 2000). Given its connections to both crude visual information from the pulvinar-collicular route as well as detailed visual information from the visual cortices (Palermo & Rhodes, 2007), this area is thought to serve a particularly important role in the integration of social information (Brothers & Ring, 1993; Young, Aggleton, Hellawell, Johnson, Broks, & Hanley, 1995). Lesions of the amygdala also impair both gaze and expression recognition (Calder, Young, Rowland, Perrett, Hodges, & Etcoff, 1996; Kawashima et al., 1999; Scott, Young, Calder, Hellawell, & Aggleton, 1997; Young et al., 1995).

The amygdala is also uniquely located to receive projections from many areas of the brain and is therefore densely interconnected with regions involved in affective, cognitive, perceptual, and behavioral responses in which exteroceptive and interoceptive information can be integrated (Adolphs, 2003; Adolphs & Tranel, 2000; Morris, Öhman, & Dolan, 1998) and is known to exert top-down modulation on extrastriate responses (George, Driver, & Dolan, 2001). It is reciprocally connected to regions involved in other forms of face perception including: 1) fusiform gyrus (FG), which is specialized for identity processing (Kanwisher et al., 1997; Kanwisher et al., 1998), 2) orbitofrontal cortex (OFC), known to be involved in adaptive behavioral responding, conceptual knowledge retrieval, and decision making during the processing of emotion information (Bechara et al., 2000; Schoenbaum et al., 1999), 3) superior temporal sulcus (STS), particularly responsive to biological movement including "changeable" aspects of the face (Hoffman & Haxby, 2000), and 4) inferior occipital gyrus (IOG), involved in low-level structural encoding of faces (Haxby et al., 2000). Other extended networks of interest to consider in the processing of compound social cues include the posterior parietal attention network thought to be involved in visual orienting (Posner & Petersen, 1990), an affective top-down attention route driven primarily through the ventromedial prefrontal cortex (VMPFC), and a cognitive top-down attention route through the dorsolateral prefrontal cortex (DLPFC; see also Palermo and Rhodes, 2007). The anterior cingulate cortex (ACC), which is connected to both the VMPFC and DLPFC (Cohen, Botvinick, & Carter, 2000; Kerns et al., 2004), is also known to play a critical role in processing of ambiguous relative to clear emotional stimuli (Nomura et al., 2003) and thus is likely involved in detecting and directing processing related to various combinations of social cues.

Conclusion

The current chapter has introduced some basic processes involved in the perception and understanding of compound social cues in the face. This approach comes with a number of assumptions. The first assumption is that facial features fundamentally signal socially relevant information. The second is that humans possess an innate propensity to extract such information from the face. The third assumption is that the decoding of facial communication is the product of an interplay of learned social signals and direct perceptual experiences triggered by the face.

The functional approach to social and emotional perception put forth in this chapter extends current models of face processing by accounting for the combinatorial nature of social perception. Faces are, after all, complex visual objects that require efficient interpretation of numerous cues. The ability of our perceptual system to utilize parallel pathways is advantageous and consistent with many two-process models that maximize efficiency via distributed processing. Our approach underscores the importance of also understanding that given the inherent social meaning conveyed by and extracted from the human face, the integration of multiple features based on shared ecological relevance is also necessary for social functioning.

From these assumptions we argue that visual features can perceptually determine social perception, both in terms of innate signaling (e.g., basic emotion) and learned stereotypes (e.g., d gender social category memberships). Vision can in turn moderate social interaction, arguably even playing a pivotal role in the development of complex social cognition (Baron-Cohen, 1995). Additionally, social factors can exert powerful influences on even low-level visual processing through attentional gating and stereotypic expectation. Finally, although this chapter focused on face processing, the functional approach to compound social cue perception can be readily applied to other visual channels (i.e., body motion, see de Gelder & Tamietto, 2010), and modalities (Beauchamp, 2010). Given the adaptive value of extracting such social information, these insights should inform social perception more broadly, including how other channels and modalities combine and interact to influence social perception. Examining the compound nature of social perception in this way has the potential to offer new insights into the origin, adaptive purpose, and the cognitive, cultural, and biological underpinnings of social perception.

References

Ackerman, J. M., Shapiro, J. R., Neuberg, S. L., Kenrick, D. T., Becker, D. V., Griskevicius, V., et al. (2006). They all look the same to me (unless they're angry): From out-group homogeneity to out-group heterogeneity. *Psychological Science, 17*, 836–840.

Adams, R.B., Jr. (2009). Facing a perceptual crossroads: Mixed messages and shared meanings in social perception. Talk presented at the annual meeting for Society for Personality and Social Psychology, Tampa, FL.

Adams, R.B., Jr., Ambady, N., Macrae, C. N., & Kleck, R. E. (2006). Emotional expressions forecast approach-avoidance behavior. *Motivation and Emotion, 30*, 177–186.

Adams, R. B., Jr., Gordon, H. L., Baird, A. A., Ambady, N., & Kleck, R. E. (2003). Effects of gaze on amygdala sensitivity to anger and fear faces. *Science, 300*, 1536.

Adams, R. B., Jr. & Kleck, R. E. (2003). Perceived gaze direction and the processing of facial displays of emotion. *Psychological Science, 14*, 644–647.

Adams, R. B., Jr. & Kleck, R. E. (2005). Effects of direct and averted gaze on the perception of facially communicated emotion. *Emotion, 5*, 3–11.

Adams, R. B., Jr., Ambady, N., Nakayama, K., & Shimojo, S. (2010). *The science of social vision.* New York: Oxford University Press.

Adams R. B., Jr. & Franklin, R. G., Jr. (2009). Influence of emotional expression on the processing of gaze direction. *Motivation & Emotion, 33*, 106–112.

Adams, R. B., Jr., Pauker, K., & Weisbuch, M. (2010). Looking the other way: The role of gaze direction in the cross-race memory effect. *Journal of Experimental Social Psychology, 46*, 478–481.

Adolphs, R. (2002). Neural systems for recognizing emotion. *Current Opinion in Neurobiology, 12*, 169–177.

Adolphs, R. (2003). Is the human amygdala specialized for processing social information? *Annals of the New York Academy of Sciences, 985*, 326–340.

Adolphs, R. & Tranel, D. (2000). Emotion recognition and the human amygdala. In J. P. Aggleton (Ed.), *The amygdala: A functional analysis* (pp. 587–630). USA: Oxford University Press.

Aggleton, J. P., Burton, M. J., & Passingham, R. E. (1980). Cortical and subcortical afferents to the amygdala of the rhesus monkey (Macaca mulatta). *Brain Research, 190*, 347–368.

Atkinson, A. P., Tipples, J., Burt, D. M., & Young, A.W. (2005). Asymmetric interference between sex and emotion in face perception. *Perception and Psychophysics, 67*, 1199–1213.

Baron-Cohen, S. (1995). Theory of mind and face-processing: How do they interact in development and psychopathology. In D. Cicchetti & D. Cohen (Eds.), *Developmental psychopathology* (Vol. 1, pp. 343–356). New York, NY: John Wiley & Sons.

Baron-Cohen, S., Wheelwright, S., Hill, J., Raste, Y., & Plumb, I. (2001). The "Reading of the Mind in the Eyes" test revised version: A study with normal adults, and adults with Asperger syndrome or high functioning autism. *Journal of Child Psychology and Psychiatry, 42*, 241–251.

Baudouin, J., Martin, F., Tiberghien, G., Verlut, I., & Franck, N. (2002). Selective attention to facial emotion and identity in schizophrenia. *Neuropsychologia, 40*, 503–511.

Beauchamp, M. S. (2010). Biological motion and multisensory integration: The role of the superior temporal sulcus. To appear in: R. B. Adams, Jr., N. Ambady, K. Nakayama, & S. Shimojo (Eds.), *The science of social vision* (pp. 409–420). New York: Oxford University Press.

Bechara, A., Damasio, H., & Damasio, A. R. (2000). Emotion, decision making and the orbitofrontal cortex. *Cerebral Cortex, 10*, 295–307.

Becker, D. V., Kenrick, D. T., Neuberg, S. L., Blackwell, K. C., & Smith, D. M. (2007). The confounded nature of angry men and happy women. *Journal of Personality and Social Psychology, 92*, 179–190.

Brothers, L. (1990). The social brain: A project for integrating primate behavior and neurophysiology in a new domain. *Concepts in Neuroscience, 1*, 27–51.

Brothers, L. & Ring, B. (1993). Mesial temporal neurons in the macaque monkey with responses selective for aspects of social stimuli. *Behavioural Brain Research, 57*, 53–61.

Brothers, L. (1997). *Friday's footprint: How society shapes the human mind.* New York: Oxford University Press.

Bruce, V. & Young, A. (1986). Understanding face recognition. *British Journal of Psychology, 77*, 305–327.

Bruck, M., Cavanagh, P., & Ceci, S. J. (1991). Fortysomething: Recognizing faces at one's 25th reunion. *Memory and Cognition, 19*, 221–228.

Calder, A. J., & Young, A. W. (2005). Understanding the recognition of facial identity and facial expression. *Nature Reviews Neuroscience, 6*, 641–651.

Calder, A. J., Young, A. W., Rowland, D., Perrett, D. I., Hodges, J. R., & Etcoff, N. L. (1996). Facial emotion recognition after bilateral amygdala damage: Differentially severe impairment of fear. *Cognitive Neuropsychology, 13*, 699–745.

Carré, J. M., McCormick, C. M., & Mondloch, C. J. (2009). Facial structure is a reliable cue of aggressive behavior. *Psychological Science, 20*, 1194–1198.

Chiao, J. Y., Adams, R. B., Jr., Tse, P. U., Lowenthal, W. T., Richeson, J. A., & Ambady, N. (2008). Knowing who's boss: fMRI and ERP investigations of social dominance perception. *Group Processes & Intergroup Relations, 11*, 201–214.

Cohen, J. D., Botvinick, M., & Carter, C. S. (2000). Anterior cingulate and prefrontal cortex: Who's in control? *Nature Neuroscience, 3*, 421–423.

Crisp, R. J., Hewstone, M., & Rubin, M. (2001). Does multiple categorization reduce intergroup bias? *Personality and Social Psychology Bulletin, 27*, 76–89.

Darwin, C. (1872/1965). *The expression of the emotions in man and animals.* New York, NY: Oxford University Press.

de Gelder, B., Morris, J. S., & Dolan, R. J. (2005). Unconscious fear influences emotional awareness of faces and voices. *Proceedings of the National Academy of Sciences, 102*, 18682–18687.

de Gelder, B. & Tamietto, M. (2010). Faces, bodies, social vision as agent vision and social consciousness. In R. B. Adams, N. Ambady, K. Nakayama, & S. Shimojo (Eds.), *The science of social vision* (pp. 51–74). New York: Oxford University Press.

Dunbar, R. I. M. (1998). The social brain hypothesis. *Evolutionary Anthropology, 6*, 178–190.

Ekman, P. & Friesen, W. V. (1971). Constants across cultures in the face and emotion. *Journal of Personality and Social Psychology, 17*, 124–129.

Emery, N. J. & Amaral, D. G. (2000). The role of the amygdala in primate social cognition. In R. D. Lane & L. Nadel (Eds.), *Cognitive neuroscience of emotion* (pp. 156–191). New York, NY: Oxford University Press.

Engell, A. D. & Haxby, J. V. (2007). Facial expression and gaze-direction in human superior temporal sulcus. *Neuropsychologia, 45*, 3234–3241.

Etcoff, N. L. (1984). Selective attention to facial identity and facial emotion. *Neuropsychologia, 22*, 281–295.

Friedman, H. & Zebrowitz, L. A. (1992). The contribution of typical sex differences in facial maturity to sex role stereotypes. *Personality and Social Psychology Bulletin, 18*, 430–438.

Ganel, T. & Goshen-Gottstein, Y. (2002). The perceptual integrality of sex and identity of faces: Further evidence for the single-route hypothesis. *Journal of Experimental Psychology: Human Perception and Performance, 28*, 854–867.

Ganel, T. & Goshen-Gottstein, Y., (2004). Effects of familiarity on the perceptual integrality of the identity and expression of faces: The parallel-route hypothesis revisited. *Journal of Experimental Psychology: Human Perception and Performance, 30*, 583–597.

Ganel, T., Goshen-Gottstein, V., & Goodale, M. A. (2005). Interactions between the processing of gaze direction and facial expression. *Vision Research, 45*, 1191–1200.

Gauthier, I. & Nelson, C. (2001). The development of face expertise. *Current Opinion in Neurobiology, 11*, 219–224.

George, N., Driver, J., & Dolan, R. J. (2001). Seen gaze-direction modulates fusiform activity and its coupling with other brain areas during face processing. *NeuroImage, 13*, 1102–1112.

George, N., Driver, J. & Dolan, R. J. (2001). Seen gaze-direction modulates fusiform activity and its coupling with other brain areas during face processing. *NeuroImage, 13*, 1102–1112.

Gibson, J. J. (1979). *The ecological approach to visual perception.* Boston, MA: Houghton-Mifflin.

Gobbini, M. I. & Haxby, J. V. (2007). Neural systems for recognition of familiar faces. *Neuropsychologia, 45*, 32–41.

Graham, R. & LaBar, K. S. (2007). Garner interference reveals dependencies between emotional expression and gaze in face perception. *Emotion, 7*, 296–313.

Gross, C. G., Bender, D. B., & Rocha-Miranda, C. E. (1969). Visual receptive fields of neurons in inferotemporal cortex of the monkey. *Science, 166*, 1303–1306.

Hasselmo, M. E., Rolls, E. T., & Baylis, G. C. (1989). The role of expression and identity in the face-selective responses of neurons in the temporal visual cortex of the monkey. *Behavioural Brain Research, 32*, 203–218.

Haxby, J. V., Hoffman, E. A., & Gobbini, M. I. (2000). The distributed human neural system for face perception. *Trends in Cognitive Sciences, 4*, 223–233.

Haxby, J. V., Hoffman, E. A., & Gobbini, M. I. (2002). Human neural systems for face recognition and social communication. *Biological Psychiatry, 51*, 59–67.

Hess, U., Adams, R. B., Jr., & Kleck, R. (2004). Facial appearance, gender, and emotion expression. *Emotion, 4*, 378–388.

Hess, U., Adams, R. B., Jr., & Kleck, R. (2005). Who may frown and who should smile? Dominance, affiliation, and the display of happiness and anger. *Cognition & Emotion, 19*, 515–536.

Heywood, C. A., Cowey, A., & Rolls, E. T. (1992). The role of the "face-cell" area in the discrimination and recognition of faces by monkeys. *Philosophical Transactions of the Royal Society B: Biological Sciences, 335*, 31–38.

Hoffman, E. A. & Haxby, J. V. (2000). Distinct representations of eye gaze and identity in the distributed human neural system for face perception. *Nature Neuroscience, 3*, 80–84.

Hugenberg, K. (2005). Social categorization and the perception of facial affect: Target race moderates the response latency advantage for happy faces. *Emotion, 5*, 267–276.

Johnson, M. H., Dziurawiec, S., Bartrip, J., & Morton, J. (1992). The effects of movement of internal features on infants' preferences for face-like stimuli. *Infant Behavior & Development, 15*, 129–136.

Kanwisher, N., McDermott, J., & Chun, M. M. (1997). The fusiform face area: A module in human extrastriate cortex specialized for face perception. *Journal of Neuroscience, 17*, 4302–4311.

Kanwisher, N., Tong, F., & Nakayama, K. (1998). The effect of face inversion on the human fusiform face area. *Cognition, 68*, 1–11.

Kawashima, R., Sugiura, M., Kato, T., Nakamura, A., Hatano, K., Ito, K., et al. (1999). The human amygdala plays an important role in gaze monitoring. A PET study. *Brain, 122*, 779–783.

Keltner, D., Ekman, P., Gonzaga, G. C., & Beer, J. (2003). Facial expression of emotion, In R. J. Davidson, K. R. Scherer, & H. H. Goldsmith (Eds.) *Handbook of affective sciences* (pp. 415–431). New York: Oxford University Press.

Kenny, D. A., Horner, C., Kashy, D. A., & Chu, L. (1992). Consensus at zero acquaintance: Replication, behavioral cues, and stability. *Journal of Personality and Social Psychology, 62*, 88–97.

Kerns, J. G., Cohen, J. D., MacDonald, A. W., Cho, R. Y., Stenger, V. A., & Carter, C. S. (2004). Anterior cingulate conflict monitoring and adjustments in control. *Science, 303*, 1023–1026.

Kveraga, K., Ghuman, A. S. & Bar, M. (2007) Top-down predictions in the cognitive brain. *Brain and Cognition, 65*, 145–168.

Kveraga, K., Boshyan, J., & Bar, M. (2007) The magnocellular trigger of top-down facilitation in object recognition. *Journal of Neuroscience, 27*, 13232–13240.

LeDoux, J. E. (1996). *The emotional brain.* New York, NY: Simon & Schuster.

Le Gal, P. M. & Bruce, V. (2002). Evaluating the independence of sex and expression in judgments of faces. *Perception & Psychophysics, 64*, 230–243.

Leventhal, A. G. (1979). Evidence that the different classes of relay cells of the cat's lateral geniculate nucleus terminate in different layers of the striate cortex. *Experimental Brain Research, 37*, 349–372.

Leventhal, A. G., Rodieck, R. W., & Dreher, B. (1981). Retinal ganglion cell classes in the Old World monkey: Morphology and central projections. *Science, 213*, 1139–1142.

Levy, Y. & Bentin, S. (2008). Interactive processes in matching identity and expressions of unfamiliar faces: Evidence for mutual facilitation effects. *Perception, 37*, 915–930.

Livingstone, M. S. & Hubel, D. H. (1987). Psychophysical evidence for separate channels for the perception of form, color, movement, and depth. *Journal of Neuroscience, 7*, 3416–3468.

Marsh, A. A., Adams, R. B., Jr., & Kleck, R. E. (2005). Why do fear and anger look the way they do? Form and social function in facial expressions. *Personality and Social Psychology Bulletin, 31*, 73.

Maurer, D. (1983). The scanning of compound figures by young infants. *Journal of Experimental Child Psychology, 35*, 437–448.

McCarthy, G., Puce, A., Gore, J. C., & Allison, T. (1997). Face-specific processing in the human fusiform gyrus. *Journal of Cognitive Neuroscience, 9*, 605–610.

McLuhan, M. (2001). *Understanding media: The extensions of man.* Cambridge, MA: MIT Press.

Meeren, H. J. M., van Heijnsbergen, C. C. R. J., & de Gelder, B. (2005). Rapid perceptual integration of facial expression and emotional body language. *Proceedings of the National Academy of Sciences, 102*, 16518–16523.

Milner, A. D. & Goodale, M. A. (1996). *The visual brain in action.* New York: Oxford University Press.

Mishkin, M., Ungerleider, L. G., & Macko, K. A. (1983). Object vision and spatial vision: Two cortical pathways. *Trends in Neurosciences, 6*, 414–417.

Morris, J. S., Öhman, A., & Dolan, R. J. (1998). Conscious and unconscious emotional learning in the human amygdala. *Nature, 393*, 467–470.

Morris, J. S., Öhman, A., & Dolan, R. J. (1999). A subcortical pathway to the right amygdala mediating "unseen" fear.

Proceedings of the National Academy of Sciences, 96, 1680–1685.

Moynihan, M. (1964). Some behavior patterns of platyrrhine monkeys: I. The night monkey (Aotus Trivirgatus). *Smithsonian Miscellaneous Collections, 146,* 1–84.

Nomura, M., Iidaka, T., Kakehi, K., Tsukiura, T., Hasegawa, T., Maeda, Y., et al. (2003). Frontal lobe networks for effective processing of ambiguously expressed emotions in humans. *Neuroscience Letters, 348,* 113–116.

Öhman, A. (2005). The role of the amygdala in human fear: Automatic detection of threat. *Psychoneuroendocrinology, 30,* 953–958.

Palermo, R. & Rhodes, G. (2007). Are you always on my mind? A review of how face perception and attention interact. *Neuropsychologia, 45,* 75–92.

Perrett, D. I. & Mistlin, A. J. (1990). Perception of facial characteristics by monkeys. In W. C. Stebbins & M. A. Berkley (Eds.), *Comparative perception* (pp. 187–215). New York, NY: John Wiley & Sons.

Perret, D. I., Rolls, E. T., & Caan, W. (1982). Visual neurons responsive to faces in the monkey temporal cortex. *Experimental Brain Research, 47,* 329–342.

Perrett, D. I., Smith, P. A. J., Mistlin, A. J., Chitty, A. J., Head, A. S., Potter, D. D., et al. (1985). Visual analysis of body movements by neurones in the temporal cortex of the macaque monkey: A preliminary report. *Behavioural Brain Research, 16,* 153–170.

Phillips, M. L., Bullmore, E. T., Howard, R., Woodruff, P. W. R., Wright, I. C., Williams, S. C. R., et al. (1998). Investigation of facial recognition memory and happy and sad facial expression perception: An fMRI study. *Psychiatry Research: Neuroimaging, 83,* 127–138.

Phillips, R. J. (1979). Some exploratory experiments on memory for photographs of faces. *Acta Psychologica, 43,* 39–56.

Posner, M. I. & Petersen, S. E. (1990). The attention system of the human brain. *Annual Review of Neuroscience, 13,* 25–42.

Pourtois, G., Sander, D., Andres, M., Grandjean, D., Reveret, L., Olivier, E., et al. (2004). Dissociable roles of the human somatosensory and superior temporal cortices for processing social face signals. *European Journal of Neuroscience, 20,* 3507–3515.

Premack, D. & Woodruff, G. (1978). Does the chimpanzee have a theory of mind? *Behavioral and Brain Sciences, 1,* 515–526.

Puce, A., Allison, T., Bentin, S., Gore, J. C., & McCarthy, G. (1998). Temporal cortex activation in humans viewing eye and mouth movements. *Journal of Neuroscience, 18,* 2188–2199.

Quinn, K. A. & Macrae, C. N. (2005). Categorizing others: The dynamics of person construal. *Journal of Personality and Social Psychology, 88,* 467–479.

Redican, W. K. (1982). An evolutionary perspective on human facial displays. In P. Ekman (Ed.), *Emotion in the human face* (pp. 212–280). New York, NY: Cambridge University Press.

Richeson, J. A., Todd, A. R., Trawalter, S., & Baird, A. A. (2008). Eye-gaze direction modulates race-related amygdala activity. *Group Processes and Intergroup Relations, 11,* 233–246.

Said, C. P., Sebe, N., & Todorov, A. (2009). Structural resemblance to emotional expressions predicts evaluation of emotionally neutral faces. *Emotion, 9,* 260–264.

Schoenbaum, G., Chiba, A. A., & Gallagher, M. (1999). Neural encoding in orbitofrontal cortex and basolateral amygdala during olfactory discrimination learning. *Journal of Neuroscience, 19,* 1876–1884.

Schweinberger, S. R., Burton, A. M., & Kelly, S. W. (1999). Asymmetric dependencies in perceiving identity and emotion: Experiments with morphed faces. *Perception & Psychophysics, 61,* 1102–1115.

Schweinberger, S. R. & Soukup, G. R. (1998). Asymmetric relationships among perceptions of facial identity, emotion, and facial speech. *Journal of Experimental Psychology: Human Perception & Performance, 24,* 1748–1765.

Scott, S. K., Young, A. W., Calder, A. J., Hellawell, D. J., & Aggleton, J. P. (1997). Impaired auditory recognition of fear and anger following bilateral amygdala lesions. *Nature, 385,* 254–257.

Trawalter, S., Todd, A., Baird, A. A. & Richeson, J. A. (2008). Attending to threat: Race-based patterns of selective attention. *Journal of Experimental Social Psychology, 44,* 1322–1327.

Van Overwalle, F., Drenth, T., & Marsman, G. (1999). Spontaneous trait inferences: Are they linked to the actor or to the action? *Personality and Social Psychology Bulletin, 25,* 450–462.

Vuilleumier, P., Armony, J. L., Driver, J., & Dolan, R. J. (2003). Distinct spatial frequency sensitivities for processing faces and emotional expressions. *Nature Neuroscience, 6,* 624–631.

Whiten, A. & Byrne, R. W. (1997). *Machiavellian intelligence II: Extensions and evaluations.* Cambridge, UK: Cambridge University Press.

Willis, J. & Todorov, A. (2006). First impressions: Making up your mind after a 100-ms exposure to a face. *Psychological Science, 17,* 592–598.

Young, A. W., Aggleton, J. P., Hellawell, D. J., Johnson, M., Broks, P., & Hanley, J. R. (1995). Face processing impairments after amygdalotomy. *Brain, 118,* 15–24.

Zebrowitz, L. A. (1997). *Reading faces: Window to the soul?* Boulder, CO: Westview Press.

Zebrowitz, L. A. (2006). Finally, faces find favor. *Social Cognition, 24,* 657–701.

Zebrowitz, L. A., Kikuchi, M., & Fellous, J. M. (2007). Are effects of emotion expression on trait impressions mediated by babyfaceness? Evidence from connectionist modeling. *Personality and Social Psychology Bulletin, 33,* 648–662.

Bruce D. Bartholow *and* Cheryl L. Dickter

Abstract

This chapter is concerned with the ways in which the use of various psychophysiological measures, and the theory that underlies their use, has advanced understanding of person perception. A social neuroscience approach can be useful for testing theory and advancing the science of person perception. In particular, event-related brain potentials (ERPs) provide a time-sensitive means of measuring and separating the rapidly unfolding cognitive and affect-related processes theorized in many models of person perception, and functional brain imaging permits a detailed picture of the neural structures that subserve these processes. Neuropsychological studies also offer important insights into the functions of particular regions of the brain that appear crucial for effective person perception. Most importantly, linking these neural indices with important psychological and behavioral outcomes can provide a more comprehensive understanding of person perception than can be gained by any self-report, behavioral, cognitive, neural, or biological approach alone.

Keywords: person perception, cognitive neuroscience, psychophysiological measures, stereotyping, perception of emotion, face perception, impression formation

In his influential 1990 text, *Interpersonal Perception*, Ed Jones nicely encapsulated the essence of person perception as how people try to determine what another person is "really like" inside. More specifically, Jones described how people "come to understand what makes a particular person—including ourselves—behave in particular ways" (p. 1). People seem innately driven to make such determinations. Indeed, given the ways in which cognitive processing is biased toward formation of and reliance on categories and expectancies (see Allport, 1954; Bruner, 1957), it is virtually impossible for social interactions to proceed in any other way. According to Jones (1990), when we perceive a person we draw conclusions about him or her, often rapidly and

automatically, sometimes thoughtfully and carefully. A brief (and nonexhaustive) list of the psychological processes involved in this pursuit includes some of the most basic, foundational issues in social psychological research: causal attribution, expectancies, assessment of situational constraint—and its converse, the correspondence bias—and various self-presentation goals and strategies. In this chapter we will be concerned with the ways in which the use of various psychophysiological measures, and the theory that underlies their use, has advanced understanding of person perception. However, given the attention paid to them in other chapters in this volume, we will only briefly consider some topics of central interest to person perception researchers, such as stereotyping, perception of emotion, face perception, and impression formation.

Why Study Person Perception from a Social Neuroscience Perspective?

Before reviewing the literature on the social neuroscience of person perception, it is important to first briefly examine what can be gained by using a social neuroscience approach to studying this topic. Person perception research has a deep and important history in social psychology. It goes without saying that the behavioral methods traditionally used in person perception research, including recall (i.e., person memory), response latency, and self-reported evaluations (among others; see Olson, Roese, & Zanna, 1996), have provided a strong foundation for advancing our understanding of how and why people attempt to draw conclusions about others' traits. However, the nature of the cognitive and affective processes thought to be important for person perception makes certain theoretical questions difficult to address when using behavioral and self-report methods alone. For example, when participants are better able to recall information about people in one condition versus another, we infer that the information in the former condition received more extensive processing than the information in the latter condition. In this sense, recall represents one *outcome* of some cognitive activity associated with memory, but a number of processes likely intervene between stimulus encoding and recall that are not well represented in a memory measure.

In contrast, augmenting a memory measure (or other measures) with one or more psychophysiological measures can provide insight into theoretically relevant intervening processes. As we review more extensively later in this chapter, for example, event-related brain potentials (ERPs) have been used in a number of studies to elucidate the stage(s) of processing at which information that violates previously formed impressions of others is processed differently (e.g., more extensively) than information that confirms prior impressions (e.g., Bartholow, Fabiani, Gratton, & Bettencourt, 2001; Bartholow, Pearson, Gratton, & Fabiani, 2003; Van Duynslaeger, Van Overwalle, & Verstraeten, 2007). Such information is important for understanding not only the timecourse of person perception processes (e.g., Ito, Thompson, & Cacioppo, 2004), but also the specific mechanisms of information processing that are involved.

More generally, it is important to consider what kinds of information can be gained by the use of particular psychophysiological and/or neuropsychological measures and methods. For example, the two primary brain-based measures used in social neuroscience research on person perception, ERPs and functional magnetic resonance imaging (fMRI), provide data relevant to quite different levels of analysis. Specifically, ERPs provide excellent temporal resolution of brain activity (on the order of milliseconds following a stimulus event), relevant to the timing of relevant psychological processes. Such data can be very useful for testing hypotheses derived from multiple-stage models of person perception, such as various dual-process models (see Chaiken & Trope, 1999). However, ERPs can provide only very limited information on the specific neural structures producing relevant information-processing activity (see Chapter 6 in this volume for more information on ERP measures). The converse is true of fMRI: the temporal resolution of the signal is quite sluggish by comparison, on the order of 4–6 seconds following an eliciting stimulus event, but spatial resolution is very good, allowing for quite specific inferences concerning the neural sources of relevant psychological processes. Such data can be very useful for both exploratory purposes, such as identifying structures involved in forming impressions (e.g., Mitchell, Cloutier, Banaji, & Macrae, 2006), and for testing hypotheses concerning differences in the activity of specific structures across experimental conditions.

Another important difference between ERP and fMRI measures is that whereas ERPs represent a fairly direct measure of the electrical activity of the brain associated with information-processing operations (see Rugg & Coles, 1995), the fMRI BOLD (blood oxygen level dependent) signal is a rather indirect measure, reflecting the dynamics of blood flow and resource utilization (represented by the ratio of oxygenated to deoxygenated hemoglobin in the blood) in various parts of the brain. In other words, fMRI highlights areas of the brain where activity is assumed to have recently increased or decreased, but does not, technically, represent the activity of neurons as the brain processes information.

Cognitive Neuroscience Studies of Person Perception

Although the social neuroscience of person perception is still a relatively new field, the literature is sufficiently large as to limit the coverage any single chapter can provide. Here, we have chosen to focus primarily on research in which measures of brain activity or brain functionality were used. This decision was purely a practical one, and is in no way intended to suggest that studies using other psychophysiological measures, such as cardiovascular and other autonomic nervous system measures, are not as useful as brain-based measures.

ERP Studies

Although the existence of bioelectrical potentials in the brain had been known for decades prior (e.g., Bartholow, 1882), Hans Berger (1929) was the first to describe a method for recording the electrical activity of the human brain (the electroencephalogram; EEG) from the surface of the head by placing a pair of electrodes on the scalp and connecting them to a differential amplifier. Other scientists (e.g., Davis, Davis, Loomis, Harvey, & Hobart, 1939) later discovered that when stimuli are presented during EEG recording, epochs of the EEG that are time-locked to stimulus onset can be defined. With repeated sampling, that portion of the EEG representing the neural response to a specific stimulus (or stimulus class) emerges from the ongoing, "background" EEG signal as a series of positive and negative voltage deflections known as components. Decades of systematic research has linked these components to specific information-processing operations (see Rugg & Coles, 1995). In general, component amplitude reflects the extent of neural activation associated with a particular cognitive operation (or set of operations), while component latency reflects the time required to carry out that operation (e.g., Gehring, Gratton, Coles, & Donchin, 1992; Fabiani et al., 2007; Rugg & Coles, 1995). However, it is important to stress that any given component likely represents numerous simultaneously occurring processes (see Coles & Rugg, 1995).

Armed with this knowledge, social psychologists began a series of fruitful collaborations with cognitive psychophysiologists in the early 1990s to better understand the information-processing operations involved in person perception (e.g., Cacioppo, Crites, Gardner, & Berntson, 1994). These early studies focused primarily on a late positive component in the ERP known as the P3 or P300, so named because of its positive voltage and peak latency (in early studies) around 300 ms post-stimulus. This component had been widely studied by cognitive psychophysiologists for many years, and had been associated with the brain's response to novelty (Friedman, Cycowicz, & Gaeta, 2001), in that P300 amplitude increases as the subjective probability of an eliciting event decreases (e.g., Donchin & Coles, 1988;

Duncan-Johnson & Donchin, 1977; Squires et al., 1975). The P300 has been described as a manifestation of context updating in working memory, based on numerous studies indicating better subsequent memory for stimuli that elicit larger P300 amplitude (e.g., Donchin, 1981; Donchin & Coles, 1988; Friedman & Johnson, 2000), and more generally as an indication of the motivational significance or relevance of an eliciting stimulus (see Nieuwenhuis, Cohen, & Aston-Jones, 2005). The peak latency of the P300 serves as a neural indicator of stimulus evaluation or categorization time, with longer latencies indicating more effortful categorization (see Coles, 1989). Despite its name, it is not uncommon for the P300 to peak substantially later than 300 ms in tasks involving complex social or emotional stimuli (see Bartholow & Amodio, 2009; Bartholow & Dickter, 2007), a fact that has led some to posit a difference between the "classic" P300 elicited in purely cognitive tasks and a "late positive potential," or LPP, elicited by stimuli that carry more social or emotional significance (e.g., Schupp et al., 2000).

Given that the P300 serves as an index of subjective probability in categorization processes (e.g., Donchin & Coles, 1988; Friedman et al., 2001), Cacioppo and his colleagues (Cacioppo et al., 1993) reasoned that it also should mark the implicit categorization of evaluatively consistent and inconsistent attitude objects. In their initial study, Cacioppo et al. (1993) developed stimulus sets consisting of valenced (i.e., positive and negative) words presented in sequences in which word valence either was evaluatively consistent or was evaluatively inconsistent. As predicted, Cacioppo et al. found that P3 amplitude was much larger to a given target type when it was preceded by words from a different evaluative category (e.g., a negative target following positive words) than when it was preceded by words from the same evaluative category (e.g., a negative target following negative words).

Using a variation of this method, Cacioppo et al. (1994) began to investigate the neural underpinnings of person perception. This work showed that P300 amplitude also indexes evaluative categorization of positive and negative personality traits, and that this effect is associated with categorization per se rather than response processes (Crites, Cacioppo, Gardner, & Berntson, 1995), suggesting that the P300 might assess implicit interpersonal attitudes. In a similar experiment, Osterhout, Bersick, and McLaughlin (1997) showed that a P300-like, late positivity in the ERP waveform is sensitive to violations of gender stereotypical noun-pronoun agreement in sentence comprehension (e.g., "Our aerobics instructor gave *himself* a break"). This effect was independent of participants' self-reported judgments of the acceptability of the sentences, further suggesting that the P300 might provide a relatively covert indication of implicit person judgments.

A more recent study conducted by Ito, Thompson, and Cacioppo (2004) further confirmed this notion. Ito and colleagues had White participants view images of White men's and Black men's faces embedded within series of positively- and negatively-valenced images from the International Affective Picture System (IAPS; Lang, Bradley, & Cuthbert, 2001). Based on previous work showing that the P300 is sensitive to changes in evaluative categorization, Ito and colleagues hypothesized that P300 amplitude elicited in the context of frequent negative images would be smaller to infrequent Black faces than to infrequent White faces, and that the P300 elicited in the context of frequent positive images would be larger to infrequent Black faces than to infrequent White faces. Their results showed only modest (and nonsignificant) differences in these predicted directions. However, the difference in P300 amplitude elicited by White compared to Black faces was correlated with scores on self-reported measures of racism, such that those with more negative attitudes toward Blacks showed larger P300 amplitude differences. Thus, these findings support the idea that the P300 elicited in tasks of person perception can serve as a sensitive measure of implicit attitudes (see also Ito & Cacioppo, 2007).

Based in part on the work of Cacioppo and colleagues and Osterhout et al. (1997), Bartholow et al. (2001) reasoned that the processing of interpersonal expectancy violations also should be manifest in P300 amplitude. Numerous studies in social and developmental psychology indicate that expectancy-violating information about people often is recalled better than expectancy-confirming information (see Stangor & McMillan, 1992). Theoretical models (e.g., Srull & Wyer, 1989) posit that this recall advantage reflects updating of working memory that occurs during *inconsistency resolution*, the process by which people attempt to reconcile the discrepancy between new information and existing "person concepts." The longstanding notion that the P300 reflects the process of working memory updating (e.g., Donchin, 1981; Donchin & Coles, 1988; Friedman & Johnson, 2000) suggests that P300 amplitude should reflect the neural processes associated with inconsistency resolution.

Bartholow and colleagues (2001; see also Bartholow et al., 2003) tested this idea in a set of experiments in which participants read paragraph descriptions of several fictitious individuals in order to form impressions of them, and then read sentences (presented one word at a time) depicting behaviors that were either consistent or inconsistent with those impressions. Consistent with the working-memory updating hypothesis of the P300 (Donchin & Coles, 1988), P300 amplitude elicited by expectancy-violating sentence-ending words was larger than that elicited by expectancy-consistent sentence-ending words. Expectancy-violating behaviors also were better recalled than expectancy-consistent behaviors, further supporting the notion that P300 amplitude reflects the extent to which stimuli are processed during memory encoding (see Fabiani & Donchin, 1995). Moreover, P300 amplitude was greater to negative than to positive expectancy-violating behaviors, consistent with research indicating that negative information about people is more informative or relevant to person perception than positive information (see Peeters & Czapinski, 1990; Reeder & Coovert, 1986; Sherman & Frost, 2000; Trafimow & Finlay, 2001; Ybarra, 2002; Ybarra, Schaberg, & Keiper, 1999). Figure 27.1 presents relevant ERP waveforms showing these effects.

Bartholow et al.'s (2001) findings indicated that the recall advantage long known to accompany expectancy violations (e.g., Stangor & McMillan, 1992) results from evaluative categorization processes occurring quite rapidly following perception, and strongly implicate a role for working memory updating—one of a host of so-called executive cognitive functions, thought to be mediated by activity in the prefrontal cortex (see Miyake et al., 2000)—in the process of inconsistency resolution (see also Macrae, Bodenhausen, Schloersheidt, & Milne, 1999). To further test the role of executive working memory in the inconsistency resolution processes reflected in the P300, Bartholow, Pearson, Gratton, and Fabiani (2003) conducted an experiment in which participants consumed either alcohol or a placebo beverage just prior to engaging in the person perception task used by Bartholow et al. (2001). Alcohol's effects on interpersonal behaviors are commonly attributed to impairment of executive cognitive functions thought mediated by the prefrontal cortex (e.g., Hoaken, Giancola, & Pihl, 1998; Peterson, Rothfleisch, Zelazo, & Pihl, 1990; Steele & Josephs, 1990). Thus, Bartholow et al. (2003) reasoned that inconsistency resolution might be

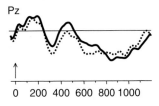

Negative trait condition

Pz

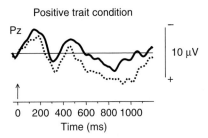

0 200 400 600 800 1000

Fig. 27.1 ERP waveforms elicited by expectancy-consistent and expectancy-violating behaviors as a function of whether targets had positive traits or negative traits. Consistency or violation with initial trait impressions was determined by the valence of relevant behaviors, for example, a negative behavior in the positive trait condition would be an expectancy violation. Reprinted from Bartholow, B. D., Fabiani, M., Gratton, G., & Bettencourt, B. A. (2001), with permission of SAGE Publications.

Expectancy-consistent ———
Expectancy-violation ···········

Positive trait condition

Pz

10 μV

0 200 400 600 800 1000
Time (ms)

impaired during intoxication, and used ERPs to track the time course and severity of hypothesized impairments.

For participants in the placebo condition, the P300 and recall data largely replicated those of the earlier report (Bartholow et al., 2001), in that expectancy violations—particularly negative behaviors—elicited larger P300 than expectancy confirmations, and recall was better for negative than positive expectancy-violating behaviors. However, for participants who consumed alcohol the opposite pattern emerged, with generally larger expectancy-violation effects associated with positive behaviors presented in a negative context, and better recall for positive than negative expectancy-violating behaviors. Bartholow et al. (2003) interpreted this reversal in terms of alcohol-induced activation of the cerebral reward system influencing processing of reward-congruent information in working memory (see London, Ernst, Grant, Bonson, & Weinstein, 2000). This study also illustrates the use of alcohol as a tool in social neuroscience research. Given that many social-cognitive phenomena are presumed to be mediated by prefrontal cortical activity, examining social cognitive processes in healthy individuals temporarily impaired by alcohol provides a method for bridging gaps between research in neuropsychology, social cognition, and cognitive neuroscience (see also Macrae et al., 1999).

The expectancy violation studies conducted by Bartholow et al. (2001, 2003) provided an initial understanding of the neural events associated with *intentional trait inferences*. Participants in those

studies were instructed to form impressions of target persons based on trait-related information provided about them. Later violations of those traits elicited enhanced neural responses, indicating that traits had been inferred from the earlier information. However, outside of the laboratory, people generally are not told to form impressions of others on the basis of their behavior; rather, this process happens spontaneously, a process known as *spontaneous trait inference* (see Uleman, 1999; Uleman et al., 1996, 2005). In a recent series of studies, Van Overwalle and his colleagues (e.g., Van Duynslaeger, Van Overwalle, & Verstraeten, 2007; Van Overwalle, Van den Eede, Baetens, & Vandekerckhove, 2009; Van Duynslaeger, Sterken, Van Overwalle, & Verstraeten, 2008) have used ERPs to investigate similarities and differences in the neural activity elicited under intentional versus spontaneous trait-inference conditions. For example, Van Duynslaeger et al. (2007) modified the paradigm developed by Bartholow et al. (2001) by telling half of their participants to simply "read the stimulus materials carefully," making no mention of forming impressions, and telling the other half of the participants to form an impression of each target (cf., Bartholow et al., 2001, 2003). Van Duynslaeger et al. found that P300 amplitude was enhanced to trait-inconsistent compared to trait-consistent behaviors in both the intentional and spontaneous trait inference conditions, indicating that the inconsistency-resolution process is very similar in both cases. However, compared to expectancy violations encountered under intentional inference instructions, source analysis indicated that expectancy violations encountered under spontaneous trait inference conditions elicited greater activation in the temporo-parietal junction, a neural region implicated in representing others' mental states (Frith & Frith, 2001) and considered a primary generator of the P300 (see Nieuwenhuis et al., 2005).

A number of person perception processes are known to be strongly affected by the social category memberships of both the perceiver and the targets. Certain very basic social categories (i.e., those that are most readily identifiable), such as gender and race, are particularly influential. In recent years, ERPs have been applied to the study of very basic attention-related and evaluative processes occurring during the perception of race (see Ito & Bartholow, 2009). ERP studies of race perception consistently show that racial information is processed very quickly and automatically. For example, Ito and Urland (2003) showed that ERP waveforms elicited by pictures of White and Black faces begin to diverge as early as around 120 ms after picture onset (i.e., the N100 component), a finding that held regardless of whether participants explicitly categorized the faces by race or according to some other social dimension (e.g., gender). The most consistent finding to emerge from studies in this literature is that the P200 (or P2) component is larger to racial outgroup than ingroup faces, and the N200 (or N2) is larger to racial ingroup than outgroup faces (e.g., Dickter & Bartholow, 2007; Ito, Thompson, & Ca-cioppo, 2004; Ito & Urland, 2003, 2005; Kubota & Ito, 2007; Walker, Silvert, Hewstone, & Nobre, 2008; Willadsen-Jensen & Ito, 2006, 2008). Precise interpretation of these patterns is still elusive given that this literature remains relatively small and only recently has emerged. However, current understanding suggests that increased P2 and N2 responses in race perception tasks reflect automatic encoding and orienting toward racial category information.

Initial studies in this literature (e.g., Ito & Urland, 2003, 2005) relied on White participants, and therefore it was unclear whether the enhanced P2 to Black targets and N2 to White targets reflected responses to features of race specifically (e.g., skin tone; facial structure) or reflected a more general distinction between outgroup and ingroup targets. Dickter and Bartholow (2007) conducted the first race perception ERP study using both Black and White participants. Their results showed the typical pattern for White participants, with larger P2 amplitude to Black than to White targets and larger N2 amplitude to White than to Black targets. Among Black participants, however, these patterns were reversed (i.e., larger P2 to White than to Black targets; larger N2 to Black than to White targets), supporting the perspective that the "race categorization" effects seen in previous studies actually represent differential outgroup and ingroup categorization effects. Similar results also have been reported by Willadsen-Jensen and Ito (2008) using Asian participants viewing Asian and White faces.

The fact that processing of ingroup faces consistently increases N2 amplitude raises questions concerning how this "ingroup categorization" N2 compares to N2 responses elicited by other stimulus conditions. For example, increased N2 amplitude has been associated in numerous studies with processes related to conflict detection, in that the N2 often is larger on trials that elicit competing response activations, such as incongruent Stroop trials (e.g., Liotti, Woldorff, Perez, & Mayberg, 2000) and incompatible trials in flanker tasks (i.e., stimulus arrays including stimuli mapped to opposing behavioral responses; see Kopp, Rist, & Mattler, 1996; van Veen & Carter, 2002). Additionally, the N2 often increases as a function of stimulus infrequency, such that low-probability stimuli elicit larger N2s than higher-probability stimuli, regardless of whether the stimuli themselves elicit competing response activations (e.g., Jones, Cho, Nystrom, Cohen, & Braver, 2002; Nieuwenhuis, Yeung, Van Den Wildenberg, & Ridderinkhof, 2003). It has been unclear whether these conflict- and infrequency-related N2s also respond to race perception, however.

Recently, Dickter and Bartholow (2010) investigated the potential interaction among these various stimulus conditions by presenting White participants with pictures of White and Black men's faces in the context of a flanker task, in which centrally presented target faces (which had to be categorized by race via button press) were flanked on either side either by same-race faces (i.e., compatible trials; e.g., Black target and Black flankers) or by other-race faces (i.e., incompatible trials; e.g., Black target and White flankers). Trial type frequency was manipulated by varying the probability of compatible trials across trial blocks, resulting in 80% compatible, 50% compatible, and 20% compatible conditions. Dickter and Bartholow found the typical ingroup categorization effect, with larger N2 to White target trials than to Black target trials. However, this effect was qualified by both compatibility and frequency conditions (i.e., a Race x Compatibility x Probability interaction). As shown in Figure 27.2, the N2 was sensitive to compatibility

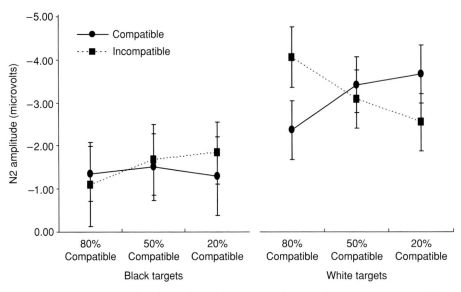

Fig. 27.2 Mean N2 amplitude (measured from frontal electrode locations) as a function of target race, trial compatibility and the probability of compatible trials. It is striking that compatibility and infrequency—stimulus conditions known to reliably affect N2 amplitude—had virtually no effect for Black target trials.
Adapted with permission from Dickter, C. L. & Bartholow, B. D. (2010).

and trial type frequency in a predictable manner (see Bartholow et al., 2005; Bartholow, Riordan, Saults, & Lust, 2009), but only on White (ingroup) target trials. Dickter and Bartholow posited that this pattern could reflect that ingroup targets elicit stronger engagement of the processes underlying generation of the N2 than outgroup targets, leading to stronger effects of compatibility and infrequency on ingroup trials. Consistent with this notion, considerable work using a variety of methods indicates that White participants spontaneously attend more to Black male than to White male faces (e.g., Trawalter, Todd, Baird, & Richeson, 2008; Cunningham et al., 2004; Dickter & Bartholow, 2007). Thus, it could be that among White participants Black targets elicit narrower, more focused attention than White targets, which would reduce the influence of both flanker compatibility and the probability of compatible arrays—factors that both rely on manipulations of (peripheral) flanker information—on Black target trials.

That the processing of ingroup faces reflected in the N2 is more sensitive to other manipulations than the processing of outgroup faces was recently demonstrated in a very different context by Henry, Bartholow, and Arndt (2010). These researchers investigated the effects of mortality salience, known to elicit preferences for ingroup members assumed to share one's cultural worldview and to intensity of ingroup identification (e.g., Solomon, Greenberg,

& Pyszczynski, 2000), on ERP responses elicited by White and Black faces displaying neutral, happy, and angry facial expressions. Henry et al. found that the ingroup N2 effect was larger and more widespread across scalp locations for participants in the mortality salience condition (who, prior to the facial expression task, were asked to write down the feelings that the thought of their own death aroused in them) compared to those in a control condition (who, prior to the task, wrote about dental pain). Moreover, whereas control participants showed a larger N2 to happy than to angry White faces, a pattern consistent with previous research (Kubota & Ito, 2007), those in the mortality salience condition showed larger N2s to angry than to happy White faces. Henry et al. posited that the preference following mortality salience to view ingroup members favorably, coupled with the sensitivity of the N2 to perceived stimulus infrequency (e.g., Nieuwenhuis et al., 2003), could lead to enhanced conflict when processing threatening/angry ingroup targets.

The cognitive neuroscience of face processing is reviewed in detail elsewhere in this volume (see Chapter 25). However, given that person perception often is studied with face stimuli, as is evident by our review, here we provide a brief overview of some the face processing research most relevant to this chapter. Given their importance for conveying social information, researchers have long been interested in understanding whether faces are accorded special status within the universe of stimuli that people encounter. ERP studies of face perception have identified a negative-going component, typically peaking around 170 ms following target onset and largest at lateral, temporo-parietal electrode locations, known as the N170, which appears particularly sensitive to faces (e.g., Eimer, 2000; Kanwisher, McDermott, & Chun, 1997). Source localization data indicate that the N170 primarily reflects activity in the fusiform gyrus (Herrmann et al., 2005), a cortical structure often associated with face processing. Indeed, some have even referred to this structure as the "fusiform face area" (e.g., Kanwisher & Yovel, 2006). Other research, however, does not support the specialization of the fusiform gyrus for face processing, indicating instead that this area is active to any stimuli with which participants have particular expertise (e.g., Gauthier et al., 1999, 2000).

Nevertheless, some researchers have tested whether social factors, such as racial ingroup/outgroup status of the targets, influence the amplitude of the N170 elicited by faces. Unfortunately, findings to date have been equivocal. For example, based on the notion that participants generally have more experience/expertise interacting with members of ingroups, the "expertise hypothesis" predicts that the N170 should be larger for racial ingroup targets than racial outgroup targets. This pattern has been found in one published report (Ito & Urland, 2005). However, other research has shown that the N170 is larger to atypical faces and inverted faces than to "typical" faces (e.g., Halit et al., 2000), an effect attributed to a disruption of the configural processing often applied to faces. Based on these ideas, some researchers have argued that N170 amplitude elicited by racial outgroup faces, which arguably are less typical for perceivers and which are thought to be processed in a less configural manner (Mitchell et al., 2006), should be larger than the amplitude elicited by racial ingroup faces. Several recent studies have found such a pattern (Stahl et al., 2008; Walker et al., 2008).

How can these seemingly contradictory findings be reconciled? Consideration of methodological differences among these studies reveals that, in each study in which the N170 was reported to be larger to racial outgroup than ingroup faces, participants had been asked to focus on face identity (e.g., by having participants detect when two consecutively presented faces matched, or by having participants try to remember the faces), whereas studies reporting different patterns have asked participants to

focus on other stimulus dimensions (e.g., by having participants scan for nonface stimuli or make valence judgments). If we assume that the N170 reflects structural face encoding, and that perceivers typically process racial outgroup faces in a less configural and shallower manner (e.g., as reflected in poorer memory for outgroups), tasks that require attention to identity may selectively increase recruitment of face processing mechanisms to racial outgroup relative to ingroup targets. However, more work is needed to understand the factors that influence the N170 and its relevance for person perception.

Functional Neuroimaging Studies
Complementing recent electrophysiological research on person perception are a number of recent reports investigating the neural structures involved in this process. The majority of such studies have employed fMRI. Unlike ERP recording, which provides a fast but spatially coarse measure of the electrical activity generated in the brain in response to some stimulus, fMRI provides a measure of the hemodynamic response (i.e., blood flow) elicited by a stimulus in very specific neural structures (see Chapter 5 in this volume for a more detailed discussion of fMRI methods).

Social categorization
Functional MRI methods have proven particularly useful for investigating the neural structures that appear to be involved in perceiving and forming judgments about individuals in a variety of situations. In typical person perception experiments involving fMRI, participants passively view faces of people from varying social categories (e.g., Cunningham et al., 2004) or make social judgments about such faces (e.g., judging personality traits; see Todorov, Baron, & Oosterhof, 2008). Not surprisingly, face stimuli consistently increase hemodynamic response in the fusiform gyrus, consistent with the ERP research reviewed previously indicating that the N170 component associated with face perception is generated in the fusiform (Herrmann et al., 2005).

Of course, perception of faces also conveys social category information. Like ERP studies, brain imaging research has shown that faces varying according to social category membership differentially activate the areas involved in face processing. For example, Golby, Gabrieli, Chiao, and Eberhardt (2001) found that both Black and White participants experienced greater activity in the fusiform gyrus when viewing pictures of racial ingroup compared to outgroup members. Similarly, Van Bavel, Packer, and Cunningham (2008) found that participants randomly assigned to one of two mixed-race teams showed greater fusiform activity to pictures of their own teammates compared to pictures of members of the other team, regardless of their own or the targets' race and regardless of whether they categorized the targets according to team status or race. These findings suggest that fusiform activity associated with ingroup bias can occur regardless of perceptual expertise or any kind of threat or reward associated with ingroup relative to outgroup members. However, recent work also suggests some specialization in the left fusiform gyrus for sex-based categorization, as activation in this area is greater when participants categorize targets along the sex dimension compared to a different dimension (Cloutier, Turk, & Macrae, 2008).

The amygdala also has been shown to be sensitive to judgments of social category membership. The amygdala is a neural structure considered part of the limbic system, often linked with emotional processes; specifically, the amygdala is thought to be instrumental in the processing of threatening stimuli (LeDoux, 1996; Liddell et al., 2005) and has been shown to be more sensitive to negative than positive information (Satpute & Lieberman, 2006; Wager, Phan, Liberzon, & Taylor, 2003; but see Cunningham, Van Bavel, & Johnsen, 2008, for a different interpretation). As with the fusiform regions, the amygdala has been shown to be involved in racial categorization. Specifically, several studies have shown greater amygdala activation to Black targets than White targets, and have demonstrated that the amount of activity in this region is correlated with race-related prejudice (Cunningham et al., 2004; Phelps et al., 2000). It appears that these effects are not limited to White participants, either; that is, both White and Black participants show greater amygdala activity to Black than to White targets, suggesting that greater amygdala activation to Blacks is not due to novelty effects but may reflect negative cultural associations of Blacks (Lieberman, Hariri, Jarcho, Eisenberg, & Bookheimer, 2005). However, it also should be noted that some recent work indicates greater amygdala activation for novel ingroup compared to novel outgroup targets (Chiao et al., 2008; Van Bavel et al., 2008), suggesting that different psychological mechanisms might be involved in mediating activity in this important neural structure depending upon the goals of the perceiver and/or the importance or significance of the target (see Van Bavel et al., 2008).

Neuropsychological research also has contributed to our understanding of the neural processes important for social categorization. For example, Mason and Macrae (2004) investigated the contributions to individuation and categorization of neural processes situated in the right and left hemispheres (left and right visual fields, respectively) in both healthy controls and a split-brain patient. Participants viewed pictures of two simultaneously-presented faces and indicated (during an individuation task) whether the pictures were of the same person or (during a categorization task) whether the pictures showed people of the same sex. All participants performed better on the individuation task when faces were presented to the right hemisphere (i.e., left visual field). Functional MRI data showed that the individuation task yielded increased activation in right inferior frontal and right occipito-temporal areas and that the categorization task yielded increased activation in the left inferior frontal and left superior temporal gyri. These findings suggest that hemispheric differences may exist during social categorization and individuation, and support a more general model of processing asymmetry in the brain (e.g., Rhodes, 1985).

Impression formation
Due to the apparent role of the amygdala in evaluating valence, recent studies have investigated how positive and negative information influences amygdala activation during impression formation (e.g., Fiske, Cuddy, & Glick, 2007). Investigations of impression formation using fMRI tend to couple self-reported judgments with neural measures, and researchers look for correlations between participants' self-reported judgments and amygdala activation. One recent area of investigation has been the evaluation of trustworthiness. Social psychological research has demonstrated that social perceivers can make judgments about a target individual's trustworthiness very quickly after viewing the target's face (e.g., Willis & Todorov, 2006). Functional imaging investigations of trustworthiness have demonstrated that amygdala activation to faces increases as the perceived trustworthiness of faces decreases, using both explicit and implicit trustworthiness evaluations (Engell, Haxby, & Todorov, 2007; Todorov, Baron, & Oosterhof, 2008; Winston, Strange, O'Doherty, & Dolan, 2002). Evidence from neuropsychological research provides further support that the amygdala is involved in perceptions of trustworthiness; specifically, patients with complete bilateral amygdala damage were less able

to judge targets on the trustworthiness dimension than normal participants, especially for untrustworthy target faces (Adolphs, Tranel, & Damasio, 1998).

Research on the role of the amygdala in impression formation has not been limited to perceptions of trustworthiness, however. For example, Todorov and Engell (2008) conducted an fMRI study in which participants viewed target faces with neutral emotional expressions. These faces had previously been rated on 14 different trait dimensions by a separate group of participants. When participants in the fMRI study viewed these faces, amygdala activation indicated general sensitivity to negativity, correlating positively with prior ratings of negative traits and negatively with prior ratings of positive traits. Additionally, amygdala activation was largest on dimensions with clear negative or positive associations (e.g., trustworthiness) and smallest on traits with ambiguous associations (e.g., dominance).

The neural correlates of facial attractiveness also have been investigated in recent fMRI work. A large number of social psychological studies have detailed the important role of facial attractiveness in person perception, with much evidence supporting a universal (i.e., cross-cultural) standard of facial beauty (e.g., Jones & Hill, 1993). Studies using neuroimaging methods have attempted to examine how the nervous system responds to variations in facial attractiveness and have identified a number of structures, especially the amygdala (Winston, O'Doherty, Kilner, Perrett, & Dolan, 2007) and the medial orbito-frontal cortex (OFC; Ishai, 2007; O'Doherty et al., 2003), that respond to facial beauty. Researchers believe that these regional activations are thought to reflect the positive emotions that attractive faces evoke; additionally, these brain regions have been previously associated with the processing of rewarding stimuli (Chatterjee, Thomas, Smith, & Aguirre, 2009). Research also has demonstrated that the brain regions associated with facial beauty may differ depending on the explicit task. For example, Chatterjee and colleagues (2009) presented participants with pictures of target faces. When participants were explicitly judging facial attractiveness, fMRI results showed greater activation in the ventral occipital, anterior insular, dorsal posterior parietal, inferior dorsolateral, and medial prefrontal cortices to attractive versus unattractive faces. However, when participants were not attending to attractiveness, only activation in the ventral occipital cortex was related to targets' facial attractiveness. Taken together, these studies indicate that brain regions associated with perceptual, decision-making, and reward processes are activated by facial attractiveness, and perhaps indicate a biological predisposition to process beauty.

Emotion perception

Social neuroscience studies of person perception also have contributed to the emerging literature on the processing of emotional faces (for a more complete treatment of neuroscience studies of emotion recognition, see Chapter 16). Early work demonstrated that the amygdala was associated with the processing of facial expressions that showed fear. In fact, healthy participants showed increased amygdala activity to fear expressions compared with other emotions (e.g., Adolphs et al., 1998), and patients with amygdala lesions showed impairment in the recognition of facial fear (Adolphs, Tranel, Damasio, & Damasio, 1994; Calder et al., 1996). Additionally, in a study of "normal" adult males, individuals who demonstrated a deficit in facial fear recognition showed reduced activation in the amygdala compared to individuals with normal facial fear recognition, providing further support that the amygdala is instrumental in the processing of facial fear (Corden, Critchley, Skuse, & Dolan, 2006). However, other studies have indicated that increased amygdala activity is not limited to the processing of fearful faces. Yang and colleagues (2002) presented participants with happy, sad, angry, fearful, and neutral faces. Functional MRI results demonstrated that amygdala activation was greater for all emotional faces compared to the neutral faces, indicating that the amygdala's role may be broader than previously assumed (Yang et al., 2002). Other recent work consistent with this notion suggests that the amygdala responds to stimuli with particular motivational significance (Cunningham et al., 2008). From this perspective, the considerable literature showing amygdala sensitivity to negative information could be re-cast in terms of negative information having more relevance or significance than positive information, a view consistent with a voluminous literature in person perception (see Bartholow et al., 2001; Peeters & Czapinski, 1990; Ybarra, 2002) and social perception more generally (e.g., Baumeister, Bratslavsky, Finkenauer, & Vohs, 2001; Ito, Larsen, Smith, & Cacioppo, 1998; Taylor, 1991).

Benuzzi and colleagues (2004) used a neuropsychological approach to examine additional areas of the brain that are instrumental in processing emotion from faces. Specifically, they compared the responses of patients with mesial temporal lobe epilepsy with those of normal controls in a series of facial recognition and matching tasks. Results indicated that patients with right-hemisphere damage showed deficits in identifying fear in target faces, as compared to the other participants. Analyses of fMRI data in control participants showed increased activation to fearful faces in the inferior frontal cortex, the fusiform gyrus, and other occipito-temporal regions. These data indicate that a number of structures besides the amygdala, especially areas in the inferior frontal lobe and right mesial temporal structures, are involved in the processing of negative facial expressions.

Conclusions

As is evident by this and other recent reviews (e.g., Amodio & Lieberman, 2009; Bartholow & Amodio, 2009; Bartholow & Dickter, 2007; Ito, Willadsen-Jensen, & Correll, 2007), the use of neuroscience methods to gain better understanding of person perception processes has increased rapidly in recent years. At the outset of this chapter, we outlined a number of reasons why a social neuroscience approach can be useful for testing theory and advancing the science of person perception. In particular, ERPs provide a time-sensitive means of measuring and separating the rapidly-unfolding cognitive and affect-related processes theorized in many models of person perception, and functional brain imaging permits a detailed picture of the neural structures that subserve these processes. Neuropsychological studies also offer important insights into the functions of particular regions of the brain that appear crucial for effective person perception. Most importantly, linking these neural indices with important psychological and behavioral outcomes can provide a more comprehensive understanding of person perception than can be gained by any self-report, behavioral, cognitive, neural, or biological approach alone (cf., Ochsner & Lieberman, 2001; Ochsner, 2004).

However, despite the promise of and interest in this relatively recent advancement, it is vital for both scientists and consumers of knowledge in this area to keep in mind that research in social neuroscience is only as valuable to advancing knowledge as the research methods and paradigms employed. In other words, the *science* component of social neuroscience is more important than the advanced technological tools we employ or the colorful and detailed images they produce. To paraphrase John Cacioppo (2003), one of the true pioneers of this field, we as social psychologists and others interested in person perception cannot stop using our heads simply because we now have the capability to image the brain. It is also important for contemporary scientists to recognize the importance of the ground-breaking work of early visionaries who first saw the potential to enhance understanding of person perception by measuring bodily responses. One of the first studies of this kind was conducted by Rankin and Campbell (1955), who realized that skin conductance (i.e., changes in the electrical properties of the skin due to perspiration, often associated with anxiety) could be a useful indication of White participants' attitudes toward Blacks, even when their self-reported evaluations were generally positive. Research using peripheral psychophysiological measures continues to make important theoretical advances in person perception to this day (e.g., Mendes, Blascovich, et al., 2007; Mendes, Gray, et al., 2007). The recent focus on central nervous system measures, such as the electrocortical and functional brain imaging research reviewed here, adds to this important tradition in social psychophysiology.

References

Adolphs, R., Tranel, D., & Damasio, A. R. (1998). The human amygdala in social judgment. *Nature, 393*, 470–474.

Adolphs, R., Tranel, D., Damasio, H., & Damasio, A. R. (1994). Impaired recognition of emotion in facial expressions following bilateral damage to the human amygdala. *Nature, 372*, 669–672.

Allport, G. W. (1954). *The nature of prejudice*. Oxford England: Addison-Wesley.

Amodio, D. M. & Lieberman, M. D. (2009). Pictures in our heads: Contributions of fMRI to the study of prejudice and stereotyping. In T. Nelson (Ed.) *Handbook of prejudice, stereotyping, and discrimination* (pp. 347–366). New York: Erlbaum Press.

Bartholow, B. D. & Amodio, D. (2009). Using event-related brain potentials in social psychological research: A review and tutorial. In E. Harmon-Jones & J. S. Beer (Eds.), *Methods in social neuroscience* (pp. 198–232). New York: Guilford Press.

Bartholow, B. D. & Dickter, C. L. (2007). Social cognitive neuroscience of person perception: A selective review focused on the event-related brain potential. In E. Harmon-Jones & P. Winkielman (Eds.), *Social neuroscience: Integrating biological and psychological explanations of social behavior.* (pp. 376–400). New York: Guilford Press.

Bartholow, B. D., Fabiani, M., Gratton, G., & Bettencourt, B. A. (2001). A psychophysiological examination of cognitive processing of and affective responses to social expectancy violations. *Psychological Science, 12*, 197–204.

Bartholow, B. D., Pearson, M. A., Gratton, G., & Fabiani, M. (2003). Effects of alcohol on person perception: A social cognitive neuroscience approach. *Journal of Personality and Social Psychology, 85*, 627–638.

Bartholow, B. D., Riordan, M. A., Saults, J. S., & Lust, S. A. (2009). Psychophysiological evidence of response conflict and strategic control of responses in affective priming. *Journal of Experimental Social Psychology, 45*, 655–666.

Bartholow, R. (1882). Medical electricity: A practical treatise on the applications of electricity to medicine and surgery (2nd ed.). Philadelphia, PA: Henry C. Lea's Son & Co.

Baumeister, R. F., Bratslavsky, E., Finkenauer, C., & Vohs, K. D. (2001). Bad is stronger than good. *Review of General Psychology, 5*, 323–370.

Benuzzi, F., Meletti, S., Zamboni, G., Calandra-Buonaura, G., Serafini, M., Lui, F., et al. (2004). Impaired fear processing in right mesial temporal sclerosis: An fMRI study. *Brain Research Bulletin, 63*, 269–281.

Berger, H. (1929). Über das elektrenkephalogramm das menchen. *Archiv für Psychiatrie, 87*, 527–570.

Cacioppo, J. T., Crites, S. L., Berntson, G. G., & Coles, M. G. (1993). If attitudes affect how stimuli are processed, should they not affect the event-related brain potential? *Psychological Science, 4*, 108–112.

Cacioppo, J. T., Crites, S. L., Gardner, W. L., & Berntson, G. G. (1994). Bioelectrical echoes from evaluative categorizations: A late positive brain potential that varies as a function of trait negativity and extremity. *Journal of Personality and Social Psychology, 67*, 115–125.

Calder, A. J., Young, A. W., Rowland, D., Perrett, D. I., Hodges, J. R., & Etcoff, N. L. (1996). Facial emotion recognition after bilateral amygdale damage: Differentially severe impairment of fear. *Cognitive Neuropsychology, 13*, 699–745.

Chaiken, S. & Trope, Y. (Eds.) (1999). *Dual-process theories in social psychology*. New York: Guilford Press.

Chatterjee, A., Thomas, A., Smith, S. E., & Aguirre, G. K. (2009). The neural response to facial attractiveness. *Neuropsychology, 23*, 135–143.

Chiao, J. Y., Iidaka, T., Gordon, H. L., Nogawa, J., Bar, M., Aminoff, E., et al. (2008). Cultural specificity in amygdala response to fear faces. *Journal of Cognitive Neuroscience, 20*, 2167–2174.

Cloutier, J., Turk, D. J., & Macrae, C. N. (2008). Extracting variant and invariant information from faces: The neural substrates of gaze detection and sex categorization. *Social Neuroscience, 3*, 69–78.

Coles, M. G. H. (1989). Modern mind-brain reading: Psychophysiology, physiology, and cognition. *Psychophysiology, 26*, 251–269.

Coles, M. G. H., & Rugg, M. D. (1995). Event-related brain potentials: An introduction. In M. D. Rugg, M. G. H. Coles, M. D. Rugg & M. G. H. Coles (Eds.), *Electrophysiology of mind: Event-related brain potentials and cognition.* (pp. 1–26). New York: Oxford University Press.

Corden, B., Critchley, H. D., Skuse, D., & Dolan, R. J. (2006). Fear recognition ability predicts differences in social cognitive and neural functioning in men. *Journal of Cognitive Neuroscience, 18*, 889–897.

Crites, S. L., Cacioppo, J. T., Gardner, W. L., & Berntson, G. G. (1995). Bioelectrical echoes from evaluative categorization: A late positive brain potential that varies as a function of attitude registration rather than attitude report. *Journal of Personality and Social Psychology, 68*, 997–1013.

Cunningham, W. A., Johnson, M. K., Raye, C. L., Gatenby, J. C., Gore, J. C., & Banaji, M. R. (2004). Separable neural components in the processing of black and white faces. *Psychological Science, 15*, 806–813.

Cunningham, W. A., Van Bavel, J. J., & Johnsen, I. R. (2008). Affective flexibility: Evaluative processing goals shape amygdala activity. *Psychological Science, 19*, 152–160.

Davis, H., Davis, P. A., Loomis, A. L., Harvey, E. N., & Hobart, G. (1939). Electrical reactions of the human brain to auditory stimulation during sleep. *Journal of Neurophysiology, 2*, 500–514.

Dickter, C. L. & Bartholow, B. D. (2007). Racial ingroup and outgroup attention biases revealed by event-related brain potentials. *Social Cognitive and Affective Neuroscience, 2*, 189–198.

Dickter, C. L. & Bartholow, B. D. (2010). Ingroup categorization and response conflict: Interactive effects of target race, flanker compatibility and infrequency on N2 amplitude. *Psychophysiology, 47*, 596–601.

Donchin, E. (1981). Surprise … surprise? *Psychophysiology, 18*, 493–513.

Donchin, E. & Coles, M. G. H. (1988). Is the P300 component a manifestation of context updating? *Behavioral and Brain Sciences, 11*, 357–427.

Duncan-Johnson, C. & Donchin, E. (1977). On quantifying surprise: The variation of event-related potentials with subjective probability. *Psychophysiology, 14*, 456–467.

Engell, A. D., Haxby, J. V., & Todorov, A. (2007). Implicit trustworthiness decisions: Automatic coding of face properties in human amygdala. *Journal of Cognitive Neuroscience, 19*, 1508–1519.

Fabiani, M. & Donchin, E. (1995). Encoding processes and memory organization: A model of the von Restorff effect. *Journal of Experimental Psychology: Learning, Memory and Cognition, 21*, 224–240.

Fabiani, M., Gratton, G., & Federmeier, K. D. (2007). Event-related brain potentials: Methods, theory, and applications. In J. T. Cacioppo, L. G. Tassinary, & G. G. Berntson (Eds.), *Handbook of psychophysiology* (3rd ed., pp. 85–119). New York: Cambridge University Press.

Fiske, S. T., Cuddy, A. J. C., & Glick, P. (2007). Universal dimensions of social cognition: Warmth and competence. *Trends in Cognitive Sciences, 11*, 77–83.

Friedman, D., Cycowicz, Y. M., & Gaeta, H. (2001). The novelty P3: An event-related brain potential (ERP) sign of the brain's evaluation of novelty. *Neuroscience & Biobehavioral Reviews, 25*, 355–373.

Friedman, D. & Johnson R., Jr. (2000). Event-related potential (ERP) studies of memory encoding and retrieval: A selective review. *Microscopy Research and Technique, 51*, 6–28.

Frith, U. & Frith, C. (2001). The biological basis of social interaction. *Current Directions in Psychological Science, 10*, 151–155.

Gauthier, I., Tarr, M. J., Anderson, A. W., Skudlarski, P., & Gore, J. C. (1999). Activation of the middle fusiform "face area" increases with expertise in recognizing novel objects. *Nature Neuroscience, 2*, 568–573.

Gauthier, I., Tarr, M. J., Moylan, J., Skudlarski, P., Gore, J. C., & Anderson, A. W. (2000). The fusiform "face area" is part of a network that processes faces at the individual level. *Journal of Cognitive Neuroscience, 12*, 495–504.

Gehring, W. J., Gratton, G., Coles, M. G. H., & Donchin, E. (1992). Probability effects on stimulus evaluation and response processes. *Journal of Experimental Psychology: Human Perception and Performance, 18*, 198–216.

Golby, A. J., Gabrieli, J. D. E., Chiao, J. Y., & Eberhardt, J. L. (2001). Differential responses in the fusiform region to same-race and other-race faces. *Nature Neuroscience, 4*, 845–850.

Halit, H., de Haan, M., & Johnson, M. H. (2000). Modulation of event-related potentials by prototypical and atypical faces. *NueroReport: For Rapid Communication of Neuroscience Research, 11,* 1871–1875.

Henry, A. E., Bartholow, B. D., & Arndt, J. (2010). Death on the brain: Effects of mortality salience on the neural correlates of ingroup and outgroup categorization. *Social, Cognitive, and Affective Neuroscience, 5,* 77–87.

Herrmann, M. J., Ehlis, A-C., Muehlberger, A., & Fallgatter, A. J. (2005). Source localization of early stages of face processing. *Brain Topography, 18,* 77–85.

Hoaken, P. N. S., Giancola, P. R., & Pihl, R. O. (1998). Executive cognitive functions as mediators of alcohol-related aggression. *Alcohol and Alcoholism, 33,* 47–54.

Ishai, A. (2007). Sex, beauty, and the orbitofrontal cortex. *International Journal of Psychophysiology, 63,* 181–185.

Ito, T. A. & Cacioppo, J. T. (2007). Attitudes as mental and neural states of readiness: Using physiological measures to study implicit attitudes. In B. Wittenbrink & N. Schwarz (Eds.), *Implicit measures of attitudes* (pp. 125–158). New York, NY US: Guilford Press.

Ito, T. A. & Bartholow, B. D. (2009). The neural correlates of race. *Trends in Cognitive Sciences, 13,* 524–531.

Ito, T. A., Larsen, J. T., Smith, K., & Cacioppo, J. T. (1998). Negative information weighs more heavily on the brain: The negativity bias in evaluative categorization. *Journal of Personality and Social Psychology, 75,* 887–900.

Ito, T. A., Thompson, E., & Cacioppo, J. T. (2004). Tracking the timecourse of social perception: The effects of racial cues on event-related brain potentials. *Personality and Social Psychology Bulletin, 30,* 1267–1280.

Ito, T. A. & Urland, G. R. (2003). Race and gender on the brain: Electrocortical measures of attention to the race and gender of multiply categorizable individuals. *Journal of Personality and Social Psychology, 85,* 616–626.

Ito, T. A. & Urland, G. R. (2005). The influence of processing objectives on the perception of faces: An ERP study of race and gender perception. *Cognitive, Affective & Behavioral Neuroscience, 5,* 21–36.

Jones, A. D., Cho, R. Y., Nystrom, L. E., Cohen, J. D., & Braver, T. S. (2002). A computational model of anterior cingulate function in speeded response tasks: Effects of frequency, sequence, and conflict. *Cognitive, Affective & Behavioral Neuroscience, 2,* 300–317.

Jones, D. & Hill, K. (1993). Criteria of facial attractiveness in five populations. *Human Nature, 4,* 271–296.

Jones, E. E. (1990). *Interpersonal perception.* New York: W H Freeman.

Kanwisher, N. & Yovel, G. (2006). The fusiform face area: A cortical region specialized for the perception of faces. *Philosophical Transactions of the Royal Society, B, 361,* 2109–2128.

Kopp, B., Rist, F., & Mattler, U. (1996). N200 in the flanker task as a neurobehavioral tool for investigating executive control. *Psychophysiology, 33,* 282–294.

Kubota, J. T., & Ito, T. A. (2007). Multiple cues in social perception: The time course of processing race and facial expression. *Journal of Experimental Social Psychology, 43,* 738–752.

Lang, P. J., Bradley, M. M., & Cuthbert, B. N. (2001). *International affective picture system (IAPS): Instruction manual and affective ratings.* Technical Report A-5, The Center for Research in Psychophysiology, University of Florida.

LeDoux, J. E. (1996). *The emotional brain.* New York: Simon and Schuster.

Liddell, B. J., Brown, K. J., Kemp, A. H., Barton, M. J., Das, P., Peduto, A., et al. (2005). A direct brainstem-amygdala-cortical "alarm" system for subliminal signals of fear. *NeuroImage, 24,* 235–243.

Lieberman, M. D., Hariri, A., Jarcho, J. M., Eisenberger, N. I., & Bookheimer, S. Y. (2005). An fMRI investigation of race-related amygdala activity in African American and Caucasian American individuals. *Nature Neuroscience, 8,* 720–722.

Liotti, M., Woldorff, M. G., Perez, R. I., II, & Mayberg, H. S. (2000). An ERP study of the temporal course of the Stroop color-word interference effect. *Neuropsychologia, 38,* 701–711.

London, E. D., Ernst, M., Grant, S., Bonson, K., & Weinstein, A. (2000). Orbitofrontal cortex and human drug abuse: Functional imaging. *Cerebral Cortex, 10,* 334–342.

Macrae, C. N., Bodenhausen, G. V., Schloerscheidt, A. M., & Milne, A. B. (1999). Tales of the unexpected: Executive function and person perception. *Journal of Personality and Social Psychology, 76,* 200–213.

Mason, M. F. & Macrae, C. N. (2004). Categorizing and individuating others: The neural substrates of person perception. *Journal of Cognitive Neuroscience, 16,* 1785–1795.

Mendes, W. B., Blascovich, J., Hunter, S., Lickel, B., & Jost, J. (2007). Threatened by the unexpected: Challenge and threat during inter-ethnic interactions. *Journal of Personality and Social Psychology, 92,* 698–716.

Mendes, W. B., Gray, H., Mendoza-Denton, Major, B., & Epel, E. (2007). Why egalitarianism might be good for your health: Physiological thriving during inter-racial interactions. *Psychological Science, 18,* 991–998.

Mitchell, J. P., Cloutier, J., Banaji, M. R., & Macrae, C. N. (2006). Medial prefrontal dissociations during processing of trait diagnostic and nondiagnostic person information. *Social Cognitive and Affective Neuroscience, 1,* 49–55.

Miyake, A., Friedman, N. P., Emerson, M. J., Witzki, A. H., & Howerter, A. (2000). The unity and diversity of executive functions and their contributions to complex "frontal lobe" tasks: A latent variable analysis. *Cognitive Psychology, 41,* 49–100.

Nieuwenhuis, S., Aston-Jones, G., & Cohen, J. D. (2005). Decision making, the P3, and the locus coeruleus-norepinephrine system. *Psychological Bulletin, 131,* 510–532.

Nieuwenhuis, S., Yeung, N., Van, D. W., & Ridderinkhof, K. R. (2003). Electrophysiological correlates of anterior cingulate function in a go/no-go task: Effects of response conflict and trial type frequency. *Cognitive, Affective & Behavioral Neuroscience, 3,* 17–26.

Ochsner, K. N. (2004). Current directions in social cognitive neuroscience. *Current Opinion in Neurobiology, 14,* 254–258.

Ochsner, K. N. & Lieberman, M. D. (2001). The emergence of social cognitive neuroscience. *American Psychologist, 56,* 717–734.

O'Doherty, J., Winston, J., Critchley, H., Perrett, D., Burt, D. M., & Dolan, R. J. (2003). Beauty in a smile: The role of orbitofrontal cortex in facial attractiveness. *Neuropsychologia, 41,* 147–155.

Olson, J. M., Roese, N. J., & Zanna, M. P. (1996). Expectancies. In E. T. Higgins & A. W. Kruglanski (Eds.), *Social psychology: Handbook of basic principles* (pp. 211–238). New York: Guilford Press.

Osterhout, L., Bersick, M., & McLaughlin, J. (1997). Brain potentials reflect violations of gender stereotypes. *Memory & Cognition, 25*, 273–285.

Peeters, G. & Czapinski, J. (1990). Positive-negative asymmetry in evaluations: The distinction between affective and informational negativity effects. *European Review of Social Psychology, 1*, 33–60.

Peterson, J. B., Rothfleisch, J., Zelazo, P. D., & Pihl, R. O. (1990). Acute alcohol intoxication and cognitive functioning. *Journal of Studies on Alcohol, 51*(2), 114–122.

Phelps, E. A., O'Connor, K. J., Cunningham, W. A., Funayama, E. S., Gatenby, J. C., Gore, J. C., et al. (2000). Performance on indirect measures of race evaluation predicts amygdala activation. *Journal of Cognitive Neuroscience, 12*, 729–738.

Rankin, R. E. & Campbell, D. T. (1955) Galvanic skin response to Negro and white experimenters. *Journal of Abnormal and Social Psychology, 51*, 30–33.

Reeder, G. D. & Coovert, M. D. (1986). Revising an impression of morality. *Social Cognition, 4*, 1–17.

Rhodes, G. (1985). Lateralized processes in face recognition. *British Journal of Psychology, 76*, 249–271.

Rosenberg, S., Nelson, C., Vivekananthan, P. S. (1968). A multidimensional approach to the structure of personality impressions. *Journal of Personality and Social Psychology, 9*, 283–294.

Rugg, M. D., & Coles, M. G. H. (1995). The ERP and cognitive psychology: Conceptual issues. In M. D. Rugg & M. G. H. Coles (Eds.), *Electrophysiology of mind: Event-related brain potentials and cognition* (pp. 27–39). New York: Oxford University Press.

Satpute, A. B. & Lieberman, M. D. (2006). Integrating automatic and controlled processes into neurocognitive models of social cognition. *Brain Research, 1079*, 86–97.

Schupp, H. T., Cuthbert, B. N., Bradley, M. M., Cacioppo, J. T., Ito, T., & Lang, P. J. (2000). Affective picture processing: The late positive potential is modulated by motivational relevance. *Psychophysiology, 37*, 257–261.

Sherman, J. W. & Frost, L. A. (2000). On the encoding of stereotype-relevant information under cognitive load. *Personality and Social Psychology Bulletin, 26*, 26–34.

Solomon, S., Greenberg, J., & Pyszczynski, T. (2000). Pride and prejudice: Fear of death and social behavior. *Current Directions in Psychological Science, 9*, 200–204.

Squires, K. C., Squires, N. K., & Hillyard, S. A. (1975). Decision-related cortical potentials during an auditory signal detection task with cued observation intervals. *Journal of Experimental Psychology: Human Perception and Performance, 1*, 268–279.

Srull, T. K. & Wyer, R. S. (1989). Person memory and judgment. *Psychological Review, 96*, 58–83.

Stahl, J., Wiese, H., & Schweinberger, S. R. (2008). Expertise and own-race bias in face processing: An event-related potential study. *NeuroReport: For Rapid Communication of Neuroscience Research, 19*, 583–587.

Stangor, C. & McMillan, D. (1992). Memory for expectancy-congruent and expectancy-incongruent information: A review of the social and social developmental literatures. *Psychological Bulletin, 111*, 42–61.

Steele, C. M. & Josephs, R. A. (1990). Alcohol myopia: Its prized and dangerous effects. *American Psychologist, 45*, 921–933.

Taylor, S. E. (1991). Asymmetrical effects of positive and negative events: The mobilization-minimization hypothesis. *Psychological Bulletin, 110*, 67–85.

Todorov, A., Baron, S. G., & Oosterhof, N. N. (2008). Evaluating face trustworthiness: A model based approach. *Social Cognitive and Affective Neuroscience, 3*, 119–127.

Trafimow, D. & Finlay, K. A. (2001). An investigation of three models of multitrait representations. *Personality and Social Psychology Bulletin, 27*, 226–241.

Trawalter, S., Todd, A. R., Baird, A. A., & Richeson, J. A. (2008). Attending to threat: Race-based patterns of selective attention. *Journal of Experimental Social Psychology, 44*, 1322–1327.

Uleman, J. S. (1999). Spontaneous versus intentional inferences in impression formation. In S. Chaiken & Y. Trope (Eds.), *Dual-process theories in social psychology* (pp. 141–160). New York: Guilford Press.

Uleman, J. S. (2005). On the inherent ambiguity of traits and other mental concepts. In B. F. Malle & S. D. Hodges (Eds.), *Other minds: How humans bridge the divide between self and others* (pp. 253–267). New York: Guilford Press.

Uleman, J. S., Blader, S. L., Todorov, A. (2005). Implicit impressions. In R. R. Hassin, J. S. Uleman, J. A. Bargh, (Eds.), *The new unconscious* (pp. 362–392). New York: Oxford University Press.

Uleman, J. S., Hon, A., Roman, R. J., & Moskowitz, G. B. (1996). On-line evidence for spontaneous trait inferences at encoding. *Personality and Social Psychology Bulletin, 22*, 377–394.

Uleman, J. S., Newman, L. S., Moskovitz, G. B. (1996). People as flexible interpreters: Evidence and issues from spontaneous trait inference. In M. P. Zanna (Ed.), *Advances in experimental social psychology* (Vol. 28, pp. 211–279). San Diego, CA: Academic Press.

Van Duynslaeger, M., Van Overwalle, F., & Verstraeten, E. (2007). Electrophysiological time course and brain areas of spontaneous and intentional trait inferences. *Social Cognitive and Affective Neuroscience, 2*, 174–188.

Van Duynslaeger, M., Sterken, C., Van Overwalle, F., Verstraeten, E. (2008). EEG components of spontaneous trait inferences. *Social Neuroscience, 3*, 164–177.

Van Duynslaeger, M., Van Overwalle, F., & Edwin Verstraeten, E. (2007). Electrophysiological time course and brain areas of spontaneous and intentional trait inferences. *Social Cognitive and Affective Neuroscience, 2*, 174–188.

Van Overwalle, F., Van den Eede, S., Baetens, K., & Vandekerckhove, M. (2009). Trait inferences in goal-directed behavior: ERP timing and localization under spontaneous and intentional processing. *Social Cognitive and Affective Neuroscience, 4*, 177–190.

van Veen, V. & Carter, C. S. (2002). The timing of action-monitoring processes in the anterior cingulate cortex. *Journal of Cognitive Neuroscience, 14*, 593–602.

Wager, T. D., Phan, K. L., Liberzon, I., Taylor, S. F. (2003). Valence, gender, and lateralization of functional brain anatomy in emotion: A meta-analysis of findings from neuroimaging. *NeuroImage, 19*, 513–531.

Walker, P. M., Silvert, L., Hewstone, M., & Nobre, A. C. (2008) Social contact and other-race face processing in the human brain. *Social Cognitive and Affective Neuroscience, 3*, 16–25.

Willadsen-Jensen, E. & Ito, T. A. (2006). Ambiguity and the timecourse of racial perception. *Social Cognition, 24*, 580–606.

Willadsen-Jensen, E. & Ito, T. A. (2008). A foot in both worlds: Asian Americans' perceptions of Asian, White, and racially ambiguous faces. *Group Processes & Intergroup Relations, 11,* 182–200.

Willis, J. & Todorov, A. (2006). First impressions: Making up your mind after a 100-ms exposure to a face. *Psychological Science, 17,* 592–598.

Winston, J. S., O'Doherty, J., Kilner, J., Perrett, D., & Dolan, R. (2007). Brain systems for assessing facial attractiveness. *Neuropsychologia, 45,* 195–206.

Winston, J. S., Strange, B. A., O'Doherty, J., & Dolan, R. J. (2002). Automatic and intentional brain responses during evaluation of trustworthiness of faces. *Nature Neuroscience, 5,* 277–283.

Wyer, R. S. Jr. & Srull, T. K. (1989). *Memory and cognition in social context.* Hillsdale, NJ: Erlbaum.

Yang, T. T., Menon, V., Eliez, S., Blasey, C., White, C. D., Reid, A. J., et al. (2002). Amygdalar activation associated with positive and negative facial expressions. *Neuroreport: For Rapid Communication of Neuroscience Research, 13,* 1737–1741.

Ybarra, O. (2002). Naive causal understanding of valenced behaviors and its implications for social information processing. *Psychological Bulletin, 128,* 421–441.

Ybarra, O., Schaberg, L., & Keiper, S. (1999). Favorable and unfavorable target expectancies and social information processing. *Journal of Personality and Social Psychology, 77,* 698–709.

Impression Formation:
A Focus on Others' Intents

Daniel L. Ames, Susan T. Fiske, *and* Alexander T. Todorov

Abstract

This chapter reviews research on social impression formation, focusing specifically on how social neuroscience has contributed to our understanding of this complex but fundamental social process. For convenience, this review organizes around three different ways that people form impressions of one another: secondhand information (being told about someone), direct behavioral experience (interacting with someone), and appearance (seeing someone's looks). While the lines between these three information sources often blur, studies focusing on one kind or another have tended to elicit different patterns of neural activity, with the more deliberative tasks involving secondhand information and direct experience most frequently recruiting medial prefrontal cortex (mPFC), temporoparietal junction (TPJ), and posterior regions of the superior temporal sulcus (pSTS); and tasks involving more automatic, appearance-based judgments most frequently recruiting the amygdala. The chapter concludes by comparing impression formation and intentional inference, and then discussing their functional relationship.

Keywords: impression formation, social cognition, attribution, theory of mind, intent, capability, dispositions, agents, warmth, competence, trustworthiness, dominance, face perception, mPFC, amygdala, Stereotype Content Model, fMRI, social neuroscience, social perception, neuroimaging

Living things need to predict their environments in order to survive. This fundamental fact of nature appears in the impressive array of predictive adaptations observed across species. For example, the archer fish, which feeds by shooting insects off branches with jets of water, predicts the 3D trajectory of its dislodged prey, allowing it to move to the splash point before its meal (or another fish) arrives (Rossel, Corlija, & Schuster, 2002). Similarly, some species of flies predict (with frustrating accuracy) the most likely trajectory of a looming flyswatter and plot an optimal escape path before the threat descends (Card & Dickinson, 2008).

While the computational challenges posed by these everyday feats of prediction are incredibly complex, the daily predictive challenges faced by human beings are orders of magnitude more complicated. This is largely because what people most

need to predict in order to obtain their desired outcomes is other people—agents whose actions arise from internal, volitional causes. Because they are intentional agents, people are notoriously difficult to predict, and often prefer it that way. How then do we predict the willfully unpredictable?

Attribution theories (e.g., Heider, 1958; Jones & Davis, 1965; Kelley, 1967) suggest that people understand each other's behavior as arising from two causes: dispositions (i.e., personalities) and situations. From this perspective, predicting how intentional agents will behave can be accomplished via simple algebra: disposition + situation = behavior (Lieberman, Gaunt, Gilbert, & Trope, 2002). By combining dispositional information about Kevin (who has a morbid fear of pachyderms) and situational information (an elephant is traipsing into the room), one should be able to make reasonable predictions about what behaviors Kevin might enact. In this example, the relationship between situation and disposition is relatively straightforward; however, in the real world, the kaleidoscopic interplay between these two factors is fantastically complex (perhaps irreducibly so; Gilbert, 1998), making it frustratingly difficult to implement the clean logic of the attributionist's equation.

Luckily, people have developed a remarkably efficient way of simplifying the calculus: They ignore the elephant in the room. A voluminous body of research has demonstrated that people tend to neglect situational information when trying to make sense of others' actions (e.g., Gilbert & Malone, 1995; Jones & Harris, 1967; Ross, 1977). One consequence of this is that when people undertake the difficult but crucial job of predicting what other agents will do, the dispositional impression is the tool of choice. That it is not always the best tool for the job does not limit people's use of it. Like other blunt instruments, dispositional inferences are easy and satisfying to apply; and they promise results (albeit imprecise ones), only occasionally causing irreparable damage in the process. In their more assiduous moments, people will complement their stable impressions of others with situational information, combining the dispositional hammer with the fine edge of a situationist's chisel to carve out detailed predictions and interpretations of others' behavior (Gilbert, Pelham, & Krull, 1988; Trope & Gaunt, 2003). Usually, however, people are contented to swing hammers freely and leave the chisel to rust. Because dispositional impressions are the tool of choice for predicting other people, impression formation plays an enormous role in determining how people think about and navigate the social world. As such, understanding the cognitive processes involved in forming these impressions has long been a primary objective of social cognition research.

The advent of social neuroscience provides a new avenue for understanding social impression formation. Capitalizing on recent technological advances, researchers have begun to characterize how the brain gives rise to coherent, stable impressions of other people, despite the complexity of people's behavior. One of the major advantages of this approach is that it affords unique opportunities for revealing areas of convergence and dissociation across cognitive processes.

Overview

This chapter reviews research on social impression formation, focusing specifically on how social neuroscience has contributed to our understanding of this complex but fundamental social process. For convenience, this review organizes around three different ways that people form impressions of one another: secondhand information (being told about someone), direct behavioral experience (interacting with someone), and appearance (seeing someone's looks). While the lines between these three information sources often blur, studies focusing on one kind or another have tended to elicit different patterns of neural activity, with the more deliberative tasks involving secondhand information and direct experience most frequently recruiting medial prefrontal cortex (mPFC), temporoparietal junction (TPJ), and posterior regions of the superior temporal sulcus (pSTS), and tasks involving more automatic, appearance-based judgments most frequently recruiting the amygdala. For the reader's convenience, these and other neural regions referenced in this chapter are illustrated in Figure 28.1 below. The chapter concludes by comparing impression formation and intentional inference, and then discussing their functional relationship.

Impression Formation via Secondhand Information

Human beings are motivated to learn about others. Indeed, our appetite for social knowledge seems to far exceed the limits of what we can absorb through direct experience. Some 65% of people's conversational time is devoted to social topics (Dunbar, Marriott, & Duncan, 1997). Consequently, social impressions often result from secondhand information. This section reviews research on the neural processes involved in forming impressions from what perceivers are told about other people (as opposed to impressions based on others' appearance or actions—topics covered in later sections). Presenting participants with this kind of secondhand information about other people has been the most popular way of investigating impression-formation processes in social neuroscience—in part because it is easy to implement. Because a wide range of studies has employed this approach, this section subdivides into four different topics. The first subsection explores how the marriage of social neuroscience with classic attribution theories has generated insights about the brain regions involved in impression formation. The second subsection considers whether social impression formation relies on different neural substrates than other kinds of impression formation. The third subsection asks how impression formation changes subsequent neural responses to other persons. The final subsection

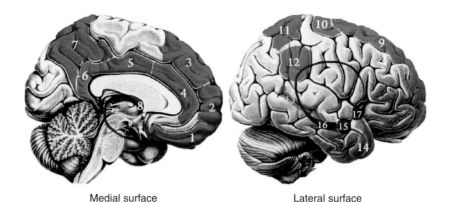

Medial surface   Lateral surface

(1) Orbitofrontal Cortex
(2) Ventral Medial Prefrontal Cortex
(3) Dorsal Medial Prefrontal Cortex
(4) Anterior Cingulate Cortex
(5) Middle Cingulate Cortex
(6) Posterior Cingulate Cortex
(7) Medial Parietal Cortex
(8) Caudate Nucleus (not actually visible)

(9) Superior Frontal Gyrus
(10) Superior Precentral Gyrus
(11) Superior Parietal Gyrus (Superior
      Parietal Lobule)
(12) Temporoparietal Junction
(13) Superior Temporal Sulcus
(14) Temporal Poles
(15) Amygdala (not actually visible)
(16) Hippocampus (not actually visible)
(17) Anterior Insula (not actually visible)

Fig. 28.1 Brain regions featured in this chapter. Those regions that are discussed most prominently are labeled with black-outlined numbers and are bolded in the figure key. Darker shades of gray are assigned to structures located *between* the lateral (side) and medial (center-line) surfaces, but which are displayed *on* the lateral or medial surface for presentation purposes (caudate, hippocampus, amygdala, anterior insula).
Adapted from Lieberman (2010).

considers whether these changes reflect content-specific representations or only general evaluations.

Attribution in the Brain

Attribution theories of person perception (Heider, 1958; Jones & Davis, 1965; Kelley, 1967) represent one of the longest and richest theoretical traditions in social cognition research, and this tradition offers many well-validated paradigms for studying how people form impressions of one another. A recent study adapted one such paradigm (McArthur, 1972) to examine what specific kinds of information trigger the neural mechanisms that give rise to dispositional attributions (Harris, Todorov, & Fiske, 2005). McArthur's original study (1972) sought to test the prediction that specific patterns of information about people's behaviors (consensus across actors, distinctiveness across entities, and consistency over time) induce people to make dispositional inferences (Kelley, 1967). For example, if Mike laughs at the comedian, observers may not know why; but if they also know that no one else laughs (low consensus), that Mike laughs at every

comedian (low distinctiveness), and that he always laughs at this comedian (high consistency), then observers will readily deduce that Mike is easily amused (a dispositional inference).

McArthur's (1972) participants read descriptions of various actions, along with eight combinations of information about those actions related to high and low consensus, distinctiveness, and consistency. Participants then indicated whether they thought each action (e.g., Mike laughing) was most likely caused by (a) something about the person (Mike), (b) something about the stimulus (the comedian), (c) something about the particular circumstances (Mike was drunk at the time), or (d) some combination thereof. As Kelley's model predicts, when actions appeared as low-consensus, low-distinctiveness, and high-consistency (as in the example involving Mike and the comedian), participants overwhelmingly chose option (a), that is, they made a dispositional inference, an impression that explained his actions.

This behavioral result was replicated when participants completed a computerized version of the task during fMRI scanning (Harris, Todorov, & Fiske,

2005). Moreover, only this specifically dispositional combination (and none of the other seven McArthur combinations) activated posterior STS (previously implicated in perceived intent and intentional trajectories; e.g., Gobbini, Koralek, Bryan, Montgomery, & Haxby, 2007; Saxe, Xiao, Kovacs, Perrett, & Kanwisher, 2004). Decades of behavioral research show, however, that people often ignore information about consensus across actors (whether only Mike laughs) (see Fiske, 2004 for review). Ignoring consensus information in this study, both the high-consistency/low-distinctiveness combinations activated mPFC above baseline, whereas the remaining six combinations did not. This work converges with research reviewed in subsequent sections, which shows that STS and mPFC play crucial roles in impression formation across a variety of tasks.

Different Systems for Secondhand Person and Object Knowledge

The introduction offered two related suggestions about the nature of social impression formation. First, because social agents' actions prominently arise from dispositions, which are *internal* causes, while nonsocial actions arise from *external* causes, understanding and predicting other people involves fundamentally distinct challenges from understanding and predicting things (e.g., bugs, flyswatter trajectories). Second, people use social impression formation as a way to meet the particular challenges involved in predicting intentional agents. These suggestions together imply that, although the term "impression formation" could describe understanding many sorts of things—couches and musical genres, as well as people—social and nonsocial impression formation are, in fact, distinct mental events with dissociable underlying processes.

Functional MRI investigations of social versus nonsocial impression formation support this distinction. For example, in one study (Mitchell, Macrae, & Banaji, 2005), participants read about both people and objects during fMRI scanning and either formed an impression of each target or performed a (perceptually identical) "sequencing" task, memorizing the order in which the information about each target appeared. Dorsal aspects of medial prefrontal cortex (dmPFC) were more active for the social impression formation task than for all other conditions (including forming impressions of objects and memorizing the order of information about people). The mPFC has been heavily implicated in a wide array of social cognitive tasks (for meta-analyses, see Amodio & Frith, 2006; Gallagher

& Frith, 2003; Van Overwalle, 2009). Thus, the preferential activation of mPFC for forming impressions about people suggests a particular role for this region in the social-cognitive components of impression formation (we hasten to add that mPFC is a large area of cortex, with various subregions involved in many kinds of processing besides social cognition; e.g., Duncan & Owen, 2000; Schacter, Addis & Buckner, 2008. While a complete review of the mPFC lies beyond this chapter's scope, some alternative theories of mPFC function are discussed toward the end of this chapter).

Even stronger support for a social/nonsocial processing distinction appears in a similar study (Mitchell, Macrae, & Banaji, 2004). In this experiment (which used the same social impression formation and relatively nonsocial "sequencing" conditions), dmPFC again engaged more for impression formation than for sequencing. A strikingly different set of regions was more active for the sequencing task than for the impression-formation task (including the caudate as well as superior frontal, parietal, and precentral gyri). This double-dissociation was echoed by a second double-dissociation in participants' memory for information in both conditions: The better participants' memory for information presented in the impression-formation condition, the more dmPFC activated during the impression formation task (but not during the nonsocial sequencing task). In contrast, memory performance for the sequencing task (but not impression formation) correlated with right hippocampus activity (a region more generally involved in memory; Squire, 1992). These memory findings imply that mPFC may be preferentially involved in a distinctly social form of processing, a suggestion corroborated by demonstrations that dmPFC activity is specifically predictive for the encoding of social versus nonsocial pictures (Harvey, Fossati, & Lepage, 2007).

Thus, while social impression formation may specifically link to dmPFC (Mitchell et al., 2005; Van Overwalle, 2009), the results could also stem from a more general social/nonsocial processing distinction. Consistent with this idea, other studies have demonstrated a division of neural architecture for applying knowledge about agents versus objects (with mPFC subserving agent knowledge; Mason, Banfield, & Macrae, 2004; Mitchell, Heatherton, & Macrae, 2002). Because such bifurcated systems are both anatomically and metabolically expensive, these findings raise the question of why these divisions might exist. One possibility is that such a system confers advantages in speed and accuracy of information processing. When different categories of knowledge are subserved by common neural architecture, competition between categories may cause interference, thus compromising information processing (Mason et al., 2004, see also Caramazza, 2000; Otten & Rug, 2001). Such interference can have dire consequences in evolutionarily important domains that require the rapid translation of knowledge into action. For human beings, social cognition is surely one such domain.

Secondhand Impression Formation Changes Subsequent Person Representations

Indeed, for impression formation to be useful, it has to change how people act toward others. If rumor has it that one cinema ticket-booth operator is perpetually surly, rarely showers, and refuses to serve every fourth customer, while the other is generally cheery, practices good hygiene, and gives away high-end electronics with each purchase, moviegoers will want to make sure to queue in the right line. To distinguish the two employees, one must link the crucial information to the appropriate person, making it accessible for later use (e.g., Goren & Todorov, 2009; Todorov & Uleman, 2002, 2003, 2004). The next experiments examine the neural substrates of this process.

In one revealing study (Delgado, Frank, & Phelps, 2005), participants read detailed information about the life events of three individuals, suggesting exemplary, neutral, or dubious moral character. Later, they played a trust game with each of these partners while undergoing fMRI scanning. Behavioral and neural data suggested that, when diagnostic information was available (in the "good" and "bad" partner conditions), participants tended to rely less on their opponents' actual behaviors in the game to predict how they intended to play future rounds—instead using their prior impressions to predict others' intentions. Behaviorally, participants persisted in trusting the "good" partner to play cooperatively, despite equivalent payouts for all trading partners. The fMRI findings showed that activity in the caudate nucleus (an important structure in reward learning; Poldrack et al., 2001) distinguished whether the outcome of each round was positive or negative for the participant, consistent with past work on neural reward-feedback systems (Delgado, Nystrom, Fissell, Noll, & Fiez, 2000). However, this pattern appeared robustly only for the neutral partner, about whom no diagnostic

information for impression-formation had been presented. Prior impressions of the "good" and "bad" partners apparently reduced reliance on the neural reward-feedback systems involved in trial-and-error learning. This result converges with the suggestion that impression formation is people's preferred method of predicting others' intentions by showing that, when people have the opportunity to use dispositional information about another person to predict intentions, they seem to use that information rather than actual behavior to guide their forecasting of what others will do. Although scores of behavioral studies have indicated people's over-reliance on social expectancies (Fiske & Taylor, 2008), these fMRI data provide clues regarding the distinct brain systems potentially involved.

While maintaining stable impressions as predictive models of other people in the face of inconsistent behavior may sometimes lead to suboptimal outcomes (in this case, over-investing in the "good" partner in an economic game), maintaining a robust impression is an adaptive strategy overall. Updating our long-term predictive models of other people following each instance of behavior could interfere with ongoing activity (McClelland, McNaughton, & O'Reilly, 1995), preventing the use of impression formation as a long-term predictive strategy. Because people are agents, they do not always behave as expected, even when expectations are sensible. For example, even if we know that chocolate is Karen's favorite flavor of ice cream, she will probably still choose other flavors with some frequency. While being too quick to write off our diagnosis of Karen as an inveterate chocoholic may not have dire consequences, the matter becomes much more serious when one considers other situations, such as how heavily to weigh evidence of recent good acts in gauging whether an individual with a history of violent crime is likely to aggress again.

How much prior information is required in order to establish an impression that alters subsequent neural responses to others? In the trust game experiment (Delgado et al., 2005), participants had access to fairly detailed information about each target prior to scanning. However, a more recent study (Todorov, Gobinni, Evans, & Haxby, 2007) based on prior behavioral experiments (Todorov & Uleman, 2002, 2003) demonstrates that, at least in some instances, a single piece of information will suffice. In the first phase of this study, participants viewed faces paired with a statement about that person's (ostensible) previous behavior. In the second phase, participants underwent fMRI scanning while viewing the faces from phase one intermixed with a set of other faces. The task that participants performed in the scanner (deciding whether or not each face was the same as the one preceding it) was perceptual and did not require the retrieval of social knowledge. Nevertheless, faces previously paired with behaviors evoked stronger responses in STS (as noted, often associated with inferred intent) and dmPFC than did novel faces, suggesting the activation of impressions irrelevant for the current task. Perhaps more surprisingly, responses to specific faces were influenced by the type of behavior with which each face had previously been associated. For example, compared with faces previously paired with aggressive behaviors, faces previously paired with disgusting behaviors reliably elicited greater response in anterior insula, a region involved in processing disgust (Philips et al., 1997). These studies suggest that impression formation does meet the usefulness criterion laid out at the beginning of this section: Because impressions change how people predict others' intentions (Delgado et al., 2005), and even simply perceive those others (Todorov et al., 2007), social impressions can usefully guide social behavior.

Content-Specific Representations or Mere Valence?

Merely thinking about or seeing another person suffices to make accessible previously learned information about that person. But whether such activations encode content-specific impressions or only general evaluations has, until recently, remained unclear. This ambiguity sparked an investigation of the neural systems responsible for the general evaluative component of first impressions (Schiller, Freeman, Mitchell, Uleman, & Phelps, 2009). During scanning, participants viewed a series of target individuals and six pieces of information about each person that varied in affective valence. In separate trials, participants also viewed each face without information. Participants then gave their overall evaluative impression of each target on a 1–8 scale. The dmPFC and several other areas were more active when the faces accompanied information about the target than when the faces of the targets appeared alone, providing additional evidence for the specific recruitment of dmPFC for social impression formation, as opposed to the mere perception of persons (Amodio & Frith, 2006; Mitchell et al., 2004). However, dmPFC did not relate to participants' evaluations of the targets, while amygdala and posterior cingulate cortex (PCC) regions (frequently implicated in emotion and valuation processes) did relate (Cunningham et al., 2008; Kable & Glimcher, 2007; Taber et al., 2004). Specifically, parametric analyses revealed greater activity in the amygdala and PCC during the viewing of positive information when participants evaluated targets positively, and during the viewing of negative information when participants evaluated targets negatively. That is, regardless of any given participant's idiosyncratic impressions, these two regions reliably tracked the affective components of their impressions. No such pattern emerged for dMPFC. Consistent with prior theories (Firth, 2007), the role of mPFC in impression formation appears dissociable from the general affective functions of evaluative subsystems in the brain—with the mPFC perhaps playing a special role in encoding higher-order representations of others' mental lives.

A Cautionary Note

Despite the growing evidence for the involvement of mPFC and STS in impression formation culled from studies employing written descriptions of people, this format may exaggerate people's dispositional inferences and therefore provide a biased depiction of the brain systems that covary with these inferences. For example, behavioral experiments show that secondhand information underemphasizes situational qualifications and results in more severe judgments (Gilovich, 1987), and leads to stereotypes more extreme than those learned via direct contact (Thompson, Judd, & Park, 2000). Hence, the next section turns to neural processes involved in impressions based on direct experience.

Impression Formation via Interaction

Reading about others is a useful way to learn about people. However, notwithstanding the best efforts of Internet search companies and social networking websites, people continue to gain some proportion of their knowledge about others by interacting with them. While interaction is perhaps the most obvious way to form impressions of other people, the neural processes underlying interaction-based impression formation have been relatively understudied to date. Emphasis on secondhand information characterizes social cognition research more generally (Fiske & Taylor, 2008); however the current limitations of functional neuroimaging research (e.g., the requirement that participants in fMRI studies lie motionless and alone inside a dark, noisy bore) make studying actual social interactions at the neural level particularly challenging.

Investigators have negotiated these impediments by simplifying social interactions to fit the scanning environment. Often, the interactions take the form of economic games. Though artificial by design (indeed, their constrained nature is what makes them useful), economic games permit participants to engage in socially meaningful actions, such as trusting, cooperating, and betraying.

Success in these games depends largely on participants' ability to predict their opponents' intentions (e.g., to cooperate or defect on the next round; Delgado et al., 2005; Van Overwalle, 2009). Consistent with the idea of impression formation as a tool for predicting others' intentional behaviors, players appear to meet the predictive challenges of economic games by forming impressions of their opponents based on their actions in previous rounds of the game (unless they have already formed an impression by other means; Delgado et al., 2005; reviewed above). These impressions reflect neural responses to opponents' faces after their interaction. In one study (Singer, Keibel, Winston, Dolan, & Frith, 2004), participants underwent fMRI scanning while judging the gender of opponents who had previously played fairly or unfairly in an ultimatum game, and likewise judged the gender of other targets for whom participants had no behavioral basis for impression formation (matched for earlier exposure). Despite the irrelevance of impressions to gender judgments, faces of participants' previous opponents in the ultimatum game elicited greater activity in the amygdala, orbitofrontal cortex, and anterior insula, regions that have frequently been implicated in forming rapid, intuitive, judgments of others' trustworthiness and approachability (Damasio, 1994; Adolphs, 2003; Winston, O'Doherty & Nolan, 2003; Todorov, in press).

Note that these activations occurred subsequent to participant-opponent interactions, outside the context that informed the impressions. Thus, impressions as models for predicting others' intentions show at least some contextual invariance—that is, people appear to use impressions to predict one another even when those impressions are formed under specific contexts that may not approximate how people will behave outside of those contexts. As suggested earlier, people rely on impression formation to predict others because people are agents: They choose to do things. Hence, contextual insensitivity in impression formation may arise partially from participants' sense (either tacit or explicit) that the opponents themselves, rather than contextual constraints, controlled their behavior. To examine this possibility, participants in the Singer et al. (2004) study were told that some of their opponents were simply following a computer's instructions rather than freely choosing their responses. As expected, the intentionality of opponents' actions impacted subsequent neural responses to those opponents' faces; for example, intentional cooperators elicited greater recruitment of OFC and posterior STS than did non-intentional cooperators. As Frith and Frith (2006a) observed,

"[s]ubjects were not simply learning which faces were associated with reward. They were learning whom to trust" (p. 38).

A second experimental game study demonstrates the relationship between experience-based impression formation and predicting others' intentions even more directly (King-Casas et al., 2005): Behavioral and neural responses to others changed as people became acquainted during an economic decision-making game. As in other studies, neural signals in the caudate nucleus apparently encoded reward value. Within the context of a trust game, where rewards related to trusting other players, this caudate reward signal reliably predicted the intention to trust one's opponent. As participants gained experience with their opponents, this "intention to trust signal" (King-Casas et al., 2005) became anticipatory, shifting earlier by 14 seconds over the course of the study. This suggests that participants were predicting their partners' intentions in the next round further in advance as they got to know their opponents. In support of this interpretation, participants became increasingly accurate in predicting other players' intentions over the same period during which this shift in neural activity took place. Cross-brain analyses examining correlations between players in "trustee" and "investor" roles yielded a strong correlation between ventral aspects of mPFC in the trustee's brain and the middle cingulate of the investor's brain (which most strongly activated when the investor made a decision). The development of such cross-brain analysis techniques (see also Hasson, Nir, Levy, Fuhrmann, & Malach, 2004) may facilitate applying neuroscience to dynamic social processes. Altogether, this study demonstrates how forming impressions of others through interaction results in neural changes that allow people to predict more accurately others' future intentions.

A recent survey of several other economic game studies (Van Overwalle, 2009) drew similar conclusions about the role of dispositional inferences in predicting partners' intentions. Fully 100% of economic game studies reviewed in this meta-analysis yielded significant activations in regions of mPFC that have been strongly implicated in social cognition, with 86% of these activations occurring in dmPFC, the region of the brain most consistently implicated in social impression formation and ascribing dispositional traits to others (e.g., Mitchell et al., 2004; 2005; Van Overwalle, 2009). The same meta-analysis observed frequent activation of STS in conjunction with the presentation of biological motion, such as human movement and glancing behavior (with such motion often being related to intentional inference; see also Macrae & Quadflieg, in press).

Although experimental games cannot (and are not intended to) recreate naturalistic human interactions, they provide social neuroscience a way to study how interpersonal experience influences social impressions. In addition, because these games motivate players to predict their opponents' intentions, they offer a particularly appropriate context for studying the relationship between impression formation and interpersonal prediction. Together, the studies reviewed in this section illustrate the neural processes through which social interactions can shape interpersonal impressions, and how these impressions, in turn, help people predict others' intentions.

Impression Formation via Appearance

In a counterpoint to the first- and secondhand impressions research, people adeptly form impressions without benefit of any behavioral information at all. The human face offers a powerful social stimulus; a fleeting glance at another's face provides a wealth of information (and misinformation) about others' transient states and stable dispositions (Macrae & Quadflieg, in press). One key finding: People judge another person's trustworthiness based on facial appearance after as little as 33 ms of exposure (Todorov, Pakrashi, & Oosterhof, in press). Although such judgments are not necessarily accurate, they nonetheless predict important social outcomes, including criminal sentencing and success in being elected to public office (Ballew & Todorov, 2007; Todorov, Mandisodza, Goren, & Hall, 2005, see also Eberhardt, Davies, Purdie-Vaughns, & Johnson, 2006).

Impressions based on appearance alone tend to be rapid, intuitive, and emotional. As such, this research contrasts with the previously reviewed studies, which lean toward slower, more deliberative impression formation processes that build on more explicit social information. Whereas mPFC and STS tend to be the most frequently observed regions in these deliberative, explicit processes, the amygdala appears to matter more for intuitive judgments based on appearance.

Perhaps the most-studied appearance-based impression in social neuroscience has been trustworthiness (Todorov, in press). Trustworthiness appears as a universal dimension of person perception, correlating with many other important social judgments (Oosterhof & Todorov, 2008; Todorov, Said, Engell, & Oosterhof, 2008; see also Fiske, Cuddy, & Glick, 2007, below). As such, trustworthiness assessment is crucial to impression formation. Neuroimaging studies implicating the amygdala in trustworthiness judgments fit neuropsychological evidence of patients with bilateral amygdala damage, who exhibit impaired performance in discriminating between trustworthy- and untrustworthy-looking faces (Adolphs, Tranel, & Damasio, 1998). Several researchers have reported increased amygdala responsivity to faces judged untrustworthy (e.g., Engell, Haxby, & Todorov, 2007; Winston, Strange, O'Doherty, & Dolan, 2002), as well as to members of racial outgroups (Hart et al., 2000; Phelps et al., 2000). Such findings align with initial views of the amygdala as a fear/threat-detection region (Phelps, 2006).

However, recent evidence suggests that the amygdala exhibits a nonlinear response pattern, activating preferentially to both highly trustworthy and highly untrustworthy faces (Said, Baron, & Todorov, 2009). This finding fits other observations of amygdala activation correlating with attitudinal intensity, rather than valence per se (Cunningham, Raye, & Johnson, 2004; Cunningham et al., 2008). One intriguing possibility is that the amygdala encodes, not threat or fear, but vigilance, directing attention to emotionally important information in one's environment (Vuilleumier, 2005). Thus, within the context of social impression formation, increased amygdala activation may help direct attention toward people who appear particularly likely to help or harm—perhaps by providing arousal cues coinciding with the perception of those individuals. Increased arousal and attention toward likely friends and foes would facilitate the efficient encoding of their behaviors. In other words, paying closer attention to what people do provides a stronger informational basis for detailed impression formation and, by extension, for the accurate prediction of behavior. The amygdala (working in conjunction with other regions) may help to serve this function by biasing attention toward particularly trustworthy and untrustworthy individuals (Adolphs, 1999; Haxby, Hoffman, & Gobbini, 2000).

This suggestion fits Todorov's recent theoretical proposal that judgments of facial trustworthiness derive from overgeneralizing facial cues signaling emotional valence (i.e., anger and happiness; Todorov & Engell, 2008). Knowing whether another person is angry or happy is useful for a number of reasons, not least because it indicates whether another's intentions are likely to be friendly or hostile. From this perspective, human beings would be highly attuned to facial features that signal these states—perhaps even to the extent that permanent features of facial geometry (e.g., low eyebrows) could imply a subtle emotional message (e.g., anger), causing the perceiver to make a dispositional inference about the target (e.g., untrustworthiness). Several studies have confirmed that even subtle manipulations of facial cues encoding happiness and anger are sufficient to impact judgments of dispositional trustworthiness (Oosterhof & Todorov, 2008). The emotion overgeneralization hypothesis (Montepare & Dobish, 2003; Oosterhof & Todorov, 2009; Said, Sebe, & Todorov, 2009) gains further support from the observation that nonlinear patterns of amygdala responses to facial trustworthiness (Said, et al., 2009; Todorov, Baron, & Oosterhof, 2008) closely mirror earlier observations that the amygdala is more responsive to both happy and fearful faces than to neutral faces (Pessoa, McKenna, Gutierrez, & Ungerleider, 2002).

Thus, people are highly sensitive to social information conveyed by facial appearance, and facial information serves as a powerful basis for rapid and intuitive impression formation. Most likely, such impressions are driven largely by extrapolation from physiognomic features encoding subtle emotional messages that are interpreted (perhaps misinterpreted) as cues about a person's trustworthiness. A second dimension of face-perception, dominance, has been identified as orthogonal to trustworthiness judgments. Just as trustworthiness judgments appear to be extrapolations from valence cues, perceptions of facial dominance appear to be driven by subtle facial features encoding masculinity and femininity (Oosterhof & Todorov, 2008). Presently, the neural correlates of dominance perception are less well understood than those pertaining to judgments of facial trustworthiness; however important social judgments (e.g., how threatening a person is) can be modeled as conjunctions of trustworthiness and dominance (Oosterhof & Todorov, 2008) (see Figure 28.2).

Besides faces, people use other aspects of appearance to judge others. Behavioral studies demonstrate the universality of two primary dimensions, accounting for about 80% of the variance in first impressions (Fiske, Cuddy, & Glick, 2007). Consistent with the Todorov et al. studies, the most rapid and apparently primary dimension assesses people's intentions as warm (trustworthy, friendly, sincere, moral, communal) or not. This dimension is predicted by cooperative or competitive relationships, such as those implicated in the experimental game literature. The second dimension reflects people's ability to enact their intentions, that is, competence (capability, skill, agency). This dimension is predicted by status, consistent with the Todorov results for perceived facial dominance. This robust behavioral literature uses stimuli ranging from personal acquaintances, to videos and photographs, to stereotypes and expectations (see Figure 28.3).

Recent neuroimaging studies investigating the dimensions of warmth and competence have capitalized on people's willingness to form impressions based on appearances. In these studies, participants view photographs of people who are easily identified, based on their appearance, as representing the four distinct combinations of people high and low on warmth and competence. One series of studies especially implicates the by-now familiar mPFC in perceptions of all combinations except one: those perceived as both low-warmth and low-competence. The lowest of the low, essentially outcasts, are poor people, especially those who appear to be homeless, as well as people apparently drug-addicted. Photographs of these individuals uniquely fail to activate mPFC above baseline (Harris & Fiske, 2006), and behavioral data fit the interpretation that observers tend to dehumanize the outcasts, reporting difficulty with perceiving their minds: intentions, thoughts, and feelings (Harris & Fiske, in press). As converging evidence for the role of the mPFC in forming social impressions, an instruction to consider the preferences of the pictured individuals suffices to bring the mPFC back online (Harris & Fiske, 2007).

In sum, appearances can inform impressions. In contrast to studies examined in earlier sections, which focused on relatively deliberative inferences based on relatively substantive information, the work reviewed in this section shows that people can form rapid and intuitive impressions based on almost no information at all. People readily extrapolate

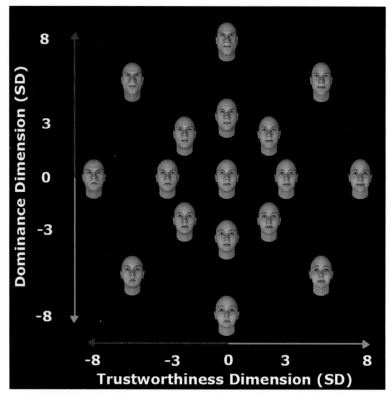

Fig. 28.2 A data-driven model of face evaluation. Human judges rated 300 emotionally neutral faces on the primary social dimensions of dominance and trustworthiness. The appearance of each face was statistically represented in terms of 50 independent principal components. Covariation between these principal components and participants' ratings revealed what aspects of facial physiognomy most strongly drive people's judgments of facial trustworthiness and dominance. Modeling extremely trustworthy/untrustworthy and dominant/submissive faces (here, up to 8 standard deviations from the mean on each dimension) strongly suggests that trustworthiness judgments derive from an overgeneralization of emotional expressions of happiness and anger. Perceptions of dominance (orthogonal to trustworthiness) correlate with perceived masculinity/femininity.

personality features from facial features, overgeneralizing features that encode socially relevant emotions. People also make direct assessments of primary social dimensions based on appearance and these assessments partially determine whether the neural mechanisms used for thinking about other minds come online. Thus, impressions formed on the basis of minimal social information can have consequences for social interaction.

Impression Formation and Intentional Inference: Theoretical and Functional Overlap

This chapter has examined three kinds of information that people use to form impressions: secondhand information, direct experience, and appearance. Across these three domains, various studies have supported the theoretical relationship suggested at the chapter's

outset between impression formation and predicting others' intentions. This final section explores this connection at a functional level, capitalizing on the ability of social neuroscience to identify areas of overlap and dissociation in cognitive processes.

The suggestion that there may be a functional relationship between impression formation and intentional prediction may seem misguided, because the neural literature often sharply dissociates these two processes, with intentional inference ascribed principally to posterior regions of STS and impression formation usually associated with mPFC. Like most clear-cut neural distinctions and pre-mixed peanut butter and jelly, this proposal sacrifices something worthwhile for the sake of convenience. At least three sets of findings support a more nuanced story in which the mPFC contributes to the representation of others' intentions (though the STS certainly does so as well).

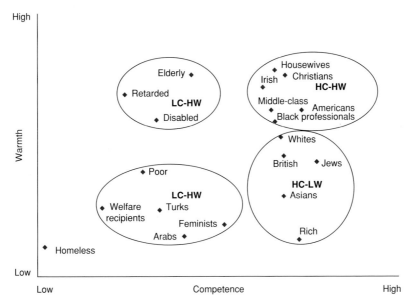

Fig. 28.3 Scatter plot and cluster analysis of competence and warmth ratings for various social groups. The Stereotype Content Model proposes that social groups are readily perceived in terms of two orthogonal dimensions: warmth and competence. Participants (in this case, US survey respondents) rated each group on warmth and competence using a 5-point scale. Ratings were then submitted to cluster analysis, yielding the four circled clusters shown here. Groups appearing near the center of clusters most reliably replicate their cluster membership across studies. Reproduced from Cuddy et al., 2007, with permission of APA.

First, intentional inference is not a monolithic mental operation and, therefore, not likely supported by a single set of neural substrates. Social neuroscience usefully distinguishes the representation of intentions at a *perceptual* level from the representation of *covert mental states* that may predict future intentional actions; the posterior STS contributes to perception of intention, while the mPFC and temporo-parietal junction (TPJ) serve the inference of intention (Gobbini et al., 2007; Saxe & Powell, 2006; Saxe et al., 2004). That is, inferring intentions from present, perceptible actions (e.g., biological motion; Saxe et al., 2004) is, to some extent, a qualitatively different process compared with inferring intentions from tacit information that is not presently perceptible (e.g., another's beliefs, Young & Saxe, 2008).

Second, mPFC shows an inconsistent pattern of engagement across intention-relevant tasks, perhaps due to a selective functional profile for different *kinds* of intention. Specifically, present evidence suggests that mPFC may be critical for representing others' *social* intentions (for example, the intention to communicate with another person), but not other kinds of intentions (Ciaramidaro et al., 2007; Kampe et al., 2003; Walter et al., 2004). In contrast, STS may represent both social and nonsocial intentions.

Third, the relative contributions of STS and mPFC to thinking about intentions vary as a function of participant age. Although both adolescents and adults recruit both regions in intentional inference tasks, adolescents rely more heavily on mPFC, while adults show greater recruitment of STS (Blakemore et al., 2007). This suggests that, while most normally developing children are able to pass theory-of-mind tasks (which typically test the ability to reason about others' beliefs) by about age 5 (Barresi & Moore, 1996), the computational strategies used to think about intention continue to be refined at least into early adulthood. In sum, both mPFC and STS contribute to the understanding of intention, with their relative involvement varying as a function of the level at which the intention is being inferred (perceptual vs. covert), the type of intention (social vs. nonsocial), and the age of the perceiver.

Of course, mPFC is a large area of cortex, and has been implicated in many different social functions (Amodio & Frith, 2006; Frith & Frith, 2001, 2006a; Van Overwalle, 2009). Note, however, that at least some studies suggest that there may be considerable neural overlap in the regions involved in impression formation and intentional prediction. For example, the region reported by Mitchell et al.

(2004; described above) for impression formation bears a striking resemblance to the activation reported by Walter et al. (2004) for the prediction of social intentions. Both sets of findings have been replicated (impression formation: Mitchell et al., 2005; predicting others' intentions: Ciaramirado et al., 2007). Although caution must accompany comparing results across studies, this overlap is echoed in meta-analyses (Amodio & Frith, 2006; Van Overwalle, 2009). The question of whether and to what extent these two processes truly rely on the same neural architecture awaits an empirical test that examines both intentional inference and impression formation in the same study.

Other studies have identified a similar region as playing an important role in imagining the future (Addis, Wong, & Schacter, 2007; Schacter, Addis, & Buckner, 2007; 2008). Perhaps, within the context of social cognition—which is subserved by a network of regions including mPFC, TPJ, STS, medial parietal cortex, and temporal poles (Fletcher et al., 1995; Gallagher et al., 2000; Gallagher, Jack, Roepstorff, & Frith, 2002; Goel, Grafman, Sadato, & Hallett, 1995; Saxe & Kanwisher, 2003; Van Overwalle, 2009)—mPFC may serve a special function in predicting others' future mental states, the better to anticipate their actions (Frith & Frith, 2006b). Such observations appear consistent with the findings reviewed herein demonstrating the important role played by impression formation in predicting others' intentions. Note, however, that this region is also implicated in remembering the past (Addis et al., 2007). Thus, the involvement of mPFC in inter-temporal construction could be entirely separable from its involvement in impression formation. Alternatively, the two processes might converge in cases where impressions formed based on past experience are marshaled for predicting one's own or others' future intentions and behaviors (see also Buckner & Carroll, 2006).

Note that this chapter does not claim the mPFC is selective for impression-formation processes or even for social cognition. Indeed, as noted, mPFC is a large, complex region of cortex with a host of different functions (Amodio & Frith, 2006). For instance, subregions of mPFC (particularly more ventral/orbitofrontal aspects) have been consistently implicated in reward processing (Montague, King-Casas, & Cohen, 2006) (though even some of these subregions are differentially responsive to social vs. nonsocial rewards; Harris, McClure, van den Bos, Cohen, & Fiske, 2007; van den Bos, McClure, Harris, Fiske, & Cohen, 2008). Nonetheless, the evidence for the involvement of mPFC in social cognitive processes including impression formation and intentional prediction is, by now quite substantial (e.g., Amodio & Frith, 2006; Gallagher & Frith, 2003; Van Overwalle, 2009). While the processes subserved by mPFC may not all be specifically social, because they can demonstrably be recruited for use in other domains, it may be that the evolutionary importance of complex social tasks has been largely responsible for causing these processes to develop in increasingly sophisticated ways (Frith, 2007).

The proposed relationship between impression formation and intentional inference outlined in this chapter bridges between what have sometimes been seen as two separate components of social cognition: inferences of transitory states and inferences of enduring characteristics (Frith & Frith, 2006a; Van Overwalle, 2009). The research reviewed here points to functional overlap between these two processes, highlighting a strength of neuroscientific approaches to social cognition research: the ability to determine whether and to what extent two apparently disparate social cognitive responses involve fundamentally similar neural processes. This capacity to force theoretical convergence meets an equally useful and opposing property: the ability to determine when two apparently similar behaviors are driven by different cognitive processes. Overall, the ability of social neuroscience to measure the extent of overlap and dissociation between processes may shed light on both novel questions and longstanding theoretical debates about social impression formation. Just as impression formation is a critical tool in understanding other people, so too is social neuroscience rapidly becoming a critical tool for understanding impression formation.

References

Addis, D., Wong, A., & Schacter, D. (2007). Remembering the past and imagining the future: Common and distinct neural substrates during event construction and elaboration. *Neuropsychologia*, *45*(7), 1363–1377.

Addis, D., Wong, A., & Schacter, D. (2008). Age-related changes in the episodic simulation of future events. *Psychological Science*, *19*(1), 33–41.

Adolphs, R. (1999). Social cognition and the human brain. *Trends in Cognitive Sciences*, *3*(12), 469–479.

Adolphs, R. (2003). Cognitive neuroscience of human social behaviour. *Nature Reviews Neuroscience*, *4*(3), 165–178.

Adolphs, R., Tranel, D., & Damasio, A. (1998). The human amygdala in social judgment. *Nature*, *393*, 470–474.

Amodio, D. M. & Frith, C. D. (2006). Meeting of minds: The medial frontal cortex and social cognition. *Nature Reviews Neuroscience*, *7*(4), 268–277.

Ballew, C. & Todorov, A. (2007). Predicting political elections from rapid and unreflective face judgments. *Proceedings of the National Academy of Sciences, 104*(46), 17948–17953.

Blakemore, S. J., Ouden, H., Choudhury, S., & Frith, C. (2007). Adolescent development of the neural circuitry for thinking about intentions. *Social Cognitive and Affective Neuroscience, 2*(2), 130–139.

Barresi, J. & Moore, C. (1996). Intentional relations and social understanding. *Behavioral and Brain Sciences, 19*(1), 107–122.

Buckner, R. L. & Carroll, D. C. (2006). Self-projection and the brain. *Trends in Cognitive Sciences, 11*, 49–57.

Bolger, D. J., Perfetti, C. A., & Schneider, W. (2005). Cross-cultural effect on the brain revisited: Universal structures plus writing system variation. *Human Brain Mapping, 25*(1), 92–104.

Caramazza, A. (2000). The organization of conceptual knowledge in the brain. In M. S. Gazzaniga (Ed.), *The new cognitive neurosciences (2nd ed.)* (pp. 901–914). Cambridge, MA: MIT Press.

Card, G. & Dickinson, M. H. (2008). Visually mediated motor planning in the escape response of drosophila. *Current Biology, 18*(17), 1300–1307.

Chiao, J. Y., Iidaka, T., Gordon, H. L., Nogawa, J., Bar, M., Aminoff, E., et al. (2008). Cultural specificity in amygdala response to fear faces. *Journal of Cognitive Neuroscience, 20*(12), 2167–2174.

Ciaramidaro, A., Adenzato, M., Enrici, I., Erk, S., Pia, L., Bara, B. G., et al. (2007). The intentional network: How the brain reads varieties of intentions. *Neuropsychologia, 45*, 3105–3113.

Cohen, D., Vandello, J., Puente, S., & Rantilla, A. (1999). "When you call me that, smile!" how norms for politeness, interaction styles, and aggression work together in southern culture. *Social Psychology Quarterly, 62*(3), 257–275.

Cuddy, A. J., Fiske, S. T., & Glick, P. (2007). The BIAS map: Behaviors from intergroup affect and stereotypes. *Journal of Personality and Social Psychology, 92*(4), 631–648.

Cunningham, W. A., Van Bavel, J. J., & Johnsen, I. R. (2008). Affective flexibility: Evaluative processing goals shape amygdala activity. *Psychological Science, 19*(2), 152–160.

Cunningham, W. A., Raye, C. L., & Johnson, M. K. (2004). Implicit and explicit evaluation: fMRI correlates of valence, emotional intensity, and control in the processing of attitudes. *Journal of Cognitive Neuroscience, 16*, 1717–1729.

Damasio, A. R. (1994). *Descartes' error*. New York: Putnam.

Delgado, M. R., Frank, R. H., & Phelps, E. A. (2005). Perceptions of moral character modulate the neural systems of reward during the trust game. *Nature Neuroscience, 8*, 1611–1618.

Delgado, M. R., Nystrom, L. E., Fissell, C., Noll, D. C., & Fiez, J. A. (2000). Tracking the hemodynamic responses to reward and punishment in the striatum. *Journal of Neurophysiology, 84*(6), 3072–3077.

Dunbar, R. I. M., Marriott, A., & Duncan, N. D. C. (1997). Human conversational behavior. *Human Nature, 8*(3), 231–246.

Duncan, J. & Owen, A. (2000). Common regions of the human frontal lobe recruited by diverse cognitive demands. *Trends in Cognitive Sciences, 23*, 475–483.

Eberhardt, J. L. & Fiske, S. T. (1998). *Confronting racism: The problem and the response*. Thousand Oaks, CA: Sage Publications.

Engell, A., Haxby, J., & Todorov, A. (2007). Implicit trustworthiness decisions: Automatic coding of face properties in the human amygdala. *Journal of Cognitive Neuroscience, 19*(9), 1508–1519.

Fiske, S. T., Cuddy, A., & Glick, P. (2007). Universal dimensions of social cognition: Warmth and competence. *Trends in Cognitive Sciences, 11*(2), 77–83.

Fiske, S. T. (2004). *Social beings: A core motives approach to social psychology*. Hoboken, NJ: Wiley.

Fiske, S. T. & Taylor, S. E. (2008). *Social cognition: From brains to culture*. Boston: McGraw-Hill Higher Education.

Fletcher, P. (1995). Other minds in the brain: A functional imaging study of "theory of mind" in story comprehension. *Cognition, 57*(2), 109–128.

Frith, C. D. (2007). The social brain? *Philosophical Transactions of the Royal Society B: Biological Sciences, 362*(1480), 671–678.

Frith, C. D. & Frith, U. (2006a). How we predict what other people are going to do. *Brain Research, 1079*, 36–46.

Frith, C. D. & Frith, U. (2006b). The neural basis of mentalizing. *Neuron, 50*(4), 531–534.

Frith, U. & Frith, C. D. (2001). The biological basis of social interaction. *Current Directions in Psychological Science, 28*(6), 151–155.

Gallagher, H. (2000). Reading the mind in cartoons and stories: An fMRI study of "theory of mind" in verbal and nonverbal tasks. *Neuropsychologia, 38*(1), 11–21.

Gallagher, H. L. & Frith, C. D. (2003). Functional imaging of "theory of mind." *Trends in Cognitive Sciences, 7*(2), 77–83.

Gallagher, H., Jack, A., Roepstorff, A., & Frith, C. (2002). Imaging the intentional stance in a competitive game. *Neuroimage, (16*, 3 Part 1), 814–821.

Gilbert, D. T. (1998). Ordinary personology. In D. T. Gilbert, S. T., Fiske, & G. Lindzey, (Eds.) *The handbook of social psychology* (4th ed.) (pp. 89–150). New York: McGraw Hill.

Gilbert, D. T. & Malone, P. S. (1995). The correspondence bias. *Psychological Bulletin, 117*, 21–38.

Gilbert, D., Pelham, B., & Krull, D. (1988). On cognitive busyness: When person perceivers meet persons perceived. *Journal of Personality and Social Psychology, 54*(5), 733–740.

Gilovich, T. (1987). Secondhand information and social judgment. *Journal of Experimental Social Psychology, 23*(1), 59–74.

Gobbini, M., Koralek, A., Bryan, R., Montgomery, K., & Haxby, J. (2007). Two takes on the social brain: A comparison of theory of mind tasks. *Journal of Cognitive Neuroscience, 19*(11), 1803–1814.

Goel, V., Grafman, J., Sadato, N., & Hallett, M. (1995). Modeling other minds. *Neuroreport, 6*(13), 1741–1746.

Goren, A. & Todorov, A. (2009). Two faces are better than one: Eliminating false trait associations with faces. *Social Cognition, 27*, 222–248.

Greicius, M. D., Srivastava, G., Reiss, A. L., & Menon, V. (2004). Default-mode network activity distinguishes Alzheimer's disease from healthy aging: Evidence from functional MRI. *Proceedings of the National Academy of Sciences, 101*(13), 4637–4642.

Gutchess, A. H., Welsh, R. C., Boduroglu, A., & Park, D. C. (2006). Cultural differences in neural function associated with object processing. *Cognitive, Affective, and Behavioral Neuroscience, 6*, 102–109.

Harris, L. T. & Fiske, S. T. (2006). Dehumanizing the lowest of the low: Neuroimaging responses to extreme out-groups. *Psychological Science, 17*(10), 847–853.

Harris, L. T. & Fiske, S. T. (2007). Social groups that elicit disgust are differentially processed in mPFC. *Social Cognitive and Affective Neuroscience*, *2*, 45–51.

Harris, L. T. & Fiske, S. T. (in press). Dehumanized perception: The social neuroscience of thinking (or not thinking) about disgusting people. In M. Hewstone & W. Stroebe (Eds.), *European review of social psychology*. London: Wiley.

Harris, L. T., McClure, S. M., Van den Bos, W., Cohen, J. D., & Fiske, S. T. (2007). Regions of the MPFC differentially tuned to social and nonsocial affective evaluation. *Cognitive, Affective & Behavioral Neuroscience*, *7*(4), 309–316.

Harris, L. T., Todorov, A., & Fiske, S. T. (2005). Attributions on the brain: Neuro-imaging dispositional inferences, beyond theory of mind. *NeuroImage*, *28*(4), 763–769.

Hart, A. J., Whalen, P. J., Shin, L. M., McInerney, S. C., Fischer, H., & Rauch, S. L. (2000). Differential response in the human amygdala to racial outgroup vs. ingroup face stimuli. *Neuroreport*, *11*(11), 2351–2351.

Harvey, P. O., Fossati, P., & Lepage, M. (2007). Modulation of memory formation by stimulus content: Specific role of the medial prefrontal cortex in the successful encoding of social pictures. *Journal of Cognitive Neuroscience*, *19*(2), 351–362.

Hasson, U., Nir, Y., Levy, I., Fuhrmann, G., & Malach, R. (2004). Intersubject synchronization of cortical activity during natural vision. *Science*, *303*(5664), 1634–1640.

Haxby, J. V., Hoffman, E. A., & Gobbini, M. I. (2000). The distributed human neural system for face perception. *Trends in Cognitive Sciences*, *4*(6), 223–232.

Heider, F. (1958). *The psychology of interpersonal relations*. Hillsdale, NJ: Lawrence Erlbaum Associates.

Eberhardt, J., Davies, P., Purdie-Vaughns. V., & Johnson, S., (2006). Looking deathworthy: Perceived stereotypicality of black defendants predicts capital-sentencing outcomes, *Psychological Science*, *17*(5), 383–386.

Jones, E. E. & Davis, K. E. (1965). From acts to dispositions: The attribution process in person-perception. *Advances in Experimental Social Psychology*, *2*, 219–266.

Jones, E. E. & Harris, V. A. (1967). The attribution of attitudes. *Journal of Experimental Social Psychology*, *3*(1), 1–24.

Kable, J. W. & Glimcher, P. W. (2007). The neural correlates of subjective value during intertemporal choice. *Nature Neuroscience*, *10*(12), 1625–1633.

Kampe, K., Frith, C. D., & Frith, U. (2003). "Hey John": Signals conveying communicative intention toward the self activate brain regions associated with "mentalizing," regardless of modality. *Journal of Neuroscience*, *23*(12), 5258–5263.

Kelley, H. H. (1967). Attribution theory in social psychology. In D. Levine (Ed.), *Nebraska Symposium on Motivation* (Vol. 15, pp. 192–238). Lincoln: University of Nebraska Press.

King-Casas, B., Tomlin, D., Anen, C., Camerer, C. F., Quartz, S. R., & Montague, P. R. (2005). Getting to know you: Reputation and trust in a two-person economic exchange. *Science*, *308*(5718), 78–83.

Lieberman, M. D. (2010). Social cognitive neuroscience. In S. T. Fiske, D. T. Gilbert & G. Lindzey (Eds.), *Handbook of social psychology* (5th ed.). New York: Wiley.

Lieberman, M. D., Gaunt, R., Gilbert, D. T., & Trope, Y. (2002). Reflection and reflexion: A social cognitive neuroscience approach to attributional inference. *Advances in Experimental Social Psychology*, *34*, 199–249.

Macrae, C. N. & Quadflieg, S. (in press). Person perception. In S. T. Fiske, D. T. Gilbert & G. Lindzey (Eds.), *Handbook of social psychology* (5th ed.). New York: Wiley.

Mason, M. F., Banfield, J. F., & Macrae, C. N. (2004). Thinking about actions: The neural substrates of person knowledge. *Cerebral Cortex*, *14*(2), 209–214.

McArthur, L. A. (1972). The how and what of why: Some determinants and consequences of causal attribution. *Journal of Personality and Social Psychology*, *22*(2), 171–193.

McClelland, J. L., McNaughton, B. L., & O'Reilly, R. C. (1995). Why there are complementary learning systems in the hippocampus and neocortex: Insights from the successes and failures of connectionist models of learning and memory. *Psychological Review*, *102*(3), 419–457.

Mitchell, J. P., Heatherton, T. F., & Macrae, C. N. (2002). Distinct neural systems subserve person and object knowledge. *Proceedings of the National Academy of Sciences*, *99*(23), 15238–15243.

Mitchell, J. P., Macrae, C. N., & Banaji, M. R. (2004). Encoding-specific effects of social cognition on the neural correlates of subsequent memory. *Journal of Neuroscience*, *24*(21), 4912–4917.

Mitchell, J. P., Macrae, C. N., & Banaji, M. R. (2005). Forming impressions of people versus inanimate objects: Social-cognitive processing in the medial prefrontal cortex. *NeuroImage*, *26*(1), 251–257.

Montague, P. R., King-Casas, B., & Cohen, J. D. (2006). Imaging valuation models in human choice. *Annual Review of Neuroscience*, *29*, 417–448.

Montepare, J. M. & Dobish, H. (2003). The contribution of emotion perceptions and their overgeneralizations to trait impressions. *Journal of Nonverbal Behavior*, *27*, 237–254.

Oosterhof, N. & Todorov, A. (2008). The functional basis of face evaluation. *Proceedings of the National Academy of Sciences*, *105*(32), 11087–11092.

Oosterhof, N. N. & Todorov, A. (2009). Shared perceptual basis of emotional expressions and trustworthiness impressions from faces. *Emotion*, *9*, 128–133.

Otten, L. J. & Rugg, M. D. (2001). Task-dependency of the neural correlates of episodic encoding as measured by fMRI. *Cerebral Cortex*, *11*(12), 1150–1160.

Pessoa, L., McKenna, M., Gutierrez, E., & Ungerleider, L. (2002). Neural processing of emotional faces requires attention. *Proceedings of the National Academy of Sciences*, *99*(17), 11458–11463.

Phelps, E. A. (2006). Emotion and cognition: Insights from studies of the human amygdala. *Annual Review of Psychology*, *57*(1), 27–53.

Phelps, E., O'Connor, K., Cunningham, W., Funayama, E. S., Gatenby et al. (2000). Performance on indirect measures of race evaluation predicts amygdala activation *Journal of Cognitive Neuroscience*. *12*(5), 729–738.

Phillips, M. L., Young, A. W., Senior, C., Brammer, M., Andrew, C., Calder, A. J., et al. (1997). A specific neural substrate for perceiving facial expressions of disgust. *Nature*, *389*, 495–498.

Poldrack, R. A., Clark, J., Pare-Blagoev, E. J., Shohamy, D., Moyano, J. C., Myers, C., et al. (2001). Interactive memory systems in the human brain. *Nature*, *414*(6863), 546–550.

Rilling, J. K., Sanfey, A. G., Aronson, J. A., Nystrom, L. E., & Cohen, J. D. (2004). The neural correlates of theory of mind within interpersonal interactions. *NeuroImage*, *22*(4), 1694–1703.

Ross, L. (1977). The intuitive psychologist and his shortcomings: Distortions in the attribution process. In L. Berkowitz (Ed.),

Advances in experimental social psychology (vol. 10), New York: Academic Press.

Rossel, S., Corlija, J., & Schuster, S. (2002). Predicting three-dimensional target motion: How archer fish determine where to catch their dislodged prey. *Journal of Experimental Biology*, *205*(21), 3321–3326.

Said, C., Baron, S., & Todorov, A. (2009). Nonlinear amygdala response to face trustworthiness: Contributions of high and low spatial frequency information. *Journal of Cognitive Neuroscience*, *21*(3), 519–528.

Said, C., Sebe, N., & Todorov, A. (2009). Structural resemblance to emotional expressions predicts evaluation of emotionally neutral faces. *Emotion*, *9*, 260–264.

Saxe, R. & Kanwisher, N. (2003). People thinking about thinking people: FMRI investigations of theory of mind. *NeuroImage*, *19*, 1835–1842.

Saxe, R. & Powell, L. J. (2006). It's the thought that counts: Specific brain regions for one component of theory of mind. *Psychological Science*, *17*(8), 692–699.

Saxe, R., Xiao, D. K., Kovacs, G., Perrett, D. I., & Kanwisher, N. (2004). A region of right posterior superior temporal sulcus responds to observed intentional actions *Neuropsychologia*, *42*(11), 1435–1446.

Schacter, D. L., Addis, D. R., & Buckner, R. L. (2007). Remembering the past to imagine the future: The prospective brain. *Nature Reviews Neuroscience*, *8*(9), 657–661.

Schacter, D. L., Addis, D. R., & Buckner, R. L. (2008). Episodic simulation of future events: Concepts, data, and applications. *Annals of the New York Academy of Sciences*, *1124*, 39–60.

Schiller, D., Freeman, J. B., Mitchell, J. P., Uleman, J. S., & Phelps, E. A. (2009). A neural mechanism of first impressions. *Nature Neuroscience*, *12*, 508–514.

Singer, T., Seymour, B., O'Doherty, J. P., Stephan, K. E., Dolan, R. J., & Frith, C. D. (2006). Empathic neural responses are modulated by the perceived fairness of others. *Nature*, *439*(7075), 466–469.

Singer, T., Winston, J., Kiebel, S., Dolan, R., & Frith, C. (2004). Brain responses to the acquired moral status of faces. *Neuron*, *41*(4), 653–662.

Squire, L. (1992). Memory and the hippocampus: A synthesis from findings with rats, monkeys, and humans. *Psychological Review*, *99*(2), 195–231.

Taber, K., Wen, C., Khan, A., & Hurley, R. (2004). The limbic thalamus. *Journal of Neuropsychiatry and Clinical Neurosciences*, *16*, 127–132.

Thompson, M. S., Judd, C. M., & Park, B. (2000). The consequences of communicating social stereotypes, *Journal of Experimental Social Psychology*, *36*(6), 567–599.

Todorov, A. (in press). Evaluating faces on social dimensions. In A. Todorov, S. T. Fiske, & D. Prentice (Eds.), *Social neuroscience: Toward understanding the underpinnings of the social mind*. Oxford University Press.

Todorov, A., Baron, S. G., & Oosterhof, N. N. (2008). Evaluating face trustworthiness: A model based approach. *Social Cognitive and Affective Neuroscience*, *3*(2), 119–127.

Todorov, A. & Engell, A. (2008). The role of the amygdala in implicit evaluation of emotionally neutral faces. *Social Cognitive and Affective Neuroscience*, *3*, 303–312.

Todorov, A., Gobbini, M. I., Evans, K. K., & Haxby, J. V. (2007). Spontaneous retrieval of affective person knowledge in face perception. *Neuropsychologia*, *45*(1), 163–173.

Todorov, A., Mandisodza, A. N., Goren, A., & Hall, C. C. (2005). Inferences of competence from faces predict election outcomes. *Science*, *308*(5728), 1623–1626.

Todorov, A., Pakrashi, M., & Oosterhof, N. (in press). Evaluating faces on trustworthiness after minimal time exposure. *Social Cognition*.

Todorov, A., Said, C. P., Engell, A. D., & Oosterhof, N. N. (2008). Understanding evaluation of faces on social dimensions. *Trends in Cognitive Sciences*, *12*(12), 455–460.

Todorov, A. & Uleman, J. S. (2002). Spontaneous trait inferences are bound to actors' faces: Evidence from a false recognition paradigm. *Journal of Personality and Social Psychology*, *83*(5), 1051–1065.

Todorov, A. & Uleman, J. S. (2003). The efficiency of binding spontaneous trait inferences to actors' faces. *Journal of Experimental Social Psychology*, *39*(6), 549–562.

Todorov, A. & Uleman, J. S. (2004). The person reference process in spontaneous trait inferences. *Journal of Personality and Social Psychology*, *87*, 482–493.

Trope, Y. & Gaunt, R. (2003). Attribution and person perception. In M. A. Hogg & J. Cooper (Eds.), *The sage handbook of social psychology* (pp. 190–209). New York: Sage Publications.

Van den Bos, W., McClure, S. M., Harris, L. T., Fiske, S. T., & Cohen, J. D. (2008). Dissociating affective evaluation and social cognitive processes in the ventral medial prefrontal cortex. *Cognitive, Affective and Behavioral Neuroscience*, *7*(4), 337–346.

Van Overwalle, F. (2009). Social cognition and the brain: A meta-analysis. *Human Brain Mapping*, *30*(3), 829–858.

Vuilleumier, P. (2005). How brains beware: Neural mechanisms of emotional attention *Trends in Cognitive Sciences*, *9*(12), 585–594.

Walter, H., Adenzato, M., Ciaramidaro, A., Enrici, I., Pia, L., & Bara, B. (2004). Understanding intentions in social interaction: The role of the anterior paracingulate cortex. *Journal of Cognitive Neuroscience*, *16*(10), 1854–1863.

Winston, J., Strange, B., O'Doherty J., & Dolan R. J. (2002). Automatic and intentional brain responses during evaluation of trustworthiness in faces. *Nature Neuroscience*, *5*, 277–283.

Young, L. & Saxe, R. (2008). The neural basis of belief encoding and integration in moral judgment. *NeuroImage*, *40*(4), 1912–1920.

The Origins of First Impressions in Animal and Infant Face Perception

Leslie A. Zebrowitz *and* Yi Zhang

Abstract

This chapter examines evidence for phylogenetic origins that is revealed in continuities between face perception in nonhuman animals and human infants and the first impressions shown by human adults. It provides four kinds of evidence pertinent to the evolutionary origins of impression formation. First, it shows a phylogenetic foundation for overgeneralization effects in a shared sensitivity across species to particular facial qualities and their affordances. Second, it shows similar sensitivities in human infants. Third, it provides direct evidence that overgeneralized reactions to these facial qualities contribute to first impressions. Finally, the chapter provides neural data concerning the arguments presented. This is done for facial qualities that convey familiarity, neoteny, emotion, fitness, and species.

Keywords: amygdala; babyface; ecological theory; evolutionary psychology; face familiarity; face overgeneralization; facial attractiveness; facial expression recognition; facial maturity; first impressions; fusiform face area; impression formation; infant face perception; reward circuit; species recognition; superior temporal sulcus

Cultural wisdom enjoins us not to "judge a book by its cover," an admonition suggesting that our natural proclivity is in fact to judge people by their appearance. Considerable social-psychological research has shown that this is so. Not only do we make judgments about people from their faces, but also there is a remarkable consensus in our judgments. A full understanding of these first impressions requires an analysis of their origins at both the phylogenetic and ontogenetic levels. In the present chapter we examine evidence for phylogenetic origins that is revealed in continuities between face perception in nonhuman animals[1] and human infants and the first impressions shown by human adults.

First impressions are fast and automatic. Brief exposure to faces yields consensual impressions of a variety of traits that have functional significance for perceivers, including aggressiveness, competence, dominance, health, sexuality, and trustworthiness, in some cases at exposures of 50 ms or less (Bar, Neta, & Linz, 2006; Rule & Ambady, 2008; Willis & Todorov, 2006; Zebrowitz & Rhodes, 2004). Moreover, subliminal priming with different facial types speeds responses to associated trait words, supporting the automaticity claim (Dovidio, Kawakami, Johnson, Johnson, & Howard, 1997). The speed and automaticity of first impressions from faces suggests that they have origins in evolutionarily adaptive systems that would be shared by animals and operate early in human development (Johnson, 2005). The ecological approach to person perception (Zebrowitz, 1997; Zebrowitz &

Montepare, 2006) offers an explanation for first impressions consistent with this analysis. Although we limit our discussion to impressions based on facial cues, similar arguments can be made for impressions based on other nonverbal cues, such as voice and movement.

In the ecological account of face perception, first impressions are grounded in the adaptive value of fast, automatic detection of cues that identify natural categories: familiar identities, infants, emotions, low fitness, and species. Consistent with the importance of these categories, functionally distinct neural populations code different ages (babies vs. adults), races (own vs. other), and species (monkey vs. human) (Little, DeBruine, Jones, & Waitt, 2008), as well as face identity and emotion expression (Haxby, Hoffman, & Gobbini, 2000; but see Calder & Young, 2005). In addition to considering when first impressions will be accurate, ecological theory proposes *overgeneralization effects* that yield systematic biases (Zebrowitz, 1996; Zebrowitz & Collins, 1997). Specifically, the preparedness to respond adaptively to familiar identities, infants, emotions, unfit individuals, and various species is overgeneralized to impressions of people whose facial structure merely resembles one of these categories.

Although first impressions are typically assessed by the verbal attribution of psychological traits, they can be construed more broadly as the perception of behavioral affordances. These are opportunities for acting or being acted upon that can be recognized without verbal mediation (Gibson, 1979). Construing first impressions this way makes it reasonable to look for phylogenetic origins in the perceptions of animals and human infants, both of whom show an interest in faces (Johnson, 2005; Tate, Fischer, Leigh, & Kendrick, 2006). Behavioral paradigms used to study face perception in these populations include: a) habituation; b) visual preference; and c) instrumental learning. Neural methods include: a) single cell recordings in animals that provide a much finer resolution than fMRI research in adult humans; b) evoked response potentials (ERP), which provide temporal information with very crude localization; and c) near-infrared spectroscopy (NIRS), which can localize cortical, but not sub-cortical brain activation.

We provide four kinds of evidence pertinent to the evolutionary origins of impression formation. First, we show a phylogenetic foundation for overgeneralization effects in a shared sensitivity across species to particular facial qualities and their affordances. Next we show similar sensitivities in human infants. Third, we provide direct evidence that overgeneralized reactions to these facial qualities contribute to first impressions. Finally, we provide neural data concerning our arguments. We do this for facial qualities that convey familiarity, neoteny, emotion, fitness, and species.[2]

Origins in Familiarity Perception
Animal Response to Face Familiarity
A fundamental aspect of face perception is to differentiate known from novel faces, and research demonstrates a keen sensitivity to face familiarity in nonhuman animals (see Tate et al., 2006, for a comprehensive review). Lambs recognize their mother's face at one- to two-months of age as do chimpanzees, looking longer at their own mother's face than an "average" chimpanzee face (Myowa-Yamakoshi, Yamaguchi, Tomonaga, Tanaka, & Matsuzawa, 2005). Adult sheep discriminate photographs of familiar and unfamiliar adult sheep faces, and even recognize familiar faces after two years. Moreover, sheep prefer the faces of familiar sheep, and pictures of them reduce stress symptoms following social isolation. Even wasps differentiate among faces of conspecifics (Gronenberg, Ash, & Tibbetts, 2008). Animals also use facial cues to differentiate familiar from unfamiliar humans. Infant gibbons do so by four weeks of age, and prefer familiar faces (Myowa-Yamakoshi & Tomonaga, 2001). Sheep also recognize individual human faces, as do cows (Hagen & Broom, 2003; Taylor & Davis, 1998) and wild crows (Marzluff, Walls, & Withey, 2008). Finally, there is evidence that primates better recognize and discriminate members of their own species than other species (see Leopold & Rhodes, 2010, for a review).

Infant Response to Face Familiarity
Two-day-old infants prefer their mother's face to that of a female stranger (Walton, Bower, & Bower, 1992), and six-month-old infants look longer at a facial composite of previously seen than unseen faces (Rubenstein, Kalakanis, & Langlois, 1999). Just as animals discriminate familiar from unfamiliar human faces, three-month-old infants discriminate familiar from unfamiliar animal faces. Interestingly, this ability declines with age (Pascalis, de Haan, & Nelson, 2002), as does the ability to discriminate familiar from unfamiliar other-race faces (Kelly et al., 2007), which may reflect a developing expertise in recognizing own-race human faces and a low adaptive utility of differentiating faces of animals or other-race humans.

Familiar Face Overgeneralization (FFO)

That animals and human infants differentiate unfamiliar from familiar faces and prefer the latter may be a precursor of adults' tendency to form more positive first impressions of familiar faces. Mere exposure to faces of strangers increases their likeability (Zajonc, 1968). Moreover, sensitivity to familiar faces yields FFO, whereby unknown faces elicit more positive impressions when they show more resemblance to familiar faces. For example, faces of strangers are judged more trustworthy when their photos are morphed to resemble the perceiver, even though that resemblance is not consciously detected (DeBruine, Jones, Little, & Perrett, 2008). Familiar face overgeneralization also contributes to negative impressions of other-race individuals. Faces of other-race strangers appear less familiar than faces of own-race strangers, and the tendency to judge own-race strangers as more likeable is mediated by impressions of familiarity (Zebrowitz, Bronstad, & Lee, 2007). In addition, racial prejudice is influenced by the similarity of faces to one's own race, even when faces are all the same race (Blair, Judd, Sadler, & Jenkins, 2002; Livingston & Brewer, 2002). The lesser familiarity of other-race faces also contributes to the strength of culturally based race stereotypes, enhancing negative stereotypes of other-race faces and diminishing positive ones (Zebrowitz et al., 2007). Furthermore, short-term exposure to increase the general familiarity of other-race faces increases the likeability of novel faces of that race (Zebrowitz, Weineke, & White, 2008), and learning to recognize other-race faces decreases implicit race biases (Lebrecht, Pierce, Tarr, & Tanaka, 2009).

Neural Response to Face Familiarity

A neural response to face familiarity in animals has been documented by single-cell recordings in temporal and frontal cortices (Hasselmo, Rolls, & Baylis, 1989; Tate et al., 2006), regions that may be analogous to the human fusiform face area (FFA), specialized for face processing (Kanwisher, McDermott, & Chun, 1997), and the orbitofrontal cortex (OFC), involved in evaluating the emotional valence of stimuli for the purpose of guiding goal-related behavioral responses (Schoenbaum, Gottfried, Murray, & Ramus, 2007). Human infants as young as three months old also show a neural response to face familiarity, with different ERPs to faces familiarized through experimental exposure versus previously unseen faces (Pascalis, de Haan, Nelson, & de Schonen, 1998). In adult humans, FFA shows a weaker response to familiarized than unseen faces (Gobbini & Haxby, 2006). This suggests a greater ease in processing familiar faces that could contribute to greater liking according to a perceptual fluency explanation for the mere exposure effect. At the same time, activation of the amygdala, which has strong anatomical connections to the OFC, is lower for familiarized faces (Gobbini & Haxby, 2006), suggesting that a reduced wariness of familiar faces could contribute to greater liking. Consistent with FFO, these responses of the FFA and amygdala to familiarized versus unfamiliar faces are paralleled by responses to faces of own-race versus other-race strangers, effects shown by both Black and White perceivers (for a review, see Eberhardt, 2005). Also consistent with FFO, the different ERPs shown by six-month olds to mother's face and a stranger's face varied depending on whether the stranger looked similar or dissimilar to the mother (de Haan & Nelson, 1997). Additional research is needed to better understand the neural substrate for valenced impressions associated with familiarity, particularly since the complex neural system underlying the response to variations in face familiarity extends beyond the FFA and amygdala (Gobbini & Haxby, 2007).

Origins in Perception of Babies
Animal Response to Babies' Faces

There are systematic differences in infantile versus mature facial qualities that show commonalities across species (Lorenz, 1942; Todd, Mark, Shaw, & Pittenger, 1980), and animals are sensitive to these differences. Female rhesus macaques show greater approach toward infantile facial features (Gerald, Waitt, & Maestripieri, 2006), rhesus monkeys reared in isolation preferred looking at pictures of infant monkeys to adult monkeys (Sackett, 1973), and nursing female mice prefer infant mice bred to have a super-normal (large) infant head shape (Csermey & Mainardi, 1983).

Infant Response to Babies' Faces

Human infants as young as four months are also sensitive to differences between infantile and mature facial qualities. They discriminate faces of adults from babies, and show a visual preference and more positive affective responses for the latter, even when other perceptual cues to age are held constant (for a review, see Zebrowitz & Montepare, 2006).

Baby Face Overgeneralization (BFO)

Differentiation of infant and adult faces by animals and human infants may be a precursor to different impressions of the two face categories as well as BFO. Compared with young adult faces, faces of babies elicit impressions of high likeability and low power, reactions that have adaptive value for species survival. Moreover, more babyfaced people of all ages also elicit impressions of high likeability and low power, a BFO effect (for a review, see Montepare & Zebrowitz, 1998). Agreement in judgments of babyfacedness and associated traits is robust and seen across cultures and in young children. Even six-month olds show visual preferences for babyfaced adults, with facial attractiveness controlled (Kramer, Zebrowitz, San Giovanni, & Sherak, 1995). Consistent with the claim that these responses are overgeneralized adaptive reactions to babies, they are predicted by the same facial features that differentiate real babies from adults. This has been demonstrated in various ways, including predicting impressions from connectionist model assessments of the extent to which adult faces structurally resemble those of babies (Zebrowitz, Fellous, Mignault, & Andreoletti, 2003)

Neural Response to Babies' Faces

Adults show more amygdala activation to photographs of babies' faces than young adult faces, consistent with evidence that the amygdala is activated by emotionally salient stimuli (Zebrowitz, Luevano, Bronstad, & Aharon, 2009). More remarkable, babyfaced men and babies elicited equally high activation, with lower activation elicited by mature-faced men of the same age. Facial qualities previously shown to elicit strong amygdala activation, such as smiling, attractiveness, and structural distinctiveness, could not account for this effect. Babyfaced and mature-faced men were distinguished only by their resemblance to babies. Thus, the preparedness to respond to infantile facial qualities generalizes to babyfaced men in perceivers' neural responses just as it does in their behavioral reactions. Additional research is needed to identify the neural substrate for the more specific impressions of babies and babyfaced adults as likeable and weak. Amygdala activation in and of itself cannot explain these impressions, since it is also higher for faces that are emotionally salient for other reasons, such looking either trustworthy or untrustworthy (Todorov, Baron, & Oosterhof, 2008).

Origins in Emotion Perception
Animal Response to Facial Expressions

Chimpanzees can accurately discriminate basic facial expressions such as a scream, bared-teeth (fear grin), pant-hoot, and relaxed open mouth expression (play face), from a neutral face, abilities that are consistent with the significance of facial expressions in their daily group living (Parr, Dove, & Hopkins, 1998; Parr, Waller, & Heintz, 2008). More surprisingly, sheep also respond to emotion cues in faces, preferring a picture of the face of a calm sheep over one stressed by social isolation, with stress validated by autonomic indicators and shown in more visible whites of the eyes and different ear position. Moreover, sheep preferred a picture of an unfamiliar calm sheep to a known stressed one, contrary to their usual preference for familiar faces. Sheep also showed a reliable preference for a smiling human face over an angry one (cf. Tate et al., 2006).

Infant Response to Facial Expressions

By two to three weeks of age, infants mimic facial gestures posed by a stranger (Meltzoff & Moore, 1977), and by 10 weeks, they match joyful and angry expressions posed by their mothers, as well as showing meaningful affective reactions to them (Haviland & Lelwica, 1987). Whereas the preceding studies combined vocal and facial cues using dynamic faces, four-month-old infants visually discriminate neutral, happy, and angry static facial expressions independently of cues such as toothiness and the particular model posing the expression (Serrano, Iglesias, & Loeches, 1995). Not only can young infants perceptually differentiate facial expressions, but also they show understanding of their affective meaning, with more approach behaviors to happy expressions and more avoidant behaviors to anger and other negative expressions (Serrano et al., 1995; Sorce, Emde, Campos, & Klinnert, 1985). Infants as young as five months also showed a stronger startle response to noise when looking at an angry face than a happy one, indicating an attunement to the dangerous meaning of the angry face (Balaban, 1995).

Emotion Face Overgeneralization (EFO)

Accurate identification of transient emotional states by human adults (Ekman, 1994) are overgeneralized to impressions of more stable traits—a *temporal extension* effect (Secord, 1958). For example, an angry person is viewed not only as likely to act momentarily in an unaffiliative or dominant way, but also as likely to possess enduring low affiliative or high dominant traits (for a review, see Zebrowitz & Montepare, 2008). In a second level of overgeneralization, trait impressions elicited by facial expressions of emotion are overgeneralized to individuals whose neutral expression facial structure resembles a particular emotional expression, an EFO effect. For example, people with an angry-looking facial structure are perceived as high in dominance and low in affiliation even when they are not feeling or expressing anger (Montepare & Dobish, 2003; Oosterhof & Todorov, 2008; Zebrowitz, Kikuchi, & Fellous, 2010), and race differences in the resemblance of neutral faces to anger expressions mediates and suppresses race-stereotyped impressions (Zebrowitz, Kikuchi et al., 2010). Animal and human infant sensitivity to the meaning of emotion expressions may be a precursor of such EFO effects.

Neural Response to Facial Expressions

Human infants as young as four months show a neural response to emotion expressions, with ERPs differentiating fear from anger or happy expressions as well as anger directed toward the self (with direct gaze) from anger directed elsewhere (Striano, Kopp, Grossmann, & Reid, 2006) (Kobiella, Grossmann, Reid, & Striano, 2008; Nelson & de Haan, 1996). Single-cell recordings also document a neural response to emotion expressions in animals. In apes and monkeys, responses are found in neurons located in the superior temporal sulcus (STS) (Tate et al., 2006), a region that also responds to expression in humans (Haxby, Hoffman, & Gobbini, 2002). In sheep, the representation of emotion cues appears to be organized by a distributed network in the temporal cortex (Tate et al., 2006). In humans, emotion perception has been shown to involve a complex network, including both cortical and subcortical structures, like the amygdala (Adolphs, 2002), with the significance of the latter shown in a response to subliminal presentations of emotion expressions (Liddell et al., 2005). Despite considerable research investigating adult humans, a distinctive neural signature for the response to different emotion expressions remains to be found. Indeed, over a dozen brain regions are reliably activated in response to multiple emotions, including facial expressions (Phan, Wager, Taylor, & Liberzon, 2004). Different patterns of connectivity between the amygdala and orbitofrontal cortex provide some clue, as they differentiate the neural response to emotions that vary in valence, those that vary in perceiver approach versus avoidance, as well as among

specific emotion categories (Liang, Zebrowitz, & Aharon, 2009). Once the neural correlates of perceiving particular emotion expressions are more clearly identified, EFO predicts similar patterns of neural response to neutral expression faces with structural features that resemble a particular emotion, like those shown to resemble sadness and anger (Neth & Martinez, 2009), as well as correlations of these neural patterns with trait impressions.

Origins in Attractiveness Perception
Animal Response to Facial Attractiveness

Animals show preferences for particular facial qualities. Female sheep prefer pictures of rams' faces to those of ewes during estrus, but not anestrus, indicating a functional preference for male facial qualities (Kendrick, et al., 1995). Rhesus macaques presented with pictures of opposite-sex conspecifics showed preferential looking at symmetrical versus asymmetrical faces (Waitt & Little, 2006), a cue that influences perceived attractiveness by humans and is a putative marker of genetic fitness (Scheib, Gangestad, & Thornhill, 1999). A preference for symmetry also was shown by monkeys viewing schematic human faces (Anderson, Kuwahata, Kuroshima, Leighty, & Fujita, 2005). In addition, infant macaques presented with pairs of schematic macaque faces showed greater-than-chance fixation on normal faces but not on faces distorted in various ways, including an increased distance between the eyes (Lutz, Lockard, Gunderson, & Grant, 1998), which is a common facial marker of genetic anomalies in humans (cf. Zebrowitz, 1997). The preference shown for facial symmetry and prototypicality supports a phylogenetic foundation for anomalous face overgeneralization (AFO), whereby adaptive responses to individuals with diseases or bad genes are overgeneralized to normal individuals whose faces resemble those who are unfit.

Infant Response to Facial Attractiveness

Infants less than three days old prefer photographs of adult faces judged by adults as more attractive, an effect driven by attention to internal facial features rather than external face shape (Slater et al., 2000). Infants also show a visual preference for infant faces judged more attractive by adults (Van Duuren, Kendell-Scott, & Stark, 2003) as well as for faces of cats and lions judged more attractive (Quinn, Kelly, Kang, Pascalis, & Slater, 2008). The preference for more attractive infant faces was lost when the faces were inverted, suggesting a response to configural qualities rather than local features. Those configural facial qualities may include high averageness and symmetry, which increase adults' judgments of attractiveness (Langlois & Roggman, 1990; Rhodes, Sumich, & Byatt, 1999), and are also discriminated by infants. In one study, six-month olds, like adults, showed a visual preference for faces high in averageness over low-attractive faces (Rubenstein et al., 1999). However, another study found that seven-month olds preferred faces low in averageness or symmetry (Rhodes, Geddes, Jeffery, Dziurawiec, & Clark, 2002). This unexpected preference may reflect a competing response to stimulus novelty. Indeed, adults judged the faces low in averageness and symmetry to be odd looking. Whereas visual preference paradigms can be ambiguous regarding the meaning of longer facial fixations, mobile infants show a behavioral aversion to unattractive faces, suggesting that they are perceived to afford negative outcomes (Langlois, Roggman, & Rieser-Danner, 1990). Since low averageness can mark disease or genetic anomalies, the infant visual preference for average faces shown by Rubenstein et al. (1999) and the behavioral aversion to atypical, unattractive faces shown by Langlois et al. (1990) may be a byproduct of a disease-avoidance mechanism, consistent with AFO.

Anomalous Face Overgeneralization (AFO)

The responses to variations in facial attractiveness shown in animals and human infants may be precursors of the well-documented attractiveness halo effect, whereby people with more attractive faces are perceived to have more positive traits, including sociability, intelligence, and health (Zebrowitz & Rhodes, 2002). Similar responses to attractiveness across species, age, and cultures (Dion, 2002), implicate some universal mechanism, consistent with AFO. On this account, the adaptive value of recognizing individuals with disease or bad genes has produced a strong preparedness to respond to unattractive facial qualities that can mark low fitness, such as asymmetry or atypicality (Scheib et al., 1999). These responses are then overgeneralized to normal individuals whose faces resemble those who are unfit. Consistent with AFO, impressions of the attractiveness, health, intelligence, and sociability of normal faces were predicted by their resemblance to anomalous ones, as assessed by a connectionist model of facial structure (Zebrowitz et al., 2003). Evidence that these effects are overgeneralizations rather than accurate impressions was supported by the fact that they could not be explained by variations in the actual health and intelligence of the

people with normal faces. Also consistent with AFO is evidence that the automatic association of facial disfigurement with disease overrides rational knowledge to the contrary (Duncan & Schaller, 2005), and that the attractiveness halo effect is driven more by the perception that "ugly is bad" than the perception that "beautiful is good" (Griffin & Langlois, 2006).[3]

Neural Response to Facial Attractiveness

More positive behavioral responses to attractive than unattractive faces has spurred investigations of neural mechanisms in a "reward circuit" that includes brain regions innervated by dopamine pathways and that functions to guide goal-related behavioral responses (Schoenbaum et al., 2007). Animal research provides some direct support for the reward value of facial attractiveness. In vivo microdialysis from the hypothalamus of female sheep revealed that pictures of preferred male sheep elicited release of dopamine similar to actual interaction with the preferred mate (Fabre-Nys, Ohkura, & M., 1997). Functional MRI data from humans also supports the reward value of variations in facial attractiveness. Attractive faces elicit greater activation in the nucleus accumbens (NAC) and medial orbitofrontal cortex (MOFC), regions that respond to rewarding stimuli (Aharon et al., 2001; O'Doherty et al., 2003; Winston, O'Doherty, Kilner, Perrett, & Dolan, 2007), while unattractive faces elicit greater activation in putamen and lateral orbitofrontal cortex (Cloutier et al., 2008; Liang et al., 2009), regions that respond to aversive stimuli (O'Doherty, Kringelbach, Rolls, Hornak, & Andrews, 2001). However, there also are nonlinear effects in these regions, with higher activation to both rewarding and aversive stimuli than neutral ones, including faces, suggesting that the neural differentiation of high, medium, and low attractive faces does not show any simple dissociation across brain regions (Liang, Zebrowitz, & Zhang, 2009). Once the neural coding of variations in facial attractiveness is better understood, it will be possible to test the AFO prediction of a more similar response to faces that are high and medium attractive than to those that are low attractive and also to determine how the neural coding of attractiveness relates to trait impressions.

Origins in the Perception of Species
Animal Response to Different Species Faces
Infant macaques just three-months old discriminated among faces of female macaques from three

different species, but only when faces were presented upright, indicating configural processing like that shown in humans (Swartz, 1983). Sheep differentiated sheep from human, dog, and goat faces as well as different breeds of sheep, preferring own species and showing impaired differentiation when faces were inverted or eyes were masked (Kendrick et al., 1995). Cows also differentiated faces of their own species from sheep, goats, horses and dogs (Coulon et al., 2007). (See Tate et al., 2006 for a review).

Infant Response to Different Species' Faces

Discrimination of different species was once crucial for human survival, and the focus on animal identification in infants' picture books suggests that animals constitute natural categories to which young children are highly attuned. Indeed, infants show a sensitivity to species differences even before any formal instruction occurs. By three months of age, they can discriminate cats, dogs, and birds (Quinn, Eimas, & Rosenkrantz, 1993), with the significance of facial cues shown in the finding that they discriminated dogs and cats in pictures of the whole animal or just the face, but not just the body (Quinn & Eimas, 1996). Further evidence for the salience of the face was shown by four-month-old infants' visual preference for a novel cat face on a dog's body over a novel dog's face on a cat's body after repeated exposure to dogs, with the reverse effect after exposure to cats (Spencer, Quinn, Johnson, & Karmiloff-Smith, 1997).

Species Face Overgeneralization (SFO)

Comparisons of impressions of animals and humans has recently been a focus of psychological research, with a special issue of *Social Cognition* (April, 2008) devoted to anthropomorphism, the attribution of human traits to animals, and the inverse dehumanization, the attribution of animal traits to humans. However, with one exception (Kwan, Gosling, & John, 2008), the role of appearance is not considered in this innovative research. In contrast, the SFO hypothesis gives facial appearance a central role in the attribution of animal traits to humans. Specifically, evolutionarily adaptive responses to various species, evident in differentiation of their faces by animals and human infants, may be overgeneralized, with people perceived to have traits associated with the animals their faces resemble.[4] While SFO may seem far-fetched, the idea that humans share traits with the animals they resemble has a long history (cf. Zebrowitz, 1997), and it persists in modern cartoonists' satire and in linguistic metaphor, such as "leonine," "foxy," and "chicken." Empirical evidence for SFO is, to our knowledge, limited to two studies. Consistent with the notion that lions are "king of the beasts," schematic human faces manipulated to have facial proportions resembling a lion were judged as more dominant than those manipulated to have facial proportions resembling a fox (Zebrowitz, 1997, pp. 60–61). In addition, connectionist modeling of the degree to which humans' facial metrics resembled those of animals revealed that neutral expression human faces with greater resemblance to lions were judged more dominant, shrewd, and cold, while those with greater resemblance to Labrador retrievers were judged more warm and intelligent, but less shrewd (Zebrowitz, Wadlinger, Luevano, et al., in press). Animal and human infant differentiation of species' faces may be a precursor to such SFO effects,

Conclusions

The foregoing research points to phylogenetic origins of first impressions from faces, and it provides insights into the functional foundations of such impressions. Greater success at replicating one's genes through successful mating, parenting, and kin-directed activities would have accrued to members of various species who solved the problems of distinguishing familiar individuals from strangers, infants from adults, angry individuals from happy ones, fit individuals from unfit ones, and lions from lambs. Non-human primates and even "lower" animals can achieve many of these discriminations from faces. Moreover, animals show evidence of attaching meaning to different types of faces that would serve adaptive behavior. The same is true for human infants. Although the discriminations made from facial information are surely not totally "prewired," the demonstration of competence by animals and human infants strongly suggests an evolutionary preparedness. Moreover, the face overgeneralization effects reveal that attunements to facial qualities that reveal adaptively significant attributes are sufficiently potent to influence first impressions of individuals who merely resemble those who actually have those attributes. The neural signatures for these first impressions should resemble those associated with actual variations in face familiarity, age, emotion, fitness, or species.[5]

Acknowledgments

This work was supported by NIH Grants MH066836 and K02MH72603 to the first author.

Notes

1 For brevity, we henceforth refer to nonhuman animals as animals.

2 There are two caveats about the evidence we present. First, our literature review is illustrative not exhaustive. Second, we do not discuss ontogenetic influences that create variability in first impressions across time and individuals.

3 A competing explanation for the preference for attractive faces is that it reflects a preference for prototypical stimuli, since nonface average stimuli are also preferred (Halberstadt & Rhodes, 2000), perhaps because they are easier for the visual system to process. Another is that it reflects a sensitivity to good genes actually associated with high attractiveness, rather than an overgeneralized reaction to bad genes (Scheib et al., 1999).

4 This hypothesis does not imply that de-humanization of outgroup members (Haslam, 2006) derives from any resemblance to nonhuman animals, although de-humanization does motivate visual images depicting such resemblance.

5 This prediction concerns the neural signature for the *contents* of first impressions in contrast to that for the *process* of first impressions, irrespective of content (Schiller, Freeman, Mitchell, Uleman, & Phelps, 2009).

References

Adolphs, R. (2002). Neural systems for recognizing emotion. *Current Opinion in Neurobiology*, *12*(2), 169–177.

Aharon, I., Etcoff, N., Ariely, D., Chabris, C. F., O'Connor, E., & Breiter, H. C. (2001). Beautiful faces have variable reward value: fMRI and behavioral evidence. *Neuron*, *32*(3), 537–551.

Anderson, J. R., Kuwahata, H., Kuroshima, H., Leighty, K. A., & Fujita, K. (2005). Are monkeys aesthetists? Rensch (1957) Revisited. *Journal of Experimental Psychology: Animal Behavior Processes*, *31*(1), 71–78.

Balaban, M. T. (1995). Affective influences on startle in five-month-old infants: Reactions to facial expressions of emotion. *Child Development*, *66*(1), 28–36.

Bar, M., Neta, M., & Linz, H. (2006). Very first impressions. *Emotion*, *6*(2), 269–278.

Blair, I. V., Judd, C. M., Sadler, M. S., & Jenkins, C. (2002). The role of Afrocentric features in person perception: Judging by features and categories. *Journal of Personality and Social Psychology*, *83*(1), 5–25.

Calder, A. J. & Young, A. W. (2005). Understanding the recognition of facial identity and facial expression. *Nature Reviews Neuroscience*, *6*(8), 641–651.

Cloutier J, Heatherton TF, Whalen PJ, et al. (2008). Are attractive people rewarding? Sex differences in the neural substrates of facial attractiveness. *Journal of Cognitive Neuroscience*, *20*(6), 941–951.

Coulon, M., Deputte, B. L., Heyman, Y., Delatouche, L., Richard, C., & Baudoin, C. (2007). Visual discrimination by heifers (Bos taurus) of their own species. *Journal of Comparative Psychology*, *121*(2), 198–204.

Csermey, D. & Mainardi, D. (1983). Infant signals. In A. Oliverio & M. Zappella (Eds.), *The behavior of human infants* (pp. 1–19). New York: Plenum Press.

de Haan, M. & Nelson, C. A. (1997). Recognition of the mother's face by six-month-old infants: A neurobehavioral study. *Child Development*, *68*(2), 187–210.

DeBruine, L., Jones, B., Little, A., & Perrett, D. (2008). Social perception of facial resemblance in humans. *Archives of Sexual Behavior*, *37*(1), 64–77.

Dion, K. K. (2002). Cultural perspectives on facial attractiveness. In G. Rhodes & L. A. Zebrowitz (Eds.), *Facial attractiveness: Evolutionary, cognitive, and social perspectives.* (pp. 239–259). Westport, CT US: Ablex Publishing.

Dovidio, J. F., Kawakami, K., Johnson, C., Johnson, B., & Howard, A. (1997). On the nature of prejudice: Automatic and controlled processes. *Journal of Experimental Social Psychology*, *33*(5), 510–540.

Duncan, L. A. & Schaller, M. (2005). *Facial disfigurement activates disease concepts despite conflicting knowledge.* Paper presented at the Annual Meeting of the Society for Personality and Social Psychology, New Orleans, LA.

Eberhardt, J. L. (2005). Imaging race. *American Psychologist*, *60*(2), 181–190.

Ekman, P. (1994). Strong Evidence For Universals In Facial Expressions - A Reply To Russell's Mistaken Critique, *Psychological Bulletin*, *115*(2), 268–287.

Fabre-Nys, C., Ohkura, S., & M., K. K. (1997). Male faces and odours evoke differential patterns of neurochemical release in the mediobasal hypothalamus of the ewe during oestrus: an insight into sexual motivation? *European Journal of Neuroscience*, *9*(8), 1666–1677.

Gerald, M. S., Waitt, C., & Maestripieri, D. (2006). An experimental examination of female responses to infant face coloration in rhesus macaques. *Behavioural Processes*, *73*(3), 253–256.

Gibson, J. J. (1979). *The ecological approach to visual perception.* Boston: Houghton Mifflin.

Gobbini, M. I. & Haxby, J. V. (2006). Neural response to the visual familiarity of faces. *Brain Research Bulletin*, *71*(1–3), 76–82.

Gobbini, M. I. & Haxby, J. V. (2007). Neural systems for recognition of familiar faces. *Neuropsychologia*, *45*(1), 32–41.

Griffin, A. M. & Langlois, J. H. (2006). Stereotype directionality and attractiveness stereotyping: Is beauty good or is ugly bad? *Social Cognition*, *24*(2), 187–206.

Gronenberg, W., Ash, L. E., & Tibbetts, E. A. (2008). Correlation between facial pattern recognition and brain composition in paper wasps. *Brain, Behavior and Evolution*, *71*(1), 1–14.

Hagen, K. & Broom, D. M. (2003). Cattle discriminate between individual familiar herd members in a learning experiment. *Applied Animal Behaviour Science*, *82*(1), 13.

Halberstadt, J. & Rhodes, G. (2000). The attractiveness of non-face averages: Implications for an evolutionary explanation of the attractiveness of average faces. *Psychological Science*, *11*(4), 285–289.

Haslam, N. (2006). Dehumanization: An integrative review. *Personality and Social Psychology Review*, *10*(3), 252–264.

Hasselmo, M. E., Rolls, E. T., & Baylis, G. C. (1989). The role of expression and identity in the face-selective responses of neurons in the temporal visual cortex of the monkey. *Behavioural Brain Research*, *32*(3), 203–218.

Haviland, J. M. & Lelwica, M. (1987). The induced affect response: 10-week-old infants' responses to three emotion expressions. *Developmental Psychology*, *23*(1), 97–104.

Haxby, J. V., Hoffman, E. A., & Gobbini, M. I. (2000). The distributed human neural system for face perception. *Trends in Cognitive Sciences*, *4*(6), 223–233.

Haxby, J. V., Hoffman, E. A., & Gobbini, M. I. (2002). Human neural systems for face recognition and social communication. *Biological Psychiatry*, *51*(1), 59–67.

Johnson, M. H. (2005). Subcortical face processing. *Nature Reviews Neuroscience*, *6*, 766–774.

Kanwisher, N., McDermott, J., & Chun, M. M. (1997). The fusiform face area: A module in human extrastriate cortex specialized for face perception. *Journal of Neuroscience*, *17*(11), 4302–4311.

Kelly, D. J., Quinn, P. C., Slater, A. M., Lee, K., Ge, L., & Pascalis, O. (2007). The other-race effect develops during infancy: Evidence of perceptual narrowing. *Psychological Science*, *18*(12), 1084–1089.

Kendrick K. M., Atkins, K., Hinton M. R., et al. (1995). Facial and vocal discrimination in sheep. *Animal Behaviour*, *49*(6), 1665–1676.

Kobiella, A., Grossmann, T., Reid, V. M., & Striano, T. (2008). The discrimination of angry and fearful facial expressions in 7-month-old infants: An event-related potential study. *Cognition & Emotion*, *22*(1), 34–146.

Kramer, S., Zebrowitz, L.A., San Giovanni, J.P., & Sherak, B. (1995) Infants' preferences for attractiveness and babyface-ness. In B.G. Bardy, R.J. Bootsma, & Y. Guiard (Eds.), *Studies in Perception and Action III* (pp. 389–392). Hillsdale, N.J.: Erlbaum Associates.

Kwan, V. S. Y., Gosling, S. D., & John, O. P. (2008). Anthropomorphism as a special case of social perception: A cross-species social relations model analysis of humans and dogs. *Social Cognition*, *26*(2), 129–142.

Langlois, J. H. & Roggman, L. A. (1990). Attractive faces are only average. *Psychological Science*, *1*(2), 115–121.

Langlois, J. H., Roggman, L. A., & Rieser-Danner, L. A. (1990). Infants' differential social responses to attractive and unattractive faces. *Developmental Psychology*, *26*(1), 153–159.

Lebrecht, S., Pierce, L. J., Tarr, M. J., & Tanaka, J. (2009). Perceptual other-race training reduces implicit racial bias. *Plos One*, *4*, 1–7.

Leopold, D.A., & Rhodes, G. (2010). A comparative view of face perception. *Journal of Comparative Psychology*, *124*(3), 233–251.

Liang, X., Zebrowitz, L. A., & Aharon, I. (2009). Effective connectivity between amygdala and orbitofrontal cortex differentiates the perception of facial expressions. *Social Neuroscience*, *4*(2), 185–196.

Liang, X., Zebrowitz, L. A., & Zhang, Y. (2009). *Neural activation in the "reward circuit" shows a nonlinear response to facial attractiveness*. Brandeis University.

Liddell, B. J., Brown, K. J., Kemp, A. H., Barton, M. J., Das, P., Peduto, A., et al. (2005). A direct brainstem-amygdala-cortical "alarm" system for subliminal signals of fear. *NeuroImage*, *24*(1), 235–243.

Little, A. C., DeBruine, L. M., Jones, B. C., & Waitt, C. (2008). Category contingent aftereffects for faces of different races, ages and species. *Cognition*, *106*(3), 1537–1547.

Livingston, R. W. & Brewer, M. B. (2002). What are we really priming? Cue-based versus category-based processing of facial stimuli. *Journal of Personality and Social Psychology*, *82*(1), 5–18.

Lorenz, K. (1942). Die angeborenen Formen moglicher Arfahrung [The innate forms of potential experience]. *Zietschrift fur Tierpsychologie*, *5*, 235–409.

Lutz, C. K., Lockard, J. S., Gunderson, V. M., & Grant, K. S. (1998). Infant monkeys' visual responses to drawings of normal and distorted faces. *American Journal of Primatology*, *44*(2), 169–174.

Marzluff, J. M., Walls, J., & Withey, J. C. (2008). *Lasting recognition of a threatening person by wild American crows*. College of Forest Resources, University of Washington.

Meltzoff, A. N. & Moore, M. K. (1977). Imitation of facial and manual gestures by human neonates. *Science*, *198*(4312), 75–78.

Montepare, J. M. & Dobish, H. (2003). The contribution of emotion perceptions and their overgeneralizations to trait impressions. *Journal of Nonverbal Behavior*, *27*(4), 237–254.

Montepare, J. M. & Zebrowitz, L. A. (1998). "Person perception comes of age": The salience and significance of age in social judgments. In M. Zanna (Ed.), *Advances in experimental social psychology* (Vol. 30, pp. 93–163). San Diego, CA: Academic Press.

Myowa-Yamakoshi, M. & Tomonaga, M. (2001). Development of face recognition in an infant gibbon (Hylobates agilis). *Infant Behavior & Development*, *24*(2), 215–227.

Myowa-Yamakoshi, M., Yamaguchi, M. K., Tomonaga, M., Tanaka, M., & Matsuzawa, T. (2005). Development of face recognition in infant chimpanzees (Pan troglodytes). *Cognitive Development*, *20*(1), 49–63.

Nelson, C. A. & de Haan, M. (1996). Neural correlates of infants' visual responsiveness to facial expression of emotion. *Developmental Psychobiology*, *29*(7), 577–595.

Neth, D. & Martinez, A. M. (2009). Emotion perception in emotionless face images suggests a norm-based representation. *Journal of Vision*, *9*, 1–11.

O'Doherty, J., Kringelbach, M. L., Rolls, E. T., Hornak, J., & Andrews, C. (2001). Abstract reward and punishment representations in the human orbitofrontal cortex. *Nature Neuroscience*, *4*(1), 95–102.

O'Doherty, J., Winston, J., Critchley, H., Perrett, D., Burt, D. M., & Dolan, R. J. (2003). Beauty in a smile: The role of medial orbitofrontal cortex in facial attractiveness. *Neuropsychologia*, *41*(2), 147–155.

Oosterhof, N. N. & Todorov, A. (2008). The functional basis of face evaluation. *PNAS Proceedings of the National Academy of Sciences of the United States of America*, *105*(32), 11087–11092.

Parr, L. A., Dove, T., & Hopkins, W. D. (1998). Why faces may be special: Evidence of the inversion effect in chimpanzees. *Journal of Cognitive Neuroscience*, *10*(5), 615–622.

Parr, L. A., Waller, B. M., & Heintz, M. (2008). Facial expression categorization by chimpanzees using standardized stimuli. *Emotion*, *8*(2), 216–231.

Pascalis, O., de Haan, M., & Nelson, C. A. (2002). Is face processing species-specific during the first year of life? *Science*, *296*, 1321–1323.

Pascalis, O., de Haan, M., Nelson, C. A., & de Schonen, S. (1998). Long-term recognition memory for faces assessed by visual paired comparison in 3- and 6-month-old infants. *Journal of Experimental Psychology: Learning, Memory, and Cognition*, *24*(1), 249–260.

Phan, K. L., Wager, T. D., Taylor, S. F., & Liberzon, I. (2004). Functional neuroimaging studies of human emotions. *CNS Spectrums*, *9*(4), 258–266.

Quinn, P. C. & Eimas, P. D. (1996). Perceptual cues that permit categorical differentiation of animals species by infants. *Journal of Experimental Child Psychology*, *63*(1), 189–211.

Quinn, P. C., Eimas, P. D., & Rosenkrantz, S. L. (1993). Evidence for representations of perceptually similar natural categories by 3-month-old and 4-month-old infants. *Perception*, *22*(4), 463–475.

Quinn, P. C., Kelly, D. J., Kang, L., Pascalis, O., & Slater, A. M. (2008). Preference for attractive faces in human infants extends beyond conspecifics. *Developmental Science, 11*(1), 76–83.

Rhodes, G., Geddes, K., Jeffery, L., Dziurawiec, S., & Clark, A. (2002). Are average and symmetric faces attractive to infants? Discrimination and looking preferences. *Perception, 31*(3), 315–321.

Rhodes, G., Sumich, A., & Byatt, G. (1999). Are average facial configurations attractive only because of their symmetry? *Psychological Science, 10*(1), 52–58.

Rubenstein, A. J., Kalakanis, L., & Langlois, J. H. (1999). Infant preferences for attractive faces: A cognitive explanation. *Developmental Psychology, 35*(3), 848–855.

Rule, N. O. & Ambady, N. (2008). Brief exposures: Male sexual orientation is accurately perceived at 50ms. *Journal of Experimental Social Psychology, 44*(4), 1100–1105.

Sackett, G. P. (1973). Monkeys reared in isolation with pictures as visual input: Evidence for an innate releasing mechanism. In T.E. McGill (Ed.) *Readings in Animal Behavior* (2nd. ed. pp. 263–269). New York: Holt, Rinehart, & Winston.

Scheib, J. E., Gangestad, S. W., & Thornhill, R. (1999). Facial attractiveness, symmetry, and cues to good genes. *Proceedings of the Royal Society of London, Series B: Biological Sciences, 266*, 1913–1917.

Schiller, D., Freeman, J. B., Mitchell, J. P., Uleman, J. S., & Phelps, E. A. (2009). A neural mechanism of first impressions. *Nature Neuroscience, 12*(4), 508–514.

Schoenbaum, G., Gottfried, J. A., Murray, E. A., & Ramus, S. J. (2007). *Linking affect to action: Critical contributions of the orbitofrontal cortex.* Malden, MA US: Blackwell Publishing.

Secord, P. (1958). Facial features and inference processes in interpersonal perception. In R. Tagiuri & L. Petrullo (Eds.), *Person perception and interpersonal behavior* (pp. 300–315). Stanford, CA: Stanford University Press.

Serrano, J. M., Iglesias, J., & Loeches, A. (1995). Infants' responses to adult static facial expressions. *Infant Behavior & Development, 18*(4), 477–482.

Slater, A., Bremner, G., Johnson, S. P., Sherwood, P., Hayes, R., & Brown, E. (2000). Newborn infants' preference for attractive faces: The role of internal and external facial features. *Infancy, 1*(2), 265–274.

Sorce, J. F., Emde, R. N., Campos, J. J., & Klinnert, M. D. (1985). Maternal emotional signaling: Its effect on the visual cliff behavior of 1-year-olds. *Developmental Psychology, 21*(1), 195–200.

Spencer, J., Quinn, P. C., Johnson, M. H., & Karmiloff-Smith, A. (1997). Heads you win, tails you lose: Evidence for young infants categorizing mammals by head and facial attributes. *Early Development & Parenting, 6*(3), 113–126.

Striano, T., Kopp, F., Grossmann, T., & Reid, V. M. (2006). Eye contact influences neural processing of emotional expressions in 4-month-old infants. *Social Cognitive and Affective Neuroscience, 1*(2), 87–94.

Swartz, K. B. (1983). Species discrimination in infant pigtail macaques with pictorial stimuli. *Developmental Psychobiology, 16*(3), 219–231.

Tate, A. J., Fischer, H., Leigh, A. E., & Kendrick, K. M. (2006). Behavioural and neurophysiological evidence for face identity and face emotion processing in animals. *Philosophical Transactions of the Royal Society, 361*, 2155–2172.

Taylor, A. A. & Davis, H. (1998). Individual humans as discriminative stimuli for cattle (Bos taurus). *Applied Animal Behaviour Science, 58*(1), 13–21.

Todd, J. T., Mark, L. S., Shaw, R. E., & Pittenger, J. B. (1980). The perception of human growth. *Scientific American, 24*, 106–114.

Todorov, A., Baron, S. G., & Oosterhof, N. N. (2008). Evaluating face trustworthiness: A model based approach. *Social Cognitive and Affective Neuroscience, 3*(2), 119–127.

Van Duuren, M., Kendell-Scott, L., & Stark, N. (2003). Early aesthetic choices: Infant preferences for attractive premature infant faces. *International Journal of Behavioral Development, 27*(3), 212–219.

Waitt, C. & Little, A. (2006). Preferences for symmetry in conspecific facial shape among Macaca mulatta. *International Journal of Primatology, 27*(1), 133–145.

Walton, G. E., Bower, N. J., & Bower, T. G. (1992). Recognition of familiar faces by newborns. *Infant Behavior & Development, 15*(2), 265–269.

Willis, J. & Todorov, A. (2006). First impressions: Making up your mind after a 100-ms exposure to a face. *Psychological Science, 17*(7), 592–598.

Winston, J. S., O'Doherty, J., Kilner, J. M., Perrett, D. I., & Dolan, R. J. (2007). Brain systems for assessing facial attractiveness. *Neuropsychologia, 45*(1), 195–206.

Zajonc, R. B. (1968). Attitudinal effects of mere exposure. *Journal of Personality and Social Psychology, 9*, 1–27.

Zebrowitz, L. A. (1996). Physical appearance as a basis for stereotyping. In N. McRae, M. Hewstone, & C. Stangor (Eds.), *Foundation of stereotypes and stereotyping* (pp. 79–120). New York: Guilford Press.

Zebrowitz, L. A. (1997). *Reading faces: Window to the soul?* Boulder, CO: Westview Press.

Zebrowitz, L. A., Bronstad, P. M., & Lee, H. K. (2007). The contribution of face familiarity to ingroup favoritism and stereotyping. *Social Cognition, 25*, 306–338.

Zebrowitz, L. A. & Collins, M. A. (1997). Accurate social perception at zero acquaintance: The affordances of a Gibsonian approach. *Personality and Social Psychology Review, 1*, 204–223.

Zebrowitz, L. A., Fellous, J. M., Mignault, A., & Andreoletti, C. (2003). Trait impressions as overgeneralized responses to adaptively significant facial qualities: Evidence from connectionist modeling. *Personality and Social Psychology Review, 7*, 194–215.

Zebrowitz, L. A., Kikuchi, M., & Fellous, J. M. (2010). *Facial resemblance to emotions: Group differences, impression effects, and race stereotypes.* Journal of Personality and Social Psychology, 98(2), 175–189.

Zebrowitz, L. A., Luevano, V. X., Bronstad, P. M., & Aharon, I. (2009). Neural activation to babyfaced men matches activation to babies. *Social Neuroscience, 4*(1), 1–10.

Zebrowitz, L. A. & Montepare, J. M. (2006). The ecological approach to person perception: Evolutionary roots and contemporary offshoots. In M. Schaller, J. A. Simpson, & D. T. Kenrick (Eds.), *Evolution and social psychology* (pp. 81–113). New York: Psychology Press.

Zebrowitz, L. A., & Montepare, J. M. (2008). Social psychological face perception: Why appearance matters. *Social and Personality Psychology Compass, 2*, 1497–1517.

Zebrowitz, L. A., & Rhodes, G. (2002). Nature let a hundred flowers bloom: The multiple ways and wherefores of attractiveness. In G. Rhodes & L. A. Zebrowitz (Eds.), *Facial attractiveness: Evolutionary, cognitive, and social perspectives* (pp. 261–293). Westport, CT: Ablex.

Zebrowitz, L. A. & Rhodes, G. (2004). Sensitivity to "Bad Genes" and the anomalous face overgeneralization effect: Cue validity, cue utilization, and accuracy in judging intelligence and health. *Journal of Nonverbal Behavior, 28,* 167–185.

Zebrowitz, L. A., Wadlinger, H., Luevano, V. X., Xing, C., White, B., & Zhang, Y. (in press). *Animal analogies in first impressions of faces. Social Cognition, in press.*

Zebrowitz, L. A., Weineke, K., & White, B. (2008). Mere exposure and racial prejudice: Exposure to other-race faces increases liking for strangers of that race. *Social Cognition, 26,* 259–275.

Using ERPs to Understand the Process and Implications of Social Categorization

Tiffany A. Ito

Abstract

This chapter focuses on research that examines the underlying process and consequences of social categorization. It reviews social neuroscience research specifically using event-related brain potentials (ERPs) to understand issues related to social categorization. Three main issues are discussed: the degree to which attention to social category information is automatic, whether such attention is malleable, and how attentional differences in response to social category information relate to behavior.

Keywords: social categorization, event-related brain potentials, neuroscience research, social category information

Humans are prodigiously talented in the realm of social perception. With very little effort, we can typically infer the intentions, motives, emotions, and traits of others and from those quickly determine implications for our well-being. Determining the conscious inferences perceivers make about an individual can often be done in a relatively straightforward way. If we want to know if someone was determined to be trustworthy, we can simply ask a perceiver if she judges the individual to be so. What can be more difficult to ascertain is how and when this judgment is made, and on what information it is based. This difficulty derives from the likelihood that person perception is governed by theoretically discrete stages (Brewer, 1988; Fiske & Neuberg, 1990), many of which operate quite quickly and outside of conscious awareness (e.g., Bargh, 1999). As a consequence, social actors may often lack conscious awareness of the separable processes that occur to produce final impressions.

More fully understanding the mechanisms that underlie social cognition has been aided by measures that can match the quick timecourse of social perception. Response latency measures have been used frequently to make inferences about quickly occurring social processes. Direct measures of physiological processes are another class of measures ideally suited to detect quickly occurring judgments. The present chapter reviews research using event-related brain potentials (ERPs) in particular. Their fine temporal sensitivity gives them the ability to quantify information processing operations online as they occur, with millisecond resolution. A growing body of research has made use of ERPs to understand aspects of social cognition, as reflected in numerous chapters in this volume. The focus in the present chapter is specifically with research that examines the underlying process and consequences of social categorization. Social judgments can be made in a piecemeal fashion by carefully attending to individual behaviors, but identifying social categories to which an individual belongs is a particularly efficient way to activate a host of expectations and assumptions based on only a single piece of information. The seeming simplicity of identifying someone as being a member of a particular group—of determining, for instance that someone is male—belies its impact on social interaction. Once categorized, beliefs and feelings associated with the group will usually be activated, and become available to influence judgments about and behaviors toward the individual. Given its critical role in mediating the activation of group-based associations, understanding the processes through which social categorization occur has implications for a wide range of outcomes. The present chapter reviews social neuroscience research specifically using ERPs to understand issues related to social categorization. Three main issues are discussed in the present chapter: the degree to which attention to social category information is automatic, whether such attention is malleable, and how attentional differences in response to social category information relate to behavior.

Automaticity of Social Categorization

It has long been assumed that we process social category information automatically, especially about salient and well-practiced dimensions such as race, gender, and age (Bodenhausen & Macrae, 1998; Brewer, 1988; Bruner, 1957; Fiske & Neuberg, 1990; Macrae & Bodenhausen, 2000; Stangor, Lynch, Duan, & Glass, 1992). This assumption has far-ranging implications, but direct empirical tests have been limited. This stems in part from the ease with which stereotypes and prejudice can be activated following social categorization, which makes it challenging to quantify the encoding of social cues independent of the beliefs and feelings they activate. As a result, inferences about categorization have often been made indirectly based on the presence of a stereotypical or prejudiced response (e.g., Macrae, Bodenhausen, & Milne, 1995). At other times, categorization has been studied more directly, for instance as reflected in categorization speed (Stroessner, 1996; Zarate, Bonilla, & Luevano, 1995; Zarate & Smith, 1990). While this clearly provides evidence about explicit categorization decisions, these data are limited to measuring a single conscious outcome of the entire categorization process. ERPs have been used to extend this past research, and in so doing, more directly examine the automaticity of social categorization and what this implies.

Mouchetant and colleagues reported some of the first studies using ERPs to examine social categorization. Participants viewed blocks of pictures containing either faces or body parts (hands and torsos) that either all came from a single gender group, or were from both males and females (Mouchetant-Rostaing, Giard, Bentin, Aguera, & Pernier, 2000). Participants performed two different tasks as ERPs were recorded, either making explicit gender categorizations in some blocks or searching for particular features in other blocks (presence of glasses in the face blocks, presence of torsos in the body parts blocks). Differences in brain activity sensitive to gender variation started at around 145 ms at central-frontal areas. Specifically, differences were obtained in a positive-going component in blocks including both male and female faces as compared to blocks containing only one gender. That is, ERPs differed when gender categorization differentiated the faces as compared to when it did not. Similar effects also occurred in blocks that were heterogenous or not with respect to age (Mouchetant-Rostaing & Giard, 2003). In both studies, the effects were restricted to the blocks in which faces were seen, and were not obtained in the blocks showing body parts, demonstrating specificity of the effects to facial stimuli.

The difference in brain responses when stimuli varied versus were homogeneous with respect to a social category is consistent with the assumption that social categorization occurs automatically. In further support, the ERP effects occurred both when participants were explicitly categorizing along gender or age, and when they were attending to other dimensions (presence of glasses). At the same time, automatic social categorization implies that a man would be categorized as such even if he is in a room of only other men or encountered on his own. That is, while context might accentuate perceived category-based differences (e.g., Tajfel, 1978; Tajfel & Wilkes, 1963; Turner, Hogg, Oakes, Reicher, & Wetherell, 1987), categorization should still occur regardless of the categorical variability within the viewing context. Subsequent research addressed this question, and also examined ERP responses as a function of the specific target group being viewed. This was done by showing participants pictures of Black and White males and females, and examining ERP components known to reflect selective attention for differences as a function of target race and gender. Specifically, Ito and Urland (2003) quantified the amplitude of the N100, P200, and N200 components, which have been shown to vary as a function of covert orienting to task-relevant and/or salient features (Czigler & Geczy, 1996; Eimer, 1997; Kenemans, Kok, & Smulders, 1993; Naatanen & Gaillard, 1983; Raney, 1993; Wijers, Mulder, Okita, Mulder, & Scheffers, 1989).

Several processing differences to Black versus White and male versus female faces were observed that together provide clear evidence of automatic social categorization. The race of the faces first modulated responses in the N100 component. Peaking with a mean latency of around 120 ms after face onset, N100s were larger to Blacks than Whites. This continued into the next component, the P200 (mean peak latency around 180 ms), with larger P200s to Blacks than Whites. Target gender did not begin to affect processing until the P200, where responses were larger to males than females. The third temporally occurring component, the N200, peaked with a latency around 260 ms. The direction of both race and gender effects was reversed in the N200, with larger N200s to Whites and females than Blacks and males, respectively. Given the association of these early components with attentional selection, these results suggest initially greater attention to Blacks and males, but subsequently greater attention to Whites and females. Of importance, all effects occurred regardless of whether participants were explicitly categorizing faces in terms of race or gender. Thus, the early attentional effects do not require an explicit focus on a social dimension, suggesting they are due more to the properties of the individual being perceived, as opposed to the goals of the perceiver.

In this study, trial structure was carefully controlled so that responses could be analyzed not only in terms of the race and gender of the target individual, but also the race and gender of the faces that preceded it. This created trials in which the target face was from both the same racial and gender group as the preceding faces, differed along only one of the dimensions, or differed along both. This structure allowed a determination of whether sensitivity to social category information is restricted to situations where the category varies among the stimulus individuals, as might be implied by Mouchetant et al. (2000; 2003). Instead, the N100, P200, and N200 race and gender effects were present even if the current face was of the same race and/or gender as the faces that immediately preceded it.

This trial structure also allowed examination of a fourth component, the P300. The P300 is associated with categorization processes, with P300 amplitude typically increasing when there is a discrepancy between a given stimulus and preceding stimuli along salient dimensions. In Ito and Urland (2003), P300s were sensitive to the explicit categorization dimension. For instance, for participants categorizing faces in terms of *gender*, P300s were larger to a male face presented after a gender-incongruent female than congruent male face. Of greater relevance to the issue of automaticity in social categorization, implicit categorization effects were also seen. P300 amplitude increased when a target picture differed from the individuals pictured in preceding pictures along the *task-irrelevant* dimension. For instance, for participants categorizing faces in terms of *gender*, P300s were larger to a Black face presented after a racially-incongruent White face relative to a race-congruent Black face.

Finally, the simultaneous variation of two group dimensions in this study also makes these data relevant to understanding how attention is directed to multiple category dimensions. The effects of both race and gender on ERPs regardless of participants' explicit focus suggest that attention to social categories occurs spontaneously for all salient social category dimensions. At the level of stereotype activation and application, there is evidence that a single category dimension dominates, while other relevant dimensions are inhibited (Gilbert & Hixon, 1991). Integrating these findings together, it appears that multiple social categorizations can be activated in parallel, but stereotype activation or application is typically restricted to a single dimension (Bodenhausen & Macrae, 1998; Macrae & Bodenhausen, 2000; Macrae, Bodenhausen, & Milne, 1995).

Effects of Perceiver and Target Group Membership

There is every reason to expect that automatic encoding of social category information is a general phenomenon that occurs regardless of perceiver characteristics. For instance, both female and male perceivers are expected to automatically encode social category information. However, within this automatic process, it is possible that perceivers react to particular *groups* in different ways. Consider race. While perceivers of any race would be expected to encode social category information quickly, the groups to which they attend most may differ depending on their own racial identity. This may arise for motivational reasons or because individuals often have more experience interacting with and perceiving members of their racial ingroup (Goldstein & Chance, 1980; Rhodes, Brennan, & Carey, 1987; Valentine, 1991; Valentine & Bruce, 1986). Ito and

Urland (2003) did record responses from male and female participants, finding no effect of perceiver gender on reactions as a function of target gender (or target race), but differences as a function of perceiver race were not systematically investigated in that study. Instead, the majority of participants were White, and none were Black.

Studies that have varied participant race find that it does affect the way in which race is processed. In a comparison of Black and White participants, Dickter and Bartholow (2007) found that both the P200 and N200 were sensitive to ingroup/outgroup status. P200s were larger to racial outgroup members and N200s were larger to racial ingroup members. That is, among White participants, P200s were larger to Blacks and N200s were larger Whites, replicating Ito and Urland (2003). Of particular interest, the Black participants showed the inverse pattern, with larger P200s to Whites and larger N200s to Blacks.

Ingroup/outgroup effects were also obtained in a sample of Asian participants, although their responses were slightly more nuanced. In this study, ERPs were recorded as Asian participants viewed pictures of ingroup Asians and outgroup Whites (Willadsen-Jensen & Ito, 2008). A contextual manipulation was employed in which the frequency of Asian and White faces varied across two blocks, with Asian faces shown more frequently in one block, and Whites in the other. This allowed an evaluation of whether racial perception among non-Whites is sensitive to the surrounding racial context. White perceivers may frequently have the experience of being in a primarily White environment (e.g. in their jobs, classrooms, and home life). By contrast, non-Whites may be more likely to experience different contexts, such as being among a large number of Whites at work or school, but more non-Whites at home or with friends. It was not known whether greater variability in the types of racial contexts that are encountered might affect the way race is encoded.

As with Bartholow and Dickter (2007), the P200 was larger to outgroup faces—in this case, larger to White faces. This occurred regardless of whether Asian or White faces were shown more frequently. The N200, though, did show an effect of context. When Asian faces were shown most frequently, N200s were larger to ingroup Asian than outgroup White faces. The opposite was obtained in the White context; N200s were larger to outgroup Whites faces.

Integrating across results obtained with White, Black, and Asian participants, two clear conclusions emerge.

The first is that quick attention to racial information is generalizable among perceivers of different races. Data has not been collected from participants of all races, but results are very consistent across the three that have been analyzed. Second, perceiver race does affect the way in which race is encoded. P200s show a consistent ingroup/outgroup effect, with larger P200s to racial outgroup members. N200s tend to be larger to racial ingroup members, although racial context can change this effect, at least for Asian perceivers. Their N200s suggest they flexibly direct attention to individuals from whatever the most numerous racial group is at the time. It is as if Asian perceivers can adopt a perspective that matches that of White perceivers when they find themselves in a context that involves primarily White individuals. This is consistent with the idea that non-Whites in the United States have experience navigating two social realms: their own and that of the White majority. This possibility is further supported by the high degree of contact with Whites reported by these particular Asian participants (Willadsen-Jensen & Ito, 2008). At present, we do not know whether context effects would also occur with other non-White perceivers as context was not manipulated in the study with Black participants. We do know that White perceivers show no such context effects (Ito & Urland, 2003, 2005; Willadsen-Jensen & Ito, 2006). Variation in racial context is therefore not sufficient on its own to alter perceptions; it appears to have effects only in certain perceivers.

It is interesting to consider why perceiver race affects reactions to targets of different races, but perceiver gender has not had parallel effects on reactions to targets of different genders. There are many similarities in the processes that govern our sensitivity to race and gender. As demonstrated here, both social dimensions are processed very quickly and implicitly, and mere perception of race and gender can implicitly activate stereotypes and evaluations (e.g., Dovidio, Kawakami, Johnson, Johnson, & Howard, 1997; Fazio, Jackson, Dunton, & Williams, 1995; Moskowitz, Gollwitzer, Wasel, & Schaal, 1999). At the same time, there are meaningful differences between the two dimensions. For one, between-gender contact is very high, whereas interracial contact is often limited. Because of its relevance to mating, the biological relevance of gender also differs from that of race. The content of the stereotypes associated with specific race and gender groups is also quite variable. Any of these may be sufficient to create a situation where one's own race affects how attention is deployed to particular racial groups, while males and females are similarly differentiated regardless of one's gender.

Sensitivity to Race and Gender, or Low Level Physical Features?

Another important issue to consider is whether the effects that have been obtained in response to variations in target race and gender in fact reflect responses to race and gender information within faces per se, or simply reflect reactions to low-level physical differences that happen to covary with race and gender. For instance, Black and White faces likely differ on average in luminance, and these physical properties could be driving the ERP effects. The degree to which the ERP effects reviewed to this point reflect social processes has been investigated in several ways. First, Ito and Urland (2003) conducted two studies, one with faces shown in full color, and the other with the faces converted to grayscale and equated for luminance across the categories. Automatic attention to race and gender occurred in both studies. That is, race and gender effects were obtained regardless of whether the faces were in color or grayscale.

In another study, color photos of Black and White men were inverted and distorted with a Gaussian blur (Kubota & Ito, 2007). This had the effect of preserving the physical features of the stimuli such as color and luminance but rendering them unrecognizable as faces. The same procedure was applied to an equal number of pictures of dog and cat faces, which served as control stimuli. Stimuli were then used in a spatial processing task, with participants asked to judge whether the picture was to the right or left of fixation. ERP waveforms had a completely different morphology as compared to Ito and Urland (2003). Moreover, there were no significant race effects elicited by these stimuli (nor any effects of whether the faces were originally of humans or pets). These results allow us to clearly conclude that differences in ERP waveforms that are observed as perceivers view members of different social groups are due to social category processes—to perceiving the individuals as being male or female, or Black or White or Asian, and not simply to physical properties that happen to covary with category membership.

Malleability of Social Categorization

These initial studies have been informative in establishing the implicit nature of social category encoding. They have also established that reactions to race are influenced by one's own racial group membership, whereas reactions as a function of gender are not. ERP research has also moved beyond these initial demonstrations of automaticity to assess issues with important implications for behavioral change. To the degree that categorization is the primary process through which group-based associations become applied to an individual, evidence that social categorization occurs automatically raises the question of whether behavioral outcomes can be changed by decreasing attention to social category information. In fact, there are numerous manipulations that have been successful in diminishing the display of bias (for a review on the malleability of implicit bias in particular, see Blair, 2002). These studies demonstrate changes in the activation of stereotypes and evaluations following various task manipulations, but have not addressed whether the manipulations have their effect by decreasing attention to category membership, or on some subsequent aspects of person perception. ERPs provide a way to examine this specific question.

Studies have been done investigating the effects of directing attention to a level either deeper or more shallow than the social category. In one study, some participants viewing pictures of Black and White males were asked to judge whether each individual liked various kinds of vegetables (Ito & Urland, 2005). The goal was to encourage them to consider the people before them in a more person-based instead of category-based way. This task was selected because it decreases implicit stereotype activation, and also attenuates differences in amygdala activation to racial outgroup as compared to ingroup faces which are thought to reflect greater negativity toward the outgroup (Wheeler & Fiske, 2005). Other participants in the study saw the same faces but determined whether a white dot was present on the picture. The goal with this task was to direct attention away from the semantic nature of the faces altogether. This task has also been associated with a decrease in implicit stereotyping (Macrae, Bodenhausen, Milne, Thorn, & Castelli, 1997; Wheeler & Fiske, 2005) and attenuation in race differences in amygdala activation (Wheeler & Fiske, 2005). After completing these tasks, both sets of participants viewed the faces again while making explicit race judgments, which allowed a direct comparison of sensitivity to race information when attention is explicitly directed to race as compared to when it is directed at other cues.

ERP waveforms across the three tasks—vegetable judgment, dot detection, and race categorization—were indistinguishable and showed the same effects as past studies in which all participants made explicit social categorization judgments (Ito & Urland, 2003). P200s from this primarily White sample were larger to Blacks, N200s were larger to Whites, and the P300 was sensitive to the match between a target's race and the race of preceding faces. A subsequent study replicated and extended these findings to the encoding of not only race but also gender. In this study, participants made introversion/extraversion judgments while viewing pictures of Black and White males and females (Ito & Urland, 2005). ERPs again looked identical to data obtained when participants were explicitly attending to race or gender (Ito & Urland, 2003). That is, N100s and P200s were larger to Blacks and males, N200s were larger to Whites and females, and the P300 was sensitive to the match between a target's race and gender and the race and gender of preceding faces.

As noted, the tasks examined in these studies were selected because they have been effective in past studies in reducing implicit stereotyping. There is no reason to think the tasks would fail to do so in the ERP studies. Still, it would be even more powerful to evaluate the effects of the tasks on encoding of social category information with direct knowledge of whether implicit bias was affected. Tomelleri and Ito (2009) addressed this in a sequential priming task in which brief presentations of either Black or White male face primes preceded pictures of guns and insects (Judd, Blair, & Chapleau, 2004). Participants made a manual response to categorize the gun and insect pictures while mentally performing one of two processing tasks with respect to the faces. They either categorized them in terms of race, or performed the dot detection task. ERP responses to the faces were used to determine task effects on the encoding of social category information, and behavioral responses to the gun and insect pictures were examined to determine task effects on implicit bias. ERP results replicated Ito and Urland (2005) by showing encoding of racial information both when participants were explicitly focused on it, and when they had attention directed away from the social nature of the stimuli through the dot task. At the behavioral level, though, priming effects were seen only in the race categorization task. When participants mentally categorized the primes in terms of race, they were faster and more accurate to respond to guns following Black than White primes. By contrast, when they were looking for dots, participants were equally fast and accurate to respond to guns following Black and White primes.

The pattern across these studies is very consistent. Directing perceivers to attend to individuals at either a deeper or more shallow level does not inhibit the perception of racial and gender information that is observed under conditions of explicit attention to the social categories. This further supports the obligatory nature of social category encoding and also provides interesting insights into the way in which attentional manipulations can affect implicit bias. These data indicate that, at least for the specific tasks tested so far, processing manipulations have their effect at stages of processing that occur after at least elementary aspects of social category information have been perceived. Generally speaking, this supports models of social cognition that assume social perception occurs in theoretically dissociable stages (e.g., Brewer 1988; Fiske & Neuberg, 1990). More specifically, it suggests that interventions might be most fruitfully focused on changing the activation and application of group-based associations. At least within the context of the particular tasks implemented thus far, ERP responses indicates it may be challenging to bring about changes in stereotyping and prejudice by blocking the encoding of category membership.

Attention to Race and Behavior

An important motivation to understanding social categorization is the link between identifying someone as belonging to a particular social group and activation of group-based associations. Given their theoretical relation, it is important to ask whether the ERP responses elicited by social category information show any relation to the activation of stereotypes and prejudice. This has been assessed in studies employing the general logic of recording ERPs that are sensitive to social category processing, then examining whether individual variation in the ERP responses predicts variability in implicit bias.

One such study measured implicit bias in a sequential priming task (Ito & Urland, 2005). Faces of Black and White males served as primes. In one block of trials, participants classified subsequently presented pictures as showing guns or insects (Judd et al., 2004). In another block, they classified pictures of guns or sports-related images. In the latter case, all images focused on sports that are stereotypically associated with African Americans (basketball and football). The two blocks allow an assessment of the degree to which Blacks versus Whites more strongly activate associations with danger and violence, compared against one category that is also negative in valence but not racially stereotypical (the insects) and another category that is also racially stereotypical but not negative in valence (the basketball and football images). In both blocks of trials, racial differentiation in the N200 predicted implicit bias. Those individuals who spontaneously showed larger N200s to Whites as compared to Blacks also showed faster responses to guns following Black primes.

Another study used the sequential priming paradigm of Fazio, Jackson, Dunton, and Williams (1995), with Black and White primes being shown before positive and negative words that participants had to categorize as such (Willadsen-Jensen & Ito, 2010). Replicating Ito and Urland (2009), racial differentiation in the N200 predicted greater racial bias. Those individuals who showed relatively larger N200s to Whites than Blacks also showed relatively greater facilitation of responses to negative words following Black primes. In this study, race differences in the P200 also predicted racial bias in response latencies, such that individuals who showed relatively larger P200s to Blacks as compared to Whites demonstrate greater racial bias in response latency to the words.

Finally, ERP responses have predicted racial bias in the Shooter paradigm, which involves making a *shoot* response to armed individuals and a *not shoot* response to unarmed ones (Correll Park, Judd, & Wittenbrink, 2002). The individuals pictured are either Black or White males. Racial effects in both the P200 and N200 predicted racial bias (Correll, Urland & Ito, 2006). Individuals who showed relatively larger P200s to Blacks or N200s to Whites showed greater bias in their responses. That is, they were relatively faster to shoot armed Blacks as compared to Whites, but faster to not shoot unarmed Whites as compared to Blacks. In this study, the magnitude of the race effect in the N100 also exhibited a marginal correlation with bias. The target race main effect was actually not significant at the mean level, when averaged across participants. Nevertheless, the correlation shows that individuals varied in their attention to race as early as 160ms (the latency at which the N100 peaked in this study), and that this variation predicted differences in racially biased behavior.

The three studies reviewed in this section used a heterogenous set of procedures involving sequential priming tasks as well as simple reaction time assessments to a focal stimulus. They also vary in their assessment of implicit racial beliefs (the gun versus insects and gun versus sports priming task, and the Shooter task) and evaluative associations.

Despite this variability, they are united in showing that differences in the way individuals attend to race predict the magnitude of racial bias they display. It is worth noting that the race differences in both the ERP effects and the behavioral responses were for the most part spontaneous. Participants did not have to make any explicit racial judgments in any of the tasks, and behavior was focused on other dimensions (classifying pictures or words). There is consistent evidence that spontaneous differences in responses to Blacks versus Whites in the N200 predict racial bias in behavior; this pattern was obtained in all three studies. There has been more variability in whether the race effects in earlier components also predict racial bias. Because of the relatively small number of studies, it is not yet clear what accounts for these differences. Nevertheless, the take-home message is clear. The spontaneous differences perceivers show in their reactions to social category information predict the implicit associations activated by social categorization.

Conclusions

Because of their non-invasive nature and ability to measure quickly occurring information-processing operations online, ERPs have been informative in the study of social perception. Research using ERPs to study aspects of social categorization suggests numerous conclusions that expand our understanding of the larger process of person perception. To date, all studies converge to demonstrate the ease and speed with which race, gender, and age are processed. Race, gender, and age all moderate ERP responses by 145 ms at the latest. There is also evidence that these effects reflect processes specialized for extracting physiognomic features from faces and not from body parts more generally (Mouchetant et al., 2000; 2003). Moreover, the ERP effects reviewed here are sensitive to the social aspects of the social category information in particular, and do not simply reflect responses to physical features such as luminance that might covary with social category membership (Ito & Urland, 2003; Kubota & Ito, 2007). It is particularly striking that sensitivity to social cues occurs across a range of tasks, including when perceivers are attending to another social dimension (e.g., race effects occur even when perceivers explicitly attend to gender), a non-social cue (searching for dots on faces), or individual characteristics that foster person-based as opposed to category-based impressions. In this way, early perceptual aspects of social categorization are occurring in a relatively obligatory manner that is sensitive more to the physical features of the individual being perceived than by the goals and intentions of the perceiver.

Studies showing a dissociation between the encoding of social category information and stereotype activation or application are particularly intriguing. In one study, performing a nonsemantic task with respect to facial primes—determining whether a small dot was present—had no effect on ERP responses as a function of race, but did eliminate racial bias in response latencies indicative of implicit stereotype activation (Tomelleri & Ito, 2009). Such a pattern indicates that this manipulation has its effects on attentional processes that operate after completion of rudimentary physical analyses of social category membership. Dissociable effects are consistent with current assumptions that aspects of person perception can be broken down into theoretically and empirically distinct stages (Brewer, 1988; Fiske & Neuberg, 1990). They also support the general conclusion that changes in behavioral outcomes such as stereotyping can occur even in instances where category boundaries are maintained (cf. Deffenbacher, Park, Judd, & Correll, 2009; Wolsko, Park, Judd, & Wittenbrink, 2000). Of course, while several studies have been done to examine the effects of particular processing manipulations on the encoding of social category information (Ito & Urland, 2005; Tomelleri & Ito, 2009), only a limited number of manipulations have been tested to date. It is possible that another manipulation could result in a change in both attention to social category information and to subsequent activation of group-based associations. Nevertheless, the basic conclusion still stands, that attention to category membership is not synonymous with the activation of group-based associations. The former so far appears to occur in a relatively unconditional way, while the latter can be affected by numerous factors (Blair, 2002).

The direction of the ERP effects has been very consistent across numerous studies. Research is still being conducted to determine the psychological implications of the effects in each particular component, but some preliminary hypotheses are possible based on extant research. The N100, P200, and N200 have all been associated with selective attention, with the amplitude of the component taken as an index of covert orienting to relevant and/or salient features (Czigler & Geczy, 1996; Eimer, 1997; Kenemans et al., 1993; Naatanen & Gaillard, 1983; Raney, 1993; Wijers et al., 1989). The larger N100s and P200s to racial outgroup members may reflect a form of coarse vigilance or wariness toward members of less familiar or more novel groups. The content of specific racial stereotype may also contribute to this effect. In the case of gender, larger P200s to males could occur because they are typically associated with power and strength, which may draw initial attention. The timecourse of these effects is consistent with other affective modulation effects on ERPs, which have been observed as early as 100 ms (Pizzagalli, Regard, & Lehmann, 1999; Smith, Cacioppo, Larsen, & Chartrand, 2003) and in particular, with findings that more negative stimuli attract more attention (Carretié, Martin-Loeches, Hinojosa, & Mercado, 2001; Carretié, Mercado, Tapia, & Hinojosa, 2001; Eimer & Holmes, 2002; Eimer, Holmes, & McGlone, 2003; Smith et al., 2003).

If attention is initially oriented to racial outgroup members and males, effects shift by the time the N200 peaks. For gender, N200s are consistently larger to females. For race, N200s are either larger to ingroup members, or sometimes are increased to Whites when Whites are in the numerical majority (as in the case of Asian participants in Willadsen-Jensen & Ito, 2008). Orienting more attention to racial ingroup members, or to racial outgroup members when they are more numerous, may represent spontaneously greater attention directed at racial ingroup members and/or members of the more culturally dominant racial group. This is consistent with the large body of research showing that Whites and racial ingroup members are spontaneously processed more deeply than other racial groups (Anthony, Cooper, & Mullen, 1992; Levin, 2000). In support of this interpretation, larger N200s have also been observed to pictures of one's own face as compared to those of strangers (Tanaka, Curran, Porterfield, & Collins, 2006), and to famous as compared with unfamiliar faces (Bentin & Deouell, 2000). In each case, larger N200s were elicited by the types of faces that would be expected to spontaneously attract more attention and possibly deeper, more individuated processing. The meaning of the larger N200s to females is less clear. Processing differences in favor of female over male targets have been obtained (Lewin & Herlitz, 2002; McKelvie, 1981; McKelvie, Standing, St. Jean, & Law, 1993; O'Toole, Deffenbacher, Valentin, McKee, Abdi, 1998), but these effects are more variable than differences in processing as a function of race. As noted, the possible interpretations are preliminary, but they do fit with many intersecting lines of research.

In closing, ERPs have demonstrated their value in understanding the complex processes that underlie social behavior. When applied to issue of social categorization, we find clear evidence that attention is modulated within the first several hundred milliseconds as a function of a target's race, gender, and age. Attention to such information occurs in a fairly obligatory way, and is relatively insensitive to task manipulations. Social category information then becomes available to influence subsequent judgment and behaviors toward the individual, with individual differences in the degree to which individuals spontaneously direct different amounts of attention to members of different social groups predicting activation of implicit bias (Ito & Urland 2006; Tomelleri & Ito, 2009; Willadsen-Jensen & Ito, 2010;). The work in this area is ongoing, so further insights into both the operation of social processes and neural organization are expected by the continued integration of social psychology and neuroscience.

References

Anthony, T., Copper, C., & Mullen, B. (1992). Cross-racial facial identification: A social cognitive integration. *Personality and Social Psychology Bulletin*, 18, 296–301.

Bargh, J. A. (1999). The cognitive monster: The case against the controllability of automatic stereotype effects. In S. Chaiken & Y. Trope (Eds.), *Dual-process theories in social psychology* (pp. 361–382). New York: The Guilford Press.

Bentin, S. & Deouell, L. Y. (2000). Structural encoding and identification in face processing: ERP evidence for separate mechanisms. *Cognitive Neuropsychology*, 17, 35–54.

Blair, I. V. (2002). The malleability of automatic stereotypes and prejudice. *Personality and Social Psychology Review*, 6, 242–261.

Bodenhausen, G. V. & Macrae, C. N. (1998). Stereotype activation and inhibition. In R. S. Wyer, Jr. (Ed.). *Stereotype activation and inhibition* (pp. 1–52). Mahwah, NJ: Lawrence Erlbaum.

Brewer, M. C. (1988). A dual process model of impression formation. In R. Wyer & T. Scrull (Eds.). *Advances in social cognition* (Vol. 1) (pp. 1–36). Hillsdale, NJ: Erlbaum.

Bruner, J. S. (1957). On perceptual readiness. *Psychological Review*, 64, 123–151.

Carretié, L., Martín-Loeches, M., Hinojosa, J. A., & Mercado, F. (2001). Emotion and attention interaction studied through event-related potentials. *Journal of Cognitive Neuroscience*, 13, 1109–1128.

Carretié, L., Mercado, F., Tapia, M., & Hinojosa, J. A. (2001). Emotion, attention, and the "negativity bias," studied through event-related potentials. *International Journal of Psychophysiology*, 41, 75–85.

Correll, J., Park, B., Judd, C. M., & Wittenbrink, B. (2002). The police officer's dilemma: Using ethnicity to disambiguate potentially threatening individuals. *Journal of Personality and Social Psychology*, 83, 1314–1329.

Correll, J., Urland, G. R., & Ito, T. A. (2006). Event-related potentials and the decision to shoot: The role of threat perception and cognitive control. *Journal of Experimental Social Psychology*, 42, 120–128.

Czigler, I. & Geczy, I. (1996). Event-related potential correlates of color selection and lexical decision: Hierarchical processing or late selection? *International Journal of Psychophysiology*, 22, 67–84.

Deffenbacher, D. M., Park, B., Judd, C. M., & Correll, J. (2009). Category boundaries can be accentuated without increasing intergroup bias. *Group Processes & Intergroup Relations*, 12, 175–193.

Dickter, C. L. & Bartholow, B. D. (2007). Event-related brain potential evidence of ingroup and outgroup attention biases. *Social, Cognitive, and Affective Neuroscience*, 2, 189–198.

Dovidio, J. F. Kawakami, K. Johnson, C., Johnson, B., & Howard, A. (1997). On the nature of prejudice: Automatic and controlled processes. *Journal of Experimental Social Psychology*, 33, 510–540.

Eimer, M. (1997). An event-related potential (ERP) study of transient and sustained visual attention to color and form. *Biological Psychology*, 44, 143–160.

Eimer, M. & Holmes, A. (2002). An ERP study on the time course of emotional face processing. *NeuroReport*, 13, 427–431.

Eimer, M., Holmes, A., & McGlone, F. (2003). The role of spatial attention in the processing of facial expression: An ERP study of rapid brain responses to six basic emotions. *Cognitive, Affective, and Behavioral Neuroscience*, 3, 97–110.

Fazio, R. H., Jackson, J. R., Dunton, B. C., & Williams, C. J. (1995). Variability in automatic activation as an unobtrusive measure of racial attitudes: A bona fide pipeline? *Journal of Personality and Social Psychology*, 69, 1013–1027.

Fiske, S. T. & Neuberg, S. L. (1990). A continuum of impression formation, from category-based to individuating processes: Influences of information and motivation on attention and interpretation. *Advances in Experimental Social Psychology*, 23, 1–73.

Gilbert, D. T. & Hixon, J. G. (1991). The trouble of thinking: Activation and application of stereotypic beliefs. *Journal of Personality and Social Psychology*, 60, 509–517.

Goldstein, A. G. & Chance, J. E. (1980). Memory for faces and schema theory. *Journal of Psychology*, 105, 47–59.

Ito, T. A. & Urland, G. R. (2003). Race and gender on the brain: Electrocortical measures of attention to race and gender of multiply categorizable individuals. *Journal of Personality and Social Psychology*, 85, 616–626.

Ito, T. A. & Urland, G. R. (2005). The influence of processing objectives on the perception of faces: An ERP study of race and gender perception. *Cognitive, Affective, and Behavioral Neuroscience*, 5, 21–36.

Ito, T.A., & Urland, G.R. (2006). The functional significance of differences in attention to Blacks and Whites. Unpublished data.

Judd, C. M., Blair, I. V., & Chapleau, K. M. (2004). Automatic stereotypes versus automatic prejudice: Sorting out the possibilities in the Payne (2001) weapon paradigm. *Journal of Experimental Social Psychology*, 40, 75–81.

Kenemans, J. L., Kok, A., & Smulders, F. T. Y. (1993). Event-related potentials to conjunctions of spatial frequency and orientation as a function of stimulus parameters and response requirements. *Electroencephalography and Clinical Neurophysiology*, 88, 51–63.

Kubota, J. T. & Ito, T. A. (2007). Multiple cues in social perception: The time course of processing race and facial expression. *Journal of Experimental Social Psychology*, 43, 738–752.

Levin, D. T. (2000). Race as a visual feature: Using visual search and perceptual discrimination tasks to understand face categories and the cross-race recognition deficit. *Journal of Experimental Psychology: General, 129*, 559–574.

Lewin, C. & Herlitz, A. (2002). Sex differences in face recognition-women's faces make the difference. *Brain and Cognition, 50*, 121–128.

Macrae, C. N. & Bodenhausen, G. V. (2000). Social cognition: Thinking categorically about others. *Annual Review of Psychology, 51*, 93–120.

Macrae, C. N., Bodenhausen, G. V., & Milne, A. B. (1995). The dissection of selection in person perception: Inhibitory processes in social stereotyping. *Journal of Personality and Social Psychology, 69*, 397–407.

Macrae, C. N., Bodenhausen, G. V., Milne, A. B., Thorn, T. M. J., & Castelli, L. (1997). On the activation of social stereotypes: The moderating role of processing objectives. *Journal of Experimental Social Psychology, 33*, 471–489.

McKelvie, S. J. (1981). Sex differences in memory for faces. *The Journal of Psychology, 107*, 109–125.

McKelvie, S. J., Standing, L., St. Jean, D., & Law, J. (1993). Gender differences in recognition memory for faces and cars: Evidence for the interest hypothesis. *Bulletin of the Psychonomic Society, 31*, 447–448.

Moskowitz, G. B., Gollwitzer, P. M., Wasel, W., & Schaal, B. (1999). Preconscious control of stereotype activation through chronic egalitarian goals. *Journal of Personality and Social Psychology, 77*, 167–184.

Mouchetant-Rostaing, Y. & Giard, M. H. (2003). Electrophysiological correlates of age and gender perception on human faces. *Journal of Cognitive Neuroscience, 15*, 900–910.

Mouchetant-Rostaing, Y., Giard, M. H., Bentin, S., Aguera, P. E. (2000). Neurophysiological correlates of face gender processing in humans. *European Journal of Neuroscience, 12*, 303–310.

Naatanen, R. & Gaillard, A. W. K. (1983). The orienting reflex and the N2 deflection of the event-related potential (ERP). In A. W. K. Gaillard & W. Ritter (Eds.), *Tutorials in ERP research: Endogenous components* (pp. 119–141). New York: North-Holland Publishing Company.

O'Toole, A. J., Deffenbacher, K. A., Valentin, D., McKee, K., & Abdi, H. (1998). The perception of face gender: The role of stimulus structure in recognition and classification. *Memory and Cognition, 26*, 146–160.

Pizzagalli, D., Regard, M., & Lehmann, D. (1999). Rapid emotional face processing in the human right and left brain hemispheres: An ERP study. *NeuroReport, 10*, 2691–2698.

Raney, G. E. (1993). Monitoring changes in cognitive load during reading: An event-related brain potential and reaction time analysis. *Journal of Experimental Psychology: Learning, Memory, and Cognition, 19*, 51–69.

Rhodes, G., Brennan, S., & Carey, S. (1987). Identification and ratings of caricatures: Implications for mental representations of faces. *Cognitive Psychology, 19*, 473–497.

Smith, N. K., Cacioppo, J. T., Larsen, J. T., & Chartrand, T. L. (2003). May I have your attention, please: Electrocortical responses to positive and negative stimuli. *Neuropsychologia, 41*, 171–183.

Smith, E. R. & Zarate, M. A. (1992). Exemplar-based model of social judgment. *Psychological Review, 99*, 3–21.

Stangor, C., Lynch, L. Duan, C., & Glass, B. (1992). Categorization of individuals on the basis of multiple social features. *Journal of Personality and Social Psychology, 62*, 207–218.

Stroessner, S. J. (1996). Social categorization by race or sex: Effects of perceived non-normalcy on response times. *Social Cognition, 14*, 247–276.

Tajfel, H. (1978). *Differentiation between social groups: Studies in the social psychology of intergroup relations*. New York: Academic Press.

Tajfel, H. & Wilkes, A. L. (1963). Classification and quantitative judgment. *British Journal of Psychology, 54*, 101–114.

Tanaka, J. W, Curran, T., Porterfield, A. L., & Collins, D. (2006). Activation of preexisting and acquired face representations: The N250 event-related potential as an index of face familiarity. *Journal of Cognitive Neuroscience, 18*, 1488–1497.

Tomelleri, S. & Ito, T. A. (2009). On the flexibility of social perception: Categorization and stereotype activation as functionally independent processes. Unpublished raw data.

Turner, J. C., Hogg, M. A., Oakes, P. J., Reicher, S. D., & Wetherell, M. S. (1987). *Rediscovering the social group: A self-categorization theory*. Oxford: Basil Blackwell.

Valentine, T. (1991). A unified account of the effects of distinctiveness, inversion, and race in face recognition. *Quarterly Journal of Experimental Psychology, 43A*, 161–204.

Valentine, T. & Bruce, V. (1986). The effect of race, inversion and encoding activity upon face recognition. *Acta Psychologica, 61*, 259–273.

Wheeler, M. E. & Fiske, S. T. (2005). Controlling racial prejudice: Social cognitive goals affect amygdala and stereotype activation. *Psychological Science, 16*, 56–63.

Wijers, A., Mulder, G., Okita, T., Mulder, L. J. M., & Scheffers, M. (1989). Attention to color: An analysis of selection, controlled search, and motor activation, using event-related potentials. *Psychophysiology, 26*, 89–109.

Willadsen-Jensen, E. C. & Ito, T. A. (2010). The Effect of Context on Responses to Racially-ambiguous Faces: Changes in Perception and Evaluation. Manuscript under review.

Willadsen-Jensen, E. C. & Ito, T. A. (2008). A foot in both worlds: Asian Americans' perceptions of Asian, White, and racially ambiguous faces. *Group Processes and Interpersonal Relations, 11*, 182–200.

Willadsen-Jensen, E. C. & Ito, T. A. (2006). Ambiguity and the timecourse of racial perception. *Social Cognition, 24*, 580–606.

Wolsko, C. V., Park, B., Judd, C. M., & Wittenbrink, B. (2000). Framing interethnic ideology: Effects of multicultural and color-blind perspectives on judgments of groups and individuals. *Journal of Personality and Social Psychology, 78*, 635–654.

Zarate, M. A., Bonilla, S., & Luevano, M. (1995). Ethnic influences on exemplar retrieval and stereotyping. *Social Cognition, 13*, 145–162.

Zarate, M. A. & Smith, E. R. (1990). Person categorization and stereotyping. *Social Cognition, 8*, 161–185.

Real-world Consequences of Social Deficits: Executive Functions, Social Competencies, and Theory of Mind in Patients with Ventral Frontal Damage and Traumatic Brain Injury

Valerie E. Stone *and* Catherine A. Hynes

Abstract

A variety of brain disorders may give rise to social deficits. Social neuroscience is in a position to help such patients by providing objective methods of defining and measuring social competencies. Such measurements can provide researchers with a more detailed picture of the components of social competencies, assist clinicians in making appropriate treatment recommendations, and provide a foundation for further research into rehabilitation programs tailored to remediating specific and well-defined social difficulties. This chapter reviews existing tools for measuring social competencies, and examines the relationships between these tools and measures of executive functions. In doing so, it discusses the need for more precise use of the terms "executive functions" and "theory of mind."

Keywords: traumatic brain injury, frontal lobes, ventral frontal cortex, orbitofrontal cortex, theory of mind, social competence, social skills, executive functioning, executive function, neuropsychological assessment

Introduction

A variety of brain disorders may give rise to social deficits. Social neuroscience is in a position to help such patients by providing objective methods of defining and measuring social competencies. Such measurements can provide researchers with a more detailed picture of the components of social competencies, assist clinicians in making appropriate treatment recommendations, and provide a foundation for further research into rehabilitation programs tailored to remediating specific and well-defined social difficulties. In this chapter, we review existing tools for measuring social competencies, and examine the relationships between these tools and measures of executive functions. In doing so, we discuss the need for more precise use of the terms "executive functions" and "theory of mind." Because neither refers to a unitary underlying function, we encourage researchers to link the use of these terms to specific tests or sub-processes, to avoid conflation of separable processes. We review several measures of social competence, focusing on tests of the ability to infer others' internal, mental states. The chapter focuses on how these measures have been used with patients who have nonpenetrating traumatic brain injuries (TBI) and/or damage to the ventral frontal cortex, because they are the largest group of patients with acquired brain damage who present with social deficits (Langlois, Rutland-Brown, & Wald, 2006). We find that only Sarcasm/Irony Detection tasks, the Recognition of Faux Pas Task, and The Awareness of Social Inference Test (TASIT) reliably differentiate these patients from healthy matched controls, and correlate with patients' real-world outcomes. Current clinical practice assesses patients with ventral frontal damage and TBI with objective, performance-based measures of *cognitive* abilities, whereas *social* competencies are often assessed with questionnaires or qualitative observations. We encourage social neuroscientists to work with neuropsychologists and neurologists to bring objective assessments of a wide range of social competencies into the clinic, where they can guide rehabilitation, and improve patients' and their loved ones' lives.

Background

As a society, we recognize that someone with a stroke affecting her motor cortex cannot help the fact that she cannot move one side of her body. We recognize that someone with Alzheimer's disease cannot help the fact that he cannot remember who came to visit this morning. With social deficits, however, our society tends not to recognize that some people with neurological damage might have difficulty reading social cues, inhibiting impulses, or being aware of how their social behavior is inappropriate. The general attitude still seems to be that someone who is socially inappropriate has a personal or moral failing.

There is little public education to broadcast a central insight of social neuroscience: Deficits in social behavior can have a neurological origin because parts of the brain are specialized for processing social and emotional information. Those parts of the brain have been called "the social brain" by social neuroscientists, and include frontal and temporal areas (Brothers, 1990). The lay public does not necessarily know about the existence of specialized systems in the brain for social information-processing. When brain injury is called "a hidden disability" (e.g., Abouhamad, 1999), one meaning of that phrase is that people cannot see the source of someone's inappropriate behavior, that they cannot see that the person now has tremendous difficulty controlling impulses, and accurately perceiving social cues. People, even family members and friends, get angry, offended, and may reject the person with a brain injury because they misunderstand the behavior's source. Such social consequences have

profound and potentially long-term effects on patients' quality of life (Langlois et al., 2006; McDonald, Flanagan, Rollins, & Kinch, 2003; Ownsworth & Fleming, 2005; Ponsford, Draper, & Schonberger, 2008). Given that some neurological patients have significant deficits in social judgment and in producing appropriate social behavior, it is imperative that social neuroscientists discuss and measure the real-world consequences of damage to the social brain, and devise and publicize new tools for assssessing problems with social competencies objectively. Social neuroscience must be science in the public interest.

What is Needed to Assess Patients with Social Deficits?

A variety of brain disorders may give rise to social deficits: traumatic brain injury (e.g., Langlois et al., 2006), damage to the amygdala (e.g., Brothers, Ring, & Kling, 1990; Broks et al., 1998; Adolphs, Tranel, & Damasio, 1998; Stone, Baron-Cohen, Calder, Keane, & Young, 2003), damage to the frontal cortex from trauma, surgery, stroke, or frontotemporal dementia (e.g., Stone, 2000; Neary, 1999; Tekin & Cummings, 2002), damage to the cerebellum (e.g., Shevell & Majnemer, 1996; Ozonoff, Williams, Gale, & Miller, 1999), or damage to the temporal lobes (Brothers, 1990; Rosen et al., 2002; Park et al., 2003). The largest group of people who are at risk for social and emotional problems is the group suffering nonpenetrating traumatic brain injuries (TBI; Langlois et al., 2006), causing damage predominantly in the ventral frontal and anterior temporal regions (e.g., Devinsky & D'Esposito, 2004; Levine et al., 2008). Accordingly, here we focus specifically on people with damage to the ventral frontal cortex, also called the orbitofrontal cortex, and people with TBI, including those with focal damage to the ventral frontal cortex. (See Figure 31.1 for diagram of frontal cortex.) The two groups of patients overlap, but are not exactly the same. In many research studies of patients with ventral frontal damage, the most common cause of damage is traumatic brain injury, though some patients may have damage from surgery for tumors, or other sources. (The term "ventromedial frontal damage" means lesions that affect *both* the ventral frontal cortex and medial frontal cortex, —often caused by removal of a tumor. See Figure 31.1.) As noted above, particularly in moderate to severe TBI, damage to the ventral frontal cortex is one of the most common lesion locations. Studies examining the physics of TBI have shown

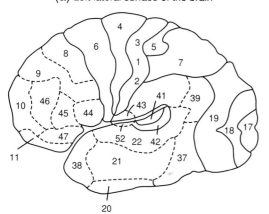
(a) Left lateral surface of the brain

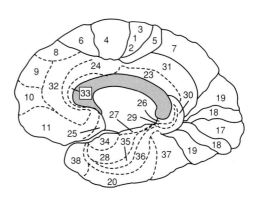
(b) Medial surface of the brain, right hemisphere

Fig. 31.1 The brain, with Brodmann areas marked (anatomical regions determined by differences in cell structure). (a) View of the left hemisphere from the outside (lateral view). Ventral frontal cortex in this view would include primarily Brodmann area 11, but also area 47 and ventral parts of area 10. Dorsolateral prefrontal cortex would include areas 6, 8, 9, and dorsal parts of 10 & 46. (b) View of the right hemisphere from the center of the brain (medial view). Ventral frontal cortex would include Brodmann areas 11, 25 and possibly ventral parts of area 32. Medial frontal cortex would include areas 24, 32, and area 33 (anterior cingulate cortex). Dorsolateral prefrontal cortex would include areas 6, 8, 9 on this medial view.

that the frontal lobes exhibit the most deformation by being compressed forward against the skull, whereas more posterior regions exhibit stretching, which shears fiber pathways (Bayly et al., 2005). Furthermore, as the brain bounces around inside the skull following a severe blow, the bony protrusions in the skull above the eyes, directly below the ventral frontal cortex, can bruise and tear neural tissue, causing focal lesions.

Patients with TBI also have diffuse axonal injury because of stretching and shearing of axons and toxic chemical events started by the trauma that unfold for hours or days after the injury (e.g., Kraus et al., 2007; McCrea, 2007; Kumar et al., 2009). Thus, while people with TBI are at high risk for ventral frontal dysfunction, they are also likely to have difficulties from multiple diffuse injuries affecting various brain regions, potentially leading to several sources of deficits in social competencies and cognition.[1] Therefore, when we say, below, "patients with ventral frontal cortex damage and/or TBI," these two groups should be understood as overlapping but not identical.

Social deficits may result from impairments in multiple cognitive and affective systems, and as yet, we do not have a precise model of all of the systems underlying social behavior. Social neuroscience is a new and burgeoning field for this precise reason: there is much to discover about how the social brain works. Defining social information-processing rigorously is a difficult problem, because so many

processes are involved. For example, patients with ventral frontal damage may suffer from both a difficulty reading other people's emotional expressions (Hornak, et al., 2003; Hornak, Rolls, & Wade, 1996) and a difficulty inhibiting inappropriate remarks in a particular social context (Berlin, Rolls, & Kischka, 2004; Cummings, 1993; Kim, 2002). Although both of these difficulties can be categorized as deficits in the *social* realm, they may result from impairments in different underlying systems, and would entail different types of treatment. In order to get a full picture of the many factors that may influence inappropriate social behavior, clinicians need to assess cognitive *and* social functions.

Psychological assessments can use any of four methods to evaluate a patient's competence in a particular domain. First, performance measures are objective tests requiring patients to demonstrate competence by solving a problem in that domain. Second, informant reports are questionnaires given to caregivers to report on patients' competence. Third, self-reports are questionnaires given to patients to report on their own competence, or are patients' own unstructured, qualitative reports of their experiences. Fourth, clinicians use their own qualitative judgments, or those produced by family and friends to assess certain behaviors.

All four of these methods have value. Some phenomena, such as emotional distress, are inherently subjective, internal experiences, making a self-report necessary to gather this information. Other behaviors, such as easily losing one's temper, may not occur in the presence of strangers or in formal settings, making the behaviors difficult to observe in the clinic or laboratory. Reports about patients' behaviors in multiple settings are a rich source of information, and should continue to be part of assessments of social and emotional problems. Nevertheless, objective, performance-based measures can more precisely describe particular abilities: for instance, does socially inappropriate behavior result from a problem with eye contact, interpreting facial expressions, or making inferences about others' intentions? A clinician's qualitative report about a patient's cognitive abilities such as "the patient seemed bright and solved everyday problems without too much effort" is not taken seriously *by itself* as an assessment of cognition; however, a qualitative report such as "the client was often socially inappropriate and made offensive remarks" is often taken more seriously. We would like to see an increase in the use of performance measures to assess social and emotional abilities, in order to increase the objectivity and utility of these assessments.

Social neuroscience has advanced enough in the last decade to be able to provide clinicians with performance measures of several social and emotional competencies: facial expression recognition, empathy, theory of mind, eye-gaze tracking, emotion regulation, understanding and using language pragmatics. Many of these measures have been used in the experimental literature more than in the clinical literature, and therefore not all measures have population norms gathered in large samples, but there are enough useful social competence tasks for researchers to begin collecting norms. We will review some of these new tasks in this chapter, and recommend some directions for research.

The Interaction of Executive Functions and Social Competencies

Social interaction is cognitively complex and requires multitasking, applying memories to a changing stream of behavior, tracking changes in social context and rewards, selecting behaviors from a range of options, and rapidly changing the focus of attention. Such situations make high demands on executive functions, a group of cognitive abilities including working memory, distraction-suppression, planning, problem-solving and the organization of behavioral output. Functional neuroimaging has revealed that tests of executive functions are associated primarily with activation in dorsolateral frontal regions (e.g., Derrfuss, 2005), rather than ventral frontal regions. (See Figure 31.1 for a diagram of ventral frontal and dorsolateral frontal regions.)

Deficits in executive abilities can cause problems in social interaction, just as they do in other complex tasks. Imagine a common social situation: a group of people are standing together at a party, talking. One man tells a political joke, and while some people in the group laugh, a couple of people frown in disapproval, and an awkward moment ensues. A socially skilled person in the group then changes the topic to something politically neutral. Suppose one woman in the group has a deficit in executive functioning, specifically, a deficit in the ability to shift her attention flexibly. She might continue to focus on the man who told the joke, without shifting her attention to the reactions of the others in the group. She might be puzzled by the change in conversational topic, or might tell another political joke, having missed important social information by not attending to it. An attentional deficit is not specifically social, but, as seen in this example, it can cause social problems. To predict social outcomes for neurological patients with social behavior difficulties, therefore, a clinician will need to assess executive functions thoroughly.

Although it is *necessary* to assess executive functions in people with social deficits caused by neurological damage, it is not *sufficient*. Clinicians must also assess social competencies per se to provide the best information to patients and their families about the difficulties they are likely to encounter, and to provide detailed recommendations for rehabilitation. Certain social competencies might be completely independent of certain executive abilities. Impaired recognition of emotion from facial expressions or voice, or the ability to tell if someone might be cheating in a deal can cause social difficulties even if some executive functions are intact (Stone et al., 2002; Hornak et al., 1996). Researchers have described patients with focal lesions to ventral frontal regions resulting in social dysfunction, but who have some spared executive abilities (e.g., Eslinger & Damasio, 1985; Dimitrov, Phipps, Zahn, & Grafman, 1999; Stone et al., 2002). (The assessments of executive functions in these patients were not exhaustive, and thus some executive deficits may have been missed.) Social and executive skills have also been dissociated in patients with the frontal variant of fronto-temporal dementia, a progressive disease first causing atrophy in the ventral frontal cortex. Such patients present with personality changes and social and emotional disruptions, but generally normal performance on some commonly used tests of executive functions (Gregory, 1999; Lough, Gregory, & Hodges, 2001). Finally, performance on some executive tests does not predict social performance in people with TBI (Milders, Fuchs, & Crawford, 2003). Thus, there is mounting evidence that social and executive functioning are at least partly independent of one another.

The Nature of Executive Functions and the Most Effective Measures

Part of the confusion about executive functions outlined here comes from a tendency in many neuropsychological studies to assess what they call "executive function" (singular), referring to the "function" as if it were the same ability tapped by different tests (e.g., Bach, Happé, Fleminger, & Powell, 2000; Lough et al., 2001; McPherson, Fairbanks, Tiken, Cummings, & Back-Madruga, 2002; Weyandt, 2005). However, the many different tasks used to assess executive functions do not all necessarily intercorrelate and do not all measure the same thing. Thus, "executive function" (singular) is a problematic term because it does not refer to a unitary ability, but rather to a *set* of cognitive abilities. The term was originally introduced to refer to the "central executive," the controller of the short-term memory system, which allocates attentional resources, and off-loads some processing demands to its "slave systems," the articulatory loop and the visuospatial sketch pad (Baddeley, 1981). Since then, "executive functions" has come to mean a collection of cognitive abilities, usually including working memory, sequencing, planning, set-shifting, cognitive flexibility, flexible control of attention, task-switching, establishing a hierarchy of goals, inhibition of competing action programs or cognitive processes, response inhibition and selection, and the application of strategic behavior. Tests of these various abilities are by no means interchangeable.

No one truly claims that there is a unitary "executive function"; it is rather that the term has come to be used as if there were. In fact, factor analyses do not show a unitary factor structure for different tests of executive functions (Pennington, 1997, Burgess, Alderman, Evans, Emslie, & Wilson, 1998; Miyake, Friedman, Emerson, Witzki, & Howerter, 2000; Busch, McBride, Curtiss, & Vanderploeg, 2005). Furthermore, because the results of any given factor analysis of executive functions depend on which particular cognitive tests are included in the analysis, there can be no definitive factor analysis of executive functions. Also, the way that factors from the analyses are named may vary from one research group to another. Nevertheless, there is some overlap in the factors discovered for executive functions. Pennington (1997) analyzed executive functions in a group of typically developing children and children with developmental disorders, and found three factors that were consistent across both groups: 1) working memory, 2) flexibility/set-shifting, and 3) motor inhibition. Researchers using somewhat different tests report a slightly different three-factor solution: 1) information updating and monitoring, 2) set shifting, and 3) inhibition (Miyake et al., 2000). In a large sample of patients with TBI, Busch and colleagues (2005) also found three factors: 1) cognitive control, particularly of material in working memory; 2) higher-order executive functions including both self-generative behavior and cognitive flexibility/set shifting; and 3) error control failures, especially of inhibition of errors. There are clear similarities in the contents of the three sets of three-factor accounts of executive functions. Others, however, have suggested a five-factor structure for executive functions, including 1) inhibition (the ability to suppress a prepotent response); 2) planning (goal-directed planning and execution of behavior, which includes insight); 3) memory organization (temporal sequencing of memory); and 4) positive and 5) negative personality changes that co-occur with the cognitive syndrome (Burgess, et al., 1998). Still others have argued that executive functions can be reduced to working memory, and that compromised working memory affects all executive functions (Braver, Cohen, & Barch, 2002; Miller, 2007).

Some of the same researchers who have investigated the factor structure of executive functions have argued that the original theoretical formulation of executive functions is no longer clinically useful, and that a new set of tests ought to be developed that are focused on functional evaluations and ecological validity (Burgess et al., 2006). We agree, and encourage, at the very least, the use of the plural "executive functions," to denote the multiplicity of cognitive processes that the concept comprises. We would also like to suggest that authors always describe the specific task or function that is implicated in the assessment of executive functions, to add clarity to both research and clinical interpretations. Rather than saying, for example, "executive function was correlated with patients' behavioral problems," a more specific statement such as "perseverative errors on the Wisconsin Card Sorting Test were correlated with patients' scores on the

Neuropsychiatric Index" would be both more accurate and more useful, and would reduce some of the conceptual confusion in the executive functioning literature. Finally, because of the plurality of cognitive abilities summed up by the term "executive functions," clinicians should use multiple tests to assess these multiple abilities (Gioia & Isquith, 2004).

Assessments of Executive Functions in Patients with Ventral Frontal Damage and TBI

Common Tests

Commonly used tests of executive functions include the Trail Making Test, Parts A & B, a test of sequencing and working memory (e.g., Reitan, 1958); verbal fluency tests, such as F-A-S or semantic fluency (e.g., Benton & Hamsher, 1989); nonverbal design fluency tests (e.g., the Design Fluency subtest of the Delis-Kaplan Executive Function System (D-KEFS)); the Stroop color-word interference test, a test of cognitive inhibition (e.g., Stroop, 1935); cognitive estimates tasks, measuring ability to estimate without strong external cues (e.g., Shallice & Evans, 1978); the Wisconsin Card Sorting Test (WCST) or the California Card Sorting Test, measuring several abilities, including set-shifting

(e.g., Berg, 1948; Milner, 1964; Delis, Kaplan, & Kramer, 2001); the Tower of London (e.g., Culbertson & Zillmer, 2001) and the Tower of Hanoi (e.g., Samet & Marshall-Mies, 1987), measuring sequencing and planning, Go/No-go tasks, measuring inhibition (e.g., Robertson, Manly, Andrade, Baddeley, & Yiend, 1997); and the Hayling Sentence Completion Test, measuring inhibition (Burgess & Shallice, 1997). There are also batteries, such as the Delis-Kaplan Executive Function Battery (D-KEFS; Delis et al., 2001), which contain a number of these tasks as subtests. Among these performance-based measures of frontal lobe functions, each task has different strengths and weaknesses (see Table 31.1).

Available norms on tests

Appropriate normative data that are stratified by age and education are available for Trail Making (Strauss et al., 2006), Verbal Fluency (Strauss, Sherman, & Spreen, 2006), and Card Sorting tests (Heaton, Chelune, Talley, Kay, & Curtiss, 1993; Delis et al., 2001). Norms stratified by age alone are available for the Stroop (e.g., Delis et al., 2001) and Tower Tests (Delis et al., 2001; Culbertson & Zillmer, 2001). Unstratified norms are available for Go/No-go (Dubois, Slachevsky, Litvan, & Pillon, 2000) and the Hayling Sentence Completion tests

Table 31.1 Comparison of Commonly Used Tests of Executive Functions

Neuropsychological Test	Normative Data Stratified By	Neuroanatomical Correlates	Links to Functional Outcome
Trail Making Test	Age, Education	Dorsolateral prefrontal cortex	Activities of Daily Living
Verbal Fluency	Age, Education	Frontal, temporal, parietal lobes	Activities of Daily Living
Stroop Test	Age	Dorsolateral and dorsomedial prefrontal cortex	Treatment Outcome Measures*
Card Sorting Tests	Age, Education	Dorsolateral prefrontal and parietal cortices	Need for Supervision, Functional Status at Hospital Discharge
Hayling Sentence Completion	Unstratified Separate norms for older adults	Frontal lobes	Caregiver Questionnaire of Functional Outcome
Tower Tests	Age	Frontal and parietal lobes.	None
Behavioral Assessment of Dysexecutive Function	Unstratified, No Scaled Scores for Subtests	Non-specific Brain Damage	+ Caregiver Questionnaire of Functional Outcome
Go/No Go Test	Unstratified	Ventral prefrontal cortex	Everyday Action Slips

Summary of neuropsychological tests of frontal lobe function in terms of the availability of appropriate norms, neuro-anatomical correlates of task performance, and correlations with measures of functional outcome. * in Modified versions of the Stroop Task; + inconsistent finding.

(Burgess & Shallice, 1997). For the Hayling, norms have been collected separately for older adults (Bielak et al., 2006). For cognitive estimates tests, norms for adults (Axelrod & Millis, 1994) and older adults (Gillespie, Evans, Gardener, & Bowen, 2002) are available.

Brain regions involved in tests

Not all of the tests have specific neuroanatomical correlates, and not all are sensitive to TBI or ventral frontal damage. There is evidence indicating no specific association between frontal damage and performance on cognitive estimates tests (Taylor & O'Carroll, 1995). Tower tests and card sorting tests have frontal *and* parietal lobe involvement, and verbal fluency tests are associated with broad networks including the frontal, temporal and parietal lobes (e.g., Baldo, Schwartz, Wilkins, & Dronkers, 2006; Barcelo, 2001). Neuroimaging and patient studies of the Stroop test suggest it is associated with superior medial frontal and inferior lateral frontal regions rather than ventral frontal cortex proper (e.g., Stuss, et al., 2001; Demakis, 2004). Patient studies of Trails A & B show that completion time on Trails B, not errors, seems to be the most sensitive measure, but even that is sensitive to damage in dorsolateral prefrontal cortex rather than ventral frontal cortex (Stuss, et al., 2001; Demakis, 2004). Several studies show sensitivity to frontal damage on most but not all subtests of the D-KEFS (e.g., Delis, Kramer, Kaplan, & Holdnack, 2004; Keil, Baldo, Kaplan, Kramer, & Delis, 2005; McDonald, Delis, Norman, Tecoma, & Iragui, 2005), and the Verbal Fluency and Category Switching subtests seem to be sensitive to TBI, with mixed results for the Design Fluency subtest (Strong Tiesma, & Donders, 2010; Varney et al., 1996) and ventral frontal damage (Boone et al., 1999). On the more positive side, the Hayling Sentence Completion Test is associated with damage to the frontal lobes generally rather than specifically ventral damage (Burgess & Shallice, 1997), but it is one of the executive tests most sensitive to TBI[1] (Ponsford et al., 2008). Poor performance on Go/No-go tests is associated with TBI and damage to the ventral frontal cortex (e.g., Gagnon, Bouchard, Rainville, Lecours, & St-Amand, 2006; Robertson et al., 1997).

Links to real-world outcomes

The most notable gap in the development of many of these executive tests is the absence of studies linking the tests with real-world functional outcomes. By functional outcome, we mean some measure of the patient's adjustment in daily life, for example, assessing the ability to drive, make friends, hold a job, or assessing real-world behavioral problems. Test manuals rarely include studies investigating these properties of the tests, in spite of how crucial such information is for clinicians. For some tests, researchers have established such links, and we hope that people developing tests in the future will investigate real-world correlates of poor test performance as a routine and necessary part of test development. To our knowledge, there are no studies establishing a link between performance on tower tests or cognitive estimates tests and real-world functioning. Only modified, treatment-specific versions of the Stroop task have been associated with treatment outcomes (Carpenter, Schreiber, Church, & McDowell, 2006; Carter, Bulik, McIntosh, & Joyce, 2000). The Trail-Making and Verbal Fluency tests have been linked to the ability to perform activities of daily living in older adults (Cahn-Weiner, Boyle, & Malloy, 2002). The Wisconsin Card Sorting Test has been linked to the need for supervision and to employment status (Benge, Caroselli, & Temple, 2007; Greve, Bianchini, Hartley, & Adams, 1999; Moritz, et al., 2005). The Hayling test correlates with patients' functional status as reported by a caregiver in a structured interview (Odhuba, van den Broek, & Johns, 2005), and the Go/No-Go task has been linked to everyday action slips (Robertson, et al., 1997).

Linking test performance to functional outcome is perhaps the most important of all aspects of test development. While the absence of norms may necessitate qualitative evaluations of test performance, and a lack of anatomical specificity may mean that corroborative neuroimaging is required for lesion-localization, an absence of a relationship between task performance and patients' real world functioning makes the value of the test questionable. When clinicians or researchers use tests of executive functions that are insensitive to ventral frontal damage or TBI, they risk failing to identify such patients' real lack of competency, or failing to find associations that might be there if more appropriate tests were used. Patients with brain injuries may be denied disability benefits if the cognitive tests used do not capture their particular difficulties. Thus, we strongly encourage clinicians and researchers to use only those executive tests most likely to be sensitive to TBI and/or ventral frontal damage with such patients.

Finally, when clinicians and researchers limit assessment of patients with ventral frontal damage or TBI to assessment only of cognitive, executive functions, they may miss one of the most important areas of disability. The limitation to cognitive assessments has serious, real-world consequences. Patients whose deficits are more social and emotional than cognitive may be denied benefits, and in some cases, they may even be accused of "malingering" because the way in which they were tested does not capture their disability (e.g., Eslinger & Damasio, 1985). Thus, more widespread use of objective measures of social competence is necessary for patients to be treated appropriately.

Performance Measures of Social Competencies in Patients with Ventral Frontal Damage and TBI

As with the assessment of executive functions (Gioia & Isquith, 2004), it will be necessary to measure multiple abilities in order to accurately assess a person's social competence. In the following section, we review some of the tasks developed for this purpose, and evaluate the clinical utility of these tests according to two criteria of central importance in neuropsychological test development (Ardila, Ostrosky-Solis, & Bernal, 2006): whether the tasks are sensitive to the difficulties present in neurological patients who present with social difficulties, specifically, ventral frontal damage or TBI, and whether performance on these tasks has been associated with real-world social functioning (Burgess et al., 2006). Our purpose here is to identify the measures that are most useful for assessments of social competencies from those that are currently available.

Theory of Mind Tasks in Patients with Ventral Frontal Damage and TBI

Several researchers have looked at theory of mind (ToM) in patients with ventral frontal damage, with the idea that deficits in ToM might underlie the patients' social difficulties. The term "theory of mind" suffers from many of the same conceptual problems as the term "executive function": 1) in practice, in the field of neuropsychology, it refers to a set of abilities rather than a unitary ability; 2) a variety of tasks are used to test it; 3) not all of these tasks measure the same ability; and 4) not everyone agrees that ToM is a distinct cognitive module (e.g., Stone & Gerrans, 2006). Furthermore, different groups of researchers use the term to mean different things. In the social neuroscience literature, ToM has often been construed broadly as "the ability to infer others' mental states" (Stone et al., 2003; Bibby & McDonald, 2005; Shamay-Tsoory & Aharon-Peretz, 2007;

Shamay-Tsoory, Tomer, Berger, Goldsher, & Aharon-Peretz, 2005; Shamay-Tsoory, Tomer, Berger, & Aharon-Peretz, 2003; Stone, 2007). "Mental states" might include intentions, thoughts, beliefs, emotions, focus of attention, and attitudes. Within developmental and cognitive psychology, however, ToM has a more narrow usage, referring *only* to the ability to do metarepresentation, that is, the ability to understand that mental states of knowledge and belief represent the world, and thus that such mental states can be mistaken (e.g., Baron-Cohen, Leslie, & Frith, 1985; Saxe, Carey, & Kanwisher, 2004; Stone & Gerrans, 2006). In the developmental/cognitive psychology view, "theory of mind" means *only* inferring others' knowledge and beliefs, and specifically excludes inferences about affective mental states (Leslie & Frith, 1990). As detailed below, there is little evidence that patients with ventral frontal damage are specifically impaired in belief understanding and metarepresentation. Their difficulties instead seem to be with understanding others' intentions and feelings.

The tasks that different researchers use to assess ToM demonstrate differences in how they use the term. With a narrow definition of ToM, as in the developmental/cognitive psychology view, the only valid task is a false belief task (see details below), in which the researcher tests whether the participant can infer when someone else's belief state is mistaken. In contrast, with the broader definition of ToM used in most social neuroscience research, tasks examining inferences about intention, attention, sarcasm, empathy, as well as false beliefs have all been used as measures of ToM (Stone, 2007; Stone & Gerrans, 2006). These tasks may involve listening to or seeing brief stories, cartoons, or pictures, and then inferring characters' intentions, feelings, focus of attention, and beliefs, or recognizing when something awkward has been said. Several different tests, besides false belief tests, are used for testing the understanding of others' mental states (see Table 31.2), and we will discuss each one in more detail below. If ToM is more broadly defined to include inferences about mental states such as intentions, feelings, and focus of attention, patients with ventral frontal damage and TBI can be shown to have ToM deficits.

False Belief Tasks-Understanding of Knowledge and Belief
Description of the Task
False belief tasks ask participants to make an inference about what a story character would think or

Table 31.2 Summary of Tests of Theory of Mind in Terms of Social Competences Measured, Sensitivity to Ventral Frontal Damage or TBI, and Correlations with Measures of Functional Outcome

Name of Test	Social Competences Measured	Test Performance Affected by TBI or Frontal Damage?	Links to Functional Outcome
False belief	Inferring contents of others' knowledge and beliefs	No	No*
Charlie & the Chocolates (Cognitive Version)	Inferring intentions or language reference from eye gaze	Maybe ventral frontal damage from FTD**	Not tested
Charlie & the Chocolates (Affective Version)	Inferring desires from eye gaze	No	Not tested
Reading the Mind in the Eyes-Original Version	Inferring cognitive & affective mental states from eyes	Ventral frontal damage from FTD	No
Happé's Strange Stories (& variants)	Inferring thoughts, beliefs, intentions	Inconsistent results, maybe ventromedial frontal damage	Not tested
Strange Stories-Affective Version	Inferring feelings	No	Not tested
Sarcasm/Irony	Detecting sarcasm or irony by inferring intentions and/or feelings	TBI, ventral frontal damage	Not tested
Faux Pas Recognition	Inferring beliefs, intentions, feelings	TBI, ventral frontal damage	Neuropsychiatric Index Scores (NPI), & maybe Neuropsychology Behavior & Affect Profile
Cartoon tests	Inferring beliefs, intentions	Inconsistent results	No

* Only second-order false belief tasks were related to Neuropsychiatric Index Scores, not first-order false belief; thus the correlation could result from the working memory demands of second-order tasks.

** FTD = frontotemporal dementia. Unknown whether FTD patients did poorly on this test because of social competence deficits or cognitive inhibitory deficits—no control condition run.

believe in a situation in which the story character's belief could be mistaken. A common type of false belief task is a "location-change" task, in which a story character puts an object away, say in a drawer, and then leaves the room. Another character moves the object when the first cannot see, and later the first character comes back into the room. The key question is where the first character now thinks the object is, or where she will look for the object. The methods involve either showing the participant the story in pictures, reading it to them, or having them read the story. Then participants answer questions about the character's belief, as well as control questions testing for memory, comprehension, and (in some cases) inferential abilities (e.g., Stone et al., 1998).

There are also different "orders" of false belief tests. In a first-order false belief test, one is simply

asked what the first character thinks or believes, testing understanding of, say, "Maria thinks that [X is true]." In a second-order task, another level of embedding is added, testing understanding of, say, "Jose thinks that Maria thinks that [X is true]." For example, if Maria put an object away and left the room, the story might depict her peeking back through a keyhole and seeing Jose move the object to another location. In that case, Maria would not hold a false belief about the object, but Jose would hold a false belief about Maria's belief, thinking that she didn't know where it was moved to (Baron-Cohen, 1995). This process can be extended to further levels of embedding. A third-order task would test understanding of statements such as "Katrin thinks that Alex believes that Katrin does not know that Alex is having an affair." Higher orders are possible, but after three levels of embedding, the working memory demands of parsing the embedded clauses make the task extremely difficult. It has not been established that second- or third-order false belief tests truly test a greater level of ability to infer *mental states*; instead, they may simply add greater linguistic and working memory demands to the first-order task (Stone, 2007).

Relationship to Ventral Frontal Damage and TBI
Results on frontal patients' performance on false belief tasks are mixed, and there is a good methodological reason for these mixed results. Sound methodology requires controlling for other, non-ToM factors involved in performance on ToM tasks (Bibby & McDonald, 2005; Stone, 2005; Stone, et al., 1998). ToM tasks require not only an intact capacity to metarepresent beliefs, but also an intact ability to make inferences, intact working memory, and inhibition of one's own belief state or personal preference to determine someone else's belief state or preference (Carlson & Moses, 2001; Henry, Phillips, Crawford, Ietswaart, & Summers, 2006; Stone, 2005; Stone et al., 1998; Stone & Gerrans, 2006).

Where the working memory demands of false belief tasks have been controlled for, for instance by placing pictures depicting the sequence of events in front of the participant throughout the session, deficits on false belief tasks are not always evident (Bibby & McDonald, 2005; Gregory, Lough, Stone, Erzinclioglu, Martin, Baron-Cohen, & Hodges, 2002; Muller, Simion, Reviriego, Galera, Mazaux, Barat, & Joseph, 2010; Stone et al., 1998). Stone et al. (1998) found that patients with orbitofrontal damage were at ceiling on false belief tasks on all conditions, and that patients with dorsolateral frontal damage had no deficits when the working memory demands were lowered. Gregory et al. (2002) found that patients with ventral frontal atrophy from frontotemporal dementia performed best on first-order false belief tasks across three different ToM tasks. Stone and Baron-Cohen tested 5 patients with ventral frontal damage on first-, second- and third-order false belief tasks with control tasks requiring first-, second- and third-order non-mentalistic inferences, and found that the patients were not specifically impaired on the false belief tasks compared to the control tasks, though higher orders of embedding were more difficult on both types of task (Stone, 2007). Bibby and McDonald (2005) tested whether TBI patients could understand false beliefs, controlling for working memory with Digit Span (backwards), and found no evidence for specific deficits on these tasks in the patient group.

Failing to control for working memory demands might include using video versions of the tasks, or versions where the action is acted out in some other way, so that the patient has to rely on working memory to keep track of what happened when and to whom. Where the working memory demands have *not* been controlled for, some studies have found deficits on false belief tasks (Stuss, 2001; Fernandez-Duque, Baird, & Black, 2008), and others have not (Shamay-Tsoory & Aharon-Peretz, 2007; Shamay-Tsoory, Tomer, et al., 2005; Snodgrass & Knott, 2006). Shamay-Tsoory, Tomer, et al. (2005) used second-order false belief tasks, and found that patients with ventromedial frontal lesions had no difficulty with these tasks.

Thus, for false belief tasks, which narrowly test for understanding of others' knowledge and belief states, there is scant evidence that patients with frontal lobe damage or TBI have deficits (Stone & Gerrans, 2006). In contrast, patients with posterior lesions in the temporal-parietal junction have specific difficulty with false belief tasks and other tests of metarepresentation, controlling for language, working memory, and inhibitory task demands (Apperly, Samson, Chiavarino, Bickerton, & Humphreys, 2007; Apperly, Samson, Chiavarino, & Humphreys, 2004; Apperly, Samson, & Humphreys, 2005).

Links to Functional Outcome
In frontotemporal dementia patients, Gregory et al. (2002) measured behavioral disturbance and functional problems using the Neuropsychiatric Index (NPI), an index of behavioral problems common in dementia patients, such as problems with inhibition, motivation, and aggression (Cummings et al., 1994). First-order false belief tasks were not related to NPI scores, but second-order false belief tasks did predict NPI scores. It is possible that second-order false belief scores reflected working memory deficits rather than ToM deficits, because of the memory load involved in parsing embedded clauses in higher-order false belief tasks (Gregory et al., 2002). To our knowledge, no other researchers have investigated the relationship between false belief understanding and patient's functioning.

The Charlie and the Chocolates Test–Inferences About Intention and Eye Gaze
Description of the Task
This test, originally designed for children who are too young to pass false belief tests, investigates whether participants can determine desire for,

intention towards, or attention to an object from the eye-gaze direction of a cartoon character (Baron-Cohen, 1995). Typically, the response is chosen from four options. A cartoon character in the center of the display, "Charlie," looks at one of four objects arrayed around him. The participant is asked, "Which one does Charlie want?" or "Which one will Charlie take?" Young children also use adults' direction of eye gaze to determine which object an unfamiliar word refers to, so in this task, if the stimuli are meaningless shapes, the experimenter can ask a question about which shape Charlie is referring to with a novel nonsense word when he looks at it, by asking, for example, "Which one does Charlie say is the bleb?" (Baron-Cohen, 1995).

Shamay-Tsoory and Aharon-Peretz (2007) created "cognitive" and "affective" versions of this task. A "cognitive" item showed the character looking at an object, and asked something like, "Yoni is thinking of _____ " (which one)? An "affective item would ask something like, "Yoni loves _____ " (which one)? They also created second-order versions of the items that probed understanding of a character thinking about a toy that another character likes, or liking/not liking a toy that another character likes.

Relationship to Ventral Frontal Damage and TBI
In addition to testing the ability to infer desire or intention from eye gaze, the Charlie and the Chocolates task has significant inhibitory demands. In order to tell the experimenter that the cartoon character intends to, say, take a particular chocolate bar he is looking at, the participant must suppress her desire for her own preferred chocolate bar (Stone, 2005). Thus, although Snowden and colleagues (2003) found that frontotemporal dementia patients were impaired on the task, it is difficult to know whether the impairment was due to deficits in inhibition or in mental state inference.

Shamay-Tsoory and Aharon-Peretz (2007) gave their version of this task to three groups of patients, one group with dorsolateral frontal lesions, one with ventromedial frontal lesions (including some lesions that extended back to temporal cortex), and one with posterior lesions, as well as age-matched healthy controls. No group differences were evident on the basic version of the task, but in the second-order condition, patients with ventromedial damage were significantly impaired relative to the healthy controls. However, no significant differences were reported between the group with ventromedial damage, and those with dorsolateral frontal or posterior damage. Patients with left frontal lesions (whether ventral or dorsolateral) scored significantly lower on the affective items on this task compared to the cognitive items. Thus, evidence that this task is sensitive and specific to ventral frontal damage is not strong.

Relationship to functional outcome
To our knowledge, no one has yet investigated the relationship between this task and behavioral problems or adjustment in patients.

The Reading the Mind in the Eyes Test—Original Version
Description of the Task
This test is often used as a ToM test (Gregory et al., 2002; Henry, Phillips, Crawford, Ietswaart, & Summers, 2006; Milders, Fuchs, & Crawford, 2003; Stone et al., 2003; Torralva et al., 2007). Some confusion in the literature results from there being two versions of the test. The *original version* of the test (Baron-Cohen et al., 1997) includes not only 17 items asking about subtle emotional states, but also 8 items asking about more cognitive mental states—intention or focus of attention (e.g., "noticing you/ignoring you," "observing/daydreaming," Stone et al., 2003). The original version also had only two response choices, making it more difficult to distinguish participants' performance from chance. The *revised version* (Reading the Mind in the Eyes-R, Baron-Cohen, Wheelwright, Hill, Raste, & Plumb, 2001) eliminates all items that ask about focus of attention or intention, and has items only about subtle emotional states. It also has four response choices instead of two. Because the revised version asks only for inferences about emotional states, researchers categorize it as a measure of emotion recognition, rather than a ToM task. Emotion recognition is not considered to be ToM by many researchers, because it is more automatic than inferences about beliefs, knowledge, or attention, develops earlier, and does not require the same kinds of representations (Leslie & Frith, 1990; Stone, 2003).

Relationship to Ventral Frontal Damage and TBI
In Gregory et al's (2002) study, using the original version of the test, patients with ventral frontal atrophy from frontotemporal dementia had deficits on both affective and nonaffective items compared to healthy controls and patients with Alzheimer's disease. Reading the Mind in the Eyes did not correlate with any other ToM tasks in this study,

neither first- and second-order false belief, nor Faux Pas Recognition (described below).

Milders, Fuchs, and Crawford (2003) and Henry et al. (2006) found that patients with TBI were impaired on the revised emotion-recognition version of the task, and Torralva et al. (2007) found that frontotemporal dementia patients were also impaired on the revised task. Although all authors used the phrase "theory of mind" in the titles of their papers, they used the *revised* version of the task, and thus these patients may have had deficits in emotion-recognition rather than deficits in other kinds of mental state inference.

Links to Functional Outcome

In frontotemporal dementia patients, Gregory et al. (2002) found no relationship between NPI scores as a measure of behavioral disturbance, and scores on the original version of Reading the Mind in the Eyes. To our knowledge, no one else has looked at the association between the original version of the Eyes task and behavioral outcomes for patients with ventral frontal damage or TBI.

Happé's Strange Stories Test and Variants–Mixed Mental State Inferences

Description of the Task

Some story-based tasks are not specific to particular kinds of inferences about others' internal states, such as belief, but instead look at participants' ability to infer several mental states from a verbal story, that is, a story characters' thoughts, feelings, and intentions (Channon, Pellijeff, & Rule, 2005; Happé, 1994; Shamay-Tsoory & Aharon-Peretz, 2007; Shamay-Tsoory, Tomer, & Aharon-Peretz, 2005a). In Happé's Strange Stories test (1994), participants read a brief story in which a character does something, such as a spy telling a lie to deceive his interrogators, or a person telling a white lie about how nice someone's awful new haircut looks. (For examples, see pp. 12–13 in Gallagher et al., 2000.) Questions following the story probe whether the participant understood the story character's intentions (e.g., Why did the person say the haircut looked good?), beliefs, or feelings. Control stories and questions about those stories require non-mentalistic inferences, for example, inferences about physical processes.

Shamay-Tsoory et al. (2007) created a version with brief stories that asked either about what a story character thinks about another character's *beliefs* (second-order false belief) or what a story character thinks about how another character *feels*, which they called second-order affective ToM,

and thus they could compare what they called "cognitive" and "affective" ToM.

Relationship to Ventral Frontal Damage and TBI

Little evidence exists that performance on this task is impaired by ventral frontal damage, specifically. Snowden et al. (2003) found that patients with ventral frontal damage from FTD were not impaired on mental-state stories compared to control stories on this task. Shamay-Tsoory and Aharon-Peretz (2007), on their affective versus cognitive mental states version of the task, found that there were no differences between patients with ventromedial frontal or posterior lesions or controls on the cognitive version, but that ventromedial frontal patients were significantly impaired relative to patients with posterior lesions on affective items.

Patients with TBI have also been tested on versions of this task. Bibby and McDonald (2005) presented TBI patients with a Stories task, controlling for working memory and language demands, but found no deficits specific to the ToM stories as opposed to control stories in patients. Channon, Pellijeff, and Rule (2005) found that TBI patients were not impaired on mentalistic items relative to healthy controls when they had to choose the correct response from four choices, but TBI patients did have selective difficulty interpreting mentalistic actions in the stories compared to physical actions. Bach et al. (2000), in a case study of a TBI patient, found that he performed as well as both older and younger controls. They note his particular strength in making affective inferences about story characters' feelings. Although their findings are of limited use because they did not compare patients to controls, Bach and David (2006) found that performance on the task predicted TBI patients' social self-awareness. Social self-awareness was measured by self-other rating discrepancies on the Patient Competency Rating Scale, a scale measuring behavioral problems and how well a patient can manage independent living.

For reported results on tasks of this type to make sense, researchers must report not just a total score for the task, but also separate scores for each type of mental state asked about, for example, a "feelings inference score," an "intentions inference score," a "beliefs inference score." Because these tasks assess the understanding of several kinds of mental states, a total score is difficult to interpret. A patient could be impaired in inferring others' intentions, for example, but not impaired in inferring feelings or vice versa. Indeed, people with TBI and people with ventral frontal damage seem to be more impaired in inferring intentions or feelings than they are in inferring others' false beliefs (Stone, 2005). As further evidence of dissociability in these abilities, evidence suggests that emotional perspective-taking is associated with ventral frontal activation, whereas nonemotional perspective-taking is not (Hynes, Baird, & Grafton, 2006). Thus, it would be useful to have results on these tasks reported by type of mental state inference.

There is only one study with clear evidence showing that tasks of this type are sensitive to ventral frontal damage or TBI (Shamay-Tsoory & Aharon-Peretz, 2007), and several studies showing that it is not (Bach, et al., 2000; Bibby & McDonald, 2005; Snowden et al., 2003). We can make sense of these different findings by considering that Shamay-Tsoory and Aharon-Peretz (2007) make distinctions between type of mental state inference in reporting their results. The patients in Shamay-Tsoory and Aharon-Peretz (2007) were required to make either cognitive or affective inferences about others' mental states, and the demonstrated deficit was only in affective inferences. Thus, the type of mental state (feeling, belief, intention) about which patients make inferences is crucial to interpreting the patients' scores or group differences. We encourage other researchers to report results on these tasks as a "feelings inference score," an "intentions inference score," a "beliefs inference score," not just a total score, so that the type of inference that is difficult for the patient is clear.

Links to Functional Outcome
Thus far, there are no indications that performance on this task relates to patients' functional outcomes, though little research has been done investigating that question. Bach and David (2006) found no significant difference in performance on Happé's Strange Stories test between "behaviorally disturbed" and "non-behaviorally disturbed participants." Behavioral disturbance was operationalized as relatives' ratings of the patients on the Patient Competency Rating Scale, a measure of behavioral problems and how well a patient can manage independent living. The absence of a strong relationship between these tasks and measures of functional outcome in TBI patients is consistent with the fact that patients with TBI are often able to perform well on the task.

Detection of Sarcasm/Irony Tasks
Description of the Tasks
These tasks are quite similar to Happé's Strange Stories task, but with the items restricted to understanding story characters' use of sarcasm (also called

irony in some studies), that is, saying the opposite of what they mean. For example, it is sarcastic to say, when someone has clumsily dropped something, "You're so graceful" or "Why don't you go into neurosurgery?" The participant reads a story, and is asked why someone said what they said, when the utterance was sarcastic, or what someone meant by such an utterance (Channon, et al., 2005; Channon, et al., 2007; McDonald & Pearce, 1996; Shamay-Tsoory & Aharon-Peretz, 2007; Shamay-Tsoory, Tomer, & Aharon-Peretz, 2005; Shamay-Tsoory, Tomer, Berger, Goldsher, & Aharon-Peretz, 2005). Control stories may contain a sincere utterance. The stories are presented in writing, so that tone-of-voice cues do not give away when a character is being sarcastic. Sarcasm comprehension may tap into an understanding of others' intentions, and the social context, because the participant has to understand the speaker's true intention, separate from the literal content of the speaker's statement. An advantage of these tasks over the Strange Stories tasks is that sarcasm-comprehension tasks test understanding of intentions, rather than many different types of mental states.

Relationship to Ventral Frontal Damage and TBI
Several studies have demonstrated that this task is sensitive to ventral frontal damage and TBI. Patients with TBI are impaired in understanding sarcasm as opposed to sincere statements, relative to healthy controls (Channon et al., 2005; McDonald & Pearce, 1996). Patients with ventral frontal lesions are also impaired in understanding sarcasm, but not sincere statements, compared to patients with posterior lesions, dorsolateral frontal lesions, or healthy controls (Shamay-Tsoory, Tomer, & Aharon-Peretz, 2005; Shamay-Tsoory, Tomer, Berger, et al., 2005). There was no significant relationship between sarcasm-comprehension deficits and frontal or posterior lesion size in another study (Shamay-Tsoory et al., 2005b) Kosmidis et al. (2008) found patients with frontotemporal dementia were impaired at using paralinguistic cues to detect sarcasm or lies, but could perform well when more verbal cues indicating sarcasm were given. Thus, many studies confirm that this task differentiates people with TBI from healthy controls, and people with ventral frontal damage from those with dorsolateral frontal lesions, posterior damage, and healthy controls.

Links to Functional Outcome
No studies, to our knowledge, have investigated the relationship of performance on sarcasm detection

tasks to patients' behavioral outcomes or ability to engage in activities of daily living. Shamay-Tsoory, Tomer, Berger, et al.(2005), however, did find that greater depression, as indicated by scores on the Beck Depression Inventory, was a strong predictor of lower sarcasm-comprehension scores, though the difference between ventral frontal patients and posterior lesion and healthy control groups could not be attributed to depression scores. This finding implies that the aspects of impaired social competence measured by sarcasm tasks may contribute to social rejection and depression.

Cartoon Tasks
Description of the Tasks
Cartoon tasks have the advantage of testing mental state inferences without requiring comprehension of a verbal story. They use a small number of visual cartoons that require an inference about a character's feelings, intentions, focus of attention, or beliefs to understand the joke (Gallagher et al., 2000; Happé et al., 1999). Control cartoons require a physical inference to get the joke, for example three (presumably blind) mice are asleep in a bed with three tiny pairs of sunglasses on the nightstand. (For examples, see page 14 in Gallagher et al., 2000.) Participants view each cartoon and explain why it is funny. Responses on each are scored from 0 to 3 points, depending on the relevance and correctness of the answer. Responses can also be scored for how many mental state terms are used in explaining the cartoon. A related task asks participants to look at a pair of cartoons, one of which is funny, the other of which is not, and choose the funny one (Happé et al., 1999). Half of the cartoons require mental state inferences to get the joke, and half do not.

As with the Strange Stories Task, these tasks examine the understanding of several types of mental states, such as intentions, beliefs, or focus of attention. One cartoon is funny because of focus of attention: a man is looking at a piano bench that has crashed onto the sidewalk, and has not noticed the piano hurtling towards him from above. Another is funny because of a character's lack of knowledge/false belief: an astronomer does not realize he has black rings around his eyes because his colleagues have put black charcoal around the eye piece of the telescope he has been looking through. Again, we encourage researchers to report scores broken down by type of mental state inference required (intentions, knowledge, belief, feelings, focus of attention). About two-thirds of the items in the version used by Happé and colleagues (1999), however,

do seem to depend on false belief. Thus, a total score on this version of the task can reasonably be interpreted as primarily reflecting false belief understanding.

Relationship to Ventral Frontal Damage and TBI
Attempts to link performance on this task to frontal lobe lesions or TBI have produced inconsistent results. Snowden et al. (2003) found that patients with ventral frontal atrophy from frontotemporal dementia produced fewer mental state verbs in their responses to this task, and made more errors in interpreting mental state cartoons versus control cartoons when compared to patients with Huntington's and to healthy controls. When Bibby and McDonald (2005) controlled for working memory deficits using digits backwards from Digit Span, TBI patients showed a deficit specific to mental state inferences on the cartoon task. Milders et al. (2006) found no deficit specific to mental state inferences in TBI patients relative to neurologically healthy controls with orthopedic injuries on the cartoon task when the patients were tested shortly after injury, but scores for the mentalistic cartoons were correlated with scores on Alternating Fluency, a test of cognitive flexibility in which participants generate words in categories, alternating between three categories. Cartoon task scores were not correlated with severity of TBI (as measured by Glasgow Coma Scale scores). One year later, the same TBI patients showed a significant improvement in performance on the mentalistic cartoons relative to the orthopedic controls. Milders et al. (2008) also used the cartoon task with only mental-state cartoons to test another group of TBI patients. TBI patients were significantly impaired relative to matched controls with only orthopedic injuries both soon after their injuries and at one-year follow-up. Bach and David (2006) found that performance on this task predicted TBI patients' social self-awareness (as measured by self-other rating discrepancies on the Patient Competency Rating Scale), but their study did not compare patients to controls, so they provide no information as to its sensitivity to TBI. They also report that performance on both Happé's Strange Stories and cartoon tasks was "associated with a limited number of executive function tests" (Bach & David, 2006 p. 407), but report neither which tests they used, nor the correlations. Because performance on cartoon-based tasks may be affected by many non-ToM factors (working memory, some executive functions, and perceptual abilities), researchers should partial out other cognitive differences in

patient groups. Because results on sensitivity of cartoon-based tasks to ventral frontal damage and TBI are mixed, clinicians may not find these tasks most useful for testing patients' social competencies.

Links to Functional Outcome

The little research that has been done testing the relationship between cartoon task performance and functional outcomes for patients indicates no relationship. Milders et al. (2006) found no relationship between a composite measure consisting of cartoon task performance and Faux Pas Recognition task performance, and informant ratings on the Katz Adjustment Scale, which measures social behavior problems, whether shortly after injury or at one-year follow-up. Bach and David (2006) found no significant difference in performance between TBI participants who were "behaviorally disturbed" and those who were not, with behavioral disturbance measured as relatives' ratings of the patients on the Patient Competency Rating Scale.

Faux Pas Recognition Task

Description of the Task

A faux pas is an awkward or insulting statement made unintentionally. The task involves reading a brief story out loud while the patients read along on their own copy. In the faux pas stories, someone says something awkward or insulting, while in the control stories a minor conflict occurs, but no faux pas (Gregory, et al., 2002; Stone, et al., 1998). The patient has a copy of the story in front of them to reduce any memory demands. Several questions are asked that assess whether the participant understands that something awkward has been said, why it was inappropriate to say it, that it was said unintentionally, and that one character might have felt bad as a result of the faux pas. Control comprehension questions test for general comprehension of story facts, apart from mental state understanding. Although this measure was originally introduced as a measure of ToM (Gregory, et al., 2002; Stone, et al., 1998), it measures multiple abilities: false belief understanding, empathy, inferences about intentions, knowledge of appropriate social behavior, as well as language comprehension. Stone (2000; 2005) has noted that ventral frontal patients typically make three types of errors: 1) *faux pas errors*: failing to detect a faux pas, or a false faux pas identification in the control stories; 2) *intentionality errors*: noticing that something awkward has been said, but stating that it was said intentionally instead

of accidentally; or 3) *appropriateness errors*: failing to identify the reason that the comment was inappropriate. As noted in the false belief section above, it seems unlikely that ventral frontal patients cannot track false beliefs, as they generally perform at or close to ceiling on false belief tasks. Their faux pas errors on the Recognition of Faux Pas Test sometimes reflect a difficulty inferring that something hurtful has been said, perhaps because they do not notice the "oohhh!" gut response that most people experience when hearing such stories, because of impaired physiological responsivity caused by TBI (e.g., de Sousa, McDonald, Rushby, Li, Dimoska, & James, 2010). At other times, their errors reflect a difficulty tracking others' intentions, resulting in the misperception that the comment was deliberate (intentionality errors), or a difficulty perceiving what would lead to others' distress (appropriateness errors), resulting in failure to detect the faux pas. Such errors are rarely made by controls without brain damage (Gregory, et al., 2002; Stone, 2000; Stone, et al., 1998).

Interpretation of the Recognition of Faux Pas Test in the literature is made more difficult by differences in how the errors are reported. Researchers do report faux pas errors (see hit rates and correct reject rates in Gregory, et al., 2002), but it is rare for researchers to report differences between intentionality errors and appropriateness errors (but see Stone, et al., 1998). These two types of errors tend to be lumped together into a "composite score" or a "follow-up questions score" (Gregory, et al., 2002; Lough & Hodges, 2002; Milders, et al., 2003; Milders, et al., 2006; Shamay-Tsoory, Tomer, Berger, et al., 2005; Torralva, et al., 2007). Detailed reporting of all responses on the test is important for determining the cause of the failure to detect the faux pas, and it appears, from studies that report information broken down by question type, that patients make appropriateness errors, that is, not understanding why the faux pas was awkward or inappropriate, and intentionality errors, that is, not understanding that the faux pas was unintentional (Stone, et al., 1998; Torralva, et al., 2007).

The faux pas task has been found to be independent of the effects of depression in patients with frontal damage (Shamay-Tsoory, Tomer, Berger, et al., 2005). It has been found to correlate with perseverative errors on the Wisconsin Card Sorting Test, but not with other scores on the Wisconsin, nor with verbal fluency (Gregory, et al., 2002). It also may measure something distinct from emotion-based decision-making, as it did not correlate with performance on the Iowa Gambling Task in frontotemporal dementia patients (Torralva, et al., 2007).

Relationship to Ventral Frontal Damage and TBI

The Recognition of Faux Pas Test has often been used in patients with ventral frontal damage from FTD, TBI, or other causes, and researchers have found that such patients are impaired on recognition of faux pas, but not items testing story comprehension (Gregory, et al., 2002; Lough & Hodges, 2002; Milders, et al., 2003; Milders, et al., 2006; Shamay-Tsoory, Tomer, & Aharon-Peretz, 2005; Stone, et al., 1998; Torralva, et al., 2007). Patients with TBI are more impaired on faux pas detection than either patients with dorsolateral prefrontal cortex lesions, those with more posterior damage, or non-brain-injured controls; they often fail to identify social faux pas, and they erroneously label non-faux pas as faux pas (Milders, et al., 2003; Shamay-Tsoory, Tomer, & Aharon-Peretz, 2005; Stone, et al., 1998). They do not, however, appear to exhibit similar impairments on comprehension of the stories in the task (Gregory, et al., 2002; Milders, et al., 2003; Milders, et al., 2006; Stone, et al., 1998). A longitudinal study showed that patients with TBI were impaired on the Recognition of Faux Pas Test an average of two months post-injury, and remained impaired relative to healthy controls one year later (Milders, et al., 2006). There was some improvement in Faux Pas scores over the year, but this improvement was equivalent in patients and controls. A second longitudinal study looked only at the intentionality question on the Faux Pas test, because that was found to best differentiate patients and controls (Milders et al., 2008). Patients with TBI were significantly impaired on the intention question both soon after TBI and at a one-year follow-up (Milders et al., 2008).

Links to Functional Outcome

Faux pas scores were significantly correlated with behavioral disturbances in frontotemporal dementia patients, as measured by the NPI, (r = −.64, Gregory, et al., 2002). Faux pas scores were substantially, but not significantly correlated with behavioral outcomes in patients with TBI (r = −.61, Milders, et al., 2003), with behavioral outcomes measured using relatives' ratings on the Neuropsychology Behavior and Affect Profile, a questionnaire rating indifference, social inappropriateness, poor communication pragmatics, depression, and

mania. However, neither soon after the occurrence of TBI nor at one-year follow-up did Milders et al. (2008) find a correlation between a composite ToM measure including Faux Pas scores and cartoon task scores, and TBI patients' informant-rated behavioral problems on three different rating scales. In patients with schizophrenia, Faux Pas scores significantly predict community functioning, and are better predictors than are cognitive measures (Pijnenborg, Withaar, Evans, van den Bosch, Timmerman, & Browner, 2009).

Conclusions about ToM Tests in Ventral Frontal and TBI Patients

Of the theory of mind tasks reviewed above, sarcasm detection tasks and the Recognition of Faux Pas Task seem to be the most sensitive to ventral frontal damage and TBI. Both are also correlated with some outcome measures: depression in the case of sarcasm tasks (Shamay-Tsoory, Tomer, Berger, et al., 2005), or behavioral disturbances, in the case of the Recognition of Faux Pas Task (Gregory et al., 2002; Milders et al., 2003). In contrast, there is no strong evidence that false belief tasks, cartoon tasks, story tasks, the Reading the Mind in the Eyes task, or the Charlie and the Chocolates task are consistently sensitive to ventral frontal damage or TBI, nor do any of these measures show correlations with patient outcomes.

In order for sarcasm detection tasks and the Recognition of Faux Pas Task to be clinically useful, the next step in research must be to develop population norms by age, gender, and ethnicity. Without norms to compare an individual client's score to, clinicians cannot tell whether that person is performing as expected or is impaired. Collecting norms for various cultures and subcultures is essential when a test measures social inferences, because subtle cultural differences can affect the way social situations are interpreted.

Theory of mind tests, however, tap into only one type of social competence. They generally use static stimuli or stories, and as such, are quite different from the demands of a dynamic social interaction, in which information is processed rapidly, online, and comes from multiple input sources, including dynamic facial, postural, and prosodic cues. Accordingly, other researchers have developed video-based social inference tasks that improve upon the ecological validity of ToM tasks. One promising video-based tool has been developed out of research on sarcasm detection.

The Awareness of Social Inference Test (TASIT)

Description of the Task

TASIT requires emotion recognition and lie- and sarcasm- detection from video-taped stimuli of actors engaged in social interactions (McDonald, Flanagan, & Rollins, 2002). The authors propose that the Emotion Evaluation Test represents an improvement over previous emotion-recognition measures because the emotional expressions on TASIT are spontaneous, rather than posed, and the dynamic nature of the stimuli allows for the complexity of real-life emotional expressions, including the natural tendency to regulate or conceal a strongly-felt emotion (McDonald, Flanagan, Rollins, & Kinch, 2003). The Social Inference portions of the task consist of short video clips of actors engaging either in sincere or counter-factual exchanges, that is, sarcasm or lies. The context of the statement indicates whether the speaker's meaning is the opposite of what was said (sarcasm or lying), or is sincere. Responses are scored according to four comprehension questions, probing aspects of intention, belief, and emotion (McDonald, et al., 2002). Questions all have yes/no/don't know responses, and are scored as correct or incorrect. Australian norms are available for all three subtests of TASIT (McDonald, Flanagan, & Rollins, 2001).

Relationship to Ventral Frontal Damage and TBI

TASIT was administered to twenty-one people with TBI, and twenty-one age- gender- and education-matched controls (McDonald, Flanagan, Martin, & Saunders, 2004). All measures of TASIT differentiated people with TBI from healthy controls, whereas people with TBI had no difficulty with comprehension of literal statements in the social inference sections of TASIT.

TASIT performance has also been associated with performance on an emotion-recognition task using photographs, a false-belief task, and a social problem-solving task, showing good convergent validity (McDonald et al., 2006). Measures of verbal and visual memory and working memory correlated with TASIT performance as well, however, suggesting that TASIT relies on basic cognitive abilities as well as socially specific skills (McDonald et al., 2006).

To our knowledge, TASIT has not yet been tested in patients with known ventral frontal damage, rather than just a diagnosis of TBI, or in patients with ventral frontal atrophy from frontotemporal dementia. We would predict it to be useful with such patients.

Links to Functional Outcome

TASIT's relationship with real-life social skills was established by demonstrating an association between TASIT scores and structured ratings of social interactions of the participants with TBI (McDonald et al., 2004). Other research has shown that TASIT performance is associated with duration of post-traumatic amnesia and post-injury employment status (McDonald & Flanagan, 2004), and with communication competence (Watts & Douglas, 2006). One social skills training intervention, however, did not improve TASIT scores (McDonald et al., 2008).

Conclusions

Overall, TASIT represents a promising beginning to the development of clinically useful and well-validated measures of social abilities. Across studies, there was variability in both the level and the quality of difficulties exhibited by people with TBI; some struggled with emotions, others struggled with sarcasm/deception inferences, emphasizing the need to have multi-dimensional assessments of social abilities (McDonald & Flanagan, 2004), as we have with cognitive abilities. Thus, although TASIT samples two or three domains of social inference abilities, it would be useful to have tasks that assess a wider range of social inferences than just emotion recognition, deception, and sarcasm.

Possible Future Directions for Applied Social Neuroscience

Social neuroscience has an opportunity to offer tremendous benefits to neurological patients suffering from social deficits, by providing objective ways to define and measure social competence. Many patients with TBI and/or ventral frontal damage suffer long-term consequences to their well-being because of their social deficits, and new developments in this field can help guide clinicians in designing effective rehabilitation programs to improve social functioning in everyday life. There has been a lag between empirical developments in social neuroscience that generate objective, performance-based measures of social competence and clinicians' making use of these measures when assessing social competence. This lag exists partly because many such measures do not have published norms. Clinicians rely on norms to tell them what the expected score on a test would be for a person of the same age, gender, socioeconomic status, and ethnicity. Of the social measures reviewed above, only The Awareness of Social Inference Test (TASIT) has norms available, for primarily white Australians, though versions of the test are now being created for North American and Dutch clients (McDonald, personal communication, 2010). Clinical assessment of patients with TBI or frontal damage instead relies heavily on cognitive performance measures of executive functions, because norms are readily available, while relying on more qualitative or questionnaire-based measures of social and emotional functioning. Clinicians doing rehabilitation, however, are well aware of the need to address social competences, and some treatment programs for TBI address social behavior particularly (e.g., Dahlberg et al., 2007). Social neuroscientists and neuropsychologists therefore have an opportunity to increase the application of their research by 1) collecting norms on social competence performance measures developed; and 2) in patient studies, including measures of real-world functional outcome, so that clinicians can prioritize tests that predict patients' level of coping in their everyday lives.

The purpose of neuropsychological assessments is to make recommendations about a patient's functional status. If a test is insensitive to TBI or ventral frontal damage and uncorrelated with patient outcomes, we should be asking ourselves, "Should this test be included in assessment batteries?" There is considerable time and cost involved in neuropsychological testing, and patients often find it unpleasant, tiring, and frustrating. Therefore, test selection should be parsimonious and the assessments should produce information that has practical, real-world relevance for the purpose of informing treatment recommendations. For these reasons, we encourage researchers and clinicians to work together to investigate the utility of currently used tests, and produce and use new neuropsychological tests that have broad, stratified normative data, empirically demonstrated neuroanatomical correlates, and empirically established associations with real-world functional difficulties. Tests that do not meet these criteria should be re-evaluated and possibly dropped from neuropsychological assessments.

There are many tests of "theory of mind" in the research literature, such as false belief tests and cartoon ToM tests, for which there is no empirical evidence of sensitivity to ventral frontal damage or TBI. In addition, more data linking performance on ToM tests to actual social performance should be gathered; tests that relate to real-world social functioning are valuable regardless of whether the tests are sensitive to specific regions of brain damage.

Despite these problems, two types of ToM tests do seem promising. TBI and ventral frontal damage do seem to impair performance on the Recognition of Faux Pas Task and Sarcasm/Irony Detection tasks, and there are some data linking these tests to functional outcomes. As an ecologically valid extension of Sarcasm tasks, the TASIT is promising as a clinical measure of some social competencies, with norms, solid validation, and links to real-world social competence. The scope of social competencies that these tests measure, however, are limited.

We encourage researchers and clinicians to work together to produce and use objective performance measures of a wide range of specific social competencies, not just the tests of inferring others' internal states reviewed here, but also, for example, the ability to track the intimacy level of the people one is interacting with before disclosing information, to track relative social status and select behavior appropriately, to monitor reciprocity and fairness in interactions, and to understand and act on conversation partner's needs for turn-taking and relevance.

For patients' and their loved ones' best interests, neuropsychological assessments should be geared towards creating treatment programs that may include 1) education for both the patient and the family about key areas of loss in competencies, 2) adopting strategies to manage any difficulties, and 3) retraining some functions. To improve care of patients with social deficits following TBI and/or ventral frontal damage, rehabilitation programs must have a detailed picture of an individual's strengths and weaknesses in a range of social competencies. The TASIT is already available for clinical use. With further research to collect norms and study how tests are related to everyday outcomes, some of the other social competence tests reviewed here could become available for clinical use in the near future, thus improving the assessment and subsequent treatment of social dysfunction following brain damage. Patients and their families would benefit enormously from such progress in social neuroscience research.

Note

1 Their study investigated long-term cognitive difficulties in 60 patients with TBI and 43 controls using logistic regression, and also found that among *non-executive* cognitive tests, the Symbol-Digit Modalities Test, the Rey Auditory Verbal Learning Test, and the Sustained Attention to Response Test best differentiated TBI patients from controls (Ponsford et al., 2008).

References

Abouhamad, J. (1999). Acquired brain injury: The hidden disability. *Literacy Broadsheet*, *54*, 31–33.

Adolphs, R., Tranel, D., Damasio, A. R. (1998). The human amygdala in social judgment. *Nature*, *393*, 470–4.

Apperly, I. A., Samson, D., Chiavarino, C., Bickerton, W.-L., & Humphreys, G. W. (2007). Testing the domain-specificity of a theory of mind deficit in brain-injured patients: Evidence for consistent performance on non-verbal, "reality-unknown" false belief and false photograph tasks. *Cognition*, *103*(2), 300–321.

Apperly, I. A., Samson, D., Chiavarino, C., & Humphreys, G. W. (2004). Frontal and temporo-parietal lobe contributions to theory of mind: Neuropsychological evidence from a false-belief task with reduced language and executive demands. *Journal of Cognitive Neuroscience*, *16*, 1773–1784.

Apperly, I. A., Samson, D., & Humphreys, G. W. (2005). Domain-specificity and theory of mind: Evaluating neuropsychological evidence. *Trends in Cognitive Sciences*, *9*(12), 572–577.

Ardila, A., Ostrosky-Solis, F., & Bernal, B. (2006). Cognitive testing toward the future: The example of Semantic Verbal Fluency (ANIMALS). *International Journal of Psychology*, *41*(5), 325–332.

Axelrod, B. N. & Millis, S. R. (1994). Preliminary standardization of the Cognitive Estimation Test. *Assessment*, *1*(3), 269–274.

Bach, L. J. & David, A. S. (2006). Self-awareness after acquired and traumatic brain injury. *Neuropsychological Rehabilitation*, *16*(4), 397–414.

Bach, L. J., Happé, F., Fleminger, S., & Powell, J. (2000). Theory of mind: Independence of executive function and the role of the frontal cortex in acquired brain injury. *Cognitive Neuropsychiatry*, *5*(3), 175–192.

Baddeley, A. (1981). The concept of working memory: A view of its current state and probable future development. *Cognition*, *10*(1-3), 17–23.

Baldo, J. V., Schwartz, S., Wilkins, D., & Dronkers, N. F. (2006). Role of frontal versus temporal cortex in verbal fluency as revealed by voxel-based lesion symptom mapping. *Journal of the International Neuropsychological Society*, *12*(6), 896–900.

Barcelo, F. (2001). Does the Wisconsin Card Sorting Test measure prefrontal function? *The Spanish Journal of Psychology*, *4*(1), 79–100.

Baron-Cohen, S. (1995). *Mindblindness: An essay on autism and theory of mind*. Cambridge, MA: MIT Press.

Baron-Cohen, S., Leslie, A. M., & Frith, U. (1985). Does the autistic child have a "theory of mind"? *Cognition*, *21*(1), 37–46.

Baron-Cohen, S., Wheelwright, S., Hill, J., Raste, Y., & Plumb, I. (2001). The "Reading the mind in the eyes" Test revised version: A study with normal adults, and adults with Asperger syndrome or high-functioning autism. *Journal of Child Psychology and Psychiatry*, *42*(2), 241–251.

Baron-Cohen, S., Wheelwright, S., & Jolliffe, T. (1997). Is there a "language of the eyes"? Evidence from normal adults, and adults with autism or Asperger syndrome. *Visual Cognition*, *4*(3), 311–331.

Bayly, P. V., Cohen, T. S., Leister, E. P., Ajo, D., Leuthardt, E. C., & Genin, G. M. (2005). Deformation of the human brain induced by mild acceleration. *Journal of Neurotrauma*, *22*(8), 845–856.

Benge, J. F., Caroselli, J. S., & Temple, R. O. (2007). Wisconsin Card Sorting Test: Factor structure and relationship to productivity and supervision needs following severe traumatic brain injury. *Brain Injury*, *21*(4), 395–400.

Benton, A. & Hamsher, K. (1989). *Multilingual aphasia examination*. Iowa City: AJA Associates.

Berg, E. A. (1948). A simple objective treatment for measuring flexibility in thinking. *Journal of General Psychology*, *39*, 15–22.

Berlin, H. A., Rolls, E. T., & Kischka, U. (2004). Impulsivity, time perception, emotion and reinforcement sensitivity in patients with orbitofrontal cortex lesions. *Brain*: *127*(5), 1108–1126.

Bibby, H. & McDonald, S. (2005). Theory of mind after traumatic brain injury. *Neuropsychologia*, *43*(1), 99–114.

Bielak, A. A. M., Mansueti, L., Strauss, E., & Dixon, R. A. (2006). Performance on the Hayling and Brixton tests in older adults: Norms and correlates. *Archives of Clinical Neuropsychology*, *21*(2), 141–149.

Boone, K. B., Miller, B. L., Lee, A., Berman, N., Sherman, D., & Stuss, D. T. (1999). Neuropsychological patterns in right versus left frontotemporal dementia. *Journal of the International Neuropsychological Society*, *5*(7), 616–622.

Braver, T, Cohen, J. D., & Barch, D. M. (2002). The role of prefrontal cortex in normal and disordered cognitive control: A cognitive neuroscience perspective. In D. T. Stuss & R. T. Knight (Eds.), *Principles of frontal lobe function*, (pp. 428–447). New York: Oxford University Press.

Broks, P., Young, A. W., Maratos, E. J., Coffey, P. J., Calder, A. J., Isaac, C. L., et al. (1998). Face processing impairments after encephalitis: Amygdala damage and recognition of fear. *Neuropsychologia*, *36*(1), 59–70.

Brothers, L. (1990). The social brain: A project for integrating primate behavior and neurophysiology in a new domain. *Concepts in Neuroscience*, *1*(1), 27–51.

Brothers, L., Ring, B., & Kling, A. (1990). Response of neurons in the macaque amygdala to complex social stimuli. *Behavioral Brain Research*, *41*(3), 199–213.

Burgess, P. W., Alderman, N., Evans, J., Emslie, H., & Wilson, B. A. (1998). The ecological validity of tests of executive function. *Journal of the International Neuropsychological Society*, *4*(6), 547–558.

Burgess, P. W., Alderman, N., Forbes, C., Costello, A., Coates, L. M., Dawson, D. R., et al. (2006). The case for the development and use of "ecologically valid" measures of executive function in experimental and clinical neuropsychology. *Journal of the International Neuropsychological Society*, *12*(2), 194–209.

Burgess, P. & Shallice, T. (1997). *The Hayling and Brixton Tests*. Bury St Edmunds: Thames Valley Test Company.

Busch, R. M., McBride, A., Curtiss, G., & Vanderploeg, R. D. (2005). The components of executive functioning in traumatic brain injury. *Journal of Clinical and Experimental Neuropsychology*, *27*(8), 1022–1032.

Cahn-Weiner, D. A., Boyle, P. A., & Malloy, P. F. (2002). Tests of executive function predict instrumental activities of daily living in community-dwelling older individuals. *Applied Neuropsychology*, *9*(3), 187–191.

Carlson, S. M. & Moses, L. J. (2001). Individual differences in inhibitory control and children's theory of mind. *Child Development*, *72*(4), 1032–1053.

Carpenter, K. M., Schreiber, E., Church, S., & McDowell, D. (2006). Drug Stroop performance: Relationships with primary substance of use and treatment outcome in a drug-dependent outpatient sample. *Addictive Behaviors*, *31*(1), 174–181.

Carter, F. A., Bulik, C. M., McIntosh, V. V., & Joyce, P. R. (2000). Changes on the Stroop test following treatment: Relation to word type, treatment condition, and treatment outcome among women with bulimia nervosa. *International Journal of Eating Disorders, 28*(4), 349–355.

Channon, S., Pellijeff, A., & Rule, A. (2005). Social cognition after head injury: Sarcasm and theory of mind. *Brain and Language, 93*(2), 123–134.

Channon, S., Rule, A., Maudgil, D., Martinos, M., Pellijeff, A., Frankl, J., et al. (2007). Interpretation of mentalistic actions and sarcastic remarks: Effects of frontal and posterior lesions on mentalising. *Neuropsychologia, 45*(8), 1725–1734.

Culbertson, W. & Zillmer, E. (2001). *Tower of London- Drexel University Technical Manual.* Toronto, Canada: Multi-Health Systems Inc.

Cummings, J. L. (1993). Frontal-subcortical circuits and human behavior. *Archives of Neurology, 50*(8), 873–880.

Cummings, J. L., Mega, M., Gray, K., Rosenberg-Thompson, S., Carusi, D. A., & Gornbein, J. (1994). The Neuropsychiatric Inventory: Comprehensive assessment of psychopathology in dementia. *Neurology, 44*, 2308–2314.

Dahlberg, C. A., Cusick, C. P., Hawley, L. A., Newman, J. K., Morey, C. E., Harrison-Felix, C. L., et al. (2007). Treatment efficacy of social communication skills training after traumatic brain injury: A randomized treatment and deferred treatment controlled trial. *Archives of Physical Medicine & Rehabilitation, 88*(12), 1561–73.

de Sousa, A, McDonald, S, Rushby, J, Li, S, Dimoska, A, & James, C (2010). Understanding deficits in empathy after traumatic brain injury: The role of affective responsivity. *Cortex*, Mar 1. (E-publication ahead of print; DOI: 10.1016/j.cortex.2010.02.004).

Delis, D. C., Kaplan, E., & Kramer, J. H. (2001). *The Delis-Kaplan Executive Function System: Technical Manual.* San Antonio: The Psychological Corporation.

Delis, D. C., Kramer, J. H., Kaplan, E., & Holdnack, J. (2004). Reliability and validity of the Delis-Kaplan Executive Function System: An update. *Journal of the International Neuropsychological Society, 10*(2), 301–303.

Demakis, G. J. (2004). Frontal lobe damage and tests of executive processing: A meta-analysis of the Category Test, Stroop Test, and Trail-Making Test. *Journal of Clinical and Experimental Neuropsychology, 26*(3), 441–450.

Derrfuss, J., Brass, M., Neumann, J., & von Cramon, D. Y. (2005). Involvement of the inferior frontal junction in cognitive control: Meta-analyses of switching and Stroop studies. *Human Brain Mapping, 25*(1), 22–34.

Devinsky, O. & D'Esposito, M. (2004). *Neurology of cognitive and behavioral disorders* (Vol. 68). New York: Oxford University Press.

Dimitrov, M., Phipps, M., Zahn, T. P., & Grafman, J. (1999). A thoroughly modern gage. *Neurocase, 5*(4), 345–354.

Dubois, B., Slachevsky, A., Litvan, I., & Pillon, B. (2000). The FAB: A frontal assessment battery at bedside. *Neurology, 55*(11), 1621–1626.

Eslinger, P. J. & Damasio, A. R. (1985). Severe disturbance of higher cognition after bilateral frontal lobe ablation: patient EVR. *Neurology, 35*(12), 1731–1741.

Fernandez-Duque, D., Baird, J. A., & Black, S. E. (2008) False-belief understanding in frontotemporal dementia and Alzheimer's disease. *Journal of Clinical and Experimental Neuropsychology, 31*(4), 489–497.

Gagnon, J., Bouchard, M.-A., Rainville, C., Lecours, S., & St-Amand, J. (2006). Inhibition and object relations in borderline personality traits after traumatic brain injury. *Brain Injury, 20*(1), 67–81.

Gallagher, H. L., Happé, F., Brunswick, N., Fletcher, P. C., Frith, U., & Frith, C. D. (2000). Reading the mind in cartoons and stories: An fMRI study of 'theory of mind' in verbal and nonverbal tasks. *Neuropsychologia, 38*(1), 11–21.

Gillespie, D. C., Evans, R. I., Gardener, E. A., & Bowen, A. (2002). Performance of older adults on tests of cognitive estimation. *Journal of Clinical and Experimental Neuropsychology, 24*(3), 286–293.

Gioia, G. A. & Isquith, P. K. (2004). Ecological assessment of executive function in traumatic brain injury. *Developmental Neuropsychology, 25*(1–2), 135–58.

Gregory, C. A. (1999). Frontal variant of frontotemporal dementia: A cross-sectional and longitudinal study of neuropsychiatric features. Psychological Medicine, 29(5), 1205–17.

Gregory, C., Lough, S., Stone, V., Erzinclioglu, S., Martin, L., Baron-Cohen, S., et al. (2002). Theory of mind in patients with frontal variant frontotemporal dementia and Alzheimer's disease: Theoretical and practical implications. *Brain, 125*(Pt 4), 752–764.

Greve, K. W., Bianchini, K. J., Hartley, S. M., & Adams, D. (1999). The Wisconsin Card Sorting Test in stroke rehabilitation: Factor structure and relationship to outcome. *Archives of Clinical Neuropsychology, 14*(6), 497–509.

Happé, F., Brownell, H., & Winner, E. (1999). Acquired "theory of mind" impairments following stroke. *Cognition, 70*(3), 211–240.

Happé, F. G. E. (1994). An advanced test of theory of mind: Understanding of story characters' thoughts and feelings by able autistic, mentally handicapped, and normal children and adults. *Journal of Autism and Developmental Disorders, 24*(2), 129–154.

Heaton, R., Chelune, G., Talley, J., Kay, G., & Curtiss, G. (1993). *Wisconsin Card Sorting Test Manual, eevised and expanded.* U.S.A.: Psychological Assessment Resources, Inc.

Henry, J. D., Phillips, L. H., Crawford, J. R., Ietswaart, M., & Summers, F. (2006). Theory of mind following traumatic brain injury: The role of emotion recognition and executive dysfunction. *Neuropsychologia, 44*(10), 1623–1628.

Hornak, J., Bramham, J., Rolls, E. T., Morris, R. G., O'Doherty, J., Bullock, P. R., et al. (2003). Changes in emotion after circumscribed surgical lesions of the orbitofrontal and cingulate cortices. *Brain, 126*(7), 1691–1712.

Hornak, J., Rolls, E. T., & Wade, D. (1996). Face and voice expression identification in patients with emotional and behavioural changes following ventral frontal lobe damage. *Neuropsychologia, 34*(4), 247–261.

Hynes, C. A., Baird, A. A., & Grafton, S. T. (2006). Differential role of the orbital frontal lobe in emotional versus cognitive perspective taking. *Neuropsychologia, 44*, 374–383.

Keil, K., Baldo, J., Kaplan, E., Kramer, J., & Delis, D. C. (2005). Role of frontal cortex in inferential reasoning: Evidence from the Word Context Test. *Journal of the International Neuropsychological Society, 11*(4), 426–433.

Kim, E. (2002). Agitation, aggression, and disinhibition syndromes after traumatic brain injury. *NeuroRehabilitation, 17*(4), 297–310.

Kosmidis, M. H., Aretouli, E., Bozikas, V.P., Giannakou, M., & Ioannidis, P. (2008). Studying social cognition in patients with schizophrenia and patients with frontotemporal dementia: Theory of mind and the perception of sarcasm. *Behavioral Neurology*, 19(1–2), 65–9.

Kraus, M. F., Susmaras, T, Caughlin, B. P., Walker, C. J., Sweeney, J. A., & Little, D. M. (2007). White matter integrity and cognition in chronic traumatic brain injury: A diffusion tensor imaging study. *Brain*, 130(10), 2508–19.

Kumar, R., Husain, M., Gupta, R. K., Hasan, K. M., Haris, M., Agarwal, A. K., et al. (2009). Serial changes in the white matter diffusion tensor imaging metrics in moderate traumatic brain injury and correlation with neuro-cognitive function. *J Neurotrauma*, 26(4), 81–95.

Langlois, J. A., Rutland-Brown, W., & Wald, M. M. (2006). The epidemiology and impact of traumatic brain injury: A brief overview. *Journal of Head Trauma Rehabilitation*, 21(5), 375–378.

Leslie, A. M. & Frith, U. (1990). Prospects for a cognitive neuropsychology of autism: Hobson's choice. *Psychological Review*, 97, 114–21.

Levine, B., Kovacevic, N., Nica, E. I., Cheung, G., Gao, F., Schwartz, M. L., & Black, S.E. (2008). The Toronto traumatic brain injury study: Injury severity and quantified MRI. *Neurology*, 70(10), 771–778.

Lough, S. & Hodges, J. R. (2002). Measuring and modifying abnormal social cognition in frontal variant frontotemporal dementia. *Journal of Psychosomatic Research*, 53(2), 639–646.

Lough, S., Gregory, C., & Hodges, J. R. (2001). Dissociation of social cognition and executive function in frontal variant frontotemporal dementia. *Neurocase*, 7(2), 123–130.

McCrea, M. A. (2007). *Mild traumatic brain injury and postconcussion syndrome: The new evidence base for diagnosis and treatment.* New York: Oxford University Press.

McDonald, C. R., Delis, D. C., Norman, M. A., Tecoma, E. S., & Iragui, V. J. (2005). Discriminating patients with frontal-lobe epilepsy and temporal-lobe epilepsy: Utility of a multilevel design fluency test. *Neuropsychology*, 19(6), 806–813.

McDonald, S. Personal communication to Valerie Stone, October 12, 2010.

McDonald, S., Bornhofen, C., Shum, D., Long, E., Saunders, C., & Neulinger, K. (2006). Reliability and validity of The Awareness of Social Inference Test (TASIT): A clinical test of social perception. *Disability and Rehabilitation: An International, Multidisciplinary Journal*, 28(24), 1529–1542.

McDonald, S. & Flanagan, S. (2004). Social perception deficits after traumatic brain injury: Interaction between emotion recognition, mentalizing ability, and social communication. *Neuropsychology*, 18(3), 572–579.

McDonald, S., Flanagan, S., Martin, I., & Saunders, C. (2004). The ecological validity of TASIT: A test of social perception. *Neuropsychological Rehabilitation*, 14(3), 285–302.

McDonald, S., Flanagan, S., & Rollins, J. (2001). *The Awareness of Social Inference Test.* Sydney, Australia: Harcourt Assessment.

McDonald, S., Flanagan, S., & Rollins, J. (2002). *The Awareness of Social Inference Test.* Bury St Edmonds, UK: Thames Valley Test Company.

McDonald, S., Flanagan, S., Rollins, J., & Kinch, J. (2003). TASIT: A new clinical tool for assessing social perception after traumatic brain injury. *Journal of Head Trauma Rehabilitation*, 18(3), 219–238.

McDonald, S. & Pearce, S. (1996). Clinical insights into pragmatic theory: Frontal lobe deficits and sarcasm. *Brain and Language*, 53(1), 81–104.

McDonald, S., Tate, R., Togher, L., Bornhofen, C., Long, E., Gertler, P., & Bowen, R. (2008). Social skills treatment for people with severe, chronic acquired brain injuries: A multicenter trial. *Archives of Physical Medicine & Rehabilitation*, 89(9), 1648–59.

McPherson, S., Fairbanks, L., Tiken, S., Cummings, J. L., & Back-Madruga, C. (2002). Apathy and executive function in Alzheimer's disease. *Journal of the International Neuropsychological Society*, 8(3), 373–81.

Milders, M., Fuchs, S., & Crawford, J. R. (2003). Neuropsychological impairments and changes in emotional and social behaviour following severe traumatic brain injury. *Journal of Clinical & Experimental Neuropsychology*, 25(2), 157–172.

Milders, M., Ietswaart, M., Crawford, J. R., & Currie, D. (2006). Impairments in theory of mind shortly after traumatic brain injury and at 1-year follow-up. *Neuropsychology*, 20(4), 400–408.

Milders, M., Ietswaart, M., Crawford, J. R., & Currie, D. (2008). Social behavior following traumatic brain injury and its association with emotion recognition, understanding of intentions, and cognitive flexibility. *Journal of the International Neuropsychological Society*, 14(2), 318–26. Erratum in: *Journal of the International Neuropsychological Society*, 2008, 14(3):508.

Miller, B. L. (2007). The human frontal lobes: An introduction. In B. L. Miller & J. L. Cummings, (Eds.), (pp. 1–11), *The human frontal lobes: Functions and disorders.* New York: Guilford Press.

Milner, B. (1964). Some effects of frontal lobectomy in man. In J. M. Warren & K. Akert (Eds.), *The frontal granular cortex and behavior: A symposium* (pp. 313–334). New York: McGraw-Hill.

Miyake, A., Friedman, N. P., Emerson, M. J., Witzki, A. H., & Howerter, A. (2000). The unity and diversity of executive functions and their contributions to complex "frontal lobe" tasks: A latent variable analysis. *Cognitive Psychology*, 41(1), 49–100.

Moritz, S., Kloss, M., Jacobsen, D., Fricke, S., Cuttler, C., Brassen, S., et al. (2005). Neurocognitive impairment does not predict treatment outcome in obsessive-compulsive disorder. *Behaviour Research and Therapy*, 43(6), 811–819.

Muller, F, Simion, A, Reviriego, E, Galera, C, Mazaux, JM, Barat, M, Joseph, PA. (2010) Exploring theory of mind after severe traumatic brain injury. *Cortex*, 46(9), 1088–99.

Neary, D. (1999). Overview of frontotemporal dementias and the consensus applied. *Dementia & Geriatric Cognitive Disorders*, 10 Suppl 1, 6–9.

Odhuba, R. A., van den Broek, M. D., & Johns, L. C. (2005). Ecological validity of measures of executive functioning. *British Journal of Clinical Psychology*, 44(2), 269–278.

Ownsworth, T. & Fleming, J. (2005). The relative importance of metacognitive skills, emotional status, and executive function in psychosocial adjustment following acquired brain injury. *Journal of Head Trauma Rehabilitation*, 20(4), 315–32.

Ozonoff, S., Williams, B. J., Gale, S., & Miller, J. N. (1999). Autism and autistic behavior in Joubert syndrome. *Journal of Child Neurology*, 14(10), 636–41.

Park, N. W., Conrod, B., Hussain, Z., Murphy, K. J., Rewilak, D., & Black, S. E. (2003). A treatment program for individuals with deficient evaluative processing and consequent impaired social and risk judgement. *Neurocase*, 9(1), 51–62.

Pennington, B. F. (1997). Dimensions of executive functions in normal and abnormal development. In N. A. Krasnegor, G. R. Lyon, & P. S. Goldman-Rakic (Eds.), *Development of the prefrontal cortex: Evolution, neurobiology, and behavior.* (pp. 265–281). Baltimore, MD: Paul H Brookes Publishing.

Pijnenborg, G. H. M., Withaar, F. K., Evans, J. J., van den Bosch, R. J., Timmerman, M. E., & Browner, W. H. (2009). The predictive value of measures of social cognition for community functioning in schizophrenia: Implications for neuropsychological assessment. *Journal of the International Neuropsychological Society, 15*(2), 239–247.

Ponsford, J., K. Draper, & M. Schonberger, (2008). Functional outcome 10 years after traumatic brain injury: Its relationship with demographic, injury severity, and cognitive and emotional status. *Journal of the International Neuropsychological Society, 14*(2), 233–42.

Reitan, R. (1958). Validity of the Trail Making Test as an indicator of organic brain damage. *Perceptual and Motor Skills, 8,* 271–276.

Robertson, I. H., Manly, T., Andrade, J., Baddeley, B. T., & Yiend, J. (1997). "Oops!": Performance correlates of everyday attentional failures in traumatic brain injured and normal subjects. *Neuropsychologia, 35*(6), 747–758.

Rosen, H. J., Perry, R. J., Murphy, J., Kramer, J. H., Mychack, P., Schuff, N., et al. (2002). Emotion comprehension in the temporal variant of frontotemporal dementia. *Brain, 125*(10), 2286–95.

Samet, M. G. & Marshall-Mies, J. C. (1987). *Expanded Complex Cognitive Assessment Battery (CCAB): Final test administrator user guide.* Alexandria, VA: Systems Research Laboratory, U.S. Army Research Institute.

Saxe, R., Carey, S., & Kanwisher, N. (2004). Understanding other minds: Linking developmental psychology and functional neuroimaging. *Annual Review of Psychology, 55,* 87–124.

Shallice, T. & Evans, M. (1978). The involvement of the frontal lobes in cognitive estimation. *Cortex, 14*(2), 294–303.

Shamay-Tsoory, S. G., & Aharon-Peretz, J. (2007). Dissociable prefrontal networks for cognitive and affective theory of mind: A lesion study. *Neuropsychologia, 45*(13), 3054–3067.

Shamay-Tsoory, S. G., Tomer, R., & Aharon-Peretz, J. (2005). The neuroanatomical basis of understanding sarcasm and its relationship to social cognition. *Neuropsychology, 19*(3), 288–300.

Shamay-Tsoory, S. G., Tomer, R., Berger, B. D., Goldsher, D., & Aharon-Peretz, J. (2005). Impaired "affective theory of mind" is associated with right ventromedial prefrontal damage. *Cognitive & Behavioral Neurology, 18*(1), 55–67.

Shamay-Tsoory, S. G., Tomer, R., Berger, B. G., & Aharon-Peretz, J. (2003). Characterization of empathy deficits following prefrontal brain damage: The role of the right ventromedial prefrontal cortex. *Journal of Cognitive Neuroscience, 15*(3), 324–337.

Shevell MI, Majnemer A. (1996). Clinical features of developmental disability associated with cerebellar hypoplasia. *Pediatric Neurology, 15*(3), 224–9.

Snodgrass, C. & Knott, F. (2006). Theory of mind in children with traumatic brain injury. *Brain Injury, 20*(8), 825–833.

Snowden, J. S., Gibbons, Z. C., Blackshaw, A., Doubleday, E., Thompson, J., Craufurd, D., et al. (2003). Social cognition in frontotemporal dementia and Huntington's disease. *Neuropsychologia, 41*(6), 688–701.

Stone, V. E. (2000). The role of the frontal lobes and the amygdala in theory of mind. S. Baron-Cohen, H. Tager-Flusberg, D. J. Cohen, (Eds.), Reprinted 2005, *Understanding other minds: Perspectives from developmental cognitive neuroscience (2nd ed.).* (pp. 253–273). New York: Oxford University Press.

Stone, V. E. (2005). Theory of mind and the evolution of social intelligence. In J. Cacioppo, S. Penny, C. L. Pickett, (Eds.), Social neuroscience: People thinking about thinking people (Vol. xiiii). Cambridge, MA: MIT Press.

Stone, V. E. (2007). An evolutionary perspective on domain specificity in social intelligence. In E. Harmon-Jones & P. Winkielman (Eds.), *Social neuroscience: Integrating biological and psychological explanations of social behavior.* (pp. 316–349). New York: Guilford Press.

Stone, V. E., Baron-Cohen, S., Calder, A., Keane, J., & Young, A. (2003). Acquired theory of mind impairments in individuals with bilateral amygdala lesions. *Neuropsychologia, 41*(2), 209–220.

Stone, V. E., Baron-Cohen, S., & Knight, R. T. (1998). Frontal lobe contributions to theory of mind. *Journal of Cognitive Neuroscience, 10*(5), 640–656.

Stone, V. E., Cosmides, L., Tooby, J., Kroll, N. & Knight, R. T. (2002). Selective impairment of reasoning about social exchange in a patient with bilateral limbic system damage. *Proceedings of the National Academy of Science, USA, 99*(17), 11531–11536.

Stone, V. E. & Gerrans, P. (2006). What's domain-specific about theory of mind? *Social Neuroscience, 1*(3–4), 309–319.

Strauss, E., Sherman, E. M. S., & Spreen, O. (2006). *A compendium of neuropsychological tests: Administration, norms, and commentary* (3rd. ed.). New York, NY: Oxford University Press.

Strong, C.A., Tiesma, D., & Donders, J. (2011). Criterion validity of the Delis-Kaplan Executive Function System (D-KEFS) Fluency subtests after traumatic brain injury. *Journal of the International Neuropsychological Society, 17*(1), 1–8.

Stroop, J. R. (1935). Studies of interference in serial verbal reactions. *Journal of Experimental Psychology, 18*(6), 643–662.

Stuss, D. T. (2001). The frontal lobes are necessary for 'theory of mind'. *Brain, 124,* 279–286.

Stuss, D. T., Bisschop, S. M., Alexander, M. P., Levine, B., Katz, D., & Izukawa, D. (2001). The Trail Making Test: a study in focal lesion patients. *Psychological Assessment, 13,* 230–239.

Tekin, S. & Cummings, J. L. (2002). Frontal-subcortical neuronal circuits and clinical neuropsychiatry: An update. *Journal of Psychosomatic Research, 53*(2), 647–654.

Taylor, R. & O'Carroll, R. (1995). Cognitive estimation in neurological disorders. *British Journal of Clinical Psychology, 34*(2), 223–228.

Torralva, T., Kipps, C. M., Hodges, J. R., Clark, L., Bekinschtein, T., Roca, M., et al. (2007). The relationship between affective decision-making and theory of mind in the frontal variant of frontotemporal dementia. *Neuropsychologia, 45*(2), 342–349.

Varney, N. R., Roberts, R. J., Struchen, M. A., Hanson, T. V., et al. (1996). Design fluency among normals and patients with closed head injury. *Archives of Clinical Neuropsychology, 11*(4), 345–353.

Watts, A. J. & Douglas, J. M. (2006). Interpreting facial expression and communication competence following severe traumatic brain injury. *Aphasiology, 20*(8), 707–722.

Weyandt, L. L. (2005). Executive function in children, adolescents, and adults with attention deficit hyperactivity disorder: Introduction to the special issue. *Developmental Neuropsychology, 27*(1), 1–10.

The Neuroscience of Moral Cognition and Emotion

Roland Zahn, Ricardo de Oliveira-Souza, *and* Jorge Moll

Abstract

The observation of profound changes in moral character after brain lesions in humans in the 19th century marked the beginning of modern moral neuroscience. These observations led to the notion that certain parts of our brains are necessary to enable moral beliefs, feelings, reasoning, knowledge, and behavior. This chapter summarizes recent evidence on the cognitive-anatomical components underlying moral values and sentiments which enable moral motivations. It then provides an overview of the neural basis of moral knowledge and the different accounts of moral reasoning and decision-making. The chapter closes with future directions for moral neuroscience research.

Keywords: moral character, moral values, moral knowledge, decision-making, moral neuroscience research, moral reasoning, moral emotions, social emotions

Introduction

The observation of profound changes in moral character after brain lesions in humans in the 19th century (reviewed in (Welt, 1888)) marked the beginning of modern moral neuroscience. These observations led to the notion that certain parts of our brains are necessary to enable moral beliefs, feelings, reasoning, knowledge and behavior. In this chapter we will summarize evidence on current models of moral cognition and emotion from studies in patients with brain lesions as well as functional neuroimaging in healthy people.

One crucial question is whether moral cognition should and can be separated from general social cognition, and how their respective neural bases relate to each other. What is special about moral cognition? The concepts "moral" or "ethical" can be defined based on their literal meaning in Latin and

Greek, as in accordance with the customs of a society. This meaning of morality already implies that moral phenomena emerge when we extend interpersonal behavior to the societal level. One could argue, however, that even at the direct inter-personal level, any kind of social behavior will have moral implications as it can be judged as "right" or "wrong" based on socio-cultural norms. Socio-cultural norms define the boundaries of legitimate self-interest and duties of the individual towards others or society. The ability to steer one's social behavior according to socio-cultural norms is uniquely human (Fehr & Fischbacher, 2003). Here, we will argue that this ability to behave morally depends on two major components: 1) knowing about socio-cultural norms and the needs of others (i.e., social knowledge) and 2) the ability to be motivated by socio-cultural norms or other people's needs (i.e., moral motivations). This definition of moral faculties points to the importance of understanding altruistic motivations as the key to enabling moral behavior in humans, a view which has been advanced by Francis Hutcheson, a pioneer of moral psychology in the 18th century (Bishop, 1996). Following this view, the important question of whether there are distinct cognitive and neural systems specialized for the moral domain should be addressed by understanding the mechanisms underlying altruistically motivated behavior and whether these can be selectively impaired while leaving other social cognitive abilities intact. Another possibility is that moral faculties emerge by integrating general social cognitive abilities, but without necessarily drawing upon domain-specific brain systems.

In order to understand moral behavior one needs to explain how altruistic motives can be tied to societal goals to enable complex moral motivations. The 18th century British philosophers Adam

Smith and David Hume have suggested that our moral behavior is guided by intuitive "moral sentiments" (often called moral emotions in the modern literature and now including, for example, compassion, guilt, shame, indignation, contempt, gratitude, certain forms of pride) which express our approval or disapproval of behavior, a point of view supported by current moral psychology (Haidt, 2001). Moral sentiments can act as powerful motivators of moral behavior, but additional social knowledge is required to specify which kind of behavior we associate with a particular type of feeling. A key to understanding how social knowledge becomes morally motivating is the understanding of values. Social or moral values (e.g. "honesty") are beliefs or concepts describing abstract norms shared across a socio-cultural group which have high motivational/emotional relevance and serve as overarching goals of behavior (Schwartz, 1992). Acting in accordance with personally relevant values

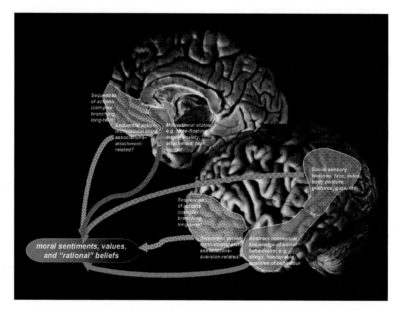

Fig. 32.1 Brain regions implicated in human moral cognition (adapted from Moll & Shulkin, 2009 and Moll et al., 2005). Cortical regions include FPC, medial and lateral ventral PFC, right anterior dorsolateral PFC, aTL, and pSTS. Subcortical structures include the extended amygdala, hypothalamus, basal forebrain (especially the septal region), basal ganglia, and midbrain regions. We have postulated that integration across these corticolimbic structures gives rise to event–feature–emotion complexes (EFEC), possibly by temporal binding mechanisms. Main components include: (1) Sequential knowledge of actions/events (provided by representations within specific PFC subregions with FPC being more involved in complex branching of consequences of actions in the future and ventral PFC regions representing associative knowledge of motivational/emotional states embedded into sequential event/action contexts (potentially there is a medial to lateral division for attachment (medial) and aversion-related (lateral) information in the ventral PFC analogous to the proposed division for reward and punishment (Kringelbach & Rolls, 2004); (2) social sensory features stored in pSTS (the role of the temporo-parietal junction in social spatial representations [Decety & Grezes, 2006] needs to be formulated more clearly in future extensions of the model) and abstract (i.e., context-independent) conceptual knowledge of social behavior stored in the anterior temporal cortex, especially in the superior sectors; (3) central motive or basic emotional states, such as "free-floating" anger, attachment, sadness, and sexual arousal (represented by the subcortical limbic structures listed above). The figure also illustrates how moral sentiments, values and "rational" beliefs, can emerge through integration across specific subcomponents of the moral cognition network, we assume by temporal binding.

or contrary to them is associated with distinct moral sentiments (Zahn, Moll, Paiva, et al., 2009). In the following sections we will summarize recent evidence on the cognitive-anatomical components underlying moral values and sentiments which enable moral motivations. We will then provide an overview of the neural basis of moral knowledge and the different accounts of moral reasoning and decision-making. This chapter closes with future directions for moral neuroscience research.

The Neural Basis of Moral Motivations
Cognitive-anatomical Definition of Moral Motivations

Moral (i.e., altruistic) motivations require a motivational force and a goal to which this motivational force can be tied. Stellar proposed that motivational forces in general are represented as "central motive states" in the brain (Stellar, 1954/1994). Inspired by this notion, we have proposed that motivational/ emotional states as represented in subcortical limbic brain regions are key ingredients of moral motivations. Motivations, however, require a second component which represents the goal of action. Socio-moral goals can take different forms: 1) Goals can be contextualized by forming the end of a sequence of actions/events (Wood & Grafman, 2003) (e.g., attaining a professorship in cognitive neuroscience after having gone through PhD, postdoc, assistant, and associate professorships); or 2) goals can describe a certain qualitative state one wants to reach across different action contexts (e.g., attaining wisdom, Zahn, Moll, Paiva et al., 2009). The latter type of goal is also known as a social or moral value (Schwartz, 1992). Goals of the first kind (contextualized action goal) require knowledge of the sequence of actions necessary to attain the goal, whereas goals of the second kind (moral value) require knowledge of the conceptual quality of the goal (Zahn et al., 2007). Moral value-related goals are often intertwined with contextualized action goals in that the latter are implementations of the former (e.g., in order to become wise one may want to become a professor in cognitive neuroscience).

Based on evidence from lesions in patients and functional neuroimaging we have proposed that contextualized social action goals are represented in the ventral prefrontal (PFC) and frontopolar cortices (FPC) and that conceptual qualities of social behavior necessary for moral value-related goals are represented in the anterior temporal lobe (aTL, see Figure 32.1; Moll, Zahn, de Oliveira-Souza, Krueger, & Grafman, 2005). Moral motivations, according to

this view, depend on integration of information across ventral PFC, FPC, and subcortical mesolimbic regions for contextualized action goals and on integration across aTL and fronto-mesolimbic regions for moral value-related goals. In the following sections we will review recent studies investigating these hypotheses.

Altruistic and Self-serving Motivations

Motivational psychology, psychiatry, and neuroscience have long held the view that motivational forces in humans are provided by self-serving drives (e.g. sex-drive, hunger, thirst) which are critical for our immediate survival (Weiner, 1992). Across species, however, there is a growing body of evidence on social attachment as a powerful motivation for mating behaviors and limited altruism towards members of kin (see second section). Furthermore, recent findings on experimental economic interactions in humans support the existence of altruistic motivations that cannot be reduced to self-interest, a view which is compatible with evolutionary models of group survival advantages through cooperation (Gintis, Henrich, Bowles, Boyd, & Fehr, 2008).

Until recently, the brain regions necessary for altruistically motivated behavior in humans were unknown. Observations in patients showed that lesions of the ventral PFC (Anderson, Bechara, Damasio, Tranel, & Damasio, 1999; Eslinger & Damasio, 1985; Welt, 1888) or atrophy of the aTL in frontotemporal neurodegeneration (Liu et al., 2004) led to behavior counter to moral and social norms. These observations were, however, not necessarily attributable to a lack of altruistic motivations. New insights into the neural bases of interpersonal altruism came from neuroeconomic studies using functional MRI in healthy people while interacting in economic experiments (see below). However, humans often sacrifice material benefits or even risk their lives to uphold abstract values far beyond the interpersonal realm. Anonymous donation to charities during functional MRI has been used to explore the anatomical basis of this far-reaching form of altruism (see Figure 32.2; Moll et al., 2006).

Both pure monetary rewards and decisions to donate to charities activated the mesolimbic reward system, in agreement with the hypothesis stating that altruistic behavior can be driven by internalized rewards, or "warm glow" feelings (Andreoni, 1990). Interestingly, when decisions to donate were pitted against the pure monetary reward condition, the subgenual cingulate cortex (SCC)-septal network,

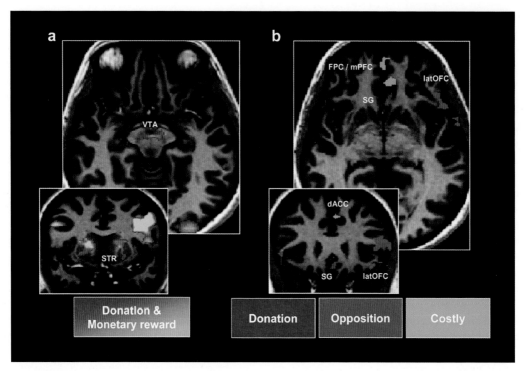

Fig. 32.2 Brain regions involved in donation and opposition to charitable organizations. Brain regions showing increased activation in a functional MRI study of charitable donations to societal causes (e.g., abortion, children's rights, nuclear energy, war, and euthanasia). (a) Both pure monetary rewards (an experimental control condition) and decisions to donate (with or without personal financial costs) activated the mesolimbic reward system, including the ventral tegmental area (VTA) and the ventral and dorsal striatum (STR). (b) The subgenual–septal area (SG), however, was selectively activated by decisions to donate, as compared with pure monetary rewards (both by costly and non-costly decisions, conjunction analysis). The lateral orbitofrontal cortex (latOFC) was activated by decisions to oppose charities. This activation extended to the anterior insula and to the inferior dorsolateral PFC, and was present both for costly and non-costly decisions (conjunction analysis). The FPC and ventral medial PFC (mPFC) were activated when volunteers made costly decisions, that is, when they voluntarily chose to sacrifice own monetary resources either to donate to a charity or to oppose to it (conjunction analysis).

which is related to social affiliative behaviors in other species (Freedman, Insel, & Smith, 2000; Young & Wang, 2004), was selectively activated. When participants opposed charities (e.g., many of them refused to make decisions that would benefit the National Rifle Association), the lateral orbitofrontal cortex (OFC), linked to indignation/anger and contempt/disgust towards others, was engaged. Furthermore, when decisions were costly to the participant—both costly donation and costly opposition—the FPC and anterior ventral PFC were activated. This could be interpreted as a result of weighing the costs and benefits of decisions, and anticipating the consequences of one's decisions for oneself and for the charities. Noteworthy, during costly donations these PFC areas showed increased functional connectivity with the SCC-septal area (unpublished results). This indicates that moral motivations depend on the co-activation of limbic systems involved in affiliative rewards and of the

more recently evolved FPC, which seem to work cooperatively (instead of competitively) during decision making.

These findings extended the role of fronto-limbic networks in social cooperation from interpersonal economic interactions, as addressed by a number of previous studies (de Quervain et al., 2004; Delgado, Frank, & Phelps, 2005; King-Casas et al., 2005; Sanfey, Rilling, Aronson, Nystrom, & Cohen, 2003; Singer, Kiebel, Winston, Dolan, & Frith, 2004), to the realm of decisions based on internalized values and preferences shaped by culture. A more recent functional MRI study on charitable donation confirmed the involvement of the septal region adjacent to the ventral striatum in altruistic behavior and showed that this region is also activated by "mandatory" donations to worthy causes (Harbaugh, Mayr, & Burghart, 2007). Furthermore, activity within the septal region was associated with the number of meals donated to orphan children (efficiency) in a more recent fMRI study (Hsu, Anen, & Quartz, 2008). Taken together, there is growing evidence for the selective involvement of parts of the septal-SCC region in altruistic decisions and a common role of ventral tegmental area and striatum in self-serving and affiliative rewards.

Moral Sentiments and Values and Their Relationship with Altruism

Philosophers of the Scottish Enlightenment in the 18th century (Francis Hutcheson, his successor Adam Smith, and David Hume) have proposed that a natural moral sense and its underlying moral sentiments allow us to intuitively approve or disapprove social behaviors in accordance to moral values (i.e., virtues). "Sympathy," defined as "man's capacity for fellow feeling with others," was considered the most important moral sentiment by Adam Smith (Lamb, 1974). Hutcheson claimed that "benevolence" motivates virtuous actions and thereby provides "moral motivations" (Bishop, 1996). In the modern psychological literature, the term "moral emotion" is usually preferred over moral sentiment and the field has developed to distinguish between different moral emotions with some controversies as to which emotions to include and how to define them (Eisenberg, 2000; Tangney, Stuewig, & Mashek, 2007). We adopt the term moral sentiments or feelings (referring to the subjective experience) in order to stress the complex cognitive information implicitly entailed in these experiences such as causal agency and prospective evaluations.

Depending on the context, different moral sentiments, such as pride, guilt, shame, embarrassment, or indignation can be associated with anticipated or completed contextualized action goals (e.g., "attaining a professorship in cognitive neuroscience") or value-related goals (e.g., "becoming wise"; see Figure 32.3) (Zahn, Moll, Paiva, et al., 2009). Early neuroimaging studies in healthy people have compared morally relevant with less morally relevant materials while controlling for overall emotional salience, arousal, and by using active or passive tasks (reviewed in Moll, Zahn, de Oliveira-Souza, Krueger, & Grafman, 2005). Morally relevant pictures or verbal descriptions of contextualized social behavior (e.g., "The judge condemned an innocent man") used in those experiments consistently evoked moral sentiments; however, only later were different moral sentiments directly investigated by asking people to label feelings they had experienced.

When reviewing the results of these functional imaging studies on specific moral sentiments, we restrict ourselves to brain regions reported in brain lesion studies (reviewed in Moll et al., 2005) to be associated with impairments of moral behavior (see Figure 32.1). Grey matter volume reductions in several areas of this moral cognition network (bilateral FPC, medial OFC, SCC, and bilateral pSTS) were correlated with the degree of callousness (indicative of a reduced ability to feel compassion and guilt) in individuals with developmental psychopathy (de Oliveira-Souza et al., 2008). It is important to consider that not all of the regions found to be associated with changes in moral behavior in patients need to be special for moral cognition. Some regions may be involved in cognitive components necessary for moral cognition, but not restricted to moral abilities (e.g., fear conditioning associated with parts of the amygdala).

Guilt

Guilt, shame and embarrassment have been extensively studied in modern psychology (Eisenberg, 2000; O'Connor, Berry, Weiss, & Gilbert, 2002; Tangney, Stuewig, & Mashek, 2007). We focus on neuroimaging investigations of guilt which allow a more consistent summary at this stage. The first neuroimaging study investigating guilt found bilateral aTL, anterior insula, and anterior cingulate activation dorsally to the genu of the corpus callosum when compared with a neutral condition (Shin et al., 2000). Guilt has been consistently associated with FPC activation when using other-critical feelings (e.g., indignation) or emotionally neutral stimuli as a control condition (Moll et al., 2007; Zahn, Moll, Paiva, et al., 2009), and when comparing guilt with embarrassment (Takahashi et al., 2004) or with anger towards oneself in a study looking at unintentional causation of harm to others (Kedia, Berthoz, Wessa, Hilton, & Martinot, 2008). Further, guilt has been correlated with SCC activation using functional MRI, but only when modeling individual differences in either frequency of guilt experience (Zahn, Moll, Paiva, et al., 2009) or individual differences in empathic concern (Zahn, de Oliveira-Souza, Bramati, Garrido, & Moll, 2009). SCC activation was selective for guilt when compared with other-critical feelings such as indignation/anger while controlling for valence and conceptual detail (Zahn, Moll, Paiva, et al., 2009). A recent study showed that prosocial moral sentiments (guilt and embarrassment) when compared with basic negative feelings led to activations in the FPC, left aTL and right pSTS/temporo-parietal junction (Burnett, Bird, Moll, Frith, & Blakemore, 2009) and that there was ongoing reorganization within this fronto-temporal network during adolescence.

Compassion

We use sympathy, pity, and compassion synonymously here to refer to emotional empathy (for the link of emotional and cognitive forms of empathy, see chapter 37 of this volume). Feelings of compassion have been associated with FPC activation when compared with anger towards oneself (Kedia, Berthoz, Wessa, Hilton, & Martinot, 2008) and towards others (Moll et al., 2007). The ventral striatum and ventral tegmental area were more active during empathic moral sentiments (compassion and guilt) than during other-critical feelings (disgust, indignation) (Moll et al., 2007).

Other-critical (Other-blaming) moral sentiments

Disapproval of moral violations of others is vital to maintaining moral standards in societies (Gintis, Henrich, Bowles, Boyd, & Fehr, 2008). Indignation/anger and contempt/disgust towards others have been associated with similar regions as nonmoral anger and disgust towards others: lateral OFC and anterior insula (Moll et al., 2007; Zahn, Moll, Paiva, et al., 2009). One study found even stronger activity in the bilateral OFC for indignation and moral disgust versus nonmoral disgust (Moll et al., 2005), whereas the right amygdala was more activated for nonmoral than moral disgust. Schaich-Borg and co-workers (Borg, Lieberman, & Kiehl, 2008) investigated different forms of moral disgust and disgust for behaviors related to health risks for the agent (pathogen disgust) versus an emotionally and morally neutral condition. They found aTLs, left lateral OFC and FPC, bilateral amygdala and basal ganglia more activated for all disgust conditions compared with neutral conditions. There was no direct comparison with prosocial moral sentiments such as guilt to investigate whether FPC activation was specific for disgust. Another study also reported FPC activity for anger towards others, but compared with a condition evoking anger towards oneself (Kedia, Berthoz, Wessa, Hilton, & Martinot, 2008). In addition, left lateral OFC and right dorsolateral PFC activity have been found when people expected punishment for violating social norms (Spitzer, Fischbacher, Herrnberger, Gron, & Fehr, 2007) versus when they did not expect punishment for those norm violations. These effects could potentially be explained by expecting other people's indignation towards ourselves to be represented in the same regions that represent our indignation towards others.

Pride

Pride was judged to be a self-interested motive by Adam Smith, though he considered the striving for "dignity" as leading to "ethical improvement" (Lamb, 1974). Hume pointed to "good and bad forms of pride" (Hume, 1777). The following studies used pride in social value-related rather than self-serving contexts. Pride-evoking sentences have been associated with right pSTS and left aTL activation in one study when compared with a neutral condition (Takahashi et al., 2008). In another study, there were activations within the mesolimbic reward system (ventral tegmental area) with its projections to the basal forebrain (posterior septum) and within the ventral FPC for social value-related pride compared with gratitude and guilt (Zahn, Moll, Paiva, et al., 2009; see Figure 32.3).

Taken together, there have been several studies showing differential activations within fronto-mesolimbic parts of the moral cognition network for different moral sentiments. FPC activations were among the most consistent for moral sentiments in general (Moll, Zahn, de Oliveira-Souza, Krueger, & Grafman, 2005). Those studies which directly compared prosocial moral sentiments (guilt, compassion, embarrassment) with other-critical moral sentiments (indignation towards others) have demonstrated selective activation for prosocial moral sentiments within the FPC. Other-critical (other-blaming) moral sentiments have been most consistently associated with lateral OFC and anterior insula activations when compared with prosocial moral sentiments (compassion, guilt, embarrassment). Few studies have investigated pride and gratitude, but mesolimbic and basal forebrain regions were found in one study (Figure 32.3).

One limitation of functional imaging studies of moral sentiments is the difficulty of controlling for confounding differences between stimulus conditions, especially when using contextualized descriptions of social behavior. Posterior STS activation found in some but not all studies for different moral sentiments could be due to different requirements of mental imagery of moral scenes in different conditions in keeping with its role in social sensory representations (Allison, Puce, & McCarthy, 2000). ATL activations were found to be selective for some moral sentiments compared with others in a number of studies. However, none of these studies controlled for the degree of conceptual detail with which stimuli described social behavior. When one controls for this variable, aTL activity is present during the experience of any type of moral sentiment and does not differ between different feelings (Zahn, Moll, Paiva, et al., 2009). Further studies need to show whether stronger FPC activation is due to more demands on detailed representations of future consequences of social actions (Moll, Zahn, de Oliveira-Souza, Krueger, & Grafman, 2005) for empathic moral sentiments (guilt, compassion) or for those related to self-agency (pride, guilt) in comparison with other-critical feelings such as indignation for others, which may not depend as much on thinking about far-reaching consequences of social behavior.

Moral and social values (e.g., "generosity") have been recently studied and the hypothesis was corroborated that they are composed of an abstract conceptual component (the conceptual knowledge of the common quality of e.g., "generous" behavior across different contexts) within the aTL, independent of emotional and action context, bound together with context-dependent representations of different moral sentiments depending on the context of agency within different parts of the fronto-mesolimbic network (see Figure 32.3) (Zahn, Moll, Paiva, et al., 2009).

Social Instincts of Attachment and Aversion as Key Ingredients of Moral Sentiments

There is a growing awareness that the primitive motivational ingredients of moral sentiments can be found in other social species as well (de Waal, 1998). Social motivations can be organized into two broad classes: one linked to approach and affiliation, and the other linked to aversion and rejection. While attachment promotes cooperation within members of a group, aversion fosters blame of others and defining out-groups (Moll, De Oliveira-Souza, & Zahn, 2008). Such primitive social-motivational dispositions find a close correspondence to the prosocial and social-aversive counterparts at work in sophisticated psychological spheres of human moral cognition. These are manifested as moral sentiments and values, which embody motivational elements of social attachment/aversion.

The cingulate gyrus, lateral septal nuclei, medial preoptic area, mediobasal hypothalamus and ventral tegmental area form a neural system implicated in pair bonding and affiliative rewards across a broad range of species (Depue & Morrone-Strupinsky, 2005; Insel & Young, 2001). Whereas parts of this mesolimbic system are well known for their role in basic self-serving rewards (e.g., ventral tegmental area), human fMRI suggests that when altruistic and self-serving choices are directly compared, the SCC and adjacent septal region are specific for anonymous altruistic decisions (Moll et al., 2006), presumably driven by affiliative feelings. Further, it

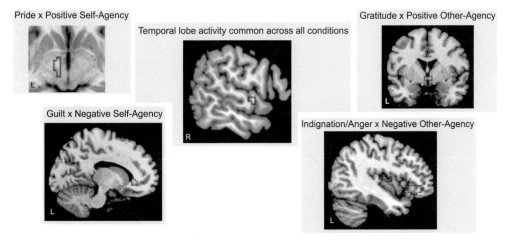

Fig. 32.3 The neural basis of human social and moral values has been studied using fMRI (Zahn, Moll, Paiva et al., 2009) and four conditions in which participants had to imagine actions in accordance with or counter to a value described by a written sentence and rate their pleasantness. After the scan they chose labels which best described their feelings (the analysis compares each moral sentiment versus visual fixation and versus two other moral sentiments, only selective effects were reported): 1) positive self-agency: for example, "Tom (first name of participant) acts generously towards Sam (first name of best friend)"—associated with pride and ventral tegmental, septal, and ventral medial FPC activation (not depicted), 2) positive other-agency: for example, "Sam acts generously towards Tom"—associated with gratitude and hypothalamic activation, 3) negative self-agency: for example "Tom acts stingily towards Sam"—associated with guilt and SCC as well as ventral medial FPC activation (not depicted), 4) negative other-agency: for example "Sam acts stingily towards Tom"—associated with indignation/anger and lateral orbitofrontal/insular activation. In the center, one can see the right superior aTL region showing equally strong activation during all moral sentiment and agency contexts, this region increased activity with increasing richness of conceptual detail describing social behavior (for comparison see Figure 32.5).

has been demonstrated that the septal region was associated with unconditional trust in economic cooperation, whereas the ventral tegmental area was activated when calculating the benefits for oneself (Krueger et al., 2007).

In addition, SCC activity was associated with the experience of guilt and was higher in individuals with high frequency of guilt (Zahn, Moll, Paiva, et al., 2009) and high empathic concern (Zahn, de Oliveira-Souza, Bramati, Garrido, & Moll, 2009). Further, this region is part of a network of regions activated when participants view pictures of romantic partners or their own infants (Bartels & Zeki, 2004). One hypothesis for activation of the SCC across those different tasks is its involvement in the representation of affiliation/attachment to other people as well as affiliation/attachment to abstract social and moral values (Moll & Schulkin, 2009).

Further studies are needed to identify SCC-septal and OFC representations of different types of affiliative rewards and punishments in interpersonal and moral value-related contexts and to confirm the hypotheses of the extended attachment model of moral cognition (Moll & de Oliveira-Souza, 2009).

The Neural Basis of Moral Knowledge
Cognitive-anatomical Definition of Moral Knowledge

From our perspective on moral neuroscience as distinguished from general social neuroscience primarily by its aim to account for moral (i.e., altruistic) motivations, there is no sharp distinction between social and moral knowledge when stripped from its motivational components. This is also true for the knowledge underlying moral or social values.

A recent review on the neural basis of social knowledge highlighted the importance of knowledge of one's own mind and other people's minds as key to understanding social cognition in general (Adolphs, 2009). Here, we take a less inclusive perspective on social knowledge by focusing on nonepisodic knowledge of sensory social information and information on social behavior (see Figure 32.4).

The representation of social knowledge in the brain is not well understood. Wood & Grafman (2003) had proposed that social knowledge arises from knowledge of the sequences of social events and actions represented in the ventral medial PFC. Other researchers, however, have stressed that when

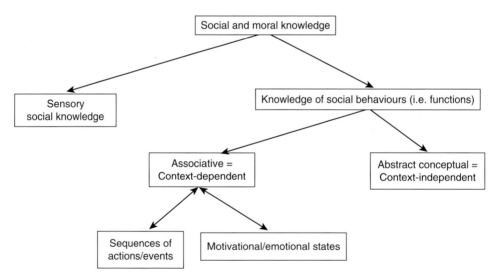

Fig. 32.4 The hypothesized neurocognitive components of social and moral knowledge are illustrated. We refer to nonepisodic long-term memory here and distinguish between sensory social knowledge presumably represented in pSTS and knowledge of social behaviors (i.e., functions). The latter is subdivided into two anatomically separable systems: 1) abstract conceptual (i.e., context-independent) knowledge of social behavior represented in the aTL and 2) associative (i.e., context-dependent) knowledge of social behavior represented in fronto-mesolimbic networks. Associative knowledge of social behavior is subdivided into a component representing knowledge of sequences of social actions (events) within FPC and ventral PFC (representing associations of action/event sequences with motivational/emotional states) and a subcortical mesolimbic component representing "free-floating" motivational/emotional states (see also Figure 32.1). Please note that context-dependent knowledge of social behavior, as defined here, only comprises sequential and motivational state contexts of actions, because we consider these to be the core components needed to represent different classes of social behavior.

abstracted from the sequential context of action, social knowledge remains largely intact in patients with damage of the ventral medial PFC (Eslinger & Damasio, 1985; Saver & Damasio, 1991). Below we will review a series of studies directly aimed at resolving these discrepancies.

Context-dependent and Context-independent Forms of Socio-moral Knowledge

Socially appropriate behavior requires knowledge of adequate social actions within a given sequential context (e.g., "to appropriately kiss a romantic partner on her/his lips after a romantic date but not the waiter/waitress after dinner in a restaurant"; Wood & Grafman, 2003), but also knowledge of the abstract conceptual quality of a given social action within a given context (e.g., enabling us to flexibly interpret not being greeted by a colleague who is passing by in a corridor at work as a sign of "disrespect," "impoliteness," "shyness" or "absent-mindedness"; Zahn, Moll, Iyengar, et al., 2009).

Using fMRI, we have demonstrated that abstract conceptual social knowledge, which is independent of the sequential context of actions and emotions, is represented in the superior aTL (see Figure 32.5) (Zahn et al., 2007). Abstract conceptual social knowledge (i.e., context-independent) allows us to define the meaning of overarching social and moral values (e.g., intelligence, ambition, honor, politeness). Preserved aTL representations of this kind of knowledge may help explain the observation of intact abstract conceptual social knowledge and normal performance on certain social cognition tasks (when the gist of the context is summarized for the patient) in patients with damage of the ventral medial PFC (Eslinger & Damasio, 1985; Saver & Damasio, 1991). In a study in patients with frontotemporal neurodegeneration we have been able to demonstrate that regional abnormalities within the right superior aTL are associated with selective impairments of social concepts when compared with less socially relevant concepts describing animal behavior (Zahn, Moll, Iyengar, et al., 2009). Interestingly, patients with selective impairments on social concepts showed more inappropriate social behaviors than patients with selective impairments on animal function concepts. These findings suggest that context-independent conceptual social knowledge is important for real-life social behavior rather than being merely necessary to understand verbal descriptions of social behavior.

Using fMRI in healthy people, we have been able to support the hypothesis that the context of agency (self vs. other) and moral sentiments tied to abstract social concepts determines which part of the fronto-mesolimbic network will be activated, whilst right superior aTL activity was equally high across different contexts (see Figure 32.3; Zahn, Moll, Paiva, et al., 2009). These results are in keeping with the hypothesis of separable neural representations of context-independent abstract conceptual knowledge of social behavior in the superior aTL and context-dependent associative-semantic knowledge of social behavior in fronto-mesolimbic networks. Lacking so far, are direct investigations of the exact type of representations within different subcortical mesolimbic, ventral PFC, and FPC brain regions.

These results on separable neural representations for context-dependent and context–independent components of knowledge of social behavior provide a neurobiological mechanism which may explain the remarkable human ability to dynamically rearrange social concepts, actions, and emotional "flavors" to produce the rich variety of personal, moral, and social values which subtly steer our social lives.

The Neural Basis of Moral Reasoning and Decision Making
Cognitive-anatomical Definition of Moral Reasoning and Decision Making

The first functional imaging studies of moral judgment and reasoning showed activation of the anterior dorsolateral PFC and FPC (Greene, Nystrom, Engell, Darley, & Cohen, 2004; Greene, Sommerville, Nystrom, Darley, & Cohen, 2001; Moll, Eslinger, & Oliveira-Souza, 2001). Decision making in the moral domain can be conceived of as either top-down control exerted primarily by the dorsal PFC onto the ventral PFC and subcortical limbic structures (Greene, Nystrom, Engell, Darley, & Cohen, 2004) or as a competition between different fronto-temporo-mesolimbic association complexes (Moll, de Oliveira-Souza, & Zahn, 2008). Another model holds that the ventral medial PFC is necessary for social decision making because it links our decisions with our autonomic nervous system (hypothalamus) and produces a fast "somatic marker" signal (Bechara, Damasio, & Damasio, 2000). The somatic marker model predicts that patients with ventral medial PFC lesions are overall less emotional and is thus compatible with the top-down control model of moral judgment. The fronto-temporo-mesolimbic integration model of moral cognition and emotion is based on

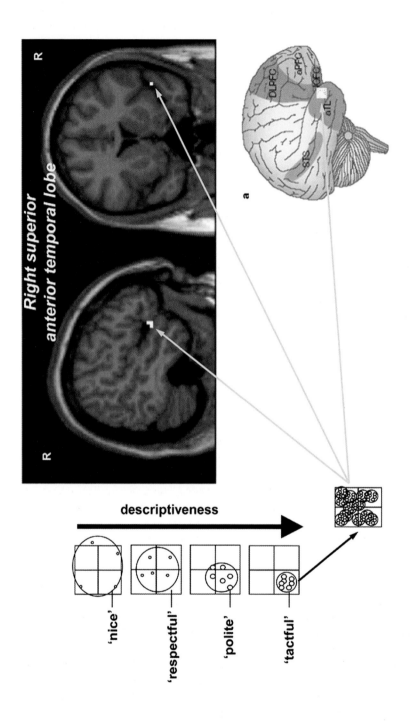

Fig. 32.5 Representations of abstract conceptual knowledge of social and moral behavior within a right superior aTL region. In this fMRI study (Zahn et al., 2007) people were asked to judge the meaning relatedness of concept pairs (e.g. social concept condition- positive: honourable-brave, negative: stingy-greedy; animal function concept condition: ridden-trainable). This whole brain image shows the only region surviving the following three criteria: 1) selective for social versus animal function concepts, 2) increases activation with meaning relatedness of word pairs, 3) increases activation with descriptiveness of social behavior (i.e., the richness of detail with which concepts describe social behavior). Psycholinguistic confounds were carefully controlled (imageability, word frequency, familiarity) and there was no difference for positive or negative concepts in the aT.. These results are in keeping with the hypothesis of a topographic coding of meaning relatedness within the aTL and with context-independent (denoted exemplar-independent) representations of abstract conceptual knowledge in this area (Ralph & Patterson, 2008).

a representational view of the frontal cortex (Wood & Grafman, 2003) and assumes a topographic map coding for different formats and contents of sequential action contexts and their associations with motivational/emotional states within the ventral frontal cortex (Moll, Zahn, de Oliveira-Souza, Krueger, & Grafman, 2005). In the sections below we will review recent lesion studies which have stimulated the debate on these different models of moral reasoning and decision making.

Fronto-limbic Top-down Control Models of Moral Reasoning and Decision-making

One view is that reasoning (often assumed to be purely "cognitive") and emotion (often equated with the subjective experience of feelings) rely on anatomically separable systems (cognition in the PFC and parietal areas, and emotion in limbic regions), and that cognition and emotion can be placed in conflict and compete with each other during decisions (McClure, Botvinick, Yeung, & Cohen, 2006). In the context of difficult moral choices, such as when one must decide whether it would be appropriate to push an innocent man to death on the tracks of a runaway trolley to save five other individuals, the emotional system would tell the decision maker to refrain from this choice, the prepotent response, whereas the cognitive system would recommend the "utilitarian" choice, the one that leads to the maximum overall benefit, the rational choice (Greene, Nystrom, Engell, Darley, & Cohen, 2004). According to this "dual-process theory," choosing to push the man means that cognitive brain areas were successful in overcoming or suppressing the emotional bias of not doing it—an extension of the influential cognitive control model (Miller & Cohen, 2001) to the sphere of moral judgment.

Recent lesion studies (Ciaramelli, Muccioli, Ladavas, & di Pellegrino, 2007; Koenigs et al., 2007) employed classical "trolley-type" dilemmas to investigate patterns of moral judgments in patients with bilateral damage to the ventral medial PFC. They demonstrated that these patients endorsed "utilitarian" decisions in high-conflict scenarios—highly emotionally aversive choices that would nonetheless lead to greater aggregate welfare (e.g., more lives saved)—more often than control subjects did. The increased preference of patients with ventral medial PFC lesions for utilitarian choices could be interpreted according to different functional-anatomic hypotheses. One possibility would be that making more "rational," utilitarian choices in difficult dilemmas might have resulted from a general

emotional blunting and reduced autonomic signaling arising from ventral medial PFC damage—an interpretation that would fit with the somatic-marker hypothesis. This possibility, however, is not supported by the results of another study (Koenigs & Tranel, 2007) investigating the performance of patients with ventral medial PFC lesions in the two-person ultimatum game. In this game (participants interact only one time, anonymously), participants must choose between accepting an unfair but financially rewarding proposal (the economically "rational" choice), or rejecting it to punish the unfair player (the "emotional" choice). Patients with ventral medial PFC lesions opted more often than controls for rejecting unfair offers (i.e., they were more "emotional"). Therefore, while patients made more utilitarian choices in trolley-type dilemmas (interpreted as "rational" responses), they opted more often for costly punishing, that is, "emotional" responses associated with anger. Thus, the choice patterns observed in these morally salient experimental settings can neither be explained by a single mechanism of overall emotional blunting as predicted by the somatic marker model, nor by the dual-process proposal, in which cognition and emotion processes compete for behavioral output in conflicting situations (Greene, Nystrom, Engell, Darley, & Cohen, 2004).

Fronto-temporo-mesolimbic Integration Models of Moral Reasoning and Decision Making

An alternative explanation for the findings of Koenigs et al. (2007) and Ciaramelli et al. (2007) would be the occurrence of a dissociation within the moral sentiment domain, with a selective impairment of prosocial moral sentiments, such as guilt and compassion, but spared other-critical sentiments such as indignation/anger towards others. As reviewed in our section on moral sentiments, there is evidence that the ventral medial PFC which includes the SCC and ventral FPC may be more critical for the experience of prosocial moral sentiments (i.e., guilt, compassion), whereas the dorsolateral PFC, lateral OFC, and anterior insular cortex could be more relevant for other-critical moral sentiments (such as indignation and contempt towards others).

The "cold-blooded" utilitarian choices and increased punishment of others observed in patients with ventral medial PFC lesions could be explained by a reduced conflict between choosing the option which saves more lives and the option requiring patients to take direct responsibility for sacrificing the life of an individual, because they feel less guilt for doing so. Thereby patients would have an increased tendency to decide for the option which saves more lives.

The evidence reviewed here suggests that moral reasoning is not solely dependent on isocortical brain regions and that emotions are unlikely to arise from isolated limbic activity (Moll, Zahn, de Oliveira-Souza, Krueger, & Grafman, 2005). Although subcortical limbic brain regions may be functionally specialized for motivational/emotional states, and isocortical regions for more complex cognitive operations, this does not imply clear boundaries or competition between cognition and emotion. Instead, competition between behavioral options will only occur when moral "rational" choices are endowed with emotional/motivational salience, a notion which has been highlighted in Francis Hutcheson's moral psychology (Bishop, 1996). The cortico-limbic integration view of moral cognition and emotion therefore predicts that temporal binding between functionally specialized brain regions within the moral cognition network gives rise to complex subjective experiences such as moral sentiments and values. The difference between a subjective experience we call "feeling" and one which we call "rational belief" would be associated with differences in the salience of activation states in different parts of the network. The hypothesis of the fronto-limbic integration model is thus that the experience of feelings is associated with neural activity within isocortical areas (FPC, aTL) in addition to classical limbic areas and that the experience of rational beliefs is associated with neural activity within subcortical limbic and ventral PFC regions in addition to isocortical areas.

Conclusions and Future Directions of Research

Taken together, there is convergent evidence from patients with brain lesions and functional neuroimaging in healthy people that moral cognition and emotion rely on a fronto-temporo-mesolimbic brain network. Current controversies mainly focus on how to describe the function of different parts of this network. Future research needs to directly probe whether the FPC represents complex sequential information including outcomes of social behavior and whether the septal-SCC region is involved in representing affiliative rewards and punishments, specified by different contexts of social actions and outcomes. The role of superior parts of the aTL in representing context-independent conceptual knowledge of social behavior is corroborated through one brain lesion and

two fMRI studies, but needs to be replicated in future research. Experiments directly probing fronto-limbic top-down suppression versus fronto-temporo-mesolimbic integration models of moral cognition are needed because current evidence does not conclusively support one model while ruling out the other. Methods other than fMRI may be needed to address these questions; electrophysiological mapping to measure temporal binding and transcranial magnetic stimulation to induce functional lesions will be particularly useful to test functional integration within the moral cognition network. The neuroscience of morality has important implications for the understanding of the pathogenesis, diagnosis, and treatment of neuropsychiatric disorders such as developmental psychopathy, major depression, bipolar disorder, and behavioral changes in patients with brain lesions. Future clinical research needs to translate insights from basic moral neuroscience into new disease models, neuropsychological assessments, and neurorehabilitation strategies to benefit patients and their families.

References

Adolphs, R. (2009). The social brain: Neural basis of social knowledge. *Annual Review of Psychology, 60*, 693–716.

Allison, T., Puce, A., & McCarthy, G. (2000). Social perception from visual cues: Role of the STS region. *Trends in Cognitive Sciences, 4*(7), 267–278.

Anderson, S. W., Bechara, A., Damasio, H., Tranel, D., & Damasio, A. R. (1999). Impairment of social and moral behavior related to early damage in human prefrontal cortex. *Nat Neurosci, 2*(11), 1032–1037.

Andreoni, J. (1990). Impure altruism and donations to public good: A theory of warm glow giving. *The Economic Journal, 100*(401), 464–477.

Bartels, A. & Zeki, S. (2004). The neural correlates of maternal and romantic love. *Neuroimage, 21*(3), 1155–1166.

Bechara, A., Damasio, H., & Damasio, A. R. (2000). Emotion, decision making and the orbitofrontal cortex. *Cerebral Cortex, 10*(3), 295–307.

Bishop, J. D. (1996). Moral motivation and the development of Francis Hutcheson's philosophy. *Journal of the History of Ideas, 57*(2), 277–295.

Borg, J. S., Lieberman, D., & Kiehl, K. A. (2008). Infection, incest, and iniquity: Investigating the neural correlates of disgust and morality. *Journal of Cognitive Neuroscience, 20*(9), 1529–1546.

Burnett, S., Bird, G., Moll, J., Frith, C., & Blakemore, S.J. (2009). Development during adolescence of the neural processing of social emotion. *Journal of Cognitive Neuroscience, 21*(9), 1736–1750.

Ciaramelli, E., Muccioli, M., Ladavas, E., & di Pellegrino, G. (2007). Selective deficit in personal moral judgment following damage to ventromedial prefrontal cortex. *Soc Cogn Affect Neurosci, 2*(2), 84–92.

de Oliveira-Souza, R., Hare, R. D., Bramati, I. E., Garrido, G. J., Azevedo Ignácio, F., Tovar-Moll, F., et al. (2008). Psychopathy as a disorder of the moral brain: Fronto-temporo-limbic grey matter reductions demonstrated by voxel-based morphometry. *NeuroImage, 40*(3), 1202–1213.

de Quervain, D. J., Fischbacher, U., Treyer, V., Schellhammer, M., Schnyder, U., Buck, A., et al. (2004). The neural basis of altruistic punishment. *Science, 305*(5688), 1254–1258.

de Waal, F. (1998). *Chimpanzee politics power and sex among apes.* Baltimore: Johns Hopkins University Press.

Decety, J. & Grezes, J. (2006). The power of simulation: Imagining one's own and other's behavior. *Brain Research, 1079,* 4–14.

Delgado, M. R., Frank, R. H., & Phelps, E. A. (2005). Perceptions of moral character modulate the neural systems of reward during the trust game. *Nat Neurosci, 8*(11), 1611–1618.

Depue, R. A. & Morrone-Strupinsky, J. V. (2005). A neurobehavioral model of affiliative bonding: Implications for conceptualizing a human trait of affiliation. *Behavioral and Brain Sciences, 28*(3), 313–350.

Eisenberg, N. (2000). Emotion, regulation, and moral development. *Annu Rev Psychol, 51,* 665–697.

Eslinger, P. J. & Damasio, A. R. (1985). Severe disturbance of higher cognition after bilateral frontal lobe ablation: Patient EVR. *Neurology, 35*(12), 1731–1741.

Fehr, E. & Fischbacher, U. (2003). The nature of human altruism. *Nature, 425*(6960), 785–791.

Freedman, L. J., Insel, T. R., & Smith, Y. (2000). Subcortical projections of area 25 (subgenual cortex) of the macaque monkey. *J Comp Neurol, 421*(2), 172–188.

Gintis, H., Henrich, J., Bowles, S., Boyd, R., & Fehr, E. (2008). Strong reciprocity and the roots of human morality. *Social Justice Research, 21*(2), 241–253.

Greene, J. D., Nystrom, L. E., Engell, A. D., Darley, J. M., & Cohen, J. D. (2004). The neural bases of cognitive conflict and control in moral judgment. *Neuron, 44*(2), 389–400.

Greene, J. D., Sommerville, R. B., Nystrom, L. E., Darley, J. M., & Cohen, J. D. (2001). An fMRI investigation of emotional engagement in moral judgment. *Science, 293*(5537), 2105–2108.

Haidt, J. (2001). The emotional dog and its rational tail: A social intuitionist approach to moral judgment. *Psychological Review, 108*(4), 814–834.

Harbaugh, W. T., Mayr, U., & Burghart, D. R. (2007). Neural responses to taxation and voluntary giving reveal motives for charitable donations. *Science, 316*(5831), 1622–1625.

Hsu, M., Anen, C., & Quartz, S. R. (2008). The right and the good: Distributive justice and neural encoding of equity and efficiency. *Science, 320*(5879), 1092–1095.

Hume, D. (1777). *An enquiry into the principles of morals* (Vol. 2). London: T. Cadell.

Insel, T. R. & Young, L. J. (2001). The neurobiology of attachment. *Nat Rev Neurosci, 2*(2), 129–136.

Kedia, G., Berthoz, S., Wessa, M., Hilton, D., & Martinot, J. L. (2008). An agent harms a victim: A functional magnetic resonance imaging study on specific moral emotions. *J Cogn Neurosci, 20*(10), 1788–1798.

King-Casas, B., Tomlin, D., Anen, C., Camerer, C. F., Quartz, S. R., & Montague, P. R. (2005). Getting to know you: Reputation and trust in a two-person economic exchange. *Science, 308*(5718), 78–83.

Koenigs, M. & Tranel, D. (2007). Irrational economic decision-making after ventromedial prefrontal damage: Evidence from the Ultimatum Game. *J Neurosci, 27*(4), 951–956.

Koenigs, M., Young, L., Adolphs, R., Tranel, D., Cushman, F., Hauser, M., et al. (2007). Damage to the prefrontal cortex increases utilitarian moral judgments. *Nature, 446*(7138), 908–911.

Kringelbach, M. L. & Rolls, E. T. (2004). The functional neuroanatomy of the human orbitofrontal cortex: Evidence from neuroimaging and neuropsychology. *Progress in Neurobiology, 72*(5), 341–372.

Krueger, F., McCabe, K., Moll, J., Kriegeskorte, N., Zahn, R., Strenziok, M., et al. (2007). Neural correlates of trust. *Proc Natl Acad Sci U S A, 104*(50), 20084–20089.

Lamb, R. B. (1974). Adam Smith's system: Sympathy not self-interest. *Journal of the History of Ideas, 35*(4), 671–682.

Liu, W., Miller, B. L., Kramer, J. H., Rankin, K., Wyss-Coray, C., Gearhart, R., et al. (2004). Behavioral disorders in the frontal and temporal variants of frontotemporal dementia. *Neurology, 62*(5), 742–748.

McClure, S. M., Botvinick, M. M., Yeung, J. D., & Cohen, J. D. (2006). Conflict monitoring in cognition-emotion competition. In J. J. Gross (Ed.), *Handbook of emotion regulation.* New York Guilford Press.

Miller, E. K. & Cohen, J. D. (2001). An integrative theory of prefrontal cortex function. *Annu Rev Neurosci, 24,* 167–202.

Moll, J. & de Oliveira-Souza, R. (2009). "Extended attachment" and the human brain: Internalized cultural values and evolutionary implications. In Verplaetse, de Schrijver, Vanneste, Braeckman, (Eds.). *The moral brain* (pp. 69–85). London: Springer.

Moll, J., de Oliveira-Souza, R., Garrido, G. J., Bramati, I. E., Caparelli-Daquer, E. M. A., Paiva, M. M. F., et al. (2007). The self as a moral agent: Linking the neural bases of social agency and moral sensitivity. *Social Neuroscience, 2*(3 & 4), 336–352.

Moll, J., de Oliveira-Souza, R., Moll, F. T., Ignacio, F. A., Bramati, I. E., Caparelli-Daquer, E. M., et al. (2005). The moral affiliations of disgust: A functional MRI study. *Cogn Behav Neurol, 18*(1), 68–78.

Moll, J., de Oliveira-Souza, R., & Zahn, R. (2008). The neural basis of moral cognition: Sentiments, concepts, and values. *Ann NY Acad Sci, 1124*(1), 161–180.

Moll, J., Eslinger, P. J., & Oliveira-Souza, R. (2001). Frontopolar and anterior temporal cortex activation in a moral judgment task: Preliminary functional MRI results in normal subjects. *Arq Neuropsiquiatr, 59*(3-B), 657–664.

Moll, J., Krueger, F., Zahn, R., Pardini, M., de Oliveira-Souza, R., & Grafman, J. (2006). Human fronto-mesolimbic networks guide decisions about charitable donation. *Proc Natl Acad Sci U S A, 103*(42), 15623–15628.

Moll, J. & Schulkin, J. (2009). Social attachment and aversion in human moral cognition. *Neuroscience and Biobehavioral Reviews, 33*(3), 456–465.

Moll, J., Zahn, R., de Oliveira-Souza, R., Krueger, F., & Grafman, J. (2005). Opinion: The neural basis of human moral cognition. *Nat Rev Neurosci, 6*(10), 799–809.

O'Connor, L. E., Berry, J. W., Weiss, J., & Gilbert, P. (2002). Guilt, fear, submission, and empathy in depression. *Journal of Affective Disorders, 71*(1–3), 19–27.

Ralph, M. A. L. & Patterson, K. (2008). Generalization and differentiation in semantic memory - Insights from semantic dementia. *Year in Cognitive Neuroscience, 2008, 1124,* 61–76.

Sanfey, A. G., Rilling, J. K., Aronson, J. A., Nystrom, L. E., & Cohen, J. D. (2003). The neural basis of economic decision-making in the Ultimatum Game. *Science, 300*(5626), 1755–1758.

Saver, J. L. & Damasio, A. R. (1991). Preserved access and processing of social knowledge in a patient with acquired sociopathy due to ventromedial frontal damage. *Neuropsychologia, 29*(12), 1241–1249.

Schwartz, S. H. (1992). Universals in the content and structure of values—Theoretical advances and empirical tests in 20 countries. *Advances in Experimental Social Psychology, 25*, 1–65.

Shin, L. M., Dougherty, D. D., Orr, S. P., Pitman, R. K., Lasko, M., Macklin, M. L., et al. (2000). Activation of anterior paralimbic structures during guilt-related script-driven imagery. *Biological Psychiatry, 48*(1), 43–50.

Singer, T., Kiebel, S. J., Winston, J. S., Dolan, R. J., & Frith, C. D. (2004). Brain responses to the acquired moral status of faces. *Neuron, 41*, 653–662.

Spitzer, M., Fischbacher, U., Herrnberger, B., Gron, G., & Fehr, E. (2007). The neural signature of social norm compliance. *Neuron, 56*(1), 185–196.

Stellar, E. (1954/1994). The physiology of motivation. *Psychological Review, 101*(2), 301–311.

Takahashi, H., Matsuura, M., Koeda, M., Yahata, N., Suhara, T., Kato, M., et al. (2008). Brain activations during judgments of positive self-conscious emotion and positive basic emotion: Pride and joy. *Cerebral Cortex, 18*(4), 898–903.

Takahashi, H., Yahata, N., Koeda, M., Matsuda, T., Asai, K., & Okubo, Y. (2004). Brain activation associated with evaluative processes of guilt and embarrassment: An fMRI study. *Neuroimage, 23*(3), 967–974.

Tangney, J. P., Stuewig, J., & Mashek, D. J. (2007). Moral emotions and moral behavior. *Annual Review of Psychology, 58*, 345–372.

Weiner, B. (1992). *Human motivation: Metaphors, theories, and research*: SAGE.

Welt, L. (1888). Über charakterveränderungen des menschen. *Dtsch Arch Klin Med, 42*, 339–390.

Wood, J. N. & Grafman, J. (2003). Human prefrontal cortex: Processing and representational perspectives. *Nat Rev Neurosci, 4*(2), 139–147.

Young, L. J. & Wang, Z. (2004). The neurobiology of pair bonding. *Nat Neurosci, 7*(10), 1048–1054.

Zahn, R., de Oliveira-Souza, R., Bramati, I., Garrido, G., & Moll, J. (2009). Subgenual cingulate activity reflects individual differences in empathic concern. *Neuroscience Letters, 457*(2), 107–110.

Zahn, R., Moll, J., Iyengar, V., Huey, E. D., Tierney, M., Krueger, F., et al. (2009). Social conceptual impairments in frontotemporal lobar degeneration with right anterior temporal hypometabolism. *Brain, 132*(Pt 3), 604–616.

Zahn, R., Moll, J., Krueger, F., Huey, E. D., Garrido, G., & Grafman, J. (2007). Social concepts are represented in the superior anterior temporal cortex. *Proc Natl Acad Sci U S A, 104*(15), 6430–6435.

Zahn, R., Moll, J., Paiva, M. M. F., Garrido, G., Krueger, F., Huey, E. D., et al. (2009). The neural basis of human social values: evidence from functional MRI. *Cereb. Cortex, 19*(2), 276–283.

Embodiment and Social Cognition

Paula M. Niedenthal, Jiska Eelen, *and* Marcus Maringer

Abstract

This chapter briefly reviews models of the conceptual system on which most research in social cognition research was based until very recently. It then outlines the principles of another account, which is the theory of embodied or grounded cognition. Relevant research findings are presented to demonstrate how several dimensions of experience, such as spatial location and temperature, can represent abstract concepts, and can be extended to account for abstract social concepts. The chapter then considers how social cognition is embedded in the social environment. One such support is suggested by the situatedness of concepts: Just like concepts of basic objects, social concepts are constructed online for use in particular situations. In addition, social cognitive processes are facilitated by off-loading onto the social environment. Consistent with the goals of the present volume, the chapter also points to the neural bases of these processes. It concludes with an example of a model that seeks to account for the interpretation of one of the most important social signals, the human smile.

Keywords: embodied cognition, embedded cognition, social cognition, conceptual system, scaffolding, associative networks, simulation, convergence zones, mirror neurons, amygdala, eye contact, Duchenne smiles, facial expression, mimicry

Up through the first half of the 20th century, *social psychology* could be defined as the scientific study of the ways in which the social environment elicits and provides structure to such complex social phenomena as discrimination, prejudice, prosocial behavior, conformity, and aggression. By the 1960s, insights from a subfield of psychology, most often called the *psychology of learning*, had begun to influence traditional social psychology (e.g., DeSoto, 1960; Zajonc & Burnstein, 1965), pushing it toward an endeavor that came to be known as *social cognition* (Wegner & Vallacher, 1977; Roloff & Berger, 1982). The pushing was later accelerated by insights from the emerging field of cognitive science

(Higgins & King, 1981; Rogers, 1981; Sherman, 1987; Smith, 1994; Srull & Wyer, 1989). Social cognition ultimately came to be most simply viewed as an approach that favored cognitive-mechanistic explanations of the social phenomena just listed (Fiske & Taylor, 1991; Kunda, 1999; Levine, Resnick, & Higgins, 1993; Schneider, 1991). Thus, research in this area examines how social behavior is mediated by mental processes involved in the translation of perceptual information into knowledge and also the manipulation of that knowledge, once acquired, for use in behaviors that rely on memory, inference, decision making, and judgment. For example, stereotype use and prejudice are complex social behaviors.

In order to understand their origins and unfoldings one not only needs to consider the environment in which they occur, but one also needs to assess how the discriminating person processes, stores, retrieves and applies social information about the target group (e.g., Brauer, Chambres, Niedenthal, & Chatard-Pannetier, 2004; Brauer, Judd, & Thompson, 2003; Devine, 1989).

A central construct in research in social cognition is thus the concept. A *concept* is a mental representation of a category, natural or artifactual, that exists in the world or in the introspective experience of the individual. So, researchers in the area of social cognition are indeed preoccupied with social concepts that refer, for example, to types of people, situations, and interactions (e.g., Cantor, 1981). Importantly, though, the manner in which concepts are represented and processed has been viewed differently over time. The models from cognitive psychology that initially impelled research in social cognition (discussed below) were strongly influenced by the metaphor of the mind as a computer. However, since the goal of social psychology is to identify the ways in which the social environment shapes people's behavior, a computer-based model of social cognition falls short, because it overlooks the fact that thinking and reasoning is a creative process that unfolds in a continuous interaction between the individual and its social environment.

Interestingly, the very same researchers who were associated with the initial forays into social cognition were the same ones who ultimately called for a less computer-like model of social cognition (e.g., Zajonc & Markus, 1984; Schwarz, 2000). In this century, social cognition research has come to rely more and more on new ideas about how social behavior is supported. While conceptual processing is still central to most who generate models of social behavior, social-cognitive models now incorporate two notions: the notion of embodied or grounded cognition, and the notion of embedded or situated information processing. These two notions integrate the original concerns of social psychology about the effects of the environment on behavior with the concerns of researchers in social cognition about the mediating mechanisms. The neural mechanisms in particular have become of great interest as theories of embodied cognition find increasing support and utility.

The present chapter briefly reviews models of the conceptual system on which most research in social cognition research was based until very recently. This is followed by an outline of the principles of another account, which is the theory of embodied or grounded cognition. We then review research findings that demonstrate how several dimensions of experience such as spatial location and temperature can represent abstract concepts, and can be extended to account for abstract social concepts. Next we consider how social cognition is embedded in the social environment. One such support is suggested by the situatedness of concepts: Just like concepts of basic objects, social concepts are constructed online for use in particular situations. In addition, social cognitive processes are facilitated by off-loading onto the social environment. Along the way we point to the neural bases of these processes. We end with an example of a model that seeks to account for the interpretation of one of the most important social signals, the human smile.

Traditional Models of the Conceptual System in Social Cognition

The human conceptual system contains the knowledge base that supports the full continuum of cognitive operations from encoding of perceptual information to inference and decision making. Two of the initially relied-upon models of the conceptual system within social cognition—imported from cognitive psychology—were associative network models (e.g., Anderson, 1981 Collins & Loftus, 1975) and exemplar models (Medin & Shaffer, 1978; Nosofsky, 1988). According to both views, when perceiving a social entity, such as for instance a group of people demonstrating during a strike, information is initially encoded in the brain's modality systems, such as the visual, auditory, and probably affective systems. The information is then extracted and stored as an abstract language-like symbol or "node." In the associative network view, the node might be the word "DEMONSTRATION." This symbol or node may be stored in some relation (for instance through associative links) to the information that was encoded in the brain's modality systems as "LOUD," "ENERGETIC," and "EXHILERATED." Later, when thinking about one's concept of demonstrations, what is extracted from memory and used to make inferences are (at least) these three pieces of information in their language-like form, that is a label for the concept and a list of its features.

Hence, according to associative network accounts, discrete nodes represent pieces of information in a symbolic way. Nodes are further interconnected by "associative links" and the patterns of associations constitute concepts. When a node is activated, all nodes linked to it are activated according to the strength of association and via a mechanism of spreading activation. That is, the more a node is interconnected, the greater the probability that it will be activated by its neighbors and influence processing. In a similar manner, exemplar models propose that each experience of a category member is preserved as a trace in memory, although not in photo-like form since conceptual and attentional influences at encoding bias the preserved memory to some degree. The entire body of exemplars associated with a category constitutes the concept. Exemplars may be points in multi-dimensional space or attribute values such as Xs and Os, but for most theorists, they are redescriptions of the original perceptual, motor, and introspective states.

The full set of the abstracted symbols thus constitutes the person's conceptual system, and it is this system that supports inference, categorization, memory, and other forms of higher cognition. A theorist can use the construct of feature lists, semantic networks, propositions, schemata, statistical vectors, and so on, to account for redescriptions of the original input. Adopting any such an approach in modeling concepts involves accepting two assumptions. One is that the processes of the mind are separate and independent of the processes of the body and the brain (Block, 1995; Dennett, 1969). Recent advances in the neurosciences, however, cast strong doubt on the validity of this assumption. A second inherent assumption is that higher-level cognitive processes operate on symbols that have been transduced (i.e., extracted and redescribed) from the perceptual system in which they were initially encoded and stored in an amodal (i.e., symbolic and non-analogical) format (Newell & Simon, 1972; Pylyshyn, 1984). Recent advances in cognitive science cast doubt on whether the transduction principle of amodal representations can fully account for most types of high-level cognition (Barsalou, 2008).

Embodied Cognition Theories

There is another possible view, and in that view an important part of the conceptual system is nonmodular and modal, using systems in the brain's modalities to represent conceptual content (Barsalou, 1999; Martin, 2001; Thompson-Schill, 2003). For example, retrieving the memory of an encounter with a bear could involve the reactivation of parts of the visual, auditory, and affective states that were active while perceiving it (Niedenthal, 2007). Indeed, researchers now work with the idea that the neural states that occur in interaction with an entity or a situation represent that entity in higher-order cognition (Barsalou, 1999, 2003, 2005, 2008; Gallese, 2003, 2005; Gibbs, 2003; Glenberg, 2007;

Niedenthal et al., 2005, Semin & Smith, 2008). A distributed circuit across the modalities represents the specific properties typically processed for a category. Thus, in this approach, the modality-specific states that occurred during a particular perceptual episode are also used to represent these ideas when the original entity or situation is not actually present, that is in "offline" cognition.

A vast amount of neuropsychological research demonstrates that mental simulations take place when processing information. For example, studies about action understanding show that, when reading action verbs or meaningful stories that imply object interactions, brain regions that are involved in motor function are activated simultaneously (Pulvermüller, 2005; Rizzolatti & Craighero, 2004; Speer, Reynolds, Swallow, & Zacks, 2009; Willems, Hagoort, & Casasanto, 2010). Also, research on emotion suggests that emotion understanding requires simulating emotional states internally. Impairments in right somatosensory cortex activation hamper recognition of emotional facial expressions (Adolphs, Damasio, Tranel, Cooper, & Damasio, 2000). A recent study of Hennenlotter et al. (2008) showed that an induced decrease of frown muscle activation (i.e., corrugator supercilii) while imitating angry faces let to a reduction in activation of left amygdala and its coupling with the dorsal brain stem. According to Wicker and colleagues (2003), both feeling disgusted and seeing others feeling disgusted activates a neural representation of this emotion in the anterior insula and the anterior cingulate cortex.

The notion of simulation is central to many theories of embodied cognition (e.g., Barsalou, 1999; Gallese, 2003; Glenberg, 2007). Simulation is a principle that stands as an alternative to the principle of transduction of perceptual symbols into amodal ones. But it does not suffice to fully implement a conceptual system.

Perceptual Symbol Systems (PSS)

Specific theories of embodied cognition have added constructs to the general notion of simulation in the brain's modality systems in order to achieve fuller functionality. Barsalou's (1999) *Perceptual Symbol Systems* (PSS) account, for instance, uses the construct of a *simulator* to implement concepts. A simulator develops for any object, event, or aspect of experience that has been repeatedly attended to. Via learning, a large number of simulators are established in long-term memory to represent this diverse experience. Once a simulator is established, it can be used to reenact interactions with the environment, thus supporting the capacity to perform conceptual tasks. The use of a given simulator, a concept, in performing a conceptual task is called *simulation*. The number of ways that a simulator can simulate a category is, in theory, unlimited. This is because in different situations, different subsets of the modality-specific knowledge in the simulator can be activated to represent the category.

For instance, when asked what typical *dentists* are like, an individual might simulate, in a number of modalities (e.g., visual, auditory, and introspective), the impressions of dentists that he or she has acquired in real life (or films). But the sampling within these modalities changes depending upon which instance of dentists drives the simulation (i.e., where it happened, why it happened, and who was there). Because dentists are associated with emotional reactions, simulations within the affective system should be quite marked and quite negative. Note that if part of knowing what a dentist signifies involves simulations within systems for negative affect, then we do not necessarily need to assume that a "tag" for the concept *dentist* is associated with another "tag" that stands for, and somehow generates, negative affect (e.g., Fiske, 1982). Because thinking about a dentist involves a multimodal simulation, the negative affect is construed as a partial grounding of the concept, not as a reaction that is activated by access to the concept's "tag" in associative memory.

In suggesting a neural architecture for conceptual processing, PSS takes as a starting point Damasio's (1989) theory of convergence zones (CZ) (see Simmons & Barsalou, 2003, for an elaborated account). This approach holds that the perception of a stimulus activates corresponding feature detectors in the brain's modality-specific systems. The populations of neurons that code featural information in a particular modality are organized in distributed hierarchically arranged feature maps (Palmer, 1999; Zeki, 1993). For example, the visual perception of a smiling face activates feature detectors that respond to the color, orientation, and planar surfaces of the face in that configuration. The low-level feature detectors process detailed perspective-based properties of the face, while higher-order detectors code its more abstract properties. The pattern of activation across corresponding feature maps represents the face in visual processing.

Convergence zones theory further holds that conjunctive neurons in the brain's association areas capture and store the patterns of activation in feature maps for subsequent use in higher cognitive processes such as memory and judgment. These association areas are the so-called convergence zones. Convergence zones are also organized hierarchically such that the CZs in a specific modality such as vision or audition capture patterns of activation within that modality and then higher-level CZs link patterns of activation across modalities. As an example, when an individual hears the sound of lightning bolt, conjunctive neurons in auditory CZs capture the pattern of activation in auditory feature maps. Other conjunctive neurons in motor CZs capture the pattern of activation caused by moving away from the location of the acute sound. At an even higher level of associative processing, conjunctive neurons in modality-specific CZs conjoin the two sets of modality-specific conjunctive neurons for the combined processing of sound and movement.

What is important about the CZ architecture as relied on by PPS is the idea that conjunctive neurons are capable of reactivating the established states in and across modalities, without input from the original stimulus. That is, the processing that occurred on a prior occasion can be reinstated. In this way, the CZ architecture implements off-line embodied cognition. For example, when thinking about a person's face, conjunctive neurons partially reactivate the visual states active while perceiving it. Similarly, when thinking about an action, conjunctive neurons partially activate the motor states that produced it. This same mechanism is viewed as supporting mental imagery in working memory (e.g., Farah, 2000; Grezes & Decéty, 2001). However, the CZ architecture and PSS do not require the reinstantiation process to be conscious (e.g., Barsalou, 1999, 2003).

In other models of embodied social cognition, simulation is proposed to be supported by specialized *mirror neurons*, or even an entire *mirror neuron system*, which map the correspondences between the observed and performed actions (Gallese, 2003, 2005). There is, however, some disagreement about the exact location of the mirror neurons, whether these neurons actually constitute a system and whether there actually are specialized neurons dedicated to mirroring or whether regular neurons can perform a mirroring function. Some of the original work on mirror neurons in monkeys emphasized the unique role of neurons located in the inferior parietal and inferior frontal cortex. These neurons discharge both when a monkey performs an action and when it observes another individual perform the same action. In extending these findings to humans, some researchers have argued that humans have a dedicated "mirror neuron area," located around the

Brodmann area 44 (human homologue of the monkey F5 region; Gallese, Keysers, & Rizzolatti, 2004, Rizzolatti & Craighero, 2004). This mirror area may compute complex operations such as mapping the correspondence between self and other (Decety, Michalska, & Akitsuki, 2008) or differentiating between goal-oriented versus nonintentional action (e.g., Decety & Sommerville, 2008).

Still, more questions about the architecture for embodied cognition have been raised than have been answered. The specifics of the underlying architecture will be one of the defining projects for neuroscience and neurophysiology in the coming years.

Examples in Social Cognition

A number of interesting findings in social cognition appear to be consistent with the embodied cognition view. Research has demonstrated, for example, that the activation of the stereotype of the elderly automatically primes stereotype-consistent behavior (e.g., reduced motor speed, Dijksterhuis & Bargh, 2001; Ferguson & Bargh, 2004). A classic study by Bargh, Chen, and Burrows (1996) showed that when students were primed with the category "elderly people," they walked more slowly when leaving the laboratory than nonprimed students. Mussweiler (2006) turned this effect around. Over a series of studies, he induced experimental participants to engage in motor movements that typified a particular social category and showed that these movements primed the use of that category in social judgment, including automatic perceptual processing. For instance, in one study individuals were led to walk around with weights on their ankles and their wrists while wearing life preservers on their upper bodies. After having this physical experience, the participants read about a hypothetical person and then rated the person on a number of traits, some of which were part of the stereotype of "overweight people." Results showed that participants who had been induced to use heavy, sluggish movements themselves rated the hypothetical person more like a typical overweight person than did control participants who had not had this physical experience.

Considering how bodily experiences shape people's understanding of others, models of social cognition that assume that the mind is separate and independent of the processes of the body lack explanatory value. Embodiment in the current psychological literature refers to the brain's modality-specific systems and how these structures are related to people's conceptual knowledge (e.g., Niedenthal, Winkielman, Mondillon & Vermeulen, 2009). The circuits in modality-specific brain systems are efficiently able to represent the complexity of a very large number of entities and experiences. Furthermore, such states can be reactivated without their output being observable in overt behavior, so that embodiment needs not to be associated with an observable bodily reenactment of a stimulus. Nevertheless, actual embodied states may arise under many circumstances, as when the motor system becomes activated or actually begins to execute expressions, movements, postures, actions, and so forth. In this sense, embodiment refers to reenactments that can include cortical reactivation of modality-specific areas, internal bodily activity associated with arousal, heart rate, and even contractions in the musculature.

Accounting for Abstraction and Embeddedness

PSS can be extended to account for two concerns that have become critical for advancing the study of social cognition: abstraction, and embeddedness. Here we define each and illustrate how they have been recently illustrated in the empirical literature.

Abstraction

Abstract concepts are concepts whose instances do not share diagnostic perceptual features, and thus are not "seen" as constituting a category. For example, it is easy to form a category of dentists based on visual (e.g., gloves and mouth protection), auditory (e.g., high speed drilling noise), and introspective experiences (e.g., negative affect), but how do the brain's modalities support a category of "moral codes" or more importantly for social cognition, "extraverts" or "glad-handing salesmen." It would appear difficult to propose that embodied responses can ground such concepts (see e.g., Mahon & Caramazza, 2008). Nevertheless, Boroditsky and Prinz (2008) suggest a number of ways in which PSS can be extended to accommodate abstract concepts. Metaphors, for instance, help people describe abstract ideas in concrete terms, and suggest that the abstract world is conceptualized physically (Lakoff & Johnson, 1980). The abstract notion of valence (i.e., positivity) has been shown to be grounded in perceptual dimensions such as spatial location (i.e., good is up and bad is down, Meier & Robinson, 2004), brightness (i.e., good is bright and bad is dark, Meier, Robinson, Crawford, & Ahlvers, 2007) and auditory pitch (i.e., high pitch sounds mean good things) (for a review, see

Crawford, 2009). Work from Boroditsky has further demonstrated that the conceptualization of time heavily depends on the dimension of space (Boroditsky, 2000, 2001; Boroditsky & Ramscar, 2002; Casasanto & Boroditsky, 2008). The idea of importance seems to be related to the physical dimension of weight (Jostmann, Lakens, & Schubert, 2009; Ackerman, Nocera, & Bargh, 2010) and the concept of numbers is represented spatially on a horizontal line (Brozzoli et al., 2008). Hence, one solution to accommodate abstract concepts is the use of perceptual dimensions of experience by analogical extension. Intuitively, such dimensions are revealed through linguistic expressions.

In the following two sections we provide further interesting evidence of how perceptual dimensions of experience also ground abstract social concepts. In particular we show how the abstract notion of social power is related to the perceptual dimension of space, and how the abstract notion of interpersonal closeness is related to the perceptual dimension of temperature.

Power
During the course of a lifetime, most people encounter individuals who have power over them, at least to a certain extent (e.g., parents, teachers, religious leaders). In interactions with powerful people, attention might be drawn to perceptual, motor, and introspective states of the situation that can serve to represent social power. For instance, one important and common feature that accompanies the experience of social power is the perception of space differences. Children experience the fact that most powerful people are taller than they are. They may also notice that the school director has an extra-large office, with an extra-large chair. Why else would he need that extra-large space other than being more powerful than other teachers? This illustrates how spatial experiences, such as experiences of size differences, can easily be incorporated into the representation of an abstract social concept like power, and also why people have names such as "Big Daddy" or "Alexander the Great."

In a series of studies, Schubert (2005) demonstrated empirically that mental representations of power include spatial location information about what is up and down. People seem to share a mental power = up schema and visualize power relationships between social groups with the powerful group (e.g., boss) on top and the powerless group (e.g., secretary) underneath. Also, judgments of power interfere with spatial cues about up and down. Across all

studies, participants recognized powerful social groups faster or more accurately when provided with an up-cue, than when provided with a down-cue, whereas the opposite was true for powerless items. Spatial power cues were both visual (i.e., names of social group appear at the top or the bottom of the computer screen) and motoric (i.e., responding with "up" and "down" arrow on the keyboard). Schubert ruled out the possibility that these effects were caused by valence, which also implies spatial information about up (good) and down (bad). Moreover, Schubert demonstrated that judgments of power can also be (erroneously) influenced by spatial power cues. Powerful items (e.g., lion) are rated even more powerful when shown at the top of the computer screen in comparison with presenting these items at the bottom.

Giessner and Schubert (2007) extended these findings and showed that information on a vertical dimension also influences power judgments of leaders. In one experiment, participants read a short text about a manager accompanied by an organization chart. Boxes at the lower level represented employees and were connected to one top box representing the manager of the company. The length of the vertical line (short or long) was manipulated between participants. Participants in the large vertical difference condition perceived the leader as more powerful than participants in the small vertical difference condition.

Conversely, Giessner and Schubert also demonstrated that thinking about leaders is externalized vertically. In another study, participants read a description about a powerful or a powerless leader. Next, participants had to move a box on the computer screen that represented the manager until its position matched his relationship to the personnel. The six pictures of the employees could not be moved. Similar to using an organization chart in a different study (which explicitly referred to verticality), participants put a more powerful leader higher up than a less powerful leader.

Zink et al. (2008) had their participants play a visual discrimination game against virtual opponents (human or inanimate). Before each round, a picture of the other involved player was shown, together with his rank (inferior or superior to participant's rank). Zink et al. observed that the occipital/parietal cortex, ventral striatum, and parahippocampal cortex were activated more strongly when participants saw a superior than an inferior player (human or inanimate), no matter whether this social hierarchy was stable or unstable over different rounds. Activation of the dorsolateral prefrontal cortex only occurred in social hierarchy situations where participants were inferior to their (human) counter players. Further research should investigate whether, as would be predicted by an embodied account of social cognition, these neural correlates represent the concept of power, and whether these brain regions also detect physical spatial differences between powerful and powerless agents.

Not only do spatial differences affect how powerful others are perceived, interestingly, holding a high power pose also makes oneself feel more powerful. Carney, Cuddy, and Yap (2010) asked participants to hold a high power pose (i.e., open and expansive) or a low power pose (i.e., closed and constrictive) and showed that these postures induced neuroendocrine and behavioral changes in power. Posing high (vs. low) power increased (vs. decreased) participants' testosterone level, decreased (vs. increased) their cortisol level and led to more (vs. less) risk taking.

The behavioral evidence just summarized suggests that the abstract social concept of power is grounded in part in the physical experience of being with powerful people. This experience can be represented by the spatial relationship between the powerless and the powerful. In this sense embodied experience has a social meaning. Another physical experience, temperature, seems to represent social meaning too.

Interpersonal warmth
A fundamental dimension of social judgment is that of "warm" versus "cold" and this judgment exerts important influences on social interaction. Recent evidence suggests that sensations of temperature can represent the basis of these social judgments and behaviors. Williams and Bargh (2008) recently demonstrated that the tactile experience of warmth affects how interpersonally warm people behave and judge others. On their way to the experimental room participants were asked by an assistant to hold his cold or hot beverage so that he could write down some information about the participant. Later, during the actual experimental session, participants who had held a hot beverage judged a hypothetical person as more interpersonally warm than participants who had held the cold beverage.

In a second experiment participants evaluated a cold or hot therapeutic pad and were later compensated for their participation by the receipt of one of two gifts. One gift was described as a treat for a friend, while the other was described as a treat for themselves. Participants who had held the hot pad previously during the session chose to treat a friend

more often than participants who touched the cold pad, suggesting that the notion of interpersonal warmth had been primed by the physical experience of warmth. Williams and Bargh note that the activation of the anterior insula underlies both the physical sensation of warmth (Craig, Chen, Bandy, & Reiman, 2000) and psychological sensations of warmth like feelings of social inclusion, trust, and empathy (Carr, Iacoboni, Dubeau, Mazziotta, & Lenzi, 2003; King-Casas et al., 2008; Rilling et al., 2008; van den Bos, van Dijk, Westenberg, Rombouts, & Crone, 2009).

IJzerman and Semin (2009) replicated and extended these findings by showing that different manipulations of physical warmth can make people feel more close to others and that concrete language use mediates this effect. In a first study participants were instructed to hold a warm or a cold beverage, while the experimenter ostensibly prepared a questionnaire. Later participants completed the Inclusion of Other in Self scale (IOS) with regard to a significant other. This scale is a measure of the extent to which an individual represents another person as part of the self. Participants who held a warm beverage felt more socially proximate to the close other, as indicated by a higher overlap between the self and the other in the IOS-scale, than those who held a cold beverage.

In a second study, ambient temperature in the room in which a participant was sitting was manipulated to be rather cold or warm. Participants watched a video about chess pieces and described what they saw. Later they completed the IOS scale, using the experimenter as the other person. Descriptions of the video were coded for concreteness (with actions being most concrete and use of adjectives being most abstract). Results showed that participants in the warm room described the chess events more concretely than participants in the cold room. Participants in the warm room also felt closer to the experimenter than participants in the cold room. Language use partially mediated the effect of temperature on social proximity.

In a final study, IJzerman and Semin (2009) showed that a warm room temperature made participants focus more on relationships between objects, whereas a cold room temperature made participants focus more on details within objects. Again, this effect was mediated by language use, as indicated by participants' descriptions of the chess video, with cold temperatures leading to abstract language use and warm temperatures leading to more concrete language use.

Zhong and Leonardelli (2008) found evidence for the reverse effect, namely that experiences of social proximity affect perceptions of temperature. Participants who recalled experiencing social exclusion reported lower perceptions of the ambient temperature than participants who recalled an inclusion experience. Furthermore, participants who were feeling excluded in a virtual gaming setting were more likely to seek warmth, as indicated by their desire for warm food and drinks, than participants who were not excluded from the video game.

The research just summarized demonstrates that abstract social concepts such as social power and social warmth have a basis in physical experiences such that the activation of this experience affects the use of these concepts in information processing. Such findings illustrate how embodied cognition can serve to represent subtle aspects of social meaning.

In addition to abstraction, PSS can be extended to account for another construct that has become critical for advancing the study of social cognition: embedded cognition. Embodiedness and embeddedness seem to go together, since that the crucial assumption of both is that the mind does not function in isolation. Whereas embodiment describes social cognition as a function of the mind and the body, embeddedness complements that view by describing how social cognition unfolds as a function of the mind and the social environment.

Embedded cognition

Embedded or situated cognition has a number of different definitions, the general one being that cognition and environment are strongly interdependent and that cognitive processes do not operate in a vacuum (Clark, 1997; Smith & Semin, 2007; Wilson, 2002). Indeed, Smith and Semin (2007) argue that cognitive processes are always determined by situational goals and motives of the actors. For instance, when studying stereotypes, researchers have assumed that people hold stable beliefs about social groups. These representations are considered to be automatically activated and consistent over situations and time. However, it has been shown that situational factors can easily alter the contentt and influence of stereotypes in social situations (Semin, de Montes, & Valencia, 2003).

Embodiedness and embeddedness seem to go together, and theories of concepts such as PSS that rely on principles of embodied cognition have been extended to accommodate the idea that cognition is linked to the environment in which it occurs. Notions that perception is embedded, cognition is off-loaded, and learning is scaffolded, furthermore, bring the environment back into social cognition in a manner that should allow it to reunite with basic principles of social psychology (Smith & Semin, 2007). Next we will show how this could be accomplished by describing relevant work from the areas of perception and learning.

Perception

One reason that cognition must be thought of as embedded in situations (or situated) is that perception itself is situated. For example, Barsalou (2008) suggests that

> "if simulation underlies conceptual processing, a potential implication of the representation of concepts follows: if a conceptual representation simulates a perceptual experience, it should simulate a situation, because situations provide the background of perceptual experience." (p. 241).

Even more radically, senses such as vision are now described by some theorists as embedded in situation as well. Researchers in animate and interactive vision see the task of vision to be a real-world, task-sensitive process that operates in the service of goals at hand, rather than providing a sort of passive film of a disembodied environment (Ballard, 1991). Consistent with this view, there is accumulating evidence that aspects of the social environment affect several types of perception.

Chambon (2009), for instance, recently showed how the embodiment of the stereotype of the elderly influences basic processes in perception. In a first study he stopped young adults walking through a park and invited them to complete a task that surreptitiously primed the stereotype of the elderly (but that made no reference to fatigue or movement) or another neutral concept. He then asked participants to estimate the incline of one of several grassy slopes. The results of their estimates as a function of the type of priming are graphed in Figure 33.1. As can be seen, individuals for whom the stereotype of the elderly had been covertly primed overestimated the incline significantly as compared to the control participants, and this effect increased over the size of the incline.

Similar to Chambon, previous research had shown modifications of perceived space when the individuals' physiological potential is reduced by age, poor health, an hour's jogging, or a heavy backpack. Chambon's results, however, demonstrate more radically the effects of embodied belief in addition to effects of real experiences. That is, stereotype

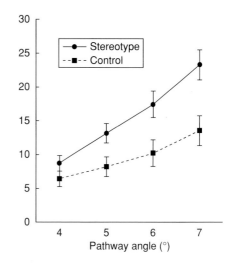

Fig. 33.1 Perceived gradient (± 1 SE) as a function of true pathway gradient for participants in whom the stereotype of the eldery was primed versus not primed. Adapted from Chambon, M. (2009). Embodied perception with others' bodies in mind: Stereotype priming influence on the perception of spatial environment. *Journal of Experimental Social Psychology*, 45, 283–287. Reprinted with permission of Elsevier.

priming affected perceptions such that the encoded information was related to the embodied meaning: Young adults primed with the elderly category estimated slopes as steeper and distances longer than their nonprimed counterparts because for them the exertion required to traverse the space in these cases was momentarily viewed as surpassing their capacity. Additional findings that illustrate the socially embedded nature of perception were provided by Chambon, Droit-Volet, and Niedenthal (2007). These authors conducted a study of time perception, in which time was represented by photographs of faces of the elderly, versus faces of young people. According to internal-clock models of time judgment (Gibbon, Church, & Meck, 1984), the raw material for subjective time comes from the number of pulses emitted by a (biologically based) pacemaker, which are accumulated in a timer during the event to be judged. Subjective time thus depends on the number of pulses accumulated during an event: the more pulses accumulated, the longer the event is perceived to last. Perceived duration can thus vary as a function of the speeding up or the slowing down of the pacemaker in certain circumstances (e.g., Drew, Fairhurst, Malapani, Horvitz & Balsam, 2003). If perceivers reproduce the sensory-motor states of "being there" with elderly people, arousal should decrease, as it does when movements are slower. This should slow the speed of the pacemaker, fewer pulses should accumulate, and time should appear shorter rather than longer (i.e., underestimated).

In the study, Chambon and colleagues employed the temporal bisection task, a task frequently used to test the predictions of the clock-based model (e.g., Droit-Volet, 2003). The task involved learning to categorize two standard durations, one short and one long, in an initial training phase. In a test phase, participants were presented with comparison stimulus durations (i.e., intermediate duration values) and the standard values and they judge the durations as representing either the short or to the long standard duration. In Chambon et al. (2007) the comparison stimulus durations in the test phase were represented by pictures of faces of elderly and young males and females (expressing neutral emotion). Results showed that female participants underestimated the time that an elderly woman's face was presented on a computer screen. This underestimation was not observed when duration was represented by faces of young women or men of any age. In addition, male participants underestimated the duration that the face of an elderly man was presented on a computer screen. This underestimation was not observed when duration was represented by faces of young women or men. The sex-specific effect could be expected to occur because the (relatively young) participants may not be sufficiently identified with the elderly of the opposite sex to internally simulate their motor behavior.

Another way in which cognition is embedded in the environment is reflected in the concepts and empirical demonstrations of off-loading cognition, to which we will turn next.

Off-loaded cognition
Clark describes off-loading cognition as the "interplay between individual reason, artifact, and culture" (1999, p. 349). A simple example of off-loading cognition is the act of calculating a number on a piece of paper, or using fingers to add up numbers. As Niedenthal and Alabali (2009) further note,

off-loading is also related to the developmental process of scaffolding.

Physical scaffolds are structures that are used temporarily to support workers and materials during construction of a tall building. The concept of psychological scaffolding was described by Wood, Bruner, and Ross (1976) to characterize, by reference to a real physical scaffold, the manner by which a tutor can support the acquisition of knowledge and skills in a pupil. The notion of a psychological scaffold has since been used to model a number of supportive learning relationships, including parent-child interactions, teacher-student interactions, and interactions between peers (e.g., Tabak & Baumgartner, 2004; Taumoepeau & Ruffman, 2008) and it has been framed in terms of Vygotsky's (1978) sociocultural theory of development. In the same way that physical scaffolds support construction workers during their labor, adults' social scaffolding supports children's task performance. Social scaffolding helps them to broaden their behavioral and cognitive repertoire, and to perform tasks that would be otherwise difficult or impossible (Greenfield, 1984). Once a new task is accomplished or skill achieved, the social scaffold can be withdrawn, just as a physical scaffold is disassembled when construction is complete.

Relatedly, in off-loading cognition, individuals use the environment consciously and unconsciously to store, represent, or manipulate ideas and operations. We think that an excellent example of off-loaded social cognition is that of transactive memory (Wegner, Giuliano, & Hertel, 1985). The general idea is that humans function in dyads and groups, and that each member of these social structures stores only some part of all the information that the structure needs to function. That is, individuals store some information themselves, and remember who has stored other useful pieces of information. They then rely on the other individual's memory when those additional pieces of information are needed. This happens, for instance, when a husband takes the wheel of the car knowing that while he has no idea how to get to the current destination, his wife has already learned that information and can guide him. The notion of transactive memory in that sense accounts for how intimate dyads and families coordinate memory and tasks, and also how groups and organizations might develop "group minds"—systems of knowledge that are more articulated and sometimes more effective than those of any of their individual members.

In a classic study, Wegner, Erber and Raymond (1991), for instance, recruited (heterosexual) dating couples for a study on memory. Some of the couples remained together as natural couples whereas other couples were separated and randomly assigned to new experimental couples. The idea was that natural couples over time have developed efficient strategies for sharing and organizing information, which experimental couples that have just been put together are lacking. Wegner and colleagues then compared the natural and experimental couples with respect to their performance on a memory task. In line with the assumption that people can enhance their cognitive recourses by organizing their memories with others, the results showed that natural couples were able to remember more items compared to experimental couples. Moreover, on the individual level participants within the natural couples outperformed participants within the experimental couples regarding memory performance. Hence, people share, or we would say off-load their memories with others and by doing so increase their individual and dyadic mental capacity.

Interestingly, transactive memory was initially linked to amodal, computer-based models of memory (Wegner, 1995). But the processes of representation and retrieval probably fit more naturally with an embodied account (Glenberg, 1997; Pecher & Zwaan, 2005) as has been noted in cultural anthropology and robotics.

Bringing it Together: Interpreting the Smile

The idea that social cognition is both embodied and embedded and that these processes serve in part to integrate classic concerns and approaches in social psychology with principles of social cognition are reflected in the Simulation of Smiles Model (SIMS) described by Niedenthal, Mermillod, Maringer, and Hess (2010). The SIMS attempts to account for the interpretation of the meanings of smiles. A functional analysis of smiles led these researchers to propose that the three primary smiles types are the *enjoyment* smile, the *affiliative* smile, and the *dominance* smile. These different displays, when accurately processed, result in the judgments that the smiling individual is "happy," "friendly," and "superior," respectively. These judgments are absolutely fundamental to social functioning; the manner in which smiles are interpreted determines the unfolding of many social interactions (see Hess, Beaupré & Cheung, 2002). Although different smiles have been described in terms of static features, such as the presence of the Duchenne marker (crows feet around the eyes) and in terms of specific dynamic characteristics (see Krumhuber, Manstead, &

Kappas, 2007 for details), these perceptual features of smiles have largely been mapped to the judgment that a smile is "true" versus "false."

The SIMS is embodied in that it suggests, in agreement with a now vast literature on the processing of facial expression, that imitation of facial expression and the reproduction of the state that corresponds to that imitated expression in the brain's systems serve to support interpretation (e.g., Adolphs, 2006; Calder & Young, 2005). The SIMS is embedded in that the interaction between the smiler and the perceiver of the smile determines how the smile is processed. Specifically, the authors propose that eye contact is one interpersonal behavior that triggers automatic imitation (i.e., it is a sufficient but not necessary condition). In addition, social factors also inhibit and facilitate imitation. Thus, although the perceptual features of smiles can be described in terms of both static and dynamic features, in social interaction the embodiment of the smile and the way in which the processing is embedded in the particular social context finally determines how any given smile is actually interpreted.

An example of how the smile is processed in a context in which an enjoyment smile has high uncertainty and salience is illustrated in Figure 33.2. Yang et al. (2002) have shown that in this case (i.e., in which the smile is unique or rare), the perception of a smile, as a significant signal (i.e., with uncertainty of meaning), is accompanied by activation in the amygdala. Consideration of the role of the amygdala in both face and gaze processing just identified support the contention that amygdala activation raises the probability that eye contact with the smiling person will be made. In the view of Niedenthal and colleagues (2010), eye contact has evolved as a sufficient trigger to embodied simulation in the sense of the construction of an internal representation of the state signaled by the perceptual input. As seen in the figure, in the case of an enjoyment smile with empirically derived authentic morphology (and/or dynamics), eye contact would produce increased activation of the reward centers of the basal ganglia and the motor brain regions (e.g., Schilbach et al., 2006), and these together enhance correspondent mimicry.

According to the model, input from the brain regions associated with smile production and the rewarding aspects of it that are used as content in the representation, or image, are produced by the somatosensory cortex. An enjoyment smile will be judged as indicating that the smiling person "is happy" on the basis of input from both facial mimicry (which provides subtle information about the characteristics of the perceived smile) and the positive feelings that such a smile produces, its reward value. When such a smile is mimicked correspondingly, the motor and reward centers will feed into a somatosensory image that provides the grounding for the judgment that the perceived smile is an enjoyment smile (that is, that the person is happy). Thus, the most straightforward case involves detection of uncertain meaning (amygdala activation), the direction of gaze accordingly (eye contact), the automatic generation of mimicry and the positive affect produced by a smile (activation of motor and limbic regions of the brain), and the feed forward of that information into the somatosensory cortex. The interpretation of the smile meaning will be grounded by that somatosensory image.

The middle panel of Figure 33.2 shows the same process that results in the judgment that a smile means that the smiling individual is "friendly," when in fact the stimulus is an empirically derived good example of such a smile. In this case, a morphologically (or dynamically) affiliative smile is perceived in a context in which amygdala activation would be expected due to the signal value of the expression (e.g., in which the smile is unique or rare). The grounding for a judgment that the smiling individual is friendly is based on inputs from regions of the brain that serve to recognize in-group members and other attachment figures, probably the orbitofrontal cortex (Nitsche et al., 2004). Finally, for the dominance smile illustrated in the bottom panel, eye contact would again be predicted to occur and to produce activation in relevant motor regions described by Schilbach and colleagues (2006). No activation of the reward-processing regions would be expected. Rather, a pattern of asymmetrical neural activation that is related to withdrawal-related negative affect (Davidson, Ekman, Saron, Senulis, & Friesen, 1990) or conflict (Wacker, Chavanon, Leue, & Stemmler, 2010) might occur. The model holds that it is the input from the specific regions associated with (dominance) smile mimicry and negative aspects of it that are used as content in the representation produced by the somatosensory cortex. A smiler will be judged as "superior" based on input from both facial mimicry and the negative feelings that it produces. In sum, this other straightforward case involves detection of significance (amygdala activation), the direction of gaze accordingly (eye contact), the automatic generation of mimicry and the more negative affect produced by the emblematic smile, and a feed forward of that

Simulation of Smiles (SIMS) Core Model

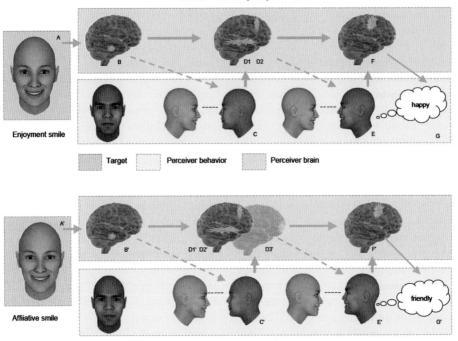

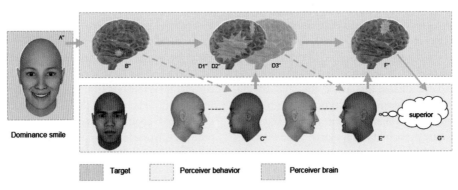

Fig. 33.2 The top panel illustrates the case of an enjoyment smile (A) presented such that the meaning is initially uncertain. The perception of the smile is accompanied by activation in the amygdala (B), which enhances the probability that eye contact with the smiling person is made (C). In the SIMS model, eye contact has evolved as a trigger for embodied simulation. Eye contact thus produces increased activation in the reward centers of the basal ganglia (D1) and in motor regions described by Schilbach and colleagues (2006) (D2) that support motor mimicry (E). These motor and limbic processes then produce bodily sensations in the somatosensory cortex (F). On this basis, the smile is judged as indicating that the smiling individual feels happy (G). The middle panel illustrates the process that results in the judgment of a smile as affiliative. The only difference between the content of the two panels (A'—G') is the additional OFC (D3') activation, which in theory supports distinctive positive affect related to attachment. The bottom panel shows the processing of a dominance smile (A"). Amygdala activation would again be expected (B") and eye contact would be predicted to occur (C"). Dominance smiles may be associated with a pattern of asymmetrical neural activation related to withdrawal-related negative affect (e.g., Davidson et al., 1990; D1") or conflict (Wacker, Chavanon, Leue, & Stemmler, 2009). Activation in relevant motor regions (D2") would be expected and output resulting in mimicry (E"). Because of the role of prefrontal cortices in processing status, OFC or contiguous regions may also be involved (D3"). Implications of these supported by somatosensory cortices (F1") will ground a judgment of a smile as a smile of superiority of some type (G").
Figure adapted from Niedenthal, Mermillod, Marginer, & Hess (in press).

502

information into the somatosensory cortex. Judgment will be grounded by that somatosensory image, and in this case it will deliver a judgment of "superior."

Niedenthal and colleagues (2010) show how the judgment process depicted in Figure 33.2 can change with social/environmental conditions, and these additional examples are beyond the scope of the present chapter. The point of the illustration here is to show how the social environment and social-cognitive processes combine to furnish a social judgment that is critical for ensuing social interaction.

Conclusion

In the present chapter we briefly reviewed some of the dominant representational models in social cognition. We then outlined the principles of and the utility of more recent theories that hold that meaning is embodied in the sensory-motor states that occur in interaction with them. These models will not suffice for accounting for all cognitive phenomena that we observe, and no one is making that argument. Language, for example, is a powerful and not always embodied code for representation and process of manipulating ideas. Notions of embodiedness and embeddedness, however, do seem to capture very well the phenomena, both social and cognitive, of interest in the area of social psychology, the models based on these two ideas do a good job of à priori predicting interactions between brain, behavior, and environment that will motivate changes and developments in theory building and links between sciences that previously were unable to communicate.

References

Adolphs, R. (2006). Perception and emotion. *Current Directions in Cognitive Science*, 15, 222–226.

Ackerman, J. M., Nocera, C. C., & Bargh, J. A. (2010). Incidental haptic sensations influence social judgments and decisions. *Science*, 328(5986), 1712–1715.

Adolphs, R., Damasio, H., Tranel, D., Cooper, G., & Damasio, A. R. (2000). A role for somatosensory cortices in the visual recognition of emotion as revealed by three-dimensional lesion mapping. *Journal of Neuroscience*, 20(7), 2683–2690.

Anderson, N. H. (1981). *Foundations of information integration theory*. New York: Academic Press.

Ballard, D. (1991). Animate vision. *Artificial Intelligence*, 48, 57–86.

Bargh, J. A., Chen, M., & Burrows, L. (1996). Automaticity of social behavior: Direct effects of trait construct and stereotype activation on action. *Journal of Personality and Social Psychology*, 71, 230–244.

Barsalou, L. W. (1999) Perceptual symbol systems. *Behavorial and Brain Sciences*. 22, 577–660.

Barsalou, L. W. (2003). Situated simulation in the human conceptual system. *Language and Cognitive Processes*, 18, 513–562. [Reprinted in H. Moss & J. Hampton, Conceptual representation (pp. 513–566). East Sussex, UK: Psychology Press.]

Barsalou, L.W. (2008). Grounded cognition. *Annual Review of Psychology*, 59, 617–645.

Barsalou, L. W., Santos, A., Simmons, W. K., & Wilson, C. D. (2008). Language and simulation in conceptual processing. In M. De Vega, A. M. Glenberg, & A. C. Graesser, (Eds.). *Symbols, embodiment, and meaning* (pp. 245–283). Oxford: Oxford University Press.

Block, N. (1995). The mind as the software of the brain. In E. E. Smith & D. N. Osherson (Eds.), *Thinking* (pp. 377–425). Cambridge, MA: MIT Press.

Boroditsky, L. (2000). Metaphoric structuring: Understanding time through spatial metaphors. *Cognition*, 75(1), 1–28.

Boroditsky, L. (2001). Does language shape thought? Mandarin and English speakers' conceptions of time. *Cognitive Psychology*, 43(1), 1–22.

Boroditsky, L. & Prinz, J. (2008). What thoughts are made of. In G. R. Semin & E. R. Smith (Eds.), *Embodied grounding: Social, cognitive, affective, and neuroscientific approaches* (pp. 98–115). New York: Cambridge University Press.

Boroditsky, L. & Ramscar, M. (2002). The roles of body and mind in abstract thought. *Psychological Science*, 13(2), 185–189.

Brauer, M., Chambres, P., Niedenthal, P. M., & Chatard-Pannetier, A. (2004). The relationship between expertise and evaluative extremity: The moderating role of experts' task characteristics. *Journal of Personality and Social Psychology*, 86, 5–18.

Brauer, M., Judd, C. M., & Thompson, M. S. (2003). The acquisition, transmission, and discussion of social stereotypes: Influences of communication on group perceptions. In V. Yzerbyt, O. Corneille, & C. M. Judd (Eds.), *The psychology of group perception: Contributions to the study of homogeneity, entitativity, and essentialism.* (pp. 237–255). New York, NY: Psychology Press.

Brozzoli, C., Ishihara, M., Göbel, S. M., Salemme, R., Rossetti, Y., & Farnè, A. (2008). Touch perception reveals the dominance of spatial over digital representation of numbers. *Proceedings of the National Academy of Sciences of the United States of America*, 105(14), 5644–5648.

Calder, A. J. & Young, A. W. (2005). Understanding the recognition of facial identity and facial expression. *Nature Review Neuroscience*, 6, 641–651.

Cantor, N. (1981). Perceptions of situations: Situation prototypes and person-situation prototypes. In D. Magusson (Ed.), *Toward a psychology of situations: An interactional perspective*. Hilldale, N.J.: Lawrence Erlbaum.

Carney, D. R., Cuddy, A. J. C., & Yap, A. J. (2010). Power posing: Brief nonverbal displays affect neuroendocrine levels and risk tolerance. *Psychological Science*, 21(10), 1363–1368.

Carr, L., Iacoboni, M., Dubeau, M.-C., Mazziotta, J. C., & Lenzi, G. L. (2003). Neural mechanisms of empathy in humans: A relay from neural systems for imitation to limbic areas. *Proceedings of the National Academy of Sciences of the United States of America*, 100(9), 5497–5502.

Casasanto, D. & Boroditsky, L. (2008). Time in the mind: Using space to think about time. *Cognition*, 106(2), 579–593.

Chambon, M. (2009). Embodied perception with others' bodies in mind: Stereotype priming influence on the perception of spatial environment. *Journal of Experimental Social Psychology*, *45*, 283–287.

Chambon, M., Droit-Volet, S., & Niedenthal, P. M. (2007). The effect of embodying the elderly on temporal perception. *Journal of Experimental Social Psychology*, *44*, 672–677.

Clark, A. (1997). *Being there: Putting brain, body and world together again*. Cambridge: MIT Press.

Clark, A. (1999). An embodied cognitive science? *Trends in Cognitive Science*, *3*, 345–351.

Collins, A. M., & Loftus, E. F. (1975). A spreading-activation theory of semantic processing. *Psychological Review*, *82*, 407–428.

Craig, A. D., Chen, K., Bandy, D., & Reiman, E. M. (2000). Thermosensory activation of insular cortex. *Nature Neuroscience*, *3*(2), 184–190.

Crawford, L. E. (2009). Conceptual metaphors of affect. *Emotion Review*, *1*(2), 129–139.

Damasio, A. R. (1989). Time-locked multiregional retroactivation: A systems-level proposal for the neural substrates of recall and recognition. *Cognition*, *33*, 25–62.

Davidson, R., Ekman, P., Saron, C., Senulis, J., & Friesen, W. (1990). Approach-withdrawal and cerebral asymmetry: Emotional expression and brain physiology: I. *Journal of Personality and Social Psychology*, *58*, 330–341.

Decety, J., Michalska, K. J., & Akitsuki, Y. (2008). Who caused the pain? A functional MRI investigation of empathy and intentionality in children. *Neuropsychologia*, *46*, 2607–2614.

Decety, J. & Sommerville, J.A. (2008). Action representation as the bedrock of social cognition: A developmental neuroscience perspective. In E. Morsella, J. Bargh, & P. Gollwitzer (Eds.). *The Oxford handbook of human action* (pp. 250–275). New York: Oxford University Press.

Dennett, D. C. (1969). *Content and consciousness*. Oxford, England: Humanities Press.

DeSoto, C. B. (1960). Learning a social structure. *Journal of Abnormal and Social Psychology*, *60*, 417–421.

Devine, P. G. (1989). Stereotypes and prejudice: Their automatic and controlled components. *Journal of Personality and Social Psychology*, *56*, 5–18.

Dijksterhuis, A. & Bargh, J. A. (2001). The perception-behavior expressway: Automatic effects of social perception on social behavior. *Advances in Experimental Social Psychology*, *33*, 1–40.

Drew, M. R., Fairhurst, S., Malapani, C., Horvitz, J. C., & Balsam, P. D. (2003). Effects of dopamine antagonists on the timing of two intervals. *Pharmacology Biochemistry and Behavior*, *75*, 9–15.

Droit-Volet, S. (2003). Temporal experience and timing in children. In W. Meck (Ed.), *Functional and neural mechanisms of interval timing* (pp. 183–208). Washington, DC: CRC Press.

Farah, M. J. (2000). The neural bases of mental imagery. In M. S. Gazzaniga (Ed), *The cognitive neurosciences* (2nd ed., pp. 965–974). Cambridge, MA: MIT Press.

Fiske, S. T. (1982). Schema-triggered affect: Applications to social perception. In M. S. Clark & S. T. Fiske (Eds.), *Cognition and affect: The 17th Annual Carnegie Symposium*. Hillsdale, NJ: Erlbaum.

Fiske, S. T. & Taylor, S. E. (1991). *Social cognition* (2nd ed.). New York: McGraw-Hill.

Ferguson, M. J. & Bargh, J. A. (2004). How social perception can automatically influence behavior. *Trends in Cognitive Sciences*, *8*, 33–39.

Gallese, V. (2003). The roots of empathy: The shared manifold hypothesis and the neural basis of intersubjectivity. *Psychopathology*, *36*, 171–180.

Gallese, V. (2005). "Being like me": Self-other identity, mirror neurons, and empathy. Perspectives on imitation: From neuroscience to social science: Vol. 1: *Mechanisms of imitation and imitation in animals* (pp. 101–118). Cambridge, MA US: MIT Press.

Gallese, V. (2007). Embodied simulation: From mirror neuron systems to interpersonal relations. *Novartis Foundation Symposium*, *278*, 3–12.

Gallese, V., Keysers, C., & Rizzolatti, G. (2004). A unifying view of the basis of social cognition. *Trends in Cognitive Science*, *8*, 396–403.

Gibbon, J., Church, R. M., & Meck, W. H. (1984). Scalar timing in memory. In J. Gibbon & L. Allan (Eds.), *Timing and time perception* (pp. 57–78). New York: The New York Academy of Sciences.

Gibbs, R. W. (2003). Embodied experience and linguistic meaning. *Brain and Language*, 84, 1–15.

Giessner, S. R., & Schubert, T. W. (2007). High in the hierarchy: How vertical location and judgments of leaders' power are interrelated. *Organizational Behavior and Human Decision Processes*, *104*(1), 30–44.

Glenberg, A. M. (1997). What memory is for? *Behavioral & Brain Sciences*, *20*(1), 1–55.

Glenberg, A. M. (2007). Language and action: Creating sensible combinations of ideas. In G. Gaskell (Ed.) *The Oxford handbook of psycholinguistics* (pp.361–370). Oxford, UK: Oxford University Press.

Greenfield, P. M. (1984). A theory of the teacher in the learning activities of everyday life. In B. Rogoff, & J. Lave (Eds.), *Everyday cognition: Its development in social context* (pp. 117–138). Cambridge, MA: Harvard University Press.

Grezes, J. & Decety, J. (2001). Functional anatomy of execution, mental simulation, observation, and verb generation of actions: A meta-analysis. *Human Brain Mapping*, *12*, 1–19.

Hennenlotter, A., Dresel, C., Castrop, F., Ceballos Baumann, A. O., Wohlschläger, A. M., & Haslinger, B. (2008). The link between facial feedback and neural activity within central circuitries of emotion—New insights from Botulinum toxin-induced denervation of frown muscles. *Cerebral Cortex*, *19*(3), 537–542.

Hess, U., Beaupré, M. G., & Cheung, N. (2002). To whom and why–cultural differences and similarities in the function of smiles. In M. Abel (Ed.) *The smile: Forms, functions, and consequences* (pp. 187–216). NY: The Edwin Mellen Press.

Higgins, E. T. & King, G. (1981). Accessibility of social constructs: Information-processing consequences of individual and contextual variability. In N. Cantor and J. F. Kihlstrom (Eds.), *Personality, cognition, and social interaction* (pp. 69–122). Hilldale, NJ: Erlbaum.

IJzerman, H. & Semin, G. R. (2009). The thermometer of social relations: Mapping social proximity on temperature. *Psychological Science*, *20*, 1214–1220.

Jostmann, N. B., Lakens, D., & Schubert, T. W. (2009). Weight as an embodiment of importance. *Psychological Science*, *20*(9), 1169–1174.

King-Casas, B., Sharp, C., Lomax-Bream, L., Lohrenz, T., Fonagy, P., & Montague, P. R. (2008). The rupture and repair of cooperation in borderline personality disorder. *Science*, *321*(5890), 806–810.

Krumhuber, E., Manstead, A. S. R., & Kappas, A. (2007). Temporal aspects of facial displays in person and expression perception. The effects of smile dynamics, head-tilt and gender. *Journal of Nonverbal Behavior, 31*, 39–56.

Kunda, Z. (1999). *Social cognition: Making sense of people*. Cambridge, MA: The MIT Press.

Lakoff, G. & Johnson, M. (1980). *Metaphors we live by*. Chicago: The University of Chicago Press.

Levine, J. M., Resnick, L. B., & Higgins, E.T. (1993) Social foundations of cognition. *Annual Review of Psychology, 44*, 585–612.

Mahon, B.Z. & Caramazza, A. (2008). A Critical Look at the Embodied Cognition Hypothesis & a New Proposal for Grounding Conceptual Content. *Journal of Physiology - Paris*, 102, 59–70.

Martin, A. (2001) Functional neuroimaging of semantic memory. In R. Cabeza & A. Kingstone (Eds.), *Handbook of functional neuroimaging of cognition* (pp. 153–186). Cambridge, MA: MIT Press.

Medin, D. L. & Shaffer, M. M. (1978). Context theory of classification learning. *Psychological Review*, 85, 207–238.

Meier, B. P. & Robinson, M. D. (2004). Why the sunny side is up: Associations between affect and vertical position. *Psychological Science, 15*(4), 243–247.

Meier, B. P., Robinson, M. D., Crawford, L. E., & Ahlvers, W. J. (2007). When "light" and "dark" thoughts become light and dark responses: Affect biases brightness judgments. *Emotion, 7*(2), 366–376.

Mussweiler, T. (2006). Doing is for thinking! Stereotype activation by stereotypic movements. *Psychological Science, 17*, 17–21.

Newell, A. & Simon, H. A. (1972). *Human problem solving*. Englewood Cliffs, NJ: Prentice Hall.

Niedenthal, P. M. (2007). Embodying emotion. *Science, 316*, 1002–1005.

Niedenthal, P. M., (2008). Emotion concepts. In M. Lewis, J. M. Haviland-Jones, and L. F. Barrett (Eds.), *Handbook of emotion, 3*rd Edition. New York: Guilford.

Niedenthal, P. M., Barsalou, L.W., Winkielman, P., Krauth-Gruber, S., & Ric, F. (2005). Embodiment in attitudes, social perception, and emotion. *Personality and Social Psychology Review, 9*, 184–211.

Niedenthal, P. M. & Maringer, M. (2009). Embodied emotion considered. *Emotion Review, 1*, 122–128.

Niedenthal, P. M., Mermillod, M., Maringer, M., & Hess, U. (2010). The simulation of smiles (SIMS) model: Embodied simulation and the meaning of facial expression. *Behavioral and Brain Sciences*, in press.

Niedenthal, P. M., Winkielman, P., Mondillon, L., & Vermeulen, N. (2009). Embodied emotion concepts. *Journal of Personality and Social Psychology, 96*, 1120–1136.

Nitsche, J. B., Nelson, E. E., Rusch, B. D., Fox, A. S., Oakes, T. R., & Davidson, R. J. (2004). Orbitofrontal cortex tracks positive mood in mothers viewing pictures of their newborn infants. *NeuroImage, 21*, 583–592.

Nosofsky, R. M. (1988). Exemplar-based accounts of relations between classification, recognition, and typicality. *Journal of Experimental Psychology: Learning, Memory, & Cognition, 14*(4), 700–708.

Palmer, S. E. (1999). *Vision science: Photons to phenomenology*. Cambridge, MA: MIT Press.

Pecher, D. & Zwaan, R. (Eds.) (2005). *The grounding of cognition: The role of perception and action in memory, language, and thinking*. Cambridge: Cambridge University Press.

Pulvermüller, F. (2005). Brain mechanisms linking language and action. *Nature Reviews Neuroscience, 6*(7), 576–582.

Pylyshyn, Z. W. (1984). *Computation and cognition: Towards a foundation for cognitive science*. MIT Press: Cambridge, MA.

Rilling, J. K., Goldsmith, D. R., Glenn, A. L., Jairam, M. R., Elfenbein, H. A., Dagenais, J. E., et al. (2008). The neural correlates of the affective response to unreciprocated cooperation. *Neuropsychologia, 46*(5), 1256–1266.

Rizzolatti, G. & Craighero, L. (2004). The mirror-neuron system. *Annual Review of Neuroscience, 27*, 169–192.

Rogers, T. B. (1981). A model of the self as an aspect of the human information processing system. In N. Cantor & J. F. Kihlstrom (Eds.), *Personality, cognition, and social interaction* (pp. 193–214). Hilldale, NJ: Erlbaum.

Roloff, M. E. & Berger, C. R. (Eds.) (1982). *Social cognition and communication*. Beverly Hills, CA: Sage.

Schilbach, L., Wohlschlaeger, A., Kraemer, N., Newen, A., Shah, N., & Fink, G., (2006). Being with virtual others: Neural correlates of social interaction. *Neuropsychologia, 44*, 718–730.

Schneider, D. J. (1991). Social cognition. *Annual Review of Psychology, 42*, 527–561.

Schubert, T. W. (2005). Your highness: Vertical positions as perceptual symbols of power. *Journal of Personality and Social Psychology, 89*(1), 1–21.

Schwarz, N. (2000). Social judgment and attitudes: Warmer, more social, and less conscious. *European Journal of Social Psychology, 30*, 149–176.

Semin, G. R., de Montes, G. L., & Valencia, J. F. (2003). Communication constraints on the linguistic intergroup bias. *Journal of Experimental Social Psychology, 39*, 142–148.

Semin, G. R. & Smith, E. R. (Eds.) (2008). *Embodied grounding: Social, cognitive, affective, and neuroscientific approaches*. New York: Cambridge University Press.

Sherman, S. J. (1987). Cognitive processes in the formation, change, and expression of attitudes. In M. P. Zanna, J. M. Olson, & C. P. Herman (Eds.), *Social influence: The Ontario Symposium*, Vol. 5 (pp. 95–106). Hillsdale, NJ: Lawrence Erlbaum Associates.

Simmons, K., & Barsalou, L.W. (2003). The similarity-in-topography principle: Reconciling theories of conceptual deficits. *Cognitive Neuropsychology, 20*, 451–486.

Smith, E. R. (1994). Procedural knowledge and processing strategies in social cognition. In R. S. Wyer & T. K. Srull (Eds.), *Handbook of social cognition, Vol. 1*. (2nd ed., pp. 99–151). Hillsdale, NJ: Lawrence Erlbaum Associates.

Smith, E. R. (1996). What do connectionism and social psychology offer each other? *Journal of Personality and Social Psychology, 70*, 893–912.

Smith, E. R. & DeCoster, J. (1998). Knowledge acquisition, accessibility, and use in person perception and stereotyping: Simulation with a recurrent connectionist network. *Journal of Personality and Social Psychology, 74*, 21–35.

Smith, E. & Semin, G. (2007). Situated social cognition. *Current Directions in Psychological Science, 16*(3), 132–135.

Speer, N. K., Reynolds, J. R., Swallow, K. M., & Zacks, J. M. (2009). Reading stories activates neural representations of visual and motor experiences. *Psychological Science, 20*(8), 989–999.

Srull, T. K. & Wyer, R. S., Jr. (1989). Person memory and judgment. *Psychological Review, 96*, 58–83.

Tabak, I., & Baumgartner, E. (2004). The teacher as partner: Exploring participant structures, symmetry, and identity work in scaffolding. Cognition & Instruction, 22, 393–429.

Taumoepeau, M., & Ruffman, T. (2008). Stepping stones to others' minds: Maternal talk relates to child mental state language and emotion understanding at 15, 24, and 33 months. Child Development, 79, 284–302.

Thompson-Schill, S. L. (2003). Neuroimaging studies of semantic memory: Inferring "how" from "where." Neuropsychologia, 41, 280–292.

van den Bos, W., van Dijk, E., Westenberg, M., Rombouts, S. A. R. B., & Crone, E. A. (2009). What motivates repayment? Neural correlates of reciprocity in the Trust Game. Social Cognitive and Affective Neuroscience, 4(3), 294–304.

Vygotsky, L. S. (1978). Interaction between learning and development. In M. Cole, V. John-Steiner, S. Scribner, & E. Souberman (Eds.) and Trans., Mind in society: The development of higher psychological processes (pp. 79–91). Cambridge, MA: Harvard University Press.

Wacker, J., Chavanon, M. L., Leue, A., & Stemmler, G. (2010). Trait BIS predicts alpha asymmetry and P300 in a go/no-go task. European Journal of Personality, 24(2), 85–105.

Wegner, D. M., Erber, R., & Raymond, P. (1991). Transactive memory in close relationships. Journal of Personality and Social Psychology, 61, 923–929.

Wegner, D. M., Giuliano, T., & Hertel, P. (1985). Cognitive interdependence in close relationships. In W. J. Ickes (Ed.), Compatible and incompatible relationships (pp. 253–276). New York: Springer-Verlag.

Wegner, D.M. & Vallacher, R.R. (1977). Implicit psychology: An introduction to social cognition. New York: Oxford University Press.

Wegner, D. M. (1995). A computer network model of human transactive memory. Social Cognition, 13, 1–21.

Wicker, B., Keysers, C., Plailly, J., Royet, J.-P., Gallese, V., & Rizzolatti, G. (2003). Both of us disgusted in My Insula: The common neural basis of seeing and feeling disgust. Neuron, 40(3), 655–664.

Willems, R. M., Hagoort, P., & Casasanto, D. (2010). Body-specific representations of action verbs: neural evidence from right- and left-handers. Psychological Science, 21(1), 67–74.

Williams, L. E. & Bargh, J. A. (2008). Experiencing physical warmth promotes interpersonal warmth. Science, 322(5901), 606–607.

Wilson, M. (2002). Six views of embodied cognition. Psychonomic Bulletin & Review, 9, 625–636.

Wood, D., Bruner, J. S.,&Ross, G. (1976). The role of tutoring in problem solving. Journal of Child Psychology and Psychiatry, 17, 89–100.

Yang, T. T., Menon, V., Eliez, S., Blasey, C., White, C. D., Reid, A. J., et al. (2002). Amygdalar activation associated with positive and negative facial expressions. Neuroreport, 13, 1737–1741.

Zajonc, R. B., Adelmann, P. K., Murphy, S. T., & Niedenthal, P. M. (1987). Convergence in the physical appearance of spouses: An implication of the vascular theory of emotional efference. Motivation and Emotion, 11, 335–346.

Zajonc, R. B. & Burnstein, E. (1965). The learning of balanced and unbalanced social structures. Journal of Personality, 33, 153–163.

Zajonc, R. B. & Markus, H. (1984). Affect and cognition: The hard interface. In C. Izard, J. Kagan, & R. B. Zajonc (Eds.), Emotions, cognition and behavior (pp. 73–102). Cambridge: Cambridge University Press.

Zeki, S. (1993). A vision of the brain. Cambridge, MA: Blackwell Scientific Publications, Inc.

Zhong, C.-B. & Leonardelli, G. J. (2008). Cold and lonely: Does social exclusion literally feel cold? Psychological Science, 19(9), 838–842.

Zink, C. F., Tong, Y., Chen, Q., Bassett, D. S., Stein, J. L., & Meyer-Lindenberg, A. (2008). Know your place: Neural processing of social hierarchy in humans. Neuron, 58(2), 273–283.

Socioemotional Functioning
and the Aging Brain

Gregory R. Samanez-Larkin *and* Laura L. Carstensen

Abstract

Effective social and emotional functioning is essential to healthy relationships at any age. Although the understanding of socioemotional functioning in late life has increased in recent decades, most of the existing research relies on information reported by individuals on questionnaires or during interviews. Social neuroscience promises to uncover important and novel information that can greatly enhance this growing area of research. In particular, social neuroscience is allowing tests of hypotheses that cannot be tested well using traditional behavioral methods. This chapter identifies the important contributions that social neuroscience has made to our understanding of the socioemotional aspects of adult development and aging. It reviews studies that utilize a variety of methods to assess autonomic and central nervous system function from peripheral physiology to electrophysiology to fMRI. It argues that brain imaging introduces a way to tease apart findings that may reflect top-down processes from ones that are bottom-up, and that the neuroscience literature to date provides surprisingly consistent support for the postulates of socioemotional selectivity theory (SST) and a motivated basis for the positivity effect.

Keywords: adult development, aging, emotion, motivation, social cognition, positivity effect, anticipation, memory, learning, reward, emotion regulation, individual differences, fMRI, ERP, psychophysiology, methods, (functional) connectivity, amygdala, caudate, anterior cingulate, medial prefrontal cortex, dorsolateral prefrontal cortex

Effective social and emotional functioning is essential to healthy relationships at any age. Although the understanding of socioemotional functioning in late life has increased in recent decades, most of the existing research relies on information reported by individuals on questionnaires or during interviews. Social neuroscience promises to uncover important and novel information that can greatly enhance this growing area of research. In particular, social neuroscience is allowing tests of hypotheses that cannot be tested well using traditional behavioral methods.

Throughout this chapter we identify the important contributions that social neuroscience has made to our understanding of the socioemotional aspects of adult development and aging.

A growing body of research suggests that the ability to regulate emotion remains stable and in some aspects may improve across the adult life span (Charles & Carstensen, 2007). Compared to their younger counterparts, older adults recover more quickly from negative emotional states, are less likely to respond to verbal slights with anger

(Charles & Carstensen, 2008), maintain positive emotional states longer than younger adults (Carstensen, Pasupathi, Mayr, & Nesselroade, 2000; Carstensen et al., 2011; Charles & Carstensen, 2008), report superior emotional control (Carstensen et al., 2011; Gross et al., 1997; Lawton, Kleban, Rajagopal, & Dean, 1992; Tsai, Levenson, & Carstensen, 2000), and display less physiological arousal when experiencing negative emotions (Levenson, Carstensen, Friesen, & Ekman, 1991; Tsai et al., 2000). A number of studies using a variety of experimental methods have found that older adults selectively attend to positive stimuli and are more likely to retrieve positive memories than negative ones (Charles, Mather, & Carstensen, 2003; Fernandes, Ross, Wiegand, & Schryer, 2008; Isaacowitz, Toner, Goren, & Wilson, 2008; Isaacowitz, Wadlinger, Goren, & Wilson, 2006a, 2006b; Kennedy, Mather, & Carstensen, 2004; Mather & Carstensen, 2003).

These somewhat surprising findings contribute to what is often called the "paradox of aging." Despite age-related losses, emotional well-being remains relatively high in old age. An important question for neuroscientists is whether the positive profile of findings emerging in the literature reflects age-related changes in brain function, such as the relative structural preservation of select emotional processing regions or even the serendipitous benefits of brain deterioration, or is instead the result of motivational and experiential changes associated with adult development and aging. For example, could less robust brain activation *account* for a slowness to anger? Or does it reflect motivation on the part of older adults to maintain strong social bonds? Given the breadth and the depth of age-related loss (in the brain and elsewhere) it is easy to be drawn to explanations rooted in dysfunction associated with physical aging. We argue, however, that the existing literature better supports claims that top-down changes in motivation play a substantial—if not primary—role in functional changes observed in the aging brain.

We come to the subject matter from the perspective of socioemotional selectivity theory (SST; Carstensen, 1992, 2006). The theory contends that as people age and time horizons imposed by mortality shrink, people place increasingly greater priority on goals related to well-being and relatively less on emotionally riskier goals associated with expanding horizons, learning, and social exploration. Consequently social and cognitive resources are more likely to be allocated to the regulation of emotion (Carstensen, 2006; Carstensen, Fung, & Charles, 2003). Strong preferences for social partners who are well known and meaningful are apparent among older adults, for example (Fredrickson & Carstensen, 1990; Fung, Carstensen, & Lang, 2001; Fung, Carstensen, & Lutz, 1999); and there is mounting evidence that attention and memory operate in support of well-being as well. Our research team has coined the term "positivity effect" to describe the developmental shift from a preference for negative information in youth to a preference for positive information at older ages (Carstensen, Mikels, & Mather, 2005). The effect is operationalized as a ratio representing the relative difference between younger and older adults. In some cases, it is driven by heightened attention to positive and in others by relatively reduced attention to negative material. This developmental pattern has been observed in memory across short periods of time, that is, across experimental sessions (Charles et al., 2003; Mather & Johnson, 2000), as well as in autobiographical memories that span many years (Kennedy et al., 2004). A preference for positive over negative is also evident in affective working memory (Mikels, Larkin, Reuter-Lorenz, & Carstensen, 2005) and in affective forecasting (Nielsen, Knutson, & Carstensen, 2008). In the last five years, the positivity effect has been widely replicated in independent laboratories (Comblain, D'Argembeau, & Van der Linden, 2005; Fernandes et al., 2008; Isaacowitz et al., 2008; Isaacowitz et al., 2006b; Kisley, Wood, & Burrows, 2007; Mather, Knight, & McCaffrey, 2005; Schlagman, Schulz, & Kvavilashvili, 2006; Spaniol, Voss, & Grady, 2008). Importantly, this preference for positive information is not impervious to context. SST maintains that chronically activated goals change with age, but of course there are circumstances when younger adults strive to regulate emotion and those when older adults pursue informational goals. Interestingly, when goals are explicitly instructed, age differences in positivity are eliminated (Löckenhoff & Carstensen, 2007). That is, all things being equal, older adults appear to focus on positive information but experimental conditions and instructions can and do eliminate age differences.

With the development of in vivo functional brain imaging techniques in humans, a growing body of research has focused on exploring age differences in cognitive function. Over the past couple of decades much progress has been made in the cognitive neuroscience of aging (Buckner, Head, & Lustig, 2006; Cabeza, Nyberg, & Park, 2005; Grady, 2008). Only relatively recently have studies of emotional and social aspects of aging received attention by neuroscientists. In the last several years, especially, attention to the neural basis of emotional functioning in older adults has burgeoned. In this chapter, we review studies across a wide range of domains including the emotional processing of social stimuli; the anticipation of, exposure to, and memory for emotional stimuli; attention to emotion; and emotion regulation. The studies reviewed in this chapter utilize a variety of methods to assess autonomic and central nervous system function from peripheral physiology to electrophysiology to fMRI. We maintain that brain imaging introduces a way to tease apart findings that may reflect top-down processes from ones that are bottom-up and that the neuroscience literature to date provides surprisingly consistent support for the postulates of SST and a motivated basis for the positivity effect. After attempting to comprehensively review and synthesize the literature on socioemotional functioning in the aging brain, we identify existing gaps in the literature and discuss potential directions for future research.

Social and Emotional Processing in the Aging Brain

By far, the most common approach to the study of age differences in neural responses associated with social and emotional stimuli are based on responses to facial expressions. In fact, the first study exploring age differences in emotional responses using fMRI asked a group of younger and older adults to make gender discriminations while viewing images of the faces of young adults expressing negative emotions (Iidaka et al., 2002). While viewing these faces, older adults, compared to younger adults, showed significantly reduced activation in the amygdala. In contrast, older adults did show significant activation in one medial prefrontal region, the cingulate, while viewing negative faces, while younger adults did not. A similar reduction in subcortical activation and increased cortical activation while viewing negative social stimuli has been replicated in a number of other studies using emotional facial expressions. This age-related decrease in amygdala activation has been observed during the passive viewing of angry faces (Fischer et al., 2005), valence discrimination of negative (sad, angry, fearful, disgusted) facial expressions (Gunning-Dixon et al., 2003), and expression matching of fearful and angry faces (Tessitore et al., 2005). Alongside this reduction in amygdala activity, the same studies found an age-related increase in insula activity (Fischer et al., 2005), an increase in lateral and dorsomedial frontal activation (Gunning-Dixon et al., 2003; Tessitore et al., 2005), and anterior cingulate activity in older but not younger adults (Gunning-Dixon et al., 2003).

In all of these studies which expose participants to mostly negative emotional facial expressions, older adults show a reduction in amygdala activation. Investigators commonly conclude that this is evidence of age-related amygdala dysfunction, although it is hard to fully reconcile this interpretation given the important role this subcortical region plays in emotional processing (Phelps, 2006; Sergerie, Chochol, & Armony, 2008; Zald, 2003) yet also the overwhelming behavioral evidence for intact emotional processing into old age (Carstensen et al., 2005). Subsequent experiments have shown that amygdala activation is relatively robust in older adults under certain conditions, raising questions about whether lesser activation in older adults reflected lesser salience of experimental tasks or stimuli as opposed to dysfunction. One study, for example, found similarly high levels of amygdala activation in younger and older adults (Wright, Wedig, Williams, Rauch, & Albert, 2006). In this study, participants were instructed to passively view but focus on the eyes of familiar and novel fearful faces while undergoing fMRI. Prior studies with young adults have shown that novelty also activates the amygdala (Dubois et al., 1999; Schwartz et al., 2003). When examining the combined effects of negative valence and novelty by contrasting the viewing of fearful novel faces with neutral familiar (pre-exposed) faces, the two age groups did not differ in amygdala sensitivity (Wright et al., 2006). Although this provides evidence that the amygdala can be equivalently activated in healthy younger and older adults, the authors did not test the independent effects of novelty and negative valence on amygdala activity in the two age groups. It is possible that the amygdala could be driven by the combination of negative valence and novelty in young but primarily novelty and not negative valence in the old. A follow up study found no age differences in amygdala responses when isolating the contrast of novel versus familiar in younger and older adults during the passive viewing of neutral faces (Wright et al., 2008). Although this result provides evidence for similar novelty responses in the amygdala, it does not address how the age groups differ in the processing of emotional valence. However, these studies do provide important evidence that the amygdala can be activated in older adults and does not suffer from global functional decline in healthy aging.[1] In contrast to the view that the amygdala dysfunctions with age, it is possible that older adults show less reactivity in the amygdala during the processing of negative emotional stimuli as a result of changing goals and shifting priorities which reduce the salience of stimuli.

Although most of the early literature focuses on age-related reductions in subcortical amygdala activity, one study explored the potential role of cortical activations in regulatory processes in social emotional tasks (Williams et al., 2006). Although prior studies have reported an increase in prefrontal activity in older adults while viewing negative stimuli, Williams and colleagues documented an age group by valence interaction in the medial prefrontal cortex during the passive viewing of happy and fearful faces using fMRI. Activity in this region was greater in older adults while viewing negative faces, but lower than younger adults while viewing positive faces.[2] The authors interpreted these results as suggesting that older adults may be engaging in more regulation while viewing negative faces than positive faces. Additional temporal support for this interpretation was provided by electrophysiological findings. A similar pattern emerged in this medial prefrontal cortical area when examining event-related potentials (ERPs). Older adults had an increased late fronto-central ERP signal during the viewing of negative faces but a decreased early fronto-central signal during the viewing of positive faces. This pattern of results suggests that older adults may have a more controlled, regulatory response to negative social stimuli but a more free, unregulated response to positive social stimuli. Providing additional support for this interpretation, both the fMRI and ERP effects in the medial prefrontal cortex correlated with individual differences in emotional stability as assessed by neuroticism (Williams et al., 2006). Individuals with greater medial prefrontal fMRI responses and increased late ERP signals to negative stimuli also had higher levels of emotional stability.

In summary, a number of studies have examined neural responses to emotional, facial stimuli in younger and older adults. The common finding across studies is an age-related decrease in amygdala activation during the perception of negative faces and an age-related increase in a number of lateral and medial prefrontal cortical regions. Yet a combination of novelty and negative valence activates the amygdala equivalently in younger and older adults. Initial evidence from one study supports the hypothesis that the increase in the medial prefrontal cortex may be playing a regulatory role even in passive viewing tasks and has linked this cortical increase to an individual difference measure of emotional stability. This interpretation of the subcortical decreases and cortical increases is consistent with the age-related positivity effect which suggests that relative positivity in older age is regulatory in nature.

Emotional Processing in the Aging Brain: Positivity Effects in Anticipation, Exposure, Memory, and Regulation
Anticipation of Emotional Stimuli
A number of studies have appeared that examine age differences in the anticipation of cued emotional stimuli. One study examined neural activity using fMRI while participants viewed symbolic cues (smile, frown, or neutral icon) that deterministically signaled an upcoming positive, negative, or neutral emotional image from the IAPS picture database. Analyses focused on the anticipation of negative stimuli. The authors reported an age-related decrease in rostral anterior cingulate activity during the anticipation of negative stimuli (Erk, Walter, & Abler, 2008), and interpreted this result as in line with older adults' reduced focus on negative future events. Not only did the researchers report a reduction in cingulate activity during negative anticipation, they also report a reduction in amygdala activity during exposure to negative images (Erk et al., 2008). Within the older participants in the sample, an individual difference analysis showed that individuals with higher scores on the reappraisal subscale of the emotion regulation questionnaire (ERQ) showed reduced amygdala activation (Erk et al., 2008). This finding provides initial direct support that the age differences in amygdala activity during negative emotional processing may be associated with regulatory efforts.

Similar age differences in the processing of negative stimuli are found in other studies focusing on anticipation using incentive-based tasks with financial gains and losses. One particular study examined the physiological anticipation of gains and losses while younger and older participants played the Iowa Gambling Task (IGT). In the IGT, participants begin by randomly selecting cards from four decks in an attempt to learn over time which decks are better (i.e., yield higher overall positive earnings or points). Two decks have high gains but larger losses leading to a negative expected value over time and the other two decks have smaller gains and smaller losses leading to a positive expected value over time. When reaching for *negative* expected value decks younger adults generate an anticipatory skin conductance response, whereas older adults generate a skin conductance response when reaching for decks with a *positive* expected value (Denburg, Recknor, Bechara, & Tranel, 2006). Important individual differences in learning emerge as well. A subset of older adults performs just as well as younger adults, but some perform much worse (Denburg, Tranel, & Bechara, 2005). What distinguishes these groups is that those who perform well have these positive anticipatory physiological markers (Denburg et al., 2006). The authors interpret these results as physiological evidence suggesting that older adults are more likely to learn in this task by seeking gains whereas younger adults learn by avoiding losses. The idea that this physiological guiding signal has been tuned over the adult life span from a focus on signaling the avoidance of negativity toward a focus on seeking positivity is consistent with SST.

A similar effect has been observed in a task that does not require learning revealing age differences in prefrontal and striatal activity using fMRI. When younger and older adults are shown explicit cues that signal a potential financial gain or loss of varying magnitudes, the age groups do not differ during the anticipation of gains in either self-reported positive affect or neural activation in the nucleus accumbens, caudate, or insula. However, when anticipating losses younger adults self-report more negative affect and show more sensitivity to loss magnitudes in the caudate and insula when compared to older adults (Samanez-Larkin et al., 2007). An age-by-valence-by-magnitude interaction in the caudate and insula suggests that these regions are not dysfunctional in old age, but instead that they respond selectively to gains and not losses in older adults. The only region where older adults showed a significant signal during loss anticipation was in a region of the medial prefrontal cortex, the anterior cingulate. In a follow-up study, the authors linked these anticipatory biases to subsequent learning performance. The individuals who showed reduced sensitivity in the insula during loss anticipation in the first task (that did not require learning) later performed worse (controlling for age) in a probabilistic loss-avoidance learning task (Samanez-Larkin, Hollon, Carstensen, & Knutson, 2008). Thus, although this reduction in anticipatory anxiety may contribute to higher well-being, there may be negative consequences especially in financial domains.

It will be important for future studies to pursue these individual differences in physiological responses and learning performance in order to further characterize the underlying explanatory variables. Are these anticipatory patterns of activity linked to regulatory efforts? If this positivity effect is goal-directed and part of regulatory efforts, the benefits of improved well-being may also come at a cost. The preliminary evidence suggests that a positivity effect in financial domains can have deleterious side effects. If older adults are sensitive to potential positive outcomes but less sensitive to potential negative consequences, this could put older adults at an elevated risk for financial scams (Denburg et al., 2007).

Exposure to Emotional Stimuli

Although age differences emerge during anticipation of rewards, younger and older adults show relatively similar responses to *actual* gains and losses on these tasks in the nucleus accumbens, caudate, and medial prefrontal cortex (Cox, Aizenstein, & Fiez, 2008; Samanez-Larkin et al., 2007). That is, older adults are not impervious to loss when it occurs but appear to respond little to the prospect of loss before it occurs. Initial evidence suggested that the error signal in the anterior cingulate is disrupted in older age (Nieuwenhuis et al., 2002), yet when behavioral performance is matched between groups the age differences in error signaling disappear (Eppinger, Kray, Mock, & Mecklinger, 2008). Nevertheless, even if older adults accurately represent and show similar physiological responses to gains, losses, and errors, there is evidence that older adults may differentially weight feedback information when making future decisions. For example, there is some evidence that older adults compared to younger adults learn better from positive than negative feedback (Denburg et al., 2006; Eppinger et al., 2008; Wood, Busemeyer, Koling, Cox, & Davis, 2005).[3]

A number of other studies have explored age differences in responses to emotional images. One study which used electrophysiology asked younger, middle-aged, and older adults to view and make valence ratings on a set of positive, negative, and neutral IAPS pictures while measuring ERPs. An age-by-valence interaction emerged in a parietal brain region (Pz). There was a stronger signal during the evaluation of negative images in the young adults, but no age differences at the Pz for positive images (Kisley et al., 2007; Wood & Kisley, 2006). This Pz site has been linked to very early attention. The authors suggest that this is evidence that the age-related positivity effect appears even at an early processing stage. However, it is important to note that such an early effect does not rule out a regulatory explanation of age-related positivity effects. Chronically activated goals in older adults could tune attentional resources and contribute to these early effects.

A similar positivity effect was reported in another study where younger and older adults viewed and made arousal ratings on positive, negative, and neutral IAPS pictures while undergoing fMRI. Again, an age-by-valence interaction emerged but this time in amygdala activity. Younger adults showed greater amygdala activation than older adults while viewing negative images. Older adults showed greater amygdala activation for positive compared to negative, whereas younger adults did not (Mather et al., 2004). This finding extends other work and provides additional evidence that the amygdala is not only activated by novelty but also by positive emotional stimuli. The authors interpret the results through the lens of socioemotional selectivity theory and suggest that the sensitivity of the amygdala may change with age and that this change may be related to a shift in emotional goals.

A similar age-by-valence interaction but with a complete age-related valence reversal was observed in the anterior cingulate using a different set of stimuli (matched in arousal across valence) while participants made nonemotional (relative physical size) judgments during picture viewing. This positivity effect (full valence reversal) emerged when participants didn't have to make an emotional judgment. The authors interpret their results as evidence for controlled processing differences during the viewing of positive and negative images (Leclerc & Kensinger, 2008). These authors have also observed age-by-valence interactions in the medial prefrontal cortex when exposed to emotional words (Leclerc & Kensinger, in press). In addition to the interactions in the medial prefrontal cortex, when exposed to emotional objects, consistent with several studies cited thus far, they also found that older adults had less amygdala activity when viewing negative compared to positive pictures (Leclerc & Kensinger, in press).

Nearly all of the studies reviewed thus far find age differences in activation of the amygdala and/or medial prefrontal cortex, but none of the studies has examined the interactions between these two regions. Are the age differences in responses in these regions related? A more recent study explored the functional connectivity of these regions that have previously shown age-by-valence interactions: the

amygdala and anterior cingulate. While younger and older adults viewed negative IAPS images and made valence ratings, older adults had greater levels of functional connectivity between the amygdala and anterior cingulate (St. Jacques, Dolcos, & Cabeza, 2010). The authors discuss a possible regulatory interpretation of their results in line with SST. They speculate that this subcortical structure, the amygdala, may be regulated during the viewing of negative stimuli by this cortical structure in the medial prefrontal cortex, the anterior cingulate. Previous studies in young adults show increases in the medial prefrontal cortex and decreases in the amygdala during successful regulation (Ochsner & Gross, 2005) lending support to this age-related regulatory hypothesis.

Emotional Memory

As cited in the introduction to this chapter, age-related positivity effects have also emerged in memory. Three recent studies have examined memory for emotional stimuli using functional neuroimaging. In one study, younger and older adults viewed and made valence ratings on a set of positive, negative, and neutral IAPS images while undergoing fMRI (St. Jacques, Dolcos, & Cabeza, 2009). In a surprise cued-recall test outside of scanner, the older adults showed a reduction in memory for negative relative to neutral images. Providing additional evidence that the amygdala is functionally intact in older age, the neuroimaging data revealed that both groups recruited greater amygdala activity during the successful encoding of negative relative to positive images. However, older adults showed higher levels of dorsolateral prefrontal activation during the successful encoding of negative images than the younger adults. Further functional connectivity analyses revealed a reduced coupling of the amygdala with the hippocampus and ventrolateral prefrontal cortex but an increased coupling between the amygdala and the dorsolateral prefrontal cortex (St. Jacques et al., 2009). Similar to the connectivity effects during picture viewing discussed above, this age-related shift in connectivity may suggest that older adults are engaging in less primary stimulus encoding (amygdala and hippocampus) and more regulation of the negative emotional stimuli (amygdala and dorsolateral prefrontal cortex). Importantly, although this interpretation is speculative and no direct evidence for differential regulatory efforts in the two age groups was provided in this particular study, this pattern of age-related differences in neural activity would be predicted by SST.

In another study using negative and neutral IAPS images that collected functional imaging data during both the encoding and retrieval phases, older adults show greater dorsolateral prefrontal activation during encoding and greater dorsolateral prefrontal and cingulate and less amygdala activity during retrieval when compared to younger adults. Replicating St. Jacques and colleagues (2009) but also extending the findings to the retrieval stage, in this study functional connectivity analyses revealed that older adults had reduced amygdala-hippocampal coupling and increased amygdala-prefrontal coupling during both encoding and retrieval (Murty et al., 2009).

Another memory study identified a common set of regions in both younger and older age groups that were activated during the successful encoding of emotional stimuli. Both younger and older adults showed significant amygdala and orbitofrontal activation during the successful encoding of all emotional stimuli (Kensinger & Schacter, 2008). However, older adults showed greater anterior cingulate activity than the younger adults during the successful encoding of positive object images (which were later correctly recognized outside of scanner) (Kensinger & Schacter, 2008). Nearby medial prefrontal regions showed a similar pattern during the successful encoding of verbal stimuli as well (Leclerc & Kensinger, in press). In this study, older adults showed greater activation during the encoding of positive relative to negative words. The older adults also showed a positivity effect in memory for the words (Leclerc & Kensinger, in press).

In summary, although a number of studies identified age differences in subcortical and mostly medial prefrontal regions during emotional anticipation and exposure, the studies focusing on emotional memory reveal both medial and dorsolateral prefrontal effects during both memory encoding and retrieval. These initial studies suggest that these prefrontal processes may mediate behavioral positivity effects in memory and provide potential evidence for the role of regulatory efforts at the encoding stage (St. Jacques, Bessette-Symons, & Cabeza, 2009).

Emotion Regulation

A number of possible regulatory suggestions and implications have been raised in the discussion of many of the studies reviewed thus far. Although initial regulatory evidence was provided above linking reappraisal (Erk et al., 2008) and emotional stability (Williams et al., 2006) to reductions in amygdala

activation and interactions in the medial prefrontal cortex, few studies have explicitly manipulated emotion regulation in older adults (Urry, van Reekum, Johnstone, & Davidson, 2009; Urry et al., 2006; van Reekum et al., 2007; Winecoff, LaBar, Madden, Cabeza, & Huettel, in press). In all four of the existing studies, older adults were instructed to intentionally decrease their emotional responses to negative pictures. In the decrease condition all four studies reported a significant reduction in amygdala activity from the control condition suggesting that (1) the amygdala can be activated by negative stimuli in older adults and (2) that amygdala activation to negative stimuli is reduced when older adults are regulating their emotional responses. In line with other studies where regulatory interpretations were speculative, when regulation was instructed these studies also found a coupling between the amygdala and both the medial (Urry et al., 2006; Winecoff et al., in press) and lateral prefrontal cortex (Winecoff et al., in press). Even more interesting, higher inverse coupling between the ventromedial prefrontal cortex and amygdala predicted more adaptive profiles of diurnal cortisol secretion in an individual difference analysis (Urry et al., 2006). The pattern of results across these studies is remarkably similar to the findings from studies without instructed regulation summarized above.

Summary and Conclusions

As described in this chapter, the growing body of research on socioemotional functioning in the aging brain reveals consistent age differences in patterns of activity in prefrontal and subcortical regions during emotional processing. The most informative and consistent findings that emerge across a wide range of studies are: (1) there is an age-related reduction in subcortical activation associated with exposure to negative affective stimuli and (2) it is often coupled with an increase in cortical activation. As reviewed above, initial evidence for reduced response to negative stimuli raised legitimate questions about the functional capacity of the aging brain. The pattern emerging in the literature, however, is inconsistent with an argument that the maintenance of well-being in old age is the serendipitous consequence of neural degradation. Rather, brain regions involved in both positive and negative emotional processing in young adulthood appear to be selectively responsive to positive material in older adults. The evidence to date suggests that older adults are effectively regulating emotional responses.

Cognitive Decline and Emotional Stability: A Paradox?

A similar age-related increase in cortical activation commonly emerges in the cognition and aging neuroimaging literature (Cabeza, 2002; Reuter-Lorenz & Lustig, 2005; Spreng, Wojtowicz, & Grady, 2010). Although there is still some unresolved debate about whether this increase in cortical activity is compensatory or the result of dedifferentiation, many studies suggest that this cortical activity is compensating for faulty age-related functioning in other regions. Are the age-related cortical increases in socioemotional tasks also due to declining functional capacity in subcortical regions?

In fact, one intriguing postulate is that age-related increases in emotional well-being are the result of functional declines in the amygdala (Cacioppo, Berntson, Bechara, Tranel, & Hawkley, 2011). However, as reviewed above, cognitive decline and neural atrophy explanations cannot account for many of the findings. Many of the studies reported above show age-by-valence interactions in the same brain regions (Gutchess, Kensinger, & Schacter, 2007; Leclerc & Kensinger, 2008, 2010, in press; Mather et al., 2004; Samanez-Larkin et al., 2007; Williams et al., 2006). These subcortical and cortical regions can be activated in some conditions, but in other conditions are not. Thus, the age differences cannot be *caused* by age-related structural or functional atrophy in these regions.

On the contrary, there is some evidence that cognitive decline or even amygdalar dysfunction would produce the opposite effects and lead to negativity biases. One recent study found greater amygdala activity in patients with mild Alzheimer's disease compared to age-matched controls (Wright, Dickerson, Feczko, Negeira, & Williams, 2007). This abnormal amygdala activity correlated with irritability and agitation/aggression symptoms. This effect could be either due to hyper-responsivity in the amygdala due to disease-related medial temporal pathology, or the result of unregulated amygdala reactivity due to damage to connections with control input from cortical regions projecting into the medial temporal lobe—or a combination of both. These results provide support for a relationship between cognitive decline, abnormal amygdala function, and negative affect (not positive affect). This speaks against cognitive decline or neural atrophy explanations of the positivity effect.

If the effects are not due to declining subcortical structures but instead subcortical activity is modulated through cortical control regions by motivation, this may create a paradox. It is well known that older adults show difficulty in tasks that require lateral prefrontal resources (Hedden & Gabrieli, 2004; West, 1996). These same regions typically emerge in studies of emotion regulation (Ochsner & Gross, 2007). If older adults are suffering from cognitive decline in controlled frontal resources, how is it neurally possible that regulation improves with age? After all, there is well-documented structural decline in older adults in many regions implicated in both emotional control and basic emotional responding including the lateral prefrontal cortex, insula, and striatum (Raz, 2005; Raz et al., 2005).

However, this may not be a paradox at all. Motivation may compensate for structural decline. It has been demonstrated that even frontal regions that suffer from relatively steep age-related structural decline can be functionally activated in older adults under supportive conditions in cognitive tasks (Logan, Sanders, Snyder, Morris, & Buckner, 2002; Lustig & Buckner, 2004). In one of the emotional tasks reported in this chapter, the authors documented relatively smaller *structural* medial prefrontal volumes, but the age by valence *functional* interaction held when controlling for structural decline in this region (Williams et al., 2006). Thus, even though prefrontal regions suffer from age-related structural decline, these same regions may be selectively functionally recruited to meet the motivational demands of older adults (Kryla-Lighthall & Mather, 2009).

Although some studies provide evidence for lateral prefrontal activity contributing to differential emotional processing in old age (Murty et al., 2009; Samanez-Larkin, Robertson, Mikels, Carstensen, & Gotlib, 2009; St. Jacques et al., 2009), a large proportion of the studies find age differences in medial prefrontal regions. A variety of brain regions near the frontal midline including the anterior cingulate and dorso- and ventromedial prefrontal cortex show age differences in responses to positive and negative affective stimuli, age by valence interactions, and age differences in connectivity with the amygdala. See Table 34.1 for a list of studies, conditions, and coordinates and Figure 34.1 for a graphical depiction of age differences in medial prefrontal activity. Interestingly, the possibility that medial versus lateral prefrontal distinctions may play a role in age differences in cognition and emotion was suggested before virtually all of these studies were published (MacPherson, Phillips, & Della Sala, 2002).

To the extent that these medial prefrontal activations reflect regulation (Ochsner & Gross, 2005;

Table 34.1 Age Effects in the Medial Prefrontal Cortex During Socioemotional Processing

Study	Condition	R	A	S
Gunning-Dixon et al., 2003	Negative Valence	0	8	44
Gutchess et al., 2007	Age × Valence (self)	11	39	35
Iidaka et al., 2002	Negative Valence	2	18	40
Kensinger & Schacter, 2008	Positive Valence	0	33	−10
	Positive Valence	−8	45	26
Leclerc & Kensinger, 2008	Age × Valence	0	39	−5
Leclerc & Kensinger, in press	Age × Valence	−4	39	9
Samanez-Larkin et al., 2007	Negative Valence	13	37	20
St Jacques et al., 2010	Amygdala Connectivity	−4	44	−2
Tessitore et al., 2005	Negative Valence	−10	31	40
Urry et al., 2006	Amygdala Connectivity	5	37	−12
	Amygdala Connectivity	−23	43	−10
Williams et al., 2006	Age × Valence	−20	37	37
	Age × Valence	8	46	35

See Figure 34.1 for an anatomical map of peak coordinates. Coordinates listed in Talairach space.

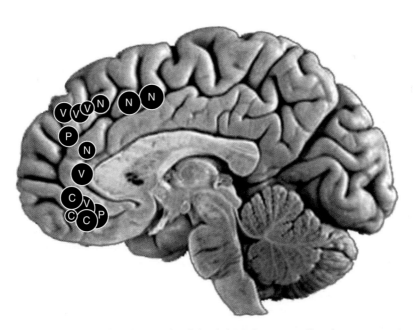

Fig. 34.1 Regions of the medial prefrontal cortex identified with fMRI showing age effects during socioemotional tasks. N = negative valence; P = positive valence; V = age by valence interaction; C = functional connectivity with the amygdala. For a list of all coordinates and studies, see Table 34.1. In the figure Talairach coordinates are projected onto the medial wall (L/R = 0). Marker diameter indicates distance from the midline (smaller markers = farther from midline).

Ochsner et al., 2004), these findings may offer evidence for important age differences in regulatory strategies. In older age, regulation may be more automatic and less cognitively effortful (Scheibe & Blanchard-Fields, 2009) due to chronically activated goals.[4] Although it is certainly possible that age-related decreases in lateral prefrontal resources (Hedden & Gabrieli, 2004) may also contribute to this lateral to medial shift in regulatory, prefrontal processing, it is also possible that this shift occurs naturally as regulatory strategies change over the adult life span. Presently, neural differences in regulatory strategies have received very little attention in social neuroscience (Goldin, McRae, Ramel, & Gross, 2008; McRae et al., 2010). As this area continues to grow, it will be essential to explore how the neural mechanisms underlying regulatory strategies may change with age.

Future Directions in the Social Neuroscience of Aging

Although a number of studies that rely on simple perceptual judgment tasks suggest that older adults are impaired (Ruffman, Henry, Livingstone, & Phillips, 2008), a vast amount of behavioral research suggests that older adults function exceptionally well in social situations (Hess, 2006). In fact, across a range of domains, older adults display intact and in some cases superior social cognitive abilities (Blanchard-Fields, 2007; Blanchard-Fields & Heckman, forthcoming; Blanchard-Fields, Horhota, & Mienaltowski, 2008). An important detail to note is that often criterion measures for accuracy in the emerging perceptual studies are based on normative data collected from younger adults. Future studies should keep with the tradition of the social cognition and aging literature and not overweigh agreement with younger adult norms but instead focus on possible implications of age differences in behavior and underlying neural processes.

In fact, one of the only studies with non-facial social stimuli examining social cognition in the aging brain reveals both an age-related positivity effect in self judgments but remarkably similar social discrimination in the medial prefrontal cortex (Gutchess et al., 2007). In this study younger and older adults evaluated positive and negative trait adjectives and decided whether the words applied to the self or a social other. When evaluating whether adjectives applied to the self, an age-by-valence interaction emerged in the dorsomedial prefrontal cortex. Activation in this region was greater for positive relative to negative adjectives in older but not

younger adults. The study also provided evidence for an intact self-versus-other representation in the medial prefrontal cortex in older adults. There were no significant age differences in the medial prefrontal cortex for self versus other judgments (Gutchess et al., 2007).

Although this suggests that older adults may show similar neural activity discriminating the self and other, interesting age differences may emerge within self-relevant thought. In some contexts older adults may be less inwardly focused even when considering highly personal agendas (Mitchell et al., 2009). When compared to younger adults, older adults showed an attenuated difference between anterior and posterior medial prefrontal regions when asked to contemplate self-relevant agendas (i.e., hopes and aspirations, duties and obligations). The authors interpreted these findings as possible evidence for an age-related change from focusing primarily on specific personal details and instead focusing on a more broad (and potentially interpersonal) picture.

One important consideration in all social cognitive studies of healthy aging (or any group comparison for that matter) is that younger and older adults may interpret tasks or stimuli differently. Future studies will need to use stimuli that are comparably socially relevant for the age groups studied. For example, most of the studies exploring facial affect processing reported in this chapter did not include older faces. Older adults, then, are often processing age out-group faces. This detail may contribute to age differences in functional activity. In fact, when authors use both younger and older adult faces as stimuli important differences emerge. Although behavioral studies have not observed differences for in- or out-group faces in identification accuracy or memory in older adults (Ebner & Johnson, 2009), in a neuroimaging study within-group responses in the amygdala were larger than out-group responses (Wright et al., 2008). These effects held when controlling for valence ratings of neutral face stimuli and novelty recognition errors. This could be a confound in prior studies that didn't use old faces and reported age differences in amygdala function.

In addition to age differences in social salience, emotional perceptions of stimuli may vary across age. Investigators should consistently attempt to categorize stimuli based on the subjective ratings of individual participants (St. Jacques et al., 2010). However, also reporting any systematic age differences in perception may uncover important effects. Interestingly, in one study reported in this chapter the rating data showed that older adults rated more negative pictures as neutral (St. Jacques et al., 2010). Many other studies have documented American, German, and Korean older adults rating the same stimuli more positively than younger adults (Grühn & Scheibe, 2008; Kwon, Scheibe, Samanez-Larkin, Tsai, & Carstensen, 2009; Mather & Knight, 2005; Smith, Hillman, & Duley, 2005).

Similarly, an interesting detail often overlooked in studies of emotion labeling of facial expressions is that although no age differences emerge in labeling happy, surprised, and neutral expressions, older adults more often disagree with young adult norms for anger, disgust, and sadness (Keightley et al., 2007). Meta-analyses of emotion recognition and aging suggest that older adults are especially "worse" at categorizing fear and anger (Isaacowitz et al., 2007; Ruffman et al., 2008). Although these are often characterized as "errors" by the authors, when the direction of this effect is more carefully explored interesting implications emerge. For example, when categorizing younger faces in one study, the older adults perceived the same faces as less angry and more sad than younger adults (Iidaka et al., 2002). This may have important social implications. If older adults systematically perceive high-arousal negative expressions, such as anger, in others as lower arousal expressions, such as sadness, they may take a less confrontational approach to the social interaction. However, this may also lead to miscommunication if the social partner feels misunderstood.

Future studies in social neuroscience should not ignore the wealth of evidence for age-related preservation and improvement in social cognitive function and should instead build upon this wealth of prior research and focus efforts on uncovering the functional implications of potential age differences (Hess, 2006).

Conclusions

In summary, the patterns of decreased subcortical but increased cortical responses to negative emotional stimuli in older adults suggest that regulatory neural processes are involved in the age-related positivity effect. The majority of the age differences in neural activity during negative processing and behavioral positivity effects cannot be explained by cognitive decline or neural atrophy theories. Both subcortical and cortical brain regions can be modulated in healthy older adults when necessary but appear to respond selectively to goal congruent stimuli. Future research should continue to directly manipulate and measure emotion regulation in

younger and older adults. Many studies speculate about the role of regulation, but direct measures of regulatory processing during the tasks are not always provided. Additionally, future research in social neuroscience should extend beyond examining age differences in the processing of facial affect and consider social cognition more broadly. Many of the original studies supporting socioemotional selectivity theory focused on age differences in social interactions as a function of limitations in future time perspective (Carstensen, 1992; Fredrickson & Carstensen, 1990; Lang & Carstensen, 1994). Understanding the neural correlates of social interaction and social understanding across the adult life span could make important contributions to the literature on socioemotional selectivity theory.

The expansiveness of this handbook suggests that research across areas in psychological neuroscience will continue to grow. In future years, emerging integrative research examining socioemotional processing in the aging brain will surely make novel and lasting contributions toward a more comprehensive understanding of the psychology of human aging.

Acknowledgments

During the preparation of this chapter, Gregory R. Samanez-Larkin was supported by National Institute on Aging pre-doctoral NRSA AG032804 and Laura L. Carstensen was supported by National Institute on Aging MERIT award AG08816. The authors thank Mara Mather and Ben Eppinger for comments.

Notes

1 An important methodological detail to acknowledge here is that small subcortical structures like the amygdala may be volumetrically smaller and poorly spatially normalized in older adults. Without careful methods this can bias between-group tests. The study described (Wright et al., 2006) documented smaller amygdala volumes in the older adults. Based on this finding, the authors used less spatial smoothing (7mm) and careful ROI definition methods to be sure that comparisons between groups in amygdala activity were reliable. It is important to consider that other studies showing reductions in amygdala activation in older adults use large smoothing kernels which may systematically reduce the signal in this small subcortical structure (Fischer et al., 2005; Gunning-Dixon et al., 2003; Tessitore et al., 2005). Like any group comparisons, careful methods in the study of adult development are vital for all investigators. Beyond the potential structural confounds described here, there are many other issues regarding subject selection, task design, and analyses that have been covered in recent reviews (D'Esposito, Deouell, & Gazzaley, 2003; Gazzaley & D'Esposito, 2005; Rugg & Morcom, 2005) with one review providing a summary of suggestions for studies using fMRI (Samanez-Larkin & D'Esposito, 2008).

2 Although Williams and colleagues documented an age-related reduction in medial prefrontal activity during the processing of positive stimuli, in the only other study using social stimuli that has attempted to isolate differences between the processing of positive and negative expressions in younger and older adults, the authors found similar ventromedial prefrontal and dorsal anterior cingulate (deactivation) activity that distinguished happy from other expressions (Keightley, Chiew, Winocur, & Grady, 2007). Thus, it does not appear that these regions cannot be modulated by positive emotional stimuli in old age.

3 Although recent studies have been interpreted as suggesting that the opposite is true, that older adults learn better from negative than positive feedback, (Eppinger & Kray, 2011; Frank & Kong, 2008; Haümmerer, Li, Muüller, & Lindenberger, in press) it is important to note that none of these studies have actually provided evidence for a robust behavioral age-related shift toward a preference for negative over positive information from young adulthood to old age. Instead these studies provide little evidence for valence effects and more consistent evidence for a general age-related reduction in learning from probabilistic feedback (Mell et al., 2005, 2009, Samanez-Larkin et al., 2010, in press).

4 However, even if it is easier it is also important to note that regulation should still take some effort for older adults, as evidenced by reversals of the positivity effect when attention is divided (Knight et al., 2007; Mather & Knight, 2005).

References

Blanchard-Fields, F. (2007). Everyday problem solving and emotion: An adult developmental perspective. *Current Directions in Psychological Science, 16*, 26–31.

Blanchard-Fields, F. & Heckman, A. (forthcoming). Social cognition and aging. In D. Park & N. Schwarz (Eds.), *Cognitive aging: A primer* (2nd ed.). New York: Psychology Press.

Blanchard-Fields, F., Horhota, M., & Mienaltowski, A. (2008). Social context and cognition. In S. Hofer & D. Alwin (Eds.), *Handbook on cognitive aging: Interdisciplinary perspectives* (pp. 614–628). Sage Press.

Buckner, R. L., Head, D., & Lustig, C. (2006). Brain changes in aging: A lifespan perspective. In E. Bialystok & F. I. M. Craik (Eds.), *Lifespan cognition: Mechanisms of change*. Oxford University Press.

Cabeza, R. (2002). Hemispheric asymmetry reduction in older adults: The HAROLD model. *Psychology and Aging, 17*(1), 85–100.

Cabeza, R., Nyberg, L., & Park, D. (2005). *Cognitive neuroscience of aging: Linking cognitive and cerebral aging*. New York, NY, US: Oxford University Press.

Cacioppo, J. T., Berntson, G. G., Bechara, A., Tranel, D., & Hawkley, L. C. (2011). Could an aging brain contribute to subjective well being?: The value added by a social neuroscience perspective. In A. Tadorov, S. T. Fiske, & D. Prentice (Eds.), *Social neuroscience: Toward understanding the underpinnings of the social mind* (pp. 249–262). New York: Oxford University Press.

Carstensen, L. L. (1992). Social and emotional patterns in adulthood: Support for socioemotional selectivity theory. *Psychology and Aging, 7*(3), 331–338.

Carstensen, L. L. (2006). The influence of a sense of time on human development. *Science, 312*(5782), 1913–1915.

Carstensen, L. L., Fung, H. H., & Charles, S. T. (2003). Socioemotional selectivity theory and the regulation of emotion in the second half of life. *Motivation and Emotion, 27*(2), 103–123.

Carstensen, L. L., Mikels, J. A., & Mather, M. (2005). Aging and the intersection of cognition, motivation and emotion. In J. E. Birren & K. W. Schaie (Eds.), *Handbook of the psychology of aging* (Sixth ed.). Academic Press.

Carstensen, L. L., Pasupathi, M., Mayr, U., & Nesselroade, J. R. (2000). Emotional experience in everyday life across the adult life span. *Journal of Personality & Social Psychology, 79*(4), 644–655.

Carstensen, L. L., Turan, B., Scheibe, S., Ram, N., Ersner-Hershfield, H., Samanez-Larkin, G. R., Brooks, K. P., Nesselroade, J. R. (2011). Emotional experience improves with age: Evidence based on over 10 years of experience sampling. *Psychology and Aging*.

Charles, S. T. & Carstensen, L. L. (2007). Emotion regulation and aging. In J. J. Gross (Ed.), *Handbook of emotion regulation*. New York: Guilford Press.

Charles, S. T. & Carstensen, L. L. (2008). Unpleasant situations elicit different emotional responses in younger and older adults. *Psychology and Aging, 23*(3), 495–504.

Charles, S. T., Mather, M., & Carstensen, L. L. (2003). Aging and emotional memory: The forgettable nature of negative images for older adults. *Journal of Experimental Psychology: General, 132*(2), 310–324.

Comblain, C., D'Argembeau, A., & Van der Linden, M. (2005). Phenomenal characteristics of autobiographical memories for emotional and neutral events in older and younger adults. *Experimental Aging Research, 31*(2), 173–189.

Cox, K. M., Aizenstein, H. J., & Fiez, J. A. (2008). Striatal outcome processing in healthy aging. *Cognitive, Affective and Behavioral Neuroscience, 8*(3), 304–317.

D'Esposito, M., Deouell, L. Y., & Gazzaley, A. (2003). Alterations in the BOLD fMRI signal with ageing and disease: A challenge for neuroimaging. *Nature Reviews Neuroscience, 4*(11), 863–872.

Denburg, N. L., Cole, C. A., Hernandez, M., Yamada, T. H., Tranel, D., Bechara, A., et al. (2007). The orbitofrontal cortex, real-world decision making, and normal aging. *Annals of the New York Academy of Sciences, 1121*, 480–498.

Denburg, N. L., Recknor, E. C., Bechara, A., & Tranel, D. (2006). Psychophysiological anticipation of positive outcomes promotes advantageous decision-making in normal older persons. *International Journal of Psychophysiology, 61*(1), 19–25.

Denburg, N. L., Tranel, D., & Bechara, A. (2005). The ability to decide advantageously declines prematurely in some normal older persons. *Neuropsychologia, 43*(7), 1099–1106.

Dubois, S., Rossion, B., Schiltz, C., Bodart, J. M., Michel, C., Bruyer, R., et al. (1999). Effect of familiarity on the processing of human faces. *NeuroImage, 9*, 278–289.

Ebner, N. C. & Johnson, M. K. (2009). Young and older emotional faces: Are there age-group differences in expression identification and memory? *Emotion, 9*(3), 329–339.

Eppinger, B. & Kray, J. (2011). To choose or to avoid: Age differences in learning from positive and negative feedback. *Journal of Cognitive Neuroscience, 23*(1), 41–52.

Eppinger, B., Kray, J., Mock, B., & Mecklinger, A. (2008). Better or worse than expected? Aging, learning, and the ERN. *Neuropsychologia, 46*(2), 521–539.

Erk, S., Walter, H., & Abler, B. (2008). Age-related physiological responses to emotion anticipation and exposure. *Neuroreport, 19*(4), 447–452.

Fernandes, M., Ross, M., Wiegand, M., & Schryer, E. (2008). Are the memories of older adults positively biased? *Psychology and Aging*, 23(2), 297–306.

Fischer, H., Sandblom, J., Gavazzeni, J., Fransson, P., Wright, C. I., & Backman, L. (2005). Age-differential patterns of brain activation during perception of angry faces. *Neuroscience Letters*, 386(2), 99–104.

Frank, M. J. & Kong, L. (2008). Learning to avoid in older age. *Psychology and Aging*, 23(2), 392–398.

Fredrickson, B. L. & Carstensen, L. L. (1990). Choosing social partners: How old age and anticipated endings make us more selective. *Psychology and Aging*, 5, 335–347.

Fung, H. H., Carstensen, L. L., & Lang, F. R. (2001). Age-related patterns in social networks among European-Americans and African-Americans: Implications for socioemotional selectivity across the life span. *International Journal of Aging and Human Development*, 52(3), 185–206.

Fung, H. H., Carstensen, L. L., & Lutz, A. M. (1999). Influence of time on social preferences: Implications for life-span development. *Psychology and Aging*, 14(4), 595–604.

Gazzaley, A. & D'Esposito, M. (2005). BOLD functional MRI and cognitive aging. In R. Cabeza, L. Nyberg, & D. Park (Eds.), *Cognitive neuroscience of aging: Linking cognitive and cerebral aging* (pp. 107–131). New York, NY: Oxford University Press.

Goldin, P. R., McRae, K., Ramel, W., & Gross, J. J. (2008). The neural bases of emotion regulation: Reappraisal and suppression of negative emotion. *Biological Psychiatry*, 63(6), 577–586.

Grady, C. L. (2008). Cognitive neuroscience of aging. *Annals of the New York Academy of Sciences*, 1124, 127–144.

Gross, J. J., Carstensen, L. L., Pasupathi, M., Tsai, J. L., Goetestam Skorpen, C., & Hsu, A. Y. C. (1997). Emotion and aging: Experience, expression, and control. *Psychology and Aging*, 12(4), 590–599.

Grühn, D. & Scheibe, S. (2008). Age-related differences in valence and arousal ratings of pictures from the International Affective Picture System (IAPS): Do ratings become more extreme with age? *Behavior Research Methods*, 40, 512–521.

Gunning-Dixon, F. M., Gur, R. C., Perkins, A. C., Schroeder, L., Turner, T., Turetsky, B. I., et al. (2003). Age-related differences in brain activation during emotional face processing. *Neurobiology of Aging*, 24(2), 285–295.

Gutchess, A., Kensinger, E. A., & Schacter, D. (2007). Aging, self-referencing, and medial prefrontal cortex. *Social Neuroscience*, 2(2), 117–133.

Haümmerer, D., Li, S., Muüller, V., & Lindenberger, U. (in press). Life span differences in electrophysiological correlates of monitoring gains and losses during probabilistic reinforcement learning. *Journal of Cognitive Neuroscience*.

Hedden, T. & Gabrieli, J. D. (2004). Insights into the aging mind: A view from cognitive neuroscience. *Nature Reviews Neuroscience*, 5(2), 87–96.

Hess, T. M. (2006). Adaptive aspects of social cognitive functioning in adulthood: Age–related goal and knowledge influences. *Social Cognition*, 24(3), 279–309.

Iidaka, T., Okada, T., Murata, T., Omori, M., Kosaka, H., Sadato, N., et al. (2002). Age-related differences in the medial temporal lobe responses to emotional faces as revealed by fMRI. *Hippocampus*, 12(3), 352–362.

Isaacowitz, D. M., Löckenhoff, C. E., Lane, R. D., Wright, R., Sechrest, L., Riedel, R., et al. (2007). Age differences in recognition of emotion in lexical stimuli and facial expressions. *Psychology and Aging*, 22(1), 147–159.

Isaacowitz, D. M., Toner, K., Goren, D., & Wilson, H. R. (2008). Looking while unhappy: Mood-congruent gaze in young adults, positive gaze in older adults. *Psychological Science*, 19(9), 848–853.

Isaacowitz, D. M., Wadlinger, H. A., Goren, D., & Wilson, H. R. (2006a). Is there an age-related positivity effect in visual attention? A comparison of two methodologies. *Emotion*, 6(3), 511–516.

Isaacowitz, D. M., Wadlinger, H. A., Goren, D., & Wilson, H. R. (2006b). Selective preference in visual fixation away from negative images in old age? An eye-tracking study. *Psychology and Aging*, 21(1), 40–48.

Keightley, M. L., Chiew, K. S., Winocur, G., & Grady, C. L. (2007). Age-related differences in brain activity underlying identification of emotional expressions in faces. *Social Cognitive and Affective Neuroscience*, 2(4), 292–302.

Kennedy, Q., Mather, M., & Carstensen, L. L. (2004). The role of motivation in the age-related positivity effect in autobiographical memory. *Psychological Science*, 15(3), 208–214.

Kensinger, E. A. & Schacter, D. L. (2008). Neural processes supporting young and older adults' emotional memories. *Journal of Cognitive Neuroscience*, 20(7), 1161–1173.

Kisley, M. A., Wood, S., & Burrows, C. L. (2007). Looking at the sunny side of life: Age-related change in an event-related potential measure of the negativity bias. *Psychological Science*, 18(9), 838–843.

Knight, M., Seymour, T. L., Gaunt, J. T., Baker, C., Nesmith, K., & Mather, M. (2007). Aging and goal-directed emotional attention: Distraction reverses emotional biases. *Emotion*, 7(4), 705–714.

Kryla-Lighthall, N. & Mather, M. (2009). The role of cognitive control in older adults' emotional well-being. In V. Berngtson, D. Gans, N. Putney, & M. Silverstein (Eds.), *Handbook of theories of aging, 2nd Edition* (pp. 323–344): Springer Publishing.

Kwon, Y., Scheibe, S., Samanez-Larkin, G. R., Tsai, J. L., & Carstensen, L. L. (2009). Replicating the positivity effect in picture memory in Koreans: Evidence for cross-cultural generalizability. *Psychology and Aging*, 24(3), 748–754.

Lang, F. R. & Carstensen, L. L. (1994). Close emotional relationships in late life: Further support for proactive aging in the social domain. *Psychology and Aging*, 9, 315–324.

Lawton, M. P., Kleban, M. H., Rajagopal, D., & Dean, J. (1992). Dimensions of affective experience in three age groups. *Psychology and Aging*, 7(2), 171–184.

Leclerc, C. M. & Kensinger, E. A. (2008). Age-related differences in medial prefrontal activation in response to emotional images. *Cognitive, Affective and Behavioral Neuroscience*, 8(2), 153–164.

Leclerc, C. M. & Kensinger, E. A. (2010). Age-related valence-based reversal in recruitment of medial prefrontal cortex on a visual search task. *Social Neuroscience*, 5(5), 560–576.

Leclerc, C. M. & Kensinger, E. A. (in press). Neural processing of emotional pictures and words: A comparison of young and older adults. *Developmental Neuropsychology*.

Levenson, R. W., Carstensen, L. L., Friesen, W. V., & Ekman, P. (1991). Emotion, physiology, and expression in old age. *Psychology and Aging*, 6(1), 28–35.

Löckenhoff, C. E. & Carstensen, L. L. (2007). Aging, emotion, and health-related decision strategies: Motivational manipulations can reduce age differences. *Psychology and Aging*, 22(1), 134–146.

Logan, J. M., Sanders, A. L., Snyder, A. Z., Morris, J. C., & Buckner, R. L. (2002). Under-recruitment and nonselective recruitment: Dissociable neural mechanisms associated with aging. *Neuron*, *33*(5), 827–840.

Lustig, C. & Buckner, R. L. (2004). Preserved neural correlates of priming in old age and dementia. *Neuron*, *42*(5), 865–875.

MacPherson, S. E., Phillips, L. H., & Della Sala, S. (2002). Age, executive function and social decision making: A dorsolateral prefrontal theory of cognitive aging. *Psychology and Aging*, *17*(4), 598–609.

Mather, M., Canli, T., English, T., Whitfield, S., Wais, P., Ochsner, K. N., et al. (2004). Amygdala responses to emotionally valenced stimuli in older and younger adults. *Psychological Science*, *15*(4), 259–263.

Mather, M. & Carstensen, L. L. (2003). Aging and attentional biases for emotional faces. *Psychological Science*, *14*(5), 409–415.

Mather, M. & Johnson, M. K. (2000). Choice-supportive source monitoring: Do our decisions seem better to us as we age? *Psychology and Aging*, *15*(4), 596–606.

Mather, M. & Knight, M. R. (2005). Goal-directed memory: The role of cognitive control in older adults' emotional memory. *Psychology and Aging*, *20*, 554–570.

Mather, M., Knight, M. R., & McCaffrey, M. (2005). The allure of the alignable: Younger and older adults' false memories of choice features. *Journal of Experimental Psychology: General*, *134*(1), 38–51.

McRae, K., Hughes, B., Chopra, S., Gabrieli, J. D. E., Gross, J. J., & Ochsner, K. N. (2010). The neural bases of distraction and reappraisal. *Journal of Cognitive Neuroscience*, *22*(2), 248–262.

Mell, T., Heekeren, H. R., Marschner, A., Wartenburger, I., Villringer, A., Reischies, F. M. (2005). Effect of aging on stimulus-reward association learning. *Neuropsychologia*, *43*(4) 554–563.

Mell, T., Wartenburger, I., Marschner, A., Villringer, A., Reischies, F. M., & Heekeren, H. R. (2009). Altered function of ventral striatum during reward-based decision making in old age. *Frontiers in Human Neuroscience*, *3*, 34.

Mikels, J. A., Larkin, G. R., Reuter-Lorenz, P. A., & Carstensen, L. (2005). Divergent trajectories in the aging mind: Changes in working memory for affective versus visual information with age. *Psychology and Aging*, *20*(4), 542–553.

Mitchell, K. J., Raye, C. L., Ebner, N. C., Tubridy, S. M., Frankel, H., & Johnson, M. K. (2009). Age-group differences in medial cortex activity associated with thinking about self-relevant agendas. *Psychology and Aging*, *24*(2), 438–449.

Murty, V. P., Sambataro, F., Das, S., Tan, H. Y., Callicott, J. H., Goldberg, T. E., et al. (2009). Age-related alterations in simple declarative memory and the effect of negative stimulus valence. *Journal of Cognitive Neuroscience*, *21*(10), 1920–1933.

Nielsen, L., Knutson, B., & Carstensen, L. L. (2008). Affect dynamics, affective forecasting, and aging. *Emotion*, *8*(3), 318–330.

Nieuwenhuis, S., Ridderinkhof, K. R., Talsma, D., Coles, M. G., Holroyd, C. B., Kok, A., et al. (2002). A computational account of altered error processing in older age: Dopamine and the error-related negativity. *Cognitive, Affective and Behavioral Neuroscience*, *2*(1), 19–36.

Ochsner, K. N. & Gross, J. J. (2005). The cognitive control of emotion. *Trends in Cognitive Sciences*, *9*(5), 242–249.

Ochsner, K. N. & Gross, J. J. (2007). The neural architecture of emotion regulation. In J. J. Gross (Ed.), *Handbook of emotion regulation* (pp. 87–109). New York: Guilford Press.

Ochsner, K. N., Knierim, K., Ludlow, D. H., Hanelin, J., Ramachandran, T., Glover, G., et al. (2004). Reflecting upon feelings: An fMRI study of neural systems supporting the attribution of emotion to self and other. *Journal of Cognitive Neuroscience*, *16*(10), 1746–1772.

Phelps, E. A. (2006). Emotion and cognition: Insights from studies of the human amygdala. *Annual Review of Psychology*, *57*, 27–53.

Raz, N. (2005). The aging brain observed in vivo: Differential changes and their modifiers. In R. Cabeza, L. Nyberg, & D. Park (Eds.), *Cognitive neuroscience of aging: Linking cognitive and cerebral aging* (pp. 19–57). New York: Oxford University Press.

Raz, N., Lindenberger, U., Rodrigue, K., Kennedy, K. M., Head, D., Williamson, A., et al. (2005). Regional brain changes in aging healthy adults: General trends, individual differences and modifiers. *Cerebral Cortex*, *15*(11), 1676–1689.

Reuter-Lorenz, P. A. & Lustig, C. (2005). Brain aging: Reorganizing discoveries about the aging mind. *Current Opinion in Neurobiology*, *15*(2), 245–251.

Ruffman, T., Henry, J. D., Livingstone, V., & Phillips, L. H. (2008). A meta-analytic review of emotion recognition and aging: Implications for neuropsychological models of aging. *Neuroscience and Biobehavioral Reviews*, *32*(4), 863–881.

Rugg, M. D. & Morcom, A. M. (2005). The relationship between brain activity, cognitive performance, and aging: The case of memory. In R. Cabeza, L. Nyberg, & D. Park (Eds.), *Cognitive neuroscience of aging: Linking cognitive and cerebral aging* (pp. 132–154). New York: Oxford University Press.

Samanez-Larkin, G. R. & D'Esposito, M. (2008). Group comparisons: Imaging the aging brain. *Social Cognitive and Affective Neuroscience*, *3*(3), 290–297.

Samanez-Larkin, G. R., Gibbs, S. E. B., Khanna, K., Nielsen, L., Carstensen, L. L., & Knutson, B. (2007). Anticipation of monetary gain but not loss in healthy older adults. *Nature Neuroscience*, *10*(6), 787–791.

Samanez-Larkin, G. R., Hollon, N. G., Carstensen, L. L., & Knutson, B. (2008). Individual differences in insular sensitivity during loss anticipation predict avoidance learning. *Psychological Science*, *19*(4), 320–323.

Samanez-Larkin, G. R., Kuhnen, C. M., Yoo, D. J., & Knutson, B. (2010). Variability in nucleus accumbens activity mediates age-related suboptimal financial risk taking. *Journal of Neuroscience*, *30*(4), 1426–1434.

Samanez-Larkin, G. R., Robertson, E. R., Mikels, J. A., Carstensen, L. L., & Gotlib, I. H. (2009). Selective attention to emotion in the aging brain. *Psychology and Aging*, *24*(3), 748–754.

Samanez-Larkin, G. R., Wagner, A. D., & Knutson, B. (in press). Expected value information improves financial risk taking across the adult life span. *Social Cognitive and Affective Neuroscience*.

Scheibe, S. & Blanchard-Fields, F. (2009). Effects of regulating emotions on cognitive performance: What is costly for young adults is not so costly for older adults. *Psychology and Aging*, *24*(1), 217–223.

Schlagman, S., Schulz, J., & Kvavilashvili, L. (2006). A content analysis of involuntary autobiographical memories: Examining the positivity effect in old age. *Memory*, *14*(2), 161–175.

Schwartz, C. E., Wright, C. I., Shin, L. M., Kagan, J., Whalen, P. J., McMullin, K. G., et al. (2003). Differential amygdalar response to novel versus newly familiar neutral faces: A functional MRI probe developed for studying inhibited temperament. *Biological Psychiatry*, 53, 854–862.

Sergerie, K., Chochol, C., & Armony, J. L. (2008). The role of the amygdala in emotional processing: A quantitative meta-analysis of functional neuroimaging studies. *Neuroscience and Biobehavioral Reviews*, 32(4), 811–830.

Smith, D. P., Hillman, C. H., & Duley, A. R. (2005). Influences of age on emotional reactivity during picture processing. *Journals of Gerontology: Series B: Psychological and Social Sciences*, 60B, 49–56.

Spaniol, J., Voss, A., & Grady, C. (2008). Aging and emotional memory: Cognitive mechanisms underlying the positivity effect. *Psychology and Aging*, 23(4), 859–872.

Spreng, R. N., Wojtowicz, M., & Grady, C. L. (2010). Reliable differences in brain activity between young and old adults: A quantitative meta-analysis across multiple cognitive domains. *Neuroscience and Biobehavioral Reviews*, 34(8), 1178–1194.

St. Jacques, P., Bessette-Symons, B., & Cabeza, C. (2009). Functional neuroimaging studies of aging and emotion: Fronto-amygdalar differences during emotional perception and episodic memory. *Journal of the International Neuropsychological Society*, 15, 819–825.

St. Jacques, P., Dolcos, F., & Cabeza, R. (2010). Effects of aging on functional connectivity of the amygdala during negative evaluation: A network analysis of fMRI data. *Neurobiology of Aging*, 31(2), 315–327.

St. Jacques, P., Dolcos, F., & Cabeza, R. (2009). Effects of aging on functional connectivity of the amygdala for subsequent memory of negative pictures. *Psychological Science*, 20(1), 74–84.

Tessitore, A., Hariri, A. R., Fera, F., Smith, W. G., Das, S., Weinberger, D. R., et al. (2005). Functional changes in the activity of brain regions underlying emotion processing in the elderly. *Psychiatry Research*, 139(1), 9–18.

Tsai, J. L., Levenson, R. W., & Carstensen, L. L. (2000). Autonomic, subjective, and expressive responses to emotional films in older and younger Chinese Americans and European Americans. *Psychology and Aging*, 15(4), 684–693.

Urry, H. L., van Reekum, C. M., Johnstone, T., & Davidson, R. J. (2009). Individual differences in some (but not all) medial prefrontal regions reflect cognitive demand while regulating unpleasant emotion. *NeuroImage*, 47(3), 852–863.

Urry, H. L., van Reekum, C. M., Johnstone, T., Kalin, N. H., Thurow, M. E., Schaefer, H. S., et al. (2006). Amygdala and ventromedial prefrontal cortex are inversely coupled during regulation of negative affect and predict the diurnal pattern of cortisol secretion among older adults. *Journal of Neuroscience*, 26(16), 4415–4425.

van Reekum, C. M., Johnstone, T., Urry, H. L., Thurow, M. E., Schaefer, H. S., Alexander, A. L., et al. (2007). Gaze fixations predict brain activation during the voluntary regulation of picture-induced negative affect. *NeuroImage*, 36(3), 1041–1055.

West, R. (1996). An application of prefrontal cortex function theory to cognitive aging. *Psychological Bulletin*, 120, 272–292.

Williams, L. M., Brown, K. J., Palmer, D., Liddell, B. J., Kemp, A. H., Olivieri, G., et al. (2006). The mellow years?: Neural basis of improving emotional stability over age. *Journal of Neuroscience*, 26(24), 6422–6430.

Winecoff, A., LaBar, K., Madden, D., Cabeza, R., & Huettel, S. (in press). Cognitive and neural contributors to emotion regulation in aging. *Social Cognitive and Affective Neuroscience*.

Wood, S., Busemeyer, J., Koling, A., Cox, C. R., & Davis, H. (2005). Older adults as adaptive decision makers: Evidence from the Iowa Gambling Task. *Psychology and Aging*, 20(2), 220–225.

Wood, S. & Kisley, M. A. (2006). The negativity bias is eliminated in older adults: age-related reduction in event-related brain potentials associated with evaluative categorization. *Psychology and Aging*, 21(4), 815–820.

Wright, C. I., Dickerson, B. C., Feczko, E., Negeira, A., & Williams, D. (2007). A functional magnetic resonance imaging study of amygdala responses to human faces in aging and mild Alzheimer's disease. *Biological Psychiatry*, 62(12), 1388–1395.

Wright, C. I., Negreira, A., Gold, A. L., Britton, J. C., Williams, D., & Barrett, L. F. (2008). Neural correlates of novelty and face-age effects in young and elderly adults. *NeuroImage*, 42(2), 956–968.

Wright, C. I., Wedig, M. M., Williams, D., Rauch, S. L., & Albert, M. S. (2006). Novel fearful faces activate the amygdala in healthy young and elderly adults. *Neurobiology of Aging*, 27(2), 361–374.

Zald, D. H. (2003). The human amygdala and the emotional evaluation of sensory stimuli. *Brain Research Reviews*, 41(1), 88–123.

PART 4

Inter-Personal Processes

The Mirror Neuron System and Social Cognition

Christian Keysers, Marc Thioux, *and* Valeria Gazzola

Abstract

For many animals, the actions of other organisms are of critical importance. For humans in particular understanding the actions of others and the capacity to learn skills by observing the actions of a teacher are necessary foundation for the evolution of human cooperation and culture. The discovery of mirror neurons has laid a foundation for a neuroscientific understanding of how the brain processes the actions of others and similar systems may contribute to how we perceive the sensations and emotions of others. This chapter introduces the key methods used to investigate this system and reviews its properties, localization, and functions in monkeys and humans together with examples of its dysfunctions.

Keywords: sensations, emotions, perception, monkeys, mirror neurons

Mirror Neurons in the Monkey

Mirror neurons have first been discovered in the premotor cortex (area F5, Figure 35.1) of the monkey (Gallese, Fadiga, Fogassi, & Rizzolatti, 1996). Neurons in this region of the brain are active while the monkey performs goal-directed actions such as grasping an object or shelling a peanut. For each premotor neuron, the execution of only a particular subset of all possible actions is linked to an increase in firing rate. This subset will be called "effective executed actions," and represents a form of tuning curve of the premotor neuron. Electrostimulation in area F5 can induce overt behavior such as grasping a nearby object (Graziano, Taylor, & Moore, 2002). This shows that neurons in F5 are part of the causal chain of neurons that triggers the actions of the monkey.

Unlike neurons in the primary motor cortex (M1) that encode the details of how the body moves,

F5 neurons resemble generals in the army that determine *what* should be done more than the precise muscles that need to be moved (Rizzolatti et al., 1988; Thioux, Gazzola, & Keysers, 2008). For instance, while very different populations of M1 neurons are involved in grasping an object with the hand and with the mouth, many F5 neurons show similar increases of firing rate in both cases, probably because the goal (grasping) is the same (Rizzolatti et al., 1988).

For a long time, neurons in F5 were thought to exclusively deal with the monkey's own actions. To the surprise of many, a significant number of F5 neurons also responds while monkeys simply view another individual perform certain actions. These actions, the observation of which triggers activity in a certain premotor neuron, form the visual tuning curve of this neuron and will be called "effective observed actions" (e.g., grasping or shelling a peanut).

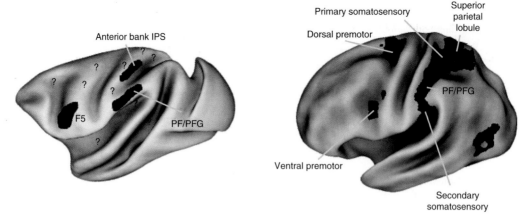

Fig. 35.1 Locations in which mirror neurons have been found in monkeys (left), with most of the brain still unexplored (question marks). Location of the putative MNS as identified using fMRI in humans (right).
Adapted from Gazzola & Keysers (2009) with permission of Oxford Journals.

According to the relationship between the visual and motor tuning curve, visuo-motor F5 neurons can be classified as non-congruent (the tuning curves do not overlap) or as "mirror neurons" (the curves do overlap). Box 35.1 specifies the main classes of visuo-motor neurons encountered in F5 and indicates the proportion of neurons falling in each class.

Neurons with overlapping visual and motor tuning curves are called mirror because when monkey A sees monkey B grasp a banana, for example, such neurons in A will activate grasping motor programs. These grasping programs in A now mirror internally the behavior of B, acting like a mirror reflection or resonance of the observed behavior. Non-congruent neurons should therefore not be called mirror neurons.

More recently, mirror neurons have also been recorded in the anterior half of the convexity of the inferior parietal lobule of the macaque (area PFG and to a lesser extent, PF (Rozzi, Ferrari, Bonini, Rizzolatti, & Fogassi, 2008), see Figure 35.1). These parietal mirror neurons have properties that are surprisingly similar to those of F5 neurons and are composed of similar proportions of non-congruent and mirror neurons. In both brain regions only 10–20% of neurons have mirror properties. A further set of mirror neurons have been reported in the anterior bank of the intraparietal sulcus (Fujii, Hihara, & Iriki, 2008). The fact that mirror neurons have not yet been found in other locations in the macaque brain, however, cannot be taken as evidence that only F5, PF, PFG, and the intraparietal sulcus contain mirror neurons, because mirror neurons have not been systematically searched for

outside of these brain regions. Studies examining the uptake of glucose in the macaque brain during action observation and execution suggest for instance that the somatosensory cortices might also contain neurons that are active during action execution and observation (Evangeliou, Raos, Galletti, & Savaki, 2009; Raos, Evangeliou, & Savaki, 2004).

Most investigators assume that mirror neurons in parietal and premotor cortices respond to the sight of actions because PF/PFG has reciprocal anatomical connections with the STS and because some STS neurons show visual responses that are similar to those of mirror neurons—although the STS neurons lack the motor properties that make mirror neurons so unique (Keysers & Perrett, 2004; Rozzi et al., 2006; Rozzi et al., 2008). This visual information is then transmitted from PF/PFG to F5 through the reciprocal connections between these regions (Keysers & Perrett, 2004; Rozzi et al., 2006).

Additional Properties of Monkey Mirror Neurons
Object Directed Actions
Most of the mirror neurons in F5 respond exclusively to *object directed* actions. A mirror neuron responding to the observation and execution of grasping a peanut for instance will not respond to the sight of someone miming the same action without the object (Gallese et al., 1996; Umilta et al., 2001). This is in holding with the motor properties of F5 neurons, the vast majority of which seem responsible for actions directed at things (i.e., "transitive" actions). A minority of mirror neurons not only respond during the execution and observation of transitive actions (e.g., grasping with the mouth)

Box 35.1

Neurons responding both during the execution and observation/audition of actions can be classified based on the relationship between their visual/auditory (dotted) and motor (solid) tuning curves. The last two columns of the table below indicate the approximate proportion of neurons in each category (as percentage of motor neurons responding to action observation) based on Gallese et al. (1996) and di Pellegrino et al. (1992) for F5 and Rozzi et al. (2008) for PFG. Broadly and strictly congruent neurons are separated by a dotted line to indicate that rather than a sharp distinction, one should see this difference as one of degree, with individual neurons varying along a continuum from very strict to very broad.

Family	Definition and example	Visual (dotted) and motor (solid) tuning curves	F5	PFG
Non-Congruent	**Non-Congruent:** There is no overlap between visual and motor tuning curves and no logical relationship **Example:** Effective executed action includes tearing an object apart but not grasping. Effective observed action includes grasping but not tearing			11%
	Logically Related: There is no overlap between visual and motor tuning curves but a logical relationship **Example:** Effective executed actions include grasping but not placing but effective observed actions include placing but not grasping. Given that an experimenter's placing food often precedes the monkey's grasping of that food, a logical relationship exists in the form of a causal chain of events		7%	6%
Mirror	**Broadly Congruent:** There is overlap between motor and visual tuning curves, but the overlap is partial, with some actions only being effective in one of the modalities **Example:** Effective executed actions restricted to a precision grip with the hand, effective observed actions include precision grip with the hand but also whole hand prehension and grasping with the mouth		61%	54%
	Strictly Congruent: The tuning curves overlap very tightly **Example:** Precision grip with the hand is the only effective action during both observation and execution		32%	29%

but also to the observation of intransitive actions that are visually similar (e.g., smacking the lips, an affiliative gesture frequently performed by monkeys) (Ferrari, Gallese, Rizzolatti, & Fogassi, 2003). These neurons may represent an important pre-adaptation for the emergence of symbolic gestures. It remains to be investigated whether neurons in other motor brain regions may have mirror properties without preferring object directed actions.

Occlusion

About half the mirror neurons that respond to the sight of a hand grasping an object but not the sight of hand miming a grasp will also respond to the sight of a hand reaching behind an occluding screen, but only if the monkey has seen previously that an object is hidden behind that screen (Kraskov et al., 2009; Umilta et al., 2001). This suggests that mirror neurons are part of a circuitry that can trigger accurate motor representation of occluded actions by combining present but incomplete visual information with past information stored in memory.

Sound

Mirror neurons also respond to the sound of their effective executed actions. Many mirror neurons responding during the execution and observation of peanut shelling will also respond to the sound of peanut shelling. Some only respond when both the sound and the vision of the effective action is presented, others will respond to either modality alone, but more to their combination, and others finally will respond maximally to either modality (Keysers et al., 2003; Kohler et al., 2002). On average, an auditory mirror neuron will start responding 120 ms after the onset of the sound of the effective action, suggesting a rapid and relatively direct route from the sensory input to mirror neurons (Keysers et al., 2003; Kohler et al., 2002).

Action Discrimination

It is possible to deduce which of two actions another individual is performing with >90% accuracy from the firing rate of mirror neurons in the brain of an observing and/or listening monkey (Keysers et al., 2003). This is remarkable given that a decade ago, the premotor cortex was considered not to have any functions in perception.

The Human Mirror Neuron System

In humans, recording single neurons is only rarely possible, making it difficult to directly test if single neurons respond both during the observation and execution of actions. However, the existence of a system that has the same properties as the mirror neurons in monkeys, and which is therefore called the mirror neuron system (MNS) is now well established in humans by more than a decade of experiments based on a variety of less invasive techniques (see Box 35.2). Taken together, these techniques have established three facts.

Existence

Measuring TMS-evoked motor potentials (Aziz-Zadeh, Iacoboni, Zaidel, Wilson, & Mazziotta, 2004; Fadiga, Craighero, & Olivier, 2005; Fadiga, Fogassi, Pavesi, & Rizzolatti, 1995) and motor reaction times (Brass, Bekkering, Wohlschlager, & Prinz, 2000) while participants perceive the actions of others has shown that viewing or hearing actions facilitates the execution of corresponding actions and interferes with the execution of antagonistic actions. This can only be the case if certain neurons involved in executing a motor program also respond to the observation of similar actions, and these findings therefore demonstrate the existence of mirror neurons somewhere in the human brain. This fact is further confirmed by the observation that perceiving the actions of others is linked with changes in the power-spectrum of the EEG and MEG signal that resemble those associated with executing similar actions. This was first observed in 1954, four decades before the discovery of mirror neurons in the monkey, by Gastaut and Bert in a surprisingly modern experiment:

> "[the rolandic mu-rhythm] is blocked when the subject performs a movement [. . .]. It also disappears when the subject identifies himself with an active person represented on the screen. [. . .] During a sequence of film showing a boxing match. [. . .] less than a second after the appearance of the boxers all type of rolandic activity disappears in spite of the fact that the subject seems completely relaxed" (Gastaut & Bert, 1954, p. 439).

Once mirror neurons were described, this phenomenon received renewed interest, with a number of experiments now confirming its existence using EEG (Cochin, Barthelemy, Lejeune, Roux, & Martineau, 1998; Cochin, Barthelemy, Roux, & Martineau, 1999; Muthukumaraswamy & Johnson, 2004a, 2004b; Muthukumaraswamy, Johnson, & McNair, 2004) and MEG (Hari et al., 1998).

Localization

Second, PET and fMRI studies that map brain activity in the same participants during (i) action execution and (ii) viewing or hearing others perform similar actions have shown that a number of brain regions respond in both cases (Figure 35.1). This network includes ventral premotor and inferior parietal cortices, which have been shown to contain mirror neurons in monkeys, and additional areas including the dorsal premotor, supplementary motor, primary and secondary somatosensory, dorsal posterior parietal cortex and the cerebellum

Based on the definition of mirror neurons in the monkey, a brain area should only be considered to be putatively mirror if it is involved *both* in action observation (or listening) *and* execution. A number of techniques have been used to establish whether this is true of some neurons and/or brain regions in humans.

TMS (transcranial magnetic stimulation): A single magnetic pulse, given on a particular location of M1's homunculus, evokes a twitch in a corresponding muscle that is measured using electromyography, leading to a "motor evoked potential" (MEP) measurement. If and only if a human MNS exists, seeing or hearing someone else perform an action involving the same muscle should increase the MEP but one involving other muscles should not (see for example Fadiga et al., 1995). Repetitive TMS (rTMS) can also be used to inhibit a restricted area of the brain shortly before using the MEP technique described above to test if this particular area is part of the MNS that causes the MEP modulation during observation (for example Avenanti et al., 2007).

Psychophysics: Instead of triggering motor programs using TMS one can also ask participants to execute certain actions in response to a cue and simultaneously show seemingly task irrelevant actions. Again, if and only if there is an MNS should the execution of a particular action be *accelerated* by viewing actions using the same muscle and be *slowed* by viewing actions using an antagonistic muscle (for example, Brass et al., 2000; Kilner et al., 2003).

PET (positron emission tomography) & fMRI (functional magnetic resonance imaging): The distribution of injected radioactive molecules of water or oxygen (PET), or the distribution of changes in the distortions of the magnetic field due to blood oxygenation (fMRI) can be used to localize brain regions activated while viewing or hearing the actions of others. The same procedure is then used to visualize the brain regions involved in action execution, preferably in the same participants. Only voxels activated both during the perception and execution of actions will be considered part of the putative MNS (for example Gazzola & Keysers, 2009).

Repetition suppression fMRI: For many neurons the repetition of the same stimulus causes a reduction of the activity to that stimulus. If action observation and execution are indeed encoded by the same (population of) neurons, asking the subject to watch the very same action he/she just performed (or the other way around) should cause a reduction of the activity similar to the one caused by the repetition of two consecutive visual stimuli. Areas showing this reduction will then be consider part of the putative MNS. If repetition suppression does not occur in a particular region, this may be due to the fact that neurons in this region do not show repetition suppression under certain conditions or that the region does not contain (enough) mirror neurons to trigger a measurable repetition suppression (for example Kilner et al., 2009).

Pattern classification fMRI: If an MNS exists, the pattern of activity across the many neurons of a mirror brain region should be similar during action perception and action execution. Accordingly, after training a pattern classifier algorithm to discriminate the brain activity when participants hear or view actions A and B, the pattern classification algorithm should automatically be able to discriminate above chance the similar patterns of brain activity associated with executing actions A and B (for example Etzel et al., 2008).

EEG/MEG (electroencephalogram or magnetoencephalogram): EEG and MEG measure, through the scalp, currents that are generated by synchronous activity of populations of neurons. Two rhythms have been associated with action execution: the mu and beta rhythm. Both rhythms have more energy while the subject is at rest and are disrupted as soon as an action is performed. If an MNS exists a similar suppression of these two rhythms should occur while perceiving the actions of others. An alternative approach is to stimulate of the median nerve, which produces a disruption of the mu and beta rhythms similar to the one produced by action execution. Studying whether this induced disruption is modified by action observation is another method to assess the existence of an MNS in humans (for a review see Pineda, 2005). Finally, using source localization, one can test if activity during action perception depends on sources that overlap with those during action execution, but the limited spatial resolution of source localization makes this approach less attractive.

(Aziz-Zadeh, Wilson, Rizzolatti, & Iacoboni, 2006; Dinstein, Hasson, Rubin, & Heeger, 2007; Filimon, Nelson, Hagler, & Sereno, 2007; Gazzola, Aziz-Zadeh, & Keysers, 2006; Gazzola, Rizzolatti, Wicker, & Keysers, 2007; Grezes, Armony, Rowe, & Passingham, 2003; Keysers & Gazzola, 2009; Ricciardi et al., 2009; Turella, Erb, Grodd, & Castiello, 2009). However, the limited spatial resolution of traditional fMRI and PET cannot show that the same neurons within a voxel are active during action execution and action perception, so it is therefore appropriate to refer to this network as the "putative MNS," where putative acknowledges the fact that in some of these regions, different neurons within a voxel could be responsible for the activity during action execution and action perception. Putative, however, does not question the existence of an MNS in humans per se, because the existence has been established using TMS and psychophysics.

Repetition suppression fMRI (see Box 35.2) has provided further evidence that at least the human premotor and posterior parietal cortex also contain mirror neurons (Chong, Cunnington, Williams, Kanwisher, & Mattingley, 2008; Dinstein et al., 2007; Kilner, Neal, Weiskopf, Friston, & Frith, 2009; Lingnau, Gesierich, & Caramazza, 2009). Repetitive TMS on the ventral premotor cortex further showed that this region seems responsible for the MEP increase during action observation (Avenanti, Bolognini, Maravita, & Agliotti, 2007), and pattern classification has shown that similar patterns of activity are indeed evoked in premotor and parietal regions during action execution and perception (Etzel, Gazzola, & Keysers, 2008).

Properties of the Human MNS

Object and Non-Object Directed Actions

In humans, there is evidence that the MNS also responds to actions not directed at objects (intransitive actions): EEG/MEG studies show a suppression of the mu-rhythm during finger movements observation (Babiloni et al., 2002; Calmels et al., 2006; Cochin et al., 1998; Cochin et al., 1999); TMS studies show an MEP facilitation during the observation of finger flexion and extension (Baldissera, Cavallari, Craighero, & Fadiga, 2001; Clark, Tremblay, & Ste-Marie, 2004; Fadiga et al., 1995); fMRI studies find premotor activity while observing finger-lifting movements (Iacoboni et al., 1999), hand gestures (Lui et al., 2008) and the pantomime of object-related actions without the object (Buccino et al., 2001; Lui et al., 2008); and psychophysical studies show that seeing another person moving their fingers (M. Brass et al., 2000) or arm (Kilner, Paulignan, & Blakemore, 2003) facilitates the execution of similar movement. Nevertheless, when intransitive and transitive actions are directly compared, transitive actions seem to elicit more putative MNS activity (Buccino et al., 2001; Muthukumaraswamy & Johnson, 2004a; Muthukumaraswamy et al., 2004; but see Rossi et al., 2002).

How and What

In the monkey, the presence of both strictly and broadly congruent mirror neurons ensures that the mirror activity triggered by the observation of actions reflects both *what* was performed (the goal) and *how* it was performed (the means). This is because the motor programs associated with strictly congruent mirror neurons will mirror the details of *how* the action was performed (e.g., precision grip), while those associated with the broadly congruent mirror neurons often differ in means but have a goal in common with the observed action (e.g., grasping with mouth or hand), and therefore reflect *what* was achieved (grasping). In humans too, there is evidence that goals and means are mirrored in the putative MNS (Thioux et al., 2008). TMS experiments show a facilitation of the specific muscles involved in the observed action (Alaerts, Swinnen, & Wenderoth, 2009; Urgesi, Moro, Candidi, & Agliotti, 2006). FMRI experiments show that observing actions with familiar goals, but means the actor cannot reproduce, still triggers the motor programs the observer would use to achieve the same goal (Gazzola, Rizzolatti et al., 2007; Gazzola, van der Worp et al., 2007), possibly allowing us to mirror at least the goal of nonhuman (robotic or animal) actions as well. Additionally, repetition suppression fMRI (Box 35.2) has shown that parts of the putative MNS respond less to the observation of an action if seen after another action that has the same goal but different means (Hamilton & Grafton, 2006, 2008), providing further evidence for goal coding in the MNS. By default, based on the fact that broadly congruent mirror neurons are twice as frequent as strictly congruent ones (Gallese et al., 1996; Rozzi et al., 2008), goals should prevail over means in the MNS. This is in holding with the fact that if asked to reproduce an action, humans will tend to reproduce the goal rather than the means (Bekkering, Wohlschlager, & Gattis, 2000) but specific tasks can bias this equilibrium (Bird, Brindley, Leighton, & Heyes, 2007).

Sounds

As in monkeys, the putative MNS is also activated by the sound of an action (Caetano, Jousmaki, & Hari, 2007; Gazzola et al., 2006; Pizzamiglio et al., 2005), even in congenitally blind participants (Ricciardi et al., 2009) showing that this system can develop independently of vision. Unlike for vision, the sound of an action often carries no information about what body part was used to perform the action (e.g., one could press a piano key with the foot, nose or hand and produce the same sound). Auditory mirror responses therefore also show the MNS's capacity to mirror what was done (press a key) without direct information about how it was done, probably by activating the motor programs the listener would use to produce the same sound. In this respect, the MNS projects the perceiver's own motor programs onto the sensory evidence of other people's actions rather than objectively mirroring the details of how the other has performed the action.

Correlation with Empathy

People that report being more empathic in life activate their MNS more strongly when hearing the actions of others, linking the MNS to empathy (Gazzola et al., 2006).

Anticipation

While observing the actions of other individuals in a predictable context, activity in the MNS seems to predict the actions of others by ~200ms. If an infant, for instance, repeatedly sees that a hand will reach and grasp a toy 1 sec after a curtain opens, the child will increasingly suppress its mu-rhythm in the 400 ms before the onset of the now predictable arm movement (Southgate, Johnson, Osborne, & Csibra, 2009). Also, when viewing a hand rhythmically flex and extend the wrist, adult observers will modulate the excitability of their own wrist muscles with the same frequency, but about 200 ms in advance of the observed movement (Borroni, Montagna, Cerri, & Baldissera, 2005). Given that it takes at least 100 ms for the brain to relay auditory and visual information to the MNS (Keysers et al., 2003; Kohler et al., 2002), this suggests that the MNS is part of a system that will anticipate predictable events.

Plasticity and Development

Expertise

FMRI experiments show that expertise in a domain is associated with increased activity in the putative MNS to the sight/sound of actions of that domain. Ballet dancers who have learned a specific dance style have a higher level of activity in the pre-motor and parietal cortex while watching that dance relative to a dance unknown to them (Calvo-Merino, Glaser, Grèzes, Passingham, & Haggard, 2005). Professional pianists activate the putative MNS more then piano novices when viewing a hand play the piano (Haslinger et al., 2005).

Training

Practice-related changes in the activation of the putative MNS can be observed after relatively short periods of training. Dancers who learned new dance sequences for five weeks showed increased activity in the putative MNS when observing the same sequences relative to other matched sequences (Cross, Hamilton, & Grafton, 2006) and this increase was correlated with the dancers' own appreciations of their ability

to reproduce the sequences. Also, although piano-naïve participants do not significantly activate their premotor cortex to the sound of piano music, after only 5 half-hour lessons of piano, they do (Lahav, Saltzman, & Schlaug, 2007). Finally, when participants first observe movies involving index and little-finger movements, MEPs increase in the index but not the little-finger for the observation of index finger abduction, and vice-versa for the observation of little-finger abduction. After being trained to perform index abductions when seeing little-finger movements and vice-versa for a couple of hours, participants in this group showed a reversed effect: facilitation of MEPs of the index abductor when viewing little finger abduction and vice-versa (Catmur, Walsh, & Heyes, 2007).

Hebbian Learning

Since an actor is also spectator and auditor of her own actions, during hand actions for instance, parietal and pre-motor neurons controlling the action fire at the same time as neurons in the STS that respond to the observation and sound of this specific hand action (some of which irrespective of the view point). These sensory and motor neurons that fire together would wire together, that is, strengthen their connections through Hebbian synaptic potentiation (Keysers & Perrett, 2004) (see also Heyes et al., 2001, for a similar model based on association learning). After repeated self-observation/audition, the motor neurons in the premotor and parietal regions would now receive such strong synaptic input from sensory STS neurons responding to the sight and sound of the action, that they would become mirror. The same pairing between execution and observation would also occur in cases in which an individual is imitated by another (Brass & Heyes, 2005; Del Giudice, Manera, & Keysers, 2009; Heyes, 2001). For instance, a child cannot observe its own facial expressions, but the adult who imitates the child's expression would serve as a mirror, triggering in the child's STS an activity pattern, representing what the expression sounds and looks like, that becomes associated with the premotor cortex activity producing the expression that was imitated (Del Giudice et al., 2009). Hebbian learning could explain the emergence of the MNS in infants and its plasticity in adulthood. This perspective does not preclude the possibility that some genetic factors may guide its development. Genetic factors could for instance canalize (Del Giudice et al., 2009) Hebbian learning by equipping the baby with a tendency to perform spontaneous and cyclic movements and to look preferentially at biological motion congruent with its actions to provide the right activity patterns for Hebbian learning to occur. What is important in this perspective is that the MNS is no longer a specific social adaptation that evolved to permit action understanding, but is a simple consequence of sensory-motor learning that has to occur for an individual to be able to visually control his own actions (Brass & Heyes, 2005; Del Giudice et al., 2009; Oztop & Arbib, 2002). Note that due to sensorimotor latencies, there is a systematic time-lag between motor activity and sensory consequences that endows this Hebbian learning with predictive properties (see below).

Neonatal Imitation

Imitative abilities in newborns are often taken to suggest that the MNS is partially genetically predetermined. Infants younger than a month tend to imitate facial expressions (Meltzoff & Moore, 1977). Tongue protrusion is the most frequently imitated behavior, but some experiments also report lips protrusion, mouth opening, eye-blinking, and finger movements imitation (Anisfeld, 1991, 1996; Meltzoff & Moore, 1997; Meltzoff & Decety, 2003). What remains unclear, is how this neonatal imitation relates to the MNS (Brass & Heyes, 2005; Heyes, 2001; Meltzoff & Moore, 1997; Meltzoff & Decety, 2003): it could represent the activity of a primitive and specialized system that is fundamentally different from the adult MNS or a genetic pre-wiring of what will become the adult MNS. Longitudinal studies that measure the neural basis of such neonatal imitation and follow it until mature imitation arises later in life will be necessary to settle this debate.

MNS Activity in Children

Few studies have measured putative MNS activity in children. EEG shows mu-suppression during action observation in children aged 4 to 10 years with the degree of mu-suppression independent of age (Lepage & Théoret, 2006). In addition, babies aged 14–16 month show more mu- and beta-suppression while they view other babies crawl (which they can do themselves) than when they see other babies walk (which they cannot yet do) (van Elk, van Schie, Hunnius, Vesper, & Bekkering, 2008). This effect was stronger in babies that had more crawling experience. The substantial change in EEG rhythms occurring during the first years of life, however, makes it difficult to extend this EEG approach to infants below the age of one year. Shimada and Hiraki (2006) therefore used near

infrared sprectroscopy, an optical method that measures the local blood oxygenation under the scalp, to test if younger children already activate their motor cortices while viewing the actions of others. They found that even 6- to 7-month-old infants already activate brain regions involved in hand-action execution while they view the hand actions of others. This suggests that action perception and execution may already be coupled by an MNS in 6-month-old babies, and that this system changes relatively little from 4 to 10 years of age.

Action Understanding in Infants

This conclusion is largely supported by recent studies investigating goal attribution in infants. By the end of the first year, infants readily recognize the goals of observed actions. For instance, 6-month-old infants were habituated to seeing an experimenter grasp one of two toys (Woodward, 1998). After habituation, the position of the toys was inverted. Infants suddenly looked longer when the experimenter started picking the other toy (despite the fact that the movement trajectory was the same as during habituation). They were less interested when the experimenter picked the old toy in the new location, suggesting that infants at that age already encore the goal of an observed action (i.e., *what* was grasped). This capacity to extract the goal of a grasping action seems to depend on the infant's ability to grasp. Three-month-old babies cannot yet reach and grasp objects by themselves, and they do not show the above-mentioned goal habituation. If they are fitted with a "sticky" glove to which toys will adhere, and become able to retrieve toys by themselves, when re-tested in the observation condition they start to show the goal habituation effect (Sommerville, Woodward, & Needham, 2005). This link between the capacity to perform an action (grasping) and the capacity to understand similar actions in others (as measured through habituation) suggests that the MNS, linking observation and execution, might be involved.

Similar Systems for Emotions and Sensations

Touch

Similarly to what occurs in the MNS for actions, fMRI experiments have shown that observing other people getting touched, activates regions of the secondary, and to a lesser extent, primary somatosensory cortex that are also activated when the same participants are touched in similar ways (Blakemore, Bristow, Bird, Frith, & Ward, 2005; Ebisch et al., 2008;

Keysers et al., 2004). In addition, Brodmann area 2, a sector of the primary somatosensory cortex responsible for the combining tactile and proprioceptive information, becomes active both when participants manipulate objects and when they see or hear other's do so (for a review see Keysers, Kaas & Gazzola, 2010). This suggests that a mechanism similar to mirror neurons in the motor domain may apply to the somatosensory domain: We activate brain regions involved in our own tactile and proprioceptive experiences when seeing those of others.

Pain

Functional MRI and EEG studies suggest that witnessing the pain of other individuals activates regions of the pain matrix involved in feeling pain, including the somatosensory, insular, and anterior cingulate cortices (for reviews see Jackson, Rainville, & Decety, 2006; Singer & Lamm, 2009). Rare single-cell recordings in epileptic patients suggest that single neurons in the anterior cingulate cortex indeed respond to both the experience of pinpricks and the observation of other individuals being pinpricked (Hutchison, Davis, Lozano, Tasker, & Dostrovsky, 1999). In addition, seeing a needle penetrate someone else's skin leads to relaxation of the muscles in the observer that corresponds to the pricked region, suggesting an interaction between the mirroring of pain and the motor system (Avenanti, Minio-Paluello, Bufalari, & Aglioti, 2009). Generally, all of these effects are stronger in more empathic individuals (Avenanti et al., 2009; Singer et al., 2004).

Emotions

Finally, when observing the emotional facial expressions of others, participants not only activate regions they would use to generate similar expressions; this motor sharing appears to trigger activity in the anterior insula of the observer in regions that become active when the observer experiences similar emotions (for a review see Bastiaansen, Thioux, & Keysers, 2009). Again this phenomenon is more pronounced in more empathic individuals (Jabbi, Swart, & Keysers, 2007).

Together, this data suggests that mirror neurons in the motor system may be a specific example of a more general phenomenon: Our brains vicariously activate representations of our own actions, sensations, and emotions while viewing those of others. Lesions in each of these systems seem to be followed by impairments in the recognition of other people's states (Adolphs, Damasio, Tranel, Cooper, & Damasio, 2000; Calder, Keane, Manes, Antoun, & Young, 2000).

Functions of the Motor MNS

Action Recognition

The property of mirror neurons to link the observation/audition of an action to motor programs for that action suggests that they may play a key role in perceiving what others do and how they are doing it (Thioux et al., 2008). Evidence that the MNS indeed contributes to our understanding of other people's actions primarily derives from studies that show that an rTMS-induced interference with the MNS or lesions in the MNS cause deficits in action understanding. Indeed, disrupting the ventral premotor cortex using rTMS impairs participants' capacity to judge how heavy a box is when seeing someone else lift the box (Pobric & Hamilton, 2006). Participants that suffer from limb aplasia have difficulties in deciding whether a hand gesture they observe is meaningful or meaningless, with performance in this perceptual task being correlated with their capacity to imitate intransitive gestures (Pazzaglia, Smania, Corato, & Aglioti, 2008). Lesion analysis showed that patients with limb apraxia who showed more action recognition difficulties were more likely to have lesions in the ventral premotor cortex. The fact that many patients with apraxia and lesions in the MNS were still able to perceive some of the gestures correctly shows that the MNS is not the only system that can help recognize actions, but the significant deficits observed in the majority of patients shows that it can significantly contribute to action recognition. In addition, participants with apraxia also have difficulties in recognizing the sound of other people's actions, with those suffering from apraxia of the mouth more impaired in recognizing mouth action sounds, and those suffering from apraxia of the limb more impaired in recognizing hand action sounds (Pazzaglia, Pizzamiglio, Pes, & Aglioti, 2008), in agreement with the somatotopic organization of the auditory MNS (Gazzola et al., 2006). Finally, the ventral premotor cortex is also involved in mirroring a very specific type of action: facial expressions (van der Gaag, Minderaa, & Keysers, 2007), and lesions to this area impair the recognition of facial expressions (Adolphs et al., 2000).

Imitation

Given their propensity to match observed actions with motor programs necessary to execute the same action, mirror neurons are thought to play a role in imitation (Brass & Heyes, 2005; Heyes, 2001; Iacoboni, 2009; Iacoboni et al., this book). Functional MRI has demonstrated that activity in the ventral premotor cortex (ventral BA44 in particular) during imitation of finger movements is higher than the combination of the activity during the observation and the execution of the same movements (Iacoboni et al., 1999; Molnar-Szakacs, Iacoboni, Koski, & Mazziotta, 2005) and rTMS-induced disruption of this region impairs imitation of an action but not its execution in response to a spatial cue (Heiser, Iacoboni, Maeda, Marcus, & Mazziotta, 2003). Imitation is likely, however, to require more than a simple matching between action perception and action execution (Gergely, Bekkering, & Király, 2002; Tessari, Canessa, Ukmar, & Rumiati, 2007) and brain systems in addition to the MNS are likely to be essential for dynamically controlling the contribution of the MNS to behavior in a social setting (Kokal, Gazzola, & Keysers, 2009).

Ethologists and developmental psychologists have introduced an important distinction between emulation and imitation. Emulation refers to replicating the goal of an observed action without necessarily copying the means while imitation in the strict sense requires that the detailed movements used to achieve this action be also copied. Considering that the majority of mirror neurons are of the broadly congruent type, observing an action should trigger a varied set of motor programs that would allow the observer to achieve the same goal. Of these, the motor system is likely to favor the most economical for the observer rather than the one chosen by the demonstrator, making emulation a more natural consequence of mirror neurons than imitation. This seems to be the case for both human infants (Bekkering et al., 2000) and monkeys (Subiaul, Cantlon, Holloway, & Terrace, 2004), both of which seem to emulate rather than imitate. True imitation using the MNS would require additional mechanisms that select the motor output of strictly congruent mirror neurons, and the necessity of these additional mechanisms may explain why adult humans can imitate while monkeys very seldom do so—despite the fact that both have mirror neurons.

Language

The MNS has also been considered to play a role in the evolution of language (Rizzolatti & Arbib, 1998). The fact that mirror neurons in the monkey were discovered in F5, which is likely to be the homologue to ventral BA6, BA44, or 45 in humans, all of which are involved in spoken language, supports this idea. Mirror neurons could facilitate language evolution in two ways:

First, the acoustic signal composing speech is ambiguous. A certain sound for instance will be perceived as a /k/ in front of an /a/, but as a /p/ in front of a /u/. The motor theory of speech perception proposes that the human brain resolves this ambiguity, at least in part, by activating the motor programs it would use to produce this sequence of sounds (Liberman, Cooper, Shankweiler, & Studdert-Kennedy, 1967). If this motor program involves pushing the tongue on the palate, we will perceive a /k/, if it involves closing the lips, a /p/. FMRI and TMS studies show that the premotor and motor cortices, respectively, that are involved in producing speech sounds, become reactivated while we listen to the sounds of other people's speech, and rTMS experiments show that interfering with this activity impairs speech perception (Iacoboni, 2008). Importantly, the regions involved correspond to those in which auditory mirror neurons were found in monkeys and encompass classical MNS areas.

Second, according to embodied semantics, the meaning of action words like "running" might in part be stored in the motor programs we use to run. Indeed, fMRI studies show than when reading sentences, the premotor cortex becomes activated in a somatotopic fashion, with words like running, grasping, and chewing activating regions involved in executing actions with the foot, hand, and mouth, respectively (Aziz-Zadeh et al., 2006). The fact that these activations fall within regions showing mirror activity to the sight of other people performing similar actions (Aziz-Zadeh et al., 2006) suggests that some neurons might link the sound of action words to the motor representations much like mirror neurons link the sound of the action itself to the motor representations (Gazzola et al., 2006; Keysers et al., 2003; Kohler et al., 2002). In evolution, onomatopeic words such as "crack" [a nut], which indeed sound like the action, may have served to recruit mirror neurons to convey action meaning through words. Modern language, with its fully arbitrary association of word and meaning may represent an evolution of this system.

Although the MNS could therefore help in language and its evolution, the MNS is not sufficient for language: Monkeys have mirror neurons but no language and many words are not about actions (e.g., "blue") and therefore cannot be embodied in our motor cortex. The scope of MNS theories of language are therefore necessarily limited to specific sub-aspects of language (Toni, de Lange, Noordzij, & Hagoort, 2008) and understanding how the MNS interacts with other systems to enable language will remain an important issue.

Prediction

In the Hebbian model presented above, for simplicity's sake, we considered that while observing oneself executing an action, activity in the premotor cortex is simultaneous with sensory representations of the same action in the STS. While this is approximately true at the time scale of entire actions, it is relevant to note that it takes a total of ~200 ms for the causal chain of events linking premotor and STS activity to unfold: A motor command in the premotor cortex needs to trigger activity in the primary motor cortex, move our body, and the visual or auditory signal from that action needs to go through the many synaptic stages of auditory and visual processing to feed back onto the synaptic connections in the parietal and premotor cortex. This means that while we reach and grasp a cup in front of us, motor programs for *grasping* will be active while the STS is still sending representations of the *reaching* phase back to parietal and premotor neurons. What gets to wire together is thus not the premotor command for grasping with the vision of grasping, but the command for *grasping* with the vision of the *reaching* that typically precedes grasping by ~200 ms. The Hebbian model thus predicts that mirror activity would anticipate actions about to occur in ~200 ms. This is exactly what seems to be the case (Borroni et al., 2005; Southgate et al., 2009) and it has important consequences for the function of the MNS. Instead of simply helping us understand actions that have occurred, it seems to trigger motor representations of the actions to come in the next hundreds of milliseconds. These anticipated motor representations then seem to be sent back to the STS (Gazzola & Keysers, 2009; Iacoboni et al., 2001), where they are compared with the future sensory input, generating a prediction error (Gazzola & Keysers, 2009). The MNS is therefore not a simple perceptual system that recognizes the action of others, but a predictive model (Kilner, Friston, & Frith, 2007), that generates hypothesis about people's future actions and dynamically compares them with people's next move to generate a dynamically adjusting model of other people's intentions (i.e., future actions). In nature, anticipating the behavior of a prey or predator can make the difference between life and death. For humans, it can provide a competitive edge in sports (Aglioti, Cesari, Romani, & Urgesi, 2008) but most importantly, it can be key to truly joint actions (Kokal et al., 2009): For two people to act in synchrony, each partner's brain has to anticipate the actions of the other partner by ~200 ms to have enough time to program and execute his own action in behavioral synchrony with those observed. To act in "real time" with someone else, our brain actually has to anticipate. Only by doing so can two people lift a set dinner table without tipping over the glasses, skillfully dance together, or even just clap in synchrony. The fact that such sophisticated computations seem to be the outcome of simple Hebbian learning is an elegant property of the synaptic plasticity in the brain.

Learning by Observation

Many have argued that the MNS can help the emergence of culture by equipping humans with the capacity to imitate. Incremental culture and technology, however, have to adopt the *successful* actions of others but not their unsuccessful attempts. The MNS alone cannot perform this filtering, as it would respond equally to successful and unsuccessful actions. The fact that similar systems exist for emotions may resolve this problem. Individual trial-and-error learning is based on the fact that when we perform an action and the outcome is more positive than expected, dopaminergic reward-prediction error signals increase the likelihood of that particular behavior in the future (Brovelli, Laksiri, Nazarian, Meunier, & Boussaoud, 2008; Schultz, 2006). Conceptually, combining MNS for actions and similar systems for emotions means that while observing the actions and outcomes of others, we would vicariously activate motor *and* emotional representation of similar actions and outcomes, respectively. Only those simulated actions that lead to unexpectedly positive simulated outcomes would then trigger vicarious dopaminergic reward-prediction signals that would consolidate those simulated behaviors that were successful. Thus, observation learning actually uses the same mechanisms that govern individual learning but operate on vicarious representations provided by MNS and similar mirror-like mechanisms for vicarious reward (Monfardini et al., 2009).

Support Mentalizing

Mentalizing refers to the capacity to *consciously* attribute mental states and beliefs to other individuals and has been associated with activity in the medial prefrontal cortex (Amodio & Frith, 2006). The tasks investigated in that literature differ from those in the literature on the MNS: Mentalizing experiments do not typically involve the movies of actions used for MNS experiments but explicitly encourage participants to *consciously* think about what other people *think*, while MNS experiments involve seeing/hearing the actions of others without being encouraged to think about the thoughts behind the actions (Keysers & Gazzola, 2007). It remains unclear how the MNS contributes to mentalizing. Some propose that the MNS could feed into the distinct mentalizing brain system when the thoughts of others need to be deduced from their actions: Much as we can mentalize about our own actions (why does my heart beat stronger each time I see her?), we could mentalize about the vicarious representations of other people's actions, sensations, and emotions (Keysers & Gazzola, 2007). Others emphasize that across many studies, the medial prefrontal cortex involved in mentalizing is only seldom found to be activated in the same studies as the MNS, suggesting that these two systems are often rather independent (Van Overwalle, 2009). Understanding when and how the MNS and mentalizing brain regions collaborate will be an important question for the future (de Lange, Spronk, Willems, Toni, & Bekkering, 2008; Thioux et al., 2008).

Dysfunctions of the MNS

Compulsive Imitation

Following frontal-lobe lesion, some patients show a tendency to imitate the behavior of others such as scratching his/her forehead, clapping his/her hands, and so on (De Renzi, Cavalleri, & Facchini, 1996; Lhermitte, 1983; Lhermitte, Pillon, & Serdaru, 1986). The patients persist in imitating the behavior of the experimenter even after being explicitly told to stop doing so. This phenomenon is observed in about 40% of patients with frontal-lobe lesions, and virtually never occurs as a consequence of post-rolandic brain lesion (De Renzi et al., 1996). Infarct to the anterior cerebral artery resulting in medial frontal lesions seems to be a frequent cause. The fact that most humans do not overtly and compulsively imitate the actions performed by others indicates the existence of a supervisory system in the brain that ensures that of all the premotor programs that mirror neurons activate, only those that are appropriate in a particular situation will be executed while the others are somehow inhibited (Shallice, Burgess,

Schon, & Baxter, 1989). The medial frontal lesions inducing compulsive imitation behavior seem to deactivate this system. The idea of such an inhibitory system finds further support from the fact that fMRI studies that measure an activation of premotor cortices during action observation sometimes simultaneously measure an inhibition of M1, as if to block the motor output of simulation (Gazzola & Keysers, 2009; Gazzola, Rizzolatti et al., 2007).

Mirror Touch Synesthesia

An intriguing phenomenon seems to represent the over-activity in one of the mirror-like networks for the simulation of touch (Blakemore et al., 2005). A little over 1% of people experience touch upon seeing someone else being touched (Banissy, Kadosh, Maus, Walsh, & Ward, 2009). Touch is typically experienced on the same body part that was seen to be touched. One of these individuals was scanned using fMRI and this revealed hyper-activation of the somatosensory cortices, the premotor cortex, and the anterior insula relative to controls during the observation of a video of a person being touched. Interestingly, participants with this form of synesthesia are particularly empathic (Banissy & Ward, 2007), further strengthening the idea that empathy, the capacity to feel what goes on in others, depends on vicarious activation of similar states in the self.

Autism Spectrum Disorders (ASD)

Some have argued that ASD could be the consequence of a deficit affecting the MNS (Iacoboni & Dapretto, 2006; Oberman & Ramachandran, 2007; Rizzolatti, Fabbri-Destro, & Cattaneo, 2009; Williams, Whiten, Suddendorf, & Perrett, 2001). The idea is that since mirror neurons are thought to support the ability to imitate and understand the intentions behind the action of others and may provide input to systems that deduce the mental states of others, an impairment in the MNS might explain the problem ASD individuals have with understanding the state of mind of other people. Empirical evidence for this idea, however, remains contradictory.

Three studies requiring the imitation of facial expressions or hand/finger movements suggest that the cerebral network involved in action imitation might be abnormal in autism, but fail to identify consistent differences in putative MNS activity. One study found a delay in the activation of the ventral premotor cortex in autism (Nishitani, Avikainen, & Hari, 2004), one study reported a complete absence of activity in this region (Dapretto et al., 2006), and one a hypo-activity of the inferior parietal lobe, along with many other areas of hypo-activation (Williams et al., 2006). The interpretation of these findings is, however, problematic, as ASD participants often foveate the actions to be imitated less, (Vivanti, Nadig, Ozonoff, & Rogers, 2008) and several well-controlled experiments actually show that autistic children demonstrate a normal tendency to imitate the goal of observed actions (Carpenter, Pennington, & Rogers, 2001; Hobson & Hobson, 2008).

Studies investigating the observation of actions without requesting imitation generated similarly inconsistent results. Three studies have measured Mu-suppression during action execution and action observation in ASD using EEG (Box 35.2). One study found significant mu-suppression in ASD, suggesting a normal MNS (Bernier, Dawson, Webb, & Murias, 2007), one found no suppression, suggesting an abnormal MNS (Oberman et al., 2005), and a third one found normal suppression only when the action was attributed to a familiar individual (Oberman, Ramachandran, & Pineda, 2008). Another study using MEG also reported normal activity in motor areas during action observation (Avikainen, Kulomäki, & Hari, 1999). In addition, psychophysical interference from observed actions (Box 35.2) seems to be normal in autism, suggesting that simulation of hand actions occurs automatically (Bird, Leighton, Press, & Heyes, 2007). Studies that record muscle activity in the face or hand while participants view the emotional facial expressions or hand actions of others additionally show that although ASD children often show facial muscle activity while viewing the expressions of other, this activity is often in a muscle not involved in that expression (McIntosh, Reichmann-Decker, Winkielman, & Wilbarger, 2006). This finding is confirmed by a more recent study that also finds that children with autism aged 7 to 12 showed abnormal facial muscle activity, but this activity improved with age (Beall, Moody, McIntosh, Hepburn, & Reed, 2008).

Altogether, there is therefore evidence that activity in the putative MNS may indeed be atypical in ASD. More research is, however, needed to understand how the age of ASD participants influences activity in the putative MNS and whether this activity reflects less specific vicarious motor program activity than in controls.

Authors' Note

CK and MT were supported by a Marie Curie Excellence Grant of the European Commission to CK, and the research was additionally funded by a VIDI grant of the Dutch Science Foundation (N.W.O.). VG was supported by a VENI grant of the N.W.O. We thank all members of the social brain lab for help with the research and Dan Arnstein for comments on the manuscript.

References

Adolphs, R., Damasio, H., Tranel, D., Cooper, G., & Damasio, A. R. (2000). A role for somatosensory cortices in the visual recognition of emotion as revealed by three-dimensional lesion mapping. *J Neurosci, 20*(7), 2683–2690.

Aglioti, S. M., Cesari, P., Romani, M., & Urgesi, C. (2008). Action anticipation and motor resonance in elite basketball players. *Nat Neurosci, 11*(9), 1109–1116.

Alaerts, K., Swinnen, S. P., & Wenderoth, N. (2009). Is the human primary motor cortex activated by muscular or direction-dependent features of observed movements? *Cortex, 45*(10), 1148–1155.

Amodio, D. M. & Frith, C. D. (2006). Meeting of minds: The medial frontal cortex and social cognition. *Nat Rev Neurosci, 7*(4), 268–277.

Anisfeld, M. (1991). Neonatal imitation. *Developmental Review, 11*, 60–97.

Anisfeld, M. (1996). Only tongue protrusion modeling is matched by neonates. *Developmental Review, 16*, 149–161.

Avenanti, A., Bolognini, N., Maravita, A., & Aglioti, S. M. (2007). Somatic and motor components of action simulation. *Curr Biol, 17*(24), 2129–2135.

Avenanti, A., Minio-Paluello, I., Bufalari, I., & Aglioti, S. M. (2009). The pain of a model in the personality of an onlooker: Influence of state-reactivity and personality traits on embodied empathy for pain. *Neuroimage, 44*(1), 275–283.

Avikainen, S., Kulomäki, T., & Hari, R. (1999). Normal movement reading in Asperger subjects. *Neuroreport, 10*(17), 3467–3470.

Aziz-Zadeh, L., Iacoboni, M., Zaidel, E., Wilson, S., & Mazziotta, J. (2004). Left hemisphere motor facilitation in response to manual action sounds. *Eur J Neurosci, 19*(9), 2609–2612.

Aziz-Zadeh, L., Wilson, S. M., Rizzolatti, G., & Iacoboni, M. (2006). Congruent embodied representations for visually presented actions and linguistic phrases describing actions. *Curr Biol, 16*(18), 1818–1823.

Babiloni, C., Babiloni, F., Carducci, F., Cincotti, F., Cocozza, G., Del Percio, C., et al. (2002). Human cortical electroencephalography (EEG) rhythms during the observation of simple aimless movements: A high-resolution EEG study. *Neuroimage, 17*(2), 559–572.

Baldissera, F., Cavallari, P., Craighero, L., & Fadiga, L. (2001). Modulation of spinal excitability during observation of hand actions in humans. *Eur J Neurosci, 13*(1), 190–194.

Banissy, M. J., Kadosh, R. C., Maus, G. W., Walsh, V., & Ward, J. (2009). Prevalence, characteristics and a neurocognitive model of mirror-touch synesthesia. *Exp Brain Res*.

Banissy, M. J. & Ward, J. (2007). Mirror-touch synesthesia is linked with empathy. *Nat Neurosci, 10*(7), 815–816.

Bastiaansen, J. A., Thioux, M., & Keysers, C. (2009). Evidence for mirror systems in emotions. *Philos Trans R Soc Lond B Biol Sci, 364*(1528), 2391–2404.

Beall, P. M., Moody, E. J., McIntosh, D. N., Hepburn, S. L., & Reed, C. L. (2008). Rapid facial reactions to emotional facial expressions in typically developing children and children with autism spectrum disorder. *J Exp Child Psychol, 101*(3), 206–223.

Bekkering, H., Wohlschlager, A., & Gattis, M. (2000). Imitation of gestures in children is goal-directed. *Q J Exp Psychol A, 53*(1), 153–164.

Bernier, R., Dawson, G., Webb, S., & Murias, M. (2007). EEG mu rhythm and imitation impairments in individuals with autism spectrum disorder. *Brain Cogn, 64*(3), 228–237.

Bird, G., Brindley, R., Leighton, J., & Heyes, C. (2007). General processes, rather than "goals," explain imitation errors. *J Exp Psychol Hum Percept Perform, 33*(5), 1158–1169.

Bird, G., Leighton, J., Press, C., & Heyes, C. (2007). Intact automatic imitation of human and robot actions in autism spectrum disorders. *Proc Biol Sci, 274*(1628), 3027–3031.

Blakemore, S. J., Bristow, D., Bird, G., Frith, C., & Ward, J. (2005). Somatosensory activations during the observation of touch and a case of vision-touch synaesthesia. *Brain, 128*(Pt 7), 1571–1583.

Borroni, P., Montagna, M., Cerri, G., & Baldissera, F. (2005). Cyclic time course of motor excitability modulation during the observation of a cyclic hand movement. *Brain Res, 1065*(1–2), 115–124.

Brass, M., Bekkering, H., Wohlschlager, A., & Prinz, W. (2000). Compatibility between observed and executed finger movements: Comparing symbolic, spatial, and imitative cues. *Brain Cogn, 44*(2), 124–143.

Brass, M. & Heyes, C. (2005). Imitation: Is cognitive neuroscience solving the correspondence problem? *Trends Cogn Sci (Regul Ed), 9*(10), 489–495.

Brovelli, A., Laksiri, N., Nazarian, B., Meunier, M., & Boussaoud, D. (2008). Understanding the neural computations of arbitrary visuomotor learning through fMRI and associative learning theory. *Cereb Cortex, 18*(7), 1485–1495.

Buccino, G., Binkofski, F., Fink, G. R., Fadiga, L., Fogassi, L., Gallese, V., et al. (2001). Action observation activates premotor and parietal areas in a somatotopic manner: An fMRI study. *Eur J Neurosci, 13*(2), 400–404.

Caetano, G., Jousmaki, V., & Hari, R. (2007). Actor's and observer's primary motor cortices stabilize similarly after seen or heard motor actions. *Proc Natl Acad Sci U S A, 104*(21), 9058–9062.

Calder, A. J., Keane, J., Manes, F., Antoun, N., & Young, A. W. (2000). Impaired recognition and experience of disgust following brain injury. *Nat Neurosci, 3*(11), 1077–1078.

Calmels, C., Holmes, P., Jarry, G., Leveque, J. M., Hars, M., & Stam, C. J. (2006). Cortical activity prior to, and during, observation and execution of sequential finger movements. *Brain Topogr, 19*(1–2), 77–88.

Calvo-Merino, B., Glaser, D. E., Grèzes, J., Passingham, R. E., & Haggard, P. (2005). Action observation and acquired motor skills: An FMRI study with expert dancers. *Cereb Cortex, 15*(8), 1243–1249.

Carpenter, M., Pennington, B. F., & Rogers, S. J. (2001). Understanding of others' intentions in children with autism. *J Autism Dev Disord, 31*(6), 589–599.

Catmur, C., Walsh, V., & Heyes, C. (2007). Sensorimotor learning configures the human mirror system. *Curr Biol, 17*(17), 1527–1531.

Chong, T. T., Cunnington, R., Williams, M. A., Kanwisher, N., & Mattingley, J. B. (2008). fMRI adaptation reveals mirror neurons in human inferior parietal cortex. *Curr Biol, 18*(20), 1576–1580.

Clark, S., Tremblay, F., & Ste-Marie, D. (2004). Differential modulation of corticospinal excitability during observation, mental imagery and imitation of hand actions. *Neuropsychologia, 42*(1), 105–112.

Cochin, S., Barthelemy, C., Lejeune, B., Roux, S., & Martineau, J. (1998). Perception of motion and qEEG activity in human adults. *Electroencephalogr Clin Neurophysiol, 107*(4), 287–295.

Cochin, S., Barthelemy, C., Roux, S., & Martineau, J. (1999). Observation and execution of movement: Similarities demonstrated by quantified electroencephalography. *Eur J Neurosci, 11*(5), 1839–1842.

Cross, E. S., Hamilton, A. F. d. C., & Grafton, S. T. (2006). Building a motor simulation de novo: Observation of dance by dancers. *Neuroimage, 31*(3), 1257–1267.

Dapretto, M., Davies, M. S., Pfeifer, J. H., Scott, A. A., Sigman, M., Bookheimer, S. Y., et al. (2006). Understanding emotions in others: Mirror neuron dysfunction in children with autism spectrum disorders. *Nat Neurosci, 9*(1), 28–30.

de Lange, F. P., Spronk, M., Willems, R. M., Toni, I., & Bekkering, H. (2008). Complementary systems for understanding action intentions. *Curr Biol, 18*(6), 454–457.

De Renzi, E., Cavalleri, F., & Facchini, S. (1996). Imitation and utilisation behaviour. *J Neurol Neurosurg Psychiatr, 61*(4), 396–400.

Del Giudice, M., Manera, V., & Keysers, C. (2009). Programmed to learn? The ontogeny of mirror neurons. *Dev Sci, 12*(2), 350–363.

di Pellegrino, G., Fadiga, L., Fogassi, L., Gallese, V., & Rizzolatti, G. (1992). Understanding motor events: A neurophysiological study. *Exp Brain Res, 91*(1), 176–180.

Dinstein, I., Hasson, U., Rubin, N., & Heeger, D. J. (2007). Brain areas selective for both observed and executed movements. *J Neurophysiol, 98*(3), 1415–1427.

Ebisch, S. J., Perrucci, M. G., Ferretti, A., Del Gratta, C., Romani, G. L., & Gallese, V. (2008). The sense of touch: Embodied simulation in a visuotactile mirroring mechanism for observed animate or inanimate touch. *J Cogn Neurosci, 20*(9), 1611–1623.

Etzel, J. A., Gazzola, V., & Keysers, C. (2008). Testing simulation theory with cross-modal multivariate classification of fMRI data. *PLoS One, 3*(11), e3690.

Evangeliou, M. N., Raos, V., Galletti, C., & Savaki, H. E. (2009). Functional imaging of the parietal cortex during action execution and observation. *Cereb Cortex, 19*(3), 624–639.

Fadiga, L., Craighero, L., & Olivier, E. (2005). Human motor cortex excitability during the perception of others' action. *Curr Opin Neurobiol, 15*(2), 213–218.

Fadiga, L., Fogassi, L., Pavesi, G., & Rizzolatti, G. (1995). Motor facilitation during action observation: A magnetic stimulation study. *J Neurophysiol, 73*(6), 2608–2611.

Ferrari, P. F., Gallese, V., Rizzolatti, G., & Fogassi, L. (2003). Mirror neurons responding to the observation of ingestive and communicative mouth actions in the monkey ventral premotor cortex. *Eur J Neurosci, 17*(8), 1703–1714.

Filimon, F., Nelson, J. D., Hagler, D. J., & Sereno, M. I. (2007). Human cortical representations for reaching: Mirror neurons for execution, observation, and imagery. *Neuroimage, 37*(4), 1315–1328.

Fujii, N., Hihara, S., & Iriki, A. (2008). Social cognition in premotor and parietal cortex. *Soc Neurosci, 3*(3–4), 250–260.

Gallese, V., Fadiga, L., Fogassi, L., & Rizzolatti, G. (1996). Action recognition in the premotor cortex. *Brain, 119 (Pt 2)*, 593–609.

Gastaut, H. J. & Bert, J. (1954). EEG changes during cinematographic presentation—Moving picture activation of the EEG. *Electroencephalogr Clin Neurophysiol, 6*(3), 433–444.

Gazzola, V., Aziz-Zadeh, L., & Keysers, C. (2006). Empathy and the somatotopic auditory mirror system in humans. *Curr Biol, 16*(18), 1824–1829.

Gazzola, V. & Keysers, C. (2009). The observation and execution of actions share motor and somatosensory voxels in all tested subjects: Single-subject analyses of unsmoothed fMRI data. *Cereb Cortex, 19*(6), 1239–1255.

Gazzola, V., Rizzolatti, G., Wicker, B., & Keysers, C. (2007). The anthropomorphic brain: The mirror neuron system responds to human and robotic actions. *Neuroimage, 35*(4), 1674–1684.

Gazzola, V., van der Worp, H., Mulder, T., Wicker, B., Rizzolatti, G., & Keysers, C. (2007). Aplasics born without hands mirror the goal of hand actions with their feet. *Curr Biol, 17*(14), 1235–1240.

Gergely, G., Bekkering, H., & Király, I. (2002). Rational imitation in preverbal infants. *Nature, 415*(6873), 755.

Graziano, M. S., Taylor, C. S., & Moore, T. (2002). Complex movements evoked by microstimulation of precentral cortex. *Neuron, 34*(5), 841–851.

Grezes, J., Armony, J. L., Rowe, J., & Passingham, R. E. (2003). Activations related to "mirror" and "canonical" neurones in the human brain: An fMRI study. *Neuroimage, 18*(4), 928–937.

Hamilton, A. F. & Grafton, S. T. (2006). Goal representation in human anterior intraparietal sulcus. *J Neurosci, 26*(4), 1133–1137.

Hamilton, A. F. & Grafton, S. T. (2008). Action outcomes are represented in human inferior frontoparietal cortex. *Cereb Cortex, 18*(5), 1160–1168.

Hari, R., Forss, N., Avikainen, S., Kirveskari, E., Salenius, S., & Rizzolatti, G. (1998). Activation of human primary motor cortex during action observation: A neuromagnetic study. *Proc Natl Acad Sci U S A, 95*(25), 15061–15065.

Haslinger, B., Erhard, P., Altenmüller, E., Schroeder, U., Boecker, H., & Ceballos-Baumann, A. O. (2005). Transmodal sensorimotor networks during action observation in professional pianists. *J Cogn Neurosci, 17*(2), 282–293.

Heiser, M., Iacoboni, M., Maeda, F., Marcus, J., & Mazziotta, J. C. (2003). The essential role of Broca's area in imitation. *Eur J Neurosci, 17*(5), 1123–1128.

Heyes, C. (2001). Causes and consequences of imitation. *Trends Cogn Sci (Regul Ed), 5*(6), 253–261.

Hobson, R. P. & Hobson, J. A. (2008). Dissociable aspects of imitation: A study in autism. *J Exp Child Psychol, 101*(3), 170–185.

Hutchison, W. D., Davis, K. D., Lozano, A. M., Tasker, R. R., & Dostrovsky, J. O. (1999). Pain-related neurons in the human cingulate cortex. *Nat Neurosci, 2*(5), 403–405.

Iacoboni, M. (2008). The role of premotor cortex in speech perception: Evidence from fMRI and rTMS. *J Physiol Paris, 102*(1–3), 31–34.

Iacoboni, M. (2009). Neurobiology of imitation. *Curr Opin Neurobiol.*

Iacoboni, M. & Dapretto, M. (2006). The mirror neuron system and the consequences of its dysfunction. *Nat Rev Neurosci, 7*(12), 942–951.

Iacoboni, M., Koski, L. M., Brass, M., Bekkering, H., Woods, R. P., Dubeau, M. C., et al. (2001). Reafferent copies of imitated actions in the right superior temporal cortex. *Proc Natl Acad Sci U S A, 98*(24), 13995–13999.

Iacoboni, M., Woods, R. P., Brass, M., Bekkering, H., Mazziotta, J. C., & Rizzolatti, G. (1999). Cortical mechanisms of human imitation. *Science, 286*(5449), 2526–2528.

Jabbi, M., Swart, M., & Keysers, C. (2007). Empathy for positive and negative emotions in the gustatory cortex. *Neuroimage, 34*(4), 1744–1753.

Jackson, P. L., Rainville, P., & Decety, J. (2006). To what extent do we share the pain of others? Insight from the neural bases of pain empathy. *Pain, 125*(1–2), 5–9.

Keysers, C. & Gazzola, V. (2007). Integrating simulation and theory of mind: From self to social cognition. *Trends Cogn Sci, 11*(5), 194–196.

Keysers, C. & Gazzola, V. (2009). Expanding the mirror: Vicarious activity for actions, emotions, and sensations. *Curr Opin Neurobiol.*

Keysers, C., Kaas, J. H., & Gazzola, V. (2010). Somatosensation in social perception. *Nat Rev Neurosci, 11*(6), 417–428.

Keysers, C., Kohler, E., Umilta, M. A., Nanetti, L., Fogassi, L., & Gallese, V. (2003). Audiovisual mirror neurons and action recognition. *Exp Brain Res, 153*(4), 628–636.

Keysers, C. & Perrett, D. I. (2004). Demystifying social cognition: A Hebbian perspective. *Trends Cogn Sci, 8*(11), 501–507.

Keysers, C., Wicker, B., Gazzola, V., Anton, J. L., Fogassi, L., & Gallese, V. (2004). A touching sight: SII/PV activation during the observation and experience of touch. *Neuron, 42*(2), 335–346.

Kilner, J. M., Friston, K. J., & Frith, C. D. (2007). Predictive coding: an account of the mirror neuron system. *Cogn Process, 8*(3), 159–166.

Kilner, J. M., Neal, A., Weiskopf, N., Friston, K. J., & Frith, C. D. (2009). Evidence of mirror neurons in human inferior frontal gyrus. *J Neurosci, 29*(32), 10153–10159.

Kilner, J. M., Paulignan, Y., & Blakemore, S. J. (2003). An interference effect of observed biological movement on action. *Curr Biol, 13*(6), 522–525.

Kohler, E., Keysers, C., Umilta, M. A., Fogassi, L., Gallese, V., & Rizzolatti, G. (2002). Hearing sounds, understanding actions: Action representation in mirror neurons. *Science, 297*(5582), 846–848.

Kokal, I., Gazzola, V., & Keysers, C. (2009). Acting together in and beyond the mirror neuron system. *Neuroimage, 47*(4), 2046–2056.

Kraskov, A., Dancause, N., Quallo, M. M., Shepherd, S., & Lemon, R. N. (2009) Corticospinal neurons in macaque ventral premotor cortex with mirror properties: A potential mechanism for action suppression? *Neuron, 64*(6), 922–930.

Lahav, A., Saltzman, E., & Schlaug, G. (2007). Action representation of sound: Audiomotor recognition network while listening to newly acquired actions. *J Neurosci, 27*(2), 308–314.

Lepage, J.-F. & Théoret, H. (2006). EEG evidence for the presence of an action observation-execution matching system in children. *Eur J Neurosci, 23*(9), 2505–2510.

Lhermitte, F. (1983). "Utilization behaviour" and its relation to lesions of the frontal lobes. *Brain, 106*(Pt 2), 237–255.

Lhermitte, F., Pillon, B., & Serdaru, M. (1986). Human autonomy and the frontal lobes. Part I: Imitation and utilization behavior: A neuropsychological study of 75 patients. *Ann Neurol*, *19*(4), 326–334.

Liberman, A. M., Cooper, F. S., Shankweiler, D. P., & Studdert-Kennedy, M. (1967). Perception of the speech code. *Psychol Rev*, *74*(6), 431–461.

Lingnau, A., Gesierich, B., & Caramazza, A. (2009). Asymmetric fMRI adaptation reveals no evidence for mirror neurons in humans. *Proc Natl Acad Sci U S A*, *106*(24), 9925–9930.

Lui, F., Buccino, G., Duzzi, D., Benuzzi, F., Crisi, G., Baraldi, P., et al. (2008). Neural substrates for observing and imagining non-object-directed actions. *Soc Neurosci*, *3*(3–4), 261–275.

McIntosh, D. N., Reichmann-Decker, A., Winkielman, P., & Wilbarger, J. L. (2006). When the social mirror breaks: Deficits in automatic, but not voluntary, mimicry of emotional facial expressions in autism. *Dev Sci*, *9*(3), 295–302.

Meltzoff, A. & Moore, M. (1977). Imitation of facial and manual gestures by human neonates. *Science*, *198*(4312), 75–78.

Meltzoff, A. & Moore, M. (1997). Explaining facial imitation: A theoretical model. *Early Development and Parenting*, *6*, 179–192.

Meltzoff, A. N. & Decety, J. (2003). What imitation tells us about social cognition: A rapprochement between developmental psychology and cognitive neuroscience. *Philos Trans R Soc Lond, B, Biol Sci*, *358*(1431), 491–500.

Molnar-Szakacs, I., Iacoboni, M., Koski, L., & Mazziotta, J. C. (2005). Functional segregation within pars opercularis of the inferior frontal gyrus: Evidence from fMRI studies of imitation and action observation. *Cereb Cortex*, *15*(7), 986–994.

Monfardini, E., Gazzola, V., Brovelli, A., Boussaoud, D., Keysers, C., & Wicker, B. (2009). I learn from what you do: an fMRI study of social learning, *Organization for Human Brain Mapping (OHBM) Meeting*. San Francisco (CA).

Muthukumaraswamy, S. D. & Johnson, B. W. (2004a). Changes in rolandic mu rhythm during observation of a precision grip. *Psychophysiology*, *41*(1), 152–156.

Muthukumaraswamy, S. D. & Johnson, B. W. (2004b). Primary motor cortex activation during action observation revealed by wavelet analysis of the EEG. *Clin Neurophysiol*, *115*(8), 1760–1766.

Muthukumaraswamy, S. D., Johnson, B. W., & McNair, N. A. (2004). Mu rhythm modulation during observation of an object-directed grasp. *Brain Res Cogn Brain Res*, *19*(2), 195–201.

Nishitani, N., Avikainen, S., & Hari, R. (2004). Abnormal imitation-related cortical activation sequences in Asperger's syndrome. *Ann Neurol*, *55*(4), 558–562.

Oberman, L. M., Hubbard, E. M., McCleery, J. P., Altschuler, E. L., Ramachandran, V. S., & Pineda, J. A. (2005). EEG evidence for mirror neuron dysfunction in autism spectrum disorders. *Brain Res Cogn Brain Res*, *24*(2), 190–198.

Oberman, L. M. & Ramachandran, V. S. (2007). The simulating social mind: The role of the mirror neuron system and simulation in the social and communicative deficits of autism spectrum disorders. *Psychol Bull*, *133*(2), 310–327.

Oberman, L. M., Ramachandran, V. S., & Pineda, J. A. (2008). Modulation of mu suppression in children with autism spectrum disorders in response to familiar or unfamiliar stimuli: the mirror neuron hypothesis. *Neuropsychologia*, *46*(5), 1558–1565.

Oztop, E. & Arbib, M. A. (2002). Schema design and implementation of the grasp-related mirror neuron system. *Biol Cybern*, *87*(2), 116–140.

Pazzaglia, M., Pizzamiglio, L., Pes, E., & Aglioti, S. M. (2008). The sound of actions in apraxia. *Curr Biol*, *18*(22), 1766–1772.

Pazzaglia, M., Smania, N., Corato, E., & Aglioti, S. M. (2008). Neural underpinnings of gesture discrimination in patients with limb apraxia. *J Neurosci*, *28*(12), 3030–3041.

Pineda, J. A. (2005). The functional significance of mu rhythms: Translating "seeing" and "hearing" into "doing". *Brain Res Brain Res Rev*, *50*(1), 57–68.

Pizzamiglio, L., Aprile, T., Spitoni, G., Pitzalis, S., Bates, E., D'Amico, S., et al. (2005). Separate neural systems for processing action- or non-action-related sounds. *Neuroimage*, *24*(3), 852–861.

Pobric, G. & Hamilton, A. F. d. C. (2006). Action understanding requires the left inferior frontal cortex. *Curr Biol*, *16*(5), 524–529.

Raos, V., Evangeliou, M. N., & Savaki, H. E. (2004). Observation of action: Grasping with the mind's hand. *Neuroimage*, *23*(1), 193–201.

Ricciardi, E., Bonino, D., Sani, L., Vecchi, T., Guazzelli, M., Haxby, J. V., et al. (2009). Do we really need vision? How blind people "see" the actions of others. *J Neurosci*, *29*(31), 9719–9724.

Rizzolatti, G. & Arbib, M. A. (1998). Language within our grasp. *Trends Neurosci*, *21*(5), 188–194.

Rizzolatti, G., Camarda, R., Fogassi, L., Gentilucci, M., Luppino, G., & Matelli, M. (1988). Functional organization of inferior area 6 in the macaque monkey. II. Area F5 and the control of distal movements. *Exp Brain Res*, *71*(3), 491–507.

Rizzolatti, G., Fabbri-Destro, M., & Cattaneo, L. (2009). Mirror neurons and their clinical relevance. *Nat Clin Pract Neurol*, *5*(1), 24–34.

Rossi, S., Tecchio, F., Pasqualetti, P., Ulivelli, M., Pizzella, V., Romani, G. L., et al. (2002). Somatosensory processing during movement observation in humans. *Clin Neurophysiol*, *113*(1), 16–24.

Rozzi, S., Calzavara, R., Belmalih, A., Borra, E., Gregoriou, G. G., Matelli, M., et al. (2006). Cortical connections of the inferior parietal cortical convexity of the macaque monkey. *Cereb Cortex*, *16*(10), 1389–1417.

Rozzi, S., Ferrari, P. F., Bonini, L., Rizzolatti, G., & Fogassi, L. (2008). Functional organization of inferior parietal lobule convexity in the macaque monkey: Electrophysiological characterization of motor, sensory and mirror responses and their correlation with cytoarchitectonic areas. *Eur J Neurosci*, *28*(8), 1569–1588.

Schultz, W. (2006). Behavioral theories and the neurophysiology of reward. *Annu Rev Psychol*, *57*, 87–115.

Shallice, T., Burgess, P. W., Schon, F., & Baxter, D. M. (1989). The origins of utilization behaviour. *Brain*, *112*(Pt 6), 1587–1598.

Shimada, S. & Hiraki, K. (2006). Infant's brain responses to live and televised action. *Neuroimage*, *32*(2), 930–939.

Singer, T. & Lamm, C. (2009). The social neuroscience of empathy. *Ann N Y Acad Sci*, *1156*, 81–96.

Singer, T., Seymour, B., O'Doherty, J., Kaube, H., Dolan, R. J., & Frith, C. D. (2004). Empathy for pain involves the affective but not sensory components of pain. *Science*, *303*(5661), 1157–1162.

Sommerville, J. A., Woodward, A. L., & Needham, A. (2005). Action experience alters 3-month-old infants' perception of others' actions. *Cognition*, *96*(1), B1–11.

Southgate, V., Johnson, M. H., Osborne, T., & Csibra, G. (2009). Predictive motor activation during action observation in human infants. *Biol Lett*, *5*(6), 769–772.

Subiaul, F., Cantlon, J. F., Holloway, R. L., & Terrace, H. S. (2004). Cognitive imitation in rhesus macaques. *Science, 305*(5682), 407–410.

Tessari, A., Canessa, N., Ukmar, M., & Rumiati, R. I. (2007). Neuropsychological evidence for a strategic control of multiple routes in imitation. *Brain, 130*(Pt 4), 1111–1126.

Thioux, M., Gazzola, V., & Keysers, C. (2008). Action understanding: how, what and why. *Curr Biol, 18*(10), R431–434.

Toni, I., de Lange, F. P., Noordzij, M. L., & Hagoort, P. (2008). Language beyond action. *J Physiol Paris, 102*(1–3), 71–79.

Turella, L., Erb, M., Grodd, W., & Castiello, U. (2009). Visual features of an observed agent do not modulate human brain activity during action observation. *Neuroimage, 46*(3), 844–853.

Umilta, M. A., Kohler, E., Gallese, V., Fogassi, L., Fadiga, L., Keysers, C., et al. (2001). I know what you are doing. A neurophysiological study. *Neuron, 31*(1), 155–165.

Urgesi, C., Moro, V., Candidi, M., & Aglioti, S. M. (2006). Mapping implied body actions in the human motor system. *J Neurosci, 26*(30), 7942–7949.

van der Gaag, C., Minderaa, R. B., & Keysers, C. (2007). Facial expressions: What the mirror neuron system can and cannot tell us. *Soc Neurosci, 2*(3–4), 179–222.

van Elk, M., van Schie, H. T., Hunnius, S., Vesper, C., & Bekkering, H. (2008). You'll never crawl alone: Neurophysiological evidence for experience-dependent motor resonance in infancy. *Neuroimage, 43*(4), 808–814.

Van Overwalle, F. (2009). Social cognition and the brain: A meta-analysis. *Hum Brain Mapp, 30*(3), 829–858.

Vivanti, G., Nadig, A., Ozonoff, S., & Rogers, S. J. (2008). What do children with autism attend to during imitation tasks? *J Exp Child Psychol, 101*(3), 186–205.

Williams, J. H., Whiten, A., Suddendorf, T., & Perrett, D. I. (2001). Imitation, mirror neurons and autism. *Neurosci Biobehav Rev, 25*(4), 287–295.

Williams, J. H. G., Waiter, G. D., Gilchrist, A., Perrett, D. I., Murray, A. D., & Whiten, A. (2006). Neural mechanisms of imitation and "mirror neuron" functioning in autistic spectrum disorder. *Neuropsychologia, 44*(4), 610–621.

Woodward, A. L. (1998). Infants selectively encode the goal object of an actor's reach. *Cognition, 69*(1), 1–34.

The Mirror Neuron System and Imitation

Marco Iacoboni

Abstract

Imitation is a pervasive behavior in humans that is central to learning and transmission of culture. Imitation seems also a 'facilitator' in many social encounters, helping not only the synchronization of body postures, gestures, voices and facial expressions, but also seemingly increasing liking between people. Some have suggested that imitation is some sort of 'social glue.' The complexity of imitative behavior, however, has not traditionally inspired the study of its neural correlates. A big impetus to the study of the neural mechanisms of imitation has been recently provided both by the growth of social cognitive neuroscience as a field and by single cell recordings in the monkey brain. This chapter discusses these recordings in detail, which have revealed the existence of some neurons that have physiological properties that seem ideal for imitation.

Keywords: imitation, neuron system, monkeys, brain, mirror neurons

Introduction

Imitation is a pervasive behavior in humans that is central to learning and transmission of culture (Hurley & Chater, 2005). Imitation seems also a "facilitator" in many social encounters, helping not only the synchronization of body postures, gestures, voices, and facial expressions, but also seemingly increasing liking between people. Some have suggested that imitation is some sort of "social glue." (Dijksterhuis, 2005) The complexity of imitative behavior, however, has not traditionally inspired the study of its neural correlates. A big impetus to the study of the neural mechanisms of imitation has been recently provided both by the growth of social cognitive neuroscience as a field and by single-cell recordings in the monkey brain. These recordings, discussed in detail below, have revealed the existence of some neurons that have physiological properties that seem

ideal for imitation. The discovery of these neurons in monkeys and the ensuing work on the neural mechanisms of imitation in humans, however, must be interpreted keeping in mind two main issues. First, the imitative abilities of monkeys and humans are largely different, to the point that some scholars have challenged the idea that monkeys are able to imitate at all (Tomasello, Kruger, & Ratner, 1993) (but see also Ferrari et al., 2006; Voelkl & Huber, 2000; 2007). Second, the neuroscience techniques adopted in monkeys and humans are also quite different, and the kind of data obtained in monkeys with depth electrode recordings are quite different from the kind of data obtained in humans with brain imaging techniques. To make sense and integrate the data from one species to another and from one technique to another, a series of key concepts must be kept in mind, as we will see further below.

Neural Precursors of Imitation: Mirror Neurons in Monkeys

In the monkey, depth electrode recordings have revealed that some cortical neurons with motor properties (that is, they discharge during the execution of goal-directed actions and are located in agranular sectors of the cortex, a structural defining feature of the motor cortex, broadly construed) also fire in absence of movement, when the monkey is perceiving the actions of other individuals (di Pellegrino, Fadiga, Fogassi, Gallese, & Rizzolatti, 1992). This population of neurons has been called mirror neurons (Gallese, Fadiga, Fogassi, & Rizzolatti, 1996), because it seems as if the monkey is watching her actions reflected by a mirror when watching somebody else's actions. There are two main categories of mirror neurons: strictly congruent and broadly congruent mirror neurons (Rizzolatti & Craighero, 2004). Strictly congruent mirror neurons discharge during the execution and the observation of the same action. In broadly congruent mirror neurons, the correspondence between the coding of the executed action and the coding of the action perceived is less strict. In general, from a motor standpoint, the coding is narrower than its perceptual counterpart. For instance, a broadly congruent mirror neuron may fire only during the execution of a precision grip (when two fingers are used to grasp a small object), from a motor standpoint. Perceptually, though, this cell may fire during the observation of a precision grip performed by somebody else, but also during the observation of a hand-to-mouth movement, and even the observation of a biting movement with the mouth. A common denominator of broadly congruent mirror neurons is that they code in motor and perceptual terms actions that either achieve the same goal or are somewhat related as if they belong to a chain of simpler acts that form a complex action.

Thus, while the term "mirror" captures a striking feature of these cells, it is also somewhat misleading. Mirror neurons are not simply monkey-see-monkey-do cells; they code the motor and perceptual aspects of the actions of the self and of other individual in a more complex way. Another property of these cells, or at least of a sub-population of these cells, is that they are perceptually multimodal. Some mirror neurons respond not only to the sight of an action, but also to the sound associated with that action (Kohler et al., 2002) (for instance, the sound of a broken peanut), even when the action is not visible. This property suggests that these cells may provide a fairly abstract coding of the actions of other individuals. Indeed, other studies have demonstrated that mirror neurons respond also to only partially visible actions (for instance, when the completion of a grasping action is hidden) (Umiltà et al., 2001). Furthermore, a well-controlled study has demonstrated that the majority of mirror neurons, approximately two-thirds of all recorded cells in the relevant experiments, code not simply the action (say, grasping), but rather the intention associated with it (say, grasping-for-eating rather than grasping-for-placing) (Fogassi et al., 2005).

A recent study has also demonstrated that some mirror neurons code differentially the perceptual aspect of actions that occur in the peri-personal space of the monkey, compared to the same actions that occur in the extra-personal space of the monkey (Caggiano, Fogassi, Rizzolatti, Thier, & Casile, 2009). This differential coding suggests that, as a population, mirror neurons clearly differentiate between the actions on which the observer can intervene versus the actions on which the observer cannot intervene. This suggests that the coding of the actions of other individuals that mirror neurons implement is not meant to simply provide a description of the action and of its associated mental states, but rather to code those actions in operative terms, in terms of the possible social interactions that they can afford.

The types of mirror neurons that have been more frequently described in the literature are mirror neurons for hand actions, especially grasping. Mirror neurons for mouth actions, both ingestive and communicative, have been described as well (Ferrari, Gallese, Rizzolatti, & Fogassi, 2003). A recent report has demonstrated the existence of mirror neurons for gaze (Shepherd, Klein, Deaner, & Platt, 2009). Indeed, all sorts of actions may be in principle coded by mirror neurons.

From an anatomical standpoint, mirror neurons for hand and mouth actions have been recorded so far in the ventral premotor cortex, in area F5 (Gallese et al., 1996), and in the anterior part of the inferior parietal lobule, in areas PF/PFG (Fogassi et al., 2005). Mirror neurons for gaze have been recently recorded also in area LIP in the lateral aspect of the intraparietal sulcus (Shepherd et al., 2009). Obviously, it is in principle possible that mirror neurons are located in many other brain regions of the monkey brain and they have simply not been recorded yet.

From Monkeys to Humans: Evolutionary and Methodological Considerations

It makes perfect sense to consider neurons that fire during both execution of an action and during observation of the same or similar action as plausibly involved in imitation. However, there are still many unclear issues related to mirror neurons in monkeys and humans and their possible role in imitation.

The first issue to consider is the issue of imitation itself. In the 19th century, it was commonly accepted that monkeys imitate all the time (Romanes, 1883). However, this view has evolved over time quite dramatically. By the mid-20th century, the dominant view was that monkeys do not imitate at all (Tomasello et al., 1993; Byrne & Russon, 1998). Quite a change from the 19th century! Obviously, the presumed lack of imitative abilities in monkeys would raise the question about the adaptive role of mirror neurons in the monkey brain. In principle, mirror neurons in monkeys may support action recognition and only in later evolutionary steps that may have presumably been involved in imitation. Recently, however, a series of studies from different labs and using quite different settings have clearly demonstrated that monkeys do imitate (Voelkl & Huber, 2007, 2000; Subiaul et al., 2004). Even infant monkeys show imitative behavior (Ferrari et al., 2006). Other studies show also that monkeys are able to recognize who is imitating them (Paukner, Anderson, Borelli, Visalberghi, & Ferrari, 2005). While none of these studies has investigated the neural mechanisms supporting these behaviors, it is reasonable to assume that mirror neurons are likely involved in them (or, to put it differently, mirror neurons are definitely the best candidates among all the neurons formally described in the literature on depth electrode recordings in the monkey).

Another important issue to consider is related to the kinds of brain investigations that are typically performed in monkeys and in humans. In monkeys, mirror neurons have been identified with depth electrode recordings; whereas in humans the neural correlates of imitation have been typically performed with brain-imaging techniques. These two approaches are quite different.

Depth electrode recordings measure the action potentials of nearby neurons. These recordings tend to be biased toward large neurons, that is, pyramidal cells (Logothetis, 2003). Thus, a specific population of neurons is most likely recorded by depth electrode recordings. Furthermore, action potentials represent the output of a neuron. Thus, the neural activity recorded by depth electrodes is the output of a specific neuronal population in the brain region in which the electrode is inserted.

On the other hand, the most widely used brain imaging technique, functional magnetic resonance imaging (fMRI), measures the level of oxygenation of cerebral blood. Blood oxygenation is typically correlated with local neural activity, making it possible to measure neural activity indirectly with fMRI. However, there are many factors that influence the BOLD signal. These factors belong to two main categories, vascular and neural factors (Logothetis & Wandell, 2004; Bartels et al., 2008). The vascular factors are unlikely to play major roles in standard activation studies on imitation. The neural factors are of three types: action potentials (AP), local field potential (LFP which represents the input to a local brain area), and global, attentional factors.

While only AP are relevant to mirror neuron activity (because that's how a mirror neuron is defined), AP and LFP tend to correlate under many circumstances (Logothetis et al., 2001). They also tend to co-localize in the cortex, making the interpretation of BOLD signal changes relatively simple, at least under many circumstances. Only when AP and LFP diverge, the fMRI signal correlates with the LFP but not with AP (Logothetis & Wandell, 2004). Thus, it is prudent to avoid that decoupling of neuronal input (LFP) and output (AP). A classical paradigm that decouples input and output is the adaptation paradigm. This paradigm employs the repeated presentation of the same stimulus or the same class of stimuli to induce habituation (or adaptation) in specific neuronal populations. Unfortunately, the interpretation of fMRI adaptation studies with respect to the activity of specific neuronal populations is largely unreliable (Bartels, Logothetis, & Moutoussis, 2008). However, while adaptation studies have become more and more popular, they have not been typically employed in imitation experiments.

Imitation in Humans: Core Circuitry

The initial fMRI studies on imitation have suggested the existence of a core imitation circuitry that comprises three main neural systems: a frontal system encompassing the ventral premotor cortex and the posterior part of the inferior frontal gyrus (pars opercularis), which would be the homologue of area F5 in the monkey brain; a parietal system located in the rostral part of the posterior parietal cortex, which would be the homologue of areas PF/PFG in the monkey brain; and a temporal system located in the posterior part of the superior temporal sulcus (STS) and adjacent cortex, which would be the homologue of neurons in monkeys' STS that respond to the sight of intentional actions and of hand-object interactions (Iacoboni, 2005; Iacoboni & Dapretto, 2006; Iacoboni et al., 2001; Iacoboni et al., 1999).

According to the properties of the neural systems belonging to the core imitation circuitry, we can speculate on what the information processing flow is between them: The temporal system most likely provides a higher order visual processing of the observed action; this information is sent to the parieto-frontal mirror neuron system. This system activates during action observation, action execution, and also during imitation. The activity profile of the parieto-frontal mirror neuron system is typically as follows. There is some activation during action observation and a higher activation during action execution. This profile is very similar to the firing rate changes observed in mirror neurons in the monkey brain. Indeed, mirror neurons typically have a stronger discharge during action execution than during action observation. During imitation, the parieto-frontal mirror neuron system shows higher activity compared to action execution. The increased activity during imitation is roughly equal to the sum of the activity during action observation and action execution (Aziz-Zadeh, Koski, Zaidel, Mazziotta, & Iacoboni, 2006; Molnar-Szakacs, Iacoboni, Koski, & Mazziotta, 2005; Koski, Iacoboni, Dubeau, Woods, & Mazziotta, 2003; Koski et al., 2002; Iacoboni et al., 1999). Indeed, during imitation there is both action observation and action execution. The functional role of the human mirror neuron system during imitation would be the mapping of the observed action onto motor representations in the imitator's brain.

It is likely that the motor plan of the imitative action is sent back to the posterior part of the STS (Iacoboni et al., 2001). This would make it possible to have a matching process between the visual description of the observed action and the anticipated outcome of the planned imitative action. If there is a good match, the action is executed. If the match is not good enough, a correction of the motor plan is implemented.

We can also speculate on how this correction is implemented computationally. Indeed, the information flow outlined above within the core imitation circuitry reminds us of a functional architecture proposed in motor control literature (Haruno, Wolpert, & Kawato, 2001), and composed of modular pairs of forward and inverse internal models (Wolpert, Miall, & Kawato, 1998).

In motor control, the role of the inverse model is to retrieve the motor plan necessary to reach a desired sensory state. The desired sensory state would be the input of the inverse model, while the motor plan necessary to reach that desired sensory state would be the output of the inverse model. During imitation, the input of the inverse model is created by sending the visual description of the observed action from the temporal STS system to the parieto-frontal mirror neuron system. The parieto-frontal mirror neuron system would produce the motor command necessary to imitate the observed action, which is the output of the inverse model.

The role of the forward model in motor control is to predict the sensory consequences of planned actions. In the core imitation circuitry, the parieto-frontal mirror neuron system may provide the input of the forward model by means of an efference copy of the motor command. The efference copy is sent to the temporal STS system, which would provide the output of the forward model by means of a match between the visual description of the action and the predicted sensory consequences of the planned imitative action.

When the prediction is confirmed by re-afferent feedback, then a "responsibility signal" (Haruno et al., 2001) would assign high responsibility for imitating that given action to that specific forward-inverse model pair. As we will see in the next section, the "responsibility signal" may originate from prefrontal areas.

Core Imitation Circuitry and its Interactions: Imitative Learning

Obviously, the core imitation circuitry is a core element of larger networks that participate in the implementation of a variety of imitative behaviors. Two main categories of imitative behaviors are imitative learning (some sort of cognitive imitation) and social mirroring (some sort of nonreflective, emotional form of imitation). Available data indeed suggest that the interactions between the core imitation circuitry and other neural systems are essential for both main categories of imitative behavior (Iacoboni, 2005), as we will see below.

However, to better understand the functional nature of these interactions, it may be useful to discuss a very recent fMRI study on imitation of hand actions (Menz, McNamara, Klemen, & Binkofski, 2009). This study used independent component analysis (ICA) to identify networks of neural systems activated during imitation. Independent CA is a multivariate statistical technique that allows the separation of a signal that depends on many sources into independent components. One of the appealing aspects of ICA is that it is completely data driven and does not rely on the assumptions of the investigator. When ICA was applied to the brain-imaging data, it demonstrated four separate networks: a network of visual areas that are most likely related to the basic visual processing of the observed actions; a network of areas including both the core imitation circuit and motor areas such as the primary motor cortex, supplementary motor area (SMA) and pre-SMA, cerebellum and putamen; and two additional complex networks of difficult interpretation. Thus, the ICA demonstrated that the core imitation circuit—which includes a purely visual neural system as pSTS—belongs to a component that includes classical motor areas. This suggests that the functional processes implemented during imitation are heavily oriented toward a motor representation of the actions to be imitated, rather than toward a visual one. This is theoretically important, because it reveals that the imitation process is embodied, or anchored to the motor and body parts representations of the cortex. Indeed, it makes little theoretical sense to think about the imitation process in abstract terms, without considering the body parts and type of actions involved.

One aspect of imitative learning that is not intuitively covered by the functional properties of neural mirroring is the imitation of novel actions that do not belong to the motor repertoire of the observer. In principle, complex actions can be decomposed in simpler acts (for which presumably there are mirroring neural mechanisms) and re-composed again to support imitative learning. Neural mechanisms of control over the core imitation circuitry may be ideally placed to support imitative learning. Practically, unfortunately, it is not easy to study imitation learning with brain-imaging techniques, because the number of actions that can be performed in the scanner is limited. Some recent fMRI studies cleverly addressed this difficult issue. In a first study, musically naïve subjects were studied while observing and subsequently executing guitar chords (Buccino et al., 2004). Perhaps not surprisingly, the fronto-parietal mirror neuron system was active during both observation and execution of the guitar chords. The imitation of novel actions, however, yielded the additional activation of the dorsolateral prefrontal cortex (DLPFC) and of cortical areas relevant to motor preparation—dorsal premotor cortex, mesial frontal cortex, and superior parietal lobule. The activity in the DLPFC seems to reflect the selection of motor acts appropriate for the task, a role that would not be specific to imitation but also critical to other forms of sensory-motor behavior.

Thus, imitative learning seems supported by a large network encompassing the core imitation circuitry, motor preparation areas, and DLPFC.

In a follow-up, event-related fMRI study on learning how to play guitar chords, after practice subjects observed both practiced and nonpracticed guitar chords (Vogt et al., 2007). Activity in the parieto-frontal mirror neuron areas was higher for nonpracticed guitar chords than for practiced guitar chords. A similar pattern of activity was also observed in the left DLPFC. In this region, activity was also higher during motor preparation for nonpracticed chords, compared to practiced chords. Taken together, these findings suggest that the left DLPFC is engaged in selecting and re-combining existing, elementary motor representations in the observer/imitator's brain. If this interpretation is correct, then parieto-frontal mirroring mechanisms are also critically involved in early stages of imitative learning. The mirroring of the elementary acts that form the novel action to be is an essential component of the imitative learning process. Such mirroring, however, is not sufficient, because it still requires the involvement of the DLPFC.

A recent model, mostly based on neuronal recordings in monkeys, is consistent with this hypothesis. The model proposes a direct mirroring pathway for automatic, reflexive imitation and an indirect mirroring pathway from mirror neuron areas to the prefrontal cortex for parsing, storing, and organizing motor representations, all essential steps for imitative learning (Ferrari, Bonini, & Fogassi, 2009).

Core Imitation Circuitry and its Interactions: Empathy

At the beginning of the last century, Theodor Lipps proposed a concept of empathy, or Einfuhlung—which can be translated as "in-feeling" or "feeling-into"—according to which we achieve the ability to share and understand the emotions and feelings of others by using some sort of projection of the self into the other. As he noted, "When I observe a circus performer on a hanging wire, I feel I am inside him" (as cited by Gallese, 2001). Lipps proposed that at the basis of our ability to empathize there is a process of inner imitation. The mirror neuron system has functional properties that seem ideally suited to support this process of inner imitation. Interestingly, social psychology research has demonstrated that being imitated increases liking and that more empathic individuals tend to imitate other people more than less empathic individuals

(Chartrand & Bargh, 1999). These psychological data suggest functional links between the human mirror neuron system and neural systems more traditionally associated with emotional processing. Anatomical connections in the primate brain suggests that the areas that form the core imitation circuitry are connected to emotional brain centers like the amygdala through the insula (Augustine, 1996; 1985). Thus, it is conceivable that empathy requires the simulation (or inner imitation) of the facial emotional expressions of other people. Mirror neurons would provide such a simulation process. Their connections with the limbic system via the insula would allow mirror neurons to send signals to limbic areas, such that the observer can feel what others are feeling. This model makes two predictions: first, there should be activation of mirror neuron areas, insula, and amygdala during both observation and imitation of facial emotional expressions; second, in this network of areas the activity during imitation should be higher than during observation, as the previous study on imitation of finger movements had shown. Furthermore, the higher activity during imitation should not be restricted to mirror neuron areas only. Indeed, if empathy requires the simulation of others' actions and functional links between mirror neurons and limbic areas, one would expect that the higher activity during imitation in mirror neuron areas would also spread to the insula and limbic areas. Empirical data from an fMRI confirmed both predictions (Carr, Iacoboni, Dubeau, Mazziotta, & Lenzi, 2003).

While this study compellingly described a large-scale neural network supporting empathy via a simulative process implemented by mirror neurons, it did not provide any direct evidence linking the activity in this neural network and individual differences in empathy, since no behavioral data were included in the study. Three recent fMRI studies have correlated behavioral data on empathy with brain-imaging data. In one study, subjects listened to action sounds. As we know, action sounds trigger a discharge in mirror neurons. This predicts that human brain areas with mirror neurons should also become activated while listening to action sounds. Indeed, the study demonstrated that action sounds increased the activity of ventral premotor and inferior frontal areas (Gazzola et al., 2006). These areas have both activity profile and anatomical localization compatible with mirror neuron activity. Furthermore, subjects with high empathy scores had higher activity in these areas than subjects with low empathy scores (Gazzola et al., 2006).

Another fMRI study measured brain activity while subjects observed grasping actions. As expected, grasping observation activated the inferior frontal cortex, where presumably human mirror neurons are located. The inferior frontal activity was also correlated with empathy scores (Kaplan & Iacoboni, 2006).

A more recent study has investigated the relationships between activity in mirror neuron areas and empathy in children (Pfeifer, Iacoboni, Mazziotta, & Dapretto, 2008). The children were asked to imitate and to simply observe facial emotional expressions displaying basic emotions. As in the previous study on adults (Carr et al., 2003), mirror neuron areas, the insula, and the amygdala activated for both observation and imitation of facial emotional expressions, with higher activity during imitation. Correlation analyses were performed between brain activity and two types of scores: empathy scores and interpersonal competence scores. Empathy was correlated with activity in mirror neuron areas during observation of facial emotional expressions. Furthermore, mirror neuron activity during imitation of facial emotional expressions correlated with interpersonal competence scores (Pfeifer et al., 2008). This makes sense, as overtly mirroring the emotions of others plays an important role in social interactions. It is through this mirroring that we communicate to other people that we understand what they are feeling. The fact that activity in mirror neuron areas maps well onto interpersonal competence during emotion imitation suggests that the mirror neuron system is a fairly nuanced bio-marker of sociality.

Imaging studies of autism support this hypothesis. A recent fMRI study of observation and imitation of facial emotional expressions has demonstrated reduced activity in mirror neuron areas in children with autism spectrum disorder compared to typically developing children. Moreover, this study also revealed a correlation between the severity of the disorder and activity in mirror neuron areas during observation and imitation of facial emotional expressions (Dapretto et al., 2006). The more severe the disorder, the more reduced was the activity in mirror neuron areas. This suggests that, in principle, interventions that may be able to re-train mirror neuron activity in children with autism (for instance, imitation-based forms of intervention) should be beneficial for these children.

Imitation and Vocal Learning

The discovery of mirror neurons in monkeys and the brain-imaging work linking imitation with the human mirror neuron system has obviously raised the issue of whether mirror neurons exist in other animals, too. For instance, imitative vocal learning is a behavior that both humans and songbirds share. The neurobiology of birdsong learning was well studied and well understood before the recent wave of studies on the neurobiological mechanisms of imitation in humans. However, a new series of studies in songbirds are testing the hypothesis that some neurons in songbirds may display precise auditory-vocal mirroring. Indeed, neurons in the swamp sparrow forebrain demonstrate this form of neural mirroring (Prather, Peters, Nowicki, & Mooney, 2008). Certain note sequences in both the songbird's repertoire and in the birdsong of other species trigger identical responses in these neurons. When the bird sings the same sequence, the same neurons display the same pattern of activity. This activity is unaltered by disruption of auditory feedback, suggesting that these neurons are concerned with production, rather than perception of the birdsong, when the bird is singing. The auditory-vocal mirror neurons of the swamp sparrow innervate striatal structures important for song learning, suggesting that the activity of these cells is essential for imitative learning.

Auditory-vocal mirroring responses have been recently reported also in the juvenile zebra finch (Keller & Hahnloser, 2009). In principle, these mirroring responses may be widespread in songbirds. The functional significance of these mirroring responses in songbirds may be to establish a correspondence between sensory and motor codes used for communication signals. A similar concept had been proposed for human speech by the motor theory of speech perception (Liberman & Whalen, 2000; Liberman & Mattingly, 1985; Liberman et al., 1967). Recent studies have demonstrated increased activity in speech motor areas during speech perception, supporting the hypothesis of mirroring speech responses in humans (Fadiga, Craighero, Buccino, & Rizzolatti, 2002; Wilson, Molnar-Szakacs, & Iacoboni, 2008; Wilson & Iacoboni, 2006; Wilson, Saygin, Sereno, & Iacoboni, 2004). These studies, however, had not demonstrated that the activity in speech motor areas during speech perception is essential to the perceptual process. A recent transcranial magnetic stimulation (TMS) study perturbed the activity of a speech motor area while subjects performed a perceptual speech task. Speech perception was indeed impaired, thus providing for the first time evidence that disrupting activity in a motor area

reduces perception (Meister, Wilson, Deblieck, Wu, & Iacoboni, 2007).

Obviously, these results do not negate the important role of classical auditory cortices in speech perception. The question, then, is to figure out what is the interplay between speech motor areas and auditory cortices during speech perception. A recent model proposes that auditory neurons in the superior temporal cortex would provide acoustic analysis of speech sounds, whereas motor speech areas would provide a "simulation" or "inner imitation" of phoneme production. This simulative process would allow the prediction of the acoustic consequences of phoneme production that would be compared in the superior temporal cortex with the acoustic analysis of the heard speech sounds. If necessary, an error signal would be generated to allow correction of the simulated phoneme production used for phoneme categorization (Wilson & Iacoboni, 2006; Iacoboni, 2008). From a functional standpoint, this information-processing flow is very similar to the one proposed in the core imitation circuitry described above.

Conclusions

The role of imitation in social behavior is widespread and complex. The mirror neuron system is the first neural system that allows us to have an experimental grip on what are most likely extremely complex neurobiological underpinnings of a complex behavior. This obviously already tells us that the mirror neuron system is only one piece of a much larger puzzle that forms the neural underpinnings of imitative behavior (see, for instance, the brain imaging work of Jean Decety on imitation) (Chaminade, Meltzoff, & Decety, 2005; Meltzoff & Decety, 2003; Decety, Chaminade, Grèzes, & Meltzoff, 2002; Chaminade, Meltzoff, & Decety, 2002; Jackson, Meltzoff, & Decety, 2006). One obvious very important question that will likely be addressed in the near future is the role of control mechanisms onto the mirror neuron system and imitation. Are these control mechanisms general-purpose ones, or especially dedicated to this specific system? A better understanding of these phenomena will greatly improve our knowledge on the neural basis of social behavior.

Acknowledgments

For generous support the author thanks the Brain Mapping Medical Research Organization, Brain Mapping Support Foundation, Pierson-Lovelace Foundation, The Ahmanson Foundation, William M.

and Linda R. Dietel Philanthropic Fund at the Northern Piedmont Community Foundation, Tamkin Foundation, Jennifer Jones-Simon Foundation, Capital Group Companies Charitable Foundation, Robson Family and Northstar Fund.

References

Augustine, J. R. (1985). The insular lobe in primates including humans. *Neurol Res, 7*(1), 2–10.

Augustine, J. R. (1996). Circuitry and functional aspects of the insular lobe in primates including humans. *Brain Res Brain Res Rev, 22*(3), 229–244.

Aziz-Zadeh, L., Koski, L., Zaidel, E., Mazziotta, J., & Iacoboni, M. (2006). Lateralization of the human mirror neuron system. *J Neurosci, 26*(11), 2964–2970.

Bartels, A., Logothetis, N. K., & Moutoussis, K. (2008). fMRI and its interpretations: An illustration on directional selectivity in area V5/MT. *Trends Neurosci, 31*(9), 444–453.

Buccino, G., Vogt, S., Ritzl, A., Fink, G. R., Zilles, K., et al. (2004). Neural circuits underlying imitation learning of hand actions: An event-related fMRI study. *Neuron, 42*(2), 323–334.

Byrne, R. W. & Russon, A. E. (1998). Learning by imitation: A hierarchical approach. *Behav Brain Sci, 21*(5), 667–684; discussion 684–721.

Caggiano, V., Fogassi, L., Rizzolatti, G., Thier, P., & Casile, A. (2009). Mirror neurons differentially encode the peripersonal and extrapersonal space of monkeys. *Science, 324*(5925), 403–406.

Carr, L., Iacoboni, M., Dubeau, M. C., Mazziotta, J. C., & Lenzi, G. L. (2003). Neural mechanisms of empathy in humans: A relay from neural systems for imitation to limbic areas. *Proc Natl Acad Sci U S A, 100*(9), 5497–5502.

Chaminade, T., Meltzoff, A. N., & Decety, J. (2002). Does the end justify the means? A PET exploration of the mechanisms involved in human imitation. *Neuroimage, 15*(2), 318–328.

Chaminade, T., Meltzoff, A. N., & Decety, J. (2005). An fMRI study of imitation: Action representation and body schema. *Neuropsychologia, 43*(1), 115–127.

Chartrand, T. L. & Bargh, J. A. (1999). The chameleon effect: The perception-behavior link and social interaction. *Journal of Personality & Social Psychology, 76*(6), 893–910.

Dapretto, M., Davies, M. S., Pfeifer, J. H., Scott, A. A., Sigman, M., et al. (2006). Understanding emotions in others: Mirror neuron dysfunction in children with autism spectrum disorders. *Nat Neurosci, 9*(1), 28–30.

Decety, J., Chaminade, T., Grèzes, J., & Meltzoff, A. N. (2002). A PET exploration of the neural mechanisms involved in reciprocal imitation. *Neuroimage, 15*(1), 265–272.

di Pellegrino, G., Fadiga, L., Fogassi, L., Gallese, V., & Rizzolatti, G. (1992). Understanding motor events: A neurophysiological study. *Exp Brain Res, 91*(1), 176–180.

Dijksterhuis, A. (2005). Why we are social animals: The high road to imitation as social glue. In S. Hurley & N. Chater (Eds.), *Perspective on imitation: From neuroscience to social science* (pp. 207–220). Cambridge, MA, US: MIT Press.

Fadiga, L., Craighero, L., Buccino, G., & Rizzolatti, G. (2002). Speech listening specifically modulates the excitability of tongue muscles: A TMS study. *Eur J Neurosci, 15*(2), 399–402.

Ferrari, P. F., Bonini, L., & Fogassi, L. (2009). From monkey mirror neurons to primate behaviours: possible "direct" and "indirect" pathways. *Philos Trans R Soc Lond B Biol Sci, 364*(1528), 2311–2323.

Ferrari, P. F., Gallese, V., Rizzolatti, G., & Fogassi, L. (2003). Mirror neurons responding to the observation of ingestive and communicative mouth actions in the monkey ventral premotor cortex. *Eur J Neurosci, 17*(8), 1703–1714.

Ferrari, P. F., Visalberghi, E., Paukner, A., Fogassi, L., Ruggiero, A., & Suomi, S. J. (2006). Neonatal imitation in rhesus macaques. *PLoS Biol, 4*(9), e302.

Fogassi, L., Ferrari, P. F., Gesierich, B., Rozzi, S., Chersi, F., & Rizzolatti, G. (2005). Parietal lobe: From action organization to intention understanding. *Science, 308*(5722), 662–667.

Gallese, V. (2001). The "shared manifold" hypothesis. *Journal of Consciousness Studies, 8*(5–7), 33–50.

Gallese, V., Fadiga, L., Fogassi, L., & Rizzolatti, G. (1996). Action recognition in the premotor cortex. *Brain, 119* (Pt 2), 593–609.

Gazzola, V., Aziz-Zadeh, L., & Keysers, C. (2006). Empathy and the somatotopic auditory mirror system in humans. *Curr Biol, 16*(18), 1824–1829.

Haruno, M., Wolpert, D. M., & Kawato, M. (2001). Mosaic model for sensorimotor learning and control. *Neural Comput, 13*(10), 2201.

Hurley, S. & Chater, N. (2005). *Perspective on imitation: From neuroscience to social science.* Cambridge, MA: MIT Press.

Iacoboni, M. (2005). Neural mechanisms of imitation. *Curr Opin Neurobiol, 15*(6), 632–637.

Iacoboni, M. (2008). The role of premotor cortex in speech perception: Evidence from fMRI and rTMS. *J Physiol Paris, 102*(1–3), 31–34.

Iacoboni, M. & Dapretto, M. (2006). The mirror neuron system and the consequences of its dysfunction. *Nat Rev Neurosci, 7*(12), 942–951.

Iacoboni, M., Koski, L. M., Brass, M., Bekkering, H., Woods, R. P., et al. (2001). Reafferent copies of imitated actions in the right superior temporal cortex. *Proc Natl Acad Sci U S A, 98*(24), 13995–13999.

Iacoboni, M., Woods, R. P., Brass, M., Bekkering, H., Mazziotta, J. C., & Rizzolatti, G. (1999). Cortical mechanisms of human imitation. *Science, 286*(5449), 2526–2528.

Jackson, P. L., Meltzoff, A. N., & Decety, J. (2006). Neural circuits involved in imitation and perspective-taking. *Neuroimage, 31*(1), 429–439.

Kaplan, J. T. & Iacoboni, M. (2006). Getting a grip on other minds: mirror neurons, intention understanding, and cognitive empathy. *Soc Neurosci, 1*(3–4), 175–183.

Keller, G. B. & Hahnloser, R. H. (2009). Neural processing of auditory feedback during vocal practice in a songbird. *Nature, 457*(7226), 187–190.

Kohler, E., Keysers, C., Umiltà, M. A., Fogassi, L., Gallese, V., & Rizzolatti, G. (2002). Hearing sounds, understanding actions: Action representation in mirror neurons. *Science, 297*(5582), 846–848.

Koski, L., Iacoboni, M., Dubeau, M. C., Woods, R. P., & Mazziotta, J. C. (2003). Modulation of cortical activity during different imitative behaviors. *J Neurophysiol, 89*(1), 460–471.

Koski, L., Wohlschläger, A., Bekkering, H., Woods, R. P., Dubeau, M. C., et al. (2002). Modulation of motor and premotor activity during imitation of target-directed actions. *Cereb Cortex, 12*(8), 847–855.

Liberman, A. M. & Mattingly, I. G. (1985). The motor theory of speech perception revised. *Cognition, 21*, 1–36.

Liberman, A. M. & Whalen, D. H. (2000). On the relation of speech to language. *Trends Cogn Sci, 4*, 187–196.

Liberman, A. M., Cooper, F. S., Shankweiler, D. P., & Studdert-Kennedy, M. (1967). Perception of the speech code. *Psychol Rev, 74*, 431–461.

Logothetis, N. K. (2003). The underpinnings of the BOLD functional magnetic resonance imaging signal. *J Neurosci, 23*(10), 3963–3971.

Logothetis, N. K. & Wandell, B. A. (2004). Interpreting the BOLD signal. *Annu Rev Physiol, 66*, 735–769.

Logothetis, N. K., Pauls, J., Augath, M., Trinath, T., & Oeltermann, A. (2001). Neurophysiological investigation of the basis of the fMRI signal. *Nature, 412*(6843), 150–157.

Meister, I. G., Wilson, S. M., Deblieck, C., Wu, A. D., & Iacoboni, M. (2007). The essential role of premotor cortex in speech perception. *Curr Biol, 17*(19), 1692–1696.

Meltzoff, A. N. & Decety, J. (2003). What imitation tells us about social cognition: A rapprochement between developmental psychology and cognitive neuroscience. *Philos Trans R Soc Lond B Biol Sci, 358*(1431), 491–500.

Menz, M. M., McNamara, A., Klemen, J., & Binkofski, F. (2009). Dissociating networks of imitation. *Hum Brain Mapp*.

Molnar-Szakacs, I., Iacoboni, M., Koski, L., & Mazziotta, J. C. (2005). Functional segregation within pars opercularis of the inferior frontal gyrus: Evidence from fMRI studies of imitation and action observation. *Cereb Cortex, 15*(7), 986–994.

Paukner, A., Anderson, J. R., Borelli, E., Visalberghi, E., & Ferrari, P. F. (2005). Macaques (Macaca nemestrina) recognize when they are being imitated. *Biol Lett, 1*(2), 219–222.

Pfeifer, J. H., Iacoboni, M., Mazziotta, J. C., & Dapretto, M. (2008). Mirroring others' emotions relates to empathy and interpersonal competence in children. *Neuroimage, 39*(4), 2076–2085.

Prather, J. F., Peters, S., Nowicki, S., & Mooney, R. (2008). Precise auditory-vocal mirroring in neurons for learned vocal communication. *Nature, 451*(7176), 305–310.

Rizzolatti, G. & Craighero, L. (2004). The mirror-neuron system. *Annu Rev Neurosci, 27*, 169–192.

Romanes, G. J. (1883). *Mental evolution in animals*. London: Kegan Paul Trench & Co.

Shepherd, S. V., Klein, J. T., Deaner, R. O., & Platt, M. L. (2009). Mirroring of attention by neurons in macaque parietal cortex. *Proc Natl Acad Sci U S A, 106*(23), 9489–9494.

Subiaul, F., Cantlon, J. F., Holloway, R. L., & Terrace, H. S. (2004). Cognitive imitation in rhesus macaques. *Science, 305*(5682), 407–410.

Tomasello, M., Kruger, A. C., & Ratner, H. H. (1993). Cultural learning. *Behav Brain Sci, 16*, 495–552.

Umiltà, M. A., Kohler, E., Gallese, V., Fogassi, L., Fadiga, L., et al. (2001). I know what you are doing. A neurophysiological study. *Neuron, 31*(1), 155–165.

Voelkl, B. & Huber, L. (2000). True imitation in marmosets. *Anim Behav, 60*(2), 195–202.

Voelkl, B. & Huber, L. (2007). Imitation as faithful copying of a novel technique in marmoset monkeys. *PLoS ONE, 2*, e611.

Vogt, S., Buccino, G., Wohlschläger, A. M., Canessa, N., Shah, N. J., et al. (2007). Prefrontal involvement in imitation learning of hand actions: Effects of practice and expertise. *Neuroimage, 37*(4), 1371–1383.

Wilson, S. M. & Iacoboni, M. (2006). Neural responses to nonnative phonemes varying in producibility: Evidence for the sensorimotor nature of speech perception. *Neuroimage, 33*(1), 316–325.

Wilson, S. M., Molnar-Szakacs, I., & Iacoboni, M. (2008). Beyond superior temporal cortex: intersubject correlations in narrative speech comprehension. *Cereb Cortex, 18*(1), 230–242.

Wilson, S. M., Saygin, A. P., Sereno, M. I., & Iacoboni, M. (2004). Listening to speech activates motor areas involved in speech production. *Nat Neurosci, 7*(7), 701–702.

Wolpert, D. M., Miall, R. C., & Kawato, M. (1998). Internal models in the cerebellum. *Trends Cogn Sci, 2*, 338–347.

Social Neuroscience of Empathy

Tania Singer *and* Jean Decety

Abstract

This chapter discusses the study of empathy in the field of social neuroscience. It also considers the role of action understanding and cognitive perspective-taking in empathic understanding. The first part of the chapter discusses different definitions of empathy, thereby comparing the construct of empathy to related constructs, such as compassion, emotion contagion, empathic concern, sympathy, cognitive perspective taking, and Theory of Mind. The second part reports evidence from social neuroscience studies on empathy and the role of the mirror neuron for empathy, the modulation of empathic brain responses, and empathy deficits in psychopathology.

Keywords: empathy, social neuroscience, action understanding, compassion, emotion contagion, empathic concern, sympathy, Theory of Mind, mirror neuron

Introduction

Being at the root of positive social interaction, empathy—the ability to share and understand other people's affective and mental states—has long been the focus of studies in social sciences and in social and developmental psychology. Recent work in social and cognitive neuroscience has now begun to tease apart the component processes of this general capacity and identify its neural underpinnings. Several functional neuroimaging studies have demonstrated that different yet interacting brain circuits underlie our ability to understand other people's a) action intentions, b) emotions and feelings, and c) beliefs and thoughts. This chapter will mainly focus on the study of empathy in the field of social neuroscience, but we will also discuss the role of action understanding and cognitive perspective-taking in empathic understanding.

In the first part of the chapter, we will discuss different definitions of empathy, thereby comparing the construct of empathy to related constructs, such as compassion, emotion contagion, empathic concern, sympathy, cognitive perspective-taking, and Theory of Mind. In the second part, we will report evidence from social neuroscience studies on empathy and the role of the mirror neuron system for empathy, the modulation of empathic brain responses, and empathy deficits in psychopathology.

Clearing up Conceptual Issues

Empathy is a commonly used word in everyday language, but there is no uniform definition for the construct. The word has its linguistic roots in ancient Greek "empatheia" (passion), which is composed of "en" (in) and "pathos" (feeling) and corresponds to the German word "Einfühlung" ("feeling into"), which has been translated into English as "empathy". Very broadly, it denotes our capacity to put ourselves in someone else's shoes. In order to examine empathy empirically, developmental and social psychologists and later social neuroscientists attempted to more clearly define it as well as distinguish it from related concepts such as mentalizing or cognitive perspective-taking, emotion contagion, sympathy, compassion, and empathic concern (e.g., Batson, 2009; Davis, 1994; Decety & Jackson, 2004; Eisenberg, 2000; Hoffman, 2000; Preston & de Waal, 2002; Singer, 2006). Taking a cognitive neuroscience approach, Decety and Jackson (2004) put forward a model of empathy involving three distinct, yet interacting, functional components: affective sharing, emotion understanding, and self-regulation. Similarly, de Vignemont and Singer (2006) identified four constitutive factors of empathy: (i) the presence of an affective state in oneself, (ii) isomorphism between one's own and another person's affective state, (iii) elicitation of one's own affective state upon observation or imagination of another person's affective state, and (iv) knowledge that the other person's affective state is the source of one's own affective state. Importantly, this latter definition differentiates empathy from the cognitive ability to understand other people's abstract beliefs and thoughts, also referred to as "theory of mind" or "mentalizing" (Frith & Frith, 2003). Accordingly, "mentalizing" refers to the drawing of inferences about other people's mental states, including their affective states, but it does not entail emotional involvement as in empathy. The specific qualia, the way it feels for the other person to be in pain or to rejoice, is missing. Such a distinction is supported by research in psychopathology. For instance, psychopaths have an understanding of other people's mental states, including their affective states, and consequently are very good at manipulating other people. At the same time, however, they lack the experience of empathy; this deficit can result in antisocial behavior. Recent neuroscientific evidence has demonstrated that the ability to empathize and to mentalize indeed relies on distinct neural networks (Blair, 2005; Hynes, Baird, & Grafton, 2006; Völlm et al., 2006).

Another important conceptual clarification is related to the distinction between empathy and sympathy (Eisenberg, 2007; Wispé, 1986). Whereas both concepts involve affective feeling states, "empathy" refers to the sharing of another person's feeling, while "sympathy" refers to an emotional response congruent with the other person's feeling, but not

necessarily isomorphic. For example, when another person is angry about something, I might share his/her anger ("empathize") or I might feel pity for him/her ("sympathize"). Even though this is not necessarily explicit in the concept itself, sympathy sometimes has a condescending quality to it: The sympathetic other feels that he/she is *above* the one feeling the emotion (see also Singer & Steinbeis, 2009).

The concepts of "empathic concern" or "compassion" are similar to that of sympathy in that they also refer to a *feeling for* another person. In addition, they involve a *motivation* to act, that is, to help the other. Thus, compassion has been defined as a "deep awareness of the suffering of another coupled with the wish to relieve it" (American Heritage) or as the "human quality of understanding the suffering of others and wanting to do something about it" (Merriam-Webster). Contemplative traditions typically refer to "loving-kindness" as the wish for happiness for others and of "compassion" as the wish to relieve others' suffering.

Furthermore, empathy is not only elicited by the observation of another person's display of emotion, but also by imagining another person's emotion (i.e., putting oneself in someone else's shoes) (de Vignemont & Singer, 2006; Decety & Grèzes, 2006; Decety & Jackson, 2004). For example, when reading a letter in which a friend describes a sad event, one cannot glean information about the friend's affective state from facial or vocal indicators, but must imagine the circumstances the friend is facing and their effect on the friend's affective state.

One last aspect of the definition pertains to the distinction between "empathy" and "emotional contagion." "Emotional contagion" refers to

> "the tendency to automatically mimic and synchronize facial expressions, vocalizations, postures, and movements with those of another person and, consequently, to converge emotionally" (Hatfield, Cacioppo, & Rapson, 1994).

and has been seen as an important precursor to empathy that is already present in infants (Hoffman, 1984). In contrast to empathy, there is no self-other distinction in emotional contagion: One is not aware that one's emotion was elicited by observing another person's emotion.

Although a distinction can be made between empathy, emotional contagion, cognitive perspective-taking, sympathy, and compassion, these different phenomena frequently occur in concert. Generally, a certain sequence is suggested, with emotional contagion being antecedent to empathy, which in turn precedes sympathy, empathic concern, and compassion, which in turn may motivate prosocial behavior. Empathy is thought to be a necessary but not sufficient condition for compassion to arise because an excess of empathy can result in personal distress and avoidance of the suffering other. On the other hand, a lack of empathy as observed in psychopaths is associated with a lack of compassionate motivation and the occurrence of antisocial behavior (Blair, Mitchell, & Blair, 2005).

Shared Neural Circuits Between Self and Other

The empirical investigation of empathy within neuroscience was strongly inspired by "simulation theory" developed in the domain of philosophy of the mind (Goldman, 2006), perception-action models originating from action research in cognitive psychology (Hommel, Müsseler, Aschersleben, & Prinz, 2001; Prinz, 1987), and by the discovery of "mirror neurons" in neurophysiological investigations of the monkey brain (Rizzolatti & Craighero, 2004). In more general terms, these accounts suggest that we come to understand others' actions, sensations, and emotions by means of the activation of the neural representations corresponding to those states: To understand what others are doing, we simulate their movements using our own motor program; to understand what others are feeling, we simulate their feelings using our own affective programs. Preston and de Waal (2002), for example, proposed a neuroscientific model of empathy which suggests that observing or imagining another person in a particular emotional state automatically activates a representation of that state in the observer, along with its associated autonomic and somatic responses. Indeed, this so-called "shared representations" account of social interaction and intersubjectivity has become the dominant explanation of the hemodynamic activation patterns observed in recent fMRI studies of empathy (Decety & Sommerville, 2003).

After reviewing neuroimaging evidence for such shared circuitry in the domain of empathy, we will critically evaluate the role of mirror neurons for empathy and the meaning of shared networks for empathy.

One first evidence for overlapping neural activation during one's own experience and the observation of another person's experience of emotion came from a study that investigated shared neural responses in the domain of olfaction (Wicker et al., 2003).

Experiencing disgust oneself upon smelling disgusting odors and observing someone else's odor-elicited expression of disgust evoked similar neural responses in the anterior insula (AI) and the anterior cingulate cortex (ACC). A more recent study revealed similar overlapping AI activation when subjects drank pleasant and unpleasant drinks and when they saw someone else drinking pleasant and unpleasant drinks and producing the corresponding facial expressions (Jabbi, Swart, & Keysers, 2007). In addition, Keysers and colleagues (2004) found evidence for overlapping neural activation in secondary somatosensory cortices (SII) when subjects were either touched themselves or watched videos in which other people were being touched.

Most studies on shared neural networks in the affective domain have been conducted on empathy for pain (Avenanti, Bueti, Galati, & Aglioti, 2005; Avenanti, Paluello, Bufalari, & Aglioti, 2006; Botvinick et al., 2005; Bufalari, Aprile, Avenanti, Di, & Aglioti, 2007; Cheng et al., 2007; Decety, Echols, & Correll, 2009; Gu & Han, 2007; Jackson, Meltzoff, & Decety, 2005; Jackson, Brunet, Meltzoff, & Decety, 2006; Lamm & Decety, 2008; Lamm, Batson, & Decety, 2007; Lamm, Nusbaum, Meltzoff, & Decety, 2007; Moriguchi et al., 2007; Morrison & Downing, 2007; Morrison, Lloyd, di Pellegrino, & Roberts, 2004; Morrison, Peelen, & Downing, 2007; Saarela et al., 2007; Singer et al., 2004, 2006; Valeriani et al., 2008). For example, in an early study, Singer and colleagues (2004) recruited couples and measured hemodynamic responses triggered by electrode-delivered painful stimulation of the hand of either the female participant or her partner, who was sitting next to the scanner. Differently colored flashes of light on a screen pointed to either the male or the female participant's hand, indicating which of them would receive the painful stimulation. Using this procedure, pain-related brain activation was measured when pain was delivered to the scanned participant (first-hand experience of pain) or to her partner (empathy for pain). The results suggested that parts of the so-called "pain matrix," which consists of the brain areas involved in the processing of pain, were activated when participants experienced pain themselves as well as when they saw a signal indicating that their loved one would be experiencing pain. These areas—in particular, bilateral AI, the rostral ACC, brainstem, and the cerebellum—are involved in the processing of the affective, but not the sensory-discriminative component of pain. In other words, these regions encode how unpleasant and aversive the subjectively felt pain is. Thus, the first-hand experience of pain and the knowledge that a beloved partner is experiencing pain activate the same pain-related affective brain circuits—suggesting that our own neural response reflects our partner's negative affect. This initial finding of shared neural activation between self and other in the insular cortex and ACC when empathizing with others who are experiencing pain has been replicated frequently and extended using a variety of paradigms and methods. More detailed analysis has also revealed that not all activated voxels in the insular cortex and ACC during the first-hand experience overlap with the vicarious experience of pain. Shared networks in the insular cortex, for example, seem to be mostly confined to parts of the AI, whereas first-hand experience of pain also involves mid and posterior parts of the insular cortices (Decety & Lamm, 2009; Jackson, 2006b; Morrison & Downing, 2007; Singer et al., 2004). Furthermore, in most empathy-for-pain studies, no evidence for shared networks was observed in the so-called sensory-discriminative components of a pain experience—typically reflected in activation in primary and secondary somatosensory cortices contralateral to the stimulated body parts (e.g., Singer et al., 2004, 2006). Some recent studies, however, suggest that under some conditions areas associated with somatosensory processing can also be activated during empathy for pain—in particular when our attention is explicitly directed to the importance of the somatosensory aspects of another person's pain experience (e.g., Bufalari, Aprile, Avenanti, Di Russo, & Aglioti, 2007; Cheng et al., 2008; Lamm & Decety, 2008; Lamm, Nusbaum et al., 2007).

In sum, a number of studies investigating empathic brain responses in the domains of touch, smell, and pain have identified networks involved in the experience of one's own emotions as well as in the vicarious experience of others' emotions. Before expounding on the nature of these shared networks, we will introduce the notion of mirror neurons and critically evaluate their relationship to the experience of empathy.

The Contribution of Mirror Neurons to Empathy

The functional imaging results in the domain of empathy have frequently been interpreted within the scope of the mirror neuron system, partly due to the above-mentioned paper by Preston and de Waal (2002) in which the authors argued for a perception-action model of empathy. In this section, we will critically examine the contribution of mirror neurons to empathy by briefly reviewing the properties and localization of these neurons in the monkey brain and then discuss the evidence for mirror neurons in humans during the perception and execution of action. Finally, we will consider their contribution to emotion processing.

Mirror neurons are a unique class of cells with sensorimotor properties that were first identified in the monkey ventral premotor cortex. In a seminal paper, Gallese and colleagues (1996) reported that approximately 17% of the neurons recorded in ventral premotor area F5 of the macaque monkey responded both when the monkey executed a particular movement—for example, grasping, placing or manipulating—and when the monkey observed someone else performing that same movement. Later, neurons with similar visuomotor properties were discovered in the anterior intraparietal area (Fogassi et al., 2005) and recently in the motor cortex (Tkach, Reimer, & Hatsopoulos, 2007). The primary function of the mirror neurons was proposed to be related to action understanding. Alternatively, it was recently suggested that the cells might only be facilitating the motor system via learned associations (see Hickok, 2009, for a critical review).

So far evidence for the existence of mirror neurons in humans is indirect and principally relies on functional neuroimaging studies that demonstrate an overlap in activation between observation and action conditions in regions homologous to areas of the monkey brain in which mirror neurons have been found. These regions include the anterior part of the inferior frontal gyrus (pars triangularis), the ventral premotor cortex (pars opercularis), the anterior and posterior intraparietal sulcus, and an area in the lateral occipital cortex (Dinstein, Hasson, Rubin, & Heeger, 2007; Etzel, 2008; Gazzola, 2006, 2007a, 2007b; Grezes & Decety, 2001). These activations are usually lateralized in the left hemisphere. Transcranial magnetic stimulation (TMS) and motor-evoked potentials (MEP) studies have demonstrated changes in the excitability of the observer's brain motor and premotor cortices that encode the execution of observed actions (Fadiga, Craighero, & Olivier, 2005). Magnetoencephalography and electroencephalographic measurements have demonstrated suppression in the mu rhythm (8–13 Hz) over the sensorimotor cortex during the observation of action that parallels the changes detected during action production (e.g., Cheng et al., 2008; Cochin, Barthelemy, Lejeune, Roux, &

Martineau, 1998). It has been hypothesized that this mu rhythm reflects downstream modulation of primary sensorimotor areas by mirror neuron activity, representing a critical information-processing function translating perception into action (Pineda, 2005).

Such a motor resonance mechanism has also been proposed to account for emotion sharing and the experience of empathy, the so-called motor theory of empathy (Carr, Iacoboni, Dubeau, Mazziotta, & Lenzi, 2003; Decety & Meyer, 2007; Leslie, Johnson-Frey, & Grafton, 2004). In the context of emotion processing, it is posited that the observer's perception of an emotion activates neural mechanisms responsible for the production of a similar emotion. It should be noted that a similar mechanism was previously proposed to account for emotion contagion. Indeed, Hatfield et al. (1994) argued that people catch the emotions of others as a result of afferent feedback generated by elementary motor mimicry of others' expressive behavior, which produces a simultaneous match in emotional experience. There is evidence that observing facial expressions of emotion elicits emotionally congruent facial electromyographic (EMG) responses and modulates reported mood (e.g., Hess & Blairy, 2001; Lamm et al., 2008). In a similar vein, Sonnby-Borgstrom and colleagues (2003) examined the relationship between facial mimicry (measured by facial EMG) and self-reported mood upon exposure to static facial expressions of anger and happiness in participants who were categorized as either high or low empathizers. They found that the high-empathy participants produced greater facial mimicry than low-empathy participants.

Overall, this mimicry mechanism, which happens very quickly and unconsciously, fits well with the mirror neuron system account of motor resonance. Nevertheless, one cannot conclude that mimicry leads to the same emotional state in the observer via a simulation process. While neuroimaging data are merely correlational, studies of neurological patients are critical for determining the causal role of a given area and its functional weight with respect to the cognitive process studied. Several neuropsychological observations speak against such a link. For instance, Keillor and colleagues (2002) reported the case of a patient suffering from bilateral facial paralysis due to Guillain-Barré syndrome (a disorder in which the body's immune system attacks part of the peripheral nervous system), who was unable to convey emotions through facial expressions. Despite her complete facial paralysis, the patient did not show deficits in the experience

of emotion or the recognition and mental imagery of facial expressions. Similarly, patients with Möbius syndrome, who suffer from bilateral and usually complete facial paralysis, have difficulty communicating with facial expressions, but their ability to recognize others' facial expressions of emotions is not impaired (Calder et al., 2002). Interestingly, no single measure of somatovisceral response is able to differentiate fully between discrete emotions such as anger, fear, happiness, sadness, or disgust. In addition, meta-analyses of psychophysiological studies indicate that while combinations of measures provide a clearer differentiation, they are clearest when positive and negative emotions are contrasted (with stronger autonomic responses for negative than positive emotions) than when discrete emotions are contrasted (Cacioppo, Berntson, Larsen, Poehlmann, & Ito, 2000).

The idea that the mirror neuron system is implicated in emotion perception is mainly based on studies that have reported activation in the inferior frontal gyrus (IFG; an area homologue to the monkey ventral premotor cortex) during the observation and imitation of facial expression of emotions (e.g., happiness, sadness, anger, disgust, and surprise) and during the imitation of these emotions (e.g., Carr et al., 2003; van der Gaag, Minderaa, & Keysers, 2007). Another study, conducted by Leslie, Johnson-Frey, and Grafton (2004) used a paradigm in which subjects had to observe and imitate hand and face actions (smile and frown condition) using film clips instead of static displays. The right ventral premotor cortex was commonly activated during observation and imitation of facial expressions. A more recent study demonstrated that even passive viewing of facial expressions activates a wide network of brain regions also involved in the execution of similar expressions, including the IFG and the posterior parietal cortex (van der Gaag et al., 2007). In a recent study, Jabbi and Keysers (2008) further explored the link between emotion recognition from facial expression and their relation to mirror-neuron-related areas (IFG and IPL) and emotion-related areas (insula), respectively. Based on analyses involving Granger causality and effective connectivity, their data suggest that IFG and IPL are relevant when observing muscle movements in faces, whereas insula comes into play when emotional quality must be inferred from facial expressions.

In this context, it is also worth mentioning that not all functional neuroimaging studies have reported activation of the IFG or other mirror neuron areas during the perception of facial expressions of emotions (see Murphy, Nimmo-Smith, & Lawrence, 2003; Phan, Wager, Taylor, & Liberzon, 2002, for meta-analyses). For instance, Chakrabarti and colleagues (2006) presented participants with video clips depicting happy, sad, angry, and disgusted facial expressions. Only the perception of happy expressions was associated with an activation of the left pars opercularis. Unfortunately, many studies claiming to have found mirror neuron system activation during action and emotion tasks did not have the appropriate experimental conditions to support such a claim (see Turella, Pierno, Tubaldi, & Castiello, 2009, for a meta-analysis).

It is also noteworthy that many of the above-mentioned empathy studies directly investigating shared networks when participants experienced their own emotions or vicariously experienced others' emotions did not report shared activation in mirror-neuron relevant networks (e.g., Jackson et al., 2005; Keysers et al., 2004; Singer et al., 2004; Singer, 2006). It seems that the observation of activation in mirror-neuron networks during empathy tasks are mostly related to paradigms involving tasks that require motor mimicry as, for example, when subjects are asked to mimic the facial expressions of other people (e.g., Carr et al., 2003). In paradigms such as the "empathy-for-pain" paradigm by Singer et al., which uses arbitrary cues rather than explicit affective displays or other potentially contagious stimuli to indicate the suffering of another person, mirror-neuron-related networks do not seem to play a crucial role.

Finally, accumulating evidence suggests that observed empathic activations do not rely on automatic simple resonance mechanisms. Thus, in the next paragraph, we will provide ample evidence suggesting that the degree to which we engage in empathic responses depends on several contextual and person intrinsic factors (for a similar argument, see de Vignemont & Singer, 2006). Another finding which speaks against simple automatic mirror-neuron-like resonance mechanisms was reported in a recent functional MRI study which demonstrated that patients unable to experience pain in themselves due to a specific neurological condition are nevertheless able to empathize with others when they are experiencing pain (Danziger, Faillenot, & Peyron, 2009). Thus, the patients showed activation in the AI and ACC when exposed to videos depicting people in painful situations. This speaks for their ability to show a negative affective response to other people's suffering even though they cannot experience nociceptive stimulation themselves.

Nevertheless, some researchers and journalists tend to interpret such shared neural representation between self and others in the domain of empathy as "mirror-like or mirror-systems" (e.g., Wicker et al., 2003). Although this mirror neuron and shared representation analogy is interesting, it neither accounts for the empirical data nor for the complexity of empathy and certainly not for sympathy and compassion as defined above. Strictly speaking, the term "mirror neuron" should be reserved for findings based on single-cell recordings and not be used for those based on neuroimaging data, which do not allow drawing conclusions about single cells as they do not measure the activity of single neurons or neural networks directly (Singer & Lamm, 2009). To our knowledge, until now, no study has provided evidence for mirror-neuron-like cells in somatosensory, insular, or anterior cingulate cortices.

In sum, we suggest that while the mirror neuron system provides an interesting physiological mechanism for motor resonance and may play a role in mimicry and perhaps in some aspects of emotion contagion and recognition, it seems unlikely that such a mechanism can explain emotion recognition, empathy, and social cognition in general (Decety, 2010). Even though activation in mirror-neuron-related brain networks may be observed when participants perform empathy tasks, especially if the tasks also involve some sort of motor action (facial expressions, body movements, etc.), this does not make the operation of mirror neurons a necessary or a sufficient condition for empathy or compassion to arise.

Modulation of Empathy

Whereas the first phase of empathy research in social neuroscience focused on the question of *how* we empathize with others, the second phase focused more on the question of *when* we empathize (de Vignemont & Singer, 2006). What are the modulatory factors influencing empathic brain responses? Previous work in social cognition has shown that empathy can be modulated by how the target person is perceived, including how similar (e.g., Batson et al., 1997, 2005) or likeable (e.g., Kozak, Marsh, & Wegner, 2006) the target person is to the observer, and by the target's group membership (e.g., Yabar, Johnston, Miles, & Peace, 2006). Understanding how such factors impact the ability to perceive and respond with care to the cognitive, affective, and motivational internal states of another is crucial for understanding the conditions under which empathy is expressed (Decety & Batson, 2007).

Accumulating evidence suggests that observed empathic brain responses depend crucially on the contextual appraisal of the situation and the affective link between the empathizer and the "object" of empathy. For instance, Singer and colleagues (2006) demonstrated in an extension of their "empathy-for-pain" paradigm that empathic pain responses were only detected in the AI when participants observed an individual in pain who had played fairly, but not when that individual had played unfairly in a preceding economic game. Instead of engaging in empathy, male participants showed reward-related activation in the nucleus accumbens when seeing dislikable and unfair players receiving painful stimulation. Moreover, the level of reward-related activation was correlated with the level of subjectively reported desire for revenge. These results suggest that the feeling of "schadenfreude" can override the feeling of empathy when male participants are confronted with the punishment of an unfair conspecific.

In a series of studies, Decety and colleagues provided further evidence for such contextual appraisal effects on empathic brain responses to the pain of others (Decety, Echols, & Correll, 2009; Lamm et al., 2007a, 2009). In two fMRI studies, Lamm and colleagues (2007a, 2009) investigated the role of cognitive appraisal and the ability to distinguish between self and other. In the first study, participants saw pictures of tissue biopsies being performed on patients. The biopsies appeared to be painful, but were actually not, as they were performed on anesthetized hands. In a follow-up study, using the same stimuli, participants were told that they would see pain being inflicted on neurological patients who reacted with no pain to surgical procedures but with pain to a soft touch. Thus, both paradigms involved observing a situation which was aversive only for the observer, but neutral for the target. This required participants to disentangle their own unpleasant response to the aversive stimulus from the actual response of the target. In both studies and similar to previous studies using painful needle injections as stimuli, watching biopsies led to signal increases in large parts of the pain matrix, including the AI and the medial and (dorsal) ACC. These empathic pain-related responses were slightly lower, but still present, even if the participant believed that the target did not actually perceive the injection as being painful. These results speak for a bottom-up affective response to a putatively harmful stimulus. On the other hand, this incongruent condition was also associated with enhanced activation in brain networks known to be crucial for self-other distinction (e.g., temporoparietal junction, TPJ) and cognitive control (e.g., right inferior frontal cortex, IFC). Interestingly, in the second study, effective connectivity between the IFC and areas implicated in affective processing was enhanced during the incongruent conditions. Hence, inferring the affective state of someone who perceives differently than we do requires that we overcome pre-reflective affective response tendencies through the involvement of brain networks responsible for the distinction between self and other and for cognitive control.

Similarly, Decety et al. (2009) exposed participants again to the same video clips featuring age-matched individuals experiencing pain who were either a) similar to the participant (healthy), b) stigmatized, but not responsible for their stigmatized condition (infected with AIDS as a result of an infected blood transfusion), or c) stigmatized and responsible for their stigmatized condition (infected with AIDS as a result of intravenous drug use). Results showed that participants were significantly more sensitive to the pain of AIDS-via-transfusion targets as compared to healthy individuals and AIDS-via-drugs targets as evidenced by significantly higher pain and empathy ratings during video evaluation and significantly greater hemodynamic activity in areas associated with pain processing (i.e., AI, aMCC, PAG). In contrast, significantly less activity was observed in the aMCC for AIDS-via-drugs targets as compared to healthy controls. Furthermore, differences in participants' behavior in the healthy versus the AIDS-via-drugs target condition were moderated by the extent to which participants blamed the AIDS-via-drugs targets for their condition. Controlling for both explicit and implicit AIDS biases, the more participants blamed the targets, the less pain they attributed to them as compared to healthy controls (Decety, Echols, & Correll, 2009).

Empathic brain responses have also been found to be modulated by a) the intensity of the stimulation or displayed emotion and b) attention. Saarela and colleagues (2007) found stronger activation in AI and ACC when participants empathized with people in acute as compared to chronic pain and Avenanti and colleagues (2006) showed that empathy-related inhibition of muscle-evoked potentials, following TMS, were only found when participants observed a needle deeply penetrating body parts of a human model, but not if the needle just scratched the surface of the skin. Further, participants showed stronger empathic brain responses in the AI and

ACC when they focused on the intensity of the other's pain as compared to when they were asked to perform a task designed to shift their attention away from the other's pain, for example, count the number of hands (Gu & Hahn, 2007; see also Hein & Singer, 2008).

Expertise has a clear impact on the neural processes involved in empathy. This was demonstrated in a study comparing physicians and non-physicians who were exposed to short video clips depicting body parts being touched by a Q-tip (non-painful stimulus) or pricked by a needle (painful stimulus). While the ACC and AI of control participants were, the same region of physicians' were not activated when they saw body parts being pricked by a needle. Instead, regions of their prefrontal cortex subserving emotion regulation were selectively involved (Cheng et al., 2007).

Finally, attribution of intentionality has also been found to have an effect on the perception of pain in others as demonstrated by a study in which participants were scanned while presented with short dynamic visual stimuli depicting painful situations either accidentally or intentionally caused by another individual (Akitsuki & Decety, 2009).

In sum, empathic brain responses are modulated by a variety of factors ranging from stimulus properties, person characteristics, and appraisal of the situation, to the affective link between empathizer and other.

The Role of Interoceptive Cortex and Insula in Empathy

If shared networks as observed in neuroimaging studies do not reflect an automatic mirror-neuron-like resonance mechanism, what is it then that is encoded or processed in shared activation areas such as the AI or the medial and anterior cingulate cortex during the vicarious observation of pain and disgust?

It has been suggested that insular cortex represents a crucial part of the human viscerosensory and interoceptive cortex (Craig, 2003) and subserves neural representations of internal bodily states such as information about temperature, lust, hunger, bodily arousal states, and information from the gut (Craig, 2002, 2003; Critchley, 2005; Critchley, Wiens, Rotshtein, Ohman, & Dolan, 2004; Damasio, 1994). Based on anatomical observations in nonhuman species, Bud Craig (2002, 2003) developed a detailed anatomical model suggesting that an image of the body's internal state is first mapped to the brain by afferents that provide input to the thalamic

nuclei, sensorimotor cortices, and posterior dorsal insula. The re-mapping of this first-order representation to anterior parts of the insular cortex then allows for the generation of conscious subjective feeling states to arise.

Based on the observation that the very same structures (AI and ACC) that play a crucial role in representing one's own subjective feeling states also seem to be crucial in processing vicarious feelings, Singer and colleagues (2004) suggested that such cortical re-representations in AI of bodily states may have a dual function. First, they may allow us to form subjective representations of our own feelings. These representations not only allow us to understand our own feelings when emotional stimuli are present, but also to predict the bodily effects of anticipated emotional stimuli to our bodies. Second, they may serve as the visceral correlate of a prospective simulation of how something may feel for others. This may then help us to understand the emotional significance of a particular stimulus and its likely consequences. Such an account predicts that impaired access to one's own emotional state will cause empathic deficits. And, indeed, Silani and colleagues were able to provide evidence that individuals with alexithymia—a personality trait associated with difficulty identifying and describing feelings despite basic awareness of bodily sensations and arousal—failed to engage the AI when asked to perceive their emotions. Furthermore, activation in the AI reflected both the degree of alexithymia and deficiencies in trait empathy (Silani et al., 2008).

Furthermore, data from several pain processing and touch studies support the view that more posterior insular regions support modality-specific, primary representations and more anterior regions support secondary representations associated with anticipatory negative affect in self and other. Thus, anticipation of pain has been found to activate more anterior insular regions, whereas the actual experience of pain recruits more posterior insular regions (Ploghaus et al., 1999). Similarly, in pain empathy studies, activity in posterior insular cortices was observed only when participants were experiencing pain themselves (Lamm et al., 2007; Singer et al., 2004, 2006) whereas activity in AI was observed when participants were experiencing pain themselves *and* when vicariously feeling someone else's pain. Whereas such a posterior-anterior organization within the insular cortex seems to apply to pain and touch (e.g., Lovero, Simmons, Aron, & Paulus, 2009), it may not generalize to other domains such as taste where the primary cortex also lies within the AI (e.g., Jabbi et al., 2007).

Singer, Critchley, and Preushhoff (2009) recently proposed a unifying model of insular function that aims to integrate recent findings showing an involvement of the AI in both uncertainty processing and affective learning. According to this model, the insula cortex more generally supports different levels of representations of current and predictive states, allowing for error-based learning of both modality-specific feeling states (e.g., pain, disgust) and of uncertainty information inherent in complex environments. This information is integrated in a general subjective feeling state in the AI, which in turn can be modulated by individual preferences and traits (e.g., risk aversion, anxiety) as well as by contextual appraisal. Such a dominant integrated feeling state that includes current and predictive feeling states and uncertainty information as well as individual preferences is putatively experienced as emotional confidence that serves to regulate bodily homeostasis and motivate and guide social interaction and decision-making behavior in complex and uncertain environments.

Despite recent efforts to clarify the functions of the human insular cortex, a brain area that had been neglected by neuroscience for quite some time, additional empirical work is needed to test existing models and specify the exact nature of representations subserved by the insular cortex. How does the insular cortex differentiate between positive and negative affective states and between different modalities such as pain, disgust, and touch? How does the insula support affective and vicarious learning? How does the brain differentiate between one's own and others' pain?

Empathy Deficits

Many psychiatric disorders are associated with deficits or even a lack of empathy. Notably, psychopathy is a disorder that encapsulates the essence of a lack of empathy. The classification of psychopathy, introduced by Hare (1993), involves both affective-interpersonal (e.g., lack of empathy and guilt) and behavioral components (e.g., criminal activity and poor behavioral control). Empathy deficits in psychopathy has been suggested to come from a reduced ability to feel other people's emotional state, and especially so for sadness and fear (Mealey, 1995). This deficit has been ascribed to a dysfunction in the amygdala and its functional connectivity with the orbitofrontal cortex (Blair, 1995). This view is compatible with the fact that individuals

with this disorder have generally intact executive functions and can successfully complete theory of mind tasks (Blair & Cipolotti, 2000). Therefore, their lack of empathy could be related to disrupted affective processing rather than an inability, for instance, to adopt the perspective of others. In fact, people with antisocial personality disorders are probably good at perceiving others' intentions, while disregarding the emotional content, and thus may take advantage of it. The individual with psychopathy cannot simulate emotions he cannot experience, and must rely exclusively on cognitive inputs to his theory of mind mechanism.

Individuals with autistic spectrum disorder (ASD) display a broad range of social communication deficits, and most scholars agree that a lack of empathy prominently figures amongst them. The underlying cause of the empathy deficit is, however, more controversial. Baron-Cohen and colleagues (1985) suggested that the social impairment in autism arises from a failure of a mentalizing mechanism (a Theory of Mind module). Other authors believe that children with autism have a hard time feeling and expressing emotions, and that this basic deficit prevents them from engaging in social interactions (Hobson, 2002). Rogers (1999) suggested a cascade model of autism in which the lack of certain aspects of interpersonal development at every previous stage disrupts certain developments in the following stage. These authors view early imitation skills, emotion sharing, and Theory of Mind as increasingly complex expressions of the ability to form and coordinate certain representations of self and other. These representations are then used to guide the planning and execution of one's own behavior. Finally, Dawson (1991) proposed that autism involves impairment in attentional functioning for social stimuli (e.g., facial expressions, speech, gestures). She hypothesized that, because social stimuli are complex, variable, and unpredictable, children with autism have difficulty processing and representing them and, therefore, their attention is not naturally drawn to such stimuli. These different views (imitation/emotions sharing vs. executive functions) are not incompatible with our model of empathy, as it remains possible that empathy deficits in autism are related to disruption of either emotion sharing or mental flexibility/self regulation components, or even both.

Burgeoning research efforts suggest that an aberrant mirror neuron system may contribute to motor and social problems experienced in autism spectrum disorder (ASD). Research with humans using transcranial magnetic stimulation (TMS) demonstrates selective changes in the amplitude of the motor-evoked (M1) potentials during action observation (e.g., Fadiga, Fogassi, Pavesi, & Rizzolati, 1995). To build on this finding, TMS was applied over the motor cortex of adults with ASD and matched healthy controls. Compared to the controls, individuals with ASD showed significantly less M1 amplitude change during the observation of transitive, meaningless finger movements (Theoret et al., 2005). In contrast, observation of the finger movements in control subjects selectively modulated the excitability of the motor cortex in areas delivering signals to the muscles concerned with the observed action. The weaker M1 modulation in individuals with ASD suggests, that the less mirror neuron activation in the motor cortex may be partly responsible for a cascade of deficits in social cognition.

Functional MRI experiments are in line with these TMS findings, and indicate abnormal activation of mirror neuron systems during imitation in adults with Asperger syndrome (Nishitani, Avikainen, & Hari, 2004) and reduced functional connectivity in mirror neuron system areas (Villalobos, Mizuno, Dahl, Kemmostsu, & Muller, 2004). In an attempt to examine a potential link between mirror neuron dysfunction and developmental delay of social cognitive skills, one fMRI study found a lack of activation in the inferior frontal gyrus in children with ASD as compared to controls during the observation and imitation of basic facial emotion expressions (Dapretto et al., 2006). However, this finding was recently challenged by Bastiaanen, Thioux, and Keysers (2008) who scanned a group of 17 adults with ASD during the observation of dynamic facial expressions, including disgust. The authors found that ASD participants activate their mirror system not less, but more strongly than controls when observing dynamic facial expressions.

Structural neuroanatomical evidence also implicates aberrations in mirror neuron systems in ASD. One morphometric study reported locally diminished gray matter in adults with high-functioning ASD in areas incorporated in the mirror neuron system compared to controls matched for sex, age, intelligence quotient, and handedness (Hadjikhani, Joseph, Snyder, & Gager-Flushber, 2005). Cortical thinning of the mirror system was correlated with ASD symptom severity (as measured with ADI-R scores), and cortical thinning was also seen in areas engaged in emotion recognition and social cognition. Thus, irregular thinning of cortical areas that

implement mirror neurons and the broader network of cortical areas subserving social cognition may contribute to the emotional deficits characteristic of autism, such as problems engaging in intersubjective transactions and displays of empathic responding. It should be noted however, that in the tables included in the paper, not only mirror neuron cortical areas, but all areas of the brain show a significant reduction of gray matter. Thus, one needs to be cautious with these new findings, as cortical thinning may not be specific to areas where mirror neurons are located. In fact, an earlier study using magnetoecephalography failed to find any differences in motor cortex activation between individuals with ASD and healthy controls while observing action (Avikainen, Kulomaki, & Hari, 1999), a result that is in contradiction with the study by Theoret and colleagues (2005).

Perhaps more convincing evidence of anomalies in the mirror neuron system in ASD derives from EEG studies that examine mu rhythm in sensorimotor areas. Robust evidence suggests that the magnitude of mu rhythm in sensorimotor areas is strongly suppressed during the execution and observation of an action in adults (e.g., Muthukumaraswamy, Johnson, & McNair, 2004) and typically developing children (Lepage & Theoret, 2006). In children and adults with high functioning ASD, however, mu rhythm suppression occurs when individuals observe their own action, however fails to suppress during the observation of other persons' actions (Oberman, Hubbard, McCleery, Altschuler, Ramachandran, & Pineda, 2005), suggesting dysfunction in mirror neuron systems. Moreover, this result did not significantly correlate with age, implicating that this deficit manifests early and shows little improvement with age. Bernier, Dawson, Webb and Murias (2007) extended these results to show that in individuals with high functioning ASD, the degree of mu wave suppression during action observation is associated with behavioral assessments of imitation ability. That is, less mu suppression correlates with poorer imitation abilities, and is most robust for facial imitation skills.

Together, these recent findings, which need to be replicated, seem to suggest that dysfunctions of the mirror neuron system may hamper the normal development of self-other connectedness, creating a cascade of deficient processes that lead to social deficits, including empathy. However, it is worth noting that this account is still debated, and that the results from a recent fMRI study do not support a global failure of the mirror neuron system in children with autism (Hamilton, Brindley, & Frith, 2007; Yang-Teng, Decety, Chia-Yen, Lui, & Cheng, 2010).

Summary and Conclusions

In this chapter, we have reviewed recent neuroscientific efforts to clarify the neural networks underlying our capacity to empathize with other people. We have defined empathy as a vicarious emotional response produced by the emotional state of another individual that occurs without the empathizer losing sight of whose feelings belong to whom. This narrow definition of empathy allows us to distinguish between empathy and related concepts such as cognitive perspective taking, emotional contagion, mimicry, empathic concern, and compassion. We have shown that these are not only conceptual distinctions, but also reflect empirical evidence suggesting that different neural circuitries underlie our ability to share and understand other people's feelings, on the one hand, and our ability to understand action intentions and abstract thoughts and beliefs, on the other hand. Whereas empathy mostly relies on brain areas relevant for interoceptive and affective processing, such as somatosensory, insular, and anterior cingulated cortices, the capacity to mentalize relies on a brain circuitry involving the mPFC, TPJ, STS, and sometimes temporal poles. Finally, evidence from animal and human studies suggests that mimicry and action understanding rely on yet another network, the so-called mirror neuron network. This network—even though very often cited in the context of empathy research—is neither a necessary nor sufficient condition for empathy to arise, but can be a useful route to trigger empathy, especially when we have to decode facial expressions or body movements to infer emotions. Another set of studies mostly focusing on the modulation of empathic brain responses to the suffering of other people identified multiple factors influencing the degree of empathic activation in interoceptive cortex, including the intensity of the displayed emotion, situational context, features of the empathizer and of the target of empathy. These studies also revealed the importance of other capacities, such as cognitive control and emotion regulation, for empathic understanding of others. Especially in situations in which the other is not experiencing the same emotions as oneself, so that a simple projection of one's own affective state onto the other (simple affect sharing) would be misleading.

Although recent research in social neuroscience has contributed substantially to our understanding of the neural underpinnings of empathy and its modulatory factors, this research is still in its beginnings and future research will have to continue to fractionate the complex phenomenon of empathy into its dissociable components, including shared neural affective representations and their relation to cognitive perspective taking, self-awareness, self-other distinction, mental flexibility, and emotion regulation. Such research may also help clarify the link between empathic brain responses and sympathy or compassion, in other words, feeling *as* and feeling *for* the other, as well as their relation to pro- and antisocial behavior.

Furthermore, a combination of genetic and developmental neuroscientific approaches may help clarify the sources of inter-individual differences in empathy. Finally, almost nothing is known about the plasticity of the empathic brain, that is, about the trainability of empathy and compassionate motivation, an issue which could have considerable practical importance in education and society in general.

References

Akitsuki, Y. & Decety, J. (2009). Social context and perceived agency modulate brain activity in the neural circuits underpinning empathy for pain: An event-related fMRI study. *NeuroImage, 47,* 722–734.

Avenanti, A., Bueti, D., Galati, G., & Aglioti, S. M. (2005). Transcranial magnetic stimulation highlights the sensorimotor side of empathy for pain. *Nature Neuroscience, 8,* 955–960.

Avenanti, A., Paluello, I. M., Bufalari, I., & Aglioti, S. M. (2006). Stimulus-driven modulation of motor-evoked potentials during observation of others' pain. *NeuroImage, 32,* 316–324.

Avikainen, S., Kulomaki, T., & Hari, R. (1999). Normal movement reading in Asperger subjects. *NeuroReport, 10,* 3467–3470.

Baron-Cohen, S., Leslie, A. M., & Frith, U. (1985). Does the autistic child have a "theory of mind"? *Cognition, 21,* 37–46.

Bastiaanen, J., Thioux, M., & Keysers, C. (2008, April). *Mirror-neuron system not broken in adults with ASD for viewing emotions of others.* Paper presented at the 15th Annual Cognitive Neuroscience Society Meeting, San Francisco.

Batson, C. D. (2009). These things called empathy: Eight related but distinct phenomena. In J. Decety & W. Ickes (Eds.), *The social neuroscience of empathy* (pp. 3–15). Cambridge, MA: MIT Press.

Batson, C. D., Lishner, D. A., Cook, J., & Sawyer, S. (2005). Similarity and nurturance: Two possible sources of empathy for strangers. *Basic and Applied Social Psychology, 27,* 15–25.

Batson, C. D., Sager, K., Garst, E., Kang, M., Rubchinsky, K., & Dawson, K. (1997). Is empathy-induced helping due to self-other merging? *Journal of Personality and Social Psychology, 73,* 495–509.

Bernier, R., Murias, M., Dawson, G., & Webb, S.J. (2007). EEG mu rhythm and imitation in autism. *Brain and Cognition*, *64*, 228–237.

Blair, J., Mitchell, D. R., & Blair, K. (2005). *The psychopath: Emotion and the brain*. Oxford, UK: Blackwell.

Blair, R. J. (1995). A cognitive developmental approach to mortality: Investigating the psychopath. *Cognition*, *57*, 1–29.

Blair, R. J. (2005). Responding to the emotions of others: Dissociating forms of empathy through the study of typical and psychiatric populations. *Consciousness and Cognition*, *14*, 698–718.

Blair, R. J. & Cipolotti, L. (2000). Impaired social response reversal: A case of "acquired sociopathy." *Brain*, *123*, 1122–1141.

Botvinick, M., Jha, A. P., Bylsma, L. M., Fabian, S. A., Solomon, P. E., & Prkachin, K. M. (2005). Viewing facial expressions of pain engages cortical areas involved in the direct experience of pain. *NeuroImage*, *25*, 312–319.

Bufalari, I., Aprile, T., Avenanti, A., Di, R. F., & Aglioti, S. M. (2007). Empathy for pain and touch in the human somatosensory cortex. *Cerebral Cortex*, *17*, 2553–2561.

Cacioppo, J. T., Berntson, G. G., Larsen, J. T., Poehlmann, K. M., & Ito, T. A. (2000). The psychophysiology of emotion. In R. Lewis & J. M. Haviland-Jones (Eds.), *The handbook of emotion* (2nd ed., pp. 173–191). New York: Guilford Press.

Calder, A. J., Keane, J., Cole, J., Campbell, R., & Young, A. W. (2000). Facial expression recognition by people with Möbius syndrome. *Cognitive Neuropsychology*, *17*, 73–87.

Calder, A. J., Lawrence, A. D., Keane, J., Scott, S. K., Owen, A. M., Christoffels, I., et al. (2002). Reading the mind from eye gaze. *Neuropsychologia*, *40*, 1129–1138.

Carr, L., Iacoboni, M., Dubeau, M. C., Mazziotta, J. C., & Lenzi, G. L. (2003). Neural mechanisms of empathy in humans: A relay from neural systems for imitation to limbic areas. *Proceedings of National Academy of Sciences, USA*, *100*, 5497–5502.

Chakrabarti, B., Bullmore, E., & Baron-Cohen, S. (2006). Empathizing with basic emotions: Common and discrete neural substrates. *Social Neuroscience*, *1*, 364–384.

Cheng, Y., Lee, P.-L., Yang, C.-Y., Lin, C.-P., Hung, D., & Decety, J. (2008). Gender differences in the mu rhythm of the human mirror-neuron system. *PLoS ONE*, *3*, e2113. doi:10.1371/journal.pone.0002113.

Cheng, Y., Lin, C., Liu, H. L., Hsu, Y., Lim, K., Hung, D., et al. (2007). Expertise modulates the perception of pain in others. *Current Biology*, *17*, 1708–1713.

Cochin, S., Barthelemy, C., Lejeune, B., Roux, S., & Martineau, J. (1998). Perception of motion and qEEG activity in human adults. *Electroencephalography and Clinical Neurophysiology*, *107*, 287–295.

Craig, A. D. (2002). How do you feel? Interoception: The sense of the physiological condition of the body. *Nature Reviews Neuroscience*, *3*, 655–666.

Craig, A. D. (2003). Interoception: The sense of the physiological condition of the body. *Current Opinion in Neurobiology*, *13*, 500–505.

Critchley, H. D. (2005). Neural mechanisms of autonomic, affective, and cognitive integration. *The Journal of Comparative Neurology*, *493*, 154–166.

Critchley, H. D., Wiens, S., Rotshtein, P., Öhman, A., & Dolan, R. J. (2004). Neural systems supporting interoceptive awareness. *Nature Neuroscience*, *7*, 189–195.

Damasio, A. (1994). Descartes' error and the future of human life. *Scientific American*, *271*, 144.

Danziger, N., Faillenot, I., & Peyron, R. (2009). Can we share a pain we never felt? Neural correlates of empathy in patients with congenital insensitivity to pain. *Neuron*, *61*, 203–212.

Dapretto, M., Davies, M. S., Pfeifer, J. H., Scott, A. A., Sigman, M., Bookheimer, S. Y., et al. (2006). Understanding emotions in others: Mirror neuron dysfunction in children with autism spectrum disorders. *Nature Neuroscience*, *9*, 28–31.

Davis, M. H. (1994). *Empathy*. Madison, WI: Brown & Benchmark.

Dawson, G. A. (1991). A psychobiological perspective on the early socioemotional development of children with autism. In D. Cicchetti & S. L. Toth (Eds.), *Rochester symposium on developmental psychology* (Vol. 3, pp. 207–234). Hillsdale, NJ: Erlbaum.

de Vignemont, F. & Singer, T. (2006). The empathic brain: How, when and why? *Trends in Cognitive Sciences*, *10*, 435–441.

Decety, J. (2010). To what extent is the experience of empathy mediated by shared neural circuits? *Emotion Review*, *2*, 204–207.

Decety, J. & Batson, C. D. (2007). Social neuroscience approaches to interpersonal sensitivity. *Social Neuroscience*, *2*, 151–157.

Decety, J., Echols, S. C., & Correll, J. (2009). The blame game: The effect of responsibility and social stigma on empathy for pain. *Journal of Cognitive Neuroscience*, *22*, 985–997.

Decety, J. & Grèzes, J. (2006). The power of simulation: Imagining one's own and other's behavior. *Brain Research*, *1079*, 4–14.

Decety, J. & Jackson, P. L. (2004). The functional architecture of human empathy. *Behavioral and Cognitive Neuroscience Reviews*, *3*, 71–100.

Decety, J. & Lamm, C. (2009). Empathy versus personal distress: Recent evidence from social neuroscience. In J. Decety & W. Ickes (Eds.), *The social neuroscience of empathy* (pp. 199–213). Cambridge, MA: MIT Press.

Decety, J. & Meyer, M. (2008). From emotion resonance to empathic understanding: A social developmental neuroscience account. *Development and Psychopathology*, *20*, 1053–1080.

Decety, J. & Sommerville, J. A. (2003). Shared representations between self and others: A social cognitive neuroscience view. *Trends in Cognitive Sciences*, *7*, 527–533.

Dinstein, H., Hasson, U., Rubin, N., & Heeger, D. J. (2007). Brain areas selective for both observed and executed movements. *Journal of Neurophysiology*, *98*, 1415–1427.

Eisenberg, N. (2000). Emotion, regulation, and moral development. *Annual Review in Psychology*, *51*, 665–697.

Eisenberg, N. (2007). Empathy-related responding and prosocial behaviour. *Novartis Foundation Symposium*, *278*, 71–80.

Etzel, J. A., Gazzola, V., & Keysers, C. (2008). Testing simulation theory with cross-modal multivariate classification of fMRI data. *PLoS One*, *3*, e3690. doi:10.1371/journal.pone.0003690.

Fadiga, L., Craighero, L., & Olivier, E. (2005). Human motor cortex excitability during the perception of others' action. *Current Opinion in Neurobiology*, *15*, 213–218.

Fadiga, L., Fogassi, L., Pavesi, G., & Rizzolatti, G. (1995). Motor facilitation during action observation: A magnetic stimulation study. *Journal of Neurophysiology*, *73*, 2608–2611.

Fogassi, L., Ferrari, P. F., Gesierich, B., Rozzi, S., Chersi, F., & Rizzolatti, G. (2005). Parietal lobe: From action organization to intention understanding. *Science, 308*, 662–667.

Frith, U. & Frith, C. D. (2003). Development and neurophysiology of mentalizing. *Philosophical Transactions of the Royal Society, London B, 358*, 459–473.

Gallese, V., Fadiga, L., Fogassi, L., & Rizzolatti, G. (1996). Action recognition in the premotor cortex. *Brain, 119*, 593–609.

Gazzola, V., Aziz-Zadeh, L., & Keysers, C. (2006). Empathy and the somatotopic auditory mirror system in humans. *Current Biology, 16*, 1824–1829.

Gazzola, V., Rizzolatti, G., Wicker, B., & Keysers, C. (2007a). The anthropomorphic brain: The mirror neuron system responds to human and robotic actions. *NeuroImage, 35*, 1674–1684.

Gazzola, V., van der Worp, H., Mulder, T., Wicker, B., Rizzolatti, G., & Keysers, C. (2007b). Aplasics born without hands mirror the goal of hand actions with their feet. *Current Biology, 17*, 1235–1240.

Goldman, A. I. (2006). *Simulating minds: The philosophy, psychology, and neuroscience of mindreading.* Oxford: Oxford University Press.

Grèzes, J. & Decety, J. (2001). Functional anatomy of execution, mental simulation, observation, and verb generation of actions: A meta-analysis. *Human Brain Mapping, 12*, 1–19.

Gu, X. & Han, S. (2007). Attention and reality constraints on the neural processes of empathy for pain. *NeuroImage, 36*, 256–267.

Hadjikhani, N., Joseph, R., Snyder, J., & Gager-Flushberg, H. (2005). Anatomical differences in the mirror neuron system and social cognition network in autism. *Cerebral Cortex, 10*, 1093.

Hamilton, A. F., Brindley, R. M., & Frith, U. (2007). Imitation and action understanding in autistic spectrum disorders: How valid is the hypothesis of a deficit in the mirror neuron system? *Neuropsychologia, 45*, 1859–1868.

Hare, R. D. (1993). *Without conscience: The disturbing world of the psychopaths among us.* New York: Simon and Schuster.

Hatfield, E., Cacioppo, J., & Rapson, R. (1994). *Emotional contagion.* New York: Cambridge University Press.

Hein, G. & Singer, T. (2008). I feel how you feel but not always: The empathic brain and its modulation. *Current Opinion in Neurobiology, 18*, 153–158.

Hess, U. & Blairy, S. (2001). Facial mimicry and emotional contagion to dynamic emotional facial expressions and their influence on decoding accuracy. *International Journal of Psychophysiology, 40*, 129–141.

Hickok, G. (2009). Eight problems for the mirror neuron theory of action understanding in monkeys and humans. *Journal of Cognitive Neuroscience, 21*, 1229–1243.

Hobson, R. P. (2002). *The cradle of thought.* London: Macmillan.

Hoffman, M. L. (1984). Interaction of affect and cognition in empathy. In C. Izard, J. Kagan, & R. Zajonc (Eds.), *Emotions, cognition, and behavior* (pp. 103–131). New York: Cambridge University Press.

Hoffman, M. L. (2000). *Empathy and moral development: Implications for caring and justice.* Cambridge, MA: Cambridge University Press.

Hommel, B., Müsseler, J., Aschersleben, G., & Prinz, W. (2001). The theory of event coding (TEC): A framework for perception and action planning. *Behavioral and Brain Sciences, 24*, 849–878.

Hynes, C. A., Baird, A. A., & Grafton, S. T. (2006). Differential role of the orbital frontal lobe in emotional versus cognitive perspective-taking. *Neuropsychologia, 44*, 374–383.

Jabbi, M. & Keysers, C. (2008). Inferior frontal gyrus activity triggers anterior insula response to emotional facial expressions. *Emotion, 8*, 775–780.

Jabbi, M., Swart, M., & Keysers, C. (2007). Empathy for positive and negative emotions in the gustatory cortex. *NeuroImage, 34*, 1744–1753.

Jackson, P. L., Brunet, E., Meltzoff, A. N., & Decety, J. (2006). Empathy examined through the neural mechanisms involved in imagining how I feel versus how you feel pain. *Neuropsychologia, 44*, 752–761.

Jackson, P. L., Meltzoff, A. N., & Decety, J. (2005). How do we perceive the pain of others? A window into the neural processes involved in empathy. *NeuroImage, 24*, 771–779.

Jackson, P. L., Rainville, P., & Decety, J. (2006). To what extent do we share the pain of others? Insight from the neural bases of pain empathy. *Pain, 125*, 5–9.

Keillor, J. M., Barrett, A. M., Crucian, G. P., Kortenkamp, S., & Heilman, K. M. (2002). Emotional experience and perception in the absence of facial feedback. *Journal of the International Neuropsychological Society, 8*, 130–135.

Keysers, C., Wicker, B., Gazzola, V., Anton, J. L., Fogassi, L., & Gallese, V. (2004). A touching sight: SII/PV activation during the observation and experience of touch. *Neuron, 42*, 335–346.

Kozak, M., Marsh, A., & Wegner, W. (2006). What do I think you're doing? Action identification and mind attribution. *Journal of Personality and Social Psychology, 90*, 543–555.

Lamm, C., Batson, C. D., & Decety, J. (2007). The neural substrate of human empathy: Effects of perspective-taking and cognitive appraisal. *Journal of Cognitive Neuroscience, 19*, 42–58.

Lamm, C. & Decety, J. (2008). Is the extrastriate body area (EBA) sensitive to the perception of pain in others? *Cerebral Cortex, 18*, 2369–2373.

Lamm, C., Meltzoff, A. N., & Decety, J. (2010). How do we empathize with someone who is not like us? A functional magnetic resonance imaging study. *Journal of Cognitive Neuroscience.* doi:10.1162/jocn.2009.21186.

Lamm, C., Nusbaum, H. C., Meltzoff, A. N., & Decety, J. (2007a). What are you feeling? Using functional magnetic resonance imaging to assess the modulation of sensory and affective responses during empathy for pain. *PLoS ONE, 2*, e1292.

Lamm, C., Porges, E. C., Cacioppo, J. T., & Decety, J. (2008). Perspective taking is associated with specific facial responses during empathy for pain. *Brain Research, 1227*, 153–161.

Lepage, J.-F., & Théoret, H. (2006). EEG evidence for the presence of an action observation–execution matching system in children. *European Journal of Neuroscience, 23*, 2505–2510.

Leslie, K. R., Johnson-Frey, S. H., & Grafton, S. T. (2004). Functional imaging of face and hand imitation: Towards a motor theory of empathy. *NeuroImage, 21*, 601–607.

Lovero, K. L., Simmons, A. N., Aron, J. L., & Paulus, M. P. (2009). Anterior insular cortex anticipates impending stimulus significance. *NeuroImage, 45*, 976–983.

Mealey, L. (1995). The sociobiology of sociopathy: An integrated evolutionary model. *Behavioral and Brain Sciences, 18*, 523–599.

Moriguchi, Y., Decety, J., Ohnishi, T., Maeda, M., Mori, T., Nemoto, K., et al. (2007). Empathy and judging others' pain: An fMRI study of alexithymia. *Cerebral Cortex, 17,* 2223–2234.

Morrison, I. & Downing, P. E. (2007). Organization of felt and seen pain responses in anterior cingulate cortex. *NeuroImage, 37,* 642–651.

Morrison, I., Lloyd, D., di Pellegrino, G., & Roberts, N. (2004). Vicarious responses to pain in anterior cingulate cortex: Is empathy a multisensory issue? *Cognitive, affective & behavioral neuroscience, 4,* 270–278.

Morrison, I., Peelen, M. V., & Downing, P. E. (2007). The sight of others' pain modulates motor processing in human cingulate cortex. *Cerebral Cortex, 17,* 2214–2222.

Muthukumaraswamy, S.D., Johnson, B.W., & McNair, N.A. (2004). Mu rhythm modulation during observation of a goal-directed grasp. *Cognitive Brain Research, 19,* 195–201.

Murphy, F. C., Nimmo-Smith, I., & Lawrence, A. D. (2003). Functional neuroanatomy of emotions: A meta-analysis. *Cognitive, Affective, & Behavioral Neuroscience, 3,* 207–233.

Nishitani, N., Avikainen, S., & Hari, R. (2004). Abnormal imitation-related cortical activation sequences in Asperger's syndrome. *Annals of Neurology, 55,* 558–562.

Oberman, L. M., Hubbard, E. M., McCleery, J. P., Altschuler, E. L., Ramachandran, V. S., & Pineda, J. A. (2005). EEG evidence for mirror neuron dysfunction in autism spectrum disorders. *Cognitive Brain Research, 24,* 190–198.

Phan, K. L., Wager, T., Taylor, S. F., & Liberzon, I. (2002). Functional neuroanatomy of emotion: A meta-analysis of emotion activation studies in PET and fMRI. *NeuroImage, 16,* 331–348.

Pineda, J. A. (2005). The functional significance of mu rhythms: Translating seeing and hearing into doing. *Brain Research Review, 50,* 57–68.

Ploghaus, A., Tracey, I., Gati, J. S., Clare, S., Menon, R. S., Matthews, P. M., et al. (1999). Dissociating pain from its anticipation in the human brain. *Science, 284,* 1979–1981.

Preston, S. D. & de Waal, F. B. M. (2002). Empathy: Its ultimate and proximate bases. *Behavioral and Brain Sciences, 25,* 1–72.

Prinz, W. (1987). Ideo-motor action. In H. Heuer & A. F. Sanders (Eds.), *Perspectives on perception and action* (pp. 47–76). Hillsdale, NJ: Erlbaum.

Rizzolatti, G. & Craighero, L. (2004). The mirror-neuron system. *Annual Review of Neuroscience, 27,* 169–192.

Rogers, S. J. (1999). An examination of the imitation deficit in autism. In J. Nadel & G. Butterworth (Eds.), *Imitation in infancy* (pp. 254–283). Cambridge, MA: Cambridge University Press.

Saarela, M. V., Hlushchuk, Y., Williams, A. C., Schurmann, M., Kalso, E., & Hari, R. (2007). The compassionate brain: Humans detect intensity of pain from another's face. *Cerebral Cortex, 17,* 230–237.

Silani, G., Bird, G., Brindley, R., Singer, T., Frith, C., & Frith, U. (2008). Levels of emotional awareness and autism: An fMRI study. *Social Neuroscience, 3,* 97–112.

Singer, T. (2006). The neuronal basis and ontogeny of empathy and mind reading: Review of literature and implications for future research. *Neuroscience and Biobehavioral Reviews, 30,* 855–863.

Singer, T., Critchley, H., & Preuschoff, K. (2009). A common role of insula in feelings, empathy and uncertainty. *Trends in Cognitive Sciences, 13,* 334–340.

Singer, T. & Lamm, C. (2009). The social neuroscience of empathy. *The Year in Cognitive Neuroscience 2009: Annals of the New York Academy of Sciences, 1156,* 81–96.

Singer, T., Seymour, B., O'Doherty, J., Kaube, H., Dolan, R. J., & Frith, C. D. (2004). Empathy for pain involves the affective but not sensory components of pain. *Science, 303,* 1157–1162.

Singer, T., Seymour, B., O'Doherty, J. P., Stephan, K. E., Dolan, R. J., & Frith, C. D. (2006). Empathic neural responses are modulated by the perceived fairness of others. *Nature, 439,* 466–469.

Singer, T. & Steinbeis, N. (2009). Differential roles of fairness- and compassion-based motivations for cooperation, defection and punishment. *Annals of the New York Academy of Sciences, 1167,* 41–50.

Sonnby-Borgstrom, M., Jonsson, P., & Svensson, O. (2003). Emotional empathy as related to mimicry reactions at different levels of information processing. *Journal of Nonverbal Behavior, 27,* 3–23.

Theoret, H., Halligan, E., Kobayashi, M., Fregni, F., Tager-Flusber, H., & Pascual-Leone, A. (2005). Impaired motor facilitation during action observation in individuals with autism spectrum disorder. *Current Biology, 15,* 84–85.

Tkach, D., Reimer, J., & Hatsopoulos, N. G. (2007). Congruent activity during action and action observation in motor cortex. *Journal of Neuroscience, 27,* 13241–13250.

Turella, L., Pierno, A. C., Tubaldi, F., & Castiello, U. (2009). Mirror neurons in humans: Consisting or confounding evidence? *Brain and Language, 108,* 10–20.

Valeriani, M., Betti, V., Le Pera, D., De Armas, L., Miliucci, R., Restuccia, D., et al. (2008). Seeing the pain of others while being in pain: A laser-evoked potentials study. *NeuroImage, 40,* 1419–1428.

Van der Gaag, C., Minderaa, R. B., & Keysers, C. (2007). Facial expressions: What the mirror neuron system can and cannot tell us. *Social Neuroscience, 2,* 179–222.

Villalobos, M. E., Mizuno, A., Dahl, B. C., Kemmotsu, N., & Muller, R. A. (2004). Reduced functional connectivity between V1 and inferior frontal cortex associated with visuomotor performance in autism. *NeuroImage, 25,* 916–925.

Völlm, B. A., Taylor, A. N., Richardson, P., Corcoran, R., Stirling, J., McKie, S. et al. (2006). Neuronal correlates of theory of mind and empathy: A functional magnetic resonance imaging study in a nonverbal task. *NeuroImage, 29,* 90–98.

Wicker, B., Keysers, C., Plailly, J., Royet, J. P., Gallese, V., & Rizzolatti, G. (2003). Both of us disgusted in my insula: The common neural basis of seeing and feeling disgust. *Neuron, 40,* 655–664.

Wispé, L. (1986). The distinction between sympathy and empathy: To call forth a concept, a word is needed. *Journal of Personality and Social Psychology, 50,* 314–321.

Yabar, Y., Johnston, L., Miles, L., & Peace, V. (2006). Implicit behavioral mimicry: Investigating the impact of group membership. *Journal of Nonverbal Behavior, 30,* 97–113.

Yang-Teng, F., Decety, J., Chia-Yen, Y., Lui, J. L., & Cheng, Y. (2010). Unbroken mirror neurons in autism spectrum disorders: An EEG study. *Journal of Child Psychology and Psychiatry, 51,* 981–988.

Altruism

Stephanie D. Preston *and* Frans B. M. de Waal

"Empathy may be uniquely well suited for bridging the gap between egoism and altruism, since it has the property of transforming another person's misfortune into one's own feeling of distress."

— (Hoffman, 1981, p. 133)

Abstract

This chapter reviews the ultimate and proximate levels of analysis on altruism in humans, hoping to create an overarching framework that places each within a larger context that can stimulate human research informed by extensive empirical research in animals. The available neuroscientific evidence will be reviewed at the end, demonstrating consistently that decisions to help are mediated through overlapping decision and reward circuits that integrate emotional and contextual information into a unified somatic state that guides decisions to help. The chapter first defines the important terms, reviews in brief the most common and widely used biological models of altruism, and then provides evidence for these models. After this, the proximate mechanism will be explicated, largely through indirect evidence regarding the motivational and neural circuits thought to underlie decisions to help. The chapter ends with recommendations for future research to provide more direct evidence for the proximate mechanism, using more ecological tasks that elicit altruistic tendencies while being amenable to concurrent recording with neuroscientific tools.

Keywords: altruism, empathy, reciprocity, consolation, prosocial behavior, sympathy, cooperation

Introduction

There has been persistent and intense debate about the nature and even existence of altruism throughout the history of formal academic discourse. For the past half-century, a theoretical tug of war has existed between those who take an ultimate perspective (i.e., focused on function and evolution) and those who view altruism from a proximate perspective (i.e., focused on motivation and intention). The first school focuses on why a behavior evolved over thousands of generations, which depends on its fitness consequences (Dugatkin & Mesterton-Gibbons, 1996;

Koenig, 1988; Trivers, 1971; Wilson, 1997). As such, they have studied the adaptive significance of individuals helping other individuals and assume that all behaviors evolved to serve the performer's long-term genetic interests, not worrying about whether the behaviors are motivationally altruistic. Even on occasions when personal, genetic interests are not served, biologists construe the behavior as the evolutionary product of self-interest, rendering its performance a "big mistake" or the product of genetic "misfiring." The second school focuses on the immediate situation that triggers behavior, and the role of learning, physiology, and neural processes—typically the domain of psychologists. As such, they have studied emotional-motivation states that underlie acts of helping, situational and trait factors that mediate the response, and the development of prosocial tendencies (Batson, 1998; Eisenberg & Strayer, 1987; Hoffman, 1981; Zahn-Waxler & Radke-Yarrow, 1982). Within this school, a large body of research has examined whether humans are truly capable of altruism, focusing their efforts on the plight of the other in the absence of personal gain or a perception of the self in the other (e.g., Batson et al., 1989; Cialdini, Brown, Lewis, Luce, & Neuberg, 1997).

The biological and psychological literatures appear to study the same topic from conflicting points of view. In point of fact, there is virtually no formal discourse between these two literatures; they represent different interpretations of the term "altruism," and they investigate different types of problems. But because they divide along proximate and ultimate levels of analysis, we view them as largely complementary. They can and should be used to inform one another (Mayr, 1961; Tinbergen, 1963). Indeed, the empirical evidence points to a continuum between nonhuman and human acts of altruism, with similar findings in each. For example, across mammals, acts of altruistic giving are directed most often to relatives, friends, and helpless others in need, particularly in response to a salient cue of need and in the context of a positive social bond. To demonstrate this continuity across species, consider the following examples:

> A juvenile vampire bat, not yet experienced at foraging, is starving and without help will not survive until the next day. The juvenile approaches a successful adult forager who is familiar to the juvenile through a social bond with his mother. The juvenile grooms the unrelated adult on the stomach and licks her face. In turn, she regurgitates a meal of blood for the young individual in need, enough for it to survive until the next day (Wilkinson, 1990).

> Rhesus monkeys trained to pull chains for differential rewards discover that pulling the more rewarding chain causes another monkey to be shocked. After witnessing this shock, two-thirds of the subjects prefer the nonshock chain, receiving half as many rewards. Of the remaining third, one stops pulling the chains altogether for 5 days and another for 12 days, starving themselves to avoid shocking another monkey (Masserman, Wechkin, & Terris, 1964).

> A 3-year old boy, walking along the edge of the gorilla enclosure at the Brookfied Zoo, falls 18 feet onto the concrete enclosure floor. Binti Jua, a female gorilla caring for her baby, picks up the unconscious boy in her arms and rocks him as she carries him to and places him next to an access door where he is retrieved by zookeepers and paramedics (BBC h2g2 contributors, December 30, 2005).

> Michael Keenan is celebrating Christmas Eve with a friend at a San Francisco yacht club when he witnesses a car plunge into the Bay. He grabs a wrench, dives into the cold water, breaks the back window and pulls one woman to safety. Six years later, he dies after returning to a burning building to save a dog for whom he was pet sitting (Allday, 2007).

The altruism literature holds many such striking similarities across cases, from widely varying taxa, looking at both anecdotal and experimental evidence. For obvious reasons, there exists hardly any systematic research on costly altruism in both humans and other animals but, increasingly, studies address and report striking examples of low-cost altruism. Prominent similarities include the role of visible distress or need, a social bond, favors exchanged for other favors, and a requirement that the giver understand the appropriate response to the other's state or situation. Thus, although little work has directly investigated the proximate mechanisms of altruism in humans, cross-species similarities offer a window into the mechanism.

This volume is dedicated to the social neurosciences, and thus deals largely with proximate mechanisms; however, the neuroscientific literature on altruism per se in humans is limited (excluding studies of empathy, covered in other chapters in this volume). As such, this chapter will review the ultimate and proximate levels of analysis equally, hoping to create an overarching framework that places each within a larger context that can spurn human research that is informed by extensive empirical research in animals. The available neuroscientific evidence will be reviewed at the end, demonstrating consistently that decisions to help are mediated through overlapping decision and reward circuits that integrate emotional and contextual information into a unified somatic state that guides decisions to help.

We first define the important terms, review in brief the most common and widely-used biological models of altruism and then provide evidence for these models. After this, the proximate mechanism will be explicated, largely through indirect evidence regarding the motivational and neural circuits thought to underlie decisions to help. We will end with recommendations for future research to provide more direct evidence for the proximate mechanism, using more ecological tasks that elicit altruistic tendencies while being amenable to concurrent recording with neuroscientific tools.

Terminology

Some have claimed that humans are the only truly altruistic species (e.g., Dawkins, 1976/2006; Fehr & Fischbacher, 2003; Kagan, 2000; Silk et al., 2005), while on the other hand, the vast majority of empirical work on altruism examines the behavior of animals, particularly nonmammals such as eusocial insects and birds, but also mammals (reviewed by Dugatkin, 1997; Gadagkar, 1997). Underlying this paradox is a differential focus on the level of analysis. These perspectives can be united by separating the term altruism into three overlapping types (cf. Sober & Wilson, 1998).

Evolutionary altruism makes no assumptions about motivations or intentions, and considers only effects; it refers to behavior that benefits the recipient at a cost to the actor. This kind of altruism is widespread, including honeybee attacks of intruders to the hive and alarm calls by birds and ground squirrels that alert conspecifics to danger. The vast majority of animal research on altruism refers to this level of analysis, which focuses on the *function* of behavior. These studies are aimed at answering the question: "How did this behavior evolve, assuming that evolution favors behavior that benefits the individual and its close kin, promoting replication of the genes responsible for the behavior?"

On the other hand, *psychological altruism* is a reaction to the signals and situation of another individual and involves an attempt to alleviate the other's negative state. It is motivated by other-directed emotions, such as nurturance or empathy, without necessarily requiring a full awareness of the effect on the other. This kind of altruism is common in mammalian species, such as monkeys who cease to pull food chains to avoid shocking a conspecific (Masserman et al., 1964), and chimpanzees who approach and console a distressed friend with an embrace (de Waal & Aureli, 1996). Most of the human work on empathy and altruism is aimed at this middle level of analysis, which focuses on the *motivation* or *causation* of the act of giving. These studies typically aim to answer the question: "What is the psychological state of an individual that reaches out to help? Are they stressed and annoyed,

seeking simply to terminate the other's display or do they truly feel compassion and sympathy for the other?" Thus, when one asks if an act is either "truly altruistic" or "selfish" it is the motivation that is at issue. Those who study evolutionary altruism do not need to know what is in the mind of the giver; they simply want to demonstrate that the behavior has potential benefits to the giver's reproductive success.

One kind of psychological altruism that goes beyond other-directed motivation is *intentional altruism*. This is a rare form that rests on an appreciation of how one's behavior benefits the other and requires knowledge of one's behavioral impact upon others. Intentional altruism is tailored to the other's specific situation, such as when dolphins save companions by biting through harpoon lines or hauling them out of nets in which they got entangled (Caldwell & Caldwell, 1966). Such so-called "targeted helping" requires perspective-taking, which may be limited to a few large-brained animals (de Waal, 2008). Most human research assumes intentional altruism, but rarely demonstrates this level, having simply measured whether helping occurred or the extent of helping, not the type or the degree to which it is tailored to the other's situation.

With a framework that separates altruism into its component levels of analysis, we assume that altruism evolved because acts of helping, on average and in the long run, return benefits to the giver or its close relatives. Therefore, we do not require that an act has no possible benefits to the self in order to be construed as altruism. We thus define altruism as *any instance where one individual helps another, in the absence of any clear, immediate benefit to the self, even though such behavior may ultimately be to the giver's evolutionary advantage.*

Empathy. In human research, empathy and altruism overlap considerably in their usage and conceptualization. This makes sense, given a multi-level model where the observer's resonating state motivates them to give. For example, the most extensive work investigating empathy and altruism in humans proposes that we are indeed capable of true altruism, because witnessing the distress of a relatable target elicits an emotional state called "empathic concern" (akin to sympathetic, softhearted compassion for the other), which is focused on the other and predisposes helping (Batson, 1986; Batson & Coke, 1981).

The definition of empathy is itself a topic of debate that has been covered in other treatments

(Preston & de Waal, 2002; Wispé, 1986) and will be addressed elsewhere in this volume. According to most researchers, *empathy* (sometimes called "*emotional empathy*") occurs when the emotional state of the observer results from perceiving the state of the object, and generates a state in the subject more applicable to the object's situation than the subject's own prior state or situation (cf. Hoffman, 2000). More cognitive forms of empathy, where the subject actively imagines him or herself in the position of the other, is usually referred to as *cognitive empathy* or *perspective taking*, while feeling sorry for the subject and wanting to alleviate their distress is usually referred to as *sympathy*. People disagree as to whether empathy or sympathy can exist without a concurrent desire to help the other. In this chapter, we assume that empathy and sympathy are emotional and motivational states that predispose helping, but reserve the terms *altruism* or *prosocial behavior* to refer specifically to acts of helping.

Biological Models of Altruism

According to *kin selection theory* one helps another in accordance with shared genetic relatedness; that is, by helping an individual who is related to you, you in turn increase the success of your own genes insofar as they are represented in the other, also known as *inclusive fitness* (Hamilton, 1964). This theory predicts that helping scales with the degree of relatedness, with more risky and costly aid being administered to closer relatives.

According to *reciprocal altruism theory* (Trivers, 1971), helping even non-kin is adaptive if it results in a future reciprocation of help by the original recipient. Reciprocal altruism predicts, in distinction to kin selection, that help will be given even to unrelated individuals who are likely to return the favor in the future, such as close friends, group members, and trusted individuals. Using game-theoretic models, reciprocal benefit has been demonstrated to be an evolutionary stable strategy (ESS; Maynard Smith, 1964) even in relatively asocial environments (Axelrod, 1984).

Group selection takes direct advantage of the natural division of social species into separate populations and colonies, postulating that it is adaptive to help individuals from one's own population, because the success of group members raises the success of the entire group relative to other groups, conferring genetic success to all members (Darwin, 1871/1982; Wilson, 1975, 1997; Wilson & Sober, 1994; Wilson, 2005). Most biologists, however, regard group selection as a variant of kin selection that

only applies to genetically isolated populations, which is a rare condition in our close relatives, the primates (Lehmann, Keller, West, & Roze, 2007).

Origins of Altruism

Emotional states such as empathy and sympathy may have evolved because of the selection pressure to evolve rapid emotional connectedness in the context of parental care, long before our species appeared (Eibl-Eibesfeldt, 1971/1974; MacLean, 1985). During mammalian evolution, females alert to and affected by their offspring's needs likely out-reproduced those who remained indifferent. Signaling their state through smiling and crying, human infants urge their caregiver to pay attention and come into action (Acebo & Thoman, 1995; Bowlby, 1958). Essentially the same mechanisms operate in all mammals. Having descended from a long line of mothers who nursed, fed, cleaned, carried, comforted, and defended their young, we should not be surprised by gender differences in human empathy, which appear well before socialization (Hoffman, 1978). The same sex difference is found in the second year of life, with girls showing more concern for others than boys (Zahn-Waxler, Radke-Yarrow, Wagner, & Chapman, 1992). The literature on adult gender differences is more equivocal, but women are better readers of subtle affective cues than men (Hall, 1978) and report stronger empathic reactions (Eisenberg & Fabes, 1998). Moreover, a recent neuroimaging study found that females were more cooperative than males, associated with greater grey matter volume in multiple regions involved in social cognition including posterior inferior frontal and left anterior medial prefrontal cortices (Yamasue et al., 2008).

The complexity and variety of needs a mammalian mother must accommodate would make a genetically encapsulated, reflex-like system for caring difficult. Conversely, a system where mothers are directly affected by offspring distress, and are subsequently motivated to help, is adaptive and can be built upon pre-existing perception-action mechanisms in the nervous system. Thus, infants and offspring in need cry, whine, and scream, which in turn creates empathic distress or sympathy in the mother, who becomes motivated to both terminate the distress and provide the necessary care to soothe the offspring. While some aspects of this model are specific to a "perception-action model" (PAM) of empathy (Preston & de Waal, 2002), most of the primary elements are shared across models. For example, mirror-neuron theories of empathy also emphasize the fact that the nervous system is designed to automatically activate the other's state in the perceiver (Gallese, 2001) and developmental theories of attachment, bonding, and social behavior (e.g., Sroufe, 1988; Ungerer, 1990; Zahn-Waxler, Radke-Yarrow, & King, 1979) as well as biological theories of altruism (e.g., de Waal, 2008; Eibl-Eibesfeldt, 1971/1974; Hirata, 2009) emphasize the importance of the mother-offspring bond in developing compassionate, prosocial behavior. Thus, models of empathy and altruism generally agree that helping is motivated by positive, other-regarding emotional states that evolved in the context of the mother-offspring bond (for an extensive treatment see Hrdy, 2009).

Once the empathic capacity evolved, it could of course be applied outside of the parental-care context and play a role in the wider network of social relationships typical of group-living animals. Here too, caring responses have high survival value. For example, primates often lick and clean each other's wounds. This form of allogrooming is so critical for healing that adult male macaques often temporarily return to their native group to receive the service (Dittus & Ratnayeke, 1989). Empathy and altruism are not necessarily bound by the original context in which they evolved, however, because the tendency to help has gained "motivational autonomy" in that one can experience empathy and want to help in cases far removed from the original context, independent from the ultimate goal of increasing fitness (de Waal, 2008).

Animal Evidence for Altruism

Altruistic behavior is found across the animal kingdom, including insects, fish, birds, and mammals. Most research has been directed at investigating the extent to which kin selection and/or reciprocal altruism can explain the existence of altruistic or cooperative behavior. The vast majority of such examples involve predator detection and defense, offspring care, foraging, and grooming, demonstrating that altruistic giving most often evolves to subserve behaviors that are advantageous, but difficult for a single individual to achieve.

For example, Belding's ground squirrels give alarm calls which are costly to the individual who attracts attention to himself, but beneficial to neighboring animals, who receive advance notice of the approaching predator. Supporting the role of kin selection, such calls occur more often when the surrounding animals are related than when they are not (e.g., Sherman, 1977). Subordinate individuals in

naked mole-rat colonies contribute greatly to the maintenance and defense of the colony even though they do not themselves reproduce (e.g., Lacey & Sherman, 1991). This feature of the colony increases the reproductive success of queens and the survival of the colony, and is thought to be due to an extremely high average relatedness among colony members (Jarvis, O'Riain, Bennett, & Sherman, 1994; Reeve, Westneat, Noon, Sherman, & Aquadro, 1990), again indicating a role for kin selection. There are many examples of inclusive fitness in birds, in which "helpers at the nest" are common, with female offspring helping to care for siblings rather than themselves mating (Stacey & Koenig, 1990).

Evidence for reciprocal altruism also tends to focus on two forms, defense and food procurement. For example, Pied wagtail birds allow intruder conspecifics to forage in their territories in exchange for cooperation in defense of the region (Davies & Houston, 1981). Guppies cooperatively engage in "predator inspection," alternating turns to move closer to a potentially dangerous source (Pitcher, 1992) and multiple unrelated queens in colonies of seed harvester ants (*Messor pergandei*) cooperate, which in turn increases the success of brood raiding (Pollock & Rissing, 1989; Rissing & Pollock, 1987).

In primates, support during aggressive encounters is the most common form of collaboration, often performed on behalf of close kin, but also distributed reciprocally among nonrelatives. Chimpanzees show evidence for so-called calculated reciprocity, that is, reciprocal exchange of favors based on mental record keeping of previous events. For example, chimpanzees have been shown to support each other reciprocally in fights (de Waal & Luttrell, 1988) and to exchange services even after delays in time (de Waal, 1997b; Koyama, Caws, & Aureli, 2006b). In contrast to claims in the literature that humans are the only primates to extensively cooperate with nonrelatives, recent testing of DNA samples from wild chimpanzees has confirmed a high frequency of collaborative partnerships between unrelated individuals (Langergraber, Mitani, & Vigilant, 2007). Reciprocity is a rapidly growing topic in and of itself, particularly in animal cognition, and has been extensively studied in primates in particular (Brosnan & de Waal, 2002; de Waal & Brosnan, 2006; de Waal & Berger, 2000; Hauser, McAuliffe, & Blake, 2009).

It is widely agreed that kin selection and reciprocal altruism can, and likely do, act in concert with each other, with maximal reinforcement in small groups where one tends to be surrounded by individuals who are either related or close friends with multiple, long-term opportunities for giving and receiving (e.g., Brown & Brown, 2006; Preston & de Waal, 2002). A recent study set out to determine if chimpanzee helping occurs outside of reciprocal altruism by creating situations with unfamiliar individuals and in the absence of return rewards. Chimpanzees spontaneously assisted humans regardless of whether doing so yielded a reward, or not, and were also willing to help fellow chimpanzees reach a room with food. One would assume that rewards, even if not strictly necessary, would at least stimulate helping; but in fact, rewards seemed to have no impact on the giving in this study. Since the decision to help did not seem to be based on a self-focused cost/benefit calculation, it may have been genuinely other-oriented at the motivational level (Warneken, Hare, Melis, Hanus, & Tomasello, 2007).

Recent studies further demonstrated spontaneous helping in marmosets (Burkart, Fehr, Efferson, & van Schaik, 2007) and capuchin monkeys. In the latter study, two monkeys were placed side by side in separate enclosures in full view of one another. One monkey could barter with small plastic tokens, exchanging them for food. Two differently colored tokens were used, with different consequences: one was "selfish," the other "prosocial." If the bartering monkey picked the selfish token, it could receive a small piece of apple upon exchange, but the partner got nothing. The prosocial token rewarded both monkeys equally. The bartering monkey was rewarded either way, so the only difference was in the partner's receipt of a reward. The stronger the social tie between partners, the more the bartering monkey would select the prosocial token. The procedures were repeated many times with different social combinations and sets of tokens, and the prosocial behavior persisted. Their choices could not be explained by fear of punishment, because the dominant monkey consistently proved to be the most prosocial (de Waal, Luttrell, & Canfield, 1993). Similar results on capuchin monkeys have been obtained by Lakshminarayanan and Santos (2008).

Exchanges Involving Food Sharing and Grooming

One of the most common ways to investigate altruism and reciprocity in animals is to study food-sharing among non-kin. There is an extensive literature on food sharing and its relation to altruism, which is beyond the scope of this paper (Brosnan & de Waal, 2002; de Waal, 1989; de Waal, 1997b; Kaplan & Hill, 1985; Moore, 1984). Importantly, food sharing with non-kin has been observed in many mammals including vampire bats (Wilkinson, 1988), lions (Pusey & Packer, 1997), chimpanzees (e.g., de Waal, 1989; Goodall, 1963; Teleki, 1973), bonobos (Hohmann & Fruth, 1993), and New World capuchin monkeys (e.g., de Waal, 1997a; Perry & Rose, 1994). Such food sharing has been specifically found to be reciprocal (with individuals sharing with those who have shared with them in the recent past) in vampire bats (Wilkinson, 1984), chimpanzees (de Waal, 1989; de Waal, 1997b), and capuchin monkeys (de Waal, 2000a).

Allogrooming is also considered an altruistic act since grooming another is risky for the giver, who is necessarily rendered less vigilant (Maestripieri, 1993; Mooring & Hart, 1995). Conversely, grooming is highly beneficial for the recipient, reducing many key physiological variables including stress and tension (Schino, Scucchi, Maestripieri, & Turillazzi, 1988), allostatic load (Liu et al., 1997), damaging ticks (Hart, 1990; Mooring, McKenzie, & Hart, 1996), heart rate (Aureli, Preston, & de Waal, 1999; Boccia, Reite, & Laudenslager, 1989; Feh & de Mazières, 1993; Smith, Astley, Chesney, Taylor, & Spelman, 1986), and increasing beta-endorphins (Keveme, Martensz, & Tuite, 1989). Allogrooming is reciprocally distributed, with individuals grooming those who previously groomed them (even among non-kin), in mice (Stopka & Graciasova, 2001), impala (Hart & Hart, 1992; Mooring & Hart, 1997), macaques (Manson, David Navarrete, Silk, & Perry, 2004) capuchin monkeys (Manson et al., 2004), and baboons (Henzi & Barrett, 1999; Silk, Seyfarth, & Cheney, 1999).

Allogrooming in particular seems to be a useful biological economy for animals (Henzi & Barrett, 1999), as it has been proven not only to increase the receipt of grooming, but to influence the future likelihood of agonistic support (Hemelrijk, 1994; Koyama, Caws, & Aureli, 2006a; Seyfarth & Cheney, 1984), food sharing (de Waal, 1982; de Waal, 1997b; Koyama et al., 2006a), and sex (Stopka & Graciasova, 2001; Stopka & Macdonald, 1999).

Importantly, descriptions of food sharing bear a remarkable similarity to each other, with data from vampire bats (Wilkinson, 1984, 1990), capuchin monkeys, and chimpanzees (Brosnan & de Waal, 2002; de Waal, 1997b) all involving a particular form of exchange whereby individuals share food with others who have previously groomed them.

For example, in a study with captive chimpanzees, with a sample of 200 food trials and 6,972 approaches to the individual endowed with a sharable leafy branch, previous grooming increased the probability of sharing and the few examples of hostile reactions to requests were directed at beggars that had not previously groomed the food possessor. In this sample, grooming was separated from food sharing by at least two hours and was specific to the individual who did the grooming, not being explainable by a general positive mood effect (de Waal, 1997b).

In studies with vampire bats, the probability of sharing can be more strictly tied to the costs and benefits of the act, with giving being greater for kin and familiar individuals, but also demonstrating reciprocity and being scaled, in a cost-benefit fashion, to the level of need of the recipient and the food supply of the giver. As with the descriptions of food sharing in chimpanzees and capuchin monkeys, food sharing in vampire bats almost always involves an older, more experienced forager sharing food with a younger, less-experienced forager, after the young individual has approached and groomed the older (Wilkinson, 1984, 1986, 1990; Figure 38.1).

Consolation Behavior

When one individual is distressed, the most common and oftentimes most necessary act of helping is to simply approach the distressed other and provide emotional support and soothing; this in turn reduces the other's distress as well as the associated negative attention. The development of concern and consolation was extensively studied in humans, looking at children's reactions to distressed family members in the home, through direct recording of behavior and indirectly through questionnaires (Zahn-Waxler et al., 1992). In these studies, they found that almost all children exhibited some form of prosocial responding to another's distress as early as one year (hugging, patting), by 18 months most showed a full repertoire of prosocial actions, and by two years nearly all children responded prosocially. Empathy and helping differed for caused than observed distress in expected ways, with caused distress involving more aggression, positive affect, and less hypothesis-testing. Supporting presumed gender differences, girls showed more empathic concern than boys, but only for naturally occurring observed distress, and they also showed more self-referential behavior (e.g., patting one's own arm when the other's arm is hurt) at 18 months. Interestingly, within individuals, prosocial behavior at 18 months was more associated with hypothesis testing than empathic concern and empathic concern with self-referential behavior, likely reflecting the different demands of helping and feeling with another; by two years, the four measures were all highly intercorrelated, supporting empathy-altruism models more generally (Batson & Coke, 1981; Hoffman, 2000).

In animal research, similar behavior has become known as "consolation," defined as a reassuring behavior by an uninvolved bystander towards one of the combatants in a previous aggressive incident (de Waal & van Roosmalen, 1979). For example, a third party approaches the loser of a fight and gently puts an arm around his or her shoulders (Figure 38.2). De Waal and van Roosmalen (1979) analyzed

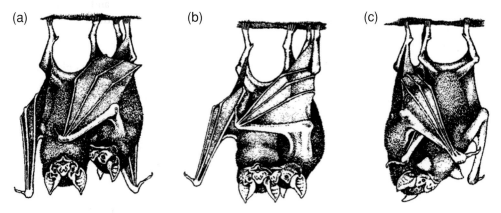

Fig. 38.1 Depiction of food-sharing between roost-mate vampire bats, a form of reciprocal altruism. During a typical sequence of events, the hungry bat would solicit a meal of regurgitated blood from a more successful roost-mate by first licking the potential donor under her wing (a) and then by licking the donor's lips (b). In turn, the receptive donor (most likely a close relative or social affiliate) would regurgitate blood into the recipient's mouth (c), greatly increasing their likelihood of survival until the next day. Reproduced from Wilkinson, 1990, with permission of Scientific American and www.patriciawynne.com.

Fig. 38.2 There has been a tendency in the literature to emphasize the competitive and aggressive side of chimpanzees, but our close relatives also often show altruistic and affectionate behavior, such as here a female with her daughter apprehensively watching a fight among others.
Photograph by Frans de Waal.

hundreds of post-conflict observations of consolation in chimpanzees, and a replication by de Waal and Aureli (de Waal & Aureli, 1996) included an even larger sample, strongly suggesting that consolation is indeed distress alleviating.

Subsequent studies have confirmed consolation in chimpanzees, gorillas, and bonobos (Cordoni, Palagi, & Tarli, 2006; Fuentes, Malone, Sanz, Matheson, & Vaughan, 2002; Palagi, Cordoni, & Borgognini, 2006; Palagi, Paoli, & Borgognini, 2004; Mallavarapu, Stoinski, Bloomsmith, & Maple, 2006), but it has not been found in monkeys despite extensive attempts using the same procedures (de Waal & Aureli, 1996; Watts, Colmenares, & Arnold, 2000). This is surprising as species after species of monkey does exhibit reconciliation (i.e., friendly reunions between former opponents) (de Waal, 2000b). The consolation gap between monkeys and the Hominoidea extends even to the one situation where consolation is most expected: Macaque mothers fail to reassure their offspring who have lost a fight (Schino, Geminiani, Rosati, & Aureli, 2004). O'Connell's (1995) content analysis of over 2,000 anecdotal reports of non-human primate empathy confirmed that comforting responses to the emotional state of others are typical of apes but rare in monkeys. Thus, the evidence suggests that apes are affected by the emotions of others and take action to reduce the target's distress. The data on consolation suggest that apes evaluate the emotions and situations of others with a greater understanding than most other nonhuman animals,

but more research is needed to determine the extent to which ape consolation is actually similar to human consolation.

Recent studies have also investigated the physiological effects of consolation. An initial report documented no stress-reducing effect of consolation (Koski & Sterck, 2007), but a more detailed follow-up study found that recipients reduced self-directed behavior (e.g., self-scratching), a behavioral response commonly associated with anxiety (Maestripieri, Schino, Aureli, & Troisi, 1992), leaving the authors to conclude that consolation is beneficial to the other (Fraser, Stahl, & Aureli, 2008). Since this behavior also occurs mostly in reaction to distress signals, it most closely resembles empathy-induced altruism in humans.

Proximate Mechanisms
The above review of the animal literature reveals that examples of altruism from across the animal kingdom support the ultimate-level models, such as kin selection and reciprocal altruism. But can these examples inform the proximate mechanisms of altruism? Some of the aforementioned forms of altruism appear to be relatively specific to the species and its ecology and, thus, are more likely to involve specific adaptations that are restricted to *evolutionary altruism* and not homologous with human giving, empathy, or sympathy.

For example, extensive research on allogrooming in impala suggests that this cooperative behavior does not reflect a general economy of exchange, but rather is a specific adaptation for removing ticks, which exists across dyads, is dependent on season, body size, and habitat, is always traded for grooming, and is visible from the first days of life (Mooring, Blumstein, & Stoner, 2004). Research on cooperation among colony members in eusocial species such as hymenoptera and the naked mole-rat suggests that their particular form of cooperation is restricted to colony members with a high degree of interrelatedness, owing to their haplo-diploid genetic structure. Such examples likely reflect an independent evolution of cooperative behavior within species, to solve particular ecological problems.

At a functional and neuroanatomic level, it is not expected that neural mechanisms underlying altruism in solitary fish and eusocial insects will bear much resemblance to that of social, diploid mammals, such as rodents, nonhuman primates, and humans. In addition, it seems that the types of altruistic giving that receive the most attention in primate and human behavior are those that are flexible, interchangeable across various forms of giving, socially embedded, and the result of a decision to help (implicit or explicit), rather than a biological destiny. Thus, in explicating the proximate mechanism of altruism in humans, we will focus on data from social mammals that depict flexible, interchangeable giving at the level of *psychological altruism*.

Emotions Guide Decisions to Help

Traditional models of altruism, similar to classical models of decision making, assumed that decisions are made through rational comparative processes that explicitly integrate pros and cons, taking into account remembered past events and projections of future outcomes. When computed explicitly, this process is relatively inefficient and slow, but does accord with the common belief that true decision making is restricted to intentional choice and restricted to humans. The overt weighting of costs and benefits surely does occur, but its contribution to behavior is probably overstated due to its disproportional availability in consciousness (Nisbett & Wilson, 1977).

The research reviewed above and current models of decision making highlight an alternative to the explicit, comparative approach. Consider the examples of animal altruism given above. Almost all involve a conspecific recipient with greater need (due to age, rank, foraging skill) given access to a valued resource (food, grooming, coalitionary support) from a group member that is socially bonded

and previously groomed or supported the potential giver. The important role of kin and friends, social bonding, and prior acts of social support and grooming imply a role for affectively driven cues that do not require explicit calculation. For example, we know that grooming and interpersonal touch are positive, relaxing experiences for the recipient (Aureli et al., 1999; Feh & de MaziËres, 1993; Kalin, Shelton, & Lynn, 1995) that predispose future giving, even in a different modality (e.g., food). We also know from work on empathic emotion that similarity, familiarity, social closeness, and positive experience with the other strengthen the empathic response across species, which is known to increase the likelihood of helping (vide Table 1 in Preston & de Waal, 2002). This is consistent with the social relationships in which biologists expect altruism to occur, which are those between close relatives and potential reciprocators. Negative social relationships or competitive situations, on the other hand, can produce counter-empathy, or *schadenfreude* (e.g., Smith et al., 1996; Takahashi et al., 2009). The empathy mechanism is therefore biased precisely the way that one would expect from an evolutionary perspective (de Waal, 2008). Thus, decisions to help must at least be influenced by positive associations with the target. While this affective information could be represented explicitly at the time of the decision in the mind of the giver, all of the data on decision processes in neuroscience and human decision-making indicate that it need not be.

For example, the "risk as feelings" model from judgment and decision making (Loewenstein, Weber, Hsee, & Welch, 2001), the "mood as information" model from social psychology (Schwarz & Clore, 2003), and the "somatic marker hypothesis" (Damasio, 1994) from cognitive neuroscience all assume and provide evidence that internal states are implicitly used to guide decisions, either by being directly and unconsciously accessed at the time of judgment (Schwarz & Clore, 2003) or by generating affective signals during conscious deliberation that are neurally integrated to bias choice on the basis of past experience. A similar argument has been proposed to specifically explain primate giving as reciprocity, called the "emotional mediation" hypothesis (Aureli & Schaffner, 2002; Aureli & Schino, 2004; Aureli & Whiten, 2003; see also, Pryce, 1996; Whiten, 1996). In this model, current physiological emotional states that reflect prior outcomes from social interaction serve as the bridge between neural processes and behavior. As evidence, heart rate (Aureli et al., 1999) and self-scratching—both indicators of anxiety—increase in the presence of a dominant individual (Castles & Aureli, 1999; Maestripieri, 1993; Pavani, Maestripieri, Schino, Turillazzi, & Scucchi, 1991; Troisi & Schino, 1987) and the frequency of post-conflict reconciliation is moderated by friendship quality (reviewed by Aureli, Cords, & van Schaik, 2002; de Waal, 2000b). Thus, the anxiety of the victim or target individual is thought to indirectly indicate the status of the relationship between individuals, which in turn predicts avoidance or a friendly reunion.

At the neural level, affective and declarative information from many subsystems are thought to converge in the orbital frontal cortex (OFC) where they are integrated to influence choice (Bechara et al., 2000; Kringelbach & Rolls, 2004). The amygdala is thought to generate the initial emotional response to rewards and punishments (Bechara, Damasio, & Damasio, 2003) while the hippocampus and associated cortical representations feed forward contextual information from past experience that can moderate the effect. In the other direction, the OFC is known to also send signals back to the amygdala (basolateral nucleus; BLA) to track expected outcomes during delays, in the absence of the cue, and in probabilistic settings (O'Doherty, 2003; Schoenbaum, Chiba, & Gallagher, 1998; Schoenbaum, Setlow, Saddoris, & Gallagher, 2003). This is important as it allows animals and people to represent situations and outcomes that are not strictly locked to the presence of the stimulus, which can be used to anticipate and plan actions. Similarly, the dorsolateral prefrontal cortex (DLPFC) is expected to be necessary for more explicit, cost-benefit tradeoffs and tracking of favors given and received, as well as for maximizing learning and performance by the more medial and emotional system (Krain et al., 2006). For example, in gambling tasks, the DLPFC is needed to develop conscious, explicit knowledge about the contingencies of the different decks of cards, even if subjects can chose advantageously without it (Bechara, Damasio, Tranel, & Anderson, 1998; Krain et al., 2006).

Both the amygdala and the OFC are highly interconnected with the ventral striatum, in particular the nucleus accumbens (NAcc), which is thought to be involved in many different, overlapping processes related to decisions about reward that should play a role in altruistic giving. The largest literature on the dopaminergic reward system focuses on addiction (for reviews, see Berridge & Robinson, 2003; Robinson & Berridge, 2003). Dopaminergic signals

in the NAcc are thought to mediate the motivation to attain rewards ("wanting") (Wyvell & Berridge, 2000) while opioid processes underlie the *hedonic pleasure* (i.e., "liking") of consuming those rewards (Peciña & Berridge, 2005). Dopamine signals in the NAcc are also thought to track the *expectation* of rewards (Berns, McClure, Pagnoni, & Montague, 2001; Fiorillo, Tobler, & Schultz, 2003; Schultz, 2002) while the neuropeptide action of oxytocin and vasopressin in the NAcc is necessary for the formation of long-term social bonds in animals (Insel & Young, 2001) and is implicated in multiple models to underlie social bonding, trust, and giving in primates and humans (Carter et al., 2008; Churchland, 2008; Hrdy, 2009; Kosfeld, Heinrichs, Zak, Fischbacher, & Fehr, 2005; Preston & Brown, submitted; Zak, 2008).

Given these findings in the decision literature, one would predict particular involvement of the NAcc, amygdala, and hippocampus to initially encode, as important and emotional, the fact that your new neighbor either called the police or brought over a bottle of wine to your first party. The OFC, acting in concert with the DLPFC, would be needed to recall these facts when your neighbor later comes over to borrow a cup of sugar. The NAcc-driven motivational systems would also be expected to motivate you to approach the neighbor who initially brought you wine when you later see him in the adjacent driveway, and as the relationship grows may even motivate you to help him bring in the groceries or shovel ice from the driveway. The DLPFC would be necessary in particular to boost explicit comparisons of past outcomes, such as may occur in a case where your neighbor of many years (with whom you had experienced both ups and downs) comes to ask you for a relatively costly favor—one that you want to really consider and be able to justify. Most substantial acts of helping probably take this form, containing an amalgam of unconscious, affective feelings associated with the other and explicit memories and analyses.

These existing models provide an excellent starting point for understanding the embodiment of decision process; however, it is hard to generalize from experimental tests of decision making to real-world empathic altruism. Decision-making experiments typically use highly constrained numbers of variables and provide relatively precise information on the expected utility of various options. In contrast, real-world decisions that have a large impact on reproductive success usually involve many conceivable options, each with multiple positive and negative consequences, all of which must be estimated from very noisy, indirect, or nonexistent past data. For example, when deciding to marry, you must estimate your intended partner's commitment to a long-term monogamous relationship; when you leave your young child with a babysitter, nanny, or relative, you must estimate the likelihood that they will vigilantly and lovingly care for your offspring; when you allow your young adult child to go to school abroad, you must estimate the likelihood that they can succeed in a large city thousands of miles from home. Such decisions require great inferential leaps from individual events that may have distant relevance to the issue at hand. It is precisely this complexity and uncertainty that supports the adaptiveness of an implicit, affectively driven decision process. Next we review the existing data on the neural substrates of altruistic giving. These studies, while consistent in their emphasis on the role of the aforementioned mesolimbocortical system, are also limited in that they refer only to very constrained forms of giving, most of which are financial. There is a large and still growing literature on the neural substrates of empathic emotion and perspective-taking, which are presumed to play an important role as the mediating psychologically felt emotion that intervenes between the perception of another's need and the decision to help. However, as other chapters in this volume are dedicated to empathy and its substrates (e.g., chapter 41), we will focus our evidence on studies that actually require giving.

Evidence for Human Altruism in Neuroimaging

The role for decision and reward circuits in interpersonal giving has been demonstrated in two recent lines of research in cognitive and affective neuroscience—trust and cooperation in behavioral economics, and the neural substrates of charitable giving. While these studies are convergent with the neuroanatomical circuits explicated above because they consistently find engagement of the same regions (OFC, NAcc, insula, amygdala), the function of each region in context with the specific task or behavior is largely speculative at this point, with the same region being implicated in opposing processes or the same process being located to different regions across studies. A detailed analysis of these data is beyond the scope of this chapter, but we provide the authors' interpretations of the activation after each finding as a guide.

A growing body of research has investigated patterns of neural activation while people play economic games designed to solicit trade-offs between keeping monetary rewards for oneself, versus giving to another, or trusting another with one's investment in order to secure a larger reward (see Camerer & Fehr, 2006; Fehr & Camerer, 2007; Walter, Abler, Ciaramidaro, & Erk, 2005; Zak, 2004 for reviews). In a study of women doing the iterated prisoner's dilemma game, both the OFC and NAcc were activated when both partners cooperated, interpreted as representing the rewards of cooperation, which enhanced and sustained cooperation over selfish decisions (Rilling et al., 2002). In a subsequent study, reciprocated cooperation was associated with activation in the ventromedial prefrontal cortex (vmPFC) while unreciprocated cooperation was associated with activation in the ventral striatum, suggesting that the striatum provided an error signal when the partner failed to reciprocate, which could inform future decisions (presumably to punish defection) (Rilling, Sanfey, Aronson, Nystrom, & Cohen, 2004). In another study, subjects played the same game outside of the scanner and subsequently viewed pictures of the hypothetical partners in the scanner (Singer et al., 2006). Pictures of former cooperators elicited activation in the amygdala, NAcc, lateral OFC, insula, fusiform gyrus, and superior temporal sulcus (STS), activating a large network associated with social cognition, memory, and associated memories. Importantly, partners classified as intentionally cooperative particularly activated the ventral striatum and lateral OFC. In contrast, activation to defectors was lower overall and only increased relative activation in the medial OFC, perhaps activating stronger representations for expected loss similar to effects in the ventromedial prefrontal cortex (VMPFC) for learning to avoid risky gambling decks (Bechara, Damasio, Tranel, & Damasio, 1997).

When the Ultimatum Game was played in the scanner against partners believed to be humans or computers, unfair offers produced higher activation in the insula, ACC, and DLPFC (Sanfey, Rilling, Aronson, Nystrom, & Cohen, 2003). Insula and ACC activity are presumed to result from the negative reaction to unfairness, motivating a change in subsequent behavior. DLPFC activation is presumed to reflect the cognitive control brought online to accept fair offers (the optimal choice) despite such negative emotional signals. As evidence for a role for the lateral frontal cortex, temporary disruption of the right DLPFC using transcranial magnetic stimulation (TMS) reduces the rejection rate of unfair offers (Knoch & Fehr, 2007;

Knoch et al., 2008; Knoch, Pascual-Leone, Meyer, Treyer, & Fehr, 2006). Conversely, patients with damage to the VMPFC reject more unfair offers than comparison groups (Koenigs & Tranel, 2007).

In the trust and reciprocity game, only subjects who cooperated with a human partner showed increased activation in the prefrontal cortex while waiting to learn the outcome of their choices, an effect not seen in noncooperators or against computer partners (McCabe, Houser, Ryan, Smith, & Trouard, 2001). This effect is similar to the effect seen in rats (above), where the OFC is needed to maintain outcome representations in the absence of the stimulus (Schoenbaum et al., 2003). In another version of the trust game, intentional and real punishment (as opposed to symbolic) was associated with activation in the dorsal striatum while punishment that was intentional and costly (as opposed to free) specifically activated the medial orbital frontal and VMPFC (de Quervain et al., 2004). In a recent reciprocal trust game where both players were scanned simultaneously (hyperscanning), conditional trust behavior increased relative activation in the VTA while unconditional trust increased activation in the septal region (Krueger et al., 2007).

Effects of agency during behavioral economic games are mirrored in two other functional imaging studies of altruism. In the first, subjects performed or watched a reaction-time task that delivered earnings to themselves and a charity. Trait altruism positively correlated with the tendency to recruit the right posterior superior temporal sulcus (r pSTS) as well as the OFC for watching more than playing (Tankersley, Stowe, & Huettel, 2007). The authors suggest that pSTS activation is associated with altruism because it encodes low-level actions, which can feed into more general empathic processes when observing the actions or state of another. These data are consistent with a perception-action model of empathy that places a bottleneck on empathic processes on the observer's attention to the other's state, necessary for downstream activation of resonating, self-related representations (Preston & de Waal, 2002). In addition, they confirm the importance of observing the others' need and being able to model the appropriate action, which has been found to play a role in helping across species and contexts.

Another study that more directly studied decisions to give to others also found an important role for agency by pitting charitable donations against money for one's self, under a condition of voluntary or mandatory transfer (resembling taxation for public goods) (Harbaugh, Mayr, & Burghart, 2007).

Supporting common neural mechanisms for rewards to the self and to others, monetary gains to both parties activated a common network in the ventral striatum. Individuals did make cost-benefit trade-offs, giving more when it cost them less, but supporting an altruistic motivation to give to the charity, individuals with higher activity in the ventral striatum during giving donated almost twice as much voluntarily. Also supporting the "warm glow" motivation for giving (for the positive affect that ensues), activation in the caudate and right NAcc, as well as satisfaction with the donation, increased when donations were made voluntarily, even after controlling for the fact that subjects earned more by rejecting proposals to give voluntarily.

A similar study had participants allocate earnings either to themselves or a variety of real causes that had differential political appeal across subjects, allowing them to differentiate giving to valued and disliked recipients (Moll et al., 2006; Figure 38.3). As in the prior study, both personal rewards and charitable donations activated a common network in the mesolimbocortical system including the VTA, and dorsal and ventral striatum. In particular, the degree of costly charitable donation was correlated with activation in the ventral striatum. The more selfless the decision, or the more costly the donation, the more anterior the activation, including frontopolar and medial frontal cortex (also correlating with real-world charitable giving). Activity in the sgACC was particularly associated with donating when contrasted with monetary reward. In an fMRI study by the same group, the subgenual region of the ACC (sgACC; BA 25) was also associated with guilt from having imagined actions against another that violated social norms while pride and gratitude were associated with additional activation in mesolimbic and basal forebrain regions (Zahn et al., 2008).

These pertinent studies by Moll and colleagues, as well as additional evidence from research on emotion and psychopathology, may suggest a particularly important role for the sgACC in mediating altruistic acts in the context of empathic concern because of its ability to mediate emotional responses and associated effects on motivation, learning, and memory. This region has extensive interconnections with the OFC, lateral hypothalamus, amygdala, nucleus accumbens, subiculum, VTA, raphe locus coeruleus, PAG, and the nucleus tractus solitarius (NTS) (reviewed in (Freedman, Insel, & Smith, 2000; Ongür & Price, 2000; Ongür & Price, 2003). Projections from the sgACC to the hypothalamic

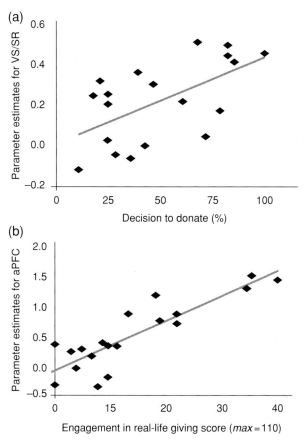

Fig. 38.3 Positive correlations between charitable giving and brain activation in the mesolimbocortical system. In the top panel (a), the frequency of costly donation (how often each participant made costly donations) increases with parameter estimates in the ventral striatum/septal region (VS/SR; x = –6, y = 11, z = 4; r = 0.58; $p < 0.01$). In the bottom panel (b), the level of self-reported engagement in real-life voluntary activities increases with the degree of aPFC activation during costly donation (peak: x = –6, y = 25, z = –14; r = 0.87; $p < 0.0001$).

Graphs reproduced from Figures 3d and 4e in: Moll, J., Krueger, F., Zahn, R., Pardini, M., de Oliveira-Souza, R., & Grafman, J. (2006). Human fronto-mesolimbic networks guide decisions about charitable donation. *Proc Natl Acad Sci U S A, 103*(42), 15623–15628. Copyright 2006, National Academy of Sciences, U.S.A.

and brainstem autonomic regions are presumed to regulate emotional arousal (reviewed in Freedman, Insel, & Smith, 2000; Barbas, Saha, Rempel-Clower, & Ghashghaei, 2003), particularly parasympathetic control (Critchley, 2004; O'Connor, Gundel, McRae, & Lane, 2007), which would be particularly germane for both a role in responding to others' distress and in the normal experience of negative emotions (Kross, Davidson, Weber, & Ochsner, 2008; van den Bos, McClure, Harris, Fiske, & Cohen, 2007), such as sadness (Damasio et al., 2000; Liotti et al., 2000; Talbot & Cooper, 2006) major depression, and bipolar disorder (reviewed by Charney & Nestler, 2005; Drevets, Savitz, & Trimble, 2008). Displays of need typically involve some form of expressed sadness or distress, which would be expected to activate the parasympathetic

system and sgACC. As evidence, this region is specifically activated when mothers listen to infant cries (Lorberbaum et al., 2002; Lorberbaum et al., 1999) and experiments consistently find an orienting response (a reduction in heart rate presumed to result from increased parasympathetic tone) when subjects attend to and are concerned about the plight of another and offer to help (Eisenberg & Fabes, 1990; Eisenberg et al., 1989). Taken together, the subgenual region may be best thought of as a region that normally mediates the ability to redirect cognitive and physiological resources (attention, metabolism, motivation, memorial processes) in response to biologically important stimuli in context. This makes it a good candidate for mediating acts of helping, which depend both on an emotionally salient distress signal, the relationship of the distressed other to the observer, and the ability/knowledge of the observer to respond appropriately. It also allows for a neural link between the assumption that empathy and altruism originated in the mother-offspring bond, which causes caregivers to respond to the cues of distress in offspring.

Thus, extensive evidence from neuroimaging supports the view that the ventral striatum and orbital frontal regions in particular are necessary for making cost-benefit trade-offs during social decisions such as cooperative investment games. However, despite being "social," compared to gambling with known or fixed probabilities, these situations are still heavily biased towards cost-benefit processes, which may not underlie typical forms of giving in the real world. For example, when someone retrieves and cuddles a distressed infant, runs to the rescue of a fallen child, or gives up their seat on the bus to an older passenger, a trade-off between helping and monetary reward is not involved. Even implicit trade-offs between the needs of the giver and the receiver may not be practically important in situations where the motivational inputs to respond are sufficiently strong that they clearly dominate processing. The involvement with monetary rewards and the explicitness of the tradeoff indicate that frontal-striatal systems may be particularly involved when giving involves a clear trade-off, such as when deciding whether to use a windfall of earning to buy an expensive accessory or donate to a charity, or when deciding to help one individual or charity over another. Activation is expected to be more anterior and involve interactions between medial and lateral portions of the frontal cortex the more abstract and cogitated the decisions, while more immediate stimuli/situations should activate more posterior, medial structures such as the amygdala, NAcc, and sgACC.

Putting it All Together

More than three decades ago, biologists deliberately removed the altruism from altruism. Now, there is increasing evidence that the brain is hard-wired for social connection, and that individuals often have an emotional stake in the emotions of others. The brain may have evolved to maximize personal fitness, but did so by running a genuine reach-out program that is at least as old as the mammals.

Mechanisms designed to subserve mating, pair bonding, offspring care, and food procurement affect and mediate our propensities towards others, predisposing us to act towards others who are socially bonded, loved, positively regarded, or sexually desired. At a proximate level, such decisions rely on the neural and physiological systems involved in reward processing and decision making, elucidated in animal and human models of bonding, maternal care, food reward, drug addiction, and economic choice. These basic mesolimbocortical mechanisms are shared across species and likely explain the vast majority of implicit behavioral investment choices, but also explain how giving does not act in a vacuum, but is highly sensitive to cost-benefit factors that make giving more or less valuable or desired. Thus, while the motivation for reward-based giving is largely implicit, it is also sensitive to context: 1) information from past experience with the individual and situation feeds into the system from association cortex and the hippocampus, 2) giving is suppressed by feelings of uncertainty, risk, fear, and vulnerability, through inputs from amygdala to ventral striatum, and 3) giving is sensitive to cost-benefit effects on resource allocation such as have been documented for food availability, group size, and relationship quality.

Indeed, as pointed out by many skeptics of a seemingly "automatic" mechanism for empathy and altruism, sometimes empathy seems wholly absent. On the opposite end of the spectrum, people can brutally hurt others in the service of personal protection or gain and even revel in another's misfortune in artificial laboratory experiments. However, consistent with the model, *schadenfreude* occurs particularly for nonbonded, nonrelatives who directly compete for resources and may be surpassing the subjects. Chimpanzees are also capable of brutally killing each other (de Waal, 1982; Wrangham & Peterson, 1996) and, hence, must be able to eliminate empathic activation in relation to conspecifics (Jane Goodall, 1986, p. 532 refers to chimpanzee victims as "dechimpized").

Originally, the mechanisms of reward and decision making were likely designed to facilitate consummatory behaviors (sex, eating, pup retrieval, allogrooming) where the incentive salience of a stimulus draws the individual toward the target, to obtain an expected reward. With increased involvement of the interconnected mesolimbocortical system and bidirectional connections between the ventral striatum and prefrontal cortex, primates can extend this act of consumption over time, such that the initial act of opening oneself up for another can occur in more abstract contexts and before any expected reward is salient. Such decisions likely rely on these interactions between expected reward as processed by the ventral striatum and control functions subserved by interconnections with the amygdala, hippocampus, anterior cingulate and orbital frontal cortex. Emotional associations with the other generate the motivation to help, with a particular moderating influence from relationship quality and situational variables (such as food supply or the presence of a dominant individual), producing behavior that maximizes inclusive fitness and reciprocal altruism with minimal demands on explicit calculation.

In cases where the recipient is a truly loved and bonded individual, reward mechanisms associated with the bond and past experience generate an incentive salience-like state to approach and comfort the other, which still need not be compulsory. For example, giving can be inhibited if fear is associated with the situation or the other or there are overriding personal needs.

In humans, even giving that is not mediated by a high-quality social relationship can occur as cognitive capacities allow individuals to override immediately obvious risks and model less immediate potential rewards. In so doing, potential givers can take control of situations in myriad ways. Individuals can actively inhibit options that are compelling, but non-optimal (such as helping individuals who are liked, but nonetheless unlikely to reciprocate), or highlight options that are not compelling, but optimal (such as helping someone unliked, but likely to reciprocate), planning long-term cooperative ventures that require multiple stages and long-term payoffs, and enacting rules or strategies that avoid manipulation while maximizing the potential for return (like stop-loss rules for social investments or tit-for-tat strategies).

Choices are likely to reflect maximization of salient variables, which were generally adaptive in our evolutionary history, but may or may not be beneficial in the individual case. For example, when your friend is standing at your doorstep, it would be all but impossible to turn them away and you will offer more than if their plight was presented indirectly. However, the friend at the door may be a freeloader (something you knew, but could not use to override the immediate salience), while the sincere friend across town harbors resentment that you did not rush to her aid (which you also knew, but which was insufficiently salient to get you out of the house). This variability in the salience of variables that are immediately or more distantly perceived is known as the "hot-cold empathy gap," and has been applied to myriad discounting

problems including drug addiction and financial investments (Loewenstein, 2000). Choices are also sensitive to costs and benefits, such that even when the person is standing at the door, a mother of five may turn them away while a single person may drive across town to comfort their friend. Adding a decision-making perspective to prosocial giving allows us to defeat misgivings about the role of empathic emotion in mediating truly altruistic giving. In this view, empathic and sympathetic emotions surely do predispose giving, but must be integrated with many simultaneous motivational and situational cues that may bias behavior in different directions.

As exemplified by this review, the vast majority of empirical evidence for altruism exists in animals, even nonprimates. The existing evidence in humans has relied on financial decisions because of our concurrent interest in financial decisions as well as the ease of demonstrating them in the lab. However, this approach biases our knowledge in favor of cost-benefit approaches and implies necessarily a trade-off between self and other rewards. In the real world, many decisions to help do not take this structure. For example, when you rush out of your home to help the boy who has fallen off of his bike, spend an evening at work to help a distressed colleague, or pick up the phone after a particularly moving plea for help on the television, the conflict between personal and other goals is minor while the compulsion to act is strong. In reality, everyone in our environment could use help and, thus, the decision is not *whether* to help, but *who* and *how much* (making an evolutionary perspective particularly productive). People even persist in giving to their detriment or reveal unfettered self-interest, demonstrating trait-like tendencies that are robust to cost-benefit information. Thus, while genetic contribution to future generations is the bottom line in evolution, the proximate mechanism is dynamic, imprecise, and highly affected by temperament and past experience. Successful models of altruism must capture this inherent complexity and variability better while being grounded in the known neural and physiological mechanisms of decision making. Creativity is needed to develop paradigms that elicit active helping in noneconomic settings in ways that are feasible during neuroscientific recording such as with PET, fMRI, ERP, and TMS. Only by taking a broader view can we understand the complexity of a behavior that can be observed in our most distant relatives and hard to demonstrate in our own species.

References

Acebo, C. & Thoman, E. B. (1995). Role of infant crying in the early mother-infant dialogue. *Physiology & Behavior, 57*(3), 541–547.

Allday, E. (February 9, 2007). 2-time hero clings to life. *San Francisco Chronicle*, p. 1. Retrieved December 31, 2008, from http://www.sfgate.com/cgi-bin/article.cgi?f=/c/a/2007/02/09/MNGEKO1R511.DTL.

Aureli, F., Cords, M., & van Schaik, C. P. (2002). Conflict resolution following aggression in gregarious animals: A predictive framework. *Animal Behaviour, 64*(3), 325–343.

Aureli, F., Preston, S. D., & de Waal, F. B. (1999). Heart rate responses to social interactions in free-moving rhesus macaques (*Macaca mulatta*): a pilot study. *J Comp Psychol, 113*(1), 59–65.

Aureli, F. & Schaffner, C. M. (2002). Relationship assessment through emotional mediation. *Behaviour, 139*(2/3), 393–420.

Aureli, F. & Schino, G. (2004). The role of emotions in social relationships. In B. Thierry, M. Singh, & W. Kaumanns (Eds.), *Macaque societies* (pp. 38–61). Cambridge: Cambridge University Press.

Aureli, F. & Whiten, A. (2003). Emotions and behavioral flexibility. In D. Maestripieri (Ed.), *Primate psychology* (pp. 289–323). Cambridge, MA: Harvard University Press.

Axelrod, R. M. (1984). *The evolution of cooperation*. New York: Basic Books.

BBC h2g2 contributors (December 30, 2005). *Binti Jua - Gorilla Heroine*. Retrieved December 27, 2008, 2008, from http://www.bbc.co.uk/dna/h2g2/A2627264.

Barbas, H., Saha, S., Rempel-Clower, N., & Ghashghaei, T. (2003). Serial pathways from primate prefrontal cortex to autonomic areas may influence emotional expression. *BMC Neuroscience, 4*, 25.

Batson, C. D. (1998). Altruism and prosocial behavior. In D. Gilbert, S. Fiske, & G. Lindzey (Eds.), *The handbook of social psychology* (4th ed., Vol. 2, pp. 282–316). New York: McGraw-Hill.

Batson, C. D., Batson, J. G., Griffitt, C. A., Barrientos, S., Brandt, J. R., Sprengelmeyer, P., et al. (1989). Negative-state relief and the empathy-altruism hypothesis. *Journal of Personality and Social Psychology, 56*(6), 922–933.

Batson, C. D., Bolen, M. H., Cross, J. A., Neuringer-Benefiel, H. E. (1986). Where is the altruism in the altruistic personality? *Journal of Personality and Social Psychology, 50*(1), 212–220.

Batson, C. D. & Coke, J. (1981). Empathy: A source of altruistic motivation for helping. In J. Rushton, J. P. & Sorrentino, R. M. (Eds.), *Altruism and helping behavior*. Hillsdale, NJ: Erlbaum.

Bechara, A., Damasio, H., & Damasio, A. R. (2000). Emotion, decision making and the orbitofrontal cortex. *Cerebral Cortex, 10*(3), 295–307.

Bechara, A., Damasio, H., & Damasio, A. R. (2003). The role of the amygdala in decision-making. *Annals of the New York Academy of Sciences, 985*, 356–369.

Bechara, A., Damasio, H., Tranel, D., & Anderson, S. (1998). Dissociation of working memory from decision making within the human prefrontal cortex. *Journal of Neuroscience, 18*, 428–437.

Bechara, A., Damasio, H., Tranel, D., & Damasio, A. R. (1997). Deciding advantageously before knowing the advantageous strategy. *Science, 275*(5304), 1293–1294.

Berns, G. S., McClure, S. M., Pagnoni, G., & Montague, P. R. (2001). Predictability modulates human brain response to reward. *The Journal of Neuroscience, 21*(8), 2793–2798.

Berridge, K. C. & Robinson, T. E. (2003). Parsing reward. *Trends Neurosci, 26*(9), 507–513.

Boccia, M. L., Reite, M., & Laudenslager, M. (1989). On the physiology of grooming in a pigtail macaque. *Physiology and Behavior, 45*, 667–670.

Bowlby, J. (1958). The nature of the child's tie to his mother. *International Journal of Psycho-Analysis, 39*, 350–373.

Brosnan, S. F., & de Waal, F. B. M. (2002). A proximate perspective on reciprocal altruism. *Human Nature, 13*(1), 129–152.

Brown, S. L. & Brown, R. M. (2006). Selective investment theory: Recasting the functional significance of social bonds. *Psychological inquiry, 17*, 1–29.

Burkart, J. M., Fehr, E., Efferson, C., & van Schaik, C. P. (2007). Other-regarding preferences in a non-human primate: Common marmosets provision food altruistically. *Proceedings of the National Academy of Sciences, 104*(50), 19762–19766.

Caldwell, M. C. & Caldwell, D. K. (1966). Epimeletic (caregiving) behavior in Cetacea. In K. Norris (Ed.), *Whales, dolphins, and porpoises* (pp. 755–789). Berkeley: University of California Press.

Camerer, C. F. & Fehr, E. (2006). When does "economic man" dominate social behavior? *Science, 311*(5757), 47–52.

Carter, C. S., Grippo, A. J., Pournajafi-Nazarloo, H., Ruscio, M. G., Porges, S. W., Inga, D. N., et al. (2008). Oxytocin, vasopressin and sociality. In *Progress in brain research* (Vol. 170, pp. 331–336): Elsevier.

Castles, D. L. & Aureli, F. (1999). Social anxiety, relationships and self-directed behaviour among wild female olive baboons. *Animal Behaviour, 58*, 1207–1215.

Charney, D. S. & Nestler, E. J. (2005). *Neurobiology of mental illness*. New York: Oxford University Press.

Churchland, P. S. (2008). The impact of neuroscience on philosophy. *Neuron, 60*(3), 409–411.

Cialdini, R. B., Brown, S. L., Lewis, B. P., Luce, C., & Neuberg, S. L. (1997). Reinterpreting the empathy-altruism relationship: When one into one equals oneness. *Journal of Personality and Social Psychology, 73*(3), 481–494.

Cordoni, G., Palagi, E., & Tarli, S. (2006). Reconciliation and consolation in captive Western gorillas. *International Journal of Primatology, 27*(5), 1365–1382.

Critchley, H. D. (2004). The human cortex responds to an interoceptive challenge. *Proceedings of the National Academy of Sciences, 101*(17), 6333–6334.

Damasio, A. (1994). *Descartes' error: Emotion, reason, and the human brain*. New York, NY: G. P. Putman's Sons.

Damasio, A. R., Grabowski, T. J., Bechara, A., Damasio, H., Ponto, L. L. B., Parvizi, J., et al. (2000). Subcortical and cortical brain activity during the feeling of self-generated emotions. *Nature Neuroscience, 3*(10), 1049–1056.

Darwin, C. (1871/1982). *The descent of man, and selection in relation to sex*. Princeton: Princeton University Press.

Davies, N. B. & Houston, A. I. (1981). Owners and satellites: The economics of territory defence in the Pied wagtail, Motacilla alba. *Journal of Animal Ecology, 50*(1), 157–180.

Dawkins, R. (1976/2006). *The selfish gene* (30th Anniversary Edition ed.). Oxford: Oxford University Press.

de Quervain, D. J., Fischbacher, U., Treyer, V., Schellhammer, M., Schnyder, U., Buck, A., et al. (2004). The neural basis of altruistic punishment. *Science, 305*(5688), 1254–1258.

de Waal, F. & Brosnan, S. (2006). Simple and complex reciprocity in primates. In P. M. Kappeler & C. P. van Schaik (Ed.), *Cooperation in primates and humans* (pp. 85–105). Berlin: Springer.

de Waal, F. B. M. (1982). *Chimpanzee politics: Power and sex among apes.* Baltimore: The Johns Hopkins University Press.

de Waal, F. B. M. (1989). Food sharing and reciprocal obligations among chimpanzees. *Journal of Human Evolution, 18,* 433–459.

de Waal, F. B. M. (1997a). Food transfers through mesh in brown capuchins. *The Journal of Comparative Psychology, 111,* 370.

de Waal, F. B. M. (1997b). The chimpanzee's service economy: Food for grooming. *Evolution & Human Behavior, 18*(6), 375–386.

de Waal, F. B. M. (2000a). Attitudinal reciprocity in food sharing among brown capuchin monkeys. *Animal Behaviour, 60*(2), 253–261.

de Waal, F. B. M. (2000b). Primates: A natural heritage of conflict resolution. *Science, 289*(5479), 586–590.

de Waal, F. B. M. (2008). Putting the altruism back into altruism: The evolution of empathy. *Annual Review of Psychology, 59*(1), 279–300.

de Waal, F. B. M. & Aureli, F. (1996). Consolation, reconciliation, and a possible cognitive difference between macaque and chimpanzee. In A. E. Russon, K. A. Bard, & S. T. Parker (Ed.), *Reaching into thought: The minds of the great apes* (pp. 80–110). Cambridge, UK: Cambridge University Press.

de Waal, F. B. M. & Berger, M. L. (2000). Payment for labour in monkeys. *Nature, 404*(6778), 563.

de Waal, F. B. M. & Luttrell, L. M. (1988). Mechanisms of social reciprocity in three primate species: Symmetrical relationship characteristics or cognition? *Ethology & Sociobiology, 9,* 101–118.

de Waal, F. B. M., Luttrell, L. M., & Canfield, M. E. (1993). Preliminary data on voluntary food sharing in brown capuchin monkeys. *American Journal of Primatology, 29*(1), 73–78.

de Waal, F. B. M. & van Roosmalen, A. (1979). Reconciliation and consolation among chimpanzees. *Behavioral Ecology and Sociobiology, 5,* 55–66.

Dittus, W. P. & Ratnayeke, S. M. (1989). Individual and social behavioral responses to injury in wild toque macaques (Macaca sinica). *International Journal of Primatology, 10*(3), 215–234.

Drevets, W. C., Savitz, J., & Trimble, M. (2008). The subgenual anterior cingulate cortex in mood disorders. *CNS Spectrums, 13*(8), 663–681.

Dugatkin, L. A. (1997). The evolution of cooperation. *BioScience, 47*(6), 355–362.

Dugatkin, L. A. & Mesterton-Gibbons, M. (1996). Cooperation among unrelated individuals: reciprocal altruism, by-product mutualism and group selection in fishes. *Biosystems, 37*(1–2), 19–30.

Eibl-Eibesfeldt, I. (1971/1974). *Love and hate* (G. Strachan, Trans. 2nd ed.). New York: Schocken Books.

Eisenberg, N. & Fabes, R. A. (1990). Empathy: Conceptualization, measurement, and relation to prosocial behavior. *Motivation and Emotion, 14*(2), 131–149.

Eisenberg, N. & Fabes, R. A. (1998). Prosocial development. In N. Eisenberg (Ed.), *Handbook of child psychology* (5th ed., Vol. 3: Social, emotional, and personality development pp. 701–778). New York: John Wiley.

Eisenberg, N., Fabes, R. A., Miller, P. A., Fultz, J., Shell, R., Mathy, R. M., et al. (1989). Relation of sympathy and personal distress to prosocial behavior: A multimethod study. *Journal of Personality and Social Psychology, 57*(1), 55–66.

Eisenberg, N. & Strayer, J. (Eds.). (1987). Empathy and its development. New York: Cambridge University Press.

Feh, C. & de Mazières, J. (1993). Grooming at a preferred site reduces heart rate in horses. *Animal Behaviour, 46*(6), 1191–1194.

Fehr, E. & Camerer, C. F. (2007). Social neuroeconomics: The neural circuitry of social preferences. *Trends Cogn Sci, 11*(10), 419–427.

Fehr, E. & Fischbacher, U. (2003). The nature of human altruism. *Nature, 425*(6960), 785–791.

Fiorillo, C. D., Tobler, P. N., & Schultz, W. (2003). Discrete coding of reward probability and uncertainty by dopamine neurons. *Science, 299*(5614), 1898–1902.

Fraser, O. N., Stahl, D., & Aureli, F. (2008). Stress reduction through consolation in chimpanzees. *Proceedings of the National Academy of Sciences, 105*(25), 8557–8562.

Freedman, L. J., Insel, T. R., & Smith, Y. (2000). Subcortical projections of area 25 (subgenual cortex) of the macaque monkey. *Journal of Comparative Neurology, 421*(2), 172–188.

Fuentes, A., Malone, N., Sanz, C., Matheson, M., & Vaughan, L. (2002). Conflict and post-conflict behavior in a small group of chimpanzees. *Primates, 43*(3), 223–235.

Gadagkar, R. (1997). *Survival strategies: Cooperation and conflict in animal societies.* Cambridge: Harvard University Press.

Gallese, V. (2001). The "Shared Manifold" hypothesis: From mirror neurons to empathy. *Journal of Consciousness Studies 8*(5–7), 33–50.

Goodall, J. (1963). Feeding behaviour of wild chimpanzees: A preliminary report. *Symposia of the Zoological Society of London, 10,* 9–48.

Goodall, J. (1986). *The chimpanzees of Gombe: Patterns of behavior.* Cambridge, MA: Harvard University Press.

Hall, J. A. (1978). Gender effects in decoding nonverbal cues. *Psychological Bulletin, 85,* 845–857.

Hamilton, W. D. (1964). The evolution of social behavior. *Journal of Theoretical Biology, 7*(1–52).

Harbaugh, W. T., Mayr, U., & Burghart, D. R. (2007). Neural responses to taxation and voluntary giving rebel motives for charitable donation. *Science, 316,* 1622–1625.

Hart, B. L. (1990). Behavioral adaptations to pathogens and parasites: Five strategies. *Neuroscience & Biobehavioral Reviews, 14,* 273–294.

Hart, B. L. & Hart, L. A. (1992). Reciprocal allogrooming in impala, Aepyceros melampus. *Animal Behaviour, 44,* 1073–1083.

Hauser, M., McAuliffe, K., & Blake, P. R. (2009). Evolving the ingredients for reciprocity and spite. *Philos Trans R Soc Lond B Biol Sci, 364*(1533), 3255–3266.

Hemelrijk, C. K. (1994). Support for being groomed in long-tailed macaques, *Macaca fascicularis. Animal Behaviour, 48,* 479–481.

Henzi, S. P., & Barrett, L. (1999). The value of grooming to female primates. *Primates, 40,* 47–59.

Hirata, S. (2009). Chimpanzee social intelligence: Selfishness, altruism, and the mother–infant bond. *Primates, 50*(1), 3–11.

Hoffman, M. L. (1978). Empathy: Its development and prosocial implications. In J. H. E. Howe & C. B. Keasey (Eds.), *Nebraska symposium on motivation: Social cognitive development* (Vol. 25, pp. 169–217). Lincoln, NE: University of Nebraska Press.

Hoffman, M. L. (1981). Is altruism part of human nature? *Journal of Personality and Social Psychology, 40*(1), 121–137.

Hoffman, M. L. (2000). *Empathy and moral development: Implications for caring and justice.* New York: Cambridge University Press.

Hohmann, G. & Fruth, B. (1993). Field observations on meat sharing among bonobos (*Pan paniscus*). *Folia Primatologica, 6*, 225–229.

Hrdy, S. B. (2009). *Mothers and others.* Cambridge: Harvard University Press.

Insel, T. R. & Young, L. J. (2001). The neurobiology of attachment. *Nat Rev Neurosci, 2*(2), 129–136.

Jarvis, J. U. M., O'Riain, M. J., Bennett, N. C., & Sherman, P. W. (1994). Mammalian eusociality: A family affair. *Trends in Ecology and Evolution, 9*, 47–51.

Kagan, J. (2000). Human morality is distinctive. *Journal of Consciousness Studies, 7*, 46–48.

Kalin, N. H., Shelton, S. E., & Lynn, D. E. (1995). Opiate systems in mother and infant primates coordinate intimate contact during reunion. *Psychoneuroendocrinology, 20*(7), 735–742.

Kaplan, H. & Hill, K. (1985). Food sharing among ache foragers: Tests of explanatory hypotheses. *Current Anthropology, 26*(2), 223.

Keveme, E. B., Martensz, N. D., & Tuite, B. (1989). Beta-endorphin concentrations in cerebrospinal fluid of monkeys are influenced by grooming relationships. *Psychoneuroendocrinology, 14*, 155–161.

Knoch, D. & Fehr, E. (2007). Resisting the power of temptations: the right prefrontal cortex and self-control. *Ann N Y Acad Sci, 1104*, 123–134.

Knoch, D., Nitsche, M. A., Fischbacher, U., Eisenegger, C., Pascual-Leone, A., & Fehr, E. (2008). Studying the neurobiology of social interaction with transcranial direct current stimulation—the example of punishing unfairness. *Cereb Cortex, 18*(9), 1987–1990.

Knoch, D., Pascual-Leone, A., Meyer, K., Treyer, V., & Fehr, E. (2006). Diminishing reciprocal fairness by disrupting the right prefrontal cortex. *Science, 314*(5800), 829–832.

Koenig, W. D. (1988). Reciprocal altruism in birds: A critical review. *Ethology and Sociobiology 9*, 73–84.

Koenigs, M. & Tranel, D. (2007). Irrational economic decision-making after ventromedial prefrontal damage: evidence from the Ultimatum Game. *J Neurosci, 27*(4), 951–956.

Kosfeld, M., Heinrichs, M., Zak, P. J., Fischbacher, U., & Fehr, E. (2005). Oxytocin increases trust in humans. *Nature, 435*(7042), 673–676.

Koski, S. E. & Sterck, E. H. M. (2007). Triadic postconflict affiliation in captive chimpanzees: does consolation console? *Animal Behaviour, 73*(1), 133–142.

Koyama, N., Caws, C., & Aureli, F. (2006a). Interchange of grooming and agonistic support in chimpanzees. *International Journal of Primatology, 27*(5), 1293–1309.

Koyama, N. F., Caws, C., & Aureli, F. (2006b). Interchange of grooming and agonistic support in chimpanzees. *International Journal of Primatology, 27*, 1293–1309.

Krain, A. L., Wilson, A. M., Arbuckle, R., Castellanos, F. X., & Milham, M. P. (2006). Distinct neural mechanisms of risk and ambiguity: A meta-analysis of decision-making. *NeuroImage, 32*(1), 477–484.

Kringelbach, M. L., & Rolls, E. T. (2004). The functional neuroanatomy of the human orbitofrontal cortex: evidence from neuroimaging and neuropsychology. *Progress in Neurobiology, 72*(5), 341–372.

Kross, E., Davidson, M., Weber, J., & Ochsner, K. (2008). Coping with emotions past: The neural bases of regulating affect associated with negative autobiographical memories. *Biol Psychiatry.*

Krueger, F., McCabe, K., Moll, J., Kriegeskorte, N., Zahn, R., Strenziok, M., et al. (2007). Neural correlates of trust. *Proc Natl Acad Sci U S A, 104*(50), 20084–20089.

Lacey, E. A. & Sherman, P. W. (1991). Social organization of naked mole-rat colonies: Evidence for divisions of labor. In P. W. Sherman, J. U. M. Jarvis & R. D. Alexander (Eds.), *The biology of the naked mole-rat* (pp. 275–336). Princeton, NJ: Princeton University Press.

Lakshminarayanan, V. R. & Santos, L. R. (2008). Capuchin monkeys are sensitive to others' welfare. *Current Biology, 18*(21), R999–R1000.

Langergraber, K. E., Mitani, J. C., & Vigilant, L. (2007). The limited impact of kinship on cooperation in wild chimpanzees. *Proceedings of the National Academy of Sciences, USA, 104*, 7786–7790.

Lehmann, L., Keller, L., West, S., & Roze, D. (2007). Group selection and kin selection: Two concepts but one process. *Proceedings of the National Academy of Sciences, USA, 104*, 6736–6739.

Liotti, M., Mayberg, H. S., Brannan, S. K., McGinnis, S., Jerabek, P., & Fox, P. T. (2000). Differential limbic—cortical correlates of sadness and anxiety in healthy subjects: Implications for affective disorders. *Biol Psychiatry, 48*(1), 30–42.

Liu, D., Diorio, J., Tannenbaum, B., Caldji, C., Francis, D., Freedman, A., et al. (1997). Maternal care, hippocampal glucocorticoid receptors, and hypothalamic-pituitary-adrenal responses to stress. *Science, 277*(5332), 1659–1662.

Loewenstein, G. (2000). Emotions in economic theory and economic behavior. *The American Economic Review, 90*(2), 426–432.

Loewenstein, G. F., Weber, E. U., Hsee, C. K., & Welch, N. (2001). Risk as feelings. *Psychological bulletin, 127*(2), 267.

Lorberbaum, J., Newman, J. D., Horwitz, A. R., Dubno, J. R., Lydiard, R. B., Hamner, M. B., et al. (2002). A potential role for thalamocingulate circuitry in human maternal behavior. *Biological Psychiatry, 51*(6), 431–445.

Lorberbaum, J. P., Newman, J. D., Dubno, J. R., Horwitz, A. R., Nahas, Z., Teneback, C. C., et al. (1999). Feasibility of using fMRI to study mothers responding to infant cries. *Depression and Anxiety, 10*(3), 99–104.

MacLean, P. D. (1985). Brain evolution relating to family, play, and the separation call. *Archives of General Psychiatry, 42*(4), 405–417.

Maestripieri, D. (1993). Vigilance costs of allogrooming in macaque mothers. *The American Naturalist, 141*(5), 744–753.

Maestripieri, D., Schino, G., Aureli, F., & Troisi, A. (1992). A modest proposal: displacement activities as an indicator of emotions in primates. *Animal Behaviour, 44*(5), 967–979.

Mallavarapu, S., Stoinski, T. S., Bloomsmith, M. A., & Maple, T. L. (2006). Postconflict behavior in captive western lowland gorillas (*Gorilla gorilla gorilla*). *American Journal of Primatology*, *68*(8), 789–801.

Manson, J. H., David Navarrete, C., Silk, J. B., & Perry, S. (2004). Time-matched grooming in female primates? New analyses from two species. *Animal Behaviour*, *67*(3), 493–500.

Masserman, J. H., Wechkin, S., & Terris, W. (1964). "Altruistic" behavior in rhesus monkeys. *American Journal of Psychiatry*, *121*(6), 584–585.

Maynard Smith, J. (1964). Group selection and kin selection. *Nature*, *201*, 1145–1147.

Mayr, E. (1961). Cause and effect in biology. *Science*, *134*(3489), 1501–1506.

McCabe, K., Houser, D., Ryan, L., Smith, V., & Trouard, T. (2001). A functional imaging study of cooperation in two-person reciprocal exchange. *Proc Natl Acad Sci U S A*, *98*(20), 11832–11835.

Moll, J., Krueger, F., Zahn, R., Pardini, M., de Oliveira-Souza, R., & Grafman, J. (2006). Human fronto-mesolimbic networks guide decisions about charitable donation. *Proc Natl Acad Sci U S A*, *103*(42), 15623–15628.

Moore, J. (1984). The evolution of reciprocal sharing. *Ethology & Sociobiology*, *5*, 5–14.

Mooring, M. S., Blumstein, D. T., & Stoner, C. J. (2004). The evolution of parasite-defence grooming in ungulates. *Biological Journal of the Linnean Society*, *81*(1), 17–37.

Mooring, M. S. & Hart, B. L. (1995). Costs of allogrooming in impala: Distraction from vigilance. *Animal Behaviour*, *49*(5), 1414–1416.

Mooring, M. S. & Hart, B. L. (1997). Self grooming in impala mothers and lambs: Testing the body size and tick challenge principles. *Animal Behaviour*, *53*(5), 925–934.

Mooring, M. S., McKenzie, A. A., & Hart, B. L. (1996). Role of sex and breeding status in grooming and total tick load of impala. *Behavioral Ecology and Sociobiology*, *39*(4), 259–266.

Nisbett, R. E. & Wilson, T. D. (1977). Telling more than we can know: Verbal reports on mental processes. *Psychological Review*, *7*, 231–259.

O'Connell, S. M. (1995). Empathy in chimpanzees: Evidence for theory of mind? *Primates*, *36*(3), 397–410.

O'Connor, M. F., Gundel, H., McRae, K., & Lane, R. D. (2007). Baseline vagal tone predicts BOLD response during elicitation of grief. *Neuropsychopharmacology*, *32*(10), 2184–2189.

O'Doherty, J. (2003). Can't learn without you: Predictive value coding in orbitofrontal cortex requires the basolateral amygdala. *Neuron*, *39*(5), 731–733.

Ongür, D. & Price, J. L. (2000). The organization of networks within the orbital and medial prefrontal cortex of rats, monkeys and humans. *Cerebral Cortex*, *10*, 206–219.

Ongür, D., Ferry, A. T., & Price, J. L. (2003). Architectonic subdivision of the human orbital and medial prefrontal cortex. *Journal of Comparative Neurology*, *460*, 425–449.

Palagi, E., Cordoni, G., & Borgognini, T. S. (2006). Possible roles of consolation in captive chimpanzees (*Pan troglodytes*). *American Journal Physical Anthropology*, *129*, 105–111.

Palagi, E., Paoli, T., & Borgognini, T. S. (2004). Reconciliation and consolation in captive bonobos (*Pan paniscus*). *American Journal of Primatololgy*, *62*, 15–30.

Pavani, S., Maestripieri, D., Schino, G., Turillazzi, P. G., & Scucchi, S. (1991). Factors influencing scratching behavior in long-tailed macaques. *Folia primatologica*, *57*, 34–38.

Peciña, S. & Berridge, K. C. (2005). Hedonic hot spot in nucleus accumbens shell: Where do μ-opioids cause increased hedonic impact of sweetness? *The Journal of Neuroscience*, *25*(50), 11777–11786.

Perry, S. & Rose, L. (1994). Begging and transfer of coati meat by white-faced capuchin monkeys, *Cebus capucinus*. *Primates*, *35*(4), 409–415.

Pitcher, T. J. (1992). Who dares, wins: The function and evolution of predator inspection behaviour in shoaling fish. *Netherlands Journal of Zoology* (42), 371–391.

Pollock, G. B. & Rissing, S. W. (1989). Intraspecific brood raiding, territoriality, and slavery in ants. *The American Naturalist*, *133*(1), 61–70.

Preston, S. D. & Brown, S. L. (submitted). The ultimate and proximate bases of active altruism.

Preston, S. D. & de Waal, F. B. M. (2002). Empathy: Its ultimate and proximate bases. *Behavioral and Brain Sciences*, *25*(1), 1–71.

Pryce, C. R. (1996). Socialization, hormones, and the regulation of maternal behaviour in nonhuman simian primates. *Advances in the Study of Behavior*, *25*, 423–473.

Pusey, A. E. & Packer, C. (1997). The ecology of relationships. In J. R. Krebs & N. B. Davies (Eds.), *Behavioral ecology: An evolutionary approach* (4th ed., pp. 254–283). Oxford: Blackwell Science.

Reeve, H. K., Westneat, D. F., Noon, W. A., Sherman, P. W., & Aquadro, C. F. (1990). DNA "fingerprinting" reveals high levels of inbreeding in colonies of the eusocial naked mole-rat. *Proceedings of the National Academy of Sciences, USA*, *87*, 2496–2500.

Rilling, J. K., Gutman, D., Zeh, T., Pagnoni, G., Berns, G., & Kilts, C. (2002). A neural basis for social cooperation. *Neuron*, *35*(2), 395–405.

Rilling, J. K., Sanfey, A. G., Aronson, J. A., Nystrom, L. E., & Cohen, J. D. (2004). The neural correlates of theory of mind within interpersonal interactions. *Neuroimage*, *22*(4), 1694–1703.

Rissing, S. W. & Pollock, G. B. (1987). Queen aggression, pleometrotic advantage and brood raiding in the ant Veromessor pergandei (Hymenoptera: Formicidae). *Animal behaviour*, *35*(4), 975–981.

Robinson, T. E. & Berridge, K. C. (2003). Addiction. *Annu Rev Psychol*, *54*, 25–53.

Sanfey, A. G., Rilling, J. K., Aronson, J. A., Nystrom, L. E., & Cohen, J. D. (2003). The neural basis of economic decision-making in the Ultimatum Game. *Science*, *300*(5626), 1755–1758.

Schino, G., Geminiani, S., Rosati, L., & Aureli, F. (2004). Behavioral and emotional response of Japanese Macaque (Macaca fuscata) mothers after their offspring receive an aggression. *Journal of Comparative Psychology*, *118*(3), 340–346.

Schino, G., Scucchi, S., Maestripieri, D., & Turillazzi, P. G. (1988). Allogrooming as a tension-reduction mechanism: A behavioral approach. *American Journal of Primatology*, *16*(1), 43–50.

Schoenbaum, G., Chiba, A. A., & Gallagher, M. (1998). Orbitofrontal cortex and basolateral amygdala encode expected outcomes during learning. *Nat Neurosci*, *1*(2), 155–159.

Schoenbaum, G., Setlow, B., Saddoris, M. P., & Gallagher, M. (2003). Encoding predicted outcome and acquired value in orbitofrontal cortex during cue sampling depends upon input from basolateral amygdala. *Neuron, 39*(5), 855–867.

Schultz, W. (2002). Getting formal with dopamine and reward. *Neuron, 36*(2), 241–263.

Schwarz, N. & Clore, G. L. (2003). Mood as information: 20 years later. *Psychological Inquiry, 14*(3/4), 296–303.

Seyfarth, R. M. & Cheney, D. L. (1984). Grooming, alliances and reciprocal altruism in vervet monkeys. *Nature, 308*, 541–542.

Sherman, P. W. (1977). Nepotism and the evolution of alarm calls. *Science, 197*, 1246–1253.

Silk, J. B., Brosnan, S. F., Vonk, J., Henrich, J., Povinelli, D., & et al. (2005). Chimpanzees are indifferent to the welfare of unrelated group members. *Nature, 427*, 1357–1359.

Silk, J. B., Seyfarth, R. M., & Cheney, D. L. (1999). The structure of special relationships among female savanna baboons in Moremi Reserve, Botswana. *Behaviour, 136*, 679–703.

Singer, T., Seymour, B., O'Doherty, J. P., Stephan, K. E., Dolan, R. J., & Frith, C. D. (2006). Empathic neural responses are modulated by the perceived fairness of others. *Nature, 439*(7075), 466–469.

Smith, O. A., Astley, C. A., Chesney, M. A., Taylor, D. J., & Spelman, F. A. (1986). Personality, stress and cardiovascular disease: Human and nonhuman primates. In B. Lown, A. Malliani, & M. Prosdomici (Eds.), *Neural mechanisms and cardiovascular disease* (pp. 471–484). Padova: Liviana Press.

Smith, R. H., Turner, T. J., Garonzik, R., Leach, C. W., Urch-Druskat, V., & Weston, C. M. (1996). Envy and schadenfreude. *Pers Soc Psychol Bull, 22*(2), 158–168.

Sober, E. & Wilson, D. S. (1998). *Unto others: The evolution and psychology of unselfish behavior.* Cambridge, MA: Harvard University Press.

Sroufe, L. A. (1988). The role of infant-caregiver attachment in development. In J. Belsky & T. Nezworski (Eds.), *Clinical implications of attachment* (pp. 18–38). Hillsdale, NJ: Erlbaum.

Stacey, P. B. & Koenig, W. D. (1990). *Cooperative breeding in birds: Long-term studies of ecology and behavior.* Cambridge, UK: Cambridge University Press.

Stopka, P. & Graciasova, R. (2001). Conditional allogrooming in the herb-field mouse. *Behav. Ecol., 12*(5), 584–589.

Stopka, P. & Macdonald, D. W. (1999). The market effect in the wood mouse, *Apodemus sylvaticus*: Selling information on reproductive status. *Ethology, 105*(11), 969–982.

Takahashi, H., Kato, M., Matsuura, M., Mobbs, D., Suhara, T., & Okubo, Y. (2009). When your gain is my pain and your pain is my gain: Neural correlates of envy and schadenfreude. *Science, 323*(5916), 937–939.

Talbot, P. S. & Cooper, S. J. (2006). Anterior cingulate and subgenual prefrontal blood flow changes following tryptophan depletion in healthy males. *Neuropsychopharmacology, 31*, 1757–1767.

Tankersley, D., Stowe, C. J., & Huettel, S. A. (2007). Altruism is associated with an increased neural response to agency. *Nat Neurosci, 10*(2), 150–151.

Teleki, G. (1973). *The predatory behavior of wild chimpanzees.* Lewisburg, Pennsylvania: Bucknell University Press.

Tinbergen, N. (1963). On aims and methods of ethology. *Zeitschrift für Tierpsychologie, 20*, 410–433.

Trivers, R. L. (1971). The evolution of reciprocal altruism. *Quarterly Review of Biology, 46*, 35–57.

Troisi, A. & Schino, G. (1987). Environmental and social influences on autogrooming behaviour in a captive group of Java monkeys. *Behaviour, 100*, 292–302.

Ungerer, J. A. (1990). The early development of empathy: Self-regulation and individual differences in the first year. *Motivation and Emotion, 14*(2), 93–106.

van den Bos, W., McClure, S. M., Harris, L. T., Fiske, S. T., & Cohen, J. D. (2007). Dissociating affective evaluation and social cognitive processes in the ventral medial prefrontal cortex. *Cogn Affect Behav Neurosci, 7*(4), 337–346.

Walter, H., Abler, B., Ciaramidaro, A., & Erk, S. (2005). Motivating forces of human actions: Neuroimaging reward and social interaction. *Brain Research Bulletin, 67*, 368–381.

Warneken, F., Hare, B., Melis, A. P., Hanus, D., & Tomasello, M. (2007). Spontaneous altruism by chimpanzees and young children. *PLoS Biol, 5*(7), e184.

Watts, D. P., Colmenares, F., & Arnold, K. (2000). Redirection, consolation, and male policing: How targets of aggression interact with bystanders. In F. Aureli & F. d. Waal (Eds.), *Natural conflict resolution* (pp. 281–301). Berkeley: University California Press.

Whiten, A. (1996). When does smart behaviour-reading become mind-reading? In P. Carruthers & P. K. Smith (Eds.), *Theories of theories of mind* (pp. 277–292). Cambridge, UK: Cambridge University Press.

Wilkinson, G. S. (1984). Reciprocal food sharing in the vampire bat. *Nature, 308*, 181–184.

Wilkinson, G. S. (1986). Social grooming in the common vampire bat, *Desmodus rotundus*. *Animal Behaviour, 34*, 1880–1889.

Wilkinson, G. S. (1988). Reciprocal altruism in bats and other mammals. *Ethology and Sociobiology, 9*(2–4), 85–100.

Wilkinson, G. S. (1990). Food sharing in vampire bats. *Scientific American, 262*, 76–82.

Wilson, D. S. (1975). A theory of group selection. *Proc Natl Acad Sci U S A, 72*(1), 143–146.

Wilson, D. S. (1997). Altruism and organism: Disentangling the themes of multilevel selection theory. *Am Nat, 150 Suppl 1*, S122–134.

Wilson, D. S. & Sober, E. (1994). Reintroducing group selection to the human behavioral sciences. *Behavioral and Brain Sciences, 17*(4), 585–654.

Wilson, E. O. (2005). Kin selection as the key to altruism: Its rise and fall. *Social Research, 72*, 159–166.

Wispé, L. (1986). The distinction between sympathy and empathy: To call forth a concept, a word is needed. *Journal of Personality & Social Psychology, 50*(2), 314–321.

Wyvell, C. L. & Berridge, K. C. (2000). Intra-accumbens amphetamine increases the conditioned incentive salience of sucrose reward: Enhancement of reward "wanting" without enhanced "liking" or response reinforcement. *The Journal of Neuroscience, 20*(21), 8122–8130.

Yamasue, H., Abe, O., Suga, M., Yamada, H., Rogers, M. A., Aoki, S., et al. (2008). Sex-linked neuroanatomical basis of human altruistic cooperativeness. *Cerebral Cortex, 18*(10), 2331–2340.

Zahn, R., Moll, J., Paiva, M., Garrido, G., Krueger, F., Huey, E. D., et al. (2008). The neural basis of human social values: Evidence from functional MRI. *Cereb Cortex.*

Zahn-Waxler, C. & Radke-Yarrow, M. (1982). The development of altruism: Alternative research strategies. In N. Eisenberg (Ed.), *The development of prosocial behavior* (pp. 133–162). New York: Academic Press.

Zahn-Waxler, C., Radke-Yarrow, M., & King, R. A. (1979). Child rearing and children's prosocial initiations toward victims of distress. *Child Development, 50*(2), 319–330.

Zahn-Waxler, C., Radke-Yarrow, M., Wagner, E., & Chapman, M. (1992). Development of concern for others. *Developmental Psychology, 28*(1), 126–136.

Zak, P. J. (2004). Neuroeconomics. *Philos Trans R Soc Lond B Biol Sci, 359*(1451), 1737–1748.

Zak, P. J. (2008). The neurobiology of trust. *Scientific American, 298*(6), 88.

Why Rejection Hurts: What Social Neuroscience Has Revealed About the Brain's Response to Social Rejection

Naomi I. Eisenberger

Abstract

This chapter reviews evidence from behavioral, pharmacological, and social neuroscience research that supports the notion that physical and social pain rely on shared neural substrates. It then reviews some of the unexpected and potentially surprising consequences that arise from such a physical-social-pain overlap. Specifically, it considers evidence showing that, even though experiences of physical and social pain seem very different from one another on the surface, individuals who are more sensitive to one kind of pain are also more sensitive to the other. It also reviews evidence demonstrating that factors that alter one kind of pain experience alter the other in a congruent manner. Finally, the chapter concludes by discussing what this shared neural circuitry means for our experience and understanding of social pain.

Keywords: social rejection, social pain, neural circuitry, physical pain, neural substrates

In 1989, Vivian Paley, a MacArthur Award-winning teacher, introduced a new rule into her kindergarten classroom: "You can't say you can't play." In other words, social exclusion or not being allowed to play with others—an experience that is almost synonymous with childhood—was banned. As simple as it sounds, Paley describes the mixed feelings that her kindergarten students had about instituting the rule and the difficulty that they had, at first, in following it (discussed in her book; Paley, 1993). However, Paley also describes the palpable sense of relief she observed in her class once this new rule was put into effect: "It was as if the children had been rescued from meanness. They were grateful for a structure that let them feel good about themselves and each other."

As we all know, being rejected or excluded is distressing and painful, even at this young age. Indeed, most of us have vivid childhood memories of the pain of social rejection and can easily imagine the relief experienced by the children in Paley's classroom who were granted at least a temporary safe haven from this dreaded experience. Yet, one question that comes to mind when reflecting on these experiences is: Why is it that social rejection exerts such a powerful effect on our emotional well-being? Or more simply put, why is it that social rejection "hurts"?

Over the past several years, social neuroscience research has transformed our understanding of this question by demonstrating that the experience of social rejection or exclusion ("social pain") is processed by some of the same neural regions that process physical pain (Eisenberger, Lieberman, & Williams, 2003; Eisenberger & Lieberman, 2004, 2005; MacDonald & Leary, 2005). In essence, individuals may describe experiences of rejection as being "painful" because they rely, in part, on pain-related neural circuitry.

In fact, it has been suggested that, because of the importance of social connection for human survival, the social attachment system—which ensures social connection—may have piggybacked directly onto the physical pain system, borrowing the pain signal itself to indicate when social relationships are threatened (Panksepp, 1998). Specifically, as a mammalian species, humans are born relatively immature without the capacity to feed or fend for themselves and must rely solely on the care and nurturance of a caregiver in order to survive. Later in life, being connected to close others as well as a social group increases chances of survival by providing access to shared resources as well as protection from predators (Axelrod & Hamilton, 1981; Buss, 1990). Thus, over the course of our evolutionary history, being separated from others significantly decreased chances of survival. Consequently, if broken social ties are experienced as "painful," an individual will be more likely to avoid situations that might threaten social ties or lead to rejection, hence increasing one's likelihood of inclusion in the social group and one's chances of survival. In short, to the extent that social rejection or exclusion is a threat to survival, feeling "hurt" by these experiences may be an adaptive way to prevent them.

In this chapter, I will review evidence from behavioral, pharmacological, and social neuroscience research that supports the notion that physical and social pain rely on shared neural substrates. I will then review some of the unexpected and potentially surprising consequences that arise from such a physical-social-pain overlap. Specifically, I will review evidence showing that, even though experiences of physical and social pain seem very different from one another on the surface, those individuals who are more sensitive to one kind of pain are also more sensitive to the other. I will also review evidence demonstrating that factors that alter one kind of pain experience alter the other in a congruent manner. Finally, I will end by discussing what this shared neural circuitry means for our experience and understanding of social pain.

Evidence for a Physical-Social Pain Overlap
Linguistic Evidence

One reason to believe that physical and social pain share overlapping mechanisms is that they share a common vocabulary. When individuals describe times when they have felt rejected or excluded, they will often describe these experiences with words typically reserved for physical pain experiences—complaining of "hurt" feelings and "broken" hearts. Indeed, there is no other way to describe socially painful experiences other than through the use of these physical pain words. Interestingly, the use of physical pain words to describe experiences of social pain is not unique to the English language and is observed across many other languages as well (MacDonald & Leary, 2005). However, while suggestive, linguistic evidence alone does not substantiate the claim that physical and social pain processes overlap. After all, it is possible that describing rejection as being "painful" may be no more than a convenient metaphor and social rejection may not actually be experienced as painful. One way to more convincingly demonstrate an overlap in the mechanisms that support physical and social pain processes is to show that they rely on shared neurochemistry or shared neural circuitry. Here, I will review pharmacological, neuropsychological, and neuroimaging research to support this overlap.

Pharmacological Evidence

Pharmacological studies provide evidence that physical and social pain rely on shared neurochemistry by showing that certain drugs have similar effects on both types of pain. For example, opiate drugs, such as morphine and heroin, known primarily for their pain-relieving qualities, have also been shown to reduce behaviors indicative of social pain in animals. Specifically, low, nonsedative doses of morphine have been shown to reduce distress vocalizations made by infants when separated from their mothers across multiple species, including monkeys, dogs, guinea pigs, rats, and chickens (Carden, Barr, & Hofer, 1991; Herman & Panksepp, 1978; Kalin, Shelton, & Barksdale, 1988; Panksepp et al., 1978; Warnick, McCurday, & Sufka, 2005). Moreover, some have suggested that in humans opiate abuse is due, in part, to its capacity to alleviate negative social experience, as opiate addiction is most common in environments where social isolation is pervasive (Panksepp, 1998). Consistent with this, animal research has demonstrated greater opiate consumption among animals who are separated from companions (Alexander, Coambs, & Hadaway, 1978). Similar to the effects of opiates, antidepressants (such as selective serotonin reuptake inhibitors or SSRIs), which are commonly prescribed to treat anxiety and depression often resulting from social stressors, also alleviate physical pain (Nemoto, Toda, Nakajima, Hosokawa, Okada, et al., 2003;

Shimodozono, Kamishita, Ogata, Tohgo, & Tanaka, 2002; Singh, Jain, & Kulkarni, 2001) and are now commonly prescribed to treat chronic pain conditions. Thus, both opiates and antidepressants seem to reduce social as well as physical pain.

Neural Evidence

Neuropsychological and neuroimaging research amassed over the past several decades has also provided support for a physical-social pain overlap by showing that some of the same neural regions that are involved in physical pain are also involved in separation distress behaviors in nonhuman mammals and social pain experience in humans.

The neural correlates of physical pain

Physical pain experience can be subdivided into two components: 1) a *sensory* component, which codes for the discriminative aspects of pain (e.g., location, intensity, duration) and 2) an *affective* component, which codes for the unpleasant aspects of pain (e.g., distressing, suffering). Because the experience of social rejection does not necessitate any direct sensory contact, the affective component of pain may be more relevant for understanding feelings of social pain and will be focused on here.

The "affective" or unpleasant component of physical pain is processed by various regions of the anterior cingulate cortex (specifically the dorsal portion: dACC) and insula (anterior insula) (Apkarian, Bushnell, Treede, & Zubieta, 2005; Peyron, Laurent, & Garcia, 2000; Price, 2000; Rainville, 2002). Thus, chronic pain patients who have undergone cingulotomy—a surgery in which a portion of the dACC is lesioned (Richter et al., 2004)—report that they can still feel and localize pain sensation (sensory component intact) but that the pain no longer "bothers" them (Foltz & White, 1968; Hebben, 1985). Similar reductions in emotional responses to painful stimuli have been observed following insular lesions as well (Berthier, Starkstein, Leiguardia, & Carrea, 1988).

Neuroimaging studies support these neuropsychological findings by showing that both the dACC and anterior insula track the affective component of pain. In one study, subjects who were hypnotized to selectively increase the "unpleasantness" of noxious stimuli (affective component) without altering the intensity (sensory component) showed increased activity in the dACC without changing activity in the primary somatosensory cortex (Rainville, Duncan, Price, Carrier, & Bushnell, 1997). Moreover, other work has shown that self-reports of pain unpleasantness correlate specifically with dACC activity (Peyron et al., 2000; Tolle et al., 1999). Similarly, the anterior insula has been shown to track the affective component of pain and self-reported pain unpleasantness correlates with bilateral anterior insular activity as well (Schreckenberger et al., 2005).

The ACC and separation distress in non-human mammals

Interestingly, the ACC—clearly implicated in perceptions of pain unpleasantness—is also a major contributor to attachment-related distress vocalizations. In many mammalian species, infants will emit distress vocalizations upon caregiver separation in order to signal the caregiver to return to the infant. These vocalizations are presumed to reflect some degree of distress due to separation and serve the adaptive purpose of reducing prolonged separation from a caregiver. Highlighting a role for the ACC in distress vocalizations, it has been shown that lesions to the ACC (that include both dorsal and ventral regions) eliminate the production of these distress vocalizations (Hadland, Rushworth, Gaffan, & Passingham, 2003; MacLean & Newman, 1988), whereas electrical stimulation of the ACC can lead to the spontaneous production of these vocalizations (Robinson, 1967; Smith, 1945). Similar findings have not been observed for the anterior insula. However, other regions that play a role in pain processing, such as the periaqueductal gray (PAG), are also known to be involved in attachment-related behaviors such as distress vocalizations (Bandler & Shipley, 1994).

The neural correlates of social pain in humans

Recent research has also started to reveal that the neural regions that are most often associated with pain unpleasantness (dACC, anterior insula) are also involved in the distressing experience of social exclusion. In the first neuroimaging study of social exclusion (Eisenberger, Lieberman, & Williams, 2003), participants were led to believe that they would be scanned while playing an interactive ball-tossing game over the Internet ("cyberball"), with two other individuals who were also in fMRI scanners. Unbeknownst to participants, they were actually playing with a preset computer program. Participants completed one round of the ball-tossing game in which they were included and a second round in which they were excluded partway through the game.

Upon being excluded from the game, compared to when being included, participants showed increased activity in both the dACC and anterior insula—a pattern very similar to what is often observed in studies of physical pain. Furthermore, individuals who showed greater activity in the dACC reported greater levels of social distress (e.g., "I felt rejected," "I felt meaningless") in response to the exclusion episode. In addition to activity in these pain-related neural regions, participants also showed significant activity (in response to exclusion vs. inclusion) in a neural region that is often associated with regulating painful or negative affective experience—the right ventral prefrontal cortex (RVPFC; Hariri, Bookheimer, Mazziotta, 2000; Lieberman, Jarcho, Berman, Naliboff, Suyenobu, Mandelkern, & Mayer, 2004; Lieberman, Eisenberger, Crockett, Tom, Pfeifer, & Way, 2007; Ochsner & Gross, 2005; Petrovic & Ingvar, 2002; Wager et al., 2004). Indeed, consistent with this region's role in emotion/pain regulatory processes, greater RVPFC activity was associated with lower levels of self-reported social distress in response to social exclusion and reduced activity in the dACC. Finally, we found that the dACC was a significant mediator of the RVPFC—distress relationship, such that the RVPFC may relate to lower levels of social distress by downregulating the activity of the dACC.

Although, we have not yet examined neural responses to physical and social pain within the same set of participants, Figure 39.1 shows the similarity in the neural responses to social pain, taken from the study of social exclusion described above (on the left; Eisenberger et al., 2003) and the neural responses to physical pain, taken from a neuroimaging study of irritable bowel syndrome patients undergoing painful visceral stimulation (on the right; Lieberman et al., 2004). Thus, not only are the general locations of the activations similar but the pattern of correlations between neural activity and self-reported pain or social distress is similar as well.

Subsequent research, using various experimental designs, has provided analogous findings. Thus, both our own group and others have found that greater self-reported social pain following the cyberball game was associated with greater activity in the dACC (Eisenberger, Taylor, Gable, Hilmert, & Lieberman, 2007; Onoda et al., 2009). Moreover, it has been shown that individual difference factors that typically moderate responses to social pain show the expected relationships with neural activity. Thus, individuals with higher levels of social support show reduced dACC activity in response to social exclusion (Eisenberger, Taylor et al., 2007).

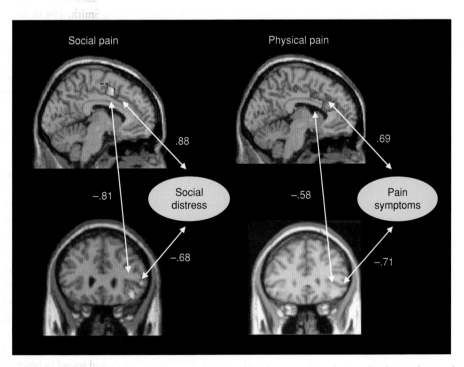

Fig. 39.1 The left side of the panel displays neural activity during social exclusion, compared to social inclusion, that correlates with self-reported social distress (from Eisenberger, Lieberman, & Williams, 2003). The right side of the panel displays the neural activity during painful visceral stimulation, compared to baseline, that correlates with self-reported pain experience. (From Lieberman, Jarcho, Berman, Naliboff, Suyenobu, Mandelkern, & Mayer, 2004. Reprinted with permission of Elsevier.)

Conversely, individuals with lower levels of self-esteem (vs. higher levels of self-esteem) report feeling more hurt in response to social exclusion (using the cyberball game) and also show greater activity in the dACC (Onoda et al., 2010). Finally, individuals who reported feeling more socially rejected or disconnected in their real-world social interactions (assessed daily across a 10-day period) showed greater activity in the dACC and PAG in response to a cyberball-exclusion episode (Eisenberger, Gable, & Lieberman, 2007), suggesting a link between real-world experiences of social rejection and pain-related neural activation.

In addition to studies examining the neural correlates underlying the experience of social pain, studies using rejection-themed images or facial expressions have shown similar effects as well. Thus, Kross and colleagues (2007) have shown both dACC and anterior insula activity in response to rejection-themed images (paintings by Edward Hopper) compared to acceptance-themed images. Moreover, we have shown that for rejection-sensitive individuals, viewing videos of individuals making disapproving facial expressions—a potential cue of social rejection—was associated with greater activity in the dACC, but not other limbic regions (e.g., amygdala), suggesting that the dACC may be specifically responsive to these cues of rejection (Burklund, Eisenberger, & Lieberman, 2007).

Finally, other types of socially painful experiences, such as bereavement, have also been shown to activate pain-related neural regions. In one study (Gundel, O'Connor, Littrell, Fort, & Lane, 2003), bereaved participants were scanned while viewing pictures of their deceased first-degree relative or pictures of a stranger. In response to viewing pictures of the deceased, compared to pictures of a stranger, participants showed greater activity in regions of the dACC and anterior insula. A subsequent study, using a similar design, replicated these findings; bereaved individuals experiencing normal or complicated grief showed greater activity in both the dACC and anterior insula in response to viewing images of the deceased vs. images of a stranger (O'Connor et al., 2008). Thus, various types of socially painful experience—not just experiences of social rejection or exclusion—may activate pain-related neural regions as well.

Summary
Across diverse languages, individuals use the same words to describe the negative feelings associated with physical injury and social rejection.

Pharmacological agents that affect one type of pain appear to have parallel effects on the other. Moreover, neural data from both animal and human subjects converge to show that some of the same neural regions support both physical and social pain experience. One of these regions, the dACC, has been shown to be involved in the experienced unpleasantness of physical pain, the elicitation of separation distress behaviors in non-human mammals, and the experience of distress following social rejection in humans. Other regions that have also been shown to play a role in these pain processes include the anterior insula and PAG, which encode physical pain experience (Aziz, Schnitzler, & Enck, 2000; Bandler & Shipley, 1994; Cechetto & Saper, 1987), as well as the RVPFC, which has been involved in regulating painful as well as generally negative affective experience (Hariri et al., 2000; Lieberman et al., 2004, 2007; Petrovic & Ingvar, 2002; Wager et al., 2004).

Taken together, these data provide convergent evidence for a physical-social pain overlap. In the next section, I will highlight some of the expected functional consequences of such an overlap and will review several studies that have examined the nature of these consequences. It should be noted, however, that even though there is evidence to support a functional overlap in physical and social pain processes, these processes certainly do not overlap completely. Intuitively, we know this to be true because we can differentiate between pain due to a relationship snub and pain due to physical injury. Moreover, research has identified specific differences between these two types of pain experience. For example, Chen and colleagues have shown that individuals can easily relive the pain of previous relationship breakups or other socially painful events; however, it is much harder, and sometimes impossible to relive the pain of physical injury (Chen, Williams, Fitness, & Newton, 2008). Nonetheless, even though there are certainly ways in which physical and social pain experiences are different, this next section will focus on ways in which these pain processes are similar and the consequences of this similarity.

Consequences of a Physical-Social Pain Overlap
One of the benefits of identifying a physical-social pain overlap is that it leads to several novel hypotheses regarding the functional consequences of such an overlap. The first hypothesis—*the individual differences hypothesis*—is that individuals who are more

sensitive to one kind of pain should also be more sensitive to the other because both of these pain processes are governed, in part, by the same underlying system. The second hypothesis—*the manipulation hypothesis*—is that factors that either increase or decrease one kind of pain should affect the other in a similar manner, because altering one pain process should alter the underlying system that supports both pain types of painful experience. Here I will review evidence for each of these hypotheses. I will then discuss several other possible consequences of a social-pain overlap that have remained largely unexplored.

Individual Differences Hypothesis: Sensitivity to One Kind of Pain Should Relate to Sensitivity to the Other

One of the intriguing consequences of a physical-social pain overlap is that individuals who are more sensitive to one kind of pain (e.g., physical pain) should also be more sensitive to a seemingly different kind of pain (e.g., social pain). To test this notion, we have investigated whether baseline sensitivity to physical pain relates to self-reported sensitivity to social rejection (Eisenberger, Jarcho, Lieberman, & Naliboff, 2006). In this study, participant's baseline sensitivity to physical pain was assessed by asking participants to rate the temperature at which they perceived a painful heat stimulus delivered to their forearm to be very unpleasant ("pain threshold"). After this, participants completed one round of the cyberball game in which they were socially excluded and were subsequently asked to rate how much social distress they felt in response to being excluded. As predicted, individuals who were more sensitive to physical pain at baseline (e.g., lower baseline pain thresholds) were also more socially distressed by the social exclusion episode. Moreover, this relationship remained significant after controlling for neuroticism, suggesting that this relationship cannot be explained solely by a general tendency to report higher levels of negative experience.

Building on this, we have also examined whether a genetic correlate of physical pain sensitivity relates to social pain sensitivity as well (Way, Taylor, & Eisenberger, 2009). Previous research has shown that a polymorphism in the mu-opioid receptor gene (*OPRM1*; *A118G*) is associated with physical pain sensitivity, such that individuals with the variant G allele tend to experience more physical pain and need more morphine to deal with the pain (Chou et al., 2006a-b; Coulbault et al., 2006;

Sia et al., 2008). To examine whether this polymorphism also related to social pain sensitivity, we examined whether allelic differences in the *OPRM1* gene related to both dispositional and neural sensitivity to social rejection. Participants (n = 125) were genotyped for the *OPRM1* gene and were asked to complete a self-report measure of trait sensitivity to rejection (Mehrabian Sensitivity to Rejection Scale; Mehrabian, 1976; e.g., "I am very sensitive to any signs that a person might not want to talk to me"). Following this, a subset of these individuals (n = 30) completed the cyberball game in the scanner in which they were socially excluded. Results demonstrated that G allele carriers—who have previously been shown to be more sensitive to physical pain—also reported significantly higher levels of rejection sensitivity. Moreover, neuroimaging analyses revealed that G allele carriers also showed greater pain-related neural activity (dACC, anterior insula) in response to social exclusion (Figure 39.2). Thus, a genetic correlate of physical pain sensitivity related to both dispositional and neural sensitivity to social pain as well.

Although less work has examined whether individual differences in social pain sensitivity relate to physical pain sensitivity, correlational research has shown that adolescents with higher levels of attachment anxiety (increased sensitivity to rejection from an attachment figure) also reported greater pain severity over a one-month assessment period (Tremblay & Sullivan, 2009). Moreover, depressed individuals who reported increases in levels of state rejection sensitivity also reported increases in symptoms of pain (e.g., chest pain, headaches, body aches and pains) (Ehnvall, Mitchel, Hadzi-Pavlovic, Malhi, & Parker, 2009). Thus, individuals who tend to be more sensitive to rejection may also be more sensitive to physical pain.

Manipulation Hypothesis: Factors that Increase or Decrease One Kind of Pain Should Affect the Other in a Similar Manner

To the extent that physical and social pain processes overlap, factors that alter one type of painful experience should affect the other type of pain in a similar manner. Thus, factors that increase or decrease social pain should have similar effects on physical pain, and, likewise, factors that increases or decrease physical pain should have parallel effects on social pain. Although few studies have directly examined this hypothesis, as it is not necessarily intuitive to measure feelings of social and physical pain in the

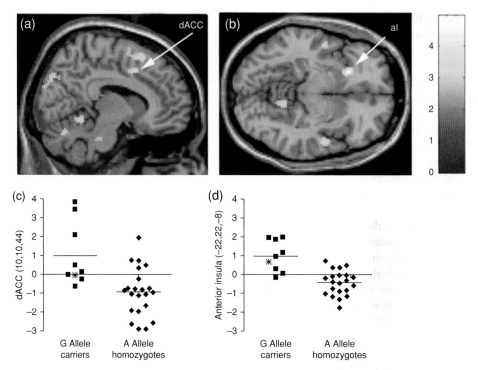

Fig. 39.2 Sagittal (a; dACC) and axial (b; anterior insula, denoted by arrow) sections of neural activations during social exclusion vs. inclusion that showed significantly greater activity (p < 0.001, 20 voxel extent) for G allele carriers than A allele homozygotes. c) Parameter estimates from the dACC (8,12,44; $t_{(24)}$ = 4.06, p < 0.001); d) Parameter estimates from the left anterior insula (–22,24,–8; $t_{(24)}$ = 5.07, p < 0.001). * denotes G allele homozygote.

same study, the number of studies that have started to explicitly test this notion is increasing. I will begin by reviewing the studies that have examined whether factors that increase or decrease social pain (social pain potentiation/regulation effects) affect physical pain and will then review the studies that have examined whether factors that increase or decrease physical pain (physical pain potentiation/regulation) affect social pain as well.

Social pain potentiation effects

To explore whether factors that increase social pain increase physical pain as well, we tested whether an episode of social exclusion increased subsequent physical pain sensitivity (Eisenberger et al., 2006). In this study, participants were randomly assigned to play a round of the cyberball game in which they were either included or excluded. Then, as participants were either being included or excluded from the game, they were exposed to three painful heat stimuli (the level of heat was customized so that each participant received heat stimuli that he/she had previously rated as "very unpleasant") and were asked to rate the unpleasantness of each. Following this, participants rated how much social distress

they felt during the cyberball game (e.g., "I felt rejected," "I felt meaningless"). Although we did not find that excluded individuals reported feeling more pain in response to the heat stimuli than included individuals, we did find that, among subjects who were excluded, those who felt the most social distress also reported the highest pain ratings in response to the heat stimuli. Moreover, this effect remained after controlling for neuroticism, suggesting that the positive correlational relationship between social distress and pain distress was not due solely to a greater tendency to report negative affect and could reflect a more specific relationship between physical and social pain processes. Thus, even though this finding is correlational, it suggests that augmented sensitivity to one type of pain is related to augmented sensitivity to the other.

It should be noted, however, that these findings are somewhat different from those of another study that examined the effect of social exclusion (using a different manipulation) on physical pain sensitivity (DeWall & Baumeister, 2006). This study was based on the observation that extreme physical pain can sometimes turn off the pain system itself, leading to temporary analgesia or numbness (Gear, Aley, &

Levine, 1999). Based on this observation, it was hypothesized that, to the extent that physical and social pain overlap, extreme forms of social exclusion should lead to numbness, not only to negative social experiences, but to physical pain as well. In this study (DeWall & Baumeister, 2006), social exclusion was manipulated by telling participants that they would be alone in the future. Participants in this "future alone" condition, compared to those who were given no feedback or who were told that they would have satisfying relationships in the future, showed a reduced (rather than an increased) sensitivity to physical pain.

Differences between these two sets of findings could be due to the underlying nature of the pain system, such that mild pain (e.g., being excluded by strangers during the cyberball game) augments pain sensitivity whereas more intense pain (e.g., being told that one will be alone in the future) leads to analgesia (Gear et al., 1999; Price, 2000). It is also possible that the "future alone" manipulation may have induced more depression-like affect, which in some cases has been associated with reduced experimental pain sensitivity (Adler & Gattaz, 1993; Dickens, McGowan, & Dale, 2003; Orbach, Mikulincer, King, Cohen, & Stein, 1997), whereas the cyberball manipulation may have induced more anxiety-like affect, which has been linked with increased experimental pain sensitivity (Cornwall & Donderi, 1988; Lautenbacher & Krieg, 1994; Melzack & Wall, 1999). Nonetheless, it is important to note that in both studies, physical and social pain sensitivity still appear to be working in parallel. In the first study, greater sensitivity to social rejection was correlated with greater sensitivity to physical pain; in the second, an extreme form of social exclusion resulted in general emotional insensitivity, both to social and physical pain.

As a final example of the effect of social pain potentiation on physical pain, Gray and Wegner (2009) examined whether an intentional interpersonal transgression (i.e., stepping on someone's toe on purpose), which is typically more emotionally "hurtful" than an accidental transgression, was also more physically painful. Participants believed that another subject, who was actually a confederate, was going to choose which of two tasks the participant was going to complete. In the intentional transgression condition, the confederate chose a task that involved the participant receiving electric shock; in the unintentional transgression condition, the confederate chose a pitch judgment task for the participant to complete, but the participant still received shock due to study constraints. Participants were told which task the confederate chose for them and then rated pain unpleasantness as they received a series of electric shocks. Results demonstrated that physical pain ratings following the intentional transgression were higher than those following the unintentional transgression. In addition, while participants in the unintentional transgression condition showed habituation to repeated painful stimulation, those in the intentional transgression condition did not. Thus, social factors that are primarily thought to increase emotional pain seem to affect physical pain in a congruent manner.

Social pain regulation effects

A great deal of correlational research has shown that factors that reduce social pain—such as social support—are associated with less physical pain as well. Thus, individuals with more social support report feeling less pain during childbirth (Chalmers, Wolman, Nikodem, Gulmezoglu, & Hofmeyer, 1995; Kennell, Klaus, McGrath, Robertson, & Hinkley, 1991), following coronary artery bypass surgery (King, Reis, Porter, & Norsen, 1993; Kulik & Mahler, 1989), and during cancer (Zaza & Baine, 2002). However, because of the correlational nature of these studies, it is not clear if social support directly reduces physical pain or whether some third variable (e.g., extraversion) explains these effects.

A few experimental studies have provided evidence to suggest that social support may directly reduce physical pain by demonstrating that participants receiving interactive support during a painful task reported less pain than participants completing the task alone or during nonsupportive interactions (Brown, Sheffield, Leary, & Robinson, 2003; Jackson, Iezzi, Chen, Ebnet, & Eglitis, 2005). However, given the nature of these studies, some of the pain-attenuating effects of social support could have been due to other factors unrelated to social support, such as distraction due to the presence of the support figure or reappraisal due to the support figure actively helping the participant to cope with the pain.

Thus, in a recent study, we examined whether a very minimal social support manipulation could directly reduce physical pain experience (Master, Eisenberger, Taylor, Naliboff, Shirinyan, & Lieberman, 2009). In this study, female participants received a series of painful heat stimuli and were asked to rate the unpleasantness of each while they went through a number of different tasks, including holding their partner's hand, a stranger's hand, or a squeeze-ball and viewing a picture of their partner, a stranger, or a neutral object (a chair). We found that participants reported significantly less pain while holding their partner's hand compared to when they were holding a stranger's hand or an object. Interestingly, participants also reported feeling significantly less pain while simply viewing pictures of their partner compared to when they were viewing pictures of a stranger or an object. Thus, simple reminders of one's social support figure may be capable of directly reducing physical pain, in addition to social pain.

Physical pain potentiation effects
Although there is not a lot of research that has directly examined whether potentiating physical pain experience potentiates social pain experience as well, there is some correlational research that supports the notion that these two experiences are related. For example, Bowlby noted that when children experience physical pain, they become much more sensitive to the whereabouts of their caregiver, experiencing distress more frequently and easily upon noting distance from a caregiver (Bowlby, 1969). Similarly, compared to healthy controls, adults with chronic pain are more likely to have an anxious attachment style, characterized by a heightened sense of concern with their partner's relationship commitment (Ciechanowski, Sullivan, Jensen, Romano, & Summers, 2003).

In the only experimental study (to our knowledge) to examine whether factors that increase physical pain also increase experiences of social pain, we examined the effect of inflammatory activity on feelings of social disconnection (Eisenberger, Inagaki, Mashal, & Irwin, 2010). Previous research has shown that pro-inflammatory cytokines, which are involved in fighting off foreign agents such as bacteria, facilitates physical pain experience as well, presumably to promote recovery and recuperation from infection or disease (Watkins & Maier, 2000). Here, we wanted to see if inflammatory processes might also increase social pain experience.

In this study, participants were randomly assigned to either receive placebo or endotoxin—a bacterial agent that has been shown to trigger an inflammatory response in a safe manner. Participants were then asked to complete hourly self-report measures of their feelings of social disconnection (e.g., "I feel disconnected from others," "I feel overly sensitive around others (e.g., my feelings are easily hurt)") for six hours. Results demonstrated that individuals in the endotoxin condition reported significantly greater increases in feelings of social disconnection (from baseline to two hours post-drug treatment) than those in the placebo condition. Thus, activating inflammatory processes, known to increase experiences of physical pain, increased self-reports of social disconnection as well.

Physical pain regulation effects
Finally, we have also examined whether factors that regulate physical pain also regulate social pain. Specifically, we have explored whether Tylenol (generic name: acetaminophen), a well-known physical pain reliever, could also reduce social pain (DeWall et al., 2010). In a first study, participants were randomly assigned to take either a daily dose of Tylenol (1000 mg/day) or placebo for 3 weeks and were asked each night to report on their daily "hurt feelings" (e.g., "Today, I rarely felt hurt by what other people said or did to me" (reverse-scored)). Results demonstrated that individuals in the Tylenol condition showed a significant reduction in hurt feelings across the 3-week period, whereas individuals in the placebo condition showed no significant change in hurt feelings over time. In fact, the average participant in the Tylenol group reported significantly lower daily hurt feelings than the average participant in the placebo group starting on Day 9 and continuing through Day 21.

To further examine the neural mechanisms that might underlie these effects, in a second study, participants were randomly assigned to take a daily dose of Tylenol (2000 mg/day) or placebo for 3 weeks and then completed the cyberball task in the scanner at the end of the 3-week period. Consistent with the results from the first study, participants in the Tylenol condition, compared to those in the placebo condition, showed significantly less pain-related neural activity (dACC, anterior insula) in response to social exclusion (Figure 39.3). Thus, Tylenol, a well-known physical pain reliever, appears to have similar effects on experiences of social pain.

Other Consequences of a Physical-Social Pain Overlap?
There are several other possible consequences of a physical-social pain overlap that have not yet been directly explored. One of these may be the aggressive behaviors that are observed following both physical and social pain. Aggressive action makes sense if one is in danger of being physically harmed, and not surprisingly, one consequence of painful stimulation in animals is aggressive attacks on a con-specific (Berkowitz, 1983). However, aggressive acts make less sense if one is being socially harmed,

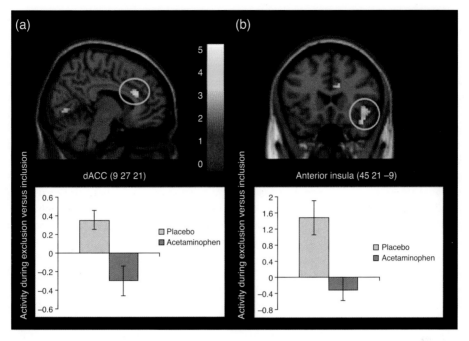

Fig. 39.3 Whole-brain, between-group analysis displaying neural activity (parameter estimates during exclusion vs. inclusion) that was greater for participants who took placebo (vs. those who took acetaminophen) in the (a) dACC and (b) right anterior insula (p < .005, 20 voxels). Bar graphs (with standard error bars) for each region show the activity during exclusion compared to inclusion, averaged across the entire cluster, for the acetaminophen and placebo groups.

as aggression is presumably not conducive to strengthening or mending social ties. Nonetheless, it has been well documented that the experience of social rejection can lead to aggressive acts as well (Twenge, Baumeister, Tice, & Stucke, 2001). Thus, it is possible that aggressive responses to rejection may be a by-product of an adaptive response to physical pain, which was subsequently co-opted by the social pain system. In other words, although aggressive responses to rejection may be maladaptive in recreating social bonds, this response may reflect a conservation of behavioral responses that are adaptive following physical pain.

Another possible consequence of this overlap may be the similar physiological stress responses that are observed to both physical threat and social threat. It is well known that physical threat induces physiological stress responses to mobilize energy and resources to deal with the threat (Taylor, 2003), and this makes good sense. Escaping a predator or navigating some other life-threatening situation may require a significant amount of physical energy. However, these same physiological responses are responsive to social threats as well, such as being socially evaluated (Dickerson & Kemeny, 2004). Although this may not seem surprising to stress researchers who have witnessed these effects

repeatedly, from a functional perspective, it makes little sense that the body would require significant energy resources to manage the stress of social evaluation. After all, how much physical energy is needed to give a public speech or to worry about one's performance? However, if the threat of social rejection is interpreted by the brain in the same manner as the threat of physical harm, biological stress responses might be triggered to both for the simple reason that these two systems overlap.

Summary

Identifying an overlap in the neural substrates that underlie physical and social pain leads to several novel hypotheses regarding the ways in which these two types of painful experiences interact. For examples, studies reviewed here demonstrated that those more sensitive to physical pain were also more sensitive to social pain and that factors that regulate or potentiate one kind of pain have similar effects on the other. There are likely many other consequences of this functional overlap and future research will be needed to further explore and uncover these effects.

Conclusions

Taken together, the research presented here puts forth a strong case for the notion that being rejected "hurts."

Indeed, social neuroscience research has fundamentally changed the way that we understand experiences of social rejection by demonstrating that some of the same neurochemistry and neural circuitry that underlies physical pain, underlies social pain too. One of the implications of these findings is that episodes of rejection or relationship dissolution can be just as damaging and debilitating to the person experiencing those events as episodes of physical pain. Thus, even though we may treat physical pain conditions more seriously and regard them as more valid ailments, the pain of social loss can be equally as distressing, as demonstrated by the activation of pain-related neural circuitry to social disconnection as well.

It is important to remember, though, that while painful in the short-term, feelings of distress and heartache following social exclusion or broken social relationships also serve a valuable function, namely to ensure the maintenance of close social ties. Thus, returning to our opening example, although the pain of social rejection on the kindergarten playground is palpable, it also serves as a reminder of our inherent need for social connection. To the extent that being rejected hurts, individuals are motivated to avoid situations in which rejection is likely. Over the course of evolutionary history, avoiding social rejection and staying socially connected to others likely increased chances of survival, as being part of a group provided additional resources, protection, and safety. Thus, the experience of social pain, while distressing and hurtful in the short-term, is an evolutionary adaptation that promotes social bonding and ultimately survival.

References

Adler, G. & Gattaz, W. F. (1993). Pain perception threshold in major depression. *Biological Psychiatry*, 15, 687–689.

Alexander, B. K., Coambs, R. B., & Hadaway, P. F. (1978). The effect of housing and gender on morphine self-administration in rats. *Psychopharmacology*, 58, 175–179.

Apkarian, A. V., Bushnell, M. C., Treede, R. -D., & Zubieta, J. -K. (2005). Human brain mechanisms of pain perception and regulation in health and disease. *Journal of Pain*, 9, 463–484.

Axelrod, R. & Hamilton, W. D. (1981). The evolution of cooperation. *Science*, 211, 1390–1396.

Aziz, Q., Schnitzler, A., & Enck, P. (2000). Functional neuroimaging of visceral sensation. *Journal of Clinical Neurophysiology*, 17, 604–612.

Bandler, R. & Shipley, M. T. (1994). Columnar organization in the midbrain periaqueductal gray: Modules for emotional expression? *Trends in Neurosciences*, 17, 379–389.

Berkowitz, L. (1983). Aversively stimulated aggression: Some parallels and differences in research with animals and humans. *American Psychologist*, 38, 1135–1144.

Berkowitz, L. (1993). *Aggression: Its causes, consequences and control*. Philadelphia, PA: Temple University Press.

Berthier, M., Starkstein, S., Leiguardia, R., & Carrea, R. (1988). Asymbolia for pain: A sensory-limbic disconnection system. *Annals of Neurology*, 24, 41–49.

Bowlby, J. (1969). *Attachment & loss, Vol. I: Attachment*. New York: Basic Books.

Brown, J. L., Sheffield, D., Leary, M. R., & Robinson, M. E. (2003). Social support and experimental pain. *Psychosomatic Medicine*, 65, 276–283.

Burklund, L. J., Eisenberger, N. I., & Lieberman, M. D. (2007). Rejection sensitivity moderates dorsal anterior cingulate activity to disapproving facial expressions. *Social Neuroscience*, 2, 238–253.

Carden, S. E., Barr, G. A., & Hofer, M. A. (1991) Differential effects of specific opioid receptor agonists on rat pup isolation calls. *Brain Research, Development, Brain Research, 62,* 17–22.

Cechetto, D. F. & Saper, C. B. (1987). Evidence for a viscerotopic sensory representation in the cortex and thalamus in the rat. *Journal of Comparative Neurology*, 262, 27–45.

Chalmers, B., Wolman, W. L., Nikodem, V. C., Gulmezoglu, A. M., & Hofmeyer, G. J. (1995). Companionship in labour: Do the personality characteristics of labour supporters influence their effectiveness? *Curationis*, 18, 77–80.

Chen, Z., Williams, K. D., Fitness, J., & Newton, N. (2008). When hurt won't heal: Exploring the capacity to relive social and physical pain. *Psychological Science*.

Chou, W-Y., Yang, L.-C., Lu, H. F., Ko, J. Y., Wang, C.H., Lin, S. H. et al. (2006a). Association of mu-opiod receptor gene polymorphism (A118G) with variations in morphine consumption for analgesia after total knee arthroplasty. *Acta Anaesthesiol Scandanavica*, 50, 787–792.

Chou, W. Y., Wang, C. -H., Liu, P. -H., Liu, C. -C., Tseng, C.- C., & Jawan, B. (2006b). Human opioid receptor A118G polymorphism, affects intravenous patient-controlled analgesia morphine consumption after total abdominal hysterectomy. *Anesthesiology*, 105334–105337.

Ciechanowski, P., Sullivan, M., Jensen, M., Romano, J., & Summers, H. (2003). The relationship of attachment style to depression, catastrophizing and health care utilization in patients with chronic pain. *Pain, 104*, 627–637.

Cornwall, A. & Donderi, D. C. (1988). The effect of experimentally induced anxiety on the experience of pressure pain. *Pain, 35*, 105–113.

Coulbalt, L., Beaussier, M., Verstuyft, C., Weikmans, H., Dubert, L., Trégouet, D., et al. (2006). Environmental and genetic factors associated with morphine response in the postoperative period. *Pharmacogenetics and Genomics, 79*, 316–324.

DeWall, C. N. & Baumeister, R. F. (2006). Alone but feeling no pain: Effects of social exclusion on physical pain tolerance and pain threshold, affective forecasting, and interpersonal empathy. *Journal of Personality and Social Psychology, 91*, 1–15.

DeWall, C. N., MacDonald, G., Webster, G. D., Masten, C., Baumeister, R. F., Powell, C., et al. (2010). Tylenol reduces social pain: Behavioral and neural evidence. *Psychological Science, 21*, 931–937.

Dickens, C., McGowan, L., & Dale, S. (2003). Impact of depression on experimental pain perception: A systematic review of the literature with meta-analysis. *Psychosomatic Medicine, 65*, 369–375.

Dickerson, S. & Kemeny, M. E. (2004). Acute stressors and cortisol responses: A theoretical integration and synthesis of laboratory research. *Psychological Bulletin, 103*, 355–391.

Eisenberger, N. I., Gable, S. L., & Lieberman, M. D. (2007). fMRI responses relate to differences in real-world social experience. *Emotion, 7*, 745–754.

Eisenberger, N. I., Inagaki, T. K., Mashal, N. M. & Irwin, M. R. (2010). Inflammation and social experience: An inflammatory challenge induces feelings of social disconnection in addition to depressed mood. *Brain, Behavior, & Immunity, 24*, 558–563.

Eisenberger, N. I., Jarcho, J. M., Lieberman, M. D., & Naliboff, B. D. (2006). An experimental study of shared sensitivity to physical pain and social rejection. *Pain, 126*, 132–138.

Eisenberger, N. I. & Lieberman, M. D. (2004). Why rejection hurts: The neurocognitive overlap between physical and social pain. *Trends in Cognitive Sciences, 8*, 294–300.

Eisenberger, N. I. & Lieberman, M. D. (2005). Broken hearts and broken bones: The neurocognitive overlap between social pain and physical pain. In K. D. Williams, J. P. Forgas, & von Hippel (Eds.), *The social outcast: Ostracism, social exclusion, rejection, and bullying* (pp. 109–127). New York: Cambridge University Press.

Eisenberger, N. I., Lieberman, M. D., & Williams, K. D. (2003). Does rejection hurt: An fMRI study of social exclusion. *Science, 302*, 290–292.

Eisenberger, N. I., Taylor, S. E., Gable, S. L., Hilmert, C. J., & Lieberman, M. D. (2007). Neural pathways link social support to attenuated neuroendocrine stress responses. *Neuroimage, 35*, 1601–1612.

Ehnvall, A., Mitchell, P. B., Hadzi-Pavlovic, D., Malhi, G. S., & Parker, G. (2009). Pain during depression and relationship to rejection sensitivity. *Acta Psychiatrica Scandinavica, 119*, 375–382.

Foltz, E. L. & White, L. E., (1968). The role of rostral cingulotomy in "pain" relief. *International Journal of Neurology, 6*, 353–373.

Gear, R. W., Aley, K. O., & Levine, J. D. (1999). Pain-induced analgesia mediated by mesolimbic reward circuits. *The Journal of Neuroscience, 15*, 7175–7181.

Gray, K. & Wegner, D. M. (2009). The sting of intentional pain. *Psychological Science.*

Gündel, H., O'Connor, M.-F., Littrell, L., Fort, C., & Richard, L. (2003). Functional neuroanatomy of grief: An fMRI study. *Journal of Psychiatry, 160*, 1946–1953.

Hadland, K. A, Rushworth, M. F. S., Gaffan, D., & Passingham, R. E. (2003). The effect of cingulate lesions on social behaviour and emotion. *Neuropsychologia, 41*, 919–931.

Hariri, A. R., Bookheimer, S. Y., & Mazziotta, J. C. (2000). Modulating emotional response: Effects of a neocortical network on the limbic system. *NeuroReport, 11*, 43–48.

Hebben, N. (1985). Toward the assessment of clinical pain. In G. M. Aronoff (Ed.), *Evaluation and treatment of chronic pain* (pp. 451–462). Baltimore: Urban & Schwarzenburg.

Herman, B. H. & Panksepp, J. (1978). Effects of morphine and naloxone on separation distress and approach attachment: Evidence for opiate mediation of social affect. *Pharmacology and Biochemical Behavior, 9*, 213–220.

Jackson, T., Iezzi, T., Chen, H., Ebnet, S., & Eglits, K. (2005). Gender, interpersonal transactions, and the perception of pain: An experimental analysis. *The Journal of Pain, 6*, 228–236.

Kalin, N. H., Shelton, S. E., & Barksdale, C. M. (1988). Opiate modulation of separation-induced distress in non-human primates. *Brain Research, 440*, 285–292.

Kennell, J., Klaus, M., McGrath, S., Robertson, S., & Hinkley, C. (1991). Continuous emotional support during labor in US hospital: A randomized control trial. *Journal of the American Medical Association, 265*, 2197–2201.

King, K. B., Reis, H. T., Porter, L. A., & Norsen, L. H. (1993). Social support and long-term recovery from coronary artery surgery: Effects on patients and spouses. *Health Psychology, 12*, 56–63.

Kirzinger, A. & Jurgens, U. (1982). Cortical lesion effects and vocalization in the squirrel monkey. *Brain Research, 233*, 299–315.

Kulik, J. A. & Mahler, H. I. (1989). Social support and recovery from surgery. *Health Psychology, 8*, 221–238.

Kross, E., Egner, T., Ochsner, K., Hirsch, J., & Downey, G. (2007). *Journal of Cognitive Neuroscience, 19*, 945–956.

Lautenbacher, S. & Krieg, J. C. (1994). Pain perception in psychiatric disorders: A review of the literature. *Journal of Psychiatric Research, 28*, 109–122.

Lieberman, M. D., Eisenberger, N. I., Crockett, M. J., Tom, S. M, Pfeifer, J. H., & Way, B. M. (2007). Putting feelings into words: Affect labeling disrupts amygdala activity to affective stimuli. *Psychological Science, 18*, 421–428.

Lieberman, M. D., Jarcho, J. M., Berman, S., Naliboff, B. D., Suyenobu, B. Y., Mandelkern, M., et al. (2004). The neural correlates of placebo effects: A disruption account. *Neuroimage, 22*, 447–455.

MacDonald, G. & Leary, M. R. (2005). Why does social exclusion hurt? The relationship between social and physical pain. *Psychological Review, 131*, 202–223.

MacLean P. D. & Newman, J. D. (1988). Role of midline frontolimbic cortex in production of the isolation call of squirrel monkeys. *Brain Research, 45*, 111–123.

Master, S. L., Eisenberger, N. I., Taylor, S. E., Naliboff, B. D., Shirinyan, D., & Lieberman, M. D. (2009). A picture's worth: Partner photographs reduce experimentally induced pain. *Psychological Science, 20*, 1316–1318.

Mehrabian, A. (1976). Questionnaire measures of affiliative tendency and sensitivity to rejection. *Psychological Reports, 38*, 199–209.

Melzack, R. & Wall, D. (1999). *Textbook of pain.* Edinburgh: Churchill Livingstone.

Nemoto, H., Toda, H., Nakajima, T., Hosokawa, S., Okada, Y., Yamamoto, K., et al. (2003). Fluvoxamine modulates pain sensation and affective processing of pain in human brain. *Neuroreport, 14*, 791–797.

Ochsner, K. N. & Gross, J. J. (2005). The cognitive control of emotion. *Trends in Cognitive Sciences, 9*, 242–249.

O'Connor, M. F., Wellisch, D. K., Stanton, A., Eisenberger, N. I., Irwin, M. R., & Lieberman, M. D. (2008). Craving love? Enduring grief activates brain's reward center. *NeruoImage, 42*, 969–972.

Onoda, K., Okamoto, Y., Nakashima, K, Nittono, H., Ura, M., & Yamawaki, S. (2009). Decreased ventral anterior cingulate cortex activity is associated with reduced social pain during emotional support. *Social Neuroscience, 4*, 443–454.

Onoda, K., Okamoto, Y., Nakashima, K, Nittoni, H., Yoshimura, S., Yamawaki, S., et al. (2010). Does low self-esteem enhance social pain? The relationships between trait self-esteem and anterior cingulate cortex activation induced by ostracism. *Social Cognitive and Affective Neuroscience, 5*, 385–391

Orbach, I., Mikulincer, M., King, R., Cohen, D., & Stein, D. (1997). Thresholds and tolerance of physical pain in suicidal and nonsuicidal adolescents. *Journal of Consulting and Clinical Psychology*, *65*, 646–652.

Paley, V. (1993). *You can't say you can't play*. Cambridge, MA: Harvard University Press.

Panksepp, J. (1998). *Affective neuroscience*. New York: Oxford University Press.

Panksepp, J., Herman, B., Conner, R., Bishop, P., & Scott, J. P. (1978). The biology of social attachments: Opiates alleviate separation distress. *Biological Psychiatry*, *13*, 607–618.

Petrovic, P. & Ingvar, M. (2002). Imaging cognitive modulation of pain processing. *Pain*, *95*, 1–5.

Peyron, R., Laurent, B., & Garcia-Larrea, L. (2000). Functional imaging of brain responses to pain. A review and meta-analysis. *Neurophysiological Clinics*, *30*, 263–288.

Price D. D. (2000). Psychological and neural mechanisms of the affective dimension of pain. *Science*, *288*, 1769–1772.

Rainville, P. (2002). Brain mechanisms of pain affect and pain modulation. *Current Opinion in Neurobiology*, *12*, 195–204.

Rainville, P., Duncan, G. H., Price, D. D., Carrier, B., & Bushnell, M. D. (1997). Pain affect encoded in human anterior cingulate but not somatosensory cortex. *Science*, *277*, 968–971.

Richter, E. O., Davis, K. D., Hamani, C., Hutchison, W. D., Dostrovsky, J. O., & Lozano, A. M. (2004). Cingulotomy for psychiatric disease: Microelectrode guidance, a callosal reference system for documenting lesion location, and clinical results. *Neurosurgery*, *54*, 622–628.

Robinson, B. W. (1967). Neurological aspects of evoked vocalizations. In S. A. Altmann (Ed.), *Social communication among primates* (pp. 135–147). Chicago, IL: The University Press.

Shimodozono, M., Kawahira, K., Kamishita, T. Ogata, A., Tohgo, S., & Tanaka, N. (2002). Reduction of central poststroke pain with the selective reuptake inhibitor fluvoxamine. *International Journal of Neuroscience*, *112*, 1173–1181.

Schreckenberger, M., Siessmeier, T., Viertmann, A., Landvogt, C., Buchholz, H.-G., Rolke, R., et al. (2005). The unpleasantness of tonic pain is encoded by the insular cortex. *Neurology*, *64*, 1175–1183.

Singh, V. P., Jain, N. K., & Kulkarni, S. K. (2001). On the anitnociceptive effect of fluoxetine, a selective serotonin reuptake inhibitor. *Brain Research*, *915*, 218–226.

Smith, W. (1945). The functional significance of the rostral cingular cortex as revealed by its responses to electrical excitation. *Journal of Neurophysiology*, *8*, 241–255.

Taylor, S. E. (2003). *Health psychology* (5th Edition). New York: McGraw Hill Publishers.

Tölle, T. R., Kaufmann, T., Siessmeier, T., Lautenbacher, S., Berthele, A., Munz, F., et al. (1999). Region-specific encoding of sensory and affective components of pain in the human brain: A positron emission tomography correlation analysis. *Annals of Neurology*, *45*, 40–47.

Tremblay, I. & Sullivan, M. J. L. (2009). Attachment and pain outcomes in adolescents: The mediating role of pain catastrophizing and anxiety. *Journal of Pain, in press*.

Twenge, J. M., Baumeister, R. F., Tice, D. M., & Stucke, T. S. (2001). If you can't join them, beat them: Effects of social exclusion on aggressive behavior. *Journal of Personality and Social Psychology*, *81*, 1058–1069.

Wager, T. D., Rilling, J. K., Smith, E. E., Sokolik, A., Casey, K. L., Davidson, R. J., et al. (2004). Placebo-induced changes in fMRI in the anticipation and experience of pain. *Science*, *303*, 1162–1167.

Warnick, J. E., McCurdy, C. R., & Sufka, K. J. (2005). Opioid receptor function in social attachment in young domestic fowl. *Behavioral Brain Research*, *160*, 277–285.

Watkins, L. R. & Maier, S. F. (2000). The pain of being sick: Implications of immune-to-brain communication for understanding pain. *Annual Review of Psychology*, *51*, 29–57.

Way, B. M., Taylor, S. E., & Eisenberger, N. I. (2009). Variation in the mu-opioid receptor gene (OPRM1) is associated with dispositional and neural sensitivity to social rejection. *Proceedings of the National Academy of Sciences*, *106*, 15079–15084.

Zaza, C. & Baine, N. (2002). Cancer pain and psychosocial factors: A critical review of the literature. *Journal of Pain and Symptom Management*, *24*, 526–542.

Neural Systems of Intrapersonal and Interpersonal Self-Esteem Maintenance

Jennifer S. Beer

Abstract

This chapter reviews social neuroscience research on the maintenance of self-esteem. Self-esteem defense is considered from both intrapersonal (i.e., internal feelings of self-worth) and interpersonal (i.e., social acceptance) perspectives. It shows that intrapersonal self-esteem defense is associated with reduced orbitofrontal cortex (OFC) and dorsal anterior cingulate cortex (dACC) activation, whereas interpersonal self-esteem defense is associated with increased dACC and amygdala activation and reduced striatal activation. Future research is needed to better understand whether these are meaningful neural distinctions between intrapersonal and interpersonal self-defense or an artifact of the currently used paradigms in each line of inquiry. Developing neural research in this area will be helpful for understanding the psychological processes involved in self-esteem defense and how aging-related changes in neural function may impact self-esteem defense.

Keywords: social cognition, self, emotion, motivation, brain, orbitofrontal cortex, anterior cingulate cortex, regulation, self-esteem

In his memoir "Immortal Class," Travis Culley (2001) states that "everyone knows" he is "untouchable" because his profession involves "saving a little bit of the world all day long" and for that he "requires at least that much respect (p. 31–32)." Readers unfamiliar with Culley and his book might be surprised to learn that Culley "saves the world a little bit everyday" in his job as a bike messenger in Chicago. Critics of Culley, including some of his co-workers, have described his lofty language as egotistical and argue that his grandiose statements actually harm public impressions of the profession he wants to champion (see Greenfield, 2001). Bike messengers provide a useful service and arguably benefit the environment, so what would Culley have to gain by exaggerating those positive aspects and

focusing so much on the respect he feels due from other people?

A host of research in social psychology posits that people are motivated to exaggerate positive aspects of the self and one's social acceptance because these intrapersonal and interpersonal factors promote self-esteem (e.g., Leary & Downs, 1995; Paulhus & John, 1998; Taylor & Brown, 1988). Researchers argue that people are motivated to view themselves in a positive light and this motivation can blur self-views in an unrealistically positive direction (Taylor & Brown, 1988). Intrapersonally, people feel good about themselves by focusing on their positive qualities more than their negative qualities (e.g., Dunning, Meyerowitz, & Holzberg, 1989). Interpersonally, individuals may feel worthy only as much as they feel they are being accepted by other people (Leary & Downs, 1995; Leary, Tambor, Terdal, & Downs, 1995).

Although intrapersonal and interpersonal self-esteem maintenance processes are fundamental aspects of social cognition and are illustrated by decades of behavioral research, most neural models of social cognition only mention these processes to note that they are important domains for future study (e.g., Blakemore, Winston, & Frith, 2004; Heatherton, Macrae, & Kelley, 2004). Currently, a literature search using terms like "self," "emotion regulation," and "social cognition" in combination with "brain" will generate a multitude of articles but few will explicitly address motivational issues surrounding the self and social perception. Social neuroscience research on self-perception has mostly focused on understanding whether (a) commonalities and differences between the neural systems underlying self-perception compared to perceptions of others, and (b) interactions between self-perception and perceptions of other people. For example, studies comparing self-perception to other kinds of perception have typically adopted self-reference paradigms in which participants make judgments about personality trait words. Judgments of the self-descriptiveness of the trait words are contrasted with other kinds of judgments such as how well the traits describe another person or whether the traits are socially desirable. Research along these lines shows strong convergence on the association between self-judgments and medial prefrontal cortex (MPFC) activation. Although it was first thought this association was specific to self-judgment, later research showed that the MPFC is also associated with making judgments about well-known others (see Beer & Ochsner, 2006; Gilihan & Farah, 2005; Heatherton, Macrae, & Kelley, 2004). Another major focus has been elucidating the neural systems that underlie simulation; that is, using the self to understand what someone else might be thinking or feeling. Research on this topic has examined this question using more varied paradigms than the self-reference research. Simulation has been examined by contrasting perceptions of other people who are similar or dissimilar to the self or looking for neural commonalities between the self's own experience and observation of that experience in another person (i.e., "mirror neurons"). These studies have identified the MPFC, temporal-parietal junction (TPJ), and the mirror neuron system as important neural components of social cognition (e.g., Mitchell, Macrae, & Banaji, 2006; Saxe, 2006; Uddin et al., 2007).

If the goal of self-esteem maintenance is to regulate feelings about the self, then neural research on emotion regulation is another potential avenue for understanding the neural basis of self-esteem maintenance processes. However, social neuroscience research on emotion regulation has been dominated by paradigms involving reappraisal and interference of emotional stimuli that do not typically have explicit relevance for self-esteem. Participants regulate their emotional reaction to pictures or films through suppressing or reappraising their meaning or regulate their attention to superfluous emotional information that is embedded in other tasks (e.g., Beer, in press; Ochsner & Gross, 2005). These studies have shown that a number of neural regions typically involved in cognitive control (Botivinick, Cohen, & Carter, 2004) are also helpful for controlling emotional experience or attention to emotional information. For example, regions such as the ventral lateral prefrontal cortex (VLPFC), dorsal lateral prefrontal cortex (DLPFC), and the ventral and dorsal anterior cingulate cortex (vACC, dACC) are involved in reappraising and ignoring emotional stimuli. Furthermore, this research has shown that the VLPFC likely down-regulates amygdala activity during emotional regulation (see Beer, 2009a; Ochsner & Gross, 2005 for reviews).

Together, these social neuroscience investigations of social cognition and emotion regulation certainly suggest a neural model of the processes that contribute to intrapersonal and interpersonal self-esteem maintenance. For example, it could be that regions associated with social cognition such as the MPFC and TPJ might be important for processing information about the self and information about how others are viewing the self. Additionally, regions associated with emotion regulation such as the VLPFC, DLPFC, and ACC should presumably be important for regulating feelings about the self as well as regulating behavior in the anticipation or aftermath of a possible social transgression. However, one advantage of social neuroscience is that it strives to bridge the social and neural levels of analysis and, if possible, avoid the need to extrapolate to the social level just because it is more complex or difficult to measure (Beer & Ochsner, 2006). So, although it is not yet a central focus of extant social neuroscience research, what is known from the small amount of current research that has more explicitly addressed intrapersonal and interpersonal self-esteem maintenance? How might that knowledge inform psychological theory about those processes?

Intrapersonal Self-Enhancement: Negative Associations with Orbitofrontal Cortex and Anterior Cingulate Cortex Activity and Positive Associations with Medial Prefrontal Cortex Activity

Social neuroscience research on intrapersonal self-enhancement began with clinical observations of frontal lobe patients. Clinicians and neurologists have long described an association between frontal lobe damage and poor self-insight (Blumer & Benson, 1975). Although not exclusively associated with damage to the frontal lobe, patients who have sustained frontal lobe injuries are often described as having little insight into the deficits arising from their brain damage (Blumer & Benson, 1975). In this way, insight might be considered to be positively biased because patients do not acknowledge impairments. More recently, empirical work involving lesion patients and neuroimaging of healthy populations has built on these clinical observations to elucidate which subregions of the frontal lobe may be helpful for accurate self-insight (see Table 40.1 and Figure 40.1).

Empirical research with patients with OFC damage has shown that their self-perceptions tend to be positively biased when compared to trained judges' perceptions of their behavior. In these studies, patients with OFC damage participated in social-interaction tasks such as making conversation, sharing autobiographical memories, and teasing (Beer et al., 2003; Beer et al., 2006). According to both verbal and non-verbal measures, OFC patients tended to interact with strangers in a manner that would have been more appropriate for interactions with familiar others. In comparison to other participants, OFC patients disclosed overly personal information and were more likely to stare at or invade the personal space of other people in the social interaction. Patients tended to be proud and unembarrassed by their inappropriate social behavior (Beer et al., 2003; Beer et al., 2006). These feelings were not accounted for by a lack of awareness or concern for social norms. OFC patients, DLPFC patients, and healthy control participants all held similar social norms for interacting with strangers (Beer et al., 2006). Instead, OFC patients were unaware of how their behavior was received by others. Specifically, their evaluations of their social behavior were much more positive than evaluations made by trained judges (Beer et al., 2006). The self-insight of patients with DLPFC damage was similar to the self-insight exhibited by neurologically intact control participants (Beer et al., 2006). Intriguingly, patients with OFC damage may be able to gain appropriate self-insight in certain circumstances. After watching a videotape of their social interactions, patients with OFC damage reported feeling embarrassed about their behavior (Beer et al., 2006). Together, these findings raise two possibilities for the role of the OFC in self-insight. The OFC may be important for monitoring one's behavior but is not the only region that can perform the processes needed to gain accurate insight. Alternatively, it is also possible that patients with OFC damage were able to gain insight after watching the videotape because the remaining OFC tissue was able to make appropriate computations after having a second chance to process information from the social interaction task.

Table 40.1 Overview of Neural Research on Intrapersonal Self-esteem Defense

Method	Paradigm	Finding
Lesion	Self-perception vs. observer perception	Patients with orbitofrontal damage have unrealistically positive self-views; patients with dorsolateral prefrontal damage have insight similar to healthy controls
fMRI	Social comparison of self to average peer; overconfidence in task performance; self-serving attributions for task performance	Medial and lateral orbitofrontal cortex associated with less positivity bias; some studies also suggest that cingulate cortex is related to reduced positivity bias
ERP	Self-serving attributions	Source localization suggest dorsal anterior cingulate cortex associated with non-self-serving attributions
TMS	Self-evaluations vs. evaluations of best friend	Only 1 study found behavioral evidence of self-enhancement; in that study, TMS to MPFC decreased self-favoring ratings whereas sham TMS did not

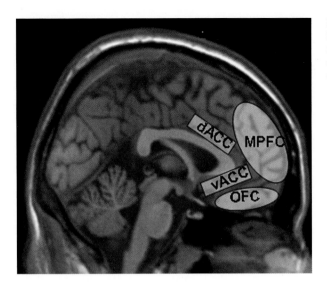

Fig. 40.1 Medial view of regions implicated in intrapersonal self-esteem processes: self-enhancement (MPFC = medial prefrontal cortex) and the reduction of self-enhancement (OFC = orbitofrontal cortex; dACC = dorsal anterior cingulate cortex).

Although behavioral studies can operationalize positively biased self-views by comparing self-perceptions to the perceptions of trained judgments, neuroimaging studies do not lend themselves to that approach. The challenge of studying self-insight (rather than self-evaluation) is evidenced by the fact that the earliest attempts to study this topic built on the widely used self-referent paradigms typically used in social neuroscience research on self-evaluation (Kelley et al., 2002; Ochsner et al., 2005). These studies have implications for understanding how motivational concerns affect self-evaluation by comparing self-evaluation of positive characteristics to self-evaluation of negative characteristics (Moran et al., 2006; Sharot et al., 2007). In these studies, participants evaluate the self-descriptiveness of traits or the likelihood of future events that are either positive or negative in nature (Moran et al., 2006, Sharot et al., 2007). Participants tend to claim more positive traits and future events than their negative counterparts. In these studies, vACC differentiates judgments of positive stimuli from judgments of negative stimuli. However, there was no way to tell whether these judgments were positively biased or accurate reflections of positive self-characteristics. Although people do claim more positive information as self-descriptive then negative information (Taylor & Brown, 1988), they also under report negative information about themselves (e.g., Dunning, Meyerowitz, & Holzberg, 1989; Taylor & Brown, 1988). Therefore, the valence of characteristics is not a reliable proxy for bias nor is it possible to measure self-insight by asking someone to rate the self-descriptiveness of a trait or an event. This method does not provide any measure to compare with the self-perception.

In order to address this issue, recent fMRI studies have adapted new paradigms from the social psychological literature to investigate the neural systems associated with accuracy and bias. For example, bias can be measured by having participants evaluate themselves in relation to an average peer across a large number of personality traits (e.g., Alicke et al., 1995; Chambers & Windschitl, 2004; Dunning, Meyerowitz, & Holzberg, 1989). Although each individual is likely to have some unique characteristics, it is unlikely that so many people in a random sample would be significantly more desirable than an average peer across such a large number of traits. Instead, it is expected that accurate self-ratings across a large number of traits should be centrally distributed around the average peer (Chambers & Windschitl, 2004). However, the majority of people judge themselves to be "above average" when asked to judge themselves in relation to their average peer which is considered to reflect positivity bias. The social-comparative approach also makes it possible to unconfound bias and valence through manipulations of the trait words. Behavioral research has shown that people make relatively accurate social comparisons when evaluating traits that have fewer associated behaviors rather than many. In other words, there are fewer ways to be "tidy" whereas there are more ways to be "talented." People tend to evaluate themselves as more similar to an average peer for specific traits like "tidy" than for broad traits like "talented" (Dunning, Meyerowitz, & Holzberg, 1989). The range of behaviors associated with traits (and therefore their likelihood of yielding biased evaluations) is independent from their valence. Therefore, accuracy can be examined through comparisons of judgments of specific versus broad traits and valence can be examined through comparisons of judgments of positive versus negative traits.

Two neuroimaging studies have used this approach to disentangle the neural system's associated bias and valence (Beer & Hughes, 2009; Hughes & Beer, 2009). These studies have found that the vACC, the region associated with self-evaluations of positive stimuli (Moran et al., 2006; Sharot et al., 2007) is most important for differentiating positive valence from negative valence than bias from accuracy. Additionally, judgments of specific traits more strongly engage the MPFC, PFCC, OFC, and dACC. However, individual differences in social comparisons only modulated activation in the OFC and dACC. The more participants evaluated themselves as similar to their average peer, the more they engaged the medial and lateral OFC and dACC (Beer & Hughes, 2009). In a follow-up study, social-comparative judgments were made for targets that varied in how much an individual might be motivated to view them in an unrealistically positive light (i.e., relationship partner, assigned roommate). Evaluations of relationship partners exhibited similar patterns of bias as self-evaluations (i.e., better than average for broad traits; about average for specific traits) whereas evaluations of dorm roommates were relatively accurate across both trait conditions. Consistent with the first study, the OFC and dACC were recruited for specific trait judgments of relationship partner and for all roommate judgments. Furthermore, the OFC was modulated by individual differences in accuracy. The more participants tended to view their relationship partner or roommate as similar to the average peer, the more they engaged the OFC (Hughes & Beer, 2009). Although the second study is not directly relevant for intrapersonal self-esteem maintenance, it provides convergent evidence and rules out the possibility that the neural activation associated with accuracy is somehow accounted for by judgments of specific traits.

Neuroimaging studies of positively biased self-evaluations have also moved beyond paradigms that involve the evaluation of general personality traits or future events. For example, bias is also evident when people's evaluation of their task performance exceeds their actual performance or they consistently take credit for their task successes but not their task failures. Studies taking these approaches have found convergent results: accuracy most strongly engages the dACC and OFC. For example, one study found that the OFC predicted positivity bias across people and across trials (Beer, Lombardo, & Bhanji, in press). Participants answered forced-choice trivia questions and then estimated how confident they were in their performance (Beer, Lombardo, & Bhanji, 2009). Just as the lesion study found that OFC damage predicts positivity bias (Beer et al., 2006), participants who failed to engage their OFC were the most likely to show overconfidence in their task performance. Additionally, a different region of OFC was negatively modulated by confidence estimates but only for trials that participants had answered incorrectly. In other words, reduced OFC activation on incorrect trials was associated with overly confident performance estimates. This finding is particularly remarkable because no feedback on task performance was provided, so the sensitivity of OFC to incorrect trials was not driven by explicit external cues.

Dorsal ACC and lateral OFC activity are also associated with reduced self-serving attributions for task performance. In one study, participants imagined positive and negative events and then made hypothetical attributions for why something like that might happen to them (Blackwood et al., 2003). Attribution choices reflected either an internal or external attribution style. For example, participants were asked to imagine that a neighbor had invited them over for a drink (positive event) or that a friend had picked a fight with them (negative event). These events had to be attributed to something about themselves (internal) or the situation (external). Participants who were likely to attribute positive events to something about the situation but negative events to something about themselves were most likely to engage the lateral OFC. In other words, their attributions were exactly opposite of the self-serving pattern of attributing positive events to the self and negative events to the situation. In another study, participants performed a working memory task, received trial-by-trial manipulated feedback on their performance, and then made an attribution for each trial's success or failure (Krusemark, Campbell, & Clementz, 2008). As above, attributions were considered to be self-serving to the extent that successes were attributed to internal factors (i.e., "I am smart") and failures were attributed to external factors (i.e., "It was bad luck"). The opposite pattern was considered to be non-self-serving. The study used ERP and found differences at 320 ms after the attribution selections had been presented. Source localization procedures suggested that a swath of medial cortex including the dACC predicted the selection of non-self-serving attributions.

Whereas lesion and neuroimaging studies implicate the dACC and OFC in accurate self-evaluations, two TMS studies implicate the MPFC in self-evaluation bias (Barrios et al., 2008; Kwan et al., 2007). In one study, participants rated themselves and their best friends on a series of personality traits. Ratings were considered to be biased to the extent that more desirable traits and less undesirable traits were ascribed to the self when compared with ratings of best friend. Participants in the sham TMS condition showed this biased self-evaluation. When TMS was delivered to the MPFC, ratings of the self and best friend tended to be similar. In contrast, TMS delivered to the somatosensory cortex did not change the biased pattern seen in the sham TMS condition. Therefore, a disruption of MPFC function impacts biased evaluations rather than disruption of brain function in general. A second study also measured bias by comparing self-ratings to ratings of best friend (Barrios et al., 2008). This study was aimed at understanding bias that is driven by a desire to inflate one's status or one's moral virtue. Egoistic traits are those traits that elevate the self's status (e.g., ambitious, popular) and are distinct from moralistic traits that reflect biased views of one's exceptional ability to adhere to social norms (e.g., moral, considerate). Surprisingly, participants in this study did not show a significant discrepancy between self-ratings and best-friend ratings in the sham TMS condition. In other words, participants did not show evidence of bias in their ratings. Although there was not overall evidence of bias, discrepancies between self-ratings and best friend ratings were somewhat larger for egoistic ratings in the sham TMS condition compared to the MPFC condition. No differences were found for ratings of moralistic traits.

Why did the lesion and neuroimaging studies find such different results than the TMS studies? More research will be needed to answer this question but several issues warrant consideration. It may be that the TMS findings are actually consistent with the findings in the other studies. The TMS studies measured bias in such a way that it included the degree to which positive and negative traits were rated differently for self and best friend. If the TMS did disrupt vACC regions that differentiate positive

and negative traits, it might be that biased evaluations are reduced because this region no longer distinguishes between positive and negative traits for either the self or best friend as it did in the social comparison studies (Beer & Hughes, in press; Hughes & Beer, 2009). It also might be that the vACC region from the social comparison study (Hughes & Beer, 2009) is overlapping or needs to communicate with the affected MPFC region in the TMS study (Kwan et al., 2008). Second, MPFC disruption may impair mentalizing processes (Mitchell, Macrae, & Banaji, 2006; Saxe, 2006; Uddin et al., 2007) These processes may be needed to differentiate the self from other people rather than reduce defensive processes contributing to self-enhancement. Ratings may become more convergent because the self is less differentiated. Finally, TMS is actually more similar to a lesion method than neuroimaging methodologies (Schutter, 2009). Therefore, the TMS study may test different aspects of brain function. While this region may not show significantly different recruitment across conditions in the neuroimaging studies, it could be that damage in this region impacts the influence of positivity motivations. Patients with focal MPFC damage are rare, even more so than patients with OFC damage (Beer, 2009a). If studies of MPFC patients could be conducted, then the TMS studies suggest that these patients would show relatively accurate self-evaluations. These finding would be especially interesting given the clinical characterizations of frontal lobe patients as having impaired self-evaluation (Blumer & Benson, 1975). As mentioned above, empirical research has shown that OFC patients have impaired insight whereas DLPFC patients do not (Beer et al., 2006). If MPFC function actually interferes with bias and damage to this region results in greater accuracy, then this suggests that not only do some frontal lobe areas not affect accuracy (i.e., DLPFC) but that damage to certain regions of the frontal lobe actually promote accuracy.

Interpersonal Self-Esteem Threat: Positive Associations with Dorsal Anterior Cingulate and Amygdala and Negative Associations with Striatum

Social neuroscience research on interpersonal self-esteem threat comes from a series of studies examining social exclusion and social acceptance as well as relevant individual differences. Whereas research on intrapersonal self-esteem maintenance most consistently found associations with reduced frontal lobe activation, the research on interpersonal self-esteem maintenance finds associations with increased

Table 40.2   Overview of Neural Research on Interpersonal Self-esteem Defense

Method	Paradigm	Finding
fMRI	Rejection in cyberball game; Individual differences in rejection sensitivity to disapproving faces; opinion that contradicts group opinion	Increased dorsal anterior cingulate cortex activity related to rejection, disapproving faces; contradictory opinion
fMRI	Cooperation in Prisoner's Dilemma; opinion that is consistent with group opinion; receiver of trust in Trust game	Increased striatum or caudate activation related to cooperation, consistent opinion, trust
fMRI	Individual differences in loneliness when viewing social vs. nonsocial stimuli	Reduced ventral striatum related to lonely people viewing social stimuli
fMRI	Individual differences in social anxiety to anticipation of public speaking; fearful faces; novel faces	Increased amygdala activity relates to high social anxiety while anticipating public speaking, viewing fearful or novel faces

frontal lobe activation and modulation of subcortical regions. More specifically, interpersonal threat is most consistently associated with increased dACC and amygdala activation and reduced striatal activation across a variety of experimental and individual difference studies (see Table 40.2 and Figure 40.2).

One of the earliest lines of inquiry that has implications for understanding interpersonal self-esteem is research on the neural correlates of social exclusion. In a hallmark study, participants believed they were playing a "cyberball" game in which they and two other participants threw a ball to each other (Eisenberger, Lieberman, & Williams, 2003). While in the scanner, they saw a depiction of two other players and a symbol that represented their "hand."

In the social exclusion condition, participants were thrown the ball a few times but after that, the other two players just threw the ball back and forth between themselves. Compared to conditions in which participants were included, the social exclusion condition elicited activation in the dACC and VLPFC. Furthermore, individual differences in social anxiety were positivity related to dACC and negatively related to VLPFC activation. The more participants felt distressed in response to their social exclusion, the more they engaged their dACC and the less they engaged their VLPFC. Drawing on parallels between their pattern of findings and neural patterns associated with physical pain, the researchers suggested that the dACC activation

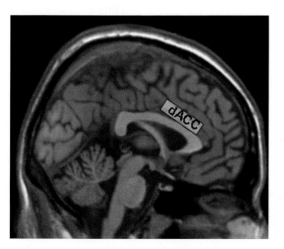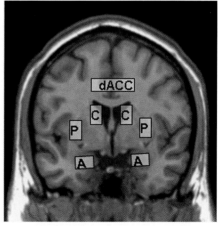

Fig. 40.2 Neural regions implicated in interpersonal self-esteem processes: social exclusion (dACC = dorsal anterior cingulate cortex; A = amygdala) and social reward (striatum is composed of caudate (C) and putamen (P)).

reflects an alarm system that something is amiss whereas the VLPFC may serve to control feelings arising from social exclusion.

Some researchers have raised the possibility that the dACC findings from the cyberball study with adults merely reflected expectancy violations rather than social "pain" (Somerville, Heatherton, & Kelley, 2006). In the cyberball study, participants were always excluded after they had been included and, therefore, the exclusion condition always included the element of surprise given the previous condition. In order to tease apart surprise and social exclusion, researchers presented participants with pictures of other people and asked them judge whether they would like the person. The participants were also presented with false feedback about whether that person had judged their picture as likable. In this way, the researchers created conditions of whether one's own expectancy about liking was congruent with another person's that were distinct from whether the participant was rejected by another person. This study found that incongruence between one's expectation of liking and feedback from the other person (i.e., expectancy violation) engaged dACC activation whereas rejection (regardless of whether the participant expected to like that individual) was associated with less vACC activation. Although this study concluded that expectancy violations, not social rejection, engage dACC activity, it is not clear whether social rejection in the feedback condition was truly comparable to the social rejection elicited in the cyberball study. Researchers have questioned whether receiving negative feedback from someone you will never meet is similar to actively being excluded from an ongoing interaction. Consistent with the view that the feedback paradigm and the cyberball paradigm create very different interpersonal contexts, the vACC behaves very differently in the feedback study than in studies that include the cyberball paradigm. Specifically, a study of adolescents playing the cyberball game found that social distress positively modulated the vACC (Masten et al., 2009).

In addition to the cyberball study conducted with adults, two more lines of research support the relation between the dACC and social exclusion. Individual differences in variables affecting concern about others' esteem for the self modulate dACC activation. For example, rejection sensitivity modulates dACC activation. Participants who varied in rejection sensitivity viewed different faces while in the scanner (Burkland, Eisenberger, & Lieberman,

2007). Some of the faces were disapproving whereas others expressed other kinds of negative emotions such as anger or disgust. Participants who tended to be more sensitive to social rejection also tended to show the most dACC activation in reaction to the disapproving faces but not other negative emotional faces. Additionally, social exclusion may not even need to be explicit in order to engage dACC activation. A study of social conformity found that a dorsal paracingulate cortex region is modulated by conflict between's one own opinion and group opinion (Klucharev et al., 2009). In this study, participants rated the attractiveness of a series of faces. On each trial, they were given feedback about the rating assigned to the face from an "average participant." All of the feedback about the average rating was experimentally manipulated and often deviated from the participant's own rating. After performing the task in the scanner, participants once again rated the photos outside of the scanner with no feedback. For the first round of ratings, a region of the paracingulate cortex activated most on the trials where there was high agreement between participant ratings and average participant ratings. Additionally, this region's activation predicted whether participants would change their rating to become more similar to the average participant rating in the post-scan rating session. The authors of the study interpreted the results as reflecting a reinforcement signal associated with group conformity. Although there was not explicit social exclusion, the changes in ratings may have been shaped by a fundamental desire to conform to the group to avoid exclusion.

In addition to the evidence for a role of the dACC in self-esteem threat, interpersonal threats may positively modulate amygdala activation and negatively modulate striatal activation. For example, socially anxious individuals tend to have low esteem for their social skills. These individuals show increased amygdala activation in relation to social stimuli. For example, social anxiety modulates amygdala activation to social threats such as anticipation of public speaking (e.g., Furmark et al., 2004; Lorberbaum et al., 2004; Tillfors et al., 2002). Furthermore, amygdala activation to harsh faces predicts social anxiety symptoms (Phan et al., 2006). The association between social anxiety and amygdala modulation is likely consistent over the lifespan. Inhibited temperament in infancy predicts amygdala hyperactivity to novel faces in adulthood (Schwarz et al., 2003). Additionally, the hyperactivity of the amygdala may also make it more difficult for socially anxious individuals to regulate their negative emotional responses to social stimuli (Goldin et al., 2009). Together, these studies suggest that the amygdala may be sensitive to social situations in which self-esteem may be compromised.

In addition to amygdala involvement, a series of studies suggests a role for the striatum in detection of interpersonal threat. For example, studies of lonely people suggest that they desire social contact but may engage in self-defeating behavior such that social interaction holds little reward. When compared to nonlonely people, lonely people show neural differences when processing social versus nonsocial stimuli (Cacioppo, Norris, Decety, Monteleone, & Nusbaum, 2008). Specifically, lonely people show reduced ventral striatum activation and increased visual cortex activation when viewing pictures of people compared to pictures of objects. In nonlonely people, social pictures elicit more ventral striatum activation as well as TPJ activation, a neural region associated with mentalizing. These findings may reflect a reduction in reward processing for social situations and an increase in vigilance because of a chronic concern about others' opinions coupled with poor social skills.

On the other side of the coin, group acceptance elicits neural activation in the striatum (i.e., King-Casas et al., 2005; Klucharev et al., 2009; Rilling et al., 2002). In the study of social conformity mentioned above, the striatum, a region associated with reward, showed the opposite pattern to the paracingulate cortex region (Klucharev et al., 2009). Specifically, the striatum activated more when participant ratings matched the average participant ratings. Additionally, studies drawing on economic theories of cooperation have shown that the striatum is modulated by cooperation and trust in dyadic exchanges. In one study, female participants played a multiple round version of what is known as the Prisoner's Dilemma game (Rilling et al., 2002). In this paradigm, participants played the game with a partner who was not being scanned. On each round, the participant's outcome will depend on the combination of their own choice as well as their partner's choice. Essentially, each player chooses whether or not to cooperate in sharing a pot of money or take money for only themselves. Activation in the caudate (part of the striatum) was strongest for rounds where there was mutual cooperation. Furthermore, it appeared that this caudate activation also predicted cooperation in subsequent trials (Rilling et al., 2002). A second study suggests that social acceptance, particularly after a social transgression, from another person also activates the caudate (King-Casas et al., 2005). In this study, participants played what is known as the Trust game. In the role of investor, participants send money to another player (i.e., the trustee). One the trustee receives the money, it is tripled and the trustee must decide how much of the sum to share with the investor. This study found that caudate activation was associated with high investment despite previous trials of low rates of repayment. In this way, caudate activation may have reflected the trustee's feeling of reward that they were still being trusted even though they had not conformed to norms of fairness in the past.

Implications and Future Directions for Research on Intrapersonal Self-Esteem Defense

People maintain self-esteem through overly positive self-evaluations and maintaining group inclusion (e.g., Leary & Downs, 1995; Paulhus & John, 1998; Taylor & Brown, 1988). Extant social neuroscience research suggests that these two self-esteem processes are handled somewhat differently at the neural level. In terms of maintaining self-esteem by bolstering self-views, lesion and neuroimaging studies found strong convergent evidence for a negative relation between overly positive self-views and OFC and dACC activation. However, no convergence was found in a neural region that was actively engaged in relation to overly positive self-views. In terms of maintaining group inclusion, neuroimaging studies suggest that the dACC and amygdala may detect instances in which group inclusion is in jeopardy and the striatum may detect instances in which group inclusion will be successful. What can the neural studies of overly positive self-evaluations and social exclusion tell us about the psychological and neural mechanisms through which people are able to maintain their self-esteem?

Intrapersonal self-esteem defense may reflect top-down processing, whereas interpersonal self-esteem defense may arise from bottom-up processing
One possibility arising from the neural distinctions in the research on overly positive self-evaluations and social exclusion is that these processes differ in the extent to which they represent top-down or bottom-up processing. For example, it is possible that overly positive self-evaluations may reflect an overuse of heuristics. The OFC and dACC have previously been associated with cognitive control in a host of other research domains (Beer, Shimamura, & Knight, 2005; Botivinick, Cohen, & Carter, 2004). From

this perspective, the negative association between biased self-evaluation and OFC and dACC function more closely parallel the findings from neural studies that have examined availability heuristics in non-social judgments (e.g., Beer, Knight, & D'Esposito, 2006; DeMartino et al., 2006) rather than emotionally regulated information-processing (Beer, 2009b; Ochsner et al., 2002). For example, neural studies examining gambling judgments that are susceptible to salient information (such as emotion or win/loss frames: Beer, Knight, & D'Esposito, 2006; DeMartino et al., 2006) have found that the OFC and dACC are helpful for integrating less salient information into gambling judgments. Furthermore, the less participants relied on salient information, the more they engaged the mOFC and lOFC (Beer, Knight, & D'Esposito, 2006; DeMartino et al., 2006). The activation of the OFC and dACC in relation to less biased self-evaluations appear to be consistent with behavioral theories that posit that bias arises from judgments made on easily available self-information which tends to be positively skewed (Dunning, Meyerowitz, & Holzberg, 1989). However, the fact that positively biased self-evaluations are negatively associated with "cognitive control" regions does not necessarily translate into the conclusion that cognitive control suppresses positivity-bias. One could argue that the increased activation in the OFC and dACC regions represent increased but failed cognitive control efforts in the conditions associated with less biased evaluations. However, an examination of cognitive load evidence in combination with the neural studies makes a cognitive control explanation of the OFC and dACC more plausible. One of the neuroimaging studies also includes data showing that cognitive load increases the extent to which people believe they are more socially desirable than the average person (Beer & Hughes, 2009). The fact the cognitive load increases positivitybias suggests that some kind of increased cognitive resource is needed to avoid positivity-bias. Future research aimed at understanding the role of the OFC and dACC in motivated self-evaluation may want to focus on their involvement in cognitive effort.

In contrast, extant research on social exclusion suggests that reward and punishment systems rather than differences in cognitive effort may be important for recognizing when interpersonal self-esteem is at stake. Although the VLPFC was implicated in the cyberball studies, presumably as a way of regulating away social distress in response to exclusion (Eisenberger, Lieberman, & Williams, 2003; Masten

et al., 2009), research across paradigms suggests roles for the dACC, amygdala, and striatum in interpersonal self-esteem maintenance. A host of research on emotional interference suggests that the dACC and amygdala are important for encoding sources of threat (Beer, 2009b; Bishop et al., 2004; Whalen, 1998). Additionally, the striatum has consistently been associated with reward processing in both humans and nonhuman animals (see Delgado, 2007, for a review). It is possible that the robust convergence on roles of the dACC, amygdala, and striatum in studies of social exclusion reflect their role in detecting when social interactions may impact self-esteem in a negative or positive manner. Further examination of the extant research suggests that neural regions associated with threat encoding may be sensitive to the certainty of threat. It is possible that the dACC may be important for detecting social exclusion that has occurred as indicated by exclusion from a cyberball game (Eisenberger, Lieberman, & Williams, 2003) or a disapproving face (Burklan, Eisenberger, & Lieberman, 2007). In contrast, the amygdala may be recruited more often for anticipating threats to self-esteem in contexts that are social. The amygdala was most often seen in studies that did not include explicit social threat but instead led participants to believe that self-esteem might be threatened by a social interaction such as giving public speeches (Furmark et al., 2004; Lorberbaum et al., 2004; Tillfors et al., 2002; but see Phan et al., 2005).

However, another explanation for the differences in the neural research on intrapersonal and interpersonal self-esteem maintenance is that these two lines of work differ quite a bit in their scope. It may be the extant research paints a very different picture of the neural systems involved in intrapersonal and interpersonal self-esteem because the extant lines of inquiry have focused on different aspects of each. The research on intrapersonal self-esteem has accumulated evidence from a diverse set of approaches (lesion, fMRI, ERP, and TMS) and has used a variety of measurements to operationalize self-evaluations that are unrealistically positive (see Table 40.1 and Figure 40.1). However, unlike neural research on interpersonal self-esteem, this body of studies does not include paradigms that explicitly threaten self-esteem nor has it examined whether the neural regions identified in these studies are modulated by relevant individual differences. In contrast, the research on interpersonal self-esteem relies heavily on fMRI approaches and has used paradigms that emphasize the difference between threatening and nonthreatening situations rather than directly examining how self-esteem is regulated in response to threat.

Future research is needed to examine the influence of explicit self-esteem threat on the neural systems involved in overly positive self-evaluation

In addition to fleshing out the extant research, manipulations that directly affect self-esteem will be helpful for more deeply understanding how the findings from the current studies fit into the debate about the underlying psychological mechanism of bias. If the studies above do reflect the self-evaluation bias that supports self-esteem maintenance, then they suggest a different interpretation of the mechanism underlying the changes in self-evaluation bias as a function of threat or affirmation. As mentioned above, threats to self-esteem elicit even greater bias (e.g., Gramzow & Willard, 2006; Paulhus et al., 2003). Bias that occurs in reaction to threat has typically been conceived as a reflection of even stronger engagement of the cognitive control used to manipulate self-relevant information in a self-serving way. This perspective contrasts with the neural findings which suggest that increased heuristic processing would give rise to even greater bias. An alternate possibility is that the current studies do not actually reflect self-evaluation bias that supports self-esteem maintenance. Instead, they may reflect baseline or default self-evaluations that arise from cognitive efficiency (Beer, 2007). Therefore, it is important to examine whether explicit self-esteem threat reveals the same or different patterns of neural activation associated with self-evaluation bias. After a self-esteem threat, bias may be associated with neural regions supporting cognitive control.

In addition to experimental manipulations of self-esteem threat, more research is needed to understand whether relevant individual differences modulate the neural systems associated with intrapersonal self-esteem processes. Narcissism and defensive coping styles predict greater self-evaluation bias. In the domains they care about, narcissists tend to have fragile self-esteem which may make them quick to experience self-esteem threat. Nonclinical levels of narcissism are associated with inflated perceptions of popularity, social status, and intellectual ability but not agreeableness or morality (Campbell, Rudich, & Sedikides, 2002; Paulhus & John, 1998; Robins & Beer, 2001). In other words, most self-evaluation tasks may be threatening to narcissists.

Therefore, studies that include experimental manipulations of self-esteem threat or individual differences in narcissism are another way to examine the neural systems mediating intrapersonal self-esteem defense. These studies will be helpful for understanding whether overly positive self-evaluations reflect similar processes when they arise in relation to threat or nonthreat. Do experimental manipulations of threat and individual differences in narcissism modulate OFC and dACC activity or some other neural system? Additionally, the inclusion of explicit self-esteem threat will provide a stronger test of whether there is commonality in the neural systems governing intrapersonal and interpersonal self-esteem defense. Do the neural regions associated with interpersonal self-esteem threat (dACC, amygdala, and striatum) show similar sensitivity to intrapersonal threat?

Future neural research is needed to understand regulation in response to interpersonal threat

The bulk of current neural research on interpersonal self-esteem processes focus on anticipation or detection of threat. Detection is helpful for understanding how people know when threat has occurred but does not provide insight into the neural systems that are recruited to preserve self-esteem in reaction to that threat. Individuals' awareness of threat and reactions to that threat are equally important components of interpersonal self-esteem maintenance. Paradigms that more directly examine the regulatory reactions to interpersonal threat will help flesh out the neural systems that support interpersonal self-esteem processes. Additionally, investigating reactions to threat may reveal more of a role for neural regions associated with top-down processing.

Implications of neural research for self-esteem maintenance across the lifespan

The identification of neural systems underlying a psychological process is also helpful for thinking about how aging-related neural changes impact processes at the psychological level of analysis. Therefore, researchers may want to investigate how aging-related neural changes affect self-esteem defense across the lifespan as a complement to the behavioral research on this topic. The neural regions identified in the extant research on intrapersonal and interpersonal self-esteem defense are affected by aging. In later life, the frontal lobes tend to atrophy (Hartel & Buckner, 2006; Raz, 2000) whereas striatal processing of reward remains intact (Samanez-Larkin et al., 2007). How might aging-related changes in these regions affect intrapersonal and interpersonal self-esteem defense across the lifespan?

Very little is known about self-evaluation bias in the very old or the very young. If bias requires correction by frontal lobe engagement, then bias may be particularly pronounced when frontal lobes have yet to mature or have begun to atrophy (Hartel & Buckner, 2006; Raz, 2000). Developmental research has shown that the frontal lobes do not fully develop until early adulthood and this accounts for the reduced executive functioning seen in children (Bunge & Wright, 2007). It may be that young children have pronounced positivity biases because they do not have full executive function capacity. The frontal lobe atrophy associated with late life does not preclude the execution of controlled processes. Older adults are just more selective about expending these processes (Hartel & Buckner, 2006; Raz, 2000). Therefore, older individuals may actually exhibit increased positivity bias in their self-evaluations because their preferred cognitive style promotes positivity bias.

Much more is known about interpersonal self-esteem processes in late life. Older individuals are known to show more selectivity in their social networks and tend to populate them mostly with individuals who are likely to reinforce self-esteem that relies on interpersonal sources (Carstensen, Isaacowitz, & Charles, 1999). Neural studies have shown that older adults tend to have preserved reward processing but are not sensitive to anticipated loss in a gambling paradigm (Samanez-Larkin et al, 2007). In particular, the relation between anticipated monetary gain and striatal activation is preserved in later life. If this relation holds in relation to social reward, then aging-related changes should not affect older adults' ability to recognize potentially rewarding social interactions. It may be this neural system that is recruited to help selectively prune social networks in a self-esteem bolstering manner.

Conclusion

Social neuroscience research on the self and emotion regulation has only recently begun to more specifically focus on questions of intrapersonal and interpersonal self-esteem defense. Currently, research suggests that intrapersonal self-esteem defense is associated with reduced OFC and dACC activation whereas interpersonal self-esteem defense is associated with increased dACC and amygdala activation and reduced striatal activation. Future research is needed to better understand whether these are meaningful neural

distinctions between intrapersonal and interpersonal self-defense or an artifact of the currently used paradigms in each line of inquiry. Developing neural research in this area will be helpful for understanding the psychological processes involved in self-esteem defense and how aging-related changes in neural function may impact self-esteem defense.

References

Adolphs, R. (2006). How do we know the minds of others? Domain-specificity, simulation, and enactive social cognition. *Brain Research, 1079*, 25–35.

Aleman, A., Agrawal, N., Morgan, K. D., & David, A. S. (2006). Insight into psychosis and neuropsychological function meta-analysis. *British Journal Psychiatry, 189*, 204–212.

Alicke, M. D. (1985). Global self-evaluation as determined by the desirability and controllability of trait adjectives. *Journal of Personality and Social Psychology, 49*, 1621–1630.

Alicke, M. D., Klotz, M. L., Breitenbecher, D. L., Yurak, T. J., & Vredenburg, D. S. (1995). Personal contact, individuation, and the above-average effect. *Journal of Personality and Social Psychology, 68*, 804–825.

Baltes, P. B. & Baltes, M. M. (1990). Psychological perspectives on successful aging: The model of selective optimization with compensation. In P. B. M. Baltes (Eds.), *Successful aging: Perspectives from the behavioral sciences* (pp. 1–34). Cambridge, England: Cambridge University Press.

Barrios, V., Kwan, V. S. Y., Ganis, G., Gorman, J., Romanowski, J., & Keenan, J. P. (2008). Elucidating the neural correlates of egoistic and moralistic self-enhancement. *Consciousness & Cognition, 17*, 451–456.

Beer, J. S. (2007). The default self: Feeling good or being right? *Trends in Cognitive Science, 11*, 187–189.

Beer, J. S. (2009a). Patient methodologies in the study of personality and social processes. In W. Harmon-Jones & J. S. Beer. (Eds). *Methods in social neuroscience*. New York: Guilford Press.

Beer, J. S. (2009b). The neural basis of emotion regulation: Making emotion work for you and not against you. In M. Gazzaniga (Ed.). *The cognitive neurosciences IV*. Cambridge: MIT Press.

Beer, J. S., Heerey, E. H., Keltner, D., Scabini, D., & Knight, R. T. (2003). The regulatory function of self-conscious emotion: Insights from patients with orbitofrontal damage. *Journal of Personality and Social Psychology, 85*, 594–604.

Beer, J. S. & Hughes, B. L. (2010). Neural systems of social comparison and the "above-average" effect. *NeuroImage, 49*, 2671–2679.

Beer, J. S., John, O. P., Scabini, D., & Knight, R. T. (2006). Orbitofrontal cortex and social behavior: Integrating self-monitoring and emotion-cognition interactions. *Journal of Cognitive Neuroscience, 18*, 871–880.

Beer, J. S., Knight, R. T., & D'Esposito, M. (2006). Integrating emotion and cognition: The role of the frontal lobes in distinguishing between helpful and hurtful emotion. *Psychological Science, 17*, 448–453.

Beer, J. S., Lombardo, M., & Bhanji, J. (2010). Roles of medial prefrontal cortex and orbitofrontal cortex in self-evaluation. *Journal of Cognitive Neuroscience, 22*, 2108–2119.

Beer, J. S., & Ochsner, K. N. (2006). Social cognition: A multi level analyses. *Brain Research, 1079*, 98–105.

Beer, J. S., Shimamura, A. P., & Knight, R. T. (2005). Frontal lobe contributions to executive control of cognitive and social behavior. In M. S. Gazzaniga (Ed.) *The newest cognitive neurosciences* (3rd Edition). Cambridge: MIT Press.

Bishop, S., Duncan, J., Brett, M., & Lawrence, A. D. 2004. Prefrontal cortical function and anxiety: Controlling attention to threat-related stimuli. *Nat Neurosci., 7*, 184–188.

Blackwood, N. J., Bentall, R. P., ffytche, D. H., Simmons, A., Murray, R. M., & Howard, R .J. (2003). Self-responsibility and the self-serving bias: An fMRI investigation of causal attributions. *NeuroImage, 20*, 1076–1085.

Blakemore, S .J., Winston, J., & Frith, U. (2004). Social cognitive neuroscience: Where are we heading? *Trends in Cognitive Science, 8*, 216–222.

Blumer, D. & Benson, D. F. (1975). Personality changes with frontal and temporal lobe lesions. In D. F. Benson, & D. Blumer (Eds.). *Psychiatric aspects of neurologic disease* (pp. 151–169). New York: Grune & Stratton.

Bodenhausen, G. V., Kramer, G. P., & Süsser, K. (1994). Happiness and stereotypic thinking in social judgment. *Journal of Personality and Social Psychology, 66*, 621–632.

Botvinick, M., Cohen, J. D., & Carter, C. S. (2004). Conflict monitoring and anterior cingulate cortex: An update. *Trends in Cognitive Sciences. 8*, 539–546.

Bunge, S. A., & Wright, S. B. (2007). Neurodevelopmental changes in working memory and cognitive control. *Current Opinion in Neurobiology, 17*, 243–250.

Burkland, L. J., Eisenberger, N. I., & Lieberman, M. D. (2007). The face of rejection: Rejection sensitivity modulates dorsal anterior cingulate activation to disapproving faces. *Social Neuroscience, 2*, 238–253.

Cacciopo, J. T. & Berntson, G. G. (1992). Social psychological contributions to the decade of the brain: Doctrine of multi-level analyses. *American Psychologist, 47*, 1019–1028.

Cacioppo, J. T., Norris, C. J., Decety, J., Monteleone, G., & Nusbaum, H. (2008). In the eye of the beholder: Individual differences in perceived social isolation predict regional brain activation to social stimuli. *Journal of Cognitive Neurscience, 21*, 83–92.

Campbell, W. K., Rudich, E. A., & Sedikides, C. (2002). Narcissism, self-esteem, and the Positivity of self-views: Two portraits of self-love. *Personality and Social Psychology Bulletin, 28*, 358–368.

Carstensen, L. L., Isaacowitz, D. M., & Charles, S. T. (1999). Taking time seriously: A theory of socioemotional selectivity. *American Psychologist, 54*, 165–181.

Chambers, J. R., & Windschitl, P. D. (2004). Biases in social comparative judgments: The role of nonmotivated factors in above-average and comparative-optimism effects. *Psychological Bulletin, 130*, 813–838.

Culley, T. H. (2001). *The immortal class* (p. 32). Villard: New York.

Delgado, M. (2007). Reward related responses in the human striatum. *Annals of the New York Academy of Sciences, 1104*, 70–88.

DeMartino, B., Kumaran, D., Seymour, B., & Dolan, R. J. (2006). Frames, biases, and rational decision-making in the human brain. *Science, 313*, 684–687.

Dunning, D. (1995). Trait importance and modifiability as factors influencing self-assessment and self-enhancement motives. *Personality and Social Psychology Bulletin, 21*, 1297–1306.

Dunning, D., Meyerowitz, J. A., & Holzberg, A. D. (1989). Ambiguity and self-evaluation: The role of idiosyncratic trait definitions in self-serving appraisals of ability. *Journal of Personality and Social Psychology, 57*, 1082–1090.

Eagleman, D. M. (2001). Visual illusions and neurobiology. *Nature Reviews Neuroscience, 2*, 920–925.

Eisenberger, N. I., Lieberman, M. D., & Williams, K. D. (2003). Does rejection hurt? An fMRI study of social exclusion. *Science, 302*, 290–292.

Furmark, T., Tillfors, M., Garpenstrand, H., Marteinsdottir, I., Langstrom, B., Oreland, L., et al (2004): Serotonin transporter polymorphism related to amygdale excitability and symptom severity in patients with social phobia. *Neuroscience Letters, 362*,189–192.

Gilihan, S. J. & Farah, M. J. (2005). Is self special? A critical review of evidence from experimental psychology and cognitive neuroscience. *Psychological Bulletin, 131*, 76–97.

Gramzow, R. H. & Willard, G. (2006). Exaggerating current and past performance: Motivated self-enhancement versus reconstructive memory. *Personality and Social Psychology Bulletin, 32*, 1114–1125.

Greenfield, J. (2001). "Shoot the Messenger" *Chicago Reader*, March 30, 2001.

Goldin, P. et al., (2009). Neural bases of social anxiety disorder: Emotional reactivity and cognitive regulation during social and physical threat, *Archives of General Psychiatry, 66*, 170–180.

Hartel, C. R. & Buckner, R. L. (2006). Utility of brain imaging methods in research on aging. In L. L. Carstensen & C. R. Hartel (Eds.) *When I'm 64* (pp. 240–246). Washington, DC: National Academic Press.

Heatherton, T. F., Macrae, C.N., & Kelley, W. (2004). What can the social brain science tell us about the self? *Current Directions in Psychological Science, 13*, 190–193.

Hess, T. M. (2006). Adaptive aspects of social cognitive functioning in adulthood: Age-related goal and knowledge influences. *Social Cognition, 24*, 279–309.

Hughes, B. L. & Beer, J.S. (2009). Orbitofrontal cortex and anterior cingulate cortex are modulated by motivated social cognition. *Under review.*

Kelley, W. M., Macrae, C. N., Wyland, C. L., Caglar, S., Inati, S., & Heatherton, T. F. (2002). Finding the self? An event-related fMRI study. *Journal of Cognitive Neuroscience, 14*, 785–794.

King-Casas, B., Tomlin, D., Anen, C., Camerer, C. F., Quartz, S. R., & Montague, P. R. (2005). Getting to know you: Reputation and trust in a two-person economic exchange. *Science, 308*, 78–83.

Klayman, J., Soll, J. B., González-Vallejo, C., & Barlas, S. (1999). Overconfidence: It depends on how, what, and whom you ask. *Organizational Behavior and Human Decision Processes, 79*, 216–247.

Klein, S. B. & Kihlstrom, J. F. (1998). On bridging the gap between social-personality psychology and neuropsychology. *Personality and Social Psychology Review, 2*, 228–242.

Klucharev, V., Hytonen, K., Rijpkema, M., Smidts, A., & Fernandez, G. (2009). Reinforcement learning signal predicts social conformity. *Neuron, 61*, 140–151.

Kruger, J. (1999) Lake Wobegon be gone! The "below-average effect" and the egocentric nature of comparative ability judgments. *Journal of Personality and Social Psychology, 77*, 221–232.

Krusemark, E. A., Campbell, W. K., & Clementz, B. A. (2008). Attributions, deception, and event related potentials: An investigation of the self-serving bias. *Psychophysiology, 45*, 511–515.

Kwan, V. S. Y., Barrios, V., Ganis, G., Gorman, J., Lange, C., Kumar, M., et al. (2007). Assessing the neural correlates of self-enhancement bias: A transcranial magnetic stimulation study. *Experimental Brain Research, 182*, 379–385.

Labouvie-Vief, G. (2003). Dynamic integration: Affect, cognition, and the self in adulthood. *Current Directions in Psychological Science, 12*, 201–206.

Leary, M. R. & Downs, D. L. (1995). Interpersonal functions of the self-esteem motive: The self-esteem system as a sociometer. In M. H. Kernis (Ed.), *Efficacy, agency, and self-esteem* (pp. 123–144). New York: Plenum Press.

Leary, M. R., Tambor, E. S., Terdal, S. K., & Downs, D. L. (1995). Self-esteem as an interpersonal monitor: The sociometer hypothesis. *Journal of Personality and Social Psychology.*

Logan G. D. & Cowan, W. B. (1984) On the ability to inhibit thought and action: A theory of an act of control. *Psychological Review, 91*, 295–327.

Masten, C. M., Eisenberger, N. I., Borofsky, L.A., Pfeifer, J. H., McNealy, K., Mazziotta, J. C. et al. (2009). Neural correlates of social exclusion during adolescence: Understanding the distress of peer rejection. *Social Cognitive and Affective Neuroscience, 4*, 143–157.

Mata, R., Schooler, R. J., & Rieskamp, J. (2007). The aging decision maker: Cognitive aging and the adaptive selection of decision strategies. *Psychology and Aging, 22*, 796–810.

Mather, M. (2006). A review of decision-making processes: Weighing the risks and benefits of aging. In L. Carstensen & C. Hartel (Eds.) *When I'm 64: Committee on Aging Frontiers in Social Psychology, Personality, and Adult Developmental Psychology* (pp. 145–173). Washington, DC: National Academies Press.

McLennan J. D., Shaw E., Shema S. J., Gardner W. P., Pope S. K., & Kelleher K. J. (1998). Adolescents' insight into heavy drinking. *Journal of Adolescent Health, 22*, 409–416.

McQueen, A. & Klein, W. M. P (2006). Experimental manipulations of self-affirmation: A systematic review. *Self and Identity, 5*, 289–354.

Metcalfe, J. (1998). Cognitive optimism: Self-deception or memory-based heuristic processing? *Personality and Social Psychology Review, 2*, 100–110.

Mitchell, J. P., Macrae, C. N., & Banaji, M. R. (2006). Dissociable medial prefrontal contributions to judgments of similar and dissimilar others. *Neuron, 50*, 655–663.

Moore, D. A., & Small, D. A. (2007). Error and bias in comparative judgment: On being both better and worse than we think we are. *Journal of Personality and Social Psychology, 92*, 972–989.

Moran, J. M., Macrae, C. N., Heatherton, T. F., Wyland, C. L., and Kelley, W. M. (2006). Neuroanatomical evidence for distinct cognitive and affective components of self. *Journal of Cognitive Neuroscience, 18*, 1586–1594.

Mroczek, D. K. (2001). Age and emotion in adulthood. *Current Directions in Psychological Science, 10*, 87–90.

Ochsner, K. N. & Lieberman, M. D. (2001). The emergence of social cognitive neuroscience. *American Psychologist, 56*, 717–734.

Ochsner, K. N., Beer, J. S., Robertson, E. A., Cooper, J., Gabrieli, J. D. E., Kihlstrom, J. F., et al. (2005). The neural correlates of direct and reflected self-knowledge. *Neuroimage, 28*, 797–814.

Ochsner, K. N., Bunge, S. A., Gross, J. J., and Gabrieli, J. D. E. (2002). Rethinking feelings: An fMRI study of the cognitive regulation of emotion. *Journal of Cognitive Neuroscience, 14*, 1215–1229.

Ochsner, K. N. & Gross, J. J. (2005). *The cognitive control of emotion. Trends in Cognitive Sciences, 9*, 242–249.

Ochsner, K. N. & Lieberman, M. D. (2001). The emergence of social cognitive neuroscience. *American Psychologist, 56*, 717–734.

Paulhus D. L., Graf, P., & Van Selst, M. (1989) Attentional load increases the positivity of self-presentation. *Social Cognition 7*, 389–400.

Paulhus, D. L., Harms, P. D., Bruce, M. N., & Lysy, D. C. (2003). The over-claiming technique: Measuring self-enhancement independent of ability. *Journal of Personality and Social Psychology, 84*, 890–904.

Paulhus, D. L. & John, O. P. (1998). Egoistic and moralistic biases in self-perception: The interplay of self-deceptive styles with basic traits and motives. *Journal of Personality, 66*, 1025–1106.

Peters, E., Hess, T. M., Vastfjall, D., & Auman, C. (2007). Adult age differences in dual information processes: Implications for the role of affective and deliberative processes in older adults' decision making. *Current Directions in Psychological Science, 2*, 1–23.

Phan, K. L, Fitzgerald, D. A., Nathan, P. J., & Tancer, M. E. (2005). Association between amygdala hyperactivity to harsh faces and severity of social anxiety in generalized social phobia. *Biological Psychiatry, 59*, 424–429.

Raz, N. (2000). Aging of the brain and its impact on cognitive performance: Integration of structural and functional findings. In F. I. M. Craik & T. A. Salthouse (Eds). *Handbook of aging and cognition* (2nd edition). Mahwah, NJ: Erlbaum.

Rilling, J., Gutman, D., Zeh, T., Pagnoni, G., Berns, G., & Kilts, C. (2002). A neural basis for social cooperation. *Neuron, 35*, 395–405.

Robins, R. W. & Beer, J. S. (2001). Positive illusions about the self: Short-term benefits and long-term costs. *Journal of Personality and Social Psychology, 80*, 340–352.

Samanez-Larkin, G. R., Gibbs, S. E. B., Khanna, K., Nielsen, L., Carstensen, L. L., & Knutson, B. (2007). Anticipation of monetary gain but not loss in healthy older adults, *Nature Neuroscience, 10*, 788–791.

Sanz, M., Constable, G., Lopez-Ibor, I., Kemp, R., & David, A. S. (1998). A comparative study of insight scales and their relationship to psychopathological and clinical variables. *Psychological Medicine, 28*, 437–466.

Saxe, R. (2006). Uniquely human social cognition. *Current Opinion in Neurobiology, 16*, 235–239.

Schutter, D. J. L. G. (2009). Transcranial magnetic stimulation. In E. Harmon-Jones & J. S. Beer, (Eds). *Methods in social neuroscience.* New York: Guilford Press.

Schwartz, C. E., Wright, C. I., Shin, L. M., Kagan, J., & Rauch, S. L. (2003). Inhibited and uninhibited infants "grown up": Adult amygdalar response to novelty. *Science, 300*, 1952–1953.

Sharot, T., Riccardi, A. M ., Raio, C. M., & Phelps, E. A. (2007). Neural mechanisms mediating optimism bias. *Nature, 450*, 102–105.

Somerville, L., Heatherton, T. F., & Kelley, W. A. (2006). Anterior cingulate responds differently to expectancy violation and social exclusion. *Nature Neuroscience. 9*, 1007–1008.

Steele, J. D., Currie, J., Lawrie, S. M., & Reid, I. (2006) Prefrontal cortical abnormality in major depressive disorder: A stereotactic meta-analysis. *Journal of Affective Disorders, 101*, 1–11.

Swann, W. B., Pelham, B. W., & Krull, D. S. (1989) Agreeable fancy or disagreeable truth? Reconciling self-enhancement and self-verification. *Journal of Personality and Social Psychology, 57*, 782–791.

Taylor, S. E. & Brown, J. D. (1988). Illusion and well-being: A social psychological perspective on mental health, *Psychological Bulletin, 103*, 193–210.

Taylor, S. E., Neter, E., & Wayment, H. A. (1995). Self-evaluation processes. *Personality and Social Psychology Bulletin, 21*, 1278–1287.

Tillfors, M., Furmark, T., Marteinsdottir, I., & Fredrikson, M. (2002). Cerebral blood flow during anticipation of public speaking in social phobia: APET study. *Biological Psychiatry, 52*, 1113–1119.

Tversky, A. & Kahneman, D. (1974) Judgement under uncertainty: Heuristics and biases. *Science, 185*, 1124–1131.

Uddin, L. Q., Iacoboni, M., Lange, C., & Keenan, J. P. (2007). The self and social cognition: The role of mirror neurons. *Trends in Cognitive Sciences, 11*, 153–157.

Volkow, N. D., Fowler, J. S., Wolf, A. P., Hitzemann, R., Dewey, S., Bendriem, B., et al (1991) Changes in brain glucose metabolism in cocaine dependence and withdrawal. *American Journal of Psychiatry, 14*8, 621–626.

Whalen, P. J. (1998). Fear, vigilance, and ambiguity: Initial neuroimaging studies of the human amygdala. *Current Directions in Psychological Science, 7*, 177–188.

The Social Regulation of Emotion

James A. Coan

Abstract

This chapter argues that links between social relationships and health are largely mediated through the impact of social relationships on emotion and emotional responding—that the social regulation of emotion not only largely accounts for these observations, but that it is indeed the baseline or default emotion regulatory strategy employed by most or all social animals, a perspective called the social baseline model. Social forms of emotion regulation can be mediational, where the presence of a social resource directly modifies an ongoing emotional response; or moderational, where socially relevant personality factors, past social experiences, or cognitive representations of either current relational partners or broader social networks modify an individual's self-regulation needs or capabilities.

Keywords: emotion, emotion regulation, social proximity, social interaction, attachment, physiology, neurobiology, behavioral ecology

Social relationships and interpersonal behaviors exert regulatory influences on our physiological, behavioral, and dispositional responses to emotionally charged situations (Berscheid, 2003; Sapolsky, 1998; Uchino, Cacioppo, & Kiecolt-Glaser, 1996). Supportive social behaviors attenuate stress-related activity in the autonomic nervous system (ANS) and hypothalamic-pituitary-adrenal (HPA) axis (Boccia, Reite, & Laudenslager, 1989; Flinn & England, 1997; Lewis & Ramsay, 1999). Maternal grooming behaviors affect glucocorticoid receptor gene expression underlying hippocampal and HPA-axis stress reactivity in rat pups (Weaver, Cervoni, et al., 2004). In novel, mildly stressful environments, rats in the company of familiar companions engage in more exploration and play than rats either alone or in the company of unfamiliar companions (Terranova, Cirulli, & Laviola, 1999). Perceived interpersonal

social support attenuates the risk of psychopathology in the wake traumatic life experiences (Moak & Agrawal, in press). All of these observations, and many similar ones, result from the security-provision and distress-alleviation regulatory functions on negative affect and arousal that social relationships afford (Bowlby, 1973; Mikulincer, Shaver, & Pereg, 2003). They are the result of the social regulation of emotion.

Importantly, the social regulation of emotion does not refer to any and all effects that one individual's behavior may have on the emotional behavior of another. For example, if one individual were to insult or compliment another, either behavior could elicit an emotional response in the receiver. By contrast, social processes *regulate* emotional responses when the behavior of one or more individuals influences another's up- or down-regulation of a current or potential emotional response to some situation or event. Emotion-regulation effects attributable to social proximity and interaction may be mediational—that is, may reflect social processes that directly impact emotional reactions to a stressful event—or moderational, where social influences modify the need for, or the implementation of, self-regulatory capabilities that manifest during subsequent emotional situations. This (somewhat simplified) distinction captures a wide variety of emotion-regulation effects attributable to social contact and provides an organizational framework for the information that follows.

Social Processes as Mediators of Emotion-Regulation

From a meditational point of view (cf., Baron & Kenny, 1986), social proximity or interaction is the mechanism through which (or partially through which) emotion-regulation effects are proximally achieved. For example, a child may be at risk for emotional distress while having blood drawn at the doctor's office, but be simultaneously calmed by the mother's presence, especially if the mother holds the child or uses soothing language and tone of voice. In a mediational model, these parental behaviors are the putative mechanisms of emotion-regulation in the child. Another way to say this is that for the child in question, and at least within the context of the blood draw, the regulation of emotional distress is somewhat *dependent* upon proximity to the parent. Figure 41.1 represents a mediational model of social emotion regulation under conditions of where 1) a situational threat causes activation of a set of behavioral and physiological responses we might call fear (cf., Coan, 2010b) and; 2) increased proximity to a social partner or network inhibits that fear response.

Many researchers have observed the stress-buffering effects of social proximity, soothing, and contact on behaviors and physiological systems related to emotional responding. This social buffering can occur at many levels (e.g., group, caregiver, familiar conspecific) and in many species, but familiarity and attachment are common factors associated with the strength of social regulation effects. In rats, the presence of familiar conspecifics (e.g., cage mates) increases exploration and attenuates HPA-axis activity under conditions of threat (Kiyokawa, Kikusui, Takeuchi, & Mori, 2004; Ruis et al., 1999; Terranova et al., 1999). Familiar conspecifics attenuate emotional stress responding in nonhuman primates during new social group formation and social conflict (Gust, Gordon, Brodie, & McClure, 1996; Weaver & de Waal, 2003). Recently, Langford and colleagues (Langford et al., 2010) have observed that in mice social proximity between familiar cage mates even attenuates pain behavior.

Humans regulate each other in similar ways. The performance of stressful tasks is associated with less negative affect in the presence of familiar friends than with strangers (Snydersmith & Cacioppo, 1992). Cardiovascular reactivity to giving a public speech is attenuated by supportive verbal behavior, even to some extent by strangers (Lepore, Allen, & Evans, 1993; O'Donovan & Hughes, 2008). Experimentally manipulated social support by relational partners has resulted in lower cortisol reactivity (Kirschbaum, Klauer, Filipp, & Hellhammer, 1995). Gottman and colleagues (Gottman, Coan, Carrere, & Swanson, 1998) have documented social regulation influences even among couples engaged in interpersonal conflict, where small moments of positive affect expressed by one partner frequently and immediately preceded a relaxation of physiological arousal in the other. And the effectiveness of these social regulation attempts held consequences for relationship outcomes. The couples who showed the strongest decreases in physiological arousal following their partner's expression of positive affect were more likely to regard their marriages as highly satisfactory 4 years later. By contrast, those couples who showed the least attenuation in arousal following their partner's positive affect were more likely to have divorced during the same period. Recently, Coan and colleagues (Coan, Schaefer, & Davidson, 2006) observed that simple hand holding was

Fig. 41.1 A mediational model representing the social regulation of emotion. In this model, a perceived threat causes both a fear response and proximity to a social resource (friend, group, romantic partner). Proximity to the social resource provides an inhibitory influence on the fear response.

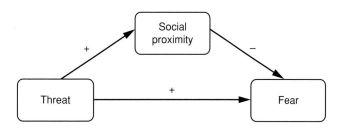

sufficient to attenuate a host of neural responses to the threat of electric shock during neuroimaging. These effects, too, corresponded with relationship quality.

Relatively little work to date has specifically identified the neural mediators of the social regulation of emotion. Coan et al. (2006) did observe that hand holding during threat of shock was, in the highest quality relationships, associated with decreased activation in the hypothalamus, providing evidence of the long suspected role the hypothalamus plays in linking social support to better health—particularly immune functioning (Kiecolt-Glaser & Newton, 2001)—but the question of what neural mechanisms translate the hand holding into reduced hypothalamic functioning remains, and this question has been more difficult to answer. Coan et al did not observe, for example, any regions of the brain that were more active during supportive hand holding than while alone, and no regions that showed negative associations with threat-responsive circuits apparently down-regulated by hand holding. In a separate attempt to address this question, Eisenberger and colleagues (Eisenberger, Taylor, Gable, Hilmert, & Lieberman, 2007) monitored associations between threat-evoked neural reactivity, threat-evoked cortisol reactivity, and self-reported levels of daily social support. Their findings were highly similar to those of Coan et al (2006) in at least one important sense: The provision of social support was not positively correlated with any threat responsive region of the brain. Rather, Eisenberger et al. observed that greater daily levels of social support were associated only with lower levels of threat-related activation in the dorsal anterior cingulate cortex (dACC) and Brodmann area 8 (BA8). It is of particular interest that no evidence of prefrontally mediated self-regulation activity was observed to covary with either the daily measures of social support monitored by Eisenberger et al. (2007), or the experimentally introduced social support of the Coan et al. (2006) study. This and other evidence has led Coan (2008; 2010a) to propose that the social regulation of emotion does not achieve its

effects via circuits ordinarily associated with self-regulation (Ochsner & Gross, 2005b). As discussed in greater detail below, the conservation of prefrontal resources achieved through these and similar nonprefrontally mediated forms of emotion regulation may be among the phylogenetic (and ontogenetic) advantages driving the formation of social groups and relationships (Coan, 2008; 2010a).

Social Processes as Moderators of Emotion Regulation

Strictly speaking, the Eisenberger study discussed above is not a mediational example of social emotion regulation, because the effects of social support were measured more globally, and not introduced as intervening variables during threat responding. This illustrates one of the many ways in which social proximity and interaction can *moderate* self-regulation needs and capabilities as third variables that create conditions under which self-regulation strategies are either called upon or maximally effective (see Figure 41.2). Ample research suggests that perceived current social support and past social experience impact an individual's self-regulation capabilities (Allen, Moore, Kuperminc, & Bell, 1998; Carter, 2005; Prinstein & La Greca, 2004; Weaver, Diorio, Seckl, Szyf, & Meaney, 2004). For example, Eisenberger et al. (2007) has suggested that part of the effect of ongoing daily social support is to modify the functioning of circuits supporting the perception of threats encountered while alone, which in turn impacts the perceived need for engaging self-regulation capabilities. Prior experience with a close relational partner may provide a form of "regulatory capital" in the face of emotional stressors; cognitive representations of one's relational partner, one's resources or status as a function of having a relational partner, or both, may alter one's sensitivity to potential threats.

The impact of social experiences on subsequent self-regulation capabilities is probably a process that continues to varying degrees throughout life (Mikulincer et al., 2003). Many have conjectured, however, that the most impactful social experiences

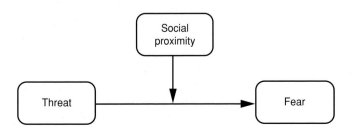

Fig. 41.2 A moderational model representing the social regulation of emotion. In this model, the causal pathway linking a perceived threat to a fear response is modified either by knowledge of the current perceived availability of social resources or by past social experiences that impact the general perception of the availability of social resources.

occur early, during a period of significant neural development. During the first year of life, the human brain grows exponentially, a process that continues well into the second year (Franceschini et al., 2007) There is a concomitant rise in brain glucose metabolism that continues until about the fourth year, but the average brain glucose metabolism remains approximately double that of adults until about age 10 (Chugani, 1998). Proteins that aid in neuron survival (neurotrophins) depend for their production on neural activity—on *use*—which is itself largely dependent upon the type and level of stimulation in the environment (Berardi & Maffei, 1999; Cancedda et al., 2004). This early rapid expansion in neural development results in an excess of axonal, dendritic, and synaptic production that is subsequently "pruned" by lack of use (Reichardt, 2006). Demands in the environment shape an early developing brain initially prepared for a wide range of possibilities, such that it is better prepared for meeting the demands it has faced—and thus "expects" to keep facing—with neural organization ultimately following the patterned and repeated activation of circuits capable of meeting those demands (Hebb, 1949; Posner & Rothbart, 2007). This developmental time, as many have documented, represents a "critical" or "sensitive" period for the impact of sensory experiences on the developing brain (cf., Briones, Klintsova, & Greenough, 2004; Hubel & Wiesel, 1970; Schauwers et al., 2004).

In most social species, including humans, filial bonding occurs rapidly, unconditionally, and primarily during this period of rapid neural development (Ainsworth, Blehar, Waters, & Wall, 1978; Bowlby, 1969/1982, 1973; Hofer, 1984; Hofer, 2006; Moriceau & Sullivan, 2005). As this process unfolds, interactions between social experiences, regulatory circuits in the prefrontal cortex (PFC), and socioemotional activity in regions such as the amygdala and nucleus accumbens, may shape different expectations about social resources, opportunities for affiliation, and the consequences of those affiliations. This may in turn set the stage for different broad strategies of engaging (or avoiding) social stimuli, perhaps especially during emotional stress. Indeed, the conditions under which the filial bond forms and develops may constitute a kind of rudimentary "pre-working model" of interdependence and affect regulation—of attachment style, for example, (Ainsworth et al., 1978; Hofer, 1995; Mikulincer et al., 2003)—that is subsequently either altered or reinforced throughout childhood (Coan, 2008).

Normal psychological development clearly depends in part on proximity to and interaction with caregivers during infancy (Harlow, Dodsworth, & Harlow, 1965; Harlow & Zimmermann, 1959). Maternal grooming of infant rats influences glucocorticoid gene receptor development in the hippocampus, in turn influencing the stress reactivity of the pups throughout their lives, and even into subsequent generations (Weaver, Cervoni, et al., 2004; Weaver, Diorio, et al., 2004). In brown capuchin monkeys, early mother/offspring behaviors predict the post-conflict reconciliation styles of offspring with nonfamilial conspecifics (Weaver & de Waal, 2003). Recently, Hofer (Hofer, 2006) proposed a process by which early interactions with caregivers evolve from the regulation of sensory-motor, thermal, and nutrient functions to the regulation of affect. Initially in this process, the infant's access to primary reinforcers (e.g., food, water, warmth, touch) is dependent upon neural circuitry that solicits the attention of the caregiver via emotional behavior. As the infant develops, the caregiver comes to regulate emotional behavior per se. Repeated exposures to the regulatory behaviors of caregivers are thought to then shape the infant's expectations about the availability of social resources—a process thought to lead to *attachment styles,* about which more is discussed below.

Unfortunately, much of what is known about the effects of early social experiences on subsequent self-regulation capabilities derives from studies of abuse and neglect, conditions associated with heightened stress reactivity, anxiety, depression, and social deviance well into adulthood (Teicher, Samson, Polcari, & McGreenery, 2006). Importantly, many regions of the brain most vulnerable to such experiences are also associated with both social behavior and emotional regulation (Teicher et al., 2003). For example, the cerebellar vermis, a portion of the cerebellum with a high density of glucocorticoid receptors, is both highly sensitive to early stress and involved in modulating activity in the hypothalamus, reticular system, locus coeruleus, ventral tegmental area, nucleus accumbens, substantia nigra, and the prefrontal cortex. Selective lesions of the vermis have in fact been observed to tame social deviance linked to early maternal deprivation stress in rhesus monkeys (Berman, 1997). Childhood neglect may also disrupt the functioning of neuropeptides critical for the kinds of social affiliation and bonding behaviors that determine the strength and frequency of opportunities for social emotion regulation (Carter, 2003; Insel, 1997; Ross et al., 2009; Uvnaes-Moberg, 1998).

For example, children who experienced social deprivation and neglect in Romanian orphanages were observed to have lower overall levels of vasopressin, as well as blunted oxytocin responses to physical contact by their caregivers (Wismer-Fries, Ziegler, Kurian, Jacoris, & Pollak, 2005). Early social isolation is a well-known risk factor for a number of neurodevelopmental and psychosocial problems, ranging from anxiety and depression, to increased risk of suicide, relational problems, and even stress-related dwarfism (Barber, Eccles, & Stone, 2001; Cacioppo et al., 2006; Kawachi, 2001; Newcomb & Bentler, 1988; Skuse, Albanese, Stanhope, Gilmour, & Voss, 1996). Experiences with peers and parents during adolescence are similarly related to levels of substance use and dysfunctional romantic relationship behavior (Prinstein & La Greca, 2004). Indeed, adolescent social experiences consistently emerge as among the strongest predictors of adult social and emotional behavior (Allen, Porter, & Tencer, 2002; Magdol, Moffitt, Caspi, & Silva, 1998). Dozens of studies have identified the negative sequelae of social isolation at any age (Uchino et al., 1996), such as increased levels of basal ANS arousal, alteration of platelet function in ways that contribute to endothelial injury, sleep dysfunction, and disturbances in both endocrine and immune systems (Cacioppo et al., 2002; Knox et al., 1998; Phillips et al., 2006).

With regard to social emotion regulation, attachment theorists (Ainsworth et al., 1978; Bartholomew & Horowitz, 1991; Mikulincer & Shaver, 2007) have had perhaps the most to say about how individuals differ in their utilization of close social relationships as emotion-regulatory resources (Mikulincer et al., 2003). Major theories of attachment posit that individuals develop relatively stable adaptations called attachment styles to cope with expected social and environmental conditions (e.g., frequent or lengthy absences by the caregiver shape the expectation that individuals must learn to depend on themselves alone). Attachment styles can be expressed as two relatively independent axes related to feelings about social relationships—anxiety and avoidance. Individuals low in both tend to hold less threatening appraisals of potentially threatening events (Mikulincer & Florian, 1998), engage in more honest emotional disclosure (Mikulincer & Nachshon, 1991; Mikulincer & Orbach, 1995), seek out more emotional support from others (Larose, Bernier, Soucy, & Duchesne, 1999; Rholes, Simpson, & Grich Stevens, 1998), and benefit more from the support they acquire (Fraley & Shaver, 2000).

Neuroscientific investigations of attachment style are rare. In one such study, 20 women were prompted during neuroimaging to ruminate on threatening relationship scenarios (Gillath, Bunge, Shaver, Wendelken, & Mikulincer, 2005). Greater trait attachment anxiety corresponded with greater activity in the dACC and temporal pole, and decreased activity in the orbitofrontal cortex. These findings partially converge with those of Eisenberger et al. (2007) described above, suggesting that the dACC in particular is sensitive to the availability of social resources, with important implications for the self-regulation of emotion. The dACC has also been implicated in the affective component of pain and distress (Eisenberger, Lieberman, & Williams, 2003; Wang et al., 2005). As noted by Eisenberger and colleagues (2007), the dACC may become desensitized by social experience through repeated exposure to endogenous opioids. The dACC has a high density of opioid receptors, and endogenous opioids are unconditionally released in response to positive social experiences (Panksepp, 1998; Panksepp, Nelson, & Siviy, 1994). These are exciting possibilities, but a detailed delineation of the neural mechanisms linking social experience to self-regulation needs and capabilities awaits further research.

The Social Baseline Model

Drawing on optimization theory and behavioral ecology (Krebs & Davies, 1993), Coan (2008; 2010a) has proposed the *social baseline model* of emotion regulation, which suggests that social proximity and interaction are not *only* strategies for emotion regulation, but also that they are the primary, default, or *baseline* emotion regulation strategies employed by many social species, not least humans. This is in part because social proximity and interaction is fundamental to human ecology, much as water is fundamental to aquatic species. That is, in contrast to specific climates, diets, landforms, or other obvious environmental characteristics, the dominant ecology for the human being is other human beings (Kudo & Dunbar, 2001). From this perspective, proximity to conspecifics is implicitly regulatory because it decreases the perceived cost of coping with dangerous environments, thus conserving neural resources. By contrast, violations of the assumption of proximity are unconditionally threatening for the opposite reason—going it alone is more costly.

According to the social baseline model, the quality of social relationships can be defined by their health- and safety-enhancing properties. In addition to distributing risk merely by increased numbers (as many species do), trusted companions devote energy of their own to activities that benefit their partners—activities like vigilance for predators, the identification and acquisition of resources, and cooperative caretaking of offspring. The emotion regulatory effects of social proximity and interaction are thus yoked to ongoing appraisals of access to social resources and personal risk as a function of proximity to them (cf., Cohen & Wills, 1985).

Of course, humans have powerful self-regulation capabilities in comparison to other animals, including other primates. For example, humans are the only animals on Earth who can regulate themselves with thoughts such as "it's only a movie." These sorts of self-regulatory activities are largely mediated through the prefrontal cortex (Ochsner & Gross, 2005a), which is a computationally and metabolically costly region of the brain (Banfield, Wyland, Macrae, Munte, & Heatherton, 2005). Indeed, long periods of self-regulation frequently result in steadily diminishing self-regulation capabilities, possibly due to the steady depletion of metabolic resources required for such sustained activity (Galliot & Baumeister, 2007; but see Kurzban, 2010, for a contrary view). The principle of *economy of action* suggests that to survive, organisms will conserve resources whenever possible in order to optimize the ratio of resources acquired to resources expended (Krebs & Davies, 1993; Proffitt, 2006). The social baseline model suggests the human prefrontal cortex is a major target of resource conservation, and that a powerful way to meet this need is via socially mediated affect regulation (Coan, 2008), a process that does not seem to achieve its effects via prefrontal activity (Coan et al., 2006; Eisenberger et al., 2007). This would explain why individuals tend to invest less effort in self-regulation in the presence of relational partners (Edens, Larkin, & Abel, 1992; Mikulincer & Florian, 1998; Robles & Kiecolt-Glaser, 2003).

An example of this latter point is illustrated in the work by Coan et al. (2006) mentioned above. Recall that for this study, women were confronted with the threat of shock while either alone, holding a stranger's hand, or holding their partner's hand. Women in the highest quality relationships showed the least threat-related brain activation overall—little more than activation of the ventromedial prefrontal cortex. Relatively greater threat-related activity—presumably reflecting the perception of more threat-related demands—was observed in women with lower quality relationships, with additional activations in the right anterior insula,

superior frontal gyrus, and hypothalamus, a suite of activity associated with steadily increasing threat salience and the release of stress hormones. Shifting from relational partner to stranger occasioned a major increase in the number of threat-related activations, now including all those previously noted in addition to the superior colliculus, right dorsolateral PFC, caudate, and nucleus accumbens, suggesting additional vigilance and self-regulation efforts were implemented. When finally alone and under threat of shock, all preceding activations were observed in addition to increased activity in the ventral ACC, posterior cingulate, supramarginal gyrus, and postcentral gyrus, suggesting that the coordination of threat-related arousal and musculoskeletal activity was then needed, too. These observations point to a steady increase in threat responsiveness as a function of proximity to social resources, with social resources themselves arranged in quasi-ordinal fashion, from stranger to relational partner, and from low to high relationship quality. Another way to construe this progression is in terms of personal resources devoted to meeting the demands of the threat. With increasing distance from a social resource comes increasing demands on one's own emotional, attentional, and neural resources. The human brain utilizes social resources to economize its activity.

Work by McComb and colleagues (2001) provides a striking example of just this sort of economy of action in elephants. These researchers observed that the reproductive success of groups of female elephants is enhanced by the presence of older females, who have more knowledge of potential threats associated with other elephant groups. When one group of elephants first encounters another, both groups frequently cluster together in a behavior termed "bunching." Bunching behavior is resource depleting in a variety of ways, not least by reducing interaction opportunities with potential mates. Because older females have more knowledge of who among elephant strangers may be more threatening versus more friendly, their own anxious behavior guides bunching within the group. Although younger females will automatically begin to bunch when encountering strange groups, the nonanxious behavior of older females (in the presence of safe strangers) is soothing, inhibiting bunching behavior and allowing for intergroup interaction. By contrast, groups of young elephants lacking an older elephant with this knowledge tend to bunch indiscriminately and much more frequently. They tend, in other words, to become emotionally disregulated, with costly results for their reproductive success.

Conclusion

Social proximity and interaction are essential components of human health and well-being. Over the past decades, a tremendous amount of research has documented that strong social relationships, access to rich social networks, high perceived social support, and positive social development correspond with measures such as decreased basal cortisol, decreased autonomic reactivity, decreased susceptibility to illness, more rapid recovery from wounds, decreased vulnerability to mental illness, and even extended longevity. In this chapter, I have argued that links between social relationships and health are largely mediated through the impact of social relationships on emotion and emotional responding—that the social regulation of emotion not only largely accounts for these observations, but that it is indeed the baseline or default emotion regulatory strategy employed by most or all social animals, a perspective I have called the social baseline model. Social forms of emotion regulation can be mediational, where the presence of a social resource directly modifies an ongoing emotional response, or moderational, where socially relevant personality factors, past social experiences, or cognitive representations of either current relational partners or broader social networks modify an individual's self-regulation needs or capabilities.

The social baseline model proposes that social forms of emotion regulation are not "down-regulatory" in the same sense as self-regulation efforts. Rather, it proposes that social resources alter perception-action links associated with intervening in the environment, such that there is less perceived alarm when perceived social resources are high, which corresponds in turn to fewer actions needed to meet demands associated with the stressor. This, I have argued, conserves metabolically costly operations in the prefrontal cortex and elsewhere, either by simply conserving neural resources or freeing them to be devoted to other problems, thus increasing the efficiency of coping with a potentially dangerous and uncertain world.

Nevertheless, there still remains the question of the neural mechanisms of social support, and these remain primarily a matter of speculation. Candidate mechanisms include oxytocinergic activity throughout nucleus accumbens, the ventral tegmentum, and perhaps portions of the hypothalamus and even amygdala. For example, intranasally administered oxytocin has been observed to attenuate amygdala activation to threat cues (Kirsch et al., 2005). Other possibilities include endogenous opioid activity, especially in the dorsal anterior cingulate cortex (dACC), a region that is rich in opioid receptors (Eisenberger et al., 2007; Gillath et al., 2005; Panksepp, 1998). Future research will have to settle these and other questions. In the meantime, research into the social regulation of emotion is rich with possibilities, and I look forward to seeing them realized.

References

Ainsworth, M. D. S., Blehar, M. C., Waters, E., & Wall, S. (1978). *Patterns of attachment: A psychological study of the strange situation.* Hillsdale, N.J: Erlbaum.

Allen, J. P., Moore, C., Kuperminc, G., & Bell, K. (1998). Attachment and adolescent psychosocial functioning. *Child Development, 69*(5), 1406–1419.

Allen, J. P., Porter, M. R., & Tencer, H. L. (2002). *New mechanisms of negative peer influence: The role of the dominant deviant.* Paper presented at the Biennial Meetings of the Society for Research in Adolescence, New Orleans, LA.

Banfield, J., Wyland, C. L., Macrae, C. N., Munte, T. F., & Heatherton, T. (2005). The cognitive neuroscience of self-regulation. In R. F. Baumeister & K. D. Vohs (Eds.), *The handbook of self-regulation* (pp. 63–83). New York: Guilford.

Barber, B. L., Eccles, J. S., & Stone, M. R. (2001). Whatever happened to the jock, the brain, and the princess? Young adult pathways linked to adolescent activity involvement and social identity. *Journal of Adolescent Research, 16*(5), 429–455.

Baron, R. M. & Kenny, D. A. (1986). The moderator-mediator variable distinction in social psychological research: Conceptual, strategic, and statistical considerations. *Journal of Personality and Social Psychology, 51*, 1173–1182.

Bartholomew, K. & Horowitz, L. M. (1991). Attachment styles among young adults: A test of a four-category model. *Journal of Personality and Social Psychology, 61*, 226–244.

Berardi, N. & Maffei, L. (1999). From visual experience to visual function: Roles of neurotrophins. *Journal of Neurobiology, 41*, 119–126.

Berman, A. J. (1997). Amelioration of aggression: Response to selective cerebellar lesions in the rhesus monkey. *International Review of Neurobiology, 41*, 111–119.

Berscheid, E. (2003). The human's greatest strength: Other humans. In U. M. Staudinger (Ed.), *A psychology of human strengths: Fundamental questions and future directions for a positive psychology* (pp. 37–47). Washington D.C.: American Psychological Association.

Boccia, M. L., Reite, M., & Laudenslager, M. (1989). On the physiology of grooming in a pigtail macaque. *Physiology & Behavior, 45*, 667–670.

Bowlby, J. (1969/1982). *Attachment and loss: Vol. 1* (2nd. ed.). New York, NY: Basic Books.

Bowlby, J. (1973). *Attachment and loss: Vol. 2. Separation: Anxiety and anger.* New York, NY: Basic Books.

Briones, T. L., Klintsova, A. Y., & Greenough, W. T. (2004). Stability of synaptic plasticity in the adult rat visual cortex induced by complex environment exposure. *Brain Research, 1018*, 130–135.

Cacioppo, J. T., Hawkley, L. C., Crawford, L. E., Ernst, J. M., Burleson, M. H., Kowalewski, R. B., et al. (2002). Loneliness and health: Potential mechanisms. *Psychosom Med, 64*(3), 407–417.

Cacioppo, J. T., Hawkley, L. C., Ernst, J. M., Burleson, M., Berntson, G. G., Nouriani, B., et al. (2006). Loneliness within a nomological net: An evolutionary perspective. *Journal of Research in Personality, 40*, 1054–1085.

Cancedda, L., Putignano, E., Sale, A., Viegi, A., Berardi, N., & Maffei, L. (2004). Acceleration of visual system development by environmental enrichment. *Journal of Neuroscience, 24*, 4840–4848.

Carter, C. S. (2003). Developmental consequences of oxytocin. *Physiology & Behavior, 79*, 383–397.

Carter, C. S. (2005). The chemistry of child neglect: Do oxytocin and vasopressin mediate the effects of early experience? *Proceedings of the National Academy of Science, 102*, 18247–18248.

Chugani, H. T. (1998). A critical period of brain development: studies of cerebral glucose utilization with PET. *Preventive Medicine, 27*, 184–188.

Coan, J. A. (2008). Toward a neuroscience of attachment. In J. C. a. P. R. Shaver (Ed.), *Handbook of attachment: Theory, research, and clinical applications, 2nd edition* (pp. 241–265). New York: Guilford Press.

Coan, J. A. (2010a). Adult attachment and the brain. *Journal of Social and Personal Relationships, 27*, 210–221.

Coan, J. A. (2010b). Emergent ghosts of the emotion machine. *Emotion Review, 2*, 274–285.

Coan, J. A., Schaefer, H. S., & Davidson, R. J. (2006). Lending a hand: Social regulation of the neural response to threat. *Psychological Science, 17*, 1032–1039.

Cohen, S. & Wills, T. A. (1985). Stress, social support, and the buffering hypothesis. *Psychological bulletin, 98*, 310.

Edens, J. L., Larkin, K. T., & Abel, J. L. (1992). The effect of social support and physical touch on cardiovascular reactions to mental stress. *Journal of Psychosomative Research, 36*, 371–382.

Eisenberger, N. I., Lieberman, M. D., & Williams, K. D. (2003). Does rejection hurt? An fMRI study of social exclusion. *Science, 302*, 290–292.

Eisenberger, N. I., Taylor, S. E., Gable, S. L., Hilmert, C. J., & Lieberman, M. D. (2007). Neural pathways link social support to attenuated neuroendocrine stress responses. *Neuroimage, 35*, 1601–1612.

Flinn, M. V. & England, B. G. (1997). Social economics of childhood glucocorticoid stress response and health. *American Journal of Physical Anthropology, 102*, 33–53.

Fraley, R. C. & Shaver, P. R. (2000). Adult romantic attachment: Theoretical developments, emerging controversies, and unanswered questions. *Review of General Psychology, 4*, 132–154.

Franceschini, M. A., Thaker, S., Themelis, G., Krishnamoorthy, K. K., Bortfeld, H., Diamond, S. G., et al. (2007). Assessment of infant brain development with frequency-domain near-infrared spectroscopy. *Pediatric Research, 61*, 546–551.

Galliot, M. T. & Baumeister, R. F. (2007). The physiology of willpower: Linking blood glucose to self-control. *Personality and Social Psychology Review, 11*, 303–327.

Gillath, O., Bunge, S. A., Shaver, P. R., Wendelken, C., & Mikulincer, M. (2005). Attachment-style differences in the ability to suppress negative thoughts: Exploring the neural correlates. *Neuroimage, 28*, 835–847.

Gottman, J. M., Coan, J., Carrere, S., & Swanson, C. (1998). Predicting marital happiness and stability from newlywed interactions. *Journal of Marriage & the Family, 60*(1), 5–22.

Gust, D. A., Gordon, T. P., Brodie, A. R., & McClure, H. M. (1996). Effect of companions in modulating stress associated with new group formation in juvenile rhesus macaques. *Physiology & Behavior, 59*, 941–945.

Harlow, H. F., Dodsworth, R. O., & Harlow, M. K. (1965). Total social isolation in monkeys. *Proceedings of the National Academy of Sciences of the United States of America, 54*, 90–97.

Harlow, H. F. & Zimmermann, R. R. (1959). Affectional responses in the infant monkey. *Science, 130*, 421–432.

Hebb, D. O. (1949). *The organization of behavior.* New York: Wiley.

Hofer, M. A. (1984). Early social relationships: A psychobiologist's view. *Child Development, 58*, 633–647.

Hofer, M. A. (1995). Hidden regulators: Implications for a new understanding of attachment, separation, and loss. In S. Goldberg, R. Muir, & J. Kerr (Eds.), *Attachment theory: Social, developmental, and clinical perspectives.* Hillsdale, NJ: Analytic Press, Inc.

Hofer, M. A. (2006). Psychobiological roots of early attachment. *Current Directions in Psychological Science, 15*, 84–88.

Hubel, D. H. & Wiesel, T. N. (1970). The period of susceptibility to the physiological effects of unilateral eye closure in kittens. *The Journal of Physiology, 206*, 419–436.

Insel, T. R. (1997). A neurobiological basis of social attachment *American Journal of Psychiatry, 154*, 726–735.

Kawachi, I. B. & Berkman, L. F. (2001). Social ties and mental health *Journal of Urban Health: Bulletin of the New York Academy of Medicine, Volume 78, Number 3, 1,* pp. 458–467(410).

Kiecolt-Glaser, J. K. & Newton, T. L. (2001). Marriage and health: His and hers. *Psychological Bulletin, 127*, 472–503.

Kirsch, P., Esslinger, C., Chen, Q., Mier, D., Lis, S., Siddhanti, S., et al. (2005). Oxytocin modulates neural circuitry for social cognition and fear in humans. *Journal of Neuroscience, 25*, 11489–11493.

Kirschbaum, C., Klauer, T., Filipp, S. H., & Hellhammer, D. H. (1995). Sex-specific effects of social support on cortisol and subjective responses to acute psychological stress. *Psychosomatic Medicine, 57*, 23–31.

Kiyokawa, Y., Kikusui, T., Takeuchi, Y., & Mori, Y. (2004). Partner's stress status influences social buffering effects in rats. *Behavioral Neuroscience, 118*, 798–804.

Knox, S. S., Siegmund, K. D., Weidner, G., Ellison, R. C., Adelman, A., & Paton, C. (1998). Hostility, social support, and coronary heart disease in the National Heart, Lung, and Blood Institute Family Heart Study. *American Journal of Cardiology, 82*, 1192–1196.

Krebs, J. R. & Davies, N. B. (1993). *An introduction to behavioural ecology* (3rd ed.). Malden, MA: Blackwell.

Kudo, H. & Dunbar, R. I. M. (2001). Neocortex size and social network size in primates. *Animal Behaviour, 62*, 711–722.

Kurzban, R. (2010). Does the brain consume additional glucose during self-control tasks? *Evolutionary Psychology, 8*, 245–260.

Langford, D. J., Tuttle, A. H., Brown, K., Deschenes, S., Fischer, D. B., Mutso, A., et al. (2010). Social approach to pain in laboratory mice. *Social neuroscience, 5*, 163–70.

Larose, S., Bernier, A., Soucy, N., & Duchesne, S. (1999). Attachment style dimensions, network orientation and the process of seeking help from college teachers. *Journal of Social and Personal Relationships, 16*, 225–247.

Lepore, S. J., Allen, K. A., & Evans, G. W. (1993). Social support lowers cardiovascular reactivity to an acute stressor. *Psychosomatic Medicine, 55*, 518–524.

Lewis, M. & Ramsay, D. S. (1999). Effect of maternal soothing on infant stress response. *Child Development, 70*(1), 11–20.

Magdol, L., Moffitt, T. E., Caspi, A., & Silva, P. A. (1998). Developmental antecedents of partner abuse: A prospective-longitudinal study. *Journal of Abnormal Psychology, 107*(3), 375.

McComb, K., Moss, C., Durant, S. M., Baker, L., & Sayialel, S. (2001). Matriarchs as repositories of social knowledge in African elephants. *Science, 292*, 491–494.

Mikulincer, M. & Florian, V. (1998). The relationship between adult attachment styles and emotional and cognitive reactions to stressful events. In J. A. Simpson & W. S. Rholes (Eds.), *Attachment theory and close relationships* (pp. 143–165). New York: Guilford.

Mikulincer, M. & Nachshon, O. (1991). Attachment styles and patterns of self-disclosure. *Journal of Personality and Social Psychology, 61*, 321–331.

Mikulincer, M. & Orbach, I. (1995). Attachment styles and repressive defensiveness: The accessibility and architecture of affective memories. *Journal of Personality and Social Psychology, 68*, 917–925.

Mikulincer, M. & Shaver, P. R. (2007). *Attachment in adulthood: Structure, dynamics, and change.* New York: Guilford Press.

Mikulincer, M., Shaver, P. R., & Pereg, D. (2003). Attachment theory and affect regulation: The dynamics, development, and cognitive consequences of attachment-related strategies. *Motivation & Emotion, 27*, 77–102.

Moak, Z. B. & Agrawal, A. (in press). The association between perceived interpersonal social support and physical and mental health: Results from the national epidemiological survey on alcohol and related conditions. *Journal of Public Health.*

Moriceau, S. & Sullivan, R. M. (2005). Neurobiology of infant attachment. *Developmental Psychobiology, 47*, 230–242.

Newcomb, M. D. & Bentler, P. M. (1988). Impact of adolescent drug use and social support on problems of young adults: A longitudinal study. *Journal of Abnormal Psychology, 97*(1), 64.

O'Donovan, A. & Hughes, B. M. (2008). Access to social support in life and in the laboratory: Combined impact on cardiovascular reactivity to stress and state anxiety. *Journal of Health Psychology, 13*, 1147–1156.

Ochsner, K. N. & Gross, J. J. (2005a). The cognitive control of emotion. *Trends in cognitive sciences, 9*, 242–249.

Ochsner, K. N. & Gross, J. J. (2005b). The cognitive control of emotion. *Trends in Cognitive Science, 9*, 242–249.

Panksepp, J. (1998). *Affective neuroscience: The foundations of human and animal emotions.* New York: Oxford University Press.

Panksepp, J., Nelson, E. E., & Siviy, S. (1994). Brain opioids and mother-infant social motivation. *Acta Paediatrica, 397*, 40–46.

Phillips, A. C., Carroll, D., Burns, V. E., Ring, C., Macleod, J., & Drayson, M. (2006). Bereavement and marriage are associated with antibody response to influenza vaccination in the elderly. *Brain, Behavior, and Immunity, 20*(3), 279.

Posner, M. I. & Rothbart, M. K. (2007). Research on attention networks as a model for the integration of psychological science. *Annual Review of Psychology, 58*, 1–23.

Prinstein, M. J. & La Greca, A. M. (2004). Childhood peer rejection and aggression as predictors of adolescent girls' externalizing and health risk behaviors: A 6-year longitudinal study. *Journal of Consulting & Clinical Psychology, 72*, 103–112.

Proffitt, D. R. (2006). Embodied perception and the economy of action. *Perspectives on Psychological Science, 1*, 110.

Reichardt, L. F. (2006). Neurotrophin-regulated signalling pathways. *Philosophical transactions of the Royal Society of London, 361*, 1545–1564.

Rholes, W. S., Simpson, J. A., & Grich Stevens, J. (1998). Attachment orientations, social support, and conflict resolution in close relationships. In Jeffry A. Simpson & W. S. Rholes (Eds.), *Attachment theory and close relationships* (pp. 166–188). New York: Guilford.

Robles, T. F. & Kiecolt-Glaser, J. K. (2003). The physiology of marriage: Pathways to health. *Physiology & Behavior, 79*, 409–416.

Ross, H. E., Freeman, S. M., Spiegel, L. L., Ren, X., Terwilliger, E. F., & Young, L. J. (2009). Variation in oxytocin receptor density in the nucleus accumbens has differential effects on affiliative behaviors in monogamous and polygamous voles. *Journal of Neuroscience, 29*, 1312–1318.

Ruis, M. A. W., te Brake, J. H. A., Buwalda, B., De Boer, S. F., Meerlo, P., Korte, S. M., et al. (1999). Housing familiar male wildtype rats together reduces the long-term adverse behavioural and physiological effects of social defeat. *Psychoneuroendocrinology*, 285–300.

Sapolsky, R. M. (1998). *Why zebras don't get ulcers.* New York, NY: Holt.

Schauwers, K., Gillis, S., Daemers, K., De Beukelaer, C., De Ceulaer, G., Yperman, M., et al. (2004). Normal hearing and language development in a deaf-born child. *Otology & Neurotology, 25*, 924–929.

Skuse, D., Albanese, A., Stanhope, R., Gilmour, J., & Voss, L. (1996). A new stress-related syndrome of growth failure and hyperphagia in children, associated with reversibility of growth-hormone insufficiency. *Lancet, 348*, 353–358.

Snydersmith, M. A. & Cacioppo, J. T. (1992). Parsing complex social factors to determine component effects: I. Autonomic activity and reactivity as a function of human association. *Journal of Social and Clinical Psychology, 11*, 263–263.

Teicher, M. H., Andersen, S. L., Polcari, A., Anderson, C. M., Navalta, C. P., & Kim, D. M. (2003). The neurobiological consequences of early stress and childhood maltreatment. *Neuroscience and Biobehavioral Reviews, 27*, 33–44.

Teicher, M. H., Samson, J. A., Polcari, A., & McGreenery, C. E. (2006). Sticks, stones, and hurtful words: Relative effects of various forms of childhood maltreatment. *American Journal of Psychiatry, 163*, 993–1000.

Terranova, M. L., Cirulli, F., & Laviola, G. (1999). Behavioral and hormonal effects of partner familiarity in periadolescent rat pairs upon novelty exposure. *Psychoneuroendocrinology, 24*, 639–656.

Uchino, B. N., Cacioppo, J. T., & Kiecolt-Glaser, J. K. (1996). The relationship between social support and physiological processes: A review with emphasis on underlying mechanisms and implications for health. *Psychological Bulletin, 119*, 488–531.

Uvnaes-Moberg, K. (1998). Oxytocin may mediate the benefits of positive social interaction and emotions. *Psychoneuroendocrinology, 23*(8), 819–835.

Wang, J., Rao, H., Wetmore, G. S., Furlan, P. M., Korczykowski, M., Dinges, D. F., et al. (2005). Perfusion functional MRI reveals cerebral blood flow pattern under psychological stress. *Proceedings of the National Academy of Sciences, 102*, 17804–17809.

Weaver, A. & de Waal, F. B. M. (2003). The mother–offspring relationship as a template in social development: Reconciliation in captive brown capuchins (cebus apella). *Journal of Comparative Psychology, 117,* 101–110.

Weaver, I. C. G., Cervoni, N., Champagne, F. A., D'Alessio, A. C., Sharma, S., Seckl, J. R., et al. (2004). Epigenetic programming by maternal behavior. *Nature Neuroscience, 7,* 847–854.

Weaver, I. C. G., Diorio, J., Seckl, J. R., Szyf, M., & Meaney, M. J. (2004). Early environmental regulation of hippocampal glucocorticoid receptor gene expression: Characterization of intracellular mediators and potential genomic target sites.

In T. Kino, E. Charmandari, & G. P. Chrousos (Eds.), *Glucocorticoid action: Basic and clinical implications* (pp. 182–212). New York NY: New York Academy of Sciences.

Wismer-Fries, A. B., Ziegler, T. E., Kurian, J. R., Jacoris, S., & Pollak, S. D. (2005). Early experience in humans is associated with changes in neuropeptides critical for regulating social behavior. *Proceedings of the National Academy of Science, 102,* 17237–17240.

From Emotion to Notion:
The Importance of Melody

Kathleen Wermke *and* Werner Mende

Abstract

This chapter presents compelling evidence for the assumption that language acquisition in human infants starts with the production of simple melodies. Although simple melody arcs of nonhuman primate calls and human infant cries seem to be rather similar in their shape properties—a systematic investigation is still pending—there remains a crucial difference: Human infants exhibit a characteristic continuous, unidirectional development from simple melodies in early emotive utterances to complex melodies that provides constituents (building blocks) for producing syllables, words, and sentences later on.

Keywords: human infants, crying, language acquisition, melody, emotive sounds

No animal infant peals its voice as persistently and vigorously as the human infant. The product of a long evolution process, the human infant's crying represents a highly effective alarm signal. It is indeed impossible to ignore the emotive utterances of a crying infant.

By courtesy of evolution, these powerful, emotionally charged utterances seem to be a compensation for the infant's motoric helplessness, itself a result of immaturity at birth ("physiological premature"; Portmann, 1969). In this regard, the human infant shares the fate of his ancient relatives from about 2 million years ago: the infants of Homo ergaster and Homo erectus (Mithen, 2006; Falk, 2004, 2009; Flinn & Ward, 2005). A ritualized mother-infant communication behavior, including a particular maternal speech pattern with an exaggerated melody, co-evolved alongside the refinement of acoustic communication to foster language evolution. Some researchers have suggested that this

was an essential step in the evolution of oral language in our hominin ancestors (e.g., Falk, 2009). The emergence of human language from primate call systems over a course of only a few hundred thousand generations of genetic and social tradition remains enigmatic. However, there is no doubt that language evolution was driven by strong emotive forces.

Contrary to orthodox interpretations, we will extend reflections on human infants' crying beyond its function as an alarm signal to its role for seeding language development. In the following, the argument will be advanced that the emotional content conveyed via melody represents the first step of a hierarchical coding of meaning into words, leading from self-evident, "body-near" messages to abstract symbols and notions. This transition may also represent a recapitulation of evolution of vocal/auditory communication at the cradle of language millions of years ago. The analysis of human infants' crying and other emotive utterances may contribute to resolving the enigma as to how language is acquired by children seemingly without effort as well as to how it may have emerged in early hominins.

The Motivation to Investigate Crying

Crying is the most peremptory expression of emotion in early infancy (Wolff, 1987). Paradoxically, the emotive content of infants' earliest sound productions is often taken as evidence for their non-linguistic nature and hence, their irrelevance for language acquisition. It is indisputable that one of the most striking similarities of both nonhuman primate calls and human infant cries is their powerful expression of emotions mediated by melodic and/or rhythmic features. "Prosodic" properties in primate vocalizations are a means of expressing emotional and affective content and of manipulating the emotional states and behavior of other individuals. There is compelling evidence for a strong evolutionary/developmental continuity between nonhuman primate vocalizations and human (pre-)speech (e.g., Hauser, 2000; Newman, 2007). However, human infants develop a spoken language quickly and seemingly without effort by forming syllables, words, and sentences, while nonhuman primates do not (even when intensively trained by humans).

Our research provides compelling evidence for the assumption that language acquisition in human infants starts with the production of simple melodies (see fifth section, below). Although simple melody arcs of nonhuman primate calls and human infant cries seem to be rather similar in their shape properties—a systematic investigation is still pending—there remains a crucial difference: Human infants exhibit a characteristic continuous, unidirectional development from simple melodies in early emotive utterances to complex melodies that provides constituents (building blocks) for producing syllables, words and sentences later on (see section 5 in this chapter).

In qualifying our sometimes naive conceptions of what makes human language special, it may be important not only to explore similarities between human neonates and nonhuman primates and other species—as frequently done—but also to investigate what precisely allows the human infant to acquire so quickly and effortlessly such a complex faculty as language.

To approach the question "Where does language come from?," human infants may indeed be better candidates than nonhuman primates. Infants share early roots of vocal language evolution with other primates, thus reflecting developmental continuity, but at the same time they exhibit an essential difference: Over a period of several million years, human individuals, as well as populations, have accumulated genetic and life-historical experience with respect to language. The corresponding selective pressures are not yet precisely identified, let alone their sequence and timing. Human infants differ from their nonhuman relatives in that they are specifically pre-adapted to acquire language (Chomsky, 1965; Deacon, 1998; Pinker, 1994). It is noteworthy, that caregivers and cultural environments are equally pre-adapted to enable language development in infants.

From a phylogenetic perspective, communicating via signed gestures is most likely an early stage of language evolution, well before vocal communication (cf. review in Gentilucci & Corballis, 2006). At a certain point in the course of language evolution, due to strong selection pressures of a still unknown origin, our hominine ancestors were compelled to abandon a well-developed multimodal communication system (facial, gestural, bodily signals; vocalizations were sparse and ancillary) and to adopt a completely different monomodal, acoustic communication system that led finally to the development of spoken language (e.g., Botha & Knight, 2009).

Most likely, vocal communication was initially only used under special circumstances, for instance in the dark or during twilight. At higher latitudes, moreover, winters brought more hours of darkness, and the need to survive the northern winters may have fostered cooperation and larger group sizes. For such ends, acoustic communication was more appropriate. Another advantage was that acoustic communication functions nondirectionally, because it does not require any visual contact or special attention on the part of the recipient of a message. Hence, acoustic communication has probably been advantageous for larger-sized social groups. Eventually it may have become so successful that it generated its own selection pressure for a stronger shift towards acoustic communication.

This modal shift represented a concentration on acoustic means of expression and probably forced our ancestors to push frequency modulation (melody) to its physical limits. The typical frequency modulation bands of the human voice lie in a range that was not heavily occupied by ambient frequency modulations. The importance of melody may therefore be a consequence of this modal shift toward acoustic communication, and we see infants' early preference for perceptive and productive "melody performances" as means of tracing this shift. Based on this phylogenetic perspective and contrary to orthodox interpretations, we will extend our reflections on human infants' crying beyond its function as an alarm signal (bio-siren) to its direct significance for the development of spoken language.

Indeed, crying "may be a missing link in theories about how language is learned and how it emerged in early hominins" (Falk, 2009, p.82). The existence of a special infant-directed speech is a strong argument in favor of this idea (see third section).

The Anticipation of Continuity

Several previous authors have postulated a continuity between animal sounds, utterances of human infants, and spoken language (e.g., Darwin, 1871; Flatau & Gutzmann, 1906; Gardiner, 1832). Free from constraints of prevailing linguistic theories, these authors may indeed have had a quite accurate concept of the continuity involved in language evolution. Of many whom we could mention here, we would like to draw special attention to William Gardiner, an English musician, who, rather intuitively, recognized and discussed the remarkable connections between animal and human infants' sounds. Furthermore, about 40 years before the publication of Darwin's theories of evolution, he observed the close relationships between infant sounds, speech sounds, and music.

While Gardiner's work was neither recognized by musicologists as being particularly valuable in describing the history of musical arts, nor by linguists as providing acceptable ideas for the evolution of speech and language or the emergence of words from melody in children, his arguments are noteworthy with respect to the exemplified relationships between natural sounds and human speech, between animal sounds and human cries, between music and language, and for its focus on the importance of melody for all these relations. His writings anticipate insights supported by modern research many years later.

In 1832, William Gardiner[1] published a book with the title:

The MUSIC OF NATURE; or an attempt to prove that what is passionate and pleasing in the art of singing, speaking, and performing upon musical instruments, is derived from the sounds of The Animated World.

Being a musician himself, he was fascinated by the enormous influences of "the sounds of nature," particularly "the cries of animals and the songs of birds" (Preface), on the evolution of voice, speech, and language as well as the art of singing (with his book containing lovely, readable discussions of the vocal practices of several leading singers of his time) and composing music: "In the busy world or in quiet and repose, he [the author] has amused himself with taking down these germs of melody" (Gardiner, 1832, Preface).

This book contains a section entitled "Human Cries", in which Gardiner demonstrates "what a fruitful source" human cries have been "in giving hints to the composer and musicians" (Gardiner, 1832, p. 195). He exemplifies this view by referring to the imitation of a sobbing child in the opera *Gazza Ladra* by Rossini, and "the endearing tone of a mother fondling her child" (ibid., p. 197) in Beethoven's Third Trio, Op. 9 along with other examples taken from compositions by Haydn and Mozart. Gardiner also puts infants' crying in the same category as animal sounds, anticipating later insights with regard to continuities of speech and language development.

Gardiner instigated later research (Flatau & Gutzmann, 1906; Ostwald, 1973; Papoušek & Papoušek, 1981) by pointing out the musical elements contained in the earliest sound productions of infants. Moreover, he already states that vocal communication does not necessarily require words and grammar and that an infant's crying may be where meaningful communication starts:

> "Children have no difficulty in expressing their
> wants, their pleasure, and pains, by their cries,
> long before they know the use or meaning of
> a word; and it is surprising to see with what energy
> they will evince the strongest passion." (Gardiner,
> 1832, p.195)

Our personal appreciation of Gardiner's thoughts is based on our view of the prehistory of music and language and the evolutionary importance of melody. This anticipative book, published thirty-nine years before Darwin's *The Descent of Man*, undoubtedly provides an interesting synopsis of melodic sounds of the animated world and human vocalizations in crying, speech, and singing.

In 1871, Charles Darwin presented a scientific theory about the origin of language that also pointed to the importance of the emotionally charged sounds of the animated world:

> ". . . language owes its origin to the imitation and
> modification of various natural sounds, the voices

of other animals, and man's own instinctive cries, aided by sign and gestures. . .It is, therefore, probable that the imitation of musical cries by articulated sounds may have given rise to words expressive of various complex emotions." (Darwin, 1871, Chapter III, p. 87)

It is speculative to ask why Darwin used the term "musical cry." Could perhaps Gardiner's book have inspired him? Or did he recognize a "musicality" in the crying of his children? At any rate, melody and rhythm, that is, prosodic features, play an essential role in Darwin's "song theory" as elements occurring in animal vocal communication as well as at the roots of spoken language. As we will outline in the next section, Darwin's "song theory" is supported by the social and communicative function of *motherese,* the special way mothers, or indeed other caring persons, speak to infants intuitively without explicit instruction.

How we communicate with infants using melody—*Motherese*

The origin of spoken language, particularly the transformation from any form of primitive song or protolanguage to a full-blown language still belongs to the enigmas of hominin evolution, despite so many years of intensive research (cf. Botha & Knight, 2009; Deacon, 1998; Falk, 2009; Gärdenfors, 2007; Hurford, Studdert-Kennedy, & Knight, 2001; Jackendoff, 2003; Mithen, 2006, 2009; Pinker, 1994).

The true origin of human oral language may lie much further back than 200,000 years ago, a date as is commonly proposed by linguists; indeed, it may be located at the beginning of hominin evolution several million years ago.[2]

In consequence of increasing fetal brain size[3] and the fact that they were born "prematurely" in a physiological sense (Portmann, 1969), hominine infants, as human infants today, required a high degree of maternal care (Key & Aiello, 1999). Hominine infants probably experienced increasing difficulty clinging and riding on their mothers' backs. Mothers were therefore forced to put their infants down temporarily, for example, during foraging. Infants probably started fussing and crying when separated from their mothers (see *putting the baby down* theory; Falk, 2004, 2009).

At first, fussing, crying, screaming, grunts, and more mitigated non-cry sounds define the boundaries of what the motorically helpless human baby is able to vocally communicate with the persons caring

for him. Like his nonhuman primate relatives he initially has to content himself with these simple sounds to express his emotions, feelings, needs, and desires. However, there is a decisive difference—a human infant's mother is far more talkative than those of his primate relatives (Falk, 2009). Beginning immediately after birth, his mother continuously talks to him in a very specific way, exaggerating the melody and simplifying the rhythm of her vocalizations ("motherese" or "baby talk"). Is this a key factor in the development of language? Some prehistoric form of motherese or infant-directed speech (IDS) may indeed have been important for the origin of spoken language in our hominine ancestors (Falk, 2009).

IDS is typical for humans and has no comparable analogue in other primates, albeit primitive precursors.[4] Mother-infant communication in apes, for example, chimpanzees or bonobos, is, apart from bodily contact, mainly based on visual signals like facial expressions and body language gestures. Nonhuman primate mothers do not encourage their infants to vocalize.

> "One of the few circumstances under which mothers routinely vocalize to their infants is during travelling and foraging. Both, the bonobo and chimpanzee mothers utter hoos to retrieve their infants for travel." (Falk 2009, p.17)

Infant-directed speech seems to be a universal trait of humans and has been observed in many different cultures in mother-infant communication (Ferguson, 1964; Fernald et al., 1989; Fernald & Simon, 1984; Garnica, 1977; Grieser & Kuhl, 1988; Papoušek & Papoušek, 1987; Papoušek, Papoušek, & Bornstein, 1985; Papoušek, Papoušek, & Symmes, 1991; Stern, Spieker, Barnett, & MacKain, 1983). It is characterized by exaggerated melodic expression,[5] and exemplifies how messages are conveyed to the preverbal human infant by melody (Fernald, 1989a, b; 1992; 1993). The contents of words and phrases are not essential to IDS: exclamations, interjections, nick names, and sound imitations predominate (Papoušek, Papoušek, & Symmes, 1991). The melodic and rhythmic properties of IDS constitute meaningful emotive sounds, albeit still lacking symbolic meaning and abstract notions (Falk, 2009). Cross-linguistic analyses, including tonal languages, proved that IDS is characterized by different melody contours, each associated with a different emotive context: approval, prohibition, attention, or comfort (Fernald, 1989; Fernald et al., 1992). Approval is expressed by relatively symmetrically rising-then-falling melody contours with a relatively large frequency modulation amplitude (FM-amplitude, FM-depth). Attention is characterized by melodies with final stress (rising fundamental frequency), while melodies of comfort have falling melody contours. Prohibition may be conveyed by markedly shorter sounds with a smaller FM-amplitude.

Motherese conveys emotional content via melody. Its primary function is thus emotional regulation and social tuning. This is related to Robin Dunbar's (2004) theory, namely that language originally functioned to regulate social behavior rather than convey information, meanings, and personal thoughts. The culture-universal existence of motherese may indeed provide supporting evidence for this theory, since emotions and feelings are tightly connected with social relations (Dissanayake, 2008; Falk, 2009; Gärdenfors, 2007; Trevarthen, 1999).

However, a functional reduction of motherese to its social regulatory power is unjustified by the accumulated evidence, which shows that it also helps infants to acquire language.

"Linguists often look at motherese from a top-down perspective. How, they ask, can mother's melodic cooing possibly help infants grasp grammar (the rules that define a language), syntax (rules for arranging words into phrases and phrases into sentences), recursion (the inclusion of phrases within phrases, ad infinitum), and semantics (the meaning of words and phrases)? From this point of view, their bewilderment seems reasonable. The problem, however, is that they are viewing language development and baby talk as two separate entities–as if they were apples and oranges–when the acquisition of language and motherese actually are related to each other like apples and apple seeds." (Falk 2009, p. 74)

Perceiving the emotional (prosodic) features of speech from an early age (cf. fourth section), infants increasingly apply this knowledge in order to segment the continuous speech stream into meaningful parts and to recognize words (Gerken, Jusczyk, & Mandel, 1994; Jusczyk et al., 1992; Jusczyk, 1999; Morgan & Demuth, 1996). "Words begin to emerge from the melody"—as Hauser aptly describes this process (Hauser, 2000, p. 335).

Neurophysiological data support the strong impact motherese has on infants by demonstrating that cortical structures participate in the processing of prosodic information, particularly frequency modulation amplitude ("normal" versus "flattened" speech). Investigating Japanese neonates ranging in age from 2 to 9 days with near-infrared spectroscopy (NIRS), it was found that IDS affected blood flow to the frontal area of the brain more than adult-directed speech (ADS). Furthermore a hemispheric asymmetry with better processing of IDS on the right side of the brain was shown (Saito et al., 2007). Examining cortical activation in 3-month-old Japanese infants using the same technique (NIRS), bilateral activation in the frontal, temporal, and temporoparietal regions was demonstrated in response to normal and flattened speech during quiet sleep. Moreover, the right temporoparietal region was found to show a more marked response to melody (Homae, Watanabe, Nakano, Asakawa, & Taga, 2006).

There is considerable evidence that human infants recognize utterances and "understand" relevant information on the basis of prosodic cues long before they become sensitive to the segmental characteristics of spoken language.

"They know about the 'prosodic,' or emotional, features of speech a very long time before they can understand its meaning. Later they use this knowledge as an attentional hook to help them hone in on the intended meaning of what they hear. The speaker's tone of voice tells the infant where and when to look and marks the significance of the utterance. The situational context usually provides the meaning. This reduces the difficulty of tracking the content hidden in words and sentences." (Donald, 2001, p. 230)

Using play-back studies, four-month-old infants were shown to be capable of both differentiating between prototypical melodic contours in motherese and reacting appropriately to them, that is, "understanding" the implied context-dependent messages conveyed (Papoušek, Bornstein, Nuzzo, Papoušek, & Symmes, 1990).

Five-month-old infants can already discriminate affective vocal expressions in infant-directed speech in several languages. Moreover, they respond to approval by smiling, and when they show negative affect, it is more likely to occur in response to prohibitions (Fernald, 1993). Fernald's experiments proved that the essential feature is the emotional content, rather than the words used. But even much younger infants perceive and appreciate the emotional content transmitted in IDS; the utterances are in a certain sense (as a holistic message) "meaningful" to them. We interpret this as a primitive first step in a coding hierarchy toward referential meaning and finally toward semantics with abstract notions (see sixth section of this chapter).

Using fMRI in infants it was found that the angular gyrus and the posteromedial portion of the parietal lobe, the precuneus, were activated more strongly by listening to forward sentences than by backward sentences (Dehaene-Lambertz, Hertz-Pannier, & Dubois, 2006). The angular gyrus is involved in lexical storage in adults. In infants, it obviously is involved in the storage of the prosodic patterns that they use to "recognize" their native language.

So, infants and older children exhibit an expressive ability to interpret the intention behind a vocal utterance. This skill is also a decisive difference between humans and apes (Bloom, 2000; Gärdenfors, 2007; Tomasello, 1998). From a phylogenetic perspective, this probably points to older layers of language, to a time when prehistoric prosodic capabilities were unfolding and only later served as scaffolding for the evolution of the referential and symbolic capabilities of spoken language.

The multimodal characteristic of mother-infant communication and the establishment of a ritualized mother-infant interaction—consisting of such temporally-coordinated interactions as facial expressions, head movements, rhythmic touches and gestural activities—evolutionarily precedes and continues to accompany the specific vocal behavior described above (Dissanayake, 2000, 2001, 2004). Early mother-infant interactions serve to balance the emotions and behaviors of both partners while reinforcing their emotional attachment (Dissanayake, 2008).

This bonding behavior seems to represent one aspect of the mysterious *humanum*, intensively sought by researchers of various disciplines. However, we focus here only on a specific aspect: to describe how words may emerge from melodies. Certainly, *motherese* helps to explain this with regard to perception and ritualized mother-infant interaction. The exaggerated melodies, the prototypical melody contours, the temporarily extended vowels, and the redundant, simple rhythmic features of typical IDS will enable the young infant to discover syntactic boundaries in the continuous speech stream of his mother, or any other person. However, this is only one side of the coin.

During the whole process of language acquisition—although being hard-wired with the ability to learn language—the human infant must modify his laryngeally produced melodies repeatedly, and tune them to the resonance frequencies of a vocal tract that continues to grow and change (see fifth section). This means, attention should also be paid to the necessary complement of perception: sound production. How do words emerge from melodies in an infant's own sound production? This question touches on two issues: It asks for this emergence with respect to speech as well as with respect to language. We will emphasize here the latter aspect, in correspondence to the language-relevant function performed by motherese.

This approach is not common. Often unjustly, the expressive power of melodic and rhythmical performances in human infant's crying goes largely unrecognized and is for that reason frequently underestimated in its importance for language development.

For example, Steven Pinker (1994) states in his book The Language Instinct, that

> "not much of linguistic interest happens during the first two months, when babies produce the cries, grunts, sighs, clicks, stops, and pops associated with breathing, feeding, and fussing, or even during the next three, when coos and laughs are added. Between five and seven months babies begin to play with sounds, rather than using them to express their physical and emotional states, and their sequences of clicks, hums, glides, trills, hisses, and smacks begin to sound like consonants and vowels." (p. 265)

However, one should not confuse "linguistic interest" with "importance for language development." As in this example, the essential criterion for the relevance of an infant's vocalization to language development has often been equated in the literature with its "speech-similarity."[6]

The significance of both infants' earliest emotive utterances and of the emotionally charged interactions between mother and infant for language acquisition is often underestimated. Similarly, the neglect of the issue of emotion in recent studies of language evolution appears to be "a serious omission" (Mithen, 2006, p. 60).

As we have tried to demonstrate, motherese substantiates the view that melody might have been a primordial communication tool at the early roots of oral language evolution.[7] Effective usage of this tool, however, requires a co-evolved perceptual sensitivity on the part of the receiver (human infant). We focus on this aspect in the next section.

Infants are Born with an Inherent Appreciation of Melody

For most of us, the term "melody" is primarily connected with singing, playing instruments, or dancing; that is, with musical culture. In listening to people talk, especially to accomplished orators, a kind of "musicality" also becomes apparent in language. Each language is characterized by very specific musical elements in the form of its prosody, that is, its intonation system and constituent rhythm. Intonation[8] is one of the most language-specific features in spoken languages (Hirst & Di Cristo, 1998). Based on prosody alone, human adults (Maidment, 1983; Ohala & Gilbert, 1981) and even newborns are able to distinguish different languages (Mehler et al., 1988; Nazzi, Bertoncini, & Mehler, 1998; Ramus, Hauser, Miller, Morris, & Mehler, 2000). Intonation is not only one of the most language-specific, but also one of the most universal features of human language (Hirst & Di Cristo, 1998).

> "While it is true that all languages have vowels and consonant systems, and even that similar patterns of vowels and consonants can be found in languages which are only very distantly related, these systems do not convey meanings directly in the way that intonation seems to. There is, for example, no systematic universal meaning which can be ascribed to the difference between front vowels and back vowels or between stops and fricatives."
> (ibid., pp. 1–2)

It is above all this universality, that is, the observation that "many of the linguistic and paralinguistic functions of intonation systems seem to be shared by languages of widely different origins" (ibid., p. 1), that sets the tone for what we will focus on here with respect to the importance of melody from a phylogenetic and ontogenetic perspective.

Newborn infants "appear to arrive in the world as eager to respond to music as they are to acquire language" (Mithen, 2009, p. 63) and are "born with a musical wisdom and appetite" (Trevarthen, 1999, p. 174, cited according to Mithen, 2009). There is considerable evidence that this "appetite" is already present prenatally. Vocal perception and learning starts by the third trimester of gestation (Al-Qahtani, 2005; Fifer & Moon, 1989; James, Spencer, & Stepsis, 2002; Morre, Perazzo, & Braun, 1995; Richards, Frentzen, Gerhardt, McCann, & Abrams, 1992; Winkler, Haden, Ladinig, Sziller, & Honing, 2009) although the brain will need months and years to develop a full auditory capacity (Morlet, Collet, Salle, & Morgon, 1993; Ponton, Eggermont, Kwong, & Don, 2000; Poulsen, Picton, & Paus, 2009). The maternal voice, along with the rhythms and noises generated by her physiological systems (heart beat, gastrointestinal noises) and by her

behavior (walking, for example) are most intensively perceived by the fetus. There is strong evidence that term-fetuses can distinguish between voices: mother versus stranger (Kisilevsky et al., 2003) or male versus female (Lecanuet, Granier-Deferre, Jacquet, Capponi, & Ledru, 1993). Music played in the external environment is also perceptible in utero (Kisilevsky, Hains, Jacquet, Granier-Deferre, & Lecanuet, 2004; Querleu, Renard, Boutteville, & Crepin, 1989). Term-fetuses can discriminate musical notes (piano D4 versus C5, Lecanuet, Granier-Deferre, Jacquet, & DeCasper, 2000) and may habituate to a brief piano sequence with changing melodic contour (Granier-Deferre, Bassereau, Jacquet, & Lecanuet, 1998).

Newborns show perceptual preferences for melodies and rhythms to which they were exposed prenatally (DeCasper & Spencer, 1986; James, Spencer, & Stepsis, 2002; Mastropieri & Turkewitz, 1999; Mehler et al., 1988; Moon, Panneton-Cooper, & Fifer, 1993). For example, they respond most intensively to their mothers' voice shortly after birth (Damstra-Wijmenga, 2009; Ockleford, Vince, Layton, & Reader, 1988; Querleu et al., 1984). Newborns are also able to discriminate between upward and downward pitch contours (Carral et al., 2005) and their brains were shown to perceive a violation of the beat in a rhythmic sound sequence (Winkler et al., 2009).

In general, human infants are well equipped with surprising musical perceptual capabilities (Trehub, 2000, 2001, 2003). The cognitive flexibility of infants is reflected in several perceptive performances, for example, their perception of pitch transpositions and tempo changes as well as in their attending to absolute-pitch cues if the task requires it (Saffran, 2003; Trainor, Wu and Tsang, 2004; Levitin, 2007).

> "Infants recognize transpositions of pitch and of time (tempo changes), indicating they are capable of relational processing, something that even the most advanced computers still can't do very well."
> (Levitin, 2007, p. 228)

Both human fetuses and newborns are "gourmets" in their "musical appetites." They prefer melodious, harmonic pieces with simple rhythms and contours, above all, relatively marked FM-amplitudes (FM-depth), features that characterize many musical pieces as well as speech prosody. There is mounting evidence that melody and rhythm are the most salient prosodic elements for both the human fetus in the last trimester and the newborn baby in perceiving speech or music (e.g., DeCasper & Spencer, 1986; Demany, McKenzie, & Vurpillot, 1977; Granier-Deferre et al., 1998; Jusczyk & Krumhansl, 1993; Mehler et al., 1988; Trehub, 1985, 1987, 1990; Trehub & Trainor, 1990; Winkler et al., 2009).

These findings suggest that pre-dispositions for "musical" sensitivity represent aspects of an innate capability for musicality as well as for speech and language performance before birth. This is particularly obvious with respect to the most salient musical feature for infants: melody contour (Dowling, 1978, 1982; Trehub, 2001, 2003). Melody contour is closely related to intonation in spoken language, and there is convincing evidence that "infants' sensitivity to musical contour parallels their sensitivity to linguistic contour."(Levitin, 2007, p. 228).

This specific sensitivity for melody is very important with regard to the function of motherese during early phases of language development, as discussed above. However, melodic contour remains also an important scaffolding or framework for temporal organization in perception and singing as well as speaking throughout childhood and beyond (cf. Deutsch, 1999; Locke, 2001).

The primary and probably the oldest function of "prosody" in music and language is the expression of emotion. While a high emotive valence is commonly ascribed to music, many people are often unaware of the emotional charge of their spoken utterances. The increasing emancipation from affective contents is only a relatively recent achievement. However, even in "modern" languages a residual affective and emotional content conveyed via melody and rhythm has "survived." The shared property of both music and language to express emotions as well as the degree of musicality of language, that is, "variations of pitch, rhythm, tone, and timbre of the voice and the equivalent with regard to movements of the body" (Mithen 2009, p. 59), are keys to understanding language evolution. Such a shared property is also the key to a better understanding of the way in which words emerge from melody during language development in children. The melody of young infants' vocalizations and older infants' talking is initially much more related to emotions, affects and bodily states than to abstract notions coded in words and grammar systems. In this sense, melody should be seen as a forerunner of codified abstract meaning in the strict linguistic sense (see sixth section). Before further elaboration on this topic, however, we will describe our findings with respect to melody of

human infants' earliest sound productions in more detail.

Melodic Development of Human Infants' Vocal Sounds

". . .human infants have evolved distinctive ways of crying to get caregivers' attention while communicating their own needs and moods. Our infants cry to get what they want."
(Falk, 2009, p. 35)

Neonates have to adapt from an "all-inclusive" intra-uterine world to an extra-uterine reality in which they have to struggle to ensure that their demands are met. The neonate emerges with a pre-programmed response repertoire and is able to support and maintain interactions with its mother immediately after birth. Both visual and very effective acoustic signals support this interaction, and the best-known and also the most powerful acoustic signal is the infant cry. In addition, several non-cry utterances, such as guttural sounds, grunts, "quasivowels" (Oller, 2000) or cooing are among human infants' earliest communicative sounds. All these sounds have high emotive and affective content (e.g., Wolff, 1987), comparable to some extent to certain nonhuman primate calls (Cheney & Seyfarth, 1982; Stewart & Harcourt, 1994, see also the review in Hauser, 2000). This feature, along with their alarming function,[9] explains why reflections on human infants' earliest sound productions often emphasize their similarity to nonhuman primate calls (e.g., Lieberman, Harris, Wolff, & Russell, 1971; McCune, Vihman, Roug-Hellichius, Delery, & Gogate, 1996; Newman, 2007). Undeniably, there are obvious acoustic similarities between human infant cries and nonhuman primate calls (e.g., "hoo" vocalizations; cf. review in Newman, 2007; Masataka, 2008), reflecting continuity from primate call systems to spoken language. However, cries are essential facilitators for human infants' rapid development toward speech.

In the 1970s, Joseph Garland, a leading pediatrician in Massachusetts, refuted an argument from the poem *In Memoriam* by the famous poet Alfred Tennyson, namely that infants having no language and so resort only to crying. To illustrate the rich facets in human infants' crying and to allude to the emerging field of systematic cry research, Garland wrote,

"Most physicians engaged to any extent in pediatric practice are aware not only that crying is one of the inalienable privileges of infancy, but that different cries may have different meanings; crying is a language in itself, based on its genesis, its volume, its pitch, its energy requirements and other characteristics." (Garland, 1972, p. 409)

In many ways, it can be argued that tremendous progress has been made since the time of Garland's writing, owing in large part to newly developed computer programs and signal analysis techniques that have enabled large scale objective analysis of early infant sounds. The field of "crydiagnosis"[10] expanded particularly throughout the 70s and 80s. Cries were found to vary with factors such as efficacy of adaptation to the external environment, occurrence of pre- or perinatal stress or integrity of vocal production circuitry in the brain (Mende, Wermke, Schindler, Wilzopolski, & Höck, 1990).

Central integration of information from different brain regions is necessary to co-ordinate all systems involved in phonation. Structures belonging to the "phonatory tract" (analogues to the auditory tract) are located in immediate vicinity to pathways and centers controlling vegetative functions such as breathing (reticular formation). These close anatomical associations might explain the vocal expression of physical and functional states of the CNS and indeed the whole body, as observed by many cry researchers. However, concerning the neural basis of infant crying in humans, the corresponding literature is still "sparse and largely inferential" (Newman, 2007, p. 157).

In contrast to the old "brainstem model" of cry production, suggesting that no structures rostral to the midbrain are required for infant crying, more recent studies recognize the involvement of cortical structures, for example, the cingulate gyrus (cf., Newman, 2007). Studies of infant rhesus macaques demonstrated another forebrain structure to be involved in cry production of nonhuman infants: the amygdala (Newman and Bachevalier, 1997). Bilateral neonatal ablation of the amygdala caused less screaming and reduced the likelihood of the infant's preferring his own mother in dyadic interactions (Baumann, Lavenex, Mason, Capitanio, & Amaral, 2004). There is reason to hypothesize that these and indeed other higher CNS structures are involved in human infants' cry production. For instance, the finding that Broca's area is active in 3-month-old infants (Dehaene-Lambertz et al., 2006), that is, during a developmental stage with a dominance of crying and cooing and before speech-like babbling, points to its regulatory function in

learning of complex motor sequences required for future speech production.

The large repertoire of melodic and rhythmic structures observable in healthy infants (see fifth section) as well as their capability to modify cry melody in response to the surrounding language (Mampe, Friederici, Christophe, & Wermke, 2009) require a high degree of laryngo-respiratory control. Furthermore, empirical evidence for the highly coordinated interactions between phonation and early articulatory activity found from about the 9th week of life, alongside the anecdotal observations about a change in cry melody structure in response to mother-infant interaction can illuminate the potential role of higher cortical brain structures in human infants' cry production.

Following a period of very intensive work in cry research at the end of the 1980s, it became obvious that cry analysis for medical diagnosis and prognosis had enormous limitations, specifically owing to the lack of longitudinal studies and adequate developmental models of crying. Regular changes in the "acoustic signature" of infant cries during ontogenesis could mask cry modifications caused by cerebral dysfunction. Overall, despite a large body of outstanding research in the field, the lack of knowledge of developmental processes influencing the acoustic signature of cries hampered the general impact of the findings. Soltis (2004), for instance, notes the highly inconsistent ranges for cry parameters provided in the relevant literature. This situation may have been caused by a lack of adequate developmental models at the time, rather than by the different analytical methods applied (Wermke & Friederici, 2004).

In several prospective and cross-sectional studies, including twin studies, conducted over the last 20 years, we have investigated more than 100.000 cries and non-cry vocalizations of human infants. Beginning in 1990, our studies concentrated on structural changes of infant cries during early ontogenesis. We focused on the identification of systematic developmental changes of cries during the first months and demonstrated a high degree of continuity in melody development from crying via cooing and babbling to word production (e.g., Mende et al., 1990; Wermke, 2002; Wermke & Mende, 1994, 2006, 2009; Wermke, Mende, Borschberg, & Ruppert, 1996; Wermke, Leising, & Stellzig-Eisenhauer, 2007).

Our personal view of human infants' crying and early non-cry sound production underwent a kind of revolution as a result of insights drawn from our study of regular changes in melodic and rhythmic properties and in light of gathered data regarding the developmental outcome of many infants after several years. We discovered that human infants' cries undergo impressive systematic modifications from initially simple to increasingly more complex signals during the first months of life, following an innate program. Complexity here refers to melody changes, rhythm variations as well as interaction patterns of laryngeal or articulatory processes. We recognized that melody is a key to understanding the continuous development from first cries, via cooing and babbling toward word production on both the level of speech and of language. In this fifth section, we outline selected developmentally important stages and their typical melodic patterns, visualizing them with frequency spectrograms and melody diagrams.

We will demonstrate that from the perspective of evolutionary theory, melody qualifies as a "developmental module" (Schlosser, 2004, p. 527) because of its relatively permanent presence during language development, itself a result of its "integrated and context-insensitive behavior in the face of local perturbations" (ibid., p. 560).

When investigated with signal analysis methods, melody remains a well-identifiable item in all stages of pre-speech and speech development despite increasing articulatory activity and simultaneous vocal tract changes.

Basic Melody Types of Neonates' Crying
Neonates' cries have often been described as essentially stereotypical with regard to their acoustic patterns, particularly in the case of cries uttered in response to a pain-eliciting situation. We excluded these "pain cries" from our developmental studies and exclusively analysed mitigated cries in a relatively "relaxed context" in the presence of the mother. In this way cry melodies[11] emerged that were in a certain sense similar to simple musical melodies and which could provide raw material for prosodic constituents of later language (Wermke & Mende, 2009).

As exemplified below, cry melodies consist mainly of ascending and descending modulations of the fundamental frequency (F0), a product of vocal fold physiology and underlying neurophysiological control. A "simple" cry melody consists of a single ascending and a descending flank of F0. Both flanks constitute together an arc-like structure ("melody arc") (Figure 42.1).

For a description of the contour of such "simple" cry melodies the term "melody type" was introduced by pioneering cry researchers (Michelsson, 1971; Wasz-Höckert, Lind, Vuorenkoski, Partanen, & Valanne, 1968) who mainly differentiated between "rising," "falling," "rising-falling," and "flat" contours. In these early studies, melody type determination was based exclusively on visual inspections of frequency spectrograms (cf. Michelsson, Raes, & Rinne, 1984; Michelsson, Raes, Thoden, & Wasz-Höckert, 1982; Michelsson, Tuppurainen, & Aula, 1980; Sirvio & Michelsson, 1976; Stark, Rose, & McLagen, 1975). In many cases melody contour can be sufficiently well determined by this method of qualitative analysis.

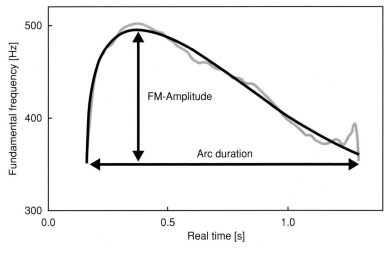

Fig. 42.1 Original and modeled ascending-then-descending melody arc of a neonate's cry. The figure shows an original cry melody arc and the corresponding model arc. The model arc is the result of a fit, which minimizes the distance between model curve and data. The fit provides six parameters describing the individual model arc uniquely.

One of the authors (WM) has developed a mathematical model (EF-Model) to facilitate a quantitative analysis of melody shapes, to control for the enormous inter- and intra-individual variability of cry melodies, and to compare melody similarities between different vocalization types (crying, cooing, babbling). Modeling removes irrelevant local variations, reduces intra- and inter-individual variability and describes each single melody arc by a few individually determined model parameters, which help preserve essential individual characteristics of a melody arc, including the onset and fading behavior on both sides of the arc. Our model describes melody arcs by six parameters: Four are necessary for linear scaling in time and frequency coordinates, and the other two for characterizing the shape of the arcs. Different scale-invariant shapes of melody arcs are described by variation of the two shape parameters: one defines the degree of asymmetry, the other the degree of convexity/concavity. Such a model allows for normalization, parametric averaging and quantitative comparisons of melody arcs which are otherwise difficult to compare. For a given group of melody arcs, a quantitatively determined "melody type" for this group can be objectively defined by parametric averaging. Applying the model to infant cries, four global categories (prototypes) were determined and are represented by bold curves in Figure 42.5.

These prototypes represent four shape classes:

• Shape Class 1, a fast ascending and slowly descending melody ÷ left-accentuated type (roughly corresponding to the "falling melody type" of above-mentioned former qualitative analysis),

• Shape class 2, a slowly ascending and fast descending melody ÷ right-accentuated type (roughly corresponding to "rising melody type" of former qualitative analysis),

• Shape class 3, a symmetrical ascending-then-descending melody ÷ symmetric type (corresponding to the "rising-falling melody type" of former qualitative analysis), and

• Shape class 4, exhibiting a relatively stable melody in the centre of the arc at a certain frequency ÷ plateau type (roughly corresponding to the "flat melody type" of former qualitative analysis, as the ascending and descending flanks are often invisible in these frequency spectrograms).

This model-based system of shape classification unambiguously assigns any modeled melody arc to one of these four categories (shape classes).

Melodies of all classes are regularly found in neonates' cries, albeit with different relative frequencies of occurrence. For example, with increasing distress a higher prevalence of shape class 1 melodies is found (Figure 42.2).[12]

Although systematic analyses have not been undertaken, the displayed frequency spectrograms of calls produced by nonhuman primates in the literature suggest that their melody arcs partially also could be assigned to the described basic melody classes (Demolin & Delvaux, 2006; Fischer, 2003; Hauser, 1992; Richman, 1987).

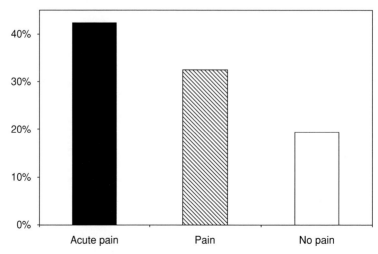

Fig. 42.2 Decrease of prevalence of shape class 1 cry melodies with decreasing distress. Frequency of occurrence of neonates' cry melodies belonging to shape class 1 in cries uttered immediately after a heel-stick for routine blood sampling (acute pain cries), cries uttered about 10 seconds after this pain stimulus (pain cries) and cries recorded in a pain-free condition. Caregivers are generally well capable of distinguishing between different levels of acuteness of discomfort based on cry features.

In our data (52,400 analyzed vocalizations), about 67% of neonates' voiced cries with identifiable melody exhibit a single ascending-descending arc belonging to one of the above-mentioned shape classes (Figure 42.3). This situation changes dramatically over the first weeks of life, when those simple, single-arc melodies become increasingly substituted by complex, that is, double- or multiple-arc melodies. Figure 42.4 displays examples of such complex melodies. In full-term, healthy neonates complex melodies may already be observed within the first few days after birth. About 50% of the cries with an identifiable melody in the second month already consist of complex melodies, and from about the eighth week the proportion of utterances (cries, "fake cries"[13], or "transitional sounds" and cooing sounds) exhibiting a single-arc melody further decreases (Figure 42.3).

Initially, cry melody shapes are generated by neural circuits that are still immature, so-called "proto-modules." This immaturity causes many irregularities and local and global variability in young infants' cry melodies. Proto-modules have to be trained and stabilized before they are available for intentional application (mature modules) (Wermke, 2002; Wermke & Mende, 1994). The difference between modules and proto-modules is that the latter result from the trial-and-error of actuating variables underlying cry production. A similar process is described by Pinker (1994), who compares a babbling infant with a "frobbing [computer] hacker" (p. 266). Ongoing maturation of proto-modules into "modules" results in a regularization of melody shapes. The functional brain modules are controlled by a fixed set of values of the actuating variables of the phonatory/articulatory system taken from an inventory of "trained" melody modules. Such modules can be interpreted as autonomous disposable entities available on request to higher systems. This organization could explain the high reproducibility of melody arc shapes observed in older infants' crying, cooing, babbling and spoken words. The general maturation of the auditory-vocal system seems to occur simultaneously on several efferent, afferent and re-afferent levels. Upon completion of these processes, modules can voluntarily and reliably function in different contexts, as for example reflected in structural changes of cry melodies in the first weeks of life. Similar network-organization is described for perception in infants (Dehaene-Lambertz et al., 2006).

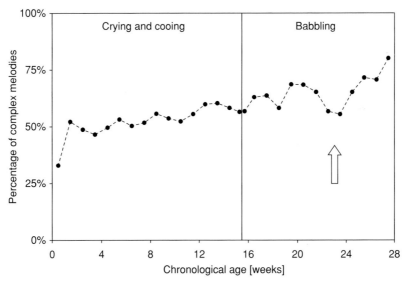

Fig. 42.3 Developmental changes of the frequency of occurrence complex, multiple-arc-melodies over the first 28 weeks of life. Shown is the percentage–share of complex melodies identified in 52400 analysed vocalizations from 450 infants across the first 7 months. The vocalizations were categorised in simple or complex melodies. From birth to the 16th week of life, fuzzing/mitigated crying (N = 45000) and cooing (N = 3400) was investigated. Babbling (N = 4000) was analysed from 16 until 28 weeks, hence two data points in week 16 (vertical line). The associated relative errors, mostly caused by categorization, are estimated to remain in all weeks under 2%. The development of melody in terms of complexity exhibits a nearly monotonous increase with age; the data confirm a continuity of development across very different pre-speech stages. The only observed marked "monotony break" occurs at about 23 weeks corresponding to the known developmental change in phonetic perception from non-native toward language specific perception beginning at about this age.

From Simple to Complex Cry Melodies

It is well known to mothers and other caretakers that infant crying changes in its sound quality (timbre) with age, at least after the third month of life (Kent & Murray, 1982). *Melody* is the most crucial feature responsible for this recognized change. Infant cries undergo dramatic developmental changes with respect to their melodic properties beginning at birth and continuing for some months (e.g. Mende et al., 1990; Wermke & Mende, 1994; Wermke et al., 1996; Wermke, 2002; Wermke & Friederici, 2004). This development from simple to complex cry melodies happens in a very regular, systematic way, and involves, among other things, a nearly monotonically increasing short-term stability of the fundamental frequency (Wermke & Mende, 1994) caused by the maturation of underlying neural circuits (modules). Such sublime maturation processes could only be revealed by modeling the melodic components and tracking systematic shape changes.

The observed high regularity and reproducibility of melody development across a number of individuals points to a universal phenomenon. Neonates and young infants are able to produce melodies of similar shape, expanded or compressed in time and varying in frequency level (melody transposition). This ability can be viewed as a necessary prerequisite for imitating simple melodies of nursery or other songs and for imitating sounds of the ambient language (Wermke & Mende, 2009). Voluntary control of time organization is crucial for synchronization of communication processes, for example, for mother-child interactions (turn-taking, babble dueting) and during musical and language-learning activities.

For a better understanding, we exemplify this developmental program by presenting melody patterns with different degrees of complexity in the following sections.

DOUBLE-ARC MELODIES IN INFANT CRIES

According to our proposed developmental model of melody, differentiation occurs phenomenologically by a simple repetition and/or concatenation of instances of the basic melody types, generating complex pattern sequences. The simplest form of *complexification* in this sense is a doubling of shape-identical melody arcs (Figure 42.4a). A doubling is either accomplished by two successive melody arcs or by two arcs separated by a short interruption (brief segmentation pause). This doubling occurs within a single expiratory sound production, that is,

a single cry.[14] The pause in segmented double-arcs is thus generated by an intentional glottal stop of vibration during the expiratory sound production, not by an inspiratory break.[15] The ability to intentionally segment melodies by brief pauses is an important skill necessary later for syllable production.

MULTIPLE-ARC MELODIES AND RHYTHMICAL VARIATIONS

Further *complexification* of cry melody is characterized by multiple repetitions or concatenations of single melody arcs or arc-like structures during the second–fourth month of life. By varying the number of successive melody arcs, in combination with a varying number and position of segmentation pauses, a large melodic and rhythmic repertoire can be generated (Figure 42.4b). Such "complex" cries may consist of two, three, four, or more melody arcs either with or without segmentation pauses within a single expiratory sound production. Segmentation pauses represent rhythmical components because they organize the "substrate" melody into subunits. While melody represents time variation of the fundamental frequency, rhythm reflects aspects of the temporal organization in vocal communication.

We interpret this process of structuring and *complexification* as a universal developmental program. Further refinement of laryngeal coordination during the first months of life and the gradual addition of upper pharyngeal and oral controls deliver several elementary abilities (building-blocks), which, once having been established by practice, are later used in speech-like vocalizations or speech utterances. From the very first vocal utterances of an infant, these building-blocks are rehearsed (learned by doing) for their use later in "real" speech. This seems to be an effective way to develop, stabilize, and provide constituents essential for speech and language acquisition. This interpretation is supported by trends within our data to show the effect that infants lacking a certain degree of melody complexity during the second month of life are at a higher risk for poorer language performance two years later (Wermke et al., 2007).

To delineate whether or not the demonstrated aptitude of human infants to generate an amazing manifold of melodies using the basic melody types distinguishes them from other primates is a task for future comparative studies. The huge diversity of melody patterns found in cries already comprises the majority of those patterns that cooing, babbling or speech will later employ and incorporate in the

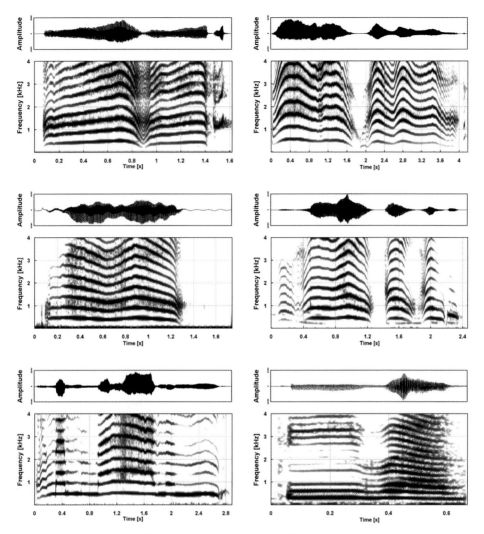

Fig. 42.4a-f Time waveforms and narrowband spectrograms displaying double- and multiple arc melodies in crying (a, b), cooing (c, d), babbling (e) and word production (f)

hierarchic recursive structures of language. In the following two sections we buttress this claim by displaying melodies from later developmental stages.

Melody Development from Crying via Cooing and Babbling Toward Word Production—How Words Emerge from Melody

"As for the intonation, the child uses the same tones in speaking his first conventional words as he had used in his own primitive speech; and as for the patterns of sound, there is no doubt that if we examine children's earliest conventional words— such as mama, papa, baba, dada, atta—we find in them the clear marks of the child's own earlier expressive cries." (Lewis, 1936)

In the analysis of melody structure in early non-cry utterances (cooing, babbling, etc.) and first words, the four basic melody types outlined above were regularly found. Occasionally, they occured in isolation, but more often also combined to form complex patterns (e.g., double arcs). Typical spectrograms of original cooing (Figure 42.4c, d) and babbling (Figure 42.4e) vocalizations as well as a two-syllabic word (Figure 42.4f) are displayed.

Moreover, an objective comparison of melody arcs in crying and babbling using the above-mentioned mathematical model demonstrated recurring similar shape characteristics in cry and babbling melodies (Figure 42.5). These data provide further evidence for the inner continuity of melody development and support the assumption that prosodic primitives (melodic building blocks) are already trained during the earliest stages of pre-speech development.

The data (Figure 42.5) indicate a striking shape similarity of melodies in crying and babbling, pointing to a smooth gradual transition from crying to subsequent pre-speech phases. The mathematical normalizations applied to the data correspond to transformations the infant brain is able to effect in both sound perception and production. The observed ability of neonates and young infants to produce melodies of similar shape, extended or compressed in time, and varying within a certain frequency range (Wermke, 2002), could be viewed as a prerequisite for the acquisition of specific prosodic features in different phonological units of the target language. This view is supported by the observation that the genesis of complex cry sounds and babbling sounds displays a striking homology in modular composition.

Comparing the frequency of occurrence of cries, coos, and babbles consisting only of simple, that is, single-arc melodies versus those consisting of complex, multiple-arc melodies, we found a continuous, nearly monotonic increase of complex melody structures from the 4th week to the 28th week of life (Figure 42.3). Note that we did not find a discontinuity in melody development between the second and fourth month, a period characterized by an increase in non-cry vocalizations, major changes of vocal tract structure and related functional changes in the vocal tract transfer function. A developmental continuity is further evident in the early babbling stage that follows from the fourth month. Figure 42.3 indicates continuity from crying/cooing to babbling in the form of an increasing share of vocalizations with complex melodies from the fourth month onward.

Interestingly, we observed only one marked break in the trend of increasing shares of babbling vocalizations with complex melodies, namely a decrease of complex melodies to 55% (Figure 42.3) during the 23rd–24th week (6 months). This is consistent with data from perceptual studies postulating a reorganization of perceptive sensitivity starting at about 6 months (Kuhl, 1991; Kuhl et al., 2006; Kuhl, Williams, Lacerda, Stevens, & Lindblom, 1992; Werker & Tees, 1984). At about this age, infants lose sensitivity to non-native vowel contrasts and exhibit greater sensitivity to prototypical vowels of their native language ("perceptual magnet effect"). Correspondingly, there are several studies that found that from 5–7 months onward, infants produce babbling which contains features of their target language (Chen & Kent, 2005; Whalen, Levitt, & Wang, 1991). As can be seen from Figure 42.3, we observed a new increase in the share of babbling sounds consisting of complex melodies from the end of the sixth month to the seventh month. The brief "continuity distortion" in our melody data may reflect this reorganization process. De Boysson-Bardies (1999) notes with respect to this developmental period:

> "Toward the end of the sixth month, babies are capable of globally coordinating phonatory and supraglottal adjustments: they begin to be able to interrupt their vocalizations at will, which is an essential condition of vocal control. . .They can also imitate simple patterns of intonation on the basis of adult examples (Masataka, 1992; see also Kuhl and Meltzoff, 1984)." (p. 39),

The described findings support our assumption that melody functions as a framework and scaffolding during pre-speech development, from the simple melodies that prevail during the first week of life to the first spoken words (and possibly beyond, as language use continues to be refined). In a section below, we outline the significance of melody for the gradual development of articulatory flexibility.

Modular Composition of Melody Complexity

The development from simple to complex cry melodies by a strategy of repetition and specialization reflects a general evolutionary principle for composing complex structures (Maynard Smith & Szathmáry, 2000; Riedl, 1975; Schlosser, 2004).

According to the principle of modular composition, initially single elements (e.g., melody shapes) develop separately, differentiate, and stabilize (phenomenologically, a kind of maturation process). After this maturation a combination of different separately "trained" elements (e.g., single arcs, double-arcs) results in an "explosion of possibilities" and leads to a completely new quality (e.g., manifold of complex melody patterns). Integration of different elements (e.g., complex melodies and tuning of melody with resonance frequencies, see next section) generates a combinatorial manifold of possibilities and the potential for new performances (e.g., cooing, babbling) which as elements of the next higher level undergo a corresponding differentiation and maturation process in turn.[16] This process of complexification is well observable in infants' pre-speech development.

A later stage of pre-speech development, babbling, is also an excellent example for the evolutionary

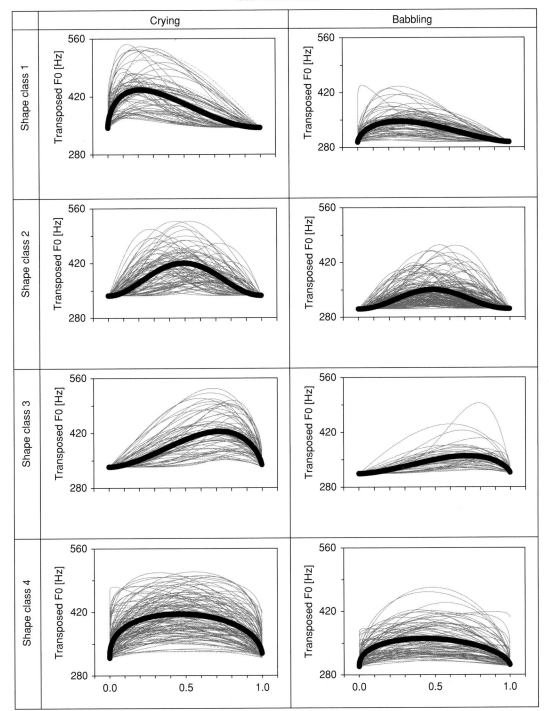

Fig. 42.5 Synopsis of basic shape classes (melody types) in infants' cries and babbling sounds. Time-normalized (1 sec) model curves of individual cry melodies (left column, N = 389) and babbling melodies (right column, N = 340) grouped in shape classes. The individual vocalizations are normalized in time and frequency in such a way that the relative frequency modulation amplitude (FM-amplitude or FM-depth) is preserved and transposed to the class-averaged socket frequency. The class-median values of the two shape parameters of the applied mathematical model and the geometric means of the class frequency intervals provide the bold standard curves (melody types) for the classes 1–4. The deviation of individual model arcs from the corresponding bold standard curve demonstrates the intra-class variability of shape and FM-amplitude. Class-depending decrease of the FM-amplitude from crying toward babbling was between 6 – 11%.

principle of repetition and specialization. After initially producing single syllables (such as [ba]) in isolation, babbling progresses to rhythmic reduplicated syllables (Elbers, 1982). In the reduplicated babbling that follows, infants utter sequences of identical consonant-vowel (CV) syllables, for example, [ma-ma-ma, da-da-da or ba-ba-ba], and in doing so they ". . . appear to concentrate on a single CV type (e.g., [ba]) for a period of time before concentrating on another" (Gerken, 2009). They then acquire alternating or concatenating contrasts (such as [da-ba, di-de]) (Fletcher, 1992); in other words, they combine building-blocks previously trained in isolation to produce a new expressive quality. During later developmental periods ("jargon babbling") they produce both types of babbling and mix them with real words, as they also still produce simple cry melodies while already exhibiting a preference for the production of complex melodies. There seems to be only one way to compose the pre-speech modules to the final mastery of language.

The Importance of Melody at the Beginning of Articulatory Development

As has been outlined in the preceding sections, melody is a key entity for characterizing infants' vocalizations. However, there is no doubt that the maturation of supralaryngeal control mechanisms, along with major developmental changes in vocal tract structure (e.g., descent of the larynx and lengthening of the pharyngeal cavity; Vorperian et al., 2005), becomes increasingly important during later pre-speech phases. Late-stage vocal development is described as "the addition of upper pharyngeal and oral modulations to an already well-developed laryngeal vocal coordination" from about the third month onward (Bosma, Truby, & Lind, 1965, p. 91). Most vocal tract structures "appear to have an ongoing growth from age 2 weeks to age 6 years 9 months with somewhat more rapid growth during approximately the first 18 months of life" (Vorperian et al., 2005, p. 344). At about 18 months, some structures "get closer to their adult mature size sooner than others" (ibid., p. 344).[17] However, the acquisition of a voluntary control of the speech organs (tongue, lips, jaw, larynx) and above all the adjustment of melody production and resonance characteristics of the SVT is a necessary precondition for the first production of speech or speech-like utterances at the end of the first year.

This view is supported by the work of Goldstein (1980) who postulates on the basis of her estimates of articulatory and acoustic prototypes of the point

vowels[18] /i/,/a/and/u/that "newborns are not prevented from speaking because of the anatomy of their vocal tracts" (p. 214).[19] Instead, she emphasizes the importance of the "development of proprioception, neuromuscular control, and intellectual capacity" (p. 214). A variety of recent simulation studies using the variable linear articulatory model developed by Maeda (Boë & Maeda, 1998) (modeling a vocal tract from birth to adulthood) confirms Goldstein's hypothesis (cf. Boë et al., 2007). The results obtained with this modeling approach showed that the maximal vowel space "of newborn infants is potentially (at least) the same as that for an adult male and it allows us to propose [i a u] midsagittal prototypes" (ibid., p. 577). The obtained formant values of these vowels are fully compatible with the formant data on vocalizations of 12–20-week-old infants as reported by Kuhl and Meltzoff (1996). Although 20-week-old infants manage to produce differentiated [i]-like, [a]-like, [u]-like vowels, they do not yet possess full control of their tongue and lips (Rvachew, Mattock, Polka, & Ménard, 2006).

Thus, the developmental (as the evolutionary) challenge seems not to be fundamentally related to the geometry and the acoustics of the vocal tract but rather to the maturation of neurophysiologic control systems enabling well-tuned operations of phonatory and articulatory mechanisms. This conclusion is further supported by findings that the average formant frequencies remain unchanged, that is, do not decrease as anticipated by the increase in the length of the vocal tract of 1.5 to 2 cm (Vorperian et al., 2005) that occurs during the first 2 years of life (Kent & Murray, 1982; Robb, Chen, & Gilbert, 1997; Stathopoulos, 1995). Robb et al. (1997) attributed the additionally found increasing range of formant values (dispersion) during the first 2 years to a greater variability of tongue movement. The intentional tongue movement in producing words and sentences is certainly based on well-developed neurophysiological control mechanisms of the articulatory system:

Below, we will sketch a scenario of how such a precise tuning between melody and resonance frequencies of the vocal tract may develop gradually in young infants.

From a neurophysiological point of view laryngeal *phonation* and vocal-tract-based *articulation* are at first independently controlled systems. However, a tuned coupling between phonation and articulation is an essential prerequisite for acquiring the intentional flexibility necessary for producing fast sequences of highly contrastive phonological structures in speech.

The acquisition of a well-tuned coordination between laryngeal (melody) and supralaryngeal activity (resonance frequencies[20]) occurs gradually beginning at about the ninth week of life. The so-called "Expansion stage" (age of onset 3–8 months) is characterized as period during which human infants typically explore the vowel space (Oller, 2000). This explorative vocal behavior represents a scrutinizing of the multi-parametric resonance characteristics of the vocal tract by playing with the articulators and thereby learning to intentionally adjust resonance frequencies and melody.

Investigating the coupling behavior and the timing between resonances and melody with the help of signal analysis methods, we were able to identify three main characteristics of early articulatory development: (1) an increasing synchronous movement of the melody and the first two resonance frequencies (R1 and R2), or a kind of "tuning"; (2) an increasing prevalence of coherent and smooth movements of R1 and/or R2 from the vicinity (defined by our analysis bandwidth) of one to that of another either higher or lower harmonic of the fundamental frequency (F0), called transition phenomena; and (3) increasingly faster transition phenomena with age (Wermke, Mende, Manfredi, & Bruscaglioni, 2002).

The voluntary mastering of such transition phenomena is an essential prerequisite for performing fast and accurate shifts between vowel formants in babbling and later speech (cf. Oller, 2000; Robb & Saxman, 1990). Temporal features, such as the speed and dynamics of these transitions, depend on the neurophysiological fitness of the underlying control systems as well as upon the intended utterance.

Based on our findings we hypothesize that the found early developmental course of articulation may be universal and may represent the only way by which the necessary tuning of nasal and vocal tract resonances and their coupling with the voice apparatus (larynx) can be explored and exercised by the infant. The hypothesis that the described stages of articulatory development are common to all infants is in agreement with the findings of Davis and MacNeilage (1990, 1995), namely that some CV sequences are more frequent than others in babbling. However, there is some evidence that babbling is ultimately shaped by the target language at some point between the age of 6–10 months (Boysson-Bardies et al., 1992; Boysson-Bardies,

Hallé, Sagart, & Durand, 1989; Boysson-Bardies & Vihman, 1991; Chen & Kent, 2005; Levitt & Wang, 1991).

The described coupling of phonatory and articulatory activities under continuous vocal activity is perhaps the fastest and most demanding tuning process between neuro-physiological maturation and physical growth processes during language acquisition.

Melody is the Message—A Coding Hierarchy

Does language acquisition therefore begin with crying? In the preceding sections we tried to explain that the language acquisition process commences on the productive side with the first melodic cries. This may seem to be far-fetched at first glance and contradicts common views. However, we contend that the production of speech-like sounds produced by the infant during later pre-speech phases that are more commonly regarded as language-relevant, for example, canonical babbling, is inevitably based on a preceding systematic melody development. Our analyses indicate that melody works like a scaffolding during all phases of early language development.

The apparent constraints of the human infant's sound producing system, that is, dominance of laryngeal mechanisms and an immature vocal tract function (see previous section), may mark the only possible route by which the infant is able to acquire an easy-to-learn "protolanguage" that bears the potential for ultimately developing a rich symbolic structure and unbounded complexity. Moreover, this route may be the only one by which this potential continues to be gradually realized during early language development. This scenario is consistent with Deacon's view about language evolution (Deacon, 1998, particularly pp. 136–137). He assumes that the passage of language through the "immature" brains of our hominine ancestors probably minimized the abyss between an object and its symbolic reference in the past at the cradle of symbolic language, and that this coding principle is repeated by each human infant acquiring language today. "Immaturity of the brain is a learning handicap that greatly aides language acquisition" (Deacon, 1998, p. 141). As we argued elsewhere (Wermke & Mende, 2006), infants from all cultures likely have to pass through the same stages of melody development at the same phase of life history. Spoken language is hereby tested and shaped by all the infants' brains of a language community, and vice versa. That means that brain development is also influenced by language tradition. Language acquisition by the immature brain is hereby a critical bottleneck (a "language pelvis") through which all evolving language has to pass, generation by generation.

With respect to ontogeny, therefore, we argue that cry melody types, observed in infants of different cultures carry specific emotional content that may represent first prosodic (melodic) primitives and the simplest pre-stage of referential coding. At this early moment of individual life-history there is not yet a deep gap between meaning and symbol: In young infants, the coding for needs and emotional states is not arbitrary, but it is closely coupled to real physiological processes and bodily states (for which we use the term "body-near"). They are expressed by highly emotionally charged vocal productions via melody. A branching that occurs much later may recapitulate the emergence of different coding processes; one leading to language faculty with definite hierarchically organized semantics and finally abstract notions and thinking, the other leading to a corresponding musical competence. Both processes are driven by different coding principles for processing one-dimensional sound streams in the brain (Roederer, 2008): on the one hand, an optimization for fast switches of highly contrastive sequences for speech signals with definite semantics, on the other hand, an optimization for highly emotionally charged sequences without adherence to an obligatory semantics.

Arguing along these lines, we suggest that the "musical" quality of the infant's crying provides evidence for the assumption that melody was and remains at the roots of both the development of spoken language and music (Wermke & Mende, 2009). This perspective supports one of three evolutionary interpretations (Brown, 2000), namely that of a shared ancestry of music and language with a still unknown time of branching. In contrast to the two other interpretations, which suggest either that one of them is a derivative of the other, or that both developed independently, the shared-ancestry-view suggests that music and language might have co-evolved for a certain time during evolution and share a primordial form of communication system (called "musilanguage" by Brown). In support of the existence of a "musilanguage" form of communication, attention should be drawn to human infants' perceptual preferences for music and musical elements of speech, namely prosody (cf. Mithen, 2009).

In human infants, simple melodic sounds heavily loaded with emotions are gradually modified and refined until they lead to utterances with ultimately definite meanings and references that still retain a degree of emotional content. As outlined above, we locate traces of the early roots of spoken language in the cry melody of human infants and its systematic change during the first months of life. Newborns are already sensitive to the expressivity both of faces and prosodic contours and unconsciously decode the "indexing function" of such (to use the definition of Deacon, 1998). This co-evolved with the typical way of mothers to talk to their young infants by exaggerating melodies and varying melody contours to express different emotive contents.

Therefore, we argue that emotional content conveyed via melody is the beginning of a hierarchical coding of meaning into words leading from body-near, self-evident messages to abstract symbols; a transition that recapitulates essential pathways in the evolution of language. This idea is related to parallels between the ontogenetic and phylogenetic unfolding of organic structures of multicellular organisms discovered by Karl Ernst von Baer (1828) and Ernst Haeckel (1866), the latter of whom coined the phrase "ontogenesis recapitulates phylogenesis." Over a century later, von Baer's and Haeckel's findings were unexpectedly corroborated by modern molecular and genetic research, particularly with respect to the hereditary, neurophysiological relationship between regions of the brain.

Overall, we claim that the systematic changes of human infants' cries that take place over the first weeks of life (outlined across the five preceding sections) already constitute language-relevant performances.

From Emotion to Notion—From Melody to Words

The developmental steps described above lend support to the hypothesis that for the production of cries, early non-cry vocalizations, speech-like babbling, and of first words, not only are the same "architectural principles" at work but that the prosodic constituents (melodic building blocks) for the later spoken language are also developed. Our data reveal a clear coherence and a strong developmental continuity from first crying via cooing and babbling toward speech and first language competence.

Our perspective on the importance of melody for the evolution of spoken language in hominine ancestors as well as for language acquisition in modern human infants, accords both with Elissa Newport's suggestion (cited by Deacon, 1998) and Deacon's view.

"Language structures may have preferentially adapted to children's learning biases and limitations because languages that are more easily acquired at an early age will tend to replicate more rapidly and with greater fidelity from generation to generation than those that take more time or neurological maturity to be mastered. . ..Languages may thus be more difficult to learn later in life only because they evolved to be easier to learn when immature." (Deacon, 1998, p. 137)

With respect to ontogeny, the aptitude of newborns and young infants to produce increasingly complex melodies by combining basic melody types and rhythmical elements, while not yet possessing the skills of intentional articulation, might represent an "incidental feature of maturation that just happened to be co-opted in languages' race" (Deacon, 1998, p. 137) during the evolution of spoken language.

From these developmental data it seems reasonable to state: "In the beginning was/is the melody." A coherent progression from emotion to notion, from melodies to words, is recapitulated in each infant's acquisition of language.

Notes

1 William Gardiner (born March 15, 1769 in Leicester, died November 16, 1853 in Leicester), an English hosiery manufacturer, musicologist, composer, and editor–was "a member of the semichorus at Victoria's coronation (1838) and trained a 100-voice chorus for the important 1827 Leicester Musical Festival . . .Procuring a copy of Beethoven's E$_b$ String Trio op. 3 in Bonn, he played the viola in a Leicester performance in 1794, three years before its London publication. He was thus regarded as the introducer of Beethoven's music to England and was asked, at the unveiling of Beethoven's statue in Bonn (1848), to sign the inauguration parchment beneath the names of Victoria and Albert" (Wilshere, 2010).

2 This time line is clearly depending on the date from which on acoustic communication is defined to be a language. From the biological perspective each human communication system deserves the status of a language if it (1) contains compositional, reproducible messages, (2) has a multi-generational tradition and (3) is meaningful to all adult members of a social group. Such a system can be holistic, iconic, and without words and grammar. One might call it *protolanguage,* but this term is extremely vague and should be used with care.

3 From a recently discovered female pelvis of Homo erectus in Gona (Ethiopia), found not far from the site were the famous Australopithecus afarensis "Lucy" was found, the researchers assert that head circumference of a Homo erectus baby could have been about 32 cm. The researchers report that this is at the lower end of the spectrum of modern day human beings (32.0–37.0 cm). They argue that this data demonstrate that "pelvic shape in H. erectus was evolving in response to increasing fetal brain size" and neither in adaptation to tropical environments nor to endurance necessary for running as primary selective factors (Simpson et al., 2008).

4 Newman points out that vocal behavior directed at the infant as well as communication in mother-infant dialogues in mammals may be the evolutionary precursors of motherese (Newman, 1985; 2007).

5 Falk (2009) remarks that "tone of voice, however, is not the only widespread feature of motherese . . ..baby talk everywhere tends to have words composed of duplicated syllables (. . .); a special vocabulary that includes a high proportion of names for body parts and functions, food, animals, and games (. . .); and special constructions, such as the compound verb 'go bye-bye'" (p. 89).

6 There is undoubtedly a close link between speech and language, but they are absolutely not synonymous. While *speech* is only a modality that can be used to convey language, *language* is a system for representing and communicating messages, ideas, moods, emotions, and other expressive or descriptive contents, irrespective of modality. Spoken language is based on produced and perceived sounds (acoustic mode, speech), while sign language, for example, is based on producing gestural signals and perceiving them by the visual system (visual mode).

7 For comprehensive hypothesis about the transition from holistic phrases to compositional language see e.g., Mithen (2006) and Deacon (1998).

8 *Intonation* refers here to variations of one or more acoustic parameters of which fundamental frequency (F0) is the primary parameter. Besides F0, also variations of intensity and segmental duration as well as rhythm (temporal organization of these quantities) are included under the term intonation. *Prosody* in its most general sense describes both a number of lexical systems (tone, stress, quantity) and a non-lexical system, i.e., intonation. For more details concerning terminology see e.g., Hirst & Di Cristo (1998) or Hewlett & Beck (2006).

9 The infant cry has typical alerting sound characteristics and a high penetrative force because of its frequency modulation content and its harmonic character (high harmonic-to-noise ratio).

10 The term "crydiagnosis" has been used in a number of studies that aimed to determine the possible diagnostic value of cry features for assessing neurophysiological states as well as developmental risks (cf. reviews in Barr, Hopkins, & Green, 2000; LaGasse, Neal, & Lester, 2005; Murry & Murry, 1980).

11 Note that cry melodies (as melodies of other pre-speech and speech sounds) have no marked step-structure, but represent glissandi smoothly slurred or swept over a certain frequency interval. This structure differs from what is commonly meant by *melody* in Western music. Melody in scale-based music is a sequence of discrete notes which represent well-determined frequency plateaus and is perceived as a single entity (gestalt). The notes can be bound by a more or less smooth transition, but the frequency steps remain well noticeable. However, from a physical point of view melody generally can be characterized by the time varying fundamental frequency, that is, by the term "frequency modulation."

12 This accords with the claim by Wasz-Höckert and colleagues (1968) that a "falling melody type" (in their case determined by a subjective evaluation of frequency spectrograms) prevails in pain cries.

13 Wolff (1987) describes "fake cries" (labelled as such by mothers) as a vocalization category intermediate between fussing and non-cry vocalizations produced "at times when the

infants gave no visible or audible evidence of being in distress .... mothers interpreted these sounds as the baby's efforts to attract attention when there was nothing wrong." (p. 178). We have elsewhere referred to this category "transitional sounds" (Übergangslaute).

14 Any kind of inspiratory crying is not considered here (Grau, Robb, & Cacace, 1995).

15 A corresponding phenomenon of such segmentation processes in non-cry vocalizations is described by Koopmans-van Beinum and van der Stelt (1986). They found "interrupted phonation" and production of glottal stops to occur in cooing beginning with two months.

16 Piaget (1966) described these principles for the cognitive development.

17 Percent of adult size achieved at 18 months: laryngeal descent (65%), tongue length (70%), hard palate length and maxillary lip thickness (80%), mandibular depth and pharyngeal length (80%)–after Vorperian et al. (2005).

18 "Point vowels" correspond to three extremes of oral-tract constriction with [u], most back-tongue/lips rounded; [i], most front-tongue/jaw closed/lips spread; and [a], most pharyngeal/jaw open (cf. Pickett, 1999).

19 For over 30 years the theory of Philip Lieberman and Edmund Crelin (1971) predominated. They postulate that apes and human infants (and Neanderthals) do not have the anatomical prerequisites for producing the full range of human speech sounds, notably the three extreme "point" or "quantal" vowels [i, a, u] found in almost all the world's spoken languages (Lieberman, 1972, 1973, 1984, 1991; followed up by Lieberman, 1994). For a recent discussion that casts doubt on fundamental aspects of this theory see Boë, Heim, Honda, & Maeda (2002), Boë et al. (2007) and a reply by Lieberman (2007).

20 During sound transmission from the glottis through the vocal tract, resonances occur that strongly affect the frequency spectrum of a sound. Resonances as properties of the vocal tract are characteristic for speech sounds, particularly vowels. They are called *formants* and are numbered in order of their frequencies as F1, F2, F3, and so on. F1 and F2 are closely tied to the shape of the vocal tract in articulating consonants and vowels, while F3 is related to only a few specific speech sounds (Pickett, 1999). The term "formants" refers to speech sounds. So, instead we use the term resonance frequencies in describing phenomena of vocal tract properties in pre-speech vocalizations.

References

Al-Qahtani, N. H. (2005). Foetal response to music and voice. *The Australian and New Zealand Journal of Obstetrics & Gynaecology, 45*, 414–417.

Baer, K. E. v. (1828). *Über Entwickelungsgeschichte der Thiere.* Königsberg: Bornträger.

Barr, R. G., Hopkins, B., & Green, J. A. (2000). *Crying as a sign, a symptom, & a signal. Clinical, emotional and developmental aspects of infant and toddler crying.* London: Mac Keith Press.

Baumann, M. D., Lavenex, P., Mason, W. A., Capitanio, J. P., & Amaral, D. G. (2004). The development of mother-infant interactions after neonatal amygdala lesions in rhesus monkeys. *Journal of Neuroscience, 24*, 711–721.

Bloom, L. (2000). *How children learn the meanings of words.* Cambridge, MA: The MIT Press.

Boë, L.-J. & Maeda, S. (1998). Modélations de la croissance du conduit vocal. *Journées d'Études Linguistiques, La Voyelle dans tous ses états*, 98–105.

Boë, L.-J., Heim, J.-L., Honda, K., & Maeda, S. (2002). The potential Neanderthal vowel space was as large as that of modern humans. *Jounal of Phonetics, 30*, 465–484.

Boë, L.-J., Heim, J.-L., Honda, K., Maeda, S., Badin, P., & Abry, C. (2007). The vocal tract of newborn humans and Neanderthals: Acoustic capabilities and consequences for the debate on the origin of language. A reply to Lieberman (2007). *Jounal of Phonetics, 35*, 564–581.

Bosma, J. F., Truby, H. M., & Lind, J. (1965). Cry motions of the newborn infant. *Acta Paediatrica Scandinavica Supplement, 163*, 61–92.

Botha, R. & C. Knight. (Eds.) (2009). *The prehistory of language. Studies in the evolution of language.* New York: Oxford University Press.

Boysson-Bardies, B. d. (1999). *How language comes to children: From birth to two years.* Cambridge, MA: The MIT Press.

Boysson-Bardies, B. d., Hallé, P., Sagart, L., & Durand, C. (1989). A cross-linguistic investigation of vowel formants in babbling. *Journal of Child Language, 16*, 1–17.

Boysson-Bardies, B. d. & Vihman, M. M. (1991). Adaption to language: Evidence from babbling and first words in four languages. *Language, 67*, 297–319.

Boysson-Bardies, B. d., Vihman, M. M., Roug-Hellichius, L., Durand, C., Landberg, I., & Arao, F. (1992). Material evidence of infant selection from the target language. A cross-linguistic phonetic study. In C. A. Ferguson, L. Menn, & C. Stoel-Gammon (Eds.), *Phonological development. Models, research, implications* (pp. 369–391). Timonium, MD: York Press.

Brown, S. (2000). The "musilanguage" model of music evolution. In N. L. Wallin, B. Merker, & S. Brown (Eds.), *The origins of music* (pp. 271–300). Cambridge, MA: The MIT Press.

Carral, V., Huotilainen, M., Ruusuvirta, T., Fellman, V., Naatanen, R., & Escera, C. (2005). A kind of auditory "primitive intelligence" already present at birth. *The European Journal of Neuroscience, 21*, 3201–3204.

Chen, L. M. & Kent, R. D. (2005). Consonant-vowel co-occurrence patterns in Mandarin-learning infants. *Journal of Child Language, 32*, 507–534.

Cheney, D. L. & Seyfarth, R. M. (1982). How vervet monkeys perceive their grunts: Field playback experiments. *Animal Behaviour, 30*, 739–751.

Chomsky, N. (1965). *Aspects of the theory of syntax.* Cambridge, MA: The MIT Press.

Damstra-Wijmenga, S. M. (2009). The memory of the new-born baby. *Midwives Chronicle, 104*, 66–69.

Darwin, C. (1871). *The descent of man, and selection in relation to sex.* (2nd ed.) London: John Murray.

Davis, B. L. & MacNeilage, P. F. (1990). Acquisition of correct vowel production: A quantitative case study. *Journal of Speech and Hearing Research, 33*, 16–27.

Davis, B. L. & MacNeilage, P. F. (1995). The articulatory basis of babbling. *Journal of Speech and Hearing Research, 38*, 1199–1211.

Deacon, T. W. (1998). *The symbolic species: The co-evolution of language and the brain.* New York: W.W. Norton & Company.

DeCasper, A. & Spencer, M. (1986). Prenatal maternal speech influences newborns' perception of speech sounds. *Infant Behavior & Development, 9*, 113–150.

Dehaene-Lambertz, G., Hertz-Pannier, L., Dubois, J., Mériaux, S., Roche, A., Sigman, M, & Dehaene, S. (2006). Functional organization of perisylvian activation during presentation of sentences in preverbal infants. *Proceedings of the National Academy of Science of the USA, 103*(38), 14240–14245.

Demany, L., McKenzie, B., & Vurpillot, E. (1977). Rhythm perception in early infancy. *Nature, 266*, 718–719.

Demolin, D. & Delvaux, V. (2006). A comparison of the articulatory parameters involved in the production of sound of bonobos and modern humans. In A. Cangelosi, A. D. M. Smith, & K. Smith (Eds.), *Proceedings of the 6th International Conference on the Evolution of Language* (pp. 67–74).

Deutsch, D. (1999). *The psychology of music.* (2nd ed.) San Diego: Academic Press.

Dissanayake, E. (2000). Antecedents of the temporal arts in early mother-infant interaction. In N. L. Wallin, B. Merker, & S. Brown (Eds.), *The origins of music* (pp. 389–410). Cambridge, Massachusetts: The MIT Press.

Dissanayake, E. (2001). An ethological view of music and its relevance to music therapy. *Journal of Music Therapy, 10*, 159–175.

Dissanayake, E. (2004). Motherese is but one part of a ritualized, multimodal, temporarily organized affiliative interaction. *Behavioral and Brain Sciences, 27*, 512.

Dissanayake, E. (2008). If music is the food of love, what about survival and reproductive success? *Musicae Scientiae, Special Issue: Narrative in Music and Interaction*, 169–195.

Donald, M. (2001). *A mind so rare: The evolution of human consciousness.* New York: Norton Company.

Dowling, W. J. (1978). Scale and contour: Two components of a theory of memory for melodies. *Psychological Review, 85*, 341–354.

Dowling, W. J. (1982). Contour in context: Comments on Edworthy. *Psychomusicology, 2*, 47–48.

Dunbar, R. I. M. (2004). *Grooming, gossip and the evolution of language* (2nd ed.). London: Faber and Faber.

Elbers, L. (1982). Operating principles in repetitive babbling: A cognitive continuity approach. *Cognition, 12*, 45.

Falk, D. (2004). Prelinguistic evolution in early hominins: Whence motherese? *Behavioural and Brain Sciences, 27*(4), 491–503.

Falk, D. (2009). *Finding our tongues. Mothers, infants and the origins of language.* New York: Basic Books.

Ferguson, C. A. (1964). Baby talk in six languages. *American Anthropologist, 66*, 103–114.

Fernald, A. (1989). Intonation and communicative intent in mothers' speech to infants: Is the melody the message? *Child Development, 60*, 1497–1510.

Fernald, A. & Simon, T. (1984). Expanded intonation contours in mothers' speech to newborns. *Developmental Psychology, 20*, 104–113.

Fernald, A., Taeschner, T., Dunn, J., Papoušek, M., de Boysson-Bardies, B., & Fukui, I. (1989). A cross-language study of prosodic modifications in mothers' and fathers' speech to preverbal infants. *Journal of Child Language, 16*, 477–501.

Fernald, A. (1992). Meaningful melodies in mothers' speech. In H. Papoušek, U. Jürgens, & M. Papoušek (Eds.), *Nonverbal vocal communication: Comparative and developmental perspectives* (pp. 262–282). Cambridge, UK: Cambridge University Press.

Fernald, A. (1993). Approval and disapproval: Infant responsiveness to vocal affect in familiar and unfamiliar languages. *Child Development, 64*, 657–674.

Fifer, W. P. & Moon, C. (1989). Psychobiology of newborn auditory preferences. *Seminars in Perinatology, 13*, 430–433.

Fischer, J. (2003). Developmental modifications in the vocal behavior of nonhuman primates. In A. A. Ghazanfar (Ed.), *Primate audition. Ethology and neurobiology* (pp. 109–125). Boca Raton: CRC Press.

Flatau, T. S. & Gutzmann, H. (1906). Die Stimme des Säuglings. *Archiv für Laryngologie und Rhinologie, 18*, 139–151.

Fletcher, S. G. (1992). *Articulation. A physiological approach.* San Diego: Singular Publishing Group.

Flinn, M. V. & Ward, C. V. (2005). Ontogeny and evolution of the social child. In B. J. Ellis & D. F. Bjorklund (Eds.), *Origins of the social mind: Evolutionary psychology and child development* (pp. 19–44). New York: Guilford.

Gärdenfors, P. (2007). *How homo became sapiens: On the evolution of thinking.* New York: Oxford University Press.

Gardiner, W. (1832). *The Music of nature.* London, Leicester: Rees et al., T. Combe and Son, A. Cockshaw.

Garland, J. (1972). No language but a cry. *New England Journal of Medicine, 287*, 409.

Garnica, O. K. (1977). Some prosodic and paralinguistic features of speech to young children. In C. E. Snow & C. A. Ferguson (Eds.), *Talking to children: Language input and acquisition* (pp. 63–88). Lanham, MD: Cambridge University Press.

Gentilucci, M. & Corballis, M. C. (2006). From manual gesture to speech: A gradual transition. *Neuroscience and Biobehavioral Review, 30*, 949–960.

Gerken, L. (2009). *Language development.* San Diego: Plural Publishing Inc.

Gerken, L., Jusczyk, P. W., & Mandel, D. R. (1994). When prosody fails to cue syntactic structure: 9-month-olds' sensitivity to phonological versus syntactic phrases. *Cognition, 51*, 237–265.

Goldstein, U. G. (1980). *An articulatory model for the vocal tract of the growing children.* MIT Cambridge, MA, Cambridge, MA. http://theses.mit.edu.

Granier-Deferre, C., Bassereau, S., Jacquet, A. Y., & Lecanuet, J. P. (1998). Fetal and neonatal cardiac orienting responses to music in quiet sleep. *Developmental Psychobiology, 33*, 372.

Grau, S. M., Robb, M. P., & Cacace, A. T. (1995). Acoustic correlates of inspiratory phonation during infant cry. *Journal of Speech and Hearing Research, 38*, 373–381.

Grieser, D. L. & Kuhl, P. K. (1988). Maternal speech to infants in a tonal language: Support for universal prosodic features in motherese. *Developmental Psychology, 24*, 14–20.

Haeckel, E. A. P. (1866). *Generelle Morphologie der Organismen.* Berlin: Reimer.

Hauser, M. D. (1992). Articulatory and social factors influence the acoustic structure of rhesus monkey vocalizations: A learned mode of production? *Journal of the Acoustical Society of America, 91*, 2175–2179.

Hauser, M. D. (2000). *The evolution of communication.* (4th ed.) Cambridge, MA: The MIT Press.

Hewlett, N. & Beck, J. (2006). *An introduction to the science of phonetics.* Mahwah: Erlbaum.

Hirst, D. & Di Cristo, A. (1998). A survey of intonation systems. In D. Hirst & A. Di Cristo (Eds.), *Intonation systems: A survey of twenty languages* (pp. 1–44). Cambridge, UK: Cambridge University Press.

Homae, F., Watanabe, H., Nakano, T., Asakawa, K., & Taga, G. (2006). The right hemisphere of sleeping infant perceives sentential prosody. *Neuroscience Research, 54*, 276–280.

Hurford, J. R., Studdert-Kennedy, M., & Knight, C. (2001). *Approaches to the evolution of language*. Cambridge, UK: Cambridge University Press.

Jackendoff, R. (2003). *Foundations of language: Brain, meaning, grammar, evolution*. New York: Oxford University Press.

James, D. K., Spencer, C. J., & Stepsis, B. W. (2002). Fetal learning: A prospective randomized controlled study. *Ultrasound in Obstetrics and Gynecology, 20*, 431–438.

Jusczyk, P. W. (1999). Narrowing the distance to language: One step at a time. *Journal of Communication Disorders, 32*, 207–222.

Jusczyk, P. W., Hirsh-Pasek, K., Nelson, D. G., Kennedy, L. J., Woodward, A., & Piwoz, J. (1992). Perception of acoustic correlates of major phrasal units by young infants. *Cognitive Psychology, 24*, 252–293.

Jusczyk, P. W. & Krumhansl, C. L. (1993). Pitch and rhythmic patterns affecting infants' sensitivity to musical phrase structure. *Journal of Experimental Psychology: Human Perception & Performance, 19*, 627–640.

Kent, R. D. & Murray, A. D. (1982). Acoustic features of infant vocalic utterances at 3, 6, and 9 months. *Journal of the Acoustical Society of America, 72*, 353–365.

Key, C. & Aiello, L. C. (1999). The evolution of social organization. In R. Dunbar, C. Knight, & C. Power (Eds.), *The evolution of culture* (pp. 15–33). Edinburgh: Edinburgh University Press.

Kisilevsky, B. S., Hains, S. M., Lee, K., Xie, X., Huang, H., Ye, H. H., et al. (2003). Effects of experience on fetal voice recognition. *Psychological Science, 14*, 220–224.

Kisilevsky, B. S., Hains, S. M., Jacquet, A. Y., Granier-Deferre, C., & Lecanuet, J. P. (2004). Maturation of fetal responses to music. *Developmental Science, 7*, 550–559.

Koopmans-van Beinum, F. J. & van der Stelt, J. M. (1986). Early stages in the development of speech movements. In B. Lindblom & R. Zetterstrom (Eds.), *Precursors of early speech* (pp. 37–50). New York: Stockton.

Kuhl, P. K. (1991). Human adults and human infants show a "perceptual magnet effect" for the prototypes of speech categories, monkeys do not. *Perception and Psychophysics, 50*, 93–107.

Kuhl, P. K. & Meltzoff, A. N. (1984). The intermodal representation of speech in infants. *Infant Behavior and Development, 7*, 361–381.

Kuhl, P. K. & Meltzoff, A. N. (1996). Infant vocalizations in response to speech: Vocal imitation and development change. *Journal of the Acoustical Society of America, 100*, 2425–2438.

Kuhl, P. K., Stevens, E., Hayashi, T., Deguchi, T., Kiritani, S., & Iverson, P. (2006). Infants show a facilitation effect for native language phonetic perception between 6 and 12 months. *Developmental Science, 9*, F13–F21.

Kuhl, P. K., Williams, K. A., Lacerda, F., Stevens, K. N., & Lindblom, B. (1992). Linguistic experience alters phonetic perception in infants by 6 months of age. *Science, 255*, 606–608.

LaGasse, L. L., Neal, A. R., & Lester, B. M. (2005). Assessment of infant cry: Acoustic cry analysis and parental perception. *Mental Retardation and Developmental Disabilities Research Reviews, 11*, 83–93.

Lecanuet, J. P., Granier-Deferre, C., Jacquet, A. Y., Capponi, I., & Ledru, L. (1993). Prenatal discrimination of a male and a female voice uttering the same sentence. *Early Development and Parenting, 2*, 217–228.

Lecanuet, J. P., Granier-Deferre, C., Jacquet, A. Y., & DeCasper, A. (2000). Fetal discrimination of low-pitched musical notes. *Developmental Psychobiology, 36*, 29–39.

Levitin, D. J. (2007). *This is your brain on music: The science of a human obsession*. New York: PLUME.

Levitt, A. G. & Wang, Q. (1991). Evidence for language-specific rhythmic influences in the reduplicative babbling of French- and English-learning infants. *Language and Speech, 34* (Pt 3), 235–249.

Lewis, M. M. (1936). *Infant speech: A study of the beginnings of language*. London: Kegan Paul, Trench, Trubner & Co. Ltd.

Lieberman, P. (1972). *The speech of primates*. The Hague: Mouton.

Lieberman, P. (1973). On the evolution of language: A unified view. *Cognition, 2*, 59–94.

Lieberman, P. (1984). *The biology and evolution of language*. Cambridge, MA: The MIT Press.

Lieberman, P. (1985). The physiology of cry and speech in relation to linguistic behavior. In B. M. Lester & C. F. Z. Boukydis (Eds.), *Infant crying* (pp. 29–57). New York: Plenum.

Lieberman, P. (1991). *Uniquely human. The evolution of speech, thought, and selfless behaviour*. Cambridge, MA: Harvard University Press.

Lieberman, P. (1994). Functional tongues and Neanderthal vocal tract reconstruction: A reply to Dr. Houghton (1993). *American Journal of Physical Anthropology, 95*, 443–450.

Lieberman, P. (2007). Current views on Neanderthal speech capabilities: A reply to Boë et al. (2002). *Journal of Phonetics, 35*, 552–563.

Lieberman, P. & Crelin, E. S. (1971). On the speech of Neanderthal man. *Linguistic Inquiry, 2*, 203–222.

Lieberman, P., Harris, K. S., Wolff, P., & Russell, L. H. (1971). Newborn infant cry and nonhuman primate vocalization. *Journal of Speech and Hearing Research, 14*, 718–727.

Locke, J. L. (2001). Social sound-making as precursor to spoken language. In J.R. Hurford, M. Studdert-Kennedy, & C. Knight (Eds.), *Approaches to the evolution of language* (pp. 190–201). Cambridge, UK: Cambridge University Press.

MacNeilage, P. F. & Davis, B. L. (2000). Deriving speech from nonspeech: A view from ontogeny. *Phonetica, 57*, 284–296.

Maidment, J. A. (1983). Language recognition and prosody: Further evidence. *Speech, Hearing and Language: Work in Progress, 1*, 131–141.

Mampe, B., Friederici, A. D., Christophe, A., & Wermke, K. (2009). Newborns' cry melody is shaped by their native language. *Current Biology, 19*(23), 1994-1997.

Masataka, N. (1992). Pitch characteristics of Japanese maternal speech to infants. *Journal of Child Language, 19*, 213–223.

Masataka, N. (2008). *The onset of language*. Cambridge, UK: Cambridge University Press.

Maskarinec, A. S., Cairns, G. F., Jr., Butterfield, E. C., & Weamer, D. K. (1981). Longitudinal observations of individual infant's vocalizations. *Journal of Speech and Hearing Disorders, 46*, 267–273.

Mastropieri, D. & Turkewitz, G. (1999). Prenatal experience and neonatal responsiveness to vocal expressions of emotion. *Developmental Psychobiology, 35*, 204–214.

Maynard Smith, J. & Szathmáry, E. (2000). *The major transitions in evolution*. Oxford: Oxford University Press.

McCune, L., Vihman, M. M., Roug-Hellichius, L., Delery, D. B., & Gogate, L. (1996). Grunt communication in human infants (Homo sapiens). *Journal of Comparative Psychology*, *110*, 27–36.

Mehler, J., Jusczyk, P., Lambertz, G., Halsted, N., Bertoncini, J., & Miel-Tison, C. (1988). A precursor of language acquisition in young infants. *Cognition*, *29*, 143–178.

Mende, W., Wermke, K., Schindler, S., Wilzopolski, K. & Höck, S. (1990). Variability of the cry melody and the melody spectrum as indicators for certain CNS disorders. *Early Child Development and Care*, *65*, 95–107.

Michelsson, K. (1971). Cry analyses of symptomless low birth weight neonates and of asphyxiated newborn infants. *Acta Paediatrica Scandinavica Supplement*, *216*, 1–45.

Michelsson, K., Raes, J., & Rinne, A. (1984). Cry score—an aid in infant diagnosis. *Folia Phoniatrica*, *36*, 219–224.

Michelsson, K., Raes, J., Thoden, C. J., & Wasz-Höckert, O. (1982). Sound spectographic cry analysis in neonatal diagnostics: An evaluative study. *Journal of Phonetics*, *10*, 79–88.

Michelsson, K., Tuppurainen, N., & Aula, P. (1980). Sound spectographic analysis of infants with karyotype abnormality. *Neuropediatrics*, *11*, 365–376.

Mithen, S. (2006). *The singing Neanderthals. The origins of music, language, mind and body*. London: Phoenix.

Mithen, S. (2009). Holistic communication and the co-evolution of language and music; Resurrecting an old idea. In R. Botha & C. Knight (Eds.), *The prehistory of language: Studies in the evolution of language* (pp. 58–76). New York: Oxford University Press.

Moon, C., Panneton-Cooper, R., & Fifer, W. P. (1993). Two-day-olds prefer their native language. *Infant Behavior & Development*, *16*, 494–500.

Morgan, J. & Demuth, K. (1996). *Signal to syntax*. Mahwah: Erlbaum.

Morlet, T., Collet, L., Salle, B., & Morgon, A. (1993). Functional maturation of cochlear active mechanisms and of the medial olivocochlear system in humans. *Acta Oto-Laryngologica*, *113*, 271–277.

Morre, J. K., Perazzo, L. M., & Braun, A. (1995). Time-course of axonal myelination in the human brain-stem auditory pathway. *Hearing Research*, *87*, 21–31.

Murry, T. & Murry, J. (Eds.) (1980). *Infant communication. Cry and early speech*. Houston, Texas: College-Hill Press.

Nazzi, T., Bertoncini, J., & Mehler, J. (1998). Language discrimination by newborns: Toward an understanding of the role of rhythm. *Journal of Experimental Child Psychology*, *24*, 756–766.

Newman, J. D. (2007). Neural circuits underlying crying and cry responding in mammals. *Behavioral and Brain Research*, *182*, 155–165.

Newman, J. D. & Bachevalier, J. (1997). Neonatal ablations of the amygdala and inferior temporal cortex alter the vocal response to social separation in rhesus macaques. *Brain Research*, *758*, 180–186.

Ockleford, E. M., Vince, M. A., Layton, C., & Reader, M. R. (1988). Responses of neonates to parents' and others' voices. *Early Human Development*, *18*, 27–36.

Ohala, J. J. & Gilbert, J. B. (1981). Listeners' ability to identify languages by their prosody. In P. R. Léon & M. Rossi (Eds.), *Problème de prosodie, II, Expérimentations* (pp. 123–131). Ottawa: Didier.

Oller, D. K. (2000). *The emergence of the speech capacity*. Mahwah: Erlbaum.

Ostwald, P. F. (1973). Musical behavior in early childhood. *Developmental Medicine and Child Neurology*, *15*, 367–375.

Papoušek, M., Bornstein, M. H., Nuzzo, C., Papoušek, H., & Symmes, D. (1990). Infant responses to prototypical melodic contours in parental speech. *Infant Behaviour and Development*, *13*, 539–545.

Papoušek, M. & Papoušek, H. (1981). Musical elements in the infant's vocalization: Their significance for communication, cognition, and creativity. In L. P. Lipsitt (Ed.), *Advances in infancy research* (pp. 163–224). Norwood, N.J.: Ablex.

Papoušek, M. & Papoušek, H. (1987). Models and messages in the melodies of maternal speech in tonal and nontonal languages. In *Paper presented at the meeting of the Society for Research in Child Development, Baltimore, MD, April 1987*.

Papoušek, M., Papoušek, H., & Bornstein, M. H. (1985). The naturalistic vocal environment of young infants. On the significance of homogeneity and variability in parental speech. In T. Field & N. Fox (Eds.), *Social perception in infants* (pp. 269–297). Norwood, NJ: Ablex.

Papoušek, M., Papoušek, H., & Symmes, D. (1991). The meaning of melodies in motherese in tone and stress languages. *Infant Behavior and Development*, *14*, 415–440.

Piaget, J. & Inhelder, B. (1966). *La psychologie de l'enfant*. Paris: Presses Universitaires de France.

Pickett, J. M. (1999). *The acoustics of speech communication: Fundamentals, speech perception theory, and technology*. Boston: Allyn and Bacon.

Pinker, S. (1994). *The language instinct*. London: Penguin Books.

Ponton, C. W., Eggermont, J. J., Kwong, B., & Don, M. (2000). Maturation of human central auditory system activity: Evidence from multi-channel evoked potentials. *Clinical Neurophysiology*, *111*, 220–236.

Portmann, A. (1969). *Biologische Fragmente zu einer Lehre vom Menschen*. Basel: Schwabe.

Poulsen, C., Picton, T. W., & Paus, T. (2009). Age-related changes in transient and oscillatory brain responses to auditory stimulation during early adolescence. *Developmental Science*, *12*, 220–235.

Querleu, D., Lefebvre, C., Titran, M., Renard, X., Morillion, M., & Crepin, G. (1984). Reaction of the newborn infant less than 2 hours after birth to the maternal voice. *Journal de Gynécologie Obstrétique et Biologie de la Reproduction*, *13*, 125–134.

Querleu, D., Renard, X., Boutteville, C., & Crepin, G. (1989). Hearing by the human fetus? *Seminars in Perinatology*, *13*, 409–420.

Ramus, F., Hauser, M. D., Miller, C., Morris, D., & Mehler, J. (2000). Language discrimination by human newborns and by cotton-top tamarin monkeys. *Science*, *288*, 349–351.

Richards, D. S., Frentzen, B., Gerhardt, K. J., McCann, M. E., & Abrams, R. M. (1992). Sound levels in the human uterus. *Obstetrics & Gynecology*, *80*, 186–190.

Richman, B. (1987). Rhythm and melody in Gelada vocal exchanges. *Primates*, *28*, 199–223.

Riedl, R. (1975). *Die Ordnung des Lebendigen: Systembedingungen der Evolution*. Hamburg: Verlag Paul Parey.

Robb, M. P., Chen, Y., & Gilbert, H. R. (1997). Developmental aspects of formant frequency and bandwidths in infants and toddlers. *Folia Phoniatrica et Logopaedica*, *49*, 88–95.

Robb, M. P. & Saxman, J. H. (1990). Syllable durations of preword and early word vocalizations. *Journal of Speech and Hearing Research*, *33*, 583–593.

Roederer, J. G. (2008). *The physics and psychophysics of music*. (4th ed.) New York: Springer Verlag.

Rvachew, S., Mattock, K., Polka, L., & Menard, L. (2006). Developmental and cross-linguistic variation in the infant vowel space: The case of Canadian English and Canadian French. *Journal of the Acoustical Society of America, 120*, 2250–2259.

Saffran, J. R. (2003). Musical learning and language development. *Annals of the New York Academy of Sciences, 999*, 397–401.

Saito, Y., Aoyama, S., Kondo, T., Fukumoto, R., Konishi, N., Nakamura, K. et al. (2007). Frontal cerebral blood flow change associated with infant-directed speech. *Archives of Disease in Childhood. Fetal and Neonatal Edition, 92*, F113–F116.

Schlosser, G. (2004). The role of modules in development and evolution. In G. Schlosser & G. P. Wagner (Eds.), *Modularity in development and evolution* (pp. 519–582). Chicago: The University of Chicago Press.

Simpson, S. W., Quade, J., Levin, N. E., Butler, R., Dupont-Nivet, G., Everett, M. et al. (2008). A female Homo erectus pelvis from Gona, Ethiopia. *Science, 322*, 1089–1092.

Sirvio, P. & Michelsson, K. (1976). Sound-spectrographic cry analysis of normal and abnormal newborn infants: A review and a recommendation for standardization of the cry characteristics. *Folia Phoniatrica (Basel), 28*, 161–173.

Soltis, J. (2004). The signal functions of early infant crying. *Behavioral and Brain Sciences, 27*, 443–458.

Stark, R. E., Rose, S. N., & McLagen, M. (1975). Features of infant sounds: The first eight weeks of life. *Journal of Child Language, 2*, 205–221.

Stathopoulos, E. T. (1995). Variability revisited: An acoustic, aerodynamic, and respiratory kinematic comparison of children and adults during speech. *Journal of Phonetics, 23*, 67–80.

Stern, D. N., Spieker, S., Barnett, R. K., & MacKain, K. (1983). The prosody of maternal speech: Infant age and context related changes. *Journal of Child Language, 10*, 1–15.

Stewart, K. J. & Harcourt, A. H. (1994). Gorillas' vocalizations during rest periods: Signals of impending departure? *Behaviour, 130*, 29–40.

Tomasello, M. (1998). Reference: Intending that others jointly attend. *Pragmatics and Cognition, 6*, 229–243.

Trainor, L. J., Wu, L., & Tsang, C. D. (2004). Long-term memory for music: Infants remember tempo and timbre. *Developmental Science, 7*, 289–296.

Trehub, S. E. (1985). Auditory pattern perception in infancy. In S. E. Trehub & B. A. Schneider (Eds.), *Auditory development in infancy* (pp. 183–195). New York: Plenum.

Trehub, S. E. (1987). Infants' perception of musical patterns. *Perception & Psychophysics, 41*, 635–641.

Trehub, S. E. (1990). Human infants' perception of auditory patterns. *International Journal of Comparative Psychology, 4*, 91–110.

Trehub, S. E. (2000). Human processing predispositions and musical universals. In N. L. Wallin, B. Merker, & St. Brown (Eds.), *The origins of music* (pp. 271–300). Cambridge, MA: The MIT Press.

Trehub, S. E. (2001). Musical predispositions in infancy. *Annals of the New York Academy of Sciences, 930*, 1–16.

Trehub, S. E. (2003). The developmental origins of musicality. *Natural Neuroscience, 6*, 669–673.

Trehub, S. E. & Trainor, L. J. (1990). Rules for listening in infancy. In J. Enns (Ed.), *The development of attention: Research and theory* (pp. 87–119). Amsterdam: Elsevier.

Trevarthen, C. (1999). Musicality and the intrinsic motive pulse: Evidence from human psychobiology and infant communication. *Musicae Scientiae, Special Issue 1999–2000 on Rhythm*, Musical Narrative, and the Origins of Human Communication, 155–215.

Vorperian, H. K., Kent, R. D., Lindstrom, M. J., Kalina, C. M., Gentry, L. R., & Yandell, B. S. (2005). Development of vocal tract length during early childhood: A magnetic resonance imaging study. *Journal of the Acoustical Society of America, 117*, 338–350.

Wasz-Höckert, O., Lind, J., Vuorenkoski, V., Partanen, T., & Valanne, E. H. (1968). *The infant cry: A spectrographic and auditory analysis*. Lavenham: Spastics International Medical Publications.

Werker, J. F. & Tees, R. C. (1984). Cross-language speech perception: Evidence for perceptual reorganization during the first year of life. *Infant Behavior and Development, 7*, 49–63.

Wermke, K. (2002). *Untersuchung der Melodieentwicklung im Säuglingsschrei von monozygoten Zwillingen in den ersten 5 Lebensmonaten*. Habilitation, Humboldt-Universität zu Berlin, http://edoc.hu-berlin.de.

Wermke, K. & Friederici, A. D. (2004). Developmental changes of infant cries—the evolution of complex vocalizations. *Behavioral and Brain Sciences, 27*, 474–475.

Wermke, K. & Mende, W. (1994). Ontogenetic development of infant cry- and non-cry vocalization as early stages of speech abilities. In R. Aulanko & A. M. Korpijaakko-Huuhka (Eds.), *Third congress of the international clinical phonetics and linguistics association* (pp. 181–189). Helsinki/Finnland: Department of Phonetics, University of Helsinki.

Wermke, K. & Mende, W. (2006). Melody as a primordial legacy from early roots of language. *Behavioral and Brain Sciences, 29*, 300.

Wermke, K. & Mende, W. Musical elements in human infants' cries: In the beginning is the melody. In O. Vitouch & O. Ladinig (Eds.), *Musicae Scientiae, Special Issue 2009–2010 on Music and Evolution* (151–175).

Wermke, K., Mende, W., Borschberg, H., & Ruppert, R. (1996). Voice characteristics of prespeech vocalizations of twins during the first year of life. In T. W. Powell (Ed.), *Pathologies of speech & language: Contributions of clinical phonetics & linguistics* (pp. 1–8). New-Orleans, LA, ICPLA.

Wermke, K., Mende, W., Manfredi, C., & Bruscaglioni, P. (2002). Developmental aspects of infant's cry melody and formants. *Medical Engineering & Physics 24(7–8)*, 501–514.

Wermke, K., Leising, D., & Stellzig-Eisenhauer, A. (2007). Relation of melody complexity in infants' cries to language outcome in the second year of life: A longitudinal study. *Clinical Linguistics and Phonetics, 21*, 961–973.

Whalen, D. H., Levitt, A. G., & Wang, Q. (1991). Intonational differences between the reduplicative babbling of French- and English-learning infants. *Journal of Child Language, 18*, 501–516.

Wilshere, J. (2010). "Gardiner, William." In *Grove Music Online*. Oxford Music Online, http://www.oxfordmusiconline.com/subscriber/article/grove/music/10664 (accessed December 16, 2010).

Winkler, I., Haden, G. P., Ladinig, O., Sziller, I., & Honing, H. (2009). Newborn infants detect the beat in music. *Proceedings of the National Academy of Sciences of the United States of America, 106*, 2468–2471.

Wolff, P. (1987). *The development of behavioral states and the expression of emotions in early infancy: New proposals for investigation*. Chicago: The University of Chicago Press.

Social Mechanisms in Early Language Acquisition: Understanding Integrated Brain Systems Supporting Language

Patricia K. Kuhl

Abstract

This chapter advances a new hypothesis—that in the earliest phases of language acquisition, infants combine a powerful set of domain-general computational skills with their equally extraordinary social skills to "crack the speech code." Further, it is hypothesized that the social brain—in ways we have yet to understand—"gates" the computational mechanisms underlying learning in the domain of language. Four levels at which the gating mechanism might work are developed. It is argued that the assertion that social factors gate language learning explains not only how typically developing children acquire language, but also why children with autism exhibit twin deficits in social cognition and language, and why nonhuman animals with impressive computational abilities do not acquire language.

Keywords: language acquisition, infants, domain-general computational skills, social skills, social brain

The earliest phases of language acquisition invoke a special fascination because they allow us to examine humans' extraordinary abilities to acquire what is arguably our most unique skill—the ability to speak. Humans' capacity for speech and language provoked classic debates on nature versus nurture by equally strong proponents of nativism (Chomsky, 1959) and learning (Skinner, 1957) as the explanation for children's remarkable abilities. While we are far beyond those debates and now informed by a great deal of data about infants, their innate predispositions, and their incredible abilities to learn once exposed to natural language (Kuhl, 2009; Saffran, Werker, & Werner, 2006), we are still at ground zero with regard to the mechanisms of language acquisition in the brain and mind of a child.

In this chapter I will advance a new hypothesis—that in the earliest phases of language acquisition, infants combine a powerful set of domain-general computational skills with their equally extraordinary social skills to "crack the speech code." Further, I hypothesize that the social brain—in ways we have yet to understand—"gates" the computational mechanisms underlying learning in the domain of language. I will develop four levels at which the gating mechanism might work.

The assertion that social factors gate language learning, I argue, explains not only how typically developing children acquire language, but also why children with autism exhibit twin deficits in social cognition and language, and why nonhuman animals with impressive computational abilities do not acquire language. Moreover, this gating hypothesis may explain why social factors play a far more significant role than previously realized in human learning across domains throughout our lifetimes (Meltzoff, Kuhl, Movellan, & Sejnowski, 2009).

In the next decade, the methods of modern neuroscience will be used to explore how the integration of information across specialized brain systems such as language and social cognition take place, and this will advance our understanding of the potent role social interaction plays in language learning. These approaches, as well as others described here, will lead us towards a transformational view of language acquisition in the human child.

The Learning Problem

Speech learning is a deep puzzle that our theories and machines struggle to solve. How do infants discover the sounds and words used in their particular language(s) when the most sophisticated computers cannot? What is it about the human mind that allows the young child, merely a year old, to understand the words that induce meaning in our collective minds, and to begin to use those words to convey their innermost thoughts and desires? Children's ability to express a thought through words is a breathtaking feat of the human mind.

In explaining a new approach to this problem, I will focus on perception of the elementary units of language, the consonants and vowels that make up words, and children's early word recognition, to show how our computational and social skills combine to form a very powerful learning mechanism. Interestingly, the new solution does not resemble Skinner's operant conditioning and reinforcement model of learning, nor Chomsky's parameter setting, but rather a view of the process that takes into account new data on children's learning via computational and social means.

Language Exhibits a "Critical Period" for Learning

A stage-setting concept for human language learning is the graph shown in Figure 43.1, redrawn from a study by Johnson and Newport on English grammar in speakers of Korean learning English (1989). The graph as rendered shows a simplified schematic of second language learning as a function of age.

The graph is surprising from the standpoint of human learning more generally. In the domain of language, infants and young children are superior learners when compared to adults, in spite of adults' cognitive superiority. Language is one of the classic examples of a "critical" or "sensitive" period in neurobiology (Bruer, 2008; Johnson & Newport 1989; Knudsen, 2004; Kuhl, 2004; Newport, Bavelier, & Neville, 2001).

Scientists are in agreement that this curve represents data across a wide variety of language-learning studies (Bialystok & Hakuta, 1994;

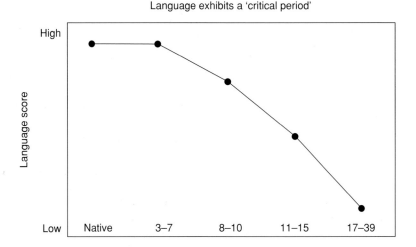

Fig. 43.1 The relationship between age of acquisition of a second language and language skill.
From Johnson and Newport (1989); reprinted with permission of Elsevier.

Birdsong & Molis 2001; Flege, Yeni-Komshian, & Liu, 1999; Johnson & Newport, 1989; Kuhl, Conboy, Padden, Nelson, & Pruitt, 2005; Kuhl et al., 2008; Maryberry & Locke, 2003; Neville et al., 1997; Newport & Supalla, 1987; Weber-Fox & Neville 1999; Yeni-Komshian, Flege, & Liu, 2000). The learning function describes our current understanding of second-language learning, though it is composed of many individual sensitive periods for phonological, semantic, and grammatical learning, over time. Given widespread agreement on the fact that we do not learn equally well over the lifespan, theory is currently focused on attempts to explain the phenomenon. What accounts for adults' inability to learn a new language with the facility of an infant?

One of the candidate explanations was Lenneberg's hypothesis that development of the corpus callosum changed the brain in a way that affected learning (Lenneberg, 1967; Newport et al., 2001). More recent hypotheses take a different perspective. Newport has raised the "less is more" hypothesis, which suggests that infants' limited cognitive capacities actually allow superior learning of the simplified language spoken to infants (Newport, 1990). Work in my laboratory has led me to advance the concept of *neural commitment*, the idea that the neural architecture is established early in infancy to detect the phonetic and prosodic patterns of speech (Kuhl, 2004; Zhang et al., 2005; Zhang et al., 2009). This architecture is designed to maximize processing for the language experienced by the infant. Once established, the neural architecture for French or Tagalog, for example, impedes learning of new patterns that do not conform. We will return to the concept of the critical period for language learning, and the role that computational and social skills may play in accounting for the relatively poor performance of adults attempting to learn a second language, later in this chapter.

Focal Example: Phoneme and Word Learning

The world's languages contain approximately 600 consonants and 200 vowels (Ladefoged, 2001). Each language uses a unique set of about 40 distinct elements, *phonemes*, which change the meaning of a word (e.g., from *bat* to *pat*). But phonemes are actually groups of nonidentical sounds, *phonetic units*, which are functionally equivalent in the language. The baby's task is to make some progress in figuring out the composition of the 40-odd phonemic categories before trying to acquire words

which depend on these elementary units. Japanese-learning infants have to group the phonetic units *r* and *l* into a single phonemic category (Japanese *r*), whereas English-learning infants must uphold the distinction to separate *rake* from *lake*. Similarly, Spanish-learning infants must distinguish phonetic units critical to Spanish words (*bano* and *pano*), whereas English-learning infants must combine them into a single category (English *b*). If infants were exposed only to the subset of phonetic units that will eventually be used phonemically to differentiate words in their language, the problem would be trivial. But infants are exposed to many more phonetic variants than will be used phonemically. Simple exposure to a category of sounds does not explain phonetic learning.

Learning to produce the sounds that will characterize infants as speakers of their "mother tongue" is equally challenging, and is not completely mastered until the age of 8 years (Ferguson, Menn, & Stoel-Gammon, 1992). Yet, by 10 months of age, differences can be discerned in the babbling of infants raised in different countries (de Boysson-Bardies, 1993), and in the laboratory, vocal imitation can be elicited by 20 weeks (Kuhl & Meltzoff, 1982). The speaking patterns we adopt early in life last a lifetime (Flege, 1991). My colleagues and I have suggested that this kind of indelible learning stems from a linkage between sensory and motor experience; sensory experience with a specific language establishes auditory patterns stored in memory that are unique to that language and these representations guide infants' successive motor approximations until a match is achieved (Kuhl & Meltzoff, 1996). The ability to imitate vocally may depend on the brain's social understanding mechanisms, those that form a human mirroring system for social understanding (Hari & Kujala, 2009), and we will revisit the brain's social understanding systems later in this chapter.

What enables the kind of learning we see in infants for speech? No machine in the world can derive the phonemic inventory of a language from natural language input (Rabiner & Huang, 1993), though models improve when exposed to "motherese," the linguistically simplified and acoustically exaggerated speech that adults universally use when speaking to infants (de Boer & Kuhl, 2003). The variability in speech input is simply too enormous; Japanese adults produce both English *r*- and *l*-like sounds, exposing Japanese infants to both sounds (Lotto, Sato, & Diehl, 2004; Werker, Pons, Dietrich, Kajikawa, Fais, & Amano, 2007). How do Japanese infants learn that these two sounds do not distinguish words, and that their differences should be ignored? Similarly, English speakers produce the Spanish *b* and *p*, exposing American infants to both categories of sound (Abramson & Lisker, 1970). How do infants learn that these sounds are not important in distinguishing words in English? An important discovery in the 1970s was that infants initially hear all these phonetic differences (Eimas, 1975; Eimas, Siqueland, Jusczyk, & Vigorito, 1971; Lasky, Syrdal-Lasky, & Klein, 1975; Werker & Lalonde, 1988). What we have to explain is how infants learn which phonetic categories make a difference in their language.

The Timing of Infant Learning

An important discovery in the 1980s identified the timing of the change in infant perception. The transition from an early universal perceptual ability for all languages to language-specific perception occurred very early in development—between 6 and 12 months of age (Werker & Tees, 1984). At this age, infants' perception of nonnative distinctions declines (Best & McRoberts, 2003; Rivera-Gaxiola, Silva-Pereyra, & Kuhl, 2005; Tsao, Liu, & Kuhl, 2006; Werker & Tees, 1984). Work in my laboratory also established a new fact: At the same time that nonnative perception declines, native language speech perception shows a significant increase. We showed that Japanese infants' discrimination of English *r-l* declined between 8 and 10 months of age, while at the same time in development, American infants' discrimination of the same sounds showed an increase (Kuhl et al., 2006) (Figure 43.2).

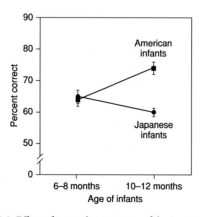

Fig. 43.2 Effects of age on discrimination of the American English /ra-la/ phonetic contrast by American and Japanese infants at 6–8 and 10–12 months of age. Mean percent correct scores are shown with standard errors indicated.
From Kuhl et al. (2006); reprinted with permission of John Wiley and Sons.

We argued that the increase observed in native-language phonetic perception represented a critical step in initial language learning (Kuhl et al., 2006; Kuhl et al., 2008). Many studies in our laboratory now show that native-language discrimination between 6 and 7 months predicts the rate of language growth between 11 and 30 months (Conboy, Rivera-Gaxiola, Klarman, Aksoylu, & Kuhl, 2005; Kuhl, Conboy, et al., 2005; Kuhl et al., 2008; Rivera-Gaxiola, Klarman, Garcia-Sierra, & Kuhl, 2005; Tsao, Liu, & Kuhl, 2004). Intriguingly, our data show that while better performance on *native* contrast discrimination predicts rapid growth in later language abilities, better performance on *non*native contrasts predicts slower language growth (Kuhl, Conboy, et al., 2005; Kuhl et al., 2008) (Figure 43.3). In other words, phonetic learning does not depend on auditory acuity, but something else. Based on these findings we argued that exposure to language commits the brain's neural circuitry to the properties of native-language speech, and that neural commitment has bi-directional effects—it increases learning for patterns (such as words) that are compatible with the learned phonetic structure, while decreasing perception of nonnative patterns that do not match the learned scheme (Kuhl, 2004).

A Computational Solution to Phonetic and Word Learning

Studies in the decade of the 1990s demonstrated that infants are capable of a surprising new form of learning, referred to as "statistical learning" (Saffran, Aslin, & Newport, 1996). Statistical learning is computational in nature, and reflects implicit rather than explicit learning. It relies on the ability to automatically pick up and learn from the statistical regularities that exist in the stream of sensory information we process, and both phonetic learning and early word learning have been shown to be strongly influenced by this form of learning.

Consider phonetic learning. What causes the developmental change in phonetic perception between the ages of 6 and 12 months? Recent studies show that infants analyze the statistical distributions of sounds that they hear in ambient language, and this affects perception. Although adult listeners hear /r/ and /l/ as either distinct (English speakers) or identical (Japanese), speakers of both languages produce highly variable sounds. Japanese adults produce both English r- and l-like sounds, so Japanese infants are exposed to both. Similarly, in Swedish there are 16 vowels, whereas English uses 10 and Japanese uses only 5, but speakers of these languages

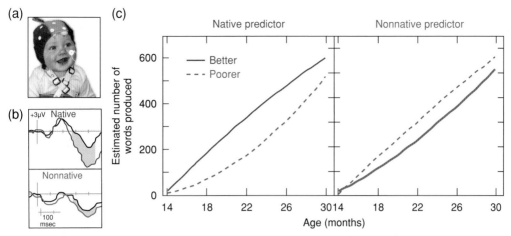

Fig. 43.3 (a) A 7.5-month-old infant wearing an ERP electrocap. (b) Infant ERP waveforms at one sensor location (CZ) for one infant are shown in response to a native (English) and nonnative (Mandarin) phonetic contrast at 7.5 months. The mismatch negativity (MMN) is obtained by subtracting the standard waveform (black) from the deviant waveform (English = red; Mandarin = blue). This infant's response suggests that native-language learning has begun because the MMN negativity in response to the native English contrast is considerably stronger than that to the nonnative contrast. (c) Hierarchical linear growth modeling of vocabulary growth between 14 and 30 months for MMN values of +1SD and −1SD on the native contrast at 7.5 months (c, left) and vocabulary growth for MMN values of +1SD and −1SD on the nonnative contrast at 7.5 months (c, right). Analyses show that both contrasts predict vocabulary growth but that the effects of better discrimination are reversed for the native and nonnative contrasts.
From Kuhl et al. (2008); reprinted with permission of Royal Society.

produce a wide range of sounds. The mere presence of a particular sound, therefore, does not account for infant learning, but the distributional patterns of such sounds differ across languages. In each language, distributional frequency is high for phonetic units at the center of phonemic categories, and low at the borders between categories. Distributional patterns of sounds thus provide clues about the phonemic structure of a language. If infants are sensitive to the relative distributional frequencies of phonetic segments in the language that they hear, this could explain native language phonetic learning.

Cross-cultural studies indicate that infants are sensitive to these statistical properties. Infants tested in Sweden and the United States at 6 months of age show a unique response to the "prototypical" vowels in their language—ones that are not only the distributional mean in productions of adults but the ones judged as perceptually preferred by adults; this response is not shown to foreign-language vowel prototypes (Kuhl, Williams, Lacerda, Stevens, & Lindblom, 1992). Moreover, when tested with very simple stimuli in the laboratory, infants can also learn from distributional patterns in language input after short-term exposure to phonetic stimuli (Maye, Werker, & Gerken, 2002). Six- and 8-month-old

infants were exposed for 2 minutes to 8 sounds that formed a series. They heard all the stimuli on the entire continuum, but experienced different distributional frequencies (Figure 43.4). A "bimodal" group heard more frequent presentations of stimuli at the ends of the continuum; a "unimodal" group heard more frequent presentations of stimuli from the middle of the continuum. After familiarization, infants in the bimodal group discriminated the two sounds, whereas those in the unimodal group did not.

Statistical learning also supports word learning. A previously unsolved problem in both human and machine language learning is how words are detected in the ongoing stream of speech. Unlike written language, spoken language has no reliable markers to indicate word boundaries in typical phrases. How do infants find words? New experiments show that before 8-month-old infants know the meaning of even a single word, they detect likely word candidates through sensitivity to the transitional probabilities between adjacent syllables. In typical words, like in the phrase, "pretty baby," the transitional probabilities between the two syllables within a word, such as those between "pre" and "tty," and those between "ba" and "by," are higher than those between syllables that cross word boundaries, such and "tty" and "ba."

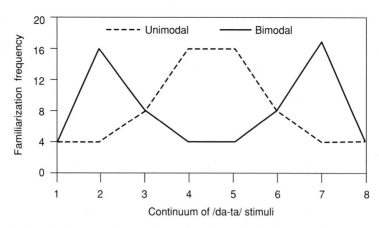

Fig. 43.4 Infants are familiarized for 2 min with a series of /da-ta/ stimuli, with higher frequencies of either stimuli 2 and 7 (bimodal group) or stimuli 4 and 5 (unimodal group). Only infants in the bimodal condition discriminated the /da-ta/ end-point stimuli.

From Maye et al. (2002); reprinted with permission of Elsevier.

Infants are sensitive to these probabilities. When exposed to a 2-min string of nonsense syllables, with no acoustic breaks or other cues to word boundaries, they treat syllables that have high transitional probabilities as "words" (Saffran et al., 1996). Statistical learning is not limited to humans (Hauser, Newport, & Aslin, 2001), nor to speech; it operates for musical and visual patterns in the same way (Fiser & Aslin, 2002; Kirkham, Slemmer, & Johnson, 2002; Saffran, Johnson, Aslin, & Newport, 1999).

Effects of Social Interaction on Computational Learning

Human infants have an intense social interest in people and their behavior, and the newly discovered statistical learning mechanisms, which provide powerful sources of leverage for early learning, appear to be strongly modulated by social interaction.

Demonstrations of statistical learning in the laboratory when infants are exposed to the speech material for only a few minutes, as well as demonstrations that the phenomenon was domain-general, suggested that statistical learning was an automatic process. However, recent studies done in this laboratory suggest that in complex natural language-learning situations social interaction may be necessary for learning. In other words, in natural language learning situations, there are constraints on infants' computational abilities.

The new experiments showing that social interaction is critical began with a simple question—can infants learn phonetically from first-time natural exposure to a foreign language at 9 months?

We wondered whether statistical learning at 9 months required a long-term history of listening to that language—we reasoned that infant learning at this age might depend on the build-up of statistical distributions over the initial 9 months of life. Alternatively, the transition might occur at 9 months because a learning process initially became available at that age.

We designed a foreign-language intervention to test whether learning the statistics of a new language would occur. Nine-month-old American infants listened to four different native speakers of Mandarin during 12 sessions scheduled over 4–5 weeks time. The foreign language "tutors" read books and played with toys in sessions that were unscripted. A control group was also exposed for 12 sessions but heard only English from native speakers. After infants in the experimental Mandarin exposure group and the English control group completed their sessions, all were tested with a Mandarin phonetic contrast that does not occur in English. Both behavioral and ERP methods were used. The results indicated that infants had a remarkable ability to learn from the live sessions—they performed significantly better on the Mandarin contrast when compared to the control group that heard only English. In fact, they performed equivalently to infants of the same age tested in Taiwan who had listened to the language for 10 months (Kuhl, Tsao, & Liu, 2003).

Learning was durable. Infants returned to the laboratory for their behavioral discrimination tests between 2 and 12 days after the final exposure session, with a median of 6 days, and for their ERP measurements between 8 and 33 days following the last exposure session, with a median of 15 days. These delays allowed us to examine whether longer periods between exposure and test resulted in poorer discrimination. A median-split approach was used to subdivide infants based on the median delay in days between exposure and test. The results indicated no significant differences between discrimination performance for infants above and below the median delay for either the behavioral or brain tests. No "forgetting" of the Mandarin contrast occurred during the 2 to 33 day delay.

Infants' remarkable learning led us to test two additional conditions. We were struck by the fact that infants exposed to Mandarin were socially very engaged in the language sessions. We began to wonder about the role of social interaction in learning, and what would happen if infants were exposed to the same information in the absence of a human being, say, via television or via an audiotape. The results of these tests were surprising. Infants exposed to the same foreign-language material, at the same time in development, and at the same rate, but via standard television or via audio-tape only, showed no learning—their performance equaled that of infants in the control group who had not been exposed to Mandarin at all (Figure 43.5).

Thus, the presence of a human being interacting with the infant during language exposure, while not required for simpler statistical-learning tasks

(a) Foreign-language exposure

(b) Mandrain Chinese phonetic discrimination

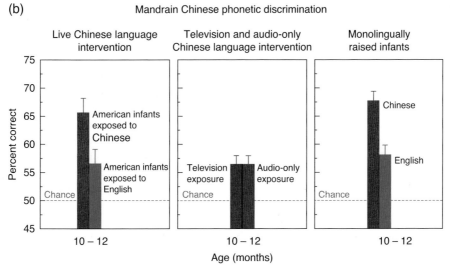

Fig. 43.5 The need for social interaction in language acquisition is shown by foreign-language learning experiments. Nine-month-old infants experienced 12 sessions of Mandarin Chinese through (a) natural interaction with a Chinese speaker (left) or the identical linguistic information delivered via television (right) or audiotape (not shown). (b) Natural interaction resulted in significant learning of Mandarin phonemes when compared with a control group who participated in interaction using English (left). No learning occurred from television or audiotaped presentations (middle). Data for age-matched Chinese and American infants learning their native languages are shown for comparison (right).
From Kuhl et al. (2003); adapted with permission of National Academy of Sciences, USA.

(Maye et al., 2002; Saffran et al., 1996), is critical for learning in complex natural language-learning situations in which infants heard, on average, 33,000 Mandarin syllables, from a total of four different talkers, over a 4–5-week period (Kuhl et al., 2003).

Explaining the Effect of Social Interaction on Language Learning

The 2003 (Kuhl et al., 2003) findings led us to develop a *social gating hypothesis* (Kuhl, 2007) that was in turn modified and expanded by interaction with an interdisciplinary group of scientists in the LIFE Center, an NSF Science of Learning Center. As expanded, the social gating hypothesis examines four concepts that may explain how social settings and interactions fundamentally alter language learning. The concepts revolve around mechanisms that support learning via: (1) attention, (2) information, (3) relationship, and/or (4) brain mechanisms linking perception and action.

The first, the *attention gate,* captures the idea that social contexts and interactions often increase arousal, and increased arousal can lead to increased attention, motivation, and encoding of content. Infant learning in the context of our "live" social exposure could be explained by increased attention and arousal produced by the social interaction. The second is the *intersubjective coordination gate*, and captures the idea that social learning is potent because of the close interaction between people which provides information that enhances learning. An example is joint visual attention—cued by gesture, bodily orientation, and speech—which signals adults' goals, intentions, desires, and emotions. These coordinated actions provide information that is not available in nonsocial learning settings. Infants' tracking of adults' eye movements could help parse speech. An adult's gaze toward a newly introduced toy, while simultaneously naming that toy, would indicate the correspondence between the object and its name. Thus, the "secret ingredient" provided by social interaction could go beyond arousal and reward and involve intersubjective coordination between people, and the information it provides in social settings.

The third concept is codified by the *sense of relationship gate*, which highlights the idea that a person's perception of self in relation to others can affect whether they learn. Infants in our social language learning experiment may require a social "tutor" that they perceive to be "like me" (Meltzoff, 2007). In this case learning may occur only from

other humans, or possibly from machines, such as robots, when they exhibit human-like social properties. Finally, a fourth option identifies something more fundamental as the explanation for the potent effects of social learning on language. The *socially adapted brain gate* describes the ways that human beings—who developed evolutionarily to learn from and adapt to others in their social group–are predisposed to place special value on human features (faces, voices), patterns of action (biological movement), and interactions (reciprocal exchanges and interactivity). The emerging field of social cognitive neuroscience is beginning to uncover the brain systems that underlie these preferences and more importantly the human brain systems linking social perception and action (Hari & Kujala, 2009). These brain systems, sometimes called shared representations or "mirroring systems" link what we see and hear others do in response to our own actions. These systems may underpin the parity between self and other that supports seamless interpersonal communication and reciprocity.

The four "gates" are not mutually exclusive. More than one could play a role in explaining the effects of a social other on early language learning. Empirical studies can identify whether a simpler more global mechanism, such as attention, is sufficient to explain these effects, or whether a more complex and fundamentally social system, such as the brain's evolved mechanisms for social interaction, are necessary. We have made some progress on elucidating these mechanisms in further experiments, as described below.

Attention and Arousal as a Mechanism

Attention and arousal affect learning in a wide variety of domains (Posner, 2004). Could they impact infant learning during exposure to a new language? Infant attention, measured in our studies, was significantly higher in response to the live person than to either inanimate source (Kuhl et al., 2003). Attention has been shown to play a role in the statistical learning studies as well. "High-attender" 10-month-olds learned from bimodal stimulus distributions when "low-attenders" did not (Yoshida, Pons, Cady, & Werker, 2006). Infant arousal, while not measured in our first tests, appeared to be enhanced in some conditions. Infants in the live exposure sessions were visibly aroused before the sessions—they watched the door expectantly, and were excited by the tutor's arrival, whereas infants in the nonsocial conditions did not. Heightened attention and arousal could produce an overall increase

Fig. 43.6 Infant interactions with a touch-screen TV result in contingent presentation of the Mandarin video clips.

in the quantity or quality of the speech information that infants encode and remember.

In recent tests we examined whether increasing infants' attention would result in learning from the same television presentations we used in the original study (Kuhl et al., 2003). The critical difference was that in these new tests, children's interactions with the TV screen resulted in contingent presentation of the Mandarin video clips (Figure 43.6). We used a touch-screen TV—in other words, the infants had control over the presentation of the language— turning it on with their own touch (Roseberry, Nash, Garcia-Sierra, & Kuhl, in preparation).

Preliminary results, measured using ERPs and the same Mandarin stimuli used in the original study, suggest that some learning does occur. This learning is not as robust as that produced during "live" exposure (Kuhl et al., 2003), but there is some evidence of learning. The group-level behavioral data do not show significant learning of the Mandarin contrast. However, the ERP data show evidence of discrimination at a left hemisphere electrode site (F7), indicating Mandarin sound discrimination after the interactive TV exposure (Roseberry, et al., in preparation). Interestingly, children's ERP responses are related to their vocalizations. Children who vocalize at the TV screen during the exposure sessions show increased negativity to Mandarin sounds at left hemisphere electrode sites. This link to vocalizations is of interest because in other work on infant word learning, infant vocalizations were linked to learning object-word correspondences, and vocalizations were interpreted as indicators of increased attention (Goldstein, Schwade, Briesch, & Syal, 2010). Our interactive TV experiment increases infants' attention—while everything else remains as it was in the original

Kuhl et al. (2003) study. The intermediate level of learning we observed may reflect the effects of attention. Interactive touch-screen TV increases infants' attention to the person on the screen and her toys, and we are currently hypothesizing that this prompts the infant to "test," through vocalizing at the screen, whether the person on the screen will react to them. Vocalizing may provide a way for infants to attempt to interact with the inanimate device.

Contingency plays a role in human vocalization learning (Bloom, 1975; Bloom & Esposito, 1975; Goldstein, King, & West, 2003), as well as in infant cognition more broadly (Watson, 1979, 2005). Interactivity, the reciprocity that is integral in social exchange, could therefore be a key component of early language learning in the experiments we have designed. Infants have a great deal of experience with people whose vocalizations are contingent on their own: Reciprocity in adult-infant language is common as infants alternate their vocalizations with those of an adult (Bloom, Russell, & Wassenberg, 1987), and the pervasive use of motherese by adults tends to encourage infant reciprocity (Kuhl & Meltzoff, 1982, 1996). Infants may have been "testing" the televised speaker by vocalizing, expecting reciprocity.

Intersubjective Coordination as a Mechanism

We raised a second hypothesis to explain the effectiveness of social interaction—our live learning situation allowed the infants and tutors to interact and this produced added information that could foster learning. During live exposure, tutors focus their visual gaze on pictures in the books or on the toys they talk about, and infants' gaze tends to follow the speaker's gaze (Baldwin, 1995; Brooks, & Meltzoff, 2002) beginning at this point in development. Referential information is present in both the live and televised conditions, but it is more difficult to pick up via television, and is totally absent during audio-only presentations. Gaze following is a significant predictor of receptive vocabulary (Baldwin, 1995; Brooks & Meltzoff, 2005; Mundy & Gomes, 1998), and may help infants segment foreign speech into word-like units that assist phonetic learning. When 9-month-old infants follow a tutor's line of regard in our foreign-language learning situation, the tutor's specific meaningful social cues, such as eye gaze and pointing to an object of reference, might help infants segment words from ongoing speech, thus facilitating phonetic learning of the sounds contained in those words.

Several key developments coincide with the ability to understand reference. By 9 months, infants begin to engage in triadic "person–person–object games"—they systematically combine attention to objects with looks that promote interest from another human, reflecting a "secondary intersubjectivity" (Trevarthen & Hubley, 1978). Shared perception of communicative intentions, which emerges at around 9 months of age, has been argued to be crucial for the acquisition of language (Akhtar & Tomasello, 1998; Tomasello, 2003a, 2003b). Attending to objects of another person's reference is linked to the infant's growing ability to understand others as intentional agents (Meltzoff, 1995; Tomasello, 2003a). The timing of these social abilities coincides with the beginnings of word comprehension. The suggestion here is that attunement to the communicative intentions of other humans enhances attention to linguistic units at several levels. Attunement to the meaning of a communicative act would be expected to enhance the uptake of units of language present in that act.

If this hypothesis is correct, then the degree to which infants in our social language-learning situation interact and engage socially with the tutor should correlate with learning. In studies testing this hypothesis, we exposed 9-month-old infants to Spanish. We wanted to extend our findings to a new language, and to examine both Spanish phonetic learning and Spanish lexical learning. To address the social question, we also designed the study to measure specific interactions between the tutor and the infant to examine whether specific kinds of interactive episodes could be related to learning of either phonemes or words.

The results confirmed Spanish learning, both of the phonetic units of the language (Conboy & Kuhl, 2010a) and the lexical units of the language (Conboy & Kuhl, 2010b). In addition, these studies answered a key question—does the degree of infants' social engagement during the Spanish exposure sessions predict the degree of language learning as shown by brain measures? Our results (Figure 43.7) show that they do (Conboy, Brooks, Meltzoff, & Kuhl, submitted; Stevens, Mehus, Mertl, Conboy, & Kuhl, submitted). Infants' eye-gaze data show that when the tutor introduced new toys, infants who shifted attention between the tutor and the toy learned more than infants who simply gazed at the tutor, or the toy.

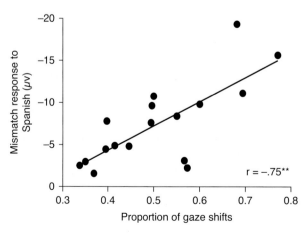

Fig. 43.7 ERP N250–450 effect (mismatch response) to Spanish phonetic contrast /d-t/, by proportion of gaze shifts during Spanish sessions.
From Conboy et al. (submitted).

A parallel set of ERP measures show that lexical learning also occurred from these Spanish exposure sessions. The ERP results show infants learned Spanish words that were presented during sessions, as opposed to those never presented, indicating that infants learned these new word patterns. The degree of infants' social engagement during sessions predicted word learning and the results mirror the phonetic findings—the more socially engaged the infant, the greater the word learning an infant showed (Conboy & Kuhl, 2010b).

There is evidence to suggest that cognitive (inhibitory) control is improved in bilingual speakers (Bialystok, 1999, 2001; Bialystok & Hakuta, 1994), and tests done both before and after the Spanish exposure sessions show an association between the degree of phonetic and/or word learning and infants' scores on tests of inhibitory control (Conboy, Sommerville, & Kuhl, in preparation). Infants who show greater learning from Spanish exposure show higher skill on tests of inhibitory control after, but not before, Spanish exposure. These results suggest that even short-term second-language exposure *may* play some role in enhancing inhibitory control skills (Conboy et al., in preparation), a finding consistent with those showing higher inhibitory control skills in bilingual adults (Bialystok, 1999, 2001; Bialystok & Hakuta, 1994).

Finally, the findings on Spanish exposure were extended to speech production and show that infants' exposure to Spanish affects their speech production as well their speech perception skills (Ward, Sundara, Conboy, & Kuhl, 2009). Infants exposed to 12 sessions of Spanish showed changes in their patterns of vocalization. After Spanish exposure, infants' vocalizations change to reflect the prosodic patterns of Spanish that are not characteristic of English when listening to a Spanish speaker but not when listening to an English speaker. This does not occur before exposure to Spanish in the laboratory or in infants who did not experience the 12-session Spanish exposure. Infants' learning from perceptual experience extends to the motor system.

The Spanish exposure experiments provide strong support for the idea that social interactivity and engagement plays an important role in initial language learning. The fact that social engagement promotes word learning has been shown in previous studies (Baldwin, 1995; Brooks & Meltzoff, 2005), but this effect has not previously been shown for phonetic learning. The findings suggest a more fundamental role for social interaction in language learning, one more akin to that seen in social learning in birds, in which conspecific song learning occurs only when engaged socially with tutor birds (Woolley & Doupe, 2008).

A Sense of Relationship as a Mechanism

The finding that social interaction is critical to learning raise a more fundamental question: What defines a "social agent" for infants? Must a social agent involve a human being (with sight, smell, and all other indicators of humanness), or would an inanimate entity, imbued with certain interactive features, induce infant perception of a social being? And if so, could infants learn language from such a socially augmented entity? Social interaction might be effective *because* it involves other humans, or because features inherent in social settings, such as interactivity and contingency, are critical for learning.

In another set of studies, we took a different approach to address the question. The interactive television experiment made only one change from the original television condition tested in Kuhl et al. (2003). Infants had control over the TV presentation, using a touchscreen to provide a contingent presentation of Mandarin. Using a different approach, we tested a more "human-like" machine, one that delivered contingencies automatically, and had certain key characteristics of a human actor.

We examined 18–24-month-old children's learning from a foreign language (Finnish) via a "social robot." The robot interacts with the children in a daycare setting by (1) orienting its head to them when they hand the robot a toy, (2) naming the toy in Finnish in a sentence context, and (3) taking the toy from the child using its pincer (Tanaka, Cicourel, & Movellan, 2007). Learning was assessed using a pre- and post-test examining children's knowledge of 10 Finnish words, with 10 English words used as controls. At the group level, English word learning did not change over the 2-week period of the intervention, while Finnish word learning increased significantly (Figure 43.8). Of most interest were the individual differences. Excellent learning was shown in some of the children, but not in all of them. Some children learned all of the 10 Finnish words and repeated these new words throughout the day in the daycare setting, as reported by the teachers. Supporting our hypothesis, learning was greatest in children who had the most sustained interaction with the robot during the learning episodes. This sustained interaction appears to be more important than overall time spent in interacting with the robot. During sustained periods of interaction, young children engage at different levels

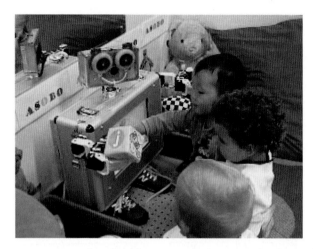

Fig. 43.8 A social robot can operate autonomously with children in a preschool setting. In this photo, toddlers play a game with the robot. One long-term goal is to engineer systems that test whether young children can learn a foreign language through interactions with a talking robot.

with the robot, and analyses of these data are continuing.

Socially Adapted Brain as a Mechanism

While attention, intersubjective coordination, and a sense of relationship may help explain our social language learning effects, it is also possible that social contexts are connected to language through more fundamental mechanisms. Social interaction may activate brain mechanisms of social understanding that link perception and action (Hari & Kujala, 2009). Neuroscience research focused on shared neural systems for perception and action have a long tradition in speech, and interest in "mirror systems" for social cognition (Kuhl, 2007; Kuhl & Meltzoff, 1996; Meltzoff & Decety, 2003; Pulvermuller, 2005; Rizzolatti, 2005; Rizzolatti & Craighero, 2004) have re-invigorated this tradition. Might the brain systems that link perception and production for speech be engaged when infants experience social interaction during language learning?

The theoretical linkage between perception and action in speech began with the motor theory (Liberman, Cooper, Shankweiler, & Studdert-Kennedy, 1967) and direct realism (Fowler, 1986), both of which posited that the mechanisms of speech production are involved in speech perception. The discovery of "mirror neurons" in monkeys that react both to the sight of others' actions and the same actions produced by themselves (Gallese 2003; Rizzolatti, Fadiga, Gallese, & Fogassi, 1996; Rizzolatti, Fogassi, & Gallese, 2002) rekindled interest in a potential mirror system for speech, as has work on the origins of infant imitation (Meltzoff & Moore, 1997). The perception-action link for speech has been viewed as potentially innate (Liberman & Mattingly, 1985) and also viewed as forged early in development through experience (Kuhl & Meltzoff, 1982, 1996).

Neuroscience studies using speech and imaging techniques have the capacity to examine whether the brain systems involved in speech production are activated when infants listen to speech. Two new infant studies take a first step towards an answer to this developmental issue. Imada et al. (2006) used magnetoencephalography (MEG) to study newborns, 6-month-old infants, and 12-month-old infants while they listened to nonspeech, harmonics and syllables (Figure 43.9). Dehaene-Lambertz, Hertz-Pannier, Dubois, Meriaux, and Roche (2006) used fMRI to scan 3-month-old infants while they listened to sentences. Both studies show activation in brain areas responsible for speech production (the inferior frontal, Broca's area) in response to auditorally presented speech. Imada et al. reported synchronized activation in response to speech in auditory and motor areas at 6 and 12 months, and Dehaene et al. reported activation in motor speech areas in response to sentences in 3-month olds. Is activation of Broca's area to the pure perception of speech present at birth? Newborns tested by Imada et al. showed no activation in motor speech areas for any signals, whereas auditory areas responded robustly to all signals, suggesting the possibility that perception-action linkages for speech develop by 3 months of age as infants produce vowel-like sounds. Further work must be done to answer the

AUDITORY (Superior temporal) WERNICKE'S AREA

Newborns   6-month-olds   12-month-olds

MOTOR (Inferior frontal) BROCA'S AREA

1 2 3 4 5 6   (Z score relative to 100 to 0 ms baseline)

Fig. 43.9 (top) Neuromagnetic signals were recorded in newborns, 6-month-old (shown) and 12-month-old infants in the MEG machine while listening to speech and nonspeech auditory signals. (bottom) Brain activation in response to speech recorded in auditory (top row) and motor (bottom row) brain regions showed no activation in the motor speech areas in the newborn in response to auditory speech, but increasing activity that was temporally synchronized between the auditory and motor brain regions was observed in 6- and 12-month-old infants when listening to speech.
From Imada et al. (2006); reprinted with permission of Wolters Kluwer Health.

question—whether binding of perception and action requires experience with the language, or is activated by speech with or without experience. This is one of the exciting questions that can now be addressed. Using the tools of modern neuroscience, we can now ask how the brain systems responsible for speech perception and speech production forge links in early development, and if these same brain areas are involved when language is presented socially, but not when language is presented through a disembodied source such as a television set.

Implications for Children with Autism Spectrum Disorder (ASD)

Scientific discoveries on the progression toward language by typically developing children are providing new insights into the language deficit shown by children with autism spectrum disorder (ASD). Neural measures of language processing in children with autism, involving both phonemes and words, when coupled with measures of social interest in speech in children with ASD, are revealing a tight coupling between social interaction skills and language acquisition. These measures hold promise as potential diagnostic markers of risk for autism in very young children, and therefore there is a great deal of excitement surrounding the application of these basic measures of speech processing as potential biomarkers in very young children with autism.

In typically developing children, behavioral and/or brain responses to a change in speech predicts the growth of language to the age of 30 months (Kuhl et al., 2008; Rivera-Gaxiola, Klarman, et al., 2005). We are therefore interested in the degree to which ERP measures of phonetic processing are sensitive to the degree of severity of autism, and also the degree to which the brain's responses to syllables can be predicted by other factors, such as a social interest in speech.

We examined phonetic perception in preschool-age children with ASD (Kuhl, Coffey-Corina, Padden, & Dawson, 2005), using ERPs to measure responses to a simple change in two speech syllables. A measure of the children's social interest in speech was also taken. The social measure was a listening choice that allowed children with autism to select between listening to "motherese" or an acoustically matched nonspeech signal. Motherese is a social signal that typical infants prefer when given a choice between infant-directed and adult-directed speech (Fernald & Kuhl, 1987; Grieser & Kuhl, 1988), and the phonetic units in motherese are acoustically stretched (Kuhl et al., 1997), a feature of maternal speech that can be linked to infants' performance on tests of phonetic perception (Liu, Kuhl, & Tsao, 2003).

In the tests on children with autism and typical controls, the nonspeech signal was created by replacing the formant frequencies of speech with pure tones at the same frequencies. The resulting signal was a computer warble that followed exactly the frequencies and amplitudes of the 5-second speech samples over time. Slight head turns to one direction versus the other allowed the children to choose their preferred signal on each trial. Our goal was to compare performance at the group level between typically developing children and children with ASD, as well as to examine the relationship between brain measures of speech perception and measures of social processing of speech in children with ASD.

The ERP measures of phonetic perception showed that, as a group, children with ASD did not exhibit the mismatched negativity (MMN) that marks discrimination of the simple change in syllables. However, when children with ASD were sub-grouped on the basis of their preference for motherese, very different results were obtained. Children with ASD who preferred motherese produced MMN responses that resembled those of typically developing children, whereas those who preferred the non-speech analog did not show an MMN response to the change in a speech syllable.

The results of auditory preference testing showed that while typically developing children listen to both motherese and non-speech analog signals, children with autism strongly preferred the non-speech analog signals. Moreover, the degree to which they did so was significantly correlated with both the severity of autism symptoms (see Figure 43.10) and MMN responses to speech syllables.

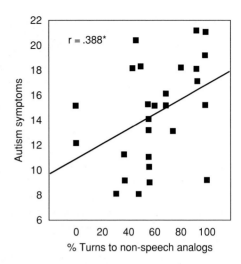

Fig. 43.10 Children with ASD: scatter plots relating autism symptoms (ADOS social-communication total) and percent head-turns to non-speech analogs (r_s = .388, p = .037, n = 29). From Kuhl, Coffey-Corina, et al. (2005); reprinted with permission of John Wiley and Sons.

These results underscore the importance of a social interest in speech early in development, especially an interest in motherese. The acoustic stretching in motherese makes phonetic units more distinct from one another (Burnham, Kitamura, & Vollmer-Conna, 2002; Englund, 2005; Kuhl et al., 1997; Liu et al, 2003; Liu, Tsao, & Kuhl, 2007). Mothers who use the exaggerated phonetic patterns to a greater extent when talking to their typically developing 2-month-old infants have infants who, months later in the laboratory, show significantly better performance in phonetic discrimination tasks (Liu et al., 2003). New data show that the potential benefits of early motherese extend to the age of 5 years (Liu, Tsao, & Kuhl, submitted). In the absence of a listening preference for motherese, children with autism would miss the benefit these exaggerated phonetic cues provide.

Infant-directed speech also produces unique brain responses in typically developing infants. Brain measures of typical infants' response to infant-directed speech, used by Pena et al. (2003) in the first study using near infrared spectroscopy (NIRS), showed more activation in left temporal areas when infants were presented with infant-directed speech as opposed to backward speech or silence. Bortfeld, Wruck, and Boas (2007) obtained analogous results using NIRS in a sample of 6–9-month-old infants presented with infant-directed speech and visual stimulation. It would be of interest to examine brain activation while children with autism listen to motherese as opposed to acoustically matched nonspeech signals. In children with ASD, brain activation to carefully controlled speech versus non-speech signals may provide clues to these children's aversion to highly intonated speech signals typical of motherese.

Neurobiological Foundations of Social Learning

Humans are not the only species in which communicative learning is affected by social interaction. Communicative learning in songbirds provides an example. Young zebra finches need visual interaction with a tutor bird to learn song in the laboratory (Eales, 1989). A zebra finch will override its innate preference for conspecific song if a Bengalese finch foster father feeds it, even when adult zebra finch males can be heard nearby (Immelmann, 1969). White-crowned sparrows, which reject the audio-taped songs of alien species, learn the same alien songs when a live tutor sings them (Baptista & Petrinovich, 1986). In barn owls (Brainard & Knudsen, 1998) and white-crowned sparrows (Baptista & Petrinovich, 1986), a richer social environment extends the duration of the sensitive period for learning. Social contexts also advance song production in birds; male cowbirds respond to the social gestures and displays of females, which affect the rate, quality, and retention of song elements in their repertoires (West & King, 1988), and white-crowned sparrow tutors provide acoustic feedback that affects the repertoires of young birds (Nelson & Marler, 1994).

In birds, social interaction can take various forms. Blindfolded zebra finches that cannot see the tutor, but can interact through pecking and grooming, learn their songs. And young birds operantly conditioned to present conspecific song to themselves by pressing a key learn the songs they hear (Adret, 1993; Tchernichovski, Mitra, Lints, & Nottebohm, 2001). In other words, in birds, interactivity and contingency play critical roles even in the absence of another bird.

Neural Underpinnings of Social Influences on Language Learning

Language evolved to address a need for social communication and evolution may have forged a link between language and the social brain in humans (Adolphs, 2003; Dunbar, 1998; Pulvermuller, 2005). Work on mirror neurons in nonhuman primates indicates a neural link between the self and other; seeing an action and producing it oneself are neurally equivalent in adult monkeys, and shared neural systems for action and perception assist imitation and social understanding (Meltzoff & Decety, 2003; Rizzolatti, 2005). Research on the development of the neural networks that constitute the "social brain" is beginning to appear (Hari & Kujala, 2009).

The fact that MEG has now been demonstrated to be feasible for developmental studies of speech perception in infants during the first year of life (Imada et al., 2006) opens up new possibilities for examining shared brain systems for action and perception involving speech in infancy. Examining brain activation using MEG with infants during social versus nonsocial language experience will allow us to test whether shared brain networks are activated differentially in the two conditions.

If social factors "gate" computational learning, infants would be protected from meaningless calculations—learning would be restricted to signals that derive from humans (or close facsimiles) rather than other sources (Doupe & Kuhl, 1999; Evans & Marler, 1995; Marler, 1991). Constraints of this kind appear to exist for infant imitation: When infants hear sounds that resemble vowels, but ones that could not be produced by human vocal tracts, they fail to imitate (Kuhl, Williams, & Meltzoff, 1991), and in action imitation experiments, infants infer and reproduce intentions displayed by humans but not by machines (Meltzoff, 1995). Our current experiments with social robots will explore the extent to which children will treat a social robot as a social agent. The data establish an interesting set of boundary conditions for language: Exposure to a new language in a live social interaction situation induces remarkable learning in 9-month-old infants, but *no* learning when the exact same language material is presented to infants by a disembodied source. We now are exploring various mechanisms that may explain this dramatic difference: attention, interactive coordination that enhances information, a sense of relationship, and evolution of a socially adapted brain.

Many questions remain about the impact of social interaction on natural speech and language learning. The idea that social interaction is integral to language learning is admittedly not entirely new because it has been linked by many to word learning; however, and importantly, previous data and theorizing have not tied early *phonetic* learning to social factors, and doing so suggests a more fundamental connection between the motivation to learn socially and the mechanisms that enable language learning. Moreover, linking early speech acquisition to social cognition places human communication solidly within the neurobiology of communication learning in nonhuman animals. Neuroscience studies over the next decade will help advance our understanding of how brain systems underlying language and social cognition interact during the earliest phases of language learning.

Acknowledgments

The author and research were supported by a grant from the National Science Foundation's Science of Learning Program to the LIFE Center (SBE-0354453), and by grants from the National Institutes of Health (HD37954, HD55782, HD02274, DC04661).

References

Abramson, A. S. & Lisker, L. (1970). Discriminability along the voicing continuum: Cross-language tests. *Proceedings of the Sixth International Conference of Phonetic Sciences in Prague* (pp. 569–573). Prague: Academia.

Adolphs, R. (2003). Cognitive neurosciences of human social behavior. *Nature Reviews Neuroscience, 4*, 165–178.

Adret, P. (1993). Operant conditioning, song learning and imprinting to taped song in the zebra finch. *Animal Behavior, 46*, 149–159.

Akhtar, N. & Tomasello, M. (1998). Intersubjectivity in early language learning and use. In S. Bråten (Ed.), *Intersubjective communication and emotion in early ontogeny* (pp. 316–335). Cambridge: Cambridge University Press.

Baldwin, D. A. (1995). Understanding the link between joint attention and language. In C. Moore & P. J. Dunham (Eds.), *Joint attention: Its origins and role in development* (pp. 131–158). Hillsdale, NJ: Lawrence Erlbaum Associates.

Baptista, L. F. & Petrinovich, L. (1986). Song development in the white-crowned sparrow: Social factors and sex differences. *Animal Behavior, 34*, 1359–1371.

Best, C. & McRoberts, G. W. (2003). Infant perception of nonnative consonant contrasts that adults assimilate in different ways. *Language and Speech, 46*, 183–216.

Bialystok, E. (1999). Cognitive complexity and attentional control in the bilingual mind. *Child Development, 70*, 636–644.

Bialystok, E. (2001). *Bilingualism in development: Language, literacy, and cognition.* New York, NY: Cambridge University Press.

Bialystok, E. & Hakuta, K. (1994). *In other words: The science and psychology of second-language acquisition.* New York, NY: Basic Books.

Birdsong, D. & Molis, M. (2001). On the evidence for maturational constraints in second-language acquisitions. *Journal of Memory and Language, 44*, 235–249.

Bloom, K. (1975). Social elicitation of infant vocal behavior. *Journal of Experimental Child Psychology, 20*, 51–58.

Bloom, K. & Esposito, A. (1975). Social conditioning and its proper control procedures. *Journal of Experimental Child Psychology, 19*, 209–222.

Bloom, K., Russell, A., & Wassenberg, K. (1987). Turn taking affects the quality of infant vocalizations. *Journal of Child Language, 14*, 211–227.

de Boer, B. & Kuhl, P.K. (2003). Investigating the role of infant-directed speech with a computer model. *Acoustic Research Letters Online (ARLO), 4*, 129–134.

Bortfeld, H., Wruck, E., & Boas, D. A. (2007). Assessing infants' cortical response to speech using near-infrared spectroscopy. *NeuroImage, 34*, 407–415.

de Boysson-Bardies, B. (1993). Ontogeny of language-specific syllabic productions. In B. de Boysson-Bardies, S. de Schonen, P. Jusczyk, P. McNeilage, & J. Morton (Eds.), *Developmental neurocognition: Speech and face processing in the first year of life* (pp. 353–363). Dordrecht, Netherlands: Kluwer.

Brainard, M. S. & Knudsen, E. I. (1998). Sensitive periods for visual calibration of the auditory space map in the barn owl optic tectum. *The Journal of Neuroscience, 18*, 3929–3942.

Brooks, R. & Meltzoff, A. N. (2002). The importance of eyes: How infants interpret adult looking behavior. *Developmental Psychology, 38*, 958–966.

Brooks, R. & Meltzoff, A. N. (2005). The development of gaze following and its relation to language. *Developmental Science, 8*, 535–543.

Bruer, J. T. (2008). Critical periods in second language learning: Distinguishing phenomena from explanation. In M. Mody and E. Silliman (Eds.), *Brain, behavior and learning in language and reading disorders* (pp72–96). New York: The Guilford Press.

Burnham, D., Kitamura, C., & Vollmer-Conner, U. (2002). What's new pussycat? On talking to babies and animals. *Science, 296*, 1435–1435.

Chomsky, N. (1959). A review of B. F. Skinner's "Verbal Behavior". *Language, 35*, 26–58.

Conboy, B. T. & Kuhl, P. K. (2010a). Impact of second-language experience in infancy: Brain measures of first- and second-language speech perception. *Developmental Science, 1–7.* Advance online publication. doi:10.1111/j.1467-7687.2010.00973x.

Conboy, B. T. & Kuhl, P. K. (2010b). Brain responses to words in 11-month-old infants after exposure to a second language. Paper presented at the American Speech, Language, and Hearing Association Convention, Philadelphia, PA, 18–20 November.

Conboy, B. T., Brooks, R., Meltzoff, A. N., & Kuhl, P. K. (submitted). Infants' social behaviors during exposure to a second language predict phonetic learning in that language.

Conboy, B., Rivera-Gaxiola, M., Klarman, L., Aksoylu, E., & Kuhl, P. K. (2005). Associations between native and nonnative speech sound discrimination and language development at the end of the first year. In A. Brugos, M. R. Clark-Cotton, & S. Ha (Eds.), *Supplement to the Proceedings of the 29th Boston University Conference on Language Development*; http://www.bu.edu/linguistics/APPLIED/BUCLD/supp29.html.

Conboy, B., Sommerville, J., & Kuhl, P. K. (in preparation). Infants' phonetic second-language learning is linked to executive control.

Dehaene-Lambertz, G., Hertz-Pannier, L., Dubois, J., Meriaux, S., & Roche, A. (2006). Functional organization of perisylvian activation during presentation of sentences in preverbal infants. *Proceedings of the National Academy of Sciences 103*, 14240–14245.

Doupe, A. J. & Kuhl, P. K. (1999). Birdsong and human speech: Common themes and mechanisms. *Annual Review of Neuroscience, 22*, 567–631.

Dunbar, R. J. M. (1998). The social brain hypothesis. *Evolutionary Anthropology, 6*, 178–190.

Eales, L. (1989). The influences of visual and vocal interaction on song learning in zebra finches. *Animal Behavior, 37*, 507–508.

Eimas, P. D. (1975). Auditory and phonetic coding of the cues for speech: Discrimination of the /r–l/ distinction by young infants. *Perception and Psychophysics, 18*, 341–347.

Eimas, P. D., Siqueland, E. R., Jusczyk, P., & Vigorito, J. (1971). Speech perception in infants. *Science, 171*, 303–306.

Englund, K. T. (2005). Voice onset time in infant directed speech over the first six months. *First Language, 25*, 219–234.

Evans, C. S. & Marler, P. (1995). Language and animal communication: Parallels and contrasts. In H. L. Roitblat & J. -A. Meyer (Eds.), *Comparative approaches to cognitive science: Complex adaptive systems* (pp. 341–382). Cambridge, MA: MIT Press.

Ferguson, C. A., L. Menn, & C. Stoel-Gammon. (Eds.) (1992). *Phonological development: Models, research, implications.* Timonium, MD: York Press.

Fernald, C. A. & Kuhl, P. K. (1987). Acoustic determinants of infant preference for motherese speech. *Infant Behavior and Development, 10*, 279–293.

Fiser, J. & Aslin, R. N. (2002). Statistical learning of new visual feature combinations by infants. *Proceedings of the National Academy of Science, USA, 99*, 15822–15826.

Flege, J. E. (1991). Age of learning affects the authenticity of voice-onset time (VOT) in stop consonants produced in a second language. *Journal of the Acoustical Society of America, 89*, 395–411.

Flege, J. E., Yeni-Komshian, G. H., & Liu, S. (1999). Age constraints on second-language acquisition. *Journal of Memory and Language, 41*, 78–104.

Fowler, C. A. (1986). An event approach to the study of speech perception from a direct-realist perspective. *Journal of Phonetics, 14*, 3–28.

Gallese, V. (2003). The manifold nature of interpersonal relations: The quest for a common mechanism. *Philosophical Transactions of the Royal Society B, 358*, 517–528.

Goldstein, M. H., King, A. P., & West, M. J. (2003). Social interaction shapes babbling: Testing parallels between birdsong and speech. *Proceedings of the National Academy of Sciences, 100*, 830–835.

Goldstein, M. H., Schwade, J., Briesch, J., & Syal, S. (2010). Learning while babbling: Prelinguistic object-directed vocalizations indicate a readiness to learn. *Infancy*, 1–30. Retrieved February 1, 2010 from http://www3.interscience.wiley.com/cgi-bin/fulltext/123237333/HTMLSTART.

Greiser, D. L. & Kuhl, P. K. (1988). Maternal speech to infants in a tonal language: Support for universal prosodic features in motherese. *Developmental Psychology, 24*, 14–20.

Hari, R. & Kujala, M. (2009). Brain basis of human social interaction: From concepts to brain imaging. *Physiological Reviews, 89*, 453–479.

Hauser, M. D., Newport, E. L., & Aslin, R. N. (2001). Segmentation of the speech stream in a nonhuman primate: Statistical learning in cotton-top tamarins. *Cognition, 78*, B53–B64.

Imada, T., Zhang, Y., Cheour, M., Taulu, S., Ahonen, A., & Kuhl, P. K. (2006). Infant speech perception activates Broca's area: A developmental magnetoenceohalography study. *NeuroReport, 17*, 957–962.

Immelmann, K. (1969). Song development in the zebra finch and other estrildid finches. In R. Hinde (Ed.), *Bird vocalizations* (pp. 61–74). London: Cambridge University Press.

Johnson, J. & Newport, E. (1989) Critical period effects in second language learning: The influence of maturation state on the acquisition of English as a second language. *Cognitive Psychology, 21*, 60–99.

Kirkham, N. Z., Slemmer, J. A., & Johnson, S. P. (2002). Visual statistical learning in infancy: Evidence for a domain general learning mechanism. *Cognition, 83*, B35–B42.

Knudsen, E. I. (2004). Sensitive periods in the development of the brain and behavior. *Journal of Cognitive Neuroscience, 16*, 1412–1225.

Kuhl, P. K. (2004). Early language acquisition: Cracking the speech code. *Nature Reviews Neuroscience, 5*, 831–843.

Kuhl, P. K. (2007). Is speech learning "gated" by the social brain? *Developmental Science, 10*, 110–120.

Kuhl, P. K. (2009). Early language acquisition: Neural substrates and theoretical models. In M. S. Gazzaniga (Ed.), *The cognitive neurosciences, 4th Edition* (pp. 837–854). Cambridge, MA: MIT Press.

Kuhl, P. K. (2009). Early language acquisition: Phonetic and word learning, neural substrates, and theoretical model. In B. C. Moore, L. K. Tyler, & W. D. Marslen-Wilson (Eds.), *The perception of speech* (pp. 103–131). New York: Oxford University Press Inc.

Kuhl, P. K., Andruski, J. E., Chistovich, I. A., Chistovich, L. A., Kozhevnikova, E. V., Ryskina, V. L., et al. (1997). Cross-language analysis of phonetic units in language addressed to infants. *Science, 277*, 684–686.

Kuhl, P. K., Coffey-Corina, S., Padden, D., & Dawson, G. (2005). Links between social and linguistic processing of speech in preschool children with autism: Behavioral and electrophysiological evidence. *Developmental Science, 8*, 1–12.

Kuhl, P. K., Conboy, B. T., Coffey-Corina, S., Padden, P., Rivera-Gaxiola, M., & Nelson, T. (2008). Phonetic learning as a pathway to language: New data and native language magnet theory expanded (NLM-e). *Philosophical Transactions of the Royal Society B., 363*, 979–1000.

Kuhl, P. K., Conboy, B. T., Padden, D., Nelson, T., & Pruitt, J. (2005). Early speech perception and later language development: Implications for the "critical period." *Language Learning and Development, 1*, 237–264.

Kuhl, P. K. & Meltzoff, A. N. (1982). The bimodal perception of speech in infancy. *Science, 218*, 1138–1141.

Kuhl, P. K. & Meltzoff, A. N. (1996). Infant vocalizations in response to speech: Vocal imitation and developmental change. *Journal of the Acoustical Society of America, 100*, 2425–2438.

Kuhl, P. K., Stevens, E., Hayashi, A., Deguchi, T., Kiritani, S., & Iverson, P. (2006). Infants show facilitation for native language phonetic perception between 6 and 12 months. *Developmental Science, 9*, 13–21.

Kuhl, P. K., Tsao, F. -M., & Liu, H. -M. (2003). Foreign-language experience in infancy: Effects of short-term exposure and social interaction on phonetic learning. *Proceedings of the National Academy of Sciences, 100*, 9096–9101.

Kuhl, P. K., Williams, K. A., Lacerda, F., Stevens, K. N., & Lindblom, B. (1992). Linguistic experience alters phonetic perception in infants by 6 months of age. *Science, 255*, 606–608.

Kuhl, P. K., Williams, K. A., & Meltzoff, A. N. (1991). Cross-modal speech perception in adults and infants using nonspeech auditory stimuli. *Journal of Experimental Psychology: Human Perception and Performance, 17*, 829–840.

Ladefoged, P. (2001). *Vowels and consonants: An introduction to the sounds of language.* Oxford: Blackwell Publishers.

Lasky, R. E., Syrdal-Lasky, A., & Klein, R. E. (1975). VOT discrimination by four to six and a half month old infants from Spanish environments. *Journal of Experimental Child Psychology, 20,* 215–225.

Lenneberg, E. (1967). *Biological foundations of language.* New York: John Wiley & Sons.

Liberman, A. M., Cooper, F. S., Shankweiler, D. P., & Studdert-Kennedy, M. (1967). Perception of the speech code. *Psychological Review, 74,* 431–461.

Liberman, A. M., & Mattingly, I. G. (1985). The motor theory of speech perception revised. *Cognition, 21,* 1–36.

Liu, H. -M., Kuhl, P. K., & Tsao, F. -M. (2003). An association between mothers' speech clarity and infants' speech discrimination skills. *Developmental Science, 6,* F1–F10.

Liu, H. -M., Tsao, F. -M., & Kuhl, P. K. (2007). Acoustic analysis of lexical tone in Mandarin infant-directed speech. *Developmental Psychology, 43,* 912–917.

Liu, H. -M., Tsao, F. -M., & Kuhl, P. K. (submitted). Lexical diversity and phonetic clarity of maternal speech in infancy predicts 5-year-olds' language skills.

Lotto, A. J., Sato, M., & Diehl, R. (2004). Mapping the task for the second language learner: The case of Japanese acquisition of /r/ and /l/. In J. Slitka, S. Manuel, & M. Matthies (Eds.), *From sound to sense* (pp. C181–C186). Cambridge, MA: MIT Press.

Marler, P. (1991). The instinct to learn. In S. Carey & R. Gelman (Eds.), *The epigenesis of mind: Essays on biology and cognition* (pp. 37–66). Hillsdale, NJ: Lawrence Erlbaum Associates.

Mayberry, R. I. & Lock, E. (2003). Age constraints on first versus second language acquisition: Evidence for linguistic plasticity and epigenesis. *Brain Language, 87,* 369–384.

Maye, J., Werker, J. F., & Gerken, L. (2002). Infant sensitivity to distributional information can affect phonetic discrimination. *Cognition, 82,* B101–B111.

Meltzoff, A. N. (1995). Understanding the intentions of others: Re-enactment of intended acts by 18-month-old children. *Developmental Psychology, 31,* 838–850.

Meltzoff, A. N. (2007). The "like me" framework for recognizing and becoming an intentional agent. *Acta Psychologica, 124,* (26–43).

Meltzoff, A. N. & Decety, J. (2003). What imitation tells us about social cognition: A rapprochement between developmental psychology and cognitive neuroscience. *Philosophical Transactions of the Royal Society B, 358,* 491–500.

Meltzoff, A. N., Kuhl, P. K., Movellan, J., & Sejnowski, T. (2009). Foundations for a new science of learning. *Science, 17,* 284–288.

Meltzoff, A. N. & Moore, M. K. (1997). Imitation of facial and manual gestures by human neonates. *Science, 198,* 75–78.

Mundy, P. & Gomes, A. (1998). Individual differences in joint attention skill development in the second year. *Infant Behavior and Development, 21,* 469–482.

Nelson, D. & Marler, P. (1994). Selection-based learning in bird song development. *Proceedings of the National Academy of Sciences, USA, 91,* 10498–10501.

Neville, H. J., Coffey, S.A., Lawson, D. S., Fischer, A., Emmorey, K., & Bellugi, U. (1997). Neural systems mediating American Sign Language: Effects of sensory experience and age of acquisition. *Brain and Language, 57,* 285–308.

Newport, E. (1990). Maturational constraints on language learning. *Cognitive Science, 14,* 11–28.

Newport, E. L., Bavelier, D., & Neville, H. J. (2001). Critical thinking about critical periods: Perspectives on a critical period for language acquisition. In E. Dupoux (Ed.), *Language, brain, and cognitive development: Essays in honor of Jacques Mehlter* (pp. 481–502). Cambridge, MA: MIT Press.

Newport, E. L. & Supalla, T. (1987). *A critical period effect in the acquisition of a primary language.* Unpublished manuscript.

Pena, M., Maki, A., Kovacic, D., Dehaene-Lambertz, G., Koizumi, H., Bouquet, F., et al. (2003). Sounds and silence: An optical topography study of language recognition at birth. *Proceedings of the National Academy of Sciences, 100,* 11702–11705.

Posner, M. I. (Ed.) (2004). *Cognitive neuroscience of attention.* New York: Guilford Press.

Pulvermuller, F. (2005). Brain mechanisms linking language to action. *Nature Reviews Neuroscience, 6,* 574–582.

Rabiner, L. R. & Huang, B. H. (1993). *Fundamentals of speech recognition.* Englewood Cliffs, NJ: Prentice Hall.

Rivera-Gaxiola, M., Klarman, L., Garcia-Sierra, A., & Kuhl, P. K. (2005). Neural patterns to speech and vocabulary growth in American infants. *NeuroReport, 16,* 495–498.

Rivera-Gaxiola, M., Silvia-Pereyra, J., & Kuhl, P. K. (2005). Brain potentials to native and non-native speech contrasts in 7- and 11-month-old American infants. *Developmental Science, 8,* 162–172.

Rizzolatti, G. (2005). The mirror neuron system and imitation. In S. Hurley & N. Chater (Eds.), *Perspectives on imitation: From neuroscience to social science–Volume 1: Mechanisms of imitation and imitation in animals* (pp. 55–76). Cambridge, MA: MIT Press.

Rizzolatti, G. & Craighero, L. (2004). The mirror-neuron system. *Annual Review of Neuroscience, 27,* 169–192.

Rizzolatti, G., Fadiga, L., Gallese, V., & Fogassi, L. (1996). Premotor cortex and the recognition of motor actions. *Cognitive Brain Research, 3,* 131–141.

Rizzolatti, G., Fogassi, L., & Gallese, V. (2002). Motor and cognitive functions of the ventral premotor cortex. *Current Opinion in Neurobiology, 12,* 149–154.

Roseberry, S., Nash, B., Garcia-Sierra, A. & Kuhl, P. K. (in preparation). Can infants learn phonetically from interactive TV?

Saffran, J., Aslin, R., & Newport, E. (1996). Statistical learning by 8-month old infants. *Science, 274,* 1926–1928.

Saffran, J. R., Johnson, E. K., Aslin, R. N. & Newport, E. L. (1999). Statistical learning of tone sequences by human infants and adults. *Cognition, 70,* 27–52.

Saffran, J. R., Werker, J. F., & Werner, L. A. (2006). The infant's auditory world: Hearing, speech, and the beginnings of language. In W. Damon & R. M. Lerner (Series Eds.) & R. Siegler & D. Kuhn (Vol. Eds.), *Handbook of child psychology: Vol. 2, Cognition, perception and language* (6th ed., pp. 58–108). New York: Wiley.

Skinner, B. F. (1957). *Verbal Behavior.* Acton, MA: Copely Publishing Group.

Stevens, R., Mehus, S., Mertl, V., Conboy, B., & Kuhl, P. K. (submitted). An Interaction analysis of joint attention and joint action in a laboratory experiment with infants: Results from an interdisciplinary collaboration across the ethnographic and experimental divide.

Tanaka, F., Cicourel, A., & Movellan, J. (2007). Socialization between toddlers and robots at an early childhood education center. *Proceedings of the National Academy of Sciences, US, 104,* 17954–17958.

Tchernichovski, O., Mitra, P., Lints, T., & Nottebohm, F. (2001). Dynamics of the vocal imitation process: How a Zebra Finch learns its song. *Science, 291,* 2564–2569.

Tomasello, M. (2003a). *Constructing a language*. Cambridge, MA: Harvard University Press.

Tomasello, M. (2003b). The key is social cognition. In D. Gentner & S. Kuczaj (Eds.), *Language and thought* (pp. 47–58). Cambridge, MA: MIT Press.

Trevarthen, C. & Hubley, P. (1978). Secondary intersubjectivity: Confidence, confiding, and acts of meaning in the first year. In A. Lock (Ed.), *Action, gesture, and symbol* (pp. 183–229). London: Academic Press.

Tsao, F.-M., Lui, H.-M., & Kuhl, P. K. (2004). Speech perception in infancy predicts language development in the second year of life: A longitudinal study. *Child Development, 75*, 1067–1084.

Tsao, F. -M., Liu, H. -M., & Kuhl, P. K. (2006). Perception of native and non-native affricate-fricative contrasts: Cross-language tests on adults and infants. *Journal of the Acoustical Society of America, 120*, 2285–2294.

Ward, N., Sundara, M., Conboy, B., & Kuhl, P. K. (2009, October). *Consequences of short-term language exposure in infancy on babbling*. Poster presented at the 158th meeting of the Acoustical Society of America, San Antonio.

Watson, J. S. (1979). Perception of contingency as a determinant of social responsiveness. In E. B. Thomas (Ed.), *The origins of social responsiveness* (pp. 33–64). New York: Erlbaum.

Watson, J. S. (2005). The elementary nature of purposive behavior: Evolving minimal neural structures that display intrinsic intentionality. *Evolutionary Psychology, 3*, 24–48.

Weber-Fox, C. M. & Neville, H. J. (1999). Functional neural subsystems are differentially affected by delays in second language immersion: ERP and behavioral evidence in bilinguals. In D. Birdsong (Ed.), *Second language acquisition and the critical period hypothesis* (pp. 23–38). Mahwah, NJ: Lawrence Erlbaum and Associates, Inc.

Werker, J. F. & Lalonde, C. (1988). Cross-language speech perception: Initial capabilities and developmental change. *Developmental Psychology, 24*, 672–683.

Werker, J.F., Pons, F., Dietrich, C., Kajikawa, S., Fais, L., & Amano, S. (2007). Infant-directed speech supports phonetic category learning in English and Japanese. *Cognition, 103*, 147–162.

Werker, J.F., & Tees, R.C. (1984). Cross-language speech perception: Evidence for perceptual reorganization during the first year of life. *Infant Behavior and Development, 7*, 49–63.

West, M. & King, A. (1988). Female visual displays affect the development of male song in the cowbird. *Nature, 334*, 244–246.

Woolley, S. C. & Doupe, A. J. (2008). Social context-induced song variation affects female behavior and gene expression. *PLos Biol 6*, e62.

Yeni-Komshian, G. H., Flege, J. E., & Liu, S. (2000). Pronunciation proficiency in the first and second languages of Korean–English bilinguals. *Bilingualism: Language and Cognition, 3*, 131–149.

Yoshida, K. A., Pons, F., Cady, J. C., & Werker, J. F. (2006). *Distributional learning and attention in phonological development*. Paper presented at International Conference on Infant Studies, Kyoto, Japan, 19–23 June.

Zhang, Y., Kuhl, P. K., Imada, T., Kotani, M., & Tohkura, Y. (2005). Effects of language experience: Neural commitment to language-specific auditory patterns. *NeuroImage, 26*, 703–720.

Zhang, Y., Kuhl, P. K., Imada, T., Iverson, P., Pruitt, J., Stevens, E., et al. (2009). Neural signatures of phonetic learning in adulthood: A magnetoencephalography study. *NeuroImage, 46*, 226–240.

Language and Communication

Howard C. Nusbaum

Abstract

This chapter argues that we can think about language in terms of communicative interaction as a psychologically significant act that was part of the basic force shaping the evolution of the brain, rather than think about language simply as a signal for transmitting information. By this construal, the listener's goal may not be to interpret the linguistic message but to interact with the interlocutor in a way that satisfies specific social goals and motives. This would suggest that communicative behavior—broadly construed—should be affected by a conversational partner's behavior, even beyond the simple process of interpretation.

Keywords: language, neurons, neural mechanism, speech perception, communication

Language is at the heart of most of human social interactions. We identify ourselves to others, and we identify our affiliates through the way we speak and use language (Kinzler, Dupoux, & Spelke, 2007: Kinzler, Shutts, Dejesus, & Spelke, 2009). We connect to others through the way we talk and what we say, either explicitly, in terms of specific messages about agreement with attitudes and ideas, or implicitly through convergence of speaking (Giles, 1979; Pardo, 2006) and physical behavior (e.g., foot tapping, chin scratching) while talking (cf. Chartrand & Bargh, 1999). We reward others with spoken praise or we distance people by cursing and criticizing. Moreover, beyond our vernacular and daily conversations, our social institutions from law to education to religion and government all depend on the written word to define their foundations and speech for daily transactions.

Much of the psychological and linguistic research on language has focused on the form and meaning of language (e.g., Gleitman & Liberman, 1996) either in terms of systematic descriptions or processing models. This modern scientific study of language has largely been shaped by Chomsky's view of a rule-based computation-theoretic linguistics (Chomsky, 1957) that divorces linguistic form from message meaning, mental representation from language use, and scientific evidence from evolutionary biology (see Margoliash & Nusbaum, 2009). While divide and conquer is a long-held and often successful approach to scientific problems, when the division of issues redefines the nature of the scientific problem radically enough, the fundamental nature of the scientific question may be lost—rather than studying language in service of communication, language is studied as a natural object independent of its function but without physical manifestation or empirically testable prediction (Chomsky, 1986, see the concept of "I language"). When this approach to the scientific study of language is imported into the neuroscience of language, putative linguistic structures become reified as neural structures. For example, in consideration of the neural mechanisms of language processing, recent debates focus on finding the neural locus for syntax (e.g., Grodzinsky & Santi, 2008) rather than understanding the complexity by which neural systems implement communication.

On the other hand, research in neuroscience has identified neural mechanisms that may be important in understanding human action and forming social connection (see Iacoboni, Chapter 36; Singer & Decety, Chapter 37, this volume). "Mirror neurons" are neurons found originally in the macaque motor system (but subsequently claimed to exist in parietal cortex beyond the traditionally defined motor system, e.g., see Meister & Iacoboni, 2007) that respond both in producing a learned and practiced action, and when observing the same action in another individual (see Rizzolatti & Craighero, 2004; Rizzolatti et al., 2001). These neurons, located in area F5 of the macaque cortex, respond in an effector-specific manner (mouth actions different from hand actions) to observed action (Gallese et al., 1996) and are putatively sensitive to the goal of the action rather than the specific motor behavior (Rizzolatti, Fogassi, & Gallese, 2001). The fact that these putative motor neurons are claimed to respond to the intention of the action, rather than the motor movement, has been used, in part, to motivate the theory that such neurons are important in understanding action (Rizzolatti & Craighero, 2004).

Evolution of Language and Neural Mechanisms

These empirical observations and theoretical speculations have led to a theory of the evolution of language as an extension of action understanding (Rizzolatti & Arbib, 1999). In essence the theory suggests a progression of development from observing others performing actions and understanding the intended action based on personal experience, to a symbolic form of such actions or manual gestures. A form of pantomime or acting out intended messages serves as a kind of bridge between observing behavior and interpreting it and a first form of some gestural language that may abstract some properties of communication away from the more simple notion of a one-to-one correspondence

between action and interpretation.[1] With increasing abstraction from real action, it is then conceivable that speech substituted for manual gestures, permitting communication over distance.

This view of the evolution of language has some conceptual appeal in its simplicity and comprehensibility. In many respects, it provides a description of evolution as comparable to individual development. However, it does ascribe to macaques the principal mechanism of action understanding in the form of mirror neurons, which is the only core competency necessary for language. By contrast, Hauser et al. (2002) view language as depending on a very different kind of mechanism. Whereas Rizzolatti and Arbib (1999) ground their theory in an empirically observed neural mechanism that may play a role in understanding others (thus fundamental to communication), Hauser et al. identify recursion as the basic computational capacity needed to license language. Recursion is of course not a biological mechanism at all, but it is a formally defined class of computational algorithms (Chabert, 2008). In attributing language to recursion, Hauser et al. assert that it is the ability to generate an infinite set of patterns from a finite set of rules that is at the heart of language. In other words, the core of language is its formal generativity (Hockett, 1960) rather than aspects of message transmission. Moreover, the assertion that this is a capacity that is unique to humans, it removes the study of language from the realm of evolutionary and organismal biology (Margoliash & Nusbaum 2009). This has the consequence of limiting the neurobiology of language to the study of humans, which is very different from the action understanding view derived from mirror neurons (Rizzolatti & Arbib, 1999).

However, there is another way to think about the evolution of language. A number of species uses vocal signals to communicate with conspecifics. These vocal signals can serve a wide range of social functions such as the organization and coordination of small groups, mating, territoriality, warning, support, and social signals. Moreover many of these functions may need to be carried out beyond the line of sight rather than in the physical and visual presence of an audience.

Although physicists have debated the possibility of action at a distance for quite some time, the biological form of action at a distance is well established, as achieved through vocal communication in an extremely broad range of behaviors and settings. Many species of fish, amphibians, reptiles, birds, and mammals commonly exchange information at a distance through their calls. The learned songs (and some calls) of songbirds are particularly rich sources of information conveying, to the receiver, individual identity and a host of other characteristics of the sender (Kroodsma & Miller, 1996). Some mammals exchange information at great distances through calling behavior. Humpback whale (Megaptera novaeangliae) vocalizations are perceived over extremely long distances and may be used to maintain social groups at distances as great as 5 km (Frankel, Clark, Herman, & Gabriele, 1995). African elephants (Loxodonta africana) can recognize friends and relatives from their calls at a distance of 2.5 km (McComb, Reby, Baker, Moss, & Sayialel, 2003). Human sheepherders keep each other company from the top of one mountain to another in the Canary Islands using a whistled language called Silbo Gomero (Busnel & Classe, 1976). Whether for purposes of mating, threat, warning, or social organization, conveying information regarding location, identity, and motivation, and directed at one individual or towards far-flung groups, vocal communication plays an important role in the social connection and behavior of a great number of vertebrate species. This affords insight into biological constraints on the evolution of vocal communication systems.

Production and Comprehension

The functional linkage between production and perception of biologically significant signals has often suggested that there should be interactions among the underlying neural systems, whether in songbirds (Marler & Peters, 1980; Margoliash, 2002), bats (e.g., Moss & Sinha, 2003), or humans (Liberman & Mattingly, 1985). When signal producers are also signal perceivers, there is a tendency to assume that some kind of common processing system may underlie aspects of both. From an engineering perspective, if one were building a device to both produce and interpret a set of signals, there needs to be a way to relate the meaning of signals, even if the generation of a signal is physically different from the sensory encoding of a signal. However, for organisms the common principles derive not only from the physical constraints of the environments and the signals (which engineers will know about), but also from evolutionary constraints (which engineers will not know about). This can have unexpected consequences. For example, in the electric fish, "timed" electric pulses are used as a kind of sonar system for perceiving the environment, and when two fish are close, their signals can

interfere. To avoid this interference, the fish that is sending signals lower in frequency reduces frequency and the higher frequency sender increases signal frequency. One might assume that part of this jamming avoidance response depends on the use of a common "pacer" or "clock" neuron both in production and perception, but this is not correct—the system is much more complicated (Heiligenberg, 1991; Nelson & MacIver, 2006). This suggests the cautionary point that the assumption of processing commonality between production and perception simply on the face of apparent similarity can be wholly misleading.

Theories of speech perception that depend on the motor system have a long history in modern speech research (at least over the past forty years). For example, Liberman and his colleagues (e.g., Liberman, Cooper, Shankweiler, & Studdert-Kennedy, 1967; Liberman & Mattingly, 1985) argued that speech *perception* could only be accounted for by the involvement of the motor system. In the most general terms, the theory was intended to account for our ability to recognize phonemes in spite of the many-to-many relationship between acoustic patterns and linguistic categories. This lack of invariance between acoustic patterns and phonetic categories is observed, for example, for vowel categories between speakers (Peterson & Barney, 1952) and for stop consonants across vowel contexts (Liberman et al., 1967) and for consonants at different rates of speech (Francis & Nusbaum, 1996). A particular acoustic pattern for a phoneme (e.g., the second formant transition for the consonant /d/) may be different in two contexts (e.g., /i/ and /u/) and yet listeners hear the same phoneme regardless of context. Moreover the same acoustic pattern (e.g., formant transition rate) may indicate two different phonemes (e.g., /b/ or /w/) depending on context (e.g., speaking rate). In theoretical terms, perhaps the most critical feature of the lack of invariance problem is that it makes speech recognition an inherently nondeterministic process (see Nusbaum & Magnuson, 1997).

Towards a New Motor Theory of Speech Perception

The neuroscience of language processing has long been shaped by studies of patients with relatively focal brain lesions. Broca (1861) described a patient Leborgne who had severe brain damage to the left side of his brain and as a result could only utter a single nonsense syllable. Broca's aphasia, widely associated with damage to the left inferior frontal gyrus (IFG, although damage is seldom confined to that region, Dronkers, Redfern, & Knight, 1999) is generally identified as "expressive aphasia." An aphasia is defined as a selective disruption of a language function and expressive aphasia was described as selective damage to the ability to produce language.

Wernicke (1874) subsequently identified damage to a posterior region of the superior temporal gyrus but extending into the parietal cortex (although cf. Bogen & Bogen, 1976) with a selective loss of comprehension or "receptive aphasia." This led to a proposed neural model of language processing in which the respective functions of talking and understanding were assigned to different cortical areas, one in the IFG and one in the posterior STG/inferior parietal region. Lichtheim (1885) developed a more elaborated model of language use that related neural mechanisms for production, comprehension, and conceptual representation and their relationships in processing. This relatively simple view of the neural mechanisms of language processing was being advocated even into the 1970s (Geschwind, 1970) suggesting little theoretical development in the neuroscience of language over a hundred years.

In many areas of cognitive and social neuroscience (e.g., memory and behavioral regulation), research has been influenced by notable patients such as HM and Phineas Gage (see Farah & Feinberg, 2000). However, this foundation has always been tempered by animal models of perception, memory, and even aspects of behavioral control and emotion that make possible neurophysiological measures and intervention that could not be carried out with human participants until recently. The dissociation of human language from any grounding in the communication systems of other species has worked against a similar penetration of comparative neuroscience into understanding the neurobiology of language use. However, the demonstration of mirror neurons described above suggests a very different view of language from the theory that traditional neural view that completely separates production and perception of language. As described by Rizzolatti and Arbib (1999), language understanding and language production may be grounded in a common system (but see Lotto, Hickok, & Holt, 2009), rooted in the motor system but extending into a more posterior network as well, for action understanding. This mirror neuron theory has been extended even more broadly to include understanding social cognition (Gallese, Keysers & Rizzolatti, 2004). While other research has suggested substantially greater limits on the role this

system may play in empathy and social cognition (e.g., Decety & Lamm, 2006), the recognition of the importance of motor mimicry (e.g., Chartrand & Bargh, 1999) in interpersonal interaction is growing, even in respect of language processing (Pickering & Garrod, 2004).

The model of language processing as grounded in action production and perception is quite different from the more traditional linguistic view of language as a conventional system of symbol use and organization that evolved from the communicative signs of other species. On a linguistic analysis, the fundamental properties of language consist of the meaningless form elements (e.g., phonemes or syllables) organized into hierarchically meaningful symbolic patterns (e.g., words and sentences). This suggests that the sound patterns of speech must be recognized and combined according to abstract rules that allow for the generativity of any novel legal utterance. Of course this view of language processing has a large group of proponents (e.g., Friederici, Bahlmann, Heim, Schubotz, & Anwander, 2006; Caplan, 1996), who espouse a view of spoken language understanding that progresses from auditory patterns to phonological analysis in the superior temporal gyrus (Hickok & Poeppel, 2004) to lexical processing in the more posterior regions proximal to traditional Wernicke's area, to syntactic processing in Broca's area (Friederici et al., 2006) and sentence understanding (Hagoort, 2005).

Indeed, this is essentially the model that Hickok and Poeppel (2004) present as the "ventral stream" in speech perception. They suggest that speech perception is mediated by networks that are similar to the ventral/dorsal pathway difference in vision (Goodale & Milner 1992; Mishkin, Ungerleider, & Macko, 1983). In vision, these two systems are respectively viewed as important for object recognition (ventral stream) and for object location or object-oriented action (dorsal stream). Although others (e.g., Rauschecker, 1998) have argued for a ventral/dorsal distinction in auditory processing, Hickok and Poeppel specifically make this distinction for speech perception. The ventral stream, projecting from primary auditory cortex ventrally and laterally to the posterior inferior temporal cortex is responsible for mapping sound onto meaning, ultimately projecting to anterior temporal cortex (aSTS) for sentence processing. This represents a bottom-up sound-to-phoneme-to-word-to-sentence mapping process that bears some general similarity to the traditional neural models of vision in which simple features map to complex features which map onto object form and then visual memory in a progression along the ventral visual stream. By contrast, the dorsal speech stream, which projects from auditory areas to the parietal cortex to the IFG and premotor cortex, is functionally more vague. Hickok and Poeppel allude to a role in language development and word learning and maintaining information in working memory through the use of the "phonological loop" to subvocalize (Baddeley & Hitch, 1974). In other words, according to this model, speech perception is fundamentally a bottom-up process of progressive interpretation within the ventral stream, while the dorsal stream projection to the premotor system plays little or no role in normal speech understanding.

Traditionally, auditory theories of speech perception(e.g., Fant, 1967; Diehl, Lotto, & Holt, 2004; Stevens & Blumstein, 1981) view speech perception as a purely auditory process in which acoustic features are coded and matched to stored representations of phonetic categories which are then mapped onto words, and so forth. On the other hand, motor theory (Liberman & Mattingly, 1985) and analysis-by-synthesis (Stevens & Halle, 1967) have viewed speech perception as involving the motor system as part of the recognition process (albeit in very different ways). In recent years, neuroimaging methods have begun to present evidence that increasingly supports the involvement of the motor system in the process of speech perception. Of course, the enthusiasm to embrace this new evidence for motor theory needs to be tempered by the fact that the same neuroimaging methods implicate broader arrays of cortical activation than previously anticipated for numerous tasks. If so, then the new data help to define language mechanisms, placing them in the context of other perceptual processes (e.g., Price, Thierry, & Griffiths, 2005).

If Rizzolatti and Arbib (1999) are correct in their view of the evolution of spoken language, then face-to-face communication is a much better match to the conditions under which language emerged than communication at a distance (as might be exemplified by the voice-only telephone model investigated in most speech research). If spoken language understanding is an abstracted form of action understanding, we might expect to see evidence of ventral premotor activity (corresponding to mouth movements) when a talking face is visible. On the other hand, the ventral stream described by Hickok and Poeppel does not involve the premotor cortex. By this view, there is no reason why seeing the face of a talker should necessarily recruit the premotor cortex in service of speech perception, given that the ventral stream is responsible for understanding spoken language.

Skipper, Nusbaum, and Small (2005) examined patterns of neural activity while listeners heard auditory-only spoken stories or watched and heard an audio-video recording of a person telling stories. Hearing and seeing someone tell stories significantly increases ventral premotor activity compared to either hearing the speech alone or seeing the talking face with no speech. In addition, hearing and seeing the talker significantly increased neural activity in the superior temporal cortex as well. Moreover, for stories with greater viseme content (visual mouth shapes that are informative about the phonetic structure of speech), premotor activity was greater than for stories with less viseme content. This suggests that the premotor activity was specifically related to phonetic information visible in the talker's mouth movements.

Fifty years ago, Sumby and Pollack (1954) demonstrated that speech presented in noise is significantly more intelligible when the talking face can be seen by listeners. Clearly there is phonetically useful information in the visible mouth movements made during speech production. In fact, McGurk and MacDonald (1976) demonstrated that visible mouth movements dramatically change the perception of the acoustic speech signal. For example, when an acoustic recording of /pa/ is dubbed onto a video recording of a face producing /ka/, listeners often perceive an illusory syllable /ta/. The increased activity in the ventral premotor region during audiovisual speech perception may indicate a mechanism by which this illusion is created. This mechanism may operate in much the same way that Stevens and Halle (1967) suggested in analysis-by-synthesis, in which the motor system is only involved to aid phonetic interpretation of more phonetically ambiguous acoustic segments.

Skipper, Nusbaum, and Small (2006) suggested that the motor system may operate as part of the active process of speech perception (see Nusbaum & Schwab, 1986). Sensory information from visual and auditory representations in the occipital and temporal cortex is decoded into motor representations in the premotor cortex. These motor representations can feed back to the sensory systems as part of a distributed recognition network. This suggests that the sensory and motor cortices may interact over time to determine the phonetic percept experienced by the observer.

To test this, Skipper, Wassenhove, Nusbaum, and Small (2007) examined patterns of neural activity during the perception of the McGurk illusion. The time course of BOLD response to audiovisual /pa/, /ta/, and /ka/ in right ventral premotor, left supermarginal, and right middle occipital cortices were measured as estimated population responses to these syllables. The correlation between the McGurk syllable (audio /ka/ and visual /pa/) and each of these population responses was measured to determine how similar the neural response to the McGurk syllable was to each of the three consistent audiovisual syllables. The results showed that in the ventral premotor region, /ta/ (consistent with the actual percept) was the best fitting representation of the McGurk syllable, whereas in the supermarginal gyrus, the initial best fitting syllable was /pa/ (consistent with the acoustic signal) which then shifted to fitting best with /ta/. In the middle occipital gyrus, the initial best fit was to /ka/ (consistent with visual information about the mouth movements) which shifted to /ta/. Thus in sensory cortex, the best fitting representations for the McGurk stimulus started out consistent with their respective sensory input signals but then shifted to fit best with the percept. However, in the ventral premotor region, the /ta/ representation fit best throughout the entire time course of processing. This is consistent with the hypothesis that visual and auditory information, when fed to the premotor cortex, give rise to an activity pattern consistent with the McGurk illusion which then may interact with sensory cortices resulting in a final activity pattern consistent across all regions with the McGurk percept.

These results are entirely consistent with an active theory of perception for which the lack of invariance between acoustic patterns and phonetic categories is resolved by an interaction between articulatory knowledge in the premotor representation of speech and the sensory representation of speech. One interpretation of this kind of interaction is the notion of covert motor simulation: The activity within the premotor region leads to associated sensory activity that would be associated with the actual act of speech production (Skipper, Nusbaum, & Small, 2006). The premotor representation can be taken as a kind of "hypothesis" regarding the phonetic interpretation of sensory input and this hypothesis can constrain the alternative interpretations possible given the sensory representations alone. This is exactly the kind of mechanism described by Nusbaum and Magnuson (1997) in considering how an active process might resolve the nondeterministic

relationship (i.e., a many-to-many mapping) between acoustic speech patterns and the possible phonetic interpretations of those patterns, although it was not clear that articulatory knowledge would provide sufficient phonetic constraint. We note that cross-modal interactions are typically poorly explored but there is increasing evidence for such interactions (e.g., Bensmaia, Killebrew, & Craig, 2006). Thus, this new perspective on language processing may be illuminating general properties of cortical organization, not those that are unique to language.

One apparent problem with this active theory of speech perception, by contrast to Hickok and Poeppel's dual pathway model, is that the supporting evidence derives largely from audiovisual speech perception. While the support from audiovisual speech is consistent with the idea that speech has evolved as face-to-face communication (and thus audiovisual speech may be the "ethologically appropriate" stimulus), the ventral stream of the dual pathway does not really use any premotor processing. Thus if the dorsal stream were modified to play a role in speech recognition when face information is present, the dual pathway model would be largely unchanged. Moreover this raises the question as to whether there is any role for premotor processing when face information is not present. Can premotor activity serve as a constraint on phonetic interpretation even without visual input about mouth movements? Part of the motivation for the revision of the motor theory proposed by Liberman and Mattingly (1985) was to assert the perceptual equivalence of mouth movements and acoustic patterns in speech perception given the McGurk effect. Although this also included the theoretically implausible claim that auditory sensory processing plays no role in speech perception, the notion was that motor knowledge should be important in speech perception whether a face is seen or not. If we take seriously the current premise that covert motor simulation (or prior associations between speech production experiences and the sensory consequences of production) provide a constraint on phonetic interpretation that can reduce acoustic-phonetic uncertainty, there should be evidence of premotor activity even without face input. Indeed, there is a substantial body of research on motor imagery that demonstrates substantial premotor activity during imagery that overlaps with motor execution (see Hanakawa, 2003; Jeannerod, 1994). Moreover, this evidence of premotor simulation during imagery has been functionally interpreted as relevant to understanding others' actions (Decety & Grezes, 2006).

Fadiga et al. (2002) showed some evidence for the involvement of the premotor system in speech perception, even without input from the mouth movements seen while watching a talker's face. Audio-only speech perception alone was not sufficient to produce peripheral EMG signals in tongue muscles, nor did single-shot TMS (transcranial magnetic stimulation) to the ventral premotor region alone produce a tongue EMG. However, the combination of speech input and premotor TMS did produce measurable tongue EMG. Fadiga et al. suggested that during audio-only speech perception, the premotor cortex is active but well below the threshold to produce a peripheral EMG in articulators. However, the addition of TMS-induced neural activity in the premotor system was sufficient to produce measurable EMG.

Wilson et al. (2004) presented acoustic speech syllables to listeners (with no visual information) and found evidence for ventral premotor activity. Subsequently, Wilson and Iacoboni (2006) presented listeners with familiar phonemes and unfamiliar phonemes from other languages and measured brain activity during passive listening (no classification task involved). They reported significantly more premotor activity for unfamiliar phonemes although this activity did not change with producibility of the speech. They interpret this result, along with activity in the superior temporal gyrus as evidence for the role of ventral premotor activity in speech perception. Specifically they interpret their data as suggesting that premotor categorizations serve as phonetic hypotheses that are tested against auditory representations in sensory areas arguing for speech perception as a neither purely sensory nor purely motor but instead a sensorimotor process (see also Skipper et al., 2006).

Spoken Language Understanding

The putative role of the motor system in speech perception is only one way in which the motor system may interact with cognition and comprehension. There is a growing body of research on embodied cognition that understanding meaning is grounded in aspects of concrete sensory-motor representation. Barsalou (1999) has argued for sensory and motor simulation as a fundamental basis for conceptual representation. Glenberg and Kaschak (2002) demonstrated that motor responses are facilitated or inhibited when they are directionally compatible versus different from the directionality inherent in the main verb of a stimulus sentence (towards or away from oneself). This suggests that the semantics of verbs are closely linked to our understanding of motor plans.

Tettamanti et al. (2005) demonstrated that listening to sentences describing action increases brain activity in the motor system in pars opercularis and the premotor cortex. Similarly Hauk, Johnsrude, and Pulvermüller (2004) showed that reading action words that are specific to the hand, foot, or mouth (e.g., grasp, kick, kiss), activate a pattern of cortical activity in the premotor cortex that displays somatotopic organization similar to the performance of those actions. These studies demonstrate that there is a close correspondence between the patterns of cortical activity seen in the motor system when understanding the meaning of action words and sentences and when engaged in motor behavior.

In the anatomical model of neural language processing derived from Broca, Wernicke, and Lichtheim, the conceptual representation of word and sentence meaning was not considered to be localized in the motor system. In the model proposed by Hickok and Poeppel (2004), within the ventral stream where sentences are understood, meaning is not represented in the motor system either. However, given the kind of evidence provided recently for motor system activity during word and sentence comprehension, it is unlikely there is a single amodal conceptual representation system. An abstract conceptual representational system alone cannot account for why the motor system would be involved in comprehending language. Barsalou's (1999) view of a sensory- and motor-grounded conceptual system seems much more consistent with recent behavioral and neural evidence regarding embodied comprehension.

Expert sports players (hockey or football) understand sentences containing sport-specific objects or actions differently from people with little or no experience in that sport (Holt & Beilock, 2006). More recently, Beilock et al. (2008) used fMRI neuroimaging data to show that the effect of hockey expertise in understanding hockey sentences is entirely mediated by premotor activity. Thus increased experience in an action domain such as sports can significantly modify the neural processing of language to recruit brain areas that are not part of the "traditional language network" (i.e., IFG and pSTG) in comprehension. Indeed, many neural models of language processing need to consider how other domains of experience and cognitive processing outside of linguistic knowledge may operate during language understanding.

However, it is clear that language processing takes place in a much broader network than has been typically considered. Speech perception may draw on the motor system and attention mechanisms (Wong, Nusbaum, & Small, 2004) that are not part of the brain networks thought of as involved in speech processing. Word and sentence understanding may also depend on the use of the motor system, although in different ways from phoneme perception. These kinds of results suggest that the basic processing of language depends broadly on neural networks subserving more general cognitive processes than would be considered under the rubric of "neural mechanisms of language comprehension."

Broadening the Neurobiology of Language

A recent theoretical paper by Bar (2003) speculated on a connection and interactions between the ventral and dorsal pathways in vision. Rather than view these pathways as playing functionally independent roles in vision, he suggested that the dorsal route may represent a coarse form route to object recognition that connects through goal-directed attention systems linked to working memory and to affective-modulation systems that may bias responses. The dorsal route projects through motor, attention, affective, and working memory systems and then projects back to the inferior temporal cortex to constrain aspects of perceptual analysis carried out in parallel by the ventral pathway. Given the proximity (even overlap) in brain systems involved in emotion, executive function, and behavioral control, working memory, and attention, and the relationship between these systems and other aspects of perceptual processing, it seems surprising that this kind of proposal has not been made previously. Moreover, it raises the possibility of thinking about language networks in much the same way.

Roland (1993) has argued that the frontal cortex can generate sensory expectations that can "tune" the sensitivity of more posterior areas. Bar's argument is that affective goals and evaluations are important in shifting attention for perception. This process of shifting attention involves frontal and prefrontal systems changing the sensitivity of posterior sensory processes, presumably by modifying receptive fields (e.g., Moran & Desimone, 1985). This could be the way in which visual information about mouth movements during speech production changes neural population responses in the superior temporal cortex during comprehension of the talker's speech.

To postulate that goals, motives, and expectations may change the processing of auditory information goes well beyond the notion that immediately available visual information about motor movements

changes phonetic perception. Goals, motivations, and expectations are not manifest in the sensory signal about the articulations underlying speech production—they are completely endogenous information. Consider that seeing the race of a talker's face (shown as a static image) can change the perception of the talker's speech (Rubin, 1992) and the gender of a talker's face can change interpretation of speech (Johnson, Strand, & D'Imperio, 1999). These effects are driven by expectations of the listener rather than the sensory information from a talker's mouth movements. Even without dynamic real-time perceptual input about a talker's mouth movements, expectations can change the interpretation of speech. Furthermore, language processing is shaped by expectations even when they do not involve information about a talker's face. Magnuson and Nusbaum (2007) showed the expectations about the importance of an acoustic fundamental frequency difference can drive a low-level perceptual process such as calibrating to the vocal characteristics of a talker.

How can we explain the role of expectations in recognizing and understanding speech? One approach would be to posit two different systems, a cognitive system for maintaining and applying expectations (e.g., working memory and attention) and a sensory system for speech perception. This approach would be consistent with the kind of theory proposed by Hickok and Poeppel in that recognition within the ventral stream (speech recognition) would then be modulated by processing within the dorsal stream (working memory and attention). Indeed the model itself does not specifically try to explain how expectations might play a role in speech perception. In general, expectations, attention, and other processes that are not specifically linguistic in nature are treated by such a model as external to a language processing system, even given the evidence that such processes might be critical to understanding language comprehension. In contrast though, social expectations (e.g., Rubin, 1992; Johnson et al., 1999) and emotional expectations (Luks, Nusbaum, & Levy, 1998) seem to interact with the basic processes of phonetic and prosodic recognition. This would suggest a more direct interaction akin to Bar's (2003) model of vision rather than the "cold cognitive" approach of Hickok and Poeppel.

The shift to consider information beyond the propositional content of utterances, such as social and emotional information, leads to a consideration of prosody. While the linguistic categories used in the "message" content of speech are considered discrete

(Hockett, 1960), speech also conveys less categorical and more continuous information in prosody. There is a general assumption that much of the processing of prosodic information is carried out by the right hemisphere separate from the left-hemisphere networks involved in word and sentence understanding, but this is probably an oversimplification. Luks, Nusbaum, and Levy (1998) investigated the cortical lateralization of intonation information relevant to emotion and syntactic judgments using a behavioral method similar to research investigating the lateralization of phonetic processing. When judging the emotional tone of a sentence, there was a reliable left-ear advantage, suggesting greater right-hemisphere processing. In contrast, when listeners decided if a sentence was a question or a statement (based on rising or falling intonation of the same declarative syntactic form), there was no advantage in processing sentences in either ear, suggesting both right and left hemispheres were contributing to processing equally. But when the same sentences differing in pitch were judged as indicating either a surprised or neutral attitude, a left-ear advantage was found. This suggests that the way listeners attend to the speech determines aspects of the neural processing of the speech.

The interaction between affective systems and cognitive systems also raises the question of understanding the relationship between cortical and subcortical mechanisms. Subcortical structures are clearly important in a number of psychological processes such as attention (thalamus), emotion and reward (ventral striatum), and motor control (basal ganglia) and are heavily connected to cortical systems that are typically studied in language processing. However, few studies have explicitly investigated the relationship between subcortical and cortical processing of language. Mussachia et al. (2006, 2007) demonstrated that auditory brainstem responses are shaped by higher order sensory inputs so that visual information such as seeing a talker's mouth produce speech sharpens the subcortical coding of auditory information such as speech. This suggests that neural theories such as Suga's corticofugal (e.g., Suga & Ma, 2003) model of bat echolocation may provide new insights about active processing in speech perception.

Conclusions

Rather than think about language simply as a signal for transmitting information, we can think about the communicative interaction itself as a psychologically significant act that was part of the basic force shaping the evolution of the brain. By this construal, the listener's goal may not be to interpret the linguistic message but to interact with the interlocutor in a way that satisfies specific social goals and motives. This would suggest that communicative behavior—broadly construed—should be affected by a conversational partner's behavior, even beyond the simple process of interpretation.

As noted previously, Giles (1973; Giles & Smith, 1979) has demonstrated speech accommodation in conversations, in which one interlocutor (or both) converges on the speech of the other, in terms of speaking patterns. This kind of vocal accommodation or indexical mimicry is increased between members of the same social group and decreased between groups (Giles & Coupland, 1991). It is also increased when one interlocutor is trying to persuade the other of something (Giles & Coupland, 1991). Moreover, this kind of behavioral convergence in a conversation is not restricted to speech patterns. Chartrand and Bargh (1999) demonstrated that other motor behaviors that are not speech related show similar accommodation between conversational partners and depend on social goals. One conversational partner tapping her foot can start the other partner tapping as well even though this is not a linguistically relevant behavior. And this can serve to socially link the interlocutors, increasing the sense of interpersonal affiliation (Lakin & Chartrand, 2003) as well as shifting attention from one's self to the broader environment (Van Baaren, Horgan, Chartrand, & Dijkmans, 2004).

It is also important to realize that there is much more information in conversations than is represented in the propositional content of utterances and the prosodic expression of speaker attitude and emotion. Besides the mouth movements that correspond to articulatory gestures, speakers routinely make manual gestures accompanying speech. McNeill (1992) has argued that these gestures present more continuous and analogical information than conventionalized linguistic words and sentences. Gestures, more than other nongesture hand movements, differentially activate the dorsal premotor and have increased connectivity to the anterior portion of the STG which is associated with sentence processing (Skipper et al., 2009). This suggests that gesture may be understood through the use of sensorimotor networks that interact with the sensorimotor networks for spoken language.

Indeed, if gestures represent a first abstraction of observed action per Rizzolatti and Arbib (1999), and the foundation of speech communication, then there should be some form of speech that is more similar to gesture. Is there a vocal signal that is descriptive and referential, as is true of the propositional content of language, but is also continuous (as opposed to the discrete representation in language) and analogical rather than arbitrary (as are words and sentences)? Speech researchers typically describe the arbitrary-discrete and analogical-continuous aspects of language as corresponding to the propositional content in words and the attitude and affect content in prosody. However, Shintel, Okrent, and Nusbaum (2006) described a third channel of spoken language that may serve as a kind of "missing link" between manual gesture and propositional speech. When speakers describe a dot moving up or down or moving fast or slow, they modulate fundamental frequency or speaking rate to describe these events. Speakers do this even without instruction and even when the propositional content is about a different aspect of the event. Speakers can say "It's going right" quickly or slowly to indicate dot speed, even when the task is to describe dot direction. Furthermore this information is communicative for listeners who can decide what the speaker was referring to. Shintel and Nusbaum (2007) have demonstrated that this kind of analog acoustic expression or spoken gesture can actually create an image in the head of the listener so that describing a horse with a fast rate of speech implies to the listener a horse in motion. Finally, listeners' interpretation of spoken gesture is not a simple motor resonance with the articulatory gestures that produced the speech. Shintel and Nusbaum (2008) show that the interpretation of spoken gesture depends on the discourse context that preceded it. Thus, as with all other aspects of spoken language, there is no unique and invariant interpretation of the acoustic signature of spoken gesture.

Spoken language understanding is not a process of determining an objectively specified meaning for a particular utterance. It is a process of construing the intended meaning of an utterance as a construction within the context of a social interaction. As such, the listener must bring to bear a broad set of mechanisms including some that are language specific and some that are more general to cognition such as attention and memory and some that are more general still to social interaction and affective evaluation. The primary function of language is as a social signal and as social communication it may share much in common with the vocal communication systems of other species, even if the evolutionary history of those systems is quite different. Although much of the research in the neuroscience of language has started from a traditional linguistic perspective that separates out the propositional content from other aspects of communication such as manual gesture, spoken gesture, and emotional information, by understanding spoken language use as social communication we may derive new insights into the neural basis of language.

Acknowledgments

This work was supported in part by a grant from the John Templeton Foundation and in part by NIH grant DC00378 to the University of Chicago.

Note

1 It is important to make clear that there is no simple one-to-one mapping between real behavior and the interpretation of that behavior (e.g., Ahn et al., 2003) which poses a serious challenge to the mirror neuron theory of understanding action.

References

Ahn, W., Novick, L., & Kim, N. S. (2003). Understanding behavior makes it more normal. *Psychonomic Bulletin and Review*, 10, 746–752.

Baddeley, A.D., & Hitch, G. (1974). Working memory. In G.A. Bower (Ed.), *The psychology of learning and motivation* (Vol. 8). NewYork: Academic Press, 47–89.

Bar, M. (2003). A cortical mechanism for triggering top-down facilitation in visual object recognition. *Journal of Cognitive Neuroscience*, 15, 600–609.

Barsalou, L. (1999). Perceptual symbol systems. *Behavioral and Brain Sciences*, 22, 577–660.

Beilock, S. L., Lyons, I. M., Mattarella-Micke, A., Nusbaum, H. C., & Small, S. L. (2008). Sports experience changes the neural processing of action language. *Proceedings of the National Academy of Sciences*, 105, 13269–13272.

Bensmaia, S.J., Killebrew, J.H. & Craig, J.C. (2006). Influence of visual motion on tactile motion perception, *Journal of Neurophysiology*, 96, 1625–1637.

Bogen, J. E. & Bogen, G. M. (1976). Wernicke's region: Where is it?. *Annals of the NY Academy of Sciences*, 280. 834–843.

Broca, P. P. (1861). Nouvelle observation d'Aphémie produite par une lesion de la partie postérieure des deuxième et troisième circonvolutions frontales. *Bull Soc Anat Paris*, 6, 398–407.

Busnel, R. G. & Classe, A. (1976). *Whistled languages*. New York: Springer-Verlag.

Caplan, D. (1996). *Language: Structure, processing, and disorders*. Cambridge: MIT Press.

Chabert, J- L. (2008). Algorithms. In T. Gowers (Ed.), *The Princeton companion to mathematics* (pp. 106–117). Princeton, NJ: Princeton University Press.

Chartrand, J. L. & Bargh, J. A. (1999). The chameleon effect: The perception-behavior link and social interaction. *Journal of Personality and Social Psychology*, 76, 893–910.

Chomsky, N. (1957). *Syntactic structures*. Mouton.

Chomsky, N. (1986). *Knowledge of language: Its nature, origins, and use*. New York: Praeger.

Decety, J. & Grezes, J. (2006). The power of simulation: Imagining one's own and other's behavior. *Brain Research*, 1079, 4–14.

Decety, J. & Lamm, C. (2006). Human empathy through the lens of social neuroscience. *The Scientific World Journal*, 6, 1146–1163.

Diehl, R. L., Lotto, A. J., & Holt, L. L. (2004). Speech perception. *Annual Review of Psychology*, 55, 149–179.

Dronkers, N. F., Redfern, B. B., & Knight, R. T. 1999. The neural architecture of language. In M. S. Gazzaniga (Ed.), *The cognitive neurosciences*. Cambridge, MA: MIT Press.

Fadiga L., Craighero L., Buccino G., & Rizzolatti G. (2002). Speech listening specifically modulates the excitability of tongue muscles: A TMS study. *European Journal of Neuroscience*, 15, 399–402.

Fant, G. (1967). Sound, features and perception. *STL-QPSR* 2–3/1967, 1–14.

Farah, M. J. & Feinberg, T. E., (Eds.) (2000). *Patient-based approaches to cognitive neuroscience*. Cambridge: MIT Press.

Frankel, A. S., Clark, C. W., Herman, L. M. & Gabriele, C. M. (1995). Spatial distribution, habitat utilization, and social interactions of humpback whales, Megaptera novaeangliae, off Hawaii, determined using acoustic and visual techniques. *Canadian Journal of Zoology*, 73, 1134–1146.

Francis, A. L. & Nusbaum, H. C. (1996). Paying attention to speaking rate. *Proceedings of the International Conference on Spoken Language Processing*, Philadelphia.

Friederici, A. D., Bahlmann, J., Heim, S., Schubotz, R. I., & Anwander, A. (2006). The brain differentiates human and non-human grammars: Functional localization and structural connectivity. Proceedings of the National Academy of Sciences, 103, 2458–2463.

Gallese V., Fadiga L., Fogassi L., Rizzolatti G. (1996). Action recognition in the premotor cortex. *Brain*, 119, 593–609.

Gallese V., Keysers C., & Rizzolatti G. (2004). A unifying view of the basis of social cognition. *Trends in Cognitive Sciences*, 8, 396–403.

Geschwind, N. (1970). The organization of language and the brain. *Science*, 170, 940–944.

Giles, H. (1973). Accent mobility: A model and some data. *Anthropological Linguistics*, 15, 87–105.

Giles, H. & Coupland, N. (1991). *Language: Contexts and consequences*. Pacific Grove: Brooks-Cole.

Giles, H. & Smith, P. (1979). Accommodation theory: Optimal levels of convergence. In H. Giles & R. N. St. Clair (Eds.), *Language and social psychology*. Baltimore: University Park Press, 45–65.

Gleitman, L. R. & Liberman, M. Y. (1969). *Invitation to cognitive science language* (Vol. 1). Cambridge, MA: MIT Press.

Glenberg, A. M. & Kaschak, M. P. (2002). Grounding language in action. *Psychonomic Bulletin & Review*, 9, 558–565.

Grodzinsky, Y. & Andrea S. 2008. The battle for Broca's region. *Trends in Cognitive Sciences*, 12, 474–480.

Goodale, M. A., & Milner, A. D. (1992). Separate visual pathways for perception and action. *Trends in Neurosciences*, 15, 20–25.

Hauk, O., Johnsrude, I., & Pulvermüller, F. (2004). Somatotopic representation of action words in human motor and premotor cortex. *Neuron*, 41, 301–307.

Hagoort, P. (2005). On Broca, brain, and binding: A new framework. *Trends in Cognitive Sciences*, 9 (9), 416–423.

Hickok, G. and Poeppel, D. (2004). Dorsal and ventral streams: A framework for understanding aspects of the functional anatomy of language. *Cognition*, 92, 67–99.

Holt, L. E. & Beilock, S. L. (2006). Expertise and its embodiment: Examining the impact of sensorimotor skill expertise on the representation of action-related text. *Psychonomic Bulletin & Review*, 13, 694–701.

Hanakawa, T., Immisch, I., Toma, K., Dimyan, M. A., Van Gelderen, P., & Hallett, M. (2003). Functional properties of brain areas associated with motor execution and imagery. *Journal of Neurophysiology*, 89, 989–1002.

Hauser, M. D., Chomsky, N., & Fitch, T. (2002). The faculty of language: What is it, who has it, and how did it evolve? *Science*, 298, 1569–1579.

Heiligenberg, W. F. (1991). *Neural nets in electric fish*. MIT Press, Cambridge.

Hockett, C. F. (1960). *The origin of speech. Scientific American*, 203, 88–96.

Jeannerod, M. (1994). The representing brain. Neural correlates of motor intention and imagery. *Behavioral and Brain Science*, 17, 187–245.

Johnson, K., Strand, E. A., & D'Imperio, M. (1999). Auditory-visual integration of talker gender in vowel perception. *Journal of Phonetics*, 27, 359–384.

Kinzler, K. D., Shutts, K., Dejesus, J., & Spelke, E. S. (2009). Accent trumps race in guiding children's social preferences. *Social Cognition*, 27, 623–634.

Kinzler, K. D., Dupoux, E., & Spelke, E. S. (2007). The native language of social cognition. *Proceedings of the National Academy of Sciences*, 104, 12577–12580.

Kroodsma, D. E. & Miller, E. H. (Eds.) (1996). *Ecology and evolution of acoustic communication in birds*. Ithaca: Cornell University Press.

Lakin, J. & Chartrand, T. L. (2003). Using nonconscious behavioral mimicry to create affiliation and rapport. *Psychological Science*, 14, 334–339.

Liberman, A. M., Cooper, F. S., Shankweiler, D. P., & Studdert-Kennedy, M. (1967). Perception of the speech code. *Psychological Review*, 74, 431–461.

Liberman, A. M. & Mattingly, I. G. (1985). The motor theory of speech perception revised. *Cognition*, 21, 1–36.

Lichtheim, L. (1885). On aphasia. *Brain*, 7:433–484.

Lotto, A. J., Hickok, G. S., & Holt, L. L. (2009). Reflections on mirror neurons and speech perception. *Trends in Cognitive Science*, 13, 110–114.

Luks, T. L., Nusbaum, H. C., & Levy, J. (1998). Hemispheric involvement in the perception of syntactic prosody is dynamically dependent on task demands. *Brain and Language*, 65, 313–332.

Magnuson, J. S. & Nusbaum, H. C. (2007). Acoustic differences, listener expectations, and the perceptual accommodation of talker variability. *Journal of Experimental Psychology: Human Perception and Performance*, 33, 391–409.

Margoliash, D. (2002). Evaluating theories of bird song learning: Implications for future directions. *Journal of Comparative Physiology A*, 188, 851–866.

Margoliash, D., & Nusbaum, H. C. (2009). Language: the perspective from organismal biology. Trends in Cognitive Sciences, 13, 505–510.

Marler, P., Peters, S. (1980). Birdsong and speech: Evidence for special processing. In: Eimas, P., Miller, J. (Eds.), *Perspectives on the study of speech*. Erlbaum, Hillsdale, 75–112.

McComb, K., Reby, D., Baker, L., Moss, C., Sayialel, S. (2003). Long-distance communication of acoustic cues to social identity in African elephants. *Animal Behaviour*, 65, 317–329.

McGurk H. & MacDonald, J. (1976). Hearing lips and seeing voices. *Nature*, 264, 746–748.

McNeill, D. (1992). *Hand and mind: What gestures reveal about thought*. Chicago: University of Chicago Press.

Meister, I. G. & Iacoboni, M. (2007). No language-specific activation during linguistic processing of observed actions. *PLoS ONE, 2*(9): e89, 1–7.

Mishkin, M., Ungerleider, L. G., & Macko, K. A. (1983).Object vision and spatial vision: Two cortical pathways. *Trends in Neurosciences, 6*, 414–417.

Moran, J. & Desimone, R. (1985). Selective attention gates visual processing in the extrastriate cortex. *Science, 229*, 782–784.

Moss, C. F. & Sinha, S. R., (2003). Neurobiology of echolocation in bats. *Current Opinion in Neurobiology, 13*, 755–762.

Musacchia, G. E., Sams, M., Nicol, T. G., & Kraus, N. (2006) Seeing speech affects acoustic information processing in the human brainstem. *Experimental Brain Research, 168*, 1–10.

Nelson, M. E. & MacIver, M. A. (2006) Sensory acquisition in active sensing systems. *Journal of Comparative Physiology A, 192*, 573–586.

Nusbaum, H. C. & Magnuson, J. S. (1997). Talker normalization: Phonetic constancy as a cognitive process. In K. A. Johnson & J. W. Mullennix (Eds.), *Talker variability in speech processing*. New York, NY: Academic Press.

Nusbaum, H. C. & Schwab, E. C. (1986). The role of attention and active processing in speech perception. In E. C. Schwab & H. C. Nusbaum (Eds.), *Pattern recognition by humans and machines: Vol. 1. Speech perception*. San Diego: Academic Press, 113–157.

Pardo, J. S. (2006). On phonetic convergence during conversational interaction, *Journal of the Acoustical Society of America, 119*, 2382–2393.

Peterson, G. & Barney, H. (1952). Control methods used in a study of the vowels. *Journal of the Acoustical Society of America, 24*, 175–184.

Pickering, M. J. & Garrod, S. (2004) Towards a mechanistic psychology of dialogue. *Behavioral and Brain Sciences, 27*, 169–226.

Price, C., Thierry, G., & Griffiths, T. (2005). Speech-specific auditory processing: Where is it? *Trends in Cognitive Sciences, 9*, 271–276.

Rauschecker, J. P. (1998). Cortical processing of complex sounds. *Current Opinion in Neurobiology, 8*, 516–521.

Rizzolatti, G. & Arbib, M. A. (1999). Language within our grasp. *Trends in Neurosciences, 21*, 188–194.

Rizzolatti, G., & Craighero, L. (2004). The mirror-neuron system. *Annual Review of Neuroscience, 27*, 169–192.

Rizzolatti, G., Fogassi, L., & Gallese, V. (2001). Neurophysiological mechanisms underlying the understanding and imitation of action. *Nature Review Neuroscience, 2*, 661–670.

Roland, P. (1993). *Brain activation*. New York: Wiley-Liss.

Rubin, D. L. (1992). Nonlanguage factors affecting undergraduates' judgments of nonnative English-speaking teaching assistants. *Research in Higher Education, 33*, 511–531.

Shintel, H., Nusbaum, H. C., & Okrent, A. (2006). Analog acoustic expression in speech communication. *Journal of Memory and Language, 55*, 167–177.

Shintel, H. & Nusbaum, H. C. (2007). The sound of motion in spoken language: Visual information conveyed by acoustic properties of speech. *Cognition, 105*, 681–690.

Shintel, H. & Nusbaum, H. C. (2008). Moving to the speed of sound: Context modulation of the effect of acoustic properties of speech. *Cognitive Science, 32*, 1063–1074.

Skipper, J. L., Goldin-Meadow, S., Nusbaum, H. C., & Small, S. L. (2009). Neural mechanisms of gesture processing during language comprehension. *Current Biology, 19*, 661–667.

Skipper, J. I., Nusbaum, H. C., & Small, S. L. (2005). Listening to talking faces: Motor cortical activation during speech perception. *NeuroImage, 25*, 76–89.

Skipper, J. I., Nusbaum, H. C., & Small, S. L. (2006). Lending a helping hand to hearing: Another motor theory of speech perception. In M. A. Arbib, (Ed.). *Action to language via the mirror neuron system*. Cambridge University Press, 250–285.

Skipper, J. I., van Wassenhove, V., Nusbaum, H. C., & Small, S. L. (2007). Hearing lips and seeing voices: How cortical areas support speech production mediate audiovisual speech perception. *Cerebral Cortex, 17*, 2387–2399.

Stevens, K. N. & Blumstein, S. E. (1981). The search for invariant acoustic correlates of phonetic features. In P. D. Eimas & J. Miller (Eds.), *Perspectives on the study of speech*. Hillsdale, NJ: Lawrence Erlbaum Associates, 1–38.

Stevens, K. N. & Halle, M. (1967). Remarks on analysis by synthesis and distinctive features. In W. Walthen-Dunn (Ed.), *Models for the perception of speech and visual form*. Cambridge: MIT Press, 88–102.

Suga, N. & Ma, X. (2003) Multiparametric corticofugal modulation and plasticity in the auditory system. *Nature Reviews Neuroscience, 4*, 783–794.

Sumby, W. H. & Pollack, I. (1954). Visual contribution of speech intelligibility in noise. *Journal of the Acoustical Society of America, 26*, 212–215.

Tettamanti, M., Buccino, G., Saccuman, M. C., Gallese, V., Danna, M., Scifo, P., et al. (2005). Listening to action-related sentences activates fronto-parietal motor circuits. *Journal of Cognitive Neuroscience, 17*, 273–281.

Van Baaren, R. B., Horgan, T. G., Chartrand, T. L., & Dijkmans, M. (2004). The forest, the trees and the chameleon: Context-dependency and mimicry. *Journal of Personality and Social Psychology, 86*, 453–459.

Wernicke, C. (1874). *Der aphasische symptomenkomplex*. Breslau: Cohn & Weigert.

Wilson, S. M., Saygin, A. P., Sereno, M. I., & Iacoboni M. (2004). Listening to speech activates motor areas involved in speech production. *Nature Neuroscience, 7*, 701–702.

Wilson, S., Iacoboni, M. (2006). Neural responses to non-native phonemes varying in producibility: evidence for the sensorimotor nature of speech perception, *NeuroImage, 33*, 316–325.

Wong, P. C. M., Nusbaum, H. C., & Small, S. L. (2004). Neural bases of talker normalization. *Journal of Cognitive Neuroscience, 16*, 1173–1184.

PART 5

Group Processes

The Neurobiology of Primate Social Behavior

Melissa D. Bauman, Eliza Bliss-Moreau, Christopher J. Machado, *and* David G. Amaral

Abstract

This chapter begins by providing a neural systems perspective to studying the social brain. It then provides a brief summary of macaque monkey social behavior before proposing a model of social processing and describing in detail research on several putative components of the social brain. These include the amygdala and the anterior cingulate cortex. It briefly discusses the mirror neuron system before returning to descriptions of the orbitofrontal and inferior temporal contributions to social function. Much of the data reported is based on lesion studies and, to a lesser extent, on electrophysiological studies. Noninvasive studies of the social brain in the nonhuman primate are beginning to appear and the chapter concludes by highlighting some future directions for research in the nonhuman primate.

Keywords: Macaque monkey, social brain, amygdala, anterior cingulate cortex, orbitofrontal cortex, inferior temporal cortex, mirror neurons

Introduction

The nonhuman primate, particularly the macaque monkey, provides a useful model system for evaluating components of the social brain. While the macaque brain is only about one tenth the size of the human brain, it appears to contain most, if not all, of the different cortical and subcortical areas that are found in the human brain. This is not to say that the organization of the macaque monkey brain is identical to that of the human brain (Preuss, 2000). There are even certain neuronal cell types in the human and great ape brains that do not appear to be present in the macaque monkey brain (Nimchinsky, et al., 1999). The choice of the macaque monkeys, in particular the rhesus macaque, as the model for much of modern biomedical

research is, in part, an artifact of the polio crisis of the previous century. Rhesus monkey kidney cells were used both in the production and testing of polio vaccines (Blume & Geesink, 2000). Because of concerns over availability of rhesus monkeys for importation from India and Asia, it was deemed in the national interest of the United States to establish a system of regional primate centers for the development of adequate supplies of rhesus monkeys (Dukelow & Whitehair, 1995). This action, combined with the burgeoning research efforts fostered by the National Institutes of Health, lead to the rhesus monkey becoming the subject for widespread biomedical research. As a result of this series of events, there is now an enormous database of neurobiological information on the structure and function of the rhesus[1] monkey brain. These data are both far more comprehensive and fine grained than is currently achievable through analyses of the human brain.

It could be argued that the rhesus monkey is not the best model for studying human social behavior. The titi monkey (*Callicebus*), for example, is a much better model of lifelong monogamy (Bales, Mason, Catana, Cherry, & Mendoza, 2007). But, Dario Maestripieri, in his book Macachiavellian Intelligence: How Rhesus Macaques and Humans Have Conquered the World (Maestripieri, 2007), argues that there are many parallels between the human and macaque monkey social systems as well as their biological underpinnings. Both live in complex, hierarchical social units that rely on emotional expression and aggression for control. Both take advantage of a situation when they think that they have the upper hand! With the publication of the rhesus monkey genome (Gibbs, et al., 2007), (which demonstrated 90–93% alignment of nucleotide sequences with the human genome), other similarities have been demonstrated. Polymorphisms in the serotonin transporter gene, for example, which have been associated with temperamental differences and susceptibility to psychiatric disorders, are similar in humans and rhesus monkeys, but not other nonhuman primates (Champoux, et al., 2002; Lesch, et al., 1997; Trefilov, Krawczak, Berard, & Schmidtke, 1999). Given these biological and behavioral similarities between humans and macaque monkeys, these animals provide an excellent tool to better understand the structures and functions of the human brain.

In the following sections, we first provide a neural systems perspective to studying the social brain. We then provide a brief summary of macaque monkey social behavior before proposing a model of social processing and describing in detail research on several putative components of the social brain. These include the amygdala and the anterior cingulate cortex. We then briefly discuss the mirror neuron system before returning to descriptions of the orbitofrontal and inferior temporal contributions to social function. Many fundamental questions remain and we are not currently able to define a social brain system like we can a visual or somatosensory system in the rhesus monkey brain. Much of the data that we report is based on lesion studies and, to a lesser extent on electrophysiological studies. Noninvasive studies of the social brain in the nonhuman primate are beginning to appear and we end the chapter by highlighting some future directions for research in the nonhuman primate.

A Neural Systems Approach to the Social Brain

Neuroscientists, who take a neural systems approach to understanding the brain, attempt to group interconnected brain regions that appear to be involved in a particular behavioral function. This approach has been most successful in the definition of sensory systems. One can track the visual system, for example, from receptors in the retina, through relays in the thalamus to primary visual cortex in the occipital lobe. From there, projections reach as much as 70% of the primate cerebral cortex that constitutes the unimodal visual processing regions of the brain. From research conducted in the nonhuman primate, more than 30 separable brain areas have been defined that carry out various component processes of visual perception (Felleman & Van Essen, 1991). These brain regions are considered "visual" based both on neuroanatomical connectivity as well as electrophysiological analyses of neuronal responsivity. Although, even these "visual" portions of the cortex can be influenced by information from other sensory modalities (Maunsell, Sclar, Nealey, & DePriest, 1991).

As one attempts to define the neural systems underlying higher cognitive functions, the ability to track from specific receptors to neural systems is lost. Memory, for example, can be unisensory but is often polysensory and is clearly not linked to any particular set of peripheral receptors. It is well accepted that structures in the medial temporal lobe are essential for forming declarative memories (conscious memories for facts and events) (Squire, Stark, & Clark, 2004). The definition of this memory system relied initially on the analysis of human patients, such as H.M. (Corkin, 2002) who have more or less selective damage to the hippocampal formation and a behavioral syndrome characterized by impairments specifically in the domain of memory. In fact, it was the finding that H.M. and similar patients with hippocampal damage (Zola-Morgan, Squire, & Amaral, 1986) have memory impairments without concomitant sensory, motor, motivational, or attentional deficits that allowed the specification of the hippocampal formation as a focal point of one memory system of the brain. Once this focal point was established, neuroanatomical studies and lesion research carried out in the nonhuman primate have identified other brain regions such as the perirhinal and parahippocampal cortices (Suzuki & Amaral, 1994, 2004) and retrosplenial cortex (Kobayashi & Amaral, 2003, 2007) as important components of the medial temporal lobe memory system.

A central question for the field of social neuroscience is whether the social brain is organized in a manner similar to memory. If it is, one would expect that the elimination or silencing of candidate social brain regions would dramatically alter normal social behavior without affecting other sensory, motor, or cognitive functions. Data in support of this notion are not overwhelming and raise the question, why would we expect that there is a social brain system in the first place?

A seminal paper in the evolution of research on the neurobiology of the social brain was published by Leslie Brothers in 1990 (Brothers, 1990). In that paper, Brothers proposed that the social brain was composed of several brain regions, including the amygdala, anterior cingulate cortex, orbitofrontal cortex, and temporal cortex (Brothers, 1990). As we will develop in more detail below, the exact role that these structures play in social processing, or even if these structures are essential for social behavior, remains unclear to this day. Moreover, recent evidence indicates that regions of the brain not previously implicated in social processing may indeed play an important role (e.g., the mirror neuron system of the ventral premotor and inferior parietal cortices).

Brother's review included a summary of arguments supporting the existence of neural networks specialized for social processing. This included evidence: 1) for a common evolution of social behavior, 2) that social knowledge is distinct from other knowledge, 3) that there is a well-defined developmental progression for the emergence of social behavior and 4) that social behavior can be selectively disrupted in disorders such as autism. We briefly summarize these main lines of evidence for the existence of a social brain.

From an evolutionary perspective, the ability to accurately interpret and produce appropriate social behavior is of paramount importance for humans and other group-living primates. Sophisticated social interactions form the basis for primate societies and are necessary for forming and maintaining long-lasting relationships with other group members, for acquiring resources, for maintaining protection from predators (and competitors) and ultimately ensuring the propagation of one's genetic material (Cheney, Seyfarth, & Smuts, 1986). In her review, Brothers highlighted the phylogeny of facial expressions in primates as one line of evidence for a common evolution of social processing. She quotes Charles Darwin:

"The community of certain expressions in distinct though allied species, as in the movements of the same facial muscles during laughter by man and by various monkeys, is rendered somewhat more intelligible, if we believe in their descent from a common progenitor" (Darwin, 1872; Brothers, 1990, p.29).

Nearly a century later, Ekman and colleagues demonstrated that a specific set of emotional facial expressions is commonly generated and widely recognized across highly divergent cultures (Ekman, 1993; Ekman & Friesen, 1971), suggesting that the ability to generate facial expressions that relate them to emotion states has been highly conserved throughout the development of human culture and likely across the phylogenetic and evolutionary spectrum. Moreover, closely related species of non-human primates display similarities in facial muscular structure and produce facial expressions believed to be homologous to several human expressions (Parr, Waller, & Fugate, 2005). Brothers suggested that as this capacity to produce social signals evolved, it is likely that neural systems evolved to facilitate the accurate processing of this information. What remains unknown, however, is the precise relationship between pressures from the social domain and corresponding changes in neural circuitry (Barrett, Henzi, & Dunbar, 2003; Dunbar, 1998; Reader & Laland, 2002). Moreover, a fundamental question is whether brain regions have become specialized for the processing of social stimuli (and therefore their loss would lead to a focal impairment of social behavior) or whether processing of social stimuli are handled by more general sensory and cognitive processing systems. The fusiform face area, for example, appears to be specialized for processing configurations of facial features (Kanwisher, McDermott, & Chun, 1997) (presumably an important part of the identification of social expressions such as fear or anger). But, the fusiform face area also appears to be involved in the identification of any complex object with which an individual is expert (Gauthier, Tarr, Anderson, Skudlarski, & Gore, 1999).

Brothers also suggested that social knowledge is operationally distinct from other domains of knowledge. She proposed that certain cognitive functions, such as making transitive inferences, operate most strongly in the context of social processing. In tests of the capacity for making transitive inference, overlapping pairs of items are trained (e.g., A + B−, B + C−, C + D−, and D + E−, where + and − indicate correct and incorrect choices). During training, terms B and D are correct and incorrect equally often. Later, participants who choose B over D when presented with novel pair BD are said to demonstrate transitive inference. Although transitive inference has been demonstrated in several primate species in the laboratory using inanimate objects as the "terms," it requires an enormous amount of training to reach criteria (McGonigle & Chalmers, 1977). In contrast, many primate species live in well-defined dominance hierarchies and are able to quickly and accurately determine the social status of other group members, mainly through understanding family relationships (Cheney & Seyfarth, 1990). To do this they are using conspecifics as the "terms" of a transitive inference paradigm and are clearly much more adept at performing these complex logical operations within a naturalistic social context. This difference suggests that at least some aspects of primate intelligence evolved specifically to solve the challenges of interacting with conspecifics (Cheney, et al., 1986). The increasing complexity of social groups may have forced the evolution of ever more sophisticated social cognitive processing.

Brothers also proposed that the distinctive and characteristic trajectory that characterizes primate social development is also evidence for the existence of a social brain. Newborn human infants, for example, display visual preferences for face-like stimuli (Goren, Sarty, & Wu, 1975; Johnson, Dziurawiec, Ellis, & Morton, 1991; Morton & Johnson, 1991) and are capable of imitating adult facial gestures immediately after birth (Meltzoff & Moore, 1977, 1983). Infant monkeys also display at least a transient ability to imitate facial gestures in the first week after birth (Ferrari, et al., 2006). These innate social predispositions suggest that components of the human and nonhuman primate genetic endowment generate brain regions that are specialized to mediate complex social interactions.

Brothers further argued that selective changes in social behavior as a result of developmental disorders such as autism support the existence of a social brain. Autism is a neurodevelopmental disorder characterized by deficits in social interactions, impaired communication, and restricted patterns of behaviors, interests, and activities. Of these three domains, the alteration in social behavior is often considered the "hallmark" feature. Brothers suggested that the "inborn selective absence of social cognition" that characterizes autism provides evidence that social processing can selectively be disrupted. Unfortunately, the neuropathology of

autism is still quite uncertain (Amaral, Schumann, & Nordahl, 2008). But, information concerning which brain regions are impaired in autism may ultimately provide suggestive evidence about what regions subserve normal social cognition. Research on other neurodevelopmental disorders that alter social behavior may provide further insight into the social brain. For example, Williams Syndrome is a rare genetic disorder caused by a hemizygous deletion in chromosome band 7q11.23. In contrast to patients with autism, individuals with Williams Syndrome display hypersociability (Bellugi, Lichtenberger, Mills, Galaburda, & Korenberg, 1999). These changes in social behavior resulting from a genetic alteration provide additional evidence of a genetic basis of social development (Doyle, Bellugi, Korenberg, & Graham, 2004) and support the notion that there is indeed a social brain.

If there is indeed a social brain, how can we determine which neural structures play a critical role in processing social information? One approach is to examine social processes in animal models which are more amenable to traditional neuroscience methodologies. The rich repertoire of social behavior described below makes macaques a particularly good model in which to study the neural basis of social processing.

Macaque Social Behavior

Among primates, the genus *Macaca* is one of the most successful primate radiations, second only to humans in geographical range. The success of macaque monkeys is due to an evolutionary history which has shaped both brain and behavior, resulting in a sophisticated social structure and the requisite neural systems needed to navigate complex social interactions (Barrett, et al., 2003; Reader & Laland, 2002; Wrangham, 1987). In the following section we will briefly describe the social structure and communication of macaque monkeys. We should point out that while we will simply refer to "macaques" throughout this chapter, this is an oversimplification as there are well-defined behavioral differences among the approximately 20 different species of macaques (Maestripieri, 2005; Thierry, 1985). It is also important to note that although we share over 90% of our genetic material with macaque monkeys, the last common ancestor of humans and macaques dates back more than 30 million years (Kay, Ross, & Williams, 1997). As a result, homologous relationships among behavior and brain regions are not always clear (Sereno & Tootell, 2005). Moreover, some aspects of human social cognition, such as theory of mind, may not be possible to study in macaque monkeys. We are, however, able to study many fundamental aspects of social behavior common to many group-living primates, including the use of species-typical social signals, the motivation to interact with group members and the ability to form and maintain life-long relationships with group members.

Macaque monkeys live in large, multi-male and female groups consisting of 10 to 100 individuals (Lindburg, 1991). Female macaques generally remain in their natal group for the duration of their lives, while males emigrate into a new group when they reach 3–5 years of age (Altmann, 1967). Each large group of macaques thus consists of several matrilines (i.e., clusters of related females and their offspring) as well as a number of unrelated males (Wrangham, 1980). Most macaque species have well-defined, stable dominance relationships among individuals within a matriline, as well as dominance relationships across matrilines (Drickamer, 1975). Macaques must therefore have knowledge of their individual rank within their own matriline, as well as the status of that matriline within the larger group. The prediction of social rank within the hierarchy (i.e., dominance rank) is closely linked to the dominance status of kin, with high-ranking mothers producing high-ranking offspring (Missakian, 1972; Sade, 1967). Within a matriline, infants will acquire rank just below their mothers and above their older siblings (Datta, 1984; de Waal, 1977). Remarkably, infant macaques quickly learn their place within the complex social structure. As early as the first year of life, infant macaques begin to express species-appropriate expressions of dominance by directing more aggression to adults that rank lower than their mothers, but not to adults that outrank their mothers (Datta, 1984).

The strong matrilinear structure of macaque society results in social networks spanning several generations of mothers, daughters, and other closely related females (Altmann, 1967). Social grooming is of paramount importance in establishing and maintaining these long-lasting social relationships (Matheson & Bernstein, 2000). The amount of time spent near, or in physical contact with, other individuals is a good indicator of the strength of their social bond. Affiliative behavior in infants and juveniles consists primarily of play behavior, often considered an important precursor for developing species-typical social behavior (Ruppenthal, Harlow, Eisele, Harlow, & Suomi, 1974). Infants spend most of their time interacting with members of their immediate social group, primarily their mother's close female kin and their offspring (Berman, 1982). The development of affiliative networks and alliances is thus profoundly influenced by the mother and further solidifies social relationships among closely related individuals (de Waal, 1996).

The complex social structure of macaques requires a sophisticated communication system that allows the conveyance of signals of dominance, submission, affiliation, mating behaviors and parental care (Maestripieri, 1997). From an ethological perspective, an animal's ability to recognize social attributes and predict the outcome of a social encounter undoubtedly serves an adaptive function of minimizing injuries that might be sustained through aggressive conflicts (Bernstein, 1981). Much like humans, macaque monkeys communicate with each other through a variety of facial expressions, body postures, and vocalizations (Lindberg, 1971). Among these social signals, the use of facial expressions is one of the most salient features of macaque social behavior and the most similar to our own social communication. Much like human infants, neonatal macaques show an early preference for social stimuli and readily attend and respond to the face of their mother (Ferrari, Paukner, Ionica, & Suomi, 2009; Kuwahata, Adachi, Fujita, Tomonaga, & Matsuzawa, 2004; Lutz, Lockard, Gunderson, & Grant, 1998; Mendelson, 1982; Mendelson, Haith, & Goldman-Rakic, 1982). Newborn macaques even demonstrate a transient ability to imitate human facial gestures (Ferrari, Paukner, Ruggiero, et al., 2009; Ferrari, et al., 2006). Facial threats (i.e., staring with mouth open, eyebrows raised, and ears flattened) commonly occur in the contexts of competition and aggression and are generally displayed by higher-ranking monkeys to lower-ranking monkeys (Bernstein & Mason, 1963). In contrast, the grimace (i.e., mouth closed, lips retracted to expose teeth) and lipsmack (i.e., rapid opening and closing of the lips) are common submissive signals given in response to threat, aggression, or approach from a dominant animal, but may also be used to convey affiliative intentions (Maestripieri, 1996). Body postures, such as presentation of hindquarters (a submissive gesture), are often seen in response to aggression and or approach from a dominant animal, while presentation of other body parts for grooming is associated with affiliative interactions (Maestripieri & Wallen, 1997). In addition to visual social signals, macaques also use a number of species-typical vocalizations to communicate (Rowell & Hinde, 1962). Common agonistic vocalizations include screams, barks, and recruitment screams which are used to elicit aid from other individuals during conflicts (Gouzoules & Gouzoules, 2000; Gouzoules, Gouzoules, & Tomaszycki, 1998), while coo calls and grunts are more often associated with affiliative interactions (Kalin, Shelton, & Snowdon, 1992).

Due to space constraints, we are only able to describe a small sampling of the rich behavioral repertoire of macaque monkeys. The use of these and other social signals provides the means for sophisticated social interactions that are dependent on the identity of the individual as well as the context in which the interaction occurs. Macaque monkeys are capable of rapidly and accurately processing a barrage of complex social information, including individual identity, dominance rank, social signals, as well as the presence or absence of allies (Deaner, Khera, & Platt, 2005; Drea, 1998; Drea & Wallen, 1999; Flombaum & Santos, 2005). What brain regions are responsible for mediating the interactions between a macaque monkey and its social world? We next provide a perspective with which to evaluate the role of candidate brain regions and then review data implicating certain brain regions as components of the social brain.

Model of Social Processing

Given the complexity of primate social behavior, we have found it useful to generate a schematic of social information processing in order to clearly define the component processes of social interactions (Bauman & Amaral, 2008). Our schematic breaks down the interpretation and production of social behavior into component processes in order to more clearly define the essential and modulatory brain functions underlying social interactions (Figure 45.1). In order to process the information conveyed in a social stimulus, such as a facial expression, the expression must first be perceived as an important source of information. The meaning of that particular expression must be evaluated and finally an appropriate social response must be generated. There is, of course, the overarching precondition that the individual must be motivated to engage in social interactions or to interpret the gestures of others as social communication. Beyond this obligatory social impetus, the fundamental components of social processing include: 1) perception of the social stimulus, 2) evaluation of its social significance, and 3) production of a species-appropriate response. The species-appropriate response could either be the production of a social response gesture or the interpretation of the disposition or intention of the other individual. The nature of that response (or whether a response will even be generated) will depend on several modulatory factors including: 1) whether emotions such as fear are generated that might modulate the response, 2) the motivation to

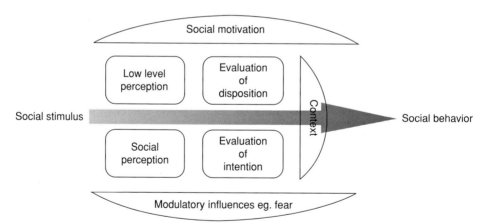

Fig. 45.1 It is useful to break down the component processes of social behavior into executable functions by different brain regions. This is a simplified model that indicates some of the facets of social behavior. There is an overarching and essential condition that the organism must be interested in engaging other conspecifics, in other words, must have social motivation. Through attentional mechanisms, a social stimulus such as a facial expression must initially be perceived at a lower level (differentiating a face from any other complex object) and then at a higher level to determine the "social" content of the expression (those features that differentiate an affiliative facial expression from a threatening one). The organism must then use the information conveyed by the gesture to interpret the disposition and intention of the other organism. Whether the perceiving organism acts and what behavior is generated is also conditioned by the context of the situation (does the perceiver have the upper hand in a potential battle or is he outnumbered) and whether other emotions such as fear are limiting potential responses. Each of these component processes are subsumed by one or more brain regions that could be said to be contributing to social behavior.

respond, and 3) whether the context is conducive to a social response. Given adequate perception, evaluation, motivation, emotion, and context, the brain must then execute an appropriate response that may take the form of thought or deed. In the remainder of this chapter, we evaluate a number of brain regions implicated as components in the social brain and summarize evidence related to which facet(s) of social cognition each may be involved.

Putative Structures of the Social Brain
Amygdala

The primate amygdala is a cytoarchitectonically complex structure buried deep within the anterior temporal lobe. The unique neuroanatomical connections of the amygdala allow it to combine highly processed sensory information from all modalities with contextual information needed to evaluate social stimuli and coordinate behavioral responses (Emery & Amaral, 2000). While the amygdala is responsive to a variety of social stimuli, its activity is particularly driven by signals that convey potential danger. Electrophysiological recording studies (Brothers & Ring, 1993; Brothers, Ring, & Kling, 1990; A. Kling, Steklis, & Deutsch, 1979; Leonard, Rolls, Wilson, & Baylis, 1985; Rolls, 1984) have demonstrated that neurons in the amygdala modulate their activity in response to a wide array of social stimuli, especially facial expressions depicting fear or anger (Gothard, Battaglia, Erickson, Spitler, & Amaral, 2007). These results have been confirmed by noninvasive functional magnetic resonance imaging (fMRI) in rhesus monkeys. Hoffman and colleagues (2007) showed that the basolateral amygdala was particularly active when animals viewed threatening facial expressions relative to appeasement gestures.

Lesion studies also implicate the amygdala in the detection of, and appropriate response to, social stimuli. Early studies using large temporal lobe resections (Rosvold, Mirsky, & Pribram, 1954) or aspiration lesions (see for review, Kling, 1992) resulted in monkeys that had drastically altered social behavior. However, the magnitude and direction (increase or decrease) of the social changes depended on many factors, including gender, age, level of positive social signals in a group, amount of pre-operative social experience, and complexity of the social environment (Bachevalier, 2000; Kling, 1992). An additional complicating factor in these early studies was the extent of lesions, which in many cases included not only the amygdala but also the adjacent temporal cortical areas which are known to regulate emotional responses (Meunier & Bachevalier, 2002), respond to various kinds of social cues (Bruce, Desimone, & Gross, 1981; Perrett, Rolls, & Caan, 1982), and associate visual stimuli with their incentive value (Liu, Murray, & Richmond, 2000; Liu & Richmond, 2000). These complications have been mitigated in more recent studies that used a neurotoxin (ibotenic acid) to selectively destroy amygdala neurons while sparing adjacent cortical areas and fibers of passage. When adult macaques with bilateral neurotoxic amygdala lesions interact either in pairs (Emery, et al., 2001) or in groups of four (Machado, et al., 2008), they show a more unrestrained pattern of social behavior (e.g., approaching to within arm's reach, physical contact and grooming) than control animals. Similarly, when $GABA_A$ antagonists are used to stimulate the nonhuman primate amygdala, animals show decreased social contact, a complete loss of social play, as well as increased passivity and active withdrawal from social interaction (Malkova, 2003). Specific deficits in behavioral responses to threat have also been demonstrated for monkeys with bilateral neurotoxic amygdala lesions in stable social groups (Machado & Bachevalier, 2006). This mounting evidence suggests that one role of the amygdala is to signal the level of danger or threat present in the social environment, and thereby modulate social behavior adaptively. This interpretation is also consistent with the human literature. Humans with amygdala lesions also demonstrate specific deficits in identifying fearful facial expressions (Adolphs, Tranel, Damasio, & Damasio, 1994), rating the magnitude of fearful expressions (Adolphs, Tranel, Damasio, & Damasio, 1995) and assessing the approachability or trustworthiness of unfamiliar individuals (Adolphs, Tranel, & Damasio, 1998).

Understanding the function of a complex neural region such as the amygdala in the adult primate is informative, but another question, particularly germane to developmental psychopathology, is how does the amygdala factor into the development of social behavior? The first studies of neonatal amygdala damage in nonhuman primates reported few changes in behavior (Kling & Green, 1967) or changes in fear-related behaviors (Thompson, 1968, 1981; Thompson, Bergland, & Towfighi, 1977; Thompson, Schwartzbaum, & Harlow, 1969). More recently, Bachevalier (1994) re-evaluated the effects of medial temporal lobe damage in neonatal rhesus monkeys. These studies included a group of six neonates that received bilateral aspiration lesions of the amygdala, resulting in damage to the amygdala, piriform cortex, rostral portion of the entorhinal cortex, and inferior temporal cortical area TE (Bachevalier, Beauregard, & Alvarado, 1999). When placed in social pairs at two months of age, the neonatal amygdala-lesioned infants showed less overall activity, exploration of the testing environment, and social behavior initiation as compared to age-matched controls. This pattern of decreased social interactions continued when the amygdala-lesioned infants were reassessed at six months of age. Given that impaired social communication and diminished social interest are hallmarks of autism, it was proposed that dysfunction of the medial temporal lobe, in particular the amygdala, might underlie some of the core behavioral deficits seen in autism (Bachevalier, 1994, 2000).

One important detail that was not considered in these previous studies was the animals' rearing condition. The results summarized above were derived from infant monkeys reared in isolation (Thompson, et al., 1969), with their mother only (Kling & Green, 1967), or with peers only (Bachevalier, 1994). Rearing nonhuman primates without access to both mothers and peers, even without any other insult to the brain, has a deleterious effect on their social development (Capitanio, 1986). Therefore, the behavioral deficits observed in those studies could have been due to the brain lesion, the rearing environment, or a combination of the two factors. To address this question, we conducted a series of experiments to evaluate the effects of neurotoxic amygdala damage in maternally and socially reared rhesus monkeys (Bauman, Lavenex, Mason, Capitanio, & Amaral, 2004a, 2004b; Prather, et al., 2001). We found that macaque monkeys that are reared by their mothers in a social environment and receive selective amygdala-lesions at two weeks of age do not demonstrate profound impairments in social development within the first year of life. The amygdala-lesioned monkeys were able to produce and respond to a variety of species-typical social signals and did not differ from control monkeys in the amount of their social interactions (Bauman, et al., 2004a, 2004b). The amygdala-lesioned monkeys did, however, show abnormal fear responses to both social and nonsocial stimuli (e.g., heightened fear of conspecifics and absence of fear to normally aversive objects) (Bauman, et al., 2004b; Prather, et al., 2001). Thus, neonatal lesions of the macaque amygdala resulted in a sparing of species-typical social behavior, while profoundly impacting fear processing abilities.

The collective results from the studies described above indicate that the amygdala is not essential for the production of social behavior in adult macaque monkeys or for the early development of fundamental components of social behavior. The current research does, however, suggest that the amygdala plays an essential role in modulating social behavior adaptively, especially in potentially threatening contexts. Thus, in relation to Figure 45.1, we would propose that the amygdala is involved in the generation of emotion to a social stimulus that, depending on the context, may either inhibit or facilitate social interaction. This is especially important for macaques and other species where evaluation of potential danger is an essential component of species-typical social behavior.

Anterior Cingulate Cortex

The cingulate cortex is a heterogeneous structure whose various subregions are broadly implicated in social, emotional, executive, and motor functions. The anterior cingulate cortex (ACC) forms the anterior portion of the cingulate gyrus and surrounds the genu of the corpus callosum. The ACC is broadly connected to structures which are known to be involved in the generation and regulation of emotion states such as the amygdala, nucleus accumbens, hypothalamus, anterior insula, and orbitofrontal cortex, as well as a host of brainstem nuclei which regulate autonomic nervous system activity (Devinsky, Morrell, & Vogt, 1995; Vogt, Hof, & Vogt, 2004). The ACC is also interconnected to brain areas that coordinate and influence behavioral action, somatovisceral regulation, and autonomic responses such as the spinal cord, primary and supplementary motor regions (Vogt, Berger, & Derbyshire, 2003; Vogt, et al., 2004), as well as the dorsolateral striatum (Devinsky, et al., 1995), the inferior paritelal cortex (Vogt, et al., 2003), and the thalamus (Devinsky, et al., 1995).

The phenomena subserved by the ACC are numerous and diverse, but many are likely involved in generating and/or regulating normal social behavior. For example, in nonhuman primates, ACC neuronal activity is associated with learning motor sequences and routines (Procyk, Tanaka, & Joseph, 2000), processing conflicting sensory arrays and inhibiting prepotent behavioral responses (Michelet, Bioulac, Guehl, Escola, & Burbaud, 2007), and receiving rewards and punishment (Koyama, Kato, Tanaka, & Mikami, 2001; Koyama, Tanaka, & Mikami, 1998). In humans, the ACC is activated when stimuli conflict with one and other, when behavioral errors are committed, and when motor plans are made (for reviews, see Botvinick, 2007; Holroyd & Coles, 2002; Yeung, Botvinick, & Cohen, 2004). Broad ACC activity is observed in humans during social rejection (Eisenberger, Lieberman, & Williams, 2003; Kross, Egner, Ochsner, Hirsch, & Downey, 2007), empathetic responses to others (Singer, et al., 2004), the experience and perception of discrete emotions (e.g., happiness, sadness, fear, etc), and global affective states (e.g., pleasantness, unpleasantness, arousal, threat, reward, etc.) (Habel, Klein, Kellermann, Shah, & Schneider, 2005; Lane, et al., 1998; Markowitsch, Vandekerckhove, Lanfermann, & Russ, 2003; Ottowitz, et al., 2004). Similarly, nonhuman primates with ACC lesions, as compared to neurologically intact animals, engage in fewer normal social interactions and show reduced social awareness (Hadland, Rushworth, Gaffan, & Passingham, 2003; Rudebeck, Buckley, Walton, & Rushworth, 2006; Ward, 1948).

Early nonhuman primate lesion studies paint a somewhat inconsistent picture of the role of anterior cingulate cortex in social behavior. A handful of early lesion studies demonstrated that monkeys showed a profound lack of "social conscience" (Ward, 1948, p. 15) following lesions to the anterior cingulate cortex. Despite appearing generally attentive and aware of their surroundings, monkeys with ACC lesions, as compared to control animals, appeared to be less reactive to social stimuli. Monkeys with ACC lesions consistently demonstrated lack of social awareness in their interactions with their cage mates by walking over them, sitting on them, taking food from them, and so forth. (Glees, Cole, Whitty, & Cairns, 1950; Kennard, 1959; Ward, 1948). Monkeys with ACC lesions were also less timid or fearful and more passive in the presence of humans (Glees, et al., 1950; Kennard, 1959; Mirsky, Rosvold, & Pribram, 1957; Ward, 1948). In contrast, other early studies suggested that lesions to the anterior cingulate cortex did not perturb social behavior. Monkeys with lesions of the entire cingulate cortex (i.e., both anterior and posterior portion) readily returned to their social groups and to normative social activity (e.g., grooming, mounting, proximity with kin) (Franzen & Myers, 1973; Mirsky, et al., 1957; Myers, Swett, & Miller, 1973). In these studies, cingulate lesions did not appear to alter animals' position in the dominance hierarchy (Mirsky, et al., 1957). Finally, animals with cingulate lesions demonstrated a normal repertoire of sexual and maternal behavior

(Franzen & Myers, 1973). A consistent picture cannot be painted from these early studies because the lesion extent varied widely as did the method for collecting behavioral observations; often reports that behavior had changed or not changed were based on impressions rather than formal ethographic data collection.

Contemporary lesion research is more consistent in suggesting that the anterior cingulate cortex is critically involved in social processing. Compared to control animals, rhesus macaques with ACC lesions spend less time engaged in social interaction with other monkeys (Hadland, et al., 2003) although the specific reasons for this lack of engagement are not clear. In a recent report by Rudebeck and colleagues (2006), aspiration lesions to the ACC sulcus or gyrus of adult male rhesus macaques were shown to differentially impair the extent to which social stimuli captured the subjects' attention. In these experiments, the dependent variable was the amount of time that it took for the animal to take a piece of food in the presence of a social stimulus. The authors' interpret this as a measure of how "valued" the social test stimulus was insofar as longer reach times indicated greater value of the test stimulus presumably because the test stimulus captures the animals' attention delaying their food retrieval. Animals with ACC lesions showed impaired interest in (or attention to) social stimuli since they were faster to take the food as compared with unoperated control animals. Notably, a similar pattern of reach times was observed on trials where a supposedly fear-inducing stimulus (a snake) was presented with the food. Another interpretation of these data is that food-reaching times were faster for ACC-lesioned animals in the presence of social and emotional stimuli because, in the absence of the ACC, there was no signal to direct attention towards the competing stimuli (the social or emotional stimulus that was introduced on each trial) in order to override the animals' prepotent response to reach for food.

Aside from the global involvement in social behavior suggested by lesion studies, the ACC is likely involved in subordinate processes that subserve normal social behavior such as the perception and encoding of value (e.g., reward or threat value of a perceived stimulus) and the execution of appropriate or sequential behavioral responses. For example, single cell studies in macaques have demonstrated that different discrete populations of ACC neurons fire when monkeys learn which series of behavioral actions are required to obtain reward and when known behavioral sequences are repeated in order to obtain rewards (Procyk, et al., 2000) suggesting that the ACC is involved in both discerning and then later generating successful sequences of behavior (insofar as they result in a desired outcome—obtaining reward). Similarly, ACC neurons fire when animals must generate a sequence of behaviors when they anticipate receiving a reward but not when they do not anticipate receiving a reward (Matsumoto, Suzuki, & Tanaka, 2003), suggesting that the ACC is involved in discriminating between contexts that do or do not predict reward. Neurons in the ACC also differentiate between primary rewarding and aversive stimuli and stimuli that predict the presence of reward or threat (Koyama, et al., 2001; Koyama, et al., 1998; Nishijo, et al., 1997). The ACC not only responds to specific types of rewards, but it also codes the proximity of reward (Shidara & Richmond, 2002) and the magnitude of reward (Amiez, Joseph, & Procyk, 2006). One hypothesis is that the ACC evaluates information about the proximity, and magnitude of reward in ambiguous contexts to determine not only the actions the organism will take to obtain the reward, but also to determine how much effort is warranted to obtain it (Rushworth, Behrens, Rudebeck, & Walton, 2007). Within the proposed model of social processing (Figure 45.1), the ACC likely plays an important role at multiple stages of processing. It is likely involved in low-level perceptual processing insofar as it serves to sort (or process) incoming representations of social stimuli and behaviors that are relevant versus nonrelevant in given contexts allowing for coherent, advantageous behavioral actions. Once coherent behavioral actions have been executed, the ACC is likely involved in evaluating the efficacy of those actions and then subtly adjusting future actions based on the success or failure of previous behaviors.

Mirror Neurons

Mirror neurons were first discovered while investigating cells specialized for hand movements in the motor cortex of pigtail macaques (di Pellegrino, Fadiga, Fogassi, Gallese, & Rizzolatti, 1992). Neurons in a portion of the inferior frontal cortex fired when the monkey reached for an object and unexpectedly fired when the monkey observed a human performing the same action (Gallese, Fadiga, Fogassi, & Rizzolatti, 1996; Rizzolatti, Fadiga, Gallese, & Fogassi, 1996). Subsequent single-cell recordings revealed another population of mirror neurons in the anterior portion of the inferior parietal lobule (Fogassi, et al., 2005). These two regions form an integrated frontoparietal mirror-neuron system that has been theorized to underlie the ability to understand actions and intentions of others (for review, see Cattaneo & Rizzolatti, 2009; Iacoboni & Dapretto, 2006; Rizzolatti & Craighero, 2004; Rizzolatti, Fabbri-Destro, & Cattaneo, 2009). Importantly, mirror neurons do not simply encode perceptual or sensory-based features of the actions, but rather appear to be sensitive to the goal or meaning of actions. For example, mirror neurons fire even when visual access to the action is partially obscured but monkeys have knowledge of the purpose or goal of the action (Umilta, et al., 2001) or if the action is represented by sounds in the absence of visual cues (Kohler, et al., 2002). Similarly, the magnitude of neuronal activity appears to be dependent on the intention of an executed action. Mirror-neuron activity was greatest for grasping actions associated with the goal of eating a piece of food as compared to grasping actions meant only to pick up a piece of food and deposit it in a container (Fogassi, et al., 2005). In addition to being dependent on the goal of actions, mirror-neuron activity appears to be dependent on the spatial proximity of actions relative to self and the likelihood that one will interact with the agent engaging in the action (Caggiano, Fogassi, Rizzolatti, Thier, & Casile, 2009).

Despite accumulating evidence about the basic functions of mirror neurons in macaques, little is known about their actual role in social behavior. A small subset of mirror neurons responds to observation and execution of macaque communicative gestures, such as lipsmacking, suggesting a possible role for mirror neurons in interpreting species-typical social signals (Ferrari, Gallese, Rizzolatti, & Fogassi, 2003). In addition, some functional imaging studies in humans have identified a putative mirror-neuron system that responds to a variety of cognitive processes related to social behavior, including action understanding, communication, imitation, and emotion processing (Chong, Cunnington, Williams, Kanwisher, & Mattingley, 2008; Dapretto, et al., 2006; Iacoboni, et al., 2005; Iacoboni, et al., 1999; Kilner, Neal, Weiskopf, Friston, & Frith, 2009). Of course, these neuroimaging studies cannot monitor the activity of a distributed class of neurons such as the mirror neurons. Moreover, not all human imaging studies have found mirror-neuron properties when expected (Lingnau, Gesierich, & Caramazza, 2009), thus calling into question the existence of a human mirror-neuron system (Dinstein, 2008; Hickok, 2009).

In contrast, macaques clearly have mirror neurons, but may not demonstrate the higher order socioemotional functions often broadly ascribed to mirror neurons. Imitation, for example, is one of the primary functions associated with mirror neurons that has not been convincingly documented in adult macaque monkeys (Ferrari, et al., 2006). While additional research is needed to further define the role of mirror neurons in macaque social behavior, the current literature certainly supports consideration of this unique class of neurons and the cortical regions they inhabit as potential components of the social brain. The proposal that mirror neurons encode action understanding (i.e., "what others are doing") and may possibly play a role in determining behavioral responses (i.e., "how I might interact with them") would suggest that mirror neurons may contribute to several component process of social perception, evaluation of intention, and generating behavioral responses (Figure 45.1).

Orbitofrontal Cortex

The nonhuman primate orbitofrontal cortex occupies the cortex on the ventral surface of the frontal lobe, and typically includes Brodmann areas 11, 12, 13 and 14. The orbitofrontal cortex is a heterogeneous region, both in terms of cytoarchitecture and its pattern of intrinsic and extrinsic connections (Barbas, 2007a, 2007b; Price, 2007). One prominent view is that the orbitofrontal cortex sits at the confluence of two separate, yet partially overlapping and interconnected, networks of the frontal lobe (Price, 2007). A "medial network" includes all areas of the medial frontal cortex (areas 9, 10, 14, 24, 25 and 32) and the most medial sectors of the orbital surface (medial sections of areas 10, 11 and 13). This network has strong connections with the amygdala, temporal cortical structures linked to memory, striatal regions associated with representation of reward, and autonomic centers in the brain that influence emotional arousal. The "orbital network" includes more lateral areas on the orbital surface (lateral sections of areas 11 and 13, a majority of area 12, and the agranular insular area). This network predominantly receives sensory information from all modalities, but also has connections with the amygdala via the agranular insular area. Given this anatomical organization, the orbitofrontal cortex is well positioned to integrate information regarding one's current physiological state with external sensory stimuli, and thereby flexibly represent the reward value or meaning of environmental stimuli, especially those of a social nature.

Evidence in support of this idea has been provided by electrophysiological and lesion studies. Similar to the amygdala, the nonhuman primate orbitofrontal cortex contains neurons that are responsive to a wide array of social signals, especially fearful or aggressive facial expressions (O'Scalaidhe, Wilson, & Goldman-Rakic, 1997, 1999). Much of what is known regarding the orbitofrontal cortex and social behavior in nonhuman primates has come from lesion studies. Early studies using large frontal lobotomies, including the orbitofrontal cortex, demonstrated profound changes in social behavior for monkeys living in a free-ranging colony on the island of Cayo Santiago near Puerto Rico (Franzen & Myers, 1973; Myers, et al., 1973). Upon re-introduction to their colony, the operated monkeys displayed an overall decrease in positive social behaviors and socially communicative facial, vocal, and postural behaviors, as well as an increase in inappropriate social interactions. Ultimately, a majority of these animals were ejected from their social groups and remained solitary for the duration of the experiment. Similarly, Butter and colleagues (1970) reported a decrease in aggressive behaviors coupled with a transient increase in avoidance responses in monkeys with lesions confined only to the orbitofrontal cortex. These behavioral disturbances appeared to be exacerbated in cases where cortical damage was localized to the posteromedial region of the orbitofrontal cortex (i.e., area 13 and the agranular insular area). Orbitofrontal cortex damage has also been shown to result in decreased grooming and huddling, the formation of fewer coalitions during aggressive bouts, and less success in aggressive encounters when animals were observed in a semi-naturalistic setting (Raleigh & Steklis, 1981; Raleigh, Steklis, Ervin, Kling, & McGuire, 1979).

These lesion studies indicate that the orbitofrontal cortex may play a role in motivating animals to engage in social interactions since damage to this region generally led to a decrease in both positive and negative social behavior. However, a different picture of orbitofrontal function was painted by Butter and Snyder (1972) when they performed a resection of the orbitofrontal cortex in monkeys that had acquired the highest dominance rank in a group of five animals. When the operated animals were recombined with their familiar peers after surgery in a laboratory setting, they displayed *increased* aggression and reacquired their dominant status over older and heavier monkeys in the group. Interestingly, after repeated interactions, these operated animals lost their dominant status; the specific reasons for this loss of status were not determined. One interpretation of this different pattern of results is that the orbitofrontal cortex may not merely motivate social behavior, but may be more involved in regulating social behavior adaptively with regard to social or contextual factors, such a dominance rank.

To address this issue, Machado and Bachevalier (2006) studied the social behavior of adult rhesus monkeys before and after selective damage confined mostly to areas 11 and 13 of the orbitofrontal cortex. These lesioned animals displayed an increased frequency of threatening gestures and also received higher levels of aggression from their group mates. Consistent with previous studies, these changes were most pronounced for the highest-ranked animals with orbitofrontal lesions. The lesioned animals also showed changes in how they typically responded to social signals received from their group mates. However, unlike amygdala-lesioned animals that show selective deficits in responding to threatening social signals, animals with orbitofrontal lesions responded abnormally to both threatening *and* affiliative social signals. When orbitofrontal cortex-damaged animals were threatened, they displayed increased affiliative social signals and decreased aggressive behaviors. Animals with orbitofrontal cortex lesions were less likely to mount their group mates when solicited.

These findings are similar to those in humans indicating that the orbitofrontal cortex, but not the amygdala, may play an important role in making judgments based on social context. More specifically, the orbitofrontal cortex is activated when subjects are required to make social judgments, such as rating the attractiveness of a face (O'Doherty, et al., 2003), using the meaning of a facial expression to guide one's own behavior (Kringelbach & Rolls, 2003), choosing to cooperate or deceive another individual (Rilling, et al., 2002), or judging whether or not another individual's behavior is morally right or wrong (Moll, de Oliveira-Souza, Bramati, & Grafman, 2002) or violated social norms (Berthoz, Armony, Blair, & Dolan, 2002).

In summary, the neuroanatomical, experimental, and clinical data suggest that the orbitofrontal cortex may be critical for the efficient modulation of aggression, affiliation, and avoidance with respect to changes in the social context. Due to its anatomical connections with sensory, visceral, and reward centers of the brain, the orbitofrontal cortex may flexibly represent the current reward value or meaning of both positive and negative social signals, thereby facilitating the selection of the most appropriate behavioral response within a given social context (Figure 45.1).

Inferior Temporal Cortex

The inferior temporal (IT) cortex is a region of the visual association cortex that, in the monkey, includes the inferior temporal gyrus and adjacent portions of the lower bank of the superior temporal sulcus (STS). The IT cortex receives highly processed visual information from a variety of occipito-temporal inputs and is reciprocally connected with a number of subcortical structures, including the amygdala (Webster, Bachevalier, & Ungerleider, 1993; Webster, Ungerleider, & Bachevalier, 1991). Converging evidence from humans and nonhuman primates suggests that the IT cortex plays a role in social perception, though direct comparisons are difficult, as homologies between human and nonhuman primate temporal cortex are not completely characterized.

Over the last three decades, single-cell recordings have identified a subset of neurons in macaque temporal cortex that are activated in response to social stimuli. For example, cells that respond to faces have been found throughout the inferior temporal gyrus, as well as along the banks and floor of the STS (Baylis, Rolls, & Leonard, 1987; Bruce, et al., 1981; Desimone, Albright, Gross, & Bruce, 1984; Perrett, et al., 1982; Rolls, 1984). Many of these "face-cells" are sensitive to particular individuals or emotional facial expressions (Hasselmo, Rolls, & Baylis, 1989; Perrett, et al., 1984), as well as gaze direction (Perrett, et al., 1985). Cells that activate during the perception of other body parts and body movements have also been found throughout the temporal cortex, though such neurons are less frequent than face-cells (Desimone, et al., 1984; Gross, Rocha-Miranda, & Bender, 1972; Jellema & Perrett, 2006; Perrett, et al., 1985).

Adult-like face selectivity is present in the IT cortex at early developmental time points, but undergoes considerable postnatal refinement (Rodman, 1994). Within the second month of life, individual IT neurons show response selectivity for faces, though cells in the infant monkeys show lower response magnitudes and longer response latencies compared to adults (Rodman, Scalaidhe, & Gross, 1993; Rodman, Skelly, & Gross, 1991). In adult macaques, neuronal activity in the IT cortex can influence the perception of social stimuli. Monkeys exposed to "face" and "nonface" stimuli were more likely to categorize all stimuli as faces when face-selective neurons were stimulated as compared to when other nearby neurons were stimulated (Afraz, Kiani, & Esteky, 2006). Interestingly, differences in response latencies within the same IT cells may carry information about complex social images. For example, face cells in the IT cortex of monkeys responded to both primate and animal faces, but respond more quickly to the primate faces (Kiani, Esteky, & Tanaka, 2005). Faces are thus discriminated from objects by activation of different groups of IT neurons, whereas different types of faces can be discriminated by differences in onset latencies of responses in the same group of cells.

Functional imaging studies have recently been used to identify clusters of STS neurons activated by faces (Hoffman, et al., 2007; Tsao, Freiwald, Knutsen, Mandeville, & Tootell, 2003), which were subsequently confirmed to be almost entirely face-selective using fMRI-guided single unit recordings (Tsao, Freiwald, Tootell, & Livingstone, 2006). Cells in these face-selective patches preferentially respond to combinations of particular facial features and are tuned to specific dimensions of each feature (i.e., distance between eyes, etc.) (Freiwald, Tsao, & Livingstone, 2009). These face-selective regions in the macaque may be homologous to the human fusiform face area which is also involved in processing face stimuli (Kanwisher, et al., 1997). While regions of the temporal cortex appear to be sensitive to social stimuli in general, the magnitude of neural activity may be modulated by the specific affective meaning of stimuli. In support of this, a recent fMRI study in monkeys has shown that the STS is activated by many types of conspecifics' body postures, but the highest activity was observed for those postures conveying social threat (de Gelder & Partan, 2009). These intriguing findings suggest that the macaque STS is involved not only in the low-level processing of biologically important stimuli, but also in the processing of more sophisticated social information.

Collectively, these studies indicate that there are a number of face-selective regions and fewer body-selective regions scattered throughout the macaque temporal cortex (Moeller, Freiwald, & Tsao, 2008; Pinsk, et al., 2009; Pinsk, DeSimone, Moore, Gross, & Kastner, 2005). Despite this wealth of information, it is still difficult to disentangle purely sensory representations in the temporal cortex from those that also include social meaning. For example, it is unclear if deficits in eye-gaze processing associated with bilateral STS lesions specifically impair processing of social information (Campbell, Heywood, Cowey, Regard, & Landis, 1990; Heywood & Cowey, 1992) or if these deficits are the result of a more general impairment in visual-discrimination learning (Eacott, Heywood, Gross, & Cowey, 1993). Future research, perhaps utilizing functional neuroimaging combined with electro-physiological recordings and/or microstimulation, should focus on both the type and affective quality of stimuli that activates particular subregions as well as the time-course and magnitude of that activation. This may provide additional insight into the role of the temporal cortex in early stages of perceptual processing of social stimuli (Figure 45.1).

Conclusion

The key regions discussed above both contribute uniquely to social behavior and work together in a distributed network to appropriately perceive, generate, and regulate social behavior. The goal of this chapter was not to provide a definitive inventory of the brain regions mediating particular social behaviors, but rather to highlight key aspects of macaque social behavior that make it an appropriate model for humans and then to discuss neural regions of particular importance in order to develop a framework for a neural-systems approach to studying the social brain. Clearly, there is still much to learn about the regions discussed here—for example, the role they play in particular classes of behavior, at what stages of processing they are required for normal social behavior, at what stages of processing they merely play a modulatory role, their role within functional neural networks, etc.

Fortunately, as technology advances, so too does our ability to investigate the social brain. Recent advances in the use of noninvasive neuroimaging techniques (e.g., MicroPET, fMRI), new molecular approaches to temporarily deactivate specific neural regions, and multi-method approaches (e.g., combining lesion studies with functional neuroimaging and naturalistic observation) will make tremendous headway in our understanding of the macaque monkey brain. This research will undoubtedly have important implications not only for understanding the neural basis of typical social behavior, but also for understanding the impairments of a host of social processing disorders ranging from autism spectrum disorders to social anxiety.

Acknowledgments

Original research reported in this paper was supported by the NIMH and conducted, in part, at the

California National Primate Research Center (RR0069).

Note

1 While much of the biomedical research that we review has been carried out using rhesus macaques (*Macaca mulatta*), other macaque species, such as the crab-eating or cynomolgus monkey (*Macaca fascicularis*), have also been employed in neuroscience research. Generally only subtle differences have been identified in the neural organization of these different macaque species.

References

Adolphs, R., Tranel, D., & Damasio, A. R. (1998). The human amygdala in social judgment. *Nature, 393*(6684), 470–474.

Adolphs, R., Tranel, D., Damasio, H., & Damasio, A. (1994). Impaired recognition of emotion in facial expressions following bilateral damage to the human amygdala. *Nature, 372*(6507), 669–672.

Adolphs, R., Tranel, D., Damasio, H., & Damasio, A. R. (1995). Fear and the human amygdala. *Journal of Neuroscience, 15*(9), 5879–5891.

Afraz, S. R., Kiani, R., & Esteky, H. (2006). Microstimulation of inferotemporal cortex influences face categorization. *Nature, 442*(7103), 692–695.

Altmann, S. (1967). The structure of primate social communication. In S. Altmann (Ed.), *Social communication among primates*. Chicago: University of Chicago Press.

Amaral, D. G., Schumann, C. M., & Nordahl, C. W. (2008). Neuroanatomy of autism. *Trends Neurosci, 31*(3), 137–145.

Amiez, C., Joseph, J. P., & Procyk, E. (2006). Reward encoding in the monkey anterior cingulate cortex. *Cereb Cortex, 16*(7), 1040–1055.

Bachevalier, J. (1994). Medial temporal lope structures and autism—a review of clinical and experimental findings. *Neuropsychologia, 32*(6), 627–648.

Bachevalier, J. (2000). The amygdala, social cognition, and autism. In J. P. Aggleton (Ed.), *The amygdala: A functional analysis* (pp. 509–543). New York: Oxford University Press.

Bachevalier, J., Beauregard, M., & Alvarado, M. C. (1999). Long-term effects of neonatal damage to the hippocampal formation and amygdaloid complex on object discrimination and object recognition in rhesus monkeys (Macaca mulatta). *Behav Neurosci, 113*(6), 1127–1151.

Bales, K. L., Mason, W. A., Catana, C., Cherry, S. R., & Mendoza, S. P. (2007). Neural correlates of pair-bonding in a monogamous primate. *Brain Res, 1184*, 245–253.

Barbas, H. (2007a). Flow of information for emotions through temporal and orbitofrontal pathways. *J Anat, 211*(2), 237–249.

Barbas, H. (2007b). Specialized elements of orbitofrontal cortex in primates. *Ann N Y Acad Sci, 1121*, 10–32.

Barrett, L., Henzi, P., & Dunbar, R. (2003). Primate cognition: From "what now?" to "what if?" *Trends Cogn Sci, 7*(11), 494–497.

Bauman, M. D. & Amaral, D. G. (2008). Neurodevelopment of social cognition. In M. L. C. A. Nelson (Ed.), *Handbook of developmental cognitive neuroscience*, 2nd Edition. Cambridge, Massachusetts: MIT Press.

Bauman, M. D., Lavenex, P., Mason, W. A., Capitanio, J. P., & Amaral, D. G. (2004a). The development of mother-infant interactions after neonatal amygdala lesions in rhesus monkeys. *J Neurosci, 24*(3), 711–721.

Bauman, M. D., Lavenex, P., Mason, W. A., Capitanio, J. P., & Amaral, D. G. (2004b). The development of social behavior following neonatal amygdala lesions in rhesus monkeys. *J Cogn Neurosci, 16*(8), 1388–1411.

Baylis, G. C., Rolls, E. T., & Leonard, C. M. (1987). Functional subdivisions of the temporal lobe neocortex. *J Neurosci, 7*(2), 330–342.

Bellugi, U., Lichtenberger, L., Mills, D., Galaburda, A., & Korenberg, J. R. (1999). Bridging cognition, the brain and molecular genetics: Evidence from Williams syndrome. *Trends Neurosci, 22*(5), 197–207.

Berman, C. M. (1982). The ontogeny of social relationships with group companions among free-ranging rhesus monkeys: I. Social networks and differentiation. *Animal Behaviour, 30*, 149–162.

Bernstein, I. S. (1981). Dominance: The baby and the bathwater. *The Behavioral and Brain Sciences, 4*, 419–457.

Bernstein, I. S. & Mason, W. A. (1963). Group formation by rhesus monkeys. *Animal Behaviour, 11*(1), 28–31.

Berthoz, S., Armony, J. L., Blair, R. J., & Dolan, R. J. (2002). An fMRI study of intentional and unintentional (embarrassing) violations of social norms. *Brain, 125*(Pt 8), 1696–1708.

Blume, S. & Geesink, I. (2000). A brief history of polio vaccines. *Science, 288*(5471), 1593–1594.

Botvinick, M. M. (2007). Conflict monitoring and decision making: Reconciling two perspectives on anterior cingulate function. *Cogn Affect Behav Neurosci, 7*(4), 356–366.

Brothers, L. (1990). The social brain: A project for integrating primate social behavior and neurophysiology in a new domain. *Concepts in Neuroscience, 1*, 27–51.

Brothers, L. & Ring, B. (1993). Mesial temporal neurons in the macaque monkey with responses selective for aspects of social stimuli. *Behavioural Brain Research, 57*(1), 53–61.

Brothers, L., Ring, B., & Kling, A. (1990). Response of neurons in the macaque amygdala to complex social stimuli. *Behav Brain Res, 41*(3), 199–213.

Bruce, C., Desimone, R., & Gross, C. G. (1981). Visual properties of neurons in a polysensory area in superior temporal sulcus of the macaque. *J Neurophysiol, 46*(2), 369–384.

Butter, C. M. & Snyder, D. R. (1972). Alterations in aversive and aggressive behaviors following orbital frontal lesions in rhesus monkeys. *Acta Neurobiol Exp (Wars), 32*(2), 525–565.

Butter, C. M., Snyder, D. R., & McDonald, J. A. (1970). Effects of orbital frontal lesions on aversive and aggressive behaviors in rhesus monkeys. *J Comp Physiol Psychol, 72*(1), 132–144.

Caggiano, V., Fogassi, L., Rizzolatti, G., Thier, P., & Casile, A. (2009). Mirror neurons differentially encode the peripersonal and extrapersonal space of monkeys. *Science, 324*(5925), 403–406.

Campbell, R., Heywood, C. A., Cowey, A., Regard, M., & Landis, T. (1990). Sensitivity to eye gaze in prosopagnosic patients and monkeys with superior temporal sulcus ablation. *Neuropsychologia, 28*(11), 1123–1142.

Capitanio, J. (1986). Behavioral pathology. In G. Mitchell & J. Erwin (Eds.), *Comparative primate biology: Behavior, conservation, and ecology* (Vol. 2A, pp. 411–454). New York: Alan R. Liss.

Cattaneo, L. & Rizzolatti, G. (2009). The mirror neuron system. *Arch Neurol, 66*(5), 557–560.

Champoux, M., Bennett, A., Shannon, C., Higley, J. D., Lesch, K. P., & Suomi, S. J. (2002). Serotonin transporter gene polymorphism, differential early rearing, and behavior in rhesus monkey neonates. *Mol Psychiatry*, *7*(10), 1058–1063.

Cheney, D., Seyfarth, R., & Smuts, B. (1986). Social relationships and social cognition in nonhuman primates. *Science*, *234*(4782), 1361–1366.

Cheney, D. L. & Seyfarth, R. M. (1990). The representation of social relations by monkeys. *Cognition*, *37*(1–2), 167–196.

Chong, T. T., Cunnington, R., Williams, M. A., Kanwisher, N., & Mattingley, J. B. (2008). fMRI adaptation reveals mirror neurons in human inferior parietal cortex. *Curr Biol*, *18*(20), 1576–1580.

Corkin, S. (2002). What's new with the amnesic patient H.M.? *Nat Rev Neurosci*, *3*(2), 153–160.

Dapretto, M., Davies, M. S., Pfeifer, J. H., Scott, A. A., Sigman, M., Bookheimer, S. Y., et al. (2006). Understanding emotions in others: Mirror neuron dysfunction in children with autism spectrum disorders. *Nat Neurosci*, *9*(1), 28–30.

Darwin, C. (1872). *The expression of the emotions in man and animals*. London: John Murray.

Datta, S. B. (1984). Relative power and the acquisition of rank. In R. A. Hinde (Ed.), *Primate social relationships: An integrated approach* (pp. 93–103). Oxford: Blackwell Scientific Publ.

de Gelder, B. & Partan, S. (2009). The neural basis of perceiving emotional bodily expressions in monkeys. *Neuroreport*, *20*(7), 642–646.

de Waal, F. B. (1977). The organization of agonistic relations within two captive groups of Java-monkeys (Macaca fascicularis). *Z Tierpsychol*, *44*(3), 225–282.

de Waal, F. B. (1996). Macaque social culture: Development and perpetuation of affiliative networks. *J Comp Psychol*, *110*(2), 147–154.

Deaner, R. O., Khera, A. V., & Platt, M. L. (2005). Monkeys pay per view: Adaptive valuation of social images by rhesus macaques. *Curr Biol*, *15*(6), 543–548.

Desimone, R., Albright, T. D., Gross, C. G., & Bruce, C. (1984). Stimulus-selective properties of inferior temporal neurons in the macaque. *J Neurosci*, *4*(8), 2051–2062.

Devinsky, O., Morrell, M. J., & Vogt, B. A. (1995). Contributions of anterior cingulate cortex to behaviour. *Brain*, *118* (*Pt 1*), 279–306.

di Pellegrino, G., Fadiga, L., Fogassi, L., Gallese, V., & Rizzolatti, G. (1992). Understanding motor events: A neurophysiological study. *Exp Brain Res*, *91*(1), 176–180.

Dinstein, I. (2008). Human cortex: Reflections of mirror neurons. *Curr Biol*, *18*(20), R956–959.

Doyle, T. F., Bellugi, U., Korenberg, J. R., & Graham, J. (2004). "Everybody in the world is my friend" hypersociability in young children with Williams syndrome. *Am J Med Genet A*, *124*(3), 263–273.

Drea, C. M. (1998). Social context affects how rhesus monkeys explore their environment. *Am J Primatol*, *44*(3), 205–214.

Drea, C. M. & Wallen, K. (1999). Low-status monkeys "play dumb" when learning in mixed social groups. *Proc Natl Acad Sci U S A*, *96*(22), 12965–12969.

Drickamer, L. C. (1975). Quantitative observation of behavior in free-ranging Macaca mulatta: methodology and aggression. *Behaviour*, *55*(3–4), 209–236.

Dukelow, W. R. & Whitehair, L. A. (1995). A brief history of the regional primate centers. *Comparative Pathology Bulletin*, *27* (3), 1–2.

Dunbar, R. I. M. (1998). The social brain hypothesis. *Evolutionary Anthropology*, *178*, 178–190.

Eacott, M. J., Heywood, C. A., Gross, C. G., & Cowey, A. (1993). Visual discrimination impairments following lesions of the superior temporal sulcus are not specific for facial stimuli. *Neuropsychologia*, *31*(6), 609–619.

Eisenberger, N. I., Lieberman, M. D., & Williams, K. D. (2003). Does rejection hurt? An fMRI study of social exclusion. *Science*, *302*(5643), 290–292.

Ekman, P. (1993). Facial expression and emotion. *Am Psychol*, *48*(4), 384–392.

Ekman, P., & Friesen, W. V. (1971). Constants across cultures in the face and emotion. *J Pers Soc Psychol*, *17*(2), 124–129.

Emery, N. J. & Amaral, D. G. (2000). The role of the primate amygdala in social cognition. In R. D. Lane & L. Nadel (Eds.), *Cognitive neuroscience of emotion. Series in affective science*. (pp. 156–191). New York: Oxford University Press.

Emery, N. J., Capitanio, J. P., Mason, W. A., Machado, C. J., Mendoza, S. P., & Amaral, D. G. (2001). The effects of bilateral lesions of the amygdala on dyadic social interactions in rhesus monkeys (Macaca mulatta). *Behav Neurosci*, *115*(3), 515–544.

Felleman, D. J. & Van Essen, D. C. (1991). Distributed hierarchical processing in the primate cerebral cortex. *Cereb Cortex*, *1*(1), 1–47.

Ferrari, P. F., Gallese, V., Rizzolatti, G., & Fogassi, L. (2003). Mirror neurons responding to the observation of ingestive and communicative mouth actions in the monkey ventral premotor cortex. *Eur J Neurosci*, *17*(8), 1703–1714.

Ferrari, P. F., Paukner, A., Ionica, C., & Suomi, S. J. (2009). Reciprocal face-to-face communication between rhesus macaque mothers and their newborn infants. *Curr Biol*, *19*(20), 1768–1772.

Ferrari, P. F., Paukner, A., Ruggiero, A., Darcey, L., Unbehagen, S., & Suomi, S. J. (2009). Inter-individual differences in neonatal imitation and the development of action chains in rhesus macaques. *Child Dev*, *80*(4), 1057–1068.

Ferrari, P. F., Visalberghi, E., Paukner, A., Fogassi, L., Ruggiero, A., & Suomi, S. J. (2006). Neonatal imitation in rhesus macaques. *PLoS Biol*, *4*(9).

Flombaum, J. I. & Santos, L. R. (2005). Rhesus monkeys attribute perceptions to others. *Curr Biol*, *15*(5), 447–452.

Fogassi, L., Ferrari, P. F., Gesierich, B., Rozzi, S., Chersi, F., & Rizzolatti, G. (2005). Parietal lobe: from action organization to intention understanding. *Science*, *308*(5722), 662–667.

Franzen, E. A. & Myers, R. E. (1973). Neural control of social behavior: Prefrontal and anterior temporal cortex. *Neuropsychologia*, *11*(2), 141–157.

Freiwald, W. A., Tsao, D. Y., & Livingstone, M. S. (2009). A face feature space in the macaque temporal lobe. *Nat Neurosci*, *12*(9), 1187–1196.

Gallese, V., Fadiga, L., Fogassi, L., & Rizzolatti, G. (1996). Action recognition in the premotor cortex. *Brain*, *119* (*Pt 2*), 593–609.

Gauthier, I., Tarr, M. J., Anderson, A. W., Skudlarski, P., & Gore, J. C. (1999). Activation of the middle fusiform "face area" increases with expertise in recognizing novel objects. *Nat Neurosci*, *2*(6), 568–573.

Gibbs, R. A., Rogers, J., Katze, M. G., Bumgarner, R., Weinstock, G. M., Mardis, E. R., et al. (2007). Evolutionary and biomedical insights from the rhesus macaque genome. *Science*, *316*(5822), 222–234.

Glees, P., Cole, J., Whitty, C. W., & Cairns, H. (1950). The effects of lesions in the cingular gyrus and adjacent areas in monkeys. *J Neurol Neurosurg Psychiatry*, *13*(3), 178–190.

Goren, C. C., Sarty, M., & Wu, P. Y. (1975). Visual following and pattern discrimination of face-like stimuli by newborn infants. *Pediatrics*, *56*(4), 544–549.

Gothard, K. M., Battaglia, F. P., Erickson, C. A., Spitler, K. M., & Amaral, D. G. (2007). Neural responses to facial expression and face identity in the monkey amygdala. *J Neurophysiol*, *97*(2), 1671–1683.

Gouzoules, H. & Gouzoules, S. (2000). Agonistic screams differ among four species of macaques: The significance of motivation-structural rules. *Anim Behav*, *59*(3), 501–512.

Gouzoules, H., Gouzoules, S., & Tomaszycki, M. (1998). Agonistic screams and the classification of dominance relationships: Are monkeys fuzzy logicians? *Anim Behav*, *55*(1), 51–60.

Gross, C. G., Rocha-Miranda, C. E., & Bender, D. B. (1972). Visual properties of neurons in inferotemporal cortex of the Macaque. *J Neurophysiol*, *35*(1), 96–111.

Habel, U., Klein, M., Kellermann, T., Shah, N. J., & Schneider, F. (2005). Same or different? Neural correlates of happy and sad mood in healthy males. *Neuroimage*, *26*(1), 206–214.

Hadland, K. A., Rushworth, M. F., Gaffan, D., & Passingham, R. E. (2003). The effect of cingulate lesions on social behaviour and emotion. *Neuropsychologia*, *41*(8), 919–931.

Hasselmo, M. E., Rolls, E. T., & Baylis, G. C. (1989). The role of expression and identity in the face-selective responses of neurons in the temporal visual cortex of the monkey. *Behav Brain Res*, *32*(3), 203–218.

Heywood, C. A. & Cowey, A. (1992). The role of the "face-cell" area in the discrimination and recognition of faces by monkeys. *Philos Trans R Soc Lond B Biol Sci*, *335*(1273), 31–37; discussion 37–38.

Hickok, G. (2009). Eight problems for the mirror neuron theory of action understanding in monkeys and humans. *J Cogn Neurosci*, *21*(7), 1229–1243.

Hoffman, K. L., Gothard, K. M., Schmid, M. C., & Logothetis, N. K. (2007). Facial-expression and gaze-selective responses in the monkey amygdala. *Curr Biol*, *17*(9), 766–772.

Holroyd, C. B. & Coles, M. G. (2002). The neural basis of human error processing: Reinforcement learning, dopamine, and the error-related negativity. *Psychol Rev*, *109*(4), 679–709.

Iacoboni, M. & Dapretto, M. (2006). The mirror neuron system and the consequences of its dysfunction. *Nat Rev Neurosci*, *7*(12), 942–951.

Iacoboni, M., Molnar-Szakacs, I., Gallese, V., Buccino, G., Mazziotta, J. C., & Rizzolatti, G. (2005). Grasping the intentions of others with one's own mirror neuron system. *PLoS Biol*, *3*(3), e79.

Iacoboni, M., Woods, R. P., Brass, M., Bekkering, H., Mazziotta, J. C., & Rizzolatti, G. (1999). Cortical mechanisms of human imitation. *Science*, *286*(5449), 2526–2528.

Jellema, T. & Perrett, D. I. (2006). Neural representations of perceived bodily actions using a categorical frame of reference. *Neuropsychologia*, *44*(9), 1535–1546.

Johnson, M. H., Dziurawiec, S., Ellis, H., & Morton, J. (1991). Newborns' preferential tracking of face-like stimuli and its subsequent decline. *Cognition*, *40*(1–2), 1–19.

Kalin, N. H., Shelton, S. E., & Snowdon, C. T. (1992). Affiliative vocalizations in infant rhesus macaques (Macaca mulatta). *J Comp Psychol*, *106*(3), 254–261.

Kanwisher, N., McDermott, J., & Chun, M. M. (1997). The fusiform face area: A module in human extrastriate cortex specialized for face perception. *J Neurosci*, *17*(11), 4302–4311.

Kay, R. F., Ross, C., & Williams, B. A. (1997). Anthropoid origins. *Science*, *275*(5301), 797–804.

Kennard, M. A. (1959). The cingulate gyrus in relation to consciousness. *Journal of Nervous and Mental Disease*, *121*, 34–39.

Kiani, R., Esteky, H., & Tanaka, K. (2005). Differences in onset latency of macaque inferotemporal neural responses to primate and non-primate faces. *J Neurophysiol*, *94*(2), 1587–1596.

Kilner, J. M., Neal, A., Weiskopf, N., Friston, K. J., & Frith, C. D. (2009). Evidence of mirror neurons in human inferior frontal gyrus. *J Neurosci*, *29*(32), 10153–10159.

Kling, A., Steklis, H. D., & Deutsch, S. (1979). Radiotelemetered activity from the amygdala during social interactions in the monkey. *Exp Neurol*, *66*(1), 88–96.

Kling, A. S. (1992). The amygdala and social behavior. In J. P. Aggleton (Ed.), *The amygdala: Neurobiological aspects of emotion, memory, and dysfunction*. New York: Wiley-Liss.

Kling, A. S. & Green, P. C. (1967). Effects of neonatal amygdalectomy in the maternally reared and maternally deprived macaque. *Nature*, *213*(5077), 742–743.

Kobayashi, Y. & Amaral, D. G. (2003). Macaque monkey retrosplenial cortex: II. Cortical afferents. *J Comp Neurol*, *466*(1), 48–79.

Kobayashi, Y. & Amaral, D. G. (2007). Macaque monkey retrosplenial cortex: III. Cortical efferents. *J Comp Neurol*, *502*(5), 810–833.

Kohler, E., Keysers, C., Umilta, M. A., Fogassi, L., Gallese, V., & Rizzolatti, G. (2002). Hearing sounds, understanding actions: Action representation in mirror neurons. *Science*, *297*(5582), 846–848.

Koyama, T., Kato, K., Tanaka, Y. Z., & Mikami, A. (2001). Anterior cingulate activity during pain-avoidance and reward tasks in monkeys. *Neurosci Res*, *39*(4), 421–430.

Koyama, T., Tanaka, Y. Z., & Mikami, A. (1998). Nociceptive neurons in the macaque anterior cingulate activate during anticipation of pain. *Neuroreport*, *9*(11), 2663–2667.

Kringelbach, M. L. & Rolls, E. T. (2003). Neural correlates of rapid reversal learning in a simple model of human social interaction. *Neuroimage*, *20*(2), 1371–1383.

Kross, E., Egner, T., Ochsner, K., Hirsch, J., & Downey, G. (2007). Neural dynamics of rejection sensitivity. *J Cogn Neurosci*, *19*(6), 945–956.

Kuwahata, H., Adachi, I., Fujita, K., Tomonaga, M., & Matsuzawa, T. (2004). Development of schematic face preference in macaque monkeys. *Behav Processes*, *66*(1), 17–21.

Lane, R. D., Reiman, E. M., Axelrod, B., Yun, L. S., Holmes, A., & Schwartz, G. E. (1998). Neural correlates of levels of emotional awareness. Evidence of an interaction between emotion and attention in the anterior cingulate cortex. *J Cogn Neurosci*, *10*(4), 525–535.

Leonard, C. M., Rolls, E. T., Wilson, F. A. W., & Baylis, G. C. (1985). Neurons in the amydgala of the monkey with responses selective for faces. *Behavioural Brain Research*, *15*(2), 159–176.

Lesch, K. P., Meyer, J., Glatz, K., Flugge, G., Hinney, A., Hebebrand, J., et al. (1997). The 5-HT transporter gene-linked polymorphic region (5-HTTLPR) in evolutionary perspective: alternative biallelic variation in rhesus monkeys. Rapid communication. *J Neural Transm, 104*(11–12), 1259–1266.

Lindberg, D. G. (1971). The rhesus monkey in North India: An ecological and behavioral study. In L. A. Rosenblum (Ed.), *Primate Behavior* (pp. 1–106). New York: Academic Press.

Lindburg, D. G. (1991). Ecological requirements of macaques. *Lab Anim Sci, 41*(4), 315–322.

Lingnau, A., Gesierich, B., & Caramazza, A. (2009). Asymmetric fMRI adaptation reveals no evidence for mirror neurons in humans. *Proc Natl Acad Sci U S A, 106*(24), 9925–9930.

Liu, Z., Murray, E. A., & Richmond, B. J. (2000). Learning motivational significance of visual cues for reward schedules requires rhinal cortex. *Nat Neurosci, 3*(12), 1307–1315.

Liu, Z. & Richmond, B. J. (2000). Response differences in monkey TE and perirhinal cortex: stimulus association related to reward schedules. *J Neurophysiol, 83*(3), 1677–1692.

Lutz, C. K., Lockard, J. S., Gunderson, V. M., & Grant, K. S. (1998). Infant monkeys' visual responses to drawings of normal and distorted faces. *Am J Primatol, 44*(2), 169–174.

Machado, C. J. & Bachevalier, J. (2006). The impact of selective amygdala, orbital frontal cortex, or hippocampal formation lesions on established social relationships in rhesus monkeys (Macaca mulatta). *Behav Neurosci, 120*(4), 761–786.

Machado, C. J., Emery, N. J., Capitanio, J. P., Mason, W. A., Mendoza, S. P., & Amaral, D. G. (2008). Bilateral neurotoxic amygdala lesions in rhesus monkeys (Macaca mulatta): Consistent pattern of behavior across different social contexts. *Behav Neurosci, 122*(2), 251–266.

Maestripieri, D. (1996). Gestural communication and its cognitive implications in pigtail macaques (*Macaca nemestrina*). *Behaviour, 133*, 997–1022.

Maestripieri, D. (1997). Gestural communication in macaques: Usage and meaning of nonvocal signals. *Evolution of Communication, 1*, 193–222.

Maestripieri, D. (2005). Gestural communication in three species of macaques (Macaca mulatta, M. nemestrina, M. arctoides): Use of signals in relation to dominance and social context. *Gesture*(5), 57–73.

Maestripieri, D. (2007). *Macachiavellian intelligence: How rhesus macaque and humans have conquered the world.* Chicago: University of Chicago Press.

Maestripieri, D. & Wallen, K. (1997). Affiliative and submissive communication in rhesus macaques. *Primates, 38*(127–138).

Malkova, L., Barrow, K. V., Lower, L. L., & Gale, K. (2003). Decreased social interactions in monkeys after unilateral blockade of GABA-A receptors in the basolateral amygdala. *Annals of the New York Academy of Sciences, 985*, 540–541.

Markowitsch, H. J., Vandekerckhove, M. M., Lanfermann, H., & Russ, M. O. (2003). Engagement of lateral and medial prefrontal areas in the ecphory of sad and happy autobiographical memories. *Cortex, 39*(4–5), 643–665.

Matheson, M. D. & Bernstein, I. S. (2000). Grooming, social bonding, and agonistic aiding in rhesus monkeys. *Am J Primatol, 51*(3), 177–186.

Matsumoto, K., Suzuki, W., & Tanaka, K. (2003). Neuronal correlates of goal-based motor selection in the prefrontal cortex. *Science, 301*(5630), 229–232.

Maunsell, J. H., Sclar, G., Nealey, T. A., & DePriest, D. D. (1991). Extraretinal representations in area V4 in the macaque monkey. *Vis Neurosci, 7*(6), 561–573.

McGonigle, B. O. & Chalmers, M. (1977). Are monkeys logical? *Nature, 267*(5613), 694–696.

Meltzoff, A. N. & Moore, M. K. (1977). Imitation of facial and manual gestures by human neonates. *Science, 198*(4312), 74–78.

Meltzoff, A. N. & Moore, M. K. (1983). Newborn infants imitate adult facial gestures. *Child Dev, 54*(3), 702–709.

Mendelson, M. J. (1982). Visual and social responses in infant rhesus monkeys. *Am J Primatol, 3*, 333–340.

Mendelson, M. J., Haith, M. M., & Goldman-Rakic, P. S. (1982). Face scanning and responsiveness to social cues in infant rhesus monkeys. *Developmental Psychology, 18*(2), 222–228.

Meunier, M. & Bachevalier, J. (2002). Comparison of emotional responses in monkeys with rhinal cortex or amygdala lesions. *Emotion, 2*(2), 147–161.

Michelet, T., Bioulac, B., Guehl, D., Escola, L., & Burbaud, P. (2007). Impact of commitment on performance evaluation in the rostral cingulate motor area. *J Neurosci, 27*(28), 7482–7489.

Mirsky, A. F., Rosvold, H. E., & Pribram, K. H. (1957). Effects of cingulectomy on social behavior in monkeys. *J Neurophysiol, 20*(6), 588–601.

Missakian, E. A. (1972). Genealogical and cross-genealogical dominance relations in a group of free ranging rhesus monkeys (Macaca mulatta) on Cayo Santiago. *Primates, 13*(2), 169–180.

Moeller, S., Freiwald, W. A., & Tsao, D. Y. (2008). Patches with links: A unified system for processing faces in the macaque temporal lobe. *Science, 320*(5881), 1355–1359.

Moll, J., de Oliveira-Souza, R., Bramati, I. E., & Grafman, J. (2002). Functional networks in emotional moral and nonmoral social judgments. *Neuroimage, 16*(3 Pt 1), 696–703.

Morton, J. & Johnson, M. H. (1991). CONSPEC and CONLERN: A two-process theory of infant face recognition. *Psychol Rev, 98*(2), 164–181.

Myers, R. E., Swett, C., & Miller, M. (1973). Loss of social group affinity following prefrontal lesions in free-ranging macaques. *Brain Res, 64*, 257–269.

Nimchinsky, E. A., Gilissen, E., Allman, J. M., Perl, D. P., Erwin, J. M., & Hof, P. R. (1999). A neuronal morphologic type unique to humans and great apes. *Proc Natl Acad Sci U S A, 96*(9), 5268–5273.

Nishijo, H., Yamamoto, Y., Ono, T., Uwano, T., Yamashita, J., & Yamashima, T. (1997). Single neuron responses in the monkey anterior cingulate cortex during visual discrimination. *Neurosci Lett, 227*(2), 79–82.

O'Doherty, J., Winston, J., Critchley, H., Perrett, D., Burt, D. M., & Dolan, R. J. (2003). Beauty in a smile: The role of medial orbitofrontal cortex in facial attractiveness. *Neuropsychologia, 41*(2), 147–155.

O'Scalaidhe, S. P., Wilson, F. A., & Goldman-Rakic, P. S. (1997). Areal segregation of face-processing neurons in prefrontal cortex. *Science, 278*(5340), 1135–1138.

O'Scalaidhe, S. P., Wilson, F. A., & Goldman-Rakic, P. S. (1999). Face-selective neurons during passive viewing and working memory performance of rhesus monkeys: Evidence for intrinsic specialization of neuronal coding. *Cereb Cortex, 9*(5), 459–475.

Ottowitz, W. E., Dougherty, D. D., Sirota, A., Niaura, R., Rauch, S. L., & Brown, W. A. (2004). Neural and endocrine correlates of sadness in women: Implications for neural network regulation of HPA activity. *J Neuropsychiatry Clin Neurosci, 16*(4), 446–455.

Parr, L. A., Waller, B. M., & Fugate, J. (2005). Emotional communication in primates: Implications for neurobiology. *Curr Opin Neurobiol, 15*(6), 716–720.

Perrett, D. I., Rolls, E. T., & Caan, W. (1982). Visual neurones responsive to faces in the monkey temporal cortex. *Exp Brain Res, 47*(3), 329–342.

Perrett, D. I., Smith, P. A., Potter, D. D., Mistlin, A. J., Head, A. S., Milner, A. D., et al. (1984). Neurones responsive to faces in the temporal cortex: studies of functional organization, sensitivity to identity and relation to perception. *Hum Neurobiol, 3*(4), 197–208.

Perrett, D. I., Smith, P. A., Potter, D. D., Mistlin, A. J., Head, A. S., Milner, A. D., et al. (1985). Visual cells in the temporal cortex sensitive to face view and gaze direction. *Proc R Soc Lond B Biol Sci, 223*(1232), 293–317.

Pinsk, M. A., Arcaro, M., Weiner, K. S., Kalkus, J. F., Inati, S. J., Gross, C. G., et al. (2009). Neural representations of faces and body parts in macaque and human cortex: A comparative FMRI study. *J Neurophysiol, 101*(5), 2581–2600.

Pinsk, M. A., DeSimone, K., Moore, T., Gross, C. G., & Kastner, S. (2005). Representations of faces and body parts in macaque temporal cortex: A functional MRI study. *Proc Natl Acad Sci U S A, 102*(19), 6996–7001.

Prather, M. D., Lavenex, P., Mauldin-Jourdain, M. L., Mason, W. A., Capitanio, J. P., Mendoza, S. P., et al. (2001). Increased social fear and decreased fear of objects in monkeys with neonatal amygdala lesions. *Neuroscience, 106*(4), 653–658.

Preuss, T. M. (2000). Taking the measure of diversity: Comparative alternatives to the model-animal paradigm in cortical neuroscience. *Brain Behav Evol, 55*(6), 287–299.

Price, J. L. (2007). Definition of the orbital cortex in relation to specific connections with limbic and visceral structures and other cortical regions. *Ann N Y Acad Sci, 1121*, 54–71.

Procyk, E., Tanaka, Y. L., & Joseph, J. P. (2000). Anterior cingulate activity during routine and non-routine sequential behaviors in macaques. *Nat Neurosci, 3*(5), 502–508.

Raleigh, M. J. & Steklis, H. D. (1981). Effect of orbitofrontal and temporal neocortical lesions of the affiliative behavior of vervet monkeys (Cercopithecus aethiops sabaeus). *Exp Neurol, 73*(2), 378–389.

Raleigh, M. J., Steklis, H. D., Ervin, F. R., Kling, A. S., & McGuire, M. T. (1979). The effects of orbitofrontal lesions on the aggressive behavior of vervet monkeys (Cercopithecus aethiops sabaeus). *Exp Neurol, 66*(1), 158–168.

Reader, S. M. & Laland, K. N. (2002). Social intelligence, innovation, and enhanced brain size in primates. *Proc Natl Acad Sci U S A, 99*(7), 4436–4441.

Rilling, J., Gutman, D., Zeh, T., Pagnoni, G., Berns, G., & Kilts, C. (2002). A neural basis for social cooperation. *Neuron, 35*(2), 395–405.

Rizzolatti, G. & Craighero, L. (2004). The mirror-neuron system. *Annu Rev Neurosci, 27*, 169–192.

Rizzolatti, G., Fabbri-Destro, M., & Cattaneo, L. (2009). Mirror neurons and their clinical relevance. *Nat Clin Pract Neurol, 5*(1), 24–34.

Rizzolatti, G., Fadiga, L., Gallese, V., & Fogassi, L. (1996). Premotor cortex and the recognition of motor actions. *Brain Res Cogn Brain Res, 3*(2), 131–141.

Rodman, H. R. (1994). Development of inferior temporal cortex in the monkey. *Cereb Cortex, 4*(5), 484–498.

Rodman, H. R., Scalaidhe, S. P., & Gross, C. G. (1993). Response properties of neurons in temporal cortical visual areas of infant monkeys. *J Neurophysiol, 70*(3), 1115–1136.

Rodman, H. R., Skelly, J. P., & Gross, C. G. (1991). Stimulus selectivity and state dependence of activity in inferior temporal cortex of infant monkeys. *Proc Natl Acad Sci U S A, 88*(17), 7572–7575.

Rolls, E. T. (1984). Neurons in the cortex of the temporal lobe and in the amygdala of the monkey with responses selective for faces. *Human Neurobiology, 3*, 209–222.

Rosvold, H. E., Mirsky, A. F., & Pribram, K. H. (1954). Influence of amygdalectomy on social behavior in monkeys. *Journal of Comparative & Physiological Psychology, 47*, 173–178.

Rowell, T. E. & Hinde, R. A. (1962). Vocal communication by the rhesus monkey (*Macaca mulatta*). *Proceedings of the Zoological Society of London, 138*(2), 279–294.

Rudebeck, P. H., Buckley, M. J., Walton, M. E., & Rushworth, M. F. (2006). A role for the macaque anterior cingulate gyrus in social valuation. *Science, 313*(5791), 1310–1312.

Ruppenthal, G. C., Harlow, M. K., Eisele, C. D., Harlow, H. F., & Suomi, S. J. (1974). Development of peer interactions of monkeys reared in a nuclear-family environment. *Child Dev, 45*(3), 670–682.

Rushworth, M. F., Behrens, T. E., Rudebeck, P. H., & Walton, M. E. (2007). Contrasting roles for cingulate and orbitofrontal cortex in decisions and social behaviour. *Trends Cogn Sci, 11*(4), 168–176.

Sade, D. S. (1967). Determinants of dominance in a group of free-ranging rhesus monkeys. In S. A. Altmann (Ed.), *Social communication among primates* (pp. 99–114). Chicago: University of Chicago Press.

Sereno, M. I. & Tootell, R. B. (2005). From monkeys to humans: What do we now know about brain homologies? *Curr Opin Neurobiol, 15*(2), 135–144.

Shidara, M. & Richmond, B. J. (2002). Anterior cingulate: Single neuronal signals related to degree of reward expectancy. *Science, 296*(5573), 1709–1711.

Singer, T., Seymour, B., O'Doherty, J., Kaube, H., Dolan, R. J., & Frith, C. D. (2004). Empathy for pain involves the affective but not sensory components of pain. *Science, 303*(5661), 1157–1162.

Squire, L. R., Stark, C. E., & Clark, R. E. (2004). The medial temporal lobe. *Annu Rev Neurosci, 27*, 279–306.

Suzuki, W. A. & Amaral, D. G. (1994). Perirhinal and parahippocampal cortices of the macaque monkey: Cortical afferents. *J Comp Neurol, 350*(4), 497–533.

Suzuki, W. A. & Amaral, D. G. (2004). Functional neuroanatomy of the medial temporal lobe memory system. *Cortex, 40*(1), 220–222.

Thierry, B. (1985). Social development in three species of macaque (Macaca mulatta, M. fascicularis, M. tonkeana): A preliminary report on the first ten weeks of life. *Behavioural Processes, 11*, 89–95.

Thompson, C. I. (1968). *Social development of infant rhesus monkeys following amygdaloid lesions.* U. Wisconsin.

Thompson, C. I. (1981). Long-term behavioral development of rhesus monkeys after amygdalectomy in infancy. In Y. Ben-Ari (Ed.), *The amygdaloid complex* (pp. 259–270). Amsterdam: Elsevier.

Thompson, C. I., Bergland, R. M., & Towfighi, J. T. (1977). Social and nonsocial behaviors of adult rhesus monkeys after amygdalectomy in infancy or adulthood.

Journal of Comparative & Physiological Psychology, 91(3), 533–548.

Thompson, C. I., Schwartzbaum, J. S., & Harlow, H. F. (1969). Development of social fear after amygdalectomy in infant rhesus monkeys. *Physiology & Behavior, 4*(2), 249–254.

Trefilov, A., Krawczak, M., Berard, J., & Schmidtke, J. (1999). DNA sequence polymorphisms in genes involved in the regulation of dopamine and serotonin metabolism in rhesus macaques. *Electrophoresis, 20*(8), 1771–1777.

Tsao, D. Y., Freiwald, W. A., Knutsen, T. A., Mandeville, J. B., & Tootell, R. B. (2003). Faces and objects in macaque cerebral cortex. *Nat Neurosci, 6*(9), 989–995.

Tsao, D. Y., Freiwald, W. A., Tootell, R. B., & Livingstone, M. S. (2006). A cortical region consisting entirely of face-selective cells. *Science, 311*(5761), 670–674.

Umilta, M. A., Kohler, E., Gallese, V., Fogassi, L., Fadiga, L., Keysers, C., et al. (2001). I know what you are doing. A neurophysiological study. *Neuron, 31*(1), 155–165.

Vogt, B. A., Berger, G. R., & Derbyshire, S. W. (2003). Structural and functional dichotomy of human midcingulate cortex. *Eur J Neurosci, 18*(11), 3134–3144.

Vogt, B. A., Hof, P. R., & Vogt, L. J. (2004). Cingulate gyrus. In G. P. J. K. Mai (Ed.), *The human nervous system*, 2nd Ed (pp. 915–949). San Diego, CA: Academic Press.

Ward, A. A. (1948). The cingular gyrus: Area 24. *J Neurophysiol, 11*, 13–23.

Webster, M. J., Bachevalier, J., & Ungerleider, L. G. (1993). Subcortical connections of inferior temporal areas TE and TEO in macaque monkeys. *J Comp Neurol, 335*(1), 73–91.

Webster, M. J., Ungerleider, L. G., & Bachevalier, J. (1991). Connections of inferior temporal areas TE and TEO with medial temporal-lobe structures in infant and adult monkeys. *J Neurosci, 11*(4), 1095–1116.

Wrangham, R. W. (1980). An ecological model of female-bonded primate groups. *Behaviour, 75*, 262–300.

Wrangham, R. W. (1987). Evolution of social structure. In B. B. Smuts, D. L. Cheney, R. M. Seyfarth, R. W. Wrangham & T. T. Struhsaker (Eds.), *Primate societies* (pp. 282–296). Chicago: University of Chicago Press.

Yeung, N., Botvinick, M. M., & Cohen, J. D. (2004). The neural basis of error detection: Conflict monitoring and the error-related negativity. *Psychol Rev, 111*(4), 931–959.

Zola-Morgan, S., Squire, L. R., & Amaral, D. G. (1986). Human amnesia and the medial temporal region: enduring memory impairment following a bilateral lesion limited to field CA1 of the hippocampus. *J Neurosci, 6*(10), 2950–2967.

Neural Representation of Social Hierarchy

Caroline F. Zink *and* Joseph W. Barter

Abstract

This chapter reviews current knowledge regarding neural systems underlying social hierarchies, focusing primarily on human and nonhuman primates. It starts with an examination of two neurotransmitter systems: 1) the involvement of the central serotonergic system in the determination and maintenance of one's hierarchical rank; and 2) the repercussions of acquiring a particular hierarchical position on the dopaminergic system. This section is followed by a discussion of various brain regions that have been implicated in the processing of perceived social status in stable and unstable hierarchical settings. It also explores the neural processing of the 'hierarchical value' associated with specific events or circumstances that potentially impact one's status (either positively or negatively) during periods of hierarchy instability. In closing, the chapter considers future research directions aimed at further elucidating the complexity of the neural representations of social hierarchies.

Keywords: social hierarchy, social status, rank, dominant, subordinate, serotonin, dopamine, brain, fMRI, human, monkey, (hierarchical) value

Introduction

Social hierarchy refers to the ranking of individuals within a group according to power, prestige, and control of resources. Social hierarchy formation is ubiquitous in virtually all social animals, such as insects (Richards, 1971; Van Honk & Hogeweg, 1981; Wilson, 1975), fish (Grosenick, Clement, & Fernald, 2007), reptiles (Brattstrom, 1974), birds (Ficken, Weise, & Popp, 1990; Lahti, Koivula, & Orell, 1994), rodents (Blanchard, Flannelly, & Blanchard, 1988), and primates, including humans (Cheney & Seyfarth, 1990; Cummins, 2000; Sapolsky & Ray, 1989). In humans, social status can be inferred automatically and efficiently (Moors & De Houwer, 2005) by implicit cues (e.g., facial features, [Buss, 1998; Keating, 1985], emotion expression [Hess, Blairy, & Kleck, 2000; Knutson, 1996], posture [Tiedens & Fragale, 2003], height, gender, age, and dress [Karafin, Tranel, & Adolphs, 2004]) and also by explicit cues (e.g., uniforms, honorifics, verbal assignment, [Zink et al., 2008]; and possession of status-related objects, [Erk, Spitzer, Wunderlich, Galley, & Walter, 2002]). The ability to recognize and transitively reason about relations within a hierarchy minimizes aggressive encounters and the corresponding stress, energy, and injury costs in animals (Barnard & Burk, 1979), as well as being critical for assimilating implicit expectations and action dispositions that drive appropriate social behavior (Cummins, 2000). How do our brains achieve this incredible feat? In other words, how do neural systems integrate social hierarchical information and context to form accurate status precepts for guiding behavior, and what are the neural implications of occupying a particular hierarchical rank? Much of our understanding of the neural underpinnings of social hierarchy come from animal studies, not only due to the permissibility of more invasive research techniques, but also because of a relatively less complex social structure in animal societies compared to human; virtually all animals, including nonhuman primates, belong to only one dominance hierarchy within their social living group, and the hierarchy is based primarily on the interplay of physical aggressive and affiliative behaviors (de Waal, 1986; Wilson, 1975). Conversely, social organization in humans is complicated by the fact that we simultaneously occupy different positions in separate hierarchies within various social environments (e.g., recreational, domestic, and professional settings). Furthermore, rather than being determined and maintained solely by physical aggressive and affiliative encounters, hierarchies in humans can be established along various dimensions according to one's skill, economic, or intellectual standing. The advent of neuroimaging techniques, for example, positron emission tomography (PET) and functional magnetic resonance imaging (fMRI), however, has enabled valuable information regarding neural correlates of social status to be obtained from humans as well.

In this chapter, we will present current knowledge regarding neural systems underlying social hierarchies, focusing primarily on human and nonhuman primates. We start with an examination of two neurotransmitter systems: 1) the involvement of the central serotonergic system in the determination and maintenance of one's hierarchical rank, and 2) the repercussions of acquiring a particular hierarchical position on the dopaminergic system. This section is followed by a discussion of various brain regions that have been implicated in the processing of perceived social status in stable and unstable hierarchical settings. We will also explore the neural processing of the "hierarchical value" associated with specific events or circumstances that potentially impact one's status (either positively or negatively) during periods of hierarchy instability. In closing, we touch on future research directions aimed to further elucidate the complexity of the neural representations of social hierarchies.

Neurotransmitter Systems Affecting and Affected by Social Hierarchy
Serotonergic Neurotransmitter System
In multiple species, a relationship has been established between activity in the brain's serotonin system and one's social status within a hierarchy. Serotonin plays a prominent role in the regulation and expression of social aggression (Lucki, 1998), overall dampening aggressive behaviors and enhancing affiliative behaviors towards others (Carrillo, Ricci, Coppersmith, & Melloni, 2009; Raleigh, McGuire, Brammer, Pollack, & Yuwiler, 1991). As such, the directionality of the relationship between serotonin and social status appears to be largely species-specific, depending substantially on the preponderance of aggressive versus affiliative behaviors in status determination and maintenance.

Several primate species (e.g., vervet monkeys, rhesus macaques, and humans) rely heavily on coalitions with others (Struhsaker, 1967), as high status is predominantly established by the ability to form affiliative relationships and by the ability to recruit allies during conflict, rather than an individual's fighting ability (de Waal, 1986; Higley et al., 1996; Raleigh et al., 1991). Here, enhanced serotonin activity is associated with heightened social hierarchical rank. In female rhesus macaques, higher baseline cerebral spinal fluid (CSF) concentration levels of the major serotonin metabolite, 5-hydroxyindoleacetic acid (5-HIAA)—an indicator of serotonin activity—predict acquisition of higher rank during hierarchy formation (Higley et al., 1996). Moreover, CSF 5-HIAA levels remain significantly elevated in the individuals holding the dominant compared to subordinate position in stable social hierarchies (Higley et al., 1996; Westergaard, Suomi, Higley, & Mehlman, 1999). Similarly, whole-blood concentrations of serotonin are significantly greater in dominant than in subordinate male vervet monkeys, and status changes from subordinate to dominant are accompanied by a rise in blood serotonin concentration, while a decline in serotonin concentration accompanies the switch from a dominant to a subordinate position or to social isolation (Raleigh, McGuire, Brammer, & Yuwiler, 1984). Furthermore, pharmacological manipulations of central serotonin function in vervet monkeys can determine social status. Specifically, during experimentally induced hierarchy instability, pharmacological dampening of central serotonin activity—via administration of cyproheptadine, a serotonin receptor antagonist, or fenfluramine, an amphetamine derivative which decreases serotonin function when given chronically—prevents occupation of the dominant position in the hierarchy, whereas pharmacological enhancement of central serotonin activity—via administration of the serotonin precursor, tryptophan, or serotonin reuptake inhibitor, fluoxetine—leads to obtainment of high social status (Raleigh et al., 1991). Dominant vervet monkeys also demonstrate heightened behavioral sensitivity to pharmacological agents that increase serotonergic neurotransmission, indicative of status-related differences within the central serotonin system, although the exact neural substrates remain unknown (Raleigh, Brammer, McGuire, & Yuwiler, 1985). In humans, linking the serotonergic system to social status is complicated by the fact that humans simultaneously occupy different positions in multiple different hierarchies (Raleigh et al., 1984); however, healthy individuals treated with citalopram, a selective serotonin reuptake inhibitor, are judged by their peers to be less submissive, display dominant patterns of eye-contact in social interactions, and engage in more affiliative and cooperative behaviors with others (Tse & Bond, 2002). These data suggest elevated serotonin levels in humans are associated with higher social status.

On the other hand, in several species, including lizards, rats, and certain primates, enhanced serotonin activity is associated with diminished social status. In female cynomolgus monkeys, baseline CSF 5-HIAA concentrations are lower in individuals who became dominant compared to subordinate and remain lower in the dominant animals in stable hierarchies (Riddick et al., 2009). Similarly, talapoin monkeys with higher levels of CSF 5-HIAA during hierarchy formation occupy subordinate positions (Yodyingyuad, de la Riva, Abbott, Herbert, & Keverne, 1985), and brain tissue levels of 5-HIAA in the preoptic area, amygdala, hippocampus, spinal cord, and entorhinal cortex of subordinate rats are higher than dominant and individually housed rats (Blanchard et al., 1991; Blanchard, Sakai, McEwen, Weiss, & Blanchard, 1993). Furthermore, pharmacologically enhancing central serotonin transmission with serotonin precursors (e.g., tryptophan and 5-hydroxytryptophan), serotonin receptor agonists (e.g., quipazine), and selective serotonin reuptake inhibitors (e.g., femoxetine and sertraline) in dominant lizards and rats negates or reverses the dominant status, that is, the dominant animals become subordinate (Kostowski, Plewako, & Bidzinski, 1984; Larson & Summers, 2001). Conversely, diminishing serotonin activity—via serotonin synthesis blockage with p-chlorophenylalanine, administration of the serotonin receptor antagonist, metergoline, or by lesioning the ralphe nucleus

where serotonergic neurons originate—transforms subordinate rats into dominant rats (Kostowski et al., 1984). While these data are seemingly contradictive to the evidence linking heightened serotonergic activity with heightened status, it is likely that the difference stems from an emphasis on fighting prowess and aggression, rather than affiliative gestures, for dominance establishment in certain animals (Larson & Summers, 2001; Westergaard et al., 1999). The exact mechanisms and neural substrates underlying the status differences within the serotonin neurotransmitter system remain to be elucidated, but there is a strong, species-specific relationship between serotonin and the acquisition and maintenance of rank in social hierarchies.

Dopaminergic Neurotransmitter System

As opposed to serotonin, the relationship between the dopamine system and social status appears to be more consequential than determinant and without a clear species-specific nature. Over a decade ago, using PET imaging and [^{18}F]4-fluoroclebopride ([^{18}F]FCP), a radioligand that binds to available dopamine D2 receptors with high affinity (Mach et al., 1996), an association was established between high social rank and heightened striatal D2 receptor availability, as indicated by greater [^{18}F]FCP uptake in dominant female cynomolgus monkeys compared to subordinate counterparts (Grant et al., 1998). A strikingly similar effect has also been determined in humans. In men and women, the availability of striatal D2 receptors—as measured by PET [11C] raclopride binding potential—is strongly correlated with an one's social rank and levels of social support (Martinez et al., 2010). Such status-related difference in binding potentials may stem from the chronic stress generally experienced by subordinates in stable hierarchies (Shively, 1998). Stress can increase striatal dopamine levels and in turn evoke the downregulation of striatal D2 receptors which would result in a relative increase in receptor availability in dominant individuals (Cabib & Puglisi-Allegra, 1996). However, by assessing PET [^{18}F]FCP-binding potentials in cynomolgus monkeys prior to establishment of a hierarchy, that is, in social isolation, and subsequently three months after group formation, it has been demonstrated that an alteration in dopamine receptor availability is evoked by occupying a dominant position. While subordinate monkeys have less striatal D2 receptor availability than dominant monkeys after hierarchy establishment, the ligand uptake measured in subordinates is not different than measurements taken during social isolation, whereas dominant monkeys demonstrate a significant increase in ligand uptake relative to isolation (Morgan et al., 2002) (Figure 46.1). From these findings, two conclusions can be drawn: 1) the social status-related effects on striatal D2 receptor availability are consequential of one's hierarchical position, rather than being a trait that predicts future status; and 2) the social status-related differences in striatal D2 receptor availability are primarily driven by changes in the dopaminergic system of the dominant rather than subordinate individual, perhaps as a result of enhanced environmental enrichment experienced in a high-status position. Deprivation of environmental enrichment, that is, isolation, is associated with elevated striatal dopamine levels and decreases in striatal receptor density (Hall et al., 1998; Rilke, May, Oehler, & Wolffgramm, 1995). As such, while individually housed and socially subordinate animals have relatively high synaptic dopamine levels, acquiring dominant rank allows animals to be in more control of environmental enrichment which may result in neurochemical changes that decrease dopamine levels in high-status individuals (Morgan et al., 2002). Interestingly, three months following experimentally induced hierarchical rearrangement, a relationship between new social rank and D2 receptor

availability does not exist; newly dominant cynomolgus monkeys (some of which were previously subordinate) do not have higher levels of D2 receptor availability compared to newly subordinate monkeys (some of which were previously dominant) (Nader, Czoty, Gould, & Riddick, 2008). Therefore, once an original rank and corresponding changes to the dopaminergic system are established, perhaps the dopaminergic neurochemical profile cannot be altered. An alternative explanation posits that following hierarchy rearrangement, updated corresponding modifications in the dopaminergic system require more time to materialize than following original hierarchy formation.

So far, in this sub-section we have focused our discussion on the effects of social status on *striatal* dopamine function, as the striatum is a major neural target of dopaminergic neurotransmission. It should be noted, however, that the aforementioned relationship between dopamine and social rank may be specific to the striatum and may not apply to other sites of dopaminergic activity, such as the prefrontal cortex which is also highly innervated by dopaminergic projections. Contrary to what would be expected based on the direction of the status-dopamine relationship demonstrated in the striatum, CSF levels of the dopamine metabolite,

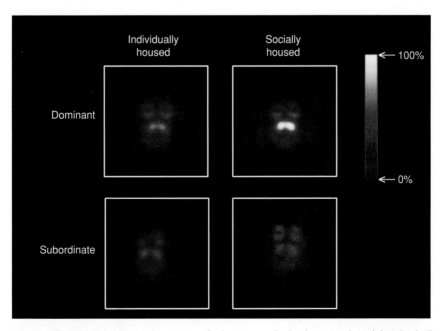

Fig. 46.1 PET images of [18F]FCP binding in the striatum of a dominant and subordinate monkey while individually (i.e., in isolation) or socially housed. Dopamine D2 receptor availability (measured by [18F]FCP binding potential) increases in dominant monkeys when status is achieved in social housing.
From Morgan et al. (2002); reproduced with permission from Nature Publishing Group.

Fig. 46.2 Stimuli in paradigms used to identify the neural representation of social hierarchy. a-b) Examples of social status cues in facial features and expressions used in EEG studies to differentiate status-related neural responses. Adapted with permission from **Chiao et al., 2008; Rudebeck, Buckley, Watson, & Rushworth, 2006;** c-d) Examples of social status cues displayed in full-body postures used in fMRI studies to differentiate status-related neural responses to dominance and subordination. Adapted with permission from **Freeman, Rule, Adams, & Ambady, 2009; Marsh, Blair, Jones, Soliman, & Blair, 2009;** e-f) Examples of video clips used to assess social status judgments after brain lesions; g) Schematic of an interactive fMRI paradigm used to assess differential neural responses to high and low status individuals in a stable hierarchy. Adapted with permission from **Zink et al., 2008;** h) schematic of an interactive fMRI paradigm used to assess differential neural responses to high and low status individuals in an unstable hierarchy, as well as neural responses to hierarchically valuable outcomes. Adapted with permission from **Zink et al., 2008.**

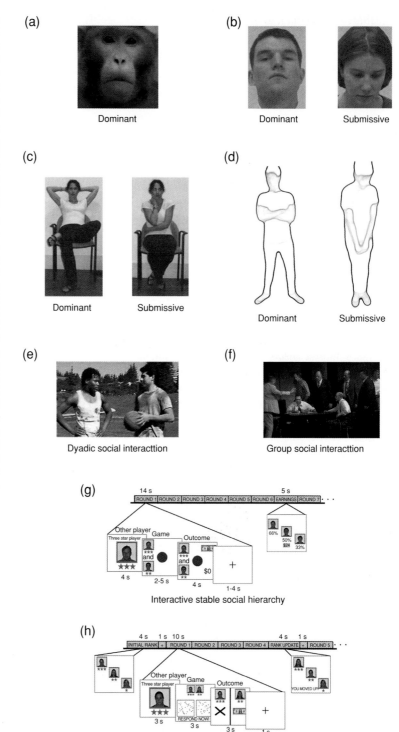

(a) Dominant

(b) Dominant   Submissive

(c) Dominant   Submissive

(d) Dominant   Submissive

(e) Dyadic social interacttion

(f) Group social interacttion

(g) Interactive stable social hierarchy

(h) Interactive unstable social hierarchy

homovanillic acid (HVA)—an indirect measure of dopamine neural activity—are greater in dominant cynomolgus monkeys than subordinate monkeys (Kaplan, Manuck, Fontenot, & Mann, 2002). CSF measures lack regional specificity, and the CSF HVA levels may be reflecting dopamine activity in the prefrontal cortex rather than the striatum. In fact, while deprivation of an enriched environment via isolation elicits dopamine hyperactivity in the striatum, dopaminergic activity in the prefrontal cortex is reduced in isolation, as measured by levels of the dopamine metabolite, dihydroxyphenylacetic acid (DOPAC) (Blanc et al., 1980). In summary, as with serotonin, the exact mechanisms and neural substrates underlying the status differences within the dopamine neurotransmitter system are unknown at this time, but there is strong evidence that the position one holds in a social hierarchy impacts the dopaminergic neurotransmitter system.

Brain Regions Implicated in the Processing of Perceived Social Status

Within a social hierarchy, animals are able to effectively discriminate between high- and low-status individuals and act accordingly. From a behavioral standpoint this is well documented, but relatively few data exist regarding neural systems that differentiate between hierarchical ranks, particularly in humans; however, in recent years, efforts have been made to identify such neural mechanisms. Utilizing EEG and fMRI technology, scientists have now identified several brain regions that respond in a status-dependent manner to visually presented expressions of social dominance cues (Chiao et al., 2008; Freeman, Rule, Adams, & Ambady, 2009; Marsh, Blair, Jones, Soliman, & Blair, 2009; Pineda, Sebestyen, & Nava, 1994) (Figure 46.2A-D). Furthermore, to assess hierarchical rank-related neural responses in the more naturalistic setting of an actual hierarchy, Zink and colleagues (2008) designed an fMRI paradigm in which a social hierarchy is created based on incidental skill in the context of a simulated, interactive game with others (Figure 46.2G-H). Results from these studies, together with relevant data from brain lesion and neuronal recording investigations, are presented in this section.

Social Status in a Stable Hierarchy

During periods of hierarchical stability, hierarchy-related conflicts are minimal, and social ranks within a hierarchy are firmly established and unchanging. In a stable hierarchical setting, four main brain regions have been identified—occipitoparietal cortex, ventral striatum, parahippocampal cortex, and lateral prefrontal cortex—in which neural activity is greater when viewing/interacting with a person of higher status than oneself compared to viewing/interacting with a lower status individual (Figure 46.3). We will consider each region separately in terms of the social hierarchical information that it may convey in its status-related differential neural signature.

The finding in the occipital/parietal cortex is the most replicable within and across multiple research approaches. An event-related potential (ERP) study in monkeys revealed that the amplitude of the N2 ERP component measured over occipital/parietal sites is larger when monkeys view photographs of familiar dominant conspecifics (Figure 46.2A) than when viewing corresponding low-status pictures (Pineda et al., 1994). A similar ERP phenomenon has been demonstrated in humans when viewing photographs of unfamiliar people displaying dominant compared to submissive facial expressions (Figure 46.2B) (Chiao et al., 2008). FMRI paradigms have also replicated these findings; both the occipital (Marsh et al., 2009) and parietal cortex (Freeman et al., 2009) are differentially activated by visually displayed social dominant cues (Figure 46.2C-D), with cues depicting higher status evoking a greater neural response. Viewing higher-ranked compared to lower-ranked individuals in an interactive hierarchy setting (Figure 46.2G) also elicits a greater occipitoparietal response (Zink et al., 2008). It should be noted that the extent of the activations expand into the temporal cortex/fusiform gyrus (Chiao et al., 2008; Marsh et al., 2009; Zink et al., 2008). These occipital/partietal activations likely underlie a greater perceptional/attentional processing (Bradley et al., 2003) of the higher status individual, consistent with behavior findings in nonhuman primates. In primates "visual observing is perhaps the most effective means of acquiring information about conspecifics" (Haude, Graber, & Farres, 1976) and is strongly related to status; the dominant animal "is the focus of attention of those holding subordinate status within the same group." (Chance, 1967). As illustrated in a choice selection paradigm, monkeys prefer to look at higher status compared to low-status monkeys and are even willing to sacrifice getting juice reward to do so (Deaner, Khera, & Platt, 2005; Klein, Deaner, & Platt, 2008). Lateral intraparietal neurons increase firing when a monkey is presented with and makes the choice to view a dominant monkey (the preferred option) but only in the context of making a decision whether or not to orient to it. This suggests that rather than coding social value per se, lateral intraparietal neurons may integrate value with the decision to orient, thus facilitating the direction of attention to important stimuli, such as those individuals with high status.

Activity in the ventral striatum increases when viewing a person of higher status than oneself compared to a person of lower status in the context of an

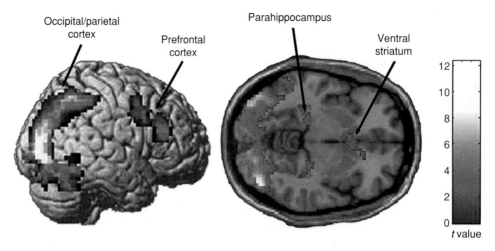

Fig. 46.3 Brain activations elicited by viewing a superior individual compared to an inferior individual in an interactive stable hierarchy. FMRI signal is increased in the occipitoparietal cortex, ventral striatum, parahippocampal cortex, and dorsolateral prefrontal cortex. Similar activation patterns are elicited by superior individuals in an unstable hierarchy. Adapted with permission from Zink et al., 2008.

interactive hierarchy (Figure 46.2G) (Zink et al., 2008). The ventral striatal activation is likely representing greater social value attributed to the higher status individual. The ventral striatum has been highly implicated in the processing of value and saliency, that is, attentional or behavioral relevance, independently of hedonic properties (Jensen et al., 2006; Zink, Pagnoni, Chappelow, Martin-Skurski, & Berns, 2006; Zink, Pagnoni, Martin, Dhamala, & Berns, 2003). While top-ranked individuals in a hierarchy may be considered behaviorally aversive due to their threatening nature, they may still carry more salience than low-ranked individuals by providing valuable information to guide behavior (Deaner et al., 2005; Klein et al., 2008). Of note, the assignment of greater value to a particular status and the corresponding striatal response can be culturally influenced (although perhaps in a more dorsal region), as demonstrated in a recent fMRI study comparing neural responses to social status cues between American and Japanese culture (Freeman et al., 2009). In both cultures, visual body displays of dominance (converted into figural outlines to remove culture membership cues; Figure 46.2D) evoke a greater parietal response compared to submissive displays, suggesting that in both cultures, dominance compels attention; however, striatal responses to dominance are culturally dependent. In Americans (who are generally taught to value dominance, independence, assertiveness, and self-elevation), dominant visual displays elicit greater striatal activity than submissive displays. Alternatively, in Japanese (who are generally

taught to value subordination, agreeability, humility, and vulnerability), dominant visual displays elicit *less* striatal activity than submissive displays.

Within the context of an interactive hierarchy (Figure 46.2G), a status-related differential neural response is also revealed in the parahippocampal cortex, where more superior individuals within the hierarchy elicit greater activity (Zink et al., 2008), indicative of differential contextual episodic encoding of the association between the hierarchical status and the particular person to whom it pertains. The parahippocampal cortex plays a central role in the mediation of contextual associative processing (Aminoff, Gronau, & Bar, 2007; Bar, Aminoff, & Ishai, 2008). Activity in the human parahippocampal cortex has been shown to increase during the viewing of faces that are highly associated with a context (e.g., famous faces) compared to faces that lack contextual association (Bar et al., 2008). Because the parahippocampal cortex is more activated by those who are ranked higher than oneself compared to those who are ranked lower, the neural processing of the contextual association between status and person is greater for high-status compared to low-status individuals. Depictions of status cues outside of a hierarchical context do not elicit differential status-related responses in the parahippocampal cortex (Freeman et al., 2009; Marsh et al., 2009) because there is no contextual association to be made between status and a particular person.

Finally, within a stable hierarchy, the dorsolateral prefrontal cortex (DLPFC) is activated more when viewing someone possessing relatively higher hierarchical status as opposed to lower status (Zink et al., 2008); a finding that has been replicated using pictures of unfamiliar people in dominant or submissive poses (Figure 46.2C) (Marsh et al., 2009). The DLPFC is involved with multiple cognitive processes (e.g., working memory, attention, decision-making, behavior selection) (Miller & Cohen, 2001), and therefore, pinning down the exact indication of the DLPFC activation to higher status is difficult. The DLPFC is, however, crucial for making inferences about nonverbal social interactions (Figure 46. 2E), including social status judgments (Mah, Arnold, & Grafman, 2004). Moreover, activity in the DLPFC is associated with the degree of social-norm compliance in the presence of an agent who can punish social-norm violations (Spitzer, Fischbacher, Herrnberger, Gron, & Fehr, 2007). Social norms describe behaviors that are "permitted, obligated or prohibited" (Cummins, 2000) and are defined and maintained by social hierarchies; the dominant figures typically take on the role of punishing social-norm violators (Cummins, 2000). As such, the DLPFC may exert cognitive control over the coordination of appropriate behavior selection (e.g., social norm compliance) within a given social context (e.g., position in social hierarchy). Specific anatomical connections with the DLPFC support this contention; the DLPFC is preferentially connected to motor system structures enabling the exertion of control over behavior (Miller & Cohen, 2001), and the DLPFC also has connection with the parahippocampal cortex (Goldman-Rakic, Selemon, & Schwartz, 1984), which may enable the integration of contextual information (Bar et al., 2008) within the DLPFC. Possibly, the DLPFC exerts greater cognitive control over behavior selection in the context of interacting with a hierarchically superior person—as indicated by a greater increase in DLPFC activity when faced with a person of higher status compared to lower status—because of the pertinence of appropriate behavior in the presence of high-status individuals. Patterns of monkey DLPFC cell firing further support a role for the DLPFC in social context discrimination and behavioral selection (Fujii, Hihara, Nagasaka, & Iriki, 2009). In the specific context of dyadic social conflict provoked by the introduction of food into a shared space, neurons in the DLPFC increase their firing rate in the dominant monkey (who usually "wins" the conflict, i.e., gets most of the food placed in a shared space), and neurons in the subordinate monkey's DLPFC decrease their firing rate. These firing patterns are context-dependent, occurring only when the monkeys are socially engaged, but not in a conflict-free, socially disengaged context. Moreover, the observed DLPFC firing rates are status-dependent; when status is switched by rearrangement of monkey pairings, the pattern of DLPFC neuron-firing also switches. In other words, when a monkey is in the dominant position, DLPFC cell-firing increases, but if that monkey becomes the subordinate in a new conflict dyadic pairing, DLPFC cell-firing decreases according to the new status, suggesting these neuronal firing patterns are not linked to the monkey per se, but rather to the appropriate behavior selection in a particular context. While the prefrontal cortex data presented so far implicate the dorsolateral region, the ventrolateral prefrontal cortex also responds to cues of dominance (Figure 46.2C) (Marsh et al., 2009), bringing into question the dorsal specificity of these lateral prefrontal cortical responses.

Of note, all of the aforementioned brain activity patterns—in the occipitopartietal cortex, striatum, parahippocampal cortex, and lateral prefrontal cortex—are increases in activity when one is viewing higher status individuals or social cues compared to lower status. No brain regions, in the current paradigms, were identified in which a low-status individual (or associated cues) evoked a greater response than a high-status individual, with the exception of the culturally defined striatal activation which, in the Japanese culture, is greater for subordinate status cues compared to dominant status cues (Freeman et al., 2009).

Social Status in an Unstable Hierarchy

Introduction or departure of group members and conflict within a stable hierarchy can induce hierarchical instability and, as a result, stimulate status rearrangement within a group. Whether competitively or circumstantially instigated, in unstable hierarchies, a subordinate can overtake a more dominant position. As such, periods of hierarchical instability evoke stress in high-status individuals due to increased competition and future status uncertainty (Sapolsky, 2005), while providing an importantly opportunity (i.e., moving up in the hierarchy) for lower-status individuals. To date, very little empirical data exist that identify neural underpinnings of status perception specifically during periods of hierarchical instability. Some neural systems have been identified, however, by assessing status-related effects of brain lesions during hierarchy formation or introduction/reintroduction into an established group. Furthermore, to investigate the influence of hierarchy stability on status-related differential neural responses in humans, Zink and colleagues (Zink et al., 2008) modified the previously mentioned fMRI paradigm in which a stable hierarchy was established based on incidental skill. Specifically, by making use of the interactive nature of the paradigm, a prolonged period of hierarchical instability was induced by allowing social ranks to repeatedly update based on performance (i.e., skill) in the simulated, interactive game (Figure 46.2H). Together these studies have shed some light on the neural representation of social hierarchy during hierarchical instability as outlined below.

In humans, the same brain regions that exhibit status-related differential responses when one is involved in a [simulated] interactive stable hierarchy—as described above—demonstrate similar responses when the hierarchy is made unstable (i.e., relative hierarchical ranks can adjust). Specifically, the occipitopartietal cortex, ventral striatum, parahippocampal cortex, and the dorsolateral prefrontal cortex are all more active when viewing someone of superior status compared to inferior status (Zink et al., 2008), suggesting that the high-status individuals command more attention (Bradley et al., 2003), salience (Zink et al., 2006), and social-cognitive processes related to contextual association (Bar et al., 2008) and behavior selection (Miller & Cohen, 2001). With hierarchical instability, however, come additional dissociable neural responses to perceived social status, related to emotion, social cognition, and behavioral motivation.

Viewing the individual currently occupying the coveted superior rank compared to an inferior rank relative to oneself in an unstable hierarchy (Figure 46.2H), elicits an increased amygdala response—a brain region critically involved with recognizing emotional salience in social environments and with the production of appropriate emotionally driven reactions (Amaral, 2002)—that is correlated with one's self-reported desire to occupy the top hierarchical position (Zink et al., 2008). This is in accordance with a previous finding in primates demonstrating that jealousy induced by social hierarchical challenge is accompanied by an increase in amygdala activity (Rilling, Winslow, & Kilts, 2004). Moreover, in young adult humans, subjective socioeconomic status is negatively correlated with amygdala activity in response to threatening, angry facial expression, as measured with fMRI (Gianaros et al., 2008). In other words, lower subjective socioeconomic status is associated with

enhanced amygdala reactivity to social dominance cues. As a testament to the crucial status-related role of amygdala in appropriate encoding of social emotion during hierarchical instability, neonatal amygdala neurotoxin lesions (which spare adjacent cortical areas and fibers of passage) increase social fear and decrease aggression, rendering an inability to achieve high status during hierarchy formation in a group of unfamiliar monkeys (Bauman, Toscano, Mason, Lavenex, & Amaral, 2006). In another study, however, neurotoxin lesions of the amygdala in adolescent monkeys followed by reintroduction into a familiar group with a previously (i.e., pre-lesion) established hierarchy did not affect hierarchical ranks; after group reintroduction, monkeys regained their original status, despite the amygdala-lesioned monkeys displaying abnormal social behaviors (e.g., increase social fear) (Machado & Bachevalier, 2006). Addition investigations are necessary to gain the a full understanding of the influence of amygdala lesions on social behaviors and consequential social rank—the directionality of which may depend on several factors, including age at time of lesion and familiarity of the group (i.e., effects during hierarchy formation versus reintroduction into a familiar group) (Bachevalier & Malkova, 2006). That said, the amygdala-lesion studies, together with the human fMRI studies, suggest that the amygdala plays an important status-related role in producing and interpreting emotional social signals necessary for appropriate displays of aggressive and affiliative behaviors (Amaral, 2002).

Like the amygdala, in humans the medial prefrontal cortex (MPFC), a brain area known to play an important role in social cognition, is preferentially activated by viewing a higher ranked individual compared to a lower ranked individual during hierarchy instability (Figure 46.2H). The MPFC is particularly involved in recognizing and reasoning about the intentions and motives of other people (i.e., "mentalizing"), forming judgments of other people ("person perception"), and understanding how others view us ("reputation") (Amodio & Frith, 2006). Greater activity in the MPFC, therefore, implies greater encoding of the agenda of a higher status person, which could then be used to predict the future actions of this individual (Amodio & Frith, 2006). Having such a cognitive ability is self-beneficial, particularly in an unstable hierarchy when interacting with a person of higher status. Interestingly, the activation patterns in the MPFC may be culturally dependent, driven by self-relevant value, as demonstrated in the aforementioned fMRI study comparing neural responses to social status cues (Figure 46.2D) between American and Japanese culture (Freeman et al., 2009). As with value/salience coding in the striatum (see previous subsection), in Americans, the MPFC is more active when viewing dominant displays than submissive displays, while, in Japanese, dominant visual displays elicit less MPFC activity than submissive displays. It should also be noted that the location of these activations are in a more dorsal than ventral region of the MPFC, and the ventral MPFC may, therefore, play a minimal role in social status-related cognition. In fact, it has been shown that human patients with ventral MPFC damage retain an accurate concept of dominance and are able to make appropriate social dominance judgments (Figure 46.2F) (Karafin et al., 2004).

In the context of an unstable hierarchy (Figure 46.2H), activity in motor-related brain areas, specifically in the sensorimotor cortex and supplementary motor area (SMA), is increased when faced with a higher status individual compared to lower status (Zink et al., 2008). Both the sensorimotor cortex and SMA are active during actual movement as well as during imagined movement, and consequently have been implicated in motor preparation (Lotze et al., 1999). It is important to note that in the paradigm used to elicit this status-driven activity, viewing a person of a particular status occurs just prior to engaging in a motor-related simulated interactive game with that individual, the outcome of which impacts future status rankings (Zink et al., 2008) (Figure 46.2H). As such, the motor area activations likely represent status-related differential degrees of motor preparation as a result of greater behavioral motivation when interacting with someone of higher status as opposed to lower status in an unstable hierarchy.

As with stable hierarchies, the brain regions implicated in processing social status in unstable hierarchical contexts all exhibit heightened responses when faced with a superior individual compared to inferior. No brain regions have been identified in the current paradigms in which lower status evokes a greater response that higher status, with the exception of the culturally dependent MPFC response, which is greater to low status cues relative to high status in Japanese but not in Americans (Freeman et al., 2009).

Neural Responses to "Hierarchically Valuable" Events

In the previous section, several brain regions were highlighted that differentially respond to perceived relative social status. In this section, we expand our discussion of neural processing of hierarchical information to include brain regions that encode the "hierarchical value" of events. Hierarchical value refers to the positive or negative impact that certain incidences or outcomes can have on one's current status relative to others. More specifically, outperforming a superior can increase one's status and thus, such an event outcome is associated with *positive* hierarchical value. On the other hand, being outperformed by an inferior can decrease one's status and, therefore, is associated with *negative* hierarchical value. Importantly, outperforming an individual of lower status than oneself and being outperformed by an individual of higher status do not carry any hierarchical value because such events cannot impact one's relative status positively or negatively, but rather these outcomes just reinforce the current hierarchical rankings (Zink et al., 2008).

In a carefully controlled investigation, human neural responses to positive and negative hierarchical value were isolated using the fMRI paradigm described above in which one's status relative to others in the hierarchy can be adjusted according to performance in an interacted game (Zink et al., 2008) (Figure 46.2H). In this paradigm, performance outcomes are presented visually and are either associated with hierarchical value or not. The occipital/parietal cortex and striatum respond to both positive and negative hierarchically valuable outcomes, as opposed to hierarchically nonvaluable outcomes, indicative of greater perceptual/attentional processing (Bradley et al., 2003) and greater saliency (Zink et al., 2006)—as described in previous sections—associated with events that carry hierarchical value. Rather than responding to all hierarchically valuable outcomes, other brain areas discriminate between positive and negative hierarchical value, as evident by differential brain activity.

The negative hierarchical value associated with performing worse than someone of inferior status is uniquely coded in the anterior insula. The anterior insula is part of the brain's pain network, activating not only during the infliction of physical pain, but also when watching a loved-one receive the same physically painful stimulus, implicating the anterior insula in coding emotional pain (Singer et al., 2004). Evidence also relates activity in the anterior insula with social rejection (Eisenberger, Lieberman, & Williams, 2003) and frustration (Abler, Walter, & Erk, 2005). The anterior insula response to negative hierarchical value, therefore, likely represents frustration and emotional pain evoked by a lower-status individual when he/she performs at a relatively superior level. Intuitively, one may peg the ability to inflict pain (physical and emotional) on someone with higher status; however, during periods of hierarchical instability, the high-status position is the only one with something to lose, meaning that a lower-ranked individual is capable of eliciting emotional pain by virtue of the threat to overtake the more superior position. In support of this interpretation is a positive correlation between anterior insula activity levels during negative hierarchically valuable outcomes and the self-reported degree to which one enjoys occupying the top position in the hierarchy (Zink et al., 2008), suggesting that being outperformed by an inferior elicits more emotional pain in those who want the superior position most.

The positive hierarchical value associated with performing better than someone of superior status is uniquely coded in several brain areas, including the anterior cingulate, dorsomedial prefrontal cortex, and motor areas such as the dorsal premotor cortex and pre-supplementary motor area (pre-SMA). The increase in anterior cingulate activity corresponding to the possibility of rising in social status is consistent with the finding that lower subjective socioeconomic status is associated with reduced gray matter volume in the anterior cingulate (Gianaros et al., 2007). The anterior cingulate gyrus is critical for mediating the valuation of social stimuli as demonstrated in nonhuman primates; monkeys with specific anterior cingulate gyrus lesions (but not with anterior cingulate sulcus or ventrolateral prefrontal cortex lesions) disregard social status-related value of stimuli as measured by a decrease in latency to retrieve food in the presence of large staring monkeys, a sign of dominance (Figure 46.2A), as well as other socially valuable cues (i.e., affiliative monkeys and female monkey perinea), suggesting a devaluating of such stimuli (Rudebeck, Buckley, Walton, & Rushworth, 2006). The anterior cingulate activation to positive hierarchical value, therefore, may represent the high social importance of outperforming a superior.

A second brain region activated by positive hierarchically valuable events is the dorsomedial prefrontal cortex, which has recently been implicated in the process of retaliating against an opponent. In an interactive fMRI study, participants were provoked by receiving an aversive physical stimulus and then given the opportunity to retaliate with a stimulus intensity of their choice administered to their opponent (Lotze, Veit, Anders, & Birbaumer, 2007). The dorsomedial prefrontal cortex was active both when picking the intensity of the retaliation stimuli and when watching the opponent receive the retaliation stimuli. As such, activation of the dorsomedial prefrontal cortex in response to positive hierarchically valuable outcomes may be related to retaliation associated with possibly overtaking the superior position from the current occupier of the top rank.

Finally, positive hierarchically valuable outcomes elicit activity in the dorsal premotor cortex and pre-SMA. These motor-related areas have been associated with higher-order action dispositions (Lotze et al., 1999; Picard & Strick, 1996), raising the intriguing possibility that event outcomes that are associated with acquiring a more superior position activate brain regions that evoke a bias toward an abstract "active," as opposed to passive, state.

Conclusions and Future Directions

In summary, from neurotransmission at the synaptic level to brain regional activity at the systems level, the extraordinarily complex neural representation of social hierarchy has begun to be elucidated. The central serotonergic and dopaminergic neurotransmitter systems play powerful roles in the determination, maintenance, and consequence of status within a social hierarchy. Furthermore, activations in multiple brain regions work in concert to form accurate precepts of social ranks and appropriate behavioral reactions. In both stable and unstable hierarchy settings, neural correlates of visual perception/attention, salience, contextual association, and behavior selection in the occipitoparietal cortex, striatum, parahippocampal cortex, and dorsolateral prefrontal cortex, respectively, respond differentially to social status, with more resources directed to high status individuals. In unstable hierarchies, those in superior hierarchical positions also evoke greater activity in the amygdala, medial prefrontal cortex, and motor-related areas associated with social emotion, "mentalization," and behavioral motivation, respectively. In addition to differential status-related neural responses, neural systems have been identified that distinguish hierarchically valuable events that can positively or negatively affect one's social status. Negative hierarchically valuable events preferentially activate the anterior insula, possibly related to the emotional pain they induce. Positive hierarchically valuable events are preferentially encoded in the anterior cingulate, medial prefrontal cortex, and motor areas, likely mediating social valuation, behavioral retaliation, and a bias toward an abstract active state, respectively. Overall, much progress has been made in our understanding of neural underpinnings of social hierarchy but much more still remains to be discovered.

As demonstrated in this chapter, functional neuroimaging, such as fMRI, has proved to be exceptionally valuable for investigating neural mechanisms underlying the representation of social hierarchy; however, these imaging techniques are limited by the inability to investigate the processing of social status in natural habitats (Figure 46.2). FMRI signals in the brain are remarkably context-dependent, and therefore, it is unclear to what extent universal conclusions can be drawn from the brain activation patterns discussed here. It will also be important to evaluate the neural similarities and differences related to the various aspects governing social-rank relationships in humans, such as power, physical, economic, and professional standings. Further cultural, gender, and age effects on the neural processing of social hierarchy are likely to exist as well. Importantly, even with evidence of brain regions and neurotransmitter systems involved with social hierarchy, the exact molecular and cellular mechanisms underlying the activation patterns remain to be discovered. The answers are sure to come as scientists continue to better research paradigms and technology that will be used to elucidate the full extent of the neural representation of social hierarchy.

Acknowledgment

This work was supported by the Intramural Research Program of the National Institute of Mental Health, NIH.

References

Abler, B., Walter, H., & Erk, S. (2005). Neural correlates of frustration. *Neuroreport, 16*(7), 669–672.

Amaral, D. G. (2002). The primate amygdala and the neurobiology of social behavior: Implications for understanding social anxiety. *Biol Psychiatry, 51*(1), 11–17.

Aminoff, E., Gronau, N., & Bar, M. (2007). The parahippocampal cortex mediates spatial and nonspatial associations. *Cereb Cortex, 17*(7), 1493–1503.

Amodio, D. M. & Frith, C. D. (2006). Meeting of minds: The medial frontal cortex and social cognition. *Nat Rev Neurosci, 7*(4), 268–277.

Bachevalier, J. & Malkova, L. (2006). The amygdala and development of social cognition: Theoretical comment on Bauman, Toscano, Mason, Lavenex, and Amaral (2006). *Behav Neurosci, 120*(4), 989–991.

Bar, M., Aminoff, E., & Ishai, A. (2008). Famous faces activate contextual associations in the parahippocampal cortex. *Cereb Cortex, 18*(6), 1233–1238.

Barnard, C. J. & Burk, T. (1979). Dominance hierarchies and the evolution of "individual recognition." *J Theor Biol, 81*(1), 65–73.

Bauman, M. D., Toscano, J. E., Mason, W. A., Lavenex, P., & Amaral, D. G. (2006). The expression of social dominance following neonatal lesions of the amygdala or hippocampus in rhesus monkeys (Macaca mulatta). *Behav Neurosci, 120*(4), 749–760.

Blanc, G., Herve, D., Simon, H., Lisoprawski, A., Glowinski, J., & Tassin, J. P. (1980). Response to stress of mesocorticofrontal dopaminergic neurones in rats after long-term isolation. *Nature, 284*(5753), 265–267.

Blanchard, D. C., Cholvanich, P., Blanchard, R. J., Clow, D. W., Hammer, R. P., Jr., Rowlett, J. K., et al. (1991). Serotonin, but not dopamine, metabolites are increased in selected brain regions of subordinate male rats in a colony environment. *Brain Res, 568*(1–2), 61–66.

Blanchard, D. C., Sakai, R. R., McEwen, B., Weiss, S. M., & Blanchard, R. J. (1993). Subordination stress: Behavioral, brain, and neuroendocrine correlates. *Behav Brain Res, 58*(1–2), 113–121.

Blanchard, R. J., Flannelly, K. J., & Blanchard, D. C. (1988). Life-span studies of dominance and aggression in established colonies of laboratory rats. *Physiol Behav, 43*(1), 1–7.

Bradley, M. M., Sabatinelli, D., Lang, P. J., Fitzsimmons, J. R., King, W., & Desai, P. (2003). Activation of the visual cortex in motivated attention. *Behav Neurosci, 117*(2), 369–380.

Brattstrom, B. H. (1974). The evolution of reptilian social behavior. *American Zoologist, 14*(1), 35–49.

Buss, D. M. (1998). *Evolutionary psychology: The new science of the mind.* Boston: Allyn and Bacon.

Cabib, S. & Puglisi-Allegra, S. (1996). Stress, depression and the mesolimbic dopamine system. *Psychopharmacology, 128*(4), 331–342.

Carrillo, M., Ricci, L. A., Coppersmith, G. A., & Melloni, R. H., Jr. (2009). The effect of increased serotonergic neurotransmission on aggression: A critical meta-analytical review of preclinical studies. *Psychopharmacology, 205*(3), 349–368.

Chance, M. R. A. (1967). Attention structure as the basis of primate rank orders. *Man, 2*(4), 503–518.

Cheney, D. L. & Seyfarth, R. M. (1990). The representation of social relations by monkeys. *Cognition, 37*(1–2), 167–196.

Chiao, J. Y., Adams, R. B., Tse, P. U., Lowenthal, L., Richeson, J. A., & Ambady, N. (2008). Knowing who's boss: fMRI and ERP investigations of social dominance perception. *Group Process Intergroup Relat, 11*(2), 201–214.

Cummins, D. D. (2000). How the social environment shaped the evolution of the mind. *Synthese, 122*(1/2), 3–28.

de Waal, F. B. (1986). The integration of dominance and social bonding in primates. *Q Rev Biol, 61*(4), 459–479.

Deaner, R. O., Khera, A. V., & Platt, M. L. (2005). Monkeys pay per view: Adaptive valuation of social images by rhesus macaques. *Curr Biol, 15*(6), 543–548.

Eisenberger, N. I., Lieberman, M. D., & Williams, K. D. (2003). Does rejection hurt? An FMRI study of social exclusion. *Science, 302*(5643), 290–292.

Erk, S., Spitzer, M., Wunderlich, A. P., Galley, L., & Walter, H. (2002). Cultural objects modulate reward circuitry. *Neuroreport, 13*(18), 2499–2503.

Ficken, M. S., Weise, C. M., & Popp, J. W. (1990). Dominance rank and resource access in winter flocks of black-capped chickadees. *Wilson Bulletin, 102*(4), 623–633.

Freeman, J. B., Rule, N. O., Adams, R. B., Jr., & Ambady, N. (2009). Culture shapes a mesolimbic response to signals of dominance and subordination that associates with behavior. *Neuroimage, 47*(1), 353–359.

Fujii, N., Hihara, S., Nagasaka, Y., & Iriki, A. (2009). Social state representation in prefrontal cortex. *Soc Neurosci*, *4*(1), 73–84.

Gianaros, P. J., Horenstein, J. A., Cohen, S., Matthews, K. A., Brown, S. M., Flory, J. D., et al. (2007). Perigenual anterior cingulate morphology covaries with perceived social standing. *Soc Cogn Affect Neurosci*, *2*(3), 161–173.

Gianaros, P. J., Horenstein, J. A., Hariri, A. R., Sheu, L. K., Manuck, S. B., Matthews, K. A., et al. (2008). Potential neural embedding of parental social standing. *Soc Cogn Affect Neurosci*, *3*(2), 91–96.

Goldman-Rakic, P. S., Selemon, L. D., & Schwartz, M. L. (1984). Dual pathways connecting the dorsolateral prefrontal cortex with the hippocampal formation and parahippocampal cortex in the rhesus monkey. *Neuroscience*, *12*(3), 719–743.

Grant, K. A., Shively, C. A., Nader, M. A., Ehrenkaufer, R. L., Line, S. W., Morton, T. E., et al. (1998). Effect of social status on striatal dopamine D2 receptor binding characteristics in cynomolgus monkeys assessed with positron emission tomography. *Synapse*, *29*(1), 80–83.

Grosenick, L., Clement, T. S., & Fernald, R. D. (2007). Fish can infer social rank by observation alone. *Nature*, *445*(7126), 429–432.

Hall, F. S., Wilkinson, L. S., Humby, T., Inglis, W., Kendall, D. A., Marsden, C. A., et al. (1998). Isolation rearing in rats: Pre- and postsynaptic changes in striatal dopaminergic systems. *Pharmacol Biochem Behav*, *59*(4), 859–872.

Haude, R. H., Graber, J. G., & Farres, A. G. (1976). Visual observing by rhesus monkeys: Some relationships with social dominance rank. *Anim Learn Behav*, *4*(2), 163–166.

Hess, U., Blairy, S., & Kleck, R. E. (2000). The influence of facial emotion displays, gender, and ethnicity on judgments of dominance and affiliation. *Journal of Nonverbal Behavior*, *24*(4), 265–283.

Higley, J. D., King, S. T., Jr., Hasert, M. F., Champoux, M., Suomi, S. J., & Linnoila, M. (1996). Stability of interindividual differences in serotonin function and its relationship to severe aggression and competent social behavior in rhesus macaque females. *Neuropsychopharmacology*, *14*(1), 67–76.

Jensen, J., Smith, A. J., Willeit, M., Crawley, A. P., Mikulis, D. J., Vitcu, I., et al. (2007). Separate brain regions code for salience vs. valence during reward prediction in humans. *Hum Brain Mapp*, *28*(4), 294–302.

Kaplan, J. R., Manuck, S. B., Fontenot, M. B., & Mann, J. J. (2002). Central nervous system monoamine correlates of social dominance in cynomolgus monkeys (Macaca fascicularis). *Neuropsychopharmacology*, *26*(4), 431–443.

Karafin, M. S., Tranel, D., & Adolphs, R. (2004). Dominance attributions following damage to the ventromedial prefrontal cortex. *J Cogn Neurosci*, *16*(10), 1796–1804.

Keating, C. F. (1985). Gender and the physiognomy of dominance and attractiveness. *Social Psychology Quarterly*, *48*(1), 61–70.

Klein, J. T., Deaner, R. O., & Platt, M. L. (2008). Neural correlates of social target value in macaque parietal cortex. *Curr Biol*, *18*(6), 419–424.

Knutson, B. (1996). Facial expressions of emotion influence interpersonal trait inferences. *Journal of Nonverbal Behavior*, *20*(3), 165–182.

Kostowski, W., Plewako, M., & Bidzinski, A. (1984). Brain serotonergic neurons: Their role in a form of dominance-subordination behavior in rats. *Physiol Behav*, *33*(3), 365–371.

Lahti, K., Koivula, K., & Orell, M. (1994). Is the social hierarchy always linear in tits? *Journal of Avian Biology*, *25*(4), 347–348.

Larson, E. T. & Summers, C. H. (2001). Serotonin reverses dominant social status. *Behav Brain Res*, *121*(1–2), 95–102.

Lotze, M., Montoya, P., Erb, M., Hulsmann, E., Flor, H., Klose, U., et al. (1999). Activation of cortical and cerebellar motor areas during executed and imagined hand movements: An fMRI study. *J Cogn Neurosci*, *11*(5), 491–501.

Lotze, M., Veit, R., Anders, S., & Birbaumer, N. (2007). Evidence for a different role of the ventral and dorsal medial prefrontal cortex for social reactive aggression: An interactive fMRI study. *Neuroimage*, *34*(1), 470–478.

Lucki, I. (1998). The spectrum of behaviors influenced by serotonin. *Biol Psychiatry*, *44*(3), 151–162.

Mach, R. H., Nader, M. A., Ehrenkaufer, R. L., Line, S. W., Smith, C. R., Luedtke, R. R., et al. (1996). Comparison of two fluorine-18 labeled benzamide derivatives that bind reversibly to dopamine D2 receptors: In vitro binding studies and positron emission tomography. *Synapse*, *24*(4), 322–333.

Machado, C. J. & Bachevalier, J. (2006). The impact of selective amygdala, orbital frontal cortex, or hippocampal formation lesions on established social relationships in rhesus monkeys (Macaca mulatta). *Behav Neurosci*, *120*(4), 761–786.

Mah, L., Arnold, M. C., & Grafman, J. (2004). Impairment of social perception associated with lesions of the prefrontal cortex. *Am J Psychiatry*, *161*(7), 1247–1255.

Marsh, A. A., Blair, K. S., Jones, M. M., Soliman, N., & Blair, R. J. (2009). Dominance and submission: The ventrolateral prefrontal cortex and responses to status cues. *J Cogn Neurosci*, *21*(4), 713–724.

Martinez, D., Orlowska, D., Narendran, R., Slifstein, M., Liu, F., Kumar, D., et al. (2010). Dopamine type 2/3 receptor availability in the striatum and social status in human volunteers. *Biol Psychiatry*, *63*(2), 275–278.

Miller, E. K. & Cohen, J. D. (2001). An integrative theory of prefrontal cortex function. *Annu Rev Neurosci*, *24*, 167–202.

Moors, A. & De Houwer, J. (2005). Automatic processing of dominance and submissiveness. *Experimental Psychology*, *52*(4), 296–302.

Morgan, D., Grant, K. A., Gage, H. D., Mach, R. H., Kaplan, J. R., Prioleau, O., et al. (2002). Social dominance in monkeys: Dopamine D2 receptors and cocaine self-administration. *Nat Neurosci*, *5*(2), 169–174.

Nader, M. A., Czoty, P. W., Gould, R. W., & Riddick, N. V. (2008). Review. Positron emission tomography imaging studies of dopamine receptors in primate models of addiction. *Philos Trans R Soc Lond B Biol Sci*, *363*(1507), 3223–3232.

Picard, N. & Strick, P. L. (1996). Motor areas of the medial wall: A review of their location and functional activation. *Cereb Cortex*, *6*(3), 342–353.

Pineda, J. A., Sebestyen, G., & Nava, C. (1994). Face recognition as a function of social attention in non-human primates: An ERP study. *Brain Res Cogn Brain Res*, *2*(1), 1–12.

Raleigh, M. J., Brammer, G. L., McGuire, M. T., & Yuwiler, A. (1985). Dominant social status facilitates the behavioral effects of serotonergic agonists. *Brain Res, 348*(2), 274–282.

Raleigh, M. J., McGuire, M. T., Brammer, G. L., Pollack, D. B., & Yuwiler, A. (1991). Serotonergic mechanisms promote dominance acquisition in adult male vervet monkeys. *Brain Res, 559*(2), 181–190.

Raleigh, M. J., McGuire, M. T., Brammer, G. L., & Yuwiler, A. (1984). Social and environmental influences on blood serotonin concentrations in monkeys. *Arch Gen Psychiatry, 41*(4), 405–410.

Richards, O. W. (1971). The biology of the social wasps. *Biological Reviews, 46*(4), 483–528.

Riddick, N. V., Czoty, P. W., Gage, H. D., Kaplan, J. R., Nader, S. H., Icenhower, M., et al. (2009). Behavioral and neurobiological characteristics influencing social hierarchy formation in female cynomolgus monkeys. *Neuroscience, 158*(4), 1257–1265.

Rilke, O., May, T., Oehler, J., & Wolffgramm, J. (1995). Influences of housing conditions and ethanol intake on binding characteristics of D2, 5-HT1A, and benzodiazepine receptors of rats. *Pharmacol Biochem Behav, 52*(1), 23–28.

Rilling, J. K., Winslow, J. T., & Kilts, C. D. (2004). The neural correlates of mate competition in dominant male rhesus macaques. *Biol Psychiatry, 56*(5), 364–375.

Rudebeck, P. H., Buckley, M. J., Walton, M. E., & Rushworth, M. F. (2006). A role for the macaque anterior cingulate gyrus in social valuation. *Science, 313*(5791), 1310–1312.

Sapolsky, R. M. (2005). The influence of social hierarchy on primate health. *Science, 308*(5722), 648–652.

Sapolsky, R. M. & Ray, J. C. (1989). Styles of dominance and their endocrine correlates among wild olive baboons (Papio anubis). *American Journal of Primatology, 18*(1), 1–13.

Shively, C. A. (1998). Social subordination stress, behavior, and central monoaminergic function in female cynomolgus monkeys. *Biol Psychiatry, 44*(9), 882–891.

Singer, T., Seymour, B., O'Doherty, J., Kaube, H., Dolan, R. J., & Frith, C. D. (2004). Empathy for pain involves the affective but not sensory components of pain. *Science, 303*(5661), 1157–1162.

Spitzer, M., Fischbacher, U., Herrnberger, B., Gron, G., & Fehr, E. (2007). The neural signature of social norm compliance. *Neuron, 56*(1), 185–196.

Struhsaker, T. (1967). Social structure among vervet monkeys. *Behavior, 29*(2), 83–121.

Tiedens, L. Z. & Fragale, A. R. (2003). Power moves: complementarity in dominant and submissive nonverbal behavior. *J Pers Soc Psychol, 84*(3), 558–568.

Tse, W. S. & Bond, A. J. (2002). Serotonergic intervention affects both social dominance and affiliative behaviour. *Psychopharmacology, 161*(3), 324–330.

Van Honk, C. & Hogeweg, P. (1981). The ontogeny of the social structure in a captive Bombus terrestris colony. *Behavioral Ecology and Sociobiology, 9*(2), 111–119.

Westergaard, G. C., Suomi, S. J., Higley, J. D., & Mehlman, P. T. (1999). CSF 5-HIAA and aggression in female macaque monkeys: Species and interindividual differences. *Psychopharmacology, 146*(4), 440–446.

Wilson, E. O. (1975). *Sociobiology: The new synthesis.* Cambridge: Belknap Press of Harvard University Press.

Yodyingyuad, U., de la Riva, C., Abbott, D. H., Herbert, J., & Keverne, E. B. (1985). Relationship between dominance hierarchy, cerebrospinal fluid levels of amine transmitter metabolites (5-hydroxyindole acetic acid and homovanillic acid) and plasma cortisol in monkeys. *Neuroscience, 16*(4), 851–858.

Zink, C. F., Pagnoni, G., Chappelow, J., Martin-Skurski, M., & Berns, G. S. (2006). Human striatal activation reflects degree of stimulus saliency. *Neuroimage, 29*(3), 977–983.

Zink, C. F., Pagnoni, G., Martin, M. E., Dhamala, M., & Berns, G. S. (2003). Human striatal response to salient nonrewarding stimuli. *J Neurosci, 23*(22), 8092–8097.

Zink, C. F., Tong, Y., Chen, Q., Bassett, D. S., Stein, J. L., & Meyer-Lindenberg, A. (2008). Know your place: Neural processing of social hierarchy in humans. *Neuron, 58*(2), 273–283.

Group Processes: Social Dominance

Paul W. Czoty, Drake Morgan, *and* Michael A. Nader

Abstract

A great deal of behavior occurs in a social context. It has become obvious that social and environmental variables can have a profound influence on behavior, neurochemistry, physiology, and the effects of drugs. This chapter highlights one facet of social neuroscience—the effects of being dominant in social environments. It focuses on animal models, describing several important independent variables using both rodent and nonhuman primate models. It focuses on adults rather than adolescents to better emphasize the powerful role of social rank in brain function and disease progression.

Keywords: social neuroscience, epigenetics, dominance, social environment, animal models

Introduction

"[A]ny disease . . . depends for its spread on the three necessities: a susceptible individual, an infecting substance and an environment where the two can meet" (Mills, 1965). The field of neuroscience has appreciated this observation for several decades, most often under the banner of "gene × environment interactions." Many behaviors occur in a social context and we are now intimately aware that social interactions produce changes in the brain that can impact ongoing behavior, as well as the incidence of disease and the prognosis of rehabilitation. When social hierarchies are formed (as described in this chapter), dominant animals represent conditions of environmental enrichment, while subordinate animals model conditions of chronic stress. Models of social behavior include ethologically relevant stressors and may have more etiological, predictive, and/or construct validity relative to animal models

of stress associated with purely physical stressors (e.g., foot shock). The study of social neuroscience has taken on even more relevance with the emphasis on developmental factors and epigenetics. However, we will not examine the roles of early-life social events (such as social isolation, maternal deprivation, peer-rearing, etc.) in this chapter. Rather, we will highlight one facet of social neuroscience—the effects of being dominant in social environments and, when possible, the changes that accompany attaining dominance. There are a number of experimental animal models of social stress, hierarchy formation, dominance and subordination, and social confrontation established and validated with regard to behavior, physiology, sensitivity to pharmacological agents, and neurobiology. To this point, much of the research has focused on rodents (rats and mice) and nonhuman primates. For the interested reader, many excellent reviews are available (for example Blanchard, Sakai, McEwen, Weiss, & Blanchard, 1993; Stefanski, 2001; Miczek, Covington, Nikulina, & Hammer, 2004; Malatynska & Knapp, 2005; Honess & Marin, 2006). Our focus will be on animal models; we will describe several important independent variables using both rodent and nonhuman primate models. We will focus on adults rather than adolescents so that we can better emphasize the powerful role of social rank in brain function and disease progression.

Animal Models of Social Hierarchy, Dominance and Rank
Formation of Social Hierarchies in Rodent Models

There are numerous laboratories studying social behavior, dominance, and social rank that use group housing to allow for the development of social hierarchies. There are an unlimited number of permutations regarding the details of the colonies of animals including the number and sex of the animals, the size of the colony, and relative abundance or lack of resources—each of these variables has been demonstrated to influence behavior and physiology (Sakai & Tamashiro, 2005). For example, it is generally accepted that large groups of all males do not necessarily form hierarchies; however, the introduction of one or more females promotes the formation of a hierarchy. However, if only three males are placed together, a triad of dominant, subdominant, and subordinate rats can form. One "simple" example is housing two rats side by side, provided with olfactory, auditory, and visual stimulation, and then pairing them for some period of time to measure dominance and submission (i.e., social confrontation tests; Stefanski, 2001). Females are typically added to each side to promote aggression between males. Another method is to introduce a particular animal into an established group. Inevitably the new animal gets attacked and becomes subordinate. A variation on that theme is to introduce individual animals one by one to a "dominance-experienced" rat. In this setting, each of the new animals becomes subordinate. A different strategy is to simply group house a number of animals and allow the natural contingencies to create a hierarchy as occurs when using the visible burrow system (VBS; Blanchard et al., 1995). The dominance hierarchies that form in the VBS have been shown to be stable for years, with little change in aggressive behavior both within the colony and when challenged with an intruder (Blanchard, Flannelly, & Blanchard, 1988). An interesting extension of group housing is the "social instability"

model: on alternate days, animals are housed individually or placed in overcrowded caging. In this situation, high frequency of physical aggression is observed that has been demonstrated to be particularly useful in creating a stress response in females (Haller, Fuchs, Halasz, & Makara, 1988). In these experiments, readily identifiable dominants and subordinates are not studied; rather, the stressed animals are compared to control animals.

In many of the experimental conditions described above, a dominant animal is "created" beforehand and the introduced animal (the intruder, socially inexperienced animal or the socially naive rodent) typically becomes subordinate. In the group-housing situations (e.g., VBS), body weight can be predictive of eventual social rank (larger animals are more likely to become dominant) and for this reason body weight is typically accounted for in a particular experiment (i.e., body weights are matched before group formation). In most cases, basal concentrations of testosterone and corticosterone do not predict dominance although these measures are always altered by hierarchy formation (see below).

Formation of Social Hierarchies in Nonhuman Primate Models

Nonhuman primate social groups have proven useful for studying social status-related differences in vulnerability and resistance to disease, with such differences linked to predictable variation in physiological, neurobiological, and behavioral characteristics. For example, socially subordinate monkeys are more susceptible to immune, cardiovascular, and reproductive dysfunction compared to dominant monkeys (Cameron, 1997; Cohen et al., 1997; Kaplan & Manuck, 1998, 2004; Sapolsky, 2005). Moreover, subordinate monkeys are more sensitive to the abuse-related effects of cocaine (Morgan et al., 2002; Czoty, McCabe, & Nader, 2005) and can serve as a model of major depressive disorder (Shively, Laber-Liard, & Anton, 1997; Shively et al., 2005). The influence of social rank on health in monkeys parallels the direct relationship between control over resources and life expectancy in humans (Wohlfarth & van den Brink, 1998; Amick et al., 2002) and the inverse relationship between socioeconomic status and susceptibility to disease (Kaplan, Manuck, Clarkson, Lusso, & Taub, 1982; Krantz & McCeney, 2002). These similarities have encouraged research into the physiological correlates and consequences of assuming a particular social rank.

The linear dominance hierarchies that characterize nonhuman primate social groups are established in large part by dyadic agonistic interactions and maintained with aggressive, submissive and affiliative behaviors (Kaplan et al., 1982). Dominant monkeys (i.e., those above the median in social rank) typically have greater control over resources and maintain their status through physical aggression and/or intimidation; subordinate monkeys often experience a shortage of resources, fewer coping strategies, and reproductive impairment (Kaplan & Manuck, 2004). Thus, one explanation put forth to explain physiological and neurobiological differences across social rank involves a relatively greater amount of stress experienced by subordinate monkeys (Henry & Stephens, 1977). The extent to which different monkeys in such hierarchies experience stress varies widely according to the particulars of the social structure, including the stability of hierarchies, the availability of social support to subordinates and style of dominance, that is, whether dominance is maintained through physical aggression or nonphysical intimidation (Clarke, Czekala, & Lindburg, 1995; Abbott et al., 2003; Sapolsky, 2005).

As was discussed with rodent models, it must be acknowledged that research into the biological correlates of social rank has taken place in numerous primate species under diverse experimental settings with varying approaches. Importantly, the social rank of the monkey that experiences the greatest amount of social stress can vary according to characteristics of the social group including sex, social structure, and stability of the hierarchy (for reviews see Kaplan & Manuck, 1998; Creel, 2001; Sapolsky, 2002, 2005; Abbott et al., 2003; Goyman & Wingfield, 2004). Dominant monkeys may experience relatively greater stress during periods of instability when dominance is being contested, and in groups in which dominance is maintained through physical aggression. Conversely, characteristics of social groups in which subordinates experience a higher amount of stress include hierarchy stability, an abundance of resources, reliance of dominant monkeys on nonphysical intimidation, inability of subordinates to avoid dominants, and a lack of social support as a means for coping with stress. Thus, it is perhaps unsurprising that apparently conflicting data exist for a number of measures, particularly between captive and free-ranging monkeys.

Resident-Intruder/Social Defeat

One of the best characterized animal models of social dominance is the resident-intruder or social defeat model (Miczek, 1979). In its most general form, the experimenter establishes a territory for the "resident" (most commonly a male rodent), and an "intruder" (most commonly a male of the same species, but sometimes different strain) is placed in the territory. These sessions typically last a short period of time (e.g., minutes). There is a clear and nearly immediate physical attack by the resident/dominant animal followed by submission from the intruder/subordinate animal. This model of dominance and submission is particularly useful, as it can permit the study of acute (one defeat), intermittent or chronic social stress (e.g., Bartolomucci, 2007). In many instances, the physical interactions of the dominant and subordinate animals are limited following the first encounter by separating the animals but allowing visual, auditory, and olfactory stimulation. This stimulation results in similar hormone and endocrine responses but limit the potential physical (e.g., wounding) interactions. This paradigm has been used to systematically investigate social variables—primarily stress—in rodents and nonhuman primates. However, the student of social neuroscience should be aware that there are individual differences in response to serving as an intruder. For example, we have observed different behavioral outcomes depending on whether the intruder was a dominant or subordinate monkey. One could hypothesize that intruder-induced aggression would be more "rewarding" to dominant intruders, while the aggression directed toward the subordinate animals would be stressful and noxious.

Behavioral and Physiological Correlates of Social Rank
Body Weight

In the resident-intruder and social confrontation models involving rodents, most studies demonstrate dramatic decreases in body weight as a consequence of social defeat. A single defeat episode can result in weight loss (or attenuated weight gain) for a number of days (de Jong, van der Begt, Buwalda, & Koolhaas, 2005; de Jong et al., 2005). These effects are more profound in males relative to females (e.g., Berton, Aguerre, Sarrieau, Mormede, & Chaouloff, 1998; Stefanski, 2001). In the "social instability" model, stressed animals showed an attenuated weight gain relative to controls (Haller et al., 1998). Changes in body weight and body composition have been extensively evaluated in the VBS; dramatic decreases were observed in subordinate rats' body weights, whereas slight decreases were seen in dominant animals (e.g., Blanchard et al., 1995). Recent studies using NMR technology suggest that the dominant animals lose subcutaneous adipose tissue and may gain lean/muscle mass, indicating a shift in body composition. In contrast, subordinate animals lose fat only (primarily subcutaneous) from eating less. During "recovery" (living outside of the VBS) subordinates become hyperphagic and gain nearly all of the fat back although as visceral fat, at which point they are hyperinsulinemic and hyperleptinemic (Tamashiro et al., 2007).

In nonhuman primates, body weight and physical appearance in general can have profound effects on social rank (e.g., Bernstein & Mason, 1962; Bernstein, Gordon, & Rose, 1974; Tokuda & Jensen, 1969). Typically, experiments related to social neuroscience will involve captive monkeys of similar ages and body weights. Nonetheless, under these conditions there still appears to be a relationship between body weight and social rank in all-male groups (Morgan et al., 2000), although it is not absolute (i.e., the heaviest monkey will not be the most dominant in every group). In contrast, body weight does not appear to be a factor influencing social rank in all-female groups of monkeys (Tokuda & Jensen, 1969; Riddick et al., 2009). These findings suggest that physical appearance (in this case body weight) may be more critical in influencing social rank for male monkeys. Recent work has shown an interaction between personality variables of the monkey and response to physical acts of aggression, as seen while watching videos (Capitanio, 2002). In this study, 12 male rhesus monkeys were first assessed for "sociability"; behaviors were recorded while monkeys lived in an outdoor pen consisting of 45 adults. The sociability scale consisted of a series of sociable adjectives (e.g., seeks companionship of others, playful, curious, etc.). High- and low-sociable monkeys watched 10-min videos of unfamiliar adult male monkeys displaying aggressive, affiliative, or nonsocial behaviors. As it relates to aggression, low-sociable monkeys had a greater tendency to "sit and stare" suggesting poorer social skills (Capitanio, 2002); such poor social behavior has functional consequences.

Hormones and HPA Axis Function

Changes in rodent housing conditions have resulted in activation of stress systems and corresponding changes in corticosterone concentrations and hypothalamic-pituitary-adrenal (HPA) axis function. For example, using the social confrontation procedure, it has been demonstrated that after 2 days of living in a familiar space, subordinate rats showed increased concentrations of the adrenal catecholamines epinephrine, norepinephrine, and corticosterone; in some cases these differences were not statistically significant between dominants and subordinates until day 7. Interestingly, females exposed to the social instability situation showed clear increases in adrenal weight and corticosterone concentrations, whereas males failed to show these changes leading to the suggestion that instability is a greater stressor in females (Haller et al., 1998). In the VBS, basal concentrations of corticosterone were increased in subordinate animals (e.g., Blanchard et al., 1995). Studies with the resident-intruder paradigm demonstrated increases in corticosterone in both males and females relative to nonhandled controls, even after just one exposure (Berton et al., 1998; Keeney, Hogg, & Marsden, 2001; Stefanski & Gruner, 2006; Marini et al., 2006). Importantly, increases in corticosterone occurred in both dominant and subordinate animals (Covington & Miczek, 2005), and although most animals tended to show a habituated response following repeated exposure to physical stressors, this did not happen readily with social defeat (e.g., Barnum, Blandino, & Deak, 2007; but see Bhatnagar, Vining, Iyer, & Kinni, 2006).

The prominent influence of social stress in the lives of socially housed monkeys has also led researchers to investigate social rank-related differences in the function of the HPA axis. Exposure to environmental stressors results in increases in release of corticotropin-releasing hormone (CRH) from the paraventricular nucleus of the hypothalamus, which acts to release ACTH from the anterior pituitary into the circulation. ACTH acts in the adrenal cortex to synthesize and release cortisol, which mediates physiological responses to stress throughout the body. When evaluating HPA axis function in monkeys, three commonly assessed variables are circulating concentrations of cortisol, sensitivity to suppression by dexamethasone (DEX), a glucocorticoid receptor agonist which acts in the pituitary to suppress ACTH release via negative feedback, and following DEX suppression, adrenal responsiveness to an injection of an amount of ACTH designed to be reflect stimulation due to exposure to a stressor. A considerable number of studies describing the relationship between glucocorticoids and social rank have been conducted in Old World monkeys. The hypothesis that differences in HPA axis function among socially housed monkeys are due to chronic stress experienced by subordinates is supported by the findings that subordinate monkeys have heavier adrenal glands and greater cortisol secretion in response to stressors than dominant monkeys (e.g., Shively & Kaplan, 1984). However, the relationship between social rank and basal cortisol concentrations is less clear, with studies reporting higher circulating cortisol in dominant monkeys (Kimura, Shimizu, Hayashi, Ishikawa, & Ago, 2000; Czoty, Gould, & Nader, 2009), subordinate monkeys (Yodyingyuad, de la Riva, Abbott, Herbert, & Keverne, 1985; Sapolsky, 1992; Sapolsky, Alberts, & Altmann, 1997; Shively et al., 1997; Shively, 1998), or a lack of a relationship between cortisol concentration and social rank (Sassenrath, 1970; McGuire, Brammer, & Raleigh, 1986; Bercovitch & Clarke, 1995; Stavisky, Adams, Watson, & Kaplan, 2001). The relationship between social status and cortisol concentration is extremely sensitive to setting and procedural details such that it may not be possible to generalize from captive to free-ranging animals.

Stimulation of the HPA axis under controlled conditions appears to unmask a more consistent pattern in which subordinate monkeys exhibit increased HPA reactivity relative to dominants. Thus, although dominant monkeys are often found to have higher circulating levels of cortisol (Leshner & Candland, 1972; Coe, Mendoza, & Levine, 1979; Mendoza, Coe, Lowe, & Levine, 1979; Gonzales, Coe, & Levine, 1982; Batty, Herbert, Keverne, & Velluci, 1986; Kimura et al., 2000; Czoty et al., 2009), the HPA axis of subordinates is more sensitive to acute stressors (Sassenrath, 1970; Kaplan et al., 1986; Shively et al., 1997). There are several factors that may contribute to the apparent discrepancies with other studies that have reported different relationships between cortisol concentrations and social rank. As with other aspects of the dominance hierarchy, these measures appear to be extremely sensitive to setting and procedural details. An interpretation which may reconcile the apparent differences between basal and stimulated cortisol concentrations involves adaptation in subordinate monkeys. In several studies, rank-related differences in basal cortisol concentrations have been observed only shortly after group formation; in some cases dissipation of those differences has been documented (Golub, Sassenrath, & Goo, 1979; Goo & Sassenrath, 1980; Clarke et al., 1995; Gust et al., 1991; Czoty et al., 2009). For example, in a recent study in male cynomolgus monkeys, we observed that cortisol concentrations were greatly elevated after the first day of social housing in monkeys that

would become subordinate despite the fact that dominant monkeys had higher average cortisol concentrations 12 weeks later (Czoty et al., 2009). Adaptation to the cortisol-elevating effect of social interaction took place within 3 days, suggesting that a reduction in circulating cortisol may have occurred as an adaptation to chronic stimulation of the HPA axis. Despite this adaptation of basal cortisol concentrations, adrenal responsiveness to a pharmacological challenge was significantly greater in subordinates. The extent to which such adaptations occur, if at all, likely depends greatly on variables related to setting, such as captive versus free-ranging, group size, and density.

Locomotor Activity

Locomotor activity in individually housed animals is an unconditioned behavior that has been shown to predict several behavioral outcomes (e.g., vulnerability to drug abuse; Piazza, Deminiere, Le Moal, & Simon, 1989). Findings regarding locomotor activity in subordinate versus dominant animals are inconsistent across studies. One potential contributor to this inconsistency is the method by which locomotion is assessed; for example, whether locomotor activity is assessed within the living space or in a separate activity chamber. In rodent models, most examples in the literature demonstrate that subordinates move around the least (e.g., Raab et al., 1986; Schaefer & Michael, 1991; Hilakivi-Clarke & Lister, 1992; Meerlo, Overkamp, Daan, Van Den Hoofdakker, & Koolhaas, 1996; Berton et al., 1998; Blanchard et al., 2001; Bartolomucci et al., 2003; Pohorecky, 2006). However, there are examples of no differences in locomotor activity due to housing conditions or social rank (e.g., Brain & Benton, 1979; Palanza, Gioiosa, & Parmigiani, 2001), or increases in locomotor activity in the subordinate animals (relative to controls) following social defeat (e.g., Keeney et al., 2001).

As has been observed in rodents, the relationship between social rank and locomotor activity in monkeys varies across studies. In our earlier work with individually housed male cynomolgus monkeys, we found that locomotor activity in an open field following a very low dose of the stimulant cocaine was predictive of eventual social rank; monkeys that eventually would be dominant had significantly lower levels of locomotion compared to monkeys that would eventually become subordinate (Morgan et al., 2000). In female cynomolgus monkeys, however, no such relationship was noted (Riddick et al., 2009). Other investigators have extended this behavioral phenotype to include other behaviors that may be considered part of an "impulsive" phenotype; high impulsivity is hypothesized to be related to social subordination. In females, novelty and stimulant-induced locomotor behavior varied as a function of estrus cycle in rats (Davis, Clinton, Akil, & Becker, 2008; Sell, Thomas, & Cunningham, 2002), suggesting a source for sex differences in this dependent measure.

Neurobiological Correlates of Social Rank
Dopaminergic Systems
Some of the earliest studies examining social subordinates in the resident-intruder model have demonstrated enhanced dopamine (DA) release in the nucleus accumbens and prefrontal cortex, but not in the dorsal striatum, in the absence of increases in locomotor activity, suggesting that the increases in dopamine were related to the threat and "stress" of the situation (e.g., Tidey & Miczek, 1996). This social defeat-enhanced dopamine release was recently replicated and measured using fast-scan cyclic voltammetry, and found to be due to increased bursting of dopaminergic neurons in the ventral tegmental area (Anstrom, Miczek, & Budygin, 2009). Several studies, however, showed that the changes in the dopaminergic system following social defeat are complex, such that the results depend on a particular history of social interactions, the sex of the aggressor, and the housing condition after the defeat (Cabib, D'Amato, Puglisi-Allegra, & Maestripieri, 2000; Isovich, Engelmann, Landgraf, & Fuch, 2001). Studies using the VBS have demonstrated relatively long-lasting changes in markers of dopaminergic activity (e.g., D2 receptor and DAT density; Lucas et al., 2004).

As it relates to social dominance, several studies have documented the effects of environmental enrichment on the DA system. For example, Bowling et al. (1993) studied two groups of rats: those living in enriched conditions (EC) defined as 12–13 rats per cage with toys in homecage, and rats living in impoverished conditions (IC), that is, individually housed with no toys. They found that EC rats had lower concentrations of DA compared to IC rats. These investigators also found differences in the behavioral effects of the indirect-acting DA agonist *d*-amphetamine, including differences in sensitivity to the conditioned and reinforcing effects as determined by conditioned place preference (Bowling & Bardo, 1994) and drug self-administration procedures (Bardo, Klebaur, Valone, & Deaton, 2001), respectively.

Relationships between various aspects of dopamine function and social rank have been documented in several nonhuman primate species. For example, Miller-Butterworth et al. (2008) identified two variants in the macaque dopamine transporter gene that were significantly associated with social rank. Moreover, cerebrospinal fluid (CSF) levels of homovanillic acid (HVA), the primary metabolite of dopamine in primates, were higher in dominant male and female cynomolgus monkeys (Kaplan, Fontenot, & Mann, 2002 and unpublished data).

We have examined the impact of environmental variables related to the social hierarchy on brain D2 receptor function using PET in socially housed monkeys (see Nader & Czoty, 2008). Initial PET imaging studies using the D2 receptor ligand [^{18}F]fluoroclebopride (FCP) found significantly lower D2 receptor availability in subordinate versus dominant female cynomolgus monkeys who had lived in a social group for over three years (Grant et al., 1998). It was not clear from these data, however, whether the difference in D2 availability pre-dated acquisition of a particular rank or was a result of long-term exposure to social stress that is unequivocally experienced by subordinate monkeys (Kaplan et al., 1982; Shively & Kaplan, 1984; Shively et al., 1988). This question was directly addressed in subsequent studies in male monkeys. Data from FCP PET scans performed on 20 experimentally naïve and individually housed male cynomolgus monkeys showed no differences in D2 receptor availability, indicating that it was not a trait that determined eventual social rank. Next, monkeys were placed in groups of 4 and were re-scanned with FCP three months later (Morgan et al., 2002). As in the previous study (Grant et al., 1998), we observed significantly higher D2 availability in dominant monkeys. However, contrary to our hypothesis, the >20% difference between dominant and subordinate monkeys was due to a significant *increase* in D2 receptor availability in dominant monkeys whereas subordinates, on average, did not change. A similar effect of attaining dominance was found in female cynomolgus monkeys under nearly identical conditions (unpublished data). These data demonstrating lower D2 receptor availability in subordinate monkeys are consistent with a diminished prolactin response to the D2 receptor antagonist haloperidol in female cynomolgus monkeys (Shively et al., 1998). The increases in D2 measures associated with attainment of social dominance were in the same direction as reported in rodent studies demonstrating the influence of environmental enrichment on DA function, including increased D2 receptor densities (e.g., Bowling, Rowlett, & Bardo, 1993; Rilke, May, Oehler, & Wolffgramm, 1995; Hall et al., 1998). Thus, we have conceptualized experience in the nonhuman primate social hierarchy as a continuum of experiences that can affect brain dopamine function ranging from chronic social stress in subordinates to chronic environmental enrichment in dominant monkeys.

Serotonergic Systems

Individual differences in brain serotonin (5-HT) function have been closely linked to variability in personality traits and behaviors that influence social function in humans, including impulsivity and aggression. In addition to DA, the serotonin neurotransmitter system has also been studied in socially housed animals. For example, social defeat resulted in increases in 5-HT release assessed using microdialysis (Keeney et al., 2006), and changes in indirect markers of 5-HT metabolism (e.g., 5-hydroxyindoleacetic acid (5-HIAA) and 5-HIAA/5-HT ratio; Berton et al., 1998). In the VBS, several studies have demonstrated increases in serotonin metabolite levels (e.g. 5-HIAA), higher levels of 5-HT2 receptors in subordinates, rank-specific changes in 5-HT1A receptor density and lower levels of 5-HT transporters (McKittrick, Blanchard, Blanchard, McEwen, & Sakai, 1995; McKittrick et al., 2000). Such findings highlight the powerful influence of social rank on brain serotonin function and make it obvious that pharmacological manipulations can (and do) produce different neurobiological effects depending on the social rank of the animal.

Fittingly, 5-HT has been the most thoroughly investigated neurotransmitter system with respect to social dominance and subordination in nonhuman primates. CSF concentrations of 5-HIAA are the most accessible measure of central nervous system 5-HT function. Relatively low concentrations of 5-HIAA, thought to reflect decreased brain 5-HT function, have been associated with aggression and impulsivity in humans and nonhuman primates (Van Praag, 1982; Asberg, 1994; Higley, King, et al., 1996; Higley, Mehlman, Higley, et al., 1996; Higley, Mehlman, Poland, et al., 1996; Fairbanks, Melega, Jorgensen, Kaplan, & McGuire, 2001). Some studies in nonhuman primates have demonstrated an inverse relationship between CSF 5-HIAA concentrations and social rank (Higley et al., 1991, 1992; Higley, King, et al.,1996; Westergaard, Suomi, Higley, & Mehlman, 1999; Kaplan et al., 2002).

The relationship of high 5-HIAA concentrations and low social status has been supported by studies that have associated impulsivity and inappropriate aggression with both measures (Higley et al., 1992, Higley, King, et al., 1996a, Higley, Mehlman, Higley, et al., 1996; Higley, Mehlman, Poland, et al., 1996; Mehlman et al., 1994, 1995, 1997; Fairbanks et al., 2001, Westergaard et al., 2003). Other studies have observed higher 5-HIAA concentrations in dominant monkeys (Yodyingyuad et al 1985; Fairbanks et al., 2004; Howell et al., 2007), whereas others have found no relationship (Fontenot, Kaplan, Manuck, Arango, & Mann, 1995). Recently, high basal CSF concentrations of 5-HIAA were predictive of eventual subordinate status in female monkeys (i.e., appeared to be a trait variable) and these differences persisted after stable group formation (Riddick et al., 2009).

More direct comparisons of 5-HT neurotransmission across social ranks arise from studies of 5-HT receptors and the 5-HT transporter (SERT). In a recent study, SERT availability as measured by PET imaging in a group of individually housed female cynomolgus monkeys did not predict social rank, nor did it differ across ranks once hierarchies were established (Riddick et al., 2009). This finding may be due to the radiotracer used or the brain regions examined. On the whole, however, the lack of a difference in SERT availability across ranks is inconsistent with studies showing differences in SERT availability, SERT mRNA levels, and polymorphisms of the SERT gene in humans and laboratory animals that correlated with differences .in impulsivity or social stress (Berton et al., 1999; Filipenko, Beilina, Alekseyenko, Dolgov, & Kuuudryavtseva, 2002; Frankle et al., 2005; Paaver et al., 2007).

Sensitivity to Pharmacological Challenges

The functional significance of the changes described above has been assessed through the use of pharmacological challenges and sensitivity to various classes of drugs. In this section, we provide some examples of how social dominance can impact drug actions. Most studies have examined sensitivity to psychostimulants, ethanol, barbiturates, and opioids, and examples of each will be provided. In rodent models, both acute and repeated social defeat induces an enhanced sensitivity to the locomotor and reinforcing effects of cocaine and amphetamine (Haney, Maccari, Le Moal, Simon, & Piazza, 1995; Covington & Miczek, 2001, 2005; de Jong et al., 2005b). It was demonstrated early on that social defeat produced an opioid-like antinociceptive effect (Miczek et al., 1982; Williams et al., 1990), and, interestingly, that repeated social defeat resulted in a long-lasting tolerance to the antinociceptive effects of morphine (Miczek, 1991). There is a long history of examining opioid self-administration and its interaction with housing conditions and social rank in rats. In many of these studies, the role of social isolation was studied without regard to rank within the colony (e.g., Alexander, Coambs, & Hadaway, 1978; Alexander, Beyerstein, Hadaway, & Coambs, 1981; Hadaway et al., 1979). Later studies demonstrated that subordinates consumed larger amounts of opioids orally compared to dominant rats (e.g., Heyne, 1996). Similar studies have been conducted with ethanol self-administration and identified a role of social status in group-housed rats (e.g., Wolffgramm & Heyne, 1991). In addition, there was enhanced voluntary ethanol intake in subordinate rats in the VBS (Blanchard, Hori, Tom, & Blanchard, 1987). Interestingly, a history of ethanol self-administration and access to ethanol during group formation eliminated evidence of a hierarchy (Duncan et al., 2006). During periods of social defeat, there was a general suppression of ethanol intake (van Erp, Tachi, & Miczek, 2001). In response to experimenter-administered ethanol, there were differential effects on locomotor activity in an open field with subordinates showing greater sensitivity to ethanol's depressant effects and differences in levels of activity in various portions of the open field (e.g., periphery versus central area movement) (Balkey & Pohorecky, 2006). From a neurochemical perspective, it has been demonstrated with voltammetry that ethanol has biphasic effects on dopamine release in subordinate/defeated animals, and no effect on dopamine release in dominant/resident mice (Yavich & Tiihonen, 2000).

Using group-housed rhesus monkeys, Crowley et al. (1974) demonstrated that ethanol, methamphetamine, pentobarbital, and morphine produced various dose-dependent changes on social behavior. Miczek and colleagues extended these studies using an intruder model in squirrel monkeys (e.g., Miczek et al. 1981; Miczek & Yoshimura, 1982; Miczek & Gold, 1983). In general, cocaine and amphetamine decreased most forms of social behavior, including aggression. These investigators also found that, at high doses, dominant monkeys change from primary initiators of aggression to recipients of aggression (Miczek & Gold, 1983). That similar patterns of amphetamine-induced alterations were not observed in the subordinate monkeys suggested that the effects of these drugs were partially dependent on the social status of the monkey receiving the drug. A somewhat different pattern was observed in macaques: amphetamine increased aggression in the highest and lowest ranking monkeys, with little effect on the mid-ranking monkeys (Smith & Byrd, 1984, 1985). Furthermore, if monkeys changed rank, responses to amphetamine matched the new rank (Martin, Smith, & Byrd, 1990). These data demonstrate that social rank can profoundly influence the effects of psychostimulants on social behavior.

A particular advantage of using nonhuman primates for non-invasive brain imaging is that brain changes and drug actions can be studied in the same animal. For example, as described above, attaining dominance was associated with an increase in D2 dopamine receptors. Based on studies in humans (Volkow et al., 1999), monkeys (Nader et al., 2006), and rodents (Dalley et al., 2007) there appears to be an inverse relationship between D2 availability and pleasurable response to psychomotor stimulants. Thus, we hypothesized that the subordinate monkeys would self-administer more cocaine than the dominant monkeys. This hypothesis was borne out. When monkeys were allowed to self-inject cocaine, subordinate monkeys were significantly more sensitive to cocaine (Morgan et al., 2002). In fact, cocaine did not initially function as a reinforcer in the dominant monkeys; although after repeated exposures to cocaine, they did eventually begin to self-administer cocaine (see Nader & Czoty, 2005 for additional discussion). Once monkeys had developed an extensive history of cocaine self-administration such that D2 receptor availability no longer differed between dominant and subordinate monkeys (see above), rates of cocaine self-administration were also similar across animals (Czoty et al., 2004). Next we examined whether there would be differences between social ranks under conditions in which cocaine was available in the context of an alternative, non-drug reinforcer (Czoty et al., 2005). We found that subordinate monkeys were significantly more sensitive to the reinforcing effects of cocaine using this procedure, such that they would choose a lower dose of cocaine over food compared to dominant monkeys. These findings highlight several important facets of organism × environmental interactions. In addition, these findings indicate that after years of living in these stable groups the influence of the social context was still apparent. Since the vast majority of studies described in this section involved males, future studies are required to determine if a similar impact of social rank on drug actions are apparent in female subjects.

Conclusions

This chapter began by highlighting the importance of considering gene × environment interactions in the study of human disease. The environmental variable that we have focused on is the social rank of the animal. In terms of developing animal models of human disease, the role of the social environment cannot be "controlled," but rather must be considered as a significant independent variable in order to begin understanding brain-behavior interactions. It should be apparent that the powerful influence of social environment is observed in mice, rats, nonhuman primates, and humans; thus, the generality of these observations is extremely strong. As social neuroscientists trying to understand behavior or as behavioral neuroscientists attempting to understand physiology and pharmacology, the findings demonstrating that outcomes can be dependent on social rank should help us appreciate why there are individual differences in treatment outcomes. Simply knowing neuronal firing patterns or how drugs bind to receptors will not provide enough information to account for the behavioral outcome.

There are consequences for including social dominance in the design of an experiment. As mentioned above, this may increase the variability of effects that are measured. As a result, including social dominance as an independent variable will require increases in sample size. For example, if 10 subjects were required to reliably observe an effect, 20 (10 dominant and 10 subordinate) would be needed if subjects were to be socially housed; this will increase the cost and, most likely, reduce productivity. The outcome, however, will likely be more valid than simply studying individually housed animals.

Acknowledgments

Preparation of this chapter and some of the research described was supported by National Institute on Drug Abuse grants R37 DA10584, DA17763 and DA21658. The authors report no conflicts of interest.

References

Abbott, D. H., Keverne, E. B., Bercovitch, F. B., Shively, C. A., Mendoza, S. P., Saltzman, W., et al. (2003). Are subordinates always stressed? A comparative analysis of rank differences in cortisol levels among primates. *Horm Behav, 43*, 67–82.

Alexander, B. K., Beyerstein, B. L., Hadaway, P. F., & Coambs, R. B. (1981). Effects of early and later colony housing on oral ingestion of morphine in rats. *Pharmacol Biochem Behav, 15*, 571–576.

Alexander, B. K., Coambs, R. B., & Hadaway, P. F. (1978). The effect of housing and gender on morphine self-administration in rats. *Psychopharmacology, 58*, 175–179.

Amick, 3rd, B. C., McDonough, P., Chang, H., Rogers, W. H., Pieper, C. F., & Duncan, G. (2002). Psychological and physical exposures in the United States labor market from 1968 to 1992. *Psychosom Med, 64*, 370–381.

Anstrom, K. K., Miczek, K. A., & Budygin, E. A. (2009). Increased phasic dopamine signaling in the mesolimbic pathway during social defeat in rats. *Neuroscience, 161*, 3–12.

Asberg, M. (1994). Monoamine neurotransmitters in human aggressiveness and violence: A selective review. *Crim Behav Mental Health, 4*, 303–327.

Bardo, M. T., Klebaur, J. E., Valone, J. M., & Deaton, C. (2001). Environmental enrichment decreases intravenous self-administration of amphetamine in female and male rats. *Psychopharmacology, 155*, 278–284.

Barnum, C. J., Blandino, Jr., P., & Deak, T. (2007). Adaptation in the corticosterone and hyperthermic responses to stress following repeated stressor exposure. *J Neuroendocrinol, 19*, 632–642.

Bartolomucci, A. (2007). Social stress, immune functions and disease in rodents. Frontiers in. *Neuroendocrinol, 28*, 28–490.

Bartolomucci, A., Palanza, P., Costoli, T., Savani, E., Laviola, G., Parmigiani, S., et al. (2003). Chronic psychosocial stress persistently alters autonomic function and physical activity in mice. *Physiol Behav, 80*, 57–67.

Batty, K. A., Herbert, J., Keverne, E. B., & Vellucci, S. V. (1986). Differences in blood levels of androgens in female talapoin monkeys related to their social status. *Neuroendocrinology, 44*, 347–354.

Bercovitch, F. B. & Clarke, S. (1962). Dominance rank, cortisol concentrations, and reproductive maturation in male rhesus macaques. *Physiol Behav, 58*, 215–221.

Bernstein, S. & Mason, W. A. (1962). The effects of age and stimulus conditions on the emotional responses of rhesus monkeys: Responses to complex stimuli. *J Genet Psychol, 101*, 279–298.

Bernstein, I. S., Gordon, T. P., & Rose, R. M. (1974). Aggression and social controls in rhesus monkey (Macaca mulatta) groups revealed in group formation studies. *Folia Primatol, 21*, 81–107.

Berton, O., Aguerre, S., Sarrieau, A., Mormede, P., & Chaouloff, F. (1998). Differential effects of social stress on central serotonergic activity and emotional reactivity in Lewis and Spontaneously Hypertensive Rats. *Neuroscience, 82*, 147–159.

Berton, O., Durand, M., Aguerre, S., Mormede, P., & Chaouloff, F. (1999). Behavioral, neuroendocrine and serotonergic consequences of single social defeat and repeated fluoxetine pretreatment in the Lewis rat strain. *Neuroscience, 92*, 327–341.

Bhatnagar, S., Vining, C., Iyer, V., & Kinni, V. (2006). Changes in hypothalamic-pituitary-adrenal function, body temperature, body weight and food intake with repeated social stress exposure in rats. *J Neuroendocrinol, 18*, 13–24.

Blakley, G. & Pohorecky, L. A. (2006). Psychosocial stress alters ethanol's effect on open field behaviors. *Pharmacol Biochem Behav, 84*, 51–61.

Blanchard, R. J., Flannelly, K. J., & Blanchard, D. C. (1988). Life-span studies of dominance and aggression in established colonies of laboratory rats. *Physiol Behav, 43*, 1–7.

Blanchard, D. C., Cholvanich, P., Blanchard, R. J., Clow, D. W., Hammer, Jr., R. P., Rowlett, J. K., et al. (1991). Serotonin, but not dopamine, metabolites are increased in selected brain regions of subordinate male rats in a colony environment. *Brain Research, 568,* 61–66.

Blanchard, R. J., Hori, K., Tom, P., & Blanchard, D. C. (1987). Social structure and ethanol consumption in the laboratory rat. *Pharmacol Biochem Behav, 28,* 437–442.

Blanchard, D. C., Sakai, R. R., McEwen, B., Weiss, S. M., & Blanchard, R. J. (1993). Subordination stress: Behavioral, brain, and neuroendocrine correlates. *Behavioral and Brain Research, 58,* 112–121.

Blanchard, D. C., Spencer, R. L., Weiss, S. M., Blanchard, R. J., McEwen, B., & Sakai, R. R. (1995). Visible burrow system as a model of chronic social stress: Behavioral and neuroendocrine correlates. *Psychoneuroendocrinology, 20,* 117–134.

Blanchard, R. J., Dulloog, L., Markham, C., Nishimura, O., Nikluna, Compton, J., et al. (2001). Sexual and aggressive interactions in a visible burrow system with provisioned burrows. *Physiol Behav, 72,* 245–254.

Bowling, S. L., & Bardo, M. T. (1994). Locomotor and rewarding effects of amphetamine in enriched, social, and isolate reared rats. *Pharmacol Biochem Behav, 48,* 459–464.

Bowling, S. L., Rowlett, J. K., & Bardo, M. T. (1993). The effect of environmental enrichment on amphetamine-stimulated locomotor activity, dopamine synthesis and dopamine release. *Neuropharmacology, 32,* 885–893.

Brain, P. & Benton, D. (1979). The interpretation of physiological correlates of differential housing in laboratory rats. *Life Science, 24,* 99–115.

Cabib, S., D'Amato, F. R., Puglisi-Allegra, S., & Maestripieri, D. (2000). Behavioral and mesocorticolimbic dopamine responses to non aggressive social interactions depend on previous social experiences and on the opponent's sex. *Behav Brain Res, 112,* 13–22.

Cameron, J. L. (1997). Stress and behaviorally induced reproductive dysfunction in primates. *Semin Reprod Endocrinol, 15,* 37–45.

Capitanio, J. P. (2002). Sociability and responses to video playbacks in adult male rhesus monkeys (Macaca mulatta). *Primates, 43,* 169–177.

Clarke, A. S., Czekala, N. M., & Lindburg, D. G. (1995). Behavioral and adrenocortical responses of male cynomolgus monkeys and lion-tailed macaques to social stimulation and group formation. *Primates, 36,* 41–56.

Coe, C. L., Mendoza, S. P., & Levine, S. (1979). Social status constrains the stress response in the squirrel monkey. *Physiol Behav, 23,* 633–638.

Cohen, S., Line, S., Manuck, S. B., Rabin, B. S., Heise, E. R., & Kaplan, J. R. (1997). Chronic stress, social status, and susceptibility to upper respiratory infections in nonhuman primates. *Psychosom Med, 59,* 213–221.

Covington, H. E. III & Miczek, K. A. (2001). Repeated social-defeat stress, cocaine or morphine. Effects on behavioral sensitization and intravenous cocaine self-administration "binges." *Psychopharmacology, 158,* 388–398.

Covington, H. E. III, & Miczek, K. A. (2005). Intense cocaine self-administration after episodic social defeat stress, but not after aggressive behavior: Dissociation from corticosterone activation. *Psychopharmacology, 183,* 331–340.

Creel, S. (2001). Social dominance and stress hormones *Trends Ecol Evol, 16,* 491–497.

Crowley, T. J., Stynes, A. J., Hydinger, M., & Kaufman, I. C. (1974). Ethanol, methamphetamine, pentobarbital, morphine and monkeys social behavior. *Arch Gen Psychiatry, 31,* 829–838.

Czoty, P. W., Gould, R. W., & Nader, M. A. (2009). Relationship between social rank and cortisol and testosterone concentrations in male cynomolgus monkeys (Macaca fascicularis). *J Neuroendocrinol, 21,* 68–76.

Czoty, P. W., Morgan, D., Shannon, E. E., Gage, H. D., & Nader, M. A. (2004). Characterization of dopamine D1 and D2 receptor function in socially housed cynomolgus monkeys self-administering cocaine. *Psychopharmacology, 174,* 381–388.

Czoty, P. W., McCabe, C., & Nader, M. A. (2005). Assessment of the relative reinforcing strength of cocaine in socially housed monkeys using a choice procedure. *J Pharmacol Exp Ther, 312,* 96–102.

Dalley, J. W., Fryer, T. D., Brichard, L., Robinson, E. S., Theobald, D. E., Laane, K., et al. (2007) Nucleus accumbens D2/3 receptors predict trait impulsivity and cocaine reinforcement. *Science, 315,* 1267–1270.

Davis, B. A., Clinton, S. M., Akil, H., & Becker, J. B. (2008). The effects of novelty-seeking phenotypes and sex differences on acquisition of cocaine self-administration in selectively bred high-responder and low-responder rats. *Pharmacol Biochem Behav, 90,* 331–338.

de Jong, J. G., van der Begt, B. J., Buwalda, B., & Koolhaas, J. M. (2005). Social environment determines the long-term effects of social defeat. *Physiol Behav, 84,* 87–95.

de Jong, J. G., Wasilewski, M., van der Vegt, B. J., Buwalda, B., & Koolhaas, J. M. (2005). A single social defeat induces short-lasting behavioral sensitization to amphetamine. *Physiol Behav, 83,* 805–811.

Duncan, E. A., Tamashiro, K. L. K., Nguyen, M. M. N., Gardner, S. R., Woods, S. C., & Sakai, R. R. (2006). The impact of moderate daily alcohol consumption on aggression and the formation of dominance hierarchies in rats. *Psychopharmacology, 189,* 83–94.

Fairbanks, L. A., Melega, W. P., Jorgensen, M. J., Kaplan, J. R., & McGuire, M. T. (2001). Social impulsivity inversely associated with CSF 5-HIAA and fluoxetine exposure in vervet monkeys. *Neuropsychopharmacology, 24,* 370–378.

Fairbanks, L. A., Jorgensen, M. J., Huff, A., Blau, K., Hung, Y. Y., & Mann, J. J. (2004). Adolescent impulsivity predicts adult dominance attainment in male vervet monkeys. *Am J Primatol, 64,* 1–17.

Filipenko, M. L., Beilina, A. G., Alekseyenko, O. V., Dolgov, V. V., & Kuuudryavtseva, N. N. (2002). Repeated experience of social defeats increases serotonin transporter and monoamine oxidase A mRNA levels in raphe nuclei of male mice. *Neurosci Lett, 321,* 25–28.

Fontenot, M. B., Kaplan, J. R., Manuck, S. B., Arango, V., & Mann, J. J. (1995). Long-term effects of chronic social stress on serotonergic indices in the prefrontal cortex of adult male cynomolgus macaques. *Brain Res, 705,* 105–108.

Frankle, W. G., Lombardo, I., New, A. S., Goodnam, M., Talpot, P. S., Huang, Y., et al. (2005). Brain serotonin transporter distribution in subjects with impulsive aggressivity: A positron emission study with [11C]McN 5652. *Am J Psychiatry, 162,* 915–923.

Golub, M. S., Sassenrath, E. N., & Goo, G. P. (1979). Plasma cortisol levels and dominance in peer groups of rhesus monkey weanlings. *Horm Behav, 12,* 50–59.

Gonzalez, C. A., Coe, C. L., & Levine, S. (1982). Cortisol responses under different housing conditions in female squirrel monkeys. *Psychoneuroendocrinology, 7,* 209–216.

Goo, G. P. & Sassenrath, E. N. (1980). Persistent adrenocortical activation in female rhesus monkeys after new breeding groups formation *J Med Primatol, 9,* 325–334.

Goymann, W. & Wingfield, J. C. (2004). Allostatic load, social status and stress hormones: The costs of social status matter. *Animal Behaviour, 67,* 591–602.

Grant, K. A., Shively, C. A., Nader, M. A., Ehrenkaufer, R. L., Line, S. W., Morton, T. E., et al. (1998). Effects of social status on striatal dopamine D2 receptor binding characteristics in cynomolgus monkeys assessed with positron emission tomography. *Synapse, 29,* 80–83.

Gust, D. A., Gordon, T. P., Wilson, M. E., Ahmed-Ansari, A., Brodie, A. R., & McClure, H. M. (1991). Formation of a new social group of unfamiliar female rhesus monkeys affects the immune and pituitary adrenocortical systems. *Brain Behav Immun, 5,* 296–307.

Hadaway, P. F., Alexander, B. K., Coambs, R. B., & Beyerstein, B. (1979). The effect of housing and gender on preference for morphine-sucrose solutions in rats. *Psychopharmacology, 66,* 87–91.

Hall, F. S., Wilkinson, L. S., Humby, T., Inglis, W., Kendall, D. A., Marsden, C. A., et al. (1998). Isolation rearing in rats: Pre- and postsynaptic changes in striatal dopaminergic systems. *Pharmacol Biochem Behav, 59,* 859–872.

Haller, J., Fuchs, E., Halasz, J., & Makara, G. B. (1998). Defeat is a major stressor in males while social instability is stressful mainly in females: Towards the development of a social stress model in female rats. *Brain Research Bulletin, 50,* 33–39.

Haney, M., Maccari, S., Le Moal, M., Simon, H., & Piazza, P. V. (1995). Social stress increases the acquisition of cocaine self-administration in male and female rats. *Brain Research, 698,* 46–52.

Henry, J. P. & Stephens, P. M. (1977). *Stress, health and the social environment: A sociobiologic approach to medicine.* New York: Springer-Verlag.

Heyne, A. (1996). The development of opiate addiction in the rat. *Pharmacol Biochem Behav, 53,* 11–25.

Higley, J. D., Hasert, M. F., Suomi, S. J., Linnoila, M. (1991). Nonhuman primate model of alcohol abuse—Effects of early experience, personality, and stress on alcohol consumption. *Proc Natl Acad Sci USA, 88,* 7261–7265.

Higley, J. D., King, S. T. Jr., Hasert, M. F., Champoux, M., Suomi, S. J., & Linnoila, M. (1996). Stability of interindividual differences in serotonin function and its relationship to severe aggression and competent social behavior in rhesus macaque females. *Neuropsychopharmacology, 14,* 67–76.

Higley, J. D., Mehlman, P. T., Higley, S. B., Fernald, B., Vickers, J., Lindell, S. G., et al. (1996). Excessive mortality in young free-ranging male nonhuman primates with low cerebrospinal fluid 5-hydroxyindoleacetic acid concentrations. *Arch Gen Psychiatry, 53,* 537–543.

Higley, J. D., Mehlman, P. T., Poland, R. E., Taub, D. M., Vickers, J., Suomi, S. J., et al. (1996). CSF testosterone and 5-HIAA correlate with different types of aggressive behaviors. *Biol Psychiatry, 40,* 1067–1082.

Higley, J. D., Mehlman, P. T., Taub, D. M., Higley, S. B., Suomi, S. J., Vickers, J. H., et al. (1992). Cerebrospinal fluid monoamine and adrenal correlates of aggression in free-ranging rhesus monkeys. *Arch Gen Psychiatry, 49,* 436–441.

Hilakivi-Clarke, L. A. & Lister, R. G. (1992). Are there preexisting behavioral characteristics that predict the dominant status of male NIH Swiss mice (Mus musculus)? *J Comp Psychol, 106,* 184–189.

Honess, P. E. & Marin, C. M. (2006). Behavioural and physiological aspects of stress and aggression in nonhuman primates. *Neuroscience and Biobehavioral Reviews, 30,* 390–412.

Howell, S., Westergaard, G., Hoos, B., Chavanne, T. J., Shoaf, S. E., Cleveland, A., et al. (2007) Serotonergic influences on life-history outcomes in free-ranging male rhesus macaques. *Am J Primatol, 69,* 851–865.

Isovich, E., Engelmann, M., Landgraf, R., & Fuch, E. (2001). Social isolation after a single defeat reduces striatal dopamine transporter binding in rats. *European Journal of Neuroscience, 13,* 1254–1256.

Kaplan, J. R. & Manuck, S. B. (1998). Status, stress, and atherosclerosis: The role of environment and individual behavior. *Ann NY Acad Sci, 896,* 145–161.

Kaplan, J. R. & Manuck, S. B. (2004). Ovarian dysfunction, stress, and disease: A primate continuum. *ILAR J, 45,* 89–115.

Kaplan, J. R., Manuck, S. B., Clarkson, T. B., Lusso, F. M., & Taub, D. M. (1982). Social status, environment, and atherosclerosis in cynomolgus monkeys. *Atherosclerosis, 2,* 359–368.

Kaplan, J. R., Fontenot, M. B., & Mann, J. J. (2002). Central nervous system monoamine correlates of social dominance in cynomolgus monkeys (Macaca fascicularis). *Neuropsychopharmacology, 26,* 431–443.

Kaplan, J. R., Adams, M. R., Koritnik, D. R., Rose, J. C., & Manuck, S. B. (1986). Adrenal responsiveness and social status in intact and ovariectomized Macaca fascicularis. *Am J Primatol, 11,* 181–193.

Keeney, A. J., Hogg, S., & Marsden, C. A. (2001). Alterations in core body temperature, locomotor activity, and corticosterone following acute and repeated social defeat of male NMRI mice. *Physiol Behav, 74,* 177–184.

Keeney, A., Jessop, D. S., Harbuz, M. S., Marsden, C. A., Hogg, S., & Blackburn-Munro, R. E. (2006). Differential effects of acute and chronic social defeat stress on hypothalamic-pituitary-adrenal axis function and hippocampal serotonin release in mice. *J Neuroendocrinol, 18,* 330–338.

Kimura, K., Shimizu, K., Hayashi, M., Ishikawa, T., & Ago, Y. (2000). Pituitary-adrenocortical responses to the first dyadic encounters in male rhesus monkeys: Effect of dominance relationship. *Am J Primatol, 50,* 247–256.

Krantz, D. S. & McCeney, M. K. (2002). Effects of psychological and social factors on organic disease: A critical assessment of research on coronary heart disease. *Ann Rev Psychol, 53,* 341–369.

Leshner, A. I. & Candland, D. K. (1972). Endocrine effects of grouping and dominance rank in squirrel monkeys. *Physiol Behav, 8,* 441–445.

Lucas, L. R., Celen, Z., Tamashiro, K. L. K., Blanchard, R. J., Blanchard, D. C., Markham, C., et al. (2004) Repeated exposure to social stress has long-term effects on indirect markers of dopaminergic activity in brain regions associated with motivated behavior. *Neuroscience, 124,* 449–457.

Malatynska, E. & Knapp, R. J. (2005). Dominant-submissive behavior as models of mania and depression. *Neuroscience and Biobehavioral Reviews, 29,* 715–737.

Marini, F., Pozzato, C., Andreetta, V., Jansson, B., Arban, R., Domenici, E., et al. (2006). Single exposure to social defeat increase corticotropin-releasing factor and glucocorticoid receptor mRNA expression in rat hippocampus. *Brain Research, 1067,* 25–35.

Martin, S. P., Smith, E. O., & Byrd, L. D. (1990). Effects of dominance rank on d-amphetamine-induced increases in aggression. *Pharmacol Biochem Behav, 37*, 493–496.

McGuire, M. T., Brammer, G. L., & Raleigh, M. J (1986). Resting cortisol levels and the emergence of dominant status among male vervet monkeys. *Horm Behav, 20*, 106–117.

McKittrick, C. R., Blanchard, D. C., Blanchard, R. J., McEwen, B. S., & Sakai, R. R. (1995). Serotonin receptor binding in a colony model of chronic social stress. *Biological Psychiatry, 37*, 383–393.

McKittrick, C. R., Magariños, A. M., Blanchard, D. C., Blanchard, R. J., McEwen, B. S., & Sakai, R. R. (2000). Chronic social stress reduces dendritic arbors in CA3 of hippocampus and decreases binding to serotonin transporter sites. *Synapse, 36*, 85–94.

Meerlo, P., Overkamp, G. J., Daan, S., Van Den Hoofdakker, R. H., & Koolhaas, J. M. (1996). Changes in behaviour and body weight following a single or double social defeat in rats. *Stress, 1*, 21–32.

Mehlman, P. T., Higley, J. D., Faucher, I., Lilly, A. A., Taub, D. M., Vickers, J., et al. (1994). Low CSF concentrations and severe aggression and impaired impulse control in nonhuman primates. *Am J Psychiatry, 151*, 1485–1491.

Mehlman, P. T., Higley, J. D., Faucher, I., Lilly, A. A., Taub, D. M., Vickers, J., et al. (1995). Correlation of CSF 5-HIAA concentration with sociality and the timing of emigration in free-ranging primates. *Am J Psychiatry, 152*, 907–913.

Mehlman, P. T., Higley, J. D., Fernald, B. J., Sallee, F. R., Suomi, S. J., & Linnoila, M. (1997). CSF 5-HIAA, testosterone, and sociosexual behaviors in free-ranging male rhesus macaques in the mating season. *Psychiatry Res, 72*, 89–102.

Mendoza, S. P., Coe, C. L., Lowe, E. L., & Levine, S. (1979). The physiological response to group formation in adult male squirrel monkeys. *Psychoneuroendocrinology, 3*, 221–229.

Miczek, K. A. (1979). A new test for aggression in rats without aversive stimulation: Differential effects of d-amphetamine and cocaine. *Psychopharmacology, 60*, 253–259.

Miczek, K. A. (1991). Tolerance to the analgesic, but not discriminative stimulus effects of morphine after brief social defeat in rats. *Psychopharmacology, 104*, 181–186.

Miczek, K. A., Woolley, J., Schlisserman, S., & Yoshimura, H. (1981). Analysis of amphetamine effects on agonistic and affiliative behavior in squirrel monkeys (Saimiri sciereus). *Pharmacol Biochem Behav, 14* S1, 89–93.

Miczek, K. A. & Yoshimura, H. (1982). Disruption of primate social behavior by d-amphetamine and cocaine: Differential antagonism by antipsychotics. *Psychopharmacology, 76*, 163–171.

Miczek, K. A. & Gold, L. H. (1983). d-Amphetamine in squirrel monkeys of different social status: Effects on social and agonistic behavior, locomotion, and stereotopies. *Psychopharmacology, 81*, 183–190.

Miczek, K. A., Covington, H. E. 3rd, Nikulina, E. M. Jr., & Hammer, R. P. (2004). Aggression and defeat: Persistent effect on cocaine self-administration and gene expression in peptidergic and aminergic mesocorticolimbic circuits. *Neuroscience and Biobehavioral Reviews, 27*, 787–802.

Miczek, K. A., Thompson, M. L., & Shuster, L. (1982). Opioid-like analgesia in defeated mice. *Science, 215*, 1520–1522.

Miller-Butterworth, C. M., Kaplan, J. R., Shaffer, J., Devlin, B., Manuck, S. B., & Ferrrell, R. E. (2008). Sequence variation in the primate dopamine transporter gene and its relationship to social dominance. *Mol Biol Evol, 25*, 18–28.

Mills, J. (1965) Needle park. *Life Magazine*, March 5.

Morgan, D., Grant, K. A., Gage, H. D., Mach, R. H., Kaplan, J. R., Prioleau, O., et al. (2002). Social dominance in monkeys: Dopamine D$_2$ receptors and cocaine self-administration. *Nature Neuroscience, 5*, 169–174.

Morgan, D., Grant, K. A., Prioleau, O. A., Nader, S. H., Kaplan, J. R., & Nader, M. A. (2000). Predictors of social status in cynomolgus monkeys (Macaca fascicularis) after group formation. *Am J Primatol, 52*, 115–131.

Nader, M. A. & Czoty, P. W. (2008). Brain imaging in nonhuman primates: Insights into drug addiction. *ILAR J, 49*, 89–102.

Nader, M. A. & Czoty, P. W. (2005). PET imaging of dopamine D2 receptors in monkey models of cocaine abuse: Genetic predisposition versus environmental modulation. *Am J Psychiatry, 162*, 1473–1482.

Nader, M. A., Morgan, D., Gage, H. D., Nader, S. H., Calhoun, T. L., Buchheimer, N., et al. (2006). PET imaging of dopamine D2 receptors during chronic cocaine self-administration in monkeys. *Nat Neurosci, 9*, 1050–1056.

Paaver, M., Nordquist, N., Parik, J., Harro, M., Oreland, L., & Harro, J. (2007). Platelet MAO activity and the 5-HTT gene promoter polymorphism are associated with impulsivity and cognitive style in visual information processing. *Psychopharmacology, 194*, 545–554.

Palanza, P., Gioiosa, L., & Parmigiani, S. (2001). Social stress in mice: Gender differences and effects of estrous cycle and social dominance. *Physiol Behav, 73*, 411–420.

Piazza, P. V., Deminiere, J. M., Le Moal, M., & Simon, H. (1989). Factors that predict individual vulnerability to amphetamine self-administration. *Science, 245*, 1511–1513.

Pohorecky, L. A. (2006). Housing and rank status of male Long-Evans rats modify ethanol's effect on open-field behaviors. *Psychopharmacology, 185*, 289–297.

Raab, A., Dantzer, R., Michaud, B., Mormede, P., Taghzouti, K., Simon, H., et al. (1986). Behavioural, physiological and immunological consequences of social status and aggression in chronically coexisting resident-intruder dyads of male rats. *Physiol Behav, 36*, 223–228.

Riddick, N. V., Czoty, P. W., Gage, H. D., Kaplan, J. R., Nader, S. H., Icenhower, M., et al. (2009). Behavioral and neurobiological correlates influencing social hierarchy formation in female cynomolgus monkeys. *Neuroscience, 158*, 1257–1265.

Rilke, O., May, T., Oehler, J., & Wolffgramm, J. (1995). Influences of housing conditions and ethanol intake on binding characteristics of D2, 5-HT1A, and benzodiazepine receptors of rats. *Pharmacol Biochem Behav, 52*, 23–28.

Sakai, R. R. & Tamashiro, K. L. K. (2005). Social hierarchy and stress. In T. Steckler, N. Kalin, & J. M. H. M. Reul (Eds.). Handbook of stress and the brain (pp. 113–132). Amsterdam, The Netherlands. Elsevier.

Sapolsky, R. M. (2005). The influence of social hierarchy on primate health. *Science, 308*, 648–652.

Sapolsky, R. M. (2002). Endocrinology of the stress response. In: J Becker, S. Breedlove, D. Crews, & M. McCarthy, (Eds.). Behavioral endocrinology, 2nd ed (pp. 409–450). Cambridge, MA: MIT Press.

Sapolsky, R. M. (1992). Cortisol concentrations and the social significance of rank instability among wild baboons. *Psychoneuroendocrinology, 17*, 701–709.

Sapolsky, R. M., Alberts, S. C., & Altmann, J. (1997). Hypercortisolism associated with social subordinance or social isolation among wild baboons. *Arch Gen Psychiatry, 54*, 1137–1143.

Sassenrath, E. N. (1970). Increased adrenal responsiveness related to social stress in rhesus monkeys. *Horm Behav, 1*, 283–298.

Schaefer, G. J. & Michael, R. P. (1991). Housing conditions alter the acquisition of brain self-stimulation and locomotor activity in adult rats. *Physiol Behav, 49*, 635–638.

Sell, S. L., Thomas, M. L., & Cunningham, K. A. (2002). Influence of estrous cycle and estradiol on behavioral sensitization to cocaine in female rats. *Drug and Alcohol Dependence, 67*, 281–290.

Shively, C. A. (1998). Social subordination stress, behavior, and central monoaminergic function in female cynomolgus monkeys. *Biological Psychiatry, 44*, 882–891.

Shively, C. & Kaplan, J. (1984). Effects of social factors on adrenal weight and related physiology of Macaca fascicularis. *Physiol Behav, 33*, 777–782.

Shively, C. A., Laber-Liard, K., & Anton, R. F. (1997). Behavior and physiology of social stress and depression in female cynomolgus monkeys. *Biol Psychiatry, 41*, 871–882.

Shively, C. A., Register, T. C., Friedman, D. P., Morgan, T. M., Thompson, J., & Lanier, T, (2005). Social stress-associated depression in adult female cynomolgus monkeys. *Biol Psychology, 69*, 67–84.

Smith, E. O. & Byrd, L. D. (1984). Contrasting effects of d-amphetamine on affiliation and aggression in monkeys. *Pharmacol Biochem Behav, 20*, 255–260.

Smith, E. O. & Byrd, L. D. (1985). d-Amphetamine induced changes in social interaction patterns. *Pharmacol Biochem Behav, 22*, 135–139.

Stefanski, V. (2001). Social stress in laboratory rats. Behavior, immune function, and tumor metastasis. *Physiol Behav, 73*, 385–391.

Stefanski, V. & Gruner, S. (2006). Gender difference in basal and stress levels of peripheral blood leukocytes in laboratory rats. *Brain, Behavior, and Immunity, 20*, 369–377.

Stavisky, R. C., Adams, M. R., Watson, S. L., & Kaplan, J. R. (2001). Dominance, cortisol and behavior in small groups of female cynomolgus monkeys (Macaca fascicularis). *Horm Behav, 39*, 232–238.

Syme, L. A. (1973). Spurious species comparisons in housing studies using laboratory rats and mice. *Psychol Rep, 33*, 507–510.

Tamashiro, K. L. K., Hegeman, M. A., Nguyen, M. M. N., Melhorn, S. J., Ma, L. Y., Woods, S. C., et al. (2007). Dynamic body weight and body composition changes in response to subordination stress. *Physiol Behav, 91*, 440–448.

Tidey, J. W. & Miczek, K. A. (1996). Social defeat stress selectively alters mesocorticolimbic dopamine release: An in vivo microdialysis study. *Brain Research, 721*, 140–149.

Tokuda, K. & Jensen, G. D. (1969). Determinants of dominance hierarchy in a captive group of pigtailed monkeys (Macaca nemestrina). *Primates, 10*, 227–236.

van Erp, A. M., Tachi, N., & Miczek, K. A. (2001). Short or continuous social stress: Suppression of continuously available ethanol intake in subordinate rats. *Behav Pharmacol, 12*, 335–342.

Van Praag, H. M. (1982). Depression, suicide and the metabolism of serotonin in the brain. *J Affective Disorders, 4*, 275–290.

Volkow, N. D., Wang, G.J., Fowler, J.S., Logan, J., Gatley, S.J., Gifford, A., Hitzemann, R., Ding, Y., S., & Pappas, N. (1999). Prediction of reinforcing responses to psychostimulants in humans by brain dopamine D2 receptor levels. *Am J Psychiatry, 156*, 1440–1443.

Westergaard, G. C., Suomi, S. J., Higley, J. D., & Mehlman, P. T. (1999). CSF 5-HIAA and aggression in female macaque monkeys: Species and interindividual differences. *Psychopharmacology, 146*, 440–446.

Westergaard, G. C., Suomi, S. J., Chavanne, T. J., Houser, L., Hurley, A., Cleveland, A., et al. (2003) Physiological correlates of aggression and impulsivity in free-ranging female primates. *Neuropsychopharmacology 28*, 1045–1055.

Williams, J. L., Worland, P. D., & Smith, M. G. (1990). Defeat-induced hypoalgesia in the rat: Effects of conditioned odors, naltrexone, and extinction. *J Exp Psychol Anim Behav Process, 16*, 345–357.

Wohlfarth, T. & van den Brink, W. (1998). Social class and substance use disorder: The value of social class as distinct from socioeconomic status. *Soc Sci Med, 47*, 51–58.

Wolffgramm, J. & Heyne, A. (1991). Social behavior, dominance, and social deprivation of rats determine drug choice. *Pharmacol Biochem Behav, 38*, 389–399.

Yavich, L. & Tiihonen, J. (2000). Ethanol modulates evoked dopamine release in mouse nucleus accumbens: Dependence on social stress and dose. *Eur J Pharmacol, 401*, 365–373.

Yodyingyuad, U., de la Riva, C., Abbott, D. H., Herbert, J., & Keverne, E. B. (1985). Relationship between dominance hierarchy, cerebrospinal fluid levels of amine transmitter metabolites (5-hydroxyindole acetic acid and homovanillic acid) and plasma cortisol in monkeys. *Neuroscience, 16*, 851–858.

Mechanisms for the Regulation of Intergroup Responses: A Social Neuroscience Analysis

David M. Amodio *and* Kyle G. Ratner

Abstract

Social neuroscience refers to the study of the brain, mind, and behavior in social contexts. The area of intergroup relations provides a particularly rich domain for examining the interplay of neural and social psychological processes at multiple levels of analysis, from the intrapsychic to the group and society. For this reason, social neuroscience research on intergroup relations has already contributed important advances to our understanding of the social brain, and this area continues to thrive as one of the most active areas in the field. In this chapter, we describe neuroscience models of control and their implications for theories of self-regulation in the domain in intergroup relations.

Keywords: social neuroscience, control mechanisms, intergroup relation, self-regulation, response regulation

Social neuroscience concerns the interacting roles of the brain, mind, and behavior in social contexts. Of the many topics studied by social neuroscientists, the area of intergroup relations stands out as a particularly rich domain for examining the interplay of neural and psychological processes at multiple levels of analysis, from the intrapsychic to the group and society. Research on this topic also provides an important connection between basic questions of neural and psychological science with real-life societal issues. For these reasons, social neuroscience research on intergroup relations has already provided many important advances in our understanding of the social brain, and this area continues to thrive as one of the most active areas in the field. In this chapter, we discuss how basic neuroscience research on the mechanisms of control can be used to inform psychological models of how intergroup responses may be regulated.

Self-Regulation in Intergroup Relations

Intergroup bias refers to the influence of stereotypic beliefs or prejudiced attitudes on one's behavior toward people from a different social group. Although people may hold stereotypic beliefs and prejudiced attitudes that they consciously endorse, stereotypes and prejudices can also operate implicitly, without one's conscious awareness (Devine, 1989; Fazio, Jackon, Dunton, & Williams, 1995). Implicit intergroup bias is a problem for egalitarian individuals who, on principle, wish to treat others equally regardless of race or social status, as well as for those who simply want to appear egalitarian when under normative pressures. In either case, self-regulation is needed to respond without the influence of such biases.

There are multiple views on how self-regulation processes operate in the intergroup context (Amodio & Devine, 2010). Some theories focus on how race-biased thoughts or emotions may be modulated within the mind (Greenwald & Banaji, 1995), such that the regulatory processes operates intrapsychically, directly targeting the source of bias (e.g., Gawronski & Bodenhausen, 2006). Other theories focus on the extent to which a bias emerges in behavior (Devine, 1989), such that regulatory processes operate by limiting the influence of bias on the expression of behavior (e.g., Amodio, Devine, & Harmon-Jones, 2008; Monteith, 1993; Payne, 2005). One's particular theoretical approach to regulation is important, as it influences the way that research studies are designed and data are interpreted. One's approach also has major implications for how discoveries in this area may be translated into applications for reducing prejudice and discrimination in society.

When discussing psychological mechanisms involved in the regulation of intergroup responses, it is useful to consider potential sources of intergroup bias. Bias may arise from learned emotional responses to members of a racial outgroup (Mackie & Elliot, 1998) or learned stereotypic trait associations that might be commonly expressed in one's culture (Devine, 1989). Other research suggests that bias may arise from perceptual processes, such that faces of ingroup and outgroup members are seen differently (Eberhardt, Goff, Purdie, & Davies, 2004; Hugenberg & Bodenhausen, 2003), or from learned behavioral tendencies that unfold without one's conscious intention (Amodio et al., 2004; Bargh et al., 1996). Of these potential sources, negative emotions and stereotypic thoughts have received the most attention in the social psychological literature, and most social psychological theories assume that these are the direct targets of control. This view is complicated, however, by research showing that people are practically incapable of directly down-regulating their thoughts and emotions (Gross & Levenson, 1993; Wegner, 1994). For the prejudice researcher interested in designing interventions to reduce discrimination, clarity on these issues is crucial. The primary goal of this chapter is to explore how neuroscience research may shed light on these critical psychological questions about the mechanisms of self-regulation.

The Neuroscience of Self-regulation

The foremost benefit of the social neuroscience approach is the ability to examine mechanism. Models of neuroanatomy from human and non-human animal studies provide a roadmap for understanding how different neural structures associated with cognition, emotion, perception, and behavior are likely to interact with structures involved in controlled processing. In this section, we review neuroscience models of these basic mechanisms of control.

Although the entire brain may be thought of as a regulatory organ, the prefrontal cortex (PFC, Figure 48.1) is believed to play a special role in intentional control (Norman & Shallice, 1986; Passingham, 1993). The PFC is richly interconnected with structures throughout the brain, with especially strong cortico-cortical connections within the frontal cortex (Figure 48.2). Evidence for the PFC's contribution to control comes from studies of brain-lesion patients and, more recently, from a large body of neuroimaging research. However, there is less clarity on what the specific targets of control include. As noted above, some theories propose that the main targets of control are stereotypic thoughts and prejudiced feelings, suggesting that the PFC should *down-regulate* the activity of structures underlying these mental processes. Other theories propose that the main targets of control are egalitarian or race-irrelevant actions and/or changes in attention or perception to facilitate such actions, such that race-biased thoughts and feelings are regulated indirectly by modulating how social targets are perceived and how the perceiver acts. Here, we review research on the putative neural pathways of control, obtained primarily from human neuroimaging data and anatomical studies of the macaque monkey brain, a close homologue of the human brain (Nakahara, Adachi, Osada, & Miyashita, 2007).

Regulation of emotions

Many contemporary studies of intergroup response regulation have focused on the control of prejudiced emotional responses, such as fear, disgust, or anger directed toward the outgroup (e.g., Cunningham et al., 2004; see Amodio, Harman-Jones, & Devine, 2003). Although "emotion" refers to a very intuitive response at an experiential level of analysis, it actually comprises a complex set of processes at the neural and physiological level of analysis (LeDoux, 1996). Nevertheless, intuitive notions of emotion as a "feeling" are often ascribed to specific neural structures. For example, negative emotion is often associated with activity in the amygdala (e.g., Davidson & Irwin, 1999; Ochsner et al., 2002), largely on the basis of animal lesion studies demonstrating the amygdala's important role in behavioral

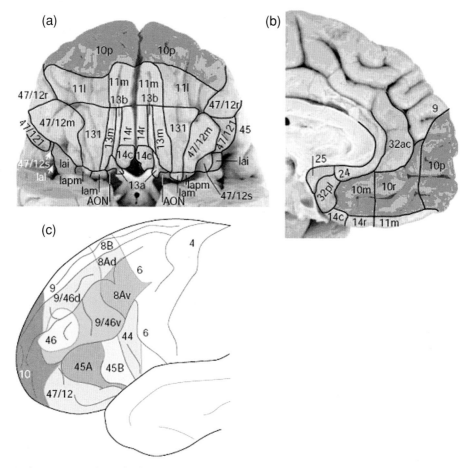

Fig. 48.1 Brodmann areas are shown for the ventral (a), medial (b), and lateral (c) surfaces of the human prefrontal cortex. Adapted from Petrides and Pandya (1994) with permission of John Wiley and Sons.

expressions of classical fear conditioning (e.g., Davis, 1992; LeDoux, 1992). Indeed, several neuroimaging studies have reported increased activity in various PFC regions along with decreased amygdala activity while subjects viewed outgroup faces—a pattern sometimes interpreted as the PFC directly "down-regulating" the amygdala response (e.g., Cunningham et al., 2004; Lieberman et al., 2005).

On the surface, PFC-amygdala correlations appear to support the notion that intergroup response regulation involves the direct control of emotion. However, a consideration of neuroanatomy reveals some complications in this interpretation. For example, although correlations between activations in the PFC and amygdala are often interpreted in a "top-down" direction in fMRI studies (i.e., PFC-to-amygdala), anatomical research

indicates that connections between these regions are bi-directional, with the densest connections running from the amygdala to the PFC (specifically to caudal areas of the OFC and subgenual ACC; Barbas & Zikopoulos, 2007; Ghashghaei & Barbas, 2002). By contrast, regions of lateral PFC that have been implicated in most fMRI studies of prejudice control have very sparse, if any, connections to the amygdala (Barbas & Zikopoulos, 2007; Carmichael & Price, 1995; Ghashghaei & Barbas, 2002; Stefanacci & Amaral, 2002). Of these PFC regions, lateral areas of BA9 and 10—areas most often implicated in fMRI studies of emotion control—have the sparsest connections, and these are *from* the amygdala to the PFC (Ghashghaei et al., 2007). Thus, the down-regulatory pathway posited in many neuroimaging studies appears to be inconsistent with anatomy. An alternative interpretation is that

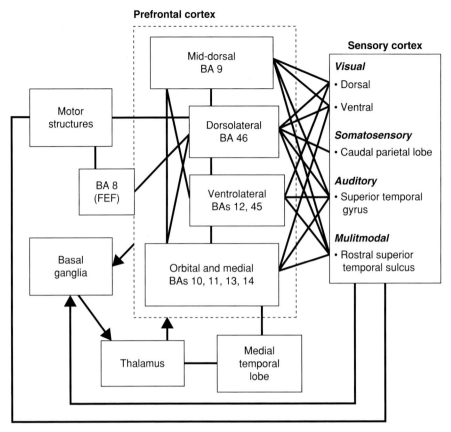

Fig. 48.2 Schematic representation of intrinsic and extrinsic connectivity involving the prefrontal cortex, labeled by Brodmann areas (BAs). Most connections are bi-direction; exceptions are indicated by arrows. The frontal eyefield (FEF) region is depicted as directly adjacent to the PFC, given that some researchers consider it to be a part of the PFC, whereas others do not. Adapted from Miller & Cohen (2001) with permission.

subcortical structures linked to emotion and attention signal PFC regions involved in control when regulation is needed.

Given the lack of anatomical evidence for a strong and direct pathway from the lateral PFC to amygdala, some researchers have suggested a revised down-regulatory model of the PFC effect on the amygdala. Based on other research implicating medial PFC regions in the extinction of fear learning (e.g., Milad & Quirk, 2002), these researchers have suggested that this lateral PFC to amygdala effect is mediated by the medial PFC (e.g., Lieberman et al., 2007). However, it is important to recognize that extinction involves the learning of new, alternative memory traces over time—a process that is very different from the intentional regulation of an emotional response in a particular moment. Therefore, it is problematic to invoke mPFC research on extinction to support a hypothesis about on-line regulation.

The PFC-amygdala down-regulation idea is further complicated when one begins to consider amygdala anatomy. The amygdala comprises multiple nuclei connected in a complex network of inhibitory connections, with different nuclei involved in coordinating different patterns of behavior. For example, the central nucleus signals sympathetic nervous system response linked to fear, whereas the basal nucleus is important for instrumental responses linked to approach motivation and action (Killcross, Robbins, & Everitt, 1997). Because it is difficult to distinguish these nuclei with fMRI, interpretations of "down-regulation" of the amygdala from fMRI data are complex and often ambiguous. Furthermore, fear-related autonomic responses triggered by the central nucleus are modulated by a network of inhibitory GABAergic intercalated masses within the amygdala (Barbas & Zikopoulos, 2007). An implication of this circuitry is that observations of increased amygdala activity using fMRI could indicate either more or less fear-related autonomic activation, depending on the role of these inhibitory connections. Given this broad set of issues, neuroscience models challenge the popular notion that regulatory mechanisms linked to the PFC have a direct effect on amygdala activity. Furthermore, the common assumption that the psychological construct of negative emotion maps onto the amygdala is too simplistic to be accurate, and thus problematic. Therefore, the idea that mechanisms of control directly down-regulate negative emotions, such as those associated with intergroup bias, does not comport well with neuroanatomy.

Control of Stereotypic Thoughts

Another important source of intergroup bias is stereotypic thought. Several theorists have suggested that regulatory processes operate directly on stereotypic associations in the mind by supressing their activation (e.g., Bodenhausen & Macrae, 1998; Monteith, Sherman, & Devine, 1998). However, like emotion, the psychological construct of "thought" is difficult to operationalize at the neural level, or even at a basic cognitive level of analysis. For the present purposes, research on the selection of conceptual knowledge is relevant, as it concerns the intentional selection of information into working memory (Gabrieli, 1998; Wagner, Maril, Bjork, & Schacter, 2001). Neuroimaging studies consistently link the process of intentional semantic selection to activity in the left inferior frontal gyrus (BAs 44, 45, and 47; Thompson-Schill, 2003). Consistent with these findings in human subjects, single-unit recordings in the macaque monkey brain have revealed activity in left PFC neurons, in an area homologous to BAs 45 and 47 in humans, when monkeys performed an active memory retrieval task (Cadoret & Petrides, 2007). Although the connectivity of these regions is complex (with input from nearly every area of the PFC), the PFC is prominently interconnected with regions of temporal cortex associated with visual processing (e.g., rostral inferotemporal cortex), auditory processing (superior temporal cortex), and, more broadly, with the processing of semantic knowledge (Gabrieli, 1998; Martin, 2007; Petrides & Pandya, 2002). This pattern of connectivity suggests that these PFC regions contribute to control by producing representations of visuospatial and auditory information to guide action.

In line with anatomical studies, neuroimaging data suggest that the "control" of thought is accomplished through this process of selection of information into working memory (Badre & Wagner, 2007; Thompson-Schill, 2003). Furthermore, it appears that "suppression" at the psychological level involves the selective activation, rather than inhibition, of semantic processes at the neural level

(Anderson et al., 2004). Research also suggests that the left PFC activity associated with conceptual knowledge is strongest for concepts linked to action (Bunge, 2004; Petersen et al., 1988), an idea consistent with the large body of evidence linking left PFC activity with approach motivation and action (Harmon-Jones, 2003). In sum, neuroimaging and anatomical data appear to be inconsistent with psychological theories of thought suppression as a mechanism for regulating stereotypic thoughts. Rather, these studies suggest a goal-directed selection process, whereby semantic information is selected to guide regulatory responses.

Regulation of Action

The PFC is most extensively interconnected with structures linked to goal-driven action (Fuster, 2001; Passingham, 1993). This includes inputs from the thalamus and sensory regions to the medial and orbital frontal cortices, which have been associated with the selection of action-relevant information. It also includes outputs from lateral PFC areas to structures associated with the planning and implementation of action, such as the basal ganglia and motor cortices (see Figure 48.2; Miller & Cohen, 2001). This evidence is relevant for understanding how intergroup responses are regulated because, as we mentioned previously, intergroup situations often impose a variety of different goals for action, such as the goal to appear nonprejudiced in front of others. Although the neural circuitry of action control is extensive and complex, research suggests three different general aspects of action control.

Goal-directed action

A major pathway for goal-directed action involves bidirectional connections between the PFC and the basal ganglia (i.e., the fronto-striatal loop), which operates in concert with thalamic and midbrain processes (Middleton & Strick, 2000; Yin & Knowlton, 2006). The implementation of a goal-directed behavioral response is associated with activity in the left PFC, via a fronto-striatal-pallidal circuit that includes the supplementary motor cortex, putamen, pallidum, thalamus, and primary motor cortex (Aron, 2007). Additionally, the premotor cortex mediates extensive connections between the PFC and primary motor cortex (Miller & Cohen, 2001). The special role of the left PFC in the control of actions is further consistent with the finding that left-lateralized frontal cortical activity, indicated by alpha-band suppression in encephalography, is associated with approach motivation and preparation for action (Amodio et al., 2007; Davidson, 1992; Harmon-Jones, 2003).

Inhibition of action

A second form of action control concerns the active inhibition of a response (Logan & Cowan, 1984). For example, in the *Stop-Signal* task, research participants initiate a response (e.g., button press) to a specific cue. On a subset of trials, a *Stop Signal* tone is presented sometime after the cue appears, so that the subject must inhibit an already-initiated response. Successful response inhibition has been associated with activity in the right inferior frontal cortex (Aron, Robbins, & Poldrack, 2004). Aron (2007) proposed that regions of the right inferior frontal cortex disrupt the motor plan at the globus pallidus pars interna, via projections to the subthalamic nucleus of the basal ganglia. In this way, the PFC controls action through motor inhibition.

Oculomotor orienting

Oculomotor networks constitute an important interface between action and perception in the context of control. The arcuate sulcus within BA8, referred to as the "frontal eyefield," has bidirectional connections with PFC regions, most prominently with BA46. How might the control of eye movements relate to neuroimaging studies of self-regulation? A recent study suggests that PFC activity interpreted as down-regulating emotion may actually reflect the control of eyegaze (van Reekum et al., 2007). The authors found that, when instructed to reduce one's affective response to aversive images, subjects' gaze avoided the most aversive parts of the image, as indicated by eye-tracking sensors. Interestingly, when subjects attempted to reduce their negative affect, increases in PFC activity (and decreases in amygdala activity) were statistically accounted for by changes in eye gaze. This finding suggests that reductions in negative affect may result from a change in behavior that limits one's exposure to an aversive stimulus (rather than indicating the direct "down-regulation" of amygdala activity).

Regulation of Sensation and Perception

Sensory input

Anatomical studies of the macaque brain show that regions of the PFC implicated in control modulate the processing of basic sensory information via major projections to the thalamic reticular nucleus and the thalamus (Barbas & Zikopoulos, 2007). Tracer studies reveal projections to the thalamus originating from BA 9, 10, and 46 in the lateral PFC, and BA 13 in the OFC, along with other connections to sensory and motor cortices (Zikopoulos & Barbas, 2006). It is believed that through these connections the PFC plays a role in selecting motivationally relevant sensory signals while suppressing irrelevant information, in the service of task goals.

Perceptual processing

The PFC influences perception through connections to visual and auditory association cortices. For example, neurons located in the frontal pole (rostral BA10) and paracingulate (rostral BA32) project to inhibitory neurons within the auditory associational cortex, which are believed to modulate auditory sensory input (Medalla, Lera, Feinberg, & Barbas, 2007). In an fMRI study of visual processing, efforts to ignore (vs. remember) a visual stimulus were associated with lower activity in the visual association cortex, and this effect was modulated by activity in the left middle frontal gyrus (Gazzaley et al., 2007). Additionally, recent studies of pain regulation suggest that PFC activity is associated with changes in the perception of pain (Salomons, Johnstone, Backonja, Shackman, & Davidson, 2007; Wager et al., 2004). Although these fMRI findings are inherently correlational, they are consistent with anatomical findings, and suggest that control regions of the PFC function to regulate sensory input as well as higher-level perceptual processes, presumably to aid the regulation of action.

Summary of Neural Models of Self-regulation

Our review of neural mechanisms for self-regulation suggests that general mechanisms of control operate primarily on behavioral actions (i.e., response output) and on sensation and perception (i.e., informational input), and that emotional and cognitive processes are part and parcel of the self-regulatory process, helping to guide behavior in the context of one's goals and situational circumstances. Interestingly, the view emerging from our discussion of the neuroscience literature contrasts with some traditional ideas of control in the social psychology literature, in the sense that emotional and cognitive processes appear to be the mechanisms of regulation, rather than the targets of regulation. That is, although inhibitory networks operate within neural systems to modulate processes at the neuronal level, evidence does not seem to support the notion of the *down-regulation* of thoughts and emotions at the psychological level of analysis. In the next section, we consider the implications of this analysis for models of the self-regulation of intergroup responses.

Relation of Neuroscience Models to the Regulation of Intergroup Bias

Now that we have reviewed neuroscience models of PFC connectivity and function as they relate to various mechanisms of self-regulation, we can consider their implications for theories of how intergroup responses may be regulated. In addition, we evaluate recent social neuroscience literature on the regulation of racial bias in light of these neuroscience models.

Regulation of Race-biased Emotion

Most social neuroscience studies on the regulation of race bias have focused on the regulation of emotion, driven by an intuitive belief that, in the brain, the regulation of emotion involves the PFC's down-regulatory control of amygdala activity. However, as reviewed above, anatomical and functional studies of the amygdala in animals challenge this view and suggest the amygdala is itself an important regulatory mechanism that recruits goal-directed control processes in the PFC. Numerous fMRI studies on the regulation of race-biased affect have reported correlations between the PFC and amygdala, which have been interpreted as evidence for a down-regulation pattern (for a review, see Stanley, Phelps, & Banaji, 2008). However, a consideration of neuroanatomy, along with methodological concerns of such studies, suggests serious potential problems with the interpretation of down-regulatory effects of the PFC on amygdala responses to race.

Most fMRI studies reporting the top-down control of amygdala activity have used variants of a passive face-viewing task in the scanner. In such studies, the participant simply views faces of ingroup and outgroup members while making either no response or a response that is irrelevant to issues of race or one's attitudes. For example, the subject might indicate which side of the screen the face appeared or whether it repeated the previous stimulus. In such cases, the task does not place any type of response in conflict with another, and thus does not create a situation that requires regulation. Because such tasks do not necessarily involve a regulated response, one cannot be sure that observed brain activity is related to mechanisms of control. Furthermore, analyses of fMRI data that relate activity from one part of the brain to another are correlational, and thus the direction of the effect is ambiguous.

A correlation between activity in regions of the PFC and amygdala could reflect signals from the PFC to the amygdala, signals from the amygdala to the PFC, or the effect of some unobserved "third" variable. Third, given that nuclei within the amygdala communicate through inhibitory connections, such that increased activity in one nucleus signals decreased activity in another, observations of a net increase or decrease in amygdala activity are problematic. This issue is compounded by the low spatial resolution of fMRI, relative to the size of individual nuclei. Finally, all of these issues must be considered in light of the broader challenge of attempting to map high-level psychological constructs onto particular brain structures (Amodio, 2010a; Cacioppo et al., 2003).

Perhaps the main difficulty with conventional social neuroscience models regarding the down-regulation of emotional responses to race concerns a lack on agreement with known neuroanatomy. For example, in fMRI studies, the lateral regions of the PFC that are typically described as down-regulating the amygdala are not actually connected to the amygdala anatomically. As noted above, most connections between the amygdala and caudal regions of the PFC are characterized by amygdala-to-PFC signaling. An alternative interpretation of such findings is that the PFC activity observed in fMRI studies of race is associated with preparation to make a task response, whereas the amygdala activity is associated with attention to cues related to intergroup bias (e.g., outgroup faces). For example, Cunningham et al. (2004) observed greater amygdala activity in participants when viewing Black vs. White faces presented quickly, near the threshold for subliminal presentation (~30 ms). But when Black vs. White faces were presented for a longer duration (525 ms), the authors observed increased activity in the lateral PFC but no activity in the amygdala. Cunningham et al. (2004) also reported that greater right lateral PFC activity to Black vs. White faces during long-duration presentation was correlated with stronger amygdala activity to Black faces during short-duration presentations, controlling for amygdala activity on long-duration trials. Given the anatomy research reviewed above, it is unlikely that this correlation reflects the effect of the PFC down-regulating the amygdala response to race. Therefore, it is useful to consider other plausible interpretations of these findings. For example, it is possible that some individuals, knowing the task concerned issues of race, were simply more engaged than others across trials. The correlation observed by Cunningham et al. (2004) could reflect that participants who showed greater amygdala activity to the short-duration trials also showed more lateral PFC activity during the long-duration trials. This interpretation would be more consistent with brain anatomy, and it does not invoke PFC-amygdala down-regulation. A similar interpretation could be used to explain other findings in this literature (e.g., Lieberman et al., 2005; Richeson et al., 2003), and it is generally consistent with papers showing that control is either not associated with amygdala activity (Beer et al., 2008) or that control is accompanied by greater amygdala activity (Wager et al, 2008). It will be important for future research to interpret patterns of brain activity related to the regulation of intergroup responses in the context of basic neuroscience models of anatomy and function, and with a consideration of whether the experimental task is designed in a way that clearly elicits regulatory processing.

One useful alternative procedure for examining fear-related amygdala activity in humans is the emotion-modulated startle-eyeblink method. This method is based on fear-potentiated startle paradigms in animals, in which the magnitude of the startle reflex, such as to a loud, startling noise, is measured in a context of threatening versus rewarding situations. When in a threatened context, the amygdala is involved in intensifying the magnitude of the defensive startle response, via input from the central-nucleus of the amygdala—the nucleus specifically involved in the fear response. Therefore, increases in the startle eyeblink response due to an experimental manipulation can be more clearly interpreted as threat-related amygdala activity, as it is known to specifically reflect activity of the central nucleus.

Amodio et al., (2003) used the startle eyeblink method to examine amygdala activity to outgroup versus ingroup faces. In this study, blink responses were measures at short (400 ms) and long (4 s) intervals following face onset, as a way to distinguish automatic and controlled aspects of affective responding. Amodio et al. (2003) observed a patterns of racial bias in blink amplitudes at both intervals, without evidence for top-down control of amygdala activity. Another startle-eyeblink study of ingroup versus outgroup face viewing found a similar, although nonsignificant, trend of larger startle responses to outgroup faces at probe latencies of 2 seconds, which was correlated with participants degree of implicit negative attitudes toward Black faces (Phelps et al., 2000). Hence, research using the startle-eyeblink method, from which a fear-related amygdala response may

be more clearly inferred, contradicts fMRI studies suggesting that simply looking at an outgroup face engages the down-regulation of amygdala activity. More research will be needed to clarify the observed pattern of results across studies. One issue that remains to be resolved is whether any fear-related responses arise from the outgroup stimulus itself or from the subject's concern about being evaluated by the experimenter whenever an outgroup stimulus appears. Nevertheless, the notion that intergroup responses are regulated through the direct down-regulation of the amygdala, or of emotion more broadly, remains debated.

Regulation of Stereotypes

Several models of intergroup bias suggest that stereotypic thoughts can be inhibited or suppressed within the mind. This type of hypothesis is difficult to test with traditional behavioral and self-report measures used in social psychology, because it is difficult to assess whether changes in behavior reflect the control of mental processes or the control of the behavior itself. Therefore, evidence for the direct regulation of stereotypic thoughts remains somewhat tentative. Interestingly, a brain-based model of control raises some complications with the notion of a stereotype inhibition mechanism. That is, at the neural level, the same neural processes involved in semantic retrieval—a substrate of stereotypes—are involved in control. That is, research on PFC function suggests that stereotypes are themselves a mechanism for guiding perception and action, in line with the traditional idea that stereotypes provide schemas for social behavior. Given that stereotypes are themselves a mechanism of control, it is problematic to conclude that stereotypes are also the target of control.

Control of Actions Related to Intergroup Responses

Early models of prejudice control emphasized the regulation of behavioral responses in a way that is generally consistent with neuroscience models of control. For example, Devine's (1989) dissociation model posited that control involves the implementation of an intended, nonbiased response, which replaces a race-biased tendency. Indeed, Devine and colleagues' research on people's motivations for responding without prejudice has also focused on how nonprejudiced responding involves making a response that does not include the influence of bias (e.g., Amodio et al., 2003, 2008; Devine, Plant, Amodio, Harmon-Jones, & Vance, 2002; Plant & Devine, 1998). Several social neuroscience studies on the regulation of prejudice are consistent with the idea that regulatory processes focus on goal-directed action. For example, Amodio, Devine, and Harmon-Jones (2007) examined the role of left-PFC activity in regulating one's behavior after being induced to feel guilty about responding in a prejudiced way. In their study, greater left-PFC activity predicted stronger intentions to engage in egalitarian behaviors, which would override any unintended race-biased tendencies. The left PFC's role in engaging a goal-direct response may be contrasted with research implicating the right PFC in inhibiting a response (Aron et al., 2004).

The Amodio et al. (2007) study examined action control processes directed at the goal to engage in egalitarian behaviors. However, the more typical scenario of prejudice control concerns the goal to complete a race-irrelevant task without being influenced by race. For example, a series of studies by Amodio and colleagues has examined responses on Payne's (2001) weapons identification task, in which the main task is to categorize target objects as handguns or handtools—a task for which race should be irrelevant. However, in the task, faces of White and Black males appear just before each target. In line with the stereotype of Blacks as dangerous, Black face primes tend to facilitate the categorization of guns while interfering with the categorization of tools (Payne, 2001). Therefore, regulation is needed on Black-tool trials to overcome the race-biased tendency to respond with "gun" on such trials. Using ERPs to assess anterior cingulate activity, these studies showed that when a Black face prime was presented prior to a handtool, causing response interference, there was greater activity in the anterior cingulate cortex (Amodio et al., 2004; Amodio, Devine, & Harmon-Jones, 2008; Amodio, Kubota, Harmon-Jones, & Devine, 2006). Conflict-related ACC activity is believed to recruit regions of the PFC to increase the top-down control of action (Miller & Cohen, 2001; Botvinick et al., 2001). Indeed, larger ERP indices of ACC activity were associated with greater response control on the task. This line of work is consistent with neuroanatomical studies of the PFC and its likely role in control, such that it is involved in the regulation of goal-directed action.

Inhibition of Action Related to Intergroup Responses

Relatively few theories of intergroup response regulation have pointed to the importance of withholding a prejudiced behavioral response. An exception is Monteith's theory of self-regulation, which posits that an important step in responding without prejudice is to halt all responses, so that a nonbiased response can be planned and then implemented in future situations (Monteith, 1993; Monteith, Ashburn-Nardo, Voils, & Czopp, 2002). Indeed, in Devine's (1989) statement of intergroup response control, she emphasized that positive intergroup interactions often involve the intentional inhibition of an unacceptable behavior (see also, Monteith, Devine, & Zuwerink, 1993). To date, social neuroscience studies have not directly examined the process of inhibiting a response that might reflect the influence of racial bias. Nevertheless, several studies using fMRI and frontal lesion patient samples have reported activity in regions of the right frontal cortex associated with response inhibition processes (Aron et al., 2004). As described above, Amodio and Potanina (2011) observed heightened right lateral PFC activity when subjects were concerned about making a stereotypical response. Lieberman et al. (2005) also found activity in this region when subjects performed a task that involved matching ethnic group labels to faces. It is possible that subjects were reluctant to make such responses, and thus engaged in some form of inhibition. Our interpretations are speculative, however, and based on a reverse inference that activity in the right lateral PFC may indicate behavioral inhibition processes. Therefore, additional research will be needed to directly examine the process of behavioral inhibition in the regulation of stereotypes.

Regulating Perception and Attention to Race

Neuroanatomical studies suggest that major targets of control-related PFC activity are processes involved in sensation, perception, and attention. Traditionally, social cognition theories have focused more on how people think about outgroup members than on how motivation and controlled processing may alter perceptions of and attention to racial cues. Nevertheless, there are interesting findings in the social cognition literature that may, in hindsight, be interpreted as supporting the notion of perceptual control. For example, research has observed reduced activation of stereotypes when attention was diverted from one task (evaluating a target's behavior) to another (rehearsing a 9-digit number; Gilbert & Hixon, 1991) or was focused on a particular aspect of a target's identity (e.g., female) as opposed to another (e.g., Chinese; Macrae, Bodenhausen, & Milne, 1995). Although these findings were originally interpreted as evidence that one's social framing modulates the automatic activation of stereotypes, the present analysis suggests that changes in social framing may reflect a regulatory process that actively changes perception as a way to promote behaviors to match one's goals (Ito & Urland, 2005; Wheeler & Fiske, 2005).

Some neuroscience studies have examined the perception of race (Golby et al., 2001), but few were designed to examine the regulatory effect of a perceiver's goals (e.g., Ito & Urland, 2005; Wheeler & Fiske, 2005). There is a large ERP literature on the perceptual processing of faces, and several studies have investigated the influence of race on early face processing by examining early ERP components such as the N170 and P200 (e.g., James, 2001; Caldera et al, 2003, 2004; Ito & Urland, 2005; Walker et al, 2008). Although the findings of ERP research on intergroup perception are rather mixed, several studies have observed different early neural responses to outgroup versus ingroup faces (Amodio, 2010b; Correll, Urland, & Ito, 2006; Dickter & Bartholow, 2007; Ito & Urland, 2003, 2005; Kubota & Ito, 2007; Ofan, Rubin, & Amodio, in press; Willadsen-Jensen & Ito, 2006, 2008). For example, several studies have found a larger P2 ERP response to outgroup faces compared with ingroup faces that peaks at approximately 180 ms after face onset. Although early ERP responses to race, like the P2, are typically interpreted as reflecting bottom-up attention processes, mounting evidence suggests that these effects are driven in large part by top-down expectancies associated with motivation and self-regulation (Amodio, 2010b; van Peer et al., 2007). Amodio (2010b) demonstrated that the magnitude of this P2 effect to race was influenced by left PFC activity—an index of approach-related motivation and controlled processing—as subjects completed Payne's (2001) weapons identification task. This effect suggested that differential attention to Black versus White faces was driven by motivation. Furthermore, Amodio (2010b) showed that PFC activity and the P2 effect predicted better behavioral control on the task, suggesting a model whereby motivational processes tuned attention to race, which in turn facilitated action control. Given this finding, previous research showing early ERP differences to ingroup versus outgroup faces might be reinterpreted as reflecting motivated top-down expectancy processes.

Summary of Neuroscience Perspective on the Regulation of Intergroup Bias

It can be very informative to consider the implications of neuroanatomy and basic neural function

for theories of intergroup response regulation, as it leads to some new and potentially counterintuitive conclusions. Foremost among these, the popular and intuitive notion that regulation operates through the direct "down-regulation" of emotional processes appears inconsistent with brain anatomy. Indeed, when the extant evidence for a down-regulatory circuit in fMRI studies is scrutinized, this interpretation becomes problematic, and alternative explanations emerge. Similarly, the traditional idea that stereotype activation can be directly inhibited in the mind also appears inconsistent with brain anatomy and function. By contrast, a neuroscience analysis supports the idea that regulatory processes target mechanisms for behavioral action and inhibition, and for sensory input and perceptual processing. These forms of self-regulation have also been described previously in the social cognition literature (e.g., Devine, 1989; Wheeler & Fiske, 2005). However, because social psychological analyses tend to focus on internal psychological processes like thoughts and feelings, the idea that perception, sensation, and behavior may be the primary targets of controlled processing may have received less attention in theories of intergroup regulation. Finally, our theoretical analysis suggests that interventions to reduce bias should focus on training in perceptual vigilance and plans for enacting goal-directed egalitarian behaviors (e.g., Mendoza, Gollwitzer, & Amodio, 2010; Monteith, 1993).

Conclusion

Questions about intergroup bias, and the processes through which it may be regulated, has provided a strong impetus for research in the burgeoning field of social neuroscience. Research in this area has made important strides in connecting low-level neural mechanisms to relatively high-level social processes, and the intergroup context continues to provide fertile ground for new discoveries at the social-cognitive-neuroscience interface. Here, we have described how research on basic neural circuitry regarding the PFC may be used to inform social cognitive models of self-regulation. Although some aspects of this analysis may be provocative and counter-intuitive, we believe that it offers a useful guide for the future development of theory and experimentation. More broadly, this analysis highlights the ways in which a consideration of neuroscience research can advance our thinking on classic social psychological questions.

Acknowledgments

Work on this article was supported by a National Science Foundation grant (BCS *0847350*) to David M. Amodio and a National Science Foundation Graduate Research Fellowship to Kyle G. Ratner.

References

Amodio, D. M. (2008). The social neuroscience of intergroup relations. *European Review of Social Psychology*, *19*, 1–54.

Amodio, D. M. (2010a). Can neuroscience advance social psychological theory? Social neuroscience for the behavioral social psychologist. *Social Cognition*, *28*, 695–716.

Amodio, D. M. (2010b). Coordinated roles of motivation and perception in the regulation of intergroup responses: Frontal cortical asymmetry effects on the P2 event-related potential and behavior. *Journal of Cognitive Neuroscience*, *22*, 2609–2617.

Amodio, D. M. & Devine, P. G. (2010). Regulating behavior in the social world: Control in the context of intergroup bias. In R. R. Hassin, K. N. Ochsner, and Y. Trope (Eds). *Self control in society, mind and brain* (pp. 49–75). New York: Oxford University Press.

Amodio, D. M. & Lieberman, M. D. (2009). Pictures in our heads: Contributions of fMRI to the study of prejudice and stereotyping. In T. Nelson (Ed.) *Handbook of prejudice, stereotyping, and discrimination* (pp. 347–366). New York: Erlbaum Press.

Amodio, D. M. & Mendoza, S. A. (2010). Implicit intergroup bias: Cognitive, affective, and motivational underpinnings. In B. Gawronski and B. K. Payne (Eds.) *Handbook of Implicit Social Cognition* (pp. 353–374). New York: Guilford.

Amodio, D. M., Devine, P. G., & Harmon-Jones, E. (2007). A dynamic model of guilt: Implications for motivation and self-regulation in the context of prejudice. *Psychological Science*, *18*, 524–530.

Amodio, D. M., Harmon-Jones, E., Devine, P. G., Curtin, J. J., Hartley, S. L., & Covert, A. E. (2004). Neural signals for the detection of unintentional race bias. *Psychological Science*, *15*, 88–93.

Amodio, D. M., Devine, P. G., & Harmon-Jones, E. (2008). Individual differences in the regulation of intergroup bias: The role of conflict monitoring and neural signals for control. *Journal of Personality and Social Psychology*, *94*, 60–74.

Amodio, D. M., Harmon-Jones, E., & Devine, P. G. (2003). Individual differences in the activation and control of affective race bias as assessed by startle eyeblink responses and self-report. *Journal of Personality and Social Psychology*, *84*, 738–753.

Amodio, D. M., Kubota, J. T., Harmon-Jones, E., & Devine, P. G. (2006). Alternative mechanisms for regulating racial responses according to internal vs. external cues. *Social Cognitive and Affective Neuroscience*, *1*, 26–36.

Anderson, M. C., Ochsner, K. N., Kuhl, B., Cooper, J., Robertson, E., Gabrieli, S. W., et al. (2004). Neural systems underlying the suppression of unwanted memories. *Science*, *303*, 232–235.

Aron, A. R., Robbins, T. W., & Poldrack, R. A. (2004). Inhibition and the right inferior frontal cortex. *Trends in Cognitive Sciences*, *8*, 170–177.

Aron, A. R. (2007). The neural basis of inhibition in cognitive control. *The Neuroscientist*, *13*, 214–228.

Badre, D. & Wagner, A. D. (2007). Left ventrolateral prefrontal cortex contributions to the control of memory. *Neuropsychologia*, *45*, 2883–2901.

Barbas, H. & Zikopoulos, B. (2007). The prefrontal cortex and flexible behavior. *The Neuroscientist*, *13*, 532–545.

Bargh, J. A., Chen, M., & Burrows, L. (1996). Automaticity of social behavior: Direct effects of trait construct and stereotype activation on action. *Journal of Personality and Social Psychology*, *71*, 230–244.

Bartholow, B. D. & Dickter, C. L. (2007). Social cognitive neuroscience of person perception: A selective review focused on the event-related brain potential. In E. Harmon-Jones & P. Winkielman (Eds.). *Social neuroscience: Integrating biological and psychological explanations of social behavior* (pp. 376–400). New York: Guilford Press.

Beer, J. S., Stallen, M., Lombardo, M. V., Gonsalkorale, K., Cunningham, W., & Sherman, J. W. (2008). The Quadruple Process Model Approach to Examining the Neural Underpinnings of Prejudice. *NeuroImage*, *43*, 775–783.

Bodenhausen, G. V. & Macrae, C. N. (1998). Stereotype activation and inhibition. In R. S. Wyer, Jr. (Ed.), *Stereotype activation and inhibition: Advances in social cognition* (Vol. 11, pp. 1–52). Mahwah, NJ: Erlbaum.

Bunge, S. A. (2004). How we use rules to select actions: A review of evidence from cognitive neuroscience. *Cognitive, Affective, and Behavioral Neuroscience*, *4*, 564–579.

Cadoret, G. & Petrides, M. (2007). Ventrolateral prefrontal neuronal activity related to active controlled memory retrieval in nonhuman primates. *Cerebral Cortex*, *17*, 27–40.

Caldara, R., Thut, G., Servoir, P., Michel, C., Bovet, P., & Renault, B. (2003). Face versus non-face object perception and the "other-race" effect: A spatio-temporal ERP study. *Clinical Neurophysiology*, *114*, 515–528.

Caldara, R., Rossion, B., Bovet, P., & Hauert, C. A. (2004). Event-related potentials and timecourse of the "other-race" face classification advantage. *NeuroReport*, *15*, 905–910.

Carmichael, S. T. & Price, J. L. (1995). Sensory and premotor connections of the orbital and medial prefrontal cortex of macaque monkeys. *Journal of Comparative Neurology*, *363*, 642–664.

Cunningham, W. A., Johnson, M. K., Raye, C. L., Gatenby, J. C., Gore, J. C., & Banaji, M. R. (2004). Separable neural components in the processing of Black and White faces. *Psychological Science*, *15*, 806–813.

Davidson, R. J. (1992). Emotion and affective style: Hemispheric substrates. *Psychological Science*, *3*, 39–43.

Davidson, R. J. & Irwin, W. (1999). The functional neuroanatomy of emotion and affective style. *Trends in Cognitive Sciences*, *3*, 11–21.

Davis, M. (1992). The role of the amygdala in fear-potentiated startle: Implications for animal models of anxiety. *Trends in Pharmacological Sciences*, *13*, 35–41.

Devine, P. G. (1989). Prejudice and stereotypes: Their automatic and controlled components. *Journal of Personality and Social Psychology*, *56*, 5–18.

Devine, P. G., Plant, E. A., Amodio, D. M., Harmon-Jones, E., & Vance, S. L. (2002). The regulation of explicit and implicit race bias: The role of motivations to respond without prejudice. *Journal of Personality and Social Psychology*, *82*, 835–848.

Dickter, C. L. & Bartholow, B. D. (2007). Racial ingroup and outgroup attention biases revealed by event-related brain potentials. *Social Cognitive and Affective Neuroscience*, *2*, 189–198.

Dovidio, J., Kawakami, K., Johnson, C., Johnson, B., & Howard, A. (1997). On the nature of prejudice: Automatic and controlled processes. *Journal of Experimental Social Psychology*, *33*, 510–540.

Dovidio, J. F., Pearson, A. R., & Orr, P. (2008). Social psychology and neuroscience: Strange bedfellows or a healthy marriage. *Group Processes & Intergroup Relations*, *11*, 247–263.

Eberhardt, J. L. (2005). Imaging race. *American Psychologist*, *60*, 181–190.

Eberhardt, J. L., Goff, P. A., Purdie, V. J., & Davies, P. G. (2004). Seeing black: Race, crime, and visual processing. *Journal of Personality and Social Psychology*, *87*, 876–963.

Fazio, R. H., Jackson, J. R., Dunton, B. C., & Williams, C. J. (1995). An individual difference measure of motivation to control prejudiced reactions. *Personality and Social Psychology Bulletin*, *23*, 316–326.

Fuster, J. M. (2001). The prefrontal cortex-An update: Time is of the essence. *Neuron*, *2*, 319–333.

Gabrieli, J. D. (1998). Cognitive neuroscience of human memory. *Annual Review of Psychology*, *49*, 87–115.

Gawronski, B. & Bodenhausen, G. V. (2006). Associative and propositional processes in evaluation: An integrative review of implicit and explicit attitude change. *Psychological Bulletin*, *132*, 692–731.

Gazzaley, A., Rissman, J., Cooney, J. W., Rutman, A., Seibert, T., Clapp, W., & D'Esposito, M. (2007). Functional interactions between prefrontal and visual association cortex contribute to top-down modulation of visual processing. *Cerebral Cortex. 17*, 125–135.

Gazzaniga, M. S. (2004). *The cognitive neurosciences III*. Cambridge, MA: MIT Press.

Ghashghaei, H. T. & Barbas, H. (2002). Pathways for emotions: Interactions of prefrontal and anterior temporal pathways in the amygdala of the rhesus monkey. *Neuroscience*, *115*, 1261–1279.

Ghashghaei, H. T., Hilgetag, C. C., & Barbas, H. (2007). Sequence of information processing for emotions based on the anatomic dialogue between prefrontal cortex and amygdala. *Neuroimage*, *34*, 905–923.

Gilbert, D. T. & Hixon, J. G. (1991). The trouble of thinking: Activation and application of stereotypic beliefs. *Journal of Personality and Social Psychology*, *60*, 509–517.

Golby, A. J., Gabrieli, J. D. E., Chiao, J. Y., Eberhardt, J. L. (2001). Differential fusiform responses to same- and other-race faces. *Nature Neuroscience*, *4*, 845–850.

Greenwald, A. G. & Banaji, M. R. (1995). Implicit social cognition. *Psychological Review*, *102*, 4–27.

Gross, J. J. & Levenson, R. W. (1993). Emotional suppression: Physiology, self-report, and expressive behavior. *Journal of Personality and Social Psychology*, *64*, 970–986.

Harmon-Jones, E. (2003). Clarifying the emotive functions of asymmetrical frontal cortical activity. *Psychophysiology*, *40*, 838–848.

Hugenberg, K. & Bodenhausen, G. V. (2003). Facing prejudice: Implicit prejudice and the perception of facial threat. *Psychological Science*, *14*, 640–643.

Ito, T. A. & Urland, G. R. (2003). Race and gender on the brain: Electrocortical measures of attention to the race and gender of multiply categorizable individuals. *Journal of Personality and Social Psychology*, *85*(4), 616–662.

Ito, T. A. & Urland, G. R. (2005). The influence of processing objectives on the perception of faces: An ERP study of race and gender perception. *Cognitive, Affective, and Behavioral Neuroscience*, *5*, 21–36.

James, M. S., Johnstone, S. J., & Hayward, W. G. (2001). Event-related potentials, configural encoding and feature-based encoding in face recognition. *Journal of Psychophysiology*, *15*, 275–285.

Killcross, A. S., Robbins, T. W., & Everitt, B. J. (1997). Different types of fear conditioned behavior mediated by separate nuclei in amygdala. *Nature*, *388*, 377–380.

Kubota, J. T. & Ito, T. A. (2007). Multiple cues in social perception: The time course of processing race and facial expression. *Journal of Experimental Social Psychology*, *43*, 738–752.

LeDoux, J. E. (1992). Emotion and the amygdala. In J. P. Aggleton (Ed.), *The amygdala: Neurobiological aspects of emotion, memory, and mental dysfunction* (pp. 339–351). New York: Wiley-Liss.

LeDoux, J. E. (1996). *The emotional brain: The mysterious underpinnings of emotional life*. New York: Simon & Schuster.

Lieberman, M. D., Hariri, A., Jarcho, J. M., Eisenberger, N. I., & Bookheimer, S. Y. (2005). An fMRI investigation of race-related amygdala activity in African-American and Caucasian-American individuals. *Nature Neuroscience*, *8*, 720–722.

Logan, G. D. & Cowan, W. B. (1984). On the ability to inhibit thought and action: A theory of an act of control. *Psychological Review*, *91*, 295–327.

Mackie, D.M. & Smith, E.R. (1998). Intergroup relations: Insights from a theoretically integrative approach. *Psychological Review*, *105*, 499–529.

Macrae, C. N., Bodenhausen, G. V., & Milne, A. B. (1995). The dissection of selection in person perception: Inhibitory processes in social stereotyping. *Journal of Personality and Social Psychology*, *69*, 397–407.

Martin, A. (2007). The representation of object concepts in the brain. *Annual Review of Psychology*, *58*, 25–45.

Medalla, M., Lera, P., Feinberg, M., & Barbas, H. (2007). Specificity in inhibitory systems associated with prefrontal pathways to temporal cortex in primates. *Cerebral Cortex*, *17*, 136–150.

Mendoza, S. A., Gollwitzer, P. M., & Amodio, D. M. (2010). Reducing the Expression of Implicit Stereotypes: Reflexive Control through Implementation Intentions. *Personality and Social Psychology Bulletin*, 36, 512–523.

Middleton, F. A. & Strick, P. L. (2000). Basal ganglia and cerebellar loops: Motor and cognitive circuits. *Brain Research Reviews*, *31*, 236–250.

Milad, M. R. & Quirk, G. J. (2002). Neurons in medial prefrontal cortex signal memory for fear extinction. *Nature*, *420*, 70–74.

Miller, E. K. & Cohen, J. D. (2001). An integrative theory of prefrontal cortex function. *Annual Review of Neuroscience*, *24*, 167–202.

Monteith, M. J. (1993). Self-regulation of prejudiced responses: Implications for progress in prejudice reduction efforts. *Journal of Personality and Social Psychology*, *65*, 469–485.

Monteith, M. J., Ashburn-Nardo, L., Voils, C. I., & Czopp, A. M. (2002). Putting the brakes on prejudice: On the development and operation of cues for control. *Journal of Personality and Social Psychology*, *83*, 1029–1050.

Monteith, M. J., Devine, P. G., & Zuwerink, J. R. (1993). Self-directed versus other-directed affect as a consequence of prejudice-related discrepancies. *Journal of Personality and Social Psychology*, *64*, 198–210.

Monteith, M. J., Sherman, J. W., & Devine, P. G. (1998). Suppression as a stereotype control strategy. *Personality and Social Psychology Review, 2*, 63–82.

Nakahara, K., Adachi, Y., Osada, T., & Miyashita, Y. (2007). Exploring the neural basis of cognition: Multi-modal links between human fMRI and macaque neurophysiology. *Trends in Cognitive Sciences, 11*, 84–92.

Norman, D. & Shallice, T. (1986). Attention to action: Willed and automatic control of behavior. In R. Davidson, G. Schwartz, and D. Shapiro, (Eds.) *Consciousness and self-regulation: Advances in research and theory*, Vol. 4 (pp. 1–18). New York: Plenum.

Ochsner, K. N., Bunge, S. A., Gross, J. J., & Gabrieli, J. D. E. (2002). Rethinking feelings: An fMRI study of the cognitive regulation of emotion. *Journal of Cognitive Neuroscience, 14*, 1215–1299.

Ofan, R. H., Rubin, N., Amodio, D. M., (in press). Seeing race: N170 responses to race and their relation to automatic racial attitudes and controlled processing. *Journal of Cognitive Neuroscience.*

Paré, D. & Smith, Y. (1993). The intercalated cell masses project to the central and medial nuclei of the amygdala in cats. *Neuroscience, 57*, 1077–1090.

Passingham, R. (1993). *The frontal lobes and voluntary action.* Oxford, UK: Oxford University Press.

Payne, B. K. (2001). Prejudice and perception: The role of automatic and controlled processes in misperceiving a weapon. *Journal of Personality and Social Psychology, 81*, 181–192.

Payne, B. K. (2005). Conceptualizing control in social cognition: How executive functioning modulates the expression of automatic stereotyping. *Journal of Personality and Social Psychology, 89*, 488–503.

Petersen, S. E., Fox, P. T., Posner, M. I., Mintun, M., & Raichle, M. E. (1988). Positron emission tomographic studies of the cortical anatomy of single-word processing. *Nature, 331*, 585–589.

Petrides, M. & Pandya, D. N. in *Handbook of Neuropsychology*, Vol. 9 (ed. Grafman, J.) 17–58 (Elsevier, Amsterdam, 1994).

Petrides, M. & Pandya, D.N. (2002). Comparative architectonic analysis of the human and the macaque ventrolateral prefrontal cortex and corticocortical connection patterns in the monkey. *European Journal of Neuroscience, 16*, 291–310.

Phelps, E. A., O'Connor, K. J., Cunningham, W. A., Funayama, E. S., Gatenby J. C., Gore, J. C., et al. (2000). Performance on indirect measures of race evaluation predicts amygdala activation. *Journal of Cognitive Neuroscience, 12*, 729–738.

Plant, E. A. & Devine, P. G. (1998). Internal and external motivation to respond without prejudice. *Journal of Personality and Social Psychology, 75*, 811–832.

Richeson, J. A., Baird, A. A., Gordon, H. L., Heatherton, T. F., Wyland, C. L., Trawalter, S., et al. (2003). An fMRI examination of the impact of interracial contact on executive function. *Nature Neuroscience, 6*, 1323–1328.

Salomons, T. V., Johnstone, T., Backonja, M. M., Shackman, A. J. & Davidson, R. J. (2007). Individual differences in the effects of perceived controllability on pain perception: Critical role of the prefrontal cortex. *Journal of Cognitive Neuroscience, 19*, 993–1003.

Schuman, H., Steeh, C., Bobo, L., & Krysan, M. (1997). *Racial attitudes in America: Trends and interpretations.* Cambridge, MA: Harvard University Press.

Stanley, D., Phelps, E. A., & Banaji, M. (2008). The neural basis of implicit attitudes. *Current Directions in Psychological Science, 17*(2), 164–170.

Stefanacci, L. & Amaral, D. G. (2002). Some observations on cortical inputs to the macaque monkey amygdala: An anterograde tracing study. *Journal of Comparative Neurology, 451*, 301–323.

Thompson-Schill, S. L. (2003). Neuroimaging studies of semantic memory: inferring "how" from "where." *Neuropsychologia, 41*, 280–292.

van Peer, J. M., Roelofs, K., Rotteveel, M., van Dijk, J. G., Spinhoven, P., & Ridderinkhof, K. R., (2007). The effects of cortisol administration on approach avoidance behavior: An event-related potential study. *Biological Psychology, 76*, 135–146.

van Reekum, C. M., Johnstone, T., Urry, H. L., Thurow, M. E., Schaefer, H. S., Alexander, A. L., et al. (2007). Gaze fixations predict brain activation during the voluntary regulation of picture-induced negative affect. *Neuroimage, 36*, 1041–1055.

Wager, T. D., Rilling, J. K., Smith, E. E., Sokolik, A., Casey, K. L., Davidson, R. J., et al. (2004). Placebo-induced changes in fMRI in the anticipation and experience of pain. *Science, 303*, 1162–1167.

Wager, T. D., Davidson, M., Hughes, B. L., Lindquist, M. A., & Ochsner, K. N. (2008). Prefrontal-subcortical pathways mediating successful emotion regulation. *Neuron, 59*, 1037–1050.

Wagner, A. D., Maril, A., Bjork, R. A., & Schacter, D. L. (2001). Prefrontal contributions to executive control: fMRI evidence for functional distinctions within lateral prefrontal cortex. *NeuroImage, 14*, 1337–1347.

Walker, P. M., Silvert, L., Hewstone, M., & Nobre, A. C. (2008). Social contact and other-race face processing in the human brain. *Social Cognitive and Affective Neuroscience, 3*, 16–25.

Wegner, D. M. (1994). Ironic processes of mental control. *Psychological Review, 101*, 34–52.

Whalen, P. J. (1998). Fear, vigilance, and ambiguity: Initial neuroimaging studies of the human amygdala. *Current Directions in Psychological Science, 7*, 177–188.

Wheeler, M. E. & Fiske, S. T. (2005). Controlling racial prejudice: Social-cognitive goals affect amygdala and stereotype activation. *Psychological Science, 16*, 56–63.

Willadsen-Jensen, E. C. & Ito, T. A. (2006). Ambiguity and the timecourse of racial perception. *Social Cognition, 24*, 580–606.

Willadsen-Jensen, E. C. & Ito, T. A. (2008). A foot in both worlds: Asian Americans' perceptions of Asian, White, and racially ambiguous faces. *Group Processes and Interpersonal Relations, 11*, 182–200.

Yin, H. H. & Knowlton, B. J (2006). The role of the basal ganglia in habit formation. *Nature Reviews Neuroscience, 7*, 464–476.

Zikopoulos, B. & Barbas, H. (2006) Prefrontal projections to the thalamic reticular nucleus form a unique circuit for attentional mechanisms. *Journal of Neuroscience, 26*, 7348–7361.

Cultural Neuroscience: Visualizing Culture-Gene Influences on Brain Function

Joan Y. Chiao

Abstract

This chapter presents an introduction to cultural neuroscience. Cultural neuroscience is an emerging research discipline that investigates cultural variation in psychological, neural, and genomic processes as a means of articulating the bidirectional relationship of these processes and their emergent properties. Research in cultural neuroscience is motivated by two intriguing questions of human nature: How do cultural traits (e.g., values, beliefs, practices) shape neurobiology (e.g., genetic and neural processes) and behavior; and how do neurobiological mechanisms (e.g., genetic and neural processes) facilitate the emergence and transmission of cultural traits?

Keywords: cultural neuroscience, transcultural neuroimaging, cultural psychology, neuroscience, individualism-collectivism, population genetics, neurogenetics, culture-gene coevolution, social neuroscience, neuroanthropology, gene-environment interaction

Introduction

The nature and scope of cultural diversity in human behavior is breathtakingly unparalleled throughout the animal kingdom. With the exception of a few primitive cultural traits shared with nonhuman primate societies (Tomasello et al., 2005; Whiten et al., 2007), humans demonstrate a rare level of cultural competence, which has subsequently led to the expansion of and control over their ecological niche. In addition to nonverbal gestures, the uniquely human ability to create and manipulate symbolic systems, such as language and numbers, has further facilitated the continuity and evolution of cultural traits across successive generations. Even more remarkably, humans have shown the ability to invent and transmit not only one, but several distinct kinds of culturally specific symbolic and nonsymbolic systems over the course of human evolution.

It is perhaps not surprising then that the nature and origin of human cultural diversity has been a rich source of intellectual curiosity for scholars since the first millennium. Early in the 7th century, Isidore of Seville observed in one of the earliest written encyclopedias, *Etymologiae,* that humans vary both in physical appearance and ways of thinking (Jahoda, 2002). Centuries later, philosophers, such as Descartes and Locke, renewed debate on the origin of human diversity in thinking and behavior. During the Age of Enlightenment, the study of human diversity accelerated with the emergence of two enormously influential, but divergent, schools of thought: evolutionary biology and modern anthropology. Darwin's theory of evolution led to the development of the field of evolutionary biology, which explained diversity in the biological world as emerging from the universal process of natural selection. By contrast, pioneering anthropologists, such as Franz Boas and Margaret Mead, favored scientific approaches to culture that emphasized relativism whereby human cultures were best understood on their own terms, rather than as products of transparent universal laws, including those of a biological nature (Lewis, 2001).

Following Darwin and Boas, the scientific study of biology and culture largely continued to diverge, even with the emergence of nexus fields, such as psychology, which would appear well positioned to formally integrate theory and methods across the social and natural sciences. Evolutionary psychologists, for instance, argue that the human mind and behavior are best understood as adaptations or functional products of natural selection and embrace neuroscience as a means uncovering universal neural circuitry specialized for solving different adaptive problems (Barkow, Cosmides, & Tooby 1992). Widely adopted by modern cognitive neuroscientists, this evolutionary approach to the study of the human brain has proved enormously fruitful for generating sound hypotheses and evidence for how discrete brain structures map onto distinct kinds of adaptive psychological functions (Caramazza & Shelton, 1998; Dehaene & Cohen, 2007; Kanwisher, Chun, & McDermott, 1997). However, this evolutionary emphasis has also steered much scientific attention within cognitive neuroscience towards the study of universal, rather than culturally specified, neural mechanisms and behavior. By contrast, cultural psychologists have largely focused on investigating the mutual constitution of culture and the human mind and have convincingly constructed theories and discovered evidence that culture shapes nearly every facet of psychology and behavior (Kitayama & Cohen, 2007). However,

as a consequence, cultural psychologists have spent less time thinking about how to meaningfully integrate theories of human culture with theories of human evolution and how cultural values, practices, and beliefs shape not only mental, but also neurobiological, processes.

The past century has witnessed a number of theoretical attempts within psychology to integrate cultural and neurobiological approaches in the study of the human mind and behavior. For instance, prominent developmental psychologists, such as D'Arcy Thompson and C. Waddington, introduced early notions of probabilistic epigenesis, whereby humans come into the world with sets of possible developmental trajectories that are then pursued or not over the course of the lifespan as a result of interactions with the cultural environment (Johnson, 1997). More recently, biocultural co-constructivism theory has emerged as a way of explaining how developmental trajectories unfold via interactions between genetic and cultural factors, and importantly, how neural plasticity may later both developmental trajectories and the end state (Li, 2003).

Culture-gene coevolution, or dual inheritance theory, stands as a particularly powerful and compelling theoretical lens for integrating the study of human culture and biology (Figure 49.1). Culture-gene coevolutionary theory proposes explaining the human mind and brain as a byproduct of two kinds of evolutionary forces: genetic and cultural (Boyd & Richerson, 1985; Cavalli-Sforza & Feldman, 1981; Lumsden & Wilson, 1981). Conventional evolutionary biology theory posits that organisms adapt to their environment and over time exhibit favorable traits or characteristics that best enable them to survive and reproduce in their given environment, through the process of natural selection (Darwin, 1859).

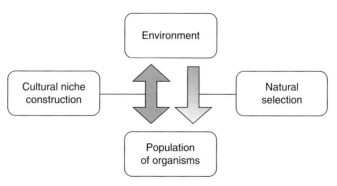

Fig. 49.1 Model of two complementary evolutionary processes, natural selection and cultural niche construction, by which the environment exerts selective pressure on organisms and organisms modify their environment in order to alter selection pressures exerted on them. Culture-gene coevolutionary theory further asserts that both genes and cultural traits may undergo selection pressure.

The concept of natural selection has been enormously influential to the study of human behavior, particularly in evolutionary psychology, which has emphasized that much of human behavior arises as a byproduct of adaptive mechanisms in the mind and brain (Barkow, Cosmides, & Tooby 1992). More recently, dual inheritance theory of human behavior proposes that akin to biological traits, cultural traits are adaptive, evolve, and influence the social and physical environments under which genetic selection operates (Boyd & Richerson, 1985). Importantly, culture-gene coevoluationary theory posits that adaptive neural machinery may arise not only via pressures of natural selection but also cultural selection. That is, neural mechanisms that facilitate the successful storage and transmission of cultural values, practices, and beliefs are also likely to endure over successive generations due to their adaptive function (Boyd & Richerson, 1985). Hence, any comprehensive understanding of the human brain and its adaptive function requires examination of how neural mechanisms emerge as a byproduct of both cultural and genetic forces.

Despite rich theoretical motivation for studying culture-biology interactions within the human brain, precise empirical demonstrations and theoretical models of bidirectional relationship between cultural and biological mechanisms (e.g., culture-gene; culture-brain; culture-brain-gene) have largely remained elusive. A number of factors have contributed to the current knowledge gap. First, empirical studies of neural substrates underlying human emotion and cognition have typically been informed first by empirical evidence in nonhuman animals (Davidson & Sutton, 1995; Gazzaniga, Ivry, Mangun, 2002). However, since cultural competence is predominantly a human achievement, it is not possible for behavioral neuroscience models of culture to inform human neuroscience investigations of culture. Second, until recently, researchers have lacked technology to study these questions in humans. For instance, the field of human neuroimaging began to flourish only within the past two decades (Figure 49.2a). Third, there is typically a lack of awareness amongst researchers about the growing research bias in the populations that they study (Arnett, 2008). Within the field of psychology, 95% of psychological samples come from countries with only 12% of the world's population (Arnett, 2008). Within the field of human neuroimaging alone, 90% of peer-reviewed neuroimaging studies come from Western countries (Figure 49.2b). Hence, our current state of knowledge of mind-brain mappings is largely restricted to scientific observations made of people living within Western industrialized nations, leaving a large empirical gap in our understanding of how diverse cultural environments affect the human mind, brain and behavior.

Cultural Neuroscience: An Overview

Cultural neuroscience is an emerging research discipline that investigates cultural variation in psychological, neural, and genomic processes as a means of articulating the bidirectional relationship of these processes and their emergent properties (Figure 49.3). Research in cultural neuroscience is

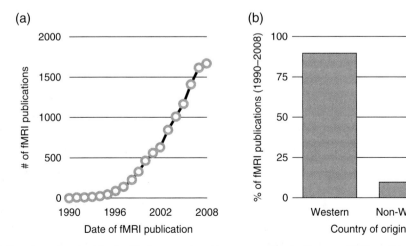

Fig. 49.2 Growth trends and publication bias in peer-reviewed human neuroimaging literature. (a) Graph illustrating the growth in peer-reviewed human neuroimaging studies from 1990–2008; (b) Graph illustrating the publication bias within the human neuroimaging literature whereby the vast majority (~90%) of publications to date originate from a Western country.

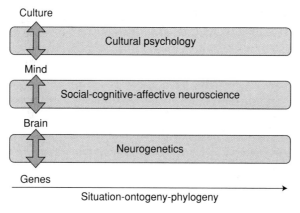

Fig. 49.3 Illustration of the cultural neuroscience framework, integrating theory from cultural psychology, social/cognitive/affective neuroscience and neurogenetics.

motivated by two intriguing questions of human nature: How do cultural traits (e.g., values, beliefs, practices) shape neurobiology (e.g., genetic and neural processes) and behavior and how do neurobiological mechanisms (e.g., genetic and neural processes) facilitate the emergence and transmission of cultural traits?

The idea that complex behavior results from the dynamic interaction of genes and cultural environment is not new (Johnson, 1997; Li, 2003; Caspi & Moffitt, 2007); however, cultural neuroscience represents a novel empirical approach to demonstrating bidirectional interactions between culture and biology by integrating theory and methods from cultural psychology (Kitayama & Cohen, 2007), neuroscience (Gazzaniga, Ivry & Mangun, 2002), and neurogenetics (Canli & Lesch, 2006; Green, et al., 2008, Hariri, Drabant, Weinberger, 2006). Similar to other interdisciplinary fields such as social neuroscience (Cacioppo, Berntson, Sheridan, McClintock, 2000) or social cognitive neuroscience (Ochsner & Lieberman, 2001), affective neuroscience (Davidson & Sutton, 1995) and neuroeconomics (Glimcher, Camerer, Poldrack, Fehr, 2008), cultural neuroscience aims to explain a given mental phenomenon in terms of a synergistic product of mental, neural, and genetic events. Cultural neuroscience shares overlapping research goals with social neuroscience, in particular, as understanding how neurobiological mechanisms facilitate cultural transmission involves investigating primary social processes that enable humans to learn from one another, such as imitative learning. However, cultural neuroscience is also unique from related disciplines in that it focuses explicitly on ways that mental and neural events vary as a function

of culture traits (e.g., values, practices and beliefs) in some meaningful way. Additionally, cultural neuroscience illustrates how cultural traits may alter neurobiological and psychological processes beyond those that facilitate social experience and behavior, such as perception and cognition.

There are at least three reasons why understanding cultural and genetic influences on brain function likely holds the key to articulating better psychological theory. First, a plethora of evidence from cultural psychology demonstrates that culture influences psychological processes and behavior (Kitayama & Cohen, 2007). To the extent that human behavior results from neural activity, cultural variation in behavior likely emerges from cultural variation in neural mechanisms underlying these behaviors. Second, cultural variation in neural mechanisms may exist even in the absence of cultural variation at the behavioral or genetic level. That is, people living in different cultural environments may develop distinct neural mechanisms that underlie the same observable behavior or recruit the same neural mechanism to varying extents during a given task. Third, population variation in the genome exists, albeit on a much smaller scale relative to individual variation, and 70% of genes express themselves in the brain (Hariri, Drabant, & Weinberger, 2006). This population variation in allelic frequency in functional polymorphisms, such as those that regulate neural activity, may exert influence on subsequent mental processes and behavior. To the extent that behavior arises from neural events and both cultural and genetic factors influence neural events, a comprehensive understanding of the nature of the human mind and behavior is impoverished without a theoretical and empirical approach that incorporates these multiple levels of analyses.

Theory and Methods in Cultural Neuroscience

The current ability to discover cultural variation across multiple levels of analysis is now possible in ways never previously imagined, due in large part, to fortuitous theoretical and methodological advances in three distinct fields: cultural psychology, brain sciences, and neurogenetics (Figures 49.3 and 49.4). In recent years, cultural psychology has made major advances in identifying cultural traits that characterize the diversity in social groups around the world as well as articulating the criteria for creating culturally appropriate behavioral measures that ensure the psychological phenomena of interest is testable in people of all cultures (Kitayama & Cohen, 2007; Norenzayan & Heine, 2005). Human neuroscience, including cognitive, social, and affective neuroscience, has revolutionized the study of the mind and brain by developing an arsenal of techniques for mapping neural processes to psychological processes at varying degrees of spatial and temporal resolution (Gazzaniga, Ivry, & Mangun, 2002; Handy, 2005; Heeger & Rees, 2002). Molecular biology has witnessed major transformations in the scope of data and techniques now available for understanding the structure and function of the human genome. From techniques for studying the association between single genes and behavior to genome-wide maps that assess the association of the entire genome to a given behavior, the development of molecular biology techniques has led to an explosion of possible ways for mapping genes to neural, mental,

and cultural processes. Taken together, the convergence of these tools enables unprecedented ability to investigate the mutual constitution of genes, brain, mind, and culture.

Cultural Psychology

Theory and methods of cultural psychology comprise the first component of the cultural neuroscience toolbox. First, cultural psychologists have developed a rich set of theoretical constructs that specify what kinds of cultural values, practices and beliefs reliably impact human behavior. For instance, Hofstede (2001) proposed that cultures could be distinguished according to five cultural dimensions: *individualism-collectivism, uncertainty avoidance, power distance, long-term/short-term orientation, and masculinity/femininity.* The cultural dimension of *individualism-collectivism*, in particular, has been shown to reliably affect a wide variety of human mental processes at a behavioral level, including self-concept, motivation, perception, emotion, and cognition (Markus & Kitayama, 1991; Triandis, 1995). Individualism refers to when individuals construe themselves as separate and autonomous from each other, whereas collectivism refers to when individuals construe themselves as highly interconnected and defined by their relations and social context. Another potent cultural construct is *holistic versus analytic cognition,* a dimension thought to characterize differences in thinking styles between Westerners and East Asians. East Asians are thought to primarily engage in holistic cognition, attending to the entire field of a scene and relying on dialectical reasoning, whereas Westerners have been shown to primarily exhibit analytic cognition, attending to objects more than their context and

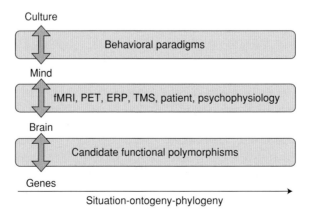

Fig. 49.4 Illustration of the cultural neuroscience toolbox, integrating methods from cultural psychology, social/cognitive/affective neuroscience, and population genotyping.

using rules, such as formal logic, to understand reason about themselves and the world (Nisbett, Peng, Choi, & Norenzayan, 2001). Finally, *socioeconomic status or social class* has been shown to serve as an important cultural lens shaping one's sense of free will, choice, and related behaviors (Snibbe & Markus, 2005; Savani, Markus, & Conner, 2008). These cultural dimensions provide a core theoretical foundation from which cultural neuroscientists can formulate novel hypotheses about how and why culture may influence brain functioning. Formulating sound hypotheses about how cultural traits modulates neural mechanisms a priori is critical to building better theories about how culture shapes neural systems and why as well as ensuring that evidence of cultural variation in neural systems is not misinterpreted as evidence for essentialist theories of race (No et al., 2008).

Second, cultural psychologists have developed a number of novel behavioral methods for investigating cultural influences on behavior. First, a popular and effective way of measuring cultural traits is via *behavioral surveys*. Indeed, a lion's share of prior cultural psychological research has been focused on creation and validation of cultural value surveys, such as those used to measure individualism and collectivism (Singelis, 1994). Importantly, cultural psychologists have discovered that people living in diverse cultural value systems demonstrate different types of response biases when completing behavioral surveys. For instance, collectivists tend to show moderacy biases, such that they respond to items using the midpoint of Likert scales, whereas individualists tend to show extremity biases, such that they typically respond to items using the endpoints of Likert scales (Heine, 2008). Understanding when and how these response biases may emerge is critical for cultural neuroscientists wishing to map cultural variation in behavior to cultural variation in neural functioning. Another important cultural psychological method is *situational sampling*. One of the hardest challenges in designing cross-cultural experiments is in ensuring that one's experimental stimuli have the intended meaning across cultures. Situational sampling refers to a technique for generating experimental stimuli that are optimized to reveal cultural variation in behavior. In experiments utilizing situational sampling, researchers ask participants from the two or more cultures of interest to generate examples of the phenomenon of interest. Then, these examples are used as stimuli in a subsequent experiment to test cultural variation in responses to the culturally specific stimuli (Heine, 2008).

A third cultural psychology technique important for conducting cultural neuroscience research is *cultural priming* (Hong et al., 2000; Oyserman & Lee, 2008). Often, cross-cultural psychologists conceptualize nation or race as a proxy for culture; however, such gross characterizations of culture are impoverished as they fail to capture the individual variability within cultures, the dynamic nature of culture, and the fact that an individual can possess awareness of and appreciation for more than one cultural system simultaneously. To address these important issues, cultural psychologists have developed cultural priming techniques to directly manipulate cultural value systems within mono- and multi-cultural individuals and to show how cultural values dynamically shape behavior. Cultural priming involves temporarily heightening individuals' awareness of a given cultural value system through either explicit (e.g., writing an essay about individualism) or implicit means (e.g., search for synonyms of individualism in a word search). A number of different types of cultural priming techniques have been successfully used to elicit cultural variation in a range of behavioral processes. Notably, prior research has revealed that not all cultural priming techniques have equivalent influence across domains; that is, some cultural priming methods are more likely to trigger cultural variation in social relative to cognitive processes and vice versa (Oyserman & Lee, 2008). Hence, when adopting cultural priming to study the direct influence of cultural values on neural mechanisms, it is important to select a cultural priming technique that is task-appropriate.

Human Neuroscience

Cognitive neuroscience theory and methods comprise the second component of the cultural neuroscience toolbox. Recent decades have brought an unprecedented array of tools for directly and indirectly measuring human brain activity and relating this brain activity to behavior. There are several neuroscience tools that psychologists can use to map neural structure to mental function such as the following: functional magnetic resonance imaging (fMRI), positron emission topography (PET), transcranial magnetic stimulation (TMS), magnetoencephalography (MEG), event-related potentials (ERP), and lesion studies. Each tool has its strengths and weaknesses, particularly when comparing each tool's spatial and temporal resolution. Neuroimaging techniques, such as fMRI and PET, record indirect neural activity and have very good spatial resolution (mm^3), but poor temporal resolution (seconds), relative to electrophysiological techniques such as ERP and EEG. By contrast, ERP and EEG record neural activity directly below the scalp and thus have excellent temporal resolution (milliseconds), but lack high spatial resolution. Newer hybrid techniques, such as MEG, combine the advantages of both brain imaging and electrophysiological techniques and it is likely that as medical technology improves, so too will our ability to accurately record neural activity while awake humans perform mental tasks.

In addition to taking into consideration the spatial and temporal resolution of human neuroscience techniques, it is equally important to consider what kinds of questions can be addressed with each technique, and what questions remain unaddressed given the limitations of current methodologies. TMS and lesion studies enable researchers to address which brain regions are necessary for a given mental function, while brain imaging and electrophysiology provide tools for associating a given neural structure or processes to a given mental function. To date, most cultural neuroscience research has utilized cross-cultural or transcultural neuroimaging to demonstrate cultural variation in the magnitude of neural response to a given stimuli (Chiao & Ambady, 2007; Han & Northoff, 2008; Park & Gutchess, 2006). However, future research may also include novel methodologies, such as cross-cultural TMS or lesion studies, that will be able to address novel questions such as whether or not a given brain region is necessary for a given mental function in one culture, but not another.

Neurogenetics

The theory and methods from neurogenetics comprise the third component of the cultural neuroscience toolbox. Genes are the fundamental physical and functional unit of heredity. Genes substantially influence every level of human biology, including regulating neurotransmission within the brain. Recent advances in neurogenetics have led to major advances in our understanding of how genes regulate brain mechanisms underlying cognitive (Green et al., 2008), emotional (Hariri & Weinberger, 2001), and social behavior (Canli & Lesch, 2008).

Cultural variation is evident in the human genome for a number of reasons, albeit on a much smaller scale relative to individual genetic variation. Cultural variation in allelic frequencies of a given gene may occur due to number of evolutionary processes, such as natural selection and genetic drift. Natural selection may lead to differential frequency of gene variants when certain genetic variants confer reproductive advantages over another. Genetic drift may also result in changes to allele frequencies within populations over time, but in a more random manner. For instance, founder effects, a type of genetic drift, can lead to a loss of genetic variation when a new population is established by a very small number of individuals from a larger population.

Due to their robust allelic variation across cultures, two genes are likely to play a key role in future cultural neuroscience research: the serotonin transporter polymorphism (5-HTTLPR) and dopamine D4 receptor (DRD4) exon III polymorphism. The 5-HTTLPR consists of a 44-base pair insertion or deletion, generating either a long (l) or a short (s) allele. Evidence from behavioral genetics indicates that the S allele of the serotonin transporter gene (5-HTTLPR) is associated with increased negative emotion, including heightened anxiety (Munafo, Clark, & Flint, 2005; Sen, Burmeister, & Ghosh, 2004), harm avoidance (Munafo et al, 2005), fear conditioning (Londsforf et al, in press), attentional bias to negative information (Beevers, Gibb, McGeary, & Miller, 2007) as well as increased risk for depression in the presence of environmental risk factors (Caspi et al., 2003; Taylor et al, 2006; Uher & McGuffin 2008, see also Munafo, Durrant, Lewis, & Flint, 2009). In particular, exposure to chronic life stress, such as interpersonal conflict, loss, or threat, is considered a well-known environmental risk factor for depression in S allele carriers of the 5-HTT (Caspi et al., 2002). The S allele of the 5-HTTLPR is extremely prevalent in East Asian populations (e.g., 70–80% s carriers) relative to other nations (e.g., 50% or less S carriers) (Chiao & Blizinsky, in press). The dopamine D4 receptor (DRD4) exon III polymorphism has been linked to novelty seeking and pathological gambling (Chen et al, 1999). Individuals with the 7-repeat allele have higher novelty seeking scores than those with other DRD4 variants (Chen et al., 1999). The 7-repeat allele is extremely prevalent in South American Indian populations (e.g., 70–80% 7-repeat carriers), but extremely rare in East Asian populations (e.g., < 1% 7-repeat carriers) (Chen et al., 1999).

Importantly, genes not only regulate brain mechanisms and behavior, but also influence and are influenced by cultural selection (Boyd & Richerson, 1985). According to culture-gene coevolutionary theory, cultural traits can possess evolutionary advantages. For instance, cultural traits, such as individualism and collectivism (Fincher et al., 2008), may serve adaptive functions and thus, culturally consistent phenotypes may become selected for over successive generations, leading to population variation in allelic frequencies for certain genes. Additionally, a central claim of culture-gene coevolutionary theory is that once cultural traits are adaptive, it is likely that genetic selection causes refinement of the cognitive and neural architecture responsible for the storage and transmission of those cultural capacities (Boyd & Richerson 1985). Hence, these evolutionary processes of cultural and genetic selection likely result in cultural variation in psychological and neural processes, which serve as endophenotypes or intermediate phenotypes of the cultural and genetic traits.

A central goal for cultural neuroscience research is to understand how these dual forces of cultural and genetic selection shape brain function and behavior. The field of neurogenetics provides the empirical means by which cultural neuroscientists can investigate similarities and differences in how genes regulate human brain function across cultures. More specifically, neurogenetics research enables cultural neuroscientists to identify neural endophenotypes or brain regions that may be influenced by culture-gene coevolutionary forces. For example, recent imaging genetics research has shown that people who carry the s allele of the *5-HTTLPR* exhibit greater amygdala response to emotional stimuli (Hariri et al., 2002) which is likely due to increased amygdala resting activation (Canli et al., 2005) and decreased functional coupling between the amygdala and subgenal cingulate gyrus (Pezawas et al., 2005), relative to individuals carrying the L allele. Future research in cultural neuroscience may examine the effect of cultural and genetic selection on amygdala response and emotional behavior. More broadly, by converging theory and methods from neurogenetics and cultural psychology, cultural neuroscientists are equipped to generate and test novel hypotheses not only about how genes or culture independently influence brain function, but also how genes and culture interact and mutually shape brain function across the lifespan and across successive generations.

Kinds of Cultural Influences on Brain Function: Neuronal Recycling, Neuroplasticity and Neurovariation

An important challenge for cultural neuroscience is to reconcile various theories for how culture influences brain function and to situate these seemingly disparate explanations within a parsimonious theoretical context. Convergent research in cognitive and cultural neuroscience to date has led to the emergence of three distinct theories for mechanisms by which culture influences brain function: *neuronal recycling, neuroplasticity, and neurovariation*. Representing the viewpoint of strong universalism in brain function, *neuronal recycling theory* (Dehaene & Cohen, 2007) posits that cultural competencies arise from evolutionarily ancient cortical maps that provide strong anatomical and connectional constraints evident from early infancy and bias subsequent learning. Basic psychological functions and even modern cultural competencies whose recent emergence is not likely due to natural selection pressures, such as reading and arithmetic, are associated with one or more specific cortical maps that are largely preserved or universal across individuals and cultures. One example of neuronal recycling is the visual word form area (VWFA). The VWFA is a cortical area of the left occipitotemporal sulcus that responds preferentially to linguistic symbols or written characters relative to other kinds complex visual stimuli, such as faces and houses, across diverse languages, including English, Japanese, and Chinese (Dehaene & Cohen, 2007). This locational and functional invariance of VWFA across cultures and languages provides strong evidence that cultural competencies, such as reading, arise from evolutionary preserved neural architecture.

The VWFA is just one of now many examples (e.g., fusiform face area (FFA) or intraparietal sulcus (IPS)) from cognitive neuroscience of cortical specialization for a given psychological function. In fact, it is not an exaggeration to note that one of the greatest contributions of cognitive neuroscience to date has been the discovery of cortical specializations of numerous mental capacities, from face perception to numerical cognition. However, these discoveries are perhaps not surprising given that mainstream cognitive neuroscientists have been motivated by influential philosophical theories of nativism (e.g., modularity of mind) (Fodor, 1983), to seek evidence for universal, rather than culturally specific, cortical specializations and that most empirical work in cognitive neuroscience to date has occurred within Western industrialized nations (Figure 49.2b). Given the population biases within the existing human neuroscience literature and the emergence of novel theories about human brain and its evolutionary origins, neuronal recycling and related theories that emphasize universal neural architecture may be premature, as any comprehensive theory of the human brain requires a way to predict and explain cultural variation in brain function.

Representing the viewpoint of strong cultural variance in brain function are *neuroplasticity* and *neurovariation theories*. *Neuroplasticity theory* proposes that neural architecture retains the ability to reorganize itself by forming new connections throughout life. For instance, prior neuroimaging research has shown that primary and secondary visual cortical areas (V1/V2) activate when blind participants read Braille, a nonvisual sensorimotor task (Sadato et al., 1996). These findings provide a remarkable demonstration of cross-modal plasticity, whereby the primary visual cortex, which typically receives visual input from the eyes through the lateral geniculate nuclei, has the capacity to reorganize itself to receive and process non-visual sensorimotor information. Unlike *neuronal recycling theory*, neuroplasticity theory suggests that cultural variation in neural structure, function and connectivity may occur due to the brain's ability to form new cortical connections throughout the lifespan, from early infancy into late adulthood (Wexler, 2006).

Here I introduce the notion of *neurovariation theory* to explain how cultural variation in neural structure, function, and connectivity may occur, not only due to environmental input shaping brain function during the lifespan, but also because of culture-gene coevolutionary forces occurring across generations. Whereas neuronal recycling theory proposes that evolution provides strong constraints for cortical organization leading to largely universal neural architecture, neurovariation theory asserts that evolutionary constraints also provide strong constraints for cultural variation in neural architecture due to genetic and cultural selection pressures. First, cultural variation in brain function may arise in cortical regions that are regulated by genes whose allelic frequencies are known to vary substantially across cultures. For instance, recent neurogenetics research has shown that the serotonin transporter gene (*5-HTTLPR*) regulates serotonergic neurotransmission within the human amygdala whereby S allele carriers show greater amygdala response relative to L allele carriers (Hariri et al., 2002). Hence, cultural variation in amygdala response between East Asians and Westerners may occur due to a greater proportion of S allele carriers living in East Asian nations compared to Western industrialized nations. Indeed, recent cross-cultural neuroimaging evidence demonstrates that native Japanese show greater bilateral amygdala response to negative emotional scenes relative to Caucasian Americans (Chiao et al, 2009).

Second, cultural variation of cortical maps may arise in brain regions that facilitate the successful storage and transmission of cultural traits that have been selected for due to their adaptive cultural function. Recent cultural psychology research has shown that cultural values of individualism-collectivism have adaptive value, serving as an anti-pathogen (Fincher et al., 2008) and anti-psychopathology defense (Chiao & Blizinsky, 2009). Recent cultural neuroscience research shows that brain regions, such as the medial prefrontal cortex and posterior cingulate cortex, respond differentially during self-evaluation as a function of cultural values (Zhu et al., 2007; Chiao et al, 2009a; Chiao et al, 2010), due to their role in facilitating the storage and transmission of individualistic and collectivistic representations of the self. Thus, genetic and cultural selection pressures allow for universality and cultural variation in neural architecture, with neuroplasticity providing an additional means by which cortical maps may continually adapt to the cultural environment across multiple time scales. Taken together, these distinct theories form a foundational conceptual spectrum from which testable hypotheses, about what kinds of cultural influences on brain function may occur, may be formulated.

Cultural Influences on Brain Function: Progress in Cultural Neuroscience

Recent research in cultural neuroscience has lead to a growing body of evidence for cultural influences on brain function across multiple time scales (Chiao, 2009; Han & Northoff, 2008; Park & Gutchess, 2006). As an earlier chapter addresses in depth the neural circuitry underlying cultural transmission via human imitation and the mirror neuron mechanisms (see chapter 38), this section highlights illustrative empirical advances of how cultural values, beliefs, and practices influence brain function in a range of psychological domains, from perception and memory to emotion and social cognition.

Visual Perception

Cultural beliefs, such as self-construal style, have been shown to influence visual perception at a behavioral level, as demonstrated by the Frame-Line Test (FLT) (Kitayama et al., 2003). The FLT measures one's capacity to both incorporate and to ignore contextual information in a nonsocial domain. Prior cultural psychology research has shown that people living in a collectivistic culture, such as Japan, are better at incorporating contextual information during perception of a focal object (e.g., relative condition) while people living in an individualistic culture, such as North America, are better at ignoring contextual information (e.g., absolute condition) when perceiving a focal object (Kitayama et al., 2003). These results suggest that cultural beliefs affect how a simple visual percept, such as a vertical line, is perceived and experienced.

Modulation of visual experience by cultural beliefs is thought to arise from frontal-parietal regions associated with high-level attentional modulation, rather than early stage primary perceptual processes associated with temporo-occipital regions (Hedden et al., 2008). Using fMRI, Hedden and colleagues (2008) measured neural activity while people completed a modified version of the FLT task. During scanning, people were asked to perform vertical-line size judgments that involved either incorporating (relative condition) or ignoring (absolute) contextual information, such as the relationship between the perceived size of the line and the surrounding square frame. Brain-imaging results showed that people recruited frontal and parietal regions associated with attentional control to a greater extent when engaged in a task that was incongruent with their cultural values (Figure 49.5). More specifically, neural activity in frontal-parietal regions increased when people of East Asian descent ignored contextual information and people of European descent incorporated contextual information during line size judgments. Moreover, degree of activation during the incongruent relative to the congruent judgments was negatively correlated with degree of individualism in people of European descent and degree of acculturation in people of East Asian descent. Hence, conscious perception of a vertical line embedded in a square frame and its underlying neural circuitry is affected by experience with and identification to a given cultural context.

Recent studies using event-related potentials have found converging evidence of cultural values of individualism-collectivism on neural substrates of visual perception. In one study, Lewis and colleagues (2008) measured event-related potentials while participants completed the oddball task, where they are shown visual stimuli in either a frequent or infrequent (i.e., oddball stimulus) manner. Results demonstrated that European-American participants showed greater novelty P3 amplitude for target events, whereas East Asians showed greater P3 amplitude to contextually deviant events. In another study, Lin and colleagues (2008) recorded electrophysiological activity in the extrastriate cortex while participants primed with either individualism or collectivism viewed compound visual stimuli in either a global or a local fashion. Results demonstrated that individualistic self-construal priming resulted in greater P1 amplitude during local relative to global processing, whereas collectivistic self-construal priming resulted in greater P1 amplitude during global relative to local processing. These results provide a novel demonstration that temporarily heightening one's awareness of cultural values can dynamically alter neural responses during visual perception. Taken together, these findings provide convergent evidence that cultural values of individualism and collectivism modulate neural and electrophysiological responses during visual perception at both macro and micro timescales.

Memory

Cultural variation in holistic versus analytic thinking styles affects how people encode and retrieve information. Several cultural psychological studies have shown that Westerners are more likely to encode and retrieve focal objects in a complex visual scene, whereas East Asians encode focal and contextual information (Chua, Boland, & Nisbett, 2005; Nisbett & Masuda, 2003; Nisbett, Peng, Choi, & Norenzayan, 2001). Recent cultural neuroscience evidence suggests that cultural variation in memory performance may occur, in part, to cultural variation in neural processing within lateral occipital regions, particularly in elderly populations (Gutchess et al., 2006; Goh et al., 2007). One cross-cultural neuroimaging study found that East Asians and Westerners vary within object-processing regions such as the bilateral middle temporal gyrus (Gutchess et al., 2006). Another neuroimaging study comparing young and elderly East Asians and Westerners found that activity within the right lateral occipital region differed between East Asian and Western elderly, but not East Asian and Western young adults, providing novel evidence that that neural regions may show cultural variation as a function of age (Goh et al., 2007, Figure 49.6).

Emotion

Numerous behavioral studies have shown that culture affects how people prefer to experience, express, recognize, and regulate their emotions (Mesquita & Leu, 2007). East Asian prefer experience low arousal relative to high arousal positive emotions (Tsai, 2007) and are more likely to suppress their emotions relative to Westerners (Butler, Lee,

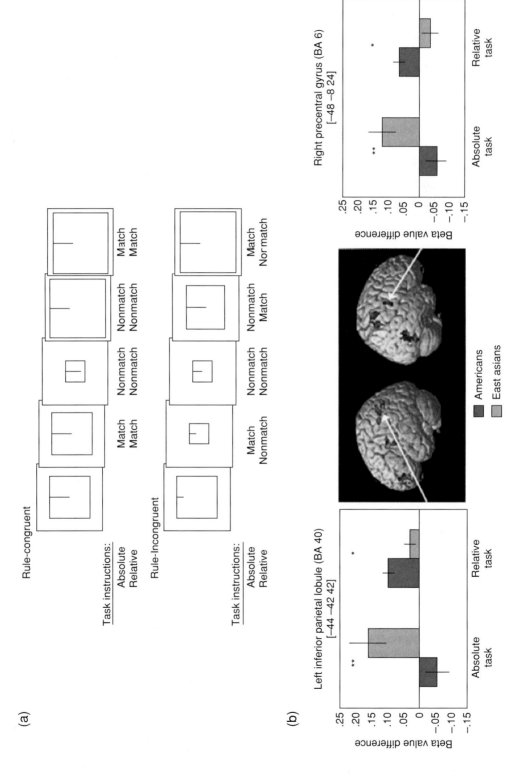

Fig. 49.5 Cultural influence on neural basis of visual attention (adapted with permission from Hedden et al, 2008). (a) Illustration of the modified Frame-Line Task; (b) East Asians show greater neural response within left inferior parietal lobe and right precentral gyrus during the absolute task whereas Caucasian Americans show greater response in the same regions during the relative task.

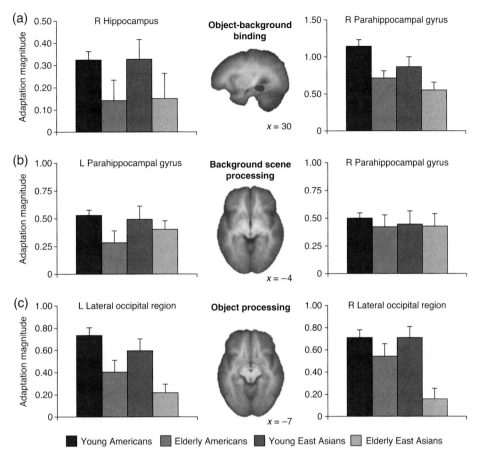

Fig. 49.6 Effects of age and culture on neural responses during encoding of complex visual scenes (adapted with permission from Goh et al., 2008). (a) Young adults show greater neural activity within the right hippocampus during object-background binding relative to older adults, irrespective of culture; (b) Younger compared to older Americans show greater neural response within left parahippocampal gyrus when processing backgrounds of complex scenes; (c) Compared to younger Americans and East Asians, as well as older Americans, elderly East Asians show significantly decreased right lateral occipital activity during object processing.

Gross, 2007). Additionally, both East Asians and Westerners demonstrate cultural specificity in emotion recognition, whereby they show greater recognition for emotions expressed by their own cultural group members relative to members of other cultural groups (Elfenbein & Ambady, 2002). Recent cultural neuroscience of emotion research has shown cultural specificity effects within a number of brain regions involved in emotion recognition. Consistent with prior behavioral findings, one recent study showed that people exhibit greater amygdala response to fear faces expressed by own-relative to other-culture members (Chiao et al., 2008, Figure 49.7). Another recent study found that people also exhibit greater superior temporal sulcus activity when inferring the emotional states specifically from the eye region of others from their own—relative to other—culture (Adams et al., in press). Taken together, these findings provide convergent evidence that culture influences how people infer emotional states from nonverbal cues, and their underlying neural substrates, possibly by tuning neural responses towards familiar stimuli in the environment during development.

Social Cognition

Cultural values, practices, and beliefs shape social behavior in profound ways. One of the most robust ways that values, such as individualism and collectivism, influence human behavior is in self-construal, or how people think about themselves in relation to others. Individualists think of themselves as autonomous from others, while collectivists think of themselves as highly interconnected with others

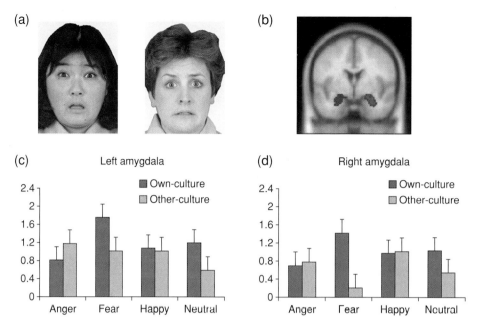

Fig. 49.7 Cultural specificity in bilateral amygdala response to fear faces (adapted from Chiao et al., 2008 MIT). (a) Examples of Japanese and Caucasian-American fear faces; (b) Illustration of bilateral amygdala; participants show greater left (c) and right (d) amygdala response to fear expressed by members of one's own cultural group.

(Markus & Kitayama, 1991; Triandis, 1995). Recent evidence from social neuroscience indicates that specific brain regions, such as the medial prefrontal cortex (MPFC) and posterior cingulate cortex (PCC) are involved in self-evaluation and self-knowledge (Amodio & Frith, 2006).

Recent cultural neuroscience evidence indicates that neural substrates of self-evaluation are modulated by cultural values of individualism and collectivism. In one study, Caucasians, but not Chinese, showed greater neural activity within the MPFC during evaluation of personality traits of one's self relative to a close other (i.e., mother), suggesting cultural variation in MPFC response during self-evaluation (Zhu et al., 2007). More recent evidence has demonstrated that cultural values (i.e., individualism-collectivism), rather than cultural affiliation (i.e., East Asian-Westerners) per se, modulate neural response during self-evaluation. In one cross-cultural neuroimaging study, people in both Japan and the United States who endorsed individualistic values showed greater MPFC activity for general relative to contextual self-descriptions, whereas people who endorsed collectivistic values greater MPFC for contextual relative to general self-descriptions (Chiao et al., 2009). Supporting this view, another study using cultural priming showed that even

temporarily heightening awareness of individualistic and collectivistic values in bicultural individuals (i.e., Asian-Americans) modulates the MPFC and PCC in a similar manner (Chiao et al., 2010, Figure 49.8). In addition to cultural values modulating neural responses during explicit self processing, a recent neuroimaging study shows that dorsal, but not ventral, regions of the MPFC are modulated by cultural priming of individualism and collectivism during implicit self processing (Harada, Li, Chiao, in press). Such findings suggest that cultural values dynamically shape neural representations during the evaluation, rather than the detection, of self-relevant information. Taken together, these studies provide convergent evidence that cultural values of individualism-collectivism shape neural representations of both implicit and explicit self-knowledge.

Culture-Gene Interactions in Brain Function: Promise of Cultural Neuroscience

Prior demonstrations of cultural influences on brain function provide evidence for the viability and utility of the cultural neuroscience approach. However, cultural neuroscience possesses even greater explanatory potential to address fundamental questions. How do cultural and genetic

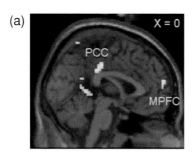

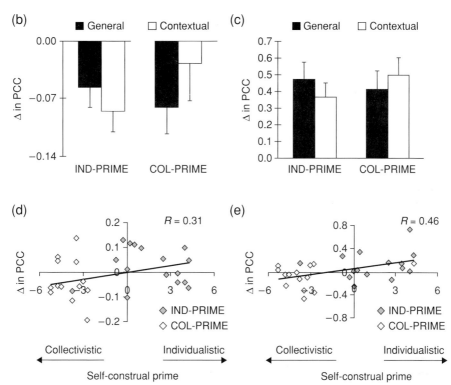

Fig. 49.8 Dynamic cultural influences on neural representations of self (adapted from Chiao et al., 2010). (a) Modulation of neural activity within cortical midline structures, including the posterior cingulate cortex (PCC) and medial prefrontal cortex (MPFC) as a function of cultural priming. Bicultural participants primed with individualistic cultural values show greater PCC (b) and MPFC (c) response to general relative to contextual self-descriptions. Bicultural participants primed with collectivistic cultural values show greater PCC (b) and MPFC (c) response to contextual relative to general self-descriptions. The degree to which a person is primed with individualistic or collectivistic values is positively correlated with neural activity within the PCC (d) and MPFC (e) to general relative to contextual self-descriptions, respectively.

factors interact in the brain and how does this culture-gene interaction affect subsequent typical and atypical behavior?

To understand the etiology of complex affective disorders, psychiatrists initially relied heavily on behavioral genetics studies associating a single gene or family of genes with a particular behavior (Figure 49.9a). However, behavioral genetics studies often produce inconsistent findings, suggesting a more complex path from gene to disease. More recently, psychiatrists have integrated endophenotypes in

pathway models of affective disorders (Figure 49.9b). Endophenotypes, such as specific psychological processes and their underlying neural substrates, are thought to serve as a more proximate measure of genetic expression, given that genes regulate neurotransmitter function within these specific neural pathways. Importantly, complex human behaviors, such as affective disorders (e.g., anxiety and depression), are now widely acknowledged as emerging as a byproduct of gene-by-environment interactions observed at both behavioral and neural levels

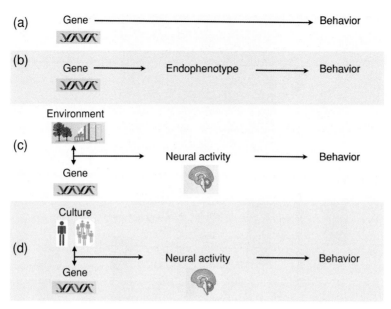

Fig. 49.9 Illustration of different models of gene-to-behavior pathways. (a) The direct linear approach to gene and behavior; (b) The endophenotype approach which assumes that the gene-to-behavior pathway is mediated by proximate or intermediate phenotypes, such as neural activity; (c) The gene-by-environment approach which assumes interaction between genetic and environmental factors influence neural activity and behavior; (d) the culture-by-gene approach which identifies specific cultural traits and genes that interact and mutually influence neural activity and subsequent behavior.

(Figure 49.9c) (Canli & Lesch, 2007; Caspi & Moffitt, 2006; Taylor et al., 2006).

Critically, cultural neuroscience may further contribute to these models by identifying specific cultural values, practices and beliefs that serve as key environmental factors in gene-by-environment interactions (Figure 49.9d). For instance, Chiao and Blizinsky (2010) recently found that cultural values of individualism and collectivism are associated with the serotonin transporter gene (*5-HTTLPR*) across nations (Figure 49.10). Collectivistic cultures were significantly more likely to be comprised of individuals carrying the S allele of the 5-HTTLPR across 29 nations. Additionally, cultural values and frequency of S allele carriers negatively predicted global prevalence of anxiety and mood disorder. Mediation analyses further indicate that increased frequency of S allele carriers predicted decreased anxiety and mood disorder prevalence due to increased collectivistic cultural values. These findings support the notion that cultural values buffer genetically susceptible populations from increased prevalence of affective disorders and suggest culture-gene coevolution between allelic frequency of 5-HTTLPR and cultural values of individualism-collectivism. A central claim of culture-gene coevolutionary

theory is that once cultural traits are adaptive, it is likely that genetic selection causes refinement of the cognitive and neural architecture responsible for the storage and transmission of those cultural capacities (Boyd & Richerson, 1985). Future research in cultural neuroscience (Chiao, 2009) may investigate the extent to which cultural values of individualism-collectivism are associated with neural response within brain regions regulated by serotonergic neurotransmission, and if so, the process by which this activity within neural pathways supports the storage and transmission of cultural values and related behaviors.

The promise of cultural neuroscience rests in the ability to visualize these kinds of culture-gene interactions in neural activity. To the extent that neural activity serves as a more proximate reflection of culture × gene interactions relative to behavior, researchers may have unprecedented ability to better understand how specific environmental and genetic factors produce complex behavior via regulation of neural activity. Similar to behavior, culture × gene interactions in neural activity may be driven by several distinct mechanisms (Figure 49.11). Genotypes may enhance the expression of a cultural trait on neural activity (Figure 49.11a). Alternatively,

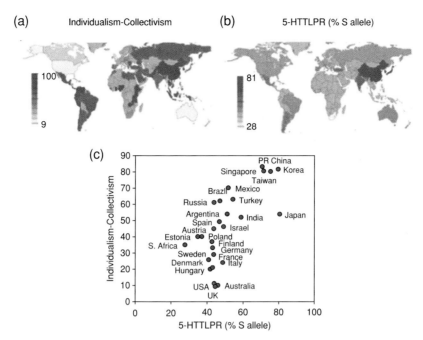

Fig. 49.10 Culture-gene coevolution of individualism-collectivism and the serotonin transporter gene (5-HTTLPR). (a) Color map of frequency distribution of IND-COL from Hofstede (2001); (b) Color map of frequency distribution of S alleles of 5-HTTLPR; (c) Collectivistic nations showed higher prevalence of S allele carriers.

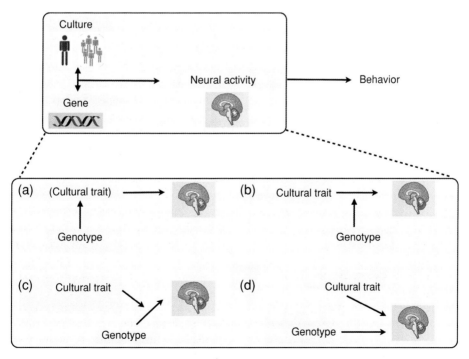

Fig. 49.11 Illustration of the variations in the culture-by-gene pathway. (a) Genotypes may enhance the expression of a cultural trait on neural activity; (b) A particular genotype may alter the culture-to-neural activity pathway; (c) A particular cultural trait may alter the gene-to-neural activity pathway. (d) Both genotype and cultural traits may simultaneously, but independently, contribute to neural activity.

a particular genotype may alter the culture-to-neural activity pathway (Figure 49.11b). Similarly, a particular cultural trait may alter the gene-to-neural activity pathway (Figure 49.11c). Finally, both genotype and cultural traits may simultaneously, but independently, contribute to neural activity (Figure 49.11d). Researchers in cultural neuroscience are just beginning to identify specific cultural and genetic associations (see Chiao & Blizinsky, 2010; Kim et al., 2010 for examples); however, as our understanding of these relationships increases, future researchers will be able to apply this improved theoretical platform towards designing novel neuroscience studies that test for culture-gene interactions in brain function, even if such interactions may not directly observable in behavior. Importantly, culture × gene interactions in neural activity and behavior may vary across multiple timescales, from phylogeny to ontogeny. Hence, future cultural neuroscience studies that tests different ways in which culture × gene interactions may emerge in patterns of neural activity, akin to behavior, will likely benefit from incorporating cross-species (Rilling, 2008), cross-sectional (Johnson, 1997; Park & Gutchess, 2006), and longitudinal (Meltzer et al., 2009) designs, as appropriate.

Implications of Cultural Neuroscience for Basic and Applied Research

It is not expected that the study of all psychological and biological phenomena will necessitate a cultural neuroscience approach. Rather, the goal and challenge for cultural neuroscience is to identify the phenomena that can be readily mapped within and across multiple levels of analysis. There are at least three foreseeable benefits of a cultural neuroscience approach for basic and applied research: 1) merging the social and natural sciences, 2) informing interethnic ideology, and 3) enhancing the condition and care of human health across diverse cultural populations.

Merging the Scientific Study of Culture and Biology

The increasing stratification of the social and natural sciences within universities and academic subfields has led to deep conceptual and methodological schisms between different communities of researchers. In a celebrated lecture, Snow, an influential British physicist and novelist (1959), famously characterized the fissure between social and natural sciences as "the two cultures." Even within the field of anthropology, which Boas

originally envisioned as simultaneously encompassing cultural and social anthropology, physical and biological anthropology, archaeology, and linguistics, there has historically been such deep intrafield antagonism that some anthropology departments within the American universities have even split into two, with one half of the department focused on cultural approaches while the other half focused on biological approaches to the same questions (Shenk, 2006). Is the gap between cultural and biological sciences too wide to be bridged within a single discipline? How might consilience be achieved (Wilson, 1998)? Psychology as a hub science (Cacioppo, 2007) stands in a natural position to merge the scientific study of culture and biology by harnessing theories and methods from every area of psychology, from evolutionary and cognitive to cultural and developmental. The empirical tools needed to investigate the links across multiple levels of analysis are available now in ways not previously imaginable. The cultural neuroscience framework represents an opportunity to transcend the confines of academic subfields and address age-old questions regarding the mutual constitution of cultural and biological influences on human behavior in novel ways.

Informing Interethnic Ideology

Research in cultural neuroscience may also inform public policy issues related to cultural diversity and interethnic justice. As a result of globalization, cultural communities of the world are becoming increasingly interdependent and interethnic, leading to an increasing urgency to understand how diverse communities of people may optimally coexist (Wolsko, Park, Judd, & Wittenbrink, 2000). On the one hand, interethnic ideologies such as colorblindness advocate treating people of different cultural heritages similarly, with no regard to interethnic differences. On the other hand, interethnic ideologies such as pluralism advocate embracing cultural differences and creating public policies that respect interethnic differences. Research in cultural neuroscience can potentially inform this important debate by studying how cultural identity affects the brain and behavior, whether or not cultural traits have adaptive value, and how changes in cultural diversity may affect the human mind, brain, and behavior. At the same time, scientific rigor and ethical care is needed when seeking to apply cultural neuroscience evidence towards larger public policy discourse regarding how best to achieve optimal coexistence of diverse cultural and ethnic groups.

Implications for Population Health

Finally, the important interplay of culture and genes in the study of population health has long been acknowledged (Shields et al., 2005; Wang & Sue, 2005). For instance, whereas Ashkenazi Jews have a greater likelihood of Tay-Sachs disease, people from Northern Europe are more likely to develop cystic fibrosis (Exner, Dries, Domanski & Cohen, 2001; Wang & Sue, 2005). Another example of population differences in health as a function of differences in allelic frequency is the gene *CYP2A6* and nicotine addiction (Shields et al., 2005). Protective forms of the CYP2A6 gene are very rare in Europeans and Africans (~3%), but more prevalent in Japanese and Koreans (~24%) (Shields et al., 2005). Cross-national epidemiological studies, including the 2008 World Health Organization cross-national survey of affective disorders, indicates significant variation in global prevalence of mental health disorders, such as anxiety and major depression (Kessler & Ustun, 2008; see also Weissman, 1996). How do differences in genetic frequencies affect brain systems and behavior underlying physical and mental health conditions? How do cultural factors influence the expression and function of these genes and their regulatory effects on brain and behavior?

The answers to these intriguing questions are finally within our empirical grasp. By using the cultural neuroscience framework to identify and investigate candidate phenomena using the multiple levels of analysis approach, we will enhance our chances of understanding how sociocultural and biological forces interact and shape each other as well as find potential ways to direct this knowledge towards timely issues in population health.

Acknowledgments

Special thanks to Tetsuya Iidaka, Ahmad Hariri, Tokiko Harada, Zhang Li, Genna Bebko, Bobby Cheon, Donna Bridge, Vani Mathur and Steve Franconeri for supportive and thoughtful discussion. This work is supported by National Science Foundation BCS-0720312 and BCS-0722326 grants to J.Y.C.

References

Adams, R. B. Jr., Rule, N. O., Franklin, R. G. Jr., Wang, E., Stevenson, M. T., Yoshikawa, S., et al. (in press). Cross-cultural reading the mind in the eyes: An fMRI Investigation. *Journal of Cognitive Neuroscience*.

Amodio, D. M. & Frith, C. D. (2006). Meeting of minds: The medial frontal cortex and social cognition. *Nature Reviews Neuroscience*, 7, 268–277.

Arnett, J. J. (2008). The neglected 95%: Why American psychology needs to become less American. *American Psychologist*, 63(7), 602–614.

Barkow, J. H., Cosmides, L., & Tooby, J. 1992 Eds. *The adapted mind: Evolutionary psychology and the generation of culture.* (Oxford University Press, New York).

Beevers, C. G., Gibb, B. E., McGeary, J. E., & Miller, I. W. (2007). Serotonin transporter genetic variation and biased attention for emotional word stimuli among psychiatric inpatients. *J. Abnorm. Psychol*, 11, 208–212.

Boyd, R. & Richerson, P. J. (1985). *Culture and the evolutionary process.* The University of Chicago Press, Chicago.

Butler, E. A., Lee, T. L., & Gross, J. J. (2007). Emotion regulation and culture: Are the social consequences of emotion suppression culture-specific? *Emotion*, 7, 30–48.

Cacioppo, J. T., Berntson, G. G., Sheridan, J. F., & McClintock, M. K. (2000). Multi-level integrative analyses of human behavior: Social neuroscience and the complementing nature of social and biological approaches. *Psychological Bulletin*, 126, 829–843.

Cacioppo, J. T. (2007). Psychology is a hub science. *Observer*, 20(8), 5 & 42.

Canli, T. & Lesch, K. P. (2007) Long story short: The serotonin transporter in emotion regulation and social cognition. *Nature Neuroscience*, 10, 1103–1109.

Caramazza, A. & Shelton, J. R. (1998). Domain-specific knowledge systems in the brain: The animate-inanimate distinction. *Journal of Cognitive Neuroscience*, 10, 1–34.

Caspi, A. & Moffitt, T. (2006). Gene-environment interactions in psychiatry: Joining forces with neuroscience. *Nature Reviews Neuroscience*, 7, 583–590.

Cavalli-Sforza, L. & Feldman, M. (1981) *Cultural transmission and evolution: A quantitative approach.* Princeton University Press, Princeton.

Chen, C., Burton, M. L., Greenberger, E., & Dmitrieva, J. (1999). Population migration and the variation of dopamine (DRD4) allele frequencies around the globe. *Evolution and Human Behavior*, 20, 309–324.

Chiao, J. Y. (2009). Cultural neuroscience: Cultural influences on brain function. *Progress in Brain Research*, Elsevier Press.

Chiao, J. Y. & Ambady, N. (2007). Cultural neuroscience: Parsing universality and diversity across levels of analysis. In Kitayama, S. & Cohen, D. (Eds.) *Handbook of cultural psychology*, Guilford Press, NY, pp. 237–254.

Chiao, J. Y. & Blizinsky, K. D. (2010). Culture-gene coevolution of individualism-collectivism and the serotonin transporter gene (5-HTTLPR). Proceedings of the Royal Society B: Biological Sciences, 277(1681):529–37.

Chiao, J. Y., Harada, T., Komeda, H., Li, Z., Mano, Y., Saito, D. N., et al. (2009). Neural basis of individualistic and collectivistic views of self. *Human Brain Mapping*.

Chiao, J. Y., Harada, T., Komeda, H., Li, Z., Mano, Y., Saito, D. N., et al. (2010). Dynamic cultural influences on neural representations of the self. *Journal of Cognitive Neuroscience*.

Chiao, J. Y., Hariri, A. R. Harada, T., Komeda, H., Li, Z., Mano, Y., et al. (2009). Cultural variation in amygdala response to emotional scenes. *Proceedings of the 16th Cognitive Neuroscience Society meeting*.

Chiao, J. Y., Iidaka, T., Gordon, H. L., Nogawa, J., Bar, M., Aminoff, E., et al. (2008). Cultural specificity in amygdala response to fear faces. *Journal of Cognitive Neuroscience*, 20(12), 2167–2174.

Chua, H. F., Boland, J. E., & Nisbett, R. E. (2005). Cultural variation in eye movements during scene perception. *Proceedings of the National Academy of Sciences, USA, 102,* 12629–12633.

Darwin, C. (1859). *On the origin of species by means of natural selection, or the preservation of favoured races in the struggle for life.* Murray, London.

Davidson, R. J. & Sutton, S. K. (1995). Affective neuroscience: The emergence of a discipline. *Current Opinion in Neurobiology, 5,* 217–224.

Dehaene, S. & Cohen, L. (2007). Cultural recycling of cortical maps. *Neuron, 56*(2), 384–398.

Elfenbein, H. A. & Ambady, N. (2002). Is there an in-group advantage in emotion recognition? *Psychological Bulletin, 128,* 243–249.

Exner, D. V., Dries, D. K., Domanski, M. J., & Cohen, J. N. (2001). Lesser response of angiotensin-converting-enzyme inhibitor therapy in black as compared with white patients with left ventricular dysfunction. *New England Journal of Medicine, 344,* 1351–1377.

Fincher, C. L., Thornhill, R., Murray, D. R., & Schaller, M. (2008). Pathogen prevalence predicts human cross-cultural variability in individualism/collectivism. *Proceedings of the Royal Society B, 275,* 1279–1285.

Fodor, J. A. (1983). *Modularity of mind: An essay on faculty psychology.* Cambridge, Mass.: MIT Press.

Fox, E., Ridgewell, A., & Ashwin, C. (2009). Looking on the bright side: biased attention and the human serotonin gene. *Proceedings of the Royal Society B: Biological Sciences.* doi: 10.1098/rspb.2008.1788.

Gazzaniga, M. S., Ivry, R., & Mangun, G. R. (2002). *Cognitive neuroscience: The biology of the mind.* New York: Norton.

Glimcher, P. W., Camerer, C. F., Fehr, E., & Poldrack, R. A. (2008). *Neuroeconomics: Decision making and the brain.* Academic Press.

Goh, J. O., Chee, M. W., Tan, J. C., Venkatraman, V., Hebrank, A., Leshikar, E. D., et al. (2007). Age and culture modulate object processing and object-scene binding in the ventral visual area. *Cognitive, Affective, and Behavioral Neuroscience, 7*(1), 44–52.

Green, A. E., Munafò, M., DeYoung, C. G., Fossella, J., Fan, J., & Gray, J. R. (2008). Using genetic data in cognitive neuroscience: From growing pains to genuine insights. *Nature Reviews Neuroscience, 9,* 710–720.

Gutchess, A. H., Welsh, R. C., Boduroglu, A., & Park, D. C. (2006). Cross-cultural differences in the neural correlates of picture encoding. *Cognitive, Affective, and Behavioral Neuroscience, 6*(2), 102–109.

Han, S. & Northoff, G. (2008). Culture-sensitive neural substrates of human cognition: A transcultural neuroimaging approach. *Nature Review Neuroscience, 9,* 646–654.

Handy, T. C. (Ed.) (2005). *Event-related potentials: A methods handbook.* Cambridge, MA: MIT Press.

Harada, T., Li, Z., Chiao, J. Y. (2010). Differential dorsal and ventral medial prefrontal representations of the implicit self modulated by individualism and collectivism: an fMRI study. *Social Neuroscience, 22,* 1–15.

Hariri, A. R., Mattay V. S., Tessitore A., Kolachana B. S., Fera F., Goldman D., et al. (2002). Serotonin transporter genetic variation and the response of the human amygdala. *Science, 297,* 400–403.

Hariri, A. R., Drabant, E. M., & Weinberger, D. R. (2006). Imaging genetics: Perspectives from studies of genetically driven variation in serotonin function and corticolimbic affective processing. *Biological Psychiatry, 59*(10), 888–897.

Hedden, T., Ketay, S., Aron, A., Markus, H. R., & Gabrieli, J. D. E. (2008). Cultural influences on neural substrates of attentional control. *Psychological Science, 19*(1), 12–16.

Heeger, D. J. & Ress, D. (2002). What does fMRI tell us about neuronal activity? *Nature Reviews Neuroscience, 3,* 142–151.

Heine, S. J. (2008). *Cultural psychology.* New York: Norton.

Hong, Y., Morris, M. W., Chiu, C., & Benet-Martinez, V. (2000). Multicultural minds: A dynamic constructivist approach to culture and cognition. *American Psychologist, 55,* 709–720.

Hofstede, G. (2001). *Culture's consequences: Comparing values, behaviors, institutions and organizations across nations.* Thousand Oaks, CA: Sage Publications.

Jahoda, G. (2002). Culture, biology and development across history. In H. Keller, Y.H. Poortinga, & A. Schoemerich (Eds.), *Between culture and biology: Perspectives on ontogenetic development* (pp. 13–29). Cambridge, UK: Cambridge University Press.

Johnson, M. H. (1997). *Developmental cognitive neuroscience: An introduction.* Oxford, UK: Blackwell.

Kessler, R. C. & Ustun, T. B. (2008). *The WHO World Mental Health Surveys: global perspectives on the epidemiology of mental disorders.* Cambridge University Press, New York.

Kanwisher, N., McDermott, J., & Chun, M. (1997). The fusiform face area: A module in human extrastriate cortex specialized for the perception of faces. *Journal of Neuroscience, 17,* 4302–4311.

Kim, H. S, Sherman, D. K., Taylor, S. E., Sasaki, J. Y., Chu, T. Q., Ryu, C., et al. (2010). Culture, the serotonin receptor polymorphism (5-HTR1A), and locus of attention. *Social Cognitive and Affective Neuroscience.*

Kitayama, S. & Cohen, D. (2007). *Handbook of cultural psychology.* Guilford Press, New York NY.

Kitayama, S., Dufy, S., Kawamura, T., & Larsen, J. T. (2003). Perceiving an object and its context in different cultures: A cultural look at New Look. *Psychological Science, 14,* 201–206.

Laland, K. N., Odling-Smee, J., & Feldman, M. W. (2000). Niche construction, biological evolution and cultural change. *Behavioural and Brain Sciences, 23*(1), 131–146.

Lewis, H. S. (2001). Boas, Darwin, science and anthropology. *Current Anthropology, 42*(3), 381–406.

Lewis, R. S., Goto, S. G., & Kong, L. L. (2008). Culture and context: East Asian American and European American differences in P3 event-related potentials and self-construal. *Personality and Social Psychology Bulletin, 34*(5), 623–634.

Lin, Z., Lin, Y., & Han, S. (2008). Self-construal priming modulates visual activity underlying global/local perception. *Biological Psychology, 77,* 93–97.

Li, S. C. (2003). Biocultural orchestration of developmental plasticity across levels: The interplay of biology and culture in shaping the mind and behavior across the life span. *Psychological Bulletin, 129*(2), 171–194.

Lonsdorf, T. B., Weike, A. I., Nikamo, P., Schalling, M., Hamm, A. O., & Ohman, A. (2009). Genetic gating of human fear learning and extinction. *Psychological Science 20*(2), 198–206.

Lumsden, C. J. & Wilson, E. O. (1981). *Genes, mind and culture: The coevolutionary process.* Harvard University Press, Cambridge.

Markus, H. R. & Kitayama, S. (1991). Culture and the self: implications for cognition, emotion and motivation. *Psychological Review, 98*, 224–253.

Meltzer, J. A., Postman-Caucheteux, W. A., McArdle, J. J., & Braun, A. R. (2009). Strategies for longitudinal neuroimaging studies of overt language production. *Neuroimage, 47*(2), 745–755.

Mesquita, B. & Leu, J. (2007). The cultural psychology of emotion. In S. Kitayama & D. Cohen (Eds.), *Handbook for cultural psychology*. New York: Guilford Press.

Munafò, M. R., Clark, T., & Flint, J. (2005). Does measurement instrument moderate the association between the serotonin transporter gene and anxiety-related personality traits? A meta-analysis. *Molecular Psychiatry, 10*, 415–419.

Munafo, M. R., Durrant, C., Lewis, G., & Flint, J. (2009). Gene x environment interactions at the serotonin transporter locus. *Biological Psychiatry 65*(3), 211–219.

Nisbett, R. E. & Masuda, T. (2003). Culture and point of view. *Proceedings of the National Academy of Sciences, 100*, 11163–11175.

Nisbett, R. E., Peng, K., Choi, I., & Norenzayan, A. (2001). Culture and systems of thought: Holistic versus analytic cognition. *Psychological Review, 108*(2), 291–310.

Norenzayan, A. & Heine, S. J. (2005). Psychological universals: What are they and how can we know? *Psychological Bulletin, 135*, 763–784.

Ochsner, K. N. & Lieberman, M. D. (2001). The emergence of social cognitive neuroscience. *American Psychologist, 56*, 717–734.

Osinsky, R., Reuter, M., Kupper, Y., Schmitz, A., Kozyra, E., Alexander, N., et al. (2008). Variation in the serotonin transporter gene modulates selective attention to threat. *Emotion, 8*(4), 584–588.

Oyserman, D. & Lee, S. W. S. (2008). Does culture influence what and how we think? Effects of priming individualism and collectivism. *Psychological Bulletin, 134*, 311–342.

Pezawas L., Meyer-Lindenberg A., Drabant E. M., Verchinski B. A., Munoz K. E., Kolachana B. S., et al. (2005). *5-HTTLPR* polymorphism impacts human cingulate-amygdala interactions: A genetic susceptibility mechanism for depression. *Nature Neuroscience, 8*(6), 828–834.

Park, D. C. & Gutchess, A. H. (2006). The cognitive neuroscience of aging and culture. *Current Directions in Psychological Science, 15*(3), 105–108.

Rilling, J. K. (2009). Neuroscientific approaches and applications within anthropology. *American Journal of Physical Anthropology, 47*, 2–32.

Sadato, N., Pascual-Leone, A., Grafman, J., Ibanez, V., Deiber, M.-P., Dold, G. et al. (1996). Activation of the primary visual cortex by Braille reading in blind subjects. *Nature, 38*, 526–528.

Savani, K., Markus, H. R., & Conner, A. L. (2008). Let your preference be your guide? Preferences and choices are more tightly linked for North Americans than for Indians. *Journal of Personality and Social Psychology, 95*, 861–876.

Sen, S., Burmeister, M. L., & Ghosh, D. (2004). Meta-analysis of the association between a serotonin transporter promoter polymorphism (5-HTTLPR) and anxiety related personality traits. *American Journal of Medical Genetics B: Neuropsychiatric Genetics, 127*(1), 85–89.

Shenk, M. K. (2006). Models for the future of anthropology. *Anthropology News*. Retrieved July 15, 2009, from http://www.aaanet.org/press/an/0106/shenk.html.

Shields, A. E., Fortun, M., Hammonds, E., King, P. A., Lerman, C., Rapp R., & Sullivan, P. F. (2005). The use of race variables in genetic studies of complex traits and the goal of reducing health disparities: A transdisciplinary perspective. *American Psychologist, 6*(1), 77–103.

Singelis, T. M. (1994). The measurement of independent and interdependent self-construals. *Personality & Social Psychology Bulletin, 20*(5), 580–591.

Snibbe, A. & Markus, H. R. (2005). You can't always get what you want: Educational attainment, agency, and choice. *Journal of Personality and Social Psychology, 88*, 703–720.

Snow, C. P. (1959). *The two cultures and the scientific revolution*. New York: Cambridge University Press.

Taylor, S. E., Way, B. M., Welch, W. T., Hilmert, C. J., Lehman, B. J., & Eisenberger, N. I. (2006). Early family environment, current adversity, the serotonin transporter polymorphism, and depressive symptomatology. *Biological Psychiatry, 60*, 671–676.

Tomasello, M., Carpenter, M., Call, J., Behne, T., & Moll, H. (2005). Understanding and sharing intentions: The origins of cultural cognition. *Behavioral and Brain Sciences, 28*, 675–691.

Triandis, H. C. (1995). *Individualism and collectivism*. Westview, Boulder.

Tsai, J. L. (2007). Ideal affect: Cultural causes and behavioral consequences. *Perspectives on Psychological Science, 2*, 242–259.

Wang, V. A. & Sue, S. (2005). In the eye of the storm: Race and the genomics in research and practice. *American Psychologist, 60*, 37–45.

Weissman, M. M., Bland, R. C., Canino, G. J., Faravelli, C., Greenwald, S., Hwu, H. G., et al. (1996). Cross-national epidemiology of major depression and bipolar disorder. *Journal of American Medical Association, 276*, 293–299.

Wexler B. E. (2006). *Brain and culture: Neurobiology, ideology and social change*. MIT Press, Cambridge.

Wilson, E. O. (1998). *Consilience: The unity of knowledge*. New York: Alfred A. Knopf, Inc.

Wolsko, C., Park, B., Judd, C. M., & Wittenbrink, B. (2000). Framing interethnic ideology: Effects of multicultural and color-blind perspectives on judgments of groups and individuals. *Journal of Personality and Social Psychology, 78*(4), 635–654.

Whiten, A., Spiteri, A., Horner, V., Bonnie, K. E., Lambeth, S. P., Schapiro, S. J., et al. (2007). Transmission of multiple traditions within and between chimpanzee groups. *Current Biology, 17*, 1038–1043.

Zhu, Y., Zhang, Li., Fan, J., & Han. S. (2007). Neural basis of cultural influence on self representation. *Neuroimage, 34*, 1310–1317.

PART 6

Social Influences on Health and Clinical Syndromes

Perceived Social Isolation: Social Threat Vigilance and Its Implications for Health

Louise C. Hawkley *and* John T. Cacioppo

Abstract

This chapter elaborates on a theory of loneliness and surveys representative evidence that chronic loneliness hijacks brain and biology to produce significant consequences for health and well-being. Feelings of loneliness are the entry point into a regulatory loop that begins with heightened vigilance for perceived social threat. Vigilance for social threat produces attentional, confirmatory, and memory biases. These biases lead to behavioral confirmation processes through which negative social interactions are perpetuated, thereby reinforcing the lonely individual's belief that he or she has little control or social value. Social pain (e.g., depressive symptoms) continues unabated, and the carrot of social reward lies just beyond reach.

Keywords: loneliness, health, well-being, social isolation, social pain

We live in the shadow of our evolutionary history. Take the human stress response as a case in point. Over the course of millennia, natural selection processes sculpted a species with finely tuned biological responses to potentially life-threatening stimuli. Responses to physical stressors (e.g., pain, blood loss, bodily attack by hostile others) and anticipated stressors (e.g., sight of a predator) evolved to reflexively elicit efficient and coordinated reactions across bodily systems and maintain physiological integrity, health, and life itself. The short-term gains of survival outweighed any long term costs that might accrue. In contemporary society, these ostensibly adaptive physiological processes are seen to work against health and longevity. Chronic, unremitting stress (e.g., caregiving for a spouse with a dementia, living in a dangerous neighborhood, working at a job with high demands and little control) goes so far as to reorganize the brain regions that control the stress response (Ulrich-Lai & Herman, 2009), and physiological responses to chronic stress contribute to physical disease, cognitive decline, and depression (Hawkley, Bosch, Engeland, Marucha, & Cacioppo, 2007; Kemeny & Schedlowski, 2007; Rozanski & Kubzansky, 2005; Siegrist, 2008; Ulrich-Lai & Herman, 2009).

There is another way we are haunted by our evolutionary history, and it is in our capacity to feel socially isolated. An individual's complete involvement in a thriving, engaged, and altruistic community is more than an extravagance. As a social species, humans create emergent organizations beyond the individual—structures that range from dyads, families, and groups to cities, civilizations, and international alliances. These emergent structures evolved hand-in-hand with supporting genetic, neural, and hormonal mechanisms because the consequent social behaviors helped humans survive, reproduce, and care for offspring sufficiently long that they too survived to reproduce. Social neuroscience concerns the study of the neural, hormonal, cellular, molecular, and genetic mechanisms underlying these emergent social structures and their relationship to cognition, emotion, and behavior.

Whereas the feeling of social isolation, or loneliness, has been described as an aversive state with no redeeming features (Weiss, 1973), we have come to view loneliness as an adaptive biological response which, like the stress response, has long term costs that are more likely to be realized in contemporary than evolutionary times. The theory is straightforward: (a) genes that promote behavior which increases the odds of the genes surviving are perpetuated; (b) when offspring have long periods of abject dependency, as exemplified in the case of *Homo sapiens*, selfish genes are more likely to act to produce social brains to ensure that individuals survive, reproduce, and support their offspring sufficiently long that they too reproduce; and (3) the feeling of loneliness evolved as an aversive biological signal to promote vigilance against (additional) social threats that endanger one's short-term survival, and reduce opportunities for the social connection necessary for one's long-term survival and for the survival of one's genes. The social structures in which hominids lived for tens of thousands of years were smaller and more stable than they are in contemporary society, and in this context the aversive feeling of being isolated from one's group promoted displays and behavior to achieve reinstatement into the group or safe entry into another group (Cacioppo & Patrick, 2008). Ostracism, the shunning of a member of a group, is fatal in most social species but typically serves to shape more positive social behavior in humans (Williams, 2007). Loneliness then, like stress or physical pain, is not inherently absent of redeeming qualities even if it has negative long-term consequences in contemporary society.

The analogy with pain is more apt than one might first think. Social pain appears to be built on the same neural pathways as subserve physical pain. Moreover, social pain, like physical pain, motivates avoidance and withdrawal from the source of pain and promotes a defensive response predisposition. Social pain is the "stick," and social reward is the "carrot." Social cooperation activates the appetitive/reward system, particularly the nucleus accumbens, the caudate nucleus, ventromedial frontal/orbitofrontal cortex, and rostral anterior cingulate cortex (Rilling et al., 2002), whereas social exclusion activates the

dorsal anterior cingulate cortex (dACC) (Eisenberger, Lieberman, & Williams, 2003). Together, the push and pull forces of social pain and reward combine to confer the survival benefits of social connections. The shadow of this evolutionary history is that the perturbations in brain and biology that were adaptive in evolutionary time can carry more deleterious effects in contemporary society. In this chapter, we elaborate on our theory of loneliness and survey representative evidence that chronic loneliness hijacks brain and biology to produce significant consequences for health and well-being.

Implications and Extensions of an Evolutionary Model of Loneliness

An evolutionary model of loneliness presumes heritable differences in the degree to which the pain of social disconnection is experienced. In some circumstances, greater sensitivity to the pain of social disconnection could be advantageous because it motivates communication, cooperation, and mutual aid and defense that enhance survival of one's genes (i.e., one's children), even if not oneself. In other circumstances, less sensitivity to the pain of social disconnection could be advantageous because it encourages extended periods of exploration and isolated adventures. Moreover, to the extent that weak aversive responses to social disconnection might enhance one's own survival and future reproductive opportunities, even if at the cost of the survival of one's current offspring, some circumstances (e.g., mass starvation, village massacres) might have favored the later offspring of those who selfishly survive and live long enough that the offspring also reproduce. Natural selection processes therefore should result in variability in social pain sensitivity to hedge the likelihood of the survival of the species. In support of this reasoning, studies of children, adolescents, and adults have shown that approximately 50 percent of the variation in loneliness is attributable to genetic factors, with the balance largely explained by unshared environmental factors (McGuire & Clifford, 2000; Boomsma, Willemsen, Dolan, Hawkley, & Cacioppo, 2005).

Knowing that there is a heritable component to loneliness does not address which specific genes are involved, however. Recent work has implicated polymorphisms in the oxytocin receptor gene (*OXTR*) as a contributor to individual differences in loneliness. Oxytocin is a key player in what has been termed the "calm and connection system" (Uvnäs-Moberg, Arn, & Magnusson, 2005). Although typically associated with labor and lactation, oxytocin is released in both men and women with salubrious social effects. Intranasal administration of oxytocin increases social approach behavior, social bonding, trust, and generosity; improves facial emotion recognition; reduces anxiety and responsiveness to social threat; and attenuates cortisol responses to psychosocial stress (Lee, Macbeth, Pagani, & Young, 2009). None of these effects is possible without an oxytocin receptor, and interindividual variation in the oxytocin receptor genotype contributes to individual differences in loneliness. Lucht et al. (2009) examined combinations of single nucleotide polymorphisms (SNPs) at each of three locations on the *OXTR* gene (rs53576, rs2254298, and rs2228485) and found that loneliness in a sample of 20–79-year-old adults was significantly higher among those with a GGC haplotype (i.e., a combination of the G alleles of rs53576 and rs2254298 and the C allele of rs2228485) than those with a GGT haplotype. Loneliness has been associated with differential sensitivity to social reward, and polymorphisms in the OXTR gene may help to explain why positive social stimuli are less satisfying for lonely than nonlonely individuals (Cacioppo, Norris, Decety, Monteleone, & Nusbaum, 2009).

Another gene of potential relevance to loneliness is the μ-opioid receptor gene. Recall that loneliness is a type of social pain, and that social pain activates aspects of the pain matrix in the brain. In animal models, the μ-opioid receptor (MOR) mediates the effect of opiates (e.g., morphine) not only on physical pain (Sora et al., 1997), but also on the social pain of infant separation from the mother (i.e., distress vocalization) (Moles, Kieffer, & D'Amato, 2004). Recent evidence from a study of humans indicates that variability in the MOR gene (*OPRM1*), and the A118G SNP in particular, is associated with variability in sensitivity to social pain (Way, Taylor, & Eisenberger, 2009). In a functional magnetic resonance imaging (fMRI) study of 31 young adults, sensitivity to the social pain of rejection was assessed by having individuals play a virtual ball-tossing game, ostensibly with two other individuals but in reality with a programmed computer. During one game of 60 throws, the subject was included; in a second game, the subject was excluded after having received the ball seven times. Dispositional sensitivity to rejection (self-reported) and activity in the pain processing region of the brain (dACC, anterior insula) during the exclusion relative to the inclusion version of the game were each significantly higher in the G allele carriers than A allele homozygotes. Moreover, the degree of

activation in the dACC was significantly associated with dispositional rejection sensitivity and mediated the association between A118G polymorphisms and rejection sensitivity (Way et al., 2009). Causal relationships cannot be inferred from these data, however, and additional research is needed to exclude the possibility, for instance, that dispositional rejection sensitivity leads to altered dACC activity, perhaps independently of A118G polymorphisms.

In sum, the overlap between physical and social pain in neural circuitry as well as in MOR gene receptor polymorphisms that are differentially associated with sensitivity to pain suggests that social pain responsivity was built on a pre-existing foundation for physical pain responsivity (Eisenberger et al., 2003). This provides a clue to understand why the primal pain of loneliness has such profound effects on biology. It is to these we turn next.

Loneliness Embodied

Terry Anderson, a former reporter in Lebanon, spent seven years as a hostage, most of that time in isolation. In his book, *Den of Lions* (1993), he describes in vivid detail the intense feelings of loneliness and their deleterious effects on his mentation and well-being. Empirical evidence now exists for various deleterious cognitive effects of loneliness including the rate of cognitive decline and the likelihood of Alzheimer's dementia in older adults (see Cacioppo & Hawkley, 2009). In population-based research, however, perceived isolation is far from synonymous with objective isolation (i.e., being alone, having no friends or family with whom to interact). Rather, loneliness reflects how people interpret their social world; the greater the discrepancy between desired and perceived degree of social connectedness, the greater the distress and pain (Peplau & Perlman, 1982). People hold intimate, relational, and collective representations of their social connections (Hawkley, Browne, & Cacioppo, 2005), and perceived shortcomings in any one of these domains (e.g., a spouse who fails to serve as a confidant, friends and relatives who don't meet a need for affirmation and support, and a lack of a sense of belonging to a meaningful group) can promote feelings of loneliness (Hawkley, et al., 2008). The fact that loneliness is "in the head" does not minimize its role in health and physiology. It is precisely because loneliness is represented in the brain that it can influence neural control of peripheral physiology. By virtue of extensive interconnections among the brain, peripheral nervous systems, endocrine glands, and even genes, the feelings of isolation and loneliness have a broad and deep reach.

Feelings of loneliness are associated with negative affective states, including depressed affect, anxiety, low self-esteem, hostility, anger, pessimism, fear of negative evaluation, perceived lack of social support, and perceived stress (Cacioppo et al., 2006; Hawkley, Masi, Berry, & Cacioppo, 2006). The neural underpinnings of negative (and positive) affective states involve the limbic system, those parts of the brain that contribute to the processing of emotion and memory (i.e., amygdala, hippocampus; cingulate, orbitofrontal, and insular cortices; basal forebrain and septal region) (Adams, Gordon, Baird, Ambady, & Kleck, 2003; Coan, Schaefer, & Davidson, 2006; Etkin et al., 2004; Killgore &Yurgelun-Todd, 2004; Liberzon, Phan, Decker, & Taylor, 2003). These same regions communicate with the brainstem and hypothalamus to regulate activity of the autonomic nervous system (ANS) and the hypothalamic-pituitary-adrenocortical (HPA) axis (Ulrich-Lai & Herman, 2009). These pathways, especially the HPA axis, provide a neural foundation for loneliness to influence peripheral physiology and, via feedback loops, to reach back again to affect the brain.

The sympathetic and vagal branches of the ANS play direct roles in regulating heart rate, cardiac contractility and stroke volume, and total peripheral resistance (TPR). Among the first studies showing an influence of loneliness on physiology were studies that found an association between loneliness and altered cardiovascular functioning indicative of differences in ANS activity. Specifically, among young adults, TPR was elevated in the lonely relative to the nonlonely group, whether measured at baseline or during laboratory stressors (Cacioppo, Hawkley, Crawford, et al., 2002; Hawkley, Burleson, Berntson, & Cacioppo, 2003). Experimental manipulations of social threat have also been observed to increase levels of TPR (Ewart, Jorgensen, Schroder, Suchday, & Sherwood, 2004), indicating that TPR differences between the lonely and nonlonely group are consistent with our theoretical conception that loneliness activates implicit hypervigilance to social threat (Cacioppo & Hawkley, 2009) on a chronic basis.

TPR, together with cardiac output, determines levels of blood pressure, and increases in TPR with age are largely responsible for age-related increases in systolic blood pressure (SBP), at least until 50 years of age (Franklin, 1997). Our studies revealed no SBP differences between lonely and nonlonely young adults (Cacioppo, Hawkley, Crawford, et al., 2002; Hawkley et al., 2003), as would be expected given blood pressure is a regulated physiological endpoint and the homeostatic mechanisms of young adults are generally quite resilient. However, over years these elevated levels of vascular resistance can contribute to elevated SBP (Franklin, 1997). The physiological changes that give rise to changes in SBP take time to exert their effects, and when we tested middle- and older age adults (50–68 years old), loneliness made a significant difference in SBP levels. A mere ten points on the loneliness scale (where totals range from 20–80 points) was associated with a 5 mm Hg higher SBP, and the older the individual, the larger the association between loneliness and SBP (Hawkley et al., 2006).[1]

Evidence of the slowly accumulating effect of loneliness was demonstrated in a longitudinal study of these same individuals. In this study, short-term (i.e., one year) fluctuations in loneliness were not significant predictors of SBP changes over one-year intervals, but a trait-like component of loneliness present at study onset contributed to greater increases in SBP over two-, three-, and four-year intervals (Hawkley et al., under review). Elevated SBP is a risk factor for chronic cardiovascular disease, and these data suggest that the effects of loneliness accrue to accelerate movement along a trajectory toward serious health consequences (Hawkley & Cacioppo, 2007).

Another mechanism through which loneliness may impact health involves alterations in HPA activity. The hypothalamus receives neural input on brain and body states (e.g., pain, anger, fear, hunger) and communicates with brain and spinal cord regions that regulate activity of the ANS (see above) and the pituitary gland. The pituitary gland releases hormones that ultimately permit modulation of almost every endocrine gland in the body, including the adrenal glands. Pituitary secretion of adenocorticotropic hormone (ACTH) stimulates synthesis and secretion of cortisol by the adrenal cortex. Any physical or psychological stimulus that requires, or might require, metabolic resources activates the HPA axis and increases circulating levels of cortisol. The finely choreographed physiological results of increased cortisol include increases in blood sugar levels and blood pressure and parallel decreases in immune responses and inflammation to maximize the amount of energy allocated to more immediate metabolic needs. Social evaluative threat is a potent stimulus that elicits an increase in cortisol (Dickerson & Kemeny, 2004), and loneliness, which we theorize is characterized by chronic threat of and hypervigilance for negative social evaluation (Cacioppo & Hawkley, 2009), is associated with chronic elevations in ACTH (Cacioppo et al., 2000) and cortisol (Kiecolt-Glaser, Ricker, George, Messick, Speicher, Garner, et al., 1984), especially in the morning (Adam, Hawkley, Kudielka, & Cacioppo, 2006; Steptoe, Owen, Kunz-Ebrecht, & Brydon, 2004). In our study of 50–68 year-old men and women, we assessed salivary cortisol upon awakening, 30 minutes after awakening (to estimate the cortisol awakening response, or CAR), and at bedtime for each of three consecutive days in their home settings. We also asked subjects to complete a mini-diary at day's end in which they endorsed the degree to which they had experienced feelings of loneliness, sadness, and threat that day. These feeling states cohered to form a single component that was associated with a higher CAR. In addition, competing causal models showed that feelings of loneliness and threat at day's end predicted a higher spike in the CAR the next morning, but the CAR in the morning did not predict feelings of loneliness and threat on the ensuing day (Adam et al., 2006). The association between loneliness and higher CAR values is not restricted to daily fluctuations in feelings of loneliness but is also evident as a function of trait differences in degree of loneliness. Steptoe et al. (2004) found that chronically high levels of trait loneliness in middle-aged adults ($M = 52.4$ yrs) predicted a greater CAR such that the CAR in individuals in the highest loneliness tertile was 21 percent greater than that in the lowest tertile.

On the face of it, higher cortisol levels should be good for health. After all, cortisol is a potent anti-inflammatory agent (consider, for example, the use of hydrocortisone cream to quell the inflammation elicited by poison ivy exposure). Many chronic diseases are diseases of chronic inflammation (e.g., hypertension, cardiovascular disease, atherosclerosis, cancer), and elevated levels of cortisol should protect against their development and progression. Paradoxically, loneliness is associated with a greater risk of chronic disease and mortality (Caspi, Harrington, Moffitt, Milne, & Poulton, 2006; Penninx, van Tilburg, Kriegsman, Deeg, Boeke, & van Eijk, 1997; Seeman, 2000; Sugisawa, Liang, & Liu, 1994; Thurston & Kubzansky, 2009). This phenomenon has a possible explanation in the fact that chronically elevated levels of cortisol may signal desensitization of target tissues to its anti-inflammatory effects.

Negative feedback control of cortisol synthesis and secretion at the hypothalamus and pituitary gland depends on optimal concentrations and functioning of the glucocorticoid receptor (GR). When GR activity is compromised, cortisol has a diminished capacity to shut off its own production through feedback at each level of the HPA axis. In addition, when GR activity is reduced, downstream anti-inflammatory effects mediated by the GR are also diminished. A number of molecular mechanisms have been shown to contribute to glucocorticoid desensitization, including decreased expression of the GR gene and increased expression of pro-inflammatory transcription factors that inhibit expression of the GR gene (Barnes & Adcock, 2009).

Some basic definitions and terminology about gene expression are in order at this point (see also, Champagne & Mashoodh, 2009, and Ochs & Golemis, 2003, for a basic tutorial on gene expression). Gene expression refers to a multi-step process through which a gene leads to a functional gene product (typically a protein). Each step—transcription, mRNA splicing, translation, and post-translational protein modification—can be regulated by internal or external influences (Jaenisch & Bird, 2003) to alter the end product. These are known as epigenetic effects because the gene itself is not altered. At the transcription step, differences in gene expression between groups of individuals are assessed by comparing the relative levels of transcribed RNA, strands of nucleotides that complement the DNA being transcribed (e.g., thymidine on the DNA is transcribed as adenine on the RNA, cytidine as guanine). High-density DNA microarrays simultaneously assess relative levels of transcribed messenger RNA (mRNA) across the entire human genome. The gene transcription process is highly complex, and interactions among signaling pathways mean that expression levels of different genes are correlated. Differentially expressed genes are therefore examined for functional commonalities by referring to existing gene function databases (e.g., Gene Ontology, or GO annotations). Additional analyses can be conducted to identify upstream transcription control pathways that mediate the gene expression differences. These analyses rely on group comparisons of transcription-factor binding motifs (TFBMs; i.e., particular nucleotide sequences on gene regulatory regions) in up- or down-regulated genes.

Recent findings indicate that psychosocial variables may have epigenetic effects (Cole, 2009; Cole et al., 2007; Miller et al., 2008; Miller, Rohleder,

& Cole, 2009), and this is where we return to the story of loneliness. We compared gene expression rates in leukocytes extracted from blood samples in a small group of chronically lonely adults (i.e., consistently highly lonely for each of three consecutive years) and a matched group of socially connected adults. Genome-wide microarray analyses revealed that 209 transcripts, representing 144 distinct genes, were differentially expressed in these two groups. Over-expressed genes in the lonely relative to the socially connected group (37% of the 209 differentially expressed transcripts) included transcription factors that share functional commonalities representing regulation of cell growth and cycling. These functions take on special significance in leukocytes that play a role in immune and inflammatory processes. Over-expressed genes in these leukocyte samples included genes for immune activation and inflammation (e.g., pro-inflammatory cytokines and inflammatory mediators). Under-expressed genes in the lonely relative to the socially connected group (63% of the differentially expressed transcripts) included markers for cell cycle inhibitors and an inhibitor of the potent pro-inflammatory NF-κB transcript, with functional implications that complement the increased expression of genes favoring increased cell cycling and inflammation. In addition, under-expressed genes in the lonely group included genes for immunoglobulins and B lymphocyte maturation and differentiation suggesting functional impairments in mature B lymphocyte activity. Differential gene expression rates were not attributable to objective indices of social isolation, nor were they explained by associated demographic, psychosocial (i.e., perceived stress, depression, hostility), or medical risk factors (Cole et al., 2007). Rather, these data suggest that chronic subjective social isolation (i.e., loneliness) is a unique risk factor associated with altered expression of genes relevant to inflammatory processes.

As noted above, one pathway to glucocorticoid resistance and over-activation of immune- and inflammation-related genes is under-expression of the GR gene (NR3C1). The lonely and socially connected groups did not differ in expression rates of NR3C1, however. Additional analyses were therefore conducted to examine whether increased transcription of immune activation genes in the lonely group could be explained by reduced GR-mediated transcriptional activity or by increased activity of the pro-inflammatory NF-κB transcriptional pathway. Consistent with a reduction in GR-mediated transcriptional activity, TFBMs for glucocorticoid

response elements (GREs) were significantly lower in genes over-expressed in the lonely group relative to genes over-expressed in the socially connected group. Cross-inhibition of GR and NF-κB target genes is well known, and a relative paucity of GREs in the lonely group suggests poorer detection of the glucocorticoid signal and therefore less effective reduction of the pro-inflammatory signaling pathway. In support of this hypothesis, TFBMs for pro-inflammatory NF-κB/Rel response elements were significantly higher in genes over-expressed in the lonely group relative to genes over-expressed in the socially connected group. Moreover, the ratio of under-expressed GREs and over-expressed NF-κB/Rel response elements (5.08) significantly exceeded that expected by chance across the whole genome (.0035) (Cole et al., 2007). The precise molecular site of GR resistance in the pro-inflammatory transcription cascade has yet to be identified, and additional longitudinal and experimental research are needed to determine the degree to which chronic feelings of social isolation play a causal role in differential gene expression. However, the association between subjective social isolation and gene expression corresponds well to gene expression differences in animal models of social isolation (e.g., Levine & Mody, 2003; Pan, Liu, Young, Zhang, & Wang, 2009), suggesting that a subjective sense of isolation, or conversely, connectedness, is important for genomic expression and normal immunoregulation in humans. We are socially attuned beings to our cellular core, sculpted by an evolutionary history that has endowed us with an exquisite sensitivity to a perceived sense of social connectedness or isolation.

The effects of loneliness on cardiovascular, neuroendocrine, and genome physiology happen outside our awareness, and convey the possibility that a realm of unconscious processes may be similarly affected. Sleep is probably one of the most telling unconscious processes shown to be influenced by loneliness. In our evolutionary history, humans were most vulnerable during sleep and relied on the presence of others to ensure a sense of safety that permitted good quality sleep. The importance of protective others for good quality sleep is evident to this day. From the carefully designed circular structure of desert villages in Africa, to the more specific example of the "circle of sleep" in which "lost boys" of Sudan took turns sleeping in the center of a circle of protective others to survive nightly threat of attack by rodents (and sometimes lions) (Eggers, 2006), sound and restorative sleep depends on a sense of safety and security which is best afforded in the company of others who can aid in our defense. Is it any wonder that the lack of a sense of security that defines the implicitly threatened lonely individual influences sleep? Notably, feelings of loneliness rarely affect the amount of sleep, but they do affect the quality of sleep. In young adults (18–25 yrs), sleep cap data were collected for one night in a hospital bed and for seven nights in participants' own beds. Results showed similar sleep duration but a greater number of micro-awakenings in the lonely than the socially connected group (Cacioppo, Hawkley, Berntson, et al., 2002). In 50–68 year-old adults, analyses of the three-day diary protocol described earlier showed that greater loneliness at the end of one day predicted poorer sleep quality that night (Hawkley, Preacher, & Cacioppo, 2009), and this effect was independent of sleep duration (which did not differ as a function of loneliness). In a seven-year follow-up study of elderly adults, feelings of loneliness at 70 years of age predicted poorer sleep quality at 77 years of age, and this effect was independent of other significant risk factors including depression, obesity, back pain, poor self-rated health, economic problems, and pre-existing poor sleep quality (Jacobs, Cohen, Hammerman-Rozenberg, & Stessman, 2006). The developing picture is that the feeling of social isolation hijacks not only peripheral biology but also the unconscious state of sleep.

Loneliness also exerts an influence on cognition in part through stealth means. At a fundamental level, loneliness impairs self-regulatory abilities indicative of executive function. For instance, lonely young adults were less successful than their non-lonely counterparts in shifting auditory attention from the dominant right ear to the non-dominant left ear (Cacioppo et al., 2000). In middle-aged and older adults, loneliness was associated with a diminished tendency to capitalize on positive emotions, a type of emotion regulation that explained why lonely individuals were less likely than nonlonely individuals to engage in physical activity (Hawkley, Thisted, & Cacioppo, 2009). At a more profound level, loneliness increases risk for the devastating effects of impaired cognitive ability and dementia. For instance, a 4-year prospective study of initially dementia-free older adults showed that the risk of Alzheimer's disease was more than twice as great in lonely than in nonlonely individuals. In addition, loneliness was associated with lower cognitive ability at baseline and with a more rapid decline in

cognition during the 4-year follow-up (Wilson et al., 2007). Similar results were reported for a sample of 75–85-year-old individuals over a 10-year follow-up (Tilvis et al., 2004). These findings are particularly disturbing in light of ongoing declines in multigenerational households worldwide (Kinsella & He, 2009) and an increase in older people living alone (U.S. Census Bureau, 2009). Living alone is itself a health risk factor, but it is not synonymous with being lonely. Living alone increases risk for feelings of loneliness, however, and for that reason the true cost of solitary living for health, cognitive and physical, is not yet fully appreciated.

The Loneliness Regulatory Loop

Loneliness imposes an additional burden to that of declining physical and mental health, and that is its impact on emotional health and well-being. The reflexive thoughts associated with implicit social threat foster a downward negative spiral evident in increased depressive symptoms (Cacioppo, Hawkley, & Thisted, 2009) and diminished life satisfaction (Cacioppo, Hawkley, et al., 2008) over time. We have posited that feelings of loneliness are the entry point into a regulatory loop that begins with heightened vigilance for perceived social threat (see Figure 50.1). For instance, in a Stroop study that pitted color against content of verbal stimuli, negative social words (e.g., rejected, alone, disliked), but not positive social words, created greater interference for lonely than nonlonely individuals (Egidi et al., 2008). Similarly, in an fMRI study, activation of the visual cortex was greater in lonely than nonlonely individuals when viewing negative social (compared to nonsocial) stimuli—a significant effect that was not observed for the positive social minus positive nonsocial contrast (Cacioppo et al., 2009). These data suggest that loneliness increases attention to negative social information and potential social threats, findings that correspond to well-substantiated characterizations of the lonely individual as distrustful, fearful of negative evaluation, and anxious (Cacioppo et al., 2006; Ernst & Cacioppo, 1999; Rotenberg, 1994). As shown in Figure 50.1, vigilance for social threat produces attentional, confirmatory, and memory biases (Cacioppo & Hawkley, 2009). These biases lead to behavioral confirmation processes through which negative social interactions are perpetuated (Hawkley, Preacher, & Cacioppo, 2007), thereby reinforcing the lonely individual's belief that he or she has little control or social value. Social pain (e.g., depressive symptoms) continues unabated, and the carrot

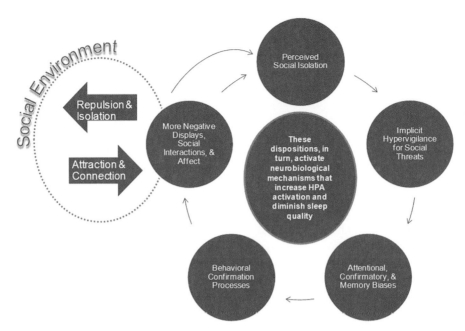

Fig. 50.1 The Loneliness Regulatory Loop. This is a reproduction of Figure III (p. 451) in: Cacioppo, J. T. & Hawkley, L. C. (2009). Perceived social isolation and cognition. Trends in Cognitive Science, 13, 447–454.

of social reward lies just beyond reach. The latter is evident in reduced activation in the reward circuitry (i.e., ventral striatum) among lonely individuals in response to positive social relative to positive nonsocial stimuli (Cacioppo et al., 2009).

It is also evident in the environmental forces of social attraction and repulsion that push the lonely person further and further toward the periphery of a social network (Cacioppo, Fowler, & Christakis, 2009), but not without first placing those around them at higher risk for becoming lonely and undermining overall trust and cohesion. We are only now beginning to truly understand the ramifications of our individualistic lifestyles, as our social brains struggle to cope with isolation, loneliness and failing communities. Our evolutionary heritage has endowed us with the capacity to feel the pain of social isolation and the rewards of social connection. Importantly, it has also endowed us with the capacity to feel others' social pain (see Decety, this volume) and the compassion to care for the sick and the elderly far beyond their reproductive or economic utility. A society that is measured by the strength of its weakest link would do well to tend to the innate need for a sense of social connectedness and belonging in each of its members. The extant myth of rugged individualism notwithstanding, the social, mental, medical, and economic costs of denying our evolutionary heritage are too great to ignore.

Acknowledgments

This research was supported by National Institute of Aging Program Project Grant No. PO1 AG18911, RO1 AG034052–01, RO1 AG036433–01, and by an award from the Templeton Foundation.

Note

1 Loneliness was also associated with greater concentrations of urinary epinephrine in an overnight sample, indicating greater cumulative activity of the sympathetic nervous system at the adrenal medulla (Hawkley et al., 2006). At high concentrations, circulating epinephrine binds α-1 receptors on vascular smooth muscle cells to elicit vasoconstriction and could thereby serve as a mechanism for increased SBP in lonely individuals. Urinary epinephrine concentrations did not explain loneliness differences in SBP in our sample, however (unpublished findings).

References

Adam, E. K., Hawkley, L. C., Kudielka, B. M., & Cacioppo, J. T. (2006). Day-to-day dynamics of experience-cortisol associations in a population-based sample of older adults. *Proceedings of the National Academy of Sciences, 103,* 17058–17063. PMC1636578.

Adams, R. B. Jr., Gordon, H. L., Baird, A. A., Ambady, N., & Kleck, R. E. (2003). Effects of gaze on amygdala sensitivity to anger and fear faces. *Science, 300,* 1536.

Anderson, T. (1993). *Den of lions.* New York: Ballantine Books.

Barnes, P. J. & Adcock, I. M. (2009). Glucocorticoid resistance in inflammatory diseases. *The Lancet, 373,* 1905–1917.

Boomsma, D. I., Willemsen, G., Dolan, C. V., Hawkley, L. C., & Cacioppo, J. T. (2005). Genetic and environmental contributions to loneliness in adults: The Netherlands Twin Register Study. *Behavior Genetics, 35,* 745–752.

Cacioppo, J. T., Ernst, J. M., Burleson, M. H., McClintock, M. K., Malarkey, W. B., Hawkley, L. C., et al. (2000). Lonely traits and concomitant physiological processes: The MacArthur Social Neuroscience Studies. *International Journal of Psychophysiology*, 35, 143–154.

Cacioppo, J. T., Fowler, J. H., & Christakis, N. A. (2009). Alone in the crowd: The structure and spread of loneliness in a large social network. *Journal of Personality and Social Psychology*, 97, 977–991.

Cacioppo, J. T. & Hawkley, L. C. (2009). Perceived social isolation and cognition. *Trends in Cognitive Science*, 13, 447–454. doi:10.1016/j.tics.2009.06.005.

Cacioppo, J. T., Hawkley, L. C., Berntson, G. G., Ernst, J. M., Gibbs, A. C., Stickgold, R., & Hobson, J. A. (2002). Do lonely days invade the nights? Potential social modulation of sleep efficiency. *Psychological Science*, 13, 385–388.

Cacioppo, J. T., Hawkley, L. C., Crawford, L. E., Ernst, J. M., Burleson, M. H., Kowalewski, R. B., et al. (2002). Loneliness and health: Potential mechanisms. *Psychosomatic Medicine*, 64, 407–417.

Cacioppo, J. T., Hawkley, L. C., Ernst, J. M., Burleson, M. H., Berntson, G. G., Nouriani, B., et al. (2006). Loneliness within a nomological net: An evolutionary perspective. *Journal of Research in Personality*, 40, 1054–1085.

Cacioppo, J. T., Hawkley, L. C., Kalil, A., Hughes, M. E., Waite, L., & Thisted, R. A. (2008). Happiness and the invisible threads of social connection: The Chicago Health, Aging, and Social Relations Study. In M. Eid & R. Larsen (Eds.), *The science of well-being* (pp. 195–219). New York: Guilford.

Cacioppo, J. T., Norris, C. J., Decety, J., Monteleone, G., & Nusbaum, H. (2009). In the eye of the beholder: Individual differences in perceived social isolation predict regional brain activation to social stimuli. *Journal of Cognitive Neuroscience*, 21, 83–92.

Cacioppo, J. T. & Patrick, W. (2008). *Loneliness: Human nature and the need for social connection*. New York: W. W. Norton & Company.

Caspi, A., Harrington, H., Moffitt, T.E., Milne, B.J., & Poulton, R. (2006). Socially isolated children 20 years later. *Archives of Pediatric Adolescent Medicine*, 160, 805–811.

Champagne, F. A. & Mashoodh, R. (2009). Genes in context: Gene-environment interplay and the origins of individual differences in behavior. *Current Directions in Psychological Science*, 18, 127–131.

Chobanian, A. V., Bakris, G. L., Black, H. R., Cushman, W. C., Green, L. A., Izzo, J. L., Jr., et al. (2003). The seventh report of the Joint National Committee on prevention, detection, evaluation, and treatment of high blood pressure. *Journal of the American Medical Association*, 289, 2560–2572.

Coan, J. A., Schaefer, H. S., & Davidson, R. J. (2006). Lending a hand: Social regulation of the neural response to threat. *Psychological Science*, 17, 1032–1039.

Cole, S. W. (2009). Social regulation of human gene expression. *Current Directions in Psychological Science*, 18, 132–137.

Cole, S. W., Hawkley, L. C., Arevalo, J. M., Sung, C. Y., Rose, R. M., & Cacioppo, J. T. (2007). Social regulation of gene expression in humans: Glucocorticoid resistance in the leukocyte transcriptome. *Genome Biology*, 8, R189.1–R189.13. PMC2375027.

Dickerson, S. S. & Kemeny, M. E. (2004). Acute stressors and cortisol responses: A theoretical integration and synthesis of laboratory research. *Psychological Bulletin*, 130, 355–391.

Eggers, D. (2006). *What is the what?* San Francisco: McSweeney's.

Ernst, J. M. & Cacioppo, J. T. (1999). Lonely hearts: Psychological perspectives on loneliness. *Applied & Preventive Psychology*, 8, 1–22.

Egidi, G., Shintel, H., Nusbaum, H. C., & Cacioppo, J. T. (2008). Social isolation and neural correlates of attention control, 20th Annual Meeting of the Association for Psychological Science. Chicago, IL.

Eisenberger, N. I., Lieberman, M., & Williams, K. D. (2003). Does rejection hurt? An fMRI study of social exclusion. *Science*, 302, 290–292.

Etkin, A., Klemenhagen, K. C., Dudman, J. T., Rogan, M. T., Hen, R., Kandel, E. R., & Hirsch, J. (2004). Individual differences in trait anxiety predict the response of the basolateral amygdala to unconsciously processed fearful faces. *Neuron*, 44, 1043–1055.

Ewart, C. K., Jorgensen, R. S., Schroder, K. E., Suchday, S., & Sherwood, A. (2004). Vigilance to a persisting personal threat: Unmasking cardiovascular consequences in adolescents with the Social Competence Interview. *Psychophysiology*, 41, 799–804.

Franklin, S. S. (1997). Hemodynamic patterns of age-related changes in blood pressure: The Framingham Heart Study. *Circulation*, 96, 308–315.

Hawkley, L. C., Bosch, J. A., Engeland, C. G., Marucha, P. T., & Cacioppo, J. T. (2007). Loneliness, dysphoria, stress and immunity: A role for cytokines. N. Plotnikoff et al., Eds. *Cytokines: Stress, & Immunity*, 2nd ed. (pp. 67–85). Boca Raton, FL: CRC Press.

Hawkley, L. C., Browne, M. W., & Cacioppo, J. T. (2005). How can I connect with thee? Let me count the ways. *Psychological Science*, 16, 798–804.

Hawkley, L. C., Burleson, M. H., Berntson, G. G., & Cacioppo, J. T. (2003). Loneliness in everyday life: Cardiovascular activity, psychosocial context, and health behaviors. *Journal of Personality & Social Psychology*, 85, 105–120.

Hawkley, L. C. & Cacioppo, J. T. (2007). Aging and loneliness: Downhill quickly? *Current Directions in Psychological Science*, 16, 187–191.

Hawkley, L. C., Hughes, M. E., Waite, L., J., Masi, C. M., Thisted, R. A., & Cacioppo, J. T. (2008). From social structural factors to perceptions of relationship quality and loneliness: The Chicago Health, Aging, and Social Relations Study. *Journal of Gerontology: Social Sciences*, 63B, S375–S384.

Hawkley, L. C., Masi, C. M., Berry, J. D., & Cacioppo, J. T. (2006). Loneliness is a unique predictor of age-related differences in systolic blood pressure. *Psychology and Aging*, 21, 152–164.

Hawkley, L. C., Preacher, K. J., & Cacioppo, J. T. (2007). Multilevel modeling of social interactions and mood in lonely and socially connected individuals: The MacArthur Social Neuroscience Studies. In A.D. Ong & M.H.M. van Dulmen (Eds.), *Oxford handbook of methods in positive psychology* (pp. 559–575). New York: Oxford University Press.

Hawkley, L. C., Preacher, K, J., & Cacioppo, J. T. (2009). Loneliness impairs daytime functioning but not sleep duration. Manuscript under review.

Hawkley, L. C., Thisted, R. A., & Cacioppo, J. T. (2009). Loneliness predicts reduced physical activity: Cross-sectional and longitudinal analyses. *Health Psychology*, 28, 354–363.

Hawkley, L. D., Thisted, R. A., Masi, C. M., & Cacioppo, J. T. (2009). Loneliness predicts increased blood pressure: Five-year cross-lagged analyses in middle-aged and older adults. *Psychology and Aging, 25*, 132–141.

Jacobs, J. M., Cohen, A., Hammerman-Rozenberg, R., & Stessman, J. (2006). Global sleep satisfaction of older people: The Jerusalem Cohort Study. *Journal of the American Geriatric Society, 54*, 325–329.

Jaenisch, R. & Bird, A. (2003). Epigenetic regulation of gene expression: How the genome integrates intrinsic and environmental signals. *Nature Genetics Supplement, 33*, 245–254.

Kemeny, M. E. & Schedlowski, M. (2007). Understanding the interaction between psychosocial stress and immune-related diseases: A stepwise progression. *Brain, Behavior, & Immunity, 21*, 1009–1018.

Kiecolt-Glaser, J. K., Ricker, D., George, J., Messick, G., Speicher, C. E., Garner, W., & Glaser, R. (1984). Urinary cortisol levels, cellular immunocompetency and loneliness in psychiatric inpatients. *Psychosomatic Medicine, 46*, 15–23.

Killgore, W. D. & Yurgelun-Todd, D. A. (2004). Sex-related developmental differences in the lateralized activation of the prefrontal cortex and amygdala during perception of facial affect. *Perceptual & Motor Skills, 99*, 371–391. [PMID. 15560325]

Kinsella, K. & He, W. (2009). *An aging world: 2008.* Washington, DC: U.S. Census Bureau, International Population Reports, P95/09–1.

Lee, H.-J., Macbeth. A. H., Pagani, J. H., & Young, W. S. 3rd (2009). Oxytocin: The great facilitator of life. *Progress in Neurobiology, 88*, 127–151.

Levine, S. & Mody, T. (2003). The long-term psychobiological consequences of intermittent postnatal separation in the squirrel monkey. *Neuroscience & Biobehavioral Reviews, 27*, 83–89.

Liberzon, I., Phan, K. L., Decker, L. R., & Taylor, S. F. (2003). Extended amygdala and emotional salience: A PET activation study of positive and negative affect. *Neuropsychopharmacology, 28*, 726–733.

Lucht, M. J., Barnow, S., Sonnenfeld, C., Rosenberger, A., Grabe, H. J., Schroeder, W., et al. (2009). Associations between the oxytocin receptor gene (OXTR) and affect, loneliness and intelligence in normal subjects. *Progress in Neuro-Psychopharmacology & Biological Psychiatry, 33*, 860–866.

McGuire, S. & Clifford, J. (2000). Genetic and environmental contributions to loneliness in children. *Psychological Science, 11*, 487–491.

Miller, G. E., Chen, E., Sze, J., Marin, T., Arevalo, J. M., Doll, R., et al. (2008). A functional genomic fingerprint of chronic stress in humans: Blunted glucocorticoid and increased NF-kappaB signaling. *Biological Psychiatry, 64*, 266–272.

Miller, G. E., Rohleder, N., & Cole, S. W. (2009). Chronic interpersonal stress predicts activation of pro- and anti-inflammatory signaling pathways 6 months later. *Psychosomatic Medicine, 71*, 57–62.

Moles, A., Kieffer, B. L., D'Amato, R. F. (2004). Deficit in attachment behavior in mice lacking the mu-opioid receptor gene. *Science, 304*, 1983–1986.

Ochs, M. F. & Golemis, E. A. (2003). The biology behind gene expression: A basic tutorial. In K. F. Johnson & S. M. Lin, (Eds.), *Methods of microarray data analysis III* (pp. 9–24). Norwell, MA: Kluwer Academic Publishers.

Pan, Y., Liu, Y., Young, K. A., Zhang, Z., & Wang, Z. (2009). Post-weaning social isolation alters anxiety-related behavior and neurochemical gene expression in the brain of mal prairie voles. *Neuroscience Letters, 454*, 67–71.

Penninx, B. W. J. H., van Tilburg, T., Kriegsman, D. M. W., Deeg, D. J. H., Boeke, A. J. P., & van Eijk, J. Th. M. (1997). Effects of social support and personal coping resources on mortality in older age: The Longitudinal Aging Study Amsterdam. *American Journal of Epidemiology, 146*, 510–519.

Peplau, L. A. & Perlman, D. (1982). Perspectives on loneliness. In L. A. Peplau & D. Perlman (Eds.), *Loneliness: A sourcebook of current theory, research and therapy* (pp. 1–20). New York: John Wiley & Sons.

Rilling, J. K., Gutman, D. A., Zeh, T. R., Pagnoni, G., Berns, G. S., & Kilts, C. D. (2002). A neural basis for social cooperation. *Neuron, 35*, 395–405.

Rotenberg, K. (1994). Loneliness and interpersonal trust. *Journal of Social and Clinical Psychology, 13*, 152–173.

Rozanski, A. & Kubzansky, L. D. (2005). Psychologic functioning and physical health: A paradigm of flexibility. *Psychosomatic Medicine, 67*, S47–53.

Seeman, T. E. (2000). Health-promoting effects of friends and family on health outcomes in older adults. *American Journal of Public Health, 14*, 362–370.

Siegrist, J. (2008). Chronic psychosocial stress at work and risk of depression: Evidence from prospective studies. *European Archives of Psychiatry and Clinical Neuroscience, 258*, 115–119.

Sora, I., Takahashi, N., Funada, M., Ujike, H., Revay, R., Donovan, D., et al. (1997). Opiate receptor knockout mice define mu receptor roles in endogenous nociceptive responses and morphine-induced analgesia. *Proceedings of the National Academy of Sciences, 94*, 1544–1549.

Steptoe, A., Owen, N., Kunz-Ebrecht, S. R., & Brydon, L. (2004). Loneliness and neuroendocrine, cardiovascular, and inflammatory stress responses in middle-aged men and women. *Psychoneuroendocrinology, 29*, 593–611.

Sugisawa, H., Liang, J., & Liu, X. (1994). Social networks, social support, and mortality among older people in Japan. *Journal of Gerontology, 49*, S3–13.

Thurston, R. C. & Kubzansky, L. D. (2009). Women, loneliness, and incident coronary heart disease. *Psychosomatic Medicine, 71*, doi: 10.1097/PSY.0b013e3181b40efc.

Tilvis, R. J., Kähönen-Väre, M. H., Jolkkonen, J., Valvanne, J., Pitkala, K. H., & Strandberg, T. E. (2004). Predictors of cognitive decline and mortality of aged people over a 10-year period. *The Journals of Gerontology Series A: Biological Sciences and Medical Sciences, 59*, M268–M274.

Ulrich-Lai, Y. M. & Herman, J. P. (2009). Neural regulation of endocrine and autonomic stress responses. *Nature Reviews Neuroscience, 10*, 397–409.

U.S. Census Bureau (2009). *America's families and living arrangements: 2008.* Washington, DC: U.S. Census Bureau, Housing and Household Economic Statistics Division, Fertility & Family Statistics Branch.

Uvnäs-Moberg, K., Arn, I., & Magnusson, D. (2005). The psychobiology of emotion: The role of the oxytocinergic system. *International Journal of Behavioral Medicine, 12*, 59–65.

Way, B. M., Taylor, S. E., & Eisenberger, N. I. (2009). Variation in the μ-opioid receptor gene (OPRM1) is associated with dispositional and neural sensitivity to social rejection.

Proceedings of the National Academy of Sciences, 106, 15079–15084.

Weiss, R.S. (1973). *The experience of emotional and social isolation.* Cambridge, MA: MIT Press.

Williams, K. D. (2007). Ostracism. *Annual Review of Psychology, 58,* 425–452.

Wilson, R. S., Krueger, K. R., Arnold, S. E., Schneider, J. A., Kelly, J. F., Barnes, L. L., et al. (2007). Loneliness and risk of Alzheimer's disease. *Archives of General Psychiatry, 64,* 234–240.

Pathways Linking Early Life Stress to Adult Health

Shelley E. Taylor

Abstract

This chapter presents a developmental model of responses to early life stress that integrates sociodemographic, genetic, psychosocial, neural, physiological, and health-related evidence concerning the pathways that may explain the often surprisingly strong relations between stress in early life and adult health. Genetic predispositions and aspects of the early environment are represented as joint predictors of the ability to develop psychosocial resources. Early life stress is known to compromise: emotion regulation; coping skills; the ability to make effective use of social support; individual differences in psychological resources; and chronic negative emotional states. These psychosocial factors, in turn, influence and are influenced by neural responses to threat in the brain that regulate autonomic, neuroendocrine, and immune responses to threatening circumstances. The cumulative impact of these inputs ultimately influences health risks. In addition, there are direct paths from genes and the early environment to compromised physiological functioning that do not route through psychosocial resources.

Keywords: early life stress, adult health, genetic predispositions, health risk, early environment

Both animal and human investigations reveal that adult mental and physical health is rooted in early experiences with threat. Early life experience helps to shape psychological and biological reactions to stress that persist across the lifespan (e.g., Liu et al., 1997; Repetti, Taylor, & Seeman, 2002) and affects the likelihood of developing stress-related health disorders (e.g., McEwen, 1998). How these early life experiences are instantiated in enduring form has consequently been an important area for research, because it is not immediately obvious why experiences in the first few years of life would affect the likelihood of early-onset chronic illness often decades later.

To address this issue, some investigators have focused heavily on the vulnerability of developing biological stress regulatory systems to extreme, recurring, or prolonged stress (e.g., Cacioppo & Patrick, 2008; McEwen, 1998; Seeman, Singer, Horwitz, & McEwen, 1997). Others have focused more heavily on the development of psychosocial factors that regulate socioemotional responses to stress (e.g., Cacioppo & Patrick, 2008; Folkman & Moskowitz, 2004; Taylor & Stanton, 2007). Genetic contributions to mental and physical health across the lifespan have been increasingly explored (e.g., Caspi et al., 2002; Caspi et al., 2003). The potential importance of critical periods in development is becoming understood as well (Meaney, 2001).

In this article, we present a developmental model of responses to early life stress that integrates sociodemographic, genetic, psychosocial, neural, physiological, and health-related evidence concerning the pathways that may explain the often surprisingly strong relations between stress in early life and adult health. The schematic model that guides our analysis is shown in Figure 51.1. We hasten to add that many other health psychologists and social neuroscientists adopt a similar model, but may emphasize somewhat different variables in the pathways to adult health. For example, Cacioppo and colleagues especially emphasize social support and loneliness (Cacioppo & Patrick, 2008), Matthews and colleagues emphasize the development of chronic emotional states and their adverse effects on health outcomes (Gallo & Matthews, 2003), and biological stress researchers focus on the accumulating damage to physiological systems (e.g., Seeman, McEwen, Rowe, & Singer, 2001).

In our approach (Figure 51.1), genetic predispositions and aspects of the early environment are represented as joint predictors of the ability to develop psychosocial resources. Early life stress is known to compromise: emotion regulation; coping skills; the ability to make effective use of social support; individual differences in psychological resources; and chronic negative emotional states. These psychosocial factors, in turn, influence and are influenced by neural responses to threat in the brain that regulate autonomic, neuroendocrine, and immune responses to threatening circumstances. The cumulative impact of these inputs ultimately influences health risks. In addition, there are direct paths from genes and the early environment to compromised physiological functioning that do not route through psychosocial resources.

As such, Figure 51.1 characterizes 1) a developmental model of stress-related health outcomes across the lifespan, 2) the metatheoretical perspective that has guided our work, and 3) the methodological procedures that have guided specific research investigations. Whether these are the primary variables and pathways linking early life experience to adult health outcomes remains to be determined by future research; at present, they represent our best efforts to identify pivotal variables. In the subsequent sections, we focus especially on our own research program, because it directly addresses the model in Figure 51.1.

Developmental Origins

Research indicates that health across the lifespan has origins in both early environmental and genetic factors. Low childhood socioeconomic status has been tied to a broad array of adult disorders, including depression, anxiety, coronary heart disease, cardiovascular disease, and immune-related disorders (e.g., Adler, Marmot, McEwen, & Stewart, 1999; Cohen, Doyle, Turner, Alper, & Skoner, 2004; Galobardes,

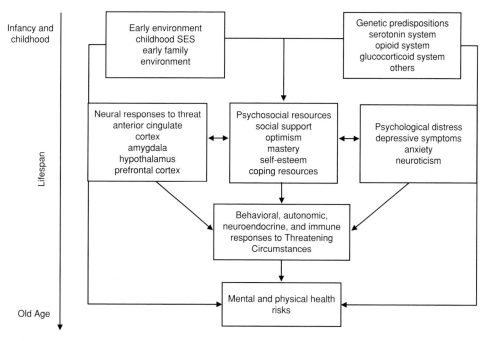

Fig. 51.1 A lifespan model of how early environment contributes to adult health risks.

Lynch, & Davey Smith, 2004; Galobardes, Davey Smith, & Lynch, 2006; Hemingway et al., 2003; Hertzman, 1999) and all-cause mortality (Kittleson et al., 2006; Kuh, Hardy, Langenberg, Richards, & Wadsworth, 2002). Similar patterns are found when an early family environment is assessed directly. A harsh family upbringing has been related to depression (Repetti et al., 2002); to acute disorders, such as susceptibility to respiratory infections (Cohen et al., 2004); to risk factors for chronic disease, including compromised metabolic functioning (e.g., Lehman, Taylor, Kiefe, & Seeman, 2005), immunologic functioning (e.g., Taylor, Lehman, Kiefe, & Seeman, 2006), and elevated blood pressure (e.g., Lehman, Taylor, Kiefe, & Seeman, 2009); and to major mental and physical health disorders (e.g., Felitti et al., 1998).

As noted, a viable hypothesis as to why these relationships exist is that early stress compromises the functioning of biological stress regulatory systems. At the physiological level, stress-related changes in autonomic and neuroendocrine functioning include: 1) activation of the sympathetic nervous system, which leads to increases in heart rate and blood pressure, among other changes and 2) activation of the hypothalamic-pituitary-adrenal axis (HPA axis), which leads to the production of corticosteroids, including cortisol, which are necessary for energy mobilization (Sapolsky, 1993). 3) Stress inductions have also been associated with changes in proinflammatory cytokine activity (e.g., Dickerson, Kemeny, Aziz, Kim, & Fahey, 2004), effects that may be driven, in part, by autonomic and HPA axis activity.

The theory of allostatic load (McEwen, 1998) maintains that stress, in conjunction with genetic risks, leads to a cascade of adverse biological changes that over time may erode the resiliency of stress systems, laying the groundwork for illness. Increasingly, researchers are identifying indicators of allostatic load that cumulatively enhance risk for disease (Seeman et al., 2001; Seeman, Singer, Ryff, Dienberg Love, & Levy-Storms, 2002).

Genetic Antecedents

Genetic factors are implicated in stress reactivity both in their own right and in interaction with a stressful early environment. For example, genes involved in the development of stress systems, such as the glucocorticoid receptor gene, in conjunction with the early environment, play a lifelong role in stress responses (Meaney & Szyf, 2005; Miller & Chen, 2007). Genes in the opioid system, such as

the μ-opioid receptor gene, and genes in the oxytocin and vasopressin systems likely play roles in both stress regulation and the deployment of psychosocial resources (Way & Taylor, 2011, for a review). Genetic factors that increase vulnerability to specific health disorders, such as diabetes, heart disease, or cancer, likely interact with stress processes to increase risk, precipitate acute events, or accelerate the course of existing health problems.

A harsh early environment contributes to lifespan risk for health disorders not only directly, but also via gene-environment interactions. For example, in rhesus monkeys, genetic variation in the promoter region of the serotonin transporter gene interacts with rearing environment to affect hypothalamic-pituitary-adrenal (HPA) axis responses to social stress (Barr et al., 2004). Specifically, reduced maternal interaction potentiates the stress response among monkeys with a short allele and also increases aggressive behavior. Related effects have now been found in humans (Miller & Chen, 2007).

Risk for depression in humans is also affected by allelic variation in the promoter region of the serotonin transporter (5-HTTLPR) gene. Recent investigations have found that people carrying at least one copy of the short (s) allele of this gene are more at risk for depression, especially if they have grown up in an environment marked by maltreatment (see Caspi et al., 2003). In a recent investigation, we examined whether a supportive early environment might reverse this risk (Taylor, Way et al., 2006). Participants completed assessments of early family environment, recent stressful events, and depressive symptomatology. A gene-by-environment interaction was observed between the 5-HTTLPR and early family environment, such that people homozygous for the short allele (s/s) had greater depressive symptomatology if they had experienced early adversity but significantly less depressive symptomatology if they reported a supportive early environment, compared to people with s/l or the l/l genotypes. This study, then, provides exciting evidence that the beneficence of the early environment can actually reverse the effects of a genetic risk.

Genetic and early environmental factors contribute to aggressive as well as depressive responses to stress. The MAOA genetic polymorphism has been linked to hostile, aggressive behavior toward others. People with low expression of MAOA (MAOA-L) have been found to be more aggressive than those with high expression (MAOA-H), particularly when they come from an adverse early environment (e.g., Caspi et al., 2002). Exactly why is not known. One possibility is that MAOA-L individuals are less socially sensitive and thus commit violent acts because they do not care about harming others or the repercussions of so doing. Alternatively, MAOA-L individuals may be more sensitive to negative social experiences and respond to such episodes with defensively aggressive behavior (Blair, Peschardt, Budhani, Mitchell, & Pine, 2006).

To evaluate these alternative accounts, we examined how allelic variation in the promoter region of the MAOA gene related to (self-reported) aggression (e.g., "having the urge to harm someone"), interpersonal hypersensitivity (e.g., "feeling very self-conscious with others"), and neural responses to an episode of social exclusion in the scanner. During this fMRI task, the participant plays catch with two other (virtual) participants, but over time, is excluded from the play; this task has previously been found to produce psychological distress and corresponding activation in the dorsal anterior cingulate cortex (dACC) (Eisenberger, Lieberman, & Williams, 2003). MAOA-L individuals reported higher levels of trait aggression than MAOA-H individuals, consistent with prior research. MAOA-L individuals also reported greater trait interpersonal hypersensitivity and showed greater dACC activity to social rejection than MAOA-H individuals. These results suggest that the MAOA-L-aggression link is the result of heightened sensitivity to negative social experiences and not insensitivity.

Psychosocial Resources
Psychosocial resources are critical for regulating responses to threat and have been demonstrated to beneficially affect both mental and physical health. Four such resources that have been consistently tied to these benefits are optimism, mastery, self esteem, and social support.

Optimism refers to outcome expectancies that good things rather than bad things will happen to the self (Scheier, Weintraub, & Carver, 1986). It predicts greater psychological well-being (e.g., Scheier & Carver, 1992), lower vulnerability to infection (Cohen, Doyle, Turner, Alper, & Skoner, 2003; Segerstrom, Taylor, Kemeny, & Fahey, 1998), faster recovery from illness (Scheier et al., 1989), and a slower course of advancing disease (Antoni & Goodkin, 1988) (see Carver & Scheier, 2002, for a review).

Personal control or mastery refers to whether a person feels able to control or influence his/her outcomes (Thompson, 1981). Studies have shown relationships between a sense of control and better

psychological health (Rodin, Timko, & Harris, 1985; Taylor, Helgeson, Reed & Skokan, 1991) and better physical health outcomes, including lower incidence of coronary heart disease (CHD) (Karasek, Theorell, Schwartz, Pieper, & Alfredsson, 1982), better self-rated health, better functional status, and lower mortality (Seeman & Lewis, 1995).

A positive sense of self or high self-esteem is also protective against adverse mental and adverse health outcomes. For example, research consistently ties a positive sense of self to lower autonomic and cortisol responses to stress (e.g., Creswell, Welch, Taylor, Sherman, Gruenewald, & Mann, 2005; Seeman & Lewis, 1995). Ties to health outcomes are modest but consistently positive (Adler et al., 1999; Taylor & Seeman, 1999).

Social support is defined as the perception or experience that one is loved and cared for by others, esteemed and valued, and part of a social network of mutual assistance and obligations (Wills, 1991). Research consistently demonstrates that social support reduces negative affect during times of stress and promotes psychological adjustment to a broad array of chronically stressful conditions (see Cacioppo & Patrick, 2008; Taylor, 2011, for reviews). Social support also contributes to physical health and survival, and the impact of social ties on health is as powerful a predictor of health and longevity as well-established risk factors for chronic disease and mortality, including smoking, lipids, obesity, and physical activity (e.g., Berkman & Syme, 1979; House, Landis, & Umberson, 1988). Thus, each of these four constructs has robust and well-documented mental and physical health effects.

Psychosocial resources may represent a vital link from genes and early environment to health outcomes across the lifespan. It has long been suspected that psychosocial resources have genetic origins. For example, twin studies indicate that approximately 25% of the variance in optimism appears to be genetically based (Plomin et al., 1992). Similarly, Kessler, Kendler, Heath, Neale, and Eaves (1992) reported a genetic basis for social support, which may reflect either the ability to perceive social support as available or the ability to make use of it, or both. An early family environment marked by harsh or conflict-ridden parenting is reliably associated with deficits in offspring psychosocial resources as well (Repetti et al., 2002) and with difficulty in managing challenging circumstances (Brody & Flor, 1998; Dishion, 1990; Repetti et al., 2002). Substantial research links economic adversity (low socioeconomic status [SES]) to problems in the enlistment or use of psychosocial resources (Adler et al., 1999; Repetti et al., 2002; Taylor & Seeman, 1999). Deficits in psychosocial resources related to early family environment may appear in latent form in early childhood and contribute to a propensity for chronic negative affect and to a lack of psychosocial resources in adulthood (Repetti et al., 2002).

Intense, chronic, or recurring biological responses to stress represent a downstream pathway by which psychosocial resources may exert adverse effects on health across the lifespan (McEwen, 1998; Repetti et al., 2002). For example, a lack of supportive contacts in early childhood has been tied to higher HPA axis responses to stressors in both children and adults (Gunnar, Larson, Hertsgaard, Harris, & Brodersen, 1992; Taylor, Lerner, Sage, Lehman, & Seeman, 2004).

Neural Regulation of Stress Responses

Is there neural evidence to connect psychosocial resources directly to the regulation of biological responses to stress? Eisenberger, Taylor, Gable, Hilmert, and Lieberman (2007) examined the neural pathways that may link the experience of social support to reduced physiological reactivity. Specifically, we examined the relation of daily experiences of social support to neural responses to social threat in the brain and to autonomic and HPA axis responses to laboratory stressors indicative of social threat. Thirty participants completed a daily experience sampling procedure over a 9-day period that assessed and averaged their experiences of social support. At the end of this 9-day period, participants took part in an fMRI investigation of neural responses to threat; specifically, the virtual social rejection task described earlier (Eisenberger et al., 2003). At a third time point, participants went through the Trier Social Stress Task (TSST) to assess autonomic and neuroendocrine activity to social stressors (Kirschbaum, Pirke, & Hellhammer, 1993). (The TSST is a standardized, widely used laboratory stress challenge known to produce social-evaluative threat (Dickerson & Kemeny, 2004). People who reported that they interacted regularly with supportive individuals showed diminished dorsal anterior cingulate cortex (dACC) and Brodmann area (BA8) reactivity to social rejection in the fMRI task; both are regions implicated in responses to social threat. People with strong social support also showed diminished cortisol reactivity to the TSST. Most important, individual differences in dACC and BA8 activity mediated the relationship between social

support and cortisol reactivity. The results imply that social support may influence downstream biological stress responses by modulating neurocognitive reactivity to social stressors, which, in turn, attenuates neuroendocrine stress responses.

Do other psychosocial resources operate via these pathways? Two brain structures, the amygdala and, as noted, the dorsal anterior cingulate cortex (dACC), are consistently associated with threat detection, serving an alarm function that mobilizes other neural regions, such as the lateral prefrontal cortex (LPFC) and hypothalamus, to promote adaptive responses to environmental threats (e.g., Hariri, Tessitore, Mattay, Fera, & Weinberger, 2002). Once activated, these neural threat detectors set in motion a cascade of responses via projections to the hypothalamus and LPFC (Botvinick, Braver, Barch, Carter, & Cohen, 2000), aimed at amplifying or attenuating the threat signal and preparing to respond to the threat. A neural region that appears critical for regulating the magnitude of these threat responses is the VLPFC (Hariri, Bookheimer, & Mazziotta, 2000; Lieberman, Hariri, Jarcho, Eisenberger, & Bookheimer, 2005).

We examined the relation of individual differences in psychosocial resources to neural responses in these regions to threat cues (fearful and angry faces) and to HPA axis and cardiovascular responses to the TSST stress tasks (Taylor et al., 2008). Specifically, participants took part in an fMRI investigation that examined 1) amygdala reactivity to threat-relevant cues, specifically observation of fearful/angry faces; 2) amygdala and right ventrolateral prefrontal cortex (RVLPFC) responses to labeling emotions displayed in these faces; and 3) the relation between RVLPFC and amygdala activity during the labeling task. Previous research had found that the face observation task evokes amygdala activity, that the labeling task evokes RVLPFC activity, and that activity in the amygdala and RVLPFC are (typically) negatively correlated in the labeling task (suggesting that the RVLPFC may be involved in the regulation of limbic responses to threat cues) (Lieberman et al., 2005; Lieberman et al., 2007). Participants then completed the TSST described earlier.

High levels of psychosocial resources (a composite of optimism, control, and self-esteem) were associated with greater right ventrolateral prefrontal cortex and less amygdala activity during the labeling task in the fMRI component of the investigation and to lower cortisol responses and lower blood pressure during the TSST. Mediational analyses suggest that the relation of psychosocial resources to low cortisol reactivity was mediated by lower amygdala activity during threat regulation (i.e., the labeling task). Results suggest that psychosocial resources are associated with lower cortisol responses to stress by means of enhanced inhibition of threat responses during threat regulation, rather than by decreased sensitivity to threat.

Taken together, these two studies suggest that social support may modulate biological stress responses by reducing emotional reactivity, whereas trait assessments of psychosocial resources (such as optimism and self-esteem) may modulate stress responses by augmenting regulatory capacity to manage stress. Whether those different patterns are a function of the particular tasks and methods used or whether they indicate that different psychosocial resources affect stress regulation in different ways remains to be seen.

Coping with Threat

Early environment, genetic factors, and psychosocial resources affect the coping processes that people use to manage stressful events. Coping processes include both actions taken (or not) to deal with stressors, as well as the regulation of emotional responses to threat. Although several frameworks for delineating coping processes have been advanced (see Skinner, Edge, Altman, & Sherwood, 2003, for a review), a particularly useful distinction is that between approach and avoidance coping. Reflecting a core motivational construct (e.g., Davidson, Jackson, & Kalin, 2000), the approach-avoidance continuum maps easily onto broader theories of biobehavioral functioning. Approach-related coping includes problem solving, seeking social support, and creating outlets for emotional expression. Coping through avoidance includes both cognitive and behavioral strategies designed to tune out the implications of a stressor. For the most part, research suggests beneficial effects of approach coping and adverse effects of avoidant coping, although there are qualifications based on type and timing of stressor (e.g., Folkman & Moskowitz, 2004; Taylor & Stanton, 2007). Approach coping strategies have been reliably tied to positive affect and to beneficial health outcomes (Taylor & Stanton, 2007). Attempting to avoid thoughts and feelings regarding stressors predicts elevated distress, physical health outcomes, chronic disease progression, and mortality (See Taylor & Stanton, 2007, for a review).

Research links a harsh family environment to the use of maladaptive coping strategies. Specifically,

offspring from harsh family environments appear to overreact to threatening circumstances, responding aggressively to situations that are only modestly stressful (Reid & Crisafulli, 1990), but may also respond by tuning out or avoiding stressful circumstances when they can, as through behavioral escape/avoidance or substance abuse (e.g., O'Brien, Margolin, John, & Krueger, 1991). Genetic factors are also implicated in the propensity to use certain coping strategies. Using twin study methodology, behavioral genetics investigations have estimated moderate genetic contributions to problem solving, emotion-focused coping, use of social support, and avoidant coping, (e.g., Kato & Pedersen, 2005; Kendler, Kessler, Heath, Neale, & Eaves, 1991). Both shared and unshared environmental factors appear to contribute to these effects (Mellins, Gatz, & Baker, 1996).

Can poor coping resulting from a non-nurturant early environment be linked directly to the neural regulation of stress responses? To examine potential neural concomitants of coping deficits, we (Taylor, Eisenberger, Saxbe, Lehman, & Lieberman, 2006) explored neural reactivity to tasks involving threat detection and regulation of responses to emotional stimuli. Participants completed an assessment of early family environment (Taylor et al., 2004) and then completed the fearful faces task described earlier. Offspring from nurturant families showed expected amygdala reactivity to observing fearful/angry faces and expected activation of the RVLPFC while labeling the emotions in the faces. Activity in these two regions was significantly negatively correlated, as expected. This pattern suggests that the RVLPFC was effective in regulating emotional responses to the tasks. Offspring from harsh families, however, showed little amygdala activation during the observation task, a strong amygdala response to the labeling task, and a strong positive correlation between RVLPFC and amygdala activation in the labeling task (Taylor et al., 2006). These patterns suggest potential dysregulation in the neural systems involved in regulating responses to threat.

Specifically, it appears that during the task that normally activates amygdala activity, participants from harsh families may instead have been tuning out the threatening stimuli, but when forced to confront the threatening stimuli in the labeling task, unexpectedly high amygdala activity was seen. Moreover, it appears that offspring from harsh families did not recruit the RVLPFC effectively for regulating amygdala responses to threatening stimuli, given the strong positive correlation between amygdala and RVLPFC responses to the tasks. Thus, offspring from harsh families appear to experience deficits in threat detection and coping responses to emotional stimuli that are evident at the neural level. These processes, in turn, have downstream effects on autonomic, neuroendocrine, and immune responses to stress.

Autonomic, Neuroendocrine, and Immune Responses to Stress

As Figure 51.1 and the research described indicates, genetic factors, early environment, psychosocial resources, and neural and coping responses to threat have downstream effects on autonomic, neuroendocrine, and immune responses to threat. These responses may represent the proximal contributors to both acute health disorders and, cumulatively, to chronic health conditions. Studies have shown connections between neural structures critical to threat detection and the hypothalamus, the origin of both sympathetic and neuroendocrine responses to threat. The amygdala has dense projections to the hypothalamus (Ghashghaei & Barbas, 2002), and the ACC projects to the paraventricular nucleus of the hypothalamus (PVN; Risold, Thompson, & Swanson, 1997), the specific region of the hypothalamus that triggers the cascade of events ultimately leading to cortisol release. Stimulation of both the amygdala and the ACC has also been associated with increases in blood pressure and cortisol levels in both animals and humans (e.g., Frankel, Jenkins, & Wright, 1978; Pool, 1954; Setekliev, Skaug, & Kaada, 1961). Stress-induced proinflammatory cytokine activity (including interleukin-6 (IL-6) and tumor necrosis factor alpha (sTNFαRII) are also implicated (Maier & Watkins, 1998).

We related aspects of the early family environment to autonomic and neuroendocrine responses to stress directly (Taylor et al., 2004). Young adults completed measures of early environment and participated in laboratory stress tasks. We found a strong relationship between childhood SES and a harsh family environment. Low childhood SES and harsh family environment were, in turn, related to an elevated and flat trajectory of cortisol across the stress tasks. For males only, those from the harshest family environments had elevated heart rate and blood pressure during the challenges and throughout the post-challenge recovery. Because risk factors for CHD and CVD frequently show up earlier in life for males than females (Allen, Matthews, & Sherman, 1997), the fact

that the results were significant only for males is not surprising. The model also significantly predicted self-rated health. This study, then, suggests that a legacy of having grown up in a harsh early environment includes the propensity to respond to new stressors with stronger biological threat responses.

Although stress-related multi-system changes such as these are protective in the short term, their chronic activation may negatively affect mental health over time, potentially elevating risk for depression and anxiety disorders and also enhancing risks for physical illnesses, including cardiovascular disease and type II diabetes (e.g., Kiecolt-Glaser, McGuire, Robles, & Glaser, 2002; Seeman et al., 1997 for reviews).

Relating the Model to Risk Factors for Disease

Evidence linking variables in the model to specific health outcomes is substantial. Childhood SES (Cohen, Doyle, Turner, Alper, & Skoner, 2004; Galobardes, Lynch, & Davey Smith, 2004; Galobardes, Davey Smith, & Lynch, 2006) and a harsh family environment (Repetti, Taylor, & Saxbe, 2007) have both been related to a broad array of risk factors for cardiovascular disease, immune-related disorders (e.g., Miller & Chen, 2007), diabetes, and some cancers. Chronic negative affect, especially hostility and depression, are tied to hypertension and coronary heart disease (CHD) (Gallo & Matthews, 2003). Social support and social isolation have profound effects on all-cause mortality and risk of and progression of many chronic disorders (Cacioppo & Patrick, 2008). Individual differences of optimism, mastery, and self-esteem have been tied to health-related outcomes, which, in turn, have been related to mental and physical health-related outcomes (e.g., Felitti et al., 1998).

This section highlights three specific examples from our laboratory that address (much of) the model detailed in Figure 51.1, specifically, early environment, social support, chronic negative affect, and health outcomes. In collaboration with investigators from the Coronary Artery Risk Factors in Young Adults investigation (CARDIA), we (Lehman, Taylor, Kiefe, & Seeman, 2005) used structural equation modeling to explore the relation of the model (Figure 51.1) to metabolic functioning, which is a composite risk factor for diabetes, coronary artery disease, and several other chronic health conditions. Participants (N = 3,225) completed our assessment of early family environment and participated in a physical exam that assessed cholesterol, insulin, glucose, triglycerides, and waist circumference (as indicators of metabolic functioning). Structural equation modeling indicated that low childhood SES and a harsh early family environment were associated with dysregulation in metabolic functioning via association with poor psychosocial resources and chronic negative affect, consistent with the model.

A second study assessed whether the model contributed to elevated C-reactive protein, a marker of inflammation and a risk factor for both mental (e.g., depression) and physical (e.g., heart disease) disorders in adulthood. Structural equation modeling supported a model whereby low SES and a harsh early environment contributed to elevated C-reactive protein via pathways involving poor psychosocial resources, chronic negative affect, and high body mass index (i.e., obesity). A third investigation explored the viability of the model for explaining variability in blood pressure as well as change in blood pressure over time (Lehman et al., 2009). Again, the model was a good fit. Although the psychosocial variables included in these three tests of the model were restricted to chronic negative emotional states and social support, the results are encouraging evidence for pathways linking early environment through psychosocial variables to health outcomes.

Conclusions and Unresolved Issues

The picture of how genes and the early environment contribute to health risks via pathways implicating psychosocial resources, coping, and the neural regulation of stress responses is sketchy. Several directions for future work are evident. A first issue concerns the role of stress in the model. The guiding framework places a heavy burden on stress processes as a primary vehicle linking early environment, genes, and psychosocial resources to health risks. Is the damage actually done primarily during stressful times? Does damage accelerate as biological stress regulatory systems are compromised? Is the damage reversible? Answers to these questions are currently unknown.

Second, the guiding framework offered in this article is still evolving, and additional probable direct paths and feedback loops are not pictured. For example, environmental factors influence neural and endocrine functioning directly, as well as through psychosocial resources. Stress hormones, cytokine responses, and environmental factors influence genetic expression. Thus, further research will add refinements, specificity, and complexity to the model.

At present, the model is a generic one that can be applied, albeit imprecisely, to a broad array of antecedents. As the specific genetic and experiential precursors of specific health disorders become increasingly well understood, it will be possible to build disease-specific models that integrate these multiple levels of analysis.

Acknowledgment

Preparation of this article was supported by a grant from the National Institute of Aging (AG030309).

References

Adler, N. E., Marmot, M., McEwen, B.S., & Stewart, J. (1999). *Socioeconomic status and health in industrial nations: Social, psychological, and biological pathways.* New York: New York Academy of Sciences.

Allen, M. T., Matthews, K. A., & Sherman, F. S. (1997). Cardiovascular reactivity to stress and left ventricular mass in youth. *Hypertension, 30,* 782–787.

Antoni, M. H. & Goodkin, K. (1988). Host moderator variables in the promotion of cervical neoplasia. I: Personality facets. *Journal of Psychosomatic Research, 32,* 327–338.

Barr, C. S., Newman, T. K., Shannon, C., Parker, C., Dvoskin, R. L., Becker, M. L., et al. (2004). Rearing condition and rh5-HTTLPR interact to influence limbic-hypothalamic-pituitary-adrenal axis response to stress in infant macaques. *Biological Psychiatry, 55,* 733–738.

Berkman, L. F. & Syme, S. L. (1979). Social networks, host resistance, and mortality: A nine-year follow-up study of Alameda County residents. *American Journal of Epidemiology, 109,* 186–204.

Blair, R. J. R., Peschardt, K. S., Budhani, S., Mitchell, D. G. V., & Pine, D. S. (2006). The development of psychopathy. *Journal of Child Psychology and Psychiatry, 47,* 262–275.

Botvinick, M. M., Braver, T. D., Barch, D. M., Carter, C. S., & Cohen, J. D. (2000). Conflict monitoring and cognitive control. *Psychological Review, 108,* 624–652.

Brody, G. H. & Flor, D. L. (1998). Maternal resources, parenting practices, and child competence in rural, single-parent African-American families. *Child Development, 69,* 803–816.

Cacioppo, J. T. & Patrick, W. (2008). *Loneliness: Human nature and the need for social connection.* New York: Norton Books.

Carver, C. S. & Scheier, M. F. (2002). Optimism. In C. R. Snyder & S. J. Lopez (Eds.), *Handbook of positive psychology* (pp. 231–243). New York: Oxford University Press.

Caspi, A., McClay, J., Moffitt, T. E., Mill, J., Martin, J., Craig, I. W., et al. (2002). Role of genotype in the cycle of violence in maltreated children. *Science, 297,* 851–854.

Caspi, A., Sugden, D., Moffitt, T. E., Taylor, A., Craig, I. W., Harrington, H., et al. (2003). Influence of life stress on depression: Moderation by a polymorphism in the 5-HTT gene. *Science, 301,* 386–389.

Cohen, S., Doyle, W. J., Turner, R. B., Alper, C. M., & Skoner, D. P. (2003). Emotional style and susceptibility to the common cold. *Psychosomatic Medicine, 65,* 652–657.

Cohen, S., Doyle, W. J., Turner, R. B., Alper, C. M., & Skoner, D. P. (2004). Childhood socioeconomic status and host resistance to infectious illness in adulthood. *Psychosomatic Medicine, 66,* 553–558.

Creswell, J. D., Welch, W. T., Taylor, S. E., Sherman, D. K., Gruenewald, T., & Mann, T. (2005). Affirmation of personal values buffers neuroendocrine and psychological stress responses. *Psychological Science, 16,* 846–851.

Davidson, R. J., Jackson, D. C., & Kalin, N. H. (2000). Emotion, plasticity, context, and regulation: Perspectives from affective neuroscience. *Psychological Bulletin, 126,* 890–909.

Dickerson, S. S. & Kemeny, M. E. (2004). Acute stressors and cortisol responses: A theoretical integration and synthesis of laboratory research. *Psychological Bulletin, 130,* 355–391.

Dickerson, S. S., Kemeny, M. E., Aziz, N., Kim, K. H., & Fahey, J. L. (2004). Immunological effects of induced shame and guilt. *Psychosomatic Medicine,* 124–131.

Dishion, T. J. (1990). The family ecology of boys peer relations in middle childhood. *Child Development, 61,* 874–891.

Eisenberger, N., Lieberman, M. D., & Williams, K. D. (2003). Does rejection hurt? An fMRI study of social exclusion. *Science, 302,* 290–292.

Eisenberger, N. I., Taylor, S. E., Gable, S. L., Hilmert, C. J., & Lieberman, M. D. (2007). Neural pathways link social support to attenuated neuroendocrine stress responses. *NeuroImage, 35,* 1601–1612.

Felitti, V. J., Anda, R. F., Nordenberg, D., Williamson, D. F., Apitz, A. M., Edwards, V., et al. (1998). Relationship of childhood abuse and household dysfunction to many of the leading causes of death in adults. *American Journal of Preventive Medicine, 14,* 245–258.

Folkman, S. & Moskowitz, J. T. (2004). Coping: Pitfalls and promise. *Annual Review of Psychology, 55,* 745–774.

Frankel, R. J., Jenkins, J. S., & Wright, J. J. (1978). Pituitary-adrenal response to stimulation of the limbic system and lateral hypothalamus in the rhesus monkey (Macacca mulatta). *Acta Endocrinologica, 88,* 209–216.

Gallo, L. C. & Matthews, K. A. (2003). Understanding the association between socioeconomic status and physical health: Do negative emotions play a role? *Psychological Bulletin, 129,* 10–51.

Galobardes, B., Lynch, J. W., & Smith, G. D. (2004). Childhood socioeconomic circumstances and cause-specific mortality in adulthood: Systematic review and interpretation. *Epidemiologic Review, 26,* 7–21.

Galobardes, B., Smith, G. D., & Lynch, J. W. (2006). Systematic review of the influence of childhood socioeconomic circumstances on risk for cardiovascular disease in adulthood. *Annals of Epidemiology, 16,* 91–104.

Ghashghaei, H. T. & Barbas, H. (2002). Pathways for emotion: Interactions of prefrontal and anterior temporal pathways in the amygdala of the rhesus monkey. *Neuroscience, 115,* 1261–1279.

Gunnar, M. R. Larson, M. C., Hertsgaard, L., Harris, M. L., & Brodersen, L. (1992). The stressfulness of separation among nine-month-old infants: Effects of social context variables and infant temperament. *Child Development, 63,* 290–303.

Hariri, A. R., Bookheimer, S. Y., & Mazziotta, J. C. (2000). Modulating emotional responses: Effects of a neocortical network on the limbic system. *Neuroreport, 11,* 43–48.

Hariri, A. R., Tessitore, A., Mattay, V. S., Fera, F. & Weinberger, D. R. (2002). The amygdala response to emotional stimuli: A comparison of faces and scenes. *NeuroImage 17,* 317–323.

Hemingway, H., Shipley, M., Mullen, M. J., Kumari, M., Brunner, E., Taylor, M., et al. (2003). Social and psychosocial influences on inflammatory markers and vascular function in civil servants (The Whitehall II Study). *The American Journal of Cardiology, 92,* 984–987.

Hertzman, C. (1999). The biological embedding of early experience and its effects on health in adulthood. *Annals of the New York Academy of Sciences, 896,* 85–95.

House, J. S., Landis, K. R., & Umberson, D. (1988). Social relationships and health. *Science, 241,* 540–545.

Karasek, R. A., Theorell, T., Schwartz, J., Pieper, C., & Alfredsson, L. (1982). Job, psychological factors and coronary heart disease: Swedish prospective findings and U.S. prevalence findings using a new occupational inference method. *Advances in Cardiology, 29,* 62–67.

Kato, K. & Pedersen, N. L. (2005). Personality and coping: A study of twins reared apart and twins reared together. *Behavior Genetics, 35,* 147–158.

Kendler, K. S., Kessler, R. C., Heath, A. C., Neale, M. C., & Eaves, L. J. (1991). Coping: A genetic epidemiological investigation. *Psychological Medicine, 21,* 337–346.

Kessler, R. C., Kendler, K. S., Heath, A. C., Neale, M. C., & Eaves, L. J. (1992). Social support, depressed mood, and adjustment to stress: A genetic epidemiological investigation. *Journal of Personality and Social Psychology, 62,* 257–272.

Kiecolt-Glaser, J. K., McGuire, L., Robles, T. F., & Glaser, R. (2002). Emotions, morbidity, and mortality: New perspectives from psychoneuroimmunology. *Annual Review of Psychology, 53,* 83–107.

Kirschbaum, C., Pirke, K. M., & Hellhammer, D. H. (1993). The "Trier Social Stress Test"—A tool for investigating psychobiological stress responses in a laboratory setting. *Neuropsychobiology, 28,* 76–81.

Kittleson, M. M., Meoni, L. A., Wang, N. Y., Chu, A. Y., Ford, D. E., & Klag, M. J. (2006). Association of childhood socioeconomic status with subsequent coronary heart disease in physicians. *Archives of Internal Medicine, 166,* 2356–2361.

Kuh, D., Hardy, R., Langenberg, C., Richards, M., & Wadsworth, M. E. J. (2002). Mortality in adults aged 26–54 years related to socioeconomic conditions in childhood and adulthood: Post war birth cohort study. *British Medical Journal, 325,* 1076–1080.

Lehman, B. J., Taylor, S. E., Kiefe, C. I., & Seeman, T. E. (2005). Relation of childhood socioeconomic status and family environment to adult metabolic functioning in the CARDIA study. *Psychosomatic Medicine, 67,* 846–854.

Lehman, B. J., Taylor, S. E., Kiefe, C. I., & Seeman, T. E. (2009). Relationship of early life stress and psychological functioning to blood pressure in the CARDIA Study. *Health Psychology, 28,* 338–346.

Lieberman, M. D., Eisenberger, N. I., Crockett, M. J., Tom, S. M., Pfeifer, J. H., & Way, B. M. (2007). Putting feelings into words: Affect labeling disrupts amygdala activity to affective stimuli. *Psychological Science, 18,* 421–428.

Lieberman, M. D., Hariri, A., Jarcho, J. M., Eisenberger, N. I., & Bookheimer, S. Y. (2005). An fMRI investigation of face-related amygdala activity in African-American and Caucasian-American individuals. *Nature Neuroscience, 8,* 720–722.

Liu, D., Dorio, J., Tannenbaum, B., Caldji, C., Francis, D., Freedman, A., et al. (1997). Maternal care, hippocampal glucocorticoid receptors, and hypothalamic-pituitary-adrenal responses to stress. *Science, 277*, 1659–1662.

Maier, S. F. & Watkins, L. R. (1998). Cytokines for psychologists: Implications of bidirectional immune-to-brain communication for understanding behavior, mood, and cognition. *Psychological Review, 105*, 83–107.

McEwen, B. S. (1998). Protective and damaging effects of stress mediators. *New England Journal of Medicine, 338*, 171–179.

Meaney, M. J. (2001). Maternal care, gene expression, and the transmission of individual differences in stress reactivity across generations. *Annual Review of Neuroscience, 24*, 1161–1192.

Meaney, M. J. & Szyf, M. (2005). Environmental programming of stress responses through DNA methylation: Life at the interface between a dynamic environment and a fixed genome. *Dialogues in Clinical Neuroscience, 7*, 103–123.

Mellins, C. A., Gatz, M., & Baker, L. (1996). Children's methods of coping with stress: A twin study of genetic and environmental influences. *Journal of Child Psychology and Psychiatry, 37*, 721–730.

Miller, G. & Chen, E. (2007). Unfavorable socioeconomic conditions in early life presage expression of proinflammatory phenotype in adolescence. *Psychosomatic Medicine, 69*, 402–409.

O'Brien, M., Margolin, G., John, R. S., & Krueger, L. (1991). Mothers' and sons' cognitive and emotional reactions to simulated marital and family conflict. *Journal of Consulting and Clinical Psychology, 59*, 692–703.

Plomin, R., Scheier, M. F., Bergeman, S. C., Pedersen, N. L., Nesselroade, J. R., & McClearn, G. E. (1992). Optimism, pessimism, and mental health: A twin/adoption study. *Personality and Individual Differences, 13*, 921–930.

Pool, J. L. (1954). The visceral brain of man. *Journal of Neurosurgery, 11*, 45–63.

Reid, R. J. & Crisafulli, A. (1990). Marital discord and child behavior problems: A meta-analysis. *Journal of Abnormal Child Psychology, 18*, 105–117.

Repetti, R. L., Taylor, S. E., & Saxbe, D. (2007). The influence of early socialization experiences on the development of biological systems. In J. Grusec and P. Hastings (Eds.), *Handbook of socialization* (pp. 124–152). New York, NY: Guilford.

Repetti, R. L., Taylor, S. E., & Seeman, T. E. (2002). Risky families: Family social environments and the mental and physical health of offspring. *Psychological Bulletin, 128*, 330–366.

Risold, P. Y., Thompson, R. H., & Swanson, L. W. (1997). The structural organization of connections between hypothalamus and cerebral cortex. *Brain Research Reviews, 24*, 197–254.

Rodin, J., Timko, C., & Harris, S. (1985). The construct of control: Biological and psychosocial correlates. *Annual Review of Gerontology and Geriatrics, 5*, 3–55.

Sapolsky, R. M. (1993). Endocrinology alfresco: Psychoendocrine studies of wild baboons. *Recent Progress in Hormone Research, 48*, 437–468.

Scheier, M. F. & Carver, C. S. (1992). Effects of optimism on psychological and physical well-being: Theoretical overview and empirical update. *Cognitive Therapy Research, 16*, 201–228.

Scheier, M. F., Matthews, K. A., Owens, J., Magovern, G. J., Sr., Lefebvre, R. C., Abbott, R. A., et al. (1989). Dispositional optimism and recovery from coronary artery bypass surgery: The beneficial effects on physical and psychological well-being. *Journal of Personality and Social Psychology, 57*, 1024–1040.

Scheier, M. F., Weintraub, J. K., & Carver, C. S. (1986). Coping with stress: Divergent strategies of optimists and pessimists. *Journal of Personality and Social Psychology, 51*, 1257–1264.

Seeman, M. & Lewis, S. (1995). Powerlessness, health, and mortality: A longitudinal study of older Men and mature women. *Social Science and Medicine, 41*, 517–525.

Seeman, T. E., McEwen, B. S., Rowe, J. W., & Singer, B. H. (2001). Allostatic load as a marker of cumulative biological risk: MacArthur studies of successful aging. *Proceedings of the National Academy of Sciences, 98*, 4770–4775.

Seeman, T. E., Singer, B. H., Ryff, C. D., Dienberg Love, G., & Levy-Storms, L. (2002). Social relationships, gender, and allostatic load across two age cohorts. *Psychosomatic Medicine, 64*, 395–406.

Seeman, T. E., Singer, B., Horwitz, R., & McEwen, B. S. (1997). The price of adaptation—allostatic load and its health consequences: MacArthur studies of successful aging. *Archives of Internal Medicine, 157*, 2259–2268.

Segerstrom, S. C., Taylor, S. E., Kemeny, M. E., & Fahey, J. L. (1998). Optimism is associated with mood, coping, and immune change in response to stress. *Journal of Personality and Social Psychology, 74*, 1646–1655.

Setekliev. J., Skaug, O. E., & Kaada, B. R. (1961). Increase of plasma 17-hydroxycorticosteroids by cerebral cortical and amygdaloid stimulation in the cat. *Journal of Endocrinology, 22*, 119–127.

Skinner, E. A., Edge, K., Altman, J., & Sherwood, H. (2003). Searching for the structure of coping: A review and critique of category systems for classifying ways of coping. *Psychological Bulletin, 129*, 216–269.

Taylor, S. E. (2011). Social support: A review. In H. S. Friedman (Ed.), *Oxford handbook of health psychology*. New York, NY: Oxford University Press.

Taylor, S. E., Burklund, L. J., Eisenberger, N. I., Lehman, B. J., Hilmert, C. J., & Lieberman, M. D. (2008). Neural bases of moderation of cortisol stress responses by psychosocial resources. *Journal of Personality and Social Psychology, 95*, 197–211.

Taylor, S. E., Eisenberger, N. I., Saxbe, D., Lehman, B. J., & Lieberman, M. D. (2006). Neural responses to emotional stimuli are associated with childhood family stress. *Biological Psychiatry, 60*, 296–301.

Taylor, S. E., Helgeson, V. S., Reed, G. M., & Skokan, L. A. (1991). Self-generated feelings of control and adjustment to physical illness. *Journal of Social Issues, 47*, 91–109.

Taylor, S. E. Lehman, B. J., Kiefe, C. I., & Seeman, T. E. (2006). Relationship of early life stress and psychological functioning to adult C-reactive protein in the Coronary Artery Risk Development in Young Adults Study. *Biological Psychiatry, 60*, 819–824.

Taylor, S. E., Lerner, J. S., Sage, R. M., Lehman, B. J., & Seeman, T. E. (2004). Early environment, emotions, responses to stress, and health. Special Issue on Personality and Health. *Journal of Personality, 72*, 1365–1393.

Taylor, S. E. & Seeman, T. E. (1999). Psychosocial resources and the SES-health relationship. In N. Adler, M. Marmot, B. McEwen, & J. Stewart (Eds.), *Socioeconomic status and* health in industrial nations: Social, psychological, and biological pathways (pp. 210–225). New York: New York Academy of Sciences.

Taylor, S. E. & Stanton, A. (2007). Coping resources, coping processes, and mental health. Annual Review of Clinical Psychology, 3, 129–153.

Taylor, S. E., Way, B. M., Welch, W. T., Hilmert, C. J., Lehman, B. J., & Eisenberger, N. I. (2006). Early family environment, current adversity, the serotonin transporter polymorphism, and depressive symptomatology. Biological Psychiatry, 60, 671–676.

Thompson, S. C. (1981). Will it hurt less if I can control it? A complex answer to a simple question. Psychological Bulletin, 90, 89–101.

Way, B. M. & Taylor, S. E. (2011). Genetic factors in social pain. In G. MacDonald and L. A. Jensen-Campbell (Eds.), Social Pain: A Neuroscientific, Social, Clinical, and Developmental Analysis (pp. 95–119). Washington, DC: American Psychological Association.

Wills, T. A. (1991). Social support and interpersonal relationships. In M. S. Clark (Ed.). Prosocial behavior (pp. 265–289). Newbury Park, CA: Sage.

Physiological Effects of Social Threat: Implications for Health

Sally S. Dickerson, Tara L. Gruenewald, *and* Margaret E. Kemeny

Abstract

This chapter examines the specific physiological parameters that may be elicited in response to social self threats in humans. Evidence is provided showing that sensitivity to social threat could have negative health effects in part because of increases in physiological activity

Keywords: social health, social self threat, health, physiological activity

Humans are inherently social, and are driven by the motive to be accepted by others and belong to social groups (e.g., Baumeister & Leary, 1995; Bowlby, 1969; James, 1890/1950). Therefore, situations in which the fundamental goal of social acceptance, status, or belonging is jeopardized are perceived as profound threats. Research has documented that these types of social threats can elicit a wide-range of effects, including psychological, physiological, and behavioral changes. This can be seen in an acute context; where instances of feeling evaluated, rejected, or criticized by others can lead to transient changes in cardiovascular, neuroendocrine, and immune parameters. Some forms of social threat can be chronic or enduring, such as occupying low socioeconomic status or exposure to a harsh, critical family. These persistent or longer-lasting experiences of social threat have also been associated with physiological changes as well as negative health-related outcomes.

Many theorists have argued that the social context is integral for eliciting and shaping physiological responses to threat (e.g., Blascovich & Mendes, 2000; Cacioppo, Berntson, Sheridan, & McClintock, 2000; Sapolsky, 2005; Seeman & McEwen, 1996). Drawing on literatures from social, biological, and health psychology, in this chapter we review evidence that the social milieu is important for understanding not only the specific conditions that may elicit certain physiological responses, but also the magnitude of the response engendered.

Our perspective is informed by *Social Self Preservation Theory* (Dickerson, Gruenewald, & Kemeny, 2004; Gruenewald, Dickerson, & Kemeny, 2007). This theory posits that situations that pose a threat to the social self (e.g., threats to one's social esteem, status, and acceptance) elicit a coordinated biobehavioral response. This response is characterized by activation of different physiological systems, including the hypothalamic-pituitary-adrenocortical (HPA) axis (which regulates the release of the hormone cortisol), and components of the immune system related to inflammation. Threats to the social self can trigger psychological changes—specifically, increases in self-conscious emotions such as shame, embarrassment, and humiliation—which can accompany the physiological changes observed under these conditions. These emotional and physiological changes may represent a coordinated, adaptive response to social-self threat in an acute context (e.g., Dickerson, Gruenewald, & Kemeny, 2009); however, if these conditions are experienced for prolonged periods of time, they may lead to physiological dysregulation with implications for health.

Acute threat to the social self includes contexts characterized by social-evaluative threat, in which the self could be negatively judged by others (Dickerson & Kemeny, 2004). Social-evaluative threat could manifest in performance situations in which negative attributes (e.g., lack of intelligence) could be revealed to others, situations characterized by the potential for or explicit rejection, or situations in which an unwanted or devalued characteristic/identity could be exposed. While these social-evaluative contexts could threaten the social self in humans, more rudimentary or less elaborated forms of social threat can be seen in nonhuman primates and other animals; specifically, threats to social status, social defeat, and social subordination may function as analogous social threats, and provide the phylogenetic roots for social self threat in humans. Therefore, examining the physiological responses to social threat in nonhuman animals could serve the important function of identifying specific physiological parameters that may be elicited in response to social self threats in humans.

Physiological Responses to Social Threat: Evidence from Nonhuman Animals

Cortisol is a hormone that is the end product of activation of the HPA axis, which is initiated when the hypothalamus receives signals from the central nervous system that triggers the release of corticotrophin-releasing hormone (CRH). This, in turn, stimulates the anterior pituitary to secrete adrenocorticotropin hormone (ACTH); when released, it triggers the adrenal cortex to secrete cortisol into the bloodstream. Cortisol then exerts effects on a number of physiological systems, and plays a critical role in maintaining normal physiological processes. It is particularly important for metabolic functioning; cortisol can release energy stores (primarily by elevating glucose levels), which provides fuel for the central nervous system and other peripheral systems. Cortisol can also regulate other physiological processes; for example, cortisol can inhibit components of the immune system and allows other

systems, such as the sympathetic nervous system, to function effectively (for reviews, see Lovallo & Thomas, 2000; Sapolsky, Romero & Munck, 2000).

Superimposed on its role of maintaining normal basal physiological processes, cortisol is also critical in shaping the body's response to acute threat. Certain types of acute stressors can elicit cortisol responses. For example, threats to physical self preservation—such as threats to safety or survival—can activate the HPA axis and lead to elevations in cortisol levels. This is thought to be adaptive in this context, as cortisol can mobilize energy resources that could be functional to deal with the demands of the acute situation.

Like threats to the goal of physical self preservation, threats to social self preservation—such as threats to social standing—may also elicit cortisol responses. Indeed, studies of acute and chronic threats to social status in nonhuman primates and other animals have demonstrated that subordinate, lower-ranking animals have higher levels of HPA hormones compared to higher-ranking, dominant peers (e.g., Sapolsky, 2005; Shively, Laber-Laird, & Anton, 1997). In social dominance contests, the "losers" typically show elevations in ACTH and corticosteroid levels not seen among the "winners" of these exchanges (e.g., Kollack-Walker, Watson, & Akil, 1997). Furthermore, the submissive display behavior of subordinates has been shown to correlate with HPA activity (e.g., Shively et al., 1997). The HPA axis is not the only system that can be activated by this type of social threat. Studies in animal models demonstrate that social subordination or threats to social status can also elicit increases in sympathetic nervous system (SNS) activity, as indexed by increases in heart rate or the hormones epinephrine and norepinephrine (e.g., Shively, et al., 2005; Stefanski, 2000). Taken together, this research demonstrates that social threat in nonhuman primates and other animals can elicit increases in cortisol and other HPA products, as well as indicators of SNS activity.

Nonhuman animal models also demonstrate a wide range of immunological effects which can result from social threat. For example, social defeat has been associated with changes in the number and/or distribution of certain classes of immune cells, including increases in granulocytes and declines in the percentage of CD4 and CD8 T-cells (e.g., Stefanski, 1998). Functional impairments have also been observed, including decreases in lymphocyte function (proliferative response to Concanavalin A) and decreases in natural killer cell activity (see Stefanski, 2001, for review).

Research has also illuminated that the important immunological process of inflammation can be impacted by social threat. In response to tissue injury or infection, the body can initiate an inflammatory reaction. This is orchestrated by proinflammatory cytokines, including tumor necrosis factor-alpha (TNFα) and interleukin-6 (Il-6). Produced primarily by macrophages and monocytes, proinflammatory cytokines can alter the production and movement of different types of immune cells, and can induce the cardinal signs of inflammation (e.g., redness, pain, edema).

Recent evidence has demonstrated that other threats besides pathogens can activate the inflammatory response. A series of studies have demonstrated that social defeat/threats to social status in nonhuman animals can also increase inflammatory processes. Specifically, animals that are subordinate or socially defeated show increases in proinflammatory cytokines (e.g., TNFα, Il-6) compared to control animals (e.g., Avitsur, Stark, & Sheridan, 2001; Quan et al., 2001; Stark, Avitsur, Padgett, & Sheridan, 2001; Stark, Avitsur, Hunzeker, Padgett, & Sheridan, 2002). Additionally, defeated animals show increases in other parameters indicative of heightened inflammation, including increases in granulocytes and levels of nerve growth factor (e.g., Avitsur et al., 2001; Stefanski & Engler, 1998). Taken together, these studies show that social threat in nonhuman animals can elicit inflammatory processes.

Social threat may also influence the relationship between physiological systems. Under basal or resting conditions, cortisol can suppress certain components of the immune system, including inflammation. However, the association between inflammatory processes and the glucocorticoid hormone cortisol may shift under social threat. Indeed, research in nonhuman animals demonstrates that social threat can lead to decreases in glucocorticoid sensitivity (see Avitsur, Padgett, & Sheridan, 2006, for review); in other words, glucocorticoids are less able to shut down or suppress inflammatory responses following social threat. Importantly, decreases in glucocorticoid sensitivity may be specific to social threat; other types of stressors, such as physical restraint, have not lead to these changes (Sheridan, Stark, Avitsur, & Padgett, 2000).

Taken together, this research in nonhuman animals points to key outcomes that may be particularly relevant to examine in the context of social threat in humans, that is, HPA activity and inflammatory processes. In the subsequent section, we review evidence that acute threats to the social self in humans elicit changes in these systems as well as other physiological parameters.

Acute Physiological Responses to Social Threat
Acute Social Threat and Cortisol Responses

In a meta-analytic review, we tested the premise that social-evaluative threat provides one set of conditions capable of eliciting cortisol responses (Dickerson & Kemeny, 2004). We identified 208 psychological stressor studies in which cortisol was assessed as an outcome, and then coded the stressors with regard to whether they had elements of social-evaluative threat (e.g., presence of an audience, video camera, or confederate/source of social comparison). Overall, we found that the stressors with social-evaluative threat were associated with greater increases in cortisol (effect size d = 0.67) compared to stressors without a social-evaluative element (d = 0.15). Importantly, these effect size estimates controlled for other methodological factors that also predicted cortisol responses (e.g., time of day, timing of cortisol assessment). This provided evidence that SET is a robust elicitor of cortisol responses in the laboratory.

Further, the meta-analysis found that the effect of social-evaluative threat on cortisol reactivity was heightened under uncontrollable conditions. Stressors were classified as "uncontrollable" if behavior could not affect outcomes or nothing could be done to change a situation; this included if participants received harassment, were exposed to inescapable noise or other stimuli, or were given unrealistic time constraints or impossible/unsolvable tasks which prevented success. The combination of social evaluation and uncontrollability lead to substantial increases in cortisol (d = 0.93), whereas stressors without either component failed to activate this system (ds < –0.03). Not only were uncontrollable, social-evaluative stressors associated with greater cortisol *reactivity*; they were also associated with delayed *recovery*. Studies that utilized uncontrollable, social-evaluative stressors showed persistent cortisol elevations. Specifically, uncontrollable, social-evaluative stressors were still associated with heightened cortisol levels 40–60 minutes post-task, whereas tasks with only one element (e.g., just social evaluation or just uncontrollability) or without either element had returned to baseline levels by this time. Additionally, uncontrollable, social-evaluative stressors also triggered greater increases in ACTH compared to tasks without both elements. Together, these findings demonstrate that uncontrollable social-evaluative threat can strongly activate the HPA axis and influence both reactivity and recovery processes.

The meta-analysis identified social-evaluative threat as an important element associated with cortisol reactivity; subsequent empirical studies have further characterized the relationship between social-evaluative threat and cortisol responses. In an experimental laboratory study, we (Gruenewald, Kemeny, Aziz, & Fahey, 2004) had all participants undergo a modified version of the Trier Social Stress Test (TSST; Kirschbaum, Pirke, & Hellhammer, 1993), which included delivering a speech and solving mental arithmetic problems (via computer). Participants were randomly assigned to complete this task in front of a 2-member panel (SET condition) or alone in a room (non-SET condition). This manipulation differentially induces feelings of social evaluation in the SET condition compared to the non-SET condition, while keeping perceptions of effort, difficulty, or task performance comparable across conditions (Dickerson, Gable, Irwin, Aziz, & Kemeny, 2009; Gruenewald et al., 2004). We found that the participants in the SET condition showed a significant cortisol response; cortisol levels increased substantially from pre- to post-task. However, participants in the non-SET condition who performed the identical task while alone in a room showed no changes in cortisol. This finding has since been replicated in several studies which have utilized a similar experimental SET manipulation (e.g., audience vs. no audience) using psychosocial stressors (speech and/or math task; Dickerson, Mycek, & Zaldivar, 2008; Het, Rohleder, Schoofs, Kirschbaum, & Wolf, 2009) or physical stressors (cold pressor; Schwabe, Haddad, & Schachinger, 2008). Taken together, this series of studies provide persuasive evidence that SET elicits robust cortisol responses compared to otherwise equivalent non-SET stressor conditions.

Other studies have compared social-evaluative and non-social-evaluative stressor conditions naturalistically. Rohleder and colleagues (2007) examined cortisol levels among ballroom dancers during judged competition (SET context) or a rehearsal day (non-SET context). The social-evaluative competition day was associated with greater increases in cortisol compared to responses on the non-evaluated rehearsal day. Furthermore, participants who appraised the competition judges as "more stressful"

showed greater cortisol responses, demonstrating that perceptions of social evaluation were correlated with reactivity to the ballroom dance competition. Overall, the results of this study parallel those observed in the laboratory in which SET conditions elicited stronger cortisol responses than non-SET conditions; further, it extends the findings to naturally occurring performance stressors.

Emotional Correlates of Cortisol Responses to SET

The experimental SET studies have provided an opportunity to also examine the emotional effects of social-evaluative threat and the potential relationships between the emotional and physiological changes. Drawing on the theoretical and empirical research linking self-conscious emotions to beliefs that others are negatively evaluating the self or judging one's social acceptability (e.g., Leary, 2007), we have proposed that this specific class of emotions are elicited when the social self is threatened, and are linked to the physiological changes observed in this context (e.g., Dickerson et al., 2004; Gruenewald et al., 2007). Consistent with this premise, we have found greater increases in self-conscious emotions (e.g., embarrassment, shame, humiliation) under SET performance contexts compared to non-SET conditions (Dickerson et al., 2008; Gruenewald et al., 2004). Importantly, although we have found that other emotions such as fear or anxiety increase in response to the performance task, the SET and non-SET conditions have shown similar changes in these emotions. This suggests that the self-conscious emotions were the most sensitive to the social context of the emotions assessed.

Further, the self-conscious emotional changes observed under SET have been associated with the increases in cortisol. In both studies (Dickerson et al., 2008; Gruenewald et al., 2004), those in the SET condition who showed greater increases in self-conscious emotion also showed greater increases in cortisol. There was no association between cortisol and the other emotions assessed (e.g., fear, sadness). Taken together, this suggests that social-evaluative threat is associated with the experience of self-conscious emotions and further, that this class of emotions may be linked with cortisol changes in this context. Negative social perceptions and cognitions have also been associated with HPA activity. For example, we have shown that social threat-induced reductions in social self-esteem are associated with greater cortisol responses (Gruenewald et al., 2004). Also supporting the link between social perceptions and HPA activation, increased vigilance to ambiguous social cues (e.g., masked threatening faces) has predicted greater cortisol responses following an acute social threat (Roelofs, Bakvis, Hermans, van Pelt, & van Honk, 2008).

Specific Elements of the SET Context Associated with Cortisol Reactivity

In the studies described above, a non-SET condition in which one was alone in a room is compared to a SET condition in which individuals are present, video cameras are often rolling, and others can negatively evaluate performance. Therefore, there are many components of a SET stressor condition that differentiate it from non-SET contexts. A series of studies have examined what element of the SET context is capable of triggering cortisol reactivity; in other words, what is the "active ingredient" that is responsible for eliciting this physiological system or what situational factors moderate the SET effects.

In one study, we examined whether the mere presence of others is enough to elicit cortisol responses, or whether others must be in an explicitly social evaluative mode to lead to changes in this system (Dickerson et al., 2008). To test this question, we randomly assigned participants to deliver a speech in a non-SET condition (alone in a room), in a SET condition (in front of a 2-member evaluative panel), or in an inattentive presence condition (PRES). In the PRES condition, a research assistant was physically present during the speech task, but was working on a computer and not paying attention to the participant's performance. Analyses demonstrated that the inattentive presence condition did not elicit a significant cortisol response. In fact, the flat cortisol profile observed in this condition was similar to the non-SET condition; both of which differed from the significant increase in cortisol observed in the SET stressor condition. This study demonstrates that the mere presence of others is not sufficient for eliciting cortisol responses in the laboratory; instead, others may need to be in an evaluative mode in order to trigger this response.

Other studies have examined whether the evaluative others must be physically present in order to elicit cortisol responses, or whether ostensible social evaluation from another location (e.g., through use of a one-way mirror, intercom, or virtual audience) can also increase cortisol levels. Several studies have found that remote evaluation during a stressor task can lead to elevations in cortisol (e.g., Andrews, et al., 2007; Het et al., 2009; Jansen, Wied, & Kahn, 2000; Kelly, Matheson, Martinez, Merali, & Anisman, 2007; Kemmer et al., 1986). However, the cortisol increases observed with "remote" evaluation have typically been smaller than those seen when an audience is visibly present (e.g., Het et al, 2009; Kelly et al., 2007; but see Andrews et al., 2007). For example, Kelly and colleagues (2007) found that the presence of a "live" audience led to increases in cortisol levels over three times the magnitude of conditions in which remote forms of evaluation were used. Taken together, this research suggests that while remote evaluation appears capable of eliciting modest cortisol responses, "live" or visible evaluation heightens reactivity.

Many of the SET studies include both the presence of an evaluative audience and a video camera (e.g., Kirschbaum et al., 1993; Gruenewald et al., 2004); therefore, it is unclear whether the threat of subsequent evaluation (captured with the video-camera) or the threat of current, real-time evaluation (captured with the audience) is driving cortisol responses. The meta-analysis found that the stressors that included real-time evaluation (e.g., audience) were associated with greater cortisol responses compared to stressors with the potential for evaluation (e.g., videotape). A subsequent study found that videotaping a participant's speech while otherwise alone in a room did not elicit a significant cortisol response (Robbins, Dickerson, Epstein, & Zaldivar, 2010). These findings suggest that real-time evaluation is associated with greater cortisol responses compared to the potential for evaluation, which may not reliably elicit changes in this parameter.

Other studies have examined whether anticipation of social evaluation can elicit increases in cortisol. In these studies, participants are given instructions that they will be delivering a speech, and then given time to prepare the speech. Then, they are told they will not have to give the speech after all, and cortisol levels are monitored throughout the session. The findings from these studies have been mixed. Some have found no changes in cortisol in response to anticipating and preparing to deliver a speech (e.g., Kelly et al., 2007; Rohrmann, Hennig, & Netter, 1999), while others have found that this type of anticipatory stressor can increase cortisol levels (e.g., Starcke, Wolf, Markowitsch, & Brand, 2008), at least in some individuals (e.g., men but not women; Kirschbaum, Wust, & Hellhammer, 1992). When cortisol responses have been observed under this anticipation of social threat, the magnitude has generally been smaller than what is typically seen when the speech is actually delivered in a SET context. This suggests that anticipation of social-evaluative threat can elicit small increases in cortisol, particularly among some individuals; but actually engaging in the social-evaluative context more reliably and robustly lead to these changes.

Taken together, these studies examining different elements of the SET context demonstrate that the real-time visual presence of an evaluative audience during a performance task is a robust and reliable way to elicit a cortisol response in the laboratory. Conditions in which this is mitigated (e.g., evaluative audience is "remote," others are present in a non-evaluative mode, participants anticipate—but do not experience—social evaluation, or only the potential for evaluation is present), appear to only minimally activate or do not activate this system. This suggests conditions in which the salience of social evaluation is maximized lead to greater cortisol elevations.

Interpersonal Evaluation and Rejection and Cortisol Responses

The studies reviewed above have all examined how social threat in a performance context may elicit increases in cortisol. However, not all social threats occur during performance situations; they can also unfold within interpersonal relationships characterized by evaluation, rejection, or criticism.

Several laboratory studies have used interpersonal rejection paradigms to examine how social exclusion and/or ostracism can influence cortisol levels. Stroud and colleagues (Stroud, Tanofsky-Kraff, Wilfley, & Salovey, 2000) found that female participants who were increasingly ignored or ostracized by confederates during a discussion task showed increases in cortisol. In another study (Blackhart, Eckel, & Tice, 2007), participants engaged in a 15-minute conversation period with 4–6 others. Following this activity, they were told that either "nobody wants to work with you" (rejection condition) or "everyone wants to work with you" (acceptance condition) on a subsequent task. Results demonstrated that the rejection condition was associated with elevated cortisol levels compared to the acceptance condition. These findings are also aligned with those reported by Gunnar and colleagues in studies of acceptance and rejection among children (Gunnar, Sebanc, Tout, Donzella, & van Dulman, 2003). They found that children who were more disliked by their peers had elevated cortisol levels compared to those who were more socially accepted or liked. Taken together, these studies demonstrate that negative interpersonal interactions characterized by rejection or exclusion are also capable of activating the HPA axis.

Other studies have examined social threat in the context of conflict discussion tasks. Couples are brought into the lab and asked to discuss a problem in their relationship, while HPA activity is assessed. In a series of studies, women who are on the receiving end of criticism, disapproval, and other evaluative, rejecting behaviors have shown increases in HPA activity, including elevations in ACTH and cortisol levels (Kiecolt-Glaser et al., 1997; Malarkey, Kiecolt-Glaser, Pearl, & Glaser, 1993). This effect has been observed in newlyweds (Malarkey et al., 1994) and in older adults married, on average, for over 40 years (Kiecolt-Glaser et al., 1997). Interestingly, this effect has only emerged among women, suggesting that there may be important gender differences in the HPA response to social threat within interpersonal interactions.

Summary of Acute Social Threat and Cortisol Responses

These studies have demonstrated that social-evaluative threat can elicit strong and substantial elevations in the laboratory (e.g., Dickerson & Kemeny, 2004; Gruenewald et al., 2004) or in naturally occurring situations (e.g., Rohleder et al., 2007). This can occur under social threat that is performance-based or in the context of negative interpersonal interactions. Importantly, this effect seems to be moderated by several factors, including uncontrollability (e.g., Dickerson & Kemeny, 2004), and the salience of the evaluative audience. Additionally, self-conscious emotions may occur in concert with the cortisol changes.

Acute Social Threat and Cardiovascular Responses

It is clear that other systems besides the HPA system can also be activated in response to social threat. For example, social-evaluative performance stressors, such as delivering a speech in front of an audience, elicit marked elevations in systolic blood pressure (SBP), diastolic blood pressure (DBP) and heart rate (HR; e.g., Kirschbaum et al., 1993). These changes are seen rapidly, and tend to dissipate more quickly than HPA responses (which typically are slower to activate and take longer to return to baseline). Other studies have shown that markers of sympathetic activity (e.g., epinephrine, norepinephrine, alpha-amylase) increase in response to social-evaluative threat (Lovallo & Thomas, 2000; Nater & Rohleder, 2009). It is not only social-evaluative performance tasks which can elicit these changes; interpersonal rejection or conflict can also lead to activation of the cardiovascular and/or sympathetic systems (e.g., Kiecolt-Glaser et al., 1993; Stroud et al., 2000).

Social factors may also influence the magnitude of cardiovascular stress responses. A number of studies have manipulated the social-evaluative context of the stressor (e.g., presence/absence of an evaluative audience, emphasizing or de-emphasizing the evaluative nature of the task, or having others display nonsupportive/evaluative behavior vs. neutral/supportive behavior). In general, the more social-evaluative conditions have resulted in greater cardiovascular and/or sympathetic reactivity compared to other comparison conditions (e.g., Christian & Stoney, 2006; Gerin, Pieper, Levy, & Pickering, 1992; Gruenewald et al., 2004; Lepore, Allen, & Evans, 1993; Sheffield & Carroll, 1994; Smith, Nealey, Kircher, & Limon, 1997); although this has not been found in all investigations (e.g., Dickerson et al., 2009; Kelsey, Blascovich, Leitten, Schneider, Tomaka, & Weins, 2000). This accentuation of reactivity in a social-evaluative context may be particularly likely when the task is difficult (e.g., Wright, Tunstall, Williams, Goodwin, & Harmon-Jones, 1995); suggesting other factors may interact with social evaluation to influence reactivity (e.g., Blascovich, Mendes, Hunter, & Salomon, 1999).

It is important to note that across these studies reviewed above, indicators of cardiovascular activity have generally increased in all conditions; in other words, both social and nonsocial threats are capable of markedly increasing blood pressure and heart rate. However, social and inter-individual difference factors may influence the *magnitude* of cardiovascular reactivity observed in these contexts. This may be different than in the case of cortisol reactivity, in which the social context may be critical for whether the response is elicited at all (e.g., Gruenewald et al., 2004; Het et al., 2009). Future studies should further elucidate the conditions under which the cardiovascular and HPA systems may be activated either concordantly and discordantly, and characterize the social factors that shape which pattern is observed (cf. Gruenewald et al., 2004; Het et al., 2009; Schommer, Hellhammer, & Kirschbaum, 2003).

Other research has investigated the effects of social evaluation on cardiovascular responses using impedance and electrocardiographic assessment, which allows for the determination of whether the increases in cardiovascular activity are attributed to myocardial or vascular changes; in other words, whether increases in blood pressure are due to the heart beating faster or harder (myocardial) or the blood vessels constricting (vascular). Several studies have demonstrated greater increases in pre-ejection period (PEP) in response to performing under social-evaluative versus nonsocial evaluative conditions (e.g., Christian & Stoney, 2006; Kelsey et al., 2000), which may indicate greater myocardial reactivity when social evaluation is present. This is also consistent with a study which found that a shame-inducing stressor condition (social evaluation in which the evaluator highlights that the participant failed to live up to expectations) resulted in greater HR and PEP responses compared to a neutral stressor condition (Herrald & Tomaka, 2002). However, this study also found greater increases in total peripheral resistance in the shame-inducing context, suggesting that vascular activity is also affected by these conditions. This cardiovascular response observed in a shame-inducing situation—marked by increases in cardiac reactivity coupled with high vascular resistance—are hallmarks of the "threat" response, which has been documented under conditions characterized by social threat (e.g., Blascovich et al., 1999; see Blascovich & Mendes, 2000, for review). Future research is needed to further delineate the complex cardiovascular responses observed under different social threat contexts.

Acute Social Threat and Immunologic Responses

Acute social threat can lead to changes in specific components of the immune system, for example, affecting the number and types of cells in circulation, as well as how these cells function. Meta-analyses have documented that acute threats, including those which are social in nature, can reliably alter immunologic parameters (Segerstrom & Miller, 2004; Steptoe, Hamer, & Chida, 2007). For example, acute threat can lead to increases in natural killer cell and T-cytotoxic lymphocyte numbers (Segerstrom & Miller, 2004) and increases in circulating levels of markers of inflammatory activity (e.g., proinflammatory cytokines interleukin-6 and interleukin-1β; Steptoe et al., 2007). There are also functional changes that can be observed in response to acute stressors; natural killer cell cytotoxicity (e.g., ability of NK cells to lyse a target cell) increases and the ability of lymphocytes to multiply and divide upon stimulation decreases (Segerstrom & Miller, 2004). This pattern of findings suggests that acute threat can up-regulate or enhance natural immunity (associated with fast mobilization to attack any pathogen) and down-regulate or reduce specific immunity (designed to respond to specific pathogens). These changes could be adaptive in the context of acute threat (Segerstrom & Miller, 2004), which may involve injury and exposure to pathogens therefore requiring a rapid mobilization of the innate immune system to control infection. Importantly, these meta-analyses included many types of acute stressors, some of which were social threats (e.g., evaluative speech task) and some which were not (e.g., watching a video). It appears as though many stressors—including those with elements of social threat—can elicit these immunologic changes.

A series of studies have also examined the immunological sequelae of one particular type of social threat—marital conflict. In these studies, couples are brought into the lab and asked to discuss a problem in their relationship. This type of discussion task can elicit a wide-range of behaviors among the couples; and, individual differences in how one reacts to conflict predict patterns of immunological changes. For example, those who displayed more negative behaviors and/or were hostile and expressed anger during the discussion task showed greater immunologic changes, including greater decreases in NK cell cytotoxicity and the proliferative response to mitogenic stimulation (Kiecolt-Glaser et al., 1993; Kiecolt-Glaser et al., 1997; Miller, Dopp, Myers, & Fahey, 1999). Thus, social conflict—particularly when characterized by high hostility or negative behaviors—is associated with immunological changes.

To compare whether social threat may elicit specific immunological responses (as opposed to all stressors more generally triggering these changes), we conducted an experimental study that examined one component of immune activity—inflammation (Dickerson et al., 2009). We focused on this immunological outcome based on findings in nonhuman animals that social threat can lead to elevations in inflammatory markers (e.g., Avitsur et al., 2001), and tested whether social-evaluative threat in humans could have similar immunologic effects. We randomly assigned healthy undergraduate females to deliver a speech and perform a computerized math task either alone in a room (non-SET condition) or in front of an evaluative audience (SET). Consistent with hypotheses, we found increases in the production of the proinflammatory cytokine TNFα in the SET condition; however, performing the task in a non-SET context led to no changes in this parameter. Further, we found that those who perceived the task as more evaluative showed greater increases in TNFα production, indicating that perceptions

of social evaluation were linked to inflammatory changes. However, there was no such relationship between other appraisals (e.g., task difficulty, effort, performance), suggesting that there was a specific association between social evaluative appraisals and inflammatory activity.

These findings—linking social-evaluative processes to inflammation—is also consistent with work demonstrating that the self-conscious emotions that can be elicited under these conditions are also associated with this immune process (Dickerson, Kemeny, Aziz, Kim, & Fahey, 2004). We found that a condition that induced self-conscious emotions (through writing about an experience of self-blame) lead to increases in the soluble receptor for TNFα, which is a marker of TNFα proinflammatory activity; however, writing about neutral topic, which did not induce self-conscious emotion to the same extent, also did not alter this parameter. Additionally, we found that those reporting greater increases in the self-conscious emotion of shame also showed greater increases in TNFα activity. This study demonstrates that the emotional states induced by social-evaluative threat may also be associated with inflammatory activity.

Acute Social Threat: Cortisol and Immune Interactions

Social threat has been shown to elicit increases in cortisol (e.g., Dickerson & Kemeny, 2004) and proinflammatory cytokine production (e.g., Dickerson et al., 2009); however, there are interactions between these two systems. Glucocorticoids (GCs) are essential regulators of the development, homeostasis, effector function, and cellular trafficking of the innate and adaptive immune system, including processes directly related to inflammation (Pitzalis, Piptone, & Perretti, 2002; Rook, 1999; Sternberg, 2001; Webster, Tonelli, & Sternberg, 2002). Glucocorticoids, including cortisol, act on the body via the glucocorticoid receptor, and are capable of altering the activity of most immune cell types (Ashwell, Lu, & Vacchio, 2000; Refojo, Liberman, Holsboer, & Arzt, 2001). While GCs are not always anti-inflammatory (e.g., depending on timing), they can have powerful anti-inflammatory effects (Rivest, 2001; Webster et al., 2002). Specifically, cortisol can inhibit the expression and production of proinflammatory cytokines. However, social threat may alter the relationship between these two parameters. Indeed, research in nonhuman animals has demonstrated that social threat can lead to decreases in glucocorticoid sensitivity; or the ability of glucocorticoids to shut down an inflammatory response (e.g., Avitsur et al., 2001), as described earlier, resulting in higher inflammatory cytokine levels in the spleen, liver, lung, and brain (Quan et al., 2001). Additionally, this effect appears specific to social threat, as other types of physical stressors have not produced these changes. Studies in humans have demonstrated that acute social threat can modulate glucocorticoid sensitivity (Rohleder, Wolf, & Kirschbaum, 2003); although it is unclear whether this effect is specific to social threat, as has been shown in the nonhuman animal literature.

To test this, in the Dickerson et al. (2009) study in which we manipulated social-evaluative threat in the laboratory we also investigated whether SET versus non-SET contexts were more likely to lead to decreased glucocorticoid sensitivity. Glucocorticoid sensitivity is examined by adding a glucocorticoid, such as cortisol, to wells which contain inflammatory cytokine producing cells and then determining the ability of the GC to suppress the production of inflammatory cytokines. Consistent with hypotheses, we found that women performing a speech and completing a math task in front of a social-evaluative panel showed decreases in the suppressive effects of glucocorticoids compared to those performing the same task alone in a room (non-SET context). This demonstrates that social threat may not only influence the elicitation of inflammatory products, but also the regulation of these processes as well by altering the expression of the GC receptor on the inflammatory cytokine producing cell which is required for GC regulation of inflammatory activity.

Chronic Social Threat: Implications for Physiology and Disease

The alterations in endocrine, immunological, and cardiovascular parameters that follow short-term exposure to social threat may have implications for health and well-being if experienced chronically or repeatedly. Chronic social threat can take different forms. For example, chronic experience of interpersonal stressors—such as conflict within close relationships—could be seen as chronic social threat, as perceptions of negative evaluation, criticism, or rejection could be central to these types of events. Other experiences, such as growing up in a harsh, critical, or rejecting family, could be considered a chronic threat to the social self. Broad social variables such as socioeconomic status can also be viewed from a chronic social threat lens, as social status can affect access to social support and resources,

exposure to prejudice and discrimination, and influence the ways in which one interprets and responds to social-environmental threat (e.g., Chen, Langer, Raphaelson, & Matthews, 2004; Williams, 1990). Thus, different types of studies from different disciplines which conceptualize "chronic social threat" in different ways can inform our knowledge of the psychological, physiological, and health sequelae of chronic threats to the social self. Chronic activation of physiological systems in response to stressor exposure is hypothesized to exact a cumulative toll on the body, what has been referred to as *allostatic load* (McEwen, 1998, 2003; McEwen & Seeman, 1999), leading to physiological changes such as altered basal levels of hormones and proteins (e.g., cortisol, inflammatory markers) of stress-responsive systems, alterations in stress system sensitivity or function (e.g., decreased sensitivity of the HPA to negative feedback signals, exaggerated or blunted reactivity), and subsequent effects on other physiological processes affected by hormones and proteins of primary stress systems, such as metabolic, reproductive, and growth processes. Such physiological consequences of chronic stress exposure are hypothesized to place individuals at greater risk of disease and dysfunction.

Several lines of evidence link chronic social stress to alterations in HPA hormone levels and activity. A meta-analysis by Miller, Chen, and Zhou (2007) indicated that chronic stressors (e.g., caregiving, loss, abuse) that were likely to threaten the social self were associated with higher morning and evening cortisol levels compared to chronic stressors that were nonsocial in nature. Evening cortisol levels were also higher in individuals exposed to chronic stressors likely to elicit shame. Additional evidence that chronic social threat is associated with elevated HPA activity comes from research on loneliness, which measures perceived deficiencies in emotional and social connections. This research indicates that greater feelings of loneliness are linked to greater cortisol responses to awakening (Adam, Hawkley, Kudielka, & Cacioppo, 2006; Steptoe, Owne, Kunz-Ebrech, & Brydon, 2004) and higher morning and evening cortisol levels (Pressman et al., 2005).

In humans, one model of chronic social threat is low socioeconomic status (SES). Socioeconomic status is one of the most powerful predictors of health and morbidity in humans (Adler, Boyce, Chesney, Folkman, & Syme, 1993). Lower SES has been associated with greater risk for cardiovascular, respiratory, and psychiatric diseases, as well as greater mortality (Adler et al., 1994; Berkman & Kawachi, 2000). Clearly, behavioral and contextual factors play a role in this relationship. For example, lack of medical care, deleterious health behaviors, such as smoking, and exposure to toxins and pathogens contribute to this relationship. But these factors explain only a small amount of this variance, and SES effects continue to be observed when controlling for these factors. One pathway through which SES may manifest negative health outcomes is via HPA activity. For example, low SES has been associated with higher basal cortisol levels (Cohen, Doyle & Baum, 2006). Duration of lifetime exposure to low SES conditions is associated higher overnight cortisol levels and other changes (Evans & Kim, 2007). These findings suggest that chronicity of exposure to low SES conditions and their psychological sequelae may be critical components in health effects.

Similar patterns of elevated HPA activity have been observed in studies of chronic social stress in animals. The chronic occupation of a low status position is associated with high basal levels of cortisol, a slower response to challenge and impaired sensitivity of the HPA to negative feedback (Sapolsky, 1993). In addition, low social status is associated with greater cortisol production in response to a pharmacological challenge in female monkeys (Shively, 1998; Shively & Kaplan, 1984). These findings suggest overall greater activity and reactivity of the HPA system in the context of low social status. These effects are most evident in species where high-ranking animals maintain dominance through social rather than physical intimidation, where hierarchies are more stable, and where low rank in the social hierarchy is associated with greater exposure to social stressors (Cavigelli, 1999; Eberhart, Keverne, & Meller, 1983; Sapolsky, 2005; Sapolsky, Romero & Munck, 2000). Primates who have difficulty distinguishing between threatening and nonthreatening encounters have elevated basal cortisol, demonstrating the importance of social perception (Manuck, Marsland, Kaplan, & Williams, 1995; Ray & Sapolsky, 1992).

In terms of effects of low social rank on other systems, socially subordinate females monkeys have higher resting heart rate and greater heart-rate reactivity to acute stress (see Shively, Register, & Clarkson, 2009), mirroring the cardiovascular patterns of reactivity that have been observed in human social stress studies. The physiological correlates of chronic social stress may have important health consequences; chronic social subordination is associated with the development of visceral obesity (Shively et al., 2009), an important risk factor for diabetes and heart disease in both human and nonhuman primates (Depres, 2009; Shively, Clarkson, Miller, & Weingand, 1987), as well as impaired ovarian function in female monkeys (Kaplan & Manuck, 2004). High cortisol levels and other physiological markers of social stress, including elevations in cholesterol and sympathetic activity, are believed to contribute to the poorer health states of socially subordinate animals (Shively et al., 2009).

Although chronic social self-threat, and the emotions experienced under such threats, have often been linked with elevated HPA activity in studies of human and nonhuman animals, not all studies have found this relationship (e.g., Rohleder, Chen, Wolf, & Miller, 2007). Future research should continue to delineate the specific contexts in which, or specific individuals for whom, the chronic experience of social self-threat and corresponding emotions results in HPA activation. In general, though, the patterns of cortisol activity observed under chronic social threat are consistent with those observed in studies of acute social threat and shame experience in both naturalistic and laboratory settings.

Other studies have linked more chronic forms of social threat to inflammatory processes. In one study (Fuligni, et al., 2009), adolescents completed questionnaires each evening for two weeks, which included questions regarding interpersonal stressors they had experienced (e.g., had arguments with friends or family, received harassment from others, or punished by parents); this daily assessment could provide a "snapshot" into the chronic interpersonal stressors experienced by these adolescents. Participants who reported greater levels of interpersonal stressors also had greater levels of C-reactive protein (CRP), a marker of systemic inflammation. Consistent with this finding, a longitudinal study of adolescent females found that greater chronic interpersonal stress predicted greater increases over time in stimulated production of the proinflammatory cytokine interleukin-6 (Il-6; Miller, Rohleder, & Cole, 2009). Further, this study also showed that chronic interpersonal stress was associated with greater expression of genes involved in transducing inflammatory signals. Others have found that lonely individuals—who may perceive and experience chronic threats to social acceptance or belonging—also show an upregulation in inflammatory signaling pathways (Cole, 2008a) and greater inflammatory responses to stress (Steptoe et al., 2004). Taken together, these studies demonstrate that the experience of chronic interpersonal stress is associated with inflammatory processes.

Other research has also examined inflammatory activity and exposure to a harsh family environment during childhood. In a sample of adolescent females, exposure to harsh family environment predicted a trajectory with increasing inflammatory responses (stimulated production of Il-6) over the two years of the longitudinal study (Miller & Chen, 2009). Interestingly, this effect was moderated by life stressors; individuals who came from a harsh family environment and experienced a major life event showed greater stimulated production of Il-6, whereas there was no relationship between inflammation and early childhood experience among those not exposed to a life stressor. This study not only demonstrates the effects of childhood experience on inflammatory processes, but also how life stressors may be particularly damaging for those with this vulnerability.

More extreme forms of chronic social threat have also been linked to inflammatory activity. Childhood maltreatment was examined as a predictor of CRP in a longitudinal study which followed participants from birth through adulthood (Danese, Pariante, Caspi, Taylor, & Poulton, 2007). Childhood maltreatment was assessed using a composite of various negative behaviors/events, including maternal rejection, exposure to harsh discipline, disruptive caregiver changes, or exposure to physical or sexual abuse, and thus would represent a severe and chronic social self threat. Childhood maltreatment was a significant predictor of CRP in adulthood; even when controlling for other early life risks (e.g., low birthweight, SES), health behaviors, and adult stress. Indeed, those exposed to childhood maltreatment were almost twice as likely to have elevated CRP levels compared to a healthy, nonmaltreated control group. Therefore, extreme forms of chronic interpersonal stressors may also be linked with inflammatory processes.

Links between inflammation and other forms of chronic social threat—such as socioeconomic status—have also been observed. Low SES individuals have been found to have higher levels of markers of inflammation in comparison to their high SES counterparts. In a number of studies, low SES has been associated with levels of C-reactive protein (CRP) levels and other markers of systemic inflammation, including inflammatory cytokines (Owen, Poulton, Hay, Mohamed-Ali, & Steptoe, 2003; Petersen, et al., 2008, Pollitt, et al., 2007). For example, in a study of a large community sample, lower community SES (based on census track information for place of residence) was associated with higher levels of IL-6 and CRP, adjusting for demographic factors and health behaviors (Petersen et al., 2008).

Childhood SES has also been found to predict inflammatory indicators. For example, Miller and colleagues (Miller, Chen, Folk, et al., 2009) selected participants who were low or high on childhood SES, but who were equivalent on adult SES. They found that the low childhood SES participants showed greater stimulated production of Il-6 compared to those with higher SES childhood backgrounds; the effect was quite robust, with low SES participants showing 35–50% greater production of the cytokine compared to the high childhood SES group. This demonstrates that early childhood social threat—as conceptualized by childhood SES—is associated with exaggerated inflammatory activity in adulthood.

Other studies have examined the relationships between early childhood SES, family environment, and inflammatory processes. Given that a harsh early family environment (e.g., "risky families") has been linked to SES, this may be one factor responsible for the relationship between childhood SES, physiological processes, and health outcomes (Repetti, Taylor, & Seeman, 2002). Consistent with this premise, low childhood SES has shown a direct relationship to elevated levels of CRP in adulthood (Taylor, Lehman, Kiefe, & Seeman, 2006). Additionally, there was also evidence of an indirect relationship between SES and CRP through early family environment and psychosocial resources; specifically, SES predicted harsh early family experiences, which in turn were associated with lower psychosocial resources (e.g., high depression, low social support, more negative social contacts) which predicted higher CRP levels. Another study found similar effects with blood pressure as an outcome (Lehman, Taylor, Kiefe, & Seeman, 2009). Childhood SES predicted both SBP and DBP in adulthood directly; and, there was an indirect relationship between childhood SES and blood pressure outcomes through early family environment and negative emotionality. Specifically, low SES predicted harsh family background, which in turn predicted greater levels of negative emotionality and higher BP levels. This is consistent with other work that has found the chronic experience of emotions experienced under social threat are associated with heightened levels of sympathetic activity (Rohleder et al., 2008).

Not only have chronic forms of social threat been associated with inflammatory responses, but also the ways in which glucocorticoids regulate this response. Similar to the acute social threat literature, in which social threat has led to decreases in the sensitivity of cells to the suppressive effects of glucocorticoids, there is evidence that chronic social threat can lead to changes in regulation as well. Specifically, elevations in glucocorticoids resulting from social threat can lead to downregulation of the glucocorticoid receptors on immune cells, leaving cells less sensitive to the suppressive effects of glucocorticoids on inflammatory processes (e.g., Miller, Chen, Fok, et al., 2009; Zhang et al., 2006).

Consistent with this premise, several studies have demonstrated that markers of chronic social threat (e.g., low childhood SES, high levels of interpersonal stress, adverse family background) have predicted decreased sensitivity to glucocorticoids. For example, Miller and colleagues (Miller, Chen, Fok, et al., 2009) found that those coming from backgrounds of low childhood SES showed greater cortisol output, and a downregulation of glucocorticoid receptors on peripheral blood mononuclear cells, relative to those from higher SES backgrounds. Similar results have been obtained in studies in which chronic social threat was conceptualized as loneliness; lonely individuals showed decreases in the sensitivity of leukocytes to cortisol (Cole, 2008a) and a downregulation of genes associated with glucocorticoid response elements (Cole, et al., 2007). Chronic social threat (unstable social hierarchies) has resulted in similar processes in rhesus monkeys (Cole, Mendoza, & Capitanio, 2009). This diminished capacity of glucocorticoids to inhibit inflammatory signals could set the stage for inflammatory disease (e.g., Miller, Chen, & Cole, 2009).

There is evidence that social threat—and its physiological sequelae—can play a role in the exacerbation of inflammatory diseases, such as rheumatoid arthritis (RA). RA is characterized by dysregulations in the inflammatory and HPA systems in both human and nonhuman animal models; specifically, disease activity and progression is driven by chronic and sustained inflammatory responses coupled with impaired anti-inflammatory responses, including HPA activity and regulation (e.g., Feldmann, Brennan, & Maini, 1996; Sternberg, 1995). Chronic social threat may influence disease-relevant physiological systems and disease activity. Consistent with this premise, chronic interpersonal stressors among patients with rheumatoid arthritis has predicted greater stimulated Il-6 production, as well as decreased sensitivity to glucocorticoids (Davis, et al., 2007). This heightened inflammatory activity, together with decreases in glucocorticoid-mediated suppression of the inflammatory response, could have implications for disease processes. Indeed, interpersonal stressors have predicted disease activity among those with rheumatoid arthritis (Smith & Zautra, 2002); an effect particularly pronounced for those high on interpersonal sensitivity.

Other inflammatory diseases, such as asthma, also have demonstrated links between chronic social threat, inflammation, and disease activity. One recent study found that social threat, conceptualized as a lack of family support, predicted greater symptoms in children with asthma (Chen, Chim, Strunk, & Miller, 2007). Additionally, low family support was associated with an immunological profile detrimental to asthma disease process (e.g., higher levels of IgE and eosinophils, greater production of Il-4). Furthermore, there was evidence that the immunological processes mediated the relationship between lack of family support and asthmatic symptoms, setting up a model in which the increased allergic inflammation associated with social threat leads to the exacerbation of disease activity. Other studies have found decreases in glucocorticoid sensitivity among children with asthma undergoing chronic social threat; not feeling supported or understood by parents was associated with resistance to hydrocortisone's anti-inflammatory effects in children with asthma (Miller, Guadin, Zysk, & Chen, 2009).

Acute stressors may also exacerbate the effects of chronic social threat on asthma-relevant physiological processes and disease activity. Children with asthma who had chronic family stressors showed greater increases in inflammatory activity (interleukins 4 and 5 and interferon-gamma) and asthma symptoms when also undergoing an acute stressor (Marin, Chen, Munch, & Miller, 2009). A similar pattern of high chronic interpersonal stressors combined with episodic stressors has also predicted greater daily cortisol output and declines the expression in glucocorticoid receptor mRNA in healthy individuals (Marin, Martin, Blackwell, Stetler, & Miller, 2007). Taken together, this suggests that those undergoing chronic social threat may be particularly vulnerable to acute threats, especially in the context of disease.

Individual differences in perception and response to social threats also appear to moderate HIV disease risk. Studies of HIV disease course in gay and bisexual men indicate that those with greater sensitivity to social rejection show poorer disease-relevant immunological function (e.g., higher viral load, faster CD4 cell decline), and faster time to AIDS diagnosis and death as compared to less rejection-sensitive men (Cole, Kemeny, Fahey, Zach, & Naliboff, 2003; Cole, Kemeny, & Taylor, 1997). Other studies have found that chronically experiencing negative self-related cognitions (which are often experienced under social threat) has also been associated with disease-relevant immunologic outcomes in the context of HIV; specifically, attributions of self-blame and self-reproach have predicted CD4 cell declines among HIV-positive men (Kemeny & Dean, 1995; Segerstrom, Taylor, Kemeny, Reed, & Visscher, 1996).

Higher levels of virus replication and faster immunologic declines in those sensitive to social threat appear to be due, in part, to increased sympathetic activity (for review, see Cole, 2008b). Individuals high on social inhibition, which is characterized by high levels of rejection sensitivity, have shown elevations in autonomic activity (e.g., skin conductance, systolic blood pressure; Cole et al., 2003), and elevations in autonomic activity have predicted greater levels of viral load and lower numbers of CD4 cells (Cole, et al., 2001). Further, these autonomic effects mediated the relationship between sensitivity to social threat and these virologic and immunologic health-relevant outcomes (Cole et al., 2003). Indeed, differences in autonomic activity between those high and low on sensitivity to social threat accounted for between 72–92% of the relationship between this trait and viral load and CD4 cells. Together, this provides evidence that sensitivity to social threat could have negative health effects in part because of increases in physiological activity.

Future research should continue to delineate the causal pathways through which social threat may subsequently influence long-term health outcomes. Acute social threat can elicit health-relevant physiological responses, including changes in cardiovascular, neuroendocrine, and immune parameters, and can also influence the regulation of these systems. Additional longitudinal research which examines how these acute responses to social threat could, over time, manifest in physiological dysregulation and influence the incidence and progression of disease could help further our understanding of the processes through which social threat could ultimately affect health.

References

Adam, E. K., Hawkley, L. C., Kudielka, B. M., & Cacioppo, J. T. (2006). Day-to-day dynamics of experience-cortisol associations in a population-based sample of older adults. *Proceedings of the National Academy of Sciences, USA, 103*, 17058–17063.

Adler, N. E., Boyce, T., Chesney, M. A., Folkman, S., & Syme, S. L. (1993). Socioeconomic inequalities in health: No easy solution. *Journal of the American Medical Association, 269*, 3140–3145.

Adler, N. E., Boyce, T., Chesney, M. A., Cohen, S., Folkman, S., Kahn, R. L., et al. (1994). Socioeconomic status and health: The challenge of the gradient. *American Psychologist, 49*, 15–24.

Andrews, J., Wadiwalla, M., Juster, R. P., Lord, C., Lupien, S. J., & Pruessner, J. C. (2007). Effects of manipulating the amount of social-evaluative threat on the cortisol stress response in young healthy men. *Behavioral Neuroscience, 121*(5), 871–876.

Ashwell, J. D., Lu, F. W., & Vacchio, M. S. (2000). Glucocorticoids in T cell development and function. *Annual Review of Immunology, 18*, 309–345.

Avitsur, R., Stark, J.L., & Sheridan, J.F. (2001). Social stress induces glucocorticoid resistance in subordinate animals. *Hormones and Behavior, 39*, 247–257.

Avitsur, R., Padgett, D. A., & Sheridan, J. F. (2006). Social interactions, stress, and immunity. *Neurology Clinics, 24*, 483–491.

Baumeister, R. F. & Leary, M. R. (1995). The need to belong: desire for interpersonal attachments as a fundamental human motivation. *Psychological Bulletin, 117*, 497–529.

Berkman, L. F. & Kawachi, I. (2000). A historical framework for social epidemiology. In L. F. Berkman & I. Kawachi (Eds.), *Social epidemiology* (p. 3–12). New York, NY: Oxford University Press.

Blackhart, G.C., Eckel, L. A., & Tice, D. M. (2007). Salivary cortisol in response to acute social rejection and acceptance by peers. *Biological Psychology, 75*(3), 267–276.

Blascovich, J. & Mendes, W. B. (2000). Challenge and threat appraisals: The role of affective cues. In J. P. Forgas (Ed.), *Feeling and thinking: The role of affect in social cognition* (pp. 59–82). New York: Cambridge University Press.

Blascovich, J., Mendes, W. B., Hunter, S. B., & Salomon, K. (1999). Social facilitation as challenge and threat. *Journal of Personality and Social Psychology, 77*, 68–77.

Bowlby, J. (1969). *Attachment and loss, Vol. 1, Attachment.* New York: Basic Books.

Cacioppo, J. T., Berntson, G., Sheridan, J. F., & McClintock, M. K. (2000). Multilevel integrative analysis of human behavior: Social neuroscience and the complementing nature of social and biological approaches. *Psychological Bulletin, 126*, 829–843.

Cavigelli, S. A. (1999). Behavioral patterns associated with faecal cortisol levels in free-ranging female ring-tailed lemurs, Lemur catta. *Animal Behavior, 57*, 935–944.

Chen, E., Langer, D. A., Raphaelson, Y. E., & Matthews, K. A. (2004). Socioeconomic status and health in adolescents: The role of stress interpretations. *Child Development, 75*(4), 1039–1052.

Chen, E., Chim, L. S., Strunk, R. C., & Miller, G. E. (2007). The role of social environment in children and adolescents with asthma. *American Journal of Respiratory and Critical Care Medicine, 176*, 644–649.

Christian, L. M. & Stoney, C. M. (2006). Social support versus social evaluation: Unique effects on vascular and myocardial response patterns. *Psychosomatic Medicine, 68*, 914–921.

Cohen, S., Doyle, W. J., & Baum, A. (2006). Socioeconomic status is associated with stress hormones. *Psychosomatic Medicine, 68*, 414–420.

Cole, S. W. (2008a). Social regulation of leukocyte homeostasis: The role of glucocorticoid sensitivity. *Brain, Behavior, and Immunity, 22*, 1049–1055.

Cole, S. W. (2008b). Psychosocial influences on HIV-1 disease progression: Neural, endocrine, and virologic mechanisms. *Psychosomatic Medicine, 70*, 562–568.

Cole, S. W., Hawkley, L. C., Arevalo, J. M., Sung, C. Y., Rose, R. M., & Cacioppo, J. T. (2007). Social regulation of gene expression in human leukocytes. *Genome Biology, 8*(9), R189.

Cole, S.W., Kemeny, M. E., & Taylor, S. E. (1997). Social identity and physical health: Accelerated HIV progression in rejection-sensitive gay men. *Journal of Personality and Social Psychology, 72*, 320–335.

Cole, S. W., Kemeny, M. E., Fahey, J. L., Zack, J. A., & Naliboff, B. D. (2003). Psychological risk factors for HIV pathogenesis: Mediation by the autonomic nervous system. *Biological Psychiatry, 54*, 1444–1456.

Cole, S. W., Mendoza, S. P., & Capitanio, J. P. (2009). Social stress desensitizes lymphocytes to regulation by endogenous glucocorticoids. Insights from in vivo cell trafficking dynamics in rhesus macaques. *Psychosomatic Medicine, 71*, 591–597.

Cole, S. W., Naliboff, B. D., Kemeny, M. E., Griswold, M. P., Fahey, J. L., & Zack, J.A. (2001). Impaired response to HAART in HIV-infected individuals with high autonomic nervous system activity. *Proceedings of the National Academy of Sciences, 98*, 12695–12700.

Davis, M. C., Zautra, A. J., Younger, J., Motivala, S. J., Attrep, J., & Irwin, M. R. (2007). Chronic stress and regulation of cellular markers of inflammation in rheumatoid arthritis: Implications for fatigue. *Brain, Behavior, and Immunity, 22*, 24–32.

Danese, A., Pariante, C. M., Caspi, A., Taylor, A., & Poulton, R. (2007). Childhood maltreatment predicts adult inflammation in a life-course study. *Proceedings of the National Academy of Sciences, 104*, 1319–1324.

Depres, J. P. (2009). Targeting abdominal obesity and the metabolic syndrome to manage cardiovascular disease risk. *Heart, 95*(13), 1118–1124.

Dickerson, S. S., Gable, S. L., Irwin, M. R., Aziz, N., & Kemeny, M. E. (2009). Social-evaluative threat and proinflammatory cytokine regulation: An experimental laboratory investigation. *Psychological Science, 20*, 1237–1244.

Dickerson, S. S., Gruenewald, T. L., & Kemeny, M. E. (2009). Psychobiological responses to social self threat: Functional or detrimental? *Self and Identity, 8*, 270–285.

Dickerson, S. S., Gruenewald, T. L., & Kemeny, M. E. (2004). When the social self is threatened: Shame, physiology, and health. *Journal of Personality, 72*(6), 1192–1216.

Dickerson, S. S. & Kemeny, M. E. (2004). Acute stressors and cortisol responses: A theoretical integration and synthesis of laboratory research. *Psychological Bulletin, 130*(3), 355–391.

Dickerson, S. S., Kemeny, M. E., Aziz, N., Kim, K. H., & Fahey, J. L. (2004). Immunological effects of induced shame and guilt. *Psychosomatic Medicine, 66*, 124–131.

Dickerson, S. S., Mycek, P. J., & Zaldivar, F. (2008). Social evaluation–but not mere social presence–elicits cortisol responses to a laboratory stressor task. *Health Psychology, 27*(1), 116–121.

Eberhart, J. A., Keverne, E. B., & Meller, R. E. (1983). Social influences on circulating levels of cortisol and prolactin in male talapoin monkeys. *Physiology and Behavior, 30*, 361–369.

Evans, G.W. & Kim, P. (2007). Childhood poverty and health: Cumulative risk exposure and stress dysregulation. *Psychological Science, 18*(11), 953–957.

Feldmann, M., Brennan, F. M., & Maini, R. N. (1996). The role of cytokines in rheumatoid arthritis. *Annual Review of Immunology, 14*, 397–440.

Fuligni, A., Telzer, E. H., Bower, J., Cole, S. W., Kiang, L., & Irwin, M. R. (2009). A preliminary study of daily interpersonal stress and c-reactive protein levels among adolescents from Latin American and European backgrounds. *Psychosomatic Medicine, 71*(3), 329–333.

Gerin, W., Pieper, C., Levy, R., & Pickering, T. G. (1992). Social support in social interaction: A moderator of cardiovascular reactivity. *Psychosomatic Medicine, 54*, 42–58.

Gruenewald, T. L., Dickerson, S. S., & Kemeny, M. E. (2007). A social function for the self-conscious emotions: Social-self preservation theory. In J. Tracy, R. Robins, & J. Tangney (Eds.), *Self-conscious emotions (2nd Ed.)*. New York: Guilford Press.

Gruenewald, T. L., Kemeny, M. E., Aziz, N., & Fahey, J. L. (2004). Acute threat to the social self: Shame, social self-esteem, and cortisol activity. *Psychosomatic Medicine, 66*, 915–924.

Gunnar, M. R., Sebanc, A. M., Tout, K., Donzella, B. & van Dulmen, M. M. H. (2003). Peer rejection, temperament, and cortisol activity in preschoolers. *Developmental Psychobiology, 43*, 346–358.

Herrald, M. M. & Tomaka, J. (2002). Patterns of emotion-specific appraisal, coping, and cardiovascular reactivity during an ongoing emotional episode. *Journal of Personality and Social Psychology, 83*, 434–450.

Het, S., Rohleder, N., Schoofs, D., Kirschbaum, C., & Wolf, O. T. (in press). Neuroendocrine and psychometric evaluation of a placebo version of the "Trier Social Stress Test." *Psychoneuroendocrinology*.

James, W. J. (1950). *The principles of psychology*. Vol. 1. New York: Dover. Originally published in 1890.

Jansen, L. M. C., Wied, C. C. G., & Kahn, R. S. (2000). Selective impairment in the stress response in schizophrenic patients. *Psychopharmacology, 149*, 319–325.

Kaplan, J. R. & Manuck, S. B. (2004). Ovarian dysfunction, stress, and disease: A primate continuum. *Institute for Laboratory Animal Research Journal, 45*(2), 89–115.

Kelly, O., Matheson, M., Martinez, A., Merali, Z., & Anisman, H. (2007). Psychosocial stress evoked by a virtual audience: Relation to neuroendocrine activity. *CyberPsychology & Behavior, 10*(5), 655–662.

Kelsey, R. M., Blascovich, J., Leitten, C., Schneider, T. R., Tomaka, J., & Weins, S. (2000). Cardiovascular reactivity and adaptation to recurrent psychological stress: The moderating effects of evaluative observation. *Psychophysiology, 37*, 748–756.

Kemeny, M. E. & Dean, L. (1995). Effects of AIDS-related bereavement on HIV progression among New York City gay men. *AIDS Education and Prevention, 7*, 36–47.

Kemmer, F. W., Bisping, R., Steingruber, H. J., Baar, H., Hardtmann, F., Schlaghecke, R., et al. (1986). Psychological stress and metabolic control in patients with type I diabetes mellitus. *New England Journal of Medicine, 314*, 1078–1084.

Kiecolt-Glaser, J. K., Malarkey, W. B., Chee, M., Newton, T., Cacioppo, J. T., Mao, H., et al. (1993). Negative behavior during marital conflict is associated with immunological down-regulation. *Psychosomatic Medicine, 55*, 395–409.

Kiecolt-Glaser, J. K., Glaser, R., Cacioppo, J. T., MacCallum, R. C., Snydersmith, M., Kim, C., et al. (1997). Marital conflict in older adults: Endocrinological and immunological correlates. *Psychosomatic Medicine, 59*, 339–349.

Kirschbaum, C., Pirke, K. M., & Hellhammer, D. H. (1993). The "Trier Social Stress Test": A tool for investigating psychobiological responses in a laboratory setting. *Neuropsychobiology, 28*, 76–81.

Kirschbaum, C., Wust, S., & Hellhammer, D. (1992). Consistent sex differences in cortisol responses to psychological stress. *Psychosomatic Medicine, 54*, 648–657.

Kollack-Walker, S., Watson, S. J., & Akil, H. (1997). Social stress in hamsters: Defeat activates specific neurocircuits within the brain. *Journal of Neuroscience, 17*, 8842–8855.

Leary, M. R. (2007). Motivational and emotional aspects of the self. *Annual Reviews of Psychology, 58*, 317–344.

Lehman, B. J., Taylor, S. E., Kiefe, C. I., & Seeman, T. E. (2009). Relationship of early life stress and psychological functioning to blood pressure in the CARDIA study. *Health Psychology, 28*, 338–346.

Lepore, S. J., Allen, K. A., & Evans, G. W. (1993). Social support lowers cardiovascular reactivity to an acute stressor. *Psychosomatic Medicine, 55*, 518–524.

Lovallo, W. R. & Thomas, T. L. (2000). Stress hormones in psychophysiological research: Emotional, behavioral, and cognitive implications. In J. T. Cacioppo, L. G. Tassinary, & G. G. Bertson (Eds.), *Handbook of psychophysiology* (pp. 342–367). Cambridge: Cambridge University Press.

Malarkey, W. B., Kiecolt-Glaser, J. K., Pearl, D., & Glaser, R. (1994). Hostile behavior during marital conflict alters pituitary and adrenal hormones. *Psychosomatic Medicine, 56*, 41–51.

Manuck, S. B., Marsland, A. L., Kaplan, J. R., Williams, J. K. (1995). The pathogenicity of behavior and its neuroendocrine mediation: An example from coronary artery disease. *Psychosomatic Medicine, 57*, 275–283.

Marin, T. J., Chen, E., Munch, J. A., & Miller, G. E. (2009). Double-exposure to acute stress and chronic family stress is associated with immune changes in children with asthma. *Psychosomatic Medicine, 71*, 378–384.

Marin, T. J., Martin, T. M., Blackwell, E., Stetler, C., & Miller, G. E. (2007). Differentiating the impact of episodic and chronic stressors on hypothalamic-pituitary-adrenocortical axis regulation in young women. *Health Psychology, 26*, 447–455.

McEwen, B. S. (1998). Stress, adaptation, and disease. Allostasis and allostatic load. *Annals of the New York Academy of Sciences, 840*, 33–44.

McEwen, B. S. (2003). Interacting mediators of allostasis and allostatic load: towards an understanding of resilience in aging. *Metabolism, 52*(10 Suppl 2), 10–16.

McEwen B. S. & Seeman, T. (1999). Protective and damaging effects of mediators of stress. Elaborating and testing the concepts of allostasis and allostatic load. *Annals of the New York Academy of Sciences, 896*, 30–47.

Miller, G. E. & Chen, E. (2009). Harsh family climate in early life presages the emergence of pro-inflammatory phenotype in adolescence. Under review.

Miller, G. E., Chen, E., & Cole, S. W. (2009). Health psychology: Developing biologically plausible models linking the social world and physical health. *Annual Review of Psychology, 60*, 501–524.

Miller, G. E., Chen, E., Fok, A. K., Walker, H., Lim, A., Nicholls, E. F., et al. (2009). Low early-life social class leaves a biological residue manifested by decreased glucocorticoid and increased proinflammatory signaling. *Proceedings of the National Academy of Sciences, 106*(34), 14716–14721.

Miller, G. E., Chen, E., & Zhou, E. (2007). If it goes up, must it come down? Chronic stress and the hypothalamic-pituitary-adrenocortical axis in humans. *Psychological Bulletin, 133*, 25–45.

Miller, G. E., Dopp, J. M., Myers, H. F., Stevens, S. Y., & Fahey, J. L. (1999). Psychosocial predictors of natural killer cell mobilization during marital conflict. *Health Psychology, 18*, 262–271.

Miller, G. E., Guadin, A., Zysk, E., & Chen, E. (2009). Parental support and cytokine activity in childhood asthma: The role of glucocorticoid sensitivity. *Journal of Allergy Clinical Immunology, 123*(4), 824–830.

Miller, G. E., Rohleder, N., & Cole, S. W. (2009). Chronic interpersonal stress predicts activation of pro- and anti-inflammatory signaling pathways 6 months later. *Psychosomatic Medicine, 71*, 57–62.

Nater, U. M. & Rohleder, N. (2009). Salivary alpha-amylase as a non-invasive biomarker for the sympathetic nervous system: Current state of research. *Psychoneuroendocrinology, 34*, 486–496.

Owen, N., Poulton, T., Hay, F. C., Mohamed-Ali, V., & Steptoe, A. (2003). Socioeconomic status, c-reactive protein, immune factors, and responses to acute mental stress. *Brain Behavior & Immunity, 7*(4), 286–295.

Petersen, K. L., Marsland, A. L., Flory, J., Votruba-Drzal, E., Muldoon, M. F., & Manuck, S. B. (2008). Community socioeconomic status is associated with circulating interleukin-6 and C-reactive protein. *Psychosomatic Medicine, 70*(6), 646–652.

Pitzalis, C., Pipitone, N., & Perretti, M. (2002). Regulation of leukocyte-endothelial interactions by glucocorticoids. *Annals of the New York Academy of Sciences, 966*, 108–118.

Pollitt, R. A., Kaufman, J. S., Rose, K. M., Diez-Roux, A.V., Zeng, D., & Heiss, G. (2007). Early-life and adult socioeconomic status and inflammatory risk markers in adulthood. *European Journal of Epidemiology, 22*, 55–66.

Pressman, S. D., Cohen, S. D., Miller, G. E., Barkin, A., Rabin, B. S., & Treanor, J. J. (2005). Loneliness, social network size, and immune response to influenza vaccination in college freshmen. *Health Psychology, 24*, 297–306.

Quan, N., Avitsur, R., Stark, J.L., He, L., Shah, M., Caligiuri, M., et al. (2001). Social stress increases the susceptibility to endotoxic shock. *Journal of Neuroimmunology, 115*, 36–45.

Ray, J. C. & Sapolsky, R. M. (1992). Styles of male social behavior and their endocrine correlates among high-ranking wild baboons. *American Journal of Primatology, 28*, 231–250.

Refojo, D., Liberman, A. C., Holsboer, F., & Arzt, E. (2001). Transcription factor-mediated molecular mechanisms involved in the functional cross-talk between cytokines and glucocorticoids. *Immunology & Cell Biology, 79*, 385–394.

Repetti, R. L., Taylor, S. E., & Seeman, T. E. (2002). Risky families: Family social environments and the mental and physical health of offspring. *Psychological Bulletin, 128*, 330–366.

Rivest, S. (2001). How circulating cytokines trigger the neural circuits that control the hypothalamic-pituitary-adrenal axis. *Psychoneuroendocrinology, 26*, 761–788.

Robbins, M. L., Dickerson, S. S., Epstein, E. B., & Zaldivar, F. (2010). *The potential for evaluation and cortisol: A preliminary investigation*. Manuscript under review.

Roelofs, K., Bakvis, P., Hermans, E. J., van Pelt, J., van Honk, J. (2007). The effects of social stress and cortisol responses on the preconscious selective attention to social threat. *Biological Psychology, 75*, 1–7.

Rohelder, N., Beulen, S. E., Chen, E., Wolf, J. M., & Kirschbaum, C. (2007). Stress on the dance floor: The cortisol stress response to social-evaluative threat in competitive ballroom dancers. *Personality and Social Psychology Bulletin, 33*, 69–84.

Rohleder, N., Chen, E., Wolf, J. M., & Miller, G. E. (2008). The psychobiology of trait shame in young women: Extending the social self preservation theory. *Health Psychology, 27*, 523–532.

Rohleder, N., Wolf, J. M., & Kirschbaum, C. (2003). Glucocorticoid sensitivity in humans: Inter-individual differences and acute stress effects. *Stress, 6*, 207–222.

Rohrmann, S., Hennig, J., & Netter, P. (1999). Changing psychobiological stress reactions by manipulating cognitive processes. *International Journal of Psychophysiology, 33*, 149–161.

Rook, G. A. (1999). Glucocorticoids and immune function. *Baillieres Best Practice and Research: Clinical Endocrinology and Metabolism, 13*, 567–581.

Sapolsky, R. M. (1993). Endocrinology alfresco: Psychoendocrine studies of wild baboons. *Recent Progress in Hormone Research, 48*, 437–448.

Sapolsky, R. M. (2005). The influence of social hierarchy on primate health. *Science, 308*, 648–652.

Sapolsky, R. M., Romero, L. M., & Munck, A. U. (2000). How do glucocorticoids influence stress responses? Integrating permissive, suppressive, stimulatory, and preparative actions. *Endocrine Reviews, 21*, 55–89.

Schommer, N. C., Hellhammer, D. C., & Kirschbaum, C. (2003). Dissociation between reactivity of the hypothalamic-pituitary-adrenal axis and the sympathetic-adrenal-medullary system to repeated psychosocial stress. *Psychosomatic Medicine, 65*(3), 450–460.

Schwabe, L., Haddad, l., & Schachinger, H. (2008). HPA axis activation by a socially evaluated cold-pressor task. *Psychoneuroendocrinology, 33*(6), 890–895.

Seeman, T. E. & McEwen, B. S. (1996). Impact of social environmental characteristics on neuroendocrine regulation. *Psychosomatic Medicine, 58*, 459–471.

Segerstrom, S. C. & Miller, G. E. (2004). Psychological stress and the human immune system: A meta-analytic study of 30 years of inquiry. *Psychological Bulletin, 130*, 601–630.

Segerstrom, S. C., Taylor, S. E., Kemeny, M. E., Reed, G. M., & Visscher, B. R. (1996). Causal attributions predict rate of immune decline in HIV-seropositive gay men. *Health Psychology, 15*, 485–493.

Sheridan, J. F., Stark, J. L., Avitsur, R., & Padgett, D. A. (2000). Social disruption, immunity, and susceptibility to viral infection. Role of glucocorticoid insensitivity and NGF. *Annals of the New York Academy of Sciences, 917*, 894–905.

Sheffield, D. & Carroll, D. (1994). Social support and cardiovascular reactions to active laboratory stressors. *Psychology & Health, 9*, 305–316.

Shively, C. A. (1998). Social subordination stress, behavior, and central monoaminergic function in female cynomolgus monkeys. *Biological Psychiatry, 44*(9), 882–891.

Shively, C. A., Clarkson, T. B., Miller, L. C., & Weingand, K. W. (1987). Body fat distribution as a risk factor for coronary artery atherosclerosis in female cynomolgus monkeys. *Arteriosclerosis, 7*(3), 226–231.

Shively, C. & Kaplan, J. (1984). Effects of social factors on adrenal weight and related physiology of Macaca fascicularis. *Physiology & Behavior, 33*(5), 777–782.

Shively, C. A., Laber-Laird, K., & Anton, R. F. (1997). Behavior and physiology of social stress and depression in female cynomolgus monkeys. *Biological Psychiatry, 41*, 871–882.

Shively, C. A., Register, T. C., Friedman, D. P., Morgan, T. M., Thompson, J., & Lanier, T. (2005). Social stress-associated depression in adult female cynomolgus monkeys (Macaca fascicularis). *Biological Psychology, 69*, 67–84.

Shively, C. A., Register, T. C., & Clarkson, T. B. (2009). Social stress, visceral obesity, and coronary artery atherosclerosis: Product of a primate adaptation. *American Journal of Primatology, 71*, 742–751.

Smith, T. W., Nealey, J. B., Kircher, J. C., & Limon, J. P. (1997). Social determinants of cardiovascular reactivity: Effects of incentive to exert influence and evaluative threat. *Psychophysiology, 34*, 65–73.

Smith, B. S. & Zautra, A. J. (2002). The role of personality in exposure and reactivity to interpersonal stress in relation to arthritis disease activity and negative affect in women. *Health Psychology, 21*, 81–88.

Stark, J., Avitsur, R., Padgett, D. A., & Sheridan, J. F. (2001). Social stress induces glucocorticoid resistance in macrophages. *American Journal of Physiology: Regulatory, Integrative, and Comparative Physiology, 280*, 1799–1805.

Stark, J. L., Avitsur, R., Hunzeker, J., Padgett, D. A., & Sheridan, J. F. (2002). Interleukin-6 and the development of social disruption-induced glucocorticoid resistance. *Journal of Neuroimmunology, 124*, 9–15.

Starcke, K., Wolf, O. T., Markowitsch, H. J., & Brand, M. (2008). Anticipatory stress influences decision-making under explicit risk conditions. *Behavioral Neuroscience, 122*(6), 1352–1360.

Stefanski, V. (1998). Social stress in loser rats: Opposite immunological effects in submissive and subdominant males. *Physiology & Behavior, 63*, 605–613.

Stefanski, V. (2000). Social stress in laboratory rats: hormonal responses and immune cell distribution. *Psychoneuroendocrinology, 25*, 389–406.

Stefanski, V. (2001). Social stress in laboratory rats: Behavior, immune function, and tumor metastasis. *Physiology & Behavior, 73*, 385–391.

Stefanski, V. & Engler, H. (1998). Effects of acute and chronic social stress on blood cellular immunity in rats. *Physiology and Behavior, 64*, 733–741.

Steptoe, A., Hamer, M., & Chida, Y. (2007). The effects of acute psychological stress on circulating inflammatory factors in humans: a review and meta-analysis. *Brain, Behavior, and Immunity, 21*(7), 901–912.

Steptoe, A., Owen, N., Kunz-Ebrecht, S. R., & Brydon, L. (2004). Loneliness and neuroendocrine, cardiovascular, and inflammatory stress responses in middle-aged men and women. *Psychoneuroendocrinology, 29*, 593–611.

Sternberg, E. M. (1995). Neuroendocrine factors in susceptibility to inflammatory disease: Focus on the hypothalamic-pituitary-adrenal axis. *Hormone Research*, *43*, 159–161.

Sternberg, E. M. (2001). Neuroendocrine regulation of auto-immune/inflammatory disease. *Journal of Endocrinology*, *169*, 4235–4239.

Stroud, L. R., Tanofsky-Kraff, M., Wilfley, D. E., & Salovey, P. (2000). The Yale Interpersonal Stressor (YIPS): Affective, physiological, and behavioral responses to a novel interpersonal rejection paradigm. *Annals of Behavioral Medicine*, *22*, 204–213.

Taylor, S. E., Lehman, B. J., Kiefe, C. I., & Seeman, T. E. (2006). Relationship of early life stress and psychological functioning to adult C-reactive protein in the Coronary Artery Risk Development in Young Adults Study. *Biological Psychiatry*, *60*, 819–824.

Webster, J. I., Tonelli, L., & Sternberg, E. M. (2002). Neuroendocrine regulation of immunity. *Annual Review of Immunology*, *20*, 125–163.

Williams, D. R. (1990). Socioeconomic differentials in, health: A review and redirection. *Social Psychology Quarterly*, *53*(2), 81–99.

Wright, R. A., Tunstall, A. M., Williams, B. J., Goodwin, J. S., & Harmon-Jones, E. (1995). Social evaluation and cardiovascular response: An active coping approach. *Journal of Personality and Social Psychology*, *69*, 530–543.

Zhang, T. Y., Bagot, R., Parent, C., Nesbitt, C., Bredy, T. W., Caldji, C., et al. (2006) Maternal programming of defensive responses through sustained effects on gene expression. *Biological Psychology*, *73*, 72–89.

Social Neuroscientific Pathways Linking Social Support to Health

Bert N. Uchino, Timothy W. Smith, Wendy Birmingham, *and* McKenzie Carlisle

Abstract

This chapter reviews recent evidence on the social neuroscience of social support in an attempt to examine the physiological pathways potentially producing such effects. It starts by examining the more established links between social support and peripheral physiological processes. This is followed by a discussion of evidence linking support to activation of specific brain processes that are implicated in stress and self-regulatory processes more generally.

Keywords: social support, social neuroscience, physiological pathways, health, stress

Disease agents are ubiquitous in the environment and most individuals are protected from these agents. Under certain conditions, however, this relationship is altered. The construct "social support" is now considered a significant factor in changing the relationship between the individual and these agents, thus transforming an innocuous, possibly symbiotic relationship to one in which disease and/or death is the outcome (Blazer, 1982, p. 684).

Social support is widely regarded as one of the most reliable psychosocial predictors of physical health outcomes (see reviews by Berkman, Glass, Brissette, & Seeman, 2000; Cohen, 1988; Uchino, 2004). It is typically conceptualized as the social functions (e.g., emotional, informational) that are perceived as available or actually received by our relationships (Dunkel-Schetter & Bennett, 1990). Importantly, Blazer (1982) was one of the first to show that perceived support predicted lower mortality rates; an effect that was statistically independent from aspects of social integration. In fact, a majority of studies has found

an association with lower morbidity and mortality, including the development/progression of cardiovascular disease (Andre-Petersson, Hedblad, Janzon, & Ostergren, 2006; Berkman et al., 1992; Orth-Gomer et al., 1993; Raikkonen, Matthews, & Kuller, 2001). There is also preliminary evidence linking support to lower cancer and infectious disease mortality (Lee & Rotheram-Borus, 2001; Weihs et al., 2005).

Despite the wealth of epidemiological evidence, an important question is what are the physiological mechanisms that link social support to such health outcomes (Cohen, 1988)? Critical data have been appearing over the last decade but an integrative understanding of such pathways remains elusive (Uchino, 2004). Given the general links between social support and physical health, it is likely that multiple, cascading physiological pathways are operating. We propose that a better understanding of such mechanisms can be gained by focusing on potential neuroscientific pathways linking social support to health.

In the present chapter, we review recent evidence on the social neuroscience of social support in an attempt to examine the physiological pathways potentially producing such effects. Although not a focus of this chapter, there are also behavioral (e.g., cooperation with medical regimens, health behaviors) and psychosocial (e.g., stress, control) pathways and the interested reader is referred to Uchino (2004) for an overview of these mechanisms. We first start by examining the more established links between social support and peripheral physiological processes. This is followed by a discussion of evidence linking support to activation of specific brain processes that are implicated in stress and self-regulatory processes more generally.

Potential Peripheral Social Neuroscientific Pathways Linking Social Support to Health

Given the diverse links between social support and physical health outcomes, there are probably multiple physiological pathways operating. As shown in Figure 53.1, these peripheral pathways include cardiovascular, neuroendocrine, and immunologic processes that may then influence disease susceptibility and/or its clinical course. These links are detailed below.

Social Support and Cardiovascular Function

Most of the evidence linking social support to biological pathways has examined the cardiovascular system (Uchino, Cacioppo, & Kiecolt-Glaser,

1996). One of these paradigms includes conceptual links to the reactivity hypothesis of disease (Kamarck, Manuck, & Jennings, 1990). According to this perspective, individuals or situations characterized by high levels of cardiovascular reactivity (usually indexed by blood pressure or heart rate) may be related to higher risk for the development and exacerbation of cardiovascular disease (Treiber et al., 2003). Thus, social support may be beneficial because it "buffers" the potentially harmful influences of stress-induced cardiovascular reactivity (Cohen & Wills, 1985). Indeed, studies that directly manipulate the supportive function of relationships appear to provide evidence for this stress-buffering hypothesis (Thorsteinnsson & James, 1999).

Social support may also be beneficial because it is associated with lower blood pressure during everyday life. This would be an important link because studies examining the prognostic value of ambulatory blood pressure suggest that it predicts future cardiovascular problems above and beyond that predicted by conventional (resting) blood pressure readings (e.g., Perloff, Sokolow, & Cowan, 1983). Existing studies are consistent with a link between social support and lower ambulatory blood pressure (Gump, Polk, Kamarck, & Shiffman, 2001; Steptoe, Lundwall, & Cropley, 2000).

More direct evidence for a role of social support on the development of cardiovascular disease can be

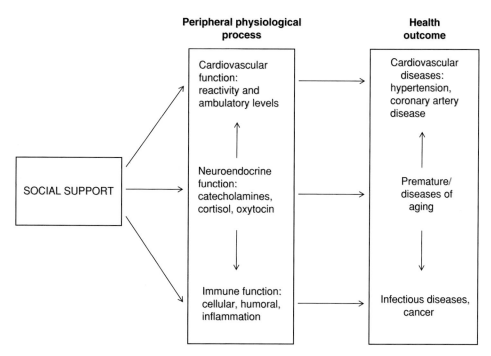

Fig. 53.1 Potential peripheral physiological processes linking social support to health outcomes.

found in data utilizing imaging techniques. To date, several of these studies have shown that social support predicts less underlying atherosclerosis (Angerer et al., 2000; Wang, Mittleman, & Orth-Gomer, 2005). For instance, the National Heart, Lung, and Blood Institute Family Heart Study examined links between social support and carotid artery atherosclerosis using B-mode ultrasonic imaging (Knox et al., 2000). Results of this study revealed that social support was related to less underlying atherosclerosis in women at high risk for the development of heart disease. In other studies, women with established coronary artery disease who were low in emotional support showed faster disease progression as indexed by angiography over a subsequent three-year period (Wang et al., 2005; also see Angerer et al., 2000). These data are consistent with the role of social support in predicting both the development and exacerbation of cardiovascular disease.

Social Support and Neuroendocrine Function

In comparison to cardiovascular function, there is much less work linking social support to neuroendocrine function. The relative lack of such data is noteworthy because hormones and neurotransmitters mediate aspects of cardiovascular and immune function (Ader, Felton, & Cohen, 2001) and thus may shed light on how these diverse physiological systems are coordinated as a function of social support. There is some evidence that social support is associated with lower catecholamine levels (Seeman, Berkman, Blazer, & Rowe, 1994; Grewen, Girdler, Amico, & Light, 2005). These associations are consistent with the beneficial effects of social support on cardiovascular function.

Another important hormone implicated in disease processes is cortisol which has well-documented immunosuppressive effects (Greenspan & Baxter, 1994). Although inconsistencies arose in earlier studies, more recent work is consistent with a link between social support and lower cortisol levels (Floyd et al., 2007). More specifically, these recent studies have improved upon prior work by measuring salivary cortisol over several time points instead of a single point in time (Heinrichs, Baumgartner, Kirschbaum, & Ehlert, 2003; Turner-Cobb et al., 2000).

At present little research exists on oxytocin responses in humans despite its potential links to social support (Knox & Uvnas-Moberg, 1998). For instance, oxytocin is linked to social processes and has anti-stress effects in both the brain and more peripheral physiological systems (Taylor et al., 2000). In one of the few human studies, perceptions of partner support were uniformly associated with higher oxytocin levels (Gwenen et al., 2005). Heinrichs and colleagues (2003) also manipulated social support (via a friend) and oxytocin levels (via a nasal spray) in men undergoing acute psychological stress. Consistent with the stress-buffering hypothesis, social support was associated with lower cortisol responses. These support effects were especially evident if combined with the oxytocin manipulation as such individuals showed the smallest increases in cortisol during stress. More research is needed to explore additional neuroendocrine mediators of social support effects given hormonal influences on multiple physiological systems.

Social Support and Immune Function

A final physiological pathway by which social support may influence physical health is via the immune system. This association is particularly noteworthy because infectious diseases are a leading cause of death in older individuals (Effros & Walford, 1987). An association between social support and better immune function was found in an earlier meta-analytic review (Uchino et al., 1996) and recent studies have confirmed such a link (Lutgendorf et al., 2005; Miyazaki et al., 2005). Moreover, the biological significance of such links is evident (Glaser, Kicolt-Glaser, Bonneau, Malarkey, & Hughes, 1992; Moynihan et al., 2004).

A patient population of particular importance given links between social support and immune function is HIV+ individuals. Although there are some inconsistencies in findings (e.g., Perry, Fishman, Jacobsberg, & Frances, 1992), several studies have reported an association between social support and higher helper T-cell counts in HIV+ men (Persson, Gullberg, Hanson, Moestrup, & Ostergren, 1994; Theorell et al., 1995). Moreover, more recent reviews suggest that longer-term studies are consistent with a protective link and that social support appears to have a more positive influence later in the disease course (Ironson & Hayward, 2008).

Currently, researchers have been actively examining links between social support and inflammation. Such work is important because immune-mediated inflammatory processes appear to play an important role in atherosclerosis (Libby, 2002) and hence can provide a bridge across multiple disease processes. Results from existing studies linking support to inflammatory responses appear to vary as a function of the cytokine. There is some evidence linking social support to lower IL-6 levels (Costanzo et al.,

2005; Friedman et al., 2005; see Hawkley et al., in press for a discussion of the complex role of IL-6 in inflammation). However, less consistent findings appear for other inflammatory cytokines including TNF-alpha (Marsland, Sathanoori, Muldoon, & Manuck, 2007) and CRP (McDade, Hawkley, & Caccioppo, 2006). These inconsistencies may be due to a variety of issues (e.g., statistical power, complex effects of cytokines). Future research will need to model the inflammatory cascade over time to provide more sensitive tests of such potential links.

Potential Central Social Neuroscientific Pathways Linking Social Support to Health

As reviewed above, most of the research on the social neuroscience of support has examined peripheral physiological pathways potentially linking it to health. The emergence of brain-imaging methodologies (e.g., fMRI) allows an investigation into the central processes potentially coordinating these diverse peripheral physiological responses. Thus far, there have been only a few relatively direct studies addressing such issues and hence only preliminary evidence is available.

Social Support and Central Neural Activation

To our knowledge, there have been two relatively direct tests of the links between social support and central activation of relevant brain structures (Coan, Schaefer, & Davidson, 2006; Eisenberger, Taylor, Gable, Hilmert, & Lieberman, 2007). In the first study, Coan and colleagues (2006) examined fMRI responses during the threat of electric shock. Women in the study were subject to this threat alone, or while holding the hand of their spouse or that of a stranger as a form of emotional support. Results revealed that spousal hand-holding was associated with attenuated neural responses to the threat in the ventral anterior cingulate cortex (vACC), left caudate, superior colliculus, posterior cingulate, left supramarginal gyrus, and right postcentral gyrus compared to the alone condition. Holding a spouse's hand was also associated with lower activation in the right dorsolateral prefrontal cortex (DLPFC) compared to holding a stranger's hand. Moreover, wives' marital satisfaction scores were directly correlated with lower neural activation in the spousal hand-holding condition (e.g., hypothalamus). The authors interpreted these findings as evidence that support from a spouse may be particularly effective in regulating neural structures involved in vigilance, evaluation, and the self-regulation of affect.

The second study examined the associations between perceptions of social support using daily experience sampling, and its links to neural activation during a social exclusion task (i.e., cyberball) and cortisol reactivity during social stress (tier social stress task, Eisenberger et al., 2007). Results replicated prior work showing that social support was associated with lower cortisol reactivity to stress. In addition, this association was statistically mediated by lower neural activity in the dorsal ACC and Brodmann's area 8 (part of frontal cortex) as evidenced during the cyberball task. There was also some evidence of further mediation via the hypothalamus. These findings were discussed in light of the modulation of neural threat responses as a function of social support

There are several important points regarding these initial studies. First, due to the lack of research, these data reflect preliminary link between social support and central brain processes. Second, although there are some broad similarities in activation (e.g., ACC), there are also differences in patterns of neural activation and these may correspond to discrepancies in the paradigms and operationalization of support. For instance, Coan and colleagues (2006) examined the receipt of support, whereas Eisenberger and colleagues (2007) focused on perceptions of support during everyday life. As will be discussed later, received support and perceptions of available support appear to be separable processes with distinct antecedent processes (Uchino, 2009). Finally, it is also the case that these preliminary data might help us better understand links between social support and peripheral physiology. For instance, there are direct projections between the ACC and subcortical brain structures important for autonomic nervous system control (Critchley et al., 2003) and neural activity in the ACC correlates with blood pressure changes during psychological stress (Gianaros et al., 2005).

Testing Conceptual Models Linking Social Support to Central Neural Processes

These two recent studies point to the potential promise of examining the central neural substrates of social support in an attempt to foster a better understanding of its links to health. A noteworthy feature of both studies is that existing conceptual models were used to make more specific predictions regarding the expected pattern of neural activation. More specifically, both of these studies utilized the stress-buffering model of support and hence the growing literature on the neural processes associated with stress (e.g., Gianaros et al., 2005; Wang et al., 2005). This approach underscores an important strength of social neuroscience studies—the ability to test the implications of conceptual models using data from multiple levels of analysis (Cacioppo, Berntson, & Nusbaum, 2008). This approach is ideal for the testing of existing models linking social support to health, while also elucidating links to more peripheral physiological processes.

The major models linking social support to health outcomes are the stress-buffering, stress-prevention, and main effects models (Uchino & Birmingham, 2010). The stress-buffering model suggests that social support is beneficial because it decreases the deleterious influences of stress (Cohen & Wills, 1985). The stress prevention model is linked to this model but specifically predicts that social support should decrease one's exposure to stress (as opposed to stress reactivity; Gore, 1981). The main effects model predicts that social support is generally beneficial to health regardless of stress levels (Cohen & Wills, 1985). Importantly, each of these models highlights overlapping, but also unique psychological processes that might then explain variance in links to health (Cohen, 1988). As a result the broader social neuroscience literature on central neural processes associated with psychosocial processes (e.g., Cacioppo et al., 2007, Lieberman, 2007) can be used as a guide to explore and/or contrast the predictions of these models. Table 53.1 outlines exemplar psychological pathways from these models and its links to potential central neural processes to be discussed below.

The stress-buffering model is the dominant model utilized in social support research. Psychological processes related to appraisals are especially important to this model (Cohen, 1988). That is, support may result in an evaluation of the context such that more benign appraisals occur, which may then dampen peripheral physiological responses (Cohen, 1988). Research by Oschner, Gross, and colleagues

(2004, 2008) suggest that reappraisal of negative stimuli results in decreased activity in the ventral lateral prefrontal cortex (VLPFC), amygdala, and dorsal ACC. The latter structures are particularly important for the processing and subsequent peripheral physiological responses associated with negative emotional states (Critchley et al., 2003; Mohanty et al., 2007). In addition, more successful self-regulatory attempts via the VLPFC appear to recruit the nucleus accumbens which is implicated in positive affective experiences, whereas less successful attempts are associated with amygdala activation (Wager, Davidson, Hughes, Lindquist, & Ochsner, 2008). These findings thus highlight a priori regions of interest relevant to an important psychological mechanism of the stress-buffering model, although the specificity of the findings would require additional work (Cacioppo & Tassinary, 1990).

The stress-prevention model highlights the role of social support in reducing exposure to stress (Gore, 1981). Appraisals are certainly important for this model. In addition, more long-term self-regulatory processes are salient via proactive coping that result in decreased exposure to stress (Aspinwall & Taylor, 1997). For instance, social support (e.g., informational support on planning for a rainy day) can help individuals make informed decisions that minimize their subsequent stress exposure. In fact, social support more generally may enhance self-esteem and personal feelings of control which are important antecedents of proactive coping (Aspinwall & Taylor, 1997).

One proactive coping strategy is planning which requires considerable cognitive control. That is, it is often necessary to maintain one's focus on goals that might reduce exposure to stress (e.g., getting adequate rest during workdays; preparing well for upcoming tasks). Importantly, research on the neural structures activated during cognitive control suggests the importance of reciprocal influences between the dorsolateral prefrontal cortex (DLPC)

Table 53.1 **Potential Links Between Salient Psychological Processes and Relevant CNS Structures Based on Major Social Support Models**

Model	Exemplar Psych. Process	Potential CNS Structures
Stress-Buffering	Appraisals	VLPFC, dorsal ACC
Stress Prevention	General Self-Regulatory Skills	DLPC, ACC
Main Effects	Positive Affect	Striatum, OFC

Abbreviations: Psych=psychological; VLPFC=ventral lateral prefrontal cortex; ACC=anterior cingulate cortex; DLPC=dorsolateral prefrontal cortex; OFC=orbital frontal cortex.

and the ACC (Kerns et al., 2004; MacDonald, Cohen, Stenger, & Carter, 2000). MacDonald and colleagues have argued that the DLPC is important for maintaining attentional demands, whereas the ACC is important in evaluating conflicts and can then signal the DLPC to increase its engagement if necessary.

Proactive coping may also involve competition between short-term versus longer-term rewards (e.g., buying that latest radiant large screen TV, waiting for it to go down in price, or saving the money for a rainy day). There appear to be separable neural structures underlying such decisions. McClure, Laibson, Loewenstein, and Cohen (2004) found that limbic structures (e.g., medial orbitofrontal cortex, ventral striatum) were more likely to be activated during immediate rewards. However, more long-term rewards that involve a consideration of trade-offs and control were more likely to be associated with greater activation of the LPFC more generally.

The main effects model of support differs from the other two models in that it highlights the importance of relationships regardless of stress. A relatively unique aspect of this model is that support may be beneficial to health because it helps individuals maintain levels of positive affect that in turn is related to well-being (Cohen, 1988). Research on the neural basis of positive affect suggests the importance of several structures. For instance, asymmetric left prefrontal activation has been associated with (a) brief exposure to positive stimuli (Herrington et al., 2005) and (b) individual differences in the tendency to experience positive affect or approach emotions (Davidson, 2004; Harmon-Jones & Allen, 1998). The basal ganglia and related areas of the striatum implicated in reward also appear more active during states of positive emotions such as happiness (Phan et al., 2002). These areas are richly innervated by dopamine neurons that may serve such motivational processes (Schultz, 2000). The orbital frontal cortex has also been suggested as responsible, in part, for the experience of positive affect (Pelletier et al., 2003), although it may have a broader role in decoding the emotional aspects of an event (Nitschke et al., 2004).

Based on these social neuroscientific data, we propose a general model linking social support to activation of central and peripheral physiological processes in Figure 53.2. The top boxes highlight the higher level (top down) central pathways that are implicated based on prior stress, affect, and self-regulatory neuroscientific research (Cacioppo et al., 2007, Lieberman, 2007). Importantly, these pathways have links to brain regions that regulate autonomic, endocrine, and immune function (Uchino et al., 2007). For instance, the amygdala has direct projections to the hypothalamus and release of

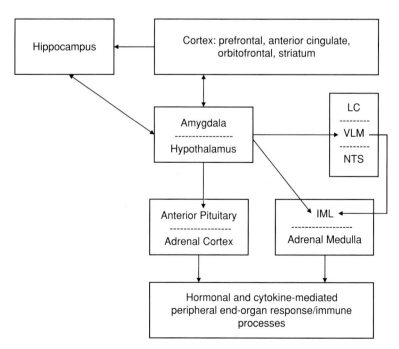

Fig. 53.2 Potential central neural processes linking social support to peripheral physiological activity and health.

CRH from the hypothalamus activates the HPA axis (Gray, 1993). The hypothalamus also has efferent projections to the ANS via the sympathetic preganglionic neurons of the intermediolateral cell column, the ventral lateral medulla, and the nucleus tractus solitarus (Menzaghi et al., 1993). In combination, the release of HPA hormones and activation of the ANS may account for many of the peripheral physiological pathways that appear to vary as a function of social support.

An understanding of the neural substrates of social support shown in Figure 53.2 may inform emerging theoretical issues in the social support and health literature. One important issue is that although measures of general perceived support have been reliably related to lower mortality, measures of received support typically have shown less consistent links and sometimes are related to higher rates of mortality (Uchino, 2004). This association does not appear to be due to the possibility that those who are most sick to begin with receiving more support than their healthier counterparts (i.e., support mobilization). These findings have led to theoretical arguments on the separability of perceived and received support (Uchino, 2009). That is, perceived available support appears more likely to reflect early family influences on social-cognitive processes and hence co-develop with other positive psychosocial factors such as self-esteem and feelings of personal control. On the other hand, received support appears to reflect more of a situational factor that arises in response to stress. As a result, the context in which support is received (e.g., relationship quality, timing of support) is critical in determining whether it has positive or negative influences on health.

One implication of these theoretical arguments is that perceived support is more likely to be related to general self-regulatory processes (e.g., proactive coping) than measures of received support. As reviewed earlier, areas of the prefrontal cortex are of particular importance for executive planning and control that are hallmarks of self-regulatory strategies. In particular, the LPFC and the dorsal ACC have been implicated in self-regulatory processes such as delaying gratification and monitoring goal progress and conflict (Kerns et al., 2004). In addition, if measures of perceived support are linked to social competencies via early, close familial relationships, then one might expect perceived support to be linked to earlier development of the frontal cortices (Yeates et al., 2007). To the best of our knowledge, these studies do not exist

but are promising areas of research based on a social neuroscientific approach to social support and health.

It is also important to emphasize that the separability of perceived and received support represents just one emerging conceptual issue in the study of social support. Such recent perspectives are serving to question/clarify the meaning of support and the specificity of its links to health. Thus, it may be necessary to cast a broader conceptual net on the set of neuroscientific processes that can then inform these emerging perspectives. For instance, activation of the ACC highlights the central pain circuits that also appears to be linked to "social pain" or exclusion. Is social support related to health due to its links to social exclusion and these specific neurobiological circuits (Eisenberger et al., 2007)? It has also been argued recently that part of the health benefits of social support may be due to its links with being a support provider (Brown, Nesse, Vinokur, & Smith, 2003; Piferi & Lawler, 2006). Social neuroscientific studies of support that are informed by these constructs and their associated mechanisms (e.g., loneliness, self-efficacy) may provide valuable tests of these emerging conceptual perspectives.

Conclusions

Social support has been reliably related to lower rates of morbidity and mortality. The last decade has witnessed an increase in studies modeling the peripheral physiological pathways via which support may influence health. In particular, social support appears to be related to the autonomic, neuroendocrine, and immune systems in ways that might confer protection to disease. We argue that a more complete understanding of such links may be obtained via the modeling of central neural structures that coordinate such diverse physiological pathways. Moreover, although direct data on the issue is scarce, such social neuroscientific inquiries can further aide in the testing of existing and emerging conceptual models that posit specific psychological, emotional, and motivational pathways by which relationships influence health. In fact, it is imperative that (a) such studies are guided by existing models, (b) findings are corroborated by data from other levels of analysis, and (c) the specificity of such associations demonstrated via strong inference (Cacioppo & Tassinary, 1990). Such an approach can help foster a more complete understanding of the complex links between social support and health outcomes.

Acknowledgment

Preparation for this review was generously supported by grant number R01 HL68862 from the National Heart, Lung, and Blood Institute.

References

Ader, R., Felton, D. L., & Cohen, N. (2001). *Psychoneuroimmunology* (3rd ed.). N. Y.: Academic Press.

Andre-Petersson, L., Hedblad, B., Janzon, L., & Ostergren, P. (2006). Social support and behavior in a stressful situation in relation to myocardial infarction and mortality: Who is at risk? Results from the prospective cohort study "Men born in 1914," Malmo, Sweden. *International Journal of Behavioral Medicine*, *13*, 340–347.

Angerer, P., Siebert, U., Kothny, W., Muhlbauer, D., Mudra, H., & von Schacky, C. (2000). Impact of social support, cynical hostility and anger expression on progression of coronary atherosclerosis. *Journal of the American College of Cardiology*, *36*, 1781–1788.

Aspinwall, L. G. & Taylor, S. E. (1997). A stitch in time: Self-regulation and proactive coping. *Psychological Bulletin*, *121*, 417–436.

Berkman, L. F., Glass, T., Brissette, I., & Seeman, T. E. (2000). From social integration to health: Durkheim in the new millennium. *Social Science and Medicine*, *51*, 843–857.

Berkman, L. F., Leo-Summers, L., & Horwitz, R. I. (1992). Emotional support and survival after myocardial infarction: A prospective, population-based study of the elderly. *Annals of Internal Medicine*, *117*, 1003–1009.

Blazer, D. G. (1982). Social support and mortality in an elderly community population. *American Journal of Epidemiology*, *115*, 684–694.

Brown, S. L., Nesse, R. M., Vinokur, A. D., & Smith, D. M. (2003). Providing social support may be more beneficial than receiving it: Results from a prospective study of mortality. *Psychological Science*, *14*, 320–327.

Cacioppo, J. T., Berntson, G. G., & Nusbaum, H. C. (2008). Neuroimaging as a new tool in the toolbox of psychological science. *Current Directions in Psychological Science*, *17*, 62–67.

Cacioppo, J. T. & Tassinary, L. G. (1990). Inferring psychological significance from physiological signals. *American Psychologist*, *45*, 16–28.

Cacioppo, J. T., Amaral, D. G., Blanchard, J. J., Cameron, J. L., Carter, C. S., Crews, D., et al. (2007). Social neuroscience: Progress and implications for mental health. *Perspectives on Psychological Science*, *2*, 99–123.

Coan, J. A., Schaefer, H. S., & Davidson, R. J. (2006). Lending a hand: Social regulation of the neural response to threat. *Psychological Science*, *17*, 1032–1039.

Cohen, S. (1988). Psychosocial models of the role of social support in the etiology of physical disease. *Health Psychology*, *7*, 269–297.

Cohen, S. & Wills, T. A. (1985). Stress, social support, and the buffering hypothesis. *Psychological Bulletin*, *98*, 310–357.

Costanzo, E. S., Lutgendorf, S. K., Sood, A. K., Anderson, B., Sorosky, J., & Lubaroff, D. M. (2005). Psychosocial factors and interleukin-6 among women with advanced ovarian cancer. *Cancer*, *104*, 305–313.

Critchley, H. D., Mathias, C. J., Josephs, O., O'Doherty, J., Zanini, S., Dewar, B.-K., et al. (2003). Human cingulated cortex and autonomic control: Converging neuroimaging and clinical evidence. *Brain*, *126*, 2139–2152.

Davidson, R. J. (2004). Well-being and affective style: Neural substrates and biobehavioural correlates. *Phil. Trans. R. Soc. Lond. B*, *359*, 1395–1411.

Dunkel-Schetter, C. & Bennett, T. L. (1990). Differentiating the cognitive and behavioral aspects of social support. In B. R. Sarason, I. G. Sarason, & G. R. Pierce, (Eds.). *Social support: An interactional view* (pp. 267–296). N. Y.: John Wiley and Sons.

Effros, R. B. & Walford, R. L. (1987). Infection and immunity in relation to aging. In E. A. Goidl (Ed.), *Aging and the immune response* (pp. 45–65). N. Y.: Marcel Dekker.

Eisenberger, N. I., Taylor, S. E., Gable, S. L., Hilmert, C. J., & Lieberman, M. D. (2007). Neural pathways link social support to attenuated neuroendocrine stress responses. *NeuroImage*, *35*, 1601–1612.

Floyd, K., Mikkelson, A. C., Tafoya, M. A., Farinelli, L., La Valley, A. G., Judd, J., et al. (2007). Human affection exchange XIV. Relational affection predicts resting heart rate and free cortisol secretion during acute stress. *Behavioral Medicine*, *32*, 151–156.

Friedman, E. M., Hayney, M. S., Love, G. D., Urry, H. L., Rosenkranz, M. A., et al. (2005). Social relationships, sleep quality, and interleukin-6 in aging women. *PNAS*, *102*, 18757–18762.

Gianaros, P. J., Derbyshire, S. W. G., May, J. C., Siegle, G. J., Gamalo, M. A., & Jennings, J. R. (2005). Anterior cingulated activity correlates with blood pressure during stress. *Psychophysiology*, *42*, 627–635.

Glaser, R., Kiecolt-Glaser, J. K., Bonneau, R., Malarkey, W., Hughes, J. (1992). Stress-induced modulation of the immune response to recombinant hepatitis B vaccine. *Psychosomatic Medicine*, *54*, 22–29.

Gore, S. (1981). Stress-buffering functions of social supports: An appraisal and clarification of research models. In B. Dohrenwend & B. Dohrenwend (Eds.), *Stressful life events and their context* (pp. 202–222). N. Y.: Prodist.

Gray, T. S. (1993). Amygdaloid CRF pathways: Role ir. Autonomic, neuroendocrine, and behavioral responses to stress. *Annals of the New York Academy of Sciences*, *697*, 53–60.

Greenspan, F. S., and Baxter, J. D. 1994. *Basic and clinical endocrinology*. Norwalk, Conn.: Appleton and Lange.

Gump, B. B., Polk, D. E., Kamarck, T. W., & Shiffman, S. M. (2001). Partner interactions are associated with reduced blood pressure in the natural environment: Ambulatory monitoring evidence from a healthy, multiethnic adult sample. *Psychosomatic Medicine*, *63*, 423–433.

Grewen, K. M., Girdler, S. S., Amico, J., & Light, K. C. (2005). Effects of partner support on resting oxytocin, cortisol, norepinephrine, and blood pressure before and after warm partner contact. *Psychosomatic Medicine*, *67*, 531–538.

Harmon-Jones, E., & Allen, J. J. B. (1998). Anger and prefrontal brain activity: EEG asymmetry consistent with approach motivation despite negative affective valence. *Journal of Personality and Social Psychology*, *74*, 1310–1316.

Hawkley, L. C., Bosch, J. A., Engeland, C. G., Marucha, P. T., & Cacioppo, J. T. (in press). Loneliness, dysphoria, stress and immunity: A role for cytokines. In N. P. Plotnikoff, R. E. Faith, & A. J. Murgo (Eds.), *Cytokines: Stress and immunity* (2nd ed.). Boca Raton, LA: CRC Press.

Heinrichs, M., Baumgartner, T., Kirschbaum, C., & Ehlert, U. (2003). Social support and oxytocin interact to suppress cortisol and subjective responses to psychosocial stress. *Biol Psychiatry, 54*, 1389–1398.

Herrington, J. D., Mohanty, A., Koven, N. S., Fisher, J. E., Stewart, J. L., Banich, M. T., et al. (2005). Emotion-modulated performance and activity in left dorsolateral prefrontal cortex. *Emotion, 5*, 200–207.

Ironson, G. & Hayward, H. (2008). Do positive psychosocial factors predict disease progression in HIV-1? A review of the evidence. *Psychosomatic Medicine, 70*, 546–554.

Kamarck, T. W., Manuck, S. B., & Jennings, J. R. (1990). Social support reduces cardiovascular reactivity to psychological challenge: A laboratory model. *Psychosomatic Medicine, 52*, 42–58.

Kerns, J. G., Cohen, J. D., MacDonald, III, A. W., Cho, R. Y., Stenger, V. A., & Carter, C. S. (2004). Anterior cingulated conflict monitoring and adjustments in control. *Science, 303*, 1023–1026.

Knox, S. S., Adelman, A., Ellison, C. R., Arnett, D. K., Siegmund, K. D., Weidner, G., et al. (2000). Hostility, social support, and carotid artery atherosclerosis in the National Heart, Lung, and Blood Institute Family Heart Study. *American Journal of Cardiology, 86*, 1086–1089.

Knox, S. S. & Uvnas-Moberg, K. (1998). Social isolation and cardiovascular disease: An atherosclerotic pathway? *Psychoneuroendocrinology, 23*, 877–890.

Lieberman, M. D. (2007). Social cognitive neuroscience: A review of core processes. *Annual Review Psychology, 58*, 259–289.

Lee, M. & Rotheram-Borus, M. J. (2001). Challenges associated with increased survival among parents living with HIV. *American Journal of Public Health, 91*, 1303–1309.

Libby, P. (2002). Inflammation in atherosclerosis. *Nature, 420*, 868–874.

Lutgendorf, S. K., Sood, A. K., Anderson, B., McGinn, S., Maiseri, H., Dao, M., et al. (2005). Social support, psychological distress, and natural killer cell activity in ovarian cancer. *Journal of Clinical Oncology, 23*, 7105–7113.

MacDonald, III, A. W., Cohen, J. D., Stenger, V. A., & Carter, C. S. (2000). Dissociating the role of the dorsolateral prefrontal and anterior cingulated cortex in cognitive control. *Science, 288*, 1835–1838.

Marsland, A. L., Sathanoori, R., Muldoon, M. F., & Manuck, S. B. (2007). Stimulated production of interleukin-8 covaries with psychosocial risk factors for inflammatory disease among middle-aged community volunteers. *Brain, Behavior and Immunity, 21*, 218–228.

McClure, S. M., Laibson, D. I., Loewenstein, G., & Cohen, J. D. (2004). Separate neural systems value immediate and delayed monetary rewards. *Science, 306*, 503–507.

McDade, T. W., Hawkley, L. C., & Cacioppo, J. T. (2006) Psychosocial and behavioral predictors of inflammation in middle-aged and older adults: The Chicago health, aging, and social relations study. *Psychosomatic Medicine, 68*, 376–381.

Menzaghi, F., Heinrichs, S. C., Pich, E. M., Weiss, F., & Koob, G. F. (1993). The role of limbic and hypothalamic corticotropin-releasing factor in behavioral responses to stress. *Annals of the New York Academy of Sciences, 697*, 142–154.

Miyazaki, T., Ishikawa, T., Nakata, A., Sakurai, T., Miki, A., Kawakami, N., et al. Association between perceived social support and Th1 dominance. *Biological Psychology, 70*, 30–37.

Mohanty, A., Engels, A. S., Herrington, J. D., Heller, W., Ho, M. R., Banich, M. T., et al. (2007). Differential engagement of anterior cingulate cortex subdivisions for cognitive and emotional function. *Psychophysiology, 44*, 343–351.

Moynihan, J. A., Larson, M. R., Treanor, J., Duberstein, P. R., Power, A., Shore, B., et al. (2004). Psychosocial factors and the response to influenza vaccination in older adults. *Psychosomatic Medicine, 66*, 950–953.

Nitschke, J. B., Nelson, E. E., Rusch, B. D., Fox, A. S., Oakes, T. R., & Davidson, R. J. (2004). Orbitofrontal cortex tracks positive mood in mothers viewing pictures of their newborn infants. *NeuroImage, 21*, 583–592.

Orth-Gomér, K., Rosengren, A., & Wilhelmsen, L. (1993). Lack of social support and incidence of coronary heart disease in middle-aged Swedish men. *Psychosomatic Medicine, 55*, 37–43.

Ochsner, K. N. & Gross, J. J. (2008). Cognitive emotion regulation: Insights from social cognitive and affective neuroscience. *Current Directions in Psychological Science, 17*, 153–158.

Ochsner, K. N., Ray, R. D., Cooper, J. C., Robertson, E. R., Chopra, S., Gabrieli, J. D. E., et al. (2004). For better or for worse: Neural systems supporting the cognitive down- and up-regulation of negative emotion. *NeuroImage, 23*, 483–499.

Piferi, R. L. & Lawler, K. A. (2006). Social support and ambulatory blood pressure: An examination of both giving and receiving. *International Journal of Psychophysiology, 62*, 328–336.

Pelletier, M., Bouthillier, A., Levesque, J., Carrier, S., Breault, C., Paquette, V., et al. (2003). Separate neural circuits for primary emotions? Brain activity during self-induced sadness and happiness in professional actors. *Neuroreport, 14*, 1111–1116.

Persson, L., Gullberg, B., Hanson, B. S., Moestrup, T., & Ostergren, P. O. (1994). HIV infection: Social network, social support, and CD4 lymphocyte values in infected homosexual men in Malmo, Sweden. *Journal of Epidemiology and Community Health, 48*, 580–585.

Perloff, D., Sokolow, M., & Cowan, R. (1983). The prognostic value of ambulatory blood pressure. *Journal of American Medical Association, 249*, 2793–2798.

Perry, S., Fishman, B., Jacobsberg, L., & Frances, A. (1992). Relationships over 1 year between lymphocyte subsets and psychosocial variables among adults with infection by human immunodeficiency virus. *Archives of General Psychiatry, 49*, 396–401.

Phan, K. L., Wager, T., Taylor, S. F., & Liberzon, I. (2002). Functional neuroanatomy of emotion: A meta-analysis of emotion activation studies in PET and fMRI. *NeuroImage, 16*, 331–348.

Raikkonen, K., Matthews, K. A., & Kuller, L. H. (2001). Trajectory of psychological risk and incident hypertension in middle-aged women. *Hypertension, 38*, 798–802.

Schultz, W. (2000). Multiple reward signals in the brain. *Neuroscience, 1*, 199–207.

Seeman, T. E., Berkman, L. F., Blazer, D., & Rowe, J. W. (1994). Social ties and support and neuroendocrine function: The MacArthur studies of successful aging. *Annals of Behavioral Medicine, 16*, 95–106.

Steptoe, A., Lundwall, K., & Cropley, M. (2000). Gender, family structure and cardiovascular activity during the working day and evening. *Social Science and Medicine, 50*, 531–539.

Taylor, S. E., Klein, L. C., Lewis, B. P., Gruenewald, T. L., Gurung, R. A. R., & Updegraff, J. A. (2000). Biobehavioral responses to stress in females: Tend-and-befriend, not fight-or-flight. *Psychological Review*, *107*, 411–429.

Theorell, T., Blomkvist, V., Jonsson, H., Schulman, S., Berntorp, E., & Stigendal, L. (1995). Social support and the development of immune function in human immuno-deficiency virus infection. *Psychosomatic Medicine*, *57*, 32–36.

Thorsteinsson, E. B. & James, J. E. (1999). A meta-analysis of the effects of experimental manipulations of social support during laboratory stress. *Psychology and Health*, *14*, 869–886.

Treiber, F. A., Kamarck, T., Schneiderman, N., Sheffield, D., Kapuku, G., & Taylor, T. (2003). Cardiovascular reactivity and development of preclinical and clinical disease states. *Psychosomatic Medicine*, *65*, 46–62.

Turner-Cobb, J. M., Sephton, S. E., Koopman, C., Blake-Mortimer, J., & Spiegel, D. (2000). Social support and salivary cortisol in women with metastatic breast cancer. *Psychosomatic Medicine*, *62*, 337–345.

Uchino, B. N. (2004). *Social support and physical health: Understanding the health consequences of relationships.* New Haven, CT: Yale University Press.

Uchino, B. N., Cacioppo, J. T., & Kiecolt-Glaser, J. K. (1996). The relationship between social support and physiological processes: A review with emphasis on underlying mechanisms and implications for health. *Psychological Bulletin*, *119*, 488–531.

Uchino, B. N., Smith, T. W., Holt-Lunstad, J. L., Campo, R., & Reblin, M. (2007). Stress and illness. In J. Cacioppo, L. Tassinary, & G. Berntson (Eds.), *Handbook of psychophysiology* (3rd edition, pp. 608–632). New York: Cambridge University Press.

Uchino, B. N. & Birmingham, W. (2010). Stress and social support processes. In R. Contrada & A. Baum (Eds.), *Handbook of stress science* (pp. 111–121). New York: Springer.

Uchino, B. N. (2009). Understanding the links between social support and physical health: A lifespan perspective with emphasis on the separability of perceived and received support. *Perspectives in Psychological Science*, *4*, 236–255.

Wager, T. D., Davidson, M. L., Hughes, B. L., Lindquist, M. A., & Ochsner, K. N. (2008). Prefrontal-subcortical pathways mediating successful emotion regulation. *Neuron*, *59*, 1037–1050.

Wang, H.-X., Mittleman, M. A., & Orth-Gomer, K. (2005). Influence of social support on progression of coronary artery disease in women. *Social Science & Medicine*, *60*, 599–607.

Wang, J., Rao, H., Wetmore, G. S., Furlan, P. M., Korczykowski, M., Dinges, D. F., et al. (2005). Perfusion functional MRI reveals cerebral blood flow pattern under psychological stress. *PNAS*, *102*, 17804–17809.

Weihs, K. L., Simmens, S. J., Mizrahi, J., Enright, T. M., Hunt, M. E., & Siegel, R. S. (2005). Dependable social relationships predict overall survival in Stages II and III breast carcinoma patients. *Journal of Psychosomatic Research*, *59*, 299–306.

Yeates, K. O., Bigler, E. D., Dennis, M., Gerhardt, C. A., Rubin, K. H., Stancin, T., et al. (2007). Social outcomes in childhood brain disorder: A heuristic integration of social neuroscience and developmental psychology. *Psychological Bulletin*, *133*, 535–556.

CHAPTER
54

Stress, Negative Emotions, and Inflammation

Jean-Philippe Gouin, Liisa V. Hantsoo, *and* Janice K. Kiecolt-Glaser

Abstract

Chronic low grade inflammation is a core pathophysiological process that may be involved in many age-related diseases. Elevations in circulating markers of inflammation have been associated with frailty and disability, osteoporosis, certain cancers, cardiovascular disorders, type II diabetes, rheumatoid arthritis, and Alzheimer's disease. Importantly, stress and negative emotions appear to promote the production of inflammatory mediators, providing a physiological mechanism by which negative psychological states may impact health. This chapter reviews the basic physiological processes of inflammation, the relationships among stress, negative emotions, social relationships, and inflammation, and the behavioral and physiological pathways linking stress, emotions, and inflammation.

Keywords: inflammation, Interleukin-6, C-Reactive protein, glucocorticoid resistance, stress, depression, caregiving, social support, social conflict, marriage, health behaviors, chronic disease, psychoneuroimmunology

Stress and negative emotions are daily occurrences that have psychological implications, but also clear endocrine and immune consequences. As such, these affective responses provide a window by which the external environment can influence the individual's physiology. Furthermore, increasing evidence suggests a bi-directional relationship between emotions and physiological systems, such that endocrine and immune changes may also modulate emotional responses. Of special interest for social neuroscience, inflammation, a component of immune function, may be a key physiological mediator of the impact of stress and negative emotions on health.

Chronic low-grade inflammation is a core pathophysiological process that may be involved in many age-related diseases. Elevations in circulating markers of inflammation have been associated with frailty and disability, osteoporosis, certain cancers, cardiovascular disorders, type II diabetes, rheumatoid arthritis, and Alzheimer's disease (Maggio, Guralnik, Longo, & Ferrucci, 2006). Importantly, stress and negative emotions appear to promote the production of inflammatory mediators, providing a physiological mechanism by which negative psychological states may impact health. The current chapter reviews the basic physiological processes of inflammation, the relationships among stress, negative emotions, social relationships and inflammation, and the behavioral and physiological pathways linking stress, emotions, and inflammation. Throughout the chapter, empirical human studies are emphasized.

Acute Inflammation: An Essential Response to Infections and Injuries

Inflammation is an essential immune response triggered by infection and injury. It is the initial, automatic, and nonspecific reaction of the innate immune system that occurs upon exposure to an antigen—a substance foreign to the host's body. Inflammation promotes the destruction and clearance of pathogens and initiates wound healing, enabling the body to cope with a range of insults, from viral infections to allergic reactions to cutaneous wounds. This process is enacted primarily by cytokines; soluble proteins that provide an intercellular signal to recruit and activate other immune cells to the affected area.

Cytokines are produced mainly by immune cells such as monocytes, macrophages, lymphocytes, and endothelial cells, but they are also secreted by non-immune cells such as osteoblasts, intestinal epithelial cells, adipocytes, and vascular smooth muscle cells. Proinflammatory cytokines, such as interleukin-6 (IL-6) or tumor necrosis factor-α (TNF-α), promote a state of inflammation while anti-inflammatory cytokines, such as interleukin-10 (IL-10), decrease the production and function of proinflammatory cytokines, thereby regulating the immune response to antigens (Parham, 2004). In addition, cytokines may be classified as Th1 type or Th2 type. Th1 cytokines are associated with the proinflammatory response, which involves killing intracellular invaders. As prolonged Th1 response may result in tissue damage, the Th2 response counteracts this, promoting anti-inflammatory activity. Furthermore, some cytokines have both proinflammatory and anti-inflammatory properties. For example, IL-6 promotes local inflammation but also restrains inflammatory response by suppressing TNF-α and interleukin-1β (IL-1β) production, increasing IL-1 receptor antagonist and soluble TNF receptor p55, and by stimulating production of cortisol, a potent anti-inflammatory hormone (Tilg, Dinarello, & Mier, 1997).

Proinflammatory cytokines trigger the release of acute-phase reactants by the liver. Plasma concentrations of positive acute-phase proteins increase in response to inflammation, while negative acute-phase proteins decrease in response to inflammation. Positive acute-phase reactants, such as CRP and serum amyloid A, play a role in the inflammatory process, engaging in processes such as opsonization of antigens (flagging an antigen as a target for phagocytosis) or recruiting immune cells. Negative acute phase reactants are important carrier and metal-binding proteins (Gabay & Kushner, 1999).

Interleukin-6, TNF-α, and C-reactive protein (CRP) are the main inflammatory mediators that have been studied in relation to stress and depression in humans. Interleukin-1β is another important proinflammatory cytokine, but is harder to detect in plasma of healthy individuals. Figure 54.1 provides an overview of the component of the innate involved in the acute inflammatory response.

Chronic Inflammation and Health

Local inflammatory responses are critical in acute infection and injury. However, exaggerated responses and/or chronic inflammation may be detrimental to health. In fact, chronic low-grade inflammation has been implicated in a number of serious medical conditions (Ershler & Keller, 2000; see Figure 54.2). In addition, both IL-6 and CRP have been prospectively associated with increased risk of all-cause of mortality, even among healthy older people (Harris et al., 1999).

Among rheumatoid arthritis patients, IL-6 and its soluble receptor are elevated in synovial fluid and in plasma, and are correlated with disease activity (Madhok, Crilly, Watson, & Capell, 1993). Moreover, among older adults, elevated serum IL-6 is positively associated with markers of physical frailty and inversely related to bone mineral density (Cesari et al., 2004; Giuliani et al., 2001). High levels of inflammatory markers have been prospectively associated with the development of frailty and disability in older adults (Ferrucci et al., 1999). Furthermore, an inverse relation between plasma IL-6 and hippocampal grey matter volume and cognitive performance has been found among healthy individuals (Marsland, Gianaros, Abramowitch, Manuck, & Hariri, 2008).

Elevated markers of inflammation may increase risk of certain cancers (Aggarwal, Shishodia, Sandur, Pandey, & Sethi, 2006). In experimental and clinical studies, inflammation in and around the tumor appears to promote cancer development and progression (Balkwill, Charles, & Mantovani, 2005). In humans, elevated inflammatory markers have also been associated with poorer prognosis and more severe cancer-related symptoms such as persistent fatigue (Collado-Hidalgo, Bower, Ganz, Cole, & Irwin, 2006; Salgado et al., 2003).

Notably, IL-6 is a prospective risk factor for type 2 diabetes (Pradhan, Manson, Rifai, Buring, & Ridker, 2001). Inflammation is also related to atherosclerotic processes and hypertension, which in turn are linked to the development of cardiovascular disorders (Amar et al., 2006; Sesso et al., 2003).

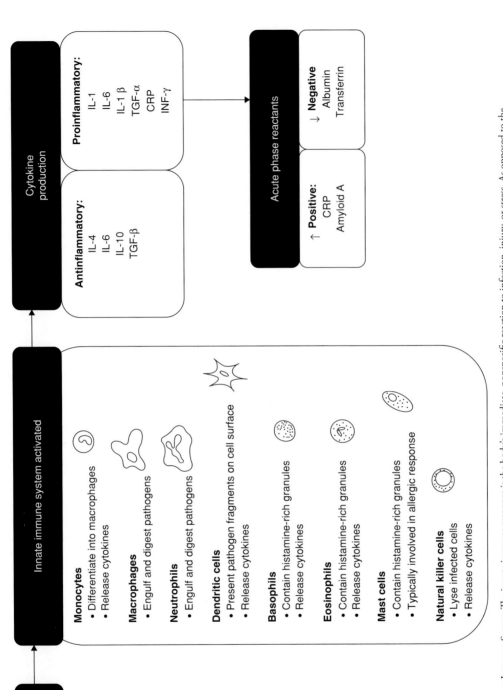

Fig. 54.1 Acute Inflammation: Innate Immune System The innate immune response is the body's immediate, nonspecific reaction to infection, injury, or stress. As opposed to the adaptive immune response, which relies on antibodies, the innate immune response relies on cytokines. Cytokines are signaling molecules which can act in an endocrine, paracrine, or autocrine manner, recruiting other immune cells to the site.

Infection, injury, stress

Innate immune system activated

Monocytes
• Differentiate into macrophages
• Release cytokines

Macrophages
• Engulf and digest pathogens

Neutrophils
• Engulf and digest pathogens

Dendritic cells
• Present pathogen fragments on cell surface
• Release cytokines

Basophils
• Contain histamine-rich granules
• Release cytokines

Eosinophils
• Contain histamine-rich granules
• Release cytokines

Mast cells
• Contain histamine-rich granules
• Typically involved in allergic response

Natural killer cells
• Lyse infected cells
• Release cytokines

Cytokine production

Antinflammatory:
IL-4
IL-6
IL-10
TGF-β

Proinflammatory:
IL-1
IL-6
IL-1 β
TGF-α
CRP
INF-γ

Acute phase reactants

↑ **Positive:**
CRP
Amyloid A

↓ **Negative**
Albumin
Transferrin

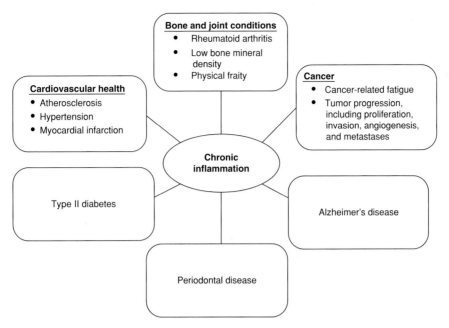

Fig. 54.2 Chronic Inflammation and Health Chronic inflammation is associated with a number of health conditions.

Indeed, plasma levels of IL-6 and CRP have been associated with an increased risk of myocardial infarction, even among apparently healthy individuals (Ridker, Rifai, Stampfer, & Hennekens, 2000; Ridker, 2000). Circulating markers of inflammation also predict a worse prognosis following an acute coronary episode (Lindmark, Diderholm, Wallentin, & Siegbahn, 2001). Moreover, individuals presenting high levels of CRP were at increased risk of developing transient myocardial ischemia during a laboratory mental stressor, a condition associated with increased risk of later, clinically relevant cardiac events (Shah et al., 2006).

Acute Stress and Inflammation

Acute stress elicits peripheral production of proinflammatory cytokines. In animal models, a range of stressors including physical restraint, foot shock, and open field exposure, provoke elevations in circulating markers of inflammation, with the magnitude of the change proportional to the intensity of the stressor (LeMay, Vander, & Kluger, 1990; Zhou, Kusnecov, Shurin, DePaoli, & Rabin, 1993). For example, the increase in circulating IL-6 was proportional to the number of foot shocks administered to the rat (Zhou et al., 1993). Furthermore, this inflammatory response to stress can be conditioned. After pairing the foot shocks with an auditory tone for several trials, the conditioned stimulus (i.e., the auditory tone) acquired the ability to elicit

an inflammatory response even in the absence of shock (Johnson et al., 2002; Zhou et al., 1993).

In humans, standardized laboratory stressors lead to increases in inflammation (Brydon, Edwards, Mohamed-Ali, & Steptoe, 2004). For example, the Trier Social Stress Test (TSST), a laboratory stressor involving mental arithmetic and a public-speaking task, elicited elevations in plasma IL-6 (Pace et al., 2006). Similarly, exposure to an experimental stressor comprising a computerized color-word interference (i.e., Stroop) task and a mirror tracing task led to an increase in IL-1β gene expression in mononuclear cells (Brydon et al., 2005). A meta-analysis of human studies on the impact of acute stress on circulating markers of inflammation suggests that elevations in plasma levels of IL-6, IL-1β, and CRP are reliably observed after exposure to a standardized psychological stressor. The increase in biomarkers of inflammation appears to be greater 30 to 120 minutes post-stress compared to immediately after the stress task (Steptoe, Hamer, & Chida, 2007). In fact, elevations in circulating markers of inflammation were observed up to 24 hours following the discussion of a marital disagreement in a well-controlled environment (Kiecolt-Glaser et al., 2005). Some null effects observed in the literature may be explained by the fact the blood samples were taken too close to the occurrence of the stressor (e.g. Heesen et al., 2002; Lutgendorf, Logan, Costanzo, & Lubaroff, 2004).

Short-term naturalistic stressors also appear to promote systemic inflammation. Psychiatry residents who gave an oral presentation before the members of their department exhibited an increase in IL-1β and sICAM, a chemokine whose presence suggest an inflammatory state, as compared to control days when they listened to colleagues giving presentations (Heinz et al., 2003). Similarly, among community-dwelling adults, the frequency of daily hassles in the past month was positively associated with elevated plasma levels of sICAM-1, and the frequency of positive events over the last month was negatively associated with higher IL-6 plasma levels (Jain, Mills, von Kanel, Hong, & Dimsdale, 2007). Self-reported perceived stress has also been cross-sectionally associated with plasma CRP levels (McDade, Hawkley, & Cacioppo, 2006). Low socioeconomic status, a condition often associated with multiple stressors, has been related to greater plasma levels of IL-6, TNF-α, and CRP, compared to higher socioeconomic status (Koster et al., 2006).

Repeated exposure to a standardized stressor does not lead to the habituation of the inflammatory response. Participants who participated in the TSST once a week for three weeks demonstrated reduced cortisol and systolic blood pressure reactivity during the second and third exposure to the stressor. However, the inflammatory responses remained the same across the three experimental sessions (von Kanel, Kudielka, Preckel, Hanebuth, & Fischer, 2005). If such lack of habituation also occurs in naturalistic settings, inflammatory responses to relatively minor but recurrent stress in daily life may contribute to increased low-grade inflammation. Importantly, stress-induced elevations in circulating inflammatory markers have been prospectively associated with the development of subclinical indicators of cardiovascular diseases (Brydon & Steptoe, 2005; Ellins et al., 2008).

In the context of autoimmune and inflammatory diseases, stress-induced increases in inflammation may exacerbate disease activity. Individuals suffering from gingivitis, a chronic inflammation of the oral gingival connective tissue, were randomly exposed to either a public-speaking task or a nonstressful control task. The stress task induced increases in IL-8 production in gingival crevicular fluid, suggesting a mechanism by which stress may promote disease progression (Weik, Herforth, Kolb-Bachofen, & Deinzer, 2008). Among women with rheumatoid arthritis, chronic interpersonal stress was associated with greater LPS-stimulated IL-6 production by peripheral blood mononuclear cells.

This increase in IL-6 production was in turn related to greater self-reported fatigue (Davis et al., 2008). Dysregulated inflammatory responses may therefore be detrimental in the context of autoimmune and inflammatory diseases.

Chronic Stress and Inflammation

Chronic stress may promote a state of chronic low-grade inflammation. Family dementia caregiving is one of the best human models of chronic stress. Caregivers must deal daily with the changes in cognitive functioning (e.g., memory loss, confusion), behaviors (e.g., agitation, aggression), and personality (e.g. apathy, inappropriate emotion) of their loved one. Caregivers have an increased risk for anxiety and depressive disorders, a greater frequency of infectious illnesses, poorer responses to vaccines, delayed wound healing, and even an increased risk of death, compared to noncaregiving controls (Gouin, Hantsoo, & Kiecolt-Glaser, 2008).

The chronic stress associated with caregiving has been related to heightened inflammation. Older women caring for a spouse with dementia exhibited higher plasma IL-6 levels compared to older women undergoing the time-limited stress of housing relocation, as well as women who were not experiencing significant life changes (Lutgendorf et al., 1999). These results were replicated in a larger study in which 116 caregivers exhibited higher plasma levels of IL-6 compared to 54 demographically similar noncaregiving controls (von Kanel et al., 2006). Chronic stress also appears to exacerbate the natural age-related increases in IL-6. In a longitudinal study, 119 caregivers exhibited on average a four-fold greater increase in IL-6 over a 6-year period, compared to 106 demographically-similar noncaregiving controls (Kiecolt-Glaser et al., 2003). This amplified age-related increase in IL-6 was not trivial. Based on the results of epidemiological studies, older adults with an IL-6 serum concentration greater than 3.19 pg/ml had a 2-fold greater risk of death. In the Kiecolt-Glaser et al. study (2003), caregivers reached this threshold on average around the age of 75, while noncaregivers were expected to cross that threshold after the age of 90.

The higher frequency of infectious illnesses, poorer responses to vaccine, and delayed wound healing in combination with chronic stress may contribute to greater production of proinflammatory cytokines among caregivers. The subsequent chronic low-grade inflammation is a physiological mechanism that might explain the association between the chronic stress of caregiving and the development and progression of age-related diseases, and even death (Black, 2006).

Depression, Mood, and Inflammation

Clinical depression and subsyndromal depressive symptoms have been related to elevated circulating markers of inflammation. Several lines of evidence support the association between depression and inflammation.

Pharmacologically-induced Inflammation is Associated with Depression

In rodents, systemic or central administration of proinflammatory cytokines, IL-1β in particular, induces a sickness behavior syndrome resembling human depression. Behavioral changes following proinflammatory cytokine administration include fever, anorexia, weight loss, psychomotor retardation, sleep disturbances, impaired cognitive abilities, and anhedonia. The fact that these symptoms disappear when the administration of cytokine is interrupted, or with the administration of cytokine antagonists or anti-inflammatory compounds, supports the role of cytokines in causing these depression-like symptoms (Dantzer, O'Connor, Freund, Johnson, & Kelley, 2008).

In humans, proinflammatory cytokines are administered therapeutically to treat certain cancers and infectious diseases such as hepatitis C. Patients undergoing IL-2 or interferon (IFN)-α treatment exhibit cognitive disturbances and neurovegetative symptoms such as loss of appetite, fatigue, or altered sleep in the first week of treatment. A few weeks later, sadness and loss of interest are experienced by 40% of the patients receiving cytokine treatment (Capuron, Gumnick et al., 2002). A notable proportion of those patients developed sufficiently severe depressive symptoms to require psychiatric treatment (Dieperink, Ho, Thuras, & Willenbring, 2003). In addition, IFN-α treatment causes increases in circulating IL-6 and TNF-α, and provokes HPA axis alterations, as well as dysregulation of serotonin metabolism (Capuron & Miller, 2004).

Vaccinations can also lead to transient mood disturbances that may be related to inflammatory responses to the immune challenge. Individuals who were vaccinated reported an increase in negative affect and a decrease in positive mood that was correlated with the elevation in serum IL-6 levels following the immune challenge (Wright, Strike, Brydon, & Steptoe, 2005). Similarly, injection of a *salmonella abortus equi* endotoxin led to a 50- to 100-fold increase in plasma IL-6 and TNF-α

concentration within 4 hours, but no such increase was observed following administration of the placebo substance. Significant elevations in anxiety and depressed mood were observed in the endotoxin group but not the placebo group (Reichenberg et al., 2001).

Depression Treatment Leads to Reduction in Inflammation

Successful pharmacological treatment of depression reduces circulating markers of inflammation, providing further evidence of an association between depression and inflammation. Antidepressant medication has been associated with reduction in plasma IL-6, TNF-α, and CRP (Lanquillon, Krieg, Bening-Abu-Shach, & Vedder, 2000; Sluzewska et al., 1995). A complementary increase in anti-inflammatory cytokines is also observed in depressed patients responding to antidepressant medication (Leonard, 2001). Furthermore, the depressive symptoms elicited by IFN-α therapy can be prevented or attenuated by antidepressant treatment (Hauser et al., 2002; Musselman et al., 2001). Conversely, some anti-inflammatory medication can have antidepressant effects. Patients with psoriasis who received etanercept, a TNF-α antagonist, exhibited reductions in depressive symptoms independent of improvement in disease activity. Such improvement in depressive symptoms was not observed among patients who received a placebo medication (Tyring et al., 2006).

Behavioral interventions targeting stress and depression may also impact inflammatory activity. A mindfulness-based stress reduction intervention with cancer patients led to reduction in proinflammatory cytokines as well as a complementary increase in anti-inflammatory cytokines (Carlson, Speca, Patel, & Goodey, 2003). Similarly, during a meditation intervention, individuals who engaged in meditation practices more frequently had a lower IL-6 response to a laboratory stressor, the TSST (Pace et al., 2009). Furthermore, a cognitive-behavioral intervention targeting stress and depression among cardiac patients led to a reduction in plasma proinflammatory cytokines (Doering, Cross, Vredevoe, Martinez-Maza, & Cowan, 2007).

Association Between Depression and Inflammation in Epidemiological and Clinical Studies

Syndromal depressive disorders as well as depressive symptoms have been associated with increased systemic inflammation. Several studies have noted an elevation of 40 to 50% in the serum concentrations of IL-6 and CRP among clinically depressed patients relative to control participants who had no psychiatric history (Ford & Erlinger, 2004; Irwin, 2002; Maes et al., 1997; Miller, Stetler, Carney, Freedland, & Banks, 2002; Pike & Irwin, 2006). In epidemiological studies, individuals presenting subsyndromal depressive symptoms also exhibited higher serum concentrations of CRP, IL-6, TNF-α and IL-1β compared to individuals reporting no or low levels of depressive symptoms (Dentino et al., 1999; Kop et al., 2002; Penninx et al., 2003; Suarez, Krishnan, & Lewis, 2003; Thomas et al., 2005). A meta-analysis confirmed the positive association between depressive symptoms, clinical depression and elevations in plasma IL-1β, IL-6, and CRP (Howren, Lamkin, & Suls, 2009).

Chronic Diseases, Inflammation, and Depression

Some authors argue that the high prevalence of depression seen in cardiovascular, cancer, diabetes, and rheumatoid arthritis patients may in part be due to the state of chronic inflammation found in these medical conditions (Raison, Capuron, & Miller, 2006). Infectious and inflammatory diseases have also been associated with behavioral alterations resembling depression such as malaise, lethargy, anorexia, hypersomnia, and anhedonia (Larson & Dunn, 2001). Indeed, high levels of proinflammatory cytokines have been associated with clinical depression among patients with diverse diseases (Bonaccorso et al., 2002).

Bidirectional Relationships Between Mood and Inflammation

Even transient mood disturbances may impact peripheral inflammatory activity. Academic examination-induced anxiety has been associated with greater production of serum TNF-α, IL-6, and IFN-γ among medical students (Maes et al., 1998). Similarly, increased anxiety in response to a laboratory stressor was associated with a higher level of IL-1β gene expression, suggesting that mood disturbance following exposure to a stressor contributes to changes in systemic inflammation (Brydon et al., 2005). Moreover, state depressive symptoms in the past week that represented a deviation from trait or typical depressive symptoms over the past 6 months were associated with elevated plasma IL-6 levels (Rohleder & Miller, 2007). Collectively, these data suggests a bidirectional relationship between mood and inflammation.

Other Negative Emotions and Inflammation

Other negative emotions have also been associated with increased inflammation. Individuals with post-traumatic stress disorder (PTSD) had greater LPS-stimulated IL-6 production, compared to individuals without such anxiety disorder (Rohleder, Loksimovic, Wolf, & Kirschbaum, 2004). Furthermore, elevated morning plasma IL-6 levels predicted the development of PTSD symptoms among children involved in motor vehicle accidents (Pervanidou et al., 2007). Anger and hostility have also been associated with increased inflammation (Graham et al., 2006; Marsland, Prather, Petersen, Cohen, & Manuck, 2008; Suarez, Boyle, Lewis, Hall, & Young, 2006). Depression and hostility appear to interact in predicting basal levels of inflammation. Individuals with high levels of both depression and hostility have higher levels of IL-6 and CRP, compared to individuals with high levels of hostility but lower levels of depressive symptoms (Stewart, Janicki-Deverts, Muldoon, & Kamarck, 2008). The self-conscious emotion of shame has been related to elevated biomarkers of inflammation. Participants assigned to write about a traumatic experience in which they blame themselves had increased TNF-α soluble receptor activity, compared to participants who wrote about neutral experiences (Dickerson, Kemeny, Aziz, Kim, & Fahey, 2004). Similarly, greater self-reported shame was also associated with elevated circulating markers of inflammation among young women (Rohleder, Chen, Wolf, & Miller, 2008). Figure 54.3 summarizes the relationship between depression and inflammation.

Cross-sensitization: Stress, Depression, and Inflammation

Stress and depression can also sensitize the immune system to the action of other stressors. Rats exposed to stressors such as inescapable tail shocks or social disruption exhibited amplified inflammatory and sickness behavior responses to the administration of a bacterial endotoxin, compared to rats that were not exposed to stressors (Gibb, Hayley, Gandhi, Poulter, & Anisman, 2008; Johnson et al., 2002). In humans, stress can also amplify inflammatory response to additional stressors. Healthy volunteers who both received a typhoid vaccination and were exposed to the psychological stressor exhibited greater increases in serum IL-6, compared to participants who were not randomized to both the active vaccine and the psychological stressor (Brydon et al., 2009).

Depression can also amplify inflammatory responses to psychological stressors. Men with a

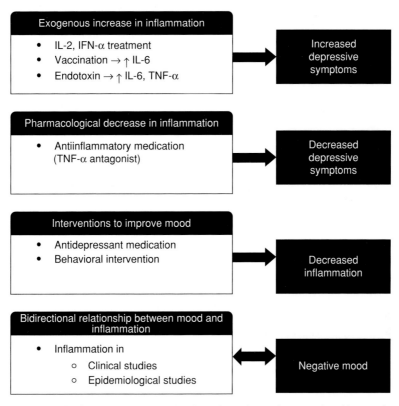

Fig. 54.3 Negative emotions and inflammation experimental and correlational research in animals and humans demonstrates bidirectional relationships between inflammation and mood.

diagnosis of major depression had significantly greater mononuclear cell NF-κB activation, a gene involved in the production of inflammatory proteins, and greater increases in plasma IL-6 following exposure to the TSST, compared to participants with no history of affective disorder (Pace et al., 2006). Depression may also exacerbate CRP response to psychological stress. Individuals without depression had a sharper increase in CRP following exposure to a laboratory stressor, but their CRP levels declined to baseline during the recovery. In contrast, depressed individuals had a smaller CRP increase following exposure to the stressor; however, CRP levels kept rising during the recovery to the levels that the controls reached immediately after the stressor (Miller, Rohleder, Stetler, & Kirschbaum, 2005). Furthermore, depressed individuals with a history of childhood maltreatment had greater basal CRP plasma levels, compared to depressed individuals who did not experience childhood adversities (Danese, Pariante, Caspi, Taylor, & Poulton, 2007).

In addition, depression may sensitize the immune response to other nonpsychological stressors. Older adults reporting depressive symptoms had an amplified IL-6 response up to two weeks after influenza immunization, compared to individuals reporting no depressive symptoms (Glaser, Robles, Sheridan, Malarkey, & Kiecolt-Glaser, 2003). This result is especially noteworthy because even relatively low levels of depressive symptoms can amplify the inflammatory response to the influenza vaccine (Glaser et al., 2003).

Social Relationships and Inflammation

There is a robust relationship between social relationships and immunity (Graham, Christian, & Kiecolt-Glaser, 2007). Social support and positive social relationships have been associated with lower circulating markers of inflammation among cancer patients and healthy volunteers (Costanzo et al., 2005; Friedman et al., 2005; Lutgendorf, Anderson, Sorosky, Buller, & Lubaroff, 2000; Lutgendorf et al., 2002). Conversely, low social support has been related to higher plasma CRP and greater LPS-stimulated IL-8 production (Coussons-Read, Okun, & Nettles, 2007; Marsland, Sathanoori, Muldoon, & Manuck, 2007). In an epidemiological study, social integration was inversely related to plasma CRP and IL-6 in men (Loucks et al., 2006). In a similar vein, socially isolated individuals presented a shift from anti- to proinflammatory gene expression (Cole et al., 2007). Furthermore, greater religious participation has also been related to lower levels of systemic inflammation (Koenig et al., 1997; Lutgendorf, Russell, Ullrich, Harris, & Wallace, 2004).

Negative social interactions have been associated with elevations in circulating markers of inflammation. Couples who exhibited more negative and hostile behaviors during the discussion of marital disagreement had greater increases in IL-6 and TNF-α, compared to less hostile couples (Kiecolt-Glaser et al., 2005). This effect was even more pronounced among individuals with higher levels of attachment avoidance (Gouin et al., in press). Moreover, healthy young women reporting chronic interpersonal difficulties exhibited a greater increase in messenger ribonucleic acid (mRNA) for the proinflammatory transcription factor NF-κB, and greater LPS-stimulated IL-6 production over the next 6 months (Miller, Rohleder, & Cole, 2009). Furthermore, in a 32-year prospective study, childhood maltreatment, a major interpersonal stressor, was associated with increased plasma CRP levels in adulthood (Danese et al., 2008).

Behavioral Pathways Linking Negative Emotions and Inflammation

Changes in health behaviors may partially mediate the relationship between stress, depression, and inflammation. Stress and depression often elicit the adoption of detrimental health behaviors, including smoking and alcohol use, reduction in physical activity, poor diet choices, and less sleep (Steptoe, Wardle, Pollard, Canaan, & Davies, 1996; Vitaliano, Scanlan, Zhang, Savage, & Hirsch, 2002). Several of these negative health behaviors have been associated with elevated biomarkers of systemic inflammation.

In population-based studies, smoking and greater alcohol intake were associated with greater plasma CRP levels (Hamer & Chida, 2009; Nazmi, Oliveira, & Victora, 2008). Acute exercise triggers transient increases in plasma IL-6 and TNF-α that are important for muscle repair, cell turnover, and regulation of lipids (Petersen & Pedersen, 2005). However, lack of regular physical activity is associated with

higher basal levels of circulating inflammatory markers (e.g., Elosua et al., 2005; Ford, 2002).

Diets high in saturated fat may fuel chronic low-grade inflammation. A high-fat meal, but not a high-carbohydrate meal, was associated with subsequent increases in plasma IL-6 (Nappo et al., 2002). In epidemiological studies, high levels of omega-3 (n-3) polyunsaturated fatty acids have been associated with lower circulating makers of inflammation (Ferrucci et al., 2006). Lower levels of n-3 appear to interact with stress and depression to promote increased inflammatory responses. Students with a higher n-6: n-3 ratio had greater inflammatory reactivity to academic examination stress, compared to students with lower n-6: n-3 ratio (Maes, Christophe, Bosmans, Lin, & Neels, 2000). Similarly, among older adults, depression interacted with the n-6: n-3 ratio to predict higher basal levels of circulating markers of inflammation (Kiecolt-Glaser et al., 2007).

Obesity, a condition associated with poor eating habits and low exercise levels, is also associated with increased plasma levels of inflammatory mediators (Vachharajani & Granger, 2009). Systemic inflammation was once thought to be primarily the result of production of IL-6 by immune cells, but recent data reveal that more than one-third of the circulating IL-6 may originate from adipocytes (Mohamed-Ali, Pinkney, & Coppack, 1998). Furthermore, abdominal fat can amplify cortisol and inflammatory responses to psychological stress (Brydon et al., 2008; Epel et al., 2000).

Finally, both objectively measured and self-reported sleep disturbances have been associated with increases in circulating markers of inflammation (Mills et al., 2007). In a large epidemiological study, greater self-reported sleep disturbances were associated with greater CRP plasma levels in men (Liukkonen et al., 2007). Among older women, objectively measured sleep efficiency was inversely related with plasma IL-6 levels (Friedman et al., 2005). Figure 54.4 summarizes the health behaviors that may be part of a behavioral mechanism linking stress and inflammation.

Physiological Pathways Linking Negative Emotions and Inflammation
Regulation of Monoamines

Cytokines and their receptors have been found in the hypothalamus, the hippocampus, the prefrontal cortex, and the brain stem (Miller, 1998). The action of cytokines may be mediated by their impact on the serotonergic and other monoamine systems.

Poor health behaviors and inflammation

- Smoking
- Alcohol intake
- Low physical activity
- Diet high in saturated fat
- Obesity
- Sleep disturbances

Fig. 54.4 Health behaviors associated with inflammation.

In rats, intraventricular injections of IFN-α reduced the level of 5-HT in the brain (Kamata, Higuchi, Yoshimoto, Yoshida, & Shimizu, 2000). Proinflammatory cytokines can decrease the availability of tryptophan (TRP) in the brain by activating the enzyme indoleamine-2,3 dioxygenase, which provokes a switch from the synthesis of TRP to the synthesis of kynurenine and quinolinic acid, thereby reducing the production of 5-HT (Schiepers, Wichers, & Maes, 2005). Decreased CSF levels of TRP have been positively correlated with the development of depressive symptoms among cancer patients treated with IFN-α (Capuron, Ravaud, et al., 2002). In addition, several proinflammatory cytokines (TNF-α, IL-1β, IFN-γ) reduced the activity of the 5-HT transporter, which may result in a decrease in extracellular levels of 5-HT (Bonaccorso et al., 2002). Cytokines may also influence the synthesis and reuptake of dopamine and norepinephrine (Kitagami et al., 2003; Moron et al., 2003). Furthermore, inflammation may reduce neural plasticity. Pharmacologically induced inflammation via LPS injection was associated with cognitive impairment, decreased hippocampal expression of brain-derived neurotrophic factor (BDNF) and its receptor, tyrosine kinase-B, as well as reduced hippocampal neurogenesis in rats (Wu et al., 2007).

Glucocorticoid Resistance

Cortisol plays an important role in regulating inflammatory responses. However, chronic low-grade levels of inflammation may excessively prolong the activation of the HPA axis. Several proinflammatory cytokines can stimulate the production of corticotropin-releasing hormone (Besedovsky et al., 1991). Usually, cortisol, the end product of HPA-axis activation, has anti-inflammatory properties. However, in the case of chronic exposure to cortisol, a downregulation of glucocorticoid receptors is observed (Miller, Pariante, & Pearce, 1999). This leads to glucocorticoid resistance, whereby immune cells are less responsive to the anti-inflammatory properties of glucocorticoids. This process can then promote chronic elevations in circulating markers of inflammation. In fact, the chronic stress of caregiving for a child with cancer has been associated with diminished inhibition of LPS-stimulated IL-6 production following administration of a synthetic glucocorticoid (Miller, Cohen, & Ritchey, 2002).

Molecular Mechanism Linking Stress and Inflammation

A direct molecular mechanism linking stress and inflammation has been detailed by Bierhaus and collaborators (Bierhaus et al., 2003). Exposure to the TSST led to an increase in the nuclear factor NF-κB from peripheral blood monocyte cells within 10 minutes among healthy volunteers. NF-κB is a transcription factor that influences the expression of the genes of several inflammatory mediators (Barnes & Karin, 1997). In humans, activation of NF-κB was correlated with stress-induced catecholamine and cortisol secretion. Animal studies specified that binding of norepinephrine, but not epinephrine, led to a downstream signaling cascade that resulted in the activation and translocation of NF-κB in the nucleus of the cells (Bierhaus et al., 2003). Therefore, stress-induced increases in norepinephrine might lead to the activation of NF-κB and, subsequently, to increased gene expression of inflammatory proteins. Individuals caring for a relative with a brain tumor exhibited higher plasma levels of CRP, greater expression of the NF-κB-related genes, as well as decreased expression of glucocorticoid receptor-related genes, suggesting that chronic stress also activates the NF-κB pathway (Miller et al., 2008). Figure 54.5 depicts different physiological pathways linking stress and inflammation.

Conclusion

Inflammation is a vital process involved in infection clearance and wound healing. However, converging evidence suggests that stress and negative emotions can promote a state of chronic low-grade inflammation, which has been associated with detrimental health outcomes. Although some studies suggest that increased inflammation may reflect simply the presence of risk factors or represent a marker of disease activity, other evidence suggests that inflammation may have a causal pathophysiological role. For social neuroscientists, inflammation may thus become a key physiological mediator of the impact of stress and negative emotions on health.

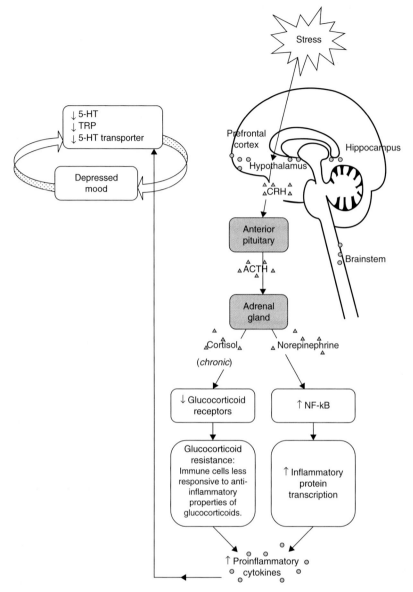

Fig. 54.5 Physiological pathways. A physiological pathway linking stress, negative emotions, and proinflammatory cytokines production. Stress lead to the production of CRH by the hypothalamamus, which in turn lead to production and ACTH by the pituitary gland. The adrenal cortex releases cortisol. Cortisol usual suppresses inflammatory activity. However, chronic cortisol production leads to glucocorticoid resistance, a state in which immune cells are less responsive to anti-inflammatory property of glucocorticoids. Upon stimulation by ACTH, the adrenal medulla releases norepinephrine. A noradrenergic-dependent mechanism activates NF-kB and leads to the transcription of a host of inflammatory proteins. Proinflammatory cytokines in circulation can cross the blood-brain barrier and bind to receptors in the brain. Cytokines impact serotonergic (5-HT) activity, which may in turn affect mood and behavior.

Acknowledgments

Work on this chapter was supported by a Doctoral Research Training Award from the Fonds de la Recherche en Santé du Québec (J-P.G.), and grants AT002971, AG025732, AG029562, CA126857, M01-RR-0034 and CA16058 from the National Institutes of Health.

References

Aggarwal, B. B., Shishodia, S., Sandur, S. K., Pandey, M. K., & Sethi, G. (2006). Inflammation and cancer: How hot is the link? *Biochem Pharmacol*, *72*(11), 1605–1621.

Amar, J., Fauvel, J., Drouet, L., Ruidavets, J. B., Perret, B., Chamontin, B., et al. (2006). Interleukin 6 is associated with subclinical atherosclerosis: A link with soluble intercellular adhesion molecule 1. *Journal of Hypertension*, *24*(6), 1083–1088.

Balkwill, F., Charles, K. A., & Mantovani, A. (2005). Smoldering and polarized inflammation in the initiation and promotion of malignant disease. *Cancer Cell*, 7(3), 211–217.

Barnes, P. J. & Karin, M. (1997). Nuclear factor-kappaB: A pivotal transcription factor in chronic inflammatory diseases. *N Engl J Med*, 336(15), 1066–1071.

Besedovsky, H. O., del Rey, A., Klusman, I., Furukawa, H., Monge Arditi, G., & Kabiersch, A. (1991). Cytokines as modulators of the hypothalamus-pituitary-adrenal axis. *J Steroid Biochem Mol Biol*, 40(4–6), 613–618.

Bierhaus, A., Wolf, J., Andrassy, M., Rohleder, N., Humpert, P. M., Petrov, D., et al. (2003). A mechanism converting psychosocial stress into mononuclear cell activation. *Proceedings of the National Academy of Sciences of the United States of America*, 100(4), 1920–1925.

Black, P. H. (2006). The inflammatory consequences of psychologic stress: Relationship to insulin resistance, obesity, atherosclerosis and diabetes mellitus, type II. *Med Hypotheses*, 67(4), 879–891.

Bonaccorso, S., Marino, V., Puzella, A., Pasquini, M., Biondi, M., Artini, M., et al. (2002). Increased depressive ratings in patients with hepatitis C receiving interferon-alpha-based immunotherapy are related to interferon-alpha-induced changes in the serotonergic system. *J Clin Psychopharmacol*, 22(1), 86–90.

Brydon, L., Edwards, S., Jia, H. Y., Mohamed-Ali, V., Zachary, I., Martin, J. F., et al. (2005). Psychological stress activates interleukin-1 beta gene expression in human mononuclear cells. *Brain, Behavior, and Immunity*, 19(6), 540–546.

Brydon, L., Edwards, S., Mohamed-Ali, V., & Steptoe, A. (2004). Socioeconomic status and stress-induced increases in interleukin-6. *Brain Behavior and Immunity*, 18(3), 281–290.

Brydon, L. & Steptoe, A. (2005). Stress-induced increases in interleukin-6 and fibrinogen predict ambulatory blood pressure at 3-year follow-up. *J Hypertens*, 23(5), 1001–1007.

Brydon, L., Walker, C., Wawrzyniak, A., Whitehead, D., Okamura, H., Yajima, J., et al. (2009). Synergistic effects of psychological and immune stressors on inflammatory cytokine and sickness responses in humans. *Brain Behav Immun*, 23(2), 217–224.

Brydon, L., Wright, C. E., O'Donnell, K., Zachary, I., Wardle, J., & Steptoe, A. (2008). Stress-induced cytokine responses and central adiposity in young women. *Int J Obes (Lond)*, 32(3), 443–450.

Capuron, L., Gumnick, J. F., Musselman, D. L., Lawson, D. H., Reemsnyder, A., Nemeroff, C. B., et al. (2002). Neurobehavioral effects of interferon-alpha in cancer patients: Phenomenology and paroxetine responsiveness of symptom dimensions. *Neuropsychopharmacology*, 26(5), 643–652.

Capuron, L. & Miller, A. H. (2004). Cytokines and psychopathology: Lessons from interferon-alpha. *Biol Psychiatry*, 56(11), 819–824.

Capuron, L., Ravaud, A., Neveu, P. J., Miller, A. H., Maes, M., & Dantzer, R. (2002). Association between decreased serum tryptophan concentrations and depressive symptoms in cancer patients undergoing cytokine therapy. *Mol Psychiatry*, 7(5), 468–473.

Carlson, L. E., Speca, M., Patel, K. D., & Goodey, E. (2003). Mindfulness-based stress reduction in relation to quality of life, mood, symptoms of stress, and immune parameters in breast and prostate cancer outpatients. *Psychosomatic Medicine*, 65(4), 571–581.

Cesari, M., Penninx, B. W. J. H., Pahor, M., Lauretani, F., Corsi, A. M., Rhys Williams, G., et al. (2004). Inflammatory markers and physical performance in older persons: The InCHIANTI study. *Journals of Gerontology. Series A, Biological Sciences and Medical Sciences*, 59(3), 242–248.

Cole, S. W., Hawkley, L. C., Arevalo, J. M., Sung, C. Y., Rose, R. M., & Cacioppo, J. T. (2007). Social regulation of gene expression in human leukocytes. *Genome Biol*, 8(9), R189.

Collado-Hidalgo, A., Bower, J. E., Ganz, P. A., Cole, S. W., & Irwin, M. R. (2006). Inflammatory biomarkers for persistent fatigue in breast cancer survivors. *Clinical Cancer Research*, 12, 2759–2766.

Costanzo, E. S., Lutgendorf, S. K., Sood, A. K., Anderson, B., Sorosky, J., & Lubaroff, D. M. (2005). Psychosocial factors and interleukin-6 among women with advanced ovarian cancer. *Cancer*, 104(2), 305–313.

Coussons-Read, M. E., Okun, M. L., & Nettles, C. D. (2007). Psychosocial stress increases inflammatory markers and alters cytokine production across pregnancy. *Brain Behav Immun*, 21(3), 343–350.

Danese, A., Moffitt, T. E., Pariante, C. M., Ambler, A., Poulton, R., & Caspi, A. (2008). Elevated inflammation levels in depressed adults with a history of childhood maltreatment. *Arch Gen Psychiatry*, 65(4), 409–415.

Danese, A., Pariante, C. M., Caspi, A., Taylor, A., & Poulton, R. (2007). Childhood maltreatment predicts adult inflammation in a life-course study. *Proc Natl Acad Sci U S A*, 104(4), 1319–1324.

Dantzer, R., O'Connor, J. C., Freund, G. G., Johnson, R. W., & Kelley, K. W. (2008). From inflammation to sickness and depression: When the immune system subjugates the brain. *Nat Rev Neurosci*, 9(1), 46–56.

Davis, M. C., Zautra, A. J., Younger, J., Motivala, S. J., Attrep, J., & Irwin, M. R. (2008). Chronic stress and regulation of cellular markers of inflammation in rheumatoid arthritis: Implications for fatigue. *Brain Behav Immun*, 22(1), 24–32.

Dentino, A. N., Pieper, C. F., Rao, M. K., Currie, M. S., Harris, T., Blazer, D. G., et al. (1999). Association of interleukin-6 and other biologic variables with depression in older people living in the community. *Journal of the American Geriatrics Society*, 47, 6–11.

Dickerson, S. S., Kemeny, M. E., Aziz, N., Kim, K. H., & Fahey, J. L. (2004). Immunological effects of induced shame and guilt. *Psychosom Med*, 66(1), 124–131.

Dieperink, E., Ho, S. B., Thuras, P., & Willenbring, M. L. (2003). A prospective study of neuropsychiatric symptoms associated with interferon-alpha-2b and ribavirin therapy for patients with chronic hepatitis C. *Psychosomatics*, 44(2), 104–112.

Doering, L. V., Cross, R., Vredevoe, D., Martinez-Maza, O., & Cowan, M. J. (2007). Infection, depression, and immunity in women after coronary artery bypass: A pilot study of cognitive behavioral therapy. *Altern Ther Health Med*, 13(3), 18–21.

Ellins, E., Halcox, J., Donald, A., Field, B., Brydon, L., Deanfield, J., et al. (2008). Arterial stiffness and inflammatory response to psychophysiological stress. *Brain Behav Immun*.

Elosua, R., Bartali, B., Ordovas, J. M., Corsi, A. M., Lauretani, F., & Ferrucci, L. (2005). Association between physical activity, physical performance, and inflammatory biomarkers in an elderly population: The InCHIANTI study. *J Gerontol A Biol Sci Med Sci*, 60(6), 760–767.

Epel, E. S., McEwen, B. S., Seeman, T., Matthews, K. A., Castellazzo, G., Brownell, K. D., et al. (2000). Stress and body shape: Stress-induced cortisol is consistently greater among women with central fat. *Psychosomatic Medicine*, 62, 623–632.

Ershler, W. & Keller, E. (2000). Age-associated increased interleukin-6 gene expression, late-life diseases, and frailty. *Annual Review of Medicine*, 51, 245–270.

Ferrucci, L., Cherubini, A., Bandinelli, S., Bartali, B., Corsi, A., Lauretani, F., et al. (2006). Relationship of plasma polyunsaturated fatty acids to circulating inflammatory markers. *Journal of Clinical Endocrinology and Metabolism*, 91, 439–446.

Ferrucci, L., Harris, T., Guralnik, J., Tracy, R., Corti, M., Cohen, H., et al. (1999). Serum IL-6 level and the development of disability in older persons. *Journal of the American Geriatrics Society*, 47, 639–646.

Ford, D. E. & Erlinger, T. P. (2004). Depression and C-reactive protein in U.S. adults. *Archives of Internal Medicine*, 164, 1010–1014.

Ford, E. S. (2002). Does exercise reduce inflammation? Physical activity and c-reactive protein among U.S. adults. *Epidemiology*, 13, 561–568.

Friedman, E. M., Hayney, M. S., Love, G. D., Urry, H. L., Rosenkranz, M. A., Davidson, R. J., et al. (2005). Social relationships, sleep quality, and interleukin-6 in aging women. *Proc Natl Acad Sci U S A*, 102(51), 18757–18762.

Gabay, C. & Kushner, I. (1999). Acute-phase proteins and other systemic responses to inflammation. *N Engl J Med*, 340(6), 448–454.

Gibb, J., Hayley, S., Gandhi, R., Poulter, M. O., & Anisman, H. (2008). Synergistic and additive actions of a psychosocial stressor and endotoxin challenge: Circulating and brain cytokines, plasma corticosterone and behavioral changes in mice. *Brain Behav Immun.* 22(4), 573–589.

Giuliani, N., Sansoni, P., Girasole, G., Vescovini, R., Passeri, G., Passeri, M., et al. (2001). Serum interleukin-6, soluble interleukin-6 receptor and soluble gp130 exhibit different patterns of age- and menopause-related changes. *Exp Gerontol*, 36(3), 547–557.

Glaser, R., Robles, T., Sheridan, J., Malarkey, W. B., & Kiecolt-Glaser, J. K. (2003). Mild depressive symptoms are associated with amplified and prolonged inflammatory responses following influenza vaccination in older adults. *Archives of General Psychiatry*, 60, 1009–1014.

Gouin, J., Hantsoo, L. V., & Kiecolt-Glaser, J. K. (2008). Immune dysregulation and chronic stress among older adults: A review. *Neuroimmunododulation*, 15, 254–262.

Gouin, J. P., Glaser, R., Loving, T. J., Malarkey, W. B., Stowell, J., Houts, C., et al. (in press). Attachment avoidance predicts inflammatory responses to marital conflict. *Brain, Behavior, and Immunity*.

Graham, J. E., Christian, L. M., & Kiecolt-Glaser, J. K. (2007). Close relationships and immunity. In R. Ader (Ed.), *Psychoneuroimmunology* (Vol. 2, pp. 781–798). Burlington, MA: Elsevier Academic Press.

Graham, J. E., Robles, T. F., Kiecolt-Glaser, J. K., Malarkey, W. B., Bissell, M. G., & Glaser, R. (2006). Hostility and pain are related to inflammation in older adults. *Brain Behav Immun*, 20(4), 389–400.

Hamer, M. & Chida, Y. (2009). Associations of very high C-reactive protein concentration with psychosocial and cardiovascular risk factors in an ageing population. *Atherosclerosis*.

Harris, T., Ferrucci, L., Tracy, R., Corti, M., Wacholder, S., Ettinger, W. J., et al. (1999). Associations of elevated interleukin-6 and C-reactive protein levels with mortality in the elderly. *American Journal of Medicine*, 106, 506–512.

Hauser, P., Khosla, J., Aurora, H., Laurin, J., Kling, M. A., Hill, J., et al. (2002). A prospective study of the incidence and open-label treatment of interferon-induced major depressive disorder in patients with hepatitis C. *Molecular Psychiatry*, 7(9), 942–947.

Heesen, C., Schulz, H., Schmidt, M., Gold, S., Tessmer, W., & Schulz, K. H. (2002). Endocrine and cytokine responses to acute psychological stress in multiple sclerosis. *Brain, Behavior, and Immunity*, 16, 282–287.

Heinz, A., Hermann, D., Smolka, M. N., Rieks, M., Graf, K. J., Pohlau, D., et al. (2003). Effects of acute psychological stress on adhesion molecules, interleukins and sex hormones: Implications for coronary heart disease. *Psychopharmacology (Berl)*, 165(2), 111–117.

Howren, M. B., Lamkin, D. M., & Suls, J. (2009). Associations of depression with C-reactive protein, IL-1, and IL-6: A meta-analysis. *Psychosom Med*, 71(2), 171–186.

Irwin, M. (2002). Psychoneuroimmunology of depression: Clinical implications. *Brain, Behavior, and Immunity*, 16, 1–16.

Jain, S., Mills, P. J., von Kanel, R., Hong, S., & Dimsdale, J. E. (2007). Effects of perceived stress and uplifts on inflammation and coagulability. *Psychophysiology*, 44(1), 154–160.

Johnson, J. D., O'Connor, K. A., Deak, T., Stark, M., Watkins, L. R., & Maier, S. F. (2002). Prior stressor exposure sensitizes LPS-induced cytokine production. *Brain, Behavior, and Immunity*, 16, 461–476.

Kamata, M., Higuchi, H., Yoshimoto, M., Yoshida, K., & Shimizu, T. (2000). Effect of single intracerebroventricular injection of alpha-interferon on monoamine concentrations in the rat brain. *Eur Neuropsychopharmacol*, 10(2), 129–132.

Kiecolt-Glaser, J. K., Belury, M. A., Porter, K., Beversdorf, D. Q., Lemeshow, S., & Glaser, R. (2007). Depressive symptoms, omega-6: Omega-3 fatty acids, and inflammation in older adults. *Psychosom Med*, 69(3), 217–224.

Kiecolt-Glaser, J. K., Loving, T. J., Stowell, J. R., Malarkey, W. B., Lemeshow, S., Dickinson, S. L., et al. (2005). Hostile marital interactions, proinflammatory cytokine production, and wound healing. *Archives of General Psychiatry*, 62, 1377–1384.

Kiecolt-Glaser, J. K., Preacher, K. J., MacCallum, R. C., Atkinson, C., Malarkey, W. B., & Glaser, R. (2003). Chronic stress and age-related increases in the proinflammatory cytokine IL-6. *Proceedings of the National Academy of Sciences of the United States of America*, 100, 9090–9095.

Kitagami, T., Yamada, K., Miura, H., Hashimoto, R., Nabeshima, T., & Ohta, T. (2003). Mechanism of systemically injected interferon-alpha impeding monoamine biosynthesis in rats: Role of nitric oxide as a signal crossing the blood-brain barrier. *Brain Res*, 978(1–2), 104–114.

Koenig, H. G., Cohen, H. J., George, L. K., Hays, J. C., Larson, D. B., & Blazer, D. G. (1997). Attendance at religious services, interleukin-6, and other biological parameters of immune function in older adults. *International Journal of Psychiatry in Medicine*, 27, 233–250.

Kop, W. J., Gottdiener, J. S., Tangen, C. M., Fried, L. P., McBurnie, M. A., Walston, J., et al. (2002). Inflammation and coagulation factors in persons >65 years of age with symptoms of depression but without evidence of myocardial ischemia. *American Journal of Cardiology, 89*, 419–424.

Koster, A., Bosma, H., Penninx, B. W., Newman, A. B., Harris, T. B., van Eijk, J. T., et al. (2006). Association of inflammatory markers with socioeconomic status. *J Gerontol A Biol Sci Med Sci, 61*(3), 284–290.

Lanquillon, S., Krieg, J. C., Bening-Abu-Shach, U., & Vedder, H. (2000). Cytokine production and treatment response in major depressive disorder. *Neuropsychopharmacology, 22*(4), 370–379.

Larson, S. J. & Dunn, A. J. (2001). Behavioral effects of cytokines. *Brain Behav Immun, 15*(4), 371–387.

LeMay, L. G., Vander, A. J., & Kluger, M. J. (1990). The effects of psychological stress on plasma interleukin-6 activity in rats. *Physiol Behav, 47*(5), 957–961.

Leonard, B. E. (2001). The immune system, depression and the action of antidepressants. *Prog Neuropsychopharmacol Biol Psychiatry, 25*(4), 767–780.

Lindmark, E., Diderholm, E., Wallentin, L., & Siegbahn, A. (2001). Relationship between interleukin 6 and mortality in patients with unstable coronary artery disease: Effects of an early invasive or noninvasive strategy. *JAMA-Journal of the American Medical Association, 286*(17), 2107–2113.

Liukkonen, T., Rasanen, P., Ruokonen, A., Laitinen, J., Jokelainen, J., Leinonen, M., et al. (2007). C-reactive protein levels and sleep disturbances: Observations based on the Northern Finland 1966 Birth Cohort study. *Psychosom Med, 69*(8), 756–761.

Loucks, E. B., Sullivan, L. M., D'Agostino, R. B., Sr., Larson, M. G., Berkman, L. F., & Benjamin, E. J. (2006). Social networks and inflammatory markers in the Framingham Heart Study. *J Biosoc Sci, 38*(6), 835–842.

Lutgendorf, S., Russell, D., Ullrich, P., Harris, T. B., & Wallace, R. (2004). Religious participation, Interleukin-6, and mortality in older adults. *Health Psychology, 23*(5), 465–475.

Lutgendorf, S. K., Anderson, B., Sorosky, J. I., Buller, R. E., & Lubaroff, D. M. (2000). Interleukin-6 and use of social support in gynecologic cancer patients. *International Journal of Behavioral Medicine, 7*, 127–142.

Lutgendorf, S. K., Garand, L., Buckwalter, K. C., Reimer, T. T., Hong, S., & Lubaroff, D. M. (1999). Life stress, mood disturbance, and elevated interleukin-6 in healthy older women. *Journals of Gerontology: Series A, Biological Sciences and Medical Sciences, 54*, M434–439.

Lutgendorf, S. K., Johnsen, E. L., Cooper, B., Anderson, B., Sorosky, J. I., Buller, R. E., et al. (2002). Vascular endothelial growth factor and social support in patients with ovarian carcinoma. *Cancer, 95*(4), 808–815.

Lutgendorf, S. K., Logan, H., Costanzo, E., & Lubaroff, D. (2004). Effects of acute stress, relaxation, and a neurogenic inflammatory stimulus on interleukin-6 in humans. *Brain, Behavior, and Immunity, 18*, 55–64.

Madhok, R., Crilly, A., Watson, J., & Capell, H. A. (1993). Serum interleukin 6 levels in rheumatoid arthritis: correlations with clinical and laboratory indices of disease activity. *Ann Rheum Dis, 52*(3), 232–234.

Maes, M., Bosmans, E., De Jongh, R., Kenis, G., Vandoolaeghe, E., & Neels, H. (1997). Increased serum IL-6 and IL-1 receptor antagonist concentrations in major depression and treatment resistant depression. *Cytokine, 9*, 853–858.

Maes, M., Christophe, A., Bosmans, E., Lin, A. H., & Neels, H. (2000). In humans, serum polyunsaturated fatty acid levels predict the response of proinflammatory cytokines to psychologic stress. *Biological Psychiatry, 47*, 910–920.

Maes, M., Song, C., Lin, A., De Jongh, R., Van Gastel, A., Kenis, G., et al. (1998). The effects of psychological stress on humans: Increased production of pro-inflammatory cytokines and a Th1-like response in stress-induced anxiety. *Cytokine, 10*, 313–318.

Maggio, M., Guralnik, J. M., Longo, D. L., & Ferrucci, L. (2006). Interleukin-6 in aging and chronic disease: a magnificent pathway. *J Gerontol A Biol Sci Med Sci, 61*(6), 575–584.

Marsland, A. L., Gianaros, P. J., Abramowitch, S. M., Manuck, S. B., & Hariri, A. R. (2008). Interleukin-6 covaries inversely with hippocampal grey matter volume in middle-aged adults. *Biol Psychiatry, 64*(6), 484–490.

Marsland, A. L., Prather, A. A., Petersen, K. L., Cohen, S., & Manuck, S. B. (2008). Antagonistic characteristics are positively associated with inflammatory markers independently of trait negative emotionality. *Brain Behav Immun, 22*(5), 753–761.

Marsland, A. L., Sathanoori, R., Muldoon, M. F., & Manuck, S. B. (2007). Stimulated production of interleukin-8 covaries with psychosocial risk factors for inflammatory disease among middle-aged community volunteers. *Brain Behav Immun, 21*(2), 218–228.

McDade, T. W., Hawkley, L. C., & Cacioppo, J. T. (2006). Psychosocial and behavioral predictors of inflammation in middle-aged and older adults: The Chicago health, aging, and social relations study. *Psychosom Med, 68*(3), 376–381.

Miller, A. H. (1998). Neuroendocrine and immune system interactions in stress and depression. *Psychiatric Clinics of North America, 21*, 443–463.

Miller, A. H., Pariante, C. M., & Pearce, B. D. (1999). Effects of cytokines on glucocorticoid receptor expression and function. Glucocorticoid resistance and relevance to depression. *Adv Exp Med Biol, 461*, 107–116.

Miller, G. E., Chen, E., Sze, J., Marin, T., Arevalo, J. M., Doll, R., et al. (2008). A functional genomic fingerprint of chronic stress in humans: Blunted glucocorticoid and increased NF-kappaB signaling. *Biol Psychiatry, 64*(4), 266–272.

Miller, G. E., Cohen, S., & Ritchey, A. K. (2002). Chronic psychological stress and the regulation of pro-inflammatory cytokines: A glucocorticoid-resistance model. *Health Psychol, 21*(6), 531–541.

Miller, G. E., Rohleder, N., & Cole, S. W. (2009). Chronic interpersonal stress predicts activation of pro- and anti-inflammatory signaling pathways 6 months later. *Psychosom Med, 71*(1), 57–62.

Miller, G. E., Rohleder, N., Stetler, C., & Kirschbaum, C. (2005). Clinical depression and regulation of the inflammatory response during acute stress. *Psychosomatic Medicine, 67*, 679–687.

Miller, G. E., Stetler, C. A., Carney, R. M., Freedland, K. E., & Banks, W. A. (2002). Clinical depression and inflammatory risk markers for coronary heart disease. *American Journal of Cardiology, 90*(12), 1279–1283.

Mills, P. J., von Kanel, R., Norman, D., Natarajan, L., Ziegler, M. G., & Dimsdale, J. E. (2007). Inflammation and sleep in healthy individuals. *Sleep, 30*(6), 729–735.

Mohamed-Ali, V., Pinkney, J. H., & Coppack, S. W. (1998). Adipose tissue as an endocrine and paracrine organ. *Int J Obes Relat Metab Disord, 22*(12), 1145–1158.

Moron, J. A., Zakharova, I., Ferrer, J. V., Merrill, G. A., Hope, B., Lafer, E. M., et al. (2003). Mitogen-activated protein kinase regulates dopamine transporter surface expression and dopamine transport capacity. *J Neurosci, 23*(24), 8480–8488.

Musselman, D. L., Lawson, D. H., Gumnick, J. F., Manatunga, A. K., Penna, S., Goodkin, R. S., et al. (2001). Paroxetine for the prevention of depression induced by high-dose interferon alfa. *The New England Journal of Medicine, 344*(13), 961–966.

Nappo, F., Esposito, K., Cioffi, M., Giugliano, G., Molinari, A. M., Paolisso, G., et al. (2002). Postprandial endothelial activation in healthy subjects and in type 2 diabetic patients: Role of fat and carbohydrate meals. *J Am Coll Cardiol, 39*(7), 1145–1150.

Nazmi, A., Oliveira, I. O., & Victora, C. G. (2008). Correlates of C-reactive protein levels in young adults: A population-based cohort study of 3827 subjects in Brazil. *Braz J Med Biol Res, 41*(5), 357–367.

Pace, T. W., Negi, L. T., Adame, D. D., Cole, S. P., Sivilli, T. I., Brown, T. D., et al. (2009). Effect of compassion meditation on neuroendocrine, innate immune and behavioral responses to psychosocial stress. *Psychoneuroendocrinology, 34*(1), 87–98.

Pace, T. W. W., Mletzko, T. C., Alagbe, O., Musselman, D. L., Nemeroff, C. B., Miller, A. H., et al. (2006). Increased stress-induced inflammatory responses in male patients with major depression and increased early life stress. *American Journal of Psychiatry, 163*(9), 1630–1632.

Parham, P. (2004). *The immune system* (2nd ed.). London: Garland Science.

Penninx, B. W. J. H., Kritchevsky, S. B., Yaffe, K., Newman, A. B., Simonsick, E. M., Rubin, S., et al. (2003). Inflammatory markers and depressed mood in older persons: Results from the health, aging, and body composition study. *Biological Psychiatry, 54*, 566–572.

Pervanidou, P., Kolaitis, G., Charitaki, S., Margeli, A., Ferentinos, S., Bakoula, C., et al. (2007). Elevated morning serum interleukin (IL)-6 or evening salivary cortisol concentrations predict posttraumatic stress disorder in children and adolescents six months after a motor vehicle accident. *Psychoneuroendocrinology, 32*(8–10), 991–999.

Petersen, A. M. & Pedersen, B. K. (2005). The anti-inflammatory effect of exercise. *J Appl Physiol, 98*(4), 1154–1162.

Pike, J. L. & Irwin, M. R. (2006). Dissociation of inflammatory markers and natural killer cell activity in major depressive disorder. *Brain Behav Immun, 20*(2), 169–174.

Pradhan, A., Manson, J., Rifai, N., Buring, J., & Ridker, P. (2001). C-reactive protein, interleukin 6, and risk of developing type 2 diabetes mellitus. *JAMA, 286*, 327–334.

Raison, C. L., Capuron, L., & Miller, A. H. (2006). Cytokines sing the blues: Inflammation and the pathogenesis of depression. *Trends in Immunology, 27*, 24–31.

Reichenberg, A., Yirmiya, R., Schuld, A., Kraus, T., Haack, M., Morag, A., et al. (2001). Cytokine-associated emotional and cognitive disturbances in humans. *Archives of General Psychiatry, 58*, 445–452.

Ridker, P., Rifai, N., Stampfer, M., & Hennekens, C. (2000). Plasma concentration of interleukin-6 and the risk of future myocardial infarction among apparently healthy men. *Circulation, 101*, 1767–1772.

Ridker, P. M., Hennekens, C. H., Buring, J. E., & Rifai, N. (2000). C-Reactive protein and other markers of inflammation in the prediction of cardiovascular disease in women. *The New England Journal of Medicine, 342*(12), 836–843.

Rohleder, N., Chen, E., Wolf, J. M., & Miller, G. E. (2008). The psychobiology of trait shame in young women: Extending the social self preservation theory. *Health Psychol, 27*(5), 523–532.

Rohleder, N., Loksimovic, L., Wolf, J. M., & Kirschbaum, C. (2004). Hypocortisolism and increased glucocorticoid sensitivity of pro-inflammatory cytokine production in Bosnian War refugees with posttraumatic stress disorder. *Biological Psychiatry, 55*, 745–751.

Rohleder, N. & Miller, G. E. (2007). Acute deviations from long-term trait depressive symptoms predict systemic inflammatory activity. *Brain Behav Immun, 22*(5), 709–716.

Salgado, R., Junius, S., Benoy, I., Van Dam, P., Vermeulen, P., Van Marck, E., et al. (2003). Circulating interleukin-6 predicts survival in patients with metastatic breast cancer. *Int J Cancer, 103*(5), 642–646.

Schiepers, O. J., Wichers, M. C., & Maes, M. (2005). Cytokines and major depression. *Prog Neuropsychopharmacol Biol Psychiatry, 29*(2), 201–217.

Sesso, H. D., Buring, J. E., Rifai, N., Blake, G. J., Gaziano, J. M., & Ridker, P. M. (2003). C-reactive protein and the risk of developing hypertension. *JAMA-Journal of the American Medical Association, 290*(22), 2945–2951.

Shah, R., Burg, M. M., Vashist, A., Collins, D., Liu, J., Jadbabaie, F., et al. (2006). C-reactive protein and vulnerability to mental stress-induced myocardial ischemia. *Mol Med, 12*(11–12), 269–274.

Sluzewska, A., Rybakowski, J. K., Laciak, M., Mackiewicz, A., Sobieska, M., & Wiktorowicz, K. (1995). Interleukin-6 serum levels in depressed patients before and after treatment with fluoxetine. *Annals of the New York Academy of Sciences, 762*, 474–476.

Steptoe, A., Hamer, M., & Chida, Y. (2007). The effects of acute psychological stress on circulating inflammatory factors in humans: a review and meta-analysis. *Brain Behav Immun, 21*(7), 901–912.

Steptoe, A., Wardle, J., Pollard, T. M., Canaan, L., & Davies, G. J. (1996). Stress, social support and health-related behavior: A study of smoking, alcohol consumption and physical exercise. *Journal of Psychosomatic Research, 41*, 171–180.

Stewart, J. C., Janicki-Deverts, D., Muldoon, M. F., & Kamarck, T. W. (2008). Depressive symptoms moderate the influence of hostility on serum interleukin-6 and C-reactive protein. *Psychosom Med, 70*(2), 197–204.

Suarez, E. C., Boyle, S. H., Lewis, J. G., Hall, R. P., & Young, K. H. (2006). Increases in stimulated secretion of proinflammatory cytokines by blood monocytes following arousal of negative affect: the role of insulin resistance as moderator. *Brain Behav Immun, 20*(4), 331–338.

Suarez, E. C., Krishnan, R. R., & Lewis, J. G. (2003). The relation of severity of depressive symptoms to monocyte-associated proinflammatory cytokines and chemokines in apparently healthy men. *Psychosomatic Medicine, 65*, 362–368.

Thomas, A. J., Davis, S., Morris, C., Jackson, E., Harrison, R., & O'Brien, J. T. (2005). Increase in interleukin-1beta in late-life depression. *American Journal of Psychiatry, 162*, 175–177.

Tilg, H., Dinarello, C. A., & Mier, J. W. (1997). IL-6 and APPs: Anti-inflammatory and immunosuppressive mediators. *Immunol Today, 18*(9), 428–432.

Tyring, S., Gottlieb, A., Papp, K., Gordon, K., Leonardi, C., Wang, A., et al. (2006). Etanercept and clinical outcomes, fatigue, and depression in psoriasis: Double-blind placebo-controlled randomised phase III trial. *Lancet, 367*(9504), 29–35.

Vachharajani, V. & Granger, D. N. (2009). Adipose tissue: A motor for the inflammation associated with obesity. *IUBMB Life, 61*(4), 424–430.

Vitaliano, P. P., Scanlan, J. M., Zhang, J., Savage, M. V., & Hirsch, I. B. (2002). A path model of chronic stress, the metabolic syndrome, and coronary heart disease. *Psychosomatic Medicine, 64*, 418–435.

von Kanel, R., Dimsdale, J. E., Mills, P. J., Ancoli-Israel, S., Patterson, T., Mausbach, B. T., et al. (2006). Effect of Alzheimer caregiving stress and age on frailty markers interleukin-6, c-reactive protein, and d-dimer. *Journal of Gerontology, 61A*(9), 963–969.

von Kanel, R., Kudielka, B. M., Preckel, D., Hanebuth, D., & Fischer, J. E. (2005). Delayed response and lack of habituation in plasma interleukin-6 to acute mental stress in men. *Brain, Behavior, and Immunity, 20*, 40–48.

Weik, U., Herforth, A., Kolb-Bachofen, V., & Deinzer, R. (2008). Acute stress induces proinflammatory signaling at chronic inflammation sites. *Psychosom Med, 70*(8), 906–912.

Wright, C., Strike, P. C., Brydon, L., & Steptoe, A. (2005). Acute inflammation and negative mood: Mediation by cytokine activation. *Brain, Behavior, and Immunity, 19*, 345–350.

Wu, C. W., Chen, Y. C., Yu, L., Chen, H. I., Jen, C. J., Huang, A. M., et al. (2007). Treadmill exercise counteracts the suppressive effects of peripheral lipopolysaccharide on hippocampal neurogenesis and learning and memory. *J Neurochem, 103*(6), 2471–2481.

Zhou, D., Kusnecov, A. W., Shurin, M. R., DePaoli, M., & Rabin, B. S. (1993). Exposure to physical and psychological stressors elevates plasma interleukin 6: Relationship to the activation of hypothalamic-pituitary-adrenal axis. *Endocrinology, 133*, 2523–2530.

Michael V. Lombardo, Simon Baron-Cohen, Matthew K. Belmonte, *and* Bhismadev Chakrabarti

Abstract

Autism is characterized by qualitative impairments in social interaction, communication, and stereotyped repetitive behaviors and/or restricted interests. Beyond these diagnostic criteria, autism is viewed as a neurodevelopmental condition with possibly several etiologies that manifest in complex patterns of atypical structural and functional brain development, cognition, and behavior. Despite the multidimensional nature of and substantial variation within the autism spectrum, impairments in social interaction remain among the most visible hallmarks of the condition. It is this profound developmental deficit in the social domain that makes autism a unique case in the field of social neuroscience. This chapter contributes to the dialogue amongst both the fields of autism research and social neuroscience by deliberately taking the stance of asking how we can understand more about the etiological mechanisms underlying social behavior in autism. It presents a multi-level overview of the literature on the behavioral, neural, and genetic underpinnings of social functioning in autism spectrum conditions (ASC). The main objective is to highlight the current state of the field regarding theory of mind/empathy difficulties in ASC, and then to suggest distinct candidate neural endophenotypes that can bridge the gap between social behavior and genetic mechanisms.

Keywords: autism, Asperger syndrome, social cognition, social behavior, theory of mind, mentalizing, empathy, face-processing, meta-analysis, neuroimaging, endophenotype, social development

Autism, as defined by ICD-10 and DSM-IV criteria, is characterized by qualitative impairments in social interaction, communication, and stereotyped repetitive behaviors and/or restricted interests (APA, 1994; ICD-10, 1994). Beyond these diagnostic criteria, autism is viewed as a neurodevelopmental condition with possibly several etiologies (Geschwind & Levitt, 2007) that manifest in complex patterns of atypical structural and functional brain development (Belmonte et al., 2004; Courchesne et al., 2007), cognition, and behavior (Baron-Cohen & Belmonte, 2005; Volkmar, Lord, Bailey, Schultz, &

Klin, 2004). Despite the multidimensional nature of and substantial variation within the autism spectrum, impairments in social interaction remain among the most visible hallmarks of the condition. It is this profound developmental deficit in the social domain that makes autism a unique case in the field of social neuroscience. However, autism research also benefits dramatically from progress in social neuroscience, since such progress informs us about the etiological mechanisms and processes underlying the social hallmarks of autism. Thus, both fields are critically locked in a bidirectional interaction and it is the dialogue amongst researchers in both fields that can help provide further advancements in our knowledge of both fields.

For the purposes of this chapter we contribute to the dialogue amongst both the fields of autism research and social neuroscience by deliberately taking the stance of asking how we can understand more about the etiological mechanisms underlying social behavior in autism. Historically, the most concretely testable and widely documented of the social impairments in autism was the ability to mentalize[1] and/or to rapidly and flexibly manifest empathy with others (Baron-Cohen, 1995; Baron-Cohen, Leslie, & Frith, 1985; Frith, 2001). An increasing body of evidence also relates autistic mentalizing deficits to computationally and developmentally prior abnormalities in social and other perceptual processes (Dawson et al., 2004; Rogers & Pennington, 1991; Schultz, 2005). However, amongst the search for explanations of autism, at the cognitive, neural, and genetic levels, some have argued that there may be no single overarching explanation for all of the phenotypic variability (Happé, Ronald, & Plomin, 2006; Ronald, Happé, Bolton, et al., 2006). Many researchers now tend to view autism as a set of subtypes that fall under the broad label of autism spectrum conditions (ASC). Thus, if we are to identify the underlying etiological mechanisms giving rise to various types of autism, there is a need to characterize individuals in terms of variables closer to these mechanisms.

Recent thinking in the field of psychiatry has led to the concept of intermediate phenotypes ("endophenotypes"; see Box 55.1) which are one step closer to the genetic mechanisms that, in interaction with environmental factors, ultimately give rise to variability within the diagnostic phenotype (Gottesman & Gould, 2003; Meyer-Lindenberg & Weinberger, 2006). For example, in different individuals with ASC, the same abnormality of neural information processing may arise from partially or wholly distinct sets of factors. Although the final common pathway underlying the diagnosis may lie at the level of neural information processing, interindividual variations in the genetic and environmental factors from which this neural abnormality arises produce corresponding inter-individual variations within and outside the common pathway. In this endophenotypic sense, a fractionable, multiple-factors view of autism is not incompatible with a unified, final common pathway account (Belmonte, Bonneh, et al., 2009).

> **Box 55.1. Endophenotype**
> Endophenotypes are defined as "measurable components unseen by the unaided eye along the pathway between disease and distal genotype" (Gottesman & Gould, 2003). Endophenotypes can be of variable depth, in that some measures (e.g., cellular activity as measured by single-unit electrophysiology) might be closer to the genetic end, whilst others such as reaction time in a behavioral task could constitute an endophenotype that is closer to the end marked by clinical diagnosis. Neural endophenotypes (as identified by structural and functional neuroimaging) lie in an intermediate position in this scale measuring the "depth of endophenotype." Meyer-Lindenberg and Weinberger (2006) were among the first to propose a framework for identifying neural endophenotypes for understanding complex psychiatric conditions.

In this chapter we present a multi-level overview of the literature on the behavioral, neural, and genetic underpinnings of social functioning in autism spectrum conditions (ASC). Our main objective is to highlight the current state of the field regarding theory of mind/empathy difficulties in ASC, and then to suggest distinct candidate neural endophenotypes that can bridge the gap between social behavior and genetic mechanisms (see Figure 55.1). We start with a review of behavioral and neuroimaging studies on theory of mind/empathy in ASC. Rather than providing an exhaustive review of all studies in ASC, we give a succinct overview of widely used and consistently replicated behavioral assays or tests of this construct in ASC. While theory of mind/empathy is a broad construct (Baron-Cohen & Wheelwright, 2004; Belmonte, 2008; Blair, 2005; Chakrabarti & Baron-Cohen, 2006; de Vignemont & Singer, 2006; Preston & de Waal, 2002) (see Box 55.2), this review highlights the most pertinent aspects of theory of mind and empathy that have been systematically addressed (see Table 55.1 for an overview).

In addition to the overview of research on theory of mind/empathy, we go one step further and suggest candidate neural endophenotypes for social impairment in ASC. To this end, we discuss results from recent meta-analyses of functional neuroimaging studies relevant to social behavior in people with and without ASC. By providing a quantitative insight into the literature relating to social behavior in autism (e.g., face perception, facial emotions, eye gaze, mentalizing, self-referential cognition), we illustrate how a "candidate neural endophenotype" should focus on the most robust and consistent

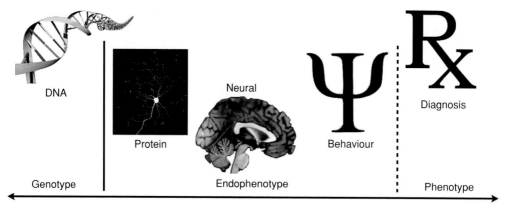

Fig. 55.1 Intermediate phenotypes (endophenotypes) in psychiatry. The far left (left of the solid vertical line) represents the primary structure of DNA, variations in which have been related to clinical phenotypes (far right) in traditional genetic association studies. The vertical line in the right is a dotted one to denote that clinical diagnoses (especially for ASC) exist along a continuum, that there is no strict distinction from the range of observed behavior. A range of intermediate phenotypes (e.g., mRNA/protein abundance and activity, cell population response, overt/covert behavior) exists between these two ends, which are all potential endophenotypes. An endophenotype could be closer to the DNA end (in which case effect sizes of genetic association would be higher), or closer to the clinical diagnostic end (which could account for why most genetic studies find multiple associations of low-medium effect size). Thus the "depth of endophenotype" (i.e., how close a particular endophenotype is to the DNA end of this continuum) can help determine the strength of a genetic association. The horizontal arrow at the bottom of the figure is bidirectional, to denote that just as DNA can influence behavior through the set of endophenotypes, the environment can in turn impact on gene expression.

neural systems that differ between groups. We also illustrate how endophenotypes may be refined by highlighting the common and distinct neural systems underlying subdomains of social behavior such as theory of mind and face processing. Finally, we discuss evidence from humans and other animals for genetic contributions to social behavior and autism and suggest directions for future research that will integrate genotypic and endophenotypic levels of analysis.

Theory of Mind in ASC

Inquiry into theory of mind began with the seminal paper by Premack and Woodruff (1978), provocatively titled "Does the chimpanzee have a theory of mind?"

We first tested theory of mind ability in ASC via a modified version of Wimmer and Perner's (1983) False Belief test. In this test children are presented a brief story involving two dolls, Sally and Ann. Sally enters a room and puts her marble into her basket and then leaves the room. Whilst she is away, "naughty" Ann takes Sally's marble out of the basket and puts it into her own box. Upon Sally's return the crucial test question to children was "Where will Sally look for her marble?" Whilst 85% of typically developing children were able to attribute a false belief to Sally (e.g., "Sally will look in her basket"), 80% of children with autism failed to attribute a false belief to Sally (Baron-Cohen et al., 1985). Various manipulations and control tasks have been

---

Box 55.2. Theory of Mind, Mentalizing, and Empathy

Theory of mind (ToM) allows us the capacity to infer the full range of mental states (beliefs, desires, goals, intentions, imagination, emotions, etc.) that cause action, in a top-down manner. In brief, having a theory of mind is to be able to reflect on the contents of one's own and other's minds (Baron-Cohen, 1995). *Mentalizing* is a synonymous term to theory of mind. *Empathy* is a superordinate category, encompassing ToM as well as automatic components of emotion perception and the ability to respond to others' emotions in an appropriate way. Empathizing is defined as the ability to identify emotions, thoughts, and other mental states in others, and to respond to these in an emotionally appropriate way (Baron-Cohen & Wheelwright, 2004). Empathy consists of three main fractions, including a) cognitive empathy (identical to ToM), b) affective empathy, which is responsible for our automatic reactions to others' emotions, and c) sympathy/prosocial behavior, which is involved in making an emotionally appropriate motor response (for a discussion, see Chakrabarti & Baron-Cohen, 2006). For the purposes of the meta-analysis reported in the *Neural Systems Involved in ASC Social Impairment* section, we have taken a broad approach, including all studies that tap the broad construct encompassing theory of mind, and empathy, either directly or indirectly.

Table 55.1   Overview of the Common Behavioral Results in the Domains of Theory of Mind/Empathy in ASC.

	Experimental paradigms	Observed differences	Primary example references
	Vocalizations		Hobson (1986)
	Body Posture	ASC<Controls	Hobson (1986)
Emotion Recognition			
	Facial Expression	ASC<Controls (accuracy)	Humphreys et al. (2007)
		ASC>Controls (reaction time)	Humphreys et al. (2007)
	Reading the Mind in the Eyes task	ASC<Controls	Baron-Cohen et al. (2001a)
	False Belief Task	ASC< Controls	Baron-Cohen et al. (1985)
			Happé (1995)
Theory of Mind	Strange Stories Task	ASC<Controls	Happé (1994)
			Happé et al. (1996)
	Faux pas test	ASC<Controls	Baron-Cohen et al. (1999)
	Animations Task	ASC<Controls	Klin (2000)
			Abell et al. (2000)
	Unexpected Contents Task		
	Smarties Task		Perner et al. (1989)
			Leslie & Thaiss (1992)
	Plasters Task		Williams & Happé (2009)
	Appearance-Reality Distinction		Baron-Cohen (1989)
	Self-Reference Effect in Memory		
	Self>Semantic	ASC<Controls	Toichi et al. (2002)
	Self>Dissimilar Non-Close Other	ASC<Controls	Lombardo et al. (2007)

(Continued)

833

Table 55.1   Continued

	Experimental paradigms	Observed differences	Primary example references
		ASC<Controls	Henderson et al. (2009)
Self	Self>Similar Close Other	ASC=Controls	Lombardo et al. (2007)
	Self-Knowledge Estimation		
	Self>Close Other	ASC<Controls	Mitchell & O'Keefe (2008)
	Alexithymia	ASC>Controls	Hill et al. (2004)
			Lombardo et al. (2007)
	Self-Conscious Emotion		
	Experience	ASC<Controls	Hobson et al. (2006)
	Recognition	ASC<Controls	Heerey et al. (2003)
			Hobson et al. (2006)

Tasks have been broadly classified into categories marked by different shades of gray. RMET in particular has been marked in a special category, as it represents an overlap of ToM and emotion-recognition paradigms.

tested and all point to a similar conclusion, that children with autism have a marked deficit in attributing beliefs to others. In a meta-analysis Happé (1995) clarified that some children with ASC do eventually acquire the ability to pass this false belief test, but only after a delay of approximately 5 years relative to typically developing children.

However, even where individuals with ASC pass traditional false belief tests, significant social disability persists, reflecting that more subtle deficits in mental state attribution exist than are measured by the standard false belief test. Traditional false belief tests yield only two outcomes: pass or fail. As the Happé (1995) meta-analysis highlighted, this limitation of a relatively simple measure of theory of mind spurred the development of more complex tests that yield greater variability. In one such test, the Strange Stories Test (Happé, 1994), participants read vignettes about everyday situations where the characters say things that aren't meant literally. Comprehension on this test requires the attribution of more complex mental states and intentions such as deception, joking, pretence, persuasion, and

sarcasm. Even more able individuals with ASC who pass both first- and second-order false belief tests are impaired at giving context-appropriate mental-state explanations for characters' nonliteral utterances.

The Strange Stories paradigm was employed in one of the first neuroimaging studies on theory of mind in autism (Happé et al., 1996). Individuals with autism show hypoactivation of the dorsomedial prefrontal cortex (dMPFC) during this task. Later fMRI studies by Wang and colleagues probed similar aspects of pragmatics in language that intersect with mentalizing ability (Wang, Lee, Sigman, & Dapretto, 2006, 2007). These studies also showed that people with ASC hypoactivate dMPFC. However, when individuals with ASC are explicitly directed to attend to social cues such as facial expression or prosody, dMPFC activation is restored to a level similar to controls' (Wang et al., 2007). This set of results highlights the role of attention to social cognitive cues in engaging intact abilities, and suggests that in many cases, skills that are assumed to be absent in autism may simply not be rapidly and flexibly activated by social cues.

As the research of Wang and colleagues demonstrates, perceptual social cues are integral for more advanced theory of mind ability. We developed an advanced theory of mind task that relies more on perceptual rather than linguistic cues. During the Reading the Mind in the Eyes task (RMET) (Baron-Cohen, Jolliffe, Mortimore, & Robertson, 1997; Baron-Cohen, Wheelwright, Hill, Raste, & Plumb, 2001a) participants are shown photos of just the eye regions of faces. Individuals are asked to judge what the person in the picture is thinking or feeling, based solely on viewing the eyes. These judgments involve complex emotion recognition and show a fairly normal distribution within the general population. This point is important because for most theory of mind tests which people with autism do not pass, typically developing control participants pass at ceiling rates. On the RMET, even the most able individuals with ASC, such as adults with Asperger syndrome, show impaired performance, suggesting that theory of mind deficits are a core characteristic of all individuals on the autistic spectrum. The RMET has also demonstrated sensitivity in detecting familial effects, as both parents and siblings of individuals with ASC perform significantly worse when compared to parents and siblings of control children (Baron-Cohen & Hammer, 1997; Dorris, Espie, Knott, & Salt, 2004; Losh & Piven, 2007; Losh et al., 2009). This concurs well with other recent demonstrations of familiality of face-processing deficits in ASC (Adolphs, Spezio, Parlier, & Piven, 2008; Losh et al., 2009).

Using fMRI we probed the neural correlates of performance on the RMET and found hypoactivation in ASC within structures important for emotion and action/perception mirroring: the frontal operculum (FO), amygdala, and insula (Baron-Cohen et al., 1999). These results differed from the earlier studies revealing dMPFC involvement in pragmatic language aspects of theory of mind in autism and highlight the possibility of dissociable neural mechanisms for theory of mind tasks that involve perceptual versus linguistic cues.

A significant drawback of many tests of theory of mind has been their reliance on verbal ability and/or an explicit focus on mental state attribution. As noted early in the study by Wang and colleagues (2007), mentalizing activation in ASC was below normal when the individual was left to process the task in whatever way was natural for them, but could be normalized by explicitly directing attention to social cues. Thus, there is a need for measures to test whether the mentalizing abnormalities that persist throughout life are indicative of an underlying deficit in spontaneously mentalizing. One such nonverbal measure of automatic mental state attribution (i.e., *implicit* mentalizing) without an explicit focus on mental states is the Social Attribution (or Animations) Test. In the Animations test, an individual watches an animation of two geometric shapes moving about on a computer screen. In one set of animations, the shapes move in such a sequence that most typically developing individuals will spontaneously anthropomorphize into a narrative full of mental state references. People with ASC, including those who demonstrate first- and second-order false belief ability, are less prone to attribute cognitive and affective mental states to these animations spontaneously. When people with autism do attribute mental states, they are often contextually inappropriate (Abell, Happé, & Frith, 2000; Klin, 2000). Similar to the study by Wang and colleagues, this paradigm demonstrates an absence of automatic attribution of mental states in the absence of explicit instructions to do so. The two fMRI studies to date employing the Animations task have shown hypoactivation of mentalizing areas such as the dMPFC and posterior superior temporal sulcus (pSTS) (Castelli, Frith, Happé, & Frith, 2002; Kana, Keller, Cherkassky, Minshew, & Just, 2009).

Convergent recent evidence further extends the notion that individuals with autism do not spontaneously engage with the mental worlds of others. In our own recent work (Barnes, Lombardo, Wheelwright, & Baron-Cohen, 2009), we wanted to see whether adults with ASC would be able spontaneously to extract rich mentalistic information from naturalistic film clips depicting moral dilemmas and to convey them through written narratives. While control participants wrote narratives full of mental state references, adults with autism produced significantly shorter and more constrained narratives that focused less on mental states. This example corroborates the results from the Animations test: Adults with autism do not spontaneously mentalize in situations that approximate naturalistic settings.

Senju, Southgate, White, and Frith (2009) demonstrated a similar phenomenon through dependent measures that are completely nonverbal. In this study, participants watched a scenario where a puppet hides a ball in one of two boxes in front of an observant other person. The other person then turns away briefly, and the puppet removes the ball from the box. Upon the test trial phase, a light flashes, indicating to the participant that the person will reach for the box in which they believe the ball is hidden. Using an eye-tracker, the researchers were able to measure anticipatory looks to the box with which participants should have associated the observer's false belief. Adults with Asperger syndrome who could pass the standard Sally-Ann false belief test showed no anticipatory gaze fixations to the false-belief location. This ability emerges as early as 2 years of age in non-ASC children (Southgate, Senju, & Csibra, 2007), yet is absent in adults with Asperger syndrome.

The Self and its Link to the Social World in Autism

The historical focus in autism research on mentalizing deficits as they relate to *other* people is complemented by more recent studies of how people with autism understand their *own* mental states. Behavioral studies suggest that people with autism are as impaired, if not more so, in explicit awareness of their own mental states (Baron-Cohen, 1989; Perner, Frith, Leslie, & Leekam, 1989; Williams & Happé, 2009) and other aspects of self-referential cognition (Hill, Berthoz, & Frith, 2004; Lombardo, Barnes, Wheelwright, & Baron-Cohen, 2007; Toichi et al., 2002). See Table 55.1. Theoretical accounts have proposed that people with autism are locked in an egocentric stance (Baron-Cohen, 1995; Frith & de Vignemont, 2005) and that deficits in self-processing are integrally linked to how individuals with autism relate to the social world (Baron-Cohen, 2005; Frith, 2003; Frith & Happé, 1999; Happé, 2003; Hobson, Chidambi, Lee, & Meyer, 2006). In the context of theoretical accounts of social cognition such as simulation theory (Goldman, 2006) and self-other narrative practice (Hutto, 2007), and the abundance of research demonstrating overlapping/shared neural representations for self and other (Keysers et al., 2004; Lombardo, Chakrabarti, Bullmore, Wheelwright et al., 2010; Mitchell, Macrae, & Banaji, 2006; Singer et al., 2004; Wicker et al., 2003), the case of autism presents a unique opportunity to test such theoretical predictions.

To date, five neuroimaging studies have examined self-referential processing in autism. In the domain of self-recognition, Uddin and colleagues (2008) asked participants to make self-recognition judgments about pictures that varied continuously in "self" or "other" facial features. Both participants with and without ASC activated a right-lateralized frontoparietal system for self-recognition judgments. However, people with ASC did not activate this system when making other-recognition judgments. Thus, while this task suggests a deficit for

recognizing others, it did not distinguish the two groups in terms of a self-referential impairment and parallels findings suggesting that individuals with autism have no difficulties in self-recognition at the appropriate age (Dawson & McKissick, 1984; Lind & Bowler, 2009).

In the realm of reflective emotional self-awareness, Silani and colleagues (Silani et al., 2008) instructed participants to rate how *they* felt after viewing emotionally charged pictures, in comparison to judging how much color was in the pictures. During emotional self-appraisal, people with autism showed hypoactivation within the dMPFC, posterior cingulate cortex/precuneus (PCC), and temporal pole. This hypoactivation in the dMPFC during emotional self-introspection is in the same area on the paracingulate sulcus where previous studies observed other-referential mentalizing difficulties (Castelli, Frith, Happé, & Frith, 2002; Happé et al., 1996; Kana, Keller, Cherkassky, Minshew, & Just, 2009; Wang et al., 2007).

In the context of reflective trait judgments about self or other, Kennedy and Courchesne (2008a) asked participants to judge the descriptiveness of internally (e.g., generous, polite) or externally focused traits (e.g., coffee drinker) about *themselves* or a *close other* (the participant's mother), and found no significant group differences in Self>Other activation. However, as the "other" person in this study was someone significantly close to the participant, the lack of group differences in this study may reflect a simple absence of any Self>Other effects in the control group. Research with typical adults shows that the vMPFC Self>Other response is most robust when the comparison "other" is a familiar but *non-close other* (Kelley et al., 2002). In contrast, when the other person is a *close other* (Ochsner et al., 2005) or someone *similar to oneself* (Mitchell et al., 2006), vMPFC response to Self and Other is nearly identical. Given that the vMPFC is highly involved in tracking self-relevant information (Moran et al., 2006), the vMPFC may be picking up on self-relevant information even when one is directed to think about others.

Another reason for the lack of a vMPFC group difference in the Kennedy and Courchesne (2008a) study may be a more pronounced egocentrism in ASC (Frith & de Vignemont, 2005). Clinical accounts from the outset, by Kanner (1943) and Asperger (1944), suggested an extreme egocentrism in autism. A study by Mitchell and O'Keefe (2008) documented that typically developing children tend to attribute more privileged self-knowledge to themselves, over and above that which they think their mother knows of them. However, people with ASC perceive themselves and their mothers to know equivalent amounts of information about themselves. These observations suggest that individuals with ASC may not automatically distinguish between self and other (Lombardo & Baron-Cohen, 2010).

Testifying to this explanation, our own study (Lombardo, Chakrabarti, Bullmore, Sadek et al., 2010) compared activation when participants made mentalizing or physical judgments about themselves or a familiar but non-close other (the British Queen). While control participants showed robust Self>Other activity in vMPFC, participants with autism showed equivalent activity in vMPFC for both Self and Other judgments. Corroborating that this lack of a neural self-other distinction is associated with social deficits, we showed that the magnitude of social impairment as measured on the Autism Diagnostic Interview–Revised (ADI-R) increased as the self-other distinction in vMPFC decreased.

Further evidence in real-time social contexts also suggests that the normative neural response for self-referential processing is atypical in ASC. Chiu and colleagues (2008) assessed agent-specific responses in the neural systems underlying decision-making in a social context (i.e., the trust game). Participants with autism showed marked reduction in an area previously shown to be sensitive specifically for self-decisions in the context of a social interaction; the middle cingulate cortex (MCC). The magnitude of MCC self-response was also strongly related to the social impairments in ASC. However, given the embedding of this task in a real-time social interaction, it is difficult to tell from this study whether the effects observed during the self-decision phase may relate to deficits in self-mentalizing, other-mentalizing, or a combination of both (Frith & Frith, 2008). Our own study (Lombardo, Chakrabarti, Bullmore, Sadek, et al., 2010) clarifies this issue, showing that participants with autism do indeed hypoactivate the MCC specifically for self-mentalizing when compared to other-mentalizing.

In sum, cognitive impairments in theory of mind are robust and consistent in ASC and occur for both self and other. False belief ability is significantly delayed by about 5 years, and even when individuals with ASC acquire such abilities, subtle deficits still exist. In this sense, theory of mind deficits could be universal to individuals on the autistic spectrum, regardless of IQ level or language level. Even in

high-functioning individuals with ASC, clear signs of theory of mind deficits remain in natural, implicit mentalizing and complex emotion perception.

From our review of the neural systems involved in theory of mind in autism, the dMPFC seems a consistent, replicable locus of abnormal neural function during theory of mind tasks that are more conceptual or require linguistic processing. However, given the wide variety of findings in the neuroimaging literature, it is difficult to say whether there is a consistent picture of atypical neural function in other regions of the brain and across a myriad of mentalizing tasks. As we have highlighted, the range of paradigms extends from visual stimuli of faces, cartoons, or ambiguous geometric shapes, to linguistic scenarios, reflective judgments, and competitive games embedded in a social context. Furthermore, the social target about whom inferences are made varies across the self and real or hypothetical others. Greater clarity among this range of stimuli, tasks, and social targets can be made via quantitative meta-analysis.

Neural Systems Involved in ASC Social Impairment

To surmount the limitations of qualitative reviews of the neural systems underlying social behavior in ASC, we recently conducted a voxel-wise whole-brain quantitative meta-analysis of all neuroimaging studies in autism to date. Collapsing across all kinds of social tasks (e.g., biological motion, face perception, emotion, theory of mind, imitation, self-referential cognition), hypoactivation in ASC occurs across a whole neural circuit implicated in the typical development of social cognition; namely the vMPFC, dMPFC, FO, anterior insula (AI), amygdala (Amyg), anterior temporal lobe (ATL), mid and posterior sections of the superior temporal sulcus (mSTS, pSTS), secondary somatosensory cortex/inferior parietal lobe (SII/IPL), and fusiform gyrus (FG). See Figure 55.2. That is, across the entire literature of "social" functional neuroimaging studies in autism, individuals with ASC consistently show reduced activation in this crucial network involved in normative social cognition.

We followed up this "social" meta-analysis by dividing studies into theory of mind or face-processing studies (here, face-processing included all studies using faces irrespective of the emotional context). Theory of mind studies highlighted a hypoactive neural circuit in ASC within the dMPFC, posterior cingulate/precuneus (PCC), pSTS, and ATL (see blue clusters in Figure 55.3a), while face-processing in ASC highlighted a nearly dissociable hypoactive circuit of Amyg, AI, and FO (see orange clusters in Figure 55.3a).

We suggest that these striking dissociations, taken together, reflect neural endophenotypes that index impairment in specific social domains. Initial validity for this suggestion comes from the observation that the neural systems crucial for normative theory of mind processes such as pSTS, ATL, dMPFC, and PCC (Frith & Frith, 2003; Saxe & Powell, 2006) all are areas of consistent hypoactivation for theory of mind in ASC, but not for face processing. In contrast, the amygdala, FO, and insula tend to be involved in emotion and facial emotion processing (Lee & Siegle, 2009; Wager et al., 2008).

Two of the distinct face-processing regions (FO and amygdala) have already been observed as possible endophenotype candidates. Our own early work demonstrated that people with ASC show reduced activity in FO during the RMET (Baron-Cohen et al., 1999). In later work we showed that parents of individuals with autism manifest a similar neural response profile (Baron-Cohen et al., 2006). Individual differences in trait empathy in the general population covary with activity in FO during facial emotion recognition and such relationships generalize regardless of the type of emotion (Chakrabarti, Bullmore, & Baron-Cohen, 2006) and across development (Pfeifer, Iacoboni, Mazziotta, & Dapretto, 2008). Furthermore, as mentioned earlier, performance on the RMET is impaired in parents and siblings of children with autism and may thus be a useful cognitive endophenotypic marker of social symptoms related to autism (Baron-Cohen & Hammer, 1997; Dorris, Espie, Knott, & Salt, 2004; Losh & Piven, 2007; Losh et al., 2009).

When participants performed the RMET in the scanner, we also found significantly reduced amygdala activity in ASC—an impetus for the amygdala theory of ASC (Baron-Cohen et al., 2000). Similarly for the amygdala, clinically unaffected siblings of children with autism exhibit intermediate activation between autistic and normal levels during face-processing (Dalton, Nacewicz, Alexander, & Davidson, 2007). The convergence of previous research with the meta-analytic result here suggests the FO and amygdala as initial endophenotypic markers of autistic deficits in face processing and emotion recognition. However, unlike the FO and amygdala, within the theory of mind system no neuroimaging studies have specifically looked for heritability or familiality of functioning. Future work should specifically address this question.

Despite this dissociation of neural systems involved in theory of mind and face-processing, we also found that the vMPFC emerged as the only *common* hypoactive region for both theory of mind and face-processing. This common area of the vMPFC may be of crucial importance in the search for neural endophenotypes of social dysfunction in autism. The vMPFC is a hub for social information processing in the typically developing brain (Amodio & Frith, 2006) and is important for self-referential processing and understanding the relationship between self and other (Mitchell et al., 2006; Ochsner et al., 2005). In a recent study we found that in autism, the vMPFC does not distinguish between self and other and this lack of distinction is related to the social impairments in autism (Lombardo, Chakrabarti, Bullmore, Sadek et al., 2010).

Aside from its role in cognition, vMPFC is also a network hub for intrinsic functional brain organization (Buckner et al., 2009) and connects much of the prefrontal cortex with subcortical limbic areas (Hagmann et al., 2008). In ASC, the vMPFC is shows decreased functional connectivity at rest and is atypical as baseline measure of brain activity (Kennedy & Courchesne, 2008b; Kennedy, Redcay, & Courchesne, 2006). Dopamine and serotonin binding in MPFC is also reduced in autism (Ernst, Zametkin, Matochik, Pascualvaca, & Cohen, 1997; Makkonen et al., 2008; Murphy et al., 2006), as are glucose metabolism (Hazlett et al., 2004; Haznedar et al., 2000) and regional cerebral blood flow (George et al., 1992; Zilbovicius et al., 1995). Concentrations of metabolites such as choline, which reflect altered membrane metabolism, are reduced in this area in ASC (Levitt et al., 2003). White matter adjacent to the vMPFC shows reduced fractional anisotropy, tract number (Barnea-Goraly et al., 2004; Cheung et al., 2009; Pardini et al., 2009, Pugliese et al., 2009), and white matter volume (Bonilha et al., 2008; McAlonan et al., 2009), while gray matter volume is increased in the vMPFC of individuals with autism (Bonilha et al., 2008; Carper & Courchesne, 2005; Waiter et al., 2004). The convergence of both the cognitive and biological significance of the vMPFC, both in social functioning and in general network organization suggests that the vMPFC is an important network node that future research in autism should target.

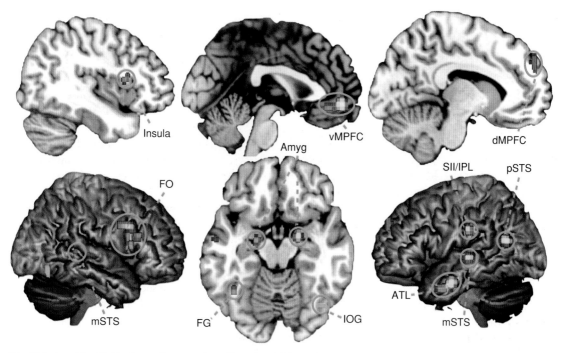

Fig. 55.2 Areas identified in the social meta-analysis. Controls>ASC (orange), ASC>Controls (blue).

In contrast to hypoactivations, during social information processing individuals with ASC may be compensating for the lack of normative engagement of social cognitive circuits by hyperactivating other areas of the brain. Our meta-analyses found evidence of such compensatory hyperactivation in the dorsal premotor cortex near the frontal eye fields (FEF) for theory of mind and in the inferior frontal sulcus (IFS) and right FG for face processing. FEF and IFS are integral areas of a hierarchical cognitive control circuit (Badre, 2008; Corbetta, Patel, & Shulman, 2008; Derrfuss, Brass, Neumann, & von Cramon, 2005). Given that high-functioning individuals with autism have certain strengths in nonsocial cognitive processing (Baron-Cohen, Richler, Bisarya, Gurunathan, & Wheelwright, 2003; Mottron, Dawson, Soulières, Hubert, & Burack, 2006), these results suggest that nonsocial cognitive strategies may be co-opted to solve problems of social information processing (Belmonte et al., 2004). These meta-analytic results are consistent with other recent findings (Belmonte, Gomot, & Baron-Cohen, 2010) contradicting the idea that people with autism always have abnormally low frontal activity and abnormally greater posterior cortical activity. Rather we suggest the more general notion that people with autism deploy alternate strategies to solve cognitive problems, via routes that may be more readily available to them than those used by typical individuals.

In conclusion, autistic abnormalities in theory of mind and face processing arise in brain regions implicated in normative functioning. The decreased recruitment of these systems is nearly completely distinct between theory of mind and face processing tasks. The exception is a common region in vMPFC, consistently hypoactivated across both theory of mind and face processing. Emerging research suggests that vMPFC may be a network hub on both cognitive and biological levels. We suggest that future work examine the possibility of reduced vMPFC response as a meaningful physiological marker for general social impairment in autism (the meta-analysis maps are available upon request). In addition, the dissociable neural systems involved in theory of mind and face processing may be meaningful biomarkers or endophenotypes for specific social subdomains. Such anatomically and functionally circumscribed endophenotypes may greatly aid genetic association studies in humans, and parallel basic research on animal models of social behavior. Thus, in the final

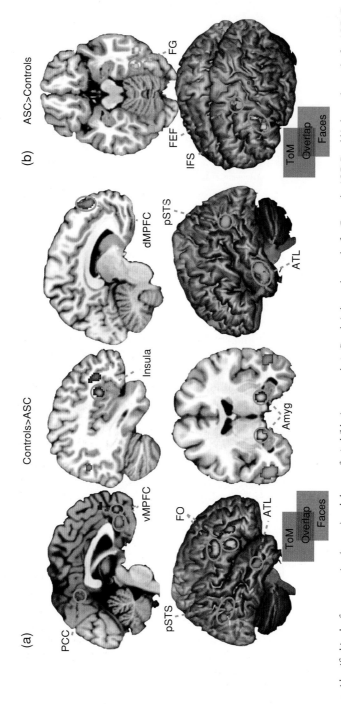

Fig. 55.3 Areas identified in the face processing (orange) and theory of mind (blue) meta-analysis. Panel a) shows the results for Controls>ASC. Panel b) shows the results for ASC>Controls.

section we provide a brief overview of genetic underpinnings of social behavior, and suggest the utility of such endophenotypes for future genetic research.

The Genetics of Social Behavior: Implications for a Neural Endophenotype for Autism

Confirming the known familiality of social behavior in ASC (Adolphs, Spezio, Parlier, & Piven, 2008; Baron-Cohen & Hammer, 1997; Baron-Cohen et al., 2006; Dorris, Espie, Knott, & Salt, 2004; Losh & Piven, 2007; Losh et al., 2009), recent research has begun to pinpoint its genetic underpinnings. Animal research suggests that basic forms of social behavior such as maternal and pair-bonding behavior have a long evolutionary history across many species. Some of these genetic mechanisms are common across species, and hence relevant to understanding social behavior in humans. The combination of knowledge of human genetic variability and techniques such as fMRI to study whole-brain activity in living humans are poised to enable a parsing of the genetic factors giving rise to complex social behaviors. To do this, it is crucial to have well-defined phenotypic measures. Given the assumption that in many cases, neural measures can be more sensitive than behavioral measures, well-defined "neural" phenotypes, as described in the previous section, represent a concrete step towards such future research (Landis & Insel, 2008).

Several studies have explicitly investigated the genetic basis of human social behavior in the general population. A standard approach so far has been to test for heritability (see Box 55.3) of trait empathy or other measures of social behavior by comparing monozygotic (MZ) and dizygotic (DZ) twins. Nearly all of these studies have shown a greater correlation of empathy measures in MZ compared to DZ twins, suggesting a genetic basis for trait empathy (Davis, Luce, & Kraus, 1994; Loehlin

& Nichols, 1976; Matthews, Batson, Horn, & Rosenman, 1981) as measured indirectly using the Questionnaire Measure of Emotional Empathy (QMEE) (Mehrabian & Epstein, 1972). Rushton et al. (1986), in a large-scale twin study in humans, suggested a heritability estimate of 68% for emotional empathy. Other twin studies, particularly in children, have used behavioral observation paradigms of empathy in a laboratory situation. These involve simulating scripted situations (e.g., the experimenter tripping on a chair, or the mother of the child getting her finger caught while closing a suitcase), while video-recording the child's reactions. A study of 14- and 20-month-old twins using this paradigm confirmed a genetic contribution to empathic concern (Zahn-Waxler, Radke-Yarrow, Wagner, & Chapman, 1992).

A recent twin study on 409 twin pairs by the same group showed that genetic effects on empathy and prosociality (measured using video-recorded behavior in a laboratory setting) increase with age and shared environmental effects decrease with age (Knafo, Zahn-Waxler, Van Hulle, Robinson, & Rhee, 2008). In the domain of autistic traits, very few behavioral phenotypes have been tested for genetic effects. A notable exception is performance on the RMET, which shows a strong degree of familiality (Baron-Cohen & Hammer, 1997; Losh & Piven, 2007). Recent questionnaire measures of social (Social Responsiveness Scale (SRS); Constantino & Todd, 2000, 2005) and emotion understanding (alexithymia; Szatmari et al., 2008), and autistic traits (Autism Spectrum Quotient (AQ); Baron-Cohen et al., 2001b) reveal strong familiality (Bishop et al., 2004) as well as heritability in twin studies (Hoekstra et al., 2007). These studies corroborate findings from the early twin studies in suggesting a genetic underpinning for social behavior relevant to ASC.

In comparison, the animal phenotypes for social behavior have primarily included indices of maternal care (e.g., licking-grooming/arched-back nursing), pair bonding behavior (e.g., mate loyalty), and social recognition. These have established a role for a set of genes involved in endogenous opioid systems (Panksepp, 1998; Panksepp, Nelson, & Bekkedal, 1997), neuroendocrine factors such as oxytocin and vasopressin (Donaldson & Young, 2008; Winslow & Insel, 2004), and sex hormones such as estrogen (Choleris, Clipperton, Phan, & Kavaliers, 2008), among others. A recent study reported testing for "empathy" in rats by measuring autonomic changes in rats who observed other rats

---

Box 55.3.   Heritability

Heritability refers to the proportion of the variance in a particular phenotype that is explained by purely genetic effects. Experiments with monozygotic (MZ) and dizygotic (DZ) twin pairs are used to estimate the heritability of particular traits. In these experiments, heritability is estimated after accounting for phenotypic variance due to shared and nonshared environments.

---

receiving electric shocks (Chen, Panksepp, & Lahvis, 2009). This study showed that such an autonomic index of "empathy" was a function of the genetic background. Developing effective assays for social behavior and empathy in rodents continues to be an active area of research (Arakawa et al., 2008; Crawley, 2007). However, there is considerable variation in the degree to which gene function is preserved across species. A common example is vasopressin, which in monogamous species of voles is involved in pair-bonding behavior such as mate-guarding and paternal care, but has no such effect in non-monogamous species of voles. Hence, whilst animal research can point toward suggestive candidate genes for social behavior, it is essential to test for genetic association with relevant human social behavioral endophenotypes.

Processing facial expressions of emotion is one of the key paradigms used to test social behavior in an experimental setting (See Table 55.1 for examples of such studies). Initial studies associating candidate gene polymorphisms with neuroimaging paradigms of facial expression processing have shown considerable promise. Hariri and colleagues (2005; 2002) showed that variability in serotonin transporter (*SLC6A4*) genotype modulates amygdala response to fear faces. Using the same paradigm, Meyer-Lindenberg and colleagues (Meyer-Lindenberg et al., 2009) showed that polymorphisms in the arginine vasopressin receptor 1A (*AVPR1A)* gene (previously linked to autism) are related to the amygdala response to faces displaying fear or anger. Work from our and other groups has shown that variations in the cannabinoid receptor (*CNR1*) gene modulate striatal response to happy faces (Chakrabarti, Kent, Suckling, Bullmore, & Baron-Cohen, 2006; Domschke et al., 2008). Future research will target such discrete "neural phenotypes" in ASC in combination with ideal candidate genes. Specifically, response from the regions identified in the meta-analysis should be analyzed for association with polymorphisms in these genes and others that have been linked to autism spectrum conditions (for a review, see Abrahams & Geschwind, 2008).

In one of the first genetic association studies of empathy (measured using EQ) and autistic traits (measured using AQ) in the general population and Asperger syndrome, we found nominally significant associations for 27 genes (Chakrabarti et al., 2009). These genes belong to three broad functional categories: a) social emotional responsivity; b) neural growth and connectivity; and c) sex steroid

synthesis, transport, and metabolism. Genes involved in social/emotional responsivity included genes coding for oxytocin and its receptor (*OXT, OXTR*), confirming their previously reported role in ASC (Wu et al., 2005) as well as animal models of social behavior (Insel, Brien, & Leckman, 1999). Genes in the group b included those coding for neuroligin receptors (particularly, *NLGN4X*), as well as neurotrophic receptor kinases (*NTRK1*), which play a central role in neuronal survival, development, and synapse stabilization. The estrogen receptor gene (*ESR2*) as well as genes involved in the functioning of sex steroids such as *CYP11B1*, and *CYP17A1* were among the significantly associated genes in group c. These genes are among the many possible candidates to explore in relation to neuroimaging endophenotypes of social behavior as discussed in the previous section.

Conclusion

In summary, we have reviewed evidence demonstrating that people with ASC have significant social deficits across development. Underlying these deficits are abnormalities across neural circuits crucial for normative social behavior. We have also reviewed evidence suggesting that social behavior has a strong genetic component. What is needed next, both in the context of normative development and in the context of the autism spectrum and other developmental conditions, is an exploration of the processes and interactions that mediate the effects of such genetic and molecular factors on social behavior. The intervening level between genetic influences and behavioral outcomes is the neural abnormalities consistently associated with social behavior in autism. In this chapter we have identified circumscribed neural systems whose atypical response in social behavioral paradigms can function as putative neural endophenotypes. These data pave the way for future genetic association studies, both for ASC as well as in the general population. Such inquiries will strengthen our understanding of neural processes underlying social cognition in autism, and provide fundamental insights into how variation within the general population can lead to extremes such as autism.

Acknowledgments

MVL was supported by the Shirley Foundation and the Cambridge Overseas Trust. BC and SBC were supported by the MRC-UK during the period of this work. MKB was supported by Autism Speaks. This work was conducted in association with the

CLAHRC for Cambridgeshire and Peterborough, and the ENSCAP Research Network for Biomarkers in Autism (N-EURO).

Note

1 The term "mentalizing" is used synonymously with the term "theory of mind."

References

Abell, F., Happé, F. G., & Frith, U. (2000). Do triangles play tricks? Attribution of mental states to animated shapes in normal and abnormal development. *Cognitive Development, 15*, 1–16.

Abrahams, B. S. & Geschwind, D. H. (2008). Advances in autism genetics: On the threshold of a new neurobiology. *Nature Reviews Genetics, 9*, 341–355.

Adolphs, R., Spezio, M. L., Parlier, M., & Piven, J. (2008). Distinct face-processing strategies in parents of autistic children. *Current Biology, 18*, 1090–1093.

Amodio, D. M. & Frith, C. D. (2006). Meeting of minds: the medial frontal cortex and social cognition. *Nature Reviews Neuroscience, 7*, 268–277.

Arakawa, H., Blanchard, D. C., Arakawa, K., Dunlap, C., & Blanchard, R. J. (2008). Scent marking behavior as an odorant communication in mice. *Neuroscience and Biobehavioral Reviews, 32*, 1236–1248.

Asperger, H. (1944). Die autistischen psychopathen im kindesalter. *Archiv fur Psychiatrie und Nervenkrankheiten, 117*, 76–136.

Association, A. P. (1994). *Diagnostic and statistical manual of mental disorders* (4 ed.). Washington, DC: American Psychiatric Association.

Badre, D. (2008). Cognitive control, hierarchy, and the rostro-caudal organization of the frontal lobes. *Trends in Cognitive Sciences, 12*, 193–200.

Barnea-Goraly, N., Kwon, H., Menon, V., Eliez, S., Lotspeich, L., & Reiss, A. L. (2004). White matter structure in autism: Preliminary evidence from diffusion tensor imaging. *Biological Psychiatry, 55*, 323–326.

Barnes, J. L., Lombardo, M. V., Wheelwright, S., & Baron-Cohen, S. (2009). Moral dilemmas film task: A study of spontaneous narratives by individuals with autism spectrum conditions. *Autism Research, 2*, 148–156.

Baron-Cohen, S. (1989). Are autistic children "behaviorists"? An examination of their mental-physical and appearance-reality distinctions. *Journal of Autism and Developmental Disorders, 19*, 579–600.

Baron-Cohen, S. (1995). *Mindblindness: An essay on autism and theory of mind.* Cambridge, MA: MIT Press.

Baron-Cohen, S. (2005). Autism—"autos': Literally, a total focus on the self? In T. E. Feinberg & J. P. Keenan (Eds.), *The lost self: Pathologies of the brain and identity.* Oxford: Oxford University Press.

Baron-Cohen, S. & Belmonte, M. K. (2005). Autism: A window onto the development of the social and the analytic brain. *Annual Review of Neuroscience, 28*, 109–126.

Baron-Cohen, S. & Hammer, J. (1997). Parents of children with Asperger syndrome: What is the cognitive phenotype? *Journal of Cognitive Neuroscience, 9*, 548–554.

Baron-Cohen, S., Jolliffe, T., Mortimore, C., & Robertson, M. (1997). Another advanced test of theory of mind: Evidence from very high-functioning adults with autism and Asperger syndrome. *Journal of Child Psychology and Psychiatry, 38*, 813–822.

Baron-Cohen, S., Leslie, A. M., & Frith, U. (1985). Does the autistic child have a "theory of mind"? *Cognition, 21*, 37–46.

Baron-Cohen, S., O'Riordan, M., Stone, V., Jones, R., & Plaisted, K. (1999). Recognition of faux pas by normally developing children and children with Asperger syndrome or high-functioning autism. *Journal of Autism and Developmental Disorders, 29*, 407–418.

Baron-Cohen, S., Richler, J., Bisarya, D., Gurunathan, N., & Wheelwright, S. (2003). The systemizing quotient: an investigation of adults with Asperger syndrome or high-functioning autism, and normal sex differences. *Philosophical Transactions of the Royal Society London B Biological Sciences, 358*, 361–374.

Baron-Cohen, S., Ring, H., Chitnis, X., Wheelwright, S., Gregory, L., Williams, S., et al. (2006). fMRI of parents of children with Asperger syndrome: A pilot study. *Brain and Cognition, 61*, 122–130.

Baron-Cohen, S., Ring, H. A., Bullmore, E. T., Wheelwright, S., Ashwin, C., & Williams, S. C. (2000). The amygdala theory of autism. *Neuroscience and Biobehavioral Reviews, 24*, 355–364.

Baron-Cohen, S., Ring, H. A., Wheelwright, S., Bullmore, E. T., Brammer, M. J., Simmons, A., et al. (1999). Social intelligence in the normal and autistic brain: An fMRI study. *European Journal of Neuroscience, 11*, 1891–1898.

Baron-Cohen, S. & Wheelwright, S. (2004). The empathy quotient: An investigation of adults with Asperger syndrome or high functioning autism, and normal sex differences. *Journal of Autism and Developmental Disorders, 34*, 163–175.

Baron-Cohen, S., Wheelwright, S., Hill, J., Raste, Y., & Plumb, I. (2001a). The "Reading the Mind in the Eyes" Test revised version: A study with normal adults, and adults with Asperger syndrome or high-functioning autism. *Journal of Child Psychology and Psychiatry, 42*, 241–251.

Baron-Cohen, S., Wheelwright, S., Skinner, R., Martin, J., & Clubley, E. (2001b). The autism-spectrum quotient (AQ): Evidence from Asperger syndrome/high-functioning autism, males and females, scientists and mathematicians. *Journal of Autism and Developmental Disorders, 31*, 5–17.

Belmonte, M. K. (2008). Does the experimental scientist have a "theory of mind"? *Review of General Psychology, 12*, 192–204.

Belmonte, M. K., Bonneh, Y. S., Adini, Y., Iversen, P. E., Akshoomoff, N. A., Kenet, T., et al. (2009). Autism overflows with syntheses. *Neuropsychology Review, 19*, 273–274.

Belmonte, M. K., Cook, E. H., Jr., Anderson, G. M., Rubenstein, J. L., Greenough, W. T., Beckel-Mitchener, A., et al. (2004). Autism as a disorder of neural information processing: directions for research and targets for therapy. *Molecular Psychiatry, 9*, 646–663. Unabridged edition at http://www.CureAutismNow.org/conferences/summitmeetings/.

Belmonte, M. K., Gomot, M., & Baron-Cohen, S. (2010). Visual attention in autism families: "Unaffected' sibs share atypical frontal activation. *Journal of Child Psychology and Psychiatry, 51*, 259–276.

Bishop, D., Maybery, M., Maley, A., Wong, D., Hill, W., & Hallmayer, J. (2004). Using self-report to identify the broad phenotype in parents of children with autistic spectrum disorders: A study using the Autism-Spectrum Quotient. *Journal of Child Psychology and Psychiatry, 45*, 1431–1436.

Blair, R. J. (2005). Responding to the emotions of others: Dissociating forms of empathy through the study of typical and psychiatric populations. *Consciousness and Cognition, 14*, 698–718.

Bonilha. L., Cendes, F., Rorden, C., Eckert, M., Dalgalarrondo, P., Li, L. M., et al. (2008). Gray and white matter imbalance—typical structural abnormality underlying classic autism? *Brain and Development, 30*, 396–401.

Buckner, R. L., Sepulcre, J., Talukdar, T., Krienen, F. M., Liu, H., Hedden, T., et al. (2009). Cortical hubs revealed by intrinsic functional connectivity: Mapping, assessment of stability, and relation to Alzheimer's disease. *Journal of Neuroscience, 29*, 1860–1873.

Carper, R. A. & Courchesne, E. (2005). Localized enlargement of the frontal cortex in early autism. *Biological Psychiatry, 57*, 126–133.

Castelli, F., Frith, C., Happé, F., & Frith, U. (2002). Autism, Asperger syndrome and brain mechanisms for the attribution of mental states to animated shapes. *Brain, 125*, 1839–1849.

Chakrabarti, B. & Baron-Cohen, S. (2006). Empathizing: Neurocognitive developmental mechanisms and individual differences. *Progress in Brain Research, 156*, 403–417.

Chakrabarti, B., Bullmore, E., & Baron-Cohen, S. (2006). Empathizing with basic emotions: Common and discrete neural substrates. *Social Neuroscience, 1*, 364–384.

Chakrabarti, B., Dudbridge, F., Kent, L., Wheelwright, S., Hill-Cawthorne, G., Allison, C., et al. (2009). Genes related to sex-steroids, neural growth, and social-emotional behavior are associated with autistic traits, empathy, and Asperger syndrome. *Autism Research, 2*, 157–177.

Chakrabarti, B., Kent, L., Suckling, J., Bullmore, E., & Baron-Cohen, S. (2006). Variations in the human cannabinoid receptor (CNR1) gene modulate striatal responses to happy faces. *European Journal of Neuroscience, 23*, 1944–1948.

Chen, Q., Panskepp, J. B., & Lahvis, G. P. (2009). Empathy is moderated by genetic background in mice. *PLoS One, 4*, e4837.

Cheung, C., Chua, S. E., Cheung, V., Khong, P. L., Tai, K. S., Wong, T. K., et al. (2009). White matter fractional anisotrophy differences and correlates of diagnostic symptoms in autism. *Journal of Child Psychology and Psychiatry, 50*, 1102–1112.

Chiu, P. H., Kayali, M. A., Kishida, K. T., Tomlin, D., Klinger, L. G., Klinger, M. R., et al. (2008). Self responses along cingulate cortex reveal quantitative neural phenotype for high-functioning autism. *Neuron, 57*, 463–473.

Choleris, E., Clipperton, A. E., Phan, A., & Kavaliers, M. (2008). Estrogen receptor beta agonists in neurobehavioral investigations. *Current Opinion in Investigational Drugs, 9*, 760–773.

Constantino, J. N. & Todd, R. D. (2000). Genetic structure of reciprocal social behavior. *American Journal of Psychiatry, 157*, 2043–2045.

Constantino, J. N. & Todd, R. D. (2005). Intergenerational transmission of subthreshold autistic traits in the general population. *Biological Psychiatry, 57*, 655–660.

Corbetta, M., Patel, G., & Shulman, G. L. (2008). The reorienting system of the human brain: From environment to theory of mind. *Neuron, 58*, 306–324.

Courchesne, E., Pierce, K., Schumann, C. M., Redcay, E., Buckwalter, J. A., Kennedy, D. P., et al. (2007). Mapping early brain development in autism. *Neuron, 56*, 399–413.

Crawley, J. N. (2007). Mouse behavioral assays relevant to the symptoms of autism. *Brain Pathology, 17*, 448–459.

Dalton, K. M., Nacewicz, B. M., Alexander, A. L., & Davidson, R. J. (2007). Gaze-fixation, brain activation, and amygdala volume in unaffected siblings of individuals with autism. *Biological Psychiatry, 61*, 512–520.

Davis, M. H., Luce, C., & Kraus, S. J. (1994). The heritability of characteristics associated with dispositional empathy. *Journal of Personality, 62*, 369–391.

Dawson, G. & McKissick, F. C. (1984). Self-recognition in autistic children. *Journal of Autism and Developmental Disorders, 14*, 383–394.

Dawson, G., Toth, K., Abbott, R., Osterling, J., Munson, J., Estes, A., et al. (2004). Early social attention impairments in autism: Social orienting, joint attention, and attention to distress. *Developmental Psychology, 40*, 271–283.

de Vignemont, F. & Singer, T. (2006). The empathic brain: how, when and why? *Trends in Cognitive Sciences, 10*, 435–441.

Derrfuss, J., Brass, M., Neumann, J., & von Cramon, D. Y. (2005). Involvement of the inferior frontal junction in cognitive control: meta-analyses of switching and Stroop studies. *Human Brain Mapping, 25*, 22–34.

Domschke, K., Dannlowski, U., Ohrmann, P., Lawford, B., Bauer, J., Kugel, H., et al. (2008). Cannabinoid receptor 1 (CNR1) gene: Impact on antidepressant treatment response and emotion processing in major depression. *European Neuropsychopharmacology, 18*, 751–759.

Donaldson, Z. R. & Young, L. J. (2008). Oxytocin, vasopressin, and the neurogenetics of sociality. *Science, 322*, 900–904.

Dorris, L., Espie, C. A. E., Knott, F., & Salt, J. (2004). Mind-reading difficulties in the siblings of people with Asperger's syndrome: Evidence for genetic influence in the abnormal development of a specific cognitive domain. *Journal of Child Psychology and Psychiatry, 45*, 412–418.

Ernst, M., Zametkin, A. J., Matochik, J. A., Pascualvaca, D., & Cohen, R. M. (1997). Low medial prefrontal dopaminergic activity in autistic children. *Lancet, 350*, 638.

Frith, C. D. & Frith, U. (2008). The self and its reputation in autism. *Neuron, 57*, 331–332.

Frith, U. (2001). Mind blindness and the brain in autism. *Neuron, 32*, 969–979.

Frith, U. (2003). *Autism: Explaining the enigma* (2nd ed.). Malden, MA: Blackwell.

Frith, U. & de Vignemont, F. (2005). Egocentrism, allocentrism, and Asperger syndrome. *Consciousness and Cognition, 14*, 719–738.

Frith, U. & Frith, C. D. (2003). Development and neurophysiology of mentalizing. *Philosophical Transactions of the Royal Society London B Biological Sciences, 358*, 459–473.

Frith, U. & Happé, F. (1999). Theory of mind and self-consciousness: What it is like to be autistic. *Mind and Language, 14*, 1–22.

George, M. S., Costa, D. C., Kouris, K., Ring, H. A., & Ell, P. J. (1992). Cerebral blood flow abnormalities in adults with infantile autism. *Journal of Nervous and Mental Disease, 180*, 413–417.

Geschwind, D. H. & Levitt, P. (2007). Autism spectrum disorders: developmental disconnection syndromes. *Current Opinion in Neurobiology, 17*, 103–111.

Goldman, A. (2006). *Simulating minds: The philosophy, psychology, and neuroscience of mind reading.* New York: Oxford University Press.

Gottesman, II & Gould, T. D. (2003). The endophenotype concept in psychiatry: Etymology and strategic intentions. *American Journal of Psychiatry, 160*, 636–645.

Hagmann, P., Cammoun, L., Gigandet, X., Meuli, R., Honey, C. J., Wedeen, V. J., et al. (2008). Mapping the structural core of human cerebral cortex. *PLoS Biology, 6*, e159.

Happé, F. (2003). Theory of mind and the self. *Annals of the New York Academy of Sciences, 1001*, 134–144.

Happé, F., Ehlers, S., Fletcher, P., Frith, U., Johansson, M., Gillberg, C., et al. (1996). "Theory of mind' in the brain. Evidence from a PET scan study of Asperger syndrome. *Neuroreport, 8*, 197–201.

Happé, F., Ronald, A., & Plomin, R. (2006). Time to give up on a single explanation for autism. *Nature Neuroscience, 9*, 1218–1220.

Happé, F. G. (1994). An advanced test of theory of mind: Understanding of story characters' thoughts and feelings in able autistic, mentally handicapped, and normal children and adults. *Journal of Autism and Developmental Disorders, 24*, 129–154.

Happé, F. G. (1995). The role of age and verbal ability in the theory of mind task performance of subjects with autism. *Child Development, 66*, 843–855.

Hariri, A. R., Drabant, E. M., Munoz, K. E., Kolachana, B. S., Mattay, V. S., Egan, M. F., et al. (2005). A susceptibility gene for affective disorders and the response of the human amygdala. *Archives of General Psychiatry, 62*, 146–152.

Hariri, A. R., Mattay, V. S., Tessitore, A., Kolachana, B., Fera, F., Goldman, D., et al. (2002). Serotonin transporter genetic variation and the response of the human amygdala. *Science, 297*, 400–403.

Hazlett, E. A., Buchsbaum, M. S., Hsieh, P., Haznedar, M. M., Platholi, J., LiCalzi, E. M., et al. (2004). Regional glucose metabolism within cortical Brodmann areas in healthy individuals and autistic patients. *Neuropsychobiology, 49*, 115–125.

Haznedar, M. M., Buchsbaum, M. S., Wei, T. C., Hof, P. R., Cartwright, C., Bienstock, C. A., & Hollander, E. (2000). Limbic circuitry in patients with autism spectrum disorders studied with positron emission tomography and magnetic resonance imaging. *American Journal of Psychiatry, 157*, 1994–2001.

Heerey, E. A., Keltner, D., & Capps, L. M. (2003). Making sense of self-conscious emotion: Linking theory of mind and emotion in children with autism. *Emotion, 3*, 394–400.

Henderson, H. A., Zahka, N. E., Kojkowski, N. M., Inge, A. P., Schwartz, C. B., Hileman, C. M., et al. (2009). Self-referenced memory, social cognition, and symptom presentation in autism. *Journal of Child Psychology and Psychiatry, 50*, 853–860.

Hill, E., Berthoz, S., & Frith, U. (2004). Brief report: Cognitive processing of own emotions in individuals with autistic spectrum disorder and in their relatives. *Journal of Autism and Developmental Disorders, 34*, 229–235.

Hobson, R. P. (1986). The autistic child's appraisal of expressions of emotion. *Journal of Child Psychology and Psychiatry, 27*, 321–342.

Hobson, R. P., Chidambi, G., Lee, A., & Meyer, J. (2006). Foundations for self-awareness: An exploration through autism. *Monographs of the Society for Research in Child Development, 71*, vii–166.

Hoekstra, R. A., Bartels, M., Verweij, C. J., & Boomsma, D. I. (2007). Heritability of autistic traits in the general population. *Archives of Pediatrics and Adolescent Medicine, 16*, 372–377.

Humphreys, K., Minshew, N., Leonard, G. L., & Behrmann, M. (2007). A fine-grained analysis of facial expression processing in high-functioning adults with autism. *Neuropsychologia, 45*, 685–695.

Hutto, D. (2007). *The narrative practice hypothesis: Origins and applications of folk psychology.* In D. Hutto (Ed.), Narrative and understanding persons (pp. 43–68). Cambridge: Cambridge University Press.

ICD-10. (1994). *International classification of diseases.* Geneva, Switzerland: World Health Organization.

Insel, T. R., O'Brien, D. J., & Leckman, J. F. (1999). Oxytocin, vasopressin, and autism: Is there a connection? *Biological Psychiatry, 45*, 145–157.

Kana, R. K., Keller, T. A., Cherkassky, V. L., Minshew, N. J., & Just, M. A. (2009). Atypical frontal-posterior synchronization of theory of mind regions in autism during mental state attribution. *Social Neuroscience, 4*, 135–152.

Kanner, L. (1943). Autistic disturbance of affective contact. *Nervous Child, 2*, 217–250.

Kelley, W. M., Macrae, C. N., Wyland, C. L., Caglar, S., Inati, S., & Heatherton, T. F. (2002). Finding the self? An event-related fMRI study. *Journal of Cognitive Neuroscience, 14*, 785–794.

Kennedy, D. P. & Courchesne, E. (2008a). Functional abnormalities of the default network during self- and other-reflection in autism. *Social Cognitive and Affective Neuroscience, 3*, 177–190.

Kennedy, D. P. & Courchesne, E. (2008b). The intrinsic functional organization of the brain is altered in autism. *Neuroimage, 39*, 1877–1885.

Kennedy, D. P., Redcay, E., & Courchesne, E. (2006). Failing to deactivate: Resting functional abnormalities in autism. *Proceedings of the National Academy of Sciences U S A, 103*, 8275–8280.

Keysers, C., Wicker, B., Gazzola, V., Anton, J. L., Fogassi, L., & Gallese, V. (2004). A touching sight: SII/PV activation during the observation and experience of touch. *Neuron, 42*, 335–346.

Klin, A. (2000). Attributing social meaning to ambiguous visual stimuli in higher-functioning autism and Asperger syndrome: The social attribution task. *Journal of Child Psychology and Psychiatry, 41*, 831–846.

Knafo, A., Zahn-Waxler, C., Van Hulle, C., Robinson, J. L., & Rhee, S. H. (2008). The developmental origins of a disposition toward empathy: Genetic and environmental contributions. *Emotion, 8*, 737–752.

Landis, S. & Insel, T. R. (2008). The "neuro" in neurogenetics. *Science, 322*, 821.

Lee, K. H. & Siegle, G. J. (2009). Common and distinct brain networks underlying explicit emotional evaluation: A meta-analytic study. *Social Cognitive and Affective Neuroscience, in press.* doi: 10.1093/scan/nsp001.

Leslie, A. M. & Thaiss, L. (1992). Domain specificity in conceptual development: Neuropsychological evidence from autism. *Cognition, 43*, 225–251.

Levitt, J. G., O'Neill, J., Blanton, R. E., Smalley, S., Fadale, D., McCracken, J. T., et al. (2003). Proton magnetic resonance spectroscopic imaging of the brain in childhood autism. *Biological Psychiatry, 54*, 1355–1366.

Lind, S. E. & Bowler, D. M. (2009). Delayed self-recognition in children with autism spectrum disorder. *Journal of Autism and Developmental Disorders, 39*, 643–650.

Loehlin, J. C. & Nichols, R. C. (1976). *Heredity, environment, and personality.* Austin, TX: University of Texas Press.

Lombardo, M. V., Barnes, J. L., Wheelwright, S. J., & Baron-Cohen, S. (2007). Self-referential cognition and empathy in autism. *PLoS One, 2*, e883.

Lombardo, M. V. & Baron-Cohen, S. (2010). Unraveling the paradox of the autistic self. *Wiley Interdisciplinary Reviews: Cognitive Science, 1*, 393–403.

Lombardo, M. V., Chakrabarti, B., Bullmore, E. T., Sadek, S. A., Wheelwright, S. J., Pasco, G., et al. (2010). Atypical neural self-representation in autism. *Brain, 133*, 611–624.

Lombardo, M. V., Chakrabarti, B., Bullmore, E. T., Wheelwright, S. J., Sadek, S. A., Suckling, J., et al. (2010). Shared neural circuits for mentalizing about the self and others. *Journal of Cognitive Neuroscience, 22*, 1623–1635.

Losh, M., Adolphs, R., Poe, M. D., Couture, S., Penn, D., Baranek, G. T., et al. (2009). Neuropsychological profile of autism and the broad autism phenotype. *Archives of General Psychiatry, 66*, 518–526.

Losh, M. & Piven, J. (2007). Social-cognition and the broad autism phenotype: identifying genetically meaningful phenotypes. *Journal of Child Psychology and Psychiatry, 48*, 105–112.

Makkonen, I., Riikonen, R., Kokki, H., Airaksinen, M. M., & Kuikka, J. T. (2008) Serotonin and dopamine transporter binding in children with autism determined by SPECT. *Developmental Medicine and Child Neurology, 50*, 593–597.

Matthews, K. A., Batson, C. D., Horn, J., & Rosenman, R. H. (1981). "Principles in his nature which interest him in the fortune of others.": The heritability of empathic concern for others. *Journal of Personality, 49*, 237–247.

McAlonan, G. M., Cheung, C., Cheung, V., Wong, N., Suckling, J., & Chua, S. E. (2009). Differential effects on white-matter systems in high-functioning autism and Asperger's syndrome. *Psychological Medicine, 9*, 1–9.

McAlonan, G. M., Cheung, V., Cheung, C., Suckling, J., Lam, G. Y., Tai, K. S., et al. (2005). Mapping the brain in autism. A voxel-based MRI study of volumetric differences and intercorrelations in autism. *Brain, 128*, 268–276.

Mehrabian, A. & Epstein, N. (1972). A measure of emotional empathy. *Journal of Personality, 40*, 525–543.

Meyer-Lindenberg, A., Kolachana, B., Gold, B., Olsh, A., Nicodemus, K. K., Mattay, V., et al. (2009). Genetic variants in AVPR1A linked to autism predict amygdala activation and personality traits in healthy humans. *Molecular Psychiatry, 14*, 968–975.

Meyer-Lindenberg, A. & Weinberger, D. R. (2006). Intermediate phenotypes and genetic mechanisms of psychiatric disorders. *Nature Reviews Neuroscience, 7*, 818–827.

Mitchell, J. P., Macrae, C. N., & Banaji, M. R. (2006). Dissociable medial prefrontal contributions to judgments of similar and dissimilar others. *Neuron, 50*, 655–663.

Mitchell, P. & O'Keefe, K. (2008). Brief report: Do individuals with autism spectrum disorder think they know their own minds? *Journal of Autism and Developmental Disorders, 38*, 1591–1597.

Moran, J. M., Macrae, C. N., Heatherton, T. F., Wyland, C. L., & Kelley, W. M. (2006). Neuroanatomical evidence for distinct cognitive and affective components of self. *Journal of Cognitive Neuroscience, 18*, 1586–1594.

Mottron, L., Dawson, M., Soulières, I., Hubert, B., & Burack, J. (2006). Enhanced perceptual functioning in autism: An update, and eight principles of autistic perception. *Journal of Autism and Developmental Disorders, 36*, 27–43.

Murphy, D. G., Daly, E., Schmitz, N., Toal, F., Murphy, K., Curran, S., et al. (2006). Cortical serotonin 5-HT2A receptor binding and social communication in adults with Asperger's syndrome: an in vivo SPECT study. *American Journal of Psychiatry, 163*, 934–936.

Ochsner, K. N., Beer, J. S., Robertson, E. R., Cooper, J. C., Gabrieli, J. D., Kihlstrom, J. F., et al. (2005). The neural correlates of direct and reflected self-knowledge. *Neuroimage, 28*, 797–814.

Panksepp, J. (1998). *Affective neuroscience: The foundations of human and animal emotions.* New York: Oxford University Press.

Panksepp, J., Nelson, E., & Bekkedal, M. (1997). Brain systems for the mediation of social separation-distress and social-reward. Evolutionary antecedents and neuropeptide intermediaries. *Annals of the New York Academy of Sciences, 807*, 78–100.

Pardini, M., Garaci, F. G., Bonzano, L., Roccatagliata, L., Palmieri, M. G., Pompili, E., et al. (2009). White matter reduced streamline coherence in young men with autism and mental retardation. *European Journal of Neurology, 16*, 1185–1190.

Perner, J., Frith, U., Leslie, A. M., & Leekam, S. R. (1989). Exploration of the autistic child's theory of mind: Knowledge, belief, and communication. *Child Development, 60*, 688–700.

Pfeifer, J. H., Iacoboni, M., Mazziotta, J. C., & Dapretto, M. (2008). Mirroring others' emotions relates to empathy and interpersonal competence in children. *Neuroimage, 39*, 2076–2085.

Premack, D. & Woodruff, G. (1978). Does the chimpanzee have a theory of mind? *Behavioral and Brain Sciences, 1*, 515–526.

Preston, S. D. & de Waal, F. B. M. (2002). Empathy: Its ultimate and proximate bases. *Behavioral and Brain Sciences, 25*, 1–72.

Pugliese, L., Catani, M., Ameis, S., Dell'acqua, F., de Schotten, M. T., Murphy, C., et al. (2009). The anatomy of extended limbic pathways in Asperger syndrome: A preliminary diffusion tensor imaging tractography study. *Neuroimage, 47*, 427–434.

Rogers, S. J. & Pennington, B. F. (1991). A theoretical approach to deficits in infantile autism. *Development and Psychopathology, 3*, 137–162.

Ronald, A., Happé, F., Bolton, P., Butcher, L. M., Price, T. S., Wheelwright, S., et al. (2006). Genetic heterogeneity between the three components of the autism spectrum: A twin study. *Journal of the American Academy of Child and Adolescent Psychiatry, 45*, 691–699.

Rushton, J. P., Fulker, D. W., Neale, M. C., Nias, D. K., & Eysenck, H. J. (1986). Altruism and aggression: The heritability of individual differences. *Journal of Personality and Social Psychology, 50*, 1192–1198.

Saxe, R. & Powell, L. J. (2006). It's the thought that counts: Specific brain regions for one component of theory of mind. *Psychological Science, 17*, 692–699.

Senju, A., Southgate, V., White, S., & Frith, U. (2009). Mindblind eyes: An absence of spontaneous theory of mind in Asperger Syndrome. *Science, 325,* 883–885.

Schultz, R. T. (2005). Developmental deficits in social perception in autism: The role of the amygdala and fusiform face area. *International Journal of Developmental Neuroscience, 23,* 125–141.

Silani, G., Bird, G., Brindley, R., Singer, T., Frith, C., & Frith, U. (2008). Levels of emotional awareness and autism: An fMRI study. *Social Neuroscience, 3,* 97–110.

Singer, T., Seymour, B., O'Doherty, J., Kaube, H., Dolan, R. J., & Frith, C. D. (2004). Empathy for pain involves the affective but not sensory components of pain. *Science, 303,* 1157–1162.

Southgate, V., Senju, A., & Csibra, G. (2007). Action anticipation through attribution of false belief by 2-year olds. *Psychological Science, 18,* 587–592.

Szatmari, P., Georgiades, S., Duku, E., Zwaigenbaum, L., Goldberg, J., & Bennett, T. (2008). Alexithymia in parents of children with autism spectrum disorder. *Journal of Autism and Developmental Disorders, 38,* 1859–1865.

Toichi, M., Kamio, Y., Okada, T., Sakihama, M., Youngstrom, E. A., Findling, R. L., et al. (2002). A lack of self-consciousness in autism. *American Journal of Psychiatry, 159,* 1422–1424.

Uddin, L. Q., Davies, M. S., Scott, A. A., Zaidel, E., Bookheimer, S. Y., Iacoboni, M., et al. (2008). Neural basis of self and other representation in autism: An fMRI study of self-face recognition. *PLoS One, 3,* e3526.

Volkmar, F. R., Lord, C., Bailey, A., Schultz, R. T., & Klin, A. (2004). Autism and pervasive developmental disorders. *Journal of Child Psychology and Psychiatry, 45,* 135–170.

Wager, T. D., Barrett, L. F., Bliss-Moreau, E., Lindquist, K., Duncan, S., Kober, H., et al. (2008). The neuroimaging of emotion. In M. Lewis (Ed.), *Handbook of emotion.*

Waiter, G. D., Williams, J. H., Murray, A. D., Gilchrist, A., Perrett, D. I., & Whiten, A. (2004). A voxel-based investigation of brain structure in male adolescents with autistic spectrum disorder. *Neuroimage, 22,* 619–625.

Wang, A. T., Lee, S. S., Sigman, M., & Dapretto, M. (2006). Neural basis of irony comprehension in children with autism: The role of prosody and context. *Brain, 129,* 932–943.

Wang, A. T., Lee, S. S., Sigman, M., & Dapretto, M. (2007). Reading affect in the face and voice: Neural correlates of interpreting communicative intent in children and adolescents with autism spectrum disorders. *Archives of General Psychiatry, 64,* 698–708.

Wicker, B., Keysers, C., Plailly, J., Royet, J. P., Gallese, V., & Rizzolatti, G. (2003). Both of us disgusted in My insula: The common neural basis of seeing and feeling disgust. *Neuron, 40,* 655–664.

Williams, D. M., & Happé, F. (2009). What did I say? Versus what did I think? Attributing false beliefs to self amongst children with and without autism. *Journal of Autism and Developmental Disorders, 39,* 865–873.

Wimmer, H. & Perner, J. (1983). Beliefs about beliefs: Representation and constraining function of wrong beliefs in young children's understanding of deception. *Cognition, 13,* 103–128.

Winslow, J. T. & Insel, T. R. (2004). Neuroendocrine basis of social recognition. *Current Opinion in Neurobiology, 14,* 248–253.

Wu, S., Jia, M., Ruan, Y., Liu, J., Guo, Y., Shuang, M., et al. (2005). Positive association of the oxytocin receptor gene (*OXTR*) with autism in the Chinese Han population. *Biological Psychiatry, 58,* 74–77.

Zilbovicius, M., Garreau, B., Samson, Y., Remy, P., Barthelemy, C., Syrota, A., et al. (1995). Delayed maturation of the frontal cortex in childhood autism. *American Journal of Psychiatry, 152,* 248–252.

Zahn-Waxler, C., Radke-Yarrow, M., Wagner, E., & Chapman, M. (1992). The development of concern for others. *Developmental Psychology, 28,* 126–136.

Developmental Disorders

Yoko Kamio, Shozo Tobimatsu, *and* Hiroki Fukui

Abstract

This chapter examines the phenomenal diversity in developmental disorders and reconsiders it from a developmental perspective on neuro-cognitive-behavioral dimensions. It focuses on autism spectrum disorder (ASD), attention-deficit/hyperactivity disorder (ADHD), developmental language disorder (DLD), and learning disabilities (LD). First, it attempts to provide a picture of atypical development beginning before diagnosis, based on the fragmented evidence obtained from ongoing research. Second, it introduces the concept of "spectrum," a concept that is key to interpreting complex phenomena that manifest across developmental disorders. Third, it describes developmental trajectories observed in individuals with developmental disorders. Finally, the chapter documents a developmental model of ASD that explains the range of phenomena seen, including weaknesses (impairments) as well as strengths (enhanced skills), from the neuro-cognitive-behavioral perspective. In this framework, social neuroscience will contribute most to untangling the complexities and diversities of social cognition, and to uncovering how social cognition comes to function and how it can be compensated for when it fails to develop in a typical way.

Keywords: developmental disorders, taxonomic categories, prototypical conditions, developmental convergence, developmental divergence, parvocellular pathway (P-pathway), magnocellular pathway (M-pathway), autism spectrum disorder (ASD), attention-deficit/hyperactivity disorder (ADHD), developmental language disorder (DLD), learning disabilities (LD), specific language impairment (SLI), multidimensional developmental model, social impairments

Introduction

In this chapter, we focus on the phenomenal diversity in developmental disorders, and reconsider it from a developmental perspective on neuro-cognitive-behavioral dimensions. Developmental disorders have heterogeneous manifestations, and their causes range from ones with identified genotype, to ones with postnatal exogenous etiology or unknown etiology. They share, however, some common features in neuro-cognitive-behavioral manifestations.

Here, we use the term "developmental disorders" in a narrow sense, referring to disorders of brain function affecting the higher-order functions of emotion, learning, memory, or social cognition without impairment of physical development. Higher-order functions progressively mature and are acquired by learning over periods longer than those required for lower-order functions. The function of social cognition is, therefore, more vulnerable to atypical events during development, and as a consequence, various dysfunctions of social cognition can occur as the final common pathway in developmental disorders. Thus, some aspects of social cognition impairment but not others might be shared by different developmental disorders.

Among the various developmental disorders, we focus our discussion here on autism spectrum disorder (ASD), attention-deficit/hyperactivity disorder (ADHD), developmental language disorder (DLD), and learning disabilities (LD). First, we attempt to provide a picture of atypical development beginning before diagnosis, based on the fragmented evidence obtained from ongoing research. Second, we introduce the concept of "spectrum," a concept that is key to interpreting complex phenomena that manifest across developmental disorders. Third, we describe developmental trajectories observed in individuals with developmental disorders, and finally, we document a developmental model of ASD that explains the range of phenomena seen, including weaknesses (impairments) as well as strengths (enhanced skills), from the neuro-cognitive-behavioral perspective. In this framework, social neuroscience will contribute most to untangling the complexities and diversities of social cognition, and to uncovering how social cognition comes to function and how it can be compensated for when it fails to develop in a typical way.

Developmental Origin of Social Impairments

Social impairments are observed in common across ASD, ADHD, DLD, and LD, although the nature and degree is varied. ASD represents developmental disorders characterized by social and communication impairments and repetitive/stereotyped behaviors. The standard diagnostic criteria of ASD, such as that provided by the Diagnostic and Statistical Manual of Mental Disorders, Fourth edition, Text Revision (DSM-IV-TR) (American Psychiatric Association, 2000), are based on clinical observations of children aged 3 to 4 years and older, and as such they cannot be applied to children under 3 years of age. However, a growing body of literature indicates that children with ASD can be reliably diagnosed as young as age 2 on the basis of various social abnormalities (Johnson, Myers, & the Council on Children with Disabilities, 2007; Landa, 2008). Although evidence of neural abnormalities suggests a prenatal origin for ASD (Kemper & Bauman, 1993; Palmen, van Engeland, Hof, & Schmitz, 2004), the social abnormalities can be observed only postnatally. Further, the symptoms of ADHD, DLD, and LD usually do not become clinically significant until school age.

One way to understand the complex social behavior of human beings is to trace its origin back to infancy. Closer inspection of young children with typical development tells us how they learn social behaviors, and examinations of atypically developing children provide us with insights into the developmental trajectory to later complex social behaviors. By this reasoning, identifying the earliest abnormalities in children who will demonstrate social impairments several years later is of particular interest from both a theoretical and a clinical viewpoint.

Developmental Origin on the Behavioral Dimension

Parents of children with ASD often report that they became aware of developmental abnormalities during their child's second year (Chakrabarti & Fombonne, 2005). Parental concerns range widely from reduced social responsivity, through language delay or loss, stereotyped movement, manipulation of objects in a stereotyped way, temper tantrums, restlessness, sleep problems, and eating problems, to sensory abnormalities (Chawarska et al., 2007). For a third of children with ASD, parents recognize reduced social responsivity or motor delay as early as the first year of life (De Giacomo & Fombonne, 1998). Home video analyses have also demonstrated the possibility that infants who subsequently develop ASD can be detected at around the age of 12 months by their reduced social behaviors (Baranek, 1999; Osterling, Dawson, & Munson, 2002), or even before the age of 6 months by reduced social attention (Maestro et al., 2005) or abnormal movement/reflex (Teitelbaum et al., 2004).

There is a more persuasive way to uncover the developmental origin of social impairments, considering the high heritability of autism, which is higher than 90%. A prospective study of high-risk siblings of children with ASD found a wide range of abnormalities in attention, affective, or sensory/motor development in 6 to 12 months infants who were later diagnosed with ASD (Bryson et al., 2007; Zwaigenbaum et al., 2005). Taken together, it appears that developmental abnormalities that are not specific to the social domain are predominant in 6- to 12-month-old infants with ASD, while from age 1 year on, socio-communication abnormalities start to manifest overtly. However, even in the second year of life, social impairments do not necessarily readily manifest in all children later diagnosed with ASD. There also seem to be different developmental trajectories during the first two years in children with this disorder, which can be characterized by developmental slowing, arrest, or regression in the socio-communication domain (Bryson et al., 2007; Landa, Holman, & Garrett-Mayer, 2007).

Developmental Origin on the Neurocognitive Dimension

In the literature on typical development, infants from birth to 2 months of age visually orient to stimuli driven by a reflexive system under subcortical influence. Then, between 3 and 6 months of age, they become able to orient voluntarily to their surroundings, as the neural network involving parietal/temporal cortices matures. From 6 months on, an anterior executive attention system, which includes the prefrontal and anterior cingulate cortices, becomes functional. Thus, between 6 to 12 months of age, joint attention behavior gradually manifests, enabling the infant to start sharing attention to object or event between him or herself and another person (Mundy & Neal, 2001). This cognitive process seems to be coincident with neural development in the typical brain, in which initial growth and subsequent regression by neuronal loss or synaptic pruning occur, leading to the organization of functional networks that underlie higher-order cognitive, social, emotional, and language functions.

In ASD, by contrast, during the first year of life when the behavioral origin is not yet overtly manifested, the underlying cognitive process, whether it is social or nonsocial—already seems atypical. Studies of brain volume suggest that abnormal brain overgrowth occurs within this period in ASD children (Courchesne, Carper, & Akshoomoff, 2003; Dawson et al., 2007; Fukumoto et al., 2008). These developmental abnormalities may result in a subsequent failure to develop highly integrative functioning, especially with regard to social cognition, and instead enhance a compensatory mechanism involving locally distributed nonsocial information processing (Müller, 2007). Thus, not only impairments (weaknesses) but also enhanced skills (strengths) in ASD can be explained by such an atypical but experience-dependent developmental process. It is for this reason that early intervention which targets these early manifestations can alter the developmental course (Pandey, Wilson, Verbalis, & Fein, 2008; Zwaigenbaum et al., 2009).

The Concept of "Spectrum": A Reconsideration of Developmental Disorders

The concept of spectrum, along which the number and intensity of behavioral features change, derives from an epidemiological study by Wing and Gould (1979). Wing found that the severity of symptoms such as impairments of social reciprocal interaction, communication, and restricted interests/repetitive behaviors (referred to as the triad) varied continuously in the target population from the severe form of classic autism to the mild form. Within the autistic spectrum, some children fit the clinical picture of the severest form of classic autism, while others fit into that of Asperger syndrome, which is characterized by high verbal abilities (Wing, 1988). More importantly, Wing addressed the fact that there are many intermediate forms in children who were not classified into any named syndromes (Wing, 1988). The discovery of this spectrum provided new insights into the autistic syndrome, and researchers have subsequently started to explore what underlies its diversity as well as what is specific to it.

The concept of the spectrum has thus been broadened. According to recent epidemiological studies, the prevalence rate of ASD has increased, particularly the proportion of "high-functioning" individuals with IQ > 70 to total ASD (Fombonne, 2003). Many of the high-functioning subgroup do not show the full set of autistic triad impairments and are perhaps near the end of the spectrum. In cases where impairments of communication, or restricted interests/repetitive behaviors are mild or absent, DSM-IV-TR (American Psychiatric Association, 2000) assigns such conditions to the miscellaneous subcategory of Pervasive Developmental Disorder Not Otherwise Specified (PDD-NOS) (Towbin, 2005).

Overlapping features exist between the ASD subcategories of autism, Asperger syndrome, and PDD-NOS in terms of symptoms (Allen et al., 2001; Prior et al., 1998; Walker et al., 2004), cognitive abilities (Kamio & Toichi, 2007; Koyama & Kurita, 2008), and brain morphology (Dager et al., 2007; Hallahan et al., 2009). Furthermore, PDD-NOS is intermediate between autism and the nonautistic group on the behavioral or cognitive dimension (Towbin, 2005). The evidence to date favors an autistic spectrum on which behavioral and cognitive impairments vary continuously, but it remains unclear how the underlying neurobiological structure and function are different or continuous among the various conditions on the spectrum.

As mentioned above, the early developmental course in children later diagnosed with ASD is diverse. This raises a question: Is the boundary of the clinical entity of ASD following a definite diagnosis around at age 3 tangible? In other words, are there any distinct features of ASD differentiating it from other developmental disorders on a behavioral, cognitive, or neurological dimension?

Blurred Boundaries: ASD and Other Disorders

Co-occurrence of ASD and ADHD, DLD, or other LDs in an individual has been reported in clinical work, and some evidence has emerged to support that this co-occurrence is not just by chance. Although typical cases of specific disorders described in a textbook can be easily differentiated, the actual boundaries between the developmental disorders are by no means clear, and social, language, motor, attention, or cognitive difficulties are common to the different disorders.

Delayed speech and various forms of language abnormalities constitute the second part of the triad of autistic features, and are striking when children also have intellectual disabilities. On the other hand, children with DLD have a clinically significant language deficit irrespective of their normal IQ. Thus, autism and DLD (also known as specific language impairment (SLI)) are traditionally regarded as distinct and exclusive disorders. On closer examination, however, it was found that more than just a few children with high-functioning ASD (HFASD) have linguistic difficulties similar to DLD (Bishop et al., 2004; Kamio, Robins, Kelly, Swainson, & Fein, 2007; Kjelgaard & Tager-Flusberg, 2001; Rapin et al., 1996), and many children are intermediate between ASD and DLD/SLI; they have subthreshold autistic symptoms and pragmatic language difficulties (Bishop & Norbury, 2002). This provides evidence of a continuum from ASD, through pragmatic language impairment, to the classic language impairment. Although it is not at present clear why ASD and DLD appear to be continuous on a socio-communication domain, etiological explanations are being sought (Bishop, 2006).

ADHD is a neurodevelopmental disorder with symptoms of hyperactivity, impulsivity, and inattention, with an early origin. Although typical cases of ADHD and ASD are defined as mutually exclusive in DSM-IV-TR, clinical studies have reported high rates of co-occurrence in clinical populations (de Bruin, Ferdinand, Meester, de Nijs, & Verheij, 2007; Hattori et al., 2006; Leyfer et al., 2006;

Mulligan et al., 2009). In comorbid cases, cognitive features as well as behavioral ones of both ADHD and ASD overlap each other: While the cognitive profile differs for each condition (Koyama, Tachimori, Osada, & Kurita, 2006), it is intermediate between them in comorbid cases (Scheirs & Timmers, 2009). According to Kinsbourne (1991), the attentional features should be considered as a core deficit of ASD and not just a co-occurring ADHD symptom. He also postulated a clinical syndrome that includes elements of both ADHD and PDD-NOS ("an overfocused child"), marked by a narrow focus of attention and social withdrawal. Deficit in attention, motor control, and perception (DAMP) syndrome is a clinical entity conventionally used in Scandinavia, and the condition includes elements of ADHD and developmental coordination disorder (DCD) (Gillberg, 2003). Epidemiological examinations demonstrated that children with DAMP frequently had autistic features, learning problems, linguistic difficulties, and tic disorders (Gillberg, 2003). There is also new evidence from family study data indicating that the co-occurrence of ADHD and ASD symptoms is due to shared familial risk factors (Mulligan et al., 2009; Ronald, Simonoff, Kuntsi, Asherson, & Plomin, 2008). Taking these findings together, ADHD and ASD might be considered to lie on a spectrum from typical ADHD, to ADHD with ASD symptoms, to ASD.

Nonverbal learning disability (NVLD), a subtype of learning difficulties, is marked by impairments in visuospatial and nonverbal problem-solving skills, reduced speech prosody, and psychomotor difficulties (Rourke et al., 2002). It is reported that the cognitive features characteristic of NVLD are observed in Asperger syndrome, the mildest form of ASD (Klin, Volkmar, Sparrow, Cicchetti, & Rourke, 1995). Furthermore, features of NVLD also manifest in acquired brain abnormalities (Erickson, Baron, & Fantie, 2001) as well as genetic syndromes (Simon, 2007). The fact that such features are not specific to particular disorders suggests that the clinical picture of NVLD might be, in part, explained as the developmental consequences of some unspecified neurodevelopmental abnormalities (Rourke et al., 2002).

In parallel with the behavioral similarities observed in ASD, DLD, and ADHD, substantial similarities in brain anatomy and metabolism (Brieber et al., 2007; Herbert & Kenet, 2007) as well as disorder-specific abnormalities (Brieber et al., 2007; Whitehouse & Bishop, 2008) have been reported by comparing age- and IQ-matched children.

Taxonomic Categories Revisited

Contrary to traditional definition, the taxonomic categories of developmental disorders can be seen to partly overlap each other and appear to constitute a spectrum on the behavioral and cognitive dimensions. Besides prototypal conditions, there are subthreshold conditions that also require treatment and call for theoretical understanding. When multiple subthreshold conditions co-occur, the clinical picture is ambiguous and the therapeutic need also varies accordingly.

The coming DSM-5, which is currently under consideration, will likely encompass dimensional measures in addition to the taxonomic categories (Helzer, Kraemer, Krueger, Wittchen, & Sirovatka, 2008). The inclusion of dimensional measures based on the concept of spectrum would not only highlight the irrelevance of taxonomic classification in relation to development disorders, but also enhance the clinical validity of developmental disorders as well as psychiatric disorders.

In order to define developmental pathology and find clues to treatment, the relations among neurocognitive-behavioral dimensions should be uncovered. To this end, a bottom-up approach starting from strictly defined cognitive phenotypes (Bishop, 2006; Dawson et al., 2002) appears to have advantages over a top-down approach starting from the taxonomic categories.

Diversity of Developmental Trajectories

Let us now address the following question: Within an individual, do diagnostic features of a developmental disorder remain stable and distinguishable on the behavioral, cognitive, or neurological dimension during the developmental course?

Developmental Convergence from Various Taxonomic Conditions

According to longitudinal studies, the language and social functioning of some individuals diagnosed as having either SLI or autism as children became closer to each other in adolescence or young adulthood. Many of the significant differences found between the two groups were quantitative rather than qualitative (Howlin, Mawhood, & Rutter, 2000; Mawhood, Howlin, & Rutter, 2000). Further follow-up in the mid-30s revealed that the majority of individuals with SLI were impaired in social functioning with a theory of mind deficit rather than a deficit of language itself (Clegg, Hollis, Mawhood, & Rutter, 2005). Thus, some features in the socio-communication domain became less

distinct with age, although they appeared to be disorder-specific when young.

On the other hand, nonsocial or domain-general neurocognitive features such as executive functioning deficits in ADHD and ASD (Bramham et al., 2009; Happé, Booth, Charlton, & Hughes, 2006) or attentional problems in ASD (Landry & Bryson, 2004; Townsend et al., 1996) have been consistently reported for different age groups, although they are not diagnostic features for these disorders. Thus, it might be that some nondiagnostic features do remain distinguishable and follow a developmental trajectory specific to the disorder from childhood into adulthood, while diagnostic features when young do not necessarily remain stable during the developmental course.

Developmental Divergence from a Childhood Disorder

Although the behavioral manifestations of SLI may change beyond the linguistic domain during the developmental course (Bishop & Norbury, 2002; Clegg, Hollis, Mawhood, & Rutter, 2005), twin data suggest that the condition is genetically distinct from other developmental disorders (Bishop, 1994). Rutter, Kim-Cohen, and Maughan (2006) questioned the starting concept that SLI is a "pure" language disorder, and instead postulated that the disorder remains the same but only its behavioral manifestations alter (referred to as "heterotypic continuity"). Cases showing a taxonomic transition from one disorder to another have been reported: some evolved from typical ASD into clear-cut ADHD (Fein, Dixon, Paul, & Levin, 2005), or into ADHD and Tourette syndrome (Zappella, 2002), and others from ADHD into ASD (Kawatani, Nakai, Mayumi, & Hiratani, 2009). When considering a spectrum on which both ADHD and ASD lie, these cases might be explained by heterotypic continuity.

As for ADHD, there is great individual variation in the adult outcome. In particular, antisocial psychopathology frequently co-occurs in both children and adults with ADHD, and confers serious impact on their social functioning. Such developmental progression follows from ADHD, through oppositional defiant disorder (ODD) and conduct disorder (CD) in childhood, to antisocial personality disorder in adulthood. Longitudinal studies have found that the progression is not related to ADHD itself, but to the concurrent ODD or CD in childhood (Biederman et al., 2008; Satterfield et al., 2007). Data from a family study (Mulligan et al.,

2009) and a cohort study (Caspi et al., 2008) suggest that there is a genetic liability for increased risk of co-occurrence with antisocial behavior. This genetic liability is suggested not only for the co-occurrence of ADHD symptoms and antisocial behavior, but also for the co-occurrence of ADHD and autistic symptoms. There might, therefore, be a partial association between antisocial behavior and autistic symptoms, although such a suggestion remains controversial.

It is known that a small group of adolescents or adults with HFASD, especially those with Asperger syndrome, conduct violent crime. However, there are few empirical data supporting the notion that an underlying cognitive profile for committing such antisocial acts is related to the cognitive features specific to ASD, and psychopathy, when defined as a deficit in social interaction and empathy, is found to be independent of autistic cognitive deficit such as mind-reading or executive function (Anckarsäter, 2005; Rogers, Viding, Blair, Frith, & Happé, 2006). Rather, it is suggested that the association can be mediated by a third factor—concurrent psychiatric disorders (Newman & Ghaziuddin, 2008) in addition to environmental factors such as a disorganized home environment and existence of physical abuse/neglect (Mukaddes & Topcu, 2006). Thus, the diversity of adult outcome may be partly explained by concurrent psychiatric or developmental disorders in ASD, which are common and frequently multiple (Leyfer et al., 2006; Simonoff et al., 2008).

Interaction between genetic and environmental factors also plays a role in the diversity of long-term outcome in ASD and involves an optimal developmental trajectory. An early detection study reported that a subgroup of children diagnosed with ASD at around 2 years of age grew out of the diagnosis at 4 years of age (Sutera et al., 2007). It is not clear why this happened in some children and not others, and the predictive factors have not yet to be identified (Sutera et al., 2007), but early intervention is probably one factor that would make a difference (Landa, 2008).

Multidimensional Model from a Developmental Perspective

According to Morton and Frith (1995), a developmental disorder should be described in terms of a causal chain. In such a model, an explanation of a disorder should start with biological factors, then specify the cognitive consequences and finally describe the behavioral manifestations. From a developmental perspective, various manifestations of developmental disorders should be explained as the downstream consequences resulting from an upstream impairment. The developmental trajectory from an upstream impairment to the downstream consequences is not simple, since it is modified by a complex gene-environmental interaction. A closer inspection of the manifestations of developmental disorders reveals that there are weaknesses and strengths; some are disorder-specific traits found across the lifespan and others are age- or experience-dependent. A good example of an epiphenomenon of atypical development involves the visual system; behavioral, cognitive, and electrophysiological studies are now producing growing evidence of deficits as well as strengths in the early processing of the visual system in developmental disorders.

Visual information is processed via two pathways: the dorsal and the ventral pathways. The dorsal pathway is dominated by input from the magnocellular lateral geniculate nucleus (LGN) and projects from V1 to (V2 to V3 to) middle temporal (MT), to medial superior temporal (MST) area. The ventral pathway, which has input from the parvocellular LGN, projects from V1 to V2, to (V3 to) V4, to inferior temporal (IT) area. Similar impairments in the dorsal pathway are observed across developmental disorders such as dyslexia, fragile X syndrome, and Williams syndrome (Braddick, Atkinson, & Wattam-Bell, 2003). This may be explained by the fact that the dorsal pathway function develops later than the ventral pathway function, and therefore the dorsal pathway is a system with progressively more complex processing and which is more susceptible to atypical experience during development (Braddick, Atkinson, & Wattam-Bell, 2003).

Individuals with ASD show superior performance in processing fine details (Happé, 1996; Happé & Frith, 2006; Ishida, Kamio, & Nakamizo, 2009; Jolliffe & Baron-Cohen, 1997), while even those with high IQ are poor at processing global structure and motion perception (Bertone, Mottron, Jelenic, & Faubert, 2003; Milne et al., 2002; Spencer et al., 2000). These features of low-level perception are considered to contribute to higher-level impairments of social cognition in ASD (Dakin & Frith, 2005; Mottron & Burack, 2001). Fine form perception is mainly processed in the parvocellular pathway (P-pathway) and spatial localization is processed in the magnocellular pathway (M-pathway). Given this background, we hypothesized that the atypical visual findings seen in ASD might derive from abnormalities at lower-level processing in the P- and

M-pathways on a basis of parallel visual information processing (Livingstone & Hubel, 1988; Tobimatsu & Celesia, 2006).

To test this hypothesis, we assessed visual evoked potentials (VEPs) at the Oz electrode by using preferential stimuli for the P- and M-pathways (Fujita, Yamasaki, Kamio, Hirose, & Tobimatsu, 2011). Twelve adults with HFASD (8 males, aged 17–38 years) and 12 control adults (7 males, aged 19–36 years) participated in this study. None of the participants had problems with color vision or visual acuity. Using chromatic sinusoidal gratings as P-stimulus and black-white gratings as M-stimulus, VEPs were recorded during a flickering stimulus presentation. It was found that the mean latency of a negative ERP occurring approximately 100 msec in the HFASD group in response to P-stimulus was significantly longer than that of the control group, while there was no difference in the response to M-stimulus between the two groups. These results suggest that adults with HFASD have lower-level (before or within V1) impairment of the P-pathway with a preserved lower-level M-pathway function in the visual stream.

The human P-pathway consists of two streams: the parvocellular-blob (P-B) and the parvocellular-interblob (P-I) stream at V1. The P-B stream is important for analyzing color information, and the P-I stream is responsible for processing fine form information (Tobimatsu & Celesia, 2006). Since we used a chromatic stimulus targeting the P-B stream, our results suggest dysfunction of the P-B stream but not the P-I stream. This finding is supported by a recent study reporting abnormalities of color perception (color memory, color search, chromatic discrimination) in children with autism (Franklin, Sowden, Burley, Notman, & Alder, 2008; Franklin et al., 2010). The P-B stream anatomically interacts with the P-I stream, and the P-B dysfunction could partially affect the P-I function through some compensatory mechanism in ASD, although the P-I function was not assessed in our study. Strength in fine form perception in ASD (Dakin & Frith, 2005) suggests heightened functioning of the P-I stream that is responsible for fine form perception (Tobimatsu & Celesia, 2006). The lack of evidence of dysfunction at the lower-level M-pathway is consistent with earlier psychological studies suggesting abnormal function of the higher-level M-pathway with intact function of the lower-level M-pathway within the higher-level visual area in ASD (Pellicano, Gibson, Maybery, Durkin, & Badcock, 2005; Pellicano & Gibson, 2008).

The reported perceptual abnormalities in ASD could be upstream impairments or downstream impairments during development. In order to determine which they are, systematic longitudinal studies are necessary. Assuming early atypical brain development in ASD (Courschesne, Carper, & Akshoomoff, 2003; Dawson et al., 2007; Fukumoto et al., 2008), these ill-timed maturational events might result in insufficiently organized frontal-posterior reciprocal interaction (Geschwind & Levitt, 2007; Müller, 2007). Such insufficient circuitry will affect higher-order processing as well as lower-order processing, since altered higher processing integrates information from different systems and sends feedback to lower-level systems.

Summary and Future Directions

Over the past several decades, extensive studies using various genetic, neurobiological, cognitive, and behavioral approaches have sought a single explanation for the heterogeneous manifestations of developmental disorders. However, research efforts were often hampered as the starting point was operationally defined behavioral features and did not correspond to the etiology. For example, it is a misleading assumption that ASD is a disorder in which only the social domain is impaired and the other domains are intact. Indeed, over time, it has become clear that there is a great diversity of clinical manifestations across and within individuals, and researchers have started seeking the reason why the manifestations of developmental disorders are so diverse (Happé, Ronald, & Plomin, 2006).

By introducing the concept of the spectrum, we have gained a clue to disentangling the seemingly complex and irregular phenomena involved—such progress cannot be successfully made only with a top-down approach starting from the operationally defined behavioral features. A bottom-up approach based on evidence from social neuroscience would contribute to uncovering what varies on the spectrum dimensionally from the neuro-cognitive-behavioral perspective, and how social cognition is associated with the other functions on the spectrum. Developmental perspectives are also required to disentangle the complex phenomena that make up, for example, social impairments; we should aim to find out what is age-dependent and what is age-independent. Exploring the earliest developmental origin of higher-order dysfunction which includes social impairments, as well as gaining a deeper knowledge of the developmental trajectories will help us to develop therapeutic intervention strategies along the life course as social policy.

We presented here our model based on neuro-cognitive-behavioral findings using a bottom-up approach. To test the clinical validity of our hypothesis on developmental disorders, the establishment of a prospective database on neuro-cognitive-behavioral dimensions is necessary. Research on these dimensions combined with longitudinal and multidimensional approaches will expand the horizon in the field of developmental disorders to reveal the underlying mechanisms of developmental diversity leading to various social impairments and to help design optimal prevention and intervention.

Acknowledgments

This work was supported by a grant from JST, RISTEX. The authors thank Professor Deborah Fein and Dr. Kiyotaka Segami for their kind efforts in helping the development of this manuscript.

References

Allen, D. A., Steinberg, M., Dunn, M., Fein, D., Feinstein, C., Waterhouse, L., et al. (2001). Autistic disorder versus other pervasive developmental disorders in young children: Same or different? *European Child and Adolescent Psychiatry, 10*, 67–78.

American Psychiatric Association. (2000). *Diagnostic and statistical manual of mental disorders*. 4th ed., Text Rev. (DSM-IV-TR). Washington, DC, American Psychiatric Publishing, Inc.

Anckarsäter, S. H. (2005). Clinical neuropsychiatric symptoms in perpetrators of severe crimes against persons. *Nordic Journal of Psychiatry, 59*, 246–252.

Baranek, G. T. (1999). Autism during infancy: A retrospective video analysis of sensory-motor and social behaviors at 9–12 months of age. *Journal of Autism and Developmental Disorders, 29*, 213–224.

Bertone, A., Mottron, L., Jelenic, P., & Faubert, J. (2003). Motion perception in autism: A "complex" issue. *Journal of Cognitive Neuroscience, 15*, 218–225.

Biederman, J., Petty, C. R., Dolan, C., Hughes, S., Mick, E., Monuteaux, M. C., et al. (2008). The long-term longitudinal course of oppositional defiant disorder and conduct disorder in ADHD boys: Findings from a controlled 10-year prospective longitudinal follow-up study. *Psychological Medicine, 38*, 1027–1036.

Bishop, D. V. (1994). Is specific language impairment a valid diagnostic category? Genetic and psycholinguistic evidence. *Philosophical Transactions of the Royal Society of London. series B: Biological Sciences, 346*, 105–111.

Bishop, D. V. M. (2006). Developmental cognitive genetics: How psychology can inform genetics and vice versa. *The Quarterly Journal of Experimental Psychology, 59*, 1153–1168.

Bishop, D. V. M., Maybery, M., Wong, D., Maley, A., Hill, W., & Hallmayer, J. (2004). Are phonological processing deficits part of the broad autism phenotype? *American Journal of Medical Genetics: (Neuropsychiatric Genetics), 128B*, 54–60.

Bishop, D. V. M. & Norbury, C. F. (2002). Exploring the borderlands of autistic disorder and specific language impairment: A study using standardized diagnostic instruments. *Journal of Child Psychology and Psychiatry and Allied Disciplines, 43*, 917–929.

Braddick, O., Atkinson, J., & Wattam-Bell, J. (2003). Normal and anomalous development of visual motion processing: motion coherence and "dorsal-stream vulnerability." Neuropsychologia, *41*, 1769–1784.

Bramham, J., Amberey, F., Young, S., Morris, R., Russell, A., Xenitidis, K., et al. (2009). Executive functioning differences between adults with attention deficit hyperactivity disorder and autistic spectrum disorder in initiation, planning and strategy formation. *Autism, 13*, 245–264.

Brieber, S., Neufang, S., Bruning, N., Kamp-Beckere, I., Remschmidt, H., Herpertz-Dahlmann., et al. (2007). Structural brain abnormalities in adolescents with autism spectrum disorder and patients with attention deficit/hyperactivity disorder. *Journal of Child Psychology and Psychiatry, 48*, 1251–1258.

Bryson, S. E., Zwaigenbaum, L., Brian, J., Roberts, W., Szatmari, P., Rombough, V., et al. (2007). A prospective case series of high-risk infants who developed autism. *Journal of Autism and Developmental Disorders, 37*, 12–24.

Caspi, A., Langley, K., Milne, B., Moffitt, T. E., O'Donovan, M., Owen, M. J., et al. (2008). A replicated molecular genetic basis for subtyping antisocial behavior in children with attention-deficit/hyperactivity disorder. *Archives of General Psychiatry, 65*, 203–210.

Chakrabarti, S. & Fombonne, E. (2005). Pervasive developmental disorders in preschool children: Confirmation of high prevalence. *American Journal of Psychiatry, 162*, 1133–1141.

Chawarska, K., Paul, R., Klin, A., Hannigen, S., Dichel, L. E., & Volkmar, F. (2007). Parental recognition of developmental problems in toddlers with autism spectrum disorders. *Journal of Autism and Developmental Disorders, 37*, 62–72.

Clegg, J., Hollis, C., Mawhood, L., & Rutter, M. (2005). Developmental language disorders—a follow-up in later adult life: Cognitive, language and psychosocial outcomes. *Journal of Child Psychology and Psychiatry, 46*, 128–149.

Courchesne, E., Carper, R., & Akshoomoff, N. (2003). Evidence of brain overgrowth in the first year of life in autism. *JAMA, 290*, 393–394.

Dager, S. R., Wang, L., Friedman, S. D., Shaw, D. W., Constanton, J. N., Artru, A. A., et al. (2007). Shape mapping of the hippocampus in young children with autism spectrum disorder. *American Journal of Neuroradiology, 28*, 672–677.

Dakin, S. & Frith, U. (2005). Vagaries of visual perception in autism. *Neuron, 48*, 497–507.

Dawson, G., Munson, J., Webb, S. J., Nalty, T., Abbot, R., & Toth, K. (2007). Rate of head growth decelerates and symptoms worsen in the second year of life in autism. *Biological Psychiatry, 61*, 458–464.

Dawson, G., Webb, S., Schellenberg, G. D, Dager, S., Friedman, S., Aylward, E., et al. (2002). Defining the broader phenotype of autism: Genetic, brain, and behavioral perspectives. *Development and Psychopathology, 14*, 581–611.

de Bruin, E. I., Ferdinand, R. F., Meester, S., de Nijs, P. F. A., & Verheij, F. (2007). High rates of psychiatric co-morbidity in PDD-NOS. *Journal of Autism and Developmental Disorders, 37*, 977–886.

De Giacomo, A. & Fombonne, E. (1998). Parental recognition of developmental abnormalities in autism. *European Child and Adolescent Psychiatry*, 7, 131–136.

Erickson, K., Baron, I. S., & Fantie, B. D. (2001). Neuropsychological functioning in early hydrocephalus: Review from a developmental perspective. *Child Neuropsychology*, 7, 199–229.

Fein, D., Dixon, P., Paul, J., & Levin, H. (2005). Brief report: Pervasive developmental disorder can evolve into ADHD: Case illustrations. *Journal of Autism and Developmental Disorders*, 35, 525–534.

Fombonne, E. E. (2003). Epidemiological surveys of autism and other pervasive developmental disorders: An update. *Journal of Autism and Developmental Disorders*, 33, 365–382.

Franklin, A., Sowden, P., Burley, R., Notman, L., & Alder, E. (2008). Color perception in children with autism. *Journal of Autism and Developmental disorders*, 38, 1837–1847.

Franklin, A., Sowden, P., Notman, L., Gonzalez-Dixon, M., West, D., Alexander, I., et al. (2010). Reduced chromatic discrimination in children with autism spectrum disorders. *Developmental Science*, 13, 188–200.

Fujita, T., Yamasaki, T., Kamio, Y., Hirose, S., & Tobimatsu, S. (2011). Parvocellular pathway impairment in autism spectrum disorder: Evidence from visual evoked potentials. *Research in Autism Spectrum Disorders*, 5, 277–285.

Fukumoto, A., Hashimoto, T., Ito, H., Nishimura, M., Tsuda, Y., Miyazaki, M., et al. (2008). Growth of head circumference in autistic infants during the first year of life. *Journal of Autism and Developmental disorders*, 38, 411–418.

Geschwind, D. H. & Levitt, P. (2007). Autism spectrum disorders: Developmental disconnection syndromes. *Current Opinion in Neurobiology*, 17, 103–111.

Gillberg, C. (2003). Deficits in attention, motor control, and perception: A brief review. *Archives of Disease in Childhood*, 88, 904–910.

Hallahan, B., Daly, E. M., McAlonan, G., Loth, E., Toal, F., O'Brien, F., et al. (2009). Brain morphometry volume in autistic spectrum disorder: A magnetic resonance imaging study of adults. *Psychological Medicine*, 39, 337–346.

Happé, F.G.E. (1996). Studying weak central coherence at low levels: Children with autism do not succumb to visual illusions: A research note, *Journal of Child Psychology and Psychiatry*, 37, 873–877.

Happé, F., Booth, R., Charlton, R., & Hughes, C. (2006). Executive function deficits in autism spectrum disorders and attention-deficit/hyperactivity disorder: Examining profiles across domains and ages. *Brain and Cognition*, 61, 25–39.

Happé, F., Ronald, A., & Plomin, R. (2006). Time to give up on a single explanation for autism. *Nature Neuroscience*, 9, 1218–1220.

Happé, F. & Frith, U. (2006). The weak coherence account: Detail-focused cognitive style in autism spectrum disorders, *Journal of Autism and Developmental Disorders*, 36, 5–25.

Hattori, J., Ogino, T., Abiru, K., Nakano, K., Oka, M., & Ohtsuka, Y. (2006). Are pervasive developmental disorders and attention-deficit/hyperactivity disorder distinct disorders? *Brain and Development*, 28, 371–374.

Helzer, J. E., Kraemer, H. C., Krueger, R. F., Wittchen, H-U., & Sirovatka, P. J. (2008). *Dimensional approaches in diagnostic classification: Refining the research agenda for DSM-V*. Washington, D. C.: American Psychiatric Association.

Herbert, M. R. & Kenet, T. (2007). Brain abnormalities in language disorders and in autism. *Pediatric Clinics of North America*, 54, 563–583.

Howlin, P., Mawhood, L., & Rutter, M. (2000). Autism and developmental receptive language disorder-a follow-up comparison in early adult life. II: Social, behavioural, and psychiatric outcomes. *Journal of Child Psychology and Psychiatry*, 41, 561–578.

Ishida, R., Kamio, Y., & Nakamizo, S. (2009). Perceptual distortions in visual illusions in children with high-functioning autism spectrum disorder. *Psychologica: An International Journal of Psychology in the Orient*, 52, 175–187.

Johnson, C., Myers, S., & the Council on Children with Disabilities of the American Academy of Pediatrics. (2007). Identification and evaluation of children with autism spectrum disorders. *Pediatrics*, 120, 1183–1215.

Jolliffe, T. & Baron-Cohen, S. (1997). Are people with autism and Asperger syndrome faster than normal on the Embedded Figures Test? *Journal Child Psychology and Psychiatry*, 38, 527–534.

Kamio, Y., Robins, D., Kelley, E., Swainson, B., & Fein, D. (2007). Atypical lexical/semantic processing in high-functioning autism spectrum disorders without early language delay. *Journal of Autism and Developmental Disorders*, 37, 1116–1122.

Kamio, T. & Toichi, M. (2007). Memory illusion in high-functioning autism and Asperger's disorder, *Journal of Autism and Developmental Disorders*, 37, 867–876.

Kawatani, M., Nakai, A., Mayumi, M., & Hiratani, M. (2009). Retrospective analysis of pervasive developmental disorder patients initially diagnosed with attention deficit/hyperactivity disorder. *Brain and Development (No to Hattatsu)*, 41, 11–16.

Kemper, T. L. & Bauman, M. L. (1993). The contribution of neuropathologic studies to the understanding of autism. *Neurologic clinics*, 11, 175–187.

Kinsbourne, M. (1991). Overfocusing: An apparent subtype of attention deficit-hyperactivity disorder. In N. Amir., I. Rapin, & D. Braski, (Eds.), *Pediatric neurology: Behavior and cognition of the child with brain dysfunction, vol. 1, Pediatric Adolescent Medicine* (pp. 18–35). Basel: Karger.

Kjelgaard, M. M. & Tager-Flusberg, H. (2001). An investigation of language impairment in autism: Implications for genetic subgroups. *Language and Cognitive Process*, 16, 287–308.

Klin, A., Volkmar, F. R., Sparrow, S. S., Cicchetti, D. V., & Rourke, B. P. (1995). Validity and neuropsychological characterization of Asperger syndrome: Convergence with nonverbal learning disabilities syndrome. *Journal of Child Psychology and Psychiatry and Allied Disciplines*, 36, 1127–1140.

Koyama, T. & Kurita, H. (2008). Cognitive profile difference between normally intelligent children with Asperger's disorder and those with pervasive developmental disorder not otherwise specified. *Psychiatry and Clinical Neurosciences*, 62, 691–696.

Koyama, T., Tachimori, H., Osada, H., & Kurita, H. (2006). Cognitive and symptom profiles in high-functioning pervasive developmental disorder not otherwise specified and attention-deficit/hyperactivity disorder. *Journal of Autism and Developmental Disorders*, 36, 373–380.

Landa, R. J. (2008). Diagnosis of autism spectrum disorders in the first 3 years of life. *Nature Clinical Practice Neurology*, 4, 138–147.

Landa, R. J., Holman, K. C., & Garrett-Mayer, E. (2007). Social and communication development in toddlers with early and later diagnosis of autism spectrum disorders. *Archives of General Psychiatry, 64*, 853–864.

Landry, R. & Bryson, S. E. (2004). Impaired disengagement of attention in young children with autism. *Journal of Child Psychology and Psychiatry, 45*, 1115–1122.

Leyfer, O. T., Folstein, S. E., Bacalman, S., Davis, N. O., Dinh, E., Morgan, J., et al. (2006). Comorbid psychiatric disorders in children with autism: Interview development and rates of disorders. *Journal of Autism and Developmental Disorders, 36*, 849–861.

Livingstone, M. & Hubel, D. (1988). Segregation of form, color, movement, and depth: Anatomy, physiology, and perception. *Science, 240*, 740–749.

Maestro, S., Muratori, F., Cavallaro, M. C., Pecini, C., Cesari, A., Paziente, A., et al. (2005). How young children treat objects and people: An empirical study of the first year of life in autism. *Child Psychiatry and Human Development, 35*, 383–393.

Mawhood, L., Howlin, P., & Rutter, M. (2000). Autism and developmental receptive language disorder-a comparative follow-up in early adult life. I: Cognitive and language outcomes. *Journal of Child Psychology and Psychiatry, 41*, 547–559.

Milne, E., Swettenham, J., Hansen, P., Campbell, R., Jeffries, H., & Plaisted, K. (2002). High motion coherence thresholds in children with autism. *Journal of Child Psychology and Psychiatry, 43*, 255–263.

Morton, J. & Frith, U. (1995). Causal modeling: A structural approach to developmental psychopathology. In D. Cicchetti & D. J. Cohen, (Eds.), *Developmental psychopathology, Vol. 1* (pp. 357–391). New York: Wiley.

Mottron, L. & Burack, J. A. (2001). Enhanced perceptual functioning in the development of autism, In J. A. Burack, T. Charman, N. Yirmiiya, & P. R. Zelazo (Eds.), *The development of autism: Perspectives from theory and research* (pp. 131–148). Mahwah: Lawrence Erlbaum.

Mukaddes, N. M. & Topcu, Z. (2006). Case report: Homicide by a 10-year-old girl with autistic disorder. *Journal of Autism and Developmental Disorders, 36*, 471–474.

Müller, R. A. (2007). The study of autism as a distributed disorder. *MR Research Reviews, 13*, 85–95.

Mulligan, A., Anney, R. J. L., O'Regan, M., Chen, W., Butler, L., Fitzgerald, M., et al. (2009). Autism symptoms in attention-deficit/hyperactivity disorder: A familial trait which correlates with conduct, oppositional defiant, language and motor disorders. *Journal of Autism Developmental Disorders, 39*, 197–209.

Mundy, P. & Neal, A. R. (2001). Neural plasticity, joint attention, and a transactional social-orienting model of autism. In L. M. Glidden (Ed.), *International review of research in mental retardation: Autism,* 23 (pp. 139–168). San Diego: Academic Press.

Newman, S. S. & Ghaziuddin, M. (2008). Violent crime in Asperger syndrome: The role of psychiatric comorbidity. *Journal of Autism and Developmental Disorders, 38*, 1848–1852.

Osterling, J., Dawson, G., & Munson, J. A. (2002). Early recognition of 1-year-old infants with autism spectrum disorder versus mental retardation. *Development and Psychopathology, 14*, 239–251.

Palmen, S. J. M., van Engeland, H., Hof, P. R., & Schmitz, C. (2004). Neuropathological findings in autism. *Brain, 127*, 2572–2583.

Pandey, J., Wilson, L., Verbalis, A., & Fein, D. (2008.) Can autism resolve? In B. K. Shapiro, & P. J. Accardo (Eds.), *Autism frontiers: Clinical issues and innovations* (pp. 191–205). Baltimore: Paul H. Brookes Publishing.

Pellicano, E. & Gibson, L. (2008). Investigating the functional integrity of the dorsal visual pathway in autism and dyslexia. *Neuropsychologia, 46*, 2593–2596.

Pellicano, E., Gibson, L., Maybery, M., Durkin, K., & Badcock, D. R. (2005). Abnormal global processing along the dorsal visual pathway in autism: A possible mechanism for weak visuospatial coherence? *Neuropsychologia, 43*, 1044–1053.

Prior, M., Eisenmajer, R., Leekam, S., Wing, L., Gould, J., Ong, B., et al. (1998). Are there subgroups within the autistic spectrum? A cluster analysis of a group of children with autistic spectrum disorders. *Journal of Child Psychology and Psychiatry, 39*, 893–902.

Rapin, I., Allen, D. A., Aram, D. M., Dunn, M. A., Fein, D., Morris, R., et al. (1996). Classification issues. In I. Rapin (Ed.), *Preschool children with inadequate communication: Developmental language disorder, autism, low IQ.* (pp. 190–213). London: Mac Keith.

Rogers, J., Viding, E., Blair, R. J., Frith, U., & Happ, F. (2006). Autism spectrum disorder and psychopathy: Shared cognitive underpinnings or double hit? *Psychological Medicine, 36*, 1789–1798.

Ronald, A., Simonoff, E., Kuntsi, J., Asherson, P., & Plomin, R. (2008). Evidence for overlapping genetic influences on autistic and ADHD behaviours in a community twin sample. *Journal of Child Psychology and Psychiatry, 49*, 535–542.

Rourke, B. P., Ahmad, S. A., Collins, D. W., Hayman-Abello, B. A., Hayman-Abello, S. E., & Warriner, E. M. (2002). Child clinical/pediatric neuropsychology: Some recent advances. *Annual Review of Psychology, 53*, 309–339.

Rutter, M., Kim-Cohen, J., & Maughan, B. (2006). Continuities and discontinuities in psychopathology between childhood and adult life. *Journal of Child Psychology and Psychiatry, 47*, 276–295.

Satterfield, J. H., Faller, K. J., Crinella, F. M., Schell, A. M., Swanson, J. M., & Homer, L. D. (2007). A 30-year prospective follow-up study of hyperactive boys with conduct problems: Adult criminality. *Journal of the American Academy of Child and Adolescent Psychiatry, 46*, 601–610.

Scheirs, J. G. M. & Timmers, E. A. (2009). Differentiating among children with PDD-NOS, ADHD, and those with a combined diagnosis on the basis of WISC-III profiles. *Journal of Autism and Developmental Disorders, 39*, 549–556.

Simon, T. J. (2007). Cognitive characteristics of children with genetic syndromes. *Child and Adolescent Psychiatric Clinics of North America, 16*, 599–616.

Simonoff, E., Pickles, A., Charman, T., Chandler, S., Loucas, T., & Baird, G. (2008). Psychiatric disorders in children with autism spectrum disorders: Prevalence, comorbidity, and associated factors in a population-derived sample. *Journal of the American Academy of Child and Adolescent Psychiatry, 47*, 921–929.

Spencer, J., O'Brien, J., Riggs, K., Braddick, O., Atkinson, J., & Wattam-Bell, J. (2000). Motion processing in autism: Evidence for a dorsal stream deficiency. *Neuroreport, 11*, 2765–2767.

Sutera, S., Pandey, J., Esser, E. L. Rosenthal, M. A., Wilson, L. B., Barton, M., et al. (2007). Predictors of optimal outcome in toddlers diagnosed with autism spectrum disorders. *Journal of Autism and Developmental Disorders, 37*, 98–107.

Teitelbaum, O., Benton, T., Shah, P. K., Prince, A., Kelly, J. L., & Teitelbaum, P. (2004). Eshkol-Wachman movement notation in diagnosis: The early detection of Asperger's syndrome. *Proceedings of the National Academy of Sciences of the United States of America, 101*, 11909–11914.

Tobimatsu, S. & Celesia, G. G. (2006). Studies of human visual pathophysiology with visual evoked potentials. *Clinical Neurophysiolgy, 117*, 1414–1433.

Towbin, K. E. (2005). Pervasive developmental disorder not otherwise specified. In F. R. Volkmar., R. Paul., A. Klin., & D. Cohen. (Eds.), *Handbook of autism and pervasive developmental disorders. Volume 1. Diagnosis, development, neurology, and behavior.* (3rd ed., pp. 165–200). Hovoken, NJ: John Wiley and Sons.

Townsend, J., Courchesen, E., & Egaas, B. (1996). Slowed orienting of covert visual-spatial attention in autism: Specific deficits associated with cerebellar and parietal abnormality. *Development and Psychopathology, 8*, 563–584.

Walker, D. R., Thompson, A., Zwaigenbaum, L., Goldberg, J., Bryson, S. E., Mahorney, W. J., et al. (2004). Specifying PDD-NOS: A comparison of PDD-NOS, Asperger syndrome, and autism. *Journal of the American Academy of Child and Adolescent Psychiatry, 43*, 172–180.

Whitehouse, A. J. O. & Bishop, D, V. M. (2008). Cerebral dominance for language function in adults with specific language impairment or autism. *Brain, 131*, 3193–3200.

Wing, L. (1988). The continuum of autistic characteristics. In E. Schopler & G. B. Mesibov (Eds.), *Diagnosis and assessment in autism* (pp. 91–110). New York: Plenum.

Wing, L. & Gould, J. (1979). Severe impairments of social interaction and associated abnormalities in children: Epidemiology and classification. *Journal of Autism Development Disorders, 9*, 11–29.

Zappella, M. (2002). Early-onset Tourette syndrome with reversible autistic behaviour: A dysmaturational disorder. *European Child and Adolescent Psychiatry 11*, 18–23.

Zwaigenbaum, J., Bryson, S., Lord, C., Rogers, S., Carter, A., Carver, L., et al. (2009). Clinical assessment and management of toddlers with suspected autism spectrum disorder: Insights from studies of high-risk infants. *Pediatrics, 123*, 1383–1391.

Zwaigenbaum, L., Bryson, S., Rogers, T., Roberts, W., Brian, J., & Szatmari, P. (2005). Behavioral manifestations of autism in the first year of life. *International Journal of Developmental Neuroscience, 23*, 143–152.

The Asperger Syndrome

Bruno Wicker *and* Marie Gomot

Abstract

This chapter reviews major recent findings in Asperger Syndrome (AS), ranging from behavior to neurobiology, and focusing both on social cognitive and executive processes and their interactions. The study of AS benefits from several lines of research on one hand, but on the other hand a lot of controversy remains as to whether the results of individual studies can be generalized to the entire AS population. This obviously highlights the need for further extensive research. But it also demonstrates a very hopeful and intense period for research aiming at : 1) better characterizing the clinical, behavioral, and cognitive phenotypes; 2) building a new conceptual framework through an integrative approach mixing emotional/social cognition and other areas of cognition; and 3) progressively supplanting the localizationism realm by applying recent massive advances in neuroimaging techniques and analysis that explore connectivity and functional interactions in large scale dynamic brain networks.

Keywords: Asperger syndrome, autism, social neuroscience, emotion, imitation, face processing, empathy, executive functions, flexibility, cognitive style, diagnosis, neuroimaging, neuroanatomy, functional connectivity

Introduction

Since the pioneer book by Temple Grandin ("Thinking in Pictures"), several books dealing with the life of or written by people with Asperger syndrome (AS) have been published in the past years. The quite unique and characteristic way of living of people with AS has also been used to shape a hero's character in recent novels and movies (e.g., Lisbeth Salander in Stieg Larsson's trilogy). These rich everyday life descriptions illustrate that some individuals with AS are extremely successful in their area of expertise and lead fulfilling lives despite or because of their condition, while others are considered failures and life for them is an endless struggle on the margins of society. For some, Asperger syndrome appears to be a gift; for others, a curse. The professional literature generally highlights deficits and weaknesses with very little emphasis on special strengths or talents, but as knowledge about AS is growing, researchers tend more and more to refer to it as a particular development of the brain rather than an abnormal development. This supports the pertinent idea that this neurodevelopmental disorder should not be considered as a handicap, but rather as a different mental life, underpinned by a different development of the brain (Baron-Cohen, 2000). This is also the reason why studying AS is an extraordinary opportunity to better understand both typical and different development of the brain, and its relation to social cognition as one of the most unique characteristic of the human brain.

Nevertheless, it has to be kept in mind that Asperger syndrome is a mild form of autism. If autism is a continuum, then Asperger syndrome is at the extreme end of this continuum. Indeed, AS and autism both belong to the pervasive developmental disorders which also includes Rett's disorder, childhood disintegrative disorder and pervasive developmental disorder not otherwise specified (PDD-NOS). People suffering from AS don't have communication delays as people with other forms of autism have; they function relatively well in terms of intelligence and social functions, and they often manage to go to school, graduate from college, and live independently. AS is thus considered as a specific type of "high-functioning autism" (HFA), characterized by poor social skills, advanced and overly formal language, and extensive, pervasive interest in a specific subject. It is often said that geniuses and people with AS share the same characteristics because they both have narrow interests and are more focused and persistent on what they are doing than normal people. Many geniuses are sometimes recalled as showing Asperger's traits, for example, Isaac Newton, Albert Einstein, George Orwell, and H. G. Wells.

Although the title of this chapter explicitly refers to Asperger syndrome, given the relatively recent emergence of considering this syndrome as a singular one, we will often expose results from studies on populations of subjects labeled as autism spectrum disorders (ASD). The clinical populations tested are indeed generally constituted of people diagnosed with AS or high-functioning autism. Furthermore, as we will discuss briefly below in the clinical presentation of the AS, there is no consensus on a distinction between these two conditions. Therefore, it is not wise, and certainly not pertinent at this point of knowledge and research, to consider the data as specific to Asperger syndrome per se, and we certainly do not intend to promote the idea of a clear distinction between Asperger syndrome and high functioning autism.

This Handbook has a focus on social neuroscience and we will therefore develop aspects of research exploring social behavior and their neural underpinnings, with a special emphasis on imitation and emotion processing. However, social behavior obviously encompasses interactions between cognition and purely socioemotional cognitive processes. This chapter would thus lack exhaustivity without some data on studies aiming at exploring nonsocial cognition such as sensory perception, attention, or memory. The last part of this chapter presents the most recent findings on neuroanatomy and brain connectivity in AS and discusses it in relation with perspectives on future research in AS.

The Diagnostic Issue

Current conceptualisations of autism actually favour an autistic spectrum of conditions in which an individual's clinical presentation is thought to be influenced by the severity of various factors including IQ and language ability (Constantino et al., 2004; Fombonne et al., 2004). At the severe end of the autism spectrum are individuals with significant intellectual disability and very limited language development along with a range of behaviors arising from the core features of autism. At the other end of the spectrum are individuals with what has been described as high functioning autism and Asperger syndrome.

Lorna Wing was the first to use the term Asperger syndrome while describing a group of children and adolescents who presented clinical features similar to those initially reported by the Austrian paediatrician Hans Asperger (Wing, 1981). Asperger's PhD dissertation published in 1944 described four boys displaying unusual social and cognitive profiles, characterized by a lack of empathy, failure to establish friendship, unilateral conversation, restrictive and intense interests, and clumsiness (Asperger, 1944). Nowadays the criteria used for the diagnosis of Asperger syndrome in the ICD-10 (WHO, 1990) and the DSM-IV-R (APA, 2000) are very similar to those of the original description of the syndrome (see Box 57.1).

Diagnostic Criteria

Complementary clinical features have repeatedly been suggested to precise Asperger diagnosis (Klin, Pauls, Schultz, & Volkmar, 2005). Motor deficits (e.g., clumsiness, dexterity, coordination, and balance difficulties) were proposed as a diagnostic feature in the first description of the syndrome and later on (Teitelbaum et al., 2004). However, the extent to which these symptoms are specific to AS remains under discussion as systematic assessment revealed that these patients were less impaired than classical autism or PDD-NOS subjects during standardized tests of motor coordination (Ghaziuddin & Butler, 1998; Ghaziuddin, Butler, Tsai, & Ghaziuddin, 1994). Discrepancy between verbal and nonverbal skills would also be characteristic of the syndrome. Some reports suggest that as a group, subjects with

AS possess a specific cognitive profile on tests of intelligence characterized by Verbal IQ > Performance IQ (Ehlers et al., 1997; Ghaziuddin & Mountain-Kimchi, 2004; Koyama & Kurita, 2008).

Differential Diagnosis

A number of diagnostic labels have been used to describe people of normal intelligence who have difficulties with social interaction. Whether these are fundamentally different syndromes or labels evolved from different areas of clinical expertise remains controversial (Woodbury-Smith & Volkmar, 2009).

High Functioning Autism vs Asperger Syndrome

Patients with HFA generally have IQs in the normal range and well-developed language, although they experience a delay in their acquisition of language in childhood. Those described as having AS, like the others on the autism spectrum, have impairments in social reciprocity and social communication and also demonstrate a restricted range of interests. However, they do not show a delay in language acquisition and often have vocabulary and grammar ability within the normal range, though displaying a somewhat pedantic, rambling, and one-sided language marked by a lack of normal prosody. Moreover, most AS people have important pragmatic deficits (Ghaziuddin & Gerstein, 1996; Klin & Volkmar, 2003). The quality of social deficits might also help to distinguish between the two diagnosis: The social dysfunction is usually milder in AS than seen in HFA; Asperger patients may be "active but odd" whereas HFA would rather be "passive and aloof" (Ghaziuddin, 2008).

Differential diagnosis from schizoid personality disorder may sometimes be difficult. The schizoid type also displays flattened or restricted range of emotions, lack of affective rapport, and diminished capacity for enjoyment, but does not feature the limited special interests that are typical of AS, nor entail the tendency towards stereotypical behaviors (Roy, Dillo, Bessling, Emrich, & Ohlmeier, 2009).

The relationship between AS and *obsessive-compulsive disorder (OCD)* is also not entirely clear. Among the repetitive and restricted activities and interests, the obsessive hyper-focusing on very specific, often odd, details is particularly characteristic of AS. These behaviors are generally referred to in terms of obsessive and compulsive traits. On the other hand, higher prevalence of autistic traits has been found in OCD samples (Bejerot, 2007), and some evidence suggests that treatment effective for OCD may be valuable for repetitive thoughts and behaviors in AS as well (Buchsbaum et al., 2001; McDougle, Kresch, & Posey, 2000). Taken together, these evidences point to a partial overlap of the two disorders. However, the application of OCD concepts to the autism spectrum in terms of diagnostic category or dimensional domain is currently controversial, mainly because AS patients tend not to show distress associated with their fixed beliefs and they have little awareness about the excessive and unreasonable nature of their repetitive thoughts and behaviors (Ruta, Mugno, D'Arrigo, Vitiello, & Mazzone, 2009).

Finally Klin et al., proposed an overlap between AS and *non-verbal learning disability* (NLD), or Rourke syndrome (Klin et al., 1995), a neuropsychological disability characterized by emotional disturbance and clumsiness, along with a significant verbal/performance discrepancy favoring the former.

Prevalence and Outcome

Asperger syndrome has not been well known by most clinicians during several decades and the progressive better characterization of the disorder has "artificially" increased the prevalence figures. Nevertheless, synthesis of prevalence studies now leads to a median prevalence estimate of 2.6/10,000 with a sex ratio of eight boys for one girl (Fombonne, Zakarian, Bennett, Meng, & McLean-Heywood, 2006 (Fombonne, Quirke, & Hagen, 2009)). Follow-up studies are limited, but most of them indicate that although the majority of people with AS improves over time, difficulties in terms of communication skills, social adjustment, and independent living continue into adulthood.

Clinical Tools

A number of screening and complementary diagnostic tools have been specifically designed to be used when a diagnosis of AS is queried: The Childhood Asperger's Screening Test (CAST) (Scott, Baron-Cohen, Bolton, & Brayne, 2002) and the Australian Scale for Asperger Syndrome (ASAS) (Attwood, 1998) have been developed specifically to screen school-age populations for behavioral symptoms indicative of AS. The Autism Spectrum Screening Questionnaire (ASSQ) (Ehlers, Gillberg, & Wing, 1999) and the Asperger Syndrome Diagnostic Scale (ASDS) (Myles, Jones-Bock, & Simpson, 2001) have been designed to assess the characteristic symptoms in children and adolescents (but see Matson & Rivet, 2008, for an exhaustive review and Campbell, 2005, for a comparison of the psychometric properties—reliability and validity—between several screening instruments). Finally, the Adult Asperger Assessment (AAA) is one of the only instruments relevant to the diagnosis of AS in adulthood (Baron-Cohen, Wheelwright, Robinson, & Woodbury-Smith, 2005).

Social Cognition and Asperger Syndrome

Social cognition is a broad term that refers to an array of behaviors ranging from basic face perception to emotional expression recognition, complex interpretation of body movements and social contexts, empathy, and decision making in moral dilemmas. Humans, and perhaps other nonhuman primate species, have developed incredibly efficient brain processes—automatic or controlled—specifically dedicated to social-information processing.

This is well illustrated by the fact that we are without any explicit effort able to recognize someone's identity from seeing his face, irrespective of its orientation or whether it is presented with full details or as caricature, or whether it is presented in full light or in the shade. Our brain is, however, typically unable to calculate quickly and without effort $1,23,237 \times 56,45,680$. We can calculate it of course, but using a very slow and explicit strategy. By contrast, a computer can calculate the operation very quickly but it will take him ages to assign the same identity to two pictures of the same face observed under different luminosity conditions or orientations, or expressing different emotional expressions. This is because the amount of information to process is too enormous compared to a serial calculation. A—very broad!—relation may be drawn with respect to AS behavior. Indeed, many individuals with AS are very good at mathematics and logic and some of them can even calculate very rapidly a complex operation such as 1237×5680, without being able to explain how they do it. However, they seem unable to automatically recognize emotional signals on a face, and seem to apply a controlled and slow strategy to do it. Our ability to automatically process social signals is fascinating. Lacking it would transform our everyday life in a nightmare, just as it is for even very high level functioning AS people.

In this section we review the most recent evidences from behavioral and neuroimaging studies on ASD, to clarify at which level deficits are observed and to which extent they are correlated to abnormal brain functioning. Social cognition in AS has been explored mainly by using theory of mind, mental state attribution, face perception, and emotional information processing tasks. As chapter 60 already deals in details with mental state attribution and theory of mind aspects in ASD, we chose here to insist on other aspects of social cognition. We will first review behavioral impairments related to some particular social cognitive processes, and then focus on the underlying brain substrates.

Face perception and recognition is obviously a crucial aspect of social cognition. Abnormal processing of faces would reflect a dramatic ignorance that it is—together with the eye region—the potential vector of crucial information about other's internal states, and should thus be the target of privileged attention. Consistent with this view, early behavioral studies that examined face processing in ASD have shown low performance on tests of incidental face learning, memory for faces, face categorization, and recognition of familiar faces. Reduced, nonexistent, or even reversed face inversion effect has been consistently reported and interpreted as reflecting a specific deficit in configural face processing (Teunisse & de Gelder, 2003). This was later confirmed by studies showing that individuals with ASD tend to process faces in terms of their component parts (Joseph & Tanaka, 2003; Rutherford, Clements, & Sekuler, 2007; Teunisse & de Gelder, 2003). Behavioral evidence from eye-tracking studies also suggests that individuals with ASD process faces by using an abnormal strategy of exploration with a tendency to look less at the inner features of the face, particularly the eyes (Joseph & Tanaka, 2003; Klin, Jones, Schultz, Volkmar, & Cohen, 2002; Pelphrey et al., 2002; Riby, Doherty-Sneddon, & Bruce, 2009; Rutherford et al., 2007). Although here again conflicting results have been reported (Dalton et al., 2005; Pelphrey et al., 2002). All these perceptual and/or attentional abnormalities in ASDs point to a diminished level of expertise for faces and lead to the premise of a deficit in face perception in this population. Yet, the picture of impairments remains somewhat confusing and suggests that the versatility and abilities in face processing in ASD have been underestimated. For example, a recent study revealed that the social judgements of the individuals with AS were just as competent and consistent as those of their matched controls, with only one exception: There was a trend for them to be less able to judge the attractiveness of faces if they were of the same sex (White, Hill, Winston, & Frith, 2006). These findings remind us that there are dissociable subcomponents to social cognition and that not all of these are compromised in AS.

At the brain level, the first neuroimaging studies on face perception reported a lack of fusiform gyrus (FG) activation (Schultz et al., 2000; Schultz et al., 2003). However, further studies revealed normal activation of the face fusiform area (FFA) to familiar faces (Pierce, Haist, Sedaghat, & Courchesne, 2004) and when the attention was explicitly directed to faces by displaying a cross between the two eyes (Hadjikhani et al., 2004). These studies nevertheless revealed atypical patterns of activation in regions forming the broader face-processing network and social brain, outside the core FFA and inferior occipital gyrus (IOG) regions (Hadjikhani, Joseph, Snyder, & Tager-Flusberg, 2007).

Facial expression of emotion is considered as one of the core element of an individual's publicly observable emotional experience, because it provides universally understandable nonverbal messages broadcasting the individual's emotional state

to others. In this context, most of the investigations on emotion perception and recognition in AS have predominantly focused on processing of facial expressions. A general impairment in emotional processing has been widely demonstrated in autism, data specific to AS are, however, less frequent and often controversial across studies. On one hand, studies report impairment in emotional information perception and recognition. For example, Aschwin et al. consistently reported impairment in the recognition of negative emotions from facial expressions (Ashwin, Baron-Cohen, Wheelwright, O'Riordan, & Bullmore, 2007; Ashwin, Chapman, Colle, & Baron-Cohen, 2006). A pictorial emotional Stroop paradigm, though, revealed normal attention biases towards threatening emotional faces (Ashwin, Wheelwright, & Baron-Cohen, 2006a) with interference effects to all facial stimuli regardless of expression or sex, suggesting that faces cause disproportionate interference in AS. These results are in line with an atypical strategy of emotional face processing in AS. Using a well-controlled attentional blink paradigm, Corden et al. showed that the typical enhancement of perception for emotionally arousing events is significantly reduced in AS at short inter-target intervals (Corden, Chilvers, & Skuse, 2008b). The same group combined eye-tracking technology with a test of facial affect recognition and a measure of self-reported social anxiety in order to explore the etiology of social-perceptual deficits in AS (Corden, Chilvers, & Skuse, 2008a). Results revealed that the AS group was impaired in the recognition of fearful and sad expressions and spent significantly less time fixating on the eye region of all faces. This correlation between impaired recognition of emotional expressions and a failure to fixate the eyes in individuals with AS was confirmed in another study (Spezio, Adolphs, Hurley, & Piven, 2007). Avoidance of emotionally arousing stimuli, such as eyes, may thus explain social-perceptual impairment in AS.

On the other hand, other studies report an intact ability of emotional processing in AS, at least in experimental—sometimes far from real life— settings. The ability of subjects with ASD to recognize emotion from black and white photography and from facial expression presented contextually was recently evaluated (Wright et al., 2008). Neither a diagnosis of ASD nor a measure of severity (Autism Quotient score) affected the ability to recognize emotional expression, except that the participants with ASD were significantly worse at recognizing angry and happy facial expressions.

Unlike the control group, most participants with ASD mirrored the facial expression before interpreting it. Authors wisely acknowledge that test conditions may lead to results different from everyday life, but alternatively suggest that deficits in emotion recognition in high-functioning ASD may be less marked than previously thought. Two studies performed in our lab also suggest that explicit perception and labeling of primary emotions does not seem to be impaired in AS (Hubert, Wicker, Monfardini, & Deruelle, 2009; Wicker et al., 2008). Interestingly, a recent study used an emotion perception test consisting of facial expressions and tone of voice cues that varied in intensity to study potential performance differences between HFA and AS. Participants with AS and the typically developing standardization sample of the emotion-perception instrument had the same mean emotion perception accuracy, whereas participants with HFA performed significantly worse (Mazefsky & Oswald, 2007).

As briefly reviewed above, most of the relevant evidence for an emotional impairment to date stems from studies assessing how individuals with AS understand and react to the emotional signals of others. The specificity of AS's behavioral impairments in emotional information processing has led researchers to consider different strategies. First, by using more naturalistic stimuli (color videos, whole context instead of black and white faces with no hair) to test subjects in conditions as close as possible to real life; second, by using more subtle experimental tasks that target more implicit and automatic processes.;third, by broadening the focus of research and assess how the emotional significance of stimuli impacts on processes that are not primarily of a social nature. This last point will be developed in another section of this chapter.

Impaired automatic processing of emotional information was explored using "modified" stimuli, such as low or high frequency filtered emotional faces. Using this approach, the ability of subjects with AS to recognize basic emotional facial expressions (anger, disgust, fear, and happiness) from static and dynamic facial expressions whose spatial frequency contents had been manipulated was investigated (Katsyri, Saalasti, Tiippana, von Wendt, & Sams, 2008). The two groups recognized emotions similarly from nonfiltered faces and from dynamic versus static facial expressions. In contrast, the participants with AS were less accurate than controls in recognizing facial emotions from very low-spatial frequencies. The results suggest intact recognition of basic facial emotions and dynamic facial information, but impaired

visual processing of global features in ASDs. Another study asked participants to categorize hybrid faces (composed of two overlapped faces of different spatial bandwidths) by gender and emotion (Santos, Rondan, Rosset, Da Fonseca, & Deruelle, 2008). Control participants exhibited a bias for low-pass information during gender categorization and a bias for high-pass information during emotion categorization. By contrast, adults with ASD showed the same low-pass bias in both tasks. Authors discuss this shift in processing style in terms of diminished top-down modulation in ASD. The incidental attentional bias to emotional stimuli has also been investigated by means of a "face in the crowd" paradigm. Results revealed that people with HFA/AS performed similarly to controls in many conditions. However, widely varying crowd sizes and inverted faces reduced the effect in the HFA/AS group, suggesting a more general difference in face processing style (Ashwin, Wheelwright, & Baron-Cohen, 2006b). Threat detection mechanisms might thus be intact in AS under simple and predictable conditions, but like other face-perception tasks, the visual search of threat faces task reveals atypical face-processing in ASD. Studies showing intact behavioral performance but abnormal automatic physiological reactions provide further support for the view that AS may be characterized by atypicalities in the integration of physiological and cognitive aspects of emotional experiences and are also good evidence that automatic processing of emotion is impaired in AS (Bolte, Feineis-Matthews, & Poustka, 2008; Hubert et al., 2009).

In summary, so far behavioral data point to the idea that individuals with AS process emotion using a different cognitive strategy, which may perform well in simple situations but is pushed to its limit in more subtle or complex social contexts (Corbett, Carmean, et al., 2009; Hubert et al., 2007; Wicker et al., 2008). From the everyday life difficulties observed in this syndrome, this alternative strategy is obviously more cognitively demanding and may explain why people with AS sometimes seem to misunderstand and then avoid complex contexts, or tend to focus on things they master well and speak seemingly without taking into account other's reactions or opinion.

Neuroscientists have begun to tackle the cerebral bases of this potential alternative strategy for emotional processing (although the primary goal was not always this one). In the recent years a number of studies have used electrophysiological or neuroimaging techniques to try to reveal functional cerebral differences while behavioral performance was identical between groups.

Adults with AS were found to exhibit delayed P1 and N170 latencies and smaller N170 amplitudes in comparison to control subjects during explicit processing of happy, sad, angry, scared, and neutral faces (O'Connor, Hamm, & Kirk, 2005). This may reflect impaired holistic and configural processing of faces in AS adults. However, these differences were not observed between AS and control children. This may result from incomplete development of the neuronal generators of these ERP components and/ or early intervention. Using fMRI, Ashwin et al. reported that HFA/AS is associated with different patterns of activation of social brain areas— especially the amygdala—during processing of varying intensity of fear (Ashwin et al., 2007). Another study examined brain activations during unconscious perception of emotional stimuli using event-related fMRI. Results failed to show differences in activation of the fusiform gyrus and extrastriate cortex between groups, suggesting that these early areas may be functionally intact in AS (Deeley et al., 2007). By contrast, Corbett et al. reported intact emotion-matching performance but diminished activation of the fusiform gyrus and the amygdala in a group of children with ASD (Corbett, Carmean et al., 2009). As attentional effect may explain impaired processing of emotional expression, Dalton et al. recorded eye movements during an emotion recognition task. Results show that activation in the fusiform gyrus and amygdala was strongly and positively correlated with the time spent fixating the eyes in the ASD group. This suggests that diminished gaze fixation may account for the fusiform hypoactivation to faces commonly reported in ASD (Dalton et al., 2005). Our group also investigated the cerebral bases of explicit emotional processing in adults with ASD. Contradictory to other studies, regions classically involved in the perceptual analysis of facial features and expression, such as STS and fusiform gyrus, were normally engaged in the ASD group. This suggests that subjects with ASD might perceive and categorize adequately emotional expressions, as further reflected by their normal behavioral performance. By contrast, a lack of activation was observed in brain regions involved in higher-order processing of perceived emotional information such as the dorso medial prefrontal cortex (dMPFC) and the right ventrolateral prefrontal cortex (Wicker et al., 2008) (see Figure 57.1).

Two studies used fMRI to examine whether such emotional impairments extend to the perception of bodily expressed emotions (Grezes, Wicker, Berthoz, & de Gelder, 2009; Hadjikhani et al., 2009). Results showed that ASD and control groups did not exhibit a differential pattern of brain activation to bodies expressing fear as compared with emotionally neutral bodies. Furthermore, ASD individuals showed normal patterns of cerebral activations in response to bodies engaged in emotionally neutral actions, with the exception of decreased activation in the inferior frontal cortex and the anterior insula in ASD, suggesting that emotion perception deficits in ASD may be due to compromised processing of the emotional component of observed actions.

Although lack of empathy has been considered a central characteristic of AS, quantitative and qualitative assessments of empathy in this syndrome are lacking. Shamay-Tsoory et al. (2002) presented two cases of adolescents with AS who showed extreme deficits on measures of both cognitive and affective empathy. Analysis of their performance on tasks assessing cognitive and affective processing did not reveal significant impairment in executive functions, nor in their ability to recognize emotions or the ability to create a mental representation of another person's knowledge. However, both patients were unable to integrate the emotional content with mental representations and deduce the other person's emotional state. These results suggest that impaired empathy in individuals with AS may be due to impaired integration of the cognitive and affective facets of the other person's mental state (Shamay-Tsoory, Tomer, Yaniv, & Aharon-Peretz, 2002). The same group tested the ability of adults with ASD to understand envy and gloating using the "fortune of others" emotion task and an additional theory-of-mind (ToM) task. Individuals with AS and HFA showed no difficulty on basic ToM conditions, but were impaired in their ability to identify envy and gloating. Furthermore, the ability to recognize these emotions was related to scores on a self-rating scale of perspective-taking ability and the ToM task (Shamay-Tsoory, 2008). Scores in the Interpersonal Reactivity Index (IRI), a multi-dimensional measure of empathy, and the Strange Stories test were assessed. The AS group scored lower on the measures of cognitive empathy and theory of mind, but were no different from controls on one affective empathy scale of the IRI (Empathic Concern), and scored higher than controls on the other (Personal Distress) (Rogers, Dziobek, Hassenstab, Wolf, & Convit, 2007). A recent study reported that when observing other's pain, participants with AS did not show any amplitude reduction of

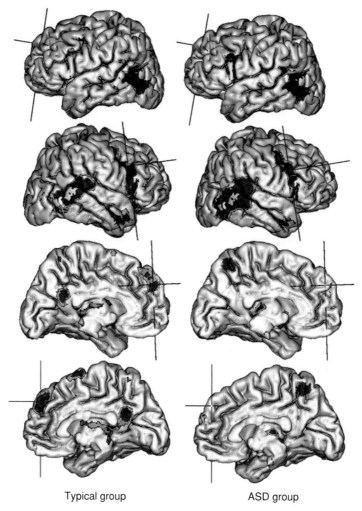

Typical group   ASD group

Fig. 57.1 Clusters of brain activations from the contrast between a condition of observation of a video sequence with the aim to recognize the emotion expressed by an actor and a condition of passive observation of a video sequence with no emotional content. Note the striking absence of activity in the dorsomedial prefrontal cortex and precuneus (medial views) in the ASD group, while other brain areas (on lateral views) are activated very similarly in both groups.

motor-evoked potentials recorded from the muscle vicariously affected by pain, nor did their neurophysiological response correlate with imagined pain sensory qualities (Minio-Paluello, Baron-Cohen, Avenanti, Walsh, & Aglioti, 2009). Participants with AS represented others' pain in relation to the self-oriented arousal experienced while watching pain videos. This finding of no embodiment of others' pain provides neurophysiological evidence for reduced empathic resonance in people with AS and indicates that their empathic difficulties involve not only cognitive dimensions but also sensorimotor resonance with others. The issue of empathy in AS still needs to be extensively visited.

This section reviewed the most recent studies investigating the behavioral and neurobiological correlates of social cognitive processes in AS.

While there is no doubt about an impairment in various domains related to social cognition in AS, results are still controversial regarding the extent of this impairment and its neural underpinnings. This is in part due to the heterogeneity of the clinical population and the fact that AS individuals are able to develop alternative cognitive strategies to deal with at least basic social information, such as explicit recognition of emotional expression. From now on, it seems therefore more and more important to head towards more ecological validity and target the automaticity of social information processing that characterizes the typical brain.

Asperger Syndrome and Imitation
Imitation has been widely demonstrated as a crucial ability for proper development of social and

communicative skills such as understanding actions of others, establishing social intersubjectivity, empathy, theory of mind, symbolic thinking, emotion sharing, and joint attention. As impairments in all of these processes have been found in individuals with AS, behavioral and neuroimaging studies have quite logically explored imitation skills and their cerebral correlates in this neurodevelopmental disorder. We review below the available corpus of research and most significant results, which prompted some theorists to suggest that imitative deficits are an important and specific feature of ASD that could be related to a dysfunction of the mirror-neuron system (Williams, Whiten, Suddendorf, & Perrett, 2001).

Imitation is a highly complex behavior (see chapter 36 of this *Handbook*) that has to be subdivided into distinct processes to be fully understood and properly investigated in a neurodevelopmental disorder such as AS. As acknowledged by a growing number of authors, it would be implausible to expect a single neurocognitive mechanism to underlie imitation in either the typical or Asperger brain (Hamilton, Brindley, & Frith, 2007). This means a need to take into account for example the meaningfulness of the gesture to imitate, the intentionality of the action to imitate, the automatic or intentional aim to imitate, and so forth. Furthermore, imitation is not restricted to simple hand or body actions; vocal, linguistic, affect, and intention imitation also exist, though more scarcely investigated.

The majority of early studies focused on complex voluntary motor imitation with a vast variety of tasks ranging from simple motor imitation to tasks involving emotional expression or goal imitation. Much of the new and informative data regarding AS have been generated in the last 10 years, with the use of more subtle experimental paradigms which aimed at dissecting the various processes in play to better specify the imitation impairments. While a quite recent review revealed that the majority of 21 considered studies found imitative deficits in the ASD groups compared to other groups (Williams, Whiten, & Singh, 2004), other studies have found no evidence of imitation impairments (e.g., Carpenter, Pennington, & Rogers, 2001; D'Entremont & Yazbek, 2007; Hamilton, Brindley, & Frith, 2007). Using a genuine test of meaningless novel gestures imitation, a recent study suggested that even when social and lexical factors are removed ASD subjects still have problems in imitating the postures adopted by others (Stieglitz Ham, Corley, Rajendran, Carletta, & Swanson, 2008). This was confirmed by

another study (Vivanti, Nadig, Ozonoff, & Rogers, 2008), but it has to be noted that both studies also reported abnormal visuomotor integration and visual attention in ASD. Individuals with AS do not seem to profit from mirror-image movements of others, and observation of mirror-image-like movements do not speed up their performance in non-imitative tasks (Avikainen, Wohlschlager, Liuhanen, Hanninen, & Hari, 2003). However, this particular pattern of a selective impairment in mirror imitation in ASD was not replicated in a subsequent study using the exact same task (Leighton, Bird, Charman, & Heyes, 2008), suggesting that the impaired performance on the imitation task was not due to a functional mirroring deficit but instead that more general factors contributed to the poor performance on this task. This idea that imitation impairments in AS arise from impairments in a range of other abilities has been proposed by a number of other authors who have found correlations between imitation performance and processes not specific to imitation, such as motor control, visuomotor integration, and social reciprocity. The fact that people with ASD might be impaired in motor imitation task has also been hypothesized to be linked to their clumsiness and potential apraxis (Haswell, Izawa, & Shadmehr, 2009). An elegant study tested the possibility that impairment in imitation could be due to abnormal generation of internal models of actions. Results showed that subjects with AS form internal models that create a stronger than normal association between the self-generated motor commands and proprioception. This suggests a greater than normal dependence on cortical regions in which movements are represented in intrinsic coordinates of motion (M1 and somatosensory cortex), and a less than normal dependence on regions in which movements are represented in extrinsic coordinates (premotor and posterior parietal) (Haswell et al., 2009).

To circumvent the voluntary essence of imitation tasks (which require socio-cognitive abilities in addition to imitation for successful performance), Bird et al. used an automatic imitation paradigm (a "cleaner" measure of imitative ability) in which participants performed a prespecified hand action in response to observed hand actions performed either by a human or a robotic hand. Both the ASD and the control group showed an automatic imitation effect: responses on compatible trials were faster than those on incompatible trials. However, ASD had a larger animacy bias than the control group; that is, the effect was greater when responses were made to human than to robotic actions (Bird, Leighton, Press, & Heyes, 2007). The core mechanisms of imitation, those that translate observed into executed actions may thus be intact in individuals with ASD. In the same trend, a systematic series of behavioral studies of the ability to understand and mirror actions, imitate goals and intentions has been recently performed by Hamilton et al. (2007). Results show no difference between groups and thus suggest that ASD children are perfectly able to imitate and understand actions (Hamilton et al., 2007).

More behavioral studies thus seem required to make sense of the conflicting findings in the literature and to fully understand the nature of observed behavioral imitation impairments in AS. To date, the study of imitation has been too much restricted to motor acts, and more subtle aspects of imitation should be explored, such as imitation of vocal stimuli or linguistic properties.

Research has quite logically investigated the neural bases of imitative behavior and their putative dysfunction in ASD. Because action understanding is a prerequisite of successful imitation, latest neuroimaging studies seek to understand if individuals with AS/HFA perform poorly on tests of imitation, in part, because they have a "functional mirroring deficit," that is, they are impaired in their capacity to match observed with executed actions ("dysfunctional mirror neurons system (MNS)"). An early MEG study by Avikainen et al. revealed on a small sample of individuals with AS that impaired mind-reading and imitation skills found in AS and autism do not seem to result from dysfunction of the motor cortex part of the action execution/observation system (Avikainen, Kulomaki, & Hari, 1999). Two studies to date used EEG recordings and analysis of mu rhythm during self-executed and observed movement to explore a potential execution/observation matching system dysfunction in individuals with ASD. The first study showed an absence of the mu suppression—considered to be an index for mirror-neuron functioning—in the ASD group (Bernier, Dawson, Webb, & Murias, 2007). The second study reported intact mu suppression to both self and observed hand movements, which does not support the hypothesis that ASD is associated with a dysfunctional MNS (Raymaekers, Wiersema, & Roeyers, 2009). Williams et al. employed a functional magnetic resonance imaging (fMRI) protocol previously used to identify the neural substrate of imitation and human mirror-neuron function (Williams et al., 2006). They report

that activity in the mirror-neuron system (MNS) parietal area and in the right temporo-parietal junction associated with "theory of mind" (ToM) function was less extensive in the ASD group in the imitation task, suggesting altered patterns of brain activity during imitation that could stem from poor integration between areas serving visual, motor, proprioceptive, and emotional functions. In the same line, Dapretto et al. recorded brain activity while participants were imitating and observing emotional expressions. Children with ASD showed no activity in the inferior frontal gyrus (pars opercularis). Authors concluded that a dysfunctional MNS may underlie the social deficits observed in ASD (Dapretto et al., 2006). Importantly, it has to be noted that both groups performed the imitation tasks equally well in these studies, adding weight to the evidence of normal imitation skills in ASD. It also suggests that individuals with ASD use an alternative strategy to imitate grounded on a different development or on plasticity of the brain. This is a more positive perspective than only referring to a dysfunction. Another explanation could be that ASD subjects have impairment in biological motion processing (although this would prevent the ability to imitate). However, rather than a specific impairment in biological motion perception, Freitag et al. reported a general impairment in movement perception, pointing towards difficulties in higher-order motion perception or in the integration of complex motion information in the association cortex (Freitag et al., 2008).

At the theoretical level, one prominent opinion has stemmed out from this literature on imitation in AS. It highlights a dysfunction of the mirror neuron system, based mainly on results of neuroimaging studies and on the role of the MNS in the perception and understanding of other's actions (Iacoboni & Dapretto, 2006; Rizzolatti, Fabbri-Destro, & Cattaneo, 2009; Williams et al., 2006; Williams et al., 2001). This "broken mirror" theory suggests that low-level problems with imitation and with matching the actions of self and other are the primary cause of difficulties with mentalizing and more complex social interactions. It emphasizes the role of simulation in understanding others (Gallese, 2003). It is not our aim here to discuss the validity of one theory over another but we believe it to be important to note that available empirical data are both supportive and unsupportive of this particular theory (see Hamilton, 2009; Hamilton et al., 2007, for an extended discussion). For instance, a recent paper based on a meta-analysis of studies exploring the neural bases of imitation challenged the role of the pars opercularis (part of the MNS) in imitation (Molenberghs, Cunnington, & Mattingley, 2009). A dysfunction of this region should thus not be an argument in favor of an impairment in imitative behavior that would in turn lead to the theory of a dysfunctional mirror-neuron system in ASD. Moreover, we would like to take this opportunity to reflect on the danger associated to the sometimes overmotivation of researchers to fit experimental data or stick their interpretation in the realm of a single theory, while ignoring results that tend to prove the contrary. The "rush" to get data that confirm a given hypothesis, without questioning results is indeed ethically problematic. More important, although lacking enough empirical evidence of its validity (Hamilton et al., 2007), the mirror neuron dysfunction theory has received considerable attention and publicity sometimes far beyond the scientific community, which may have give unjustified hopes to families. The fact that the keywords "mirror neurons" were almost implicitly required in any research project related to autism may also have led research on other aspect of social cognition in ASD to restrict interpretation of data.

Asperger Syndrome and Nonsocial Cognition

People with AS exhibit many cognitive and behavioral peculiarities that could not be exclusively explained by a deficit in social cognition. In this section are exposed findings from nonsocial cognition research that are potentially crucial for a full understanding of AS functioning.

Sensory Processing

Individuals with AS often exhibit behaviors such as auditory self stimulation or conversely noisy environment avoidance, distress due to constant touching in a crowd . . . that suggest unusual sensory processing. The emergence of some autistic behaviors may stem from these sensory impairments (see Gerrard & Rugg, 2009, for a comprehensive review). Self-reports commonly mention abnormal sensory responses (Bogdashina, 2003; Williams, 1992), especially during childhood, and systematic review of the literature indicates that rates of sensory processing dysfunction may be as high as 90% in individuals with ASD (Baker, Lane, Angley, & Young, 2008; Baranek, David, Poe, Stone, & Watson, 2006; Leekam, Nieto, Libby, Wing, & Gould, 2007; Tomchek & Dunn, 2007). These specific sensory abnormalities seem to affect all sensory modalities and

include enhanced perceptual function such as visual hyperacuity (Ashwin, Ashwin, Rhydderch, Howells, & Baron-Cohen, 2009), hyperacusis (Khalfa et al., 2004) and acute tactile sensitivity (Blakemore et al., 2006). Hyporeactivity to sensory stimuli has also been extensively reported in all sensory modes (reviews; Ben-Sasson et al., 2009; Reynolds & Lane, 2008). Sensory modulation symptoms have even been evidenced in the olfactory domain in ASD. Relative to control subjects, AS subjects were not impaired at odor detection but were significantly impaired at olfactory identification (Suzuki, Critchley, Rowe, Howlin, & Murphy, 2003). These paradoxical responses to sensory stimuli lead to a lack of consensus on the exact nature of the underlying sensory dysfunction. A more recent study assessed sensory processing in adults with ASD using the Adult/ Adolescent Sensory Profile (AASP), a self-report questionnaire assessing levels of sensory processing in everyday life (Crane, Goddard, & Pring, 2009). Results demonstrated that sensory abnormalities were prevalent in ASD, with 94.4% of the ASD sample reporting extreme levels of sensory processing on at least one sensory quadrant of the AASP. Furthermore, analysis of the patterns of sensory processing impairments revealed striking within-group variability in the ASD group, suggesting that individuals with ASD could experience very different, yet similarly severe, sensory processing abnormalities. Moreover, in people with AS especially, performance in the adaptive behaviors of community use and socials skills has been shown to decrease as symptoms of dysfunction in sensory modulation increase (Pfeiffer, Kinnealey, Reed, & Herzberg, 2005). Taken together, these results suggest that unusual sensory processing in ASD extends across the lifespan and have implications regarding both the treatment and the diagnosis of ASD in adulthood.

Executive Functioning

Executive functioning (EF) is a global term that stands for any neuropsychological processes that enable physical, cognitive, and socio-emotional self-control. Executive dysfunction in autism has been a particularly active topic of investigation since the pioneer studies (Horwitz, Rumsey, Grady, & Rapoport, 1988; Ozonoff, Pennington, & Rogers, 1991; Russell, Saltmarsh, & Hill, 1999) to such an extent that an executive dysfunction model has been proposed (Hill, 2004; Hill & Bird, 2006) and is still being reinforced (Corbett, Constantine, Hendren, Rocke, & Ozonoff, 2009; Happe, Booth, Charlton, & Hughes, 2006; Ozonoff et al., 2004). Some authors argue that executive dysfunction can explain the main symptoms of ASD (Hill, 2004). By instance, the social interaction deficit might be due to a lack of flexibility leading to difficulties in taking another's perspective, whereas the repetitive behaviors may stem from a lack of generative ability or a difficulty in set shifting to a new behavior (Turner, 1999). Because most studies that compared executive skills of patients with HFA and AS concluded that both groups show relatively equivalent profiles (Verte, Geurts, Roeyers, Oosterlaan, & Sergeant, 2006), we illustrate this section with reports on results from studies on ASD, which generally mix HFA and AS subjects. Research on executive functioning suggests that individual with AS generally experience difficulties on problem-solving tasks, although some inconsistent findings are apparent (Hill, 2004). Planning (Ozonoff & Jensen, 1999), inhibition (Ozonoff & Strayer, 1997; Russell, Jarrold, & Hood, 1999), and especially cognitive flexibility (Kaland, Smith, & Mortensen, 2008; Ozonoff & Jensen, 1999) have also been found affected in people with ASD. Synthesis of behavioral EF studies in ASD suggests that impairments on tests requiring flexibility of thought and generation occur at all ages and across a range of autistic disorders including AS (Ambery, Russell, Perry, Morris, & Murphy, 2006).

Only few functional magnetic resonance imaging studies investigated the neural substrates of executive functions in ASDs, and none of them has been specifically performed in Asperger syndrome patients. The majority of neuroimaging studies on attention shifting, response inhibition, working memory, and so on, have shown an overall reduction in brain activation in regions normally associated with these functions. Di Martino recently conducted a meta-analysis of 15 neuroimaging studies examining nonsocial cognition (including attention control, working memory . . .) in ASD (Di Martino et al., 2009). Group comparisons revealed greater likelihood of activation for the ASD group in the rostral anterior cingulated cortex (ACC) that is typically suppressed during attentionally demanding tasks. Just et al. (2007) used the Tower of London task to explore brain activation associated with planification. Behavioral results showed that ASD individuals displayed similar error rates but longer reaction time than controls when the number of moves required to perform the task increases. During this planification task the two groups activated the same area to similar degrees. However, the degree of synchronization between frontal and parietal areas was lower in ASD than in controls. Authors concluded that the neural basis of altered planification in ASD entails a lower degree of integration of information across certain cortical areas resulting from reduced intracortical connectivity (Just, Cherkassky, Keller, Kana, & Minshew, 2007). In a working memory task using a n-back paradigm, (Koshino et al., 2005) found that ASD exhibited more neural activity in the posterior regions relative to controls, and showed a different pattern of temporal connectivity between prefrontal and parietal regions. Behavioral result showed comparable performance suggesting that individuals with ASD used a different strategy to perform working memory task, based on the over-recruitment of posterior regions at the expenses of more integrative frontal areas. Similarly, functional connectivity analysis performed during a cognitive control task (while subjects were preparing to overcome prepotent response) revealed lower levels of functional connectivity and less network integration between frontal, parietal, and occipital regions in the ASD group, associated with higher error rate in response to the most difficult trials that need greater involvement of cognitive control process (Solomon et al., 2009). Kana et al. (2007) used a go-no-go task to investigate the neural basis of response inhibition in autism (Kana, Keller, Minshew, & Just, 2007). Although both groups showed similar performances, the inhibition circuitry (namely anterior cingulate gyrus, middle cingulate gyrus, and insula) in the ASD group was activated atypically and was less synchronized, leaving inhibition to be accomplished by strategic control rather than automatically. Taken together, these results from functional connectivity analysis during EF tasks provide converging evidence in line with the long range under connectivity hypothesis proposed by Just et al. (Just, Cherkassky, Keller, & Minshew, 2004) (see next section for more detail).

Cognitive flexibility deficit appears to be central to ASD. This would yield routines, restricted, idiosyncratic and intense interests, and lack of generalization, which are particularly incapacitating for several daily life activities Parents and clinicians report that it is the most troubling, consistent and resistant-to-intervention characteristic of the autistic disorder. As this aspect of the AS cognition prevents any flexible adaptation to unexpected or changing events, it might have a fundamental role in the social interaction deficit revealed in the highly unpredictable social world. Researchers and clinicians assume that inflexible everyday behaviors in autism are directly related to cognitive flexibility deficits as assessed by clinical and experimental measures. However, there is a large gap between the day-to-day behavioral flexibility and that measured with cognitive flexibility tasks (Geurts, Corbett, & Solomon, 2009).

Only a small number of studies has explored the relationships between executive functioning performances and the repetitive and rigid behaviors. Lopezdemonstrated that repetitive behaviors in adults with ASD were associated with deficits in some executive function (cognitive flexibility, working memory) but not others (planning and fluency) (Lopez, Lincoln, Ozonoff, & Lai, 2005). In a study examining the relationship between everyday repetitive behaviors and performance on neuropsychological tests of executive function and central coherence, South et al. evidenced partial support in the ASD group for the link between repetitive behaviors and Wisconsin Card Sorting Task performance (South, Ozonoff, & McMahon, 2007). Conversely, there was no support for a link between repetitive behaviors and measures of central coherence (Gestalt Closure test and Embedded Figures Test).

The neural correlates of set shifting were investigated using fMRI in ASD subjects (Shafritz, Dichter, Baranek, & Belger, 2008). Results showed lower accuracy on response-shifting trials along with reduced activation in frontal, striatal, and parietal regions during these trials in ASD. In addition, the severity of restricted, repetitive behaviors was negatively correlated with activation in anterior cingulate and posterior parietal regions, suggesting that executive deficits and, by extension, repetitive behaviors associated with ASD might reflect a core dysfunction within the brain's executive circuitry. Other results suggest that the lack of flexibility might be related to more basic dysfunction involving perception and attention. Using an active auditory oddball task, Gomot et al. showed superior activation of the inferior parietal and prefrontal regions in ASD in response to novel targets (Gomot, Belmonte, Bullmore, Bernard, & Baron-Cohen, 2008). Moreover, this atypical pattern of activation in the fronto-parietal network during novelty detection was associated with high scores on the Autism Quotient, raising the possibility of links between these brain regions and autistic traits. Authors suggested that this over-focused attention on specific events may be counterproductive during flexible social interactions and may play a role in the development of narrow patterns of interests or activities. Interestingly, using the same auditory oddball

sequence but presented in passive condition we found that the inferior parietal lobule in children with autism was hypo-activated in response to novel stimuli, whereas this same region was found hyperactivated during the active run (Gomot et al., 2006). Therefore, depending on the context (instruction), individuals with autism may have an abnormally narrow or an abnormally broad focus of attention toward changing events. Similar attention impairments have been demonstrated in the spatial domain, in a task that required stimulus discrimination following a spatial cue that preceded the target presentation either with a long (voluntary spatial attention) or a short (automatic attention) inter stimulus interval (Haist, Adamo, Westerfield, Courchesne, & Townsend, 2005). The pattern of fMRI findings suggests that ASD is associated with a profound deficit in automatic spatial attention and abnormal voluntary spatial attention skills.

These findings on EF showing roughly similar performances between control and ASD groups but differences in the temporal connectivity of the different brain areas involved in the cognitive task, favor the hypothesis of the development of alternative strategies in ASD rather than a cognitive deficit per se.

Weak Central Coherence

Central coherence is defined as the ability to draw together diverse information in order to construct higher-level meanings in context. It involves the ability to move from a local to global level of processing. People with ASD demonstrate a unique profile of perceptual and cognitive abilities, characterized by over-focus on the local level at the expense of the global view. Evidence of a pattern of weak central coherence has been examined with respect to visual processing (i.e. people with ASD display better performance in the embedded figures tasks; Jolliffe & Baron-Cohen, 1997—and are not fooled by visual illusions such as Tichener Circles, which depend on the context being taking into account or not (Happe, 1999), as well as to a conceptual deficit as originally demonstrated in reading tasks (Snowling, Goulandris, Bowlby, & Howell, 1986). Moreover, it has been shown that subjects with ASD are not affected by interfering visual (Jolliffe & Baron-Cohen, 1997) or auditory (Foxton et al., 2003) "gestalts" and this lack of interference has been interpreted as reflecting a deficit in the "coherent whole" representation. Rather than a deficit in global processing, it has then been proposed, mostly on the basis of study of auditory attention processes that revealed enhanced pitch processing (Bonnel et al., 2003; Heaton, Hudry, Ludlow, & Hill, 2008), that low-level information processing systems for sensory stimuli would be over-developed in autism (Mottron, Peretz, & Menard, 2000; Plaisted, Saksida, Alcantara, & Weisblatt, 2003), but see further conceptualization with the Enhanced Perceptual Processing Model (Mottron, Dawson, Soulieres, Hubert, & Burack, 2006).

Few brain-imaging studies have investigated the neural correlates of context processing in AS. In a study employing fMRI while subjects performed the Embedded Figures Tasks, Ring et al. tested local/global processing through the visual search of a simple shape in a complex figure (Ring et al., 1999). Whereas typical subjects preferentially activated prefrontal areas, subjects with ASD demonstrated greater activation of ventral occipito-temporal regions, associated with superior task performances. Authors concluded that the ASD group strategy depends to an abnormally large extent on visual systems for objects features analysis, at the expenses of more integrative processing. Hypo-activation of prefrontal areas during visuo-spatial context processing has recently been confirmed by other groups (Manjaly et al., 2007; Lee et al., 2007).

Another study has addressed brain activity associated with global information processing, in which context was given by gaze direction (Pelphrey et al., 2002). Findings suggested that gaze processing impairments in ASD are not due to gaze discrimination per se, but rather linked to deficits in using information from gaze direction to solve social situations that demand awareness of contextual subtleties.

More recently, the hypersystemizing theory of ASD (Baron-Cohen, 2002, 2006) has been proposed, based on the empathizing-systemizing model that postulates the existence of two distinct psychological dimensions: Systemizing is the drive to analyze the variables in a system, to derive the underlying rules that govern the behavior of a system. This allows one to predict the behavior of a system, and to control it. "Empathizing" is the drive to identify another person's emotions and thoughts, and to respond to these with an appropriate emotion. Empathizing in this model permits one to predict a person's behavior, and to care about how others feel. A large body of evidence suggests that, on average, males spontaneously systemize to a greater degree than do females while females spontaneously empathize more than do males (Lawson, Baron-Cohen, & Wheelwright, 2004).

Systemizing and empathizing may thus be two key dimensions defining the male and female brain which conceptualization has led Baron-Cohen et al., to propose the extreme male brain theory of ASD (Baron-Cohen, 2002), while underlining that this theory of autism was first informally suggested by Hans Asperger in 1944:

"The autistic personality is an extreme variant of male intelligence. . . . In the autistic individuals the male pattern is exaggerated to the extreme" (Asperger, 1944).

Finally, Baron-Cohen and Belmonte (2005) argue that Empathizing-Systemizing and Weak Central Coherence should not be considered as mutually exclusive explanations of ASD behaviors, but as complementary ones that can be developmentally unified. Specifically, the attention to detail described by weak central coherence may be one of the earliest manifestations of a strong drive toward systemizing or, vice-versa, interest in systemizing may arise as a consequence of attention to detail.

Memory

Autobiographical memory comprises both personally experienced events (personal episodic memories) and self-related information (personal semantic memories). It serves several important social functions, aiding in solving social problems (Goddard, Dritschel, & Burton, 1996), in the formation and maintenance of social relationships and in providing information for social communication and interaction. Considering these pertinent social aspects of autobiographical memory, some research groups considered of strong theoretical interest to examine autobiographical memory in neurodevelopmental disorders characterized by impairments in the social domain. Likewise, in one of the few studies of autobiographical memory in adults with ASD, Goddard et al. (2007) examined personal episodic memory using a cueing methodology in which participants were required to generate memories of specific autobiographical events in response to cue words at speed. Results demonstrated that the adults with ASD recalled significantly fewer specific autobiographical memories and took considerably longer to do so than an age, gender, and IQ-matched control group. Taken together, these two studies suggest that an autobiographical memory deficit is characteristic of ASD and that this deficit persists across the lifespan.

Episodic and semantic autobiographical memories were examined in a group of adults with ASD and a control group matched for age, gender, and IQ. Results demonstrated a personal episodic memory deficit in the ASD group in the absence of a personal semantic memory deficit, suggesting dissociation between these two components of memory in ASD. Further analysis of memories across different lifetime periods revealed the adolescent and early adult lifetime periods to facilitate memory recall in the control group, but not in the ASD group. These findings suggest a distinctive pattern of remembering in ASD (Crane & Goddard, 2008).

Specific Cognitive Style vs. Socio-emotional Disorder

Current research into the field of ASD is basically/traditionally dissociated into two main domains: emotion and cognition. Such dichotomy is possibly due to the prevalent view of the brain as organized into either affective or cognitive components (see the meta-analysis of social and nonsocial processes in ASD by Di Martino et al., 2009 as an illustration). However, as a pervasive developmental disorder, ASD should certainly not be reduced to deficits in one restricted domain. Based on the proposition that the neural basis of emotion and cognition should be view as strongly non-modular (Pessoa, 2008), some recent studies have attempted to integrate these two fields.

ASD individuals are characterized by cognitive control deficits as well as impairment in social interaction, but only few studies have addressed the interactive effects of these deficits. Using fMRI (Dichter & Belger, 2007) showed that processing social stimuli interferes with the (decreased) functioning of brain regions recruited during cognitive control tasks in ASD. Eye movement analysis and computational model of visual saliency argue that the peculiar bias for fixating the mouth in ASD would be related to an abnormal top-down strategy for allocating visual attention (Neumann, Spezio, Piven, & Adolphs, 2006). Many behavioral observations indicate that in healthy people attention is modulated by the emotional salience of stimuli (Vuilleumier, 2005). Attentional Blink paradigm was used to determine whether emotional words could capture attention similarly in ASD and in controls (Gaigg & Bowler, 2009a). Whilst the emotionality of words facilitates attention in typical comparison participants, this effect was attenuated in ASD. Decision-making processes are typically influenced by the emotional/motivational significance of the choice. A crucial issue is whether such relationships of motivation and cognition are observed in ASD. This was investigated using a financial task in which the monetary prospects were presented either as loss or gain. Results showed that ASD patients display a more consistent pattern of choice and tend to less incorporate emotional contextual cues into their decision process than controls. This somewhat enhanced rationality possibly comes at a cost of reduced behavioral flexibility (De Martino, Harrison, Knafo, Bird, & Dolan, 2008). To assess whether the emotional valence of visual scenes affects recall skills in high-functioning individuals with ASD, a recent study compared recall performance of neutral and emotional pictures with that of typically developing adults. While typically developing individuals showed enhanced recall skills for negative relative to positive and neutral pictures, individuals with ASD recalled the neutral pictures as well as the emotional ones (Deruelle, Hubert, Santos, & Wicker, 2008). This points to a reduced influence of emotion on memory processes in ASD, possibly owing to amygdala dysfunctions. In a series of studies, Gaigg et al. used various tasks to target the influence of emotional processing on other areas of cognition such as memory and conditional learning. Results of a first study showed that ASD subjects exhibit a pattern of abnormality in differentially acquiring fear, suggesting that their fear responses are atypically modulated by conditioned and nonconditioned stimuli (Gaigg & Bowler, 2007). A second study showed that although individuals with ASD, like typical individuals, exhibit a free recall advantage for emotionally arousing and semantically related neutral as compared to unrelated neutral words, they do not show reduced forgetting rates for arousing stimuli as do typical individuals (Gaigg & Bowler, 2008, 2009b).

Accurate processing of social stimuli typically challenges the impaired skills of individuals with ASD: they are complex, multisensorial, move and change rapidly, and are highly unpredictable. In view of the ASDs' cognitive peculiarities highlighted in this chapter, one can logically expect that people with AS will fail to efficiently process such information. Recent research has turned to investigate interplay between the cognitive and emotional dimensions. Altogether results reveal the potential interest of exploring functional links between these two domains in ASD. Further studies need now to be carried out to determine whether ASDs undergo a specific socio-emotional impairment involving, for example, a motivational dysfunction rooted in amygdala connectivity abnormalities that leads to a deficient ignition of the attentional frontal circuitry during processing of relevant social information, or a more general cognitive style that would not be efficient in the frame of social interactions.

Asperger Syndrome, Brain Anatomy and Connectivity

Autism being a neurodevelopmental disorder of genetic origin, researchers have quite early on investigated if discrete brain structural abnormalities could explain behavioral impairments. For a long time, studies were confined to post-mortem brain anatomy or basic MRI explorations, which for various reasons yielded often controversial findings. The recent advent of innovative imaging technologies and analysis methods, such as voxel-based morphometry (VBM), fiber tracking with diffusion tensor imaging (DTI), and morphometrical measures of cortical thickness and folding have addressed several of the limitations of previous research and now begin to highlight key neuroanatomical abnormalities more consistently. Results of neuroanatomical studies performed in autism have been reviewed elsewhere (Brambilla et al., 2003; Penn, 2006), and we will thus restrict this section to recent data obtained from AS populations.

Voxel-based morphometry (VBM) gives probabilistic information about grey and white matter volume and is the most often used technique. McAlonan et al. (2005) have shown generalized as well as localized grey matter reduction in the fronto-striatal, parietal, and temporal cortex in high-functioning autistic children, pointing to an early structural abnormality of the "social brain"(McAlonan et al., 2005). Local white matter volume deficits have been described in the corpus callosum, left middle temporal, right middle frontal, and left superior frontal gyri (McAlonan et al., 2005; Waiter et al., 2005). Ke et al. found a significant decrease of the white matter density in the right frontal lobe, left parietal lobe, and right anterior cingulate and a significant increase in the right frontal lobe, left parietal lobe, and left cingulate gyrus in a group of ASD children compared with a control group (Ke et al., 2009). Using an automated technique of analysis that accurately measures the thickness of the cerebral cortex, Hadjikhani et al. (2006) found cortical thinning in cerebral areas involved in emotion and social information processing, including the STS, the inferior frontal gyrus, inferior parietal lobule, anterior cingulate, and prefrontal cortex (Hadjikhani, Joseph, Snyder, & Tager-Flusberg, 2006). This result has been confirmed by a combination of cortical thickness analyses and VBM, which revealed grey matter

increases in brain areas implicated in social cognition, communication, and repetitive behaviors (Hyde, Samson, Evans, & Mottron, 2009). Cortical shape abnormalities in the intraparietal sulcus correlating with age, intelligence quotient, and Autism Diagnostic Interview-Revised social and repetitive behavior scores have also been reported (Nordahl et al., 2007). Interestingly, grey matter increases were also found in auditory and visual primary and associative perceptual areas, which were interpreted as structural brain correlates of atypical auditory and visual perception in ASD, supporting the enhanced perceptual functioning model (Hyde et al., 2009).

Potential anatomical differences between HFA and AS were recently investigated. While HFA and AS exhibited a common pattern of decreased grey matter density in the ventromedial regions of the temporal cortex (right inferior temporal gyrus, entorhinal cortex, and rostral fusiform gyrus) in comparison with an age-matched comparison group, the AS group had specifically less grey matter density in the body of the cingulate gyrus (Kwon, Ow, Pedatella, Lotspeich, & Reiss, 2004). Another study reported that compared to controls, children with HFA had smaller grey matter volumes in predominantly fronto-pallidal regions, while children with Asperger's had less grey matter in mainly bilateral caudate and left thalamus. Combination of data from both groups confirmed a mixed picture of smaller grey matter volumes in frontal, basal ganglia, temporal, and parietal regions (McAlonan et al., 2008). White-matter volumes around the basal ganglia were also reported higher in AS than in controls (McAlonan et al., 2008). Children with AS also had less frontal and corpus callosal white matter in the right hemisphere with more white matter in the left parietal lobe. Taken together, these results suggest that AS thus affects predominantly right hemisphere white-matter systems and that the underlying neurobiology in HFA and AS is at least partly discrete.

Structural Connectivity

A technique that (in part) overcomes the limitations of VBM approaches is tractography applied to diffusion tensor magnetic resonance imaging (DT-MRI or DTI) datasets. Indeed, DTI-tractography is the only technique that allows the simultaneous quantification of the white matter volume and microstructural integrity within specific tracts in the living human brain. Focusing on the cerebellum, Catani et al. measured mean diffusivity and fractional anisotropy within the inferior, middle, superior cerebellar peduncles, and short intracerebellar fibers (Catani et al., 2008). No group differences were observed in mean diffusivity but people with AS had significantly lower fractional anisotropy in the short intracerebellar fibers and right superior cerebellar peduncle compared to controls. These findings suggest a vulnerability of specific cerebellar neural pathways in people with AS. The localized abnormalities in the main cerebellar outflow pathway may prevent the cerebral cortex from receiving those cerebellar feedback inputs necessary for a successful adaptive social behavior (Schmahmann, Weilburg, & Sherman, 2007). Another study compared the micro-structural integrity in the extended limbic pathways between subjects with AS and healthy controls (Pugliese et al., 2009). The dissected limbic pathways included the inferior longitudinal fasciculus, inferior frontal occipital fasciculus, uncinate, cingulum, and fornix. Compared to healthy controls, individuals with AS had a significantly higher number of streamlines in the right and left cingulum, and in the right and left inferior longitudinal fasciculus. In contrast, people with AS had a significantly lower number of streamlines in the right uncinate. These preliminary findings suggest that people with AS have significant differences in the anatomy, and maturation, of some (but not all) limbic tracts and other tracts connecting sensory areas to temporal and orbitofrontal limbic regions. Anterior cingulate cortex microstructural integrity of the white matter and function during response monitoring were recently investigated using fMRI and measures of fractional anisotropy (FA) (Thakkar et al., 2008). Relative to controls, ASD participants showed reduced activity in the rostral ACC during discrimination between error and correct responses, and reduced FA in the white matter underlying ACC. Furthermore, these differences were related to higher ratings of repetitive behavior. Structural and functional abnormalities of the ACC in ASD may thus compromise response monitoring and thereby contribute to behavior that is rigid and repetitive rather than flexible and responsive to contingencies.

Functional Connectivity

As described above and in previous sections, research into the neural bases of ASD has largely focused on the identification of structural or functional abnormalities in specific structures or "modules" within large scale networks underpinning aspects of social-emotional or executive functioning. However, there has recently been a shift from focus on discrete brain regions to emphasis on reasoning in terms of network of brain areas acting together to enable a specific, simple or very complex function. Hence, the issue of how different brain regions are connected functionally, that is, how the interplay of different areas subserves cognitive function, has become a key concern. Most recent research has thus now turned to investigating the more dynamic processes of brain functional connectivity. In fact, the concept of autism as a functional disconnection syndrome originates in one of its earliest neurobiological accounts (Damasio & Maurer, 1978) that was later supported by data reporting abnormalities of inter-regional correlation between frontal, parietal, and neostriatal metabolic rates for glucose measured by positron emission tomography (PET) (Horwitz et al., 1988).

Functional connectivity MRI (fcMRI) typically investigates whole brain connectivity with a number of predefined seed brain regions of interest. The method is to examine interregional correlations of activity ("synchronization") and it has been applied to fMRI data collected during performance of various tasks.

Results supporting the hypothesis of underconnectivity in ASD are the most common. Abnormally reduced correlation of activity between extrastriate and superior temporal cortices at the temporoparietal junction, an area associated with the processing of biological motion as well as with mentalizing, was observed during attribution of mental states from movements of animated shapes. This finding suggested a physiological cause for the mentalizing dysfunction in ASD: a bottleneck in the interaction between higher-order and lower-order perceptual processes (Castelli, Frith, Happe, & Frith, 2002). Decreased functional connectivity between Wernicke's and Broca's areas during language processing and reduced functional connectivity between V1 and inferior frontal cortex in a visuomotor task was also reported (Just et al., 2004; Kana, Keller, Cherkassky, Minshew, & Just, 2006; Villalobos, Mizuno, Dahl, Kemmotsu, & Muller, 2005). More recently, abnormally low functional connectivity between frontal and parietal areas was evidenced during a cognitive control task (Solomon et al., 2009) and during the performance of a Tower of London task (Just et al., 2007). Interestingly, this study also revealed that relevant parts of the corpus callosum—through which many of the bilaterally activated cortical areas communicate—were smaller and that the size of the genu of the corpus callosum was correlated with frontal-parietal functional connectivity (Just et al., 2007). Using the fusiform face area as a seed region, functional connectivity during face processing indicated that whereas FFA-amygdala and FFA-superior temporal sulcus functional connectivity was found in both the ASD and control participants, there was lower functional connectivity of the fusiform face area with frontal areas (Kleinhans et al., 2008; Koshino et al., 2008). Moreover, greater social impairment was associated with reduced FFA-amygdala connectivity and increased FFA-right inferior frontal connectivity in ASD. Evidence for significant abnormality of functional integration of amygdala and parahippocampal gyrus in people with AS during fearful face processing was also reported (Welchew et al., 2005). Functional underconnectivity in the connections between frontal and posterior areas was recently reported during the attribution of mental states, providing new evidence that underconnectivity between frontal regions and more posterior areas may be the biological basis of atypical processing of ToM in ASD (Kana, Keller, Cherkassky, Minshew, & Just, 2009). Whole-brain connectivity with three seed regions of interest located in the left middle frontal, left superior parietal, and left middle occipital cortices was also evaluated using fMRI datasets acquired during performance of a source recognition task (Noonan, Haist, & Muller, 2009). Functional cMRI patterns were found to be largely similar across clinical and control groups, including many common areas. Moreover, effects for the ASD group were generally more extensive. Although inconsistent with underconnectivity in ASD, these results are compatible with a model of aberrant connectivity in which the nature of connectivity disturbance (i.e., increased or reduced) may vary across regions.

Altogether, these findings suggest that the neural basis of altered cognition in AS entails a lower degree of integration of information across certain cortical areas resulting from reduced intracortical connectivity. Several possibilities have been proposed: a bottom-up failure of feed-forward visual signals reaching the superior temporal sulcus (STS) from extrastriate cortices such as the fusiform gyrus; or a top-down failure of feedback signals reaching STS from the anterior components of the mentalizing system; that is, dorso-medial and lateral prefrontal cortices (DMPFC and LPFC). The theoretical formulation that draws together much of these data is that ASD may be characterized by dysfunctioning functional interactions between networks of distributed brain regions important for socio-emotional cognition.

Recent research has now focused on connectivity associated to the "default mode" of the brain. From existing studies, the "default mode network" (DMN) has been associated indirectly with the pattern of evoked activity that is observed with tasks involving self-judgments, autobiographical memory recall, moral dilemma, and prospective thinking, among others (Buckner, Andrews-Hanna, & Schacter, 2008). In general terms, a common feature of these tasks is that they enhance subjects' attention toward themselves—a presumed behavioral correlate of resting-state imaging conditions and the spontaneous thought processes, or "mind-wandering," that accompany it. The DMN is composed of multiple interacting subsystems and includes the prefrontal medial cortex, the precuneus/posterior cingulate cortex, the lateral and inferior parietal cortex, and the medial temporal lobe (Raichle et al., 2001). These areas are deactivated during task performance and active in the resting brain with a high degree of functional connectivity between regions. The more demanding the task, the stronger the deactivation appears to be (Singh, Mukherjee, & Chung, 2008). Because of its relation with various processes involved in social cognition, research has begun to explore the relationship of the DMN to mental disorders including autism, schizophrenia, and Alzheimer's disease (Broyd et al., 2009; Buckner et al., 2008). Altered intrinsic connectivity within the default network may underlie offline processing that may actuate ASD impairments. Kennedy and colleagues recently used fMRI to directly explore the functional integrity of the default network in ASD (Kennedy, Redcay, & Courchesne, 2006). While the control participants showed the typical pattern of activity in the default network during the passive tasks, direct comparison between the groups revealed absence of activation in the ventromedial prefrontal cortex and in the posterior parietal cortex in the ASD group. Moreover, in an exploratory analysis of individual differences within the ASD group, those individuals with the greatest social impairment (measured using a standardized diagnostic inventory) were those with the most atypical vMPFC activity levels. Weaker intrinsic functional correlations in the default network, particularly between the posterior cingulate cortex and superior frontal gyrus in ASD added weight to the evidence (Cherkassky, Kana, Keller, & Just, 2006; Monk et al., 2009). An intriguing possibility suggested by the authors and extended by Iacoboni (2006) is that the failure to modulate the default network in ASD is driven by differential cognitive mentation during rest, specifically a lack of self-referential processing. Of note, the fronto-parietal dysfunction concerns a network that has been recently hypothesized to control interactions between the default network and brain systems linked to external attention (Vincent et al., 2007). In this line, no abnormal patterns of connectivity in the task-positive network, but reduced connectivity in the DMN mainly associated with the MPFC, were recently reported (Kennedy & Courchesne, 2008). As the MPFC is thought to mediate a dynamic interplay between emotional processing and cognition functions which map on to the ventral and dorsal regions, this imbalance between the task-positive and DMN networks may bias an individual with ASD toward nonsocial and emotional processing styles. Moreover, it is suggested that such a neural bias may exist from a young age, affecting the developmental trajectory of social and emotional processing (Kennedy & Courchesne, 2008). In summary, DMN activity in ASD is thought to be low at rest, with reduced connectivity between anterior and posterior DMN regions probably reflecting a disturbance of self-referential thought. Developmental disruption of the default network, in particular disruption linked to the MPFC, might result in a mind that is environmentally focused and absent a conception of other people's thoughts. The inability to interact with others in social contexts would then be an expected behavioral consequence. It is important to note that dysfunction of the default network and associated symptoms may emerge as an indirect consequence of early developmental events that begin outside the network.

Several explanations were proposed to address the question of the origin of abnormal functional connectivity in AS. Early brain overgrowth in the form of reduced long-distance connections between structurally remote but functionally connected networks, with additionally enhanced or exaggerated connectivity within local network nodes, that is, local "overconnectivity," has been the most influential (Belmonte et al., 2004; Courchesne & Pierce, 2005). Recent modeling results support this hypothesis that the deviant growth trajectory in ASD may lead to a disruption of established patterns of functional connectivity during development, with potentially negative behavioral consequences, and a subsequent reduction in physical connectivity (Lewis & Elman, 2008).

Unfortunately, functional connectivity only refers to temporal correlations between remote neurophysiological events and is therefore simply a statement about observed correlations and does not provide any direct insight into how these correlations are mediated. Another method to study brain connectivity is modeling effective connectivity through structural equation modeling (SEM) or dynamic causal modeling (DCM). This methodology has been recently applied and revealed abnormal pattern of effective connectivity in the ASD brain. Attentional modulation for social (face) and nonsocial (house) stimuli was investigated and results of effective connectivity analysis indicated that this impairment was due to a failure of attention to modulate connectivity between extrastriate areas and V1. This particular result may explain the reduced processing of social stimuli in ASD (Bird, Catmur, Silani, Frith, & Frith, 2006). Distinct patterns of effective connectivity during explicit processing of emotional expressions of anger and happiness were also recently reported, with direct evidence of abnormal long-range connectivity between the brain structures implicated in the socioemotional network in ASD (Wicker et al., 2008). This is in line with the idea of reduced long-distance anterior to posterior cortico-cortical connectivity (Courchesne, 2004), which impairs the fundamental frontal function of integrating information from widespread and diverse systems (emotional, language, sensory, autonomic, etc.) and providing complex context-rich feedback, guidance, and control to lower-level systems (Taylor & Fragopanagos, 2005). Furthermore, these data suggest that this abnormal modulation most likely has its origins in abnormal activation, and effective connectivity, of the medial and lateral prefrontal cortices. This adds a functional relevance and value to recent data from histopathological, voxel-based morphometry, MRI volumetric analysis, and diffusion tensor imaging studies suggesting abnormal development and abnormal local connectivity in the medial part of the prefrontal cortex (Waiter et al., 2005). Another study suggests that while the brain resources involved in motor representation of perceived action are functional in ASD subjects, their failure to grasp action-related emotional content has its origin in abnormal activation and reduced effective connectivity of the amygdala with other areas comprising the emotional brain (Grezes et al., 2009).

The next step towards a full understanding of abnormal connectivity in ASD is now to combine data from structural, functional, and effective connectivity, to build more pertinent models that take into account anatomical constraints in extended large scale brain network modeling. Several research team have begun to follow this line of research in controls (Damoiseaux & Greicius, 2009; Stephan, Tittgemeyer, Knosche, Moran, & Friston, 2009), and the replication of such data analysis approach in ASD is very promising.

Conclusion

This chapter has reviewed major recent findings in AS, ranging from behavior to neurobiology, and focusing both on social cognitive and executive processes and their interactions. It revealed that the study of AS benefits from several lines of research on one hand, but that on the other hand a lot of controversy remains as to whether the results of individual studies can be generalized to the entire AS population. This obviously highlights the need for further extensive research. But it also evidences a very hopeful and intense period for research aiming at : 1) better characterizing of the clinical, behavioral, and cognitive phenotypes; 2) building a new conceptual framework through an integrative approach mixing emotional/social cognition and other areas of cognition; and 3) progressively supplants the localizationism realm by applying recent massive advances in neuroimaging techniques and analysis that explore connectivity and functional interactions in large scale dynamic brain networks. This is obviously particularly encouraging and pertinent when dealing with a pervasive neurodevelopmental disorder like Asperger syndrome.

References

Ambery, F. Z., Russell, A. J., Perry, K., Morris, R., & Murphy, D. G. (2006). Neuropsychological functioning in adults with Asperger syndrome. *Autism, 10*(6), 551–564.

American Psychiatric Association. (2000). *Diagnostic and statistical manual of mental disorders, Fourth Edition, Text Revision.* Washington DC: American Psychiatric Association.

Ashwin, C., Baron-Cohen, S., Wheelwright, S., O'Riordan, M., & Bullmore, E. T. (2007). Differential activation of *the* amygdala and the "social brain" during fearful face-processing in Asperger syndrome. *Neuropsychologia, 45*(1), 2–14.

Ashwin, C., Chapman, E., Colle, L., & Baron-Cohen, S. (2006). Impaired recognition of negative basic emotions in autism: A test of the amygdala theory. *Soc Neurosci, 1*(3–4), 349–363.

Ashwin, C., Wheelwright, S., & Baron-Cohen, S. (2006a). Attention bias to faces in Asperger syndrome: A pictorial emotion Stroop study. *Psychol Med, 36*(6), 835–843.

Ashwin, C., Wheelwright, S., & Baron-Cohen, S. (2006b). Finding a face in the crowd: Testing the anger superiority effect in Asperger syndrome. *Brain Cogn, 61*(1), 78–95.

Ashwin, E., Ashwin, C., Rhydderch, D., Howells, J., & Baron-Cohen, S. (2009). Eagle-eyed visual acuity: An experimental investigation of enhanced perception in autism. *Biol Psychiatry, 65*(1), 17–21.

Asperger, H. (1944). Die "autistichen psychopathen" *Archives für Psychiatrie und Nervenkraun kheiten, 117*, 76–136.

Attwood, T. (1998). *Asperger's syndrome: A guide for parents and professionals.* London: Jessica Kingsley Publishers.

Avikainen, S., Kulomaki, T., & Hari, R. (1999). Normal movement reading in Asperger subjects. *Neuroreport, 10*(17), 3467–3470.

Avikainen, S., Wohlschlager, A., Liuhanen, S., Hanninen, R., & Hari, R. (2003). Impaired mirror-image imitation in Asperger and high-functioning autistic subjects. *Curr Biol, 13*(4), 339–341.

Baker, A. E., Lane, A., Angley, M. T., & Young, R. L. (2008). The relationship between sensory processing patterns and behavioural responsiveness in autistic disorder: A pilot study. *J Autism Dev Disord, 38*(5), 867–875.

Baranek, G. T., David, F. J., Poe, M. D., Stone, W. L., & Watson, L. R. (2006). Sensory Experiences Questionnaire: Discriminating sensory features in young children with autism, developmental delays, and typical development. *J Child Psychol Psychiatry, 47*(6), 591–601.

Baron-Cohen, S. (2000). Is Asperger syndrome/high-functioning autism necessarily a disability? *Dev Psychopathol, 12*(3), 489–500.

Baron-Cohen, S. (2002). The extreme male brain theory of autism. *Trends Cogn Sci, 6*(6), 248–254.

Baron-Cohen, S. (2006). The hyper-systemizing, assortative mating theory of autism. *Prog Neuropsychopharmacol Biol Psychiatry, 30*(5), 865–872.

Baron-Cohen, S. & Belmonte, M. K. (2005). Autism: A window onto the development of the social and the analytic brain. *Annu Rev Neurosci, 28*, 109–126.

Baron-Cohen, S., Richler, J., Bisarya, D., Gurunathan, N., & Wheelwright, S. (2003). The systemizing quotient: An investigation of adults with Asperger syndrome or high-functioning autism, and normal sex differences. *Philos Trans R Soc Lond B Biol Sci, 358*(1430), 361–374.

Baron-Cohen, S., Wheelwright, S., Robinson, J., & Woodbury-Smith, M. (2005). The Adult Asperger Assessment (AAA): A diagnostic method. *J Autism Dev Disord, 35*(6), 807–819.

Bejerot, S. (2007). An autistic dimension: A proposed subtype of obsessive-compulsive disorder. *Autism, 11*(2), 101–110.

Belmonte, M. K., Allen, G., Beckel-Mitchener, A., Boulanger, L. M., Carper, R. A., & Webb, S. J. (2004). Autism and abnormal development of brain connectivity. *J Neurosci, 24*(42), 9228–9231.

Ben-Sasson, A., Hen, L., Fluss, R., Cermak, S. A., Engel-Yeger, B., & Gal, E. (2009). A meta-analysis of sensory modulation symptoms in individuals with autism spectrum disorders. *J Autism Dev Disord, 39*(1), 1–11.

Bernier, R., Dawson, G., Webb, S., & Murias, M. (2007). EEG mu rhythm and imitation impairments in individuals with autism spectrum disorder. *Brain Cogn, 64*(3), 228–237.

Bird, G., Catmur, C., Silani, G., Frith, C., & Frith, U. (2006). Attention does not modulate neural responses to social stimuli in autism spectrum disorders. *Neuroimage, 31*(4), 1614–1624.

Bird, G., Leighton, J., Press, C., & Heyes, C. (2007). Intact automatic imitation of human and robot actions in autism spectrum disorders. *Proc Biol Sci, 274*(1628), 3027–3031.

Blakemore, S. J., Tavassoli, T., Calo, S., Thomas, R. M., Catmur, C., Frith, U., et al. (2006). Tactile sensitivity in Asperger syndrome. *Brain Cogn, 61*(1), 5–13.

Bogdashina, O. (2003). *Sensory perceptual issues in autism and Asperger syndrome.* London & Philadelphia: Jessica Kingsley.

Bolte, S., Feineis-Matthews, S., & Poustka, F. (2008). Brief report: Emotional processing in high-functioning autism—physiological reactivity and affective report. *J Autism Dev Disord, 38*(4), 776–781.

Bonnel, A., Mottron, L., Peretz, I., Trudel, M., Gallun, E., & Bonnel, A. M. (2003). Enhanced pitch sensitivity in individuals with autism: A signal detection analysis. *J Cogn Neurosci, 15*(2), 226–235.

Brambilla, P., Hardan, A., di Nemi, S. U., Perez, J., Soares, J. C., & Barale, F. (2003). Brain anatomy and development in autism: Review of structural MRI studies. *Brain Res Bull, 61*(6), 557–569.

Broyd, S. J., Demanuele, C., Debener, S., Helps, S. K., James, C. J., & Sonuga-Barke, E. J. (2009). Default-mode brain dysfunction in mental disorders: A systematic review. *Neurosci Biobehav Rev, 33*(3), 279–296.

Buchsbaum, M. S., Hollander, E., Haznedar, M. M., Tang, C., Spiegel-Cohen, J., Wei, T. C., et al. (2001). Effect of fluoxetine on regional cerebral metabolism in autistic spectrum disorders: A pilot study. *Int J Neuropsychopharmacol, 4*(2), 119–125.

Buckner, R. L., Andrews-Hanna, J. R., & Schacter, D. L. (2008). The brain's default network: anatomy, function, and relevance to disease. *Ann N Y Acad Sci, 1124*, 1–38.

Campbell, J. M. (2005). Diagnostic assessment of Asperger's disorder: A review of five third-party rating scales. *J Autism Dev Disord, 35*(1), 25–35.

Carpenter, M., Pennington, B. F., & Rogers, S. J. (2001). Understanding of others' intentions in children with autism. *J Autism Dev Disord, 31*(6), 589–599.

Castelli, F., Frith, C., Happe, F., & Frith, U. (2002). Autism, Asperger syndrome and brain mechanisms for the attribution of mental states to animated shapes. *Brain, 125*(Pt 8), 1839–1849.

Catani, M., Jones, D. K., Daly, E., Embiricos, N., Deeley, Q., Pugliese, L., et al. (2008). Altered cerebellar feedback projections in Asperger syndrome. *Neuroimage, 41*(4), 1184–1191.

Cherkassky, V. L., Kana, R. K., Keller, T. A., & Just, M. A. (2006). Functional connectivity in a baseline resting-state network in autism. *Neuroreport, 17*(16), 1687–1690.

Constantino, J. N., Gruber, C. P., Davis, S., Hayes, S., Passanante, N., & Przybeck, T. (2004). The factor structure of autistic traits. *J Child Psychol Psychiatry, 45*(4), 719–726.

Corbett, B. A., Carmean, V., Ravizza, S., Wendelken, C., Henry, M. L., Carter, C., et al. (2009). A functional and structural study of emotion and face processing in children with autism. *Psychiatry Res*.

Corbett, B. A., Constantine, L. J., Hendren, R., Rocke, D., & Ozonoff, S. (2009). Examining executive functioning in children with autism spectrum disorder, attention deficit hyperactivity disorder and typical development. *Psychiatry Res, 166*(2–3), 210–222.

Corden, B., Chilvers, R., & Skuse, D. (2008a). Avoidance of emotionally arousing stimuli predicts social-perceptual impairment in Asperger's syndrome. *Neuropsychologia, 46*(1), 137–147.

Corden, B., Chilvers, R., & Skuse, D. (2008b). Emotional modulation of perception in Asperger's syndrome. *J Autism Dev Disord, 38*(6), 1072–1080.

Courchesne, E. (2004). Brain development in autism: early overgrowth followed by premature arrest of growth. *Ment Retard Dev Disabil Res Rev, 10*(2), 106–111.

Courchesne, E. & Pierce, K. (2005). Why the frontal cortex in autism might be talking only to itself: local over-connectivity but long-distance disconnection. *Curr Opin Neurobiol, 15*(2), 225–230.

Crane, L., & Goddard, L. (2008). Episodic and semantic autobiographical memory in adults with autism spectrum disorders. *J Autism Dev Disord, 38*(3), 498–506.

Crane, L., Goddard, L., & Pring, L. (2009). Sensory processing in adults with autism spectrum disorders. *Autism, 13*(3), 215–228.

Dalton, K. M., Nacewicz, B. M., Johnstone, T., Schaefer, H. S., Gernsbacher, M. A., Goldsmith, H. H., et al. (2005). Gaze fixation and the neural circuitry of face processing in autism. *Nat Neurosci, 8*(4), 519–526.

Damasio, A. R. & Maurer, R. G. (1978). A neurological model for childhood autism. *Arch Neurol, 35*(12), 777–786.

Damoiseaux, J. S. & Greicius, M. D. (2009). Greater than the sum of its parts: A review of studies combining structural connectivity and resting-state functional connectivity. *Brain Struct Funct, 213*(6), 525–533.

Dapretto, M., Davies, M. S., Pfeifer, J. H., Scott, A. A., Sigman, M., Bookheimer, S. Y., et al. (2006). Understanding emotions in others: Mirror neuron dysfunction in children with autism spectrum disorders. *Nat Neurosci, 9*(1), 28–30.

D'Entremont, B., & Yazbek, A. (2007). Imitation of intentional and accidental actions by children with autism. *J Autism Dev Disord, 37*(9), 1665–1678. doi: 10.1007/s10803-006-0291-y.

De Martino, B. Harrison, N. A., Knafo, S., Bird, G., & Dolan, R. J. (2008). Explaining enhanced logical consistency during decision making in autism. *J Neurosci, 28*(42), 10746–10750.

Deeley, Q., Daly, E. M., Surguladze, S., Page, L., Toal, F., Robertson, D., et al. (2007). An event related functional magnetic resonance imaging study of facial emotion processing in Asperger syndrome. *Biol Psychiatry, 62*(3), 207–217.

Deruelle, C., Hubert, B., Santos, A., & Wicker, B. (2008). Negative emotion does not enhance recall skills in adults with autistic spectrum disorders. *Autism Res, 1*(2), 91–96.

Di Martino, A., Ross, K., Uddin, L. Q., Sklar, A. B., Castellanos, F. X., & Milham, M. P. (2009). Functional brain correlates of social and nonsocial processes in autism spectrum disorders: An activation likelihood estimation meta-analysis. *Biol Psychiatry, 65*(1), 63–74.

Dichter, G. S., & Belger, A. (2007). Social stimuli interfere with cognitive control in autism. *Neuroimage, 35*(3), 1219–1230.

Ehlers, S., Gillberg, C., & Wing, L. (1999). A screening questionnaire for Asperger syndrome and other high-functioning autism spectrum disorders in school age children. *J Autism Dev Disord, 29*(2), 129–141.

Ehlers, S., Nyden, A., Gillberg, C., Sandberg, A. D., Dahlgren, S. O., Hjelmquist, E., et al. (1997). Asperger syndrome, autism and attention disorders: A comparative study of the cognitive profiles of 120 children. *J Child Psychol Psychiatry, 38*(2), 207–217.

Fombonne, E. (2003). The prevalence of autism. *JAMA, 289*(1), 87–89.

Fombonne, E., Heavey, L., Smeeth, L., Rodrigues, L. C., Cook, C., Smith, P. G., et al. (2004). Validation of the diagnosis of autism in general practitioner records. *BMC Public Health, 4*, 5.

Fombonne, E., Quirke, S., & Hagen, A. (2009). Prevalence and interpretation of recent trends in rates of pervasive developmental disorders. *Mcgill J Med, 12*(2), 73.

Fombonne, E., Zakarian, R., Bennett, A., Meng, L., & McLean-Heywood, D. (2006). Pervasive developmental disorders in Montreal, Quebec, Canada: Prevalence and links with immunizations. *Pediatrics, 118*(1), e139–150.

Foxton, J. M., Stewart, M. E., Barnard, L., Rodgers, J., Young, A. H., O'Brien, G., et al. (2003). Absence of auditory "global interference' in autism. *Brain, 126*(Pt 12), 2703–2709.

Freitag, C. M., Konrad, C., Haberlen, M., Kleser, C., von Gontard, A., Reith, W., et al. (2008). Perception of biological motion in autism spectrum disorders. *Neuropsychologia, 46*(5), 1480–1494.

Gaigg, S. B., & Bowler, D. M. (2007). Differential fear conditioning in Asperger's syndrome: Implications for an amygdala theory of autism. *Neuropsychologia, 45*(9), 2125–2134.

Gaigg, S. B. & Bowler, D. M. (2008). Free recall and forgetting of emotionally arousing words in autism spectrum disorder. *Neuropsychologia, 46*(9), 2336–2343.

Gaigg, S. B. & Bowler, D. M. (2009a). Brief report: Attenuated emotional suppression of the attentional blink in autism spectrum disorder: Another non-social abnormality? *J Autism Dev Disord, 39*(8), 1211–1217.

Gaigg, S. B. & Bowler, D. M. (2009b). Illusory memories of emotionally charged words in autism spectrum disorder: Further evidence for atypical emotion processing outside the social domain. *J Autism Dev Disord, 39*(7), 1031–1038.

Gallese, V. (2003). The roots of empathy: the shared manifold hypothesis and the neural basis of intersubjectivity. *Psychopathology, 36*(4), 171–180. doi: 10.1159/000072786 PSP2003036004171 [pii].

Gerrard, S. & Rugg, G. (2009). Sensory impairments and autism: A re-examination of causal modelling. *J Autism Dev Disord, 39*(10), 1449–1463.

Geurts, H. M., Corbett, B., & Solomon, M. (2009). The paradox of cognitive flexibility in autism. *Trends Cogn Sci, 13*(2), 74–82.

Ghaziuddin, M. (2008). Defining the behavioral phenotype of Asperger syndrome. *J Autism Dev Disord, 38*(1), 138–142.

Ghaziuddin, M. & Butler, E. (1998). Clumsiness in autism and Asperger syndrome: A further report. *J Intellect Disabil Res, 42*(Pt 1), 43–48.

Ghaziuddin, M., Butler, E., Tsai, L., & Ghaziuddin, N. (1994). Is clumsiness a marker for Asperger syndrome? *J Intellect Disabil Res, 38*(Pt 5), 519–527.

Ghaziuddin, M. & Gerstein, L. (1996). Pedantic speaking style differentiates Asperger syndrome from high-functioning autism. *J Autism Dev Disord, 26*(6), 585–595.

Ghaziuddin, M. & Mountain-Kimchi, K. (2004). Defining the intellectual profile of Asperger Syndrome: Comparison with high-functioning autism. *J Autism Dev Disord, 34*(3), 279–284.

Goddard, L., Dritschel, B., & Burton, A. (1996). Role of autobiographical memory in social problem solving and depression. *J Abnorm Psychol, 105*(4), 609–616.

Goddard, L., Howlin, P., Dritschel, B., & Patel, T. (2007). Autobiographical memory and social problem-solving in Asperger syndrome. *J Autism Dev Disord, 37*(2), 291–300.

Gomot, M., Belmonte, M. K., Bullmore, E. T., Bernard, F. A., & Baron-Cohen, S. (2008). Brain hyper-reactivity to auditory novel targets in children with high-functioning autism. *Brain, 131*(Pt 9), 2479–2488.

Gomot, M., Bernard, F. A., Davis, M. H., Belmonte, M. K., Ashwin, C., Bullmore, E. T., et al. (2006). Change detection in children with autism: An auditory event-related fMRI study. *Neuroimage, 29*(2), 475–484.

Grezes, J., Wicker, B., Berthoz, S., & de Gelder, B. (2009). A failure to grasp the affective meaning of actions in autism spectrum disorder subjects. *Neuropsychologia, 47*(8–9), 1816–1825.

Hadjikhani, N., Joseph, R. M., Manoach, D. S., Naik, P., Snyder, J., Dominick, K., et al. (2009). Body expressions of emotion do not trigger fear contagion in autism spectrum disorder. *Soc Cogn Affect Neurosci, 4*(1), 70–78.

Hadjikhani, N., Joseph, R. M., Snyder, J., Chabris, C. F., Clark, J., Steele, S., et al. (2004). Activation of the fusiform gyrus when individuals with autism spectrum disorder view faces. *Neuroimage, 22*(3), 1141–1150.

Hadjikhani, N., Joseph, R. M., Snyder, J., & Tager-Flusberg, H. (2006). Anatomical differences in the mirror neuron system and social cognition network in autism. *Cereb Cortex, 16*(9), 1276–1282.

Hadjikhani, N., Joseph, R. M., Snyder, J., & Tager-Flusberg, H. (2007). Abnormal activation of the social brain during face perception in autism. *Hum Brain Mapp, 28*(5), 441–449.

Haist, F., Adamo, M., Westerfield, M., Courchesne, E., & Townsend, J. (2005). The functional neuroanatomy of spatial attention in autism spectrum disorder. *Dev Neuropsychol, 27*(3), 425–458.

Hamilton, A. F. (2009). Goals, intentions and mental states: Challenges for theories of autism. *J Child Psychol Psychiatry, 50*(8), 881–892.

Hamilton, A. F., Brindley, R. M., & Frith, U. (2007). Imitation and action understanding in autistic spectrum disorders: How valid is the hypothesis of a deficit in the mirror neuron system? *Neuropsychologia, 45*(8), 1859–1868.

Happe, F. (1999). Autism: Cognitive deficit or cognitive style? *Trends Cogn Sci, 3*(6), 216–222.

Happe, F., Booth, R., Charlton, R., & Hughes, C. (2006). Executive function deficits in autism spectrum disorders and attention-deficit/hyperactivity disorder: Examining profiles across domains and ages. *Brain Cogn, 61*(1), 25–39.

Haswell, C. C., Izawa, J., L R. D., S, H. M., & Shadmehr, R. (2009). Representation of internal models of action in the autistic brain. *Nat Neurosci, 12*(8), 970–972.

Heaton, P., Hudry, K., Ludlow, A., & Hill, E. (2008). Superior discrimination of speech pitch and its relationship to verbal ability in autism spectrum disorders. *Cogn Neuropsychol, 25*(6), 771–782.

Hill, E. L. (2004). Executive dysfunction in autism. *Trends Cogn Sci, 8*(1), 26–32.

Hill, E. L. & Bird, C. M. (2006). Executive processes in Asperger syndrome: Patterns of performance in a multiple case series. *Neuropsychologia, 44*(14), 2822–2835.

Horwitz, B., Rumsey, J. M., Grady, C. L., & Rapoport, S. I. (1988). The cerebral metabolic landscape in autism. Intercorrelations of regional glucose utilization. *Arch Neurol, 45*(7), 749–755.

Hubert, B., Wicker, B., Moore, D. G., Monfardini, E., Duverger, H., Da Fonseca, D., et al. (2007). Brief report: Recognition of emotional and non-emotional biological motion in individuals with autistic spectrum disorders. *J Autism Dev Disord, 37*(7), 1386–1392.

Hubert, B. E., Wicker, B., Monfardini, E., & Deruelle, C. (2009). Electrodermal reactivity to emotion processing in adults with autistic spectrum disorders. *Autism, 13*(1), 9–19.

Hyde, K. L., Samson, F., Evans, A. C., & Mottron, L. (2009). Neuroanatomical differences in brain areas implicated in perceptual and other core features of autism revealed by cortical thickness analysis and voxel-based morphometry. *Hum Brain Mapp*.

Iacoboni, M. (2006). Failure to deactivate in autism: The co-constitution of self and other. *Trends Cogn Sci*, *10*(10), 431–433.

Iacoboni, M. & Dapretto, M. (2006). The mirror neuron system and the consequences of its dysfunction. *Nat Rev Neurosci*, *7*(12), 942–951.

Jolliffe, T. & Baron-Cohen, S. (1997). Are people with autism and Asperger syndrome faster than normal on the Embedded Figures Test? *J Child Psychol Psychiatry*, *38*(5), 527–534.

Joseph, R. M. & Tanaka, J. (2003). Holistic and part-based face recognition in children with autism. *J Child Psychol Psychiatry*, *44*(4), 529–542.

Just, M. A., Cherkassky, V. L., Keller, T. A., Kana, R. K., & Minshew, N. J. (2007). Functional and anatomical cortical underconnectivity in autism: Evidence from an FMRI study of an executive function task and corpus callosum morphometry. *Cereb Cortex*, *17*(4), 951–961.

Just, M. A., Cherkassky, V. L., Keller, T. A., & Minshew, N. J. (2004). Cortical activation and synchronization during sentence comprehension in high-functioning autism: Evidence of underconnectivity. *Brain*, *127*(Pt 8), 1811–1821.

Kaland, N., Smith, L., & Mortensen, E. L. (2008). Brief report: Cognitive flexibility and focused attention in children and adolescents with Asperger syndrome or high-functioning autism as measured on the computerized version of the Wisconsin Card Sorting Test. *J Autism Dev Disord*, *38*(6), 1161–1165.

Kana, R. K., Keller, T. A., Cherkassky, V. L., Minshew, N. J., & Just, M. A. (2006). Sentence comprehension in autism: Thinking in pictures with decreased functional connectivity. *Brain*, *129*(Pt 9), 2484–2493.

Kana, R. K., Keller, T. A., Cherkassky, V. L., Minshew, N. J., & Just, M. A. (2009). Atypical frontal-posterior synchronization of theory of mind regions in autism during mental state attribution. *Soc Neurosci*, *4*(2), 135–152.

Kana, R. K., Keller, T. A., Minshew, N. J., & Just, M. A. (2007). Inhibitory control in high-functioning autism: Decreased activation and underconnectivity in inhibition networks. *Biol Psychiatry*, *62*(3), 198–206.

Katsyri, J., Saalasti, S., Tiippana, K., von Wendt, L., & Sams, M. (2008). Impaired recognition of facial emotions from low-spatial frequencies in Asperger syndrome. *Neuropsychologia*, *46*(7), 1888–1897.

Ke, X., Tang, T., Hong, S., Hang, Y., Zou, B., Li, H., et al. (2009). White matter impairments in autism, evidence from voxel-based morphometry and diffusion tensor imaging. *Brain Res*, *1265*, 171–177.

Kennedy, D. P. & Courchesne, E. (2008). Functional abnormalities of the default network during self- and other-reflection in autism. *Soc Cogn Affect Neurosci*, *3*(2), 177–190.

Kennedy, D. P., Redcay, E., & Courchesne, E. (2006). Failing to deactivate: resting functional abnormalities in autism. *Proc Natl Acad Sci U S A*, *103*(21), 8275–8280.

Khalfa, S., Bruneau, N., Roge, B., Georgieff, N., Veuillet, E., Adrien, J. L., et al. (2004). Increased perception of loudness in autism. *Hear Res*, *198*(1–2), 87–92.

Kleinhans, N. M., Richards, T., Sterling, L., Stegbauer, K. C., Mahurin, R., Johnson, L. C., et al. (2008). Abnormal functional connectivity in autism spectrum disorders during face processing. *Brain*, *131*(Pt 4), 1000–1012.

Klin, A., Jones, W., Schultz, R., Volkmar, F., & Cohen, D. (2002). Visual fixation patterns during viewing of naturalistic social situations as predictors of social competence in individuals with autism. *Arch Gen Psychiatry*, *59*(9), 809–816.

Klin, A., Pauls, D., Schultz, R., & Volkmar, F. (2005). Three diagnostic approaches to Asperger syndrome: Implications for research. *J Autism Dev Disord*, *35*(2), 221–234.

Klin, A. & Volkmar, F. R. (2003). Asperger syndrome. *Child Adolesc Psychiatr Clin N Am*, *12*(1), xiii–xvi.

Klin, A., Volkmar, F. R., Sparrow, S. S., Cicchetti, D. V., & Rourke, B. P. (1995). Validity and neuropsychological characterization of Asperger syndrome: Convergence with nonverbal learning disabilities syndrome. *J Child Psychol Psychiatry*, *36*(7), 1127–1140.

Koshino, H., Carpenter, P. A., Minshew, N. J., Cherkassky, V. L., Keller, T. A., & Just, M. A. (2005). Functional connectivity in an fMRI working memory task in high-functioning autism. *Neuroimage*, *24*(3), 810–821.

Koshino, H., Kana, R. K., Keller, T. A., Cherkassky, V. L., Minshew, N. J., & Just, M. A. (2008). fMRI investigation of working memory for faces in autism: Visual coding and underconnectivity with frontal areas. *Cereb Cortex*, *18*(2), 289–300.

Koyama, T. & Kurita, H. (2008). Cognitive profile difference between normally intelligent children with Asperger's disorder and those with pervasive developmental disorder not otherwise specified. *Psychiatry Clin Neurosci*, *62*(6), 691–696.

Kwon, H., Ow, A. W., Pedatella, K. E., Lotspeich, L. J., & Reiss, A. L. (2004). Voxel-based morphometry elucidates structural neuroanatomy of high-functioning autism and Asperger syndrome. *Dev Med Child Neurol*, *46*(11), 760–764.

Lawson, J., Baron-Cohen, S., & Wheelwright, S. (2004). Empathising and systemising in adults with and without Asperger syndrome. *J Autism Dev Disord*, *34*(3), 301–310.

Lee, P. S., Foss-Feig, J., Henderson, J. G., Kenworthy, L. E., Gilotty, L., & Gaillard, W. D. (2007). Atypical neural substrates of Embedded Figures Task performance in children with Autism Spectrum Disorder. *Neuroimage*, *38*(1), 184–193. doi: S1053-8119(07)00610-6 [pii] 10.1016/j.neuroimage.2007.07.013.

Leekam, S. R., Nieto, C., Libby, S. J., Wing, L., & Gould, J. (2007). Describing the sensory abnormalities of children and adults with autism. *J Autism Dev Disord*, *37*(5), 894–910.

Leighton, J., Bird, G., Charman, T., & Heyes, C. (2008). Weak imitative performance is not due to a functional "mirroring" deficit in adults with autism spectrum disorders. *Neuropsychologia*, *46*(4), 1041–1049.

Lewis, J. D. & Elman, J. L. (2008). Growth-related neural reorganization and the autism phenotype: A test of the hypothesis that altered brain growth leads to altered connectivity. *Dev Sci*, *11*(1), 135–155.

Lopez, B. R., Lincoln, A. J., Ozonoff, S., & Lai, Z. (2005). Examining the relationship between executive functions and restricted, repetitive symptoms of Autistic Disorder. *J Autism Dev Disord*, *35*(4), 445–460.

Manjaly, Z. M., Bruning, N., Neufang, S., Stephan, K. E., Brieber, S., Marshall, J. C., et al. (2007). Neurophysiological correlates of relatively enhanced local visual search in autistic adolescents. *Neuroimage*, *35*(1), 283–291.

Matson, J. L. & Rivet, T. T. (2008). Characteristics of challenging behaviours in adults with autistic disorder, PDD-NOS, and intellectual disability. *J Intellect Dev Disabil*, *33*(4), 323–329.

Mazefsky, C. A. & Oswald, D. P. (2007). Emotion perception in Asperger's syndrome and high-functioning autism: The importance of diagnostic criteria and cue intensity. *J Autism Dev Disord*, *37*(6), 1086–1095.

McAlonan, G. M., Cheung, V., Cheung, C., Suckling, J., Lam, G. Y., Tai, K. S., et al. (2005). Mapping the brain in autism. A voxel-based MRI study of volumetric differences and intercorrelations in autism. *Brain*, *128*(Pt 2), 268–276.

McAlonan, G. M., Suckling, J., Wong, N., Cheung, V., Lienenkaemper, N., Cheung, C., et al. (2008). Distinct patterns of grey matter abnormality in high-functioning autism and Asperger's syndrome. *J Child Psychol Psychiatry*, *49*(12), 1287–1295.

McDougle, C. J., Kresch, L. E., & Posey, D. J. (2000). Repetitive thoughts and behavior in pervasive developmental disorders: Treatment with serotonin reuptake inhibitors. *J Autism Dev Disord*, *30*(5), 427–435.

Millward, C., Powell, S., Messer, D., & Jordan, R. (2000). Recall for self and other in autism. Children's memory for events experienced by themselves and their peers. *J Autism Dev Disord*, *30*(1), 15–28.

Minio-Paluello, I., Baron-Cohen, S., Avenanti, A., Walsh, V., & Aglioti, S. M. (2009). Absence of embodied empathy during pain observation in Asperger syndrome. *Biol Psychiatry*, *65*(1), 55–62.

Molenberghs, P., Cunnington, R., & Mattingley, J. B. (2009). Is the mirror neuron system involved in imitation? A short review and meta-analysis. *Neurosci Biobehav Rev*, *33*(7), 975–980.

Monk, C. S., Peltier, S. J., Wiggins, J. L., Weng, S. J., Carrasco, M., Risi, S., et al. (2009). Abnormalities of intrinsic functional connectivity in autism spectrum disorders. *Neuroimage*, *47*(2), 764–772.

Mottron, L., Dawson, M., Soulieres, I., Hubert, B., & Burack, J. (2006). Enhanced perceptual functioning in autism: An update, and eight principles of autistic perception. *J Autism Dev Disord*, *36*(1), 27–43.

Mottron, L., Peretz, I., & Menard, E. (2000). Local and global processing of music in high-functioning persons with autism: Beyond central coherence? *J Child Psychol Psychiatry*, *41*(8), 1057–1065.

Myles, B., Jones-Bock, S., & Simpson, R. (2001). *The Asperger Syndrome Diagnostic Scale*. Pro-Ed Publishers.

Neumann, D., Spezio, M. L., Piven, J., & Adolphs, R. (2006). Looking you in the mouth: abnormal gaze in autism resulting from impaired top-down modulation of visual attention. *Soc Cogn Affect Neurosci*, *1*(3), 194–202.

Noonan, S. K., Haist, F., & Muller, R. A. (2009). Aberrant functional connectivity in autism: evidence from low-frequency BOLD signal fluctuations. *Brain Res*, *1262*, 48–63.

Nordahl, C. W., Dierker, D., Mostafavi, I., Schumann, C. M., Rivera, S. M., Amaral, D. G., et al. (2007). Cortical folding abnormalities in autism revealed by surface-based morphometry. *J Neurosci*, *27*(43), 11725–11735.

O'Connor, K., Hamm, J. P., & Kirk, I. J. (2005). The neurophysiological correlates of face processing in adults and children with Asperger's syndrome. *Brain Cogn*, *59*(1), 82–95.

Ozonoff, S., Cook, I., Coon, H., Dawson, G., Joseph, R. M., Klin, A., et al. (2004). Performance on Cambridge Neuropsychological Test Automated Battery subtests sensitive to frontal lobe function in people with autistic disorder: Evidence from the Collaborative Programs of Excellence in Autism network. *J Autism Dev Disord*, *34*(2), 139–150.

Ozonoff, S. & Jensen, J. (1999). Brief report: Specific executive function profiles in three neurodevelopmental disorders. *J Autism Dev Disord*, *29*(2), 171–177.

Ozonoff, S., Pennington, B. F., & Rogers, S. J. (1991). Executive function deficits in high-functioning autistic individuals: Relationship to theory of mind. *J Child Psychol Psychiatry*, *32*(7), 1081–1105.

Ozonoff, S. & Strayer, D. L. (1997). Inhibitory function in nonretarded children with autism. *J Autism Dev Disord*, *27*(1), 59–77.

Pelphrey, K. A., Sasson, N. J., Reznick, J. S., Paul, G., Goldman, B. D., & Piven, J. (2002). Visual scanning of faces in autism. *J Autism Dev Disord*, *32*(4), 249–261.

Penn, H. E. (2006). Neurobiological correlates of autism: A review of recent research. *Child Neuropsychol*, *12*(1), 57–79.

Pessoa, L. (2008). On the relationship between emotion and cognition. *Nat Rev Neurosci*, *9*(2), 148–158.

Pfeiffer, B., Kinnealey, M., Reed, C., & Herzberg, G. (2005). Sensory modulation and affective disorders in children and adolescents with Asperger's disorder. *Am J Occup Ther*, *59*(3), 335–345.

Pierce, K., Haist, F., Sedaghat, F., & Courchesne, E. (2004). The brain response to personally familiar faces in autism: Findings of fusiform activity and beyond. *Brain*, *127*, 2703–2716.

Plaisted, K., Saksida, L., Alcantara, J., & Weisblatt, E. (2003). Towards an understanding of the mechanisms of weak central coherence effects: Experiments in visual configural learning and auditory perception. *Philos Trans R Soc Lond B Biol Sci*, *358*(1430), 375–386.

Pugliese, L., Catani, M., Ameis, S., Dell'acqua, F., de Schotten, M. T., Murphy, C., et al. (2009). The anatomy of extended limbic pathways in Asperger syndrome: A preliminary diffusion tensor imaging tractography study. *Neuroimage*. *47*(2), 427–434.

Raichle, M. E., MacLeod, A. M., Snyder, A. Z., Powers, W. J., Gusnard, D. A., & Shulman, G. L. (2001). A default mode of brain function. *Proc Natl Acad Sci U S A*, *98*(2), 676–682.

Raymaekers, R., Wiersema, J. R., & Roeyers, H. (2009). EEG study of the mirror neuron system in children with high functioning autism. *Brain Res*.

Reynolds, S. & Lane, S. J. (2008). Diagnostic validity of sensory over-responsivity: A review of the literature and case reports. *J Autism Dev Disord*, *38*(3), 516–529.

Riby, D. M., Doherty-Sneddon, G., & Bruce, V. (2009). The eyes or the mouth? Feature salience and unfamiliar face processing in Williams syndrome and autism. *Q J Exp Psychol (Colchester)*, *62*(1), 189–203.

Ring, H. A., Baron-Cohen, S., Wheelwright, S., Williams, S. C., Brammer, M., Andrew, C., et al. (1999). Cerebral correlates of preserved cognitive skills in autism: A functional MRI study of embedded figures task performance. *Brain*, *122*(Pt 7), 1305–1315.

Rizzolatti, G., Fabbri-Destro, M., & Cattaneo, L. (2009). Mirror neurons and their clinical relevance. *Nat Clin Pract Neurol*, *5*(1), 24–34.

Rogers, K., Dziobek, I., Hassenstab, J., Wolf, O. T., & Convit, A. (2007). Who cares? Revisiting empathy in Asperger syndrome. *J Autism Dev Disord*, *37*(4), 709–715.

Roy, M., Dillo, W., Bessling, S., Emrich, H. M., & Ohlmeier, M. D. (2009). Effective methylphenidate treatment of an adult Asperger's syndrome and a comorbid ADHD: A clinical investigation with fMRI. *J Atten Disord*, *12*(4), 381–385.

Russell, J., Jarrold, C., & Hood, B. (1999). Two intact executive capacities in children with autism: Implications for the core executive dysfunctions in the disorder. *J Autism Dev Disord*, *29*(2), 103–112.

Russell, J., Saltmarsh, R., & Hill, E. (1999). What do executive factors contribute to the failure on false belief tasks by children with autism? *J Child Psychol Psychiatry*, *40*(6), 859–868.

Ruta, L., Mugno, D., D'Arrigo, V. G., Vitiello, B., & Mazzone, L. (2009). Obsessive-compulsive traits in children and adolescents with Asperger syndrome. *Eur Child Adolesc Psychiatry*.

Rutherford, M. D., Clements, K. A., & Sekuler, A. B. (2007). Differences in discrimination of eye and mouth displacement in autism spectrum disorders. *Vision Res*, *47*(15), 2099–2110.

Santos, A., Rondan, C., Rosset, D. B., Da Fonseca, D., & Deruelle, C. (2008). Mr. Grimace or Ms. Smile: Does categorization affect perceptual processing in autism? *Psychol Sci*, *19*(1), 70–76.

Schmahmann, J. D., Weilburg, J. B., & Sherman, J. C. (2007). The neuropsychiatry of the cerebellum—insights from the clinic. *Cerebellum*, *6*(3), 254–267.

Schultz, R. T., Gauthier, I., Klin, A., Fulbright, R. K., Anderson, A. W., Volkmar, F., et al. (2000). Abnormal ventral temporal cortical activity during face discrimination among individuals with autism and Asperger syndrome. *Arch Gen Psychiatry*, *57*(4), 331–340.

Schultz, R. T., Grelotti, D. J., Klin, A., Kleinman, J., Van der Gaag, C., Marois, R., et al. (2003). The role of the fusiform face area in social cognition: Implications for the pathobiology of autism. *Philos Trans R Soc Lond B Biol Sci*, *358*(1430), 415–427.

Scott, F. J., Baron-Cohen, S., Bolton, P., & Brayne, C. (2002). The CAST (Childhood Asperger Syndrome Test): preliminary development of a UK screen for mainstream primary-school-age children. *Autism*, *6*(1), 9–31.

Shafritz, K. M., Dichter, G. S., Baranek, G. T., & Belger, A. (2008). The neural circuitry mediating shifts in behavioral response and cognitive set in autism. *Biol Psychiatry*, *63*(10), 974–980.

Shamay-Tsoory, S. G. (2008). Recognition of "fortune of others' emotions in Asperger syndrome and high functioning autism. *J Autism Dev Disord*, *38*(8), 1451–1461.

Shamay-Tsoory, S. G., Tomer, R., Yaniv, S., & Aharon-Peretz, J. (2002). Empathy deficits in Asperger syndrome: A cognitive profile. *Neurocase*, *8*(3), 245–252.

Singh, V., Mukherjee, L., & Chung, M. K. (2008). Cortical surface thickness as a classifier: Boosting for autism classification. *Med Image Comput Comput Assist Interv Int Conf Med Image Comput Comput Assist Interv*, *11*(Pt 1), 999–1007.

Snowling, M., Goulandris, N., Bowlby, M., & Howell, P. (1986). Segmentation and speech perception in relation to reading skill: A developmental analysis. *J Exp Child Psychol*, *41*(3), 489–507.

Solomon, M., Ozonoff, S., Ursu, S., Ravizza, S., Cummings, N., Ly, S., et al. (2009). The neural substrates of cognitive control deficits in autism spectrum disorders. *Neuropsychologia*.

South, M., Ozonoff, S., & McMahon, W. M. (2007). The relationship between executive functioning, central coherence, and repetitive behaviors in the high-functioning autism spectrum. *Autism*, *11*(5), 437–451.

Spezio, M. L., Adolphs, R., Hurley, R. S., & Piven, J. (2007). Abnormal use of facial information in high-functioning autism. *J Autism Dev Disord*, *37*(5), 929–939.

Stephan, K. E., Tittgemeyer, M., Knosche, T. R., Moran, R. J., & Friston, K. J. (2009). Tractography-based priors for dynamic causal models. *Neuroimage*, *47*(4), 1628–1638.

Stieglitz Ham, H., Corley, M., Rajendran, G., Carletta, J., & Swanson, S. (2008). Brief report: Imitation of meaningless gestures in individuals with Asperger syndrome and high-functioning autism. *J Autism Dev Disord*, *38*(3), 569–573.

Suzuki, Y., Critchley, H. D., Rowe, A., Howlin, P., & Murphy, D. G. (2003). Impaired olfactory identification in Asperger's syndrome. *J Neuropsychiatry Clin Neurosci*, *15*(1), 105–107.

Taylor, J. G. & Fragopanagos, N. F. (2005). The interaction of attention and emotion. *Neural Netw*, *18*(4), 353–369.

Teitelbaum, O., Benton, T., Shah, P. K., Prince, A., Kelly, J. L., & Teitelbaum, P. (2004). Eshkol-Wachman movement notation in diagnosis: The early detection of Asperger's syndrome. *Proc Natl Acad Sci U S A*, *101*(32), 11909–11914.

Teunisse, J. P. & de Gelder, B. (2003). Face processing in adolescents with autistic disorder: The inversion and composite effects. *Brain Cogn*, *52*(3), 285–294.

Thakkar, K. N., Polli, F. E., Joseph, R. M., Tuch, D. S., Hadjikhani, N., Barton, J. J., et al. (2008). Response monitoring, repetitive behaviour and anterior cingulate abnormalities in autism spectrum disorders (ASD). *Brain*, *131*(Pt 9), 2464–2478.

Tomchek, S. D. & Dunn, W. (2007). Sensory processing in children with and without autism: A comparative study using the short sensory profile. *Am J Occup Ther*, *61*(2), 190–200.

Turner, M. A. (1999). Generating novel ideas: Fluency performance in high-functioning and learning disabled individuals with autism. *J Child Psychol Psychiatry*, *40*(2), 189–201.

Verte, S., Geurts, H. M., Roeyers, H., Oosterlaan, J., & Sergeant, J. A. (2006). Executive functioning in children with an autism spectrum disorder: Can we differentiate within the spectrum? *J Autism Dev Disord*, *36*(3), 351–372.

Villalobos, M. E., Mizuno, A., Dahl, B. C., Kemmotsu, N., & Muller, R. A. (2005). Reduced functional connectivity between V1 and inferior frontal cortex associated with visuomotor performance in autism. *Neuroimage*, *25*(3), 916–925.

Vincent, J. L., Patel, G. H., Fox, M. D., Snyder, A. Z., Baker, J. T., Van Essen, D. C., et al. (2007). Intrinsic functional architecture in the anaesthetized monkey brain. *Nature*, *447*(7140), 83–86.

Vivanti, G., Nadig, A., Ozonoff, S., & Rogers, S. J. (2008). What do children with autism attend to during imitation tasks? *J Exp Child Psychol*, *101*(3), 186–205.

Vuilleumier, P. (2005). How brains beware: Neural mechanisms of emotional attention. *Trends Cogn Sci*, *9*(12), 585–594.

Waiter, G. D., Williams, J. H., Murray, A. D., Gilchrist, A., Perrett, D. I., & Whiten, A. (2005). Structural white matter deficits in high-functioning individuals with autistic spectrum disorder: A voxel-based investigation. *Neuroimage*, *24*(2), 455–461.

Welchew, D. E., Ashwin, C., Berkouk, K., Salvador, R., Suckling, J., Baron-Cohen, S., et al. (2005). Functional disconnectivity of the medial temporal lobe in Asperger's syndrome. *Biol Psychiatry*, *57*(9), 991–998.

White, S., Hill, E., Winston, J., & Frith, U. (2006). An islet of social ability in Asperger Syndrome: Judging social attributes from faces. *Brain Cogn, 61*(1), 69–77.

Wicker, B., Fonlupt, P., Hubert, B., Tardif, C., Gepner, B., & Deruelle, C. (2008). Abnormal cerebral effective connectivity during explicit emotional processing in adults with autism spectrum disorder. *Soc Cogn Affect Neurosci, 3*(2), 135–143.

Williams, D. (1992). *Nobody nowhere: The remarkable autobiography of an autistic girl.* London: Jessica Kingsley.

Williams, J. H., Waiter, G. D., Gilchrist, A., Perrett, D. I., Murray, A. D., & Whiten, A. (2006). Neural mechanisms of imitation and "mirror neuron' functioning in autistic spectrum disorder. *Neuropsychologia, 44*(4), 610–621.

Williams, J. H., Whiten, A., & Singh, T. (2004). A systematic review of action imitation in autistic spectrum disorder. *J Autism Dev Disord, 34*(3), 285–299.

Williams, J. H., Whiten, A., Suddendorf, T., & Perrett, D. I. (2001). Imitation, mirror neurons, and autism. *Neurosci Biobehav Rev, 25*(4), 287–295.

Wing, L. (1981). Asperger's syndrome: A clinical account. *Psychol Med, 11*(1), 115–129.

WHO, W. H. O. (1990). *The ICD-10, Classification of Mental and Behavioural Disorders : Clinical descriptions and diagnostic guidelines.* Geneva: Switzerland: Author.

Woodbury-Smith, M. R. & Volkmar, F. R. (2009). Asperger syndrome. *Eur Child Adolesc Psychiatry, 18*(1), 2–11.

Wright, B., Clarke, N., Jordan, J., Young, A. W., Clarke, P., Miles, J., et al. (2008). Emotion recognition in faces and the use of visual context in young people with high-functioning autism spectrum disorders. *Autism, 12*(6), 607–626.

58 | Antisocial Personality Disorders

Andrea L. Glenn *and* Adrian Raine

Abstract

Neuroscience research is beginning to uncover significant neurobiological impairments in antisocial, violent, and aggressive groups. The neurophysiologic basis of antisocial behavior is complex—many structures have been implicated, each of which may be related to antisocial behavior in different ways. Research in social neuroscience is helping us to better understand the role of many of these regions in normal social behavior, and thus why abnormality would result in a disruption of appropriate social behavior. This chapter highlights neuroscience data on antisocial individuals and provides interpretation based on the knowledge that has been gained in recent years in the field of social neuroscience.

Keywords: antisocial personality disorder, conduct disorder, empathy, moral decision-making, prefrontal cortex, amygdala, violence, aggression

Antisocial Personality

Antisocial personality disorder (APD), as outlined in the DSM-IV, is a categorization of individuals who consistently fail to conform to social norms and display criminal or antisocial behavior. Studies have estimated that approximately 75% of the prison population has APD (Hare, 1991). The construct of APD is very heterogeneous; since antisocial behavior is broadly defined, individuals may vary greatly on the type and severity of antisocial behavior they exhibit. For example, a common distinction in the type of antisocial behavior is between "reactive" and "proactive" forms of aggression. Reactive or "hot" aggression is aggression in response to a perceived threat or frustration. Proactive or "cold" aggression is planned, purposeful aggression used to achieve a goal (e.g., to obtain possessions). Psychopathic individuals fall into the category of individuals with APD who engage in high rates of

proactive aggression, though most engage in reactive aggression as well. Psychopathy is a more specific type of antisocial personality and is discussed in chapter 59 and therefore will not be included in the present review. Although some studies have focused on more specific types of antisocial behavior (e.g., Raine et al., 1998), studies commonly define antisocial or violent groups in a broad sense. As such, neuroscience findings appear to implicate a wide range of brain regions and mechanisms. However, it is likely that there are multiple biological pathways that lead to antisocial behavior and that not all antisocial individuals demonstrate the same brain abnormalities.

The major childhood precursor to antisocial personality disorder is conduct disorder (CD) (Lahey et al., 2005). Conduct disorder is described as a longstanding pattern of violations of rules and laws, including aggressive behavior, manipulativeness, deceitfulness, theft, forced sex, bullying, running away from home, and property destruction. Conduct disorder is typically diagnosed in older children and adolescents. Antisocial behavior in younger children may be diagnosed as oppositional defiant disorder (ODD), which involves persistently hostile, defiant, and disruptive behavior, as well as low frustration tolerance, occurring outside of the normal range of behavior. In the present chapter, we will focus on studies that implement these clinical definitions of antisocial personality in adults and youth, as well as studies of criminal, delinquent, or violent groups.

Social Neuroscience and Antisocial Personalities

There is strong evidence suggesting that brain abnormalities, whether developmental or as a result of injury, may serve as precursors to antisocial behavior. Paralleling the increasing use of brain-imaging techniques to examine brain functioning during normal social processing, many studies have begun using brain imaging to identify the brain regions that are disrupted in antisocial individuals. The knowledge gained by social neuroscience studies has been crucially important in our ability to interpret how deficits in specific brain regions may lead to antisocial behavior. Research on constructs such as empathy, emotion regulation, response inhibition, and moral decision-making has begun to illuminate the neurobiological underpinnings of these processes, thus helping to explain why disruptions to regions involved in these processes could potentially result in disrupted social behavior. However, these processes are also extremely complex and interrelated, and there are likely a large number of potential sources of disruption that could lead to antisocial behavior.

Perhaps the most complex and highest-level construct that is directly relevant to antisocial behavior is moral decision-making. Several studies in social neuroscience have begun to examine the brain regions that are involved when people contemplate moral dilemmas (e.g., Greene et al., 2001) or make moral judgments (e.g., Moll, Oliveira-Sousa, et al., 2002; Oliveira-Sousa & Moll, 2000). It has been argued that regions important in moral decision-making and the processes that underlie it may play an especially central role in the development of antisocial personality (Raine & Yang, 2006). Moral decision-making relies on several underlying processes, including the experience of empathy and guilt, theory of mind, and decision-making capabilities. Each of these processes in turn require further

capabilities; for example, empathy itself is a complex construct that requires affective sharing between the self and other, self awareness, mental flexibility, and emotion regulation (Decety & Moriguchi, 2007), all of which are still quite complex and have been shown to recruit multiple brain regions. Thus, it is possible that the impairments in higher-order construct of moral decision-making observed in antisocial individuals may result from disruption in any number of different underlying processes. Furthermore, disruptions of different processes may lead to different forms of antisocial behavior.

As an example, reduced empathy is a common feature of antisocial individuals. This reduction in empathy may result from disruption to one or more of the relatively lower-level processes that underlie it. In some individuals, the deficit may come from a reduced ability to share other people's emotional state, primarily in the domains of sadness and fear, which has been found to be associated with activity in the amygdala (Blair, 2007; Blair et al., 2001). Such deficits may result in increased proactive, unprovoked aggression. In contrast, other individuals may exhibit deficits in the ability to self-regulate emotions, as many antisocial individuals perform poorly on tests of executive functioning (Morgan & Lilienfeld, 2000) and inhibitory control (Vollm et al., 2004). This may be due to impairments in orbitofrontal or dorsolateral prefrontal regions. As a result, individuals may be prone to engage in more reactive aggression.

Despite the enormous complexity of studying the neurobiology of antisocial behavior, research has identified several regions which appear to be consistently implicated. These regions are primarily in the prefrontal and temporal cortices. The following will provide a review of several of the regions implicated in antisocial behavior along with the insights gained from social neuroscience about why these regions are likely involved.

The Neural Basis of Antisocial Personality

The best-replicated abnormality across a wide range of antisocial groups and across different imaging methodologies is in the prefrontal cortex. Within the frontal lobe, both structural and functional abnormalities have been observed. Using PET, reduced frontal functioning has been observed in impulsive aggressive individuals (New et al., 2002), murderers (Raine et al., 1997), and violent psychiatric patients (Volkow et al., 1995). Using SPECT, reduced blood flow in the prefrontal cortex has been observed in violent offenders (Soderstrom et al.,

2000) and alcoholics with APD (Kuruoglu et al., 1996). Structurally, Raine et al. (2000) found individuals with APD show an 11% reduction in gray matter volume in the prefrontal cortex compared with controls. Additional studies have further localized these abnormalities to specific areas of the prefrontal cortex. Laakso et al. (2002) reported reduced gray matter volume in dorsolateral, orbitofrontal, and medial prefrontal cortex in alcoholics with APD compared to controls. In a recent study using voxel-based morphometry, Tiihonen et al. (2008) found reduced gray matter in the frontopolar and orbitofrontal cortex bilaterally in persistently violent offenders. Regional cortical thinning has been observed in the ventromedial prefrontal cortex in violent individuals with APD (Narayan et al., 2007). A functional imaging study found reduced activity in the orbitofrontal cortex of antisocial individuals during inhibitory control (Vollm et al., 2004). Within the prefrontal cortex, the medial and orbitofrontal/ventromedial regions appear to be the most commonly implicated.

Studies from social neuroscience have provided insight into the functions of regions within the prefrontal cortex and thus why they might be involved in antisocial behavior. The orbitofrontal/ventromedial region is thought to play a role in affective theory of mind (Shamay-Tsoory et al., 2005), processing reward and punishment information (Rolls, 2000), inhibiting responses (Aron et al., 2004; Vollm et al., 2006), and regulating emotions (Ochsner et al., 2005). Unsurprisingly, the orbitofronal cortex is also important in moral decision-making (Borg et al., 2006; Moll, Oliveira-Souza, et al., 2002; Oliveira-Sousa & Moll, 2000). It has been suggested that dysfunction in the orbitofrontal region results in poor response inhibition (Aron et al., 2004) and poor decision-making (Bechara, 2004). This also applies to the moral domain, as recent studies of patients with damage to the orbitofrontal/ventromedial prefrontal cortex have demonstrated impairments in moral decision-making (Ciaramelli et al., 2007; Koenigs et al., 2007). Additional studies of patients with brain injury are discussed in Box 58.1.

The medial prefrontal cortex has been implicated in the prosocial emotions of guilt, embarrassment, and compassion (Moll et al., 2007; Takahashi et al., 2004), the cognitive appraisal of emotion (Ochsner et al., 2002), and in self-reflection (Gusnard et al., 2001). This region has also been implicated in moral judgment (Greene et al., 2001) as well as in the regulation of moral emotions (Harenski & Hamann,

2006). Impaired functioning in the medial region of the prefrontal cortex may lead to disruptions in one or more of these processes that are important in appropriate social behavior and moral judgment.

Finally, within the prefrontal cortex, several studies have found the dorsolateral region to be impaired. In contrast to the orbitofrontal and medial prefrontal regions, which play a large role in emotion and moral decision-making, the dorsolateral prefrontal cortex is likely associated with antisocial behavior because of its role in executive functions. The dorsolateral prefrontal cortex is involved in processes such as planning and organization (Smith & Jonides, 1999), attentional set shifting and cognitive flexibility (Dias et al., 1996), cognitive reappraisal of emotional experience (Ochsner et al., 2002), and response perseveration (Lombardi et al., 1999). Thus, dysfunction in the dorsolateral prefrontal cortex may impair planning and other executive functions (Smith & Jonides, 1999) that may predispose to outcomes such as occupational failure and hence low income, repetition of maladaptive antisocial responses, or a failure to consider alternative strategies to resolve conflict. In antisocial groups, reduced gray matter volume of the dorsolateral prefrontal cortex has been observed in alcoholics with antisocial personalities (Laakso et al., 2002), and reduced bloodflow has been found in aggressive patients (Hirono et al., 2000). Abnormal dorsolateral prefrontal cortex functioning has been observed in two fMRI studies of individuals with APD (Schneider et al., 2000; Vollm et al., 2004).

In addition to the prefrontal cortex, there is substantial evidence for structural and functional impairments in the amygdala in antisocial groups. Reduced volume of the amygdala has been reported in violent offenders (Tiihonen et al., 2000). Functional asymmetries of the amygdala have been observed in murderers (Raine et al., 1997), showing reduced left and increased right amygdala activity. However, two studies have reported *increased* amygdala activation in antisocial individuals while viewing negative visual content (Muller et al., 2003) and during aversive conditioning (Schneider et al., 2000). Deficits have also been observed in the adjacent temporal cortex in antisocial individuals. Volume reductions in the temporal lobe have been observed in patients with APD (Barkataki et al., 2006) and impulsive-aggressive personality-disordered patients (Dolan et al., 2002). Reduced metabolism in the temporal cortex has been observed in violent patients (Seidenwurm et al., 1997; Volkow et al., 1995) and reduced blood flow has been

Studies of patients with damage to particular brain regions have helped to further confirm the importance of some of the brain regions implicated in antisocial behavior. Lesion studies have shown that damage to the orbitofrontal/ventromedial prefrontal cortex produces personality traits and behaviors strikingly similar to those observed in APD (Damasio, 1994). Individuals with lesions in this region display significant rule breaking, lying, impulsivity, failure to hold jobs, failure to plan for the future or form goals, and financial irresponsibility. They are described as lacking empathy, guilt, remorse, and fear, and are unconcerned with their behavioral transgressions. They also show disturbances in moral behavior and decision making. In moral decisions involving highly conflicting considerations of aggregate welfare versus emotionally aversive behaviors (e.g., smothering one's baby to save a group of people), patients with ventromedial prefrontal cortex damage demonstrate an abnormally utilitarian pattern of judgments compared to controls (Koenigs et al., 2007). It is suggested that the ventromedial prefrontal cortex is crucial for the generation of emotional responsiveness to the aversive acts. While the patients show intact explicit knowledge of social and moral norms, their moral decisions are not guided by emotion to the same degree as normal controls.

Lesion studies have found that individuals who incur brain damage to the ventromedial prefrontal cortex very early in life have even more pronounced antisocial traits. Anderson et al. (1999) found that patients who incurred damage before the age of 16 months developed irresponsible and criminal behavior, abusive behavior towards others, and a lack of empathy or remorse. These antisocial characteristics and behaviors were more severe than those observed in patients who suffered damage in adulthood. It has been suggested that intact functioning of the ventromedial prefrontal cortex early in life is important for moral development (Anderson, 1999). When this region is damaged early on, the process of moral socialization may be disrupted. Indeed, the study found that these individuals demonstrated an immature stage of moral reasoning.

Individuals with lesions to the amygdala have also exhibited some of the same impairments that are observed in antisocial individuals, including impairments in aversive conditioning (Bechara et al., 1999), augmentation of the startle reflex to visual threat primes (Angrilli et al., 1996), and recognizing fearful facial expressions (Adolphs, 2002). However, patients with lesions to the amygdala do not closely resemble individuals with antisocial personality. This may be because amygdala abnormalities in antisocial individuals are not as widespread or severe as those of lesion patients.

Antisocial behavior has also been observed in individuals with frontotemporal dementia (FTD) (Mendez, 2006), a neurodegenerative disorder that affects the frontal lobes, temporal lobes, or both. The transgression of social norms is a core feature of FTD; patients engage in behaviors such as stealing, shoplifting, inappropriate sexual behavior, physical violence, and poor financial decision making (Mendez et al., 2005). Such a demonstration of pervasive disregard for social and moral standards closely resembles that of individuals with APD, and suggests that impairment in the prefrontal and temporal cortices likely play a significant role in antisocial behavior.

observed in aggressive patients (Hirono et al., 2000) and violent offenders (Soderstrom et al., 2000). Functional impairments in the temporal lobe have been shown in aggressive patients (Amen et al., 1996; Volkow & Tancredi, 1987) and in violent offenders (Raine et al., 2001).

The disruption of amygdala functioning may interfere with processes that have been found to be important to normal socialization and social behavior. Amygdala dysfunction impairs classical conditioning (LeDoux, 2000) which is hypothesized to form the basis of conscience and the anticipatory fear that normally deters individuals from committing antisocial acts (Blair, 2004). More specifically, the amygdala is necessary for the formation of stimulus-reinforcement associations, which are necessary for an individual to learn to associate their harmful actions with the pain and distress of others,

thus facilitating empathy for victims and discouraging antisocial behavior (Blair, 2006). It is also involved in the production of emotional states (Phillips et al., 2003), and enhancing attention to emotional stimuli, such as facial expressions of emotion (Adolphs et al., 1999). Finally, the amygdala has been identified as a region important in moral judgment (Greene et al., 2004), the experience of moral emotions (Moll, Oliveira-Souza, et al., 2002), and has also been found to respond during one's own moral violations (Berthoz et al., 2006).

There are two additional regions that are commonly implicated in moral decision-making that have also been associated with antisocial behavior— the angular gyrus (posterior superior temporal gyrus) and the posterior cingulate. Deficits in the angular gyrus have been observed in murderers (Raine et al., 1997) and in impulsive, violent criminals

(Soderstrom et al., 2000). Reduced volume of the posterior cingulate has been observed in persistently violent offenders (Tiihonen et al., 2008). The angular gyrus is implicated in the experience of guilt and embarrassment (Takahashi et al., 2004), which are secondary emotions motivating rule-breaking individuals to desist from future antisocial behaviors. It has also been found to be involved in reasoning about social contracts (Fiddick et al., 2005). The posterior cingulate is involved in self-referencing (Ochsner et al., 2005) and reflecting on one's duties and obligations (Johnson et al., 2006). Both the posterior cingulate and angular gyrus are involved in aspects of social cognition that are important to moral decision-making, and have been found to be active in studies of moral judgment (Greene et al., 2004; Greene et al., 2001).

There are additional areas that have been implicated in antisocial behavior that have not commonly been associated with moral judgment. For example, the functional integrity of the hippocampus has been found be abnormal in murderers (Raine et al., 1997), and in violent offenders (Soderstrom et al., 2000). It has been suggested that abnormalities in this region may reflect disrupted neurodevelopmental processes (Raine et al., 2004). The hippocampus is also important in the retrieval of emotional memories and is involved in contextual fear conditioning (Fanselow, 2000; LeDoux, 1998). Thus, hippocampal impairments may disrupt learning in the social context, rendering antisocial individuals insensitive to environmental cues of future punishment.

In sum, numerous brain regions involved in social processes have been implicated in antisocial behavior. Given the heterogeneity of the categorization of antisocial individuals, it is likely that different brain impairments underlie different forms of antisocial personality. However, a core feature of antisocial personality disorders is immoral behavior. This may result from a disruption to one or more brain regions underlying moral decision-making, including the medial prefrontal and orbitofrontal cortices, amygdala, angular gyrus, and posterior cingulate. As highlighted in a recent review (Raine & Yang, 2006), the regions frequently activated in moral decision-making tasks demonstrate significant overlap with the brain regions structurally and functionally compromised in antisocial populations. By juxtaposing these two sets of empirical data, the commonalities become apparent (see Figure 1 in Raine & Yang, 2006). This overlap may give rise to the hypothesis that some of the brain impairments observed in antisocial individuals disrupt moral emotions and decision-making, in turn predisposing to antisocial behavior (Raine & Yang, 2006).

Antisocial Personality in Youth

Childhood antisocial behavior is an especially important area of study because it can give insight into the developmental pathways that lead to long-term antisocial behavior. Although brain-imaging methods in youth were previously limited due to potential hazards of administering radioactive isotopes or ionizing radiation, the development of MRI techniques have allowed for the extension of brain imaging studies to youth. Studies of youth with conduct disorder have produced results that are largely similar to those in antisocial adults, suggesting that the brain impairments observed in adults likely exist at an early age. However, some inconsistencies in findings do exist.

The first structural MRI study of conduct disordered youth did not produce significant results (Bussing et al., 2002); however, this study was limited by a small sample size of seven individuals. Later, Kruesi et al. (2004) found that youth with conduct disorder and a history of ADHD demonstrated significantly reduced volumes of the temporal lobes; volumes of the prefrontal cortex also tended to be smaller in subjects with CD, but results did not reach statistical significance. In a recent study using voxel-based morphometry, Huebner et al. (2008) found that boys with conduct disorder, most of whom had comorbid ADHD, demonstrated a 6% decrease in overall gray matter. Specific reductions were observed in the orbitofrontal cortex and temporal lobes, including the hippocampus and amygdala. Symptoms of conduct disorder correlated primarily with reduced gray matter in limbic brain regions.

Several functional MRI studies have demonstrated reduced activity in the amygdala of youth with conduct disorder. Sterzer et al. (2005) found reduced activation in the amygdala in aggressive children with conduct disorder while viewing negative emotional pictures. Jones et al. (2009) found that boys with conduct problems and callous-unemotional traits demonstrated reduced activity in the amygdala when viewing fearful faces compared to control participants. Similarly, Marsh et al. (2008) found that children with callous-unemotional traits demonstrate reduced amygdala activity to fearful facial expressions, but not to neutral or angry expressions. Furthermore, these children demonstrated reduced connectivity between the amygdala and ventromedial prefrontal cortex;

the severity of symptoms in the callous-unemotional traits groups was found to be negatively correlated with the degree of connectivity between these regions. It is suggested that the connectivity between these regions is important because it allows for input from the amygdala to guide behavioral selection processes in the ventromedial prefrontal cortex.

Additional regions that have demonstrated reduced functioning fMRI studies of youth with conduct disorder include the orbitofronal cortex, insula, hippocampus, and anterior cingulate during a rewarded continuous performance task (Rubia et al., 2009), and the posterior cingulate and temporal-parietal regions during an inhibition task (Rubia et al., 2008). Reduced activity in the medial and orbitofrontal prefrontal cortex and temporo-parietal junction has been observed in adolescents with conduct disorder when viewing scenes of pain being intentionally inflicted on another individual (Decety et al., 2009). Adolescents with CD also exhibited less amygdala/prefrontal coupling when perceiving others in pain, which may reflect impairment in the ability to regulate emotions.

However, some discrepancies remain. Herpertz et al. (2008) found *increased* left-sided amygdala activity in boys with conduct disorder when viewing negative pictures, and no evidence of reduced functioning in orbitofrontal, anterior cingulate, or insular cortices. Similarly, Decety et al. (2009) found greater activity in the amygdala and temporal pole in adolescents with aggressive conduct disorder compared to healthy adolescents when perceiving other individuals in pain. It is hypothesized that this activation may reflect an aroused state of enjoyment or excitement at viewing others in pain.

For the most part, findings from neuroimaging studies in antisocial youth tend to parallel those of adult antisocial individuals. This suggests that brain abnormalities likely exist early in life and thus affect socialization.

Conclusion and Implications

The findings of brain abnormalities in antisocial youth and adults raise an intriguing forensic question. There is little doubt that most criminal and delinquent individuals *know* the difference between right and wrong—the question is whether they have the *feeling* of what is right and wrong. Moral decision-making is viewed as heavily predicated on affect (Greene & Haidt, 2002; Moll et al., 2005). This "moral feeling," based on the functioning of the moral neural circuit, is thought to translate the cognitive recognition that an act is immoral into behavioral inhibition; in normal individuals, these emotional experiences inhibit aggressive impulses (Davidson et al., 2000). This system may function less well in antisocial individuals. This issue raises the question, if a criminal offender has disruption to this neural circuitry, are they fully accountable for their immoral behavior? This issue is further discussed in Box 58.2.

Despite an exponential increase in brain imaging research on antisocial populations implicating multiple brain systems, neuroscience research on this important social and clinical construct is far from complete. With the continual development of imaging techniques, as well as unique paradigms from social neuroscience, our understanding of the neurobiological bases of antisocial personality will become more sophisticated. The application of neuroscience methods to the study of antisocial personality has the potential to lead to new approaches for treatment by providing an understanding of the mechanisms that underlie the development of antisocial personalities. Given the heterogeneous nature of the disorder, it is likely that different biological risk factors underlie different manifestations of the disorder. Although the neurobiological impairments currently seem widespread, it is likely that different biological risk factors may lead to antisocial behavior in different ways. In the future, it may be possible to develop individualized treatments that target specific neurobiological risk factors.

Advances in this field will also need to take increasing cognizance of the environmental context within which neurobiological predispositions give expression to antisocial behavior. There is initial evidence that environmental factors may moderate brain-violence relationships. Surprisingly, integrative biosocial research in this imaging field is almost nonexistent. Another future direction will be the delineation of the specific genes that give rise to the brain impairments found in antisocial groups. For example, a common polymorphism in the MAOA gene has been implicated in antisocial behavior (Caspi et al., 2002), and in males this same polymorphism is associated with an 8% reduction in the volume of the amygdala, anterior cingulate, and orbitofrontal cortex (Meyer-Lindenberg et al., 2006), structures compromised in antisocial individuals. Given the evidence that 90% of the variability in prefrontal gray volume is attributable to genetics (Thompson et al., 2001), a "genes-to-brain-to-antisocial behavior" approach is likely to increasingly

provide an important conceptual framework for
future empirical research of this important societal
problem (Raine, 2008).

References

Adolphs, R. (2002). Neural systems for recognizing emotion.
  Current Opinion in Neurobiology, 12, 169–177.

Adolphs, R., Tranel, D., Young, A. W., Calder, A. J., Phelps, E. A.,
  & Anderson, A. K. (1999). Recognition of facial emotion
  in nine individuals with bilateral amygdala damage.
  Neuropsychologia, 37, 1111–1117.

Amen, D. G., Stubblefield, M., Carmichael, B., & Thisted, R.
  (1996). Brain SPECT findings and aggressiveness. *Annals of
  Clinical Psychiatry, 8*, 129–137.

Anderson, S. W., Bechara, A., Damasio, H., Tranel, D., &
  Damasio, A. R. (1999). Impairment of social and moral
  behavior related to early damage in human prefrontal cortex.
  Nature Neuroscience, 2, 1031–1037.

Angrilli, A., Mauri, A., Palomba, D., Flor, H., Birbaumer, N., &
  Sartori, G. (1996). Startle reflex and emotion modulation impairment after a right amygdala lesion. *Brain, 119*,
  1991–2000.

Aron, A. R., Robbins, T. W., & Poldrack, R. A. (2004). Inhibition
  and the right inferior frontal cortex. *Trends in Cognitive
  Science, 8*(4), 170–177.

Barkataki, I., Kumari, V., Das, M., Taylor, P., & Sharma, T.
  (2006). Volumetric structural brain abnormalities in men
  with schizophrenia or antisocial personality disorder.
  Behavioral Brain Research, 15, 239–247.

Bechara, A. (2004). The role of emotion in decision-making:
  Evidence from neurological patients with orbitofrontal
  damage. *Brain and Cognition, 55*(1), 30–40.

Bechara, A., Damasio, H., Damasio, A. R., & Lee, G. P. (1999).
  Different contributions of the human amygdala and ventro-
  medial prefrontal cortex to decision-making. *Journal of
  Neuroscience, 19*, 5473–5481.

Berthoz, S., Grezes, J., Armony, J. L., Passingham, R. E., &
  Dolan, R. J. (2006). Affective response to one's own moral
  violations. *NeuroImage, 31*, 945–950.

Blair, R. J. (2004). The roles of the orbital frontal cortex in the
  modulation of antisocial behavior. *Brain and Cognition, 55*,
  198–208.

Blair, R. J. (2006). Subcortical brain systems in psychopathy. In
  C. J. Patrick (Ed.), *Handbook of psychopathy* (pp. 296–312).
  New York: Guilford.

Blair, R. J. (2007). The amygdala and ventromedial prefrontal
  cortex in morality and psychopathy. *Trends in Cognitive
  Sciences, 11*(9), 387–392.

Blair, R. J., Colledge, E., Murray, L., & Mitchell, D. G. V.
  (2001). A selective impairment in the processing of sad and
  fearful facial expressions in children with psychopathic tendencies. *Journal of Abnormal Child Psychology, 29*, 491–498.

Borg, J. S., Hynes, C., Van Horn, J., Grafton, S., &
  Sinnott-Armstrong, W. (2006). Consequences, action, and
  intention as factors in moral judgments: An fMRI investigation. *Journal of Cognitive Neuroscience, 18*, 803–817.

Bussing, R., Grudnik, J., Mason, D., Wasiak, M., & Leonard, C.
  (2002). ADHD and conduct disorder: An MRI study in a
  community sample. *The World Journal of Biological Psychiatry,
  3*, 216–220.

Caspi, A., McClay, J., Moffitt, T. E., Mill, J., Martin, J., Craig, I. W., et al. (2002). Role of genotype in the cycle of violence in maltreated children. *Science, 297*, 851–854.

Ciaramelli, E., Muccioli, M., Ladavas, E., & di Pellegrino, G. (2007). Selective deficit in personal moral judgment following damage to ventromedial prefrontal cortex. *Social Cognitive and Affective Neuroscience, 2*, 84–92.

Damasio, A. R. (1994). *Descartes' error: Emotion, reason, and the human brain*. New York: GP Putnam's Sons.

Davidson, R. J., Putnam, K. M., & Larson, C. L. (2000). Dysfunction in the neural circuitry of emotion regulation—a possible prelude to violence. *Science, 289*, 591–594.

Decety, J., Michalska, K. J., Akitsuki, Y., & Lahey, B. B. (2009). Atypical empathic responses in adolescents with aggressive conduct disorder: A functional MRI investigation. *Biological Psychology, 80*, 203–211.

Decety, J. & Moriguchi, Y. (2007). The empathic brain and its dysfunction in psychiatric populations: Implications for intervention across different clinical conditions. *Biopsychosocial Medicine, 1*, 22.

Dias, R., Robbins, T. W., & Roberts, A. C. (1996). Dissociation in prefrontal cortex of affective and attentional shifts. *Nature, 380*, 69–72.

Dolan, M., Deakin, J. F. W., Roberts, N., & Anderson, I. M. (2002). Quantitative frontal and temporal structural MRI studies in personality-disordered offenders and control subjects. *Psychiatry Research Neuroimaging, 116*, 133–149.

Fanselow, M. S. (2000). Contextual fear, gestalt memories, and the hippocampus. *Behavioral Brain Research, 110*, 73–81.

Fiddick, L., Spampinato, M. V., & Grafman, J. (2005). Social contracts and precautions activate different neurological systems: An fMRI investigation of deontic reasoning. *NeuroImage, 28*(4), 778–786.

Greene, J. D. & Haidt, J. (2002). How (and where) does moral judgment work? *Trends in Cognitive Science, 6*, 517–523.

Greene, J. D., Nystrom, L. E., Engell, A. D., Darley, J. M., & Cohen, J. (2004). The neural bases of cognitive conflict and control in moral judgment. *Neuron, 44*, 389–400.

Greene, J. D., Sommerville, R. B., Nystrom, L. E., Darley, J. M., & Cohen, J. (2001). An fMRI investigation of emotional engagement in moral judgment. *Science, 293*, 2105–2108.

Gusnard, D. A., Akbudak, E., Shulman, G. L., & Raichle, M. E. (2001). Medial prefrontal cortex and self-referential mental activity: Relation to a default mode of brain function. *Proceedings of the National Academy of Sciences of the United States of America, 98*(7), 4259–4264.

Hare, R. D. (1991). *Manual for the Hare Psychopathy Checklist-Revised*. Toronto: Multi-Health Systems.

Harenski, C. L. & Hamann, S. (2006). Neural correlates of regulating negative emotions related to moral violations. *NeuroImage, 30*, 313–324.

Herpertz, S. C., Huebner, T., Marx, I., Vloet, T. D., Fink, G. R., Stoecker, T., et al. (2008). Emotional processing in male adolescents with childhood-onset conduct disorder. *Journal of Child Psychology & Psychiatry, 49*, 781–791.

Hirono, N., Mega, M. S., Dinov, I. D., Mishkin, F., & Cummings, J. L. (2000). Left frontotemporal hypoperfusion is associated with aggression in patients with dementia. *Archive of Neurology, 57*, 861–866.

Huebner, T., Vloet, T. D., Marx, I., Konrad, K., Fink, G. R., Herpertz, S. C., et al. (2008). Morphometric brain abnormalities in boys with conduct disorder. *Journal of*

the American Academy of Child and Adolescent Psychiatry, *47*, 540–547.

Johnson, M. K., Raye, C. R., Mitchell, K. J., Touryan, S. R., Greene, E. J., & Nolen-Hoeksema, S. (2006). Dissociating the medial frontal and posterior cingulate activity during self-reflection. *Social, Cognitive and Affective Neuroscience, 1*, 64.

Jones, A. P., Laurens, K. R., Herba, C. M., Barker, G. J., & Viding, E. (2009). Amygdala hypoactivity to fearful faces in boys with conduct problems and callous-unemotional traits. *American Journal of Psychiatry, 166*, 95–102.

Koenigs, M., Young, L., Adolphs, R., Tranel, D., Cushman, F., Hauser, M., et al. (2007). Damage to the prefrontal cortex increases utilitarian moral judgments. *Nature, 446*(7138), 908–911.

Kuruoglu, A. C., Arikan, Z., Vural, G., & Karatas, M. (1996). Single photon emission computerised tomography in chronic alcoholism: Antisocial personality disorder may be associated with decreased frontal profusion. *British Journal of Psychiatry, 169*, 348–354.

Laakso, M. P., Gunning-Dixon, F., Vaurio, O., Repo-Tiihonen, E., Soininen, H., & Tiihonen, J. (2002). Prefrontal volumes in habitually violent subjects with antisocial personality disorder and type 2 alcoholism. *Psychiatry Research Neuroimaging, 114*, 95–102.

Lahey, B. B., Loeber, R., Burke, J. D., & Applegate, B. (2005). Predicting future antisocial personality disorder in males from a clinical assessment in childhood. *Journal of Consulting and Clinical Psychology, 73*, 389–399.

LeDoux, J. E. (1998). *The emotional brain*. New York: Weidenfeld & Nicolson.

LeDoux, J. E. (2000). Emotion circuits in the brain. *Annual Review of Neuroscience, 23*, 155–184.

Lombardi, W. J., Andreason, P. J., Sirocco, K. Y., Rio, D. E., Gross, R. E., Umhau, J. C., et al. (1999). Wisconsin Card Sorting Test performance following head injury: Dorsolateral fronto-striatal circuit activity predicts perseveration. *Journal of Clinical and Experimental Neuropsychology, 21*, 2–16.

Marsh, A. A., Finger, E. C., Mitchell, D. G. V., Reid, M. E., Sims, C., Kosson, D. S., et al. (2008). Reduced amygdala response to fearful expressions in children and adolescents with callous-unemotional traits and disruptive behavior disorders. *American Journal of Psychiatry, 165*, 712–720.

Mendez, M. F. (2006). What frontotemporal dementia reveals about the neurobiological basis of morality. *Medical Hypotheses, 67*(2), 411–418.

Mendez, M. F., Chen, A. K., Shapira, J. S., & Miller, B. L. (2005). Acquired sociopathy and frontotemporal dementia. *Dementia and Geriatric Cognitive Disorders, 20*, 99–104.

Meyer-Lindenberg, A., Buckholtz, J. W., Kolachana, B., Hariri, A. R., Pezawas, L., Blasi, G., et al. (2006). Neural mechanisms of genetic risk for impulsivity and violence in humans. *Proceedings of the National Academy of Sciences of the United States of America, 103*, 6269–6274.

Moll, J., de Oliveira-Souza, R., Garrido, G. J., Bramati, I. E., Caparelli-Daquer, E. M., Paiva, M. L., et al. (2007). The self as a moral agent: Linking the neural bases of social agency and moral sensitivity. *Social Neuroscience, 2*, 336–352.

Moll, J., Oliveira-Sousa, R., Bramati, I. E., & Grafman, J. (2002). Functional networks in emotional moral and non-moral social judgments. *NeuroImage, 16*, 696–703.

Moll, J., Oliveira-Souza, R., Eslinger, P. J., Bramati, I. E., Mourao-Miranda, J., Andreiuolo, P. A., et al. (2002).

The neural correlates of moral sensitivity: A functional magnetic resonance imaging investigation of basic and moral emotions. *The Journal of Neuroscience: The Official Journal of the Society for Neuroscience, 22*(7), 2730–2736.

Moll, J., Oliveira-Souza, R., Moll, F. T., Ignacio, F. A., Bramati, I. E., Caparelli-Daquer, E. M., et al. (2005). The moral affiliations of disgust: A functional MRI study. *Cognitive Behavioral Neurology, 18*, 68–78.

Morgan, A. B. & Lilienfeld, S. O. (2000). A meta-analytic review of the relation between antisocial behavior and neuropsychological measures of executive function. *Clinical Psychology Review, 20*, 113–136.

Muller, J. L., Sommer, M., Wagner, V., Lange, K., Taschler, H., Roder, C. H., et al. (2003). Abnormalities in emotion processing within cortical and subcortical regions in criminal psychopaths: Evidence from a functional magnetic resonance imaging study using pictures with emotional content. *Psychiatry Research Neuroimaging, 54*, 152–162.

Narayan, V. M., Narr, K. L., Kumari, V., Woods, R. P., Thompson, P. M., Toga, A. W., et al. (2007). Regional cortical thinning in subjects with violent antisocial personality disorder or schizophrenia. *American Journal of Psychiatry, 164*, 1418–1427.

New, A. S., Hazlett, E., Buchsbaum, M. S., Goodman, M., Reynolds, D., Mitropoulous, V., et al. (2002). Blunted prefrontal cortical 18-fluorodeoxyglucose positron emission tomography response to meta-chlorophenylpiperazine in impulsive aggression. *Archives of General Psychiatry, 59*, 621–629.

Ochsner, K. N., Beer, J. S., Robertson, E. R., Cooper, J. C., Gabrieli, J. D. E., Kihsltrom, J. F., et al. (2005). The neural correlates of direct and reflected self-knowledge. *NeuroImage, 28*(4), 797–814.

Ochsner, K. N., Bunge, S. A., Gross, J. J., & Gabrieli, J. D. E. (2002). Rethinking feelings: An fMRI study of the cognitive regulation of emotion. *Journal of Cognitive Neuroscience, 14*(8), 1215–1229.

Oliveira-Sousa, R. & Moll, J. (2000). The moral brain: Functional MRI correlates of moral judgment in normal adults. *Neurology, 54*, 252.

Phillips, M. L., Drevets, W. C., Rauch, S. L., & Lane, R. (2003). Neurobiology of emotion perception I: The neural basis of normal emotion perception. *Biological Psychiatry, 54*, 504–514.

Raine, A. (2008). From genes to brain to antisocial behavior. *Current Directions in Psychological Science, 17*, 323–328.

Raine, A., Buchsbaum, M. S., & Lacasse, L. (1997). Brain abnormalities in murderers indicated by positron emission tomography. *Biological Psychiatry, 42*, 495–508.

Raine, A., Ishikawa, S. S., Arce, E., Lencz, T., Knuth, K. H., Bihrle, S., et al. (2004). Hippocampal structural asymmetry in unsuccessful psychopaths. *Biological Psychiatry, 55*, 185–191.

Raine, A., Lencz, T., Bihrle, S., LaCasse, L., & Colletti, P. (2000). Reduced prefrontal gray matter volume and reduced autonomic activity in antisocial personality disorder. *Archives of General Psychiatry, 57*, 119–127.

Raine, A., Meloy, J. R., Bihrle, S., Stoddard, J., Lacasse, L., & Buchsbaum, M. S. (1998). Reduced prefrontal and increased subcortical brain functioning assessed using positron emission tomography in predatory and affective murderers. *Behavioral Sciences & the Law, 16*, 319–332.

Raine, A., Park, S., Lencz, T., Bihrle, S., Lacasse, L., Widom, C. S., et al. (2001). Reduced right hemisphere activation in severely abused violent offenders during a working memory task: An fMRI study. *Aggressive Behavior, 27*, 111–129.

Raine, A. & Yang, Y. (2006). Neural foundations to moral reasoning and antisocial behavior. *Social, Cognitive, and Affective Neuroscience, 1*, 203–213.

Rolls, E. T. (2000). The orbitofrontal cortex and reward. *Cerebral Cortex, 10*, 284–294.

Rubia, K., Halari, R., Smith, A. B., Mohammad, M., Scott, S., Giampietro, V., et al. (2008). Dissociated functional brain abnormalities of inhibition in boys with pure conduct disorder and in boys with pure attention deficit hyperactivity disorder. *American Journal of Psychiatry, 165*, 889–897.

Rubia, K., Smith, A. B., Halari, R., Matsukura, F., Mohammad, M., Taylor, E., et al. (2009). Disorder-specific dissociation of orbitofrontal dysfunction in boys with pure conduct disorder during reward and ventrolateral prefrontal dysfunction in boys with pure ADHD during sustained attention. *American Journal of Psychiatry, 166*, 83–94.

Schneider, F., Habel, U., Kessler, C., Posse, S., Grodd, W., & Muller-Gartner, H. W. (2000). Functional imaging of conditioned aversive emotional responses in antisocial personality disorder. *Neuropsychobiology, 42*, 192–201.

Seidenwurm, D., Pounds, T. R., Globus, A., & Valk, P. E. (1997). Abnormal temporal lobe metabolism in violent subjects: Correlation of imaging and neuropsychiatric findings. *American Journal of Neuroradiology, 18*, 625–631.

Shamay-Tsoory, S. G., Tomer, R., Berger, B. D., Goldsher, D., & Aharon-Peretz, J. (2005). Impaired "affective theory of mind" is associated with right ventromedial prefrontal damage. *Cognitive Behavioral Neurology, 18*(1), 55–67.

Smith, E. E. & Jonides, J. (1999). Storage and executive processes in the frontal lobes. *Science, 283*(1657–1661).

Soderstrom, H., Tullberg, M., Wikkelso, C., Ekholm, S., & Forsman, A. (2000). Reduced regional cerebral blood flow in non-psychotic violent offenders. *Psychiatry Research: Neuroimaging, 98*, 29–41.

Sterzer, P., Stadler, C., Krebs, A., Kleinschmidt, A., & Poustka, F. (2005). Abnormal neural responses to emotional visual stimuli in adolescents with conduct disorder. *Biological Psychiatry, 57*, 7–15.

Takahashi, H., Yahata, N., Koeda, M., Matsuda, T., Asai, K., & Okubo, Y. (2004). Brain activation associated with evaluative processes of guilt and embarrassment: An fMRI study. *NeuroImage, 23*(3), 967–974.

Thompson, P. M., Cannon, T. D., Narr, K. L., van Erp, T., Poutanen, V. P., & Huttunen, M. (2001). Genetic influences on brain structure. *Nature Neuroscience, 4*, 1253–1258.

Tiihonen, J., Hodgins, S., & Vaurio, O. (2000). Amygdaloid volume loss in psychopathy. *Society for Neuroscience Abstracts*, 20017.

Tiihonen, J., Rossi, R., Laakso, M. P., Hodgins, S., Testa, C., Perez, J., et al. (2008). Brain anatomy of persistent violent offenders: More rather than less. *Psychiatry Research: Neuroimaging, 163*, 201–212.

Volkow, N. D. & Tancredi, L. R. (1987). Neural substrates of violent behavior: A preliminary study with positron emission tomography. *British Journal of Psychiatry, 151*, 668–673.

Volkow, N. D., Tancredi, L. R., Grant, C., Gillespie, H., Valentine, A., Mullani, N., et al. (1995). Brain glucose metabolism in violent psychiatric patients: A preliminary study. *Psychiatry Research Neuroimaging, 61*, 243–253.

Vollm, B., Richardson, P., McKie, S., Elliot, R., Deakin, J., & Anderson, I. M. (2006). Serotonergic modulation of neuronal responses to behavioural inhibition and reinforcing stimuli: An fMRI study in healthy volunteers. *European Journal of Neuroscience, 23*(2), 552–560.

Vollm, B., Richardson, P., Stirling, J., Elliot, R., Dolan, M., Chaudhry, I., et al. (2004). Neurobiological substrates of antisocial and borderline personality disorders: Preliminary result of a functional MRI study. *Criminal Behavior and Mental Health, 14*, 39–54.

Psychopathy from the Perspective of Social and Cognitive Neuroscience

James Blair

Abstract

This chapter focuses on psychopathy, paying particular attention to some of the social aspects of the disorder. It first considers the nature of psychopathy and what is understood regarding the pathophysiology of this disorder from a cognitive neuroscience perspective. Following this, it considers whether psychopathy might be caused by social/environmental factors before concluding with a brief description of the implications of findings with patients with psychopathy for social cognitive neuroscience, particularly regarding the development of morality.

Keywords: psychopathy, callous and unemotional traits, amygdala, orbitofrontal cortex, instrumental aggression, reactive aggression, morality

The goal of this chapter is to consider psychopathy, paying particular attention to some of the social aspects of the disorder. As such, I will first consider the nature of psychopathy and what is understood regarding the pathophysiology of this disorder from a cognitive neuroscience perspective. Following this, I will consider whether psychopathy might be caused by social/environmental factors, before concluding with a brief description of the implications of findings with patients with psychopathy for social cognitive neuroscience, particularly regarding the development of morality.

What is Psychopathy?

The disorder of *psychopathy* characterizes an individual who shows pronounced problems in emotional processing and who is at increased risk for displaying antisocial behavior (Frick, 1995; Hare, 2003). The problems in emotional processing involve reduced guilt, empathy, and attachment to significant others

(callous and unemotional [CU] traits). The antisocial behavior component involves an increased risk for displaying antisocial behavior from an early age.

Psychopathy is a developmental disorder. Recent work has confirmed the stability of CU traits in particular and the disorder more generally from child- into adult-hood (Lynam, Caspi, Moffitt, Loeber, & Stouthamer-Loeber, 2007; Munoz & Frick, 2007; Obradovic', Pardini, Long, & Loeber, 2007). Moreover, CU traits indexed in adolescents have been shown to predict adult measures of psychopathy in early adulthood (Burke, Loeber, & Lahey, 2007; Lynam et al., 2007). In addition, the functional impairments seen in adults with psychopathy (e.g., in responding to emotional expressions, aversive conditioning, passive avoidance learning, reversal learning, extinction) are also seen in adolescents with psychopathic tendencies.

Assessment scales for psychopathy include the Psychopathy Checklist-Revised (Hare, 2003) for adults and the Antisocial Process Screening Device (Frick & Hare, 2001) and Psychopathy Checklist–Youth Version (Forth, Kosson, & Hare, 2007) for adolescents. These typically identify three dimensions of behavior (Cooke, Michie, & Hart, 2006; Frick, Bodin, & Barry, 2000; Neumann, Kosson, Forth, & Hare, 2006) though it should be noted that the exact number, particularly for adult samples, is debated (Cooke et al., 2006). These three dimensions include: (1) an emotional factor that focuses on the presence or absence of callous-unemotional (CU) traits; that is, a lack of guilt and empathy and the callous use of others for personal gain; (2) an arrogant and deceitful interpersonal style involving a narcissistic view of one's self and conning and manipulative behavior and; (3) an impulsive and irresponsible behavioral style involving poorly planned behavior and proneness to boredom (Cooke et al., 2006; Frick et al., 2000; Neumann et al., 2006).

It should be noted that three (or more) factor solutions of psychopathy assessment measures does not imply that individuals with psychopathy show a triad of impairments. The strong assumption underlying this chapter is that there is an underlying impairment that gives rise to the presence of CU traits and that this impairment increases the risk for antisocial behavior and presumably leads to the arrogance and narcissism (though the relationship of CU traits to arrogance/narcissism remains underspecified). Neuro-cognitive impairments may be identified that are associated with all three factors. Indeed, neuro-cognitive impairments have been associated with both CU traits and impulsive behavior (none have yet been independently associated with arrogance/narcissism). But this does not mean that the disorder of psychopathy is necessarily associated with both forms of impairment. Indeed, while individuals with psychopathy show the impairments that are associated with CU traits (see below), they do not show the impairments associated with impulsive behavior. An increased risk for impulsive behavior is associated with impairments in "cold" (non-affect driven) executive functions—those relating to working memory and "inhibitory control" that are mediated by dorsomedial and lateral frontal cortices (Kerns et al., 2004). However, individuals with psychopathy, as youths or adults, show no significant impairment in these forms of executive function (Blair, Newman, et al., 2006; Hart, Forth, & Hare, 1990; LaPierre, Braun, & Hodgins, 1995). In short, the argument here is that psychopathy is associated with elevated CU

traits and that these traits put the individual at increased risk for antisocial behavior. However, individuals can also be at risk for (more impulsive) antisocial behavior if they show "cold" executive dysfunction.

It should also be noted that the disorder of psychopathy is not equivalent to the DSM-IV diagnoses of conduct disorder (CU) or antisocial personality disorder or their ICD-10 counterparts. These psychiatric diagnoses concentrate on the antisocial behavior rather than any potential cause for its expression such as the emotion dysfunction seen in psychopathy (Blair, Mitchell, & Blair, 2005). In fact, whereas CD has long been associated with cold executive dysfunction (Moffitt, 1993), psychopathy, as noted above, has not (Blair, Newman, et al., 2006; Hart et al., 1990; LaPierre et al., 1995). This again reinforces the idea that there are many developmental routes to an elevated risk for antisocial behavior (Blair, 2004; Frick & Marsee, 2006). As such, individuals meeting the criteria for CD and antisocial personality disorder are more heterogeneous in their pathophysiology than individuals meeting criteria for psychopathy (Karnik, McMullin, & Steiner, 2006).

One of the major strengths of the classification of psychopathy is its utility in risk assessment. Considerable work has shown the predictive power of the PCL-R with respect to recidivism (Hare, Clark, Grann, & Thornton, 2000; Hart, Kropp, & Hare, 1988; Kawasaki et al., 2001). The classification is important with respect to treatment also. Hawes and Dadds found that boys with conduct problems and high CU traits were less responsive to treatment than boys with conduct problems but low CU traits (Hawes & Dadds, 2005).

Instrumental and Reactive Aggression
A phenomenon that is worth considering, and which adds to the distinctness of CU traits, is the distinction between reactive (a.k.a. affective, impulsive, or defensive or RAID; cf. Steiner, Saxena, & Chang, 2003) and proactive (a.k.a. instrumental or premeditated or PIP; cf. Steiner et al., 2003) aggression (Barratt, Stanford, Dowdy, Liebman, & Kent, 1999; Berkowitz, 1993; Crick & Dodge, 1996; Linnoila et al., 1983). Reactive aggression is triggered by a frustrating or threatening event and involves unplanned, enraged attacks on the object perceived to be the source of the threat/frustration. This aggression type is often accompanied by anger. Critically, it is initiated without regard for any potential goal. In contrast, instrumental aggression

is *purposeful and goal directed* (e.g., to obtain the victim's possessions). Furthermore, instrumental aggression need not be accompanied by an emotional state, such as anger, and can be considered "cold" (Steiner et al., 2003).

Considerable amounts of data strongly support the existence of two relatively separable populations of aggressive individuals: individuals who present with mostly reactive aggression and individuals who present with high levels of mostly proactive and some reactive aggression (Barratt et al., 1999; Connor, 2002; Crick & Dodge, 1996; Linnoila et al., 1983). Some psychiatric conditions are associated with an increased risk for reactive aggression (e.g., post-traumatic stress disorder, childhood bipolar disorder, and intermittent explosive disorder). Elevated CU traits/psychopathy is unique as a clinical condition in that it is associated with not only an increased risk for reactive but also instrumental aggression (Cornell et al., 1996; Frick, Stickle, Dandreaux, Farell, & Kimonis, 2005).

The Cognitive Neuroscience of Psychopathy

One of the exciting features of research on psychopathy is the current relative consensus within the field. While attention-based models were dominant in the late 80s and early 90s and remain influential (Hiatt & Newman, 2006; MacCoon, Wallace, & Newman, 2004), there is now relatively general agreement that specific forms of emotional processing are compromised in psychopathy (Blair et al., 2005; Frick & Marsee, 2006; Kiehl, 2006; Lykken, 1995; Patrick, 1994); for a recent critique of the attention-based models, see Blair & Mitchell (2009).

At the neural level, there is relative consensus that the amygdala is dysfunctional (Blair, 2001; Kiehl, 2006; Patrick, 1994; Viding, 2004). This position is supported by both neuropsychological and neuro-imaging data. Thus, youth with CD+CU and adults with psychopathy show impairment in the recognition of fearful emotional expressions (Marsh & Blair, 2008), aversive conditioning (Birbaumer et al., 2005), augmentation of startle reflex by threat primes (Levenston, Patrick, Bradley, & Lang, 2000), and passive avoidance learning tasks (Newman & Kosson, 1986). These impairments are seen in human patients (Adolphs, 2002; Bechara, Damasio, Damasio, & Lee, 1999) and in animals with amygdala lesions (Ambrogi Lorenzini, Baldi, Bucherelli, Sacchetti, & Tassoni, 1999; Schoenbaum & Roesch, 2005). Moreover, fMRI studies with youth with CD+CU have shown reduced amygdala

responses to fearful expressions (Jones, Laurens, Herba, Barker, & Viding, 2009; Marsh et al., 2008) while fMRI studies with adults with psychopathy have shown reduced amygdala responses during aversive conditioning and emotional memory paradigms (Birbaumer et al., 2005; Kiehl et al., 2001).

There is also relative consensus that orbital frontal cortex (OFC) is dysfunctional (Blair et al., 2005; Kiehl, 2006). Thus, youth with CD+CU and adults with psychopathy show impairment in decision-making tasks requiring the OFC (Blair, Colledge, & Mitchell, 2001; Mitchell, Colledge, Leonard, & Blair, 2002) and in reversal learning (Budhani & Blair, 2005; Budhani, Richell, & Blair, 2006). The findings of impairments in reversal learning are particularly important as lesions of the amygdala do not compromise reversal learning (Murray & Izquierdo, 2007). In short, because reversal relearning relies on OFC, but not amygdala functioning, the reversal learning impairment in psychopathy indicates that OFC functioning is dysfunctional rather than OFC functioning is compromised by atypical input from the amygdala. FMRI work with youth with CD+CU has indicated reduced amygdala-OFC functional connectivity during expression viewing (Marsh et al., 2008). More importantly, this work has indicated that the impairment in reversal learning relates to atypical reinforcement outcome signaling in the OFC (Finger et al., 2008). FMRI studies with adults with psychopathy have similarly reported reduced OFC activity during aversive conditioning and emotional memory (Birbaumer et al., 2005; Kiehl et al., 2001).

On the basis primarily of fMRI results, Kiehl (2006) has suggested that the insula, anterior and posterior cingulate cortex, parahippocampal gyrus, and anterior superior temporal gyrus may also all be dysfunctional in psychopathy. There is no doubt that reduced superior temporal cortex activity is consistently observed in fMRI studies with CD+CU and adults with psychopathy (Finger et al., 2008; Jones et al., 2009; Kiehl et al., 2001; Marsh et al., 2008) though data with respect to the other regions is far sparser. However, it remains unknown whether the reduced superior temporal cortex activity reflects a secondary effect of the amygdala/OFC dysfunction or whether there is dysfunction within this system also. Currently, there is no neuropsychological data supporting superior temporal cortex dysfunction in psychopathy. With respect to some of the other regions implicated, the neuropsychological data suggests *no* dysfunction in psychopathy. Thus, aspects of executive attention attributed to the dorsal anterior cingulate cortex appear intact in psychopathy as assessed by Stroop performance (Blair, Newman, et al., 2006; Hiatt, Schmitt, & Newman, 2004). Indeed, fMRI work indicates appropriate dorsal anterior cingulate/dorsomedial prefrontal cortex activity in youth with CD+CU in response to punished errors during reversal learning (Finger et al., 2008). Similarly, neuropsychological data indicate no memory or spatial processing impairment in psychopathy (Hart et al., 1990); dysfunctions that would be expected following hippocampus dysfunction (Burgess, Maguire, & O'Keefe, 2002).

One additional region that should be considered, though, is the caudate. The caudate is of particular relevance given its importance in aspects of instrumental learning (O'Doherty et al., 2004). Interestingly, both fMRI studies examining instrumental learning in youth with CD+CU (this has not yet been examined in adults with psychopathy) have shown atypical caudate activity (Finger et al., 2008; in preparation). Of course, it is currently impossible to conclude whether the atypical caudate activity reflects caudate dysfunction or is the product of disrupted processing within the amygdala/OFC.

At the cognitive level, it has long been argued that psychopathy reflects problems processing punishment information (Lykken, 1957). Recent data suggest, though, that the deficit is more subtle than this. One notable feature of punishment information is that it makes individuals stop doing the response that received the punishment and try an alternative response. Youth with CD+CU and adults with psychopathy are as likely to change their response immediately following a punishment as comparison individuals (Budhani & Blair, 2005; Budhani et al., 2006). Indeed, the anterior cingulate cortex and inferior prefrontal cortex, which appear critical for organizing this change in behavior (Budhani, Marsh, Pine, & Blair, 2007), show appropriate responding to punishment in youth with CD+CU (Finger et al., 2008).

Rather than a problem in processing punishment per se, it is argued that youth with CD+CU and adults with psychopathy show problems with stimulus-reinforcement learning; that is, associating stimuli with punishment *or* reward (R. J. R. Blair, 2004). Importantly, stimulus-reinforcement learning is a critical function of the amygdala (Everitt, Cardinal, Parkinson, & Robbins, 2003) and is crucial for aversive conditioning, augmentation of startle reflex by threat primes, and passive avoidance

learning tasks. Fearful expressions importantly initiate stimulus-reinforcement learning (Blair, 2003) and recent work has demonstrated the critical role of the amygdala in this expression-initiated learning (Hooker, Germine, Knight, & D'Esposito, 2006). It is argued that stimulus-reinforcement learning is critical for socialization; the individual needs to learn whether representations of objects or actions are associated with reward or punishment and that an important "punishment" in socialization is the distress of the victim; their sadness or fear (Blair, 2004). One of the reasons of the efficacy of empathic induction (Hoffman, 1988) is its role in increasing attention to the victim and thus increasing the "punishment" strength of the victim's distress.

The OFC is critically involved in the representation of reinforcement expectancies (Blair, Marsh, et al., 2006; Hampton, Bossaerts, & O'Doherty, 2006; Rushworth, Behrens, Rudebeck, & Walton, 2007). This function of the OFC appears compromised in children with CD+CU/adults with psychopathy. Thus, the OFC shows decreased activity when expecting reward but receiving punishment. This is seen in healthy adults (Budhani et al., 2007), healthy youth, and youth with ADHD (Finger et al., 2008). However, this is not seen in youth with psychopathic traits (Finger et al., 2008). The suggestion is that these representations of reinforcement expectancies allow successful decision making to occur; the individual is able to choose the best option because he/she can represent the values of the different options. Damage to the OFC disrupts this form of decision making (Bechara, Tranel, & Damasio, 2000) and this form of decision making is disrupted in youth and adults with psychopathic traits (Blair et al., 2001; Mitchell et al., 2002).

Is Psychopathy Socially Determined?

There have been suggestions that psychopathy might be due to early physical/sexual abuse or early neglect (Rutter, 2005). Thus, Bowlby attributed "affectionless psychopathy" to family adversity that especially involved family disruption (Bowlby, 1946) and "impaired empathy" is considered an aspect of the "disinhibited attachment" that is characteristic of some children experiencing profound early institutional deprivation (O'Connor & Rutter, 2000); see also (Rutter, 2005). Work indicates high rates of trauma such as physical/sexual abuse and neglect in the early lives of many individuals with psychopathy (Hare, 2003). Moreover, high rates of such traumas are associated with an increased risk for aggression whether they occur in child- or adult-hood

(Rutter, 2005). However, Polythress et al. (2006) examined the effect of childhood maltreatment on the different dimensions of psychopathy and found that maltreatment is only associated with an increased risk for an impulsive and irresponsible lifestyle. Maltreatment is not associated with the core emotional dysfunction in psychopathy (Poythress et al., 2006). In addition, work by Pollak and colleagues suggest that maltreated children show hyper-reactivity to anger (Pollak & Sinha, 2002). Hyper-activity to anger is not seen in psychopathy which, in contrast, is associated with *hypo*-reactivity to fear and sadness (Marsh & Blair, 2008). Moreover, it should be noted that considerable animal and human work has examined the impact of extreme stressors on the development of the brain. For example, animal work has precisely shown that neglect and other stressors increase emotional responsiveness to threatening stimuli (Bremner & Vermetten, 2001a; Rilling et al., 2001). In particular, animals exposed to extreme stressors and neglect show increased amygdala responsiveness to threat stimuli (Nelson et al., 2009). Similarly, in humans, early physical/sexual abuse leads to increases in emotional responsiveness to threat stimuli and is a significant risk factor for the emergence of post-traumatic stress disorder (PTSD) (Rauch, Shin, & Phelps, 2006). PTSD is also associated with *increased* amygdala responsiveness to threat stimuli (Liberzon & Martis, 2006).

In striking contrast to the increased amygdala responsiveness to threat stimuli seen following extreme stressors and neglect, psychopathy is associated with decreased amygdala responsiveness to threat stimuli (Birbaumer et al., 2005; Jones et al., 2009; Kiehl et al., 2001; Marsh et al., 2008). As such, social factors do not appear promising as the basis of a causal account of psychopathy at the present time. Of course, it is possible that specific gene-environment interactions will be identified whereby specific environments, coupled with specific genes, can give rise to decreased amygdala responsiveness. However, such gene-environment interactions have not yet been identified.

There is, however, evidence for a genetic contribution to the disorder (Blonigen, Hicks, Krueger, Patrick, & Iacono, 2005; Viding, Blair, Moffitt, & Plomin, 2005). In one of the largest of these studies involving around 3500 twin pairs, CU traits were shown to be strongly heritable (67% heritability) at 7 years (Viding et al., 2005). However, an understanding of psychopathy at the molecular genetic level remains in its infancy. Importantly, though,

our increased understanding of the pathophysiology of psychopathy, and in particular the recognition of the dysfunction within the amygdala and medial OFC, allows for some suggestive possibilities. Recent work has shown that several different genetic polymorphisms impact on the functioning of these structures (Hariri et al., 2002; Meyer-Lindenberg et al., 2006; Pezawas et al., 2005). For example, several studies have reported that individuals who are ll homozygotes for the serotonin transporter (5-HTTLPR) gene show significantly reduced amygdala responding to emotional expressions relative to those who have the short form polymorphism of the gene (see Brown & Hariri, 2006). In addition, such individuals show behavioral impairment on some emotional learning tasks reliant on the interaction of the amygdala and medial frontal cortex (Finger et al., 2006). It is possible that there is an array of genes whose polymorphisms increase/decrease the functional integrity of the amygdala and medial frontal cortex. The basic genetic risk for psychopathy may emerge if an individual possesses a sufficient number of polymorphisms predisposing the individual to reduced emotional and amygdala responsiveness.

Of course, arguing that current data do not support the idea that trauma/neglect causes psychopathy in the face of data that trauma, neglect, and exposure to violence in the home or neighborhood are associated with an increased risk for aggression (Dodge, Pettit, Bates, & Valente, 1995; Farrington & Loeber, 2000; Miller, Wasserman, Neugebauer, Gorman-Smith, & Kamboukos, 1999; Schwab-Stone et al., 1999). This begs the question as to why they *are* associated with aggression. We believe the answer to this question rests in the form of aggression that is associated with trauma/neglect/exposure to violence; reactive aggression (Dodge et al., 1995).

Reactive aggression is part of the mammalian gradated response to threat. Low levels of danger from distant threats induce freezing. Higher levels of danger from closer threats induce attempts to escape the immediate environment. Higher levels of danger still, when the threat is very close and escape is impossible, initiate reactive aggression (Blanchard, Blanchard, & Takahashi, 1977). Animal work indicates that this progressive response to threat is mediated by a basic threat system that runs from medial amygdaloidal areas downward, largely via the stria terminalis to the medial hypothalamus, and from there to the dorsal half of the periaqueductal gray (PAG) (Gregg & Siegel, 2001; Panksepp, 1998).

This neural system, the amygdala-hypothalamus-PAG. is thought to mediate reactive aggression in humans also (Blair, 2004; Gregg & Siegel, 2001; Panksepp, 1998).

Animal work clearly shows that prolonged threat/stress leads to a long term potentiation of the neural and neurochemical systems that respond to threat; that is, the individual becomes more responsive to aversive stimuli (Bremner & Vermetten, 2001b; King, 1999). Moreover, animal work shows that poor parenting is also associated with increased responsiveness to aversive stimuli (Rilling et al., 2001; Sanchez et al., 2005). Importantly, this concurs with much of the human literature (e.g., Pollak & Sinha, 2002). In short, the suggestion is that threat/stress augment the responsiveness of the neural system, amygdala-hypothalamus-PAG, that is thought to mediate reactive aggression in humans (Blair, 2004). It is this which leads to the association between threat/stress and an increased risk for (reactive) aggression.

While it is clear that psychopathy is under considerable genetic influence, this does not imply that social factors do not influence how it presents. They clearly do. For example, socioeconomic status is associated with the emergence of the full syndrome; it is significantly less likely to appear in individuals of higher social status (Silverthorn & Frick, 1999). Indeed, lower socio-economic status (SES) and lower IQ are both associated with an increased risk for antisocial behavior, including the antisocial behavior component of psychopathy (Frick, O'Brien, Wootton, & McBurnett, 1994; Hare, 2003). The SES data suggest a social contribution to at least the behavioral manifestation of psychopathy. Importantly, some antisocial behavior shown by individuals with psychopathy is instrumental in nature; it has the goal of gaining another's money, sexual favors, or "respect" (Cornell et al., 1996; Williamson, Hare, & Wong, 1987). Individuals can attempt to achieve these goals through a variety of means. Having a higher SES (or higher IQ) enables a wider choice of available routes for achieving these goals than having a lower SES/IQ. SES is also likely to impact on the probability of displaying instrumental aggressions by determining relative reward levels for particular actions. If the individual already has $100,000, the subjective value of the $50 that could be gained if the individual mugged another person on the street is low. In contrast, if the individual is penniless, the subjective value of the $50 will be high.

Implications of Psychopathy for Social Cognitive Neuroscience

There are two main disorders of social cognition: autism and psychopathy (Blair, 2008). Work with autism has been highly informative with respect to social cognitive neuroscience, particularly with respect to the neural systems implicated in theory of mind and the developmental implications of their breakdown (Frith & Frith, 2006). Work with psychopathy is likely to be as informative with respect to moral judgments (Blair, 2007).

Early models of moral socialization suggested unitary accounts of social rule learning, stressing, for example, cultural transmission (Shweder & Much, 1987). However, such accounts struggle to explain the distinction made in individuals' judgments between moral and conventional transgressions from the age of 39 months (Smetana & Braeges, 1990) and across cultures (Nucci, Turiel, & Encarnacion-Gawrych, 1983). Moral transgressions (e.g., one person hitting another) are defined by their consequences for the rights and welfare of others. Social conventional transgressions are defined as violations of the behavioral uniformities that structure social interactions within social systems (e.g., dressing in opposite gender clothing). Moral transgressions are judged to be less rule-contingent than are conventional transgressions; individuals are less likely to state that moral, rather than conventional, transgressions are permissible in the absence of prohibiting rules (Nucci et al., 1983; Smetana & Braeges, 1990; Turiel, Killen, & Helwig, 1987).

Early discussions of the development of morality, including the development of the moral/conventional distinction itself suggested that it emerged as a function of abstract reasoning processes (Turiel et al., 1987). Such positions predicted that a population who failed the moral/conventional distinction should show impaired abstract reasoning processes. Individuals with psychopathy show significantly less of a moral/conventional distinction than do healthy individuals (Blair, 1995). However, they show no impairment in abstract reasoning and/or executive dysfunction—unless the executive function has an affective component (Blair, Newman, et al., 2006; LaPierre et al., 1995).

Considerable recent work has suggested the importance of emotional responses for moral development (Blair, 1995; Greene, Sommerville, Nystrom, Darley, & Cohen, 2001; Haidt, 2001; Moll, De Oliveira-Souza, Bramati, & Grafman, 2002;

Nichols, 2002; Prinz, 2007). I have argued that healthy individuals are predisposed to find the distress of others aversive and that we learn to avoid actions associated with this distress (i.e., acts that harm others) (Blair, 1995). This position predicted that a population who failed the moral/conventional distinction should show reduced responsiveness to the distress of others. In line with this, individuals with psychopathy show reduced arousal to the distress of others (Blair, Jones, Clark, & Smith, 1997), reduced processing of others' distress (Kimonis, Frick, Fazekas, & Loney, 2006) and reduced recognition of fearful expressions (Marsh & Blair, 2008). The position assumes that appropriate moral socialization relies upon appropriate emotional responding to the distress of others. This predicts that individuals with psychopathy, who show impaired emotional responding to the distress of others, should show difficulties with socialization. In line with the position, individuals with psychopathy are less influenced by parental socialization strategies than are healthy individuals (Oxford, Cavell, & Hughes, 2003; Wootton, Frick, Shelton, & Silverthorn, 1997).

With respect to the neural level, I have presented data above that the amygdala is critical for stimulus-reinforcement learning. In short, the amygdala enables the individual to learn the goodness and badness of objects and actions. In humans and other primates, the fearful expression serves as a reinforcer, stimuli associated with expression are avoided, and this type of stimulus-reinforcement learning relies on the amygdala, too (Adolphs, 2002; Hooker et al., 2006). The argument here is that learning the basics of care-based morality—learning that some actions harm others and because of this are to be avoided—relies on this crucial role of the amygdala in stimulus-reinforcement learning. In psychopathy, stimulus-reinforcement learning, as indexed by aversive conditioning (Birbaumer et al., 2005) and the response to another individual's fear (Marsh & Blair, 2008) is compromised and thus the individual is significantly more difficult to socialize (Oxford et al., 2003; Wootton et al., 1997).

As noted above, the amygdala provides expected reinforcement (both positively and negatively valenced) information to the OFC. Other systems then use this information to select appropriate responses (Blair, Marsh, et al., 2006). This information is crucial for reinforcement expectancy-based decision-making, including moral reasoning. The disruption in the amygdala and OFC in psychopathy means that moral and other forms of reinforcement-based decision-making are disrupted (Blair, 1995; Newman & Kosson, 1986). Indeed, recent fMRI work has shown reduced amygdala and OFC activity in individuals with psychopathy during moral reasoning (Glenn, Raine, & Schug, 2008).

Conclusions

In conclusion, psychopathy is a developmental disorder associated with specific forms of emotional dysfunction and an increased risk for instrumental and reactive aggression.

From the perspective of cognitive neuroscience, psychopathy is associated with dysfunction in the amygdala's ability to form stimulus-reinforcement associations and the representation of reinforcement expectancy information within the OFC. It is possible that this disorder may also be associated with dysfunction in prediction error signaling within the striatum but future work is required to determine whether there is a primary dysfunction within this region or whether, alternatively, indications of dysfunction as indexed by fMRI reflect deficient activity within connected regions such as the amygdala and OFC. The suggestion is that these forms of dysfunction in the neuro-cognitive architecture mediating these specific forms of emotional learning and decision-making interfere with typical socialization practices, putting the individual at greater risk of learning antisocial strategies to achieve their goals.

Evidence strongly suggests a genetic contribution to the neuro-affective deficits that are at the heart of psychopathy. However, as yet, there are no data to suggest a social contribution (e.g., via abuse/social threat/neglect) to these neuro-affective deficits. Maltreatment *does* increase the risk for aggression and behaviors corresponding to the impulsive/irresponsible dimension assessed by psychopathy measures. However, maltreatment does *not* have an association with the emotion dysfunction seen in psychopathy when assessed clinically. Moreover, while maltreatment is associated with increased amygdala responsiveness and increased responsiveness to anger expressions, psychopathy is associated with *decreased* amygdala responsiveness and *decreased* responsiveness to fearful expressions. Maltreatment and other social factors (e.g., SES) are, of course, likely to have an impact on the expression of these neuro-affective deficits; that is, whether they represent as antisocial behavior or not.

With respect to social neuroscience, psychopathy has clear implications for our understanding of moral development. Psychopathy represents a developmental neuro-psychiatric condition where at least some forms of moral processing—particularly those concerning moral judgments based on victim outcomes—are profoundly compromised. Data from work with patients with psychopathy firmly suggest that appropriate moral development requires appropriate emotional processing.

References

Adolphs, R. (2002). Neural systems for recognizing emotion. *Curr Opin Neurobiol, 12*(2), 169–177.

Ambrogi Lorenzini, C. G., Baldi, E., Bucherelli, C., Sacchetti, B., & Tassoni, G. (1999). Neural topography and chronology of memory consolidation: A review of functional inactivation findings. *Neurobiology of Learning and Memory, 71,* 1–18.

Barratt, E. S., Stanford, M. S., Dowdy, L., Liebman, M. J., & Kent, T. A. (1999). Impulsive and premeditated aggression: A factor analysis of self-reported acts. *Psychiatry Research, 86*(2), 163–173.

Bechara, A., Damasio, H., Damasio, A. R., & Lee, G. P. (1999). Different contributions of the human amygdala and ventromedial prefrontal cortex to decision-making. *Journal of Neuroscience, 19,* 5473–5481.

Bechara, A., Tranel, D., & Damasio, H. (2000). Characterization of the decision-making deficit of patients with ventromedial prefrontal cortex lesions. *Brain, 123*(Pt 11), 2189–2202.

Berkowitz, L. (1993). *Aggression: Its causes, consequences, and control.* Philadelphia: Temple University Press.

Birbaumer, N., Veit, R., Lotze, M., Erb, M., Hermann, C., Grodd, W., et al. (2005). Deficient fear conditioning in psychopathy: A functional magnetic resonance imaging study. *Arch Gen Psychiatry, 62*(7), 799–805.

Blair, K. S., Marsh, A. A., Morton, J., Vythilingham, M., Jones, M., Mondillo, K., et al. (2006). Choosing the lesser of two evils, the better of two goods: Specifying the roles of ventromedial prefrontal cortex and dorsal anterior cingulate cortex in object choice. *Journal of Neuroscience, 26*(44), 11379–11386.

Blair, K. S., Newman, C., Mitchell, D. G., Richell, R. A., Leonard, A., Morton, J., et al. (2006). Differentiating among prefrontal substrates in psychopathy: Neuropsychological test findings. *Neuropsychology, 20*(2), 153–165.

Blair, R. J. R. (1995). A cognitive developmental approach to morality: Investigating the psychopath. *Cognition, 57,* 1–29.

Blair, R. J. R. (2001). Neuro-cognitive models of aggression, the antisocial personality disorders and psychopathy. *Journal of Neurology, Neurosurgery & Psychiatry, 71,* 727–731.

Blair, R. J. R. (2003). Facial expressions, their communicatory functions and neuro-cognitive substrates. *Philos Trans R Soc Lond B Biol Sci, 358*(1431), 561–572.

Blair, R. J. R. (2004). The roles of orbital frontal cortex in the modulation of antisocial behavior. *Brain and Cognition, 55*(1), 198–208.

Blair, R. J. R. (2007). The amygdala and ventromedial prefrontal cortex in morality and psychopathy. *Trends Cogn Sci, 11*(9), 387–392.

Blair, R. J. R. (2008). Fine cuts of empathy and the amygdala: Dissociable deficits in psychopathy and autism. *Quarterly Journal of Experimental Psychology, 61*(1), 157–170.

Blair, R. J. R., Colledge, E., & Mitchell, D. G. (2001). Somatic markers and response reversal: Is there orbitofrontal cortex dysfunction in boys with psychopathic tendencies? *J Abnorm Child Psychol, 29*(6), 499–511.

Blair, R. J. R., Jones, L., Clark, F., & Smith, M. (1997). The psychopathic individual: A lack of responsiveness to distress cues? *Psychophysiology, 34,* 192–198.

Blair, R. J. & Mitchell, D. G. (2009). Psychopathy, attention, and emotion. *Psychological Medicine, 39,* 543–55.

Blair, R. J. R., Mitchell, D. G. V., & Blair, K. S. (2005). *The psychopath: Emotion and the brain.* Oxford: Blackwell.

Blanchard, R. J., Blanchard, D. C., & Takahashi, L. K. (1977). Attack and defensive behaviour in the albino rat. *Animal Behavior, 25,* 197–224.

Blonigen, D. M., Hicks, B. M., Krueger, R. F., Patrick, C. J., & Iacono, W. G. (2005). Psychopathic personality traits: Heritability and genetic overlap with internalizing and externalizing psychopathology. *Psychological Medicine, 35,* 637–648.

Bowlby, J. (1946). *Forty-four juvenile thieves: Their home life.* London: Bailliere, Tindall & Cox.

Bremner, J. D. & Vermetten, E. (2001a). Stress and development: Behavioral and biological consequences. *Development and Psychopathology, 13,* 473–489.

Bremner, J. D. & Vermetten, E. (2001b). Stress and development: Behavioral and biological consequences. *Development and Psychopathology, 13,* 473–489.

Brown, S. M. & Hariri, A. R. (2006). Neuroimaging studies of serotonin gene polymorphisms: Exploring the interplay of genes, brain, and behavior. *Cogn Affect Behav Neurosci, 6*(1), 44–52.

Budhani, S. & Blair, R. J. (2005). Response reversal and children with psychopathic tendencies: Success is a function of salience of contingency change. *J Child Psychol Psychiatry, 46*(9), 972–981.

Budhani, S., Marsh, A. A., Pine, D. S., & Blair, R. J. R. (2007). Neural correlates of response reversal: Considering acquisition. *Neuroimage, 34*(4), 1754–1765.

Budhani, S., Richell, R. A., & Blair, R. J. (2006). Impaired reversal but intact acquisition: probabilistic response reversal deficits in adult individuals with psychopathy. *J Abnorm Psychol, 115*(3), 552–558.

Burgess, N., Maguire, E. A., & O'Keefe, J. (2002). The human hippocampus and spatial and episodic memory. *Neuron, 35*(4), 625–641.

Burke, J. D., Loeber, R., & Lahey, B. B. (2007). Adolescent conduct disorder and interpersonal callousness as predictors of psychopathy in young adults. *Journal of Clinical Child and Adolescent Psychology, 36,* 334–346.

Connor, D. F. (2002). *Aggression and anti-Social behaviour in children and adolescents. Research and treatment.* New York: The Guilford Press.

Cooke, D. J., Michie, C., & Hart, S. (2006). Facets of clinical psychopathy: Toward clearer measurement. In C. J. Patrick (Ed.). *The handbook of psychopathy.* New York: Guilford Press.

Cornell, D. G., Warren, J., Hawk, G., Stafford, E., Oram, G., & Pine, D. (1996). Psychopathy in instrumental and reactive violent offenders. *Journal of Consulting and Clinical Psychology, 64,* 783–790.

Crick, N. R. & Dodge, K. A. (1996). Social information-processing mechanisms on reactive and proactive aggression. *Child Development, 67*(3), 993–1002.

Dodge, K. A., Pettit, G. S., Bates, J. E., & Valente, E. (1995). Social information-processing patterns partially mediate the effect of early physical abuse on later conduct problems. *Journal of Abnormal Psychology*, 104, 632–643.

Everitt, B. J., Cardinal, R. N., Parkinson, J. A., & Robbins, T. W. (2003). Appetitive behavior: Impact of amygdala-dependent mechanisms of emotional learning. *Annual New York Academy of Sciences*, 985, 233–250.

Farrington, D. P. & Loeber, R. (2000). Epidemiology of juvenile violence. *Child Adolesc Psychiatr Clin N Am*, 9(4), 733–748.

Finger, E. C., Marsh, A. A., Buzas, B., Kamel, N., Rhodes, R., Vythilingham, M., et al. (2006). The impact of tryptophan depletion and 5-HTTLPR genotype on passive avoidance and response reversal instrumental learning tasks. *Neuropsychopharmacology*, 32, 206–215.

Finger, E. C., Marsh, A. A., Mitchell, D. G. V., Reid, M. E., Sims, C., Budhani, S., et al. (2008). Abnormal ventromedial prefrontal cortex function in children with psychopathic traits during reversal learning. *Archives of General Psychiatry*, 65(5), 586–594.

Forth, A. E., Kosson, D. S., & Hare, R. D. (2007). *The Psychopathy Checklist: Youth Version*. Toronto, Ontario, Canada: Multi-Health Systems.

Frick, P. J. (1995). Callous-unemotional traits and conduct problems: A two-factor model of psychopathy in children. *Issues in Criminological and Legal Psychology*, 24, 47–51.

Frick, P. J., Bodin, S. D., & Barry, C. T. (2000). Psychopathic traits and conduct problems in community and clinic-referred samples of children: Further development of the psychopathy screening device. *Psychol Assess*, 12(4), 382–393.

Frick, P. J. & Hare, R. D. (2001). *The antisocial process screening device*. Toronto: Multi-Health Systems.

Frick, P. J. & Marsee, M. A. (2006). *Psychopathy and developmental pathways to antisocial behavior in youth handbook of psychopathy* (pp. 353–374). New York: Guilford.

Frick, P. J., O'Brien, B. S., Wootton, J. M., & McBurnett, K. (1994). Psychopathy and conduct problems in children. *Journal of Abnormal Psychology*, 103, 700–707.

Frick, P. J., Stickle, T. R., Dandreaux, D. M., Farell, J. M., & Kimonis, E. R. (2005). Callous-unemotional traits in predicting the severity and stability of conduct problems and delinquency. *Journal of Abnormal Child Psychology*, 33, 471–487.

Frith, C. D. & Frith, U. (2006). The neural basis of mentalizing. *Neuron*, 50(4), 531–534.

Glenn, A. L., Raine, A., & Schug, R. A. (2008). The neural correlates of moral decision-making in psychopathy. *Molecular Psychiatry*, 14, 5–6.

Greene, J. D., Sommerville, R. B., Nystrom, L. E., Darley, J. M., & Cohen, J. D. (2001). An fMRI investigation of emotional engagement in moral judgment. *Science*, 293, 1971–1972.

Gregg, T. R. & Siegel, A. (2001). Brain structures and neurotransmitters regulating aggression in cats: Implications for human aggression. *Prog Neuropsychopharmacol Biol Psychiatry*, 25(1), 91–140.

Haidt, J. (2001). The emotional dog and its rational tail: A social intuitionist approach to moral judgment. *Psychol Rev*, 108(4), 814–834.

Hampton, A. N., Bossaerts, P., & O'Doherty, J. P. (2006). The role of the ventromedial prefrontal cortex in abstract state-based inference during decision making in humans. *J Neurosci*, 26(32), 8360–8367.

Hare, R. D. (2003). *Hare Psychopathy Checklist-Revised (PCL-R*; 2nd Ed*)*. Toronto: Multi-Health Systems.

Hare, R. D., Clark, D., Grann, M., & Thornton, D. (2000). Psychopathy and the predictive validity of the PCL-R: An international perspective. *Behavioral Sciences and the Law*, 18, 623–645.

Hariri, A. R., Mattay, V. S., Tessitore, A., Kolachana, B., Fera, F., Goldman, D., et al. (2002). Serotonin transporter genetic variation and the response of the human amygdala. *Science*, 297(5580), 400–403.

Hart, S., Kropp, P. R., & Hare, R. D. (1988). Performance of male psychopaths following conditional release from prison. *Journal of consulting and clinical psychology*, 56, 227–232.

Hart, S. D., Forth, A. E., & Hare, R. D. (1990). Performance of criminal psychopaths on selected neuropsychological tests. *Journal of Abnormal Psychology*, 99, 374–379.

Hawes, D. J. & Dadds, M. R. (2005). The treatment of conduct problems in children with callous-unemotional traits. *J Consult Clin Psychol*, 73(4), 737–741.

Hiatt, K. D. & Newman, J. P. (2006). Understanding psychopathy: The cognitive side. In C. J. Patrick (Ed.), *Handbook of psychopathy* (pp. 334–352). New York, NY: Guilford Press.

Hiatt, K. D., Schmitt, W. A., & Newman, J. P. (2004). Stroop tasks reveal abnormal selective attention among psychopathic offenders. *Neuropsychology*, 18, 50–59.

Hoffman, M. L. (1988). Moral development. In M. Bornstein & M. Lamb (Eds.), *Developmental psychology: An advanced textbook* (pp. 497–548). Hillsdale, NJ: Erlbaum.

Hooker, C. I., Germine, L. T., Knight, R. T., & D'Esposito, M. (2006). Amygdala response to facial expressions reflects emotional learning. *J Neurosci*, 26(35), 8915–8922.

Jones, A. P., Laurens, K. R., Herba, C. M., Barker, G. J., & Viding, E. (2009). Amygdala hypoactivity to fearful faces in boys with conduct problems and callous-unemotional traits. *American Journal of Psychiatry*, 166, 95–102.

Karnik, N. S., McMullin, M. A., & Steiner, H. (2006). Disruptive behaviors: Conduct and oppositional disorders in adolescents. *Adolesc Med Clin*, 17(1), 97–114.

Kawasaki, H., Kaufman, O., Damasio, H., Damasio, A. R., Granner, M., Bakken, H., et al. (2001). Single-neuron responses to emotional visual stimuli recorded in human ventral prefrontal cortex. *Nat Neurosci*, 4(1), 15–16.

Kerns, J. G., Cohen, J. D., MacDonald, A. W., Cho, R. Y., Stenger, V. A., & Carter, C. S. (2004). Anterior cingulate conflict monitoring and adjustments in control. *Science*, 303, 1023–1026.

Kiehl, K. A. (2006). A cognitive neuroscience perspective on psychopathy: Evidence for paralimbic system dysfunction. *Psychiatry Res*.

Kiehl, K. A., Smith, A. M., Hare, R. D., Mendrek, A., Forster, B. B., Brink, J., et al. (2001). Limbic abnormalities in affective processing by criminal psychopaths as revealed by functional magnetic resonance imaging. *Biological Psychiatry*, 50, 677–684.

Kimonis, E. R., Frick, P. J., Fazekas, H., & Loney, B. R. (2006). Psychopathy, aggression, and the processing of emotional stimuli in non-referred girls and boys. *Behav Sci Law*, 24(1), 21–37.

King, S. M. (1999). Escape-related behaviours in an unstable, elevated and exposed environment. II. Long-term sensitization after repetitive electrical stimulation of the rodent midbrain defence system. *Behav Brain Res, 98*(1), 127–142.

LaPierre, D., Braun, C. M. J., & Hodgins, S. (1995). Ventral frontal deficits in psychopathy: Neuropsychological test findings. *Neuropsychologia, 33,* 139–151.

Levenston, G. K., Patrick, C. J., Bradley, M. M., & Lang, P. J. (2000). The psychopath as observer: Emotion and attention in picture processing. *Journal of Abnormal Psychology, 109,* 373–386.

Liberzon, I. & Martis, B. (2006). Neuroimaging studies of emotional responses in PTSD. *Ann N Y Acad Sci, 1071,* 87–109.

Linnoila, M., Virkkunen, M., Scheinin, M., Nuutila, A., Rimon, R., & Goodwin, F. K. (1983). Low cerebrospinal fluid 5-hydroxy indoleacetic acid concentration differentiates impulsive from nonimpulsive violent behavior. *Life Sciences, 33,* 2609–2614.

Lykken, D. T. (1957). A study of anxiety in the sociopathic personality. *Journal of abnormal and social psychology, 55,* 6–10.

Lykken, D. T. (1995). *The antisocial personalities.* Hillsdale, New Jersey: Erlbaum.

Lynam, D. R., Caspi, A., Moffitt, T. E., Loeber, R., & Stouthamer-Loeber, M. (2007). Longitudinal evidence that psychopathy scores in early adolescence predict adult psychopathy. *J Abnorm Psychol, 116*(1), 155–165.

MacCoon, D. G., Wallace, J. F., & Newman, J. P. (2004). Self-regulation: The context-appropriate allocation of attentional capacity to dominant and non-dominant cues. In R. F. Baumeister & K. D. Vohs (Eds.), *Handbook of self-regulation: Research, theory, and applications* (pp. 422–446). New York: Guilford.

Marsh, A. A. & Blair, R. J. R. (2008). Deficits in facial affect recognition among antisocial populations: A meta-analysis. *Neuroscience and Biobehavioral Reviews, 32*(3), 454–465.

Marsh, A. A., Finger, E. C., Mitchell, D. G. V., Reid, M. E., Sims, C., Kosson, D. S., et al. (2008). Reduced amygdala response to fearful expressions in children and adolescents with callous-unemotional traits and disruptive behavior disorders. *American Journal of Psychiatry, 165*(6), 712–720.

Meyer-Lindenberg, A., Buckholtz, J. W., Kolachana, B., A, R. H., Pezawas, L., Blasi, G., et al. (2006). Neural mechanisms of genetic risk for impulsivity and violence in humans. *Proc Natl Acad Sci U S A, 103*(16), 6269–6274.

Miller, L. S., Wasserman, G. A., Neugebauer, R., Gorman-Smith, D., & Kamboukos, D. (1999). Witnessed community violence and antisocial behavior in high-risk, urban boys. *Journal of Clinical Child Psychology, 28*(1), 2–11.

Mitchell, D. G. V., Colledge, E., Leonard, A., & Blair, R. J. R. (2002). Risky decisions and response reversal: Is there evidence of orbitofrontal cortex dysfunction in psychopathic individuals? *Neuropsychologia, 40,* 2013–2022.

Moffitt, T. E. (1993). The neuropsychology of conduct disorder. *Development and Psychopathology, 5,* 135–152.

Moll, J., De Oliveira-Souza, R., Bramati, I. E., & Grafman, J. (2002). Functional networks in emotional moral and non-moral social judgments. *Neuroimage, 16,* 696–703.

Munoz, L. C. & Frick, P. J. (2007). The reliability, stability, and predictive utility of the self-report version of the Antisocial Process Screening Device. *Scandinavian Journal of Psychology, 48,* 299–312.

Murray, E. A. & Izquierdo, A. (2007). Orbitofrontal cortex and amygdala contributions to affect and action in primates. *Ann N Y Acad Sci, 1121,* 273–96.

Nelson, E. E., Herman, K. N., Barrett, C. E., Noble, P. L., Wojteczko, K., Chisholm, K., et al. (2009). Adverse rearing experiences enhance responding to both aversive and rewarding stimuli in juvenile rhesus monkeys. *Biological Psychiatry, 66*(7), 702–704.

Neumann, C. S., Kosson, D. S., Forth, A. E., & Hare, R. D. (2006). Factor structure of the Hare Psychopathy Checklist: Youth Version (PCL: YV) in incarcerated adolescents. *Psychological Assessment, 18,* 142–154.

Newman, J. P. & Kosson, D. S. (1986). Passive avoidance learning in psychopathic and nonpsychopathic offenders. *Journal of Abnormal Psychology, 95,* 252–256.

Nichols, S. (2002). Norms with feeling: Towards a psychological account of moral judgment. *Cognition, 84*(2), 221–236.

Nucci, L. P., Turiel, E., & Encarnacion-Gawrych, G. E. (1983). Children's social interactions and social concepts: Analysis of morality and convention in the Virgin Islands. *Journal of Cross-Cultural Psychology, 4,* 469–487.

O'Connor, T. G. & Rutter, M. (2000). Attachment disorder behavior following early severe deprivation: Extension and longitudinal follow-up. English and Romanian Adoptees Study Team. *J Am Acad Child Adolesc Psychiatry, 39*(6), 703–712.

O'Doherty, J., Dayan, P., Schultz, J., Deichmann, R., Friston, K., & Dolan, R. J. (2004). Dissociable roles of ventral and dorsal striatum in instrumental conditioning. *Science, 304,* 452–454.

Obradovic´, J., Pardini, D., Long, J. D., & Loeber, R. (2007). Measuring interpersonal callousness in boys from childhood to adolescence: An examination of longitudinal invariance and temporal stability. *Journal of Clinical Child and Adolescent Psychology, 36,* 276–292.

Oxford, M., Cavell, T. A., & Hughes, J. N. (2003). Callous-unemotional traits moderate the relation between ineffective parenting and child externalizing problems: A partial replication and extension. *Journal of Clinical Child and Adolescent Psychology, 32,* 577–585.

Panksepp, J. (1998). *Affective neuroscience: The foundations of human and animal emotions.* New York: Oxford University Press.

Patrick, C. J. (1994). Emotion and psychopathy: Startling new insights. *Psychophysiology, 31,* 319–330.

Pezawas, L., Meyer-Lindenberg, A., Drabant, E. M., Verchinski, B. A., Munoz, K. E., Kolachana, B. S., et al. (2005). 5-HTTLPR polymorphism impacts human cingulate-amygdala interactions: A genetic susceptibility mechanism for depression. *Nat Neurosci, 8*(6), 828–834.

Pollak, S. D. & Sinha, P. (2002). Effects of early experience on children's recognition of facial displays of emotion. *Developmental Psychology, 38,* 784–91.

Poythress, N.G., Skeem, J. L., & Lilienfeld, S. O. (2006). Associations among early abuse, dissociation, and psychopathy in an offender sample. *Journal of Abnormal Psychology, 115,* 288–97.

Prinz, J. (2007). *The emotional construction of morals.* New York: Oxford University Press.

Rauch, S. L., Shin, L. M., & Phelps, E. A. (2006). Neurocircuitry models of posttraumatic stress disorder and extinction: Human neuroimaging research—past, present, and future. *Biological Psychiatry, 60*(4), 376–382.

Rilling, J. K., Winslow, J. T., O'Brien, D., Gutman, D. A., Hoffman, J. M., & Kilts, C. D. (2001). Neural correlates of maternal separation in rhesus monkeys. *Biol Psychiatry, 49*(2), 146–157.

Rushworth, M. F., Behrens, T. E., Rudebeck, P. H., & Walton, M. E. (2007). Contrasting roles for cingulate and orbitofrontal cortex in decisions and social behaviour. *Trends Cogn Sci, 11*(4), 168–176.

Rutter, M. (2005). Commentary: What is the meaning and utility of the psychopathy concept? *J Abnorm Child Psychol, 33*(4), 499–503.

Sanchez, M. M., Noble, P. M., Lyon, C. K., Plotsky, P. M., Davis, M., Nemeroff, C. B., et al. (2005). Alterations in diurnal cortisol rhythm and acoustic startle response in non-human primates with adverse rearing. *Biol Psychiatry, 57*(4), 373–381.

Schoenbaum, G. & Roesch, M. (2005). Orbitofrontal cortex, associative learning, and expectancies. *Neuron, 47*(5), 633–636.

Schwab-Stone, M., Chen, C., Greenberger, E., Silver, D., Lichtman, J., & Voyce, C. (1999). No safe haven II: The effects of violence exposure on urban youth. *Journal of the American Academy of Child and Adolescent Psychiatry, 38*(4), 359–367.

Shweder, R. A. & Much, N. C. (1987). *Moral development through social interaction.* New York: Wiley.

Silverthorn, P. & Frick, P. J. (1999). Developmental pathways to antisocial behavior: The delayed-onset pathway in girls. *Dev Psychopathol, 11*(1), 101–126.

Smetana, J. G. & Braeges, J. L. (1990). The development of toddlers' moral and conventional judgments. *MPQ, 36,* 329–346.

Steiner, H., Saxena, K., & Chang, K. (2003). Psychopharmacologic strategies for the treatment of aggression in juveniles. *CNS Spectrum, 8,* 298–308.

Turiel, E., Killen, M., & Helwig, C. C. (1987). Morality: Its structure, functions, and vagaries. In J. Kagan & S. Lamb (Eds.). *The emergence of morality in young children* (pp. 155–245). Chicago: University of Chicago Press.

Viding, E. (2004). Annotation: Understanding the development of psychopathy. *Journal of Child Psychology & Psychiatry & Allied Disciplines, 45*(8), 1329–1337.

Viding, E., Blair, R. J. R., Moffitt, T. E., & Plomin, R. (2005). Evidence for substantial genetic risk for psychopathy in 7-year-olds. *Journal of Child Psychology and Psychiatry, 46,* 592–597.

Williamson, S., Hare, R. D., & Wong, S. (1987). Violence: Criminal psychopaths and their victims. *Canadian Journal of Behavioral Science, 19,* 454–462.

Wootton, J. M., Frick, P. J., Shelton, K. K., & Silverthorn, P. (1997). Ineffective parenting and childhood conduct problems: The moderating role of callous-unemotional traits. *Journal of Consulting and Clinical Psychology, 65,* 301–308.

Alexithymia from the Social Neuroscience Perspective

Sylvie Berthoz, Lydia Pouga, *and* Michele Wessa

Abstract

Alexithymia is a multifaceted personality construct characterized by the impaired ability to reflect on and regulate one's own emotions. This chapter refers to a wide range of domains of investigation in the field of social neuroscience to capture and specify the processes that could account for the observed associations between such an inability to monitor and self-regulate emotions and altered social understanding and interactions. To this end, it provides empirical support for considering alexithymia as a relevant model to investigate the links between brain, cognition and behavior, notably not only to delineate potential pathways between dysfunctional cerebral circuits, poor emotional insight, and intersubjectivity, but also to further explore their links with self-oriented and other-oriented harming behaviors.

Keywords: alexithymia, psychosomatic disorders, psychopathy, autism spectrum disorders, post-traumatic stress disorder, empathy, interpersonal functioning, emotional awareness, emotion regulation, medial prefrontal cortex, anterior cingulate cortex, amygdala, insula, connectivity, voxel based morphometry

Emergence of the Alexithymia Construct

Alexithymia is a personality construct which has emerged from several clinical descriptions of different types of patients that seemed to share common cognitive-affective styles suggesting impaired affect regulation abilities.

In the sixties, two French psychoanalysts, Marty and de M'Uzan (Marty & de M'Uzan, 1963), used the term "*pensée opératoire*" to describe a thinking style devoid of emotional content that they observed in many patients for whom psychodynamic therapy was ineffective. Marty and de M'Uzan attributed this utilitarian thinking style to a lack of mental elaboration of internal conflicts.

At the beginning of the seventies, the term *alexithymia*, meaning "a lack of words for emotion," was coined by Sifnéos and Nemiah, two psychoanalysts of the Boston group of Psychosomatic, to define a set of deficits they believed to be involved in self-oriented and other-oriented harming behaviors (Nemiah & Sifneos, 1970; Sifneos, 1973).

As pointed out by Lesser (1981) "*although [alexithymia is a] new word, it does not embody a novel idea*" (p. 532). Indeed, in line with the idea that deficits in the capacity for experiencing and symbolizing emotion can have adverse effects on well-being, Sifnéos and Nemiah suggested alexithymia is associated with:

– impaired capacity for self-care and self-regulation that could be involved in the onset and the course of certain somatic disorders (the so-called psychosomatic disorders),

– a variety of altered socio-affective skills including a propensity for impulsive behaviors, as well as discomfort and/or avoidance of social relationships (Nemiah & Sifneos, 1970; Sifneos, 1967/1973).

Though some authors argued initially that alexithymia could be considered as a secondary state reaction, resulting from severe psychological distress or chronic psychopathological and somatic disorders (Freyberger, 1977), numerous empirical studies in normal as well as clinical individuals revealed alexithymia is a stable personality trait (e.g., De Rick & Vanheule, 2007; Luminet, Bagby, & Taylor, 2001; Salminen et al., 2006).

Alexithymia's Most Salient Features

In one of Sifnéos' seminal articles on alexithymia (1975), he describes alexithymic individuals as having:

> "an impoverishment of fantasy life, a constriction of emotional functioning, and a difficulty in interpersonal relations; a striking inability to find appropriate words to describe emotions and a tendency to describe endless situational details or symptoms instead of feelings; a preference for using action to avoid conflicting situations; rigid postures, including sitting in such a way as to give the impression that the person is frozen into one position"[1] (p. 67).

All clinical experts of alexithymia agree that this personality construct encompasses both affective and cognitive dimensions. Yet, the exact number of essential features of alexithymia has been debated. A summary of the dimensions that have been suggested to be crucial or characteristic are presented in Box 60.1.

Oddly enough, though Sifnéos and Nemiah insisted on several interpersonal dimensions of alexithymia, very few studies attempted to objectively investigate whether these deficits are part of the core alexithymia features. Nonetheless, these authors considered the stress and frustration resulting from the alexithymic impaired interpersonal skills to be crucially involved in the biological reactions that could lead notably to psychosomatic lesions (Sifneos, Apfel-Savitz, & Frankel, 1977).

In the '90s, Bermond and colleagues suggested that reduced capacities for emotionalizing (the ease by which one experiences an emotional feeling or becomes emotionally aroused by emotion-inducing events) should be reconsidered as an essential element of the alexithymia phenomenon. They developed the Bermond-Vorst Alexithymia Questionnaire (BVAQ; Bermond, Vorst, Vingerhoets, & Gerritsen, 1999) to measure this dimension in addition to the four prototypic alexithymia features. Moreover, on the basis of neuropsychological data concerning emotional experience, Bermond (Bermond, 1997; Bermond et al., 2007) proposed a typology into different subtypes of alexithymic individuals, depending on the balance between these five core alexithymic dimensions (see Box 60.1). Bermond initially distinguished two subtypes: an "alexithymia type I" characterized by severe reductions in both emotionalizing and emotion-accompanying cognitions; an "alexithymia type II" characterized by the unreduced (full-blown) presence of the emotional feeling in combination with severe reductions in the cognitions normally accompanying the emotional feeling. He later introduced two additional subtypes: an "alexithymia type III" characterized by low affective and high cognitive capacities, and a "lexithymic type" characterized by high affective and high cognitive capacities, that is, the antonym of alexithymia (Bermond, 1997; Bermond et al., 2007).

It has been shown that each of these four extreme groups are linked to specific other personality traits and to various personality disorders (Moormann et al., 2008).

Social self-sufficiency, that is, the satisfaction with oneself, disinterest in others, and shyness (including difficulties in relating with others), predicts type I alexithymia, which is in line with a positive relationship between this subtype and schizoid personality disorder; both alexithymia and schizoid personality disorder share a limited drive for social support and companionship and can be characterized as *Einzelgänger* (loner).

Type II alexithymia is predicted by inadequate emotional personality traits (emotional instability, neuroticism) and social inadequacy (i.e., the feeling of incompetence in comparison to others). Furthermore, it is predicted by feelings of depression, tension and emotional instability, and is linked to borderline personality disorder.

Type I and type II alexithymia are not equally distributed in men and women, with type I being more prevalent in men, whereas type II is more frequent in women. This sex-ratio effect also fits the sex ratios observed in epidemiological studies in schizoid and borderline personality disorder.

Type III alexithymia is predicted by socially adequate behavior, whereas lexithymia (the opposite of type I alexithymia) is predicted by emotional

Box 60.1.   Core affective and cognitive features of alexithymia (and most widely used related self-report questionnaires)

Sifnéos et al. (*adapted from Psychother Psychosom 1977; 28:47–57*) listed several psychological characteristics of patients with alexithymic defects they observed in a psychiatric clinical setting during the years 1954–1967:

- Presenting complaints: endless description of physical symptoms;
- Other complaints: tension, irritability, frustration, pain, boredom, void, restlessness, agitation, nervousness;
- Thought content: striking absence of fantasies and elaborate description of trivial environmental details;
- Language: marked difficulty in finding appropriate words to describe feelings;
- Crying: rare; cry copiously at times, but crying seems not related to any appropriate feelings such as sadness or anger;
- Dreaming: rare;
- Affect: inappropriate;
- Activity: tendency to take action impulsively; action seems to be a predominant way of life;
- Interpersonal relations: usually poor, with a tendency at marked dependency of preference for being alone, avoiding people;
- Personality: narcissistic, withdrawn, passive-aggressive or passive-dependent, psychopathic;
- Posture: rigid;
- Countertransference: the interviewer or the therapist is usually bored by the patient whom they find frightfully "dull."

Taylor, Bagby & Parker (see *Bagby R.M. & Taylor G.J.: Measurement and validation of the alexithymia construct. In G. J. Taylor, R. M. Bagby, & J. D. A. Parker (Eds.). Disorders of affect regulation: Alexithymia in medical and psychiatric illness (pp. 46–66). Cambridge University Press, 1997,* for a detailed description of the research conducted by this group) focused on several features which were considered the most prototypic in the process of creating a self-report instrument to measure alexithymia:

- difficulties in describing feelings;
- difficulties in distinguishing between feelings and bodily sensations that accompany states of emotional arousal;
- lack of introspection;
- social conformity;
- impoverished fantasy life;
- poor dream recall;
- the tendency to use action rather than reflection.

A series of factor and item analyses of the responses of 542 undergraduate university students lead the authors to select four factors (and their corresponding 26 items) they considered theoretically congruent with the alexithymia construct:

- difficulties in identifying feelings and distinguishing between feelings and bodily sensations of emotional arousal;
- difficulties in describing feelings to other people;
- reduced daydreaming and constricted imaginal processes;
- a stimulus-bound, externally oriented, cognitive style.

This yielded to the selection of a 26-item self-report they named the Toronto Alexithymia Scale (TAS). However, few years later, the authors revised the TAS. Their research resulted first in the elaboration of the TAS-R (a 23-item scale which eliminated all items assessing imaginal activity). Finally, they developed a 20-item version of the scale (TAS20) which measures:

- difficulties in identifying feelings;
- difficulties in describing feelings to other people;
- externally oriented thinking style.

This latter version is the most widely used instrument to measure alexithymia.

Bermond and colleagues (1999) conceptualized alexithymia as being composed of five latent continuous traits:

- reduced ability to differentiate between various emotional feelings;
- reduced ability to verbalize emotional experiences;
- reduced ability to fantasize, to create hypotheses about what is going on at the emotional level;

- reduced ability to emotionalize, degree of difficulty by which an emotional feeling is induced by internal or external stimuli;
- reduced tendency to reflect upon feelings.

The corresponding self-report questionnaire is the Bermond-Vorst Alexithymia Questionnaire (BVAQ). The original BVAQ is a Dutch 40-item self-report questionnaire that evolved from the Amsterdam Alexithymia Scale (Bermond et al., 1999). Researchers commonly use one of its two short versions: the BVAQ-A (items 1 to 20) or the BVAQ-B (items 21 to 40), but several studies have demonstrated that the BVAQ-B has better psychometric properties than the BVAQ-A.

The four types of alexithymia described by Bermond and colleagues are operationalized by two cut-off scores drawn from the BVAQ. The first score represents an affective component (A) and is built from the scales "reduced ability to fantasize" and "reduced ability to experience emotional feelings"; the second score represents the cognitive (C) component of alexithymia and is built from the scales "reduced ability to differentiate between emotional feelings," "reduced ability to verbalize emotional feelings" and "reduced ability to reflect upon emotional feelings" (Type I: A > 70, C > 70; Type II: A < 30, C > 70; Type III: A > 70, C < 30; Lexithymia: A < 30, C < 30; cf. Moormann et al., 2008).

Haviland & Reise (1996) asked 13 experts on alexithymia to use a standard instrument designed for Q-sort evaluation of personality, the California Adult Q-set (CAQ; which encompasses 100 standard items covering a broad range of personality descriptors) to list the characteristic and uncharacteristic features of a prototypic alexithymic individual.

Most characteristic features
Is emotionally bland; has flattened affect; Is disorganized and adopts maladaptive behaviors when under stress or trauma; Anxiety and tension find outlet in bodily symptoms; Is concerned with own body and the adequacy of its physiological functioning; Emphasizes communication through action and nonverbal behavior; Keeps people at distance, avoids close interpersonal relationships.

Most uncharacteristic features
Engages in personal fantasy and daydreams, fictional speculations; Has insights into own motives and behavior; Has warmth, has the capacity for close relationships, is compassionate; Is skilled in social techniques of imaginative play, pretending and humor; Is socially perceptive of a wide range of interpersonal cues; Is facially and/or gesturally expressive.

warmth of the mother. Both types go along with good coping skills and high self-esteem and are related to intact affect regulation. They are relatively rare in psychiatric patients compared to type I and type II alexithymia (Moormann et al., 2008). Regarding related personality disorders, type III alexithymia is linked to narcissistic personality disorder, and lexithymia to histrionic personality disorder.

Early Etiological Considerations
Since its early conceptualization, the alexithymia construct has been considered either as a psychological or as a neurobiological deficit and a variety of studies were conducted on alexithymia in the last 30 years. The authors, whether they adopted a psychodynamic or a neuropsychological approach, interpreted their results according to the theoretical field they were referring to. Psychoanalytical conceptualizations of alexithymia emphasize mainly on a critical role of intrapsychic conflicts and of early caregiver-infant relationships (see Taylor, Bagby, & Parker, 1997). Besides, and in line with the idea that

individual variability in emotional responsiveness reflects personality traits and are associated with variance of brain activity, another etiological model favored biological malfunctions as being the primary underlying cause of alexithymia.

Within this neurobiological framework, the evaluation of the cognitive, autonomic, and central nervous systems' correlates of alexithymia has preoccupied an increasing number of investigators. This line of research has greatly benefited from the theoretical and methodological advances of the affective neuroscience domain of expertise.

Yet, most of the initial discussions attempting to explain the etiology of alexithymia focused on the mechanisms that could account for psychosomatic phenomena or symptom formation.

Following James Papez' theory of emotion, MacLean referred to his *"triune brain model"* (MacLean, 1949), and speculated alexithymia is related to faulty exchange between the "visceral"/paleomammalian and "word"/neomammalian brains (MacLean, 1977). In alexithymia, emotional signals originating in the limbic system would not be relayed by the neocortex and finding expression in the symbolic use of words, but would find immediate expression through autonomic channels only.

Similarly, Nemiah considered disturbances in the pathway between cerebral structures underlying emotion processing (the limbic system) and that for mental elaboration (the neocortex) to be a particularly promising model for alexithymia, notably to account for an increased arousal of the somatic components of affect (Nemiah, 1977). Moreover, Nemiah, Sifnéos, and Apfel-Savitz (1977) investigated the association between alexithymia and autonomic nervous system responses to laboratory-based stressors and found smaller increases in oxygen consumption during mental arithmetic and emotional imagery in seven alexithymic patients than in their controls. These results were interpreted as

"a discontinuity between the somatic component of affect (emotion) and the psychic component of affect (feeling and fantasy)"

which were related to a *"lack of neuronal connections between the limbic system and hypothalamus and the neocortex"* (p. 170).

In parallel to these "vertical" neurophysiological etiological hypotheses, other "horizontal" models were introduced. Hoppe and Bogen (1977) reported alexithymic characteristics in patients who had undergone surgical commissurectomy for intractable epilepsy (the so-called "split-brain" patients); they hypothesized a "functionnal commissurectomy" (or a lack of interhemispheric communication) in alexithymia (see Tabibnia & Zaidel, 2005, for a critical review). Moreover, Kaplan and Wogan (1977) suggested a right hemisphere dysfunction: Unable to use their right hemisphere to fantasize or verbalize their emotional experience, alexithymic individuals would have greater physical distress and bodily symptoms (*see* de Timary, Roy, Luminet, Fillée, & Mikolajczak, 2008; Pedrosa Gil et al., 2008 for recent literature on this topic).

In addition to these neuropsychophysiological considerations, a possible genetic contribution was introduced by Heiberg and Heiberg (Heiberg & Heiberg, 1977) who compared observer-rated alexithymia scores in twins (15 pairs of monozygotic and 18 pairs of dizygotic) and reported less intra-pair difference among the monozygotic than among the dizygotic twins as well as high values for different estimates of heritability of alexithymic traits.

More recently, specific associations between some of the alexithymia dimensions and cerebral activity have been formulated by Bermond's group (Bermond, 1997; Bermond, Vorst, & Moormann, 2006). Alexithymia type I (i.e., reductions in both emotionalizing and emotion-accompanying cognitions) would be linked notably to a deficit of orbitofrontal and prefrontal functioning. Alexithymia type II (i.e., presence of emotional feelings in the absence of normally accompanying cognitions) would result from a reduced functioning of the corpus callosum. Alexithymia type III (i.e., low emotionality and a poor fantasy life, but well-developed cognitions accompanying the emotional experience) would be related to a dysfunction of the anterior commissure. However, no direct empirical evidence is in support of the above-mentioned hypotheses about different alexithymia types and their respective anatomic-functional dysregulations.

Finally, regarding the last type of alexithymia, that is "lexithymia" (characterized by rich fantasy life, high emotionality, and well-developed cognitions about emotional experiences; considered the opposite of full-blown alexithymia), no hypotheses about anatomical and functional dysregulation have been formulated. We will present in our next paragraphs that the anterior cingulate (ACC) seems to be a structure differentiating alexithymic from lexithymic individuals. Interestingly, increased dorsal ACC activation to emotion-inducing stimuli was observed in individuals with high emotional awareness (Lane et al., 1998; McRae, Reiman, Fort, Chen, & Lane, 2008). Additionally, and in line with the result that lexithymia is more frequent in women than in men, the relationship between ACC activation and emotional awareness scores was found higher in women than in men (McRae et al., 2008). Finally, women have greater emotional awareness scores (Barrett, Lane, Sechrest, & Schwartz, 2000) and higher dorsal ACC activation in response to emotional stimuli (Wrase et al., 2003).

See Box 60.2 for clinical vignettes of individuals that are considered presenting several affective and cognitive alexithymic dimensions.

Alexithymia and Affective Neuroscience

Since the '70s, among the advances that occurred in the field of social neuroscience, the alexithymia construct has benefited in particular from the increasing knowledge on the underlying mechanisms of normal and pathological emotion (verbal, facial, and body) recognition and understanding. Emotional expressions, through their signal functions, are suggested to promote the forging of relationships between individuals within a social group

Lesser (*Psychosom Med* 1981) Mr, a., a 34-year-old engineer, married and father of three children, was referred to a psychiatric clinic by his internist. He had a 7-year history of intractable headaches. Multiple diagnostic procedures and a questionable diagnosis of hydrocephalus resulted in his having a ventriculo-peritoneal shunt four years previously. His internist believed he was depressed and began tricyclic antidepressant therapy. When questioned about the depression, the patient replied. "I guess I was depressed. Those pills stopped me from crying but I don't feel differently, I still have headaches." The headaches thwarted his life-long ambition to be an airline pilot. When asked how this made him feel, he replied, "I told you, I have headaches. I don't know what you expect me to say when you ask how I feel." He was unable to elaborate any fantasies and claimed he did not dream. Sessions consisted of details of his work and sterile reports of conversations with those around him. Psychotherapy became increasingly frustrating for both the patient and therapist until a decision was made to begin conjoint therapy. With his wife's help, he was able to deal more effectively with some interpersonal difficulties, but no progress was made with his chronic headaches.

Lumley et al. (*J Pers Assessment* 2007; *89*, 230–246)

Two brief cases

Mr. A., a 50-year-old, obese man with hypertension, was referred by his physician for psychological assessment after the patient experienced an atypical panic attack in the clinic waiting room. The patient reported that the walls seemed to close in, and the voices of the other patients became a buzz. He reported experiencing no fear or apprehension, mental images, or fantasies associated with the event, and he could identify no precipitants other than the waiting room. The man was well educated and married, but he had few close friends, was compulsive and detail oriented, and had difficulty taking others' perspectives. He displayed little emotion other than mild irritability. He showed minimal insight into his feelings or psychological life, and he focused primarily on external factors (e.g., the weather, light, diet, job, his wife) as potential symptom triggers. Psychotherapy was rather boring and ended some months later with little progress, even though the patient reliably attended all sessions and even took notes.

Ms. B., a 45-year-old woman, was referred by her physician for treatment of the chronic pain condition, fibromyalgia, as well as other health problems including irritable bowel syndrome and depression. When emotional topics such as her punitive childhood were explored in therapy, Ms. B expressed facially and nonverbally various negative emotions—particularly sadness, shame, and fear—but she had difficulty labeling her feelings and linking them to her psychological experience and memories. In particular, she had difficulty identifying anger—indeed, she was surprised when a chiropractor told her how much "anger" she carried in her muscles. When her negative feelings became intense, she typically shifted focus to her body and talked only of somatic pain rather than emotional pain. Interestingly, she was very attuned to and concerned about others' feelings, including those of the therapist, and appeared to accurately identify the feelings of others. Therapy proceeded slowly over several years, but rapport was easily established, the therapeutic alliance was quite strong, and the patient eventually showed some gains. Behavioral exercises, particularly assertiveness training regarding communicating with family, and experiential exercises designed to help her access and then verbally express anger led to some improvement in pain and dysfunction.

(Grèzes, Pichon, & de Gelder, 2007; Pichon, de Gelder, & Grèzes, 2009). This suggests that there could be a link between poor emotion-identification skills and poor social skills. Addressing this question from the alexithymia perspective, Bagby and Taylor stated that alexithymic characteristics

> "*reflect deficits both in the cognitive-experiential domain of emotion response system and at the level of interpersonal regulation of emotion. [...] Lacking knowledge of their own emotional experiences, alexithymic individuals cannot readily imagine themselves in another person's situation and are consequently unempathetic and ineffective in modulating the emotional states of others.*"

They further reported the existence of previous clinical reports of alexithymic individuals describing "*restricted gestures and near expressionless faces*" and cited their own results suggesting that "*alexithymia may involve deficits in the behavioural-expressive domain of emotion response systems as well*" (Bagby & Taylor, 1997, pp. 30–31).

Three domains of research have gathered particularly informative data on the links between alexithymia and socio-cognitive skills:[2]

1. The investigation of the association between alexithymia and emotional stimuli processing, mainly by the use of pictures and static faces.

Results were obtained both in normal and clinical individuals with high alexithymia scores. Yet, the potential confounding effect of dysphoric affects (depression and anxiety) has been taken into account in the most recent studies only;

2. Several neuroimaging studies inspected the cerebral correlates of alexithymia. Though their number has increased massively in the past five years, no statistical meta-analysis has been published yet. Nevertheless, and despite the fact that they employed heterogeneous experimental designs, these studies have provided important information on the cerebral structures (and their connectivity) that may play a crucial role in alexithymia;

3. Studies on three types of psychiatric disorders associated with abnormal social adaptation and emotional stimuli processing: post-traumatic stress disorders, sociopathic disorders (antisocial and borderline personality and psychopathy) and autism spectrum disorders.

Emotional Stimuli Processing

Regarding the links between alexithymia and emotional processing in normal individuals, some studies have reported no effect on: facial expression recognition and evaluation of the induced emotional impact (Mayer, DiPaolo, & Salovey, 1990; McDonald & Prkachin, 1990; Parker, Prkachin, & Prkachin, 2005); the interpretation of the emotional content of narratives (Berenbaum & Prince, 1994); the estimation of the pleasantness/unpleasantness of emotional stimuli (Mueller, Alpers, & Reim, 2006; Roedema & Simons, 1999; Wehmer, Brejnak, Lumley, & Stettner, 1995). However, high alexithymia scorers provided fewer emotional words when they were asked to describe their emotional experience induced by emotional pictures, although they rated the pleasantness and unpleasantness of these pictures similarly to low alexithymia scorers (Roedema & Simons, 1999).

Other studies suggest alexithymia is related to abnormal emotional stimuli processing, in particular: the evaluation of the negative emotional impact induced by unpleasant stimuli (Ouellet et al., 1996; Luminet, Rimé, Bagby, & Taylor, 2004); the recognition of facial expressions of primary emotions in general (Jessimer & Markham, 1997; Mann, Wise, Trinidad, & Kohanski, 1994; Parker, Taylor, & Bagby, 1993a) or under rapid/effortful presentation conditions only (Parker et al., 2005; Prkachin,

Casey, & Prkachin, 2009); the spontaneous facial mimicry of negative emotions and the reproduction of angry and happy facial expressions (McDonald & Prkachin, 1990).

Importantly, Lane et al. (1996) were the first who demonstrated that alexithymia is not limited to an incapacity to put emotion into words, and instead conceptualized alexithymia as a deficit in the conscious experience of emotion. They asked 380 healthy young adults to complete the 20-item Toronto Alexithymia Scale (TAS20) and the Perception of Affect Task (PAT), a measure of the ability to match emotional stimuli. The PAT subtasks include matching emotional sentences and words (verbal-verbal), emotional faces and words (nonverbal-verbal), emotional sentences and faces (verbal-nonverbal), and emotional faces and pictures (nonverbal-nonverbal). Results showed that, compared to low TAS20 scorers, high TAS20 scorers had lower accuracy rates on each of the PAT subtasks. Lane et al. suggested that alexithymia is characterized by a deficit which may include, but is not limited to, a difficulty in verbalizing emotions. This has been further demonstrated in a recent Chinese comparative study (Gong, 2008): High TAS20 scorers were slower on judging the congruency/incongruency of word-picture pairs, and their mean congruency/incongruency judgment latencies were positively correlated with their subjective evaluations of the task difficulty.

With respect to the interaction between emotional and cognitive processing, empirical results have been inconsistent, with high alexithymia scorers having a greater attentional bias towards negative emotion words (Parker, Taylor, & Bagby, 1993b) or illness-related words (Lundh & Simonsson-Sarnecki, 2002), or conversely, showing a reduced emotional bias for emotionally negative words and bodily-symptom words (Mueller et al., 2006). Moreover, using an affective priming paradigm (testing the effect of the subliminal presentation of an emotional face presented before the occurrence of an emotional target word displayed subliminally), the classical facilitatory effect of the prime on the valence-judgement of a congruent word was observed among the low TAS20 scorers (smaller reaction times for congruent prime-target pairs), but not in the high TAS20 scorers when an angry face served as the prime (Vermeulen, Luminet, & Corneille, 2006). Additionally, alexithymia has been associated with difficulties in consciously recollecting emotional words (Luminet, Bagby, Taylor, Vermeulen, & Demaret, 2002; Luminet, Vermeulen, Demaret,

Taylor, & Bagby, 2006; Vermeulen & Luminet, 2009). As discussed by Vermeulen et al., both studies suggest that those scoring high on alexithymia scales may have a deficit in the automatic/associative processing of emotional cues, but not in the type of emotional processing that occurs in focal awareness.

Most of the above-mentioned studies examined the effect of alexithymia in general, that is, considering alexithymia as a unidimensional construct. Nevertheless, results of the few studies which tested the influence of the various alexithymia dimensions separately revealed specific associations. On this note, although Wehmer and colleagues (Wehmer et al., 1995) have observed no main effect of alexithymia on the valence ratings of emotional stimuli, significant negative associations between the levels of "Difficulties Describing Feelings" (DDF; TAS20 second factor) and of "Externally Oriented Thinking" (EOT; TAS20 third factor) and the percentages of emotional words produced in response to the presentation of emotional stimuli. The EOT score was also the dimension that accounted for lower subjective unpleasantness induced by negative videos (Luminet et al., 2004),[3] and for the impaired capacity to process angry, fearful, and sad faces (Prkachin et al., 2009).

Vermeulen and Luminet also highlighted specific links between the different TAS20 factors and memory rates (independently of the level of processing): DDF was associated with a reduction in remembering emotional words, whereas EOT was positively associated with the recognition rates for joyful and disgusting words (Vermeulen & Luminet, 2009). Regarding priming studies, a lack of contextual affective priming in high alexithymia scorers was mainly driven by DDF scores (Suslow & Junghanns, 2002).

Nevertheless, all alexithymia dimensions may affect some processes, as illustrated in Gong's study (2008), in which the three TAS20 factor scores were positively correlated with the mean response latencies for emotional word valence-judgment processing.

Whereas all the results presented above were obtained in normal individuals, similar findings have been found in somatoform and mental disorders (e.g., Pedrosa Gil et al., 2009).

Together, the above-mentioned literature further support that alexithymia is associated with poor emotional insight, which is the first neuro-psychophysiological model of alexithymia that has been investigated with fMRI.

Anatomical and Functional Neuroimaging Findings
Functional Neuroimaging Studies in Healthy Participants

The very first study on the neural bases of alexithymia was designed to test the "blindfeel model" introduced by Lane and colleagues (1997).

In the late 1980s, Lane and Schwartz proposed that an individual's ability to recognize and describe emotion in oneself and others, or "*emotional awareness,*" is a cognitive skill that undergoes a developmental process (Lane & Schwartz, 1987). They posited the existence of five ascending "levels of emotional awareness" with similar characteristics to Piaget's stages of general cognition development (from level 1, at which emotions are experienced as somatic sensations, to level 5, at which there's a high capacity for appreciating complex emotions of self and others). The authors developed and validated a psychometric instrument to measure emotional awareness: the Level of Emotional Awareness Scale (LEAS; Lane, Quinlan, Schwartz, Walker, & Zeitlin, 1990).

After having shown that alexithymic individuals exhibit an impaired ability to recognize emotions when both the stimulus and the response are nonverbal, Lane et al. further proposed to consider alexithymia as a deficit in emotional awareness (Lane et al., 1996). They suggested that alexithymia is linked to poor degrees of differentiation and integration of the schemata used to process emotional information. They conceptualized alexithymia as a poor capacity to consciously experience emotional feelings and introduced the term "blindfeel" (i.e., the emotional equivalent of blindsight; Lane, Ahern, Schwartz, & Kaszniak, 1997).

This hypothesis was first tested in 379 healthy young adults who completed the TAS20, the PAT, and the LEAS (Lane, Sechrest, Riedel, Shapiro, & Kaszniak, 2000). The LEAS includes 20 scripts depicting interpersonal emotional situations in 2 to 4 sentences, and measures the participant's ability to describe what he/she would feel in the situation described, as well as what the other story protagonist would feel. In line with Lane and Schwartz' emotional awareness model (1987), individuals with low LEAS scores had poorer PAT performances. Regarding the blindfeel model of alexithymia, results of this study showed a negative correlation between TAS20 and LEAS scores. This negative association between self-report alexithymia scores and LEAS scores was further confirmed in psychiatric groups (e.g., Berthoz, Ouhayoun, Perez-Diaz, Consoli, & Jouvent, 2000; Bydlowski et al., 2005).

In addition to their behavioral studies, Lane et al. attempted to identify brain regions associated with conscious experience of emotion by correlating blood flow changes induced by emotional stimuli with LEAS scores (Lane et al., 1998). The area of maximum correlation was located in the anterior cingulate cortex (ACC). On the basis of the findings that emotional awareness is correlated with blood flow in the ACC, and that the ACC is one of the structures involved in emotional experience (Lane, Fink, Chau, & Dolan, 1997), Lane et al. speculated that blindfeel (or alexithymia) would be associated with a dysfunction of the ACC during emotional processing.

We used fMRI to test this hypothesis in a comparative study investigating blood oxygen level dependent (BOLD) response changes during passive viewing of emotional stimuli in individuals scoring high and low on alexithymia (Berthoz et al., 2002). We expected to observe group differences in structures implicated in higher-level processing of the emotional significance of complex stimuli, that is, the anterior cingulate and prefrontal cortices. Two groups of eight men each were selected from a set of 437 healthy subjects on the basis of their high or low TAS20 scores, and low Hospital Anxiety and Depression Scale scores. These 16 study participants completed these self-reports on the study day again, to make sure that their alexithymia scores were stable and that they were not depressed and not anxious. The stimuli consisted of positive, negative, and neutral pictures selected from the International Affective Picture System (IAPS) (Lang, Bradley, & Cuthbert, 1997). Control stimuli were created by scrambling the initial pictures to suppress their emotional tenor. BOLD response changes in response to positive, negative, or neutral pictures were contrasted with those for their corresponding control/scrambled stimuli, allowing us to assess specific cerebral patterns associated with neutral pictures, too. With respect to the valence ratings that were provided after the scanning session (using a nonverbal visual analogue scale), no group differences for any of the emotional or neutral stimuli were found. Regarding BOLD response changes, we observed a group effect for the emotional pictures only. The two groups showed similar patterns of brain activation in the reference experimental condition (neutral pictures). In contrast, negative high-arousal pictures induced less activation in the high TAS20 scorers in the left mediofrontal-paracingulate gyrus. Conversely, this group showed greater bilateral ACC, mediofrontal, and middle frontal gyri activations with positive high-arousal pictures. These were the only regions showing between-group differences.

Since no explicit recognition or categorization of emotional valence was required during the fMRI task, we suggested that the results were not contingent on introspective attentional effort, but were instead related to spontaneous emotional experience. Our results provided the first set of functional brain imaging data in favor of Lane's "blindfeel" model. Yet, they were only partially in line with this model, which does not predict a differential effect of alexithymia depending on the positive or negative valence of the stimuli.

Since then, ten studies in normal samples (Eichmann, Kugel, & Suslow, 2008; Kano et al., 2003; Kano, Hamaguchi, Itoh, Yanai, & Fukudo, 2007; Karlsson, Naatanen, & Stenman, 2008; Kugel et al., 2008; Mantani, Okamoto, Shirao, Okada, & Yamawaki, 2005; Meriau et al., 2006; Moriguchi et al., 2009; Moriguchi et al., 2006), and six others on clinical population (Frewen, Dozois, Neufeld, & Lanius, 2008; Frewen, Pain, Dozois, & Lanius, 2006; Huber et al., 2002; Leweke et al., 2004; Li & Sinha, 2006; Silani et al., 2008) have been conducted in order to further investigate the neuroanatomical basis of alexithymia (see Box 60.3).

Using group comparisons or correlation analyses, all these studies revealed associations between ACC activation and alexithymia (see Figure 60.1). Yet, it should be noted that results were mixed, with 50% of the studies reporting a negative link, 40% a positive link, and 10% showing both type of associations (i.e., alexithymics activated more the rostral part of the ACC, whereas non-alexithymics activated more the dorsal part; Moriguchi et al., 2007). These discrepancies might refer to the wide range of experimental variables, including experimental tasks, stimulus material, the variety of technical approaches, and the gender of study participants (see Box 60.3).

Interestingly, these studies suggest that alexithymia is not related to only one structure (i.e., the ACC), but various prefrontal as well as subcortical regions. In fact, in those studies that measured BOLD response changes in response to emotional stimuli across the entire brain (whole brain analysis), alexithymia was associated with different patterns of activation in the medial prefrontal cortex (mPFC)—that comprises the ACC but not only—, the

Box 60.3.   Summary of the neuroimaging studies that have been published between 2002 and 2008

• **ROI**: The authors extracted the mean contrast values from specific regions in order to perform comparison or correlation analyses. In some articles, reported "ROI" or "SVC" results have been highlighted using a different threshold. Here this distinction is not taken into account. Nevertheless, for one study (Karlsson et al., 2008), we reported such clusters in italics because of the really low threshold (p uncorrected = 0.05).

• WB: Whole-brain analyses.

• †: PET; *: fMRI; ††: no information regarding gender is indicated in the article; α: no information regarding the participants TAS20 scores are presented in the article.

• (1): Here we report results from the comparisons between the emotional (angry, sad, and happy) and control conditions (neutral) only.

• **Abbreviations**: HA: high alexithymics; LA: low alexithymics; ♂: male; ♀: female; L: left, R: right; ACC: anterior cingulate cortex; AMG: amygdala; FG: fusiform gyrus; IFG: inferior frontal gyrus; dlPFC: dorso-lateral prefrontal cortex; mPFC: medial prefrontal cortex; occ: occipital gyrus; PM: premotor cortex, STS: superior temporal sulcus; TP: temporal pole; vlPFC: ventro-lateral prefrontal cortex. ASD: autism spectrum disorder; PTSD: post-traumatic stress disorder. Cat. App: categorical approach corresponds to between-group comparisons; Dim. App.: dimensional approach corresponds to the investigation of associations between alexithymia scores and brain activity; WB: Whole-brain analysis; ROIs: Regions of Interest analysis; ToM: theory of mind; DIF: TAS20 score reflecting difficulties in identifying feelings; DDF: TAS20 score reflecting difficulties in describing feelings to others. TAS26: 26-item Toronto Alexithymia Scale. BVAQ-B: Bermond & Vorst Alexithymia Questionnaire B-version.

• **Passive viewing**: Subjects were instructed to maintain their attention as long as the stimuli were displayed.

• **Implicit and Explicit tasks**: During an implicit task, subjects were instructed to perform a task that was not related to the emotional content of the stimuli (e.g., gender decision). During an explicit task, subjects were instructed to process the emotional content (e.g., emotion recognition).

• **Script-driven imaginary**: subjects were instructed to remember a personal pleasant, unpleasant/traumatic or neutral souvenir.

Studies	Participants	Stimuli	Tasks	Cat. App.	Dim. App.	WB	ROIs ˣ	Main Results
Berthoz et al. 2002*	16 ♂ - 8 LA: TAS20: 33.1 ± 3.4 - 8 HA: TAS20: 61.1 ± 5.2	- negative, positive, and neutral IAPS pictures with 2 emotional intensity (low and high arousal); - corresponding scrambled pictures	Passive viewing	yes	no	yes	no	- **Negative high-arousal vs. Same scrambled**: • LA > HA: L mPFC (BA9) - **Positive high-arousal vs. Same scrambled**: • HA > LA: ACC (BA24, BA32, BA31), mPFC (BA9), medial frontal gyrus (BA6)

(Continued)

Studies	Participants	Stimuli	Tasks	Cat. App.	Dim. App.	WB	ROIs [x]	Main Results
Kano et al. 2003[†](1)	24 ♂ - 12 LA: TAS < 51 - 12 HA: TAS > 61	angry, sad, happy, and neutral faces with 3 levels of intensity (33%, 67%, 100%).	Implicit: gender decision	yes	yes	yes	no	**- Angry vs. Neutral:** • LA > HA: R insula, R ACC (BA32), R superior temporal gyrus • HA > LA: L temporal sub-lobar **- Sad vs. Neutral:** • LA > HA: R insula **- Happy vs. Neutral:** • LA > HA: R mPFC (BA10), R insula **- Negative correlations** between brain activity (Angry vs. baseline & Sad vs. baseline) and TAS20 scores in R orbitofrontal cortex (BA11) and R IFG44/45
Mantani et al. 2005[*]	20 participants - 10 LA (7♂, 3♀): TAS20 ≤ 44 - 10 HA (7♂, 3♀): TAS20 ≥ 56	happy (H), sad (S), and neutral (N) fictive episodes in 2 ways - regarding a past event (P), - regarding a future event (F).	Script-driven imaginary	yes	yes	yes	no	**- FH vs. baseline:** • LA > HA: PCC **- PH vs. baseline:** • LA > HA: PCC **- Negative correlations** between brain activity (PH vs. baseline, FH vs. baseline & FH vs. FN) and TAS20 scores in PCC
Meriau et al. 2006[*]	23 ♀ - 12 LA: TAS26 = 35 - 11 HA: TAS26 = 46	angry and fearful faces	- Implicit: gender decision - Explicit: emotion recognition - Control: evaluation of geometric shapes	yes	yes	yes	yes	**- Positive correlations** between brain activity (implicit vs. control) and TAS20 scores in L dACC **- Connectivity** between L dACC and other regions: • LA > HA: dlPFC, vlPFC • HA > LA: L AMG

(Continued)

Studies	Participants	Stimuli	Tasks	Cat. App.	Dim. App.	WB	ROIs [x]	Main Results
Moriguchi et al. 2006[*]	20 participants - 16 LA (2♂, 14♀): TAS20 < 39 - 14 HA (3♂, 11♀): TAS20 > 60	- ToM animations with two triangles acting like humans - control animations with two triangles moving randomly	Explicit: intention attribution	yes	no	yes	no	- **ToM vs. control:** • LA > HA: R mPFC (BA10), R STS
Moriguchi et al. 2007[*]	20 participants - 16 LA (2♂, 14♀): TAS20 < 39 - 14 HA (3♂, 11♀): TAS20 > 60	- pictures: hands and feet in painful situations - control pictures: hands and feet in neutral situations	Explicit: evaluation of pain	yes	no	yes	no	- **Painful vs. Neutral:** • LA > HA: L dlPFC (BA8/9/10), cerebellum, dorsal pons, dorsal ACC • HA > LA: R anterior insula, R IFG (BA45), ventral ACC, R STS
Kano et al. 2007[†]	45 participants - 28 LA (22♂ + 6♀): TAS20 < 51 - 10 HA (5♂ + 5♀): TAS20 > 61	- visceral stimulations with 2 pressures (20 and 40 mmHg) - no visceral stimulation	Explicit: evaluation of pain induced by stimulations	yes	yes	yes	no	- **40mmHG vs. no stim.:** • LA > HA: L IFG (BA45), inferior parietal lobe, R cerebellum, L cuneus • HA > LA: R insula, R middle frontal gyrus (BA6), midbrain, ACC (BA32), R postcentral gyrus (BA3) - **Positive correlations** between brain activity (40mmHg vs no stim) and TAS20 scores in L orbital gyrus (BA47), R insula, L STS, R precentral gyrus (BA6), cerebellum - **Negative correlations** between brain activity (40mmHg vs no stim) and TAS20 scores in R superior parietal lobe, L cuneus, L precuneus, L middle frontal gyrus (BA6), cerebellum

(Continued)

Studies	Participants	Stimuli	Task	Cat. App.	Dim. App.	Whole-brain	ROIs [x]	Main results
Kugel et al. 2008*	21 participants (13♂, 8♀): TAS20 = 43.2 ± 13.7	sad, happy and neutral faces (33 ms) masked by neutral faces (467 ms)	valence evaluation of the mask neutral face	no	yes	no	AMG	- **Negative correlations** between AMG activity (Sad vs. Neutral) and: • TAS20 total score • DIF score • DDF score (L AMG)
Eichmann et al. 2008*	22 participants (14♂, 8♀): TAS20 = 43.9 ± 10.9	sad, happy and neutral faces (33 ms) masked by neutral faces (467 ms)	valence evaluation of the mask (neutral face)	no	yes	no	FG	- **Negative correlations** between FG activity (Sad vs. Neutral) and: • TAS20 total score • DIF score
Karlsson et al. 2008†	21 ♀ - 11 LA: TAS20 = 38.5 ± 5.3 - 10 HA: TAS20 = 62.4 ± 1.6	sad, amusing and neutral films	Explicit: evaluation of the induced emotional state	yes	no	yes	no	- **Sad + Amusing vs. Neutral**: • LA > HA: occ. areas (cuneus, BA18/19), *ACC and middle frontal gyrus (BA8, BA6).* • HA > LA: L precentral gyrus (BA4), L temporal lobe, L insula, L superior frontal gyrus (BA6)
Moriguchi et al. 2008*	20 participants - 16 LA (2♂, 14♀): TAS20 < 39 - 14 HA (3♂, 11♀): TAS20 > 60	- goal-directed hand actions video clips - control: artificial hand movements video clips	Passive viewing	yes	no	yes	no	- **Goal-directed actions vs. control**: • HA > LA: R superior parietal lobule, L postcentral gyrus (BA3), R superior frontal gyrus (BA6), L precentral gyrus (BA6), R middle temporal gyrus

(Continued)

Studies	Participants	Stimuli	Tasks	Cat. App.	Dim. App.	WB	ROIs [x]	Main Results
Huber et al. 2002[†]	19 participants - 10 LA (10 ♂): TAS20 = 38.5 ± 8.2 - 9 alexithymic psychosomatic patients (4♂, 5♀): TAS20 = 69.2 ± 4.9	unpleasant, pleasant, and neutral souvenirs	Script-driven imaginary	yes	no	yes	no	- **Pleasant vs. Neutral:** • LA > HA: corpus callosum, cingulate gyrus (BA31, BA29), mPFC (BA8), parahipp. gyrus • HA > LA: cuneus, precuneus, L middle temporal gyrus, cerebellum, R PM, R Brain stem - **Unpleasant vs. Neutral :** • LA > HA: corpus callosum, cingulate gyrus (BA24, BA31, BA29), mPFC (BA8, BA10), parahipp. gyrus, L IFG (BA44) • HA > LA: cuneus, precuneus, cerebellum, R Brain stem, L Thalamus, L IFG (BA47)
Leweke et al. 2004[*]	16 psychosomatic patients - 8 LA (4♂, 4♀): TAS20 = 43.2 ± 6 - 8 HA (5♂, 3♀): TAS20 = 68.1 ± 7	sad, disgusting, and neutral pictures	Passive viewing	yes	no	yes	no	- **Disgust vs. Neutral:** • LA > HA: R mPFC, R AMG
Frewen et al. 2006[*]	42 participants - 16 controls[††] - 26 PTSD[††] TAS20α	- traumatic souvenirs - baseline: monitoring breathing	Script-driven imaginary	no	yes	no	yes	- **Positive correlations** between brain activity (Traumatic vs. baseline) and TAS20 scores: • controls: mPFC, • PTSD: insula, PCC, thalamus. - **Negative correlations** between brain activity (Traumatic vs. baseline) and TAS20 scores: • controls: ACC, thalamus. • PTSD: ACC

(Continued)

Studies	Participants	Stimuli	Task	Cat. App.	Dim. App.	Whole-brain	ROIs [x]	Main results
Frewen et al. 2008[*]	26 participants - 26 PTSD (8♂, 18♀): TAS20 = 59.4 ± 13.7	traumatic and neutral personal memory scripts	Listening personal memory scripts	no	yes	yes	no	**- Positive correlations** between brain activity (Traumatic vs. neutral) and TAS20 scores: R post. insula, PCC, L STS **- Negative correlations** between brain activity (Traumatic vs. neutral) and TAS20 scores: ACC/mPFC, R IFG (BA47), anterior insula
Li et al. 2006[*]	27 cocaine-dependent patients (10♂, 17♀): TAS♂ = 63.2 ± 13.8 TAS♀ = 68.1 ± 10.4	traumatic and neutral personal memory scripts	Script-driven imaginary	no	yes	yes	no	**- Positive correlations** between brain activity (Traumatic vs. neutral) and TAS20 scores: • male patients: R putamen, R middle and superior frontal cortex (BA8) **- Negative correlations** between brain activity (Traumatic vs. neutral) and TAS20 scores: • female patients: R middle and superior temporal cortex, L frontal cortex (BA 6), L IFG (BA 47), R thalamus, R AMG, parahippocampal gyrus, R putamen

(Continued)

Studies	Participants	Stimuli	Task	Cat. App.	Dim. App.	Whole-brain	ROIs [x]	Main results
Silani et al. 2008*	30 participants - 15 ASD (13♂, 2♀): TAS20 = 55.6 ± 9.7 BVAQ-B = 53.2 ± 8.7 - 15 controls (13♂, 2♀): TAS20 = 43.7 ± 12.7 BVAQ-B = 47 ± 11.1	unpleasant, pleasant and neutral pictures	- Implicit: color discrimination - Explicit: evaluation of the induced emotional state	yes	yes	yes	no	**- Explicit vs. Implicit:** • controls > ASD: mPFC (BA9/10), ACC, L precuneus, L TP, cerebellum • ASD > controls: L parietal cortex, occ. cortex **- Unpleasant vs. Pleasant:** • controls > ASD: L inferior orbitofrontal cortex **- Unpleasant Explicit vs. Unpleasant Implicit:** • controls > ASD: R corpus callosum, insula **- Negative correlations** between brain activity (Unpleasant Explicit vs. Unpleasant Implicit) and TAS20 scores: • controls: anterior insula • ASD: anterior insula, L AMG

Note: Only results discussed by the authors were reported here.

dorsolateral prefrontal cortex, and the inferior frontal gyrus. Moreover, studies on pain perception or induction (using pictures depicting painful actions, Moriguchi et al., 2007; or painful stimulations induced by intestinal distensions, Kano et al., 2007) revealed greater anterior insula activity in alexithymics. This structure has been involved in subjective feelings of the body state (Craig, 2009). In the case of alexithymia, the anterior insula response could reflect altered own body-state representation. In addition, alexithymia has been associated with greater activity in somato-motor areas using heterogeneous type of stimuli (IAPS pictures, Berthoz et al., 2002; videos, Karlsson et al., 2008; Moriguchi et al., 2009; direct painful stimulations, Kano et al., 2007), suggesting that alexithymic individuals could experience increased bodily sensations when confronted with emotional events. This hypothesis is in line with the fact that alexithymics report greater

physical distress and bodily symptoms. Yet, the same result has also been interpreted as a tendency for alexithymic individuals to over-simulate other's actions, which could account for their difficulties in distinguishing their own feelings from that of others (Moriguchi et al., 2009). Both mechanisms, that is, an altered own body state representation and a disruption in self-other distinction during emotional situations, could explain why alexithymic individuals have impaired capacity for self-care and self-regulation.

The question whether there are specific associations between all or some of the alexithymia dimensions and cerebral activity has been addressed only recently in two studies which focused on circumscribed, preselected, brain regions (using ROI analyses: Eichmann et al., 2008; Kugel et al., 2008). The level of difficulty in identifying feelings (DIF) was negatively linked to the amygdala (AMG) and the

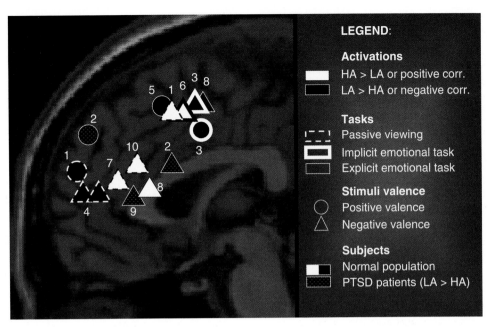

Fig. 60.1 Alexithymia-related activations during emotional tasks. Medial frontal cortex activations (x = 0; peaks), revealed in studies using either direct comparison between alexithymia and non-alexithymia groups or correlation analyses with alexithymia scores (BVAQ or TAS), were superimposed on sagittal sections of the MNI brain. HA: High Alexithymic; LA: Low Alexithymic. For LA > HA activations; the dotted patterns correspond to patients, whereas the black patterns were obtained in normal samples. 1- Berthoz et al., 2002; 2- Huber et al., 2002; 3- Kano et al., 2003; 4- Leweke et al., 2004; 5- Mantani et al., 2005; 6- Mériau et al., 2006; 7- Kano et al., 2007; 8- Moriguchi et al., 2007; 9- Frewen et al., 2008; 10- Pouga et al. (2010). corr.: correlation analyses.

fusiform gyrus in response to subliminal presentations of sad faces. A negative correlation was also found between the AMG activity and the level of difficulty in describing feelings (DDF). Hence, these studies not only highlight a specific link between the affective alexithymia dimensions and structures crucially involved in socio-affective cues processing, but further reveal that these effects occur already at an early, automatic processing stage. Unfortunately, both studies had a priori hypotheses on specific regions and did not perform whole-brain analyses. Moreover, as both used the TAS20, they provided information on only three of the alexithymia dimensions.

These limits were taken into account in our last study. We used fMRI in order to investigate the links between BVAQ scores and whole brain activity associated with the perception of threatening stimuli (fearful bodily expressions, Pouga, Berthoz, deGelder, & Grèzes, 2010). Two groups of men were selected from a set of 201 healthy subjects on the basis of their scores on the BVAQ-B: 13 high BVAQ-B scorers and 12 low BVAQ-B scorers. The sample of participants also included nine men who had intermediate BVAQ-B scores. Besides, all participants completed questionnaires measuring depression (BDI-13) and anxiety (Trait & State STAI). The experimental stimuli consisted of videos depicting actors opening doors in a fearful or neutral manner (see Grèzes et al., 2007 for a detailed description of the stimuli). In order to determine a "fear network," that is, the regions involved in the perception of fearful bodily expressions, we contrasted fearful videos with neutral ones. Using a dimensional approach in the whole sample (n = 34), we showed that the level of difficulty in identifying emotions (BVAQ Identifying factor) was negatively correlated with right AMG activity in response to fearful stimuli, and that reduced subjective emotional reactivity (BVAQ Emotionalizing factor) was linked to lower right premotor cortex (PM) activity. Then, using a categorical approach (13 high BVAQ-B scorers versus 12 low BVAQ-B scorers), high alexithymics showed greater activity in the ACC than the low alexithymics. We further observed in the entire sample that this increased ACC activity was more particularly linked to the BVAQ Emotionalizing factor. Hence, by combining two complementary approaches, we were able to specify more precisely the links between alexithymia and ACC activity, and to further propose that ACC hyperactivation to threatening stimuli in alexithymics might reflect an abnormal regulation mechanism by which they may over-control the expected negative consequences of an emotional event. Indeed, the down-regulation of emotions has been shown to activate a prefrontal network (Beauregard, Levesque, & Bourgouin, 2001; Eippert et al., 2007; Levesque et al., 2003; Ochsner, Bunge, Gross, & Gabrieli, 2002; Phillips, Ladouceur, & Drevets, 2008), including, amongst others, the ACC. This region has also been implicated in cognitive control (Miller & Cohen, 2001), emotional awareness (Lane et al., 1998; McRae et al., 2008), and the online-monitoring of performance (Botvinick, Braver, Barch, Carter, & Cohen, 2001). More recent studies using functional connectivity have also highlighted the role of the ACC in the top-down regulation of emotional states (Etkin & Wager, 2007).

Moreover, after dichotomizing their sample of participants into two groups of alexithymic and non-alexithymic (median split of the initial sample TAS20 scores), Mériau et al. (2006) found that, when faced to angry and fearful faces, only the alexithymic had an increased connectivity between ACC and AMG (psychophysiological interaction method, PPI). This result was interpreted as an increased affective influence of the AMG by enhancing information processing and guiding attention to salient emotional cues. In our own study, we used ROIs and performed correlation analyses between the ACC, AMG, and PM activities in the high and low BVAQ-B scorers separately. Unlike Mériau et al., we found no significant correlation between ACC and AMG activity in high BVAQ-B scorers. Yet, we found a negative link between ACC and PM activities in high BVAQ-B scorers only, which could reflect an altered control of adaptive behavioral response to emotional signals in these individuals. This result is also consistent with our previous hypothesis of a different regulation strategy used by alexithymics. Moreover, on the behavioral level, this neural mechanism could account for the descriptions of the "cold-blooded" personality and "stiff wooden posture" of prototypic alexithymic individuals. Nonetheless, the question whether the apparent discrepancy between Mériau et al.'s results and ours is related to experimental parameters (e.g., explicit and implicit versus passive viewing instructions; PPI analyses versus correlations between global brain regions activities; female versus male participants) should be addressed in future studies using not only normal but also clinical alexithymic participants.

Functional Neuroimaging Studies in Clinical Population

With respect to neuroimaging studies on alexithymia conducted in clinical populations (see Box 60.3), the majority used script-driven imagery, except Leweke and colleagues (2004) and Silani and colleagues 2008) who both used IAPS pictures. A first major finding is that, whereas studies on alexithymia in healthy subjects reported either an over- or an under-activation of the mPFC, those conducted in clinical populations found a negative link between alexithymia level and activity in medial prefrontal regions.

Moreover, differential activations according to the level of alexithymia were found in limbic structures, such as the AMG and parahippocampal gyrus. This was particularly salient in Silani et al.'s study (2008) that showed a negative correlation between TAS20 scores and AMG activity during the evaluation of emotions induced by unpleasant pictures in autism spectrum disorder (ASD) patients, whereas this was not the case among the controls. In addition, reduced AMG activations were documented in high-alexithymic psychosomatic patients (Leweke et al., 2004) and cocaine-dependent women (Li & Sinha, 2006).

Another interesting finding among the cocaine-dependent patients is the negative association between alexithymia scores and the striatum's (putamen) level of activation, a structure that has been implicated in motor emotional response (Saper, 1996) and addictive neural circuits (Kalivas & Volkow, 2005).

Finally, Huber and colleagues investigated the relationship between alexithymia and brain correlates of emotional processing in alexithymic patients with somatoform disorders and non-alexithymic healthy controls using a script-driven imagery paradigm. This study revealed that, relative to non-alexithymic participants, alexithymic had increased activation in the thalamus, visual cortices and language-associated areas, but decreased activity in limbic brain structures (Huber et al., 2002). In a similar study that investigated high- and low-alexithymic patients with somatoform disorders using an emotional passive viewing paradigm, a reverse pattern was observed; that is, an increased thalamus activity for low-alexithymic as compared to high-alexithymic patients (Leweke et al., 2004). Due to the role of the thalamus in the regulation of arousal (McCormick & Bal, 1997) and as it has been recently suggested that it might modulate the somatosensory and motor simulation of emotional states of others (Nummenmaa, Hirvonen, Parkkola,

& Hietanen, 2008), it is possible that thalamic differential activation shown in patients with high levels of alexithymia reflects again a dysfunction in emotional regulation processes when faced with others' emotions.

In sum, these clinical studies provide additional evidence for linking alexithymia with abnormal activity in regions involved in emotion generation and regulation. However, on an important note, in some of these studies it is difficult to disentangle the effect of alexithymia from that of the diagnosis, as high-alexithymic patients were compared to low-alexithymic healthy controls. Moreover, none of them examined the effects of the different alexithymia dimensions.

The Case of Posttraumatic Stress Disorder

Interesting findings come from studies in posttraumatic stress disorder (PTSD), which is characterized by involuntary re-experiencing of the traumatic event, avoidance, hyperarousal, and a type of emotional numbing that includes alexithymia-like features (e.g., restricted range of affect).

First, in a recent meta-analysis investigating the prevalence of alexithymic individuals among PTSD patients, a large effect size was found associating PTSD with alexithymia (Frewen et al., 2008). Moreover, in line with the functional neuroimaging studies on clinical groups with alexithymia reviewed above, under-activation in the dorsal and rostral ACC and the ventromedial prefrontal cortex have been reported consistently in PTSD patients. These cerebral patterns have been considered to reflect an inability to relate to emotional experience and a deficit in reflexive emotion-regulation processes occurring in the absence of self-reflection about emotion or deliberate attempts at emotional control (Etkin & Wager, 2007). Therefore, these deficits resemble the cognitive dimension of alexithymia, that is, an analytic reasoning or poor reflection about emotions. Finally, with respect to anatomical brain changes in PTSD patients, reduced dorsal ACC volume has been found (Kitayama, Quinn, & Bremner, 2006; Rauch et al., 2003). By means of a more automated technique (i.e., voxel-based morphometry, VBM), a reduction of grey matter in the rostral/pregenual ACC was found (Yamasue et al., 2003). A more recent study (Kasai et al., 2008) investigated combat-exposed Vietnam veterans with and without PTSD and their unexposed twins who were classified in "high-risk" if their combat-exposed sibling had PTSD or "low-risk" if their combat-exposed sibling had no PTSD.

Using VBM, the authors observed significant gray matter density reductions in combat-exposed twins with PTSD in the pregenual ACC and the insula as compared to the combat-exposed twins without PTSD. As we report below, similar morphological abnormalities have been observed in healthy alexithymic individuals. However, to our knowledge, no functional or anatomical studies on PTSD explored to which extent alexithymia could account for the observed cerebral deficits.

Anatomical Neuroimaging Findings in Alexithymia

Gündel and colleagues (2004) examined the link between alexithymia and anterior cingulate gyrus (ACG) morphology (outlined by manual tracing of sagittal MRIs) in 100 healthy university graduates (51 female, 49 male). They found that only the right ACG surface was positively linked to the TAS20 score. Yet, whereas in men this correlation remained after controlling for temperament and character scores (as measured by the Temperament and Character Inventory), this was not the case in women.

More recently, using VBM, Borsci and colleagues (2009) tried to replicate these results in two groups of healthy women (age range 26–76 years; with similar levels of depression): 14 high TAS20 and 30 low TAS20 scorers. Contrary to Gündel and colleagues (2004), high TAS20 scorers had reduced grey matter volume in the anterior cingulate cortex (anterior and posterior part, BA 24 and 32), as well as in other regions: the anterior insula and orbitofrontal cortex, which have been involved in emotion processing; the superior temporal sulcus, which is considered to be part of the human mirror-neuron system and to play a role in social cognition; and finally in the precuneus, which has been implicated in self-related mental representation. As underlined by the authors, the question on the origin of theses structural differences (developmental or acquired) remains unsolved.

The question whether the discrepancy between these two studies could be attributed to the different techniques they used (the first one used a technique based on surface measurement, whereas the other was based on differences between a template brain and subject's brain), or to the participants they included (mean and women vs. women only) should be addressed in future studies.

From a methodological perspective, these studies highlight a crucial issue concerning neuroimaging data in general. In fact, studies reporting higher activation as well as those showing lower activation in ACC for alexithymic subjects never controlled for the possible morphological differences in this region between these subjects and their controls. Hence, abnormal neural activity might be an effect of local differences in brain tissue volume. Such a "partial volume effect" has been found to account for altered neural activity in the subgenual ACC in patients with depression (Drevets et al., 1997/2000).

Alexithymia as a Lack of Socio-affective Skills

We mentioned in the beginning of this chapter that though some characteristics reflecting poor socio-affective skills have been documented by the first clinicians who supported the alexithymia construct, they haven't been considered as essential features in research on alexithymia up to now. Several recent psychometric studies in normal individuals, as well as in two types of psychiatric disorders associated with abnormal social adaptation and facial expression processing, offer additional evidence that alexithymia is marked by deficits in interpersonal functioning.

Psychometrical Approach in Healthy Individuals

Here, we report the research that investigated the hypothesis of an empathic deficit in alexithymia. Most of them used the Interpersonal Reactivity Index (IRI; Davis, 1983) to measure empathy. The dimensions measured by this questionnaire can be divided into two main categories: two dimensions referring to cognitive processes (Perspective Taking, PT; Fantasy, F) and two dimensions mainly referring to affective factors (Personal Distress, PD; Empathic Concern, EC).

Guttman and Laporte (Guttman & Laporte, 2002) were the first to examine associations between alexithymia and empathy. Participants in their study were recruited in six different populations (women with anorexia nervosa or with a borderline personality disorder and healthy women; mothers and fathers of these three groups) and two sets of analyses were conducted in order to investigate the association between TAS20 and IRI scores. The first set of analyses retained two groups of participants presenting the highest (n = 100) and lowest (n = 104) TAS20 scores. Group comparisons (controlling for age and level of education) revealed that the high alexithymia group scored lower on PT and EC, but higher on PD, than the low alexithymia one. No differences were found for F scores. Further, multivariate analyses, controlling for depression and family role

(i.e., daughter, mother, father), revealed similar results. In addition, the IRI F score became significantly positively associated with alexithymia (greater for the high alexithymia group). The second set of analyses regressed the three TAS20 scores on the four IRI scores (as well as demographic factors and psychopathology indices) and revealed the following: IRI PD and PT were significant predictors of DIF; IRI PD and IRI EC were significant predictors of DDF; IRI PT, FS, and EC were significant predictors of EOT (all were negative relationships).

Two recent fMRI studies on the neural correlates of alexithymia in different experimental settings, also provide psychometric results on the links between TAS20 and IRI scores (Box 60.3). These two studies compared 16 high versus 14 low TAS20 scorers. First, Moriguchi and colleagues (2006) observed the expected group difference for the IRI PD, PT, and EC scores, but not for the IRI F one. Moreover, the authors analyzed the participants' ratings on the pain experienced by a person depicted in pictures displaying painful (mechanical, thermal, and pressure-induced pain) and nonpainful situations: High TAS20 scorers rated the pain they thought the person on the picture would feel as significantly less intense than low TAS20 scorers (Moriguchi et al., 2007).

Finally, in another neuroimaging study examining the neural correlates of autism spectrum disorder (ASD), TAS20 and IRI scores were collected in 15 ASD and 15 matched controls (Silani et al., 2008) (Box 60.3). In the control group, a significant negative correlation was reported between the TAS20 total score and the IRI EC and PT scores. Additionally, in the ASD group, a highly significant negative correlation was found between the TAS20 total score and IRI scores, specifically for EC.

The research reviewed above provides cumulative convergent evidence for the impairing impact of alexithymia on empathic abilities. Yet, none examined specific associations that may exist between the different dimensions of both alexithymia and empathy. Of interest here is whether the cognitive (vs. affective) dimensions of alexithymia would show privileged relations with the cognitive (vs. affective) dimensions of empathy. Perhaps even more important, these studies did not examine whether associations between alexithymia and empathy persist after controlling for the participants' level of anxiety and depression, which have been shown to be associated with alexithymia (Parker, Bagby, & Taylor, 1991) and empathy (specifically for IRI PD scores, Berthoz, Wessa, Kedia, Wicker, & Grèzes, 2008).

We addressed this question and analyzed the responses of 645 students to alexithymia (TAS20), empathy (IRI), depression (BDI-13), and anxiety (STAI) self-report questionnaires (Grynberg, Luminet, Corneille, Grèzes, & Berthoz, In Press). Partial correlation analyses (adjusting for BDI-13 and STAI scores) revealed that, among the three TAS20 factors, DDF and DIF were positively correlated with the IRI PD score, whereas EOT was negatively correlated with IRI F, PT, and EC scores. Regression analyses showed that EOT and DDF were essentially predicted by PT. Hence, our set of findings offers further evidence for the impairing impact of alexithymic pragmatic way of thinking on interpersonal skills.

Moreover, we hypothesized low empathy scorers (using Baron-Cohen et al.'s Empathic Quotient) to display high alexithymia. We collected the responses of 410 normal young adults (see Berthoz, Wessa, et al., 2008 for a detailed description of the sample) and to self-report questionnaires of alexithymia (TAS20, BVAQ), empathy (IRI, EQ), depression (BDI-13), and anxiety (STAI). Even after controlling for dysphoric affects' scores (BDI-13 and STAI scores), we indeed found a main effect of Empathy category: low EQ scorers (n = 68) had lower TAS20 Total and subfactors' scores, as well as BVAQ Total and subfactors' scores (except for the BVAQ Poor Fantasizing score) (Berthoz, Kédia, & Grèzes, 2008).

In addition to being associated with a lack of empathy, alexithymia has been demonstrated to relate to specific interpersonal problems. For instance, in a recent study on the responses of 404 patients (presenting a variety of mental disorders) and of 157 psychology students to the TAS20 and the 64-item Inventory of Interpersonal Problems (IIP-64) (Vanheule, Desmet, Rosseel, Verhaeghe, & Meganck, 2007), linear multiple regression analyses showed that Cold/Distant and Non-Assertive IIP-64 scores were predictors of the TAS20 total scores. Hence, low degrees of affection for and connection with others, as well as problems in taking initiative in relation to others and in coping with social challenges (measured, respectively, by the Cold/Distant and Non-Assertive IIP-64 factors) are part of the alexithymic poor socio-affective skills.

Moreover, in a sample of 100 psychology students who completed measures of alexithymia (TAS20), empathy (Empathy Scale for Adults, ESA), morality (Tests of Self-Conscious Affect, TOSCA), and Machiavellianism (Mach-4), the TAS20 total and three factor scores were negatively correlated with the ESA and the TOSCA Guilt scores (except for the TAS20 DIF), but positively with the Mach-4 score (Wastell & Booth, 2003). Linear regressions indicated that TAS20 DIF and EOT were significant predictors of Machiavellianism. In addition, the negative association between empathy (ESA) and Machiavellianism (Mach-4) scores was reduced when alexithymia (TAS20 scores) was introduced as a mediating variable.

Furthermore, Fossati and colleagues (2009) studied the links between attachment styles, mentalized affectivity[4] (Fonagy et al., 2002), and impulsive aggressiveness in a sample of 637 undergraduate students of various academic areas (Arts, Economics, Education, Environmental Sciences, Law, Motor Sciences, Natural Sciences, Pharmacy, Political Sciences, Psychology and Social Sciences). Regression analyses indicated that TAS20 DIF factor was a significant predictor of the impulsive aggression index; there was also a minor contribution of the TAS20 EOT factor.

Finally, two recent studies further suggest that some alexithymia dimensions that are not measured by the TAS20 are linked to poor prosociality. Bekker and colleagues (Bekker, Bachrach, & Croon, 2007) investigated the relationships among alexithymia, antisocial behavior, attachment styles, and autonomy-connectedness among 202 college students in psychology (67 men and 135 women). Interestingly, reduced subjective emotional reactivity scores (BVAQ Emotionalizing factor) were linked to greater antisocial behavior scores, to lower sensitivity to others, and preoccupations with relationships scores. Moreover, the less one was inclined to fantasize (BVAQ Fantasizing factor), the less one reported having preoccupations with relationships. Finally, the BVAQ score that corresponds to the TAS20 total score (BVAQ Verbalizing + Identifying + Analyzing scores) was positively correlated with the discomfort with closeness score. De Rick and Vanheule (2007) examined the relationships between alexithymia (BVAQ scores) and personality disorder traits (ADP-IV scores) in clinical (101 alcoholic patients between 21 and 65 years old; 70% male) and non-clinical adults (101 individuals of the general population, matched with the clinical group with regard to age, gender, and highest level of education). Regarding the normal adults, the alexithymia dimensions that are not measured by the TAS20 (BVAQ Emotionalizing + Fantasizing scores) were found positively related to paranoid, schizoid, and antisocial disorder traits. The associations were not affected by age, gender, or depression and anxiety scores.

Hence, we consider that, taken together, the above-mentioned studies suggest that healthy alexithymics are characterized by a failure to connect emotionally with others, a lack of interpersonal warmth and empathy, and a greater feeling of suspicion when facing others.

Antisocial and Borderline Personality Disorders and Psychopathy

In their early descriptions of prototypic alexithymic individuals, Sifnéos and colleagues (1977) reported that in addition to their poor interpersonal relations, these individuals had passive-aggressive psychopathic personalities. Krystal (1979) underlined that the unawareness of feelings in alexithymics may contribute to engagement in uncontrollable, aggressive behaviors. Indeed, acting-out has been considered as a central component of criminal conduct (Kernberg, 1970), and acting-out (including impulsivity, irritability, and proneness to act aggressively) appears particularly in persons who have a defect in their capability to fantasize and in mentalized affectivity (Bateman & Fonagy, 2004; Jurist, 2005; Tuovinen, 1973).

The few studies that aimed at examining this question experimentally in clinical samples further suggest that alexithymia may be considered as a vulnerability factor for delinquent behavior.

Keltikangas-Järvinen (1982) investigated cognitive and affective features (by the mean of two projective tests, the Rorschach and the Thematic Apperception Test) in 68 males who had been convicted of homicide or aggravated assault (all were recidivists) and in 64 controls. This author reported the group of offenders was unable to fantasize or express imagined thoughts and emotions, and concluded they were alexithymic. In a study aimed at validating the TAS20, Kroner and Forth (1995) used also a measure of psychopathy (Hare's Psychopathy Checklist-revised, PCL-R) in a sample of 508 male inmates incarcerated for sexual and violent offenses. They observed a positive association between some of the TAS20 items (grouped in a factor they labeled "importance of emotions" on the basis of a factorial analyses of the TAS20) and the PCL-R second factor (measuring chronic instability, antisocial lifestyle, and social deviance). Further, in a study on the prevalence and co-occurrence of alexithymia and psychopathy in 37 female prison inmates (Louth, Hare, & Linden, 1998), 12 individuals were categorized as alexithymic (TAS scores), 11 as psychopathic (PCL–R scores), 3 as both, and 11 as neither. Moreover, they observed a positive correlation between the TAS total and DIF scores and the PCL-R second factor score (i.e., chronic instability, antisocial lifestyle, and social deviance). In addition, high TAS scores were also observed in a comparative study of 40 soldiers diagnosed with antisocial personality disorder who were recruited in a general military hospital (relative to 50 normal soldiers) (Sayar, Ebrinc, & Ak, 2001).

Other studies on the relationships between alexithymia and delinquent behaviors were conducted in adolescents. Langevin and Hare (2001) examined the links between alexithymia, the capacity for symbolization, and psychopathy in 40 juvenile offenders and 20 adolescent controls. Juvenile offenders had higher TAS20 scores, and TAS20 scores were correlated with psychopathy scores. Similar results were observed in a comparative study of 36 offender adolescents and 46 control adolescents (Zimmermann, 2006). The prevalence of alexithymic individuals was higher in the group of offenders, and this group had higher DIF scores. In addition, hierarchical regression analyses revealed the TAS20 was one of the two main predictors of juvenile delinquency (poor family structure was the second, but independent of the TAS20). Strikingly, in this data set the likelihood of being in the delinquent group increased by approximately 40% for each five-point increase in the TAS20 total score.

The studies mentioned above clearly show emotional regulation skills influence social behavior. In the domain of morality, we have mentioned that alexithymia has been related to Machiavellianism (Wastell & Booth, 2003). Moreover, Sifnéos presented his analyses on the "emotional profile" of what he considered the most famous criminal politicians of the 20th century: Rudolph Hoess, Adolph Eichmann, and Adolph Hitler (Sifneos, 2000). After reviewing trial transcripts and books, he noted that each man's self-description—particularly the responses of each to killing—was strikingly devoid of feelings and fantasy, which Sifnéos thought reflected alexithymia. Based on these evaluations and the research summarized previously, Haviland and colleagues (2004) further investigated the most salient characteristics in political leaders with prototypic alexithymic and psychopathic characteristics. They hypothesized that alexithymic and psychopathic features would be more prominent among controversial leaders (e.g., Adolph Hitler, Joseph Stalin, Francisco Nguema) than in a broad range of leaders and political figures. This latter group concerned 29 leaders who rose to power as skilled politicians and were generally respected, particularly at the heights of their careers (e.g., Dwight Eisenhower, John F. Kennedy, Mikhail Gorbachev, Edouard Schevardnadze, Jacques Delors, Nelson Mandela). Specific associations between the alexithymia and psychopathy constructs in the sample of controversial leaders were expected. Using experts' judgment ratings instead of self-reports[5], Haviland and colleagues (2004) discovered that individuals who were attributed high levels of both alexithymia and psychopathy lack empathy and insight and are unable to use introspection as a means to regulate their behavior. These leaders received high scores on items such as "*keeps people at a distance, avoids close interpersonal relationships*" and low scores on "*has warmth, has the capacity for close relationships, is compassionate.*"

In their paper, Haviland et al. (2004; p. 313) report that alexithymia and psychopathy share a few characteristic features that likely reflect deficits in the experience and expression of emotion as well as disturbances in interpersonal relationships. The expressions of alexithymia and psychopathy, however, appeared different. For example, the prototypic alexithymic person is considered basically anxious and overcontrolled (excessive impulse containment). In contrast, the prototypic psychopath is considered calm and relaxed (anxiety free), undercontrolled (poor impulse containment), rebellious/nonconforming, and to express hostile feelings directly.

Interestingly, experts in antisocial personality disorders made similar connections between alexithymia and psychopathy. In their review on psychopathy, Rogstad & Rogers[6] have presented converging experimental evidence for shared cognitive-affective dimensions between alexithymic and psychopathic individuals, notably a lack of awareness and use of emotional information in guiding their communication and behavior and a deficient interhemispheric integration (Rogstad & Rogers, 2008).

Moreover, on the cerebral level, psychopathic individuals present grey matter reductions in frontopolar and orbitofrontal regions, as well as in anterior temporal cortices and superior temporal sulcus (de Oliveira-Souza et al., 2008). A reduced orbitofrontal activity has been repeatedly found in association with psychopathy, for example, during cooperative interactions (Rilling et al., 2007) or during lying (Fullam, McKie, & Dolan, 2009). In addition, reduced responses of face-processing areas (e.g., fusiform gyrus) and emotion-processing structures (e.g., amygdala) were found during exposure of fearful faces in criminal psychopaths (Deeley et al., 2006), as well as in schizophrenic patients

with high psychopathy scores (Dolan & Fullam, 2009). Moreover, a lack of activation in a limbic-prefrontal circuit (including the AMG, OFC, ACC, and the insula) and no significant skin conductance response were found in psychopaths during the acquisition of fear (Birbaumer et al., 2005). However, they showed normal contingency and arousal ratings, indicating that they are capable of reflecting about the negative emotional feeling, here, acquired fear. This pattern resembles that on type III alexithymia.

Finally, the similarity between psychopathy and alexithymia in gender prevalence rates (rates of both syndromes are higher in males than in females) constitutes a supplementary link between the two traits.

In sum, functional and anatomical neuroimaging findings in psychopaths or in healthy individuals with high psychopathic traits resemble those observed in high alexithymic individuals. From a clinical perspective, psychopathic individuals might share most features of type III alexithymia. These overlaps again highlight the significance and usefulness of a typology of alexithymia as introduced by Bermond and colleagues (Bermond, 1997; Bermond et al., 2007) but this has not been explored to date.

Autism Spectrum Disorders

In ASD, too, problems in taking initiative in relation to others and in coping with social challenges have been documented using psychometric, cognitive, and anatomo-functional approaches (notably in high-functioning/Asperger syndrome individuals; see chapter 57 of this *Handbook*). Moreover, comorbid aggressive pathologies have been reported in ASD (e.g., Rogers, Viding, Blair, Frith, & Happe, 2006).

Alexithymic features have also been considered to fit descriptions of high functioning/Asperger syndrome patients who mainly have difficulties in understanding one's own and other's emotions, in expressing their internal state, and reading that of others. Their imagination is limited and they tend to have preoccupation with factual information (Fitzgerald & Molyneux, 2004).

We have conducted studies investigating the presence of alexithymia-type symptoms in groups of high-functioning adults with ASD, many of whom had a specific diagnosis of Asperger syndrome. In the first of these studies, we assessed levels of alexithymia using the TAS20. We reported the responses of 27 ASD adults in comparison to 35 controls (matched for age and gender) and 49 relatives of people with ASD (Hill, Berthoz, & Frith, 2004). In addition to showing that adults with high-functioning forms of ASD are able to report their own emotional processes, we also observed that these individuals had significantly higher TAS20 scores than the control group. Furthermore, the individuals with ASD had significantly higher alexithymia scores than the group of relatives. Moreover, when the TAS20 was dichotomized into low, intermediate, and high alexithymics (using previously established cut-off scores; Bagby, Parker, & Taylor, 1994), adults with ASD fell overwhelmingly into the intermediate and high groups, while few of the controls or relatives fell into the intermediate group, and none were represented among the high alexithymics. The hypothesis that the results may be explained by between-group differences in depression scores was ruled out. Similar results were found concurrently by Tani et al. (2004).

In another study, we demonstrated that alexithymia is stable over time in ASD, with TAS20 test-retest reliability being high for both the total score and for each of the three factors (Berthoz & Hill, 2005). Furthermore, the results observed with the TAS20 were replicated using the Bermond-Vorst Alexithymia Questionnaire (BVAQ-B). More specifically, ASD adults showed difficulties verbalizing their emotional experiences and analyzing their own emotional states and reactions, and had poor insight into their emotional experiences. This corresponds to type II alexithymia. In addition, in a study including 4 high-functioning autism and 26 Asperger syndrome patients and 30 matched controls, Lombardo and colleagues (2007) reported greater TAS20 total and subfactor scores in the ASD group. Interestingly, they also observed that, regardless of diagnosis, TAS20 scores were positively associated with autistic traits scores (Autism Spectrum Quotient scores) and were negatively related to empathizing performances (Reading the Mind in the Eyes test), suggesting that increased alexithymia is related to more endorsement of autistic traits and worse empathizing skills.

Moreover, Szatmari and colleagues (2008) further explored the construct of alexithymia as a potential part of the "Broader Autism Phenotype." First, they found significant higher TAS20 and DIF scores in parents of children affected with ASD (n = 439) than in parents of children with Prader-Willi syndrome (n = 45). Moreover, within the ASD group, the children of fathers categorized as high alexithymics had higher restricted, repetitive behaviors and interests scores (as measured by the ADI-R). The same pattern was observed for the children of mothers categorized as high alexithymics, but more marginally.

Finally, another similarity between ASD and alexithymia refers to gender differences in prevalence rates, as research has consistently demonstrated that rates of both syndromes are higher in males than in females.

Hence, the findings provide clear support for the view that individuals with ASD are likely to show symptoms of alexithymia. Moreover, as alexithymia has been identified in ASD family members, and as the heritability of alexithymia has been further demonstrated in two recent twin studies (Jorgensen, Zachariae, Skytthe, & Kyvik, 2007; Valera & Berenbaum, 2001), alexithymia traits could be useful in an endophenotype-based approach of ASD (Gottesman & Gould, 2003). In our opinion, there are at least three important aspects that could be addressed in such future studies. One is to investigate alexithymia in ASD using observer-rated measures, either by the Q-sort methodology (Haviland & Reise, 1996) and/or the Observer Alexithymia Scale (e.g., Haviland, Warren, & Riggs, 2000; Berthoz, Perdereau, Godart, Corcos, & Haviland, 2007). The second is to examine more systematically the relationships between the alexithymia dimensions and ASD symptoms at the behavioral and cognitive levels. The third is to compare directly alexithymic and non-alexithymic ASD and investigate their behavioral performances on emotion-processing tasks as well as in terms of their neural activity while performing these tasks (Bird et al., 2006).

Conclusion and Prospects

A massive set of evidence has been gathered recently which demonstrates that poor socio-affective skills should be considered core aspects of alexithymia. In addition, an increasing number of experimental results suggest there could be several "*alexithymias.*"

It should be noted that as early as in the beginning of the 1980s, Lesser and Lesser (1983) highlighted the fact that many authors may have inferred hastily the existence of specific etiological links between alexithymia and somatic disorders on the one hand, and that they used the generic term of "alexithymia" while they referred more specifically to some of its features, notably to its emotional characteristics (i.e., difficulties in identifying and verbalizing feelings), on the other hand. Nonetheless, alexithymia encompasses a constellation of both emotional and cognitive features, and it is likely that they each have different underlying mechanisms and distinct effects on self-oriented and other-oriented harming behaviors.

From a psychopathological point of view, a typological approach of alexithymia could allow, for example, to better characterize the phenotypic overlap we presented between ASD, alexithymia, and psychopathy. Moreover, in accordance with the criteria useful for the identification of endophenotypes (Gottesman & Gould, 2003), the extent to which there are common alexithymia typologies between these patient groups and their first-degree relatives should be further addressed via psychometric, cognitive, and anatomo-functional approaches.

Regarding methodological issues, functional connectivity analyses, which allow exploring the links between several brain regions activities under different conditions, constitute a promising approach. In fact, abnormal activations of different brain regions that have been reported in alexithymia could be related to dysfunctional regulatory systems. Concerning emotion regulation circuitry, it is particularly interesting that at least two mechanisms might be incriminated: one automatic, unconscious, and based on primitive areas such as limbic ones (e.g., amygdala, ventral anterior cingulate cortex), and another one voluntary, sustained by prefrontal areas (e.g., orbitofrontal cortex, medial prefrontal cortex) (Phillips et al., 2008). Nonetheless, there is also a need for further exploring the anatomical correlates of alexithymia. This point is crucial as morphological abnormalities may affect the interpretation of functional data.

Besides, with respect to other potential confounding factors, it seems essential to control more systematically for the effects of depression and anxiety when studying alexithymia.

With these recommendations in mind, we believe that it is possible to take advantage of the heterogeneity of the alexithymia construct and that it constitutes a relevant model to investigate the interactions between cognition and emotion. For instance, the study of alexithymia(s) in healthy individuals could allow bypassing major experimental biases associated with clinical groups, such as comorbidity, chronicity, or pharmacological treatments. Hence, it may offer new perspectives for determining the development of pathological mechanisms leading to emotional disorders and their predisposing factors.

In line with this suggestion, Sifnéos stated that

"the value of the concept of alexithymia lies in its ability to help us cut across our familiar nosological boundaries,

build bridges between neurobiology and psychology, and bring together clinicians and non clinician scientists so that they may develop appropriate therapies to alleviate the difficulties that are faced by patients with alexithymic characteristics" (Sifneos, 1996, p. 140).

Notes

1 Sifnéos used the word "feeling" to describe the subjective fantasies and thoughts associated with emotions.
2 In the large majority of these studies, the level of alexithymia was quantified by the 20-item Toronto Alexithymia Scale (TAS20). Few used the original Toronto Alexithymia Scale (TAS26; 26 items; 4 subscores), or the Bermond-Vorst Alexithymia Questionnaire (BVAQ; 5 subscores).
3 In this study, EOT scores correspond to the BVAQ fifth factor (i.e., Analyzing) scores.
4 Which is defined by Peter Fonagy and colleagues (2002) as the capacity to know that one has an agentive mind and to recognize the presence and importance of mental states in others, as well as the capacity for symbolic representation of one's own mental states, in the face of emotional arousal.
5 Using Q-Sort Methodology (Haviland & Reise, 1996).
6 Paper review on psychopathy that has an extremely well documented and synthesized section on the patterns of affective, cognitive, and interpersonal functioning shared by the two constructs.

References

Bagby, R. M., Parker, J. D., & Taylor, G. J. (1994). The twenty-item Toronto Alexithymia Scale—I. Item selection and cross-validation of the factor structure. *J Psychosom Res, 38*, 23–32.

Bagby, R. M. & Taylor, G. J. (1997). Affect dysregulation and alexithymia. In G. J. Taylor, R. M. Bagby, & J. D. A. Parker (Eds.), *Disorders of affect regulation: Alexithymia in medical and psychiatric illness* (pp. 26–45). Cambridge: Cambridge University Press.

Barrett, L. F., Lane, R., Sechrest, L., & Schwartz, G. (2000). Sex differences in emotional awareness. *Personality and Social Psychology Bulletin, 26*, 1027–1035.

Bateman, A. W. & Fonagy, P. (2004). Mentalization-based treatment of BPD. *J Pers Disord, 18*, 36–51.

Beauregard, M., Levesque, J., & Bourgouin, P. (2001). Neural correlates of conscious self-regulation of emotion. *J Neurosci, 21*, RC165.

Bekker, M. H. J., Bachrach, N., & Croon, M. A. (2007). The relationships of antisocial behavior with attachment styles, autonomy-connectedness, and alexithymia. *J Clin Psychol, 63*, 507–527.

Berenbaum, H. & Prince, J. D. (1994). Alexithymia and the interpretation of emotion-relevant information. *Cogn Emot, 8*, 231–244.

Bermond, B. (1997). Brain and alexithymia. In A. Vingerhoets, F. Bussel, & J. Boelhouwer (Eds.), *The (non)expression of emotions in health and disease* (pp. 115–130). Tilburg, The Netherlands: Tilburg University Press.

Bermond, B., Clayton, K., Liberova, A., Luminet, O., Maruszewski, T., Ricci Bitti, P. E., et al. (2007). A cognitive and an affective dimension of alexithymia in six languages and seven populations. *Cogn Emot, 21*, 1125–1136.

Bermond, B., Vorst, H. C., & Moormann, P. P. (2006). Cognitive neuropsychology of alexithymia: implications for personality typology. *Cogn Neuropsychiatry, 11*, 332–360.

Bermond, B., Vorst, H. C., Vingerhoets, A. J., & Gerritsen, W. (1999). The Amsterdam Alexithymia Scale: Its psychometric values and correlations with other personality traits. *Psychother Psychosom, 68*, 241–251.

Berthoz, S., Artiges, E., Van De Moortele, P. F., Poline, J. B., Rouquette, S., Consoli, S. M., et al. (2002). Effect of impaired recognition and expression of emotions on frontocingulate cortices: An fMRI study of men with alexithymia. *Am J Psychiatry, 159*, 961–967.

Berthoz, S. & Hill, E. L. (2005). The validity of using self-reports to assess emotion regulation abilities in adults with autism spectrum disorder. *Eur Psychiatry, 20*, 291–298.

Berthoz, S., Kedia, G., & Grèzes, J. (2008). Comportement social et introspection émotionnelle: étude des relations entre l'empathie et l'alexithymie. Paper presented at the 6ème Congrès de l'Encéphale, Paris, France, 24–26 Janvier 2008, *Encephale, 34,106*.

Berthoz, S., Ouhayoun, B., Perez-Diaz, F., Consoli, S. M., & Jouvent, R. (2000). Comparison of the psychometrical properties of two self-report questionnaires measuring alexithymia: Confirmatory factor analysis of the 20-item Toronto Alexithymia Scale and the Bermond-Vorst-Alexithymia Questionnaire. *Eur Rev Appl Psychol, 13*, 359–368.

Berthoz, S., Perdereau, F., Godart, N., Corcos, M., & Haviland, M. G. (2007). Observer- and self-rated alexithymia in eating disorder patients: Levels and correspondence among three measures. *J Psychosom Res, 62*, 341–347.

Berthoz, S., Wessa, M., Kedia, G., Wicker, B., & Grèzes, J. (2008). Cross-cultural validation of the empathy quotient in a French-speaking sample. *Can J Psychiatry, 53*, 469–477.

Birbaumer, N., Veit, R., Lotze, M., Erb, M., Hermann, C., Grodd, W., et al. (2005). Deficient fear conditioning in psychopathy: A functional magnetic resonance imaging study. *Arch Gen Psychiatry, 62*, 799–805.

Bird, G., Silani, G., Brindley, R., Singer, T., Frith, C., & Frith, U. (2006). *Alexithymia in autism spectrum disorders*. Paper presented at the Human Brain Mapping, Florence, Italy, 11th–15th June 2006.

Borsci, G., Boccardi, M., Rossi, R., Rossi, G., Perez, J., Bonetti, M., et al. (2009). Alexithymia in healthy women: A brain morphology study. *J Affect Disord, 114*, 208–215.

Botvinick, M. M., Braver, T. S., Barch, D. M., Carter, C. S., & Cohen, J. D. (2001). Conflict monitoring and cognitive control. *Psychol Rev, 108*, 624–652.

Bydlowski, S., Corcos, M., Jeammet, P., Paterniti, S., Berthoz, S., Laurier, C., et al. (2005). Emotion-processing deficits in eating disorders. *Int J Eat Disord, 37*, 321–329.

Craig, A. D. (2009). How do you feel—now? The anterior insula and human awareness. *Nat Rev Neurosci, 10*, 59–70.

Davis, M. H. (1983). Measuring individual differences in empathy: Evidence from a multi-dimensional approach. *J Pers Soc Psychol, 44*, 113–126.

de Oliveira-Souza, R., Hare, R. D., Bramati, I. E., Garrido, G. J., Azevedo Ignacio, F., Tovar-Moll, F., et al. (2008). Psychopathy as a disorder of the moral brain: Fronto-temporo-limbic grey matter reductions demonstrated by voxel-based morphometry. *Neuroimage, 40*, 1202–1213.

de Timary, P., Roy, E., Luminet, O., Fillée, C., & Mikolajczak, M. (2008). Relationship between alexithymia, alexithymia factors and salivary cortisol in men exposed to a social stress test. *Psychoneuroendocrinology, 33*, 1160–1164.

Deeley, Q., Daly, E., Surguladze, S., Tunstall, N., Mezey, G., Beer, D., et al. (2006). Facial emotion processing in criminal psychopathy. Preliminary functional magnetic resonance imaging study. *Br J Psychiatry, 189*, 533–539.

De Rick, A. & Vanheule, S. (2007). Alexithymia and DSM-IV personality disorder traits in alcoholic inpatients: A study of the relation between both constructs. *Pers Ind Diff, 43*, 119–129.

Dolan, M. C. & Fullam, R. S. (2009). Psychopathy and functional magnetic resonance imaging blood oxygenation level-dependent responses to emotional faces in violent patients with schizophrenia. *Biol Psychiatry, 66*, 570–577.

Drevets, W. C. (2000). Neuroimaging studies of mood disorders. *Biol Psychiatry, 48*, 813–829.

Drevets, W. C., Price, J. L., Simpson, J. R., Jr., Todd, R. D., Reich, T., Vannier, M., et al. (1997). Subgenual prefrontal cortex abnormalities in mood disorders. *Nature, 386*, 824–827.

Eichmann, M., Kugel, H., & Suslow, T. (2008). Difficulty identifying feelings and automatic activation in the fusiform gyrus in response to facial emotion. *Percept Mot Skills, 107*, 915–922.

Eippert, F., Veit, R., Weiskopf, N., Erb, M., Birbaumer, N., & Anders, S. (2007). Regulation of emotional responses elicited by threat-related stimuli. *Hum Brain Mapp, 28*, 409–423.

Etkin, A. & Wager, T. D. (2007). Functional neuroimaging of anxiety: A meta-analysis of emotional processing in PTSD, social anxiety disorder, and specific phobia. *Am J Psychiatry, 164*, 1476–1488.

Fitzgerald, M. & Molyneux, G. (2004). Overlap between alexithymia and Asperger's syndrome. *Am J Psychiatry, 161*, 2134–2135.

Fonagy, P., Gergely, G., Jurist, E. L., & Target, M. (2002). *Affect regulation, mentalization, and the development of the self*. New York: Other Press, 577 pp.

Fossati, A., Acquarini, E., Feeney, J. A., Borroni, S., Grazioli, F., Giarolli, L. E., et al. (2009). Alexithymia and attachment insecurities in impulsive aggression. *Attach & Hum Devel, 11*, 165–182.

Frewen, P. A., Dozois, D. J., Neufeld, R. W., & Lanius, R. A. (2008). Meta-analysis of alexithymia in posttraumatic stress disorder. *J Trauma Stress, 21*, 243–246.

Frewen, P. A., Pain, C., Dozois, D. J., & Lanius, R. A. (2006). Alexithymia in PTSD: Psychometric and FMRI studies. *Ann N Y Acad Sci, 1071*, 397–400.

Freyberger, H. (1977). Supportive psychotherapeutic techniques in primary and secondary alexithymia. *Psychother Psychosom, 28*, 337–342.

Fullam, R. S., McKie, S., & Dolan, M. C. (2009). Psychopathic traits and deception: Functional magnetic resonance imaging study. *Br J Psychiatry, 194*, 229–235.

Gong, H.-L. (2008). Characteristics of emotion schemas in high-alexithymics. *Acta Psychologica Sinica, 40*, 1250–1257.

Gottesman, II, & Gould, T. D. (2003). The endophenotype concept in psychiatry: Etymology and strategic intentions. *Am J Psychiatry, 160*, 636–645.

Grèzes, J., Pichon, S., & de Gelder, B. (2007). Perceiving fear in dynamic body expressions. *Neuroimage*, *35*, 959–967.

Grynberg, D., Luminet, O., Corneille, O., Grèzes, J., & Berthoz, S. (2009). Alexithymia in the interpersonal domain: A general deficit of empathy. *Pers & Indiv Diff*, In Press.

Gündel, H., Lopez-Sala, A., Ceballos-Baumann, A. O., Deus, J., Cardoner, N., Marten-Mittag, B., et al. (2004). Alexithymia correlates with the size of the right anterior cingulate. *Psychosom Med*, *66*, 132–140.

Guttman, H. A. & Laporte, L. (2002). Alexithymia, empathy and psychological symptoms in a family context. *Compr Psychiatry*, *43*, 448–455.

Haviland, M. G. & Reise, S. P. (1996). A California Q-set alexithymia prototype and its relationship to ego-control and ego-resiliency. *J Psychosom Res*, *41*, 597–608.

Haviland, M. G., Warren, W. L., & Riggs, M. L. (2000). An observer scale to measure alexithymia. *Psychosomatics*, *41*, 385–-392.

Haviland, M. G., Warren, W. L., Riggs, M. L. & Nitch, S. R. (2002). Concurrent validity of two observer-rated alexithymia measures. *Psychosomatics*, *43*, 472–477.

Haviland, M. G., Sonne, J. L., & Kowert, P. A. (2004). Alexithymia and psychopathy: comparison and application of California Q-set Prototypes. *J Pers Assess*, *82*, 306–316.

Heiberg, A. & Heiberg, A. (1977). Alexithymia—an inherited trait? *Psychother Psychosom*, *28*, 221–225.

Hill, E., Berthoz, S., & Frith, U. (2004). Brief report: Cognitive processing of own emotions in individuals with autistic spectrum disorder and in their relatives. *J Autism Dev Disord*, *34*, 229–235.

Hoppe, K. D. & Bogen, J. E. (1977). Alexithymia in twelve commissurotomized patients. *Psychother Psychosom*, *28*, 148–155.

Huber, M., Herholz, K., Habedank, B., Thiel, A., Muller-Kuppers, M., Ebel, H., et al. (2002). [Different patterns of regional brain activation during emotional stimulation in alexithymics in comparison with normal controls]. *Psychother Psychosom Med Psychol*, *52*, 469–478.

Jessimer, M. & Markham, R. (1997). Alexithymia: A right hemisphere dysfunction specific to recognition of certain facial expressions? *Brain Cogn*, *34*, 246–258.

Jorgensen, M. M., Zachariae, R., Skytthe, A., & Kyvik, K. (2007). Genetic and environmental factors in alexithymia: A population-based study of 8,785 Danish twin pairs. *Psychother Psychosom*, *76*, 369–375.

Jurist, E. L. (2005). Mentalized affectivity. *Psychoanal Psychol*, *22*, 426–444.

Kalivas, P. W. & Volkow, N. D. (2005). The neural basis of addiction: A pathology of motivation and choice. *Am J Psychiatry*, *162*, 1403–1413.

Kano, M., Fukudo, S., Gyoba, J., Kamachi, M., Tagawa, M., Mochizuki, H., et al. (2003). Specific brain processing of facial expressions in people with alexithymia: An H2 15O-PET study. *Brain*, *126*, 1474–1484.

Kano, M., Hamaguchi, T., Itoh, M., Yanai, K., & Fukudo, S. (2007). Correlation between alexithymia and hyper sensitivity to visceral stimulation in human. *Pain*, *132*, 252–263.

Kaplan, C. D. & Wogan, M. (1977). Management of pain trough cerebral activation: An experimental analogue of alexithymia. *Psychother Psychosom*, *27*, 144–153.

Karlsson, H., Naatanen, P., & Stenman, H. (2008). Cortical activation in alexithymia as a response to emotional stimuli. *Br J Psychiatry*, *192*, 32–38.

Kasai, K., Yamasue, H., Gilbertson, M. W., Shenton, M. E., Rauch, S. L., & Pitman, R. K. (2008). Evidence for acquired pregenual anterior cingulate gray matter loss from a twin study of combat-related posttraumatic stress disorder. *Biol Psychiatry*, *63*, 550–556.

Keltikangas-Järvinen, L. (1982). Alexithymia in violent offenders. *J Pers Assess*, *45*, 462–467.

Kernberg, O. (1970). Factors in the psychoanalytic treatment of narcissistic personalities. *J Am Psychoanal Ass*, *18*, 51–85.

Kitayama, N., Quinn, S., & Bremner, J. D. (2006). Smaller volume of anterior cingulate cortex in abuse-related posttraumatic stress disorder. *J Affect Disord*, *90*, 171–174.

Kroner, D. G. & Forth, A. E. (1995). The Toronto Alexithymia Scale with incarcerated offenders. *Pers Ind Diff*, *19*, 625–634.

Krystal, H. (1979). Alexithymia and psychotherapy. *Am J Psychother*, *33*, 17–13.

Kugel, H., Eichmann, M., Dannlowski, U., Ohrmann, P., Bauer, J., Arolt, V., et al. (2008). Alexithymic features and automatic amygdala reactivity to facial emotion. *Neurosci Lett*, *435*, 40–44.

Lane, R. D., Ahern, G. L., Schwartz, G. E., & Kaszniak, A. W. (1997). Is alexithymia the emotional equivalent of blindsight? *Biol Psychiatry*, *42*, 834–844.

Lane, R. D., Fink, G. R., Chau, P. M., & Dolan, R. J. (1997). Neural activation during selective attention to subjective emotional responses. *Neuroreport*, *8*, 3969–3972.

Lane, R. D., Quinlan, D. M., Schwartz, G. E., Walker, P. A., & Zeitlin, S. B. (1990). The Levels of Emotional Awareness Scale: A cognitive-developmental measure of emotion. *J Pers Assess*, *55*, 124–134.

Lane, R. D., Reiman, E. M., Axelrod, B., Yun, L. S., Holmes, A., & Schwartz, G. E. (1998). Neural correlates of levels of emotional awareness. Evidence of an interaction between emotion and attention in the anterior cingulate cortex. *J Cogn Neurosci*, *10*, 525–535.

Lane, R. D. & Schwartz, G. E. (1987). Levels of emotional awareness: A cognitive-developmental theory and its application to psychopathology. *Am J Psychiatry*, *144*, 133–143.

Lane, R. D., Sechrest, L., Reidel, R., Weldon, V., Kaszniak, A., & Schwartz, G. E. (1996). Impaired verbal and nonverbal emotion recognition in alexithymia. *Psychosom Med*, *58*, 203–210.

Lane, R. D., Sechrest, L., Riedel, R., Shapiro, D. E., & Kaszniak, A. W. (2000). Pervasive emotion recognition deficit common to alexithymia and the repressive coping style. *Psychosom Med*, *62*, 492–501.

Lang, P. J., Bradley, M. M., & Cuthbert, B. N. (1997). *International affective picture system (IAPS): Technical manual and affective ratings*. Gainesville, University of Florida: The Center for Research in Psychophysiology.

Langevin, R. & Hare, R. D. (2001). Psychopathie et alexithymie chez un groupe de jeunes contrevenants. *Rev Can Psycho-Éducation*, *30*, 227–236.

Lesser, I. M. (1981). A review of the alexithymia concept. *Psychosom Med*, *43*, 531–543.

Lesser, I. M. & Lesser, B. Z. (1983). Alexithymia: Examining the development of a psychological concept. *Am J Psychiatry*, *140*, 1305–1308.

Levesque, J., Eugene, F., Joanette, Y., Paquette, V., Mensour, B., Beaudoin, G., et al. (2003). Neural circuitry underlying voluntary suppression of sadness. *Biol Psychiatry, 53*, 502–510.

Leweke, F., Stark, R., Milch, W., Kurth, R., Schiele, A., Kirsch, P., et al. (2004). [Patterns of neuronal activity related to emotional stimulation in alexithymia]. *Psychother Psychosom Med Psychol, 54*, 437–444.

Li, C. S., & Sinha, R. (2006). Alexithymia and stress-induced brain activation in cocaine-dependent men and women. *J Psychiatry Neurosci, 31*, 115–121.

Lombardo, M. V., Barnes, J. L., Wheelwright, S. J., & Baron-Cohen, S. (2007). Self-referential cognition and empathy in autism. *PLoS One, 2*, e883.

Louth, S. M., Hare, R. D., & Linden, W. (1998). Psychopathy and alexithymia in female offenders. *Can J Behav Sci, 23*, 125–132.

Luminet, O., Bagby, R. M., & Taylor, G. J. (2001). An evaluation of the absolute and relative stability of alexithymia in patients with major depression. *Psychother Psychosom, 70*, 254–260.

Luminet, O., Bagby, R. M., Taylor, G. J., Vermeulen, N., & Demaret, C. (2002). Alexithymia and the processing of emotional information: Evidence for a deficit in the recall of emotion. *Psychosom Med, 64*, 87–88.

Luminet, O., Rimé, B., Bagby, R. M., & Taylor, G. J. (2004). A multimodal investigation of emotional responding in alexithymia. *Cogn Emot, 18*, 741–766.

Luminet, O., Vermeulen, N., Demaret, C., Taylor, G. J., & Bagby, R. M. (2006). Alexithymia and levels of processing: Evidence for an overall deficit in remembering emotion words. *J Res Pers, 40*, 713–733.

Lundh, L.-G. & Simonsson-Sarnecki, M. (2002). Alexithymia and cognitive bias for emotional information. *Pers Ind Diff, 32*, 1063–1075.

MacLean, P. D. (1949). Psychosomatic disease and the visceral brain; Recent developments bearing on the Papez theory of emotion. *Psychosom Med, 11*, 338–353.

MacLean, P. D. (1977). The triune brain in conflict. *Psychother Psychosom, 28*, 207–220.

Mann, L. S., Wise, T. N., Trinidad, A., & Kohanski, R. (1994). Alexithymia, affect recognition, and the five-factor model of personality in normal subjects. *Psychol Rep, 74*, 563–567.

Mantani, T., Okamoto, Y., Shirao, N., Okada, G., & Yamawaki, S. (2005). Reduced activation of posterior cingulate cortex during imagery in subjects with high degrees of alexithymia: A functional magnetic resonance imaging study. *Biol Psychiatry, 57*, 982–990.

Marty, P., & De M'Uzan, M. (1963). [Functional aspects of the dream life. "Operative Thinking."]. *Rev Fr Psychanal, 27*, SUPPL345–356.

Mayer, J. D., DiPaolo, M., & Salovey, P. (1990). Perceiving affective content in ambiguous visual stimuli: A component of emotional intelligence. *J Pers Assess, 54*, 772–781.

McCormick, D. A. & Bal, T. (1997). Sleep and arousal: Thalamocortical mechanisms. *Annu Rev Neurosci, 20*, 185–215.

McDonald, P. W. & Prkachin, K. M. (1990). The expression and perception of facial emotion in alexithymia: A pilot study. *Psychosom Med, 52*, 199–210.

McRae, K., Reiman, E. M., Fort, C. L., Chen, K., & Lane, R. D. (2008). Association between trait emotional awareness and dorsal anterior cingulate activity during emotion is arousal-dependent. *Neuroimage, 41*, 648–655.

Mériau, K., Wartenburger, I., Kazzer, P., Prehn, K., Lammers, C. H., van der Meer, E., et al. (2006). A neural network reflecting individual differences in cognitive processing of emotions during perceptual decision making. *Neuroimage, 33*, 1016–1027.

Miller, E. K. & Cohen, J. D. (2001). An integrative theory of prefrontal cortex function. *Annu Rev Neurosci, 24*, 167–202.

Moormann, P. P., Bermond, B., Vorst, H. C. M., Bloemendaal, A. E. T., Tejin, S. M., & Rood, L. (2008). New avenues in alexithymia research: The creation of alexithymia types. In A. Vingerhoets, I. Nyklicek & J. Denollet (Eds.), *Emotion regulation* (pp. 27–42). New York: Springer.

Moriguchi, Y., Decety, J., Ohnishi, T., Maeda, M., Mori, T., Nemoto, K., et al. (2007). Empathy and judging other's pain: An fMRI study of alexithymia. *Cereb Cortex, 17*, 2223–2234.

Moriguchi, Y., Ohnishi, T., Decety, J., Hirakata, M., Maeda, M., Matsuda, H., et al. (2009). The human mirror neuron system in a population with deficient self-awareness: An fMRI study in alexithymia. *Hum Brain Mapp, 30*, 2063–2076.

Moriguchi, Y., Ohnishi, T., Lane, R. D., Maeda, M., Mori, T., Nemoto, K., et al. (2006). Impaired self-awareness and theory of mind: An fMRI study of mentalizing in alexithymia. *Neuroimage, 32*, 1472–1482.

Mueller, J., Alpers, G. W., & Reim, N. (2006). Dissociation of rated emotional valence and Stroop interference in observer-rated alexithymia. *J Psychosom Res, 61*, 261–269.

Nemiah, J. C. (1977). Alexithymia. Theoretical considerations. *Psychother Psychosom, 28*, 199–206.

Nemiah, J. C. & Sifneos, P. E. (1970). Affect and fantasy in patients with psychosomatic disorders. In O. W. Hill, (Ed.), *Modern trends in psychosomatic medicine* (Vol. 2, pp. 26–35). London: Butterworths.

Nemiah, J. C., Sifneos, P. E., & Apfel-Savitz, R. (1977). A comparison of the oxygen consumption of normal and alexithymic subjects in response to affect-provoking thoughts. *Psychother Psychosom, 28*, 167–171.

Nummenmaa, L., Hirvonen, J., Parkkola, R., & Hietanen, J. K. (2008). Is emotional contagion special? An fMRI study on neural systems for affective and cognitive empathy. *Neuroimage, 43*, 571–580.

Ochsner, K. N., Bunge, S. A., Gross, J. J., & Gabrieli, J. D. (2002). Rethinking feelings: An fMRI study of the cognitive regulation of emotion. *J Cogn Neurosci, 14*, 1215–1229.

Ouellet, L., Nielsen, T. A., Montplaisir, J., Cartier, A., Malo, J. L., & Lassonde, M. (1996). L'alexithymie, réponse affective et rêves: investigation en laboratoire de trois caractéristiques sous-jacentes au déficit de l'expression des émotions. *Rev Int Psychopathol, 23*, 491–503.

Parker, J. D., Taylor, G. J., & Bagby, R. M. (1993a). Alexithymia and the recognition of facial expressions of emotion. *Psychother Psychosom, 59*, 197–202.

Parker, J. D., Taylor, G. J., & Bagby, R. M. (1993b). Alexithymia and the processing of emotional stimuli: An experimental study. *New Trends Exp Clin Psychol, 9*, 9–14.

Parker, J. D. A., Bagby, R. M., & Taylor, G. J. (1991). Alexithymia and depression: Distinct or overlapping constructs? *Compr Psychiatry, 32*, 387–394.

Parker, P. D., Prkachin, G. C., & Prkachin, K. M. (2005). Processing of facial expressions of negative emotion in alexithymia: The influence of temporal constraint. *J Pers, 73*, 1087–1107.

Pedrosa Gil, F., Bidlingmaier, M., Ridout, N., Scheidt, C. E., Caton, S., Schoechlin, C., et al. (2008). The relationship between alexithymia and salivary cortisol levels in somatoform disorders. *Nord J Psychiatry, 62,* 366–373.

Pedrosa Gil, F., Ridout, N., Kessler, H., Neuffer, M., Schoechlin, C., Traue, H. C., et al. (2009). Facial emotion recognition and alexithymia in adults with somatoform disorders. *Depress Anxiety, 26,* E26–33.

Phillips, M. L., Ladouceur, C. D., & Drevets, W. C. (2008). A neural model of voluntary and automatic emotion regulation: Implications for understanding the pathophysiology and neurodevelopment of bipolar disorder. *Mol Psychiatry, 13,* 829, 833–857.

Pichon, S., de Gelder, B., & Grèzes, J. (2010). Two different faces of threat. Comparing the neural systems for recognizing fear and anger in dynamic body expressions. *Neuroimage, 47,* 1873–1883.

Pouga, L., Berthoz, S., deGelder, B., & Grèzes, J. (2009). Individual differences in socioaffective skills influence the neural bases of fear processing: the case of alexithymie. Hum Brain Mapp, *31,* 1469-1481.

Prkachin, G. C., Casey, C., & Prkachin, K. M. (2009). Alexithymia and perception of facial expressions of emotion. *Pers Ind Diff, 46,* 412–417.

Rauch, S. L., Shin, L. M., Segal, E., Pitman, R. K., Carson, M. A., McMullin, K., et al. (2003). Selectively reduced regional cortical volumes in post-traumatic stress disorder. *Neuroreport, 14,* 913–916.

Rilling, J. K., Glenn, A. L., Jairam, M. R., Pagnoni, G., Goldsmith, D. R., Elfenbein, H. A., et al. (2007). Neural correlates of social cooperation and non-cooperation as a function of psychopathy. *Biol Psychiatry, 61,* 1260–1271.

Roedema, T. M. & Simons, R. F. (1999). Emotion-processing deficit in alexithymia. *Psychophysiology, 36,* 379–387.

Rogers, J., Viding, E., Blair, R. J., Frith, U., & Happe, F. (2006). Autism spectrum disorder and psychopathy: Shared cognitive underpinnings or double hit? *Psychol Med, 36,* 1789–1798.

Rogstad, J. E. & Rogers, R. (2008). Gender differences in contributions of emotion to psychopathy and antisocial personality disorder. *Clin Psychol Rev, 28,* 1472–1484.

Salminen, J. K., Saarijärvi, S., Toikka, T., Kauhanen, J., & Aärelä, E. (2006). Alexithymia behaves as a personality trait over a 5-year period in Finnish general population. *J Psychosom Res, 61,* 275–278.

Saper, C. B. (1996). Role of the cerebral cortex and striatum in emotional motor response. *Prog Brain Res, 107,* 537–550.

Sayar, K., Ebrinc, S., & Ak, I. (2001). Alexithymia in patients with antisocial personality disorder in a military hospital setting. *Isr J Psychiatry Relat Sci, 32,* 81–87.

Sifneos, P. E. (1967). Clinical observations on some patients suffering from a variety of psychosomatic diseases. *Acta Medica Psychosomatica, 7,* 1–10.

Sifneos, P. E. (1973). The prevalence of "alexithymic" characteristics in psychosomatic patients. *Psychother Psychosom, 22,* 255–262.

Sifneos, P. E. (1975). Problems of psychotherapy of patients with alexithymic characteristics and physical disease. *Psychother Psychosom, 26,* 65–70.

Sifneos, P. E. (1996). Alexithymia: Past and present. *Am J Psychiatry, 153,* 137–142.

Sifneos, P. E. (2000). Alexithymia, clinical issues, politics and crime. *Psychother Psychosom, 69,* 113–116.

Sifneos, P. E., Apfel-Savitz, R., & Frankel, F. H. (1977). The phenomenon of "alexithymia." Observations in neurotic and psychosomatic patients. *Psychother Psychosom, 28,* 47–57.

Silani, G., Bird, G., Brindley, R., Singer, T., Frith, C., & Frith, U. (2008). Levels of emotional awareness and autism: An fMRI study. *Soc Neurosci, 3,* 97–112.

Suslow, T. & Junghanns, K. (2002). Impairments of emotion situation priming in alexithymia. *Pers Ind Diff, 32,* 541–550.

Szatmari, P., Georgiades, S., Duku, E., Zwaigenbaum, L., Goldberg, J., & Bennett, T. (2008). Alexithymia in parents of children with autism spectrum disorder. *J Autism Dev Disord, 38,* 1859–1865.

Tabibnia, G. & Zaidel, E. (2005). Alexithymia, interhemispheric transfer, and right hemispheric specialization: A critical review. *Psychother Psychosom, 74,* 81–92.

Tani, P., Lindberg, N., Joukamaa, M., Nieminen-von Wendt, T., von Wendt, L., Appelberg, B., et al. (2004). Asperger syndrome, alexithymia and perception of sleep. *Neuropsychobiology, 49,* 64–70.

Taylor, G. J., Bagby, R. M., & Parker, J. D. A. (1997). *Disorders of affect regulation: Alexithymia in medical and psychiatric illness.* Cambridge: Cambridge University Press.

Tuovinen, M. (1973). [Criminal patients]. *Duodecim, 89,* 950–954.

Valera, E. M. & Berenbaum, H. (2001). A twin study of alexithymia. *Psychother Psychosom, 70,* 239–246.

Vanheule, S., Desmet, M., Rosseel, Y., Verhaeghe, P., & Meganck, R. (2007). Alexithymia and interpersonal problems. *J Clin Psychol, 63,* 109–117.

Vermeulen, N. & Luminet, O. (2009). Alexithymia factors and memory performances for neutral and emotional words. *Pers Ind Diff, 47,* 305–309.

Vermeulen, N., Luminet, O., & Corneille, O. (2006). Alexithymia and the automatic processing of affective information: Evidence from the affective priming paradigm. *Cogn & Emot, 20,* 64–91.

Wastell, C. & Booth, A. (2003). Machiavellianism: An alexithymic perspective. *J Soc Clin Psychol, 22,* 730–744.

Wehmer, F., Brejnak, C., Lumley, M., & Stettner, L. (1995). Alexithymia and physiological reactivity to emotion-provoking visual scenes. *J Nerv Ment Dis, 183,* 351–357.

Wrase, J., Klein, S., Gruesser, S. M., Hermann, D., Flor, H., Mann, K., et al. (2003). Gender differences in the processing of standardized emotional visual stimuli in humans: A functional magnetic resonance imaging study. *Neurosci Lett, 348,* 41–45.

Yamasue, H., Kasai, K., Iwanami, A., Ohtani, T., Yamada, H., Abe, O., et al. (2003). Voxel-based analysis of MRI reveals anterior cingulate gray-matter volume reduction in posttraumatic stress disorder due to terrorism. *Proc Natl Acad Sci U S A, 100,* 9039–9043.

Zimmermann, G. (2006). Delinquency in male adolescents: The role of alexithymia and family structure. *J Adolesc, 29,* 321–332.

Theory of Mind Deficits in Neurological Patients

Tal Shany-Ur *and* Simone G. Shamay-Tsoory

Abstract

This chapter reviews lesion studies that have been increasingly capable in clarifying the relationship between brain structures and social-cognitive functions, specifically emphasizing the role of the prefrontal cortex (PFC) in this domain. Accumulating lesion-based evidence suggests that the behavioral and social difficulties witnessed in patients with prefrontal neuropathologies are related, in part, to impaired theory of mind (ToM). For instance, deficits in taking another's perspective, recognizing people's social emotional expressions, or understanding when someone is being sarcastic may all result from difficulties making inferences about mental states, and consequently affect real-life social interactions. More specifically, patients with prefrontal lesions often display a specific deficit in making affective mental state attributions, and ToM tasks involving affective processing appear to depend on a distinct neural network involving the ventromedial prefrontal (VM) region and subcortical limbic structures. Since affective ToM seems to be understood at a later age than cognitive ToM, probably relating to neurodevelopmental patterns, future lesion studies should aim to compare between early and adult neurological patients, and perform longitudinal studies.

Keywords: theory of mind, social cognition, lesion, prefrontal cortex, emotion, ventromedial prefrontal cortex, affective ToM, cognitive ToM, development, executive functions, empathy

For over a century, lesion studies have been providing evidence for a biological basis of social cognitive abilities, amongst them the capacity to understand other people's minds, defined as *theory of mind* (ToM) (Premack & Woodruff, 1978) or *mentalizing*. Understanding how others' mental states (i.e., beliefs, desires, and emotions) affect their behavior is an essential skill for one's social understanding and interaction with others. Lesion studies which examine the impact of specific brain damage on social understanding and functioning in individuals with neuropathologies, have enabled making inferences about the neural basis of these skills. Such studies typically demonstrate loss of function following specific brain damage, thus providing different and complementary evidence for the correlational functional neuroimaging data, which independently do not enable inferring that an activated region is necessary or sufficient for a certain mental process (Fellows et al., 2005; Poldrack, 2008). Thus, lesion studies have been increasingly capable in clarifying the relationship between brain structures and social-cognitive functions, specifically emphasizing the role of the prefrontal cortex (PFC) in this domain.

Frontal lobe lesions have long been associated with alterations in personality and behavior (e.g., Schwab, 1927). Harlow (1868) presented one of the first descriptions of impaired social cognition following such damage. In a famous case report he described Phineas Gage, who survived and physically recovered after an iron bar penetrated his frontal lobes, causing severe damage. Although many of his cognitive abilities remained intact, Gage's social behavior was dramatically impaired. Significantly disturbing was his diminished consideration for others, which led his acquaintances to state he was "no longer Gage" (Harlow, 1868).

Following the proposal that an understanding and consideration of others requires making inferences about their mental states (Premack & Woodruff, 1978), ToM ability could be directly tested among patients with pathologies similar to Gage's. As will be discussed, lesion research since that time has demonstrated that impaired ToM abilities among people with prefrontal brain pathologies may account for some of their social and behavioral disturbances.

Theory of Mind

Theory of mind (ToM) was defined as a system of inferences used in order to attribute mental states and predict others' behavior (Premack & Woodruff, 1978). The process of understanding others' minds is thought to involve "theory making" because concepts (or mental states) such as belief and desire combine through a system of learned rules in order to explain and predict behaviors, thoughts, and feelings of other people (Olson, Astington, & Harris, 1988). It was hypothesized that people achieve a coherent understanding of others' minds using these theoretical constructs (Wellman, 2002), or alternatively by simulating the other's mental activity (Gallese & Goldman, 1999).

Developmental research has pointed to gradual, continuous, and universal stages in ToM development, that emerge in infancy and continue to progress during childhood and into early adolescence. For instance, children exhibit joint attention, participate in pretend play, and recognize basic emotions before they represent false beliefs (Frith & Frith, 2004; Leslie, 1987; Wellman & Liu, 2004). Research has also shown that ToM may be impaired following developmental (e.g., Baron-Cohen, Leslie, & Frith, 1985) or acquired (e.g., Stone, Baron-Cohen, & Knight, 1998; Stuss, Gallup, & Alexander, 2001) neurological pathologies. There are different views, however, regarding the domain specificity of ToM.

Baron-Cohen et al. (1985), who found that children with autism perform poorly on the false-belief paradigm, suggested this is due to a specific deficit in a ToM module. The modularity of ToM was subsequently supported by neuroscience research linking ToM with specific brain regions (e.g., Frith & Frith, 2004; Saxe & Kanwisher, 2003; Stuss et al., 2001). Similarly, Brothers (2002) proposed that our perception of the dispositions and intentions of others is the key feature of our "social cognition" module, which relies on a distinct neural system. Others, however, have argued against a domain-specific ToM ability, pointing out that ToM impairments simply reflect deficits in executive functions (EF). For instance, Stone and Gerrans (2006) proposed that the emergence of ToM depends on an interaction between domain-specific capacities for perceiving and processing social stimuli (e.g., gaze detection and monitoring) and domain-general abilities such as EF. We will address this issue further in this chapter's final section.

The Effect of Frontal Lobe Lesions on Social Cognition

The frontal lobes, especially regions of the PFC, have been associated with executive aspects of cognition, and social and moral behavior ever since description of frontal lobe syndromes-related changes in personality, social behavior, and emotional regulation emerged in the nineteenth century (Eslinger, Flaherty-Craig, & Benton, 2004). The case report of Phineas Gage, which provided preliminary evidence for this connection, was supported by similar clinical reports that emphasized the role of the frontal lobes in emotion regulation and social cognition (e.g., Damasio, Tranel, & Damasio, 1991; Stuss & Benson, 1986). Eslinger and Damasio (1985) described a patient (EVR) who, like Phineas Gage, presented with extensive behavioral changes following ventromedial prefrontal (VM) damage. Though previously successful in his occupational and personal life, after a VM ablation EVR lost his job and his marriage and presented with behavioral problems and inappropriateness, yet he was described as having intact intellectual abilities, knowledge of social norms, and moral judgment (Saver & Damasio, 1991).

In accordance with single case studies, group studies of adult patients with VM damage have described them as having personality changes, including blunted or inappropriate affect, apathy, low frustration tolerance, impaired goal-directed behavior, poor social judgment and decision making, social inappropriateness, and lack of insight, when compared to patients with other prefrontal or non-prefrontal lesions (Barrash, Tranel, & Anderson, 2000). Correspondingly, behavioral symptoms in patients with neurodegenerative diseases, especially those with frontotemporal dementia, are related to cortical atrophy in regions of the right medial PFC. In particular, apathy is correlated with tissue loss in the right ventromedial superior frontal gyrus, and disinhibition with tissue loss in the subgenual cingulate gyrus of the right VM (Rosen et al., 2005). Also, patients with either VM or orbital PFC (OFC) damage often exhibit indifference, deficient social judgment and pragmatics, and lack of self regulation. Despite these difficulties, they usually perform normally on tests of executive and other cognitive functions (e.g., Stone, 2000; Stuss et al., 2001).

Early-onset Prefrontal Lesions and Their Effect on Social Cognition

Pediatric lesion studies have accordingly been providing evidence for impaired social cognition following prefrontal damage. Early-onset PFC lesions often lead to altered development of social behavior, suggesting that intact maturation of the PFC is important for developing self regulation, social self-awareness, and perspective-taking abilities (Eslinger, Biddle, & Grattan, 1997).

Price, Daffner, Stowe, and Mesulam (1990) described two patients who suffered early bilateral prefrontal damage and were under psychiatric attention due to incidents of aberrant behavior. A neuropsychological examination of these patients revealed deficits in moral and social judgment, lack of insight, impaired empathy, and difficulties with complex reasoning. Accordingly, Anderson et al. (1999) characterized the long-term consequences of early lesions in two adults who suffered PFC damage as infants. Although these patients had preserved basic cognitive abilities they showed insensitivity to future consequences of decisions, defective autonomic responses to punishment contingencies, and failure to respond to behavioral interventions.

It was hypothesized that prefrontal (VM) damage in adulthood may leave social knowledge intact, but impair the ability to apply this knowledge when needed, whereas similar damage during childhood may disrupt the acquisition of social knowledge and the ability to develop adaptive social responses (Anderson, Barrash, Bechara, & Tranel, 2006).

Why do Prefrontal Lesions Impair Social Cognition and Behavior?

Several theories have tried to account for the behavioral profile described above, which often characterizes patients with prefrontal, especially VM and OFC, lesions. These include explanations concentrating on deficits in decision making, emotional information processing, empathy, and ToM abilities.

Damasio (1996) proposed that the behavioral difficulties of patients with VM lesions reflect abnormal, disadvantageous social decisions, and insensitivity to future consequences of their choices, later manifested by their impaired performance on a gambling task (Bechara, Tranel, & Damasio, 2000). Thus, it was proposed that the VM participates in emotional arousal prior to making risky decisions, supporting the "somatic marker hypothesis," which posits that physical reactions evoked by rewards or punishments signal potential outcomes, and consequently guide behavior (Bechara et al., 2000; Damasio, 1996). In accordance, Anderson et al. (2006) have shown that after damage to the VM, emotional disturbances (hyper- or hypo-emotional reactivity) contribute to impaired daily-life competencies, suggesting that impaired emotional reactivity may affect decision making and, consequently, social behavior (Anderson et al., 2006).

Patients with VM lesions were also reported to have deficits in understanding nonverbal social clues, such as facial expressions, gestures, and body postures, which may further impair their social cognition and behavior (Adolphs, 2009). Indeed, this region's role in social-emotional cognition can be attributed to its part in an intrinsic connectivity network involved in emotional salience processing (Seeley et al., 2007).

The behavioral descriptions in the aforementioned case studies also imply that PFC damage may jeopardize ToM and empathic abilities. This idea has been extensively examined by studying ToM among neurological patients.

The Neural Correlates of Theory of Mind: Evidence from Lesion Studies

In recent years, a growing number of lesion studies examined the effect of neurological damage on ToM abilities. Social-cognitive neuroscience has been characterized by frequent updates regarding the neural correlates of ToM, supporting the hypothesis that ToM is not a unitary module, and is probably not localized in one brain region (Baron-Cohen, 1995).

In accordance with reports concerning the behavioral consequences of prefrontal damage, lesion studies have commonly demonstrated ToM difficulties among patients who suffered frontal-lobe brain damage, especially in orbital or medial regions (e.g., Rowe, Bullock, Polkey, & Morris, 2001; Shamay-Tsoory, Tomer, Berger, Goldsher, & Aharon-Peretz, 2005; Stone et al., 1998; Stuss et al., 2001). Impaired ToM and empathic abilities have also been reported among patients with the frontal/behavioral variant of frontotemporal dementia (bvFTD), whose symptoms include deficient social and emotional functioning (Adenzato, Cavallo, & Enrici, 2010; Kipps & Hodges, 2006).

Several studies reported that individuals with lesions involving left or right PFC regions are impaired in performing false belief tests, and thus have difficulties taking the other's perspective (e.g., Bibby & McDonald, 2005; Rowe et al., 2001). Others, however, reported that patients with PFC lesions display intact false-belief understanding, alongside impaired performance on more advanced ToM measures such as understanding of "faux pas," a situation in which someone says something that should not have been said. To succeed in this task, one must understand that another person was offended or embarrassed by what was said and that the speaker did not intend to offend or embarrass anyone (Baron-Cohen et al., 1999a). Stone et al. (1998) found that patients with OFC lesions failed to recognize a faux pas, but could pass false-belief tests, compared to controls and to patients with dorsolateral prefrontal damage. Similar results were indicated among patients with right VM lesions, compared to controls and to patients with other prefrontal or posterior lesions (Shamay-Tsoory et al., 2005). Accordingly, patients with bvFTD were impaired in detecting faux pas, but not false beliefs, compared to controls and to patients with Alzheimer's disease (Gregory et al., 2002).

Difficulties with more advanced ToM measures have also been manifested by the ability of patients with frontal lobe injuries to detect sarcasm. These patients can correctly comprehend the literal meaning of a sarcastic remark, but not infer the speaker's real intention and meaning (McDonald & Pearce, 1996). Shamay-Tsoory, Tomer, and Aharon-Peretz (2005) described impaired understanding of sarcasm among participants with PFC lesions, especially ones involving the right VM. In contrast, Channon and Crawford (2000) reported that patients with *left*, but not right, frontal lesions, were impaired in comprehension of nonliteral meaning in stories (such as sarcasm). However, most lesion studies have linked *right* hemisphere damage with ToM deficits (Griffin et al., 2006). Deficits in understanding sarcasm have also been demonstrated

among patients with bvFTD (Kipps, Nestor, Acosta-Cabronero, & Hodges, 2009).

It was further reported that impaired perspective taking and deception recognition, which require advanced ToM abilities, are related to damage in the right medial frontal lobe and right anterior cingulate cortex (ACC) (Stuss et al., 2001). In another study, patients with diffuse frontal lobe lesions displayed impaired performance on the "reading the mind in the eyes" task (assessing recognition of affective mental states based on eye gaze) and on the "character intention task" (assessing attribution of intentions to illustrated characters) (Havet-Thomassin, Allain, Etcharry-Bouyx, & Le Gall, 2006).

While several studies have associated ToM impairments with prefrontal lesions, particularly in medial PFC (MPFC) regions, Bird, Castelli, Malik, Frith, and Husain (2004) described a patient with MPFC damage who exhibited intact performance on ToM tasks such as picture sequences, strange stories, and animations, leading the authors to question the role of the MPFC in ToM. Similarly, in another case study, a patient with OFC damage and disturbed social behavior displayed normative performance on Happé's strange stories and cartoons tasks, suggesting that regions other than the OFC may be related to ToM (Bach, Happé, Fleminger, & Powell, 2000). In a further study, Baird et al. (2006) examined advanced ToM abilities of three patients with MPFC lesions, which included the ACC. They reported impaired performance in a patient with bilateral damage, but not among patients with right damage, suggesting that unilateral right ACC damage is not sufficient to impair ToM.

Supporting the above, several lesion studies reported that neural regions outside the PFC contribute to ToM abilities. For instance, Samson, Apperly, Chiavarino, and Humphreys (2004) reported that the left temporo-parietal junction (TPJ) is necessary for reasoning about others' beliefs, in addition to the frontal lobes. More recently, it was suggested that the TPJ may be responsible for a domain general ability of meta-representation, not only for reasoning about mental states (Stone & Gerrans, 2006).

Additionally, there is lesion-based evidence for the involvement of the amygdala in ToM: Patients with damage to the amygdala have displayed deficits in understanding false beliefs, jokes, and sarcasm (Fine, Lumsden, & Blair, 2001) as well as in performing the "faux pas" and "reading the mind in the eyes" tasks (Stone, Baron-Cohen, Calderc, Keanec,

& Young, 2003). Another study that demonstrated deficits in various advanced ToM tests among patients with amygdalar lesions pointed out that such deficits are especially evident when the lesion occurred early in life (Shaw et al., 2004). These authors further reported that intact ToM performance among some of the patients with amygdalar lesions raises the possibility that the amygdala underlies domain-general emotional processes that only support certain ToM reasoning tasks, but is not a core component of ToM.

The reviewed lesion literature has been supported by neuroimaging studies linking ToM processing with activation in the MPFC, STS (Frith & Frith, 2004, 2006), TPJ (Saxe & Kanwisher, 2003), and the amygdala (Baron-Cohen, Ring, et al., 1999). Furthermore, neuroimaging studies of children with autism indicate abnormal white matter patterns between the VM, ACC, TPJ, STS and the amygdala (Barnea-Goraly et al., 2004). These regions, also referred to as "the social brain" (Brothers, 2002) have been shown to undergo significant functional and structural developments during adolescence (Blakemore, 2008), pointing out the importance of pediatric lesion studies in this field.

ToM Abilities in Patients with Early-onset Lesions

Deficits in social functioning following early-onset frontal lobe lesions have, as in adults, been attributed to impairments in social problem solving skills, recognition and interpretation of emotions, pragmatic communication, and ToM (e.g., Dennis, Barnes, Wilkinson, & Humphreys, 1998; Janusz, Kirkwood, Yeates, & Taylor, 2002; Snodgrass & Knott, 2006).

Supporting the adult literature, Snodgrass and Knott (2006) reported that 6- to- 12-year-old children with frontal lobe damage were impaired relative to controls on the "reading the mind in the eyes" task, but not on a false belief task. Accordingly, we recently found that 6- to- 10-year-old children with frontal lobe lesions were impaired in performing ToM tasks which involve affective processing, when compared to controls and to children with posterior lesions (Shany-Ur & Shamay-Tsoory, submitted).

In another recent study, school-aged children with traumatic brain injuries (TBI) had significantly lower scores on the "speech acts" ToM task, compared to the normative data (Dennis, Agostino, Roncadin, & Levin, 2009). However, using path analyses, this study demonstrated that the relation between frontal injury and ToM was mediated by working memory.

Patients with early damage to the amygdala were also shown to display impaired performance on advanced ToM tasks, such as detecting tactless or ironic comments (Shaw et al., 2004). Structural and functional abnormalities of the amygdala have been reported in autistic populations, thus suggesting that the amygdala's role in interpreting others' emotional expressions is a developmental aspect that underlies our reactions in social situations (Skuse, Morris, & Lawrence, 2003). However, while some claim that the amygdala is necessary for both ToM development and later on-line ToM processing (Stone et al., 2003), others suggested that it only supports the development of ToM capacities, and that possibly as these skills develop into the ability to *reason* about mental states, they become more dependent on frontal cortical regions (Shaw et al., 2004).

To date, pediatric lesion studies have been restricted in their ability to link ToM with specific regions of the frontal lobes, compared to adult studies. Still, they emphasize that TBI in children may disturb the development of ToM abilities, increasing the risk for social cognitive deficits (Dennis et al., 2009).

The great variety in findings regarding the neural correlates of ToM, described above, has been attributed to different task demands and, consequently, mentalizing processes involved. For instance, faux pas identification involves an empathic understanding of an emotional state, and not only understanding of the difference between the speaker's knowledge and that of the listener (i.e., false belief) (Shamay-Tsoory et al., 2005). These different task demands seem to be related to activity in overlapping but different neural networks.

Cognitive and Affective Theory of Mind: Differential Findings in Patients with Brain Lesions

ToM traditionally dealt with what people know and think, and how they refer to people's cognitive mental states, as tested by false belief tasks (Wellman & Liu, 2004). However, while one dimension of ToM relates to others' beliefs and desires, another dimension concerns the emotional and social meaning of others' intentions (Brothers & Ring, 1992). Brothers and Ring (1992) referred to these dimensions as "cold" and "hot" aspects of ToM, and suggested that both forms of cognition contribute to understanding others' actions.

The distinction between "cold" aspects of mental representations as opposed to "hot" aspects of mental representations has been further extended and examined in lesion studies (e.g., Shamay-Tsoory et al., 2005; Shamay-Tsoory & Aharon-Peretz, 2007) and functional imaging studies (Hynes, Baird, & Grafton, 2006; Völlm et al., 2006). These have differentiated between *cognitive* and *affective* ToM, referring to reasoning about beliefs versus reasoning about emotions, respectively. For instance, while cognitive false belief requires understanding what someone thinks about what someone else *thinks* (belief about belief), affective false belief refers to understanding what someone thinks about what someone else *feels* (belief about emotions). Affective ToM may also refer to making inferences about belief-emotion relationships.

Cognitive versus affective ToM has been previously tested using the false belief versus faux pas tasks, indicating that patients with OFC or VM lesions were able to complete the former task, but impaired in understanding the latter one (Shamay-Tsoory et al., 2005; Stone et al., 1998). Since the faux pas task requires making an inference about someone else's emotional reaction, it was speculated that the VM area (especially in the right) has a unique role in the network mediating affective ToM (Shamay-Tsoory et al., 2005). In accordance, patients with bvFTD displayed impaired performance on the faux pas and empathy tasks, suggesting that the OFC and MPFC degeneration among these patients could account for this deficit (Kipps & Hodges, 2006). Also, bvFTD patients were rated as having poor cognitive empathy (emotional perspective taking) but not emotional empathy, compared with controls (Rankin, Kramer, & Miller, 2005). Nonetheless, a limitation of lesion studies comparing between false belief and faux pas tasks is that the latter depends on awareness of social norms, in addition to ToM and affective processing.

In order to address this issue, more recent lesion studies entailed giving adult participants comparable versions of false belief, false attribution, and irony tasks, which were designed to specifically assess understanding of cognitive versus affective ToM, but were equated for difficulty in all other requirements. Cognitive ToM stories entailed making inferences about mental states concerning neutral, nonemotional matters (e.g., physical states), while affective ToM stories entailed making inferences about mental states involving emotions (for detailed examples please refer to Shamay-Tsoory, Tibi-Elhanani, & Aharon-Peretz, 2006; Shamay-Tsoory

& Aharon-Peretz, 2007). The results indicated that patients with VM lesions made more errors in the affective conditions, but not in the cognitive conditions, when compared to patients with posterior lesions (Shamay-Tsoory & Aharon-Peretz, 2007), to patients with TPJ lesions and to healthy controls (Shamay-Tsoory et al., 2006), indicating that affective ToM processing depends on a neural network that involves separate cortical regions in the VM. In accordance, recent imaging studies using comparable cognitive and affective ToM tasks (stories and cartoons) demonstrated selective activation in the MPFC when performing the affective versus cognitive task (Hynes et al., 2006; Völlm et al., 2006). Accordingly, Hooker, Verosky, Germine, Knight, and D'Esposito (2008) examined the neural regions involved in predicting an emotional response based on false belief, and found activation in regions involved in both ToM and emotional processing: the STS, MPFC, temporal poles, somatosensory related cortices, inferior frontal gyrus, and thalamus. However, this study did not include an affective-neutral condition.

Mitchell, Macrae, and Banaji (2006), using functional imaging, found that the VM is related to making mental state attributions about similar versus dissimilar others. These authors proposed that people use self-reference processes when understanding/simulating the mental states of similar others. Furthermore, mentalizing about affective states may rely on such self-reference mechanisms, subserved by the VM, while mentalizing about beliefs and knowledge may rely on other cognitive processes, therefore cognitive and affective ToM rely on dissociated networks (Mitchell et al., 2006).

The Development of Affective Versus Cognitive ToM

Few developmental studies have utilized ToM tasks which involve affective processing. For instance, it was reported that detecting a faux pas, or distinguishing between real and apparent emotions, is understood at a later age than understanding false beliefs (Baron-Cohen, O'Riordan, et al., 1999; Wellman & Liu, 2004), suggesting that affective ToM is more advanced than cognitive ToM. We recently administered several types of ToM tasks (false belief, false attribution, sarcasm, and deception), each consisting of a cognitive and an affective version, to 90 children of three age groups (grades 1, 3, and 6). As we expected, performance on all tasks improved with increasing age, but cognitive task scores were always better than matched affective scores. Furthermore, we found an interaction between group and task type, so that the difference between cognitive and affective ToM scores decreased between grades (Shany-Ur & Shamay-Tsoory, submitted). We speculate that the integration between ToM and affective understanding progresses with increasing age since it depends on maturation of specific neural circuits.

Indeed, it was previously hypothesized that a specific circuit involving the OFC and medial-temporal regions, including the amygdala, is responsible for decoding emotional mental states (Baron-Cohen, 1995). While early imaging studies of ToM suggested that the MPFC is generally involved in ToM (Frith & Frith, 2004), more recent literature suggests that the VM region is uniquely involved in affective ToM or "monitoring of emotions in self and others," while the dorsal MPFC is involved in "monitoring of actions in self and others" (Frith & Frith, 2006).

The proposal that the VM region is uniquely involved in affective ToM is supported by the reciprocal connections existing between the VM and sub-cortical limbic structures that are critical for understanding emotions. These connections, together with the role of the MPFC in mentalizing, make this region anatomically suited for the integration of affective and cognitive information (Beer, Shimamura, & Knight, 2004; Happaney, Zelazo, & Stuss, 2004).

Given the developmental lag between cognitive and emotional ToM, it is suggested that the network mediating affective ToM might depend upon VM cortical developments that occur during the school years. This is supported by developmental imaging studies showing that between childhood and late adolescence, frontal lobe maturation progresses from back to front and from lateral to medial regions, with the medial- orbital frontal region continuing to mature into adolescence (Gogtay et al., 2004). Furthermore, developmental functional connectivity (FC) studies show that children lack parts of the VM-centered ACC networks which are displayed among adults, and that their frontal FC is more diffuse compared to that of adults (Kelly et al., 2009). It should be noted that advancements in affective ToM during these years could also be related to developments in emotional competence (Saarni, 1999) and to environmental factors (real-life experiences).

Moreover, the distinction between cognitive and affective ToM is supported by studies of empathic abilities. Empathy, the emotional understanding of another, is a process which integrates a cognitive component (taking another's perspective), an affective component (feeling and responding to what the other is feeling), as well as a regulatory mechanism that takes into account self and other's feelings (Decety & Jackson, 2004; Shamay-Tsoory, Aharon-Peretz, & Perry, 2009). It was recently demonstrated that cognitive empathy, the ability to understand others' emotional mental states, which is related to affective ToM, is impaired in patients with VM lesions. It was further suggested that emotional empathy is an early developing system, evident among infants, while cognitive empathy is more advanced and probably develops around childhood to adolescence (Shamay-Tsoory et al., 2009). In accordance, Hooker et al. (2008) reported that activity in neural regions associated with predicting others' emotional response (affective ToM) was correlated with self-reports of empathy. Altogether is may be speculated that emotional perspective taking (cognitive empathy) is a higher-order process that relies on developing emotional empathy as well as cognitive perspective taking, and later on integrating these abilities.

The Relationship Between ToM Abilities and Executive Functions in Lesion Studies

As mentioned earlier, an ongoing concern in the ToM literature relates to whether ToM is a domain-specific ability or rather part of a general executive functioning (EF) domain. Some lesion studies have indicated no causal relationship between coexisting impairments in ToM and EF. For instance, Rowe et al. (2001) reported that patients with frontal lobe lesions were impaired in completing false belief, as well as various EF tasks (Stroop, Trail-Making, and Wisconsin Card Sorting), but that these were not causally related. Similarly, Havet-Thomassin et al. (2006) found no causal relationship between ToM and EF deficits in patients with frontal lobe lesions: Their performance on the Stroop and Trail-Making Tests did not predict performance on "reading the mind in the eyes" and "character intention" tests.

Henry and colleagues (2006) found that among patients with TBI, but not healthy controls, ToM performance was correlated with performance on a phonemic fluency task. These authors suggested that EF impairments may have lead to ToM impairments, but that these could also be separate functions depending on adjacent neuroanatomical systems.

Yet, other lesion studies have described impairments in only one of these domains: In one study, a patient with amygdalar damage displayed impaired ToM, but intact EF abilities (Fine et al., 2001). In another study, patients with PFC lesions displayed deficits in EF, but not in ToM functioning, indicating that executive dysfunction may account for some of the social behavior disturbances commonly found among these patients (Bach et al., 2000). Moreover, Apperly, Samson, and Humphreys (2005) pointed out that existing lesion data do not provide compelling evidence for domain specificity of ToM, which is commonly accompanied by and could be the result of deficits in EF or language domain-general abilities.

Merging these different perspectives, Beer, Shimamura, and Knight (2004) suggested that the orbital-medial regions of the PFC mediate different processes that all contribute to social-behavioral regulation. These include the ability to make inferences about others' mental states (ToM), monitoring behavior (an aspect of EF), and integrating emotional and cognitive information. Thus, the correlation between ToM and EF, often found in frontal lobe lesion studies, is not of functional dependency, but may rather result from their mediation by adjacent and overlapping networks, and common contribution to a "self regulation" construct (Beer et al., 2004).

Coexistence of ToM and EF deficits has also been reported among children with TBI, and it was suggested that deficits in EF are the cause for ToM impairments in this population (Dennis et al., 2009). Indeed, developmental theorists emphasize that typically developing children begin to understand false beliefs at the same age as they improve on tasks that require suppression of a previous response in favor of a new one (Perner & Lang, 1999). Thus, some theorists attribute ToM developments to advances in EF, emphasizing that a successful social cognition depends on the ability to represent several perspectives in mind (working memory) and suppress irrelevant information (inhibition) (e.g., Carlson et al., 2004). Stone and Gerrans (2006) proposed that ToM deficits may results from either impairment in domain-specific low-level input systems (such as joint attention in autism) or in domain-general high-level capacities (such as EF or metarepresentation in certain types of brain injuries), but not from damage to a separate ToM module.

Others have argued that although EF skills impact children's understanding of mental states, EF developments alone cannot account for ToM development (Wellman, 2002) and these functions may simply be correlated since they are mediated by common brain structures (Perner & Lang, 1999). Saxe, Schulz, and Jiang (2006) ruled out this possibility when, using fMRI, they found no overlap in the brain regions involved in EF and ToM. They suggest that although executive control is necessary for adult performance on some ToM tasks, the construction of mentalizing ability relies on independent domain-specific cognitive and neural substrates.

Undoubtedly, different findings regarding the relationship between ToM and EF in lesion studies may be attributed to task, age, and lesion differences. Developmental social-cognitive neuroscience research may clarify these issues.

Conclusions

Accumulating lesion-based evidence, reviewed in this chapter, suggests that the behavioral and social difficulties witnessed in patients with prefrontal neuropathologies are related, in part, to impaired ToM. For instance, deficits in taking another's perspective, recognizing people's social emotional expressions, or understanding when someone is being sarcastic may all result from difficulties making inferences about mental states, and consequently affect real life social interactions. More specifically, patients with prefrontal lesions often display a specific deficit in making affective mental state attributions, and ToM tasks involving affective processing appear to depend on a distinct neural network involving the VM region and sub-cortical limbic structures. Since affective ToM seems to be understood at a later age than cognitive ToM, possibly relating to neurodevelopmental patterns, future lesion studies should aim to compare between early and adult neurological patients, or perform longitudinal studies.

Alongside the increased application of functional neuroimaging in cognitive neuroscience research, it has been recognized that lesion studies are essential for supporting the necessity of brain structures to cognitive and behavioral functions. Nevertheless, lesion studies are subject to neuroanatomical reorganization concerns, due to individual differences and to the fact that the brain may have several ways to perform a cognitive process. They are additionally limited in their ability to show how a neuronal *network* is necessary for certain tasks (Fellows et al., 2005; Poldrack, 2008). Future social-cognitive lesion studies should aim to examine the effect of environmental variables on functioning after brain injuries. Additionally, more studies should apply neuroimaging to patients with lesions.

A final concern raised by this review is that lesion ToM studies should always aim to include measures of EF, and examine the role of these in ToM performance.

References

Adenzato, M., Cavallo, M., & Enrici, I. (2010). Theory of mind ability in the behavioural variant of frontotemporal dementia: An analysis of the neural, cognitive, and social levels. *Neuropsychologia, 48*(1), 2–12.

Adolphs, R. (2009). The social brain: Neural basis of social knowledge. *Annual Review of Psychology, 60*, 693–716.

Anderson, S. W., Barrash, J., Bechara, A., & Tranel, D. (2006). Impairments of emotion and real-world complex behavior following childhood- or adult-onset damage to ventromedial prefrontal cortex. *Journal of the International Neuropsychological Society, 12*, 224–235.

Anderson, S.W., Bechara, A., Damasio, H., Tranel, D., & Damasio, A. R. (1999). Impairment of social and moral behavior related to early damage in human prefrontal cortex. *Nature Neuroscience, 2*, 1032–1037.

Apperly, I. A., Samson, D., & Humphreys, G. W. (2005). Domain specificity and theory of mind: Evaluating neuropsychological evidence. *Trends in Cognitive Sciences, 9*(12), 572–577.

Bach, L. J., Happé, F., Fleminger, S., & Powell, J. (2000). Theory of mind: Independence of executive function and the role of the frontal cortex in acquired brain injury. *Cognitive Neuropsychiatry, 5*(3), 175–192.

Baird, A., Dewar, B. K., Critchley, H., Dolan, R., Shallice, T., & Cipolotti, L. (2006). Social and emotional functions in three patients with medial frontal lobe damage including the anterior cingulate cortex. *Cognitive Neuropsychiatry, 11*(4), 369–388.

Barnea-Goraly, N., Hower, K., Menon, V., ELiez, S., Lotspeich, L., & Reiss, A. L. (2004). White matter structure in autism: Preliminary evidence from diffusion tensor imaging. *Biological Psychiatry, 55*, 323–326.

Baron-Cohen, S. (1995). *Mindblindness: an essay on autism and theory of mind.* Cambridge, MA: MIT Press.

Baron-Cohen, S., Leslie, A., & Frith, U. (1985). Does the autistic child have a "theory of mind"? *Cognition, 21*, 37–46.

Baron-Cohen, S., O'Riordan, M., Stone, V., Jones, R., & Plaisted, K. (1999). Recognition of faux pas by normally developing children and children with Asperger syndrome or high-functioning autism. *Journal of Autism and Developmental Disorders, 29*(5), 407–418.

Baron-Cohen, S., Ring, H. A., Wheelwright, S., Bullmore, E. T., Brammer, M. J., Simmons, A., & Williams, S. C. R. (1999). Social intelligence in the normal and autistic brain: An fMRI study. *European Journal of Neuroscience, 11*(6), 1891–1898.

Barrash, J., Tranel, D., & Anderson, S.W. (2000). Acquired personality disturbances associated with bilateral damage to the ventromedial prefrontal region. *Developmental Neuropsychology, 18*(3), 355–381.

Bechara, A., Tranel, D., & Damasio, H. (2000). Characterization of the decision-making deficit of patients with ventromedial prefrontal cortex lesions. *Brain, 123*, 2189–2202.

Beer, J. S., Shimamura, A. P., & Knight, R. T. (2004). Frontal lobe contributions to executive control of cognitive and social behavior. In M.S. Gazzaniga, & E. Bizzi (Eds.), *The cognitive neurosciences, 3rd Edition* (pp. 1091–1104). Cambridge, MA: MIT Press.

Bibby, H. & McDonald, S. (2005). Theory of mind after traumatic brain injury. *Neuropsychologia, 43*(1), 99–114.

Bird, C. M., Castelli, F., Malik, O., Frith, U., & Husain, M. (2004). The impact of extensive medial frontal lobe damage on "Theory of Mind" and cognition. *Brain, 127*(4), 914–928.

Blakemore, S. J. (2008). The social brain in adolescence. *Nature Reviews Neuroscience, 9*, 267–277.

Brothers, L., & Ring, B. (1992). A neuroethological framework for the representation of minds. *Journal of Cognitive Neuroscience, 4*, 107–118.

Brothers, L. (2002). The social brain: A project for integrating primate behavior and neurophysiology in a new domain. In J. T. Cacioppo et al. (Eds.), *Foundations in social neuroscience* (pp. 367–386). Cambridge, MA: MIT Press.

Carlson, S. M., Moses, L. J., & Claxton, L J. (2004). Individual differences in executive functioning and theory of mind: An investigation of inhibitory control and planning ability. *Journal of Experimental Child Psychology, 87*(4), 299–319.

Channon, S. & Crawford, S. (2000). The effects of anterior lesions on performance on a story comprehension test: Left anterior impairment on a theory of mind-type task. *Neuropsychologia, 38*(7), 1006–1017.

Damasio, A. R. (1996). The somatic marker hypothesis and the possible functions of the prefrontal cortex. *Philosophical Transactions of the Royal Society of London, 351*, 1413–1420.

Damasio, A. R., Tranel, D., & Damasio, H. C. (1991) Somatic markers and guidance of behavior: Theory and preliminary testing. In H. S. Levin, H. M. Eisenberg, & A. L. Benton (Eds.) *Frontal lobe function and dysfunction* (pp. 217–229). New York: Oxford University Press.

Decety, J. & Jackson, P. L. (2004). The functional architecture of human empathy. *Behavioral and Cognitive Neuroscience Reviews, 3*, 71–100.

Dennis, M., Barnes, M. A., Wilkinson, M., & Humphreys, R. P. 1998. How children with head injury represent real and deceptive emotions in short narratives. *Brain and Language, 61*, 450–483.

Dennis, M., Agostino, A., Roncadin, C., & Levin, H. (2009). Theory of mind depends on domain general executive functions of working memory and cognitive inhibition in children with traumatic brain injury. *Journal of Clinical and Experimental Neuropsychology, 31*:835–847.

Eslinger, P. J., Biddle, K. R., & Grattan, L. M. (1997). Cognitive and social development in children with prefrontal cortex lesions. In N. A. Krasnegor, G. R. Lyon & P. S. Goldman-Rakic (Eds.), *Development of the prefrontal cortex: Evolution, neurobiology, and behavior* (pp. 295–335). Baltimore, MD: Paul H. Brookes Publishing.

Eslinger, P. J. & Damasio, A. R (1985). Severe disturbance of higher cognition after bilateral frontal lobe ablations: Patient EVR. *Neurology, 35*, 1731–1741.

Eslinger, P. J., Flaherty-Craig, C. V., & Benton, A. L. (2004). Developmental outcomes after early prefrontal cortex damage. *Brain and Cognition, 55*(1), 84–103.

Fellows, L. K., Heberlein, A. S., Morales, D. A., Shivde, G., Waller, S., & Wu, D. H. (2005). Method matters: An empirical study of impact in cognitive neuroscience. *Journal of Cognitive Neuroscience, 17*(6), 850–858.

Fine, C., Lumsden, J., & Blair, R. J. (2001). Dissociation between "theory of mind" and executive functions in a patient with early left amygdala damage. *Brain, 124*, 287–298.

Frith, U. & Frith, C. D. (2004). Development and neurophysiology of mentalizing. In C. D. Frith & D. M. Wolpert (Eds.), *The neuroscience of social interaction: Decoding, imitating, and influencing the actions of others* (pp. 45–75). New York: Oxford University Press.

Frith, C. D., & Frith, U. (2006). The neural basis of mentalizing. *Neuron, 50*, 531–534.

Gallese, V. & Goldman, A. (1999). Mirror neurons and the simulation theory of mind-reading. *Trends in Cognitive Sciences, 12*, 493–501.

Gogtay, N., Giedd, J. N., et al. (2004). Dynamic mapping of human cortical development during childhood through early adulthood. *Proceedings of the National Academy of Sciences of the USA, 101*(21), 8174–8179.

Gregory, C., Lough, S., Stone, V., Erzinclioglu, S., Martin, L., Baron-Cohen, S., et al. (2002). Theory of mind in patients with frontal variant frontotemporal dementia and Alzheimer's disease: Theoretical and practical implications. *Brain, 125*, 752–764.

Griffin, R., Friedman, O., Ween, J., Winner, E., Happé, F., & Brownell, H. (2006). Theory of mind and the right cerebral hemisphere: Refining the scope of impairment. *Laterlity, 11*(3), 195–225.

Harlow, J. M. (1868). Recovery from the passage of an iron bar through the head. *Publications of the Massachusetts Medical Society, 2*, 327–347.

Happaney, K., Zelazo, D. P., & Stuss, D. T. (2004). Development of orbitofrontal function: Current themes and future directions. *Brain and Cognition, 55*, 1–10.

Havet-Thomassin, V., Allain, P., Etcharry-Bouyx, F., & Le Gall, D. (2006). What about theory of mind after severe brain injury? *Brain Injury, 20*(1), 83–91.

Henry, J. D., Phillips, L. H., Crawford, J. R., Ietswaart, M., & Summers, F. (2006). Theory of mind following traumatic brain injury: The role of emotion recognition and executive dysfunction. *Neuropsychologia, 44*(10), 1623–1628.

Hooker, C. I., Verosky, S. C., Germine, L. T., Knight, R. T., & D'Esposito, M. (2008). Mentalizing about emotion and its relationship to empathy. *Social Cognitive and Affective Neuroscience, 3*(3), 204–217.

Hynes, C. A., Baird, A. A., & Grafton, S. T. (2006). Differential role of the orbital frontal lobe in emotional versus cognitive perspective-taking. *Neuropsychologia, 44*(3), 374–383.

Janusz, J. A., Kirkwood, M. W., Yeates, K. O., & Taylor, H. G. (2002). Social problem-solving skills in children with traumatic brain injury: Long-term outcomes and prediction of social competence. *Child Neuropsychology, 8*(3), 179–194.

Kelly, A. M., Di Martino, A., et al. (2009). Development of anterior cingulate functional connectivity from late childhood to early adulthood. *Cerebral Cortex, 19*(3), 640–657.

Kipps, C. M. & Hodges, J. R. (2006). Theory of mind in frontotemporal dementia. *Social Neuroscience, 1*(3–4), 235–244.

Kipps, C. M., Nestor, P. J., Acosta-Cabronero, J., Arnold, R., & Hodges, J. R. (2009). Understanding social dysfunction in the behavioural variant of frontotemporal dementia: The role of emotion and sarcasm processing. *Brain : A Journal of Neurology, 132*(3), 592–603.

Leslie, A. M. (1987). Pretense and representation: The origins of "theory of mind." *Psychological Review, 94*(4), 412–426.

McDonald, S. & Pearce, S. (1996). Clinical insights into pragmatic theory: Frontal lobe deficits and sarcasm. *Brain and Language, 53*(1), 81–104.

Mitchell, J. P., Macrae, C. N., & Banaji, M. R. (2006). Dissociable medial prefrontal contributions to judgments of similar and dissimilar others. *Neuron, 50*, 655–663.

Olson, D. R., Astington, J. W., & Hariis, P. L. (1988). Introduction. In J. W. Astington, P. L. Harris & D. R. Olson, *Developing theories of mind* (pp. 1–15). Cambridge, England: Cambridge University Press.

Perner, J. & Lang, B. (1999). Development of theory of mind and executive control. *Trends in Cognitive Science, 3*(9), 337–344.

Poldrack, R. A. (2008). The role of fMRI in cognitive neuroscience: Where do we stand? *Current Opinion in Neurobiology, 18*, 223–227.

Premack, D. & Woodruff, G. (1978). Does the chimpanzee have a theory of mind? *The behavioral and brain sciences, 4*, 515–526.

Price, B. H., Daffner, K. R., Stowe, R. M., & Mesulam, M. M. (1990). The comportmental learning disabilities of early frontal lobe damage. *Brain, 113*, 1383–1393.

Rankin, K. P., Kramer, J. H., & Miller, B. L. (2005). Patterns of cognitive and emotional empathy in frontotemporal lobar degeneration. *Cognitive and Behavioral Neurology: Official Journal of the Society for Behavioral and Cognitive Neurology, 18*(1), 28–36.

Rosen, H. J., Allison, S. C., Schauer, G. F., Gorno-Tempini, M. L., Weiner, M. W., & Miller, B. L. (2005). Neuroanatomical correlates of behavioural disorders in dementia. *Brain : A Journal of Neurology, 128*(11), 2612–2625.

Rowe, A. D., Bullock, P. R., Polkey, C. E., & Morris, R. G. (2001). "Theory of mind" impairments and their relationship to executive functioning following frontal lobe excisions. *Brain : A Journal of Neurology, 124*(3), 600–616.

Saarni, C. (1999). *The development of emotional competence.* New York: The Guilford Press.

Saver, J. L., & Damasio, A. R. (1991). Preserved access and processing of social knowledge in a patient with acquired sociopathy due to ventromedial frontal damage. *Neuropsychologia, 29*(12), 1241–1249.

Saxe, R. & Kanwisher, N. (2003). People thinking about thinking people: The role of the temporo-parietal junction in "theory of mind." *Neuroimage, 19*, 1835–1842.

Saxe, R., Schulz, L. E., & Jiang, Y. V. (2006). Reading minds versus following rules: Dissociating theory of mind and executive control in the brain. *Social Neuroscience, 1*(3–4), 284–298.

Samson, D., Apperly, I. A., Chiavarino, C., & Humphreys, G. W. (2004). Left temporoparietal junction is necessary for representing someone else's belief. *Nature Neuroscience, 7*(5), 499–500.

Seeley, W. W., Menon, V., Schatzberg, A. F., Keller, J., Glover, G. H., Kenna, H., Reiss, A.L., & Greicius, M. D. (2007). Dissociable intrinsic connectivity networks for salience processing and executive control. *The Journal of Neuroscience: The Official Journal of the Society for Neuroscience, 27*(9), 2349–2356.

Schwab, S. I. (1927). Changes in personality in tumours of the frontal lobe. *Brain, 50*(3–4), 480–487.

Shamay-Tsoory, S. G. & Aharon-Peretz, J. (2007). Dissociable prefrontal networks for cognitive and affective theory of mind: A lesion study. *Neuropsychologia, 45*, 3054–3067.

Shamay-Tsoory, S. G., Aharon-Peretz, J., & Perry, D. (2009). Two systems for empathy: A double dissociation between emotional and cognitive empathy in inferior frontal gyrus versus ventromedial prefrontal lesions. *Brain*, *132*(3), 617–627.

Shamay-Tsoory, S. G., Tibi-Elhanani, Y., & Aharon-Peretz, J. (2006). The ventromedial prefrontal cortex is involved in understanding affective but not cognitive theory of mind stories. *Social Neuroscience*, *1*(3–4), 149–166.

Shamay-Tsoory, S. G., Tomer, R., & Aharon-Peretz, J. (2005). The neuroanatomical basis of understanding sarcasm and its relationship to social cognition. *Neuropsychology*, *19*(3), 288–300.

Shamay-Tsoory, S. G., Tomer, R., Berger, B. D., Goldsher, D., & Aharon-Peretz, J. (2005). Impaired "affective theory of mind" is associated with right ventromedial prefrontal damage. *Cognitive and behavioral neurology*, *18*(1), 55–67.

Shany-Ur, T. & Shamay-Tsoory, S. G. Developmental progression of affective versus cognitive theory of mind among school-aged children. (submitted).

Shaw, P., Lawrence, E. J., Radbourne, C., Bramham, J., Polkey, C. E., & David, A. S. (2004). The impact of early and late damage to the human amygdale on "theory of mind" reasoning. *Brain*, *127*, 1535–1548.

Skuse, D., Morris, J., & Lawrence, K. (2003). The amygdala and development of the social brain. *Annals of the New York Academy of Sciences*, *1008*, 91–101.

Snodgrass, C. & Knott, F. (2006). Theory of mind in children with traumatic brain injury. *Brain Injury*, *20*(8), 825–833.

Stone, V. E. (2000). The role of the frontal lobes and the amygdala in theory of mind. In S. Baron-Cohen, H. Tager-Flusberg, & D. J. Cohen, (Eds.), *Understanding other minds: Perspectives from developmental cognitive neuroscience, 2nd Edition* (pp. 253–273). New York: Oxford University Press.

Stone, V. E., Baron-Cohen, S., & Knight, R. T. (1998). Frontal lobe contributions to theory of mind. *Journal of Cognitive Neuroscience*, *10*(5), 640–656.

Stone, V. E. Baron-Cohen, S., Calderc, A., Keanec, J., & Young, A. (2003). Acquired theory of mind impairments in individuals with bilateral amygdala lesions. *Neuropsychologia*, *41*(2), 209–220.

Stone, V. E., & Gerrans, P. (2006). What's domain-specific about theory of mind? *Social Neuroscience*, *1*(3–4), 309–319.

Stuss, D. T. & Benson, D. F. (1986). *The frontal lobes*. New York: Raven Press.

Stuss, D. T., Gallup, G. G. Jr., & Alexander, M. P. (2001). The frontal lobes are necessary for "theory of mind." 2001. *Brain*, *124*, 279–286.

Völlm, B. A., Taylor, A. N. W., Richardson, P., Corcoran, R., Stirling, J., McKie, S., Deakin, J. F. W., & Elliott, R. (2006). Neuronal correlates of theory of mind and empathy: A functional magnetic resonance imaging study in a nonverbal task. *Neuroimage*, *29*, 90–98.

Wellman, H. M. (2002). Understanding the psychological world: developing a theory of mind. In U. Goswami (Ed.), *Blackwell handbook of childhood cognitive development* (pp. 167–187). Oxford: Blackwell Publishing.

Wellman, H. M. & Liu, D. (2004). Scaling of theory-of-mind tasks. *Child Development*, *75*(2), 523–541.

PART 7

Applications

The Cognitive Neuroscience of Strategic Thinking

Meghana Bhatt *and* Colin F. Camerer

Abstract

This chapter focuses on some emerging elements of a neuroscientific basis for behavioral game theory. The premise of this chapter is that game theory can be useful in helping to elucidate the neural basis of strategic thinking. The great strength of game theory is that it offers precision in defining what players are likely to do and suggesting algorithms of reasoning and learning. Whether people are using these algorithms can be estimated from behavior and from psychological observables (such as response times and eye tracking of attention), and used as parametric regressors to identify candidate brain circuits that appear to encode those regressors.

Keywords: game theory, theory of mind, strategic thinking, insula, cingulate, precuneus, medial prefrontal cortex

Game theory is the mathematical analysis of strategic interaction. It has become a standard tool in economics and theoretical biology, and is increasingly used in political science, sociology, and computer science. Game theory has had less impact in psychology and neuroscience so far, partly because many of the analytical concepts used to derive predictions about human behavior do not seem to correspond closely to human thinking. But recently, an approach called behavioral game theory has been developed which specifically attempts to understand strategic computations people actually make, in order to explain both choices in many different games, and various measures of biological activity (Camerer, 2003).

This chapter is about some emerging elements of a neuroscientific basis for behavioral game theory. The premise of this chapter is that game theory can be useful in helping to elucidate the neural basis of strategic thinking. The great strength of game theory is that it offers some precision in defining what players are likely to do and suggesting algorithms of reasoning and learning. Whether people are using these algorithms can be estimated from behavior and from psychological observables (such as response times and eyetracking of attention) and used as parametric regressors to identify candidate brain circuits that appear to encode those regressors. This general approach has been quite successful in studying simpler choice decisions (Glimcher, 2008) but has been used less frequently to study games.

A game is mathematically defined as a set of players, descriptions of their information, a fixed order of the sequence of choices by different players, and a function mapping players' choices and information to outcomes. It is important to note that outcomes are consequences which are not always automatically represented numerically (e.g., they might represent intangibles like political gain, status, or reproductive opportunities as well as tangibles like corporate profits or poker winnings). However, the specification of a game is completed by the assumption that players order outcomes by how much they value them (or, equivalently following some simple assumptions, they attach a numerical value or "utility" to different outcomes).

Analysis in behavioral game theory separates mathematical aspects of games into different elements which are likely to correspond, at least loosely, to distinct cognitive activity. These elements are:

1. *Strategic awareness* that outcomes are affected by actions of other players;

2. *Social preferences* over the outcomes that other players receive;

3. *Beliefs and iterated beliefs* about what other players will do and think you will do;

4. *Strategic teaching*, the valuation and adjustment of behavior by anticipating the effects of one's current action on another player's beliefs and future behavior.

5. *Learning* about the value of strategies by reinforcement or counterfactual "fictive" (model-based) feedback.

These elements are typically mixed and matched for different kinds of analysis. In games with no expectation of future interaction or reputational publicity, for example, strategic teaching plays no role. Learning, strategic teaching, and social preferences can be combined so that players anticipate how their choices will "teach" players with particular social preferences reflecting, for example, reciprocity.

Strategic Awareness

When applied to individual people, most analyses assume that players are aware their outcomes depend on choices by other players, and may try to compute what other players will do.

Evidence: Several neural studies have shown differential activation when playing a game against a computer compared to a randomized opponent (e.g., Gallagher et al., 2002: McCabe et al., 2001; Coricelli & Nagel, 2009). These papers are methodologically challenging, and some imperfect by modern standards, because it is crucial to control for comparability of the behavior of humans and computers in the presence of feedback. Nonetheless, taken together they show a clear pattern of evidence that at least some agents are using different neural processes when playing other humans.

Social Preferences

When players in a game value strategic outcomes they can legitimately include a preference for what other players get (although self-interest and indifference to what others get is often a useful simplifying benchmark with substantial predictive power). A wide range of experiments, and some field data, suggest that people exhibit a variety of "social preferences." These include: an aversion to receiving outcomes which are lower or higher than what others get ("inequality-aversion"; perhaps accompanied by social emotions such as envy and guilt; Fehr & Schmidt, 1999); a Rawls-itarian concern for both the worst-off player and the payoff total (Charness & Rabin, 2002); a desire to reciprocate kind and mean treatment by others (Dufwenberg & Kirchsteiger, 2004; Rabin, 1993); and a desire to appear to be a prosocial person (Rotemberg, 2008; Bernheim & Andreoni, 2007).

Evidence: A flurry of recent studies support the general hypothesis that these social preferences are generated by neural circuitry in the anterior cingulate cortex (ACC), insula,[1] and dorsolateral prefrontal cortex (DLPFC), which compare and blend selfish and social components (Sanfey et al., 2003). The resulting values seem to be encoded in activity in the medial OFC and/or striatal regions that reliably respond to other types of reward (Fehr & Camerer, 2007; Izuma, Saito, & Sadato, 2008). Tricomi et al. (2010) show evidence that inequality-reduction activates mOFC. Social emotions such as envy and schadenfreude (taking pleasure in harm to high-status others) are shown in Takahashi et al. (2009). Izuma shows that a sensation of being observed (by a static face "watching" you) modestly increases charitable giving, as well as fMRI activity in striatum, which is consistent with a value for social image (Izuma, Saito, & Sadato, 2010).

Important evidence comes from causal experiments that use brain stimulation or pharmacological treatments to change behavior. For example, Kosfeld et al. showed that administering synthetic oxytocin, a hormone associated with social bonding, to subjects increased trusting behavior. In another study Knoch et al. found that inhibiting activity in the right DLPFC, an area generally associated with cognitive control, using transcranial magnetic stimulation increased acceptances of ultimatum offers (Knoch et al., 2006). Crockett et al. (2008) found that tryptophan depletion increased ultimatum rejections

Other evidence comes from behavioral studies in monkeys. These data suggest that a mixture of self-interest is often the default state for most monkeys. Studies with children suggest that young children (e.g., 2–3) are generally selfish then seem to acquire a preference for equality as they age and develop (Harbaugh, Krause, & Liday, 2003).

Beliefs, Iterated Beliefs, and Strategic Choice

Assuming that players have strategic awareness and valuations of outcomes that express social preferences, the next step is the heart of game theory: What strategic choices do players make?

Choices are typically assumed to follow from some belief about what other players will do. Beliefs can be developed from experience (as in learning models) or created by analysis and introspection.

Given their beliefs, players are typically assumed to choose the strategy which has the greatest expected valuation, called a "best response." However, it is psychologically appealing and mathematically easy to relax this assumption and instead assume that choice probabilities are a "softmax" or noisy function of expected valuations (sometimes called "better response").

It is often useful to think about an iterated hierarchy of beliefs. A first-order belief is a player's guess about what the other player will do. A "second-order" belief is player A's belief about another player B's belief about what all other players will do. This concept can be naturally iterated so that n-th order beliefs are beliefs about (n-1)-th order beliefs, ad infinitum.

Note that in games with bluffing and deception, a player's planned choice and her second-order belief about what she thinks the other player expects her to do could differ. For example, a military commander might plan an attack but believe that the enemy doesn't expect an attack.

At the other extreme, it is possible that all higher-order beliefs match up with lower-order beliefs and with actual choices. This restriction is called "equilibrium." An equilibrium belief about what another player will do matches accurately what that player *will* do; it is a "no surprise" condition.

For situations that are unfamiliar or particularly complex, the idea that players are in equilibrium is not especially plausible. As a result, non-equilibrium models have been developed in which some players may systematically misperceive what others are likely to do. A widely applied class is called "cognitive hierarchy" or "level-k" models (Nagel, 1995; Stahl, 1995, Camerer, Ho, & Chong, 2004). In these models, beliefs are generated by an initial assumption that players are naïve (level-0 players). Level-1 players will then best respond to these naïve players. This leads to the iterative generation of level-n players who believe that they are playing either level-(n-1) players (in level-k variants (Nagel, 1995; Costa-Gomes, Crawford, & Broseta, 2001)), or a normalized mixture of all lower-level thinkers from 0 to k-1 (Camerer, Chong, & Ho, 2004). Starting with an initial assumption about level-0 behavior allows these models to make precise and unique predictions on how a player of a particular level will play the game.

Direct cognitive evidence supporting these theories comes from eyetracking studies. These studies indicate limited searching among future possible outcomes (Camerer et al., 1993), and patterns of search and comparison of possible payoffs which often conform rather closely to thinking steps (Costa-Gomes, Crawford, & Broseta, 2001; Costa-Gomes & Crawford, 2006; Wang, Spezio, & Camerer, 2010; Brocas et al., 2009).

However, there are only a small number of neuroimaging studies that explore the neural underpinnings of belief formation and depth of thinking.

Bhatt and Camerer considered the processes of choice and first and second order belief formation in two-player, dominance-solvable matrix games with 2–4 strategies (varying in complexity) (Bhatt & Camerer, 2005). Subjects were presented with two matrices, one showing their own payoffs and the other showing their opponent's payoffs. They were asked to choose a row, understanding that the other player would choose a column and they would both get the rewards corresponding to that row-column position in their respective matrices.

Each trial presented one of three different tasks: Making a choice in the game, guessing what the opponent would choose (first-order beliefs), or guessing what the opponent thought the other player's first order beliefs about her own choice were (second-order beliefs). Subjects were rewarded at the end of the experiment for their choices, correctly guessing the opponent's strategy, and correctly guessing their opponent's first-order beliefs.

A primary goal of the study was to compare activity during the process of making a choice and the process of stating a belief. We defined equilibrium game trials as those in which the subject's choice was a best response to first-order belief, her first-order belief was a best response to her second-order belief (i.e., she guessed as if she thought the other subject was best-responding), and her second-order belief match her own actual choice.

Table 62.1 shows an example of finding the equilibrium through elimination of dominated strategies using a game from Bhatt and Camerer. Player 1 chooses a row and player two chooses a column. Notice that choosing B is better than choosing C for Player 1 regardless of Player 2's choice, so Player 1 should never choose it. This means that C is a "dominated" strategy for Player 1 and it can be eliminated. Eliminating C makes AA dominated by BB for Player 2 (assuming C is played with low or zero probability). But eliminating AA makes A the iteratedly dominant strategy for Player 1. Thus the only equilibrium for the game is for Player 1 to choose A and Player 2 to choose BB. In equilibrium Player 1 would choose A, her first-order belief would be that Player 2 will pick BB and her second-order belief should be that Player 2 knows that she will pick A. However, notice how these predictions depend sensitively on steps of iterated reasoning and on beliefs that others are rational (and think you are rational. . .).

Activation patterns during choice and belief elicitation trials were not significantly different during equilibrium trials except in a small area of the ventral striatum (probably associated with differential rewards in the two types of trials). On the other hand, when subjects' beliefs and choices were out of equilibrium, the choice task elicited significantly more frontal lobe activations, particularly in the medial prefrontal cortex (mPFC). In many of these subjects, the chain of belief broke down at the second-order belief level, that is, first-order beliefs were not best responses to second-order beliefs, but second-order beliefs matched choices (i.e., subjects thought their choices were predicted

by other subjects). This pattern is consistent with the hypothesis that subjects think choices are more transparent than they actually are or, alternatively, that they tend to make choices first and then espouse those choices as second-order beliefs.

In addition, individual differences were probed in order to assess how differences in skill might correlate to neural activity. We defined a measure of "strategic intelligence" (SIQ) based on the average payoff the player would have received given his choices, and the average correctness of his first- and second-order beliefs. High SIQ subjects had significantly greater activation in both the precuneus and the caudate. Conversely, people who were worse at these games had significantly more activation in the left insular cortex.

In a more recent study, Kuo et al. focused on two classes of games, each of which was subdivided into two types (Kuo et al., 2009). First they studied dominance solvable games that required different numbers of iterations removing dominated strategies in order to arrive at the Nash solution. These games were generally asymmetric and required an individual to shift back and forth between two different incentive schemes (one's own and one's opponents') in order to solve them. They were also explicitly spatially organized in that subjects were given targets that were either spatially or arithmetically related to the other players' choices. In one type of game that they call "box games," people were shown grids of various shapes and sizes and given spatial targets on the grid; for example, to pick the space to the left of the space chosen by their opponent. In the other, which they called number games, subjects were shown number lines and similarly given targets that depended on the other player's choice; for example, to choose a number that was as close as possible to twice the other player's choice. The games were structured so that if both players made the Nash predicted choice they would both receive a payoff. Most players did manage to find the Nash solution in both types of games. They found that activation in the precuneus scaled with the difficulty of these games.

They also studied simple matching games that had the same format as the dominance solvable games, but where your target was simply to choose the same option as your opponent. They found that the middle insula correlated with a measure of how focal a game was, essentially whether there was an "obvious" choice that would tend to draw people's attention. This measure was also correlated with the average payoff from each game.

Table 62.1 A game "solvable" by iterated deletion of dominated strategies (Bhatt, Camerer 1995)

Player 1 Payoffs		Player 2 Payoffs		
AA	BB	AA	BB	
A 43	86	A 10	37	
B 84	57	B 44	60	Dominated by A if BB is played
C 68	39	C 73	6	Dominated by B
		Dominated by BB if C is not played		

Coricelli and Nagel focused on a game called the "p-beauty contest" in which people attempt to choose a number between 0 and 100 that is closest to p (e.g., 2/3) times the average number chosen (Coricelli & Nagel, 2009). Their subjects played a series of games with different values of the multiplier p. The Nash equilibrium for these games is to choose 0 when p < 1 and 100 when p > 1 (when p = 1 any choice is an equilibrium). This is a symmetric game, so considering another player's action is, in theory, the same as considering one's own.

Notice that the Nash equilibrium is not generally the best way to play the game, because the ideal choice is just one step below the average of all choices (i.e., p times the average); so 0 is too low of a number if others are not all choosing the Nash equilibrium as well. For example, if p = 2/3, the first natural impulse may be to choose 2/3 * 50 = 33. However, if you believe that most people will arrive at the same conclusion, you may wish to go another step to 2/3 * 33 = 22. Repeating this process will eventually lead to the Nash solution of 0. While the populations studied in Kuo et al. almost all reached the unique Nash solution (possibly due to the spatial nature of their games), in numerous studies of the p-beauty contest the optimal strategy against a population of players is an intermediate value rather than the extrema predicted by the Nash solution. Coricelli and Nagel classified people according to the average number of "steps of thinking" in the games according to a version of the cognitive hierarchy model, and found that there was a significantly less activation in the mPFC in level-1 players than in level-2 and above thinkers. They also found that the superior temporal sulcus (STS) and temporoparietal junction (TPJ) were more active when subjects played other people when compared to playing a computer, but were not modulated by steps of thinking.

Both Kuo et al. and Coricelli and Nagel address "depth" of processing in games, but find completely different areas. Kuo et al. find that the precuneus correlates with the difficulty of a game (a proxy for the number of steps of thinking required). On the other hand, Coricelli and Nagel find that activity in the mPFC correlates with "levels of thinking" in the multiperson guessing game. These differences are most likely related to the differences between the classes of games themselves. Of particular note is the asymmetry of the Kuo et al. games versus the symmetry of the p-beauty contest. Reasoning in an asymmetric game requires constant shifts of attention between payoff structures in order to generate

higher order beliefs, while in a symmetric game reasoning can continue without such shifts.

Yoshida et al. (2008) create a recursive-belief model similar to the cognitive hierarchy approaches and apply it to the game of stag hunt (Yoshida, Dolan, & Friston, 2008). In their games, two low-value rabbits are present on a two-dimensional grid. A high-value stag is also present. Two players make sequential one-step moves either toward the stag (who also moves) or toward a rabbit. The game ends when either of the players reaches a rabbit target or when the two players end up adjacent to the stag, "capturing" it.

They formalize a Bayesian notion of steps of recursive anticipation. The model creates trial-by-trial computational regressors. Using fMRI, they find that entropy about opponent thinking steps (strategic uncertainty) activates the medial prefrontal cortex (paracingulate) and posterior cingulate. The level of strategy the subject seems to use is correlated with DLPFC (-50,28,32), as well as frontal eye field and superior parietal lobule. They suggest that the paracingulate is activated in mentalizing to determine an opponent's strategic thinking type, and the DLPFC is involved in implementing planning ahead and working memory during "deep" strategic thinking' (planning ahead several moves, as in chess).

Strategic Teaching and Influence Value

In the studies discussed above, beliefs were formed in a vacuum without any input from the other player. However, when two or more players are paired together in a "repeated game," it can pay for one player to take actions which deliberately manipulate beliefs of the other player. A common example of this sort of "strategic teaching" is bluffing in poker: Bluffing is betting aggressively to make opponents believe you have a winning hand, so they should quit betting and fold their cards. Another example is taking actions in one period that will influence what others will choose in future periods (Chong, Camerer, & Ho, 2006). The two studies discussed below deal explicitly with these types of belief manipulation.

Hampton, Bossaerts, and O'Doherty study strategic teaching in a two-player game (Hampton, Bossaerts, & O'Doherty, 2008). In the game an "employee" chooses to either "work" or "shirk" and an employer simultaneously chooses to "inspect" or not to inspect. The payoffs were as follows (see Table 62.2):

The employee's and the employer's incentives are completely misaligned—when the employee makes

Table 62.2 Inspection game payoff matrix

	Inspect	Don't inspect
Work	50, 0	0, 100
Shirk	0, 25	50, 0

money, the employer makes nothing and vice versa. There is no combination of strategies for each player so that each strategy is a best response to the other—in game theory terms, there is no "pure strategy equilibrium." Instead, if the employer chooses inspect with 50% probability, and the employee chooses shirk with 80% probability, then those percentages yield (weak) best responses and form a mixed strategy equilibrium.

The authors compared the actual data from this study to the predictions of three different models. The first model was a simple reinforcement learning task which assumes that people will tend to play a strategy more when it is rewarding and less when it is not rewarding. This model has been most successfully applied to "model-free" learning in non-strategic decisions in which players learn reward likelihoods but there is not another player with incentives involved.

The second model they considered was a fictitious play model where players formed expectations about likely opponent play rather than about the reward value of an action. This adds one level of belief formation since players consider and learn about opponent action, but it does not take into account the incentives of the opponent.

The third model is an "influence model" where players not only form expectations about opponent play via their history, but assume that opponents are trying to do the same, so that their current actions will influence how the opponent plays in future periods. In the influence model an employee might expect that after working several periods in a row the employer will stop inspecting, and then the employee may safely shirk. The influence model incorporates second-order belief, allowing players to make inferences about how their actions might affect the opponent's beliefs.

Hampton et al. (2008) found that for most subjects, the influence model was the best predictor of behavior in this task. They analyzed two areas generally thought to be part of the "theory of mind" or mentalizing circuit, the superior temporal sulcus (STS) and medial prefrontal cortex (mPFC), and found that these areas correlated with different aspects of the influence model. mPFC activity correlated to

predicted reward in the influence model, while the STS correlated to the component of prediction error related to second-order belief, specifically this area correlated with the amount that the model predicted the opponent should adapt his behavior based on your action. Notice that both this error signal and predicted reward are largest when surprise is involved. Predicted reward in the influence model is largest when the subject switches strategies; that is, when the subject surprises his opponent. Similarly, the influence update signal is largest when a player's own action is in opposition to his second-order belief. The difference in the finding is in the timing of the signals—the mPFC correlates to the decision to surprise your opponent, while the STS fires when the feedback is seen about the trial.

An interesting type of strategic deception emerged in a study of bargaining by Bhatt, Lohrenz, Camerer, and Montague (2010). In the game, two players, a buyer and a seller, play 60 rounds of the game. At the beginning of each round the "buyer" is informed of her private value v, which is an integer drawn with uniform probability between 1 and 10. She is then asked to "suggest a price" s to the seller, an integer between 1 and 10. The seller sees this suggestion and sets a price p. If the seller's price is less than the value (known only to the buyer), the trade executes and the seller receives p while the buyer receives $v-p$ (the difference between the true value and the sell price, also called the economic surplus). If the seller's price exceeds the buyer's value, the trade does not execute and both parties receive nothing. Importantly, *no feedback* about whether the trade occurred is provided to either player.

In this game, Bhatt et al. identified a particular behavioral type of buyer who employs the counter-intuitive strategy of sending high suggestions when they have low values, and sending low suggestions when they have high values. In fact, this behavior is predicted as level-2 and above behavior by a modified version of the cognitive hierarchy model. The basic reasoning is that level-1 sellers will attempt to make inferences about how "honest" a buyer is by considering the history of suggestions they see in the game. If those sellers see only low suggestions they will infer that the buyer is dishonest and will then ignore the suggestion.[2] However, if they see a relatively uniform mixture of suggestions, they will tend to "trust" the suggestions, choosing low prices when they see low suggestions and high prices when they see high suggestions. Level-2 buyers will realize this and use low-value rounds, where they don't stand to earn much anyway, to generate credibility so that they can reap all the rewards from very low prices during the high-value rounds. The reasoning suggested by the hierarchy model was confirmed by the self-report of strategists during debriefing. We found that several areas of the brain, including the right DLPFC, left frontopolar cortex (Brodmann area 10, or BA10), and the retrosplenial cortex are much more active in the strategic deceivers than in the other subjects.

As mentioned before, the DLPFC has been implicated widely as an area involved in cognitive control (Sanfey et al., 2003; Knoch et al., 2006), and lateral frontopolar cortex has been implicated in goal maintenance and prospective thinking, all necessary for the strategic deceivers behavior (Burgess et al., 2007; Reynolds et al., 2009).

Learning

Many empirical studies have examined how human (and monkey) agents learn to adjust their strategies in games (see Camerer, 2003, chapter 6, for a review). Little understanding has yet emerged from neuroscience about which of these learning models is on the right track, so we will review this important topic only briefly.

Two popular theories are reinforcement and belief learning (e.g., fictitious play). In reinforcement learning, strategies which are chosen are reinforced according to their payoff (possibly normalized by an aspiration level). In belief learning, players adjust beliefs about how others are expected to play then choose strategies with high expected payoffs given those adjusted beliefs. Notice that these two models correspond to the first two models considered in Hampton et al.

Camerer and Ho first pointed out a surprising subtle kinship between these two types of models (Camerer & Ho, 1999). Suppose beliefs are updated according to "weighted fictitious play," in which updated beliefs are simply a (weighted) running average of an opponent's past play (Fudenberg & Levine, 1998). Belief learning of this type is exactly mathematically equivalent to a generalized type of reinforcement in which strategy values are reinforced by their actual payoff (if they were chosen) or their "fictive" or foregone payoff (if they were not chosen). This insight invites a general model in which foregone payoffs are weighted δ times as much as received payoffs. Then $\delta = 0$ corresponds to reinforcement and $\delta = 1$ corresponds to fictitious play belief learning (akin to "model based" learning in computer science language). Empirical estimates

from behavior in many games suggest that the fictive learning weight δ is substantial, clearly between 0 and 1.

The available neuroscience studies also clearly reject the simple base case in which $\delta = 0$. Lohrenz et al. show fictive learning signals in VStr similar to prediction error signals from actual rewards (Lohrenz et al., 2007). Hayden, Pearson, and Platt (2009) also record fictive learning signals from individual neurons. Mobbs et al. (2009) show activation in response to rewards earned by similar others, which suggests a more general model in which learning is both fictive and dependent on "social distance" from others.

King-Casas et al. (2008) and Chiu et al. (2008) consider behavior and neural activity during the trust game in subjects with borderline personality disorder and autism, respectively. Borderline personality disorder (BPD) is characterized by emotional disregulation, including some level of paranoia, often leading to unstable personal relationships. In the King-Casas experiment, subjects with BPD were paired as trustees with healthy investors matched on education, IQ, and socioeconomic status, and played 10 rounds of the trust game.

The major behavioral finding is that pairs that included BPD subjects earned significantly less money in total than those involving two healthy subjects. This appears to be due to markedly lower levels of investment in the later rounds of the game when the trustee had BPD. In healthy pairs, breakdowns of cooperation were often followed by "coaxing" behavior by the trustees: Trustees would repay all or most of the money they received during the trial. This signaled trustworthiness to the investor and often restored a cooperative interaction. Investments appeared to decrease in these pairs because BPD subjects failed to effectively signal their trustworthiness to the investors via this coaxing behavior.

The study found that people with BPD had significantly decreased activation in the anterior insula in response to low investments as compared to controls. Activity in the anterior insula has often been linked to subjects experiencing a violation of social norms (low offers in the ultimatum game). A lack of activity here when BPD subjects see low investment implies a failure to interpret low offers as violations. The authors hypothesize that this failure to detect a violation of social norms impairs their ability to respond appropriately with coaxing. In turn this failure to coax leads to decreased cooperation throughout the experiment and fewer returns to both parties.

Chiu et al. (2008) find that autistic subjects had much weaker signals in regions of the cingulate specialized to "self" signals about payoffs and actions of oneself, and possibly how these actions might be interpreted by others.

Discussion

The interpretation of the neural data from any of these experiments is, by necessity, fairly speculative. This field of study is relatively new, and little is known about cognition in general. It is possible, and even likely, that the ways in which we a priori decompose these tasks bears little resemblance to how the brain actually performs computations in games. However, by taking the results of these studies and others together, we may be able to form a more coherent picture of these processes. There are several areas that appear in multiple studies: the mPFC, the precuneus, the insula, and cingulate cortex. We will summarize evidence and speculate about each of these areas next.

mPFC

Activation in the dorsal part of the mPFC was found in three of the five studies reviewed above. Bhatt and Camerer (2005) found that the area was more active when people were making choices in an out-of-equilibrium game as opposed to simply giving their beliefs about what the other player's choice might be in such a game. Coricelli and Nagel (2009) found that the area was more active in level-2 as opposed to level-1 thinkers and correlated with strategic intelligence. Yoshida et al. (2008) found that the area correlates to uncertainty about the sophistication of another player. And Hampton et al. (2008) found that the area correlated with predicted reward using a model that explicitly incorporates second-order beliefs.

The dorsal mPFC (and the mPFC more generally), has been implicated in a variety of social cognition tasks including self-knowledge and perspective taking (Amodio & Frith, 2006; D'Argembeau et al., 2007). The area has also been implicated in nonsocial tasks where cognitive control is required (Ridderinkhof et al., 2004; Li et al., 2006). Amodio and Frith hypothesize that the region is involved with modulating behavior based on anticipated value, with the most posterior areas dealing with simple action values, and representations getting increasingly abstract and complex as you approach the frontal pole.

Both the social cognition and cognitive control literatures about this area can be understood under this rubric. For example, perspective taking can be viewed as a specific aspect of predicting the value of various actions, especially when these actions may have social consequences. The prediction is that as those consequences become more complex and contingency dependent, they will be represented in more and more anterior areas of the mPFC. So, simple action values would be represented in posterior parts of the mPFC, while more complex strategy values would be represented in the anterior parts of the mPFC.

Interestingly, the three activations mention above lie in different regions of this spectrum, with the Bhatt and Camerer activation at y = 36, the activation in Coricelli and Nagel at y = 48, and the Hampton et al. activation at y = 63. The Bhatt and Camerer activation pertained to situations when they were out of equilibrium, which in these games generally implied a shallow belief-formation process yielding a simple valuation procedure. The Coricelli and Nagel activation, on the other hand, corresponds to higher-level thinkers who best respond in a one-shot game to a population, implying a deeper and more complex understanding of the game. Finally, the Hampton et al. activation corresponds to high-predicted-value trials in a repeated game where subjects understand not only how their current action will affect their payoff, but how their history of actions have affected it, adding yet another layer of complexity.

Precuneus

The precuneus is another area that appears to have a relation to strategic thinking in games. It is seen in Bhatt and Camerer (2005), Kuo et al. (2009), and Bhatt et al. (2010), all of which considered computations in asymmetric games. Bhatt and Camerer (2005), found that activity in the area correlates between subjects with a measure of the subject's strategic intelligence; and Kuo et al. found that activation in the area correlates within subject with the difficulty of the game. The precuneus has reciprocal connections with many of the other areas mentioned in this chapter, including the mPFC, the cingulate (including both the ACC and retrosplenial cortices), and the dorsolateral prefrontal cortex.

The precuneus has been implicated in a host of tasks, including episodic memory retrieval (Shallice et al., 1994; Fletcher et al., 1995; Lundstrom et al., 2003; Addis et al., 2004), attention guidance and switching (both between objects, and among object features) (Culham et al., 1998; Le, Pardo, & Hu,

1998; Nagahama et al., 1999; Simon et al., 2002), a variety of imagery tasks (Cavanna & Trimble, 2006), and perspective taking (Vogeley et al., 2004; Vogeley et al., 2001; Ruby & Decety, 2001), in addition to being one of the most active areas of the "default network" of the brain (i.e., areas that are unusually active when subjects are conscious and at rest) (Raichle et al., 2001).

It seems unlikely that episodic memory retrieval is involved in playing a series of one shot games, since the history of play is irrelevant to both current and future payoffs. However, the precuneus' possible role in perspective taking and attentional control both suggest interesting interpretations. The fact that activation in the precuneus is only seen in asymmetric games, rather than the similarly dominance-solvable, but symmetric p-beauty contest game, suggests that in strategic situations the precuneus may have something to do with attentional control. In order to make good choices in asymmetric games, subjects need to switch their attention between two distinct sets of incentives: one's own, and one's opponent's. This is also consistent with the correlation of activation in the area with task difficulty in Kuo et al. since "task difficulty" in their games is defined as the number of iterative attentional switches required to reach the equilibrium solution.

The between-subject correlation of activation in the precuneus with strategic intelligence (SIQ) found in Bhatt and Camerer (2005) is consistent with the view that strategic ability should be related to one's ability to "think about the other guy," that is, the ability to consider the other players incentives in addition to your own. Several studies show that the precuneus is more active when people take third-person as opposed to first-person perspective in a situation (Vogeley et al., 2004; Ruby & Decety, 2001; Farrer & Frith, 2002). Thus, subjects with high SIQ may earn more in these games, be more likely to take a more objective third-person perspective in the game in order generate more accurate beliefs, and thereby play more effectively.

Insula
The middle insula also appears in Bhatt and Camerer, and Kuo et al., though in the latter the activation is found in a different set of games. Bhatt and Camerer find that the middle insula correlates negatively between subjects with SIQ, while Kuo et al. find that it correlates positively within subject with how focal a matching game is.

The insula is generally thought to be responsible for interoception, that is, the perception of one's own internal state. It has been proposed that the information received in the posterior insula is processed and re-represented in the anterior insula as subjective emotion, and is important for the feeling of self (Craig, 2002; Critchley, 2005). While most insula activations in the neuroeconomics literature are in the anterior insula (Sanfey et al., 2003; King-Casas et al., 2008, Preuschoff, Quartz, & Bossaerts, 2008), the activations from Bhatt and Camerer and Kuo et al. sit in the middle insula around $y = 0$. Activations in these more posterior regions are thought to correspond to more basic, less contextualized, visceral sensations, while the anterior insula is important for processing and reflecting on these sensations via its connection to more midline structures (Critchley, 2005; Keysers & Gazzola, 2007). These posterior, pre-reflective representations may correspond to more subconscious, fast, decision making.

This corresponds again to the idea that people with low SIQ are less thoughtful about their payoffs, responding more to first impulses rather than considering the opponents actions thoughtfully. It is equally relevant to the matching games studied by Kuo, where following one's first impulse is likely to be the best route to coordination.

Cingulate
Like the insula and mPFC, different positions within the cingulate appear to correspond to different types of representations. It has been proposed that the cingulate contains a "self-other" mapping wherein the anterior and posterior sections correspond to representations of others and the middle section corresponds to representations of the self (Tomlin et al., 2006). In addition, the ACC has been implicated in cognitive control and error detection (Carter, 1998), and paired with the insula in discussions of representation of the self (Craig, 2002).

The area found in Bhatt et al. is further posterior and inferior to most of the other posterior cingulate activations found in neuroeconomic studies, in the retrosplenial cortex (RSpl). The RSpl has dense connections to the neighboring parahippocampal gyrus and the precuneus discussed above and has been implicated mainly in studies of episodic memory and navigation, and is often consider part of a "spatial working memory" system. It has also been conjectured as part of a shared network used to both consider the past and imagine the future (Addis, Wong, & Schacter, 2007; Luhmann et al., 2008), and thinking about other people's thoughts (Saxe &

Powell, 2006). It has also been correlated with skill and difficulty in non-navigational problem solving tasks (Baker et al., 1996; Unterrainer et al., 2004).

Two of the key components of the strategic deceiver's play are his interest in future payoffs and his ability to understand how the seller might process his suggestions (thinking about the seller's thoughts). The activation of this portion of the cingulate specifically in these types may relate to the fact that they are considering their future credibility when they send suggestions.

Conclusion

Game theory has emerged as a standard language in social sciences and theoretical biology. It could also be a useful organizing framework in cognitive neuroscience. An influential new approach is to use algorithmic or computational models to generate numerical quantities, either inferred from choices or measured directly, which can then be used as regressors in standard fMRI GLM (and in analyses of other data). Game theory is generally well equipped to supply computational models, and cognitive hierarchy models are especially useful. In addition, these models might organize observations about cognitive development across the lifecycle, individual differences, and psychiatric disorders. Disorders can be seen as deficits in strategic computation (as exemplified by the studies of King-Casas et al., 2008, and Chiu et al., 2008), lending precision to the understanding of their organic basis and possible treatments.

Notes

1 Chapman et al. (2009) show that facial muscles which wrinkle when people are disgusted also wrinkle when they evaluate unfairly low ultimatum offers, and facial EMG measures correlate with rejection of those offers.

2 Note that the unique Nash equilibrium is for no information to be translated (called "babbling" in game theory jargon). The reason is that if sellers reacted to the specific suggestion s* as if it indicated value v(s*), they would set a price of p=v(s*). But buyers anticipating this seller policy would then announce the price s* for all values higher than v, disconfirming the seller's belief. It is easy to extend this logic and show that there is no credible announcement s which conveys information about v.

References

Addis, D. R., McIntosh, A. R., Moscovitch, M., Crawley, A. P., & McAndrews, M. P. (2004). Characterizing spatial and temporal features of autobiographical memory retrieval networks: A partial least squares approach. *NeuroImage, 23*(4), 1460–1471.

Addis, D. R., Wong, A. T., & Schacter, D. L. (2007). Remembering the past and imagining the future: Common and distinct neural substrates during event construction and elaboration. *Neuropsychologia, 45*(7), 1363–1377.

Amodio, D. M. & Frith, C. D. (2006). Meeting of minds: The medial frontal cortex and social cognition. *Nature Reviews Neuroscience, 7*(4), 268.

Baker, S. C., Rogers, R. D., Owen, A. M., Frith, C. D., Dolan, R. J., Frackowiak, R. S. et al. (1996). Neural systems engaged by planning: A PET study of the Tower of London task. *Neuropsychologia, 34*(6), 515–526.

Bernheim, B. D. & Andreoni, J. (2007). *Social image and the 50–50 norm: Theory and experimental evidence.* Econometrica 2009.

Bhatt, M. & Camerer, C. F. (2005). Self-referential thinking and equilibrium as states of mind in games: fMRI evidence. *Games and Economic Behavior, 52*(2), 424.

Bhatt, M., Lohrenz, T., Camerer, C., & Montague, R. (2010). Neural signatures of strategic types in a two-person bargaining game. *Proceedings of the National Academy of Sciences, 107*(46), 19720–19725.

Brocas, I., Carrillo, J. D., Wang, S., & Camerer, C. F. (2009). *Measuring attention and strategic behavior in games with private information.* Available at SSRN: http://ssrn.com/abstract=1496997.

Burgess, P. W., Dumontheil, I., & Gilbert, S. J. (2007) The gateway hypothesis of rostral prefrontal cortex (area 10) function. *Trends in Cognitive Science, 11*, 290–298.

Camerer, C. & Ho, T. H. (1999). Experience-weighted attraction learning in normal form games. *Econometrica, 67*(4), 827–874.

Camerer, C. F. (2003). *Behavioral game theory,* Princeton, NJ: Princeton University Press.

Camerer, C. F., Ho, T. H., & Chong, J. K. (2004). A cognitive hierarchy model of games, *Quarterly Journal of Economics, 119*(3), 861–898.

Camerer, C. F., Johnson, E., Rymon, T., & Sen, S. (1993). Cognition and framing in sequential bargaining for gains and losses. In K. G. Binmore, A. P. Kirman, & P. Tani (Eds.). *Frontiers of game theory* (pp. 27–47). Cambridge: MIT Press.

Carter, C. S. (1998). Anterior cingulate cortex, error detection, and the online monitoring of performance. *Science, 280*(5364), 747–749.

Cavanna, A. E. & Trimble, M. R. (2006). The precuneus: A review of its functional anatomy and behavioural correlates. *Brain: A journal of neurology, 129*(3), 564–583.

Chapman, H. A., Kim, D. A., Susskind, J. M., & Anderson, A. K. (2009). In bad taste: Evidence for the oral origins of moral disgust. *Science, 323*(5918), 1222–1226.

Charness, G. & Rabin, M. (2002). Understanding social preferences with simple tests. *Quarterly Journal of Economics, 117*(3), 817–869.

Chiu, P. H., Kayali, M. A., Kishida, K. T., Tomlin, D., Klinger, L. G., Klinger, M. R., et al. (2008). Self responses along cingulate cortex reveal quantitative neural phenotype for high-functioning autism. *Neuron, 57*(3), 463–473.

Chong, J., Camerer, C. F., & Ho, T. H. (2006). A learning-based model of repeated games with incomplete information. *Games and Economic Behavior, 55*(2), 340–371.

Coricelli, G. & Nagel, R. 2009. Neural correlates of depth of strategic reasoning in medial prefrontal cortex. *PNAS, 106*(23), 9163–9168.

Costa-Gomes, M., Crawford, V. P., & Broseta, B. (2001). Cognition and behavior in normal-form games: An experimental study. *Econometrica, 69*(5), 1193–1235.

Costa-Gomes, M. A. & Crawford, V. P. (2006). Cognition and behavior in two-person guessing games: An experimental study. *American Economic Review*, 96(5), 1737–1768.

Craig, A. D. (2002). How do you feel? Interoception: The sense of the physiological condition of the body. *Nature Reviews. Neuroscience*, 3(8), 655–666.

Critchley, H. D. (2005). Neural mechanisms of autonomic, affective, and cognitive integration. *The Journal of Comparative Neurology*, 493(1), 154–166.

Crockett, M. J., Clark, L., Tabibnia, G., Lieberman, M. D., & Robbins, T. W. (2008). Serotonin modulates behavioral reactions to unfairness. *Science*, 320(5884), 1739.

Culham, J. C., Brandt, S. A., Cavanagh, P., Kanwisher, N. G., Dale, A. M., & Tootell, R. B. (1998). Cortical fMRI activation produced by attentive tracking of moving targets. *Journal of Neurophysiology*, 80(5), 2657–2670.

D'Argembeau, A., Ruby, P., Collette, F., Degueldre, C., Balteau, E., Luxen, A., et al. (2007). Distinct regions of the medial prefrontal cortex are associated with self-referential processing and perspective taking. *Journal of Cognitive Neuroscience*, 19(6), 935–944.

Dufwenberg, M. & Kirchsteiger, G. (2004). A theory of sequential reciprocity. *Games and Economic Behavior*, 47, 268–298.

Farrer, C. & Frith, C. D. (2002). Experiencing oneself vs another person as being the cause of an action: The neural correlates of the experience of agency. *NeuroImage*, 15(3), 596–603.

Fehr, E. & Camerer, C. F. (2007). Social neuroeconomics: The neural circuitry of social preferences. *Trends in Cognitive Sciences*, 11(10), 419–427.

Fehr, E. & Schmidt, K. M. (1999). A theory of fairness, competition, and cooperation. *Quarterly Journal of Economics*, 114(3), 817–868.

Fletcher, P. C., Frith, C. D., Baker, S. C., Shallice, T., Frackowiak, R. S., & Dolan, R .J. (1995). The mind's eye—precuneus activation in memory-related imagery. *NeuroImage*, 2(3), 195–200.

Fudenberg, D. & Levine, D. (1998). *Theory of learning in games*. Cambridge, MA: MIT Press.

Gallagher, H. L., Jack, A. I., Poepstorff, A., & Frith, C. D. (2002). Imaging the intentional stance in a competitive game. *NeuroImage*, 16, 814–821.

Glimcher, P. W., Camerer, C., Fehr, E., & Poldrack, R. (Eds.) (2008). *Neuroeconomics: Decision making and the brain*. London: Academic Press.

Hampton, A., Bossaerts, P., & O'Doherty, J. (2008). Neural correlates of mentalizing-related computations during strategic interactions in humans. *PNAS*, 105(18), 6741–6746.

Harbaugh, W. T., Krause, K., & Liday, S. (2003). Bargaining by children. *http://papers.ssrn.com/sol3/papers.cfm?abstract_id=436504*.

Hayden, B., Pearson, M., & Platt, M. L. (2009). Fictive learning signals in anterior cingulate cortex. *Science*, 324(5929), 948–950.

Izuma, K., Saito, D. N., & Sadato, N. (2010). Processing of the incentive for social approval in the ventral striatum during charitable donation. *Journal of Cognitive Neuroscience*, 22(4), 621–631.

Izuma, K., Saito, D. N., & Sadato, N. (2008). Processing of social and monetary rewards in the human striatum. *Neuron*, 58(2), 284–294.

Keysers, C. & Gazzola, V. (2007). Integrating simulation and theory of mind: From self to social cognition. *Trends in Cognitive Sciences*, 11(5), 194–196.

King-Casas, B., Sharp, C., Lomax-Bream, L., Lohrenz, T., Fonagy, P., & Montague, P. R. (2008). The rupture and repair of cooperation in borderline personality disorder. *Science*, 321(5890), 806–810.

Knoch, D., Pascual-Leone, A., Meyer, K., Treyer, V., & Fehr, E. (2006). Diminishing reciprocal fairness by disrupting the right prefrontal cortex. *Science*, 314(5800), 829–832.

Kosfield, M., Heinrichs, M., Zak, P., Fischbacher, U., & Fehr, E. (2005) "Oxytocin increases trust in humans" *Nature, 435*, 673–676.

Kuo, W. J., Sjostrom, T., Chen, Y. P., Wang, Y. H., & Huang, C. Y. (2009). Intuition and deliberation: Two systems for strategizing in the brain. *Science*, 324(5926), 519–522.

Le, T. H., Pardo, J. V., & Hu, X. (1998). 4 T-fMRI study of nonspatial shifting of selective attention: Cerebellar and parietal contributions. *Journal of Neurophysiology*, 79(3), 1535–1548.

Li, C. S., Huang, C., Constable, R. T., & Sinha, R. (2006). Imaging response inhibition in a stop-signal task: Neural correlates independent of signal monitoring and post-response processing. *The Journal of Neuroscience: The Official Journal of the Society for Neuroscience*, 26(1), 186–192.

Lohrenz, T., McCabe, K., Camerer, C. F., & Montague, P. R. (2007). Neural signature of fictive learning signals in a sequential investment task. *PNAS*, 104(22), 9493–9498.

Luhmann, C. C., Chun, M. M., Yi, D. J., Lee, D., & Wang, X. J. (2008). Neural dissociation of delay and uncertainty in intertemporal choice. *The Journal of Neuroscience*, 28(53), 14459–14466.

Lundstrom, B., Petersson, K. M., Andersson, J., Johansson, M., Fransson, P., & Ingvar, M. (2003). Isolating the retrieval of imagined pictures during episodic memory: activation of the left precuneus and left prefrontal cortex. *NeuroImage*, 20(4), 1934.

McCabe, K., Houser, D., Ryan, L., Smith, V., & Trouard, T. (2001). A functional imaging study of cooperation in two-person reciprocal exchange. *Proceedings of the National Academy of Sciences of the United States of America*, 98(20), 11832–11835.

Mobbs, D., Yu, R., Meyer, M., Passamonti, L., Seymour, B., Calder, A. J., et al. (2009). A key role for similarity in vicarious reward. *Science*, 324, 900.

Nagahama, Y., Okada, T., Katsumi, Y., Hayashi, T., Yamauchi, H., Sawamoto, N., et al. (1999). Transient neural activity in the medial superior frontal gyrus and precuneus time locked with attention shift between object features. *NeuroImage*, 10(2), 193–199.

Nagel, R. (1995). Unraveling in guessing games: An experimental study. *The American Economic Review*, 85(5), 1313–1326.

Preuschoff, K., Quartz, S. R., & Bossaerts, P. (2008). Human insula activation reflects risk prediction errors as well as risk. *Journal of Neuroscience*, 28(11), 2745–2752.

Rabin, M. (1993). Incorporating fairness into game theory and economics. *American Economic Review*, 83(5), 1281–1302.

Raichle, M. E., MacLeod, A. M., Snyder, A. Z., Powers, W. J., Gusnard, D. A., & Shulman, G. L. (2001). A default mode of brain function. *Proceedings of the National Academy of Sciences of the United States of America*, 98(2), 676–682.

Reynolds, J. R., West, R., & Braver, T. (2009) Distinct neural circuits support transient and sustained processes in prospective memory and working memory. *Cerebral Cortex, 19*, 1208–1221.

Ridderinkhof, K. R., Ullsperger, M., Crone, E. A., & Nieuwenhuis, S. (2004). The role of the medial frontal cortex in cognitive control. *Science, 306*(5695), 443–447.

Rotemberg, J. J. (2008). Minimally acceptable altruism and the ultimatum game. *Journal of Economic Behavior & Organization, 66*(3–4), 457–476.

Ruby, P. & Decety, J. (2001). Effect of subjective perspective taking during simulation of action: A PET investigation of agency. *Nature Neuroscience, 4*(5), 546–550.

Sanfey, A. G., Rilling, J. K., Aronson, J. A., Nystrom, L. E., & Cohen, J. D. (2003). The neural basis of economic decision-making in the ultimatum game. *Science, 300*(5626), 1755–1758.

Saxe, R. & Powell, L. J. (2006). It's the thought that counts: Specific brain regions for one component of theory of mind. *Psychological Science, 17*(8), 692–699.

Shallice, T., Fletcher, P. C., Frith, C. D., Grasby, P., Frackowiak, R. S., & Dolan, R. J. (1994). Brain regions associated with acquisition and retrieval of verbal episodic memory. *Nature, 368*(6472), 633.

Simon, O., Mangin, J., Cohen, L., Le Bihan, D., & Dehaene, S. (2002). Topographical layout of hand, eye, calculation, and language-related areas in the human parietal lobe. *Neuron, 33*(3), 475.

Stahl, D. (1995). On players' models of other players: Theory and experimental evidence. *Games and Economic Behavior, 10*(1), 218.

Takahashi, H., Kato, M., Matsuura, M., Mobbs, D., Suhara, T., & Okubo, Y. (2009). When your gain is my pain and your pain is my gain: Neural correlates of envy and schadenfreude. *Science, 323*(5916), 937–939.

Tomlin, D., Kayali, M. A., King-Casas, B., Anen, C., Camerer, C. F., Quartz, S. R., et al. (2006). Agent-specific responses in the cingulate cortex during economic exchanges. *Science, 312*(5776), 1047–1050.

Tricomi, E., Rangel, A., Camerer, C. F., & O'Doherty, J. P. (2010). Neural evidence for inequality-averse social preferences. *Nature, 463*(7284), 1089–1091.

Unterrainer, J. M., Rahm, B., Kaller, C. P., Ruff, C. C., Spreer, J., Krause, B. J., et al. (2004). When planning fails: Individual differences and error-related brain activity in problem solving. *Cerebral Cortex, 14*(12), 1390–1397.

Vogeley, K., Bussfeld, P., Newen, A., Herrmann, S., Happe, F., Falkai, P., et al. (2001). Mind reading: neural mechanisms of theory of mind and self-perspective. *NeuroImage, 14*(1)Pt 1, 170–181.

Vogeley, K., May, M., Ritzl, A., Falkai, P., Zilles, K., & Fink, G. R. (2004). Neural correlates of first-person perspective as one constituent of human self-consciousness *Journal of Cognitive Neuroscience, 16*(5), 817–827.

Wang, J. T., Spezio, M., & Camerer, C. F. (2010). Pinocchio's pupil: Using eye tracking and pupil dilation to understand truth-telling and deception in games. *American Economic Review*, June.

Yoshida, W., Dolan, R. J., & Friston, K. J. (2008). Game theory of mind. *PLoS Computational Biology, 4*(12), e1000254.

Functional Magnetic Resonance Imaging of Deception

Jonathan G. Hakun, David Seelig, *and* Daniel D. Langleben

Abstract

The use of blood oxygenation level dependent (BOLD) functional magnetic resonance imaging (fMRI) to detect or study deception was first proposed in the lay, scientific, and technical publications in the early 2000s and reported in the peer-reviewed literature shortly thereafter. The initial experiments were based on the hypothesis that lying is an executive process requiring contributions from the cortex, responsible for response planning, execution, and inhibition, as well as the expectation that measures of central processing such as BOLD fMRI, would be a more accurate assay of deception than peripheral markers such as the polygraph. Despite a number of important advances such as differentiation of deception in single-subjects, the fMRI researchers encountered problems of validity and relevance of the experimental design already well-known to their psychophysiology and electrophysiology predecessors. This chapter will review recent progress and consider strategies for future research on the fundamental translational and theoretical issues in fMRI deception research, including ecological validity, generalizability of observed fMRI deception patterns to different deception scenarios, effects of countermeasures on detection accuracy, and potential forensic applications of fMRI-based lie-detection.

Keywords: fMRI, functional magnetic resonance imaging, deception, lie, repression, inferior frontal cortex, ventrolateral prefrontal cortex, response inhibition, lie-detection, polygraph, CIT, GKT, CQT

The use of blood-oxygenation-level dependent (BOLD) functional magnetic resonance imaging (fMRI) to detect or study deception was first proposed in the lay, scientific, and technical publications in the early 2000s (Kozel, 2000; Holden, 2001) and reported in the peer-reviewed literature shortly thereafter (Langleben et al., 2001; Spence et al., 2001; Lee et al., 2002). These studies were conceived outside of mainstream forensic and psychological science and approached experimental deception as more or less virgin territory (Langleben et al., 2001; Spence et al., 2001; Lee et al., 2002).

These early efforts progressed under the framework of two primary hypotheses: 1) Lying is an executive process requiring contributions from systems responsible for planning, response execution, and response inhibition, and 2) Measurement of central processing (i.e., BOLD fMRI signal) is a more sensitive deception assay than peripheral markers, such as the polygraph. Despite the undisputed novelty of this new biological marker, the fMRI lie-detection pioneers encountered problems well-known to their psychophysiology, electrophysiology and psychology predecessors (Rosenfeld et al., 1988;

Stern, 2003a). These problems centered around issues concerning ecological and external validity of experimental design and specificity of the observed fMRI pattern to deception. The latter bears strong resemblance to the great GKT-CIT (see "Models of Deception" section) debate in psychophysiology (Lykken, 1991). Construct validity and the reliability of using fMRI to study deception continues to be one of the most controversial topics in neuroethics (Schauer, 2010), dividing the stakeholders into those who defend the methodology, those who doubt its technical merits, and those who remain wary of the ethical implications of its application (Greely & Illes, 2007).

Models of Deception

The "Comparison Question Test" (CQT) and the "Guilty Knowledge" or "Concealed Information Test" (GKT or CIT) are the two main formats of deception-generating models in psychophysiology (Kleiner, 2001; Raskin & Honts, 2001; Stern, 2003c). Both formats have their enthusiastic proponents, with the CQT preferred by practitioners in the US, and the GKT preferred by most academics as well as forensic practitioners in Japan (Kleiner, 2001). Briefly, the CQT and its many variants (Furedy, Gigliotti, & Ben-Shakhar, 1994) postulate psychophysiological differences between a lie and either the truth or another lie of less relevance. Questions administered under the CQT are selected in a manner that attempts to balance the relative salience (i.e., familiarity and complexity) of all probe questions in order to control arousal across questions. Thus, the CQT relies heavily on the proper selection of the control or comparison conditions against which the suspected lie is tested. Selection of CQT questions by the polygraph examiner is a subjective and rather imprecise art and is the main target of the CQT's critics (Ben-Shakhar, 1991; Ben-Shakhar et al., 2002). In contrast to the CQT, the GKT format relies on soliciting a uniform denial response (usually "No") to a series of questions: while such responses will result solely in truth-telling by an innocent subject, a deceptive subject will be forced occasionally to lie in the course of maintaining uniform denial to all questions. The GKT assumes that deceptive denials will be associated with a greater psychophysiological response to an item's salience than the truthful denials. As it is difficult to physiologically distinguish salience-based responses associated with lying about an item vs. simple familiarity with it, the GKT is not generally considered appropriate in situations where the suspect may have been either a witnesses or the perpetrator of the crime or action under investigation.

The selection of baseline items to be used as contrasts for the target items is critical in both question formats when used with a physiological measure based upon relative comparison such as BOLD fMRI. For example, contrasting a BOLD fMRI signal during exposure to an image of heroin injection with a signal during exposure to a "fixation screen" without a picture would produce a statistically significant brain "activation" pattern; however, this pattern may not differentiate heroin addicts from healthy controls, because an image of heroin injection would be more salient than the crosshair to both subject groups, even if for different reasons (Langleben et al., 2008). On the other hand, comparing an image of heroin injection with an image of an empty syringe inserted into a normal antecubital vein may generate differences that would be specific to a heroin addict, by exerting a level of experimental control over brain-response variability. Using these differences to diagnose heroin addiction would require validating the specific task in the relevant population.

The above analogy applies to the fundamental difference between CQT and GKT/CIT; the CQT assumes a physiological difference between lie and control items, while the GKT assumes a difference between more or less familiar items (Stern, 2003c). Hence, of the two, only the CQT attempts "lie detection" (Raskin & Honts, 2001), while interpretation of the GKT requires an inference about the significance of a subject's familiarity with a particular item (Lykken, 1998; MacLaren, 2001). This fundamental difference is amplified when translated from a four-channel modality (polygraph) to a 20,000 to 30,000 channel 3D modality (i.e., the number of individual voxels analyzed in fMRI). Another distinction between the CQT and GKT, particularly in the context of fMRI, involves the dichotomy of "mind reading" and "lie-detection" (Haynes & Rees, 2006; Haynes, 2009). Administering a GKT in the scanner could be conceptualized as the simplest example of "mind reading," while using a modified CQT (Furedy et al., 1994) would amount to lie detection.

Seminal fMRI Studies of Deception

The three initial fMRI studies of deception differed by scenario and experimental design. Spence et al. (2001) used directed deception about autobiographical information and a block design, Lee et al.

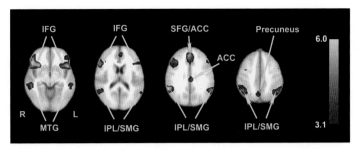

Fig. 63.1 Meta-analysis (N = 40) of two GKT/CIT studies (Langleben et al., 2002; Langleben et al., 2005), of the Lie > Truth activation contrast. The bilateral inferior frontal gyri (IFG), bilateral inferior parietal lobules (IPL), and the dorsal aspect of the anterior cingulate (ACC) are the regions most commonly associated with deception in the literature.

(2002) studied instructed malingering of memory deficits, and Langleben, Schroeder, et al. (2002) used an event-related GKT model involving a scenario of lying about concealed playing cards, adapted from psychophysiological studies (Elaad & Ben-Shakhar, 1991; Elaad, Ginton, & Jungman, 1992; Elaad & Ben-Shakhar, 1997) and forensic practice (Matte, 1996). Subjects in the Lee (2002) and Langleben (2002) studies had more leeway in choosing to lie than in Spence et al. (2001), imparting them a somewhat higher ecological validity. Despite these significant differences, the three studies revealed a similar pattern of contrasts between lie and the designated baseline condition, comprising activity in the lateral prefrontal, anterior cingulate, and inferior parietal cortices (Figure 63.1). The findings from these three studies were also similar in their failure to find areas outside the visual cortex that were more active during truth-telling than baseline (Lee et al., 2002) or lying (Spence et al., 2001; Langleben, Schroeder, et al., 2002).

The similarities between the functional anatomic pattern of experimental deception and the "Go-No-Go" task, which engages "pre-potent" response inhibition (Konishi et al., 1998; Konishi et al., 1999; Rubia et al., 2003), suggested that this basic process was also involved in deception (Langleben, Schroeder, et al., 2002). Further elaboration of this hypothesis led to predictions that the lateral prefrontal cortex (Brodmann areas 44, 45, 46, 47), an area active during response inhibition (Aron, Robbins, et al., 2004; Aron & Poldrack, 2005; Thompson-Schill et al., 2005), was a brain region critical for deception, and that deception was an executive process. There was a degree of uncertainty as to the exact anatomy, as the region associated with motor response inhibition was in the ventrolateral prefrontal cortex (VLPFC, BA 45,– 47), while some of the studies of deception reported

findings in the adjacent dorsolateral prefrontal cortex (DLPFC). The apparent lack of any executive region which was more active during truth-telling than lying suggested that lying required more of the brain's executive resources than telling the truth. Taken together, these mechanistic assumptions led to a morally-laden (and probably oversimplified) conclusion that honesty may be the baseline state of mind, at least in the normal subject population used in these initial studies (Spence, 2004; Spence et al., 2004).

Publication of these early reports generated both significant lay interest and vigorous criticism by three groups of stakeholders. A group focused on ethics and civil rights interests were concerned that the new lie-detection technology might be too effective, potentially violating freedom of thought (Boire, 2005; Tovino, 2007). Highlighting the myriad of limitations in the existing studies and citing the lay over-assessments of fMRI's capability to "read" minds, a vocal group in the neuroscience community suggested that the technology could never become effective enough to justify the ethical risks of its continued pursuit (Halber, 2007). Finally, the polygraph community circled their wagons around traditional physiological lie-detection technologies in which they had invested their trust and livelihood. A less passionate review of the data available at the time suggested a more specific set of issues of immediate relevance to what appeared to be a new topic in social neuroscience that was here to stay. First was the need to clarify the terminology. For example, it was important to distinguish between the *trait* of dishonesty and an *act* of lying (Yang et al., 2005b; Yang et al., 2007). Lie-detection (i.e., CQT) and salience detection (i.e., GKT) and the discrimination between lie and truth also had to be separated out from the positive identification of deception. These finer points were gradually recognized and addressed by a new generation of deception studies which also demonstrated the limitations of the "prepotency of truth" hypothesis (Langleben et al., 2005; Hakun et al., 2008; Gamer, Klimecki, et al., 2009; Gamer, Kosiol, et al., 2009).

Another unaddressed need was to merge concepts from existing psychology and psychophysiology work on deception with the newer concepts from experimental neuroscience and functional brain imaging. Three key parameters are used describe an fMRI deception experiment or test: the task *scenario*, the deception-generating *model*, and the fMRI *paradigm design*. As examples, a deception scenario may be "mock crime" or "resume query"; a model may be GKT, CQT, or a hybrid of the two (Langleben et al., 2005); and a paradigm design may be "event-related" or "block" (Aguirre & D'Esposito, 1999). In addition, the degree to which a subject's behavior has been dictated by the investigator is critical to the ecological validity of the experiment. This aspect of experimental deception can be described in terms of whether the deception is "endorsed," "unendorsed," or "directed" (Miller, 1993). For example, some experiments direct participants to lie by a visual or auditory command accompanying each task stimulus (Spence et al., 2001). The behavior produced by such tasks has a strong element of rule following, rather than deception per se. At the next level of ecological validity, a participant may be given an instruction to lie about a certain item (before the experiment has commenced) and provided with an incentive to maintain this behavior throughout the experiment (Langleben, Schroeder, et al., 2002). An important refinement is to separate between the individual endorsing the deceptive behavior ("confederate") and the individual administering the deception task or test (Langleben, Schroeder, et al., 2002; Abe et al., 2007). Employing "endorsement" in this fashion begins to approach real-life situations in the context of an experimental design. Finally, the risk-benefit ratio of deception is of considerable importance. Denying having committed a murder, or even lying on one's resume, entails a significantly greater penalty if the deceit is detected (and ultimately, a far greater benefit if the deceit is successful) than simply denying that one holds a five of clubs card in one's pocket for a $20 reward. So far, there has been no scientific confirmation of the assumption that data from the low risk-benefit experiments can not be extrapolated to the high risk-benefit situations (Halber, 2007). Additionally, there have been no well-controlled, peer-reviewed studies of the effect

of risk and benefit involved in deception and its associated brain response patterns.

Recent Explanatory Research

The similarity in the brain response pattern across a range of deception-generating paradigms and scenarios in the early fMRI studies of deception has been more suggestive of a lack of specificity than the existence of a "lying center" in the brain. Recent work has elaborated on this lack of specificity by comparing activity during deceptive responding to matched conditions that lack an overt deceptive response, demonstrating that CIT and related paradigms may confound a deceptive pattern of brain response with odd-ball processing (Nose et al., 2009), familiarity (Langleben et al., 2005), memory recall (Gamer, Klimecki, et al., 2009), and endogenous orientation of attention (Hakun et al., 2008). Functional anatomical overlap between these cognitive processes and deceptive responding indicates that the latter relies on a distributed network of the former, consistent with the executive process model of deception hypothesis. Variability in brain response patterns across recent studies utilizing different model parameters (i.e., higher or lower memory load demands, variability in response affordances, and frequency of lie-items) (Abe et al., 2007; Hakun et al., 2009) further supports a distributed processing account and emphasizes the need to constrain investigation of deception with respect to these processes. The robust overlap of findings in the lateral prefrontal, anterior cingulate, and inferior parietal cortices (see Hakun et al., 2008 for meta-analysis) with studies on error- (Brown & Braver, 2005) and conflict-signaling (Badre & Wagner, 2004; Botvinick et al., 2004), as well as working memory (see Owen et al., 2005 for review), rule processing (Ravizza & Carter, 2008; Bode & Haynes, 2009), and cognitive control (Cole & Schneider, 2007) justify further elaboration of the executive control model of deception.

An important study bridging the peripheral and central nervous system activity in deception has demonstrated a linear relationship between skin conductance response (SCR) amplitudes and fMRI signal in a number of brain regions, including the right inferior frontal cortex (Gamer et al., 2007). This study serves as an example of an approach to probing the specificity of a brain region to deception through multi-modality experiments. The question of specificity of brain systems or regions to deception is a special case of the larger picture of focal and distributed systems governing behavior

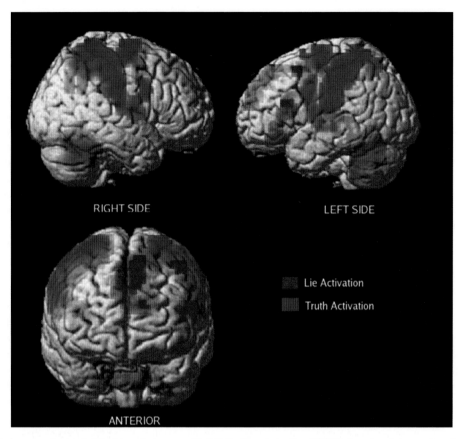

Fig. 63.2 Average activation in 22 subjects during a modified Guilty Knowledge Test (GKT2). Areas in red show regions for Lie > Truth contrast at uncorrected threshold of p = 0.05 and cluster spatial extent > 8 voxels. Areas in blue show regions for Truth > Lie contrast, corrected at p = 0.001, clusters > 100 voxels (based on data from Langleben et al., 2005).

(Haxby et al., 2001) and individual variability of the brain-behavior correlation.

With increasing sophistication and quantity of data on deception, the left VLPFC (BA 45,–47 and small parts of BA 11 and 10) has begun to emerge as potentially the most specific if not the most sensitive region involved in deception. Multiple studies have reported VLPFC activation during deceptive responding (Davatzikos et al., 2005; Kozel et al., 2005; Langleben et al., 2005; Lee et al., 2005; Phan et al., 2005; Turner et al., 2008; Baumgartner et al., 2009). In at least one study, this area remained associated with deception in a task where salience of the baseline item had been very closely matched to the lie items (Figure 63.2) (Langleben et al., 2005). The role of VLPFC has been progressively expanded and refined from simple motor response inhibition to other domains such as task-set switching (Konishi et al., 1998; Konishi et al., 1999; Liddle et al., 2001; Rubia et al., 2003; Aron, Monsell, et al., 2004; Aron & Poldrack, 2005; Aron & Poldrack, 2006;

Aron et al., 2007; Robbins, 2007; Ambach et al., 2008). The format of current models of deception generation share many features with task-set switching in that they require subjects to frequently repeat response sets (truth telling) in series with occasional switches of contingency (to lie telling). Even in the case of the CIT (where all button responses are "No"), a switch in response contingency (from truth to lie) may constitute a task-set switch akin to goal and response-rule switches in models of task-switching.

An emerging topic of considerable importance is the interaction between the functional neuroanatomy of deception and personality. Preliminary support for this possibility was provided by a series of studies by Yang et al. (2005a, 2007) which found that subjects who engaged in habitual lying showed evidence of increased white matter in orbital, medial, and inferior frontal cortex compared with other antisocial and normal controls. In a recent study by Greene and Paxton (2009), subjects were given a task in which they were told to indicate whether or not they correctly predicted the results of a coin flip, where one of the outcomes would yield them a reward. Dishonest subjects were defined as those who reported predicting the rewarding outcome a significant majority of the time (i.e. completely honest subjects would be expected to report the rewarding outcome in equal measure with the non-rewarding outcome). Deceptive subjects showed greater activity in the prefrontal cortex when they lied, but also when they told the truth. The authors used this finding to suggest that truth-telling in circumstances where lying will yield tangible rewards (at the cost of violating explicit instructions) relies on the absence of a temptation to lie rather than upon the active resistance of this temptation. This study also suggests that processing during deception (and even truth-telling) might be different depending upon the subject's own tendency to tell lies.

The improving precision in the use of terminology as well as the effective spatial resolution of fMRI studies makes it difficult to compare results across studies without formal meta-analysis of the data using a uniform system of coordinates; thus, several anatomical landmarks of the VLPFC need to be considered together in the search for a key task-independent brain region in deception. The highest peak activations from a recent meta-analysis of two CIT studies (see Figure 63.1) were found in a portion of the left VLPFC known as the anterior insula (AI). The connectivity across sensory modalities (primary, somatosensory, vestibular, and visceral) and systems (limbic, motor, sensory) in the AI (Augustine, 1996), and its cytoarchitecture (Allman et al., 2005), has led researchers to propose the AI as the seat of consciousness in the human brain (Craig, 2004; Crick & Koch, 2005; Goldstein et al., 2009). The AI is thought to be informed about the state of almost every part of the body relative to the outside world, and in the case of deception might reflect a task-independent source of information regarding a subject's internal state during deceptive responding. Taken together, the left VLPFC region corresponding to Brodmann areas 45 through 47 and overlapping the AI appears to be a strong candidate for a generalizable lie-indicator in translational studies aimed at predicting deceptive responding in individual subjects across response modalities.

Translation to Individual Subjects

The key applied question facing the field after the initial proof of concept studies was whether the reported group average findings could be translated to single subjects and if so, whether one could achieve a practical level of lie-detection accuracy in a single subject. This question was independently answered in two 2005 studies (Kozel et al., 2005; Langleben et al., 2005). Using an event-related hybrid CIT-CQT paradigm that contained multiple control items of decreasing salience, Langleben et al. (2005) and Davatzikos et al. (2005) reported an accuracy of discrimination between lie and truth of 78 to 85% with a logistic regression, and over 88% with multi-voxel pattern analysis (Davatzikos et al., 2005). This study was conducted in young healthy controls, using a hybrid deception model that allowed CIT- and CQT-type contrasts during the analysis, involving a scenario of concealed playing cards. The deception model contained a single directed lie condition and a number of control truth conditions of decreasing salience such that one class of control Truth stimuli was of either equal or greater salience to the participant than the Lie condition. The inferior prefrontal and inferior parietal cortices were the most informative in separating truth from lie during classification (Figure 63.2). In another study, Kozel et al. (2005) used a mock crime scenario with a CQT paradigm and event-related fMRI design to arrive at 90% accurate lie-detection with a logistic regression type analysis. This accuracy calculation had one significant caveat—subjects whose classification was uncertain were treated as "inconclusive" and excluded from the accuracy calculation. If they were included, the accuracy of lie-detection in this study would have been similar to the Langleben (2005) and Davatzikos (2005) findings. Considering the relative novelty of single subject studies at the time and the low ecological validity of the paradigms, these studies met their goal of demonstrating feasibility of differentiating lie and truth in individual subjects with an above chance accuracy. However, these studies left unanswered the questions of safety and efficacy which mark the point of divergence between translational research, aimed at developing a clinically viable lie-detector, and the academic study of deception.

Emotion and Deception

System neuroscience studies of deception have made significant progress in extending and confirming some of the early hypotheses and have begun to anchor the functional neuroanatomy of deception in the context of cognitive control, salience, memory, and intent. In a series of studies, Abe et al. (2006; 2009) provided physiological evidence of a functional distinction between false memory and deception using lesion evidence from Parkinson's disease patients, supporting a role of the prefrontal cortex in deception. Anxiety during deception has been postulated to be a principle mechanism of increased SCR response during polygraph examination in CQT designs, though anti-anxiety medication seems to be ineffective in reducing the polygraph lie-detection rates (Iacono et al., 1992). One of the arguments against the polygraph has been the presumably reduced SCR reactivity in psychopaths (House & Milligan, 1976; Verschuere et al., 2005). Anxiety and fear are commonly associated with activation of the extended limbic system that usually includes the anterior cingulate, orbitofrontal cortex (OFC), amygdala, insula, and the hippocampus (Chua et al., 1999). Remarkably, functional brain imaging studies of deception do not consistently report lie-related activation in these regions, perhaps due to the endorsed nature and low risk associated with lying in most of the experimental settings used in this research. However, one fMRI case report and one Positron Emission Tomogrpahy (PET) study have demonstrated limbic activation during lying in experimental settings (Abe et al., 2007; Hakun et al., 2009). In the fMRI case study, Hakun et al. (2009) reported a subject who displayed amygdala activity to a concealed item of high emotional relevance to the subject, despite not activating the typical prefrontal and parietal regions (Figure 63.1). In a PET study, Abe et al. (2007) studied the effects of endorsed deception vs. violation of investigators' instructions, which they termed "dishonesty." Briefly, participants were given the initial instruction to tell the truth or lie on two pairs of tasks. In half of the study blocks, the subjects were then put in a conflicting situation by a confederate who asked them to do the reverse of what they were originally instructed, essentially deceiving the investigator who provided their initial instructions and who questioned them during the task. The authors found that deception was associated with activation of the DLPFC and the ACC, while violating the original instructions of the investigator was associated with increased activity in the left amygdala and the ventromedial prefrontal cortex (VMPFC) (Abe et al., 2007). This study demonstrates the key role of instruction and perceived rules in deception task design, execution, and brain response, further suggesting that the brain response pattern of deception is likely to be largely task specific. Studies of behaviors that may share processing demands similar to deception, such as

making a promise that is subsequently broken (Baumgartner et al., 2009) and inferring deceit in others (Grezes et al., 2004), have reported insula and amygdala activation. While it is possible that anxiety is not as common in or specific to deception as has been traditionally assumed, the lack of an fMRI pattern suggestive of fear and anxiety during experimental deception could be explained by the low ecological validity of the laboratory paradigms. Experiments focused on increasing the ecological validity of deception paradigms and evaluating subjective anxiety during deception could help answer this question.

Translation to Clinical Populations

Feigning disease is a complex phenomenon that includes both conscious (malingering) and unconscious (i.e. factitious and conversion disorders) behaviors and states, all of which are of high importance to both clinical medicine and the health and disability insurance industry. Malingering of disorders that have no objective and pathognomonic diagnostic signs is particularly difficult to detect. Most psychiatric and a good number of neurological symptoms are based entirely on self-report, which is an example of a test without a readily available "ground truth" (Valenstein, 1990). A series of studies of feigned memory impairment (Lee et al., 2002), revealed the prefronto-parietal pattern common to studies involving CIT- or CQT-style paradigms as well as a distinction between errors and intentional false responses (Lee et al., 2009) in the precuneus. Subsequent studies by the same group had more variable results that included the precuneus, VLPFC, and the posterior cingulate, presumably due to the presence of self-referential processes (Lee et al., 2002; Lee et al., 2009). Preliminary studies comparing feigned and true hysterical paralysis and other conditions involving unconsciously false responding revealed a pattern of differences that so far, have been too variable to summarize (Spence et al., 2000; Ward et al., 2003; Lee et al., 2005; Spence et al., 2008). fMRI studies of malingered sadness, hallucinations or pain have not been reported, though the high incidence and clinical significance of these symptoms makes them prime candidates for further translational research on malingering.

Countermeasures to Lie-detection

Cognitive efforts to defeat a lie detector, referred to as countermeasures, are a long-standing topic of research (Elaad & Ben-Shakhar, 1991; Kleiner, 2001; Raskin & Honts, 2001; Rosenfeld, 2004).

While seemingly technical, the topic of counter-measures is closely linked to two fundamental topics in neuroscience: memory and learning. If the pre-potent response inhibition hypothesis of deception was true, then lying about forgotten information may not engage the executive functions as much as lying about information that is accessible to the conscious mind. Studies of false and true memory and memory suppression suggest that true memories are distinguishable from false memories and their suppression engages the brain's executive functions (Schacter et al., 1996; Anderson & Green, 2001; Wade et al., 2002; Okado & Stark, 2003; Gonsalves et al., 2004).

Consistent with these basic studies, at the group-average level, deception could be distinguished from false recognition with fMRI, though the brain regions involved do not overlap the regions reported with deception (Abe et al., 2008). Rehearsal has also been shown to attenuate and alter the brain fMRI response associated with deception (Ganis et al., 2003). Together, these data suggest that learning and memory could significantly affect the expected brain fMRI pattern of deception, making fMRI-based lie-detection more or less sensitive to countermeasures. On the other hand, the purpose of forced-choice deception models is to constrain subjects' behavior, potentially reducing any effects of rehearsal and moti-vated forgetting types of countermeasures. Another type of countermeasure is the intentional shift of attention from the target (suspected lie) to a select irrelevant item or class of items. This countermeasure has been studied with EEG and its uninstructed use has been reported by a significant proportion of par-ticipants in a modified GKT fMRI study that found higher prefronto-parietal activation associated with truthful rather than deceptive responses in all areas except the left ventrolateral frontal cortex (Rosenfeld, 2004; Davatzikos et al., 2005). An apparent violation of the earlier hypothesis of prepotency of lie over truth (Spence et al., 2001; Langleben et al., 2002) did not preclude differentiation between the two condi-tions, with an accuracy ranging from 86 to 90% (Davatzikos et al., 2005). These data suggest that while countermeasures are likely to significantly impact the deception-related pattern, they could be identified and addressed during data analysis, in a test or an experiment aimed at differentiation between two classes of stimuli, rather than positive identifica-tion of a stimulus class. Absent a methodical experi-mental study that would address individual variability as well as a range of different countermeasures, this remains an educated guess. Ganis et al., 2011 recently found that covert motor movements designed to act as a countermeasure during deceptive responding were effective at reducing differentiation of lie from truth using machine-learning fMRI pattern analysis methods. While this study demonstrated that activity in regions that maximally distinguish lie from truth (e.g. inferior frontal gyri) is reduced by such a countermeasure, the study did not explore other regions of the brain to discern whether the counter-measures themselves could be classified as their own type of activation pattern separate from lie or truth conditions.

The Problem of Ecological Validity

Inferring clinical feasibility from laboratory experi-ments of low to negligible ecological validity became one of the key problems of translational research on deception, as ecologically valid experi-ments in deception are likely to involve deception of the participants, lack of a verifiable ground truth, or both (Spence & Kaylor-Hughes, 2008; Hakun et al., 2009). Critics proposed that there is not an ethical way to conduct such experiments (Halber, 2007).

However, establishing the clinical value of a diag-nostic system is a well-known process. Two issues make deception unique among conditions to be "diagnosed" or detected; one is the need for "ground truth" to be compared with responses that may be lies, while the other is the difficulty in achieving the risk/benefit ratio of real-life situations, whether in the laboratory or in the field. For example, using fMRI to detect deception in an accused prisoner could be potentially damaging or problematic for the participant. Neither the accused nor convicted individuals are likely to provide a reliable self-report. Common civil offenses, such as lying on one's resume, could be a safer but still useful source of ecologically valid scenarios (Spence & Kaylor-Hughes, 2008; Hakun et al., 2009). Thus, though technically feasible, "real-life" clinical trials of an fMRI-based lie detector are likely to be technically challenging, expensive, and academically unreward-ing; such drawbacks may explain why they have yet not been conducted in the academic setting. Criticism of fMRI-based lie-detection for the lack of ecologically valid support is unlikely to yield the required data in the absence of an industry or government sponsor (Langleben & Dattilio, 2008; National Research Council, 2008).

Forensic Applications

While determining whether there are brain regions specific to deception is an important challenge to basic research, it is not a prerequisite for progress in the use of fMRI for forensic lie-detection. In the context of applied use, the deception-generating model is used to constrain individual variability. The task of detecting deception is then reduced to discrimination between a few pre-planned items, leaving the decision about a subject's honesty to a human evaluator who interprets the difference between conditions that have been identified by automated analysis. Not finding evidence of guilt is often sufficient for acquittal; however, the value of negative fMRI findings will remain unclear until the effect size of a lie in a particular combination of a deception task and target population has been established. The use of negative findings in forensic fMRI lie-detection has been attempted by commercial entities that are locked in a vicious cycle not uncommon in medical device development: they are unable to attract investors until the clinical feasibility of the methodology is demonstrated in court, which in turn is not possible without investors to sponsor the extensive clinical trials required to establish courtroom validity (Langleben & Dattilio, 2008). Considering the pivotal social importance of deception, it is in the public interest that such trials are conducted with as little bias as possible. Remarkably, the commercial forensic fMRI start-ups may be holding a relatively small stake in the outcome of research that may impact jurisprudence, medical diagnosis, intelligence, and ethics (Wolpe et al., 2005; Appelbaum, 2007; Canli et al., 2007; Langleben & Dattilio, 2008; Wolpe & Langleben, 2008). In the absence of research data, the utility of fMRI lie-detection evidence in the courtroom remains under debate. This debate has been highlighted by the recent unsuccessful attempt to introduce fMRI expert testimony about a defendant's veracity in the case of *US v Semrau*. The court determined that such evidence did not have a "known error rate" and had not met with "general acceptance by the scientific community", two of the five criteria established as requirements by the US Supreme Court decision in the Daubert v. Merrell Dow Pharmaceuticals (1993) and the Federal Rules of Evidence for admissibility of scientific evidence. (US v Semrau, W.D. Tenn, Eastern Division, No.: No. 07-10074 M1/P (May 31, 2010). The Semrau case highlights the problem of negative results in fMRI-based lie-detection test: so long as error rates remain unknown, a negative test result will have no value despite the lay attempts to argue the opposite (Stone, 2007). Hypothetically, a test could be designed in such a way that a positive finding would indicate innocence.

The great enthusiasm of the lay press for fMRI-based lie-detection has led to an automatic assumption that fMRI is superior to polygraph and EEG for this application. Though possible and theoretically likely, this question can only be answered with comprehensive controlled clinical trials (Wolpe et al., 2005; Langleben & Dattilio, 2008).

The opinion that scientific standards for reliability and validity should be the basis of the admissibility decision has recently been challenged on the grounds that even evidence considered "marginal" by the scientific community could still be of value in situations which only require proof (of guilt) beyond reasonable doubt (Schauer, 2010). That is, a modestly accurate test of veracity that may not be of sufficient specificity for a jury to convict could still retain enough sensitivity to satisfy legal standards for acquittal. This scenario recently came to the forefront in the death penalty hearing of Ben Dugan in Illinois, where the judge allowed the defense to present the testimony of an fMRI expert to describe to the jury evidence of the defendant's psychopathy, rather than his veracity.

It is important to consider the risk of fMRI evidence being over-interpreted by juries that are not trained in critical evaluation of scientific data. Furthermore, scientific evidence may over-simplify the motivational context of a defendant or witness's testimony- the field has not yet reached the point of discerning the complex and subtle variations between different types of lies, intents to deceive, and the influence of personality factors and is likely to be incapable of detecting misinformation provided in good conscience (Langleben & Dattillio, 2006, Spence & Kaylor-Hughes, 2008). Nonetheless, current methods of veracity determination in the courtroom are purely subjective judgments by judge and jury, and experimental evidence suggests that normal individuals (i.e., potential jury members) rarely perform better than chance at detecting lies based on social cues (Bond & DePaulo, 2006). Thus, notwithstanding the importance of maintaining a no-harm principle in introducing new forms of evidence, neuroscience methods of veracity determination with better-than-chance accuracy rates could serve to improve the legal system and stand to provide more benefit than risk to the accused (Schauer, 2010).

Applications in Psychiatry and Psychotherapy

In addition to the translational questions in fMRI-based lie-detection, there is a number of important systems neuroscience questions that could be answered though the study of deception. For example, would a response about the content of a psychotic delusion register as lie or truth (Langleben et al., 2006)? Based on the apparent relationship between rehearsal or depth of encoding and the categorization of behavior as deceptive with fMRI (Ganis et al., 2003; Gamer & Berti, 2009; Gamer, Kosiol, et al., 2009), it is possible that the degree to which an inaccurate response to a question about a delusion appears as a lie may depend on the severity of the delusion, offering a potential marker of illness when controlled for information exposure. Denial and self-deception are important phenomena in psychiatry and psychotherapy. Delusion could be conceptualized as an extreme case of self-deception. Self-deception (Gur, 1979; Trivers, 2000) may be a significant contributor to the overall act of deception, warranting a study of the latter as an important element in understanding both processes (Monterosso & Langleben, 2008; Goldstein et al., 2009). Another clinical field that might benefit from basic neuroscience research on deception is psychotherapy. Denial and repression are key defense mechanisms that may be characterized as more or less severe by comparison with the pattern of intentional deception (Loughead et al., 2010). Finally, insight is a concept overlapping clinical medicine and psychotherapy that, similarly to deception, may also be modulated by the VLPFC and anterior insula (Goldstein et al., 2009).

Conclusion

Over the last decade, significant progress has been made in the basic and translational fMRI-based research on deception. This progress stops short of propelling this fMRI application into the courtroom, but it suggests a potential for applications in forensics, jurisprudence, and medicine that justifies further research. The left VLPFC is presently the strongest candidate for a region specific to deception across models; however, the majority of evidence suggests that the brain fMRI pattern of deception is model-specific and that deception is mediated by a distributed network that overlaps with more basic cognitive processes. Clinical trials are required to identify and validate performance parameters of specific combinations of deception models and target populations that may be suitable for legal use.

References

Abe, N., Fujii, T., et al. (2009). Do Parkinsonian patients have trouble telling lies? The neurobiological basis of deceptive behaviour. *Brain, 132*(Pt 5), 1386–1395.

Abe, N., Okuda, J., et al. (2008). Neural correlates of true memory, false memory, and deception. *Cereb Cortex, 18*(12), 2811–2819.

Abe, N., Suzuki, M., et al. (2007). Deceiving others: Distinct neural responses of the prefrontal cortex and amygdala in simple fabrication and deception with social interactions. *J Cogn Neurosci, 19*(2), 287–295.

Abe, N., Suzuki, M., et al. (2006). Dissociable roles of prefrontal and anterior cingulate cortices in deception. *Cereb Cortex, 16*(2), 192–199.

Aguirre, G. K. & D'Esposito, M. (1999). Experimental design for brain fMRI. In C. T. W. Moonen & P. A. Bandettini (Eds.). *Functional MRI* (pp. 369–380). New York, Springer.

Allman, J. M., Watson, K. K., et al. (2005). Intuition and autism: A possible role for von Economo neurons. *Trends Cogn Sci, 9*(8), 367–373.

Ambach, W., Stark, R., et al. (2008). An interfering Go/No-go task does not affect accuracy in a Concealed Information Test. *Int J Psychophysiol, 68*(1), 6–16.

Anderson, M. C. & Green, C. (2001). Suppressing unwanted memories by executive control. *Nature, 410*(6826), 366–369.

Appelbaum, P. S. (2007). Law & psychiatry: The new lie detectors: neuroscience, deception, and the courts. *Psychiatr Serv, 58*(4), 460–462.

Aron, A. R., Behrens, T. E., et al. (2007). Triangulating a cognitive control network using diffusion-weighted magnetic resonance imaging (MRI) and functional MRI. *J Neurosci, 27*(14), 3743–3752.

Aron, A. R., Monsell, S., et al. (2004). A componential analysis of task-switching deficits associated with lesions of left and right frontal cortex. *Brain, 127*(Pt 7), 1561–1573.

Aron, A. R. & Poldrack, R. A. (2005). The cognitive neuroscience of response inhibition: Relevance for genetic research in attention-deficit/hyperactivity disorder. *Biol Psychiatry, 57*(11), 1285–1292.

Aron, A. R. & Poldrack, R. A. (2006). Cortical and subcortical contributions to Stop signal response inhibition: Role of the subthalamic nucleus. *J Neurosci, 26*(9), 2424–2433.

Aron, A. R., Robbins, T. W., et al. (2004). Inhibition and the right inferior frontal cortex. *Trends Cogn Sci, 8*(4), 170–177.

Augustine, J. R. (1996). Circuitry and functional aspects of the insular lobe in primates including humans. *Brain Res Brain Res Rev, 22*(3), 229–244.

Badre, D. & Wagner, A. D. (2004). Selection, integration, and conflict monitoring; Assessing the nature and generality of prefrontal cognitive control mechanisms. *Neuron, 41*(3), 473–487.

Baumgartner, T., Fischbacher, U., et al. (2009). The neural circuitry of a broken promise. *Neuron, 64*(5), 756–770.

Ben-Shakhar, G. (1991). Clinical judgment and decision-making in CQT-polygraphy. A comparison with other pseudoscientific applications in psychology. *Integrative Physiological and Behavioral Science, 26*(3), 232–240.

Ben-Shakhar, G., Bar-Hillel, M., et al. (2002). Trial by polygraph: Reconsidering the use of the guilty knowledge technique in court. *Law and Human Behavior, 26*(5), 527–541.

Bode, S. & Haynes, J. D. (2009). Decoding sequential stages of task preparation in the human brain. *Neuroimage, 45*(2), 606–613.

Boire, R. G. (2005). Searching the brain: The Fourth Amendment implications of brain-based deception-detection devices. *Am J Bioeth, 5*(2), 62–3; discussion W5.

Bond, C. F., Jr. & DePaulo, B. M. (2006). Accuracy of deception judgments. *Pers Soc Psychol Rev, 10*(3), 214–234.

Botvinick, M. M., Cohen, J. D., et al. (2004). Conflict monitoring and anterior cingulate cortex: An update. *Trends Cogn Sci, 8*(12), 539–546.

Brown, J. W. & Braver, T. S. (2005). Learned predictions of error likelihood in the anterior cingulate cortex. *Science, 307*(5712), 1118–1121.

Canli, T., Brandon, S., Casebeer, W., Crowley, P. J., Du Rousseau, D., Greely H. T., et al. (2007). Neuroethics and national security. *Am J Bioeth, 7*(5), 3–13.

Chua, P., Krams, M., Toni, I., Passingham, R., & Dolan, R. (1999). A functional anatomy of anticipatory anxiety. *Neuroimage, 9*(6 Pt 1), 563–571.

Cole, M. W. & Schneider, W. (2007). The cognitive control network: Integrated cortical regions with dissociable functions. *Neuroimage, 37*(1), 343–360.

Craig, A. D. (2004). Human feelings: Why are some more aware than others? *Trends Cogn Sci, 8*(6), 239–241.

Crick, F. C. & Koch, C. (2005). What is the function of the claustrum? *Philos Trans R Soc Lond B Biol Sci, 360*(1458), 1271–1279.

Davatzikos, C., Ruparel, K., Fan, Y., Shen, D. G., Acharyya, M., Loughead, J. W., et al. (2005). "Classifying spatial patterns of brain activity with machine learning methods: Application to lie-detection." *Neuroimage, 28*(3), 663–668.

Elaad, E. & Ben-Shakhar, G. (1991). Effects of mental countermeasures on psychophysiological detection in the guilty knowledge test. *Int J Psychophysiol, 11*(2), 99–108.

Elaad, E. & Ben-Shakhar, G. (1997). Effects of item repetitions and variations on the efficiency of the guilty knowledge test. *Psychophysiology, 34*(5), 587–596.

Elaad, E., Ginton, A., & Jungman, M. (1992). Detection measures in real-life criminal guilty knowledge tests. *J Appl Psychol, 77*(5), 757–767.

Furedy, J. J., Gigliotti, F. & Ben-Shakhar, G. (1994). Electrodermal differentiation of deception: The effect of choice versus no choice of deceptive items. *Int J Psychophysiol, 18*(1), 13–22.

Gamer, M., Bauermann, T., Stoeter, P., & Vossel, G. (2007). Covariations among fMRI, skin conductance, and behavioral data during processing of concealed information. *Hum Brain Mapp, 28*(12), 1287–1301.

Gamer, M. & Berti, S. (2009). Task relevance and recognition of concealed information have different influences on electrodermal activity and event-related brain potentials. *Psychophysiology, 47*(2), 355–364.

Gamer, M., Klimecki, O., Bauermann, T., Stoeter, P., & Vossel, G. (2009). fMRI-activation patterns in the detection of concealed information rely on memory-related effects. *Soc Cogn Affect Neurosci,* (Epub ahead of print).

Gamer, M., Kosiol, D., & Vossel, G. (2009). Strength of memory encoding affects physiological responses in the Guilty Actions Test. *Biological Psychology, 83*(2), 101–107.

Ganis, G., Kosslyn, S. M., et al. (2003). Neural correlates of different types of deception: an FMRI investigation. *Cereb Cortex, 13*(8), 830–836.

Ganis, G., Rosenfeld, J.P., et al. (2011). Lying in the scanner: Covert countermeasures disrupt deception detection by functional magnetic resonance imaging. *Neuroimage,* 1; *55*(1), 312–9.

Goldstein, R. Z., Craig, A. D., et al. (2009). The neurocircuitry of impaired insight in drug addiction. *Trends Cogn Sci, 13*(9), 372–380.

Gonsalves, B., Reber, P. J., et al. (2004). Neural evidence that vivid imagining can lead to false remembering. *Psychol Sci, 15*(10), 655–660.

Grezes, J., Frith, C., et al. (2004). Brain mechanisms for inferring deceit in the actions of others. *J Neurosci, 24*(24), 5500–5505.

Greely, H. T. & J. Illes (2007). Neuroscience-based lie detection: The urgent need for regulation. *Am J of Law & Medicine 33*(2–3), 377–431.

Gur, R. & Sackeim, H. A. (1979). Self-deception: A concept in search of a phenomenon. *Journal of Personality and Social Psychology, 37*, 147–169.

Greene, J., Paxton, D. J. M. (2009). Patterns of neural activity associated with honest and dishonest moral decisions. *Proc Natl Acad Sci* U S A. Jul 28, *106*(30), 12506–12511.

Hakun, J. G., Ruparel, K., et al. (2009). Towards clinical trials of lie-detection with fMRI. *Soc Neurosci, 4*(6), 518–527.

Hakun, J. G., Seelig, D., et al. (2008). fMRI investigation of the cognitive structure of the Concealed Information Test. *Neurocase, 14*(1), 59–67.

Halber, D. (2007). Scientists swear a good lie detector is hard to find. *MIT Tech Talk.* Cambridge. *51.*

Haxby, J. V., Gobbini, M. I., et al. (2001). Distributed and overlapping representations of faces and objects in ventral temporal cortex. *Science, 293*(5539), 2425–2430.

Haynes, J. D. (2009). Decoding visual consciousness from human brain signals. *Trends Cogn Sci, 13*(5), 194–202.

Haynes, J. D. & Rees, G. (2006). Decoding mental states from brain activity in humans. *Nature Reviews Neuroscience, 7*(7), 523–534.

Holden, C. (2001). Polygraph screening. Panel seeks truth in lie detector debate. *Science, 291*(5506), 967.

House, T. H. & Milligan, W. L. (1976). Autonomic responses to modeled distress in prison psychopaths. *J Pers Soc Psychol, 34*(4), 556–560.

Iacono, W. G., Cerri, A. M., et al. (1992). "Use of antianxiety drugs as countermeasures in the detection of guilty knowledge." *J Appl Psychol, 77*(1), 60–64.

Kleiner, M. (Ed.). (2001). *Handbook of polygraph testing* London and San Diego: Academic Press.

Konishi, S., Nakajima, K., et al. (1999). Common inhibitory mechanism in human inferior prefrontal cortex revealed by event-related functional MRI. *Brain, 122*(Pt 5), 981–991.

Konishi, S., Nakajima, K., et al. (1998). No-go dominant brain activity in human inferior prefrontal cortex revealed by functional magnetic resonance imaging. *Eur J Neurosci, 10*(3), 1209–1213.

Kozel, F., Revell, L., Lorberbaum, J. P., Shastri, A., Nahas, Z., Bohning, D. E., et al. (2000). *Regional brain correlates of deception: A pilot fMRI study in healthy young adults.* American College of Neuropsychopharmacology 39th Annual Meeting, San Juan, Puerto Rico.

Kozel, F. A., Johnson, K. A., et al. (2005). Detecting deception using functional magnetic resonance imaging. *Biol Psychiatry, 58*(8), 605–613.

Langleben, D., Dattilio, F., et al. (2006). True lies. *Psychiatry and Law, 34*(3), 351–370.

Langleben, D. D. & Dattilio, F. M. (2008). Commentary: The future of forensic functional brain imaging. *Journal of the American Academy of Psychiatry and the Law, 36*(4), 502–504.

Langleben, D. D., Loughead, J. W., et al. (2005). Telling truth from lie in individual subjects with fast event-related fMRI. *Hum Brain Mapp, 26*(4), 262–272.

Langleben, D. D., Ruparel, K., et al. (2008). Acute effect of methadone maintenance dose on brain FMRI response to heroin-related cues. *American Journal of Psychiatry, 165*(3), 390–394.

Langleben, D. D., Schroeder, L., et al. (2002). Brain activity during simulated deception: an event-related functional magnetic resonance study. *Neuroimage, 15*(3), 727–732.

Langleben, D. D., Schroeder, R. M., Maldjian, J., Gur, S., O'Brien, C. P., & Childress, A. R. (2001). *Functional magnetic resonance imaging of the brain during deception.* 31st Annual Meeting of the Society for Neuroscience, San Diego, CA, Society for Neuroscience.

Lee, T. M., Au, R. K., et al. (2009). Are errors differentiable from deceptive responses when feigning memory impairment? An fMRI study. *Brain Cogn, 69*(2), 406–412.

Lee, T. M., Liu, H. L., et al. (2005). Neural correlates of feigned memory impairment. *Neuroimage, 28*(2), 305–313.

Lee, T. M., Liu, H. L., et al. (2002). Lie-detection by functional magnetic resonance imaging. *Hum Brain Mapp, 15*(3), 157–164.

Liddle, P. F., Kiehl, K. A., et al. (2001). Event-related fMRI study of response inhibition. *Hum Brain Mapp, 12*(2), 100–109.

Loughead, J. W., Luborsky, L., et al. (2010). Brain activation during autobiographical relationship episode narratives: A core conflictual relationship theme approach. *Psychother Res,* 1–16.

Lykken, D. T. (1998). *A tremor in the blood: Uses and abuses of the lie detector,* New York, NY: Plenum Press.

Lykken, D. T. (1991). Why (some) Americans believe in the lie detector while others believe in the guilty knowledge test. *Integr Physiol Behav Sci, 26*(3), 214–222.

MacLaren, V. V. (2001). A quantitative review of the guilty knowledge test. *J Appl Psychol, 86*(4), 674–683.

Matte, J. A. (1996). The Control-Stimulation Test. *Forensic psychophysiology using the polygraph: Scientific truth verification - lie detection.* Williamsville, NY: JAM Publications. *1,* 307–321.

Miller, G. R. & Stiff, J. B. (1993). Investigating deceptive communication. In *Deceptive communication* (pp. 32–39). Newbury Park, CA: Sage Publications.

Monterosso, J. & Langleben, D. (2008). Homo Economicus' soul. Commentary on The dishonesty of honest people: A theory of self-concept maintenance. *Journal of Marketing Research,* in press.

National Research Council. (2008). *Emerging cognitive neuroscience and related technologies.* Washington, DC: National Academy Press.

Nose, I., J. Murai, et al. (2009). "Disclosing concealed information on the basis of cortical activations." *Neuroimage, 44*(4), 1380–1386.

Okado, Y. & Stark, C. (2003). Neural processing associated with true and false memory retrieval. *Cogn Affect Behav Neurosci, 3*(4), 323–334.

Owen, A. M., McMillan, K. M., et al. (2005). N-back working memory paradigm: A meta-analysis of normative functional neuroimaging studies. *Hum Brain Mapp, 25*(1), 46–59.

Phan, K. L., Magalhaes, A., et al. (2005). Neural correlates of telling lies: A functional magnetic resonance imaging study at 4 Tesla. *Acad Radiol, 12*(2), 164–172.

Raskin, D. C. & Honts, C. R. (2001). The Comparison Question Test. In M. Kleiner (Ed.). *Handbook of polygraph testing* (pp. 14–15). London and San Diego: Academic Press.

Ravizza, S. M. & Carter, C. S. (2008). Shifting set about task switching: Behavioral and neural evidence for distinct forms of cognitive flexibility. *Neuropsychologia, 46*(12), 2924–2935.

Robbins, T. W. (2007). Shifting and stopping: Fronto-striatal substrates, neurochemical modulation and clinical implications. *Philos Trans R Soc Lond B Biol Sci, 362*(1481), 917–932.

Rosenfeld, J. P., Cantwell, B., et al. (1988). A modified, event-related potential-based guilty knowledge test. *Int J Neurosci, 42*(1–2), 157–161.

Rosenfeld, P. J. (2004). Simple, effective countermeasures to P-300-based tests of detection of concealed information. *Psychophysiology, 41,* 205–219.

Rubia, K., Smith, A. B., et al. (2003). Right inferior prefrontal cortex mediates response inhibition while mesial prefrontal cortex is responsible for error detection. *Neuroimage, 20*(1), 351–358.

Schacter, D. L., Reiman, E., et al. (1996). Neuroanatomical correlates of veridical and illusory recognition memory: Evidence from positron emission tomography. *Neuron, 17*(2), 267–274.

Schauer, F. (2010). Neuroscience, lie-detection, and the law: Contrary to the prevailing view, the suitability of brain-based lie-detection for courtroom or forensic use should be determined according to legal and not scientific standards. *Trends Cogn Sci, 14*(3), 101–103.

Spence, S. A. (2004). The deceptive brain. *J R Soc Med, 97*(1), 6–9.

Spence, S. A., Crimlisk, H. L., et al. (2000). Discrete neurophysiological correlates in prefrontal cortex during hysterical and feigned disorder of movement. *Lancet, 355*(9211), 1243–1244.

Spence, S. A., Farrow, T. F., et al. (2001). Behavioural and functional anatomical correlates of deception in humans. *Neuroreport, 12*(13), 2849–2853.

Spence, S. A., Hunter, M. D., et al. (2004). A cognitive neurobiological account of deception: evidence from functional neuroimaging. *Philos Trans R Soc Lond B Biol Sci, 359*(1451), 1755–1762.

Spence, S. A. & Kaylor-Hughes, C. J. (2008). Looking for truth and finding lies: The prospects for a nascent neuroimaging of deception. *Neurocase, 14*(1), 68–81.

Spence, S. A., Kaylor-Hughes, C. J., et al. (2008). "Munchausen's syndrome by proxy' or a 'miscarriage of justice'? An initial application of functional neuroimaging to the question of guilt versus innocence." *Eur Psychiatry, 23*(4), 309–314.

Stern, P. C. (2003a). Lie detection and the polygraph. In P. C. Stern (Ed.). *The polygraph and lie detection. Report of The National Research Council Committee to Review the Scientific Evidence on the Polygraph* (pp. 27–28). Washington, DC: The National Academies Press.

Stern, P. C. (2003b). Physiological processes measured by the polygraph. In P. C. Stern (Ed.). *The Polygraph and Lie-detection. Report of The National Research Council Committee to Review the Scientific Evidence on the Polygraph* (pp. 286–290). Washington, DC: The National Academies Press.

Stern, P. C., (Ed.) (2003c). *The Polygraph and Lie Detection. Report of The National Research Council Committee to Review the Scientific Evidence on the Polygraph.* Washington, DC:, The National Academies Press (pp. 253–258).

Stone, G. (2007). See a lie inside the brain: Harvey Nathan is on a mission to prove he's not a liar. Retrieved 8.24.2008, from http://abclocal.go.com/wpvi/story?section=news/technology&id=5621892.

Thompson-Schill, S. L., Bedny, M., et al. (2005). The frontal lobes and the regulation of mental activity. *Curr Opin Neurobiol*, *15*(2), 219–224.

Tovino, S. A. (2007). Functional neuroimaging and the law: Trends and directions for future scholarship. *Am J Bioeth*, *7*(9), 44–56.

Trivers, R. (2000). The elements of a scientific theory of self-deception. *Ann N Y Acad Sci*, *907*, 114–131.

Turner, M. S., Cipolotti, L., et al. (2008). Confabulation: damage to a specific inferior medial prefrontal system. *Cortex*, *44*(6), 637–648.

Valenstein, P. N. (1990). Evaluating diagnostic tests with imperfect standards. *Am J Clin Pathol*, *93*(2), 252–258.

Verschuere, B., Crombez, G., et al. (2005). Psychopathic traits and autonomic responding to concealed information in a prison sample. *Psychophysiology*, *42*(2), 239–245.

Wade, K. A., Garry, M., et al. (2002). A picture is worth a thousand lies: using false photographs to create false childhood memories. *Psychon Bull Rev*, *9*(3), 597–603.

Ward, N. S., Oakley, D. A., et al. (2003). Differential brain activations during intentionally simulated and subjectively experienced paralysis. *Cognit Neuropsychiatry*, *8*(4), 295–312.

Wolpe, P. & Langleben, D. (2008). Lies, damn lies, and lie detectors. *Harvard Business Review: Breakthrough Ideas for 2008*, *86*(2), 1.

Wolpe, P. R., Foster, K. R., & Langleben D. D. (2005). Emerging neurotechnologies for lie-detection: Promises and perils. *Am J Bioeth*, *5*(2), 39–49.

Yang, Y., A. Raine, A., Lencz, T., Bihrle, S., Lacasse, L., & Colletti, P. (2005a). Prefrontal white matter in pathological liars. *Br J Psychiatry.* Oct, *187*, 320–325.

Yang, Y., Raine, A., Narr, K. L., Lencz, T., LaCasse, L., & Colletti, P. (2005b). Volume reduction in prefrontal gray matter in unsuccessful criminal psychopaths. *Biol Psychiatry*, *57*(10), 1103–1108.

Yang, Y., Raine, A., Lencz, T., Birhle, S., LaCasse, L., & Colletti, P. (2007). Localisation of increased prefrontal white matter in pathological liars. *British Journal of Psychiatry*, *190*, 174–175.

Mutual Benefits of Using Humanoid Robots in Social Neuroscience

Thierry Chaminade *and* Mitsuo Kawato

Abstract

The prospect of closer ties between social cognitive neuroscience and robotics is gaining momentum in both communities. First, as artificial anthropomorphic agents, such as humanoid robots and computer-animated characters, are on the verge of being accessible for casual use, it has become important to understand humans' reactions towards these agents in social cognitive neuroscience terms. Besides, humanoid robots provide new tools to investigate human social cognitive neuroscience, the study of the brain processes underlying everyday interactions between individuals. Finally, social cognitive neurosciences can participate in enhancing the social competence of companion robots. The interdisciplinary approach used to test hypotheses pertaining to motor control, from low-level control to social aspects of motor cognition such as imitative learning, will be presented in a first section. Then, we will review studies in which humanoid robots and robotic parts were used to assess the framework of social resonance, grounded on the finding of an overlap between behavioral and neural processes recruited when experiencing an event and when perceiving another individual experiencing the same event. Finally, we will discuss how results and models from social cognitive neurosciences can be combined with resources from computer and robotic sciences to enhance the social competence of artificial agents.

Keywords: robotics, humanoid robots, social cognitive neuroscience, artificial agents, social resonance

Introduction

Ten years ago, Japan promoted the "Century of the Brain." The phrase "understanding the brain by creating the brain" was coined to synthesize how humanoid robots and computational neurosciences could contribute to progresses in naturalizing human psychology and its underlying neurophysiology (Miyamoto, Kawato, Setoyama, & Suzuki, 1988; Asada, MacDorman, Ishiguro, & Kuniyoshi et al., 2001; Brooks, 1997; Cheng et al., 2007; Kawato, 2008). Reproducing the hypothesized principles underlying how the human brain and body solve a given task with artifacts, artificial neural networks and humanoid robots, is crucial to the validation of these hypotheses. Embodiment of the artificial brain in an agent, that is, an entity able to produce actions and to have perceivable effects on the world, is overriding to investigate its functions, such as vision or motor control: the artificial brain has to be connected to sensors and a motor apparatus so that it can interact with its environment (see Clark, 1999, for the importance of embodiment). Here, we will discuss how this adage is applicable to the investigation of embodied social interactions. The underlying assumption is that by implementing mechanisms postulated to intervene in certain social behaviors in an artificial brain controlling a humanoid robot, the researcher can validate, or eventually amend, the hypothesis.

A robot has to be designed to resemble a human body if it is used to explore social neuroscience theories. Humanoid robots are robots whose appearance resembles that of a human body, that is, a robot with two arms and a head attached to a trunk, as well as two legs in the case of walking humanoid robots. Because of this anthropomorphism, they provide relevant testbeds for hypotheses pertaining to human cognition. They are used for researching how global human-like appearance influences our perception of other agents, in comparison to real humans and at the other end of the anthropomorphism spectrum, to industrial robotic arms. This is even more true of androids, a specific type of humanoid robots that attempt to reproduce the human appearance not only in their overall shape, but also in their fine-grained details such as form (artificial skin used for cover, hair, and other body parts such as hands), movement (biological motion), and behaviors (see Figure 64.1, bottom left). Androids indistinguishable from humans in terms of form, motion, and behavior would be invaluable for research by providing fully controlled confederates in experiments pertaining to embodied social interactions: this is one of the objectives of the emerging field of android science (MacDorman & Ishiguro, 2006).

Achieving perfect androids, undistinguishable from humans, is a goal not unlike the Total Turing Test, which grounded the linguistic aspects of the Turing Test in nonsymbolic sensorimotor embodied functions, referred to as *"our robotic capacities–our ability to interact bodily with the things in the world in the many nonverbal ways we do [. . .]"* (Harnad, 1989). While artificial conversational abilities at the core of the original Turing Test (Turing, 1950), including language, semantics, and symbolism, are beyond the scope of the present chapter, the concept of a robot "passing" a Total Turing Test highlights the possible outcomes of bidirectional exchanges between the development of androids and research in human social cognitive neurosciences.

Human emotional reactions towards androids has been described by the "Uncanny Valley" hypothesis proposed by Japanese roboticist Masahiro Mori (Mori, 1970). While one would expect that social acceptance of humanoid robots would increase with anthropomorphism, Mori proposed that artificial agents attempting, but imperfectly, to impersonate humans, as is the case with modern-day androids, would induce a negative emotional response (MacDorman & Ishiguro, 2006; Mori, 1970). While this hypothesis has proved itself impractical, as neither anthropomorphism nor emotional response easily lend themselves to being described by one-dimensional variables, understanding the cognitive mechanisms underlying the feeling of uncanniness, that one does experience when facing an android, will be invaluable to highlight the relevant cues in human natural social interactions.

In this chapter we will first review how humanoid robotics can be used to investigate human motor control, including social behaviors such as learning by imitation or reinforcement. A second part will provide examples of the use of humanoid robots to test hypotheses pertaining to one specific framework of social cognitive neuroscience: motor resonance. A last part will provide insights on how social cognitive neuroscience can, in return, help explain our reactions towards robotic devices and contribute to enhancing the social competence of future companion robots.

Humanoid Robots and Human Motor Cognition
A Brief Overview of Humanoid Robots
Fundamental developments in humanoid research started with the investigation of bipedal walk as early as the mid-1960s (Waseda Lower-Limb series), before using full body humanoids as the embodied platform necessary for certain applications, with actuators and sensors approximating human motor and sensory processes in order to simulate human cognition (Brooks, 1997).

The end of the 20th century has seen the emergence of increasingly autonomous humanoids. Honda's humanoids P2, in 1996, followed by P3 in 1997 and ASIMO in 2000 (Hirai, Hirose, Haikawa, & Takenaka, 1998; Sakagami et al., 2002), were among the first humanoids walking on their legs and feet and eventually climbing stairs and navigating autonomously, that stunned the world by going public: human-like robots were on their way from fiction to reality. SONY produced QRIO for entertainment purposes (Nagasaka, Kuroki, Suzuki, Itoh, & Yamaguchi, 2004), and the Humanoid Robotics Project investigated practical applications of humanoid robots (HRP series) cooperating with humans (Hirukawa et al., 2004).

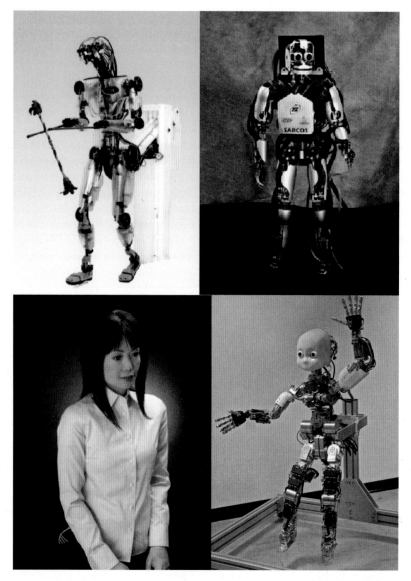

Fig. 64.1 Top: The humanoid robots DB (left) and CB-I (right) developed by Kawato and collaborators. Bottom: The humanoid robot iCub (left) and the android Repliee Q2 (right). Further details are available in the text.

Most of these projects, though some said to be "biologically inspired," had little direct input from biological sciences. Robotic implementation of walk illustrates this well: most of the existing humanoids use locomotion engineered by zero-moment-point control, a traditional control method for biped robots (details in Bezerra & Zampieri, 2004), usually resulting in a low center of gravity and bent knees, clearly distinct from the human walking pattern. In contrast, the humanoid robot DB (Dynamic Brain, Atkeson et al., 2000) was developed with the aim of most closely replicating a human body (Figure 64.1, top left): DB possesses 30 degrees-of-freedom and human-like size and weight. From the mechanical

point of view, DB behaves like a human body that is mechanically compliant since its hydraulic actuators are powerful enough to avoid the necessity of using reduction mechanisms at the joints, unlike most electric-motor-driven and highly geared humanoid robots. Within its head, DB is equipped with an artificial vestibular organ (gyro sensor), which measures head velocity, and four cameras with vertical and horizontal degrees-of-freedom. Two of the cameras have telescopic lenses corresponding to foveal vision, while the other two have wide-angle lenses corresponding to peripheral vision.

The same group subsequently developed a humanoid robot called CB-i (Computational Brain

Interface, Cheng et al., 2007), more accurate in recreating a human body than DB (Figure 64.1, top right). To maintain the mechanical compliance of the body, CB-i also utilizes hydraulic actuators for most of its actuators. The biggest improvement of CB-i over DB is its autonomy. Dynamic Brain is mounted at the pelvis because it needs to be powered by an external hydraulic pump, through oil hoses arranged around the mount. The computer system controlling DB is remote and connected by wires. In contrast, CB-i carries both onboard power supplies (electric and hydraulic) and a computing system on its back, and thus it can function fully autonomously. It is equipped with a total of 51 degrees-of-freedom (DOF): 2×7 DOF legs, 2×7 DOF arms, 2×2 DOF eyes, 3 DOF neck/head, 1 DOF mouth, 3 DOF torso, and 2×6 DOF hands.

CB-i is designed to have similar configurations, range of motion, power, and strength to a human body, allowing it to better reproduce natural human-like movements, in particular for posture control, locomotion, and object manipulation. A similar development is RoboCub, a European project investigating human cognition, and in particular developmental psychology, through the realization of a humanoid robot the size of a 3.5-year-old child, iCub (Sandini, Metta, & Vernon, 2004; see Figure 64.1, bottom right). These technical improvements illustrate that robotic devices available for research in human cognition, including but not limited to social neuroscience, are just becoming accessible.

Investigating Motor Cognition with Humanoid Robots

The use of robotic devices allows the validation of hypotheses pertaining to biological motor control, from low-level controllers, such as central pattern generators and their use in walking, to high-level cognition, such as learning by imitation (Miyamoto et al., 1996; Schaal, 1999). For instance, computational models of eye movements (Shibata, Schaal, & Kawato, 2005) are used to implement the vestibulo-ocular reflex (Shibata & Schaal, 2001), smooth and saccadic eye movements in the humanoid robot DB. Central pattern generators (CPG) are neural circuits that can spontaneously generate spatiotemporal movement patterns even if afferent inputs are absent and descending commands to the generators are temporally constant. CPG concepts were formed in the 1960s through neurobiological studies of invertebrate rhythmic movements, and they are key to understanding most rhythmic movements. Furthermore, it was shown using fMRI that these rhythmic movements use neural circuitry distinct from discrete movement in the human cerebral cortex (Schaal, Sternad, Osu, & Kawato, 2004), hence validating the use of CPG neural networks in robotic implementation of human rhythmic movements, as in the case of drumming, paddling a ball behaviors (Schaal, Peters, Nakanishi, & Ijspeert, 2003), or CB-i walking (Morimoto et al., 2006).

Another aspect of human behavior that has been described by computational neural network models before being implemented in robotic devices is reward-based reinforcement learning (Barto, Sutton, & Anderson, 1983). Animals in general and humans in particular adapt their actions to maximize rewards. Several models describe how learning can be achieved using mechanisms based on reward, including reinforcement learning. And as for CPG, animal neurophysiology and human brain imaging have identified the main actors in this model, including midbrain dopamine neurons encoding reward prediction error (Hollerman & Schultz, 1998; Haruno et al., 2004; Pessiglione, Seymour, Flandin, Dolan, & Frith, 2006), or the orbitofrontal cortex in the representation of the reward (Tremblay & Schultz, 1999; O'Doherty, Kringelbach, Rolls, Hornak, & Andrews, 2001). Validated by neurophysiology, reward-based reinforcement learning algorithms have been used to implement complex behaviors in robotic devices, as the air-hockey playing by DB, which makes use of a reinforcement-learning algorithm with reward (a puck enters the opponent's goal) and penalty (a puck enters the robot's goal), as well as imitation learning (Bentivegna, Atkeson, Ude, & Cheng, 2004). Research on the acquisition of internal models in the cerebellum (Kawato, 1999; Imamizu et al., 2000) supported a supervised learning scheme (Schaal & Atkeson, 1998) used in robotic implementations of pole-balancing and visually guided arm reaching toward a target (Atkeson et al., 2000). Approaches described until here make use of models of action control derived from neurosciences to develop algorithms for a number of behaviors that are, in turn, validated by their robotic implementation.

Learning by Observation of Conspecifics

A similar approach can be used for social aspects of motor behavior, exemplified by imitative learning (Miyamoto et al., 1996; Schaal, 1999). Compared to animals, humans, in particular infants, show an uncanny ability to learn about the world by observing others' actions (Csibra & Gergely, 2006). But for a humanoid robot, learning new motor behaviors usually requires hours of tedious programming.

As humanoids are expected to perform tasks also performed by humans, learning from observation could provide a fast, intuitive, and versatile way to control a humanoid robot. It also provides an interesting testbed for models of imitation learning derived from social neuroscience. One major issue that needs to be solved is the correspondence problem; that is, how can a perceived body part, coded in external coordinates, be mapped onto same body part in the controller, and ultimately in motor control, coded in internal coordinates? As actions can be viewed as a concatenation of motor primitives (Atkeson et al., 2000), the implementation chosen with DB in the mid-1990s has been to consider that a perceived action is mapped onto a set of motor primitives and the best predictor of the next step of the action "wins" the competition and is selected as the action to imitate. This approach allows programming behaviors such as dancing (Riley, Ude & Atkeson, 2000) and juggling (Atkeson et al., 2000). It nevertheless lacks aspects of human imitation, such as bidirectionality (Breazeal & Scassellati, 2002; Marin, Issartel, & Chaminade, 2009). We'll later discuss biomimetic approaches to imitation that have been applied to a robotic hand.

In conclusion to this first section, algorithms developed for DB and CB-i to achieve a number of motor tasks are roughly based on principles derived from neurosciences, and many utilize some or all of three learning elements described previously: reinforcement learning, supervised learning, and imitation learning. For example, biologically inspired control algorithms for locomotion utilize imitation learning and a central pattern generator. First, a neural network model (Schaal et al., 2003) learns locomotion trajectories correctly demonstrated by humans. The limit-cycle oscillator is utilized as a central pattern generator controlling a mechanical oscillator in the robot body that is phase-reset by foot-ground-contact, guaranteeing stable synchronization of neural and mechanical oscillators with respect to phase and frequency. The achieved locomotion is robust against different surfaces with various frictions and slopes, and it is human-like in the sense that the robot body's center of gravity is high while the knee is almost nearly fully extended at the foot contact. In other words, biologically inspired algorithms allow achievement of human-like locomotion by humanoid robots.

Humanoid Robots as Testbeds for Social Neuroscience

In this section, we will provide examples of how robots can be used to test hypotheses pertaining to human social neuroscience (Chaminade & Hodgins, 2006) both in behavioral and neuroimaging experiments. We will rely on one theoretical framework that fueled a series of work, motor resonance, particularly relevant for the motor foundations of embodied social interactions (Decety & Chaminade, 2003). After a brief description of this framework, we will present pertinent experiments using robotic devices.

Motor Resonance in Social Cognition

Theories of social behaviors using concepts of resonance have flourished in the scientific literature following the finding that the same neural structures show an increase of activity both when executing a given action and when observing another individual executing the same action (Blakemore & Decety, 2001; Gallese, Keysers, & Rizzolatti, 2004; Rizzolatti, Fogassi, & Gallese, 2001). Neuropsychological findings that use action production, perception, naming, and imitation for diagnosis of apraxia, hinted, in the early 1990s, that limb praxis and gesture perception share parts of their cortical networks (Rothi, Ochipa, & Heilman, 1991). Similarly in language, the motor theory of speech perception claimed, on the basis of experimental data, that the objects of speech perception are not sounds, but the phonetic gestures of the speaker, whose neural underpinnings are motor commands (Liberman & Mattingly, 1985). We will refer to these processes under the header of motor resonance, which is defined, at the behavioral and neural levels, as the automatic activation of motor control systems during perception of actions.

Mirror neurons offer the first physiological demonstration that motor resonance is valid at the cellular level. Mirror neurons are a type of neuron found in the macaque monkey brain and characterized by their response recorded by single cell electrophysiological recordings. First reported in 1992 by Giacomo Rizzolatti's group in Parma (di Pellegrino, Fadiga, Fogassi, Gallese, & Rizzolatti, 1992), "a particular subset of F5 neurons [which] discharge[s] when the monkey observes meaningful hand movements made by the experimenter" were called mirror neurons (Gallese, Fadiga, Fogassi, & Rizzolatti, 1996). The importance of this discovery stems from the known function of area F5, a premotor area in which neurons discharge when monkeys execute distal goal-directed motor acts such as grasping, holding, or tearing an object. These neurons are activated both during the execution of a given goal-directed action and during the observation of the same action made in front of the monkey. Mirror properties have also been reported in neurons of the monkey's primary motor cortex (Tkach, Reimer, & Hatsopoulos, 2007), supporting that resonance between neuronal response to observation and execution of actions is a general feature of the motor system. The human neurophysiology, investigated using the brain imaging techniques which emerged in the last decades such as positron emission tomography (PET), functional magnetic resonance imagery (fMRI), electroencephalography (EEG), magnetoencephalography (MEG), and transcranial magnetic stimulation (TMS), entails an expected conclusion on the basis of the mirror neuron literature in macaque monkey: premotor cortices, originally considered to be exclusively concerned with motor control, are also active during observation of actions in the absence of any action execution (Chaminade & Decety, 2001). Accumulating human neuroimaging data does confirm in humans what mirror neurons demonstrated beyond doubt in macaque monkeys at the cellular level: Neurophysiological bases for the perception of other individuals' behaviors makes use of the neurophysiological bases for the control of the self's behavior.

Motor resonance is evident in behaviors like action contagion, motor priming (the facilitation of the execution of an action by seeing it done; Edwards, Humphreys, & Castiello, 2003), and motor interference (the hindering effect of observing incompatible actions during the execution of actions; Kilner, Paulignan, & Blakemore, 2003). But, does the motor resonance described in a laboratory environment have a significant impact in everyday life? Past social and developmental psychological research on social interactions has demonstrated that people's movements are coordinated, reflecting a natural "entrainment" processes between agents watching each other (Schmidt et al., 2008). Social psychologists investigating this coordination in social interactions since the 1960s have found that it embodies functionally important dyadic psychological characteristics such as rapport (Bernieri & Rosenthal, 1991; Feldman, 2007; Semin, 2007). For instance, studies have shown that the traditional social and personality properties of a dyad (rapport, liking, social competence) relate to the dynamical properties of a dyad's coordinated movements and how, in return, the coordination of movements enhances the sociability of interpersonal interactions (Chartrand & Bargh, 1999; Lakin & Chartrand, 2003). The chameleon effect was introduced to describe the unconscious reproduction of "postures,

mannerisms, facial expressions and other behaviors of one's interacting partner" (Chartrand & Bargh, 1999). Subjects unaware of the purpose of the experiment interacted with an experimenter performing one of two target postures: rubbing the face or shaking the foot. Analysis of the behavior showed a significant increase of the tendency to engage in the same action. In addition, this imitation made the interacting partner more likable even though participants were not aware of this imitation (Chartrand & Bargh, 1999). Altogether, these results support the hypothesis that motor resonance, investigated at the behavioral or neural level, underlies a number of social behaviors involving action, such as action understanding (Chaminade, Meary, Orliaguet, & Decety, 2001) and imitation (Rizzolatti et al., 2001), but also more generally in the social domain, such as empathy and social bonding (Decety & Chaminade, 2003).

Resonance Applied to Humanoid Robotics

We've briefly described motor resonance, a well-studied mechanism involved in social interactions. The methods that have been developed to investigate the motor bases of human social interactions can be extended to investigate how humans react to anthropomorphic artificial agents such as humanoid robots. The underlying assumption is that the amplitude of the resonance indicates the extent to which an artificial agent is treated as a social, human-like inter-actor.

Behavioral Experiments

As a consequence of motor resonance, perception of another individual's actions influences the execution of actions by the self: Observing an action facilitates the execution of the same action (motor priming), and hinders the execution of a different action (motor interference). These behavioral effects can be investigated experimentally to provide objective measures of the magnitude of motor resonance depending on the nature of the agents.

In one experiment, this effect was investigated with two actions, hand opening and hand closing, in response to the observation of a hand opening and closing, with the hand being either a realistic human hand or a simple robotic hand having the appearance of an articulated claw with two opposite fingers (Press, Bird, Flach, & Heyes, 2005). Here, anthropomorphism is reduced to the overall function of a specific part of the body, the opposable fingers of the human hand. Volunteers in the experiment were required to make a prespecified response (to open or to close their right hand) as soon as a stimulus appears on the screen. Response time is recorded and analyzed as a function of the content of the stimulus, either a human or a robotic hand, in a posture congruent or incongruent with the pre-specified movement (e.g., opened or closed hand when the prespecified action is opening the hand). Results show an increased response time in incongruent compared to congruent conditions, in response to both human and robotic hand, suggesting that the motor priming effect is not restricted to human stimuli but generalizes to robotic stimuli (Press et al., 2005). The amplitude of the effect, taking the form of the time difference between response to incongruent and congruent stimuli, is larger for human (~30 ms) than for robotic stimuli (~15 ms).

A follow-up experiment tested whether the effect is better explained by a bottom-up process due to the overall shape of the agent or a top-down process caused by the knowledge of the intentionality of humans compared to robotic devices. Human hands modified by the addition of a metal and wire wrist are perceived as less intentional than the original hands. Nevertheless, no significant differences is found between the priming effect of the original and of the robotized human hand (Press, Gillmeister, & Heyes, 2006), in favor of the bottom-up hypothesis that the overall hand shape, and not its description as a human or robotic hand, affects the priming effect.

A series of experiments (Chaminade et al., 2005; Oztop, Franklin, Chaminade, & Cheng, 2005) using the humanoid robot DB described previously was motivated by Kilner et al.'s (2003) study of motor interference. Volunteers in this study produce a vertical or horizontal rhythmic arm movement while facing another agent, a real human being or an industrial robotic arm, producing spatially congruent (i.e., vertical when vertical, horizontal when horizontal) or spatially incongruent (horizontal when vertical and vertical when horizontal) rhythmic movements. The interference effect is measured by the increase of the variance in the movement, and it has since been shown that this variance is in fact an automatic coordination: In incongruent conditions, the movement is "pulled" in the plane orthogonal to the movement by the observed movement (Richardson, 2009). Such interference is found when volunteers watch an arm movement spatially incongruent with the one they are producing, for example, vertical versus horizontal (Kilner et al., 2003). Interestingly, this study does not reveal any interference effect when the other agent is an industrial robotic arm moving at a constant velocity, suggesting that motor interference is specific to interactions between human agents.

The original experimental paradigm was adapted to investigate how humanoid robots interfere with humans (Figure 64.2). In this series of experiments, subjects perform rhythmic arm movements while observing either a human agent or the humanoid robot DB standing approximately 2 m away from them performing either congruent or incongruent rhythmic arm movements. The robot is programmed to track the endpoint Cartesian trajectories of rhythmic top-left to bottom-right and top-right to bottom-left hand movements involving elbow, shoulder, and torso movements by commanding the right arm and the torso joints of the robot. Subjects are instructed to be in phase with the other agent's movements. During each 30-second trial, the kinematics of the endpoint of the subject's right index finger is recorded with a motion capture device. The variance of the executed movements is used as a measure of motor interference caused by the observed agent.

In the first experiment (Oztop, Franklin, et al., 2005), trajectories are derived from captured motion of the same movements performed by the human agent used in for the experiment. The movements are performed at 0.5 Hz, while the experimenter listens to a 1 Hz beep on headphones to keep the frequency constant. Results (Figure 64.2) show that in contrast to the industrial robotic arm, the humanoid robot executing movements based on motion-captured data causes a significant change of the variance of the movement depending on congruency (Oztop, Franklin, et al., 2005b). The ratio between the variance in the incongruent and in the congruent conditions increases from the industrial robotic arm (r = 1, no increase in incongruent condition, as reported in Kilner et al. 2003) and the human (r~2), both in ours and in Kilner et al.'s study. A humanoid robot does trigger an interference effect, but this interference is weaker (r~1.5) than with a human.

In a follow-up experiment, we have investigated the effect of the movement kinematics on the interference. The humanoid robot moves either with a biological motion based, as previously, on recorded trajectories, or with an artificial motion implemented by a 1-DOF sinusoidal movement of the elbow. We find a significant effect of the factors defining the experimental conditions. The increase in incongruent conditions is only significant when

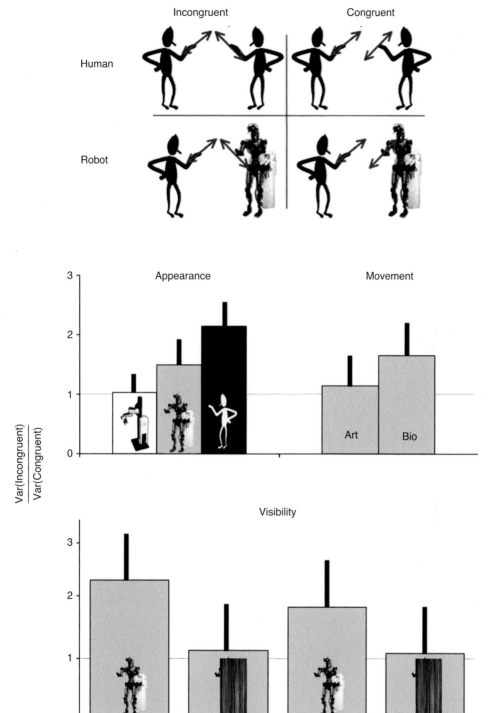

Fig. 64.2 Top: Factorial plan showing the 4 canonical condition of motor interference experiment: horizontally, the spatial congruency between the volunteers and the tested agent movement; vertically, the human control and the agent being tested, in this case the humanoid robot DB. Bottom: Summary of the results from the three experiments described in the text. Bars represent the ratio between the variance for incongruent and congruent movements (error: standard error of the mean). Effect of appearance: Results are given for three agents, an industrial robot on the left (Kilner et al., 2003), a humanoid robot with biological motion at the center (Oztop et al., 2005b) and a human on the right (Kilner et al., 2003; Oztop et al., 2005b). Effect of the motion: The humanoid robot DB displays artificial (ART) or biological (BIO) motion (Chaminade et al., 2005). Effect of visibility the humanoid robot displays artificial (ART) or biological (BIO) motion while its body is visible or hidden by a cloth (unpublished observations).

the robot movements reproduce biological motion (Chaminade et al., 2005). A similar trend for artificial motion was not significant. The ratio that can be calculated on the basis of the results is, in the case of biological motion, comparable to the ratio reported in the previous experiment, ~1.3. Note the importance of having internal controls, in this case a human, to compare the ratio between agents within groups.

A final experiment assessed whether seeing the full body or only body parts of the other agent influences motor resonance (Chaminade, Franklin, Oztop, & Cheng, unpublished results). The effect of interference could be due merely to the appearance of the agent, which would predict a linear increase of the ratio between the variance for incongruent and congruent movements with anthropomorphism. Alternatively it could be influenced by the knowledge we have about the nature of the other agent. To test whether appearance was the main factor, we cover the body and face of the humanoid robot with a black cloth leaving just the moving arm visible, and compare the results of the interference paradigm between covered and uncovered agents. Preliminary results indicate that increased variance can not be measured in the absence of body visibility. This implies that humanoid robot arm movements in isolation do not provide sufficient cues about the nature of the agent being interacted with to elicit motor resonance (bottom-up effect of the stimulus). In addition, knowledge about the aspect of the agent being interacted with is not sufficient to elicit motor resonance (top-down effect of the knowledge). These results confirm the conclusions of the motor priming experiment described previously, in favor of a bottom-up effect due to the anthropomorphic appearance of the agent being interacted with.

Overall, these examples illustrate how humanoid robots can be used to address questions pertaining to social cognition, in this case, factors influencing motor resonance. First, these experiments allow us to confirm that motor resonance is a bottom-up process involved in the perception of other agents. Second, it is modulated by the anthropomorphism of the agent being tested. And in addition, this paradigm provides an objective measure of the social bonding with the humanoid robot DB that could be extended to other robots.

Neuroimaging Experiments

Motor resonance has been extensively studied with neuroimaging in humans, and it is possible to use similar approaches to the perception of anthropomorphic robots. Neuroimaging experiments comparing the observation of humans versus robots have so far yielded mixed results. A first series of experiments has focused on hand actions. In a PET study, subjects are presented with a grasping action performed by a human or by a robotic arm. The authors report that the left ventral premotor activity found in previous experiments of action observation responded to human, but not robot, actions (Tai, Scherfler, Brooks, Sawamoto, & Castiello, 2004). However, results of a recent fMRI study indicate that a robotic arm and hand elicits motor resonance, in the form of increased activity in regions activated by the execution of actions during the observation of object-directed actions compared to simple movements (Gazzola, Rizzolatti, Wicker, & Keysers, 2007). Furthermore, the trend is of an increased activity in response to robot compared to human stimuli, though this increase is not reported as significant. How can we reconcile these two sets of results? One possibility, the different techniques used in these experiments, PET and fMRI, cannot explain the dramatic reversal of the results. Another possibility derives from differences in anthropomorphism of the robotic arms and hands used in the two studies, yet it is difficult to draw a conclusion: according to both reports, the robotic arms and hands and their motions were not attempting to be realistic. Another source of discrepancy between the two studies comes from the experimental instructions. Indeed, instructions can have significant effects on the brain structures involved in a given cognitive task. This has been clearly shown in fMRI studies in which subjects interacted with a similar random program but were presented their partner as varying in anthropomorphism (Gallagher, Jack, Roepstorff, & Frith, 2002). Regions involved in mentalizing were more active when subjects believed they were interacting with the human compared to an unintentional, artificial agent, even though the partner's responses were random in all conditions. This highlights the importance of the experimental instructions, in particular when using artificial agents. While it is the robot embodiment that is manipulated in both Tai et al. and Gazzola et al. studies, their instructions do differ. In the first report, "subjects were instructed to carefully observe the human (experimenter) or the robot model," while in the second, "subjects were instructed to watch the movies carefully, paying particular attention to the relationship between the agents and the objects."

Differences between these instructions, in particular the focus on the goal of the actions, could explain discrepancies in the results. In order to investigate the involvement of motor resonance during the observation of a humanoid robot, participants of an fMRI experiment observed video clips of human and humanoid robot depictions of facial expressions of simple emotions while rating the emotion or the motion of the agent (see details in Chaminade & Cheng, 2009; Chaminade et al., 2010). A subset of the facial Action Units (AU, described in Ekman & Friesen, 1978) is used for a simplified but realistic reproduction of the facial expression of emotions used in this experiment (Itoh et al., 2004).

We are particularly interested in the response of the left ventral premotor cortex, a region involved in motor resonance that was found in the main effect of action observation, illustrated in Figure 64.3 and in Chaminade et al. (2010). Response to the robot increases significantly when attention is directed to the action content of the stimulus compared to attending to the motion, while the same difference is not significant for human stimuli. This result comforts that resonance processes taking place when perceiving human stimuli are automatic (Rizzolatti & Craighero, 2004). In contrast, these processes are modulated by attention in the case of robot stimuli, and the reduced response in the implicit task suggests this could be explained by the absence of pre-existing representation of robots' actions. The interaction between task and agent would thus derive from an interaction between bottom-up processes, influenced by the nature of the agent (automatic for human, but not for robot), and top-down processes, depending on the object of attention. If this interpretation is correct, motor resonance towards artificial agents would be enhanced when the agents' actions are explicitly processed as actions, and not mechanical movements, by the observer.

This finding offers an interesting solution to the question raised earlier: When asking subjects to pay "particular attention to the relationship between the agents and the objects," Gazzola et al. oriented their subjects' attention to process the robot's movement as transitive goal-directed actions, hence reinforcing a top-down activation of motor resonance. In contrast, Tai et al.'s instructions to "carefully observe" the agent did not impose focusing the attention on the goal of the action, hence relying exclusively on bottom-up processes to activate motor resonance, that is reduced towards humanoid robots. An important conclusion with regards to the use of humanoid robots in social cognitive neuroscience is that the way they are perceived, either as mechanical devices or as goal-directed agents, is significantly modulated by the task, a finding that can dramatically influence the results of an experiment.

Insights from Social Neuroscience for Designing Socially Competent Humanoids Robots

While robots appear to be pertinent to investigate motor resonance, the last part of this chapter focuses

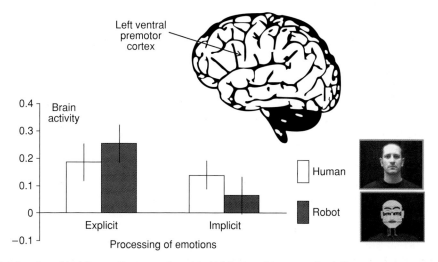

Fig. 64.3 Top: Location of the left ventral premotor cluster in which brain activity was analyzed. Bottom: graphs presenting brain activity in response to human (white) and robot (grey) agents presented on the right depending on the Task (error bar represent standard error of the mean). Note the larger increase between implicit and explicit for robot than for human stimuli.

on the complementary question: Can social cognitive neuroscience be useful to enhance the social competence of humanoid robots?

Humanoid Robot Design

Artificial anthropomorphic agents such as humanoid robots are likely to be increasingly present in our societies. Aichi 2005 exposition broadcasted internationally tens of robots, from task-specialized robots to social androids welcoming the visitors. They are embedded with an increasing number of functionalities derived from various aspects of robotic and human-computer interaction research (e.g., autonomous mobility, speech recognition and synthesis) allowing them to assist in a range of taxing tasks such as care giving (Kiesler & Hinds, 2004). Kokoro company's simroid, a feeling and responsive android patient, is now being used as a training tool for dentists because its realistic appearance and behaviors, in particular expressing pain if a nerve is hit while poking teeth, motivate dental trainees to treat it like a human being. Acceptability of robotic companions has been tested with toddlers, showing that after period of familiarization with QRIO (SONY's bipedal humanoid entertainment robot) in the classroom, children came to treat it as a peer, for example multiplying haptic contact, especially when the robot's actions were congruent with the children's and displayed variability (Tanaka, Cicourel, & Movellan, 2007). A nonhumanoid robot, designed after a baby seal, has been shown to comfort elderly people in care houses (Wada & Shibata, 2007), and is now marketed, supporting the potential use of robotic platforms in eldercare, as well as for therapies such as for autistic patients (Robins & Dautenhahn, 2006).

Personal robots intended to live and work in our environment are required to communicate with humans in a smooth and natural way, using verbal communication but also nonverbal communication like body movements, postures, and facial expressions (Bernieri et al., 1991). To optimize the social competence of humanoid robots, it is important to understand not only the processes underlying humans' automatic and unintentional reactions to these agents, but also how the robots' characteristics (form, movement, and behavior) influence these reactions. The first question, and how humanoid robots can help investigate it, has been the topic of the previous section with the example of resonance. The second question has a longstanding history in robotics circles, but often relies on introspective judgments or implicit assumptions. A number of studies have addressed the issue of the form a humanoid robot should have in order to be socially accepted. For instance, DiSalvo, Gemperle, Forlizzi, and Kiesler (2002) used questionnaires asking participants to rate human likeliness of humanoid robots as well as their functionalities.

The "Uncanny Valley of Eeriness"

The most famous introspection that has served for years as a guideline for robots designers is the "Uncanny Valley," (illustrated Figure 64.4) from the famous Japanese roboticist Masahiro Mori. This hypothesis postulates that artificial agents imperfectly attempting to impersonate humans induce a negative emotional response (MacDorman & Ishiguro, 2006; Mori, 1970). In other words, as a robot starts to resemble a human in its fine-grained details (as is the case with androids), the perceiver has strong negative emotional reactions towards tiny flaws, that is, it is more particular about its details. As Toshitada Doi, an official representative commenting the design of Sony's humanoid robot QRIO, explained,

> "We suggested the idea of an 'eight year-old space life form' to the designer—we didn't want to make it too similar to a human. In the background, as well, lay an idea passed down from the man whose work forms the foundation of the Japanese robot industry, Masahiro Mori: "the valley of eeriness." If your design is too close to human form, at a certain point it becomes just too . . . uncanny. So, while we created QRIO in a human image, we also wanted to give it little bit of a "spaceman" feel."

Nowadays though, people like David Hanson build realistic anthropomorphic robots under the assumption that the uncanny valley is an illusion caused by the poor quality of aesthetic designs (Hanson, 2005), not an insurmountable limit.

Anthropomorphism indeed influences the perception of actions from artificial agents. The bias towards perceiving a computer-animated agent's running motion as biological decreases when the agent's anthropomorphism increases (Chaminade et al., 2007). Using fMRI, we have shown that this bias negatively correlates with activity in the ventral premotor cortex, which belongs to the motor resonance system. Thus, it may be possible to explain the phenomenon of the uncanny valley in social neuroscience terms. As the motor resonance network results from Hebbian learning of associations between visual and motor representations of human actions (Keysers & Perrett, 2004), observing an

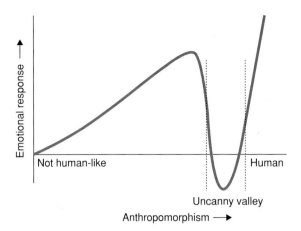

Fig. 64.4 Sketch of the Uncanny Valley adapted from Mori (1970). The Valley represents the negative emotional response hypothesized by Masahiro Mori in response to realistic albeit imperfect anthropomorphic agent.

action engages motor resonance in a bottom-up fashion for humans, but not for artificial agents (see the conclusions of the previous section). In addition, the driving inputs to the resonance system increase with anthropomorphism. But the uncanny valley hypothesis describes the case of realistic albeit imperfect anthropomorphic agents, that is, their imperfections are perceivable—to put it differently, when the agent is indistinguishable from a real human, then it is out of the uncanny valley. In the case of contemporary androids, the realistic human appearance triggers bottom-up processes as for real humans. But because of flaws in their appearance or motion (such as plastic texture and imperfect transluminance of the skin, or lack of degrees of freedom in the face or mouth, or shaky motion), the system outputs an error that triggers brain processes to re-assess the visual input. Behaviorally, this leads to doubt the humanness of the agent, leading to the feeling of uncanniness.

Recent fMRI data support this interpretation (Saygin, Chaminade, Ishiguro, Driver and Frith, 2011). We recorded brain response to the perception of actions performed by the android Repliee Q2, by the human after whom the android was developed, and by a humanoid robot obtained by removing the android cover skin, using repetition priming to isolate regions specifically responding to each agent's actions. The main results come from comparing repetition priming results for the three agents: while the human and robot actions activate a limited number of circumscribed regions, the response to android's actions is much larger and widespread across the cortex. Cortical networks are more engaged in making sense of an android movement than a human (having the same shape than the android) or humanoid robot (having the same motion than the android) movement.

In this interpretation of the uncanny valley, as we get closer to human appearance, the perceptual system, tuned by design for recognizing human actions, becomes particular to the tiniest flaws in the android form and motion. Such a view comforts David Hanson's argument: the uncanny valley is mainly a result of poor aesthetic design. This is a particularly important line of development in the perspective of the design of companion robots. By extension, it is possible that a similar uncanniness will result from interacting with anthropomorphic robots having imperfect social behaviors. For example, the addition of random micro-behaviors in one of Hiroshi Ishiguro's androids has proven beneficial to avoid it falling into the uncanny valley (Minato et al., 2004). Thus, using results from social neurosciences to enhance the social competence of companion robots is an interesting direction to design more socially competent companion robots.

Implementing a Model of Social Cognition

How can insights coming from social cognitive neurosciences be used to foster humanoid robots' social acceptability? The attribution of mental states, such as goals and beliefs, when observing other people's behavior is automatic, and this perception of internal states is known as the ability to mentalize (or theory of mind, Frith & Frith, 1999), central to human social cognition. A "mentalizing" robot would provide new grounds for human-robot social interactions. It could learn from an observer as children do, and react more accurately to the emotional, attentional, and intentional states of the agent it is interacting with, therefore reacting accurately to their behavior.

Scassellati (2001) proposed that

"to build machines that interact naturally with people, our machines must both interpret the behavior of others

according to [these] social rules and display the social cues that will allow people to naturally interpret the machine's behavior."

Such an approach amounts to a biomimetism of social cognition similar to the approach described for motor control in the first section. A model describing the developmental origin of theory of mind was proposed by Baron-Cohen (1995). In this model, an Eye-Direction Detector (EDD) and an Intentionality Detector (ID) provide a Shared Attention Module (SAM) with both the object of attention of the observed agent (from the EDD) and its current intentional state (through the ID). This model has been used to enhance the social skills of the humanoid robot Cog (Scassellati, 2002). The objective was to use the low-level perceptual abilities of a humanoid robot to reproduce the high-level cognitive abilities described in Baron-Cohen's model.

First, the system uses its visual input to build saliency maps inspired by a model of human visual attention (Wolfe, 1994), processing the input image by a variety of low-level perceptual filters (motion, depth, color, and in particular skin color) which produce individual feature maps then combined into a single activation maps. Peaks in these maps correspond to potential points of interest, and one is selected depending of the overall goal (top-down control of the allocation of attention). Objects of interest can then be tracked in real-time, for instance tracking a person's movement if the top-down influence biases the system towards social interactions. Similar tracking systems have been developed on other robotic platforms including DB (Ude & Atkeson, 2003). Once tracked, the objects' trajectories are used to classify the object into two categories: inanimate and animate. The discrimination is based purely on spatiotemporal characteristics of the movement by applying the first level of Leslie's model of agency, the theory of body mechanism (ToBy) that characterizes the physical aspects of agents and objects and their interactions, for example dynamics, trajectory and collision (Leslie, 1984). Animate objects can be the source of information about other agents' intentional stance. Using color filters to detect faces, head orientation and eyeball position can be extracted to infer objects of attention of the observed agent. At this point, the Eye Direction Detector and the Intentionality Detector of Baron-Cohen's model are available on the robotic platform Cog (Scassellati, 2001).

The focus of the previous paragraph on the development of EDD and ID illustrates how existing theories of cognitive architecture can participate in the design of socially acceptable robots. Needless to say, many other developments related to social cognition have been made by this group, including (but not limited to) shared attention (Thomaz, Berlin, & Breazeal, 2005), perspective-taking (Gray, Breazeal, Berlin, Brooks, & Lieberman, 2005), theory of mind (Breazeal, Gray, & Berlin, 2007), and empathy (Smith & Breazeal, 2007). All these abilities, together with the impressive range of facial and bodily expressions of emotions their robotic platform can achieve, make Leonardo one of the most socially competent robots to date (see Figure 64.5).

Implementing a Mechanism Involved in Social Cognition

While in the previous examples, it is mainly the modular architecture of the system that's being reproduced to control the robot, one can even think of using biomimetic features at the level of low-level computational mechanisms. In the example given here, human-like motor resonance is implemented in a humanoid robotic hand (Chaminade, Oztop, Cheng, & Kawato, 2008; Oztop, Chaminade, Cheng, & Kawato, 2005). The hypothesis is that synchronized sensory feedback of executed actions could drive Hebbian learning in associative brain networks, forming motor resonance networks from which contagion of actions could emerge. This hypothesis is inspired by the theoretical proposal that motor resonance networks can result from Hebbian learning of associations between visual and motor representations of actions (Keysers & Perrett, 2004), as well as developmental psychology observations that synchronized action and sensory feedback are available to neonate during motor babbling with their hands (Heyes, 2001; Van de Meer, van der Weel, & Lee, 1995).

A simple associative network linking a 16 degrees of freedom robotic hand and a simple visual system consisting of a camera is fed simultaneously by the motor commands sent to the robotic hand to achieve a posture and by the visual feedback of this posture captured by a camera (Chaminade et al., 2008). Embodiment of the system, that is using a robotic hand instead of a virtual simulation, brings ecologically valid noise in the training and testing phases, validating the applicability of the results in the real world. The associative memory, a modified Hopfield net, is a connectionist architecture relying on Hebbian-like learning mechanisms with units resembling neurons; it can be considered as a credible biological simulation. The network is kept

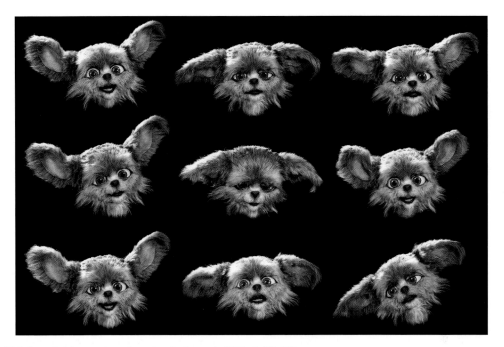

Fig. 64.5 Some facial expressions of emotions by Leonardo (© Fardad Faridi).

minimal to limit the hypotheses required to describe the homologies between this artificial and biological systems. A preprocessing step isolates the static hand posture from the background and forms the retina of the system. The motor bits control the movements of the fingers of the Gifu robotic hand. The retina and motor code form the input to the HHOP network (Figure 64.6). During a training phase, the network is fed simultaneously by the motor commands sent to the robotic hand to perform gestures and by the visual feedback of the robotic hand. During a testing phase, the system is presented with the same or new hand postures, or with hand postures from another agent.

The main results from the robotic implementation are that the associative network trained by self-observation of hand postures is capable of action contagion, and depicts two important features of imitation: generalization to new agents and to new postures. In a first experiment, response of the associative network is assessed with either visual input from itself or from other hands. Hands used in the experiment differ in relative size and shape of fingers, but their general aspect is similar to the robotic hand. The network is always correct when tested with its own visual input, and largely above chance when tested with another hand. This behavior can be described as a robotic form of automatic action contagion as the system has not been designed *in order to* imitate, but to reproduce the ontogenic

origin of resonance system. Similar results were obtained with a non-anthropomorphic robotic arm (Nadel, Revel, Andry, & Gaussier, 2004).

The system is also able to reproduce some new postures (Chaminade et al., 2008), that is to imitate hand postures the associative network hasn't been trained with initially and thus has no memory of. In behavioral terms, this suggests that motor resonance could be used to learn new gestures. Thus, in addition to action contagion, the resonance system depicts the generalization characteristics of more elaborate forms of imitation, a result which could guide research on the development of action contagion in infants.

Building on this "proof-of-concept," a similar associative learning could be used to develop a realistic architecture with full-body motor resonance abilities at the core of the robotic platform, akin to providing the humanoid robot with a sensorimotor body schema. This architecture could subtend realistic human behaviors. For instance, studies of natural interactions between humans have demonstrated that as a consequence of motor resonance, interacting agents align their behaviors (Schmidt & Richardson, 2008): two persons walking together in the street synchronize their step frequency unconsciously (Courtine & Schieppati, 2003), and crowds applaud synchronously when one starts clapping at the end of a show (Neda, Ravasz, Brechet, Vicsek, & Barabasi, 2000). As bi-directionality is a hallmark

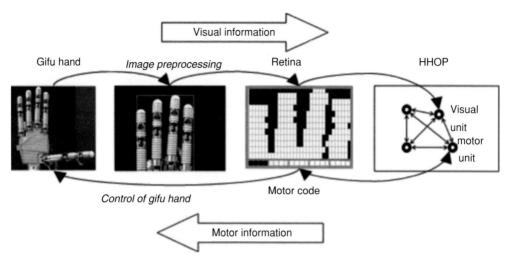

Fig. 64.6 Sketch of the robotic implementation testing the emergence of motor resonance form self observation. The hand was controlled with the motor code at the bottom of the retina, and the captured image was preprocessed and projected onto a binary matrix to form the retina. The HHOP associative network was trained with retina/motor codes patterns.

of social interactions, implementing bidirectional coordination of behaviors in humanoid robots by incorporating motor resonance abilities to the platform may lead to dramatic improvements of their social competence (Marin, Issartel, & Chaminade, 2009), though such a conclusion still awaits demonstration.

Conclusions

The fields of humanoid robotics and of social cognitive neuroscience both benefit from mutual exchanges. Robots provide tools to investigate social cognition, as in the examples derived from the motor resonance hypothesis described in this chapter. In return, social cognition could inspire epigenetic robotics, as in the example of implementing bidirectional motor resonance to improve social competence of future robotic companions. These reciprocal influences between social cognition and humanoid robotics thus promise a better understanding of man-robot interactions that will ultimately lead to a better understanding of the mechanisms involved in social interactions, and to improving the social acceptability of virtual agents.

Acknowledgment

This research was partly supported by the Strategic Research Program for Brain Sciences (SRPBS).

References

Asada, M., MacDorman, K. F., Ishiguro, H., & Kuniyoshi, Y. (2001). Cognitive developmental robotics as a new paradigm for the design of humanoid robots. *Robotics and Autonomous System, 37*, 185–193.

Atkeson, C. G., Hale, J. G., Pollick, F., Riley, M., Kotosaka, S., Schaal, S., et al. (2000). Using humanoid robots to study human behavior. *IEEE Intelligent Systems, 15*, 46–56.

Baron-Cohen, S. (1995), *Mindblindness.* Cambridge, MA: MIT Press.

Bentivegna, D. C., Atkeson, C. G., Ude, A., & Cheng, G. (2004). Learning to act from observation and practice. *International Journal of Humanoid Robotics, 1*, 585–611.

Barto, A. G., Sutton, R. S., & Anderson, C. W. (1983). Neuron-like elements that can solve difficult learning control problems. *IEEE Trans. Syst. Man. Cybern, 13*, 835–846.

Bernieri, F. J. & Rosenthal, R. (1991). Interpersonal coordination: Behavior matching and interactional synchrony. In R. S. Feldman & B. Rime (Eds.), *Fundamentals of nonverbal behavior. Studies in emotion & social interaction* (pp. 401–432). New York: Cambridge University Press.

Bezerra, C. A. D. & Zampieri, D. E. (2004) Biped robots: The state of art. In: M. Ceccarelli (Ed.), *International symposium on history of machines and mechanisms proceedings* HMM2004 (pp. 371–389). Dordrecht/Boston/London: Kluwer Academic Publishers.

Blakemore, S. J. & Decety, J. (2001). From the perception of action to the understanding of intention. *Nature Review Neuroscience, 2*, 561–567.

Breazeal, C. & Scassellati, B. (2002). Robots that imitate people. *Trends in Cognitive Sciences, 6*(11), 481–487.

Breazeal, C., Gray, J., & Berlin, M. (2007). Mindreading as a foundational skill for socially intelligent roots. *Proceedings of the 2007 International Symposium on Robotics Research (ISRR-07).* Hiroshima, Japan.

Brooks, R. A. (1997). The cog project. *Advanced Robotics, 15*, 968–970.

Chaminade, T. & Cheng, G. (2009). Social cognitive neuroscience and humanoid robotics. *Journal of Physiology (Paris),* doi: 10.1016/j.jphysparis.2009.08.011.

Chaminade, T. & Decety, J. (2001). A common framework for perception and action: neuroimaging evidence. *Behavioral and Brain Science, 24*, 879–882.

Chaminade, T., Franklin, D., Oztop, E., & Cheng, G. (2005). Motor interference between humans and humanoid robots: Effect of biological and artifical motion. *Paper presented at: International Conference on Development and Learning*, Osaka, Japan.

Chaminade, T. & Hodgins, J. (2006) Artificial agents in social cognitive sciences. *Interaction Studies, 7*(3), 347–353.

Chaminade, T., Hodgins, J., & Kawato, M. (2007). Anthropomorphism influences perception of computer-animated characters' actions. *Social Cognitive Affective Neuroscience, 2*, 206–216.

Chaminade, T., Meary, D., Orliaguet, J. P., & Decety, J. (2001). Is perceptual anticipation a motor simulation? A PET study. *Neuroreport, 12*, 3669–3674.

Chaminade, T., Oztop, E., Cheng, G., & Kawato, M. (2008). From self-observation to imitation: Visuomotor association on a robotic hand. *Brain Research Bulletin, 75*, 775–784.

Chaminade, T., Zecca, M., Blakemore, S-J., Takanishi, A., Frith, C. D., et al. (2010). Brain response to a humanoid robot in areas implicated in the perception of human emotional gestures. *PLoS ONE, 5*(7).

Chartrand, T. L. & Bargh, J. A. (1999). The chameleon effect: The perception-behavior link and social interaction. *Journal of Personality and Social Psychology, 76*, 893–910.

Cheng, G., Hyon, S.-H., Morimoto, J., Ude, A., Hale, J., Colvin, G., et al. (2007). CB: A humanoid research platform for exploring neuroscience. *Journal of Advanced Robotics, 21*, 1097–1114.

Clark, A. (1999). An embodied cognitive science? *Trends in Cognitive Sciences, 3*, 345–351.

Courtine, G. & Schieppati, M. (2003). Human walking along a curved path. I. Body trajectory, segment orientation and the effect of vision. *European Journal of Neuroscience, 18*, 177–190.

Csibra, G. & Gergely, G. (2006) Social learning and social cognition: The case for pedagogy. In: Y. Munakata & M. H. Johnson (Eds.). *Processes of change in brain and cognitive development. Attention and performance, XXI* (pp. 249–274). Oxford: Oxford University Press.

Decety, J. & Chaminade, T. (2003). When the self represents the other: A new cognitive neuroscience view on psychological identification. *Consciousness and Cognition, 12*, 577–596.

di Pellegrino, G., Fadiga, L., Fogassi, L., Gallese, V., & Rizzolatti, G. (1992). Understanding motor events: A neurophysiological study. *Experimental Brain Research, 9*, 176–180.

DiSalvo, C., Gemperle, F., Forlizzi, J., & Kiesler, S. (2002). All robots are not created equal: The design and perception of humanoid robot heads. *Paper presented at: 4th Conference on Designing Interactive Systems*, London, UK.

Edwards, M. G., Humphreys, G. W., & Castiello, U. (2003). Motor facilitation following action observation: A behavioural study in prehensile action. *Brain and Cognition, 53*, 495–502.

Ekman, P. & Friesen, W. V. (1978). *Facial action coding system: A technique for the measurement of facial movement*. Palo Alto, CA: Consulting Psychologists Press.

Feldman, R. (2007). Parent–infant synchrony and the construction of shared timing; physiological precursors, developmental outcomes, and risk conditions. *Journal of Child Psychology and Psychiatry, 48*, 329–354.

Frith, C. D. & Frith, U. (1999). Interacting minds—a biological basis. *Science, 286*, 1692–1695.

Gallagher, H., Jack, A., Roepstorff, A., & Frith, C. (2002). Imaging the intentional stance in a competitive game. *Neuroimage, 16*(3 Pt 1), 814.

Gallese, V., Fadiga, L., Fogassi, L., & Rizzolatti, G. (1996). Action recognition in the premotor cortex. *Brain, 119*(2), 593–609.

Gallese, V., Keysers, C., & Rizzolatti, G. (2004). A unifying view of the basis of social cognition. *Trends in Cognitive Sciences, 8*, 396–403.

Gazzola, V., Rizzolatti, G., Wicker, B., & Keysers, C. (2007). The anthropomorphic brain: The mirror neuron system responds to human and robotic actions. *Neuroimage, 35*, 1674–1684.

Gray, J., Breazeal, C., Berlin, M., Brooks, A., & Lieberman, J. (2005). Action parsing and goal inference using self as simulator. In: *Proceedings of Fourteenth IEEE Workshop on Robot and Human Interactive Communication (Ro-Man05)*, Nashville, TN. 202–209.

Hanson, D. (2005). Expanding the aesthetics possibilities for humanlike robots. *Paper presented at: Proc. IEEE Humanoid Robotics Conference, special session on the Uncanny Valley*, Tsukuba, Japan.

Harnad, S. (1989). Minds, machines and Searle. *Journal of Experimental and Theoretical Artificial Intelligence, 1*, 5–25.

Haruno, M., Kuroda, T., Doya, K., Toyama, K., Kimura, M., Samejima, K., et al. (2004). A neural correlate of reward-based behavioral learning in caudate nucleus: A functional magnetic resonance imaging study of a stochastic decision task. *Journal of Neuroscience, 24*, 1660–1665.

Heyes, C. (2001). Causes and consequences of imitation. *Trends in Cognitive Sciences, 5*, 253–261.

Hirai, K., Hirose, M., Haikawa, Y., & Takenaka, T. (1998). The development of Honda humanoid robot. *Paper presented at: IEEE International Conference on Robotics and Automation*, Leuven, Belgium.

Hirukawa, K., Kaneko, K., Kajita, S., Fujiwara, K., Kawai, Y., Tomita, F., et al. (2004). Humanoid robotics platforms developed in HRP. *Robotics and Autonomous System, 48*, 165–175.

Hollerman, J. R. & Schultz, W. (1998). Dopamine neurons report an error in the temporal prediction of reward during learning. *Nature Neuroscience, 1*, 304–309.

Imamizu, H., Miyauchi, S., Tamada, T., Sasaki, Y., Takino, R., Puetz, B., et al. (2000). Human cerebellar activity reflecting an acquired internal model of a new tool. *Nature, 403*, 192–195.

Itoh, K., Miwa, H., Matsumoto, M., Zecca, M., Takanobu, H., Roccella, S., et al. (2004). Various emotional expressions with emotion expression humanoid robot WE-4RII. *Paper presented at: First IEEE Technical Exhibition Based Conference on Robotics and Automation (TExCRA '04)*, Tokyo, Japan.

Kawato, M. (1999). Internal models for motor control and trajectory planning. *Current Opinion in Neurobiology, 9*, 718–727.

Kawato, M. (2008). From "understanding the brain by creating the brain" towards manipulative neuroscience. *Philosophical Transactions of the Royal Society of London: B Biological Sciences, 363*, 2201–2214.

Keysers, C. & Perrett, D. I. (2004). Demystifying social cognition: A Hebbian perspective. *Trends in Cognitive Sciences, 8*, 501–507.

Kiesler, S. & Hinds, P. (2004). Introduction to this special issue on human–robot interaction. *Human-Computer Interaction, 19*, 1–8.

Kilner, J. M., Paulignan, Y., & Blakemore, S. J. (2003). An interference effect of observed biological movement on action. *Current Biology, 13*, 522–525.

Lakin, J. L. & Chartrand, T. L. (2003). Using nonconscious behavioral mimicry to create affiliation and rapport. *Psychological Science*, 14, 334–339.

Leslie, A. M. (1984). Spatiotemporal continuity and the perception of causality in infants. *Perception*, 13, 287–305.

Liberman, A. M. & Mattingly, I. G. (1985). The motor theory of speech perception revised. *Cognition*, 21, 1–36.

MacDorman, K. F. & Ishiguro, H. (2006). The uncanny advantage of using androids in cognitive and social science research. *Interaction Studies*, 7, 297–337.

Marin, L., Issartel, J., & Chaminade, T. (2009). Interpersonal motor coordination: From human-human to human-robot interactions. Interaction Studies, 10(3), 479–504.

Minato, T., Shimada, M., Ishiguro, H., & Itakura, S. (2004). Development of an android robot for studying human-robot interaction. In: *Innovations in applied artificial intelligence* (pp. 424–434), Berlin: Springer.

Miyamoto, H., Kawato, M., Setoyama, T., & Suzuki, R. (1988). Feedback-error-learning neural network for trajectory control of a robotic manipulator. *Neural Networks*, 1, 251–265.

Miyamoto, H., Schaal, S., Gandolfo, F., Gomi, H., Koike, Y., Osu, R., et al. (1996). A Kendama learning robot based on dynamic optimization theory. *Neural Networks*, 9, 1281–1302.

Mori, M. (1970). The valley of eeriness. *Energy*, 7, 33–35.

Morimoto, J., Endo, G., Nakanishi, J., Hyon, S., Cheng, G., Bentivegna, D. C., et al. (2006). Modulation of simple sinusoidal patterns by a coupled oscillator model for biped walking. *IEEE International Conference on Robotics and Automation (ICRA2006) Proceedings*, 1579–1584, Orlando, USA, May 15–19.

Nadel, J., Revel, A., Andry, P., & Gaussier, P. (2004). Toward communication: First imitations in infants, low-functioning children with autism and robots. *Interaction studies*, 5, 45–74.

Nagasaka, K., Kuroki, Y., Suzuki, S., Itoh, Y., & Yamaguchi, J. (2004). Integrated motion control for walking, jumping and running on a small bipedal entertainment robot. *Paper presented at: IEEE Int. Conf. on Robotics and Automation*, New Orleans: LA.

Neda, Z., Ravasz, E., Brechet, Y., Vicsek, T., & Barabasi, A. L. (2000). The sound of many hands clapping. *Nature*, 403, 849–850.

O'Doherty, J., Kringelbach, M. L., Rolls, E. T., Hornak, J., & Andrews, C. (2001). Abstract reward and punishment representations in the human orbitofrontal cortex. *Nature Neuroscience*, 4, 95–102.

Oztop, E., Chaminade, T., Cheng, G., & Kawato, M. (2005). Imitation bootstrapping: Experiments on a robotic hand. In: *5th IEEE-RAS International Conference on Humanoid Robots*, Tsukuba: Japan, 189–195.

Oztop, E., Franklin, D., Chaminade, T., & Cheng, G. (2005). Human-humanoid interaction: Is a humanoid robot perceived as a human. *International Journal of Humanoid Robotics*, 2, 537–559.

Pessiglione, M., Seymour, B., Flandin, G., Dolan, R. J., & Frith, C. D. (2006). Dopamine-dependent prediction errors underpin reward-seeking behaviour in humans. *Nature*, 442, 1042–1045.

Press, C., Bird, G., Flach, R., & Heyes, C. (2005). *Robotic movement elicits automatic imitation*. Brain Research: Cognitive Brain Research, 25, 632–640.

Press, C., Gillmeister, H., & Heyes, C. (2006). Bottom-up, not top-down, modulation of imitation by human and robotic models. *European Journal of Neuroscience*, 24, 2415–2419.

Richardson, M. J., Campbell, W. L., & Schmidt, R. C. (2009). Movement interference during action observation as emergent coordination. *Neuroscience Letters*, 449, 117–122.

Riley, M., Ude A., & Atkeson, C. G. (2000). Methods for motion generation and interaction with a humanoid robot: Case studies of dancing and catching. In: *Proceeding of 2000 Workshop on Interactive Robotics and Entertainment (WIRE-2000)*, Pittsburgh: PA, 35–42.

Rizzolatti, G. & Craighero, L. (2004). The mirror-neuron system. *Annual Review of Neuroscience*, 27, 169–192.

Rizzolatti, G., Fogassi, L., & Gallese, V. (2001). Neurophysiological mechanisms underlying the understanding and imitation of action. *Nature Review Neuroscience*, 2, 661–670.

Robins, B. & Dautenhahn, K. (2006). Does appearance matter in the interaction of children with autism with a humanoid robot? *Interaction Studies*, 7(3), 479–512.

Rothi, L. J. G., Ochipa, C., & Heilman, K. M. (1991). A cognitive neuropsychological model of limb praxis. *Cognitive Neuropsychology*, 8, 443–458.

Sakagami, Y., Watanabe, R., Aoyama, C., Matsunaga, S., Higaki, N., & Fujimura, K. (2002). The intelligent ASIMO: System overview and integration. *Paper presented at: IEEE/RSJ International Conference on Intelligent Robots and Systems*, Lausanne: Switzerland.

Sandini, G., Metta, G., & Vernon, D. (2004). RobotCub: An open framework for research in embodied cognition. *Paper presented at: IEEE International Conference on Humanoid Robots*, Los Angeles: CA.

Saygin, A., Chaminade, T., Ishiguro, H., Driver, J., & Frith, C. (2011). The thing that should not be: the perception of human and humanoid robot actions. *Social Cognitive Affective Neuroscience*, in press.

Scassellati, B. (2001). Foundations for a theory of mind for a humanoid robot. Doctoral dissertation, MIT, Department of Electronic Engineering and Computer Sciences.

Scassellati. B. (2002). Theory of mind for a humanoid robot. *Autonomous Robots*, 12, 13–24, 2002.

Schaal, S. (1999). Is imitation learning the route to humanoid robots? *Trends in Cognitive Science*, 3, 233–242.

Schaal, S. & Atkeson, C. G. (1998). Constructive incremental learning from only local information. *Neural Computation*, 10, 2047–2084.

Schaal, S., Peters, J., Nakanishi, J., & Ijspeert, A. (2003). Control, planning, learning and imitation with dynamic movement primitives. In: *IEEE/RSJ International Conference on Intelligent Robots and Systems (IROS2003) Workshop on Bilateral Paradigms of Human and Humanoid*, 39–58, Las Vegas, USA.

Schaal, S., Sternad, D., Osu, R. & Kawato, M. (2004). Rhythmic arm movement is not discrete. *Nature Neuroscience*, 7, 1136–1143.

Shibata, T. & Schaal, S. (2001). Biomimetic gaze stabilization based on feedback-error learning with nonparametric regression networks. *Neural Networks*, 14, 201–216.

Shibata, T., Schaal, S., & Kawato, M. (2005). A model of smooth pursuit in primates based on learning the target dynamics. *Neural Networks*, 18(3), 213–224.

Schmidt, R. C. & Richardson, M. J. (2008). Dynamics of interpersonal coordination. In A. Fuchs & V. Jirsa (Eds.). *Coordination: Neural, behavioural and social dynamics*, Heidelberg: Springer-Verlag.

Smith, L. & Breazeal, C. (2007). The dynamic life of developmental process. *Developmental Science*, 10(1), 61–68.

Semin, G. R. (2007). Grounding communication: Synchrony. In A. Kruglanski & E. T. Higgins (Eds.), *Social psychology: Handbook of basic principles 2nd Edition* (630–649). New York: Guilford Publications.

Tanaka, F., Cicourel, A., & Movellan, J. R. (2007). Socialization between toddlers and robots at an early childhood education center. *Proceedings of the National Academy of Sciences, 104*(46), 17954–17958.

Tai, Y. F., Scherfler, C., Brooks, D. J., Sawamoto, N., & Castiello, U. (2004). The human premotor cortex is 'mirror' only for biological actions. *Current Biololgy, 14*, 117–120.

Thomaz, A. L., Berlin, M. & Breazeal, C. (2005). An embodied computational model of social referencing. In: *Proceedings of Fourteenth IEEE Workshop on Robot and Human Interactive Communication (Ro-Man-05)*, Nashville, TN, 591–598.

Tkach D., Reimer J., & Hatsopoulos, N.G. (2007). Congruent activity during action and action observation in motor cortex. *Journal of Neuroscience, 27*, 13241–13250.

Tremblay, L. & Schultz, W. (1999). Relative reward preference in primate orbitofrontal cortex. *Nature, 398*, 704–708.

Turing, A. (1950). Computing machinery and intelligence. *Mind, 59*, 433–460.

Ude, A. & Atkeson, C. G. (2003). Online tracking and mimicking of human movements by a humanoid robot. *Journal of Advanced Robotics, 17*, 165–178.

van der Meer, A. L., van der Weel, F. R., & Lee, D. N. (1995). The functional significance of arm movements in neonates. *Science, 267*, 693–695.

Wada, K. & Shibata, T. (2007). Social effects of robot therapy in a care house—change of social network of the residents for two months. In: *Proceedings of IEEE International Conference on Robotics and Automation (ICRA)*, 1250–1255, Roma, Italy.

Wolfe, J. M. (1994). Guided Search 2.0: A revised model of visual search. *Psychonomic Bulletin & Review, 1*(2), 202–238.

The Social Brain in Adolescence and the Potential Impact of Social Neuroscience on Education

Sarah-Jayne Blakemore

Abstract

This chapter describes research demonstrating that the social brain continues to develop and change during adolescence. The study of the development of the brain beyond childhood is a new but rapidly evolving field with potential applications in education and social policy. The finding that changes in brain structure continue into adolescence and early adulthood has challenged accepted views and has given rise to a recent spate of investigations into the way cognition (including social cognition) might change as a consequence. Research suggests that adolescence is a key time for the development of regions of the brain involved in social cognition and self-awareness. This is likely to be due to the interplay between a number of factors, including changes in the social environment and in hormonal functioning, structural and functional brain development, and improvements in social cognition.

Keywords: social brain, adolescence, brain development, brain structure, social neuroscience

Introduction

"Neuroscience has the potential to make important contributions to education. These potential contributions are of at least three kinds: novel understanding about the biological and environmental processes determining learning; the identification of early neural markers for educational risk; and neural methods for evaluating different teaching approaches, remediation packages or educational debates" (UK Government Foresight Project Report SR-E1, p. 2).

Knowledge of how the brain learns could, and will, have a great impact on education. Understanding the brain mechanisms that underlie learning and memory, and the effects of genetics, the environment, emotion, and age on learning could transform educational strategies and enable us to design programs that optimize learning for people of all ages and of all needs. Only by understanding how the brain acquires and lays down information and skills will we be able to reach the limits of its capacity to learn. Neuroscience can now offer some understanding of how the brain learns new information and processes this information throughout life (see Blakemore & Frith, 2005).

Understanding the brain basis of social functioning and social development is crucial to the fostering of social competence inside and outside the classroom. Social functioning plays a role in shaping learning and academic performance (as well as vice versa), and thus social neuroscience can contribute to understanding the origins and process of schooling success and failure. It can also facilitate an understanding of how children with additional socio-emotional needs can be included in mainstream schools and how to reduce exclusion.

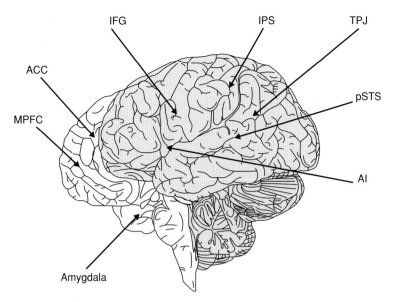

Fig. 65.1 Regions on the lateral surface of the brain that are involved in social cognition include the medial prefrontal cortex (MPFC) and temporo-parietal junction (TPJ), which are involved in thinking about mental states, and the posterior superior temporal sulcus (pSTS), which is activated by observing faces and biological motion. Other regions of the social brain on the lateral surface are the inferior frontal gyrus (IFG) and interparietal sulcus (IPS). Regions on the medial surface involved in social cognition include the amygdala, anterior cingulate cortex (ACC), and anterior insula (AI).
Adapted from Frith & Frith (2007) with permission from Elsevier.

In this chapter, I describe a specific example of an area within social neuroscience that might one day have profound implications for education; that is, the development of the social brain during adolescence.

The Social Brain

The social brain is defined as the network of brain regions subserving social cognition, that is, those enabling us to recognize others, and to evaluate our own and others' mental states (intentions, desires, beliefs), feelings, enduring dispositions, and actions (Frith & Frith, 2007). Many different brain regions are involved in social cognition, including the medial prefrontal cortex (MPFC), anterior cingulate cortex (ACC), inferior frontal gyrus, posterior superior temporal sulcus (pSTS), temporo-parietal junction (TPJ), the amygdala, and anterior insula (see Figure 65.1). Some of these brain regions are activated during the attribution of mental states to oneself and to others. This ability, known as mentalizing, or theory of mind, enables us to understand other people's behavior and actions.

Using functional imaging and a wide range of stimuli, several studies have shown remarkable consistency in identifying the brain regions that are involved in mentalizing. These studies have used

stimuli such as stories (Fletcher et al., 1995; Gallagher et al., 2000; Saxe & Kanwisher, 2003), sentences (den Ouden, Frith, Frith, & Blakemore, 2005), cartoons (Brunet, Sarfati, Hardy-Bayle, & Decety, 2000; Gallagher et al., 2000) and animations (Castelli, Happé, Frith, & Frith, 2000) designed to elicit the attribution of mental states. In each case, the mentalizing task resulted in the activation of a network of regions including the amygdala, pSTS/TPJ, the temporal poles, and the MPFC.

Many social brain regions undergo protracted structural development in humans. In this chapter, I start by briefly describing mechanisms in early brain development and then move on to what is known about structural brain development during adolescence. I then describe recent imaging studies looking at functional development of the social brain during adolescence and examples of behavioral studies on social cognitive development during this period of life. Finally, I suggest some speculative implications of this research for education.

Early Brain Development and "Sensitive Periods" for Learning

Early in development, the brain begins to form new synapses, so that synaptic density (the number of synapses per unit volume of brain tissue) greatly

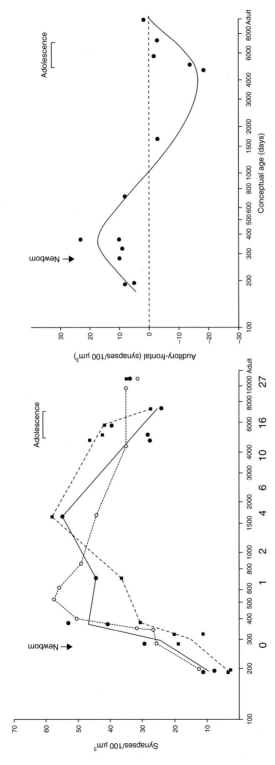

Fig. 65.2 The graph on the left shows the mean synaptic density in the primary auditory cortex (filled circles), primary visual cortex (open circles), and prefrontal cortex (middle frontal gyrus; crosses) in post-mortem human brains at different ages. The x axis shows conceptual age in days from 200 days post-conception to 10,000 days post-conception (approximately 27 years). This illustrates that synaptic density increases in all three regions in early childhood, but that synaptogenesis is most prolonged in PFC. This is further demonstrated in the graph on the right, which shows the difference in synaptic density in the auditory cortex and middle frontal gyrus (synaptic density in auditory cortex minus synaptic density in middle frontal gyrus) plotted against conceptual age. The dotted line represents the line of zero difference in time course of synaptogenesis and synaptic elimination between the two cortical regions. The solid line represents a curve of best fit for the data. Thus, while the peak synaptic density in auditory cortex occurs early (at around three months), the peak synaptic density in PFC occurs significantly later

From Huttenlocher (1979); reproduced with permission of Elsevier.

exceeds adult levels. This process of synaptic proliferation, called synaptogenesis, lasts up to several months, depending on the species of animal. The increase in the number of synapses is followed by a period of synaptic elimination (synaptic pruning) in which excess synapses are eliminated. This experience-dependent process, which occurs over a period of years, reduces the overall synaptic density to adult levels, usually by the time of sexual maturity.

Experiments on animals, starting in the 1950s, showed that sensory regions of the brain go through critical periods soon after birth, during which time environmental stimulation appears to be crucial for normal brain development and for normal perceptual development to occur (Wiesel & Hubel, 1965). This research showed that early visual deprivation has detrimental consequences on brain development and on visual perception. This research is often cited as evidence for the importance of stimulation in the first few years of a baby's life. This claim assumes that the time course of synaptogenesis and critical periods are the same for humans as for the animals. However, first of all, development in humans is much more protracted than in other animals. Second, the claim assumes that the period of synaptogenesis and synaptic pruning is the same in regions of the brain other than visual cortex. Third, the claim often implies that no learning or brain development can occur after an early critical period.

Subsequent research by Wiesel and Hubel and others has suggested that some recovery of function is possible depending on the specific period of deprivation and the circumstances following deprivation. Thus, critical periods are no longer considered rigid and inflexible. Rather, they are interpreted as sensitive periods, comprising subtle changes in the brain's ability to be shaped and changed by experiences that occur over a lifetime. For some functions to develop normally, the animal must receive appropriate sensory input from the environment at some stage during development. However, this input tends to be very general in nature, including patterned visual stimuli, the ability to move and manipulate objects, noises, and speech sounds and social interaction for human babies. It seems fair to say that the natural environment of most children contains sufficient sensory stimulation for normal brain development. There is no evidence that extra stimulation aids brain development in children who are brought up in typical environments.

Sensitive periods occur at different stages of development for different brain regions. Whereas sensitive periods for sensory brain regions are early-occurring,

the parts of the human brain that underlie complex cognitive capacities, such as language, planning, decision making, and social cognition, seem to have several sensitive periods, many of which continue into adolescence and even early adulthood.

Cellular Development During Adolescence: Post-mortem Studies

In the 1970s, research studies carried out at the University of Chicago investigated synaptic development in post-mortem human brains of different ages (Huttenlocher, 1979). This research revealed that, while in sensory brain areas synaptogenesis and synaptic pruning occur relatively early, synaptic reorganisation in the prefrontal cortex (specifically, the middle frontal gyrus), continues for several decades (Huttenlocher, 1979). Huttenlocher found that synaptic density in the PFC increases during childhood and peaks at an age that approximately corresponds to the onset of puberty, after which synaptic density decreases (due to synaptic pruning) throughout adolescence (Figure 65.2).

Another developmental mechanism that occurs for many decades in the frontal cortex is myelination. Whereas sensory and motor brain regions become fully myelinated in the first few years of life, axons in the human frontal cortex continue to be myelinated well into adolescence (Yakovlev & Lecours, 1967).

Brain Development During Adolescence: MRI Studies

There are no tools to look directly at synaptic pruning and myelination in the human brain. However, in the past decade, a number of large-scale MRI studies looking at brain development across the lifespan have provided further evidence of the ongoing maturation of the frontal cortex, and other regions, into adulthood (Giedd et al., 1999; Sowell et al., 1999; Paus, 2005). These studies have revealed a linear increase in white matter volume, which occurs across the brain throughout childhood and adolescence and beyond. This increase in white matter volume is thought to reflect ongoing maturation of neuronal axons, including myelination as well as increasing axonal caliber (Benes, Turtle, Khan, & Farol, 1994; Paus, Keshavan, & Giedd, 2008).

At the same time, in the frontal and parietal lobes, grey matter increases in volume during childhood, reaching its peak at around puberty onset (approximately 11 years in girls and 12 years in boys). This is followed by a reduction in grey matter

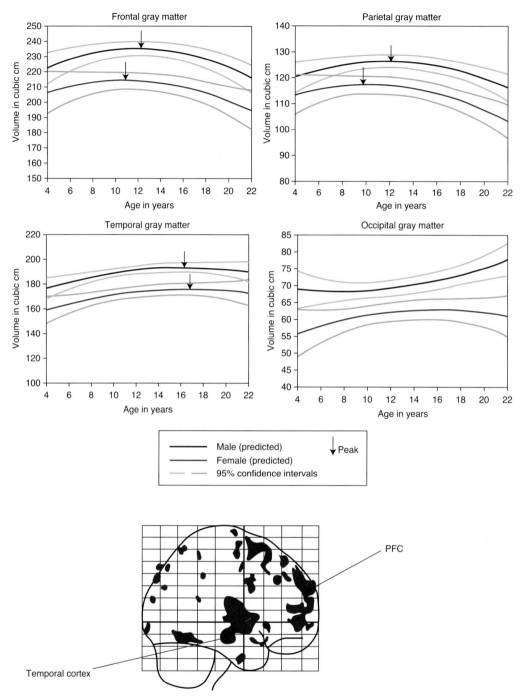

Fig. 65.3 Top: Predicted size with 95% confidence intervals for cortical gray matter in frontal, parietal, temporal, and occipital lobes for 243 scans from 89 males and 56 females, ages 4 to 22 years. The arrows indicate peaks of the curves, in other words the age at which grey matter density was maximal. Note that grey matter volume in the PFC peaks at around the age of puberty onset: age 11 in girls (red lines) and 12 in boys (blue lines). In the temporal cortex, the peak is not reached until about age 16. Bottom: Areas of grey matter volume reductions observed between adolescence and young adulthood. Anatomical MRI scans from a group of 12–16-year olds were compared with scans from a group of young adults aged 23–30. The figure shows brain regions (including PFC and temporal cortex) in which grey matter volume was higher in the adolescent group than in the adult group.
From Giedd et al. (1999).

From Sowell et al. (1999); reprinted with permission of Elsevier.

during adolescence (Figure 65.3). This is in contrast to basic sensory regions of the brain, in which peak grey matter volume is attained during childhood (Giedd et al., 1999; Sowell et al., 1999; Giedd, 2004; Paus, 2005; Paus et al., 2008). It has been suggested the regional increases in grey matter volume up to and around puberty are due to synaptic proliferation, and that subsequent grey matter thinning reflects the elimination of synapses.

Both cellular and MRI studies suggest that some brain regions are still developing well into the adolescent years. Many brain regions that are relatively late-developing in humans are involved in social cognition. For example, a recent developmental MRI study that measured cortical thickness in a sample of 375 participants aged 4 to 21 found that MPFC is one of the latest regions to mature, with a peak in cortical thickness at around age 14 years (Shaw et al., 2008).

Functional Development of the Social Brain During Adolescence

Recent functional neuroimaging studies have investigated social brain development during adolescence. There is some indication that, for social cognitive

tasks, activity in MPFC decreases between adolescence and adulthood. A recent fMRI study investigated the development of this ability by asking participants to think about what action they would take given a particular intention (Blakemore, den Ouden, Choudhury, & Frith, 2007; blue dots Figure 65.4). Adolescents (aged 12–18) and adults (aged 22–37) were scanned while answering questions about intentional causality (e.g., "You want to see what's on at the cinema; do you look in a newspaper?"), or physical causality (e.g., "A huge tree suddenly comes crashing down in a forest; does it make a loud noise?"). Adolescents activated part of the dorsal MPFC more than did adults when thinking about their own intentions compared to during physical causality judgments. In contrast, in the same comparison (intentional–physical), adults activated part of the right STS more than did adolescents.

A different fMRI study investigated the development of high-level communication using an irony comprehension task and found that children (aged 9–14) engaged frontal regions (MPFC and left inferior frontal gyrus) more than did adults (Wang, Lee, Sigman, & Dapretto, 2006; green dots Figure 65.4). A similar result was found in an fMRI

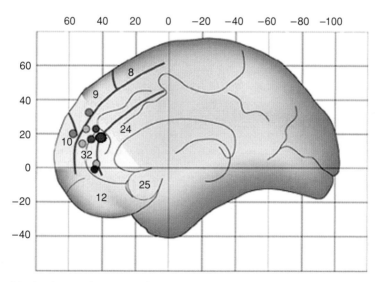

Fig. 65.4 A section of the dorsal MPFC that is activated in studies of mentalizing is shown between red lines: Montreal Neurological Institute (MNI) "y" coordinates range from 30 to 60, and "z" coordinates range from 0 to 40 (Amodio & Frith, 2006). Colored dots indicate voxels of decreased activity during social cognition tasks between late childhood and adulthood. The red dot represents higher activation in adolescents than in adults during an animations mentalizing task (Moriguchi et al., 2007). Green dots represent higher activation in adolescents than in adults in an irony comprehension task (Wang et al., 2006). Blue dots represent higher activation in adolescents than in adults during intention understanding (Blakemore et al., 2007). Yellow dots represent higher activation in children than in adults in a task comparing self and other evaluation (Pfeifer et al., 2007). Pink dots represent higher activation in adolescents than in adults during social emotion (Burnett et al., 2009). Blue lines indicate approximate borders between Brodmann areas, which are numbered on the diagram.
Adapted from Blakemore (2008) with permission of Nature Publishing Group.

study that investigated changes during adolescence of the neural processing of social emotion in the first- or third-person perspective (Burnett, Bird, Moll, Frith, & Blakemore, 2009; pink dot Figure 65.4). Adult (age 22–32) and adolescent (age 10–18) participants read scenarios that described either social emotions (guilt or embarrassment) or basic emotions (fear or disgust), and were asked to imagine these scenarios happening either to themselves (self condition) or to someone else (their mother – other condition). Activity in the dorsal MPFC during social relative to basic emotion was higher in the adolescent group than in the adult group. In another recent fMRI study of self-knowledge, 12 ten-year-olds and 12 adults underwent brain scanning while they judged whether a series of statements such as "I like to read just for fun" applied to them (Pfeifer, Lieberman, & Dapretto, 2007; yellow dots Figure 65.4). The children activated the anterior dorsal MPFC more strongly than did the adults.

Together, these studies suggest that adolescents use social brain regions differently to adults in a variety of situations that require social understanding. There are a number of possible explanations for these developmental differences in functional activity within social brain regions (see Blakemore, 2008, for review). One explanation has to do with neuroanatomical development. It could be the case that adolescents activate these developing social brain regions more strongly than adults do because the less "efficient" neural circuits need more oxygen and energy to power them. This might mean that adolescents can do just as well as adults in certain tasks requiring social understanding, but that parts of their brain require more energy to do so. Another possibility is that adolescents are actually approaching social tasks using different cognitive strategies. Perhaps teenagers are still "working out" social situations—due to accumulating experience or developing social skills. This may mean that they require more effortful, online social cognitive processing. With age, this may become less effortful, more automatic and perhaps more reliant on stored social knowledge. An unexplored implication of this could be that the period of life when the MPFC and other social brain regions are still developing—the teens and early twenties—might be a period of particular open-mindedness to new ideas and different types of people.

Behavioral Development of Mentalizing During Adolescence

In the developmental neuroimaging studies of mentalizing reviewed above, which showed that activity

in the MPFC decreases between adolescence and adulthood, task performance was equated across age groups. Equating performance between groups is critical for the interpretation of the functional neuroimaging data: If performance between groups were significantly different, it would be impossible to know whether a group difference in neural activity was the cause, or simply a consequence of, the difference in performance. However, matching performance in this way negates important differences between adolescents and adults in terms of social cognition. If the neural substrates for social cognition change during adolescence, what are the consequences for social cognitive behavior? Most developmental studies of social cognition focus on early childhood, possibly because children perform adequately in even quite complex mentalizing tasks by age four or five (Frith & Frith, 2007). It is a challenge therefore to design a task on which older children and adolescents do not perform at ceiling.

Recently, we used a computerized version of a mentalizing task on which even adults make significant errors (Keysar, Lin, & Barr, 2003). We gave our version of this task to 177 female participants divided into five age groups: Child I (7.3–9.7 years); Child II (9.8–11.4); Adolescent I (11.5–13.9); Adolescent II (14.0–17.7); Adults (19.1–27.5) (Dumontheil, Apperly, & Blakemore, in press). Participants viewed a set of shelves containing objects which they were instructed to move by a "director" who could see some but not all of the objects. In the critical condition, participants need to use the director's perspective and move only objects that the director can see, in order to make the correct response. The task involves both mentalizing (taking another's perspective), and executive functions (the need for speeded response selection). The results demonstrated improvement on this task even between the Adolescent II and Adult groups. Thus, while theory of mind tasks are passed by age four, these new data indicate that the interaction between theory of mind and executive functions continues to develop in late adolescence (Dumontheil et al., in press).

Gender Differences and the Influence of Hormones

How adolescent brain development differs between the sexes, how it is affected by hormonal changes, and how this interaction affects social cognition, are still empirical questions. Anecdotal evidence suggests that relationships with peers and other social behaviors, and the way these develop during puberty and adolescence, differ between males and females. An early MRI study demonstrated significant sex differences in grey matter changes in a range of cortical regions (Giedd et al., 1999; see Figure 65.3). Specifically, there was a delay of approximately two years in the peak total brain grey matter density in males relative to females. The arrows in Figure 65.3 indicate the age at which grey matter density was maximal. Note that grey matter density in the frontal cortex peaks at around the age of puberty onset: age 11 in girls (red lines) and 12 in boys (blue lines). In the temporal cortex, the peak is not reached until about age 16. Although no measure of puberty was taken in this study, it suggests that puberty (rather than age) might be the trigger for neuroanatomical changes, at least in frontal and parietal regions (Romeo, 2003).

Sex hormones influence a range of neurodevelopmental processes in animals including neuronal survival, neurogenesis, synaptogenesis, receptor expression, neurotransmitter synthesis, and neuronal excitability. Research in animals (Shultz et al., 2004) and humans has shown that sex hormones also influence social behavior. In humans, affective responses to male faces vary across the menstrual cycle in women (Penton-Voak et al., 1999). In men and women, sex hormone levels are associated with differential emotional responses to infants. For example, changes in female sex hormones during pregnancy in women predict postpartum attachment feelings to infants (Fleming, Ruble, Krieger, & Wong, 1997), and lower testosterone levels in men are associated with higher levels of sympathy and a higher need to respond to infant cries (Fleming, Corter, Stallings, & Steiner, 2002). In addition, sex hormones affect sexual behavior through binding to receptors in limbic areas including the hypothalamus and amygdala. In monkeys, the amygdala has a predominance of androgen receptors (Clark, MacLusky, & Goldman-Rakic, 1988), whereas the hippocampus has a predominance of estrogen receptors (Morse, Scheff, & DeKosky, 1986). This difference might account for the finding that in humans, amygdala volume increased between age 4–18 only in males, whereas hippocampal volume increased only in females (Giedd et al., 1996).

Implications for Education

In this chapter, I have described research demonstrating that the social brain continues to develop and change during adolescence. The study of the development of the brain beyond childhood is a new but rapidly evolving field with potential applications in education and social policy. The finding that changes in brain structure continue into adolescence and early adulthood has challenged accepted views and has given rise to a recent spate of investigations into the way cognition (including social cognition) might change as a consequence. Research suggests that adolescence is a key time for the development of regions of the brain involved in social cognition and self-awareness. This is likely to be due to the interplay between a number of factors including changes in the social environment and in hormonal functioning, structural and functional brain development. Future research should investigate how these factors account for behavioral phenomena that are typical of adolescence.

If early childhood is seen as a major opportunity—or a "sensitive period"—for teaching, so too should the teenage years. During both periods, particularly dramatic brain reorganization is taking place. The idea that teenagers should still go to school and be educated is relatively new. And yet the research on brain development suggests that education during the teenage years is vital. The brain is still developing during this period; it is adaptable and needs to be molded and shaped. Perhaps the aims of education for adolescents might change to include abilities that are controlled by the parts of the brain that undergo most change during adolescence. These abilities might include internal control, multi-tasking, planning, and social cognitive skills.

An important next step is to extend these efforts to the pastoral side of education in order to inform anti-bullying and extra-curricular policies. One purely speculative possibility is that, just as the environment influences synaptic pruning in the first few years of life, so might it have an impact on the pruning that occurs in the frontal cortex during adolescence. There are no tools as yet to look at pruning in the living human brain. However, if the environment influences synaptic pruning during adolescence, this has implications for what kind of experiences adolescents should encounter, both academically and socially. Secondary school is often socially stressful, just at the time when the social brain is undergoing profound development. It might be fruitful to include in the curriculum some teaching on the changes occurring in the brain during adolescence. Adolescents might be very interested in, and benefit from, learning about the changes that are going on in their brains.

Acknowledgments

My group's research is funded by the Royal Society, the Wellcome Trust and the BBSRC. I am grateful to J. Cook and O. Kuster for commenting on a previous version of this manuscript.

References

Amodio, D. M. & Frith, C. D. (2006). Meeting of minds: The medial frontal cortex and social cognition. *Nature Reviews Neuroscience, 7*(4), 268–277.

Benes, F. M., Turtle, M., Khan, Y., & Farol, P. (1994). Myelination of a key relay zone in the hippocampal formation occurs in the human brain during childhood, adolescence, and adulthood. *Arch. Gen. Psychiatr, 51*, 477–484.

Blakemore, S. J., den Ouden, H., Choudhury, S., & Frith, C. (2007). Adolescent development of the neural circuitry for thinking about intentions. *Social Cogn. Affect. Neurosci, 2*, 130–139.

Blakemore, S-J. & Frith, U. (2005). *The learning brain: Lessons for education.* Oxford UK: Blackwell.

Blakemore, S-J. (2008). The social brain in adolescence. *Nature Reviews Neuroscience, 9*(4), 267–277.

Brunet, E., Sarfati, Y., Hardy-Bayle, M. C., & Decety, J. (2000). A PET investigation of the attribution of intentions with a nonverbal task. *Neuroimage, 11*(2), 157–166.

Burnett, S., Bird, G., Moll, J., Frith, C., & Blakemore, S. J. (2009). Development during adolescence of the neural processing of social emotion. *J. Cogn. Neurosci, 21*(9), 1736–1750.

Castelli, F., Happé, F., Frith, U., & Frith, C.D. (2000). Movement and mind: A functional imaging study of perception and interpretation of complex intentional movement pattern. *Neuroimage, 12*, 314–325.

Clark, A. S., MacLusky, N. J., & Goldman-Rakic, P. S. (1988). Androgen binding and metabolism in the cerebral cortex of the developing rhesus monkey. *Endocrinology, 123*, 932–940.

den Ouden, H. E., Frith, U., Frith, C., & Blakemore, S. J. (2005). Thinking about intentions. *Neuroimage, 28*(4), 787–796.

Dumontheil, I., Apperly, I. A., & Blakemore, S-J. (2010). Online usage of theory of mind continues to develop in late adolescence. *Developmental Science, 13*(2), 331–338.

Fleming, A. S., Ruble, D., Krieger, H., & Wong, P. Y. (1997). Hormonal and experiential correlates of maternal responsiveness during pregnancy and the puerperium in human mothers. *Horm Behav, 31*(2), 145–158.

Fleming A.S., Corter, C., Stallings, J., & Steiner, M. (2002). Testosterone and prolactin are associated with emotional responses to infant cries in new fathers. *Horm Behav. 42*(4), 399–413.

Fletcher, P. C., et al. (1995). Other minds in the brain: A functional imaging study of "theory of mind" in story comprehension. *Cognition, 57*(2), 109–128.

Cooper, C. L., Goswami, U., & Sahakian, B. J. (2009). Mental capital and wellbeing. Foresight, UK Government Office for Science: Wiley.

Frith, C. D. & Frith, U. (2007). Social cognition in humans. *Curr Biol, 17*(16), 724–732.

Gallagher, H. L, Happe, F., Brunswick, N., Fletcher, P. C., Frith, U., & Frith, C. D. (2000). Reading the mind in cartoons and stories: An fMRI study of "theory of mind" in verbal and nonverbal tasks. *Neuropsychologia, 38*(1), 11–21.

Giedd, J. N., et al. (1996). Quantitative MRI of the temporal lobe, amygdala, and hippocampus in normal human development: Ages 4–18 years. *J Comp Neurol, 366*(2), 223–230.

Giedd, J. N., Blumenthal, J., Jeffries, N. O., Castellanos, F. X., Liu, H., Zijdenbos, A., et al. (1999). Brain development during childhood and adolescence: A longitudinal MRI study. *Nature Neuroscience, 2*(10), 861–863.

Giedd, J. N. (2004). Structural magnetic resonance imaging of the adolescent brain. *Annals of the New York Academy of Sciences, 1021*, 77–85.

Huttenlocher, P. R. (1979). Synaptic density in human frontal cortex—developmental changes and effects of aging. *Brain Research, 163*, 195–205.

Keysar, B., Lin, S., & Barr, D. J. (2003). Limits on theory of mind use in adults. *Cognition. 89*(1), 25–41.

Moriguchi, Y., Ohnishi, T., Mori, T., Matsuda, H., & Komaki, G. (2007). Changes of brain activity in the neural substrates for theory of mind during childhood and adolescence. *Psychiatry Clin Neurosci, 61*(4), 355–363.

Morse, J. K., Scheff, S. W., & DeKosky, S. T. (1986). Gonadal steroids influence axonal sprouting in the hippocampal dentate gyrus: A sexually dimorphic response. *Exp. Neural, 94*, 649–658.

Paus, T., Keshavan, M., & Giedd, J. N. (2008). Why do many psychiatric disorders emerge during adolescence? *Nat. Rev. Neurosci, 9*, 947–957.

Paus, T. (2005). Mapping brain maturation and cognitive development during adolescence. *Trends in Cognitive Sciences, 9*, 60–68.

Penton-Voak, I. S., et al. (1999). Menstrual cycle alters face preference. *Nature, 399*, 741–742.

Pfeifer, J. H., Lieberman, M. D., & Dapretto, D. (2007). "I know you are but what am I?!": Neural bases of self- and social knowledge retrieval in children and adults. *J. Cogn. Neurosci, 19*, 1323–1337.

Romeo, R. D. (2003). Puberty: A period of both organizational and activational effects of steroid hormones on neurobehavioural development. *J Neuroendocrinol, 15*(12), 1185–1192.

Saxe, R. & Kanwisher, N. (2003). People thinking about thinking people. The role of the temporo-parietal junction in "theory of mind." *Neuroimage, 19*(4), 1835–1842.

Shaw, P., et al. (2008). Neurodevelopmental trajectories of the human cerebral cortex. *J. Neurosci. 28*(14), 3586–3594.

Schulz, K. M., Richardson, H. N., Zehr, J. L., Osetek, A. J., Menard, T. A., & Sisk, C. L. (2004). Gonadal hormones masculinize and defeminize reproductive behaviors during puberty in the male Syrian hamster. *Horm Behav, 45*(4), 242–249.

Sowell, E. R., Thompson, P. M., Holmes, C. J., Batth, R., Jernigan, T. L., & Toga, A. W. (1999). Localizing age-related changes in brain structure between childhood and adolescence using statistical parametric mapping. *Neuroimage, 6*(1), 587–597.

Wang, A. T., Lee, S. S., Sigman, M., & Dapretto, M. (2006). Developmental changes in the neural basis of interpreting communicative intent. *Soc Cogn Affec Neurosci, 1*, 107–121.

Wiesel, T. N. & Hubel, D. H. (1965). Extent of recovery from the effects of visual deprivation in kittens. *Journal of Neurophysiology, 28*, 1060–1072.

Yakovlev, P. A. & Lecours, I. R. (1967). The myelogenetic cycles of regional maturation of the brain. In A. Minkowski (Ed.) *Regional development of the brain in early life* (pp. 3–70). Oxford: Blackwell.

The Influence of Video Games on Social, Cognitive, and Affective Information Processing

Kira Bailey, Robert West, *and* Craig A. Anderson

Abstract

This chapter first reviews literature examining the effects of video games from the perspective of social, cognitive, affective, and education science. It also considers how knowledge from social and cognitive neuroscience may serve to enhance our understanding of the effects of video game experience. The literature reveals some paradoxical effects wherein experience with the same types of games can lead to an increase in aggression, a decrease in cognitive control, and an increase in visuospatial abilities. A consideration of the behavioral, neuroanatomical, and physiological bases of the effects of video games leads to the suggestion that exposure to these media is associated with plasticity within neural networks supporting high level vision, emotion processing, cognitive control, and social decision making. Future investigations focusing on within and between domain comparisons using behavioral and neuromonitoring techniques are likely to provide greater insight into neural basis of the effects of video games.

Keywords: attention, cognition, cognitive control, emotion, executive control, individual differences, negativity bias, video games, video game violence, visuospatial cognition

Introduction

Computer and console-based video games represent a pervasive form of leisure activity in industrialized nations beginning in early to middle childhood and continuing through adulthood. A recent representative sample of U.S. teens found that 99% of boys and 94% of girls had played video games (Lenhart, et al., 2008). Boys typically play more than girls (Rideout, Roberts, & Foehr, 2005). For example, a survey of over 600 eighth and ninth grade students found that boys averaged 13 hours per week and girls averaged 5 hours per week (Gentile, Lynch, Linder, & Walsh, 2004). In addition to the entertainment value of video games, evidence from a growing number of studies demonstrates that video

games can produce positive pedagogical outcomes related to the development of health-related knowledge and behaviors (Baranowski, Buday, Thompson, & Baranowski, 2008; Barlett, Anderson, & Swing, 2009) and military training (Gopher, Weil, & Bareket, 1994).

Widespread use of video games begs the question of what intended and unintended effects they may produce. There is not a simple answer to this question. For instance, exposure to a specific type of game (e.g., violent action games) might have multiple effects including increases in aggression (Anderson & Bushman, 2001) and improvements in visuospatial cognition (Green & Bavalier, 2003). Because games differ on a range of dimensions and engage various cognitive, affective, and behavioral systems, it is reasonable to expect that they will influence multiple information processing systems (Gentile & Gentile, 2008). Indeed, there is growing evidence for a wide range of video game effects that influence social and antisocial behaviors, cognitive styles, and affective processing (Barlett et al., 2009). Furthermore, some of these effects may be moderated by personal characteristics (e.g., gender) or by social circumstances (e.g., parental involvement). Thus, the potential positive or negative effects of video game experience must be considered within the socio-cognitive-cultural context where the individual is embedded. With this in mind, the goals of the current chapter were twofold. First, we provide a review of the literature examining the effects of video games from the perspective of social, cognitive, affective, and education science. Second, we briefly consider how knowledge from social and cognitive neuroscience may serve to enhance our understanding of the effects of video game experience.

Video Games: Social, Cognitive, Affective, and Education Science
Social Science

Building on a nearly 50-year tradition considering the effects of violence in television and film, the last decade has witnessed the blossoming of research examining the impact of video game violence (VGV) on aggression. At least some of this interest seems to be motivated by the commonly observed association between high levels of consumption of VGV and violent crime sprees committed by adolescents (e.g., West Paducah, Kentucky (December, 1997); Littleton, Colorado (April, 1999); Wellsboro, Pennsylvania (June, 2003)). Laboratory studies of the relationship between exposure to VGV and aggression demonstrate that brief exposure (e.g., 15–30 minutes) to violent content during game play can result in increases in aggressive thoughts and actions (Anderson, et al., 2004). Complementing this evidence, cross-sectional and longitudinal studies demonstrate that chronic exposure to VGV may represent a unique predictor of instances of aggression outside the laboratory (Anderson et al., 2004; Anderson, Gentile, & Buckley, 2007; Anderson et al., 2008).

The research examining the effects of VGV on aggression can be understood within the context of the *general aggression model* (GAM; Anderson & Bushman, 2002). GAM is a bio-social-cognitive theory designed to account for both short-term and long-term effects of exposure to media violence (Figure 66.1). Repeated exposure to, and reinforcement of, aggression that is embodied in violent video games can lead to the development of aggressive beliefs and attitudes, perceptual schemata, expectations, behavior scripts, and desensitization to aggression (Figure 66.2). Together, the development of these knowledge structures can lead to an

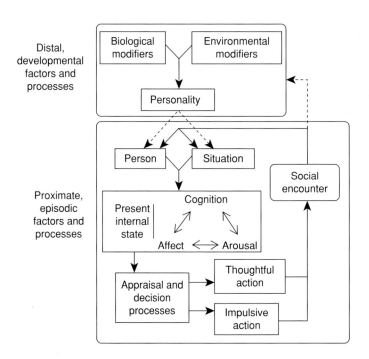

Fig. 66.1 The General Aggression Model: Overall View.
Adapted from Anderson & Carnagey (2004) with permission of Elsevier.

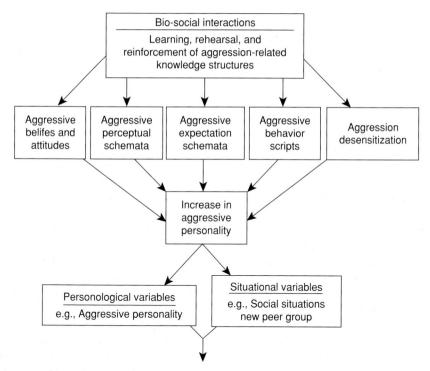

Fig. 66.2 The General Aggression Model: Developmental and Personality Processes.
Adapted from Anderson & Carnagey (2004) with permission of Elsevier.

increase in aggressive personality as well as changes in situational variables including peer groups and social activities (Anderson & Bushman, 2002).

One of the fundamental predictions derived from the GAM is that short-term or long-term exposure to VGV should lead to changes in a constellation of thoughts and actions. Consistent with this prediction, meta-analyses demonstrate that exposure to VGV is associated with an increase in physical aggression, aggressive cognition, aggressive affect, and physiological arousal, and a decrease in helping behavior (Anderson et al., 2004). Furthermore, the magnitude of the effect of VGV on measures of aggression appears to be similar in experimental and cross-sectional studies. More recent longitudinal studies also find the expected relative increase in aggression over time in those who consume high levels of VGV (Anderson et al., 2008; Moller & Krahe, 2009; Wallenius & Pnamaki, 2008).

The robust effect of VGV on aggressive behavior, thought, and affect leads to the question of what factors may give rise to this effect. This question has been examined in two types of investigations. Some studies have examined the effect of various experimental manipulations (i.e., situational variables) on the magnitude of the violent video game effect while

other studies have examined the influence of individual differences (i.e., personological variables) on the violent video game effect.

Studies examining situational variables have considered variation in characteristics of the games that are used to prime aggression. Based upon available evidence, the violent video game effect appears to be insensitive to the story line, the nature of the aggression (e.g., first person shooter, driving, and hand-to-hand combat), and the humanness of the target (Anderson et al., 2004; Bushman & Anderson, 2002). The level of aggression may also be similar for screen-based and more immersive technologies (Arriaga, Esteves, Carneiro, & Monteiro, 2008). There are, however, other characteristics of games that occasionally moderate the violent video game effect. For instance, the level of blood that is associated with in-game aggression moderates aggression both during and after game play (Barlett, Harris, & Bruey, 2008). The type of reinforcement that is associated with in-game aggression also seems to moderate the level of aggression (Carnagey & Anderson, 2005). Specifically, an increase in aggressive thoughts and actions is observed for individuals who are rewarded for violence during game play, but not for individuals who are punished for violence or play a nonviolent version of the game.

Furthermore, punishing violent actions within a game leads to a dramatic decrease in the number of such actions. Consistent with the GAM, the evidence from the two later studies indicates that positive reinforcement for aggression represents one source of violent video game effects.

Various individual difference and personality variables occasionally moderate or partially mediate the violent video game effect on aggression, though such cases are rare. For example, the violent video game effect is sometimes stronger for males than females (Bartholow & Anderson, 2002), although violent video games clearly lead to increased aggression in females (Anderson & Murphy, 2003). Trait aggression also occasionally moderates violent video game effects, but again such interactions are rare. Furthermore, when found in correlational studies, such moderation may be a methodological artifact because trait aggression is itself influenced by repeated exposure to VGV. A more consistent moderator variable is level of parental involvement in media use (Anderson et al., 2007). Children whose parents are highly involved in the child's media choices and use are less affected by VGV. This moderation effect was observed in a short-term experimental setting (Study 1), a cross-sectional analysis of trait aggression (Study 2), and a longitudinal study (Study 3; Anderson et al., 2007). The effect of trait aggression on VGV may be partially mediated by revenge motivation (Anderson et al., 2004; Bushman & Anderson, 2002) or the perception of hostility (Bartholow, Sestir, & Devic, 2005) that is experienced in response to provocation.

There is some evidence that individual differences in empathy may partially mediate the violent video game effect (Bartholow et al., 2005). The findings of this study are consistent with the GAM (Anderson & Bushman, 2002), as exposure to VGV would be expected to activate schemata that could bias the individual toward interpreting the actions of others as being more hostile and acting on this perceived threat in a more aggressive manner. Furthermore, evidence from a pair of studies demonstrates desensitization to real violence may be the locus of the influence of empathy on the VGV effect. In one experiment (Carnagey, Anderson, & Bushman, 2007), participants played either a violent or a nonviolent game and then viewed scenes of real violence while heart rate and skin conductance were measured. Those who played a nonviolent game experienced increases in heart rate and skin conductance while later viewing the real violence, whereas those who had played a violent game did

not. A second experiment (Bushman & Anderson, 2008, Experiment 1) used the same basic experimental procedures but considered helping behavior directed towards the victim of a (staged) fight outside the lab room. Those who had played a violent game were less likely to provide help and took longer to help than those who had played a nonviolent game.

The findings of studies examining neural recruitment during video game play are also consistent with the GAM, and have generally revealed that playing video games activates neural networks associated with reward processing and addiction (Koepp et al., 1998; Mathiak & Weber, 2006). Significant activation of the orbitofrontal cortex was observed when individuals played a computer game that involved capturing territory from an opponent (Hoeft, Watson, Kesler, Bettinger, & Reiss, 2008). This region is often associated with the encoding of reward value. Males demonstrated greater activation in the orbitofrontal cortex and the mesocorticolimbic system, indicating that they may have found the competitive aspects of the game more rewarding than females. A second study found that dopamine levels were elevated during video game play and that this elevation was similar to that associated with the administration of amphetamine that is known to activate the reward system (Koepp et al., 1998). Studies using functional MRI also reveal what may be desensitization to violence. During violent video game play, the rostral anterior cingulate cortex and amygdala are deactivated (Mathiak & Weber, 2006), and these neural structures are known to be related to the evaluation of the emotional content of stimuli.

Cognitive Science
VISUOSPATIAL COGNITION

Evidence from a number of studies demonstrates that the same types of video games that lead to increased aggression can serve to enhance visuospatial cognition. This enhancement can be seen in individual differences between video game players (VGPs) and non-players (NVGPs; Green & Bavelier, 2003, 2007; Lintern & Kennedy, 1984; Yuji, 1996) and in NVGPs after as little as 10 hours of training (Dorval & Pepin, 1986; Green & Bavelier, 2006). This research has revealed improvements in several domains including hand-eye coordination (Griffith, Voloschin, Gibb, & Bailey, 1983), visual attention (Castel, Pratt, & Drummond, 2005; Green & Bavelier, 2003), and flight simulation (Lintern & Kennedy, 1984).

Early studies in this area of inquiry examined the utility of video games in training pilots. Two studies using the Atari video game *Air Combat Maneuvering* revealed that the game was useful for identifying military personnel who would be successful pilots (Jones, Kennedy, & Bittner, 1981). In a similar study, Gopher et al. (1994) compared the flight performance of Israeli Air Force cadets who had been trained on *Space Fortress II* and an untrained group. This study revealed that trained cadets performed better in almost all aspects of flight performance, resulting in the game being adopted as a part of the training program.

Green and Bavelier (2003) have systematically investigated the basis of the video game effect on visuospatial cognition. These authors have reported positive effects of video game experience in a number of tasks examining visual enumeration, the useful field of view, the attentional blink, multiple object tracking, and the spatial resolution of vision (Green & Bavelier, 2003, 2006, 2007). Together, the findings of these studies demonstrate that video game experience can enhance the spatial and temporal resolution of visuospatial cognition for both static and dynamic displays.

In a series of studies, Green and Bavelier (2006) have examined the locus of the video game effect on the span of apprehension, which reflects the number of stimuli that can be extracted from a brief exposure to a visual display. As measured in the visual enumeration task the span of apprehension is typically 1.5 items greater for VGPs relative to NVGPs. Foundational work by Trick and Pylyshyn (1993) reveals that the output of two processes (i.e., subitizing and counting) gives rise to the span of apprehension. Subitizing represents the rapid, relatively automatic, extraction of 1 to 3 items from a visual display; in contrast, counting represents a slow, resource demanding, process that supports the extraction of 4 or more items from a visual display. By examining differences in response time and accuracy in the visual enumeration task under different conditions, Green and Bavelier were able to determine that the limit of subitizing was similar in VGPs and NVGPs, and that counting was more efficient in VGPs relative to NVGPs. These findings indicate that the expansion of the span of apprehension results from an increase in the efficiency of resource demanding cognitive processes rather than an increase in the number of items that can be automatically extracted from a display (Green & Bavelier, 2006).

EXECUTIVE FUNCTION AND COGNITIVE CONTROL

Evidence from a growing number of studies reveals that experience with the same types of games that produce benefits to visuospatial cognition may also be associated with disruptions of executive function or controlled attention. Two studies have reported that video game experience is positively correlated with attention deficits related to impulsivity and hyperactivity (Gentile, 2009; Swing, 2008). Gentile (2009) observed that adolescents reporting pathological video game consumption were 2.77 times more likely to be diagnosed with ADD or ADHD than were adolescents who reporting non-pathological video game consumption. Evidence reported by Swing (2008) replicates this basic finding and demonstrates that the relationship between video game experience and attention pathology remains significant even after controlling for the overall level of exposure to films and television, indicating that there is a unique effect of video game experience on attention.

Other work in this domain has focused on the relationship between video game experience and cognitive control in the Stroop task. Kronenberger et al. (2005) reported a moderate positive correlation between video game experience and the Stroop interference effect. Complimenting this finding, a study using fMRI found that VGPs failed to recruit anterior cingulate and lateral prefrontal cortex on incongruent trials during performance of the Stroop task, whereas these structures were recruited by low video game players (LVGs; Mathews, et al., 2005). This finding led to the suggestion that video game experience is associated with a disruption in the ability to engage the cognitive control network (Mathews et al., 2005).

A limitation of the study by Mathews et al. (2005) is that the task design makes it impossible to determine whether there is a general effect of video game experience on cognitive control or whether the influence is limited to specific control processes. We recently addressed this question using behavioral and event-related brain potential (ERPs) measures to examine the influence of video game experience on proactive and reactive cognitive control (Bailey, West, & Anderson, 2010). Proactive control represents a future-oriented form of control that serves to optimize task preparation; reactive control represents a just-in-time form of control that serves to resolve conflict within a trial (Braver, Gray, & Burgess, 2007). Bailey et al. found that the conflict adaptation effect (a behavioral measure of proactive control) was attenuated in HVGs relative to LVGs when there was a long delay between trials, and that this effect was associated with an attenuation of the medial frontal negativity and frontal slow wave (ERP indices of proactive control) in HVGs (Figure 66.3). In contrast, there was no difference between HVGs and LVGs for behavioral or neural indices of reactive control. These findings complement evidence revealing an association between attention deficits/hyperactivity and lead to the suggestion that video game experience may have a selective effect on proactive cognitive control processes that serve to maintain optimal goal-directed information processing. Of course, additional research using experimental and longitudinal designs is required to establish the causal nature of the effect of video game experience on cognitive control.

Affective Science

Violent video games have been shown to increase aggression (Anderson & Bushman, 2001), but less is known about how VGV affects the processing of positively and negatively valenced stimuli. At the behavioral level, Kirsh and colleagues (Kirsh & Mounts, 2007; Kirsh, Mounts, & Olczak, 2006; Kirsh, Olczak, & Mounts, 2005) have reported an increase in the bias toward processing angry faces and a decrease in the bias toward processing positive faces associated with exposure to VGV and other violent media. These studies suggest that exposure to VGV may lead to alterations in the experience of both positive and negative affect.

Autonomic Measures

One method of assessing the effects of video games on affect is to measure physiological arousal.

Research has shown that playing video games can lead to an increase in arousal as measured by heart rate, blood pressure, and skin conductance (Arriaga, Esteves, Carniero, & Monteiro, 2006; Bushman & Huesmann, 2006; Schneider, Lang, Shin, & Bradley, 2004). As an example of this effect, Ballard and Weist (1996) reported an increase in heart rate in males while playing Mortal Kombat compared to playing a billiards video game. They also found that systolic blood pressure was increased in participants playing a more graphically violent level (i.e., more blood) of Mortal Kombat compared to a less graphically violent level or billiards. Increased arousal can be associated with greater aggression and hostility following exposure to VGV (Anderson & Bushman, 2001). However, VGV has been found to lead to an increase in aggressive behavior even when physiological arousal is equated in the violent and nonviolent video game conditions (Anderson et al., 2004). This finding is important as it indicates that increased arousal is not the cause of the VGV effect on aggression.

Several attributes of video games have been shown to influence physiological arousal. Increases in heart rate are observed after playing games with greater amounts of blood compared to the same game with less blood or no blood (Barlett, Harris, & Baldassaro, 2007). Using a light gun rather than a standard controller to play a video game also produces a greater increase in heart rate (Barlett et al., 2008). Similarly, the addition of virtual reality to the game increased heart rate compared to playing the same video game on a computer monitor, and this is true for both violent and nonviolent games (Arriaga et al., 2008). In an interesting study, Schneider et al. (2004) demonstrated that the

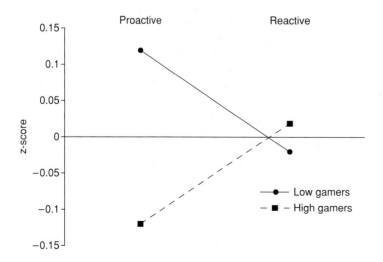

Fig. 66.3 The effect of video game experience on proactive, but not reactive, cognitive control collapsing across behavioral and ERP measures of these two types of control.
From Bailey et al. (2010) with permission of John Wiley and Sons.

presence of a storyline increased skin conductance levels in four different violent video games relative to the same games played without a storyline. Together, these findings lead to the suggestion that physiological arousal is influenced by the graphic and immersive nature of video games, as well as the violent content.

Cortical Measures

Two studies have examined the effects of VGV on the neural correlates of affective picture processing using ERPs. Bartholow, Bushman, and Sestir (2006) examined the influence of individual differences in exposure to VGV on the negativity bias. The negativity bias represents an enhanced positivity over the parietal region of the scalp associated with the processing of negative images relative to positive or neutral images that is thought to reflect an automatic orienting of attention to motivationally significant information in the environment (Ito, Larsen, Smith, & Cacioppo, 1998). Based on the GAM, Bartholow et al. (2006) predicted that the amplitude of the P3 (i.e., negativity bias) would be attenuated in VGPs relative to NVGPs for violent images, resulting from desensitization. In this study males viewed violent, negative nonviolent, and neutral images. As predicted, an increase in exposure to VGV was associated with a decrease in the amplitude of the P3 for violent images (Figure 66.4). In contrast, there was no effect of exposure to VGV on negative nonviolent images. Based upon these data the authors concluded that desensitization associated with exposure to VGV had a relatively selective effect on the processing of violent images.

In an extension of Bartholow et al. (2006), Bailey, West, and Anderson (2009) examined the effects of individual differences in exposure to VGV on the processing of positive and negative pictures using ERPs. This comparison was motivated by work demonstrating that exposure to VGV influences the processing of both positive and threatening faces (Kirsh et al., 2006). In this study VGPs and NVGPs rated neutral, positive, negative nonviolent, and violent images on three dimensions (i.e., pleasantness, how threatening, and colorfulness; Bailey et al., 2009b). Consistent with the findings of Bartholow et al. (2006), the amplitude of the negativity bias was attenuated for violent images in VGPs relative to NVGPs. Comparison of the ERPs elicited by positive stimuli revealed a second interesting effect that reflected a modulation of the P3 in addition to slow wave activity over the occipital-parietal region of the scalp. In the pleasantness rating condition this effect distinguished positive images from neutral images in the NVGPs, and positive and violent images from neutral images in the VGPs. In contrast, in the threat rating condition this effect was not observed in either group. This finding is consistent with GAM and may indicate that exposure to VGV results in violent and positive images taking on similar affective valence.

Education Science

One application of video games that may produce positive outcomes for children is in educational settings. The popularity of this medium among young children and adolescents makes video games a prime vehicle for educational and health-related

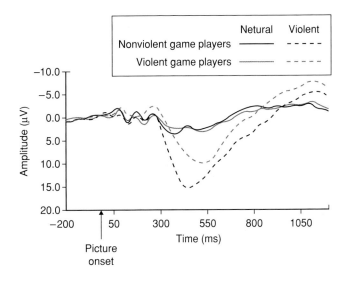

Fig. 66.4 The effect of video game violence on the amplitude of the P3 elicited by violent images, but not negative nonviolent images. Adapted from Bartholow et al. (2006) with permission of Elsevier.

messages. Video games may change behavior through the development of new skills and knowledge structures leading to the enhancement of self-efficacy (Baranowski et al., 2008; Lieberman, 2001). To date, research has investigated the utility of educational video games in the treatment of cancer (Beale, Kato, Marin-Bowling, Guthrie, & Cole, 2007; Kato & Beale, 2006), diabetes (Aoki et al., 2004; Brown et al., 1997), obesity (Lanningham-Foster et al., 2006), fetal alcohol syndrome (Padgett, Strickland, & Coles, 2006), and asthma (McPherson, Glazebrook, Forster, & Smith, 2006).

The management of childhood obesity is one promising area of investigation. Obesity has become a major health risk for many children in the United States. Active video games may be one way of combating this problem among children who prefer these media to traditional sports. Supporting this idea, one study found that the energy expended while playing games like *Dance Dance Revolution* is equivalent to that expended during physical activities like running and playing basketball (Straker & Abbott, 2007). Therefore, this evidence, coupled with the increasing popularity of physically interactive games like Wii Sports and Wii Fitness may represent a positive front in the battle against childhood obesity.

Implications of Social and Cognitive Neuroscience

(De)sensitizaton and Video Games

A curious aspect of the data reviewed in the previous sections is that exposure to VGV appears to result in desensitized responses in some contexts (Bartholow et al., 2006; Carnagey et al., 2007) and sensitized responses in other contexts (Kirsh et al., 2006). These findings lead to the natural question of how opposite effects may arise from the same set of experiences. An answer to this question may be found in a consideration of the influence of VGV on the neural systems that are likely recruited in the service of these tasks.

A number of studies examining the neural basis of affective information processing have revealed a modulation of the ERPs (i.e., early posterior negativity or EPN) over the occipital region of the scalp beginning around 250 ms after stimulus onset that is elicited by pictures of stimuli that are "high in evolutionary significance" (e.g., erotica and mutilations) (Junghöfer, Bradley, Elbert, & Lang, 2001; Schupp, Junghöfer, Weike, & Hamm, 2003). Most relevant to the current discussion, the amplitude of the EPN is greater for images of threatening faces than for images of neutral or friendly faces (Schupp, et al., 2004). In contrast, threat did not appear to influence the amplitude of the N170 (Schupp et al., 2004) that reflects a relatively early stage of face processing supported by the fusiform gyrus. Based on this finding it may be that the increased sensitivity to threatening faces associated with VGV results from enhanced processing of facial features in higher-level visual areas that occurs shortly after identification of the stimulus as a face. The adaptive benefit of this effect becomes clear within the context of first person shooter games where the rapid discrimination between friend and foe has significant survival value.

Based on data published by Bartholow et al. (2006) it appears the effects of desensitization emerge at a stage of information processing that is later than is reflected by the EPN. Specifically, Bartholow observed that the amplitude of the P3 component was attenuated in HVGs relative to LVGs. The cognitive processes reflected by the P3 have been intensively studied over the last 30 years (Polich, 2007). The P3 is commonly thought to arise from the engagement of neural processes associated with the allocation of attentional or mental resources to stimulus processing during motivated decision-making processes (Duncan-Johnson & Donchin, 1977) that involve dopaminergic modulation of the locus coeruleus-norepinephrine system (Nieuwenhuis, Aston-Jones, & Cohen, 2005). Based on these ideas related to the origin of the P3 component it may be that the desensitizing effect of VGV on the processing of violent images results from a reduction in the allocation of attention or a decrease in the degree that these stimuli are deemed motivationally significant (Cacioppo et al., 1994; Ito et al., 1998). Furthermore, together the evidence reviewed in this and the previous paragraphs leads to the suggestion that VGV may be associated with the enhancement of relatively early processing of threatening stimuli supported by visual association areas, and a reduction in activation of higher cortical areas associated with decision making.

Attention Deficit/Hyperactivity

From a public health perspective, one of the more alarming observations emerging from the literature is the relationship between video game experience and ADHD. At an anecdotal level, parents of children with ADHD often report that one of the few activities their child can engage in for an extended period of time is playing video games. Several recent findings may call the wisdom of this practice into question. Bioulac, Arfi, and Bouvard (2008) found that children with ADHD who also reported problem video game playing demonstrated higher levels of disorder-related symptoms, and higher levels of delinquency and aggression. Consistent with this finding, Gentile (2009) found that 8–18 year olds with pathological video game habits reported a higher incidence of diagnosis with ADD or ADHD, greater difficulty paying attention at school, and lower grades. Also, recent work by Swing (2008) indicates that there may be an interaction between nonpathological variation in impulsivity and hyperactivity and video game experience when predicting grade point average. Together these findings reveal what appears to be a nontrivial relationship between video game experience and disorders of attention.

How might the confluence of video game experience and ADHD be understood within the context of what is known about the cognitive neuroscience of these two domains? As described earlier, exposure to violent video games may be associated with a disruption in the ability to recruit neural structures that support proactive cognitive control (Bailey et al., 2010). Disruption in the recruitment of these same structures is often implicated in the behavioral pathology of individuals with ADHD (Barkley, 1997; Nigg & Casey, 2005) and conduct disorders (Kronenberger et al., 2005; Mathews et al., 2005). Together these findings lead to the suggestion that ADHD in combination with high levels of video game experience may have a negative synergistic effect on the neural architecture that supports cognitive control and self-regulation. Importantly, other recent evidence demonstrates that playing strategy-based video games may lead to enhancements in cognitive control (Basak, Boot, Voss, & Kramer, 2008). This finding then leads to the suggestion that directing individuals toward games that exercise specific executive processes could in fact lessen, rather than magnify, the effects of ADHD.

Conclusions

Here we have reviewed the literature examining the effects of video game experience in the domains of social, cognitive, affective, and education science. This literature reveals some paradoxical effects wherein experience with the same types of games can lead to an increase in aggression, a decrease in cognitive control, and an increase in visuospatial abilities. A consideration of the behavioral, neuroanatomical, and physiological bases of the effects of video games leads to the suggestion that exposure to these media is associated with plasticity within neural networks supporting high level vision, emotion processing, cognitive control, and social decision making. Future investigations focusing on within and between domain comparisons using behavioral and neuromonitoring techniques are likely to provide greater insight into the neural basis of the effects of video games.

References

Anderson, C. A. & Bushman, B. J. (2001). Effects of violent video games on aggressive behavior, aggressive cognition, aggressive affect, physiological arousal, and prosocial behavior: A meta-analytic review of the scientific literature. *Psychological Science, 12*, 353–359.

Anderson, C. A. & Bushman, B. J. (2002). Human aggression. *Annual Review of Psychology, 53*, 27–51.

Anderson, C. A., Carnagey, N. L., Flanagan, M., Benjamin, A. J., Eubanks, J., & Valentine, J. C. (2004). Violent video games: Specific effects of violent content on aggressive thoughts and behavior. *Advances in Experimental Social Psychology, 36*, 199–249.

Anderson, C. A., Gentile, D. A., & Buckley, K. E. (2007). *Violent videogame effects on children and adolescents: Theory, research, and public policy.* New York: Oxford University Press.

Anderson, C. A. & Murphy, C. R. (2003). Violent video games and aggressive behavior in young women. *Aggressive behavior, 29*, 423–429.

Anderson, C. A., Sakamoto, A., Gentile, D. A., Ihori, N., Shibuya, A., Yukawa, S., et al. (2008). Longitudinal effects of violent video games aggression in Japan and the United States. *Pediatrics, 122*, e1067–e1072.

Aoki, N., Ohta, S., Masuda, H., Naito, T., Sawai, T., Nishida, K., et al. (2004). Edutainment tools for initial education of type-1 diabetes mellitus: Initial diabetes education with fun. *MEDINFO*, 855–859.

Arriaga, P., Esteves, F., Carneiro, P., & Monteiro, M. (2008). Are the effects of unreal violent video games pronounced when playing with a virtual reality system? *Aggressive Behavior, 34*, 521–538.

Arriaga, P., Esteves, F., Carneiro, P., & Monteiro, M. (2006). Violent computer games and their effects on state hostility and physiological arousal. *Aggressive Behavior, 32*, 146–158.

Bailey, K., West, R., & Anderson, C. A. (2010). A negative association between video game experience and proactive cognitive control. *Psychophysiology, 47*, 34–2.

Bailey, K., West, R., & Anderson, C. A. (2009). The influence of video game violence on the processing of positive, negative, and violent images. Unpublished data.

Ballard, M. E. & Wiest, R. (1996). Mortal Kombat: The effects of violent videogame play on males' hostility and cardiovascular responding. *Journal of Applied Social Psychology, 26*, 717–730.

Baranowski, T., Buday, R., Thompson, D. I., & Baranowski, J. (2008). Playing for real: Video games and stories for health-related behavior change. *American Journal of Preventive Medicine, 34*, 74–82.

Barkley, R. A. (1997). *ADHD and the nature of self control.* New York: Guildford Press.

Barlett, C. P., Anderson, C. A., & Swing, E. L. (2009). Video game effects confirmed, suspected and speculative: A review of the evidence. *Simulation & Gaming, 40*, 377–403.

Barlett, C. P., Harris, R. J., & Bruey, C. (2008). The effect of the amount of blood in a violent video game on aggression, hostility, and arousal. *Journal of Experimental Social Psychology*, *44*, 539–546.

Barlett, C. P., Harris, R. J., & Baldassaro, R. (2007). Longer you play, the more hostile you feel: Examination of first person shooter video games and aggression during video game play. *Aggressive Behavior*, *33*, 486–497.

Bartholow, B. D. & Anderson, C. A. (2002). Effects of violent video games on aggressive behavior: Potential sex differences. *Journal of Experimental Social Psychology*, *38*, 283–290.

Bartholow, B. D., Bushman, B. J., & Sestir, M. A. (2006). Chronic violent video game exposure and desensitization to violence: Behavioral and event-related brain potential data. *Journal of Experimental Social Psychology*, *42*, 532–539.

Bartholow, B. D., Sestir, M. A., & Davic, E. B. (2005). Correlates and consequences of exposure to video game violence: Hostile personality, empathy, and aggressive behavior. *Personality and Social Psychology Bulletin*, *31*, 1573–1586.

Basak, C., Boot, W. R., Voss, M. W., & Kramer, A. F. (2008). Can training in real-time strategy video game attenuate cognitive decline in older adults? *Psychology and Aging*, *23*, 765–777.

Beale, I. L, Kato, P. M, Marin-Bowling, V. M., Guthrie, N., & Cole, S. W. (2007). Improvement in cancer-related knowledge following use of a psychoeducational video game for adolescents and young adults with cancer. *Journal of Adolescent Health*, *41*, 263–270.

Bioulac, S., Arfi, L., & Bouvard, M. P. (2008). Attention deficit/ hyperactivity disorder and video games: A comparative study of hyperactive and control children. *European Psychiatry*, *23*, 134–141.

Braver, T. S., Gray, J. R., & Burgess, G. C. (2007). Explaining the many varieties of working memory variation: Dual mechanisms of cognitive control. In Conway, A. R. A., M. J. Kane, A. Miyake, & J. Towse (Eds.), *Variation in working memory* (pp. 76–106). Oxford, UK: Oxford University Press.

Brown, S. J., Lieberman, D. A., Gemeny, B. A., Fan, Y. C., Wilson, D. M., & Pasta, D. J. (1997). Educational video games for juvenile diabetes: Results of a controlled trial. *Med Informatics*, *22*, 77–89.

Bushman, B. J. & Anderson, C. A. (2002). Violent video games and hostile expectations: A test of the general aggression model. *Personality and Social Psychology Bulletin*, *28*, 1679–1686.

Bushman, B. J. & Anderson, C. A. (2008). Comfortably numb: Desensitizing effects of violent media on helping others. *Psychological Science*.

Bushman, B. J. & Huesmann, L. R. (2006). Short-term and long-term effects of violent media on aggression in children and adults. *Archives of Pediatrics and Adolescent Medicine*, *160*, 348–352.

Cacioppo, J. T., Crites, S. L., Gardner, W. L., & Bernston, G. G. (1994). Bioelectrical echoes from evaluative categorization: I. A late positive brain potential that varies as a function of trait negativity and extremity. *Journal of Personality and Social Psychology*, *67*, 115–125.

Castel, A. D., Pratt, J., & Drummond, E. (2005). The effects of action video game experience on the time course of inhibition of return and the efficiency of visual search. *Acta Psychologica*, *119*, 217–230.

Carnagey, N. L. & Anderson, C. A. (2005). The effects of reward and punishment on violent video games on aggressive affect, cognition, and behavior. *Psychological Science*, *16*, 882–889.

Carnagey, N. L., Anderson, C.A., & Bushman, B. J. (2007). The effect of video game violence on physiological desensitization to real-life violence. *Journal of Experimental Social Psychology*, *43*, 489–496.

Dorval, M. & Pepin, M. (1986). Effect of playing a video game on a measure of spatial visualization. *Perceptual and Motor Skills*, *62*, 159–162.

Duncan-Johnson, C. C. & Donchin, E. (1977). On quantifying surprise: The variation in event-related potentials with subjective probability. *Psychophysiology*, *14*, 456–467.

Gentile, D. A. (2009). Pathological video game use among youth 8 to 18: A national study. *Psychological Science*, 20, 594–602.

Gentile, D. A. & Gentile, J.R. (2008). Video games as exemplary teachers: A conceptual analysis. *Journal of Youth and Adolescence*, *37*, 127–141.

Gentile, D. A., Lynch, P. L., Linder, J. R., & Walsh, D. A. (2004). The effects of violent video game habits on adolescent hostility, aggressive behaviors, and school performance. *Journal of Adolescence*, *27*, 5–22.

Gopher, D., Weil, M., & Bareket, T. (1994). Transfer of skill from a computer game trainer to flight. *Human Factors*, *36*, 387–405.

Green, C. S. & Bavelier, D. (2003). Action video game modifies visual selective attention. *Nature*, *423*, 534–537.

Green, C. S. & Bavelier, D. (2006). Enumeration versus multiple object tracking: The case of action video game players. *Cognition*, *101*, 217–245.

Green, C. S. & Bavelier, D. (2007). Action-video-game experience alters the spatial resolution of vision. *Psychological Science*, *18*, 88–94.

Griffith, J. L., Voloschin, P., Gibb, G. D., & Bailey, J. R. (1983). Difference in eye-hand motor coordination of video-game users and non-users. *Perceptual and Motor Skills*, *57*, 155–158.

Hoeft, F., Watson, C. L., Kesler, S. R., Bettinger, K. E., & Reiss, A. L. (2008). Gender differences in the mesocorticolimbic system during computer game-play. *Journal of Psychiatric Research*, *42*, 253–258.

Ito, T. A., Larsen, J. T., Smith, N. K., & Cacioppo, J. T. (1998). Negative information weighs more heavily on the brain: The negativity bias in evaluative categorizations. *Journal of Personality and Social Psychology*, *75*, 887–900.

Jones, M. B., Kennedy, R. S., & Bittner, Jr., A. C. (1981). A video game for performance testing. *The American Journal of Psychology*, *94*, 143–152.

Junghofer, M., Bradley, M. M., Elbert, T. R., & Lang, P. J. (2001). Fleeting images: A new look at early emotion discrimination. *Psychophysiology*, *38*, 175–178.

Kato, P. M. & Beale, I. L. (2006). Factors affecting acceptability to young cancer patients of a psychoeducational video game about cancer. *Journal of Pediatric Oncology Nursing*, *23*, 269–275.

Kirsh, S. J. & Mounts, J. R. W. (2007). Violent video game play impacts facial emotion recognition. *Aggressive Behavior*, *33*, 353–358.

Kirsh, S. J., Mounts, J. R. W., & Olczak, P. V. (2006). Violent media consumption and the recognition of dynamic facial expressions. *Journal of Interpersonal Violence*, *21*, 571–584.

Kirsh, S. J., Olczak, P. V., & Mounts, J. R. W. (2005). Violent video games induce an affect processing bias. *Media Psychology*, *7*, 239–250.

Koepp, M. J., Gunn, R. N., Lawrence, A. D., Cunningham, V. J., Dagher, A., Jones, T., et al. (1998). Evidence for striatal dopamine release during a video game. *Nature*, *393*, 266–268.

Kronenberger, W. G., Matthews, V. P., Dunn, D. W., Wang, Y., Wood, E. A., Giauque, A. L., et al. (2005). Media violence exposure and executive functioning in aggressive and control adolescents. *Journal of Clinical Psychology, 61,* 725–737.

Lanningham-Foster, L., Jensen, T. B., Foster, R. C., Redmond, A. B., Walker, B. A., Heinz, D., et al. (2006). Energy expenditure of sedentary screen time compared with active screen time for children. *Pediatrics, 118,* 2535.

Lenhart, A., Kahne, J., Middaugh, E., Macgill, E. R., Evans, C., & Vitak, J. (2008, Sept 16). Teens, video games, and civics. Washington, DC: Pew Internet & American Life Project.

Lieberman, D. A. (2001). Management of chronic pediatric diseases with interactive health games: Theory and research findings. *Journal of Ambulatory Care Management, 24,* 26–38.

Lintern, G. & Kennedy, R. S. (1984). Video game as a covariate for carrier landing research. *Perceptual and Motor Skills, 58,* 167–172.

Mathiak, K. & Weber, R. (2006). Toward brain correlates of natural behavior: fMRI during violent video games. *Human Brain Mapping, 27,* 948–956.

Mathews, V. P., Kronenberger, W. G., Wang, Y., Lurito, J. T., Lowe, M. J., & Dunn, D. W. (2005). Media violence exposure and frontal lobe activation measured by functional magnetic resonance imaging in aggressive and nonaggressive adolescents. *Journal of Computer Assisted Tomography, 29,* 287–292.

McPherson, A. C., Glazebrook, C., Forster, D., James, C., & Smyth, A. (2006). A randomized, controlled trial of an interactive educational computer package for children with asthma. *Pediatrics, 117,* 1046–1054.

Moller, I. & Krahe, B. (2009). Exposure to violent video games and aggression in German adolescents: A longitudinal analysis. *Aggressive Behavior, 35,* 75–89.

Nieuwenhuis, S., Aston-Jones, G., & Cohen, J. D. (2005). Decision making, the P3, and the locus coeruleus-norepinephrine system. *Psychological Bulletin, 131,* 510–532.

Nigg, J. T. & Casey, B. J. (2005). An integrative theory of attention-deficit/hyperactivity disorder based on the cognitive and affective neurosciences. *Developmental Psychopathology, 17,* 785–806.

Padgett, L. S., Strickland, D., & Coles, C. D. (2006). Case study: Using a virtual reality computer game to teach fire safety skills to children diagnosed with fetal alcohol syndrome. *Journal of Pediatric Psychology, 31,* 65–70.

Polich, J. (2007). Updating P300: An integrative theory of P3a and P3b. *Clinical Neurophysiology, 118,* 2128–2148.

Rideout, V., Roberts, D. F., & Foehr, U. G. (2005). *Generation M: Media in the lives of 8–18 year-olds.* Menlo Park: The Henry J. Kaiser Family Foundation.

Schneider, E. F., Lang, A., Shin, M., & Bradley, S. D. (2004). Death with a story: How story impacts emotional, motivational, and physiological responses to first-person shooter video games. *Human Communication Research, 30,* 361–375.

Schupp, H. T., Junghofer, M., Weike, A. I., & Hamm, A. O. (2003). Emotional facilitation of sensory processing in the visual cortex. *Psychological Science, 14,* 7–13.

Schupp, H. T., Ohman, A., Junghofer, M., Weike, A. I., Stockburger, J., & Hamm, A. O. (2004). The facilitated processing of threatening faces: An ERP analysis. *Emotion, 4,* 189–200.

Straker, L. & Abbott, R. (2007). Effect of screen-based media on energy expenditure and heart rate in 9-to12-year-old children. *Pediatric Exercise Science, 19,* 459–471.

Swing, E. L. (2008). *Attention abilities, media exposure, school performance, personality, and aggression.* Unpublished master's thesis, Iowa State University, Ames, Iowa.

Trick, L. M. & Pylyshyn, Z. W. (1993). What enumeration studies can show us about spatial attention: Evidence for limited capacity preattentive processing. *Journal of Experimental Psychology: Human Perception and Performance, 19,* 331–351.

Wallenius, M. & Punamäki, R. (2008). Digital game violence and direct aggression in adolescence: A longitudinal study of the roles of sex, age, and parent–child communication, *Journal of Applied Developmental Psychology, 29,* 286–294.

Yuji, H. (1996). Computer games and information processing skills. *Perceptual and Motor Skills, 83,* 643–647.

PART 8

Societal
Significance

Ethical, Legal, and Societal Issues in Social Neuroscience

Martha J. Farah

Abstract

This chapter reviews the neuroethical issues that are most closely related to social neuroscience. The next two sections address the issues that emerge from neuroscience-based technologies; in other words, relatively pragmatic issues concerning how the fruits of social neuroscience can and should be applied. These include ethical, legal, and social challenges raised by newfound abilities to image the brain and thereby obtain information about mental states and personal traits, as well as by our growing ability to intervene in individuals' brain function to alter these states and traits. The final section addresses neuroethical issues that emerge from the impact of social neuroscience on our understanding of human beings. In this section it is the knowledge per se, not its technological applications, that is the focus of the review. This section includes the ways in which our evolving understanding of the human person challenges our long-held beliefs about morality and spirituality.

Keywords: social neuroscience, neuroethical issues, neuroscience-based technologies, human beings

The Emergence of Neuroethics and Social Neuroscience

"Neuroethics" has become the short-hand term for the wide array of ethical, legal, and societal issues raised by progress in neuroscience. Social neuroscience has contributed many of the most interesting and important of these issues because of its direct relevance to our personal lives. Consider the ways in which the emergence of social neuroscience has multiplied the roles that neuroscience can play in society.

The achievements of human neuroscience in the 20th century primarily concerned nonsocial neuroscience. Tremendous progress was made in understanding the perceptual, motor and elementary memory systems of the brain (e.g., Kandel, Schwartz, & Jessell, 2000). This progress certainly

had the potential to influence human life. For example, it had consequences for the diagnosis and treatment of neurological and psychiatric disorders, and opened the door to the investigation of genetic and pharmacologic manipulations of learning and memory in healthy brains (Marshall, 2004). Nevertheless, much of what we care about as human beings—our personalities, moods, relationships, and our lives outside of the medical context—were relatively untouched by these advances. In contrast, neuroscience that addresses the mechanisms of social processes, including person perception and memory, personality, motivation, moral judgment, attachments and biases, presents many more opportunities to affect human life.

Presumably for these reasons, neuroethics has emerged as a field more or less in tandem with social neuroscience. The first meetings on neuroethics were held at the University of Pennsylvania and Stanford University in February and May of 2002, just following the first meeting on "Social Cognitive Neuroscience" at UCLA in April of 2001. The first journals devoted to neuroethics, *American Journal of Bioethics–Neuroscience* and *Neuroethics*, were established in 2007 and 2008, respectively, just following the inaugural issues of *Social Neuroscience* and *Social, Cognitive and Affective Neuroscience* in 2006.

This chapter reviews the neuroethical issues that are most closely related to social neuroscience. The next two sections will address the issues that emerge from neuroscience-based technologies; in other words, relatively pragmatic issues concerning how the fruits of social neuroscience can and should be applied. These include ethical, legal, and social challenges raised by newfound abilities to image the brain and thereby obtain information about mental states and personal traits, as well as by our growing ability to intervene in individuals' brain function to alter these states and traits. The final section will address neuroethical issues that emerge from the impact of social neuroscience on our understanding of human beings. In this section it is the knowledge per se, not its technological applications, that is the focus of the review. This section will include the ways in which our evolving understanding of the human person challenges our long-held beliefs about morality and spirituality.

Neuroimaging of Socially Relevant Traits and States

Discussions of imaging in neuroethics often seem to suffer from split personality. On the one hand, one finds claims of imminent mind-reading and the end of mental privacy, especially in the popular press. On the other, functional neuroimaging is frequently denigrated as misleading, oversold, and incapable of delivering true information about an individual's psychology. Not surprisingly, the truth about neuroimaging falls somewhere in between. Challenges to mental privacy and the dangers of uncritical acceptance are both important neuroethical issues. We begin by reviewing the state of the art in imaging mental traits and mental states.

"Images of Mind:" From Cognitive to Social Neuroscience and From Groups to Individuals

The now ubiquitous use of functional brain imaging in human neuroscience began in the late 1980s with PET studies of language and memory (e.g., Petersen,

Fox, Posner, Mintun, & Raichle, 1989; Squire, et al., 1992). As described in the book "Images of Mind" (Posner & Raichle, 1994), within ten years PET was largely displaced by the more widely available and noninvasive fMRI, which was quickly applied to a wide range of cognitive processes. By the turn of the 20th century this work had extended to include affective and social processes. Landmark studies of such topics as theory of mind (see Stone, this volume), empathy (see Singer & Decety, this volume), unconscious attitudes (see Cunningham, this volume) and emotion regulation (see Ochsner, this volume) ushered in the era of social neuroscience.

The ethical, legal, and social implications of this research did not become significant until the focus shifted from groups of subjects, studied in order to generalize about typical brain function, to individual subjects, studied to understand individual variation. Typical of the earlier studies were findings that localized a mental process, for example the experience of empathic pain, by comparing the brain activation of a group of subjects in an empathic pain condition with the brain activation of the same subjects in a control condition (see Singer & Decety, this volume). Prospects for applying this research to the measurement or classification of individuals are, of course, inherently limited. However, within a few years the same researchers had begun to relate degrees of brain activation differences or effects in these experimental paradigms to individual differences in personal traits of potentially great interest to society. Although the statistical basis for some of these analyses has been criticized (Vul et al., 2009), there is no doubt that moderately strong correlations have been documented in many cases between imaging measures and psychological traits.

Imaging Psychological Traits

A number of socially relevant psychological traits have been found to correlate moderately strongly with brain activity in fMRI studies, including aggression, altruism, and racial attitudes. For example, an early and influential study by Liz Phelps and collaborators found that White subjects' amygdala activation correlates with the degree of unconscious negative evaluation of Black faces (Phelps et al., 2000). Specifically, the discrepancy between amygdala activation to Black and White faces correlated $r = 0.576$ with the magnitude of unconscious bias against Blacks measured in the Implicit Association Test (Greenwald, McGhee, & Schwartz, 1998).

Coccaro et al. (2007) showed subjects with and without a history of impulsive aggression photos of faces displaying different emotions, while measuring neural responses to these photos with fMRI. In addition to finding overall differences between aggressive and nonaggressive subjects in their response to the sight of an angry face, including greater activation of the amygdala and less activation of the presumably regulatory orbitofrontal cortex, they also found a correlation between amygdala activation and aggression. The more aggressive one's behavior, measured over one's lifetime, the higher the activation of the left amygdala to angry faces, r = 0.546.

Turning to a more desirable trait, altruistic cooperation, Rilling et al. (2002) scanned subjects while they played an iterated "Prisoner's Dilemma" game and assessed the relationship between the tendency to prolong mutually cooperative play and the activation of reward-related brain areas by such cooperation. They found a correlation of r = 0.70 between cooperative behavior in the scanner and the activation it evoked in the ventral striatum, an area associated with the enjoyment of rewards from money to chocolate (O'Dougherty, 2004).

These studies and others like them involve what Poldrack (2008) has called "forward inference." That is, the direction of inference is from psychological process (manipulated by the researcher experimentally or by selection of subject characteristics) to brain activation (measured by the researcher; see Cacioppo & Tassinary, 1990). Each of these studies was part of a research program aimed at understanding the neural bases of the particular psychological construct under study. This can be contrasted with research whose aim is detecting or measuring personality traits or attitudes, which would be a form of "reverse inference," going from brain activity to psychological trait. Nevertheless, the data collected in these studies are also applicable to the goal of measurement. A recent review of the published literature and statistical reanalysis of published data concluded that a modest degree of measurement ability already resides in the experimental paradigms of social neuroscience research (Farah, Smith, Gawuga, Lindsell, & Foster, 2008). To the extent that neuroimaging can be used to measure traits of personal or social significance, it raises issues of privacy, which will be addressed in more detail in the final part of this section.

Imaging Mental States

Whereas the studies of trait-related differences in brain activation have generally been undertaken within the context of basic research programs, imaging studies of mental states often have a closer relationship to applied research goals such as the measurement or detection of specific states with real-world relevance. The field of neuromarketing is a prime example of the use of reverse inference for an applied goal.

The emotions and motivations of consumers are crucial for many marketing decisions, from brand identity to pricing, but consumers are notoriously poor at reporting these aspects of their own psychology. The prospect of directly "reading" consumers' brain states is therefore of great interest to marketers. In addition, brain imaging is relatively well suited to this type of reverse inference. Compared to some psychological states, states of liking and wanting have a relatively straightforward relation to patterns of brain activity. EEG and fMRI have therefore become widely used tools in market research.

Published research in the field of neuromarketing has illuminated the ways in which packaging design, price, brand identity, spokesman celebrity, and other marketing factors separate from the product itself affect neural responses to the product, and how accurately those neural responses predict purchasing decisions (for reviews see Hubert & Kenning, 2008; Lee, Broderick & Chamberlain, 2006). The success of neuromarketing as a business tool is harder to assess, but the list of companies paying for neuromarketing suggests that many corporate decision-makers have faith in it. Forbes Magazine reported that this list includes Chevron, Disney, Ebay, Google, Hyundai, Microsoft, Pepsico, and Yahoo (Burkitt, 2009).

The techniques of neuromarketing are not limited to selling products and services. They have also been used to study preferences for health behaviors (Langleben et al., 2009) and political candidates (Westen et al., 2006). The firm FKF Applied Research published advice to American presidential candidates for the 2008 election in the New York Times Op Ed pages, based on their fMRI studies (Iacoboni et al., 2007). Their advice received widespread attention in the media and online (Aron et al., 2007; Farah, 2007; see also Iacoboni, 2008, Poldrack, 2008). Less public attempts to understand voters' reactions to candidates based on measures of brain function have reportedly been carried out at the request of specific political campaigns (Linstrom, 2008).

Another type of mental state that researchers have attempted to read from brain activation is the state of intentional deception. Early studies of deception were aimed at the basic science goal of characterizing the differences in brain activation between lying and truth-telling (e.g., Langleben et al., 2002), and showed that the anterior cingulate cortex (ACC) as well as regions of prefrontal and parietal cortex were more active during lies (see Bles & Haynes, 2008; Christ et al., 2009, for reviews). More recent research on deception with fMRI has been aimed at explicitly at the reverse inference of determining the truth value of statements based on brain activation (e.g., Davatzikos et al., 2005) and at least two companies offer fMRI lie detection services. Among the potential applications cited by them are reduction of "risk in dating"; vindication "if your word, reputation or freedom is in dispute"; and a substitute for drug screening, resume validation, and security background checks in employment screening (Cephos, No Lie MRI urls).

To date, such methods have not been admitted as evidence in a court of law. A different type of brain-based lie detection, based on event-related potentials (ERPs) has been admitted as evidence in the US (Harrington v State of Iowa), and in India. Indeed, in India the method has helped convict at least two defendants of murder (Aggarwal, 2009).

Ethical, Legal, and Societal Issues in Brain Imaging

Concerns about the ethics of brain imaging generally focus either on privacy concerns or concerns about the illusory accuracy and objectivity of brain imaging. To the extent that brain imaging can actually deliver information about a person's mental states or traits, the issue of privacy is important. To the extent that it cannot, but people believe that it can, the issue of public misunderstanding is important.

A number of writers have commented on the potential threat to privacy posed by functional neuroimaging (e.g., Committee on Science and Law, ABCNY, 2005; Hyman, 2004). On the face of things, brain imaging poses a novel challenge to privacy in that it can in principle deliver information about thoughts, attitudes, beliefs and traits, even when someone offers no behavioral responses. More concretely, and perhaps more importantly, imaging-based psychological investigations lend themselves to stealth uses in ways that more conventional paper-and-pencil or other low-tech methods do not. Both structural and functional brain images can be obtained with consent for one purpose but later analyzed for other purposes. Furthermore, in many studies the stimuli and instructions do not reveal the nature of the psychological information being

sought. For example, in two of the studies cited earlier, unconscious racial attitudes and impulsive aggression were both correlated with brain activity evoked by simply viewing pictures of faces (Coccaro et al., 2007; Phelps et al., 2000). Hence, in principle it seems possible to obtain information about racial attitudes and aggressive tendencies without subjects' knowledge or consent, by misleading them into thinking the study concerns face perception.

At present the problem of public misunderstanding of neuroimaging is a more immediate challenge than the problem of mental privacy. A number of authors have suggested that laypersons may attribute greater objectivity and certainty to brain images than to other types of information about the human mind (Dumit, 2004; McCabe & Castell, 2008; Racine, Bar-Ilan, & Illes, 2005; Roskies, 2008). This may contribute to the premature commercialization of brain imaging for various real-world applications, including lie detection.

Different applications of brain-based lie detection call for different levels of protection for the consumers or citizens involved (Farah et al., submitted). Although laboratory research with the kinds of methods used by these companies documents impressively high levels of accuracy approaching 90% under laboratory conditions, this is not sufficient accuracy for high-stakes decision making in contexts such as employment screening, business disputes, legal cases, or national security, the very contexts for which the companies recommend their methods. In addition, the accuracies reported in the fMRI literature are based on laboratory tasks that differ in many ways from the real-world situations in which lie detection is employed. These include the participation of cooperative subjects (especially important for pattern classification methods that require extensive training of the system; see Haynes & Rees, 2006), the artificiality of the situation (e.g., subjects lie because they are instructed to), and the inconsequential nature of the lies.

Within the field of neuromarketing, demonstrations of good performance predicting simple buying decisions (e.g., Knutson et al., 2007) may not extend to more complex social decision making. Yet, as already mentioned, neuromarketers are venturing into the prediction of preferences in more complex situations such as political campaigns.

The risks of premature adoption of these methods, encouraged by the aura of cutting-edge science that surrounds them, can be grave. Qualified people may be denied job opportunities, guilty people may be exonerated and innocent people may be found guilty. At the same time, the more frightening aspects of science fiction mind-reading should not be allowed to cloud our judgment regarding efforts to develop and validate these methods.

Manipulation of Socially Relevant Brain Traits and States

Although most developments in psychopharmacology and brain stimulation have been motivated by the need to treat neurological and psychiatric illnesses, some drugs can also be used to improve or change aspects of healthy brain function. The use of psychoactive drugs for manipulating normal brain function has been of interest and concern within neuroethics mainly in connection with neurocognitive enhancement (e.g., see Farah et al., 2004; Greely et al., 2008). What about the enhancement of traits and states that are more directly relevant to social phenomena?

Neuroscientists have succeeded in manipulating normal levels of mood, personality, empathy, trust, aggression, and so forth, although most of this work has yet to be translated into practically useful methods. The history of what could be called social-emotional brain enhancement goes back at least as far as the mid-20th century, with medications such as Miltown and Dexadrine, also known as "mother's little helpers." These drugs were explicitly marketed in medical journals and elsewhere for the enhancement of social and emotional functioning. Ads touted them as solutions to the problems of modern life, helping housewives better handle the stresses of their 24/7 responsibilities and helping hen-pecked husbands assert themselves at home and at the office. Yet they proved to be addictive and are now rarely prescribed to enhance social or emotional functioning of healthy individuals.

The introduction of Prozac in the 1980s, followed by a string of other selective serotonin reuptake inhibitors (SSRIs), offered a much needed new treatment option for patients suffering from depression and anxiety disorders, but had wider societal effects as well. Peter Kramer foretold much of current neuroethics in his book *Listening to Prozac* (1993), in which he discussed the use of Prozac by patients who appreciated the drug's effect on their personalities, puzzled over the relationship between brain and self, and coined the term "cosmetic psychopharmacology."

Any discussion of brain enhancement must address the question of where to draw the line between enhancement and treatment. For cognitive enhancement, the question is usually framed in terms of diagnostic boundaries between everyday distractibility and ADHD, or between normal cognitive aging and dementia. In the case of SSRIs for social-emotional enhancement the question is more complex, partly because there are so many therapeutic uses of SSRIs—including depression, premenstrual dysphoria, general anxiety, social anxiety, obsessive-compulsive disorder—and partly because the relevant diagnostic boundaries appear to have shifted because of the SSRIs themselves. In the case of depression, antidepressant medications before Prozac had more troublesome side effects and were therefore reserved for patients with major depression. The greater tolerability of SSRIs, combined with pharma's energetic marketing to patients and doctors, led to a larger number of less ill patients using these drugs and to a revision of diagnostic categories (Healy, 2004). As the line between pathology and health moves to include more people on the pathological side of the line, uses of medication that would have been considered enhancement become therapy.

Ultimately, whether one labels the use of SSRIs by functional and seemingly well-adjusted people as therapy or enhancement, this definitional issue matters less than the fact that large numbers of people are using them. A recent study reported that antidepressants are now the most widely used class of drugs in the US, with an estimated 10% of the population having received a prescription for them in the year 2005 (Olfson & Marcus, 2009). This is particularly relevant to the neuroethics of social neuroscience because SSRIs subtly alter personality. A recent study in depressed patients found that the SSRI paroxetine affects personality above and beyond its effect on depression (Tang et al., 2009). The most pronounced effect on personality was on the trait of neuroticism, the tendency to experience negative emotions. In studies that have examined the effects of SSRIs in nondepressed subjects, their main effect appears to be the diminution of negative affect or neuroticism (Furlan et al., 2004 Knutson, 1998). For example, Knutson and colleagues (1998) administered paroxetine or placebo for 4 weeks and assessed the effects of the drug on personality and social behavior. The drug reduced negative affect, particularly hostility, and increased affiliative behaviors. For example, subjects on the drug spoke fewer commands and instead made more suggestions to their partners in a problem-solving exercise. Among the subjects who received the drug, plasma levels correlated with changes in negative affect and social behavior.

In subjects selected for criminal behavior rather than psychiatric diagnosis or lack thereof, SSRIs have demonstrated potential for another socially relevant use: promotion of prosocial and law-abiding behavior. Impulsive violence is associated with abnormalities in seratonergic systems, and SSRIs reliably decrease aggression in individuals prone to violence (Berman, McCloskey, Fanning, Schumacher & Coccaro, 2009; Walsh & Dinan, 2001). SSRIs have been found to decrease repeat offending in sex offenders and are used for this purpose, along with hormonal treatments to decrease sex drive (Bourget & Bradford, 2008).

Love, romance, and sexuality in healthy normal people constitute another realm for brain enhancements. Drugs that affect these aspects of life through central nervous system mechanisms have not achieved the success of, for example, Viagra, but more limited successes have been reported. The drug known as "ecstasy" (MDMA) increases feelings of closeness and interpersonal connection and can be used to enhance relationships, although serious risks accompany its use (Sessa, 2007). Hormone supplementation has been used by low-testosterone men and postmenopausal women to increase libido. A number of new drugs, including the serotonin agonist flibanserin, show promise for improving sexual function in young women suffering from low libido, and are under review for this purpose with the US Food and Drug Administration (Fitzhenry & Sandberg, 2005).

In recent years, a wealth of new findings has emerged on the role of the hormones oxytocin and vasopressin in human trust, altruism, and bonding. Building on basic research with animals, correlational studies have shown that several aspects of interpersonal behavior are related to levels of these hormones or variations in genes governing their action. For example, mothers with higher levels of plasma oxytocin during pregnancy showed better bonding with their infants by several measures of their behavior and thought patterns (Feldman et al., 2007). Players of an economic game who showed more trust of other players and more trustworthiness themselves had higher levels of circulating oxytocin (Zak, Kurzban, & Matzner, 2005). Whereas quality of pair-bonding correlates with oxytocin levels in women, it correlates with vasopressin levels in men (Taylor, Saphire-Bernstein, & Seeman, 2009).

More relevant to the topic of this section, intravenous or inhaled doses of these hormones have been shown to alter the same range of behaviors.

Intranasal oxytocin improves recognition of facial expressions, consistent with a role in social cognition (Domes et al., 2007). Oxytocin has been shown to engender more trusting and generous strategies in economic games (Kosfeld et al., 2005; Zak, Stanton, & Ahmadi, 2007). Furthermore, oxytocin appears to interfere with normal responses to maltreatment. Subjects who are betrayed by a partner in a trust game normally reduce their investment on the next trial, an understandable precaution against a selfish or untrustworthy partner. However, no such reduction of investment occurred for subjects on oxytocin (Baumgartner, et al., 2008).

In addition to providing experimental tests of the hypothesis that oxytocin plays a causal role in the behaviors with which it has been correlated in observational studies, this research has obvious potential for translation into a number of applied domains. It provides a proof of concept that could be used to alter the interpersonal relationships between spouses, parents and children, and business associates. It could also be used in diplomatic, forensic, and security contexts. Not surprisingly, a quick search online will turn up numerous companies selling oxytocin, although without evidence that the formulation being offered is effective.

Ethical, Legal and Societal Issues in Manipulating the Brain

Although the technologies just reviewed are a far cry from mind control, they do offer a number of new ways to influence the feelings and behaviors of others. We should therefore consider how these technologies could be used, what kinds of uses we would consider socially acceptable, and how we might discourage unacceptable uses.

For example, the results of research on oxytocin suggest that neuroendocrine manipulation could be a profitable, if unethical, business strategy. By increasing trust, generosity, and forgiveness in one's opponents, it appears possible to influence the outcomes of financial, political, or other negotiations. This technology also has the potential to enhance interrogation in law enforcement and national security contexts. Could the benefits ever outweigh the harms in any of these cases? Drugging an unsuspecting business associate for financial advantage seems clearly wrong, but what if we could obtain socially valuable information from an unwilling informant without causing physical or psychological pain?

What about encouraging a successful resolution of difficult negotiations by enhancing feelings of bonding and brotherhood in both parties? With their informed consent? What if we chose to increase our own resistance to the natural persuasion of others by defensively blocking our own hormonal capacity for trust and altruism?

From a consequentialist point of view, sufficiently high benefits to society should tip the balance in favor of oxytocinizing interrogees or opponents in a political conflict, even without their consent. Yet most of us sense a troubling violation of personhood in these scenarios. It is not just the assault on autonomy inherent in influencing people without their knowledge, but the co-opting of our highest moral emotions for instrumental purposes. After all, part of what makes these emotions so precious, to individuals and society, is precisely that they guide us away from selfishness, from the pursuit of our own selfish ends. The prospect of someone else harnessing them for their own ends is therefore especially repugnant.

Pharmacologic treatment of criminal offenders presents us with another set of tradeoffs between benefits and risks. If SSRIs or hormone treatments can enable offenders to live outside of prison and can protect society against crime, then the "benefit" side of the equation is substantial. However, state-imposed psychopharmacology poses a relatively new kind of risk to offenders' autonomy and privacy, different in kind from the restrictions on autonomy and privacy imposed by incarceration.

Although the most obvious neuroethical issues concern the imposition of brain interventions on others, there are also issues that arise with voluntary self-enhancement. The SSRIs have been the subject of two critiques that focus on the ways in which enhancing mood and personality in oneself can harm oneself and society. The first of these is by Carl Elliott, the best-known critic of treating the angst of normal life with medications such as SSRIs. In a number of thoughtful essays he has written of the value of such angst or alienation in alerting one to the need for a more meaningful life (e.g., Elliott, 2004). Whereas Elliott focuses on the dangers of pacifying oneself rather than experiencing misgivings about the true state of one's life or one's world, Fukuyama (2002) has expressed concern over the possibility that SSRIs could inappropriately raise the self esteem of the user, undermining an important source of motivation. He asks if Caesar and Napoleon would have created their empires had they been able to raise their self esteem simply by popping a pill (Fukuyama, 2002, p. 46)! In both cases, the risks seen by these authors have consequences for the individual user and for society.

The user is deprived of an authentic view of reality. By failing to see just how problematic the world is, or just how lacking one's own accomplishments are, we will be less motivated to improve these things for the benefit of all.

Social Neuroscience: Enlightenment or Nihilism?

Some of the most profound ethical challenges from social neuroscience come not from new technologies, but from new understandings. In place of the folk psychology with which we have traditionally understood ourselves and each other, neuroscience is offering us increasingly detailed physical mechanisms. Personality, empathy, altruism, and love have all become subjects of study in neuroscience. Starting with the Enlightenment in the 18th century, the natural sciences have become the dominant way of understanding the world around us. In this century it seems likely that neuroscience will complete this process by naturalizing our understanding of ourselves.

As scientists we of course welcome this progress. Yet this progress will pose challenges. The idea that human beings are no more than physical objects, albeit very complex objects containing powerful computational networks, seems to threaten our most fundamental beliefs about the value of human life and the possibility of human agency. The final type of neuroethical issue to be reviewed in this chapter is the challenge of assimilating neuroscience's increasingly complete physical explanation of human behavior without lapsing into nihilism.

At the root of the neuroethical challenges discussed in this final section is the erosion, by neuroscience, of a fundamental distinction that underlies many of our moral intuitions: the distinction between persons and objects. Advances in basic science are revealing the necessary and sufficient neural processing that underlies our mental life, the aspect of persons that most definitively distinguishes them from objects. Advances in applied science, including the manipulation of mental states and traits, reinforce the view that we are physical objects. As we increasingly manipulate our own and each others' brain functions in order to change abilities, moods and personality traits, we will be living with increasingly frequent reminders of the physical nature of the human person.

Moral Responsibility

The person-object distinction is more than just a metaphysical abstraction; it is central to our intuitions about morality. We view persons as having agency and therefore generally hold them responsible for their actions. Although many people believe that, in principle, human behavior is the physical result of a causally determined chain of biophysical events, we tend to put that aside when making moral judgments. We do not say, "But he had no choice—the laws of physics made him do it!" However, as the neuroscience of decision making and impulse control begins to offer a more detailed and specific account of the physical processes leading to irresponsible or criminal behavior, the amoral deterministic viewpoint will probably gain a stronger hold on our intuitions. Criminal law is largely consistent with our intuitions about human behavior, and as such Greene and Cohen (2004) have argued that progress in neuroscience will eventually force changes to the law. They suggest that the difficulty of assigning moral blame may supplant retributive punishment by incentive-based punishments and therapies.

There is already ample evidence for the idea that physical, neuroscience explanations of negative behavior can change attitudes towards them. Most readers of this chapter will be too young to remember first-hand the stigma carried by mental illness before widespread use of psychiatric drugs. In the course of marketing drugs for mental illnesses, the pharmaceutical industry introduced the public to the idea that these conditions have a neurochemical basis. Organizations such as the National Alliance on Mental Illness (NAMI) have fought against stigma in large part based on the biological bases of these illnesses. As a result, depressed individuals are less likely to face blame for being lazy or unwilling to pull themselves out of it, and children with ADHD are less likely to be viewed as bad boys and girls who refuse to behave. The role of neuroscience in shifting discourse from blame to the need for therapy is nowhere more apparent than in society's view of addiction. In 1997, while he was director of the National Institute of Drug Abuse, Alan Leshner wrote an article entitled "Addiction Is a Brain Disease–and It Matters." In it, he cited neuroscience to argue against the view that "drug addicts are weak or bad people, unwilling to lead moral lives and to control their behavior and gratifications." Of course, the public has yet to fully absolve addicts from responsibility for their behavior, but the disease model of addiction has nevertheless been influential in reducing the amount of blame born by addicts.

Human Rights

In addition to viewing persons as having agency and hence responsibility, we also view them as having special moral status and hence certain rights. Whereas we value objects for what they can do—a car because it transports us, a book because it contains information, a painting because it looks beautiful—the value of persons transcends their abilities, knowledge, or attractiveness. Persons have what Kant called "dignity," meaning a special kind of intrinsic value that trumps the value of any use to which they could be put (Kant, 1996). One way of expressing this is to say that persons have rights just because they are persons. However, the categorical distinction between persons and objects is difficult to maintain on the view that human beings are no more than physical objects. In that case, why should it matter what becomes of any of us? Why should the fate of objects containing human brains matter more than the fate of other natural or manmade objects?

Religion and Spirituality

One way in which people have traditionally justified the special status of human beings, apart from other objects in the natural world, is in terms of the spiritual. Most religions include the belief that a human person is part physical and part nonphysical, the latter part referred to as a soul or spirit. This accords well with our intuition that each of us has some essence above and beyond the hundred or two pounds of matter that we can see and touch. However, if we extrapolate the ongoing progress of neuroscience towards explaining all aspects of our mental lives in terms of physical processes, there is no logical reason to believe in any immaterial aspect of human beings. Neuroscience may therefore contribute to a shift in religious belief away from dualist conceptions of the human person (Farah & Murphy, 2009).

Self and Personal Identity

Finally, our intuitive understanding of persons includes the idea that they have a unique essence that persists over time. The changes wrought by normal development and life experience are understood as elaborations on a foundational personal identity that is constant throughout life. Yet this belief does not fit with the idea that a person is just his or her brain. As physical objects, brains can and do change in countless ways in response to injury, disease, and drugs and, less commonly but no less realistically, implants, grafts, and other surgical interventions. There is no principled limit to the ways in which a brain can physically change, and thus no immutable core to the neural substrates of a person. How can this fact be squared with the notion of an enduring personal identity or essence?

In sum, neuroscience is calling into question our age-old understanding of the human person. Our traditional ways of thinking about responsibility and blame, human rights, spirituality, and personal identity will all undergo change in the process of accommodating neuroscience's view of humanity. Whether the result is nihilism or enlightenment remains to be seen. Folk psychology and dualism do not necessarily make the world more humane. The disease model of drug addiction has not so far given addicts a free pass for their destructive behavior but rather has increased society's commitment to providing therapy to addicts. Nancy Murphy (2010) has suggested that Christianity's focus on saving souls may have detracted from its incentive to improve life for those suffering in the physical world of here-and-now. There is thus reason to hope that the insights of neuroscience we will help make us more, not less, able to understand, appreciate, and care for one another.

References

Aron, A. (2007). "Politics and the Brain." November 14, 2007. *New York Times*.

Baumgartner, T. (2008). Oxytocin shapes the neural circuitry of trust and trust adaptation in humans. *Neuron, 58*(4), 639–650.

Bles, M. & *Haynes*, J. D. (2008). Detecting concealed information using brain-imaging technology. *Neurocase, 14*(1), 82–92.

Burkitt, L. (2009). "Neuromarketing: Companies Use Neuroscience for consumer Insights." *Forbes*.

Cacioppo, J. T. & *Tassinary*, L. G. (1990). Inferring psychological significance from physiological signals. *American Psychology, 45*(1), 16–28.

Coccaro, E.F., et al. (2007). Amygdala and orbitofrontal reactivity to social threat in individuals with impulsive aggression. *Biological Psychiatry, 62*(2), 168–178. Epub 2007 Jan 8.

Christ, S. E., et al. (2009). The contributions of prefrontal cortex and executive control to deception: evidence from activation likelihood estimate meta-analyses. *Cereb Cortex, 19*(7), 1557–1566. Epub 2008 Nov 2.

Committee on Science and Law. National Bar Association. (2005). Are your thoughts your own? Neuroprivacy and the legal implications of brain imaging. New York.

Davatzikos, C., et al. (2005). Classifying spatial patterns of brain activity with machine learning methods: Application to lie detection. *Neuroimage, 28*(3), 663–668. Epub 2005 Oct 5.

Domes, G., et al. (2007). Oxytocin improves "mind-reading" in humans. *Biological Psychiatry, 61*(6), 731–733.

Dumit, J. (2004). *Picturing personhood: Brain scans and biomedical identity*. Princeton, NJ: Princeton University Press.

Farah, M. J., et al. (2004). Neurocognitive enhancement: What can we do and what should we do? *Nat Rev Neurosci, 5*(5), 421–425.

Farah, M. (2007). "This is Your Brain on Politics?" *Neuroethics and Law Blog*. A. Kolber. 2009.

Farah, M. J. & Murphy, N. (2009). Neuroscience and the soul. *Science, 323*(5918), 1168.

Fitzhenry, D. & Sandberg, L. (2005). Female sexual dysfunction. *Nature Reviews Drug Discovery, 4*(2), 99–100.

Feldman, R., Weller, A., Zagoory-Sharon, O., & Levine, A. (2007). Evidence for a neuroendocrinological foundation of human affiliation: Plasma oxytocin levels across pregnancy and the postpartum period predict mother-infant bonding. *Psychol Sci,18*(11), 965–970.

Furlan, P.M., et al (2004). SSRIs do not cause affective blunting in healthy elderly volunteers. *Am J Geriatr Psychiatry, 12*(3), 323–330.

Greely, H., Sahakian, B., Harris, J., Kessler, R. C., Gazzaniga, M., Campbell, P., et al. (2008). Towards responsible use of cognitive-enhancing drugs by the healthy. *Nature, 456*(7223), 702–705.

Greene, J., & *Cohen*, J. For the law, neuroscience changes nothing and everything. *Philos Trans R Soc Lond B Biol Sci, 359*(1451), 1775–1785.

Haynes, J. D. & Reese, G. (2006). Decoding mental states from brain activity in humans. *Nature Reviews Neuroscience, 7*(7), 523–534.

Healy, D. (2004). *Let them eat Prozac*. New York University Press: New York.

Hyman, S. E. (2004). Introduction: The brain's special status. *U, 6*(4), 9–12.

Iacobani, M. (2007). "This is you brain on politics." *New York Times*. New York, November 11, 2007.

Iacoboni, M. (2008). Iacoboni responds to neuropolitics criticism. *Neuroethics and Law Blog*. A. Kolber.

Kandel, E. R., Schwartz, J.H., & Jessell, T. M. (2000). *Principles of neural science, 4th ed*. New York: McGraw-Hill.

Kant, I. (1996). *Critique of pure reason*. Indianapolis: Hackett Publishing Company.

Kosfeld, M., Heinrichs, M., et al. (2005). Oxytocin increases trust in humans. *Nature, 435*(7042), 673–676.

Knutson, B., et al. (2007). Neural predictors of purchases. *Neuron, 53*(1),147–156.

Knutson, B., Momenan, R., Rawlings, R. R., Fong, G. W., & Hommer, D. (2001). Negative association of neuroticism with brain volume ratio in healthy humans. *Biological Psychiatry, 50*, 685–690.

Kramer, P. D. (1993). *Listening to Prozac*. New York: Penguin Books.

Langleben, D. D., et al. (2002). Brain activity during simulated deception: An event-related functional magnetic resonance study. Neuroimage, *15*(3), 727–732.

Lindström, M. (2008). *Buy ology: Truth and lies about why we buy*. New York: Doubleday.

Marshall, I., et al (2004). Repeatability of motor and working-memory tasks in healthy older volunteers: Assessment at functional MR imaging. *Radiology, 233*(3), 868–877. Epub 20Oct 04, 21.

McCabe, D. P. & Castel., A. D. (2008). Seeing is believing: The effect of brain images on judgments of scientific reasoning. *Cognition, 107*, 343–352.

Olfson, M. & Marcus, S. (2009). National patterns in antidepressant medication treatment. *Arch Gen Psychiatry, 66*(8), 848–856.

Phelps, E. A., et al. (2000). Performance on indirect measures of race evaluation predicts amygdala activation. *Journal Cognitive Neuroscience, 12*(5), 729–738.

Poldrack, R. (2008a). Poldrack replies to Iacoboni neuropolitics discussion. *Neuroethics and Law Blog*. A. Kolber. 2010.

Poldrack, R. A. (2008b). The role of fMRI in cognitive neuroscience: Where do we stand? *Current Opinion Neurobiology*, *18*(2), 223–227. Epub 2008 Aug 7.

Posner, M. I. & Raichle, M. E. (1994). *Images of mind*. Scientific American Books.

Posner, M. I. & Petersen, S. E. (1990). The attention system of the human brain. *Annual Review Neuroscience*, *13*, 25–42.

Rilling, J. A. Neural basis for social cooperation. *Neuron*, *35*(2), 395–405.

Racine, E., Bar-Ilan, O., & Illes, J. FMRI in the public eye. *Nature Reviews Neuroscience*, *6*(2), 159–164.

Roskies, A. (2006). Neuroscientific challenges to free will and responsibility. Trends in Cognitive Science, *10*(9), 419–423. Epub 2006 Aug 8.

Sessa, B. (2007). Is there a case for MDMA-assisted psychotherapy in the UK? *Journal of Psychopharmacology*, 2007 Mar;21(2), 220–224.

Tang, T. Z., et al. (2009). Personality change during depression treatment: A placebo-controlled trial. *Arch Gen Psychiatry*, *66*(12), 1322–1330.

Taylor, S. E., Saphire-Bernstein, S., & Seeman, T. E. (2010). Are plasma oxytocin in women and plasma vasopressin in men biomarkers of distressed pair-bond relationships? *Psychological Science*, *21*, 3–7.

Vul, E., et al (2009). Puzzlingly high correlations in fMRI studies of emotion, personality, and social cognition. *Perspectives on Psychological Science*, *4*(3), 274–290 DOI: 10.1111/j.1745–6924.2009.01125.x.

Zak, P. J., Kurzban, R., & Matzner, W. T. (2005). Oxytocin is associated with human trustworthiness. *Horm Behav*, *48*(5), 522–527. Epub 20Aug 05, 18.

Zak, P. J., Stanton, A. A. et al. (2007). Oxytocin increases generosity in humans. *PLoS One*, *2*(11): e1128.

PART 9

Conclusions

Epilogue

John T. Cacioppo *and* Jean Decety

Abstract

This chapter discusses the various aspects of social neuroscience as covered in this Handbook. Social neuroscience spans diverse species, disciplines, methods, and topics. Social species create organizations beyond the individual. These superorganismal structures evolved hand in hand with psychological, neural, hormonal, cellular, and genetic mechanisms to support them because the consequent social behaviors helped these organisms survive, reproduce, and care for offspring sufficiently long that they too reproduced. Social neuroscience seeks to specify the neural, hormonal, cellular, and genetic mechanisms underlying social behavior, and in so doing to understand the associations and influences between social and biological levels of organization. Social neuroscience, therefore, is a complex interdisciplinary perspective that demands theoretical, methodological, statistical, and inferential rigor to effectively integrate basic, clinical, and applied perspectives on the nervous system and brain.

Keywords: social neuroscience, brain, behavior, social processes, nervous system

Neuroscience refers to the collection of sciences that deal with the structure and function of the nervous system and brain. Neuroscience is a deeply interdisciplinary pursuit because the structure and function of the nervous system and brain are such complex topics of study and require so many disparate basic, clinical, and applied disciplines to cover the terrain.

Cross-cutting these diverse disciplinary perspectives are a set of foundational perspectives. In behavioral neuroscience, for instance, the nervous system and brain are viewed as instruments of sensation and response. Behavioral neuroscience therefore tends to emphasize topics such as reward, punishment, learning, sensation, hunger, thirst, pain, predation, thermoregulation, and reproduction—and on the neural mechanisms underlying these

functions. Cognitive neuroscience emerged as a distinct perspective in which the brain is viewed as a solitary computer, with a focus on representations and processes such as attention, memory systems, heuristics, reasoning, decision making, and executive functioning—and on the mechanisms in the human brain that underlie these representations and processes. This *Handbook of Social Neuroscience* represents the maturation of a third broad perspective, one in which the emphasis is on the functions that emerge through the coaction and interaction of conspecifics, the neural mechanisms underlying these functions, and the commonality and differences across social species in these structures, processes, and functions. If cognitive neuroscience views the brain and nervous system as a solitary computer, social neuroscience views these structures as wide-band connected, mobile information processing devices in a highly interconnected network.

As clearly illustrated in the *Handbook*, social neuroscience spans diverse species, disciplines, methods, and topics. Social species create organizations beyond the individual. These superorganismal structures evolved hand in hand with psychological, neural, hormonal, cellular, and genetic mechanisms to support them because the consequent social behaviors helped these organisms survive, reproduce, and care for offspring sufficiently long that they too reproduced. Social neuroscience seeks to specify the neural, hormonal, cellular, and genetic mechanisms underlying social behavior, and in so doing to understand the associations and influences between social and biological levels of organization. Social neuroscience, therefore, is a complex interdisciplinary perspective that demands theoretical, methodological, statistical, and inferential rigor to effectively integrate basic, clinical, and applied perspectives on the nervous system and brain.

Social neuroscience is not a hegemony so much as a confederation of scientists, clinicians, and practitioners who have shared a perspective, interests, and foundational questions but who have differed in species, technical and analytical methods, levels of analysis, and disciplinary training. The contributors to this *Handbook* illustrate the potential synergies that exist by bringing these scholarly efforts into contact. This is very important because many of the social behaviors exhibited by simple animals (such as mating, aggression, foraging, learning, and memory) are reminiscent of social behaviors in more complex animals including humans. These similarities do not mean that the underlying mechanisms are identical, but both similarities and differences in these mechanisms can contribute significantly to theory and research in social neuroscience. The same is true for the differences in the social behavior of human and nonhuman animals.

Social neuroscientists generally, but especially those who are thinking about or who have only recently entered the field may find these potential synergies to be particularly productive to pursue. The social environment affects biology and behavior, and biology and behavior affect the social environment. Recognizing these reciprocal relationships are at the heart/core of social neuroscience, and calls for increase exchanges across disciplines. Success in the field is not measured in terms of the contributions to any single parent discipline, but rather in terms of the specification of the biological mechanisms underlying social interactions and behavior—one of the major problems for the neurosciences to address in the 21st century. As these mechanisms are specified, there may well be ramifications for the parent disciplines that lead to advances there, as well.

Within its brief history, social neuroscience has received considerable attention, both within the academic world and in the media. Typically, this attention has shed a positive light on the advances, opportunities and challenges in the field, but occasionally the focus is on the obstacles, errors, or problems in the field. Although some of this is inevitable, our motivation for doing this *Handbook* is to take stock of where we are as a collective field, highlight best practices and discuss standards that are needed for the field, identify some of the major questions and challenges that lie ahead, and provide materials for use in science education of young students and the public as well as for the training of the next generation of social neuroscientists.

What might some of these interesting questions be? Each contributor to this *Handbook*, and each person in the field, has their own answer to this question, and we do not mean to speak for them. We nevertheless leave students in the field, or those who are thinking about entering the field, with a few to ponder. Does social behavior differ from individual behavior at the mechanistic level? Are there neural organizations and functions that are common across all species? What differences in neural, hormonal, or genetic organization account for cross-species differences? What might analyses of social species across evolutionary timescales contribute to our understanding of the structure and function of the brain and nervous system of social species within their lifetime today? Why are elements of social behavior conserved across species? Do social behaviors have distinct signatures in the brain or the genome? How has culture shaped the brains and genes of human and nonhuman species? What are the reciprocal influences in the evolution of genes and human culture, and are similar influences found in nonhuman animals for which something like culture has been identified? Are social neural processes distinct than nonsocial processes— and in cases in which the answer is no, has one (e.g., the nonsocial process of intra-categorical discrimination? been derived from the other (e.g., the social process of facial perception and recognition)? The medial prefrontal cortex is systematically associated with social understanding in humans, but what computations are subserved, and how are those computations interfaced with those produced in other regions that are part of a functional neural circuit? If the dissection of two social processes reveals the same neural region to be operating in two different neural circuits, do the sum of the parts differ because the computations performed by the elements differ, the individual computations of the elements in these circuits simply sum to a different total, or the computations of the elements include properties that make the total more than the sum of the parts? What are the neural structures and processes that make it possible for us to know that when readers peruse the preceding sentence, they may think they understand what we intended to convey but that they may not understand what we actually meant to convey until they understand some of the material covered in the *Handbook*, while also appreciating that what some readers think we meant to say could be more interesting and fruitful than what we actually meant to convey? As you can perhaps tell, we believe that the questions in social neuroscience are complex but are also among the most interesting scientific questions to address this century.

In sum, traditional neuroscience has for many years considered the nervous system as an isolated entity and largely ignored influences of the social environments in which humans and many animal species live. We now increasingly recognize the considerable impact on brain and body function of social structures that range from dyads, families, neighborhoods and groups to cities, civilizations, and international alliances. These factors operate on the individual through a continuous interplay of neural, neuroendocrine, metabolic and immune factors on brain and body, in which the brain is the central regulatory organ and also a malleable target of these factors. Thus, social neuroscience investigates the nervous system and its manifestations at many interacting levels—from molecules to societies—and brings together multiple disciplines and methodologies to define the emergent structures that define social species, generally, and which underlie human health and behavior, in particular. It is essential to unravel this complexity as we contemplate the future welfare of life on earth.

AUTHOR INDEX

Bennett, M. R., 14
Bennett, N. C., 569
Bennett, S. M., 181, 217
Bennett, T. L., 804
Ben-Sasson, A., 869
Ben-Shakhar, G., 962, 963, 967
Bensmaia, S. J., 673
Benson, D. F., 216, 362, 601, 604, 936
Bentall, R. P., 34
Bentin, S., 380, 385, 394, 395, 446, 452
Bentivegna, D. C., 977
Bentler, P. M., 618
Bentley, A., 31
Benton, A., 460, 936
Benton, D., 720
Benuzzi, F., 413
Beran, M. J., 44
Berard, J., 684
Berardi, N., 617
Berberich, S. L., 144
Bercovitch, F. B., 720
Berenbaum, H., 911, 928
Berg, E. A., 460
Berger, B. D., 60, 462, 938
Berger, B. G., 462, 467, 468, 469, 470
Berger, C. R., 156, 491
Berger, G. R., 690
Berger, H., 406
Berger, M. L., 569
Bergland, R. M., 689
Bergman, H., 180
Bergman, T. J., 34
Berke, R. L., 196
Berkman, L. F., 779, 796, 804, 806
Berkowitz, L., 594, 896
Berlin, H. A., 247, 248, 457
Berlin, M., 986
Berman, A. J., 617
Berman, C. M., 687
Berman, S., 589
Bermond, B., 907, 908, 909, 910, 914, 927, 928, 929
Bermudez, P., 181
Bernal, B., 462
Bernard, F. A., 871
Berne, S. A., 338
Bernheim, B. D., 950
Bernier, A., 618
Bernier, R., 537, 560, 868
Bernieri, F. J., 979, 984
Berns, G. S., 73, 183, 184, 215, 366, 574, 708
Bernstein, I. S., 687, 719
Bernstein, S., 719
Bernston, G. G., 49, 51, 65
Berntsen, D., 328
Berntson, G. G., 4, 5, 6, 14, 71, 164, 165, 166, 168, 169, 170, 171, 172, 173, 174, 197, 214, 219, 278, 406, 514, 555, 745, 768, 771, 787, 807
Berridge, K. C., 157, 164, 165, 169, 170, 171, 189, 195, 197, 199, 201, 204, 206, 222, 338, 574

Berry, J. D., 50, 768
Berry, J. W., 481
Berscheid, E., 614
Bersick, M., 406
Bert, J., 528
Berthier, M., 588
Berthoz, S., 330, 349, 354, 481, 482, 694, 836, 865, 888, 906, 913, 914, 915, 921, 925, 928
Berti, A., 337, 338
Berti, S., 970
Berton, O., 718, 719, 720, 722
Bertoncini, J., 630
Bertone, A., 853
Bertrand, O., 112, 119
Besedovsky, H. O., 823
Bessette-Symons, B., 513
Bessling, S., 861
Best, C., 652
Bester-Meredith, J. K., 154
Bettencourt, B. A., 405, 408
Bettinger, K. E., 1004
Bettman, J. R., 206
Bever, J., 31
Beyerstein, B. L., 723
Bezerra, C. A. D., 976
Bhanji, J., 603
Bhatia, J., 144, 145
Bhatnagar, S., 719
Bhatt, M., 182, 255, 949, 951, 952, 954, 956, 957
Bialystok, E., 651, 659
Bianchi, L., 363
Bianchini, K. J., 461
Bibby, H., 462, 464, 466, 467, 468, 938
Bickerton, W.-L., 464
Biddle, K. R., 937
Bidzinski, A., 704
Biederman, J., 852
Bielak, A. A. M., 461
Bielsky, I. F., 158
Bienvenu, O. J., 244
Bierhaus, A., 823
Bignolas, G., 142
Bindra, D., 336
Binkofski, F., 545
Binsted, G., 338
Bioulac, B., 690
Bioulac, S., 1008
Birbaumer, N., 712, 897, 899, 901, 927
Bird, A., 769
Bird, C. M., 869, 938
Bird, G., 481, 530, 532, 537, 867, 868, 873, 877, 929, 979, 998
Birdsong, D., 651
Birmaher, B., 237
Birmingham, W., 807
Birn, R. M., 78
Bisarya, D., 840
Biscaldi, M., 230
Bishop, D. V. M., 841, 851, 852
Bishop, J. D., 478, 481, 488

Bishop, S. J., 235, 236, 280, 281, 285, 286, 608
Bittner, A. C., Jr., 1005
Bjork, J. M., 183, 187, 303
Bjork, R. A., 733
Black, P. H., 819
Black, S. E., 464
Blackburn, T. M., 28
Blackhart, G. C., 792
Blackman, M. C., 245
Blackwell, E., 798
Blackwell, K. C., 396
Blagov, P. S., 221
Blair, I. V., 436, 449, 450, 452
Blair, J., 553
Blair, K. S., 188, 553, 706, 707, 896, 898, 900, 901
Blair, R. J., 60, 215, 218, 349, 552, 559, 694, 706, 707, 779, 831, 853, 886, 888, 896, 897, 898, 899, 900, 901, 928, 938
Blairy, S., 555, 702
Blake, P. R., 569
Blake, R., 256, 338
Blakemore, S.-J., 13, 14, 317, 321, 429, 481, 530, 532, 536, 600, 869, 939, 978, 979, 992, 993, 997, 998
Blanc, G., 707
Blanchard, D. C., 702, 704, 717, 719, 722, 723, 899
Blanchard, R. J., 702, 704, 717, 720, 722, 723, 899
Blanchard-Fields, F., 516
Blandino, P., Jr., 719
Blank, C. C., 382
Blanke, O., 326, 327
Blanken, G., 336
Blanton, R. E., 299
Blascovich, J., 414, 787, 793
Blazer, D. G., 804, 806
Blehar, M. C., 151, 617
Bles, M., 1018
Blizinsky, K. D., 748, 750, 756, 758
Block, N., 342, 493
Blonigen, D. M., 899
Blood, A. J., 181, 187, 248
Bloom, K., 657
Bloom, L., 629
Bloomsmith, M. A., 572
Blume, S., 683
Blumenschine, R. J., 28
Blumenthal, J. A., 134
Blumer, D., 362, 601, 604
Blumstein, D. T., 573
Blumstein, S. E., 672
Boas, D. A., 662
Boccia, M. L., 570, 614
Bodamer, J., 380
Bode, S., 964
Bodenhausen, G. V., 43, 407, 446, 447, 449, 730, 733, 737
Bodin, S. D., 896
Bodis-Wollner, I., 335

Bruss, J., 53, 57
Bryan, R., 422
Brydon, L., 769, 795, 817, 818, 819, 820, 822
Bryon, S., 337
Bryson, S. E., 228, 230, 231, 849, 850, 852
Buccino, G., 530, 546, 548
Buchanan, T. W., 64, 171
Buchel, C., 73, 188, 349
Bucher, S. F., 335
Bucherelli, C., 897
Buchsbaum, M. S., 861
Buchwald, J. S., 169
Buck, J. R., 108
Buck, R., 268
Buckholtz, J. W., 349, 356
Buckley, K. E., 1002
Buckley, K. M., 122, 126
Buckley, M. J., 691, 706, 712
Buckner, R. L., 77, 78, 422, 430, 508, 514, 609, 610, 838, 876
Bucy, P. C., 213
Buday, R., 1001
Budhani, S., 779, 897, 898
Budygin, E. A., 721
Bueti, D., 553
Bufalari, I., 533, 553, 554
Buhl, E. H., 271
Buhle, J., 228, 233
Bulik, C. M., 461
Buller, R. E., 821
Bullmore, E. T., 113, 836, 837, 838, 842, 863, 871
Bullock, P. R., 938
Bülthoff, H. H., 337
Bunge, M., 14
Bunge, S. A., 215, 216, 283, 302, 370, 610, 618, 733, 922
Buracas, G. T., 80
Burack, J. A., 231, 234, 840, 853, 872
Burbaud, P., 690
Burger, O., 31
Burgess, G. C., 1005
Burgess, N., 898
Burgess, P. W., 363, 364, 459, 460, 461, 462, 536, 955
Burghart, D. R., 480, 576
Buring, J. E., 815
Burk, T., 702
Burkart, J. M., 570
Burke, J. D., 895
Burkitt, L., 1017
Burkland, L. J., 606
Burklund, L. J., 590
Burleson, M. H., 768
Burley, R., 854
Burmeister, M. L., 748
Burnett, S., 481, 997, 998
Burnham, D., 662
Burns, V. E., 134, 138, 139
Burnstein, E., 491
Burrows, A. M., 41, 46

Burrows, C. L., 508
Burrows, L., 340, 495
Burt, D. M., 395
Burton, A., 395, 872
Burton, M. J., 213, 399
Busch, R. M., 459
Busemeyer, J., 511
Busey, T. A., 273
Bush, E. C., 32
Bush, G., 215, 219, 366
Bushman, B. J., 1001, 1002, 1003, 1004, 1006, 1007
Bushnell, M. C., 588
Bushnell, M. D., 588
Bushong, S. C., 294
Busnel, R. G., 670
Buss, D. M., 702
Bussing, R., 889
Butcher, P. R., 229, 230
Butler, E., 860
Butler, E. A., 751
Butter, C., 183, 693
Buttet, J., 381
Buwalda, B., 718
Buxton, R. B., 80, 94
Byatt, G., 439
Bydlowski, S., 913
Byrd, L. D., 723
Byrne, R. B., 34
Byrne, R. W., 29, 33, 39, 46, 397, 544

C

Caan, W., 399, 689
Cabanac, M., 198
Cabeza, C., 513
Cabeza, R., 64, 171, 268, 328, 508, 512, 513, 514
Cabib, S., 704, 721
Cacace, A. T., 644
Cacioppo, J. T., 3, 4, 5, 6, 7, 12, 13, 14, 17, 20, 49, 50, 51, 65, 71, 134, 141, 152, 164, 165, 168, 169, 170, 171, 173, 174, 196, 205, 214, 219, 278, 331, 341, 348, 405, 406, 407, 409, 413, 414, 452, 514, 552, 555, 607, 614, 615, 618, 745, 758, 765, 766, 767, 768, 769, 771, 772, 776, 777, 779, 782, 787, 795, 805, 806, 807, 808, 809, 810, 818, 1007, 1008, 1017
Cador, M., 183
Cadoret, G., 733
Cady, J. C., 656
Caetano, G., 530
Caggiano, V., 543, 692
Cahill, L., 64, 246, 271
Cahn-Weiner, D. A., 461
Caine, S. B., 366
Cairns, H., 364, 691
Calder, A. J., 213, 253, 257, 399, 413, 435, 456, 501, 533, 555
Calderc, A., 938
Caldwell, D. K., 567
Caldwell, M. C., 567

Calhoun, V. D., 92
Call, J., 34, 44
Callejas, A., 228
Calmels, C., 530
Calvo-Merino, B., 531
Calzavara, R., 180
Cambrosio, A., 17
Camen, C., 385
Camerer, C. F., 73, 180, 182, 255, 575, 745, 949, 950, 951, 952, 953, 954, 955, 956, 957
Cameron, J. L., 717
Campadelli-Fiume, G., 143
Campanella, S., 386
Campbell, C. B. G., 46
Campbell, D. T., 414
Campbell, J. M., 862
Campbell, L., 232
Campbell, R., 695
Campbell, W. K., 603, 609
Campos, J. J., 437
Canaan, L., 822
Cancedda, L., 617
Candidi, M., 530
Candland, D. K., 720
Canessa, N., 534
Canfield, M. E., 570
Canli, T., 64, 220, 248, 745, 748, 749, 756, 969
Cannistraci, C. J., 220
Cannon, T. D., 35
Cannon, W. B., 203
Canter, G. J., 381
Cantlon, J. F., 534
Cantor, N., 492
Capell, H. A., 815
Capitanio, J. P., 632, 690, 719, 798
Caplan, D., 671
Capponi, I., 630
Capuron, L., 819, 820, 823
Caramazza, A., 18, 340, 423, 495, 530, 692, 743
Card, G., 419
Carden, S. E., 51, 587
Cardillo, S., 158
Cardinal, R. N., 214, 216, 898
Carelli, R. M., 366
Carey, S., 303, 447, 462
Carletta, J., 867
Carlson, J. M., 232
Carlson, L. E., 819
Carlson, S. M., 228, 236, 464, 942
Carmant, L., 336
Carmean, V., 864, 865
Carmichael, D. W., 98
Carmichael, S. T., 180, 365, 731
Carnagey, N. L., 1002, 1003, 1004, 1008
Carne, R. P., 246
Carneiro, P., 1003
Carney, D. R., 497
Carney, R. M., 144, 820
Caron, A., 229
Caron, R., 229

Ciaramelli, E., 487, 887
Ciaramidaro, A., 575
Ciarocco, N. J., 368, 371
Cicchetti, D. V., 851
Cicchetti, P., 216
Cichocki, A., 106
Cicourel, A., 659, 984
Ciechanowski, P., 594
Cimatti, Z., 100, 107
Cipolotti, L., 559
Cirulli, F., 614
Cisler, J. M., 232
Clark, A. S., 439, 498, 499, 974, 999
Clark, C. W., 670
Clark, D., 896
Clark, F., 901
Clark, R. E., 684
Clark, S., 530
Clark, T., 748
Clarke, A. S., 718, 720
Clarke, E., 9
Clarke, S., 385, 720
Clarkson, T. B., 717, 796
Classe, A., 670
Claus, E. D., 217, 218, 219
Claypool, H. M., 331
Clegg, J., 852
Clement, T. S., 702
Clementz, B. A., 106, 603
Clerc, M., 118
Clinton, S. M., 721
Clipperton, A. E., 841
Cloninger, C. R., 245
Clore, G. L., 196, 197, 204, 205, 573
Cloutier, J., 366, 405, 412
Clutton-Brock, T. H., 28, 40
Coambs, R. B., 587, 723
Coan, J. A., 614, 615, 616, 617, 618,
    619, 768, 807
Coats, S., 331
Coccaro, E. F., 1016, 1018, 1020
Cochin, S., 528, 530, 554
Coe, C. L., 720
Cofer, C. N., 164
Coffey-Corina, S., 662
Cohen, A., 771
Cohen, D., 101, 119, 593, 743, 745, 746,
    859, 863, 872
Cohen, H. J., 820, 823
Cohen, J. D., 35, 58, 61, 182, 188,
    215, 219, 221, 246, 284, 327,
    340, 349, 360, 364, 368, 394,
    400, 406, 409, 430, 459, 480,
    485, 487, 575, 577, 600, 607,
    691, 709, 710, 732, 733, 737,
    780, 805, 806, 807, 809, 900,
    922, 925, 1022
Cohen, J. N., 759
Cohen, L., 743, 749
Cohen, N., 806
Cohen, R. A., 364
Cohen, R. M., 830, 831, 832, 835, 836,
    838, 840, 841

Cohen, S., 134, 138, 139, 349, 619, 717,
    777, 778, 779, 782, 796, 804, 805,
    807, 808, 809, 820, 823
Cohrs, R. J., 143
Coke, J., 567, 571
Cole, J., 691
Cole, M. W., 964
Cole, S. W., 769, 770, 796, 798,
    799, 1008
Coles, C. D., 1008
Coles, M. G. H., 219, 405, 406, 407, 691
Collado-Hidalgo, A., 815
Colle, L., 863
Colledge, E., 897
Collet, L., 630
Collins, A. M., 492
Collins, D. L., 296, 452
Collins, M. A., 435
Collins, R. L., 371
Colmenares, F., 572
Colombo, J., 229
Coltheart, M., 6, 71
Colvert, E., 234
Comair, Y. G., 337
Comblain, C., 508
Company, T., 180
Conboy, B. T., 651, 652, 658, 659
Conel, J. L., 305
Conger, K., 221
Conner, A. L., 747
Connolly, C. I., 218
Connor, D. F., 897, 898
Connors, C. M., 328
Consoli, S. M., 913
Constable, R. T., 76, 82, 248
Constantine, L. J., 228, 869
Constantino, J. N., 841, 860
Constantino, P., 319
Conty, L., 111
Convit, A., 865
Conway, M. A., 327
Cook, M. J., 246
Cooke, D. J., 896
Cooney, N. L., 370
Cooney, R. E., 285
Cooper, F. S., 534, 660, 670
Cooper, G., 253, 493, 533
Cooper, J. C., 181, 182
Cooper, S. J., 577
Coovert, M. D., 407
Coppack, S. W., 822
Coppersmith, G. A., 703
Corato, E., 533
Corballis, M. C., 625
Corbett, B. A., 228, 234, 864, 865,
    869, 871
Corbett, D., 179
Corbetta, M., 77, 98, 840
Corcoran, M. E., 366
Corcos, M., 928
Corden, B., 413, 863
Cordoni, G., 572
Cords, M., 574

Corfield, D. R., 335
Coricelli, G., 183, 950, 953, 956
Corkin, S., 364, 684
Corley, M., 867
Corlija, J., 419
Corneille, O., 912, 925
Cornell, D. G., 897, 900
Cornwall, A., 593
Corp, N., 33
Corr, P. J., 173
Correa, M., 157
Correll, J., 451, 452, 553, 557
Corter, C., 999
Cosgrove, K. P., 246
Cosmides, L., 16, 171, 198, 328, 349,
    350, 351, 354, 357, 743, 744
Costa, A., 340
Costa, P. T., Jr., 243, 244, 245, 246
Costa-Gomes, M., 951
Costantini, M., 327
Costanzo, E. S., 806, 817, 821
Couch, R. B., 138
Coulon, M., 440
Coupland, J., 341
Coupland, N., 341, 676
Courchesne, E., 231, 235, 830, 836, 837,
    838, 840, 850, 863, 871, 876, 877
Coureaud, G., 338
Courtine, G., 987
Coussons-Read, M. E., 822
Cover, T. M., 86
Covington, H. E. III, 717, 719, 722
Cowan, G. A., 14
Cowan, M. J., 819
Cowan, R., 805
Cowan, W. B., 734
Cowey, A., 399, 695
Cox, C. R., 511
Cox, K. M., 511
Crabbe, F., 390, 391
Craig, A. D., 201, 202, 259, 260, 327,
    493, 495, 497, 553, 554, 558, 914,
    957, 966
Craig, J. C., 669, 673
Craighero, L., 259, 321, 493, 495, 528,
    530, 543, 548, 553, 554, 660, 669,
    692, 983
Craik, F. I. M., 268, 328
Crane, L., 869, 873
Craske, M. G., 281
Crawford, J. R., 459, 464, 465, 466
Crawford, L. E., 495, 496, 768
Crawford, S., 938
Crawford, V. P., 951
Crawley, J. N., 842
Creel, S., 718
Creem, S. H., 337
Crelin, E. S., 644
Crepin, G., 630
Creswell, J. D., 779
Crick, F. C., 207, 966
Crick, N. R., 896, 897
Crilly, A., 815

de Lange, F. P., 535, 536
de la Riva, C., 704, 720
Delery, D. B., 631
Delgado, M., 608
Delgado, M. R., 178, 180, 181, 182, 183, 184, 185, 186, 187, 188, 189, 217, 285, 286, 366, 423, 424, 425, 480
Del Giudice, M., 531, 532
Delis, D. C., 460, 461
Della Sala, S., 337, 514
Delong, M. R., 364
Delorme, A., 110
DelParigi, A., 367
Delpuech, C., 112
Delvaux, V., 634
Demakis, G. J., 461
Demany, L., 631
Demaret, C., 912
Demaria, C., 41
De Martino, B., 608, 873
de MaziÈres, J., 573
Deminiere, J. M., 720
Demler, O., 369
Demolin, D., 634
Demoment, G., 123
de Montes, G. L., 498
Demos, K. E., 260, 367, 371
Demuth, K., 628
Denburg, N. L., 50, 63, 363, 511
Denckla, M. B., 302
de Nijs, P. F. A., 851
Dennett, D. C., 202, 207, 493
Dennis, M., 939, 942
den Ouden, H. E., 993, 997
Dentino, A. N., 820
de Oliveira-Souza, R., 479, 481, 482, 483, 484, 485, 487, 577, 694, 900, 927
Deouell, L. Y., 112, 452, 517
DePaoli, M., 817
DePaulo, B. M., 969
Depres, J. P., 796
DePriest, D. D., 684
Depue, R. A., 483
de Quervain, D. J., 187, 480, 576
Derakshan, N., 236
Derbyshire, S. W., 690
De Renzi, E., 536
Derffuss, J., 341
De Rick, A., 907, 926
De Rosa, E., 281
Derrfuss, J., 458, 840
Derringer, J. L., 340
Derryberry, D., 229, 235
Deruelle, C., 864, 873
de Ruiter, A. J., 155
Descartes, R., 202
de Schonen, S., 436
DeSimone, K., 695
Desimone, R., 675, 689, 694
Desmet, M., 925
DeSoto, C. B., 491
DeSoto, M. C., 340, 342
de Sousa, A., 469

Desportes, C., 41
DeSteno, D., 58
de Timary, P., 910
Detre, J. A., 81
Deutsch, D., 631
Deutsch, G. K., 302
Deutsch, S., 689
de Vignemont, F., 552, 556, 831, 836, 837
Devine, E. C., 141
Devine, P. G., 341, 368, 492, 729, 730, 733, 736, 737, 738
Devinsky, O., 364, 456, 690
Devlin, J. T., 247
DeVries, A. C., 152, 155, 158
De Vries, G. J., 155
DeVries, M. B., 155
Devue, C., 327
de Waal, F. B. M., 17, 40, 41, 43, 60, 261, 349, 483, 552, 553, 554, 565, 567, 568, 569, 570, 571, 572, 573, 574, 576, 578, 615, 617, 687, 703, 831
DeWall, C. N., 592, 593, 594
Dewey, J., 360
DeYoung, C. G., 246
Dhabhar, F. S., 142
Dhamala, M., 708
Di, R. F., 553, 554
Diamond, A., 234
Dias, E. C., 229
Dias, R., 887
Di Chiara, G., 179, 366
Dichter, G. S., 235, 871, 873
Dickens, C., 593
Dickerson, B. C., 514
Dickerson, S. S., 595, 768, 778, 780, 787, 788, 789, 790, 791, 792, 793, 794, 795, 820
Dickinson, M. H., 419
Dickter, C. L., 405, 406, 407, 408, 409, 410, 413, 414, 448, 738
Di Cristo, A., 630, 643
Diderholm, E., 817
Diehl, R. L., 651, 672
Dienberg Love, G., 778
Dieperink, E., 819
Dietrich, C., 651
DiFrischia, D. S., 188
DiGirolamo, G. J., 229
Dijkmans, M., 676
Dijksterhuis, A., 340, 341, 495, 542
Dillo, W., 861
DiLollo, V., 207
Di Martino, A., 870, 873
Dimberg, U., 197, 257
Dimitrov, M., 458
Dimoska, A., 469
Dimsdale, J. E., 818
Dinarello, C. A., 815
Ding, J., 106
Ding, W., 142
Dinno, N., 231
Dinstein, H., 554

Dinstein, I., 529, 530, 692
Dion, K. K., 439
Diorio, J., 616, 617
DiPaolo, M., 911
di Pellegrino, G., 17, 487, 527, 543, 553, 692, 978
DiPietro, L. A., 142
DiSalvo, C., 984
Dishion, T. J., 779
Dissanayake, C., 326
Dissanayake, E., 628, 629
Ditman, T., 349
Dittrich, W. H., 261
Dittus, W. P., 569
Dixon, P., 852
Djikic, M., 317
Dobish, H., 427, 438
Dobkin, B. H., 381
Dobson, S. D., 45, 46
Dodge, K. A., 896, 897, 899
Dodsworth, R. O., 617
Doering, L. V., 819
Dogdas, B., 118
Doherty, M. J., 336
Doherty-Sneddon, G., 863
Dolan, C. V., 766
Dolan, J. D., 327
Dolan, M. C., 887, 927
Dolan, R. J., 60, 73, 181, 182, 184, 186, 188, 200, 213, 216, 257, 260, 280, 281, 282, 284, 349, 354, 366, 396, 398, 400, 412, 413, 425, 426, 439, 480, 558, 694, 873, 913, 953, 977
Dolcos, F., 512
Dolgov, V. V., 722
Domanski, M. J., 759
Domes, G., 156, 1020
Domschke, K., 842
Don, M., 630
Donald, M., 628
Donaldson, Z. R., 841
Donchin, E., 406, 407, 1008
Donderi, D. C., 593
Donders, L., 461
Donegan, N. H., 370
Donzella, B., 792
Dopp, J. M., 794
Dorris, L., 835, 838, 841
Dorval, M., 1004
Dostrovsky, J. O., 533
Douglas, J. M., 471
Doupe, A. J., 659, 663
Dove, T., 437
Dovidio, J. F., 434, 448
Dowdy, L., 896
Dowling, W. J., 631
Downes, J. J., 268, 270, 272
Downey, G., 691
Downing, P. E., 380, 553, 554
Downs, D. L., 599, 600, 607
Doya, K., 182
Doyle, T. F., 686
Doyle, W. J., 777, 779, 782, 796

Ganellen, R. J., 340
Gangestad, S. W., 438
Ganis, G., 319, 326, 968, 970
Ganz, P. A., 815
Garamszegi, L. Z., 31
Garavan, H., 214, 366, 367
Garcia, L. M., 111
García-Fiñana, M., 35
Garcia-Sierra, A., 652
Gardener, E. A., 461
Gärdenfors, P., 627, 628, 629
Gardiner, W., 626, 627, 643
Gardner, H. E., 17
Gardner, W. L., 168, 406
Garg, A., 142
Garland, J., 631, 632
Garner, M., 232
Garner, W., 769
Garnero, L., 117, 121
Garnica, O. K., 627
Garrido, G. J., 481, 484
Garrido, L., 381
Garrido, M. I., 113
Garrod, S., 671
Gartner, B. C., 144, 145
Gaser, C., 307
Gastaut, H. J., 528
Gatenby, C., 216
Gatenby, J. C., 188, 282
Gattaz, W. F., 593
Gattis, M., 530
Gatz, M., 781
Gaunt, R., 419, 420
Gaussier, P., 987
Gauthier, I., 253, 394, 411, 685
Gawronski, B., 371, 730
Gazzaley, A., 92, 517, 734
Gazzaniga, M. S., 744, 745, 746
Gazzola, V., 525, 529, 530, 531, 533,
    534, 535, 536, 547, 554, 957,
    982, 983
Gear, R. W., 592, 593
Geary, D. C., 340
Geczy, I., 447, 452
Geddes, K., 439
Geddes, L. A., 119
Geddes, L. P. T., 349
Geesink, I., 683
Gegenfurtner, K. R., 337
Gehlert, D. R., 271
Gehring, W. J., 364, 406
Gehrke, J., 342
Geiger, T., 11
Geman, D., 123
Geman, S., 123
Geminiani, S., 572
Gemperle, F., 984
Gemroth, P., 271
Gentile, D. A., 1001, 1002, 1005, 1009
Gentile, J. R., 1002
Gentilucci, M., 625
George, J. S., 119, 769
George, K., 156

George, M. S., 838
George, N., 111, 400
Georgiou, G. A., 233
Georgopoulos, A. P., 341
Gerald, M. S., 436
Gerardi-Caulton, G., 233
Gerena, D., 155
Gerfen, C. R., 219
Gergely, G., 534, 977
Gerhardt, K. J., 630
Gerig, G., 297
Gerin, W., 793
Gerken, L., 628, 640, 653
Germine, L. T., 898, 940
Gerrans, P., 462, 464, 936, 938, 942
Gerrard, S., 869
Gerritsen, W., 907
Gerstein, L., 861
Gervais, H., 382, 383, 384
Geschwind, D. H., 830, 842, 854
Geschwind, N., 671
Geselowitz, D. B., 116
Gesierich, B., 18, 530, 692
Getz, L. L., 152
Geurts, H. M., 234, 870, 871
Geuze, R. H., 229, 230
Gezeck, S., 230
Ghashghaei, H. T., 731, 782
Ghashghaei, T., 365, 577
Ghazanfar, A. A., 382, 386
Ghaziuddin, M., 853, 860, 861
Ghaziuddin, N., 860
Ghosh, D., 748
Ghuman, A. S., 396
Gianaros, P. J., 710, 712, 807, 815
Giancola, P. R., 407
Giard, M. H., 119, 446
Gibb, B. E., 748
Gibb, G. D., 1004
Gibb, J., 820
Gibbon, J., 499
Gibbs, R. A., 684
Gibbs, R. W., 493
Gibson, J. J., 43, 398, 435
Gibson, K. R., 28
Gibson, L., 854
Giedd, J. N., 233, 296, 297, 298, 299,
    995, 996, 997, 999
Giessner, S. R., 496
Gifford, J. J., 229
Gigerenzer, G., 350, 351, 354, 357
Gigliotti, F., 962
Gilbert, D. T., 419, 420, 447, 737
Gilbert, H. R., 640
Gilbert, J. B., 630
Gilbert, P., 481
Gil-da-Costa, R., 352
Gilden, D. H., 143
Giles, H., 341, 668, 676
Gilihan, S. J., 600
Giljohann, S., 329, 331
Gillath, O., 618, 620
Gillberg, C., 851, 862

Gillespie, D. C., 461
Gillihan, S. J., 331
Gillis, M. M., 189, 285
Gilliver, S. C., 142
Gillmeister, H., 980
Gilmour, J., 618
Gilovich, T., 424
Gingrich, B. S., 157
Gintis, H., 479, 482
Ginton, A., 963
Gioia, G. A., 460, 462
Gioiosa, L., 720
Giraud, A. L., 387, 388, 389
Girdler, S. S., 806
Gitelman, D. R., 229
Giuliani, N., 815
Giuliano, T., 500
Glahn, D. C., 307
Glaser, D. E., 531
Glaser, J., 340
Glaser, R., 134, 138, 139, 140, 142, 143,
    144, 782, 792, 794, 806, 821, 822
Glass, B., 446
Glass, T., 804
Glazebrook, C., 1008
Glees, P., 691
Gleitman, L. R., 668
Glenberg, A. M., 493, 500, 674
Glenn, A. L., 901
Glick, P., 412, 426, 427
Glickman, S., 237
Glimcher, P. W., 180, 182, 424, 745, 949
Glotzer, L. D., 365
Glover, G. H., 69, 79, 85, 366
Gluck, M. A., 183
Gobbini, M. I., 253, 326, 395, 399, 422,
    427, 429, 435, 436, 438
Godart, N., 928
Goddard, L., 272, 869, 872, 873
Goebel, R., 92
Goel, V., 349, 354, 430
Goff, P. A., 730
Gogate, L., 631
Gogolushko, K., 205
Gogtay, N., 302, 941
Goh, J. O., 751, 753
Golby, A. J., 411, 738
Gold, L. H., 723
Goldberg, E., 360
Goldin, P. R., 285, 286, 370, 516, 607
Golding, C., 236
Goldman, A. I., 258, 260, 321, 322, 553,
    836, 936
Goldman-Rakic, P. S., 304, 352, 687,
    693, 709, 999
Goldsher, D., 60, 462, 467, 938
Goldsmith, D. J., 266
Goldstein, A. G., 447
Goldstein, K., 10
Goldstein, M. H., 657
Goldstein, R. Z., 966, 970
Goldstein, U. G., 640
Golemis, E. A., 769

Holland, R. W., 340
Holland, S. K., 297, 302, 303
Hollenbeck, A. R., 184
Hollerman, J. R., 366, 977
Holliday, I. E., 122
Holliday, J. E., 143
Hollis, C., 852
Hollon, N. G., 511
Holloway, R. L., 534
Holman, K. C., 850
Holmes, A. P., 73, 111, 126, 452
Holmes, C. J., 296
Holroyd, C. B., 181, 219, 691
Holsboer, F., 794
Holt, C., 229
Holt, D. D., 235
Holt, L. E., 671, 674
Holt, L. L., 671, 672
Holyoak, K. J., 350
Holzberg, A. D., 599, 602, 603, 608
Homae, F., 628
Homan, R. W., 268
Hommel, B., 553
Hommer, D. W., 181, 183, 187, 217
Honda, K., 644
Honess, P. E., 717
Honey, C. J., 113
Hong, S., 818
Hong, Y., 747
Honing, H., 630
Honts, C. R., 962, 967
Hood, B. M., 229, 230, 870
Hoogenboom, N., 112
Hooker, C. I., 898, 901, 940, 941
Hope, P. L., 295
Hopkins, B., 643
Hopkins, W. D., 437
Hoppe, K. D., 910
Horgan, T. G., 676
Horhota, M., 516
Hori, K., 723
Horn, J., 841
Hornak, J., 181, 215, 217, 218, 254, 257,
    349, 439, 457, 458, 977
Horner, C., 394
Horowitz, L. M., 618
Horvitz, J. C., 499
Horwitz, B., 92, 869, 875
Horwitz, R., 776
Hosokawa, S., 587
Houk, J. C., 219
Houle, S., 268
House, J. S., 134, 779
House, T. H., 967
Houser, D., 576
Houston, A. I., 569
Howard, A., 434, 448
Howell, P., 871
Howell, S., 722
Howells, J., 869
Howerter, A., 459
Howes, S. R., 183
Howlin, P., 852, 869

Howren, M. B., 820
Hrdy, S. B., 569, 574
Hsee, C. K., 573
Hsu, A. Y., 50
Hsu, M., 182, 255, 481
Hu, P., 370, 371
Hu, S. B., 158
Hu, X., 956
Huang, B. H., 651
Huang, M. X., 118, 126
Hubbard, E. M., 560
Hubel, D. H., 398, 617, 854, 995
Huber, E., 45
Huber, L., 198, 542, 544
Huber, M., 914, 918, 921, 922, 923
Hubert, B., 840
Hubert, B. E., 864, 872, 873
Hubley, P., 658
Hudry, K., 872
Huebner, T., 889
Huesing, B., 23
Huesmann, L. R., 1006
Huettel, S. A., 182, 356, 366, 367,
    513, 576
Hug, K., 350, 351, 354, 357
Hugenberg, K., 395, 730
Hughes, B. L., 93, 278, 603, 604,
    608, 808
Hughes, B. M., 615
Hughes, C., 233, 852, 869
Hughes, J. N., 806, 901
Hughes, K. R., 386
Hughlings Jackson, J., 10
Huizenga, H. M., 121
Hume, D., 478, 481, 482
Humphrey, N. K., 40
Humphrey, N. L., 28
Humphreys, G. W., 464, 938,
    942, 979
Humphreys, K., 833
Humphreys, R. P., 939
Hunnius, S., 230, 532
Hunt, C., 232
Hunt, L. T., 33, 189
Hunter, S. B., 793
Hunyadi, E., 328
Hunzeker, J., 789
Hurford, J. R., 627
Hurley, R. S., 863
Hurley, S., 542
Hursh, J. B., 294
Husain, M., 335, 336, 938
Hutcherson, C. A., 282
Hutchison, W. D., 260, 533
Huttenlocher, P. R., 304, 994, 995
Hutto, D., 836
Hutton, C., 82
Hutton, S. B., 229
Huttunen, M., 35
Hwang, J. H., 246
Hyde, J. S., 329
Hyde, K. L., 874
Hyder, F., 97

Hyman, S. E., 1018
Hynes, C. A., 467, 552, 940

I

Iacoboni, M., 18, 221, 319, 321, 322,
    326, 327, 341, 497, 528, 529, 530,
    534, 535, 536, 542, 545, 547, 548,
    555, 669, 692, 838, 868, 876, 1017
Iacono, W. G., 899, 967
Ida Gobbini, M., 380
Ietswaart, M., 464, 465
Iezzi, T., 593
Iglesias, J., 437
Iidaka, T., 509, 515, 517
Ijames, S. G., 366
Ijspeert, A., 977
IJzerman, H., 497
Ikemoto, S., 170
Illes, J., 1018
Ilmoniemi, R., 102
Imada, T., 660, 661, 663
Imamizu, H., 977
Imbens-Bailey, A., 318
Immelmann, K., 663
Imperato, A., 366
Inagaki, T. K., 594
Inati, S., 183
Ingvar, M., 589, 590
Insel, T. R., 153, 154, 157, 201, 480, 483,
    574, 576, 577, 617, 841, 842
Insley, S. J., 379
Ionica, C., 687
Iragui, V. J., 461
Iriki, A., 259, 526, 709
Irino, T., 387
Ironson, G., 806
Irwin, M. R., 143, 594, 790, 815, 820
Irwin, W., 730
Isaac, G., 349
Isaacowitz, D. M., 508, 517, 610
Isaacs, J. E., 331
Isenberg, N., 213
Ishai, A., 413, 708
Ishida, R., 853
Ishiguro, H., 974, 975, 984, 985
Ishikawa, T., 720
Isler, K., 28, 29
Isovich, E., 721
Isquith, P. K., 460, 462
Issartel, J., 978, 988
Ito, R., 183
Ito, T. A., 278, 405, 407, 409, 410, 411,
    413, 414, 446, 447, 448, 449, 450,
    451, 452, 454, 555, 738, 1007, 1008
Itoh, K., 983
Itoh, M., 913
Itoh, Y., 975
Ivinskis, A., 229
Ivry, R., 744, 745, 746
Ivy, G., 271
Iyengar, V., 485
Iyer, V., 719
Izawa, J., 867

Kandel, E. R., 1015
Kang, L., 438
Kanner, L., 231, 837
Kano, M., 913, 914, 915, 917, 921
Kant, I., 1022
Kanwisher, N., 253, 261, 380, 394, 399,
   400, 411, 422, 430, 462, 530, 685,
   692, 695, 743, 936, 939, 993
Kaplan, C. D., 910
Kaplan, E., 460, 461
Kaplan, H., 570
Kaplan, J., 134
Kaplan, J. R., 705, 717, 718, 720, 721,
   722, 796
Kaplan, J. T., 221, 319, 320, 326,
   327, 547
Kaplan, R. F., 364
Kapogiannis, D., 357
Kappas, A., 501
Kapur, S., 268
Karafin, M. S., 702, 711
Karama, S., 366
Karasek, R. A., 779
Karbowski, J., 28
Karin, M., 823
Karlsson, H., 913, 914, 918
Karmiloff-Smith, A., 440
Karnath, H. O., 50, 56
Karnik, N. S., 896
Karp, P. J., 116
Kasai, K., 923
Kaschak, M. P., 674
Kasel, J. A., 138
Kashy, D. A., 394
Kastner, S., 71, 257, 695
Kaszniak, A. W., 206, 913
Katcher, A. H., 143
Katila, T. E., 116
Katkin, E. S., 207
Kato, J., 221
Kato, K., 690, 781
Kato, M., 187
Kato, P. M., 1008
Katsyri, J., 864
Katz, D., 469
Kaube, H., 60
Kaufman, J. A., 28
Kaufman, L., 116, 121
Kaufman, M. J., 366
Kavaliers, M., 841
Kawachi, I. B., 618, 796
Kawahara, H., 387
Kawakami, K., 434, 448
Kawakubo, Y., 232
Kawasaki, H., 213, 896
Kawashima, R., 399
Kawatani, M., 852
Kawato, M., 545, 974, 976, 977, 986
Kay, A. C., 340
Kay, G., 460
Kay, L. E., 17
Kay, R. F., 686
Kay, S. M., 112, 126

Kaye, K., 229
Kaylor-Hughes, C. J., 968, 969
Ke, X., 874
Keane, J., 213, 253, 456, 533, 938
Keating, C. F., 702
Kedia, G., 481, 482, 925
Keefe, K. A., 188
Keeley, L., 51
Keenan, J. P., 13, 315, 316, 317, 318,
   319, 320, 326, 328
Keeney, A. J., 719, 720, 722
Keightley, M. L., 517, 518
Keil, K., 461
Keillor, J. M., 555
Keiper, S., 407
Keller, E., 815
Keller, G. B., 548
Keller, L., 568
Keller, T. A., 235, 835, 836, 870,
   875, 876
Kellermann, T., 691
Kelley, A. E., 222, 278
Kelley, H. H., 419, 421
Kelley, K. W., 135, 819
Kelley, W.M., 600
Kelley, W. A., 606
Kelley, W. K., 328
Kelley, W. M., 260, 319, 329, 330, 366,
   367, 368, 602, 836
Kelly, A. M., 941
Kelly, D. J., 435, 438
Kelly, J. L., 851
Kelly, O., 791
Kelsey, R. M., 793
Kelso, E. W., 169
Keltikangas-Järvinen, L., 926
Keltner, D., 215, 218, 394
Kemeny, M. E., 595, 765, 768, 778, 779,
   780, 787, 788, 789, 790, 792, 794,
   799, 820
Kemmer, F. W., 791
Kemmerer, D., 54
Kemmotsu, N., 875
Kemner, C., 235
Kemper, T. L., 849
Kendell-Scott, L., 438
Kendler, K. S., 247, 779, 781
Kendrick, K. M., 152, 154, 157, 435,
   438, 440
Kenemans, J. L., 447, 452
Kenet, T., 851
Kennard, C., 236
Kennard, M. A., 691
Kennedy, D. P., 235, 836, 837, 838,
   876, 877
Kennedy, Q., 508
Kennedy, R. S., 1004, 1005
Kennell, J., 593
Kenny, D. A., 318, 394, 615
Kenrick, D. T., 396
Kensinger, E. A., 512, 513, 514, 515
Kent, L., 842
Kent, R. D., 636, 638, 640, 641

Kent, T. A., 896
Keogh, E., 232
Keramatian, K., 349
Keriven, R., 118
Kern, M. K., 335, 336
Kernberg, O., 926
Kerns, J. G., 248, 364, 400, 809,
   810, 896
Kesek, A., 215
Keshavan, M., 995
Kesler, S. R., 1004
Kessler, R. C., 247, 369, 759, 779, 781
Ketelaar, T., 244
Keverne, E. B., 152, 154, 156, 157, 570,
   704, 720, 796
Key, C., 627
Keysar, B., 998
Keysers, C., 18, 60, 495, 525, 526, 528,
   529, 530, 531, 533, 534, 535, 536,
   553, 555, 556, 560, 836, 957, 978,
   982, 984, 986
Khalfa, S., 869
Khamassi, M., 216
Khan, Y., 995
Khateb, A., 171
Khera, A. V., 688, 707
Kiani, R., 695
Kiebel, S. J., 113, 126, 186, 480
Kiecolt-Glaser, J. K., 134, 138, 139, 140,
   141, 142, 143, 144, 614, 619, 769,
   782, 792, 793, 794, 805, 814, 817,
   818, 821
Kiefe, C. I., 778, 782, 783, 797
Kiehl, K. A., 482, 897, 899
Kiesler, S., 984
Kihlstrom, J. F., 6, 197
Kikuchi, M., 397, 438
Kikusui, T., 615
Killcross, A. S., 732
Killebrew, J. H., 673
Killen, M., 900
Killgore, W. D., 768
Kilner, J. M., 413, 439, 529, 530, 535,
   692, 979, 980, 981
Kilts, C. D., 213, 221, 302, 710
Kim, A. J., 154
Kim, C., 794
Kim, E., 457
Kim, H. S., 215, 370, 758
Kim, I. J., 71
Kim, K. H., 778, 794, 796, 820
Kim, K. S., 180
Kim, P., 796
Kim, S. E., 246
Kim, S. H., 246, 283, 284
Kim-Cohen, J., 852
Kimonis, E. R., 897, 901
Kimura, K., 720
Kimura, M., 182
Kinch, J., 456, 471
Kinderman, P., 34
Kindt, M., 228
King, A. P., 657, 663

Makkonen, I., 838
Malach, R., 73, 385, 387, 425
Malapani, C., 499
Malarkey, W. B., 140, 142, 143, 792, 806, 821
Malaspina, D., 246
Malatynska, E., 717
Malhi, G. S., 591
Malik, O., 938
Malkova, L., 689, 710
Mallat, S., 112
Mallavarapu, S., 572
Malloy, P. F., 461
Malone, N., 572
Malone, P. S., 420
Mampe, B., 632
Mandel, D. R., 628
Mandelkern, M., 589
Mandeville, J. B., 380, 695
Mandisodza, A. N., 426
Manera, V., 531
Manes, F., 213, 253, 533
Manfredi, C., 641
Mangin, J. F., 127
Mangun, G. R., 744, 745, 746
Manjaly, Z. M., 872
Manly, T., 460
Mann, H. B., 56
Mann, J. J., 705, 721, 722
Mann, L. S., 911
Mann, T., 371, 779
Manson, J., 815
Manson, J. H., 43, 570
Manstead, A. S. R., 500
Mantani, T., 914, 915, 921
Mantini, D., 98
Mantovani, A., 815
Manuck, S. B., 138, 705, 717, 718, 722, 796, 805, 806, 815, 820, 822
Mao, H., 214
Mao, X., 144
Maple, T. L., 572
Maravita, A., 530
Marcel, A. J., 197, 206, 207
Marchetti, C., 337
Marcus, J., 534
Marcus, S., 1019
Margoliash, D., 668, 669, 670
Margolin, G., 781
Maril, A., 733
Marin, C. M., 717
Marin, G., 117
Marin, L., 978, 988
Marin, T. J., 798
Marin-Bowling, V. M., 1008
Maringer, M., 500
Marini, F., 719
Marino, L., 31
Marino, R. Jr., 364
Mark, L. S., 436
Markham, R., 911
Markowitsch, H. J., 271, 319, 691, 791
Markus, H. R., 329, 492, 746, 747, 754

Marler, C. A., 154
Marler, P., 44, 663, 670
Marmot, M., 777, 779, 780
Marner, L., 294
Marois, R., 106
Marriott, A., 420
Marsden, C. A., 719
Marsee, M. A., 896, 897
Marsh, A. A., 396, 397, 556, 706, 707, 708, 709, 889, 897, 898, 899, 901
Marshall, I., 1015
Marshall-Mies, J. C., 460
Marsland, A. L., 138, 796, 806, 815, 820, 822
Marsman, G., 394
Martel, F. L., 156
Marten, K., 316
Martensz, N. D., 570
Martin, A., 297, 302, 387, 493, 733
Martin, C. D., 380
Martin, F., 395
Martin, I., 471
Martin, L., 464
Martin, M. E., 708
Martin, R. D., 29
Martin, S. P., 723
Martin, T. M., 798
Martineau, J., 528, 555
Martinerie, J., 98, 113
Martinez, A. M., 438, 791
Martinez, D., 704
Martinez, M. J., 349
Martinez-Garcia, F., 198
Martinez-Marcos, A., 198
Martinez-Maza, O., 819
Martinot, J. L., 481, 482
Martin-Skurski, M. E., 183, 708
Martis, B., 899
Marty, P., 906
Marucha, P. T., 134, 140, 141, 142, 765
Maruya, K., 338, 339
Marzetti, L., 113
Marzluff, J. M., 435
Masataka, N., 631, 638
Mascagni, F., 365
Mashal, N. M., 594
Mashek, D. J., 481
Mashoodh, R., 769
Masi, C. M., 50, 768
Mason, M. F., 412, 422, 423
Mason, W. A., 632, 684, 687, 690, 710, 719
Masserman, J. H., 566, 567
Masten, C. M., 606, 608
Master, S. L., 593
Mastropieri, D., 630
Masuda, T., 751
Mather, M., 50, 220, 508, 512, 514, 517, 518
Matheson, M. D., 572, 687, 791
Mathevon, N., 379
Mathews, A., 232, 233, 237
Mathews, V. P., 1005, 1009

Mathiak, K., 1004
Mathias, C. J., 182
Matochik, J. A., 838
Matson, J. L., 862
Matsumoto, K., 692
Matsuzawa, M., 230
Matsuzawa, T., 435, 687
Mattay, V. S., 64, 254, 281, 370, 780
Matte, J. A., 963
Mattes-von Cramon, G., 341
Matthews, J., 318
Matthews, K. A., 777, 782, 795, 804, 841
Matthews, P. M., 335, 336
Mattingley, J. B., 341, 530, 692, 869
Mattingly, I. G., 379, 548, 660, 670, 672, 673, 978
Mattler, U., 409
Mattock, K., 640
Mattson, R. H., 336
Matzner, W. T., 1020
Maughan, B., 852
Mauk, M. D., 169
Maunsell, J. H., 684
Maurer, D., 395
Maurer, R. G., 875
Maurice, M., 106
Maus, G. W., 536
Mawhood, L., 852
May, T., 705, 722
Mayberg, H. S., 409
Maybery, M., 854
Maye, J., 653, 654, 656
Mayer, B., 233
Mayer, J. D., 911
Mayes, L. C., 257
Maylor, E. A., 268
Maynard Smith, J., 349, 350, 351, 354, 357, 568, 638
Mayr, E., 566
Mayr, U., 480, 508, 576
Mayumi, M., 852
Mazaheri, A., 111
Mazaika, P. K., 85
Mazaux, J. M., 464
Mazefsky, C. A., 864
Mazure, C. M., 246
Mazziotta, J. C., 230, 281, 497, 528, 534, 545, 547, 555, 589, 780, 838
Mazzone, L., 861
Mazzoni, P., 337
McAlonan, G. M., 840, 874
McArthur, L. A., 421, 422
McAuliffe, K., 569
McBride, A., 459
McBurnett, K., 900
McCabe, C., 717
McCabe, D. P., 1018
McCabe, K., 576, 950
McCaffrey, M., 508
McCandliss, B. D., 228, 229
McCann, M. E., 630

McCarthy, G., 182, 253, 261, 302, 356, 380, 385, 394, 482
McCeney, M. K., 134, 717
McCleary, R. A., 197
McCleery, J. P., 560
McClelland, J. L., 340, 423
McClernon, F. J., 367
McClintock, M. K., 51, 745, 787
McCloskey, D. I., 339, 342
McClure, H. M., 615
McClure, S. M., 73, 182, 184, 188, 366, 430, 487, 574, 577, 809
McComb, K., 619, 670
McConnell, A. R., 331
McConnell, B. A., 228, 230
McCormick, C. M., 396
McCormick, D. A., 923
McCrae, R. R., 243, 244, 245, 246, 248
McCrae, V., 364
McCrea, M. A., 457
McCullough, L. D., 188
McCune, L., 631
McDade, T. W., 144, 145, 806, 818
McDermott, J. M., 228, 237, 253, 380, 394, 685, 743
McDonald, A. J., 365
McDonald, C. R., 461
McDonald, N., 237
McDonald, P. W., 911
McDonald, S., 456, 462, 464, 466, 467, 468, 469, 471, 472, 938
McDougle, C. J., 861
McDowell, D., 461
McEvoy, R. E., 234
McEwen, B. S., 704, 717, 722, 776, 777, 778, 779, 780, 787, 795
McFee, R., 101
McGaugh, J. L., 219, 271
McGeary, J. E., 748
McGhee, D. E., 368
McGivern, R. F., 303
McGlone, F., 181, 452
McGonigle, B. O., 686
McGowan, J. C., 296
McGowan, L., 593
McGrath, J., 215, 218, 349
McGrath, S., 593
McGraw, A. P., 173
McGraw, K. M., 221
McGreenery, C. E., 617
McGuire, L., 134, 141, 782
McGuire, M. T., 693, 703, 704, 720, 722
McGuire, S., 766
McIntosh, A. R., 92, 126
McIntosh, D. N., 200, 537
McIntosh, V. V., 461
McIntyre, M. C., 280
McKee, K., 453
McKelvie, S. J., 453
McKenna, M., 280, 427
McKenzie, A. A., 570
McKenzie, B., 631
McKeown, M. J., 92

McKie, S., 927
McKinnon, M. C., 328
McKissick, F. C., 836
McKittrick, C. R., 722
McLagen, M., 633
McLaughlin, J., 406
McLean, K. C., 327
McLean-Heywood, 862
McLuhan, M., 395
McMahon, W. M., 234, 235, 871
McMillan, D., 407
McMullin, M. A., 896
McNair, N. A., 528, 560
McNamara, A., 545
McNaughton, B. L., 423
McNaughton, N., 173
McNeill, D., 676
McPherson, A. C., 1008
McPherson, S., 459
McRae, K., 283, 285, 286, 370, 516, 577, 910, 922
McRoberts, G. W., 652
Mead, N. L., 340
Meador, K. J., 335, 342
Mealey, L., 559
Meaney, M. J., 14, 160, 616, 776, 778
Meary, D., 979
Mechelli, A., 78, 307
Meck, W. H., 499
Mecklinger, A., 511
Medalla, M., 734
Medin, D. L., 492
Meeren, H. J. M., 396
Meerlo, P., 720
Meester, S., 851
Meesters, C., 235
Meganck, R., 925
Mehler, J., 630, 631
Mehlman, P. T., 703, 722
Mehrabian, A., 591, 841
Mehta, A. P., 144
Mehta, S. K., 53, 57, 58, 144
Mehu, M., 41
Mehus, S., 658
Meier, B. P., 495
Meister, I. G., 548, 669
Melega, W. P., 722
Melis, A. P., 570
Mell, T., 518
Meller, R. E., 796
Mellers, B. A., 173
Mellins, C. A., 781
Melloni, L., 112
Melloni, R. H., 703
Meltzer, D., 14
Meltzer, J. A., 758
Meltzoff, A. N., 231, 341, 437, 532, 548, 553, 638, 640, 650, 651, 656, 657, 658, 659, 660, 663, 686
Melzack, R., 593
Menard, E., 872
Mende, W., 624, 632, 633, 635, 636, 641, 642

Mendelson, E., 145
Mendelson, M. J., 687
Mendes, W. B., 414, 787, 793
Mende-Siedlecki, P., 277
Mendez, M. F., 888
Mendoza, S. A., 738
Mendoza, S. P., 684, 720, 798
Meng, L., 862
Menon, V., 69, 181, 302, 303
Menz, M. M., 545
Menzaghi, F., 810
Merali, Z., 791
Mercado, A. M., 140
Mercado, F., 452
Mériau, K., 921, 922
Meriaux, S., 660
Merikangas, K. R., 369
Merikle, P. M., 203
Mermillod, M., 500, 502
Mertl, V., 658
Mesquita, B., 751
Messick, G., 769
Mesterton-Gibbons, M., 565
Mesulam, M. M., 180, 229, 366, 937
Metcalf, D., 230
Metcalfe, J., 372
Metta, G., 977
Metzinger, T., 325, 326, 327, 332
Meunier, G., 117
Meunier, M., 535, 689
Meunier, S., 121
Meyer, E., 268
Meyer, J., 831, 836, 842
Meyer, K., 34, 349, 576
Meyer, M., 555
Meyer-Lindenberg, A., 831, 842, 890
Meyerowitz, J. A., 599, 602, 603, 608
Meyn, L. A., 145
Mezulis, A. H., 329
Miall, R. C., 545
Micco, D. J., 169, 170
Michael, R. P., 716, 720
Michalska, K. J., 495
Michel, A., 156
Michel, C. M., 124
Michelet, T., 690
Michelsson, K., 633
Michie, C., 896
Miczek, K. A., 717, 718, 719, 721, 722, 723
Middleton, F. A., 733
Mienaltowski, A., 516
Mier, J. W., 815
Miettunen, J., 34
Miezin, F. M., 78
Mignault, A., 437
Mikami, A., 690
Mikati, M. A., 337
Mikels, J. A., 508, 514
Mikolajczak, M., 910
Mikulincer, M., 593, 614, 616, 617, 618, 619
Mikulis, D., 295

Moskowitz, J. T., 776, 781
Moss, C. F., 670
Mottron, L., 840, 853, 872, 874
Mount, M. K., 244, 248
Mounts, J. R. W., 1006
Moutoussis, K., 544
Movellan, J. R., 650, 659, 984
Mowrer, S. M., 215
Moynihan, J. A., 806
Moynihan, M., 397
Muccioli, M., 487
Much, N. C., 900
Mueller, J., 911, 912
Mufson, E. J., 180
Mugno, D., 861
Muhlberger, A., 236
Mukaddes, N. M., 853
Mukesh, T. M. S., 106
Mukherjee, L., 876
Mulder, G., 447
Mulder, L. J. M., 447
Muldoon, M. F., 806, 820, 822
Mullen, B., 452
Mullennix, J. W., 386
Muller, F., 464
Muller, H. K., 144
Muller, J. L., 887
Müller, R. A., 560, 850, 854, 875, 876
Mulligan, A., 851, 852
Mumford, J. A., 75, 89
Munafo, M. R., 748
Munch, J. A., 798
Munck, A. U., 788, 796
Mundy, P., 235, 658, 850
Munoz, D. P., 229, 335
Munoz, L. C., 895
Munson, J. A., 231, 849
Munte, T. F., 619
Munzel, U., 56
Murakami, S., 100
Muraven, M., 220, 368, 371
Murias, M., 537, 560, 868
Muris, P., 233, 235
Murnighan, J. K., 61
Murphy, A. Z., 157, 159, 160
Murphy, B. C., 236
Murphy, C. A., 188
Murphy, C. R., 1004
Murphy, D. G., 838, 869, 870
Murphy, F. C., 556
Murphy, N., 1022, 1023
Murphy, S. T., 197, 207
Murray, A. D., 636, 640
Murray, E. A., 215, 216, 436, 689, 897
Murray, M. M., 385
Murry, J., 643
Murry, T., 643
Murty, V. P., 513, 514
Müsseler, J., 553
Musselman, D. L., 819
Mussweiler, T., 495
Muthukumaraswamy, S. D., 528, 530, 560

Muüller, V., 518
Mycek, P. J., 790
Myers, C. E., 183
Myers, H. F., 794
Myers, R. D., 179, 183
Myers, R. E., 691, 693
Myers, S., 849
Myerson, J., 182
Myles, B., 862
Myowa-Yamakoshi, M., 435
Myrick, H., 366, 367

N

Naatanen, P., 913
Naatanen, R., 447, 452
Nacewicz, B. M., 838
Nachshon, O., 618
Nadel, J., 987
Nader, M. A., 705, 716, 717, 720, 721, 723
Nadig, A., 537, 867
Nagae-Poetscher, L. M., 165
Nagahama, Y., 957
Nagasaka, K., 975
Nagasaka, Y., 709
Nagel, E., 7, 13, 14
Nagel, R., 950, 951, 953, 956
Nakahara, K., 730
Nakai, A., 852
Nakajima, T., 587
Nakamizo, S., 853
Nakamura, W., 85
Nakanishi, J., 977
Nakano, T., 628
Nakayama, K., 381, 394, 397
Naliboff, B. D., 589, 591, 593, 799
Nappo, F., 822
Narayan, V. M., 887
Narr, K. L., 35
Narumoto, J., 261
Nash, B., 657
Nater, U. M., 792
Nathan, P. J., 254, 370
Naumann, L. P., 247
Nava, C., 707
Navarrete, E., 340
Naybar, N., 60
Nazarian, B., 535
Nazmi, A., 822
Nazzi, T., 630
Neal, A. R., 530, 643, 692, 850
Neale, M. C., 247, 779, 781
Nealey, J. B., 793
Nealey, T. A., 684
Nearing, K. I., 180, 217, 285
Neary, D., 456
Neda, Z., 987
Needham, A., 532
Neelin, P., 296
Neels, H., 822
Neely, K. A., 338
Negeira, A., 514
Nehorai, A., 121

Neisser, U., 326
Nelson, C. A., 230, 394, 435, 436, 438
Nelson, D., 663
Nelson, E. E., 618, 841, 899
Nelson, J. D., 529
Nelson, M. E., 670
Nelson, T., 651
Nemeth, C., 387
Nemiah, J. C., 906, 907, 910
Nemoto, H., 587
Nesse, R. M., 810
Nesselroade, J. R., 508
Nester, E. W., 143
Nester, M. T., 143
Nestler, E. J., 577
Nestor, P. J., 938
Neta, M., 434
Neth, D., 438
Netter, P., 791
Nettles, C. D., 822
Neuberg, S. L., 396, 445, 446, 450, 452, 566
Neubert, K., 56
Neufeld, R. W., 914
Neugebauer, R., 899
Neumann, C. S., 896
Neumann, D., 873
Neumann, I. D., 154, 156, 157, 159
Neumann, J., 840
Neumann, O., 339
Neuner, F., 381
Neville, H. J., 650, 651
Nevison, C. M., 156
New, A. S., 361, 370, 886
Newcomb, M. D., 618
Newell, A., 493
Newman, C., 896, 898, 900
Newman, J. D., 154, 588, 625, 631, 632, 643
Newman, J. L., 181, 215
Newman, J. P., 897, 901
Newman, S. S., 853
Newport, E. L., 650, 651, 652, 654
Newton, N., 590
Newton, T. L., 616
Nicastro, N., 29
Nichols, R. C., 841
Nichols, S., 901
Nichols, T. E., 71, 75, 76, 80, 87, 89, 90, 126
Niedenthal, P. M., 196, 202, 340, 351, 352, 492, 493, 495, 499, 500, 501, 502, 503
Niedermeyer, E., 110, 116
Nielsen, L., 206, 508
Nielsen, M., 326
Nienhaus, K., 371
Niessing, J., 112
Nieto, C., 869
Nieuwenhuis, S., 181, 215, 406, 409, 410, 511
Nigg, J. T., 1009
Niki, H., 179

Nikodem, V. C., 593
Nikulina, E. M. Jr., 717
Nimchinsky, E. A., 683
Nimmo-Smith, I., 556
Nir, Y., 425
Nisbett, R. E., 573, 747, 751
Nishijo, H., 692
Nishitani, N., 536, 560
Nitsche, J. B., 501
Nitschke, J. B., 809
Nobre, A. C., 215, 229, 409
Nocera, C. C., 496
Noelle, D. C., 219, 221
Noftle, E. E., 244
Noll, D. C., 74, 78, 80, 82, 181,
    366, 423
Nolte, G., 110, 113, 116
Nomikos, G. G., 366
Nomura, M., 400
Noon, W. A., 569
Noonan, S. K., 876
Noordzij, M. L., 535
Norbury, C. F., 851, 852
Nordahl, C. W., 686, 874
Norenzayan, A., 746, 747, 751
Norman, D., 730
Norman, M. A., 461
Norman, R. J., 164, 169
Norris, C. J., 205, 607, 767
Norsen, L. H., 593
Northoff, G., 215, 748, 750
Nose, I., 964
Nosofsky, R. M., 492
Notman, L., 854
Nottebohm, F., 663
Noveck, I. A., 349, 354
Nowak, M. A., 348
Nowicki, S., 548
Nucci, L. P., 900
Numan, M., 155, 157
Nummenmaa, L., 923
Nunez, P. L., 113
Nusbaum, H. C., 553, 554, 607, 668,
    669, 670, 672, 673, 675, 676, 677,
    767, 807
Nuzzo, C., 628
Nyberg, L., 268, 508
Nye, R. M., 331
Nystrom, L. E., 58, 61, 181, 349, 366,
    409, 423, 480, 485, 487, 575, 900

O

Oakes, P. J., 446
Oberman, L. M., 200, 536, 537, 560
Obleser, J., 382
Obradovic´, J., 895
Obrig, H., 112
Ochipa, C., 978
Ochs, M. F., 769
Ochsner, K. N., 12, 41, 93, 189, 201,
    207, 215, 277, 278, 279, 283, 284,
    286, 328, 330, 360, 369, 370, 414,
    512, 514, 516, 577, 589, 600, 602,

608, 616, 619, 691, 730, 745, 808,
    836, 838, 887, 889, 922
Ockleford, E. M., 379, 630
Odhuba, R. A., 461
Oehler, J., 705, 722
Oeltermann, A., 94, 295
Ogata, A., 588
Ogawa, S., 81, 156
Ohala, J. J., 630
Ohkura, S., 439
Ohlmeier, M. D., 861
Öhman, A., 171, 172, 197, 200, 207,
    257, 340, 398, 400
Okada, G., 914
Okada, Y. C., 100, 121, 587, 968
Okamoto, Y., 914
Okita, T., 447
Okon-Singer, H., 340
Okrent, A., 677
Okun, M. L., 822
Okuno-Fujiwara, M., 61
Olazabal, D. E., 154, 157
Olczak, P. V., 1006
Olfson, M., 1019
Oliveira, I. O., 822
Oliveira-Souza, R., 481, 483, 484, 485,
    886, 887, 888
Olivier, E., 528, 554
Oller, D. K., 631, 641
Ollinger, J. M., 77, 78
Olson, C. R., 181
Olson, D. R., 936
Olson, J. M., 405
Olson, M. A., 339
Olsson, A., 217
Ongür, D., 180, 365, 366, 576
Onlaor, S., 183
Onoda, K., 589, 590
Oosterhof, N. N., 411, 412, 426, 427,
    437, 438
Oosterlaan, J., 870
Oppenheim, A. V., 108
Oppenheim, H., 362, 371
Orbach, I., 593, 618
Orban, G. A., 74
Orell, M., 702
Orendi, J. L., 234
Orliaguet, J. P., 979
Ormel, J., 328
Orr, S. P., 156
Orth-Gomer, K., 804, 805
Ortinski, P., 335, 342
Osada, H., 851
Osada, T., 730
Osaka, M., 329
Osaka, N., 329
Osborne, T., 531
Osherson, D. N., 349, 356
Ossadtchi, A., 123
Ostergren, P. O., 804, 806
Osterhout, L., 406, 407
Osterling, J., 231, 849
Ostlund, S. B., 183, 219

Ostrosky-Solis, F., 462
Ostry, D., 302
Ostwald, P. F., 626
Osu, R., 977
Oswald, D. P., 864
Otten, L. J., 423
Ottowitz, W. E., 691
Ouellet, L., 911
Ouhayoun, B., 913
Overkamp, G. J., 720
Ow, A. W., 874
Owen, A. M., 73, 351, 353, 356,
    422, 964
Owen, N., 769, 797
Ownsworth, T., 456
Owren, M. J., 379
Oxford, M., 901
Oyserman, D., 747
Ozbay, E. Y., 186
Ozdamar, O., 106
Ozer, D. J., 243
Ozonoff, S., 35, 228, 234, 235, 456, 537,
    867, 869, 870, 871
Oztop, E., 532, 980, 981, 982, 986

P

Paaver, M., 722
Pace, T. W., 817, 819, 821
Pacherie, E., 335, 336
Packard, M. G., 219
Packer, C., 570
Packer, D. J., 216, 221
Padden, D., 651, 662
Padgett, D. A., 789
Padgett, L. S., 1008
Padmala, S., 281
Padoa-Schioppa, C., 215
Paetau, R., 121
Pagani, J. H., 767
Pagnoni, G., 183, 366, 574, 708
Pain, C., 914
Paiva, M. M. F., 479, 481, 482, 483,
    484, 485
Pakrashi, M., 426
Palagi, E., 45, 572
Palanza, P., 720
Palermo, R., 398, 399, 400
Paley, V., 586
Palfai, T., 234
Palmen, S. J. M., 849
Palmer, S. E., 494
Palokangas, T., 230
Palomero-Gallagher, N., 294
Pals, J. L., 327
Paluello, I. M., 553
Pan, B. A., 318
Pan, Y., 770
Pandey, J., 850
Pandey, M. K., 815
Pandya, D. N., 352, 365, 366, 731, 733
Panitz, D., 281
Panksepp, J., 157, 170, 196, 587, 618,
    620, 841, 899, 900

Pannetier-Lecoeur, M., 102
Panneton-Cooper, R., 630
Pantazis, D., 125, 126, 128
Panzica, G. C., 155
Paoli, T., 572
Papadopoulo, T., 118
Papagno, C., 336
Papoušek, H., 626, 627, 628
Papoušek, M., 626, 627, 628
Pardini, D., 895
Pardini, M., 577, 840
Pardo, J. S., 668
Pardo, J. V., 171, 213, 956
Parent, A., 180
Parham, P., 815
Pariante, C. M., 144, 797, 821, 823
Paris, J., 245
Park, B., 424, 451, 452, 758
Park, D. C., 508, 748, 750, 758
Park, H. S., 247
Park, N. W., 456
Parker, G., 591
Parker, J. D. A., 908, 909, 911, 912, 925, 928
Parker, P. D., 911
Parkes, L. M., 112
Parkinson, J. A., 216, 898
Parkkola, R., 923
Parkkonen, L., 106
Parlier, M., 835, 841
Parmigiani, S., 720
Parr, L. A., 39, 41, 43, 45, 437, 685
Parsons, L. M., 349
Partan, S., 44, 695
Partanen, T., 633
Parviainen, T., 121
Pascalis, O., 43, 435, 436, 438
Pascual-Leone, A., 34, 319, 321, 326, 349, 576
Pascualvaca, D., 838
Pasley, B. N., 257
Passingham, R. E., 213, 327, 330, 399, 529, 531, 588, 691, 730, 733
Pasupathi, M., 50, 327, 508
Patel, G., 840
Patel, K. D., 819
Patrick, C. J., 897, 899
Patrick, W., 766, 776, 777, 779, 782
Patterson, K., 486
Patterson, R. D., 351, 387
Pauker, K., 395
Paukner, A., 544, 687
Paul, C., 50
Paul, J., 852
Paul, R. H., 243
Paulhus, D. L., 599, 607, 609
Pauli, P., 236
Paulignan, Y., 530, 979
Pauls, D., 860
Pauls, J., 94, 295
Paulus, M. P., 205, 558

Paus, T., 294, 296, 297, 298, 299, 302, 303, 304, 305, 306, 307, 308, 366, 630, 995, 997
Pausova, Z., 297, 298, 299
Pavani, S., 574
Pavesi, G., 528, 560
Pawowski, B. P., 33
Paxton, D. J. M., 965
Payne, B. K., 368, 730, 737, 738
Pazzaglia, M., 533
Peace, V., 556
Pearce, B. D., 823
Pearce, S., 467, 938
Pearl, D. K., 143, 792
Pearl, J., 92
Pearson, M. A., 405, 407, 955
Pecher, D., 500
Pecina, S., 171, 199, 201, 574
Pecker, J., 364
Pedatella, K. E., 874
Pedersen, B. K., 822
Pedersen, N. L., 781
Pedrosa Gil, F., 910, 912
Peelen, M. V., 553
Peeters, G., 407, 413
Pegna, A. J., 171, 380
Pelham, B., 420
Pelletier, M., 809
Pellicano, E., 854
Pellijeff, A., 466
Pelphrey, K. A., 863, 872
Peltola, M. J., 230
Peltonen, L., 34
Pena, M., 662
Penfield, W., 363
Peng, K., 747, 751
Penn, H. E., 874
Pennington, B. F., 234, 459, 537, 831, 867, 869
Penninx, B. W., 769, 820
Penny, W. D., 92, 125, 126
Penton-Voak, I. S., 999
Pepin, M., 1004
Peplau, L. A., 767
Perani, D., 340
Perazzo, L. M., 630
Perdereau, F., 928
Pereg, D., 614
Peretz, I., 381, 872
Perez, E., 380, 385
Pérez, J. J., 110, 913
Perez, R. I., II, 409
Pérez-Barbería, F. J., 31
Perez-Edgar, K., 235, 236
Pergamin, L., 228
Perkins, A. S., 349
Perlman, D., 767
Perlmutter, J. S., 201
Perloff, D., 805
Perner, J., 41, 318, 337, 833, 834, 836, 942
Pernet, C. R., 390, 391
Pernier, J., 112, 119

Perret, E., 363
Perrett, D. I., 254, 380, 394, 399, 413, 422, 436, 439, 526, 531, 536, 689, 694, 867, 984, 986
Perretti, M., 794
Perrin, F., 119
Perrin, J. S., 298, 299, 306
Perrucci, M. G., 98
Perry, D., 941
Perry, K., 870
Perry, S., 43, 570, 806
Persson, L., 806
Pervanidou, P., 820
Pes, E., 533
Peschardt, K. S., 779
Pessiglione, M., 339, 977
Pessoa, L., 200, 257, 280, 281, 285, 357, 427, 873
Peters, J., 977
Peters, S., 548, 670
Peters, T. M., 296
Petersen, A. M., 822
Petersen, K. L., 797, 820
Petersen, S. E., 78, 228, 229, 230, 233, 398, 400, 733, 1016
Peterson, G., 670
Peterson, J. B., 246, 317, 407
Peterson, J. R., 298
Peterson, R., 366
Petkov, C. I., 382, 383, 388, 389
Petrides, M., 247, 302, 363, 365, 731, 733
Petrie, K. J., 140
Petrinovich, L., 663
Petro, L. S., 256
Petrovic, P., 589, 590
Pettit, G. S., 899
Petty, R. E., 219
Peyron, R., 202, 556, 588
Pezawas, L., 254, 307, 899
Pezze, M. A., 188
Pfaff, D. W., 156
Pfaus, J. G., 366
Pfefferbaum, A., 69
Pfeifer, J. H., 328, 547, 589, 838, 997, 998
Pfeiffer, B., 869
Pfeuffer, J., 97
Pfurtscheller, G., 111
Phan, A., 841
Phan, K. L., 201, 206, 254, 258, 279, 281, 283, 285, 370, 412, 438, 556, 606, 608, 768, 809, 965
Phelps, E. A., 171, 172, 180, 183, 186, 188, 189, 200, 213, 216, 217, 220, 221, 255, 278, 285, 339, 369, 412, 423, 424, 426, 441, 480, 509, 735, 736, 899, 1016, 1018
Phelps, M. E., 230
Phillips, A. C., 138, 139, 140, 618
Phillips, A. G., 179
Phillips, B. M., 233
Phillips, C., 125

Schmithorst, V. J., 297, 298, 299, 302, 303
Schmitt, W. A., 898
Schmittberger, R., 61
Schmitz, C., 849
Schmitz, T. W., 328
Schneider, D. J., 279, 491
Schneider, E. F., 1006
Schneider, F., 691, 887
Schneider, T. R., 793
Schneider, W., 964
Schnitzler, A., 590
Schoenbaum, G., 179, 215, 399, 400, 436, 439, 574, 576, 897
Schoenemann, P. T., 365
Schoffelen, J. M., 112
Scholz, J., 261
Schommer, N. C., 793
Schon, F., 536
Schonberg, T., 184
Schonberger, M., 456
Schooler, J. W., 202, 206, 268, 270, 271
Schorr, A., 278
Schotter, A., 186, 187
Schreckenberger, M., 588
Schreiber, C. A., 206
Schreiber, E., 461
Schroder, K. E., 768
Schroeder, L., 963, 964
Schroers, M., 273
Schryer, E., 508
Schubert, T. W., 496
Schubotz, R. I., 349, 671
Schug, R. A., 901
Schulkin, J., 484
Schultz, D. W., 339, 340
Schultz, J., 179, 180, 181, 183
Schultz, R. T., 257, 328, 830, 831, 860, 863
Schultz, W., 181, 219, 366, 535, 574, 977
Schulz, J., 508
Schulz, L. E., 942
Schuman, H. R., 364
Schumann, C. M., 686
Schupp, H. T., 406, 1008
Schuster, S., 419
Schutter, D. J. L. G., 604
Schütz-Bosbach, S., 327
Schüz, A., 294
Schwab, E. C., 672
Schwab, S. I., 936
Schwabe, L., 790
Schwade, J., 657
Schwartz, C. E., 509
Schwartz, D. P., 116
Schwartz, G. E., 910, 912, 913
Schwartz, J., 779
Schwartz, J. H., 1015, 1016
Schwartz, J. L., 368
Schwartz, M. L., 709
Schwartz, S. H., 461, 478, 479
Schwartzbaum, J. S., 689

Schwarz, A., 316
Schwarz, N., 197, 204, 492, 573
Schwarze, B., 61
Schweinberger, S. R., 381, 395
Schwerdtfeger, W. L., 271
Schwiedrzik, C. M., 112
Schyns, P. G., 254, 256
Sclar, G., 684
Scott, D. J., 73
Scott, F. J., 862
Scott, S. K., 382, 399
Scucchi, S., 570, 574
Searle, J., 207
Sebanc, A. M., 792
Sebe, N., 397, 427
Sebestyen, G., 707
Sechrest, L., 910, 913
Seckl, J. R., 160, 616
Secord, P., 437
Sedaghat, F., 863
Sedikides, C., 317, 320, 609
Seeck, M., 327
Seeley, W. W., 937
Seelig, D., 961
Seelos, K. C., 335
Seeman, M., 779
Seeman, T. E., 769, 776, 777, 778, 780, 782, 783, 787, 795, 797, 804, 806, 1020
Seger, C. A., 328
Segerstrom, S. C., 134, 135, 143, 779, 793, 794, 799
Seghier, M. L., 171
Seidenwurm, D., 887
Sejnowski, T., 110, 650
Selemon, L. D., 709
Seligman, M. E. P., 371
Sell, S. L., 721
Semin, G. R., 493, 497, 498, 979
Seminowicz, D. A., 280
Sen, S., 748
Seneta, E., 56
Senju, A., 836
Senulis, J., 501
Serdaru, M., 536
Sereno, M. I., 123, 127, 296, 529, 548, 686
Sergeant, J. A., 870
Sergent, C., 98, 106, 125
Sergent, J., 380
Sergerie, K., 509
Serrano, J. M., 437
Sessa, B., 1020
Sesso, H. D., 815
Sestir, M. A., 1004, 1007
Sethi, G., 815
Setlow, B., 574
Setoyama, T., 974
Seyfarth, R. M., 34, 43, 570, 631, 685, 686, 702
Seymour, B., 60, 188, 977
Shackman, A. J., 734
Shadmehr, R., 867

Shaffer, M. M., 492
Shafritz, K. M., 871
Shah, J. Y., 340
Shah, N. J., 691
Shah, R., 817
Shair, H., 152
Shaker, R., 335
Shallice, T., 216, 363, 364, 460, 461, 536, 730, 956
Shamay-Tsoory, S. G., 60, 462, 464, 465, 466, 467, 468, 469, 470, 865, 887, 935, 938, 939, 940, 941
Shamosh, N., 372
Shamseddine, A. N., 337
Shankle, W. R., 305
Shankweiler, D. P., 534, 660, 670
Shany-Ur, T., 935, 939, 941
Shapiro, D. E., 913
Sharot, T., 602, 603
Shattuck, D. W., 118
Shaver, P. R., 614, 618
Shaw, P., 297, 298, 302, 939, 997
Shaw, R. E., 436
Shear, K., 152
Sheehan, M. J., 365
Sheese, B. E., 228, 233, 234, 235
Sheffield, D., 593, 793
Shelton, J. N., 368
Shelton, J. R., 743
Shelton, K. K., 901
Shelton, S. E., 573, 587, 688
Shenk, M. K., 758
Shepard, S. A., 236
Shepherd, S. V., 543
Shepp, L., 79
Sherak, B., 437
Sheridan, J. F., 51, 745, 787, 789, 821
Sherman, D. K., 779
Sherman, E. M. S., 460
Sherman, F. S., 782
Sherman, J. C., 875
Sherman, J. W., 407, 733
Sherman, P. W., 569
Sherman, S. J., 491
Sherrington, C. S., 166, 168
Sherwood, A., 768
Sherwood, C. C., 41, 46
Sherwood, H., 781
Shibata, T., 977, 984
Shidara, M., 179, 692
Shields, A. E., 759
Shiffman, S. M., 805
Shimada, S., 532
Shimamura, A. P., 607, 941, 942
Shimizu, K., 720
Shimizu, T., 823
Shimodozono, M., 588
Shimojo, S., 215, 230, 397
Shin, L. M., 188, 370, 481, 899
Shin, M., 1006
Shintel, H., 677
Ship, I., 143
Shipley, M. T., 588, 590

Shirao, N., 914
Shirinyan, D., 593
Shishodia, S., 815
Shivde, G., 50
Shively, C. A., 704, 717, 720, 721, 788, 796
Shizgal, P., 181
Shoda, Y., 371, 372
Shohamy, D., 183
Sholl, D. A., 294
Shulman, G. L., 77, 284, 840
Shulman, R. G., 97
Shultz, S., 28, 30, 31, 33, 34, 35, 43, 46
Shur, S., 60
Shurin, M. R., 817
Shutts, K., 668
Shweder, R. A., 900
Sidaros, K., 89
Siddiqui, F., 204
Siegbahn, A., 817
Siegel, A., 899, 900
Siegle, G. J., 838
Siegrist, J., 765
Sifneos, P. E., 906, 907, 927, 929
Sigman, M., 835, 997
Signoret, J.-L., 380
Silani, G., 558, 836, 877, 914, 920, 922, 924
Silbersweig, D., 370
Silk, J. B., 33, 34, 349, 567, 570
Siltanen, P., 116
Silva, F. L. da., 110, 111, 116
Silva, P. A., 618
Silvert, L., 409
Silverthorn, P., 900, 901
Simion, A., 464
Simmons, A. N., 558
Simmons, K., 494
Simmons, W. K., 351, 352
Simola, J., 110
Simon, H., 720, 722
Simon, H. A., 493
Simon, O., 957
Simon, T. J., 627, 851
Simonoff, E., 851, 853
Simons, D. J., 207
Simons, R. F., 237, 911
Simonsson-Sarnecki, M., 912
Simpson, G. G., 336
Simpson, J. A., 618
Simpson, J. R., 284
Simpson, M. D. A., 156
Simpson, R., 862
Simpson, S. W., 643
Singelis, T. M., 747
Singer, B. H., 776, 777, 778
Singer, H. S., 302
Singer, T., 60, 186, 188, 260, 330, 425, 480, 533, 551, 552, 553, 554, 556, 557, 558, 559, 575, 691, 711, 831, 836
Singer, W., 111, 112, 332
Singewald, N., 156

Singh, K. D., 122
Singh, T., 867
Singh, V. P., 588, 876
Singleton, I., 33
Sinha, P., 899, 900
Sinha, R., 189, 914, 922
Sinha, S. R., 670
Sinigaglia, C., 341
Siqueland, E. R., 652
Sirevaag, A. M., 307
Sirovatka, P. J., 852
Sirvio, P., 633
Sivers, H., 248
Siviy, S., 618
Skaug, O. E., 782
Skelly, J. P., 694
Skinner, B. F., 316, 342, 649, 650
Skinner, E. A., 781
Skipper, J. I., 672, 673, 674, 676
Skoien, P., 229
Skokan, L. A., 779
Skoner, D. P., 777, 779, 782
Skorpen, C. G., 50
Skrandies, W., 121
Skudlarski, P., 76, 685
Skuse, D., 413, 618, 863, 939
Skytthe, A., 928
Slachevsky, A., 460
Slagter, H. A., 181
Slater, A. M., 438
Slemmer, J. A., 654
Slocombe, K., 43
Sloman, S. A., 357
Sluming, V., 307
Sluzewska, A., 819
Small, D. M., 214
Small, S. L., 672, 673, 675
Smania, N., 533
Smetana, J. G., 900
Smetana, Z., 145
Smith, B. H., 9, 11
Smith, B. S., 798
Smith, D. M., 396, 810
Smith, D. P., 517
Smith, D. R., 387
Smith, E. E., 71, 80, 229, 248, 280, 284, 887
Smith, E. O., 723
Smith, E. R., 331, 446, 452, 491, 493, 498
Smith, G. D., 778, 782
Smith, K. S., 168, 170, 174, 200, 201, 413
Smith, K. W., 349
Smith, L., 870, 986
Smith, M. L., 256, 901
Smith, N. K., 168, 170, 174, 197, 452, 1007, 1008
Smith, O. A., 570
Smith, P., 676
Smith, R., 197, 207, 349, 356
Smith, S. E., 413
Smith, S. M., 296

Smith, T. D., 46
Smith, T. W., 793, 804
Smith, V., 576
Smith, W., 588
Smith, Y., 478, 480, 481, 482, 576, 577
Smulders, F. T. Y., 447
Smuts, B., 685
Snibbe, A., 747
Snodgrass, C., 464, 939
Snow, C. P., 758
Snowden, J. S., 465, 466, 467, 468
Snowdon, C. T., 688
Snowling, M., 871
Snyder, A. Z., 284, 514
Snyder, D. R., 693
Snyder, J., 560, 863, 874
Snydersmith, M. A., 615
Soares, J. J. F., 197, 207
Sobel, N., 337
Sober, E., 567, 568
Soderstrom, H., 886, 888, 889
Sokolow, M., 805
Sol, D., 28
Soliman, N., 706, 707
Solinas, M., 366
Solomon, M., 234, 870, 871, 875
Solomon, S., 410
Soltis, J., 632
Somerville, L. H., 370, 606
Sommer, T., 228
Sommerville, J. A., 35, 326, 495, 532, 553, 659
Sommerville, R. B., 58, 485, 900
Song, A. W., 182, 356
Sonnby-Borgstrom, M., 555
Soon, C. S., 338
Sora, I., 767
Sorce, J. F., 437
Sorensen, L. T., 142
Sornette, D., 31
Sorosky, J. I., 821
Soto, C. J., 247
Soucy, N., 618
Soukup, G. R., 395
Soulières, I., 840, 872
South, M., 234, 871
Southgate, V., 322, 531, 535, 836
Souza, T., 269
Sowden, P., 854
Sowell, E. R., 297, 302, 995, 996, 997
Spampinato, M. V., 221, 349
Spaniol, J., 508
Sparrow, B., 341
Sparrow, S. S., 851
Speca, M., 819
Speer, N. K., 493
Speicher, C. E., 143, 769
Spekreijse, H., 71
Spelke, E. S., 668
Spelman, F. A., 570
Spence, S. A., 961, 962, 963, 964, 967, 968, 969
Spencer, C. J., 630

Svoboda, E., 328
Swainson, B., 851
Swallow, K. M., 493
Swanson, C., 615
Swanson, L. W., 782
Swanson, S., 867
Swart, M., 60, 533, 553
Swartz, K. B., 440
Swazey, J. P., 14
Sweeney, J. A., 234
Swett, C., 691
Swettenham, J., 234
Swick, D., 284
Swing, E. L., 1001, 1005, 1009
Swinnen, S. P., 335, 336, 530
Syal, S., 657
Syme, S. L., 779, 795
Symmes, D., 627, 628
Symons, C. S., 329, 331
Syrdal-Lasky, A., 652
Szathmáry, E., 638
Szatmari, P., 841, 928
Szegda, K. L., 158
Székely, T., 28
Sziller, I., 630
Szpaderska, A. M., 142
Szyf, M., 160, 616, 778

T

Tabak, I., 500
Taber, C. S., 221
Taber, K., 424
Tabibnia, G., 186, 187, 281, 910
Tachi, N., 723
Tachimori, H., 851
Tadi, T., 327
Tag, B., 23
Taga, G., 628
Tager-Flusberg, H., 851, 863, 874
Tai, Y. F., 982, 983
Tajfel, H., 446
Takahashi, H., 184, 186, 187, 481, 482, 573, 887, 889, 950
Takahashi, L. K., 899
Takahashi, Y. K., 184, 186, 187
Takayanagi, Y., 158
Takenaka, T., 975
Takeuchi, Y., 615
Talbot, P. S., 577
Talley, J., 460
Tallon-Baudry, C., 112, 126
Talos, I. F., 53
Tamashiro, K. L. K., 717, 719
Tambor, E. S., 600
Tamietto, M., 400
Tamm, L., 302
Tanaka, F., 659, 984
Tanaka, J. W., 436, 452, 863
Tanaka, K., 254, 692, 695
Tanaka, M., 435
Tanaka, N., 588
Tanaka, Y. L., 690
Tanaka, Y. Z., 690

Tancredi, L. R., 888
Tanenbaum, R., 121
Tang, T. Z., 1019
Tangney, J. P., 371, 481
Tani, P., 928
Tankersley, D., 576
Tanno, Y., 233
Tanofsky-Kraff, M., 792
Tapia, M., 452
Tarantola, A., 114, 115, 124, 129
Tarkka, I. M., 106
Tarli, S., 572
Tarr, M. J., 253, 436, 685
Tasker, R. R., 260, 533
Tassinary, L. G., 7, 71, 808, 810, 1017
Tassoni, G., 897
Tate, A. J., 435, 436, 437, 438, 440
Taub, D. M., 717
Taulu, S., 110
Taumoepeau, M., 500
Taylor, A., 797, 821
Taylor, A. A., 435
Taylor, A. R., 184
Taylor, C. S., 525
Taylor, D. J., 570
Taylor, G. J., 907, 908, 909, 911, 912, 925, 928
Taylor, H. G., 939
Taylor, J., 366
Taylor, J. G., 877
Taylor, J. L., 339, 342
Taylor, J. R., 366
Taylor, M. J., 303
Taylor, R., 461
Taylor, S. E., 184, 321, 329, 413, 423, 424, 491, 589, 591, 593, 595, 599, 602, 607, 616, 748, 756, 767, 776, 778, 779, 780, 781, 782, 783, 797, 799, 806, 807, 808, 1020
Taylor, S. F., 201, 258, 281, 282, 412, 438, 556, 768
Taymans, S. E., 155
Tchernichovski, O., 663
Tecoma, E. S., 461
Tees, R. C., 638, 652
Teicher, M. H., 617
Teitelbaum, O., 849, 860
Tejedor, J., 180
Tekin, S., 456
Teleki, G., 570
Temple, R. O., 461
Tencer, H. L., 618
Tennes, K., 230
Tepperberg, M., 145
Terdal, S. K., 600
Terracciano, A., 244, 245
Terrace, H. S., 534
Terranova, M. L., 614, 615
Terris, W., 566
Tesche, C. D., 100, 117
Tessari, A., 534
Tessitore, A., 64, 254, 281, 370, 509, 515, 517, 780

Tettamanti, M., 674
Teunisse, J. P., 863
Thakkar, K. N., 235, 875
Thaler, R., 61
Theeuwes, J., 340
Theorell, T., 806
Theoret, H., 560
Thier, P., 686, 692
Thierry, B., 41
Thierry, G., 380, 672
Thilo, K. V., 257
Thioux, M., 60, 525, 530, 533, 536, 560
Thoden, C. J., 633
Thoman, E. B., 568
Thomas, A., 413
Thomas, J. A., 86
Thomas, M. L., 721
Thomas, T. L., 788, 792
Thomaz, A. L., 986
Thompson, E., 405, 407, 409
Thompson, M. S., 424, 492, 493
Thompson, P. M., 35, 380, 890
Thompson, R. F., 169
Thompson, R. R., 156
Thompson, W. L., 71
Thompson-Schill, S. L., 493, 963
Thomson, J. J., 349, 356
Thomson, J. W., 327
Thorell, L., 236
Thorn, T. M. J., 449
Thorndike, E. L., 216, 336
Thornhill, R., 438
Thornton, D., 896
Thorpe, S. J., 181
Thorpe, W. H., 338
Thunberg, M., 197, 257
Tian, B., 382
Tibbetts, E. A., 435
Tiberghien, G., 395
Tibi-Elhanani, Y., 940
Tice, D. M., 220, 368, 595, 792
Tidey, J. W., 721
Tiedens, L. Z., 702
Tiesma, D., 461
Tiffany, S. T., 338
Tiihonen, J., 723, 887, 889
Tiippana, K., 864
Tiken, S., 459
Tikhonov, A., 115
Tilg, H., 815
Tillfors, M., 606, 608
Tilvis, R. J., 771
Timko, C., 779
Timmerman, M. E., 470
Timmermans, S., 28
Timmers, E. A., 851
Tinbergen, N., 41, 42, 566
Tindell, A. J., 201
Tingate, T. R., 144, 145
Tipples, J., 395
Titone, D., 349
Tittgemeyer, M., 878
Titze, I. R., 379, 388, 389

SUBJECT INDEX

Note: Page numbers followed by "*f*" and "*t*" denote figures and tables, respectively.

A

Abstraction, 495–98, 669, 676
  in trait judgments, 328
Acoustic communication, 625, 643*n*2.
     See also Communication
Action(s)
  expressed, 336
  influenced by stimuli, 338–39
  integrated versus un-integrated,
    341–42
  irrational, 342
  overt, 336
  and perception, dissociation between,
    337–38
  prompted by supraliminal stimuli,
    339–41
  rational, 342
  recognition, of motor neuron
    system, 533
  self-regulation of
    goal-directed action, 733–34
    inhibition of, 734
    oculomotor orienting in, 734
  unconscious, 336–38
Adenocorticotropic hormone (ACTH),
    719, 768–69, 788, 790, 792
Adolescence, 992–99
  brain development during, 293–308,
    995–97, 996*f*
    age-related changes in, 297–99*t*
    causality, 307
    cortical grey matter and thickness,
      volume of, 304–5
    functional activations, 306–7
    functional connectivity, 303
    genes and environment, role of,
      307–8
    intelligence and functional
      connectivity, relationship
      between, 303–4
    myelination in white matter,
      volume of, 305–6
    peer-peer interactions, 302–3
    resistance to peer influences, 304
    risk-taking behavior, 303
    sensation-seeking
      behavior, 303
    task performance, 302
  cellular development during,
    994*f*, 995

disengagement, development of,
    230–31
early brain development and sensitive
    periods for learning, 993–95
executive function
    development of, 234
mentalizing, behavioral
    development of, 998
orienting, development of, 230
sex hormones, influence of, 998–99
social brain, functional
    development of, 997–98, 997*f*
Adult(s/hood)
  Alzheimer's dementia in, 767
  Asperger syndrome in, 835, 865
  autism spectrum disorder in, 232
    autobiographical memory deficits
      associated with, 872–73
  callous and unemotional
    traits in, 895, 896
  disengagement, development of,
    230–31
  executive function
    development of, 234
  orienting, development of, 230
  psychopathy in, 895
  ventromedial prefrontal cortex effect
    on social cognition, 937
Adult/Adolescent Sensory
    Profile (AASP), 869
Adult Asperger Assessment (AAA), 862
Adult-directed speech (ADS), 627.
    See also Speech
Affect, 158, 171, 196
  defined, 196
  unconscious, 197
    challenges to, 205–6
    limits of, 206
    unnoticed, 206
    unverbalized, 206
Affective components, of reward system,
    181–82. *See also* Human
    reward system; Rewards
Affective neuroscience, 69
  alexithymia and, 910–11
  video games influence on, 1006
Affective sharing, 551
Affective states, unconscious, 197
Afference binding, 342, 343*f*.
    See also Binding

Aggression
  instrumental, 896–97
  proactive, 885
  reactive, 885, 886, 896–97, 899
  video game violence effects on, 1002–4
Aging
  brain, socioemotional functioning in,
    507–17
  and decision-making behavior, 50
  paradox of, 508
  -related changes in neural function,
    609–10
Agreeableness, 244. *See also* Five-factor
    model, of personality
Air Combat Maneuvering, 1005
Alcoholism
  associated with alexithymia, 926
  associated with antisocial personality
    disorder, 887
  associated with chronic low-grade
    inflammation, 822
  effects on interpersonal behavior,
    407–8
Alerting system, 228–29
Alexithymia, 906–29
  affective and cognitive features of,
    907–9
  and affective neuroscience, 910–11
  anatomical neuroimaging findings in,
    923–24
  associated with lack of empathy, 925
  construct, emergence of, 906–7
  and emotional stimuli processing,
    links between, 911–12
  etiological considerations of, 909–10
  functional commissurectomy in, 910
  functional neuroimaging studies
    in clinical population, 922–23
    in healthy participants, 912–22
  as lack of socio-affective skills, 924–29
  Machiavellianism and, 926–27
  with posttraumatic stress disorder, 923
  psychometrical approach in healthy
    individuals, 924–26
  versus psychopathy, 927
  and socio-cognitive skills, links
    between, 911
  with somatoform disorders, 922–23
  types of, 907–8, 910
Alien hand syndrome, 337

Allogrooming, 569, 570–71, 572. *See also* Altruism
Alloparental behavior, 154. *See also* Behavior; Maternal behavior
Allostatic load, 570, 778, 795
Altruism, 40, 565–79. *See also* Empathy
  allogrooming, 570–71, 572
  animal evidence for, 569–70
  biological models of, 568
  consolation behavior, 571–72
  decision making and, 573–75
  defined, 567
  evolutionary, 567, 572
  food sharing, 570–71, 571*f*
  human altruism in neuroimaging, evidence for, 575–78
  intentional, 567
  origins of, 568–69
  psychological, 567, 573
  reciprocal, 568, 569
  relationship with moral sentiments, 481–83
  terminology of, 567–68
Altruistic motivations, 479–81. *See also* Motivation
Alzheimer's disease, 320, 456, 767, 938
American Journal of Bioethics–Neuroscience, 1016
Amphetamine, 703
  effects on primate behavior, 6
  effects on reward system, 1004
  effects on social dominance, 721–23
Amsterdam Alexithymia Scale, 909
Amygdala, 82, 199*f*, 421*f*, 993*f*
  activity associated with alexithymia, 921, 922
  activity associated with antisocial behavior, 887, 888
  activity associated with conduct disorder, 889
  activity associated with fear recognition, 413
  activity associated with impulsive aggression, 1016–17
  activity associated with interpersonal self-esteem defense, 605*f*, 606–7
  activity associated with racial categorization, 411–12, 735–36
  activation, modulation of, 213
  activity associated with deception, 967
  bilateral neonatal ablation of, 632
  damage associated with alterations in personality and behavior, 938–39
  experimental odor activation in, 269, 269*f*, 369
  extended, 200
  hypoactivation associated with autism spectrum conditions, 835, 838
  -prefrontal cortex down-regulation, 730–33, 735–36

primate, 684, 689–90
  responsiveness to threat stimuli, 899, 901
  role in attitude expression, 213–15
  role in attitude formation, 216–17, 261
  role in emotion recognition, 200, 254–58, 256*f*
  role in emotion regulation, 278, 750, 753, 754*f*, 781
  role in facial expression, 200, 399–400, 501
  role in impression formation, 412–13, 424, 426–29
  role in memory retrieval process, 328
  role in regulating appetitive behaviors, 366
  role in thought suppression, 368
  secondary to herpes simplex encephalitis, bilateral lesion of, 171, 172*f*
  sex-related functional asymmetry in, 64–65
  during socioemotional processing, age effects in, 509–10, 512–14, 516
  in subcortical circuits, 171
  in thalamocortical-limbic circuits, 171
Analysis of variance (ANOVA), 56
Anarchic hand syndrome, 337, 341
Anger, 61, 142, 197, 200, 206, 252, 257, 260, 261, 281, 286, 302–3, 395–97, 427, 428*f*, 437, 438, 478*f*, 480–82, 483*f*, 487, 507, 517, 552, 555, 606, 685, 689, 730, 754*f*, 794, 820, 842, 864, 877, 896, 897, 899, 901. *See also* Emotion(s)
Angular gyrus
  activity associated with antisocial behavior, 888–89
  activity associated with language acquisition, 629
Anhedonia, 155, 819
Animals. *See also individual species*
  altruism in, 569–70
  pair bonding in, 152–53
  physiological responses to social threat, 788–89
  response to babies' faces, 436
  response to face familiarity, 435
  response to facial attractiveness, 438
  response to facial expressions, 437
  reward system in
    motivational components of, 182
    neural circuitry of, 179–80
Anomalous face overgeneralization (AFO), 439. *See also* Face overgeneralization
Anterior attention networks, 229, 233
Anterior attention system, 229–33. *See also* Attention

Anterior cingulate cortex (ACC), 60, 72, 201, 229, 235, 421*f*, 993*f*. *See also* Cortex
  activation in response to emotional stimuli, 910
  activity associated with alexithymia, 913, 914, 922, 924
  activity associated with autism spectrum disorder, 870
  structural and functional abnormalities, 875
  activity associated with deception, 963, 963*f*
  activity associated with distancing, 284
  activity associated with facial expression, 400
  activity associated with reinterpretation, 283
  activity associated with response control on task, 737
  activity associated with social preferences, 950
  activity associated with strategic thinking, 957
  damage associated with alterations in personality and behavior, 364, 938
  dorsal. *See* Dorsal anterior cingulate cortex
  dorsomedial, 281
  functional neuroanatomy of, 365–66
  personality traits and, 246–49
  primate, 684, 690–92
  role in attitude change, 215–16, 219
  role in distress vocalization, 588
  role in emotion recognition, 260
  role in maintaining positive self-image, 329–30
  role in regulating appetitive behaviors, 367
  role in regulating racial bias, 369
  role in selective construal, 281, 282
  role in self-recognition, 327
  role in task distraction, 280
  role in thought suppression, 368
  during socioemotional processing, age effects in, 510–12, 514
  ventral, 329–30
  ventrolateral, 281
Anterior insula (AI), 60, 72, 421*f*, 993*f*
  activity associated with deception, 966, 970
  hypoactivation associated with autism spectrum conditions, 835
  role in self-recognition, 327
Anterior temporal lobe (aTL)
  activity associated with sentence processing, 671
  role in moral motivations, 479
Anterolateral prefrontal cortex, 352. *See also* Lateral prefrontal cortex

contributions to goal-directed social behavior, 356

goal-directed social behavior, evolutionarily adaptive neural architecture for, 355*f*

ontogenetic map of, 353, 353*f*

Anthropomorphism, 440, 835, 975, 979, 982, 984, 985

Anticipation
of continuity, 626–27
of emotional stimuli, 280, 510–11
human motor neuron system, 531
of pain, 327, 558
of public speaking, 606
recursive, 953
of rewards, 181–82, 187, 188, 214, 511
of social evaluation, 791
of threat, 609, 791–92

Antidepressants, 587–88
for depression, 819, 1019

Antisocial personality disorder (APD), 885–91, 896, 926
implications of, 890–91
neural basis of, 886–89
social neuroscience and, 886
in youths, 889–90

Antisocial Process Screening Device, 896

Ants, altruistic behavior in, 569

Anxiety, 72, 156, 171–73, 196, 197, 207, 244, 254, 593, 618, 748, 756, 790, 929
academic examination-induced, 820
anticipatory, 511
associated with behavioral inhibition, 236, 573–74
associated with skin conductance, 414
attachment, 591, 618
attention disengagement deficits and, 231–32
during deception, 967
executive function deficits and, 234–35
orienting and, 231–32
pain-related, 285
social, 155, 236–37, 286, 605, 606, 863
trait, 236, 237, 280, 281

Appearance-based impression formation, 426–28. *See also* Impression formation

Appetitive behaviors, self-regulation of, 366–68. *See also* Behavior

Appraisal, 274, 278, 808, 836. *See also* Reappraisal
cognitive, 557
critical, 11, 14–15
of MEG/EEG source models, 125–29
psychological processes related to, 808
statistical, 115, 119

Approach-avoidance disposition, 169–70, 169*f*, 174*f*, 198, 205

Approach-avoidance systems, higher neutral substrates mediating approach and, 170–74

Arginine vasopressin (AVP)
within central nervous system, behavioral effects of, 155
effect on social bonding, 154, 155, 157, 158, 159*f*, 160
endogenous, 155
exogenous, 155
intranasal administration of, 156

Arginine vasopressin receptor 1A (*AVPR1A*), 842

Arousal, 41, 155, 158, 197, 306, 365–67, 426, 499, 508, 517, 558, 614, 615, 866, 913
competitive, 201
emotional, 171, 214, 577, 751, 937
impact on learning, 656–57
physiological, 615
sexual, 201
video games influence on, 1006–7

Arterial spin labeling (ASL), 81–82

Articulatory development
importance of melody at the beginning of, 640–41

Artificial neural networks, 974

ArtRepair, 85

ASIMO, 975. *See also* Humanoid robots

Asperger syndrome, 835, 842, 850, 859–78, 928
associated with dysfunctional mirror neuron system, 868
associated with impairments in biological motion processing, 868
autobiographical memory deficits associated with, 872–73
cognitive style vs. socio-emotional disorder, 873–74
diagnostic criteria for, 860–61
differential diagnosis of, 861–62
executive dysfunction associated with, 869–71
functional connectivity abnormalities associated with, 875–78
versus high-functioning autism, 860, 861–62
imitation and, 866–69
outcome of, 862
prevalence of, 862
screening instruments for, 862
sensory processing abnormalities associated with, 869
social cognition and, 862–66
structural connectivity abnormalities associated with, 874–75
weak central coherence associated with, 871–72, 872–73

Asperger Syndrome Diagnostic Scale (ASDS), 862

Attachment
hidden regulators in, 151
mother-infant, 153
social, 151–60
theories of, 618

Attention
anterior, 229, 233–37
disengagement of, 228
executive, 227, 228–29, 233–37
impact on learning, 656–57
joint, 230, 234
obligatory, 229
perturbations in, 232–33
posterior, 229–33
re-engaging of, 228
selective, 280–81
shifting of, 228
visual, 229, 255

Attention deficit hyperactivity disorder (ADHD), 889, 898
social impairments, developmental origin of, 849
spectrum on behavioral and cognitive impairments, 851
video games and, 1008–9

Attention deployment, 278, 279. *See also* Emotion:regulation of
distraction, 279–80
selective attention, 280–81
selective construal, 281–82

Attention Network Task, 233

Attentional Blink paradigm, 873

Attitude, 212–22
change, 217–19, 895, 897, 898
expression, 212–16
formation, 216–17
political, 221–22

Attribution theories, of person perception, 419, 421–22

Auditory cortex, temporal voice area in. *See* Temporal voice area

Auditory-evoked potentials (AEPs), 385

Australian Scale for Asperger Syndrome (ASAS), 862

Autism Diagnostic Interview–Revised (ADI-R), 837

Autism spectrum conditions (ASC)
egocentrism in, 837
empathy in, 832
neural endophenotypes of social behavior in, 830–42
implications for, 841–42
social impairment, neural systems involved in, 837–40, 839*f*, 840*f*
theory of mind in, 832–36, 833–34*t*

Autism spectrum disorder (ASD), 152, 155, 200, 231–32, 322, 536–37, 559–60, 686, 922, 924–25, 927–29
abnormal cerebral voice processing in, 383–85, 384*f*

Autism spectrum disorder (*Continued*)
attention disengagement deficits and, 231–32
in children, 661–63, 662*f*
default mode network activity in, 876–77
diagnostic criteria for, 849
executive function deficits and, 234–35
high-functioning. *See*
High-functioning autism spectrum disorder
hypersystemizing theory of, 872
orienting and, 231
prevalence of, 850
social impairments, developmental origin of
on behavioral dimension, 849–50
on neurocognitive dimension, 850
spectrum on behavioral and cognitive impairments, 851
Autism Spectrum Quotient (AQ), 841
Autism Spectrum Screening Questionnaire (ASSQ), 862
Autobiographical memories (AMs), 327–28. *See also* Memory(ies)
deficits associated with autism spectrum disorder, 872–73
Automatic imitation, 341. *See also* Imitation
Autonomic nervous system, 152, 153
activity associated with loneliness, 768
regulated by neuroendocrine factors, 158–59
stress-related activity in, 614
Aversive conditioning, 257, 887, 895, 897, 898, 901. *See also* Conditioning
Avoidance behavior, 155. *See also* Behavior

B
Babbling, 635*f*, 637–40, 637*f*, 639*f*
Babies' faces
animal response to, 436
infant response to, 436
neural response to, 437
Baby face overgeneralization (BFO), 437. *See also* Face overgeneralization
Backward masking, 339
Bared-teeth display, 41. *See also* Facial expression
Baroreceptor cardiac reflexes, 165–66, 167*f*
Basal ganglia, 180, 229, 809
activity associated with Asperger syndrome, 874
damage associated with disgust, 257, 482
role in attitude change, 219
role in emotion recognition, 257
role in habit formation, 218–19
role in reinforcement learning, 217, 218
Beamformers, 122–23

Beck Depression Inventory, 63
BDI-13, 921, 925
Bed nucleus of the stria terminalis (BNST), 156, 172
Behavior
adaptive prosocial, 43
alloparental, 154
appetitive behaviors, self-regulation of, 366–68
approach, 155
avoidance, 155
bunching, 619
complex, in social neuroscience, 4–7
consolation, 571–72
consumption, 205
emotional. *See* Emotion(s)
evaluation of, 41
evolution of, 40–41
expectancy-consistent, 407–8, 408*f*
expectancy-violating, 407–9, 408*f*
goal-directed, 178–81, 348–57
male parental, 154
maternal, 154
positive, 152
preferential, 152
primate behavior, amphetamine effects on, 6
prosocial, 184, 568
repetitive, 871
risk-taking, 303
sensation-seeking, 303
sickness, 137
social, 152, 206–8
Behavioral Assessment of Dysexecutive Function, 460*t*
Behavioral development, of mentalizing during adolescence, 998
Behavioral experiments, in humanoid robots, 979–82
appearance of the agent, 982
motor interference effect, 980
motor priming effect, 980
movement kinematics effect on interference, 980, 983
rhythmic arm movements, 980, 981*f*
Behavioral game theory, 949. *See also* Game theory
Behavioral neuroscience, 1027
Behavioral surveys, 747
Behavioral variant of frontotemporal dementia (bvFTD), 938, 940
Behavior dysregulation
anterior cingulate damage and, 364
lateral PFC damage and, 363–64
ventromedial PFC damage and, 361–63
Belief learning, 955. *See also* Learning
Beliefs, 951–53. *See also* Iterated beliefs
equilibrium, 951
Benevolence, 481
Bermond-Vorst Alexithymia Questionnaire (BVAQ), 907, 909, 921–22, 925–26, 928

Bibliometry, 10
Big Five Inventory, 248
Binding, 342–43
efference, 342, 343*f*
efference-efference, 342, 343*f*
perceptual or afference, 342, 343*f*
Biocultural co-constructivism theory, 743
Biological models, of altruism, 568. *See also* Altruism
Biological motion processing
impairment in, associated with autism spectrum disorder, 868
Biological origins, of personality, 244–45. *See also* Personality
Blister model of wound healing, 142. *See also* Dermal wound healing; Wound healing
Blood oxygenation level-dependent (BOLD) signal, 72, 76–80, 76*f*, 295, 302, 303. *See also* Functional magnetic resonance imaging
contrast-to-noise ratio, 83
hemodynamic response functions of, 77–78, 78*f*
influence of hemodynamic response on T_2*-weighted signal in, 77, 77*f*
to measure regional brain activity, 81
rest intervals and jitter, 78–80
Blood oxygen-level dependent (BOLD) activity, 218
Body posture, 261
Body weight
effects on social rank, 719
Borderline personality disorder (BPD), 907, 926, 955
Boundary element method (BEM), 117–19
Box games, 952
Brain. *See also* Socioemotional functioning, in aging brain
activity
induced, 106, 112
ongoing, 103, 111, 112
anatomy of, 293–94
computational neuroanatomy of, 295–96
connectivity
analysis, using MEG/EEG, 112–13
connectome, 113
development, during adolescence, 995–97, 996*f*
evolution of relative brain size, in primates. *See under* Primates
function, 302–4
psychoactive drugs for manipulating, 1019–20
imaging, 1016. *See also* Functional magnetic resonance imaging; Magnetic resonance imaging; Positron emission tomography

preferences, prediction of, 1018
premature adoption, risks of, 1018–19
threat to privacy, 1018
maturation, imaging-based evidence of, 304–7
mechanisms, neural basis of, 3–7
networks, 113, 128*f*
as organ of the soul, 9
regions involvement in moral cognition, 478*f*
social. *See* Social brain
socially adapted, 660–61
social visual, 398–400
structure-function correlation, 302
structure of
grey matter, age differences in, 299, 302
imaging, 294–95
white matter, age differences in, 296, 299, 300*f*, 301*f*
Brain-based lie detection, 1018
Brainstem
decerebration of, 169–70
model of cry production, 632
role in affective reactions, 199, 199*f*
Brainvox system, 54–55
Broca's aphasia, 670–71
Broken mirror theory, 868
Brunner-Munzel test, 56
Bubbles method, 254–55, 255*f*
Bunching behavior, 619. *See also* Behavior

C

California Adult Q-set (CAQ), 909
Callous-unemotional traits, 890, 895–98
Canvas, 141
Cardiovascular disease (CVD), 152, 782
Cardiovascular function
social neuroscientific pathways linking social support to, 805
Card Sorting Tests, 460, 460*t*
Caregiving, chronic stress associated with, 818
Cartoon tasks, 463*t*
description of task, 468
links to functional outcome, 469
relationship to traumatic brain injury, 468–69
relationship to ventral frontal damage, 468–69
Caudate nucleus, 421*f*
effect on human reward system, 179, 179*f*, 180, 182, 184, 186
role in impression formation, 423
during socioemotional processing, age effects in, 511
Causality, 113
CB-i (Computational Brain Interface), 976–77, 976*f*, 978. *See also* Humanoid robots
Cell phone, 5

Cellular development, during adolescence, 994*f*, 995. *See also* Adolescence
Central coherence
weak, associated with autism spectrum disorder, 871–72
Central pattern generators (CPG), 977
Cerebral cortex, 293. *See also* Cortex
cellular composition of, 294, 294*f*
Cerebral spinal fluid (CSF), 703
Chameleon effect, 979
Charlie & the Chocolates Test, 463*t*
description of task, 464–65
relationship to functional outcome, 465
relationship to traumatic brain injury, 465
relationship to ventral frontal damage, 465
Child(ren/hood)
Asperger syndrome in, 868
autism spectrum disorder in, 231–32, 322, 661–63, 662*f*, 537, 834, 849–50, 936
bipolar disorder in, 897
brain development during, 293–308
age-related changes in, 297–99*t*
casuality, 307
cortical grey matter and thickness, volume of, 304–5
functional activations, 306–7
genes and environment, role of, 307–8
myelination in white matter, volume of, 305–6
conduct disorder in, 852, 886
developmental disorders in, 459
disengagement, development of, 230–31
disintegrative disorder in, 860
disorder, developmental divergence from, 852–53
executive function
development of, 234
maltreatment effect on psychopathy, 899
mirror neuron system activity in, 532
mirror self-recognition of, 316–17
with negative temperamental reactivity, 235–36
oppositional defiant disorder in, 852
orienting, development of, 230
social preferences of, 951
traumatic brain injury in, 939
ventromedial prefrontal cortex effect on social cognition, 937
Childhood Asperger's Screening Test (CAST), 862
Chimpanzee(s). *See also* Animals; Mammals; Monkeys
altruistic behavior in, 569
facial expression in, 44, 45–46
individuals and relationships, recognition of, 43

mirror self-recognition of, 316
social affordances, recognition of, 43
social cognition in, 40, 42
traits or behavior in, 40–41
Chi-square test, 56
Chronic diseases, 769
inflammation associated with, 820
Classical conditioning, 4, 216, 217, 271, 339, 888. *See also* Conditioning
CNR1 gene, 842
Cocaine
effects on social dominance, 722, 723
Cog, 986. *See also* Humanoid robots
Cognition
behavioral patterns associates with, 33–34
embedded, 492, 498–500
embodied, 492, 498
and emotion, 196
holistic versus analytic, 746–47
influence of loneliness on, 771
moral cognition, brain regions involvement in, 478*f*
motor, 977
off-loading, 499–500
social. *See* Social cognition
visuospatial, 1004–5
Cognitive appraisal. *See also* Appraisal
effects on brain response to other people's suffering, 557
Cognitive change, 278, 282–84
distancing, 284
reappraisal, 283
reinterpretation, 283–84
Cognitive control
deficits associated with autism spectrum disorder, 873–74
video game effects on cognition associated with, 1005–6
Cognitive neuroscience, 69, 1027–28
of person perception, 405–11
of psychopathy, 897–98
of strategic thinking, 949–58
beliefs and strategic choice, 951–53
social preferences, 950–51
strategic awareness, 950
strategic teaching and influence value, 953–54
Cognitive self, 326, 327–29. *See also* Self
Coke®, 182
Collective unconscious, 315
Communication, 40, 668–77
acoustic, 625, 643*n*2
face-to-face, 318, 672, 673
mother-infant, 627–29
social cognition and, 44–45
vocal, 625
Comparison Question Test (CQT), 962–64, 966, 967
Compassion, 59, 349, 478, 481–83, 487, 552, 553, 561, 567, 772, 887

content-specific
representations, 424
subsequent neural responses to
others, changing, 423–24
social versus nonsocial, 422–23
Inclusion of Other in Self scale (IOS), 497
Inclusive fitness, 568
Independent component analysis (ICA),
92, 110, 545–46
Indignation, 478, 480–83, 483f, 487
Individualism-collectivism, 746, 748,
750, 754
culture-gene coevolution of, 756, 757f
Individuals, recognition of, 42–43
Induced brain activity, 106, 112. See also
Brain activity
Infants. See also Human infants' crying;
Human infants' vocal sounds,
melodic development of;
Newborn infants
autism spectrum disorder in, 231, 849
communicate with, using melody,
627–29
disengagement, development of, 230
effect of ventromedial prefrontal
cortex on social cognition, 937
executive function development of,
233–34
hominine, 627
melody, inherent appreciation of,
629–31
mirror neuron system activity in, 532
orienting, development of, 229–30
response to babies' faces, 436
response to face familiarity, 435
response to facial attractiveness,
438–39
response to facial expressions, 437
Infant-directed speech (IDS), 627–29.
See also Speech
Inferior frontal gyrus (IFG), 840, 993f
activity associated with deception,
963, 963f, 968
role in emotion perception, 555
role in self-face recognition, 319
role in self-recognition, 327
Inferior frontal sulcus (IFS), 840
Inferior occipital cortex, role in self-face
recognition, 320. See also
Cortex
Inferior occipital gyrus (IOG), role in face
expression, 400
Inferior parietal lobe
activity associated with deception,
963, 963f
role in self-face recognition, 319–20
Inferior temporal cortex. See also Cortex
primate, 694–95
role in emotion recognition, 254
Infinite impulse response (IIR), 108
Inflammation, 814–24
acute, 814, 815f
associated with depression, 819–21

associated with chronic
diseases, 820
depression treatment,
impact of, 819
in epidemiological and clinical
studies, association between,
819–20
pharmacologically-induced, 819
associated with negative emotions,
820, 821f
behavioral pathways linking, 822
physiological pathways linking,
822–23
associated with social relationships,
821–22
associated with stress, 820–21
acute, 817–18
chronic, 818–19
modular mechanisms linking, 823
physiological pathways
linking, 824f
chronic, 814, 816, 816f
health behaviors associated with, 823f
and mood, bidirectional relationships
between, 820
Influence model, 954
Innate immune cells, 136
Institute for Scientific
Information (ISI), 23
Instrumental aggression, 896–97. See also
Aggression
Insula, 201–2
activity associated with social
preferences, 950
activity associated with strategic
thinking, 956–57
in empathy, role of, 558–59
role in body posture and
movement, 261
role in emotion recognition,
257–61
role in task distraction, 280
Insular cortex, 199f. See also Cortex
role in attitude expression, 213
Intelligence, 302, 320, 381, 837,
860, 900
and functional connectivity,
relationship between, 303–4
Machiavellian, 29, 30, 39–40, 46
strategic, 952, 956, 957
Intentional altruism, 567. See also
Altruism
Intentional deception, 1017–18
Intentionality competencies, in primates,
34–35, 35f. See also Primates
Intentional trait inferences, 408
Intentionality Detector (ID), 986
Interaction-based impression formation.
See also Impression
formation
experience-based, 425–26
for predicting others' intentions,
424–26

Interethnic ideology, 758
Interferon (IFN)-α, 819, 823
Interferon (IFN)-γ, 820
Interleukin-1β (IL-1β), 793, 815,
817–20, 823
Interleukin-2 (IL-2), 819
Interleukin-6 (Il-6), 789, 793, 796–98,
806, 815, 817–23
Interleukin-8 (IL-8), 818, 822
Interleukin-10 (IL-10), 815
Intermediate phenotypes, 831, 832f.
See also Endophenotypes
Intermittent explosive disorder, 897
International Affective Picture System
(IAPS), 282, 407, 510–13,
913, 914, 922
Interoceptive cortex in empathy, role of,
558. See also Cortex
Interparietal sulcus (IPS), 993f
Interpersonal behavior, alcohol's effects on,
407–8. See also Behavior
Interpersonal Reactivity Index
Perspective Taking subscale, 62
Interpersonal self-esteem defense, 604–7
future directions of, 609
implications of, 609–10
negative associations with striatum,
605f, 607
positive associations with amygdala,
605f, 606–7
positive associations with dorsal
anterior cingulate cortex,
605–6, 605f
on positive self-evaluations, 607–8
on social exclusion, 608
Interpersonal warmth, 497–98. See also
Warmth
Intersubjective coordination
impact on learning, 657–59, 657f
Intonation, 630, 631, 637, 643n8, 676.
See also Language; Speech
Intraparietal sulcus (IPS), 749
Intrapersonal self-esteem defense, 601–4
future directions of, 609
implications of, 609–10
negative associations with dorsal
anterior cingulate cortex
activity, 602–4, 602f
negative associations with
orbitofrontal cortex activity,
601, 602f, 603, 604
positive associations with medial
prefrontal cortex activity, 602f,
603, 604
on positive self-evaluations, 607–8
on social exclusion, 608
Inverse modeling problem, MEG/EEG
source estimation, 114–15
ill-posed, 115
Iowa Gambling Task (IGT), 64, 510
Iowa Scales of Personality Change, 63
Iterated beliefs, 951–53. See also Beliefs
Iterative-reprocessing model, 173–74

Miltown, for manipulating normal brain function, 1019

Minimum-norm (MN) model, 124–25

Minnesota Multiphasic Personality Inventory-2, 63

Mirror neuron system (MNS), 321–22, 341, 494, 525–37, 669, 978–79
  activity in children, 532
  activity in infants, 532
  dysfunctions of, 536
    associated with autism spectrum disorder, 868–69
  emotions and, 533
  for empathy, role of, 554–56, 568–69
  in humans
    existence of, 528
    localization of, 528–30
  in monkeys, 525–28, 526f
    action discrimination, 528
    auditory, 528
    object directed actions of, 526–27
    occlusion of, 528
  motor
    action recognition, 533
    imitation, 533–34
    language, evolution of, 534–35
    learning by observation, 535
    prediction, 535
    support mentalizing, 535–36
  object and non-object directed actions of, 530
    anticipation, 531
    auditory, 530–31
    correlation with empathy, 531
    goals and means of, 530
  pain and, 533
  plasticity and development
    expertise, 531
    Hebbian learning, 531–32
    neonatal imitation, 532
    training, 531
  primate, 692–93
  touch and, 532–33

Mirror-recognition, 316–17, 320

Mirror touch synesthesia, 536–37

Mobius syndrome, 555

Moderational model, of emotion regulation, 616–18, 616f. See also Emotion:regulation of

Modular composition, of melody complexity, 638, 640

Monkeys. See also Animals; Chimpanzee; Cynomolgus monkeys; Macaque monkey; Mammals; Rhesus macaque; Squirrel monkeys; Titi monkey
  altruistic behavior in, 569
  consolation behavior in, 571
  formation of social hierarchy in, 717, 718
  imitative behavior in

evolutionary and methodological considerations of, 543–44
  neural precursors of, 543
  vocal learning and, 547–48
impact of social isolation on, 5
mirror neuron system in, 525–28, 526f
  action discrimination, 528
  auditory, 528
  object directed actions, 526–27
  occlusion of, 528
motor neuron system in, localization of, 554
sensitivity to speaker's vocal identity, in right anterior temporal lobe, 388
social preferences of, 950–51
traits or behavior in, 40–41
voice selectivity in auditory cortex, 382, 383f

Monte-Carlo simulation, 126

Mood and inflammation, bidirectional relationships between, 820

"Mood as information" model, 573

Moral versus psychopathy, 22f

Moral judgment, 58–59

Moral knowledge
  cognitive-anatomical definition of, 484–85, 484f
  context-dependent and -independent forms of, 485, 485f

Moral motivations, 479–84. See also Motivation
  altruistic and self-serving motivations, 479–81
  cognitive-anatomical definition of, 479

Moral reasoning
  cognitive-anatomical definition of, 485, 487
  fronto-limbic top-down control models of, 487
  fronto-temporo-mesolimbic integration models of, 487–88

Moral responsibility, 1021–22

Moral sentiments, 478
  functional imaging studies of, 482–83, 483f
  other-critical, 482
  relationship with altruism, 481–83

Moral value, 479

Morphine
  effects on social dominance, 723

Motherese, social and communicative function of, 627–29

Mother-infant attachment, 153. See also Attachment

Motion correction, preprocessing fMRI data, 86

Motivation
  altruistic, 479–81
  moral, 479–84
  self-serving, 479–81

Motivational components, of reward system, 182–83. See also Human reward system; Rewards

Motor interference effect, 980

Motor priming effect, 980

Motor resonance, in social cognition, 978

Motor theory, of empathy, 555. See also Empathy

μ-Opioid receptor gene, 767, 778

Mu rhythm suppression
  over sensorimotor cortex during action perception, 554–55

Multicolinearity, 77

Multilevel analysis, 12

Multiple-arc melodies and rhythmical variations, 636–37, 637f

Multiple determinism, 6, 12

Multiple signal classification (MUSIC), 122–23

Music and language, relationship between, 626–27. See also Melody

N

Naloxone, 156

Narcissism, 317

National Alliance on Mental Illness (NAMI), 1022

National Institutes of Health, 683

Natural selection, 743f, 744, 748

Near infrared spectroscopy (NIRS), 435, 628, 662

Negativity bias, 168, 169f, 170

Neglect and psychopathy, 898, 899

Neocortex
  behavioral patterns associates with, 33–34
  volume, executive function competencies associated with, 34–35, 35f

NEO Five-Factor Inventory, 247

Neonatal imitation, 532. See also Imitation

Neonates' crying, basic melody types of, 633–35, 633f, 635f

NEO Personality Inventory (NEO-PI-R), 246–48

Neophobia, 155

Neural basis, of emotional processing, 198–99. See also Emotion(s)

Neural commitment, 651

Neural endophenotypes. See also Endophenotypes
  of social behavior in autism spectrum conditions, 830–42

Neural generators models, 116

Neural network, 325, 326, 328, 330, 331, 978

Neural response
  to babies' faces, 437
  to face familiarity, 436
  to facial attractiveness, 439
  to facial expressions, 437

Neuroeconomics, 69

Neuroendocrine function
social neuroscientific pathways linking social support to, 805–6
Neuroethics, 1015–23
of brain imaging, 1016, 1018–19
emergence of, 1015–16
of human rights, 1022
of imaging mental states, 1017–18
of imaging psychological traits, 1016–17
of moral responsibility, 1021–22
of neuroendocrine manipulation, 1020–21
psychopharmacology and brain stimulation, developments in, 1019–20
of religion and spirituality, 1022
of self and personal identity, 1022–23
Neuroethics, 1016
Neurogenetics, 748–49
Neuroimaging experiments, in humanoid robots, 982–83
arms and hand movements, 982
facial expressions of emotions, 983, 983*f*
Neuroimaging Informatics Tools and Resources Clearinghouse (NITRC), 94
Neuroimaging studies, of social rewards, 184, 186. *See also* Social rewards
Neuromarketing, 1017
Neuronal recycling theory, 749–50
Neuropeptide hormones, 154
Neuroplasticity theory, 750
Neuropsychological perspectives, of social neuroscience, 49–65
Neuroticism, 244–46, 249. *See also* Five-factor model, of personality
Neurovariation theory, 750
Newborn infants. *See also* Infants
perceptual preferences for melodies and rhythms, 630–31
NF-κB, 770, 821, 823
Nihilism, 1021–23
NLGN4X, 842
Nonadditive determinism, 6, 12
Non-congruent neuron system, 526, 527
Nonhuman primates, social cognition in, 41–42. *See also* Primates
Non-rapid eye movement (NREM) parasomnias, 203
Non-verbal learning disability, 851
versus Asperger syndrome, 861–62
Normalization, preprocessing fMRI data, 86–87
NR3C1 gene, 770
NTRK1, 842
Nucleus accumbens (NAcc), 157, 171, 158, 199*f*
effect on human reward system, 179–81, 179*f*

role in affective reactions, 200, 201
role in attitude expression, 214, 215
role in body posture and movement, 261
role in memory retrieval process, 328
role in regulating appetitive behaviors, 366, 367
Nucleus of the solitary tract (NTS), 158

O

Obsessive-compulsive disorder (OCD), 861
Occipitoparietal cortex. *See also* Cortex
status-related differential neural response in, 707
Oculomotor orienting, in self-regulation of action, 734. *See also* Action(s)
Odor-evoked memory, 265–75. *See also* Memory
characteristics of, 269–74
emotionality, 270–72
evocativeness, 270–72
rarity, 272–73
vividness, 270
methodology and findings, history of, 266–69
phenomenology of, 274
Off-loading cognition, 499–500. *See also* Cognition
Olfaction, 265, 553
and emotion, neuroanatomical connection between, 272
Ongoing brain activity, 103, 111, 112. *See also* Brain activity
Ontogeny explanation, for trait/behavior, 41
Openness to experience, 244–49. *See also* Five-factor model, of personality
Operant conditioning, 339. *See* Conditioning
Opiates, 587–88
Opioids
effects on social dominance, 723
and pair bonding, 156–57
Oppositional defiant disorder (ODD), 852, 886
Optimism, 779, 781
Oral wound healing, 141. *See also* Wound healing
comparison with dermal wound healing, 142–43
Orbital prefrontal cortex. *See also* Prefrontal cortex
damage associated with alterations in personality and behavior, 937
Orbitofrontal cortex (OFC), 82, 421*f*. *See also* Cortex
activity associated with antisocial behavior, 887, 888

activity associated with intrapersonal self-esteem defense, 601, 602*f*, 603, 604
activity associated with reversal learning, 897
dorsolateral, 218
effect on human reward system, 179–83, 179*f*
medial, 950
personality traits and, 247
primate, 693–94
response to face familiarity, 436
role in attitude change, 218–19
role in attitude expression, 213
associated with subjective evaluation, 215
role in attitude formation, 217
role in body posture and movement, 261
role in emotion recognition, 253–54
role in face expression, 399, 400
role in reward-based reinforcement learning, 977
role in selective attention, 281
ventromedial, 218
Orienting, 227, 228–29
in clinical populations, 231–33
development of
in adolescence, 230
in adulthood, 230
in childhood, 230
in infancy, 229–30
endogenous, 228
exogenous, 228
impaired, 232
nonsocial, 231
perturbations in, 232–33
reflexive, 230
social, 231
volitional, 230
Overt actions, 336. *See also* Action(s)
Oxytocin (OT), 154, 186, 842, 1020–21
effect on social bonding, 154, 155, 158–60, 159*f*
exogenous, 156, 160
intranasal administration of, 155–56
Oxytocin receptor (*OXTR*), 766–67, 842

P

P2, 975. *See also* Humanoid robots
P3, 975. *See also* Humanoid robots
Pain
empathic brain responses to, 553–54, 556, 557
cognitive appraisal effects on, 557
and mirror neuron system, 533
Pair bonding, 33. *See also* Social bonding
Paired-associate cross-modal paradigm, 267, 267*f*, 271
PANAS scale, 200
Parabrachial nucleus (PBN), 199, 199*f*

role in attitude expression, 213
  associated with subjective
    evaluation, 215–16
role in emotion regulation, 369–70
role in facial expression, 400
role in intentional control, 730, 731*f*
role in maintaining positive self-image,
  329–30
role in memory retrieval process, 328
role in regulating racial bias, 369
role in selective attention, 280
role in selective construal, 281
role in self-awareness, 320
role in task distraction, 280
role in thought suppression, 368–69
ventral, 479
ventromedial. *See* Ventromedial
  prefrontal cortex
ventrolateral, 280, 281, 283, 512,
  963, 965
Prejudice, 13, 219–21, 340, 341, 368,
  369, 371, 412, 436, 446, 450,
  491, 729–31, 736–38, 795
Pretend play, 326
Pride, 184, 196, 206, 252, 317, 478, 481,
  482–83, 483*f*, 576. *See also*
  Emotion(s)
Primary reinforcers, 178, 181. *See also*
  Rewards
Primary visual cortex, 71. *See also* Cortex
Primate social behavior, neurobiology of,
  683–95
  neural systems approach to social
    brain, 684–86
  social brain, putative structures of
    amygdala, 689–90
    anterior cingulate cortex, 690–92
    inferior temporal cortex, 694–95
    mirror neurons, 692–93
    orbitofrontal cortex, 693–94
  social processing,
    model of, 688–89, 688*f*
Primates
  behavior, effects of amphetamine on, 6
  evolution of large brains in, 28–29,
    29*f*
    ontogenetic hypotheses, 29
    ecological hypotheses, 29
    social hypotheses, 29, 30
    testing of hypotheses, 30–33, 32*f*
  behavioral patterns associated with
    cognitive mechanisms, 33–34
  executive function competencies
    associated with relative
    neocortex volume, 34–35, 35*f*
  evolution of relative brain size in, 46
  evolution of social vision in, 397
  model, formation of social hierarchy
    in, 717–18
  nonhuman primates, social cognition
    in, 41–42
  vocalization, prosodic
    properties in, 625

Priming
  cultural, 747, 754
  sequential, 450–51
  supraliminal, 340, 341
Principal Components Analysis (PCA),
  92, 110, 122
Prisoner's Dilemma, 40, 1017
Private self-awareness, 316–17. *See also*
  Self-awareness
Proactive aggression, 885. *See also*
  Aggression
Production, 670
Proliferation assays, 135
Prosocial behavior, 184, 568. *See also*
  Behavior
Prosociality, genetic effects on, 841
Prosody, 643*n*8
Prosopagnosia, 380
  and expressive agnosia, dissociation
    between, 399
Protolanguage, 641. *See also* Language
Prozac, for major depressive disorder,
  1019
Psychiatry, fMRI-based lie-detection in,
  969–70
Psychoactive drugs, for manipulating
  normal brain function,
  1019–20
Psycho-education. *See also* Education
  for stress induced by wound
    healing, 141
Psychological altruism, 567, 573. *See also*
  Altruism
Psychological scaffolding, 500
Psychological traits, imaging, 1016
Psychology
  emotion research in, 196–97
  experimental, 204
  of learning, 491
  social, 491
Psychoneuroimmunology (PNI), in vivo
  assessment of, 134–45
Psychopathy, 895–902
  alexithymia versus, 927
  cognitive neuroscience of, 897–98
  defined, 895–96
  due to early physical/sexual
    abuse, 898
  due to early neglect, 898
  moral versus, 22*f*
  for social cognitive neuroscience,
    implications of, 900–901
Psychopathy Checklist–Revised (PCL-R),
  895, 926
Psychopathy Checklist–Youth
  Version, 896
Psychophysics studies, of human mirror
  neuron system, 529
Psychophysiological interaction method
  (PPI), 922
Psychosomatic disorders, 922
Psychotherapy, fMRI-based
  lie-detection in, 969–70

Public self-awareness, 317–18. *See also*
  Self-awareness
Punch biopsies, 141–42. *See also* Dermal
  wound healing; Wound
  healing
Putamen
  effect on human reward system, 179,
    179*f*, 180, 182

Q

QRIO, 975, 984. *See also* Humanoid
  robots
Quantitative polymerase chain reaction
  (qPCR), 145
Questionnaire Measure of Emotional
  Empathy (QMEE), 841

R

Rabbit. *See also* Animals; Mammals
  impact of social isolation on, 5
Race, 369, 409–11, 410*f*
  bias in response latencies, 450–51
  effects on event-related brain
    potentials, 447
  perceiver and target group
    membership, effects of,
    447–49
Race-biased emotion, self-regulation of,
  735–36
Racial categorization
  amygdala activity associated with, 412
  fusiform gyrus activity associated with,
    411–12
Racial discrimination, 220–21
Random field theory (RFT), 87
Rank order test, 56
Rapid serial visual presentation (RSVP),
  106
Rarity and odor-evoked memory, 272–73
Rats. *See also* Animals; Mammals
  altruistic behavior in, 569
  dopamine receptor effects on pair
    bonding, 157
  impact of opiates on separation
    distress, 157
  impact of social isolation on, 5
Reactive aggression, 885, 886, 896–97,
  899. *See also* Aggression
Reading the Mind in the Eyes Test, 463*t*,
  835, 838, 841
  description of task, 465
  links to functional outcome, 466
  relationship to traumatic brain injury,
    465–66
  relationship to ventral frontal damage,
    465–66
Reappraisal, 283. *See also* Appraisal
Reasoning, 953
Recall information, 405
Reciprocal altruism, 569–70. *See also*
  Altruism
  theory of, 568
Reciprocal determinism, 6, 12

Reciprocal innervation, 168
Reciprocity
    impact on learning, 657
Recognition of Faux Pas Task, 456
Recursion, 669
Region of interest analysis (ROI), 55
Regularization, 115
Reinforcement learning, 954, 955. *See also*
    Learning
Reinterpretation, 283–84
Relationships, recognition of, 42–43
Relaxation techniques
    for stress induced by wound
        healing, 141
Religion, 1022
Repeated Fixed Opponent Ultimatum
    Game, 61–62, 62*f*
Repliee Q2, 976*f*. *See also* Humanoid
    robots
    perception of actions, 985
Repression, 970
Resident-intruder/social defeat model, 718
Response inhibition, 302, 365, 368, 459,
        734, 963, 965, 968
    in autism, neural basis of, 870
    in patients with antisocial personality
        disorders, 886, 887
    right frontal cortex associated
        with, 737
Response modulation, 278
Resting-state neural correlates, of
        personality, 246–47. *See also*
        Personality
Restricted maximum
        likelihood (ReML), 89
Retrosplenial cortex (RSpl). *See also*
        Cortex
    activity associated with strategic
        thinking, 957
Rett's disorder, 860
Reversal learning, 218, 895, 897, 898.
        See also Learning
Reverse inference, 1017
Reward-based reinforcement learning,
        977. *See also* Learning
Rewards
    circuit, 439
    defined, 178, 181
    human. *See* Human reward system
    monetary, 178, 181, 188*f*
    predicted, 954
    primary, 178, 187*t*, 188*f*
    processing, 178
    secondary, 178, 187*t*, 188*f*
    social. *See* Social rewards
Rhesus macaque (*Macaca mulatta*).
        See also Monkeys
    early life stress induced by
        gene-environment
        interactions, 778
    social behavior of, 683–84
    social brain, putative structures of
        amygdala, 689, 690

anterior cingulate cortex, 691
    orbitofrontal cortex, 694
Rheumatoid arthritis, 815, 818
Right anterior temporal lobe, sensitivity
        to speaker's vocal identity in,
        387–88
Right medial frontal lobe
    damage associated with alterations in
        personality and behavior, 938
Right ventrolateral prefrontal cortex
        (RVLPFC). *See also* Prefrontal
        cortex
    activity in regulating emotional
        responses to tasks, 781–82
    responses to stress, 780
Right-hemisphere dominance, for self-face
        recognition, 326. *See also*
        Self-face recognition
"Risk as feelings" model, 573
Risk-taking behavior, 303. *See also*
        Behavior
RoboCub, 977
Rodent models, formation of social
        hierarchy in, 717
Rorschach Apperception Test, 926
Rourke syndrome, 861–62
Rubber-hand illusion (RHI), 327

S

Sadness, 184, 196, 197, 206, 244, 252,
        260, 261, 283, 286, 438, 517,
        555, 559, 577,
691, 769, 790, 819, 886, 898, 899, 967.
        See also Emotion(s)
Sarcasm/Irony Tasks, 463*t*
    description of task, 467
    links to functional outcome, 467–68
    relationship to traumatic brain
        injury, 467
    relationship to ventral frontal
        damage, 467
Schadenfreude, 186, 557, 573, 578, 950.
        See also Emotions
Schizoid personality disorder, 907
    versus Asperger syndrome, 861
Schizophrenia, 246
Science Citation Index (SCI), 23
Secondary reinforcers, 178, 181. *See also*
        Rewards
Secondhand information-based impression
        formation, 420–24. *See also*
        Impression formation
    content-specific representations, 424
    subsequent neural responses to others,
        changing, 423–24
Selective attention, 280–81. *See also*
        Attention; Attention
        deployment
Selective construal, 281–82. *See also*
        Attention deployment
Selective serotonin reuptake inhibitors
        (SSRIs)
    for depression, 1021

for manipulating normal brain
        function, 1019
Self, 256, 325–32, 779, 1022–23
    cognitive, 326, 327–29
    cultural influences on neural
        representations of, 754, 755*f*
    defined, 326
    distinguished from other, 836–37
    embodied, 326–27
    emotional, 326, 329–30
    as a unifying and unique entity,
        330–31
Self-appraisal, emotional, 836. *See also*
        Appraisal
Self-awareness, 314–22
    defined, 315–16
    emotional, 836
    private, 316–17
    public, 317–18
    role of brain regions in, 320
Self-deception, 970. *See also* Deception
Self-enhancement, 320
Self-esteem, 317, 318, 590, 599–610,
        768, 779–82, 790, 808, 810,
        909. *See also* Interpersonal
        self-esteem defense;
        Intrapersonal self-esteem
        defense
Self-evaluation, 320–21
Self-face recognition, 326–27. *See also*
        Self-recognition
    left-hemisphere dominance for, 326
    right-hemisphere dominance for, 326
Self-introspection, emotional, 836
Self-photograph recognition, 320
Self-recognition, 316, 319–20
Self-reference effect (SRE), 329
Self-referential processing
    in autism spectrum conditions, 834*t*,
        836–37
Self-reflection, 887
Self-regulation, 360–72, 551, 729–38
    of action
        control of, 736–37
        goal-directed action, 733–34
        inhibition of, 734, 737
        oculomotor orienting in, 734
    of appetitive behaviors, 366–68
    attention to racial cues, 737–38
    of emotions, 730–33
    emotion regulation, 369–70
    failure of, 371–72
    intergroup bias, 738
    in intergroup relations, 729–30
    neural models of, 734–35
    of perceptual processing, 734
        to racial cues, 737–38
    of race-biased emotion, 735–36
    relies on a domain general
        resource, 371
    of sensory input, 734
    stereotypic thoughts,
        control of, 733

of stereotypes, 736
of thought, 368–69
Self-report paradox, 339
Self-serving motivations, 479–81.
    See also Motivation
Sensation-seeking behavior, 303.
    See also Behavior
Sense of relationship
    impact on learning, 659–60
SENSE, 83
Sensor array modeling, 116
Sensory input, self-regulation of, 734
Sensory processing abnormalities, in
    patients with Asperger
    syndrome, 869
Sensu stricto hypothesis, 30. *See also* Social
    brain hypothesis
Serotonergic neurotransmitter system,
    703–4
Serotonergic systems
    effect of social defeat on, 722
Sex differences, 63–65
    functional asymmetry of amygdala
        and, 64–65
    functional asymmetry of ventromedial
        prefrontal cortex and, 63–64
    in pair bonding, 154–55
    in personality traits, 245
Sex hormones, influence in adolescence,
    998–99
Shame, 206, 244, 252, 317, 478, 481,
    788, 790, 793, 794, 796. *See
    also* Emotion(s)
    associated with inflammation, 820
Shared attention, 986
Shared Attention Module (SAM), 986
Shared representation, 553
SICAM-1, 818
Signal classification approaches, 122–23
Signal space separation (SSS), 110
Signal-to-noise ratio (SNR), 101, 122
Simulation, 493–95, 553, 836
Simulation of Smiles Model (SIMS),
    500–503, 502*f*
Situation modification, 278
Situation selection, 278
Situational information, 419–20
Situational sampling, 747
64-item Inventory of Interpersonal
    Problems (IIP-64), 925
SLC6A4 gene, 842
Sleep murders, 204
Slice timing correction, preprocessing
    fMRI data, 86
Smell, 265, 267, 269, 272
    empathic brain responses to, 553
Smile(s). *See also* Facial expression
    affiliative, 500, 502*f*
    dominance, 500, 501, 502*f*
    enjoyment, 500, 502*f*
Smoothing, preprocessing fMRI data, 87
Social affordances, recognition of, 43–44
Social anxiety, 155. *See also* Anxiety

Social attachment, 151–60. *See also*
    Attachment
Social baseline model, of emotion
    regulation, 618–19. *See also*
    Emotion:regulation of
Social behavior, 152. *See also* Behavior
    adaptive, 227, 233
    associates with cognitive mechanisms,
        33–34
    conscious emotions in, 206–8
    unconscious emotions in, 206–8
Social bonding, 30, 31, 34, 151–60
    autonomic nervous system,
        regulation of, 158–59
    consequences of, 152
    dopamine and, 157
    early experiences and, 160
    formation of, 153
    impact of developmental factors on,
        159–60
    maternal behavior and, 154
    measurement of, 152–53
    opioids and, 156–57
    proximity and, 153–54
    social engagement and, 153–54
    social isolation, effect of, 155
    social recognition and
        engagement, 158
    stress and gender differences in,
        154–55
    stress hormones and, 157–58
Social brain, 9–10, 184, 186–87, 456,
    684, 939. *See also* Brain
    defined, 993
    evolutionary basis of, 28–35
    functional development of,
        997–98, 997*f*
    neural systems approach to, 684–86
Social brain hypothesis, 30. *See also Sensu
    stricto* hypothesis
Social categorization, 411–12
    automaticity of, 446–47
    malleability of, 449–50
    social group and activation of
        group-based associations link
        between, 450–51
Social class, 747
Social cognition, 491–503. *See also*
    Cognition
    abstraction, 495–98
    and Asperger syndrome, 862–66
    biomimetism of, 986
    cultural influence on, 753–54, 755*f*
    defined, 39
    effect of frontal lobe lesions on,
        936–37
    embedded cognition, 492,
        498–500
    embodied cognition theories, 493
    evolution of, 39–47
        communication, role of, 44–45
        facial expressions, importance of,
            45–46

individuals and relationships,
    recognition of, 42–43
in nonhuman primates, 41–42
social affordances, recognition of,
    43–44
traits or behavior, 40–41
examples in, 495
Machiavellian view of, 39–42, 46
model, implementation of, 985–86
motor resonance in, 978–79
perceptual symbol systems,
    493–95, 498
Social cognitive neuroscience, 12, 69.
    See also Cognitive
    neuroscience
Social contract, 350
Social deficits, 455–72. *See also* Traumatic
    brain injury; ventral frontal
    cortex damage
    assessment of, 456–58
    in executive functions. *See* Executive
        functions
Social dominance, 716–24
    animal models of, 717–18
    resident-intruder/social defeat
        model, 718
    sensitivity to pharmacological
        challenges, 722–24
Social engagement
    social bonding and, 153–54, 158
Social entities, 11–12
    connections between biological
        entities and, 11
Social events and biological events,
    relationship between, 7
Social exchange, evolutionary
    foundations of, 349–51
Social exclusion
    intrapersonal/interpersonal self-esteem
        defense, 608
Social face, 395–97
Social feedback, 187
Social function
    of facial displays, in chimpanzee's,
        45–46. *See also* Chimpanzee;
        Monkeys
Social gating hypothesis, 656
Social hierarchy
    neural representation of, 702–13
        dopaminergic neurotransmitter
            system, 704–7, 705*f*, 706*f*
        future directions of, 712–13
        neural responses to hierarchically
            valuable events, 711–12
        serotonergic neurotransmitter
            system, 703–4
        social status in stable hierarchy,
            707–9, 708*f*
        social status in unstable hierarchy,
            709–11
    in nonhuman primate models,
        formation of, 717–18
    in rodent models, formation of, 717

Social instability model, 717, 718
Social interaction, 615, 620
    effects on language learning, 656
    effects on statistical learning,
      654–56, 655f
Social isolation, 5, 765–72. See also
    Loneliness
    effects on pair bonding, 155
Social learning, neurobiological
    foundations of, 663
Social learning hypothesis, 30
Social looking, 230. See also Political
    attitude
Social neuroscience, 3–7, 1027–29
    as an academic discipline,
      emergence of, 9–23
      critical appraisal, 14–15
      discipline building, 23
      impact analysis, 21–23, 22f,
        24–25
      innovations, 17–18, 18f
      in 1990s, roots of, 15
      pioneers, 18–20
      thought styles, changing, 15–17
      social brain, 9–10
      social entities, 11–12
    and antisocial personality
      disorders, 886
    background of, 3–4
    complex behavior underlying, 4–7
    defined, 3, 12–14
    neuropsychological
      perspective of, 49–65
    principles of, 6
    publication quantification and
      vocabulary identification,
      23–24
Social ostracism, 184
Social pain, 766. See also Pain
Social preferences, 950–51
Social proximity, 615, 620
Social psychology, 491. See also Psychology
Social rank
    behavioral and physiological
      correlates of
      body weight, 718–19
      hormones and HPA axis function,
        719–20
      locomotor activity, 720–21
    neurobiological correlates of
      dopaminergic systems, 721–22
      serotonergic systems, 722
Social rejection, brain's response to,
    586–96
    physical-social pain overlap
      aggressive behaviors, 594–95
      individual differences
        hypothesis, 591
      linguistic evidence, 587
      manipulation hypothesis, 591–94
      neural evidence, 588–90, 589f
      pharmacological evidence, 587–88
      physiological stress responses, 595

Social relationships, inflammation
    associated with, 821–22
Social Responsiveness Scale (SRS), 841
Social rewards, 187t, 188f, 766. See also
    Human reward system;
    Rewards
    modulation of, 186–87
    neuroimaging studies of, 184, 186
    overview of, 184
    processing, shared neural substrates
      for, 187
Social robot, 659, 660f
Social science, video games influence on,
    1002–6
Social self preservation theory, 787
Social status
    effect on prefrontal cortex, 705–7
    effect on striatum, 705
    in stable hierarchy, 707–9, 708f
    in unstable hierarchy, 709–11
Social support, 804–10, 805t
    effect on early life stress, 779, 22
    to health, social neuroscientific
      pathways linking, 804–10,
      808f, 809f
      cardiovascular function, 805
      central neural activation, 807
      immune function, 806
      main effects model of, 807, 809
      neuroendocrine function, 805–6
      stress-buffering model of,
        807, 808
      stress prevention model of, 807,
        808–9
    inflammation associated with, 821–
Social vision, evolution of, 397
Social visual brain, 398–400. See also
    Brain
Social visual face processing, evolution of,
    397–98
Social-evaluative threat, physiological
    effects to, 787–99. See also
    Threat
    cortisol and immune interactions,
      794–95
    effect on cardiovascular responses,
      792–93
    effect on cortisol reactivity, 789–90
      elements of, 791–92
      emotional correlates of,
        790–91
      interpersonal evaluation and
        rejection, 792
    effect on immunologic responses,
      793–94
    implications for, 795–99
    in nonhuman animals, 788–89
Socially adapted brain. See also Brain
    impact on learning, 660–61
Socio-cognitive skills and alexithymia,
    links between, 911
Socioeconomic status (SES), 245, 710,
    712, 717, 795–98, 900

Socioemotional functioning, in aging
    brain, 507–17. See also Brain
    amygdala activity associated with,
      509–10
    cognitive decline and emotional
      stability, 514–16, 515f, 515t
    emotion regulation, 513
    emotional memory, 512–13
    emotional stimuli, anticipation of,
      510–11
    exposure to emotional stimuli,
      511–12
    future directions in, 516–17
Socioemotional selectivity theory (SST),
    508, 509, 511, 512
Somatic marker hypothesis, 573, 937
Somatoform disorders, alexithymia with,
    922–23
Somatosensory cortex, 199f.
    See also Cortex
    role in affective reactions, 201–2
    role in emotion recognition, 257–61
    role in task distraction, 280
Song theory, 627
Source localization vs. source imaging,
    119, 120f
Space Fortress II, 1005
Spatial-filters, 122–23
Species face overgeneralization (SFO),
    440. See also Face
    overgeneralization
Species recognition
    animal response to, 439–40
    infant response to, 440
    neural response to, 439
Specific language impairment (SLI), 851
Spectrum, 850–52
Speech, 378, 379, 570
    adult-directed, 627
    infant-directed, 627–29
    new motor theory of, 670–74
    ventral/dorsal pathway difference in,
      671–72
Spinal cord, decerebration of, 169–70
Spinal reflex networks, 166–69
    cutaneous, 168
    extensor reflexes, 168, 170
    flexor (pain) withdrawal reflexes,
      168, 170
    pre-motivational, 170
Spiral imaging, 81
Spirituality, 1022
Spoken language, understanding of,
    674–75. See also Language
Spontaneous trait inference, 408
Squirrel monkeys. See also Monkeys
    impact of opiates on separation
      distress, 157
Squirrels, altruistic behavior in, 569
Statistical inference, 126–28, 128f
    hypothesis testing, 126–28
    non-parametric approaches to, 126
    parametric approaches, 126

Statistical parametric map (SPM), 89–90, 93
Stereotype Content Model, 429f
Stereotypes, self-regulation of, 736
Stereotypic thoughts, control of, 733
Stereotyping, 406, 491, 495
Stimulus-reinforcement learning, 898. *See also* Learning
Strange Stories-Affective Task, 463t, 834–35
Strategic awareness, 950
Strategic choice, 951–53
Strategic intelligence, 952, 956, 957. *See also* Intelligence
Strategic teaching and influence value, 953–54
Strategic thinking, cognitive neuroscience of, 949–58
Stress
    hormones and pair bonding, 157–58
    induced by wound healing
        massage therapy for, 141
        psycho-education for, 141
        relaxation techniques for, 141
    inflammation associated with, 820–21
        acute, 817–18
        chronic, 818–19
    in pair bonding, 154–55
    responses, neural regulation of, 780–81
Stress prevention model, of social support, 805, 805t, 807, 808–9
Stress-buffering model, of social support, 805, 805t, 807, 808
Striatum, 180
    activity, modulation of, 181–82
    activity associated with interpersonal self-esteem defense, 605f, 607
    dorsal, 182, 184, 186, 188, 217
    role in attitude formation, 216–17
    role in emotion regulation, 278
    ventral, 183, 186, 188, 216–17
Stroop Test, 220, 234–36, 280, 302, 339, 361, 363, 366, 368, 369, 409, 460, 460t, 461, 771, 817, 863, 898, 941, 1005
Structural connectivity
    abnormalities associated with Asperger syndrome, 874–75
Structural equation modeling (SEM), 92, 113, 783, 877
Structured event complexes (SECs), 351
Subgenual cingulate cortex (SCC). *See also* Cortex
    role in altruistic/self-serving motivations, 479–81
Subliminal stimuli, 197, 207, 231
Superconducting quantum interference devices (SQUIDs), 101
Superior colliculus, 229
Superior frontal gyrus, 421f
Superior parietal gyrus, 421f
Superior precentral gyrus, 421f

Superior temporal gyrus (STG)
    sensitivity to speaker's vocal identity in, 387
Superior temporal sulcus (STS), 302, 381–82, 421f
    activity associated with predicted reward, 954
    activity associated with strategic thinking, 953
    posterior, 835, 993f
    posterior regions of, 420, 428
    role in body posture and movement, 261
    role in emotion recognition, 254, 261
    role in face expression, 396, 399, 400
    role in impression formation, 422, 424, 428–30
Supplementary motor area, 229
Supraliminal stimuli, 231
    unconscious activation of action plans through, 339–40
    unconscious modulation of behavioral dispositions through, 340–41
Surprise, 252, 255f, 261, 266, 267, 329, 370, 397, 512, 555. *See also* Emotion(s)
Sympathetic nervous system (SNS), 788
Sympathy, 244, 482, 552–53, 567, 568, 572, 999
    defined, 481
    distinguished from empathy552
Synaptic pruning, 302, 850, 995, 999
    cortical grey matter and, 304–5, 305f
Synaptogenesis, 993–95, 994f
Systolic blood pressure (SBP), 792
    loneliness effects on, 768

T

T1-weighted imaging (T1W), 295
T2-weighted imaging (T2W), 295
Tape stripping, 142. *See also* Dermal wound healing; Wound healing
Task switching, 71–72
Taste hedonics
    associated with intake/rejection responses, 169, 170
Tay-Sachs disease, 759
Temperament, 41, 159, 227, 235, 236, 244, 362, 579, 606, 684
Temperament and Character Inventory, 246, 923
Temporal cortex. *See also* Cortex
    activity associated with antisocial behavior, 887–88
Temporal poles, 421f
Temporal voice area (TVA), 381–85
    abnormal activation, in autism, 383–85, 384f
    involvement in voice processing, 382–83
    species-specificity of, 382

voice selectivity in macaque auditory cortex, 382, 383f
voice-selective neuronal activity in, 381, 381f
Temporoparietal junction (TPJ), 261, 421f, 993f
    activity associated with strategic thinking, 953
    damage associated with alterations in personality and behavior, 938
    role in impression formation, 429
    role in self-recognition, 327
Tenth cranial nerve, 152
Tests of Self-Conscious Affect (TOSCA), 925
Thalamo-amygdala pathway, 171–72, 173f
Thalamo-cortico-amygdala pathway, 171–72, 173f
The Awareness of Social Inference Test (TASIT), 456, 472
    description of task, 471
    relationship to functional outcome, 471
    relationship to traumatic brain injury, 471
    relationship to ventral frontal damage, 471
Thematic Apperception Test, 926
Theory of body mechanism (ToBy), 986
Theory of mind (ToM), 33–35, 40, 46–47, 234, 259, 318–19, 429, 472, 552, 865, 986, 993
    abilities in patients with early-onset frontal lobe lesions, 939
    in autism spectrum conditions, 832–36, 833–34t
    behavioral development of, 998
    cognitive versus affective, 939–41
        development of, 940–41
    defined, 936
    deficits in neurological patients, 935–43
        effect of frontal lobe lesions on social cognition, 936–37
        neural correlates of, 937–39
    dysfunction associated with Asperger syndrome, 874–78
    executive function, 941–42
    false-belief task, 41–42
    robot, 985
    role of motor neuron system in, 535–36
    tasks
        in patients with traumatic brain injury, 464
        in patients with ventral frontal damage, 462
Third person perspective (3PP), 330, 331
Thought suppression, 368–69
Threat
    coping with, 781–82
    neural responses to, 780
    social-evaluative, 787–99

effect on humans reward system, 180

functional neuroanatomy of, 365

hypoactivation associated with autism spectrum conditions, 838–40

lesion overlap map of, 58–59, 59f

online empathic response of patients with damage to, 62–63, 63f

role in emotion regulation, 369–70

role in face expression, 400

role in memory retrieval process, 328

role in regulating appetitive behaviors, 367

self-other distinction in, 836–37

sex-related functional asymmetry in, 63–64

during socioemotional processing, age effects in, 516

Verbal Fluency Test, 460, 460t, 461

Viagra, 1020

Video games, 1001–9

attention deficit/hyperactivity disorder and, 1008–9

autonomic measures of, 1006–7

cortical measures of, 1007, 1007f

effects of desensitization, 1008

influence on affective science, 1006

influence on cognitive science, 1004–6, 1006f

influence on education science, 1007–8

influence on social science, 1002–4

violence, 1002–4, 1007f

Violence, 450

and antisocial personality disorder, 889

impulsive, 1020

video game, 1002–4, 1007f

Viral reactivation. See also Latent herpes viruses, Monitoring reactivation of

clinical relevance of, 136t

costs for, 136t

labor and, 136t

training for, 136t

Visceral efferent pathways, 154

Visible burrow system (VBS), 717, 718

Visual perception. See also Perception

cultural influence on neural basis of, 750–51, 752f

Visual word form area (VWFA), 749

Visualization and artifact reduction, preprocessing fMRI data, 85–86

Visuospatial cognition, video game effect on, 1004–5. See also Cognition

associated with cognitive control, 1005–6

associated with executive function, 1005–6

Vividness, of odor-evoked memory, 270

Vocal communication, 625. See also Communication

Vocal learning. See also Learning

imitative behavior and, 547–48

Voice gender, cerebral sensitivity to, 388–91, 390f

Voice Perception Assessment (VPA), 385

Voice perception, 378–91. See also Perception; Temporal voice area

assessment, 385

as auditory faces, 378–79

cerebral sensitivity to voice gender, 388–91, 390f

defined, 379

fronto-temporal positivity to, 385–86, 386f

identity information, cerebral processing of, 386–91

sensitivity to speaker's vocal identity, in right anterior temporal lobe, 387–88

model of, 386, 387f

production of, 380f

speed of processing, 385

Voice-specific response (VSR), 385

Voxel-based lesion-symptom mapping, 53–57, 57f

Voxel-based morphometry (VBM), 874, 923

W

Warmth, 427, 429f

interpersonal, 497–98

Whales, 31. See also Animals; Mammals

brain mechanisms in, 5

White matter, 294

age differences in, 296, 299, 300f, 301f

myelination and, 305–6

Wilcoxon-Mann-Whitney test, 56

Williams syndrome, 686

Wisconsin Card Sorting Task, 234, 459, 871, 941

Word learning, 651–52. See also Learning

Word production, 637–38, 637f, 639f

World Wide Web, 49

Wound healing

clinical relevance of, 136t

costs for, 136t

dermal, 141–43

impaired, 140

labor and, 136t

oral, 141, 142–43

post healing period, 142–43

principle and relevance of, 140–41

training for, 136t

Y

Youths

antisocial personality disorders in, 889–90

attention deficit hyperactivity disorder in, 898

callous and unemotional traits in, 898

conduct disorder in, 898